THE

GENEALOGIST'S ADDRESS BOOK

Fifth Edition

Elizabeth Petty Bentley

ISBN: 0-8063-1757-4
Library of Congress Catalogue Card Number 2005922158

Introduction

The information in each edition of *The Genealogist's Address Book* is based largely upon data received in response to direct-mail questionnaires and emails, supplemented by information from printed and Internet sources. In my letters to libraries, archives, genealogical and historical societies, publishers, and other vendors across the country, I requested name and address , voice phone and FAX numbers, email address, website (URL), contact person (with title), hours of operation (local time), periodical title, frequency of publication, costs of subscription, membership, research-by-mail fees, and comments regarding the organization's specialty. Of course, some responses were more expansive than others, and some organizations did not respond, presumably because the information was correct as it appeared in my letter. Naturally, all information is subject to change. Because of the length of time required to compile this list, I suggest that readers verify the information with a phone call or a letter before visiting. For instance, this paperback edition (March 2005) has been updated somewhat from the CD version (October 2004).

Even though the same information may be included in *The County Courthouse Book*, some county and municipal archives have been included, because they appeared to house more than just official government documents. Also, some historical societies may not have extensive library facilities of use to genealogists, but exist solely to maintain or preserve house museums, or battlefields or historical sites, or to serve as professional organizations. Where I was able to determine that this was the case, I've relegated those societies to the miscellaneous category. Many more strictly historical organizations have been included, making this edition of increasing use to historians as well as genealogists.

I'm glad to note that very few new organizations requested that their addresses be withheld, and some which had requested so previously, have changed their policy. Still, a few organizations, especially religious archives, cited the inability of their limited staffs to cope with the mounting demands of genealogists—hobbyists, in their view, rather than serious scholars. Others seem to be discouraging inquiries, either by citing exorbitant search fees or by simply referring queries directly to professional researchers who must charge by the hour, plus travel time and expenses. To avoid having even more facilities resort to these tactics, all mail inquiries should be as brief and concise as possible, asking only for specific information, and including a self-addressed, stamped envelope and a generous donation to offset copying, postage, and research costs or else requesting an estimate or fee schedule before any work is undertaken.

I'm grateful to the thousands of correspondents who generously took the time to answer my own inquiries. I'm especially indebted to Marian R. Hoffman, who spent many a tedious hour checking and verifying data, and to Dr. Michael Tepper, who originally perceived a need for this book and its companion volumes, and provided me the opportunity to have a part in compiling it. I'd appreciate if readers who find omissions or errors in the text would send any additions or corrections to me directly.

Elizabeth Petty Bentley
PO Box 58
Woodsboro, MD 21798
(301) 845-7040

epbentley@hotmail.com
http://www.geocities.com/epbentley

Table of Contents

Table of Contents

Part 1. National Addresses

National Archives

National Archives and Records Administration (NARA)—Archives I
Seventh St. and Pennsylvania Ave., N.W.
Washington, DC 20408
(202) 501-5400; (202) 501-5410
(Genealogy); (202) 523-3218; (202) 523-3286; (866) 325-7208 (Customer Service); (301) 713-6905 FAX
inquire@arch1.nara.gov
http://www.archives.gov
Research Room: Mon & Wed 8:45–5:00, Tue & Thur–Fri 8:45 A.M.–9:00 P.M.; Sat 8:45–4:45; Exhibits: Mon–Sun (1 Apr–Labor Day) 10:00–9:00, Mon–Sun (winter) 10:00–5:30
Pub. *Prologue*, quarterly, $15.00 per year subscription; *News from the Archives*; *Guide to Genealogical Research in the National Archives* (Washington, DC, third edition, 2000.)
(Form for any surname's Soundex code; catalog of resources on American Indians, Black studies, census records, federal court records, genealogical and biographical research, immigrant and passenger arrivals, military service records; searchable database; genealogy, naturalization records, post office records. Ship passenger arrival records, 1820–1959, census records, 1790–1920, Eastern Cherokee application records, 1906–1909, land entry files, military pension and bounty land warrant records, 1775–1916, military service records, 1775–ca 1916, military service records, ca 1917–present.)

National Archives and Records Administration (NARA)—Archives II
The National Archives at College Park (8601 Adelphi Road, College Park, MD 20740-6001—location)
Seventh Street and Pennsylvania Avenue, N.W. (mailing address)
Washington, DC 20408
(301) 713-6800 (User Services); (301) 713-7040 (Cartographic Reference Branch); (866) 272-6272 (Customer Service)
inquire@arch2.nara.gov
http://www.archives.gov
Mon–Fri 8:45–5:00; Research Rooms: Mon & Wed 8:45–5:00, Tue & Thur–Fri 8:45–9:00 P.M., Sat 8:45–4:45
Pub. *Archives II Researcher Bulletin*, quarterly
(Some records from the Washington, DC, and Suitland, MD, archives buildings have been transferred to this new facility. There are no genealogy records here. Archives II reference branches include Nixon Presidential Materials; Research Rooms; Center for Electronic Records; Cartographic Reference Branch; Motion Picture, Sound and Video Branch; and Still Picture Branch.)

Washington National Records Center (WNRC)
4205 Suitland Road
Suitland, MD 20746-8001
(403) 788-1600; (301) 778-1621 FAX; (301) 778-1501 FAX (Reference Requests)
suitland.center@nara.gov
http://www.archives.gov/facilities/md/suitland.html
Alan Kramer, Director

Mon–Sat 8:00–4:00
(Area served: Maryland, Virginia, DC, area and West Virginia; 600,000+ cubic feet of federal records, more than any other archival entity in the U.S.: Bureau of Land Management 1790–1960—land entry files, e.g., homesteads; War Relocation Authority 1940–1945—Japanese-Americans interned during WW II; Department of State 1906–1925—passports; U.S. District Court for the District of Columbia 1800–1960; Patent and Trademark Office 1836–1918)

National Archives and Records Administration (NARA)
Center for Electronic Records
Electronic and Special Media Records Services Division (NWRE)
National Archives at College Park
8601 Adelphi Road, Room 6050
College Park, MD 20740-6001
(301) 837-1474; (301) 837-0470 (Reference); (301) 837-3681 FAX
cer@nara.gov
http://www.archives.gov/research_room/center_for_electronic_records/about_the_center.html
Mon–Fri 8:45–5:00
(Casualty lists of Korean and Vietnam conflicts by state.)

NARA's National Personnel Records Center
Civilian Personnel Records
111 Winnebago Street
Saint Louis, MO 63118-4126
(314) 801-9250; (314) 801-9269 FAX
cpr.center@nara.gov
http://www.archives.gov/facilities/mo/st_louis/civilian_personnel_records.html
Paul D. Gray, Assistant Director for Civilian Records
Mon–Fri 7:45–3:45
(Civilian Personnel Records has personnel records for the Coast Guard and for most former civilian federal government employees whose service terminated after 1900.)
cannot accept requests by telephone or email due to the provisions of the Privacy Act of 1974, which require a written request, signed and dated by an authorized requester, but inquiries may be transmitted via FAX

NARA's National Personnel Records Center
Military Personnel Records
9700 Page Avenue
Saint Louis, MO 63132-5100
(314) 801-0800; (314) 801-9195 FAX
center@stlouis.nara.gov
http://www.archives.gov/facilities/mo/st_louis.html
Clifford G. Amsler, Jr., Assistant Director for Military Records
Mon–Fri 7:30–4:00
(For records in the National Archives relating to early military service, use NATF Form 26. Requests for later personnel should be sent on Standard Form 180—Army, Navy and Marines. Forms available upon request.)
cannot accept requests by telephone or email due to the provisions of the Privacy Act of 1974 and Department of Defense directives, which require a written

request, signed and dated by an authorized requester, but inquiries may be transmitted via FAX, using Standard Form 180 if at all possible

National Archives and Records Administration (NARA)
Calendar of Events (NPOL)
8601 Adelphi Road
College Park, MD 20740-6001
http://www.archives.gov/about_us/calendar_of_events
Pub. *Calendar of Events*, monthly, free
(pictorial calendar of events, including genealogical workshops, courses and presentations)

Regional Records Services Facilities
(formerly known as Regional Branches and/or Archives Records Centers)

NARA's Pacific Alaska Region (Anchorage)
Federal Office Building
654 West Third Avenue
Anchorage, AK 99501-2145
(907) 271-2441; (907) 271-2442 FAX
steven.edwards@nara.gov;
alaska.archives@nara.gov
http://www.archives.gov/facilities/ak/anchorage.html
Steven Edwards, Regional Administrator
(Area served: Alaska)

NARA's Pacific Region (Laguna Niguel)
(24000 Avila Road, First Floor-East Entrance, Laguna Niguel, CA 92677-3497—location)
PO Box 6719 (mailing address)
Laguna Niguel, CA 92607-6719
(949) 360-2641; (949) 360-2624 FAX
center@laguna.nara.gov
http://www.archives.gov/facilities/ca/laguna_niguel.html
Diane S. Nixon, Director
Mon–Fri & first Sat 8:00–4:30
(Areas served: Arizona, the southern California counties of Imperial, Inyo, Kern, Los Angeles, Orange, Riverside, San Bernardino, San Diego, San Luis Obispo, Santa Barbara and Ventura, and Clark County, Nevada)

NARA's Pacific Region-San Francisco
1000 Commodore Drive
San Bruno, CA 94066-2350
(650) 238-3501; (650) 238-3511 FAX
sanbruno.archives@nara.gov
http://www.archives.gov/facilities/ca/san_francisco.html
Daniel Nealand, Director
Mon–Fri 7:30–4:00, Wed 7:30 A.M.–8:00 P.M.
(Area served: northern California, Guam, Hawaii, Nevada [except Clark County], American Samoa, Trust Territory of the Pacific Islands; "federal court records, Bureau of Indian Affairs records, Bureau of Land Management records, Chinese immigration records, U.S. census 1790–1930, etc.")

NARA's Great Lakes Region (Chicago)
7358 South Pulaski Road
Chicago, IL 60629-5898
(773) 948-9019; (773) 948-9050 FAX
chicago.archives@nara.gov
http://www.archives.gov/facilities/il/chicago.html

Peter W. Bunce, Director of Archival
Operations
Mon–Fri 8:00–4:15 (Call for additional
hours)
(Area served: Illinois, Indiana, Michigan,
Minnesota, Ohio, Wisconsin)

NARA's Rocky Mountain Region
Building 48, Denver Federal Center
PO Box 25307
Denver, CO 80225-0307
(303) 407-5700; (303) 407-5707 FAX
denver.archives@nara.gov
http://www.archives.gov/facilities/co/
denver.html
Eileen Bolger, Director, Archival Operations
Microfilm research: Mon, Wed & Fri
7:30–3:45, Tue & Thur 7:30 A.M.–8:45
P.M., 1st & 3rd Sat 8:30–4:45; Textual
Research Room in Building 48: Mon–Fri
7:30–3:45
(Area served: Colorado, Montana, New
Mexico, North Dakota, South Dakota,
Utah, Wyoming)
copies: 25¢ per page

NARA's Southeast Region
1557 Saint Joseph Avenue
East Point, GA 30344-2593
(404) 763-7477; (404) 763-7059 FAX
archives@atlanta.nara.gov
http://www.archives.gov/facilities/ga/
atlanta.html
Charles Reeves, Director, Archival
Operations
Mon & Wed–Fri 7:00–4:00, Tue 7:00
A.M.–8:00 P.M. (reservations for microfilm
readers required)
Pub. *The Civil History*, quarterly newsletter
of the Friends of the National
Archives—Southeast Region
(Area served: Alabama, Florida, Georgia,
Kentucky, Mississippi, North Carolina,
South Carolina, Tennessee)
$10.00 per year membership in Friends of
the National Archives—Southeast Region

NARA's Northeast Region (Boston)
Frederick C. Murphy Federal Center
Attn: Paul Palermo, Director
380 Trapelo Road
Waltham, MA 02154-6399
(781) 647-8100; (781) 647-8460 FAX
archives@waltham.nara.gov
http://www.archives.gov/facilities/ma/
boston.html
Stuart Culy, Director of Archival Operations
Mon–Tue & Fri 8:00–4:30, Wed–Thur 8:00
A.M.–9:00 P.M., first & third Sat
(June–Dec) 8:00–4:30 (microfilm
research only)
(Area served: Connecticut, Maine,
Massachusetts, New Hampshire, Rhode
Island, Vermont)

NARA's Northeast Region (Pittsfield)
10 Conte Drive
Pittsfield, MA 01201-8230
(413) 236-3604; (413) 236-3509 FAX
archives@pittsfield.nara.gov;
jean.nudd@nara.gov
http://www.archives.gov/facilities/ma/
pittsfield.html
Jean Nudd, Archivist
Wed 8:00 A.M.–9:00 P.M., first Sat
8:00–4:00
("over 75,000 rolls of microfilmed Federal
records such as census, immigration and
military records")

NARA's Central Plains Region (Kansas

City)
2312 East Bannister Road
Kansas City, MO 64131-3011
(816) 268-8000; (816) 268-8037 FAX
KansasCity.Archives@nara.gov;
Mary.Burtzloff@nara.gov
http://www.archives.gov/facilities/mo/
kansas_city.html
Mary Burtzloff, Reference Supervisor
Microfilm Room: Mon & Thur–Fri
8:00–4:00, Tue 7:30–5:30, Wed 7:30
A.M.–8:30 P.M., third Sat (Jan–Nov)
9:00–4:00
(Area served: Iowa, Kansas, Missouri,
Nebraska)

**NARA's Central Plains Region (Lee's
Summit, Missouri)**
200 Space Center Drive
Lee's Summit, MO 64064-1182
(816) 268-8150; (816) 268-8159 FAX
reed.whitaker@nara.gov
http://www.archives.gov/facilities/mo/
lees_summit.html
Reed Whitaker, Regional Administrator
Mon–Fri 8:00–4:00
(Area served: New Jersey, New York, Puerto
Rico and the U.S. Virgin Islands
[temporary records])

**NARA's Northeast Region (New York
City)**
201 Varick Street
New York, NY 10014-4811
(212) 401-1620; (212) 401-1638 FAX
newyork.archives@nara.gov
http://www.archives.gov/facilities/ny/
new_york_city.html
Robert C. Morris, Director
Mon, Wed & Fri 8:00–4:30, Tue & Thur
8:00–8:00, first & third Sat 8:30–4:00;
evenings 4:30–8:00, Sat (microfilm only,
not naturalization records)
Pub. *The American Archivist*; *American
Heritage: The Journal of American
History*
(Areas served: New Jersey, New York,
Puerto Rico and the U.S. Virgin Islands
[permanent records]; federal census
records for all states and New York
passenger arrivals on microfilm, also
naturalization records for New York, New
Jersey and Puerto Rico; houses microfiche
guides to the older vital records of New
York State [except New York City]: births
1880–1921, deaths and marriages from
1880 to 1946)

NARA's Great Lakes Region (Dayton)
3150 Springboro Road
Dayton, OH 45439-1883
(937) 425-0672; (937) 425-0640 FAX
galen.wilson@nara.gov;
dayton.reference@nara.gov
http://www.archives.gov/facilities/oh/
dayton.html
Galen Wilson, Archivist
(Area served: Indiana, Michigan, Minnesota,
Ohio; no microfilm or microfilm reading
room; stores noncurrent records for
federal offices in Ohio, Indiana and
Michigan, as well as some nationwide
programs)

**NARA's Mid-Atlantic Region (Center City
Philadelphia)**
(entrance on Chestnut Street on the side of
the U.S. Court House, between Ninth and
10th Streets—location)
900 Market Street (mailing address)
Philadelphia, PA 19107-4292

(215) 606-0100; (215) 606-0116 FAX
philadelphia.archives@nara.gov
http://www.archives.gov/midatlantic/
public_services/public_services.html
Robert J. Plowman, Archivist
Mon–Fri 8:00–5:00, second & fourth Sat
8:00–4:00
(Area served: Delaware, Maryland,
Pennsylvania, Virginia, West Virginia;
primarily genealogical records)

**NARA's Mid-Atlantic Region (Northeast
Philadelphia)**
14700 Townsend Road
Philadelphia, PA 19154-1096
(215) 305-2000; (215) 305-2038 FAX
philadelphia.archives@nara.gov
http://www.archives.gov/midatlantic/fed_
agency_services/fed_agency_services.
html
Patrick Connelly, Genealogy
Mon–Fri 8:00–4:30
(Area served: Delaware, Maryland,
Pennsylvania, Virginia, West Virginia)

NARA's Southwest Region
(501 West Felix Street, Building 1, Fort
Worth, TX 76115-3405—location)
PO Box 6216 (mailing address)
Fort Worth, TX 76115-0216
(817) 831-5620 (Archival Research); (817)
831-5920 (Genealogy); (817) 831-5900
(Court Records); (817) 831-5611 FAX
ftworth.reference@nara.gov (Reference
Services); kent.carter@nara.gov
http://www.archives.gov/facilities/tx/
fort_worth.html
Kent C. Carter, Director
Mon–Fri 8:00–4:00
(Area served: Arkansas, Louisiana,
Oklahoma, Texas)

NARA's Pacific Alaska Region (Seattle)
6125 Sand Point Way, N.E.
Seattle, WA 98115-7999
(206) 336-5115; (206) 336-5112 FAX
patty.mcnamee@nara.gov;
seattle.archives@nara.gov
http://www.archives.gov/facilities/wa/
seattle.html
Patty McNamee, Genealogy
Mon–Fri 7:45–4:15, first & second Tue 7:45
A.M.–8:00 P.M., first & second Sat
9:00–4:00
(Area served: Idaho, Oregon, Washington;
federal census for all states; regional
federal records)
no admission charge; copies: 25¢ each from
microform originals

Government Departments and Agencies

Bureau of Indian Affairs
Office of Public Affairs
1849 C Street, N.W.
Washington, DC 20240-0001
(202) 343-1334; (202) 208-3710 (General
BIA Information); (202) 208-3711 (Tribal
Leaders Directory); (202) 343-1334 FAX;
(202) 501-1516 FAX
http://www.doi.gov/bureau-indian-affairs.html

Bureau of Land Management
1849 C Street, N.W.
Washington, DC 20240
(202) 343-9435; (202) 343-4152 FAX
http://www.blm.gov

Bureau of Land Management
5001 Southgate Drive
Billings, MT 59107
(406) 896-5000; (406) 896-5298 FAX
http://www.mt.blm.gov

Bureau of Land Management (Sante Fe)
(1474 Rodeo Road—location)
PO Box 27115 (mailing address)
Santa Fe, NM 87502-0115
(505) 438-7400; (505) 438-7435 FAX
(has microfiche of New Mexico, Kansas and
Oklahoma public land records, including
original patents, tract books and survey
plats)

Bureau of Land Management
Eastern States Office
General Land Office (GLO) Automated
Records System
7450 Boston Boulevard
Springfield, VA 22153-3121
(703) 440-1600; (703) 440-1609 FAX
tmayfiel@es.blm.gov
http://www.es.blm.gov
Pam Mozina, Acting Lead for GLO Records
Mon–Fri 8:00–4:30
Pub. *Federal Land Patents 1787–1960*
(has automated patent index 1820–1908 for
Alabama, Arkansas, Florida, Louisiana,
Michigan, Minnesota, Mississippi, Ohio,
Indiana and Wisconsin; can locate
documents through any one of six
categories: land description, patentee
name, patent authority, land office,
certificate number, or county; has
brochure on how researchers can use their
resources; collection includes federal land
surveys and field notes, and land patents
from the late 1820s to 1908)

U.S. Census Bureau
Personal Census Search Unit
(1201 East 10th Street, Building
48—location)
PO Box 1545 (mailing address)
Jeffersonville, IN 47131-0001
(812) 218-3046
http://www.census.gov/genealogy/www/
agesearch.html
Jean Ann Banet, Technical Supervisor
Mon–Fri 7:00–4:30
("searches census records for 1910–2000
census years")
$40.00 per search

Department of Defense
Defense Finance and Accounting Service
Cleveland Center (DFAS-CL/RO)
PO Box 99191
Cleveland, OH 44199-1126
(pay records of all DOD military retirees and
former spouses of all DOD military
retirees)

Department of Defense
Defense Finance and Accounting Service
Denver Center
Denver, CO 80279
(pay records for widows and dependants of
all DOD deceased military retirees)

Department of Homeland Security
U.S. Citizenship and Immigration Service
I&N Historical Reference Library
Chester Arthur Building, 425 I Street, N.W.,
Room 1100A
Washington, DC 20536
(202) 514-2837 (Historical Office/Library);
(202) 514-3278 (FOIA/PA Unit); (202)
633-3296 FAX
http://uscis.gov/graphics/aboutus/history/
library.htm; http://uscis.gov/graphics/
aboutus/history/natzrec/natrec.htm
(Naturalization Records)
Marian L. Smith, Historian
Mon–Fri 8:00–4:30 (all but immigration
visitors should call for an appointment)
(The Citizenship and Immigration Service
has duplicate records of all naturalizations that occurred after 26 September
1906, has records documenting the arrival
and later naturalization of millions of
American immigrants. Requests for
information must be made through a
Freedom of Information Act and Privacy
Act request, sent to the attention of
"FOIA/PA" at the District Office where
the records are maintained, if known, or to
the office serving the area where you live.
Form G-639 is available from the
FOIA/PA Unit, Second Floor ULLB. For
naturalization records, supply full name,
date and country of birth. For arrival
records, supply port and date of arrival
and, if possible, the name of the ship.)

Department of Homeland Security
U.S. Customs and Border Protection
1300 Pennsylvania Avenue, N.W.
Washington, DC 20229
(202) 354-1000
http://www.customs.ustreas.gov
("Q. How can I find out if, when and where
my relative entered the United States? A.
The United States Customs and Border
Protection does not have those records.
You may want to consult with the
National Archives for further
information." For an overview of the
types of information the CBP *does*
collect, use the web site's link to "forms"
issued, including "Vessel Entrance or
Clearance Statement," "Crew's Effects
Declaration," "Application for
Identification Card," "FAST Commercial
Driver Application," etc. To contact a
specific port or preclearance station, use
the web site's link to "ports," which lists
contact information.)

Department of State
Passport Correspondence Branch
1111 19th Street, N.W., Suite 510
Washington, DC 20522-1705
(202) 955-0307
William Crawford, Branch Chief
(certification of report of birth, consular
report of death, certificate of witness to
marriage, certification of citizenship at
birth of persons born abroad, $30.00

each)

Freedom of Information and Privacy Acts Unit (FOIA/PA)
Administrative Center, Dallas
Southern Regional Office
7701 North Stemmons Freeway
Dallas, TX 75247-9998

Government Printing Office (GPO)
Washington, DC 20401
(888) 293-6498; (202) 512-1530; (202) 512-1262
gpoaccess@gpo.gov
http://www.gpoaccess.gov

National Park Service
Office of Library, Archives and Graphics
Research
Harpers Ferry Center
Harpers Ferry, WV 25425-0050
(304) 535-6261; (304) 535-6492 FAX
David Nathanson, Chief
Mon–Fri 8:00–4:30
(employees and alumni of the National Park
Service)

Social Security Administration
Department of Health and Human Services
Office of Public Inquiries
6401 Security Boulevard
Baltimore, MD 21235
http://www.ssa.gov
Delmar D. Dowling, Director
(researchers must supply Social Security
Number or person's full name, date and
place of birth, and parents' full names)
research: $7.00 if SSN is known, $16.00 if
number is unknown

U.S. Geological Survey (USGS)
Earth Science Information Center (ESIC)
12201 Sunrise Valley Drive
Reston, VA 20192
(703) 648-5920 (for earth science
information); (888) ASK-USGS (275-
8747) (24-hour message recording
system); (703) 648-4544 (for geographic
names information)
ask@usgs.gov; gnis_manager@usgs.gov
http://www.usgs.gov; http://erg.usgs.gov/isb/
pubs/factsheets/fs09902.html (Using
Maps in Genealogy); http://mapping.usgs.
gov/esic/prices/maps.html (price list of
maps); http://geonames.usgs.gov
(mapping information, geographic names)
9:00–5:00
(over-the-counter sales of U.S.G.S.
topographic maps)

U.S. Geological Survey Library
2255 North Gemini Drive
Flagstaff, AZ 86001
(928) 556-7272; (928) 556-7156
flag_lib@usgs.gov
http://library.usgs.gov/flaglib.html

U.S. Geological Survey Library
345 Middlefield Road, MS 955
Menlo Park, CA 94025-3591
(650) 329-5027 (Reference Desk); (415)
329-5132 FAX
men_lib@usgs.gov
http://library.usgs.gov/menlib.html
Angelica Bravos, Reference Librarian
Mon–Fri 8:30–4:30

United States Geological Survey Field Records Library
United States Geological Survey
Photographic Library

Building 20, Room C-2006
Denver Federal Center
MS 914, Box 25046, Federal Center
Denver, CO 80225-0046
(303) 236-1005 (Field Records Library);
    (303) 236-1010 (Photographic Library);
    (303) 236-0015 FAX
den_lib@usgs.gov
http://library.usgs.gov/denlib.html
Mon–Fri 8:00–4:00
("Both collections reflect earth science
    research activities of the U.S. Geological
    Survey; Photo Library includes extensive
    portraits collection of USGS personnel
    only.")

United States Geological Survey
Map Distribution Center
Federal Center Building 810
Box 25286
Denver, CO 80225-0286
(303) 236-7477
8:00–4:00
(for "Quadrangles" of states; first order a free
    "Index Map" of the state)

Veterans Administration
National Cemetery Administration (402E)
810 Vermont Avenue, N.W.
Washington, DC 20420
(800) 697-6947
mps.headstones@mail.va.gov
http://www.cem.va.gov
8:00–4:30
("Provides government headstones and
    markers and Presidential Memorial
    Certificates.")

Vital Records Offices

Vital Records
feedback@vitalrec.com
http://www.vitalrec.com
Elizabeth Orsay
(up-to-date information on where and how to
    obtain copies of vital records such as birth
    certificates, death records, marriage
    records and divorce decrees from states,
    territories, counties and some cities and
    towns in the U.S.; includes order forms
    for these records for most of the state
    offices and many of the county offices;
    also links to official state and county vital
    records web sites)

Alabama Center for Health Statistics
PO Box 5625
Montgomery, AL 36103-5625
(334) 206-5418
http://adph.org
Mon–Fri 8:00–5:00
("Birth and death records begin in 1908.
    Marriage records begin in Aug 1936.
    Divorce records begin in 1950. Birth
    records have restricted access for 125
    years from date of event. Death records
    have restricted access for 25 years.")
searches: $12.00 per record (ten-year period)

**Alaska Department of Health and Social
Services**
Bureau of Vital Statistics
5441 Commercial Boulevard
Juneau, AK 99801
(907) 465-3392; (907) 465-3391 (recorded
    message); (907) 465-3618 FAX
BVSOFFICE@health.state.ak.us (Records
    Processing Unit)
http://www.hss.state.ak.us/dph/bvs
Mon–Fri 8:00–5:00
Pub. *Annual Report* (statistical analysis),
    $10.00 per issue
("Birth records are strictly confidential for
    100 years; marriage, divorce and death
    records are strictly confidential for 50
    years." Records from 1913.)
$20.00 per certified copy of birth, marriage,
    divorce or death

Arizona Department of Health Services
Office of Vital Records
(1818 West Adams—location)
PO Box 3887 (mailing address)
Phoenix, AZ 85030-3887
(602) 364-1300
http://www.hs.state.az.us/vitalrcd/index.htm
(Births and deaths from 1909)

Arkansas Department of Health
Division of Vital Records
4815 West Markham Street
Little Rock, AR 72205-3867
(501) 661-2174
http://www.healthyarkansas.com
(Births and deaths from 1914, marriages
    from 1917)

California Department of Health Services
Office of Vital Statistics
M.S. 5103
(1501 Capitol Avenue, Suite 71.1110,
Sacramento, CA 95814—location)
PO Box 997410 (mailing address)
Sacramento, CA 95899-7410
(916) 445-2684
http://www.dhs.ca.gov/hisp/chs/OVR/
    Ordercert.htm
(Records from 1905)

**Colorado Department of Public Health
and Environment**
Vital Records Division, HSVRD-VR-A1
4300 Cherry Creek Drive, South
Denver, CO 80246-1530
(303) 692-2200
vital.records@state.co.us
http://www.cdphe.state.co.us/hs/certs.asp
Mon–Fri 8:30–4:30, except holidays
(Index to marriage records 1900–1939 and
    1975–1985; request certificates from
    County Clerk, County Courthouse of
    county where marriage took place)

**State of Connecticut Department of Public
Health**
Vital Records Section
(410 Capitol Avenue—location)
PO Box 340308, MS#: 11VRS (mailing
    address)
Hartford, CT 06134-0308
(860) 509-7896; (860) 509-7964 FAX
http://www.dph.state.ct.us/OPPE/
    hpvital.htm
Public service counter: 8:30–4:30
("Because birth certificates are
    'Confidential' in Connecticut, a full
    certified copy of a certificate can be
    obtained only by registrant 18 or over,
    parent, legal representative, or member of
    a legally incorporated genealogical
    society which is registered with the
    Secretary of State and authorized to do
    business in Connecticut. A copy of the
    current, signed membership card and a
    copy of a photo ID must accompany all
    requests from genealogists for requests for
    certificates." Records from 1 July 1897.)

Office of Vital Statistics (Delaware)
Division of Public Health
(Corner of Federal and Water
Streets—location)
PO Box 637 (mailing address)
Dover, DE 19903-0637
(302) 744-4549; (302) 736-1862 FAX
http://www.state.de.us/dhss/dph/ss/
    vitalstats.html
Michael L. Richards, Vital Statistics
    Director
Mon–Fri 8:00–4:20
(has births from 1925, deaths from 1957,
    marriages from 1957, and divorces from
    1976; however the records are
    confidential and the office may only
    confirm whether a divorce has taken
    place, or it may issue birth and marriage
    records only to the individual named in
    them, or a death record only to a family
    member of someone named in it, or to an
    attorney or to someone who demonstrates
    "the need to obtain said records"; vital
    records through the early 20th century are
    open to the public at the Delaware Public
    Archives, Hall of Records; divorce
    records prior to 1976 are obtained from
    the county seat where the divorce was
    granted)
$6.00 for five-year search and certified copy

**State of Florida Department of Health and
Rehabilitative Services**
Vital Statistics
(1217 Pearl Street—location)
PO Box 210 (mailing address)
Jacksonville, FL 32231-0042
(904) 359-6900 (Information); (904) 359-
    6931 FAX
VitalStats@doh.state.fl.us
http://www.doh.state.fl.us/planning_eval/

vital_statistics
(Births from 1865, deaths from 1877, marriages from 1927)

Georgia Department of Human Resources
2600 Skyland Drive N.E.
Atlanta, GA 30319-3640
(404) 679-4701
http://www.ph.dhr.state.ga.us/programs/
vitalrecords/birth.shtml
(Births and deaths from 1919, marriages from 1952; for marriage records prior to June 9, 1952, contact the Office of the Probate Judge in the county where the license was issued)

Hawaii State Department of Health
Research and Statistics Office
Vital Records Section
(1250 Punchbowl Street, Room 103, Honolulu, HI 96813—location)
PO Box 3378 (mailing address)
Honolulu, HI 96801-9984
(808) 961-7327; (808) 586-4539; (808) 586-4542
http://www.hawaii.gov/health/vital-records/index.html
(Records from the mid-19th century.)

Bureau of Vital Records and Health Statistics (Idaho)
(450 West State, First Floor, Boise, ID 83702—location)
PO Box 83720 (mailing address)
Boise, ID 83720-0036
(208) 334-5988 (recorded message)
http://www.state.id.us/dhw
Mon–Fri 8:00–4:30
(Births and deaths from 1911, marriages from 1947; requires signature of person named in birth or marriage records and ID required.)

Illinois Department of Public Health
Division of Vital Records
605 West Jefferson Street
Springfield, IL 62702-5097
(217) 782-6553; (217) 785-3209 FAX
http://www.idph.state.il.us/vitalrecords/
index.htm
8:30–4:00
$15.00 for full certified copies of births or deaths from 1916 (birth certificates available only to the person named, a parent or other legal representative, or upon court order), $5.00 for verifications of marriages (from 1962) or divorces

Indiana State Department of Health
Vital Records Department
6 West Washington Street
Indianapolis, IN 46204
(317) 233-2700
http://www.in.gov/isdh/bdcertifs/birth_
and_death_certificates.htm
(Births from 1907, deaths from 1900, index to marriages from 1958; request marriage certificates from Clerk of the Court in the county where marriage took place)

Iowa Department of Public Health
Vital Records Bureau
Lucas State Office Building, 321 East 12th Street
Des Moines, IA 50319-0075
(515) 281-4944 (credit card orders, 7:00–4:45); (515) 281-4956 (Supervisor)
webmaster@idph.state.ia.us
http://www.idph.state.ia.us/admin/vital_
records.asp
Pat McClure, Supervisor

7:00–5:00
(Records from 1880; registration was not made mandatory until 1921)

Kansas Department of Health and Environment
Curtis State Office Building
1000 S.W. Jackson, Suite 120
Topeka, KS 66612-2221
(785) 296-1400
http://www.ink.org/public/kdhe/ovs.html
Mon–Fri 9:00–4:00
$12.00 for five-year search and certified copy of births and deaths from 1 July 1911 and marriages and divorces from 1 May 1913 (if not an immediate family member, proof of direct interest is required by the OVS, but marriage and divorce records can be obtained from the county where the event occurred without restriction)

Commonwealth of Kentucky Cabinet for Health Services
Vital Statistics Branch
275 East Main Street
Frankfort, KY 40621-0001
(502) 564-4212; (502) 227-0032 FAX
http://chs.state.ky.us/publichealth/vital.htm
Barbara F. White, State Registrar
Mon–Fri 8:00–4:30
(births and deaths from 1911, marriages and divorces from June 1958)
Births $10.00; deaths, marriages and divorces $6.00

Vital Records Registry (Louisiana)
(325 Loyola Avenue, Room 102, New Orleans, LA 70112—location)
PO Box 60630 (mailing address)
New Orleans, LA 70160-0630
(504) 568-5152; (800) 454-9570
Vitalweb@dhh.la.gov
http://www.oph.dhh.state.la.us/
recordsstatistics/vitalrecords
Lorraine A. Stuart, Archivist
Mon–Fri 8:00–4:00
(Holds one hundred years of birth records and fifty years of deaths and Orleans Parish marriages; records are confidential and require statement of relationship or a release.)
$9.00 for birth card, $15.00 for long form of births, $5.00 for deaths or Orleans marriages, $25.00 for adoption, correction or delay (only certified copies issued)

Maine Department of Human Services
Office of Vital Statistics
221 State Street
11 State House Station
Augusta, ME 04333-0011
(207) 287-3181; (207) 287-1093 FAX
http://www.state.me.us/dhs/vitalrecords.htm
Mon–Fri 8:00–5:00
(Vital records from "1923 to present. Records prior to 1923 are located at the Maine State Archives.")
$10.00 for a five-year search (two years before and two years before the year of the event. $10.00 for a certified copy, $6.00 for an uncertified copy. $9.95 for credit card orders placed through Vitalcheck Network using a credit card

State of Maryland Department of Health and Mental Hygiene
Division of Vital Records
6550 Reisterstown Road
Reisterstown Road Plaza

Baltimore, MD 21215
(410) 764-3038; (800) 832-3277
http://mdpublichealth.org/vsa/html/
apps.html
David L. Johnson, Deputy Chief
Mon–Fri & third Sat 8:00–4:00
(birth and marriage records are generally available only to the individual(s) named in the record, or to a person designated in writing as a representative of the individual(s) named; city births from 1875, county births from 1898, marriages from June 1951, divorces from July 1961, county deaths from 1911 to 1968, city deaths from 1950 to the present)

Registry Division (Massachusetts, City of Boston)
1 City Hall Plaza, Room 213
Boston, MA 02201
(617) 635-4175; (617) 635-3775 FAX
Registry@ci.boston.ma.us
http://www.cityofboston.gov/registry

Registry of Vital Records (Massachusetts)
Bureau of Health Statistics, Research and Evaluation
150 Mount Vernon Street, First Floor
Dorchester, MA 02125-3105
(617) 740-2600; (617) 740-2617 (Registrar)
vital.recordsrequest@state.ma.us
http://www.mass.gov/dph/bhsre/rvr/rvr.htm
Stanley E. Nyberg, Ph.D., Registrar
Mon–Fri 8:45–4:45
(records from 1901)

Michigan Department of Public Health
(3423 Martin Luther King Jr. Boulevard—location)
PO Box 30721 (mailing address)
Lansing, MI 48909
(517) 335-8666
http://www.michigan.gov/mdch
Mon–Fri 9:00–4:30
(Births and deaths from 1867, marriages from 1867)

Minnesota Department of Health
Center for Health Statistics
Office of the State Registrar
(717 Delaware Street, S.E.—location)
PO Box 9441 (mailing address)
Minneapolis, MN 55440-9441
(612) 676-5120; (612) 331-5776 FAX
Linda.Loftus@health.state.mn.us (withheld)
http://www.health.state.mn.us/divs/chs/osr/
index.html
("Death records may be searched by appointment. Birth and death certificates can be requested by FAX or by mail. Births from 1900 and deaths from 1908 for the entire state; marriages and divorces available only from the county of occurrence.")
search: $20.00 per hour, prorated; $13.00 for certified birth record, $10.00 for uncertified birth record or either certified or uncertified death record, $8.00 for verification of information

Mississippi State Department of Health
Public Health Statistics Division
(571 Stadium Drive—location)
PO Box 1700 (mailing address)
Jackson, MS 39215-1700
(601) 576-7960
http://www.msdh.state.ms.us/phs
(Births and deaths from 1912, marriages 1916–1938 and from 1942)
five-year search of records: $6.00, special search (genealogy): $20.00 per hour,

$10.00 minimum, certified birth record $12.00 (abstract $7.00), death and marriage records $10.00

Missouri Department of Health
Bureau of Vital Records
(Broadway State Office Building, 930 Wildwood, Jefferson City, MO 65101—location)
PO Box 570 (mailing address)
Jefferson City, MO 65102-0570
(573) 751-6400; (573) 526-3846 FAX
http://www.dhss.mo.gov/BirthAndDeath
    Records/BirthAndDeathRecords.html
Gary L. Shipley, Vital Records
    Administrator
Mon–Fri 8:00–5:00
(Births and deaths from 1910, plus index to marriages from 1948; request marriage records from Recorder of Deeds, County Courthouse or the county in which the marriage took place.)
no search without fees required by law: $10.00 for births or deaths since 1910 (includes five-year search and certificate) to Fee Receipts Unit

Missouri State Archives
(see Missouri, Part 2)

Office of Vital Statistics
Department of Public Health and Human Services
(11 North Sanders, Room 209—location)
PO Box 4210 (mailing address)
Helena, MT 59604
(406) 444-2685; (406) 444-1803 FAX
dphhstech@state.mt.us
http://vhsp.dphhs.state.mt.us/dph_12.htm
(birth and death certificates from late 1907; marriages from each county)

Nebraska Health and Human Services System
Vital Records
(301 Centennial Mall, South, Lincoln, NE 68508—location)
PO Box 95065 (mailing address)
Lincoln, NE 68509-5066
(402) 471-2872
http://www.hhs.state.ne.us/ced/bicert.htm
Mon–Fri 8:00–5:00
(births and deaths from 1904, marriages from 1909)
births $8.00 each; deaths, marriages and divorces $7.00 each

Nevada State Department of Human Resources
State Health Division
Bureau of Health Planning and Statistics
Office of Vital Records
505 East King Street, #102
Carson City, NV 89701-4749
(775) 684-4242; (775) 684-4156 FAX
vitalrecords@nvhd.state.nv.us
http://health2k.state.nv/vital
(Births and deaths from 1911)

New Hampshire Bureau of Vital Records
29 Hazen Drive
Concord, NH 03301-6527
(603) 271-4650
Stephen Wurtz, Supervisor Vital Records
Mon–Fri 8:30–4:00
("Births before 1901, deaths, marriages and divorces before 1948 are 'open nonrestricted' records. Others the requestor must have a 'direct and tangible interest.' Application can also be made to the town in which the event took place.")
$12.00 for certified copy (includes search), plus $8.00 for each additional copy ordered at the same time

New Jersey Department of Health and Senior Services
Office of Vital Statistics
(Warren and Market Streets—location)
PO Box 370 (mailing address)
Trenton, NJ 08625-0370
(609) 292-4087; (609) 777-1337 FAX
http://www.state.nj.us/health/vital/
    vital.shtml
Donald L. Lipira, State Registrar of Vital Statistics
8:30–5:00
$4.00 per record for search when the exact year is known (records from 1878)

New Mexico Department of Health
Bureau of Vital Records and Health Statistics
(1105 Saint Francis Drive—location)
PO Box 26110 (mailing address)
Santa Fe, NM 87502
(505) 827-0121
http://dohewbs2.health.state.nm.us/
    VitalRec/default.htm
Mon–Fri 8:30–4:00
Pub. *Selected Health Statistics*, annually
("New Mexico's records are restricted access." Births and deaths from 1920; request marriage records from County Clerk, County Courthouse of county where marriage took place)

Archives Division (New York City)
(see The City of New York Department of Records and Information Services, Municipal Archives—New York, City, County and Regional Archives and Libraries, Part 2)

New York City Department of Health
Office of Vital Records
125 Worth Street
New York, NY 100013-4090
(212) 788-4520; (212) 619-4530 (recorded message)
http://www.ci.nyc.ny.us/html/doh/html/vr/
    vr.html; http://www.vitalrec.com/ ny.html
(births from 1910, deaths from 1949 in Manhattan, Brooklyn, Bronx, Queens and Staten Island boroughs)
$15.00 for births and deaths

New York City
(see National Archives, Regional Records Services Facilities, New York City, Part 1)

City Clerk's Office
1780 Grand Concourse
Bronx, NY 10457
(Bronx Borough marriages from 1866 to 1907, and after 1907 if the borough was the bride's residence or if the license of nonresidents was obtained in the borough)
$10.00 each

City Clerk's Office
Municipal Building
Brooklyn, NY 11201
(Brooklyn Borough marriages from 1866 to 1907, and after 1907 if the borough was the bride's residence or if the license of nonresidents was obtained in the borough)
$10.00 each

City Clerk's Office
Municipal Building
New York, NY 10007
(Manhattan Borough marriages from 1866 to 1907, and after 1907 if the borough was the bride's residence or if the license of nonresidents was obtained in the borough)
$10.00 each

City Clerk's Office
120-55 Queens Boulevard
Kew Gardens, NY 11424
(Queens Borough marriages from 1866 to 1907, and after 1907 if the borough was the bride's residence or if the license of nonresidents was obtained in the borough)
$10.00 each

City Clerk's Office
Staten Island Borough Hall
Staten Island, NY 10301
(Staten Island Borough [no longer called Richmond Borough] marriages from 1866 to 1907, and after 1907 if the borough was the bride's residence or if the license of nonresidents was obtained in the borough)
$10.00 each

New York State Department of Health
Vital Records Section
(800 North Pearl Street, Menands, NY 12204—location)
PO Box 2602 (mailing address)
Albany, NY 12220-2602
(518) 474-3077; (518) 486-1863
nyhealth@health.state.ny.us
http://www.health.state.ny.us/nysdoh/
    consumer/vr.htm
L. Julien Rivers, Genealogy Unit, Vital Records Section
(vital records for New York State, exclusive of New York City; births 1881–1922, marriages 1881–1947, deaths 1881–1947, otherwise applicant must be a direct descendant of the person named in the record; processing time is six months for genealogy requests, but may be obtained more rapidly from the local registrar/clerk of the district where the event occurred)
$30.00 for certified copies, $22.00 for a three-year search (includes an uncertified copy, if found), $42.00 for a four- to ten-year search, and $20.00 for each additional decade searched

North Carolina Department of Health and Human Services
Vital Records Unit
(225 North McDowell Street, Raleigh, NC 27603-1382—location)
1903 Mail Service Center (mailing address)
Raleigh, NC 27699-1903
(919) 733-1511; (800) 669-8310 (automated order service); (919) 733-3526
http://vitalrecords.dhhs.state.nc.us
Glenn Cutler, State Registrar and Director of Vital Records
Mon–Fri 8:00–4:00
(births from 1913, marriages from 1962, deaths from 1930 and divorces from 1958)
$15.00 per request, $5.00 for additional copies of the same certificate

North Dakota Department of Health
Division of Vital Records
State Capitol
600 East Boulevard Avenue

Bismarck, ND 58505-0200
(701) 328-2360; (701) 328-1850 FAX
http://www.vitalnd.com
Mon–Fri 7:30–5:00
(Births and deaths from 1893, marriages
from 1925)

Ohio Department of Health/Vital Statistics
(246 North High Street, First Floor Revenue
Room—location)
PO Box 15098 (mailing address)
Columbus, OH 43215-0098
(614) 466-2531
WebMaster@gw.odh.state.oh.us
(Webmaster)
http://www.odh.state.oh.us
Herman C. Butler, State Registrar; J. Nick
Baird, M.D., Director
Mon–Fri 7:45–4:30
("Birth records 20 December 1908 to
present, whole state. Death records
January 1945 to present, whole state";
county health departments also issue
certified birth and death records)
uncertified copies 5¢ each plus postage,
certified $15.00 each

Oklahoma Department of Health
Bureau of Vital Records
(1000 N.E. 10th Street, Oklahoma City, OK
73117—location)
PO Box 53551 (mailing address)
Oklahoma City, OK 73152-3551
(405) 271-4040
http://www.health.state.ok.us/program/
vital/brec.html
Mon–Fri 8:30–4:00 (8:00–4:30 for phone
service)
(Births and deaths from 1908; request
marriage records from County Clerk,
County courthouse of the county where
the marriage took place.)

Oregon Vital Records
(800 N.E. Oregon Street, Suite 205, #23,
Portland, OR 97232—location)
PO Box 14050 (mailing address)
Portland, OR 97293-0050
(503) 731-4095 (recorded message); (503)
731-4108 (operator); (503) 731-8417
FAX
http://www.healthoregon.org
Mon–Fri 8:00–4:30
$15.00 (payable to DHS/Vital Records) for
certified copies of births (available to
immediate family, including
grandchildren), deaths or marriages,
includes a five-year search, additional
search for $1.00 per year, noncertified
copies available for births over 100 years
old or deaths over 50 years old

Pennsylvania Department of Health
Division of Vital Records
(101 South Mercer Street—location)
PO Box 1528 (mailing address)
New Castle, PA 16101
(724) 656-3100
http://www.health.state.pa.us/vitalrecords
8:00–4:30
(birth and death records from 1906; request
marriage records from County Clerk at the
County Courthouse of the county in
which the marriage took place)
births: $20.00 plus SASE, deaths: $9.00 plus
SASE

Division of Vital Records (Pennsylvania)
1910 West 26th Street
Erie, PA 16508-1148

(birth and death records from 1906; request
marriage records from County Clerk at the
County Courthouse)
births: $20.00 plus SASE, deaths: $9.00 plus
SASE

Division of Vital Records (Pennsylvania)
Room 129, Health and Welfare Building
Harrisburg, PA 17120-0012
(717) 772-3480
(birth and death records from 1906; request
marriage records from County Clerk at the
County Courthouse)
births: $20.00 plus SASE, deaths: $9.00 plus
SASE

Division of Vital Records (Pennsylvania)
1400 West Spring Garden Street, Room
1009
Philadelphia, PA 19130-4090
(215) 560-3054
(birth and death records from 1906; request
marriage records from County Clerk at the
County Courthouse)
births: $20.00 plus SASE, deaths: $9.00 plus
SASE

Division of Vital Records (Pennsylvania)
300 Liberty Avenue, Room 512
Pittsburgh, PA 15222-1210
(412) 565-5113
(birth and death records from 1906; request
marriage records from County Clerk at the
County Courthouse)
births: $20.00 plus SASE, deaths: $9.00 plus
SASE

Division of Vital Records (Pennsylvania)
100 Lackawanna Avenue
Scranton, PA 18503-1928
(570) 963-4595
(birth and death records from 1906; request
marriage records from County Clerk at the
County Courthouse)
births: $20.00 plus SASE, deaths: $9.00 plus
SASE

State of Rhode Island and Providence Plantations Department of Health
Division of Vital Records
Cannon Building
3 Capitol Hill, Room 101
Providence, RI 02908-5097
(401) 222-2811 (recorded message); (401)
277-2812
findit@mail.state.ri.us
http://www.healthri.org/management/vital/
home.htm
Roberta A. Chevoya, State Registrar, Vital
Records
Mon–Fri 8:30–4:00 (for in-person
application for certified copies)
(births and marriages from 1895, deaths from
1945; may also be obtained from
the town in which the event occurred)
$15.00 for two-year search and one certified
copy (if found), 50¢ for each additional
year searched, $10.00 for each additional
certified copy ordered at the same time,
payable to General Treasurer, State of
Rhode Island

South Carolina Department of Health and Environmental Control
Division of Vital Records
2600 Bull Street
Columbia, SC 29201-1797
(803) 898-3630; (877) 284-1008 (expedited
service, credit cards only); (803) 898-
3761 FAX
goodinj@dhec.sc.gov

http://www.scdhec.net/vr
JoAnn Gooding, Director of Vital Records
8:30–4:30
(Births and deaths from 1915, marriages
from 1950)

South Dakota Department of Health
600 East Capitol
Pierre, SD 57501-2536
(605) 773-4961; (605) 773-5683 FAX
http://www.state.sd.us/doh/VitalRec/
Vital.htm
search for birth, death, marriage, or divorce
record (from 1905): $10.00 (includes
certified copy, if found)

Tennessee Vital Records
Central Services Building, First Floor
421 Fifth Avenue North
Nashville, TN 37247-0450
(615) 741-1763; (615) 741-9860; (615) 741-
0778 (Orders); (615) 726-2559 FAX
(Orders)
http://www2.state.tn.us/health/vr/index.htm
Mon–Fri 8:00–4:00
(marriage, divorce and death records from
1914 to fifty years from the present, and
birth records from 1914)
$12.00 for certified birth, marriage and
divorce certificates, $7.00 for certified
death certificate, $12.00 for verification
of information on certificate, which is
public information and available to
anyone

Texas Department of Health
Bureau of Vital Statistics
(1100 West 49th Street, Austin, TX
78756—location)
PO Box 12040 (mailing address)
Austin, TX 78711-2040
(512) 458-7111 (for fee verification only);
(512) 458-4751
register@tdh.state.tx.us
http://www.tdh.state.tx.us/bvs/t_bvs.htm
Mon–Fri 8:00–5:00
(For birth records less than fifty years old or
death records less than twenty-five years
old, "If the requester is not an immediate
family member or properly qualified
applicant, an authorization from the
registrant or an immediate family member
must also be enclosed." Indexes to deaths
1903–1976, and delayed birth indexes
may be borrowed through interlibrary loan
from the Texas State Library, and the
library will consult the index of births for
a fee.)

Utah Department of Health
Office of Vital Records and Statistics
(288 North 1460 West, Salt Lake City, UT
84145-0500—location)
PO Box 14102 (mailing address)
Salt Lake City, UT 84114-1012
(801) 538-6105
vrequest@utah.gov
http://health.utah.gov/vitalrecords
Mon–Fri 8:00–5:00
(Births and deaths from 1905; request
marriage records from County Clerk,
County Courthouse of the county in
which the marriage took place.)

Vermont Department of Health
Vital Records Unit
(108 Cherry Street—location)
PO Box 70 (mailing address)
Burlington, VT 05402-0070
(802) 863-7275
Webkeeper@vdh.state.vt.us

http://www.healthyvermonters.info/hs/
vital/vitalhome.shtml
7:45–4:15
("Latest 5 years kept here.")
$7.00 per certified copy

Vermont General Services Department
Public Records Division
(U.S. Route 2, Middlesex—location)
PO Drawer 33 (mailing address)
Montpelier, VT 05633-7601
(802) 828-3286 (Reference); (802) 828-2794
    (Public Records); (802) 828-3288; (802)
    828-3710 FAX
http://www.bgs.state.vt.us/gsc/pubrec/
    referen/index.html
Angela Hallock, Records Research
    Specialist
Mon–Fri 8:00–4:00
(records more than ten years old)
search: $3.00; certified copies: $9.50

Virginia Department of Health
Office of Vital Records
(1601 Willow Lawn Drive, Suite 275,
Richmond, VA 23220—location)
PO Box 1000 (mailing address)
Richmond, VA 23218-1000
(804) 662-6200
http://www.vdh.state.va.us/vitalrec/
    index.asp
Mon–Fri 8:30–4:45
(Records from 1853; births and deaths were
    not routinely filed 1896–1912.)

**Washington Department of Health/Center
for Health Statistics**
(101 Israel Road S.E., Tumwater,
WA—location)
PO Box 9709 (mailing address)
Olympia, WA 98507-9709
(360) 236-4300 (Main number); (360) 236-
    4313 (Credit Card Orders)
http://www.doh.wa.gov/Topics/chs-cert.html
Wendy Kinswa, Manager, Customer Services
8:00–4:30
(Births and deaths from 1907, marriages
    from 1968)
search fee: $17.00 for ten-year span (includes
    copy of record if found) for death,
    marriage or divorce records; must have
    exact information for a birth

Vital Registration Office (West Virginia)
350 Capitol Street, Room 165
Charleston, WV 25301-3701
(304) 558-2931; (304) 558-1051 FAX
http://www.wvdhhr.org/bph/oehp/hsc/vr/
    birtcert.htm
8:30–5:00
(births and deaths from 1917, marriages from
    1964)
$5.00 per year search

**State of Wisconsin Department of Health
and Family Services**
Division of Health
(1 West Wilson Street, Room 158, Madison,
WI 53702—location)
PO Box 309 (mailing address)
Madison, WI 53701-0309
(608) 266-1371 (recording); (608) 266-1372
http://www.dhfs.state.wi.us/VitalRecords/
    index.htm
Mon–Fri 8:00–4:15
(Records from 1814, but incomplete before
    1907)

Wyoming State Vital Records Services
Hathaway Building

Cheyenne, WY 82002
(307) 777-7591; (307) 635-4103 FAX
http://wdhfs.state.wy.us/vital_records/
    certificate.htm
(Births and deaths from July 1909, marriages
    from 1941)
births and marriages: $12.00 each, deaths
    $9.00 each

Libraries and Archives
(National Focus)

Allen County Public Library
(see Indiana, Part 2)

Arizona State University
(see Arizona, Part 2)

**The Burdick International Ancestry
Library**
(see Florida, Part 2)

**Public Library of Cincinnati and Hamilton
County**
(see Ohio, Part 2)

**Clayton Library, Center for Genealogical
Research**
(see Texas, Part 2)

Clements Library Associates
(see Michigan, Part 2)

Cleveland Public Library
(see Ohio, Part 2)

College of William and Mary
Omohundro Institute of Early American
History and Culture
Earl Gregg Swem Library Building
(see Virginia, Part 2)

Dallas Public Library, Genealogy Section
J. Erik Jonsson Branch
(see Texas, Part 2)

**National Society, Daughters of the
American Revolution (D.A.R.)**
Library
(see Lineage, Hereditary and Patriotic
Societies—Revolutionary War, Part 4)

Denver Public Library
(see Colorado, Part 2)

Detroit Public Library
Burton Historical Collection
(see Michigan, Part 2)

**Family History Library of The Church of
Jesus Christ of Latter-day Saints**
(see Utah, Part 2)

Genealogical Center Library
(see Georgia, Part 2)

**Heritage Quest Research Library and
Bookstore**
(see Washington, Part 2)

Laramie County Library System
(see Wyoming, Part 2)

Library of Congress
(see District of Columbia, Part 2)

Los Angeles Public Library
(see California, Part 2)

Mid-Continent Public Library
(see Missouri, Part 2)·

National Genealogical Society (NGS)
(see Virginia, Part 2)

**The New England Historic Genealogical
Society (NEHGS)**
(see Massachusetts, Part 2)

New York Genealogical and Biographical Society Library
(see New York, Part 2)

The New York Public Library
The Irma and Paul Milstein Division of United States History, Local History and Genealogy
(see New York, Part 2)

Newberry Library
(see Illinois, Part 2)

Saint Louis Public Library
History and Genealogy Department
(see Missouri, Part 2)

Seattle Public Library
(see Washington, Part 2)

Genealogical Research Center and Library of Southeast Texas
(see Texas, Part 2)

Steward University System Library
(see Alabama, Part 2)

Sutro Library
(see California, Part 2)

Tree Trackers Library
(see Missouri, Part 2)

The University of Texas at Austin
Eugene C. Barker Texas History Center
The Center for American History
(see Texas, Part 2)

Wisconsin Historical Society
(see Wisconsin, Part 2)

Historical Societies
(National Focus)

American Antiquarian Society
(see Massachusetts, Part 2)

College of William and Mary
Omohundro Institute of Early American History and Culture
Earl Gregg Swem Library Building
(see Virginia, Part 2)

National Historical Society
(see Cowles Magazines, Independent Publications)

The New England Historic Genealogical Society (NEHGS)
(see Massachusetts, Part 2)

New York Genealogical and Biographical Society Library
(see New York, Part 2)

Smithsonian Institution
(see District of Columbia, Part 2)

The Urban History Association
(see Illinois, Part 2)

The Western Reserve Historical Society Library
Case Western Reserve University
(see Ohio, Part 2)

Genealogical Societies
(National Focus)

American Genealogical Society
(see Samford University, American Genealogical Society Depository and Headquarters, Alabama, Part 2)

National Society, Daughters of the American Revolution (D.A.R.)
(see Lineage, Hereditary and Patriotic Societies—Revolutionary War, Part 4)

Federation of Genealogical Societies
FGS Business Office
PO Box 200940
Austin, TX 78720-0940
(512) 336-2731; (512) 336-2732; (888) FGS-1500; (708) 467-0142 FAX (Editorial Office); (888) 380-0500 FAX
fgs-office@fgs.org
http://www.fgs.org
Dean J. Hunter, President; Sandra Hargreaves Luebking, Editor
Mon–Fri
Pub. *The FGS Forum*, quarterly, $15.00 per year members subscription, $18.00 per year nonmember subscription
membership for organizations or institutions based on the number of members in the organization: $25.00 per year for 0-50 members or associate organizations (includes two complimentary issues of *FGS Forum*); items for inclusion in the *FGS Forum* should be sent to the Editorial Office, PO Box 271, Western Springs, IL 60558-0271

Genealogical Association of English Speaking Researchers in Europe
(address withheld upon request)
Pub. *Family Finder*, monthly

National Genealogical Society (NGS)
3108 Columbia Pike, Suite 300
Arlington, VA 22204-4304
(703) 525-0050, ext. 225; (800) 473-0060; (703) 5841-9065 (Library); (703) 525-0052 FAX
ngs@ngsgenealogy.org
http://www.ngsgenealogy.org
Francis J. Shane, Executive Director
Library: Mon & Wed 10:00–9:00, Fri–Sat 10:00–4:00; Offices: daily 9:00–5:00
Pub. *NGS Quarterly*; *NGS Newsletter*, bimonthly; *NGS/CIG Digest*, bimonthly (extensive family files and Bible records collection)
$40.00 per year membership

National Genealogical Society (NGS)
(see Virginia, Part 2)

National Institute on Genealogical Research
(see Professional Bodies, Part 4)

The New England Historic Genealogical Society (NEHGS)
(see Massachusetts, Part 2)

New York Genealogical and Biographical Society Library
(see New York, Part 2)

Independent Publications
(Unrelated to a Geographic Region)

Aceto Bookmen
5721 Antietam Drive
Sarasota FL 34231-4903
(941) 924-9170
Charles Delmar Townsend, Owner
by appointment
Pub. *Chips from Many Trees and Growing Roots*, four times per year, $20.00 per year subscription
(genealogy and local history)

The American Genealogist (TAG)
PO Box 398
Demorest, GA 30535
(706) 865-6440 voice & FAX
amgen@alltel.net
http://www.americangenealogist.com
David L. Greene, Co-editor and Publisher
Pub. *The American Genealogist (TAG)*, quarterly, $30.00 per year subscription
(Colonial U.S.; "We focus on critical problem-solving articles and short compiled genealogies.")

Ancestry, Inc.
Ancestry
(see Publishers, Part 4)

AntiqueWeek
(see Antiquarian Book Dealers, Part 4)

Armchair Publications
Armchair Researcher
(see Georgia, Part 2)

Cemetery Q & A's
PO Box 8003
Janesville, WI 53547-8003
Peggy Rockwell Gleich, Editor
Pub. *Cemetery Q & A's (Queries & Anecdotes)*, four times per year, (Mar, June, Sept, Dec), $20.00 per year subscription
(regarding cemeteries anywhere in the world, tips on copying, cleaning, gravestone rubbings, special columns by well-known cemetery enthusiasts, etc.)
queries free to subscribers

Claudette's
Current Genealogical Publications
(see Vermont, Part 2)

Cowles Magazines
6405 Flank Drive
Harrisburg, PA 17105
(717) 657-9555
Ed Holm, Editor
Pub. *American History Illustrated*, bimonthly, $20.00 per year subscription

F&W Publications, Inc.
4700 East Galbraith Road
Cincinnati, OH 45236
(888) 419-0421 (Customer Service)
ftmedit@fwpubs.com (freelance queries); ftmletters@fwpubs.com (feedback); genealogy-newsletter@fwpubs.com (newsletter); datac@fwpubs.com (order)
http://www.familytreemagazine.com
Pub. *Family Tree Magazine*, bimonthly, $19.96 per year subscription

Family History Network
Everton's Family History Magazine
(see Publishers, Part 4)

The Genealogical Institute, Inc.
d.b.a. Family History World
(56 West Main Street, Tremonton—research library location)
PO Box 129 (mailing address)
Tremonton, UT 84337-0129
(800) 377-6058; (888) 405-1105; (435) 257-8622 FAX
genealogy@utahlinx.com
http://www.genealogysearchonline.com
Arlene H. Eakle; JoAnn Jackson, Office Manager
Mon–Fri 10:00–4:00
Pub. *Research News*, monthly, $3.00 per issue plus postage and handling, Vol. I (1982–1997) and Vol. II (1998–2001), $25.00 per volume; *Immigration Digest* (sources and strategies to link American immigrants to places of origin in the British Isles and Europe), occasionally, $16.00 per issue plus postage and handling
(publishes resource and how-to books, especially on Virginia, New York, Kentucky, southern research, immigration and Native Americans)

Genealogical Queries Magazine
169 Melody Lane
Tonawanda, NY 14150
Robert J. Wilson, Editor
Pub. *Genealogical Queries Magazine*

Genealogical Research Directory
xguyot@attglobal.net
http://membres.geneaguide.com/grd (in French)
Xavier Guyot, Agent
Pub. *Genealogical Research Directory*, annually, $29.75 postpaid for current year
(150,000 surname entries worldwide with names and addresses of worldwide listing of libraries, archives, and genealogical societies)

Genealogy Times Newsletter
PO Box 911
New Providence, NJ 07974
(908) 963-1277
webmaster@genealogytimes.com
http://genealogytimes.com
Illya D'Addezio
Mon–Fri 10:00–6:00
Pub. *Genealogy Times Newsletter*, free
(covers a single research topic in each issue)

Heritage Creations
425 North 400 West, Suite 1A
North Salt Lake, UT 84054
(801) 677-0048; (866) 783-7899; (801) 677-0049 FAX
sales@heritagecreations.com
http://www.heritagecreations.com
Leland K. Meitzler, CEO
daily 8:00–5:00
Pub. *Heritage Quest Magazine*, bimonthly, $28.00 per year subscription (genealogical articles and columns; queries; advertising); *Genealogy Bulletin*, bimonthly, $18.00 per year subscription (genealogical articles and columns; queries; advertising)

Journal of the West, Inc.
(1531 Yuma—location)
PO Box 1009 (mailing address)
Manhattan, KS 66505-1009
(785) 539-1888; (785) 539-2233 FAX
pub@sunflower-univ-press.org
http://www.sunflower-univ-press.org

Angela L. Dawdy, Director of Operations
Mon–Fri 9:00–5:00
Pub. *Journal of the West*, quarterly, $45.00 per year subscription

Lost and Found National Genealogical Query Newsletter
PO Box 207
Wathena, KS 66090
(785) 989-3117
Ethel M. Weber, Publisher/Editor
Pub. *Lost and Found National Genealogical Query Newsletter*, bimonthly, $15.00 per year subscription
(U.S. and Canada)

National Council on Public History
327 Cavanaugh Hall
Indiana University Purdue University
425 University Boulevard
Indianapolis, IN 46202-5140
(317) 274-2716; (317) 278-5230 FAX
ncph@iupui.edu
David G. Vanderstel, Ph.D., Director
Pub. *The Public Historian*, quarterly; *Public History News*, quarterly
(Historic preservation, oral history; museums, archives, historical societies. "Although the organization is geared towards professional historians, we invite any and all people who are interested in public history to become members and to assist us in our efforts to make history understood and more appreciated among the larger public.")
$60.00 per year membership

Petunia Press
1602 Belle View Boulevard #545
Alexandria, VA 22307-6531
juliecase@prodigy.net
http://www.petuniapress.com
Julia M. Case
Pub. *Missing Links: A Magazine for Genealogists*; *Somebody's Links: Genealogical Treasures Found*

Reunions Magazine
PO Box 11727
Milwaukee, WI 53211-0727
(414) 263-4567; (414) 263-6331 FAX
reunions@execpc.com
http://www.reunionsmag.com
Edith Wagner, Editor; Jeffrey P. Wallman, Publisher
Mon–Fri 9:00–5:00
Pub. *Reunions Magazine* (reunions—family, class, military—genealogy and others), bimonthly (June/July, Aug/Sept, Oct/Nov, Dec/Jan, Feb/Mar, Apr/May), $9.99 per year subscription

Society for Historians of the Early American Republic
University of Pennsylvania Press
4200 Pine Street
Philadelphia, PA 19104
http://jer.pennpress.org
John L. Larson and Michael Morrison, Editors
Pub. *Journal of the Early Republic*, quarterly
(history and culture 1789–1850)
$15.00–$30.00 per year membership

Part 2. State Addresses

Alabama

Archives and Libraries with Holdings in Genealogy

State Archives and Library

Alabama Department of Archives and History
624 Washington Avenue
Montgomery, AL 36130-0100
(334) 242-4435 (Reference Room); (334) 242-4441 (Newspaper Program); (334) 242-4452 voice & FAX (Government Records Division); (334) 242-4452 FAX
Debbie.Pendleton@archives.alabama.gov
http://www.archives.state.al.us
Tue–Fri 8:30–4:30, one Sat each month
research: $25.00 for out-of-state mail requests

State Historical Society

Alabama Historical Association
c/o Alabama Department of Archives and History
624 Washington Avenue
Montgomery, AL 36130-0100
dpendlet@archives.state.al.us
http://www.archives.state.al.us/aha/aha.html
Debbie Pendleton, Alabama Department of Archives and History, Membership Secretary
Pub. *The Alabama Review: A Quarterly Journal of Alabama History*, quarterly (Jan, Apr, July, Oct), $20.00 per year subscription for nonmembers; *Newsletter* $25.00 per year membership; research: no research staff, facilities, archives library, or resources for genealogical research

City, County and Regional Archives and Libraries
(A more exhaustive list of public and academic libraries can be found at http://www.apls.state.al.us/webpages/resources/publiclibraries.html.)

Abbeville Memorial Library
History Room
301 Kirkland Street
Abbeville, AL 36310-2419
(334) 585-2818 voice & FAX
abbmem@snowhill.com
Linda Floyd, Director
Mon–Fri 9:00–5:00, Sat 9:00–noon

Aliceville Public Library
416 Third Avenue, NE
Aliceville, AL 35442-2207
(205) 373-6691 vice and FAX
apl@pickens.net
http://www.pickens.net/~apl
Nelda Hudgins

Andalusia Public Library
212 South Three Notch Street
Andalusia, AL 36420-3799
(334) 222-6782; (334) 222-6612 FAX
andylib@alaweb.com
http://www.andylibrary.com
Karin Taylor, Director; Linda Davis, Genealogy Librarian
Mon–Fri 8:00–5:00, Sat 8:00–noon
("Extensive local information—Echos and Visions, local recording of information or VHS and audio of interesting things in Covington County.")
$2.00 charge for requested searches and limited copying

Ashville Museum and Archives
(Saint Clair County Courthouse, Sixth Avenue, Room 104—location)
PO Box 1570 (mailing address)
Ashville, AL 35953
(205) 594-2128
Charlene Simpson, Archivist
Mon–Fri 8:00–noon & 1:00–5:00

Auburn University
Special Collections and Archives
Ralph Brown Draughon Library
231 Mell Street
Auburn, AL 36849-5606
(334) 844-1732 (Reference); (334) 844-1707 (Head); (334) 844-4424 FAX
coxdway@auburn.edu
http://www.lib.auburn.edu/sca
Dwayne Cox, Head of Special Collections and Archives
Mon–Thur 7:45 A.M.–9:00 P.M., Fri 7:45–6:00, Sat 9:00–6:00, Sun 1:00–9:00 (materials for use on evenings and weekends must be requested prior to 4:00 Mon–Fri)

Birmingham Public Library
Tutwiler Collection of Southern History and Literature
2100 Park Place
Birmingham, AL 35203-2794
(205) 226-3665; (205) 226-3663; (205) 226-3743 FAX
sou@bham.lib.al.us
http://www.bplonline.org
Anne F. Knight, Coordinator for Research Services
Mon–Tue 9:00–8:00, Wed–Sat 9:00–6:00, Sun 2:00–6:00
(includes Alabama, Florida, Georgia, Mississippi, Tennessee)

H. Grady Bradshaw-Chambers County Library and Cobb Memorial Archives
3419 20th Avenue
Valley, AL 36854-3299
(334) 768-2161; (334) 768-7272 FAX
Miriam Ann K. Syler, Archivist Assistant to Director
Mon–Fri 10:00–6:00, Sat 10:00–5:00

Brent-Centreville Public Library
153 Walnut Street
Centreville, AL 35042-1322
(205) 926-4736 voice & FAX
bcpl@dbtech.net
Flo Franklin, Librarian
Mon 9:00–8:00, Tue–Fri 9:00–5:00, Sat 9:00–noon
(genealogy section, microfilm of early county records, newspapers, census)

Carrollton Public Library
(225 Commerce Avenue—location)
PO Box 92 (mailing address)
Carrollton, AL 35447-0092
(205) 367-2142 voice & FAX
cpl@pickens.net
http://www.pickens.net/~cpl
Sue Yarbrough

Chattahoochee Valley Community College
Learning Resources Center
2606 Savage Drive
Phenix City, AL 36867
(334) 291-4979
Cathy Woolbright, Director, Learning Resources Center
Mon–Thur 8:00–9:00, Fri 8:00–5:00, Sun (except summer) 2:00–6:00
("self-directed research only; a research assistant is not available at this time")

Cullman County Public Library System
200 Clark Street, N.E.
Cullman, AL 35055-2997
(256) 734-1068; (256) 734-6902 FAX
myrickj@ccpls.com
http://www.ccpls.com
John Paul Myrick

The Carl Elliott Regional Library
Genealogy Department
98 East 18th Street East
Jasper, AL 35501-5491
(205) 221-2568; (205) 221-2584 FAX

Escambia County Library
700 East Church Street
Atmore, AL 36502-2694
(251) 368-4130 voice & FAX
escolib@frontiernet.net
Patricia Hetzel

Evergreen Conecuh Public Library
201 Park Street
Evergreen, AL 36401-2903
(251) 578-2670; (251) 578-2316 FAX
Vern Steenwyk

Fayette County Memorial Library
326 Temple Avenue North
Fayette, AL 35555-2383
(205) 932-6625; (205) 932-4152 FAX
Gwendolyn Lacey, Director
Mon–Tue & Thur 9:00–6:00, Fri 9:00–5:00, Sat 9:00–1:00

Florence-Lauderdale Public Library
Genealogy-Local History Room
350 North Wood Avenue
Florence, AL 35630-4707
(256) 764-6564; (256) 764-6629 FAX
library@florence.org
http://www.library-florence.org
Lee Freeman, Local History/Genealogy Librarian
Mon–Fri 9:00–8:00, Sat 9:00–5:00, Sun 1:00–5:00
(northwest Alabama)
costs for copies and extensive searches

Foley Public Library
319 East Laurel Avenue
Foley, AL 36535-2680
(251) 943-7665; (251) 943-8637 FAX
fpllib@hotmail.com
http://www.gulftel.com/bclc/bclibraries/foley.html
Jeanette Bornholt, Library Aide and Genealogical Society Member
Mon & Wed 9:00–9:00, Tue & Thur 1:00–9:00, Fri–Sat 9:00–6:00

Gadsden-Etowah County Public Library
254 College Street
Gadsden, AL 35901-4135

(256) 549-4699, ext. 30 (Genealogy); (256)
   549-4699, ext. 29 (Reference); (256) 549-
   4766 FAX
gpl@gadsden.com
http://www.library.gadsden.com
Barbara Reed, Reference Librarian
Mon–Thur 8:00–8:00, Fri–Sat 9:00–5:00,
   Sun 1:00–5:00; summer: Mon–Thur
   8:00–7:00

Gordo Public Library
(Main Street—location)
PO Box 336 (mailing address)
Gordo, AL 35466-0336
(205) 364-7148 voice & FAX
gordolib@pickens.net
Melba Hollingsworth

Hacksma House Genealogy Library
(see Washington, Part 2)

Heritage Hall
PO Box 1118
Talladega, AL 35160
Mary Nelson

Historic Mobile Preservation Society, Inc.
300 Oakleigh Place
Mobile, AL 36604
(334) 432-6161
Carole M. Perez, Executive Director
(2,000 books in Archives)

Horseshoe Bend Regional Library
207 North West Street
Dadeville, AL 36853-1355
(256) 825-9232; (256) 825-4314 FAX
hbrl@mindspring.com
http://www.mindspring.com/~hbrl/hbrl.html
Susie R. Anderson, Director

Houston-Love Memorial Library
(212 West Burdeshaw Street, Dothan, AL
   36302—location)
PO Box 1369 (mailing address)
Dothan, AL 36303-1369
(334) 793-9767; (334) 793-6645 FAX
blforbus@yahoo.com
http://www.houstonlovelibrary.org
Susan Veasey, Reference Librarian; Bettye
   Forbus
Mon–Thur 9:00–9:00, Fri 9:00–6:00, Sat
   9:00–5:00, Sun 1:00–5:00
("southern states genealogical holdings;
   family history")
15¢ per photocopy, minimum $3.00 prepaid

**Huntsville-Madison County Public
Library**
Huntsville Heritage Room
(915 Monroe Street, S.W., Huntsville, AL
   35801-5007—location)
PO Box 443 (mailing address)
Huntsville, AL 35804
(256) 532-5969; (256) 532-5997 FAX
dterry@hpl.lib.al.us
http://www.hpl.lib.al.us
Annewhite T. Fuller, Department Head,
   Heritage Room
Mon–Thur 9:00–9:00, Fri–Sat 9:00–5:00,
   Sun 1:00–5:00
(library deals with eastern U.S., especially
   the southeast: Alabama, Arkansas,
   Florida, Georgia, Kentucky, Louisiana,
   Maryland, Mississippi, North Carolina,
   South Carolina, Tennessee, Virginia;
   archives deals with northern Alabama and
   the Civil War)
copies: $3.00 minimum; list of local
   researchers available

Interstate Library Contract

6030 Monticello Drive
Montgomery, AL 36130
(334) 213-3900

Jackson George Regional Library System
(see Mississippi, Part 2)

Landmarks of DeKalb County, Inc.
Landmarks of DeKalb Museum, Inc.
(500 Gault Avenue, North—location)
PO Box 518 (mailing address)
Fort Payne, AL 35967
Walter Weatherly, President
Pub. *Landmarks Bulletin*, biannually
   (genealogical services)
$10.00 per year membership

Liles Memorial Library
Public Library of Anniston-Calhoun County
Alabama Room
(108 East 10th Street—location)
PO Box 308 (mailing address)
Anniston, AL 36202-0308
(256) 237-8501; (256) 237-8503 FAX
alroom@anniston.lib.al.us;
   reference@anniston.lib.al.us
http://www.anniston.lib.al.us/index.htm
Thomas B. Mullins
Mon–Fri 9:00–6:300, Sat noon–4:00, Sun
   1:00–5:00

Limestone County Archives
310 West Washington Street
Athens, AL 35611
(256) 233-6404
preyer@pclcable.com
Philip Reyer, Archivist
Mon–Fri 8:00–4:30
("publish census records, indexes and
   abstracts")

Museums of the City of Mobile
PO Box 2068
Mobile, AL 36652-2068
(334) 434-7569
Charles Torrey, Museum Researcher
Research: Mon–Fri 9:00–5:00; Three
   museums: Tue–Sat 9:00–5:00, Sun
   1:00–5:00
free admission

Mobile Public Library
Local History and Genealogy
704 Government Street
Mobile, AL 36602-1402
(334) 434-7093
mobilepl@acan.net
http://www.mplonline.org
George H. Ewert, Manager
Mon–Sat 9:00–6:00

Monroe County Heritage Museums
(Old Monroe County Courthouse—location)
PO Box 1637 (mailing address)
Monroeville, AL 36461-1637
(251) 575-7433; (251) 575-2513 FAX
Dawn Crook, Assistant Director
Mon–Fri 8:00–noon & 1:00–4:00, Sat
   10:00–2:00
Pub. *Legacy*, biannually, $20.00 per year
   subscription
$35.00 per year museum membership

Montgomery County Archives
PO Box 223
Montgomery, AL 36101-0223
(334) 832-1238

Morgan County Archives
624 Bank Street
Decatur, AL 35601
(256) 351-4726

Ohoopee Regional Library
(see Georgia, Part 2)

Old Cahawba Historic Site
A division of the Alabama Historical
   Commission
9518 Canaba Road
Orrville, AL 36767
(334) 872-8058 (Park); (334) 877-4253 FAX
http://www.cahawba.org
Linda Derry, Site Archaeologist
Park: Mon–Sun 9:00–5:00; genealogical
   research: by appointment only
Pub. *Old Cahawba Newsletter*, irregularly
   ("We only maintain files on historic families
   and soldiers connected to Cahawba [also
   spelled Cahaba]. We can't help with
   general research in Dallas County."
   Alabama's first state capital 1820–1826,
   Dallas County seat 1819–1866, Civil War
   prison)
$10.00 per year membership; free search of
   Cahawba family files

Pickens County Cooperative Library
(Post Office Building, Highway 17
   South—location)
PO Box 489 (mailing address)
Carrollton, AL 35447-0489
(205) 367-8407 voice & FAX
pccl@pickens.net
Susan Wolfe

Reform Public Library
(216 First Street South—location)
PO Box 819 (mailing address)
Reform, AL 35481-0819
(205) 375-6240 voice & FAX
rlibrary@pickens.net
Virginia Barton

Samford University
Alabama Genealogical Society Depository
   and Headquarters
Samford University Library
Special Collection Department
800 Lakeshore Drive
Birmingham, AL 35229-7008
(205) 726-2198
ighr@samford.edu; mbthomas@samford.edu
http://www.samford.edu/schools/ighr/
   ighr.html
Jean Thomason, Director
Mon–Fri 8:00–4:30
(university offers genealogical short courses)

Scottsboro-Jackson Heritage Center
(208 South Houston Street—location)
PO Box 53 (mailing address)
Scottsboro, AL 35768
(256) 259-2122
Melanie Bradford, Director
Tue–Fri 11:00–4:00
(records dating as far back as 1820, such as
   Orphan's Court, Deed Books,
   Commissioner's Court, Chancery Court
   and Circuit Court, many medical and store
   ledgers)

Scottsboro Public Library
Genealogy and Local History Room
1002 South Broad Street
Scottsboro, AL 35768-2512
(256) 574-4335; (256) 259-4457 FAX
rpalmer@scottsboro.org
http://www.scottsborolibrary.com
Gloria Balentine

Steward University System Library
Route 5, Box 109
Piedmont, AL 36272-8709
(256) 447-2939

Part 2. Alabama

Mrs. Frank Ross Stewart, Sr.
8:00–5:00
Pub. *numeroos*, irregularly, free
(county, family, church, etc., worldwide)

Troy Public Library
300 North Three Notch Street
Troy, AL 36081-2022
(334) 566-1314; (334) 670-6208 FAX
mstewart@publiclibrary.troy.al.us
http://publiclibrary.troy.al.us:81 (online
  catalog)
Margaret Stewart, Director
Summer: Mon–Tue 9:00–5:30, Fri
  9:00–5:00, Sat 9:00–noon; Sept–May:
  Mon–Wed 9:00–5:30, Tue–Thur
  9:00–5:00, Sat 9:00–noon
("Genealogy Room: largest collections on
  Alabama, Georgia, North Carolina, South
  Carolina and Virginia")

Tuscaloosa Public Library
1801 River Road
Tuscaloosa, AL 35401-1099
(205) 345-5820; (205) 752-8300 FAX
npack@tuscaloosa-library.org
http://www.tuscaloosa-library.org
Glen A. Johnson; Dr. Nancy Pack
Mon–Thur 9:00–9:00, Fri–Sat 9:00–5:00,
  Sun 2:00–6:00

University of Alabama
William Stanley Hoole Special Collections
Library
PO Box 870266
Tuscaloosa, AL 35487-0266
(205) 348-0500
http://www.ua.edu

University of Mississippi
Center for the Study of Southern Culture
(see Mississippi, Part 2)

University of Southern Alabama
History Department
Humanities Building 344, USA
Mobile, AL 36688
(334) 460-6210; (334) 460-6750 FAX
Dr. Michael Thomason, Editor
Pub. *Gulf Coast Historical Review*,
  semiannually, $14.00 per year
  subscription, $25.00 for two years
(focuses on Gulf Coast history, Florida to
  Texas)

Wallace State Community College Library
Family and Regional History Program
(801 Main Street—location)
PO Box 2000 (mailing address)
Hanceville, AL 35077-2000
(256) 352-8265 (office); (256) 352-8228
  FAX
genws@hiwaay.net
Robert Scott Davis, Jr., M.Ed., M.A.,
  Director
Mon–Thur 7:30 A.M.–8:30 P.M., Fri
  7:30–4:00
(Alabama and surrounding states,
  Confederate records, Native American
  sources; houses collection of North
  Central Alabama Genealogical Society;
  also offers college courses and research
  field trips in genealogy)

Historical Societies—Local and Regional

Aliceville Historical Preservation, Inc.
103 Fourth Avenue, N.E.
Aliceville, AL 35442
(205) 373-6364

Auburn Heritage Association
(159 North College Street—location)
PO Box 2248 (mailing address)
Auburn, AL 36830

Autauga County Heritage Association
102 East Main Street
Prattville, AL 36067-3114
(334) 361-0961
http://www.autaugaheritage.com
Nancy Laforte, Executive Director
Mon–Fri 10:00–4:00
Pub. *ACHA Newsletter*, four times per year
$20.00 per year membership

Baldwin County Historic Society
PO Box 69
Stockton, AL 36579
(251) 937-9464
Pub. *Baldwin County Historic Quarterly*
$15.00 per year membership

Bibb County Heritage Association
Route 1, Box 147
Brierfield, AL 35035
(205) 665-1856

Birmingham Historical Society
1 Sloss Quarters
Birmingham, AL 35222
(205) 251-1880
Marjorie L. White, Chairman
Pub. *Birmingham Historical Society Journal*,
  semiannually

Blount County Historical Society
Blount County Memorial Museum
PO Box 45
Oneonta, AL 35121
(256) 625-6905
C. Warren Weaver, Archivist
hours: various
Pub. *BCHS Newsletter*, quarterly
$10.00 per year membership

Bullock County Historical Society
PO Box 563
Union Springs, AL 36089
Susan C. Anderson, President
Pub. *Quarterly Newsletter*
$5.00 per year membership; research: "local
  historian and genealogical researcher,
  Dean Spratlan, can be reached at above
  address for any local inquiries"

Butler County Historical and Genealogical Society
(309 Fort Dale Road, Public
  Library—location)
PO Box 561 (mailing address)
Greenville, AL 36037
(334) 383-9564
Judy Taylor, Librarian and Editor
Pub. *Butler County Historical and
  Genealogical Quarterly*
$12.00 per year membership

Chattahoochee Valley Historical Society, Inc.
H. Grady Bradshaw-Chambers County
Library and Cobb Memorial Archives
3419 20th Avenue
Valley, AL 36854
(334) 768-2161 (Library-Archives); (334)
  768-7272 FAX (Library-Archives)
Miriam Ann K. Syler, Society Representative
  and Archivist Assistant to Director
Library-Archives: Mon–Fri 10:00–6:00, Sat
  10:00–5:00 (appointments preferred on
  Sat)
Pub. *The Voice*, quarterly
(Chattahoochee Valley, Chambers and
  surrounding counties, Alabama, Troup
  and Harris counties, Georgia)
$10.00 per year membership

Chilton County Historical Society and Archives, Inc.
Chilton/Clanton Public Library
PO Box 644
Clanton, AL 35045
(205) 755-1768
B. D. Roberts; Marian Mills
Pub. *Quarterly*
$12.00 per year membership

Citronelle Historical Preservation Society
(18990-19000 South Center
  Street—location)
PO Box 384 (mailing address)
Citronelle, AL 36522
(251) 866-7730
Nell Fisher, President
$10.00 per year membership

Clarke County Historical Society
PO Box 131
Jackson, AL 36545

Coosa River Valley Historical and Genealogical Society
PO Box 295
Centre, AL 35960
(256) 447-2939

Covington Historical Society
PO Box 1582
Andalusia, AL 36420
Glen E. Powell, President
Sat 9:00–noon, Sun 2:00–4:30
Pub. *Newsletter*, quarterly
$12.00 per year membership

Cullman County Historical Society
1505 Pinecrest, N.W.
Cullman, AL 35055

Eleventh Circuit Historical Society, Inc.
(see Georgia, Part 2)

Escambia County Historical Society
PO Box 276
Brewton, AL 36427
Barbara Jones, Editor of Publications
Jefferson Davis Community College Library:
  8:00–4:00; summer: Mon–Thur
  7:30–6:30, Fri 7:30–1:30
Pub. *Escambia County Historical Society
  Journal*, semiannually (July, Dec);
  Escambia Echoes, monthly
$7.50 per year membership

Eufaula Heritage Association, Inc.
340 North Eufaula Avenue
Eufaula, AL 36027
(334) 687-3793
Hilda Chang Sexton, Executive Director

Fayette County Historical Society
PO Box 309
Fayette, AL 35555-0309
(205) 932-3255

Forney Historical Society
(3084 Sterling Road—location)
Samford University, S-215 (mailing address)
Birmingham, AL 35229
(205) 870-2784

Free State of Winston Historical Society
PO Box 26
Double Springs, AL 35553-0026

Greene County Historical Society

PO Box 746
Eutaw, AL 35462

Henry County Historical Society
(Abbeville Memorial Library, History Room,
301 Kirkland Street—location)
PO Box 222 (mailing address)
Abbeville, AL 36310
(334) 585-3020
William W. Nordan, Executive Director
Pub. *Henry County Historical Society
Newsletter*, monthly
(Henry County was formed from Alabama
territory and comprised all of southeast
Alabama, now known as the "Wiregrass,"
and produced all or parts of nine other
counties: Barbour 1832, Bullock 1866,
Coffee 1841, Covington 1822, Crenshaw
1866, Dale 1824, Geneva 1868, Houston
1903, Pike 1821)
limited membership presently closed

Historic Chattahoochee Commission
(211 North Eufaula Avenue—location)
PO Box 33 (mailing address)
Eufaula, AL 36072-0033
(334) 687-9755; (334) 687-6631 voice &
FAX
Douglas C. Purcell, Executive Director
Mon–Fri 8:00–5:00
Pub. *Chattahoochee Tracings*, quarterly
(history, art, architecture, preservation of
lower Chattahoochee Valley of Alabama
and Georgia)
free memberships available

Jackson County Historical Association
Route 1
Langston, AL 35755

Jefferson County Historical Commission
2027 First Avenue North, Suite 801
Birmingham, AL 35203
(205) 324-0988
Barbara B. King, Executive Secretary
Tue–Thur

**Lawrence County Archives and Historical
Commission, Inc.**
(698 Main Street—location)
PO Box 728 (mailing address)
Moulton, AL 35650
(256) 974-1757; (256) 974-2538
http://members.aol.com/lchc35650
Myra Borden, Archivist
Mon–Fri 9:00–4:00
Pub. *Old Lawrence Reminiscences*, quarterly
(family files, vertical files, census, court
records, library section and a large
collection of microfilm)
$15.00 per year membership; marriage
license research only: $5.00 each for out-
of-town members, $7.00 for nonmembers

Lee County Historical Society
PO Box 206
Loachapoka, AL 36865
Pub. *Trails in History*, quarterly

Limestone County Historical Society
PO Box 82
Athens, AL 35612
Doyle Lovelace, President
Pub. *Limestone Legacy*, quarterly
$15.00 per year membership

Lowndes County Historical Society
300 Cantelou Road
Montgomery, AL 36108-6000
Alice M. Lee
Pub. *Lowndes County Historical Society
Publications*, quarterly

$6.00 per year membership

Marengo County Historical Society
(407 North Commissioner
Avenue—location)
PO Box 159 (mailing address)
Demopolis, AL 36732
(334) 289-1666
Mrs. J. C. P. Turner, President
Pub. *MCHS Newsletter*, biannually

Montgomery County Historical Society
(512 South Court Street—location)
PO Box 1829
Montgomery, AL 36102
(334) 264-1837; (334) 834-9292 FAX
mchs@mont.mindspring.com
http://www.mindspring.com/~mchs
Pub. *The Herald*, quarterly
$25.00 per year membership

**Pea River Historical and Genealogical
Society**
(108 South Main—location)
PO Box 310628 (mailing address)
Enterprise, AL 36331
(334) 393-2901
Clayton G. Metcalf, President and Editor
Mon–Fri 10:00–4:00
Pub. *Pea River Trails*, quarterly
$15.00 per year membership

**Piedmont Historical and Genealogical
Society**
PO Box 47
Spring Garden, AL 36275

**Pike County Historical and Genealogical
Society**
Route 2, Box 272
Goshen, AL 36035
(334) 484-3314
Mrs. Henry W. Folmar, Treasurer and Book
Committee Chairman; Karen Bullard,
Assistant Reference Librarian
Pub. *Pike County Historical and
Genealogical Society Papers*, usually
semiannually (Apr, Oct)
$13.00 per year membership

Society of Pioneers of Montgomery, Inc.
PO Box 413
Montgomery, AL 36101

Pleasant Grove Historical Commission
501 Park Road
Pleasant Grove, AL 35127

Russell County Historical Commission
801 Dillingham Street
Phenix City, AL 36867
(334) 298-9735

St. Clair Historical Society
1734 Lynn Circle
Odenville, AL 35120
(256) 699-3760
phall@inline.com; arielle@coosahs.net
(Webmaster, Jeannie Laurance)
http://st-clair-
historic.dyndns.org/welcome.htm
Pat Hall, Third Vice President
10:00–3:00
Pub. *Cherish*, quarterly
$20.00 per year membership; copies: $5.00
each

Shelby County Historical Society, Inc.
Shelby County Museum and Archives
(1854 Courthouse, Main Street—location)
PO Box 457 (mailing address)
Columbiana, AL 35051

(205) 669-3912
schs1854@bellsouth.net
http://www.rootsweb.com/~alshelby/
shelby.html
Bobby Joe Seales
Mon–Fri 9:00–3:00
Pub. *Shelby County Historical Society Inc.
Quarterly* (Mar, June, Sept, Dec)
("Museum and Archives. Housed in the 1854
'old' courthouse on National Register of
Historic Places.")
$20.00 per year membership

Southern Studies Institute
(see Louisiana, Part 2)

Talladega County Historical Association
106 Broome Street
Talladega, AL 35160
(256) 362-2219
Pub. *Talladega County Historical
Association Newsletter*
$10.00 per year membership

Tennessee Valley Historical Society
PO Box 149
Sheffield, AL 35660
sheridanrc@aol.com
Richard C. Sheridan, Editor
Pub. *Newsletter*, quarterly; *Journal of
Muscle Shoals History*, occasionally, price
varies
(northwest Alabama)
$5.00 per year membership (includes
Newsletter but not *Journal*)

**West Jefferson County Historical Society,
Inc.**
(1740 Eastern Valley Road, Bessemer, AL
35020—location)
PO Box 184 (mailing address)
Bessemer, AL 35021
(205) 426-6604
Pub. *Journal of History*, semiannually
$10.00 per year membership

Genealogical Societies

State Genealogical Societies

**Alabama Genealogical Society, Inc.
(AGS)**
American Genealogical Society Depository
and Headquarters
Samford University
Harwell Goodwin Davis Library
Special Collection Department
(800 Lakeshore Drive—location)
PO Box 2296 (mailing address)
Birmingham, AL 35229
(205) 726-4009 voice & FAX (Director
IGHR)
mbthomas@samford.edu
http://www.samford.edu/schools/ighr/
ighr.html (Institute of Genealogy and
Historical Research)
Elizabeth C. Wells, Librarian; Jean
Thomason, Director IGHR
Library: Mon 8:00–9:00, Tue–Fri 8:00–4:30
Pub. *Alabama Genealogical Society
Newsletter*, quarterly; *Alabama
Genealogical Society Magazine*, quarterly
$20.00 per year membership

Southern Society of Genealogists, Inc.
Stewart University
PO Box 295
Centre, AL 35960
(256) 447-2939
(Southern states: Arkansas, Florida, Georgia,
Kentucky, Louisiana, Maryland,
Mississippi, North Carolina, South

Carolina, Tennessee, Texas, Virginia)

Genealogical Societies—Local & Regional

AlaBenton Genealogical Society
Liles Memorial Library
Public Library of Anniston and Calhoun
County
Alabama Room
(108 East 10th Street—location)
PO Box 308 (mailing address)
Anniston, AL 36202
Thomas B. Mullins
$15.00 per year membership

Autauga Genealogical Society (AGS)
PO Box 680668
Prattville, AL 36068-0668
jkbrown2@knology.net
http://www.rootsweb.com/~alags
John K. Brown, Editor
meetings: quarterly
Pub. *Autauga Ancestry*, quarterly
$20.00 per year membership

Baldwin County Genealogical Society
c/o Foley Public Library
319 East Laurel Avenue
Foley, AL 36535
Jeanette Bornholt, Library Aide and
Genealogical Society Member
$10.00 per year membership

Birmingham Genealogical Society, Inc.
PO Box 2432
Birmingham, AL 35201
Pub. *Pioneer Trails*, quarterly; *Birmingham
Genealogical Society Newsletter*, monthly
$10.00 per year membership

**Butler County Historical and Genealogical
Society**
(see Historical Societies—Local and
Regional, above)

**Coosa River Valley Historical and
Genealogical Society**
(see Historical Societies—Local and
Regional, above)

**Delta Genealogical Society (northeast
Alabama)**
(see Georgia, Part 2)

**The Genealogical Society of East Alabama,
Inc.**
(909 Avenue A, Opelika, AL
36801—location)
PO Box 2892 (mailing address)
Opelika, AL 36803
James Noel Baker, President
Pub. *Tap Roots*, quarterly (Apr, July, Oct,
Jan)
("Bible records, family histories, cemeteries,
church histories, items of community
interest, tax and courthouse records;
serving Chambers, Lee, Macon, Russell
and Tallapoosa counties")
$15.00 per year membership

Jackson County Genealogical Society
PO Box 1494
Scottsboro, AL 35768
Pub. *Jackson County Chronicles*, quarterly
$10.00 per year membership

Lamar County Genealogical Society
PO Box 357
Vernon, AL 35592

Marion County Genealogical Society
PO Box 1527

Winfield, AL 35594
(205) 487-2484
Loree Lindsey, Editor; Joel Palmer, President
Mon–Fri 9:00–5:00
Pub. *Marion County Alabama Tracks*,
quarterly
$15.00 per year membership

Mobile Genealogical Society, Inc.
(Woman's Club House, 1200 Government
Street—location)
PO Box 6224 (mailing address)
Mobile, AL 36660
(334) 626-6573
Dolores F. "Dee" Rhodes, President
Mon 11:00–2:00, Thur noon–4:00, second
Sat
Pub. *Deep South Genealogical Quarterly*
(Feb, May, Aug, Nov); *Deep South
Genealogical Society Newsletter*, monthly
$20.00 per year membership; research for
members only: $15.00 per hour

Montgomery Genealogical Society, Inc.
PO Box 230194
Montgomery, AL 36123-0194
Pub. *Montgomery Genealogical Society
Quarterly*
$10.00 per year membership

Natchez Trace Genealogical Society
PO Box 420
Florence, AL 35631-0420
Darrell A. Russel, Ph.D., Publications
Chairperson
Pub. *Natchez Trace Newsletter*, quarterly,
$20.00 per year subscription; *Natchez
Trace Traveler*, five times per year
(Colbert, Franklin and Lauderdale counties,
Alabama)

North Alabama Genealogical Society
3327 Danville Road, S.W.
Decatur, AL 35603-9027

**North Central Alabama Genealogical
Society**
PO Box 13
Cullman, AL 35056-0013
Carolina Nigg, Editor and Vice President
Wallace State Community College Library:
Mon–Thur 7:30 A.M.–8:30 P.M., Fri
7:30–4:00
Pub. *Alabama Family History and
Genealogy News*, quarterly, $15.00 per
year subscription
(Blount, Cullman, Marshall, Walker and
Winston counties, and Alabama families)
$15.00 per year membership

**Northeast Alabama Genealogical Society,
Inc.**
(Howard Gardner Nichols Memorial Library,
1 Cabot Avenue, Gadsden, AL
35904—location)
PO Box 8268 (mailing address)
Gadsden, AL 35902-8268
neags2001@yahoo.com
http://www.rootsweb.com/~alneags/
index.html
Georgia Brackett, Librarian
Thur 10:00–3:00, first & third Sat 9:00–1:00
Pub. *Northeast Alabama Settlers*, quarterly
(July, Oct, Jan, Apr)
$15.00 per year membership (before 15 June,
$18.00 thereafter)

**Pea River Historical and Genealogical
Society**
(see Historical Societies—Local and
Regional, above)

**Piedmont Historical and Genealogical
Society**
(see Historical Societies—Local and
Regional, above)

**Pike County Historical and Genealogical
Society**
(see Historical Societies—Local and
Regional, above)

**Southeast Alabama Genealogical Society
(SEAGS)**
PO Box 246
Dothan, AL 36302-0246
(334) 794-7480
Mrs. Ceya Minder, Corresponding Secretary
meetings: third Tue (except Dec)
Pub. *Southeast Alabama Genealogical
Society Quarterly*
(southeast Alabama counties, upper
bordering counties of Florida and lower
bordering counties of Georgia)
$12.00 per year Associate membership

Tennessee Valley Genealogical Society
PO Box 1568
Huntsville, AL 35807-0567
(256) 728-2788
ginkob1@comcast.net
http://www.tvgs.org
Pub. *Valley Leaves*, quarterly; *TVGS News*
(meeting announcements only)
(nine north Alabama counties that border on
the Tennessee River)
$25.00 per year membership

**Morning Group Tuscaloosa Genealogical
Society**
29 DuBois Terrace
Tuscaloosa, AL 35401
Mrs. Billie Lockard, Research
meetings at Tuscaloosa Public Library: first
Thur 10:00
Pub. *Roots and Branches*, three times per
year
$8.00 per year membership

**Tuscaloosa Genealogical Society, Night
Group**
PO Box 020802
Tuscaloosa, AL 35406

Walker County Genealogical Society
PO Box 3408
Jasper, AL 35502

**Genealogical Society of Washington
County**
PO Box 399
Chatom, AL 36518
http://members.aol.com/JORDANJM2/
WCGS.htm

Independent Publications and Miscellany

Society of Alabama Archivists
Auburn University
Auburn University Archives
Auburn, AL 36849-5637
(334) 826-4465
Jessica Lacher-Feldman, Newsletter Editor
Pub. *Newsletter*

Alabama Department of Transportation
Attention: Map Sales
(1409 Coliseum Boulevard, Room R-
109—location)
PO Box 303050 (mailing address)
Montgomery, AL 36130-3050
(334) 242-6071

aldotinfo@dot.state.al.us
http://www.dot.state.al.us/Bureau/
Equipment/maps.htm

Alabama Heritage
500 Margaret Drive
Tuscaloosa, AL 35487-0342
(205) 348-7434
Sara Martin, Marketing/Advertising
Director
8:00–4:45
Pub. *Alabama Heritage* (Alabama and the
South), quarterly, $16.95 per year
subscription
"Genealogy in Alabama" queries: $30.00 for
50-word listing

AlGenWeb
Part of The USGenWeb Project
elsi@augustmail.com
http://www.rootsweb.com/~algenweb
Leigh Compton, State Coordinator
(links to other Alabama resources)

Ancestor Files Library
PO Box 249
Lanett, AL 36863-0249
(334) 576-2797
Lynda S. Eller, Heard County, Georgia,
Historian
by appointment
Pub. *Heard Heritage, Heard County,
Georgia*, semiannually (May, Nov), $8.00
per year subscription
(covers Clay, Cleburne, Randolph,
Talladega and Tallapoosa counties,
Alabama; Carroll, Chambers, Coweta,
Harris, Heard, Meriwether and Troup
counties, Georgia)

Arkansas Ancestors
(see Arkansas, Part 2)

**Baldwin County Historic Development
Commission**
(1100 Fairhope Avenue, Fairhope, AL
36532—location)
PO Box 86 (mailing address)
Montrose, AL 36559
(251) 928-3002; (251) 580-2590 FAX
Jack Thomas, Chairman
Mon–Fri 8:00–4:30
(preserving and protecting historic districts
and the maintenance of the distinctive
characters of these districts)

Center for Appalachian Studies
(see North Carolina, Part 2)

Clayton Historical Preservation Authority
PO Box 385
Clayton, AL 36016
(334) 775-3542

Discovery Place of Birmingham
1320 22nd Street, South
Birmingham, AL 35205

Genealogical Institute
(see Virginia, Part 2)

Genealogy Books and Consultation
(see Texas, Part 2)

Historic Huntsville Foundation, Inc.
PO Box 786
Huntsville, AL 35804
(256) 539-0097
Lynne Lowery, Director
Pub. *Historic Huntsville: Quarterly of Local
Architecture and Preservation*
("We don't keep any genealogy records. We

do architectural preservation, don't even
keep historical files on buildings, give all
that to the public library.")
from $20.00 per year membership

**Hunting for Bears Genealogical and
Historical Society**
(3878 West 3200 South, Salt Lake City, UT
84120-2154—location)
PO Box 25593 (mailing address)
Salt Lake City, UT 84125-0593
(801) 966-1611; (801) 957-1612 FAX
genealogy@juno.com
http://www.geocities.com/huntingforbears
Dixie Murray
hours: various
Pub. *Bear Tracks* (an electronic newsletter),
monthly, free
(Alabama, Arkansas, Georgia, Illinois,
Indiana, Kentucky, Louisiana, Maryland,
Mississippi, Missouri, Ohio, North
Carolina, South Carolina, Tennessee,
Texas and Virginia; marriage records)
surname search of marriage records on a
statewide basis: $5.00 per search

MLH Research
3916 Bramble Road
Anniston, AL 36201
MariLee Beatty Hagness, Owner
Pub. *Alabama-Georgia Queries*, bimonthly,
$16.00 per year subscription
(queries, court records, Bible records,
military listings)
research: $10.00 per hour; queries

Mobile DAR
15 Gaywood Circle
Birmingham, AL 35213
Alice Merchant

Mountain Press
(see Tennessee, Part 2)

"Old Courthouse"
PO Box 153
Somerville, AL 35670
(256) 778-8282; (256) 778-8277
Imogene J. Williams, Town Clerk
weekdays 9:00–5:00

The Source Historical and Adventure
PO Box 656
Russellville, AL 35653
Pub. *The Source Historical and Adventure*,
$5.00 per year subscription

**The Southern Genealogist's Exchange
Society, Inc.**
(see Florida, Part 2)

Southern Historical Press, Inc.
(see Publishers, Part 4)

Tracking Your Roots
contribute@trackingyourroots.com
http://www.trackingyourroots.com
Lisa R. Franklin, R.N.
(links to other Alabama resources)

Tracks
280 Sierra Vista
Mobile, AL 36607
Pub. *Tracks*, quarterly, $15.00 per year
subscription

Traveller Southern Families
(see Virginia, Part 2)

Washington County Museum
Washington County Courthouse
PO Box 52

Chatom, AL 36518
Dr. Claire W. Duncan, Chairman, Museum
Board

Alaska

Archives and Libraries with Holdings in Genealogy

State Archives and Library

Alaska Collection and Archives
4101 University Drive
Anchorage, AK 99508
(907) 561-1265

Alaska State Archives
Reference Desk
141 Willoughby Avenue
Juneau, AK 99801-1720
(907) 465-2270; (907) 465-2465 FAX
archives@eed.state.ak.us
http://www.archives.state.ak.us
Reference Desk
Mon–Fri 9:00–5:00
(Alaska State and Territorial Government
  Agency records)
minimal photocopy charge

Alaska State Library
State Office Building, Eighth Floor
PO Box 110571
Juneau, AK 99811-0571
(907) 465-2921 (Reference); (907) 465-2665
  FAX
asl@eed.state.ak.us
http://www.library.state.ak.us
Karen R. Crane, Director
Reference Services: Mon–Fri 9:00–5:00;
  Historical Collections: Mon–Fri
  1:00–5:00 and by appointment

Alaska State Library, Alaska Historical Collections
Historical Reference
(State Office Building, 333 Willoughby
  Avenue, Eighth Floor—location)
PO Box 110571 (mailing address)
Juneau, AK 99811-0571
(907) 465-2925; (907) 465-2919
  (Newspaper Project); (907) 465-2990
  FAX
asl@eed.state.ak.us
http://www.library.state.ak.us/hist/hist.html
Kathryn H. Shelton, Librarian III, Head of
  Historical Collections
Mon–Fri 1:00–5:00
(book and print collection, newspapers and
  periodicals, maps, photographs,
  manuscripts, microfilm, etc.)

State Historical Societies

Alaska Association for Historic Preservation
645 West Third Avenue
Anchorage, AK 99501-2124
(907) 272-2119
Bill Coghill, Executive Director
Pub. *The Alaska Association for Historic
  Preservation*, quarterly
(not primarily genealogical)
$15.00 per year membership

Alaska Historical Society
(1489 C Street, Suite 202—location)
PO Box 100299 (mailing address)
Anchorage, AK 99510-0299
(907) 276-1596 voice & FAX
Nancy Gross, Assistant to the President
by appointment
Pub. *Alaska History*, semiannually, $12.00
  per year subscription; *Alaska History
  News*, quarterly

$35.00 per year membership

State of Alaska Office of History and Archaeology
3601 C Street, Suite 1278
Anchorage, AK 99503-5721
(907) 762-2622; (907) 762-2628 FAX
State Historian

City, County and Regional Archives and Libraries
(A more exhaustive list of public and
academic libraries can be found at http://
www.library.state.ak.us/dev/aslld99.html.)

Alpine Historical Park
Mile 61.5 Glenn Highway
General Delivery
Sutton, AK 99674
(907) 745-7000

Anchorage Municipal Libraries
Z. J. Loussac Public Library
3600 Denali Street
Anchorage, AK 99503-6093
(907) 261-2975; (907) 562-1244 FAX
Peg Thompson, Social Sciences Librarian
Mon–Thur 11:00–9:00, Fri–Sat 10:00–6:00,
  Sun 1:00–5:00

Heritage Library and Museum
(National Bank of Alaska, 301 West
  Northern Lights Boulevard—location)
PO Box 100600 (mailing address)
Anchorage, AK 99510-0600
(907) 265-2834; (907) 265-2002 FAX
Lea Worcester, Curator/Librarian

Juneau-Douglas City Museum
(Fourth and Main Streets—location)
155 South Seward Street (mailing address)
Juneau, AK 99801
(907) 586-3572; (907) 586-3203 FAX
http://www.ptialaska.net/~cbjhelp/
  museum.htm
Mary Pat Wyatt, Curator
summer: daily; winter: Fri–Sat
(reference assistance, cemetery and records,
  high school yearbooks, telephone books,
  vital statistic newspaper records; local
  Juneau-Douglas, Alaska, information)

Klondike Gold Rush National Historical Park
(Second and Broadway—location)
PO Box 517 (mailing address)
Skagway, AK 99840
(907) 983-2921; (907) 983-9249 FAX
Theresa Thibault, Chief of Resources
Mon–Fri 8:00–5:00
("Park retains Gold Rush Stampeder
  files—people who participated in the
  Gold Rush, as well as historic photos and
  archives from the Gold Rush period.")

Klondike Gold Rush National Historical Park—Seattle Unit
(see Washington, Part 2)

Carrie M. McLain Memorial Museum
(223 East Front Street—location)
PO Box 53 (mailing address)
Nome, AK 99762-0053
(907) 443-6630; (907) 443-7955 FAX
museum@ci.nome.ak.us
Laura Samuelson, Director
Tue–Sat noon–6:00
(bibliography of famous people, early 20th
  century, all copies of *Nome Nugget*,
  oldest newspaper in Alaska; gold mining,
  Bering Strait Eskimon culture)

research: $25.00 per hour

Elmer E. Rasmuson Library
Alaska and Polar Regions Department
University of Alaska, Fairbanks
PO Box 756800
Fairbanks, AK 99701
(907) 474-7261
fydir@uaf.edu
http://www.uaf.alaska.edu/library/libweb
David Hales, Head
Mon–Fri 9:00–5:00
("Rare books, archives, manuscripts, rare
  maps, oral histories, archival films,
  historical photographs," newspapers;
  materials deal with Alaska and Polar
  regions)

Sheldon Museum and Cultural Center
(11 Main Street, just above boat
  harbor—location)
PO Box 269 (mailing address)
Haines, AK 99827
(907) 766-2366; (907) 766-2368 FAX
curator@sheldonmuseum.org
http://www.sheldonmuseum.org
Cynthia Jones, Director/Curator
winter: Mon, Wed & Sun 1:00–4:00, Tue &
  Thur–Fri 3:00–5:00; summer: daily
  1:00–5:00
(pioneer history, Tingit Indian art and
  culture)
museum admission: $3.00; photocopies 25¢
  per page

Sitka National Historical Park
(103 Monastery Street—location)
PO Box 738 (mailing address)
Sitka, AK 99835
(907) 747-6281; (907) 747-5938 FAX
http://www.nps.gov/sitk
Mitzi Frank, Chief of Interpretation
Mon–Fri 8:00–5:00

University of Alaska, Anchorage
Consortium Library
3211 Providence Drive
Anchorage, AK 99508
(907) 786-1874 (Government Documents);
  (907) 786-1849 (Archives and
  Manuscripts Department); (907) 786-
  6050 FAX
AYLIB@uaa.alaska.edu
Professor Alden Rollins, Government
  Documents Librarian; Dennis Walle,
  Archivist
call ahead, hours vary with university
  calendar
(national scope collection of biographies,
  journals, diaries, local histories,
  gazetteers, plus archival and manuscript
  collections on Alaska, the northern
  Pacific area and the Arctic, with an
  emphasis on southcentral and
  southwestern Alaska, also pre-1900
  Canadiana)

The Valdez Museum and Historical Archive
(217 Egan Drive—location)
PO Box 8 (mailing address)
Valdez, AK 99686-0008
(907) 835-2764; (907) 835-4597 FAX; (907)
  835-5800 FAX
vldzmuse@alaska.net
http://www.alaska.net/vldzmuse/index.html
M. Joseph Leahy, Director
9:00–5:00
(Valdez, Prince William Sound, Copper
  River Valley regional history; gold rush
  1898–1910)

research: first ½ hour free, $20.00 per hour
thereafter

Wrangell Museum
(318 Church Street—location)
PO Box 1050 (mailing address)
Wrangell, AK 99929
(907) 874-3770; (907) 874-3785 FAX
Theresa Thibault, Director/Curator
winter: Tue–Fri 10:00–4:00; summer:
    Mon–Fri 10:00–5:00, Sat 1:00–5:00
(over 3,000 photos relating to Wrangell and
    the immediate surrounding area)
research: $5.00 minimum, $10.00 per hour
    after the first half-hour; photo
    reproduction fees vary

Historical Societies—Local and Regional

American Historical Association, Pacific Coast Branch
(see California, Part 2)

Bristol Bay Historical Society
PO Box 36
Naknek, AK 99633
(907) 246-4406
John Knutsen, President

Chilkat Valley Historical Society
c/o Sheldon Museum and Cultural Center
(11 Main Street, just above boat
harbor—location)
PO Box 269 (mailing address)
Haines, AK 99827
(907) 766-2366 (Museum); (907) 766-2368
    FAX (Museum)
Jim Heaton, President
Museum: winter: Mon, Wed & Sun
    1:00–4:00, Tue & Thur–Fri 3:00–5:00;
    summer: daily 1:00–5:00
Pub. *Chilkat Valley Historical Society
    Newsletter*, quarterly
$10.00 per year membership; museum
    admission: $3.00

Circle District Historical Society, Inc.
(Circle District Museum, Mile 127 Steese
Highway—location)
PO Box 30189 (mailing address)
Central, AK 99730
(907) 520-1893
Hannelore Wilde, Secretary
Memorial Day–Labor Day: noon–5:00
Pub. *Newsletter*, one or two times per year
(mining history, gold display 1893–1950+)
$10.00 per year membership

Cook Inlet Historical Society
Anchorage Museum of History and Art
121 West Seventh Avenue
Anchorage, AK 99501
(907) 343-6189 (Archives); (907) 343-4326
    (Museum); (907) 343-6149 FAX
JBarnett@alaska.com
http://www.powelldesign.net/cookinlet
James K. Barnett, President; M. Diane
    Brenner, Museum Archivist
Museum: Mon–Fri 10:00–noon, afternoons
    by chance or appointment

Copper Valley Historical Society
(George Ashby Memorial Museum, Mile 101
Rich Highway—location)
PO Box 84 (mailing address)
Copper Center, AK 99573
(907) 822-5285
Fred T. Williams, President
Mon–Sat (1 June–1 Sept) 1:00–5:00

Cordova Historical Society, Inc.
(Cordova Historical Museum, 622 First
Street-Centennial Building—location)
PO Box 391 (mailing address)
Cordova, AK 99574
(907) 424-6665; (907) 424-6000 FAX (City
    Hall)
Cathy Sherman, Museum Director
Tue–Sat 1:00–5:00
Pub. *The Discoverer*, somewhat quarterly
(specializes in information on Cordova,
    Katalla, Kennicott, Prince William
    Sound)
$10.00 per year membership

Eagle Historical Society
(Third and Chamberlain—location)
PO Box 23 (mailing address)
Eagle City, AK 99738
(907) 547-2230; (907) 547-2232 FAX
Elva Scott, President
Pub. *Eagle Wireless*, three times per year
$10.00 per year membership; research:
    $15.00 per hour

Gastineau Channel Historical Society
PO Box 21264
Juneau, AK 99802
(907) 586-5235

Kenai Historical Society, Inc.
PO Box 1348
Kenai, AK 99611
(907) 283-7618

Kodiak Historical Society
101 Marine Way
Kodiak, AK 99615
(907) 486-5920; (907) 486-3166 FAX
Marian Johnson, Director
winter 11:00–3:00 (five days); summer:
    Mon–Sun 10:00–4:00

Resurrection Bay Historical Society Museum
(336 Third Avenue—location)
PO Box 55 (mailing address)
Seward, AK 99664-0055
(907) 224-3902
Lee E. Poleske, President
1 May–30 Sept: 10:00–5:00, and by
    appointment
Pub. *Resurrection Bay Historical Society
    Newsletter*, nine times per year
$10.00 per year membership

Sealaska Heritage Foundation
1 Sealaska Plaza, Suite 201
Juneau, AK 99801
(907) 463-4844

Sitka Historical Society/Isabel Miller Museum
(Harrigan Centennial Hall, 330 Harbor
Drive—location)
PO Box 6181 (mailing address)
Sitka, AK 99835
(907) 747-6455; (907) 747-6588
webmaster@web4wise.com
http://www.sitka.org/historicalmuseum
Dr. Orriene First Denslow, Administrator
15 May–15 Sept: 8:00–5:00; Oct–Apr:
    Tue–Sat 10:00–4:00
Pub. *SHS Newsletter*, two to three times per
    year, $15.00 per year subscription
$25.00 per year membership

Soldotna Historical Society and Museum, Inc.
(Centennial Park Road—location)
PO Box 1986 (mailing address)

Soldotna, AK 99669
(907) 262-3756; (907) 262-8466 FAX

Talkeetna Historical Society
(First Alley and Village Airstrip—location)
PO Box 76 (mailing address)
Talkeetna, AK 99676
(907) 733-2487; (907) 733-2484 FAX
Alice Johannewes-Tobiason, Museum
    Coordinator
Jan & Dec: Sat 11:00–5:00; Feb–Mar &
    Oct–Nov: Sat–Sun 11:00–5:00; Apr &
    Sept: Fri–Sat 11:00–6:00, Sun
    11:00–5:00; May–Aug: Mon–Sun
    10:00–6:00
Pub. *Newsletter*, annually
(oral history projects, humanities research
    and projects, state and local history;
    books, documents, photos, scrapbooks
    and newspapers)
$10.00 per year membership; membership;
    museum admission, Memorial Day–Labor
    Day: $1.00 for adult nonmembers

Tanana-Yukon Historical Society
(Wickersham House Museum, Alaskaland
Park, Airport Way—location)
PO Box 71336 (mailing address)
Fairbanks, AK 99707
(907) 455-TYHS
tyhs@polarnet.com
http://www2.polarnet.com/~tyhs
Renee Blahuta, President
Pub. *TYHS Newsletter*, monthly, $12.00 per
    year subscription
(local history/historic preservations)
$10.00 per year membership

Valdez Historical Society, Inc.
"Archives Alive"
(705 North Glacier Drive—location)
PO Box 6 (mailing address)
Valdez, AK 99686
(907) 835-4367
Dorothy I. Clifton, Director
9:00–5:00
(Valdez from earliest dates)
$5.00 per year membership

Wasilla-Knik-Willow Creek Historical Society
Dorothy Page Museum and Old Wasilla
Townsite Park
323 Main Street
Wasilla, AK 99687
(907) 376-2005; (907) 373-9072 FAX
Dorothy Page, President

Genealogical Societies

State Genealogical Society

Alaska Genealogical Society
7030 Dickerson Drive
Anchorage, AK 99504

Genealogical Societies—Local & Regional

Fairbanks Genealogical Society
PO Box 60534
Fairbanks, AK 99706-0534
GGSLookup@hotmail.com (to query the
    society for resources)
http://www.ptialaska.net/~fgs
meetings at the Noel Wien Library
    conference room, Fairbanks: fourth Thur
    (Jan–May & Sept–Nov) 7:00 P.M.
Pub. *The Taproot*, nine times per year
    (monthly, Sept–May)
$15.00 per year membership; research: first
    hour free except for copying costs, $15.00

per hour thereafter

Forget-Me-Not Genealogical Society
(705 North Glacier Drive—location)
PO Box 6 (Secretary-Treasurer's mailing
address)
Valdez, AK 99686
(907) 835-4367 (Secretary-Treasurer); (907)
835-4451 (Board Member)
Dorothy I. Clifton, Secretary-Treasurer;
Minnie La Page, Board Member
9:00–5:00
$5.00 per year membership

Gastineau Genealogical Society
3270 Nowell Avenue
Juneau, AK 99801
(907) 586-3695
O. R. Kent, President
no membership dues

Genealogical Society of Southeast Alaska
PO Box 6313
Ketchikan, AK 99901
monthly meetings
Pub. *Genealogical Society of Southeast
Alaska Newsletter*, monthly
$15.00 per year membership

Wrangell Genealogical Society
Wrangell Museum
(318 Church Street—location)
PO Box 1050 (mailing address)
Wrangell, AK 99929
(907) 874-3770 (Museum); (907) 874-3785
FAX (Museum)
Theresa Thibault, Museum Director/Curator
Museum: winter: Tue–Fri 10:00–4:00;
summer: Mon–Fri 10:00–5:00, Sat
1:00–5:00

Independent Publications and Miscellany

AkGenWeb
Part of The USGenWeb Project
Capt.Pat@RootsQuest.com
http://www.rootsweb.com/~akgenweb
Pat Smith and Sarah Ligon, Co-State
Coordinators
(links to other Alaska resources)

**Alaska Department of Transportation and
Public Facilities**
3132 Channel Drive
Juneau, AK 99801
(907) 465-3900
webmanager@dot.state.ak.us
http://www.dot.state.ak.us/stwdplng/
mapping/web/Traffic_maps

Alaska State Museum
395 Whittier Street
Juneau, AK 99801-1718
(907) 465-2901; (907) 465-2976 FAX
bruce_kato@eed.state.ak.us
http://www.museums.state.ak.us/
asmhome.html
Bruce Kato, Chief Curator
summer (mid-May to mid-Sept) Mon–Fri
9:00–6:00, Sat–Sun 10:00–6:00; winter:
Tue–Sat 10:00–4:00
admission: up to $3.00

**Alutiq Museum and Archaelogical
Repository**
215 Mission Road, Suite 101
Kodiak, AK 99615
(907) 486-7004 voice & FAX; (907) 486-
7048 voice & FAX

Baranof Museum
Kodiak Historical Society
101 Marine Way
Kodiak, AK 99615
(907) 486-5920; (907) 486-3166 FAX
Eunice Neseth, Curator
Pub. *News from the Baranof Museum*,
irregularly

Clausen Memorial Museum
Museum Society of Petersburg
(203 Fram Street—Clausen Memorial
Museum location
Second and F Street—Museum Society of
Petersburg location)
PO Box 708 (mailing address)
Petersburg, AK 99833
(907) 772-3598
Michale Edgington, Director

Duncan Cottage Museum
(Duncan Street—location)
PO Box 282 (mailing address)
Metlakatla, AK 99926
(907) 886-7363 voice & FAX

Ghosts of the Klondike Gold Rush
Filson's Pan for Gold Database
www@tiger.ab.ca
http://www.gold-rush.org/filson/index.html
(includes "information on individuals who
were in the Yukon during the Gold Rush
years")

Homer Society of Natural History
Pratt Museum
3779 Bartlett Street
Homer, AK 99603
(907) 235-8635; (907) 235-2764
Betsy Pitzman, Museum Director
Pub. *HSNH Newsletter* (not genealogical;
natural and cultural history of the Kenai
Peninsula, primarily biological, geological
and anthropological)

Kotzebue Museum, Inc.
PO Box 73
Kotzebue, AK 99752

**Museums Alaska: The Statewide
Association**
PO Box 242323
Anchorage, AK 99524
(907) 243-4714 voice & FAX
info@museumsalaska.org
http://www.museumsalaska.org
Pub. *Network* (online)
(service organization, no archives)
$30.00 per year membership

National Park Service
Cultural Resources Division, Alaska Region
2525 Gambell Street
Anchorage, AK 99503-2892
(907) 257-2543
Leslie Starr Hart, Chief, Cultural Resources

Sheldon Jackson Museum
104 College Drive
Sitka, AK 99835-7657
(907) 747-8981; (907) 747-3004 FAX
http://ccl.alaska.edu/local/museum/
home.html

Trail of '98 Museum
(Seventh and Spring Streets—location)
PO Box 415 (mailing address)
Skagway, AK 99840
(907) 983-2420; (907) 983-2151 FAX

University of Alaska, Fairbanks
College of Arts and Science

University of Alaska Museum
907 Yukon Drive
Fairbanks, AK 99701
(907) 474-7505; (907) 474-5469 FAX
http://www.uaf.alaska.edu/museum

**Yupiit Piciryarait Cultural Center and
Museum**
(420 Chief Eddie Hoffman State
Highway—location)
AVCP, Inc.
PO Box 219 (mailing address)
Bethel, AK 99559
(907) 520-5312; (907) 543-3596 FAX

Arizona

Archives and Libraries with Holdings in Genealogy

State Archives and Library

Arizona State Library, Archives and Public Records
History and Archives Division
Research Division
State Capitol
1700 West Washington
Phoenix, AZ 85007
(602) 542-3942; (602) 542-4159 (History Archives Division); (602) 542-3701 (Research Division); (602) 542-4500 FAX; (602) 542-4402 FAX (History and Archives Division)
archive@dlapr.lib.az.us (History and Archives Division); rerefde@dlapr.lib.az.us (Research Division); feddocs@dlapr.lib.az.us (Federal Documents)
http://www.dlapr.lib.az.us
Melanie I. Sturgeon, Ph.D., Director, History and Archives Division
Mon–Fri 8:00–5:00 (closed state holidays)
("The History and Archives Division includes the State Archives [we have thousands of county records, as well as other state and local government records and some manuscript collections], the Arizona Collection (a wonderful collection of books about Arizona and the Southwest including several thousand biographical vertical files, the largest collection in the state of Arizona newspapers, rare books on early Arizona, and many Arizona community histories. We also have a photo archives. The Research Division has a genealogy library, a state and federal documents area, and a law library.")

Arizona State University
University Libraries
Department of Archives-Manuscripts
Box 871006
Tempe, AZ 85287-1006
(480) 965-4932; (480) 965-3145; (480) 965-0776 FAX
archives@mainex1.asu.edu
http://www.asu.edu/lib/archives
Patricia A. Etter, Associate Archivist for Information Services
Mon 11:00–7:00, Tue–Wed 8:00–7:00, Thur–Fri 8:00–5:00, Sat 1:00–5:00
("The Department of Archives and Manuscripts at Arizona State University and the Manuscript Society have established the Manuscript Society Information Exchange Database, which lists collections of manuscripts, documents, and letters held by private individuals throughout the United States. The database contains a broad range of material, national and international in scope. The database can be searched for documents *by* an individual or *about* an individual. In addition to name searches, the database is accessible by subject. The American Revolution and the Civil War are heavily represented.")
$26.50 for each name or subject search, which includes cost of printout containing citation and descriptive information to documents meeting the search criteria (photocopies of original documents will be included when available), $10.00 for a printout showing names and subjects

currently in the database

State Historical Societies

The Arizona Historical Foundation
Charles Trumbull Hayden Library, Fourth Floor
Arizona State University
Box 871006
Tempe, AZ 85287-1006
(480) 966-8331; (480) 965-2531; (480) 965-6164 (Library)
askalib@asu.edu
http://www.asu.edu/lib
Dr. Evelyn Cooper, Director
hours: various (check web site for seasonal hours and holiday closings)
(research facility and archives; primary and secondary sources for Arizona and southwest history)
$20.00 per year membership

Arizona Historical Society
949 East Second Street
Tucson, AZ 85719
(520) 617-1157; (520) 628-5695 FAX
dshelton@vms.arizona.edu
http://www.arizonahistoricalsociety.org
Deborah Shelton, Interim Museum Director, Library and Archives Department Head
Mon–Fri 10:00–4:00, Sat 10:00–1:00
Pub. *Journal of Arizona History*, quarterly
$40.00 per year membership

Arizona Historical Society, Central Division
Museum at Papago Park
1300 North College
Tempe, AZ 85281
(480) 929-0292, ext. 172; (480) 967-5450 FAX
dnave@azhs.gov
http://www.arizonahistoricalsociety.org
Dawn Nave, Archivist

Arizona Historical Society/Pioneer Museum
2340 North Fort Valley Road
Flagstaff, AZ 86001
(928) 774-6272
Joseph M. Meehan, Director; Bonnie Greer, Archivist
Mon–Sat 9:00–5:00; Archives, Cline Library Special Collections, Northern Arizona University: Mon–Fri 8:00–5:00, Sat 10:30–1:00
$25.00 per year membership (includes the Arizona Historical Society's *Journal of Arizona History*)

Arizona Historical Society—Yuma Branch
Sanguinetti House Museum and Garden
240 South Madison Avenue
Yuma, AZ 85364
(928) 782-1841; (928) 783-0680 FAX
azhistyuma@cybertrails.com
http://www.arizonahistoricalsociety.org
Megan Reid, Director; Carol Brooks, Curator
Museum: Tue–Sat 10:00–4:00; Library: by appointment
Pub. *Newsletter*, bimonthly
("Lower Colorado River, including Yuma County, Arizona, southeast Imperial County, California, and Sonora, Mexico; we have photos, maps, family histories, voter registers, tax records, business directories, phone books, coroner's records, high school yearbooks.")
$40.00 per year membership (includes the Arizona Historical Society's *Journal of*

Arizona History)

City, County and Regional Archives and Libraries
(A more exhaustive list of public and academic libraries can be found at http://www.azla.org/azinfo/libraries.html#ACAD.)

Bisbee Mining and Historical Museum
(No. 5 Copper Queen Plaza—location)
PO Box 14 (mailing address)
Old Bisbee, AZ 85603
(520) 432-7071; (520) 432-7800 FAX
boyd@bisbeemuseum.org
http://www.amdest.com/az/Bisbee/bmining.html
Boyd Nicholl, History Curator
daily 10:00–4:00
("The Museum houses The Shattuck Memorial Research Library [noncirculating].")

Flagstaff City-Coconino County Public Library
300 West Aspen Avenue
Flagstaff, AZ 86001
(928) 779-7670; (928) 774-9573 FAX
kwhitake@ci.flagstarr.az.us
http://www.flagstaffpubliclibrary.com
Kay Whitaker, Public Services Manager
Mon–Thur 10:00–9:00, Fri 10:00–7:00, Sat 10:00–6:00, Sun noon–7:00
(extensive U.S. genealogy collection of 1,500 volumes, and Arizona research collection of 11,000 volumes; also City of Flagstaff Archives of 300 cubic feet)

Fort Lewis College
(see Colorado, Part 2)

Heard Museum Library and Archives
22 East Monte Vista Road
Phoenix, AZ 85004-1480
(602) 252-8840; (602) 252-9757 FAX
http://www.heard.org/library

Mesa Public Library
Local History Archives & Special Collections
86 East First Street
Mesa, AZ 85201
(480) 644-5421 (Mesa Room); (480) 644-2207 (General Information); (480) 644-3490 FAX
anna.uremovich@cityofmesa.org; mesalib.info@cityofmesa.org
http://www.mesalibrary.org
Anna Uremovich, Archivist, Head of Mesa Room

Mojave River Valley Museum Association
(see California, Part 2)

Museum of Northern Arizona
(Fort Valley Road—location)
Route 4, Box 720 (mailing address)
Flagstaff, AZ 86001
(928) 774-5211
Hermann K. Bleibtreu, Director; Katherine Bartlett, Archivist; Dorothy A. House, Librarian
(primarily historical, not genealogical)

Phoenix Museum of History
105 North Fifth Street
Phoenix, AZ 85004
(602) 253-2734
Cindy Myers, Executive Director
Wed–Sun 11:00–4:00
Pub. *Phoenix Museum of History Newsletter*, quarterly
$15.00–$1,000.00 per year membership

Phoenix Public Library
Burton Barr Central Library
Arizona Room
1221 North Central Avenue
Phoenix, AZ 85004
(602) 262-4636
http://www.ci.phoenix.az.us/library.html
Fay Freed, Arizona Room Librarian
Library: Mon–Wed 9:00–9:00, Thur–Sat
    9:00–6:00, Sun 1:00–5:00; Arizona
    Room: Tue 5:00–9:00, Wed & Sat
    10:00–6:00
(materials on Arizona; James H. McClintock
    Collection)
fee-based research available at library
    through Facts To Go

Prescott Public Library
215 East Goodwin Street
Prescott, AZ 86303
(928) 777-1500; (928) 777-1500, ext. 115
    (Director); (928) 445-8110; (928) 445-
    1851 FAX
toni.kaus@cityofprescott.net
http://yavanet.prescottlib.lib.az.us/
    libmain.html
Toni Kaus, Library Director
Mon & Fri–Sat 9:00–5:30, Tue–Thur
    9:00–9:00

**Saint Michaels Mission: Historical
Museum and Provincial Archives**
PO Box 680
Saint Michaels, AZ 86511
(928) 871-4171
Fr. Ron Walters, OFM, Provincial Archivist
9:00–5:00

Scottsdale Public Library
Civic Center Library
3839 North Drinkwater Boulevard
Scottsdale, AZ 85251-4467
(480) 312-READ
http://library.ci.scottsdale.az.us
Becky Henry, Reference Coordinator
Mon–Thur 10:00–9:00, Fri–Sat 10:00–6:00,
    Sun 1:00–5:00

Southern Methodist University
Clements Center for Southwest Studies
(see Texas, Part 2)

State Capitol Museum
Arizona Department of Library, Archives
and Public Records
1700 West Washington
Phoenix, AZ 85007
(602) 542-4675 (Museum Division); (602)
    542-4690 FAX
(no genealogy function)

Sun City Library and Cultural Center
16828 North 99th Avenue
Sun City, AZ 85351-1299
(623) 974-2569
chuck@sclib.com
http://www.sclib.com
Mon–Tue & Thur–Fri 10:00–4:00, Wed &
    Sat 10:00–1:00

Tempe Historical Museum
809 East Southern Avenue
Tempe, AZ 85282
(480) 350-5100; (480) 350-5150 FAX
john_akers@tempe.gov
http://www.tempe.gov/museum
John H. Akers, Curator of History
Mon–Fri 10:00–5:00 by appointment
(Tempe and Arizona history; "also have
    Tempe Biographical Database, list of
    residents through 1920+")
copies: 10¢ per page

University of Arizona Library
(1510 East University Boulevard—location)
PO Box 210055 (mailing address)
Tucson, AZ 85721-0055
(520) 621-6441
http://dizzy.library.arizona.edu

University of Utah Marriott Library
(see Utah, Part 2)

Western Heritage Center
(see Montana, Part 2)

Historical Societies—Local and Regional

**American Historical Association, Pacific
Coast Branch**
(see California, Part 2)

**American West Research Center and
Historical Society, Inc.**
(see Ohio, Part 2)

Apache County Historical Society
(180 West Cleveland—location)
PO Box 146 (mailing address)
Saint Johns, AZ 85936
(928) 337-4737
Ethel Smith, Director
Mon–Fri 9:00–5:00
$5.00 per year membership

**Arizona Archaeological and Historical
Society**
Arizona State Museum, University of
Arizona
Tucson, AZ 85721
(520) 621-3656
Tobi Taylor, Editor
Pub. *Kiva: The Journal of Southwestern
    Anthropology and History*, quarterly
    (archaeology, anthropology, history)
$40.00 per year membership

**Casa Grande Valley Historical Society,
Inc.**
110 West Florence Boulevard
Casa Grande, AZ 85222
Craig Ringer, Executive Director
Mon–Fri 9:00–noon
Pub. *Historical Happenings*, one to two
    times per month

Chandler Historical Society
Chandler Museum
(178 East Commonwealth
Avenue—location)
PO Box 926 (mailing address)
Chandler, AZ 85244
(480) 786-2842

Chloride Historical Society
PO Box 294
Chloride, AZ 86431
(928) 565-3619
Joyce Herbst, President

Cochise County Historical Society
(1001 North D Avenue—location)
PO Box 818 (mailing address)
Douglas, AZ 85608-0818
(520) 364-5226
cchsaz@earthlink.net
Liz Ames, Treasurer
Tue 1:00–4:00
Pub. *Cochise County Historical Society
    Journal*, biannually
$20.00 per year membership

**Eastern Arizona Museum and Historical
Society**
(2 North Main Street—location)
PO Box 274 (mailing address)
Pima, AZ 85543
(928) 485-9400
Mrs. Edres Bryant Barney, Curator/Manager
Wed–Fri 2:00–4:00, Sat 1:00–5:00
$5.00 per year membership

El Paso County Historical Society
(see Texas, Part 2)

Gila County Historical Society
(1330 North Broad Street—location)
PO Box 2891 (mailing address)
Globe, AZ 85501
(928) 425-7385
W. A. Haak, President
Mon–Fri 10:00–4:00, Sat 11:00–3:00
$25.00 per year membership

Graham County Historical Society
(3430 West Highway 70, Thatcher, AZ
85552—location)
PO Box 127 (mailing address)
Safford, AZ 85546
(928) 348-0470; (928) 348-0069 (President)
rfg@mstar2.net
http://www.rootsweb.com/~azgraham/
    histsoc.html
Raydene Cluff, Museum Director; Chris
    Angle, President; Ron Gonzales
Mon–Tue & Sat 10:00–5:00
Pub. *Graham County Historical Society
    Symposium Publication*, annually, $5.00
    per year subscription
("Our Museum represents
    history/pictures/artifacts of Graham and
    Greenlee counties, especially, and
    southeast Arizona.")
$15.00 per year membership

Jerome Historical Society
(200 Main Street—location)
PO Box 156 (mailing address)
Jerome, AZ 86331
(928) 634-1066; (928) 634-7349
Jeannette Duke, Director
Museum: Mon–Fri 9:00–5:00
Pub. *Chronicle*, quarterly
    (history of town of Jerome)
$15.00 per year membership

Maricopa County Historical Society
21 North Frontier Street
Wickenburg, AZ 85358
(520) 684-2272
Cheryl A. Taylor, Director
Mon–Sat 10:00–4:00, Sun 1:00–4:00

Mohave County Historical Society, Inc.
Mohave Museum of History and Arts
400 West Beale Street
Kingman, AZ 86401
(928) 753-3195 voice & FAX
mocohist@citlink.net
http://www.ctaz.com/~mocohist/museum
Mr. Shannon Rossiter, Director
Mon–Fri 9:00–5:00, Sat–Sun 1:00–3:00
("We have a research library and several
    permanent exhibits pertaining to Mohave
    County.")

Navajo County Historical Society
Holbrook Branch Museum
100 East Arizona
Holbrook, AZ 86025
(928) 524-6558
Garnette Franklin, Museum
    Director/President
Pub. *NCHS Newsletter*

Northern Arizona University
Center for Colorado Plateau Studies
PO Box 5613
Flagstaff, AZ 86011
(928) 523-2562

Oracle Historical Society, Inc.
Acadia Ranch Museum
PO Box 10
Oracle, AZ 85623
(520) 896-9609; (520) 896-9037 (President)
Evaline J. Auerbach, President
Sat 1:00–5:00, except holidays

Pimeria Alta Historical Society
(126 Grand Avenue, Nogales, AZ
85621—location)
PO Box 2281 (mailing address)
Nogales, AZ 85628-2281
(520) 287-4621
Patricia B. Molina, Museum Administrator
Museum: Fri 10:00–5:00, Sat 10:00–4:00,
Sun 1:00–4:00; Office: Mon–Fri
9:00–5:00

Pinal County Historical Society, Inc.
Pinal County Historical Society Museum
(715 South Main Street—location)
PO Box 851 (mailing address)
Florence, AZ 85232
H. Christine Reid
Tue–Sat 11:00–4:00, Sun noon–4:00
Pub. *Our Heritage*, monthly (except Aug)
("Extensive research library for Pinal
County")
$15.00 per year membership; research: $5.00
per hour for private use, $15.00 per hour
for profit, $25.00 per hour for businesses;
photocopies: 25¢ per page (10¢ for
students), $2.00 for color copies;
photographs: from $7.00–$17.00

Prescott Historical Society
Sharlot Hall Museum
415 West Gurley Street
Prescott, AZ 86301
(928) 445-3122; (928) 776-9053 FAX
webmaster@sharlot.org
http://www.sharlot.org/archives
Michael Wurtz, Archivist
Tue–Fri noon–4:00, Sat 10:00–2:00
Pub. *New Directions*, bimonthly; *Cactus on
a Pine*, annually
$25.00 per year membership

**San Pedro Valley Arts and Historical
Society**
(180 South San Pedro Street—location)
PO Box 1090 (mailing address)
Benson, AZ 85602
(520) 586-2844
Lucille Kowalczyk, President
winter: Tue–Sat 10:00–4:00; May–Sept:
Tue–Sat 10:00–2:00
(artifacts and history of Benson and the San
Pedro Valley in southeast Arizona)
$10.00 per year membership

Scottsdale Historical Society, Inc.
Scottsdale Historical Museum
(7333 Scottsdale Mall, Scottsdale, AZ
85251—location)
PO Box 143 (mailing address)
Scottsdale, AZ 85252
(602) 945-4499
JoAnn Handley, Secretary
Sept–June: Wed–Sat 10:00–5:00, Sun
noon–4:00
Pub. *Scottsdale Historical Society
Newsletter*, five times per year
(artifacts, documents and photographs about
the history of Scottsdale and the

surrounding area)

Sun Cities Area Historical Society
10801 Oakmont Drive
Sun City, AZ 85351
(623) 974-2568
Tue–Fri 1:30–3:30

Superstition Mountain Historical Society
PO Box 1535
Apache Junction, AZ 85220

Tubac Historical Society
PO Box 3261
Tubac, AZ 85646
(520) 398-2919

**White Mountain Historical Society and
Historical Park**
PO Box 12
Springerville, AZ 85938
(928) 333-3322
Ginger Williams, President

Genealogical Societies

State Genealogical Societies

Arizona Genealogical Advisory Board
PO Box 5641
Mesa, AZ 85211-5641
(480) 256-6372 FAX

Arizona State Genealogical Society, Inc.
PO Box 42075
Tucson, AZ 85733-2075
(520) 275-2747
aviceandwarren.boss@worldnet.att.net
(Research Committee Chair);
rjvint@cox.net (Membership);
bcook@gbronline.com (President)
http://www.rootsweb.com/~asgs
Betty Cook, President
Pub. *Copper State Journal*, quarterly, $14.00
per year subscription
$22.00 per year membership; research:
$10.00 minimum

Family History Society of Arizona
PO Box 63094
Phoenix, AZ 85082-3094
(602) 978-3656
ssiders@cox.net
http://www.fhsa.org
Suzanne Siders, President
Pub. *FHSA Newsletter*, quarterly
(Published *The 1910 Arizona Territory
Census Index*, $44.00 ppd.)
$20.00 per year membership

Family History Society of Arizona Chapters

Family History Society of Arizona
East Valley Chapter
c/o Fellowship Square, Building 4
6945 East Main
Mesa, AZ
(480) 649-6060
meetings: first Wed 7:00

Family History Society of Arizona
Fountain Hills Chapter
(480) 837-2183
Martha Craner
meetings at New Fountain Hills Community
Center, 13001 North La Montana Drive,
Fountain Hills: second Mon 10:00 A.M.
(except June–Aug)

Family History Society of Arizona
Glendale Chapter
(602) 841-7037

Shirley Young
meetings at the Glendale Public Library,
5959 West Brown, Glendale, AZ: last
Mon 7:00

Family History Society of Arizona
Paradise Valley Chapter
(602) 991-6168
dfsum@earthlink.net
Diane Sumrall
meetings at the Chaparral Christian Church,
6451 East Shea Boulevard, Scottsdale,
AZ: third Tue 7:00

Family History Society of Arizona
Phoenix North Chapter
(602) 978-3656
ssiders@cox.net
Suzanne Siders
meetings at Phoenix North Family History
Center, 8710 North Third Avenue: second
Thur 10:00 A.M.

Family History Society of Arizona
Scottsdale Chapter
(602) 840-8835
Sharon Leezer, President
meetings at the Shepherd of the Hills
Congregational Church, Room 2, 5524
East Lafayette Boulevard, Phoenix, AZ:
fourth Tue 7:30

Family History Society of Arizona
Tempe Chapter
(480) 820-6201
Sue Clark, Secretary/Treasurer
meetings at the Pyle Adult Recreation
Center, 655 East Southern Avenue,
Tempe, AZ: second Mon 7:00

Genealogical Societies—Local & Regional

Cochise Genealogical Society
(Douglas Williams House, 1001 D Avenue,
Douglas, AZ 85607—office/library location)
PO Box 68 (mailing address)
Pirtleville, AZ 85626
(520) 364-7370 (Library Director)
Alice Percell, Library Director; J. L.
Johnson, President
Wed–Thur & Sat 1:00–4:00
Pub. *The Tombstone*, three times per year
(specializes in southwest Arizona and
Cochise County)
$10.00 per year membership

Coconino County Genealogical Society
649 East Edison
Williams, AZ 86046

Green Valley Genealogical Society
PO Box 1009
Green Valley, AZ 85622-1009
(520) 625-3065
Lou Anne Bunnel, Secretary
meetings at The Church of Jesus Christ of
Latter-day Saints, 17699 Comino de la
Quintas, Schuarite, AZ: Oct–Apr
Pub. *Past Tracks*, quarterly
$10.00 per year membership

Lake Havasu Genealogical Society, Inc.
(2126 McCulloch Boulevard, Suite
17—location)
PO Box 953 (mailing address)
Lake Havasu City, AZ 86405-0953
(928) 855-7105; (928) 855-3607; (928) 854-
5447 (meeting information)
gloharr@rraz.net
http://www.rootsweb.com/~azlhgs

Gloria Harrington, Library Manager
Tue noon–4:00, Wed 9:00–5:00, Thur
    1:00–9:00, Sat 9:00–1:00; meetings: third
    Fri 7:00
Pub. *Lake Havasu Genealogical Society, Inc.
    Newsletter*, six times per year
("Library has about 3,000 books, over 200
    CDs, fiche, about 5,000 periodicals, local
    cemetery listings.")
$15.00 per year membership; research: $5.00
    for requests found on our web site

Genealogical Workshop of Mesa, Inc.
PO Box 6052
Mesa, AZ 85206-6052
(480) 985-0250 (recorded message); (480)
    985-0250 (Statutory Agent)
Doris Miller-Redwine, Statutory Agent
mid-Sept to mid-May: second & fourth Fri
    8:15–11:45
$12.00 per year membership

Mohave County Genealogical Society
400 West Beale Street
Kingman, AZ 86401
(928) 753-3195
mocohist@citlink.net
http://www.ctaz.com/~mocohist/
    museum/geneal.htm
meetings at Mohave County Historical
    Society's Mohave Museum of History and
    Arts: second Wed 1:00
("Not affiliated with the Mohave County
    Historical Society, Inc. or the Mohave
    Museum of History and Arts")

Monte Vista Genies
Monte Vista Village Resort
Pueblo Room
8865 East Baseline Road
Mesa, AZ 85208-5309

Northern Arizona Genealogical Society
PO Box 695
Prescott, AZ 86302
(928) 776-8745
John Paulsen, Editor
Sharlot Hall Museum: Tue–Fri 9:00–4:00
Pub. *The Bulletin*, quarterly
$12.00 per year membership; research: on
    contract basis with individual members

Northern Gila County Genealogical
Society, Inc.
(Rooms 104 and 106, Payson Care Center,
    107 East Lone Pine Drive, Payson, AZ
    85541—location)
PO Box 952 (mailing address)
Payson, AZ 85547-0952
(928) 474-2139
Neil Savage, President
Thur–Sat 9:00–noon
Pub. *Gila Heritage*, quarterly, $8.00 per year
    subscription
$10.00 per year membership

Ohio Genealogical Society
Arizona Chapter
(see Ohio, Part 2)

Phoenix Genealogical Society
6220 North 35th Drive
Phoenix, AZ 85019
(602) 841-0739
Frances Hortsch, President

Sedona Genealogy Club
PO Box 4258
Sedona, AZ 86340
Pub. *Newsletter*, nine times per year
    (monthly, except July–Aug & Dec)

$10.00 per year membership

Tri-State Genealogical Society
PO Box 6045
Mohave Valley, AZ 86440

West Valley Genealogical Society
(12222 North 111th Avenue,
    Youngtown—library location)
PO Box 1448 (mailing address)
Sun City, AZ 85372-1448
(623) 933-4945; (623) 974-3415
    (Administrator)
azdaly@att.net (Membership Chairman)
http://www.rootsweb.com/~azwvgs/
    WVHome.htm
Peggy Morphew, Library Administrator
Tue & Thur–Sat 9:00–4:00
Pub. *Desert Tracker*, biannually; *Tidbits*,
    nine times per year (monthly, Sept–May)
("Frequent genealogical workshops;
    computer-use groups." "Opened new free-
    standing/membership-owned library.")
$25.00 per year membership; admission:
    $5.00 donation for nonmembers

Genealogical Society of Yuma, Arizona
(3117 West 17th Street—location)
PO Box 2905 (mailing address)
Yuma, AZ 85364
(928) 783-7982 (President's home)
Earl Mathews, President
Family History Center: Tue & Wed
    9:00–4:00 & 6:30–9:00, Thur 6:30
    P.M.–9:00 P.M., Fri–Sat 9:00–1:00
Pub. *Newsletter*, four to six times per year
(specializes in Germans to America, index of
    local newspaper, *Arizona Sentinel*,
    1872–1899)
$10.00 per year membership

Independent Publications and Miscellany

Arizona Department of Transportation
206 South 17th Avenue
Mail Drop 101A, Room 135
Phoenix, AZ 85007
(602) 712-7011 (Information)
info@dot.state.az.us
http://map.azfms.com/maps/index.html
    (Maps)

Arizona Genealogy Computer Interest
Group (AGCIG)
PO Box 51498
Phoenix, AZ 85076-1498
(480) 759-5171
webmaster@agcig.org
http://www.agcig.org
Jeannie Rogers; Rusty Perry
meetings: second Sat every other month
    except in summer 9:30–12:30
Pub. *Boot Your Roots*, five times per year

AzGenWeb
Part of The USGenWeb Project
Mjarvis@Pobox.com
http://www.rootsweb.com/~azgenweb
Mike Jarvis, State Coordinator
(links to other Arizona resources)

Center for Southwest Research
(see New Mexico, Part 2)

State Board on Geographic and Historic
Names
Arizona Department of Library, Archives and
Public Records
State Capitol
1700 West Washington

Phoenix, AZ 85007
aznames@dlapr.lib.az.us

State Historic Preservation Office (SHPO)
Arizona State Parks
1300 West Washington
Phoenix, AZ 85007
(602) 542-7115
http://www.pr.state.az.us/partnerships/
    shpo/shpo.html

Texas State Historical Association
Southwestern Historical Quarterly
(see Texas, Part 2)

University of Arizona Press
c/o Joe Wilder
Little Chapel
(350 North Main Avenue—location)
PO Box 210185 (mailing address)
Tucson, AZ 85701
Karen E. Seger, Managing Editor (JSW)
Pub. *Journal of the Southwest* (multi-
    disciplinary, southwest U.S. and northern
    Mexico), quarterly; *Arizona Quarterly*,
    $6.00 per issue
$18.00 per year membership

Tucson Corral of the Westerners
3936 East Guaymas Place
Tucson, AZ 85711
(520) 325-9874; (520) 327-8599 FAX
Bill White, Sales of the *Smoke Signal*; Jarvis
    Harriman, Editor; Richard Hughes,
    Sheriff
meetings: first Mon (Oct–May), second Mon
    (Sept)
Pub. *Smoke Signal*, semiannually
("history and lore of the West, particularly
    the Southwest)
$12.00 per year membership

Arkansas

Archives and Libraries with Holdings in Genealogy

State Archives and Library

Arkansas History Commission
1 Capitol Mall
Little Rock, AR 72201
(501) 682-6900
http://www.ark-ives.com
John L. Ferguson, State Historian
Mon–Sat 8:00–4:30
(Arkansas history and genealogy)

Arkansas State Library
Department of Education
1 Capitol Mall
Little Rock, AR 72201-1081
(501) 682-1527
jmulkey@asl.lib.ar.us
http://www.asl.lib.ar.us
Jack C. Mulkey, State Librarian

State Historical Societies

Arkansas Historical Association
Department of History, Old Main #416
University of Arkansas
Fayetteville, AR 72701
(479) 575-5884; (479) 575-2775 FAX
dludlow@uark.edu
http://www.uark.edu/depts/arkhist/home
Jeannie M. Whayne, Secretary-Treasurer and
    Editor; Gretchen Gearhardt, Assistant
    Editor
8:00–4:30
Pub. *Arkansas Historical Quarterly*;
    *Arkansas Historical Association
    Newsletter*, quarterly
(no library, archives or research staff,
    specializes in "Arkansas and the region")
$16.00 per year membership

**City, County and Regional Archives and
Libraries**
(A more exhaustive list of public and
academic libraries can be found at http://
www.state.ar.us/asl, http://www.asl.lib.ar.
us/PublicL/Libraries.PDF, http://www.
anythingarkansas.com/arts/Libraries.html, or
http:/www.arlib.org/Webpage.html.)

Arkansas State University Museum
Museum/Library Building
PO Box 490
Jonesboro, AR 72467-0490
(870) 972-2074; (870) 972-2793
Charlott Jones, Ph.D., Director
Mon–Fri 9:00–4:00, Sat–Sun 1:00–4:00
Pub. *A Different Drummer*, two times per
    year
(specializes in Arkansas history and
    American Indians)
$25.00 per year membership

Ashley County Library
211 East Lincoln Street
Hamburg, AR 71646-3217
(870) 853-2078; (870) 853-2079 FAX
ashlib@cei.net
Henrietta Thompson, Director
Mon–Fri 9:00–5:30

Baxter County Library
Headquarters
424 West Seventh Street
Mountain Home, AR 72653-4393
(870) 425-3598; (870) 425-7226 FAX
penny.e@cox-internet.com;

baxter.library@centurytel.net
http://www.baxtercountylibrary.org
Penny Ellis, Genealogy and Reference
Mon–Fri 10:00–6:30, Sat 10:00–4:00

Bentonville Public Library
125 West Central, Room 100
Bentonville, AR 72712-5298
(479) 271-3194; (479) 271-3192
    (Circulation); (479) 271-9051 FAX
csuter@bentonvillear.com
http://www.bentonvillear.com/Library.html
Cindy Suter, Librarian

Boone County Public Library
221 West Stephenson Street
Harrison, AR 72601-4298
(870) 741-5913 voice & FAX
boonecolibrary@hotmail.com
http://bcl.state.ar.us
Donna Phillips, Genealogy
Tue–Wed & Fri–Sat 10:00–5:00, Thur
    10:00–7:00
copies at 10¢ per page

Booneville Public Library
419 North Kennedy
Booneville, AR 72927-3630
(501) 675-2735 voice & FAX
bblog@cswnet.com
http://www.arvrls.com/logan2.htm
Patricia L. Curry, Librarian
Mon 11:00–7:00, Tue–Thur 9:00–5:00
(Logan County history and genealogy)
research: $3.00 plus copies and postage

**Richard C. Butler, Sr. Center for
Arkansas Studies**
Central Arkansas Library System
100 Rock Street
Little Rock, AR 72201
(501) 918-3056
http://www.cals.lib.ar.us/butlercenter/
    index.html
Tom W. Dillard, Curator of Special
    Collections; Timothy G. Nutt, Deputy
    Curator
Mon–Thur 9:00–8:00, Fri–Sat 9:00–6:00,
    Sun 1:00–5:00
Pub. *Butler Banner*, free
(Arkansas and southern states)

Central Arkansas Library System
(see Richard C. Butler, Sr. Center For
Arkansas Studies, above)

Clark County Public Library
609 Caddo Street
Arkadelphia, AR 71923-6099
(870) 246-2271; (870) 246-4189 FAX
Judy Golden, Librarian

**William J. Clinton Presidental Materials
Project**
1000 LaHarpe Boulevard
Little Rock, AR 72201
(501) 244-9756; (501) 244-9764 FAX
clinton.library@nara.gov
http://www.clinton.nara.gov
research by appointment only

Conway County Library
101 West Church Street
Morrilton, AR 72110-3305
(501) 354-5204; (501) 354-5206 FAX
Zoe Butler, Librarian

Corning Public Library
613 Pine Street
Corning, AR 72422-2752
(870) 857-3453 voice & FAX
clibrary@eudoramail.com

http://www.corninglibrary.com
Kathy Buchanan, Director
Mon–Tue & Thur 9:00–6:00, Wed & Fri
    9:00–5:00, Sat 9:00–1:00
("We currently have 312 titles in our
    genealogy section as well as microfilmed
    census and local newspapers.")

Crowley Ridge Regional Library
Craighead County-Jonesboro Public Library
Information Services
315 West Oak Avenue
Jonesboro, AR 72401-3513
(870) 935-5133; (870) 935-7987 FAX
elvis@libraryinjonesboro.org
http://www.librarinjonesboro.org
Phyllis Burkett, Librarian
Mon 11:30–8:30, Tue–Fri 9:30–6:00, Sat
    9:30–5:00, Sun 1:00–5:00

Delta Cultural Center
95 Missouri Street
Helena, AR 72342
(870) 338-4350; (870) 338-4358 FAX
http://www.heritage.state.ar.us/her_doc.html

Desha County Museum Society
(Highway 165, East—location)
PO Box 141 (mailing address)
Dumas, AR 72639
(870) 382-4222
Mary C. Martin, Director
Tue, Thur & Sun 2:00–4:00
no cost

East Arkansas Community College
Forrest City, AR 72335-9598

Fayetteville Public Library
(see Grace Keith Genealogy Collection,
below)

Fort Smith Public Library
3201 Rogers Avenue
Fort Smith, AR 72903
(479) 783-0229; (479) 783-8275 FAX
genealogy@fspl.lib.ar.us
http://www.fspl.lib.ar.us/genmain.html
Sheila M. Brushes, Genealogy Librarian
Genealogy Department: Mon & Wed–Fri
    9:00–5:30, Tue 9:00–8:00, Sat
    10:00–4:00, Sun 1:00–5:00
research: $10.00 per hour (minimum $10.00
    in advance), copies 25¢ per page from
    paper original, 50¢ per page from
    microform original

The Gann Museum of Saline County
218 South Market Street
Benton, AR 72015
(501) 778-5513
http://www.museumusa.org/data/
    museums/AR/116762.htm
Mrs. Ike Sharp, Director
Tue–Sat 10:00–2:00, Sun 1:30–4:00
Pub. *Newsletter*
(genealogical services)

Garland County Library
1427 Malvern Avenue, Room 144
Hot Springs, AR 71901-6316
(501) 623-4161; (501) 623-3943; (501) 623-
    6356 FAX; (501) 623-5647 FAX
gclhsar@hotmail.com
John Wells, Interim Director, Librarian

Hacksma House Genealogy Library
(see Washington, Part 2)

Helena Public Library
Arkansas Room
623 Pecan Street

Helena, AR 72342-3298
(870) 338-3537; (870) 338-7732 FAX
reflib@hnb.com
http://www.geocities.com/Athens/Ithaca/
4022
Pat Ward, Circulation Clerk, Genealogy;
Susan Hamilton, County Library Director
Mon–Sat 9:00–5:00

Hempstead County Library
500 South Elm Street
Hope, AR 71801-5289
(870) 777-4564; (870) 777-2957 FAX
Judy Sooter, Librarian
Mon noon–9:00, Tue–Fri 9:00–5:30, Sat
9:00–noon

Hot Spring County Public Library
Ash and E Streets
Malvern, AR 72104
(501) 332-5441; (501) 332-6679 FAX
hotspringcountylibrary@yahoo.com
http://www.hsc.lib.ar.us
Mary Ann Griggs, Librarian
8:30–5:00, until 8:30 on certain evenings

Huntsville-Madison County Public Library
(see Alabama, Part 2)

Grace Keith Genealogy Collection
Fayetteville Public Library
217 East Dickson Street
Fayetteville, AR 72701
(479) 442-2242, ext. 20; (501) 442-5723
FAX
genealogy@fayettevillelibrary.org;
fpl@fayettevillelibrary.org
http://www.fayettevillelibrary.org
Jean Boyer; Peggy Hackler
Main Library: Mon–Thur 9:30–8:00, Fri–Sat
9:30–5:00, Sun 1:00–4:00; Genealogy:
Mon 9:30–8:00, Tue–Sat 9:30–5:00, Sun
1:00–4:00
(Microfilm of federal censuses, Arkansas
1830–1930, all states 1880–1920;
Fayetteville, Arkansas, newspapers from
1868; index to "Flashback," a
Washington County Historical Society
publication, from 1951; Washington
County, Arkansas, probate, wills and
marriage records on microfilm (with
indexes)
research: $2.50 per hour, limit two hours,
plus copies at 25¢ each

S.S. Lipscomb Arkansas History and Genealogy Room
Northeast Arkansas Regional Library
Greene County Library
120 North 12th Street
Paragould, AR 72450-4155
(870) 236-8711 (no extension in genealogy
room; no research queries taken by phone,
only basic questions about holdings);
(501) 236-1442 FAX
library@paragould.net
http://www.paragouldlibrary.com
Bettye Busby
Library: Mon–Thur 9:00–6:00, Fri
9:00–4:00, Sat 9:00–1:00; Lipscomb
Room open same hours as library but not
always staffed, usually staffed by
volunteers 1:00–4:00
(extensive section on Greene County with
census; marriage and tombstone indexes;
family and community histories; and local
newspapers on microfilm; rest of
collection focuses on Arkansas and
southeastern states from which early
settlers migrated, especially Tennessee)
queries regarding indexed materials will be

answered by volunteers from the Greene
County Historical and Genealogical
Society as time permits for SASE & copy
costs at 20¢ per page

Lyon College
Regional Studies Center
Mabee Library
Batesville, AR 72501
(870) 698-4330
Nancy S. Griffith, Director
Mon–Fri 8:00–3:00
("Collection focuses on Arkansas history and
genealogy, particularly Independence and
neighboring counties.")
free admission, photocopies 10¢ per page

Marianna-Lee County Museum
PO Box 584
Marianna, AR 72360
(870) 295-2469

Heritage House Museum of Montgomery County, Arkansas
(819 Luzerne Street—location)
PO Box 1362
Mount Ida, AR 71957
(870) 867-4422
order@hhmmc.org
http://home.earthlink.net/
~heritagehousemuseum
Fred Standridge, Genealogist; Diane
Breashears, Director
Mon, Wed & Fri 9:00–4:00, Thur 4:00–8:00,
Sat–Sun 1:00–4:00
Pub. *Newsletter*
("It is Fred's goal to have a file 'for every
family having lived in Montgomery
County.'")
$25.00 per year membership; admission: free
to members

Nevada County Depot Museum Association
(400 West First Street, South—location)
PO Box 10 (mailing address)
Prescott, AR 71857
(870) 887-5821
http://wolfden.swsc.k12.ar.us/
depot_museum
J.W. Teeter and Mrs. Jim Miner, Board
Members
Mon–Fri 10:00–noon & 2:00–5:30
Pub. *News Letter: Events & Projects*,
quarterly
(family histories [written and audio tapes],
cemetery records 1790–1950,
photographs, letters, documents, school
and church histories, Civil War Battle of
Prairie De Ann; some material online)
$10.00 per year membership; SASE for
information, no fees

Piggott Public Library
361 West Main Street
Piggott, AR 72454-2099
(870) 598-3666 voice & FAX
piggottlibrary@centurytel.net
http://www.piggottlibrary.com
Gay Johnson, Librarian
Mon–Tue & Thur–Fri 9:00–5:00, Sat
9:00–noon

Pine Bluff/Jefferson County Public Library
Main Library
200 East Eighth Avenue
Civic Center Complex
Pine Bluff, AR 71601-5092
(870) 534-4802; (870) 534-2159
(Reference); (870) 534-8707 FAX
pbjc-lib@pbjc-lib.state.ar.us

http://www.pbjclibrary.org
Gwen Shelton, Reference Librarian
Mon–Tue & Thur 9:00–8:00, Wed
9:00–6:00, Fri–Sat 9:00–4:00

Polk County Library
410 Eighth Street
Mena, AR 71953-3240
(501) 394-2314 voice & FAX
genealogy@fletcher.net
Shirley Philpot, Librarian

Pope County Library
Russellville Heritage Room
116 East Third Street
Russellville, AR 72801-5198
(479) 968-4368 voice & FAX (Library)
ark@popelib.state.ar.us
http://www.gorussellville.com/Business_Dire
ctory/Community/Newcomers_Guide/Libr
aries.htm
Katie Murdoch, Local History Librarian
("Genealogy and Arkansas titles. Large
collection.")

Randolph County Library
111 West Everett Street
Pocahontas, AR 72455
(870) 892-5617; (870) 892-1142 FAX
racolib@yahoo.com
http://www.randolphcountylibrary.com
Brenda White, Librarian
Mon–Tue 10:00–7:00, Wed–Fri 9:00–5:00,
Sat 10:00–2:00

Rector Public Library
121 West Fourth Street
Rector, AR 72461-1309
(870) 595-2410 voice & FAX
rectorpubliclibrary@yahoo.com
http://www.rectorlibrary.com
Geraldine Wagster, Librarian
Mon–Tue & Thur 9:00–6:00, Wed & Fri
9:00–5:00

Rogers Historical Museum
322 South Second Street
Rogers, AR 72756
(479) 621-1154; (479) 621-1155 FAX
museum@rogersarkansas.com
http://www.rogersarkansas.com/museum
Gaye Bland, Director
Tue–Sat 10:00–4:00

Searcy County Museum
(Center—location)
PO Box 233 (mailing address)
Marshall, AR 72650
(870) 448-5786
Veda Clemons, Director
Pub. *Marshall Mountain Wave*

Shiloh Museum of Ozark History
118 West Johnson Avenue
Springdale, AR 72764
(479) 750-8165; (479) 750-8693
shiloh@springdaleark.org
http://www.uark.edu/ALADDIN/shiloh
Bob Besom
Mon–Sat 10:00–5:00
Pub. *Shiloh Scrapbook*, quarterly
(Seven buildings, including 22,000 square
foot main building. "Our focus is on the
six counties in the northwest corner of
Arkansas. We have an especially strong
photograph collection.")
$10.00–$1,000.00 per year membership; free
admission

Southwest Arkansas Regional Archives (SARA)
Old Washington Historic State Park

PO Box 134
Washington, AR 71862
(870) 983-2684 (Mon–Fri); (870) 983-2633
(Sat–Sun)
http://www.gorp.com/gorp/location/ar/
parks/old/htm
Mon–Sun 9:00–4:00
$5.00 per year membership

**Bessie Boehm Moore Stone County
Library**
(326 West Washington Street—location)
PO Box 1105 (mailing address)
Mountain View, AR 72560-1105
(870) 269-3100 voice & FAX
sclibrary99@hotmail.com
http://rootsweb.com/~arscgs/library.htm
Miriam Miller, Librarian
Tue–Wed 10:00–5:00, Thur 11:00–7:00, Fri
11:00–5:00, Sat 9:00–1:00

Stuttgart Public Library
2002 South Buerkle Street
Stuttgart, AR 72160-6508
(870) 673-1966; (870) 673-4295 FAX
http://www.ar-
net.com/sttg/library/library.htm
Ted T. Campbell, Librarian
Mon, Wed & Fri 9:00-6:00, Tue, Thur & Sat
1:00-6:00

Texarkana Museums System
(see Texas, Part 2)

University of Arkansas
Special Collections Division
University of Arkansas Libraries
Mullins Library
Fayetteville, AR 72701-1201
(501) 575-5577; (501) 575-6656 FAX
http://www.uark.edu/campus-
resources/libinfo (Library);
http://cavern.uark.edu/libinfo/speccoll/ind
ex.html (Special Collections Division)
Andrea Cantrell, Head of Research Services
Mon–Fri 8:00–5:00, Sat 9:00–1:00 (hours
vary at holidays and between semesters)
Pub. *Books and Letters*, semiannually
$25.00 per year membership in Friends of
the Library; no extensive search services

**University of Central Arkansas Archives
and Special Collections**
Torreyson Library
Conway, AR 72032
(501) 450-3418
http://www2.uca.edu/archives/main–
Tom W. Dillard, Director
Mon–Fri 8:00–5:00
(Faulkner County genealogy)

University of Mississippi
Center for the Study of Southern Culture
(see Mississippi, Part 2)

Van Buren County Library
(111 North 12th Street, Van Buren, AR
72957—location)
PO Box 724 (mailing address)
Van Buren, AR 72956-0724
(501) 474-6045; (501) 471-3226 FAX
ewhite44@hotmail.com
http://www.crawfordcountylib.org
Eva White, Librarian
Mon–Thur 9:00–7:00, Fri–Sat 9:00–5:30,
Sun 1:00–4:00
(microfilm and a few publications put out by
historical society)

Historical Societies—Local and Regional

**American West Research Center and
Historical Society, Inc.**
(see Ohio, Part 2)

**Arkansas River Historical Society
Museum**
(see Oklahoma, Part 2)

Ashley County Historical Society
Museum
300 North Cherry Street
Hamburg, AR 71646
(870) 853-5796
J. Edward White, Chairman

**Baxter County Historical and
Genealogical Society**
PO Box 1611
Mountain Home, AR 72654
calamity@mymtnhome.com
http://www.baxtercountyonline.com/bchgs
Jane Andrewson
Pub. *The History*, quarterly
$15.00 per year membership

Bella Vista Historical Society and Museum
1885 Bella Vista Way
Bella Vista, AR 72714
(501) 855-2335
Durand Young, President
Mar–Nov: daily 1:00–4:00
Pub. *BVHSM Newsletter*, bimonthly (Feb,
Apr, June, Aug, Oct, Dec)
$10.00 per year membership; no research
help except on Bella Vista topics

Benton County Historical Society
(400 South Walton Boulevard—location)
PO Box 1034 (mailing address)
Bentonville, AR 72712
(501) 273-3890
Win Logue, President
Mon, Wed & Fri 1:30–4:00
Pub. *Benton County Pioneer*, quarterly
$10.00 per year membership

**Boone County Historical and Railroad
Society, Inc.**
Boone County Heritage Museum
(Corner of Central and Cherry—location)
PO Box 1094 (mailing address)
Harrison, AR 72601
(870) 741-3312
Virginia Phillips, Corresponding Secretary
for Historical and Genealogy Affairs
Mon–Fri 10:00–4:00 (Mar–Nov); Thur
10:00–4:00 (Dec–Feb)
Pub. *Boone County Historian*, quarterly
$15.00 per year membership; $2.00
admission to museum

**Carroll County Historical Society and
Heritage Center**
(1880 Court House—location)
PO Box 249 (mailing address)
Berryville, AR 72616
(870) 423-6312
Pub. *Carroll County Historical Society
Quarterly*
$12.00 per year membership

Clark County Historical Association
Ouachita Baptist University
Riley-Hickingbotham Library
Special Collections
(410 Ouachita—location)
OBU Box 3729 (mailing address)
Arkadelphia, AR 71923
(870) 245-5332
richterw@obu.edu
http://www.obu.edu/library
Wendy Richter, Archivist

Mon–Fri 8:00–4:00
Pub. *Clark County Historical Journal*,
annually
$15.00 per year membership

**Clay County Genealogical and Historical
Society**
(see Genealogical Societies—Local and
Regional, below)

Cleburne County Historical Society
PO Box 794
Heber Springs, AR 72543
Pub. *Cleburne County Historical Quarterly*

Cleveland County Historical Society
PO Box 342
Rison, AR 71665

Craighead County Historical Society
PO Box 1011
Jonesboro, AR 72403-1011
(870) 935-6838
http://www.couchgenweb.com/society
Mrs. Frank F. Sloan, Corresponding
Secretary
Pub. *Craighead County Historical Quarterly*
(Jan, Apr, July, Oct)
("History and some genealogies of Craighead
County, formed 1859 from Greene,
Mississippi and Poinsett counties.")
$10.00 per year membership; queries: $7.00
for nonmembers

Crawford County Historical Society
PO Box 1317
Van Buren, AR 72956
(501) 474-2218
Doris West, President
Pub. *The Heritage*, annually
$10.00 per year membership

Crittenden County Historical Society, Inc.
401 Gibson
West Memphis, AR 72301
(870) 735-1659
Melanie Newton Sims, Past President

Cross County Historical Society
(Cross County Courthouse, 705 East
Union—office location)
PO Box 943 (mailing address)
Wynne, AR 72396-0943
Mrs. Jimmie S. James, Secretary
Mon–Fri 11:00–4:00
("Census records of Cross County, histories,
newspaper files for past and present Cross
County")
$4.00 per year membership

Drew County Historical Society
404 South Main
Monticello, AR 71655
(870) 367-7446
Roy A. Grizzell, Ph.D., President
Fri–Sun 2:00–5:00
Pub. *Drew County Historical Journal*,
annually, $10.00 per copy

Faulkner County Historical Society
PO Box 731
Conway, AR 72032
(501) 327-7788
http://www.users.intellinet.com/
~wmeriwet/faulkner.htm
Robert W. Meriwether, President
Pub. *Faulkner County Historical Society
Newsletter*, quarterly; *Faulkner Facts and
Fiddlings*, quarterly
$10.00 per year membership

Fort Smith Historical Society, Inc.

c/o Fort Smith Public Library
3201 Rogers Avenue
Fort Smith, AR 72903
(501) 783-1237
Amelia Martin, Editor
Library, Genealogy Department: Mon &
Wed–Fri 9:00–5:30, Tue 9:00–8:00, Sat
10:00–4:00, Sun 1:00–5:00
Pub. *Journal*, semiannually
$15.00 per year membership

Garland County Historical Society
(328 Quapaw Avenue—location)
222 McMahan Drive (mailing address)
Hot Springs, AR 71913-6243
(501) 623-6766 voice & FAX
Bobbie Jones McLane, Executive Director
and Co-editor
Mon–Fri 8:00–noon
Pub. *The Record*, annually
(primarily Hot Springs and Garland County)
$18.00 per year membership

Grand Prairie Historical Society
203 South Monroe Street
DeWitt, AR 72042
(870) 946-1336
Ellen West, Mailing Secretary
Pub. *Grand Prairie Historical Society
Bulletin*, semiannually (Apr, Oct)
("Back copies kept in DeWitt Public
Library.")
$10.00 per year membership; copies of
requested pages available

**Greene County Historical and
Genealogical Society**
120 North 12th Street
Paragould, AR 72450
(870) 239-4328 (President)
Lynda Bryant, President
Greene County Library: Mon–Tue
9:00–6:00, Fri 9:00–4:00, Sat 9:00–1:00;
S. S. Lipscomb Arkansas History and
Genealogy Room open same hours as
library but not always staffed, usually
staffed by volunteers 1:00–4:00
Pub. *The Greene County Historical and
Genealogical Quarterly*; *The GCHGS
Newsletter*, nine times per year (monthly
Sept–May)
$20.00 per year membership; research in
indexed material: cost of photocopies plus
postage

Hempstead County Historical Society
149 Highway 32E
Hope, AR 71801
(870) 777-2491 (Editor)
turnermn@arkansas.net
Mary Nell Turner, Editor
Pub. *The Journal of the HCHS*, annually
$10.00 per year membership; some search
service

Hot Spring County, AR, Historical Society
PO Box 674
Malvern, AR 72104
(501) 337-7488
Bonnie D. Stanley, Editor
Pub. *The Heritage*, annually, $22.50
postpaid per issue for nonmembers
(Specializes in Hot Spring County, Arkansas,
history and genealogy. "Our data is
housed in Hot Spring County Public
Library for research.")
$17.50 per year membership

Independence County Historical Society
PO Box 2722
Batesville, AR 27503-2722
(870) 793-2383

http://fly.hiwaay.net/~ichs.htm
Bertha Perkey, President; Nancy Britton,
Editor
8:00–4:00
Pub. *The Independence County Chronicle*,
quarterly (Jan, June); *Newsletter*, two
times per year (Apr, Oct)
$15.00 per year membership

**The Izard County Historical and
Genealogical Society**
PO Box 306
Pineville, AR 72566
(870) 499-3237
nita@centurytel.net
Juanita Stowers, Editor/Treasurer
by appointment
Pub. *The Izard County Historian*, quarterly
(Jan, Apr, July, Oct)
$15.00 per year membership; queries and
surnames researching for members

Jackson County Historical Society
7 Pickens Street
Newport, AR 72112
(870) 523-5150
Wayne Boyce, Editor
9:00–5:00
Pub. *Stream of History*, quarterly
(specializes in Jackson County history)
$10.00 per year membership

Johnson County Historical Society
PO Box 505
Clarksville, AR 72830
(501) 754-8539
Annita M. Powell, Editor
Johnson County Library: Mon 1:30–8:30,
Tue–Fri 9:30–5:30, Sat 9:00–noon
Pub. *Johnson County Historical Society
Journal*, semiannually (Apr, Oct)
$15.00 per year membership

Lafayette County Historical Society
(201 Hope Road, Stamps, AR
71860—location)
PO Box 91 (mailing address)
Lewisville, AR 71845
(870) 921-4785
Eugene D. Smith, President
Pub. *Lafayette Lookback*, semiannually
$7.00 per year membership

Lawrence County Historical Society
PO Box 93
Powhatan, AR 72458
Pub. *Lawrence County Historical Journal*,
semiannually
$10.00 per year membership

Logan County Historical Society
PO Box 40
Magazine, AR 72943-0040
Patricia L. Curry, Secretary
Pub. *Wagon Wheels*, quarterly
$15.00 per year membership; research: $3.00
plus copies

Lonoke County Historical Society
PO Box 14
Lonoke, AR 72086
(501) 676-6988
Ruby Gagliano, Co-Editor, Membership
volunteer
Pub. *Newsletter-Lonoke County Historical
Society*, three times per year
$15.00 per year membership

**Madison County Genealogical and
Historical Society**
(see Genealogical Societies—Local and
Regional, below)

**Marion County, Arkansas, Historical and
Genealogical Society**
Marion County Library
PO Box 554
Yellville, AR 72687

Montgomery County Historical Society
(Highway 270—location)
PO Box 578 (mailing address)
Mount Ida, AR 71957-0520
(870) 867-3121
director@mtidachamber.com (Chamber of
Commerce)
http://mtidachamber.com/Historical/
History.htm
Debbie Baldwin
hours: various
("We have various county books for sale.")

**Newton County Historical Society/Bradley
House Museum**
(403 Clark Street—location)
PO Box 360 (mailing address)
Jasper, AR 72641
(870) 446-6247
newtoncountyar@yahoo.com
http://www.newtoncountyar.com
Donna Dodson, Secretary-Hostess
Tue–Thur (Apr–Oct) 11:00–4:00, Tue
(Nov–Dec)
Pub. *Newsletter*, quarterly
$15.00 per year membership; research:
$15.00 per hour

Ouachita County Historical Society
926 Washington, N.W.
Camden, AR 71701
(870) 836-9243
Hubert Boddie, Docent
Wed–Sat (mid-Mar to mid-Nov)9:00–4:00
Pub. *Ouachita County Historical Society
Quarterly*
(primarily historical, not genealogical)
$20.00 per year membership; no staff-
conducted research

Phillips County Historical Society
Helena Public Library
623 Pecan Street
Helena, AR 72342
(870) 338-3271; (870) 338-3481
Ivey S. Gladin and Nancee James, Editors
Library: Mon–Sat 9:00–5:00
Pub. *Phillips County Historical Review*,
semiannually (spring and fall), $5.00 per
issue plus mailing
(history of eastern Arkansas)
$10.00 or $15.00 per year membership

Poinsett County Historical Society
PO Box 424
Harrisburg, AR 72432
Donna Bell, Treasurer
$5.00 per year membership

Pope County Historical Association
4200 A Street
Little Rock, AR 72205-4046
(501) 663-3301
Elaine Weir Cia, Editor
Pub. *Pope County Historical Quarterly*
$10.00 per year membership

**Pope County Historical Foundation
(Pottsville)**
c/o Pope County Library
Russellville Heritage Room
116 East Third
Russellville, AR 72801
ark@popelib.state.ar.us
Katie Murdoch, Local History Librarian
Russellville Heritage Room: Mon–Wed &

Fri 9:00–6:00, Thur 11:00–8:00
Pub. *Pope County Historical Quarterly*,
$10.00 per year subscription

Prairie County Historical Society
PO Box 451
Hazen, AR 72064
(870) 255-4522

Saline County Historical Commission
The Gann Museum of Saline County
218 South Market Street
Benton, AR 72015
(501) 778-5513 (Museum)
Ann Wheat Bryan, Librarian, Saline County
History and Heritage Society
Museum: Tue–Sat 10:00–2:00, Sun
1:30–4:00
Pub. *Newsletter: The Gann Museum of
Saline County*, quarterly

**Saline County History and Heritage
Society, Inc.**
PO Box 1712
Benton, AR 72018-1712
(501) 778-3770 (Tue–Wed 9:00–noon);
(501) 778-3335
http://www.rootsweb.com/~arsaline/
schhs.html
Eddie G. Landreth, Editor and Treasurer;
Ann Wheat Bryan, Librarian
The Archives and Research Center, Room
102 of the ULAR Learning Center on
River Street, Benton: Tue–Wed
9:00–noon and by appointment; meetings
in the Conference Room of the Benton
Fire Department: third Thur 7:00
Pub. *The Saline*, quarterly
$15.00 per year membership

**Scott County Historical and Genealogical
Society**
(West Second Street, Old Jail—location)
PO Box 1560 (mailing address)
Waldron, AR 72958-1560
(479) 637-2466
bettyl@ipa.net
Betty Leeper, President; Delaine Edwards,
Secretary
Mon 10:00–5:00, and by appointment for
out-of-town visitors
Pub. *Echoes*, four times per year
(publishes numerous Scott County records:
census, marriages, obituaries, etc.; contact
society for complete list)
$15.00 per year membership

Sevier County Historical Society
(717 North Maple Street—location)
PO Box 288 (mailing address)
DeQueen, AR 71832
(870) 642-6642 (Museum)
June King, Museum Director
Tue–Sat 10:00–4:00, Sun 2:00–4:00
Pub. *Sevier County Historical Society
Newsletter*, about quarterly
$5.00 per year membership

Sharp County Historical Society
PO Box 185
Ash Flat, AR 72513
(870) 257-2323
Rose Thompson, Secretary and Treasurer
meetings at the Sharp County Bank, Ash
Flat, AR
Pub. *Sharp County Historical Society*,
quarterly; occasional journals
(historical events, towns and people; "We
answer what queries we can, or point
them in the direction of someone who
may be able to help them.")
$10.00 per year membership

South Sebastian County Historical Society
PO Box 523
Greenwood, AR 72936
Roger W. McConnell, Secretary-Treasurer
Pub. *The Key*
$10.00 per year membership

Southern Studies Institute
(see Louisiana, Part 2)

Stone County Historical Society
PO Box 210
Mountain View, AR 72560
http://rootsweb.com/~arscgs/historical.htm
Pub. *Heritage of Stone*, semiannually
$12.00 per year membership

Van Buren County Historical Society
(1123 Third Street—location)
PO Box 1023 (mailing address)
Clinton, AR 72031-1023
(501) 745-4066
http://www.ntanet.net/nta/historical.html
Betty Gay, President; Sharon Baker,
Secretary
Mon–Fri 10:00–4:00
Pub. *Van Buren County Historical Journal*,
quarterly
$12.50 per year membership

Washington County Historical Society
118 East Dickson Street
Fayetteville, AR 72701
(501) 521-2970
Ann Sugg, President
usually Thur 1:00–4:00, Sat 10:00–noon
(call to confirm hours)
Pub. *Flashback & Flashforward*, quarterly
(specializes in Fayetteville, Washington
County and northwest Arkansas books
and products)
$15.00 per year membership; research
requests referred to Genealogy Section,
Fayetteville Public Library

White County Historical Society
PO Box 537
Searcy, AR 72143
(501) 268-1100; (501) 279-7896
leach@cswnet.com; ebest@ipa.net
http://www.rootsweb.com/~arwhite
Bill Leach, President; Eddie Best, Editor
Pub. *White County Heritage*, annually
$12.00 per year membership; queries
accepted

White River Valley Historical Society
(see Missouri, Part 2)

**Yell County Arkansas Historical and
Genealogical Association**
PO Box 622
Dardanelle, AR 72834
Pub. *Yell County Historical and
Genealogical Association Bulletin*,
quarterly
$10.00 per year membership

Genealogical Societies

State Genealogical Society

Arkansas Genealogical Society, Inc.
(1411 Shady Grove Road, Hot Springs, AR
71901—shipping location)
PO Box 908 (mailing address)
Hot Springs, AR 71902-0908
(501) 262-4513 voice & FAX
AskAGS@comcast.net
http://www.rootsweb.com/~args
Margaret Harrison Hubbard, Editor
Pub. *Arkansas Family Historian*, quarterly

$20.00 per year membership

Southern Society of Genealogists, Inc.
(see Alabama, Part 2)

Genealogical Societies—Local & Regional

Ancestors Unknown
PO Box 164
Conway, AR 72033
(501) 329-2868 (weekdays); (501) 329-3404
(evenings); (501) 329-3093 FAX
evatt@cswnet.com
Linda Evatt, Treasurer
meetings at Faulkner County Library, 1900
Tyler, Conway, AR: second Mon 6:30
Pub. *Ancestors Unknown Newsletter*,
monthly
$15.00 per year membership

Ark-La-Tex Genealogical Association, Inc.
Randle T. Moore Senior Citizen Center
PO Box 4462
Shreveport, LA 71134-0462
(318) 868-0036 (President)
aga@softdisk.com
http://www.softdisk.com/comp/aga
Reed Mathews, President
meetings at the Randle: second Sat
(Sept–July) 1:00
Pub. *The Genie*, quarterly
(Arkansas, Louisiana and Texas)
$12.50 per year membership

Ashley County Genealogical Society
PO Drawer R
Crossett, AR 71635-1819
(870) 364-2885
Mary Spainhour, President
Pub. *Kin Kollecting*, quarterly, $6.50
postpaid per issue; *News, Etc.*, monthly
$20.00 per year membership

Batesville Genealogical Society
PO Box 3883
Batesville, AR 72503-3883
Pub. *Bits of Bark from the Family Tree*,
quarterly
$10.00 per year membership

**Baxter County Historical and
Genealogical Society**
(see Historical Societies—Local and
Regional, above)

Bradley County Genealogical Society
PO Box 837
Warren, AR 71671-0837

**Carthage Genealogical Society and
Southwest Missouri Genealogical Library**
(see Missouri, Part 2)

**Clay County Genealogical and Historical
Society**
Piggott Public Library
361 West Main Street
Piggott, AR 72454-2099
(870) 598-3666 FAX
ccghs1985@yahoo.com
http://www.piggottlibrary.com/cc_gen_
hist_soc.htm
Gay Johnson, Librarian; Camilla Bricker
Cox, Corresponding Secretary
Library: Mon–Tue & Thur 9:00–6:00, Wed
& Fri 9:00–5:00; meetings: third Sun 2:00
Pub. *Quarterly Newsletter*
$10.00 per year membership

Crawford County Genealogical Society
(314 Fayetteville Street—location)
PO Box 276 (mailing address)

Alma, AR 72921
Lucille Titsworth, President
Tue & Thur 9:00–3:00
Pub. *Panning for Nuggets of Old*, two times
    per year (spring and fall)
$15.00 per year membership

Frontier Researchers Genealogical Society
PO Box 2123
Fort Smith, AR 72902-2123
Sherryh10@aol.com
Valerie Lewis, Corresponding Secretary;
    Sherry Hall, President
Fort Smith Public Library, Genealogy
    Department: Mon & Wed–Fri 9:00–5:30,
    Tue 9:00–8:00, Sat 10:00–4:00, Sun
    1:00–5:00
Pub. *Frontier Research*, annually
(emphasis on Oklahoma and Arkansas)
$15.00 per year membership

Grand Prairie Genealogical Society
c/o Stuttgart Public Library
2002 South Buerkle Street
Stuttgart, AR 72160-6508
http://www.rootsweb.com/~ararkans/
    grandpra.htm
meetings: second Tue 7:00
$15.00 per year membership

**Greene County Historical and
Genealogical Society**
(see Historical Societies—Local and
Regional, above)

Hempstead County Genealogical Society
(Hempstead County Library—location)
PO Box 1158 (mailing address)
Hope, AR 71802-1158
hempsteadgen@yahoo.com
http://www.geocities.com/hempsteadgen/
    HEMPSTEADGEN.html
Mon noon–8:30, Tue–Fri 9:00–5:30
Pub. *Hempstead Trails*, semiannually
$15.00 per year membership

Heritage Seekers Genealogy Club
William F. Laman Public Library
2800 Orange Street
North Little Rock, AR 72114
Richard Butler, President
fourth Mon 7:00 P.M.–9:00 P.M.
$10.00 per year membership

Howard County Heritage Club
218 West Howard Street
Nashville, AR 72852
John Reuther

**The Izard County Historical and
Genealogical Society**
(see Historical Societies—Local and
Regional, above)

Jefferson County Genealogical Society
PO Box 2215
Pine Bluff, AR 71613

**Madison County Genealogical and
Historical Society**
(Corner of Highway 74 West and
Mitchusson Park Road—location)
PO Box 427 (mailing address)
Huntsville, AR 72740
(479) 738-6408
JRussell44@aol.com
http://members.aol.com/madcounty/
    mcghs/mcghsinf.htm
Virginia Threet, President
10:00–3:00
Pub. *The Madison County Musings*,
    quarterly

$12.50 per year membership

**Marion County, Arkansas, Historical and
Genealogical Society**
(see Historical Societies—Local and
Regional, above)

Melting Pot Genealogical Society
(223A Hazel Street—location)
PO Box 936 (mailing address)
Hot Springs National Park, AR 71901
(501) 624-0229 (Library); (501) 767-5831
    (Librarian)
Barbara Stainback, Librarian
Mon, Fri & second Sat 10:00–2:00, second
    & fourth Mon 4:30–8:00; meetings at
    Garland County Library, Williams Hall:
    fourth Tue (Sept–May) 1:30
Pub. *The Melting Pot Genealogical Society
    Quarterly* (Apr, Nov)
$15.00 per year membership

**Northeast Arkansas Genealogical
Association**
North Central Arkansas Genealogical Society
314 Vine Street
Newport, AR 72112
Pub. *Arkansas Genealogical Register*,
    quarterly

Northwest Arkansas Genealogical Society
(400 South Walton, Bentonville,
AR—location)
PO Box 796 (mailing address)
Rogers, AR 72757-0796
(479) 273-3890
nags2@juno.com
Mary Crabtree, Corresponding Secretary
Tue–Sat 10:00–4:00
Pub. *The Backtracker*, quarterly
(Benton, Washington, Madison and Carroll
    counties)
$15.00 per year membership

Ouachita-Calhoun Genealogical Society
PO Box 2092
Camden, AR 71711-2092
(870) 836-5083 (Library)
Mon–Fri 9:30–5:30, Sat 9:00–noon;
    meetings at Camden-Ouachita County
    Public Library: fourth Sun 2:00
Pub. *Researchin' Ouachita-Calhoun
    Counties, Arkansas*, two times per year
("We concentrate on original
    records—courthouse, cemeteries, U.S.
    census, Bible, school, church,
    newspapers, letters, diaries and limited
    personal research.")
$15.00 per year membership; queries for
    South Arkansas families only

Polk County Genealogical Society (PCGS)
(Eighth Street and Port Arthur—location)
PO Box 1525 (mailing address)
Hatfield, AR 71945
(479) 394-2314
woodbrw@ipa.net
Col. (Ret.) Billy R. Wood, President
Library: Mon–Fri 11:00–5:30, Sat
    10:00–2:00
Pub. *Polk County Pioneers*, biannually
$12.00 per year membership; research:
    priced upon request

**Scott County Historical and Genealogical
Society**
(see Historical Societies—Local and
Regional, above)

Sevier County Genealogical Society, Inc.
(717 North Maple Street—location)
PO Box 288 (mailing address)

DeQueen, AR 71832
June King, Museum Director
Tue–Sat 10:00–4:00, Sun 2:00–4:00
Pub. *Footprints*, quarterly
$12.00 per year membership; no research
    services

Southwest Arkansas Genealogical Society
523 East Union
Magnolia, AR 71753
Pub. *SO-WE-AR*, semiannually (Columbia
    County)
$7.50 per year membership

**Stone County Arkansas Genealogical
Society**
PO Box 1477
Mountain View, AR 72560
cdjudy2@mvtel.net
http://rootsweb.com/~arscgs/index.htm
Judy Sulephen, Secretary-Treasurer

Texarkana U.S.A. Genealogy Society
(see Texas, Part 2)

Tri-County Genealogical Society
(Davidson Civic Center, 406 South Midway
    Street—location)
PO Box 580 (mailing address)
Marvell, AR 72366-0580
(870) 829-2772; (870) 829-2147 (Treasurer)
cndavison@centurytel.net;
    joenglish@centurytel.net
http://www.rootsweb.com/~armonroe/
    index.htm
Rose White; Carrie Davison, Treasurer;
    Claire English, Secretary and Editor
Library: Thur 1:00–4:00, Sun 2:00–5:00
Pub. *Tri-County Genealogy*, three times per
    year (Spring, Summer, Fall), $5.00 per
    issue
(Monroe, Lee and Phillips counties)
$15.00 per year membership; queries
    accepted

Union County Genealogical Society
Barton Library
200 East Fifth
El Dorado, AR 71730
(870) 863-5447; (870) 862-3944 FAX
Charlotte Burgess, President
Mon, Wed & Fri 9:30–5:30, Tue & Thur
    1:00–9:00, Sat 1:00–5:00
Pub. *Tracks and Traces*, semiannually
$10.00 per year membership

Village Genealogical Society
6 Aguila Way
Hot Springs Village, AR 71909

**Yell County Arkansas Historical and
Genealogical Association**
(see Historical Societies—Local and
Regional, above)

Independent Publications and Miscellany

Altus Heritage House Museum
(106 North Franklin—location)
PO Box 197 (mailing address)
Altus, AR 72821
(501) 468-4684
http://www.museumusa.org/data/
    museums/AR/116881.htm
Linda Ross

ArGenWeb
Part of The USGenweb Project
betsym@1starnet.com
http://www.rootsweb.com/~argenweb

Betsy Mills, State Coordinator
(links to other Arkansas resources)

Arkansas Ancestors
222 McMahan Drive
Hot Springs, AR 71913-6243
(501) 623-6766 voice & FAX
bjmclane@cablelynx.com
http://home.cablelynx.com/~bjmclane
Bobbie Jones McLane, Publisher
daily 8:00–4:00
(Catalog available: books on Arkansas and
Alabama)

Arkansas Department of Heritage Services
1500 Tower Building
323 Center Street
Little Rock, AR 72201
(501) 324-9150; (501) 324-9154 FAX
http://www.heritage.state.ar.us/dahhome.
html
(vital statistics)

Arkansas Genealogical Research
(805 East Fifth Street—location)
PO Box 1889 (mailing address)
Russellville, AR 72801
(479) 967-7792
Rhonda S. Norris, C.G.R.S.
Pub. *Arkansas Links: A Comprehensive
Guide to Genealogical Research in the
Natural State*, $40.00 ppd.
("Arkansas research, specializing in Pope
County, Arkansas")

Arkansas Municipal League
PO Box 38
North Little Rock, AR 72115
(501) 374-3484; (501) 374-0541
http://www.aiea.ualr.edu/dina/mleague/
publications/publications.html

Arkansas Records Association
314 Vine Street
Newport, AR 72112
(870) 523-3736; (870) 523-6611 FAX
James Logan Morgan
Pub. *Arkansas Record Survey*, three times
per year

Arkansas Research
PO Box 303
Conway, AR 72033
(501) 470-1120 voice & FAX
desmond@ipa.net; desmond@intellinet.com
http://www.arkansasresearch.com/index.
html
Desmond Walls Allen, Editor
(publishes death record indexes, census
transcriptions, county records, military
records, family histories, marriage
records, newspaper abstracts, etc.)
free catalog

**Arkansas State Highway and
Transportation Department**
Map Sales, Room 205
(10324 Interstate 30, Little Rock, AR
72209—location)
PO Box 2261 (mailing address)
Little Rock, AR 72203-2261
(501) 569-2444 (Preprinted Paper Map
Sales); (501) 569-2205 (Digital Media
Sales)
http://www.ahtd.state.ar.us/maps.htm
(areal photographs and 1936 historical maps)

Arkansas Territorial Restoration
200 East Third Street
Little Rock, AR 72201-1608
(501) 324-9351; (501) 324-9345; (501) 324-
9811 FAX

http://www.heritage.state.ar.us/atr/
her_atr.html

**Counts Genealogical Research and
Publishing**
3812 Glenmere Road
North Little Rock, AR 72116
Pub. *Arkansas Genealogical Research Aid*,
irregularly

Elk River Current
(see Missouri, Part 2)

Genealogical Institute
(see Virginia, Part 2)

Genealogy Books and Consultation
(see Texas, Part 2)

**Hunting for Bears Genealogical and
Historical Society**
(see Alabama, Part 2)

The Looking Glass
PO Box 885
Nederland, TX 77627-0885
Cate
Pub. *The Looking Glass* (Ouachita),
monthly, $12.00 per year subscription

Lum and Abner Museum
(Highway 88—location)
PO Box 38 (mailing address)
Pine Ridge, AR 71966
(870) 326-4442 voice & FAX
Kathryn Stucker, Owner/Operator
1 Mar–1 Nov: Tue–Sun 9:00–5:00
("I try to help people who stop at the Lum
and Abner Museum, but do not consider
myself to be a genealogist. A better source
for researching Montgomery County
families is the Heritage House Museum.")

Mountain Press
(see Tennessee, Part 2)

The Old Time Chronicle
PO Box 15
Antoine, AR 71922
Karron Cot, Editor
8:00–5:00
Pub. *The Old Time Chronicle* (Pike County;
folk history), bimonthly, $14.50 per year
in-state subscription, $16.00 per year out-
of-state subscription, $22.00 (U.S.) per
year Canadian subscription

The Original Arkansas Genealogy
(870) 932-5803
bcouch@couchgenweb.com
http://www.couchgenweb.com/arkansas
Bill Couch
Pub. *Craighead Co. History*

Pike County Archives
1684 Highway 26E
Delight, AR 71940
DeWayne Gray, President

Professional Genealogists of Arkansas, Inc.
PO Box 1807
Conway, AR 72033-1807
(501) 470-1120 voice & FAX
desmond@intellinet.com
http://biz.ipa.net/arkresearch
Desmond Walls Allen, Editor
Pub. *Arkansas Historical and Genealogical
Magazine*, bimonthly (odd-numbered
months)
("PGA is a loose network of genealogists,
family historians, researchers, teachers,
librarians, archivists, publishers and

professionals interested in promoting the
field of genealogy in Arkansas.")
$12.00 per year membership

*Searcy County Ancestor Information
Exchange*
2333 East Oaks Drive
Fayetteville, AR 72703
(501) 442-3691
johnston@ipa.net
James J. Johnston
Pub. *Searcy County Ancestor Information
Exchange*, bimonthly, $10.00 per year
subscription
(sponsors North Arkansas Ancestor Fair)

Seeking Your Heritage
(4511 North Schaer Street—location)
PO Box 2074 (mailing address)
North Little Rock, AR 72115-2074
(501) 758-8351 voice & FAX
Arlene Ryan, Editor/Publisher
Mon–Fri 8:00–5:00
Pub. *Seeking Your Heritage*, quarterly (Oct,
Jan, Apr, July), $15.00 per year
subscription

**The Southern Genealogist's Exchange
Society, Inc.**
(see Florida, Part 2)

Southern Historical Press, Inc.
(see Publishers, Part 4)

Traveller Southern Families
(see Virginia, Part 2)

California

Archives and Libraries with Holdings in Genealogy

State Archives and Libraries

California State Archives
Office of the Secretary of State
1020 "O" Street
Sacramento, CA 95814
(916) 653-2246; (916) 653-7363 FAX
archivesweb@ss.ca.gov
http://www.ss.ca.gov/archives/archives.htm
Walter P. Gray III, Director, Archives and
    Museum
Mon–Fri 9:30–4:00, first Sat 10:00–4:00
copies: 25¢ per page

California State Library
California History Room
(900 N Street, Room 200, Sacramento, CA
95814—location)
PO Box 942837 (mailing address)
Sacramento, CA 94237-0001
(916) 654-0176 (California History Room,
    Reference Desk); (916) 654-8777 FAX
cslcal@library.ca.gov
http://www.library.ca.gov
Mon–Fri 9:30–4:00
list of private researchers available

Sutro Library
Branch of the California State Library
480 Winston Drive
San Francisco, CA 94132-1777
(415) 731-4477; (415) 557-9325 FAX
sutro@library.ca.gov
http://www.onelibrary.com/Library/
    calslsut.htm
Clyde Janes, Director; Martha Whitaker,
    Reference Librarian; Peter Dolgenos,
    Reference Librarian
Library: Mon–Sat 10:00–5:00
(collection covers whole U.S.)

State Historical Societies

California Historical Society
678 Mission Street
San Francisco, CA 94105
(415) 357-1848, ext. 10; (415) 357-1850
    FAX
info@calhist.org
http://www.calhist.org
Judith Deaton, Director of Operations
Library: by appointment only; Other:
    Tue–Sat 11:00–5:00
Pub. *California Chronicle*, quarterly;
    California History, quarterly
$55.00 per year membership; admission:
    $5.00 for nonmembers

**Conference of California Historical
Societies**
University of the Pacific
301 Pacific Avenue
Stockton, CA 95211
(209) 946-2169; (209) 946-2578 FAX
http://ets.uop.edu/muir
Ronald Limbaugh, Executive Director
8:30 A.M.–12:30 P.M.
Pub. *California Historian*, quarterly, $20.00
    per year subscription
$25.00 per year membership

City, County and Regional Archives and
Libraries
(A more exhaustive list of public and
academic libraries can be found at
http://www.library.ca.gov/html/main.cfm.)

Alpine County Museum
(School Street—location)
PO Box 517 (mailing address)
Markleeville, CA 96120
(530) 694-2317; (530) 694-1087 FAX
acm@gbis.com
Richard C. Edwards, Director
Memorial Day–Oct: Mon & Thur–Sun
    10:00–4:00 and by appointment
Pub. *The Alpine Review*, quarterly
("The museum has an extensive photo
    collection of pioneer members of the
    Alpine County area, plus documentation
    and 19th-century newspapers of the
    area.")
$10.00 per year membership

Anderson Valley Historical Museum
(Highway 128 North—location)
PO Box 676 (mailing address)
Boonville, CA 95415
(707) 895-3207

Arcadia Public Library
20 West Duarte Road
Arcadia, CA 91006-6999
(626) 821-4364; (626) 447-8050 FAX
http://library.ci.arcadia.ca.us
Mary Beth Hayes, Librarian
Mon–Thur 10:00–9:00, Fri–Sat 10:00–6:00
(Arcadia history)

**Mary M. Arron Memorial Museum
Association**
704 D Street
Marysville, CA 95901
(530) 743-1004

Auburn-Placer County Library
350 Nevada Street
Auburn, CA 95603-3789
(530) 889-4111 (Reference Librarian; (530)
    886-4555 FAX
http://www.placer.ca.gov/library
James R. Hickson, Reference Librarian
Mon & Thur 10:00–6:00, Tue & Wed
    10:00–8:00, Fri–Sat 10:00–5:00
(Placer County history; genealogy
    department within the library organized
    and operated by Placer County
    Genealogical Society)

Autry Museum of Western Heritage
4700 Western Heritage Way
Los Angeles, CA 90027-1462
(213) 667-2000; (213) 666-9030 FAX
Joanne D. Hale, President and CEO
Tue–Sun 10:00–5:00
Pub. *Spur* (not primarily genealogical,
    emphasis on the history and myth of the
    American West)

R. C. Baker Memorial Museum, Inc.
297 West Elm Street
Coalinga, CA 93210
(559) 935-1914
Helen Cowan, Curator
Mon–Fri 10:00–noon & 1:00–5:00, Sat
    11:00–5:00, Sun 1:00–5:00

Bruggemeyer Memorial Library
City of Monterey Park
318 South Ramona Avenue
Monterey Park, CA 91754-3399
(626) 307-1368; (626) 288-4251 FAX
library@montereypark.ca.gov
http://ci.monterey-park.ca.us/Library
Dana Lubow, Reference/Adult Services
Mon–Tue noon–9:00, Wed 10:00–9:00,
    Thur–Fri 10:00–6:00, Sat 9:00–5:00
Pub. *Footnotes*, quarterly

Butte County Library
1820 Mitchell Avenue
Oroville, CA 95966-5387
(530) 538-7240; (530) 538-7642
    (Reference); (530) 538-7235 FAX
lib@buttecounty.net
http://buttecounty.net/library
Nancy Brower, Director of Libraries
Tue & Sat 10:00–5:00, Wed 2:00–9:00, Thur
    2:00–5:00, Sat 10:00–4:00

Calaveras County Archives
(Fricot Building, 46 North Main
Street—location)
PO Box 1281 (mailing address)
San Andreas, CA 95249
(209) 754-3918
Lorrayne Kennedy, Archivist
Mon & Thur–Fri 8:30–4:30 by appointment
(birth records, marriage records, cemetery
    records, Great Registers, probates,
    inquests, abstracts of judgments, co-
    partnerships, attachments—Lis Pendens,
    court cases, articles of incorporation,
    deeds, bills of sale, homesteads, mining
    claims, patents, newspapers, assessment
    rolls, mortgages, declarations of intention,
    naturalization, Frances Bishop Research
    Carts, "Las Calaveras," divorces,
    mechanic's liens, bonds, letters, wills,
    agreements, power of attorney and census;
    early Goldrush history, 1852–present,
    Calaveras County)
research: $10.00 per hour plus copies and
    postage

California Heritage Museum
2612 Main Street
Santa Monica, CA 90405
(310) 392-8537
Tobi Smith, Director
Wed–Sat 11:00–4:00, Sun 10:00–4:00
(archives/library, historical decorative arts
    exhibitions)

California History Center Foundation
21250 Stevens Creek Boulevard
Cupertino, CA 95014
(408) 864-8712; (408) 864-5486 FAX
Kathi Peregrin, Director
Mon–Thur 8:30–noon & 1:00–4:30
Pub. *The Californian*, three times per year
$30.00 per year membership; archive
    admission: $3.00 for nonstudents or
    nonmembers

California State Capitol Museum
State Capitol, Room 124
Sacramento, CA 95814
(916) 324-0312
John Knott, Director
(not primarily genealogical)

California State University, Chico Library
400 West First Street
Chico, CA 95929
(530) 898-5710
http://www.csuchico.edu/lbib/spc/
    netpages/home.htm
William A. Jones, Head, Special Resources
Mon–Fri 10:00–5:00
(northeastern California archives)

California State University, Fresno
June English, Local History and Genealogy
Collection
Henry Madden Library
Fresno, CA 93740
specialc@listserv.csufresno.edu
http://duchess.lib.csufresno.edu/
    specialcollections/englishcollection.html
Tammy Lau, Head, Special Collections

Library

California State University, Los Angeles, Library
5151 State College Drive
Los Angeles, CA 90032

California State University, Northridge
Special Collections Department
Oviatt Library, Room 4
Northridge, CA 91330-1600
(818) 677-2832
tgardner@csun.edu
http://www.csun.edu/~spcoll/hbspcoll.html

California State University, Stanislaus
Library
801 West Monte Vista Avenue
Turlock, CA 95382
(209) 667-3233; (209) 667-3164 FAX
blsantos@stan.csustan.edu
http://www.library.csustan.edu
Bob Santos, University Archivist
Library: Mon–Thur 7:30–11:00, Fri
   7:30–5:00, Sat 9:00–5:00, Sun 1:00–9:00;
   Archives: Mon–Fri 8:00–4:00 and by
   appointment
(regional history; CSUS history)

Campbell Historical Museum
51 North Central Avenue
Campbell, CA 95008
(408) 866-2119

Capitola Historical Museum
410 Capitola Avenue
Capitola, CA 95010-3318
(831) 464-0322

Carlsbad City Library
Georgina Cole Library
1250 Carlsbad Village Drive
Carlsbad, CA 92008-1991
(760) 434-2931
librarian@ci.carlsbad.ca.us
http://ci.carlsbad.ca.us/library/index.html
Mary Van Orsdol, Librarian
Mon–Thur 9:00–9:00, Fri–Sat 9:00–5:00;
   Sun 1:00–5:00
(36,000 volumes, genealogy and local
   history collection)

Carmichael Regional Library
Capital Area Joint Genealogical Library
Genealogy Room
5605 Marconi Avenue
Carmichael, CA 95608-4499
(916) 483-6055
Mary Pitts, Librarian, Root Cellar; Lorraine
   Lineer, Librarian, Genealogical
   Association of Sacramento
Mon & Thur noon–9:00, Tue 10:00–9:00,
   Wed 10:00–6:00, Fri & Sat 1:00–5:00

Carnegie Cultural Arts Center
424 South C Street
Oxnard, CA 93030
(805) 984-4649
(primarily a history and art museum, not
   genealogy)

Casa de Rancho Cucamonga
Rains' House
8810 Hemlock
Rancho Cucamonga, CA 91730
(909) 989-4970

Catalina Island Museum Society, Inc.
(Cassino Building, 1 Casino Way—location)
PO Box 366 (mailing address)
Avalon, Santa Catalina Island, CA 90704
(310) 510-2414

http://www.catalina.com/museum.html
Patricia Anne Moore, Director/Curator

Chabot College
South County Community College District
25555 Hesperian Boulevard
Hayward, CA 94545
(510) 786-6764; (510) 786-6600
Mon–Thur 7:45–10:00, Fri 7:45–5:00, Sat
   9:30–2:00

**Chaffey Communities Cultural Center and
Cooper History Museum**
(525 West 18th Street and 217 East A
   Street—location)
PO Box 772 (mailing address)
Upland, CA 91785-0772
(909) 982-8010
mavb@worldnet.att.net
http://www.culturalcenter.org
Max A. van Balgooy, Curator
by appointment only
Pub. *Record*, quarterly
("Records, photographs and artifacts related
   to Upland, Ontario, Rancho Cucamonga,
   Montclair, Mount Baldy, California, from
   1880–1980; museum and archive
   catalogue available on History
   Database.")
$15.00 per year membership; research:
   $25.00 per hour

Chaffey-Garcia House
7150 Etiwanda Avenue
Rancho Cucamonga, CA 91739
(909) 899-1209

Chico Museum
141 Salem Street
Chico, CA 95928
(530) 891-4336; (530) 891-4336 FAX
chicomuseum@chico.com
http://www.chicomuseum.com
Paul Russell, Curator
Wed–Sun noon–4:00
Pub. *Museum Notes*, quarterly
("History museum [local Chico and Butte
   County history]. Have both permanent
   and rotating exhibits, Chico time line
   1830-2000. Chico's Taoist Chinese
   Temple.")
$20.00 per year membership

Chula Vista City Library
Fourth and F Streets
Chula Vista, CA 91910
(619) 691-5069 (Reference); (619) 427-4246
   FAX
webmaster@chulavista.lib.ca.us
http://chulavista.lib.ca.us
Library: Mon–Thur 10:00–9:00, Fri–Sat
   10:00–6:00, Sun 1:00–5:00; Manned
   help: Mon 10:00–noon, Wed 11:00–2:00,
   Thur noon–2:00
("Library with all states covered, some very
   well.")

City of San Buenaventura
PO Box 99
Ventura, CA 93002
(805) 654-7837

Clarke Historical Museum
240 East Street
Eureka, CA 95501
(707) 443-1947
Pam Service, Director/Curator
Tue–Sat 11:00–4:00
Pub. *Members News*
("Museum with photographic and documents
   holdings.")

Colton Hall Museum and Old Monterey
Pacific Street Between Madison and
Jefferson
Monterey, CA 93940
(831) 375-9944
Donna Penwell, Museum Manager
Pub. *Historic Monterey* (not primarily
   genealogical)

Columbia State Historic Park
PO Box 151
Columbia, CA 95310
(209) 532-4301
http://www.sierra.parks.state.ca.us
Sherrin Grout, Ranger
8:00–5:00
(collection includes documents on 19th-
   century inhabitants)

**Community Memorial Museum of Sutter
County**
PO Box 1555
Yuba City, CA 95991

Contra Costa County Library
1750 Oak Park Boulevard
Pleasant Hill, CA 94523-4497
(925) 646-6423; (925) 646-6434
   (Reference); (925) 646-6461 FAX
libadmin@ccclib.org
http://www.cclib.org
Anne Cain, County Librarian

Cooper History Museum
(see Chaffee Communities Cultural Center
and Cooper History Museum, above)

Corona Public Library
Heritage Room
650 South Main Street
Corona, CA 91720-3417
(909) 736-2386; (909) 736-2499 FAX
library@ci.corona.ca.us
http://www.ci.corona.ca.us/library/index.htm
Gloria Freel, Heritage Room Librarian
Mon–Tue 5:00–9:00, Wed–Thur & Sat
   1:00–5:00
(Corona/Riverside County history books,
   pamphlets and memorabilia; Southern
   California history)
copies: 15¢ per page

**Defense Language Institute Historical
Holding (Museum)**
Presidio of Monterey
Area Studies Department, DLIFLC
Presidio of Monterey, CA 93944
(831) 647-5565
Chaplain (Major) Gene E. Ahlstrom
closed to the general public

Downey City Library
11121 Brookshire Avenue
Downey, CA 90241-7015
(562) 904-7358; (562) 923-3256; (562) 923-
   3763 FAX
questions@downeyca.org
http://downey.lib.ca.us
Maury McCord, Senior Librarian
Mon–Thur 10:00–8:00, Fri–Sat 10:00–5:00

Eastern California Museum
(155 Grant Street—location)
PO Box 206 (mailing address)
Independence, CA 93526
(760) 878-0364; (760) 878-0258
William Michael, Director
Mon & Wed–Sun 10:00–4:00
(county subject and family history files,
   regional reference library)

El Dorado County Library

345 Fair Lane
Placerville, CA 95667-4196
(530) 621-5540; (530) 622-3911 FAX
lib-pl@eldoradolibrary.org
http://eldoradolibrary.org
Bonnie Battaglia, Reference Librarian
Mon–Wed 1:00–8:00, Thur–Sat 10:00–5:00
(California, gold rush era, local history)

El Dorado County Museum
104 Placerville Drive
Placerville, CA 95667
(530) 621-5865; (530) 621-6644 FAX
Denis Witcher, Director
Mon–Sat 10:00–4:00
(research library; probate, early court
    records, naturalizations, voting registers,
    county directories)
copies: 25¢ per page plus postage and
    donation

El Segundo Public Library
111 West Mariposa Avenue
El Segundo, CA 90245-2299
(310) 524-2722; (310) 524-2728
    (Reference); (310) 648-7560 FAX
refdesk@elsegundo.org
http://elsegundo.org
Debra Brighton, Library Director
Mon–Thur 9:00–9:00, Fri 9:00–6:00, Sat
    9:00–5:00, Sun 1:00–5:00

Escondido Public Library
Pioneer Room
247 South Kalmia Street
Escondido, CA 92025
(760) 839-4315; (760) 746-9327 FAX
nsalisbury@ci.escondido.ca.us
http://www.ci.escondido.ca.us/library/
    pioneer
Alexa Clausen, Historian; Nancy Salisbury,
    Library Assistant
Tue & Thur noon–6:00, Wed & Sat
    10:00–2:00
("Finding aids to genealogy collections and
    local history on web site.")
research: fees available on request

Falkirk Cultural Center
(Robert Dollar Estate, 1408 Mission Street,
San Rafael, CA 94901—location)
PO Box 151560 (mailing address)
San Rafael, CA 94915-1560
(415) 485-3328
Jane Lange, Director
("We are not involved in genealogical
    research.")

Ferndale Museum, Inc.
(Shaw and Third Streets—location)
PO Box 431 (mailing address)
Ferndale, CA 95536
(707) 786-4466 voice & FAX
Jerry Lesandro, Director
Tue (summer) 11:00–4:00, Wed–Sat
    11:00–4:00, Sun 1:00–4:00
("Ferndale Enterprise on microfilm 1878 to
    present, Ferndale Cemetery register on
    microfilm.")
research: $7.50 per hour plus copy costs

Fillmore Historical Museum
(350 Main Street, Fillmore, CA
93015—location)
PO Box 314 (mailing address)
Fillmore, CA 93016
(805) 524-0948; (805) 524-0516 FAX
Rochelee Mekinnon, Executive Director;
    Ynez Haase, Historian
Mon–Fri 9:00–noon
Pub. *Newsletter*, quarterly
membership and research fees vary

Doris Foley Historical Library
(see Nevada County Public Library)

Fortuna Depot Museum
3 Park Street
Fortuna, CA 95540
(707) 725-7645
http://www.springville.com/~fortuna/
    museum.htm
Caroline Weed, Curator
June–Aug: Mon–Sun 9:00–4:30; Sept–May:
    Wed–Sun noon–4:30
(research material: Fortuna, Eel River
    Valley, Humboldt County)
free admission; research copies: 10¢ each

Fresno County Free Library
California History and Genealogy Room
2420 Mariposa Street
Fresno, CA 93721-2285
(559) 488-3185; (559) 488-3195 (California
    History and Genealogy Room); (559)
    488-1971 FAX
http://fresnolibrary.org
Linda Sitterding, County Historian; Karen
    Bosch-Cobb, Interim County Librarian
California History and Genealogy Room:
    Mon–Wed & Fri noon–6:00, Thur
    noon–8:00, Sat 10:00–5:00

Fresno Metropolitan Museum
1515 Van Ness
Fresno, CA 93721
(559) 441-1444

Gilroy Museum
195 Fifth Street
Gilroy, CA 95020
(408) 848-0470; (408) 846-0445 FAX
Lucy Solórzano, Museum Coordinator
Mon–Tue & Thur–Fri 10:00–5:00, first Sat
    10:00–2:00
(houses the South Santa Clara Valley
    Archives)
research: first hour free, $10.00 per hour
    thereafter; copies: 20¢ each

Harrison Memorial Library
Local History Department
(Park Branch, Sixth at Mission—location)
PO Box 800 (mailing address)
Carmel, CA 93921-0800
(831) 624-1615
Denise Sallee, Librarian/Archivist
Tue–Fri 1:00–5:00, and by appointment
("Carmel history; photographs, books,
    periodicals, artwork, personal papers,
    memorabilia")

**Holt-Atherton, Department of Special
Collections**
University of the Pacific Library
Stockton, CA 95211
(209) 946-2404
http://library.uop.edu/depthltmuir.html
Ms. Daryl Morrison, Department Head
Mon–Fri 10:00–5:00
Pub. *Library Associates Newsletter*,
    quarterly, $5.00 per year subscription

The Honnold/Mudd Library
Special Collections
800 North Dartmouth Avenue
Claremont, CA 91711-3991
(909) 621-8045; (909) 621-8681
http://voxlibris.claremont.edu/speccoll.html
Jean Beckner, Special Collections Librarian
Mon–Fri 9:00–noon & 1:00–5:00
(history only, not an open browsing
    collection; serves as the central library for
    the five undergraduate colleges and the
    Claremont Graduate School; genealogy is

not a subject taught at any of the colleges,
    so the library does not collect in that area
    and cannot undertake genealogical
    research)

Humboldt County Library
Main Library—Eureka
The Humboldt Room 1313 Third Street
Eureka, CA 95501-0533
(707) 269-1900; (707) 269-1905
    (Reference); (707) 269-1997 FAX; (707)
    269-1999 FAX
http://www.co.humboldt.ca.us/library
Carolyn Stacey, County Librarian and
    Director of Library Services
(local history collection, rare books and
    documents)

Humboldt State University Library
Humboldt County Collection
Arcata, CA 95521
(707) 826-3419
http://library.humboldt.edu/infoservices/
    humco.html
Joan Berman, Special Collections Librarian
Mon–Fri 10:00–5:00, Mon 6:00 P.M.–9:00
    P.M., Sun (during academic year)
    1:00–5:00
(northwestern California, especially Del
    Norte and Humboldt counties)

Huntington Beach Public Library
7111 Talbert Avenue
Huntington Beach, CA 92648-1296
(714) 960-8836, ext. 2227
library@hbpl.org
http://hbpl.org
Betty Zulianai, Librarian
Mon 1:00–9:00, Tue–Thur 9:00–9:00,
    Fri–Sat 9:00–5:00, Sun 1:00–5:00

Huntington Library
(address withheld upon request)
(historical collection; does not, as a general
    policy, allow genealogists access to the
    library)

Johnston House Foundation
(Higgins-Purissima Road—location)
PO Box 789 (mailing address)
Half Moon Bay, CA 94019
(650) 641-9102

Jurnpa Mountains Cultural Center
7621 Granite Hill Drive
Riverside, CA 92509
(909) 685-5818

**Kern County Library, Beale Memorial
Library**
Genealogical Room
(701 Truxtun Avenue, Bakersfield, CA
93301-4800—location)
PO Box 2214 (mailing address)
Bakersfield, CA 93303
(661) 868-0700; (661) 868-0701; (661) 868-
    0799 FAX
kclweb@kerncountylibrary.org
http://www.kerncountylibrary.org
Mon–Thur 10:00–9:00 Fri–Sat 10:00–6:00
(houses Kern County Genealogical Society's
    collection of books, microfiche and
    periodicals)

Kern County Museum
3801 Chester Avenue
Bakersfield, CA 93301
(661) 861-2132; (661) 322-6415 FAX
http://www.kruznet.com/kcmuseum
Jeff Nickell, MA, Curator
General operating: Mon–Fri 8:00–5:00, Sat
    10:00–5:00, Sun noon–5:00

Pub. *Newsletter*, quarterly
(photograph collection of over 250,000
   photo images, Kern County)
$50.00 per year membership; search fees for
   photos only under $20.00 plus cost of
   reproduction

Kings County Library
401 North Douty Street
Hanford, CA 93230-3908
(559) 582-0261; (559) 583-6163 FAX
Louise.Hodges@kingscountylibrary.org;
   Amy.Lowe@kingscountylibrary.org
http://www.kingscountylibrary.org
Louise Hodges, County Librarian; Amy
   Lowe, Reference Librarian
Mon–Wed 10:00–8:00, Thur 10:00–6:00,
   Fri–Sat noon–5:00

Klamath National Forest
1312 Fairlane Road
Yreka, CA 96097
(530) 842-6131
Gilbert W. Davies
(maintains historical research library)

La Cañada-Flintridge Library
County of Los Angeles Public Library
4545 North Oakwood Avenue
La Canada-Flintridge, CA 91011-3358
(818) 790-3330; (818) 952-1754 FAX
http://colapublib.org/libs/lacanada
Sue Renyer, Community Library Manager

Landmark Conservators
d.b.a. Cabot's Old Indian Pueblo Museum
67-616 East Desert View Avenue
Desert Hot Springs, CA 92240
(760) 329-7610
Colbert H. Eyraud, Curator
Oct–June: Wed–Sun 10:00–4:00; July–Sept:
   Sat–Sun 10:00–4:00
$20.00 per year membership

Lompoc Public Library
501 East North Avenue
Lompoc, CA 93436-3498
(805) 736-3477 (Reference); (805) 736-6440
   FAX
lref@rain.org
http://rain.org/~lomplynx
Nina Taylor, Director
Mon–Wed noon–8:00, Thur 10:00–8:00,
   Fri–Sun 1:00–5:00

Long Beach Public Library
(Ocean at Pacific Avenue—location)
101 Pacific Avenue (mailing address)
Long Beach, CA 90822-1097
(562) 570-7500 (Reference)
bterrell@lbpl.org
http://lbpl.org
Robert Brasher, Volunteer
Mon 10:00–8:00, Tue–Sat 10:00–5:30, Sun
   noon–5:00; volunteer hours: Wed & Sat
   1:00–5:00
(2,700 books and other items; "Genealogical
   collection supported by Questing Heirs
   Genealogical Society.")

Los Angeles Public Library
History and Genealogy Department
630 West Fifth Street
Los Angeles, CA 90071-2097
(213) 228-7400; (213) 228-7000 (to verify
   hours); (213) 228-7409 FAX
history@lapl.org
http:///www.lapl.org
Michael Kirley, Genealogy Librarian
Mon & Thur–Sat 10:00–5:30, Tue–Wed
   noon–8:00, Sun 1:00–5:00, hours subject
   to change

Marin County Free Library
Anne Kent California Room
Civic Center, 3501 Civic Center Drive
San Rafael, CA 94903
(415) 499-7419
library@co.marin.ca.us
http://countylibrary.marin.org
Jocelyn A. Moss, Senior Library Assistant
Mon, Wed & Fri 10:00–6:00, Tue & Thur
   10:00–9:00, Sat 10:00–5:00

Marin History Museum
1125 B Street
San Rafael, CA 94901
(415) 454-8538; (415) 454-6137 FAX
http://www.marinhistory.org
Jocelyn A. Moss, Librarian
Research: Tue–Fri 9:00–noon by
   appointment; open to public: Tue–Thur
   noon–3:00, third Sat
Pub. *Marin County Historical Society
   Magazine*, annually; *MCHS Bulletin*,
   biannually; *Newsletter*, quarterly
("Marin County history-genealogy. San
   Quentin, Louise Boyd.")
$30.00 per year Friend membership;
   research: $5.00

**Mariposa Museum and History Center,
Inc.**
(5119 Jessie Street—location)
PO Box 606 (mailing address)
Mariposa, CA 95338
(209) 966-2429
Muriel L. Powers, Curator/Executive
   Secretary
Nov–Dec & Feb: Sat–Sun 10:00–4:00;
   Mar–Oct: Mon–Sun 10:00–4:30
Pub. *Dear Charlie Letters*
(49er local history)
$10.00 per year membership

**Marshall Gold Discovery Park
Museum/State Park**
(310 Back Street—location)
PO Box 265 (mailing address)
Coloma, CA 95613
(530) 622-3470
Jim Grady, Research Library Manager
Mon 10:00–2:00, and by appointment
("Historical research library—primary
   emphaiss on Gold Rush era; extensive
   collection of California and Western U.S.
   history books plus mining methods and
   equipment. Approximately 2,000
   publications. Extensive genealogical
   records of Coloma residents.")

Maturango Museum
100 East Las Flores
Ridgecrest, CA 93555
(760) 375-6900; (760) 375-0479 FAX
matmus@ridgecrest.ca.us
http://www.ridgecrest.ca.us/~matmus
Richard L. Senn, Administrator
Wed–Sun 10:00–5:00
Pub. *Maturango News*, eleven times per year
$30.00 per year membership

**Mayo Hayes O'Donnell Library (of the
Monterey History and Art Association)**
(155 Van Buren Street—location)
5 Custom House Plaza (mailing address)
Monterey, CA 93940
(831) 372-2608; (831) 626-9364 FAX
   (Chairperson)
Faye Messinger, Chairperson
Wed & Fri–Sun 1:30–3:45
Pub. *Noticias del Puerto de Monterey*,
   quarterly (for Association)
(2,000 books on maritime history, 2,200
   books on local history)

$35.00 per year membership; copies: 50¢
   each

Mendocino County Museum
Mendocino County Heritage Network
400 East Commercial
Willits, CA 95490
(707) 459-2736; (707) 459-7836 FAX
Daniel Taylor, Director/Coordinator
Wed–Sun 10:00–4:30
(Mendocino County archives)

Menlo Park Public Library
800 Alma Street
Menlo Park, CA 94025-3460
(415) 858-3460; (650) 858-3463
   (Reference); (415) 858-3466 FAX
mplcirc@plsinfo.org
http://www.menloparklibrary.org
Karen Fredrickson, Director of Library
   Services

Merced County Library
2100 O Street
Merced, CA 95340-3637
(209) 385-7597; (209) 385-7484; (209) 385-
   7643 (Reference); (209) 726-7912 FAX
li05@co.merced.ca.us
http://library.co.merced.ca.us/library/
   index.html
Catherine McCullough, Reference Librarian
Mon–Thur 9:00–9:00, Fri–Sat 9:00–6:00

Mill Valley Public Library
Lucretia Little History Room
375 Throckmorton Avenue
Mill Valley, CA 94941-2698
(415) 389-4292 (Reference); (415) 388-8929
   FAX
http://www.millvalleylibrary.org
Joyce Crews, History Room Librarian; Anne
   Montgomery, City Librarian
Library: Mon–Thur 10:00–9:00, Fri
   noon–6:00, Sat 10:00–5:00, Sun
   1:00–5:00; History Room: Mon–Thur
   10:00–noon & 2:00–4:00 & 7:00–9:00,
   Fri 2:00–4:00, Sat 10:00–noon &
   2:00–4:00, Sun 2:00–4:00

Ralph L. Milliken Museum
PO Box 2294
Los Banos, CA 93635

Mission Santa Cruz
126 High Street
Santa Cruz, CA 95060
(831) 426-5686

Mojave River Valley Museum Association
(southwest corner of Barstow Road at
   Virginia Way—location)
PO Box 1282 (mailing address)
Barstow, CA 92312-1282
(760) 252-4681 (for history and genealogy);
   (760) 256-5452 (MRVM, specialty old
   data)
Germaine L. Moon, Historian/Researcher
11:00–4:00
Pub. *Monthly Newsletter*
(specializes in entire Mojave Desert of San
   Bernardino County, also parts of southern
   Nevada and western Arizona)
$20.00 per year membership; research:
   donation and postage plus copies at
   25¢–$1.00 per page

Monrovia Public Library
Reference Desk
321 South Myrtle Avenue
Monrovia, CA 91016-2848
(626) 358-0174
http://ci.monrovia.ca.us/city_hall/library/

library.htm
winter: Mon–Wed 10:00–9:00, Thur–Sat
10:00–5:00; summer: Mon 10:00–9:00,
Tue–Wed 10:00–6:00, Thur–Sat
10:00–5:00
(Monrovia archives/history)

Montclair Branch Library
9955 Fremont Avenue
Montclair, CA 91763-3223
(909) 624-4671; (909) 391-7775 FAX
James Moore, Librarian

Monterey County Free Libraries
26 Central Avenue
Salinas, CA 93901-2628
(831) 424-3244; (831) 755-5839 FAX
611-Seaside-Ref@co.monterey.ca.us
http://www.co.monterey.ca.us/library
Martha Clark, Librarian
Mon–Fri 8:00–5:00

Morgan Hill Museum
40 El Toro Avenue
Morgan Hill, CA 95037
(408) 779-5755; (408) 778-0355
Mary Dutra, Curator

Museum of Art and History
The McPherson Center
705 Front Street
Santa Cruz, CA 95060-4508
(831) 429-1964; (831) 429-1954 FAX
http://www.cruzio.com/~scva/mcpherson.
html (McPherson Center)
Rachel McKay, Research Librarian
Museum: Tue–Thur & Sat–Sun noon–5:00,
Fri noon–7:00; Archives Library:
Tue–Thur noon–5:00
Pub. *Calendar*, quarterly; *Santa Cruz County
History Journal*, annually, $14.95 per
issue
(Evergreen Cemetery files, a Protestant
cemetery, started in 1850s; clipping files
on places and people; early voter
registration records, Porter family papers,
Knight family papers; books on Santa
Cruz County)
$35.00 per year membership; research:
donation plus 10¢ per photocopy

Museum of History and Art, Ontario
225 South Euclid Avenue
Ontario, CA 91761
(909) 983-3198
Lou Ann Svenson, Director
four afternoons per week

Napa City-County Library
580 Coombs Street
Napa, CA 94559-3396
(707) 253-4241; (707) 253-4235
(Reference); (707) 253-4615 FAX
jmccoy@co.napa.ca.us
http://co.napa.ca.us/library
Janet McCoy, Acting Library Director
Mon, Tue, Fri 10:00–5:30, Wed–Thur
10:00–9:00, Sat 10:00–5:00, Sun
1:00–5:00

National City Public Library
Hollingsworth Local History Room
200 East 12th Street
National City, CA 91950-3314
(619) 336-4350; (619) 336-4351
(Reference); (619) 336-4368 FAX
locoref@sdcoe.k12.ca.us
http://sdcoe.k12.ca.us/ncpl
Anne Campbell, City Librarian

Nevada County Public Library
(Doris Foley Historical Research Library,

211 North Pine Street—location)
980 Helling Way (mailing address)
Nevada City, CA 95959-2592
(530) 265-4606; (530) 265-1407
libraryreference@co.nevada.ca.us
http://new.mynevadacounty.com/library
Maria Brower, Library Technician
Mon–Wed & Fri–Sat 10:00–4:00
("Local history, mining, Gold Rush,
California history, local newspaper going
back 150 years.")

Newbury Park Branch Library
2331 Borchard Road
Newbury Park, CA 91320-3206
(805) 498-2139; (805) 498-7034 FAX
http://www.toaks.org/library
Roxanne Burg, Library Services Supervisor

Novato History Museum and Archives
(815 Delong Avenue—location)
901 Sherman Avenue (mailing address)
Novato, CA 94945
(415) 897-4320

Oakland History Room
Oakland Public Library
125 14th Street
Oakland, CA 94612-4310
(510) 238-3222; (510) 238-2232 FAX
http://www.oaklandlibrary.org/seasonal/
sections/oakhr.html
Steven Lavoie, Librarian II
Mon–Tue & Sat 10:00–5:30, Wed–Thur
noon–8:00, Fri noon–5:30, Sun 1:00–5:00
(city directories, voting registers, county
histories, Oakland births and deaths, etc.)
research: $2.00 copying, name searches, by
mail only

Oakland Museum of California
1000 Oak Street
Oakland, CA 94607
(510) 238-6579
Deborah Cooper, Collections Manager
Pub. *The Museum of California*, four times
per year, $5.00 per issue
$25.00 per year membership

Occidental College
1600 Campus Road
Los Angeles, CA 90041-3314
(213) 259-2814; (213) 259-2818
(Reference); (213) 341-4991 FAX
http://oxy.edu/departments/library
Alfred Gonsalves, Acting College Librarian
(Diverse library collection in Occidental
College Library)

Oceanside Public Library
330 North Coast Highway
Oceanside, CA 92054-2595
(760) 966-4690
public.library@ci.oceanside.ca.us
http://library.ci.oceanside.ca.us
Deborah Polich, Library Director

Old Mission San José Museum
(43300 Mission Boulevard—location)
PO Box 3159 (mailing address)
Fremont, CA 94539
(510) 657-1797
Dolores Ferenz, Administrator
daily 10:00–5:00
(small reference library; also stories of the
local Ohlone natives; "our genealogy
(church) records are not open, but we will
research as time allows.")
research: $10.00 per hour

Ontario City Library
Model Colony History Room

215 East C Street
Ontario, CA 91764-4198
(909) 988-8481
library@ci.ontario.ca.us
http://ci.ontario.ca.us/library
Terry Carter, Library Assistant
Tue–Sat 1:00–5:00, Tue 5:30–8:30

Orange County Library
Cypress Branch
5331 Orange Avenue
Cypress, CA 90630-2985
(714) 826-0350; (714) 828-1103 FAX
Helen Richardson, Senior Administrative
Librarian

Orange County Library
El Toro Branch
24672 Raymond Way
Lake Forest, CA 92630-4489
(949) 855-8173; (949) 586-7412 FAX
Phyllis Brown, Senior Administrative
Librarian

Orange County Library
Garden Grove Regional Library
11200 Stanford Avenue
Garden Grove, CA 92640-5398
(714) 530-0711; (714) 530-0961 FAX
Su Chay, Principal Admin. Librarian

Orange County Library
Tustin Branch Library
345 East Main Street
Tustin, CA 92680-4491
(714) 544-7725; (714) 832-4279 FAX
Emily Moore, Senior Administrative
Librarian

Palm Springs Public Library
300 South Sunrise Way
Palm Springs, CA 92262-7699
(760) 323-8294; (760) 320-8294 FAX
Library@ci.palm-springs.ca.us
http://ci.palm-springs.ca.us/library.html
Josette McNary, Reference Coordinator
Mon–Tue 9:00–8:00, Wed–Thur & Sat
9:00–5:30, Fri 10:00–5:30

Palmdale City Library
700 East Palmdale Boulevard
Palmdale, CA 93550-4742
(661) 267-5600; (661) 267-5601; (661) 267-
5647 (Reference); (661) 267-5606 FAX
pcl@qnet.com
http://palmdalelibrary.org
Nancy Quelland, City Librarian

Palo Alto City Library
1213 Newell Road
Palo Alto, CA 94303-2999
(650) 329-2436; (650) 329-2516; (650) 329-
2664 (Reference); (650) 327-7568 FAX
pa_library@city.palo-alto.ca.us
http://city.palo-alto.ca.us/library
Mary Jo Levy, Director

Palos Verdes Library District
Local History Room
(2400 Via Campesina, Palos Verdes
Estates—location)
650 Deep Valley Drive, PO Box 8000
(mailing address)
Rolling Hills Estates, CA 90274
(310) 377-9584, ext. 250
lswallow@pvld.org
http://www.pvld.org
Lenore M. Blume; Lanny Swallow,
Reference Department Manager
Tue–Thur 1:00–7:00, Sat 10:00–5:00

Pasadena Public Library

Pasadena Centennial Room
285 East Walnut Street
Pasadena, CA 91101-1598
(626) 405-4052; (626) 796-3818
http://www.ci.pasadena.ca.us/library
Carolyn L. Garner, Librarian II
Mon–Thur 9:00–9:00, Fri–Sat 9:00–6:00,
    Sun 1:00–5:00

Petaluma Historical Library and Museum
20 Fourth Street
Petaluma, CA 94952
(707) 778-4398; (707) 762-3923 FAX
petmuseum@iscweb.com
http://petalumamuseum.com
Lucy Kortum, in research
Wed–Sat 10:00–4:00, Sun noon–3:00
Pub. *Update:PMA*, bimonthly
("We are a history museum but have a
    research library that has city directories,
    biographical files and local histories.")
$15.00 per year membership

Governor Pico Mansion Society
14216 Neargrove Road
La Mirada, CA 90638

**Placer County Archives and Research
Center (Department of Museums)**
(11437 D Avenue—location)
101 Maple Street (mailing address)
Auburn, CA 95603
(530) 889-7994
http://www.placer.ca.gov/museum
Carmel Barry-Schweyer, Archivist
Mon–Tue 9:00–noon & 1:00–4:00, Thur
    8:00–noon
(besides Placer County Museum location,
    includes Gold Country Museum (mining),
    1273 High Street, Auburn, CA 95603,
    (530) 887-0690, Tue–Sun 10:00–4:00;
    Bernhard Museum Complex (winery),
    291 Auburn-Folsom Road, Auburn, CA
    95603, (530) 888-6891, Tue–Fri
    10:30–3:00, Sat–Sun noon–4:00; Griffith
    Quarry Museum (granite), corner of
    Taylor and Rock Springs Road, Penryn,
    CA, (530) 663-1837, Sat–Sun noon–4:00;
    Golden Drift Museum (mining and
    railroads), 32820 Main Street, Dutch Flat,
    CA, (530) 389-2126, Memorial Day–mid-
    Sept: Wed & Sat–Sun noon–4:00; and
    Forest Hill Divide Museum (local history
    of Foresthill and Iowa Hill Divides),
    24601 Harrison Street, Foresthill, CA,
    (530) 367-3988, Sat–Sun noon–4:00)
copies: 50¢ for the first page, 25¢ for each
    additional page

Pleasanton Library
400 Old Bernal Avenue
Pleasanton, CA 94566-7012
(925) 931-3400; (925) 846-8517 FAX
circadm@ci.pleasanton.ca.us
http://ci.pleasanton.ca.us/library.html
Judy Person, Librarian
Mon–Tue 1:00–8:00, Wed–Thur
    10:00–6:00, Sat 2:00–6:00, Sun
    1:00–5:00

Plumas County Museum Association, Inc.
500 Jackson Street
Quincy, CA 95971
(530) 283-6320; (530) 283-6081
pcmuseum@psln.com
http://www.plumas.ca.us
Scott Lawson, Director
Mon–Sat 8:00–5:00
Pub. *Association Newsletter*, quarterly
(regional and local history)
$10.00 per year membership; research: $5.00
    minimum

Pomona Public Library
Special Collections Department
(625 South Garey Avenue, Pomona, CA
91766-3322—location)
PO Box 2271 (mailing address)
Pomona, CA 91769-2271
(909) 620-2043; (909) 620-3713 FAX
library@ci.pomona.ca.us
http://www.ci.pomona.ca.us
Pat Lambert, Senior Librarian, Adult
    Reference Services
Mon–Thur 9:00–8:00, Fri–Sat noon–5:00
("Seaphus W. and Ethel M. Curtiss
    Genealogical Collection. Approximately
    4,000 titles for genealogy, some
    periodicals and microfilm.")

Porterville Historical Museum
(257 North D Street—location)
Porterville Chamber of Commerce
93 North Main Street #A (mailing address)
Porterville, CA 93257-3711
(559) 784-2053
Beverly Faul, Curator
Tue–Sat 10:00–4:00
Pub. *Porterville Historical Museum
    Newsletter*, quarterly
$20.00 per year membership; museum
    admission: $1.00 for nonmember adults

Porterville Public Library
41 West Thurman Avenue
Porterville, CA 93257-3652
(559) 784-0177; (559) 781-4396 FAX
parks_leisure@ci.porterville.ca.us
http://www.ci.porterville.ca.us
Melanie Wells
Genealogy: Mon–Sat 9:00–5:00; Local
    History: Mon–Thur 10:00–noon

Potrero-East County Museum Society
PO Box 70
Potrero, CA 92063

Ramona Museum of California History
4580 North Figueroa Street
Los Angeles, CA 90065
(213) 222-0012

Rancho Cordova Community Library
9845 Folsom Boulevard
Sacramento, CA 95827-1397
(916) 264-2700; (916) 228-2114 FAX
Haleh Motiey, Branch Supervisor

Redding Museum and Art Center
(56 Quartz Hill Road, Redding, CA
96003—location)
PO Box 427 (mailing address)
Redding, CA 96099
(530) 225-4155; (530) 243-8801; (530) 243-
    8929 FAX
http://www.shastalink.k12.ca.us/rmah/
    RMAHmain.html
Keith Foster, Director
(local history)

Redwood City Public Library
Local History Collection
1044 Middlefield Road
Redwood City, CA 94063-1868
(650) 780-7030; (650) 780-7000; (650) 780-
    7026 (Library Reference); (650) 780-7069
    FAX; (650) 780-7225 (Library) FAX
relinfo@plsinfo.org
http://www.redwoodcity.org/library/
    index.html
Jeanne Thivierge, Local History Specialist
Mon–Thur 10:00–9:00, Fri–Sat 10:00–5:00,
    Sun 1:00–4:00; Local History Room: Tue
    & Thur 1:00–5:00, Wed 5:00–9:00
Pub. *Archives Committee Newsletter*,

quarterly
$5.00 per year membership

Richmond Museum Association
(400 Nevin Avenue—location)
PO Box 1267 (mailing address)
Richmond, CA 94802
(510) 235-7387; (510) 620-6845 FAX
dbastin@msn.com
http://www.richmondmuseumofhistory.
    org/aboutus.htm
Lois Boyle, President
Wed-Sun 1:00-4:00 (except holidays)
$25.00 per year membership

Richmond Public Library
Richmond Collection
325 Civic Center Plaza
Richmond, CA 94804-1659
(510) 620-6561 (Reference); (510) 620-
    6555; (510) 620-6850 FAX
http://www.ci.richmond.ca.us/~library/
    richmond_collection.htm
Emma Clark, Head, Reference Department
Mon–Thur 9:00–9:00, Fri–Sat 9:00–6:00,
    Sun 1:00–5:00

Rio Vista Museum Association
16 North Front Street
Rio Vista, CA 94571
(707) 374-5169
Sat–Sun 1:30–4:30

Riverside Local History Resource Center
Riverside Public Library
3581 Mission Inn Avenue
Riverside, CA 92501-3377
(909) 826-5736; (909) 788-1528
wswafford@ci.riverside.ca.us
http://www.ci.riverside.ca.us/library
William M. A. Swafford, Local
    History/Special Collections Librarian
Mon–Tue 10:00–8:00, Wed–Sat 10:00–6:00

City of Riverside Municipal Museum
3580 Mission Inn Avenue
Riverside, CA 92501
(909) 826-5273; (909) 369-4970 FAX
http://www.museumpress.com
Dr. Vince Moses, Interim Director
Mon 9:00–1:00, Tue–Fri 9:00–5:00, Sat
    10:00–5:00, Sun 11:00–5:00
Pub. *Newsletter of the Riverside Museum
    Associates*, monthly
$10.00 per year membership

Rosemead Library
8800 Valley Boulevard
Rosemead, CA 91770-1788
(626) 573-5220; (626) 280-8523 FAX
http://colapublib.org/libs/rosemead
Lisa Castaneda, Library Manager
Tue–Wed noon–8:00, Thur 10:00–6:00, Fri
    noon–5:00, Sat 11:00–5:00

Roseville Public Library
225 Taylor Street
Roseville, CA 95678-2681
(916) 774-5221; (916) 774-5231
    (Reference); (916) 773-5594 FAX
library@roseville.ca.us
http://roseville.ca.us/library/library.htm
Susan L. Nickerson, Library Director
Mon–Thur 9:00–9:00, Fri 9:00–6:00, Sat
    9:00–5:00, Sun 1:00–5:00

**Sacramento Archives and Museum
Collection Center**
551 Sequoia Pacific Boulevard
Sacramento, CA 95814-0229
(916) 264-7072
Charlene Gilbert Noyes, Archivist

Wed–Fri 8:15–noon by appointment
(Sacramento city and county)

Sacramento Branch Genealogical Library
5343 Halsted Avenue
Carmichael, CA 95608
Verl F. Weight
Pub. *Sacramento Branch Genealogical Library Newsletter*, monthly

Sacramento City Cemetery Archives
Old City Cemetery Committee
1000 Broadway
Sacramento, CA 95818
(916) 448-5665; (916) 554-7508 FAX
John Bettencourt, Volunteer Staff Coordinator
Mon–Fri 10:00–3:00
(deaths and burials 1850–1927, cemetery records from 1927)

Sacramento Historical Museum
101 I Street
Sacramento, CA 95814
(916) 449-2057

Sacramento Public Library
Special Collections, Central Library, Sacramento Room
828 I Street
Sacramento, CA 95814-2589
(916) 264-2920; (916) 264-2854 FAX
Ruth Ellis, Sacramento Room Librarian
Tue–Thur & Sun 1:00–5:00
("Collection includes Sacramento and California history, a local authors collection, Sacramento city directories and a book arts collection; genealogy collection is presently housed at the Carmichael Regional Branch of the Sacramento Public Library.")

Sacramento Valley Museum
(1491 "E" Street—location)
PO Box 1437 (mailing address)
Williams, CA 95987
(530) 473-2978
Kathy Manor, Operations Manager
Mar–Nov: Thur–Sat 10:00–4:00, and by appointment
Pub. *Newsletter*, annually; "other letters announcing special events"
(no genealogy, but historical records in and of the Colusa County area)
$10.00 per year membership

San Bernardino County Archives
777 East Rialto Avenue
San Bernardino, CA 92415-0795
(909) 387-2030
James D. Hofer, Archivist/Records Manager
Mon–Fri 9:00–5:00
("official records of San Bernardino County, 1853–present")

Law Library for San Bernardino County
402 North D Street
San Bernardino, CA 92401
(909) 885-3020; (909) 885-1869 FAX
Carolyn J. Poston, County Law Librarian

San Bernardino County Museum
2024 Orange Tree Lane
Redlands, CA 92374
(909) 798-8570
http://www.co.san-bernardino.ca.us/ccr/museum/museums. htm
Allen D. Griesemer, Ph.D., Director
Tue–Thur 9:00–5:00
Pub. *Museum Quarterly*, $40.00 per year subscription
(cultural and natural history)

San Bernardino County Museum
701 West Angus Avenue
San Bruno, CA 94066

San Carlos Historical Museum
533 Laurel Street
San Carlos, CA 94070
(415) 595-5842

San Carlos Library
San Mateo County Genealogical Collection
610 Elm Street
San Carlos, CA 94070-3013
(650) 591-0341; (650) 591-1585 FAX
http://sancarloslibrary.org
Mon–Wed 10:00–9:00, Thur–Fri 10:00–6:00, Sat 10:00–5:00, Sun 1:00–5:00

San Diego Public Library
Genealogy Room
820 E Street
San Diego, CA 92101-6478
(619) 236-5834
weblibrary@sandiego.gov
http://www.sannet.gov/public-library
Mary Allely, Section Supervisor
Mon–Thur 10:00–9:00, Fri–Sat 9:30–5:30, Sun 1:00–5:00
("DAR Materials, census microfilm, original 13 colonies")
copies: 15¢ per page (from paper or microform originals)

Museum of the City of San Francisco
(address withheld upon request)
(San Francisco history museum/archives, refers genealogy inquiries elsewhere)

San Francisco Public Library
Genealogy Collection
Civic Center
100 Larkin Street
San Francisco, CA 94102-4796
(415) 557-4400 (Reference); (415) 557-4239 FAX
webmail@sfpl.org
http://sfpl.org
Susan Hildreth, City Librarian

San Francisco State University
Labor Archives and Research Center
480 Winston Drive
San Francisco, CA 94132
(415) 564-4010; (415) 564-3606 FAX
larc@sfsu.edu
http://www.library.sfsu.edu/special/larc.html
Susan Sherwood, Acting Director
Mon–Fri 1:00–5:00, and by appointment

San Jacinto Valley Museum Association, Inc.
(181 East Main Street—location)
PO Box 922 (mailing address)
San Jacinto, CA 92383
Madenia Freitas, President
Tue–Sat noon–4:00
$10.00 per year membership

San Joaquin County Historical Museum
(11793 North Micke Grove Road, Lodi, CA 95240—location)
PO Box 30 (mailing address)
Lodi, CA 95241-0030
(209) 331-2055; (209) 331-2057 FAX
http://www.imon.com/sjmuseum
Michael W. Bennett, Director
Wed–Sun 1:00–4:45
Pub. *News and Notes*; *San Joaquin Historian*, quarterly
(indexed newspaper, reclamation district and county records, business records)

$4.00 per year membership; research: $25.00 per hour for nonmembers

San Jose Historical Museum Archives
1600 Senter Road
San Jose, CA 95112-2599
(408) 287-2290; (408) 277-3890 FAX
Leslie Masunaga, Archivist
Archives: Mon–Fri by appointment, Wed 1:00–4:00
(San Jose, Santa Clara Valley, New Almaden Mines)
museum admission: $4.00 for adults; copies: 15¢ per page

San Jose Public Library
California Room
180 West San Carlos Street
San Jose, CA 95113-2005
(408) 277-4867; (408) 277-4868 FAX
bob.johnson@ci.sj.ca.us
http://www.sjpl.lib.ca.us/Calif (California Room)
Bob Johnson, Reference Librarian
Mon & Thur 2:00–5:00, Tue–Wed 3:00–9:00, Fri 10:00–1:00, Sat 1:00–6:00
(local history, but no specialized genealogy collection; "useful only to those researching individuals who had lived in San Jose and Santa Clara County")
copies: $3.00 for one to three pages, 75¢ for each additional page

San Leandro Public Library
San Leandro History Room
300 Estudillo Avenue
San Leandro, CA 94577-4706
(510) 577-3971; (510) 597-3987 FAX
jprince@ci.san-leandro.ca.us
http://www.sanleandrolibrary.org
Janet Prince, Genealogy Librarian; Cindy Simons, San Leandro History Room Librarian
call for hours of operation
(San Leandro history; San Leandro historical photo collection; Alameda County history; California history)

San Rafael Public Library
1100 E Street
San Rafael, CA 94901-1900
(415) 485-3319; (415) 485-3323; (415) 485-3321 (Reference); (415) 485-3112 FAX
srf@marinet.lib.ca.us
http://marin.org/libs/srf
Catherine Wright, Reference Librarian
Tue–Thur 10:00–9:00, Fri–Sat 10:00–5:00

Santa Ana Public Library
Santa Ana History Room
26 Civic Center Plaza
Santa Ana, CA 92701-4010
(714) 647-5280
http://www.santa-ana.org/library/as/hr.asp
Mon–Sat 10:00–6:00
("Orange County, California, local history collection with Santa Ana materials; book collection on California history")
research: $10.00 for out-of-county inquiries

Santa Barbara Public Library
(40 East Anapamu Street, Santa Barbara, CA 93101-2722—location)
PO Box 1019 (mailing address)
Santa Barbara, CA 93102
(805) 962-7653 (Reference); (805) 962-6304 FAX
ckeator@santabarbaraca.gov
http://www.sbplibrary.org
Carol L. Keator, Library Director
Mon–Thur 10:00–9:00, Fri–Sat 10:00–5:30, Sun 1:00–5:00

("We provide access to materials in person; staff cannot answer research inquiries by mail.")

Santa Clara County Central Library
2635 Homestead Road
Santa Clara, CA 95051-5387
(408) 984-3236; (408) 248-8205
library@ci.santa-clara.ca.us
http://library.ci.santa-clara.ca.us
Mon–Thur 9:00–9:00, Fri–Sat 9:00–6:00,
    Sun 1:00–5:00
(international genealogy collection)

Santa Clara County Library
1095 North Seventh Street
San Jose, CA 95112-4446
(408) 293-2326 (Reference); (408) 287-9826
    FAX
webmaster@scinet.co.santa-clara.ca.us
http://santaclaracountylib.org
Susan Fuller, County Librarian

Central Branch Public Library
Local History and California Room
224 Church Street
Santa Cruz, CA 95060-3873
(831) 429-3526
Tue–Thur 10:00–8:00, Fri–Sat 10:00–5:00

Santa Cruz County Historical Museum
118 Cooper Street
Santa Cruz, CA 95060
(831) 425-2540
(primarily historical, not genealogical)

Santa Fe Springs City Library
11700 East Telegraph Road
Santa Fe Springs, CA 90670-3600
(562) 868-7738 (Reference); (562) 929-3680
    FAX
library@sfs.org
http://santafesprings.org/libindex.htm
Monica Penninger, Director
Mon–Thur 10:00–9:00, Fri 10:00–6:00, Sat
    10:00–5:00

Santa Maria Public Library
Genealogical Collection
420 South Broadway
Santa Maria, CA 93454-5107
(805) 925-0994
http://ci.santa-maria.ca.us/library
Colleen Beck, Reference Librarian
Mon–Thur 10:00–9:00, Fri–Sat 10:00–6:00
(passenger lists, general finding aids)

Searls Historical Library
214 Church Street
Nevada City, CA 95959
(530) 265-5910
Edwin L. Tyson
Mon–Sat 1:00–4:00
(Nevada County, California, with some
    material on adjoining areas)

Seaver Center for Western History Research
Natural History Museum of Los Angeles County
900 Exposition Boulevard
Los Angeles, CA 90007
(213) 744-3359 (Seaver Center); (217) 763-3565 FAX
jcahoon@nhm.org
http://www.nhm.org/research/seaver
Jonathan Spaulding, Curator
Thur by appointment

Sharpsteen Museum
(1311 Washington—location)
PO Box 573 (mailing address)

Calistoga, CA 94515
(707) 942-5911
Mary Elizabeth Cumpston, President

Shasta College Museum and Research Center
(1065 North Old Oregon Trail, Redding, CA
    96001—location)
PO Box 496006 (mailing address)
Redding, CA 96049
(530) 225-4754
Edward Clewett, Director
Mon, Wed & Fri 11:00–2:00 (volunteer
    staff)
(northern California local history,
    photographs, coroner records through the
    1930s, etc.; special events)

Sherman Library and Gardens
(2647 East Coast Highway—location)
614 Dahlia Avenue (mailing address)
Corona Del Mar, CA 92625
(949) 673-1880 (Library)

Sierra Madre Public Library
440 West Sierra Madre Boulevard
Sierra Madre, CA 91024-2399
(626) 355-7186; (626) 355-7187
    (Reference); (626) 355-6218 FAX
ref@sierramadre.lib.ca.us
http://sierramadre.lib.ca.us
Toni Gollands Buckner, Director of Library
    Services

Siskiyou County Museum
910 South Main Street
Yreka, CA 96097
(530) 842-3836; (530) 842-3166 FAX
hismus@inreach.com
http://www.snowcrest.net/fueston/
    museum.html
Michael Hendryx, Director
Tue–Fri 9:00–5:00, Sat 9:00–4:00, by
    appointment only, no research on Wed
    (closed major holidays)
Pub. *The Siskiyou Pioneer*, annually
("History museum with research library
    $20.00 per year membership; research: initial
    search (not more than ½ hours) free,
    $20.00 per hour thereafter

Siskiyou County Public Library
719 Fourth Street
Yreka, CA 96097-3381
(530) 841-4175 (Reference); (530) 842-7001
    FAX
siskiyoulibrary@snowcrest.net
http://www.snowcrest.net/fueston/index.
    html
Kathy Fueston, Reference
Mon 10:00–7:00, Tue–Wed 10:00–6:00,
    Thur noon–5:00, Sat (school year)
    1:00–5:00

Jedediah Smith Society
The John Muir Center
Wendell Phillips Center
University of the Pacific
Stockton, CA 95211
(209) 946-2169; (209) 946-2945 (Special
    Collections); (209) 946-2578 FAX; (650)
    432-1552 FAX
http://library.uop.edu/depthltmuir.html
Dr. Clover, Executive Secretary; Daryl
    Morrison, Head of Special Collections
Mon–Fri 9:00–midnight
Pub. *Castor Canadensis*, quarterly
(collection, deposited with the Holt-Atherton
    Pacific Center for Western Studies,
    emphasizes the Mountain Man era)
$10.00 per year membership; queries on
    Jedediah Smith should be addressed to

Holt-Atherton, Department of Special
    Collections

Solano County Historical Records Commission
c/o Central Services
1745 Enterprise Drive, Building 2, Suite A
Fairfield, CA 94533
Nadine Stevenson
Tue & Fri 9:00–1:00
(county archives)
research: none at present

Sonoma County Library
Local History and Genealogical Annex
Third and E Streets
Santa Rosa, CA 95404-4400
(707) 545-0831 (Reference); (707) 545-
    0831, ext. 562 (Annex); (707) 525-9563
    FAX
molly@sonoma.lib.ca.us
http://sonomalibrary.org
Thomas Trice, Library Director
Wed–Sat 10:00–5:00

Sonoma County Museum
425 Seventh Street
Santa Rosa, CA 95401
(707) 579-1500
John Z. Lofgren, Ph.D., Executive Director
Pub. *The Muse* (primarily historical, not
    genealogical)

Sonoma State University
Finley McFarling Genealogy Collections
Special Collections
Ruben Salazar Library
1801 East Cotati Avenue
Rohnert Park, CA 94928-3609
(707) 664-4152 (Special Collections)
paula.hammett@sonoma.edu
http://libweb.sonoma.edu/special.html
Paula Hammett, Head of Collections,
    Reference Librarian
by appointment

South San Francisco Public Library
South San Francisco History Room
Grand Avenue Branch Library
306 Walnut Avenue
South San Francisco, CA 94080-2700
(650) 877-8533; (650) 877-8530
ssfpladm@plsinfo.org
http://www.ssf.net/depts/library
Kathleen Kay, Historian
Mon & Wed 1:00–7:00, Tue & Thur
    1:00–4:00, Fri 10:00–2:00

Southern Methodist University
Clements Center for Southwest Studies
(see Texas, Part 2)

Stanford University
Green Library
Stanford, CA 94035-6004
(650) 725-1064
http://www-
    sul.stanford.edu/depts/green/index.html

Stanislaus County Free Library
1500 I Street
Modesto, CA 95354-1166
(209) 558-7814; (209) 558-8097 FAX
refquest@scfl.lib.ca.us
http://stanislauslibrary.org
Library: Mon–Thur 10:00–9:00, Fri–Sat
    10:00–5:00, Sun noon–5:00; Special
    Collections Room: Mon–Wed
    10:00–3:00, Thur–Sat 10:00–5:00

Stockton-San Joaquin County Public Library

605 North El Dorado Street
Stockton, CA 95202-1999
(209) 937-8221
Karen.Ramos@ci.stockton.ca.us
http://www.stockton.lib.ca.us
Karen Ramos, Reference Librarian
Mon–Thur 10:00–8:00 (closed first Wed of
    Mar, June, Sept, Dec), Fri 10:00–6:00,
    Sat 10:00–5:00
("Local genealogical collection, U.S.
    genealogy—over 1,000 titles, California
    census, 1850–1920. Very limited ILL of
    genealogical materials; no loan of
    microfilm.")

Tehama County Museum Foundation, Inc.
(275 C Street—location)
PO Box 275 (mailing address)
Tehama, CA 96090
(530) 384-2420

Temecula Library
41000 County Center Drive
Temecula, CA 92591
(909) 600-6262; (909) 600-6265 FAX
Special hours for Temecula Valley
    Genealogical Society members to assist

Thousand Oaks Library
(1401 East Janss Road, Thousand Oaks, CA
91362-2199—location)
PO Box 1228 (mailing address)
Thousand Oaks, CA 91358-0228
(805) 449-2660 (Reference); (805) 497-
    6282; (805) 373-6858 FAX
InfoChoice@mx.tol.lib.ca.us;
    sbrogden@mx.tol.lib.ca.us
http://www.toaks.org/library;
    http://www.tol.lib.ca.us/_tol/tol_gr.htm
    (Genealogy Reading Room)
Mon–Thur 10:00–9:00, Fri 10:00–6:00, Sat
    10:00–5:00, Sun 1:00–5:00

Tomales Regional Local History Center
(26700 Highway 1—location)
PO Box 262 (mailing address)
Tomales, CA 94971
(707) 878-2398
Lois Parks, President
by appointment
Pub. *Bulletin*, quarterly
(photographs, North Pacific Coast Railroad,
    family histories)
$15.00 per year membership; search: $5.00
    per hour plus copies at 10¢ per page

Tulare County Free Library System
Annie Mitchell Local History Room
200 West Oak Street
Visalia, CA 93291-4993
(559) 733-6954; (559) 730-2524 FAX
blewis@sjvls.lib.ca.us
http://sjvls.lib.ca.us/tulareco
Sheila Caskey Holder, Volunteer; Brian G.
    Lewis, County Librarian
History Room: Mon–Thur 1:00–5:00, Tue
    10:00 A.M.–noon, Wed 6:00 P.M.–8:00
    P.M.
(emphasis on Tulare County, San Joaquin
    Valley and Sequoia National Park; "Our
    'archival' material is strictly Tulare
    County [and Kern and Kings counties,
    which came off Tulare County]; book
    material encompasses all California.")
copies/search: $1.00 or 15¢ per sheet (if
    seven or more copies are made)

Tulare Public Library
Genealogy Room
113 North F Street
Tulare, CA 93274-3803
(559) 685-2342

http://www.sjvls.org/tularepub/services/
    genealogy.htm
Ronad W. Gilstrap, Genealogy Librarian
Mon & Wed 10:00–6:00, Tue & Thur
    10:00–8:30, Sat 10:00–2:00
$4.50 per surname for out-of-town research
    requests

Tuolumne County Library
480 Greenley Road
Sonora, CA 95370-5956
(209) 533-5507; (209) 533-0936 FAX
libref@mlode.com
http://libraryfriends1.homestead.com/
    files/Start_the_INTERNET.htm
Joan Rutty, Librarian Assistant II
Mon–Wed 10:00–9:00, Thur–Sat 10:00–5:30
(Tuolumne County only)
copies: 15¢ per page

University of California—Berkeley
The Bancroft Library
(address withheld upon request)
(does not collect general genealogical works;
    has some resources which may be used to
    carry out research, especially on western
    North America; pictorial collection, oral
    history, archival collections, newspaper
    and periodical indexes)

University of California—Davis
Department of Special Collections
Shields Library
Davis, CA 95616-5292
(530) 752-1621; (530) 754-5758 FAX
jlskarstad@ucdavis.edu
http://www.lib.ucdavis.edu/specol/index.
    html
Mon–Fri 10:00–4:00
(history collection, manuscripts)

**UCLA Fowler Museum of Cultural
History**
(see Ethnic Archives, Libraries and Societies,
Part 3)

University of California—Los Angeles
University Research Library
405 Hilgard Avenue
West Los Angeles, CA 90024

University of California—Riverside
Rivera Library
Special Collections
(3401 Watkins Drive, Riverside, CA
92521—location)
PO Box 5900 (mailing address)
Riverside, CA 92517-5900
(909) 787-3233
melissa.conway@ucr.edu
http://library.ucr.edu
Melissa Conway, Ph.D., Head
Mon–Fri 9:00–5:00
(Local History Collection)

University of California—Santa Barbara
Department of History
Graduate Program in Public Historical
Studies
Public History Information Unit
Santa Barbara, CA 93106
(805) 961-2224
Otis L. Graham, Ph.D., Director/Editor
Pub. *The Public Historian*
(not primarily genealogical, maintains
    archive)

University of California—Santa Cruz
Special Collections Library
Santa Cruz, CA 95064
(831) 459-2547
school year: Mon–Sun 10:00–noon &

1:00–4:00; quarter break & summer: by
    appointment only

University of La Verne
Elvin and Betty Wilson Library
2040 Third Street
La Verne, CA 91750
(909) 593-3511, ext. 4300; (909) 593-3511,
    ext. 4305; (909) 593-3511, ext. 4306;
    (909) 593-3511, ext. 6039 (Hours; (800)
    866-4858
heckmanm@ulv.edu
http://www.ulaverne.edu/~library/libs.htm
Dr. Marlin Heckman, University Librarian
academic year: Mon–Fri 8:00–5:00; summer:
    Mon–Fri 8:30–4:30, except as posted

University of Utah Marriott Library
(see Utah, Part 2)

University of Washington Libraries
(see Washington, Part 2)

Upland Public Library
450 North Euclid Avenue
Upland, CA 91786-4732
(909) 931-4200; (909) 931-4205
    (Reference); (909) 931-4209 FAX
http://uplandpl.lib.ca.us
Linda Yao, Library Director

**Vacaville Museum, A Center for Solano
County History**
213 Buck Avenue
Vacaville, CA 95688
(707) 447-4513; (707) 447-2661 FAX
vacmuseum@aol.com
Ruth Gardner Begell, Museum Director
Wed–Sun 1:00–4:30
Pub. *Vacaville Museum News & Notes*,
    quarterly
(Solano County history)
$20.00 per year membership

**Ventura County Museum of History and
Art**
(see Ventura County Historical Society,
Historical Societies—Local and Regional,
below)

Victorville Branch Library
15011 Circle Drive
Victorville, CA 92392-3998
(760) 245-4222; (760) 245-2273 FAX
http://vvo.com/comm/sbclvv.htm
Suzanne Oliver, Librarian

Vintage Hall, Inc.
473 Main Street
Saint Helena, CA 94574
(707) 963-7411

Western Heritage Center
(see Montana, Part 2)

Whittier College Library
7031 Founders Hill Road
Whittier, CA 90608
(562) 907-4245; (562) 907-4247
    (Reference); (562) 698-7168 FAX
pobrien@whittier.edu
http://whittier.edu
Philip M. O'Brien, College Librarian

Whittier Public Library
7344 South Washington Avenue
Whittier, CA 90602
(562) 464-3750; (562) 464-3569 FAX
cbirt@whittierpl.org
Cynthia Birt, Head of Reference
Mon–Wed 10:00–9:00, Thur–Fri
    10:00–6:00, Sat 10:00–5:00, Sun

1:00–5:00

Willow Creek-China Flat Museum
PO Box 102
Willow Creek, CA 95573
mwooden@juno.com
Margaret Wooden
first weekend in May to first weekend in Oct:
   Fri–Sun & holidays 10:00–4:00
Pub. *Footprints in the Sands of Time*,
   quarterly
("Featuring local Indian tribes [Hupa, Yurok,
   Karok], mining, farming, logging,
   Bigfoot.")
$10.00 per year membership

Workman and Temple Family Homestead Museum
15415 East Don Julian Road
City of Industry, CA 91745-1029
(626) 968-8492; (626) 968-2048 FAX
info@homesteadmuseum.org
http://homesteadmuseum.org
Paul R. Spitzzeri, Collections Manager
Mon–Fri 9:00–4:00
Pub. *Homestead*, three times per year; *San
   Gabriel Valley Historian*, annually
("specializing in southern California history
   from 1830–1930, plus history of the
   Workman and Temple families")

Yolo County Archives and Record Center
226 Buckeye Street
Woodland, CA 95695-2600
(530) 666-8010; (530) 666-8006 FAX
Mel Russell, Archives Co-ordinator
Tue 9:00–noon & 12:30–3:00, and by
   appointment
(Yolo County history from 1850)

Yolo County Historical Museum
512 Gibson Road
Woodland, CA 95695
(530) 666-1045
Antonina "Monika" Stengert,
   Director/Curator
Mon–Tue 9:00–5:00, Sat–Sun noon–4:00
(archival material; "library, ephemera
   collection," northern California, Yolo
   County)

Yosemite National Park Research Library
PO Box 577
Yosemite National Park, CA 95389
(209) 372-4461, ext. 280

Yuba County Library
California Room
303 Second Street
Marysville, CA 95901-6011
(530) 749-7380
library@co.yuba.ca.us
http://www.co.yuba.ca.us
Heather Moldenhauer
Mon–Wed 10:00–8:00, Thur 10:00–6:00,
   Sat noon–4:00
("Our California Room index dates back to
   1850.")

Historical Societies—Local and Regional

Alameda County Historical Society
5461 Fernhoff Road
Oakland, CA 94619-3111
(510) 531-0222

Amador County Archives
1220-A Airport Road
Jackson, CA 95642
(209) 223-6389 voice & FAX

ArchivesDept@co.amador.ca.us
http://www.co.amador.ca.us/depts/
   archives/index.htm
Larry Cenotto, County Archivist
Tue–Fri 10:00–noon & 1:00–4:00
very limited research by staff, but referrals
   available

Amador County Historical Society
PO Box 761
Jackson, CA 95642
Larry Cenotto, Treasurer
$12.00 per year membership; no research
   services

Amador Livermore Valley Historical Society Museum
603 Main Street
Pleasanton, CA 94566
(925) 462-2766
Archives: Wed–Fri 11:00–4:00; Museum:
   Wed–Sat 11:00–4:00, Sun 1:00–4:00
Pub. *Quarterly Newsletter*
$25.00 per year membership

American Historical Association, Pacific Coast Branch
Department of History
Loyola Marymount University
Los Angeles, CA 90045
(310) 338-2805; (310) 338-7662
Lawrence J. Jelinek, Secretary-Treasurer
Pub. *Pacific Historical Review*, quarterly
(specializes in "frontier West, post frontier
   West, Pacific rim": Alaska, Arizona,
   California, Colorado, Hawaii, Idaho,
   Montana, New Mexico, Nevada, North
   Dakota, Oregon, South Dakota, Utah,
   Washington, Wyoming and the Pacific
   trust territories)
$21.00 per year membership

American West Research Center and Historical Society, Inc.
(see Ohio, Part 2)

Anaheim Historical Society
(Anaheim Boulevard at Broadway—location)
PO Box 927 (mailing address)
Anaheim, CA 92815
(714) 778-3301

Association for Northern California Records and Research
PO Box 3024
Chico, CA 95927
Clarence F. McIntosh, President
Pub. *ANCRR Newsletter*

Atascadero History Society
(6600 Palma—location)
PO Box 1047 (mailing address)
Atascadero, CA 93423
(805) 466-1811
Marj Mackey, Curator
Mon–Sat 1:00–4:00
$10.00–$15.00 per year membership

Atherton Heritage Association
Atherton Town Hall
91 Ashfield Road
Atherton, CA 94027
(650) 688-6540
Marion E. Oster, President
Tue 10:00–noon
accepts donation

Azusa Historical Society, Inc.
City Hall Complex
213 East Foothill Boulevard
Azusa, CA 91702

Belmont Historical Society
Historical Room
1225 Ralston Avenue
Belmont, CA 94002
http://www.belmont.gov/hist/index.html

Berkeley Historical Society
(1325 Grant Street, Berkeley, CA
   94703—location)
PO Box 1190 (mailing address)
Berkeley, CA 94701-1190
(510) 524-9880
http://www.ci.berkeley.ca.us/histsoc
Carl C. Wilson, President

Big Bear Valley Historical Society
(In the northeast portion of Big Bear City
   Park, east of the airport—location)
PO Box 513 (mailing address)
Big Bear City, CA 92314
(909) 585-8100
Neil Nickle, President
Wed & Sat–Sun 10:00–4:00
$10.00 per year membership

Bishop Museum and Historical Society
(Laws Narrow Gauge Railroad Museum, off
   Silver Canyon Road, Laws, CA—location)
PO Box 363 (mailing address)
Bishop, CA 93515
(760) 873-5950
Alice J. Boothe, Administrator
daily 10:00–4:00
(has quite a lot of pioneer information for the
   area)

Burlingame Historical Society
Washington Park
PO Box 144
Burlingame, CA 94011
(650) 340-9960
http://www.best.com/~spectrum/history/
   history.html

Butte County Historical Society
(Ehmann Home, 1480 Lincoln
   Street—location)
PO Box 2195 (mailing address)
Oroville, CA 95965
(530) 533-5316
flexible
Pub. *Diggin's*, quarterly; *Butte County
   Historical Society Slickens*, irregularly
$15.00 per year membership

Cabrillo Historical Association
Cabrillo National Monument
1800 Cabrillo Memorial
San Diego, CA 92106
(619) 557-5450

Calaveras County Historical Society
(30 North Main Street—location)
PO Box 721 (mailing address)
San Andreas, CA 95249
(209) 754-1058; (209) 754-1086 FAX
cchs@goldrush.com
Elizabeth Braydis, Manager
Mon–Fri 9:00–4:00
Pub. *Las Calaveras*, quarterly
$16.00 per year membership

Carpinteria Valley Historical Society and Museum of History
956 Maple Avenue
Carpinteria, CA 93013
(805) 684-3112
David W. Griggs, Director/Curator
Tue–Sat 1:00–4:00, mornings by
   appointment
Pub. *Grapevine*, bimonthly
("Research library and archives.")

$20.00 per year membership

Historical Society of Centinela Valley
4513 West 138th Street
Hawthorne, CA 90250
(310) 676-4363; (310) 839-7021 (Historian)
James Robertson, Historian
Mon 10:00–3:00 by appointment
Pub. *Historical Society News Letter*, monthly
(Inglewood history, Machado family history
and Daniel Freeman history; large
collection of prominent early settlers in
the area. "We have books on Inglewood
and schools in Centinela Valley.")
$20.00 per year membership; research:
$19.00 per hour on pictures and
California history

**Century House Museum (Imperial
County, CA)**
(see Arizona Historical Society—Yuma
Branch, Arizona, Part 2)

Chino Valley Historical Society
(Old Schoolhouse Museum, 5493 "B"
Street—location)
PO Box 972 (mailing address)
Chino, CA 91708
(909) 627-6464
first Wed & first Sat 1:30–4:00
(local history)

**City of San Bernardino Historical and
Pioneer Society**
(796 North D Street—location)
PO Box 875 (mailing address)
San Bernardino, CA 92402
(909) 384-5211

Claremont Heritage, Inc.
(590 West Bonita Avenue—location)
PO Box 742 (mailing address)
Claremont, CA 91711
(909) 621-0848
Ginger Elliott, Executive Director
Pub. *Heritage News*

Coachella Valley Historical Society
PO Box 555
Indio, CA 92202-0505
(760) 342-6651

Colusa County Historical Society
Route 1, Box 510
Glen, CA 95943

Concord Historical Society
(1601 Sutter Street, Suites E and F, Concord,
CA 94520—location)
PO Box 404 (mailing address)
Concord, CA 94522
(925) 827-3380
http://conhistsoc.org
Paul Larson, President
Tue 1:00–4:00
Pub. *Concord Historian*, four times per year
("Genealogical information limited to long-
time prominent families of Concord,
California.")
$5.00–$250.00 per year membership

Contra Costa County Historical Society
610 Main Street
Martinez, CA 94553-1129
(925) 229-1042
cchistry@ix.netcom.com
http://www.cocohistory.com
Betty J. Maffei, Director
Tue–Thur 9:00–4:00
Pub. *CCCHS Bulletin*, quarterly
(court records, obituaries, maps, photos,
naturalizations)

$15.00 per year membership

Costa Mesa Historical Society
(see SAAAB Wing, Costa Mesa Historical
Society, below)

Covina Valley Historical Society, Inc.
125 East College Street
Covina, CA 91723

Cypress College Local History Association
Cypress, CA 90630
(714) 826-2220, ext. 294

Del Mar Historical Society
1442 Camino del Mar
Del Mar, CA 92014
(619) 259-0421

Del Norte County Historical Society
577 H Street
Crescent City, CA 95531
(707) 464-3922 (Main Museum/Research
Center); (707) 464-3089 (Lighthouse
Museum on Battery Point Island)
Sean Smith, Vice President; Mary Lu
Saunier, Treasurer
Main Museum: Mon–Sat (May–Sept)
10:00–4:00; Lighthouse: Wed–Sun
(Apr–Sept) times governed by tides
Pub. *Del Norte County Historical Society
Bulletin*, quarterly
("Historical exhibits and photo collection
and written research on local area. We
have no paid staff, but are open all
summer with volunteers.")
$15.00 per year membership; admission:
$2.00 and $2.00 per hour for researchers;
research: $5.00 per hour

**Delano Historical Society and Heritage
Park**
330 Lexington Street
Delano, CA 93215
(661) 725-6730

The Diocese of San Diego
Mission San Diego de Alcala—Archive-
Library
Mission San Diego Historical Society
(see Religious Archives and
Organizations—Roman Catholic, Part 3)

**Downey Historical Society/Downey
History Center**
(12540 Rives Avenue, Downey, CA
90242—location)
PO Box 554 (mailing address)
Downey, CA 90241
(562) 862-2777
Barbara Callarman, Director
Wed–Thur 9:00–2:00, and by appointment
Pub. *DHS Newsletter*, nine times per year
(monthly, Sept–June, combined Nov/Dec
issue)
("Local history, including law, education,
agriculture and genealogy; large photo
collection.")
$10.00 per year membership

**Duarte Historical Society, Museum, and
Friends of the Duarte Library**
(777 Encanto Parkway—location)
PO Box 263 (mailing address)
Duarte, CA 91009
(626) 357-3419
Claudia Heller, President; Jim Kirchner,
Editor; Irwin Margiloff, Curator
Wed 1:00–3:00, Sat 1:00–4:00
Pub. *The Branding Iron*, bimonthly
$10.00 per year membership

Eagle Rock Valley Historical Society
2035 Colorado Boulevard
Eagle Rock, CA 90041

El Cajon Historical Society
(Magnolia and Park—location)
PO Box 1173 (mailing address)
El Cajon, CA 92022
(619) 444-3800
Dorothy Maranda, President
Tue & Thur 11:00–3:30, Sun 1:00–3:30
Pub. *The Heritage*, quarterly
$10.00 per year membership

El Monte Historical Society
3150 North Tyler Avenue
El Monte, CA 91731
(626) 444-3813
Helen E. Huffines, Museum Curator
Pub. *The Landmark*, quarterly
$6.00 per year membership

Elk Grove Historical Society
PO Box 562
Elk Grove, CA 95759-0562
(916) 687-7713
Dorothy Hrepich
meetings second Mon at Elk Grove Hotel,
Elk Grove

Encino Historical Society
16756 Moorpark Street
Encino, CA 91436

Escondido Historical Society
(321 North Broadway, Escondido, CA
92025—location)
PO Box 263 (mailing address)
Escondido, CA 92033
(760) 743-8207; (760) 743-8267 FAX
Wendy Barker, Executive Director
Mon–Fri 8:00–4:00

Fair Oaks Historical Society
PO Box 2044
Fair Oaks, CA 95628
(916) 961-0637; (916) 961-6912

Fallbrook Historical Society
PO Box 1375
Fallbrook, CA 92028

Folsom Historical Society
Wells Fargo Building Museum
823 Sutter Street
Folsom, CA 95630
(916) 985-2707 (Museum)
Karen Mehring, Director
Wed–Sun 11:00–4:00

Fontana Historical Society
(8459 Wheeler Avenue—library location)
PO Box 426 (mailing address)
Fontana, CA 92334
(909) 823-1733

Fort Crook Historical Society
(Fort Crook Avenue and Highway
299—location)
PO Box 397 (mailing address)
Fall River Mills, CA 96028
(530) 336-5110

Galt Historical Society
PO Box 782
Galt, CA 95632

Glendora Historical Society
Glendora Historical Society Museum
(314 North Glendora Avenue—location)
PO Box 532 (mailing address)
Glendora, CA 91740

(626) 963-6485 (Society); (626) 963-0419
(Museum)
Kay Hall, Co-curator; Linda Price, Co-
curator
Sun 1:00–4:00, and by appointment
Pub. *Newsletter*, bimonthly, free

Goleta Valley Historical Society
304 North Los Carneros Road
Goleta, CA 93117
(805) 964-4407
Ron Nye, President
by appointment
Pub. *Goleta Valley History*, two times per
year; *Newsletter*, quarterly
(some Santa Barbara County records)
$25.00 per year membership

Hayward Area Historical Society
22701 Main Street
Hayward, CA 94541
(510) 581-0223; (510) 581-0217 FAX
http://www.hawardareahistory.org
Bernard Golumb, Librarian
Museum: Tue–Sat 11:00–4:00; Library: Wed
11:00–2:00, Sat noon–4:00
Pub. *Adobe Trails*, quarterly
("Hayward, Castro Valley, and San Lorenzo
[Eden Township]; our archive/library is
not dedicated to genealogical research but
we have many resources (both primary
and secondary) which genealogists find
useful [i.e., cemetery records for several
local cemeteries].")
$15.00 per year membership

**Healdsburg Museum and Historical
Society**
Healdsburg Museum
221 Matheson Street
Healdsburg, CA 95448
(707) 431-3325
Marie Djordjevich, Curator
Tue–Sun 11:00–4:00
Pub. *Russian River Recorder*, four times per
year
("newspapers indexed, genealogical research
by mail, photograph archive, family
ephemera files, history of northern
Sonoma County")
$20.00 per year membership; museum
admission: free; research: $5.00

Held Poage Research Library
Mendocino County Historical Society
603 West Perkins Street
Ukiah, CA 95482-4726
(707) 462-6969
mchs@Pacific.net
Lila J. Lee, Held Poage Director
Tue–Sat 1:00–4:00
Pub. *Newsletter of MCHS*, quarterly (Feb,
May, July, Oct)
$15.00 per year membership; research:
donation plus 15¢ per photocopy

**Heritage Association of El Dorado County,
Inc.**
PO Box 62
Placerville, CA 95667
(530) 622-1121 (President); (530) 622-0712
mfergie@d-web.com
Shirley Pont, President; Marilyn Ferguson
("We specialize in El Dorado County [the
site of James Marshal Gold Discovery
Park] history and the Gold Rush history,
which includes title searches of land
deeds, mining claims, probates, birth,
marriage and death records, etc.
Secondary sources—newspapers, letters,
journals, etc.")

Humboldt County Historical Society
(703 Eighth Street, Eureka, CA
95501—location)
PO Box 8000 (mailing address)
Eureka, CA 95502-8000
(707) 445-4342; (707) 445-4146 FAX
hchs@reninet.com
Matina Kilkenny, Research and Collections
Manager
Tue–Wed & Fri noon–4:00, Thur 4:00–8:00
Pub. *The Humboldt Historian*, quarterly
(research library—local history; also
historical book publisher)
$25.00 per year membership

Huntington Beach Historical Society
19820 Beach Boulevard
Huntington Beach, CA 92648
(714) 962-5777

Idyllwild Area Historical Society
(54470 North Circle Drive, corner
Oakwood—location)
PO Box 3320 (mailing address)
Idyllwild, CA 92549
(951) 659-2717
info@idyllwildareahistoricalsociety.org
http://www.idyllwildareahistoricalsociety.
org
Museum: Sat 11:00-4:00, Thur-Fri 11:00-
4:00 (Apr–Nov), Sun 11:00-4:00 (Apr-
Dec)

Irvine Historical Society and Museum
5 Rancho San Joaquin
Irvine, CA 92715
(949) 786-4112

Julian Historical Society
PO Box 513
Julian, CA 92036
(760) 765-0436
John Mattias, Treasurer
hours: various
Pub. *Julian Historical Society Reporter*,
bimonthly
$10.00 per year membership

Kern County Historical Society
PO Box 141
Bakersfield, CA 93302
Historical Research Committee
Pub. *Historic Kern*, quarterly, $10.00 per
year subscription; *Kern Grapevine
Newsletter*, ten times per year (principally
for meeting announcements)
("We do not have a library. Historical
material is placed at Beale Library.")
$10.00 per year membership; research:
search fees depend on request

Kern River Valley Historical Society
PO Box 651
Kernville, CA 93238
(760) 379-5895

La Habra Old Settlers Historical Society
600 Linden Lane
La Habra, CA 90631
(562) 697-1271
Esther Cramer, Historian
Pub. *Old Settler's Newsletter*, two times per
year
("Caboose Museum at La Habra Children's
Museum. Oldest Historical Society in
Orange County, California.")
$5.00 per year membership

La Jolla Historical Society
(7846 Eads Avenue—location)
PO Box 2085 (mailing address)
La Jolla, CA 92038

(858) 459-5335 voice & FAX
http://www.iaco.com/features/lajolla/
lifeinlj/history/ljhs.html
Sandra Zarcades, Archivist
Tue & Thur noon–4:00
Pub. *La Jolla Historical Society Quarterly
Newsletter*
(photographs and documents relating to La
Jolla's history, dating from the 1860s)
$20.00 per year membership

La Mesa Historical Society
(8369 University Avenue, La Mesa, CA
92041—location)
PO Box 882 (mailing address)
La Mesa, CA 92044-0882
(619) 460-0882
Gordon Jones, President
Sat noon–3:00, and by appointment
Pub. *Lookout Avenue*, quarterly
$10.00 per year membership

La Puente Valley Historical Society
(16021 East Gale Avenue, City of Industry,
CA 91748—location)
PO Box 522 (mailing address)
La Puente, CA 91747
(626) 336-7644; (626) 336-2382
Harold Rogers, President
Museums: first and third Wed & Sun
Pub. *The Bridge*, bimonthly
$6.00 per year membership

Lafayette Historical Society
PO Box 133
Lafayette, CA 94549
(925) 283-6822
Bill Wakeman
$10.00 per year membership

Lake County Historical Society
PO Box 1011
Lakeport, CA 95453
(707) 279-4466
Pub. *POMO Bulletin*, quarterly
$7.50 per year membership

Lake Tahoe Historical Society
(3058 Lake Tahoe Boulevard—location)
PO Box 404 (mailing address)
South Lake Tahoe, CA 96156
(530) 541-5458
Bob Corkill, President
winter: Sat–Sun noon–4:00; summer: daily
11:00–4:00
Pub. *Lake Tahoe Historical Society
Quarterly*
(Lake Tahoe archives, artifacts, photos,
books, oral histories)
$25.00 per year membership

Lakeside Historical Society
9906 Maine Avenue
Lakeside, CA 92040
(619) 561-1886

Las Virgenes Historical Society
(30473-50 Mulholland Highway—location)
PO Box 124 (mailing address)
Agoura, CA 91301
(818) 889-0836

Lassen County Historical Society
(Lassen Historical Museum, 105 North
Weatherlow Street—location)
PO Box 321 (mailing address)
Susanville, CA 96130
(530) 257-3292
Gail Bengard, President
1 May–31 Oct: Mon–Fri 10:00–4:00, Sat
11:00–3:00
$10.00 per year membership

Leisure World Historical Society of Laguna Hills
(23522 Paseo de Valencia—location)
PO Box 2220 (mailing address)
Laguna Hills, CA 92654
(949) 951-2330
Claire Still, President
Pub. *LWHSLH Newsletter*

The Lemon Grove Historical Society
(3185 Oliver Street—location)
PO Box 624 (mailing address)
Lemon Grove, CA 91946
(619) 460-4353; (619) 462-6494; (619) 462-8266 FAX
lghistorical@yahoo.com
http://lemongrovehistoricalsociety.com
Pub. *Newsletter* (online)
$10.00 per year membership

Little Landers Historical Society
(Bolton Hall Museum, 10110 Commerce Avenue, Tujunga, CA 91042—location)
PO Box 203 (mailing address)
Tujunga, CA 91043-0203
(818) 352-3420
LandMHitt@CS.com
W. Lloyd Hitt, President
Tue & Sun 1:00–4:00, second Sat 1:00–4:00
Pub. *Little Landers Historical Society Newsletter*, monthly
$15.00 per year membership

Livermore Heritage Guild
(2155 Third Street—location)
PO Box 961 (mailing address)
Livermore, CA 94551-0961
(925) 449-9927
http://www.lhg.org
Barbara S. Bunshah, Curator/Secretary
Wed–Sun 11:30–4:00
Pub. *Newsletter*, monthly
("Our collections include books, maps, microfilmed newspapers, etc.")
$7.00 per year membership

Lomita Historical Society
City Hall
24300 Narbonne Avenue
Lomita, CA 90717

Lompoc Valley Historical Society, Inc.
(207 North L Street—location)
PO Box 88 (mailing address)
Lompoc, CA 93438
(805) 735-4626; (805) 736-5304
myra@best1.net
http://lompoconline.com
Myra Manfrina, Historian
Mon & Thur 9:00–11:00 A.M. & fourth Sun
Pub. *Lompoc Legacy*, quarterly, $1.00 per issue
(genealogical files, local history and genealogy of old families)
$15.00 per year membership; research: $15.00 basic; printing family genealogy: $10.00–$20.00, up to $50.00

Historical Society of Long Beach
(The Breakers, Arcade Level, 210 East Ocean Boulevard—location)
PO Box 1869 (mailing address)
Long Beach, CA 90801
(562) 495-1210; (562) 495-1281 FAX
Dominique Brummond, Collections Manager
Tue–Fri 1:00–5:00, Thur 1:00–7:00
Pub. *Long Beach Historian*, quarterly
$30.00 per year membership; limited research: $3.50

Los Altos Hills Historical Society
27200 Elena Road

Los Altos Hills, CA 94022
(650) 948-8470
Daniel Alexander, President
Pub. *LAHHS Newsletter*

Los Altos Historical Commission
1 North San Antonio Road
Los Altos Hills, CA 94022
(650) 948-1491

Los Angeles City Historical Society
PO Box 41046
Los Angeles, CA 90041
(213) 891-4600
http://www.lacityhistory.org
Daniel T. Muñoz, President
Pub. *Los Angeles City Historical Society Newsletter* (not genealogical in content), quarterly
$25.00 per year membership

Madera County Historical Society
(210 West Yosemite Avenue, Madera, CA 93637—location)
PO Box 478 (mailing address)
Madera, CA 93639
(559) 673-0291
Dorothy Foust, Curator
Tue 9:00–noon
Pub. *Newsletter & Historian*, quarterly
("History of Madera County and early families
$10.00 per year membership

McHenry Museum and Historical Society
1402 I Street
Modesto, CA 95354-1402
(209) 577-5366
Wayne A. Mathes, Cultural Services Manager
Tue–Sun noon–4:00
Pub. *Stanislaus Stepping Stones*, quarterly
$10.00 per year membership

Mendocino County Historical Society
(see Held Poage Research Library, above)

Menlo Park Historical Association
Menlo Park Library
800 Alma Street
Menlo Park, CA 94025

Merced County Historical Society
Merced County Courthouse Museum
Old County Courthouse
21st and N Streets
Merced, CA 95340
(209) 385-7426
Andrea Metz, Director
Wed–Sun 1:00–4:00
Pub. *For the Record*, quarterly
(Jail registers 1900–40, assessor records 1880s–1950, some funeral records, school registers 1890s–1950s; "our research room is just in progress.")
research: $10.00 donation

Mill Valley Historical Society
Mill Valley Public Library
Lucretia Little History Room
375 Throckmorton Avenue
Mill Valley, CA 94941
(415) 389-4292 (Library); (415) 388-8929 FAX (Library)
http://millvalleylibrary.org (Library)
Joyce Crews, History Room Librarian; Anne Montgomery, City Librarian
Pub. *Mill Valley Historical Review* (Mill Valley and Marin County), annually, $8.00 per issue
$15.00 per year membership

Millbrae Historical Society
(621-A Magnolia, Constitution Square—location)
PO Box 511 (mailing address)
Millbrae, CA 94030
(650) 697-5786; (415) 692-3720
Alma Massolo, Curator
Sat noon–4:00

Mission San Diego Historical Society
(see The Diocese of San Diego, Religious Archives and Organizations—Roman Catholic, Part 3)

Modoc County Historical Society and Museum
600 South Main Street
Alturas, CA 96101
(530) 233-2944
Ann Odgers, Curator
Pub. *Modoc County Historical Society Journal*, annually
$6.50 per year membership

Mohave Historical Society
PO Box 21
Victorville, CA 92392
http://vvo.com/comm/mhs.htm

Mokelumne Hill Historical Society
8367 Center Street
Mokelumne Hill, CA 95245
(209) 286-1770

Montecito History Committee
1469 East Valley Road
Montecito, CA 93108
(805) 969-1597

Monterey County Historical Society
(333 Boronda Road, Salinas, CA 93906—location)
PO Box 3576 (mailing address)
Salinas, CA 93912
(831) 757-8085
Mona Gudgel, Administrator
Pub. *MCHS Newsletter*

Monterey History and Art Association
(see Mayo Hayes O'Donnell Library, City, County and Regional Archives and Libraries, above)

The Historical Society of Monterey Park, Inc.
(781 South Orange Avenue—museum location)
PO Box 272 (mailing address)
Monterey Park, CA 91754
(626) 281-3015
Bea Rexius, President
Museum: Sat–Sun 2:00–4:00
Pub. *Newsletter*, nine times per year (monthly, except July–Aug & Dec)
$10.00 per year membership

Moraga Historical Society and Archives
(1500 Saint Mary's Road—location)
PO Box 103 (mailing address)
Moraga, CA 94556
(925) 377-8734
mhistory@silcon.com
http://www.moragahistory.org
Elsie Mastick, Archivist
Mon, Wed & Fri 1:00–3:00, and by appointment
Pub. *El Rancho Moraga Newsletter*, quarterly
("Genealogy—of Moraga Family only!")
$15.00 per year membership

Morgan Hill Historical Society, Inc.

PO Box 1258
Morgan Hill, CA 95037
(408) 779-5755
Susan Locarnini, President
Pub. *Historically Speaking*

Mount Lassen Historical Society
PO Box 291
Shingletown, CA 96088
(530) 474-3061

Mountain Empire Historical Society
PO Box 394
Campo, CA 92006
(619) 478-5707

Mountain View Historical Association
(Mountain View Library, 585 Franklin
Street, Mountain View, CA
94041—location)
PO Box 252 (mailing address)
Mountain View, CA 94042
(650) 968-6595; (950) 903-6890
Barbara Kinchen, City Historian; June
Casey, Membership Chairman
Tue, Thur & Sat 1:00–5:00, Wed 5:00–9:00;
meetings at Adobe Building, Moffett
Boulevard: first Sun (Feb, May, Aug,
Nov)
Pub. *Historical Assn. Newsletter*, quarterly
$7.00 per year membership

Napa County Historical Society
Goodman Library Building, 1219 First Street
Napa, CA 94559
(707) 224-1739; (707) 224-5933 FAX
Diane S. Ballard, Executive Director
Tue & Thur noon–4:00; special tours by
appointment
Pub. *Tidings*, monthly
$12.00 per year membership; museum and
library admission: free

Nevada County Historical Society
(214 Main Street—location)
PO Box 1300 (mailing address)
Nevada City, CA 95959
(530) 265-5468; (530) 265-3754 (President)
http://www.nccn.net/orgsclbs/history/
histsoc/welcome.htm
Jim Rose, President
Mon–Sun 11:00–4:00
Pub. *Nevada County Historical Society
Bulletin*, quarterly; *Newsletter*
(pre-gold rush and gold rush mining history;
operates three museums and two research
libraries)
$12.00 per year membership

Newport Beach Historical Society
Sherman Library and Gardens
(2647 East Coast Highway—location)
614 Dahlia Avenue (mailing address)
Corona Del Mar, CA 92625
(949) 673-1880

Norco Historical Society
PO Box 159
Norco, CA 91760
(909) 734-9739

North Lake Tahoe Historical Society
(130 West Lake Boulevard—location)
PO Box 6141 (mailing address)
Tahoe City, CA 96145
(530) 583-1762; (530) 583-8992 FAX
nlths@aol.com
http://www.tahoecountry.com/nlths
Sara Larson, Director of Museums
11 May–1 Oct: 11:00–5:00
Pub. *NLTHS Newsletter*, quarterly, not
available by subscription

$30.00 per year membership

**Ojai Valley Museum and Historical
Society**
(130 West Ojai Avenue—location)
PO Box 204 (mailing address)
Ojai, CA 93024
(805) 640-1390
Sherry Smith, Director
Wed–Sun 1:00–4:00, and mornings by
appointment
Pub. *OVMHS Newsletter*, quarterly
$20.00 per year membership

Orange County Historical Commission
Federation of Orange County Historical
Organizations
c/o Environmental Management Agency
(2002 North Main—location)
PO Box 4048 (mailing address)
Santa Ana, CA 92702
(714) 834-4741 (Commission); (714) 834-
5560 (Federation)
(primarily historical, not genealogical)

Orange County Historical Society
(Dr. Howe-Waffle Victorian House, 120
Civic Center Drive West, Santa Ana, CA
92701—office location)
PO Box 10984 (mailing address)
Santa Ana, CA 92711
(714) 543-8282; (714) 525-4879
HistoryOC@aol.com
http://www.orangecountyhistory.org
Betsy Vigus, Newsletter Editor; Richard
Vining, President
by appointment only
Pub. *County Courier*, ten times per year
(monthly, Sept–June)
(local history and education, publishing
program)
$15.00 per year membership; research: no
genealogy research done but will answer
inquiries if information is available

Orange County Pioneer Council
2320 North Towner Street
Santa Ana, CA 92706

Orland Historical and Cultural Society
PO Box 183
Orland, CA 95963
(530) 865-1444

Pacific Beach Historical Society
PO Box 9200
San Diego, CA 92169
(619) 272-6655

Pacific Grove Heritage Society
(Laurel Avenue at 17th Street—location)
PO Box 1007 (mailing address)
Pacific Grove, CA 93950
(831) 372-2898
Sat 1:00–4:00
Pub. *Board and Batten*, bimonthly
$10.00 per year membership

Pacific Palisades Historical Society
PO Box 1299
Pacific Palisades, CA 90272
Fred Blum, Treasurer
Pub. *PPHS Newsletter*

Palm Springs Historical Society
(Village Green Heritage Center, 221 South
Palm Canyon Drive, Palm Springs, CA
92262—location)
PO Box 1498 (mailing address)
Palm Springs, CA 92263
(760) 323-8297; (760) 320-2561 FAX
palmspgshistory@aol.com

http://www.palmsprings.com/history
Sally Hall McManus, Director/Curator
mid-Oct–May: Wed & Sun noon–3:00,
Thur–Sat 10:00–4:00
Pub. *Whispering Palms*, three times per year
$20.00 per year membership; research:
$25.00 per hour; admission: free to
members, $2.00 general admission (to see
both museums)

Palo Alto Historical Association
(Palo Alto Main Library—location)
PO Box 193 (mailing address)
Palo Alto, CA 94302
(650) 329-2664 (Library)
http://www.commerce.digital.com/palo-
alto/historical-assoc/home.html
Steven Staiger, Historian
Tue 6:00–9:00, Thur 2:00–5:00
Pub. *Tall Tree*, ten times per year (monthly,
Sept–June)
$15.00 per year membership

Paradise Historical Society
PO Box 1696
Paradise, CA 95967
(530) 873-0769
Lois McDonald, Editor
Pub. *Tales of Paradise Ridge*, semiannually
$9.00 per year membership

**Pasadena Historical Society Research
Library**
470 West Walnut Street
Pasadena, CA 91103
(626) 577-1660
Tim Gregory, Archivist
Thur–Sun 1:00–4:00
Pub. *Newsletter*, quarterly
no library use fee

Patterson Township Historical Society
(#1 Plaza—location)
PO Box 15 (mailing address)
Patterson, CA 95363
(209) 892-8664
Bob Kimball, Curator
Tue–Fri 10:00–1:00
Pub. *The Gateway*, annually
$7.00 per year membership

**Perris Valley Historical Museum and
Association**
PO Box 343
Perris, CA 92572
(909) 657-0274
hulstrom@pe.net
http://www.angelfire.com/ca2/PVHMA
Sat 12:00-3:00

Pioneer Historical Society of Riverside
PO Box 246
Riverside, CA 92502
(909) 684-4074 (President)
Alan Curl, President
Pub. *Journal of the Riverside Historical
Society*, annually, $5.00 per issue
$10.00 per year membership

Plumas County Historical Society
(500 Jackson Street—location)
PO Box 695 (mailing address)
Quincy, CA 95971
(530) 283-4379
Edward C. Brown, Director
Pub. *Plumas Memories*, annually
$5.00 per year membership

Historical Society of Pomona Valley
1569 North Park Avenue
Pomona, CA 91768
(909) 623-2198

ogallivan@earthlin.net
http://www.osb.net/Pomona
Beth Page, President
Pub. *News Notes*, four to five times per year
(society maintains three historical sites and a
pioneer cemetery, refers genealogical
inquiries to Special Collections
Department, Pomona Public Library)
$7.50 per year membership

Poway Historical and Memorial Society
(Old Poway Park, 14114 Midland Road,
Poway, CA 92064—location)
PO Box 19 (mailing address)
Poway, CA 92074
(858) 679-8587 (Sat–Sun only); (858) 485-
0106
Cecilia Burr, Secretary
Sat 9:00–2:00, Sun 11:00–2:00
Pub. *Poway Echoes*, varies
$15.00 per year membership; research: no
fee

**Ramona Pioneer Historical Society and
Guy B. Woodward Museum**
(645 Main Street—location)
PO Box 625 (mailing address)
Ramona, CA 92065
(760) 789-1062
Geneva Woodward, President

**The City of Rancho Cucamonga Historical
Program**
(10500 Civic Center Drive—location)
PO Box 807 (mailing address)
Rancho Cucamonga, CA 91729
(909) 477-2750; (909) 477-2847 FAX
Larry Henderson, Principal Planner

Rancho Santa Fe Historical Society
PO Box 2424
Rancho Santa Fe, CA 92067-2414
(760) 756-3464

Redlands Area Historical Society, Inc.
Genealogical Branch
PO Box 1024
Redlands, CA 92373
(909) 307-6060
genealogy@rahs.org
http://www.rahs.org/genealogy.htm
Liz Beguelin, President and Genealogist
Pub. *R.A.H.S. Newsletter*, ten times per year
(monthly, Sept–June)
$10.00 per year membership

Redondo Beach Historical Society
PO Box 978
Redondo Beach, CA 90277

Reedley Historical Society
(1752 10th Street—location)
PO Box 877 (mailing address)
Reedley, CA 93654
(559) 638-1913

Rialto Historical Society
(205 North Riverside Avenue—location)
PO Box 413 (mailing address)
Rialto, CA 92377
(909) 875-1750
Elizabeth Hughbanks, President
Pub. *RHS Newsletter*

Rio Linda/Elverta Historical Society
PO Box 478
Rio Linda, CA 95673-0478
(916) 332-0355
Martha Glidden
meetings at Calvary Lutheran Church, Fifth
and L Streets, Rio Linda: third Sun
(except Aug & Nov)

Pub. *The Eggspress*, semiannually
(building an extensive collection of historical
material, with a great deal of genealogical
material included in this collection)
$15.00 per year membership

Riverside County Historical Commission
4600 Crestmore Drive
Riverside, CA 92519
(909) 955-4558
http://www.co.riverside.ca.us
Cindy Thomack, Historic Preservation
Officer
(Publishes *Guide to the Historic Landmarks
of Riverside County, California*, 1993,
$9.00 each)

Roseville Historical Society
c/o Carnegie Museum
557 Lincoln Street
Roseville, CA 95678
(916) 773-3003
meetings third Sat 10:00

**SAAAB Wing, Costa Mesa Historical
Society**
(1870 Anaheim Avenue—location)
PO Box 1764 (mailing address)
Costa Mesa, CA 92628
(949) 631-5918
Alvin "Bud" Anderson; Art Lambert; Gladys
Refakes
Thur 10:00–3:00, and by appointment
Pub. *Fairview Register*, ten times per year
(monthly, except July–Aug); *Santa Ana
Army Air Base "CADET,"* three to four
times per year
("We have a few old directories and we keep
finding things for people who phone and
write.")
$10.00 per year membership; research:
donation accepted

Sacramento County Historical Society
PO Box 160065
Sacramento, CA 95816-0065
(916) 443-6265
Melinda A. Peak, President
Pub. *Golden Notes*, quarterly; *Golden
Nuggets* (newsletter)
$25.00 per year membership

**Genealogical and Historical Council of
Sacramento Valley**
(see Genealogical Societies—Local and
Regional, below)

Saddleback Area Historical Society
(25151 Seranno Road—location)
PO Box 156 (mailing address)
El Toro, CA 92630
(949) 586-8488

San Antonio Valley Historical Association
(216 Grove Place, King City, CA
93930—location)
PO Box 184 (mailing address)
Lockwood, CA 93932
(831) 385-3587

**San Antonio Valley Historical
Society/Museum**
PO Box 21
Lodi, CA 95241

**San Benito County Historical Society
(Museum)**
498 Fifth Street
Hollister, CA 95023
(831) 635-0335
Sharlene Van Rooy, Museum Director
Sat–Sun 1:00–3:00; meetings at Dunne Park

clubhouse: last Wed
(historical museum with access to county
records, audio history, coroner's reports,
vital records, court listings, maps and
other documents)
$20.00 per year membership; research for
cost of photocopies

San Clemente Historical Society
PO Box 283
San Clemente, CA 92672
(949) 492-4716
Jim Kempton, President

San Diego Historical Society
Research Archives
(1649 El Prado, Balboa Park—location)
PO Box 81825 (mailing address)
San Diego, CA 92138-1825
(619) 232-6203
http://edweb.sdsu.edu/sdhs/histsoc.html
John Panter, Archivist
Thur–Sat 10:00–4:00
Pub. *Journal of San Diego History*,
quarterly; *SDHS Times*, quarterly
$50.00 per year membership

San Francisco Historical Society
PO Box 569
San Francisco, CA 94101
(415) 567-2725

San Gabriel Historical Association
546 West Broadway
San Gabriel, CA 91776
(626) 308-3223
Sat 1:00–4:00, and by appointment
Pub. *San Gabriel Historical News*, five times
per year (Jan, Mar, May, Sept, Nov)
(local history, Gabrielino Indians, California
missions, etc.)
$10.00–$99.00 per year membership

**San Joaquin Pioneer and Historical
Society**
The Haggin Museum
Alameda May Petzinger Library of
Californiana
1201 North Pershing Avenue
Stockton, CA 95203-1699
(209) 940-6300
info@hagginmuseum.org
http://www.hagginmuseum.org
Tod Ruhstaller, Director and Curator of
History; Susan Benedetti,
Librarian/Archivist
Tue–Sun 1:30–5:00; Archivist: by
appointment only
Pub. *The Haggin Museum Bulletin*, quarterly
admission: $5.00 for adults, free on first Tue

San Juan Bautista Historical Society
(308 Third Street—location)
PO Box 1 (mailing address)
San Juan Bautista, CA 95045
(831) 623-4542

San Juan Capistrano Historical Society
31831 Los Rios Street
San Juan Capistrano, CA 92675
(949) 493-8444

**San Luis Obispo County Historical Society
Museum**
(696 Monterey Street, San Luis Obispo, CA
93401—location)
PO Box 1391 (mailing address)
San Luis Obispo, CA 93406
(805) 543-0638
slochs@slonet.org
Ronald E. Clarke, Society Manager
Wed–Sat 10:00–4:00

$20.00 per year membership

San Marino Historical Society
(2701 Huntington Drive—location)
PO Box 80222 (mailing address)
San Marino, CA 91108
(626) 568-0119
Peggy Winkler, Librarian; Lillian Colle-
  Campbell, President
by appointment
Pub. *Grape Vine*, semiannually
$15.00 per year membership; no research
  fees unless extensive

San Mateo County Historical Association
San Mateo County History Museum
College of San Mateo Campus
1700 West Hillsdale Boulevard
San Mateo, CA 94402
(650) 574-6441; (650) 574-6468 FAX
carol@samhist.com
http://www.sanmateocountyhistory.com
Marion C. Holmes, Archivist
Mon–Thur 9:30–4:30, Sun 12:30–4:30
Pub. *La Peninsula*, semiannually
(San Mateo County history)
$35.00 per year membership

San Pablo Historical and Museum Society
Alvarado Adobe
1 Alvarado Square
San Pablo, CA 94806
(510) 236-7373; (510) 215-3080; (510) 222-
  3519
Ann Roberts, Curator
(local history reference service)

San Ramon Valley Historical Society
PO Box 521
Danville, CA 94526
(925) 837-0369
Mary Anne Iarussi, President
Pub. *Record*, five times per year, *Roster*,
  annually
$10.00 per year membership

Santa Ana Mountain Historical Society
(28192 Silverado Canyon Road—location)
PO Box 301 (mailing address)
Silverado, CA 92676
(714) 649-2216

Santa Barbara Historical Society
(136 East De La Guerra Street—location)
PO Box 578 (mailing address)
Santa Barbara, CA 93102
(805) 966-1601; (805) 966-1603 FAX
Michael Redmon, Librarian
Tue–Sat 10:00–5:00, Sun noon–5:00;
  Gledhill Library: Tue–Fri 10:00–4:00,
  first Sat 10:00–1:00
Pub. *Noticias*, quarterly; *Santa Barbara
  Historical Museum Newsletter*, monthly
$40.00 per year membership

**Santa Clara County Historical and
Genealogical Society**
Santa Clara County Central Library
2635 Homestead Road (location until 2004,
  when new library building will be
  completed)
Santa Clara, CA 95051-5387
(408) 984-3236 (Library); (408) 248-8205
  (Library)
SCCHGS@hotmail.com
http://www.rootsweb.com/~cascchgs
Micki Mistretta, President
Library: Mon–Thur 9:00–9:00, Fri–Sat
  9:00–6:00, Sun 1:00–5:00; Society: third
  Thur (except Aug and Dec) 7:00
Pub. *Santa Clara County Connections*,
  semiannually, $5.00 per year subscription;

Newsletter, monthly (except Aug & Dec)
  (library has international genealogy
  collection)
$15.00 per year membership; research: fees
  vary

**Santa Clara County Historical Heritage
Commission**
70 West Hedding Street
San Jose, CA 95110
(408) 299-4321
Janis Kuechenmeister, Deputy Clerk of the
  Board

Santa Clarita Valley Historical Society
(24107 San Fernando Road, Newhall, CA
  91321—location)
PO Box 221925 (mailing address)
Newhall, CA 91322-1925
(661) 254-1275
http://www.scvnet.com/~highlites/scvhs/
  index.html

Santa Fe Springs Historical Committee
(Santa Fe Springs Public Library, 11710
  Telegraph Road—location)
10146 Gridley Road (mailing address)
Santa Fe Springs, CA 90670
(562) 864-4538

Santa Maria Valley Historical Society
616 South Broadway
Santa Maria, CA 93454
(805) 922-3130

**Santa Monica Historical Society and
Museum**
(1539 Euclid Street—location)
PO Box 3059, Will Rogers Station (mailing
  address)
Santa Monica, CA 90408
(310) 394-2605
Louise Gabriel, President
second & fourth Sun 1:00–4:30, library and
  group tours by appointment
Pub. *Santa Monica Historical Society
  Newsletter*, bimonthly
("Resource library [California and Santa
  Monica-Westside history], photo archives
  [7,000 photos, 3,000 slides]; our library
  also has a collection of early phone
  directories and early street maps.")
$20.00 per year membership

Santa Ynez Valley Historical Society
(3596 Sagunto—location)
PO Box 181 (mailing address)
Santa Ynez, CA 93460
(805) 688-7889
Richard S. Sims, Executive Director
Pub. *The Gates of Memory*

Saratoga Historical Foundation
(20450 Saratoga Los Gratos Road—location)
PO Box 172 (mailing address)
Saratoga, CA 95071
(408) 867-4311
Louise Cooper, President
Wed–Sun 1:00–4:00
$30.00 per year membership

Sausalito Historical Society
(420 Litho Street, Sausalito, CA
  94965—location)
PO Box 352 (mailing address)
Sausalito, CA 94966

Searles Valley Historical Society
Old Guest House Museum
(13193 Main Street, corner of Main and
  Searles Streets—location)
PO Box 630 (mailing address)

Trona, CA 93592
(760) 372-5222 (Museum)
Margaret Brush, Curator
Mon & Wed–Sat 9:00–noon, Tue
  10:00–1:00
Pub. *Searles Valley Historical Society
  Newsletter*, quarterly
("We have an excellent research library.")
$15.00 per year membership

Shafter Historical Society
(150 Central Valley Highway—location)
PO Box 1088 (mailing address)
Shafter, CA 93263
(661) 746-1557
Helen Gaede, President
first Sat 10:00–2:00, and by appointment
("Museum is a restored Santa Fe Depot built
  in 1917; railroad artifacts, farm
  equipment")
$10.00 per year membership

Shasta Historical Society
Redding Museum of Art and History
56 Quartz Hill Road, Caldwell Park
Redding, CA 96099
(530) 225-4155
http://www.shastalink.k12.ca.us/rmah/
  SHS.html
Hazel McKim, Librarian
when Museum is open, and by appointment
Pub. *Covered Wagon* (Shasta County
  pioneers), annually, price varies by
  edition
("Shasta County pioneers; material limited to
  Shasta County and California related")

Sierra County Historical Society
(Kentucky Mine Museum, Highway
  49—location)
PO Box 260 (mailing address)
Sierra City, CA 96125
(530) 862-1310 voice & FAX
Karen Donaldson, Museum Curator
Wed–Sun 10:00–5:00, weekends in Oct,
  closed till Memorial Day
Pub. *The Sierran*, semiannually
$10.00 per year membership

**Sierra Madre Historical Preservation
Society**
(440 West Sierra Madre Boulevard, Sierra
  Madre, CA 91024-2399—library location)
PO Box 202 (mailing address)
Sierra Madre, CA 91025-0202
(626) 355-8129; (626) 355-7187 (Archives)
dhenders@sierramadre.lib.ca.us (Archives)
Dave Lenton, President
Sierra Madre Historical Archives at the
  Library: Tue & Thur 11:00–5:00, Fri
  10:00–1:00
Pub. *Sierra Madre Historical Preservation
  Society Newsletter*, two to four times per
  year
("In 1999 SMHPS and The Sierra Madre
  Public Library assumed joint ownership
  of the Sierra Madre Historical Archives.
  The collection is housed at the library
  under the stewardship of archivist Debbie
  Henderson.")
$10.00 per year membership

Simi Valley Historical Society
Strathearn Historical Park
(137 Strathearn Place—location)
PO Box 351 (mailing address)
Simi Valley, CA 93065
(805) 526-6453
Patricia Havens, Museum Director
Office: Tue–Fri 9:00–1:00
Pub. *Mail Cart*

Solano County Historical Society
(Fairfield, CA—location)
PO Box 922 (mailing address)
Vallejo, CA 94590
(707) 426-2081
Mary Higham, Recording Secretary
Pub. *Solano Historian*, biannually
$10.00 per year membership

Sonoma County Historical Society
PO Box 1373
Santa Rosa, CA 95402
(707) 539-1786 (Archivist)
H. A. Lapham, Archivist
Pub. *The Journal of the Sonoma County Historical Society*, quarterly
$10.00 per year membership

Sonoma Valley Historical Society
Depot Park Museum
(270 First Street West—location)
PO Box 861 (mailing address)
Sonoma, CA 95476
(707) 938-1762 voice & FAX
depot@vom.com
http://www.vom.com/depot
Diane Smith, Manager
Pub. *Sonoma Valley Notes*, bimonthly
("Serves Sonoma Valley, San Francisco Bay north to Kenwood on Highway 12. For Sonoma County, contact Sonoma County Public Library.")
$25.00 per year membership; research: varies, ask in advance

South Humboldt Historical and Genealogical Society
PO Box 656
Garberville, CA 95440
Pub. *Southern Humboldt Roots and Trails*, quarterly
$5.00 per year membership

Historical Society of Southern California
200 East Avenue 43
Los Angeles, CA 90031
(213) 222-0546
HSSC@socalhistory.org
http://www.socalhistory.org
Tom Andrews, Executive Director
Pub. *Southern California Quarterly*; *Southern Californian*, quarterly, $35.00 per year subscription for both periodicals

Spanishtown Historical Society
(505 Johnson Street—location)
PO Box 62 (mailing address)
Half Moon Bay, CA 94019
(650) 726-7084
marinaf@gene.com;
  spanishtownhs@int8.com
http://www.spanishtownhs.org
Marina Frasier, President

Sunnyvale Historical Society and Museum Association
(235 East California—location)
PO Box 61301 (mailing address)
Sunnyvale, CA 94088
(408) 749-0220
Jan Camp, President
Tue & Thur 12:30–3:30, Sun 1:00–4:00, and by appointment
Pub. *SHSMA Newsletter*, monthly
(local history resources, museum)
$15.00 per year membership

Sutter County Historical Society
PO Box 1004
Yuba City, CA 95992
(530) 673-2721
Linda Leone, Treasurer/Co-editor

Pub. *SCHS News Bulletin*, quarterly (Jan, Apr, July, Oct)
$15.00 per year membership

Tehama County Genealogical and Historical Society
(see Genealogical Societies—Local and Regional, below)

Temple City Historical Society
(9659½ Las Tunas Drive—location)
PO Box 1379 (mailing address)
Temple City, CA 91780
(626) 279-1784 (Museum)

Topanga Historical Society
PO Box 1214
Topanga, CA 90290
(310) 455-1111
http://www.topangaonline.com/hsociety.html

Torrance Historical Society
1345 Post Avenue
Torrance, CA 90501

Trinity County Historical Society
(508 Main Street—location)
PO Box 333 (mailing address)
Weaverville, CA 96093-0333
(530) 623-5211
http://www.tcoek12.org/~museum
Hal Goodyear, Museum Director
1 Jan–31 Mar: Tue & Sat 1:00–4:00, 1 Apr–30 Apr & 1 Nov–31 Dec: daily 1:00–4:00, 1 May–31 Oct: daily 10:00–5:00
Pub. *Trinity*, annually (Dec), $4.95 per issue
$10.00 per year membership

Truckee-Donner Historical Society, Inc.
PO Box 893
Truckee, CA 95734
(530) 587-2876
http://www.tahoenet.com/tdhs/tpnewslt.html#intro

Tulare County Historical Society
(Tulare County Museum, Mooney Grove, 27000 Mooney Boulevard, Visalia—museum location)
PO Box 295 (mailing address)
Visalia, CA 93279
(559) 732-5829
Terry L. Ommen, President
Pub. *Los Tulares*, quarterly
(extensive historical information on families, events and places in Tulare County)
$15.00 per year membership

Tuolumne County Historical Society
(158 West Bradford Avenue—county museum location)
PO Box 695 (mailing address)
Sonora, CA 95370-0695
(209) 532-1317
http://www.tchistory.org
Jack Gallagher, Book Sales Agent
Mon–Fri & Sun 10:00–4:00, Sat 10:00–3:30
Pub. *Chispa*, quarterly, $3.00 per issue subscription; *Historian*, monthly (except summer)
$25.00 per year membership

Tustin Area Historical Society
(395 El Camino Real—location)
PO Box 185 (mailing address)
Tustin, CA 92681
(714) 731-5701

Twentynine Palms Historical Society
(6760 National Park Drive—location)

PO Box 1926 (mailing address)
Twentynine Palms, CA 92277
(760) 367-2366
29palmshistoricalsociety@www.msnusers.com
http://www.msnusers.com/29palmshistoricalsociety
Margot Spangenberg, Board Member
Museum and Gift Shop: Wed–Sun 1:00–4:00
Pub. *News & Notes*, quarterly (Mar, June, Sept, Dec)
(Morongo Basin area historical society)
$12.50 per year membership

Historical Society of the Upper Mojave Desert
Maturango Museum

100 East Las Flores
Ridgecrest, CA 93555
(760) 375-5249 (Membership)
http://www.ridgecrest.ca/us/~matmus/Hist.html
Fred Weals, Membership
meetings: third Tue 7:30
Pub. *Newsletter*; *Bulletin*
$10.00 per year membership (Fred Weals, Treasurer, 554 East Dana, Ridgecrest, CA 93555)

Ventura County Historical Society
Ventura County Museum of History and Art
100 East Main Street
Ventura, CA 93001-2698
(805) 653-0323; (805) 653-5267 FAX
http://www.vcmha.org
Charles Johnson, Librarian
Museum: Mon–Fri 10:00–5:00, Sat 10:00–1:00
Pub. *Heritage and History*, monthly; *The Ventura County Historical Society Quarterly*, $4.00 per issue
$45.00 per year membership

Vista Ranchos Historic Society, Inc.
(651 East Vista Way, Suite A—location)
PO Box 1032 (mailing address)
Vista, CA 92085-1032

Walnut Creek Historical Society
Shadelands Ranch Historical Museum
2660 Ygnacio Valley Road
Walnut Creek, CA 94598
(925) 935-7871
Elizabeth Isles
Office: Mon–Thur 9:00–4:00, Sun 1:00–4:00; Museum: Wed–Thur 11:30–4:00, Sun 1:00–4:00
Pub. *Shadelands Newsletter*, quarterly
(Walnut Creek history)
$10.00 per year membership

Washington Township Historical Society
(43263 Mission Boulevard, Fremont, CA 94538—location)
PO Box 3045 (mailing address)
Fremont, CA 94539
(510) 656-3761

Western Sonoma County Historical Society
West County Museum
261 South Main Street
Sebastopol, CA 95472
(707) 829-6711; (707) 829-7041 FAX
http://www.wschs-grf.pon.net
Rae Swanson, Co-President
Research Room: Thur–Sun 1:00–4:00 and by appointment
Pub. *Apple Press*, monthly
$10.00 per year membership

Whittier Historical Society
6755 Newlin Avenue
Whittier, CA 90601
(562) 945-3871
Rosalie Dannenbaum, President
Tue–Fri 9:00–3:00, Sat–Sun 1:00–4:00
Pub. *Whittier Gazette*, quarterly

Winchester Historical Society of Pleasant Valley
PO Box 69
Winchester, CA 92596
(909) 926-4039
winchestermuseum@earthlink.net
http://www.homestead.com/winchester
    CAhistory/home.html
Sat–Sun 11:00–3:00 (except holiday
    weekends)

Windsor Square-Hancock Park Historical Society
137 North Larchmont Boulevard, #135
Los Angeles, CA 90004
(213) 243-8182
Fluff McLean, President
by appointment

Yolo County Historical Society
PO Box 1447
Woodland, CA 95776-1447
(530) 661-2212 (information line only)
Pub. *YCHS Newsletter*, ten times per year
(local history books, church records)
$12.00 per year membership

Yuba Historical Society
330 Ninth Street
Marysville, CA 95901
(530) 741-0509

Genealogical Societies

State Genealogical Societies

California Genealogical Society and Library
1611 Telegraph Avenue, Suite 100
Oakland, CA 94612-2154
(510) 663-1358; (510) 663-1358 FAX
cgsresrch@calgensoc.org;
    library@calgensoc.org (General
    Information)
http://www.calgensoc.org
Rick Sherman, Research Services
Thur—Sat 9:00–4:00
Pub. *CGS News*, bimonthly; *The Nugget*
    (general genealogy), semiannually
(specializes in California and San Francisco)
$30.00 per year membership; research:
    $12.00 per hour for members, $15.00 per
    hour for nonmembers; admission: $5.00
    for nonmembers, first Sat free

California State Genealogical Alliance
PO Box 3113
Danville, CA 94526-0113
(925) 278-2101 FAX
JanLVgsCsga@aol.com
http://www.csga.com
Janice Ramsey Lear, Secretary; Peter Carr,
    President
Pub. *CSGA Newsletter*, monthly; *CSGA
    Speakers Director*, biannually; *California
    County Recorders Source Book*,
    biannually; *CSGA Society Directory*,
    annually
(statewide organization with annual meetings
    in conjunction with seminars)
$20.00 per year membership

East LA/Orange County Region
California State Genealogical Alliance

norma@yfcgensearch.com
Norma Keating, Regional Contact
(Orange County and Los Angeles County,
    east of Highway 605)

North Bay Region
California State Genealogical Alliance
ljrussell@earthlink.net
Jo Russell, Regional Contact
(Lake, Mendocino, Napa and Sonoma
    counties)

North Central Region
California State Genealogical Alliance
Tkashuba@aol.com
Melinda Kashuba, Regional Contact
(Shasta County, Siskiyou County, east of
    Coastal Range, and Trinity County, east
    of Coastal Range)

North Central Valley Region
California State Genealogical Alliance
info@csga.com
Blanche Sack
(Butte, Colusa, Glenn, Sutter, Tehama and
    Yuba counties)

North East Region
California State Genealogical Alliance
(vacant)
(Lassen, Modoc, Plumas and Sierra counties)

North San Joaquin Valley Region
California State Genealogical Alliance
(vacant)
(Calaveras, Mariposa, Merced, San Joaquin,
    Stanislaus and Tuolumne counties)

North West Region
California State Genealogical Alliance
(vacant)
(Del Norte and Humboldt counties, Siskiyou
    County, west of Coastal Range, and
    Trinity County, west of Coastal Range)

Riverside/San Bernardino Region
California State Genealogical Alliance
(vacant)
(Riverside and San Bernardino counties)

Sacramento Valley Region
California State Genealogical Alliance
Pam Dallas, Regional Contact
(Alpine, Amador, El Dorado, Nevada,
    Placer, Sacramento, Solano and Yolo
    counties)

San Diego/Imperial Region
California State Genealogical Alliance
PO Box 500407
San Diego, CA 92150-0407
(619) 454-7046 (Lowrey); (858) 485-7684
    (Ireland)
jlowrey@connectnet.com
Joan Lowrey, Regional Contact; Everett B.
    Ireland, CGRS, Regional Contact
(Imperial and San Diego counties)

San Fernando Valley Region
California State Genealogical Alliance
(818) 846-2532
John and Nillah O'Neill, Regional Contacts
(Los Angeles County [San Fernando])

San Francisco Bay Region
California State Genealogical Alliance
(address withheld upon request)
(Alameda, Contra Costa, Marin, San
    Francisco, San Mateo and Santa Clara
    counties)

South Central Coast Region

California State Genealogical Alliance
(vacant)
(Monterey, San Benito and Santa Cruz
    counties)

South San Joaquin Valley Region
California State Genealogical Alliance
(209) 226-7993
Lea Mitchem, Regional Contact
(Fresno, Inyo, Kern, Kings, Madera, Mono
    and Tulare counties)

South West Los Angeles Region
California State Genealogical Alliance
(vacant)
(Los Angeles County, west of Highway 605,
    south of San Fernando Valley)

Tri-counties Region
California State Genealogical Alliance
Al Hardy, Regional Contact
(San Luis Obispo, Santa Barbara and
    Ventura counties)

Genealogical Societies—Local & Regional

Amador County Genealogical Society
42 Via Verde
Sutter Creek, CA 95685
Choice M. Glover, President

Antelope Valley Genealogical Society
PO Box 1049
Lancaster, CA 93584-1049
thegenealogists@sbcglobal.net
http://www.rootsweb.com/~caavgs
Karla Archuleta, President
Pub. *Prospector Quarterly*, $8.00 per year
    subscription; *Antelope Valley
    Genealogical Society Surname Index*,
    annually
$12.00 per year membership

Calaveras Genealogical Society
(753 Main Street—location)
PO Box 184 (mailing address)
Angels Camp, CA 95222-0184

Chester Genealogy Club
PO Box 107
Chester, CA 96020

Chula Vista Genealogical Society
(Chula Vista City Library, Fourth and F
    Streets, Chula Vista, CA 91910—location)
PO Box 3024 (mailing address)
Chula Vista, CA 91902-3024
(619) 690-1188 (President)
SusiCP@aol.com; skncr@cox.net
Susi Pentico, President; Shirley Becker,
    Secretary
Library: 10:00–9:00; Manned help: Mon
    10:00–noon, Wed 11:00–2:00, Thur
    noon–2:00
Pub. *Chula Vista Genealogical Society
    Newsletter*, monthly
$12.00 per year membership; research: $5.00
    for simple search, inquire for more
    extensive search

**Clan Diggers Genealogical Society, Inc., of
the Kern River Valley (Kern County)**
PO Box 531
Lake Isabella, CA 93240
(760) 376-6210
Pub. *Clan Gleanings Newsletter*, quarterly

Genealogical Society of Coachella Valley
PO Box 124
Indio, CA 92202
(760) 837-9923
Pat Westcott, Newsletter Editor

meetings at Indio Library, 200 Civic Center Mall on Towne Street: last Sat 10:00–noon
Pub. *Desert Diggins'*, eight times per year (monthly, Oct – May)
$15.00 per year membership

Colorado River-Blythe-Quartzite Genealogical Society
411 South Fifth Street
Blythe, CA 92225-2816

Conejo Valley Genealogical Society, Inc.
(Thousand Oaks Library, 1401 East Janss Road, Thousand Oaks, CA 91362—location)
PO Box 1228 (mailing address)
Thousand Oaks, CA 91358-0228
(805) 449-2660 (Library)
cvgsweb@verizon.net
http://www.rootsweb.com/~cacvgs
Emma Lee Price, Corresponding Secretary; Lois Burlo, President
Library: Mon–Thur 10:00–9:00, Fri 10:00–6:00, Sat 10:00–5:00, Sun 1:00–5:00; meetings at library: second Tue
Pub. *Rabbit Tracks*, quarterly; *The Genealogist*, monthly
(Ventura County censuses and voter registration, ahnentafel charts and family histories)
$20.00 per year membership, plus one-time $4.00 registration fee

Contra Costa County Genealogical Society
PO Box 910
Concord, CA 94522
(925) 937-5774
cccgs_ca@hotmail (Queries)
http://www.rootsweb.com/~cacccgs
Kathy Castro, Corresponding Secretary
Pub. *Diablo Descendants* (Contra Costa County, California), monthly
$15.00 per year membership; queries $5.00 each

Davis Genealogy Club and Library
Davis Senior Center
646 A Street
Davis, CA 95616
(530) 753-2672
Mon, Wed & Fri 1:00–4:00; meetings last Mon 1:00

Delta Genealogical Interest Group
PO Box 157
Knightsen, CA 94548
Carolyn Sherfy

East Bay Genealogical Society
(405 14th Street, Terrace Level—library location)
PO Box 20417 (mailing address)
Oakland, CA 94620-0417
(510) 451-9599 (Library)
Gretchen Kohl, President
Mon 9:00–4:00
Pub. *The Live Oak*, bimonthly
$12.50 per year membership

East Kern Genealogical Society
PO Box 961
North Edwards, CA 93523
(619) 769-4345; (619) 769-4166
Ray Young, President; Penny Kailer, Vice President
Library: Tue 5:00–9:00, Wed 9:00–1:00 & 5:00–9:00, Thur–Fri 9:00–1:00; meetings: second Sat 9:00–noon
Pub. *Tortoise Tracks*, monthly
$10.00 per year membership

Escondido Genealogical Society
PO Box 2190
Escondido, CA 92033
BW4662@aol.com
Barbara Wickham, President
meetings in the Turrentine Room, Escondido Public Library: third Sat (except July–Aug) 10:15
(Also Genealogical Computer Interest Group)

Fresno Genealogical Society
PO Box 1429
Fresno, CA 93716-1429
(559) 488-3195 (option 5)
Fresno County Free Library, California History and Genealogy Room: Mon–Wed & Fri noon–6:00, Thur noon–8:00, Sat 10:00–5:00; meetings first Tue 6:30–9:00
Pub. *Ash Tree Echo*, two times per year (Mar, Sept); *The Jotted Line*, monthly
$15.00 per year membership

Genealogical Society of North Orange County California (GSNOCC)
PO Box 706
Yorba Linda, CA 92885-0706
(714) 993-2448
ricega@aol.com
http://www.cagenweb.com/gsnocc
Grace Rice, President
meetings at Bradford House, 136 Palm Circle, Placentia, CA 92870: third Wed (Jan–Nov) 7:00 (beginners and computer help at 6:30)
Pub. *GSNOCC Newsletter*, eleven times per year
$15.00 per year membership

Glendora Genealogy Group
PO Box 1141
Glendora, CA 91740
lorman@adelophia.net
http://www.geocities.com/ccstone_us/ GlenGenGrp.htm
Pat Chavarria, President
meetings: fourth Tue 7:00
Pub. *Newsletter*, monthly
$15.00 per year membership

Glenn Genealogy Group
c/o COUCH
745 Santiago Court
Chico, CA 95973-8781

HEFA Kinseekers
PO Box 3310
Fullerton, CA 92634

Hayward Area Genealogical Society
PO Box 754
Hayward, CA 94543

Hemet-San Jacinto Genealogical Society
(1779 East Florida Avenue, Unit C-4, Hemet, CA 92544—location)
PO Box 2516 (mailing address)
Hemet, CA 92546-2516
(909) 652-9304; (909) 658-1962 (Library)
budman5104@earthlink.net
Rose M. Hodgerson, Librarian; Bud Miner, President
Library-Headquarters: Mon–Wed & first & third Sat 10:00–3:00; meetings at First Presbyterian Church, 515 East Kimball Street, Hemet: first Tue (except June–Aug) 7:00
Pub. *Past Finder*, four times per year (Aug, Oct, Jan, May)
(approximately 10,000 quarterlies and 3,000 hardbound books in library)
$18.00 per year membership

Hi Desert Genealogical Society
PO Box 1271
Victorville, CA 92392
(760) 247-8835
http://www.vvo.com/comm/sbcvv.htm (Victorville Branch Library)
Victorville Branch Library: Mon 6:00-7:45, Tue 1:00–3:00, Fri 10:00–noon; meetings: fourth Tue 7:00
Pub. *Desert Diggings*, quarterly
$10.00 per year membership

Imperial County Genealogical Society
1573 Elm Street
El Centro, CA 92243-3133

Indian Wells Valley Genealogical Society
(131 Los Flores—location)
PO Box 2047 (mailing address)
Ridgecrest, CA 93555

Kern County Genealogical Society
PO Box 2214
Bakersfield, CA 93303
(661) 831-7527 (Librarian's home)
Joyce Bayless, Librarian
meetings at Beale Library: third Tue 1:00–3:00
Pub. *Kern-Gen*, quarterly
$12.00 per year membership

Lake County Genealogical Society
PO Box 1323
Lakeport, CA 95453
Pub. *Lake County Genealogical Society Newsletter*, quarterly
(Lake County genealogy)
$7.50 per year membership

LEGS Lake Elsinore Genealogical Society
PO Box 807
Lake Elsinore, CA 92531-0807
(909) 244-0547
dague@linkline.com
http://www.bakerfamily.org
Jane M. Dague, President
meetings at Wildomar Library: second Wed 1:00 (except Dec); workshops at Wildomar Library: fourth Wed (except Nov–Dec)
Pub. *LEGS Newsletter*, bimonthly
$15.00 per year membership

Leisure World Genealogical Workshop
Leisure World Library
PO Box 2069
Seal Beach, CA 90740
Susan Montgomery, President
Mon–Thur 9:00–6:00, Fri–Sat 9:00–5:00
$2.00 per year membership

Livermore-Amador Genealogical Society (LAGS)
PO Box 901
Livermore, CA 94551-0901
(925) 447-9652
president@l-ags.org
http://www.l-ags.org
Richard Finn, President
Library: Mon–Tue 1:00–8:00, Wed–Thur 10:00–6:00, Sat 2:00–6:00, Sun 1:00–5:00; weekly meetings
Pub. *Roots Tracer*, quarterly
(web page has surname index, registers of local cemeteries)
$18.00 per year membership; research: $1.00

Lompoc Valley Genealogical Society (formerly Vandenberg Genealogical Society)
PO Box 81
Lompoc, CA 93438-0081

JanLvgsCsga@aol.com
http://www.rootsweb.com/~calvgs
Janice Ramsey Lear, President
meetings at LDS Church, 1312 West Prune:
    third Tue 7:00–9:00 (except Dec)
Pub. *SearchNotes*, monthly (except Dec)
("The LVGS is a nonprofit organization,
    serving the Lompoc and Santa Ynes
    Valleys and Vandenberg Air Force Base.
    The LVGS emphasis is on helping
    individuals get started on their family
    genealogy.")
$15.00 per year membership

Los Angeles Westside Genealogical Society
PO Box 10447
Marina Del Rey, CA 90295-6447
thomaslane@earthlink.net
http://www.genealogy-la.com/lawgs.shtml
Thomas Lane, President
Pub. *Newsletter*, eleven times per year
    (monthly, except Dec)
$18.00 per year membership

Los Banos Genealogical Society, Inc.
(16778 South Place—location)
PO Box 2525 (mailing address)
Los Banos, CA 93635
(209) 826-4882 (Library); (209) 826-0763
    (President); (209) 826-8085 (Secretary)
Betty Bettencourt, Membership; Josie
    Bosworth, President; Scott Black,
    Secretary
by appointment
Pub. *The Tree Shakers*, monthly
("Society has published Cemetery Book for
    Los Banos and Birth, Marriage & Death
    Record Books for the county of Merced.")
$15.00 per year membership

Genealogical Society of Madera County
(Madera County Main Library, across from
courthouse—library location)
PO Box 495 (mailing address)
Madera, CA 93639-0495
Sandra Williams, Editor
Pub. *Madera Heritage Quarterly* (Feb, May,
    Aug, Nov)
(cemetery records of Madera County;
    genealogical books and publications)
$12.00 per year membership

Maidu Genealogical Society
(see Roseville Genealogical Society, below)

Marin County Genealogical Society
PO Box 1511
Novato, CA 94948-1511
(415) 435-2310
MarinGenSoc@juno.com
http://www.rootsweb.com/~camargs/
    index.html
Pat Friesen
Pub. *Marin Kin Tracer*, quarterly
$15.00 per year membership; research:
    $10.00 per hour

Mendocino Coast Genealogical Society
PO Box 762
Fort Bragg, CA 95437
Alice Holmes, Editor
Wed–Sat 10:00–4:30 by appointment
Pub. *Under Construction*, quarterly (Feb,
    May, Aug, Nov), $7.50 per year
    subscription
$15.00 per year membership

Merced County Genealogical Society
(Merced County Library, 2100 O Street,
Merced, CA 95340—location)
PO Box 3061 (mailing address)
Merced, CA 95344

(209) 723-9019
Lois Jimenez
Library: Mon–Thur 9:00–9:00, Fri–Sat
    9:00–6:00
Pub. *The Family Snoop*, monthly
$10.00 per year membership

Mission Oaks Genealogy Club
(Mission Oaks Community Center, 4701
Gibbons Drive, Carmichael—location)
PO Box 216 (mailing address)
Carmichael, CA 95609-0216
(916) 482-8531
Elizabeth Kohler
meetings third Thur 1:00; PAF® User's
    Group meetings first Thur 1:00–4:00
Pub. *Mission Oaks Genealogy Club
    Newsletter*, quarterly

Monterey County Genealogical Society
PO Box 8144
Salinas, CA 93912-9144
http://www.mocogenso.org
meetings at LDS Church, Noche Buena and
    Plumas, Seaside, CA: first Thur
Pub. *Monterey County Genealogical Society*,
    monthly
$15.00 per year membership

Genealogical Society of Morongo Basin
PO Box 234
Yucca Valley, CA 92286
pauli734@msn.com (Site Administrator)
http://www.yuccavalley.com/genealogy
Dick Moran, President
meetings in the Cholla Room at the Yucca
    Valley Community Center: third Tue
    10:00
$15.00 per year membership

Mount Diablo Genealogical Society
(1910 Tice Valley Boulevard [California
Savings Bank]—location)
PO Box 4654 (mailing address)
Walnut Creek, CA 94596
(925) 682-3958
JCBED@aol.com
John Bedecarré, Newsletter Editor
Library: third Thur 1:00–3:00
Pub. *The Digger*, eleven times per year
    (monthly, except Aug)
$15.00 per year membership

**Napa Valley Genealogical and
Biographical Society**
1701 Menlo
Napa, CA 94559
(707) 252-2252
nvgbs@napanet.net
http://www.napanet.net/~nvgbs
Sandy Hoover
Tue 10:00–9:00, Wed–Thur 10:00–4:00,
    second & fourth Sat 10:00–2:00
Pub. *Wine Press Monthly Newsletter*,
    monthly
("resources of many foreign countries and
    many U.S. states")
$25.00 per year membership; research:
    $10.00 per hour

Nevada County Genealogical Society
PO Box 176
Cedar Ridge, CA 95924
(530) 272-2119
svgross@infs.com
http://www.rootsweb.com/~cancgs
Maria Brower, Founder and Editor; Sue
    Gross
meetings at Nevada County Public Library
Pub. *Kith & Kin*, monthly
(early mining records and maps, great
    registers, Nevada County records resource

guide)
$12.00 per year membership

Newberry Springs Genealogy Club
701 Montara Road, #27
Barstow, CA 92311-5742

**North San Diego County Genealogical
Society, Inc.**
(Carlsbad City Library, Georgina Cole
Library, 1250 Carlsbad Village Drive,
Carlsbad, CA 92008-1991—location)
PO Box 581 (mailing address)
Carlsbad, CA 92018-0581
(858) 481-8511 (President)
marread@aol.com
http://www.cagenweb.com/nsdcgs
Marvin Read, Corresponding Secretary
Business meeting and sharing: second Tue
    10:00; Computer Genealogy Group:
    second Tue 1:15; Program: fourth Tue
    10:00
Pub. *Paths to the Past*, monthly
$15.00 per year membership

Ohio Genealogical Society
Southern California Chapter
(see Ohio, Part 2)

**Orange County California Genealogical
Society (OCCGS)**
(Huntington Beach Public Library, 7111
Talbert Avenue, Huntington Beach, CA
92648-1296—location)
PO Box 1587 (mailing address)
Orange, CA 92856-1587
lilwind@speakeasy.net
http://www.occgs.com
Joan Rambo, President; Breeze Erwin,
    Secretary
Pub. *OCCGS Journal*, two times per year
    (Apr, Oct), $12.00 per year subscription
    for members, $15.00 per year subscription
    for nonmembers
$16.00 per year for new membership; $14.00
    per year renewal membership

Pajaro Valley Genealogical Society
53 North Drive
Freedom, CA 95019
Grace Marie Hackwell

Palm Springs Genealogical Society
(Palm Springs Public Library and Cathedral
City [CA] Public Library—collections
location)
PO Box 2093 (mailing address)
Palm Springs, CA 92263-2093
MarieScr@aol.com; pady2@juno.com;
    byronwinings@email.com;
    PSGS@dc.rr.com
Marie Scruggs, President; Mary Faith
    Cripps, Treasurer (Membership)
meetings at Cathedral City (CA) Public
    Library: first Sat (Oct–May) 10:00
Pub. *Pedigree Searchers*, eight times per
    year (monthly, except June–Sept)
$12.00 per year membership

Paradise Genealogical Society
(5587 Scottwood Road, Paradise, CA
95969—location)
PO Box 460 (mailing address)
Paradise, CA 95967
(530) 877-2330
pargenso@pacbell.net
http://www.pargenso@pacbell.net
Earl Cowden, Membership Chair
Mon & Fri 10:00–4:00, Wed 10:00–8:00, Sat
    10:00–2:00
Pub. *Genealogical Goldmine*, annually (fall)
("Also many publications on Butte County,

California, data. Births, deaths, cemetery, probates, $9.00–$25.00.")
$25.00 per year membership

Pasadena Genealogy Society
1080 North Holliston Avenue
Pasadena, CA 91104-3014
kathryn@bassett.net
("Defunct society. Send SASE for brochure: *Pasadena Research: How to Do It Yourself*, with addresses of library, mortuaries, etc., or email for PDF file of brochure.")
$10.00 per year membership

Genealogical Friends of the Pasadena Public Library
Pasadena Public Library
Pasadena Centennial Room
285 East Walnut Street
Pasadena, CA 91101

Placer County Genealogical Society
PO Box 7385
Auburn, CA 95604-7385
(530) 887-2646
http://www.pcgenes.com/pcgs.html
meetings at the Beecher Room of the Auburn-Placer County Library (collection location): fourth Thur 7:00 (except Dec)
Pub. *Placer Trails*, nine times per year
$11.00 per year membership

Pocahontas Trails Genealogical Society
3628 Cherokee Lane
Modesto, CA 95356
P. Bullocik
Pub. *Pocahontas Trails Quarterly* (winter, spring, summer, fall)
$10.00 per year membership

Pomona Valley Genealogical Society
PO Box 286
Pomona, CA 91768-0286
(909) 593-6786 (Editor)
AnneLarkin@adelphia.net
http://home.earthlink.net/~hazefam/PVGS.html
Anne Larkin, Newsletter Editor
Meetings at Claremont Library: second Sat (Sept–May) 1:30
Pub. *Pomona Valley Genealogical Society Newsletter*, nine times per year (monthly, Sept–May)
(Publications from California State Assembly Records from 1851 on—"serves Pomona Valley since 1955")
$12.00 per year membership (monies support Genealogical Collection of the Pomona Public Library); queries: free for members, $1.00 for nonmembers; research: $10.00 donation

Questing Heirs Genealogical Society, Inc.
PO Box 15102
Long Beach, CA 90815-0102
QuestHeirs@aol.com; lizstookes@cs.com
http://www.cagenweb.com/questing
Elizabeth Myers, Corresponding Secretary
Pub. *Questing Heirs Genealogical Society, Inc., Newsletter*, monthly, $12.00 per year subscription
$18.00 per year membership

Rancho Bernardo Genealogy Group
Rancho Bernardo Branch
San Diego Public Library
820 E Street
San Diego, CA 92101-6478

Redlands Area Historical Society, Inc.
Genealogical Branch

(see Historical Societies—Local and Regional, above)

Redwood Genealogical Society, Inc.
(Rohner Recreation Building, Rohner Park—location)
PO Box 645 (mailing address)
Fortuna, CA 95540-0645
(707) 725-4307 (Librarian); (707) 764-5583 (Treasurer)
barbmore@northcoast.com
http://www.qworld.net/humboldt/rgs.html
Ruth Teasley, Librarian; Barbara Morehead, Treasurer
Wed 9:00–10:00, and by appointment
Pub. *Redwood Researcher*, quarterly (Aug, Nov Feb, May)
$12.00 per year membership; queries welcome; research: "minimum donation of $5.00—depends on how much research has to be done and how many times the researcher has to travel to the county seat"

Renegade Root Diggers
9171 Fargo Avenue
Hanford, CA 93230

Genealogical Society of Riverside
PO Box 2557
Riverside, CA 92516
gaubuchon@aol.com
http://www.rootsweb.com/~cagsor
G. Aubuchon, President
Riverside Public Library
Pub. *Lifeliner*, quarterly, $10.00 per year subscription; research: $10.00 per hour plus copies and SASE
$20.00 per year membership

Root Diggers Genealogy Association
(33103 Old Women Springs Road—location)
PO Box 408 (mailing address)
Lucerne Valley, CA 92356
(760) 248-7521
Martha Rader, Treasurer
meetings: first Thur 10:00–noon
$3.00 per year membership

Roseville Genealogical Society
PO Box 459
Roseville, CA 95678
http://www.rootsweb.com/~carvgs/rgs.htm
Marilyn Larson, President
meetings at the Maidu Community Center, 1550 Maidu Drive, Roseville: second & fourth Tue 1:00–3:00 (except no fourth Tue in Dec)
Pub. *Newsletter*, eleven times per year (Dec/Jan combined issue)
(formerly known as the Maidu Genealogical Society)

Genealogical Association of Sacramento
(Belle Cooledge Library, 5600 South Lane Park Drive, Sacramento—location)
PO Box 292145 (mailing address)
Sacramento, CA 95829-2145
(916) 682-8004 (President)
Esther McAllister, President
Mon & Thur noon–9:00, Tue–Wed 10:00–9:00, Fri–Sat 1:00–5:00; meetings third Wed (except July–Aug & Dec) 12:30 at Belle Cooledge Library, 5681 Freeport Boulevard, Sacramento
Pub. *G.A.S. Lites*, semiannually; *Lamplighter*, monthly
$15.00 per year membership

Sacramento Genealogical Society—Root Cellar
(California State Archives, 1020 "O" Street, Sacramento—collection location)
PO Box 265 (mailing address)
Citrus Heights, CA 95611-0265
(916) 481-4930 (Library Chair)
samihud@aol.com
http://www.rootcellar.org
Sammie Hudgens, Library Chair
Archives: Mon–Fri 9:30–4:00; Library: first Sat 9:30–4:00; meetings at Citrus Heights Elementary School, 7085 Auburn Building, Citrus Heights: second Wed (Sept–June) 6:30
Pub. *Root Cellar Preserves*, triannually (worldwide holdings and large periodical collection)
$16.00 per year membership

Genealogical and Historical Council of Sacramento Valley
PO Box 214749
Sacramento, CA 95821-0749
(916) 331-4349
pbdallas@earthlink.net; ijones@accessbee.com
http://www.rootsweb.com/~caghcsv
Iris Carter Jones
meetings: every other month
Pub. *Newsletter*, monthly; *Speakers Directory*, $10.25 ppd. for members, $12.75 ppd. for nonmembers)
("an umbrella group for local genealogical, historical, lineage and heraldry associations and libraries in the greater Sacramento Valley area; sponsors workshops for societies, is active in legislation issues, offers channels of communication for the local societies and the genealogical community and promotes ethical and professional standards in genealogical and historical research")
$15.00 per year membership

San Bernardino Valley Genealogical Society
(Norman Feldheyon Library, Mary Kellogg Room—location)
PO Box 2220 (mailing address)
San Bernardino, CA 92406-2220
(909) 883-7468
sbvgs@sbpl.org
http://www.sbpl.org/genealogy.html
Blanche Tompkins, President
meetings: second Sat 10:30–12:30 (Jan–June & Sept–Nov)
Pub. *Valley Quarterly*
(local history)
$10.00 per year membership; research: $5.00 per hour

San Diego County Genealogical Association
PO Box 422
Ramona, CA 92065
(760) 789-2534; (760) 789-7043; (760) 789-2534
jqbeck@prodigy.net
Jacqueline Beck, President
meetings at the Ramona Library Community Room, 1406 Monticito: second Wed 7:30 (except July–Aug & Dec)
$10.00 per year membership

San Diego Genealogical Society
1050 Pioneer Way, Suite E
El Cajon, CA 92020-1943
(619) 588-0065; (619) 296-4456 (President)
sdgs@genealogy.org
http://www.rootsweb.com/~casdgs/index.html
Peter Steelquist, President
Thur 10:00–4:00, evenings by appointment; meetings at Saint Dunstan's Episcopal

Church Parish Hall, 6556 Park Ridge Boulevard, San Carlos area: second Sat (except Jan or Feb [month of annual luncheon] & Dec) noon; Reunion/Generations Group meetings: fourth Wed 10:00; FTM Group: first Sat 10:00

Pub. *San Diego Leaves and Saplings*, quarterly, $10.00 per year subscription (San Diego County, public and private records)

admission: $2.00 donation requested

San Fernando Valley Genealogical Society
(Balboa Mission Town Hall, 16916 San Fernando Mission Boulevard—location)
PO Box 3486 (mailing address)
Winnetka, CA 91396
eburrelle@netzero.net
http://www.rootsweb.com/~casfvgs
Elizabeth Burrelle-Fowler
meetings: third Fri (Except Aug) 7:30–9:30 P.M.
Pub. *SFVGS Bulletin*, monthly
$18.00 per year membership; research: no individual assistance available

San Gorgonio Genealogical Society
1050 Brinton Avenue
Banning, CA 92220
Joan Carpenter Covington, President

San Joaquin Genealogical Society
PO Box 4817
Stockton, CA 95204-0817
aappls@aol.com
http://www.rootsweb.com/~sjgs
Cheri A. Pillsbury, President
Mon–Sat 10:00–9:00; meetings third Thur 1:30 at Stockton Public Library, Park and Oak Streets, Stockton
Pub. *San Joaquin Genealogical Society*, five times per year
$10.00 per year membership; research: $10.00 per hour

San Luis Obispo County Genealogical Society, Inc.
PO Box 4
Atascadero, CA 93423-0004
(805) 237-2455
okie-italiano@tcsn.net (Foy Roberto, Membership); slogen@slonet.org (Research Queries)
http://home.kcbx.net/~slogen
Guy Kuncir, President
The South County Branch in Arroyo Grande Library, South County Regional Center, 800 West Branch: Mon 6:00 P.M.–8:00 P.M., Tue & Thur 1:00–4:00, and by appointment; The North County Branch in Paso Robles Historical Society Carnegie Library, 800 12th Street, Paso Robles: Wed–Sun 1:00–4:00; meetings at the IOOF Hall, 520 Dana Street, San Luis Obispo: first Sat (Jan–June & Sept–Nov) 1:00
Pub. *Bulletin of the San Luis Obispo County Genealogical Society*, two times per year (May and Nov); *Newsletter*, bimonthly (publishes records of San Luis Obispo County)
$22.00 per year membership; research: $13.00 per hour for nonmembers ($10.00 per hour for members), plus copies at 10¢ per page for members, $10.00 per hour plus copies for nonmembers

San Ramon Valley Genealogical Society
PO Box 305 (mailing address)
Diablo, CA 94528-8308
(925) 837-8858

Barbara Dittig, President
third Tue 10:00–noon
Pub. *San Ramon Valley Genealogical Society Newsletter*, monthly
$15.00 per year membership

Santa Barbara County Genealogical Society
(711 Santa Barbara Street—library location)
PO Box 1303 (mailing address)
Santa Barbara, CA 93116-1303
(805) 965-7423
sbcgs@msn.com
http://www.cagenweb.com/santabarbara/sbcgs
Janice G. Cloud, President
library: Tue, Thur–Fri & Sun 1:00–4:00
Pub. *Ancestors West*, quarterly; *Tree Tips, Newsletter*, monthly
$17.00 per year membership

Santa Clara County Historical and Genealogical Society
(see Historical Societies—Local and Regional, above)

Genealogical Society of Santa Cruz County
Central Branch Public Library
(224 Church Street, Santa Cruz, CA 95060—location)
PO Box 72 (mailing address)
Santa Cruz, CA 95063-0072
(831) 420-5794
Library: Mon–Thur 10:00–9:00, Fri 10:00–6:00, Sat 10:00–5:00, Sun 1:00–5:00
Pub. *Newsletter—The Genealogical Society of Santa Cruz County*, bimonthly (odd-numbered months)
(Sponsors speakers program, annual seminar, compilation of local records. "Large nonlending library.")
$15.00 per year membership; research: donation

Santa Maria Valley Genealogical Society
PO Box 1215
Santa Maria, CA 93456
(805) 925-4093
Mary McBride Munding, President
Meetings at Oak Knolls Haven, 4845 South Bradley Road, Santa Maria: third Thur 3:30
Pub. *Santa Maria Valley Genealogical Society Quarterly* (spring, summer, fall, winter)
(Santa Maria Valley early births, deaths, marriages; Knights of Pythias records; local pioneer families)
$15.00 per year membership; research donation

Sequoia Genealogical Society, Inc.
Tulare Public Library
113 North F Street
Tulare, CA 93274-3803
(559) 685-2342 (Library)
Mary De Luz, Library Assistant
Library: Mon & Wed 10:00–5:00, Tue & Thur 10:00–9:00, Sat 10:00–5:00
Pub. *Sequoia Genealogical Society, Inc., Newsletter*, eight times per year (monthly, Mar–Nov)
("San Joaquin Valley scope")
$20.00 per year membership

Shasta County Genealogical Society
PO Box 994652
Redding, CA 96099-4652
sgs106@hotmail.com
http://www.rootsweb.com/~cascogs

Karen Taylor, Corresponding Secretary
Pub. *The Shasta Genealogical Society*, monthly
("The society maintains a library at the Shasta County Library.")
$15.00 per year membership; research: $10.00 per hour plus costs

Genealogical Society of Siskiyou County
PO Box 225
Yreka, CA 96097
(530) 842-6018 (President)
Sharon Youngs, President
meetings: last Tue 7:30
Pub. *Heir Lines*, quarterly
$12.00 per year membership

Solano County Genealogical Society
(Old Town Hall, 620 East Main Street, Vacaville—location)
PO Box 2494 (mailing address)
Fairfield, CA 94533-0249
scgs@cwnet.com
http:www.rootsweb.com/~cascgsi
Nancy Morebeck, President
Mon & third Sat 10:00–2:00, except federal holidays; meetings at Senior Center, 1200 Civic Center Drive, Fairfield: first Sat 11:00
Pub. *Solano County Genealogical Society Newsletter*, ten times per year (monthly, except July–Aug); *The Root Digger*, quarterly
$15.00 per year membership

Sonoma County Genealogical Society
(Santa Rosa, CA—location)
c/o 8330 Blue Spruce Way (mailing address)
Windsor, CA 95492
(707) 838-1311; (707) 838-3635
chuckadoo@aol.com
http://web.wco.com/~hwmiller/genealogy/scgs.htm
Charles H. Warner, President
daily 9:00–5:00
Pub. *The Sonoma Searcher*, quarterly, $10.00 per year subscription
("Special interest groups: British, German, Irish, southern states, computers")
$15.00 per year membership; nonmember queries: $2.00

South Bay Cities Genealogical Society
PO Box 11069
Torrance, CA 90510-1069
sbcgs@hotmail.com
http://www.rootsweb.com/~casbcgs
Tue & Thur 10:00–2:00, third Wed 5:30–7:30
Pub. *Newsletter*, bimonthly
$10.00 per year membership

South Humboldt Historical and Genealogical Society
(see Historical Societies—Local and Regional, above)

South Orange County California Genealogy Society (SOCCGS)
PO Box 4513
Mission Viejo, CA 92690-4513
(949) 470-8498 (Library)
mcqueenmaryjo@aol.com (Mary Jo Nuttall, Treasurer and Newsletter Editor)
http://www.rootsweb.com/~casoccgs
Herb Abrams, Webmaster
Mission Viejo Library, corner of La Paz and Parguerite Parkway: Mon & Thur 10:00–9:00, Tue–Wed 10:00–7:00, Sat 10:00–4:00, Sun 1:00–3:00; meetings at the Mission Viejo Family History Center: third Sat 10:00–noon

Pub. *SOCCGS Newsletter*
$20.00 per year membership

Southern California Genealogical Society and Family Research Library
417 Irving Drive
Burbank, CA 91504
(818) 843-7247; (818) 843-7262 FAX
scgs@earthlink.net
http://www.scgsgenealogy.com
John M. O'Neill, President; Jennifer Weber, Editor
Mon & Wed–Fri 10:00–4:00, Tue, first & second Sun, third & fourth Sat 9:00–4:00
Pub. *The Searcher*, monthly
("Research Team: Revolutionary War, colonial wars, Irish famine immigrants, Virginia ancestry, Massachusetts town vital records"; Turner Collection; 18,000 books, *The American Genealogist* and many state periodicals, CDs, annual jamboree)
$22.00 per year membership; research fees vary

Genealogical Society of Stanislaus County, Inc.
(1229 East Fairmont Avenue, Modesto, CA 95350—location)
PO Box A (mailing address)
Modesto, CA 95352-3660
(209) 571-3227 (President)
gssc@worldnet.att.net
http://cagenweb.com/lr/stanislaus/gssc.html
meetings at Geneva Presbyterian Church: third Tue 7:00; Book Nook (Society-owned research center): Fri 10:00–3:00; Special Collections Room, Stanislaus County Free Library: Mon–Wed 10:00–3:00, Thur 10:00–5:00
Pub. *Stanislaus Researcher*, monthly
("The Society is committed to providing at least two low-cost seminars or workshops yearly.")
$15.00 per year membership

TRW Genealogical Society
One Space Park S-1156
Redondo Beach, CA 90278
(310) 813-6171
snminer@aol.com
Mike O'Rell, President
Pub. *Montage*, quarterly
membership limited to employees and family members of TRW

Taft Genealogical Society
PO Box 1411
Taft, CA 93268
Mzjckson@aol.com
http://www.rootsweb.com/~catgs/taft_ca_index.html
Donna Jackson
monthly business meeting
$12.00 per year membership

Tehama County Genealogical and Historical Society
PO Box 415
Red Bluff, CA 96080-0415
rssroots@pacbell.nethttp://www.tco.net/tehama/museum/tcmgene.html
Pub. *Memories*, annually (yearbook on County of Tehama history)
$10.00 per year membership

Temecula Valley Genealogical Society
27475 Ynez Road, Suite 291
Temecula, CA 92591
StuartBorok@aol.com
Beverlee Stuart-Borok, President
meetings at Temecula Library Community

Room: second Mon 6:30–8:45
$18.00 per year membership

Tracy Area Genealogical Society
Tracy Historical Museum
1141 Adam Street
Tracy, CA 95376
(209) 832-1106
dttoth@pacbell.net
http://www.rootsweb.com/~catags
Tue & Fri 9:00-1:00, second Wed 6:00-9:00; Sun 1:00-4:00; meetings at Lolly Hansen Senior Center, 375 East Ninth Street: fourth Thur (Except July) 7:00-9:00Michael Davis, President; Margaret Toth, Vice-President

Tule Tree Tracers
Porterville Public Library
41 West Thurman Avenue
Porterville, CA 93257
(559) 784-0177 (Library)
Melanie Wells
Genealogy: Mon–Sat 9:00–5:00; Local History: Mon–Thur 10:00–noon

Tuolumne County Genealogical Society
(158 West Bradford Street—location)
PO Box 3956 (mailing address)
Sonora, CA 95370
(209) 532-1317
lal@lodelink.com
http://www.tcgsonline.org
Louise Leedy, Library Director
Tue & Thur 10:00–4:00, Sat 10:00–3:30
Pub. *Golden Roots of the Mother Lode*, semianually, $3.00 each for back issues; *Gold Digger*, bimonthly
("Specialize in Tuolumne County vital records, voter registrations, censuses, cemetery records, local history and genealogy. Some records for surrounding Mother Lode counties.")
$18.00 per year membership; research: $10.00 for the first hour, $6.00 for each additional hour

Universal Genealogical Society of Bellflower
9512 Cedar Street
Bellflower, CA 90706

Genealogy Society of Vallejo-Benicia
734 Marin Street
Vallejo, CA 94590
clydenefred@juno.com (President)
http://www.rootsweb.com/~cagsv

Vandenberg Genealogical Society
(see Lompoc Valley Genealogical Society, above)

Ventura County Genealogical Society
E. P. Foster Branch
The Ventura County Library Services Agency
(651 East Main—location)
PO Box 24608 (mailing address)
Ventura, CA 93002
(805) 648-2715 (Library); (805) 642-1242 (Society President)
vcgswk@knappfamily.org
http://www.rootsweb.com/~cavcgs
Betty Johnsen, President
Mon–Thur 10:00–9:00, Fri–Sat 10:00–5:00, Sun 1:00–4:00
Pub. *Ventura County Genealogical Society Quarterly*
$12.00 per year membership

Whittier Area Genealogical Society
(13502 Suite "J," Quad Shopping Center,

Whittier Boulevard and Central—location)
PO Box 4367 (mailing address)
Whittier, CA 90607-4367
(562) 946-1758 (President)
darlenedcampbell@aol.com
http://www.cagenweb.com/kr/wags
Darlene Campbell, President
Santa Fe Springs Public Library: Mon–Thur 10:00–9:00, Fri 10:00–6:00, Sat 10:00–5:00
Pub. *Whittier Area Genealogical Society Newsletter*, monthly
$15.00 per year membership

Yucaipa Valley Genealogical Society
PO Box 32
Yucaipa, CA 92399
Pub. *Yucaipa Valley Family Finders Quarterly*
$5.00 per year membership

Independent Publications and Miscellany

Anderson Marsh State Historic Park
Clear Lake District
5300 Soda Bay Road
Kelseyville, CA 95451
(707) 994-0688
Stephen Hill, District Superintendent

Angel Island State Park
PO Box 318
San Francisco, CA 94920
(415) 435-1915
Ronald Brean, Superintendent, Marin District
(not genealogical: Civil War military base, also contains immigration station)

Belvedere-Tiburon Landmarks Society Archives
PO Box 134
Belvedere-Tiburon, CA 94920
(415) 435-5490
lmsarchivist@earthlink.net
Piper Berger, Archivist
by appointment
(archives department)
search: $30.00 per hour

Bidwell Mansion State Historic Park
Bidwell Mansion Association
525 Esplanade
Chico, CA 95926
(530) 895-6144
Paul Holman, Ranger I
Kenneth Wilber, District Superintendent
(primarily site preservation, not genealogy)

CaGenWeb
Part of The USGenWeb Project
wilson@cagenweb.com
http://www.cagenweb.com
Richard Wilson, State Coordinator
(links to other California resources)

California Council for the Humanities
312 Sutter Street, Suite 601
San Francisco, CA 94108
(415) 391-1474
Morton Rothstein, Chair; James Quay, Executive Director

California Council for the Promotion of History
PO Box 221476
Sacramento, CA 95822
Pub. *California History Action*, quarterly
(public history and history action in California, professional organization)

$35.00 per year membership

California Department of Parks and Recreation
San Joaquin Valley District
PO Box 205
Friant, CA 93626
(559) 822-2332

California Department of Transportation
Publication Distribution Unit
1900 Royal Oaks Drive
Sacramento, CA 95815-3800
(916) 323-5606; (916) 445-3520; (916) 324-8997 FAX
Publications@dot.ca.gov
http://www.caltrans.ca.gov/publicat.htm
(some interesting maps, but more at California Division of Tourism)

California Division of Tourism
caltour@commerce.ca.gov
http://visitcalifornia.com/state/tourism/tour_homepage (Maps)

California Genealogy Index
Mines Road Books
PO Box 3185
Fremont, CA 94539
(510) 656-2240
minesrb@pacbell.net
http://cmug.com/~minesroad/genealogy.html (California Genealogy Index);
http://cmug.com/~minesroad (Mines Road Books)
Dan Mosier
(Mines Road Books publishes history and genealogy and sponsors "California Genealogy Index [which] is a fee-based research service where users can choose an item from an index of over 140,000 names. Orders and retrievals are conducted by mail only.")

California Pioneers of Santa Clara Valley
(661 Empey Way—location)
PO Box 8208 (mailing address)
San Jose, CA 95155
(408) 998-1174
Pub. *Trailblazer*, quarterly
$4.00 per year membership

California State University, Bakersfield
Walter W. Stiern Library
Special Collections, Room 102
9001 Stockdale Highway
Bakersfield, CA 93311-1099
(661) 664-3372; (661) 664-3339 FAX
http://www.lib.csubak.edu/html/Special_collections.html

California Views Historical Photo Collection
469 Pacific Street
Monterey, CA 93940-2702
(831) 373-3811
hathaway@mbay.net
http://www.caviews.com
Mr. Pat Hathaway, Photo Archivist
Tue–Sat 11:00–5:00

Center for Mennonite Brethren Studies
(see Religious Archives and Organizations—Mennonite, Part 3)

Center for San Diego Studies
Department of History/Political Science
2900 Lomaland Drive
San Diego, CA 92106
(619) 221-2200
Dwayne Little, Department Chair
(historical databases)

Center for Southwest Research
(see New Mexico, Part 2)

Discovery Museum of Orange County
3101 West Harvard Street
Santa Ana, CA 92704
(714) 540-0404
Karen O. Johnson, Executive Director
(primarily historical, not genealogical)

El Pueblo de Los Angeles Historic Park
845 North Alameda
Los Angeles, CA 90012
(213) 628-1274
Jerry T. Smart, Director
Pub. *EPPAGRAM*
(site conservation, not primarily genealogical)

Fort Ross State Historic Park
19005 Coast Highway 1
Jenner, CA 95450
(707) 847-3286
Daniel F. Murley, State Park Ranger II
(historical site operation, not genealogical)

Friends of the Adobes, Inc.
South Mission Street
San Miguel, CA 93451
(805) 467-3311
Joyce A. Herman, Treasurer
Pub. *Caledonia Enterprise* (primarily historical, not genealogical)

Friends of the Carrillo Adobe
PO Box 2843
Santa Rosa, CA 95405
(707) 539-9598
Barbara Crossland, President
(primarily historical, not genealogical)

Genealogy Resources for California
James Stevenson Publisher Bookstore
(707) 469-0237
james_stevenson_publisher@jspub.com
http://www.jspub.com/genresor.html
James Stevenson, Publisher

H-California
Study of California History
542 Filbert Street
San Francisco, CA 94133
H-California-request@h-net.msu.edu
http://h-net2.msu.edu/~cal
Bruce Melendy, Web Editor
(history discussion network)

Historic Preservation Commission
501 Poli Street
Ventura, CA 93001
(805) 654-7849
Monica Nolan, Administrative Assistant II
(primarily historical, not genealogical)

Historical Shrine Foundation
2482 San Diego Avenue
San Diego, CA 92110
(primarily not genealogical)

Huntington Westerners
PO Box 80241
San Marino, CA 91118
(626) 284-2130
Midge Sherwood, Editor and Founder
(authentic history of the American frontier west, 1850–1900)
$20.00 per year membership

Indian Grinding Rock State Historic Park
14881 Pine Grove-Volcano Road
Pine Grove, CA 95665
(209) 269-7488

The K.A.R.D. Files
19305 S.E. 243rd Place
Kent, WA 98042-4820
(253) 432-1659
Judy K. Dye, Owner/Compiler
Pub. *Siskiyou County, California, Series*, irregularly

Krans-Buckland Family Association Library
(see Ethnic Archives, Libraries and Societies—English, Part 3)

Lake Oroville State Historic Site
400 Glen Drive
Oroville, CA 95965
(530) 538-2200
Harold Bradshaw, District Superintendent
(primarily historical, not genealogical)

Los Californianos, Hispanic Ancestors of Alta California
(see Ethnic Archives, Libraries and Societies, Spanish, Part 3)

Los Fundadores, The Founders and Friends of Santa Clara County
(City of Santa Clara Civic Center, 1509 Warburton Avenue, Santa Clara, CA 95050—location)
1053 South White Road (mailing address)
San Jose, CA 95127
(408) 926-1165; (408) 248-ARTS (24-hour message)
meetings: first Sun
Pub. *Los Fundadores* (California's Spanish/Mexican period, genealogy of early California; articles about the Hispanic progenitors of California; early American pioneers, recognition of Native Americans), quarterly
$11.00 per year membership; free queries for members

Los Pobladores 200
2830 East 56th Way
Long Beach, CA 90805

Mendocino Historical Research, Inc.
Kelley House Museum
(45007 Albion Street—location)
PO Box 922 (mailing address)
Mendocino, CA 95460
(707) 937-5791
Pat Turner, Executive Director
Museum: Mon & Fri–Sun 1:00–4:00; Office: Tue–Fri 9:00–4:00
Pub. *Mendocino Historical Review*, annually, $15.00 per issue
(Mendocino Coast, Mendocino and adjacent coastal towns; archival materials, genealogical records)
$35.00 per year membership

Mission Inn Foundation
Mission Inn Museum
3739 Sixth Street
Riverside, CA 92501
(909) 781-8241
Knox Mellon, Ph.D., Executive Director
Pub. *Atrio* (primarily historical, not genealogical)

Mission San Miguel
(801 Mission Street—location)
PO Box 69 (mailing address)
San Miguel, CA 93451
(805) 467-3256
(primarily historical, not genealogical)

Modern Ancestors
PO Box 1217

Salida, CA 95368
(209) 521-9830
Susan K. Park

Mother Colony Household, Inc.
(685 North Helena, Anaheim, CA
92805—location)
PO Box 3246 (mailing address)
Anaheim, CA 92803
(949) 854-1115
Harold Bastruf, President
Pub. *The Grapefine*, three times per year
(preserves Anaheim history by support of
museums, history rooms, history
programs, construction of historical place
markers)
$240.00 membership

William Penn Mott, Jr., Training Center
(837 Asilomar Boulevard—location)
PO Box 699 (mailing address)
Pacific Grove, CA 93950
(831) 649-2954

NORCAL Genealogy Index
yvonne@sonic.net
http://hompages.rootsweb.com/~yvonne/
NORCAL_index
Yvonne Bowers
(hosts email exchange subscription)

Old Mission San Luis Obispo de Tolosa
782 Monterey
San Luis Obispo, CA 93401
(805) 543-1034
(primarily historical, not genealogical)

Olompali State Historic Park
PO Box 510
Novato, CA 94948
(415) 892-3383
Ronald Brean, District Superintendent
(primarily site preservation, rather than
genealogical)

Oregon-California Trails Association
(see Miscellaneous, Part 4)

The Pardee Home Foundation
672 11th Street
Oakland, CA 94607
(510) 444-2187
David Casebolt, Historic Site Administrator
(primarily historical, not genealogical)

Petaluma Adobe State Historic Park
3325 Adobe Road
Petaluma, CA 94952
(707) 762-4871
Larry Costa, State Park Ranger I
10:00–5:00
(not primarily genealogical)

Portola Expedition Foundation
(1700 West Hillsdale Boulevard, San Mateo,
CA 94402—location)
355 Erica Drive (mailing address)
South San Francisco, CA 94080-4131
(650) 583-0424
Judge E. J. de Larios, Retired
(temporarily inactive)

Rancho Los Cerritos Historic Site
4600 Virginia Road
Long Beach, CA 90807
(562) 424-9423
Ellen Calomiris, Museum Administrator
(primarily site operation, not genealogical)

**The Ronald Reagan Presidential Library
and Museum**
40 Presidential Drive

Simi Valley, CA 93065
(805) 522-8444; (800) 410-8354; (805) 522-
9621 FAX
library@reagan.nara.gov
http://www.reagan.utexas.edu
Museum: Mon–Sun 10:00–5:00; Library
Research Room: Mon–Fri 9:00–5:00
(primarily historical, not genealogical)
museum admission: $5.00

**Sacramento Trust for Historic
Preservation**
710 Coronado Boulevard
Sacramento, CA 95825
(primarily historical, not genealogical)

San Francisco Genealogy
ron@sfgenealogy.com
http://www.sfgenealogy.com/sf
Pamela Storm Wolfskill; Ron Filion

**Santa Barbara Trust for Historic
Preservation**
(123 East Canon Perdido, Santa Barbara, CA
93101—location)
PO Box 388 (mailing address)
Santa Barbara, CA 93102
(805) 965-0093; (805) 568-1999 FAX
http://www.sbthp.org
Jarrell C. Jackman, Ph.D., Executive Director
daily 10:30–4:30
Pub. *La Campana*, quarterly ("Scholarly
publication covering a range of historical
subjects," not primarily genealogical.)
$30.00–$1,000.00 per year membership

Santa Cruz Mission State Historic Park
144 School Street
Santa Cruz, CA 95060-3726
(831) 425-5849

Shasta State Historic Park
PO Box 2430
Shasta, CA 96087

Society of California Archivists
ASUC Store, Box 605, Telegraph Avenue
and Berkeley Way
Berkeley, CA 94720-4510
(714) 278-7288
dhansen@wahoo.sjsu.edu
http:www.calarchivists.org
Dr. Debra Hansen
Mon–Fri 8:30–5:00
Pub. *Directory of Archival and Manuscript
Repositories in California* (lists more than
1,000 repositories throughout the state),
about every five years, $49.00 postpaid
for fourth edition, allow four to six weeks
for delivery

Sonoma League for Historic Preservation
Sonoma State Historic Park
(129 East Spain Street—location)
PO Box 766 (mailing address)
Sonoma, CA 95476
(707) 938-1519
Larry Ferri, District Superintendent
(primarily historical, not genealogical)

**Sourisseau Academy for California State
and Local History**
San Jose State University
San Jose, CA 95192
(408) 924-6510
glaffey@email.sjsu.edu
Glory Anne Laffey, Executive Secretary
by appointment

Stanford House State Historic Park
802 N Street
Sacramento, CA 95814

(916) 324-7405
Patricia Turse, Lead Guide
Pub. *Stanford House Post* (primarily
historical, not genealogical)

Sutter's Fort State Historic Park
2701 L Street
Sacramento, CA 95814
(916) 445-4422
Jeffery Jones, Lead Ranger
(primarily historical, not genealogical)

Texas State Historical Association
Southwestern Historical Quarterly
(see Texas, Part 2)

University of Arizona Press
Journal of the Southwest
(see Arizona, Part 2)

University of California Press
2120 Berkeley Way
Berkeley, CA 94720
(510) 642-4262 (Customer Service); (510)
642-4247 (Office); (800) 822-6657
(Orders); (510) 643-7127 FAX
Judy Lucietta, Customer Service Manager
Pub. *Pacific Historical Review*, quarterly

**Weaverville Joss House State Historic
Park**
PO Box 1217
Weaverville, CA 96093-1217
Fred Meyer, State Park Ranger I
(primarily historical, not genealogical)

Wells Fargo Bank History Department
475 Sansome Street
San Francisco, CA 94111
(415) 396-4157
(primarily historical, not genealogical)

**San Francisco Corral, Westerners
International**
201 Homer Avenue
Palo Alto, CA 94301
(650) 327-2717

Los Angeles Corral of Westerners
1506 Linda Rosa Avenue
Los Angeles, CA 90041

Stockton Corral of Westerners
PO Box 1315
Stockton, CA 95201
Joseph C. Elliff, Jr., Sheriff
Pub. *The Far Westerner*

zpub San Francisco
editor@zpub.com
http://www.zpub.com/sf/history (History of
San Francisco: Index)
Richard Petersen
(links, Q&A forum, and San Francisco-
history email list)

Colorado

Archives and Libraries with Holdings in Genealogy

State Archives and Library

Colorado State Archives
Department of Personnel
1313 Sherman Street, Room #1B-20
Denver, CO 80203
(303) 866-2358; (303) 866-2390; (303) 866-2257 FAX
archives@state.co.us
http://www.colorado.gov/dpa/doit/archives
Terry Ketelsen, State Archivist
Mon–Fri 9:00–4:45 except holidays
research: $25.00 for first item, $10.00 for each additional item, plus copying costs

Colorado State Library
State Office Building, 201 East Colfax Avenue
Denver, CO 80203-1799
(303) 866-6728; (303) 830-0793 FAX
crocker_m@cde.state.co.us
http://www.cde.state.co.us/index_library.htm
Maureen K. Crocker, State Publications Librarian
Mon–Fri 8:00–5:00
(not a statewide library or archives, does not have materials of use to genealogists; refer to Division of Archives and Public Records)

State Historical Society

Colorado Historical Society
Stephen H. Hart Library
1300 Broadway
Denver, CO 80203-2137
(303) 866-2305; (303) 866-3682
information@chs.state.co.us;
  membership@chs.state.co.us,
  research@chs.state.co.us
http://www.coloradohistory.org
Rebecca Lintz, Acting Director, Collections Services
Tue–Sat 10:00–4:30
Pub. *Colorado Heritage*, quarterly; *History NOW*, monthly; *Colorado History*, irregularly
$40.00 per year membership; research: $20.00 for ½ hour search time (includes copies and postage)

City, County and Regional Archives and Libraries
(A more exhaustive list of public and academic libraries can be found at http://www.cde.state.co.us/edulibdir/directory_10.pdf, http://www.public libraries. com/colorado.htm, or http://www.stuttersfa.org/library/ref_co.htm.)

Adams State College Library
Nielsen Library
San Luis Valley Room
208 Edgemont Boulevard
Alamosa, CO 81102
(719) 587-7781; (719) 587-7590 FAX
dlmachad@adams.edu; asclib3@adams.edu
http://www.library.adams.edu/library
Dianne Machado, Library Director
Mon–Thur 8:00–10:00, Fri 8:00–5:00, Sat 10:00–6:00, Sun 1:00–9:00
(Colorado, San Luis Valley, northern New Mexico)

Alamosa/Southern Peaks Public Library

423 Fourth Street
Alamosa, CO 81101-2601
(719) 589-6592; (719) 589-3786 FAX
gen2sppl@yahoo.com; sppl@amigo.net
Edith Woodward, Genealogy Clerk;
  Margaret Morris, Director

Arvada Center for the Arts and Humanities Museum
6901 Wadsworth Boulevard
Arvada, CO 80003
(303) 431-3080

Auraria Library
Lawrence at 11th Street
Denver, CO 80204
(303) 556-8373; (303) 556-3528 FAX
ftapp@carbon.cudenver.edu
http://www.cudenver.edu/public/library
(archives and special collection; manuscript collections)

Aurora History Museum
15001 East Alameda Parkway
Aurora, CO 80012
(303) 739-6660
http://www.ci.aurora.co.us/community/history_Museum/History_Museum.cfm

Aurora Public Library
14949 East Alameda Parkway
Aurora, CO 80012-9003
(303) 739-6600; (303) 739-6579 FAX
library@auroragov.org;
  byager@ci.aurora.co.us
http://auroralibrary.org
Bette Yager, Information Services Librarian
Mon–Thur 9:00–9:00, Fri–Sat 9:00–5:00, Sun 12:30–6:00

Littleton/Edwin A. Bemis Public Library
6014 South Datura Street
Littleton, CO 80120-2636
(303) 795-3961; (303) 795-3996 FAX
libms@littletongov.org
http://www.littletongov.org/bemis
Phyllis Larison, Head of Adult Services
Mon–Thur 9:00–9:00, Fri–Sat 9:00–5:00
(genealogy collection includes books, microfilm, periodicals)

Buena Vista Heritage Museum
(109 West Main—location)
PO Box 1414 (mailing address)
Buena Vista, CO 81211
(719) 395-2572; (719) 395-8458
Suzanne Kelley, Treasurer

Buena Vista Public Library
(131 Linderman Avenue—location)
PO Box 2019 (mailing address)
Buena Vista, CO 81211-2019
(719) 395-8700; (719) 395-6426 FAX
Gail Nottingham, Director

Cañon City Public Library
Local History Center
516 Macon Avenue
Cañon City, CO 81212-3380
(719) 269-9020; (719) 269-9031 FAX
localhistorycenter@canoncity.org
http://ccpl.lib.co.us/lhc.html

Carnegie Branch Library for Local History
1125 Pine Street
Boulder, CO 80302
(303) 441-3110 voice & FAX
hallw@boulder.lib.co.us
http://www.boulder.lib.co.us
Wendy Hall, Manager
Mon 1:00–9:00, Tue & Thur–Sat

11:00–5:00, Wed 9:00–5:00
("200,000 photographs, 700,000 documents, 4,500 books, 75 periodicals. Photograph and document collections pertain to Boulder County history including diaries, letters, maps, newspaper clippings, papers of pioneer families and businesses, records of churches, clubs and mining districts. Over 1,000 oral history interviews of long-time Bounder County residents. The Carnegie Library also houses the collection of Boulder Genealogical Society. Resources include military, foreign, immigration and individual state materials and family publications. Current and past publications from various genealogical societies.")

Colorado Chautauqua Association
Archive and History Room
Administration Building
900 Baseline Road
Boulder, CO 80302
(303) 442-3282; (303) 545-6924; (303) 440-7666; (303) 449-0790 FAX
bob@chautauqua.com
http://www.chautauqua.com
Bob D'Alessandro, Executive Director

Colorado City Historical Museum
183 West Third Street
Colorado City, CO 79512
(915) 728-8285

Colorado College
Charles Leaming Tutt Library
Special Collections and Archives
1021 North Cascade
Colorado Springs, CO 80903-2165
(719) 389-6668; (719) 389-6859 FAX
http://www.cc.colorado.edu/library/specialcollections/special.html
Virginia R. Kiefer, Curator
weekdays 9:00–noon & 1:00–4:00
(specializes in "persons who have been on the Colorado College faculty or in some way connected to the Colorado College"; Colorado and Pikes Peak Region Collection)

Colorado Springs Museum
215 South Tejon Street
Colorado Springs, CO 80903
(719) 578-6650; (719) 578-6718
Leah M. Davis, Archivist
Pub. *Update*
(35,000 historic photographs; manuscript repository)

Colorado State University
Morgan Library
Archives/Special Collections
Fort Collins, CO 80523
(970) 491-3977 (Information; (970) 491-1841 (Social Sciences/Humanities; (970) 491-1882 (Government Documents); (970) 491-1844 (Archives); (970) 491-1838 (Interim Assistant Dean); (970) 491-1195 FAX
cbush@manta.colostate.edu
http://manta.library.colostate.edu
Carmel Bush, Interim Assistant Dean, Library Operations
Mon–Fri 7:00–5:00

Cripple Creek District Museum, Inc.
(Fifth and Bennett Avenue—location)
PO Box 1210 (mailing address)
Cripple Creek, CO 80813
(719) 689-2634
Erik C. Swanson, Director

summer 9:30–5:50; winter: weekends only
("county cemetery records, city directories:
Cripple Creek, Victor, Teller County")
research done for a donation

Denver Public Library
Western History and Genealogy
10 West 14th Avenue Parkway
Denver, CO 80204-2731
(720) 865-1820 (Reference); (720) 865-1880
voice & FAX
http://www.denver.lib.co.us
James K. Jeffrey, Genealogy Collection
Specialist; Jim X. Kroll, Manager
Mon–Wed 10:00–9:00, Thur–Sat
10:00–5:30, Sun 1:00–5:00
(national in scope; specialty: Colorado,
Rocky Mountain West, Hispanic, Native
American)

Lula W. Dorsey Museum
2515 Tunnel Road
Estes Park, CO 80517
(970) 586-3341, ext. 1137

Douglas Public Library District
Local History Collection
(Phillips S. Miller Library—location)
100 South Wilcox (mailing address)
Castle Rock, CO 80104
(303) 814-0795; (303) 660-1942 FAX
sboyd@dclibraries.org
http://history.dpld.org
Shaun Boyd, Archivist; Johanna Harden,
Archivist
Mon–Fri 9:00–5:00, and by appointment

Estes Park Public Library
(335 East Elkhorn Avenue—location)
PO Box 1687 (mailing address)
Estes Park, CO 80517-1687
(970) 586-8116; (970) 586-0189 FAX
evolz@estes.lib.co.us
http://estes.lib.co.us
Ed Volz, Director

Fort Collins Museum
Colorado-Wyoming Association of Museums
200 Mathews Street
Fort Collins, CO 80524
(970) 221-6738
(primarily historical, not genealogical)

**Fort Collins Public Library—Local
History Archive**
201 Peterson Street
Fort Collins, CO 80524-2990
(970) 221-6688 (Local Historian); (970)
221-6380 (Reference); (970) 416-2140
FAX
massey@julip.fcgov.com
http://fcgov.com/library
Rheba Massey, Local History Librarian
by appointment Mon noon–4:30
& 6:00–9:00, Wed & Fri 10:00–5:00
(specializes in Fort Collins, Larimer County
and Colorado history: city directories,
newspapers, oral history transcripts,
historic photograph collection,
biographical and subject files, historical
maps, Colorado books and magazines,
cemetery records, obituary/anniversary
files, yearbooks, tax assessor records)
copies: 10¢ each ($2.00 minimum)

Fort Lewis College
Center of Southwest Studies
The Robert Delaney Southwest Research
Library
1000 Rim Drive
Durango, CO 81301-3999
(970) 247-7456

Ellison_T@fortlewis.edu
http://swcenter.fortlewis.edu
Todd Ellison, Archivist; Richard N. Ellis,
Ph.D., Archivist/Assistant Professor
Mon–Thur 11:00–8:00, Fri 11:00–4:00, Sun
3:00–7:00 (more limited hours during
academic breaks, May–Aug)
("Collection strengths include ethnographic
and historic records and artifacts relating
to Native Americans [especially their U.S.
government relations] and other peoples
of the southwest; local and regional
historic newspapers, U.S. census records
for the Four Corners States, census
records for Indians of North America, and
records of businesses and organizations of
southwest Colorado; center's holdings
include over 13,000 volumes of published
research material concerning the
southwest, over 1,200 linear shelf feet of
manuscripts and unbound printed
materials, over 5,000 rolls of historic
microfilm, and more than 15,000 historic
photos; we require a weekday's advance
notice for retrieval of microfilm
materials")

Fort Morgan Museum
(414 Main Street—location)
PO Box 184 (mailing address)
Fort Morgan, CO 80701
(970) 867-6331
Marne Jurgemeyer, Director
Pub. *Museum Monitor*
(genealogical services)

Friend Genealogy Library
1448 Que Street
Penrose, CO 81240

Gem Village Museum
Route 1
Bayfield, CO 81122
(970) 884-2811

**Golden Library Branch of Jefferson
County Public Library**
1019 10th Street
Golden, CO 80401
(303) 279-4585; (303) 277-0109 FAX
kathyh@jefferson.lib.co.us
http://jefferson.lib.co.us
Kathy Husband, Library Manager
Mon–Thur 10:00–9:00, Fri–Sat 10:00–5:00,
Sun noon–5:00
("local newspaper, *Golden Transcript*, on
microfilm, holdings back to 1867")

City of Greeley Museums
City Complex at Seventh Street
Greeley, CO 80631
(970) 350-9220
Peggy Ford, Acting Supervisor
(genealogical services)

Gunnison County Public Library
Ann Zugelder Public Library Building
307 North Wisconsin
Gunnison, CO 81230-2627
(970) 641-3485; (970) 641-4653 FAX
webmaster@co.gunnison.co.us
http://www.co.gunnison.co.us/library/
library.html
Peggy Martin, Director
Mon, Wed & Fri 10:00–5:30, Tue & Thur
10:00–8:00, Sat 10:00–4:00

Lakewood Library
Jefferson County Public Library
10200 West 20th Avenue
Lakewood, CO 80215-1483
(303) 232-7833; (303) 232-9507; (303) 275-

2234 FAX
brettl@jefferson.lib.co.us
http://jefferson.lib.co.us
Brett Lear, Library Manager
Mon–Thur 10:00–9:00, Fri–Sat 10:00–5:00,
Sun noon–5:00
(collection supported by Foothills
Genealogical Society of Colorado)

Lakewood's Heritage Center
797 South Wadsworth Boulevard
Lakewood, CO 80215
(303) 987-7850; (303) 987-7851 FAX
hca@lakewood.org
http://www.lakewood.org/index.cfm?&
includ=/Culture/heritagecenter.cfm
Kristen Anderson, Site and Collection
Administrator
Tours on the hour, Tue–Fri 10:00–3:00,
Sat–Sun noon–3:00
("History museum; [photo and document]
archives have local interest.")
$40.00+ per year membership; admission:
$3.00 for adults

Littleton Historical Museum
6028 South Galleys
Littleton, CO 80120
(303) 795-3850
Robert McQuarie, Director
(reference library)

Longmont Public Library
409 Fourth Avenue
Longmont, CO 80501-6006
(303) 651-8470; (303) 651-8911 FAX
tony.brewer@ci.longmont.co.us
http://ci.longmont.co.us/library/index.htm
E. A. Brewer, Library Director
Mon–Thur 9:00–9:00, Fri–Sat 9:00–6:00
(Longmont and Saint Vrain Valley)

Loveland Museum/Gallery
Fifth and Lincoln
Loveland, CO 80537
(970) 962-2410; (970) 962-2910 FAX
Susan P. Ison, Director of Cultural Services
Tue–Wed & Fri 10:00–5:00, Thur
10:00–9:00, Sat 10:00–4:00, Sun
noon–4:00

Loveland Public Library
300 North Adams
Loveland, CO 80537-5754
(970) 962-2665; (970) 962-2905 FAX
schmit@ci.loveland.co.us
http://www.ci.loveland.co.us/library/
libmain.htm
Carol Hammang, Reference Librarian
Mon–Thur 10:00–9:00, Fri–Sat 10:00–6:00,
Sun (Sept–May) 1:00–5:00

McAllister House Museum
(see National Society of the Colonial Dames,
Colorado, Lineage, Hereditary and Patriotic
Societies, Part 4)

Mesa County Public Library District
(530 Grand Avenue—location)
PO Box 20000-5019 (mailing address)
Grand Junction, CO 81502-5019
(970) 241-5251; (970) 243-4744 FAX
mcpldref@colosys.net
http://www.mcpld.org
Kay Oxer, Head Reference Librarian
Mon–Thur 9:00–9:00, Fri–Sat 9:00–5:00,
Sun (Sept–May) 1:00–5:00

Museum of Northwest Colorado
590 Yampa Avenue
Craig, CO 81625
(970) 824-6360; (970) 824-7175 FAX

http://www.nadga.com/museum
Dan Davidson, Director
Mon–Sat 10:00–5:00
(local history museum; obituaries, marriages, some births, some land records, photos)

Museum of the Great Plains
(see Oklahoma, Part 2)

Museum of Western Colorado
Archives and Library
(233 South Fifth, Grand Junction, CO 81501—location)
PO Box 20000-5020 (mailing address)
Grand Junction, CO 81502-5020
(970) 242-0971; (970) 242-3960 FAX
judypa@colosys.net
http://www.mwc.mus.co.us
Judy A. Prosser-Armstrong, Librarian/Archivist; Janice V. McLean, Director
Tue–Sat 10:00–4:00, and by appointment
Pub. *Museum Times*, monthly
(genealogy and western Colorado history)
$25.00 per year membership

Pikes Peak Library District
Local History and Genealogy
Penrose Public Library-Palmer Wing
(20 North Cascade, Colorado Springs, CO 80903-1690—location)
PO Box 1579 (mailing address)
Colorado Springs, CO 80901
(719) 531-6333, ext. 2252; (719) 528-5289 FAX
http://library.ppld.org
Ree Mobley, Local History and Genealogy Librarian
Mon–Thur 10:00–9:00, Fri–Sat 10:00–6:00
(Colorado Springs, El Paso County, Pikes Peak region and Colorado)
copies: 10¢ each for 8½" x 10" sheets, 20¢ each for 11" x 14" or 11" x 17" sheets, plus postage and handling

Pueblo City-County Library District
100 East Abriendo Avenue
Pueblo, CO 81004-4290
(719) 562-5626; (719) 562-5610 FAX
noreen@pueblolibrary.org
http://pueblolibrary.org
Noreen Riffe, Special Collections Librarian
Mon–Thur 9:00–9:00, Fri–Sat 9:00–6:00, Sun 1:00–5:00
("Specializes in southeastern Colorado history. We are at a temporary location until probably Sept. 2003, as a new building is being built on the old site. Phone numbers remain the same. Temporary address is 701 Court Street, Pueblo, CO 81003.")

Rio Grande County Museum and Cultural Center
580 Oak Street
Del Norte, CO 81132
(719) 657-2847; (719) 657-2627 FAX
rgcm@amigo.net
http://www.rgcm.org
Dr. A. J. Taylor and Fred M. Oglesby, Co-Directors
winter: Tue–Sat noon–5:00; summer: Tue–Sat 10:00–5:00
Pub. *The Museum Muse*, bimonthly
("Although the Museum does have a reference library with local holdings, staff size is limited. Advance notice of at least two weeks of your planned arrival date and time, and your research interests is advisable.")
$10.00 per year membership; admission: $1.00 for adults

Salida Museum
Salida Chamber of Commerce
406 West Rainbow Boulevard
Salida, CO 81201
(719) 539-2068

Salida Regional Library
405 East Street
Salida, CO 81201
(719) 539-4826; (719) 539-2318 FAX
jdonlan@salidalibrary.org
http://www.salidalibrary.org
Jeffrey P. Donlan, Library Director

San Luis Museum Cultural and Commercial Center
401 Church Place
San Luis, CO 81152
(719) 672-3611
Juanita Gurule, Director
(research center)

Ruby M. Sisson Memorial Library
Genealogy Section
(811 San Juan—location)
PO Box 849 (mailing address)
Pagosa Springs, CO 81147-0849
(970) 264-2208; (970) 264-4764 FAX
lbright@frontier.net
http://www.frontier.net/~ruby
Lenore Bright, Director
Mon–Fri 10:00–5:00
$10.00 per year membership

Stagecoach Library for Genealogical Research
(see Lending Libraries, Part 4)

Standley Lake Library
Jefferson County Public Library
8485 Kipling Street
Arvada, CO 80004-1237
(303) 456-0806; (303) 940-4501 FAX
elenar@jefferson.lib.co.us
http://jefferson.lib.co.us
Elena Rosenfeld, Library Manager

University of Colorado, Boulder
University Libraries
Archives
Norlin Library
(1157 18th Street—location)
Campus PO Box 184 (mailing address)
Boulder, CO 80309-0184
(303) 492-7242; (303) 492-3960 FAX
montgomb@spot.colorado.edu
http://www-libraries.colorado.edu
Mon–Fri 11:00–5:00
(Western American Collection collects manuscript material on the settlement and growth of the west; Labor Collection; Politics Collection; University of Colorado Archives)

University of Northern Colorado
James A. Michener Library
Archives/Special Collections
Greeley, CO 80639-0091
(970) 351-2854; (970) 351-2540
http://www.unco.edu/library/archives.htm
Archivist
Mon–Fri 1:00–5:00
Pub. *Archives Studies*

University of Utah Marriott Library
(see Utah, Part 2)

Weld Library District
Centennial Park Branch Library
2227 23rd Avenue
Greeley, CO 80634-6632
(970) 506-8600 (Main number); (970) 506-

8601 FAX
mrlangle@weld.lib.co.us
http://www.weld.lib.co.us
Margaret Langley, Reference Librarian
Mon–Fri 9:00–9:00, Sat 9:00–6:00
(Collection of materials on German Russians. Also houses Weld County Genealogical Society's resources.)

Wellington Public Library
(3800 Wilson Avenue—location)
PO Box 416 (mailing address)
Wellington, CO 80549-0416
(970) 568-3040; (970) 568-9713 FAX
Diane Montgomery, Director

Western Heritage Center
(see Montana, Part 2)

Historical Societies—Local and Regional

Adams County Historical Society
Adams County Museum and Cultural Center
9601 Henderson Road
Brighton, CO 80601
(303) 659-7103
Patricia Erge, Administrator
10:00–4:30
Pub. *Hi-Story News*, bimonthly

American Historical Association, Pacific Coast Branch
(see California, Part 2)

American West Research Center and Historical Society, Inc.
(see Ohio, Part 2)

Arkansas River Historical Society Museum
(see Oklahoma, Part 2)

Arvada Historical Society
PO Box 419
Arvada, CO 80001
Robert C. Walker, Secretary
Pub. *Arvada Historian*, quarterly
$10.00 per year membership

Aspen Historical Society
620 West Bleeker Street
Aspen, CO 81611
(970) 925-3721
Carl Bergman, President, Board of Directors
Pub. *AHS Newsletter*
(Pitkin County)

Aurora Historical Society
415 Oswego Street
Aurora, CO 80010
(303) 360-8545
Gladys Metcalf
Pub. *AHS Newsletter*

Aurora History Museum
14949 East Alameda Parkway
Aurora, CO 80012
(303) 739-6640; (303) 739-6586 FAX
CulturalServices@auroragov.org
http://www.auroragov.org/stellent/idcplg?
IdcService=SS_GET_PAGE&nodeId=745&ssSourceNodeId=621

Berthoud Historical Society, Inc.
(see Little Thompson Valley Pioneer Museum, below)

Boulder Historical Society and Museum
Boulder Museum of History
1206 Euclid Avenue

Boulder, CO 80302
(303) 449-3464; (303) 938-8322 FAX
info@boulderhistory.org;
 ngeyer@boulderhistory.org
http://www.boulderhistorymuseum.org
Nancy Geyer, Executive Director
Tue–Fri 11:00–4:00, Sat–Sun noon–4:00
Pub. *Newsletter*, quarterly
("Select photographs and manuscripts from
 the Boulder Historical Society's
 remarkable collections are displayed in
 Museum's exhibits; however, the bulk of
 these collections are housed at the
 Carnegie Branch Library for Local
 History.")
$20.00 per year membership; museum
 admission: $1.00 donation

**Cherry Creek Valley Historical Society,
Inc.**
4950 South Laredo Street
Aurora, CO 80015
(303) 699-5145
Michael McCarthy, President
by appointment
Pub. *The Quill*, quarterly
$5.00 per year membership

**Clear Creek Canyon Historical Society of
Chaffee County, Inc.**
PO Box 2181
Granite, CO 81228
(719) 486-2942

**Columbine Genealogical and Historical
Society, Inc.**
(see Genealogical Societies—Local and
Regional, below)

Comanche Crossing Historical Society
PO Box 647
Strasburg, CO 80136-0647
(303) 622-4668

Creede Historical Society
PO Box 608
Creede, CO 81130
Janis Jacobs, President
Library: Tue 10:00–2:00, Wed (summer)
 10:00–2:00, and by appointment;
 Museum: Memorial Day–Labor Day:
 Mon–Sun 10:00–4:00
(Creede and Mineral County)
$10.00 per year membership; research:
 donation

Deer Trail Pioneer Historical Society
PO Box 176
Deer Trail, CO 80105
(303) 769-4577
Clara Hanks, Curator

Delta County Historical Society
251 Meeker Street
Delta, CO 81416
(970) 874-8721
deltamuseum@aol.com
http://deltamuseum.com
Bernice Musser, President; James K. Wetzel,
 Director
Museum: May–Sept: Tue–Sat 10:00–4:00;
 Oct–Apr: Wed & Sat 10:00–4:00
museum admission: $2.00 for adults

Douglas County Historical Society
620 Lewis
Castle Rock, CO 80104

Eagle Valley Historical Society
PO Box 192
Eagle, CO 81631
(970) 845-7741

japotter@vail.net
Joann Potter, Genealogist for Three Bells
 Genealogy and Eagle Valley Historical
 Society
Pub. *Eagle Valley Enterprise*

East Yuma County Historical Society
(205 East Third Street—location)
PO Box 161 (mailing address)
Wray, CO 80758
(970) 332-5063
Patricia E. Walborn, Director
Tue–Sat 10:00–5:00
Pub. *Pictorgraph*, bimonthly
$5.00 per year membership, additional $5.00
 per year membership in genealogical
 society; admission: $1.00 for adults

**Eastern Colorado Historical Society
(Cheyenne County)**
85 West Second Street
c/o 43433 Road CC
Cheyenne Wells, CO 80810
(719) 767-5907
Karlene McKean, Librarian
afternoons, Memorial Day–Labor Day

Estes Park Area Historical Museum
(200 Fourth Street—location)
PO Box 1691 (mailing address)
Estes Park, CO 80517
(970) 586-6256; (970) 577-3768 FAX
blatanich@estes.org
http://www.estesnet.com/museum
Betty Kilsdonk, Director; Becky Latanich,
 Curator
May–Oct: daily, and by appointment
Pub. *Museum Pieces*, quarterly
$15.00 per year membership; research: cost
 of photocopies

**Florence Pioneer Museum and Historical
Society**
Price Pioneer Museum
Pikes Peak Avenue and Front Street
Florence, CO 81226

Fort Collins Historical Society
121 North Grant Avenue
Fort Collins, CO 80521

Fort Sedgewick Historical Society
114 East First
Julesburg, CO 80737

Fremont-Custer Historical Society, Inc.
PO Box 965
Canon City, CO 81212

Friends of Historic Trinidad, Inc.
1208 Logan
Denver, CO 80203
(303) 832-7165

Frisco Historical Society
(120 Main Street—location)
PO Box 820 (mailing address)
Frisco, CO 80443
(970) 668-3428
Karen Mack, Museum Manager
Tue–Sat 11:00–4:00, Sun (after Memorial
 Day) 11:00–4:00
Pub. *Frisco Historical Society Newsletter*,
 quarterly
$10.00 per year membership

**Frontier Historical Society (Garfield
County)**
1001 Colorado Avenue
Glenwood Springs, CO 81601
(970) 945-4448; (970) 384-2477 FAX
history@rof.net

Cindy Cochran, Director
1 Oct–30 Apr: Mon & Thur–Sat 1:00–4:00;
 1 May–1 Oct: Mon–Sat 11:00–4:00
$25.00 per year membership; research:
 $10.00 per hour

The Gilpin County Historical Society
Gilpin County Museum
PO Box 247
Central City, CO 80427-0247
(303) 582-5283
James J. Prochaska, P.E., Executive Director
Memorial Day–Labor Day: Mon–Sun
 11:00–4:00; winter: Mon & Fri 8:00–6:00

Grand County Historical Association
(110 Byers Avenue—location)
PO Box 165 (mailing address)
Hot Sulphur Springs, CO 80451
(970) 725-3939; (970) 725-0129 FAX
gcha@grandcountymuseum.com
http://grandcountymuseum.com
Don Woster, Director
summer: Tue–Sat 10:00–5:00, Sun
 1:00–5:00; winter: Tue–Sat 10:00–5:00
Pub. *Grand County Historical Association
 Journal*, annually
("Best exhibits available in small museum
 setting!" "Historic buildings, history
 exhibits, photo collection")
$20.00–$100.00 per year membership;
 search fees depend on subject

Grand Lake Area Historical Society
(Pitkin Street—location)
PO Box 656 (mailing address)
Grand Lake, CO 80447
(970) 627-9277
Dr. Richard Leinbach, President
Memorial Day to Labor Day: 11:00–5:00
Pub. *GLAHS Newsletter*, annually
$5.00 per year membership

**Gunnison County Pioneer and Historical
Society**
(South Adams Street—location)
696 County Road 16 (mailing address)
Gunnison, CO 81230
(970) 641-0740
Gus Grosland, President
summer 9:00–5:00
("family research-limited; we do not have
 staff for general research")
research: expenses only

Hinsdale County Historical Society
(Second and Silver Streets—location)
PO Box 353 (mailing address)
Lake City, CO 81235

Hotchkiss-Crawford Historical Society
(Second and Hotchkiss Avenue—location)
PO Box 727 (mailing address)
Hotchkiss, CO 81419
(970) 872-4858
Julie Littlefield, President
summer: Fri 1:00–4:00; tours by
 appointment
$10.00 per year membership; admission:
 $10.00

Huerfano County Historical Society
PO Box 428
Laveta, CO 81055
Christine R. Schmidt, President, Board of
 Directors
("We have no staff who specifically do
 genealogy; requests are done by
 volunteers when available; we can not
 offer this service as always available.")

Jefferson County Historical Commission

PO Box 659
Morrison, CO 80468
Pub. *Historically Jeffco*, semiannually

Jefferson County Historical Society
(Hiwan Homestead Museum, 4208 South
Timbervale Drive—location)
PO Box 703 (mailing address)
Evergreen, CO 80439
(303) 674-5934; (303) 674-6262 (Museum)
Jo Ann Dunn, President; Jennifer Karber,
Museum Administrator
Wed–Thur (June–Aug) 10:00–2:00;
Museum: Tue–Sun noon–5:00, Tue–Sun
(summer) 11:00–5:00
Pub. *The Record*, quarterly
$10.00 per year membership

La Plata County Historical Society
Animas Museum
(31st Street and West Second
Avenue—location)
PO Box 3384 (mailing address)
Durango, CO 81302
(970) 259-2402
Robert McDaniel, Museum Director
May–Oct: Mon–Sat 10:00–6:00; Oct–Apr:
by appointment
Pub. *Artifacts*, quarterly
(photo archives and research library:
Durango, La Plata County, southwest
Colorado; gift shop specializing in used,
out-of-print and rare books)
$150.00–$1,500.00 per year membership;
museum admission: $1.75 for adults;
research: negotiable fees

**Lake County Civic Center Association,
Inc.**
(100-102 East Ninth Street—location)
PO Box 962 (mailing address)
Leadville, CO 80461
(719) 486-1878

Leadville Historical Association
206 West Third Street
Leadville, CO 80461
(719) 486-0425
Leroy Wingenbach, President
1:00–4:00; meetings: fifth Mon 7:00
$5.00 per year membership

Lincoln County Historical Society
Lincoln County Hedlund House Museum
(615 Third Avenue—location)
PO Box 115 (mailing address)
Hugo, CO 80821
(719) 743-2485 (weekdays); (719) 743-2233
(after hours); (719) 743-2447 FAX
twbndee@yahoo.com
Terry W. Blevins, Lead Volunteer
Memorial Day–Labor Day: Fri 4:00–7:00,
Sat 1:00–7:00, Sun 1:00–4:00, and off-
hours by appointment
("The museum also is open for private
tours.")
$3.00 per year membership: research:
expenses and additional donation
appreciated

Little Thompson Valley Pioneer Museum
(228 Mountain Avenue—location)
PO Box 225 (mailing address)
Berthoud, CO 80513
(970) 532-2149; (970) 532-2147; (970) 484-
3905 (for appointment)
tvaughan@ci.berthoud.co.us
http://berthoudhistoricalsociety.org/
index.html
Tom Vaughan, Director
Wed–Sun 1:00–5:00
(operated by the Berthoud Historical

Society)

Logan County Historical Society, Inc.
(see Overland Trail Museum [Logan County
Historical Society, Inc.], below)

Lyons Historical Society
(d.b.a. Lyons Redstone Museum)
(340 High Street—location)
PO Box 9 (mailing address)
Lyons, CO 80540
(303) 823-6692; (303) 823-5271; (303) 443-
0084 FAX
LaVern M. Johnson, President
July–Sept: Mon–Sat 9:30–4:30, Sun
12:30–4:30
("Files of the area of Lyons, Colorado; we
are continually working on them and hope
to have more each year.")
$10.00 per year membership; research:
$10.00 for first half hour, $20.00 per hour
thereafter; copies: 50¢ each

Manitou Springs Historical Society
9 Capitol Hill Avenue
Manitou Springs, CO 80829
(719) 685-1011
Robert Yager, Executive Director
summer: 10:00–5:00; spring & fall:
11:00–4:00; winter: noon–3:00

Marble Historical Society
Marble Historical Museum
412 West Main Street
Marble, CO 81623
(970) 945-2824
Oscar D. McCollum, President
Pub. *Marble Chips*, quarterly
(Gunnison County)

Mesa County Historical Society
PO Box 841
Grand Junction, CO 81502
jmoston@aol.com
K. Don Thompson, 1997 President; Juanita
Moston, 1998 President
Pub. *Mesa County Historical Society
Newsletter*, bimonthly
$7.50 per year membership

North Fork Historic Preservation Society
(1600 Highway 187—location)
PO Box 622 (mailing address)
Paonia, CO 81428
(970) 527-3970
Judy Livingston, President
Tue & Thur–Fri 1:00–4:00, and by
appointment
$7.50 per year membership

**Overland Trail Museum (Logan County
Historical Society, Inc.)**
(21053 County Road 26-5/10 [Junction of
Highway 6 and I-76]—location)
PO Box 4000 (mailing address)
Sterling, CO 80751
(970) 522-3895 (Museum); (970) 521-0632
FAX
Anna Mae Hagemeier, Superintendent
1 Apr–31 Oct: Mon–Sat 9:00–5:00, Sun
1:00–5:00, holidays 10:00–5:00; 1
Nov–31 Mar: Tue–Sat 10:00–4:00
("Have some pioneer files and newspapers;
local history museum and files on local
pioneers. Records the greatest migration
of people our country has ever
experienced.")

Palmer Lake Historical Society
PO Box 662
Palmer Lake, CO 80133
Emory Hightower, President

Pioneer Historical Society
(East Ninth Street—location)
PO Box 68 (mailing address)
Las Animas, CO 81054
(719) 456-2005
Ann Smith, Curator
Memorial Day–Labor Day: Mon–Sun
1:00–5:00
research: $10.00

Prowers County Historical Society
Big Timbers Museum
(7515 U.S. Highway 50—location)
PO Box 362 (mailing address)
Lamar, CO 81052
Jeanne Clark, Curator
Mon–Sun 1:30–4:30, and by appointment
$7.00 per year membership

Pueblo County Historical Society
217 South Grand Avenue
Pueblo, CO 81003
(719) 543-6772
pchs_h@yahoo.com
http://griffon.mwsc.edu./~edtch/pueblo.html
George R. Williams, President
Tue–Sat 1:00–4:00
Pub. *Pueblo Lore*, monthly
("The PCHS operates a museum and a
research library, conducts ten monthly
meetings with programs of historical
interest, conducts tours, publishes books,
etc. Historical records, city directories,
school annuals and images of Pueblo,
Southern Colorado and the West are the
library's primary resources. There are also
extensive records of personalities who
have lived or visited this area.")
$20.00 per year membership; research:
queries are answered if possible or routed
to other local sources for assistance

**Rimrock Historical Society of West
Montrose County**
PO Box 305
Naturita, CO 81424
(970) 864-7837
L. S. Zatterstrom, Curator

The Saint Vrain Historical Society, Inc.
(312 Terry Street, Longmont, CO
80501—location)
PO Box 705 (mailing address)
Longmont, CO 80502-0705
(303) 776-1870; (303) 776-5778 FAX
svhsstaff@peakpeak.com
http://stvrainhistoricalsociety.org
Dale S. Bernard, Executive Director
Mon–Thur 8:30–2:30
Pub. *SVHS Newsletter*, bimonthly
("We do not have primary source materials
for genealogical research.")
$20.00 per year membership

San Juan County Historical Society
(1567 Greene Street—location)
PO Box 154 (mailing address)
Silverton, CO 81433
(970) 387-5838
Allen Nossaman, Archive Director
Mon 1:00–6:00, Wed noon–6:00, and by
appointment (recommended)
("General archive and research facility for
San Juan County, Colorado, only")

San Miguel County Historical Society
PO Box 476
Telluride, CO 81435

South Park Historical Foundation
South Park City Museum
(100 Fourth Street [Fourth and Front

Streets]—location)
PO Box 634 (mailing address)
Fairplay, CO 80440
(719) 836-2387
Carol Davis, Director/Curator
Mon–Fri (15 May–15 Oct) 9:00–5:00
(specializes in Park County, Colorado)

Trinidad Historical Society
(1102 Corant Avenue—location)
PO Box 176 (mailing address)
Trinidad, CO 81082

Genealogical Societies

State Genealogical Societies

Colorado Council of Genealogical Societies
PO Box 40270
Denver, CO 80204-0270
(303) 688-9652
charweiler@yahoo.com
http://www.rootsweb.com/~coccgs/index.
htm
Charlotte Weiler, Second Vice President
Pub. *Colorado Council of Genealogical
Societies Newsletter*, quarterly, $10.00 per
year subscription
(a cooperative organization of many
Colorado groups, does not offer direct
services to genealogists)
$10.00 per year Associate membership (open
to all genealogical and historical societies
in Colorado)

Colorado Genealogical Society
PO Box 9218
Denver, CO 80209-0218
(303) 571-1535
info@cogensoc.us
http://www.rootsweb.com/~cocgs
Vern Tomkins, President
Denver Public Library, Western History and
Genealogy: Mon–Wed 10:00–9:00,
Thur–Sat 10:00–5:30, Sun 1:00–5:00
Pub. *The Colorado Genealogist*, quarterly;
*Colorado Genealogical Society
Newsletter*, ten times per year
$20.00 per year membership

Genealogical Societies—Local & Regional

Archuleta County Genealogical Society
PO Box 1611
Pagosa Springs, CO 81147
(970) 264-2645
Margo Butner
Sisson Public Library, Genealogy Section:
Mon–Fri 10:00–5:00
$10.00 per year membership

**The Aurora Genealogical Society of
Colorado**
(1298 Peoria Street—location)
PO Box 31732 (mailing address)
Aurora, CO 80041-0732
(303) 363-8257 (Secretary)
steve@chisp.net
Paul Rawls, Corresponding Secretary; Bill
Stephens, Newsletter Editor
Wed 10:00–4:00; summer and holidays: Wed
10:00–1:00
Pub. *The Aurora Genealogical Society of
Colorado Newsletter*, five times per year
("*Aurora Democrat Newspaper* indexed; we
maintain library")
$8.00 per year membership

Boulder Genealogical Society
PO Box 3246
Boulder, CO 80307-3246
(303) 441-3110 (Library)

boardergensociety@earthlink.net;
bouldergensociety@comcast.net (Carl
Taplin, Webmaster)
http://www.rootsweb.com/~bgs
Mary Ann Looney, President
Carnegie Branch Library for Local History:
Mon 1:00–9:00, Tue & Thur–Sat
11:00–5:00, Wed 9:00–5:00; meetings at
Mountain View Methodist Church, 355
Ponca Place, Boulder, CO 80301
Pub. *Boulder Genealogical Society
Quarterly*; *Boulder Genealogical Society
Newsletter*, quarterly
(worldwide genealogical research)
$20.00 per year membership

Boulder Genealogy Group
856 Applewood Drive
Lafayette, CO 80026
Vella May Blazzard

Brighton Genealogical Society
343 South 21st Avenue
Brighton, CO 80601
beckyburnham@aol.com
Becky Burnham, President

Broomfield Genealogy Society
Broomfield Historical Depot Museum
2201 West 10th Avenue
Broomfield, CO 80020
Gennylarry@att.net
http://www.rootsweb.com/~cobgs
Larry Beck, Secretary
meetings at Broomfield Senior Center: third
Tue 7:00
$12.00 per year membership

**Columbine Genealogical and Historical
Society, Inc.**
PO Box 2074
Centennial, CO 80161-2074
(303) 792-9315 (President)
charpage@attbi.com (Newsletter);
gjmacd2@attbi.com (President)
http://www.rootsweb.com/~cocghs/index.htm
George MacDonald, President
meetings at Lutheran Church of the Holy
Spirit, 6400 South University Boulevard,
Littleton: second & third Tue 1:00
Pub. *Newsletter*, quarterly
$15.00 per year membership

Genealogical Research Society of Durango
2720 Delwood
Durango, CO 81212

**Foothills Genealogical Society of Colorado,
Inc.**
PO Box 150382
Lakewood, CO 80215-0382
(303) 642-7262; (303) 642-3646 FAX
Donna J. Porter, President; Patricia A.
Kemper, Past President and Editor
Pub. *Newsletter*, five times per year; *The
Inquirer*, quarterly
(emphasis on Clear Creek, Gilpin, Jefferson
and Park counties)
$10.00 per year membership

Fore-Kin Trails Genealogical Society
4458 North Townsend
Montrose, CO 81401
(970) 249-8140
Fay Brewer, Corresponding Secretary
Pub. *Uncompahgre Valley Chronicle* (Feb,
May, Aug, Nov), $1.50 per issue
(Montrose County, Colorado)
$12.50 per year membership

Four Corners Genealogy Society
PO Box 2636

Durango, CO 81302

High Country Genealogical Society
601 Willow Wood Lane
Delta, CO 81416-3037
Nadine Lillpop

**High Plains Heritage Genealogical Society
(Morgan County)**
Morgan County Genealogical Society
5775 East El Camino Quinto
Apache Junction, AZ 85219-8808
Elaine V. Rouse-Haskin, President

Historic Georgetown, Inc.
PO Box 667
Georgetown, CO 80444
(303) 569-2840 Denver Metro Live; (303)
674-2625
Jonathan Held, Curator, Collections and
Properties
Mon–Fri 9:00–4:00
(local, county, regional, family, property,
genealogical research)

Larimer County Genealogical Society
(Masonic Temple, 225 West Oak—location)
PO Box 9502 (mailing address)
Fort Collins, CO 80524
(970) 226-6146 (answering machine)
hstetser@direcway.com;
ralarson100@msn.com
http://dick.jymis.com/~lcgs
Carol Stetser, Corresponding Secretary; Bob
Larson, Newlsetter Editor
Pub. *Larimer County Genealogical Society
Newsletter*, bimonthly
$12.00 per year membership; research:
$10.00

Logan County Genealogical Society
PO Box 294
Sterling, CO 80751
Evelyn Camblin

Longmont Genealogical Society
PO Box 6081
Longmont, CO 80501-2077
car_olo7@yahoo.com
http://www.rootsweb.com/~colgs
Carrie Olson, Secretary
meetings at Bethlehem Lutheran Church,
1000 15th Avenue, Longmont: second
Wed 1:00
Pub. *Longmont Heritage*, quarterly
$10.00 per year membership; queries free for
members, $10.00 for nonmembers;
research: requests limited to Longmont or
Boulder County for expenses plus
donation

Mesa County Genealogical Society
PO Box 1506
Grand Junction, CO 81502-1506
Pub. *Mesa Dwellers*, quarterly
$10.00 per year membership

Mountain Genealogists
19637 Hill Drive
Morrison, CO 80465

Ohio Genealogical Society
Colorado Chapter
(see Ohio, Part 2)

Pikes Peak Genealogical Society
PO Box 1262
Colorado Springs, CO 80901
J. Richards, President
Pub. *Pikes Peak Genealogical Society
Newsletter*, quarterly
$10.00 per year membership; research: up to

two hours for $10.00 per hour suggested donation

Prowers County Genealogical Society
(Big Timers Museum and Historical Society, 7515 U.S. Highway 50—location)
PO Box 928 (mailing address)
Lamar, CO 81052-0928
(719) 336-2472
Jeanne Clark, Member/Curator
Mon–Sun 1:30–4:30 (closed Good Friday, Thanksgiving, Christmas and New Year's)
Pub. *Prowers County Genealogical Society Newsletter*, quarterly
$10.00 per year membership

San Luis Valley Genealogical Society
PO Box 911
Alamosa, CO 81101-0911
(719) 589-6592
Dorothy Wilson, Librarian
Tue–Sat 9:00–5:00
Pub. *San Luis Valley Genealogical Journal*, semiannually
(Conejos, Costilla, Alamosa, Rio Grande, Mineral and Saguache counties)
$10.00 per year membership

Sedgewick County Genealogical Society
PO Box 89
Julesburg, CO 80737

Southeastern Colorado Genealogical Society, Inc.
PO Box 4207
Pueblo, CO 81003-0207
(719) 564-2479 (President)
Esther Nesslage, President
meetings at McClelland Library, 100 East Abriendo, Pueblo, CO: fourth Sat 2:00–4:00
Pub. *Pinon Whispers*, quarterly, $12.00 per year subscription for members, $20.00 per year subscription for nonmembers
("alphabetized cemeteries, marriages, 1885 Colorado State Census, alphabetized deaths in *Pueblo Chieftain*, 1940–1992"; serving Baca, Bent, Crowley, Custer, Fremont, Huerfano, Kiowa, Las Animas, Otero, Prowers, and Pueblo counties)
research: $5.00 per hour

Weld County Genealogical Society
PO Box 278
Greeley, CO 80632
gen@weld.lib.co.us
http://www.rootsweb.com/~cowcgs
Jackie Glavinick, Editor
Weld County Library: Tue & Thur 9:00–noon & 1:00–4:00
Pub. *Weld County Genealogical Society Quarterly* (Aug, Nov, Feb, May)
$12.50 per year membership

Western Trails Genealogical Society
1570 South Knox Court
Denver, CO 80219

White River Trace Genealogical Society
1268 Hill Street
Meeker, CO 81641-3102
Ola Keller

Independent Publications and Miscellany

CoGenWeb
Part of The USGenWeb Project
MHet703234@aol.com;
GenealogyBug@Gustafson.net

http://www.rootsweb.com/~cogenweb/comain.htm
Mary Ann Hetrick, State Coordinator; Leona Gustafson, Assistant Coordinator
("We are a group of volunteer genealogists who provide our time and talents to help others with their research. We provide state- and county-level resources. We appreciate any help with transcriptions of census records and obits, etc. We are also looking for others who would like to join our fun and friendly group of coordinators. There is no charge to join, just the desire to help others.")

Colorado Department of Transportation
Info@dot.state.co.us
http://www.dot.state.co.us/TravelInfo/Maps (Maps)

El Pueblo Museum
119 Central Plaza
Pueblo, CO 81003-3239

Genealogical Advisor
PO Box 535
Farmington, MI 48332
Andrew J. Morris
Pub. *Genealogical Advisor*

Connecticut

Archives and Libraries with Holdings in Genealogy

State Archives and Library

Connecticut State Archives
231 Capitol Avenue
Hartford, CT 06106-1537
(860) 566-5650
MJones@cslib.org
http://www.cslib.org/archives.htm
Mark H. Jones, State Archivist
Mon–Fri 9:30–5:00; Archives Research Area within the History and Genealogy Reading Room: Mon–Fri 10:00–1:00 & 2:00–4:15
(records from more than 70 state agencies, manuscripts, photographs, posters, postcards)

Connecticut State Library
History and Genealogy Unit
231 Capitol Avenue
Hartford, CT 06106-1537
(860) 566-3690; (860) 566-3692; (860) 566-4452 (to arrange for handicapped parking and access); (860) 566-2133 FAX
isref@cslib.org
http://ww.cslib.org
Richard C. Roberts, Unit Head
Mon–Fri 9:30–5:00; Archives Research Area within the History and Genealogy Reading Room: Mon–Fri 10:00–1:00 & 2:00–4:15
(Barbour Collection of town vital records, family and Bible records, federal and state censuses, newspaper marriage and death notice abstracts, Hale Collection of cemetery inscriptions, church records abstracts, probate estate papers, extensive collection of local histories and genealogies, most town vital, land and probate record books to the early 1900s, church records on microfilm, naturalization papers index on microfilm, atlases and maps, city directories, passenger lists, etc.)
research: a limited genealogical index search service for an individual name in the seven major indexes in the collection, plus up to ten pages of photocopying, $5.00 for Connecticut residents, $15.00 plus long SASE for non-Connecticut residents, additional photocopy charges to be billed (no inquiries by phone, allow six weeks for a response)

State Historical Societies

Connecticut Historical Commission
59 South Prospect Street
Hartford, CT 06106-1901
(860) 566-3005; (860) 566-5078 FAX
archnet@spirit.lib.uconn.edu
http://www.chc.state.ct.us
John W. Shannahan, Director
Mon–Fri 8:30–4:30
(Connecticut architecture, historic landscapes, women's history, no archives or library)

Connecticut Historical Society (CHS)
1 Elizabeth Street at Asylum Avenue
Hartford, CT 06105
(860) 236-5621; (860) 236-2664 FAX
ask_us@chs.org; libchs@chs.org (Library and Genealogy)
http://www.chs.org
Judith Ellen Johnson, Reference Librarian

and Genealogist; David M. Kahn,
Director
Library: Tue–Sat 9:00–4:45
Pub. *The Connecticut Historical Society
Bulletin*, semiannually, $16.00 per year
subscription for members, $20.00 per year
subscription for nonmembers;
*Connecticut Historical Society Annual
Report*; *Connecticut Historical Society
Collections*, irregularly; *Notes and News*,
three times per year; *Loan Catalog*
(16,000 volume Loan Collection available
to members of The Connecticut Historical
Society or The Society of Mayflower
Descendants in the State of Connecticut),
$7.00 postpaid (Connecticut residents add
30¢ tax)
$30.00 per year membership (includes *CHS
Annual Report* and *Notes and News*, and
access to Loan Collection); admission:
$3.00 for nonmembers; research: nominal
charge

Connecticut League of Historical Societies
2105 Chester Village West
Chester, CT 06412-1040
Janet G. Jainschigg
Pub. *League Bulletin*

**City, County and Regional Archives and
Libraries**
(A more exhaustive list of public and
academic libraries can be found at
http://www.cslib.org/cln/publib.asp or
http://www.iconn.org/lib_hp.html.)

**Raymond E. Baldwin Museum of
Connecticut History**
231 Capitol Avenue
Hartford, CT 06106-1537
(860) 566-3056; (860) 566-2133 FAX
http://www.cslnet.ctstateu.edu/museum.htm
Dean Nelson, Museum Administrator
(primarily historical, not genealogical)

**Beardsley and Memorial Library of
Winsted**
40 Munro Place
Winsted, CT 06098-1423
(860) 379-6043 (Library); (860) 379-2158
(Genealogy Librarian)
newman@esslink.com (Genealogy Librarian)
http://www.beardsleyandmemorial.org
Dr. Newman A. Hall, Genealogy Librarian;
Mary Pitt, History Research Assistant
Library: Tue–Thur 10:30–8:00, Fri
10:30–4:00, Sat 10:00–1:00; Genealogy
Library: Thur 10:30–noon, and by
appointment
(focus on Connecticut and western
Massachusetts; correspondence inquiries
welcomed)

Bennington Museum
(see Vermont, Part 2)

Berkshire Athenaeum
(see Massachusetts, Part 2)

Berlin-Peck Memorial Library
Local History Room
234 Kensington Road
Berlin, CT 06037-2694
(860) 828-7125; (860) 829-1848 FAX
http://www.berlinpeck.lib.ct.us
Sarah Munson, Library Director
Local History Room: Wed 10:00–noon and
by appointment

James Blackstone Memorial Library
758 Main Street
Branford, CT 06405

(203) 488-1441; (203) 481-6077 FAX
library@blackstone.lioninc.org
http://www.blackstone.lioninc.org
Barbara Cangiano, Reference Supervisor
Mon–Thur 9:00–8:00, Fri–Sat 9:00–5:00,
Sat (July–Aug) 9:00–1:00
("Library has a collection of materials on the
history of Branford, Connecticut, and
selected Branford family genealogies.")

Cyrenius H. Booth Library
25 Main Street
Newtown, CT 06470
(203) 426-4533 (Adult Circulation); (203)
426-8552 (Reference); (203) 426-2196
FAX
boothref@biblio.org
http://www.biblio.org/chbooth/index.htm
Beryl Harrison, Reference Librarian
Mon–Tue 10:00–8:00, Wed–Thur
10:00–6:00, Fri noon–5:00, Sat
10:00–5:00, Sun 1:00–5:00
(family histories of many Fairfield County
people)

Bridgeport Public Library
Historical Collections
925 Broad Street
Bridgeport, CT 06604
(203) 576-7417; (203) 576-8255 FAX
http://www.bridgeportpubliclibrary.org
Mary K. Witkowski, Head
Mon–Sat (call for hours); closed Sat from
Memorial Day to Labor Day
(includes P.T. Barnum and circus collection;
Family Search on CD, census microfilm
for Connecticut 1790–1930, plus
Soundex, extensive genealogy
publications)
research: $5.00 plus photocpies, send request
in writing only

Bristol Public Library
Bristol History Room
(5 High Street—location)
PO Box 730 (mailing address)
Bristol, CT 06010
(860) 584-7787; (860) 584-7696 FAX
BristolLibraryRefDept@ci.bristol.ct.us
http://www.ci.bristol.ct.us/3374/default.aspx
Robert G. Robles, Historical Research
Librarian
Library: Mon–Thur 8:30–8:00, Fri–Sat
8:30–5:00; Bristol History Room: Tue
2:00–4:00, Wed 6:00–7:45
(City of Bristol archives)

Silas Bronson Library
The Public Library for the City of Waterbury
267 Grand Street
Waterbury, CT 06702
(203) 574-8222; (203) 574-8055 FAX
sblmrr@bronsonlibrary.org;
admin1@bronsonlibrary.org
http://www.biblio.org/bronson/silas.htm
Ellen Gambini, Head, Main Reading Room
Mon–Wed 9:00–9:00, Thur–Fri 9:00–5:30,
Sat 9:00–5:00, Sun 1:00–5:00; closed Sat
& Sun in summer
(genealogy and local history of New England
states)

**The David M. Roth Center for
Connecticut Studies**
Fourth Floor, J. Eugene Smith Library
Eastern Connecticut State University
Willimantic, CT 06226
(860) 465-4512; (877) 353-3278, ext. 54412
Tuckerb@easternct.edu
http://www.esternct.edu/depts/ctstudies
Dr. Barbara Tucker
9:00–noon & 1:00–4:00

Pub. *Center for CT Studies Newsletter*,
annually (fall)
("Connecticut history, research, census,
directories, newspapers, open to the
public")

Cheshire Public Library
104 Main Street
Cheshire, CT 06410
(203) 272-2245; (203) 272-7714 FAX
cshrefmail@leaplibraries.org
http://www.cheshirelib.org
Mary Beeckman, Co-Head, Reference
Department
Mon–Thur 10:00–9:00, Fri–Sat 10:00–5:00

Connecticut College Library
(address withheld upon request)
(does not specialize in genealogy)

Connecticut Valley Historical Museum
(see Massachusetts, Part 2)

Danbury Public Library
170 Main Street
Danbury, CT 06810
(203) 797-4505; (203) 797-4527; (203) 797-
4501 FAX
http://www.danburylibrary.org
Diana Nolan, Reference Librarian
Library and Local History Room: Mon &
Thur 9:00–8:00, Tue & Fri–Sat
9:00–5:00, Wed 1:00–5:00, Sun (Labor
Day–Memorial Day) 1:00–5:00
(Local History Room specializing in
Danbury history and local genealogy:
microfilm, periodicals, atlases, maps,
town and county histories)

Darien Library
35 Leroy Avenue
Darien, CT 06820-4497
(203) 655-1234; (203) 655-2568; (203) 655-
1547 FAX
lberry@darien.lib.ct.us;
AskUs@darien.lib.ct.us
http://www.darien.lib.ct.us
Louise Berry, Director

East Granby Public Library
Betty Guinan/Alice Newman Historical
Room
(24 Center Street—location)
PO Box G (mailing address)
East Granby, CT 06026
(860) 653-3002; (860) 653-3936 FAX
eastgranbylibrary@eastgranbylibrary.org;
east.granby.pub.lib@snet.net
http://www.eastgranbylibrary.org/
alicenewmanhistoricalroom.htm
Paula Davino, Director

East Hartford Public Library System
Raymond Library
840 Main Street
East Hartford, CT 06108
(860) 289-6429; (860) 291-9166 FAX
sjarush@connect.crlc.org
http://www.easthartford.lib.ct.us
Patrick Jones, Director
Mon–Tue 9:00–9:00, Fri–Sat 9:00–5:00, Sun
(Oct–May) 1:00–4:00

Eastern Connecticut State University
(see Center for Connecticut Studies, above)

Fairfield Public Library
1080 Old Post Road
Fairfield, CT 06430
(203) 256-3160; (203) 256-3155; (203) 256-
3162 FAX
tgeoffino@fplct.org

http://www.fairfieldpubliclibrary.org
Tom Geoffino, Town Librarian
Mon–Thur 9:00–9:00, Fri 9:00–6:00, Sat
9:00–5:00
("We refer all genealogy questions to either
our local Historical Society or the Pequot
Library in Southport.")

The Farmington Library
West End Annex
(17 School Street, Unionville, CT
06085—temporary location)
PO Box 407 (mailing address)
Farmington, CT 06034-0407
(860) 673-6791; (860) 675-7148 FAX
bgibson@farmington.lib.ct.us;
flref@farmington.lib.ct.us (Reference);
tmatava@farmington.lib.ct.us
(Webmaster)
http://www.farmington.lib.ct.us
Ann J. Arcari, Farmington Room Librarian;
Barbara H. Gibson, Director
Mon 9:00–9:00, Tue–Fri 9:00–5:00, Sat
9:00–1:00
(archives and history of Farmington and
daughter towns: Avon, Berlin, Bristol,
Burlington, New Britain, Plainville and
Southington)
can answer only brief questions over the
phone, send letter for more: $10.00 per
hour plus copies at 10¢ each

The Ferguson Library
1 Public Library Plaza
Stamford, CT 06904
(203) 964-1000
yelena@flvax.ferg.lib.ct.us
http://www.futuris.net/ferg
Yelena Klompus, Local History Librarian
Mon–Thur 10:00–9:00, Fri 10:00–6:00, Sat
10:00–5:00, Sun (Sept to mid-May)
1:00–5:00
(a large collection of genealogical
periodicals; focus is on Stamford, on
Connecticut and on New England
collection of history and genealogy
materials)

Friends of Boothe Park, Inc.
(Main Street and Putney—location)
PO Box 902 (mailing address)
Stratford, CT 06497
(203) 381-2046
Bessie Burton, Director of Volunteers
Tue & Fri 8:30–1:30, and tour hours
Pub. *Boothe Museum Newsletter*, two times
per year
$10.00 per year membership

Godfrey Memorial Library
134 Newfield Street
Middletown, CT 06457
(860) 346-4375; (860) 347-9874 FAX
library@godfrey.org
http://www.godfrey.org
Nancy Doane, Director
Mon 9:00–8:00, Tue–Fri 9:00–4:00
Pub. *American Genealogical-Biographical
Index*
("Library specializes in genealogy and local
history, mainly covering the original
thirteen colonies but does have material
for most of the U.S. Friends of the
Godfrey Memorial Library sponsors
programs.")
membership in Friends available; admission:
donation

Greenwich Library
101 West Putnam Avenue
Greenwich, CT 06830-5387
(203) 625-6560

mcuff@greenwichlibrary.org;
vlibrarian@greenwichlibrary.org
http://www.greenwich.lib.ct.us
Mary Cuff, Local History/Genealogy
Librarian
Mon–Fri 9:00–9:00, Sat 9:00–5:00, Sun
(except summer) 1:00–5:00
$15.00 for locating, copying and sending
obituaries, articles, etc.

Groton Public Library
52 Route 117, Newtown Road
Groton, CT 06340
(860) 441-6750; (860) 448-0363 FAX
groton.public.lib@snet.net
http://www.town.groton.ct.us/library/
index.asp
Barbara Clark-Greene, Reference Librarian
Mon–Thur 9:00–9:00, Fri 9:00–5:30, Sat
9:00–5:00, Sun (Sept–June) noon–5:00

Guilford Free Library
The Historical Room
67 Park Street, on the Green
Guilford, CT 06437
(203) 453-8282; (203) 453-8288 FAX
refdesk@guilford.lib.ct.us;
sruoff@guilford.lib.ct.us
http://www.guilford.lib.ct.us
Sandra J. Ruoff, Director
Winter: Mon–Thur 9:00–8:00, Fri
9:00–6:00, Sat 9:00–5:00, Sun (Oct–Mar)
1:00–4:00; summer: Mon & Thur
9:00–8:00, Tue–Wed & Fri 9:00–5:00,
Sat 9:00–1:00

Gunn Memorial Library and Museum
(5 Wykeham Road—location)
PO Box 1273 (mailing address)
Washington, CT 06793
(860) 868-7756 (Museum); (860) 868-7586
(Library); (860) 868-7247 FAX
gunnlib@nai.net; gunnlib@biblio.org
http://www.biblio.org/gunn
Sarah Griswold, Curator; Kristine Dyson,
Librarian
(some family and local histories, photos,
archival material; library has the
Connecticut Room, a reference library
with published genealogies, histories, etc.)

Hartford Public Library
Central Library
500 Main Street
Hartford, CT 06103
(860) 695-6300; (860) 695-6295
(Reference); (860) 722-6897 FAX
(Reference); (860) 722-6900 FAX
(Administrative)
reference@hartfordpl.lib.ct.us;
lblalock@hartfordpl.lib.ct.us
http://www.hartfordpl.lib.ct.us
Louise Blalock, Chief Librarian
Library: Mon–Thur 10:00–8:00, Fri–Sat
10:00–5:00, Sun (Oct–May) 1:00–5:00;
Hartford Collection: Mon–Fri noon–5:00

Hill-Stead Museum
671 Farmington Avenue
Farmington, CT 06032
(860) 677-4787

Kent Memorial Library
50 North Main Street
Suffield, CT 06078-2117
(860) 668-3896
director@suffield-library.org
http://www.suffield-library.org
Anne W. Borg, Assistant; Anthony Bernardo,
Director
Library: Tue–Thur 10:00–8:30, Fri
10:00–6:00, Sat 10:00–5:00, Sat

(July–Aug) 10:00–1:00; Historical Room:
by appointment
(Suffield genealogy and local history)

Living Museum of Avon
8 East Main Street
Avon, CT 06001
(860) 678-7621

Manchester Community College
Institute of Local History
60 Bidwell Street
Manchester, CT 06040
(860) 647-6101

Mattatuck Museum
144 West Main Street
Waterbury, CT 06702
(203) 753-0381; (203) 7565-6283 FAX
Carey McDougall, Assistant Curator
Tue–Sat 10:00–5:00, Sun (except July–Aug)
noon–5:00
(history specific to the greater Waterbury
region)
research: $25.00 per hour

Meriden Public Library
(105 Miller Street—location)
PO Box 868 (mailing address)
Meriden, CT 06450
(203) 238-2346
http://www.cityofmeriden.org/services/
library/default.asp
Janis L. Franco, Local History Librarian
Mon–Wed 10:00–9:00, Thur–Sat 10:00–5:00

Mystic and Noank Library
40 Library Street
Mystic, CT 06355-2418
(860) 536-7721; (860) 536-3019; (860) 536-
2350 FAX
mnl@juno.com
http://mysticnoanklibrary.com
Joanna M. Case, Library Director
Mon–Wed 10:00–9:00, Thur–Fri
10:00–5:00, Sat (winter) 10:00–5:00, Sat
(summer) 9:00–1:00

Mystic Seaport Museum
G. W. Blunt White Library
(75 Greenmanville Avenue—location)
PO Box 6000 (mailing address)
Mystic, CT 06355
(860) 572-0711 (Main Desk); (860) 572-
5367 (Library)
http://www.mysticseaport.org
Mon–Sat 10:30–5:00
Pub. *Log of Mystic Seaport*, quarterly
(some abstracts of manuscript collections and
ships plans on the web)
research: $20.00 per hour

New Britain Public Library
Local History Room
20 High Street
New Britain, CT 06051-4226
(860) 224-3155, ext. 16; (860) 223-6729
FAX
nbpllhr@netscape.net
http://www.nbpl.lib.ct
Arlene C. Palmer, Curator
Local History Room: open Mon–Fri or
Mon–Thur & Sat on alternate weeks (call
to verify hours): Mon noon–5:00 &
6:00–8:00, Tue 9:00–1:00 & 2:00–6:00
(or 5:00 on weeks open on Sat), Wed
1:00–noon, Thur 9:00–1:00 & 2:00–6:00,
Fri 9:00–1:00 & 2:00–5:00 or Sat
10:00–1:00 & 2:00–4:00
$10.00 for any search requiring more than ½
hour, photocopying 50¢ per page plus
$1.00 processing for 1-5 pages, 25¢ per

page plus $2.00 processing for 6 or more pages

New Hartford Historical Museum
New Hartford Library
(Route 44—location)
PO Box 247 (mailing address)
New Hartford, CT 06057-0247
(860) 379-6626 (Museum); (860) 379-7235 (Library)

New Haven Free Public Library
Local History Department
133 Elm Street
New Haven, CT 06510-2033
(203) 946-8130 (Local History Department); (203) 946-7430
khurley@nhfpl.org
http://www.nhfpl.lib.ct.us
Janet Zigadto, Reference Librarian
Mon–Thur 9:00–9:00, Fri–Sat 9:00–5:00
(patrons must have identification to get into the room when it's not staffed)

The Public Library of New London
Genealogy and History Room
63 Huntington Street
New London, CT 06320-6194
peterc@lioninc.org
http://www.lioninc.org/newlondon
Peter Ciparelli, Director
Mon–Thur 9:00–9:00, Fri–Sat 9:00–5:00
(closed Sat during schools' summer vacation, June–Labor Day); reference assistance is available in the room Tue–Fri 9:00–3:00
(genealogy and local history of southeastern Connecticut; "single query answered by mail only, for a fee")

Norfolk Historical Museum
13 Village Green
Norfolk, CT 06058
(860) 542-5761
Sat–Sun (June–Sept) 1:00–4:00 by appointment
(museum and research library/archives)

Old Lyme-Phoebe Griffin Noyes Library
2 Library Lane
Old Lyme, CT 06371
(860) 434-1684; (860) 434-9547
cgiles@oldlyme.lioninc.org;
mfiorell@oldlyme.lioninc.org
http://www.oldlyme.lioninc.org
C. E. Giles, Head Adult Services; Mary Fiorelli, Director
Mon, Wed & Fri 10:00–8:00, Tue, Thur & Sat 10:00–5:00
(southeastern Connecticut, particularly Lyme and Old Lyme, genealogy and local history)
no longer has staff to support genealogical searches

Otis Library
261 Main Street
Norwich, CT 06360
(860) 889-2365, ext. 13; (860) 886-4744 FAX
lsummers@otis.lioninc.org
http://www.otis.lib.ct.us
Diane Norman, Assistant Reference Librarian; Linda Summers, Director
Oct–Apr: Mon–Thur 8:30–8:30, Fri–Sat 8:30–5:00, Sun 1:00–5:00; summer: Mon & Thur 8:30–8:30, Tue–Wed & Fri 8:30–5:00
(New London County and Norwich history and genealogy, NLC census; architectural, industrial history of Norwich)

The Pequot Library
720 Pequot Avenue
Southport, CT 06490
(203) 259-0346; (203) 259-5602 FAX
freedman@pequotlibrary.com
http://www.pequotlibrary.com
Mary Freedman, Director
winter: Mon & Wed 9:00–8:30, Tue & Thur–Fri 9:00–5:30, Sat 9:00–5:00, Sun 1:00–5:00; summer (4 July–Labor Day): Mon–Tue & Thur–Fri 9:00–5:30, Wed 9:00–8:30, Sat 9:00–1:00
Pub. *Bookmark*, quarterly, free
(Americana, New England local history)

Rathbun Free Memorial Library
(36 Main Street—location)
PO Box G (mailing address)
East Haddam, CT 06423
(860) 873-8210; (860) 873-3601 FAX
http://www.rathbun.lioninc.org
Martha T. Monte, Library Director
Tue–Wed & Fri 10:00–5:00, Thur 10:00–7:00, Sat (except summer) 10:00–noon
(genealogies, town history, cemetery records, church records, scrapbooks, account books and old photographs; "known over the entire U.S.A. for having the most complete material on East Haddam")

Russell Library
123 Broad Street
Middletown, CT 06457
(860) 347-2520; (860) 347-4048 FAX
russlib@russelllibrary.org
http://www.russelllibrary.org
Denise Mackey-Russo, Reference Library Specializing in Genealogy and Local History
Mon–Thur 9:00–9:00, Fri noon–9:00, Sun (Oct–May) 1:00–5:00
("The Middletown Room Collection specializes in genealogies and histories of Middletown and northern Middlesex County. The collection includes vital records of Melilli, Sicily, maps, ephemera, architectural material, census records, newspapers, city directories, the Hale Collection, the Barbour Collection and genealogies.")

E. C. Scranton Memorial Library
(801 Boston Post Road—location)
PO Box 631 (mailing address)
Madison, CT 06443
(203) 245-7365; (203) 245-7821 FAX
longsr@madisonct.org
http://www.scrantonlibrary.com
Sandra R. Long, Library Director; Marcia Sokolnicki
Mon & Wed 9:00–9:00, Tue & Thur–Fri 9:00–5:30, Sat 9:00–5:00; summer: closed Mon at 5:30, closed Sat at noon

Seymour Public Library
46 Church Street
Seymour, CT 06483-2612
(203) 888-3903; (203) 888-4099 FAX
webmaster@seymourpubliclibrary.org
http://www.seymourpubliclibrary.org
Mon–Wed 9:30–8:00, Thur–Fri 9:30–5:00, Sat 10:00–4:00

South Windsor Public Library
1550 Sullivan Avenue
South Windsor, CT 06074
(860) 644-1541; (860) 644-7645 FAX
refswpl@libraryconnection.info
http://www.ctconnect.com/swlibrary
Mary Etter, Director
Mon–Thur 9:00–9:00, Fri 9:00–4:30, Sat

(school year) 9:00–4:30, Sat (July–Aug) 9:00–1:00, Sun (Oct–May) 1:00–4:30

Southington Public Library and Museum
255 Main Street
Southington, CT 06489-2509
(860) 628-0947
johnston@southington.org
http://library.southington.org
James Johnston, M.S., M.A., Library Director
Mon–Tue 9:15–9:00, Fri–Sat 9:15–5:00 (closed Sat, July–Aug)

Stanley-Whitman House
37 High Street
Farmington, CT 06032
(860) 677-9222; (860) 677-7758 FAX
lisa@stanleywhitman.org
http://www.stanleywhitman.org
Deborah Feinstein, Executive Director
May–Oct: Wed–Sun noon–4:00; Nov–Apr: Sat–Sun noon–4:00
$15.00 per year membership

Stratford Library Association
Reference Department
2203 Main Street
Stratford, CT 06615
(203) 385-4161; (203) 385-4164 (Reference)
gerry@stratford.lib.ct.us (Reference)
http://www.stratford.lib.ct.us/home.html
Gerald Gillespie, Reference Department
Mon–Thur 10:00–8:00, Fri 10:00–5:00

Tree Farm Archives
272 Israel Hill Road
Shelton, CT 06484
(203) 929-0126
Philip H. Jones
9:00–5:00
(archive of human interest, historical letters)

University of Connecticut
Dodd Research Center
405 Babbidge Road
Box U-205
Storrs, CT 06269-1205
doddref@lib.uconn.edu
http://www.lib.uconn.edu/DoddCenter/index.html

Wadsworth Atheneum
600 Main Street
Hartford, CT 06103
(860) 278-2670; (860) 527-0803 FAX
info@wadsworthatheneum.org
http://www.wadsworthatheneum.org
John Teahan, Head Librarian
Tue, Thur & Sat 11:00–5:00
(very limited Connecticut materials)

Wallingford Public Library
200 North Main Street
Wallingford, CT 06492
(203) 265-6754; (203) 269-5698 FAX
http://www.wallingford.lioninc.org
Amy Humphries, Assistant Director
Mon–Fri 10:00–9:00, Sat 10:00–5:00 (except summer)
("Collection includes books, pamphlets and clippings on Wallingford and Connecticut; the Connecticut Collection is not open for browsing; materials will be retrieved for patron use outside the room.")

Watkinson Library
(see English, Ethnic Archives, Libraries and Societies, Part 3)

Noah Webster House

227 South Main Street
West Hartford, CT 06107
(860) 521-5362
Sally Whipple, Executive Director
House: Mon–Fri 8:00–4:00, and weekends
    by appointment; researchers call for
    appointment
(archival material about West Hartford;
    Webster genealogy, West Hartford
    probate records)

Welles-Turner Memorial Library
2407 Main Street
Glastonbury, CT 06033
(860) 652-7720 (Reference); (860) 652-7721
    FAX
bailey@glasct.org
http://www.wtmlib.com
Barbara Bailey, Library Director
Mon–Tue & Thur 9:00–9:00, Wed
    noon–9:00, Fri 9:00–6:00, Sat 9:00–5:00,
    Sun 1:00–5:00; summer: Sat 9:00–1:00
(specializes in Glastonbury history)

Wesleyan University
Olin Memorial Library
Special Collection and Archives
Church Street
Middletown, CT 06459
(860) 685-3863
eswaim@wesleyan.edu;
    dperron@wesleyan.edu
http://www.wesleyan.edu/libr/olinhome/
    olinhome.htm

West Hartford Public Library
(address withheld upon request)

(some materials of interest to local
    genealogists, but reduced collection to
    serve local residents only)
no search services

Western Connecticut State College
181 White Street
Danbury, CT 06810

Henry Whitfield State Museum
(Old Whitfield Street—location)
PO Box 210 (mailing address)
Guilford, CT 06437-0210
(203) 453-2457; (203) 453-7544 FAX
Michael A. McBride, Curator
Research library: by appointment; Museum:
    Apr–14 Dec: Wed–Sun 10:00–4:30
(small history/genealogy library)

Wilton Library Association, Inc.
Friends of the Wilton Library
137 Old Ridgefield Road
Wilton, CT 06897-3000
(203) 762-3950; (203) 834-1166 FAX
http://www.wiltonlibrary.org
Carol Russell, Archivist
Wilton History Room: Mon–Wed & Fri
    10:00–6:00, Thur 10:00–9:00, Sat
    10:00–5:00, Sun (Oct–Apr) 1:00–5:00
(Wilton, Connecticut, families)
contributions accepted

Oliver Wolcott Library
(160 South Street—location)
PO Box 187 (mailing address)
Litchfield, CT 06759
(860) 567-8030; (860) 567-4784
owlibrary@owlibrary.org
http://www.owlibrary.org
Ann Marie White, Library Director
Mon noon–5:00, Tue–Thur 10:00–9:00, Sat
    10:00–5:00
("We do have a small but quality historical
    collection and oral history transcripts.

This was a project where local people
    discussed history of the town, memories,
    etc.")

Wood Memorial Library
(783 Main Street—location)
PO Box 131 (mailing address)
South Windsor, CT 06074
(860) 289-1783; (860) 289-4178 FAX
wood.memorial.lib@snet.net
http://pages.cthome.net/wood.memorial.lib
Virginia Macro, Library Director
Mon & Thur 10:00–8:00, Sat (Sept–June)
    noon–4:00

Yale University Library
Manuscripts and Archives
PO Box 208240
New Haven, CT 06520-8240
mssa.assist@yale.edu
http://www.library.yale.edu/mssa/home1.
    htm

Yale University
Sterling Memorial Library
120 High Street
New Haven, CT 06511
http://www.library.yale.edu/sml.html

Historical Societies—Local and Regional

Amity and Woodbridge Historical Society
Thomas Darling House
Litchfield Turnpike
Woodbridge, CT 06525
Don Menzies, President
June–Oct: Sun 2:00–4:00

Andover Historical Society
Bunker Hill Road
Andover, CT 06232
(860) 742-6796

Aspinock Historical Society of Putnam, Inc.
(206 School Street—location)
PO Box 465 (mailing address)
Putnam, CT 06260
(860) 928-6128
Robert J. Miller, Town Historian; Robert
    Chicoine, President
Pub. *Aspinock Newsletter*, three or four times
    per year
$10.00 per year membership

Bantam Historical Society, Inc.
PO Box 436
Bantam, CT 06750-0436
R. C. Schele, Chairman of Board

Barkhamsted Historical Society, Inc.
PO Box 94
Pleasant Valley, CT 06063

Beacon Falls Historical Commission
10 Maple Avenue
Beacon Falls, CT 06403
(203) 729-4340
Leonard Damico, First Selectman
Pub. *Beacon Falls Historical Commission*

Branford Historical Society
(124 Main Street—location)
PO Box 504 (mailing address)
Branford, CT 06405
(203) 488-4828
William B. Davis, President
1 June–1 Oct: Fri–Sat 2:00–5:00, and by
    appointment
$10.00 per year membership; admission:

donation

Bridgewater Historical Society
Main Street
Bridgewater, CT 06752

Brookfield Historical Society, Inc.
(Whisconier Road—location)
PO Box 5231 (mailing address)
Brookfield, CT 06804
(203) 740-8140
brookfieldhistsoc@snet.net
http://www.brookfieldhistory.org
Marilyn Whittlesey, Town Historian
Sat noon–4:00, first Sun noon–4:00, by
    appointment (May–Dec), and by
    appointment only (Dec–Apr)
Pub. *Brookfield Historical Society
    Newsletter*, quarterly
$10.00 per year membership; limited
    research: donation

Brooklyn Historical Society
(address withheld upon request)
(Primarily historical, not genealogical: "We
    have no genealogical records.")
$5.00 per year membership

Canton Historical Society
11 Front Street
Collinsville, CT 06022
(860) 693-2793
Jane Goedecke, Librarian
Wed–Sun 1:00–4:00 (weekends only,
    Dec–Mar), call for appointment if a
    librarian's help is required
(printed and pictorial material dealing with
    the history of Canton and Collinsville)
$10.00 per year membership; admission:
    $2.00 for adult nonmembers

**Chatham Historical Society of East
Hampton, Connecticut**
Bevin Boulevard
East Hampton, CT 06424
Walter Olsen, President

Chester Historical Society
PO Box 204
Chester, CT 06412
Dawn Burr, President

Colchester Historical Society
243 Old Hebron Road
Colchester, CT 06415
(860) 537-2925 (President); (860) 537-2253)
    (Town Historian)
Jennie Boluck Lenkiewicz, President;
    Stanley Moroch, Colchester Town
    Historian

Colebrook Historical Society, Inc.
(Colebrook Center, 558 Colebrook
    Road—location)
PO Box 85 (mailing address)
Colebrook, CT 06021
(860) 738-3142
weekends (Memorial Day–Columbus Day)
    2:00–4:00
(Colebrook-related only)
from $2.00 per year membership

The Columbia Historical Society, Inc.
486 Route 66
Columbia, CT 06237
(860) 228-9385
Belle Robinson, President
research: SASE appreciated

Cornwall Historical Society
(Pine Street—location)
PO Box 115 (mailing address)
Cornwall, CT 06753

Coventry Historical Society, Inc.
(South Street—location)
PO Box 307 (mailing address)
Coventry, CT 06238

Danbury Scott-Fanton Museum and Historical Society, Inc.
43 Main Street
Danbury, CT 06810-7835
(203) 743-5200 voice & FAX
Kathleen Zuris, Assistant Director
Wed–Sun 2:00–5:00; Office: Tue–Fri 10:00–5:00
Pub. *The Scott-Fanton Museum Newsletter—The Pahquidque Packet*, quarterly
(Danbury local history, published genealogies, genealogy files, city directories, cemetery inscriptions, etc., hatting, Charles Ives)
$15.00 per year membership

The Darien Historical Society, Inc.
Bates-Scofield Homestead
45 Old Kings Highway, North
Darien, CT 06820
(203) 655-9233; (203) 656-3892 FAX
http://historical.darien.org
Judith Groppa, Executive Director
Tue & Fri 9:00–2:00, Wed–Thur 9:00–4:00; tours: Wed–Thur 2:00–4:00
Pub. *Darien Historical Society Annual*
(archival material pertaining to Darien and its residents; local history in addition to quilt and costume collections)
$25.00+ per year membership

The Denison Society, Inc.
(120 Pequotsepos Road—location)
PO Box 42 (mailing address)
Mystic, CT 06355
(860) 536-9248 voice & FAX
Kitty Von Rump, Administrative Assistant; Wayne L. Denison, President
Office: Mon–Fri 4-5 hours per day; Museum: Memorial Day–Columbus Day: Thur–Sun 1:00–4:00
$15.00 per year membership (application required); admission: $4.00 for nonmembers

Derby Historical Society, Inc.
(37 Elm Street, Ansonia, CT 06401—location)
PO Box 331 (mailing address)
Derby, CT 06418
(203) 735-1908

Durham Historical Society
(Main Street—location)
PO Box 345 (mailing address)
Durham, CT 06422

East Haddam Historical Society
PO Box 27
East Haddam, CT 06423

East Haven Historical Society
(133 Main Street—location)
PO Box 120052 (mailing address)
East Haven, CT 06512
(203) 467-1766
William Anderson, Genealogist
Wed 11:00–2:00

East Windsor Historical Society, Inc.
(115 Scantic Road—location)
PO Box 551 (mailing address)
East Windsor, CT 06088
Bobbi Mazvrek, Vice President
by appointment

Eastford Historical Society
Eastford, CT 06242
Pub. *Eastford Historical Society Quarterly*
$4.00 per year membership

Historical Society of Easton, Inc.
(Easton Center in Public Library—location)
PO Box 121 (mailing address)
Easton, CT 06612
(203) 261-2090
Jerry L. Gabert, President
by appointment
Pub. *The Schoolhouse Sentinel*, quarterly
(only relating to the Town of Easton; open for "independent research but no staff to handle searches")
$25.00 per year membership

Enfield Historical Society, Inc.
1294 Enfield Street
Enfield, CT 06082
(860) 745-1729
Anthony Secondo, President

Essex Historical Society, Inc.
Hills Academy
(Prospect Street—location)
PO Box 261 (mailing address)
Essex, CT 06426
(860) 767-8269
Donald Malcarne, President
Pub. *Quarterly Newsletter*
$15.00 per year membership

Fairfield Historical Society
636 Old Post Road
Fairfield, CT 06430-6647
(203) 259-1598; (203) 255-2716 FAX
Barbara E. Austen, Librarian/Archivist
Mon–Fri 9:30–4:30, Sat–Sun 1:00–5:00
Pub. *Chronicle*, quarterly
$25.00 per year membership; research: $10.00 plus photocopies and postage

Falls Village-Canaan Historical Society
(Main Street—location)
PO Box 206 (mailing address)
Falls Village, CT 06031
(860) 824-0707
Marion L. Stock, Curator
Fri 2:00–4:00
(local history, some genealogical materials)
donation

Farmington Historical Society
PO Box 1645
Farmington, CT 06034

Franklin Historical Society
Route 32
North Franklin, CT 06254

Gaylordsville Historical Society
PO Box 25
Gaylordsville, CT 06755
(860) 350-0300; (860) 354-1715 FAX
webmaster@gaylordsville.org
http://www.gaylordsville.org
Richard T. Kosier, President
July–Aug: Sun 1:00–5:00
$5.00 per year membership

The Historical Society of Glastonbury
(Museum on the Green, 1944 Main Street—location)
PO Box 46 (mailing address)
Glastonbury, CT 06033
(860) 633-6890 voice & FAX
Nancy W. Berlet, Executive Director
Mon & Thur 10:00–4:00, and by appointment
Pub. *The Publick Post*, annually

(Connecticut, Glastonbury [central Connecticut River Valley towns] genealogy, recent search for descendants of Glastonbury founders complete and computerized)
$12.00 per year membership: research for members: $8.00 for up to two hours, $4.00 for each additional hour, plus photocopies at 10¢ per page; research for nonmembers: $12.00 for up to two hours, $6.00 for each additional hour, plus photocopies at 25¢ per page; admission: $2.00 for nonmembers

Goshen Historical Society
21 Old Middle Street
Goshen, CT 06756-2001
(860) 491-9610
N. Terry Hall, President
Tue 10:00–noon, and by appointment; volunteer workshops: Tue 10:00–noon; presentations: Sat afternoon during summer and early fall

The Greater Bristol Historical Society, Inc.
(54 Middle Street—location)
PO Box 1393 (mailing address)
Bristol, CT 06010
(860) 583-6309
Laurie Larue, President

The Historical Society of the Town of Greenwich
39 Strickland Road
Cos Cob, CT 06807
(203) 869-6899; (203) 869-6727 FAX
Mrs. Meriwether Schmid, Genealogy; William E. Finch, Jr., Town Historian; Susan Richardson, Archivist
Tue & Thur 10:00–4:00
Pub. *HSTG Post*, six times per year; *Greenwich History*, annually
$30.00 per year membership

Guilford Keeping Society, Inc.
(171 Boston Street—location)
PO Box 363 (mailing address)
Guilford, CT 06437

Haddam Historical Society, Inc.
(14 Hayden Hill Road—location)
PO Box 97 (mailing address)
Haddam, CT 06438-0097
(860) 345-2400
Janet Sweet, Director
open during office hours, please call for schedule
$15.00 per year membership

Hamden Historical Society, Inc.
(The Hamden Historical Society Library, Miller Memorial Cultural Center, 2901 Dixwell Avenue—location)
PO Box 5512 (mailing address)
Hamden, CT 06518-0512
(203) 248-8001; (203) 562-1483
Ann Reddington
by appointment only
(volunteer by project/no staff)

Hampton Antiquarian and Historical Society
(Main Street—location)
PO Box 12 (mailing address)
Hampton, CT 06247

Hartland Historical Society, Inc.
(Route 20, West Hartland, CT 06091—location)
PO Box 221 (mailing address)
East Hartland, CT 06027

(860) 379-9722 (President)
Joan Stoltze, President
first Sun 2:00–4:00, and by appointment
Pub. *The Chronicler*, three times per year
$5.00 per year membership

Harwinton Historical Society, Inc.
PO Box 84
Harwinton, CT 06791
(860) 485-1202; (860) 485-0610
Beverly Mosher, Curator
by appointment
("1840 Schoolhouse, Barn Museum, Country
Store, Blacksmith Shop, Shingle Mill.
Store, Blacksmith Shop and Shingle Mill
are located at Harwinton Fairgrounds. For
genealogical info, contact Town Hall, 100
Bentley Drive, Harwinton.")

Killingly Historical Society
Killingly Historical Center
(196 Main Street—location)
PO Box 6000 (mailing address)
Danielson, CT 06239
(860) 779-7250
Edwin Ledogar, Director
Wed & Sat 10:00–4:00
(vital records 1700–1903, census, gravestone
inscriptions, the *Windham County
Transcript*, etc.)

Lebanon Historical Society
(856 Trumbull Highway—location)
PO Box 151 (mailing address)
Lebanon, CT 06249
(860) 642-6579; (860) 642-6583 FAX
museum@LebanonCtHistSoc.org
http://www.lebanontownhall.org/
townhall/visitor.asp
Stacia Caplanson, Curator/Director
year-round Wed 9:00–1:00, Sat 1:00–5:00
research by Genealogy Committee: $15.00
per request

Litchfield Historical Society
Corner East and South Street
Litchfield, CT 06759
(860) 567-4501
Catherine Keene, Director
Pub. *The Portico*

Lyme Historical Society, Inc.
96 Lyme Street
Old Lyme, CT 06371-1426
(860) 434-5542
Jeffrey W. Andersen, Director
Pub. *Lyme Ledger*

Madison Historical Society
(853 Boston Post Road—location)
PO Box 17 (mailing address)
Madison, CT 06443
(203) 245-4567
achard@cshore.com
A. M. Chard, President
Wed & Fri–Sat (28 May–27 Sept)
1:00–4:00, and by appointment
Pub. *Madison Now & Then*, five times per
year
(Madison, Connecticut, history, houses,
genealogy)
$12.00 per year membership

Manchester Historical Society, Inc.
106 Hartford Road
Manchester, CT 06040
(860) 643-5588

Mansfield Historical Society
(954 Storrs Road, Route 195—location)
PO Box 145 (mailing address)
Storrs, CT 06268

(860) 429-6575
mansfield.historical@snet.net
http://www.mansfield.history.org
Ann Galonska, Museum Director
June–Sept: Thur & Sun 1:30–4:30, and by
appointment
(genealogical and archival materials relating
to Mansfield history)

The Marlborough Historical Society
PO Box 281
Marlborough, CT 06447
(860) 295-8106 (President's home)
Sandra Soucy, President
$5.00 per year membership

Middlesex County Historical Society
151 Main Street
Middletown, CT 06457
(860) 346-0746
Ms. Dione Longley, Director
Tue–Thur by appointment only
Pub. *Historical Observer*, bimonthly
$15.00 per year membership

Milford Historical Society
34 High Street
Milford, CT 06460
(203) 874-2664
Arthur W. Stowe, President
Pub. *Wharf Lane Newsletter*

Monroe Historical Society, Inc.
Wheeler and Old Tannery Roads
Monroe, CT 06468

Morris Historical Society, Inc.
(12 South Street—location)
PO Box 234 (mailing address)
Morris, CT 06763
(860) 567-1776
Marilyn Birkett, President; Walter France,
Historian
Sat (first weekend in June–last weekend in
Sept) 1:00–4:30, and by appointment
Pub. *MHS Newsletter*

Mystic River Historical Society, Inc.
(74 High Street—location)
PO Box 245 (mailing address)
Mystic, CT 06355
(860) 536-4779
MRHS5@juno.com
Tue 9:00–noon, Wed–Thur 1:00–4:00
Pub. *Portersville Press*, eight times per year
(monthly Sept–May, combined issue in
Nov/Dec)
("Collection strength is local history, not
genealogy; some information on Mystic
families.")
$8.00 per year membership

Naugatuck Historical Society
(87 Church Street, Naugatuck Savings
Bank—location)
PO Box 317 (mailing address)
Naugatuck, CT 06770
(203) 729-3235
Ann Simons, President
Thur 2:00–5:00
Pub. *Naugatuck Historical Society News*,
bimonthly
(artifacts and material from many early local
industries, large manuscript and picture
files, early maps, original bound
newspapers, local census, city directories,
high school yearbooks, memorabilia,
books)
$10.00 per year membership

New Canaan Historical Society
13 Oenoke Ridge

New Canaan, CT 06840
(203) 966-1776
Sharon L. Turo, Librarian
Tue–Sat 9:30–12:30 & 2:00–4:30
(genealogical research by appointment)
Pub. *New Canaan Historical Annual*,
biannually
(primarily New Canaan local history, not
genealogical, but features Silliman,
Noyes, Weed surname collections)
$35.00 per year membership; research:
$25.00 per hour, possibly plus copies and
mailing costs

**The New England Historic Genealogical
Society**
(see Massachusetts, Part 2)

New Fairfield Historical Society, Inc.
(Lower level of New Fairfield Public
Library, Route 39—location)
PO Box 8156 (mailing address)
New Fairfield, CT 06812
(203) 746-3289; (203) 775-3223
Linda Decker and Carol Ballard, Co-
Curators
Wed 1:00–4:00
("Our files include information about early
residents of New Fairfield as well as
history of town to date.")
$10.00 per year membership

New Haven Colony Historical Society
Whitney Library
114 Whitney Avenue
New Haven, CT 06510-1025
(203) 562-4183
James W. Campbell, Librarian and Curator
of Manuscripts
Tue–Fri & first Sat 1:00–4:45
Pub. *New Haven Colony Historical Society
Journal*
$35.00 per year membership; admission:
$2.00 for nonmembers

**New London County Historical Society,
Inc.**
The Shaw-Perkins Mansion
11 Blinman Street
New London, CT 06320
(860) 443-1209 voice & FAX
nlchsinc@aol.com
Alice D. Sheriff, Director/Curator
Wed–Fri 1:00–4:00, Sat 10:00–4:00, by
appointment for research
("historical/genealogical primary-secondary
resources")
$20.00 per year membership; research:
$15.00 for nonmembers

New Milford Historical Society, Inc.
(6 Aspetuck Avenue—location)
PO Box 566 (mailing address)
New Milford, CT 06776
(860) 354-3069
Elizabeth Michelson, Curator
Apr–Nov: Thur–Sat 1:00–4:00, and by
appointment
("We have extensive genealogical files on
New Milford people.")

**Newington Historical Society and Trust,
Inc.**
679 Willard Avenue
Newington, CT 06111
(860) 666-7118
Pamela Toma, Director/Curator

Newtown Historical Society
(44 Main Street—location)
PO Box 189 (mailing address)
Newtown, CT 06470

(203) 426-5937; (203) 426-3313 FAX
Sallie S. Meffert, President
Sun (May–June & Sept–Oct) 2:00–5:00, and
by appointment
Pub. *The Rooster's Crow*, five times per year
$10.00 per year membership; research: fees
by arrangement

Noank Historical Society, Inc.
(17 Sylvan Street—museum location
Latham-Chester Store Exhibition Hall, 108
Main Street—location)
PO Box 9454 (mailing address)
Groton, CT 06340
(860) 536-3021; (860) 536-7026 (Curator);
(860) 572-9000 (President)
Mary C. Anderson, Curator; Patricia White,
President
summer: Wed & Sat–Sun 2:00–5:00, and by
appointment
Pub. *Noank Ledger*, four times per year
$5.00 per year membership

North Haven Historical Society
27 Broadway
North Haven, CT 06473
(203) 239-7722
Mary K. Cervoni, President
winter: Tue & Thur 1:00–4:30; summer:
Thur 1:00–4:30
(archives and museum of local history,
including family history of North Haven
only)
$7.00 per year membership

North Stonington Historical Society, Inc.
(1 Wyassup Road—location)
PO Box 134 (mailing address)
North Stonington, CT 06359-0134
(860) 535-9448 (Library)
Library: Tue 2:00–4:00
Pub. *Newsletter*, nine times per year
(monthly, except July–Aug & Dec)
$10.00 per year membership

Norwalk Historical Commission
141 East Avenue
Norwalk, CT 06851
(203) 866-0202
Ralph C. Bloom, Curator
Mon–Fri 9:00–noon & 1:00–5:00
("all written and visual forms of local
history")
research: copy fee, research fees if required

Norwalk Historical Society
PO Box 335
Norwalk, CT 06852
(203) 846-0525
Richard A. Booth, President

The Old Bethlehem Historical Society, Inc.
North Main Street, The Green
Bethlehem, CT 06751
(203) 266-5188
Doris B. Nicholls, President

The Old Saybrook Historical Society
Archival Section
(Gen. Wm. Hart House, 350 Main
Street—location)
PO Box 4 (mailing address)
Old Saybrook, CT 06475
(860) 388-2622
Hart House library: Wed (seasonally)
10:30–noon; Archives, Main Street
School: Fri 9:30–noon, and by
appointment
(Archives consists of printed and manuscript
data on the history and genealogy of the
Saybrook Plantation, which became the
Connecticut towns of Old Saybrook,

Essex, Deep River, Chester and
Westbrook; Hart House library has bound
books on Connecticut and Saybrook
history)

Old Woodbury Historical Society
PO Box 705
Woodbury, CT 06798
Vera T. Elsenboss, President

Orange Historical Society
(615 Orange Center Road—location)
PO Box 784 (mailing address)
Orange, CT 06477
(203) 795-3106; (203) 795-9466 (President)
questions@orangehistory.org
http://www.orangehistory.org
Harry W. Jones, President
Sun (Apr–Oct) 1:00–3:00, and by
appointment
Pub. *OHS Newsletter*, five times per year
$4.00 per year membership

Oxford Historical Society, Inc.
154 Bowers Hill Road
Oxford, CT 06478
(203) 888-0363
Jane Fertig

Plainville Historical Society, Inc.
Plainville History Center
Farmington Canal Room
29 Pierce Street
Plainville, CT 06062
(860) 747-6577
Ruth Hummel, President
May–mid-Dec: Wed & Sat noon–3:30;
Office: usually Wed–Fri mornings
(before 1869 was part of Farmington, which
has older holdings)
$6.00 per year membership

Plymouth Historical Society
(572 Main Street—location)
PO Box 176 (mailing address)
Plymouth, CT 06782
(860) 283-8229
Marie MacDermid, Registrar
by appointment

Pomfret Historical Society, Inc.
(11 Town House Road—location)
PO Box 152 (mailing address)
Pomfret Center, CT 06259
(860) 974-3950 FAX
Elizabeth Carter, President; Mary G. Page,
Municipal Historian
hours: various
research fees depend on scope of search

Portland Historical Society, Inc.
PO Box 98
Portland, CT 06480

Prospect Historical Society
(Center Street—location)
6 Maria Hotchkiss (mailing address)
Prospect, CT 06712

Redding Historical Society, Inc.
Redding Center, CT 06875

**Ridgefield Library and Historical
Association**
Historical Collection
472 Main Street
Ridgefield, CT 06877
(203) 438-2282
Anita T. Daubenspeck, Director
Mon, Wed & Fri 10:00–6:00, Tue & Thur
10:00–9:00

Rocky Hill Historical Society
Academy Hall Museum
785 Old Main Street
Rocky Hill, CT 06067
(860) 379-6704

Rowayton Historical Society
(177 Rowayton Avenue—location)
PO Box 106 (mailing address)
Rowayton, CT 06853
fanders@optonline.net
http://www.rowayton.org
Fred Anderson, President

Roxbury Historical Society
Blue Stone Ridge
Roxbury, CT 06783

Salisbury Association (Historic Group)
(Scoville Library History Room, 38 Main
Street—location)
PO Box 516 (mailing address)
Salisbury, CT 06068-0516
(860) 435-9440
Virginia Moskowitz, Salisbury Town
Historian
by appointment
research fees depend on requests and what is
involved

Salmon Brook Historical Society
(208 Salmon Brook Street—location)
16 Hummingbird Lane (mailing address)
Granby, CT 06035
(860) 653-9713 (Society); (860) 653-3965
(Home)
http://www.salmonbrookhistorical.org
Carol Laun, Archivist/Genealogist
Tue & Thur 9:00–noon, and by appointment
Pub. *Collections of Salmon Brook Historical
Society*, every three to four years, cost
varies
(genealogy of Granby-Simsbury families,
Granby history)
$10.00 per year membership; research:
$20.00 per hour plus copies and mailing
costs

**Saybrook Colony Founders Association,
Inc.**
(see Lineage, Hereditary and Patriotic
Societies, Part 3)

Seymour Historical Society
(59 West Street—location)
PO Box 433 (mailing address)
Seymour, CT 06483
(203) 888-7471; (203) 888-0037
seymourhistsoc@aol.com
David Kummer, President; Alese Kummer,
Curator
Museum: first Sun by appointment; Office:
Thur
$10.00 per year membership

Shelton Historical Society
(70 Ripton Road—location)
PO Box 2155 (mailing address)
Shelton, CT 06484
(203) 925-1803
Mary Solomon, Director
Mon 10:00–4:00, seasonally two Sun per
month, and by appointment
Pub. *Shelton Historical Society News*,
quarterly
(local history of the City of Shelton, small
genealogical collection)
$15.00 per year membership; research: $8.00
plus copies at 25¢ per page

Sherman Historical Society and Museum
10 Route 37 Center

Sherman, CT 06784
(860) 354-3083; (860) 350-1187 FAX
shermanhistsoc@worldnet.att.net
http://www.shermanhistorical.org
Karen Borneman, Archivist
June–Oct: Sat–Sun 2:00–4:00, and daily by
    appointment
Pub. *S.H.S. Newsletter*, quarterly
(local genealogy and resource library)
$15.00 per year membership; research: copy
    and mail

Simsbury Historical Society
Phelps Tavern Museum and Homestead
(800 Hopmeadow Street—location)
PO Box 2 (mailing address)
Simsbury, CT 06070
(860) 658-2500; (860) 651-4354 FAX
simsburyhistory@aol.com
http://www.Simsbury_History.org
Stephen E. Simon, Librarian
Tue–Sat noon–4:00
Pub. *The Phelps Post*, quarterly
$15.00 per year membership; admission
    (includes tour and/or use of research):
    $6.00 for adults

South Windsor Historical Society, Inc.
PO Box 216
South Windsor, CT 06074

Southbury Historical Society, Inc.
PO Box 124
Southbury, CT 06488
(203) 264-2993
Richard C. Perry, President
Pub. *SHS Newsletter*, bimonthly
(local history and genealogy)
$10.00 per year membership

Southington Historical Society
Southington Historical Center
239 Main Street
Southington, CT 06489
(860) 621-4811

Sprague Historical Society
1 Main Street
Baltic, CT 06330

Stafford Historical Society, Inc.
(2 Main Street, Haymarket Square, Stafford
Springs, CT 06076—location)
PO Box 56 (mailing address)
Stafford Springs, CT 06075
David Bartlett, President
Sept–June: second Sun 2:00–4:00;
    July–Aug: Thur 2:00–4:00
Pub. *Newsletter*, quarterly
(local history, some regional and state
    history)
$5.00 per year membership

The Stamford Historical Society
1508 High Ridge Road
Stamford, CT 06903
(203) 329-1183; (203) 322-1607 FAX
history@stamfordhistory.org
http://www.stamfordhistory.org
Ron Marcus, Librarian
Tue–Sun noon–4:00
$35.00 per year membership; research:
    $25.00 contribution

The Stonington Historical Society
(Capt. Nathaniel B. Palmer House, 40
Palmer Street—location)
PO Box 103 (mailing address)
Stonington, CT 06378-0103
(860) 535-1131; (860) 535-0888 (Librarian);
    (860) 535-8445 (Palmer House); (860)
    535-1440 (Lighthouse)

Michael H. Davis, President; Robert D.
    Farwell, Librarian; Connie Colom, N. B.
    Palmer House-Manager; Louise Pittaway,
    Lighthouse Museum Curator
Palmer House: Tue–Sun (May–Nov)
    10:00–4:00; Lighthouse: Mon (July–Aug)
    & Tue–Sun (May–Nov) 10:00–5:00;
    Library: Wed 1:00–5:00, by appointment
Pub. *Historical Footnotes*, quarterly
("Genealogy and history of the Stonington
    area; also operate The Old Lighthouse
    Museum in Stonington.")
$10.00 per year membership; admission
    charge

The Stratford Historical Society
(Judson House and Catharine B. Mitchell
Museum, 967 Academy Hill—location)
PO Box 382 (mailing address)
Stratford, CT 06615
(203) 378-0630; (203) 378-2562
judsonhousestfd@aol.com
Carol W. Lovell, Curator
Office: Tue & Thur 9-2
Pub. *SHS Update*, bimonthly
(Stratford genealogy, manuscripts, photos,
    history of Stratford; "Very small library
    may be used for reference only; books not
    available for circulation.")
$12.00 per year membership

Suffield Historical Society
232 South Main Street
Suffield, CT 06078
(860) 668-5256
Roger C. Loomis, President

Thomaston Historical Society, Inc.
Town Hall, 158 Main Street
Thomaston, CT 06787
(860) 283-2159
Joseph Wassong, Curator
by appointment
$10.00 per year membership

The Thompson Historical Society
(339 Thompson Road—location)
PO Box 47 (mailing address)
Thompson, CT 06277
(860) 923-5728
jiamartino@charter.net
http://www.thompsonhistorical.org
Joseph Iamartino, President; Susan Vincent,
    Genealogist and Member Board of
    Directors
Museum shop: first Sat
Pub. *Newsletter*, four times per year
$10.00 per year membership

Tolland Historical Society, Inc.
PO Box 107
Tolland, CT 06084

Torrington Historical Society, Inc.
192 Main Street
Torrington, CT 06790
(860) 482-8260
Mark McEachern, Executive Director
Pub. *THS Newsletter*

Municipal Historian (Torrington)
City Hall, Room 209
140 Main Street
Torrington, CT 06790
Ernest Ceder

Totoket Historical Society, Inc.
(1 Library Place—location)
PO Box 563 (mailing address)
North Branford, CT 06471
(203) 488-0423
M. Grace Marx, President

Wed 2:00–4:00, first Sun 2:00–4:00
$7.00 per year membership

Trumbull Historical Society
PO Box 312
Trumbull, CT 06611-0312
(203) 377-6620 (answering machine)
http://www.trumbullhistory.org
Jean Rabinow, Managing Director, Betty
    Tracy, Genealogist
by appointment: Mon–Fri 9:30–1:30; walk-
    in: Thur 10:00–1:00, Sun 2:00–4:00
Pub. *Gristmill*, five times per year (Sept,
    Nov, Jan, Mar, May)
$10.00 per year membership

Union Historical Society, Inc.
(Town Hall Road—location)
1099 Buckley Highway (mailing address)
Union, CT 06076
(860) 684-7078
Jeannine M. Upson, President
by appointment
$3.00 per year membership

Wallingford Historical Society
(180 South Main Street—location)
PO Box 73 (mailing address)
Wallingford, CT 06492
(203) 294-1996
Robert N. Beaumont, President
Sun (Memorial Day–Labor Day) 2:00–4:30,
    and by appointment
$5.00 per year membership; research:
    donation plus expenses

Warren Historical Society
151 Melius Road
Warren, CT 06754
(860) 868-6724
Ellen Paul, Warren Town Historian
by appointment
(inactive society, whose collection, however,
    is still on display)

Waterford Historical Society, Inc.
(Jordan Green, Rope Ferry Road—location)
PO Box 117 (mailing address)
Waterford, CT 06385
Pub. *Crier*, irregularly

Watertown Historical Society, Inc.
22 DeForest Street
Watertown, CT 06795
(860) 274-1634

Weston Historical Society
(104 Weston Road—location)
PO Box 1092 (mailing address)
Weston, CT 06883

Westport Historical Society
Wheeler House
25 Avery Place
Westport, CT 06880
(203) 221-0981
Sheila O'Neill, Executive Director
Office: Mon–Fri 9:00–5:00; Museum:
    Tue–Sat 10:00–3:00
Pub. *News Notes*

Wethersfield Historical Society
150 Main Street
Wethersfield, CT 06109
(860) 529-7656; (860) 529-2609 FAX
weth.hist.society@snet.net
http://www.wethhist.org
Wesley Christensen, Research Associate
Tue–Fri 9:00–4:00, Sat 1:00–4:00
$23.00 per year membership

Dorothy Whitfield Historic Society, Inc.

Part 2. Connecticut

(84 Boston Street—location)
PO Box 229 (mailing address)
Guilford, CT 06437

Willington Historical Society
48 Red Oak Hill
West Willington, CT 06279
(860) 429-2656
Isabel Weigold, Town Historian
daily 9:00–3:00
Pub. *Hourglass*, quarterly
(Willington's early families, also Tolland
  County vital records and history)
$5.00 per year membership; research: $10.00
  per hour

Wilton Historical Society
224 Danbury Road
Wilton, CT 06897
(203) 762-3950; (203) 762-7257
Marilyn Gould, Director
Wilton History Room at the Wilton Library:
  Mon–Wed & Fri 9:00–5:30, Thur
  9:00–9:00, Sat 9:00–5:00, Sun (Oct–Apr)
  1:00–5:00
(local history and genealogy)

The Windsor Historical Society, Inc.
96 Palisado Avenue
Windsor, CT 06095
(860) 688-3813; (860) 687-1633 FAX
Robert T. Silliman, Director
1 Apr–31 Oct: Tue–Sat 10:00–4:00; 1
  Nov–31 Mar: Mon–Fri 10:00–4:00
Pub. *Windsor Historical Society News*,
  bimonthly
("Windsor, Connecticut, genealogy and
  history; Connecticut history. Repository
  for library of the Descendants of the
  Founders of Ancient Windsor.")
$18.00 per year membership; admission:
  $3.00 per day; research: fee negotiable

Windsor Locks Historical Society, Inc.
(Noden-Reed Park, 58 West
Street—location)
PO Box 733 (mailing address)
Windsor Locks, CT 06096
(860) 623-6686
Ruth Bonito, Curator; Joseph D. Bonito,
  President
Wed by appointment, Sun 1:00–5:00
Pub. *Windsor Locks Journal*
$5.00 per year membership; research:
  donation

Wintonbury Historical Society, Inc.
PO Box 7454
Bloomfield, CT 06002
fgabriel1@juno.com
Fannie R. Gabriel, President
$10.00 per year membership

Woodstock Historical Society
(523 Route 169—location)
PO Box 65 (mailing address)
Woodstock, CT 06281
$10.00 per year membership

Genealogical Societies

State Genealogical Society

Connecticut Society of Genealogists, Inc.
(175 Maple Street, East Hartford, CT
06118—library location)
PO Box 435 (mailing address)
Glastonbury, CT 06033-0435
(860) 569-0002; (860) 569-0339 FAX
csg@csginc.org
http://www.csginc.org
Helen H. Hodge, Office Manager

Mon–Fri 9:30–4:00 (except postal holidays)
Pub. *The Connecticut Nutmegger*, quarterly;
  CSG Newsletter, bimonthly
(Published *Connecting to Connecticut*.
  "Primarily Connecticut but New England
  also.")
$3.00 registration fee, $35.00 per year
  membership

Genealogical Societies—Local & Regional

American-Canadian Genealogical Society
(see New Hampshire, Part 2)

Connecticut Ancestry Society, Inc.
PO Box 249
Stamford, CT 06904-0249
(203) 457-9383 (Vice President)
Frederick C. Hart, Jr., C.G., Vice President
Pub. *Connecticut Ancestry*, quarterly
$25.00 per year membership

**Descendants of the Founders of Ancient
Windsor**
(see Lineage and Hereditary Societies, Part
3)

Middlesex Genealogical Society
PO Box 1111
Darien, CT 06820-1111
(203) 655-2734
sdshillinglaw@prodigy.net
http://mgs.darien.org/default.htm
Dorothy Shillinglaw, Newsletter Editor
Pub. *Middlesex Genealogical Society*

**The New England Historic Genealogical
Society**
(see Massachusetts, Part 2)

**New York Genealogical and Biographical
Society Library**
(see New York, Part 2)

**Palm Beach County Genealogical Society,
Inc.**
(see Florida, Part 2)

Southington Genealogical Society
Southington Historical Center
239 Main Street
Southington, CT 06489
(860) 628-7831
bahai999@aol.com
Raymond L. Thomas, President
fourth Tue 7:30 P.M. (about two hours)
Pub. *SGS Newsletter*, semiannually
$5.00 per year membership

Yankee Genealogical Society
Minnesota Genealogical Society
(see Massachusetts, Part 2)

Independent Publications and Miscellany

**Association for the Study of Connecticut
History**
Emerson College
100 Beacon Street
Boston, MA 02116
Pub. *Association for the Study of
  Connecticut History Newsletter*, quarterly;
  Connecticut History, annually, $10.00 per
  issue

**Association of Northeastern Connecticut
Historical Societies**
PO Box 104
Central Village, CT 06332
Alvin P. Ridgway, Jr., President

Pub. *News and Notes*
(publishes information about area history)

Canton Historic District Commission
Town Hall
Collinsville, CT 06022

**Connecticut Department of
Transportation**
2800 Berlin Turnpike
Newington, CT 06131-7546
(860) 594-2000
http://www.dot.state.ct.us/pub/maps/
  index.htm (Maps)

CtGenWeb
Part of The USGenWeb Project
George@Waller.Org
http://www.rootsweb.com/~ctgenweb
George Waller, State Coordinator
(links to other Connecticut resources)

Historical Ink's Old Maps
(see New York, Part 2)

**The Indian and Colonial Research Center,
Inc.**
(see Ethnic Archives, Libraries and
Societies—Native American, Part 3)

New England Connexion
PO Box 621
Goshen, NY 10924
Pub. *New England Connexion*
(specializing in New England genealogy:
  Connecticut, Maine, Massachusetts, New
  Hampshire, Rhode Island, and Vermont)

The New England Quarterly
(see Massachusetts, Part 2)

Old State House Association
800 Main Street
Hartford, CT 06103

Pioneer Publications
PO Box 1179
Tumtum, WA 99034-1179
(509) 276-1740
Shirley Penna-Oakes, Editor
Pub. *New England Queries and Reviews*,
  $6.00 plus $1.75 postage per issue

**Society for the Preservation of New
England Antiquities—Archives**
(see Massachusetts, Part 2)

Trumbull Bicentennial Page
http://trumbull.ct.us/history

Delaware

Archives and Libraries with Holdings in Genealogy

State Archives and Library

Delaware Public Archives
Hall of Records
(Corner of Duke of York and Legislature
Avenues, Dover, DE 19901—location)
PO Box 1401 (mailing address)
Dover, DE 19903
(302) 739-5318; (302) 739-2578 FAX
archives@state.de.us;
    joanne.mattern@state.de.us
http://www.archives.state.de.us
Joanne Mattern, Deputy State Archivist
Mon–Fri 8:30–4:15
(holdings include records collected by the
    Office of Vital Statistics and its
    predecessor from the mid-19th century
    until 1925 for births and 1957 for deaths
    and marriages)

Delaware State Library
Delaware Division of Libraries
43 South Dupont Highway
Dover, DE 19901
(302) 736-4748; (302) 739-6787 FAX
anorman@lib.de.us; webmaster@lib.de.us
http://www.state.lib.de.us
Annie Norman, Director

State Historical Society

Historical Society of Delaware
505 North Market Street
Wilmington, DE 19801-3091
(302) 655-7161; (302) 656-0637 (Museum);
    (302) 655-7844 FAX
hsd@hsd.org
http://www.hsd.org
Administrative Offices: Mon–Fri 9:00–5:00;
    Research Library: Mon 1:00–9:00,
    Tue–Fri 9:00–5:00
Pub. *Delaware History*, semiannually
(Delaware and Delaware families. "Research
    staff: three librarians")
$35.00 per year membership; research:
    $30.00 for nonmembers, $20.00 for
    members, plus photocopy costs

City, County and Regional Archives and Libraries
(A more exhaustive list of public and
academic libraries can be found at
http://.lib.de.us/search.shtml.)

**Brandywine Hundred Branch, New Castle
County Library**
(1300 Foulk Road, Wilmington, DE
19803–location)
87 Reads Way (mailing address)
New Castle, DE 19720
(302) 477-3150; (302) 477-4545 FAX
tweaver@co.new-castle.de.us
Thomas M. Weaver & Jean Kaufman,
    Directors
Mon–Fri 10:00–9:00, Sat 10:00–5:00, Sun
    1:00–9:00

Corbit-Calloway Memorial Library
(115 High Street—location)
PO Box 128 (mailing address)
Odessa, DE 19730
(302) 378-8838; (302) 378-7803 FAX
corbit@infionline.net;
    library@corbitlibrary.org
http://www.corbitlibrary.org
Steve Welch, Director

Mon & Thur 1:00–9:00, Tue & Fri
    10:00–5:00, Wed 10:00–9:00, Sat
    9:00–1:00, Sun 1:00–5:00

Delaware State University
William C. Jason Library-Learning Center
1200 North Dupont Highway
Dover, DE 19901-2277
(302) 736-5111; (302) 739-3571
    (Reference); (302) 739-3560 FAX
http://www.dsc.edu/library/library.html
Mon–Thur 8:00–midnight, Fri 8:00–8:00,
    Sat 9:00–5:00, Sun 2:00–10:00

**Research Center for Delmarva History
and Culture**
(see Maryland, Part 2)

Dover Public Library
45 South State Street
Dover, DE 19901
(302) 736-7030
sanderso@lib.de.us
http://www.kentnet.org
Sheila B. Anderson, Director
Mon–Thur 9:00–9:00, Fri–Sat 9:00–5:00,
    Sun 1:00–5:00

Hagley Museum and Library
(298 Buck Road East—location)
PO Box 3630 (mailing address)
Wilmington, DE 19807
(302) 658-2400; (302) 658-0568 FAX
mmcninch@hagley.org; lgross@hagley.org
http://www.hagley.lib.de.us
Marge McNinch, Reference Archivist; Linda
    Gross, Imprints Department
Mon–Fri 8:30–4:30, second Sat 9:00–4:30
(regional business and industrial records)

Laurel Public Library
101 East Fourth Street
Laurel, DE 19956
(302) 875-3184; (302) 875-4519 FAX
tlambert@lib.de.us
http://www.sussexcounty.net/libraries/
    index.html
Tamatha Lambert, Director
Mon–Thur 10:00–8:00, Fri 10:00–5:00, Sat
    10:00–2:00

Lewes Public Library
111 Adams Avenue
Lewes, DE 19958
(302) 645-2733; (302) 645-6235 FAX
cdudbrid@lib.de.us; info@leweslibrary.org
http://www.leweslibrary.org
Chris Dudbridge, Director

Milford Public Library
11 S.E. Front Street
Milford, DE 19963-1941
(302) 422-8996; (302) 422-9269 FAX
hudson@lib.de.us

    http://www.sussexcounty.net/libraries/ind
    ex.html
Kay M. Hudson
Mon, Wed & Fri 9:00–8:00, Tue & Thur
    9:00–6:00, Sat (Sept–May) 9:00–2:00;
    Sat (June–Aug) 9:00–noon)

New Castle Public Library
424 Delaware Street
New Castle, DE 19720
(302) 328-1995; (302) 328-4412 FAX
Sally Brown, Director
Mon–Tue 10:00–9:00, Wed–Thur 2:00–9:00,
    Fri 10:00–5:00, Sat 10:00–5:00

Old Swedes' Foundation
Holy Trinity (Old Swedes') Church

Foundation, Inc.
Hendrickson House Museum and Old
Swedes' Church
(see Ethnic Archives, Libraries and
Societies—Swedish, Part 3)

Rockwood Museum
610 Shipley Road
Wilmington, DE 19809-3609
(302) 761-4340

Seaford District Library
402 North Porter Street
Seaford, DE 19973
(302) 629-2524; (302) 629-9181 FAX
http://www.seaford.lib.de.us
Leigh Ann DePope, Director

Smyrna Public Library
107 South Main Street
Smyrna, DE 19977
(302) 653-4579; (302) 653-2650 FAX
smypublib58@yahoo.com
http://smyrnapubliclibrary.mybravenet.com
Mon, Wed & Fri 9:00–6:00, Tue & Thur
    11:00–8:30, Sat (Labor Day–Memorial
    Day) 9:00–2:00

University of Delaware
Morris Library
South College Avenue (Route 896)
Newark, DE 19717-5267
(302) 831-2965 (Reference); (302) 831-
    BOOK (Library); (302) 831-6952
    (Special Collections Department); (302)
    831-1046 FAX
timothy.murray@mvs.udel.edu;
    lrjm@udel.edu
http://www.lib.udel.edu;
    gopher://gopher.lib.udel.edu/11/ud/spec
admission: collection available for on-site
    use, but no individualized genealogical
    assistance available

Wesley College
Parker Library
College Square
Dover, DE 19901
(302) 736-2413; (302) 736-2301 FAX
http://www.wesley.edu/geninfo.htm

Widener University School of Law
Legal Information Center
Brandywine Valley Historical Collection
(4601 Concord Pike—location)
PO Box 7475 (mailing address)
Wilmington, DE 19803
(302) 477-2063; (302) 477-2240 FAX
http://www.widener.edu/law/lic/dir.htm

Wilmington Public Library
(10th and Market Streets—location)
PO Box 2303-19899 (mailing address)
Wilmington, DE 19801
(302) 571-7400; (302) 654-9132 FAX
wilmweb@lib.de.us
http://www.wilmlib.org
David Burdash, Director
Mon–Thur 9:00–8:00, Fri–Sat 9:00–5:00
copies: 15¢ each from paper originals, 25¢
    each from microfilm originals

**Winterthur Museum, Gardens, and
Library**
Winterthur Museum Archives
Winterthur, DE 19735
(302) 888-4701; (302) 888-4699; (302) 888-
    4870 FAX
http://www.libertynet.org/~pacscl/
    winterthur/index.html

Historical Societies—Local and Regional

Bethel Historical Society
PO Box 55
Bethel, DE 19931
(302) 875-5425

Bridgeville Historical Society
PO Box 306
Bridgeville, DE 19933
(302) 337-7823; (302) 327-7125

Duck Creek Historical Society
(227 East Mount Vernon Street—museum mailing address, 11 South Main Street—museum location)
PO Box 335 (mailing address)
Smyrna, DE 19977
(302) 653-8844; (302) 653-7023 (Museum)
George L. Caley, Secretary; Katherine D. Bailey, Museum
Sat 1:00–4:00, and by appointment
$10.00 per year membership

Fort Delaware Society
(122 Washington Street, Corner of Washington and Williams Streets—location)
PO Box 553 (mailing address)
Delaware City, DE 19706
(302) 834-1630; (302) 834-1630 FAX
FtDSociety@del.net
http://www.del.net/org/fort

Frederica Historical Society
Rural Delivery 2, Box 161AA
Lewes, DE 19958
(302) 945-0680
Dorothy Hudson

Georgetown Historical Society
Georgetown Chamber of Commerce
(37 The Circle—location)
PO Box 1 (mailing address)
Georgetown, DE 19947
(302) 856-1544; (302) 856-1577 FAX
Helen J. Kruger, Executive Director
Mon–Sat 8:30–4:30
$125.00 per year

The Greater Harrington Historical Society
(108-110 Fleming Street—location)
PO Box 64 (mailing address)
Harrington, DE 19952
(302) 398-3698
Grace C. Welch, Museum Manager
Mon–Fri 9:00–5:00, and by appointment
Pub. *Newsletter*, semiannually
(a small but growing genealogy section)
$5.00 per year membership

The Laurel Historical Society, Inc.
PO Box 102
Laurel, DE 19956
(302) 875-5678
Kendal T. Jones, President

The Lewes Historical Society
110 Shipcarpenter Street
Lewes, DE 19958-1210
(302) 645-7670; (302) 645-2375 FAX
research@historicLewes.org
http://www.historicLewes.org
Michael DiPaolo, Curator
Mon–Fri 9:00–5:00, appointment preferred
Pub. *Journal of the Lewes Historical Society*,
annually, $5.00 per year nonmember subscription
$15.00 per year membership

Milford Historical Society

(501 N.W. Front Street—location)
PO Box 352 (mailing address)
Milford, DE 19963
(302) 422-3569
Marvin Schelhouse, President; Brooke Clendaniel, Trustee
May–Oct: Sat–Sun 2:00–4:00, by appointment
Pub. *Milford Historical Society Newsletter*, semiannually (spring and fall), not available by subscription
("We have documents, photos, books, museum collections, artifacts.")
$10.00 per year membership

Milton Historical Society
210-212 Union Street
Milton, DE 19968
(302) 684-8851; (302) 684-8676

New Castle Historical Society
2 East Fourth Street
New Castle, DE 19720
(302) 322-2794
Kathleen Bidwell, Director

Newark Historical Society
PO Box 711
Newark, DE 19711
(302) 731-0955

Port Penn Historical Society
PO Box 120
Port Penn, DE 19731
(302) 834-2464; (302) 834-2421

Rehoboth Beach Historical Society, Inc.
Anna Hazzard Museum
Christian Street
Rehoboth Beach, DE 19971
(302) 841-0162
info@rehomain.com (Rehoboth Beach Main Street)
http://www.rehomain.com/museum.htm

Genealogical Societies

State Genealogical Society

Delaware Genealogical Society
505 North Market Street
Wilmington, DE 19801-3091
tdoherty@magpage.com
http://www.delgensoc.org
Historical Society of Delaware: Mon 1:00–9:00, Tue–Fri 9:00–5:00
Pub. *Delaware Genealogical Society Journal*, semiannually, $20.00 subscription for four issues; *Delaware Genealogical Society Newsletter*, five times per year (Jan, Mar, May, Sept, Nov); *Delaware Genealogical Guide*, $11.50 postpaid for nonmembers
$15.00 per year membership (includes both publications)

Genealogical Societies—Local & Regional

Downstate Delaware Genealogical Society
PO Box 1787
Dover, DE 19903

Lower Delmarva Genealogical Society
(see Maryland, Part 2)

Yankee Genealogical Society
Minnesota Genealogical Society
(see Massachusetts, Part 2)

Independent Publications and Miscellany

Cindy's Genealogy on the Eastern Shore of Maryland, Delaware, and Virginia
(see Maryland, Part 2)

Colonial Roots
217 Schley Avenue
Lewes, DE 19958
(302) 644-2798; (800) 576-8608; (302) 644-0484 FAX
customerservice@delmarvaroots.com
http://www.colonialroots.com
Holly Wright
Wed–Sat 10:00–5:00
("We publish and sell genealogy books for the mid-atlantic region. Visit our website and search our surname index to determine whether we have any books containing your family history.")

DeGenWeb
Part of The USGenWeb Project
degenweb@tyaskin.com
http://www.degenweb.org
Shari Handley, State Coordinator
(links to other Delaware resources)

Delaware Geographic Names Committee
rockman@udel.edu

Delaware Society for the Preservation of Antiquities
606 Stanton-Christiana Road
Newark, DE 19713
(302) 998-3792

Genealogy and History of the Eastern Shore (GHOTES)
(see Virginia, Part 2)

Fisher Martin House
Lewes Chamber of Commerce
(120 Kings Highway—location)
PO Box 1 (mailing address)
Lewes, DE 19958
(302) 645-8073; (302) 645-8412 FAX
http://www.leweschamber.com
Betsy Reamer, Executive Director
Mon–Fri 10:00–4:00, Sat (Memorial Day–Labor Day) 9:00–3:00, Sun (Memorial Day–Labor Day) 10:00–2:00
("historical site, no library")

Meetinghouse Galleries
316 South Governors Avenue
Dover, DE 19904-6706

Pioneer Publications
PO Box 1179
Tumtum, WA 99034-1179
(509) 276-1740
Shirley Penna-Oakes, Editor
Pub. *Mid-Atlantic Queries & Reviews (DE-NJ-MD-PA)*, $6.00 plus $1.75 postage per issue

District of Columbia

Archives and Libraries with Holdings in Genealogy

District Archives and Libraries

District of Columbia Archives
1300 Naylor Court, N.W.
Washington, DC 20001-4225
(202) 727-2054
Dorothy Provine, Archivist
by appointment
(DC original wills; marriage records)

District Historical Societies

U.S. Capitol Historical Society
200 Maryland Avenue, N.E.
Washington, DC 20002
(202) 543-8919
(no archives, no records of genealogical
interest)

The Historical Society of Washington, DC
1307 New Hampshire Avenue, N.W.
Washington, DC 20036-1507
(202) 785-2068; (202) 887-5785 FAX
Gail Redmann, Reference Librarian
Wed–Sat 10:00–4:00, Thur noon–4:00
(members only)
Pub. *Washington History*, two times per
year, $7.95 per issue
(over 14,000 volumes, vertical files,
microform collection, over 500 individual
manuscript collections, photographs,
prints, maps)
$40.00 per year membership; admission:
$3.00 for nonmembers; research: $30.00
per hour (half-hour minimum), including
up to 20 photocopies; copies: 20¢ per
exposure from paper originals for
nonmembers (15¢ for members), 50¢ per
exposure from microform originals (40¢
for members), plus minimum $5.00
postage and handling

City and Regional Archives and Libraries

**National Society, Daughters of the
American Revolution (D.A.R.)**
Library
(see Lineage, Hereditary and Patriotic
Societies—Revolutionary War, Part 4)

District of Columbia Public Library
Martin Luther King Memorial Library
Washingtoniana Division
901 G Street, N.W.
Washington, DC 20001
(202) 727-1213; (202) 727-1129 FAX
wash.dcpl@dc.gov
http://www.dclibrary.org
Susan Malbin, Chief
Mon–Thur 10:00–9:00, Fri–Sat 10:00–5:30,
Sun (Sept to mid-June) 1:00–5:00

Folger Shakespeare Library
201 East Capitol Street, S.E.
Washington, DC 20003-1094
(202) 544-4600
(17th-century immigration lists)

Georgetown University
Lauinger Library
Special Collections
PO Box 571174
Washington, DC 20057-1174
http://gulib.lausun.georgetown.edu

Library of Congress
Local History and Genealogy Reading Room
Humanities and Social Sciences Division
Thomas Jefferson Building, Room LJ42
101 Independence Ave., S.E.
Washington, DC 20540-5554
(202) 707-5537
lhgref@loc.gov
http://www.loc.gov/rr/genealogy
Judith Prowse Roach, Head
Mon & Wed–Thur 8:30–9:30, Tue & Fri–Sat
8:30–5:00, Sun 1:00–5:00
(published genealogies and U.S. local
histories)

Smithsonian Institution
1000 Jefferson Drive
Washington, DC 20560
(202) 357-2700
info@si.edu
http://www.si.edu
Mon–Sat 9:00–4:00

White House Historical Association
740 Jackson Place, N.W.
Washington, DC 20503
Bernard R. Meyer, Executive Vice President
Mon–Fri 9:00–4:30
Pub. *White House History Journal*,
occasionally, $6.00 per copy
(history relating to the White House)

Genealogical Society

Ohio Genealogical Society
National Capital Buckeye Chapter
(see Ohio, Part 2)

Independent Publications and Miscellany

Advisory Council on Historic Preservation
1100 Pennsylvania Avenue, N.W., Suite 809
Washington, DC 20004

DCGenWeb
Part of The USGenweb Project
genealogyldy@cs.com
http://www.rootsweb.com/~dcgenweb/
about.html
Debi Remer, State Coordinator
(links to other DC resources)

Florida

Archives and Libraries with Holdings in Genealogy

State Archives and Library

Florida State Archives
Bureau of Archives and Records
Management
Division of Library and Information Services
R. A. Gray Building
500 South Bronough Street
Tallahassee, FL 32399-0250
(850) 487-2073 (State Archives); (850) 488-
4894 FAX
barm@mail.dos.state.fl.us
http://dlis.dos.state.fl.us/barm/fsa.html
Miriam Gan-Spalding, Reference
Coordinator
Mon–Fri 8:00–5:00, Sat 9:00–3:00 (closed
on state holidays and holiday weekends)

State Library of Florida
Florida Collection
Division of Library and Information Services
R. A. Gray Building, Second Floor
500 South Bronough Street
Tallahassee, FL 32399-0250
(850) 245-6600; (850) 487-2651 (State
Library); (850) 488-2746 (Florida
Collection)
info@mail.dos.state.fl.us
http://dlis.dos.state.fl.us/stlib
Elaine Martin Dickinson, Librarian
Specialist
Mon–Fri 8:00–5:00, Sat 9:30–3:30

WebLUIS!
Florida Center for Library Automation
http://webluis.fcla.edu/cgi-bin/cgiwrap/
fclwlv3/wlv3/CM02/DGgen/DBwebluis/P
1home (or via link at http://www. fcla.
edu/index.html)
(statewide online library catalog)

State Historical Society

Florida Historical Society
1320 Highland Avenue
Melbourne, FL 32935
(321) 254-9855
Flahistoricalsoc@aol.com
http://www.florida-historical-soc.org
Debra Wynne, Archivist
Research Library at 435 Brevard Avenue,
Cocoa, FL 32922: Tue–Sat 10:00–5:00 by
appointment
Pub. *Florida Historical Quarterly*
$40.00 per year membership; research $5.00
per hour or part thereof, plus 10¢ per copy
for first 50 copies and 5¢ per copy over 50
copies, plus postage, invoiced prior to
shipment of materials

Florida History Associates
R. A. Gray Building
500 South Bronough Street
Tallahassee, FL 32399-0250
(850) 488-1484
M. Diane Lewis, Secretary
Pub. *Newsletter*

City, County and Regional Archives and Libraries
(A more exhaustive list of public and
academic libraries can be found at http://
librarydata.dos.state.fl.us/PLQuerResults.
cfm, http://dlis.dos.state.fl.us/fgils/fl_lib.
html, http://www.rrc.usf.edu/publib/index.
html, or http://dlis.dos.state.fl.us/bld/)

Research_Office/2002LibraryDirectory/
Public_Libraries.pdf.)

Alachua County Library District
401 East University Avenue
Gainesville, FL 32601
(352) 334-3934
bpowell@exchange.acld.lib.fl.us
http://www.acld.lib.fl.us;
   http://heritage.acld.lib.fl.us (Heritage
   Collection)
Bobby Ruth Powell, Librarian
Mon–Thur 10:00–9:00, Fri–Sat 10:00–5:00,
   Sun 1:00–5:00

Amelia Island Museum of History
Research Room for Florida and Georgia
Family History
233 South Third Street
Fernandina Beach, FL 32034
(904) 261-7378; (904) 261-9701 FAX
http://ameliaislandmuseumofhistory.org
David Mallery, Curator
10:00–5:00

Bay County Public Library
(25 West Government Street, Panama City,
   FL 32402—location)
PO Box 59625 (mailing address)
Panama City, FL 32412-0625
(850) 872-7500; (850) 872-7508 FAX
kleback@nwrls.lib.fl.us
http://www.nwrls.lib.fl.us
Linda Pazics Kleback, Genealogy Specialist
Mon–Wed 9:00–8:00, Thur–Sat 9:00–5:00,
   Sun 1:00–5:00

Birmingham Public Library
(see Alabama, Part 2)

Bonita Springs Public Library
26876 Pine Avenue
Bonita Springs, FL 33923
(239) 992-0101; (239) 992-6680 FAX
mpollock@leegov.com
http://www.lee-county.com/library
Maureen Pollock, Librarian
Mon, Wed & Fri 10:00–6:00, Tue & Thur
   10:00–8:00, Sat 9:00–5:00

Boynton Beach City Library
208 South Seacrest Boulevard
Boynton Beach, FL 33435
(561) 742-6395; (561) 742-6381 FAX
coupb@co-op.pbcl.lib.fl.us
http://coala.org/boynton
William Coup, Reference Librarian
Mon–Thur 9:00–8:30, Fri–Sat 9:00–5:00
("We have the *Palm Beach Post* online from
   1989 and the *South Florida Sun-Sentinel*
   [Fort Lauderdale] online from 1986.")

Bradford County Public Library
105 East Jackson Street
Starke, FL 32091-3396
(904) 964-6400; (904) 964-9463 FAX
bradford@neflin.org
http://www.neflin.org/bradford
Phalbe Henriksen, Director
Mon 9:00–8:00, Tue–Thur 9:00–7:00,
   Fri–Sat 9:00–5:00

Brevard Community College
Learning Resource Centers/Genealogy
Department
Cocoa Campus
BCC/UCF Joint Use Library
1519 Clearlake Road
Cocoa, FL 32922-6597
(321) 632-1111 ext. 62963 (Genealogy);
   (321) 634-3734 FAX
boonstram@brevardcc.edu

http://web2010.brevard.cc.fl.us/library/
   genealogy.html
Michael J. Boonstra, C.G.
Tue & Thur–Fri 8:00–5:00, Wed noon–8:00,
   Sat 9:00–5:00
("Diverse genealogy collection with
   approximately 370 CD-ROMs and six
   computers for public use.")

**The Brevard Museum of History and
Natural Science**
2201 Michigan Avenue
Cocoa, FL 32926
(321) 632-1830
Rachel C. Moehle, Director
(primarily historical, not genealogical)

**The Burdick International Ancestry
Library**
2317 Riverbluff Parkway, #249
Sarasota, FL 34231-5032
(941) 922-7931
Frank P. Mueller, Executive Director and
   Editor
daily 9:00–4:00

Cape Coral Public Library
(see Fort Myers-Lee County Public Library,
below)

**Central Brevard Library and Reference
Center**
308 Forrest Avenue
Cocoa, FL 32922-7781
(407) 633-1792; (321) 633-1964 FAX
dvosatka@manatee.brev.lib.fl.us
http://www.brev.org/locations/central_
   brevard/index.htm
Diane Vosatka, Adult Services

Clearwater Public Library
Main Library
100 North Osceola Avenue
Clearwater, FL 33755-4083
(727) 562-4970; (727) 562-4977 FAX
jszabo@clearwater-fl.com;
   library@public.lib.ci.clearwater.fl.us;
   treed@clearwater-fl.com (Webmaster)
http://www.clearwater-fl.com/cpl
John F. Szabo, Library Director

Collier County Museum
Collier County Government Center
3301 Tamiami Trail East
Naples, FL 34112
(941) 774-8476; (941) 774-8580 FAX
Carrie Lee Welch, Curator of Collections
Museum: Mon–Fri 9:00–5:00; Library: by
   appointment only
(documents from the pioneer era and
   Seminole Indian culture)

Collier County Public Library
Headquarters Division
2385 Orange Blossom Drive
Naples, FL 34109
(239) 593-0177; (239) 591-3784 FAX
hqref@collier-lib.org
http://www.collier-lib.org
Harriet K. Protos
Mon–Thur 9:00–8:00, Fri–Sat 9:00–5:00
(growing genealogy collection; *Naples Daily
   News* Obituary Index online)
Library card free to county residents,
   available to nonresidents for a fee, but
   genealogy collection is noncirculating

Cooper Memorial Library
620 Montrose Street
Clermont, FL 34711-2166
(904) 394-4265; (352) 394-6359 FAX
jseery@lakeline.lib.fl.us

http://www.lakeline.lib.fl.us
John Seery, Regional Branch Manager

Cornell Museum
Delray Beach Historical Society Archives
51 North Swinton Avenue
Delray Beach, FL 33444
(561) 243-7922

DeLand Area Public Library
130 East Howry Avenue
DeLand, FL 32724-5517
(386) 734-2424; (386) 822-6430
kmann@co.volusia.fl.us
http://merlin.vcpl.lib.fl.us
Kathleen Mann, Regional Librarian
Mon & Wed 10:00–6:00, Tue & Thur
   10:00–8:00, Fri 10:00–5:00, Sat
   9:00–5:00

Eaton Florida History Room
Manatee County Central Library
1301 Barcarrota Boulevard West
Bradenton, FL 34205-7599
(941) 748-5555; (941) 749-7155 FAX
reference@co.manatee.fl.us
http://www.co.manatee.fl.us/service/library
Pamela N. Gibson, Eaton Room Librarian;
   Judy Mullen, Librarian for Genealogy
   Department
Mon–Thur 9:00–9:00, Fri–Sat 10:00–5:00,
   Sun 1:00–5:00
(Florida and local Manatee County history,
   description and travel; books, maps,
   magazines, 30,000 archival negatives,
   microfilm of old newspapers and Florida
   census; main concentration is on both the
   area covered by Old Manatee County,
   stretching to the Peace River and Lake
   Okeechobee, and the history taking place
   within the current boundaries of the
   county. "New 'Floridiana-on-the-web'
   site from the University of South Florida
   now includes 212 of our old negative
   views, can be printed or downloaded
   free.")

Elmer's Genealogy Library
203 South Range Street
Madison, FL 32340-2437
(850) 973-3282; (850) 929-2970 FAX
espear@elmerslibrary.com
http://www.elmerslibrary.com
Elmer Spear, Founder; Sandra Norris,
   Librarian
Mon–Fri 10:00–4:00
Pub. *Library News*, quarterly (Jan, Apr, July,
   Oct)
(19,460 books, 3,840 rolls of microfilm, 28
   cabinet drawers of vertical files, over 160
   CDs, newsletters from 140 genealogy
   societies.)
$30.00 per year membership; admission:
   $8.00 per day; research: limited servic
   available; copies: 20¢ per page from paper
   originals, 50¢ per page from microform
   originals

Florida Folklife Archives
500 South Bronough Street
Tallahassee, FL 32399-0250

Florida State Museum
Museum Drive
Gainesville, FL 32611
(352) 392-1721

Florida State University Libraries
105 Dogwood Way
Tallahassee, FL 32306-2047
(850) 644-2706; (850) 644-5016 FAX
http://www.fsu.edu/library

hours: various according to the semester (see web site)

Fort Myers Historical Museum
2300 Peck Street
Fort Myers, FL 33901
(941) 322-5955
Patricia Bartlett, Director

Fort Myers-Lee County Public Library
2050 Central Avenue
Fort Myers, FL 33901-3917
(239) 479-4635; (941) 479-4634 FAX
bmulcahy@leegov.com;
  bryanmulcahy@hotmail.com
http://www.lee-county.com/library
Bryan L. Mulcahy, Librarian
Mon–Thur 9:00–9:00, Fri–Sat 9:00–6:00;
  "[P]atrons seeking any assistance beyond
  directional information must make an
  appointment with either the genealogy
  librarian or visit the collection on a day
  when one of our genealogy volunteers is
  available: usually Mon 9:00–4:00, Tue
  noon–4:00, Thur (Oct–May) 11:00–4:00,
  Fri–Sat 1:00–4:00
(basic research materials covering states east
  of the Mississippi River; consolidated
  collections formerly in Lee County
  Branches in Cape Coral, Pine Island and
  Lehigh Acres; received collection of Cape
  Coral Public Library)

Heritage Museum of Northwest Florida
(115 Westview Avenue—location)
PO Box 488 (mailing address)
Valparaiso, FL 32580-0488
(850) 678-2615; (850) 678-4547 FAX
http://heritage-museum.org
Barbara Lee Moss, Director
Tue–Sat 11:00–4:00
(local history, Florida history, family history)

Helen B. Hoffman Library
501 North Fig Tree Lane
Plantation, FL 33317
(954) 797-2140; (954) 797-2767 FAX
dmerritt@excite.com
Dee Anne Merritt, Director
Mon 6:30–8:00, Wed–Thur 9:00–1:00, Sat
  10:00–2:00

Homestead Branch Library
(50-52 SE 4 Road—temporary location)
700 North Homestead Boulevard (mailing
address)
Homestead, FL 33030
(305) 246-0168; (305) 248-7817 FAX
http://www.mdpls.org/info/locations/al.asp
Pamela Hogue, Librarian
Mon–Thur 9:30–6:00, Sat 9:30–6:00

**Huntsville-Madison County Public
Library**
(see Alabama, Part 2)

Indian River County Main Library
The Julian W. Lowenstein History and
Genealogy Department
1600 21st Street
Vero Beach, FL 32960
(772) 770-5060; (772) 770-5066 FAX
pcooper@indian-river.lib.fl.us
http://indian-river.lib.fl.us
Pamela J. Cooper, Supervisor, Florida
  History and Genealogy Department
Mon–Thur 10:00–8:00, Fri 10:00–5:00, Sat
  10:00–4:00
(specializes in states east of the Mississippi,
  large microform collection which includes
  manuscripts and British directories,
  extensive Florida collection which is

located in a separate room)

Jackson County Public Library
2929 Green Street
Marianna, FL 32446
(850) 482-9631; (850) 482-9632 FAX
http://www.rrcusf.edu/publib/jackson/
  index.html

Jacksonville Public Libraries
Main Library, Florida and Genealogy Room
122 North Ocean Street
Jacksonville, FL 32202-3314
(904) 630-2409 (Genealogy); (904) 630-
  2410 (Florida Collection); (904) 630-
  2431 FAX
http://jpl.coj.net
Mr. Carol Harris, Florida Curator; Arden
  Brugger, Genealogy Librarian
Mon 10:00–8:00, Tue–Thur 10:00–5:30,
  Fri–Sat 10:00–6:00

Jefferson County Public Library
260 North Cherry Street
Monticello, FL 32344
(850) 997-3712; (904) 342-0205; (850) 342-
  0207 FAX
http://www.jefferson.lib.fl.us
Mary Laverty, Director
Tue 11:00–8:00, Wed–Fri 9:00–5:30, Sat
  9:00–3:00
("All of our genealogy information
  collection, etc., has been turned over to
  Keystone Genealogy Society.")

Lakeland Public Library
Special Collections (Lakeland) Room
100 Lake Morton Drive
Lakeland, FL 33801
(941) 284-4269 (Special Collections); (863)
  834-4280; (863) 834-4271 (City
  Librarian); (941) 284-4327 FAX
http://www.lakelandgov.net/library
Kevin Logan, Special Collections Librarian
Mon–Fri 9:00–5:00, and by appointment

Largo Library
351 East Bay Drive
Largo, FL 33770-3793
(727) 587-6748; (727) 586-7410 (Genealogy
  Line); (727) 587-6738 FAX
largolib@yahoo.com (Reference questions)
http://www.largo.com/library.html
Mercedes Bleattler, Special Collections
  Director; Barbara Murphey, Director
Mon–Thur 9:30–9:00, Fri–Sat 9:30–5:00,
  Sun 1:00–5:00; genealogy volunteer on
  duty Mon–Sat 9:30–3:30
("Specializing in the New England,
  Southeastern, and Mid-Atlantic regions,
  with a sizable European and Canadian
  collection. Information on early Pinellas
  County settlers. Most federal censuses;
  D.A.R. and S.A.R. Repository for local
  chapters." Received entire collection of
  Saint Petersburg Public Library)

Leesburg Public Library
204 North Fifth Street
Leesburg, FL 34748
(352) 728-9790; (352) 728-9794 FAX
chaines@ci.leesburg.fl.us
http://www.lakeline.lib.fl.us
Barbara Morse, Director; Cathy Haines,
  Assistant Library Director
Mon–Thur 9:00–9:00, Fri 9:00–6:00, Sat
  9:00–3:00, Sun 1:00–5:00
(collection includes local history and
  genealogy material on Leesburg and Lake
  County, Florida; also material on Sumter
  and Marion County, Florida, federal
  census for Florida through 1920;

reference collection focuses on all states
east of the Mississippi)

Maitland Historical Museum
(221 Packwood Avenue—location)
PO Box 941001 (mailing address)
Maitland, FL 32794
(407) 644-2451
http://sundial.net/~bayston/Maitland/
  histsoc.html

Manatee County Central Library
(see Eaton Florida History Room, above)

**Manatee County Historical Records
Library**
1405 Fourth Avenue, West
Bradenton, FL 34205-7507
(941) 741-4070
cathy.slusser@manateeclerk.com;
  cindy.russell@manateeclerk.com
  (Research Requests)
http://www.manateeclerk.com
Cathy Slusser, Supervisor
8:30–5:00
(houses all of Manatee County's
  governmental records from 1855 to the
  mid-1970s and into the 1990s)

Melbourne Public Library
540 East Fee Avenue
Melbourne, FL 32901
(321) 952-4514; (321) 952-4518 FAX
http://www.brev.org/locations/melbourne/
  index.htm
Jeri Prieth, Director

Miami Beach Public Library
2100 Collins Avenue
Miami, FL 33139
(305) 535-4219; (305) 673-7535; (305) 535-
  4224 FAX
http://www.mdpls.org

Miami-Dade Public Library
Genealogy Collection
101 West Flagler Street
Miami, FL 33130-1523
(305) 375-5580
alpertp@mdpls.org
http://www.mdpls.org
Renee Pierce, Genealogy Librarian
Mon–Wed & Fri–Sat 9:00–6:00, Thur
  9:00–9:00, Sun (Oct–May) 1:00–5:00

Monroe County-May Hill Russell Library
Florida Reference Room
700 Fleming Street
Key West, FL 33040
(305) 292-3595; (305) 295-3626 FAX
kula-norma@monroecounty-fl.com
http://www.keyslibraries.org
Lynda Hambright, Genealogist; Norma Kula,
  Director
Mon 11:00–8:00, Tue & Thur–Sat
  10:00–6:00, Wed 9:00–8:00
(specializes in Florida Keys and Bahamas)

Museum of Florida History
Florida Museum Association
R. A. Gray Building
500 South Bronough Street
Tallahassee, FL 32399-0250
(850) 488-1484; (850) 921-2503 FAX
http://www.dos.state.fl.us./dhr/museum
Wanda Richey, Publicity Coordinator
Mon–Fri 9:00–4:30, Sat 10:00–4:30, Sun
  noon–4:30
Pub. *The Associate*, bimonthly
(history of Florida)

North Brevard Public Library

2121 South Hopkins Avenue
Titusville, FL 32780-4725
(321) 264-5026; (321) 264-5030 FAX
http://www.brev.org/locations/north_
brevard/index.htm
Nancy C. Sieck, Volunteer Genealogist
Mon–Thur 9:00–9:00, Fri–Sat 9:00–5:00,
Sun 1:00–5:00; Ms. Sieck on duty Tue
10:00–2:00
(genealogy collection)

**Orange County Library System/Orlando
Public Library**
Genealogy Department
101 East Central Boulevard
Orlando, FL 32801
(407) 835-7323; (407) 835-7649 FAX
gronlund@ocls.info
http://www.ocls.info
Gregg B. Gronlund, Department Head
Mon–Thur 9:00–9:00, Fri–Sat 9:00–6:00,
Sun 1:00–6:00
(all 1790–1930 federal censuses (no
Soundex), passenger list indexes, the state
DAR collection; states east of the
Mississippi, on-site access to full
subscription Ancestry Plus)

Orange County Regional History Center
65 East Central Boulevard
Orlando, FL 32801
(407) 836-8500; (800) 965-2030
membership@ocfl.net
http://www.thehistorycenter.org/home.html
Mon–Sat 10:00–5:00, Sun noon–5:00
Pub. *The Historian*
$40.00 per year membership; admission:
$7.00 for adult nonmembers

Orlando Public Library
(see Orange County Library System, above)

Ormond Beach Public Library
30 South Beach Street
Ormond Beach, FL 32174-6380
(386) 673-0163; (386) 676-4191; (386) 676-
4194 FAX
wjubinsky@co.volusia.fl.us
http://merlin.vcpl.lib.fl.us
Walter Jubinsky, Regional Librarian
Mon & Wed 10:00–8:00, Tue & Thur
10:00–6:00, Fri 10:00–5:00, Sat
9:00–5:00

Palm Harbor Library
2330 Nebraska Avenue
Palm Harbor, FL 34683
(727) 784-3332; (727) 784-6772 FAX
coppolg@tblc.org (Director)
http://www.palmharborlibrary.org
Mitzi Streeter, Head of Reference; Gene
Coppola, Director
Mon–Thur 10:00–8:00, Fri–Sat 10:00–5:00;
volunteer assistance: Mon–Fri 1:00–4:00

**Polk County Historical and Genealogical
Library**
100 East Main Street
Bartow, FL 33830-4629
(863) 534-4380; (863) 534-4382 FAX
jspann@pclc.lib.fl.us
http://www.polk-county.net/library.html
Joseph E. Spann, Jr., Library Manager
Tue–Sat 10:00–5:00; closed first Tue
(over 30,000 books, 7,000 microfilms, focus
on southeastern United States)
copies: 15¢ per page from paper originals,
50¢ per page from microform originals

Putnam County Library System
Palatka Public Library
Headquarters Library

Attn: Stephen J. Crowley, Library Director
601 College Road
Palatka, FL 32177-3873
(386) 329-0126; (386) 329-1240 FAX
crowles@gbso.net
http://www.putnam-fl.com/lib

**Safety Harbor Museum of History and
Fine Arts**
329 South Bayshore
Safety Harbor, FL 34695
(727) 726-1668; (727) 725-9938
shmuseum@ij.net
http://www.safety-harbor-museum.org
Betty Quibell, Director
Wed–Fri 10:00–4:00, Sat–Sun 1:00–4:00
("Safety Harbor, Pinellas County, West
Central Florida local history and
archeology.")
$25.00+ per year membership; research:
$25.00 per hour, one-hour minimum

Safety Harbor Public Library
101 Second Street, North
Safety Harbor, FL 34695
(727) 724-1525; (727) 724-1533 FAX
bullial@tblc.org
http://www.tblc.org/shpl
Lana Bullian, Director
Mon–Thur 9:00–8:00, Fri–Sat 9:00–6:00,
Sun 1:00–5:00

Saint Johns County Public Library
Main Branch Library
1960 North Ponce de Leon Boulevard
Saint Augustine, FL 32084-2620
(904) 823-2651; (904) 823-2656 FAX
libm@co.st-johns.fl.us
http://www.sjcpls.org; mjlittle@co.st-
johns.fl.us
Mary Jane Little, Library System Director

Saint Lucie County Library System
Fort Pierce Library and Library System
Administration
124 North Indian River Drive
Fort Pierce, FL 34950-4402
(772) 468-1615; (772) 462-2750 FAX
http://www.st-lucie.lib.fl.us
John Byrn, Reference Coordinator
Mon–Wed 9:00–8:30, Thur–Fri 9:00–6:00,
Sat 9:00–5:00, Sun 1:00–5:00

Saint Petersburg Public Library
(see Largo Library, above)

Sanford Museum
(520 East First Street, Sanford, FL
32771—location)
PO Box 1788 (mailing address)
Sanford, FL 32772-1788
(407) 302-1000; (407) 330-5666 FAX
Alicia Clarke, Curator
Tue–Fri 11:00–4:00, Sat 1:00–4:00
(local history; Henry S. Sanford papers of the
Civil War, the U.S. State Department,
Belgian Congo, Florida development,
Swedish American colony)

Sanibel Public Library
770 Dunlop Road
Sanibel, FL 33957-4016
(239) 472-2483; (239) 472-9524 FAX
pallen@sanlib.org; reference@sanlib.org
http://www.sanlib.org
Patricia J. Allen, Director

Sarasota County Library System
Selby Public Library
1331 First Street
Sarasota, FL 34236
(941) 861-1100; (941) 316-1181; (941) 316-

1188 FAX
lnolan@sarasota.lib.fl.us
http://suncat.co.sarasota.fl.us
Liz Nolan, Head Librarian

South Florida Museum
PO Box 9265
Bradenton, FL 34206-9265
Jennifer M. Hamilton

Historical Museum of Southern Florida
101 West Flagler Street
Miami, FL 33130-1523
(305) 375-1492
ARCHIVES@HISTORICAL-
MUSEUM.ORG
http://www.historical-museum.org/index.htm
Dawn Hugh, Archives Manager
Museum: Mon–Sat 10:00–5:00, Sun
noon–5:00; Research Center: Mon–Fri
10:00–4:30
Pub. *Currents-Historical Museum of
Southern Florida*, quarterly; *South
Florida History Magazine*, quarterly;
Tequesta, annually
(southern Florida and Caribbean history,
folklife and archaeology; research center,
archives and exhibitions)
$35.00 per year membership

Suwannee River Regional Library System
Headquarters
1848 Ohio Avenue South
Live Oak, FL 32064
(386) 362-2317; (386) 364-6071 FAX
dhales@neflin.org
http://www.neflin.org/srrl
John D. Hales, Jr., Library Director

Tampa Bay Historical Center
(225 South Franklin Street—location)
PO Box 948 (mailing address)
Tampa, FL 33601-0948
(813) 228-0097; (813) 223-7021 FAX
http://tampabayhistorycenter.org
Barbara Ware, Archivist/Librarian
Center: Tue–Sat 10:00–5:00; Library:
Tue–Fri 10:00–5:00
("For genealogical purposes we have a
collection of family and subject files
pertaining to local area and pioneer
families.")
costs: for printing, handling and mailing,
plus research after the first half hour

Tampa Bay Library Consortium
10002 Princess Palm Avenue, Suite 124
Tampa, FL 33619
(813) 622-8252; (813) 628-4425 FAX
http://snoopy.tblc.lib.fl.us

**Tampa-Hillsborough County Public
Library System**
History and Genealogy Department
900 North Ashley Drive
Tampa, FL 33602-3788
(813) 273-3652
http://www.hcplc.org
Lisa Wagner, Senior Librarian
Mon–Thur 9:00–9:00, Fri 9:00–6:00, Sat
9:00–5:00, Sun 10:00–6:00
("Genealogical holdings include southeastern
U.S., the original thirteen colonies, and
those states bordering the Mississippi
River; collection also includes Florida
history and Burgert Brothers
Photographic Collection.")

Tampa Museum
601 Doyle Carlton Drive
Tampa, FL 33602-4395
R. Andrew Maass

University of Central Florida Library
PO Box 160000
Orlando, FL 32816
http://pegasus.cc.ucf.edu/~library/special.
   htm

University of Florida Libraries
404 Library West
Gainesville, FL 32611
(352) 392-0319
Elizabeth Alexander, Librarian/Chair
(Florida and the southeast)

University of Florida
P. K. Yonge Library of Florida History
208 Smathers Library
Gainesville, FL 32611
(352) 392-0319; (352) 392-9075, ext. 306
   (Department of Special Collections)
jamcusi@mail.uflib.ufl.edu
http://web.uflib.ufl.edu/spec/pkyonge/
   index.html
James Cusick, Curator, Florida History
(biographical materials, church records,
   manuscripts, maps)

University of Miami
Archives and Special Collections
Department
Otto G. Richter Library
Coral Gables, FL 33124
(305) 284-3247; (305) 665-7352 FAX
(also Cuban collection)

University of Mississippi
Center for the Study of Southern Culture
(see Mississippi, Part 2)

University of South Florida
USF Library, LIB 407
Special Collections Department
4204 East Fowler Avenue
Tampa, FL 33620-5400
(813) 974-2731; (813) 974-5153 FAX
admmail@dudley.lib.usf.edu
http://www.lib.usf.edu/spccoll/genea.html
   (Genealogy Resources);
   http://www.lib.usf.edu/virtual/ldc/floridia
   na/index.html (Floridiana on the Web)

University of Southern Alabama
Gulf Coast Historical Review
(see Alabama, Part 2)

University of West Florida
John C. Pace Library
Special Collections Department
11000 University Drive
Pensacola, FL 32514-5750
(850) 474-2213; (850) 474-3338 FAX
ddebolt@uwf.edu
http://library.uwf.edu
Dean DeBolt, University Librarian
Mon–Fri 8:00–noon & 12:30–4:30;
   Mon–Thur 5:00–9:00 (fall/spring
   semesters), other hours by appointment
("We are a regional history collection
   covering West Florida from earliest
   settlement to the present with over 700
   collections of family, business,
   organization, government, church, and
   personal papers and records. In addition
   we have the largest holding of Panhandle
   Florida newspapers in existence, some
   300 papers, from as early as 1821, with
   ongoing subscriptions to currently
   published periodicals. There are also
   photograph collections (30,000+) of
   places, people, and buildings; map
   collections including Sanborn Insurance
   maps for all Florida cities; census records
   for Florida and the South; runs of city

directories for Florida cities in the
   Panhandle. We also have a unique multi-
   volume index titled *Bibliography of West
   Florida*, which is an annotated
   bibliography to any published information
   about the people, history, and areas of the
   Panhandle (government documents,
   journal articles, books, etc.")
will undertake modest reference service,
   including copying newspaper obituaries,
   for example, for costs for photocopying or
   photograph reproduction

University School Library
7500 S.W. 36th Street
Fort Lauderdale, FL 33066

**Venice Archives and Area Historical
Collection**
351 South Nassau Street
Venice, FL 34285
(941) 486-2487
Dorothy Korwek, Director of Historical
   Resources
Mon & Wed 10:00–4:00

Vizcaya Museum and Gardens
3251 South Miami Avenue
Miami, FL 33129
(305) 579-2708

Volusia County Archives
252 South Beach Street
Daytona Beach, FL 32014
(386) 254-4647
James M. Wheeler, Director

Volusia County Public Library
Volusia County Library Center
City Island
Daytona Beach, FL 32114
(386) 257-6036; (386) 255-3765
mknievel@co.volusia.fl.us
http://merlin.vcpl.lib.fl.us
Mary E. Gasparry, Reference Librarian;
   Michael J. Knievel, Library Director
Mon & Wed 9:30–5:30, Tue & Thur
   9:30–8:00, Fri 9:30–5:00, Sat 9:00–5:00

West Florida Regional Library System
200 West Gregory Street
Pensacola, FL 32501-4878
(850) 436-5063; (850) 436-5039 FAX
gfischer@ci.pensacola.fl.us
http://www.wfrl.lib.fl.us
Dolly Pollard, Librarian; Gene Fisher,
   Director, Library System
Tue–Thur 9:00–8:00, Fri–Sat 9:00–5:00
("Mostly southeastern states, Native
   American genealogy, mainly Creek,
   Cherokee, Choctaw and tri-racial
   clusters")
minimum research; copies: 15¢ per page

West Palm Beach Public Library
100 Clematis Street
West Palm Beach, FL 33401
(561) 868-7700; (561) 653-2632 FAX
smithp@wpbpl.com; Request@wpbpl.com
http://www.wpbpl.com
Lorraine M. Lentsch, Librarian
Mon–Sat 10:00–4:00

Historical Societies—Local and Regional

Alachua County Historical Commission
(30 East University Avenue, Gainesville, FL
32601—location)
PO Box 17 (mailing address)
Gainesville, FL 32602-0017

(352) 374-5260; (352) 377-4217
Melanie Barr
Mon–Fri 9:00–5:00
Pub. *Historical Driving Tours of Alachua
   County*, irregularly, free
(Alachua County and Gainesville history;
   also places historic markers; the Historical
   Commission is appointed by the County
   Commission to oversee the historical
   aspects of the county)

Apalachicola Area Historical Society
PO Box 75
Apalachicola, FL 32320
(850) 653-9524

Archer Historical Society, Inc.
(Corner of Magnolia and West Main
   Street—location)
PO Box 39 (mailing address)
Archer, FL 32618
Jane Behringer, President
Archer Depot: third Thur

Historical Society and Avon Park Museum
PO Box 483
Avon Park, FL 33825
(863) 453-3938

Baker County Historical Society
PO Box 856
MacClenny, FL 32063
Alice Williams, President
Tue noon–5:00, Sat 3:00–7:00
$10.00 per year membership

Beaches Area Historical Society
PO Box 50646
Jacksonville Beach, FL 32250

Boca Raton Historical Society
71 North Federal Highway
Boca Raton, FL 33432-3919
(561) 395-6766; (561) 395-4049 FAX
Peg McCall, Archivist; Kristen Hamre,
   Director
Office, gift shop, exhibit: Tue–Fri 9:00–4:00
   (archivist available Mon & Thur
   1:00–5:00, and by appointment)
Pub. *Spanish River Papers*, irregularly,
   $1.50 plus postage per copy
("local history, pioneer settlers, buildings
   and general area history, oral histories,
   some genealogical information, especially
   on early settlers [1895])
research: cost of copies and postage, plus an
   hourly rate for extensive searches

**Bradford County Historical Board of
Trustees**
(West Call and Court Streets—location)
PO Drawer A (mailing address)
Starke, FL 32091
(904) 964-6305
E. L. Matthews, Chairman
Mon–Fri 9:00–5:00
Pub. *Bradford County Telegraph*, weekly,
   $10.17 for six-month subscription, $18.19
   for one-year subscription

Broward County Historical Commission
151 S.W. Second Street
Fort Lauderdale, FL 33301
(954) 765-4670
Dorothy Bryan, Administrative Secretary
8:00–4:30
Pub. *Broward Legacy*, semiannually, $6.00
   plus 6% tax per year subscription
("Research collection includes microfilm,
   oral history tapes, photographs,
   documents, manuscripts, library, artifacts
   and maps")

Calusa Valley Historical Society
439 Hickpochee
LaBelle, FL 33935
(863) 675-1616

Cedar Key Historical Society
(Second Street and State Road 25—location)
PO Box 222 (mailing address)
Cedar Key, FL 32625
(352) 543-5549
John Andrews, President
Mon–Fri & Sun 1:00–4:00, Sat 11:00–5:00
Pub. *The Beacon Newsletter*, two times per
    year
$20.00 per year membership

Citrus County Historical Society, Inc.
The Old Courthouse, Room 111
1 Courthouse Square
Inverness, FL 34450-4802
(352) 637-9928
D. Dale Hughes, Public Relations

Clearwater Historical Society
PO Box 175
Clearwater, FL 34617
clwplumbhouse@juno.com
http://www.rootsweb.com/~flchs
$10.00 per year membership

**The Coastal Heritage Preservation
Foundation, Inc.**
203 Sanford Road
Andalusia, AL 36420-4113
Mr. Cory
Pub. *CHPF Newsletter*

Collier County Historical Society
(137 12th Avenue, South—location)
PO Box 201 (mailing address)
Naples, FL 33939
(941) 261-8164
Charles J. Dauray, President
tours Mon–Fri 2:00–4:00
Pub. *Collier County Historical Society
    Membership Directory*, annually; *The
    Timepiece*, semiannually
(southwest Florida history and artifacts)
$3.00 per year membership

Delray Beach Historical Society
(Cornell Museum, Delray Beach Historical
Society Archives, 51 North Swinton Avenue,
Delray Beach, FL 33444—location)
5 N.W. First Street (mailing address)
Delray Beach, FL 33444
(561) 243-0223; (561) 243-7922 (Archives)
Margie Miller, Executive Director
Pub. *The Quarterly Newsletter*

Duncan Lamont Clinch Historical Society
PO Box 7
Fernandina Beach, FL 32034

Dunedin Historical Society/Museum
(349 Main Street—location)
PO Box 2393 (mailing address)
Dunedin, FL 34697-2393
(727) 736-1176; (727) 529-3307

East Hillsborough Historical Society
The Quintilla Geer Bruton Archives Center
605 North Collins Street
Plant City, FL 33566-3321
(813) 757-9226; (813) 754-7031 (Volunteer
    Director); (813) 757-9252 FAX
Shelby R. Bender, Volunteer Director;
    Adrienne M. Shoffstall, Historic Site
    Administrator
Tue 10:00–8:00, Wed–Fri 1:00–5:00, Sat
    1:00–5:00
Pub. *The Pen & Quill*, bimonthly

$10.00 per year membership

Eleventh Circuit Historical Society, Inc.
(see Georgia, Part 2)

Florida Supreme Court Historical Society
(Florida Supreme Court Building, Room
268D—location)
PO Box 11344 (mailing address)
Tallahassee, FL 32302
(850) 222-3703; (850) 222-2865
Nancy Dobson, Executive Director
Mon–Fri 9:00–4:30
Pub. *Review*
$25.00 per year membership

Fort Lauderdale Historical Society
(219 S.W. Second Avenue, Fort Lauderdale,
FL 33301—location)
PO Box 14043 (mailing address)
Fort Lauderdale, FL 33302
(954) 463-4431
Daniel T. Hobby, Executive Director
Pub. *New River News*

**Geneva Historical and Genealogical
Society**
PO Box 145
Geneva, FL 32732

The Glades Historical Society
PO Box 1662
Belle Glade, FL 33430-1662
(561) 996-5198; (561) 996-7099 FAX
Dr. Joseph R. Orsenigo, Chair
by appointment
(published *Cracker History of Okeechobee,
    Okeechobee Hurricane, From Swamp to
    Sugar Bowl, Okeechobee Boats and
    Skippers, Okeechobee Catfishing,
    Dredgeman of Cape Sable*)

Gulf Coast Heritage Association, Inc.
(Historic Spanish Point, 337 North Tamiami
Trail—location)
PO Box 846 (mailing address)
Osprey, FL 34229
(941) 966-5214; (941) 966-1355 FAX
gcha2@qte.net;
    diane@historicspanishpoint.org
http://www.historicspanishpoint.org
Scott Stroh, Curator
Research Library: Mon–Fri 9:00–5:00 by
    appointment only
Pub. *Vision Newsletter*, quarterly
("Florida history, museum, historic site,
    archaeology, environment")
$35.00 per year membership

Gulfport Historical Society
PO Box 5152
Gulfport, FL 33737-5152

Halifax Historical Society Museum
252 South Beach Street
Daytona Beach, FL 32114-4407
(386) 255-6976
Elizabeth B. Baker, Director
Tue–Sat 10:00–4:00
Pub. *Halifax Historical Herald*, quarterly;
    Halifax Historical Society Newsletter,
    bimonthly
(local archives, over 10,000 early photos,
    documents, etc.)
$20.00 per year membership; research:
    $10.00; museum admission: $2.00

**Hillsborough County Historical Museum
and Library**
Historical Commission
3705 West San Rafael Street
Tampa, FL 33629-5124

Elizabeth Jones, Treasurer
Mon–Fri 10:00–4:00
(early Florida material and families, special
    local history
limited research is free, charges for copies

**Indian River County Historical Society,
Inc.**
(Vero Station, 2336 14th Avenue—location)
PO Box 6535 (mailing address)
Vero Beach, FL 32961
(772) 778-3435
Carolyn Short, Executive Director
Wed 10:00–3:00, Sat 10:00–noon, Sun
    2:00–4:00
Pub. *IRCHS Newsletter*
$15.00 per year membership

Jefferson County Historical Association
PO Box 496
Monticello, FL 32344
(850) 997-2565

Key West Art and Historical Society
East Martello Museum
3501 South Roosevelt Boulevard
Key West, FL 33040
(305) 296-3913; (305) 296-6206 FAX
Susan Olsen, Director
daily 9:30–5:00
Pub. *Martello*, quarterly
$25.00 per year membership

Lake County Historical Society, Inc.
(Main Street—location)
PO Box 7800 (mailing address)
Tavares, FL 32778-7800
(352) 343-9802; (352) 343-9814 FAX
Donna Jean Hayes, Office Manager,
    Secretary
Mon–Fri 9:00–4:00
Pub. *Tangelo*, quarterly
$10.00 per year membership

Lake Wales Depot Museum
325 South Scenic Highway
Lake Wales, FL 33853
(863) 678-9209; (863) 678-4299 FAX
http://www.TheDepotSocietyofLake
    Wales.com
Mimi Hardman, Director
Mon–Fri 7:00–5:00, Sat 10:00–4:00
("Lake Wales history and preservation.
    Helpful for those researching folks in the
    area.")
$30.00 per year membership

Largo Area Historical Society
805 South Palm Drive
Largo, FL 33770
(727) 584-3480

**Lemon Bay Historical and Genealogical
Society**
PO Box 1245
Englewood, FL 34295-1245

Loxahatchee Historical Society, Inc.
at the Florida History Center and Museum
805 North U.S. Highway 1
Jupiter, FL 33477
(561) 747-6639; (561) 575-3299 FAX
Michael Zaidman, Curator
Mon–Fri 10:00–5:00 (for research only)
Pub. *River Update*, bimonthly
$25.00+ per year membership

**Manatee County Historical Commission,
Inc.**
604 15th Street, East
Bradenton, FL 34208
(941) 749-7165

Peggy Somerville, Coordinator
Mon–Fri 8:30–4:30, Sun 1:30–4:30
free admission to museum and eight restored
   buildings

Manatee County Historical Society
604 15th Street, East
Bradenton, FL 34208
(941) 741-4070
$8.00 per year membership

Marion County Historical Society
801 N.E. Sanchez Avenue
Ocala, FL 34470-5821
Pub. *MCHS Newsletter*

Historical Society of Martin County
825 N.E. Ocean Boulevard
Stuart, FL 34996-1696
(772) 225-1961; (772) 255-2333 FAX
http://www.classicar.com/museums/
   histmart/histmart.htm

Micanopy Historical Society
(706 N.E. Cholokka Boulevard—museum
   and archive location)
PO Box 462 (mailing address)
Micanopy, FL 32667
(352) 466-3200
micanopy@afn.org
http://www.afn.org/~micanopy
Diana Cohen, Archivist
daily 1:00–4:00; archives by appointment
Pub. *Newsletter*
("The society also has an archive. The
   collections therein are indeed local in
   scope. However Micanopy [founded
   1821] is where the presence of Old
   Families is handed down as family
   tradition. People come here regularly to
   look up their ancestors. They provide the
   archives with extensive genealogical
   information, photographs, etc. We have
   copies of original data from Fort
   Micanopy [Second Seminole War] and
   one can put together an impressive picture
   of social and economic life of the region
   over a long period of time.")

North Brevard Historical Society
(301 South Washington Avenue—location)
PO Box 6199 (mailing address)
Titusville, FL 37282-6199
(321) 269-6199
http://www.nbbd.com/godo/history
Joe L. Merckson, President
Tue–Sat 10:00–3:00
Pub. *Newsletter*, eight times per year
(North Brevard Historical Museum)

Oakland Park Historical Society
3976 N.E. Sixth Avenue
Oakland Park, FL 33334
(954) 566-4284
Midge Turpen, Historian

Osceola County Historical Society, Inc.
Museum
Spence-Lanier Pioneer Enrichment Center
1750 Palmetto Drive
Kissimee, FL 32743-8960
Andrew W. Herrmann, Curator
Pub. *The Osceola Journal*
$10.00 per year membership

Pensacola Historical Society
Lelia Abercrombie Historical Library
117 East Government Street
Pensacola, FL 32501
(850) 433-1559
Sandra Johnson, Curator
Tue–Thur & Sat 10:00–noon & 1:00–3:00
Pub. *Pensacola History Illustrated*, two

times per year (no scheduled times)
$25.00 per year membership

Pinellas County Historical Society
Heritage Park—Pinellas County Historical
   Museum
11909 125th Street, North
Largo, FL 33774
(727) 462-3474
Ernest F. Dibble, Ph.D., President; Kendrick
   T. Ford, Museum Director
Pub. *Punta Pinal*

Polk County Historical Association
(180 North Central Avenue—location)
PO Box 2749 (mailing address)
Bartow, FL 33831-2749
(863) 533-3710
Sue Sellers, Secretary
Pub. *Polk County Historical Quarterly* (Mar,
   June, Sept, Dec); *Newsletter, Polk County
   Historical Association*, twelve times per
   year
$20.00 per year membership

Saint Augustine Historical Society
(6 Artillery Lane—location)
271 Charlotte Street (mailing address)
Saint Augustine, FL 32084-5033
(904) 824-2872
sahs@aug.com
Charles Tingley, Library Manager
Tue–Fri 9:00–4:30
Pub. *East Florida Gazette*, quarterly; *El
   Escribano*, annually
("Spanish Colonial Florida, Menorca, St.
   Augustine, St. Johns County, Florida.")
$35.00 per year membership

Saint Lucie County Historical Society
Saint Lucie County Historical Museum
Saint Lucie Historical Commission
414 Seaway Drive
Fort Pierce, FL 34949
(772) 462-1795 (Museum); (772) 464-6635
   (Commission)
maddoxi@co.st-lucie.fl.us
http://www.st-lucie.lib.fl.us/museum.htm
Richard Schmidt, President; Iva Jean
   Maddox, Superintendent
Tue–Sat 10:00–4:00, Sun noon–4:00
Pub. *Historical Quarterly*

Saint Petersburg Historical Society
335 Second Avenue, N.E.
Saint Petersburg, FL 33701
(813) 894-1052
Pub. *Sea Breeze*, quarterly
$20.00 per year membership

Sebastian Area Historical Society
PO Box 781348
Sebastian, FL 32978-1348

South Brevard Historical Society, Inc.
PO Box 1064
Melbourne, FL 32902-1064
(321) 723-6835 voice & FAX (Chair)
Betty Preece, Chair

Historical Association of Southern Florida
Society of Florida Archivists
14220 Leaning Pine Drive
Miami Lakes, FL 33014
baltman@mailer.fsu.edu
http://mailer.fsu.edu/~baltman/sfa.html

Southern Studies Institute
(see Louisiana, Part 2)

Southwest Florida Historical Society, Inc.
(1001 McGregor Boulevard, Fort Myers, FL

33919—location)
PO Box 1381 (mailing address)
Fort Myers, FL 33902-1381
(941) 939-4044
Jean Meola, President
Wed (Sept–May) 10:00–noon, and by
   appointment
Pub. *PastFinder*, quarterly
$12.00 per year membership

Tallahassee Historical Society
History Department
Florida State University
Tallahassee, FL 32306
jdbarret@mailer.fsu.edu
Julie Barrett
Pub. *Apalachee*, semiannually
$2.70 per year membership

Tampa Historical Society
245 South Hyde Park Avenue
Tampa, FL 33606
(813) 259-1111

Genealogical Societies

State Genealogical Societies

Florida Genealogical Society, Inc.
PO Box 18624
Tampa, FL 33679-8624
Scott L. Peeler, Jr., President; Mrs. Ceta
   Armitage, Editor
Pub. *Journal*, semiannually (Mar, Oct);
   Newsletter, five times per year (Feb, Apr,
   June, Aug, Dec), $10.00 per year
   subscription
$15.00 per year membership

Florida Society for Genealogical Research
8461 54th Street, North
Pinellas Park, FL 33565
(727) 391-2914

Florida State Genealogical Society, Inc.
PO Box 10249
Tallahassee, FL 32302-2249
mpparker@ix.netcom.com
http://www.rootsweb.com/~flsgs
Pamela Cooper, President; Mary Parker,
   Membership
Pub. *The Florida Genealogist*, quarterly;
   Florida Lines, four times per year
$25.00 per year membership

Southern Society of Genealogists, Inc.
(see Alabama, Part 2)

Genealogical Societies—Local & Regional

Alachua County Genealogical Society
PO Box 12078
Gainesville, FL 32604-0078
(352) 332-2065
jpowelljr@gru.net
http://www.afn.org/~acgs
Jim Powell, Jr., President; Mary Singley,
   Vice-President
meetings at Highlands Presbyterian Church,
   1001 N.E. 16th Avenue, Gainesville: third
   Mon 7:00 (Sept–May)
Pub. *'Latchua Country News*, quarterly;
   'Latchua Notes, as needed (newsletter)
$18.00 per year membership

Amelia Island Genealogical Society
PO Box 6005
Fernandina Beach, FL 32035-6005
(904) 261-2139 (President); (904) 277-7365
   (Library)
Winkie Robinson, President
Fernandina Library: Mon, Wed & Fri

10:00–noon
Pub. *The Geneline*, ten times per year; *The Nassau Genealogist*, quarterly (winter, spring, summer, fall)
$15.00 per year membership

Bay County Genealogical Society (BCGS)
PO Box 662
Panama City, FL 32402-0662
(850) 872-9882 voice & FAX
bander6477@knology.net
http://www.rootsweb.com/~flbcgs/index.htm
Berniece Loper, President
meetings at Bay County Library Meeting Room: first Sat (except second Sat in Dec) 1:00
Pub. *The County Line*, quarterly (Jan, Apr, July, Oct)
$15.00 per year membership; limited local research only; queries accepted

Bonita Springs Genealogical Club
25311 Paradise Road
Bonita Springs, FL 33923-7620
Mrs. Cecil D. Harvard, Secretary

Brevard Genealogical Society
PO Box 1123
Cocoa, FL 32922
(321) 632-6570
Hilda Mayo, Corresponding Secretary
9:00–9:00
Pub. *Newsletter*, quarterly
$12.00 per year membership

Genealogical Society of Broward County, Inc.
(6500 Parkside Circle, Parkland, FL—library location)
PO Box 485 (mailing address)
Fort Lauderdale, FL 33302
(954) 463-8834
Lillian Trubey, Editor
Tue 10:00–4:00, Thur 1:00–4:00, Sat 10:00–2:00
Pub. *Imprints*, quarterly (Jan, Apr, July, Oct), $12.00 per year subscription
$25.00 per year membership

Central Florida Genealogical Society, Inc.
PO Box 177
Orlando, FL 32802-0177
(407) 894-8518; (407) 228-4842 FAX
lknorr@magicnet.net
http://www.magicnet.net/~paulench/cfgs.html
Lynne Knorr, President
Pub. *Buried Treasures*, quarterly; *Treasure Chest News*, ten times per year
$20.00 per year membership

Charlotte County Genealogical Society, Inc.
PO Box 494707
Port Charlotte, FL 33949-4707
(941) 766-1985
LBKCCGS@aol.com
http://www.rootsweb.com/~flccgs
Jo Sommerville, Editor
Port Charlotte Library: Mon–Wed 9:00–9:00 (Mon nights during summer only), Thur 1:00–5:00, Fri–Sat 9:00–5:00
Pub. *Geneagram*, ten times per year (monthly, except July–Aug)
$12.00 per year membership

Citrus County Genealogical Society
PO Box 2211
Inverness, FL 34451-2211
(352) 746-0027 (President); (352) 637-6482 FAX
Robbie Joiner, Recording Secretary, Dr.

Bernie O'Neil, President
9:00–5:00
Pub. *CCGS Newsletter*, four times per year (Feb, Apr, Oct, Dec), $10.00 per year subscription
$10.00 per year membership

Clay County Genealogical Society
PO Box 1071
Green Cove Springs, FL 32043

Genealogical Society of Collier County
PO Box 7933
Naples, FL 33941-7933
(941) 793-1066
http://www.naples.net/presents/gscc
W. R. "Bob" Holbrook, President
$10.00 per year membership

Geneva Historical and Genealogical Society
(Historical Societies—Local and Regional, above)

Genealogical Society of Greater Miami, Inc.
PO Box 162905
Miami, FL 33116-2905
VDBJFB@bellsouth.net
http://www.rootsweb/~FLGSGM
Joan F. Bond
Miami-Dade Public Library: Mon–Wed & Fri–Sat 9:00–6:00, Thur 9:00–9:00, Sun (Oct–May) 1:00–5:00
Pub. *The Heritage*, quarterly, $20.00 per year subscription
research: call or write for search fees

Halifax Genealogical Society
Ormond Beach Public Library
30 South Beach Street
Ormond Beach, FL 32174
(386) 673-0163 (Library)

The Genealogy Society of Hernando County
PO Box 1793
Brooksville, FL 34605-1793
(352) 596-2642
Sharon A. Abbe, Corresponding Secretary; Kathleen Marsh, President
fourth Tue (Jan–Nov) 6:30
Pub. *Links and Bridges*, monthly
$15.00 per year membership; queries: free

Highlands County Genealogical Society
Avon Park Library
100 North Museum Avenue
Avon Park, FL 33825
(863) 382-4112 (Genealogical Society); (863) 453-4842 (Library)
Janis Grove, President
Library: Mon 9:30–8:00, Tue–Thur 9:30–5:30, Fri 9:30–3:30, Sat 9:30–noon
Pub. *Highlands County Genealogical Society Newsletter*, four times per year (Jan, Mar, May, Nov)
$12.00 per year membership

Historic Ocala/Marion County Genealogical Society
(18 S.E. 14th Avenue—location)
PO Box 1206 (mailing address)
Ocala, FL 32678-1206
Marguerite L. Dillman, Secretary
Pub. *Past Times*
$15.00 per year membership

Huxford Genealogical Society, Inc.
(see Georgia, Part 2)

Imperial Polk Genealogical Society

(Lakeland, FL—location)
PO Box 10 (mailing address)
Kathleen, FL 33849-0045
Joyce L. Bode, Treasurer
Pub. *IPGS Newsletter*, monthly
$7.50 per year membership

Indian River Genealogical Society
(Indian River County Main Library—location)
PO Box 1850 (mailing address)
Vero Beach, FL 32961-1850
(561) 770-5060, ext. 18 (Library)
George Gross, President
second Tue (Sept–May) 10:00–noon; Advanced BK/PAF® Users Group: first Thur
Pub. *IRGS Newsletter*, nine times per year (monthly, Sept–May)
$15.00 per year membership

Jacksonville Genealogical Society, Inc.
PO Box 60756
Jacksonville, FL 32205-0756
Robert Carlton Smith, Editor
Pub. *Jacksonville Genealogical Society Newsletter*, quarterly; *Jacksonville Genealogical Society Quarterly*, $5.00 per issue plus postage subscription for nonmembers

Keystone Genealogical Society
(950 East Washington—location)
PO Box 50 (mailing address)
Monticello, FL 32344
(850) 997-2559; (904) 997-3304 (Editor)
Donna Jean Wiehaus, President; Bonney McClellan, Editor
Pub. *The Keystone Kin*, quarterly (Jefferson County and surrounding counties in FL and GA)
$12.00 per year membership

Kinseekers Genealogical Society of Lake County
PO Box 492711
Leesburg, FL 32749-2711
http://members.aol.com/LakeCo1887
Jeannette Phethean, Corresponding Secretary
Pub. *Kinseekers Quarterly*
(Lake County data only)
$10.00 per year membership; research: fees negotiable

Lee County Genealogical Society, Inc.
PO Box 150153
Cape Coral, FL 33914-0153
Pub. *Lee County Genealogical Society Newsletter*, quarterly
$15.00 per year membership

Lehigh Acres Genealogical Society
PO Box 965
Lehigh Acres, FL 33970-0965
East County Regional Library: Mon–Thur 9:00–9:00, Fri–Sat 9:00–6:00; meetings at library: third Tue 1:00–3:00 (Oct–May)
(Lee County)
$2.00 per year membership

Lemon Bay Historical and Genealogical Society
(see Historical Societies—Local and Regional, above)

Madison County Genealogy Society
PO Box 136
Madison, FL 32341-0136
mgreeson@cfl.rr.com
http://www.rootsweb.com/~flmadiso/index.html
Sandra Norris, President

Mon–Fri 10:00–4:00
Pub. *Madison County, Florida Genealogical News*, quarterly
$20.00 per year membership; research: donation

The Manasota Genealogical Society, Inc.
6023 26th Street West PMB 269
Bradenton, FL 34207
DearMYRTLE@aol.com (Webmaster);
MANASOTAGEN-Lt@rootsweb.com
(Message Board not open yet)
http://www.rootsweb.com/~flmgs
Pat Richley Foy, President
9:00–5:00; meetings at the Auditorium of the
Manatee County Central Auditorium,
1301 Barcarrota Boulevard West,
Bradenton: first Wed (Oct–May) 10:00
Pub. *Cracker Crumbs*, quarterly (Sept, Nov, Jan, Mar)
(Manatee County)
$12.00 per year membership

Martin County Genealogical Society, Inc.
Main Branch c/o Blake Library
2351 S.E. Monterrey Road
Stuart, FL 34996
(772) 288-4606
rshep70683@aol.com
http://www.rootsweb.com/~flmcgs
Lawrence I. Shepard, Past President
Martin County Public Library, Armstrong
Room: third Fri 1:00
Pub. *Martin County Genealogical Society Newsletter*, three to four times per year
(Martin County cemetery project in process)
$12.00 per year membership

Genealogical Society of North Brevard (GSNB)
PO Box 897
Titusville, FL 32781-0897
http://www.rootsweb.com/~flbrevar
Randall J. Hill, President
meetings at North Brevard Public Library:
first Tue (except July–Aug) 7:00
Pub. *The Register*, monthly
$15.00 per year membership

Ohio Genealogical Society
Florida Chapter
(see Ohio, Part 2)

Genealogical Society of Okaloosa County
PO Drawer 1175
Fort Walton Beach, FL 32549
(850) 689-1535
Florence Lembeck, President
Pub. *A Journal of Northwest Florida*, three times per year
$12.00 per year membership

Genealogical Society of Okeechobee
PO Box 371
Okeechobee, FL 34973-0371
(863) 467-1400 (Secretary); (863) 467-2482
(President)
maryk@okeechobee.com (Secretary)
Mary E. Kelchner, Secretary; Joy Morley, President
Presbyterian Church: second Mon 1:30
Pub. *Okeechobee Genealogist*, quarterly
$10.00 per year membership

Palm Beach County Genealogical Society, Inc.
West Palm Beach Public Library
(100 Clematis Street, West Palm Beach, FL 33401—location)
PO Box 1746 (mailing address)
West Palm Beach, FL 33402-1746
(561) 832-3279

Lorraine M. Lentsch, Librarian
Library: Mon–Sat 10:00–4:00
Pub. *Ancestry*, quarterly (Jan, Apr, July, Oct), $20.00 per year subscription
(specializes in Massachusetts, Connecticut, Pennsylvania, Virginia, North Carolina; 1920 Florida census, Florida marriage and divorce records 1927–1991, Florida death records 1877–1991)
$35.00 per year membership; research: $10.00 minimum, one name, one year, one copy

Pinellas Genealogy Society, Inc.
PO Box 1614
Largo, FL 33779-1614
http://rootsweb.com/~flpgs
Society members volunteer at the Largo
Library Mon–Sat 9:30–3:30
Pub. *The Pinellas Genealogist*, quarterly.
$16.00 per year membership; search fee: $5.00 per name; Pinellas County cemetery books available for purchase

Putnam County Genealogical Society
(Putnam County Library Headquarters, 601 College Road—location)
PO Box 2354 (mailing address)
Palatka, FL 32177
Bobby B. Morris, President
Pub. *Putnam County Genealogical Society Newsletter*, monthly; *Putnam County Genealogical Society Journal*, quarterly
$25.00 per year membership (c/o PO Box 1305, Palatka, FL 32078)

Ridge Genealogical Society
PO Box 477
Babson Park, FL 33827
(863) 638-1616
Virginia Johnston, President
Lake Wales Public Library: second Thur (Sept–May)
Pub. *The Root Digger*, three times per year (Jan, May, Sept)
$3.00 per year membership

Saint Augustine Genealogical Society
Saint Johns County Public Library
1960 North Ponce de Leon Boulevard
Saint Augustine, FL 32084-2620

Genealogical Society of Sarasota, Inc.
(Selby Public Library—location)
PO Box 1917 (mailing address)
Sarasota, FL 34230-1917
(941) 923-7791
info@geekgirltraining.com (Webmaster)
http://www.rootsweb.com/~flgss
Winn L. Taplin, President
monthly meetings: Oct–May; collection at library open daily, year-round
Pub. *GSS Newsletter*, quarterly
$15.00 per year membership

South Bay Genealogy Club
PO Box 5202
Sun City Center, FL 33571

Genealogical Society of South Brevard County
(Melbourne Public Library—location)
PO Box 786 (mailing address)
Melbourne, FL 32902-0786
(321) 255-2791
Susanvan@aol.com
Sue van Vonno, Corresponding Secretary
Pub. *The Bulletin*, quarterly
(published *Two Cemeteries of Melbourne*, $20.00 ppd., and a supplement for $5.00, and *Hartford Times* index of the paper's weekly "Genealogical Exchange" for

$110.00)
$20.00 per year membership; research: donation

South Georgia Genealogical Society
(see Georgia, Part 2)

Southeast Alabama Genealogical Society
(see Alabama, Part 2)

Suwannee Valley Genealogical Society, Inc.
c/o Historical Museum
208 North Ohio Avenue
Live Oak, FL 32060

Tallahassee Genealogical Society, Inc.
PO Box 4371
Tallahassee, FL 32315-4371
(850) 878-2900
Nellie Bird Mims, President
Pub. *The Tallahassee Genealogist*, quarterly; *TGS Bulletin*, monthly
$15.00 per year membership

Treasure Coast Genealogical Society
PO Box 12582
Fort Pierce, FL 34979-2582
Pub. *Treasure Coast Genealogical Society Bulletin*, quarterly
$10.00 per year membership

Volusia County Genealogical Society, Inc.
(Volusia County Library Center, City Island—location)
PO Box 2039 (mailing address)
Daytona Beach, FL 32015
(386) 255-3765
Louise Schutt, President
Mon–Sat 10:00–5:00, Tue & Thur 5:00–8:00

West Florida Genealogical Society
PO Box 947
Pensacola, FL 32594-0947
Pub. *West Florida Footprints*, irregularly
$6.00 per year membership

West Pasco County Genealogical Society
(First Christian Church, 6219 River Road, New Port Richey, FL 34653—location)
PO Box 1142 (mailing address)
Port Richey, FL 34673
(727) 848-0112
dhagner@attglobal.net
Debbe Ann Hagner, President
last Wed 2:00–4:00
$10.00 per year membership

Roots and Branches Genealogical Society of West Volusia County
DeLand Public Library
130 East Howry Avenue
DeLand, FL 32724-5517
(386) 734-2424 (Library); (386) 822-6430 (Library)
Charles Baker, President
Library: Mon, Wed & Fri–Sat 10:00–5:00, Tue & Thur 10:00–8:00
Pub. *Newsletter*, three times per year

Independent Publications and Miscellany

Armchair Publications
Florida Armchair Researcher
(see Georgia, Part 2)

FlGenWeb
Part of The USGenWeb Project
drdarrel@lani.net; jpowelljr@gru.net
http://www.rootsweb.com/~flgenweb/

index.html
Darrel Bell, State Coordinator; Jim Powell,
    Assistant Coordinator; Barb Lavin,
    Assistant Coordinator
(links to other Florida resources)

Florida Department of Transportation
Maps and Publications Sales
Mail Station 12
605 Suwannee Street
Tallahassee, FL 32399-0450
(850) 414-4050; (850) 414-4915 FAX
mapsandpubs@dot.state.fl.us
http://www11.myflorida.com/
    mapsandpublications (Maps)
Lillie Tinsley; Ed McMillon
Mon–Fri 8:00–5:00

Florida Historical Research Foundation
2301 East 148th Avenue
Lutz, FL 33549
(813) 971-2968

Genealogical Institute
(see Virginia, Part 2)

Genealogy Books and Consultation
(see Texas, Part 2)

Kingdom of the Sun
4911 N.E. Seventh Street
Ocala, FL 32671
(352) 236-4740

Metro-Dade Cultural Resource Center
111 N.W. First Street
Miami, FL 33128-1902
(305) 375-4635

Mission San Luis de Apalachee
Division of Historical Resources
2020 West Mission Road
Tallahassee, FL 32304-1624
(850) 487-3711; (850) 488-6186 FAX
http://www.flheritage.com/archaeology/
    sanluis
Tue–Sun 10:00–4:00

Mountain Press
(see Tennessee, Part 2)

Osceola County Department
Genealogical Research
326 Eastern Avenue
Saint Cloud, FL 32769
Marjorie B. Bright

**Sarasota County Department of Historical
Resources**
701 North Tamiami Trail
Sarasota, FL 34236-4899
(941) 316-1115; (941) 316-1117 FAX
Ann Shank, Historical Librarian; Mark
    Smith, Archivist
Office: Mon–Fri 8:00–5:00; Research:
    Mon–Thur 9:00–4:00
(indexed obituary file, newspapers, journals,
    maps, plats, architectural drawings,
    photographs, family and organization
    manuscript files related to Sarasota
    County history)

**The Southern Genealogist's Exchange
Society, Inc.**
(6215 Sauterne Drive,
    Jacksonville—location)
PO Box 2801 (mailing address)
Jacksonville, FL 32203-2801
Jon R. Ferguson, President
Tue–Thur 10:00–4:00, Sat 1:00–5:00
Pub. *Southern Genealogist's Exchange
    Quarterly*, $20.00 per year subscription

(emphasis on, but not limited to, Southern
    US: "Our library contains over 4,000
    books, films, quarterlies, etc.")
$25.00 per year membership; research: $5.00
    minimum plus expenses

Traveller Southern Families
(see Virginia, Part 2)

University of South Florida
College of Arts and Sciences
Department of History
4202 East Fowler Avenue, SOC 107
Tampa, FL 33620-8100
(813) 974-2807
Gail Smith, Administrative Assistant
Mon–Fri 8:00–5:00
Pub. *Tampa Bay History*, semiannually
    (June, Dec)
(general history of central and southwest
    Florida, including the fifteen counties
    surrounding Tampa: Charlotte, Collier,
    DeSoto, Glades, Hardee, Hendry,
    Hernando, Highlands, Hillsborough, Lee,
    Manatee, Pasco, Pinellas, Polk and
    Sarasota counties)
$18.00 per year membership

University of South Florida
Oral History Center
4202 East Fowler Avenue
Tampa, FL 33620

Georgia

Archives and Libraries with
Holdings in Genealogy

State Archives and Library

The Georgia Archives
5800 Jonesboro Road
Morrow, GA 30260
(678) 364-3700; (678) 364-3710 (Reference)
http://www.GeorgiaArchives.org
David W. Carmichael, Director
Tue–Sat 8:30–5:00

Georgia Public Library Service
156 Trinity Avenue, S.W.
Atlanta, GA 30303-3652
(404) 656-2461
webmaster@georgialibraries.org
http://www.public.lib.ga.us

Georgia State Law Library
(244 Washington Street—location)
40 Capitol Square (mailing address)
Atlanta, GA 30334
(404) 656-3468
Martha Lappé, State Law Librarian
Mon–Fri 8:30–5:00
(strictly Georgia law and legal history, no
    genealogy materials)

State Historical Society

Georgia Historical Society
501 Whittaker Street
Savannah, GA 31499
(912) 651-2125; (912) 651-2831 FAX
ghslib@georgiahistory.com (Library and
    Archives)
http://www.georgiahistory.com
Tue–Sat 10:00–5:00
Pub. *Georgia Historical Quarterly*; *G.H.S.
    Footnotes*
(Georgia genealogy, manuscripts, rare books)
$35.00 per year membership (includes both
    publications)

**City, County and Regional Archives and
Libraries**
(A more exhaustive list of public and
academic libraries can be found at
http://www.gpls.public.lib.ga.us/pls/publibs/
directory.)

Amelia Island Museum of History
(see Florida, Part 2)

Andrew College Archives
Pitts Library
413 College Street
Cuthbert, GA 31740
(229) 732-5944; (229) 732-5957 FAX
karanpittman@andrewcollege.edu
Karan Ann Berryman, Director of Library
    Services
Mon–Fri 8:30–noon
(Southwest Georgia, Andrew College)
photocopy charge

Appling County Heritage Center
(Thomas and Harvey Streets—location)
PO Box 87 (mailing address)
Baxley, GA 31513
(912) 367-7791; (912) 367-8104 FAX

Armstrong State College
Center for Low Country Studies
11935 Abercorn Street
Savannah, GA 31419-1997
Peter Scardino

Athens Regional Library
(Corner of Baxter Street and Dudley
Drive—location)
2025 Baxter Street (mailing address)
Athens, GA 30606-6331
(706) 613-3650; (706) 613-3661 FAX
kames@mail.clarke.public.lib.ga.us
http://www.clarke.public.lib.ga.us
Laura W. Carter, Heritage Room Specialist;
Kathryn S. Ames, Director
Mon–Thur 9:00–9:00, Fri–Sat 9:00–6:00,
Sun 2:00–6:00
(specializes in Athens, Clarke County and
the Civil War, local African-American
history and genealogy)

Atlanta University Center
Special Collections and Archives
Robert W. Woodruff Library
111 James P. Brawley Drive, S.W.
Atlanta, GA 30314-2870
(404) 522-8980, ext. 1217; (404) 522-5158
FAX
kjefferson@auctr.edu
http://www.auctr.edu
Karen Jefferson, Head, Archives/Special
Collections
Mon, Wed & Fri 9:00–5:00, Tue & Thur
9:00–7:00, Sat 2:00–5:00
(African-American archival collections)

Auburn Avenue Research Library
101 Auburn Avenue, N.E.
Atlanta, GA 30303
(404) 659-4008

Augusta-Richmond County Public Library
902 Greene Street
Augusta, GA 30901-2294
(706) 821-2600; (706) 821-2629 FAX
beckl@mail.richmond.public.lib.ga.us
http://www.ecgrl.public.lib.ga.us
Linda Beck, Local History Librarian
Mon–Thur 9:00–9:00, Fri–Sat 9:00–5:30,
Sun 2:00–5:30
(Georgia local history)

Augusta State University
Reese Library
Special Collections
2500 Walton Way
Augusta, GA 30904-2200
(706) 737-1745

Austell City Museum
2716 Broad Street
Austell, GA 30001
(770) 944-4309
Rosa Mary Johnson

Bartow County Public Library System
429 West Main Street
Cartersville, GA 30120-3400
(770) 382-4203; (770) 386-3056 FAX
csims@mail.bartow.public.lib.ga.us
http://www.innerx.net/~library
Carmen Sims, Director
Mon, Wed & Fri 9:00–5:30, Tue & Thur
9:00–7:30, Sat 1:00–4:30

Bartow County/Roselawn Museum
PO Box 128
Cartersville, GA 30120
Mary Siniard

Bartow History Center
13 Wall Street
Cartersville, GA 30120
(770) 382-3818; (770) 383-9314 FAX
http://www.bartowhistorycenter.org
Michele Rodgers, Director
Tue–Sat 10:00–4:00, Sun 1:00–5:00

(a Bartow County, Georgia, history museum,
with exhibits and archives; houses some
local county records: wills, deeds, letters,
personal papers, photographs, etc.)
$25.00 per year membership

Bartram Trail Regional Library
204 East Liberty Street
Washington, GA 30673-1746
(706) 678-7736; (706) 678-1474 FAX
Shoemakj@wilkes.public.lib.ga.us
http://wilkes.public.lib.ga.us
Mon, Wed & Fri 8:30–5:30, Tue & Thur
8:30–8:00, Sat 10:00–4:00

Birmingham Public Library
(see Alabama, Part 2)

W. C. Bradley Memorial Library
Chattahoochee Valley Regional Library
Genealogical and Historical Room
1120 Bradley Drive
Columbus, GA 31906-2800
(706) 649-0780, ext. 130; (706) 649-1914
FAX
Virginia Stola, Genealogy Librarian
Mon–Thur 9:00–9:00, Fri–Sat 9:00–6:00,
Sun 1:30–6:30

Brunswick-Glynn Regional Library
Reference Department
208 Gloucester Street
Brunswick, GA 31520-7007
(912) 267-1212; (912) 267-9597 FAX
jdarby@trrl.org
Jim Darby, Director
Mon & Wed–Sat 9:00–5:00, Tue 9:00–9:00

Chattahoochee Valley Regional Library
(see W. C. Bradley Memorial Library, above)

**Chattahoochee Valley State Community
College**
(see Alabama, Part 2)

Chattooga County Library
Georgia Room
360 Farrar Drive
Summerville, GA 30747-2017
(706) 857-2553; (706) 857-7841 FAX
hutsellb@mail.chattooga.public.lib.ga.us;
chatrep@chattoogacountylibrary.org

http://www.chattooga.public.lib.ga.us/ind
ex.pl/home
Barbara Hutsell, Director

Cherokee Regional Library
Georgia History and Genealogy Room
(LaFayette-Walker County Library, 305
South Duke Street—location)
PO Box 707 (mailing address)
LaFayette, GA 30728-2936
(706) 638-2992; (706) 638-4028 FAX

http://www.walker.public.lib.ga.us/ghr/gh
r1.htm (Georgia History and Genealogy
Room)
Betty Johnson, Manager
Tue 11:15–8:00, Wed 9:00–6:00, Thur–Sat
9:00–5:00
$5.00 for 30 minutes research, 25¢ each for
copies

Chipley Historic Center of Pine Mountain
PO Box 1055
Pine Mountain, GA 31822
(706) 663-4044
Franklin Davenport

Clarkesville/Habersham County Library
(178 East Green Street—location)

PO Box 2020 (mailing address)
Clarkesville, GA 30523
(706) 754-4413; (706) 754-3479 FAX
richardm@mail.habersham.public.lib.ga.us
http://www.co.habersham.ga.us/html/
directory/directory2.html
Martha Richardson, Library Manager
Mon 9:00–8:00, Tue–Fri 9:00–6:00, Sat
9:00–1:00
research: "Our staff is limited, but we can do
some research for you. We charge $15.00
per hour for research and 15¢ for
photocopies from books, 25¢ for
microfilm copies. Before we can start, we
need authorization for a number of hours
of research and number of anticipated
copies. A $16.00 minimum is charged.
Allow 2 to 3 weeks for most research. If
you need help in estimating the scope of
the research, you may call Frances Black
at (706) 754-4412, ext. 227."

**Clayton County Library System
Headquarters**
865 Battlecreek Road
Jonesboro, GA 30236-1919
(770) 473-3850; (770) 473-3858 FAX
stewartc@mail.clayton.public.lib.ga.us
http://www.clayton.public.lib.ga.us
Carol J. Stewart, Director
Mon–Thur 9:00–9:00, Fri 9:00–6:00, Sat
9:00–5:00

Coastal Plain Regional Library
(214 Chestnut Street, Tifton, GA 31794-
3108—location)
PO Box 7606 (mailing address)
Tifton, GA 31793-7606
(229) 386-3400; (229) 386-7007 FAX
colet@mail.tift.public.lib.ga.us
http://www.tift.public.lib.ga.us
Teresa Cole, Director

Cobb County Public Library
Central Library
Georgia Room
266 Roswell Street, S.E.
Marietta, GA 30060-2004
(770) 528-2333; (770) 528-2367 FAX
http://www.cobbcat.org/aboutgarm.htm
Carolyn M. Crawford
Mon–Thur 9:00–9:30, Fri–Sat 9:00–6:00
fees for photocopies and postage

Collections of Life and Heritage
135 Auburn Avenue, N.E.
Atlanta, GA 30308
Deborah Strahorn

Collins-Callaway Library
1235 15th Street
Augusta, GA 30910-2799
(706) 821-8253
Cassandra M. Norman, Head Librarian
7:45–10:00

Columbus College
Chattahoochee Valley Historical Collections
and Columbus College Archives
School Library
Columbus, GA 31993
(706) 568-2247
Craig Lloyd, Ph.D., Associate Professor of
History/Archives

Commerce Public Library
Heritage Room
1344 South Broad Street
Commerce, GA 30529
(706) 335-5946; (706) 335-6879 FAX
Susan R. Harper, Director of Library
Services

Mon–Wed & Fri 10:00–6:00, Thur
10:00–8:00, Sat 10:00–5:00

Conyers Rockdale Library System
Nancy Guinn Memorial Library
864 Green Street, S.W.
Conyers, GA 30207
(770) 388-5041; (770) 388-5043 FAX
libraryc@mail.rockdale.public.lib.ga.us
http://www.rockdale.public.lib.ga.us
(Library);
http://mtf.home.mindspring.com/newsltr.htm (Newsletter)
Holly R. Heitman, Adult Services Specialist
Mon–Thur 10:00–8:00, Fri–Sat 10:00–5:00,
Sun 1:00–5:00
Pub. *Newsletter*

Cordele-Crisp Carnegie Library
115 East 11th Avenue
Cordele, GA 31015
(229) 276-2644
Jane Hendrix

Dahlonega Courthouse Gold Museum
Department of Natural Resources
(Public Square—location)
PO Box 2042 (mailing address)
Dahlonega, GA 30533
(706) 864-2257
http://georgiamagazine.com/tosee/
goldmus.htm
Sharon Johnson, Superintendent
Mon–Sat 9:00–5:00, Sun 10:00–5:00
(genealogical and mining files)
museum admission fee; donation charged for
research material that is available

Dawson County Library—Chestatee Regional Library
342 Allen Street
Dawsonville, GA 30534
(706) 344-3690; (706) 344-3691 FAX
dawson@gcpl.net
http://www.chestatee.public.lib.ga.us
Rebecca Stuckey, Branch Manager

DeKalb County Public Library
Decatur Library
Genealogy and Special Collections Room
215 Sycamore Street
Decatur, GA 30030-3413
(404) 370-3070; (404) 370-3073 FAX
wrightn@dekalblibrary.org;
tuckerd@dekalblibrary.org
http://www.dekalb.public.lib.ga.us/
services/REF.HTM#geneo
Beth Starkey, Special Collections Librarian
Mon–Thur 9:00–9:00, Fri–Sat 9:00–5:00,
Sun 1:00–5:00
$45.00 per year for nonresidents, free to
residents

DeSoto Trail Regional Library
145 East Broad Street
Camilla, GA 31730-1898
(229) 336-8372; (229) 336-9353 FAX
mitchelg@mail.mitchell.public.lib.ga.us
Ray Mitchell, Director

Dougherty County Public Library
300 Pine Avenue
Albany, GA 31701-2533
(912) 430-1900; (912) 431-2915 FAX
duganm@mail.dougherty.public.lib.ga.us
James F. Forsyth, Genealogical Reference
Librarian
Mon–Wed 10:00–9:00, Thur–Sat
10:00–6:00

Elbert County Public Library
345 Heard Street

Elberton, GA 30635-2436
(706) 283-5375; (706) 283-5456 FAX
johnsonp@mail.elbert.public.lib.ga.us
Peggy Johnson, Acting Director

Emory University
Robert W. Woodruff Library
Special Collections Department
540 Asbury Circle
Atlanta, GA 30322
(404) 727-6887; (404) 727-0053 FAX
speccollref@emory.edu (Special Collections)
http://web.library.emory.edu/libraries/
woodruff
Linda M. Matthews, Head, Special
Collections Department
Mon–Fri 8:30–5:30, Sat 10:00–4:00
(Georgia and the South, the Civil War, and
Methodists)

Fitzgerald-Ben Hill County Library
123 North Main Street
Fitzgerald, GA 31750-2591
(229) 423-3642; (229) 423-4493 FAX
Bernice Bacon, Director
Mon, Wed & Fri–Sat 9:00–6:00, Tue & Thur
9:00–9:00

Forsyth County Heritage Association
Forsyth County Government Building
PO Box 762
Cumming, GA 30028
(770) 887-1626
donshadburn@webtv.net
Don L. Shadburn, County Historian and
Director
by appointment only
("extensive historical/genealogical files, early
photo prints, family records, and certain
documents and memorabilia"; pioneer
families and Cherokee mixed-blood
families, and Confederate periods of
Forsyth County)

Forsyth County Public Library
585 Dahlonega Road
Cumming, GA 30040-2109
(770) 781-9840; (770) 781-8089 FAX
http://www.forsyth.public.lib.ga.us
Jon McDaniel, Director
(no genealogist on staff at this time)

Fulton County/Atlanta-Fulton Public Library
(Corner of Carnegie Way and
Forsythe—location)
1 Margaret Mitchell Square (mailing
address)
Atlanta, GA 30303-1089
(404) 688-4636, ext. 212 and 292
Referenceline@co.fulton.ga.us
http://www.af.public.lib.ga.us
Janice W. Sikes, Curator; Joyce E. Jelks,
Assistant Curator
Mon & Fri 9:00–6:00, Tue–Thur 9:00–8:00,
Sat 10:00–6:00, Sun 2:00–6:00

Genealogical Center Library
PO Box 71343
Marietta, GA 30007-1343
Barbara A. Geisert, Director
(over 9,000 books and periodicals, mail
order only)
$25.00 per year membership in GUILD,
includes book catalog and book loan
forms; $3.00 per book plus $4.00
handling fee per order of up to five books

Georgia College and State University
Center for Georgia Studies
CBX 047
Milledgeville, GA 31061

(478) 445-7382
http://www.gcsu.edu/acad_affairs/
coll_artsci/hist_geo/Center/center.html
Dr. Craig Pascoe, Department of History and
Geography, Director

Georgia College and State University
Old Governor's Mansion
120 South Clark Street, CPO 092
Milledgeville, GA 31061
Mary Jo Thompson

Georgia College and State University
Ina Dillard Russell Library
(231 West Hancock Street—location)
PO Box 43 (mailing address)
Milledgeville, GA 31061
(478) 445-4047 (Main Library); (478) 445-
5573 (Main Library); (478) 454-0988;
(478) 445-6847 FAX
scinfo@gcsu.edu
http://library.gcsu.edu/~sc
Nancy Davis Bray
Library during regular university sessions:
Mon–Thur 7:30–10:00, Fri 7:30–5:00, Sat
noon–5:00, Sun 1:00–10:00; Special
Collections: Mon–Fri 9:00–noon &
1:00–4:00; Intercession hours may vary
(Baldwin County and surrounding counties)

Georgia Institute of Technology
Archives Department
Price Gilbert Memorial Library
Atlanta, GA 30332
Anne Bartlow

Georgia Southern University
Zach S. Henderson Library
Special Collections
(address withheld upon request)
("Our Special Collections here—and indeed
the Library—does not seek to collect
genealogical material or publications.
That is the function of the Statesboro
Regional Library. They know about the
little genealogical material we have; we
make sure that they are informed so that
they can direct people here who might
want to see what we have.")

Georgia State University
William Russell Pullen Library
Special Collections Department
(address withheld upon request)
("Academic administrative records primarily
comprise our University archives
holdings; popular music and labor
archives are our other principal core
strengths.")

Gwinnett History Museum
Lawrenceville Female Seminary Building
455 Perry Street, S.W.
Lawrenceville, GA 30245
(770) 822-5178; (770) 237-5612 FAX
Angela Trigg, Director
Mon–Thur 10:00–4:00, Sat noon–5:00
Pub. *Gwinnett Muse*, quarterly
(history museum dedicated to the history of
Gwinnett County and its people; small,
growing archives)
$15.00 per year membership; museum
admission: $1.00

Hacksma House Genealogy Library
(see Washington, Part 2)

Hall County Library System
127 Main Street, N.W.
Gainesville, GA 30501-3699
(770) 532-3311; (770) 532-4305 FAX
sstewart@mail.hall.public.lib.ga.us

http://www.hall.public.lib.ga.us
Ruth Sanders, Library Assistant; Susan Stewart, Director
Mon–Thur 9:00–9:00, Fri–Sat 9:00–5:30, Sun 1:30–5:30
("Microfilm of the Federal Census of Georgia from 1820–1930 [excluding 1890]; corresponding Soundex and published indexes for the Federal censuses of Georgia when available. Georgia State Census of 1864 also known as the Joe Brown Census. Microfilm of some surrounding states' Federal censuses and corresponding published indexes. Microfilm of courthouse, church, and other miscellaneous Hall County materials. Microfilm of Gainesville newspapers starting sporadically in the late 1800s and running to current day [no index is available at this time]. Published and unpublished Hall County family histories and other local histories. Printed marriage, death, probate records, and county histories from Georgia, Virginia, North Carolina, and South Carolina. The library maintains a photographic history of Hall County on its home page. *Georgia Death Index 1919–1994, Georgia Marriage Index 1964–1994. Roster of the Confederate Soldiers of Georgia 1861–1865. Roster of Confederate Soldiers 1861–1865. Roster of Union Soldiers 1861–1865* [CD]. *Cherokee By Blood,* Vols. 1–9. *Georgia Commissary General's Record of Families with Salt 1862–1864* [CD]. *A copy of General James Longstreet's papers from when he became a resident of Gainesville.*")

Hamburg State Park Museum
Route 1, Box 233
Mitchell, GA 30820
(706) 552-2393
Russell Hinson, Site Manager
8:00–5:00; Museum: daily tours but only grinding on an as-needed basis
(operating grist mill and museum)
$2.00 parking fee

Houston County Public Library
1201 Washington Avenue
Perry, GA 31069-2599
(478) 987-3050; (478) 987-4572 FAX
goldenj@mail.houston.public.lib.ga.us
Judith A. Golden, Director
Mon & Wed–Sat 9:00–6:00, Tue 9:00–9:00

Huntsville-Madison County Public Library
(see Alabama, Part 2)

Jefferson County Library System
306 East Broad Street
Louisville, GA 30434-1624
(478) 625-3751; (478) 625-7683 FAX
Charlotte Rogers, Director
Mon 9:00–5:30, Tue–Fri 8:30–5:30, Sat 9:00–1:00

Jekyll Island Museum
375 Riverview Drive
Jekyll Island, GA 31527
(912) 635-2119; (912) 635-4420
Mon–Fri 8:00–5:00

James G. Kenan Research Center
Atlanta History Center
130 West Paces Ferry Road N.W.
Atlanta, GA 30305-1366
(404) 814-4040; (404) 814-4175 FAX
reference@atlantahistorycenter.com
http://www.atlantahistorycenter.com

Michael Rose, Director, Archives and Research Services
Tue–Fri 9:00–5:00, Sat 10:00–5:00
Pub. *Atlanta History: A Journal of Georgia and the South,* quarterly
$25.00 per year membership

Kennesaw State University
Horace W. Sturgis Library
(1000 Chastain Road, Kennesaw, GA 30144—location)
PO Box 444 (mailing address)
Marietta, GA 30061
(770) 423-6186; (770) 499-3376 FAX
rwilliam@ksumail.kennesaw.edu
Robert Williams
Mon–Thur 7:00 A.M.–midnight, Fri 7:00–5:00, Sat 8:00–6:00, Sun 2:00–10:00
Pub. *Recent Acquisitions,* semiannually, free

Kinchafoonee Regional Library
913 Forrester Drive, S.E.
Dawson, GA 31742-2106
(229) 995-6331; (229) 995-3383 FAX
messerf@mail.terrell.public.lib.ga.us
Frances P. Messer, Director

LaGrange College
William and Evelyn Banks Library
601 Broad Street
LaGrange, GA 30240
(706) 812-7233
lpinkerman@lagrange.edu
http://www.lagrange.edu/primary.cfm?linkid=195
Steve G. Weaver, Reference Librarian; Loren Pinkerman, Director
Jan term: Mon–Thur 8:00 A.M.–9:00 P.M., Fri 8:00–5:00, Sat 1:00–5:00, Sun 2:00–9:00; fall/spring session: Mon–Thur 8:00 A.M.–11:00 P.M., Fri 8:00–5:00, Sat 1:00–5:00, Sun 2:00–10:00; summer session: Mon–Thur 8:00 A.M.–9:00 P.M., Fri 8:00–5:00, Sun 6:00 P.M.–9:00 P.M.; nonsession: Mon–Fri 8:00–5:00
Pub. *Banks News* (online)

Lake Blackshear Regional Library
307 East Lamar Street
Americus, GA 31709-3699
(229) 924-8091; (229) 928-4445 FAX
hendrixj@mail.sumter.public.lib.ga.us
http://www.lbrl.org
Jeanine Bruce, Genealogy Clerk; Jane Hendrix, Director
Mon–Sat 10:00–6:00, Tue 10:00–8:00

Bryan Lang Historical Library
PO Box 715
Woodbine, GA 31569
(912) 576-5841
John H. Christian, Librarian
Mon–Fri 8:00–5:00

Lee-Steizer Heritage Research Museum
372 Sisson Avenue, N.E.
Atlanta, GA 30317
M. L. Walker

Live Oak Public Libraries
Kaye Kole Genealogy and Local History Room
2002 Bull Street
Savannah, GA 31401
(912) 652-3697; (912) 652-3635 FAX
http://www.liveoakpl.org/Genealogy.htm
Erick Erickson, Head of Reference; Bill Johnson, Executive Director
Mon–Thur 9:00–9:00; Fri–Sat 9:00–6:00; Sun 2:00–6:00
Pub. *Savannah Morning News Index,*

annually, $50.00 per issue

Neva Lomason Memorial Library
710 Rome Street
Carrollton, GA 30117-3046
(770) 836-6711; (770) 836-4787 FAX
cooperj@mail.carroll.public.lib.ga.us
http://www.carroll.public.lib.ga.us
James P. Cooper, Director; Roni L. Willis, Assistant Director
Mon–Thur 9:00–8:00, Fri 9:00–5:30, Sat 9:00–4:30, Sun 2:00–6:00

Lumpkin County Library—Chestatee Regional Library System
342 Courthouse Square
Dahlonega, GA 30533
(706) 864-3668; (706) 864-3937 FAX
lumpkin@gcpl.net
http://www.chestatee.public.lib.ga.us
Kathleen Walker, Branch Manager
Mon, Wed & Fri 10:00–6:00, Tue & Thur 10:00–8:00, Sat 10:00–2:00

Madison-Morgan Cultural Center
434 South Main Street
Madison, GA 30650
(706) 342-4743; (706) 342-1154 FAX
Cassandra E. Baker, Executive Director
Tue–Sat 10:00–4:30, Sun 2:00–5:00
Pub. untitled newsletter, quarterly (Piedmont, Georgia, History Museum)
$20.00 per year membership

Massie Heritage Interpretation Center
207 East Gordon Street
Savannah, GA 31401
(912) 651-7022
Francis W. Smith, Heritage Education Teacher

Medical College of Georgia
Special Collections Program
Medical College of Georgia Library
Laney-Waler Boulevard
Augusta, GA 30912-0300
Dorothy H. Mims

Mercer University
Main Library
1300 Edgewood Avenue
Macon, GA 31207-0001
(478) 752-2960
http://atl1.mercer.edu/~mainlib

Mercer University
Tift College Archives
1400 Coleman Avenue
Macon, GA 31207
Ann G. Park

Middle Georgia College
Roberts Memorial Library
Cochran, GA 31014
Raj Ambardekar

Midway Museum, Inc.
(U.S. Highway 17—location)
PO Box 195 (mailing address)
Midway, GA 31320
(912) 884-5837

Moultrie-Colquitt County Library
204 Fifth Street, S.E.
Moultrie, GA 31776-2828
(229) 985-6540; (229) 985-0936 FAX
jenkinsm@mail.colquitt.public.lib.ga.us
Melody S. Jenkins, Director
Mon–Sat 8:30–5:00

Mountain Regional Library
(698 Miller Street—location)

PO Box 159 (mailing address)
Young Harris, GA 30582-4016
(706) 379-3732; (706) 379-2047 FAX
haymoret@mail.towns.public.lib.ga.us
http://pines.lib.ga.us (webcat of most of the
   libraries in Georgia)
Teresa P. Haymore, Director
Mon–Fri 8:30–5:00, Sat 10:00–2:00
(local Georgia and special Appalachian
   collections)
only minimal staff-conducted research

Newton County Library System
7116 Floyd Street, N.E.
Covington, GA 30014-1572
(770) 787-3231; (770) 784-2092 FAX
gheid@mail.newton.public.lib.ga.us
Greg Heid, Director

North Georgia College
Old North Georgia College Museum
Student Center
Dahlonega, GA 30597
Alan Theriault

Northwest Georgia Regional Library
310 Cappes Street
Dalton, GA 30720-4123
(706) 278-4507; (706) 278-7519 FAX
forseej@mail.whitfield.public.lib.ga.us
http://www.whitfield.public.lib.ga.us
Joe B. Forsee, Director; Linda Litton,
   Reference Librarian
Mon–Thur 9:00–8:00, Fri 9:00–6:00, Sat
   9:00–5:00

Ocmulgee Regional Library System
(505 Second Avenue, Eastman, GA 31023-
   6107—location)
PO Box 4369 (mailing address)
Eastman, GA 31203
(478) 374-5646
Mon & Wed 9:00–5:00, Tue & Thur
   9:00–8:00, Fri 9:00–4:00, Sat 10:00–2:00
(special collections)

Oconee County Library
(1080 Experiment Station Road—location)
PO Box 837 (mailing address)
Watkinsville, GA 30677
(706) 769-3950
Laureen Alford Adams, Reference Librarian
Mon–Thur 10:00–9:00, Fri–Sat 10:00–6:00,
   Sun 2:00–6:00

Oconee Regional Library
(801 Bellevue Avenue, Dublin, GA 31021-
   4847—location)
PO Box 100 (mailing address)
Dublin, GA 31021
(478) 272-5710; (478) 272-5381
heritage@mail.laurens.public.lib.ga.us
   (Heritage Center Librarian)
http://www.laurens.public.lib.ga.us/
   geneal.htm
$15.00 per request about one person,
   includes photocopying up to ten pages,
   $5.00 for each additional name, 25¢ per
   page for each additional photocopy

Ellen Payne Odom Genealogy Library
(Moultrie-Colquit County Library—location)
PO Box 2828 (mailing address)
Moultrie, GA 31776-2828
(229) 985-6540; (229) 985-0936 FAX
http://www.scottishtales.com/familytree
   (*Family Tree*)
Beth Gay, DCTJ, Public Relations Director
   and Editor
Mon–Sat 8:30–5:00
Pub. *The Family Tree: The Ellen Payne
   Odom Genealogy Library*, bimonthly

("the largest Scottish and the largest
   genealogical publication in the world"),
   $6.00 per year subscription
("The Odom Library is archival and
   genealogical 'home' to 116 [at this date]
   Scottish Clan organizations and other
   ethnic groups. The core collection, in
   addition to a very large Scottish
   collection, is the eastern seaboard of the
   United States and the migration routes
   west. We have a very comprehensive War
   Between the States collection as well as
   the Scottish materials.")

Ohoopee Regional Library System
Headquarters: Vidalia-Toombs County
   Library
610 Jackson Street
Vidalia, GA 30474-4746
(912) 537-9283; (912) 537-3735 FAX
vidalial@mail.toombs.public.lib.ga.us
http://www.toombs.public.lib.ga.us
(Ladson Genealogy Library: 21,000
   monographs and 2,863 microfilm items
   with concentrations in New Hampshire,
   Massachusetts, New York, Pennsylvania,
   Virginia, Alabama, North Carolina, South
   Carolina, Georgia and Tennessee; system
   also includes Montgomery County
   Library, Nelle Brown Memorial Library
   [Lyons], Tattnall County Library
   [Reidsville], and Glennville Public
   Library)

Okefenokee Regional Library
(401 Lee Avenue—location)
PO Box 1669 (mailing address)
Waycross, GA 31501-3010
(912) 287-4978; (912) 287-4981 FAX
http://www.ware.public.lib.ga.us
James Britton, Reference Librarian
Mon & Thur 10:00–9:00, Tue–Wed
   10:00–6:00, Fri–Sat 10:00–4:00

Oxford College of Emory University
O'Kelley Memorial Library
Oxford, GA 30267
Margaret McPherson

Peach Public Libraries
315 Martin Luther King Jr. Drive
Fort Valley, GA 31030-4906
(478) 825-1640; (478) 825-2061 FAX
stanberg@mail.peach.public.lib.ga.us
http://www.peach.public.lib.ga.us
Gilda Stanbery-Cotney, Director

Piedmont Regional Library
189 Bell View Street
Winder, GA 30680-1706
(770) 867-2762; (770) 867-7483 FAX
rayn@mail.barrow.public.lib.ga.us
http://library.barrow.public.lib.ga.us
Nancy Ray, Director

Pine Mountain Regional Library
(218 Perry Street—location)
PO Box 709 (mailing address)
Manchester, GA 31816-1317
(706) 846-2186; (706) 846-8455 FAX
geec@mail.meriwether.public.lib.ga.us
Charles B. Gee, Director
Mon–Wed & Fri 8:30–5:00, Thur 8:30–8:00,
   Sat 9:00–1:00
copies: 25¢ per page

Roddenbery Memorial Library
320 North Broad Street
Cairo, GA 31728-2199
(229) 377-3632; (229) 377-7204 FAX
rml@rmlibrary.org
http://www.rmlibrary.org

Carolyn Chason
Genealogy: Wed 1:00–5:00

Rome-Floyd County Library
Special Collections Department
205 Riverside Parkway
Rome, GA 30161-2913
(706) 236-4607; (706) 236-4631 FAX
broomes@mail.floyd.public.lib.ga.us
http://www.floyd.public.lib.ga.us
Sandra Broome, Curator
Mon–Thur 8:30–8:30, Fri 8:30–6:00, Sat
   9:00–4:00, Sun 1:30–5:30
("Will respond to brief mail queries.")

Rossville Public Library
504 McFarland Avenue
Rossville, GA 30741
(706) 866-1368; (706) 858-0251 FAX
cclark@mail.walker.public.lib.ga.us
http://www.walker.public.lib.ga.us/
   branches/rossville.html
Mon–Wed 9:00–5:00, Thur 1:00–8:00,
   Fri–Sat 9:00–noon

San Souci Library
PO Box 167
Adairsville, GA 30103

Satilla Regional Library
Genealogy and Local History Department
201 South Coffee Avenue
Douglas, GA 31533
(912) 384-6450
Winifred Merier Gourley
Mon–Thur 10:00–6:00, Fri 10:00–3:00
(local and Georgia family history, local
   archives)

Screven-Jenkins Regional Library
106 South Community Drive
Sylvania, GA 30467-1917
(912) 564-7526; (912) 564-7580 FAX
youlesk@mail.screven.public.lib.ga.us
http://www.sjrls.public.lib.ga.us
Kathryn Youles, Interim Director

Sequoyah Regional Library
116 Brown Industrial Parkway
Canton, GA 30114-8085
(770) 479-3090; (770) 479-3069 FAX
http://tlc.library.net/sequoyah
Emma Ingle, ILL/Genealogy Coordinator
Mon–Thur 9:00–8:00, Fri–Sat 9:00–5:00

South Georgia Regional Library
300 Woodrow Wilson Drive
Valdosta, GA 31602-2592
(229) 333-0086, ext. 18; (229) 333-7669
   FAX
lizan@mail.lowndes.public.lib.ga.us
http://www.valdosta.peachnet.edu/
   ~dpeeples/sgrl.html
Liza Newsom, Director
Mon–Thur 10:00–9:00, Fri–Sat 10:00–5:30,
   Sun 2:30–5:30

Southern College of Technology Library
1112 Clay Street
Marietta, GA 30060
John W. Pattillo

**Southwest Georgia Regional Library
System**
Headquarters: Decatur County-Gilbert H.
   Gragg Library
301 South Monroe Streets
Bainbridge, GA 39819-4029
(229) 248-2665; (229) 248-2670 FAX
mchapman@mail.decatur.public.lib.ga.us;
   s_whittle@mail.decatur.public.lib.ga.us
http://www.swgrl.org

Susan S. Whittle, Director; Mandy Chapman, System Analyst
Mon 10:00–8:00, Tue–Wed & Fri 9:00–6:00, Thur 9:00–8:00, Sat 10:00–4:00
(Branches: James W. Merritt Library, 259 East Main Street, Colquitt, GA 39837, (229) 758-3131, Mon–Fri 9:30–5:30; Seminole County Public Library, 103 West Fourth Street, Donalsonville, GA 39845, (229) 524-2665, Mon–Sat 9:30–5:30. Publications: *Decatur County Past & Present* $25.00, *Jones History of Decatur County* $35.00, *Marriage Records of Miller County* $20.00, *Cornerstone of Georgia, Seminole County* $47.50.)

State University of West Georgia
A. B. Weaver Special Collections
Ingram Library
Carrollton, GA 30118
(770) 830-2350
http://www.westga.edu/library
Myron W. House

Statesboro Regional Library
Genealogy Department
124 South Main Street
Statesboro, GA 30458-5246
(912) 681-0940; (912) 764-2861 FAX
Henrietta Royal, Genealogy Librarian
Mon–Thur 9:00–8:00, Fri–Sat 9:00–6:00

Stone Mountain Park
Memorial Hall Museum
Antebellum Plantation
PO Box 778
Stone Mountain, GA 30086
Jack Bearden

Thomas College Library Archives
1501 Millpond Road
Thomasville, GA 31792
(229) 226-1621

Thomas County Museum of History
(725 North Dawson Street, Thomasville, GA 32792—location)
PO Box 1922 (mailing address)
Thomasville, GA 31799
(229) 226-7664
Charles T. Hill, Curator
Mon–Fri 9:00–5:00, Sat 10:00–5:00, Sun 2:00–5:00
$20.00 per year membership

Thomas County Public Library System
201 North Madison Street
Thomasville, GA 31792-5414
(229) 225-5252; (229) 225-5258 FAX
nancy@tcpls.org
http://tcpls.org
Nancy Tillinghast, Director

Thomaston-Upson Archives
(301 South Center Street—location)
PO Box 1137 (mailing address)
Thomaston, GA 30286-0015
(706) 646-2437; (706) 646-3524 FAX
Winston E. Walker, III, Archivist
Mon–Fri 8:00–5:00, Sat 9:00–1:00
Pub. *The Hickory Nut*, bimonthly; *Upson Vigil*, six times per year
no fee for limited research requests only, more in-depth requests referred to local independent researchers

Thomasville Genealogical, History and Fine Arts Library, Inc.
(135 North Broad Street, Thomasville, GA 31792—location)

PO Box 1597 (mailing address)
Thomasville, GA 31799
(229) 226-9640; (229) 226-3199 FAX
glibrary@rose.net
http://www.rose.net/~glibrary
Kathy Smith Mills, Director
Mon–Fri 9:00–5:00, Sat 9:00–4:00
Pub. *Origins*, quarterly, $5.00 per issue
("Genealogical library with a major emphasis on the southeastern states")
from $25.00 per year membership; research: $10.00 per hour

Troup-Harris-Coweta Regional Library
115 Alford Street
LaGrange, GA 30240-3041
(706) 882-7784; (706) 883-7342 FAX
joellen@gcpl.net;
    bechamg@mailbox.troup.public.lib.ga.us
http://lagrange.troup.public.lib.ga.us
JoEllen Ostendorf, Director

Troy Public Library
(see Alabama, Part 2)

Uncle Remus Regional Library
1131 East Avenue
Madison, GA 30650-1496
(706) 342-4974; (706) 342-4510 FAX
steve@uncleremus.org;
    schaefer@mail.morgan.public.lib.ga.us
http://www.morgan.public.lib.ga.us
Steve W. Schaefer, Director

University of Georgia
Department of Archives and Records Management
Main Library
Fourth Floor Old Building
Athens, GA 30606
(706) 542-8151; (706) 542-2131 (Photographic Services); (706) 542-4144 FAX
http://www.libs.uga.edu/darchive
Gilbert Head, Archival Associate I
Mon–Fri 8:00–5:00

University of Georgia
Hargrett Rare Book and Manuscript Library
Athens, GA 30602-1641
(706) 542-7123; (706) 542-7131; (706) 542-4144 FAX
web_editor@mail.libs.uga.edu
http://www.libs.uga.edu/hargrett/speccoll.html
Linda Aaron, Archivist
Mon–Fri 8:00–5:00, Sat 9:00–5:00

University of Georgia
Instructional Resources Center
South P-J Auditorium
Athens, GA 30602
John R. Stephens, Jr.

University of Georgia
Map Collection
Science Library
Athens, GA 30602
John Sutherland

University of Georgia Libraries
Richard B. Russell Memorial Library
Athens, GA 30602-1641
(706) 542-5788; (706) 542-4144 FAX
http://www.libs.uga.edu/russell/russell.html
Sheryl B. Vogt, Department Head

University of Mississippi
Center for the Study of Southern Culture
(see Mississippi, Part 2)

Valdosta State College

Archives of Contemporary South Georgia History
Valdosta, GA 31698
Jay Evatt

Mary Vinson Memorial Library
North Jefferson Street
Milledgeville, GA 31061
(genealogy room)

Washington Memorial Library
Genealogical and Historical Room
1180 Washington Avenue
Macon, GA 31201-1790
(478) 744-0820 (Library); (478) 744-0893 FAX
mgrlgh@bibblib.org
http://www.co.bibb.ga.us/library/GH.htm
Willard L. Rocker, Department Chief, Genealogical and Historical Room; Muriel McDowell Jackson, SLIS, Genealogy Librarian; Christopher Stokes, Ph.D., Historian; Peer Ravnen, Archivist
Mon 9:00–9:00, Tue–Sat 9:00–6:00
("More than 28,000 books and 17,500 microfilms on the thirteen original colonies, British and pre-colonial history, and southern history and genealogy. The books and microforms within the genealogy department represent a strong collection of records for thirteen colonies, subsequently states, from settlement through 1850 and an excellent collection of resources for southern states, particularly Virginia, the Carolinas and Georgia. Highlights include Georgia Confederate service records and pension records; Stevens-Davis Memorial Collection of Foreign Records [mostly British, especially English, records]; J. W. Burke imprints; and the records of Leonardo Andrea. In addition, since 1967, the Genealogical and Historical Room has proudly served as a depository for records of the Georgia Society Daughters of the American Revolution. Middle Georgia Archives is the other department within the Genealogical and Historical Room. The Middle Georgia Archives contains more than 11,000 linear feet of materials documenting the history of Macon and middle Georgia, including literary manuscripts of Harry Stilwell Edwards, Sidney Lanier, and other middle Georgia authors; records of Christ Episcopal Church; records of the Macon Volunteers; papers of Macon Mayor W. A. Huff; papers of Macon Mayor Buckner Melton; the Douglass Theatre collection of cinema and burlesque papers, financial records, and other materials relating to African Americans in vaudeville; records of the Republican Party of Bibb County; Macon photographs; records of the Bibb County Board of Education; the Steele-Tracy-Johnston Family Letters collection; and other materials of local and regional interest.")

Wesleyan College
Willet Library
Forsyth Road
Macon, GA 31297
Tena Roberts

Young Harris College
Duckworth Libraries
PO Box 39
Young Harris, GA 30582
(706) 379-4313; (706) 379-4314 FAX
http://www.yhc.edu
Bob Richardson

Historical Societies—Local and Regional

Albany-Daugherty Historic Area Commission
1108 Maryland Drive
Albany, GA 31707
Mackey R. Saunders

Historical Society of Alma-Bacon County
(201 North Pierce Street—location)
406 Mercer Street (mailing address)
Alma, GA 31510
(912) 632-8450; (912) 632-4512 FAX

Alpharetta Historical Society
1835 Old Milton Parkway
Alpharetta, GA 30004-1823
(770) 475-4663; (770) 475-0091 FAX

Ansley Park Civic Association
PO Box 7775, Station "C"
Atlanta, GA 30357
Jane P. Harmon

Appling County Historical Society, Inc.
Appling County Community Education Center
PO Box 1063
Baxley, GA 31513-7063
(912) 367-2433

Arts and Heritage Council of Pelham
(415 West Railroad Street—location)
PO Box 389 (mailing address)
Pelham, GA 31779

Ashburn Historic Preservation Commission
(121 East Madison Avenue—location)
PO Box 766 (mailing address)
Ashburn, GA 31714
(229) 567-3431; (229) 567-9284 FAX
Sandra J. Lumpkin, City Clerk
8:00–5:00

Athens-Clarke Heritage Foundation
Fire Hall 2
489 Prince Avenue
Athens, GA 30601
(706) 353-1801

Athens Historical Society
PO Box 7745
Athens, GA 30604-7745

Atlanta Historical Society
(3099 Andrews Drive—location)
PO Box 12423 (mailing address)
Atlanta, GA 30355

Banks County Historical Society
PO Box 473
Homer, GA 30547
(706) 677-2108
Richard Chambers
Mon–Fri 10:00–4:00

Barnesville-Lamar County Historical Society
(888 Thomaston Street—location)
PO Box 805 (mailing address)
Barnesville, GA 30204
(770) 358-7905; (770) 358-0150 (Museum)

Barrow County Historical Society, Inc.
(Barrow County Museum, 74 East Athens Street—location)
PO Box 277 (mailing address)
Winder, GA 30680
(770) 307-1183

W. Michael Strickland, President
Mon–Fri 1:00–4:00; two meetings: spring and fall
("The purpose of the society is to bring people together who have a particular interest in the history of Barrow County. The mission of the society shall be to preserve, protect and enhance the historical heritage of Barrow County for the enjoyment of future generations.")
$10.00 per year membership

Beach Institute Historic Neighborhood Association
9520 Ferguson Avenue
Savannah, GA 31405
W. W. Law

Bleckley County Historical Society
Middle Georgia College
Cochran, GA 31014
(478) 934-6221

Blue and Gray Memorial Association
(Blue and Gray Museum—location)
Municipal Building (mailing address)
Fitzgerald, GA 31750
(229) 423-5375
Beth M. Davis, Executive Director
1 Mar–31 Oct: Mon–Fri 2:00–5:00
(museum mirrors the history of this former Union veterans' colony in former Confederate territory)
$5.00 per year membership

Bonaventure Historical Society
1317 East 55th Street
Savannah, GA 31404-4615

Bowdon Area Historical Society
PO Box 277
Bowdon, GA 30108
Jackie Jackson

Brantley County Historical and Preservation Society
PO Box 1096
Nahunta, GA 31553

Brooks County Historical Society
(404 Tallokas Road—location)
PO Box 676 (mailing address)
Quitman, GA 31643
(229) 263-4412; (229) 263-8002 FAX
Wilma G. Knight

Bulloch County Historical Society
(address withheld upon request)
("We are not able to serve with so many members nationwide and so few local volunteers.")
$15.00 per year membership

Burke County Historical Association
Quaker Road
Waynesboro, GA 30830
Mrs. Alden Dye

Burke County Historical Society
Burke County Museum
536 Liberty Street
Waynesboro, GA 30830
(706) 554-4889 (Museum); (706) 554-4815 FAX
Robert L. Hammond, Sr., Curator
Museum: Wed–Fri 10:00–5:00, Sat 10:00–4:00, Sun 1:00–4:00
(historical information, genealogical information—Burke County and Georgia; private database of many local families)

Butts County Historical Society

(Highway 42, Indian Spring—location)
PO Box 215 (mailing address)
Jackson, GA 31233
(770) 775-6734
Mrs. Deryle Lamb, President

Byron Area Historical Society
PO Box 755
Byron, GA 31008
(478) 956-3600; (478) 956-5299 FAX

Carroll County Historical Society
(West Avenue—location)
PO Box 1308 (mailing address)
Carrollton, GA 30117
(770) 836-6494; (770) 836-6626 FAX
chestnut185@aol.com
Myron W. House, President; Gwyn Chestnut

Catoosa County Historical Society
(Old Stone Church, corner of U.S. 41 and GA 2—location)
PO Box 113 (mailing address)
Ringgold, GA 30736
(706) 935-4875
JOYWM@catt.com
Joy W. Mahan, President
Museum: Thur–Sun 1:00–5:00; meetings second Mon 7:00–8:30 (except July–Aug)
Pub. *Catoosa County Historical Society Newsletter*, monthly
("We have a museum [Civil War and Native American]. We have some family histories, census records and a full set of *The Cherokee Phoenix*.")
$5.00 per year membership

Cave Spring Historical Society, Inc.
(13 Cedartown Road—location)
PO Box 715 (mailing address)
Cave Spring, GA 30124
(706) 777-8865
Mary Jo Posey

Charlton County Historical Society Library
(100 Cypress Street—location)
PO Box 575 (mailing address)
Folkston, GA 31537-0575
(912) 496-4578
Lois B. Mays, President
by appointment
(Charlton County local history, pioneer family histories; abstracts of 1908–1938 *Charlton County Herald*, weekly county paper; microfilm census of county)
$5.00 per year membership

Chattahoochee Valley Historical Society, Inc.
(see Alabama, Part 2)

Chattooga County Historical Society
(119 East Washington Street—location)
PO Box 626 (mailing address)
Summerville, GA 30747
(706) 973-2050; (706) 397-8235
Steve32861@hotmail.com
http://www.rootsweb.com/~gahatto/index.htm
Steven Strickland, Past President and Editor
Georgia Room, Chattooga County Library: Mon–Fri 9:00–5:00
Pub. *The Chattooga County Historical Society Quarterly*
$12.00 per year membership; research: a nominal fee

Cherokee County Historical Society, Inc.
Crescent Farm Historical Center
PO Box 1287
Canton, GA 30114

(770) 479-4741
robertsfar@aol.com
http://www.rockbarn.comhttp://www.tib.
　　com/cchm/cchmpict.htm
Mary H. Free, Genealogist; Judson Roberts
Pub. *Crescent Chronicle*, monthly
$15.00 per year membership

Coastal Georgia Historical Society
(101 12th Street-location)
PO Box 21136 (mailing address)
Saint Simons Island, GA 31522-0636
(912) 638-4666; (912) 638-6609 FAX

Coastal Heritage Society, Inc.
303 Martin Luther King, Jr., Boulevard
Savannah, GA 31401
(912) 651-6840; (912) 651-6971 FAX
Sandra Godwin, Director's Assistant
Mon–Fri 9:00–5:00
Pub. *CHS Update*, quarterly
(Savannah's history, Georgia railroad
　history, military history, especially Civil
　War)
$25.00 per year membership

Cobb Landmarks and Historical Society
145 Denmeade Street
Marietta, GA 30060
(770) 426-4982
Ginger B. McPherson, Director

Colbert Improvement Club
PO Box 245
Colbert, GA 30628
(706) 788-2904
BBR12OAKS@aol.com
Barbarianne Russell, President
(publishes local history, including *History of
　Colbert*, $10.00 plus postage)

College Park Historical Society, Inc.
(3336 East Main Street—location)
PO Box F (mailing address)
College Park, GA 30337
(404) 767-6202

Colquitt County Historical Society
214 16th Avenue, S.E.
Moultrie, GA 31778
(229) 985-3413

Columbia County Historical Society
PO Box 203
Appling, GA 30802
Julia D. Prather

Cook County Historical Society
PO Box 497
Sparks, GA 31647
Dillard Ensley

Cordele-Crisp County Historical Society
Route 2, Box 995
Cordele, GA 31015
Sarah Summers

**Coweta Chatter Genealogical and
Historical Society**
(see Genealogical Societies—Local and
　Regional, below)

Crawford County Historical Society
(Crawford County Business Development
　Center—location)
PO Box 1028 (mailing address)
Roberta, GA 31078
(478) 836-3158; (478) 836-2355 FAX
Sara W. Paravis

Dade County Historical Society, Inc.
(New England Road—location)

PO Box 512 (mailing address)
Trenton, GA 30752
sueforrester@hotmail.com (Chairman)
Sonny McMahan, President; Sue Forrester,
　Chairman of Board
Pub. *NEWSLETTER*, two times per year
$10.00 per year membership; research: small
　searches for $5.00 per request, such as
　one marriage, one probate or one
　cemetery look-up (contact the society for
　fees for more extensive research)

Dahlonega Club, Inc.
Vickery House Museum
(West Main and Vickery Drive—location)
PO Box 785 (mailing address)
Dahlonega, GA 30533
(706) 864-4197; (706) 864-3365
Helyn Brooks, President
4 July, first week of Dec, and by appointment

Dahlonega Historical Commission
106 Moores Drive
Dahlonega, GA 30533
Steve Gallant

**Dawson County Historical and
Genealogical Society**
PO Box 1074
Dawsonville, GA 30534

Decatur County Historical Society
(119 West Water Street—museum location)
PO Box 682 (mailing address)
Bainbridge, GA 31718
(229) 248-1719
Jim Lillethun, Treasurer/Curator
Museum: Sat–Sun 1:00–5:00
$10.00 per year membership

DeKalb Historical Society, Inc.
101 East Court Square
Decatur, GA 30030
(404) 373-1088; (404) 373-3076; (404) 378-
　8287 FAX
dhs@dekalbhistory.org
http://www.dekalbhistory.org
Robert J. Kothe, Executive Director
Pub. *DeKalb Historical Society Newsletter*
(family records, census records, some court
　records and some land records)
$25.00 per year membership

Douglas County Historical Society
(8562 Campbellton Street—location)
PO Box 2018 (mailing address)
Douglasville, GA 30133

Early County Historical Society, Inc.
PO Box 564
Blakely, GA 31723
Chesley N. Wiger

East Point Historical Society, Inc.
(1685 Norman Berry Drive—location)
PO Box 90675 (mailing address)
East Point, GA 30364-0675

**Eatonton-Putnam County Historical
Society, Inc.**
104 Church Street
Eatonton, GA 31024
(706) 485-6442 (home); (404) 679-5277
　(work)
Jim Marshall, President and Primary
　Genealogical Researcher
by appointment
(compiling marked and unmarked
　graves/cemeteries index, published history
　of Putnam County which includes four
　surrounding county tidbits, maintains
　300+ family files)

$10.00 per year membership; search fees at
　cost and donation

Elbert County Historical Society
(1 Deadwyler Street—location)
PO Box 1033 (mailing address)
Elberton, GA 30635
J. W. Hyde, Chair-Executive Committee
monthly, except July–Aug
Pub. *Historic Echoes*, monthly
(located in a restored 1910 seaboard airline
　passenger depot)
$12.00 per year membership

**The Eleventh Circuit Historical Society,
Inc.**
PO Box 1556
Atlanta, GA 30301
(404) 335-6395
Wanda W. Lamar, Executive Director
("Projects: videotaped oral histories of our
　federal judges; writing and publishing the
　histories of the district courts of Alabama,
　Florida, and Georgia, and the history of
　the Eleventh Circuit Court of Appeals,
　portraits of our senior federal judges")

Etoway Valley Historical Society
(1903 Bartow County Courthouse, 115 West
　Cherokee Avenue—location)
PO Box 1886 (mailing address)
Cartersville, GA 30120
(770) 606-8862
evhs@evhsonline.org (not for genealogical
　queries)
http://www.evhsonline.org (Allatoona Pass
　Battlefield official web site)
President
Mon–Fri 1:30–4:30, first & third Sat
　1:00–5:00; monthly meetings
Pub. *EVHS Newsletter*, bimonthly
("Also incorporated as the Bartow County
　Historical Society.")
$15.00 per year membership; research:
　limited look-ups, check web site

Fayette County Historical Society, Inc.
(195 Lee Street—location)
PO Box 495 (mailing address)
Fayetteville, GA 30214
(770) 461-7152 (President); (770) 716-9230
　FAX
cccary@aol.com
Carolyn Cary, President, Co-founder,
　Official County Historian
Tue 6:00–9:00, Thur 10:00–1:00, Sat
　9:00–1:00
("Fairly complete Civil War research section,
　1,000 family file folders on Fayette
　Countians.")
$10.00 per year membership; search fee: 25¢
　per page for copies

Fort Gaines Historical Society, Inc.
(308 East Jefferson Street—location)
PO Box 6 (mailing address)
Fort Gaines, GA 31751

Franklin County Historical Society
(Gainesville Street—location)
PO Box 541 (mailing address)
Carnesville, GA 30521
Anna Belle Tabor

Gainesville Heritage Group
Brenau College
Gainesville, GA 30501

Gordon County Historical Society, Inc.
(335 South Wall Street—location)
PO Box 342 (mailing address)
Calhoun, GA 30701

(706) 629-4570 FAX
Mary Thomas, Secretary
Mon–Fri 10:00–4:00

Grady County Historical Society
Roddenbery Memorial Library
310 North Broad Street
Cairo, GA 31728
Wessie Connell

Greene County Historical Society
(201 Green Street—location)
PO Box 238 (mailing address)
Greensboro, GA 30642
(706) 453-2588; (706) 453-4970 FAX
V. T. Newsom

Griffin Historical and Preservation Society
(633 Meriwether Street, Griffin, GA
    30223—location)
PO Box 196 (mailing address)
Griffin, GA 30224
(770) 229-2432; (770) 227-5586
Elizabeth L. Thomas, Executive Director

Guale Historical Society
PO Box 398
Saint Marys, GA 31558
(912) 882-4587 (Vice President)
Eloise B. Thompson, Vice President
Pub. *Guale News*, seven times per year
    (before each meeting or ramble)
$8.00 per year membership

Guyton Historical Society
(Central Boulevard—location)
PO Box 15 (mailing address)
Guyton, GA 31312
(912) 772-3344

Gwinnett Historical Society, Inc.
(185 Clayton Street, Lawrenceville, GA
    30045—location)
PO Box 261 (mailing address)
Lawrenceville, GA 30046
(770) 822-5174; (770) 237-5616 FAX
gwhissoc@bellsouth.net
http://www.adsd.com/ghs
Elaine Roberts, President
Mon–Fri 9:30–1:30
Pub. *The Heritage*, quarterly
(history and genealogy of Gwinnett and
    surrounding counties)
$15.00 per year membership

Hahira Historical Society
202 East Lawson Street
Hahira, GA 31632
(229) 794-2274

Hall County Historical Society
892 Chattahoochee Drive, N.W.
Gainesville, GA 30506
(770) 532-2242; (770) 536-7072 FAX
Eula Pierce

Hancock County Foundation for Historic Preservation
703 Burwell Street
Sparta, GA 31087
Larry Gulley

Hapeville Historical Society, Inc.
PO Box 82055
Hapeville, GA 30354
Gene Norton

Haralson County Historical Society, Inc.
(Van Wert Street—location)
PO Box 585 (mailing address)
Buchanan, GA 30113
(770) 646-3369

Daisy H. Sargent, President

Hart County, Georgia Historical Society
40 Bailey Place Road
Lavonia, GA 30553-9561
(706) 377-5612
Travis Parker, President
9:00–4:00
Pub. *Pioneers of Hart County, Georgia*,
    quarterly
(Hart, Franklin, and Elbert counties, Georgia;
    records before 1865)
$21.00 per year membership; research: free
    search of all Historical Society records by
    surname for members

Hawkinsville-Pulaski County Chamber of Commerce
(100 Lumpkin Street—location)
PO Box 447 (mailing address)
Hawkinsville, GA 31036
(478) 783-1717; (478) 783-1700 FAX
Chris Clark, Executive Director
Mon–Fri 9:00–5:00
("This is the Chamber office and we do make
    referrals as needed.")

Heard County Historical Society
Heard County Historical Center and Museum
(161 Shady Street—location)
PO Box 990 (mailing address)
Franklin, GA 30217
(706) 675-6507 (Museum); (706) 675-0819
    FAX
Selma Bowen, Museum Coordinator; Lela
    Craft, Museum Coordinator
Museum: Tue & Thur 8:30–5:00, and by
    appointment
Pub. *Heard and Scene*, quarterly (Jan, Apr,
    July, Oct)
$15.00 per year membership

Historic Chattahoochee Commission
(see Alabama, Part 2)

Historic Effingham Society
(Pine and Early Streets—location)
PO Box 665 (mailing address)
Springfield, GA 31329
(912) 826-4976
Milton H. Rahn

Jackson County Historical Society
(Heritage Room of the Commerce Public
    Library, 1344 South Broad Street—location)
PO Box 1234 (mailing address)
Commerce, GA 30529
(706) 335-5946 (Library)
tina313@mindspring.com
http://www.amdatel.com/cyberplaza/
    dcrwford
Jean Booth, Editor
Library: Mon–Wed & Fri 10:00–6:00, Thur
    10:00–8:00, Sat 10:00–5:00
Pub. *Jackson County Historical Society
    Newsletter*, quarterly
(genealogy, history, library, archives)
$10.00 per year membership; research:
    $15.00

Jasper County Historical Foundation, Inc.
College Street
Monticello, GA 31064
(706) 468-6637
Marcia Carnes, President

Jefferson County Historical Society
PO Box 491
Louisville, GA 30434-0491

Jenkins County Historical Society
Chamber of Commerce

548 Cotton Street
Millen, GA 30442
(478) 982-5595; (478) 982-5112 FAX

Johnson County Historical Society, Inc.
PO Box 87
Wrightsville, GA 31096
deshistpub@hotmail.com
Donald E. Smith, President
$10.00 per year membership

Kennesaw Historical Society
2829 Cherokee Street
Kennesaw, GA 30144
(770) 975-0887

Kennesaw Mountain Historical Association
Kennesaw Mountain National Battlefield
    Park
905 Kennesaw Mountain Drive
Kennesaw, GA 30152
(770) 427-4686; (770) 528-8399 FAX
http://www.nps.gov/kemo

Keystone Genealogical Society
(see Florida, Part 2)

Laurens County Historical Society
Dublin-Laurens Museum
(Bellevue and Academy at Church, Dublin,
    GA 31021—location)
PO Box 1461 (mailing address)
Dublin, GA 31040
(478) 272-9242
Scott B. Thompson, Sr., Director
Tue–Fri 1:00–4:30
Pub. *LCHS Newsletter*, quarterly
(Laurens County history and genealogy)
$25.00 per year membership

Lee County Historical Society
PO Box 393
Leesburg, GA 31763

Liberty County Historical Society
PO Box 982
Hinesville, GA 31310

Lincoln County Historical Society, Inc.
2357 Highway 220 East
Lincolnton, GA 30817
Marion M. Glover

Lower Altamaha Historical Society
PO Box 1405
Darien, GA 31305
(912) 437-4687; (912) 485-2251; (912) 485-
    2141 FAX
Buddy Sullivan, President; Mattie R.
    Gladstone, Genealogist
Ida Hilton Public Library: third Thur except
    Dec
Pub. *Altamaha Echoes*, biannually; *LAHS
    Newsletter*, quarterly
(Scots of McIntosh [list of original settlers],
    McIntosh County cemeteries)
$10.00 per year membership

Lowndes County Historical Society and Museum
305 West Central Avenue
Valdosta, GA 31601
(229) 247-4780; (229) 247-2840 FAX
director@valdostamuseum.org
http://valdostamuseum.org
Renate K. Milner, Director
Mon–Fri 10:00–5:00, Sat 10:00–2:00
Pub. *Yesterday & Today*, monthly
(Lowndes County history)
$25.00 per year membership; admission:
    donation

Lumpkin County Historical Society
PO Box 894
Dahlonega, GA 30533
(706) 864-3668
info@dahlonega.org
Pub. newsletter, quarterly

Macon County Historical Society
(North Dooly Street—location)
PO Box 571 (mailing address)
Montezuma, GA 31063
Betty Anne Souter

Madison County Heritage Foundation, Inc.
PO Box 74
Danielsville, GA 30633
(706) 795-2017
Albert L. Stone, Jr.

Marble Valley Historical Society
(Main Street-location)
PO Box 815 (mailing address)
Jasper, GA 30143
(706) 692-6327
$10.00 per year membership

McDuffie County Historical Society
(633 Hemlock Drive—location)
PO Box 1816 (mailing address)
Thomson, GA 30824
(706) 595-5584; (706) 595-4710 FAX

Meriwether Historical Society
PO Box 741
Greenville, GA 30222
Nan F. Tidwell

Metcalfe Historical Society
Route 4, Box 219
Thomasville, GA 31792
Sarah C. Johnson

Middle Georgia Historical Society, Inc.
(Sidney Lanier Cottage, 935 High Street,
Macon, GA 31201—location)
PO Box 13358 (mailing address)
Macon, GA 31208-3358
(478) 743-3851
Katherine C. Oliver, Executive Director
Mon–Fri 9:00–1:00 & 2:00–4:00, Sat
9:30–12:30
Pub. *MGHS Newsletter*, quarterly
(Sidney Lanier, Macon, Georgia)
$15.00 per year membership; research: all
requests for genealogy turned over to
Willard Rocker at Washington Memorial
Library, where society's collection is kept

Monroe County Historical Society
PO Box 401
Forsyth, GA 31029
(478) 994-5070
Saundra Cleveland, Manager
Tue–Fri 10:00–5:00
(genealogy files and museum, also two
members who will help with genealogy
for SASE)
$5.00 per year membership

Original Montgomery County Historical Society, Inc.
PO Box 105
Mount Vernon, GA 30445
(912) 583-4401
Dwight Newsome, President

Moreland Community Historical Society
PO Box 128
Moreland, GA 30259
Sara T. Skinner, President

Morgan County Historical Society, Inc.
277 South Main Street
Madison, GA 30650
(706) 342-9627
June Whittaker, Director
Mon–Sat 10:00–4:30, Sun 1:30–4:30
Pub. *Heritage News*, nine times per year

Newnan-Coweta Historical Society
c/o Male Academy Museum
30 Temple Avenue
Newnan, GA 30263
(770) 251-0207
nchs@newnanbiz.net
http://www.nchistoricalsociety.org
Daniel R. Dietz, President
Tue–Thur 10:00–noon & 1:00–3:00,
Sat–Sun 2:00–5:00

Newton County Historical Society
(Chamber of Commerce Building, 2100
Washington Street—location)
PO Box 2415 (mailing address)
Covington, GA 30210
(770) 786-7310; (770) 786-1294 FAX

Northeast Georgia Historical and Genealogical Society
PO Box 907085
Gainesville, GA 30501-0902
Bob Conner, President
Pub. *Newsletter*, quarterly
$10.00 per year membership

Northwest Georgia Historical and Genealogical Society, Inc.
PO Box 5063
Rome, GA 30162-5063
(706) 236-4607; (706) 236-4605 FAX
patmillican@comcast.net
http://www.rootsweb.com/~ganwhags/
index.html
Pat Millican, President and Editor
Rome-Floyd County Library: Mon–Thur
8:30–8:30, Fri 8:30–6:00, Sat 9:00–4:00,
Sun 1:30–5:30
Pub. *Northwest Georgia Historical and
Genealogical Society Quarterly*
(people, newspaper excerpts, church
histories, queries, scannings of exchange
publications, five-generation charts,
community histories, Confederacy,
Indians, schools)
$15.00 per year membership; $10.00 for
topical index; free queries

Oglethorpe University Library
4484 Peachtree Road, N.E.
Atlanta, GA 30319
George G. Stewart

Okefenokee Heritage Center
(North Augusta Avenue—location)
Route 5, Box 406A (mailing address)
Waycross, GA 31501
(912) 285-0733; (912) 285-4260
Lin Owen, Executive Director
Pub. *OHC Newsletter*

Old Campbell County Historical Society, Inc.
PO Box 342
Fairburn, GA 30213-0342
(770) 997-3385; (770) 996-6796

Old Capital Historical Society
PO Box 4
Milledgeville, GA 31061
(478) 453-9049; (478) 452-4637
Ray Olivier
(museum house, no genealogy department)
$10.00 per year membership

Old Clinton Historical Society, Inc.
Rural Free Delivery 5, Box 143
Gray, GA 31032-9207
(478) 986-3384
Earlene Hamilton, President

Paulding County Historical Society, Inc.
(295 North Johnston Street—location)
PO Box 333 (mailing address)
Dallas, GA 30132
(770) 505-3485
lagroon@bellsouth.net
Johnnie Lester, President; LaGroon
Redmond, Vice President
Museum: Tue, Thur & Sat noon–4:00, or
special tours; Research Room available
(sells books about Paulding County)
$5.00 per year membership; admission:
$2.00 for adults

Pebble Hill Foundation, Inc.
PO Box 830
Thomasville, GA 31799
Joseph Kitchens

Perry Area Historical Society
1138 Macon Street
Perry, GA 31069
(478) 987-2588 (home answering machine);
(478) 987-1823 (office, 8:30–5:30)
Pauline Lewis, Past President

Pioneer Historic Society
815 College Street
McRae, GA 31055
(229) 868-6377
Ruth Mizell

Polk County Historical Society
(205 North College Street—location)
PO Box 203 (mailing address)
Cedartown, GA 30125
(770) 749-0073; (770) 748-5276 (President)
Mary Brewster, President
fourth Sun 2:00–5:00, and special occasions
$10.00 per year membership

Portal Heritage Society
Route 1, Box 318
Moultrie, GA 31768-9711
Denver Hollingsworth

Rabun County Historical Society
PO Box 155
Dillard, GA 30537
Sue B. Pennington

Randolph Historical Society, Inc.
PO Box 472
Cuthbert, GA 39840
(229) 679-5165
$10.00 per year membership

Richmond County Historical Society
c/o Augusta State University, Reese Library,
Special Collections
2500 Walton Way
Augusta, GA 30904-2200
(706) 737-1532; (706) 667-4415 FAX
vgreene@aug.edu
Vicki H. Greene, Executive Director
Mon–Tue & Thur–Fri 9:00–1:00
Pub. *Augusta Richmond County Journal*,
biannually, $6.50 per issue, $15.00 per
year subscription
(Richmond County archives)
$35.00 per year membership; research: $5.00
plus SASE

Rockdale County Historical Society
(967 Milstead Avenue—location)
PO Box 351 (mailing address)

Conyers, GA 30012
(770) 483-4398

Rome Area Heritage Foundation
PO Box 6181
Rome, GA 30162-6181
Mary J. McGuffey, President
$25.00 per year membership

Roopville Historical Society and Archives
(Highway 27 South—location)
PO Box 165 (mailing address)
Roopville, GA 30170
(770) 854-4460
Nancy Bell

Roswell Historical Society
(Roswell Cultural Arts Center, 950 Forrest
Street, Second Floor, Roswell, GA
30075—location)
PO Box 1636 (mailing address)
Roswell, GA 30077
(770) 594-6405 (Research Library and
Archives); (770) 992-1665
(Administrative Offices)
rhsla@earthlink.net (Research Library and
Archives); SocietyRHA@aol.com
(Administrative Offices)
http://www.roswellhs.org
Darlene Walsh, Newsletter Editor; Elaine
DeNiro, Archivist; Sherron Lawson,
Administrator
Mon & Thur 1:00–4:30
Pub. *Historic Roswell: Roswell Historical
Society Newsletter*
("materials concerning the history and
genealogy of Roswell, Georgia, and
environs")

San Souci Club
San Souci Historical Committee
San Souci Library
PO Box 167
Adairsville, GA 30103
Carol Adams

Schley County Preservation Committee
(Schley County Courthouse—location)
PO Box 326 (mailing address)
Ellaville, GA 31806
(229) 937-2689; (229) 937-5588
Pam Register, Schley County Tax
Commissioner
8:00–noon & 1:00–5:00
(family histories of residents, 1860 census,
cemetery list, published *History of Schley
County, Georgia*, $43.00 ppd.)

**Screven County Historical and
Genealogical Society**
384 Penrose Drive West
Savannah, GA 31410-1234
Elizabeth Lee

Seminole County Historical Society
PO Box 713
Donalsonville, GA 31759

Senoia Area Historical Society
PO Box 301
Senoia, GA 30276
Jack Thompson

Seven Springs Historical Society Museum
3901 Brownsville Road
Powder Springs, GA 30073

**Smyrna Historical and Genealogical
Society**
825 Austin Drive
Smyrna, GA 30082-3305
(770) 435-7549; (770) 431-2858 FAX

Harold Smith, Executive Director
Smyrna Museum: Tue 10:00–4:00, Wed &
Fri 10:00–noon, Sat 10:00–2:00
Pub. *Lives and Times*, bimonthly
$20.00 per year membership

Southern Studies Institute
(see Louisiana, Part 2)

Sparta-Hancock County Historical Society
PO Box 762
Sparta, GA 31087-0762
(706) 444-6411

Stephens County Historical Society
(313 South Pond Street—location)
PO Box 125 (mailing address)
Toccoa, GA 30577
(706) 282-5055

Stewart County Historical Commission
(Corner Broad and Cotton Streets—location)
PO Box 817 (mailing address)
Lumpkin, GA 31815
(229) 838-4201

Stewart County Historical Society
PO Box 818
Lumpkin, GA 31815
W. E. Cannington

Suwanee Historical Association
PO Box 815
Suwanee, GA 30174

Taliaferro County Historical Society, Inc.
(Broad Street—location)
PO Box 32 (mailing address)
Crawfordville, GA 30631
(706) 456-2339; (706) 456-2294
Ian Macfie, President
hours: various
Pub. *Taliaferro County, Georgia, Records &
Notes*, quarterly
(locally significant old photos, papers,
periodicals, and artifacts)
$5.00 per year membership

**Taylor County Historical-Genealogical
Society**
PO Box 1925
Butler, GA 31006
(478) 862-3410
nodlu2@aol.com

Thronateeska Heritage Center
100 Roosevelt Avenue
Albany, GA 31701
(229) 432-6955; (229) 435-1572 FAX
info@heritagecenter.org
http://www.heritagecenter.org
Tommy Gregors, Executive Director
Thur–Sat noon–4:00
Pub. *Journal of South Georgia History*,
annually, $20.00 per year subscription for
universities, colleges, libraries, etc.
$25.00 per year membership

Toombs County Historical Society
PO Box 2825
Vidalia, GA 30474
(912) 537-4383

**Towns County Historical and Genealogical
Society**
PO Box 101
Young Harris, GA 30582-0101
(706) 379-3150
Jerry A. Taylor

Treutlen County Historical Society, Inc.
Treutlen County Courthouse

PO Box 235
Soperton, GA 30457
(912) 529-6711; (912) 529-6062 FAX

**Troup County Historical
Society—Archives**
(136 Main Street—location)
PO Box 1051 (mailing address)
LaGrange, GA 30241
(706) 884-1828; (706) 884-1838 FAX
info@trouparchives.org
http://www.trouparchives.org
Kaye Laning Minchew, Director
Archives: Mon & Wed–Fri 9:00–5:00, Tue
9:00–8:00, Sat 9:00–1:00
Pub. *Newsletter*, quarterly

Tybee Island Historical Society
(30 Meddin Drive, Fort Screven—location)
PO Box 366 (mailing address)
Tybee Island, GA 31328
(912) 786-5801; (912) 786-6538 FAX
tybeeLH@bellsouth.net
http://www.tybeelighthouse.org
Robert Adkins, Acting Director
summer: 10:00–6:00; winter (Oct–Mar):
noon–4:00
$25.00 per year membership

Union County Historical Society
(Courthouse Square—location)
PO Box 35 (mailing address)
Blairsville, GA 30512
(706) 745-5441
history1@alltel.net
http://www.ngeorgia.com/uchs.html
Maurice Farabee, President
June–Oct: Wed–Sat 10:00–4:00
Pub. *Union County Historical Society
Newsletter*, quarterly
$10.00 per year membership

Upson Historical Society
PO Box 363
Thomaston, GA 30286-0005
(706) 647-3425
uhswebmaster@alltel.net
http://www.rootsweb.com/~gauhs
James McKinley; Mary B. Williams
(Webmaster)
Thomaston-Upson Archives: Mon–Fri
8:00–5:00, Sat 9:00–1:00
Pub. *Newsletter*, about eight times per year
$15.00 per year membership

Walker County GA Historical Society
PO Box 707
LaFayette, GA 30728
David Boyle, President; Margaret
McWhorter, Corresponding Secretary
Pub. *Walker County Historical Society
Newsletter*, quarterly
$8.00 per year membership

Historical Society of Walton County, Inc.
238 North Broad Street
Monroe, GA 30655

Washington County Historical Society
(129 Jones Street—location)
PO Box 6088 (mailing address)
Sandersville, GA 31082
(478) 552-6965; (478) 552-1449

**Washington-Wilkes Historical Foundation,
Inc.**
308 East Robert Toombs Avenue
Washington, GA 30673
(706) 678-2105

Wayne County Historical Society
125 N.E. Broad Street

Jesup, GA 31545-5516
(912) 427-3233

Weston Woman's Club
PO Box 127
Weston, GA 31832
(229) 828-2555
Mrs. C. R. Merritt, Book Orders
(family histories, cemeteries, communities,
census, churches, memorials, early
history; published *History of Webster
County, Georgia*, $40.00 ppd.)

White County Historical Society
(Town Square—location)
PO Box 1139 (mailing address)
Cleveland, GA 30528
(706) 865-3225
http://www.georgiamagazine.com/
chamber/white/wchs
$10.00 per year membership

Whitfield-Murray Historical Society, Inc.
Crown Garden and Archives
715 Chattanooga Avenue
Dalton, GA 30720
(706) 278-0217 voice & FAX
Marcelle White, Director
Tue–Fri 10:00–5:00, Sat 10:00–1:00
Pub. *Whitfield-Murray Historical Quarterly*
(Whitfield and Murray counties and some
northwest Georgia materials)
$15.00 per year membership

Worth County Historical Society
PO Box 5073
Sylvester, GA 31791
nelldt@planttel.net
Nell D. Thompson

Genealogical Societies

State Genealogical Society

Georgia Genealogical Society
PO Box 54575
Atlanta, GA 30308-0575
ggs@gagensociety.org
http://www.gagensociety.org
Sharon Tate Moody, CGRS, President 2003-
2004
Pub. *The Georgia Genealogical Society
Quarterly*; *The Scribe*, quarterly
$30.00 per year membership

Southern Society of Genealogists, Inc.
(see Alabama, Part 2)

Genealogical Societies—Local & Regional

Augusta Genealogical Society, Inc.
(1025 Chafee Avenue—location)
PO Box 3743 (mailing address)
Augusta, GA 30904-3743
(706) 738-2241
tdirksen@mail.mcg.edu
http://interoz.com/ags/index.htm
Corrie M. Adamson, Honorary President; Dr.
Tom Dirksen
Mon & Wed 9:00–4:00, Sat 9:00–1:00, Sun
2:00–5:00
Pub. *Ancestoring*, semiannually, $6.50 per
issue; *Echoes*, monthly, $10.00 per
volume
$25.00 per year membership

Bartow County Genealogical Society
(425 West Main Street, the yellow brick
building behind the Public
Library—location)
PO Box 993 (mailing address)
Cartersville, GA 30120-0993

(770) 382-6676; (770) 606-0706
Jean Belew, Board Chairman
Mon–Wed & Fri 10:00–3:30, Wed
5:00–7:00, Thur 1:00–4:00, and by
appointment
Pub. *Bartow County Quarterly* (Mar, June,
Oct, Dec)
$20.00 per year membership

Carroll County Genealogical Society
PO Box 576
Carrollton, GA 30117
(770) 832-7746
mfword@aol.com
http://ccgs.westgeorgia.org
Mary F. Word, Corresponding Secretary
Pub. *Carroll County Genealogical Quarterly*
$20.00 per year membership; queries for
members

Central Georgia Genealogical Society, Inc.
(Warner Robins, GA—location)
319 North Houston Lake Boulevard (mailing
address)
Centerville, GA 31028
(478) 953-3114
Addie P. Howell, Corresponding Secretary
and Membership
Pub. *Central Georgia Genealogical Society
Quarterly*
$20.00 per year membership

**Clarke-Oconee Genealogical Society of
Athens, Georgia**
PO Box 6403
Athens, GA 30604
Pub. *COGS Quarterly*
$10.00 per year membership

Coastal Georgia Genealogical Society
283 Moss Oak Lane
Saint Simons Island, GA 31522-1147
(912) 638-4383
Jim C. Wroton, Jr., President
Wesley United Methodist Church, Saint
Simons Island opposite Fort Frederica:
second Sun 3:00
Pub. *CGGS NewsLetter*, monthly
$12.00 per year membership

Cobb County Genealogical Society, Inc.
PO Box 1413
Marietta, GA 30061-1413
(770) 428-5172
mjhb@mindspring.com
http://www.rootsweb.com/~gaccgs
Mimi Jo Butler; Joe Tillman, Sr.
Pub. *Family Tree Newsletter*, monthly
(except Dec); *Family Tree Quarterly*
$25.00 per year membership

**Coweta Chatter Genealogical and
Historical Society**
8031 Highway 54, Route 1
Sharpsburg, GA 30277
Norma Gunby

Coweta County Genealogical Society
(5 West Broad Street, Grantville, GA
30220—location)
PO Box 1014 (mailing address)
Newnan, GA 30264
corley@mail3.newnanutilities.org
http://members.tripod.com/~CowetaGS/
index.html
Frances Christopher, President
Tue–Thur 10:00–4:00
Pub. *The Coweta Courier*, quarterly
(information for Coweta and Campbell
counties)
$18.00 per year membership; simple
research: no charge

**Dawson County Historical and
Genealogical Society**
(see Historical Societies—Local and
Regional, above)

The Decatur County Genealogical Society
Southwest Georgia Regional Library System
Gilbert H. Gragg-Decatur County Library
301 South Monroe Streets
Bainbridge, GA 31717
(229) 248-2665 (Library)
branchroot@aol.com
Shirley Fleming, President
meetings at Gilbert H. Gragg-Decatur County
Library: fourth Mon 7:00

Genealogy Study Group of DeKalb County
c/o Life Enrichment Center
1340 McConnell Drive
Decatur, GA 30033

Delta Genealogical Society
c/o Rossville Public Library
504 McFarland Avenue
Rossville, GA 30741
(706) 866-1368 (Library); (706) 858-0251
FAX (Library)
James Douthat, President; Betty P. Corliss,
Corresponding Secretary
Library: Mon–Wed 9:00–5:00, Thur
1:00–8:00, Fri–Sat 9:00–noon
Pub. *Southern Roots and Shoots*, quarterly
(northwest Georgia, northeast Alabama,
southeast Tennessee)
$12.00 per year membership; free queries

East Georgia Genealogical Society
PO Box 117
Winder, GA 30680-0117
gaeggs@email.com

EVHS Family Tree Climbers
c/o Etoway Valley Historical Society
(1903 Bartow County Courthouse, 115 West
Cherokee Avenue—location)
PO Box 1886 (mailing address)
Cartersville, GA 30120
(770) 606-8862
evhs@evhsonline.org (not for genealogical
queries)
http://www.evhsonline.org (Allatoona Pass
Battlefield official web site)
Linda Gossett Cochran

**The Genealogical Society of Henry and
Clayton Counties, Inc.**
Henry County Historical Society Building
(71 Macon Street—location)
PO Box 1296 (mailing address)
McDonough, GA 30253
(770) 366-3686; (770) 954-1456; (770) 474-
8465 (President)
R. Swann, President
Mon, Wed & Fri 10:00–3:00
Pub. *Ancestor Update*, quarterly
$15.00 per year membership; search fee:
$10.00

Huxford Genealogical Society, Inc.
(101 College Avenue, Homerville Municipal
Complex Building—location)
PO Box 595 (mailing address)
Homerville, GA 31634
(912) 487-2310; (912) 487-3881 FAX
huxford@planttel.net
http://www.huxford.com
Violet Bennett, Library Manager; Bridgette
Coley, Staff; JoAnn Gardner, Staff
Mon–Fri 9:00–5:00, Sat 10:00–4:00
Pub. *Huxford Genealogical Society
Quarterly* (Mar, June, Sept, Dec), $25.00
per year subscription for libraries and

other societies
("Genealogical research materials."
Emphasis on Georgia, South Florida,
North and South Carolina, etc.)
$30.00 per year membership; research fee:
$10.00 plus 15¢ per copy for nonmembers

Muscogee Genealogical Society
PO Box 761
Columbus, GA 31902
(706) 561-5831 voice & FAX
Pub. *Muscogiana: Journal of the Muscogee
Genealogical Society*, semiannually
(Columbus/original Muscogee County,
Georgia, area consisting of Harris, Talbot,
Marion, Chattahoochee and current
Muscogee counties)
$15.00 per year membership

**Northeast Georgia Historical and
Genealogical Society**
(see Historical Societies—Local and
Regional, above)

**Northwest Georgia Historical and
Genealogical Society, Inc.**
(see Historical Societies—Local and
Regional, above)

Piedmont Regional Genealogy Society
Athens Street
Auburn, GA 30203
(770) 963-5877

**Quitman-Brooks County Genealogical
Society**
121 North Culpepper Street
Quitman, GA 31643

Rockdale County Genealogical Society
c/o Conyers Rockdale Library System
Nancy Guinn Memorial Library
864 Green Street
Conyers, GA 30207
(770) 388-5040; (770) 388-5043 FAX
(Library)
mtf@mindspring.com; sherpi@juno.com
http://www.rootsweb.com/~garockda;
http://mtf.home.mindsrping.com/newsltr.ht
m (Newsletter)
Marian T. Farmer, Newsletter; Sherry Pierce,
Program Chairman
meetings: second Sun 3:00
Pub. *Jeans & Genes,* quarterly

Savannah Area Genealogical Society
PO Box 15385
Savannah, GA 31416
(periodical "in planning stages")
$15.00 per year membership

**Screven County Historical and
Genealogical Society**
(see Historical Societies—Local and
Regional, above)

**Smyrna Historical and Genealogical
Society**
(see Historical Societies—Local and
Regional, above)

South Georgia Genealogical Society
PO Box 602
Thomasville, GA 31799
(229) 574-5349
James A. Rollins, Treasurer and Editor
Pub. *Pine Barrens,* quarterly
(genealogical source information for south
Georgia and bordering Florida)
$10.00 per year membership; limited
research for members

Southeast Alabama Genealogical Society
(see Alabama, Part 2)

**Southwest Georgia Genealogical Society,
Inc.**
(Dougherty County, Central
Library—location)
PO Box 4672 (mailing address)
Albany, GA 31706
(912) 430-1918
Marie DeLamar, Editor
Mon–Wed 10:00–9:00, Thur–Sat 10:00–6:00
Pub. *Genealogy Gazette,* quarterly
$15.00 per year membership; queries free for
members, $3.00 for nonmembers

**Taylor County Historical-Genealogical
Society**
(see Historical Societies—Local and
Regional, above)

**Towns County Historical and Genealogical
Society**
(see Historical Societies—Local and
Regional, above)

Warren County Genealogical Society
(103 Memorial Drive—location)
PO Box 47 (mailing address)
Warrenton, GA 30828

**West Central Georgia Genealogical
Society, Inc.**
PO Box 2291
LaGrange, GA 30241
Mr. Julian Harris, President
Pub. *West Central Georgia Genealogical
Society Newsletter,* quarterly

Independent Publications and Miscellany

Ancestor Files Library
(see Alabama, Part 2)

Andersonville
(see Miscellaneous, Military, Part 4)

Armchair Publications
810 McDonough Road
Hampton, GA 30228
Joel Dixon Wells
Pub. *Armchair Researcher,* quarterly, $12.50
per year subscription; *Florida Armchair
Researcher,* quarterly, $15.00 per year
subscription; *Georgia Armchair
Researcher,* quarterly, $15.00 per year
subscription

Austell Historic Preservation Society
Austell City Hall
Broad Street
Austell, GA 30001
Rosa Mary Johnson

Bartram Trail Society
6688 Marsh Avenue
Lithia Springs, GA 30057

Bethesda Home for Boys
Bethesda Museum
Cunningham Historic Center
9520 Ferguson Avenue
Savannah, GA 31499
Lorane H. Minis

**Brasstown Bald Visitor Information
Center**
PO Box 9
Blairsville, GA 30514
Frances Mason

Jimmy Carter Library and Museum
441 Freedom Parkway
Atlanta, GA 30307-1498
(404) 331-3942; (404) 730-2215 FAX
carter.library@nara.gov
http://www.jimmycarterlibrary.org
Robert Bohanan, Chief Archivist
Museum: Mon–Sat 9:00–4:45, Sun
noon–4:45; Library: Mon–Fri 9:00–4:45
(primarily historical, no genealogical
records)
admission: $5.00 for adults

Emanuel Historic Preservation Society
PO Box 1101
Swainsboro, GA 30401

Foxfire Fund, Inc.
PO Box 541
Mountain City, GA 30562-0541
(706) 746-5828; (706) 746-5829 FAX

GaGenWeb
Part of The USGenWeb Project
tstowell@chattanooga.net;
kg04@giddeon.com
http://www.rootsweb.com/~gagenweb
Tim Stowell, State Coordinator; Keith
Giddeon, Assistant Coordinator
(links to other Georgia resources)

Genealogical Institute
(see Virginia, Part 2)

Genealogy Books and Consultation
(see Texas, Part 2)

Georgia Agrirama Development Authority
PO Box Q
Tifton, GA 31793
(229) 386-3344; (229) 386-3386 FAX

Georgia Association of Historians
Clayton State College
Morrow, GA 30260
Bradley R. Rice

Georgia Genealogical Information
Beverly S. Roden

The Georgia Salzburger Society
2980 Ebenezer Road
Rincon, GA 31326-3716
(912) 754-7001
info@GeorgiaSalzburgers.com;
Stuart@GASalzburgers.org
http://www.georgiasalzurgers.com
Stuart Exley, President
12 Mar & Labor Day
Pub. *The Georgia Salzburger Society
Newsletter* (perpetuates the memory of
Lutherans who emigrated from Salzburg
and Germany from 1734–1752 to the
Colony of Georgia, and updates the
genealogy of their descendants; settled by
General Edward Oglethorpe thirty miles
north of Savannah on the Savannah River
as a buffer with the Uchee Indians)

Historic Acworth
4468 Dallas Street
Acworth, GA 30101
Scott Evans

Historic Augusta, Inc.
(111 10th Street, Augusta, GA
30901—location)
PO Box 37 (mailing address)
Augusta, GA 30903
(706) 724-0436; (706) 724-3083 FAX
Erick Montgomery, Executive Director
Mon–Fri 9:00–5:00

Pub. *Historic Augusta Newsletter*, quarterly
(maintains files of historic buildings in
    Augusta and Richmond County, Georgia)
$35.00 per year membership

Historic Decatur
726 South Candler Street
Decatur, GA 30030
Lyn Deardoff

Historic Oakland Cemetery, Inc.
248 Oakland Avenue, S.E., AH
Atlanta, GA 30312
oaklandsexton@atlantaga.gov,
    sreed@atlantaga.gov
Samuel Reed, Sexton
Mon–Fri 9:00–5:00

Historic Oglethorpe County, Inc.
PO Box 1793
Lexington, GA 30648
Jerry Titus

**Historic Preservation Society of Social
Circle**
PO Box 772
Social Circle, GA 30279
Jane McDaniel

Historic Talbotton
Route 1, Box 101
Talbotton, GA 31827
Gary D. Page

Historical Jonesboro, Inc.
PO Box 922
Jonesboro, GA 30236

**Hunting for Bears Genealogical and
Historical Society**
(see Alabama, Part 2)

Jarrell Plantation State Historic Site
711 Jarrell Plantation Road
Juliette, GA 31046
(478) 986-5172
jarrell_plantation_park@mail.dnr.state. ga.us
http://www.mylink.net/~jarrell
Tue–Sat 9:00–5:00

MLH Research
(see Alabama, Part 2)

Mountain Press
(see Tennessee, Part 2)

Old Athens Cemetery Foundation, Inc.
145 Pendleton Drive
Athens, GA 30606
Patricia Cooper

**Old Town Brunswick Preservation
Association**
1229 Newcastle Street
Brunswick, GA 31520
Phyllis Taunton

Plains Historic Preservation Trust, Inc.
PO Box 136
Plains, GA 31780
P. J. Wise

Root Hunters
PO Box 546
Thomasville, GA 31799
Pub. *Root Hunters*, quarterly

Roswell Historic Preservation Commission
City of Roswell
PO Box 1309
Roswell, GA 30075
Barbara S. Gross

**Saint Marys Historic Preservation
Commission**
418 Osborne Street
Saint Marys, GA 31558
(912) 882-6926
Wiley B. King, CBO
8:00–5:00

**The Southern Genealogist's Exchange
Society, Inc.**
(see Florida, Part 2)

Southern Historical Press, Inc.
The Georgia Genealogical Magazine
(see Publishers, Part 4)

Sumter Historic Trust
(318 East Church Street—location)
PO Box 961 (mailing address)
Americus, GA 31709
Malcolm Argo, Executive Vice President
Pub. *Views from the Verandah*, quarterly

**Tattnall County Historic Preservation,
Inc.**
PO Box 392
Reidsville, GA 30453
(912) 557-4802

**Terrell County Council for Historic
Preservation**
PO Box 63
Dawson, GA 31742
(229) 995-2125; (229) 995-4000 FAX
Edgar W. Duskin

Thomasville Landmarks
(312 North Broad Street—location)
PO Box 1285 (mailing address)
Thomasville, GA 31799
(229) 226-6016; (229) 226-6672 FAX
tli@rose.net

Traveller Southern Families
(see Virginia, Part 2)

Vann House State Historical Park
Georgia Highways 52 and 225, North
Chatsworth, GA 30705
(706) 695-2598
http://www.ngeorgia.com/cgi-bin/park/Chief

West Georgia Museum of Tallapoosa
(185 Mann Street—location)
PO Box 725 (mailing address)
Tallapoosa, GA 30176
(770) 574-3125
William B. Craig, Jr., Director
Mon–Fri 9:00–4:00, Sat 9:00–5:00
admission: $2.00 for adults

Wynne-Russell House
City of Lilburn
76 Main Street
Lilburn, GA 30247
Jean Cole

Hawaii

Archives and Libraries with Holdings in Genealogy

State Archives and Library

Hawaii State Archives
Iolani Palace Grounds
Honolulu, HI 96813
(808) 586-0329; (808) 586-0316; (800) 486-
    4644 (in Hawaii only); (808) 586-0330
    FAX
archives@hawaii.gov
http://www.state.hi.us/dags/archives
Mon–Fri 9:00–4:00

Hawaii State Library
Hawaii and Pacific Section
478 South King Street
Honolulu, HI 96813-2901
(808) 586-3535
http://www.hawaii.gov/hidocs
Joyce Miyamoto, Section Head
Mon, Wed & Fri–Sat 9:00–5:00, Tue & Thur
    9:00–8:00
(specializing in "Hawaii genealogy of long
    resident families, especially Hawaiian
    ethnic group")

Hawaii State Library
Language, Literature and History Section
478 South King Street
Honolulu, HI 96813
(808) 586-3499
http://www.hcc.hawaii.edu/hspls/llhov.html
Sandra Ann Kolloge, Section Head
Mon, Wed & Fri–Sat 9:00–5:00, Tue & Thur
    9:00–8:00
(material for tracing family lines
    internationally with emphasis on early
    U.S. immigrants into the colonies and
    original states; "especially eastern U.S.,
    British and western European ancestry")

State Historical Society

Hawaiian Historical Society
560 Kawaiahao Street
Honolulu, HI 96813
(808) 537-6271
bedunn@lava.net
http://www.hawaiianhistory.org
Barbara Dunn, Administrative Director
Library Reading Room: Mon–Fri 10:00–4:00
Pub. *The Hawaiian Journal of History*,
    annually, $12.00 per issue; *Hawaiian
    Historical Society Newsletter*; *Annual
    Report*
(Library collection includes early voyages to
    Hawaii and the Pacific, Hawaiian-
    language books, over 64 newspapers,
    manuscript collections, photographs,
    maps, broadsides, pamphlets, journals and
    periodicals, newspaper clipping file, etc.)
$25.00 per year membership; research fee:
    $5.00 plus photocopies

**City, County and Regional Archives and
Libraries**
(A more exhaustive list of public and
academic libraries can be found at http://
www.hcc.hawaii.edu/hspls, http://www.
hcc.hawaii.edu/library/hawaiilibs.html or
http://www.stuttersfa.org/library/ref_hi. htm.)

**Alu Like, Inc. (Native Hawaiian Library
Project)**
456 Keawe Street
Honolulu, HI 96813-5125
(808) 535-6750; (808) 524-2776

Mahealani Merryman, Project Administrator
Mon–Fri 8:00–5:00

Bernice Pauahi Bishop Museum Library
1525 Bernice Street
Honolulu, HI 96817-0916
(808) 848-4148 (Library); (808) 8488-4182
(Archives); (808) 847-8241 FAX (Library
and Archives)
library@bishopmuseum.org;
archives@bishopmuseum.org
http://www.bishopmuseum.org/research/
cultstud/libarch/index.html
Duane Wenzel, Library Chairman
Tue–Fri noon–3:00, Sat 9:00–noon, except
holiday weekends

Brigham Young University, Hawaii Campus
Joseph F. Smith Library
55-220 Kulanui Street
Laie, HI 96762-1266
(808) 293-3878; (808) 293-3850 (Director);
(808) 293-3877 FAX
perritoj@byuh.edu
http://www.byuh.edu/library
Jocelyn Perriton, Circulation/University
Librarian's Office
Mon–Thur 7:00 A.M.–midnight, Fri
7:00–6:00, Sat 10:00–9:00
Pub. *Pacific Studies* (emphasis on Pacific
islands and Mormonism), semiannually
$5.00 per year membership

Hana Cultural Center and Museum
(4974 Uakea Road—location)
PO Box 27 (mailing address)
Hana, HI 96713-0027
(808) 248-8622; (808) 248-8620 FAX
http://www.planet-hawaii.com/hana

Hanalei Museum
PO Box 91
Hanalei, HI 96714
(808) 826-7387

Hawaiian Mission Children's Society Library
553 South King Street
Honolulu, HI 96813-3002
(808) 531-0481; (808) 545-2280 FAX
mreppun@missionhouses.org
http://www.lava.net/~mhm/lib.htm
Marilyn L. Reppun, Head Librarian
Mon–Fri 10:00–4:00
("19th-century Hawaiiana; Congregational
Church records beginning 1820;
unpublished letters, journals, reports of
Protestant missionaries to Hawaii,
personal as well as business; Hawaiian-
language books; Micronesian-language
books; early voyages to Hawaii and the
Pacific; early photographs and drawings
of Hawaii")
no library admission fees

Kauai Museum Association, Ltd.
(4428 Rice Street—location)
PO Box 248 (mailing address)
Lihue, HI 96766
(808) 245-6931; (808) 245-6864 FAX
museum@kauaimuseum.org
Margaret Lovett, Curator; Carol Lovell,
Director
Mon–Fri 9:00–3:00, Sat 10:00–2:00
Pub. *Kauai Museum Newsletter & Calendar
of Events*, quarterly
$25.00 per year membership

Lyman House Memorial Museum
276 Haili Street
Hilo, HI 96720
(808) 969-7685
info@lymanmuseum.org
http://www.lymanmuseum.org
Lynne Wolforth, Librarian
by appointment
(publications, photos, newspapers,
manuscripts, maps)

Municipal Reference and Records Center Archives
City Hall Annex
558 South King Street
Honolulu, HI 96813-3006
(808) 523-4577; (808) 523-4985 FAX
library@co.honolulu.hi.us
http://www.co.honolulu.hi.us/csd/lrmb/
index.htm
Anne K. Pulfrey, Records Management
Analyst

Punahou School
Cooke Library
1601 Punahou Street
Honolulu, HI 96822
(808) 944-5711
http://www.punahou.edu/eg.agci/
facilities.html

University of Hawaii at Manoa
Center for Oral History
2424 Maile Way
Saunders Hall 724
Honolulu, HI 96822
(808) 956-6259; (808) 956-9794 FAX
wnishimo@hawaii.edu
http://www.oralhistory.hawaii.edu
Warren S. Nishimoto, Center Director
8:00–4:30
Pub. *Oral History Recorder*, quarterly

University of Hawaii at Manoa
Hamilton Library
Hawaiian Collection
2550 The Mall
Honolulu, HI 96822
(808) 956-7203; (808) 956-8264; (808) 956-
5968 FAX
speccoll@hawaii.edu; jimc@hawaii.edu
http://www2.hawaii.edu/~speccoll/
hawaii.html
James F. Cartwright, University Archivist
Mon–Thur 9:00–5:00, Fri 9:00–4:45

Wailoa Arts and Cultural Center
Department of Land and Natural Resources,
State Parks, Hawaii
(200 Piopio Street—location)
PO Box 936 (mailing address)
Hilo, HI 96721
(808) 933-0416; (808) 933-0417 FAX
Codie M. King, Director
Mon–Tue & Thur–Fri 8:00–4:30, Wed
noon–4:30
(exhibits changing every month, a center for
cultural events, art displays of local, as
well as international artists and groups;
serves as a visitor center)

Historical Societies—Local and Regional

American Historical Association, Pacific Coast Branch
(see California, Part 2)

Kona Historical Society
(Kona District, Hawaii Island/Kalu
Kalu—location)
PO Box 398 (mailing address)
Captain Cook, HI 96704
(808) 323-3222; (808) 323-2398 FAX

Jill R. Olson, Executive Director; Sheree
Chase, Curator
Mon–Fri 9:00–3:00, Sat 9:00–1:00
Pub. *Newsletter*, three times per year
(extensive photo archives, land use records,
artifact collection, library; historic site)
$20.00 per year membership

Maui Historical Society Museum
(Bailey House, 2375-A Main
Street—location)
PO Box 1018 (mailing address)
Wailuku, HI 96793
(808) 244-3326; (808) 244-3920 FAX
info@mauimuseum.org
http://www.mauimuseum.org
Hokulani Holt-Padilla, Administrative
Assistant
Mon–Fri 9:00–4:00
Pub. *Maui News Index*
("We assist people in starting genealogical
work but retain only the family genealogy
of Edward & Caroline Bailey; we have no
unpublished genealogical information nor
are we a repository of any family, county,
or state records.")
$10.00 per year membership

Mormon Pacific Historical Society
Brigham Young University
Hawaii Campus
PO Box 1887
Laie, HI 96762
(808) 393-3837
Dr. Lance D. Chase, Executive Secretary
9:00–6:00
Pub. *MPHS Proceedings*, annually, $10.00
per issue
$5.00 per year membership

Genealogical Societies

Genealogical Societies—Local & Regional

Hawaii County Genealogical Society
Lyman House Memorial Museum
276 Haili Street
Hilo, HI 96720
(808) 969-7685 (Museum); (808) 244-3920
FAX (Museum)
info@lymanmuseum.org (Museum)

http://www.lei.net:8080/lei/DigitalHI/hilt
onwaikoloa/bigisland/museums/lyman.ht
ml
Charlene Dahlquist, Librarian
Library: Mon–Wed 9:00–4:00, and by
appointment

Honolulu County Genealogical Society
PO Box 235039
Honolulu, HI 96823-3500
wwreamy@hawaii.rr.com (President);
hcgs@hawaii.rr.com (Editor)
http://www.rootsweb.com/~hihcgs
Pub. newsletter, bimonthly
(forerly the Sandwich Islands Genealogical
Society)
$12.00 per year membership

Maui Genealogical Society
38A Alania Place
Kihei, HI 96753
irishjilly2002@yahoo.com
http://www.onealwebsite.com/oneall/mgs.
htm
Pub. $15.00 per year membership

Okinawan Genealogical Society of Hawaii
(808) 676-5400 (Hawaii Okinawa Center)
http://www.hawaiiokinawa.com/genealogy

Nobu Takeno, President
meetings at the Hawaii Okinawa Center:
    third Sat 9:00

Independent Publications and Miscellany

D.A.R. Memorial Library
1914 Makiki Heights Drive
Honolulu, HI 96822
(808) 949-7256
darhonolulu@hotmail.com (State Society)
http://geocities.com/darhawaii/
    index_nn4.html (State Society)
Mary Louise Cloyd, Librarian
Sat 9:00–4:00
(colonial and pre-1850 American genealogy,
    some Hawaiian)

Hawaiian Genealogy
hawaiianroots@aol.com; msz_hi@ev1.net
http://www.rootsweb.com/~higenweb/
    hawaii.htm
Maggie Stewart, State Coordinator
(Basic instruction and resources)

Hawaiian Sugar Planters Association
(99-193 Aiea Heights Road—location)
PO Box 1057 (mailing address)
Aiea, HI 96701-1057
(808) 487-5561

HiGenWeb
Part of The USGenWeb Project
swimref@cmc.net; msz_hi@ev1.net
http://www.rootsweb.com/~higenweb/
    hawaii.htm
Kevin Fraley, State Coordinator; Maggie
    Stewart, Assistant Coordinator
(links to other Hawaii resources)

Lahaina Restoration Foundation
Hale Pa'i Reading Room
1022 Front Street
Lahaina, HI 96767
(808) 661-3262; (808) 661-9309 FAX
http://www.cfws.org/WHATLES/lahaina.
    htm

Polynesian Voyaging Society
1250 Lauhala Street, Apartment 314
Honolulu, HI 96813
(808) 547-4172
dennisk@hawaii.edu
http://leahi.kcc.hawaii.edu/org/pvs

University of California Press
Pacific Historical Review
(see California, Part 2)

University of Hawaii at Hilo
Edwin H. Mookini Library
Special Collections
(address withheld upon request)
(not primarily genealogical)

Idaho

Archives and Libraries with Holdings in Genealogy

State Archives and Library

Idaho State Library
325 West State Street
Boise, ID 83702
(208) 334-2150; (800) 458-3271 (in-state);
    (208) 334-4016 FAX
cmfowles@isl.state.id.us
http://www.lili.org
Charlotte Fowles
(No collections of historical or genealogical
    value; see The Idaho State Historical
    Society, Library and Archives.)

State Historical Society

**Idaho State Historical Society Library and
Archives**
450 North Fourth Street
Boise, ID 83702
(208) 334-3356; (208) 334-3357; (208) 334-
    3198 FAX
sbarrett@ishs.state.id.us
http://www.idahohistory.net/library_
    archives.html
Linda Morton-Keithley, Administrator;
    Phyllis Lyons, Library Assistant 3; Steve
    Barrett, Library Assistant 2
Wed–Sat 9:00–5:00
Pub. *The Mountain Light: A Newsletter of
    the Idaho State Historical Society*,
    quarterly
research: $15.00 per hour (first 30 minutes
    free, then 1 additional hour maximum),
    plus 50¢ per photocopy ($5.00 minimum)

City, County and Regional Archives and Libraries
(A more exhaustive list of public and
academic libraries can be found at
http://www.LiLI.org/isl/il1a.htm#a.)

Aberdeen District Library
(76 East Central Avenue—location)
PO Box 207 (mailing address)
Aberdeen, ID 83210-0207
(208) 397-4427
aberdeenlib@hotmail.com
http://www.lili.org/aberdeen
Kathy Blaker, Director

Ada Community Library
10664 West Victory Road
Boise, ID 83709
(208) 362-0181; (208) 362-0303 FAX
askit@adalib.org; ill@adalib.org;
    twear@adalib.org
http://www.adalib.org
Terri Wear, Head of Reference

Albertson College of Idaho
N. L. Terteling Library
College Campus
Caldwell, ID 83605
(208) 459-5505; (208) 459-5299 FAX
http://www.albertson.edu/library

Appaloosa Museum and Heritage Center
2720 West Pullman Road
Moscow, ID 83843
(208) 882-5578, ext. 279; (208) 882-8150
    FAX
museum@appaloosa.com
http://www.appaloosamuseum.org
Stacey Garretson, Director
Tue–Fri 10:00–5:00, Sat 10:00–4:00

by donation

Bicentennial Historical Museum
305 North College Street
Grangeville, ID 83530
(208) 983-2573

Bingham County Historical Museum
190 North Shilling Avenue
Blackfoot, ID 83221
(208) 785-8065; (208) 785-8040

Blackfoot Public Library
(129 North Broadway—location)
PO Box 610 (mailing address)
Blackfoot, ID 83221-0610
(208) 785-8628; (208) 785-8602 FAX (City
    Hall)
blackft@ida.net
Robert Wright

Blaine County Historical Museum
(North Main Street—location)
PO Box 124 (mailing address)
Hailey, ID 8333-0124
(208) 788-2809; (208) 788-4185

Boise Basin District Library
Valley Mountain Library Consortium
(404 Montgomery Street—location)
PO Box 228 (mailing address)
Idaho City, ID 83631
(208) 392-4558; (208) 392-4974 FAX
director@boisebasin.lib.id.us
http://boisebasin.lib.us.id

Boise Public Library
715 South Capitol Boulevard
Boise, ID 83702
(208) 384-4441; (208) 384-4021 FAX
askalibrarian@cityofboise.org
http://www.boisepubliclibrary.org
James Jatkevicius, Librarian
Mon–Thur 10:00–9:00, Sat 10:00–5:00, Sun
    (Sept–May) noon–5:00
research: photocopies at 10¢ per page, plus
    postage, other fees listed on web site

Boise State University
Albertsons Library
Special Collections Department
1910 University Drive
Boise, ID 83725-1430
(208) 385-1235
avirta@boisestate.edu
http://library.boisestate.edu
Alan Virta, Head of Special Collections
(Idaho history; Archives of the Episcopal
    Diocese of Idaho [donated 1989])

Boundary County Public Library
(6370 Kootenai—location)
PO Box Y (mailing address)
Bonners Ferry, ID 83805-1276
(208) 267-3750; (208) 267-5231 FAX
Sandy Ashworth

BYU Idaho
David O. McKay Library
25 South Center Street
Rexburg, ID 83460-0405
(208) 356-2377
milesm@byui.edu (Webmaster)
http://www.lib.byui.edu
Blaine R. Bake, Archivist
winter: Mon–Fri 7:00–10:00, Sat 9:00–6:00,
    Sun 3:00–7:00; summer: Mon & Fri
    8:00–5:00, Tue–Thur 8:00–9:00, Sat
    10:00–2:00, Sun 3:00–6:00
(LDS church material, especially southeast
    Idaho; also Idaho local history)

Caldwell Public Library
1010 Dearborn
Caldwell, ID 83605-4195
(208) 459-3242; (208) 459-7344 FAX
caldwellpl@yahoo.com
Ollie Cossman; Elaine Leppert

Cascade Public Library
(105 Front Street—location)
PO Box 10 (mailing address)
Cascade, ID 83611
(208) 382-4757 voice & FAX
casclib@ctcweb.net
http://www.lili.org/cascade
Alyce Kelley

Castle Museum
(Second and State Street—location)
PO Box 454 (mailing address)
Juliaetta, ID 83535
(208) 276-3081
Onal or Donna Cope
by appointment, closed 1 Oct–1 Mar

Coeur d'Alene Public Library
201 Harrison Avenue
Coeur d'Alene, ID 83814-2373
(208) 769-2315; (208) 769-2381 FAX
cdapl@my180.net
http://www.dmi.net/cdalibrary
Julie Meier

College of Southern Idaho Library
315 Falls Avenue
Twin Falls, ID 83303-1238
(208) 733-9554, ext. 2509; (208) 736-3087
    FAX
wbeale@csi.edu
http://www.csi.cc.id.us/13.cfm?Library
William Beale

Craigmont Branch Library
(112 West Main Street—location)
PO Box 144 (mailing address)
Craigmont, ID 83523-0144
(208) 924-5510; (208) 924-4410 FAX
Sandy Riggers

Eagle Public Library
100 North Stierman Way
Eagle, ID 83616-5162
(208) 939-6814; (208) 939-1359 FAX
eaglib@hotmail.com
http://www.eaglepubliclibraary.org
Ann Gallinger

Garden City Public Library
9115 Chinden Boulevard, Suite 104
Boise, ID 83714
(208) 672-0433; (208) 672-0436 FAX
slewis@gardencitylibrary.org
http://www.gardencitylibrary.org
Heather Clark

Garden Valley Library
342 Village Circle
Garden Valley, ID 83622
(208) 462-3317; (208) 462-3758 FAX
kathrynmsmith@yahoo.com;
    grdnvaly@micron.net
http://www.lili.org/gardenvalley
Kathy Smith

Glenns Ferry Historical Museum
211 West Cleveland
Glenns Ferry, ID 83623
(208) 366-2760

Grangeville Centennial Library
215 West North Street
Grangeville, ID 83530-1729
(208) 983-0951

Linda Ruthruff
Mon, Wed & Fri noon–5:00, Tue & Thur
    noon–7:00

Heritage Hall Museum
(Reynolds Street, Old Highway 91, Dubois,
ID 83423—location)
HC 62, Box 41 (mailing address)
Dubois, ID 83446
(208) 374-5359; (208) 374-5799 FAX
Joy Myers, Secretary
by appointment; summer: Fri afternoons
(family histories of the settlers of the Silver
    Sage, Clark County; numerous
    scrapbooks, pictures, etc.)

Horseshoe Bend District Library
392 Highway 55
Horseshoe Bend, ID 83629-9701
(208) 793-2460; (208) 793-2871 FAX
June Brown

Idaho City Historical Museum
(402 Montgomery—location)
PO Box 325 (mailing address)
Idaho City, ID 83631
(208) 392-4550

Idaho State University
Eli M. Oboler Library
(850 South Ninth Street—location)
PO Box 8089 (mailing address)
Pocatello, ID 83209-0009
(208) 236-3249; (208) 236-2997; (208) 236-
    4295 FAX
http://www.isu.edu/departments/library/
    home.htm
Mon–Fri 8:00–4:30

Kamiah Branch Library
Prairie River Library District
(505 Main—location)
PO Box 846 (mailing address)
Kamiah, ID 83536-0846
(208) 935-0428 voice & FAX
kamlib@camasnet.com
Fran Woods, Branch Manager

Community Library Association
(Ketchum)
Regional History Department
(415 Spruce Avenue, North—location)
PO Box 2168 (mailing address)
Ketchum, ID 83340-2168
(208) 726-3493; (208) 726-0756 FAX
reghist@thecommunitylibrary.org
http://www.thecommunitylibrary.org/
    regionalhistory
Sandra Hofferber, Regional History
    Librarian
Tue–Sat 9:00–1:00 & 2:00–6:00

Kootenai-Shoshone Area Libraries
Hayden Branch
8385 North Government Way
Hayden Lake, ID 83835-9280
(208) 772-5612; (208) 772-2498 FAX
lalmeida@cin.kcl.org;
    hayden@ksalibraries.org;
    hay@cin.kcl.org
http://hayden.ksalibraries.org
Larry Almeida, Branch Manager
Mon–Sat 9:00–5:00

Kuna Library
(457 North Locust—location)
PO Box 129 (mailing address)
Kuna, ID 83634
(208) 922-1025; (208) 922-1026 FAX
kuna_libdir@mindspring.com
http://www.lili.org/kuna
Anne Hankins

Lewis-Clark State College Library
500 Eighth Avenue
Lewiston, ID 83501-2698
(208) 792-2396; (208) 799-2230; (208) 792-
    2227; (208) 799-2831 FAX
lbidwell@lcsc.edu
http://www.lcsc.edu/library
JoAnn Boyd, Assistant to the Director
hours: change with school year and holidays
(back files of local daily newspaper,
    Lewiston Morning Tribune; Idaho and
    Pacific Northwest history)

Lewiston-Nez Perce County Library
Lewiston City Library
428 Thain Road
Lewiston, ID 83501-5399
(208) 743-6519; (208) 798-4446 FAX
lewcitlib@CI.lewiston.id.us
http://www.cityoflewiston.org/library
Dawn Wittman

McCall Public Library
(218 Park Street, McCall, ID 83638-
3832—location)
PO Box 848 (mailing address)
McCall, ID 83638-0848
(208) 634-5522; (208) 634-3038 FAX
akantola@mccall.id.us
Gloria Cantrell, Librarian; Anne Kantola
Mon–Fri 11:00–6:00

Middleton Public Library
(307 Main Street—location)
PO Box 519 (mailing address)
Middleton, ID 83644-0519
(208) 585-3931
midlib@homeinternet.net
Elaine Mathiasen

Mountain Home Public Library
790 North 10th East
Mountain Home, ID 83647-2830
(208) 587-4716; (208) 587-6645 FAX
lhouse@ci.mountain-home.id.us
http://www.mhlibrary.org
Luise House

Museum of North Idaho
(115 Northwest Boulevard—location)
PO Box 812 (mailing address)
Coeur d'Alene, ID 83816-0812
(208) 664-3448
museumni@nidlink.com
http://www.museumni.org
Dorothy Dahlgren, Director
Tue–Sat 10:00–5:00
Pub. *Museum of North Idaho Newsletter*,
    quarterly
$15.00 per year membership

Nampa Public Library
101 11th Avenue, South
Nampa, ID 83651-3995
(208) 465-2263; (208) 465-2277
nampa@idaho-lynx.org
http://www.lili.org/nampa
Tamera LeBeau, Reference Supervisor
Mon–Thur 10:00–8:00, Fri 10:00–6:00, Sat
    10:00–5:00
(collects Nampa, Canyon County and Idaho
    history, not specifically genealogical
    material)

North Bingham County District Library
197 West Locust
Shelley, ID 83274
(208) 357-7801; (208) 357-2272 FAX
nbcdl@ida.net; heidir@ida.net
http://www.lili.org/bingham
Heidi Riddoch

North Idaho College
Molstead Library
1000 West Garden Avenue
Coeur d'Alene, ID 83814
(208) 769-3355; (208) 769-3428 FAX
andy_finney@nic.edu
http://www.nic.edu/library/lib
David Remington, Information Librarian;
    Andy Finney, Webmaster
Fall–Spring: Mon–Thur 7:30–10:00, Fri
    7:30–4:00, Sat 10:00–4:00, Sun
    1:00–9:00; Summer: Mon–Thur
    8:00–7:30, Tue–Wed 8:00–5:00, Fri
    8:00–3:00

North Idaho History Center
1000 West Garden Avenue—Fort Sherman
Officers' Quarters
Coeur d'Alene, ID 83814
(208) 769-3300
Judith A. Sylte, Director

Payette Public Library
24 South 10th
Payette, ID 83661-2861
(208) 642-6029; (208) 6542-6046 FAX
Janet Moore

Prairie Community Library
(508 King Street—location)
PO Box 65 (mailing address)
Cottonwood, ID 83522
(208) 962-3714
pclcotid@camasnet.com
Nancy Hood

Snake River Heritage Center
(2295 Paddock Avenue—location)
PO Box 307 (mailing address)
Weiser, ID 83672
(208) 549-0205
Carol Odoms, Manager
by appointment only
Pub. *Snake River Heritage Center
    Newsletter*, quarterly
("Our research library contains only
    materials donated to the museum,
    therefore, it is not a complete library.")
$15.00 per year membership

University of Idaho
University Library
Special Collections
(Rayburn Street—location)
PO Box 442350 (mailing address)
Moscow, ID 83844-2350
(208) 885-7951; (208) 885-6817 FAX
speccoll@drseuss.lib.uidaho.edu (Special
    Collections)
http://www.uidaho.edu/special-
    collections/Other.Repositories.html
    (Repositories of Primary Sources)
(repositories of Primary Sources lists over
    4,800 web sites, worldwide, describing
    holdings of manuscripts, archives, rare
    books, historical photographs, and other
    primary sources for the research scholar)

University of Utah Marriott Library
(see Utah, Part 2)

Wallace District Mining Museum
(509 Bank Street—location)
PO Box 469 (mailing address)
Wallace, ID 83873
(208) 556-1592
John Amonson, Executive Director
summer: Mon–Sun 8:00–8:00; spring & fall:
    Mon–Sun 8:00–6:00, winter: Mon–Sat
    9:00–4:00
("We are in the process of accumulating
    cemetery records and maps, payroll

records, etc.; research time is very
    limited.")
museum admission: $1.50 for adults;
    archives admission: free

Western Heritage Center
(see Montana, Part 2)

Wilder Public Library
(207 A Avenue East—location)
PO Box 128 (mailing address)
Wilder, ID 83676-0128
(208) 482-7880 voice & FAX
Susan Waldemer

Historical Societies—Local and Regional

Adams County Historical Society
PO Box 352
New Meadows, ID 83654

**American Historical Association, Pacific
Coast Branch**
(see California, Part 2)

**American West Research Center and
Historical Society, Inc.**
(see Ohio, Part 2)

Bannock County Historical Society
(Bannock County Historical Museum, 3000
Alvord Loop—location)
PO Box 253 (mailing address)
Pocatello, ID 83204-0253
(208) 233-0434
Mary Lien, Curator
Memorial Day–Labor Day: daily 11:00–6:00;
    Labor Day–Memorial Day: Tue–Sat
    10:00–2:00
(local and county history)
$10.00 per year membership

Bonner County Historical Society
609 South Ella Avenue
Sandpoint, ID 83864
(208) 263-4949
$10.00 per year membership

Bonneville County Historical Society
(Corner of Northeastern Avenue and
Elm—location)
PO Box 1784 (mailing address)
Idaho Falls, ID 83401
(208) 522-1400
Judy House, Librarian
Mon–Fri 10:00–5:00, Sat 1:00–5:00
(Idaho Falls area)
$10.00 per year membership; research: fees
    by the hour done by private arrangement
    with Ms. House

Boundary County Historical Society
(7229 Main Street—location)
PO Box 808 (mailing address)
Bonners Ferry, ID 83805
(208) 267-7720

Camas County Historical Society
PO Box 125
Fairfield, ID 83327

Canyon County Historical Society
Canyon County Historical Museum
(1200 Front Street—location)
PO Box 595 (mailing address)
Nampa, ID 83651
(208) 467-7611

Caribou Historical Society, Inc.
2253 Lago-Liberty Road

Grace, ID 83241
(208) 427-6274

Cassia County Historical Society, Inc.
(Highland and Main Streets—location)
PO Box 331 (mailing address)
Burley, ID 83318
(208) 678-7172
1 Apr–15 Nov: Tue–Sat 10:00–5:00

Clearwater County Historical Society
Clearwater County Historical Museum
(315 College Avenue—location)
PO Box 1154 (mailing address)
Orofino, ID 83544
(208) 476-5033
Evelyn Welter, Director
Tue–Sat 1:30–4:30
("We do not have a lot of genealogy
    information here, but do have some old
    records and newspapers—also old
    photos.")

Crane Historical Society
(Crane House, Main Street—location)
PO Box 152 (mailing address)
Harrison, ID 83833
(208) 689-3519

Elmore County Historical Foundation
180 South Third East
Mountain Home, ID 83647-3019
(208) 587-9041 (City Hall)
Patti McGrath, President
Mon–Tue 11:00–4:30, Fri–Sat 1:30–4:30
Pub. *Heritage*, quarterly
$4.00 per year membership

Gem County Historical Society
(501 East First—location)
PO Box 312 (mailing address)
Emmett, ID 83617
(208) 365-9530, (208) 365-2990
Jessie Goodwin, Co-ordinator
Sat–Sun (June–Sept) 2:00–5:00; group and
    private tours

Gooding County Historical Society
(North Main—location)
PO Box 580 (mailing address)
Gooding, ID 83330
Sharon Kelley, Secretary
summer: Fri–Sat 1:00–5:00
$5.00 per year membership; research for
    Gooding, Lincoln and Twin Falls counties

Hagerman Valley Historical Society
PO Box 86
Hagerman, ID 83332

Jefferson County Historical Society
(110 North State—location)
PO Box 284 (mailing address)
Rigby, ID 83442
(208) 745-8423
Gae Lynne Hinckley, President

Jerome County Historical Society
(220 North Lincoln—location)
PO Box 50 (mailing address)
Jerome, ID 83338
(208) 324-5641 (Museum Office)
info@historicaljeromecounty.com
http://www.historicaljeromecounty.com
Marguerite Roberson, Secretary
Tue–Sat 1:00–5:00
Pub. *Jerome County Historical Society
    Newsletter*, monthly
("Historical places, buildings, Hunt
    [Minidoka Relocation Center].")
$10.00 per year membership; research: fees
    vary

Latah County Historical Society
327 East Second Street
Moscow, ID 83843
(208) 882-1004; (208) 882-0759 FAX
lchlibrary@moscow.com
http://www.latah.id.us/Dept/Historical_
    Main.htm
Marilyn Sandmeyer, Curator, Mary Reed,
    Director
Tue–Fri 9:00–noon & 1:00–5:00
Pub. *Latah Legacy*, semiannually
$10.00 per year membership; admission:
    $2.00 for nonmember adults

Lemhi County Historical Society
210 Main
Salmon, ID 83467

Lewis County Historical Society
Route 2, Box 512
Kamiah, ID 83536
Mildred Ivie, Secretary

Minidoka County Historical Society, Inc.
(100 East Baseline—location)
PO Box 21 (mailing address)
Rupert, ID 83350
(208) 436-0336

Nez Perce County Historical Society
0306 Third Street
Lewiston, ID 83501
(208) 743-2535 voice & FAX
Lora Feucht, Registrar
Tue–Sat 10:00–4:00 (closed winter)
Pub. *Golden Age*, semiannually
("Focus is on Nez Perce County history,
    limited genealogical info." Operates the
    Nez Perce County Museum.)
call for fees

Nez Perce Historical Society
PO Box 86
Nezperce, ID 83542

Old Fort Boise Historical Society
(Old Fort Boise Park, corner of Highway
    20/26 and Parma Road—location)
PO Box 942
Parma, ID 83660
(208) 722-7608
atk@widaho.net
Jack Atkeson, President
Museum: Fri–Sun 1:00–3:00 (June–Aug),
    and by appointment (May–Sept)
("We are a private organization that operates
    a Museum Replica on City of Parma
    Property.")
$5.00 per year membership; museum
    admission: $1.00 for adults

Owyhee County Historical Society
Owyhee County Historical Complex
(Bassey Street—location)
PO Box 67 (mailing address)
Murphy, ID 83650
(208) 495-2319
Kristen Mercer, Museum Director
Wed–Fri 10:00–4:00, Sat–Sun (May–Aug)
    noon–5:00
Pub. *Owyhee Outpost*, annually
$10.00 per year membership

Pacific Northwest Historians Guild
(see Washington, Part 2)

Payette County Historical Society
(90 South Ninth Strteet—location)
PO Box 476 (mailing address)
Payette, ID 83661
(208) 642-4883

Sawtooth Interpretive and Historical Association
(Highway 75—location)
PO Box 75 (mailing address)
Stanley, ID 83278
(208) 774-3517
Ruth Niece, President
Memorial Day weekend–15 Sept: Mon–Fri
    & Sun 11:00–5:00, Sat 11:00–6:00

South Bannock County Historical Center and Museum
(110 East Main Street—location)
PO Box 387 (mailing address)
Lava Hot Springs, ID 83246
(208) 776-5254
http://www.ohwy.com/id/s/sbchcm.htm
Ruth Ann Olson, Director
daily noon–5:00
(files of family history available for research,
    local and South Bannock County area)

South Custer County Historical Society
PO Box 355
Mackay, ID 83251

Spirit Lake Historical Society
PO Box 186
Spirit Lake, ID 83869

Upper Snake River Valley Historical Society
(51 North Center—location)
PO Box 244 (mailing address)
Rexburg, ID 83440
(208) 356-9101
Louis Clements, Director
Mon–Fri 11:00–4:00
Pub. *Snake River Echoes*, biannually
(local history)
$10.00 per year membership

Genealogical Societies

State Genealogical Society

The Idaho Genealogical Society, Inc.
9846 Westview Drive
Boise, ID 83704
(208) 384-0542
idahogenealogy@hotmail.com
http://www.lili.org/idahogenealogy
Adrien Taylor, Vice President
Pub. *Idaho Genealogical Society Quarterly*
(sponsors Oregon Trail Project: certificates
    given to descendants of Oregon Trail
    pioneers [families who came west
    1811–1911], to descendants of pioneers
    [residing in Idaho on or before 3 July
    1890], and to descendants of early settlers
    [settled in Idaho between 4 July 1890 and
    31 December 1900])
$20.00 per year membership; $10.00
    application fee for Oregon Trail
    certificate; research $10.00 per hour

Genealogical Societies—Local & Regional

Bonner County Genealogical Society
(Sandpoint, ID—location)
PO Box 221 (mailing address)
Kootenai, ID 83840-0221
Pub. *Bonner County Genealogical Society
    Newsletter*, ten times per year (monthly,
    Jan–Oct)
$10.00 per year membership; reasonable
    research requests free to members

Caldwell Genealogy Group
3504 South Illinois Street
Caldwell, ID 83605
Carol A. Murphy

The Family Historical and Research Organization, Inc.
122 North Front Street
Sugar City, ID 83448
(208) 356-7072
Dan S. Hemsley, President
$20.00 per year membership

Kamiah Genealogical Society
PO Box 322
Kamiah, ID 83536

Kootenai County Genealogical Society
Kootenai-Shoshone Area Library
Hayden Branch
8385 North Government Way
Hayden Lake, ID 83835-9280
(208) 772-5778 (Secretary's home)
Lelah Achey, Corresponding Secretary
Library: Mon–Sat 9:00–5:00
("census for the state of Idaho, obituaries,
    over fifty research books, history books,
    old newspapers for four northern counties
    of Idaho, etc.")
$10.00 per year membership; research: fees
    vary

Latah County Genealogical Society
327 East Second Street
Moscow, ID 83843
(208) 882-5943
Dorothy Schell, Editor
Pub. *Latah County Genealogical Society
    Quarterly*
$8.00 per year membership

Pocatello Branch Genealogical Society
PO Box 4272
Pocatello, ID 83201

Shoshone County Genealogical Society
904 South Division Street
Kellogg, ID 83837-2651
Oradell Triplett, President (PG)
Osburn Public Library
$5.00 per year membership

Snake River Genealogical Society of Southeastern Idaho
122 North Front Street
Sugar City, ID 83448
(208) 356-7072
Dan S. Hemsley, President
$20.00 per year membership

Twin Rivers Genealogical Society
PO Box 386
Lewiston, ID 83501
Margaret Nell Longeteig

Valley County Genealogical Society
(Cascade Public Library, 105 Front
    Street—location)
PO Box 697 (mailing address)
Cascade, ID 83611
(208) 382-4757 voice & FAX (Library)
Ruth Redmon, Secretary; Bea Snyder,
    President
Mon–Fri noon–6:00, Sat 10:00–2:00
Pub. *Valley County Heritage*, semiannually
    (Jan, July)
("Valley County courthouse records, news
    clippings, etc.")
$10.00 per year membership; queries: free to
    members, 10¢ per word for nonmembers

Independent Publications and Miscellany

Idaho Transportation Department
Geographic Information Systems (GIS)

(3311 West State Street, Boise, ID 83703-
5881—location)
PO Box 7129 (mailing address)
Boise, ID 83707-1129
(208) 334-8000 (Headquarters Information)
http://www3.state.id.us/itd_gis (Maps)

IdGenWeb
Part of The USGenweb Project
gassaway@juno.com
http://www.rootsweb.com/~idgenweb
Rhonda Smith, State Coordinator
(links to other Idaho resources)

Massacre Rocks State Park
3592 North Park Lane
American Falls, ID 83211
(208) 548-2672

Nez Perce National Historical Park
Route 1, Box 100
Lapwai, ID 83540
http://www.nps.gov/nepe

Northwest Pioneer
(see Washington, Part 2)

Our Memories Museum
1122 Main Street
Caldwell, ID 83605
(208) 459-1413

Three Island Crossing State Park
PO Box 609
Glenns Ferry, ID 83623
http://www.wvi.com/users/TIC/tic.htm

Valley County Museum, Roseberry
13131 Farm to Market Road
Donnelley, ID 83615
(208) 325-8628; (208) 325-8383

Winchester Museum
Route 2, Box 28
Winchester, ID 83524
(208) 924-7772

Illinois

Archives and Libraries with Holdings in Genealogy

State Archives and Library

Illinois State Archives
Office of the Secretary of State
Margaret Cross Norton Building
Capitol Complex
Springfield, IL 62756-0001
(217) 782-4682; (217) 782-3556; (217) 785-
1266 (IRAD); (217) 524-3930 FAX

http://www.sos.state.il.us/departments/arc
hives/archives.html
David A. Joens, Director
Mon–Fri 8:00–4:30, Sat 8:00–3:30 (except
holiday weekends)
Pub. *Newsletter of the Illinois State Archives*,
semiannually, free to institutions and
societies

Eastern Illinois University
Illinois Regional Archives Depository
(IRAD)
Booth Library
University Archives, Room 1700
600 Lincoln Avenue
Charleston, IL 61920
(217) 581-6093
cfrvh@eiu.edu
http://www.eiu.edu/~booth
Bob Hillman
Mon–Fri 9:00–noon, 1:00–4:00
(serves Clark, Clay, Coles, Crawford,
Cumberland, Douglas, Edgar, Edwards,
Effingham, Jasper, Lawrence, Moultrie,
Richland, Shelby, Wabash, and Wayne
counties)

Illinois State University
Illinois Regional Archives Depository
(IRAD)
Milner Library
Campus Box 8900
Normal, IL 61761-8900
(309) 452-6027
jarayfi@ilstu.edunmkauth@ilstu.edu
http://www.mlb.ilstu.edu/archives/home.htm
Jo Rayfield, Archives Specialist; Nancy M.
Kauth, Chief Library Clerk
Mon–Fri 9:00–noon, 1:00–4:00
(serves Champaign, DeWitt, Ford, Grundy,
Iroquois, Kankakee, Livingston, Logan,
Marshall, McLean, Piatt, Tazewell,
Vermilion, and Woodford counties)

Northeastern Illinois University Library
Illinois Regional Archives Depository
(IRAD)
Ronald Williams Library
5500 North Saint Louis
Chicago, IL 60625-4699
(773) 442-4506
http://www.neiu.edu/~neiulib/about/
libcollections/irad.html
Mon–Fri 9:00–4:00
(serves Cook County and City of Chicago;
vital records, naturalizations, probate
records, court case files)
submit inquiries by mail or phone only

Northern Illinois University
Illinois Regional Archives Depository
(IRAD)
c/o Regional History Center
Founders Memorial Library, Room 400
DeKalb, IL 60115
(815) 753-1807

jmetzger@niu.edu
http://www.niulib.niu.edu/dept-reghist.cfm
Joan Metzger, Assistant University Archivist
Mon–Fri 8:00–4:30
(serves Boone, Bureau, Carroll, DeKalb,
DuPage, Jo Daviess, Kane, Kendall, Lake,
LaSalle, Lee, McHenry, Ogle, Putnam,
Stephenson, Whiteside, Will, and
Winnebago counties; history, genealogy,
local government records)

Southern Illinois University at Carbondale
Illinois Regional Archives Depository
(IRAD)
Morris Library Special Collections (SIU-
C)—6632
Carbondale, IL 62901-6632
(618) 453-3040 (IRAD)
speccoll@lib.siu.edu
http://www.lib.siu.edu/spcol/irad.shtml
Katharine Salzmann, Curator of Manuscripts
and IRAD Supervisor
Mon–Fri 8:30–4:30
("IRAD has noncurrent records for
Alexander, Clinton, Franklin, Gallatin,
Hamilton, Hardin, Jackson, Jefferson,
Johnson, Madison, Marion, Massac,
Monroe, Perry, Pope, Pulaski, Randolph,
Saint Clair, Saline, Union, Washington,
White, and Williamson counties"; some
genealogical material, but no separate
genealogical collection in IRAD or
Special Collections)

University of Illinois at Springfield
Illinois Regional Archives Depository
(IRAD)
Depository Library, Room 144
1 University Plaza, MS BRK 140
Springfield, IL 62794-5407
(217) 786-6520; (217) 786-6633 FAX
wood@uis.edu
http://www.uis.edu/archives
Thomas J. Wood, University Archivist
Mon–Fri 9:00–5:00
(serves Bond, Cass, Christian, Fayette,
Greene, Jersey, Macon, Macoupin,
Mason, Menard, Montgomery, Morgan,
Sangamon, and Scott counties; University
archives, local government records, local
history)

Western Illinois University Library
Illinois Regional Archives Depository
(IRAD)
Archives and Special Collections Unit
1 University Circle
Macomb, IL 61455-1391
(309) 298-2717
MC-Vizdal@wiu.edu
http://www.wiu.edu/library/units/archives
Marla Vizdal, Archives Specialist
Mon–Fri 8:00–4:30
("Collection includes materials from Adams,
Brown, Calhoun, Fulton, Hancock,
Henderson, Henry, Knox, McDonough,
Mercer, Peoria, Pike, Rock Island,
Schuyler, Stark, and Warren counties.
Holdings include county histories,
directories, newspapers, photographs, oral
history tapes, manuscripts, as well as
official county records housed by the
IRAD section of the unit.")

Illinois State Library
300 South Second Street
Reference Department
Springfield, IL 62701-1796
(217) 782-7596; (217) 524-0041 FAX
mragen@ilsos.net
http://www.cyberdriveillinois.com/
departments/library/home.html

Mike Ragen, Acting Director
Mon–Fri 8:00–4:30
(circulating collections of state and federal
documents; no genealogy section)

Abraham Lincoln Presidential Library
1 Old State Capitol Plaza
Springfield, IL 62701-1507
(217) 524-7219; (217) 524-6358; (217) 785-
7941 (Newspaper Library)
http://www.state.il.us/hpa/lib/default.htm
Kathryn M. Harris, Director, ISHL; Jane
Ehrenhart, Supervisor, Reference and
Technical Services
Mon–Fri 8:30–5:00
(family histories, county histories, and
indexes to vital records held elsewhere)
genealogical and newspaper research: see
web site for fees

State Historical Society

**Association of Illinois Museums and
Historical Societies (AIMHS)**
210½ South Sixth
Springfield, IL 62701-1503
(217) 525-2781; (217) 525-2783 FAX
ishs@eosinc.com
http://www.historyillinois.org
Mary Turner, Coordinator; Karen E.
Everingham, Programs Assistant
8:30–4:30
Pub. *IAM News*, quarterly; *Directory of
Illinois Museums*, biannually, free
(statewide association of Museums,
Historical and Genealogical Societies;
directory lists about 900 agencies and
institutions)
$35.00 per year membership

Illinois Historic Preservation Agency
1 Old State Capitol Plaza
Springfield, IL 62701-1507
(217) 785-7949; (217) 785-7937 FAX
evelyn_taylor@ihpa.state.il.us
http://www.state.il.us/hpa
Evelyn R. Taylor, Managing Editor
Mon–Fri 8:00–4:30
Pub. *Journal of Illinois History: Quarterly of
the Illinois State Historical Library*,
$18.00 per year subscription

Illinois State Historical Society
210½ South Sixth
Springfield, IL 62701-1503
(217) 525-2781; (217) 525-2783 FAX
ishs@eosinc.com
http://www.historyillinois.org
Jon Austin, Executive Director
9:00–5:00
Pub. *Dispatch/News*, quarterly; *Illinois
Historical Journal*, quarterly
(promotes research, writing and participation
in Illinois history)
$35.00 per year membership

**City, County and Regional Archives and
Libraries**
(A more exhaustive list of public and
academic libraries can be found at
http://eliillinois.org or http://www.
cyberdriveillinois.com/library/systems/
sys_dir.html.)

**Jane Addams' Hull House Museum at
University of Illinois—Chicago**
800 South Halsted Street
Chicago, IL 60607-7017
(312) 413-5354
Mary Johnson, Director
Mon–Fri 10:00–4:00, Sun noon–5:00
(local history, women's history)

Algonquin Area Public Library
Eastgate Branch
115 Eastgate Drive
Algonquin, IL 60102-3097
(847) 458-6060; (847) 458-9359 FAX
http://www.aapld.org
Randall Vlcek, Administrative Librarian

Arlington Heights Memorial Library
500 North Dunton Avenue
Arlington Heights, IL 60004-5966
(847) 506-2639; (847) 506-2636 FAX
http://www.ahml.info
Michal Mulholland, Local
History/Genealogy Librarian
Mon–Fri 9:00–10:00, Sat 9:00–5:00, Sun
noon–5:00
(Illinois and midwest states, 1900 and 1910
census microfilm for seven states,
passenger list microfilm 1820–1897 for
major eastern ports)

Assumption Public Library
205 North Oak Street
Assumption, IL 62510-1137
(217) 226-3915 voice & FAX
sestraw@yahoo.com
Anna Adermann

Atlanta Public Library District
(100 Race Street—location)
PO Box 568 (mailing address)
Atlanta, IL 61723-0568
(217) 648-2112; (217) 648-5269 FAX
atlanta.library@verizon.net
http://npinil.circ.uiuc.edu/resource/logan/
atlantpl.html
Mrs. Carol Begolka, Director; Christine
Horner
Tue–Wed & Fri 12:30–4:30, Thur
12:30–8:00, Sat 9:00–1:00
(local history)

Augustana College Library
Special Collections
3435 9½ Avenue
Rock Island, IL 61201-2210
(309) 794-7643; (309) 794-7230 FAX
specialcollections@augustana.edu
http://www.augustana.edu/library
Donna Hill, Archives Assistant
Librarian/Archivist
Mon–Fri 1:00–5:00 (closed during some
school breaks, please call ahead)

Barrington Area Library
505 North Northwest Highway
Barrington, IL 60010-3399
(847) 382-1300; (847) 382-1261 FAX
bsugden@barringtonarealibrary.org
http://www.barringtonarealibrary.org
Rose M. Faber, Head, Adult Services; Marie
Thomas, Reference Librarian; Barbara L.
Sugden, Executive Director
Mon–Fri 9:00–9:00, Sat 9:00–5:00, Sun
1:00–5:00
(Barrington genealogy and local history
information; the *Barrington Courier-
Review* indexed for births, deaths,
marriages, 1890–1929, 1994–1996 on
home page site)

Belleville Public Library
121 East Washington Street
Belleville, IL 62220-2205
(618) 234-0441, ext. 22; (618) 234-9474
FAX
baa@lcls.org; louannj@mailman.lcls.org
http://www.compu-
type.net/rengen/stclair/stchome.htm
Lou Ann James, Archivist
Mon–Thur 9:00–8:00, Fri–Sat 9:00–5:00

("Depository for St. Clair County
Genealogical Society." Emphasis on
Illinois and family history; oldest
continuing library in Illinois)
research: "no extensive family research but
will look up obituaries ($2.50 each), main
indexes ($10.00 per hour plus copies and
postage)

Bellwood Public Library
600 Bohland Avenue
Bellwood, IL 60104
(708) 547-7393; (708) 547-9352 FAX
wootenj@sls.lib.il.us; bws@sls.lib.il.us
http://www.bellwoodlibrary.org
Jimmi Wooten, Director
Mon–Thur 9:30–9:00, Fri 9:30–6:00, Sat
9:30–4:00

Benton Public Library
502 South Main Street
Benton, IL 62812-1712
(618) 438-7511; (618) 439-4476; (618) 439-
6139 FAX
mscanlan@hotmail.com
http://www.benton.lib.il.us
Mary Eubanks, Society for the Historic
Preservation of Franklin County; Molly
Scanlan, Director
Mon–Thur 9:00–8:00, Fri–Sat 9:00–5:00,
Sun 1:00–5:00

Village of Bethalto
213 North Prairie
Bethalto, IL 62010
(618) 377-8723
Arvel Fowler
Sat afternoons by appointment
(local history)

Bishop Hill State Historic Site
(Bishop Hill Road—location)
PO Box 104 (mailing address)
Bishop Hill, IL 61419-0104
(309) 927-3345; (309) 927-3343
bishophill@winco.net
Martha Jane Downey, Site Manager
Mar–Oct: 9:00–5:00; Nov–Feb: 9:00–4:00

Bloomington Public Library
(205 East Olive Street, Bloomington, IL
61701—location)
PO Box 3308 (mailing address)
Bloomington, IL 61702-3308
(309) 828-6091; (309) 821-9314 FAX
mattk@bloomingtonlibrary.org
Lois Wood, Library Associate II (Local
History); Matthew Kubiak
Mon–Thur 9:00–9:00, Fri–Sat 9:00–5:00,
Sun 1:00–5:00 (Sept–May)
(specializes in Bloomington-Normal, Illinois,
McLean County, Illinois, and Illinois state
local history, as opposed to genealogy)
research: $5.00 minimum plus 15¢ per copy

Blue Island Public Library
2433 York Street
Blue Island, IL 60406-2094
(708) 388-1078; (708) 388-1143 FAX
bis@sls.lib.il.us
http://www.blueislandlibrary.org
Lynne Ingersoll, Reference Librarian; David
J. Seleb, Director
Mon–Thur noon–8:00, Fri–Sat 9:00–5:00
(history of Blue Island, Illinois)

Gail Borden Public Library District
270 North Grove Avenue
Elgin, IL 60120
(847) 742-2411; (847) 742-0485 FAX
wblohm@nslsilus.org
http://www.gailborden.info

William R. Blohm, Reference Librarian
Mon–Thur 9:00–9:00, Fri–Sat 9:00–5:30,
Sun 1:00–5:30; summer: Mon–Thur
9:00–9:00, Fri–Sat 9:00–5:30
(Elgin and Kane County genealogy and
history)
$5.00 for basic search and photocopies from
microfilm

Bourbonnais Public Library
250 West John Casey Road
Bourbonnais, IL 60914
(815) 933-1727; (815) 933-1961 FAX
ddillinger@htls.lib.il.us
http://bourbonnais.lib.il.us
Diana Dillinger, Director
Mon–Thur 9:00–9:00, Fri 9:00–6:00, Sat
9:00–5:00

**Louisa H. Bowen University Archives and
Special Collections**
Lovejoy Library
Southern Illinois University at Edwardsville
Box 1063, SIUE
Edwardsville, IL 62026-1063
(618) 692-2665
Dr. Stephen Kerber
Mon–Fri by appointment
(Madison County naturalization records)

Bradley University
Special Collections Center/Cullum Davis
Library
1501 West Bradley
Peoria, IL 61625
(309) 677-2822; (309) 677-2823; (309) 677-
2827 FAX
Charles Frey
Mon–Fri 9:00–noon & 1:00–4:30

**C. E. Brehm Memorial Public Library
District**
Genealogy Department
101 South Seventh Street
Mount Vernon, IL 62864-4187
(618) 242-6322; (618) 242-0810 FAX
kendik@shawls.lib.il.us
http://www.mtvbrehm.lib.il.us
Maggie Kirwan, Interlibrary Loan-
Genealogy Librarian; Kendi Kelley,
Administrative Librarian
Mon & Fri 9:00–5:00, Tue–Thur 9:00–8:00,
Sat 10:00–4:00, Sun (Sept–May)
1:00–5:00
(emphasis on southern Illinois, $5.00 for
loans to libraries outside Illinois, who
should address requests to Shawnee
Library System—see below)

Brenner Library of Quincy College
1800 College Avenue
Quincy, IL 62301-2670
(217) 228-5350; (217) 228-5354 FAX
Patricia Tomczak, Librarian
Mon–Thur 8:00 A.M.–11:00 P.M., Fri
8:00–8:00, Sat 11:00–5:00, Sun
1:00–11:00
(local history collection)

Bridgeview Public Library
7840 West 79th Street
Bridgeview, IL 60455-1496
(708) 458-2880; (708) 458-3553 FAX
bvs@sls.lib.il.us
http://www.bridgeviewlibrary.org
Elsie Mikrut; Kari Hanson, Director
Mon–Thur 9:00–8:00, Fri–Sat 9:00–5:00,
Sun 10:00–2:00

**Mr. & Mrs. Alfred A. Brown Memorial
Museum**
PO Box 152

Sparta, IL 62286
(618) 443-2897
Fred Gerlach, Chair
Wed & Sat 2:00–4:00
(local history)

Bryan-Bennett Library
217 West Main Street
Salem, IL 62881-1599
(618) 548-7784; (618) 548-9593 FAX
tschafer@shawls.lib.il.us
http://www.salembbl.lib.il.us
Theresa Schaefer, Library Director
Mon–Thur noon–8:00, Fri–Sat 9:00–2:00

Byron Museum District
(106 North Union Street—location)
PO Box 186 (mailing address)
Byron, IL 61010-0186
(815) 234-5031; (815) 234-4447 FAX
ByronMuseum@byronil.net
http://www.byronillinois.org (choose
Museum link)
Dawn Johnson, Executive Director
Tue–Fri 8:30–3:30, Sat–Sun (Memorial
Day–Labor Day) 1:00–4:00
("Illinois—local history museum with small
research center, materials specific to local
and area history—no loans.")

Cairo Public Library
(1609 Washington Avenue—location)
PO Box 151 (mailing address)
Cairo, IL 62914-0151
(618) 734-1840; (618) 734-9346 FAX
Monica L. Smith
Mon–Fri 10:00–5:00, Sat 9:00–noon

**Canal and Regional History Collection of
Lewis University**
1 University Parkway
Romeoville, IL 60446
(815) 838-0500, ext. 5579; (815) 838-9456
FAX
John Lamb, Director
11:00–4:00
Pub. *Annual Report on Collection*, $10.00
per year subscription
("Material on canals, photos,
correspondence, annual reports, also local
histories of northern Illinois and other
materials such as complete files of local
Chamber of Commerce and regional
Chamber of Commerce.")
research: $5.00 plus $1.00 per page
photoduplication

Carthage Public Library District
538 Wabash Avenue
Carthage, IL 62321-1360
(217) 357-3232; (217) 357-2392 FAX
cartlib@adams.net
http://www.carthage.lib.il.us
Diana Robison, Director; Susan Hunt
Summer: Mon–Thur noon–6:00, Fri
noon–5:00, Sat 9:00–5:00; fall–spring:
Mon–Thur noon–9:00, Fri noon–5:00, Sat
9:00–5:00
(local history)

**Champaign County Historical Museum,
Inc.**
111 East University Avenue
Champaign, IL 61820
(217) 356-1010
cchmus@c-u.net
http://www.m-
crossroads.org/cchmus/index.html
Barbara Peckham, President
collection in temporary storage
$15.00 per year membership

Charleston Public Library
Genealogy Room
712 Sixth Street
Charleston, IL 61920
(217) 345-3896; (217) 348-5616 FAX
crngenealogy@yahoo.com
http://www.charlestonlibrary.org
Sheryl Snyder, Director
Mon–Thur 10:00–8:00, Fri–Sat 10:00–6:00,
Sun noon–5:00
(houses the collection of the Coles County,
Illinois, Genealogical Society)

Chicago Heights Free Public Library
25 West 15th Street (15th and Chicago
Road)
Chicago Heights, IL 60411-3488
(708) 754-0323; (708) 754-0325 FAX
paulb@sls.lib.il.us; chs@sls.lib.il.us
http://www.sls.lib.il.us/chs
Barbara Paul, Director
Mon–Thur 9:00–9:00, Fri–Sat 9:00–5:00,
Sun (during the school year) 1:00–5:00

Chicago Lawn Library
6120 South Kedzie Avenue
Chicago, IL 60629-4638
(312) 747-0639; (312) 747-0081; (312) 747-
6182 FAX
http://www.chipublib.org/002branches/
chicagolawn/chlhgh.html
Mon–Thur 9:00–8:00, Fri–Sat 9:00–5:00

Chicago Public Library
Special Collections and Preservation
Division
9N-15, 400 South State Street
Chicago, IL 60605-1203
(312) 747-4876; (312) 747-4890 FAX
comments@chipublib.org
http://www.chicagopubliclibrary.org
Sophia K. Jordan, Division Chief
Mon–Wed noon–6:00, Sat noon–4:00
(Civil War; Chicago area history)

Coal City Public Library District
Attn: Jolene Franciskovich, Director
85 North Garfield Street
Coal City, IL 60416
(815) 634-4552; (815) 634-2950 FAX
jfranciskovich@coalcity.lib.il.us
http://coalcity.lib.il.us
Mon–Thur 9:00–8:00, Fri–Sat 9:00–4:00

Collinsville Historical Museum
Collinsville Memorial Public Library, Lower
Level
408 West Main Street
Collinsville, IL 62234-3018
(618) 344-1112; (618) 345-6401 FAX
cve@lcls.org
http://www.collinsvillelibrary.org
Floyd Sperino, Museum Curator
Mon–Sat noon–4:00
(Collinsville and adjacent area of Madison
and Saint Clair counties)

Cook Memorial Public Library
413 North Milwaukee Avenue
Libertyville, IL 60048-2280
(847) 362-2330; (847) 362-2354 FAX
jules@cooklib.org
http://www.cooklib.org
Aileen Hapke, Genealogy; Eileen
Kloberdanz, Local History
Mon–Thur 9:00–9:00, Fri–Sat 9:00–5:00,
Sun (during school year) 1:00–5:00

**J. T. & E. J. Crumbaugh Memorial Public
Library**
(405 East Center Street—location)
PO Box 129 (mailing address)

LeRoy, IL 61752-0129
(309) 962-3911
crumbaughlibrary@yahoo.com
http://www.geocities.com/crumbaughlibrary
Lois Evans, Librarian
Mon–Sat 10:00–5:00
(*Tracing Your Roots*, updated every two
years, $2.00 ppd., "contains what the
library has available for searching family
histories, mostly in this area. Also
includes local history.")

Crystal Lake Public Library
126 West Paddock Street
Crystal Lake, IL 60014-6194
(815) 459-1687; (815) 459-5845 FAX
kmartens@crystallakelibrary.org
http://www.crystallakelibrary.org
Alice Hayes, Reference
Mon–Fri 9:00–9:00, Fri–Sat 9:00–5:00
("local history, genealogy")

Danville Public Library
319 North Vermilion Street
Danville, IL 61832-4787
(217) 477-5228; (217) 477-5230 FAX
dplind@dpl.lib.in.us
http://www.danville.lib.il.us/archives.htm
Roberta D. Allen, Director of Reference and
Director of Archives
Mon–Thur 9:00–8:00, Fri–Sat 9:00–5:30
(emphasis on Vermilion County, Illinois)

Decatur Public Library
Local History Room
247 East North Street
Decatur, IL 62523
(217) 424-2900; (217) 423-5741 FAX
http://www.decatur.lib.il.us
Bev Hackney, Periodicals Librarian; Dayle
Irwin, Local History Library Assistant
Mon–Thur 9:00–5:00, Mon 6:00–8:00, Sat
10:30–noon & 1:00–3:00 (staffing may
depend on volunteer availability, call
first)
(newspaper microfilm from the 1860s,
obituary index from 1868, city directories
from the 1870s, biographical and
historical information focusing on
Decatur)
research: $5.00 plus copies at 50¢ each

DeKalb Public Library
309 Oak Street
DeKalb, IL 60115-3369
(815) 756-9568; (815) 756-7837 FAX
mdhatter2000@yahoo.com
http://www.dkpl.org
Elaine Fulton, Adult Services Librarian;
Paula Torgeson
Mon–Thur 9:00–9:00, Fri 9:00–6:00, Sat
9:00–5:00, Sun (Sept–May) 1:00–4:00

DePaul University Archives
2323 North Seminary
Chicago, IL 60614
(773) 341-8088

Des Plaines Public Library
1501 Ellinwood Street
Des Plaines, IL 60016-4553
(847) 827-8551; (847) 827-7974 FAX
http://www.desplaines.lib.il.us/index.html
Sandra K. Norlin, Director
Mon–Fri 9:00–9:00, Sat 9:00–5:00, Sun
1:00–5:00

DeWitt County Museum Association
219 East Woodlawn Street
Clinton, IL 61727-1052
(217) 935-6066 (after 1:00)
Jill Fostervold, Resident Manager

1 Apr–31 Dec: Tue–Sun 1:00–5:00

Downers Grove Park District Museum
831 Maple Avenue
Downers Grove, IL 60515-4904
(630) 963-1309; (630) 963-0496 FAX
Mark S. Harmon, Museum Supervisor
Office/Research: Mon–Fri 8:30–4:30
Pub. *The Plank*, quarterly
("family history; atlases; census records;
birth, death and cemetery indices; phone
directories; school yearbooks, etc.")

Dundee Township Library
555 Barrington Avenue
Dundee, IL 60118-1496
(847) 428-3661; (847) 428-0521 FAX
jnielsen@nsls.info
http://www.dundeelibrary.info
Abbey LaVell, Local History; Joyce Nielsen,
Interim Director
Mon–Thur 9:00–9:00, Fri–Sat 9:00–5:30

DuQuoin Public Library
28 South Washington Street
DuQuoin, IL 62832-1396
(618) 542-5045; (618) 542-4735 FAX
purban@shawls.lib.il.us
http://www.sirin.lib.il.us/docs/dpl/docs/
mail_page.htm
Pam Urban, Library Director
Mon & Wed–Fri noon–6:00, Tue noon–8:00,
Sat 9:00–3:00

Early American Museum
(Route 47 North, Lake of the Woods
Park—location)
PO Drawer 1040 (mailing address)
Mahomet, IL 61853
(217) 586-2612
Cheryl Kennedy, Director
weekends (May & Sept) 10:00–5:00; daily
(June–Aug) 10:00–5:00
(east central Illinois)
$15.00 per year membership; admission:
$3.50 for adults

Edgar County Genealogy Library
408 North Main (Edgar County Historical
Museum Annex)
Paris, IL 61944-1549
(217) 463-4209
ecgl@tigerpaw.com
http://www.tigerpaw.com/ecgl
Linda Cary and A. Joyce Brown, Co-
Directors
Wed–Fri 9:00–4:00
(Holdings include Illinois marriages, public
domain land records, Paris newspapers,
county cemetery records, family and
county histories, military records, vertical
files, scrapbooks, surname exchange files,
and computer databases, including LDS
FamilySearch; Edgar County archives,
genealogies, plus many records for other
states of Indiana, Ohio, Pennsylvania,
Kentucky, North Carolina, Virginia, etc.)
research: $5.00 per hour

Edwardsville Public Library
112 South Kansas Street
Edwardsville, IL 62025
(618) 692-7556; (618) 692-9566 FAX
ede@lcls.org
http://edwardsvillelibrary.org
Deanne Holshouser
Mon–Thur 9:00–9:00, Fri–Sat 9:00–5:00,
Sun 1:00–5:00

Eisenhower Public Library District
4652 North Olcott Avenue
Harwood Heights, IL 60706-4697

(708) 867-7828; (708) 452-8989; (708) 867-
1535 FAX
stochr@sls.lib.il.us; ess@sls.lib.il.us
http://www.eisenhowerlibrary.org/index.
html
Ronald Stoch, Director
Mon–Thur 10:00–9:00, Fri 10:00–6:00, Sat
10:00–5:00
(stronger in local history than genealogy)

Ellwood House Museum (DeKalb County)
509 North First Street
DeKalb, IL 60115-3232
(815) 756-4609; (815) 756-4645 FAX
Gerald J. Brauer, Executive Director

Elmhurst Historical Museum
120 East Park Avenue
Elmhurst, IL 60126-3420
(630) 833-1457; (630) 833-1326 FAX
http://www.elmhurst.org/elmhurst/museum
Nancy Wilson, Archivist
Tue–Sun 1:00–5:00, and by appointment
admission: free

Elmwood Park Public Library
1 Conti Parkway
Elmwood Park, IL 60707-4599
(708) 453-7645; (708) 453-4671 FAX
eps@sls.lib.il.us
http://www.epcusd.w-cook.k12.il.us/eppl
Russell Parker, Librarian; Shawn Strecker,
Director
Mon–Thur 9:00–9:00, Fri 9:00–6:00, Sat
9:00–5:00
(emphasis on Elmwood Park, Galewood,
Montclare and Chicago)

Evans Public Library
215 South Fifth Street
Vandalia, IL 62471-2206
(618) 283-2824; (618) 283-4705 FAX
evanspl@shawls.lib.il.us
http://www.sirin.lib.il.us/docs/epl/docs/
lib/index.html
Candy Zeman, Librarian
Mon–Thur 10:00–7:00, Fri–Sat 10:00–5:00

Evanston Public Library
(address withheld upon request)

Forest Park Library
7555 Jackson Avenue
Forest Park, IL 60130
(708) 366-7171; (708) 366-7293 FAX
fps@sls.lib.il.us
http://www.forestparklibrary.lib.il.us
Mary Forbes, Director

Fort Sheridan Museum
Building 33
Fort Sheridan, IL 60037-5000
(847) 926-5519
(archives)

Fossil Ridge Public Library
386 West Kennedy Road
Braidwood, IL 60408
(815) 458-2187; (815) 458-2042
ljvotta@fossilridge.org
http://www.fossilridge.org
Beverley Craig; Janie Votta, Director
Mon–Thur 9:00–9:00, Fri 9:00–6:00, Sat
9:00–3:00, Sun (Oct–May) 1:00–5:00
(emphasis on local and Illinois
history/genealogy; houses library
collection of Will/Grundy Counties [IL]
Genealogical Society)

Gladys Fox Museum
Lockport Township Park District
1911 South Lawrence

Lockport, IL 60441-4498
(815) 838-1183; (815) 838-4974 FAX
Robert Paddock
Tue–Wed & Fri 11:00–3:00, Sun 1:00–4:00
(local history)

Franklin Park Public Library District
10311 West Grand Avenue
Franklin Park, IL 60131
(847) 455-6016, ext. 234; (847) 455-6299
FAX
mjohnson@linc.lib.il.us
http://www.franklinparklibrary.org
Mark Johnson, Head of Local History
Department
Mon–Thur 9:00–9:00, Fri–Sat 9:00–5:00,
Sun 1:00–5:00
(Franklin Park, some Leyden Township)

Freeport Public Library
314 West Stephenson Street
Freeport, IL 61032
(815) 233-3000; (815) 233-1099 FAX
frnovak@rocketmail.com
http://www.freeportpubliclibrary.org
John Locascio; Frank Novak
Stephenson County Genealogical Society
members volunteer in local history room:
Mon 9:00–5:00 & 6:00–8:45, Wed & Fri
9:00–noon, Thur 1:00–5:00, other hours
covered by library staff with 5:00 as the
closing hours, no Sun hours

Galena Public Library
Historical Collections Room
601 South Bench Street
Galena, IL 61036
(815) 777-0200; (815) 777-0219 FAX
coatesm@galenalink.com
H. Scott Wolfe, Historical Librarian; Maren
Coates
Mon–Fri 3:00–5:00, Sat 1:00–4:00, or by
special appointment
(history and genealogy of the upper
Mississippi lead region)

Galesburg Public Library
40 East Simmons Street
Galesburg, IL 61401-4591
(309) 343-6118; (309) 343-4877 FAX
pamv@galesburglibrary.org
http://www.galesburglibrary.org
Patricia Mosher, Archivist
Mon–Thur 9:00–9:00, Fri–Sat 9:00–5:00,
Sun (Sept–May) 1:00–5:00
("Large genealogy section covering many
Illinois counties, census on CD-ROM.
Large collection of plat maps.")

Geneva Public Library District
127 James Street
Geneva, IL 60134-2277
(630) 232-0780; (630) 232-0881 FAX
jhintz@geneva.lib.il.us
Jeanne Hintz, Director
Mon–Thur 9:00–9:00, Fri–Sat 9:00–5:00,
Sun (Sept–May) noon–4:00
charge for photocopies

Glenview Public Library
1930 Glenview Road
Glenview, IL 60025-2899
(847) 729-7500, ext. 152; (847) 729-7682
FAX
butta@CLSN3046.glenview.lib.il.us
http://www.glenview.lib.il.us
Deena Butta, Reference Librarian
Mon–Fri 9:00–9:00, Sat 9:00–5:00, Sun
1:00–5:00

**G.A.R. Memorial and Veterans' Military
Museum**

(see Lineage, Hereditary and Patriotic
Societies, Part 3)

Granite City Public Library District
2001 Delmar Avenue
Granite City, IL 62040
(618) 452-6238; (618) 876-6317 FAX
jeanettek@mailman.lcls.org
http://www.lcls.lib.il.us/gce
Jeanette L. Kampen, Assistant Director
Sept–May: Mon–Thur 9:00–9:00, Fri–Sat
9:00–5:00; June–Aug: Mon & Wed
9:00–9:00, Tue & Thur–Sat 9:00–5:00

Green Hills Public Library District
8611 West 103rd Street
Palos Hills, IL 60465
(708) 598-8446; (708) 598-0856 FAX
armstrong@greenhills.lib.il.us;
ghpld@greenhills.lib.il.us
http://www.greenhills.lib.il.us
Annette Armstrong, Director
Mon–Fri 9:00–8:30, Sat 9:00–5:00 (except
June–Aug: Sat 9:00–3:00)

Greenville Public Library
414 West Main
Greenville, IL 62246
(618) 664-3115; (618) 664-9442 FAX
gve@lcls.org
http://greenvilleillinois.com
Ted Thies, Library Director; Cindy Sayler
Mon–Thur noon–8:00, Fri 10:00–6:00, Sat
10:00–5:00

Gretna Station and Caboose Museums
391 Illini Drive
Carol Stream, IL 60188
(630) 260-7863; (630) 665-2311; (630) 665-
9045 FAX
Mary Brosious
hours: various
(Railroad memorabilia, Fire Protection
District display, bicentennial display)
free tours

Gridley Public Library District
(320 Center Street—location)
PO Box 370 (mailing address)
Gridley, IL 61744-0370
(309) 747-2284; (309) 747-3195 FAX
Perry Klopfenstein; M. Lynn McKinley

Hacksma House Genealogy Library
(see Washington, Part 2)

Harrisburg Public Library District
2 West Walnut Street
Harrisburg, IL 62946-1704
(618) 253-7455; (618) 252-1239 FAX
shinant@shawls.lib.il.us
http://www.sirin.lib.il.us/docs/mcl/docs/
lib/index.html
Sherry L. Hinant, Librarian
Assistant/Genealogist
Mon–Fri 10:00–8:00, Sat 10:00–6:00, Sun
2:00–5:00

Harvey Public Library District
15441 Turlingon Avenue
Harvey, IL 60426-3683
(708) 331-0757; (708) 331-2835 FAX
reference@harvey.lib.il.us;
has@harvey.lib.il.us (General
Information)
http://www.harvey.lib.il.us
Terry van de Berg, Reference Librarian
Mon–Thur 9:30–8:00, Fri–Sat 9:30–5:30,
Sun (Sept–May) 1:00–5:00
(Harvey local history. "Will accept email
requests.")

Havana Public Library District
201 West Adams Street
Havana, IL 62644-1321
(309) 543-4701; (309) 543-2715 FAX
hpld@casscomm.com
http://www.havana.lib.il.us/library/index.
html
Virginia Barrett
Mon–Thur 11:00–8:00, Fri 1:00–6:00; Sat
10:00–5:00

Hayner Public Library District
401 State Street
Alton, IL 62002
(618) 462-0651
haynergen@lcls.org
http://www.haynerlibrary.org
Cathie Lamere, Genealogy Services
Mon–Fri 8:00–5:00
("Illinois library with local and genealogy
holdings.")

Heritage Cultural Center
(125 South Webster—location)
200 West Douglas (mailing address)
Jacksonville, IL 62650-2012
(217) 243-7488
Wed 1:00–4:00 by appointment
(local history)

Homewood Public Library
17917 Dixie Highway
Homewood, IL 60430
(708) 798-0121; (708) 798-0662 FAX
hws@sls.lib.il.us
http://homewoodlibrary.org
Cindy Rauch, Administrator
Mon–Fri 9:30–9:00, Sat 9:30–5:00

Illinois Veteran's Home Library
1707 North 12th Street
Quincy, IL 62301
(217) 222-8641, ext. 248; (217) 222-0139
FAX

Joliet Public Library
Information Services Department
150 North Ottawa Street
Joliet, IL 60432
(815) 740-2660; (815) 740-6161 FAX
http://joliet.lib.il.us
Mon–Fri 9:00–9:00, Sat 9:00–4:00, Sun
(except summer) 1:00–5:00

Kankakee Public Library
304 South Indiana Avenue
Kankakee, IL 60901
(815) 939-4564; (815) 939-9057 FAX
cfuerst@lions-online.org
http://www.lions-online.org
Cynthia Fuerst, Director
Mon–Thur 9:00–9:00, Fri 9:00–6:00, Sat
9:00–5:00

Knox College
Seymour Library
(2 Cedar Street—location)
PO Box 500x (mailing address)
Galesburg, IL 61401-0500
(309) 341-7246, ext. 491; (309) 343-9292
FAX
http://wwwlib.knox.edu

La Grange Public Library
10 West Cossitt
La Grange, IL 60525
(708) 352-0576, ext. 10; (708) 352-1620
FAX
moskals@lagrangelibrary.org;
lgs@lagrangelibrary.org
http://www.lagrangelibrary.org
Steve Moskal, Director

(specializes in La Grange, Illinois)

Lake County Museum
(At 176 and Fairfield Road—location)
27277 North Forest Preserve Drive (mailing address)
Wauconda, IL 60084-2016
(847) 525-7878; (847) 526-0024 FAX
Janet Gallimore
Pub. *The Postcard Journal* (not genealogical: popular culture)
(regional history archives)

Lake Villa Public Library District
1001 East Grand Avenue
Lake Villa, IL 60046
(847) 356-7711; (847) 265-9595 FAX
pkaplan@lvdl.org
http://www.lvdl.org
Michael Chatlien, Librarian; Paul Kaplan
Mon–Thur 9:00–9:00, Fri–Sat 9:00–5:00,
    Sun (except summer) 1:00–5:00
(local history)

Lewis University
(see Canal and Regional History Collection of Lewis University, above)

Lincoln Courtroom and Museum
101 West Third Street
Beardstown, IL 62618-1142
(217) 323-4191
Kermit Pilger
weekends by appointment
(local history)

Lincoln Library
Sangamon Valley Collection
326 South Seventh Street
Springfield, IL 62701-1691
(217) 753-4900; (217) 753-4910; (217) 753-5329 FAX
nancyh@rpls.lib.il.us

    http://lincolnlibrary.rpls.lib.il.us/llhome5.htm
Edward J. Russo, City Historian; Nancy Huntley
Mon–Thur 9:00–9:00, Fri 9:00–6:00, Sat 9:00–5:00
(central Illinois)

Lincolnwood Public Library District
4000 West Pratt Avenue
Lincolnwood, IL 60712
(847) 677-5277; (847) 677-1937 FAX
jhurwitz@lincolnwoodlibrary.org
http://www.lincolnwoodlibrary.org
Ruth Whitney; Jack Hurwitz, Director
Mon–Fri 10:00–5:00

Litchfield Carnegie Public Library
(400 North State Street—location)
PO Box 212 (mailing address)
Litchfield, IL 62056-0212
(217) 324-4841; (217) 324-3866; (217) 324-3884 FAX
Sara Zumwalt
Mon–Thur 10:00–8:00; Fri 10:00–5:00, Sat 10:00–2:00
("Repository of the collection of the late Walter R. Sanders, some 20,000 pages of research on the Sanders-Saunders family and on Montgomery County, Illinois, and surrounding area.")

Loyola University Archives
(see Women and Leadership Archives, Miscellaneous, Part 4)

Lyons Public Library
4209 Joliet Avenue

Lyons, IL 60534-1597
(708) 447-3577; (708) 447-3589 FAX
horns@sls.lib.il.us; lys@sls.lib.il.us
http://www.lyons.lib.il.us
Sarah Horn, Director
Mon–Fri 10:00–9:00, Sat 10:00–4:00, Sun (during school year) 1:00–4:00
(Illinois, local history/New England genealogy/passenger lists)

Macomb Public Library District
Local History/Genealogy Room
(235 South Lafayette Street—location)
PO Box 220 (mailing address)
Macomb, IL 61455-2231
(309) 833-2714 voice & FAX
library@macomb.com
Dennis Danowski

Manhattan Public Library
(240 Whitson—location)
PO Box 53 (mailing address)
Manhattan, IL 60442-0053
(815) 478-3374; (815) 478-3987; (815) 478-3988
jpet@manhattan.lib.il.us
http://www.manhattan.lib.il.us
Judy Pet, Director
Mon–Fri 9:00–4:00

Matson Public Library
15 Park Avenue West
Princeton, IL 61356-1927
(815) 875-1331; (815) 872-1376 FAX
birdcs@matsonpubliclibrary.org
http://www.matsonpubliclibrary.org
Carol Bird, Librarian
Mon–Thur noon–9:00, Tue–Thur (summer) noon–6:00, Fri 9:00–5:00, Sat noon–5:00;
    Museum: Mon & Wed–Sun 1:00–5:00, closed 24 Dec–31 Jan, Easter, Mother's Day, Thanksgiving
(houses collection of the Bureau County Genealogy Society)

Helen Matthes Library
100 Market Street
Effingham, IL 62401-3499
(217) 342-2413; (217) 342-2464 voice & FAX
amandas@effinghamlibrary.org
http://www.effinghamlibrary.org
Normalie Strickland, Director; Amanda Standerfer
winter: Mon–Thur 10:00–9:00, Fri 10:00–5:00, Sat 10:00–4:00; summer: Mon–Thur 10:00–8:00, Fri 10:00–5:00, Sat 10:00–1:00; genealogy assistance: Tue 1:00–3:00, Thur 10:00–noon
(emphasis on local and Illinois genealogy; houses DAR and genealogical society collections)

Mattoon Public Library
(1600 Charleston Avenue—location)
PO Box 809 (mailing address)
Mattoon, IL 61938-0809
(217) 234-2621; (217) 234-2660 FAX
Larry Oathout
Library: Sept–May: Mon–Fri 9:00–8:00, Sat 9:00–5:00; Local History Room: Mon–Sat 1:00–5:00, and by appointment
(limited access to items during temporary relocation for renovation)
research: $2.00 minimum; copies: 10¢ each

McHenry Public Library
809 North Front Street
McHenry, IL 60050-5528
(815) 385-0036; (815) 385-7085 FAX
akaspik@mchenrylibrary.org
http://www.mchenrylibrary.org

Arlene M. Kaspik, Executive Director

Mitchell Museum at Cedarhurst
(Richview Road—location)
PO Box 923 (mailing address)
Mount Vernon, IL 62864
(618) 242-1236; (618) 242-9530 FAX
Liz Hinman, Communications/Grants
Tue–Sat 10:00–5:00, Sun 1:00–5:00

Moline Public Library
(collection moved elsewhere)

Moody Bible Institue Library
820 North LaSalle
Chicago, IL 60610
(312) 329-4140

Morris Area Public Library
604 Liberty Street
Morris, IL 60450
(815) 942-6880; (815) 942-6415 FAX
pwilson@library.mornet.org
http://morris.lib.il.us
Deborah Steffes; Pamela Wilson, Librarian
Mon–Fri 10:00–9:00, Sat 10:00–4:00
("We collect basically information relative to Grundy County, Illinois.")

Morton Grove Public Library
6140 Lincoln Avenue
Morton Grove, IL 60053-2989
(847) 965-4220; (847) 965-7903 FAX
refdesk@webrary.org
http://www.webrary.org
Reference Coordinator
Mon–Thur 9:00–9:00, Fri 9:00–6:00, Sat 9:00–5:00, Sun (Sept–May) 1:00–5:00

John Mosser Public Library
106 West Meek Street
Abingdon, IL 61410-1451
(309) 462-3129 voice & FAX
j_mosser_pld@hotmail.com
Betsy Kisler

Mount Prospect Public Library
10 South Emerson Street
Mount Prospect, IL 60056-3251
(847) 253-5675; (847) 253-0642 FAX
annes@mppl.org
http://www.mppl.org
Anne V. Shaughnessy, Reference Librarian, History/Genealogy
Mon–Fri 9:00 A.M.–10:00 P.M., Sat 9:00–5:00, Sun noon–5:00
("Collection includes books, periodicals, microform, CD-ROMs, clippings, pamphlets, and online sources.")

Mundelein College Archives
(see Women and Leadership Archives, Miscellaneous, Part 4)

Museum Association of Douglas County
Douglas County Museum
700 South Main Street
Tuscola, IL 61953-1822
(217) 253-2535
lynnita@tuscola-il.com
http://www.dcmuseum-tuscola.org
Lynnita Brown, Administrator
Mon–Thur 9:00–4:00
Pub. *Cabin Chatter*, semiannually
(Douglas County history; genealogical materials and research assistant available; Korean War oral history interviews)
$15.00 per year membership

Naperville Public Libraries
Nichols Library
200 West Jefferson Avenue

Naperville, IL 60540-5374
(630) 961-4100; (630) 961-4119 FAX
dziedzic@lib.naperville.il.us
Margaret A. Brown, Head of Reference
  Services; Donna Dziedzic
Mon–Fri 9:00–9:00, Sat 9:00–5:00, Sun
  1:00–5:00

Newberry Library
60 West Walton Street
Chicago, IL 60610-3305
(312) 943-9090; (312) 255-3506
  (Reference); (312) 255-3512 (Genealogy)
genealogy@newberry.org
http://www.newberry.org/genealogyhome.
  html
David T. Thackery, Curator of Local and
  Family History
Tue–Thur 10:00–6:00, Fri–Sat 9:00–5:00
Pub. *Newberry Newsletter*, quarterly;
  *Origins: A Newsletter of the Local &
  Family History Section and the Family &
  Community Center at the Newberry
  Library*, quarterly
("North American local and family history;
  areas of strength include history of
  cartography and history of Native
  Americans.")
research: $7.0 for "Quick" search

North Park College
Archives Department
Library
3225 West Foster Avenue
Chicago, IL 60625
(312) 244-6224; (312) 267-2362 FAX
http://www.northpark.edu

Northwestern University Library
Special Collections-Archives
Evanston, IL 60201
(847) 492-3635

Oak Lawn Public Library
9427 South Raymond Avenue
Oak Lawn, IL 60453
(708) 422-4990; (708) 422-5061 FAX
drjbc92@lib.oak-lawn.il.us
http://www.lib.oak-lawn.il.us
Dr. James B. Casey, Director

Oak Park Public Library
834 Lake Street
Oak Park, IL 60301
(708) 383-8200; (708) 383-6384 FAX
ebyers@oppl.org
http://www.oppl.org
William Jerousek; Edward Byers, Director
Mon–Fri 9:00–9:00, Sat 9:00–5:00, Sun
  (Sept–May) 1:00–5:00

Odell Public Library
Whiteside County Genealogy Room
307 South Madison Street
Morrison, IL 61270
(815) 772-READ voice & FAX
odellpld@yahoo.com
Sharon Stahler
Mon–Sun

Oregon Township Library
Genealogy Room
300 Jefferson Street (South Third and
Jefferson Streets)
Oregon, IL 61061-1697
(815) 732-2724; (815) 732-6643 FAX
Beth McCormick
Mon–Thur 9:00–8:00, Fri–Sat 9:00–4:00
(houses material from the Ogle County
  Genealogical Society)

Oswego Public Library District

32 West Jefferson Street
Oswego, IL 60543-9078
(630) 554-3150; (630) 554-2975 FAX
saskil@oswego.lib.il.us;
  laheath@oswego.lib.il.us (Webmaster)
http://www.oswego.lib.il.us
Sarah Skilton, Director
Mon–Fri 9:00–9:00, Sat 9:00–5:00, Sun
  noon–4:00
(has genealogy and local history collections;
  depository for the Fox Valley
  Genealogical Society)

Park Forest Public Library
400 Lakewood Boulevard
Park Forest, IL 60466-1684
(708) 748-3731; (708) 748-8829 FAX
pfs@sslic.net
http://www.pfpl.org
Gretchen Falk, Head, Reference Department;
  Marcella Lucas, Administrative Librarian,
  Director
Mon–Thur 10:00–9:00, Fri 10:00–6:00, Sat
  10:00–5:00, Sun (Sept–May) 2:00–5:00

Parlin-Ingersoll Library
205 West Chestnut Street
Canton, IL 61520-2472
(309) 647-0328; (309) 647-8117 FAX
rwilson@parliningersoll.org
http://www.rsa.lib.il.us/~kbunner/parlin.htm
W. Randall Wilson
Mon–Fri 9:00–8:00, Sat 9:00–4:00, Sun
  1:00–4:00

Pekin Public Library
301 South Fourth Street
Pekin, IL 61554-4284
(309) 347-7111; (309) 347-6587 FAX
Laurie Hartshorn, Reference Librarian
Mon–Thur 9:00–9:00, Fri 9:00–6:00, Sat
  9:00–5:00; June–Aug: Mon–Thur
  9:00–8:00, Fri 9:00–6:00; June–July: Sat
  9:00–1:00
(emphasis on Tazewell County)
$5.00 fee for searches, but "extensive
  genealogical research is not available via
  mail"

Peoria Public Library
107 N.E. Monroe Street
Peoria, IL 61602-1070
(309) 497-2000; (309) 674-0116 FAX
http://www.peoria.lib.il.us/genealogy.htm
Susan Herring
Mon–Thur 9:00–9:00, Fri–Sat 9:00–6:00;
  summer: closed Sat
(Peoria and area history and genealogy
  collections)

Piatt County Museum
315 West Main
Monticello, IL 61856
(217) 762-4731
Lila Miller, Vice President
June–Oct: Sat–Sun 1:00–4:00
$15.00 per year membership

Plainfield Public Library
705 North Illinois Street
Plainfield, IL 60544
(815) 436-6639; (815) 439-2878 FAX
jmmilavec@plainfield.lib.il.us
http://plainfield.lib.il.us
Julie Milavec, Director
Mon–Thur 9:00–9:00, Fri–Sat 9:00–5:00,
  Sun (Labor Day–Memorial Day)
  1:00–5:00

Plano Community Library District
15 North Center Avenue
Plano, IL 60545

(630) 552-8003; (630) 552-1008
dhoward@plano.lib.il.us
http://plano.lib.il.us
Alesia Hacker, Assistant Director; Deanna
  Howard, Head Librarian
Mon–Thur 10:00–8:00, Fri 10:00–6:00, Sat
  10:00–4:00
photocopies: 10¢ each

Poplar Creek Public Library
1405 South Park Avenue
Streamwood, IL 60107-2997
(630) 837-6800; (630) 837-6823 FAX
p-hogan@poplarcreek.lib.il.us
Patricia M. Hogan, Director
Mon–Thur 9:00–9:30, Fri–Sat 9:00–5:00,
  Sun noon–5:00
(a small genealogical collection with a few
  local histories, no archival materials)

Quincy Museum
1601 Maine Street
Quincy, IL 62301-4264
(217) 224-7669; (217) 218-2817
Steve Adams
(county history)

Quincy Public Library
526 Jersey Street
Quincy, IL 62301-3996
(217) 223-1309; (217) 222-3052 FAX
sbeach@quincylibrary.org
Nancy Dolan, Head, Reference Department;
  Sue Beach
Tue after Labor Day to Sat before Memorial
  Day: Mon–Thur 9:00–9:00, Fri–Sat
  9:00–6:00, Sun 1:00–5:00; June–Aug:
  Mon 9:00–9:00, Tue–Sat 9:00–6:00

Randolph County Archives and Museum
1 Taylor Street
Chester, IL 62233-0332
(618) 826-3743; (618) 826-3750 FAX
Emily B. Lyons, Curator
Mon, Thur–Fri & Sun 12:30–3:30 by
  appointment
(Kaskaskia manuscripts, Native American,
  town and county artifacts)

Raupp Memorial Museum
(901 Dunham Lane—location)
530 Bernard Drive (mailing address)
Buffalo Grove, IL 60089
(847) 459-2318 (call ahead for hours of
  operation)
http://www.bgparkdistrict.org (then click on
  Raupp Museum)
Debbie Fandrei, Museum Coordinator
("Buffalo Grove is on the Lake County-Cook
  County dividing line, so some records
  may not be readily available." "Local
  history archives with information on local
  families, especially the Raupp and
  Weidner families.")
charges for copies

Sharon Reason-Keithsburg Museum
(14th and Washington—location)
PO Box 79 (mailing address)
Keithsburg, IL 61442-0079
(309) 374-2659
shareail@mcics.com
Sharon Reason, Founder and Curator (Also
  Mayor of the City of Keithsburg)
Mon–Fri 8:00–noon, Sun 1:00–4:00, and by
  appointment
("local history and Civil War history and
  cemetery records of all Mercer County
  cemeteries")
donation accepted

Reddick Library

1010 Canal Street
Ottawa, IL 61350-4998
(815) 434-0509; (815) 434-2634 FAX
vtrupiano@reddicklibrary.org
http://www.reddicklibrary.org
Vicky Trupiano, Director

Rend Lake College
Southern Illinois Room
Learning Resource Center
Rural Route 1
Ina, IL 62845-9801
(618) 437-5321, ext. 275
David Patton
Mon–Thur 7:45 A.M.–9:30 P.M., Fri
7:45–4:30, Sat 8:00–noon

Richland Heritage Museum Foundation
Carnegie Building Museum
(401 East Main Street—location)
PO Box 153 (mailing address)
Olney, IL 62450-1548
(618) 395-3893; (618) 397-5491
E. L. Bosomworth, President
(local and midwest artifacts history)

Robinson Public Library District
606 North Jefferson Street
Robinson, IL 62454-2699
(618) 544-3273; (618) 544-7172 FAX
rpladmin@shawls.lib.il.us
http://www.sirin.lib.il.us/docs/rob/docs/
lib/index.html
Marilyn Manning, Assistant Director
Mon–Thur 10:00–8:00, Fri–Sat 10:00–5:30;
summer: Mon 10:00–8:00, Tue–Sat
10:00–5:30
("A large collection of source materials for
Crawford County, Illinois, including
county histories, census, family histories,
historical folders, and a significant
number of books for other states.")

Rock Island Public Library
401 19th Street
Rock Island, IL 61201-8143
(309) 788-7627; (309) 788-6591 FAX
illrip@rbls.lib.il.us
http://www.rbls.lib.il.us/rbls/index.html
Katy Powers, Reference; Ava Ketter,
Director
winter: Mon–Thur 9:00–9:00, Fri–Sat
9:00–5:30; summer: Mon–Wed
9:00–9:00, Fri 9:00–5:30, Sat 9:00–1:00
research: $10.00 per hour plus copies and
postage

Rockford Public Library
215 North Wyman Street
Rockford, IL 61101-1023
(815) 965-6731, ext. 163; (815) 965-0866
FAX
webpage@rockfordpubliclibrary.org;
kvandrie@rockfordpubliclibrary.org
http://www.rpl.rockford.org
John L. Molyneaux; Karen Van Drie,
Executive Director
Mon–Wed & Fri 9:00–noon & 1:00–6:00,
Thur noon–5:00 & 6:00–9:00, Sat
1:00–5:00
(specializes in Illinois and the U.S., east of
the Mississippi)

Saint Charles Public Library District
1 South Sixth Avenue
Saint Charles, IL 60174-2195
(630) 584-0076; (630) 584-3448 FAX
dbrown@linc.lib.il.us
http://www.st-charles.lib.il.us (Genealogy
search requests can be made via this site)
Jill L. Culbertson, Adult Services Librarian
Mon–Thur 9:00–9:00, Fri 9:00–8:00, Sat

9:00–5:00, Sun noon–5:00, Sun
(June–Aug) 1:00–4:00; Kane County
Genealogical Society volunteers available
first and third Sat 2:00–4:00
("Collection emphasis on Saint Charles,
Kane County and Illinois.")

Sangamon Valley Collection
(see Lincoln Library, Part 2)

Sauk Valley Community College (SVCC)
Learning Resource Center (LRC)
173 Illinois Route 2
Dixon, IL 61021-9112
(815) 288-5511, ext. 306 or 247; (815) 288-
5651 FAX
Robert Thomas, Coordinator
(local history)

Schaumburg Township District Library
Local History Digital Archive
130 South Roselle Road
Schaumburg, IL 60193
(847) 985-4000; (847) 985-1454 FAX
akierna@stdl.org; mmadden@stdl.org
http://www.stdl.org
Tony Kierna, Genealogy; Michael J.
Madden, Director

Schuyler Jail Museum
Schuyler County Historical Museum and
Genealogical Center
200 South Congress
Rushville, IL 62681
(217) 322-6975
Evelyn Eifert, President
1 Apr–1 Nov: Mon–Sun 1:00–5:00; 1 Nov–1
Apr: Sat–Sun 1:00–5:00
Pub. *The Schuylerite*, quarterly
(much genealogical information on Schuyler
County, other counties and many states)
$15.00 per year membership; search: $5.00
per hour

Matthew T. Scott House
227 North First Street
Chenoa, IL 61726-1019
(815) 945-4555
Elaine Augspurgen, Caretaker
Thur & Sun 2:00–4:00, and by appointment
(local history)

Shabbona-Lee-Rollo Historical Museum
(119 West Comanche—location)
PO Box 334 (mailing address)
Shabbona, IL 60550
(815) 824-2759 voice & FAX
slrmuseum@aol.com
Carol Bend, Curator
Tue–Thur 9:00–11:00 & 1:00–3:00, Sat
9:00–11:00
Pub. *Shabbona-Lee-Rollo Historical
Museum Newsletter*, quarterly
(local history)
$5.00 per year membership

Spertus Museum
618 South Michigan Avenue
Chicago, IL 60605-1901
(312) 922-9012; (312) 922-6406 FAX

Staunton Public Library
George and Santina Sawyer Genealogy
Room
306 West Main
Staunton, IL 62088
(618) 635-3852; (618) 635-2246 FAX
ste@lcls.org
Judy Rosenthal
Mon–Thur 1:00–8:00, Fri–Sat 9:00–5:00

Conrad Sulzer Regional Library

Helen Zatterberg Historical Room
4455 North Lincoln Avenue
Chicago, IL 60625-2192
(312) 744-7616; (312) 744-2899 FAX
http://www.chipublib.org/002branches/
sulzer/sulzer.html
Glenn E. Humphreys, Special Collections
Librarian
by appointment
(emphasis on north side communities that
once made up the townships of Jefferson
and Lake View, annexed to Chicago in
1889, and those neighborhoods further
north and west that were annexed a few
years later, such as Rogers Park, Edison
Park, and Norwood Park)

Sycamore Library
Joiner History Room
103 East State Street
Sycamore, IL 60178
(815) 895-7271
joinerhistoryroom@co.de-kalb.il.us
Phyllis Kelley, County Historian
Tue & Thur 10:00–3:00
Pub. *The Joiner Room Journal*, three times
per year
(Atlases, maps, plat books, cemetery records,
church histories, city directories, county
and township histories, printed census,
Civil War discharges, commissioner's
papers 1837–1935, miscellaneous school
records, nurse's registry 1877–1983, poll
books 1859–1872, poor farm records,
family files and genealogies, Grand Army
of the Republic Roster Book, Illinois
Adjutant General's reports, obituaries
1860–1930, photo collection, manuscript
materials, newspapers 1867–1965; "A
cooperative effort of the DeKalb County
Board, DeKalb County Judiciary, DeKalb
County Finance Office, DeKalb County
Central Plant, and the DeKalb County
citizens concerned with safeguarding their
heritage as represented by the historical
documents in the collection.")

Thomson Depot Museum
(Main Street—location)
PO Box 392 (mailing address)
Thomson, IL 61285-0392
(815) 259-2155
Marian McKee
23 May–31 Oct: Sat–Sun 1:00–4:00 by
appointment
(historical library)

Three Rivers Public Library District
Local History Collection
Minooka Branch Library
(109 North Wabena—location)
PO Box 370 (mailing address)
Minooka, IL 60447
(815) 467-1600; (815) 467-1632 FAX
hkinder@htls.lib.il.us
http://three-rivers-library.org
Michele Houchens, Local History Clerk;
Herb Kinder, Branch Director
("Collection consists of information from the
local area only: Aux Sable Township,
Grundy County, Channahon Township,
Will County, and the villages of Minooka
and Channahon.")

University of Chicago
John Crerar Library
35 West 33rd Street
Chicago, IL 60616
(312) 225-2526
http://www.lib.uchicago.edu/e/crerar

University of Chicago

Joseph Regenstein Library
1100 East 57th Street
Chicago, IL 60637-1502
(773) 702-8442
http://www.lib.uchicago.edu/e/su/rel

University of Illinois
Illinois Historical Survey
346 Library
1408 West Gregory Drive
Urbana, IL 61801
(217) 333-1777; (217) 333-2214 FAX (care
of the Library)
jmhoffma@ux1.cso.uiuc.edu
http://gateway.library.uiuc.edu/ihx
John Hoffmann, Illinois Historical Survey
Librarian
Mon–Fri 8:30–5:00

University of Illinois
University Archives
1408 West Gregory Drive
Urbana, IL 61801
(217) 333-0798 (Archives); (217) 333-8400
(General Information); (217) 333-2579
(Newspaper Library); (217) 333-2214
FAX
illiarch@uiuc.edu; s-clark3@uiuc.edu
(Newspapers)
http://www.library.uiuc.edu
William Maher, University Archivist
Mon–Fri 8:30–5:00

Urbana Free Library
Champaign County Historical Archives
201 South Race Street
Urbana, IL 61801-3283
(217) 367-4057 (Executive Director); (217)
367-4025; (217) 367-4061 FAX
jkoch@ltnet.ltls.org; fschli@ltnet.ltls.org
http://urbanafreelibrary.org
Jean E. Koch, Archives Director; Frederick
A. Schlipf, Executive Director
Mon–Sat 9:00–5:00, Sun 1:00–5:00
Pub. *Champaign County Historical Archives
Historical Publications Series*, irregularly
(local history and genealogy, especially of
east-central Illinois)

Vermilion County Museum
116 North Gilbert Street
Danville, IL 61832-8506
(217) 442-2922; (217) 442-2001 FAX
Susan E. Richter, Curator
Tue–Sat 10:00–5:00, Sun 1:00–5:00
Pub. *Vermilion County Museum Society
Newsletter*, bimonthly; *Heritage of
Vermilion County Illinois*, quarterly
(local county history; Lincoln site on
National Register)
$20.00 per year membership

Vogel Genealogical Research Library
(305 North First Avenue—location)
PO Box 132 (mailing address)
Holcomb, IL 61043-0132
(815) 393-4110
Doris Glade Vogel, Librarian
daily 9:00–4:00 by appointment
("Ogle County, Illinois, holdings only.")
admission: donation

Warren County Public Library
60-62 Public Square
Monmouth, IL 61462-1756
(309) 734-3166; (309) 734-5955 FAX
wcpl@monmouthnet.net
http://www.misslink.net/warrenlibrary
Julian Bruening

Warren Newport Public Library
224 North O'Plaine Road

Gurnee, IL 60031-2696
(847) 244-5150; (847) 244-3499 FAX
sbero@wnpl.info
http://www.wnpl.alibrary.com
Ms. Lourdes Mordini, Head of Adult
Services; Stephen Bero, Director
Mon–Thur 9:00–9:00, Fri 9:00–6:00, Sat
9:00–5:00, Sun (Sept–May) 1:00–5:00

West Chicago City Museum
132 Main Street
West Chicago, IL 60185-2835
(630) 231-3376
sdefauw@westchicago.org
Sally DeFauw, Archivist
Mon–Fri 8:00–4:30, research by appointment
(specializes in greater West Chicago area:
selected individual family genealogy,
obituary files, cemetery transcriptions,
Civil War records, railroad workers
information, some census material,
newspapers)

**Western Illinois University, Western
Museum**
900 West Adams Street
Macomb, IL 61455-1396
(309) 298-1808
Mary McMullen, Supervisor
Mon–Fri 9:00–noon & 1:00–4:00
(local and university history)

Wheaton Public Library
225 North Cross Street
Wheaton, IL 60187-5376
(630) 668-1374; (630) 668-8950 FAX
http://www.wheaton.lib.il.us/library
Donna Freymark, Reference Librarian
Mon–Fri 9:00–9:00, Sat 9:00–5:00, Sun
(Sept–May) 1:00–5:00

Willard Library
(see Indiana, Part 2)

Wilmette Public Library
1242 Wilmette Avenue
Wilmette, IL 60091-2597
(847) 256-5025; (847) 256-6911 FAX
wilref@wilmette.lib.il.us
http://www.wilmette.lib.il.us
Ellen B. Clark, Head of Adult Services
Mon–Fri 9:00–9:00, Sat 9:00–5:00, Sun
1:00–5:00
("Some of the library's photographs are
available on the web at
www.digitalpast.org.")

Wilmington Public Library
201 South Kankakee Street
Wilmington, IL 60481
(815) 476-2834; (815) 476-7805
mjsoucie@wilmingtonlibrary.org
http://wilmingtonlibrary.org
Mary J. Soucie, Director
Mon–Thur 9:00–8:30, Fri–Sat 9:00–5:00
(Illinois Collection contains genealogical
materials, microfilm file of local
newspaper with index to obituaries)

**Winnetka-Northfield Public Library
District**
768 Oak Street
Winnetka, IL 60093-2583
(847) 446-7220; (847) 446-5085 FAX
barbaron@wpld.alibrary.com
http://www.wpld.alibrary.com
Barbara J. Aron
Mon–Thur 9:00–9:00, Fri–Sat 9:00–5:00,
Sun 1:00–5:00 (during school year)

Woodson Regional Library
Chicago Public Library

9525 South Halsted
Chicago, IL 60628
(312) 747-6900; (312) 747-3396 FAX
http://www.chipublib.org

Zion-Benton Public Library
2400 Gabriel Avenue
Zion, IL 60099-2297
(847) 623-3501; (847) 872-4680; (847) 872-
4942 FAX
nbhilyard@zblibrary.org
http://www.zblibrary.org
Nann Blaine Hilyard, Director
Mon–Thur 9:00–9:00, Fri 9:00–6:00, Sat
9:00–5:00

Historical Societies—Local and Regional

Addison Historical Commission
(operates Addison Historical Museum and
Century House)
Addison Historical Society
(129 and 135 Army Trail Road—location)
1 Friendship Plaza (mailing address)
Addison, IL 60101-2786
(630) 628-1433; (630) 543-5593 FAX
voa@AddisonAdvantage.org
http://www.AddisonAdvantage.org
Dolores Nielsen, Addison Historical
Commission Chairperson and Addison
Historical Society Board Member
Wed (June–Aug) noon–3:00, Sat 10:00–2:00
Pub. *The Salt Creek Tattler*, bimonthly
("Some family genealogies of this area,
census books for DuPage County 1840-
70, Soul registry from old Lutheran
churches, old county record books and
atlases, etc.")
$8.00 per year membership

Alton Area Historical Society, Inc
(239 West Elm Street—location)
PO Box 971 (mailing address)
Alton, IL 62002-0971
(618) 466-5853 (President)
Maitland A. Timmermiere, President
Pub. *AAHS Newsletter*, three times per year
$5.00 per year membership

**American West Research Center and
Historical Society, Inc.**
(see Ohio, Part 2)

Andover Historical Society
(418 Locust Street—location)
340 Fourth Street, Box 197 (mailing address)
Andover, IL 61233-0197
(309) 476-8378; (309) 476-8501
Doris L. Anderson
June–Aug: Sun 1:00–4:00, and by
appointment

**Historical Society and Museum of
Arlington Heights**
Arlington Heights Historical Museum
(110 West Fremont Street, Arlington Heights
60004-5912—museum location)
500 North Vail Avenue (society location and
mailing address)
Arlington Heights, IL 60004
(847) 255-1225 (Historial Society); (847)
255-1893 (Museum); (847) 255-1570
FAX (Museum)
Susan P. English, Museum Administrator
Library: Thur 1:00–4:00, Fri 9:00–noon
Pub. *Dunton Post*, monthly
$10.00 per year membership

Augustana Historical Society
Augustana College Library

Seventh Avenue and 35th Street
Rock Island, IL 61201-2210
(309) 794-7266
Loryann Eis, President
Pub. *Augustana Historical Society
Publications* (monograph series); *AHS
Newsletter*

Aurora Historical Society and Museum
(305 Cedar Street, corner of Oak and Cedar
Streets, Aurora, IL 60506—location)
317 Cedar Street (mailing address)
Aurora, IL 60507
(630) 897-9029
John Jaros, Director
Wed & Sat–Sun 1:00–5:00, and by
appointment
Pub. *McCarty Mills Gazette*
$35.00 per year membership

Avon Historical Society
(Avcom Park—North Edge of
Avon—location)
PO Box 483 (mailing address)
Avon, IL 61415-0483
(309) 465-3189; (309) 465-3043
Margaret Hickerson, President
first two weekends of Oct: 9:00–5:00

Barrington Area Historical Society
The Heritage Research Center
212 West Main Street
Barrington, IL 60010
(847) 381-1730
Michael J. Harkins, Executive Director;
Dean Maiben, Director Heritage Research
Center
Office: Mon–Fri 9:00–4:00 by appointment;
Museum: Thur–Fri 10:00–4:00, Sat
10:00–1:00
Pub. *Landmark Living Journal*
(area family and institutional manuscripts)

Bartlett Historical Society
(228 South Main Street—location)
PO Box 8257 (mailing address)
Bartlett, IL 60103-8257
Thomas Perkins, Jr.
Memorial Day–Labor Day: Mon–Fri
8:30–4:30, Sat 9:00–noon
(local history of Bartlett, Ontarioville and
some of Elgin)

Batavia Historical Society
(Batavia Depot Museum, 155 Houston
Street—location)
PO Box 14 (mailing address)
Batavia, IL 60510-0014
(630) 406-5274 Historical Society); (630)
879-5235 (Museum); (630) 879-9537
FAX (Museum)
Carla Hill
Mar–30 Nov: Mon, Wed & Fri–Sun
2:00–4:00 by appointment
Pub. *Historic Batavia*
(local history)

Beecher Community Historical Society
(Washington Township Museum, 673
Penfield—location)
PO Box 1469 (mailing address)
Beecher, IL 60401-1469
(708) 946-2198 (Society); (708) 946-6218
(Museum)
Paula Franke, President; Virginia Bath,
Museum
Wed 6:00 P.M.–8:00 P.M., Sat 9:00–11:00
(local history)

**Bellflower Genealogical and Historical
Society**
(see Genealogical Societies—Local and

Regional, below)

Bensenville Historical Society
(900 West Wood—location)
c/o Bensenville Library, 200 South Church
Road (mailing address)
Bensenville, IL 60106-2303
(630) 595-3742; (630) 766-4642 (Historical
Commission)
Patricia Johnson

Berwyn Historical Society
(Piper School, 2435 Kenilworth—location)
PO Box 479 (mailing address)
Berwyn, IL 60402-0479
(708) 484-0020
Sue Svec, President
by appointment
(local history)

Bishop Hill Heritage Association
Bishop Hill Heritage Museum
(103 North Bishop Hill Street—location)
PO Box 92 (mailing address)
Bishop Hill, IL 61419-0092
(309) 927-3899; (309) 927-3010 FAX
Crystle D. Clark, Museum Director
Mon–Fri 10:00–4:00
Pub. *Heritage Newsbulletin*, three to four
times per year
("Information on Bishop Hill and the
Swedish immigrants who founded it; we
have a library and an archives which
contains many documents and
photographs.")
$25.00–$500.00 membership; research fees
vary by time involved

Bloomingdale Historical Society
(Bloomingdale Public Library, 101 Fairfield
Way—location)
241 Driftwood Lane (mailing address)
Bloomingdale, IL 60108-1902
(630) 529-0787
Dolores P. Howe
June–Aug: Mon–Thur 9:00–9:00; Sept–May:
Fri–Sat 9:00–5:00, 1:00–5:00

Blue Island Historical Society
Blue Island Public Library
2433 York Street
Blue Island, IL 60406-2094
(708) 371-8546; (708) 388-1078 (Library);
(708) 388-1143 FAX (Library)
Richard May
Library: Mon–Thur noon–8:00, Fri–Sat
9:00–5:00
(history of Blue Island, Illinois)

Bolingbrook Historical Society
162 North Canyon Drive
Bolingbrook, IL 60440-1526
(630) 759-4974
Philip Hanson, President

Bond County Historical Society
1014 Asbury
Greenville, IL 62246-0172
(618) 664-3054
Dean Anthony, President
Library: Mon–Thur 2:00–8:00, Fri
noon–6:00, Sat 10:00–5:00
(Bond County, Illinois, research)
$10.00 per year membership

Boone County Historical Society
311 Whitney Boulevard
Belvidere, IL 61008-3609
(815) 544-8391 (Tue & Thur)
George A. Thomas, Museum Coordinator
Museum: Tue & Thur 9:00–3:00; May–Oct:
third Sun 2:00–5:00

Bourbonnais Grove Historical Society
(Stratford Drive at Illinois Route
102—location)
PO Box 311 (mailing address)
Bourbonnais, IL 60914-0311
(815) 933-2308; (815) 933-6452
James V. Johnson
first & third Sun 1:00–4:00 by appointment
(French-Canadian heritage, county pioneer
history)

Brimfield Historical Society
Brimfield Public Library
111 South Galena
Brimfield, IL 61517
(309) 446-3631; (309) 446-3670
Alfred Arnold
Tue–Fri 3:00–6:00, Wed 9:00–noon &
3:00–7:00, Thur 3:00–7:00

Brookfield Historical Society
8820½ Brookfield Avenue
Brookfield, IL 60513
(708) 485-3420
Sun 1:00–4:00; summer: second & fourth
Sun
Pub. *Grossdale Gazette*, quarterly
$7.50 per year membership

Bureau County Historical Society
Matson Public Library
109 Park Avenue, West
Princeton, IL 61356-1927
(815) 875-2184; (815) 875-1331 (Library);
(815) 875-1376 FAX (Library)
Barbara Hansen, Museum Director
Museum: Mon & Wed–Sun 1:00–5:00,
closed 24 Dec–31 Jan, Easter, Mother's
Day, Thanksgiving; Library: Mon–Thur
noon–9:00, Tue–Thur (summer)
noon–6:00, Fri 9:00–5:00, Sat noon–5:00

Bushnell Historical Society
Bushnell Recreation and Cultural Center
300 Miller Street
Bushnell, IL 61422
(309) 772-3782; (309) 772-3612
Donna Tracy, President
Mon–Fri 9:00–4:00 by appointment

Cairo Historical Association
Magnolia Manor
826 Charles Street
Cairo, IL 62914-1458
(618) 734-0201; (618) 734-3807
Carolyn Mayberry
Wed–Sat 9:00–5:00, Sun 1:00–5:00

Calhoun County Historical Society
(County Road, Second Floor of Farm Bureau
Building—location)
PO Box 46 (mailing address)
Hardin, IL 62047
(618) 576-2660 (after 5 P.M.)
Tina Pluester, Secretary-Treasurer
Wed 9:00–3:00
Pub. *Newsletter*, quarterly
$5.00 per year membership; research: $5.00
per hour

Calumet City Historical Society Museum
(760 Wentworth Avenue—location)
PO Box 1917 (mailing address)
Calumet City, IL 60409-3515
(708) 862-8662
Florence Steffel, President
Tue–Thur 1:00–4:00 by appointment

Cambridge Historical Society
Rural Route 2, Box 96
Cambridge, IL 61238-9633
(309) 937-2233 (Library)

Deb Edmund
meetings: last Wed

Carroll County Historical Society
107 West Broadway
Mount Carroll, IL 61053
(815) 244-3474
Susan Appel, President
by appointment

Cass County Illinois Historical/Genealogical Society
(109 South Front Street—location)
PO Box 91 (mailing address)
Virginia, IL 62691-0011
cchgs2002@hotmail.com
http://www.rootsweb.com/~ilcchgs
Linda Sinnock, President
Tue 1:00–4:00, Thur 6:00–9:00, Sat
    (May–Sept) 10:00–3:00
Pub. *The Historian*, quarterly (Mar, June,
    Sept, Dec)
(Cass County marriages, cemeteries, land
    records, 1840, 1850 and 1880 censuses,
    etc.)
$10.00 per year membership; research:
    donation plus copy cost

Catlin Historical Society
Catlin Heritage Museum
(210 North Paris Street—location)
PO Box 658 (mailing address)
Catlin, IL 61817-0658
(217) 427-5766
johncast@advancenet.net
http://www.rootsweb.com/~ilchs
Shirley Nesbitt, Museum Director; Sara Cast,
    President
Mon, Wed & Sat 9:00–noon & 1:00–4:00
Pub. *Catlin Historical Society Newsletter*,
    quarterly
(much genealogical information on the local
    level: obituaries, pictures, oral histories,
    history of people in the area, etc.)
$10.00 per year membership

Cedarville Area Historical Society
(Cherry Street—location)
PO Box 46 (mailing address)
Cedarville, IL 61013-0046
(815) 563-4523
Jane Goodspeed
Apr–Nov: Sat–Sun 1:00–4:00
(local history library)

Champaign County Historical Society
Urbana Free Library
201 South Race Street
Urbana, IL 61801-3283
(217) 367-4025 (Library)
Jean Gordon; Doris K. Hoskins, President
Library: Mon–Sat 9:00–5:00, Sun 1:00–5:00
$40.00 per year membership

Chapin Community Historical Society
Superior Street
Chapin, IL 62628
(217) 472-6216
Mary Smith
by appointment
(local and family history)

Chatsworth Historical Society
(424 East Locust Street—location)
PO Box 755 (mailing address)
Chatsworth, IL 60921-0755
(815) 635-3124
Richard A. Pearson, Chairman/President

Chicago and Northwestern Historical Society
8703 North Olcott Avenue

Niles, IL 60648-2023
(847) 794-5633
Walter Feret, Chair
(local history and genealogy)

Chicago Heights Historical Society
Chicago Heights Free Public Library
15th and Chicago Road
Chicago Heights, IL 60411
(708) 754-0323 (Library); (708) 754-0325
Barbara Paul
Library: Mon–Thur 9:00–9:00, Fri–Sat
    9:00–5:00, Sun (during the school year)
    1:00–5:00

Chicago Historical Society
1601 Clark Street at North Avenue
Chicago, IL 60614-9990
(312) 642-4600; (312) 642-5035, ext. 356;
    (312) 266-2077 FAX
info@chicagohistory.org
http://www.chicagohs.org
Library: Tue–Sat 9:30–4:30, subject to
    change, call for current hours
Pub. *Chicago History*, quarterly; *CHS Quick
    Hits* (free email subscription)
$40.00 per year membership; research: only
    very limited genealogical reference
    services via mail requests, but may change
    policy to discontinue this service

Chicago Lawn Historical Society
Chicago Lawn Library
6120 South Kedzie Avenue
Chicago, IL 60629-4638
(312) 582-8778; (312) 434-4790
Jack Klaus, President

Chillicothe Historical Society
(Old Rock Island Depot, Cedar and Third
Street—location)
PO Box 181 (mailing address)
Chillicothe, IL 61523-0181
(309) 274-2247; (309) 274-3440
Tom Landes
Mar–Dec: first Sat–Sun 1:00–4:00

Christian County Historical Society
(Route 29 and Route 48 East—location)
PO Box 254 (mailing address)
Taylorville, IL 62568-0254
(217) 824-6922; (217) 824-5807
Mary Ann E. Durbin, President
Apr–Nov: Wed–Sat 10:00–4:00, Sun
    1:00–4:00

Historical Society of Cicero
2423 South Austin Boulevard
Cicero, IL 60650-2695
(708) 652-8305; (708) 652-0156
Norma F. Zbasnik
by appointment during school hours,
    8:30–2:30

Clark County Historical Society and Museum
(Fourth and Maple—location)
PO Box 207 (mailing address)
Marshall, IL 62441-0207
(217) 826-6027; (217) 826-8089
Eleanor Macey
mid-May to mid-Sept: Sun 1:00–4:00

Clinton County Historical Society
1091 Franklin Street
Carlyle, IL 62231-1820
Memorial Day–Labor Day: second, third &
    fourth Thur 10:00–3:00, Sun 1:00–4:00
Pub. *Clinton County Historical Society
    Quarterly*; *Museum Newsletter*, quarterly
$8.00 per year membership

Coles County Historical Society
Greenwood School Museum
(800 Hayes Avenue—location)
PO Box 225 (mailing address)
Charleston, IL 61920-0441
(217) 345-6690; (217) 581-3310
Robert E. Hennings, President
Apr–May: Sat–Sun 1:00–3:00
Pub. *CCHS Newsletter*

Columbia Historical Society, Inc.
11562 Bluff Road
Columbia, IL 62236
(618) 281-5734; (618) 939-6652
Linda Maus, President

Crawford County Historical Society, Inc.
(North Lincoln Trail College Campus, on
Prison Road—location)
PO Box 554 (mailing address)
Robinson, IL 62454-0554
(618) 544-3087
oldcrawf@frsb.net
http://www.rootsweb.com/~ilcchs/index.
    html
Sue Jones, Secretary
Sun 2:00–4:00, and by appointment
Pub. *Ole Crawford*, quarterly
$10.00 per year membership

Cumberland County Historical and Genealogical Society of Illinois
PO Box 393
Greenup, IL 62428
Pub. *Happy Hunter*, semiannually

Cumberland County Historical Society
(address withheld upon request)
(almost no material for research)

Arnold Damen Historical and Preservation Society
1076 West Roosevelt Road
Chicago, IL 60608-1519
(312) 421-5900
Donald F. Rowe, President
by appointment
(archives)

Danvers Historical Society
118 West Park
Danvers, IL 61732
(309) 392-2042
Robert McAllister

Darien Historical Society
7422 Cass Avenue
Darien, IL 60561
(630) 969-5171, (630) 969-8257, (630) 964-
    7033
Edward Miller, President
first Sun 2:00–4:00
Pub. *Newsletter*, quarterly
("Official center of City of Darien"; one-
    room schoolhouse)
$6.00 per year membership

Deerfield Area Historical Society
(450 Kipling Place—location)
PO Box 520 (mailing address)
Deerfield, IL 60015
(847) 948-0680
Barbara McMahon
(local history, genealogy)

DeKalb County Historical-Genealogical Society
PO Box 295
Sycamore, IL 60178-0295
Henry Leonard, President
Pub. *"Cornsilk" of DeKalb County, Illinois*,
    quarterly

(Society works with the Joiner History
Archives in the county courthouse)
$15.00 per year membership

Des Plaines Historical Society
Museum
789 Pearson Street
Des Plaines, IL 60016-4506
(847) 391-5399; (847) 297-1710
Joy A. Matthiessen, Director
Mon–Fri 9:00–4:00, Sun 1:00–4:00
Pub. *Cobweb*, bimonthly
(City of Des Plaines and Maine Township in
Cook County, Illinois)
$12.50 per year membership

Dundee Township Historical Society, Inc.
426 Highland Avenue
Dundee, IL 60118-1225
(847) 428-6996 voice & FAX
Jack Wendt
Wed & Sun 2:00–4:00
$15.00 per year membership

DuPage County Historical Society
DuPage County Historical Museum
102 East Wesley Street
Wheaton, IL 60187-5321
(630) 682-7343
Patricia A. Wallace, Director
Pub. *DuPage Roots*

Dwight Historical Society
120 East Chippewa
Dwight, IL 60420
(815) 584-1865; (815) 584-2091
Tony Thorsen

Earlville Community Historical Society
(Earl Township Public Library, 205
Winthrop Street—location)
PO Box 420 (mailing address)
Earlville, IL 60518-0420
(815) 246-9543; (815) 246-9543 FAX
Maureen Corrigan, Librarian
(local history)

East Side Historical Society
(James P. Fitzgibbons Historical Museum,
9800 Avenue and Calumet Park
Fieldhouse—location)
3658 East 106th Street (mailing address)
Chicago, IL 60617-6611
(312) 721-7948; (312) 221-7349
Frank W. Stanley
Thur 1:00–4:00

Edgar County Historical Society
408-414 North Main Street
Paris, IL 61944-1549
(217) 463-5305
Linda A. Cary, President
Wed–Fri 9:00–4:00, Sun 1:30–3:30
Pub. *Tense Past Present Future*, quarterly
(spring, summer, fall, winter)
$7.50 per year membership

Edgebrook Historical Society
6173 North McClellan
Chicago, IL 60646-4013
(312) 631-2854; (312) 774-3914; (312) 631-
2379 FAX
Janet Stessl

Edgewater Historical Society
5358 North Ashland Avenue
Chicago, IL 60640
(773) 506-4849
bmayian@rcn.com
http://www.edgewaterhistory.org
Elizabeth Mayian, President
Sat 1:00–4:00 and selected Sun

$20.00 per year membership

Edwards County Historical Society
Edwards County Genealogical Society
212 West Main Street
Albion, IL 62806
(618) 445-2631; (618) 445-3969
Terry L. Harper, President
Thur 6:00 P.M.–10:00 P.M.
Pub. *Edwards County Historical Society
Publication*, quarterly
$7.00 per year membership

Effingham Regional Historical Society
PO Box 1166
Effingham, IL 62401

Elburn and Countryside Historical Society
(525 North Main—location)
PO Box 115 (mailing address)
Elburn, IL 60119-0115
(630) 365-6655 (Community Center)
Larry Kelly

Elgin Area Historical Society
360 Park Street
Elgin, IL 60120-4455
(847) 742-4248
Ann-Macon Smith, Museum Director
Wed–Sat noon–4:00; group tours and
research requests by appointment
Pub. *Crackerbarrel*, bimonthly
$20.00 per year membership; cost of
reproduction of photographs or
documents provided upon specific request

Elk Grove Historical Society
399 Biesterfield Road
Elk Grove Village, IL 60007-3625
(847) 439-3994
Philip H. Barry, Chairman
Pub. *EGHS Newsletter*

Elkhart Historical Society
(116 North Latham—location under
restoration)
PO Box 255 (mailing address)
Elkhart, IL 62634-0255
(217) 947-2238
Gillette Ransom

Elmwood Historical Society
Lorado Taft Museum
302 North Magnolia
Elmwood, IL 61529
(309) 742-7791; (309) 742-2431
Gene Shissler, President
Wed noon–4:00
$10.00 per year membership

Historical Society of Elmwood Park
Elmwood Park Public Library
1 Conti Parkway
Elmwood Park, IL 60707
(708) 395-1219
Russell Parker, President
Library: Mon–Thur 9:00–9:00, Fri 9:00–6:00
cost for copies

Evanston Historical Society
Charles Gates Dawes House
225 Greenwood Street
Evanston, IL 60201-4713
(847) 475-3410; (847) 475-3599 FAX
evanstonhs@northwestern.edu
http://www.evanstonhistorical.org
Lee Cabot, Director
House: Thur–Sun 1:00–5:00; Research:
Thur–Sat 2:00–5:00
Pub. *Time Lines*, quarterly
(Evanston newspapers from 1872, city
directories 1879–1963, manuscript

collections, city records)
$25.00 per year membership; house
admission: $5.00; research: $5.00

Evergreen Park Historical Society
3538 West 98th Street
Evergreen Park, IL 60642
Mathilda May

Fairmount-Jamaica Historical Society
116 South Main Street
Fairmount, IL 61841-9601
(217) 288-9278; (217) 733-2171
Edna Underwood, President
first Sat 9:00–11:00, and by appointment;
meetings: third Mon (except Aug)
$5.00 per year membership; admission: free

**Farmer City Genealogy and Historical
Society**
(see Genealogical Societies—Local and
Regional, below)

**Fayette County Genealogical and
Historical Society**
(see Genealogical Societies—Local and
Regional, below)

Fern Dell Historic Association
(502 Chicago Road—location)
PO Box 254 (mailing address)
Newark, IL 60541-0254
(815) 695-5328
Van Mathre, Treasurer
Pub. *FHA Newsletter*

Flagg Creek Historical Society
PO Box 227
Burr Ridge, IL 60525
(630) 246-6169; (630) 246-7365; (630) 246-
4142 (for Museum's seasonal hours)
Martha Mees, President
Flagg Creek Historical Museum,
Pleasantdale Park District, 7425 South
Wolf Road, Burr Ridge: first & third Sat
10:00–1:00

**Flagg Township Historical Society and
Museum**
(Sixth Street and Fourth Avenue—location)
1060 Westview Drive (mailing address)
Rochelle, IL 61068-1204
(815) 562-7423; (815) 562-4693
David Guest, President; Marguerite Thomas
Memorial Day–Labor Day: Sun 2:00–4:30,
and by appointment

Ford County Historical Society
(201 West State Street—location)
PO Box 115 (mailing address)
Paxton, IL 60957
(217) 379-4192
rabbit@illicom.net
http://genforum.genealogy.com/il/ford
Florence Elliott, Genealogist
by appointment
Pub. *Ford County Historical Messenger*,
bimonthly
(Ford County obituaries and microfilm of
newspapers from 1859)
$3.00 per year membership; research: contact
Florence Elliott at 351 South Market
Street, Paxton, IL 60957

Historical Society of Forest Park
(7555 Jackson Boulevard—location)
519 Jackson Boulevard (mailing address)
Forest Park, IL 60130-1896
(708) 771-7716
Frank Orland, President

Historical Society of the Fort Hill Country

(Fort Hill Heritage Museum, 601 Noel
Drive—location)
PO Box 582 (mailing address)
Mundelein, IL 60060
(847) 526-7566
Leonard J. Schmitt, President
Sat 1:00–4:00, and by appointment
Pub. *Newsletter*, monthly
(specializes in local history of the Fort Hill
area and other history: all of Fremont
Township, parts of Avon Township and
Libertyville Township)
$5.00 per year membership

**Fort LaMotte Genealogical and Historical
Society**
(see Genealogical Societies—Local and
Regional, below)

**Frankfort Area Historical Society and
Museum**
2000 East Saint Louis Street
West Frankfort, IL 62896-1647
(618) 932-6159 (Museum); (618) 937-4458
(Home)
Mary Alyce Kern
16 Dec–31 Jan: Wed–Thur 9:00–4:00, Sun
1:30–4:00

**Frankfort Area Historical Society of Will
County**
(132 Kansas Street—location)
PO Box 546 (mailing address)
Frankfort, IL 60423-0546
(815) 469-4534; (815) 469-6541
Judy K. Herder, President
Pub. *Frankfort Newsletter*

Franklin County Historical Society
803 North McLeansboro Street
Benton, IL 62812-2732
(618) 435-6947
Bobbie Armstrong, Secretary
(materials are in storage at this time)

Franklin Grove Area Historical Society
historical.society@franklingroveil.org
http://www.franklingroveil.org/histsoc.htm

**Freeburg Historical and Genealogical
Society**
(407 South Belleville—library location)
PO Box 69 (mailing address)
Freeburg, IL 62243-0069
(618) 539-5454
Kay Marshall
11:00–7:00
Pub. *Freeburg Historical Quarterly*
("Concentrate on area history.")
$10.00 per year membership

**Fulton County Historical and Genealogical
Society**
(45 North Park Drive—location)
PO Box 583 (mailing address)
Canton, IL 61520
(309) 647-0771
Marjorie R. Bordner, Ph.D., President
Parlin-Ingersoll Library: Mon–Fri
9:00–8:00, Sat 9:00–4:00, Sun 1:00–4:00
Pub. *Fulton County Historical and
Genealogical Society Newsletter*,
quarterly, $12.00 per year subscription
("Long list of published records available.")

**Galena/Jo Daviess County Historical
Society and Museum**
211 South Bench Street
Galena, IL 61036-2297
(815) 777-9129; (815) 777-9131 FAX
Daryl Watson, Ph.D., Executive Director
Museum: Mon–Sun 9:00–4:30

Pub. *Miners' Journal*, quarterly
(no research facilities, most genealogical
research materials kept at the Galena
Public Library)
$15.00 per year membership

Galewood-Mont Clare Historical Society
1705 North Nashville Avenue
Chicago, IL 60707-3904
(708) 395-1219
Russell N. Parker, Director
by appointment
(Chicago neighborhood history)

Gallacia Historical Society
PO Box 489
Gallacia, IL 62935
Jonathan Russell

Gallatin County Historical Society
PO Box 693
Shawneetown, IL 62984
(618) 269-3716
Lucille Lawler, Executive Director and
Secretary
Pub. *Gallatin County History and Families*

**Galva Historical Society/Wiley House
Museum**
(906 West Division Street—location)
PO Box 24 (mailing address)
Galva, IL 61434-0004
(309) 932-8992
http://galva.com/historicalsociety.php
Irving Anderson, President; Sally Nelson,
Corresponding Secretary
Mon–Tue & Thur–Fri 11:00–4:00, Sun
(Memorial Day to Labor Day) 1:00–4:30
Pub. *Historical Society Newsletter*, quarterly
(online)
$10.00 per year membership

**Garden Prairie Genealogical and
Historical Society**
(see Genealogical Societies—Local and
Regional, below)

Garfield Heritage Society
444 South LaGrange Road
LaGrange, IL 60525-2448
(708) 584-8485
Jerome Johnson, Executive Director
(local history)

Geneseo Historical Association
Geneseo Historical Museum
216 North State
Geneseo, IL 61254
(309) 944-3043; (309) 944-3248 (Curator's
home)
Donald Stocks, Curator
Mar–Dec: Sat–Sun 1:30–4:30, and by
appointment

Geneva Historical Society
(400 Wheeler Drive—location)
PO Box 345 (mailing address)
Geneva, IL 60134-0345
(630) 232-4951; (630) 232-4561
Lockett Ford Ballard, Jr., Executive Director
Apr–Oct: Wed–Sun 1:00–4:00; Research
Library: Mon–Fri 9:00–4:00

Glen Ellyn Historical Society
(557 Geneva Road, Glen Ellyn, IL
60137—location)
PO Box 283 (mailing address)
Glen Ellyn, IL 60138
(630) 858-8696 voice & FAX (Museum);
(630) 469-1867 (Archives)
historical@glen-ellyn.com
http://www.glen-ellyn.com/historical

Keith McClow, Executive Director
Museum: Tue, Wed & Sun 1:30–4:30;
Archives: Wed 1:00–5:00, Thur
7:00–9:00, and by special appointment
Pub. *The Messenger*, five times per year
(An 1850s-era museum called "Stacys
Tavern")
$15.00 per year membership

Glencoe Historical Society
(305 Randolph Street—location)
999 Green Bay Road (mailing address)
Glencoe, IL 60022-1263
(847) 835-4935; (847) 835-2638
Alice Glicksberg
Sept–Apr: second Sun 2:00–4:00; May: third
Sun 2:00–4:00, and by appointment

Glenview Area Historical Society
1121 Waukegan Road
Glenview, IL 60025-3036
(847) 724-2235
Tue 1:00–3:00, Sun 1:00–4:00
(Glenview area history only, limited
genealogy information; Naval Air Station-
Glenview, history when it was Curtiss-
Wright, 1929–1937, and as Naval Air
Station, 1937–1995)
$15.00 per year membership; research:
$25.00–$100.00

Golden Historical Society
PO Box 148
Golden, IL 62339-0148
(217) 696-4672; (217) 696-2583 (Curator)
Lois Reason, President
June–early Sept: Sun 1:00–4:00, and by
appointment

**Goode-Barren Historical-Genealogical
Society**
(201 East Callie Street—location)
PO Box 1024 (mailing address)
Sesser, IL 62884-0944
(618) 625-2851; (618) 625-5762
Clara Brown
Mon 10:00–1:00, Wed 10:00–3:00 by
appointment

Grayslake Historical Society
Grayslake Municipal Historical Museum
(164 Hawley Street—location)
PO Box 185 (mailing address)
Grayslake, IL 60030-0185
(847) 223-7663
Charlotte K. Renehan, President
Thur 9:00–2:00, second Sun 1:30–3:30
(local history)
$5.00 per year membership; admission:
donation to museum

**Greater Harvard Area Historical Society
(McHenry County)**
(308 North Hart Street—location)
PO Box 505 (mailing address)
Harvard, IL 60033-0505
(815) 943-6141
Elaine Fiducci, Curator; Selma Davidson,
President
18 May–16 Nov: Wed 9:30–11:30, Sun
1:30–4:00
Pub. *Newsletter*, semiannually
$10.00 per year membership

Historical Society of Greater Peotone
PO Box 87
Peotone, IL 60468-00087
(708) 258-3436; (708) 258-3320
Michael R. Morrison, President
research: donation plus copying

Greene County Historical and

Genealogical Society
(532 North Main Street—location)
PO Box 137 (mailing address)
Carrollton, IL 62016-0137
Barbara B. Daum, President
Wed & Fri 9:00–3:00, and by appointment
("historical museum and genealogical
library, local scope")
$10.00 per year membership; research: no
search fee; copies 50¢ from files

**Griggsville Area Genealogical and
Historical Society**
(see Genealogical Societies—Local and
Regional, below)

Grove Heritage Association
PO Box 484
Glenview, IL 60025-0484
(847) 299-6096

Grundy County Historical Society
PO Box 224
Morris, IL 60450-2329
Henry Barschdorf, President

Hamilton County Historical Society
205 North Washington Street
McLeansboro, IL 62859-1048
(618) 643-4203
Eugene Van Winkle
Museum on second floor of McCoy
    Memorial Library: Fri 1:00–4:00, and by
    appointment
(local history and genealogy)

Hampton Historical Society
(601 First Avenue—location)
PO Box 68 (mailing address)
Hampton, IL 61256
(309) 755-0362
Merlin A. Nelson, President
Museum: Sat–Sun (summer) 2:30–4:30
Pub. *Hampton Historical Society News*,
    quarterly
$10.00 per year membership

Hancock County Historical Society
(306 Walnut Street—location)
PO Box 68 (mailing address)
Carthage, IL 62321-0068
hancockhistory@yahoo.com
Donald Parker, Correspondent
Mon–Fri 9:00–3:00
Pub. *News of Yesteryear*, quarterly (Feb,
    Apr, July, Oct)
(local history and genealogy)
$10.00 per year membership; research: $8.00
    per hour plus 25¢ per copy

**The Hanover Park Ontarioville Historical
Commission**
2121 West Lake Street
Hanover Park, IL 60103-4398
(630) 372-4200
Cathy-Ann Romero, Assistant to the Village
    Manager

**Hardin County Historical and
Genealogical Society**
PO Box 72
Elizabethtown, IL 62931-0072
(618) 287-2361
Noel E. Hurford, Secretary
$9.00 per year membership

**Henderson County Historical Society
Museum**
Rural Route 1, Box 130
Oquawka, IL 61469-9711
Bill Allaman
Memorial Day–Labor Day: Sun & 4 July

1:30–4:40
(local history and genealogy)

Henry County Historical Society
PO Box 48
Bishop Hill, IL 61419-9999
(309) 927-3528
Maurice Martin, President
Museum: Mon–Sun 10:00–4:00

Henry Historical and Genealogical Society
610 North Street
Henry, IL 61537-1226
(309) 364-3272
Connie Swanson, President
City Library: Mon–Sat 1:00–5:00, Wed
    1:00–8:00
Pub. *Newsletter*, quarterly
(specializes in Marshall County, especially
    city of Henry)
$5.00 per year membership

Highland Historical Society
(1739 Broadway and 1464 Old Trenton
Road—location)
PO Box 51 (mailing address)
Highland, IL 62249-0051
(618) 654-6781; (618) 654-4259
Lynn Rehberger, President

Highland Park Historical Society
(326 Central Avenue—location)
PO Box 56 (mailing address)
Highland Park, IL 60035-0056
(847) 432-7090
Betty M. Mills, Executive Director
Tue–Fri 10:00–3:00, Sat–Sun 2:00–4:00
(local history)
$25.00 per year membership; research fees
    vary

Hinsdale Historical Society
(15 South Clay—location)
PO Box 336 (mailing address)
Hinsdale, IL 60521-0366
(630) 789-2600
info@HinsdaleHistory.org
http://www.hinsdalehistory.org
Sandy Williams, Archives Chairman
Wed 10:00–2:00, and by appointment
(people, places and events in Hinsdale)
research: donation

Historic Elsah Foundation
(51 Mills Street—location)
PO Box 117 (mailing address)
Elsah, IL 62028-0117
(618) 374-1059
Thur–Sun (Apr–Nov) 1:00–4:00
Pub. *Elsah History*, biannually
(no genealogy focus)
$10.00 per year membership

Homer Historical Society
(105 North Main Street—location)
Rural Route 1 (mailing address)
Homer, IL 61849-9801
(217) 896-2538
Crystal Allen, President

Homewood Historical Society
(2035 West 183rd Street—location)
PO Box 1144 (mailing address)
Homewood, IL 60430-1044
(708) 799-1896 (Museum); (708) 798-9535
    (Home)
Gerald Egdorf; Elaine Egdorf
Tue & Sat 1:00–3:00 by appointment

Hoopeston Historical Society
617 East Washington
Hoopeston, IL 60942-1659

(217) 283-7898
Tommy McMillan

**Hutsonville Historical Society and
Memorial Village**
10953 East 1825th Avenue
Hutsonville, IL 62433
http://www.rootsweb.com/~ilcchs/
    hutson_historical.html

Hyde Park Historical Society
5529 South Lake Park
Chicago, IL 60637-1718
(312) 493-1893; (312) 643-8053
information@hydeparkhistory.org
http://www.hydeparkhistory.org
Alice Schlessinger, President
Sat–Sun 2:00–4:00
Pub. *Hyde Park History*, quarterly
$25.00 per year membership; all volunteer
    organization

Illiana Genealogical and Historical Society
(see Genealogical Societies—Local and
Regional, below)

Iroquois County Historical Society
Old Courthouse Museum
103 West Cherry Street
Watseka, IL 60970-1524
(815) 432-2215
Marie Hanford, Executive Secretary
Mon–Fri 10:30–4:30, Sat–Sun 1:00–4:00
Pub. *Iroquois County Historical Society
    Newsletter*, monthly; *The Iroquois
    Stalker*, quarterly
(Iroquois County Genealogical Society is a
    division of the Iroquois County Historical
    Society.)
$5.00 per year membership (in Historical
    Society only)

Irving Park Historical Society
4200 West Irving Park Road
Chicago, IL 60641
(773) 777-2750
Richard Lang, President
first and third Sun 1:00–4:00
Pub. *Irving Park Review*, quarterly
(local history)
$15.00 per year membership

Itasca Historical Society
Itasca Historical Depot Museum
101 North Catalpa Avenue
Itasca, IL 60143-2050
(630) 773-3363; (630) 773-2257 (Society);
    (630) 250-7938 (Museum)
Joan Stinton, Curator
Summer: Sun 1:00–4:00; Sept–May: Sun
    1:00–3:00, and by appointment

Jackson County Historical Society
1616 Edith Street
Murphysboro, IL 62966-2543
(618) 684-3455
JCHS@globaleyes.net
http://home.globaleyes.net/loganmus
Kenneth Cochran, President
Wed–Fri noon–3:00, Thur 6:30–9:00 P.M.
Pub. *Jacksonian Ventilator*, quarterly
$18.00 per year membership

**Jacksonville Area Genealogical and
Historical Society**
(see Genealogical Societies—Local and
Regional, below)

**Jasper County Historical and Genealogical
Society, Inc.**
Newton Public Library
100 South Van Buren Street

Newton, IL 62448-1559
(618) 783-8141 (Library)
pencilpusher@psbnewton.com
Patty Huston, Genealogist; Sheryl Brinson,
   President
Mon–Sat 10:00–5:00
Pub. *Our Heritage*, monthly
$15.00 per year membership

Jefferson County Historical Society
PO Box 106
Mount Vernon, IL 62864-0106
(618) 242-5423; (618) 242-4337
John Howard

Jersey County Historical Society
601 North State Street
Jerseyville, IL 62052
(618) 498-3514
iriscot@yahoo.com
http://www.jerseyusa.net
$15.00 per year membership

Joliet Area Historical Society and Museum
(17 East Van Buren Street—location)
PO Box 477 (mailing address)
Joliet, IL 60431-1211
(815) 722-7003; (815) 726-7171
Dale T. Evans, President
Tue–Fri noon–3:00, Sat 10:00–2:00

Kankakee County Historical Society
801 South Eighth Avenue
Kankakee, IL 60901-4744
(815) 932-5279
museum@daily-journal.com
http://www.kankakeecountymuseum.com
Norman Stevens
Tue–Fri 10:00–4:00, Sat–Sun 1:00–4:00
Pub. *The Museum Journal*, quarterly
$10.00 per year museum membership

Kendall County Historical Society
(107 West Center Street—location)
PO Box 123 (mailing address)
Yorkville, IL 60560-0123
(630) 553-6777
Marilyn Seaton, Librarian
Wed 9:00–noon
Pub. *Historical Notes, The Newsletter of the
   KCHS*, quarterly, not available by
   subscription
$10.00 per year membership; research: $8.00
   for the first hour, $5.00 for each
   additional hour, plus postage and copies
   at 15¢ each

The Kenilworth Historical Society
415 Kenilworth Avenue
Kenilworth, IL 60043-1134
(847) 251-2565
kenilworthhistory@earthlink.net
Ray F. Drexler, President
Mon 9:00–4:30, Thur 9:00–noon, and by
   appointment
("History of village and its people, not a
   genealogical collection. We have some
   biographical information on Kenilworth
   residents.")
$25.00 per year membership

Kewanee Historical Society, Inc.
211 North Chestnut Street
Kewanee, IL 61443-2019
(309) 854-9701; (309) 853-4572
llock@hotmail.com
Larry Lock, Museum Director
Thur & Sat 1:30–4:00
(local history)

Kishwaukee Valley Heritage Society
(700 West Park Avenue, Highway 72

West—location)
PO Box 63 (mailing address)
Genoa, IL 60135
(815) 784-5498
Jo Ann Watson, President
1 May–1 Oct: Wed & Sat 1:00–4:00;
   Apr–Nov: second Sun 2:00–4:00
$5.00 per year membership

Knox County Historical Society
PO Box 1757
Galesburg, IL 61402-1757
jward@knox.edu
http://knoxchs.homestead.com
Joel Ward, President
Pub. *Bulletin*, quarterly
$10.00 per year membership

LaGrange Area Historical Society
444 South LaGrange Road
LaGrange, IL 60525-2448
(708) 482-4248
Alice Petrik
Wed 9:30–noon, last Sun 1:00–4:00

**LaHarpe Historical and Genealogical
Society**
(East Main Street—location)
PO Box 289 (mailing address)
LaHarpe, IL 61450
Ada Hubbard, Vice President; Lois
   Bradshaw, Secretary
Museum: Mon & Sat 9:00–11:00 &
   1:00–4:00
Pub. *Historical Society Newsletter*, quarterly
$9.00 per year membership

Lake Forest College Library
Archives and Special Collections
Donnelley Library
Sheridan and College Roads
Lake Forest, IL 60045-2399
(847) 735-5064; (847) 735-5056 or 5074
   (for hours)
amiller@lakeforest.edu
Arthur Miller, Archivist and Librarian for
   special Collections
hours: change with academic calendar
("Family histories [Scotish; Chicago & Lake
   Forest social elite]; alumni & faculty,
   Lake Forest Univ./Col. 1857 to present")

Lake Forest-Lake Bluff Historical Society
361 East Westminster
Lake Forest, IL 60045
(847) 234-5253; (847) 234-5236 FAX
info@lflbhistory.org
http://www.lflbhistory.org
Janna Bennett, Collections Manager
Tue–Thur & Sun 1:00–4:00
$20.00 per year membership

Lakes Region Historical Society
(817-965-977-983 Main Street—location)
PO Box 240 (mailing address)
Antioch, IL 60002-0240
(847) 395-0899
Robert M. Lindblad, President
Sat 11:00–3:00
Pub. *Newsletter*, six times per year (Feb,
   Apr, May, June, Sept, Oct)
("Restoring oldest building in Antioch [1863
   church] to original look.")
$3.00 per year membership; research: $10.00
   minimum

Lansing Historical Museum and Society
(2750 Indiana Avenue—location)
PO Box 1776 (mailing address)
Lansing, IL 60438-2226
(708) 474-6160; (708) 474-9384
Betty Humphrey, Curator; Richard W.

Tereba, President
Mon 6:00–8:00, Wed 10:00–noon, Sun
   (Sept–May) 10:00–noon

LaSalle County Historical Society
(Museum, Canal and Union Streets, along
   Illinois/Michigan Canal—location)
PO Box 278 (mailing address)
Utica, IL 61373-0278
(815) 667-4861
Mary Toraason, Director
Winter: Fri–Sun noon–4:00; summer:
   Wed–Fri 10:00–4:00, Sat–Sun noon–4:00
(library)

Lawrence County Historical Society
(11th and State—location)
PO Box 511 (mailing address)
Lawrenceville, IL 62439-0511
(618) 943-2300
Michael Neal, President
$3.00 per year membership

Lebanon Historical Society
309 West Saint Louis Street
Lebanon, IL 62254-1516
(618) 537-4498
Harrison Church

Lee County Historical Society
(113 Madison Avenue—location)
PO Box 58 (mailing address)
Dixon, IL 61021-0058
(815) 284-1134
http://www.leecountyhistory.com
Stella Grobe, Treasurer
Tue, Thur & Sat 9:00–3:00
Pub. *Memories of Yesteryear*, annually;
   Historical Society Newsletter, nine times
   per year (monthly, except June–Aug)
$25.00 per year membership; research:
   $12.00 per hour

Lee County Iowa Historical Society
(see Iowa, Part 2)

Lemont Area Historical Society Museum
(306 Lemont Street—location)
PO Box 126 (mailing address)
Lemont, IL 60439-0126
(630) 257-2972 voice & FAX
knovak1111@aol.com
http://www.township.com/lemont/historical
Barbara Bannon; Kenneth Novak, Head of
   Committee
Tue (Summer only) & Thur–Fri 10:00–2:00,
   Sat–Sun 1:00–4:00
Pub. *'Cornerstone'*, bimonthly
(local history, genealogy)
$10.00 per year membership; library
   admission: $5.00 for nonmembers, plus
   $5.00 per hour for use of microfilm
   reader, photocopies: 25¢ per page, photos:
   $15.00 per print (8" x 11" or smaller;
   research: $5.00 per item or $20.00 for first
   three hours, $10.00 for each additional
   hour (includes travel time to other
   facilities)

Lena Area Historical Society
(427 West Grove Street—location)
PO Box 620 (mailing address)
Lena, IL 61048
(815) 369-2215; (815) 369-4555
Wieland Kayser; Margaret Scholtz
Sat–Sun 1:00–4:00 by appointment

LeRoy Historical Society
301 East Cedar
LeRoy, IL 61752
John Tompkins, President
Pub. *Heritage of the Prairie*

Lexington Genealogical and Historical Society
(see Genealogical Societies—Local and Regional, below)

Leyden Historical Society
PO Box 506
Franklin Park, IL 60131
(847) 678-1929; (847) 455-4269
Daniel Pritchett

Libertyville-Mundelein Historical Society, Inc.
Cook Memorial Library
413 North Milwaukee Avenue
Libertyville, IL 60048-2280
(847) 362-3130; (847) 362-2330 (Library); (847) 362-2354 FAX (Library)
jules@cooklib.org (Library)
http://www.cooklib.org (Library)
Douglass D. Getchell, Jr.
Sun (June–Aug) 2:00–4:00, first two weekends in Dec: 1:00–5:00
Pub. *Newsletter*, monthly
(interested in The Ansel B. Cook Victorian Museum)
from $5.00 per year membership

The Lisle Heritage Society
Lisle Station Park
919 Burlington
Lisle, IL 60532
(630) 968-2747
Edgar L. Land, President

Livingston County Historical Society
(Jones House, 314 East Madison Street and Catherine V. Yost Museum, 298 West Water Street—location)
PO Box 680 (mailing address)
Pontiac, IL 61764-0999
(815) 844-3457
Laura Sellmyer, President

Lombard Historical Society
23 West Maple Street
Lombard, IL 60148-2512
(630) 629-1885
Joel Van Haaften, Interim Director
staffed full-time; Tours: Wed–Sat & Sun 1:00–4:00, and by appointment
Pub. *Lombard Historical Society Newsletter*, quarterly
$10.00 per year membership

Long Grove Historical Society
Historical Lane
Long Grove, IL 60047
(847) 634-6155
May–Dec: second Wed & third Sun 10:00–2:00

Lyndon Historical Society
(405 First Street—location)
PO Box 112 (mailing address)
Lyndon, IL 61261-0112
(815) 778-4511
L. Gene Harrington, President

Lyons Historical Commission
(3910 Barry Point Road—location)
PO Box 392 (mailing address)
Lyons, IL 60534-0392
(708) 447-4215
Catherine Bergman, Secretary
by appointment
(local history)

Mackinaw Historical Society
Rural Route 1, Box 260
Mackinaw, IL 61755-9637
(309) 359-4001

Ross Coil, President

Macon County Historical Society
5580 North Fork Road
Decatur, IL 62521-1859
(217) 422-4919
Mary C. Talbott, Director
Museum: Tue–Sun 1:00–4:00; Office: Mon–Fri 8:00–4:30
Pub. *MCHS Newsletter*, monthly
(Macon County and Decatur)
$15.00 per year membership

Macoupin County Historical Society
(Breckenridge Street—location)
PO Box 432 (mailing address)
Carlinville, IL 62626-0432
(217) 854-3939; (217) 854-8916

http://www.rootsweb.com/~ilmacoup/m_h
stsoc.htm
Lucy Klaus
Wed (Mar–Nov) 10:00–2:00, Sun (June–Aug) 1:00–5:00

Madison County Historical Society
Madison County Historical Museum
715 North Main Street
Edwardsville, IL 62025
(618) 656-7562
http://library.wustl.edu/~spec/archives/
aslaamadison-historical.html
Mrs. Marion Sperling, Librarian
Wed–Fri 9:00–4:00, Sun 1:00–4:00, and groups by appointment
Pub. *Museum News*, two times per year
(Madison County area history and genealogy)
$10.00 per year membership in Historical Society, $100.00 per year membership in James Madison Society

Maine West Historical Society
Main West High School
Socieal Science Department
1755 South Wolf Road
Des Plaines, IL 60018-1994
(847) 827-6176

Manhattan Township Historical Society
(Manhattan Public Library—location)
15921 West Baker Road (mailing address)
Manhattan, IL 60442
Janet Werner, President
meetings: Apr, May, Sept, Oct
("Preserve artifacts, history of village. Near nonexisting—lack of interest among youth.")

Manito Historical Society
PO Box 304
Manito, IL 61546-0304
(309) 968-6985
Donna Thompson, President
Pub. *Jail House Key*, monthly
$5.00 per year membership

Manteno Historical Society
192 West Third
Manteno, IL 60950-1104
(815) 468-3480; (815) 468-8002
Wendell Marr, President
by appointment
(local history and genealogy)

Maquon Historical Association
(South end of West Street—location)
PO Box 93 (mailing address)
Maquon, IL 61458-0093
(309) 875-3481; (309) 875-3342
Beulah Donaldson, Secretary; Robert Bird

Marion County Genealogical and Historical Society
(see Genealogical Societies—Local and Regional, below)

Marissa Historical and Genealogical Society
(610 South Main Street—location)
PO Box 47 (mailing address)
Marissa, IL 62257-0047
(618) 295-2562
Elda L. Jones, Vice President
Wed 1:00–4:00, and anytime by appointment
Pub. *Branching Out from Saint Clair County, Illinois*, quarterly (Nov, Feb, May, Aug)
$15.00 per year membership

Marshall County Historical Society
(314 Fifth Street—location)
PO Box 123 (mailing address)
Lacon, IL 61540-0123
(309) 246-2349; (309) 246-6565
http://www.rootsweb.com/~ilmarsha/
mphs.htm
Eleanor H. Bussell, Curator
Mon–Fri mornings
Pub. *Newsletter*, quarterly
(genealogy searches for Marshall County)
$10.00 per year membership

Mascoutah Historical Society
(3 West Main Street—location)
504 North Jefferson Street (mailing address)
Mascoutah, IL 62258-1421
Carol Klopmeyer, President
Pub. *Newsletter*, intermittently

Mason County Genealogical and Historical Society
(see Genealogical Societies—Local and Regional, below)

Massac County Historical Society
405 Market Street
Metropolis, IL 62960
Paul E. Fellows, Secretary
Mon & Fri–Sun noon–5:00
Pub. *News Letter*, semiannually
$10.00 per year membership; research: "We do not do genealogical research. I will, personally, search newspapers (only) for family data as I have a thorough knowledge of the county newspaper files. My fee is $5.00 per hour plus copying costs."

Matteson Historical Society
813 School Avenue
Matteson, IL 60443-1849
(708) 748-3033; (708) 748-2326 FAX
lrmathis@lincolnnet.net
Deanna M. Lovell, Director
Mon–Tue 9:00–5:00, Sat 1:00–3:00
Pub. *The Matteson Bell*, four times per year
$7.50 per year membership

McDonough County Historical Society
(address withheld upon request)

McHenry County Historical Society
(6422 Main Street—location)
PO Box 434 (mailing address)
Union, IL 60180-0434
(815) 923-2267; (815) 923-2271 FAX
info@mchsonline.org
http://www.mchsonline.org
Nancy J. Fike, Museum Administrator
Library: Tue–Fri 9:00–4:30 by appointment; Museum (May–Oct): Tue–Fri & Sun 1:00–4:00
Pub. *The Tracer*, quarterly

("Strictly McHenry County history and genealogy: obituary files, biography files, maps, pictures, abstracts, Bibles, club/organization history, diaries.")
$12.50 per year membership; library admission: $1.00 per hour plus copy costs for nonmembers; research: no extensive genealogy research by mail

McLean County Historical Society
Genealogical Library
Old Courthouse, 200 North Main Street
Bloomington, IL 61701-3912
(309) 827-0428; (309) 827-0100 FAX
mcmh@mchistory.org;
    library@mchistory.org
http://www.mchistory.org (McLean County Museum of History)
Greg Koos, Executive Director; Bill Steinbacher-Kemp (Library)
Museum: Mon & Wed–Sat 10:00–5:00, Tue 10:00–9:00, Sun (Sept–May) 1:00–5:00
$30.00 per year membership; museum admission: $2.00 for nonmember adults

Melrose Park Historical Society
801 Broadway
Melrose Park, IL 60160
(708) 343-3391
Pat Italia; Carmilla Pope
meetings: third Wed 1:50
$7.00 per year membership

Menard County Historical Society
125 South Seventh Street
Petersburg, IL 62675-1554
(217) 632-7363; (217) 636-8310
Jeanne Crain Weaver, Genealogist
Mon, Wed & Fri 8:30–1:00

Mercer County Historical Society
1406 S.E. Second Avenue
Aledo, IL 61231-2504
(309) 582-2280; (309) 582-7463 (Curator)
Ruth Giffin, Curator
Apr–Oct: Wed & Sat–Sun 1:00–5:00, and by appointment
$5.00 per year membership

Meredosia Area Historical Society
(Main Street—location)
PO Box 304 (mailing address)
Meredosia, IL 62665-0304
(217) 584-1356; (217) 584-1281; (217) 584-1571 FAX
Dora Dawson
Tue–Wed & Fri–Sun 1:00–5:00

Midlothian Historical Society
(14609 Springfield—location)
14801 Pulaski (mailing address)
Midlothian, IL 60445
(708) 389-0200; (708) 389-0055; (708) 389-0255 FAX
Deborah J. McAdams
first & third Sat 11:00–2:00

Monroe County Historical Society
(700 South Church Street—location)
PO Box 48 (mailing address)
Waterloo, IL 62298-0048
(618) 281-8789
Patricia Vaseska, President
by appointment
(local history and genealogy)

Historical Society of Montgomery County
Solomon Harkey House
(South Broad Street—location)
904 South Main (mailing address)
Hillsboro, IL 62049-1738
(217) 532-3329; (217) 532-2958

Idabel Evans

Morrison Historical Society
PO Box 1
Morrison, IL 61270-0001
(815) 772-3287
Sat–Sun 1:00–4:00, and by appointment
(most of genealogical collection is duplicated by Odell Public Library)
$10.00 per year membership

Morrisonville Historical Society
(606 Carlin Street—location)
PO Box 227 (mailing address)
Morrisonville, IL 62546-0227
(217) 526-3543
Dorothy Bullard, President
by appointment

Morton Grove Historical Society
Morton Grove Historical Museum (Haupt-Yehl House)
(Harrer Park, 6240 Dempster Street—location)
PO Box 542 (mailing address)
Morton Grove, IL 60053-2946
(847) 965-7185; (847) 965-7447 (Park)
Fred N. Huscher, Coordinator
Wed 11:00–3:00, Sun 2:00–4:00

Moultrie County Historical and Genealogical Society
Moultrie County Historical and Genealogical Research Library
(Heritage Center, 117 East Harrison—location)
PO Box 588 (mailing address)
Sullivan, IL 61951-0588
(217) 728-4085
Sue Durbin, Genealogist
Mon & Sat 1:00–5:00
Pub. *Moultrie County Heritage*, quarterly; *Moultrie County Historical and Genealogical Society Newsletter*, monthly
$9.00 per year membership

Mound City Civic and Historical Association
314 Main Street
Mound City, IL 62963-1128
Frederick Winkler

Mount Greenwood Historical Society
11010 South Kedzie Avenue
Chicago, IL 60655-2222
(312) 239-2805; (847) 747-0148 (Library)
Bonnie Azeling, President
(local history library)

Mount Prospect Historical Society Museum
(1100 South Linneman Road—location)
101 South Maple (mailing address)
Mount Prospect, IL 60056-0081
(847) 392-9006; (847) 956-6777
Michelle Oberly

Mount Pulaski Township Historical Society
(108 South Washington Street—museum location)
104 East Cooke Street (mailing address)
Mount Pulaski, IL 62548
Phyllis Bryson, President; Tom and Waneta Stephens, Editors
Sept–May: Thur–Sat 1:00–4:00; June–Aug: Tue–Sat 1:00–4:00
Pub. *Mt. Pulaski Township Historical Society*, quarterly
$15.00 per year membership; free queries

Moweaqua Area Historical Society

(130 West Main Street—location)
103 Birch Street (mailing address)
Moweaqua, IL 62550-1301
(217) 768-3228
Howard Knight, Secretary
by appointment; meetings at Society Building: third Tue 7:00
("There are two separate museums: (1) Coal Mine, (2) Historical Society.")
$10.00 per year membership

Mulkeytown Area Historical Society
PO Box 485
Mulkeytown, IL 62865
Sarah Furlow, Secretary

Nauvoo Historical Society
(1380 Mulholland Street—location)
PO Box 69 (mailing address)
Nauvoo, IL 62354-0338
(217) 453-2528
Mary Logan, President
1 May–31 Oct: 9:00–5:00
Pub. *Nauvoo Historical Society Newsletter*, quarterly
(operates three facilities: restored home museum, Resource Center, and a museum undergoing restoration)
$5.00 per year membership; research: $4.00 per hour

Neponset Township Historical Society/Museum
Neponset, IL 61345
(309) 594-2197

New Boston Historical Society and Museum
(202 Main Street—location)
PO Box 284 (mailing address)
New Boston, IL 61272-0284
(309) 587-8640; (309) 587-8181 voice & FAX
Peggie Puckett; Cindy Marston
Apr–Oct: Sat–Sun 1:00–5:00

New Lenox Area Historical Society
205 West Maple Street
New Lenox, IL 60451-1741
(815) 485-9647; (815) 485-5576
Mark C. Batson, President
by appointment
Pub. *New Lenox Then and Now*, monthly
$12.00 per year membership

Newport Township Historical Society
(Wadsworth Road—location)
PO Box 98 (mailing address)
Wadsworth, IL 60083-0098
(847) 623-0939
Grace Shields, President

Niles Historical Society
8970 Milwaukee Avenue
Niles, IL 60714-1737
(847) 390-0160; (847) 647-0185 (fourth Sun)
Marilyn Brumbach, President
Wed & Fri 10:30–3:00, fourth Sun (Feb–Oct) 2:00–4:00
Pub. *Niles Historical Society Newsletter*, ten times per year

Northbrook Historical Society
(1776 Walters Avenue—location)
PO Box 2021 (mailing address)
Northbrook, IL 60065-2021
(847) 498-3404
Judith Hughes, President
Thur 10:00–2:00, Sun 2:00–4:00
("Extensive local sources, genealogy.")

Heritage League of Northwest Illinois
c/o Stockton Public Library-Lower Level
140 West Benton Street
Stockton, IL 61085-1312
(815) 947-2435; (815) 947-2030 (Library)
Patricia Nagel, Curator
Sat 1:00–3:00, and by appointment

Norwood Park Historical Society
5624 North Newark Avenue
Chicago, IL 60631-3533
(773) 631-4633
Susan Kroll, President
Sat noon–4:00, and by appointment
Pub. *The Journal of the Norwood Park
   Historical Society*, quarterly
$20.00 per year membership

Oak Brook Historical Society
PO Box 3821
Oak Brook, IL 60522-3821
(630) 654-2982; (630) 833-8154
Arlene Birkhahn, President

Oak Forest Historical Society
15440 South Central Avenue
Oak Forest, IL 60452-2104
(708) 687-4050
LaVerne Schultz

Oak Lawn Historical Society
(9526 South Cook Avenue—location)
4332 West 109th Street (mailing address)
Oak Lawn, IL 60453

**Historical Society of Oak Park and River
Forest**
(217 Home Avenue, Oak Park, IL
   60302—location)
PO Box 771 (mailing address)
Oak Park, IL 60303-0771
(708) 848-6755
Frank Lipo, Executive Director
Research: Tue & Thur; Tours: Thur–Sun
   P.M.
Pub. *Village Yesteryears*, bimonthly
$25.00 per year membership

Oakland Historical Foundation
(Corner of Washington and Walnut
Streets—location)
PO Box 431 (mailing address)
Oakland, IL 61943-0431
(217) 346-3274; (217) 346-3365
June Johnson; Zora Moore
May–Sept: Sat–Sun 1:00–4:00, and by
   appointment
(history from churches)

**Odell Prairie Trails Genealogical and
Historical Society**
(see Genealogical Societies—Local and
Regional, below)

O'Fallon Historical Society
PO Box 344
O'Fallon, IL 62269-0344
(618) 632-5216 (President)
http://www.ofallon.com/museum/index.
   shtml
Berneice T. Reidelberger, President

Ogle County Historical Society
(Sixth and Franklin Streets—location)
PO Box 183 (mailing address)
Oregon, IL 61061-0183
(815) 732-6876 (Mrs. Wood)
Mrs. Leonard Wood, Board Member
May–Oct: Thur 9:00 A.M.–11:00 A.M., Sun
   1:00–4:00; tours by request
Pub. *Ogle County Historical Society
   "Gazette,"* quarterly

$10.00 per year membership; research: $5.00
   plus copy costs

Oglesby Historical Society
(128 West Walnut Street—location)
100 Oak Street (mailing address)
Oglesby, IL 61348
(815) 883-3619
Evelyn Moyle
Mon, Wed & Fri 10:00–5:00, Tue, Thur &
   Sat 12:30–5:00, Tue–Thur 6:00–8:00

Old Six Mile Historical Society
(3279 Maryville Road—location)
PO Box 483 (mailing address)
Granite City, IL 62040-0483
Georgia Engelke, Curator
Sun 1:00–4:00, special tours by appointment

Olmsted Historical Society
PO Box 64
Olmsted, IL 62970-0064
(618) 342-6416; (618) 742-8194
Jeanne Edwards

Orland Historical Society
PO Box 324
Orland Park, IL 60462-0324
(708) 349-0065
Don Gee

Oswegoland Heritage Association
(72 Polk Street—location)
PO Box 23 (mailing address)
Oswego, IL 60543
(630) 554-2999
Judith A. Wheeler, President of the Board
(collection for genealogical research on
   Kendall County families; Oswego history
   and genealogy, school material)
$5.00 per year membership

Palatine Historical Society
(Clayson House Museum, 224 East Palatine
Road, Palatine, IL 60067—location)
PO Box 134 (mailing address)
Palatine, IL 60078-0134
(847) 991-6460
Marilyn Pedersen, Museum Coordinator
Tue & Thur 10:00–4:00, Sun 1:30–4:30
Pub. *Palatine Palaver*, four times per year
$10.00 per year membership

Palestine Historical Society
413 South Lincoln
Palestine, IL 62451

Palos Heights Historical Society
City of Palos Heights
7607 College Drive
Palos Heights, IL 60463

Palos Historical Society
c/o Palos Park Library
12330 Forest Glen Boulevard
Palos Park, IL 60464
(708) 361-3118; (708) 448-1410
John Rogers, Curator
Tue 9:00–1:00, and by appointment
$7.50 per year membership

Park Forest Historical Society
Park Forest Public Library
400 Lakewood Boulevard
Park Forest, IL 60466-1684
(708) 748-3731 (Library); (708) 748-8829
   FAX (Library)
Jane Nicoll, Archivist; Mr. Magne B. Olson,
   President
Library: Mon–Thur 10:00–9:00, Fri
   10:00–6:00, Sat 10:00–5:00, Sun
   (Sept–May) 2:00–5:00

Pub. *Prologue*, occasionally
$10.00 per year membership

Park Ridge Historical Society
41 West Prairie Avenue
Park Ridge, IL 60068
(847) 696-1973
Mar–Dec: Sat 10:00–1:00
$10.00 per year membership

Pecatonica Historical Society
PO Box 298
Pecatonica, IL 61063-0599
Jane Nabor, Treasurer

Peoria Historical Society
c/o Bradley University
Special Collections Center/Cullum Davis
Library
1501 West Bradley
Peoria, IL 61625
(309) 677-2822 (Library); (309) 677-2823
   (Library); (309) 677-2827 FAX (Library)
Charles Frey
Library: Mon–Fri 9:00–noon & 1:00–4:30
Pub. *PHS Newsletter*

Perry County Historical Society
Perry County Jail Museum
108 West Jackson Street
Pinkneyville, IL 62274
(618) 357-2225
http://www.fnbpville.com/perrycounty.html
Jean Ibendahl
Mon 9:00–4:00, Sat 10:00–3:00, Sun
   1:30–5:00
Pub. *Newsletter*, monthly
$10.00 per year membership

**Piatt County Historical and Genealogical
Society**
(Courthouse Annex, 301 South Charter
Street—location)
PO Box 111 (mailing address)
Monticello, IL 61856-0111
http://www.monticello.net/genealogy.html
Librarian
Mon & Wed 1:00–4:00
Pub. *Piatt County Historical and
   Genealogical Society Newsletter*,
   quarterly
("Mostly Piatt County.")
$10.00 per year membership; research:
   $10.00 plus copies at 15¢ per page

**Pike County Historical Society and
Museum**
(400 Block of East Jefferson—location)
PO Box 44 (mailing address)
Pittsfield, IL 62363-0044
(217) 285-4618
Elizabeth L. Lacy, Museum Director
Fri–Sat 10:00–4:00, Sun 1:00–4:00, and by
   appointment
Pub. *Pike County Historical Society
   Newsletter* ("does not cover genealogy at
   this time")
$10.00 per year membership; donation for
   search (not included in membership)

Piper City Community Historical Society
39 West Main
Piper City, IL 60959
(815) 686-2414; (815) 686-9234
Skip Ficklin, Curator
first Sat (June–Sept) 9:30–11:30, and by
   appointment

Plainfield Historical Society Museum
217 East Main Street
Plainfield, IL 60544
(815) 436-4073

Miette Rutten, Museum Director
Sat 1:00–4:00

Polo Historical Society
125 North Franklin Street
Polo, IL 61064-1506
(815) 946-2716
Keith McGuire, President

Pope County Historical Society
(Main Street—location)
PO Box 837 (mailing address)
Golconda, IL 62938-0387
(618) 683-7551; (618) 683-3050
Paul Trovillion; Mabel Trovillion

Prairie Historians
PO Box 301
Waltonville, IL 62894
meetings in the Waltonville Universalist
    Church: fourth Tue (Mar, June, Sept) 7:30
    P.M., first Tue (Dec) 7:30 P.M.
Pub. *Prairie Historian*, quarterly (Mar, June,
    Sept, Dec)
$6.00 per year membership

Historical Association of Princeville
(130 North Walnut—location)
325 North Ostrom Avenue (mailing address)
Princeville, IL 61559-9538
(309) 385-2394
Finch Stowell
May–Oct: Sat 9:00–11:00, and by
    appointment

Prophetstown Area Historical Society
320 Washington Street
Prophetstown, IL 61277
(815) 537-2818; (815) 537-2668
Dick Sommers; Mary Sommers
Sat 10:00–noon by appointment
(local history and genealogy)

Putnam County Historical Society
Route 26 and Power Road
Hennepin, IL 61327
(815) 925-7560
Julia S. Edgerley, President
Tue–Wed & Fri 9:00–3:00
Pub. *Putnam Past Times*, quarterly ("mostly
    current happenings")
(30,000 indexed names for genealogists)
$10.00 biyearly membership; research: $5.00
    per hour

**Historical Society of Quincy and Adams
County**
425 South 12th Street
Quincy, IL 62301-4303
(217) 222-1835
http://library.wustl.edu/~spec/archives/
    aslaa/quincy.html
Philip Germann, Executive Director
Mon–Fri 10:00–2:00

Randolph County Historical Society
104 Hillcrest Drive
Chester, IL 62233-2250
(618) 826-2667 voice & FAX
Emily B. Lyons, Curator, Randolph County
    Archives and Museum
by appointment
Pub. *Footprints*
(Charter Oak School; Fr & Am Creole House
    in Prairie du Rocher)
$10.00 per year membership; research:
    donation if possible

**Ravenswood-Lake View Historical
Association**
Conrad Sulzer Regional Library
Historical Room

4455 North Lincoln Avenue
Chicago, IL 60625-2192
(312) 744-7616; (312) 744-2899 FAX
Glenn E. Humphreys, Special Collections
    Librarian
by appointment
Pub. *RLVHA Newsletter*, irregularly
(history of neighborhoods on Chicago's
    North Side)
$3.00 per year general membership

**Richland County Illinois Genealogical and
Historical Society**
(see Genealogical Societies—Local and
Regional, below)

Ridge Historical Society
10621 South Seeley Avenue
Chicago, IL 60643-2618
(773) 881-1675 (recorded message)
Sue H. Delves, President
Thur & Sun 2:00–5:00, and by appointment
Pub. *RHS NewsLetter*, bimonthly
(stories of people in Beverly/Morgan Park in
    Chicago's far southwest corner, 1850
    onward; research into community's rich
    architectural heritage)
from $20.00 per year membership

River Grove Historical Commission
(2621 Thatcher Avenue—location)
2561 North Budd Street (mailing address)
River Grove, IL 60171-1736
(708) 453-8000
Loretta Page

Riverdale Historical Society
c/o Riverdale Library
208 West 144th Street
Riverdale, IL 60627-2788
(708) 841-3311
Mary Thillman
Mon & Wed–Thur 9:30–8:00, Tue
    10:00–2:00, Fri 9:30–6:00, Sat 9:30–4:00,
    Sun 11:00–3:00

Riverside Historical Commission
Riverside Historical Museum
27 Riverside Road
Riverside Village, IL 60546-2264
(708) 447-2542 (Museum)
riversidehistory@aol.com
Suzanne Bartholomew, Chairman
Sat 10:00–2:00
charge for copies

Robbins Historical Society
(13822 South Central Park
    Avenue—location)
PO Box 1561 (mailing address)
Robbins, IL 60472-1561
(708) 389-5393; (708) 385-8940
Tyrone Haymore
10:00–4:30

Rock Island County Historical Society
Rock Island County Historical Research
Library
822 11th Avenue
Moline, IL 61266-0632
(309) 764-8590
Lloyd Efflandt, President; N. Lucille
    Sampson, Archivist
Mon & Thur–Sat 9:00–5:00, Sun (last Sun in
    May–first Sun in Dec) 1:30–4:30, closed
    Christmas and New Year's weeks
Pub. *Rock Island County Historical Society
    Newsletter*, semiannually
("John H. Hauberg Collection, Belgian Book
    Collection, oral tapes, photographs,
    family collections, books and manuscripts
    that fit our purpose: to collect, preserve

and disseminate Rock Island County
    history.")
$15.00 per year membership; research:
    $10.00 per hour plus photocopying

Rockford Historical Society
Rockford Museum Association
6799 Guilford Road
Rockford, IL 61107-2613
(815) 962-6993
Eldora Ozanne, Secretary

Rockton Township Historical Society
PO Box 22
Rockton, IL 61072
(815) 624-4541
Hester Bigelow
1 June–15 Sept: Sun 1:00–4:00; Dec: first
    Sun by appointment

Rogers Park/West Ridge Historical Society
6424 North Western
Chicago, IL 60645-5422
(312) 764-4078; (312) 764-2401; (312) 274-
    7297 FAX
Mary Jo Doyle, Executive Director
Mon, Wed & Fri 10:00–5:00, Thur 7:00
    P.M.–9:00 P.M.

Romeoville Historical Society
Fountaindale Library
Romeo Road
Romeoville, IL 60441
Dorothy Hassert
first & fourth Thur 7:00 P.M.–9:00 P.M., and
    by appointment

Roselle Historical Foundation
102 South Prospect Street
Roselle, IL 60172-2026
(630) 351-5300; (630) 351-5417
Joseph L. Devlin, Administrator
10:00–3:00; Museum: Sun 2:00–4:00, and
    by appointment
Pub. *Etched in Time*, every five to six years,
    $20.00 per issue for hardcover, $12.00 per
    issue for paperback

Rossville Historical Society
(108 West Attica Street—location)
PO Box 263 (mailing address)
Rossville, IL 60963
(217) 748-6194 (President); (217) 748-6625
    (First Vice President)
Eva V. Neeland, President; Tom Cornell,
    First Vice President
Tue–Sat noon–4:00; monthly meetings
Pub. *Ross/South Ross Ramblings*, quarterly
(family local histories, cemetery books)
$2.00 per year membership; quries: free for
    members; research: $5.00 per hour

Saint Charles Heritage Center
(Dunham Hunt Museum of the Saint Charles
Heritage Center, 304 Cedar
Avenue—location)
2 East Main Street (mailing address)
Saint Charles, IL 60174
(630) 584-6967; (630) 443-6733 (Museum);
    (630) 377-4487 FAX
Karen Ponton, Administrator
Tue–Sun (June–Aug) noon–4:00, and by
    appointment
Pub. *The Charlemange*, quarterly
$25.00 per year membership; Junior
    Historical Society for children aged 7-14
    years, free with family membership, or
    $10.00 per year; admission: free; local
    historical research service:
    $100.00–$150.00 minimum

Saint Clair County Historical Society

(602 Fulton Street—location)
Victorian Museum-Home
701 East Washington Street (mailing address)
Belleville, IL 62220-3846
(618) 234-0600
http://library.wustl.edu/~spec/archives/aslaa/stclair_historical.html
Norma Walker, Office Administrator
Museum: Mon–Fri 10:00–2:00, Sun 2:00–4:00
Pub. *Saint Clair County Historical Society Journal*

Sandwich Historical Society
(Lafayette and Railroad Streets—location)
PO Box 82 (mailing address)
Sandwich, IL 60548
(815) 786-7936; (815) 786-2092
Roger Peterson, President
May–Oct: Sun 1:00–4:00

Sangamon County Historical Society
308 East Adams
Springfield, IL 62701
(217) 522-2500

Schiller Park Historical Society
(4200 Old River Road—location)
9526 Irving Park Road (mailing address)
Schiller Park, IL 60176
(847) 671-8513; (847) 678-6444; (847) 678-0567 FAX (Schiller Park Library)
June Oulund, Chairman
Mon 9:00–noon by appointment, second Sun 1:00–5:00
research: $10.00 per hour

Scott County Historical Society
PO Box 85
Winchester, IL 62694-0085
(217) 742-5575
John Rutherford
10:00–4:00

Sheffield Historical Society
Washington and Cook Streets
Sheffield, IL 61361
(815) 454-2788; (815) 454-2686
Margaret B. Schmitt
Tue–Sun noon–4:00

Shelby County Historical and Genealogical Society
(151 South Washington Street—location)
PO Box 286 (mailing address)
Shelbyville, IL 62565
(217) 774-2260
shgensoc@bmmhnet.com
http://www.bmmhnet.com/shgensoc
June McCain, Vice President and Librarian
Apr–Oct: Mon–Sat 10:00–4:00; Nov–Mar: Mon & Fri–Sat 10:00–4:00
Pub. *Shelby County Ancestors*, quarterly; *Shelby County Historical and Genealogical Society Newsletter*, four times per year
$15.00 per year membership

Sidell Community Historical Society
PO Box 42
Sidell, IL 61876
(217) 288-9030
Clifford Guthrie
by appointment

Sidney Historical Society
1985 CR 600 North
Sidney, IL 61877
(217) 688-2974
Carol Erb
by appointment

Skokie Historical Society
8031 Floral Avenue
Skokie, IL 60077
(847) 673-1888
Tue–Sat noon–4:00
Pub. *Bell Ringer*, quarterly
research: $10.00 per hour

South Beloit Historical Society
440 Oak Grove Avenue
South Beloit, IL 61080-1949
Charles Novachek

South Holland Historical Society
(16250 Wausau Avenue—location)
PO Box 48 (mailing address)
South Holland, IL 60473-0048
(708) 596-2722
Pauline Schaap, President
Sat 1:00–4:00
Pub. *Ohionskin*, quarterly
$5.00 per year membership

South Shore Historical Society
7566 South Shore Drive
Chicago, IL 60649
(773) 375-1699

South Suburban Genealogical and Historical Society
(see Genealogical Societies—Local and Regional, below)

The South Suburban Heritage Association
17130 67th Court
Tinley Park, IL 60477
(708) 614-8713
June M. Staackmann, Executive Director
Pub. *The Heritage Trail*, semiannually
(for the "preservation and dissemination of the history and heritage of Chicago's south and southwest suburbs")
$15.00 per year membership

Stark County Historical Society
(318 West Jefferson Street—location)
PO Box 524 (mailing address)
Toulon, IL 61483
(309) 286-7139; (309) 896-4532
Norman Black
June–Aug: Sun 1:00–5:00 by appointment
(historical home)

Stephenson County Historical Society
1440 South Carroll Avenue
Freeport, IL 61032-6530
(815) 232-4819
Lyall Taubert, President
Fri–Sun 1:00–4:00
(museum only, no archives)

Stephenson County Historical Society
1440 South Carroll Avenue
Freeport, IL 61032
(815) 232-8419; (815) 297-0313 FAX
Director@stephCoHS.org
http://www.stephcohs.org/index.htm

Sterling-Rock Falls Historical Society Museum
(1005 East Third Street—location)
PO Box 65 (mailing address)
Sterling, IL 61081-0065
(815) 622-6215
Terence Buckaloo, Museum Curator; Tim Keller, President of Society
Museum: Tue, Thur & Sat 10:00–noon & 1:00–4:00, Sun 1:00–5:00
Pub. *Newsletter*, monthly (except Dec & summer)
(Whiteside County history)
$10.00 per year membership

Stone Park Historical Association
1629 North Mannhiem Road
Stone Park, IL 60165-1118
(708) 345-2272
George Danda, Chair
(local history)

Streamwood Historical Society
777 West Bartlett Road
Streamwood, IL 60107-1394
(630) 289-3276

Streatorland Historical Society, Inc.
306 South Vermillion Street
Streator, IL 61364-2940
(815) 672-2443
Patricia Breen, Director
Mon–Fri 10:00–3:00, Sun 1:00–4:00
Pub. *Unionville Dispatch*, monthly
from $12.00 per year membership

Sugar Grove Historical Society
(259 Main Street—location)
PO Box 102 (mailing address)
Sugar Grove, IL 60554-0102
(630) 466-9726
Ruth B. Frantz, Treasurer
by appointment
("Sugar Grove Township, Kane County, Illinois, history and genealogy. We have the records of the two cemeteries in the township.")

Tazewell Genealogical and Historical Society
(see Genealogical Societies—Local and Regional, below)

Thebes Historical Society
PO Box 14
Thebes, IL 62990-0014
(618) 764-2600

Thornton Township Historical Society
Genealogical Section
(154 East 154th Street, Harvey, IL 60426—location)
66 Water Street (mailing address)
Park Forest, IL 60466
(708) 596-2000, ext. 356; (708) 481-6628
Dave Bartlett, President
Oct–June: first Sat
$5.00 per year membership

Tilton Historical Society
201 West Fifth Street
Tilton, IL 61833-7427
(217) 354-4832 (Charles Montgomery) (217) 442-7312 (Oscar Boyd)
Betty Montgomery; Charles Montgomery; Oscar Boyd
Thur 9:00–noon, and by appointment
(local history and genealogy)
$3.00 per year

Tinley Park Historical Society
(formerly Bremen Historical Society of Tinley Park)
(6727 West 174th Street—location)
PO Box 325 (mailing address)
Tinley Park, IL 60477-0325
(708) 429-4210
lrtphist@lincolnnet.net
Brad L. Bettenhausen, President
Wed 10:00–2:00, and by appointment
Pub. *New Bremen News* (formerly *Tinley Towne Crier*), quarterly
("Museum and research materials related primarily to the history of the Village of Bremen (a.k.a. New Bremen, now Tinley Park) and surrounding area in Bremen, Orland, and Rich townships in Cook

County, and Frankfort Township in Will
County.")
$20.00 per year membership

Tremont Museum and Historical Society
(Madison and South Sampson
Streets—location)
PO Box 738 (mailing address)
Tremont, IL 61568-0738
(309) 925-5262; (309) 925-3453
Janis Lee, President
second Sun 2:00–4:00, and by appointment
Pub. *Tales and Trails*, five times per year
(archives)
$10.00 per year membership

Tri-Township Heritage Association
306 Lime Street
Albany, IL 61230
Helen Hanson, Secretary
(genealogical services)

Triton Community History Organization
Triton College
2000 Fifth Avenue
River Grove, IL 60171-1995
(708) 456-0300, ext. 245
Florence Weese
Mon–Fri 8:00–4:00
(local history, college archives)

**Union County Historical and Genealogy
Society**
104 Clemens
Cobden, IL 62920
Patrick Brumleve, President
Pub. *Friends of the Union County Historical
and Genealogy Society*, three times per
year
$10.00 per year membership

The Urban History Association
c/o Department of History
Lake Forest College
Lake Forest, IL 60045
Michael H. Ebner, Executive Secretary

Vandalia Historical Society
307 North Sixth
Vandalia, IL 62471-2236
(618) 283-0024
Mary Burtschi, Vice President

**Versailles Area Genealogical and
Historical Society**
(see Genealogical Societies—Local and
Regional, below)

Villa Park Historical Society, Inc.
220 South Villa Avenue
Villa Park, IL 60181-2222
(630) 941-0223; (630) 834-9278
Gail McGrew
Tue–Fri 2:00–6:00, Sat–Sun 10:00–4:00

Village of Thornton Historical Society
(208 Schwab Street—location)
PO Box 34 (mailing address)
Thornton, IL 60476-0034
(708) 877-9394; (708) 877-8942
Freda Rietveld, Curator
May–Oct: Sat 1:00–4:00 by appointment

Warren County Historical Society
RR 2
Avon, IL 61415
(309) 465-3361
parrish@maplecity.com
30 May–1 Sept: Mon–Sun 1:00–5:00 by
appointment

Warrenville Historical Society

(3 South 530 Second Street—location)
PO Box 311 (mailing address)
Warrenville, IL 60555-0311
(630) 393-3335
Marge Duller
Mar–Dec: Wed & Sat–Sun 1:00–4:00;
Jan–Feb: by appointment

Warsaw Historical Society and Museum
401 Main Street
Warsaw, IL 62379-1246
Martha Zumwalt, President; Helen Seggelke,
Secretary
1 Apr–1 Nov: 2:00–5:00, and special
occasions, and by appointment
$3.00 per year membership

Historical Society of Washington County
(326 South Kaskaskia Street—location)
PO Box 9 (mailing address)
Nashville, IL 62263-0009
(618) 327-8953
Harrl Beatty

Washington Historical Society
(101 and 105 Zinser Place—location)
PO Box 54 (mailing address)
Washington, IL 61571
(309) 444-4239; (309) 444-2668
Marguerite Lucas, President
Wed–Sat 10:00–4:00

Wauconda Township Historical Society
(711 North Main Street—location)
PO Box 256 (mailing address)
Wauconda, IL 60084-0256
(847) 526-9303
Helen Funk, President
Sun afternoons in summer by appointment
Pub. *WTHS Newsletter*
(Lake County, Illinois, history)
$10.00 per year membership

Waukegan Historical Society
The Haines Museum
1917 North Sheridan Road
Waukegan, IL 60087-5131
(847) 336-1859 (Museum); (847) 360-4772
(Research Library)
Deb Fandrei, Volunteer Coordinator
Museum: Wed–Fri 10:00–2:30, third
weekend 1:00–3:00
Pub. *Historically Speaking*, quarterly
(also large photo archives)
$15.00 per year membership; photocopies:
25¢ per page; research: time free

**Waverly Genealogical and Historical
Society**
(see Genealogical Societies—Local and
Regional, below)

Wayne County Historical Society
300 S.E. Second Street
Fairfield, IL 62837
(618) 842-4701 (evening); (618) 842-5323
Carl Meeks

West Chicago Historical Society
Kruse House Museum
(527 Main Street—location)
PO Box 246 (mailing address)
West Chicago, IL 60186
(630) 231-0564; (630) 231-8472
Merle L. Burleigh, Public Relations
Coordinator
Sat (May–Sept) 11:00–3:00
("House Museum—Kruse/Burchert
Families")
$7.00 per year membership

West Side Historical Society

115 South Pulaski Road
Chicago, IL 60624

Westchester Historical Society
10332 Bond Street
Westchester, IL 60154-4361
(708) 865-1972
Luella Seida

Western Springs Historical Society
(Tower Green, 840 Hillgrove
Avenue—museum location; Grand Avenue
School, 4211 Grand Avenue—archives
location)
PO Box 139 (mailing address)
Western Springs, IL 60558-0139
(708) 246-9230
Ann Vance, Office Manager
Museum: Sat 11:00–1:00, first Sun
1:00–3:00
(local history, photos, tapes, slides,
genealogy)
$10.00 per year membership

Westmont Historical Society
William L. Gregg House Museum
(115 South Linden Avenue—location)
231 East Dallas Street (mailing address)
Westmont, IL 60559-1894
(630) 964-4174
Silvia Santillan-Baranek, Curator
Wed & Sun 1:00–3:00
("Local history of Westmont, Illinois, area.")
$15.00 per year membership

Wheeling Historical Society
Wheeling Park District
(251 North Wolf Road in Chamber
Park—location)
PO Box 3 (mailing address)
Wheeling, IL 60090-0003
(847) 537-3119; (847) 537-1450; (847) 537-
2930 (Park District); (847) 520-0512
FAX
ARCHLLR@aol.com
Linda Reading, Curator; Patti Hancock,
Secretary
Mar–Oct: Sun 2:00–4:00, except holidays
Pub. *WHS Newsletter*, monthly
("Local Wheeling history.")
$10.00 per year membership

White County Historical Society
(203 North Church—location)
PO Box 121 (mailing address)
Carmi, IL 62821-0121
(618) 382-8425
cbconly@midwest.net
http://www.rootsweb.com/~ilwcohs
Pat Davis, Librarian
Mary Smith Fay Genealogy Library: Tue–Sat
(Feb–Dec) 10:00–2:00
Pub. *White County Historian*, quarterly
(maintains four museums: the Robinson-
Stewart House, The L. Haas Store
Museum, the Ratcliff Inn, and Matsel
Cabin)
$15.00 per year membership

Will County Historical Society
(Off Route 7, 1 block west of 171—location)
803 South State Street (mailing address)
Lockport, IL 60441-3433
(815) 838-5080
Rose Bucciferro, Director
Pub. *WCHS Quarterly*; *Newsletter*, nine
times per year
$5.00 per year membership; research: $10.00
per surname

Williamson County Historical Society
105 South Van Buren Street

Marion, IL 62959-2509
(618) 997-5863
charla@shawneelink.net
http://www.thewchs.com
Charla Murphy, President
Thur (Apr–Nov) 9:00–3:00
Pub. *Footprints In Williamson Co., IL,*
quarterly
$15.00 per year membership; library
admission: free; museum tour: $2.00 for
adults; research: $7.50 per hour plus copy
costs

Wilmette Historical Society
The Wilmette Historical Museum
609 Ridge Road
Wilmette, IL 60091
(847) 853-7666; (847) 853-7706 FAX
husseyk@wilmette.com
http://www.wilmette/com/museum
Kathy Hussey-Arntson, Museum Director
Tue & Thur 10:00–noon & 1:00–4:00, Wed
& Sun 1:00–4:00
Pub. *Ouilmette Heritage,* quarterly
(archives focus on Wilmette and Gross
Point)

Wilmington Area Historical Society
(100 North Water Street—location)
PO Box 1 (mailing address)
Wilmington, IL 60481-0001
(815) 476-6330
Dorthea Smith, Curator
Sat–Sun 1:00–4:00

Winfield Historical Society
(555 Winfield Road—location)
PO Box 315 (mailing address)
Winfield, IL 60190
(630) 653-1489; (630) 665-0358
Adrienne Rose
by appointment

Winnetka Historical Society
Winnetka Historical Museum
(1140 Elm Street—location)
PO Box 142 (mailing address)
Winnetka, IL 60093-0142
(847) 501-6025
Carol Meeske, President; Jeannette Scott,
Museum Director
Tue, Thur & Sat 1:00–4:00, and by
appointment

Wood Dale Historical Society
(850 North Wood Dale Road—location)
PO Box 13 (mailing address)
Wood Dale, IL 60191-0013
(630) 595-8777; (630) 766-1768
Robert H. Doane, Curator

Woodford County Historical Society
203 South Main Street
Eureka, IL 61530-1618
milemaster@hotmail.com
http://www.eureka.lib.il.us/community/wchs
Richard Miller, Webmaster
Summer: Wed & Fri 1:00–4:00; Winter: Fri
$7.50 per year membership

Woodridge Area Historical Society
2628 Mitchell Drive
Woodridge, IL 60517-2929
(630) 985-9423
Joanie Mimhaugh

Wyanet Historical Society
(109 East Main Street—location)
PO Box 169 (mailing address)
Wyanet, IL 61379-0169
(815) 699-2531
Maxine Trotter, President and Curator

Wed–Sat 11:00–4:00
Pub. *Newsletter,* annually
("We hold an ice cream social every
Memorial Day after services [10:00 A.M.]
at the cemetery. Wyanet Vet. Park
[Walnut St.]. Family histories on file, also
obituaries, cemetery information," book,
newspapers, high school alumni books
1879–1976, display of canal, railroad,
military memorabilia, hotel register
1875–1879, Civil War diary of Emmerson
Pomeroy, minutes and pictures, records of
Wyanet War Mothers, slide presentation
of early businesses.)
$5.00 per year membership; research:
donation

Zion Historical Society
1300 Shiloh Boulevard
Zion, IL 60099
(847) 746-2427; (847) 746-2427
Alice Marshall

Genealogical Societies

State Genealogical Society

Illinois State Genealogical Society
(Margaret Cross Norton Building, Second
and Edwards—location)
PO Box 10195 (mailing address)
Springfield, IL 62791-0195
isgsoffice@a5.com
http://www.rootsweb.com/~ilsgs
Martha Dever Pulliam, President; Mary Lou
Johnsrud, Executive Secretary
Mon–Fri 8:00–4:30
Pub. *Illinois State Genealogical Society
Quarterly; Illinois State Genealogical
Society Newsletter,* bimonthly
(Does not maintain a research facility. "Also
Genealogical Institute of Mid-America
every July on the University of Illinois
campus at Springfield.")
$25.00 per year membership; research:
genealogist on staff to answer letters

**Council of Northeastern Illinois
Genealogical Societies**
820 Lisdowney Drive
Lockport, IL 60441
(coordinates society activities)

Genealogical Societies—Local & Regional

**Bellflower Genealogical and Historical
Society**
(210 North Latcha Street—location)
407 West Center Street (mailing address)
Bellflower, IL 61724
(309) 722-3457 (Woliung); (309) 722-3458
(Kumler)
Dorothy Woliung and Phyllis Kumler,
Presidents
by appointment
Pub. *Bellflower Highlights,* annually (July),
subscription by donation

**Blackhawk Genealogical Society of Rock
Island and Mercer Counties, Illinois**
PO Box 3912
Rock Island, IL 61204-3912
(309) 787-1826
bgsweb@hotmail.com; rujan2000@aol.com
http://www.rootsweb.com/~ilbgsrim/
index.html
Judy Rueckert, President; Lorraine
Hathaway, Editor
collection housed at the Rock Island Public
Library
Pub. *Blackhawk Genealogical Society
Quarterly*

$15.00 per year membership

Bond County Genealogical Society
PO Box 172
Greenville, IL 62246-0172
(618) 664-3054 (President); (618) 664-3308
FAX
Dean Anthony, President
8:00–5:00
Pub. *B.C.G.S. News,* quarterly
(census, family histories, probate records,
cemetery records, veterans records, etc.)
$15.00 per year membership; research: $7.00
per hour plus postage and copies at 25¢
per page

Bureau County Genealogical Society
(629 South Main Street—location)
PO Box 402 (mailing address)
Princeton, IL 61356-0402
(815) 875-8491
http://www.rootsweb.com/~ilbcgs
Carol McGee, Board Member
Pub. *Newsletter,* bimonthly
(Bureau County records, extensive marriage,
cemetery and church records)
$8.00 per year membership; research: for a
fee

Carroll County Genealogical Society
(Savanna Public Library, History Room, 326
Third Street—location)
PO Box 354 (mailing address)
Savanna, IL 61074-0347
(815) 273-7406
ahaliotis@internetni.com
http://www.internetni.com/~ahaliotas
Mary Falls, Secretary/Treasurer
by appointment only; meetings at Savanna
Township Library: second Fri (except
Dec)
Pub. *Carroll County Genealogical Society
Newsletter,* four times per year
("primarily Carroll County, with some
information on Jo Daviess and Whiteside
counties; county cemetery readings, burial
records, and 1910 and 1920 census
indexes for sale")
$10.00 per year membership; research:
$10.00 per hour, plus copies at 25¢ per
page

**Cass County Illinois
Historical/Genealogical Society**
(see Historical Societies—Local and
Regional, above)

Champaign County Genealogical Society
Urbana Free Library
201 South Race Street
Urbana, IL 61801-3283
(217) 367-4025 (Library)
j-lund@uiuc.edu
http://www.rootsweb.com/~ilccgs
Joan Black Lund, Editor of the Quarterly
Library: Mon–Sat 9:00–5:00, Sun 1:00–5:00
Pub. *Champaign County Genealogical
Society Quarterly; Champaign County
Genealogical Society Newsletter,*
quarterly
$20.00 per year membership

Chicago Genealogical Society
PO Box 1160
Chicago, IL 60690-1160
(312) 725-1306 (recorded message); (312)
834-7491 (library)
chgogs@chgogs.org (subject CGS
Corresponding Secretary)
http://www.chgogs.org
Jeanne Bloom, Editor, *Newsletter;* Mildred
R. Smith, Librarian

Library: by appointment, for use by members
only
Pub. *Chicago Genealogist*, quarterly;
*Newsletter of the Chicago Genealogical
Society*, eleven times per year
(Cook County and Chicago, Illinois)
$20.00 per year membership

Christian County Genealogical Society
PO Box 28
Taylorville, IL 62568
Nelvin Sloman, President
Pub. *Christian County Genealogical
Quarterly*; *Christian County
Genealogical Society Newsletter*,
quarterly
$10.00 per year membership

Clay County Genealogical Society
(West side of square—location)
PO Box 94 (mailing address)
Louisville, IL 62858-0094
(618) 665-4544
Jean Bailey, Treasurer
summer: every Mon noon–4:00, Sat
9:00–4:00; winter: second Mon
noon–4:00, Sat 9:00–4:00
Pub. *Clay Roots*, quarterly
("Large collection of family histories.")
$15.00 per year membership

**Coles County, Illinois, Genealogical
Society**
PO Box 592
Charleston, IL 61920-0592
crngenealogy@yahoo.com
Karen Zike, Corresponding Secretary
Charleston Public Library: Mon–Thur
10:00–8:00, Fri–Sat 10:00–6:00
Pub. *Among the Coles*, bimonthly
("Local and immediate surrounding
counties.")
$12.00 per year membership

Crawford County Genealogical Society
803 North Madison
Robinson, IL 62454
Sue Jones, Secretary; King Schmalhausen,
President
Robinson Public Library District: Mon–Thur
10:00–8:00, Fri–Sat 10:00–5:30; summer:
Mon 10:00–8:00, Tue–Sat 10:00–5:30
Pub. *Crawford County Genealogical Society
Newsletter*, semiannually
(state census of Illinois, DAR lineage books,
cemetery records, marriages, obituaries,
U.S. censuses of Crawford and
surrounding counties; Crawford County
history and records)
$8.00 per year membership

**Genealogical Society of Cumberland and
Coles County**
1816 Walnut
Mattoon, IL 61938

**Cumberland County Historical and
Genealogical Society of Illinois**
(see Historical Societies—Local and
Regional, above)

Decatur Genealogical Society
(356 North Main Street—location)
PO Box 1548 (mailing address)
Decatur, IL 62526-1548
(217) 429-0135
DecaturGenealogicalSociety@msn.com
http://www.rootsweb.com/~ildecgs
Cheri Hunter, Librarian
Mon 10:00–6:00, Wed & Sat 10:00–4:00
Pub. *Central Illinois Genealogical
Quarterly*; *Central Illinois News*,

semimonthly
("Our holdings cover the entire United States
with emphasis on Central Illinois."
Sponsors Macon County Pioneer
Certificates to direct descendants of
pioneers residing in Macon County prior
to 1880.)
$15.00 per year membership

**DeKalb County Historical-Genealogical
Society**
(see Historical Societies—Local and
Regional, above)

DeWitt County Genealogical Society
(Warner Library—location)
PO Box 632 (mailing address)
Clinton, IL 61727-0632
Nettie Davenport, President
Mon–Thur 9:00–9:00, Fri 9:00–6:00, Sat
9:00–4:00
Pub. *DeWitt County Genealogical Quarterly*
$15.00 per year membership; research: $5.00
per surname

Douglas County Genealogical Society
PO Box 1829
Springfield, IL 62705-1829
(217) 529-0542
Dbutton2@aol.com
Daniel W. Dixon, President
by appointment only
Pub. *Circuit Rider*, quarterly
$15.00 per year membership

**Dubuque County-Key City Genealogical
Society Chapter (IGS)**
(see Iowa, Part 2)

DuPage County Genealogical Society
PO Box 3
Wheaton, IL 60189-0003
jeffb@anet.com; judyweldon@kwom.com
http://www.dcgs.org
Jeff Bockman, GEN WEBmaster; Judy
Johnson, Corresponding Secretary
third Wed 7:30 at Wheaton Public Library
Pub. *The Review*, eight times per year
(bimonthly plus summer and winter)
$18.00 per year membership

**Edgar County, Illinois Genealogical
Society**
PO Box 304
Paris, IL 61944-0304
(217) 463-4209 (Library)
ecgl@tigerpaw.com
http://www.tigerpaw.com/ecgl
Debbie Wilson, Editor
Edgar County Genealogy Library: Wed–Fri
9:00–4:00
Pub. *Edgar County Genealogical Society
Quarterly* (Aug, Nov, Feb, May)
$12.50 per year membership

Edwards County Genealogical Society
(see Edwards County Historical Society,
Historical Societies—Local and Regional,
above)

Effingham County Genealogical Society
(Helen Matthes Library, 100 Market
Street—location)
PO Box 1166 (mailing address)
Effingham, IL 62401-1166
(217) 342-2210
Arnetia Osborn, Corresponding Secretary
Library: winter: Mon–Thur 10:00–9:00, Fri
10:00–5:00, Sat 10:00–4:00; summer:
Mon–Thur 10:00–8:00, Fri 10:00–5:00,
Sat 10:00–1:00; genealogy assistance: Tue
1:00–3:00, Thur 10:00–noon

Pub. *Crossroad Trails*, quarterly; *Effingham
County Genealogical Society Newsletter*,
monthly
$10.00 per year membership

Elgin Genealogical Society
PO Box 1418
Elgin, IL 60121-1418
(847) 697-5683
egs@listserv.nslsilus.org
http://nsn.nslsilus.org/elghome/egs/index.
html
Daniel DuBois
Pub. *Newsletter—Elgin Genealogical Society
Quarterly*
(research of probation records of Elgin)
$10.00 per year membership

Genealogical Forum of Elmhurst, Illinois
Elmhurst Historical Museum
120 East Park Avenue
Elmhurst, IL 60126-3420
appointment; meetings first Sun (odd-
numbered months) 3:00–5:00
Pub. *Newsletter of the Genealogical Forum
of Elmhurst*, five times per year (Aug,
Oct, Dec, Feb, Apr)
(Elmhurst cemeteries prior to 1916)
$10.00 per year membership; research: $5.00
and up, free to members

**Farmer City Genealogy and Historical
Society**
(Franklin School, 400 East
Market—location)
PO Box 173 (mailing address)
Farmer City, IL 61842-0173
(309) 928-9547; (309) 928-2113
Sharon Stiger

**Fayette County Genealogical and
Historical Society**
Evans Public Library
(215 South Fifth Street—location)
PO Box 177 (mailing address)
Vandalia, IL 62471-0177
(618) 423-2625; (618) 283-2824 (Library);
(618) 283-2705 FAX (Library)
webmastr@swetland.net
http:/www.swetland.net/users/fcgs
Linda Hanabarger, Editor; Jonette Eddy, Site
Coordinator
Library: Mon–Thur 10:00–7:00, Fri–Sat
10:00–5:00
Pub. *Fayette Facts*, quarterly
$5.00 per issue to members, $6.00 per issue
to nonmembers, $15.00 per year
membership

**Fort LaMotte Genealogical and Historical
Society**
Palestine Public Library
116 South Main
Palestine, IL 62451-1244
(618) 586-5580
Tue–Fri 9:00–4:30, Sat 8:30–10:30

Fox Valley Genealogical Society
PO Box 5435
Naperville, IL 60567-5435
(630) 369-2152 (President)
fvgs1@aol.com
http://members.aol.com/fvgs1/index.html
Harold Workman, President
Pub. *Fox Tales*, bimonthly
(DuPage, Kane, Kendall and Will counties;
holdings at Oswego Public Library)
$15.00 per year membership

Frankfort Area Genealogy Society
(1200 East Saint Louis Street—location)
PO Box 427 (mailing address)

West Frankfort, IL 62896-0427
Mary Rea Eubank, President
Pub. *Facts and Findings*, quarterly
$10.00 per year membership

Franklin County Genealogical Society
PO Box 524
West Frankfort, IL 62896

Freeburg Historical and Genealogical Society
(see Historical Societies—Local and Regional, above)

Fulton County Historical and Genealogical Society
(see Historical Societies—Local and Regional, above)

Garden Prairie Genealogical and Historical Society
PO Box 115
Garden Prairie, IL 61038-0115
(815) 597-1109
Carla Vassmer

Genealogical Questers
Des Plaines Historical Society
Museum
789 Pearson Street
Des Plaines, IL 60016-4506
temporarily not meeting on a regular basis

Goode-Barren Historical-Genealogical Society
(see Historical Societies—Local and Regional, above)

Great River Genealogical Society
Quincy Public Library
526 Jersey Street
Quincy, IL 62301-3996
(217) 222-0226
jeankay@adams.net;
    grgswebmaster@insightbb.com
http://www.outfitters.com/~grgs
Jean Kay
Library: Tue after Labor Day to Sat before
    Memorial Day: Mon–Thur 9:00–9:00,
    Fri–Sat 9:00–6:00, Sun 1:00–5:00;
    June–Aug: Mon 9:00–9:00, Tue–Sat
    9:00–6:00
Pub. *The Yellowjacket*, quarterly
(Adams County indexes to deaths, land
    records, cemeteries, surname index;
    Quincy newspapers on microfilm 1838 to
    date; German-American Historical Papers;
    tax lists, will indexes, coroners inquests
    indexes, and divorce index)
$10.00 per year membership

Green Hills Genealogical Society
Green Hills Public Library
8611 West 103rd Street
Palos Hills, IL 60465
(708) 598-8446 (Library); (708) 598-0856
    FAX (Library)
Darline Filis
Library: Mon–Fri 9:00–8:30, Sat 9:00–5:00
    (except June–Aug: Sat 9:00–3:00)

Greene County Historical and Genealogical Society
(see Historical Societies—Local and Regional, above)

Griggsville Area Genealogical and Historical Society
PO Box 22
Griggsville, IL 62340-0022
(217) 833-2308; (217) 285-6672
June Johnson

Mon–Fri 1:00–5:00, and by appointment

Hardin County Historical and Genealogical Society
(see Historical Societies—Local and Regional, above)

Henry County Genealogical Society
(102 South Tremont Street, lower level of
    Kewanee Public Library—location)
PO Box 346 (mailing address)
Kewanee, IL 61443-0346
srmorrison@bwsys.net
http://www.rootsweb.com/~ilhenry
Steve Morrison, President
Library: after Labor Day to Memorial Day:
    Mon–Thur 9:00–8:00, Fri 9:00–6:00, Sat
    9:00–5:00, Sun (Oct–Memorial Day)
    1:00–4:00; after Memorial Day to Labor
    Day: Mon–Fri 9:00–6:00, Sat 9:00–5:00
Pub. *The Henry County Genie*, quarterly
(how-to materials; U.S. general, foreign,
    family surnames, U.S. by state and
    county; issues Pioneers of Henry County,
    Illinois Certificates for direct descendants)
$14.00 per year membership; research: fees
    online, policy and contact person, Mary
    Jane Skoglund, skoge@bwsys.net

Henry Historical and Genealogical Society
(see Historical Societies—Local and Regional, above)

Illiana Genealogical and Historical Society
(19 East North—location)
PO Box 207 (mailing address)
Danville, IL 61834-0207
(217) 431-8733
Sally Powell, President
Mon & Wed–Sat 10:00–4:00, Tue
    10:00–8:00
Pub. *Illiana Genealogist*, quarterly (Mar,
    June, Sept, Dec)
(includes bordering counties of Vermilion
    County, IL)
$15.00 per year membership; research:
    $18.00 for two hours

Iroquois County Genealogical Society
A Division of the Iroquois County Historical
Society
Old Courthouse Museum
103 West Cherry Street
Watseka, IL 60970-1524
(815) 432-3730
iroqgene@techinter.com
http://www.rootsweb.com/~ilicggs/index.
    htm
Cheryl Gocken, Librarian/Researcher
Mon–Fri 12:30–4:30
Pub. *Newsletter*, monthly
("Also states of the migration path to
    Illinois")
$18.00 per year membership; searches: $5.00
    per hour

Jacksonville Area Genealogical and Historical Society
416 South Main Street
Jacksonville, IL 62650-2904
(217) 673-4241 (Librarian); (217) 245-5911
    (for appointment)
jaghs@caj.net
http://www.csj.net/~jaghs
Mary Frances Alkire, Volunteer Librarian
Mon–Fri 10:00–4:00, Sat by appointment
Pub. *Jacksonville Area Genealogical and
    Historical Society*, four times per year
$18.00 per year membership; research:
    donation plus any cost

Jasper County Historical and Genealogical

Society, Inc.
(see Historical Societies—Local and
Regional, above)

Jefferson County Genealogical Society
PO Box 1131
Mount Vernon, IL 62864
Secretary
Pub. *Quarterly*
$15.00 per year membership

Jersey County Genealogical Society
PO Box 12
Jerseyville, IL 62052

Kane County Genealogical Society
PO Box 504
Geneva, IL 60134-0504
bowl12x@aol.com
http://www.rootsweb.com/~ilkcgs
Susan Lye, Editor/President
meetings at the Saint Charles Public Library:
    fourth Thur (Jan–Oct), first Thur (Dec)
Pub. *The Kane County Chronicles*, quarterly
(Kane County and Illinois; database
    containing over 750,000 names from over
    160 Kane County resources)
$8.00 per year membership; research of
    database for a husband and wife
    (including wife's maiden name):
    nonrefundable $10.00 plus #10 SASE

Kankakee Valley Genealogical Society
PO Box 442
Bourbonnais, IL 60914-0442
(815) 932-7567
research@kvgs.org
http://kvgs.org
Marcia Stang, President; Dorothy Riegel,
    Research Committee Chair
Bourbonnais Public Library: Mon–Thur
    9:00–9:00, Fri 9:00–6:00, Sat 9:00–5:00
Pub. *The-a-Kiki*, quarterly
$14.00 per year membership; research:
    $10.00 plus expenses

Kishwaukee Genealogists
PO Box 5503
Rockford, IL 61125-0503
(815) 874-2706
Betty Nye, *Newsletter* Editor
meetings: second Sat (Sept–May) 1:30
Pub. *Kishwaukee Genealogists Newsletter*,
    five times per year (bimonthly, except
    June/Aug)
(Boone and Winnebago counties)
$10.00 per year membership

Knox County Genealogical Society
(Galesburg Public Library—collection
location)
PO Box 13 (mailing address)
Galesburg, IL 61402-0013
(309) 343-1466
http://www.rootsweb.com/~ilknox/
    knindexhtm
Kathy Hale, Corresponding Secretary
meetings at the Trinity Lutheran Church in
    Galesburg: second Mon 7:30
Pub. *Knox County Genealogical Society
    Quarterly* (Mar, June, Sept, Dec)
$14.00 per year membership; research:
    $12.50 for nonmembers, $6.00 per hour
    for members

LaHarpe Historical and Genealogical Society
(see Historical Societies—Local and
Regional, above)

Lake County (IL) Genealogical Society
(1170 Midlothian, Mundelein, IL

60060—location)
PO Box 721 (mailing address)
Libertyville, IL 60048-0721
(847) 918-3208
lcigs@yahoo.com
http://www.rootsweb.com/~illcgs
James E. Swab, President
Mon 1:00–9:00, Tue–Thur 9:00–9:00, Fri
1:00–5:00, Sat 9:00–5:00, Sun (during
school year) 1:00–5:00
Pub. *LCIGS Quarterly*
$205.00 per year membership

LaSalle County Genealogy Guild
115 Glover Street
Ottawa, IL 61350
(815) 433-5261
dpc@mtco.com
http://genealogy.org/~dpc
Jenan Jobst, Corresponding Secretary
Mon & Sat 9:00–4:00
Pub. *Pastfinder*, two times per year; *Genies
View*, bimonthly
$10.00 per year membership

Lawrence County Genealogical Society
Route 1, Box 44
Bridgeport, IL 62417
(618) 945-7181
Geraldine Satterthwaite, Corresponding
Secretary
Pub. *Lawrence County Genealogical Society
Newsletter*, quarterly
(books of obituaries from Lawrence County
area)
$10.00 per year membership

Lee County Genealogical Society
(Family Tree Center, 213 South Peoria
Avenue—location)
PO Box 63 (mailing address)
Dixon, IL 61021-0063
(815) 288-6702
http://www.rootsweb.com/~illee/
genealogical_society.htm
Millie Dutchoff, President; Bob Boward,
Vice President; Gordon Johnson, Web
Site Coordinator
Tue & Sat 9:00–3:00, Thur 5:00–8:00, and
by appointment
Pub. *Lee County Genealogical Society
Newsletter*, monthly
(information on Lee, Whiteside, Ogle and
other surrounding counties)
$15.00 per year membership; research:
$10.00 for initial search, plus $10.00 per
hour for extensive research, plus copy
costs for nonmembers

**Lexington Genealogical and Historical
Society**
318 West Main Street
Lexington, IL 61753-1328
(309) 365-4591
Verda Gerwick, President
Tue–Sat 9:00–4:00
(McLean, Livingston and Woodford County,
Illinois, cemetery records)
$20.00 per year membership

Macoupin County Genealogical Society
PO Box 95
Staunton, IL 62088-0095
(618) 635-8506 (Secretary's home); (618)
635-3852 (Library)
mmckenzie@madisontelco.com
http://www.rootsweb.com/~ilmacoup/
m_gensoc.htm
Cindy Leonard, Corresponding Secretary;
Mary McKenzie, Coordinator
Staunton Public Library: Mon–Thur
1:00–8:00, Fri–Sat 9:00–5:00; meetings at

First United Baptist Church, 604 North
Franklin, Staunton: third Mon (except
Dec) 7:30
Pub. *Macoupin County Searcher*, quarterly
$10.00 per year membership

Madison County Genealogical Society
PO Box 631
Edwardsville, IL 62025-0631
(618) 656-2299 (MCGS Librarian)
mcgsil@hotmail.com
http://www.rootsweb.com/~ilmadcgs
Elsie M. Wasser, Librarian
Edwardsville Public Library: Mon–Thur
9:00–9:00, Fri–Sat 9:00–5:00, Sun
1:00–5:00
Pub. *Madison County Genealogical Society
Newsletter*, nine times per year; *Madison
County Genealogical Society Stalker*,
quarterly
("Early birth, death, marriage, probate
printed indexes 1810–1920, census
records, biographical index of all history
books." "Madison County, Illinois, and
surrounding counties and states of
migration.")
$20.00 per year membership

**Marion County Genealogical and
Historical Society**
(Bryan-Bennett Library—location)
PO Box 342 (mailing address)
Salem, IL 62881
Harold Boyles, Archivist
Archives: Wed noon–4:00
Pub. *Footprints in Marion County*, quarterly
$15.00 per year membership; free queries

**Marissa Historical and Genealogical
Society**
(see Historical Societies—Local and
Regional, above)

**Mason County Genealogical and
Historical Society**
PO Box 446
Havana, IL 62644
library@casscomm.com
http://www.havana.lib.il.us/community/
mcghs.html
Virginia Barrett
meetings at Havana Public Library: third Sun
(Feb, May, Aug, Nov) 2:00
$12.00 per year membership

Massac County Genealogical Society
PO Box 1043
Metropolis, IL 62960-1043
deena@hcis.net (submect:
MCGS_Contact_US)
http://www.rootsweb.com/~ilmcgs
Deena Harris, Secretary/Treasurer
meetings in the Metropolis Public Library
basement: third Sat (except Oct & Dec)
1:00
Pub. *Massac County Genealogical Society
Quarterly* (Mar, June, Sept, Dec)
$15.00 per year membership; research: $5.00
per surname for members, $10.00 per
surname plus $1.00 postage and copies at
50¢ each for nonmembers

McDonough County Genealogical Society
PO Box 202
Macomb, IL 61455-0202
(309) 837-4558
mcgs@macomb.com
http://www.macomb.com/mcgs
Sarah Semonis
Macomb District Public Library: Mon–Tue,
Thur & Sat 9:00–6:00, Wed & Fri
9:00–9:00

Pub. *McDonough County Genealogical
Society News Quarterly*
$10.00 per year membership

**McHenry County Illinois Genealogical
Society (MCIGS)**
(McHenry Library, 1011 Green Street,
McHenry, IL 60050—location)
PO Box 184 (mailing address)
Crystal Lake, IL 60039-0184
(815) 385-0686
mcigs@mcigs.org
http://www.mcigs.org
Craig Pfarmkuche, Corresponding Secretary
Pub. *McHenry County Illinois Connection*,
quarterly
$15.00 per year membership

The McLean County Genealogical Society
(Second Floor, McLean County Courthouse,
200 North Main, Bloomington, IL 61701-
3912—location)
PO Box 488 (mailing address)
Normal, IL 61761-0488
Joy Craig, Corresponding Secretary; Laurel
Quaid, Quarterly Editor
Mon & Wed–Sat 10:00–5:00, Tue
10:00–9:00
Pub. *Gleanings from the Heart of the
Cornbelt*, quarterly; *McLean County
Genealogical Society Newsletter*, monthly
$15.00 per year membership

Monroe County Research Group
6104 State Route 156
Waterloo, IL 62298
Mr. Weilbacker

Montgomery County Genealogical Society
(Litchfield Carnegie Public Library, 400
North State Street—library location)
PO Box 212 (mailing address)
Litchfield, IL 62056-0212
(217) 324-4841 (Library)
Nola M. Eskra, President
Library: Mon–Thur 10:00–8:00; Fri
10:00–5:00, Sat 10:00–2:00
Pub. *Montgomery County Genealogical
Society Quarterly*
$12.50 per year membership

Morgan County Genealogical Association
PO Box 84
Jacksonville, IL 62651-0084
Florence Hutchison, Corresponding
Secretary
Pub. *Star Genealogical Journal*, quarterly
$10.00 per year membership

**Moultrie County Historical and
Genealogical Society**
(see Historical Societies—Local and
Regional, above)

North Central Illinois Genealogical Society
5208 Sherwood Forest Road
Rockford, IL 61109-2736
meetings second Sat (Sept–May)
Pub. *Twigs and Branches*, quarterly
$12.50 per year membership; research: $7.50
per hour

North Suburban Genealogical Society
Winnetka Public Library District
768 Oak Street
Winnetka, IL 60093-2583
(847) 446-7220 (Library); (847) 446-5085
FAX (Library)
PLS218@aol.com
http://www.fgs.org/~fgs/soc0139.htm
Pegeen Soare, President
Library: Mon–Thur 9:00–9:00, Fri–Sat

9:00–5:00, Sun 1:00–5:00 (during school year)
Pub. *Newsletter*, bimonthly
$15.00 per year membership

Northern Will County Genealogical Society
603 Derbyshire Lane
Bolingbrook, IL 60439

Northwest Suburban Council of Genealogists
PO Box AC
Mount Prospect, IL 60056-9019
(847) 398-8565
Rita Hodgetts, President
Pub. *News from the Northwest*, five times per year
$10.00 per year membership

Northwest Territory Genealogical Society
(see Indiana, Part 2)

Odell Prairie Trails Genealogical and Historical Society
PO Box 82
Odell, IL 60460-0082
(815) 998-2324
Lorraine Hare, Secretary
by appointment
(Livingston and local history)
$5.00 per year membership

Ogle County Illinois Genealogical Society
PO Box 251
Oregon, IL 61061-0251
(815) 734-6818 (Secretary)
Judith Ehnen, President
meetings at Ogle County Senior Services Conference Room, 215 Washington Street, Oregon, IL: first Tue (Mar–Dec) 7:00
Pub. *The Ogle County Links Newsletter*, four times per year
("Write for lists of records for sale. Genealogical Library is housed at The Oregon Public Library.")
$10.00 per year membership; queries: free for members

Peoria County Genealogical Society
PO Box 1489
Peoria, IL 61655-1489
Donna Schlatter, Corresponding Secretary
Peoria Public Library: Mon–Thur 9:00–9:00, Fri–Sat 9:00–6:00; summer: closed weekends
Pub. *Prairie Roots*, quarterly; *PCGS News*, monthly
(specializes in Peoria County)
$19.00 per year membership; research: $7.50 for basic search plus copy charages

Piatt County Historical and Genealogical Society
(see Historical Societies—Local and Regional, above)

Pike and Calhoun Counties Genealogical Society
(207 North Main Street—location)
PO Box 104 (mailing address)
Pleasant Hill, IL 62366-0104
(217) 734-2221 (Office); (217) 734-2736 (President)
Virginia R. Hart, President and Editor
Pub. *A Peek at Pike*, quarterly
$10.00 per year membership

Randolph County Genealogical Society
First State Bank Building
600 State Street, Room 306

Chester, IL 62233-1633
(618) 826-3807 (Mon–Tue); (618) 763-4427 (President); (573) 547-1881 (Vice President)
Virginia Mansker, President; Lola Crowder, Vice President
Mon–Tue 9:00–2:30
Pub. *The Trails*, quarterly (Mar, June, Sept, Dec), $4.50 per issue
$20.00 per year membership

Richland County Illinois Genealogical and Historical Society
(Olney Central College, Anderson Library—library location)
PO Box 202 (mailing address)
Olney, IL 62450-0202
(618) 869-2425 (Editor)
Jan Doan, President
when college library is open: Mon–Thur 8:00–7:30, Fri 8:00–4:00
Pub. *Footprints Past and Present*, quarterly; *Richland County Genealogical Society Newsletter*, occasionally (lists acquisitions and news only, no genealogy)
$20.00 per year membership

Saint Clair County Genealogical Society
(Saint Luke's Parish Center—location)
PO Box 431 (mailing address)
Belleville, IL 62222-0431
Dennis Hermann, President
collection housed at Belleville Public Library; meetings at Saint Luke's
Pub. *Saint Clair County Genealogical Society Quarterly*; *Saint Clair County Genealogical Society Newsletter*, monthly
$16.00 per year membership

Saline County Genealogical Society
(Room 24, City Hall—location)
PO Box 4 (mailing address)
Harrisburg, IL 62946-0004
(618) 252-1216 (Treasurer); (618) 252-1096
Karen Stilley, Treasurer
fourth Tue 9:00–3:00, and by appointment
Pub. *The Shawnee*, quarterly, $4.00 per issue; *Newsletter*, monthly
$12.00 per year membership

Sangamon County Genealogical Society
PO Box 1829
Springfield, IL 62705-1829
(217) 529-0542
Daniel W. Dixon, President
Pub. *Circuit Rider*, quarterly
(Sangamon County genealogical interest)
$12.00 per year membership

Schaumburg Genealogical Society
Schaumburg Township District Library
32 West Library Lane
Schaumburg, IL 60194
(847) 885-3373 (Library); (847) 885-7348 FAX (Library)

Shelby County Historical and Genealogical Society
(see Historical Societies—Local and Regional, above)

South Suburban Genealogical and Historical Society
(320 East 161st Place—location)
PO Box 96 (mailing address)
South Holland, IL 60473-0096
(708) 333-9474
ssghs@usa.net
http://www.rootsweb.com/~ssghs
Paula Malak, Librarian
Mon 10:00–4:00, Tue 1:00–5:00, Wed 10:00–11:30 & 12:30–4:00, Fri

10:30–3:30, first and second Sat
11:00–4:00
Pub. *Where the Trails Cross*, quarterly; *Newsletter*, monthly
(Pullman Car Company employment records, ca 1890–1940)
$20.00 per year membership; research: $10.00 per hour

The Genealogy Society of Southern Illinois
c/o John A. Logan College
Route 2, Box 145
Carterville, IL 62918-9599
(618) 985-6213
tullyne2@yahoo.com
http://www.rootsweb.com/~ilgssi/index.html
Tullyne Johns Oliver, *Newsletter* Editor
subject to college hours
Pub. *Newsletter*, monthly; *Saga of Southern Illinois*, quarterly
$16.00 per year membership

Stark County Genealogical Society
(207 West Main—location)
PO Box 32 (mailing address)
Toulon, IL 61483
Tue 1:00–4:00, Sat 10:10-noon, and by appointment
Pub. *Stark County Genie Quarterly*
(local history, indexed scrapbooks, diaries, letters, newspapers, oral history)
$12.00 per year membership

Stephenson County Genealogical Society
PO Box 514
Freeport, IL 61032-0514
stephcogensoc@yahoo.com
http://www.rootsweb.com/~ilstephe/historyandmuseums/gensociety.html
Gary Price, Corresponding Secretary
Genealogical Society members volunteer in Freeport Public Library local history room: Mon 9:00–5:00 & 6:00–8:45, Wed & Fri 9:00–noon, Thur 1:00–5:00, other hours covered by library staff with 5:00 as the closing hours, no Sun hours
Pub. *Stephenson County SWOGHEN*, quarterly
$8.00 per year membership

Tazewell Genealogical and Historical Society
(719 North 11th Street—location)
PO Box 312 (mailing address)
Pekin, IL 61555-0312
(309) 477-3044; (309) 579-2732 (President)
Margaret Bush, President
Wed 1:00–4:00, Thur 9:00–noon, Sun 2:00–4:30 (closed holiday weekends)
Pub. *Tazewell Genealogical and Historical Monthly*
(specializes in Tazewell County and surrounding counties)
$12.00 per year membership

Tinley Moraine Genealogists
PO Box 521
Tinley Park, IL 60477

Tri-State Genealogical Society
(see Indiana, Part 2)

Union County Historical and Genealogy Society
(see Historical Societies—Local and Regional, above)

Versailles Area Genealogical and Historical Society
(113 West First Street—location)
PO Box 92 (mailing address)
Versailles, IL 62378

(217) 225-9091 (President); (217) 225-3227 (Second Vice President)
vaghs83@adams.net
http://www.geocities.com/vaghs83
Mary Logsdon, President; Michael DeWitt, Vice President
Mon, Wed & Fri 1:30–5:00 (weather permitting); winter: Wed & Fri only
Pub. *The Versailles Area Genealogical & Historical Society Newsletter*, quarterly (Mar, June, Sept, Dec), contribution for subscription
(many family histories, census, marriages, obituaries, cemeteries, maps, scrapbooks, photo albums; research center, historical library and museum)
$10.00 per year membership

Warren County Illinois Genealogical Society
PO Box 761
Monmouth, IL 61462-0761
(309) 734-2763
Ethel Trego, Researcher
8:30–5:00
Pub. *Prairie Pioneer*, quarterly, $2.50 per issue
$9.00 per year membership

Washington County Genealogical Society
14502 County Highway 1
Nashville, IL 62263
Mr. Groennert

Waverly Genealogical and Historical Society
(Congregational Church, Waverly—location)
359 East Tremont (mailing address)
Waverly, IL 62692-1026
(217) 435-4961
Myra Martin, Historian
every other Mon, and by appointment
Pub. *Newsletter*, quarterly
$6.00 per year membership

Western Springs Genealogical Society
c/o Western Springs Historical Society
PO Box 139
Western Springs, IL 60558-0139
(708) 246-7073

Whiteside County Genealogists
PO Box 145
Sterling, IL 61081-0145
(815) 625-8750
genealogy@sterlingpubliclibrary.org
Marilyn Huffman-Anderson, President and Sterling Public Library's Genealogy/Local History Librarian
Sterling Public Library: Mon–Thur 9:00–8:00, Fri 9:00–5:00, Sat 8:00–5:00, Sun (during school year) 1:00–4:00
Pub. *Whiteside Genealogical News*, quarterly
$10.00 per year membership

Will/Grundy Counties (IL) Genealogical Society
(Coal City Public Library—collection location)
PO Box 24 (mailing address)
Wilmington, IL 60481-0024
Kwaz79@aol.com
http://www.wggs.org
Alice Dinger, Genealogist; Nancy Crilly, President
Mon–Thur 9:00–9:00, Fri 9:00–6:00, Sat 9:00–3:00, Sun (Oct–May) 1:00–5:00
Pub. *Will/Grundy Counties Genealogical Society Newsletter*, monthly; *Will/Grundy Genealogical Society Quarterly*
(gathering and publishing local records and statistics)

$15.00 per year membership; research in our collection free, county research for a fee plus expenses

Winnebago/Boone Counties Genealogical Society
PO Box 10166
Rockford, IL 61131-0166
Ruth N. Lunde, Corresponding Secretary
Pub. *Newsletter*, five times per year
$10.00 per year membership

Zion Genealogical Society
Zion-Benton Public Library
2400 Gabriel Avenue
Zion, IL 60099-2296
(847) 360-0360; (847) 623-3501 FAX
ScrptScrbe@aol.com
http://NSN.ORG/WKKHome/ZION
Joanne I. Layne, President
Library: Mon–Thur 9:00–9:00, Fri 9:00–6:00, Sat 9:00–5:00
Pub. *The Illuminator*, quarterly
(emphasis on southern research)
$15.00 per year membership

Independent Publications and Miscellany

AASR Valley of Chicago
915 North Dearborn Street
Chicago, IL 60610
(312) 787-7605, ext. 9

Chicago Tribune Archives
Tribune Tower
435 North Michigan Avenue, Room 1231
Chicago, IL 60611
(312) 222-3026

Cottonwood Hill Publishing Company
PO Box 82
Benton, WI 53803
Stephen Calvert, Editor
Pub. *Galena Genealogy* (Galena and Jo Daviess County, Illinois), quarterly; $13.95 per year subscription

Family Tree Resource Network, Inc.
(112 First Grand Avenue—location)
PO Box 107 (mailing address)
Cowden, IL 62422-0107
(217) 783-2610 voice & FAX
Helen Cox Tregillis, CEO
Mon–Fri 1:00–5:00
Pub. *Illinois Sources/Resources*, published on demand
("Extensive family files available/genealogical learning seminars available. Also Illinois Native American resources.")

Garfield Farm Museum
PO Box 403
LaFox, IL 60147
(630) 584-8485
info@garfieldfarm.org
http://www.garfieldfarm.org/index.html

Genealogy-Family History Research in Illinois
(address withheld upon request)
http://www.outfitters.com/illinois
(Web consulting company which incidentally provides links to Illinois sources.)

Grove National Historic Landmark
1421 Milwaukee Avenue
Glenview, IL 60025-1436
(847) 299-6096

Hazel Crest Historical Trust Fund
3102 West 175th Street
Hazel Crest, IL 60429-1623
(708) 335-0929

Jacob and Bernard Hostert Log Cabins
(West Avenue and 147th Street—location)
14228 Union Avenue (mailing address)
Orland Park, IL 60462-2011
(708) 349-0046

Hunting for Bears Genealogical and Historical Society
(see Alabama, Part 2)

IlGenWeb
Part of The USGenweb Project
illinois@usroots.com;
    gingerh@shawneelink.com;
    rainelane@earthlink.net
http://www.rootsweb.com/~ilgenweb
Richard Howland, State Coordinator; Ginger Hayes, Assistant Coordinator; Lorraine S. Newsome, Assistant Coordinator
(links to other Illinois resources)

Illinois Association for the Advancement of History
Northern Illinois University
Department of History
DeKalb, IL 60115-2302
(815) 753-6818
Otto Olsen, Secretary/Treasurer
Mon–Fri 8:30–4:30

Illinois Department of Transportation
Map Sales, Room 121
2300 South Dirksen Parkway
Springfield, IL 62764
(217) 782-0834
http://www.dot.state.il.us/mapsales2.html

Illinois Heritage Association
602½ East Green Street
Champaign, IL 61820
(217) 359-5600
plmxiha@prairienet.org
http://www.prairienet.org/iha
Patricia L. Miller, Executive Director
Pub. *IHA Newsletter*
(museum service organization and wholesaler of archival products)

Illinois Labor History Society
28 East Jackson Boulevard
Chicago, IL 60604-2215
(312) 663-4107

Illinois Postal History Society
PO Box 1513
Des Plaines, IL 60017-1513
(847) 443-4442

Malcolm X College
1900 West Van Buren Street
Chicago, IL 60612-3145
(312) 738-5845

Mason County History Project
14454 North State Route 78
Havana, IL 62644
Hugh McHarry
(primarily deals with Mason County)

Masonic Lodge, Office of the Grand Secretary
PO Box 4147
Springfield, IL 62708
send SASE

Michiana History Publications
(see Indiana, Part 2)

Midwest Archives Conference (MAC)
(address withheld upon request)
("We are really not a source for genealogists, other than having an occasional session at our meetings centering on how to serve the genealogical community.")

Mississippi Valley French Research
(see Ethnic Archives, Libraries and Societies—French, Part 3)

The North Eastern Illinois Historical Council (NEIL)
7007 Fargo Avenue
Niles, IL 60714-3719
(847) 390-0160; (847) 647-0185 (Chairman)
Marilyn Brown, Chairman
("An organization of societies and libraries who gather in an attempt to learn more in order to create better historical societies with amateur or volunteer help and little money; it does not serve the genealogist's needs though individual members may.")

Ohio River Valley Families
(see Ohio, Part 2)

Paarlberg Farmstead Homestead
(172nd Place and Paxton Avenue—location)
PO Box 48 (mailing address)
South Holland, IL 60473-0048
(708) 596-2722

Poplar Creek Newsletter
63 Golfview Lane
Carpentersville, IL 60110
Pub. *Poplar Creek Newsletter*, quarterly

Reppert Publications
(112 Lafayette Street—location)
PO Box 529 (mailing address)
Anna, IL 62906
(618) 833-2158; (618) 833-5813 FAX
reppert@midwest.net
Mike Newell, Editor
8:00–5:00
Pub. *Antique and Collectible News*, monthly, $12.00 per year subscription
(covers Illinois, Indiana, Kentucky, Missouri, and Tennessee)

Carl Sandburg College
2232 South Lake Storey Road
Galesburg, IL 61401
(309) 344-2518
http://csc.techcenter.org/~mcneill/csc.html
(genealogy classes and workshops)

Trailside Museum
738 Thatcher Avenue
River Forest, IL 60305
(708) 366-6530

Weaver Genealogical Publications
27 Timber Valley
Petersburg, IL 62675
(217) 632-3543
wgp1987@yahoo.com
http://pages.prodigy.net/jdcweaver
Jeanne Crain
Weaver, Publisher/Genealogist/Historian
Office: 8:00–7:00
Pub. *Menard County Heritage Newsletter*, quarterly (Jan, Apr, July, Oct), $9.00 per year subscription, free queries for subscribers
(publishes county and court records, cemetery records, history, biographies, etc.)
research (specializing in Menard County, IL: $20.00 per hour

Indiana

Archives and Libraries with Holdings in Genealogy

State Archives and Library

Indiana State Archives
6440 East Thirtieth Street
Indianapolis, IN 46219
(317) 591-5222
arc@icpr.state.in.us
http://www.state.in.us/icpr/archives
Alan F. January, Head
Mon–Fri 8:00–4:30
Pub. *Archives/Current: Newsletter of the Friends of the Indiana State Archives*, quarterly
(25,000 cubic feet of records dating from the territorial period to the present)
research: $10.00 per half-hour for out-of-state residents; copies: from 25¢ each from paper originals, $1.00 each from microform originals

Society of Indiana Archivists
State Library and Historical Building
140 North Senate Avenue
Indianapolis, IN 46204-2296
(317) 232-2537
cawley.1@nd.edu
http://cawley.archives.nd.edu/sia

Indiana State Library
140 North Senate Avenue
Indianapolis, IN 46204-2296
(317) 232-3689 (Genealogy Division); (317) 232-3664 (Newspaper Section); (317) 232-3670 (Indiana Reference Section); (317) 232-3671 (Manuscript Section)
http://www.statelib.lib.in.us
Diane Sharp, Coordinator, Genealogy Division; Cynthia Faunce, Consultant/Senior Subject Specialist, Indiana Division
Genealogy Division: Mon, Wed & Fri 8:00–4:30, Tue & Thur 8:00–8:00, Sat 8:30–4:00 (call to confirm hours); Indiana Division (housing the Newspaper, Manuscript and Indiana Reference sections): Mon–Fri 8:00–4:30
("The Genealogy Section contains many items pertaining to family history useful to genealogists. Most of the materials relate to families in Indiana although material from the eastern seaboard and southern states is also collected. The staff is not able to perform research but can assist those who come in to use the collections. The Newspaper Section contains newspapers from around the state, both historical and present day. The Reference Section contains many volumes pertaining to the history of the state of Indiana and biographical information about Indiana people. It also includes the depository for state documents. The Manuscript Section holds unpublished items relating to Indiana people, places and events. Civil War materials are one strength of the collection.")
photocopy charge, postage charge

State Historical Society

Indiana Historical Bureau
State Library and Historical Building
140 North Senate Avenue, Room 408
Indianapolis, IN 46204-2296
(317) 232-2535; (317) 232-3728 FAX
ihb@statelib.lib.in.us
http://www.statelib.lib.in.us/www/ihb/ihb.html
Judy A. Rippel, Administrative Assistant
Mon–Fri 8:00–4:30
Pub. *Indiana History Bulletin*, quarterly, $5.00 per year subscription; *The Indiana Historian*, quarterly, $5.00 per year subscription

Indiana Historical Society
450 West Ohio Street
Indianapolis, IN 46202-3269
(317) 234-0071 (Editor); (317) 232-1874 (Membership); (317) 234-0321 (Reference Services); (800) 447-1830; (317) 233-3109 FAX; (317) 234-0168 FAX (Reference Services)
tbaer@indianahistory.org
http://www.indianahistory.org; http://www.indianahistory.org/edu/localhistory/cohist.html (Indiana County Historians)
M. Teresa Baer, Editor; Tom Mason, Vice President, Indiana Historical Society Press
Library: Tue–Sat 10:00–5:00
Pub. *The Hoosier Genealogist*, quarterly ("single issues available for sale")
(library specializes in Indiana and The Old Northwest)
$35.00 per year membership

City, County and Regional Archives and Libraries
(A more exhaustive list of public and academic libraries can be found at http://www.statelib.lib.in.us/www/isl/lib/publib.html or http://www.statelib.lib.in.us/www/isl/ldo/libdir.html.)

Akron Carnegie Public Library
(205 East Rochester Street—location)
PO Box 428 (mailing address)
Akron, IN 46910-0428
(574) 893-4113 voice & FAX
http://www.akron.lib.in.us
Velma Bright, Director
(online searchable database of vital statistics)

Alexandria-Monroe Public Library
117 East Church Street
Alexandria, IN 46001-2005
(765) 724-2196
nnorris@alex.lib.in.us
http://www.alex.lib.in.us
Nancy L. Norris, Director

Alexandrian Public Library
115 West Fifth Street
Mount Vernon, IN 47620-1869
(812) 838-3286; (812) 838-9639 FAX
alexpl@evansville.net
http://www.apl.lib.in.us
Stephen Cochran, Director
Mon–Thur 9:00–8:00, Fri–Sat 9:00–5:00, Sun 1:00–5:00
Pub. *A~P~L Core* (Friends publication), quarterly, $10.00 per year
(Posey County, Indiana, local history and genealogy collections)

Allen County Public Library
Fred J. Reynolds Historical Genealogy Department
(900 Webster Street—location)
PO Box 2270 (mailing address)
Fort Wayne, IN 46801-2270
(219) 424-7241, ext. 3315
ncompton@acpl.lib.in.us; webmaster@acpl.lib.in.us; cwitcher@acpl.lib.in.us
http://www.acpl.lib.in.us
Curt B. Witcher, Manager

Mon–Thur 9:00–9:00, Fri–Sat 9:00–6:00,
Sun 1:00–6:00 (Labor Day–Memorial
Day)
Pub. *Periodical Source Index* (PERSI),
annually, $40.00 per year subscription
(North American genealogy and local
history: 183,000 volumes, 123,470 pieces
of microtext, approximately 3,500
periodicals)
$50.00 per year membership; up to six
articles copied for $7.50 plus 20¢ per
page to be billed, allow 6-8 weeks

Anderson Public Library
Local History and Genealogy Department
Indiana Room
111 East 12th Street
Anderson, IN 46016-2701
(765) 641-2442; (765) 641-2468 FAX
webmaster@and.lib.in.us
http://www.andersonlibrary.net
Beth E. Oljace, Local History and Genealogy
Librarian
Mon–Thur 9:00–9:00, Fri–Sat 9:00–5:30,
Sun 1:00–5:00
(Madison and Wayne counties, Indiana)

Andrews-Dallas Township Public Library
(30 East Madison Street—location)
PO Box 367 (mailing address)
Andrews, IN 46702-0367
(260) 786-3574 voice & FAX
Susan Anderson, Director

Attica Public Library
305 South Perry Street
Attica, IN 47918-1494
(765) 764-4194; (765) 764-0906 FAX
aplibnfink@netscape.net
http://www.attica.lib.in.us
Norma Fink, Director

Aurora Public Library
414 Second Street
Aurora, IN 47001-1384
(812) 926-0646; (812) 926-0665 FAX
webmaster@dearborncounty.org
http://www.dearborncounty.org/aurlib
Mary Alice Horton, Director

**Avon-Washington Township Public
Library**
498 North State Road 267
Avon, IN 46123-8478
(317) 272-4818; (317) 272-7302 FAX
awtpl@avon.lib.in.us
http://www.avon.lib.in.us
Laurel Setser, Director

Ball State University
Bracken Library
Muncie, IN 47306
(765) 285-1101; (765) 285-5078 (Archives
and Special Collections)
http://www.library.bsu.edu/index.html

Bartholomew County Public Library
536 Fifth Street
Columbus, IN 47201-6225
(812) 379-1255; (812) 379-1275 FAX
library@barth.lib.in.us
http://www.barth.lib.in.us
Elizabeth Booth Poor, Director
Mon–Thur 8:30–9:00, Fri–Sat 8:30–6:00,
Sun (Sept–Apr) 1:00–4:00
Pub. *Footnotes*, quarterly

Batesville Memorial Public Library
131 North Walnut Street
Batesville, IN 47006-4815
(812) 934-4706; (812) 934-6288 FAX
genealogy@ebatesville.com;

mkruse@ind.net; bmpl@cnz.com
http://www.bmpl.cnz.com
Judy Tonges, Genealogy and Local History
Specialist; Michael J. Kruse, Director
Mon–Thur 10:00-9:00, Fri–Sat 10:00–5:00;
Sat 1:00–5:00; Judy Tonges: Mon–Tue

Bedford Public Library
1323 K Street
Bedford, IN 47421-3297
(812) 275-4471; (812) 277-1145 FAX
bpl@bedlib.org
http://www.bedlib.org
Susan A. Miller, Director
Mon–Thur 9:00–8:00, Fri–Sat 9:00–5:00,
Sun 1:00–5:00
(local newspaper on microfilm, not indexed)
no research or copies

Beech Grove Public Library
1102 West Main Street
Beech Grove, IN 46107-1522
(317) 788-4203; (317) 788-0489 FAX
diane@bgpl.lib.in.us
http://www.bgpl.lib.in.us
Diane L. Burns, Director

Bell Memorial Public Library
(306 North Broadway—location)
PO Box 368 (mailing address)
Mentone, IN 46539-0368
(219) 353-7234; (574) 353-1307 FAX
bellib1@bell.lib.in.us
http://www.bell.lib.in.us
Eileen Bowser, Librarian's Assistant
Mon–Wed & Fri–Sat 9:00–5:00, Thur
9:00–8:00

Benton County Public Library
102 North Van Buren Avenue
Fowler, IN 47944-1299
(765) 884-1720 voice & FAX
bentoncountypl@hotmail.com
Sandra Furr, Director
Mon & Wed–Fri 8:00–5:00, Tue 8:00–7:30,
Sat 8:00–2:00, Sun 1:00–4:00

Berne Public Library
Heritage Room
166 North Sprunger Street
Berne, IN 46711-1595
(260) 589-2575; (260) 589-2940 FAX
bpl@bernepl.lib.in.us
http://www.bernepl.lib.in.us
Karen Adams, Heritage Room Manager
Mon–Wed & Fri–Sat 10:00–4:00, Thur
noon–8:00
("Primarily Adams County, Indiana, much
on local Swiss genealogy.")

Bicknell-Vigo Township Public Library
201 West Second Street
Bicknell, IN 47512-2109
(812) 735-2317; (812) 735-2018 FAX
bducharm@hotmail.com
http://www.bicknell-vigo.lib.in.us
Betty Jo Ducharme
Mon–Thur 10:00–8:00, Fri 10:00–5:00, Sat
10:00–3:00

**Bloomfield-Eastern Greene County Public
Library**
125 South Franklin Street
Bloomfield, IN 47424-1406
(812) 384-4125; (812) 384-0820
bloomfield@bloomfield.lib.in.us
http://www.bloomfield.lib.in.us
Carolyn Konnert, Library Director
Mon–Thur 10:00–8:00, Fri–Sat 10:00–5:00

Boonville Public Library
Indiana Room

611 West Main Street
Boonville, IN 47601-1544
(812) 897-1500; (812) 897-1508 FAX
Lois Aigner, Director

Boswell-Grant Township Public Library
(101 South Main Street—location)
PO Box 315 (mailing address)
Boswell, IN 47921-0315
(765) 869-5428 voice & FAX
boswelllib@hotmail.com
http://www.boswell.lib.in.us
Danielle Payne, Director

Bourbon Public Library
307 North Main Street
Bourbon, IN 46504-1521
(574) 342-5655; (574) 342-5001 FAX
Ramona Baer, Director

Brazil Public Library
204 North Walnut Street
Brazil, IN 47834-2297
(812) 448-1981; (812) 446-3215 FAX
jill@brazil.lib.in.us
http://www.brazil.lib.in.us
Jill E. Scarbrough, Director

Bremen Public Library
(304 North Jackson Street—location)
PO Box 130 (mailing address)
Bremen, IN 46506-0130
(574) 546-2849; (574) 546-4938 FAX
bremenpl@bremen.lib.in.us
http://www.bremen.lib.in.us
Marsha L. Patterson, Director

Bristol Public Library
505 West Vistula Street
Bristol, IN 46507-9464
(574) 848-7458; (574) 848-4391 FAX
webmaster@bristol.lib.in.us
http://www.bristol.lib.in.us
Sarah Bard, Director

Brook-Iroquois Township Public Library
(100 West Main—location)
PO Box 155 (mailing address)
Brook, IN 47922-0155
(219) 275-2471 voice & FAX
jwhaley@enterprise.palni.edu
http://www.brook.lib.in.us
Joyce Whaley, Director
Mon & Wed 9:00–7:00, Tue & Fri
9:00–5:00, Sat 9:00–1:00

Brookston-Prairie Township Library
111 West Second Street
Brookston, IN 47923
(765) 563-6511; (765) 563-6833 FAX
bptpl@dcwi.com
http://dcwi.com/~bptpl
Nancy H. Hartman, Director
Mon–Tue & Thur 1:00–8:00, Wed
9:00–8:00, Fri 1:00–5:00, Sat 9:00–1:00

Brown County Public Library
(205 Locust Lane—location)
PO Box 8 (mailing address)
Nashville, IN 47448-0008
(812) 988-2850; (812) 988-8119 FAX
yoliger@www.browncounty.lib.in.us
http://browncounty.lib.in.us
Yvonne Oliger, Director
Mon–Thur 9:00–8:00, Fri–Sat 9:00–5:00,
Sun 1:00–5:00

Brownsburg Public Library
450 South Jefferson Street
Brownsburg, IN 46112-1310
(317) 852-3167; (317) 852-7734 FAX
reference@brownsburg.lib.in.us

http://www.brownsburg.lib.in.us
Wanda Pearson, Director

Brownstown Public Library
120 East Spring Street
Brownstown, IN 47220-1403
(812) 358-2853; (812) 358-4116 FAX
http://www.brownstown.lib.in.us
Sherri L. May, Director

Butler Public Library
340 South Broadway
Butler, IN 46721-1308
(260) 868-2351; (260) 868-5491 FAX
ellen@butler.lib.in.us; mary@butler.lib.in.us
http://www.butler.lib.in.us
Ellen Stuckey, Director; Mary Marshall,
    Reference
Mon–Thur 9:00–7:00, Fri–Sat 9:00–1:00

Cambridge City Public Library
33 West Main Street
Cambridge City, IN 47327-1117
(765) 478-3335; (765) 478-6144 FAX
cambridgecitypubliclibrary@yahoo.com
http://www.cclib.lib.in.us
Vicki Rivers, Director
Mon & Wed 9:00–7:30, Tue & Thur–Fri
    9:00–5:00, Sat 10:00–5:00; History
    Room: Tue 2:00–4:00, and by
    appointment
("Have local history—Indiana, Wayne
    County, Cambridge City, Milton, Dublin,
    East Germantown.")

**Camden-Jackson Township Public
Library**
(183 West Main Street—location)
PO Box 24 (mailing address)
Camden, IN 46917-0024
(219) 686-2120 voice & FAX
cpl@tds.net
Shirley Schock, Director

Cannelton Public Library
210 South 8th Street
Cannelton, IN 47520-1218
(812) 547-6028; (812) 547-8590 FAX
cannpublib@hotmail.com
Sally L. Walker, Director

Carmel Clay Public Library
55 Fourth Avenue S.E.
Carmel, IN 46032-2278
(317) 844-3361 (Circulation); (317) 844-
    3362 (Reference)
askref@carmel.lib.in.us
http://www.carmel.lib.in.us
Wendy A. Phillips, Director
Mon–Thur 9:00–9:00, Fri–Sat 9:00–5:00,
    Sun 1:00–5:00

**Centerville Center Township Public
Library**
126 East Main Street
Centerville, IN 47330-1206
(765) 855-5223; (765) 855-2009 FAX
marie.bunch8@gte.net
http://www.cctpl.lib.in.us
Marie N. Bunch, Director
Mon, Wed & Fri 10:00–5:00, Tue & Thur
    10:00–8:00, Sat 10:00–2:00

Charlestown-Clark County Public Library
Sellersburg Library
Indiana Room
430 North Indiana
Sellersburg, IN 47172
(812) 246-4493; (812) 246-4382 FAX
mbundy@clarkco.lib.in.us;
    webmaster@clarkco.lib.in.us
http://www.clarkco.lib.in.us/sellersburg.htm

Carol Haas; Martha Bundy, Branch Manager
Mon–Thur 9:00–8:00, Fri–Sat 9:00–5:00
(mainly local history plus cemetery and
    church listings)

Charlestown-Clark County Public Library
Clarlestown Library
51 Clark Road
Charlestown, IN 47111-1997
(812) 256-3337; (812) 256-3890 FAX
tmeurer@clarkco.lib.in.us;
    webmaster@clarkco.lib.in.us
http://www.clarkco.lib.in.us/charlestown.
    htm
Susan Bennett, Researcher; Linda Lossner,
    Researcher; Tamsie Meurer, Director
Mon–Thur 9:00–8:00, Fri–Sat 9:00–5:00
(main genealogy source for the county)

Churubusco Public Library
116 North Mulberry Street
Churubusco, IN 46723-1701
(260) 693-6466 voice & FAX
buscolibrary@kconline.com
http://buscolibrary.whitleynet.org
Carol M. Scherer, Director
Mon, Wed & Fri 10:00–7:00, Tue & Thur
    3:00–7:00, Sat 9:00–2:00

Clayton-Liberty Township Public Library
(5199 Iowa Street—location)
PO Box E (mailing address)
Clayton, IN 46118-0405
(317) 539-2991; (317) 539-2050 FAX
cltpl@tds.net
http://personalpages.tds.net/~cltpl/index.htm
Jonnie J. Wallis, Director

Clinton Public Library
313 South Fourth Street
Clinton, IN 47842-2398
(765) 832-8349; (765) 832-3823 FAX
betty@clintonpl.lib.in.us
http://www.clintonpl.lib.in.us
Betty Lientz, Genealogy Assistant
Mon–Thur 9:00–8:00, Fri 9:00–5:00, Sat
    9:00–2:00
research: no charge for inquiries, but a
    nominal fee for copying and
    postage/handling

Coatesville Public Library
(4928 North Milton Street—location)
PO Box 147 (mailing address)
Coatsville, IN 46121-0147
(765) 386-2355; (765) 386-6177 FAX
Cheryl Steinborn, Director

Colfax Public Library
(207 South Clark Street—location)
PO Box 308 (mailing address)
Colfax, IN 46035-0308
(765) 324-2915; (765) 324-2689 FAX
colfaxplib@yahoo.com
http://www.colfax.lib.in.us
Judy J. Hemmerling, Director

Covington-Veedersburg Public Library
622 Fifth Street
Covington, IN 47932-1137
(765) 793-2572 voice & FAX
covlib@k-inc.com
http://www.covingtonlibrary.org
Rose Parrish, Interim Director

Covington-Veedersburg Public Library
408 North Main Street
Veedersburg, IN 47987
(765) 294-2808
Vpublib@k-inc.com
http://www.k-inc.com/~veedersburg

Crawford County Public Library
(203 Indiana Avenue—location)
PO Box 159 (mailing address)
English, IN 47118-0159
(812) 338-2606; (812) 338-3034 FAX
libstaff@cccn.net
http://www.crawfordco.lib.in.us
Catherine Ramsey, Director
summer: Tue & Thur 10:00–7:00, Wed &
    Fri–Sat 10:00–4:00
("We have old county newspapers and
    cemetery records and various other
    information for genealogy.")

Crawfordsville District Public Library
222 South Washington Street
Crawfordsville, IN 47933-2444
(765) 362-2242; (765) 362-7986 FAX
gen@cdpl.lib.in.us
http://www.cdpl.lib.in.us
Dian Moore, Local History Librarian

Crown Point Community Library
214 South Court Street
Crown Point, IN 46307-3975
(219) 663-0270; (219) 663-0403 FAX
bhouk@cyberz.net
http://www.icongrp.com/~refcpcl
Elizabeth Anstak; Barbara Houk, Special
    Services Librarian
Mon–Thur 9:00–8:00, Fri–Sat 9:00–5:00
(specializes in Indiana, especially Crown
    Point history)

Culbertson Mansion State Historic Site
914 East Main Street
New Albany, IN 47150
(812) 944-9600
Bill Brockman, Curator
Tue–Sat 9:00–5:00, Sun 1:00–5:00
(genealogical services)
donation accepted

Culver-Union Township Public Library
107 North Main Street
Culver, IN 46511-1313
(574) 842-2941; (574) 842-3441 FAX
spletka@culver.lib.in.us
http://www.culver.lib.in.us
Scott Pletka, Director

Danville Public Library
101 South Indiana Street
Danville, IN 46122-1809
(317) 745-2604; (317) 718-8003 FAX
dplind@dpl.lib.in.us
http://www.dpl.lib.in.us
Cindy Rutledge, Indiana Room
Mon–Thur 9:00–8:00, Fri–Sat 9:00–5:00,
    Sun 2:00–5:00

Darlington Public Library
(203 West Main Street—location)
PO Box 248 (mailing address)
Darlington, IN 47940-0248
(765) 794-4813 voice & FAX
John G. Dale, Director

**Daughters of the American Revolution,
Francis Vigo Chapter DAR Genealogical
Library**
(see Lineage, Hereditary and Patriotic
Societies, Part 3)

Decatur Public Library
128 South Third Street
Decatur, IN 46733-1691
(260) 724-2605; (260) 724-2877 FAX
dpldirector@mail.com
http://www2.decaturpl.lib.in.us
Kelly A. Ehinger, Director

Delphi Public Library
222 East Main Street
Delphi, IN 46923-1593
(765) 564-2929; (765) 564-4746 FAX
kelly@carlnet.orgdplibrar@carlnet.org
http://www.carlnet.org/dpl
Kelly Currie, Director
Mon–Thur 10:00–8:30, Fri 10:00–6:00, Sat
    10:00–5:00; Summer: Mon–Thur
    10:00–7:00, Fri 10:00–6:00, Sat
    10:00–4:00

DeMotte Public Library
901 Birch Street, S.W.
DeMotte, IN 46310
(219) 987-2221; (219) 987-2220 FAX

DePauw University
Roy O. West Library
Archives of DePauw University and Indiana
United Methodism
(400 South College Avenue—location)
PO Box 37 (mailing address)
Greencastle, IN 46135
(765) 658-4406; (765) 658-4423 FAX
archives@depauw.edu
http://www.depauw.edu/library/archives
Wesley W. Wilson, Coordinator of Archives
    and Special Collections
Mon–Fri 8:00–5:00, Tue 6:00–9:00;
    summer: Mon–Fri 8:00–4:00
Pub. *Newsletter*, semi-annually, free
(Includes members of the former Church of
    the United Brethren in Christ and
    Evangelical Church in Indiana. North
    Indiana Conference and South Indiana
    Conference.)
fee schedule available upon request

Dublin Public Library
(2249 East Cumberland—location)
PO Box 188 (mailing address)
Dublin, IN 47335-0188
(765) 478-6206 voice & FAX
dublinpubliclibrary@yahoo.com
Kamala Narayanan, Director

Earl Park Public Library
(102 East 5th Street—location)
PO Box 97 (mailing address)
Earl Park, IN 47942-0097
(219) 474-6932 voice & FAX
eplib@ffni.com
http://www.earlpark.lib.in.us
Theresia Hoover, Director

East Chicago Public Library
East Chicago History Room
2401 East Columbus Drive
East Chicago, IN 46312-2998
(219) 397-2453; (219) 397-6715 FAX
jmrajchel@ecpl.org
http://www.ecpl.org
Jennifer Beiriger, Archivist; Dr. James. M.
    Rajchel, Director
Library: Mon–Fri 9:00–8:00, Sat 9:00–5:30;
    East Chicago History Room: Mon &
    Wed–Fri 9:00–5:00

Eckhart Public Library
(William H. Willennar Genealogy Center,
    700 South Jackson Street—location)
603 South Jackson Street (mailing address)
Auburn, IN 46706-2298
(219) 925-2414, ext. 23; (260) 925-3635
    FAX
genealogy@epl.lib.in.us
http://www.epl.lib.in.us
Janelle H. Graber, Director
Library: Mon–Thur 9:00–8:00, Fri
    9:00–7:00, Sat 9:00–5:00; Genealogy
    Center: Tue 9:00–5:00, Wed noon–8:00,

Thur–Sat 9:00–5:00

Edinburgh Public Library
119 West Main Cross Street
Edinburgh, IN 46124-1499
(812) 526-5487; (812) 526-7057 FAX
chamm@edinburgh.lib.in.us
http://www.edinburgh.lib.in.us
Cathy Hamm, Director

Elkhart Public Library
300 South Second Street
Elkhart, IN 46516-3184
(574) 522-3333; (219) 522-5669; (219) 293-
    9213 FAX; (574) 522-2174 FAX
cjo@elkhart.lib.in.us
http://www.elkhart.lib.in.us
Marsha J. Eilers, Associate Director,
    Reference Services; Connie Jo Ozinga,
    Director
Mon–Thur 9:00–9:00, Fri–Sat 9:00–6:00
("Collection development centers on Elkhart
    and surrounding counties.")

**Elwood-North Madison County Public
Library**
1600 Main Street
Elwood, IN 46036-2023
(765) 552-5001; (765) 552-0955 FAX
baustin@elwood.lib.in.us
http://www.elwood.lib.in.us
Beverly Austin, Director

Evansville Museum of Arts and Science
411 S.E. Riverside Drive
Evansville, IN 47713
(812) 425-2406
John W. Streetman, III, Director
(local and regional history collection)

Evansville Vanderburgh Public Library
22 S.E. Fifth Street
Evansville, IN 47708-1694
(812) 428-8218; (812) 428-8215 FAX
Choose "Ask a Librarian!" at the web site
http://www.evpl.org
Sharon Olson, Reference Services Supervisor
Mon 9:00–8:00, Tue–Fri 9:00–6:00, Sat
    9:00–5:00, Sun (Sept–June) 1:00–5:00
(small DAR collection, available to the
    public on Friday afternoons)

Fairmount Public Library
(205 South Main Street—location)
PO Box 27 (mailing address)
Fairmount, IN 46928-0027
(765) 948-3177 voice & FAX
fairlib@frontiernet.net
Linda Magers, Director

Farmland Public Library
(116 South Main Street—location)
PO Box 189 (mailing address)
Farmland, IN 47340-0189
(765) 468-7292; (765) 468-7383 FAX
Monica R. Roberts, Director

Fayette County Historical Museum
103 South Vine Street
Connersville, IN 47331
(765) 825-0946
Harry Smith, Curator; Jim Wicker, Co-
    Curator
Sun 2:00–5:00, and by appointment

Fayette County Public Library
828 Grand Avenue
Connersville, IN 47331-2098
(765) 827-0883; (765) 825-4592 FAX
fcplgenealogy@yahoo.com
http://www.fcplibrary.lib.in.us
Paulette Hayes, Local History/Genealogy

Mon–Fri 9:00–8:00, Sat 9:00–5:00

Flora-Monroe Township Public Library
109 North Center Street
Flora, IN 46929-1004
(574) 967-3912; (574) 967-3671 FAX
floralib@carlnet.org
http://www.carlnet.org/floralib
Melissa Bishop, Director
Mon–Fri 10:00–6:00, Sat 10:00–4:00

Fort Branch Public Library
Main Library
107 East Locust Street
Fort Branch, IN 47648-1499
(812) 753-4212; (812) 753-4799 FAX
fblib@evansville.net
http://library.gibsoncounty.net
Lois Kissel, Director
Mon & Wed–Thur 9:00–5:00, Tue
    12:30–8:30, Fri–Sat 12:30–5:00

**Francesville-Salem Township Public
Library**
(201 West Montgomery Street—location)
PO Box 577 (mailing address)
Francesville, IN 47946-0577
(219) 567-9433; (219) 567-9433 FAX
francesvillelibrary@yahoo.com
Helen Vollmer, Director

**Frankfort Community/Clinton County
Contractual Public Library**
208 West Clinton Street
Frankfort, IN 46041-1899
(765) 654-8746; (765) 654-8747 FAX
fcpl@accs.net
http://www.accs.net/fcpl
Helen E. Grove, Genealogist
Mon–Thur 9:00–8:00, Fri–Sat 9:00–5:00
(genealogy of Clinton County and the
    surrounding area)
research: $5.00 for first request, $3.00 for
    each subsequent request within the same
    inquiry, plus copies

Franklin College Library
501 East Monroe Street
Franklin, IN 46131-2598
(317) 738-8162; (317) 736-6030 FAX
Archivist
hours: various (call or write to confirm)
("Archives, American Baptist churches of
    Indiana; Archives, Franklin College;
    David Demaree Banta Indiana History
    Collection.")
fee for photocopies mailed to patrons

Fremont Public Library
(205 West North Street—location)
PO Box 7 (mailing address)
Fremont, IN 46737-0007
(260) 495-7157; (260) 495-7127 FAX
Hope Wilson, Director

**Fulton County-Johnson Township Public
Library**
320 West Seventh Street
Rochester, IN 46975-1332
(219) 223-2713; (219) 223-5102 FAX
ref@fulco.lib.in.us
http://www.fulco.lib.in.us
Krystal Smith, Reference Librarian

Garrett Public Library
107 West Houston Street
Garrett, IN 46738-1494
(260) 357-5485; (260) 357-5170 FAX
Tillie@gpl.lib.in.us (subject: Reference
    Question)
http://www.gpl.lib.in.us
Kate Birdseye, Director

Mon–Thur 9:00–8:00, Fri 11:00–6:00, Sat 9:00–4:00

Gary Public Library
Indiana Room
220 West Fifth Avenue
Gary, IN 46402-1270
(219) 886-2484, ext. 315; (219) 882-9528 FAX; (219) 886-6829 FAX
http://www.gary.lib.in.us
David Hess, Indiana Room Librarian
Mon–Thur 9:00–8:00, Fri–Sat 9:00–5:00

Gas City-Mill Township Public Library
135 East Main Street
Gas City, IN 46933-1496
(765) 674-4718; (765) 674-5176 FAX
gascitypl@yahoo.com
http://www.gcmtpl.lib.in.us
Nancy Bryant, Library Director
Mon–Thur 10:00–8:00, Fri–Sat 10:00–5:00, closed Sat in summer

Geneva Public Library
(305 East Line Street—location)
PO Box 189 (mailing address)
Geneva, IN 46740-0189
(260) 368-7270; (260) 368-9776 FAX
genevalibrary@yahoo.com
http://www.genevapl.lib.in.us
Rose Bryan, Director

Goodland and Grant Township Public Library
(111 South Newton Street—location)
PO Box 405 (mailing address)
Goodland, IN 47948-0405
(219) 297-4431; (219) 297-4431 FAX
mitten@ffni.com
http://www.mwprairienet.lib.in.us/ Social_Services/goodlib.html
Joyce Crane, Director

Goshen Public Library
601 South Fifth Street
Goshen, IN 46526-3994
(574) 533-9531; (574) 533-5211 FAX
awaters@goshenpl.lib.in.us; gpl@goshenpl.lib.in.us
http://www.goshenpl.lib.in.us
Andrew Waters, Director

Gosport History Museum
(19 North Fourth Street—location)
PO Box 50 (mailing address)
Gosport, IN 47433
trotman@indiana.edu
Sue Trotman, Curator
Fri 9:00–4:00, Sat (Apr–Dec) 9:00–11:30
Pub. *Ten O'Clock News*, quarterly (Mar, June, Sept, Dec), $3.50 each for back issues
$10.00 per year membership; research: no service available, but "try to be helpful with inquiries"

Greentown Public Library
421 South Harrison Street
Greentown, IN 46936-1496
(765) 628-3534; (765) 628-3597 FAX
margi.bontrager@eastern.k12.in.us
http://www.eastern.k12.in.us/gpl/ grentown.htm
Marjorie Bontrager, Director
Mon, Wed & Fri 8:00–4:00, Tue & Thur 8:00–8:00, Sat 9:00-1:00

Greenwood Public Library
310 South Meridian
Greenwood, IN 46143-1699
(317) 881-1953; (317) 881-1963 FAX
mhamilton@mail.greenwood.lib.in.us;

reflib@mail.greenwood.lib.in.us
http://www.greenwood.lib.in.us
Margaret L. Hamilton, Director

Hacksma House Genealogy Library
(see Washington, Part 2)

Hagerstown-Jefferson Township Public Library
10 West College Street
Hagerstown, IN 47346-1295
(765) 489-5632; (765) 489-5808 FAX
Linda Mettler, Director

Hammond Public Library
564 State Street
Hammond, IN 46320-1532
(219) 931-5100; (219) 852-2230; (219) 931-3474 FAX
evansm@hammond.lib.in.us
http://www.hammond.lib.in.us
Kathryn Thegze, Information Services Librarian; Margaret M. Evans, Director
Mon & Wed 1:00–4:00
(Hammond area history)

Hancock County Public Library
700 North Broadway
Greenfield, IN 46140-1741
(317) 462-5141; (317) 462-5711 FAX
hcpl@hancockpub.lib.in.us
http://www.hancockpub.lib.in.us
Dianne Osborne, Director

Harrison County Public Library
105 North Capitol Avenue
Corydon, IN 47112-1144
(812) 738-4110; (812) 738-5408 FAX
hcpl@hcpl.lib.in.us
http://www.hcpl.lib.in.us
Violet (Vi) Eckart, Director

Hartford City Public Library
314 North High Street
Hartford City, IN 47348-2143
(765) 348-1720; (765) 348-5090 FAX
Vicki Cecil, Director

Hebron Public Library
(201 East Sigler Street—location)
PO Box 97 (mailing address)
Hebron, IN 46341
(219) 996-3684
http://www.pcpls.lib.in.us
Pamela Ferber, Branch Manager
Mon & Wed noon–9:00, Tue & Thur–Fri 10:00–6:00, Sat 9:00–5:00
("Our genealogy information is limited to a few family history books on local families.")

Henry Henley Public Library
(102 North Main Street—location)
PO Box 35 (mailing address)
Carthage, IN 46115-0035
(765) 565-6631
Denise Walker, Director

Huntingburg Public Library
419 North Jackson Street
Huntingburg, IN 47542-1301
(812) 683-2052; (812) 683-2056 FAX
klett@huntingburg.lib.in.us
http://www.huntingburg.lib.in.us
Kathleen Lett, Director
Mon–Wed 9:00–8:00, Thur–Sat 9:00–5:00, Sat (Memorial Day–Labor Day) 9:00–1:00

Huntington City-Township Public Library
Indiana Room
200 West Market Street

Huntington, IN 46750-2655
(260) 356-0824; (260) 356-3073 FAX
library@huntingtonpub.lib.in.us
http://www.huntingtonpub.lib.in.us
B. Joan Keefer, Department Head and County Historian
Mon–Thur 9:00–8:00, Fri–Sat 9:00–5:00
(extensive local history and genealogy)

Hussey-Mayfield Memorial Public Library
(250 North 5th Street—location)
PO Box 840 (mailing address)
Zionsville, IN 46077-1324
(317) 873-3149; (317) 873-8339 FAX
askalib@zionsville.lib.in.us
http://www.zionsville.lib.in.us
Martha E. Catt, Director
Mon–Thur 10:00–8:30; Fri–Sat 10:00–5:00, Sun (Sept–May) 1:00–5:00

Indiana State University
Cunningham Memorial Library
Department of Rare Books-Special Collections
Terre Haute, IN 47809
(812) 237-2610; (812) 237-2567 FAX
librbsc@isugw.indstate.edu
http://odin.indstate.edu/levell.dir/cml/ rbsc/index.html
Mon–Fri 8:30–noon & 1:00–4:00
(county histories, Civil War accounts, etc.)
no research services

Indiana University—Bloomington
Main Library
1320 East 10th Street
Bloomington, IN 47405-1801
(812) 855-8028 (Reference); (812) 855-8084 (Subject and Area Librarians); (812) 855-3722 (Government Publications); (812) 855-5672 (Newspapers)
http://www.indiana.edu/~librcsd

Indiana University-Purdue University at Fort Wayne
Walter E. Helmke Library
2101 East Coliseum Boulevard
Fort Wayne, IN 46805-1499
(219) 481-6514; (219) 481-6509 FAX
http://www-lib.ipfw.indiana.edu/index.html

IUPUI
University Library
Ruth Lilly Special Collections and Archives
755 West Michigan Street
Indianapolis, IN 46202-5195
(317) 274-0464
http://www.lib.iupui.edu/ecollects/ archives.html

Indianapolis-Marion County Public Library
Social Sciences Service Section
(40 East Saint Clair, Indianapolis, IN 46204—location under renovation
202 North Alabama Street—temporary location)
PO Box 211 (mailing address)
Indianapolis, IN 46206
(317) 269-1700; (317) 269-5229 FAX
ceo@imcpl.org
http://www.imcpl.lib.in.us
Laura Johnson, Interim Director
Mon–Fri 9:00–9:00, Sat 9:00–5:00, Sun 1:00–5:00
Pub. *Reading in Indianapolis*, monthly (only basic, introductory guides to doing genealogical research)

Jackson County Public Library
Seymour Library
303 West Second Street

Seymour, IN 47274-2147
(812) 522-3412; (812) 522-5456 FAX
jaker@japl.lib.in.us
http://www.japl.lib.in.us
Julia Aker, Library Director
Mon–Thur 8:30–8:30, Fri 8:30–6:00, Sat
    9:00–5:00, Sun 1:00–5:00

Jasper County Public Library
208 West Susan Street
Rensselaer, IN 47978-2447
(219) 866-5881; (219) 866-7378 FAX
jevers@jasperco.lib.in.us
http://www.jasperco.lib.in.us
Lynn E. Daugherty, Director; Jen Evers

Jasper Public Library
116 Main Street
Jasper, IN 47546-2899
(812) 482-2712; (812) 482-7123 FAX
Rita C. Douthitt, Director
Mon–Thur 9:00–8:00, Fri–Sat 9:00–5:00;
    Sun (Sept–Apr) noon–5:00

Jay County Public Library
Indiana Room
315 North Ship Street
Portland, IN 47371-2192
(219) 726-7890; (219) 726-7317 FAX
http://www.jaycpl.lib.in.us
Marcia Ford, Adult Services Librarian
Mon–Fri 8:00–8:00, Sat 8:00–5:00
(specializes in Jay County history)
research: $10.00 per hour

Jeffersonville Township Public Library
(211 East Court Avenue—location)
PO Box 1548 (mailing address)
Jeffersonville, IN 47131-1548
(812) 282-7765; (812) 285-5632
news@jefferson.lib.in.us
http://jefferson.lib.in.us
Ilona Franck, Manager, Adult Services
Mon–Thur 9:00–9:00, Fri 9:00–5:30, Sat
    9:00–5:00
(Clark County)

Jennings County Public Library
2375 North State Highway Three
North Vernon, IN 47265-7483
(812) 346-2091; (812) 346-2127 FAX
djg1816@hotmail.com
http://www.jenningscounty.lib.in.us
Denise Shafer, Assistant Librarian
Mon–Thur 9:00–9:00, Fri 9:00–6:00, Sat
    9:00–4:00
search: no search fee, except reimbursement
    of mailing costs, plus copies at 10¢ each,
    minimum $3.00

Johnson County Public Library
401 South State Street
Franklin, IN 46131-2545
(317) 738-2833; (317) 738-9635 FAX
frlref@jcplin.org
http://www.jcplin.org
Historical Room Librarian
Mon–Thur 9:00–8:00, Fri 9:00–6:00, Sat
    9:00–5:00, Sun (Labor Day–Memorial
    Day) 1:00–5:00
(Johnson County, Indiana, archives)
limited research by staff for a small fee (call
    or check the web site for details)

Jonesboro Public Library
124 East Fourth Street
Jonesboro, IN 46938-1105
(765) 674-8716; (765) 677-9080
jonesborolibrary@bpsinet.com
Carol Jones, Director

Kendallville Public Library

126 West Rush Street
Kendallville, IN 46755-1740
(260) 347-2768; (260) 347-5314 FAX
kpl@kendallvillelibrary.org;
    janderson@kendallvillelibrary.org
http://www.kendallvillelibrary.org
Jenny Draper, Director; Jenna Anderson,
    Community Relations Assistant

**Kentland-Jefferson Township Public
Library**
201 East Graham Street
Kentland, IN 47951-1233
(219) 474-5044; (219) 474-5351 FAX
Roberta Dewing, Director

Kewanna-Union Township Public Library
(210 East Main Street—location)
PO Box 365 (mailing address)
Kewanna, IN 46939-0365
(574) 653-2011; (574) 653-2130 FAX
kewannapublib@yahoo.com
Linda Hawkey, Director

Kirklin Public Library
(115 North Main Street—location)
PO Box 8 (mailing address)
Kirklin, IN 46050-0008
(765) 279-8308; (765) 279-8258 FAX
http://www.kirklinlibrary.com
Nancy Rogers, Director
Mon & Wed noon–7:00, Tue & Thur
    10:00–5:00; Fri noon–5:00, Sat
    10:00–3:00

**Knox County Public Library Historical
Collection**
(McGrady-Brockman House, 614 North
Seventh Street—location)
502 North Seventh Street (mailing address)
Vincennes, IN 47591-2101
(812) 886-4380; (812) 886-0342 FAX
bspangle@kcpl.lib.in.us;
    publib@kcpl.lib.in.us
http://www.kcpl.lib.in.us
Brian Spangle, Historical Collection
    Administrator
Mon noon–4:00 & 5:00–9:00, Tue–Wed &
    Fri–Sat 8:30–noon & 1:00–5:30
(includes many of the records of the Knox
    County Records Library)

Knox County Records Library
(see The Knox County Public Library
Historical Collection, above)

Kokomo-Howard County Public Library
Genealogy-Local History Services
Department
220 North Union Street
Kokomo, IN 46901-4614
(765) 457-3242, ext. 1601
genroom@kokomo.lib.in.us
http://www.kokomo.lib.in.us
Michele McNabb, Head
Mon–Thur 9:00–9:00, Fri–Sat 9:00–5:30,
    Sun (Labor Day–Memorial Day)
    2:00–5:30
research: $2.00 plus copies at 10¢ per page;
    as Old Richardville Publications,
    publishes material of local and statewide
    scope

Ladoga-Clark Township Public Library
(128 East Main Street—location)
PO Box 248 (mailing address)
Ladoga, IN 47954-0248
(765) 942-2456; (765) 942-2457 FAX
ladoga@ladoga.lib.in.us
http://www.ladoga.lib.in.us
Wanda Bennett, Director
Mon noon–5:00, Tue & Thur 1:00–7:00,

Wed & Fri 10:00–5:00, Sat 9:00–noon

LaGrange County Library
203 West Spring Street
LaGrange, IN 46761-1899
(260) 463-2842; (260) 463-2841 FAX
info@lagrange.lib.in.us
http://www.lagrange.lib.in.us
Mary A. Ball Hooley, Director
Mon–Thur (summer) 9:00–6:00, Mon–Thur
    (winter) 9:00–8:00, Fri–Sat 9:00–5:00

Lake County Public Library
Indiana Room Local History and Genealogy
1919 West 81st Avenue
Merrillville, IN 46410-5382
(219) 769-3541; (219) 769-0690 FAX
webmastr@lakeco.lib.in.us
http://www.lakeco.lib.in.us/indianaroom.
    html
Lawrence A. Acheff, Director
Mon–Thur 9:00–9:00, Fri 9:00–6:00, Sat
    9:00–5:00

LaPorte County Public Library
904 Indiana Avenue
LaPorte, IN 46350-3464
(219) 362-6156; (219) 362-6158 FAX
reference@lcpl2.lpco.lib.in.us
http://www.lapcat.org
Judy R. Hamilton, Director
Mon–Thur 9:00–8:00, Fri 9:00–6:00; Sat
    9:00–5:00

Lawrenceburg Public Library
123 West High Street
Lawrenceburg, IN 47025-1995
(812) 537-2775; (812) 537-2810 FAX
lawplib@seidata.com
http://www.lpld.lib.in.us
Sally Stegner, Director
Mon–Thur 10:00–8:00, Fri–Sat 10:00–5:00
("Have family histories, county histories,
    cemetery records, census records, local
    newspapers from 1819.")
enclose SASE with written inquiry; copies:
    25¢ per page from paper original, 50¢ per
    page from microfilm original

Lebanon Public Library
104 East Washington Street
Lebanon, IN 46052-2298
(765) 482-3460; (765) 873-5059 FAX
lplgen@bccn.boone.in.us
http://www.bccn.boone.in.us/LPL
Jamey Hickson, Heritage Librarian
Mon–Fri 9:00–5:00, Sat 10:00–2:00
research: $3.00–$10.00 plus copy and
    postage costs

**The Byron R. Lewis Historical Collection
Library**
LRC-22
Vincennes University
Vincennes, IN 47591
(812) 888-4330
gstevens@vunet.vinu.edu;
    rking@indian.vinu.edu
http://www.vinu.edu/PageWorks/servlet/
    PageMill?pageid=109&tempid=0
Robert R. Stevens, Director and Knox
    County Historian; Richard King,
    Reference Librarian (Florence Gould
    Watts Collection)
Mon–Fri 8:30–4:30

Ligonier Public Library
300 South Main Street
Ligonier, IN 46767-1812
(260) 894-4511; (260) 894-4509 FAX
Jerry L. Nesbitt, Director

Linden Carnegie Public Library
(102 South Main Street—location)
PO Box 10 (mailing address)
Linden, IN 47955-0010
(765) 339-4239; (765) 339-4239 FAX
Lisa Whipple, Director

Logansport-Cass County Public Library
616 East Broadway
Logansport, IN 46947-3187
(574) 753-6383; (574) 722-5889 FAX
http://www.logan.lib.in.us
Philip C. Shih, Director
Mon–Fri 9:00–9:00, Sat 9:00–5:00

Loogootee Public Library
410 North Line Street
Loogootee, IN 47553-1263
(812) 295-3713 voice & FAX
lplib@dmrtc.net
Mary Ringwald, Director

Lowell Public Library
1505 East Commercial Avenue
Lowell, IN 46356-1899
(219) 696-7704; (219) 696-5280 FAX
referenc@lowellpl.lib.in.us
http://www.lowellpl.lib.in.us
Francine Shreffler, Director
Mon–Thur 9:00–8:00; Fri–Sat 9:00–5:00

Madison-Jefferson County Public Library
420 West Main Street
Madison, IN 47250-3796
(812) 265-2744; (812) 265-2217 FAX
genealogy@madison-jeffco.lib.in.us
http://www.madison-jeffco.lib.in.us
Janice Barnes, Library Assistant
Genealogy Department open during regular
    business hours; Assistant: Mon & Wed
    1:00–5:00, Thur 4:00–9:00, Sat
    9:00–5:00
research: $5.00 per surname or subject for
    nonresidents; copies: 10¢ for nonresidents

Marion Public Library
Indiana Room
600 South Washington Street
Marion, IN 46953-1992
(765) 668-2900; (765) 668-2911 FAX
mpl@marion.lib.in.us;
    mplih@marion.lib.in.us
http://www.marion.lib.in.us
Rhonda Stoffer, Head of Indiana History and
    Genealogy
Mon, Wed & Fri 9:00–5:30; Tue & Thur
    9:00–9:00, Sat 9:00–5:00, Sun 1:00–5:00;
    summer: Mon, Wed & Fri 9:00–5:30, Tue
    & Thur 9:00–8:00, Sat 1:00–5:00
(Marion and Grant County history)
handling $1.00; copies: 10¢ each from paper
    originals, 15¢ each from microfilm
    originals, plus postage

William Hammond Mathers Museum
601 East Eighth Street
Bloomington, IN 47405
(812) 335-6873

Alameda McCollough Library and Archives
Wetherill Historical Resource Center
(see Tippecanoe County Historical Society,
    Historical Societies—Local and Regional,
    below)

Melton Public Library
8496 West College Street
French Lick, IN 47432-1068
(812) 936-2177; (812) 936-7524 FAX
carol@melton.lib.in.us
http://www.melton.lib.in.us

Carol Thornton-Anderson, Director
Mon & Fri 10:00–5:00, Tue & Thur
    10:00–7:00, Sat 10:00–3:00

Mennonite Historical Library
Goshen College
1700 South Main Street
Goshen, IN 46526
(219) 535-7418; (219) 535-7438 FAX
mhl@goshen.edu
http://www.goshen.edu/mhl
John D. Roth, Director
Mon–Fri 8:00–5:00, Sat 9:00–1:00
Pub. *Mennonite Quarterly Review* (a
    scholarly historical publication)
(strong in genealogy of Amish and
    Mennonite families from Switzerland,
    Germany, The Netherlands, West Prussia
    and Russia; U.S., European and Canadian
    records)
$30.00 per year membership in Mennonite
    Historical Society includes periodical

Michigan City Public Library
1 Library Plaza
Michigan City, IN 46360-3393
(219) 873-3063; (219) 873-3040; (219) 873-
    3475 FAX
reference@mclib.org
http://www.mclib.org
Vivianne L. Crowley, Library Genealogist
Library: Mon–Thur 9:00–8:00, Fri–Sat
    9:00–6:00, Sun 1:00–5:00; Genealogy:
    Wed & Fri–Sat noon–5:00
(Michigan City and Indiana family history)

Middletown Fall Creek Township Public Library
780 High Street
Middletown, IN 47356-1315
(765) 354-4071; (765) 354-9578 FAX
Jana Whitesel, Director

Milford Public Library
(101 North Main Street—location)
PO Box 269 (mailing address)
Milford, IN 46542-0269
(574) 658-4312; (574) 658-9454 FAX
milford@milford.lib.in.us
http://www.milford.lib.in.us
Linn M. Landis, Director
Mon & Thur 10:00–8:00, Tue–Wed & Fri
    10:00–6:00, Sat 10:00–2:00; Memorial
    Day–Labor Day: opens 9:00

Minnetrista Cultural Center
1200 North Minnetrista Parkway
Muncie, IN 47303-2925
(765) 282-4848
Karen Vincent, Director of Collections
Library: Mon–Sat 10:00–5:00
(archival material from east central Indiana)

Mishawaka-Penn-Harris Public Library
209 Lincoln Way, East
Mishawaka, IN 46544-2084
(574) 259-5277; (574) 255-8489 FAX
heritage@mppl.lib.in.us
http://www.mppl.lib.in.us
Olga Nazaroff
winter: Mon–Fri 9:00–9:00, Sat 9:00–6:00;
    summer: Mon–Thur 9:00–9:00, Fri
    9:00–6:00, Sat 9:00–1:00

Mitchell Community Public Library
804 West Main Street
Mitchell, IN 47446-1308
(812) 849-2412; (812) 849-2665 FAX
mitlib@mitlib.org
http://www.mitlib.org
Susan Medland, Director
Mon–Thur 9:00–8:00, Fri–Sat 9:00–5:00

Monon Town and Township Public Library
(427 North Market Street—location)
PO Box 305 (mailing address)
Monon, IN 47959-0305
(219) 253-6517; (219) 253-8373 FAX
jminnick@urhere.net
http://dcwi.com/~nhartman/monon.htm
Jo A. Minnick, Director

Monroe County Public Library
Indiana Room
303 East Kirkwood Avenue
Bloomington, IN 47408-3534
(812) 349-3080; (812) 349-3050; (812) 349-
    3051 FAX
pgrayove@monroe.lib.in.us
http://www.monroe.lib.in.us
Reann Lydick, Indiana Room Librarian
Mon–Thur 9:00–9:00, Fri 9:00–6:00, Sat
    9:00–5:00, Sun 1:00–5:00
(Local history, genealogy, Indiana history;
    "We have Bloomington/Monroe County
    newspapers microfilmed 1824–present,
    vital statistics, cemetery records, census
    records.")

Monterey-Tippecanoe TownshipPublic Library
(6260 East Main Street—location)
PO Box 38 (mailing address)
Monterey, IN 46960-0038
(574) 542-2171 voice & FAX
Renita Potthoff, Director

Montpelier-Harrison Township Public Library
301 South Main Street
Montpelier, IN 47359-1428
(765) 728-5969; (765) 728-5969 FAX
mhtpl@hotmail.com
Laura Lee, Director

Mooresville Public Library
Indiana Room
220 West Harrison
Mooresville, IN 46158-1633
(317) 831-7323; (317) 831-7383 FAX
wecare@mooresville.lib.in.us
http://web.incolsa.net/~mvillepl/
    indianaroom/indianaroom.htm
Wanta Potts, Indiana Room Librarian
Mon–Thur 9:00–8:00, Fri 9:00–5:00, Sat
    9:00–4:00

Morgan County Public Library
110 South Jefferson Street
Martinsville, IN 46151-1999
(765) 342-3451; (765) 342-9992 FAX
morglib@scican.net
http://morg.lib.in.us
Janice Kistler, Reference Librarian
Mon–Thur 9:00–8:30, Fri–Sat 9:00–5:30,
    Sun 1:00–5:00
Pub. morglib@scican.net
http://www.scican.net/~morglib/genasist/
    genasist.html

Morrisson-Reeves Library
80 North Sixth Street
Richmond, IN 47374-3079
(765) 966-8291; (765) 962-1318 FAX
library@mrl.lib.in.us
http://www.mrl.lib.in.us
Marilyn Nobbe, Reference Librarian
Sept–May: Mon–Thur 9:00–9:00, Fri–Sat
    9:00–5:30; June–Aug: Mon–Thur
    9:00–7:00, Fri–Sat 9:00–5:30
("This is a relatively small collection which
    focuses on Wayne and contiguous
    counties; index of Richmond newspapers
    from 1822.")

copies: 10¢ each plus cost of mailing

Muncie Public Library
Local History and Genealogy Center
201 South Jefferson Street
Muncie, IN 47305
(765) 747-8208
mgentis@munpl.org
http://www.munpl.org
Mary Lou Gentis, Supervisor
Mon–Fri 9:00–6:00, Sat 9:00–1:00

Nappanee Public Library
157 North Main Street
Nappanee, IN 46550-1956
(574) 773-7919; (574) 773-7910 FAX
lyoder@nappanee.lib.in.us
http://www.nappanee.lib.in.us
Linda Yoder, Director
Mon–Thur 9:00–9:00, Fri 9:00–5:00, Sat
    9:00–5:00, Sun 1:00–5:00
Pub. *The Insider*
("The Nappanee Public Library houses a
    large local history collection in the Evelyn
    Lehman Culp Heritage Center. Included is
    a complete file of the *Nappanee Advance
    News* and predecessors, 1879 to date; an
    extensive index file providing easy access
    to all aspects of local history in those
    papers; an indexed picture file 1874 to
    date of local personalities, businesses,
    building, and scenes; diaries and
    recollections of pioneers 1860 to date;
    cemetery records, census records of
    Elkhart County on microfilm, and
    hundreds of other important source
    materials.")

New Albany-Floyd County Public Library
Stuart Barth Wrege Indiana History Room
180 West Spring Street
New Albany, IN 47150-3692
(812) 949-3527
http://www.nafcpl.lib.in.us
Lynn B. Rueff, Department Manager
Mon–Thur 9:00–8:30, Fri–Sat 9:00–5:30
(Floyd County history and southern Indiana
    genealogy)

**New Carlisle and Olive Township Public
Library**
(408 South Bray—location)
PO Box Q (mailing address)
New Carlisle, IN 46522-0837
(574) 654-3046; (574) 654-8260 FAX
Stephen Boggs, Director

New Castle-Henry County Public Library
(376 South 15th Street—location)
PO Box J (mailing address)
New Castle, IN 47362-1050
(765) 529-0362; (765) 521-3581 FAX
kathiew@nchcpl.lib.in.us (Genealogy)
http://www.nchcpl.lib.in.us
Bertha Snell, Genealogy Librarian; Kathie
    Ward
Mon–Thur 8:30–9:00, Fri 8:30–6:00, Sat
    8:30–5:00, Sun (Sept–May) 1:00–5:00
copies: 10¢ per page

**New Harmony Workingmen's Institute
Library and Museum**
(407 West Tavern Street—location)
PO Box 368 (mailing address)
New Harmony, IN 47631
(812) 682-4806
Bonnie Smith, Director
Tue–Sat 10:00–4:30
("Extensive local history file.")
research: $4.00

Newport-Vermillion County Library

(385 East Market Street—location)
PO Box 100 (mailing address)
Newport, IN 47966-0100
(765) 492-3555; (765) 492-4553 FAX
Newport_library@hotmail.com
http://members.aol.com/KFether123/
    verlib.html
Bright Steinbrenner, Genealogy Department
Mon–Fri 8:30–6:00, Sat 10:00–2:00

Noble County Public Library
Genealogy Room
813 East Main Street
Albion, IN 46701-1302
(260) 636-7197; (260) 636-3321 FAX
http://www.nobleco.lib.in.us
Sandra Petrie, Director
Mon–Thur 8:30–8:30, Fri 8:30–5:30, Sat
    8:30–3:30
(cemetery records, obituary files, census,
    newspapers)

Noblesville-Southeastern Public Library
Indiana Room
1 Library Plaza
Noblesville, IN 46060-5639
(317) 773-1384; (317) 770-3206
masseyn@hepl.lib.in.us
http://www.hepl.lib.in.us/ref/
    indiana_room.html
Nancy Massey, Indiana Room Assistant
Mon–Thur 9:00–9:00, Fri–Sat 9:00–5:30,
    Sun 1:30–5:30
(emphasis on Hamilton County histories and
    genealogical records; obituary file index
    of Hamilton County newspapers on
    microfilm)

**North Judson-Wayne Township Public
Library**
208 Keller Avenue
North Judson, IN 46366-1208
(574) 896-2841; (574) 896-2892 FAX
Jane Ellen Felchuk, Director

North Manchester Public Library
405 North Market Street
North Manchester, IN 46962-1526
(219) 982-4773; (260) 982-6342 FAX
nmpl@nman.lib.in.us
http://www.nman.lib.in.us
Davonne Rogers, Director

**Oakland City-Columbia Township Public
Library**
210 South Main Street
Oakland City, IN 47660-1538
(812) 749-3559 voice & FAX
Patsy Creasey, Director
Mon–Fri 10:00–6:00, Sat 10:00–5:00

Odon Winkelpleck Public Library
202 West Main Street
Odon, IN 47562-1218
(812) 636-4805; (812) 636-4949 voice &
    FAX
staff@odon.lib.in.us
http://www.odon.lib.in.us
Marsha Lynn, Director

Ohio County Public Library
100 North High Street
Rising Sun, IN 47040-1092
(812) 438-2257; (812) 438-2257 FAX
ohiopubl@seidata.com
http://www.ohioco.lib.in.us
Amy C. Ketzer, Director

Ohio Township Public Library System
23 West Jennings Street
Newburgh, IN 47630-1211
(812) 853-5468; (812) 853-6377 FAX; (812)

853-0509 FAX
http://www.ohio.lib.in.us
Janet Weideman, Local History/Genealogy
    Librarian
Mon noon–4:00, Tue–Fri 9:00–5:00, Sat
    10:00–5:00

**Orleans Town and Township Public
Library**
(174 North Maple Street—location)
PO Box 142 (mailing address)
Orleans, IN 47452-0142
(812) 865-3270; (812) 865-2320 FAX
orleanslibrary@hotmail.com
http://www.orleans.lib.in.us
Deborah Stone, Director
Mon–Tue & Thur–Fri 10:00–6:00, Sat
    9:00–noon

Osgood Public Library
(136 West Ripley Street—location)
PO Box 235 (mailing address)
Osgood, IN 47037-0235
(812) 689-4011 voice & FAX
http://www.geocities.com/osgoodlibrary
John J. Castleman, Director
Mon noon–8:00, Tue–Fri noon–6:00, Sat
    noon–4:00

Otterbein Public Library
(29 South Main Street—location)
PO Box 550 (mailing address)
Otterbein, IN 47970-0550
(765) 583-2107; (765) 583-2107 FAX
Cynthia M. Rifner, Director

Owen County Public Library
10 South Montgomery Street
Spencer, IN 47460-1738
(812) 829-3392; (812) 829-6165 FAX
genealogy@owenlib.org
http://www.owenlib.org
Vickey Freeland, Director
Mon–Thur 9:00–8:00, Fri 9:00–5:00, Sat
    9:00–3:00

Owensville Carnegie Public Library
(110 South Main Street—location)
PO Box 219 (mailing address)
Owensville, IN 47665-0219
(812) 724-3335; (812) 724-3336 FAX
Peggy Callis, Director

Oxford Public Library
(201 East Smith Street—location)
PO Box 6 (mailing address)
Oxford, IN 47971-0006
(765) 385-2177; (765) 385-2313 FAX
oxlib@localline.com
http://www.oxford.lib.in.us
Julia A. Frew, Director

Paoli Public Library
10 East Court
Paoli, IN 47454-1321
(812) 723-3841 voice & FAX
paolilibrary@hotmail.com
Carol Vance, Librarian
Mon & Thur–Fri 12:30–5:30, Tue
    11:00–7:00, Sat 9:00–1:00

Peabody Public Library
(1160 East Highway 205—location)
PO Box 406 (mailing address)
Columbia City, IN 46725-0406
(260) 244-5541; (260) 244-5653 FAX
Christine@peabody.whitleynet.org
    (Webmaster)
http://www.ppl.lib.in.us
Janet M. Scank, Director

Penn Township Public Library

(195 North Union—location)
PO Box 206 (mailing address)
Pennville, IN 47369-0206
(219) 731-3333 voice & FAX
Carla Mae Wilson, Director

Peru Public Library
102 East Main Street
Peru, IN 46970-2300
(765) 473-3069; (765) 473-3060 FAX
ppl@peru.lib.in.us
http://www.peru.lib.in.us
Charles A. Wagner, Director
Mon–Thur 9:00–9:00, Fri–Sat 9:00–5:30

**Pierceton and Washington Township
Public Library**
(101 Catholic Street—location)
PO Box 328 (mailing address)
Pierceton, IN 46562-0328
(574) 594-5474
piercetonlibrary@kconline.com
Pamela Myers, Director

Pike County Public Library
Barrett Memorial Library
1104 Main Street
Petersburg, IN 47567-1337
(812) 354-6257; (812) 354-6259 FAX
genealogy_pikeco@hotmail.com
http://www.pikeco.lib.in.us
Shirley R. Behme, Genealogy Department;
    Elaine Young, Genealogy Department
Mon–Thur 9:00–8:00, Tue–Wed & Fri–Sat
    9:00–5:00

**Plainfield-Guilford Township Public
Library**
Guilford Township Historical Collection
1120 Stafford Road
Plainfield, IN 46168-2230
(317) 839-6602; (317) 838-3807 FAX
scarter@plainfield.lib.in.us
http://history.plainfield.lib.in.us
Susan Miller Carter, Department Head
Mon–Thur 9:00–8:00, Fri–Sat 9:00–5:00,
    Sun (Sept–May) 1:00–5:00

Plymouth Public Library
201 North Center Street
Plymouth, IN 46563
(219) 936-2324; (219) 936-7423 FAX
genealogy@plymouth.lib.in.us
http://www.plymouth.lib.in.us
Linda Hindman, Genealogy Librarian
Sept–May: Mon–Thur 9:00–9:00, Fri
    9:00–8:00, Sat 9:00–5:30, Sun 1:00–5:00;
    June–Aug: Mon–Fri 9:00–8:00, Sat 9:00-
    5:30
(repository for the Pioneer Society of
    Marshall County lineages)
research: $2.00 minimum, plus 15¢ per page
    for copies, plus SASE or postage charge

Porter County Public Library System
107 East Jefferson Street
Valparaiso, IN 46383-4820
(219) 462-0524; (219) 477-4866 FAX
http://www.pcpls.lib.in.us/index.html
Larry J. Clark, Genealogy Department Head
Mon–Fri 9:00–9:00, Sat 9:00–5:00
(Indiana, Midwest, eastern and southeastern
    United States, Canada, and some
    European information)

Poseyville Carnegie Public Library
(55 South Cale Street—location)
PO Box 220 (mailing address)
Poseyville, IN 47633-0220
(812) 874-3418 voice & FAX
library2@ccsi.tds.net
http://www.angelfire.com/in/carnegielibrary

Stanley Campbell, Director
Tue 9:00–9:00, Thur 5:00–8:30, Sat
    9:00–5:00

Princeton Public Library
124 South Hart Street
Princeton, IN 47670-2198
(812) 385-4464; (812) 386-1662 FAX
http://www.princetonpl.lib.in.us
Shellie Krantz, Director
Library: Mon–Thur 9:00–8:00, Fri–Sat
    9:00–5:00, Sun (Sept–May) 1:00–5:00;
    Genealogy: Mon 9:00–8:00, Tue–Fri
    9:00–5:00, second & fourth Sat 9:00–5:00

Pulaski County Public Library
121 South Riverside Drive
Winamac, IN 46996-1596
(219) 946-3432; (574) 946-6598 FAX
Lynda Irving, Pulaski County Historian
Mon 9:00–8:00, Tue–Sat 9:00–6:00

Putnam County Public Library
(103 East Poplar Street—location)
PO Box 116 (mailing address)
Greencastle, IN 46135-0116
(765) 653-2755; (765) 653-2756 FAX
director@putnam.lib.in.us;
    library@putnam.lib.in.us
http://www.putnam.lib.in.us
Alice Greenburg, Director
Mon & Fri 9:00–5:30, Tue–Thur 9:00–8:00,
    Sat 9:00–5:00; Genealogy volunteer/staff
    assistance: Mon–Sat 9:30–noon &
    1:00–5:00, Tue–Thur 6:00–8:00

**Remington-Carpenter Township Public
Library**
(105 Ohio Street—location)
PO Box 65 (mailing address)
Remington, IN 47977-0065
(219) 261-2543; (219) 261-3800 FAX
Nan E. McGlynn, Director

Ridgeville Public Library
(308 North Walnut Street—location)
PO Box 63 (mailing address)
Ridgeville, IN 47380-0063
(765) 857-2025 voice & FAX
rplibrary@jayco.net
Marcella McCormick, Director
Tue 12:30–8:00, Wed 1:00–5:00, Thur
    12:30–7:00
("We do not have a genealogical society. Our
    files are maintained by local interested
    patrons.")

**Roachdale-Franklin Township Public
Library**
(100 East Washington Street—location)
PO Box 399 (mailing address)
Roachdale, IN 46172-0399
(765) 522-1491 voice & FAX
roachdalepl@tds.net
Debra Sillery, Director

Roann-Paw Paw Township Public Library
(245 South Chippewa Street—location)
PO Box 248 (mailing address)
Roann, IN 46974-0248
(765) 833-5231 voice & FAX
roannlibrary@yahoo.com
http://www.geocities.com/roannlibrary
Joy A. Harber, Director

Roanoke Public Library
(126 North Main Street—location)
PO Box 249 (mailing address)
Roanoke, IN 46783-0249
(260) 672-2989; (260) 672-3306 FAX
Daryl K. Shrock, Director

Rockville Public Library
106 North Market Street
Rockville, IN 47872-1718
(765) 569-5544; (765) 569-5546 FAX
Cindy Hein, Director
Mon–Fri 9:00–6:00, Sat 9:00–2:00
research: $8.00 per family (queries
    forwarded to Parke County Historical
    Society)

**Royal Center-Boone Township Public
Library**
(203 North Chicago Street—location)
PO Box 459 (mailing address)
Royal Center, IN 46978-0459
(574) 643-3185; (574) 643-5003 FAX
royalcenterlib@myvine.com
Phyllis J. Gray, Director

Rushville Public Library
130 West Third Street
Rushville, IN 46173-1899
(765) 932-3496; (765) 932-4528 FAX
sueotte@rpl.lib.in.us; rpl@rpl.lib.in.us
http://www.rushcounty.com/library
Sue Prifogle Otte, Director
Mon & Wed 9:00–8:00, Tue & Thur
    9:00–6:00, Fri–Sat 9:00–5:00

Saint Joseph County Public Library
304 South Main Street
South Bend, IN 46601-2230
(219) 282-4621; (219) 282-4679 FAX
donald.napoli@sjcpl.org;
    d.matthews@gmail.sjcpl.lib.in.us (Dawn
    Matthews, Reference);
    webmaster@sjcpl.org
http://sjcpl.lib.in.us
Mary Waterson, Local History/Genealogy;
    Donald Napoli, Director
Mon–Thur 9:00–9:00, Fri–Sat 9:00–6:00,
    Sun (Oct–Apr) 1:00–5:00

Salem Public Library
212 North Main Street
Salem, IN 47167-9167
(812) 883-5600; (812) 883-5604; (812) 883-
    1609 FAX
http://www.salemlib.lib.in.us/index.htm
Eric Magness-Eubank, Director
Mon–Thur 9:30–8:00, Fri–Sat 9:30–5:00,
    Sun 1:00–5:00

Scott County Public Library
108 South Main Street
Scottsburg, IN 47170-1892
(812) 752-2751; (812) 752-2878 FAX
ishmael@scottsburg.com
http://www.scott.lib.in.us
Andrew H. Rowden, Director
Mon & Thur 9:00–8:00, Tue–Wed & Fri
    9:00–6:00, Sat 9:00–5:00

Shelbyville-Shelby County Public Library
Genealogy and History Room
57 West Broadway, Suite 4
Shelbyville, IN 46176-1294
(317) 398-7121; (317) 398-4480
    (Reference); (317) 398-8144 (Genealogy);
    (317) 835-2653 FAX; (317) 398-4430
    FAX (Reference)
jcheatham@sscpl.lib.in.us
http://www.sscpl.lib.in.us/library/
    Genealogy.htm
Ann Herold-Short, Director
Library: Mon–Thur 9:00–9:00, Fri
    9:00–7:00, Sat 9:00–5:00; Genealogy and
    History Room: Mon–Thur 10:00–8:00,
    Fri–Sat 9:00–5:00

Sheridan Public Library
214 Main Street

Sheridan, IN 46069-1142
(317) 758-5201 voice & FAX
ann@sheridan.lib.in.us
http://www.sheridan.lib.in.us
Ann Emery, Director
Mon–Thur 10:00–7:00, Fri 10:00–5:30, Sat
    9:00–noon

Shoals Public Library
(402 North High Street—location)
PO Box 909 (mailing address)
Shoals, IN 47581-0909
(812) 247-3838 voice & FAX
shoalspl@hotmail.com
http://www.shoals.lib.in.us
Linda G. Jones, Director

Speedway Public Library
5633 West 25th Street
Speedway, IN 46224-3899
(317) 244-8959; (317) 243-9373 FAX
webmaster@speedway.lib.in.us
http://www.speedway.lib.in.us
Darsi Bohr, Director; Tony Zishka,
    Webmaster

Spencer County Public Library
210 Walnut Street
Rockport, IN 47635-1398
(812) 649-4866, ext. 12; (812) 649-4018
    FAX
reference@rockport-spco.lib.in.us
http://www.rockport-spco.lib.in.us
Becky Middleton, Genealogy Room
    Librarian
Mon & Fri 9:00–5:00, Tue–Thur 9:00–9:00,
    Sat 9:00–3:00
(microfilm copies of probate records
    November 1833–December 1921,
    guardianships 1871–1885, wills
    1833–1933, marriages March
    1818–December 1921, naturalizations
    July 1852–1903, indentures 1836–1855,
    deeds November 1818–1886,
    grantor/grantee indexes 1818–1888, index
    of birth records 1882–1920, death records
    1882–1936)

Spiceland Town-Township Public Library
(106 West Main Street —location)
PO Box 445 (mailing address)
Spiceland, IN 47385-0445
(765) 987-7472; (765) 987-8840 FAX
Teresa Janney, Director

Carnegie Public Library of Steuben County
(25 South Public Square—temporary
    location)
322 South Wayne Street (mailing address)
Angola, IN 46703-1956
(260) 665-3362; (260) 665-8958 FAX
info@steuben.lib.in.us;
    reference@steuben.lib.in.us
http://www.cpl.cnz.com
Kay Lash, Reference Librarian
Mon–Thur 9:00–8:00, Fri 9:00–5:00, Sat
    9:00–3:00
genealogy research requested by those
    outside of Pleasant and York townships in
    Steuben County: $2.00 each for correctly
    dated records, $2.00 for first faxed page,
    $1.00 for each additional page, 25¢ per
    page for copies, $1.00 postage (or SASE)

Sullivan County Public Library
Genealogy/Local History Department
100 South Crowder Street
Sullivan, IN 47882-1750
(812) 268-4957; (812) 268-5370 FAX
dadams@sullivan.lib.in.us
http://www.sullivan.lib.in.us

Donna K. Adams, Sullivan County Historian
    and Head of Genealogy/Local History
    Department
Mon–Fri 9:00–5:00, Sat noon–5:00
("Always willing to help people find their
    local ties.")
basic charge: $2.00 plus postage, included up
    to twelve copies

Patrick Henry Sullivan Museum and Genealogy Library
225 West Hawthorne Street
Zionsville, IN 46077
(317) 873-4900
http://www.artcom.com/museums/nv/mr/
    46077-16.htm

Swayzee Public Library
(301 South Washington—location)
PO Box 307 (mailing address)
Swayzee, IN 46986-0307
(765) 922-7526; (765) 922-4538 FAX
swaypub@comteck.com
Dianna King, Director

Switzerland County Public Library
(205 Ferry Street—location)
PO Box 133 (mailing address)
Vevay, IN 47043-0133
(812) 427-3363; (812) 427-3654 FAX
info@switzcpl.lib.in.us
http://www.switzcpl.lib.in.us
Kristi D. Harms, Director
Mon–Fri 9:00–6:00, Sat 9:00–5:00

Syracuse Public Library
115 East Main Street
Syracuse, IN 46567-1189
(574) 457-3022; (574) 457-8971 FAX
http://www.syracuse.lib.in.us
Rosalyn Jones, Director
Mon–Wed 10:00–8:00, Thur noon–7:00, Fri
    10:00–6:00, Sat 10:00–5:00

Thorntown Public Library
124 North Market Street
Thorntown, IN 46071-1144
(765) 436-7348; (765) 436-7011 FAX
niemeyer@bccn.boone.in.us;
    tpl@bccn.boone.in.us
http://www.bccn.boone.in.us/tpl
Karen K. Niemeyer, Director
Mon & Fri 10:00–6:00, Tue–Thur
    10:00–8:00, Sat 10:00–4:00

Tippecanoe County Public Library
Reference Department
627 South Street
Lafayette, IN 47901-1470
(765) 429-0100; (765) 429-0150
jholman@tcpl.lib.in.us
http://www.tcpl.lib.in.us
Jos Holman, Director
Mon–Thur 9:00–9:00, Fri–Sat 9:00–6:00,
    Sun 1:00–6:00
$10.00 per name for search of newspapers
    from 1854 (must have exact dates)

Tipton County Public Library
127 East Madison Street
Tipton, IN 46072-1993
(765) 675-8761; (765) 675-4475 FAX
tipton@tiptonpl.lib.in.us
http://www.tiptonpl.lib.in.us
Julie Brown, Head of Information Services
Mon–Thur 9:30–8:00, Fri–Sat 9:30–5:00

Union City Public Library
408 North Columbia Street
Union City, IN 47390-1410
(765) 964-4748 voice & FAX
Virginia M. Hiatt, Director

("Local newspapers 1873–present on
    microfilm [indexed in book form] Darke
    and Preble counties, Ohio. Census on
    microfilm for Randolph, Jay and Wayne
    counties, Indiana, and Darke and Preble
    counties, Ohio.")
search: $10.00 per hour, including copies

Union County Public Library
2 East Seminary Street
Liberty, IN 47353-1398
(765) 458-5355; (800) 694-6300; (765) 458-
    9375 FAX
UCheritage@hotmail.com
http://www.union-county.lib.in.us
Karen Coffey
Mon–Wed 9:00–8:00, Tue & Thur–Fri
    9:00–6:00, Sat 9:00–3:00
copies: 10¢ per page plus postage

University of Notre Dame
Rare Books and Special Collections
102 Hesburgh Library
Notre Dame, IN 46556
(219) 631-5636; (219) 631-6772
library.rarebook.1@nd.edu
http://www.nd.edu

University of Southern Indiana
David L. Rice Library
Special Collections/University Archives
8600 University Boulevard
Evansville, IN 47712-3595
(812) 464-1896
http://www.usi.edu/library/library.htm
Gina Walker, Certified Archivist
Mon–Fri 8:00–noon & 1:00–4:30

Vigo County Public Library
Special Collections/Archives
1 Library Square
Terre Haute, IN 47807-3609
(812) 232-1113, ext. 212 or 292; (812) 232-
    3208 FAX
http://www.vigo.lib.in.us
Nancy Sherrill, Genealogy; Susan Dehler,
    Archives
Mon–Thur 9:00–9:00, Fri 9:00–6:00, Sat
    9:00–5:00, Sun 1:00–5:00 (Labor
    Day–Memorial Day)

Wabash Carnegie Public Library
188 West Hill Street
Wabash, IN 46992-3048
(260) 563-2972; (260) 563-0222 FAX
general@wabash.lib.in.us
http://www.wabash.lib.in.us/wcpl
Helen M. Bruss, Technical Services
Mon–Thur 9:00–8:00, Fri–Sat 9:00–5:00
("We have a great deal of Wabash County
    genealogy information.")

Wakarusa Public Library
(124 North Elkhart Street—location)
PO Box 485 (mailing address)
Wakarusa, IN 46573-0485
(574) 862-2465; (574) 862-4156 FAX
lhartman@wakarusa.lib.in.us
http://www.wakarusa.lib.in.us
Linda Hartman, Historical Librarian
Mon–Tue & Thur 9:00–8:00, Wed & Fri
    9:00–5:30, Sat 9:00–2:00

Walkerton-Lincoln Township Public Library
300 Michigan Street
Walkerton, IN 46574-1296
(574) 586-2933; (574) 586-2933 FAX
Connie Jo Swanson, Director

Walton and Tipton Township Public Library

(103 East Bishop—location)
PO Box 406 (mailing address)
Walton, IN 46994-0406
(574) 626-2234 voice & FAX
waltonlibrary@hotmail.com
http://www.walton.lib.in.us
Robert Moore, Library Director
Tue–Fri 10:00–6:00, Sat 9:00–noon
Pub. *Library Newsletter*, monthly

Wanatah Public Library
(104 North Main Street—location)
PO Box 299 (mailing address)
Wanatah, IN 46390-0299
(219) 733-9303; (219) 733-2763 FAX
wanatahl@msn.com
Patricia Baum, Director

Warren Public Library
(123 East Third Street—location)
PO Box 327 (mailing address)
Warren, IN 46792-0327
(260) 375-3450; (260) 375-3450 FAX
warrenpl@warren.lib.in.us
http://www.warren.lib.in.us
Rosalie Walter, Director

Warrick County Museum, Inc.
(117 South First Street—location)
PO Box 581 (mailing address)
Boonville, IN 47601
(812) 897-3100
Virginia S. Allen, Director
Mon–Thur 11:00–2:00, Sun 1:00–4:00
free admission, tours arranged

Warsaw Community Public Library
310 East Main Street
Warsaw, IN 46580-2882
(574) 267-6011; (574) 269-7739; (574) 267-3959 FAX
refdesk@wcpl.lib.in.us
http://www.wcpl.lib.in.us
Mon–Thur 9:00–9:00, Fri–Sat 9:00–6:00
(materials on Kosciusko County, Indiana)

Washington Carnegie Public Library
300 West Main Street
Washington, IN 47501-2698
(812) 254-4586; (812) 254-4585 FAX
Attn: Elizabeth Dowling, Director

Waveland Brown Township Public Library
(115 East Green Street—location)
PO Box 158 (mailing address)
Waveland, IN 47989-0158
(765) 435-2700; (765) 435-2434 FAX
wavelib@wico.net
Karen D. Moser, Director
Mon–Fri 1:00–5:00, Tue & Thur 6:30–8:30, Sat 9:30–12:30
("Copies of old *Waveland Independent*, newspaper with list of obituaries.")

Wayne County Historical Museum
1150 North A Street
Richmond, IN 47374
(765) 962-5756; (765) 939-0909 FAX
anteckjan@aol.com
Mar–10 Dec: Tue–Fri 9:00–4:00, Sat–Sun 1:00–4:00
admission: $5.00 for adults

Wells County Public Library
220 West Washington Street
Bluffton, IN 46714-1999
(219) 824-2315; (260) 824-1612; (260) 824-3129 FAX
wellscopl@parlorcity.com
http://www.wellscolibrary.org
Barbara Elliott

Mon–Thur 9:00–8:00, Fri 9:00–6:00, Sat (June–Oct) 9:00–5:00, Sat (Sept–May) 9:00–noon

West Lafayette Public Library
(200 Northwestern Avenue and the Morton Community Center—temporary quarters)
208 West Columbia Street (mailing address)
West Lafayette, IN 47906-3096
(765) 743-2261; (765) 743-2063 FAX
nick@wlaf.lib.in.us
http://www.wlaf.lib.in.us
E. Nicholas Schenkel, Director
Mon–Thur 9:30–9:00, Fri 9:30–6:00, Sat 9:30–5:00, Sun 1:00–5:00

Westchester Public Library
Thomas Library
200 West Indiana Avenue
Chesterton, IN 46304-3122
(219) 926-7696; (219) 926-6424 FAX
http://wpl.lib.in.us
Philip D. Baugher, Director

Westfield Public Library
333 West Hoover Road
Westfield, IN 46074-9283
(317) 896-9391; (317) 896-3702 FAX
sheryl@westfieldlibrary.lib.in.us
http://www.westfieldlibrary.lib.in.us
Sheryl Sollars, Director

Westville-New Durham Township Public Library
(153 Main Street—location)
PO Box 789 (mailing address)
Westville, IN 46391-0789
(219) 785-2015; (219) 785-2015 FAX
wvpubliclibrary@csinet.net
Sara U. Johnson, Director

Whitewater Valley Community Library District
Brookville Library
(919 Main Street—location)
PO Box 402 (mailing address)
Brookville, IN 47012-1498
(765) 647-4031; (765) 647-0278 FAX
wvcl@wvcl.org
http://www.wvcl.org
Linda L. Bruns, Director
Mon–Thur 9:00–8:00, Fri 9:00–6:00, Sat 9:00–1:00

Whitewater Valley Community Library District
Laurel Community Library
(200 North Clay Street—location)
PO Box 402 (mailing address)
Laurel, IN 47024
(765) 698-2626 voice & FAX
wvcl@wvcl.org
http://www.wvcl.org
Linda Bruns, Director
Mon–Thur 9:00–8:00, Fri 9:00–6:00, Sat 9:00–1:00

Whiting Public Library
1735 Oliver Street
Whiting, IN 46394-1722
(219) 473-4700; (219) 659-5833 FAX
http://www.whiting.lib.in.us
Christina Young, Director
Mon–Thur 9:00–8:00, Fri–Sat 9:00–5:00

Willard Library
Regional and Family History Center
21 First Avenue
Evansville, IN 47710-1294
(812) 425-4309; (812) 425-4303 FAX
willard@willard.lib.in.us
http://www.willard.lib.in.us

Lyn Martin, Special Collections
Mon–Tue 9:00–8:00, Wed–Fri 9:00–5:30, Sat 9:00–5:00, Sun 1:00–5:00

Williamsport-Washington Township Public Library
28 East Second Street
Williamsport, IN 47993-1299
(765) 762-6555; (765) 762-6588 FAX
wwtpl@incolsa.net
http://www.wwtpl.lib.in.us
Christopher Brown, Director

Winchester Community Public Library
125 North East Street
Winchester, IN 47394-1604
(765) 584-4824 voice & FAX
wincomlib@yahoo.com
Jenny Stonerock, Director

Wolcott Community Library
(101 East North Street—location)
PO Box 376 (mailing address)
Wolcott, IN 47995-0376
(219) 279-2695; (219) 279-2692 FAX
wolclib@ffni.com
http://www.ffni.com/~wolclib
Deanna Dreblow, Director
Mon noon–6:00, Tue & Thur 9:00–6:00, Fri noon–5:00, Sat 9:00–1:00

Worthington Jefferson Township Public Library
26 North Commercial Street
Worthington, IN 47471-1415
(812) 875-3815 voice & FAX
Andrea Fuller, Director
Mon & Wed noon–4:00, Tue & Thur noon–8:00, Fri 9:00–4:00, Sat 10:00–2:00

York Township Public Library
8475 North, 885th West
Raub, IN 47976
(219) 474-5689

Historical Societies—Local and Regional

Adams County Historian
6929 North Piqua Road
Decatur, IN 46733
(260) 724-1187 (Office); (260) 724-4954 (Home); (260) 728-9445 FAX
jko@adamswells.com
Julie O. Beirne

Adams County Historical Society
(420 West Monroe Street—location)
PO Box 262 (mailing address)
Decatur, IN 46733-0262
(219) 724-2341
Gordon Gregg, President
Sun (June–Sept) 1:00–4:00, and by appointment
Pub. *The Trumpeter*, quarterly
$10.00 per year membership

Alexandria Monroe Township Historical Society
313 North Harrison Street
Alexandria, IN 46001-1624
Pub. *Alexandria Monroe Township Historical Society Newsletter*

Allen County-Fort Wayne Historical Society
302 East Berry Street
Fort Wayne, IN 46802
(219) 426-2882; (219) 424-4419 FAX
histsociety@comcast.net
http://www.fwhistorycenter.com

Donn P. Werling, Executive Director
Feb–Dec: Tue–Fri 9:00–5:00, Sat–Sun
    noon–5:00
Pub. *Allen County-Fort Wayne Historical
    Society Bulletin*, bimonthly; *The Old Fort
    News*, annually
$25.00 per year membership

Allen County Historian
13707 Brook Hollow Court
Fort Wayne, IN 46814
(260) 625-5987 (Office); (260) 625-5987
    (Home)
tlcastaldi@aol.com
Thomas Castaldi

Anson Wolcott Historical Society
(500 North Range Street—location)
PO Box 417 (mailing address)
Wolcott, IN 47995-0417
(219) 279-2123; (219) 279-2167 FAX
Richard Wheeler, President
by appointment
Pub. *AWHS News*, annually, free

Bartholomew County Historian
1130 Franklin
Columbus, IN 47201
(812) 379-5620 (Office); (812) 376-8826
    (Home)
harry@therepublic.com

Bartholomew County Historical Society
McEwen-Samuels-Marr House
524 Third Street
Columbus, IN 47201
(812) 372-3541
John Hamblem, Volunteer Librarian; Laura
    Moses, Director
Tue & Thur 2:00–4:00, and by appointment
Pub. *Quarterly Connection*, quarterly
$15.00 per year membership

Beiger Heritage Corporation
317 Lincoln Way, East
Mishawaka, IN 46544
(219) 256-0365

Benton County Historian
711 East Third Street
Fowler, IN 47944-1343
(765) 884-1764 (Office and Home); (765)
    884-2013 FAX
fhfurr@localline.com
Freeman Harold Furr
Mon–Fri 8:00–4:00

Benton County Historical Society
(404 East Sixth Street—location)
PO Box 341 (mailing address)
Fowler, IN 47944-0341
http://benton.k12.in.us/fowler/
    community/bchs/bhs.htm
Thelma Glaspie, President

Besancon Historical Society
15533 Lincoln Highway East
New Haven, IN 46774
(219) 749-4525
violette@fwa.cioe.com
http://www.ipfw.edu/ipfwhist/historgs/
    besanco.htm
Ralph Violette
Pub. meetings at the St. Louis Parish
    Conference Room: fourt Sat (Mar, June,
    Sept & Nov)
$10.00 per year membership

Blackford County Historian
227 West Seventh Street
Hartford City, IN 47348
(765) 348-2726 (Home)

Dr. Dwight Mikkelson

Blackford County Historical Society
(321 North High Street—location)
PO Box 264 (mailing address)
Hartford City, IN 47348
sacastelo@hotmail.com
http://www.bchs-in.org
Sinuard Castelo, President
Sun 1:00–4:00, and by appointment
(houses the Cecil Beeson Genealogical
    Library)
$2.00 per year membership

Boone County Historian
635 West Pine Street
Zionsville, IN 46077
(317) 873-4900 (Office); (317) 873-2547
    (Home)
mhdoyle361@aol.com
Marianne Heath Doyle

Boone County Historical Society, Inc.
(404 West Main Street—location)
PO Box 141 (mailing address)
Lebanon, IN 46052-0141
(765) 483-9414
http://www.bccn.boone.in.us/bchs/index.htm
Marilyn Wall, Treasurer
Pub. *BCHS Newsletter*, three to four times
    per year
$10.00 per year membership

Brown County Historian
5028 North State Route 135
Sub One Office
Nashville, IN 47448
(812) 988-4629 (Office); (812) 988-4556
    (Home); (812) 988-0603 FAX
Jack McDonald

Brown County Historical Society, Inc.
(1934 State Road 135 North—archives
location
Museum Lane—museum location)
PO Box 668 (mailing address)
Nashville, IN 47448
(812) 988-6089 (answering machine)
http://www.browncounty.org/bchistoric.html
Rob Coulter, Archivist and Chair of the
    Archives and Genealogy Committee
Archives: Tue 9:00–1:00, and by
    appointment; Museum: weekends and
    holidays (May–Oct) 1:00–5:00, and by
    appointment
Pub. *Newsletter*, quarterly (Feb, May, Aug,
    Nov)
$15.00 per year membership

Carmel-Clay Historical Society
211 First, S.W.
Carmel, IN 47201
(317) 846-4564

Carroll County Historian
1512 Old Camden Road
Delphi, IN 46923
(765) 564-3634 (Home)
cchs@dcwi.com
Mrs. Don R. (Phyllis Davis) Moore, Curator

**Carroll County Historical Society
(Museum)**
(Carroll County Courthouse, 101 West Main
Street, Ground Floor—location)
PO Box 277 (mailing address)
Delphi, IN 46923-0277
(765) 564-3152; (765) 564-3634; (765) 564-
    6161
cchs@dewi.com; phyllismoore@ffni.com
http://www.carrollcountymuseum.org/
    index.html

Mrs. Don R. (Phyllis Davis) Moore, Curator
Mon–Tue & Thur–Fri 8:00–5:00, Wed
    8:00–noon, and by appointment
Pub. *Newsletter*, quarterly
$10.00 per year membership

Cass County Historian
723 Wheatland
Logansport, IN 46947
(574) 732-1875 (Home)
Richard B. Copeland

Cass County Historical Society
1004 East Market Street
Logansport, IN 46947
(574) 753-3866
Bryan Looker, Curator
Tue–Sat 1:00–5:00, first Mon 1:00–7:00
(Cass County information only)
research: donation

Cedar Lake Historical Association
Lake of the Red Cedars Museum
PO Box 421
Cedar Lake, IN 46303
(219) 374-6157

Clark County Historian
5807 Stacy Road
Charlestown, IN 47111
(812) 256-4685 (Home); (812) 256-4615
    FAX
jeanne_b@hotmail.com
Jeanne Burke

**Clark County Historical Society and
Howard Steamboat Museum, Inc.**
(1101 East Market Street—location)
PO Box 606 (mailing address)
Jeffersonville, IN 47131-0606
(812) 283-3728; (812) 283-6049 FAX
Yvonne B. Knight, Administrator
Museum: Tue–Sat 10:00–3:00, Sun
    1:00–3:00; Library: by appointment
(steamboats, Ohio River history, the
    Howards of Jeffersonville, steamboat
    builders)
$15.00 per year membership; admission:
    charge for mansion tour

Clark's Grant Historical Society
PO Box 423
Charlestown, IN 47111

Clay County Historian
2544 North County Route 200 East
Centerpoint, IN 47840
(812) 835-4891 (Home)
koehler@netusa1.net
Jeffrey Koehler

Clay County Historical Society
100 East National Road
Brazil, IN 47834
(812) 446-4036

**Clay Township Library and Museum
Society**
c/o Marion Pike
10855 North College Avenue
Indianapolis, IN 46280

Clinton County Historical Society, Inc.
Historical Museum
301 East Clinton Street
Frankfort, IN 46041
(765) 654-7773
Nancy Hart, Registrar/Curator and Director
Mon–Fri 8:00–4:00
Pub. *Historical Notes*, bimonthly
$15.00 per year membership

Clinton County, Indiana, Historian
4641 East County Road 250 North
Frankfort, IN 46041-8256
(765) 659-2030 (Office); (765) 249-2616
(Home)
jrmmem@geetel.net
Mary Ellen Mattingly

Crawford County Historian
866 North Sycamore Road
Taswell, IN 47175
(812) 338-2057
Richard Eastridge

**Crawford County Historical and
Genealogical Society**
PO Box 133
Leavenworth, IN 47137
(812) 739-2358
rockman@disknet.com
Sharon Morris, Secretary/Treasurer; Jim
Kaiser, President
Pub. *Crawford Countian*, quarterly
$10.00 per year membership

Daviess County Historian
812 East National Highway
Washington, IN 47501
(812) 254-2627 (Home)
myers812@galaxyinternet.net
L. Rex Myers

Daviess County Historical Society
(Museum, Old Jefferson School, Donaldson
Road between Highway 57 South and Troy
Road—location)
PO Box 2341 (mailing address)
Washington, IN 47501
(812) 254-5122
http://www.artcom.com/museums/nv/af/
47501.htm
Tue–Sat 11:00–3:00

Dearborn County Historian
14684 Wilson Creek
Lawrenceburg, IN 47025
(812) 537-2775 (Office); (812) 926-2006
(Home)
cmchenry@seidata.com
Chris McHenry

Dearborn County Historical Society
508 West High Street
Lawrenceburg, IN 47025-1916
(812) 537-4075 voice & FAX
history@seidata.com
Frances Egner
http://www.dearborninhistorical.org
Tue–Wed 9:00–4:00, Thur 9:00–3:00, Fri
10:00–3:00
Pub. *Doorway to History*, six times per year
$10.00 per year membership; research: $5.00
per hour

Decatur County Historian
407 North Webster
Saint Paul, IN 47272
(765) 525-4847 (Office); (765) 525-6357
(Home)
Ruth Dorrel

Historical Society of Decatur County, Inc.
PO Box 143
Greensburg, IN 47240
(812) 663-2832; ((812) 663-4275 FAX
gchamber@hsonline.net
Ruth Cash, President
Pub. *Historical Society of Decatur County
Bulletin*, quarterly
$5.00 per year membership

Decatur Township Historical Society

PO Box 42
West Newton, IN 46183
(317) 856-6567

De Kalb County Historian
PO Box 686
Auburn, IN 46706-0686
(219) 925-4560 (Office); (219) 925-5714
(Home); (219) 925-4563 FAX
inmemories@mchsi.com
John Martin Smith

De Kalb County Historical Society
PO Box 686
Auburn, IN 46706-0686
(219) 925-4560; (219) 925-4563
John Martin Smith, De Kalb County
Historian
research: donation

Delaware County Historian
(address withheld upon request)
("Can be reached through the Indiana
Historical Society web site.")

Delaware County Historical Society
Moore-Youse Historical Museum
120 East Washington Street
Muncie, IN 47305-1734
(765) 282-1550; (765) 282-1058 FAX
dchs@tmcsmail.com
http://www.dchsmunciein.org
Jim Lee, President
Tue–Fri noon–4:00, and by appointment

Dolan Historical Society
New Prospect Baptist Church
6055 North Old State Road 37
Dolan, IN 47401

DuBois County Historian
737 West Eighth Street
Jasper, IN 47546-2605
(812) 482-3074 (Office and Home)
John Fierst

DuBois County Historical Society, Inc.
737 West Eighth Street
Jasper, IN 47546
(812) 482-3074
John J. Fierst, Secretary

Dyer Historical Society
Dyer Town Hall
1 Town Square
Dyer, IN 46311
(219) 865-6108

East Chicago Historical Society
East Chicago Public Library
East Chicago History Room
2401 East Columbus Drive
East Chicago, IN 46312
Pub. *Memory Lane* (department newsletter),
seasonally, free

Elkhart County Historian
71346 State Highway 19
Nappanee, IN 46550
John Stahly

Elkhart County Historical Society, Inc.
Elkhart County Historical Museum
(304 West Vistula—location)
PO Box 343 (mailing address)
Bristol, IN 46507
(219) 848-4322 (Museum); (219) 848-5703
FAX
echm@juno.com
Tina Mellott, Director/Curator
Museum: Wed–Fri 10:00–4:00, Sun
1:00–5:00

Pub. *Elkhart County Historical Society
Newsletter*, bimonthly
$5.00 per year membership

Elwood-Pipe Creek Historical Society, Inc.
Elwood Public Library
1600 Main Street
Elwood, IN 46036-2023
hwaymire@indy.net
Wilma Romingen, President

Fayette County Historian
660 South County Road 450E
Connersville, IN 47331
(765) 825-9262
phayes@webworks2000.net (Museum)
W. Paulette Hayes
by appointment

Ferdinand Historical Society
PO Box 194
Ferdinand, IN 47532
(812) 367-1803 (President)
rpjohann@psci.net
Phyllis A. Johanneman, President

Floyd County Historian
(address withheld upon request)
("I do not do genealogy. We have a local
society that takes care of those types of
requests.")

Floyd County Historical Society
PO Box 455
New Albany, IN 47150
Stephen Pierce
$20.00 per year membership

Fort Benjamin Harrison Historical Society
1028 North Delaware Street
Indianapolis, IN 46202
(317) 636-4646

Fountain County Historian
3219 East New Richmond Road
Wingate, IN 47994
(765) 295-2604
Robert Quirk

Fountain County Historical Society
3219 East New Richmond Road
Wingate, IN 47994
(765) 295-2604
Robert Quirk, Fountain County Historian
Pub. *Fountain County History*

Franklin County Historian
11043 State Road 1
Brookville, IN 47012
(765) 647-4763 (Home)
dunaway@si-net.com
Don Dunaway
("County historians in Indiana are unpaid
volunteers and receive no compensation
for their services or expenses. I will
answer queries to the best of my ability,
but will not do extensive research.")

Franklin County Historical Society
(Fifth and Mill Streets—location)
PO Box 342 (mailing address)
Brookville, IN 47012-0342
(765) 647-5413
brookgen@juno.com
http://www.franklinchs.com
Martha Shea, President
by appointment
("Franklin County Indiana Territory was
formed from Dearborn County, December
1811. Technically probably aslo from
Clark County.")
$8.00 per year membership

Franklin Township Historical Society
PO Box 39015
Indianapolis, IN 46239
Sylvia422@aol.com
http://fths.org
Sylvia Henricks, President
$10.00 per year membership

Fulton County Historical Society, Inc.
(4 miles north of Rochester on U.S.
31—location)
37 East 375 North (mailing address)
Rochester, IN 46975-8384
(219) 223-4436
fchs@rtcol.com
http://www.icss.net/~fchs
Mon–Sat 9:00–5:00
Pub. *Fulton County Folk Finder*,
semiannually, $6.00 per year subscription;
Fulton County Images, biannually, $15.00
per issue subscription; *Fulton County
Historical Society Newsletter-scrapbook*,
semiannually
(specializes in Potawatomi Indians)
$15.00 per year membership in Fulton
County Historical Society, $5.00 per year
membership in Indian Awareness Center;
research: $5.00 per hour (no charge if
nothing found), copies: 10¢ per page

Garrett Historical Society
(Quincy and Franklin Streets—location)
PO Box 225 (mailing address)
Garrett, IN 46738
(219) 357-5575; (219) 357-5582

Gary Historical and Cultural Society, Inc.
(1 East Gateway Park in Downtown
Gary—location)
PO Box 64603 (mailing address)
Gary, IN 46401
(219) 882-6873
ghcsinc@yahoo.com
D. H. Millender, Founder-CEO
by appointment
Pub. *GHCS Newsletter*, two times per year
("We give tours to school groups and city
visitors or citizens. We sponsor a number
of [mostly free] community programs for
all ages.")
$25.00 per year general membership

Gas City Historical Society
(501 East South F Street—location)
PO Box 192 (mailing address)
Gas City, IN 46933
(765) 674-1892
gascitymuseum@hotmail.com
Jerry L. Long, President

Gibson County Historian
530 West Washington Street
Oakland City, IN 47660
Alvetta S. Wallace

Gibson County Historical Society
PO Box 516
Princeton, IN 47670
Kanda Walden, Editor
Pub. *Gibson County Lines*, monthly
("Gibson County family genealogy as well as
history of county.")
$10.00 per year membership; queries: $3.00

Goshen Historical Society, Inc.
124 South Main Street
Goshen, IN 46526
(219) 533-1053
rnofziger@aol.com
Earlene Nofziger, President of the Board
Sat 10:00–1:00
Pub. *Goshen Historical Society Newsletter*,

bimonthly
$10.00 per year membership; no research
available by mail

Grant County Historian
715 Berkley Drive
Marion, IN 46952
(765) 664-2150 (Home)
Richard Simons

Grant County Historical Society
(1713 North Quarry Road—location)
PO Box 1951 (mailing address)
Marion, IN 46952

Greene County Historian
Rural Route 3, Box 500
Bloomfield, IN 47424
(812) 384-4350 (Home)
James K. Letsinger

Greene County Historical Society
PO Box 301
Bloomfield, IN 47424-0301
Charlis Crays, Treasurer
Pub. *Newsletter*, bimonthly (Feb, Apr, June,
Aug, Oct, Dec)
$10.00 per year membership

Griffith Historical Society
PO Box 678
Griffith, IN 46319
(219) 924-7246

Guilford Township Historical Society
100 East Lincoln Street
Plainfield, IN 46168
James V. Gilbert, President
$2.00 per year membership

Hamilton County Historian
384 North 11th Street
Noblesville, IN 46060-2146
(317) 773-3454
Joe H. Burgess
anytime

Hamilton County Historical Society
(818 Conner Street—location)
PO Box 397 (mailing address)
Noblesville, IN 46061
hamcohmsn@aol.com
http://www.rootsweb.com/~inhchs
Irving M. Heath, Treasurer
Noblesville-Southeastern Public Library:
Mon–Thur 9:30–8:30, Fri–Sat 9:30–5:30,
Sun 1:30–5:30; Museum, 810 Conner
Street: Sat 9:00–2:00
Pub. *Newsletter*, bimonthly
$10.00 per year membership

Hammond Historical Society
c/o Hammond Public Library
564 State Street
Hammond, IN 46320
(219) 931-5100 (Library); (219) 852-2230
(Library)
Kathryn Thegze, Information Services
Librarian
Library: Mon & Wed 1:00–4:00
Pub. *Hammond Historical Society
Newsletter*, (Jan–May, Sept–Nov)
(Hammond area history)
$5.00 per year membership

Hancock County Historian
523 North Swope Street
Greenfield, IN 46140-1640
(317) 298-6257 (Office); (317) 467-4835
(Home); (317) 293-8037 FAX
jskvarenina@nbacares.org
Joe Skvarenina

Hancock County Historical Society
(28 North Apple Street—location)
PO Box 375 (mailing address)
Greenfield, IN 46140
(317) 462-7780
Joseph L. Skvarenina, President
Sat–Sun (1 Mar–1 Dec) 1:00–5:00
Pub. *Old Log Chain*, biannually
$10.00 per year membership

Hancock County Historical Society
PO Box 375
Greenfield, IN 46140
(317) 462-7780
Debtaxi@hotmail.com; bscjones@msn.com

http://brandywine.newpal.k12.in.us/bjhs/h
ancock_county_historical_society.htm
Debbie Elsbury, Secretary; Brigette Jones,
Curator
$10.00 per year membership

Hanover Historical Association
PO Box 157
Hanover, IN 47243
(812) 866-2901
Frank S. Baker, Historian
$15.00 per year

Harrison County Historian
161 Ponder Lane, N.E.
Corydon, IN 47112
(812) 738-3570
danbayshistorian@hotmail.com
Daniel Lee Bays

Harrison County Historical Society
117 West Beaver Street
Corydon, IN 47112

Hebron Historical Society, Inc.
PO Box 675
Hebron, IN 46341

Hendricks County Historian
Plainfield-Guilford Township Public Library
Guilford Township Historical Collection
1120 Stafford Road
Plainfield, IN 46168-2230
(317) 839-6602 (Library); (317) 839-3807
FAX (Library)
scarter@plainfield.lib.in.us
http://www.plainfield.lib.in.us (Library)
Susan Miller Carter, Department Head
Library: Mon–Thur noon–5:00 & 6:00–8:30,
Sat 9:00–noon & 1:00–5:00

Hendricks County Historical Society
Hendricks County Historical Museum
170 South Washington Street
Danville, IN 46122
(317) 745-9617
pwalters@plainfield.lib.in.us
http://history.plainfield.lib.in.us/
Museum/Hendricks_County_Historical_
Museum.htm
Phyllis Walters
Museum: Thur 10:00–4:00, Sat 1:00–4:00
Pub. *Hendricks County Historical Society
Bulletin*, quarterly (Feb, May, Aug, Nov)
$10.00 per year membership

Henry County Historian
303 South Pearl Street
Spiceland, IN 47385
(765) 987-7182 (Home)
ratcliff@nxco.com
Richard P. Ratcliff

Henry County Historical Society
606 South 14th Street
New Castle, IN 47362

(765) 529-4028
hchisoc@kiva.net
http://www.kiva.net~hchisoc/museum
John Paul, Museum Curator
Mon–Sat 1:00–4:30
Pub. *Henry County Historical Log*,
    semiannually
$10.00 per year membership; admission:
    $2.00 for adults

Hessville Historical Society
7205 Kennedy Avenue
Hammond, IN 46323
(219) 844-5666

Highland Historical Society, Inc.
2611 Highway Avenue
Highland, IN 46322

Hobart Historical Society, Inc.
(Mariam Pleak Library, 706 East Fourth
    Street—location)
PO Box 24 (mailing address)
Hobart, IN 46342
(219) 942-0970 (no long distance return
    calls)
Dorothy Ballantyne, Museum Director
Sat 10:00–3:00
Pub. *Hobart History News*, three times per
    year; *Hobart History Advocate*,
    irregularly
(specializes in Hobart and Hobart Township
    information)
research: contribution for postage and
    copying costs

Howard County Historian
2310 West King Street
Kokomo, IN 46901-5080
director@howardcountymuseum.org
Fred C. Odiet

**Howard County Historical Society and
Museum**
1200 West Sycamore Street
Kokomo, IN 46901
(765) 452-4314
director@howardcountymuseum.org
http://www.howardcountymuseum.org
Kelly Thompson, Executive Director
Museum: Tue–Sun 1:00–4:00; Office:
    Mon–Fri 9:00–4:00
Pub. *Museum Highlights*
$20.00 per year membership; museum
    admission: $4.00

Huntington County Historian
Huntington City-Township Public Library
Indiana Room
200 West Market Street
Huntington, IN 46750
(260) 356-0824
B. Joan Keefer, Department Head and
    County Historian

Huntington County Historical Society
(County Courthouse, Fourth
    Floor—location)
1041 South Jefferson (mailing address)
Huntington, IN 46750
(219) 356-5874
William Abbott, President
Tue–Fri 1:00–4:00
Pub. *Newsletter*, monthly
$10.00 per year membership

Illiana Genealogical and Historical Society
(see Illinois, Part 2)

Indiana Junior Historical Society
450 West Ohio Street
Indianapolis, IN 46202-3269

(317) 232-4549
pgillogly@indianahistory.org
http://www.indianahistory.org
Patricia D. Gillogly, School Services
    Coordinator
8:30–4:30
Pub. *IJrHS Notes*, monthly during school
    year
("We are a privately-run history organization
    for students in grades 4-12 that offers
    camps, workshops, teacher workshops,
    etc.; approximately 150 chapters with
    over 5,000 members throughout the
    state.")
$5.00 per year membership

Indiana University Northwest
Calumet Regional Archives
3400 Broadway
Gary, IN 46408
(219) 980-6628
Stephen G. McShane, Archivist/Curator
Mon–Fri 8:00–4:30
Pub. *CRA Newsletter*; *Steel Shavings*,
    annually, $5.00 per year subscription
(northwest Indiana history)

Irvington Historical Society
Benton House
312 South Downey Avenue
Indianapolis, IN 46219
(317) 357-0318

Jackson County Historian
439 East 100 South
Brownstown, IN 47220-9587
(812) 522-3412 (Office); (812) 358-5649
    (Home); (812) 522-5456 FAX
Charlotte Sellers

Jackson County Historical Society
(207 East Walnut, Box 215—location)
401 East Walnut Street
Brownstown, IN 47220
(812) 358-2182
Loren W. Noblitt, Ph.D., Secretary and
    County Historian
9:00–3:00
Pub. *Newsletter*, monthly; *Annual History
    Book*, $25.00 each
(county/national history and genealogical
    charts; "original/primary historical
    research")
$10.00 per year membership

Jasper County Historian
128 South Augusta Street
Rensselaer, IN 47978
(219) 866-5433
Beulah Arnott

Jasper County Historical Society
475 North Van Rensselaer Street
Rensselaer, IN 47978
(219) 866-5433
Beulah Arnott, Jasper County Historian

Jay County Historian
774 South 350 West
Portland, IN 47371
(260) 726-2537 (Home)
Martha Ring

Jay County Historical Society, Inc.
(903 East Main Street—location)
PO Box 1282 (mailing address)
Portland, IN 47371
(219) 997-6749 (President)
Roseamond Scott, President
Museum: by appointment
$5.00 per year membership; no research fees
    at this time

Jefferson County Historian
735 West Main Street
Madison, IN 47250
(812) 265-4472
Paul Konkle
"almost anytime"

Jefferson County Historical Society
Madison Railroad Station
615 West First Street
Madison, IN 47250
(812) 265-2335; (812) 273-5023 FAX
jchs@seidata.com
http://jcohs.org
Lee Rogers, Chairman, Local History; Ron
    Grimes, Archivist
Mon–Fri 10:00–4:30; Library: Wed 10:00-
    2:00
("We have the county archives.")
$25.00 per year membership

Jennings County Historian
1090 East 50 North
North Vernon, IN 47265-1090
(812) 346-8989 (Office); (812) 346-2534
    (Home)
Bret Caldwell

Johnson County Historian
1100 North Drive
Franklin, IN 46131
(317) 639-0330 (Office); (317) 736-8862
    (Home)
Nd1100@aol.com
Dr. Noel C. Baker

Johnson County Museum of History
Johnson County Historical Society
135 North Main Street
Franklin, IN 46131
(317) 736-4655; (317) 736-5451 FAX
map@inetdirect.com;
    maplummer@netdirect.net
Mary Ann Plummer, Director
Mon–Fri 9:00–4:00; second Sat 10:00–3:00
Pub. *Nostalgia News*, quarterly
$10.00 per year membership

Kennard Historical Society
PO Box 227
Kennard, IN 47351

Knox County Historian
2742 South Hickory Corner Road
Vincennes, IN 47591
(812) 882-1776 (Office); (812) 726-5333
    (Home)
dlatta@vincennes.net
Dennis Latta

Kosciusko County Historian
1010 North Huntington
Syracuse, IN 46567
(574) 457-3891 (Home)
Ronald Sharp

**Genealogy Section, Kosciusko County
Historical Society**
(Kosciusko County Historical Museum and
    Library, Corner of Indiana and Main
    Streets—location)
PO Box 1071 (mailing address)
Warsaw, IN 46581-1071
(574) 269-1078
http://culture.kconline.com/kchs
Margaret Warren, Genealogy Section
    Chairman; Douglas Mayer, Librarian;
    William G. "Jerry" Frush, Kosciusko
    County Historical Society President
Thur–Sat 10:00–4:00, Sun 1:00–4:00
Pub. *Kosciusko County Newsletter*
("The Research Library and Archives,

located in the Historical Museum, emphasizes research for Kosciusko County and several of the surrounding counties. This repository contains a large number of volumes of county records [e.g. Assessor's Plat Books, Guardianship Records, County Informary Records, etc.] and extensive genealogy resource materials.")
$12.00 per year membership with the Historical Society (includes newsletter only)

LaGrange County Historian
(MacKan House Museum, 405 Poplar Street—location)
3970 South 200 East (mailing address)
LaGrange, IN 46761
(260) 499-4111
J. Scott McKibben
Sun (summer) 2:00–4:00, and year-round by appointment

LaGrange County Historical Society, Inc.
(MacKan House Museum, 405 Poplar Street—location)
3970 South 200 East (mailing address)
LaGrange, IN 46761
(260) 499-4111
J. Scott McKibben, LaGrange County Historian
Sun (summer) 2:00–4:00, and year-round by appointment
Pub. *LaGrange County Historical Society Newsletter*, quarterly
$5.00 per year membership

Lake County Historian
3606 Belshaw Road
Lowell, IN 46356
(219) 696-0769 (Office); (219) 696-6015 (Home)
becky696@juno.com
Rebecca Crabb

Lake County Historical Society/Museum
(Court House Square, Crown Point, IN 46307—location)
5131 Canterbury Avenue (mailing address)
Portage, IN 46368
(219) 662-3975
Bruce L. Woods, President
Museum: May–Oct: Thur–Sat 1:00–4:00; meetings second Sat (even-numbered months)
$5.00 per year membership

Lapel Historical Society
PO Box 149
Lapel, IN 46051

La Porte County Historian
5817 West Johnson Road
La Porte, IN 46350-8586
(219) 326-6458
netster@csinet.net
Fern Eddy Schultz

La Porte County Historical Society
La Porte County Complex
La Porte, IN 46350-3430
(219) 326-6808, ext. 276
http://www.adsnet.com/MichiganCity/ Activities/HomePages/LPMuseum/ LPMuseum.html
Fern Eddy Schultz, President
Mon–Fri 10:30–4:00
Pub. *The Oldletter*, quarterly
$2.50 per year membership

Lawrence County Tourism Commission/Lawrence County Historian

(1315 Buddha Road—location)
1116 16th Street, PO Box 1193 (mailing address)
Bedford, IN 47421
(812) 275-7651; (812) 275-7637 (Office); (812) 849-9938 (Home)
mkruse@kiva.net
Maxine Kruse, Executive Director and Historian
Mon–Fri 8:00–4:00
(Lawrence County history, cemeteries, limestone carvings and famous Lawrence county people)
no charge

Lawrence County Historical Genealogical Society
931 15th Street
Bedford, IN 47421
(812) 278-8575
lchgs@hpcisp.com
Joyce Shepherd

Legonier Historical Society
300 South Main Street
Ligonier, IN 46767-1812

Lexington Historical Society, Inc.
(8060 East State Road 356—location
Highway 203, Cherry Street, next to the Post Office, corner of Walnut Street, in the Penny Pincher Shoppe—museum location)
PO Box 238 (mailing address)
Lexington, IN 47138-0238
(812) 889-2044 (Editor)
Jeannie Noe Carlisle, Secretary, Treasurer and Editor
meetings fourth Mon (except May, Nov & Dec) 7:00 P.M.; Museum: by appointment only
Pub. untitled newsletter, quarterly
(specializes in Scott County, Indiana, Lexington Township area)
$5.00 per year membership; museum admission: free

Linden-Madison Township Historical Society
PO Box 154
Linden, IN 47955
(765) 339-7245

Town of Lowell
1303 Hilltop Drive
Lowell, IN 46356
http://www.lowellpl.lib.in.us/ltschmal.htm (includes historian's "Pioneer Histories" monthly column from the *Lowell Tribune*)
Richard C. Schmal, Town Historian

Madison County Historian
3634 Woodglen Way
Anderson, IN 46011-1675
(765) 644-0407 (Home)
JBN3634@aol.com
Dr. Jack Nicholson

Madison County Historical Society, Inc.
2009 Brown, Suite 3
Anderson, IN 46016-4215
(765) 683-0052
JBN3634@aol.com; dickbo@netdirect.net
http://www.rootsweb.com/~inmadiso/ mchs.htm
Richard Bowman, President
Mon 9:00–4:00, Wed 9:00–noon
Pub. *Madison County Historical Gazette*, ten times per year; *Searchlight* (for adoptees in search); *Camp Stilwell* (on the Civil War)
$4.00 per year membership

Marion County Historian
4415 Broadway
Indianapolis, IN 46205
(317) 274-2718 (Office); (317) 962-6752 (Home); (317) 278-5230 FAX
dvanders@iupui.edu
David G. Vanderstel, Ph.D.

Marion County/Indianapolis Historical Society
735 Woodruff Place, East Drive
Indianapolis, IN 46201
(317) 635-7278
reboomer@iquest.net
http://www.iquest.net/~reboomer/mcihs.htm
Ray Brown, President
Pub. *The Circular*

Marshall County Historian
430 Clark Street
Plymouth, IN 46562
mchistory@mchistoricalsociety.org
http://www.mchistoricalsociety.org
Linda Lou Rippy
search fees available upon request through Marshall County Historical Society

Marshall County Historical Society, Inc.
123 North Michigan Street
Plymouth, IN 46563-2132
(574) 936-2306
mchistory@mchistoricalsociety.org
http://www.mchistoricalsociety.org
Judy McCollough, Research Librarian
Museum: Mon–Fri 9:00–5:00, Sat 10:00–4:00 (research library is not always open on weekends, call to confirm)
Pub. *Musings*, quarterly; *Marshall County Historical Society Quarterly*
$10.00 per year museum membership; research: $10.00 per hour one-hour minimum

Martin County Historian
PO Box 58
Shoals, IN 47581
(812) 247-2293 (Home)
NBAKER@DMRTC.NET
Nancy Baker

Martin County Historical Society, Inc.
PO Box 564
Shoals, IN 47581
(812) 247-2351

Merrillville-Ross Township Historical Society
6975 Broadway
Merrillville, IN 46410

Miami County Historian
(14 West Sixth Street—location)
PO Box 414 (mailing address)
Peru, IN 46970
(765) 472-3987 (Home); (765) 472-3702 FAX
kreig@weekendoutdoors.com
Kreig Adkins

Miami County Historical Society
Miami County Museum
51 North Broadway
Peru, IN 46970
(765) 473-9183; (765) 473-3880 FAX
mchs@netusa1.net
http://www.miamicountymuseum.org
Cinnamon Catlin-Legutko, Director
Museum: Tue–Sat 9:00–5:00
Pub. *Miami County History Bulletin*, quarterly
("Predominantly Miami County history which includes Miami Indians, railroad,

circus, pioneers, Cole Porter, large
archives.")
$15.00 per year membership

Michigan City Historical Society, Inc.
Old Lighthouse Museum
(Heisman Harbor Road, Washington
Park—location)
PO Box 512 (mailing address)
Michigan City, IN 46360-0512
(219) 872-6133
Pub. *Old Lighthouse Museum News*
(no longer answers genealogical queries)

Middletown-Fall Creek Township Historical Society
707 West Mill Street
Middletown, IN 47356
(765) 354-2791

Monon Historical Society
PO Box 193
Monon, IN 47959

Monroe County Historian
4792 Conti Street
Bloomington, IN 47404
(812) 876-1212 (Office); (812) 876-8081
(Home)
rbaldwin@bluemarble.net
Ron Baldwin

Monroe County Historical Society
Monroe County History Center
202 East Sixth Street
Bloomington, IN 47408
(812) 332-2517 (Office/Museum/Store);
(812) 355-5588 (Genealogy Library);
(812) 355-5593 FAX
mchm@kiva.net (Museum Office);
monroehistsoc@hotmail.com (Library
Director)
http://ww.kiva.net/~mchm/monroe.html
Museum and Store: Tue–Sat 10:00–4:00,
Sun 1:00–4:00; Genealogy Library: Tue
10:00–4:00, Wed–Fri 1:00–4:00, Sat
10:00–4:00
Pub. *Monroe County Historian*, six times per
year
$25.00 per year membership

Montgomery County Historian
PO Box 235
Waveland, IN 47989
(765) 435-2843 (Home)
kzacho@qserve.net
http://www.rootsweb.com/~inmontgo/
index.html
Karen Zach

Montgomery County Historical Society
212 South Water Street
Crawfordsville, IN 47933
(765) 362-3416
mchs@wico.net
http://www.lane-mchs.org
Tamara Hemmerlein, Executive Director
April–May & Sept–Oct: Tue–Sun 1:00–4:00;
June–Aug: Tue–Sat 10:00–4:00, Sun
1:00–4:00
admission: $3.00

Montpelier Historical Society, Inc.
109 West Huntington Street
Montpelier, IN 47359
(765) 728-8642

Morgan County Historian
3540 East Mahalasville Road
Martinsville, IN 46151-6565
(765) 342-8711 (Office); (765) 342-8647
(Home); (765) 342-0413 FAX

scline@hoosierweb.org
Samuel M. Cline

Morgan County History & Genealogy Association (MCHAGAI)
(59 North Jefferson Street—location)
PO Box 1012 (mailing address)
Martinsville, IN 46151-0012
(765) 349-9936
scline@hoosierweb.org
http://www.rootsweb.com/~inmchaga/
mchagai.html
Sam Cline, President
Pub. *Morgan County History & Genealogy*,
quarterly
$12.00 per year membership; queries with
Morgan County connections free to
members, $3.00 for nonmembers; research
in Morgan County records: $8.00 per hour
for members, $12.00 per hour for
nonmembers

Munster Historical Society
Town Hall
1005 Ridge Road
Munster, IN 46321
(219) 836-8810

Newton County Historian
PO Box 86
Morocco, IN 47963
(219) 285-2861
hlacosse@netnitco.net
Donna Lacosse

Newton County Historical Society, Inc.
(224 North Third—location)
PO Box 303 (mailing address)
Kentland, IN 47951
newtonhs@ffni.com
Sue Humphrey, President
$5.00 per year membership

Noble County Historian
PO Box 11
Albion, IN 46701
(260) 636-7871 (Home)
Robert C. Gagen, Jr.

Noble County Historical Society
(Old Jail Museum, Corner of West Main and
Oak Streets, two blocks west of only traffic
light—location)
PO Box 152 (mailing address)
Albion, IN 46701-0152
(260) 636-3929
Martha Ayres, President
first Sat in June to last Sun in Aug: Sat–Sun
1:30–4:30
Pub. *Pioneer Echoes*, quarterly (Jan, Apr,
July, Oct)
("Artifacts and exhibits focus on Noble
County. Old Jail Museum was entered on
the National Register of Historic Places
December 27, 1982.")
$7.00 per year membership

Northern Indiana Historical Society
Northern Indiana Center for History
808 West Washington
South Bend, IN 46601
(574) 235-9664; (574) 235-9059 FAX
director@centerforhistory.org;
education@centerforhistory.org
http://www.centerforhistory.org
Cheryl Taylor Bennett, Executive Director
Tue–Sat 10:00–5:00, Sun noon–5:00
Pub. *Saint Joseph Valley Record* (not
specifically genealogical), semiannually
$35.00 per year membership

Historical Society of Ogden Dunes

101 Ogden Dunes
Portage, IN 46368-1268
(219) 762-1268

Ohio County Historian
602 Main Street
Rising Sun, IN 47040
(812) 438-3264 (Office); (812) 438-2182
(Home); (812) 438-2182 FAX
keithbjohio@yahoo.com
Bobby Joe Keith

Ohio County Indiana Historical Society and Museum
212 South Walnut
Rising Sun, IN 47040
(812) 438-4915; (812) 438-4925 FAX
ohiocohist@seidata.com;
museum@ohiocountyINmuseum.org
http://www.ohiocountyinmuseum.org
Wayne Chipman, President
Mon–Tue & Thur–Sat 11:00–4:00, Sun
1:30–4:30
Pub. *Newsletter*, annually
$10.00 per year membership; admission:
$2.50 for adults

Orange County Historian
311 West Main Street
Paoli, IN 47454-1033
(812) 723-3437 (Home)
evjo@kiva.net
Wilma Davis

Orange County Historical Society
Thomas Elwood Lindley House
PO Box 454
Paoli, IN 47454

Osceola Historical Society
PO Box 14
Osceola, IN 46561-0014
(219) 674-9410
Kaye Solliday, President

Our Heritage, Inc., Jennings County Historical Society
(134 East Brown Street [corner of Pike and
Brown]—location)
PO Box 335 (mailing address)
Vernon, IN 47282
(812) 346-8989; (812) 346-7071 FAX
jencohissoc@seidata.com
http://jenningscohs.org
Lori Ammerman; Mr. Bret Caldwell
Mon–Tue 11:00–4:00, Wed–Fri 9:00–4:00
no extensive, personal research

Owen County Historian
35 West Hillside
Spencer, IN 47460
Linda Simmerman

Owen County Historical and Genealogical Society
PO Box 569
Spencer, IN 47460
KeeslingKB@aol.com
http://www.owen.in.us/owenhist/owen.htm
Becky Keesling, Secretary

Palmyra Historical Society
Palmyra Historical Museum
Palmyra Commercial Building
Palmyra, IN 47164

Parke County Historian
(215 West High Street—location)
PO Box 187 (mailing address)
Rockville, IN 47872
(765) 569-3978 (Office)
Mary Jo Harney

Parke County Historical Society
(503 West Ohio—location)
PO Box 332 (mailing address)
Rockville, IN 47872
(765) 569-2223 (during season)
Jim Meece, President
Museum: Memorial Day–the end of the
    Covered Bridge Festival in Oct: Tue–Sun
    1:00–4:00
Pub. *Newsletter*, four times per year
("The museum is dedicated to artifacts and
    manuscripts from Parke County history")
$10.00 per year membership

Perry County Historian
Rural Route 1, Box 196
Highway 37
Tell City, IN 47586
(812) 547-3957
Mike Rutherford

Pike County Historian
709 Locust Street
Petersburg, IN 47567
(812) 354-1043 (Home)
mcbeth@sigecom.net
Sandra McBeth

Pike County Historical Society and Museum
PO Box 216
Petersburg, IN 47567
mcbeth@sigecom.net
Sandy McBeth, Secretary
Sat 10:00–3:00
Pub. *Pike County Historical Society
    Newsletter*, bimonthly
(Pike county history and genealogy)
$10.00 per year membership

Portage Community Historical Society
2100 Willowcreek Road
Portage, IN 46368
(219) 762-4218

Porter County Historian
107 East Jefferson Street
Valparaiso, IN 46383
(219) 462-0524
Larry J. Clark

**Historical Society of Porter County, Inc.
(Old Jail Museum)**
153 Franklin Street
Valparaiso, IN 46383
(219) 465-3595
Bonnie Cuson, Curator
Tue–Wed & Fri 1:00–4:00
Pub. *Muse News*, quarterly
(naturalization books 1854–1955, marriage
    index 1836–1905, 1880 census)
$5.00 per year membership

Posey County Historian
9016 Schroeder Court
Mount Vernon, IN 47620-9695
(812) 985-9346
Glenn Curtis
("For sixteen years appointed county
    historian by Indiana Historical Society.")

Posey County Historical Society
PO Box 171
Mount Vernon, IN 47620
Wanda L. Griess, President
Mon 1:00–3:00
Pub. *The Posey*, quarterly
$10.00 per year membership; research:
    $10.00 per hour plus copy costs

Pulaski County Historian
Pulaski County Public Library

121 South Riverside Drive
Winamac, IN 46996
(219) 946-3432 (Library)
Lynda Irving
Library: Mon 9:00–8:00, Tue–Sat 9:00–6:00

Pulaski County Historical Society, Inc.
(123 South Riverside—museum location)
PO Box 135 (mailing address)
Winamac, IN 46996
(219) 946-3712; (219) 946-4411 FAX
Christine Smith
Museum: Fri 1:00–4:00
$5.00 per year membership

Putnam County Historian
4565 East 650 North
Bainbridge, IN 46105
(765) 522-6869 (Home)
Susan Huber

Putnam County Historical Society
PO Box 801
Greencastle, IN 46135
(765) 658-4445
shuber2@indy.tds.net
Don Brattain, President

Randolph County Historian
2212 East Greenville Pike
Winchester, IN 47394-9429
(765) 584-4323 (evenings); (765) 584-1155,
    ext. 10 (days)
Monisa Wisener

Randolph County Historical/Genealogical Society
Randolph County Historical Museum
416 South Meridian Street
Winchester, IN 47394
(765) 584-1334 (Museum); (765) 584-4323
    (evenings); (765) 584-1155, ext. 10 (days)
Monisa Wisener, Randolph County Historian
Mon–Fri 8:00–4:00 to 10:00–noon &
    1:30–4:30
Pub. *Historical and Genealogical Society of
    Randolph County Newsletter*, annually
(genealogical library and museum)
$10.00 per year membership; research:
    postage, copies and expenses for members

Randolph Southern Historical Society
PO Box 127
Lynn, IN 47355
(765) 874-2267
Linda L. Black

Ripley County Historian
610 North Buckeye
Osgood, IN 47037-1124
(812) 689-4755 (Home)
Helen Einhaus

Ripley County Indiana Historical Society, Inc.
(Main and Water Street—location)
PO Box 525 (mailing address)
Versailles, IN 47042
(812) 689-3031
rchslib@seidata.com
http://www.seidata.com/~rchslib
Alice McCoy
Mon–Fri 1:00–4:00
Pub. *Ripley County Historical Society
    Bulletin*, quarterly
$10.00 per year membership; research: $3.00
    plus copies & postage

Rush County Historian
1744 North 450 East
Rushville, IN 46173
(765) 932-5204 (Home)

Eleanor Arnold

Rush County Historical Society
(614 North Jackson—location)
PO Box 302 (mailing address)
Rushville, IN 46173

Saint John Historical Society
PO Box 134
Saint John, IN 46373
(219) 365-8550

Saint Joseph County Historian
7982 East Potato Hole Court
New Carlisle, IN 46552
(574) 284-5282 (Office); (574) 654-7983
    (Home); (574) 284-4791 FAX
knucksie1@aol.com
John Kovach

Schererville Historical Society
PO Box 333
Schererville, IN 46375
(219) 322-1699

Scotland Historical Society, Inc.
PO Box 173
Scotland, IN 47457

Scott County Historian
4898 Wind Drift Farm
Scottsburg, IN 47170-8420
(812) 794-4205 (Home)
Carol Susnick

Scott County Historical Society
(Scottsburg Heritage Station, Archive Room,
    Suite D, 90 North Main Street—location)
PO Box 245 (mailing address)
Scottsburg, IN 47170-0245
Mon 10:00–1:30, and by appointment

Shawnee Historical Association
5501 East 200 North
Lafayette, IN 47905
(765) 589-8049

Shelby County Historian
914 South Tompkins Street
Shelbyville, IN 46176
(317) 398-8150 (Office); (317) 398-3351
    (Home)
slough@svs.net
David Craig

Shelby County Historical Society
Louis and Lena Firn Grover Museum
52 West Broadway
Shelbyville, IN 46176-1256
(317) 392-4634
grover@shelbynet.net
June Barnett, Director
Tue–Sat 9:00–4:00, Sun 1:00–4:00
Pub. *Echos of Old Shelby*, six times per year
$15.00 per year membership

Sheridan Historical Society
308 Main Street
Sheridan, IN 46069-1113
(317) 758-5765
SherHistSoc@aol.com;
    sherhistsociety@wmconnect.com
http://www.sheridannews.net/
    historicalsociety
James H. Pickett, Executive Director
Tue & Fri 1:00–4:00

Shirley Centennial Historical Society, Inc.
Historic Shirley Museum
PO Box 69
Shirley, IN 47384-0069
(765) 737-6119

Southwestern Indiana Historical Society
435 South Spring Street
Evansville, IN 47714-1550
(812) 477-6777
Vivian M. Taylor, Secretary-Treasurer
(not a genealogical group)
research: $10.00 per hour

Spencer County Historian
6277 North County Road, 550 E
Grandview, IN 47615
(812) 649-4866 (Office); (812) 362-8573
   (Home); (812) 649-4018 FAX
middletonb@rockport-spco.lib.in.us
Becky Middleton
Historian: Mon–Fri 9:00–5:00; Library and
   Genealogy Room: Mon & Fri 9:00–5:00,
   Tue–Thur 9:00–9:00, Sat 9:00–3:00, Sun
   (during the school year) 1:00–5:00

Spencer County Historical Society
Spencer County Public Library
210 Walnut Street
Rockport, IN 47635-1398
Steve Sisley, President; Mary Anne Parker,
   Treasurer; Becky Middleton, Genealogy
   Room Librarian
Pub. *Newsletter*, quarterly
(Spencer County and surrounding area)
$10.00 per year membership; research: $5.00
   per hour plus cost of copies

Starke County Historical Society
3750 East 500 North
Knox, IN 46534
(219) 772-4311; (574) 772-2033 FAX
shilling@nitline.com
http://www.in-
   map.net/counties/STARKE/government/h
   istorical_society
Melba Shilling, Starke County Historian
Museum, 401 South Main, Knox, IN:
   afternoons; Office: Tue–Fri noon–4:00

Steuben County Historian
127 Powers Street
Angola, IN 46703
(260) 665-2434
Charles D. Skove

Stones Trace Historical Society
407 Johnson Street
Ligonier, IN 46767

Sugar Creek Historical Society
Thorntown Heritage Museum
124 West Main Street
Thorntown, IN 46071
(765) 436-2202
thm@countyhistory.com
http://www.countyhistory.com/thorntown/
   index.html

Sullivan County Historian
Sullivan County Public Library
Genealogy/Local History Department
100 South Crowder Street
Sullivan, IN 47882
(812) 268-4957 (Library); (812) 268-5370
   FAX (Library)
dadams@sullivan.lib.in.us
http://www.sullivan.lib.in.us
Donna K. Adams, Sullivan County Historian
   and Head of Genealogy/Local History
   Department
Library: Mon–Fri 9:00–5:00, Sat noon–5:00

Sullivan County Historical Society
Sullivan County Genealogical Society
Historical Museum
(10 South Court—location)
PO Box 326 (mailing address)

Sullivan, IN 47882
(812) 268-6253 (812) 268-4836 FAX
imrzip@aol.com
http://www.rootsweb.com/~inschs
Steve Tucker, President
Mon–Fri 10:00–4:00
Pub. *Sullivan County Historical Society
   Newsletter*, bimonthly
$10.00 per year membership

**Summitville Van Buren Township
Historical**
PO Box 242
Summitville, IN 46070
(765) 536-4222 FAX
chazc@netdirect.net
Charles Coates, President

Switzerland County Historian
59 Knox Ford Road
Vevay, IN 47043
(812) 427-2272 (Home)
jhendric@switzerland.k12.in.us
Janet Hendricks

Switzerland County Historical Society
(115 Tapps Ridge Road—location)
PO Box 201 (mailing address)
Vevay, IN 47043
(812) 427-3560; (812) 427-3921 (Secretary)
Ellyn Kern, Secretary
Mon–Fri noon–4:00, Sat 10:00–4:00
Pub. *The Grapevine*, two times per year, 25¢
   per copy
$8.00 per year membership; research:
   donation

Tell City Historical Society
(516 Main Street—location)
PO Box 728 (mailing address)
Tell City, IN 47586
(812) 547-8907 (Treasurer, Home); (812)
   547-3441 (Treasurer, Work)
Tony Collignon, Treasurer
by appointment only
$10.00 per year membership

Three Creeks Historical Association
c/o Lowell Public Library
1505 Commercial Avenue
Lowell, IN 46356-1899
(219) 696-9234
Bill Peterson, President

Tippecanoe County Historian
1001 South Street
Lafayette, IN 47901
(765) 476-8411 (Office); (765) 476-8414
   FAX
paul@tcha.mus.in.us
Paul Schueler

**Tippecanoe County Historical Association
(TCHA)**
Alameda McCollough Library and Archives
Wetherill Resource Center
1001 South Street
Lafayette, IN 47901
(765) 476-8407 (Library); (765) 742-8411
   (General Information); (765) 476-8414
   FAX
mail@tcha.mus.in.us;
   library@tcha.mus.in.us
http://www.tcha.mus.in.us
Kevin O'Brien, Executive Director
Pub. *Weatenotes*, monthly
$$35.00 per year membership

Tipton County Historian and Genealogist
124 North Conde
Tipton, IN 46072
(765) 675-7781

de@netusa1.net
Donna Jean Ekstrom

Tipton County Historical Society
323 West South Street
Tipton, IN 46072
(765) 675-5828
tchs@nupoint.net
http://tiptonhistorical.org
Tue–Sat 1:00–5:00
$5.00 per year membership; research fees
   vary

Topeka Area Historical Society
(123 Indiana Street—location)
PO Box 33 (mailing address)
Topeka, IN 46571
(219) 593-3613

Union County Historian
101 Maple Court
Liberty, IN 47353
(765) 458-5294 (Home)
a.redinger@gte.net
Arthur M. Redinger

Union County Indiana Historical Society
(Railroad Street—location)
PO Box 9 (mailing address)
Liberty, IN 47353
Marcellene O'Toole, Union County
   Historian
Sun (Apr–Oct) 2:00–4:00
$5.00 per year membership

Upland Area Historical Society
PO Box 577
Upland, IN 46989

Upper Whitewater Historical Association
302 East Main
Cambridge City, IN 47327

Vanderburgh County Historian
University of Southern Indiana
8600 University Boulevard
Evansville, IN 47712
(812) 465-7014 (Office); (812) 953-6147
   (Home); (812) 465-7061 FAX
dbigham@usi.edu
Darrel E. Bigham, Ph.D.

Vermillion County Historian
1850 West State Road 32
Perrysville, IN 47974
(765) 793-3022 (Office); (765) 793-4079
   (Home)
Norman Skinner

Vermillion County Historical Society
(220 East Market Street—location)
PO Box 273 (mailing address)
Newport, IN 47966
(765) 492-4417
http://vcihs.homestead.com
Jim McFall, President; Becky Gosnell, Vice
   President, Reva Weller, Treasurer, Diann
   McIntosh, Secretary
$5.00 per year membership

Vigo County Historian
236 McKinley Boulevard
Terre Haute, IN 47803-1914
(812) 232-3800 (Office); (812) 232-2034
   (Home); (812) 234-3709 FAX
res02gwi@gte.net
B. Michael McCormick

Vigo County Historical Society
Wabash Valley Historical Museum
1411 South Sixth Street
Terre Haute, IN 47802

(812) 235-9717; (812) 235-4998 FAX
vchs@vigohistory.com
http://web.indstate.edu/community/vchs/
    index.php
Marylee Hagan, Executive Director
Pub. *Leaves of Thyme*
("We combined all of our resources with the
    Vigo County Public Library.")

**Vincennes Historical and Antiquarian
Society**
PO Box 487
Vincennes, IN 47591
(812) 735-3800
Dr. Alan Snyder, President
Pub. *Knox County History*

Wabash County Historian
574 Ferry Street
Wabash, IN 46992
(260) 563-2794 (Home)
dwoodward@kconline.com
Ronald L. Woodward

Wabash County Historical Society
Wabash County Historical Museum
(89 West Hill Street—location)
PO Box 8 (mailing address)
Wabash, IN 46992
(219) 563-0661
http://www.ohwy.com/in/w/wabcohmu.htm
Tue–Sat 9:00–1:00
Pub. *Wabash County Historical Newsletter*,
    quarterly
$5.00 per year membership

Wakarusa Historical Society
PO Box 2
Wakarusa, IN 46573

Warren County Historian
10828 North 875 East
Otterbein, IN 47970
(765) 583-2976 (Home); (765) 583-0576
    FAX
mannsmith1@aol.com
Marilyn Smith Mann

Warren County Historical Society
(16 Midway—location)
PO Box 176 (mailing address)
Williamsport, IN 47993
wchs@warrencohistory.org
Terri Wargo, President
winter: by appointment; summer: varies
Pub. *Warren County Reflections*, quarterly
$10.00 per year membership

Warrick County Historian
6000 Lincoln Avenue
Evansville, IN 47715
(812) 476-2604 (Home); (812) 476-3874
    FAX
kayzeelant@aol.com
Kay F. Lant

Washington County Historian
407 West Market Street
Salem, IN 47167
(812) 883-3567 (Home)
Willie Harlen

**Washington County Historical Society,
Inc.**
Stevens Museum
307 East Market Street
Salem, IN 47167
(812) 883-6495
jmounts@peoplepc.com;
    j2mead@blueriver.net
http://165.138.44.13/washington/
    wacohiso.htm

Martha Bowers, Library Assistant; Jerry
    Morris Mounts; John Walter Mead
Library: Tue–Sat 9:00–5:00
Pub. untitled newsletter, quarterly
("Genealogy library plus museum of local
    artifacts.")
$15.00 per year membership; research:
    $10.00 per hour plus copies; admission:
    $2.00 for nonmembers

Wayne County Historian
14030 W. E. Oler Road
Hagerstown, IN 47346-9726
(765) 489-5429 (Home)
celafever-hagerstown@juno.com
Carolyn Lafever
("I do not do genealogy. Whenever I receive
    requests I have to refer them to the
    genealogy society.")

Wayne Township Historical Society
1220 South High School Road
Indianapolis, IN 46241

Wells County Historian
5211 S.E. State Road 116
Bluffton, IN 46714
(260) 824-0214 (Office); (260) 824-4010
    (Home); (260) 824-3290 FAX
cleonard@parlorcity.com
cleonard@parlorcity.com
Craig S. Leonard

Wells County Historical Society
(420 West Market Street—location)
PO Box 143 (mailing address)
Bluffton, IN 46714-0143
(219) 824-9956
cleonard@parlorcity.com
http://wchs-museum.org
Craig S. Leonard, Wells County Historian
Museum: Sun (June–Oct) 1:00–4:00, Wed
    (Apr–Aug) 1:00–4:00, and by
    appointment
Pub. *Newsletter*, quarterly
$10.00 per year membership

West Baden Historical Society
PO Box 6
West Baden Springs, IN 47469
(812) 936-9630

Western Wayne Heritage, Inc.
(800 National Road—location)
PO Box 254 (mailing address)
Cambridge City, IN 47327
(765) 478-5993
Jack O'Malley, President
daytime

Westfield-Washington Historical Society
PO Box 103
Westfield, IN 46074
(317) 896-5000

president@wwhs.us
http://www.wwhs.us

White County Historian
1173 Montgomery Street
West Lafayette, IN 47906
(574) 583-3998; (765) 497-3731 (Home);
    (574) 583-3998 FAX
Connie Cascales

**White County Historical Society and
Museum**
101 South Bluff Street
Monticello, IN 47960-2308
(574) 583-3998; (317) 497-3731 FAX
ccascales@hotmail.com
http://www.buffaloindiana.org/

whitecountyindiana/hist.htm
Connie Cascales
Mon, Wed & Fri 8:00–2:00
$5.00 per year membership; admission: free

**Whiting-Robertsdale Historical Society
Museum**
1610 119th Street
Whiting, IN 46394-1702
(219) 659-1432
Elizabeth Gehrke, Director
Tue–Wed & Sat 1:00–4:00
Pub. *Whiting-Robertsdale Historical Society
    Newsletter*, quarterly (fall, winter, spring,
    summer)
(Whiting newspapers from 1894, obituaries
    from 1894, city directories and telephone
    directories, artifacts and vertical files)
$5.00 per year membership

Whitley County Historian
1385 East County Route 900S
Columbia City, IN 46725
(260) 244-6372 (Office); (260) 396-2738
    (Home); (260) 244-6384 FAX
wchist@yahoo.com
Jeanette Brown

Whitley County Historical Museum
108 West Jefferson Street
Columbia City, IN 46725
(219) 244-6372; (219) 244-6384 FAX
WCMuseum@whitleynet.org;
    shrichey@haoo.com
http://historical.whitleynet.org
Susan Richey, Museum Director
Mon–Wed 9:00–2:00, and by appointment
Pub. *The Bulletin of the Whitley County
    Historical Society*, quarterly
$15.00 per year membership; research:
    donation

Zionsville Historical Society, Inc.
714 Sugarbush Drive
Zionsville, IN 46077

Genealogical Societies

State Genealogical Society

Indiana Genealogical Society, Inc.
PO Box 10507
Fort Wayne, IN 46852-0507
(260) 421-5631, ext. 1226
kinfindrb@comcast.net
http://www.indgensoc.org
Elizabeth Brokop, Corresponding Secretary
Pub. *Indiana Genealogist*, quarterly; *Indiana
    Genealogical Society Newsletter*,
    bimonthly
$20.00 per year membership

**Allen County Genealogical Society of
Indiana (ACGSI)**
Chapter IGS
PO Box 12003
Fort Wayne, IN 46862
katiebf2144@cs.com
http://www.ipfw.edu/ipfwhist/historgs/
    acgsi.htm
Kathryn Bloom
Pub. *Allen County Lines*, quarterly
$15.00 per year membership

Bartholomew County Genealogical Society
Chapter IGS
PO Box 2455
Columbus, IN 47202-2455
Judy Scholtz, President; Jane Johnson,
    Editor
Pub. *Bartholomew County (Indiana)
    Ancestors*, quarterly

Part 2. Indiana

149

$10.00 per year membership

Elkhart County Genealogical Society
Chapter IGS
(First Presbyterian Church, Beardsley
Street—library location)
PO Box 1031 (mailing address)
Elkhart, IN 46515
joybel@michiana.org;
    michsearcher2@aol.com
http://www.rootsweb.com/~inelkhar/ecgs.
    htm
Joyce Bellows, Membership; Donna Cooper,
    Michiana Searcher
Library: Thur 1:00–6:00; meetings: fourth
    Thur
Pub. *Michiana Searcher*, quarterly
$12.00 per year membership

Genealogical Society of Marion County
Chapter IGS
PO Box 2292
Indianapolis, IN 46206-2292
KarenBeid@aol.com; engel@iquest.net
http://www.rootsweb.com/~ingsmc
Karen Beidelman, Journal Director; Fred
    Engelking, Newsletter Director
Sat 9:30–noon, fourth Sat 1:00–4:00, and by
    appointment
Pub. *Journal*; *Newsletter*
$20.00 per year membership

Northwest Indiana Genealogical Society
Chapter IGS
(Valparaiso Public Library—location)
103 Jefferson Street (mailing address)
Valparaiso, IN 46383
http://rootsweb.com/~inlake/nwigs.htm
Michael Sutton
Pub. *Twigs*, bimonthly
(various publications available for Lake and
    Porter counties)
$10.00 per year membership

Northwest Territory Genealogical Society
Chapter IGS
c/o Knox County Public Library
502 North Seventh Street
Vincennes, IN 47591
dbeeson@vunet.vinu.edu
Donna Beeson, Editor
Library: Mon–Fri 8:30–4:30
Pub. *Northwest Trail Tracer*, quarterly
(Northwest Territory: Illinois, Indiana,
    Michigan, Ohio, Wisconsin and part of
    Minnesota; specializes in Knox County,
    Indiana, genealogical listings)
$12.00 per year membership

Wayne County (IN) Genealogical Society
Chapter IGS
PO Box 2599
Richmond, IN 47374-2599
(765) 935-0614 (late evenings); (765) 962-
    5756 (Museum)
waynet@waynet.org
http://www.waynet.org/nonprofit/WCGS.
    htm
Arnold L. Dean, President
Mon 9:00–11:00, 2:00–4:00 & 6:30–8:30;
    meetings in the Educational Building of
    Saint John Lutheran Church, 501 South
    Seventh Street, Richmond: second Tue
    (except July & Dec) 7:00
Pub. *Family Pathways*, quarterly (Mar, June,
    Sept, Dec)
(Wayne County, Indiana and Preble and
    Darke counties, Ohio)
$15.00 per year membership

Genealogical Societies—Local & Regional

**Alexandria Monroe Township Genealogy
Society**
302 West Tyler Street
Alexandria, IN 46001

Benton County Genealogical Society
711 East Third Street
Fowler, IN 47944-2343
(765) 884-1764
Freeman Harold Furr, Benton County
    Historian
Mon–Fri 8:00–4:00
(war veterans of Benton County, from the
    Revolutionary War to the Gulf War; vital
    records, cemeteries, wills and deeds, etc.)

Blackford-Wells Genealogy Society
PO Box 54
Bluffton, IN 46714-0054
cbrubaker@coolsky.com
Connie Brubaker

Brown County Genealogical Society
PO Box 1202
Nashville, IN 47448-1202
(812) 988-4297
hughams@aol.com
http://www.rootsweb.com/~inbcgs/title.htm
Peggy Scrougham, President
meetings at Brown County Public Library:
    second Tue 7:00
Pub. *Brown County Genealogical Society
    Newsletter*, quarterly, $1.00 per issue for
    nonmembers
("Focus is on Brown County families.")
$10.00 per year membership

Cass County Genealogical Society
PO Box 373
Logansport, IN 46947
bougher1@netusa1.net
Betty Burke

Clay County Genealogical Society, Inc.
(309 Main Street—location)
PO Box 56 (mailing address)
Centerpoint, IN 47840-0056
(812) 835-5005
fred@indiana.net
http://indiana.net/clay/ccgs.htm
Patricia Wilkinson, President
Wed & Sat 1:00–4:00
Pub. *The Researcher*, quarterly
$12.00 per year membership; queries printed;
    research: $5.00 per hour

Clinton County Genealogical Society
609 North Columbia Street
Frankfort, IN 46041

County Seat Genealogical Society
52 West Broadway
Danville, IN 46122
Pub. *County Seat Scraps*, quarterly
(Hendricks County)
$12.00 per year membership

**Crawford County Historical and
Genealogical Society**
(see Historical Societies—Local and
Regional, above)

**De Kalb County Indiana Genealogy
Society**
PO Box 6085
Auburn, IN 46706
alwells@locl.net
http://www.rootsweb.com/~indkigs/
    main_page.html
Amanda Wells, President
meetings at Eckhart Public Library: second
    Mon: 6:00

$10.00 per year membership; research: brief
    queries for cost of copies

DuBois County Genealogical Society
PO Box 84
Ferdinand, IN 47532-0084
genauto@psci.com
http://www.rootsweb.com/~indubois/
    dubgen.htm
Rosemary Stewart, Secretary
meetings at Jasper Public Library: first Mon
Pub. *Dubois County Genealogical Society
    Newsletter*, quarterly
("Census, marriage, death index, cemetery
    inscriptions, naturalization records
    publications for sale.")
$10.00 per year membership

Fountain County Genealogical Society
(405 North Mill Street—location)
PO Box 273 (mailing address)
Veedersburg, IN 47987
(765) 294-4954
focogensoc@netscape.net
http://glenmar.com/~emoyhbo/fcgs.html
Mon & Fri–Sat 11:00–4:00, and by
    appointment
Pub. *Newsletter*, bimonthly
$10.00 per year membership

Grant County Genealogy Club
1419 West 11th Street
Marion, IN 46953
June Shields, President
Pub. *Grant County Beacon*, quarterly
$8.00 per year membership; research: for
    contribution

Greene County Genealogical Society
PO Box 164
Bloomfield, IN 47424-0164
ddrogich@viaduct.custom.net
http://www.greenecountyin.org/gcgs.htm
Diane Drogich
Pub. newsletter, quarterly
$10.0 per year membership

Hancock County Genealogical Society
c/o Hancock Public Library
700 North Broadway
Greenfield, IN 46140-1741
(317) 462-4715
BAndr20896@aol.com
Bonnie Andrews

Hendricks County Genealogical Society
Danville Public Library
101 South Indiana Street
Danville, IN 46122

**Genealogical Society of Henry County
Indiana**
6884 North North Prairie Road
Springport, IN 47386
lljsnyder@juno.com
http://www.rootsweb.com/~ingshc/index.
    html
Lola Snyder, Secretary
Pub. *Rose City Quarterly*
$15.00 per year membership

Howard County Genealogical Society
PO Box 2
Oakford, IN 46965-0002
http://www.rootsweb.com/~inhoward/
    hcgs/index.html
Tracey Morris, President
Library: Mon–Thur 9:00–9:00, Fri–Sat
    9:00–5:30, Sun (Labor Day–Memorial
    Day) 2:00–5:30
Pub. *Howard County (IN) Genealogical
    Society Newsletter*, quarterly

(Indiana counties, Howard County, Indiana)
$15.00 per year membership; free queries in newsletter

Illiana Genealogical and Historical Society
(see Illinois, Part 2)

Jackson County Genealogical Society, Inc.
415½ South Poplar Street
Brownstown, IN 47220-1939
(812) 358-2118
Bill Day, President
Mon–Tue & Fri 9:00–4:00, Thur 9:00–8:00, first & third Sat 9:00–4:00, and by appointment if residence is over 50 miles
Pub. *Genealogy Jottings*, quarterly
$10.00 per year membership; research: $10.00 minimum for mailing and up to one hour and up to ten photocopies on one surname, accompanied by nonreturnable pedigree and ancestral charts that organize the known information and indicate the needed information

Jasper-Newton Counties Genealogical Society
Route 1, Box 307
Wheatfield, IN 46392
Kathy Lund
Pub. *Jasper-Newton Counties Genealogical Society—Genealogy Trails*, quarterly

Jay County Genealogical Society
109 South Commerce Street, Suite E
Portland, IN 47371
(260) 726-4323
jaycogen@jayco.net
http://www.rootsweb.com/~injay/jaygene.htm
Rick Hambrock, Office Manager
Mon–Fri 10:00–4:00
Pub. *Genealogical Times*, bimonthly
$10.00 per year membership; research for members; copies: 10¢ each plus postage

Jefferson County Genealogy Society
735 West Main Street
Madison, IN 47250
(812) 265-4472
pgkonkle@seidata.com
Paul Konkle, President and County Historian
hours: "almost anytime"
Pub. *Newsletter*, monthly

Jennings County Genealogical Society
PO Box 863
North Vernon, IN 47265
meetings at Farm Bureau Insurance Building, North Vernon: fourth Mon (Jan–Nov) 7:00
Pub. *Newsletter*, annually
$10.00 per year membership; search for donation

Kosciusko County Area Genealogist Researchers
1134 South Ferguson
Warsaw, IN 46580
Mrs. Willodean Metzger Andrew
(Mayer, Warren and Andrew Family Association)

Genealogy Section, Kosciusko County Historical Society
(see Historical Societies—Local and Regional, above)

LaPorte County Genealogical Society
LaPorte County Public Library
904 Indiana Avenue
LaPorte, IN 46350-3464

(219) 326-6458; (219) 362-6156 (Library)
hazeller@csinet.net
http://www.rootsweb.com/~inlcigs
Allan Zeller, Secretary
Library: Mon–Thur 9:00–9:00, Fri–Sat 9:00–6:00
Pub. *Newsletter*, quarterly
("Not affiliated with Indiana Genealogical Society.")
$7.00 per year membership

Lawrence County Historical Genealogical Society
(see Historical Societies—Local and Regional, above)

Marshall County Genealogical Society
Marshall County Historical Society
123 North Michigan Street
Plymouth, IN 46563-2132
punchnjudy@kconline.com
Judy McCollough, Editor
meetings: second Tue (Mar, May, Sept, Nov)
Pub. *Marshall County Roots and Branches*, quarterly
$8.00 per year membership

Martin County Genealogical Society
PO Box 45
Shoals, IN 47581
ljsmith7@pop3.concentric.net
Lynda Smith

Miami County Genealogical Society
PO Box 542
Peru, IN 46970
(765) 985-3435 (President)
wilson@netusa1.net
http://www.rootsweb.com/~inmiami/gensoc.html
Jean A. Musselman, President
meetings at the Peru Family History Center: second Thur 7:00
Pub. *Miami County Trakker*, quarterly
$10.00 per year membership

Monroe County Historical and Genealogical Society
(see Historical Societies—Local and Regional, above)

Genealogy Club of Montgomery County
c/o Crawfordsville District Public Library
222 South Washington Street
Crawfordsville, IN 47933-2444
gen@cdpl.lib.in.us
Dian Moore, Local History Librarian
$10.00 per year membership

Morgan County History & Genealogy Association
(see Historical Societies—Local and Regional, above)

Noble County Genealogical Society, Inc.
Noble County Public Library
813 East Main
Albion, IN 46701
(219) 636-7197 (Library); (219) 636-3321 FAX
Linda J. Shultz, Executive Secretary
Library: Mon–Thur 8:30–8:30, Fri 8:30–5:30, Sat 8:30–3:30
Pub. *The Noble News*, quarterly (Mar, June, Sept, Nov)
$5.00 per year membership

North Central Indiana Genealogical Society
1404 Zartman Road
Kokomo, IN 46902-3263
R. Tetrick

Northwest Indiana Genealogy Society
PO Box 595
Griffith, IN 46319
sdp2609@sbcglobal.net
http://www.rootsweb.com/~innwigs
Sally Phillips, Secretary

Orange County Genealogical Society
(301 West Main Street—location)
PO Box 344 (mailing address)
Paoli, IN 47454
(812) 723-3437
http://www.usgennet.org/usa/in/county/orange/gensoc.htm
Everett or Wilma Davis
by appointment; meetings: second Tue 7:00
Pub. *Orange Peelings*, quarterly (Mar, June, Sept, Dec)
$10.00 per year membership

Owen County Historical and Genealogical Society
(see Historical Societies—Local and Regional, above)

Pulaski County Genealogical Society
Pulaski County Public Library
121 South Riverside Drive
Winamac, IN 46996
Lynda Irving, Pulaski County Historian
Library: Mon 9:00–8:00, Tue–Sat 9:00–6:00
Pub. *Pulaski County Genealogical Newsletter*, quarterly
$5.00 per year membership

Randolph County Historical/Genealogical Society
(see Historical Societies—Local and Regional, above)

Scott County Genealogical Society
(Research Rooms, Scott County Heritage Center and Museum, 1050 South Main Street—location)
PO Box 23 (mailing address)
Scottsburg, IN 47170-0023
(812) 752-3388; (812) 889-2071 FAX
steve@scottinhistory.com; SCGSI@c3bb.com
http://SCGSI.com
Steve and Jeannie Noe Carlisle, Librarians
Library: Mon–Sat 10:00–4:00; meetings in the Jim Byrer Room, Scottsburg City Hall, East Main Street: first Thur 6:30
Pub. *The Scott County Genealogical Society Newsletter*, quarterly
$10.00 per year membership; newsletter queries free to members and nonmembers

Shelby County, Indiana Genealogical Society
PO Box 434
Shelbyville, IN 46176-0434
Marjorie Roberts, Secretary-Treasurer
meetings at Louis and Lena Firn Grover Museum, 52 West Broadway, Shelbyville, IN 46176-1256: third Sat 10:00 A.M.
Pub. *Fore Bears Paws*, quarterly (Feb, May, Aug, Nov)
$10.00 per year membership

Sheridan Historical and Genealogical Society
(see Historical Societies—Local and Regional, above)

South Bend Area Genealogical Society
c/o Mishawaka-Penn-Harris Public Library
209 Lincoln Way, East
Mishawaka, IN 46544-2084
meetings at First Christian Church of South Bend, 1101 East Jefferson Boulevard:

fourth Mon (except June–Aug & Dec)
7:00
Pub. *South Bend Area Genealogical
Quarterly*
$12.00 per year membership; research: new
members may receive two hours of free
research

Southern Indiana Genealogical Society
PO Box 665
New Albany, IN 47151-0665
spcarpenter@ka.net
http://www.ka.net/spcarpenter/SIGserve.htm
Mary Stauble, President
New Albany-Floyd County Public Library:
Mon–Thur 9:00–8:30, Fri–Sat 9:00–5:30
Pub. *Southern Indiana Genealogical Society
Quarterly*, $4.00 per back issue; *Southern
Indiana Genealogical Society Newsletter*,
irregularly
(covers only Floyd, Clark, Harrison,
Washington, Crawford, Scott and Perry
counties)
$15.00 per year membership; nonmember
query, $2.00 per fifty words

Starke County Genealogical Society
152 West Culver Road
Knox, IN 46534
(574) 772-3411
starkegen@myvine.com
http://www.rootsweb.com/~inscgs/index.
html
Peg Brettin, President
$10.00 per year membership

Sullivan County Historical Society
Sullivan County Genealogical Society
(see Historical Societies—Local and
Regional, above)

**Tippecanoe County Area Genealogical
Society (TIPCOA)**
PO Box 2464
West Lafayette, IN 47996
(765) 476-8420
tipcoa@yahoo.com; mam@gtemail.net
http://www.rootsweb.com/~intcags
Mary Ann McCarty, Secretary
Pub. *TIPCOA Newsletter*, quarterly
$8.00 per year membership

Tri-County Genealogical Society
(23184 Pocket Road, West—location)
PO Box 118 (mailing address)
Batesville, IN 47006
meetings at Batesville Memorial Public
Library: second Wed
(Decatur, Franklin, and Ripley counties)

Tri-State Genealogical Society
Chapter IGS
Willard Library
Regional and Family History Center
21 First Avenue
Evansville, IN 47710
(812) 425-4309 (Library); (812) 425-4303
FAX (Library)
mylines@evansville.net
http://www.rootsweb.com/~intsgs
Virginia Aldridge, President
Library: Mon–Tue 9:00–8:00, Wed–Fri
9:00–5:30, Sat 9:00–5:00, Sun 1:00–5:00;
meetings second Tue (Sept–June)
Pub. *Tri-State Packet*, quarterly
(southwestern Indiana, western Kentucky,
southeastern Illinois; "We conduct an
annual genealogical seminar, provide help
sessions monthly.")
$12.00 per year membership

Twin Oaks Genealogy

PO Box 94
Ossian, IN 46777-0094

Wabash County Genealogy Society
PO Box 825
Wabash, IN 46992-0825
Ronald L. Woodward, Editor and Wabash
County Historian
Pub. *Family Branches*, monthly
$15.00 per year; free queries; research: fees
vary

Wabash Valley Genealogy Society
PO Box 236
Terre Haute, IN 47808-0236
wvgs@inwvgs.org
http://www.inwvgs.org
meetings at the Vigo County Public Library,
Room "C": second (odd-numbered
months) Mon 6:30
Pub. *Sycamore Leaves*, quarterly
$15.00 per year membership

White County Genealogical Society
White County Historical Society and
Museum
101 South Bluff Street, Basement
Monticello, IN 47960-2308
(219) 583-3998; (219) 583-9109
http://www.buffaloindiana.org/
whitecountyindiana/whgen.htm
Linda Hintz
$10.00 per year membership; research: $5.00
per hour

Genealogical Society of Whitley County
PO Box 224
Columbia City, IN 46725-0224
BevH@myvine.com
ocraig@whitleynet.org (Kay Craig)
http://genealogy.whitleynet.org
Beverly Henley, President
meetings at Peabody Public Library: third
Thur 6:30
Pub. newsletter
$10.00 per year membership

Independent Publications and
Miscellany

Book Publisher
4641 East County Road 250 North
Frankfort, IN 46041-8256
(765) 659-2030 (Office); (765) 249-2616
(Home)
jrmmem@geetel.net
Mary Ellen Mattingly, Publisher
(specializes in family histories and Clinton
County, Indiana)

Canal Society of Indiana
(304 East Berry Street, Fort Wayne, IN
46802—location)
PO Box 40087 (mailing address)
Fort Wayne, IN 46804
(219) 432-0279
indcanal@aol.com
http://user.centralnet.net/zepp/canal.html
Carolyn Schmidt, Editor
Mon–Sat 8:00–5:00
Pub. *Indiana Canals*, quarterly, $15.00 per
year subscription; *Newsletter*, monthly

Crawford County Indiana Museum
Route 1
Leavenworth, IN 47137

Direct Line Software
Land Record Reference
(see Miscellaneous, Part 4)

H-Indiana
H-Indiana-request@h-net.msu.edu (Editors)
http://www2.h-net.msu.edu/~indiana
(history discussion network)

President Benjamin Harrison Home
1230 North Delaware Street
Indianapolis, IN 46202
(317) 631-1888 (Research Library)
harrison@surf-ici.com
http://www.surf-ici.com/harrison
Library: Tue–Sat 10:00–4:00; Museum:
Mon–Sat 10:00–3:30, Sun 12:30–3:30

Hartman Museum
901 West Maumee Street
Angola, IN 46703

Hayden Historical Museum, Inc.
PO Box 58
Hayden, IN 47245
(812) 346-8212

Historic Forks of the Wabash, Inc.
(3010 West Park Drive—location)
PO Box 261 (mailing address)
Huntington, IN 46750
(219) 356-1903 voice & FAX
dericsson@huntington.edu
http://www.historicforks.org
Lynn Brown
May–Sept: Thur–Sun 1:00–5:00
Pub. *Newsletter*, quarterly
("We deal with events on the frontier in
Indiana 1800–1850. This was a time when
people of European origin, mostly
immigrants, were settling the land, and a
time when the Native Americans were
being removed. We interpret the interplay
of cultures during a rather tumultuous
period in U.S. history and show how the
two cultures blended at the same time that
they were clashing. We have 100 acres,
three historic buildings and a Visitors'
Center.")

Historic Genealogical Magazine
(406½ North Main Street—location)
PO Box 168 (mailing address)
Michigantown, IN 46057-0168
Joan C. Bohm, Genealogist
Pub. *Historic Genealogical Magazine*,
semiannually (spring & summer, fall &
winter), $20.00 per year subscription
(specializing in Boone and Clinton counties,
Indiana)
research: $10.00 per hour plus postage and
copies

**Historic Hagerstown, Inc., and Nettle
Creek Museum**
(96½ East Main Street—location)
PO Box 126 (mailing address)
Hagerstown, IN 47346-0126
(765) 489-4005
ncvmuseum1@aol.com
Steve St. John, President

Hoosier Journal of Ancestry
(7718 Franklin Bottoms Road, Scottsburg,
IN 47170—location)
PO Box 33 (mailing address)
Little York, IN 47139
(812) 752-2051
hjasexton@scottsburg.com
Naomi Keith Sexton, Editor
Pub. *Hoosier Journal of Ancestry*, ceased
publication, but back issues still for sale
(source records from thirty counties of
southeastern Indiana)

Hunting for Bears Genealogical and

Historical Society
(see Alabama, Part 2)

Indiana Department of Transportation
100 North Senate Avenue
Room IGCN 755
Indianapolis, IN 46204
(317) 232-5533
indot@ai.org
http://www.state.in.us/dot/indot_maps.html
     (Maps)

Indiana University Folklore Institute
504 North Fess
Bloomington, IN 47408-3890
(812) 855-1027; (812) 855-4008 FAX
http://www.indiana.edu/~folklore
Ruth Aten, Administrative Secretary
8:00–5:00
Pub. *Journal of Folklore Research*, three
     times per year
$18.00 per year membership

InGenWeb
Part of The USGenweb Project
ingen@migrations.org
http://www.ingenweb.org
Patrick Hays, State Coordinator; Gene
     Andert, Assistant Coordinator
(links to other Indiana resources)

Lost Creek Lineage Company
1408 North Thirtieth Street
Terre Haute, IN 47803
(812) 466-7845
jshep@abcs.com
Vicki Norton Brown

Michiana History Publications
PO Box 1537
South Bend, IN 46634
(574) 291-3955
rockingk@michiana.org
http://dogbert.abebooks.com/abe/
     ClientHome?clientId=954241
("genealogical materials on Midwestern
     states including Illinois, Indiana,
     Kentucky, Michigan, Ohio, and selected
     other states; family histories; genealogies;
     county histories; maps")

**Morgan County Historic Preservation
Society**
PO Box 1377
Martinsville, IN 46151

Ohio River Valley Families
(see Ohio, Part 2)

Old Northwest Corporation
PO Box 1979
Vincennes, IN 47591
(812) 885-4173
Richard Day, President
Pub. *ONC Newsletter*

Pioneer Publications
PO Box 1179
Tumtum, WA 99034-1179
(509) 276-1740
Shirley Penna-Oakes, Editor
Pub. *Indiana Queries*, $6.00 plus $1.75
     postage per issue; *OH-IN-IA Queries &
     Reviews*, $6.00 plus $1.75 postage per
     issue

Reppert Publications
Antique and Collectible News
(see Illinois, Part 2)

**Indiana Society, Sons of the American
Revolution**

Hoosier Patriot
(see Lineage, Hereditary and Patriotic
Societies, Part 4)

Thompson Enterprises
2005 State Road 55, North
Crawfordsville, IN 47933
(765) 362-4169
stephent@wico.net
Stephen Jay Thompson
("Great Lakes Region: genealogical
     consulting, seminars, workshops. Over
     thirty years' experience assisting with
     genealogical research.")

University of Southern Indiana
Historic Southern Indiana
405 Carpenter Street
Evansville, IN 47708
(812) 428-7592
Darrel E. Bigham, Ph.D., Director
(not genealogical: alliance of historical
     organizations)

Iowa

Archives and Libraries with Holdings in Genealogy

State Archives and Library

State Archives of Iowa
State Historical Society of Iowa
State of Iowa Historical Building
600 East Locust, Capitol Complex
Des Moines, IA 50319-0290
(515) 281-3007; (515) 282-0502 FAX
ghendri@max.state.ia.us
http://www.iowahistory.org/library
Gordon O. Hendrickson, State Archivist
Library: Tue–Sat 9:00–4:30 (except state
     holidays and Saturdays preceding or
     following state holidays); Archives:
     Tue–Fri 9:00–4:30
(Iowa government records, statewide history
     sources)

State Library of Iowa
East 12th and Grand Streets
Des Moines, IA 50319
(515) 281-4102; (515) 281-3384 FAX; (515)
     281-6191 FAX
nhaigh@mail.lib.state.ia.us
http://www.silo.lib.ia.us

State Historical Societies

State Historical Society of Iowa
Library/Archives Bureau
State of Iowa Historical Building
600 East Locust, Capitol Complex
Des Moines, IA 50319-0290
(515) 281-6200 (Library); (515) 281-3007
     (Archives); (515) 281-5111
dm.library@iowa.gov
http://www.iowahistory.org/index.html
Library: Tue–Sat 9:00–4:30 (except state
     holidays and Saturdays preceding or
     following state holidays); Archives:
     Tue–Fri 9:00–4:30
Pub. *The Iowa Heritage Illustrated*, quarterly
     (free to active members); *The Annals of
     Iowa*, quarterly, $20.00 per year
     subscription ($18.00 per year subscription
     to active members); *The Goldfinch*,
     quarterly, $10.00 per year subscription
     ($9.00 per year subscription to active
     members); *Iowa Historian*, bimonthly
     (free to all members)
$50.00–$59.00 per year membership

State Historical Society of Iowa
Library/Archives
Centennial Building
402 Iowa Avenue
Iowa City, IA 52240-1806
(319) 335-3916
libstu@blue.weeg.uiowa.edu
http://www.iowahistory.org/index.html
Karen Laughlin, Reference Librarian
Tue–Sat 9:00–4:30 (except state holidays
     and Saturdays preceding or following
     state holidays)
Pub. *The Palimpsest*, quarterly, $15.00 per
     year subscription (free to active
     members); *The Annals of Iowa*, quarterly,
     $20.00 per year subscription ($18.00 per
     year subscription to active members); *The
     Goldfinch*, quarterly, $10.00 per year
     subscription ($9.00 per year subscription
     to active members); *Iowa Historian*,
     bimonthly (free to all members)
$20.00–$59.00 per year membership

City, County and Regional Archives and

Libraries
(A more exhaustive list of public and
academic libraries can be found at http://
silo.lib.ia.us/for-ia-libraries/directories.)

Ames Public Library
515 Douglas Avenue
Ames, IA 50010-6215
(515) 233-2115; (515) 232-4571 FAX
gmillsap@ames.lib.ia.us
http://www.ames.lib.ia.us
Mike Quinn, Information Services; Gina
Millsap, Administrator
Mon–Thur 9:00–9:00, Fri–Sat 9:00–6:00,
Sun 1:30–5:00 (Sept–May)

Mary J. Barnett Memorial Library
400 Grand
Guthrie Center, IA 50115-1328
(641) 747-8110 voice & FAX
library@guthriecenter.com
Pat Sleister, Administrator

Burlington Public Library
501 North Fourth Street
Burlington, IA 52601-5279
(319) 753-1647; (319) 753-5316 FAX
kweiss@aea16.k12.ia.us
http://www.burlington.lib.ia.us
Kay M. Weiss, Director
Mon–Thur 9:00–9:00, Fri–Sat 9:00–5:00,
call for holiday and summer hours
("Burlington was the territorial capitol of the
Wisconsin and Iowa territories. Holdings
include Territorial Papers, Draper papers,
federal census, etc.")
copies: 25¢ per page

Carnegie-Eldon Public Library
(608 West Elm Street—location)
Box 430 (mailing address)
Eldon, IA 52554-0430
(641) 652-7517 voice & FAX
Gail Potts, Administrator

Carnegie-Evans Library
203 Benton Avenue, East
Albia, IA 52531-2036
(641) 932-2469 voice & FAX
albialibrary@netscape.net
Marilyn M. Woods, Administrator
Mon–Fri noon–6:00, Sat 10:00–4:00

Carnegie-Montezuma Public Library
(200 South Third—location)
PO Box 158 (mailing address)
Montezuma, IA 50171-0158
(641) 623-3417; (641) 623-3339 FAX
montepl@netins.net
Diane Hester, Administrator

Carnegie-Stout Public Library
(11th and Bluff Streets—location)
360 West 11th Street (mailing address)
Dubuque, IA 52001-4697
(563) 589-4225; (563) 589-4217 FAX
cspl@stout.dubuque.lib.ia.us
http://http://www.dubuque.lib.ia.us
Betty Baule, Adult Services Librarian
Mon–Thur 9:00–9:00, Fri 9:00–6:00, Sat
9:00–5:00

Carroll Public Library
118 East Fifth Street
Carroll, IA 51401-2717
(712) 792-3432; (712) 792-0141 FAX
carrollpublic@yahoo.com
Gordon S. Wade
Mon–Thur 10:00–8:30, Fri 10:00–6:00, Sat
10:00–5:00
(local newspaper on microfilm, 1870 to the
present)

research: $5.00 per request

Cedar Falls Public Library
524 Main Street
Cedar Falls, IA 50613-2889
(319) 273-8643; (319) 268-5540 (Business);
(319) 273-8648 FAX
cfpl@iren.net; cfpljohn@iren.net
http://www.iren.net/cfpl
Carol F. Johnson, Administrator
(newspapers on microfilm, county histories,
local history)

Cedar Rapids Historical Archives
1201 Sixth Street, S.W.
Cedar Rapids, IA 52404
(319) 398-0419

Cedar Rapids Public Library
500 First Street, S.E.
Cedar Rapids, IA 52401-2095
(319) 398-5123; (319) 398-0476 FAX
webmaster@mail.crlibrary.org
http://www.crlibrary.org
Mon–Thur 9:30–9:00, Fri–Sat 9:30–5:00,
Sun 1:00–5:00

Chariton Public Library
803 Braden Avenue
Chariton, IA 50049-1742
(641) 774-5514; (641) 774-8695 FAX
Roberta Reynolds, Director
noon–6:00

Cherokee Area Archives, Inc.
(228 West Main—location)
215 South Second (mailing address)
Cherokee, IA 51012
(712) 225-6414
Nov–Apr: Mon, Wed & Fri 2:00–4:00,
May–Oct: Mon–Fri 2:00–4:00
(local history and genealogy material)

Clarksville Public Library
103 West Green Street
Clarksville, IA 50619-0039
(319) 278-1168 voice & FAX
clarksvillelib@butler-bremer.com
http://www.butler-bremer.com/web/lcld
Lola Clark, Library Director
Mon & Wed 10:00–7:00, Tue & Thur
10:00–5:00, Fri 10:00–4:00, Sat
10:00–2:00

Clermont Historical Society Museum
PO Box 372
Clermont, IA 52135
(563) 423-7173
Henry Follett, Site Manager

Clinton Public Library
306 Eighth Avenue, South
Clinton, IA 52732-5699
(563) 242-8441; (563) 242-8162 FAX
Dan Horwath, Administrator

Conrad Public Library
(102 East Grundy—location)
PO Box 189 (mailing address)
Conrad, IA 50621-0189
(641) 366-2583; (641) 366-3105 FAX
conradpl@netins.net
Susan Blythe, Administrator
Mon–Tue & Thur 2:00–8:00, Wed
9:00–8:00, Fri 2:00–6:00, Sat 9:00–noon

Davenport Public Library
Richardson-Sloane Special Collections
Center
321 Main Street
Davenport, IA 52801-1490
(563) 326-7902; (563) 326-7809 FAX

agroskop@libby.rbls.lib.il.us
http://www.davenportlibrary.com
Amy Groskopf, Archivist and Special
Collections Supervisor
Mon–Thur 9:00–8:30, Fri–Sat 9:00–5:00,
Sun (winter only) 1:00–3:30
call for information about research fees

Decorah Public Library
202 Winnebago
Decorah, IA 52101-1812
(563) 382-8559; (563) 382-3717; (563) 382-4524 FAX
dpllib@decorah.lib.ia.us;
lborowsk@decorah.lib.ia.us
http://www.decorah.lib.ia.us
Lorraine Borowski, Director
Mon–Thur 10:00–8:00, Fri–Sat 10:00–5:00,
Sun 1:00–4:00

Public Library of Des Moines
100 Locust Street
Des Moines, IA 50309-1791
(515) 283-4152
pldmdirector@desmoineslibrary.com;
librarywebmaster@desmoineslibrary.com
http://www.pldminfo.org
M. J. Scott, Research Requests
Mon–Wed 10:00–9:00, Thur–Fri
10:00–6:00, Sat 10:00–5:00
(Polk County, Des Moines, history, plus
National Bar Association Archives)
research: $90.00 per hour plus 25¢ per page
for photocopies, payable in advance,
$10.00 minimum per request

Dexter Historical Museum
Dexter, IA 50070

Donnellson Public Library
Family History Department
(500 Park—location)
PO Box 290 (mailing address)
Donnellson, IA 52625-0290
(319) 835-5545 voice & FAX
donpulib@interl.net
Brenda Knox, Administrator

Drake University
Cowles Library
28th and University
Des Moines, IA 50311
(515) 271-3993; (515) 271-3933 FAX
http://www.drake.edu/lib.html

Center for Dubuque History
Loras College
PO Box 178
Dubuque, IA 52004-0178
(563) 588-7163
Michael D. Gibson, Archivist
hours: various, call in advance for
appointment
(specializes in Dubuque and Dubuque
County, Iowa)
research: write for details

Eckles Memorial Library
(206 South Highway—location)
Box 519 (mailing address)
Oakland, IA 51560-0519
(712) 482-6668 voice & FAX
Patrice Vance, Administrator
Mon & Thur 1:00–5:00, Tue 9:00–noon &
1:00–5:00, Fri 7:00–9:00, Sat 1:00–5:00
$5.00 per year membership

Elgin Public Library
(214 Main Street—location)
Box 36 (mailing address)
Elgin, IA 52141-0036
(563) 426-5313 voice & FAX

elginlib@alpinecom.net
Beverly Strong, Administrator
Tue 1:00–5:00, Wed 9:30–11:30 &
  1:00–5:00, Thur 6:30–8:30, Fri
  1:00–5:30, Sat 9:00–2:00
(*Elgin Echo* newspaper on microfilm from
  September 1891)

Elliott Public Library
(401 Main Street—location)
PO Box 306 (mailing address)
Elliott, IA 51532-0306
(712) 767-2355 voice & FAX
eliotlib@netins.net
Candace Tischer, Administrator

Emmetsburg Public Library
707 North Superior
Emmetsburg, IA 50536-2410
(712) 852-4009; (712) 852-3785 FAX
publib@ilcc.cc.ia.us
Sue Kroesche, Administrator

Ericson Public Library
702 Greene Street
Boone, IA 50036-2853
(515) 432-3727; (515) 432-1103 FAX
ericson@boone.lib.ia.us
Cynthia Watson, Director
Mon–Thur 10:00–8:30, Fri 10:00–6:00, Sat
  10:00–5:00
(Boone, Iowa, history)
research: $5.00 per hour

Estherville Public Library
Special Collections
613 Central Avenue
Estherville, IA 51334-2294
(712) 362-7731; (712) 362-3509 FAX
estpub@ncn.net;
  main@esthervillepubliclibrary.com
http://www.esthervillepubliclibrary.com
Carolyn Walz, Administrator
Mon noon–8:00, Tue–Wed 10:00–6:00,
  Thur 10:00–8:00, Fri 10:00–5:00, Sat
  10:00–2:00

Fairfield Public Library
104 West Adams Avenue
Fairfield, IA 52556-3433
(641) 472-6551; (641) 472-3249 FAX
fplib@fairfield.lib.ia.us
http://www.fairfield.lib.ia.us
Judy Bar-Shimon
Mon–Thur 9:30–8:30, Fri 9:30–6:00, Sat
  9:30–4:30, Sun 1:30–4:30
research: inquiries will be answered by
  genealogy society's corresponding
  secretary, fee for copies and postage

Forest City Municipal Library
115 East L Street
Forest City, IA 50436-1401
(641) 585-4542; (641) 585-2939 FAX
fcpublib@wctatel.net
Christa Cosgriff, Administrator

Fort Dodge Public Library
424 Central Avenue
Fort Dodge, IA 50501-3738
(515) 573-8167; (515) 573-5422 FAX
fdplinfo@fortdodge.lib.ia.us
LaWanda C. Roudebush, Administrator
Mon–Thur 10:00–9:00 (summer until 8:00),
  Fri–Sat 10:00–5:30
("Iowa archives; Webster County histories;
  Fort Dodge Messenger on microfilm")

Fort Madison Public Library
Idol Rashid Memorial Branch
Rose Reynolds, Administrator
3421 Avenue L

Fort Madison, IA 52627
(319) 372-2071; (319) 372-5726 FAX
rashid@ft-madison.lib.ia.us
Mon, Wed & Fri noon–5:00, Tue & Thur
  noon–8:00, Sat 9:00–1:00
(houses Iowa and genealogy collection)

Frontier Heritage Library
Broadway and Main Streets, Second Floor
Council Bluffs, IA 51501
(712) 322-1171

Garner Public Library
(416 State Street—location)
PO Box 406 (mailing address)
Garner, IA 50438-0406
(641) 923-2850; (641) 923-2339 FAX
garnerpl@sswireless.net; garnerpl@ncn.net
Ellen Petty, Administrator
winter: Mon 10:00–5:30 & 7:00–8:00,
  Tue–Wed 10:00–5:30, Thur noon–8:00,
  Fri noon–4:00, Sat 10:00–noon &
  1:00–3:00; summer: Mon–Wed
  10:00–5:00 & 7:00–8:00, Thur
  noon–8:00, Fri noon–4:00, Sat
  10:00–noon

Matilda J. Gibson Memorial Library
200 West Howard Street
Creston, IA 50801-2339
(641) 782-2277; (641) 782-4604 FAX
clibrary@iowatelecom.net
Mon & Wed 10:00–8:00, Tue & Thur–Fri
  10:00–6:00, Sat 10:00–4:00

Glenwood Public Library
109 North Vine Street
Glenwood, IA 51534-1516
(712) 527-5252; (712) 527-3619 FAX
denise@netins.net
Betty Jo Budd, Interlibrary Loan and
  Genealogy Department
Mon–Tue & Thur–Fri 10:00–6:00, Wed
  10:00–8:00, Sat 10:00–4:00
("Will do research for Mills County, Iowa")

Grand Meadow Heritage Center
Route 1, Box 45
Washta, IA 51061
(712) 375-5117

Greenfield Public Library
(202 South First Street—location)
Box 328 (mailing address)
Greenfield, IA 50849-0328
(641) 743-6120
greenpl@mddc.com
Lynn Heinbuch Lorraine Schneider,
  Administrator

Grinnell Historical Museum
(1125 Broad Street—location)
610 Broad Street, #10 (mailing address)
Grinnell, IA 50112
(641) 236-5005
Elizabeth H. Ernst, Archivist
1 June–31 Aug: Tue–Sun 2:00–4:00; 1
  Sept–31 May: Sat 2:00–4:00
("1895 house; 30,000+ obituaries; Iowa and
  local history")
no admission charge (unless large groups)

Grout Museum of History and Science
Hans J. Chryst Archival Library
503 South Street
Waterloo, IA 50701
(319) 234-6357; (319) 236-0500 FAX
Jan Taylor, Archivist/Volunteer Coordinator
Tue–Sat 10:00–4:30, Sun 1:00–4:30
(genealogy, Iowa history, local history)

Hacksma House Genealogy Library

(see Washington, Part 2)

Hampton Public Library
4 Federal Street, South
Hampton, IA 50441-1934
(641) 456-4451; (641) 456-2377 FAX
hplibrary@sswireless.net;
  Hampublib@hampton-dumont.k12.ia.us
Judy Harper, Administrator

Harlan Community Library
718 Court Street
Harlan, IA 51537
(712) 755-5934; (712) 755-3952 FAX
harlanpl@harlannet.com
http://www.harlan.lib.ia.us
Mon–Wed & Fri 9:30–5:30, Thur 9:30–8:30,
  Sat 9:30–4:30

**Louise & Lucile Hink - Tama Public
Library**
(401 Siegel Street—location)
PO Box 308 (mailing address)
Tama, IA 52339-0308
(641) 484-4484 voice & FAX
Julie Shook, Administrator

Humboldt Public Library
30 Sixth Street, North
Humboldt, IA 50548-1799
(515) 332-1925; (515) 332-1926 FAX
Nikki Ehlers, Administrator

Independence Public Library
210 Second Street, N.E.
Independence, IA 50644-1910
(319) 334-2470; (319) 334-9527 FAX
indeelib@indytel.com

Indianola Public Library
207 North B Street
Indianola, IA 50125-2448
(515) 961-9418; (515) 961-9419 FAX
info@indianola.lib.ia.us
http://www.indianola.ia.us/library
Joyce Godwin, Administrator

Iowa City Public Library
123 South Linn Street
Iowa City, IA 52240-1820
(319) 356-5200; (319) 356-5494 FAX
comment@icpl.org
http://www.jeonet.com/city/library.htm
Susan Craig, Administrator

Iowa State University
Parks Library, Room 403
Ames, IA 50011
(515) 294-6672; (515) 294-5525 FAX
twalters@iastate.edu
http://www.iastate.edu/spcl/spcl.html
  (Special Collections Department)
Mon–Fri 8:00–11:50 & 1:00–5:00

Janesville Public Library
(227 Main Street—location)
PO Box 328 (mailing address)
Janesville, IA 50647-0328
(319) 987-2925 voice & FAX
bs10923@cedarnet.org
http://www.cedarnet.org/library/janesvil.htm
Beth Ann Scott, Administrator

Jefferson Public Library
200 West Lincolnway
Jefferson, IA 50129-2185
(515) 386-2835; (515) 386-8163 FAX
jeflib@netins.net
Jane Millard, Administrator
Reference Room: Wed 2:00–5:00, Sat
  9:00–1:00

Keokuk Museum Commission
(Johnson Street—location)
226 High Street (mailing address)
Keokuk, IA 52632
(319) 524-4765

Keokuk Public Library
210 North Fifth Street
Keokuk, IA 52632-5614
(319) 524-1483; (319) 524-2320 FAX
Shirley Dick, Director
Mon–Thur 9:30–9:00, Fri–Sat 9:30–6:00

Keosauqua Public Library
(First and Van Buren—location)
PO Box 158 (mailing address)
Keosauqua, IA 52565-0158
(319) 293-3766 voice & FAX
keolib@netins.net
http://showcase.netins.net/web/keolibrary
Kathy Fisher, Administrator
Mon–Tue & Fri 1:00–5:00, Wed 1:00–8:00,
    Thur 10:00–5:00, Sat 10:00–1:00
("Surname card file, obituary file, cemetery
    inscriptions, county-wide")

Kinney Memorial Library
(214 Main Street—location)
PO Box 58 (mailing address)
Hanlontown, IA 50444-0058
(641) 896-2888; (641) 896-2890 FAX
redhawks@wctatel.net
Mary Frisbie, Administrator

Kling Memorial Library
708 Seventh Street
Grundy Center, IA 50638-1430
(319) 825-3607; (319) 825-5863 FAX
KlingLibrary@yahoo.com
Carol Thompson, Administrator

Knoxville Public Library
213 East Montgomery
Knoxville, IA 50138-2296
(641) 828-0585 voice & FAX
knoxlib@harenet.net; Knoxlib@se-iowa.net
Janet Behrens, Administrator
Mon–Thur 10:00–8:00, Fri 10:00–5:00, Sat
    10:00–3:00

Lamoni Public Library
301 West Main
Lamoni, IA 50140-1241
(641) 784-6686; (641) 784-6693 FAX
lamonipl@grm.net
Barbara L Houston, Administrator

Le Mars Public Library
46 First Street, S.W.
Le Mars, IA 51031-3696
(712) 546-5004; (712) 546-5797 FAX
lemarspl@frontiernet.net
Beth Hartman, Administrator
Mon–Thur 10:00–8:00, Fri–Sat 10:00–5:00

Karl Miles LeCompte Memorial Library
110 South Franklin Street
Corydon, IA 50060-1518
(641) 872-1621 voice & FAX
lecompte@grm.net
http://www.corydon.swilsa.lib.ia.us
Kay Milner, Administrator
Mon–Wed & Fri noon–5:00, Thur
    noon–5:30, Sat 10:00–2:00

John L. Lewis Commission, Inc.
John L. Lewis Mining and Labor Museum
(102 Division Street—location)
PO Box 3 (mailing address)
Lucas, IA 50151
(641) 766-6831; (641) 766-6443
Jean Hager, President

mid-Apr to mid-Oct: Tue–Sat 9:00–3:00, and
    by appointment
("Many photographs, artifacts and
    documents pertaining to Mr. Lewis,
    mining and labor")
admission: $1.00

Livermore Public Library
(402 Fifth Street—location)
PO Box 18 (mailing address)
Livermore, IA 50558-0018
(515) 379-2078 voice & FAX
livplib@trvnet.net
http://www.trvnet.net/~livplib
Pansy Streit, Administrator

Loras College
(see Center for Dubuque History, above)

Lost Nation Public Library
301 Pleasant Street
Lost Nation, IA 52254-0397
(563) 678-2114 voice & FAX
Margaret Rasmussen, Administrator

Lucas County Museum
17th Street and Braden Avenue
Chariton, IA 50049
(641) 774-4464

Manchester Public Library
304 North Franklin Street
Manchester, IA 52057-1520
(563) 927-3719; (563) 927-3058 FAX
manchpl@manchester.lib.ia.us;
    mnchst00@iren.net
Dan Bakke, Administrator

Marshalltown Public Library
36 North Center Street
Marshalltown, IA 50158-4911
(641) 754-5738; (641) 754-5708 FAX
library@marshallnet.com
Carole B. Winkleblack, Administrator
Sept–May: Mon–Thur 9:00–7:30, Fri–Sat
    9:00–5:00, Sun 1:00–4:00; June–Aug:
    Mon–Sat 9:00–6:00

Mason City Public Library
225 Second Street, S.E.
Mason City, IA 50401-3999
(641) 421-3668; (641) 423-2615 FAX
admin@mcpl.org
Ernest Kallay, Administrator
Mon, Wed & Fri 9:00–noon & 1:00–4:00,
    Mon 6:00–8:00, Sat 9:00–noon

Merry Brook School Museum
210 Lincoln Way
Woodbine, IA 51579
(712) 647-2593
Thur & Fri 1:00–4:40
(houses collection of the Harrison County
    Genealogical Volunteers Chapter, Iowa
    Genealogical Society)

Montgomery Memorial Library
(711 Main—location)
PO Box 207 (mailing address)
Jewell, IA 50130-0207
(515) 827-5112 voice & FAX
jewell-library@globalccs.net;
    jewell_public.lib@s-hamilton.k12.ia.us
Kris Koehnk, Administrator

Musser Public Library
304 Iowa Avenue
Muscatine, IA 52761-3875
(563) 263-3472; (563) 264-1033
mus@libby.rbls.lib.il.us;
    illmus@rbls.lib.il.us
http://www.rbls.lib.il.us/mus/index.html

Diane Mayer Day, Library Assistant
Mon–Thur 10:00–9:00, Fri 10:00–6:00, Sat
    10:00–4:00
(Muscatine City and County history)

New Hampton Public Library
Genealogy Section
20 West Spring Street
New Hampton, IA 50659-2130
(641) 394-2184; (641) 394-5482 FAX
nhpl@iowatelecom.net
Patricia Ipsen, Administrator

Nishna Heritage Museum
(117-119 North Main—location)
3878 Hickory Road (mailing address)
Oakland, IA 51560
Merle Davis, Curator
6 days per week
Pub. *Curator*
(history and preservation)
admission: $2.00 per person

Nodaway Valley Historical Museum
(420 South 16th Street—location)
PO Box 393 (mailing address)
Clarinda, IA 51632
(712) 542-3073
Betty J. Ankeny, Curator
daily 1:00–5:00
(good area genealogy library)
research: $10.00 per hour plus copies and
    postage

Northwestern College
Ramaker Library
101 Seventh Street
Orange City, IA 51041
(712) 737-4821
Cornelia B. Kennedy, Curator
Mon–Sat 8:00 A.M.–midnight (closes at 4:30
    during holidays)

Oelwein Public Library
22 First Avenue, N.W.
Oelwein, IA 50662-1604
(319) 283-1515 voice & FAX
vpetrik@trxinc.com; oelpublib@trxinc.com
http://www.oelwein.com;
    http://www.fayettecountyia.com/educat_li
    braries.html
Vivian Petrik, Administrator
Mon–Thur 10:00–8:30, Fri 10:00–5:30, Sat
    noon–5:30, Sun (Jan–Mar) 1:00–4:00

Onawa Public Library
Genealogy Department
707 Iowa Avenue
Onawa, IA 51040-1627
(712) 423-1733; (712) 423-3828 FAX
onawalib@pionet.net; onawa00@iren.net
Lori Beck, Administrator
Mon–Fri 1:00–5:00

Orange City Public Library
112 Albany Street, S.E.
Orange City, IA 51041
(712) 737-4302; (712) 737-4431 FAX
orange00@iren.net
http://www.orangecity.lib.ia.us
Mon–Thur 8:00 A.M.–9:00 P.M., Fri
    8:00–5:00, Sat 10:00–5:00

Osage Public Library
406 Main Street
Osage, IA 50461-1125
(641) 732-3323; (641) 732-4419 FAX
osagepl@osage.net
Cindi Youngblut, Administrator

Osceola Public Library
Genealogy and Local History Room

Attn: Judy Coe, Administrator
300 South Fillmore Street
Osceola, IA 50213-1414
(641) 342-2237; (641) 342-6057 FAX
jcoe@osceola.lib.ia.us

Oskaloosa Public Library
301 South Market Street
Oskaloosa, IA 52577-3399
(641) 673-0441; (641) 673-6237 FAX
Randy Bellinger, Director
Mon–Thur 10:00–8:00, Fri–Sat 10:00–4:00

Ottumwa Public Library
102 West Fourth Street
Ottumwa, IA 52501-2509
(641) 682-7563; (641) 682-4970 FAX
Mary Ann Lemon, Adult Services Librarian
winter: Mon–Thur 8:30–8:30, Fri–Sat
9:00–5:00, Sun 1:00–5:00; summer:
Mon–Wed 9:00–6:00, Thur 9:00–9:00,
Fri–Sat 9:00–5:00

Pella Public Library
603 Main Street
Pella, IA 50219-1592
(641) 628-4268; (641) 628-1326 FAX
cvpublib@central.edu
Mon–Thur 10:00–9:00, Fri 10:00–6:00, Sat
10:00–5:00

Pioneer Heritage Public Library
(204 North Vine Street—location)
PO Box 188 (mailing address)
Le Grand, IA 50142-0188
(641) 479-2122 voice & FAX
pioner00@marshallnet.com
Shelley Barron, Administrator

Pocahontas Public Library
Pocahontas, IA 50574-1611
(712) 335-4471 voice & FAX
pokypl@ncn.net
http://www.ncn.net/~pokypl
Rita Samuelson, Administrator

Prairie Trails Museum of Wayne County Iowa
(Highway 2, East—location)
PO Box 104 (mailing address)
Corydon, IA 50060
(641) 872-2211; (641) 872-2483
Wilma West, Librarian
15 Apr–15 Oct: Mon–Sun 1:00–5:00;
June–Aug: Mon–Fri 10:00–5:00
("Cemetery records, obituary books, county
newspaper clippings, census records,
county marriages, Dr. Hinkle's birth and
death records 1880–1920, historical
articles, microfilms; the Mormon Trail
crossed Wayne County 1846;
sesquicentennial of Mormon Trail and
Iowa Statehood in 1996; big Mormon
exhibit at museum.")
$10.00 per year membership in Wayne
County Historical Society; admission:
$3.00 for nonmembers; research: fees
nominal

Putnam Museum Library
1717 West 12th Street
Davenport, IA 52804
(563) 324-1933; (563) 324-6638 FAX
Michael J. Smith, Director

Red Oak Public Library
400 North Second Street
Red Oak, IA 51566-2251
(712) 623-6516; (712) 623-6518 FAX
Karen McClendon, Library Director
Mon–Thur 10:00–8:00, Fri–Sat 10:00–5:00
(good regional archives and local history

collection, some biographies)
research: no research done by staff, will
supply list of researchers

Richardson-Sloane Genealogical Library
(1019 Mound Street, Suite 301, Davenport,
IA 52803-3923—location)
PO Box 4077 (mailing address)
Davenport, IA 52808-4077
(563) 383-0007; (800) 828-4363; (563) 383-
0008 FAX
L. Ted or Alice R. Sloane
Mon–Fri 10:00–4:00, by appointment only
(all federal census indexes and all Illinois
censuses 1850–1920; IGI, SS death index,
military, US phone listings, approximately
11,000 volumes in area's major
genealogical resource library)
$1.00 per year for library use; copies: 10¢
each plus $1.00 annual library users
charge requested

Robey Memorial Library
401 First Avenue, N.W.
Waukon, IA 52172-1803
(563) 568-4424; (563) 568-5026 FAX
robeylib@sbtek.net
Callie Irons, Administrator

Scott County Library System
215 North Second Street
Eldridge, IA 52748-1284
(563) 285-4794; (563) 285-4743 FAX
infosel@rbls.lib.il.us; illsel@rbls.lib.il.us
Anne Conner, Administrator

Sidney Public Library
(604 Clay Street—location)
PO Box 479 (mailing address)
Sidney, IA 51652-0479
(712) 374-2223; (712) 374-2821 FAX
bfinnig@sidney.heartland.net
Bev Finnigan, Administrator

Sioux Center Public Library
327 First Avenue, N.E.
Sioux Center, IA 51250-1801
(712) 722-2138; (712) 722-1235 FAX
scplsilo@mtcnet.net
Karen Bjorkman, Administrator
Mon–Fri 10:00–9:00, Sat 10:00–5:00

Public Library, Sioux City
529 Pierce Street
Sioux City, IA 51101-1203
(712) 255-2933; (712) 279-6432 FAX
questions@mail.sc.lib.ia.us
http://www.siouxcitylibrary.org
Nancy A. Neumann, Local History and
Genealogy Librarian
Mon–Thur 9:00–9:00, Fri–Sat 9:00–6:00,
Sun (Sept–May) 1:00–5:00
Pub. None
(local history collection with an emphasis on
northwest Iowa, genealogy collection with
an emphasis on Woodbury and
surrounding counties)
research: copies at 25¢ each, $1.00 handling
fee, plus postage if SASE not enclosed

Spencer Public Library
Charlotte Brett Memorial Collection of
Genealogical Books and Magazines
21 East Third Street
Spencer, IA 51301-4131
(712) 264-7290; (712) 580-7468 FAX
spencerpl@ncn.net;
vickim@spencerlibrary.com
http://www.pionet.net/~nwiowa/spencer/
library/hmpagfrt.htm
Vicki Myron, Director; Esther Connell,
Secretary, Iowa Lakes Genealogical

Society Chapter (IGS)
Mon–Thur 9:00–9:00, Fri–Sat 9:00–5:00
Pub. None

Storm Lake Public Library
609 Cayuga Street
Storm Lake, IA 50588-2239
(712) 732-8026; (712) 732-7609 FAX
slpl@stormlake.org
http://pionet.net/~nwiowa/stormlake/
City/sl_lib.htm
Susan Stone, Administrator
Sept–May: Mon–Thur 9:00–8:00, Fri–Sat
9:00–5:00; June–Aug: Mon noon–5:30,
Tue–Wed 10:00–5:30, Thur 10:00–9:00,
Fri 10:00–5:00, Sat 10:00–2:00

University of Iowa
Department of Special Collections
Main Library
Iowa City, IA 52242-1420
(319) 335-5921; (319) 335-5900 FAX
david-mccartney@uiowa.edu; lib-
spec@uiowa.edu
http://www.lib.uiowa.edu/spec-coll
David F. McCartney, University Archivist

University of Northern Iowa Library
Special Collections and University Archives
Rod Library, Third Floor
Cedar Falls, IA 50613-3675
(319) 273-6307; (319) 273-2913 FAX
gerald.peterson@uni.edu
http://www.library.uni.edu/depts/
speccoll/index.html
Gerald Peterson, University Archivist
Mon–Fri 8:00–4:00
(Iowa census, Cedar Falls, Waterloo and Des
Moines newspapers on microfilm, county
history books for most counties, excellent
collection of maps)

Urbandale Public Library
3520 86th Street
Urbandale, IA 50322-4056
(515) 278-3945; (515) 278-3918 FAX
spearson@urbandale.org
Sara Pearson, Administrator
Mon–Thur 9:30–9:00, Fri–Sat 9:30–5:30

Washington Public Library
120 East Main Street
Washington, IA 52353-1941
(319) 653-2726; (319) 653-2097 FAX
washlib@washlib.net;
reference@washlib.net
http://washlib.net/genealogy.html
Patrick Finney, Administrator
Mon & Wed 10:00–8:00, Tue & Thur
10:00–8:00, Fri–Sat 10:00–5:00

Waterloo Public Library
415 Commercial Street
Waterloo, IA 50701-1386
(319) 291-4521; (319) 291-4476
(Information); (319) 291-6736 FAX
infowiz@wplwloo.lib.ia.us
http://www.wplwloo/index.html
Carol F. Johnson, Administrator
(federal and state census, newspapers and
city directories, county histories, maps,
genealogical books)

Webb Shadle Memorial Library
(301 West Dallas—location)
PO Box 338 (mailing address)
Pleasantville, IA 50225-0338
(515) 848-5617
LConn27769@aol.com
Larry A. Conn, Administrator

Kendall Young Public Library

1201 Willson Avenue
Webster City, IA 50595-2246
(515) 832-9100; (515) 832-9102 FAX
info@kendall-young.lib.ia.us
http://kendall-young.lib.ia.us
Cynthia Weiss, Administrator
Mon–Thur 10:00–8:00, Fri 10:00–6:00, Sat
    10:00–5:00

Historical Societies—Local and Regional

Adair County Historical Society
(Highway 92 West—location)
PO Box 214 (mailing address)
Greenfield, IA 50849
May–Sept: 1:00–4:30
Pub. *Adair County Historical Society
    Newsletter*, quarterly
$10.00 per year membership

Adel Historical Society
2160 312th Street
Adel, IA 50003
(515) 993-4124

Albert City Historical Association, Inc.
(212 North Second Street—location)
2226 510 Street (mailing address)
Albert City, IA 50510
(712) 843-5684
Marilyn Bolte, Registrar/Curator

Allamakee County Historical Society
(North Allamakee Street—location)
400 Fourth Avenue, S.W. (mailing address)
Waukon, IA 52172
(563) 568-4680

Amana Heritage Society
PO Box 81
Amana, IA 52203
(319) 622-3567
Lanny Haldy, Executive Director

American West Research Center and Historical Society, Inc.
(see Ohio, Part 2)

Audubon County Historical Society
1745 160th Street
Audubon, IA 50025
(712) 563-3984
Betty Sievers, Secretary
Court House Museum: Sun (June–Sept)
    2:00–4:00; Nathaniel Hamlin Museum
    Mon–Sun (June–Oct) 2:00–4:00
Pub. None
(two museums: Court House Museum at
    Exira and Nathaniel Hamlin Park and
    Museum at Audubon)
$2.00 per year membership

Benton County Historical Society
204 Riverview Drive
Vinton, IA 52349

Big Sioux River Valley Historical Society
1934 410th Street
Hawarden, IA 51023
(712) 552-2985
Diana Oldenkamp, President

Bloomfield Historical Society
Castalia, IA 52133
(319) 567-8470
Gwenn R. Koenig
8:00 A.M.–8:00 P.M.
Pub. None

Boone County Historical Society

602 Story Street
Boone, IA 50036
(515) 432-1907
bchs@opencominc.com
Charles W. Irwin, Executive Director
Nov–Apr: Tue–Sun 1:00–5:00; May–Oct:
    Tue–Sun 10:00–5:00
Pub. *Trail Tales*, three times per year
$30.00 per year membership; research:
    $15.00 per hour

Bremer County Historical Society
(Waverly, IA 50677—museum location)
PO Box 218 (mailing address)
Plainfield, IA 50666-0218
(319) 276-4674
J. W. "Bill" Lynes, Sr., President
Tue–Fri 1:30–4:00, Sun 2:00–4:00

Buena Vista County Historical and Genealogical Society
221 West Railroad
Storm Lake, IA 50588
(712) 732-7111
bvcogen@ncn.net
Janice Danielson, President
Mon–Fri 9:00–noon, and by appointment
Pub. *The Rootdigger*, quarterly
(genealogical research available, historical
    museum and genealogical library)
$10.00 per year membership; research: $5.00
    per hour plus costs

Butler County Historical Society
420 West Jefferson Street
Clarksville, IA 50619
(319) 278-4479; (319) 267-2255 (Ms.
    Poppen for appointments)
Betty Jane McElhaney, President; Judy
    Poppen
by appointment

Calhoun County Historical Society
(150 High Street—museum location)
858 Lake (mailing address)
Rockwell City, IA 50579
(712) 297-8139
Judy Webb, Curator
Mon–Thur 8:00–11:30, Tue, Thur &
    Sat–Sun (May–Oct) 1:30–5:00, and by
    appointment
("The three-story former high school is full
    of Calhoun County memorabilia. The
    former seven-stall bus barn and fenced-in
    lap area are full of early farm equipment."
    "Plat maps 1884 & 1901, histories,
    cemetery records, obituaries, personal
    stories")
$5.00 per year membership

Camanche Historical Society
(12th Avenue and Second Street—location)
City Hall, Second Street (mailing address)
Camanche, IA 52730
(563) 259-1268

Carroll County Historical Society
704 West 15th Street
Carroll, IA 51401
Marie Hackett, Museum Curator
(*History of Carroll County IA* (1912), $45.00
    ppd.)

Cass County Historical Society and Museum
(Corner of Main and Cass Street—location)
PO Box 254 (mailing address)
Griswold, IA 51535
(712) 778-2695 (President); (712) 778-4182
    (Vice President)
Marjorie Sothman, President; Bob Brandt,
    Vice President

Sun 1:30–4:30, and by appointment
(Cass County history books and old atlases,
    local school books)
$5.00 per year membership

Cedar County Historical Society
607 Orange Street
Tipton, IA 52772
(563) 886-2740 (9:00 A.M.–8:00 P.M.)
Dorothy Stout, Corresponding Secretary
8:00–4:00
Pub. *The Cedar County Review*, annually
    (July)
(local history)
$11.00 per year membership (includes book,
    add $1.50 if mailed)

Cedar Falls Historical Society
(308 West Third Street—location)
303 Franklin Street (mailing address)
Cedar Falls, IA 50613
(319) 266-5149; (319) 268-1812 FAX
http://www.cedarfallshistorical.org
Erica Schultz, Director of Education
Museum: Wed–Sat 10:00–4:00, Sun
    1:00–4:00; research: Mon–Fri by
    appointment only
("Cedar Falls history, Bess Streeter Aldrich
    memorabilia and writings, probate records
    of Black Hawk County 1852–1932")
research: $10.00 per hour plus copies at 25¢
    each, $10.00 probate fee with 24-hour
    notice required

Central Community Historical Society
(628 Sixth Avenue—location)
2503 340th Avenue (mailing address)
De Witt, IA 52742
(563) 659-3686
Ann Soenksen, President
Mon (Jan–Dec) 8:30–11:30, Sun (Apr–Dec)
    1:00–4:30
("Reference for Clinton County, Iowa")
$10.00 per year membership

Cherokee County Historical Society
(105 East Front Street—location)
PO Box 247 (mailing address)
Cleghorn, IA 51014-0247
(712) 436-2624
Ann Wilberding, President
by appointment only
Pub. *Cherokee County Historical Society
    Newsletter*, sporadically
("The Cherokee County Chapter [IGS],
    known as the Tree Stumpers, is a part of
    the Cherokee County Historical Society.")

Chickasaw County Historical Society
Rural Route
Nashua, IA 50658
(641) 435-4701

Clinton County Historical Society
(601 South First Street—location)
PO Box 2435 (mailing address)
Clinton, IA 52733-2435
(563) 242-1201
Donald Dethmann, President
Wed 1:00–3:00, Sat–Sun 1:30–4:30
$10.00 per year membership; research:
    donation to cover expenses

The Community Historical Society
(Maxwell, IA 50161—location)
512 E Avenue (mailing address)
Nevada, IA 50201
(515) 382-4085
Robert Swanson, President
Sun & holidays 1:00–4:00, and by
    appointment
$25.00 per year membership

Crawford County Historical Society
2134 Rocky Run
Denison, IA 51442

Davis County Historical Society
(302 East Franklin Street—location)
Route 6 (mailing address)
Bloomfield, IA 52537
(641) 664-2408
summer hours, and by appointment

Decatur County Historical Society
Main Street
Leon, IA 50144
(641) 446-4186

Delaware County Historical Society
PO Box 70
Hopkinton, IA 52237-0070
(563) 926-2639
Kene Bacon, President

Des Moines County Historical Society
The Apple Trees
1616 Dill Street
Burlington, IA 52601
(319) 753-2449 voice & FAX
Debra S. Olson, Executive Secretary
Office: Mon–Fri 9:00–noon; The Apple
    Trees: May–Oct: Wed & Sun 1:30–4:30;
    Phelps House Museum, 521 Columbia
    Street, Burlington: May–Oct: Sat–Sun
    1:30–4:30; Hawkeye Log Cabin, 2915
    South Main Street, Crapo Park,
    Burlington: May–Sept: Wed & Sun
    1:30–4:30
$8.00 per year membership

**Dickinson County Historical Society and
Dickinson County Museum, Inc.**
PO Box 532
Spirit Lake, IA 51360
(712) 338-2138
Faye Peterson, Secretary and Museum
    Curator

Dover Historical Society
213 West Main
New London, IA 52645
(319) 367-2573; (877) 468-7700
Caroline Lehman, Curator
Mid-May–Nov: Fri–Sun 1:00–4:00

Dyersville Historical Society
120 Third Street S.E.
Dyersville, IA 52040
(563) 875-2504
Mon & Thur 10:00–4:00
$5.00 per year membership

Elkader Historical Society
Elkader, IA 52043
(563) 245-2622

Emmet County Historical Society, Inc.
(1720 Third Avenue, South—location)
PO Box 101 (mailing address)
Estherville, IA 51334
David L. Kaltved, President
Mon–Sun (June–Aug) 2:00–5:00
$5.00 per year membership

**Fayette County Helpers Club and
Historical Society**
Fayette County Genealogical Society
Chapter (IGS)
100 North Walnut Street
West Union, IA 52175
(563) 422-5797
http://www.rootsweb.com/~iafayett/
    iafirst6.htm
Frances R. Graham, Administrator

Mon–Fri (May–Oct) 10:00–4:00, Mon–Fri
    (Nov–Apr) 10:00–3:00; genealogical
    society meetings: fourth Mon (Jan–Oct)
    7:30
Pub. *The Fayette County Connection*,
    quarterly
(Fayette County historical and genealogical
    material)
$10.00 per year membership in historical
    society; $7.00 per year membership in
    genealogical society; admission: $2.00 for
    nonmembers; research by center
    personnel: $5.00 per surname plus copies

Floyd County Historical Society Museum
500 Gilbert Street
Charles City, IA 50616
(641) 228-1099 (Museum and Library)
fchs@fiai.net
http://www.floydcountymuseum.org
Frank McKinney, Director; Mary Ann
    Townsend, Collections Manager
Museum: Mon–Fri 9:00–4:30, Sat–Sun
    1:00–4:00
Pub. *Floyd County Heritage Newsletter* (not
    genealogical), quarterly
$7.50 per year membership

Franklin County Historical Society
(Fairgrounds west on Highway 3—location)
PO Box 114 (mailing address)
Hampton, IA 50441
(641) 456-5777
Virginia Fredericks
Mon 2:00–4:00, Tue–Fri noon–4:00,
    Sat–Sun (summer) 1:00–4:00
Pub. *Franklin County Historical Newsletter*,
    quarterly
("History of Franklin County, Iowa, in
    displays. We have school-cemetery-land
    record.")
membership: $5.00 single, $10.00 doubles,
    $50.00 annual single, $100.00 annual
    double, $25.00 supportive; research:
    $5.00 per hour

Garnavillo Historical Society
Garnavillo, IA 52049

Gowrie Historical Society
(Beek Street—location)
PO Box 297 (mailing address)
Gowrie, IA 50543
Yvonne Lungren, President
Sun (30 May–7 Sept) 2:00–4:00
$2.00 per year membership

Grafton Heritage Depot
Main Street
Grafton, IA 50440
(641) 748-2337
Connie Bruesewitz, Director
Sun 1:30–5:00; tours during the week
no charge

Greene County Historical Society
106 East State Street
Jefferson, IA 50129
(515) 386-8544 (Museum); (515) 386-9322
    (Voice mail)
Bessie Mcclelland, Curator; Valeir Ogren,
    President
18 Apr–24 Dec: Wed–Sat 2:00–5:00, Sun
    2:00–4:00
$5.00 per year membership

Grundy County Historical Society
Route 1
Grundy Center, IA 50638
(319) 824-3585

Guthrie County Historical Society

901 Grand
Guthrie Center, IA 50115
(641) 747-3403

Hardin County Historical Society
(1603 South Washington Street—location)
PO Box 187 (mailing address)
Eldora, IA 50627
Gene Farmer, Curator
by appointment

Harrison County Historical Society
119 West Fourth Street
Logan, IA 51546
(712) 644-2941
Faye Marie Dow, Secretary
Pub. *Harrison County Historical Society*

Honey Creek Church Preservation Group
30293 O Avenue
New Providence, IA 50206-8008
(641) 497-5458
Vera Cutler, Historian, Library
by appointment
Pub. *Newsletter*, annually
(local Iowa history, Quaker records,
    genealogy; Honey Creek Friends
    Meetinghouse on Registry of National
    Historic Places)
free membership

Howard County Historical Society
(324 Fourth Avenue, West—location)
722 Gillette Avenue (mailing address)
Cresco, IA 52136
(563) 547-5593
Mary A. Billmyer
30 May to Labor Day: Sun & holidays
    1:00–4:00 by appointment

Humboldt County Historical Association
(East edge of Dakota City—museum
location)
PO Box 162 (mailing address)
Humboldt, IA 50548
(515) 332-5280
Mon–Tue & Thur–Sat 10:00–4:30, Sun
    (June–Sept) 1:30–4:30
$5.00 per year membership

Ida County Historical Society
(Grant Center School, Moorehead Pioneer
    Park, Ida Grove, IA 51445—location)
c/o Good Samaritan
505 West Second Street (mailing address)
Holstein, IA 51025
Walter Voge

Iowa County Historical Society
Pioneer Heritage Museum
(675 East South Street—location)
PO Box 288 (mailing address)
Marengo, IA 52301
(319) 642-7018
Marilyn Rodgers, Secretary
mid-May–mid-Sept: Thur–Sat P.M. by
    appointment
Pub. *Pioneer Heritage News*, quarterly
("Historical Society/Resource Library: Iowa
    County")
$8.00 per year membership

Jackson County Historical Society
(Pearson Memorial Center, Fair
Grounds—location)
PO Box 1245 (mailing address)
Maquoketa, IA 52060
(563) 652-5020
Mrs. Toni Kracke, Curator
Tue–Fri 10:00–4:00, Sat–Sun noon–4:00
Pub. *Timelines*, quarterly
$15.00 per year membership

Jasper County Historical Society of Iowa
Jasper County Historical Museum
(1700 South 15th Avenue, West—location)
PO Box 834 (mailing address)
Newton, IA 50208
(641) 792-9118
Hans J. Brosig, Museum Director
Mon–Fri business hours
Pub. *The Newsletter*, five times per year
(Jasper County, Iowa, history only)
$5.00 per year membership

Jefferson County Historical Society
304 East Broadway
Fairfield, IA 52556
(641) 472-8071
Scott Reneker, Treasurer
second Tue 7:00 P.M.
$5.00 per year membership

Johnson County Historical Society
Heritage Museum
(310 Fifth Street—location)
PO Box 5081 (mailing address)
Coralville, IA 52241
(319) 351-5738; (319) 351-5310 FAX
Laurie Robinson, Executive Director
Museum: Wed–Sat 1:00–5:00, Sun
   1:00–4:00
Pub. *Newsletter*, bimonthly
from $15.00 per year membership;
   genealogical inquiries are referred to Iowa
   City Genealogical Society

Kellogg Historical Society
(218 High Street—location)
PO Box 295 (mailing address)
Kellogg, IA 50135-0295
(641) 526-8734
Mary Parsons, Secretary
Memorial Day–Labor Day: Mon–Fri
   9:00–4:00, Sun 1:30–5:00, and by
   appointment
Pub. *The Kellogg Enterprise*, quarterly (Jan,
   Apr, July, Oct)
(houses library with genealogy and cemetery
   records)
$10.00 per year membership; research fees
   vary

Keokuk County Historical Society
(Corner of East and Elm Streets—location)
PO Box 123 (mailing address)
Sigourney, IA 52591-0123
(641) 622-3005
Margaret Hollingsworth, Treasurer
Wed–Thur 9:00–4:00
Pub. *Newsletter*, at least two times per year
("Obits, marriage records, large museum. In
   addition: Stone House—oldest in
   Sigourney and furnished with 1900
   furnishings.")
$5.00 per year membership; copies: 25¢ each
   from paper originals, 50¢ each from
   reader-printer of newspapers

Kingsley Historical Society
Kingsley, IA 51028
(712) 378-2636
Helen K. Hager
summer and fall weekends, and summer
   holidays

Lee County Iowa Historical Society
(318 North Fifth Street—location)
PO Box 125 (mailing address)
Keokuk, IA 52632
Douglas Atterberg, Archivist
summer weekends, and by appointment
("Lee County and adjacent Iowa, Illinois,
   and Missouri counties." Mark Twain and
   family, Civil War, Medical College, River

history; topical and family history
   requests expedited)
$10.00 per year membership; research: by
   donation

Linn County Historical Society
(101 Eighth Avenue, S.E., Cedar Rapids, IA
   52401—location)
PO Box 175 (mailing address)
Cedar Rapids, IA 52406
(319) 369-1501
William R. Kreuger, Executive Director
Mon–Fri 9:00–4:00, Sat–Sun 1:00–4:00
Pub. *Communique*, monthly
$15.00 per year membership

Louisa County Historical Society
Louisa County Heritage Center
609 James L. Hodges Avenue (Highway 61)
Wapello, IA 52653
(319) 523-8381; (319) 523-5247
cbeck@louisacomm.net
Frank Best, President
Tue–Fri 10:00–3:00
$10.00 per year membership

Lowden Historical Society
(Main Street next to City Hall—location)
2199 155th Street (mailing address)
Lowden, IA 52255-9543
Virgil Kruckenberg, President
by appointment
Pub. *Lowden Historical Society Annual
   Report*
(local history and newspaper pictures)
$10.00 per year membership

Lyon County Historical Society
Rock Rapids, IA 51246

Madison County Historical Society
(815 South Second Avenue—location)
PO Box 15 (mailing address)
Winterset, IA 50273
(515) 462-2134
Wendell Spencer, Manager
1 May–31 Oct: Mon–Sat 11:00–4:00, Sun
   1:00–5:00
$5.00 per year membership

Mahaska County Historical Society
PO Box 578
Oskaloosa, IA 52577
(641) 672-2989
12 May–12 Oct: 9:30–4:30, and by
   appointment in winter
Pub. *NCHS Newsletter*

Marble Rock Historical Society Museum
313 Bradford Street
Marble Rock, IA 50653
(641) 397-2216 (President)

Marion County Historical Society
Marion County Park
Route 3
Knoxville, IA 50138

Historical Society of Marshall County
(202 East Church Street—location)
PO Box 304 (mailing address)
Marshalltown, IA 50158
(641) 752-6664
Michael W. Vogt
Wed–Sat 10:00–noon & 1:00–5:00
Pub. *Then & Now*, bimonthly
(specializes in historical items)
$10.00 per year membership

McGregor Historical Society
(254 Main Street—location)
217 Ann Street (mailing address)

McGregor, IA 52157
(563) 873-3450
Mae Huebsch, Curator
regular summer hours, winter by
   appointment

Monona Historical Society
(210 South Egbert Street—location)
PO Box 434 (mailing address)
Monona, IA 52159
(563) 539-2640
Elmer L. Marting, President
late May to early Oct: Sun 1:00–4:00, and by
   appointment

Monroe County Historical Society
114-116A Avenue, East
Albia, IA 52531
(641) 932-7046
E. St. Clair Gantz, President
Sat–Sun (May–Sept) 1:00–4:00, and by
   appointment
("We have a modest library.")

Moulton Historical Society
(Highway 202 North—location)
111 East Fourth Street (mailing address)
Moulton, IA 52572
(641) 642-3684 (President)
Don E. Newland, President
1 June–Labor Day: Sun 1:00–4:30, and by
   appointment
$5.00 per year membership

North Iowa Historical Society
Kinney Pioneer Museum
(Highway 18 West, Airport
Entrance—location)
PO Box 421 (mailing address)
Mason City, IA 50402-0421
(641) 423-1258; (641) 357-2980 (off-season)
Fran Tagesen, Director
Wed–Fri & Sun (May–Sept) noon–5:00; Sat
   (June–Aug) noon–5:00
$10.00 per year membership

North Lee County Historical Society
(Historic Museum, Ninth and Avenue
H—location)
PO Box 285 (mailing address)
Fort Madison, IA 52627-0285
(319) 372-7661
Nellie Foster, President

O'Brien County Historical Society
(First Street, N.E., and Heritage Park
Road—location)
PO Box 385 (mailing address)
Primghar, IA 51245
(712) 757-1511
Kurt Brown, President
Sun (May–Aug) 2:00, and by appointment
(historical library)

Oelwein Area Historical Society
(900 Second Avenue, S.E.—location)
PO Box 445 (mailing address)
Oelwein, IA 50662
(319) 283-5322
Oelwein_Area_Historical_Society@
   hotmail.com
http://www.rootsweb.com/~iaoahs
David Moore, President; Lora Saunders,
   Secretary
first weekend in June–first weekend in Oct:
   Sun 1:00–4:00
$10.00 per year membership

Osceola County Historical Society
McCallum Museum
724 Third Avenue
Sibley, IA 51249

(712) 754-3882
Jan Stofferan, Museum Curator
Memorial Day–Labor Day: Sun 1:30–4:30
  (call ahead)

Parker Historical Society of Clay County
(300 East Third Street—location)
PO Box 91
Spencer, IA 51301
(712) 262-3304
parkermuseum@evertek.net
http://parkermuseum.org
Cindy McGanahan, Director
Tue–Fri 11:30–3:30, and by appointment
Pub. untitled newsletter, three to four times
  per year ("mostly things happening at the
  museum but does include one major
  article related to a local history topic")
dues from $20.00

Pella Historical Society
Pella Historical Village
507 Franklin
Pella, IA 50219
(641) 628-2409; (641) 628-9192 FAX
pellatt@kdsi.net
http://www.pellatuliptime.com
Patsy Sadler
Mon–Fri 9:00–5:00, Sat (Apr–Dec)
  9:00–5:00

Pioneer Historical Society, Inc.
203 South Fourth Street
Farmington, IA 52626

Pocahontas County Historical Society
Route 2, Box 12
Rolfe, IA 50581
(712) 848-3342
Florence MacVey, President
Pub. *PCHS Newsletter*

Polk County Historical Society
317 S.W. 42nd Street
Des Moines, IA 50312
(515) 255-6657
LeRoy G. Pratt, Editor
Pub. *PCHS Newsletter*, ten times per year
  (monthly, except July–Aug)
(no genealogical library)
$7.00–$12.00 per year membership

Postville Historical Society
205 West Williams Street
Postville, IA 52162
(563) 864-3818
Edward W. Kozelka, Register Agent

**Historical Society of Pottawattamie
County, Iowa**
PO Box 2
Council Bluffs, IA 51502-0002
(712) 323-2509; (712) 323-2509 FAX
info@TheHistoricalSociety.org
http://www.thehistoricalsociety.org

**Poweshiek County Historical and
Genealogical Society**
(206 North Mill Street—location)
PO Box 280 (mailing address)
Montezuma, IA 50171-0280
(641) 623-3322 (Office); (641) 236-6407
fernor@pcpartner.net
Ferne Hart Norris, President
Mon, Thur & Wed 9:00–4:00, and by
  appointment
Pub. *The Searcher*, quarterly
(mainly genealogical)
$10.00 per year membership; research: $7.00
  per hour ($5.00 minimum)

Ringgold County Historical Society, Inc.

Mount Ayr, IA 50854
(641) 464-2140

Shelby County Historical Society
(Morse and Pine Streets—location)
837 Orange Road (mailing address)
Harlan, IA 51537
(712) 755-2437
Thelma Heflin, Public Relations Secretary
Sun (June–Aug) 2:00–5:00, and by
  appointment
Pub. *Wagon Tracks on Prairie Trails*,
  quarterly
$3.00 per year membership

Sheldon Historical Society
Prairie Museum
Sheldon, IA 51201

**Sioux City Public Museum and Historical
Association**
2901 Jackson Street
Sioux City, IA 51104
(712) 279-6174; (712) 252-5615 FAX
Craig R. Olson
Mon–Sat 9:00–5:00, Sun 2:00–5:00
(museum archives/research library)

Sloan Historical Society
Sloan, IA 51055

Strawberry Point Historical Society
Strawberry Point, IA 52076
(563) 933-4461

Tama County Historical Society
Museum Library
200 North Broadway Street
Toledo, IA 52342
(641) 484-6767
Joyce Wiess
Tue–Sat 1:00–4:30, and by appointment
Pub. *Tama County Museum News*, quarterly,
  $10.00 per year subscription
(extensive genealogical library)

Taylor County Historical Society
Taylor County Museum
(1001 West Pollock Avenue, Bedford, IA
50833—location)
PO Box 8 (mailing address)
Gravity, IA 50848
(712) 539-2475; (712) 523-2041 (Museum)
http://www.rootsweb.com/~iataylor/tci93.
  htm
Helen Janson, President of Museum
Museum: Tue–Sun (1 Apr–25 Dec)
  1:00–5:00

Union County Historical Society
(in McKinley Park—location)
1101 North Vine Street (mailing address)
Creston, IA 50801
Marcella M. Howe, Treasurer; Paul Roeder
Mon–Sun (June–Aug) 1:00–5:00, and by
  appointment
$1.00 per year membership

Wapello County Historical Society
Wapello County Historical Museum
Amtrak Depot
201 West Main
Ottumwa, IA 52501

Washington County Historical Society
(903 East Washington—museum location)
PO Box 364 (mailing address)
Washington, IA 52353
(319) 653-3125
Mary Levy, President
Sun (June–Aug) 1:00–5:00, first two
  weekends in Dec: 1:00–5:00

(Washington County history artifacts, no
  genealogy)

Wayne County Historical Society
(see Prairie Trails Museum of Wayne County
Iowa, City, County and Regional Archives
and Libraries, above)

West Bend Historical Society
4473 550th Avenue
West Bend, IA 50597
(515) 887-3241 (Treasurer)

West Des Moines Historical Society
Historic Jordan House
2001 Fuller Road
West Des Moines, IA 50265
(515) 225-1286
Joyce Grabinski, President
May–Oct: Wed & Sat–Sun, and private
  group tours
admission: $2.00 for adults

West Liberty Historical Society
600 East Fourth Street
West Liberty, IA 52776

Winnebago Historical Society
(336 North Clark Street—location)
PO Box 27 (mailing address)
Forest City, IA 50436

Winneshiek County Historical Society
Decorah Public Library
202 Winnebago Street
Decorah, IA 52101-1812
(563) 382-1009
Shan Thomas, President
Library: Mon–Thur 10:00–8:00, Fri–Sat
  10:00–5:00, Sun 1:00–4:00
(local county historical documents and
  records, includes county governmental
  records)

**Wright County Historical Society
(Clarion)**
615 Fifth Avenue
Clarion, IA 50525
(515) 532-3669

**Wright County Historical Society, Eagle
Grove Chapter**
(Broadway and North Iowa
Streets—location)
917 West Broadway (mailing address)
Eagle Grove, IA 50533
(515) 448-4220

**Wright County Historical Society
(Goldfield)**
PO Box 3
Goldfield, IA 50542
(515) 825-3641

Genealogical Societies

State Genealogical Society

Iowa Genealogical Society (IGS)
(6000 Douglas—location)
PO Box 7735 (mailing address)
Des Moines, IA 50322-7735
(515) 276-0287; (515) 727-1824 FAX
igs@iowagenealogy.org
http://www.iowagenealogy.org
Billy Murano, Librarian
Mon & Fri–Sat 10:00–4:00, Tue–Thur
  10:00–9:00
Pub. *Hawkeye Heritage*, quarterly; *Iowa
  Genealogical Society Newsletter*,
  bimonthly
$30.00 per year membership

Clinton County Gateway Genealogical Society Chapter (IGS)
(Camanche Historical Society Building, 13th Avenue and South Washington Boulevard, Camanche, IA—library location)
PO Box 2256 (mailing address)
Clinton, IA 52733-2256
(563) 259-1285
erevans@clinton.net
Ruth Evans
Library: third Wed 6:00–10:00, and by appointment; meetings: third Wed 7:30
Pub. *Clinton County Gateway Genealogical Society Newsletter*
$10.00 per year membership

Fayette County Genealogical Society Chapter (IGS)
(see Fayette County Helpers Club and Historical Society, Historical Societies—Local and Regional, above)

Genealogical Societies—Local & Regional

Adair County Anquestors Genealogical Society
Genie Bug Club Genealogical Society
Sherry Foresman Library
2787 335th Street
Menlo, IA 50164
(641) 524-5110 (Library)
Sherry Foresman

Adair County Anquestors Genealogy
Greenfield Library
(202 South First—location)
PO Box 328 (mailing address)
Greenfield, IA 50849
(641) 743-6120 (Library)
Millie Clayton, President
10:00–5:00
Pub. *Newsletter*, quarterly
("Extensive collection of family histories and microfilm")
$5.00 per year membership

Adams County Genealogical Society
PO Box 117
Prescott, IA 50859
(641) 335-2352
Cathy Eggleston, Vice President
Mon–Tue & Thur 9:00–4:00, Wed 9:00–6:30, Fri 9:00–noon
Pub. *Treetender*, quarterly
$5.00 per year membership

Ankeny Genealogical Society
1110 N.W. Second Street
Ankeny, IA 50021-2320
(Polk County)

Appanoose County Genealogical Society
1020 Shamrock Lane, Apartment 107
Centerville, IA 52544-1147
(641) 437-4077
Loretta Crow, Vice President
Oct–June: noon–8:00, July–Sept: noon–6:00, Sat 10:00–6:00
Pub. *Pages from the Past*, quarterly
$5.00 per year membership

Audubon County Chapter (IGS)
c/o Ballou
Exira, IA 50076

Benton County Genealogical Society
1808 Ninth Avenue
Belle Plaine, IA 52208
http://www.rootsweb.com/~iabenton/bcgs.htm
Donnette Gossen
meetings at Family History Center, Belle

Plaine: first Wed
Pub. *The Benton County Backtracker*, quarterly
$10.00 per year membership; research: $5.00 per hour for members, $7.00 per hour for nonmembers (plus SASE)

Boone County Genealogical Society
PO Box 453
Boone, IA 50036
bakelly@dmacc.cc.ia.us
Bruce A. Kelly, President
Boone County Historical Society, Historical Building, Lower Level, Research Room: by appointment
Pub. *Boone County Genealogical Society Newsletter*, quarterly
$7.50 per year membership; free queries for members, $2.00 each for nonmembers

Botna Valley Chapter (IGS)
PO Box 633
Oakland, IA 51560-0633
(712) 482-3209
Opal Palmer, President
Mon–Tue, Thur & Sat 1:00–5:00, Tue 9:00–noon, Fri 7:00–9:00
Pub. *Botna Valley Genealogical Society News*, quarterly
(Pottawattamie County)
$5.00 per year membership

Bremer County Genealogical Society
426 Washington Street
Denver, IA 50622
ehebell@trxinc.com
http://www.rootsweb.com/~iabremer/GenealogicalSociety.html
Elvira Hebell, Corresponding Secretary; Bernice Kimball, President
meetings at Waverly Civic Center: first Tue (except Jan & June–Aug) 7:00
Pub. *Bremer County Browsings*, quarterly (usually Feb, May, Aug, Nov)
$10.00 per year membership; research: $5.00 per hour plus expenses, one-hour minimum

Buchanan County Genealogical Society
(331 First Street East, Basement of City Hall, side entrance—location)
PO Box 4 (mailing address)
Independence, IA 50644-0004
Ann M. Gitsch, President
Mon 10:00–2:00, Thur 4:00–7:00, and by appointment
Pub. *Newsletter*, two times per year
("Focus: Buchanan County and surrounding counties family research; outstanding collection of obituary files; probates from 1850s; all census records for the county and the surrounding counties; extensive microfilm collection of newspapers from 1867; cemetery book, etc.")
$7.50 per year membership; research: $10.00 per hour plus copy fees at 30¢ each; $5.00 donation to open during unscheduled hours

Buena Vista County Historical and Genealogical Society
(see Historical Societies—Local and Regional, above)

Butler County Genealogical Society
(Clarksville Public Library—location)
PO Box 177 (mailing address)
Parkersburg, IA 50665
hfreese@netins.net; rgersema@aol.com
Herb Freese, President; Rick Gersema, Queries
Pub. *Butler Branches*, quarterly

Calhoun County Chapter (IGS)
Carnegie Public Library
426 Fifth Street
Rockwell City, IA 50579
$5.00 per year membership; research: donation

Calhoun County Genies
(150 High Street—museum location)
226 North Grant (mailing address)
Rockwell City, IA 50579
(712) 297-7237 (President); (712) 297-8307 (Museum Curator)
Beverly Courter, President
by appointment
(only Calhoun County records)
$5.00 per year membership

Carroll County Genealogical Society
(Genealogical Library at Lidderdale—location)
PO Box 21 (mailing address)
Carroll, IA 51401-0021
Neoma Hagge, Corresponding Secretary
Library: Wed 9:00–4:00, some Saturday mornings; meetings at Methodist Church in Carroll: second Mon 7:30
Pub. *Carroll County Genealogical Society Newsletter*, bimonthly
$8.00 per year membership; queries: free

Cass County, Iowa Genealogical Society
706 Hazel Street
Atlantic, IA 50022
(712) 781-2227
Marietta Petresen, President
meetings at the Atlantic Library: fourth Thur (Feb–Nov) 7:00
Pub. *Cass County Newsletter*, quarterly
$5.00 per year membership; research: $5.00 per hour, $1.00 for nonmember queries

Central Iowa Genealogical Society
PO Box 945
Marshalltown, IA 50158
Jo Ann Naumann, President
Pub. *Central Iowa Genealogical Society*, irregularly
(Marshall County)
$5.00 per year membership

Cherokee County Chapter (IGS)
Tree Stumpers
(105 East Front Street—location)
PO Box 247 (mailing address)
Cleghorn, IA 51014-0247
(712) 436-2624
Pat Behrens, Cherokee County Historical Society Treasurer and Tree Stumpers Chairman
by appointment in summer
(part of the Cherokee County Historical Society)

Chickasaw County Genealogical Society
New Hampton Public Library—library location)
PO Box 434 (mailing address)
New Hampton, IA 50659-0434
(641) 394-4343
http://www.chickasawcoia-geniesoc.org
Carol Bottin, Vice President
Pub. *Chickasaw County Genealogical Society Newsletter*, quarterly
$8.00 per year membership; research: $5.00 per hour for members, $10.00 per hour for nonmembers, plus copies and postage

Clarke County Genealogical Society
c/o Osceola Public Library
300 South Fillmore Street
Osceola, IA 50213-141

http://www.rootsweb.com/~iaclarke/ccgs.
  html
Evelyn Pritchard, Secretary; Diane Shough,
  Librarian-Historian
meetings: first Wed 7:00
Pub. newsletter, quarterly
$7.50 per year membership; research: $7.50
  plus SASE

Clayton County Genealogical Society
PO Box 846
Elkader, IA 52043-0846
(563) 245-1065
Myra Voss, Corresponding Secretary
Elkader Public Library: Mon, Wed & Fri
  9:30–5:00, Tue noon–5:00, Thur
  noon–7:00, Sat 9:30–2:00
("The Society continues to compile and print
  Clayton County, Iowa, history!"
  Published *1984 History of Clayton
  County, IA*, $56.00 ppd.)
$4.00 per year membership

Crawford County Chapter (IGS)
c/o Norelius Community Library
1403 First Avenue South
Denison, IA 51442
Dawn Boettger, President
Pub. *Crawford County Iowa Genealogical
  Society Newsletter*, quarterly
$5.00 to $7.50 per year membership

Dallas County Genealogical Society
(Dallas Center Library—location)
PO Box 264 (mailing address)
Dallas Center, IA 50063-0264
(515) 992-3185
IADCGS@yahoo.com
http://www.rootsweb.com/~iadcgs
Michelle Fox, President
Mon & Fr 9:00–noon & 1:00–5:00,
  Tue–Thur 9:00–noon & 1:00–7:00, Sat
  9:00–noon
(Holdings include card index to Dallas
  County newspapers for births, deaths,
  marriages, probate index 1850–1990. "We
  now have all fifty-four Dallas County
  cemeteries transcribed and available for
  purchase on CD or hard copy.")
$5.00 per year membership

Davis County Genealogical Society
(Bloomfield Public Library—location)
PO Box 94 (mailing address)
Bloomfield, IA 52537-0094
Dorothy Goldizen, Corresponding Secretary
Library: Tue–Fri 10:00–6:00, Sat
  10:00–2:00
Pub. *Davis County Genealogical Newsletter*,
  quarterly
$7.50 per year membership; research:
  "depends on what records, sometimes
  nothing"

Decatur County Chapter (IGS)
c/o Lamoni Public Library
Lamoni, IA 50140

Decorah Genealogy Association
Decorah Public Library
202 Winnebago
Decorah, IA 52101-1812
ddiggers@hotmail.com
http://rootsweb.com/~iawinnes/dga.htm
Stan Jeffers, President
Library: Mon–Thur 10:00–8:00, Fri–Sat
  10:00–5:00, Sun 1:00–4:00
Pub. *Decorah Area Diggers*, quarterly
  (genealogy, northeast Iowa)
$10.00 per year membership; research: $5.00
  per year plus copies and postage

Delaware County Chapter (IGS)
823 Howard Street
Manchester, IA 52057

Delaware County Genealogical Society
Manchester Public Library
300 North Franklin
Manchester, IA 52057
(563) 927-3719 (Library); (563) 927-3058
  FAX (Library)
mnchst00@iren.net (Library)

Des Moines County Genealogical Society
PO Box 493
Burlington, IA 52601
dmcgs@yahoo.com
http://www.dmcgs.com
Phyllis Rothlauf, President
Pub. *The Quarterly* (Feb, May, Aug, Nov)
$8.00 per year membership

**Dubuque County-Key City Genealogical
Society**
PO Box 13
Dubuque, IA 52004-0013
dckcgs_library@hotmail.com (Library
  Committee); dckcgs@hotmail.com
  (President/Corresponding Secretary)
http://www.rootsweb.com/~iadckcgs
Society Library: members only, and by
  appointment
Pub. *Dubuque County-Key City
  Genealogical Society Newsletter*,
  quarterly (Mar, June, Sept, Dec)
(Dubuque County, Iowa, Jo Daviess County,
  Illinois, and Grant County, Wisconsin;
  publishing cemetery readings for
  Dubuque County)
$8.00 per year membership; queries: $2.00
  for nonmembers (maximum of two per
  issue)

Emmet County Genealogical Society
Estherville Public Library
613 Central Avenue
Estherville, IA 51334-2294

Franklin County Chapter (IGS)
PO Box 335
Chapin, IA 50427
Judy Dannen
Pub. *Newsletter,* quarterly
$6.00 per year membership

**Franklin County Genealogical Society of
Hampton, Iowa**
c/o Hampton Public Library
4 Federal Street, South
Hampton, IA 50441
hbrandt@frontiernet.net
http://www.iowagenealogy.org/Counties/
  franklin.htm
Helen Brandt, Editor
Pub. *Franklin Record*, quarterly
$10.00 per year membership

Fremont County Genealogical Society
PO Box 671
Sidney, IA 51652

**Greater Sioux County Genealogical
Society**
Sioux Center Public Library
327 First Avenue, N.E.
Sioux Center, IA 51250-1801
query@mtcnet.net
http://www.rootsweb.com/~iasioux/gscgs/
  gscgs.htm
Wilma J. Vande Berg
meetings in the Robert Frost Room (lower
  level) of the library: fourth Monday
  (except May & Dec) 7:00 winter, 7:30

summer
Pub. *GSCGS Newsletter*, annually
(Lyon, Sioux and O'Brien counties and
  Dutch and various Northern European
  genealogy)
$7.50 per year membership (includes one
  hour research); research: donation

Greene County Genealogical Society
PO Box 133
Jefferson, IA 50129-0133
vjogren@netins.net
http://www.rootsweb.com/~iagreene/
  gcgs.htm
Valerie Ogren, Web Page Coordinator
Pub. *Greene Gleanings*, six times per year
  (county history, county vital statistics and
  cemeteries)
$7.50 per year membership

Grundy County Genealogical Society
18419 205th Street
Grundy Center, IA 50638-8733
$8.50 per year membership

Guthrie County Genealogical Society
PO Box 96
Jamaica, IA 50128-0096
(641) 429-3362; (641) 429-3362 FAX
Dana Lowry, Librarian
Mon–Wed 1:00–6:00, Thur 9:00–11:00
Pub. *Guthrie County Genealogical Society
  Newsletter*, quarterly
$7.00 per year membership

Hamilton Heritage Hunters
PO Box 364
Webster City, IA 50595-2001
(515) 832-5784 (President)
Norma Jeane Bell, President
Pub. *Hamilton Heritage Hunters Newsletter*,
  quarterly (Mar, June, Sept, Dec)
(genealogy in Hamilton County)
$7.00 per year membership; research: $5.00
  per hour

Hancock County Genealogical Society
PO Box 81
Klemme, IA 50449-0081
(641) 587-2324 (President and Researcher)
Gail C. Linahon, President and Researcher
$5.00 per year membership; research $5.00
  per hour plus expenses

Harrison County Genealogical Society
(Merry Brook School Museum, Research
  Library, Lower Level, 212 Lincoln
  Way—location)
c/o Linda Dickman, Corresponding Secretary
2810 190th Trail (mailing address)
Woodbine, IA 51579-9658
(712) 642-4191
hcgs51579@aol.com; VLKing1@aol.com
http://www.rootsweb.com/~iaharris/hcgs
Vicki King, President
Pub. *HCGS Newsletter*, quarterly
$10.00 per year membership; research
  $10.00 per hour plus copies

Harrison County Genealogical Volunteers
(Merry Brook School Museum—location)
2810 190th Train (mailing address)
Woodbine, IA 51579
(712) 647-2454; (712) 647-2593 (Museum)
DMLJLL426@netzero.com;
  VLKing1@aol.com
http://www.rootsweb.com/~iaharris/hcgs/
  index.htm
Linda Dickman, Corresponding Secretary;
  Janette Lager; Vicki King, President
Museum: Thur 1:30–4:30, Fri–Sat by
  appointment

Pub. *Harrison County Happenings*, quarterly
("3,000 early 1890s obituaries handwritten
for Harrison County, Iowa, newspapers,
Missouri Valley Times, Woodbine Twiner,
and *Logan Observer*")
$10.00 per year membership; research: $5.00
per hour

Henry County Genealogical Society
PO Box 81
Mount Pleasant, IA 52641-0081
Doris Sharp, President
Pub. *HCGS Newsletter*, quarterly
$8.00 per year membership

Howard-Winnieshieck Genealogy Society
(Cresco Public Library, 320 North
Elm—collection location)
PO Box 362 (mailing address)
Cresco, IA 52136
djsowers@powerbank.net
http://www.pafways.org/genealogy/
societes/howard_winnieshiek.htm
Janice Sowers, President
Pub. *Questions and Ancestors*, quarterly
$8.00 per year membership; research: $5.00
per hour plus cost of copies and postage

Humboldt County Genealogical Society
c/o Humboldt Public Library
30 Sixth Street, North
Humboldt, IA 50548
(515) 332-1925 (Library, 10:00–5:00)
Martha Schmidt, Corresponding Secretary
Pub. *Humboldt County Genealogical Society
Newsletter*, three times per year
("GEDCOM in/out; cemetery records,
indexed census, obituary file, indexed
county history 1963 & 1884")
$5.00 per year membership; research:
beginning at $5.00

Ida County Genealogical Society
506 Moorehead Street
Ida Grove, IA 51445-1631

Iowa City Genealogical Society
Johnson County Chapter (IGS)
PO Box 822
Iowa City, IA 52244
http://www.rootsweb.com/~iajohnso/
icgensoc.htm
Peter J. Seaba, President
meetings at the State Historical Society,
Manuscript Reading Room: last Sat 9:30
A.M.
Pub. *I.C.G.S. Newsletter*, ten times per year
$12.00 per year membership

Iowa County Genealogy Society
(Marengo Public Library, 1026 Marengo
Avenue—location)
PO Box 372 (mailing address)
Marengo, IA 52301
(319) 642-7903
iacogen@netins.net
Netha M. Meyer, President
Mon 6:30–8:00, Tue–Fri 1:00–4:00, Sat
11:00–2:00
Pub. *Iowa County Byways*, quarterly
("Genealogy queries, research in Iowa
County.")
$10.00 per year membership; research:
donation to cover cost of copies

Iowa Lakes Genealogical Society
600 West 11th Street
Spencer, IA 51301-3235
(712) 262-1318
donpaul@rconnect.com;
mnrohan@netins.net
http://www.pionet.net/~nwiowa/spencer/

clubs/ilgs.htm
Esther J. Connell, Newsletter
Pub. *ILGS Teaser*, quarterly
("Collection is at the Spencer Public Library.
We have good research capabilities and
resources for Clay County and all eight
surrounding counties in Iowa: Palo Alto,
Pocahontas, Buena Vista, O'Brien,
Osceola, Dickinson, Cherokee, and
Emmet. Also have a Clay County
Cemetery Book for sale at $10.00.")
$10.00 per year membership; research:
$10.00 per hour, plus copy fees, etc.

Jackson County Genealogical Chapter (IGS)
(Jackson County Historical Museum,
Pearson Memorial Center, Fair
Grounds—location)
PO Box 1065 (mailing address)
Maquoketa, IA 52060
(563) 652-5020 (Museum)
http://www.rootsweb.com/~iajackso/
JCGenie.html
Lucille E. Sorensen, President
Museum: Tue–Fri 10:00–4:00, Sat–Sun
noon–4:00; genealogists available: Tue &
Fri 10:00–4:00; meetings: third Mon 1:30
Pub. *Genie Gems*, quarterly
$5.00 per year membership; queries: free for
members; research: $5.00 per hour plus
copies at 10¢ each for members, 25¢ each
for nonmembers

Jasper County Genealogical Society
(113 West Second Street South—location)
PO Box 163 (mailing address)
Newton, IA 50208-2707
(641) 792-1522
http://www.usgennet.org/usa/ia/county/
jasper1/jcgs
Ernie Braida, President
Wed–Fri 10:00–3:00, first Sat 9:00–noon
Pub. *Gleaner*, four times per year
$10.00 per year membership; research: $5.00
per hour (two surnames), plus copy costs
and SASE

Jefferson County Genealogical Society
2791 240th Street
Fairfield, IA 52556-8518
(641) 472-4667
jandosse@ksdi.net
http://www.rootsweb.com/~iajeffer/jcgs.htm
Verda Baird, Corresponding Secretary; Jan
Hunerdosse
$5.00 per year membership; research: $8.00
per hour; send SASE for list of county
publications

Johnson County Chapter (IGS)
(see Iowa City Genealogical Society, above)

Jones County Genealogy Society
(100 Park Avenue, basement HACAP
Building—location)
PO Box 174 (mailing address)
Anamosa, IA 52205
(563) 462-3911; (563) 432-6389
laverta@netins.net
http://www.rootsweb.com/~iajones/
research/research.htm#jcgs
LaVerta Langenberg, Secretary
Wed 9:00–3:00, and by appointment
Pub. *News & Notes*, bimonthly
$10.00 per year membership; admission:
$2.00 for nonmembers and out-of-county
residents; research: $10.00 per hour plus
copies

Keo-Mah Genealogical Society
(103 North Third Street—location)

PO Box 616 (mailing address)
Oskaloosa, IA 52577-0616
(641) 673-9373
mabgenank@lisco.net
http://www.geocities.com/Heartland/
Acres/2263
Mabel Daniels, Librarian/President
Mon–Thur 10:00–4:00, Fri–Sat 10:30–1:30
Pub. *Keo-Mah Tracers*, quarterly
("Keo-May Library consists of many
counties in Iowa as well as in other states,
indexes, microfilm census and
newspapers.")
$15.00 per year U.S. membership;
admission: fee for nonmembers; research:
done for a nominal fee

Laurens Genies Chapter (IGS)
273 North Third Street
Laurens, IA 50554-1215
(Pocahontas County)

Lee County Genealogical Society of Iowa
PO Box 303
Keokuk, IA 52632-0303
(319) 524-4121
dasprung@interl.net
Frances E. Sprunger, Corresponding
Secretary
Mon–Thur 9:00–7:00, Fri–Sat 9:00–5:00
Pub. *Gleanings, The Lee County
Genealogical Society of Iowa Newsletter*,
quarterly
("Census microfilm; Clark, Lee, Hancock;
courthouse records; marriages, obituaries,
scrapbooks, etc.")
$8.00 per year membership; research: $6.00
per hour plus copies and postage

Lime Creek/Winnebago County Genealogical Society
Forest City Municipal Library
115 East L Street
Forest City, IA 50436-1401
http://www.pafways.org/genealogy/
societies/winnebago.htm
Ruth Leibrand, President
(Winnebago County)

Genealogical Society of Linn County, Iowa
(813 First Avenue S.E.—location)
PO Box 175 (mailing address)
Cedar Rapids, IA 52406
(319) 362-0022
http://www.usgennet.org/usa/ia/county/
linn/gen_soc.htm
Marilyn J. Walsh, President
Library: Tue–Sat 10:00–4:00; meetings:
fourth Thur (except Nov–Jan), third Thur
(Nov)
Pub. *Linn County Heritage Hunters*,
quarterly
$15.00 per year membership; research:
$10.00 per hour plus copies for
nonmembers

Louisa County Genealogical Society
(Louisa County Heritage Center, 607
Highway 61 North—location)
PO Box 202 (mailing address)
Wapello, IA 52653
(319) 523-8381
ialouisa9@yahoo.com; njennings@lisco.net
http://www.rootsweb.com/~ialcgs
Norma Jennings
$5.00 per year membership

Lucas County Genealogical Society
c/o Chariton Public Library
803 Braden Avenue
Chariton, IA 50049
(641) 535-2704 (Secretary)

lucasgene@hotmail.com
Betty M. Cross, Corresponding Secretary
Library: Mon–Fri (Sept–June) noon–6:00,
Sat 10:00–4:00
Pub. *Lucas County Notes and Shakin' The
Family Tree*, quarterly
("Many indexed resources, all available local
censuses on microfilm, newspapers on
microfilm, large obituary file, many
family histories and much more; our files
are open for research all library hours,
with limited help for searchers; more
extended research done for reasonable
fees by contacting the society.")
$10.00 per year membership; research:
$10.00 basic research

Madison County Genealogical Society
PO Box 26
Winterset, IA 50273-0026
(515) 462-1731 (Winterset Public Library);
(515) 462-4318 (Corresponding
Secretary)
Lorraine Kile, Corresponding Secretary
Mon–Thur 10:00–8:00, Fri–Sat 10:00–5:00;
meetings at Winterset Public Library
Pub. *Newsletter*, quarterly
$5.00 per year membership; research: $8.00
per hour plus postage and copies

Marion County Genealogical Society
(Research Room, Knoxville Public Library,
Second Floor)
PO Box 385 (mailing address)
Knoxville, IA 50138
(641) 842-0585 voice & FAX (Library)
jean2gen@se-iowa.net; jeanlee@harnet.net
http://www.rootsweb.com/~iamcgs/index.
html
Jean Leeper, President and Newsletter Editor
Pub. *Marion County Newsletter*, quarterly
$10.00 per year membership

Mills County Genealogical Society
c/o Glenwood Public Library
109 North Vine Street
Glenwood, IA 51534-1516
Linda Rose, President
Library: Mon–Tue & Thur–Fri 10:00–6:00,
Wed 10:00–8:00, Sat 10:00–4:00
Pub. *Mills County Genealogical Society
Newsletter*, quarterly
$4.00 per year membership

Monona County Genealogical Society
(901 12th Street—location)
PO Box 16 (mailing address)
Onawa, IA 51040-0016
Emma Lou Stanislav, Secretary
$3.00 per year membership; research: $10.00

Monona County Genealogist
Onawa Public Library
Genealogy Department
707 Iowa Avenue
Onawa, IA 51040
(712) 423-1167
Ariel E. Wonder, Historian and Genealogist

Monroe County Genealogical Society
Carnegie-Evans Library
203 Benton Avenue, East
Albia, IA 52531-2036
(641) 932-5477 (Editor); (641) 932-2593
(Secretary)
http://www.iamonroe.org/monroeco.htm
Vivian Shelquist, Editor; Sarah Hindman,
Correspondence Secretary
meetings: second Sat 1:00
Pub. *Monroe County Genealogical Society
News*, quarterly
$8.00 per year membership; research: $10.00

per hour (two-hour minimum)

Montgomery County Genealogical Society
320A Coolbaugh
Red Oak, IA 51566-2416

Muscatine County Genealogical Society
323 Main Street
Muscatine, IA 52761-2867
Gladys Mittman

Nishnabotna Genealogical Society
847 Road M 56
Harlan, IA 51537
(712) 782-3400
http://www.rootsweb.com/~iashelby/scgs.
htm
Margaret Anderson, President; Annabelle
Petersen, Secretary; Mae Petersen,
Genealogy Research
Harlan Community Library: Mon–Sat
9:30–5:30
(Shelby County marriage records,
1853–1880, and some cemeteries; records
in Library and in Museum in Harlan)
$2.00 per year membership

North Central Iowa Genealogical Society
(Mason City Public Library, 225 Second
Street, S.E., Mason City, IA
50401—location)
PO Box 237 (mailing address)
Mason City, IA 50402-0237
cbpcpapc@netins.net
http://pafways.org/genealogy/societies/
northcentraliowa/index.htm
Beth McBride, President
Library: Mon, Wed & Fri 9:00–noon &
1:00–4:00, Mon 6:00–8:00, Sat
9:00–noon
Pub. *The Genie Bug*, quarterly
(Cerro Gordo County)
$10.00 per year membership; research:
$10.00 per hour

Northeast Iowa Genealogical Society
c/o Grout Museum of History and Science
Hans J. Chryst Archival Library
503 South Street
Waterloo, IA 50701
(319) 234-6357 (Museum); (319) 236-0500
FAX (Museum)
allaireg7@mchsi.com; rutucker@cfu.net
http://www.rootsweb.com/~iablackh/
neigsbooklist.html
Allaire George, Researcher; Ruth Tucker,
Librarian
Museum: Tue–Sat 10:00–4:30, Sun
1:00–4:30
Pub. *Cedar Tree Branches*, quarterly
(Black Hawk County only; "indexes for most
cemeteries, early probates, naturalizations,
early marriages, deaths.")
$8.00 per year membership; research: $10.00
per hour

Northwest Iowa Genealogical Society
Le Mars Public Library
46 First Street, S.W.
Le Mars, IA 51031-3696
John L. Winterringer, Correspondence
Assistant
Library: Mon–Thur 10:00–8:00, Fri–Sat
10:00–5:00
Pub. *Northwest Iowa Root Diggers*, quarterly
(provides research for Plymouth County and
a few surrounding counties)
$7.50 per year membership; research: $10.00
per hour plus postage and photocopies

Oelwein Area Genealogical Society
c/o Oelwein Public Library

22 First Avenue N.W.
Oelwein, IA 50662
(319) 283-5601; (319) 283-1515 voice &
FAX (Library)
Viola Sims, Treasurer; Hazel Short,
President
Pub. *Newsletter*, quarterly
(Fayette County; material at Oelwein Public
Library)
$5.00 per year membership; research: $5.00
per hour plus copy costs

Old Fort Chapter (IGS)
Old Fort Genealogical Society, Inc.
PO Box 1
Fort Madison, IA 52627
(319) 463-7208 (President)
Pat Morrison, President
Rashid Memorial Library: Mon, Wed & Fri
noon–5:00, Tue & Thur noon–8:00, Sat
9:00–1:00
Pub. *Quarterly*
(North Lee County)
$8.00 per year membership

Palo Alto County Genealogical Society
Emmetsburg Public Library
707 North Superior
Emmetsburg, IA 50536-2410
third Wed evening (except Dec), and by
appointment
Pub. *Page One Newsletter*, quarterly
$10.00 per year membership

**Pioneer Sons and Daughters Chapter
(IGS)**
PO Box 13133
Des Moines, IA 50310-0133
Pub. *Pioneer Trails*, quarterly
(Polk County records)
$6.00 per year membership

**Pottawattamie County Genealogical
Society**
PO Box 394
Council Bluffs, IA 51502
(712) 322-1171
pcgs@pcgs.omhcoxmail.com;
geniebuff1@novia.net
http://www.rootsweb.com/~iapottaw/
PCGS.htm
Marsha Pilger, President
meetings at the U.S. Bank building,
northwest corner of Broadway and Main:
second Tue 7:00
Pub. *The Frontier Chronicle*, quarterly
$17.50 per year membership

**Poweshiek County Historical and
Genealogical Society**
(see Historical Societies—Local and
Regional, above)

Ringgold County Genealogy Society
Route 2, Box 67 C, 301 Amy Lane
Mount Ayr, IA 50854
(641) 464-3594
Earle M. Schad
meetings fourth Wed (except Dec)
Pub. *Ringgold Roots*, quarterly
$5.00 per year membership

Sac County Genealogical Society
PO Box 54
Sac City, IA 50583-0054
(712) 662-4094
Janice Larsen, President
by appointment
Pub. *SACOGE News*, quarterly
$7.50 per year membership; research: $10.00
per hour

Scott County Iowa Genealogical Society
PO Box 3132
Davenport, IA 52808-3132
(563) 326-7902
Pub. *Scott County Iowan*, quarterly
(collection placed with local library)
$12.00 per year membership

Story County Genealogical Society
PO Box 692
Ames, IA 50010-0692
http://www.rootsweb.com/~iastory/
   chapter.htm
Lucille Wahrenbrock, Librarian
meetings in the Ames Public Library: second
   Mon (Jan–May & Sept–Nov) 7:00
Pub. *Newsletter*
$7.50 per year membership

**Tama County Tracers Genealogical
Society**
Tama County Historical Museum Library
200 North Broadway Street
Toledo, IA 52342-0084
(641) 484-6767
Museum Library: Tue–Sat 1:00–4:30, and by
   appointment
Pub. *Tama County Museum News*, quarterly
$10.00 per year membership

Taylor County, Iowa Genealogical Society
(102 Washington—location)
PO Box 8 (mailing address)
Gravity, IA 50848-0008
(712) 539-2475 (President); (712) 523-2041
   (Museum)
Helen Janson, President
Taylor County Museum: Tue–Sun (1 Apr–25
   Dec) 1:00–5:00
Pub. *Taylor County, Iowa Genealogical
   Society*, semiannually
$4.00 per year membership

Tree Shakers Chapter (IGS)
1009 Woodland Ridge Court
Louisville, KY 40245-5209
Judy Stacey
(Polk County)

Union County Genealogical Society, Inc.
Matilda J. Gibson Memorial Library
200 West Howard
Creston, IA 50801
(641) 782-2277 (Library); (641) 782-4604
   FAX (Library)
imm@mddc.com
Irma M. Miller, Corresponding Secretary
Library: Mon & Wed 10:00–8:00, Tue &
   Thur–Fri 10:00–6:00, Sat 10:00–4:00
Pub. *Union Roots*, quarterly
$5.00 per year membership; research: $6.00
   per hour plus copies and postage

Van Buren County Genealogy Society
Keosauqua Public Library
(First and Van Buren—location)
PO Box 158 (mailing address)
Keosauqua, IA 52565
http://www.rootsweb.com/~iavanbur/app.
   htm
Melva Jane Workman, President
meetings: second Thur 7:00
Pub. *Van Buren County Quill*, quarterly
("Surname card file, obituary file, cemetery
   inscriptions, county-wide")
$7.50 per year membership

Wapello County Genealogical Society
(Amtrak Depot, 210 West Mail
   Street—library location)
PO Box 163 (mailing address)
Ottumwa, IA 52501

(641) 682-8676
http://www.rootsweb.com/~iawapegs
Ruth Ferdig, Secretary
Tue–Fri noon–3:30, Sat 10:00–3:30, Sun
   1:00–3:30
Pub. *Wapello County Genealogical Society
   Newsletter*, quarterly
$10.00 per year membership; research: $5.00
   per name for members, $10.00 per name
   for nonmembers

Warren County Genealogical Society
306 West Salem Street
Indianola, IA 50125-2438
(515) 961-4409
hallross@aol.com
Thelma Pehrson, Corresponding Secretary
Pub. *Warren County Genealogical Society
   Newsletter*, bimonthly
(collection in Indianola Public Library)
$6.00 per year membership

Washington County Genealogical Society
(Washington Public Library—location)
PO Box 446 (mailing address)
Washington, IA 52353
Margie Lasek, President; Wilma Atkinson,
   Corresponding Secretary; Sally Reighard,
   Editor
Pub. *Newsletter*, quarterly
("Washington County information plus
   adjoining counties.")
$8.00 per year membership; research: actual
   cost of research such as copy fees, postage

Wayne County Genealogical Society
Karl Miles LeCompte Memorial Library
110 South Franklin Street
Corydon, IA 50060-1518
Susie DeVore, President; Roberta Amdor,
   Vice President
Mon–Fri 12:30–5:00, Sat 10:00–2:00;
   meetings: first Thur (except July–Aug)
   7:30
Pub. *Wayne County Genie News*, quarterly
$8.00 per year membership; research: $5.00
   minimum

Webster County Genealogical Society
(424 Central Avenue—location)
PO Box 1584 (mailing address)
Fort Dodge, IA 50501-1584
Tue–Thur 11:00–4:00, Sat 10:00–2:00
Pub. *Genie Gleaners*, quarterly
$10.00 per year membership; research:
   $15.00 per hour plus costs

Woodbury County Genealogical Society
PO Box 624
Sioux City, IA 51102-0624
Janet P. Jolin
Public Library, Sioux City: Mon–Thur
   9:00–9:00, Fri–Sat 9:00–5:00, Sun
   (Sept–May) 1:00–5:00
Pub. *Waukaw*, quarterly
$12.00 per year membership; research:
   $10.00 per hour

Wright County Genealogical Searchers
PO Box 225
Clarion, IA 50525-0225
Rosella Gramstad, President
$7.50 per year membership; research: $5.00
   per hour, plus copying costs and postage

Independent Publications and Miscellany

**Audubon County, Iowa Genealogical
Research Services**
1019 Tekamah Lane

Papillion, NE 68128-6245
(402) 339-7291; (402) 339-0051
Donna M. Christensen Thomas
(publishes compilations of local records)

**Mamie Doud Eisenhower Birthplace
Museum and Library**
(709 Carroll Street—location)
PO Box 55 (mailing address)
Boone, IA 50036

Sherry Foresman Library
(see Lending Libraries, Part 4)

**The Herbert Hoover Presidential Library
and Museum**
(210 Parkside Drive—location)
PO Box 488 (mailing address)
West Branch, IA 52358
(563) 643-5301
hoover.library@nara.gov
http://hoover.nara.gov
Archivist
Research Room: Mon–Fri 9:00–4:45
(primarily historical; has only Hoover
   genealogical materials)

IaGenWeb
Part of The USGenweb Project
donkelly@grovenet.net;
   IAStory@genloc.com;
   gkilgore@primenet.com
http://IAGenWeb.org
Don Kelly, State Coordinator; Mark
   Christian, Assistant Coordinator; Gail
   Meyer Kilgore, Assistant Coordinator
(links to other Iowa resources)

Iowa Department of Transportation
800 Lincoln Way
Ames, IA 50010
(515) 239-1200
hank.zaletel@dot.state.ia.us
http://dot.state.ia.us/sitemap.htm#maps
   (Maps)
Hank Zaletel, Librarian

Iowa Historical Information
http://www.iowa-
   counties.com/historical/index.shtml
(links to other Iowa resources)

Liberty Hall Historic Center
1300 West Main Street
Lamoni, IA 50140
(641) 784-6133
Norma Derry Hiles, Director/Curator
Pub. *Restoration Trail Forum* (not
   genealogical)

Living History Farms
2600 N.W. 111th Street
Urbandale, IA 50322
(515) 278-5286; (515) 278-2400 (event
   information)
http://www.ioweb.com/lhf

Museum of Missouri River History
(see Nebraska, Part 2)

New Sweden, Iowa, Descendants
3623 North 37th Street
Arlington, VA 22207-4821
(703) 276-8228; (703) 276-8236 FAX
BAnnMunsey@aol.com
Bernice Wilson Munsey
(assisting those beginning to search their
   own families)

PAF-Ways
pafways@trekster.us
http://www.pafways.org/index.html

Jay Lehmann, Secretary
meetings at Hamilton College: third Sat 1:00
("A group of north central Iowans with an
interest in genealogy and learning to use
computers to obtain and organize their
records.")

Pages from Our Past
Route 2
Clarinda, IA 51632
B. Hartman and B. Ankenny, Editors
Pub. *Pages from Our Past*

Peterson Heritage, Inc.
PO Box 222
Peterson, IA 51047
(712) 295-6401
Judy Bang, President
$5.00 per year membership

Pioneer Publications
PO Box 1179
Tumtum, WA 99034-1179
(509) 276-1740
Shirley Penna-Oakes, Editor
Pub. *Iowa Queries*, $6.00 plus $1.75 postage
per issue; *OH-IN-IA Queries & Reviews*,
$6.00 plus $1.75 postage per issue

Pioneer Village Commission
City Hall
Cedar Rapids, IA 52401
(319) 398-5104

Plymouth County Historical Museum
335 First Avenue, S.W.
Le Mars, IA 51031
(712) 546-7002
Judy Bowman, Administrator
Tue–Sun 1:00–5:00

**Spillville Historic Action Group, Inc.
(SHAG)**
PO Box 187
Spillville, IA 52168-0187
(563) 562-3186 (Secretary)
Juanita J. Loven, Secretary
(Spillville history, including Antonin Dvorak
in Spillville, and Spillville's Czech
heritage)
$5.00 per year membership

Kansas

Archives and Libraries with Holdings in Genealogy

State Archives and Library

Library and Archives Division
(see Kansas State Historical Society, State
Historical Society, below)

Kansas State Library
State Capitol Building, Third Floor
Topeka, KS 66612
(785) 296-3296; (800) 432-3919 (from
within Kansas); (785) 296-6650 FAX
eric@kslib.info
http://skyways.lib.ks.us/kansas/KSL
Marc Galbraith, Reference Librarian; Cindy
Roupe, Reference Librarian; Eric Hansen
Mon–Fri 8:00–5:00
("The State Library's collection consists
primarily of social science and public
policy material. However, we do have
some biographical information about
people who served in the legislature and
the executive branch.")

State Historical Society

Kansas State Historical Society
Kansas State Archives
6425 S.W. Sixth Avenue
Topeka, KS 66615-1099
(785) 272-8681, ext. 116; (785) 272-8681,
ext. 117; (785) 272-8681, ext. 282 (Head
of Reference); (785) 272-8682 FAX
reference@kshs.org; lfredericksen@kshs.org
http://www.kshs.org
Lin Fredericksen, Head of Reference
Tue–Sat 9:00–4:30
Pub. *Kansas History: A Journal of the
Central Plains*, quarterly; *Kansas
Heritage*, quarterly
("Most microfilm holdings are available
through interlibrary loan. A great deal of
information about holdings is available at
the web site": Kansas newspapers, census,
family histories, photographs, maps, state
archives, manuscripts.)
$25.00 per year membership; research:
$15.00 for approximately a half hour,
including five copies for all mail,
telephone, and email inquiries (limited
information about holdings will be
supplied at no charge); admission: no
charge for in-person researchers, except
for photocopies

**City, County and Regional Archives and
Libraries**
(A more exhaustive list of public and
academic libraries can be found at http://
skyways2.lib.ks.us/kld or http://skyways.lib.
ks.us/KSL/admin/publiclibrarydirectory.
pdf.)

Anthony Public Library
624 East Main
Anthony, KS 67003-2738
(620) 842-5344; (620) 842-5684 FAX
library@wiredks.com
http://skyways.lib.ks.us/towns/Anthony/
library.html
Sandy Trotter, Director
Mon–Thur 9:00–11:00 & 1:00–7:30, Fri
9:00–11:00 & 1:00–5:30, Sat 1:00–5:30
("We cannot do extensive searches but can
do look-ups when names and dates are
given.")
research: no fee but copies at 25¢ each

Arkansas City Public Library
120 East Fifth Avenue
Arkansas City, KS 67705-2695
(620) 442-1280; (620) 442-4277 FAX
mswain@acpl.org
http://www.acpl.org
Michelle Swain, Director; Lesly M. Smith,
Head Librarian
Mon–Thur 9:00–8:00, Fri–Sat 9:00–6:00

Ashland Public Library
Dorothy Berryman Collection
(604 Main—location)
PO Box 397 (mailing address)
Ashland, KS 67831-0397
(620) 635-2589; (620) 635-2931 FAX
mcminimy@ucom.net; ashlib@ucom.net
http://skyways.lib.ks.us/towns/Ashland/
library.html
Eldora McMinimy, Director
Mon & Fri–Sat 1:30–5:30, Tue & Thur
11:00–5:30, Wed 1:30–5:30 & 7:00–9:00,
Sun 2:00–4:00

Atchison Public Library
401 Kansas Avenue
Atchison, KS 66002-2495
(913) 367-1902; (913) 367-2717 FAX
pjcapps@atchison.lib.ks.us
http://www.atchisonlibrary.org
P. J. Capps Director
Mon–Thur 9:00–8:00, Fri–Sat 9:00–5:00,
Sun 1:00–5:00

Atwood Public Library
102 South Sixth Street
Atwood, KS 67730-1998
(785) 626-3805; (785) 626-3670 FAX
http://skyways.lib.ks.us/genweb/rawlins/
library.html
Pamela A. Luedke, Director
Mon–Fri 9:00–5:00, Wed 7:00–8:30, Sat
9:00–1:00

Baker University Archives
PO Box 65
Baldwin, KS 66006
(785) 594-6451, ext. 380

Boot Hill Museum
Front Street
Dodge City, KS 67801
(620) 227-8188; (620) 227-7673 FAX
David Kloppenborg, Curator; Shirley
McLoughlin, President and CEO
Mon–Fri 9:00–5:00
(Ford County District Court records (except
probate records which have been returned
to the county); historic photographs;
archives)
copies: 25¢ each

Frank Carlson Library
702 Broadway
Concordia, KS 66901
(785) 243-2250
Denise DeRochefort-Reynolds, Head
Librarian
Mon–Thur 9:00–9:00, Fri–Sat 9:00–5:00;
June–Aug: Mon & Thur 9:00–8:00,
Tue–Wed 9:00–5:30, Fri–Sat 9:00–5:00
(genealogy archives of Cloud County
Genealogical Society; newspaper
microfilm of all towns of Cloud County,
1870–1950)

Cassoday Historical Museum
Washington and Beaumont
Cassoday, KS 66842
(620) 735-7286

Center for Great Plains Studies
Emporia State University
1200 Commercial
Emporia, KS 66801-5087
(620) 341-5574
johnsonj@esumail.emporia.edu
http://www.emporia.edu/S/www/cgps/grplsst.htm
Julie Johnson, Managing Editor
Mon, Wed & Fri 8:00–4:00
Pub. *Heritage of the Great Plains*, semiannually, $7.00 per year subscription
(refereed journal dealing with Great Plains topics; Kansas, Montana, Nebraska, North Dakota, Oklahoma, South Dakota, Texas)

Center for Great Plains Study
(see Nebraska, Part 2)

Cherokee Strip Land Rush Museum
(South Summit Street Road—location)
PO Box 1002 (mailing address)
Arkansas City, KS 67005
(620) 442-6750
Tue–Sun
(Cowley County genealogy library)
admission: $2.50 for adults

Chetopa Historical Museum
Route 1, Box 135
Chetopa, KS 67336
(620) 236-7195

Chisholm Trail History and Genealogy Center
(502 North Washington—location)
PO Box 402 (mailing address)
Wellington, KS 67152
(620) 326-3820; (620) 326-7315 (Sherri Theurer); (620) 326-3044 (Lora Topinka)
ltheurer@sutv.com; ltopinka@sutv.com
http://www.rootsweb.com/~kscthgc/cthgc.htm
Richard M. Gilfillan, President Board of Directors; Sherri Theurer; Lora Topinka
Tue & Fri–Sat 10:00–4:00 and by appointment
("Ours is a museum of domestic life in south central Kansas rather than specifically a cowboy museum, but does include information about frontier life and the famous Chisholm Trail as well. We do have an archives in which for about 30 years we have filed and kept considerable information about local people and the surrounding area.")
admission: donation

Columbus Public Library
205 North Kansas Avenue
Columbus, KS 66725-1297
(620) 429-2086; (620) 429-1950 FAX
collib@columbus-ks.com
http://skyways.lib.ks.us/library/columbus
Catherine VanGilder, Director
Mon–Thur 1:30–5:00 & 6:00–8:00, Fri–Sat 10:00–noon & 1:30–5:00

Mary Cotton Public Library
(915 Virginia—location)
PO Box 70 (mailing address)
Sabetha, KS 66534-0070
(785) 284-3160; (785) 284-3605 FAX
marycotton2@netscape.net
Kim Priest, Director
Mon & Wed 10:00–8:00, Tue & Thur–Fri 10:00–5:30, Sat 10:00–4:00

Council Grove Public Library
829 West Main Street
Council Grove, KS 66846-1785
(620) 767-5716; (620) 767-7312 FAX

cglib@cgtelco.net
http://www.skyways.lib.ks.us/norcen/cgrove
Anne Teghtmeyer, Director
Mon–Wed 10:00–6:00, Thur 10:00–8:00, Fri 10:00–5:00, Sat 10:00–2:00

Crawford County Genealogy Library
(Pittsburg Public Library—location)
211 West Fourth (mailing address)
Pittsburg, KS 66762
genealogy@pittsburg.lib.ks.us

http://skyways.lib.ks.us/library/pittsburg/genealogy.htm
Mon 9:00–8:00, Tue–Fri 9:00–1:00
Pub. *Seeker*, quarterly
$13.00 per year membership; research: SASE, "keep inquiry short, please"

Dodge City Public Library
1001 Second Avenue
Dodge City, KS 67801-4484
(620) 225-0248; (620) 225-0252 FAX
maryt@trails.net
http://trails.net/dcpl
Mary Tuytschaevers, Director
Mon–Thur 9:00–8:00, Fri 9:00–6:00, Sat 10:00–5:00, Sun 1:00–5:00; summer: Mon–Wed & Fri 9:00–6:00, Thur 9:00–8:00, Sat 10:00–5:00, Sun 1:00–5:00

Library District #1, Doniphan County
(105 North Main—location)
PO Box 220 (mailing address)
Troy, KS 66087-0220
(785) 985-2597; (785) 985-2602 FAX
librarydist1@carsoncomm.com
http://skyways.lib.ks.us/library/doniphan
Tina Murphy; Jorgine Drake; Carla Watkins
Mon–Tue & Thur 8:00–6:00, Wed 8:00–8:00, Fri 8:00–5:00, Sat 8:00–1:00
research: postage and copy fees ("All searching is done as time allows so do not be discouraged if you don't get a reply right away.")

Douglass Historical Museum
(312-314 South Forest Street—location)
PO Box 35 (mailing address)
Douglass, KS 67039
(316) 747-2319
Jean Valentine, Curator
Mon–Wed & Fri 10:30–2:00, most Thur
(Town of Douglass, people of Douglass and area; family history files, cemetery records, some birth and death records of the City, local newspaper, *The Douglass Tribune*, 1884–1977 on microfilm)

Downs Carnegie Library
504 South Morgan Avenue
Downs, KS 67437-2019
(785) 454-3958; (785) 454-3821; (785) 454-6606 FAX
dowcarlib@nckcn.com

http://skyways2.lib.ks.us/kld/LibraryDetail.asp?LibraryID=110
Helen Seaman, Director
Mon 1:00–5:00 & 6:00–8:00, Tue–Sat 1:00–5:00

Emporia Public Library
110 East Sixth Avenue
Emporia, KS 66801-3960
(620) 342-6524; (620) 342-2633 FAX
blechls@carrollsweb.com
http://skyways.lib.ks.us/library/emporia
Sue Blechl, Director; Katharine Commerford, Genealogist
Mon–Thur 9:00–9:00, Fri 9:00–6:00, Sat 9:00–5:00, Sun 2:00–5:00; Memorial

Day–Labor Day: closes at 6:00 on Mon–Tue & Thur
(genealogy of Lyon County, general genealogy)

Finney County Public Library
605 East Walnut
Garden City, KS 67846-5755
(620) 272-3680; (620) 272-3682 FAX
http://fcpl.homestead.com
Todd Humble, Director
Mon–Thur 9:00–9:00 (summer 9:00–7:00); Fri–Sat 9:00–6:00, Sun 1:00–6:00

Fort Hays State University
Special Collections/University Archives
Forsyth Library
600 Park Street
Hays, KS 67601-4099
(785) 628-5901 (Archives); (785) 628-4096 FAX (Library)
pnichola@fhsu.edu; refserv@fhsu.edu (Reference)
http://www.fhsu.edu/forsyth_lib/arch.shtml
Patty Nicholas
Library: Mon–Thur 7:30–midnight, Fri 7:30–7:00, Sat 9:00–4:30, Sun 1:00–midnight; Archives: Mon–Fri (including Jan intermission) 8:00–4:30, Mon–Thur (summer) 7:30–5:00, Fri (summer) 7:30–11:30 A.M.

Friends University
Pioneer Historical Museum
Fellow-Reeve Museum of History and Science
2100 West University Avenue
Wichita, KS 67213
(316) 261-5800, ext. 794
Philip Nagley, Director
Pub. *Museum Chatter*

Galena Mining and Historical Museum Association, Inc.
(319 West Seventh Street—location)
PO Box 372 (mailing address)
Galena, KS 66739
(620) 783-2192 (Museum)
Gene Russell, President
1 May–1 Nov: 9:00–11:30 & 1:00–3:00
(museum contains mining tools, artifacts, paintings and pictures of mines, smelter and mineral specimens, horse drawn hearse, etc.)

Galena Public Library
City Municipal Building
315 West Seventh Street
Galena, KS 66739-1211
(620) 783-5132
galenapubliclibrary@yahoo.com
Nellie Hoskins, Director

Geneseo City Museum
Silver Avenue
Geneseo, KS 67444
Earl Alexander, President of Board

Girard Public Library
128 West Prairie Avenue
Girard, KS 66743-1498
(620) 724-4317; (620) 724-8374
girardpl@ckt.net
http://skyways.lib.ks.us/towns/Girard/library
Terri R. Harley, Director
Mon–Tue 10:00–7:00, Wed–Thur 10:00–6:00, Fri 10:00–5:00, Sat 10:00–3:00
("Our genealogy/history room is not staffed full time, but we are always willing to assist." An extensive obituary card index and many local genealogical and historical

materials, mostly for Girard and Crawford counties.")
research: $5.00 plus postage and copies at 25¢ each

Grant County Library
215 East Grant Street
Ulysses, KS 67880-2958
(620) 356-1433; (620) 356-1344 FAX
frances@pld.com
Norma Jean Bricker, Adult Librarian; Frances Roberts, Director
Mon–Sat 9:30–5:30

Great Bend Public Library
1409 Williams Street
Great Bend, KS 67530-4090
(620) 792-2409; (620) 793-7270 FAX
gbref@ckls.org
http://www.ckls.org/~gbpl
Jim Swan, Director
Mon noon–9:00, Tue–Thur 10:00–9:00, Fri–Sat 10:00–5:00, Sun 1:00–5:00

Hamilton County Library
(102 West Avenue C—location)
Box 1307 (mailing address)
Syracuse, KS 67878-1307
(620) 384-5622; (620) 384-5623 FAX
1952@pld.com; hamcolib@yahoo.com

http://www.skyways.lib.ks.us/library/hamilton
Joyce Armstrong, Director
Mon–Thur 9:00–7:00 Fri 8:00–1:00

Harper Public Library
Harper City Building
1002 Oak
Harper, KS 67058-1233
(620) 896-2959; (620) 896-7832 FAX
harperlib@cyberlodge.com

http://www.skyways.lib.ks.us/towns/Harper/library.html
Cara Vanderee, Director; Imogene Van Dolah, Librarian

Haun Museum
Jetmore, KS 67854

Hays Public Library
Kansas Room
1205 Main Street
Hays, KS 67601-3693
(785) 625-9014; (913) 625-8683 FAX
hayspublib@spidome.net
http://www.hayspublib.org
Mary Ann Thompson, Kansas Room Librarian
winter: Mon–Thur 9:00–9:00, Fri 9:00–6:00, Sat 9:00–5:00, Sun 1:00–5:00; summer: Mon–Thur 9:00–7:00, Fri 9:00–6:00, Sat 9:00–5:00
(Kansas, Western U.S., genealogy)

Hesperian Library
(802 Locust Street, second floor of City Building, Cawker City, KS 67430-9231—location)
PO Box 136 (mailing address)
Cawker City, KS 67430
(785) 781-4925 (for appointment only, no research over the phone)
cawkerlib@nckcn.com
http://skyways.lib.ks.us/kansas/towns/Cawker/library.html
Celia Norton Kincheloe, Librarian
Mon, Thur & Sat 1:00–5:00, Tue 10:00–noon, Wed 1:00–7:00

High Plains Museum

1717 Cherry
Goodland, KS 67735
(785) 899-4595
Linda Holton, Director
(primarily Sherman County)

Hutchinson Public Library
901 North Main Street
Hutchinson, KS 67501-4401
(620) 663-5441; (620) 663-1583 FAX
http://www.hplsck.org
Cheryl L. Canfield, Head of Reference
Mon–Fri 9:00–9:00, Sat 9:00–6:00, Sun 1:00–5:00
limited research

Independence Public Library
220 East Maple Street
Independence, KS 67301-3899
(620) 331-3030; (620) 331-3912 FAX
pete.daniels@iplks.org
http://www.terraworld.net/indlib2
Pete Daniels, Director
Mon–Wed 9:00–8:00, Mon–Wed (summer) 9:00–6:00, Thur–Sat 9:00–5:30, Sun 1:00–4:00
(DAR, Kansas independent newspapers and census, city directories, marriage licenses)
search: $5.00 minimum per search

Iola Public Library
218 East Madison
Iola, KS 66749-3384
(620) 365-3262; (620) 365-5137 FAX
http://www.iola.lib.ks.us
Roger Carswell, Director
Sept–May: Mon–Thur 9:30–8:00, Fri–Sat 9:00–5:00; June–Aug: Mon–Thur 9:30–5:30, Fri–Sat 9:00–5:00
$1.50 per item for interlibrary loan out-of-state (genealogy bibliography available)

Johnson County Archives and Records Management
Johnson County Administration Building
111 South Cherry Street, Suite 500
Olathe, KS 66061-3441
(913) 715-0400; (913) 715-0405 FAX
Archives@jocoks.com
Gina Alvarez, Archivist Technician
9:00–4:30

Johnson County Library
(9875 West 87th Street—location)
PO Box 2933 (mailing address)
Shawnee Mission, KS 66201-1333
(913) 495-2400; (913) 495-2460 FAX
http://www.jocolibrary.org
Barbara Baker, Local History and Genealogy Supervisor
Mon–Thur 9:00–9:00, Fri 9:00–6:00, Sat 9:00–5:00, Sun 1:00–5:00
(a collection of items pertaining to the history of Johnson County, Kansas; the Otham Meeker Papers, the Isaac McCoy Papers, Johnson County state and federal census films, individual histories of Johnson County cities, and the Johnson County Obituary file from 1977)

Johnson County Museum of History
6305 Lackman Road
Shawnee Mission, KS 66217
(913) 631-6709; (913) 631-6359 FAX
Janet Bruce Campbell, Director
Tue–Sat 10:00–4:00, appointments recommended
(Johnson County manuscripts and printed materials)
from $25.00 per year membership

Johnston Public Library

210 West 10th
Baxter Springs, KS 66713
(620) 856-5591; (620) 856-4498 FAX
Muriel E. Burrows, Director
Mon & Thur 10:00–6:00, Tue–Wed & Fri 1:00–6:00

Kansas City Public Library
625 Minnesota
Kansas City, KS 66101-2805
(913) 551-3280; (913) 551-2033 FAX; (913) 551-3221 FAX
tgarrison@kckpl.lib.ks.us
http://www.kckpl.lib.ks.us
Eleanor Fox, Reference Librarian; Teresa Garrison, Assistant Director
Mon–Fri 3:00–5:00, and by appointment
("A part of the William E. Connelley manuscript collection that pertains to the Wyandotte Indians and early local history.")

Kansas Heritage Center
(1000 Second Avenue—location)
PO Box 1207 (mailing address
Dodge City, KS 67801
(620) 227-1616; (620) 227-1701 FAX
info@ksheritage.org
http://ksheritage.org
Janice Scott
Mon–Fri 8:00–5:00
Pub. *Newsletter*, quarterly
(media resource center for Kansas, the Great Plains, the Old West, and Dodge City history; Dodge City newspapers on microfilm from 1876, also many area newspapers; census records and Fort Dodge correspondence; birth, marriage, death records; videos; other reference materials; and photographs)

Kansas State University
Seaton Memorial Library
323 Seaton Hall
Manhattan, KS 66506
(785) 532-5968

Kansas State University
Morse Department of Special Collections
506 Hale Library
Manhattan, KS 66506-1200
(785) 532-7456
archives@ksu.edu
http://www.lib.ksu.edu/depts/spec
Cindy Von Elling
Mon–Fri 8:00–5:00, closed state holidays and Christmas–New Year's Day

Emmett Kelly Historical Museum
202-204 East Main
Sedan, KS 67361
(620) 725-3470
Roger Floyd, Chairman of the Board
Tue–Sat 10:00–5:00, Sun 1:00–5:00
("Clown and Chautauqua County History Museum")

Kingman Carnegie Library
455 North Main Street
Kingman, KS 67068-1395
(620) 532-3061; (620) 532-2528 FAX
kingc1lb@websurf.net
http://skyways.lib.ks.us/kansas/library/kingman
Linda L. Slack, Director
Mon–Thur 10:00–8:00, Fri 10:00–6:00, Sat 10:00–2:00

Kingman County Historical Museum
(400 North Main—location)
PO Box 281 (mailing address)
Kingman, KS 67068

(620) 532-5274; (620) 532-2627
June Walker, Curator
Fri 9:00–4:00, and by appointment
$10.00 per year membership

Kinsley Public Library
208 East Eighth Street
Kinsley, KS 67547-1422
(620) 659-3341; (620) 659-3613 FAX
kinlib@kl.kscoxmail.com;
    illkinsley@kl.kscoxmail.com (Assistant
    Librarian)
Joan Weaver, Director; Rosetta Graff,
    Assistant Librarian
Mon & Wed 9:30–11:00 & 1:00–8:00, Tue
    & Thur–Fri 9:30–11:00 & 1:00–5:00, Sat
    1:00–5:00
(Kinsley newspapers)
limited research if specific information is
    given (date within a month, name, etc.),
    send SASE & cost of copies at 25¢ each

Last Indian Raid Museum
258 South Penn Avenue
Oberlin, KS 67749
(houses the collection of the Decatur County
    Genealogical Society)

Lawrence Public Library
707 Vermont Street
Lawrence, KS 66044-2371
(785) 843-3833; (785) 843-3368 FAX
bflanders@lawrence.lib.ks.us
http://www.lawrencepubliclibrary.org
Bruce Flanders, Director; Cecilia Jecha May,
    Head, Reference Department
Mon–Fri 9:30–9:00, Sat 9:30–6:00, Sun
    2:00–5:00

Leavenworth Public Library
Kansas Room
417 Spruce Street
Leavenworth, KS 66048-2729
(913) 682-5666; (913) 682-1248 FAX
kimbaker@leavenworth.lib.ks.us
http://skyways.lib.ks.us/library/
    leavenworth/KSR/ksr.hm
Kimberly A. Baker, Director
Mon–Thur 9:00–9:00, Fri–Sat 9:00–5:00,
    Sun (Sept–May) 1:00–4:00

Liberal Memorial Library
519 North Kansas
Liberal, KS 67901
(620) 626-0180; (620) 626-0182 FAX
http://www.skyways.lib.ks.us/library/liberal
Ida Eatmon, Genealogy/Reference Research
    Manager
Mon–Thur 9:00–8:00, Fri–Sat 9:00–5:00,
    Sun 1:00–5:00
("Seward County newspapers from 1886 to
    present on microfilm, Seward County
    rural school records on microfilm")
research: $15.00 per hour (one hour
    minimum), plus copies at 25¢ each

Lindsborg Community Library
111 South Main
Lindsborg, KS 67456-2417
(785) 227-2710
lindsborglibrary@ks-usa.net
Karen J. Olson, Director

Lyndon Carnegie Library
(127 East Sixth—location)
PO Box 563 (mailing address)
Lyndon, KS 66451-0563
(785) 828-4520; (785) 828-4565 FAX
lyndonlibrary@nekls.org
http://skyways.lib.ks.us/kansas/towns/
    lyndon/library.html
Sarah Walker-Hitt, Director

Marion Historical Museum
625 East Main
Marion, KS 66861
(620) 382-2287; (620) 382-3432

McPherson County Old Mill Museum
(120 Mill Street—location)
PO Box 94 (mailing address)
Lindsborg, KS 67456
(785) 227-3595; (785) 227-2810 FAX
http://www.oldmillmuseum.org
Lenora Lynam, Archivist
Mon–Sat 9:00–5:00, Sun 1:00–5:00
Pub. *McPherson County Genealogical
    Resource Guide*, annually
(Houses collection of McPherson County
    Genealogical Society.)

Morrill Public Library
431 Oregon Street
Hiawatha, KS 66434-2290
(785) 742-3831; (785) 742-2054 FAX
cnewland@hiawatha.lib.ks.us
http://skyways.lib.ks.us/kansas/towns/
    Hiawatha/library.html
Catherine Newland, Director
Mon–Thur 9:00–8:00, Fri 9:00–5:00, Sat
    10:00–4:00, Sun 1:00–4:00

Museum of the Great Plains
(see Oklahoma, Part 2)

Northwest Kansas Library System
(2 Washington Square—location)
PO Box 446 (mailing address)
Norton, KS 67654-0046
(785) 877-5148; (800) 432-2858 (in
    Kansas); (785) 877-5697 FAX
illoan@ruraltel.net
http://skyways.lib.ks.us/nwkls/norwest.html
Linda Keith, Interlibrary Loan and Reference
    Clerk
Mon–Fri 8:00–5:00

Oakley Public Library
700 West Third
Oakley, KS 67748-1256
(785) 672-4776; (785) 672-4399 FAX
oakleypublib@colbyweb.com
Joyce Homm, Director
Mon & Wed 10:00–7:00; Tue & Thur–Sat
    10:00–5:00

Oketo Community Museum
Oketo, KS 66518
(785) 744-3516
Mrs. Marvin Argo
Apr–Nov: by appointment
(early photographs)

Olathe Public Library
201 East Park Street
Olathe, KS 66061-3456
(913) 764-2259; (913) 829-1706
ebaker@olatheks.org
http://olathe.lib.ks.us
Valerie Vogt, Library Assistant; Emily
    Baker, Director
Mon–Thur 9:00–9:00, Fri 9:00–6:00, Sat
    9:00–5:00, Sun 1:00–5:00
research: written request of specific
    information for donation

Osborne Public Library
325 West Main Street
Osborne, KS 67473-2425
(785) 346-5486; (785) 346-2888 FAX
osbor1lb@ruraltel.net
http://www.osbornepubliclibrary.org
Kay Coop, Director
Mon & Thur 1:00–8:00, Tue 1:00–5:00,
    Wed & Fri 10:00–5:00, Sat 10:00–2:00

Oswego Historical Museum
410 Commercial
Oswego, KS 67356
(620) 795-4500
Jerry Barnard, President
1 June–31 Oct: 1:00–5:00

Ottawa County Historical Museum
110 South Concord
Minneapolis, KS 67467-2320
(913) 392-3621
otcomu@networksplus.net
http://www.ottawacounty.org/page.asp?
    type=4&pageid=121313481
Jim Anderson, Museum Advisory Board
    Member
Tue–Sat 10:00–noon & 1:00–5:00
admission: donation

Ottawa Library
105 South Hickory Street
Ottawa, KS 66067-2306
(785) 242-3080; (785) 242-8789 FAX
staff@ottawa.lib.ks.us
http://ottawa.lib.ks.us
Barbara Dew, Library Director
Mon–Thur 9:00–8:00, Fri–Sat 9:00–5:00,
    Sun (Sept–May) 2:00–5:00
("Local history collection includes Franklin
    County newspapers on microfilm and the
    files of First Families of Franklin County,
    a library-historical society project to
    collect unpublished information about
    early Franklin County residents.
    Genealogical searches referred to Franklin
    County Genealogy Society.")

Phillipsburg City Library
888 Fourth Street
Phillipsburg, KS 67661-1699
(785) 543-5325; (785) 543-5374 FAX
pblib1@ruraltel.net
http://www.phillipsburgks.us/community/
    library/index.htm
Tonya Long, Director
Mon–Fri 10:00–6:00, Sat 10:00–4:00
("Area newspapers on microfilm from 1800s,
    obituary clippings, approximately 400
    volumes in the Marjorie Goode Collection
    on New England; also Kansas collection
    of historical materials.")
copying charges and postage appreciated

Pittsburg Public Library
308 North Walnut
Pittsburg, KS 66762-4732
(620) 231-8110; (620) 231-2258 FAX
pclement@pittsburg.lib.ks.us;
    jlewis@pittsburg.lib.ks.us (Webmaster)
http://skyways.lib.ks.us/library/pittsburg
Patricia A. Clement, Director

**Pottowatomie-Wabaunsee Regional
Library**
Saint Marys Branch
306 North Fifth
Saint Marys, KS 66536-1404
(785) 437-2278 voice & FAX
dobbinsf@oct.net
http://www.skyways.lib.ks.us/library/
    pottwablib/index.htm
Freda J. Dobbins, Director
Mon–Wed & Fri 8:30–5:00, Thur 8:30–8:00,
    Sat 9:00–1:00
(historical records relating to the Jesuit St.
    Mary's College from circa 1870–1930)

W. A. Rankin Memorial Library
502 Indiana
Neodesha, KS 66757-1532
(620) 325-3275 voice & FAX
rankin.library@neodesha.com

http://www.telepath.com/sysjer/rankin.htm
Barbara Shoop, Director
Mon 9:30–8:00, Tue–Fri 9:30–5:30, Sat
   9:00–noon
(Neodesha and Wilson County information;
   cemetery records of Neodesha City,
   Altoona City and a few rural cemeteries in
   Wilson County, index to Wilson County
   census, 1885 and 1895; estate records,
   1866–1912, obituaries, *Neodesha*
   Register, 1883–1911; tax lists 1890;
   collection of the former Heritage
   Genealogical Society)
research: $5.00 plus copies at 20¢ each

Saint Mary College
Special Collections
De Paul Library
4100 South Fourth Street
Leavenworth, KS 66048-5082
(913) 758-6306; (913) 682-2406 FAX
http://www.smcks.edu/lib/index.html
Penelope Lonergan, Director
by appointment

Salina Public Library
Campbell Room of Kansas Research
301 West Elm Street
Salina, KS 67401-2358
(785) 825-4624; (785) 823-0706 FAX
joemcken@salpublib.org
http://www.salpublib.org
Judy Lilly, Kansas Librarian; Joe McKenzie,
   Director
Mon–Fri noon–5:00, Wed 6:00–9:00, Sat
   1:00–5:00
(Kansas and Saline County history collection
   includes vertical files on Saline County
   people and subjects, Saline County
   newspapers, Kansas census)

Scandia Museum
(Main Street—location)
PO Box 153 (mailing address)
Scandia, KS 66966
(785) 335-2339 (Larson); (785) 335-2506
   (Loring)
Thelma Larson; Gwen Loring
Sept–May: 2:00–4:00, and by appointment
("The museum contains items from the
   Homesteaders as well as many other
   displays and genealogy.")

Seneca Free Library
606 Main Street
Seneca, KS 66538-1930
(785) 336-2377; (785) 336-3699 FAX
Karen Holthaus, Library Director
Mon–Thur 10:00–8:00, Fri 10:00–5:00, Sat
   10:00–2:00

Smoky Hill Museum
(211 West Iron Avenue—location)
PO Box 101 (mailing address)
Salina, KS 67402-0101
(785) 309-5776
museum@salina.org
http://www.smokyhillmuseum.org
Tom Pfannenstiel, Director
Tue–Fri noon–5:00, Sat 10:00–5:00, Sun
   1:00–5:00
Pub. *Heritage Express*, bimonthly, free

Southeast Kansas Library System
(see Iola Public Library, above)

Stevens County Gas and Historical
Museum
PO Box 87
Hugoton, KS 67951
(620) 544-8751

Thomas County Museum
75 West Fourth Street
Colby, KS 67701
(785) 462-6301

Tonganoxie Public Library
(303 Bury Street—location)
Box 890 (mailing address)
Tonganoxie, KS 66086-0890
(913) 845-3281; (913) 845-2962 FAX
director@tonganoxielibrary.org
http://www.tongie.org/Library/
   LibraryHome.htm
Winifred Turner, Librarian
Mon & Fri 9:00–noon & 1:00–5:00, Wed
   9:00–noon & 2:00–7:00, Sat 9:00–1:00

Topeka and Shawnee County Public
Library
1515 S.W. 10th Avenue
Topeka, KS 66604-1304
(785) 580-4400; (785) 233-2040; (913) 233-
   2055 FAX; (785) 580-4496 FAX
dleamon@tscpl.lib.ks.us
http://www.tcspl.org/index.html
David Leamon, Director; Warren E. Taylor
Mon–Fri 9:00–9:00, Sat 9:00–6:00, Sun
   (during school year) 2:00–6:00

University of Kansas
Kansas Heritage Center for Family and Local
   History
Kansas Data and Links
Lawrence, KS 66045-2800
http://history.cc.ukans.edu/hertiage/
   heritage_main.html

University of Kansas
Thomas R. Smith Map Collection and
   GeoMedia Services
103 Anschutz Library
1301 Hoch Auditoria Drive
Lawrence, KS 66045-7537
(785) 864-4420; (785) 864-5705 FAX
http://www.ku.edu/~anschutz
Mon–Fri 9:00–5:00 (somewhat longer during
   the semester, but call first)

University of Kansas
Kansas Collection
Spencer Research Library, Room 220
Lawrence, KS 66045-2800
(785) 864-4274; (913) 864-3855 FAX
husker@sky.net
http://www.ukans.edu/carrie/kancoll
Pub. *Voices* (online magazine)

Washburn University of Topeka
Mabee Library
1700 College
Topeka, KS 66621
(785) 231-1179; (785) 357-1240 FAX
Wilma Rife, Library Director
by appointment
(college archives)

Wichita Public Library
223 South Main Street
Wichita, KS 67202-3795
(316) 261-8509; (316) 261-8500; (316) 262-
   4540 FAX
ref-glh@wichita.lib.ks.us
http://www.wichita.lib.ks.us
Mon–Thur 10:00–9:00, Fri–Sat 10:00–5:30,
   Sun 1:00–5:00
(U.S. genealogy and Kansas history;
   affiliated with the Wichita Genealogical
   Society, a support group to the library)
obituary and other lookups for a fee (but no
   census research), send SASE Attn. Mail
   research

Wichita/Sedgwick County Historical
Museum Association
204 South Main Street
Wichita, KS 67202
(316) 265-9314
Robert A. Puckett, Director
Pub. *Heritage*
(local history archives)
$10.00 per year membership

Wichita State University
Ablah Library
Special Collections
Wichita, KS 67260
http://www.twsu.edu/library/
   specialcollections/sc.html

Young Historical Library
2770 Avenue I
Little River, KS 67457
(620) 897-6236; (620) 897-6757

Historical Societies—Local and Regional

Albany Historical Society
415 Grant
Sabetha, KS 66534
(785) 284-3323
Marvin Moore, Treasurer
Memorial Day–Labor Day: Sat–Sun
   1:00–4:00, and by appointment
(local history)

Allen County Historical Society
207 North Jefferson
Iola, KS 66749
(620) 365-3051
Betsy C. Pyle, Curator/Director
Pub. *Gaslight*
$10.00 per year membership

American West Research Center and
Historical Society, Inc.
(see Ohio, Part 2)

Anderson County Historical Society
(Sixth and Maple—location)
13538 West First Street (mailing address)
Garnett, KS 66032-2830
(785) 448-5962; (785) 448-5881
Ona Mae Hunt, President
Tue–Sat 1:00–4:00
Pub. *Anderson County Historical Society*
$5.00 per year membership

Argonia and West Sumner County
Historical Society and Museum
221 West Garfield
Argonia, KS 67004
(620) 435-6733

Arkansas City Historical Society
1400 North Third
Arkansas City, KS 67005
(620) 442-0333

Arkansas River Historical Society
Museum
(see Oklahoma, Part 2)

Atchison County Historical Society
(200 South 10th Street—location)
PO Box 201 (mailing address)
Atchison, KS 66002
(913) 367-6238
GoWest@atchisonhistory.org
http://atchisonhistory.org
Chris Taylor, Executive Director
Mon–Fri 8:00–5:00, Sat 10:00–4:00, Sun
   noon–4:00, and by appointment

Pub. *Go West*, bimonthly
("Lewis & Clark, weapons collection, railroads")
$15.00 per year membership; museum admission: donation

Barton County Historical Society
(85 South Highway 281—location)
PO Box 1091 (mailing address)
Great Bend, KS 67530
(620) 793-5125; (620) 792-2204
http://homepage.midusa.net/~shorock/
 bchs.htm

Baxter Springs Historical Society
(Eighth and East Avenue—location)
Route 2, Box 314 (mailing address)
Baxter Springs, KS 66713
(620) 856-9860

Black Jack Historical Society
163 East 2000 Road
Wellsville, KS 66092
(785) 883-2584

Historic Preservation Association of Bourbon County, Inc.
117 South Main
Fort Scott, KS 66701
(620) 223-5443
Pub. *HPA Happenings* (primarily historical, not genealogical)

Brown County Historical Society
(Agricultural Museum, 302 East Iowa—second museum location)
Headquarters, 611 Utah Street
Hiawatha, KS 66434
(785) 742-3330 (Museum)
Donna Thonen
June–Oct: Mon–Fri 10:00–3:30, and by appointment
Pub. *Brown County Historical Society Newsletter*, quarterly
$10.00 per year membership; admission: $3.00 for nonmembers

Bunker Hill Historical Society
PO Box 112
Bunker Hill, KS 67626
(785) 483-3637

Burns Community Historical Society
Main Street
Burns, KS 66840
(620) 726-5528; (620) 732-5277

Butler County Historical Society
(383 East Central, home of the Kansas Oil Museum—location)
PO Box 696 (mailing address)
El Dorado, KS 67042
(316) 321-9333; (316) 321-3619
bchs@powwwer.net
http://www.skyways.org/museums/kom
Rebecca Matticks, Director
Mon–Sat 9:00–5:00, Sun (Apr–Oct) 1:00–5:00
Pub. *The Crown Block*, quarterly
("Kansas Oil history, Butler County. We now have the Rolla A. Clymer Research Facility.")
$10.00 per year membership

Butterfield Trail Association and Historical Society of Logan County, Kansas, Inc.
(315 Hilts—location)
PO Box 383 (mailing address)
Russell Springs, KS 67755-0383
(785) 751-4242
Joye Rogge, Curator

first Tue of May–first Tue of Sept: Tue–Sat 9:00–noon & 1:00–5:00, Sun 1:00–5:00
(a few family histories on file and some old photographs and school memorabilia, besides the usual pioneer artifacts)
$10.00 per year membership

Caney Valley Historical Society
(321 West Fourth—location)
PO Box 354 (mailing address)
Caney, KS 67333
(620) 879-5198; (620) 879-5131
Mrs. Darrel (Nancy) Roe
Mon & Fri 8:00–3:00, Tue–Thur 9:00–3:00
(local and S.E. Kansas)

Cedar Vale Historical Society
600 Cedar Street
Cedar Vale, KS 67024

Chase County Historical Society, Inc.
(301 Broadway—location)
PO Box 375 (mailing address)
Cottonwood Falls, KS 66845
(620) 273-8500
Patty J. Donelson, Curator
Tue–Sat 1:00–5:00
(published *Sketches*, $30.00 plus postage and handling")
$25.00 life membership; research and copy fees subject to change

Chautauqua County, Kansas Historical and Genealogical Society
(603 West Main—location)
PO Box 227 (mailing address)
Sedan, KS 67361-0227
(620) 725-3408 (President); (620) 725-3101 (Vice President)
millerv@kans.com
http://skyways.lib.ks.us/genweb/
 chautauq/cchgs.html
Vera Miller, President; Del Huggins, Vice President
meetings: first Tue 6:30

Cherokee County Kansas Genealogical-Historical Society, Inc.
(see Genealogical Societies—Local and Regional, below)

Cheyenne County Historical Society
Cheyenne County Museum
PO Box 611
Saint Francis, KS 67756
(785) 332-2504
Marilyn Holzwarth
Mon–Fri 1:00–4:00
Pub. *Newsletter*
("Cheyenne County family genealogy")
$2.00 per year membership

Clark County Historical Society
d.b.a. Pioneer-Krier Museum
(430 West Fourth Street, Highway 160 West—location)
PO Box 862 (mailing address)
Ashland, KS 67831-0862
(620) 635-2227
pioneer@ucom.net
http://www.artcom.com/museums/nv/mr/
 67831-08.htm
Floretta Rogers, Curator
Mon–Sat 10:00–noon & 1:00–5:00, Sun 1:00–5:00
$10.00 life membership; research: $10.00 plus copies

Clay County Historical Society Museum
2121 Seventh Street
Clay Center, KS 67432-1509
Cathy Haney, Curator

Tue–Sat 10:00–5:00, Sun (Apr–Oct) 2:00–4:00
Pub. *News Letter*, quarterly
(has some naturalization records from 1869, marriages from 1867, court records from 1889)
$10.00 per year membership

Clearwater Historical Society/Museum
(149 North Fourth—location)
PO Box 453 (mailing address)
Clearwater, KS 67026
(620) 584-2444; (620) 584-2323
recreate@sktc.net
http://www.clearwaterhistoricalsociety.com
Jacke Eckel, Director
Museum: Sun 1:00–4:00, except holiday weekends, and by appointment
(We have started a reference area in our museum and have obituaries, birth announcements, wedding/engagement announcements, . . . books on local families, all the local papers from 1886 to 1840s on microfilm, . . . family file folders, . . . the assessment microfilm rolls from Sedgwick County, KS, from 1879-98, . . . some neighboring Viola, KS, newspapers, . . . gazetteers, . . . cemetery burial location records, old burial books maintained by the city.")
admission: donation; research: donation and requests that correspondents "send us their family histories (even incomplete ones) and continue to add information as they find it"

Clifton Historical Society
(108 Clifton Street—location)
Box 205 (mailing address)
Clifton, KS 66937
Alvin Vessart, President
Sun 2:00–4:00, and by appointment
Pub. *Courier*, four times per year
$5.00 per year membership

Clinton Lake Historical Society, Inc.
Route 2, Box 99
Overbrook, KS 66524
(785) 748-9836
Martha J. Parker, Director

Cloud County Historical Society and Museum
635 Broadway
Concordia, KS 66901
(785) 243-2866
Brad Chapin, Curator
Tue–Sat 1:00–5:00
Pub. *Cloud Comments*, quarterly
$5.00 per year membership

Coffey County Historical Society and Museum
1101 Neosho
Burlington, KS 66839
(620) 364-2653; (888) 877-2653; (620) 364-8933 FAX
artifacts@kans.com
http://www.coffeycountymuseum.org
Deborah Kennamore, Director
Mon–Fri 10:00–5:00, Sat–Sun 1:00–4:00
Pub. *Dob's and Data*
research: $6.00 per hour

Coffeyville Historical Society, Inc.
(113 East Eighth—location)
PO Box 843 (mailing address)
Coffeyville, KS 67337
(620) 251-0550
Gary Misch, President

Comanche County Historical Society, Inc.

(410 South Baltimore—location)
PO Box 177 (mailing address)
Coldwater, KS 67029
(620) 582-2679

Cowley County Historical Society
1011 Mansfield Street
Winfield, KS 67156
(620) 221-4811
Bruce Hedvick, Director
Tue 9:00–11:00, Sat–Sun 2:00–5:00, and by
    appointment
("We are a pioneer museum housing articles,
    items used, and documents for the period
    from approximately 1869 to the present
    showing the history of the development of
    this county.")
$10.00 per year membership; research:
    donation

**Crawford County Historical Society and
Museum**
651 South 69 Highway
Pittsburg, KS 66762
(620) 231-1440
Wed–Sun
Pub. *Pioneer Times*

Dickinson County Historical Society
Heritage Center of Dickinson County
412 South Campbell Street
Abilene, KS 67410-2905
(785) 263-2681; (785) 263-0380 FAX
heritagecenter@access-one.com
http://heritagecenterdk.com
Jeff Sheets, Director
Mon–Fri 9:00–4:00
Pub. *The Gazette*, quarterly
$15.00 per year membership; research:
    $15.00 general, $10.00 per hour in depth

Doniphan County Historical Society
PO Box 220
Troy, KS 66087-0220
(785) 985-2597

Douglas County Historical Society
Watkins Community Museum of History
1047 Massachusetts Avenue
Lawrence, KS 66046-0664
(785) 841-4109; (785) 842-9547
wcmhist@sunflower.com
http://www.dchsks.org
Steven Jansen, Ph.D., Historian
Tue–Sat 10:00–4:00, Sun 1:30–4:00;
    Research facilities: Tue–Sat 10:00–4:00
Pub. *Douglas County Historical Society
    Newsletter*, bimonthly
(Douglas County genealogical research and
    Quantrill's Raid research material)
$10.00 per year membership; research:
    $10.00 minimum if search is successful,
    $5.00 minimum if search is unsuccessful

Historical Society of Downs
416 South Morgan Avenue
Downs, KS 67437-2017
$5.00 per year membership; research: $7.00
    per hour

Edwards County Historical Society
Highway 56
Kinsley, KS 67547
(620) 659-2420

Elk County Historical Society
PO Box 1033
Howard, KS 67349
(620) 374-2266

Ellinwood Community Historical Society
PO Box 111

Ellinwood, KS 67526

Ellis County Historical Society
100 West Seventh Street
Hays, KS 67601-4429
(785) 628-2624
http://www.elliscountyhistoricalmuseum.org
Carla Barber, Executive Director
Tue–Fri (mid-May to mid-Sept) 10:00–5:00,
    Tue–Fri (mid-Sept to mid-May)
    10:00–3:00, Sat (mid-May to mid-Sept)
    1:00–5:00
Pub. *Homesteader*, quarterly
("Several local photographers' collections;
    Volga-German and Bukovina Germans.")
$15.00 per year membership

Ellsworth County Historical Society
PO Box 144
Ellsworth, KS 67439-0144
(785) 472-3059
Tue–Sat 9:00–noon & 1:00–5:00, Sun (1
    May–1 Oct) 1:00–5:00
Pub. *Sharing History*, quarterly
$7.50 per year membership; research: $5.00
    donation and SASE

Eudora Area Historical Society
Eudora Public Library
PO Box 370
Eudora, KS 66025
(785) 542-2496; (785) 542-2298
six days a week
Pub. *Eudora Area Newsletter*

Everest Community Historical Society
Seventh and Chestnut Streets
Everest, KS 66424
(785) 548-7792
Dorothy Selland, Treasurer
by appointment
(a small group of volunteers, running a small
    community museum in a small town)

Finney County Historical Society
(Finney County Historical Museum, 403
    South Fourth Street—location)
PO Box 796 (mailing address)
Garden City, KS 67846-0796
(620) 272-3664
http://www.finneycounty.org/books.asp
Mary Regan Wildeman, Executive Director
winter: 1:00–5:00; summer: 10:00–5:00, Sun
    1:00–5:00
Pub. *The Sequoyan*, quarterly
$10.00 per year membership

Florence Historical Society
(221 Marion—location)
408 West Seventh Street (mailing address)
Florence, KS 66851
(620) 878-4296
Pub. *Florence*, quarterly

Ford County Historical Society, Inc.
(112 East Vine—location)
PO Box 131 (mailing address)
Dodge City, KS 67801
(620) 227-6791; (620) 227-3400
Charles Wycoff, President
Mon–Sat 9:00–5:00, Sun (June–Aug)
    2:00–5:00
$6.00 per year membership

Fort Larned Historical Society, Inc.
Santa Fe Trail Center
Rural Route 3
Larned, KS 67550
(620) 285-2054; (620) 285-7491 FAX
trailctr@larned.net
http://www.awav.net/trailctr
Betsy Crawford-Gore, Curator

Mon–Sun 9:00–5:00, closed Mon Labor Day
    to Memorial Day
Pub. *Trail Ruts*
(Larned and Pawnee County, Kansas,
    history; Civil War records; complete set
    of *War of the Rebellion*, Pawnee County
    records; research library.)
admission: $4.00 for nonmember adults

Franklin County Historical Society, Inc.
(Franklin County Courthouse—location)
PO Box 145 (mailing address)
Ottawa, KS 66067-0145
(785) 242-1232
history@ott.net
http://www.nkans.edu/~hisite/franklin/fchs
by appointment only

**Geary County Historical Society
(Museum)**
(530 North Adams Street—location)
PO Box 1161 (mailing address)
Junction City, KS 66441-1161
(785) 238-1666
Marilyn Heldstab, Director
Tue–Sun 1:00–4:00
Pub. *Geary Glimmers*, bimonthly
("Preserving Geary (Davis) County and
    Junction City history; docent tours on
    request, research room, museum displays.
    Research done by Family Researchers,
    'friends' group of the society.")
$15.00 per year membership; research: $5.00
    minimum donation plus plus copies at 10¢
    per page

Gove County Historical Association
Gove, KS 67736

Graham County Historical Society
414 North West Street
Hill City, KS 67642
(785) 674-5601

Grant County Historical Society, Inc.
Grant County Museum
(300 East Oklahoma Avenue—location)
PO Box 906 (mailing address)
Ulysses, KS 67880-0906
(620) 356-3009
Ginger Anthony, Director
Tue–Fri 10:00–5:00, Sat–Sun 1:00–5:00
(county history, early county records)

Greeley County Historical Society
(Horace Greeley Museum, 214 East
Harper—location)
PO Box 231 (mailing address)
Tribune, KS 67879-0231
(620) 376-4996
http://www.lasr.net/leisure/kansas/
    greeley/tribune/att1.html
Nadine Cheney, Curator
10:00–4:00 by appointment
(census, newspaper, homestead, school,
    county school, cemetery records)
$6.00 per year membership; admission:
    donation

Greenwood County Historical Society, Inc.
120 West Fourth
Eureka, KS 67045-1445
(620) 583-6682
drwaff@mail.aros.net
http://skyways.lib.ks.us/kansas/genweb/
    greenwoo/gchs.htm
Helen Bradford; Jeff Hoakanson
Mon–Sat 9:00–noon & 1:00–4:00
Pub. *News Letter*, semiannually (June, Dec)
(family histories; best source for Greenwood
    County information)
$5.00 per year membership; research:

donation

Halstead Historical Society
(116 East First—location)
PO Box 88 (mailing address)
Halstead, KS 67056
(316) 835-2267
http://www.halsteadkansas.com/
historical.html
Sat–Sun 2:00–5:00 and by appointment;
meetings: third Tue
$10.00 per year membership; admission:
donation

Harper City Historical Society
Harper Public Library
1002 Oak
Harper, KS 67058-1233
(620) 896-2959 (Library)

Harvey County Historical Society
(203 Main Street—location)
PO Box 4 (mailing address)
Newton, KS 67114
(316) 283-2221 voice & FAX
archivist@hchm.org
http://www.hchm.org
Jane Jones, Archivist; Roger Wilson,
Director
Wed–Sun 1:00–4:00, except holiday
weekends
Pub. *Historical Notes*, bimonthly
(Harvey County history: tax records, census,
marriage licenses (1872–1913), county
population books (1911–1979), county
newspapers through 1930, Newton City
directories; Santa Fe Railroad collection
and memorabilia as pertains to Newton,
once a rail hub for SFRR)
$15.00 per year membership; research:
$10.00 for the first hour, $5.00 for each
additional hour, plus copy costs

The Haskell County Historical Society and Museum
(North side of Haskell County
Fairgrounds—location)
PO Box 101 (mailing address)
Sublette, KS 67877
(620) 675-8344
Janice McClure, Curator
Wed–Sun 1:00–5:00
(local history of Haskell County)
$5.00 per year membership; no research
services but visitors welcome

High Plains Historical Association
Northwest Kansas Heritage Center
(401 Kansas—location)
PO Box 284 (mailing address)
Brewster, KS 67732-0284
(785) 694-2891; (785) 694-2401
Betty Wolfe, Director
Mon–Wed 1:00–4:00, Sat 9:00–11:00

Hillsboro Historical Society and Museum
501 South Ash Street
Hillsboro, KS 67063
(620) 947-3775
David F. Wiebe, Director
Mar–Dec: daily
(Dutch/German research center)

Hodgeman County Historical Society
PO Box 128
Jetmore, KS 67854
(620) 357-8794
http://skyways.lib.ks.us/towns/Jetmore/
museum.html
Charles W. Guthrie, President; Mary Ford,
Secretary
Fri & Sun 1:00–5:00, Sat 11:00–5:00

Humboldt Historical Society
Po Box 63
Humboldt, KS 66748
(620) 473-2886

Inman Heritage Association
PO Box 217
Inman, KS 67546
(620) 585-6748

Jackson County Historical Society
(327 New York—museum location)
216 New York Avenue (mailing address)
Holton, KS 66436
(785) 364-2087; (785) 364-4991
alwilhelm@holtonks.net; jchs@holtonks.net
http://www.holtonks.net/jchs
Anna Wilhelm, Tour Director
Fri–Sat 10:00–4:00, Sun
(Apr–Dec)2:00–4:00; tours by
appointment
Pub. *Jackson County Historical Society
Newsletter*, quarterly
("We maintain historical and genealogical
materials related to Jackson County.")
$15.00 per year membership

Jefferson County Historical Society
(Old Jefferson Town, Highway 59—location)
PO Box 146 (mailing address)
Oskaloosa, KS 66066
(785) 863-2070
May–Sept: Sat 1:00–5:00, Sun 1:30–5:00
Pub. *Yesteryears*, semiannually (Apr, Oct)
$10.00 per year membership

Jewell County Historical Society
201 North Commercial Street
Mankato, KS 66956-2005
(785) 378-3692
http://skyways.lib.ks.us/towns/Mankato/
museum.html
Museum: Thur–Sat (15 Apr–15 Oct)
1:00–5:00
admission: donation

Kansas State University Historical Society
1724 Fairchild Avenue
c/o History Department, Eisenhower Hall
Kansas State University
Manhattan, KS 66506
(785) 532-6730
Caroline Peine, President
(not genealogical: history of the University)

Kearny County Historical Society
(101-111 South Buffalo—location)
PO Box 329 (mailing address)
Lakin, KS 67860
(620) 355-7448
Patricia Heath, Museum Director
10¢ per page for copies

Lake Region Historical Society
Lake Region RCGD Area Office
121 East Second Street
Ottawa, KS 66067
(785) 242-2073
8:00–5:00
Pub. *Lake Region Historical Society
Association Newsletter*, quarterly

Lane County Historical Society
Lane County Historical Museum
(333 North Main Street—location)
PO Box 821 (mailing address)
Dighton, KS 67839
(620) 397-5652
Virginia Johnston, Director
Tue–Sat 1:00–5:00, Sun (Memorial
Day–Labor Day) 2:00–5:00
Pub. *Friends of the Museum*, quarterly

("newspapers from 1880 to the present,
census, cemetery books, some marriage
licenses, county history books and family
histories; working on book of obituaries
for the county")
$10.00 per year membership; research:
$10.00 per hour plus 15¢ per page for
copies

Lanesfield School Historical Society
Route 1
Edgerton, KS 66021
(913) 882-6645

Lansing Area Historical Society
115 East Kansas Avenue
Lansing, KS 66043
(913) 727-3731

Leavenworth County Historical Society and Museum
1128 Fifth Avenue
Leavenworth, KS 66048-3213
(913) 682-7759; (913) 682-2089 FAX
http://leavenworth-net.com/lchs
Robert A. Holt, Museum Administrator
Sept–Apr: Mon–Sun 1:00–4:30; May–Aug:
Mon–Sat 10:30–4:30, Sun 1:00–4:30 and
by appointment
Pub. *Historical Society Gazette*, quarterly
$10.00 per year membership; research:
$10.00 per hour, limit of two hours

Lecompton Historical Society
(609 Woodson—location)
393 North 1900 Road (mailing address)
Lecompton, KS 66050
(785) 887-6148 voice & FAX
lanemuseum@aol.com
http://www.LecomptonKansas.com
Paul M. Bahnmaier, President
Wed–Sat 11:00–4:00, Sun 1:00–5:00
Pub. *Bald Eagle*, quarterly
("Museum contains artifacts from the
Territorial Period through Lane University
to 2003.")
$6.00 per year membership

Lenexa Historical Society
14907 West 87th Street Parkway
Lenexa, KS 66215-4135
(913) 492-0038

Lincoln County Historical Society
(214 West Lincoln Avenue—location)
PO Box 85 (mailing address)
Lincoln, KS 67455
(785) 524-4614
Ruby Ahring, President
Sun (30 May–1 Sept) P.M., and by
appointment
Pub. *Newsletter*, annually
$5.00 per year membership; research: $5.00

Linn County Historical and Genealogical Society
Linn County Museum
History/Genealogy Library
Dunlap Park
PO Box 137
Pleasanton, KS 66075-0137
(913) 352-8739 voice & FAX
Ola May Earnest, President
winter: Tue & Thur 9:00–5:00, Sat–Sun
1:00–5:00; summer: Tue–Thur 9:00–5:00,
Fri–Sun 1:00–5:00
Pub. *Linn County Historical Society
Newsletter*, quarterly
(holdings include state and federal census
records, mortality schedules, all Linn
County newspapers from 1864, funeral
records from 1910, cemetery records,

The Genealogist's Address Book

military records, vital statistics, D.A.R.
lineage books, index to probate court
records)
$5.00 per year membership in Historical
Society, $5.00 per year membership in
Genealogical Society

Luray Historical Society/Library
(505 North Fairview Avenue—location)
PO Box 216 (mailing address)
Luray, KS 67649
(785) 698-2371

Lyon County Historical Society
Lyon County Historical Museum
118 East Sixth Avenue
Emporia, KS 66801
(620) 342-0933
http://www.emporia.edu/S/www/slim/
resource/lchs/lyonco.htm
Carol Miguelino, M.L.S., Librarian/Archivist
Tue–Sat 9:30–5:00, call for appointment on
weekends
Pub. *Lyon County Lines*, quarterly
$10.00 per year membership

Marquette Historical Society, Inc.
202 North Washington
Marquette, KS 67464
(785) 546-2252; (785) 546-2205

Marshall County Historical Society
1207 Broadway
Marysville, KS 66508
(785) 562-5012
Barbara Fenstermacher, Librarian
Mon–Fri 1:00–4:00
Pub. *Magpie*, quarterly
(specializes in Marshall County genealogy;
library received the research material of
the former Blue Vallen Genealogical
Society)
$5.00 per year membership; admission: free;
research: usually $5.00 plus copies

McPherson County Historical Society, Inc.
540 East Hill Street
McPherson, KS 67460-3527
(620) 241-2699
Mr. Linn Peterson, President
$10.00 and $25.00 per year membership

Meade County Historical Society
(200 East Carthage—location)
PO Box 893 (mailing address)
Meade, KS 67864
(620) 873-2359

Medicine Lodge Historical Society
Highway 160
Medicine Lodge, KS 67104
(620) 886-3417

**Miami County Genealogy and Historical
Societies**
(see Genealogical Societies—Local and
Regional, below)

**Midwest Historical and Genealogical
Society**
(1203 North Main—location)
PO Box 1121 (mailing address)
Wichita, KS 67201-1121
(316) 264-3611
mhgs1203@hotmail.com
http://skyways.lib.ks.us/genweb/mhgs/
index.html
Donna Woods, Librarian
Tue & Sat 9:00–4:00, Thur (during Daylight
Savings Time) 4:30–8:00
Pub. *Midwest Historical and Genealogical
Register*, quarterly

("The Midwest Historical and Genealogical
Library is the largest society-owned
library in the state. MHGS holdings
include over 21,000 volumes and issues of
books, magazines, manuscripts,
collections, and CD-ROMS. These are
varied and include many items of genuine
interest to the beginning genealogist as
well as those farther along in their
research.")
$20.00 per year membership; library
admission: $4.00 per half day for
nonmembers; in-house staff research:
$5.00 per hour; outside staff research:
$10.00 per hour

Milan Historical Association
(Monroe and Market Streets—location)
PO Box 144 (mailing address)
Milan, KS 67105
(620) 435-6423; (620) 435-6632

**Mitchell County Historical
Society/Museum**
(402 West Eighth Street—location)
PO Box 472 (mailing address)
Beloit, KS 67420-0472
(785) 738-5355
http://members.nckcn.com/mchs
Marla Evert, Curator
Tue–Wed & Fri 1:00–4:00, Sat 1:30–5:00,
Sun by appointment
Pub. *Mitchell County Historical Society
Newsletter*, monthly
("We are very strong in the research for this
area.")
$15.00 per year membership; research:
donation

Morris County Historical Society
Council Grove Library
303 West Main Street
Council, KS 66846
(602) 767-5716 (Library)

Morton County Historical Society
(U.S. Highway 56—location)
PO Box 1248 (mailing address)
Elkhart, KS 67950
(620) 345-8420

Moundridge Historical Association
PO Box 69
Moundridge, KS 67107
(620) 345-8420

Mulvane Historical Society
(Mulvane Historical Museum, 300-West
Main—location)
PO Box 117 (mailing address)
Mulvane, KS 67110
(316) 777-0506 (Museum)
Vicki D. Lee, Receptionist
Tue–Sat 10:00–4:00
Pub. *Mulvane Historical Society News*,
semiannually
(Sumner County, Kansas)
$5.00 per year membership

Nemaha County Historical Society, Inc.
113 North Sixth Street
Seneca, KS 66538
(785) 336-3645 (Editor); (785) 336-3160
(President)
http://www.ukans.edu/kansas/seneca/
histsoc/nemcohis.html
Marcia Philbrick, Editor; Lillian Engelken,
President
Museum: Memorial Day weekend–Labor
Day weekend: Mon–Fri afternoons, Sat by
appointment
Pub. *Pioneer Press*, quarterly

(museum located in sheriff's home/county
jail)
$5.00 per year membership

Ness County Historical Society
Ness County Historical Museum
123 South Pennsylvania Avenue
Ness City, KS 67560-1907
(785) 798-3298
ncmuseum@gbta.net
http://skyways.lib.ks.us/towns/NessCity/
museum.html
Margery Frusher, President
Tue–Fri 10:00–11:00 & 1:00–5:00, and by
appointment
(Ness County history and genealogical
information)
$25.00 life membership

Nicodemus Historical Society
PO Box 131
Bogue, KS 67625
(785) 674-3311

**Norman #1 Oil Well and Museum
Historical Society**
109 Mill
Neodesha, KS 66757
(620) 325-5316
Nancy J. Wilson, President

**Northwest Kansas Genealogical and
Historical Society**
(see Genealogical Societies—Local and
Regional, below)

Norton County Historical Society
(105 East Lincoln Street—location)
PO Box 303 (mailing address)
Norton, KS 67654
(785) 877-2475
Kevin M. Bailey, Director
1 May–30 Sept: Wed & Sat 2:00–4:00
Pub. *Annual Newsletter* (irregular
publication date)
$3.00 per year membership

Olathe Historical Society
12466 Twilight
Olathe, KS 66062
(913) 782-5918

Onaga Historical Society
310 East Second Street
Onaga, KS 66521
(785) 889-4457
Marjorie Labbe, President
by appointment

**Osage County Historical Society Museum
and Research Center**
(631 Topeka Avenue—location)
PO Box 361 (mailing address)
Lyndon, KS 66451-0361
(785) 828-3477; (785) 528-4960
research@kanza.net; marhaw@kansas.net
http://www.osagechs.org
Margaret Hawley, President
Wed–Sat (Apr–Oct) 1:00–5:00
Pub. *Hedge Post*, quarterly
$10.00 per year membership

**Osage Mission/Neosho County Historical
Society**
PO Box 113
Saint Paul, KS 66771

Osawatomie Historical Society
420 16th Street
Osawatomie, KS 66064
(913) 755-4330 (Fisher Law Office)
Richard Fisher, President

Mon–Fri 9:00–5:00
Pub. *Osawatomie and Its People*, biannually,
$6.00 postpaid per issue
("Most of our records are at the Osawatomie
Public Library, 527 Brown Street, as well
as county cemetery listings, mortuary
listings, and other county and state
records, including local newspaper
microfilm, census records—state and
federal for Miami County.")
$5.00 per year membership

**Osborne County Genealogical and
Historical Society**
(see Genealogical Societies—Local and
Regional, below)

Parsons Historical Society
401 South Corning
Parsons, KS 67357
(620) 421-3382

The Peabody Historical Society
Rural Route 2
Peabody, KS 66866
(620) 983-2815 (President); (620) 983-2174
(City Hall)
Marilyn Jones, President
Thur–Sun (June–Aug) 1:00–4:00, and by
appointment
Pub. *The Peabody Historical Society
Newsletter*, semiannually
$10.00 per year membership

**Phillips County Historical Society at Fort
Bissell**
(at the west edge of Phillipsburg—location)
Route 2, Box 18A (mailing address)
Phillipsburg, KS 67661
darrum@phillipsburg.net
Darlene Rumbaugh, Acting President
May–Sept: 11:00–noon & 1:00–6:00

Pratt County Historical Society
208 South Ninnescah
Pratt, KS 67124
Dorothy Giannangelo, Office Manager
Mon–Sun 2:00–4:00, and by appointment
Pub. *P.C.H.S. Newsletter*, bimonthly
(genealogical information on settlers in Pratt
County)

Rawlins County Historical Society
308 State Street
Atwood, KS 67730
(785) 626-3885

**Frederic Remington Area Historical
Society**
Frederic Remington High School
PO Box 133
Whitewater, KS 67154
(316) 799-2470
Theodore J. Regier, President
Sept–May (during school year)
("We are a historical society that collects
local history.")
$5.00 per year membership

Reno County Historical Society
(100 South Walnut Street—location)
PO Box 664 (mailing address)
Hutchinson, KS 67504-0664
(620) 662-1184; (620) 662-0236 FAX
Barbara Ulrich-Hicks, Curator of Collections
Tue–Sat 9:00–5:00, Sun 1:00–5:00
Pub. *Legacy: The Journal of the Reno
County Historical Society*, quarterly,
$5.00 per year subscription

Republic County Historical Society
(Republic County Historical Museum, West

U.S. Highway 36, East of Junction U.S. 36
and U.S. 81—location)
PO Box 218 (mailing address)
Belleville, KS 66935-0218
(785) 527-5971
repcomuse@nckcn.com;
lpwalter@nckcn.com
http://www.nckcn.com/repco/repmus.htm
Patricia Walter, Curator/Director
Mon–Fri 1:00–5:00, Sun 1:30–4:30
Pub. *Illumination*, bimonthly
(Republic County cemetery grave marker
list)
$5.00 per year membership; research:
donation ("When anyone wishes us to do
a search, they would need to contact us.
Because our hours are limited and we
have other tasks to do, it sometimes takes
a little longer to get the research
accomplished"); free queries for members

Rice County Historical Society, Inc.
Coronado-Quivira Museum
105 West Lyon Street
Lyons, KS 67554-2703
(620) 257-3941
Janel Cook, Museum Director
Mon–Fri 9:00–5:00, Sun 1:00–5:00
(archive resources)
$10.00 per year membership; research: $6.00
per hour plus copies at 25¢ each

**Riley County Historical Society and
Museum**
(Goodnow House Museum and Historical
Site, 2301 Claflin—location)
2309 Claflin Road (mailing address)
Manhattan, KS 66502-3421
(785) 565-6490 (Museum)
D. Cheryl Collins, Director/Curator
Museum: Tue–Fri 8:30–5:00, Sat–Sun
2:00–5:00; Library: by appointment
Pub. *RCHS Newsletter*, ten times per year
(Goodnow family related artifacts)
$5.00 to $125.00 per year membership; no
charge for library use; no charge for
museum tour

**Rock Creek Valley Historical Society and
Museum**
(Sixth and State Streets—location)
PO Box 13 (mailing address)
Westmoreland, KS 66549
(785) 457-3578
Rose Wahl
by appointment

Rooks County Historical Society
(921 South Cedar—location)
PO Box 43 (mailing address)
Stockton, KS 67669
(785) 425-7217; (785) 425-7396
Vinta Butler, Curator
Mon–Wed 9:00–4:00; meetings: third Sun
(Jan–Nov) 2:00–4:00
(genealogical services)
$5.00 per year membership

Rush County Historical Society, Inc.
(201 West First Street—location)
PO Box 473 (mailing address)
LaCrosse, KS 67548-0473
(785) 222-2719
Betty I. Janke, Secretary-Treasurer
("Rush County Historical Museum and Post
Rock Museum")
$5.00 per year membership

Russell County Historical Society
PO Box 245
Russell, KS 67665-0245
(785) 483-3637
rchs@russellks.net

http://www.rchs.rwisp.com
Jeff McCoy, President
Memorial Day weekend–Labor Day
weekend: 1:00–4:00, and by appointment

Saint Marys Historical Society
711 Elm
Saint Marys, KS 66536
(785) 437-6600
Joan J. Doyle; Rita Muckenthaler, President
Memorial Day–Labor Day: Tue–Sun
1:00–4:00

Santa Fe Trail Historical Society
(1314 Eighth Street—location)
PO Box 443 (mailing address)
Baldwin City, KS 66006
(785) 594-6595
John C. Doudna
Pub. *Santa Fe Trail Rider*, semiannually
$10.00 per year membership

Scott County Historical Society
PO Box 155
Scott City, KS 67871-0155
(620) 872-3708

Seward County Historical Society, Inc.
567 East Cedar
Liberal, KS 67901
(620) 624-7624

Shawnee County Historical Society
PO Box 2201
Topeka, KS 66601-2201
Dr. Bill Wagnon, Treasurer
Pub. *The Shawnee County Historical Society
Newsletter*; *Shawnee County Historical
Society Bulletin*, annually
$15.00 per year membership

Shawnee Historical Society, Inc.
Old Shawnee Town
(11501 West 57th Street—location)
PO Box 3042 (mailing address)
Shawnee Mission, KS 66203
(913) 268-8772

Sheridan County Historical Society, Inc.
(1224 Oak Avenue—location)
PO Box 274 (mailing address)
Hoxie, KS 67740-0274
(785) 675-3501
schs@ruraltel.net
Marilyn Carder, Office Director
Tue–Fri 8:30–noon & 1:30–4:00
Pub. *Newsletter*, annually
(births, marriages, deaths, homestead, school,
mortuary, etc.)
$10.00 per year membership; research:
$10.00 per hour

**Sherman County Historical and
Genealogical Society**
PO Box 684
Goodland, KS 67735-0684
(785) 899-5461
Clarence Scheopner, President Historical
Society
10:00–7:00
Pub. *Quarterly*
$5.00 per year membership

Smith County Historical Society
PO Box 247
Kensington, KS 66952-0247
(785) 476-3214

Smoky Valley Historical Association
Lindsborg Community Library
111 South Main
Lindsborg, KS 67456

(785) 227-2710 (Library)

Stafford County Historical and Genealogical Society
(100 South Main, corner of Main and Broadway—location)
PO Box 249 (mailing address)
Stafford, KS 67578-0249
(620) 234-5664
mjhathaway61@earthlink.net
http://home.earthlink.net/mjhathaway61
Michael Hathaway, Curator
Office: Mon–Fri 9:00–3:30; Museum: Tue–Thur 1:30–3:30, Sat 1:00–3:00; Library: by appointment
Pub. *Reflections*, two times per year
(excellent collection of family histories, obits, cemetery records, census, local history, family files)
$10.00 per year membership; research: $2.50 per look-up, $7.50 over 30 minutes, plus postage and copies at 10¢ per page

Stanton County Historical Society
Stanton County Museum
(104 East Highland—location)
PO Box 806 (mailing address)
Johnson, KS 67855
(620) 492-1526
Katie Herrick, Curator
Mon–Fri 9:00–5:00
("County records are at Museum and Registrar of Deeds at Stanton County Courthouse.")

Stevens County History Association
1601 South Monroe Street
Hugoton, KS 67951-3033
Pauline Peachey

Sumner County Historical and Genealogical Society
Box 402
Wellington, KS 67152-0402
(316) 777-1434
dellasha@juno.com; scgs67152@yahoo.com
http://www.rootsweb.com/~ksscgs
Della Shafer, Corresponding Secretary
Pub. *Heritage Harvester*
$10.00 per year membership

Sumner County Historical Society
PO Box 402
Mulvane, KS 67110
(316) 777-1434
Ruth Swan, President
meetings at Wellington Steakhouse, Wellington: fourth Mon (Jan–Apr & Aug–Nov) 6:30
(land patents, Sumner County story)
$2.00 per year membership; some research: donation

Tescott Historical Society
109 Sunset Lane
Tescott, KS 67484-9725
Arliene Berkley Matthews

Thomas County Historical Society
(1905 South Franklin Street—location)
PO Box 465 (mailing address)
Colby, KS 67701-0465
(785) 462-4590
Sue Ellen Taylor, Director
Tue–Fri 9:00–5:00, Sat–Sun 1:00–5:00, extended summer hours
Pub. *Prairie Winds*, quarterly
("We are a historical society but we do handle written or first person requests about our county; history of Thomas County, some assistance with surrounding counties.")

$10.00 per year membership; research: donation

Tonganoxie Community Historical Society
PO Box 785
Tonganoxie, KS 66086-0785
(913) 369-3007
glcooper20@earthlink.com
http://www.tongie.org/organizations.html
(Welcome to Tonganoxie page lists historical society)
George Cooper, President
Mon–Sat 8:00–5:00
("Our Historic Site started with a donation of a barn and milk house, on 6+ acres, part of the Fairchild-Knox dairy. We have added two other historic buildings: The Reno Methodist Church and the Honey Valley One-room Schoolhouse.")
$5.00 per year membership

Trading Post Historical Society
Trading Post Historical Museum
(U.S. 69 Highway, 96 milemarker 6 miles north of Pleasanton, KS—location)
Route 2, Box 145A (mailing address)
Trading Post, KS 66075-9479
(913) 352-6441
Alice Widner, Curator and Researcher
Tue–Sat 9:00–5:00, Sun 1:00–5:00
(specializes in Valley Township, Linn County, Kansas, history and other areas as well; many old records and access to county records)
research: $6.00 per hour, 25¢ per mile, plus copying costs

Trego County Historical Society
(Trego County Fairgrounds, Wakeeney, KS 67672—location)
614 Chase (mailing address)
Wakeeney, KS 67672-1713
(785) 743-2964
Nadine Kroeger, Curator
Tue & Fri 1:00–4:00, Sun 1:30–4:30; meetings fourth Sun 2:30

Tri-County Historical Society
800 South Broadway
Herington, KS 67449-3060
(785) 258-2842
trimusda@ikansas.com
Virginia Brunner, Director
10:00–noon & 1:15–4:00
Pub. *Tri-County Newsletter*, quarterly
$5.00 per year membership; research: $2.00–$5.00

Valley Center Historical and Cultural Society
(112 North Meridian—location)
PO Box 173 (mailing address)
Valley Center, KS 67147
(785) 755-0275
Blondie Roark, President
$5.00 per year membership

Valley Falls Historical Society
310 Broadway
Valley Falls, KS 66088
(913) 945-6698

Wabaunsee County Historical Society Museum
(227 Missouri—location)
PO Box 387 (mailing address)
Alma, KS 66401
(785) 765-2200
Rayonna Mock, Curator
Tue–Sat 10:00–4:00, Sun 1:00–4:00, closed holidays
Pub. *Wabaunsee County Historical Society*

Newsletter, semiannually (spring and fall)
("1928 Reo Firetruck, Indian Artifacts, Main St. U.S.A., Marine General Walt Display, Old Farm Implements.")
$10.00 per year membership; genealogy research: $5.00 donation

Wamego Historical Society
Old Dutch Mill Museum Complex
PO Box 84
Wamego, KS 66547
(785) 456-2040
Jan Nicklus
third weekend in Apr–Labor Day: Mon–Sat 9:30–3:30, Sun 12:30–3:30; Labor Day–31 Oct: Mon–Fri 1:00–4:00, Sat 10:00–4:00, Sun 1:00–4:00, and by appointment
Pub. *WHS Newsletter*

Washington County Historical and Genealogical Society
(208 Ballard—location)
PO Box 31 (mailing address)
Washington, KS 66968-0031
(785) 325-2198 (Historical Society)
Blaine Wells, Historical Society President

Wichita County Historical Society, Inc.
(201 North Fourth Street—location)
PO Box 1561 (mailing address)
Leoti, KS 67861
(620) 375-2316
museum@wichitacountymuseum.org; jrfrench@wbsnet.org
http://wichitacountymuseum.org
Jeanene French, Editor
Tue–Fri (winter) 1:00–5:00, Tue–Fri (summer) 10:00–5:00, Sat–Sun 2:00–5:00, and by appointment
Pub. *Quarterly*

Wilson County Historical Society and Genealogical Chapter
420 North Seventh Street
Fredonia, KS 66736-1315
(620) 378-3965
Jean Vorhees, President WCGS
weekdays 12:30–4:30
Pub. *Yesteryears*, three times per year
("We have a Wilson County obituary index from 1873 to the present time.")
$8.00 per year membership in Historical Society, $12.00 per year membership in Historical Society and WCGS; research: $10.00 per hour plus copies at 25¢ per page

Woodson County Historical Society/Library
(Route 1—location)
602 South Kalida Street (mailing address)
Yates Center, KS 66783
(620) 625-2929

Wyandotte County Historical Society and Museum
631 North 126th Street
Bonner Springs, KS 66012
(913) 721-1078; (913) 721-1394 FAX
http://www.kumc.edu/wcedc/museum/wcmuseum.html
Paul Goudy, Executive Director
Tue–Sat 10:00–5:00, Sun 1:00–5:00, closed third Sat in Dec until 2 Jan
Pub. *Newsletter*
$10.00 per year membership; admission: free

Genealogical Societies

State Genealogical Societies

Kansas Council of Genealogical Societies, Inc. (KCGS)
PO Box 3858
Topeka, KS 66604-6858
fulkerson@juno.com
http://skyways.lib.ks.us/genweb/kcgs/
index.html
Shirley Fulkerson O'Toole, Corresponding and Membership Secretary
Pub. *Kansas Review*, quarterly
(sponsors a state certificate program to honor the settlers of Kansas and the *Forgotten Settlers of Kansas* series: Territorial Certificate for direct descendants of ancestors who lived in Kansas prior to 29 January 1861, Pioneer Certificate for direct descendants of ancestors who lived in Kansas between 29 January 1861 and 31 December 1880, and Early Settler Certificate for direct descendants of ancestors who lived in Kansas between 1 January 1881 and 31 December 1900)
$15.00 per year membership

Kansas Genealogical Society, Inc.
(Village Square Mall, 2601 Central—location)
PO Box 103 (mailing address)
Dodge City, KS 67801-0103
(620) 225-1951
skmug1@pld.com (Webmistress)
http://www.dodgecity.net/kgs
Betty J. Herrman, Executive Director; Kris Ball, Webmistress)
Mon–Fri 1:30–5:00, first & third Sat 10:45–4:00
Pub. *The Treesearcher*, quarterly
$15.00 per year membership; rsearch: $10.00 in advance plus LSASE

Genealogical Societies—Local & Regional

Anderson County Genealogical Society
PO Box 194
Garnett, KS 66032-0194
(785) 448-6621
welda@grapevine.net
http://www.grapevine.net/~swguinn/acgs.html
Bertha Staadt; Bob Meliza
meetings at the Town Hall Center, Garnett: second Mon 7:00
$10.00 per year membership

Atchison County Kansas Genealogical Society (ACKGS)
(Atchison Public Library, 401 Kansas Avenue—location)
PO Box 303 (mailing address)
Atchison, KS 66002-0303
(913) 367-1902 (Library)
ackgs2@yahoo.com
http://skyways.lib.ks.us/genweb/society/atchison/ackgs.htm
Mae Stirton, Corresponding Secretary/Historian
meetings in the Kansas Room at the Library: first Tue 6:30
Pub. *The Atchison Connection*, quarterly
$10.00 per year membership

Blue Valley Genealogical Society
(see Marshall County Historical Society, Historical Societies—Local and Regional, above)

Branches and Twigs Genealogical Society
c/o Kingman Carnegie Library
455 North Main Street
Kingman, KS 67068-1395
(620) 532-3061 (Library)
Kingc1lb@websurf.net (Library);

ospec@terraworld.net
http://www.kingman.ks.net
Opal Specht, President; Letha Mitchell, Corresponding Secretary
meetings: first Wed (Sept–May)
(Kingman County marriage books, obituary index, many county publications, all Kingman newspapers on microfilm, most county papers)
$5.00 per year membership; research: donation

Brown County Genealogical Society
116 South Seventh street
Hiawatha, KS 66434-2307
bcgs@jbntelco.com

Chanute Genealogical Society
800 West 14th Street
Chanute, KS 66720-2699
(620) 431-1563
aolson@chanuteks.com
http://www.rootsweb.com/~kscgs
Dee Fouch, Corresponding Secretary; Ann Olson, President
meetings at NCCC Library, 800 West 14th Street, Chanute, KS 66720-2699: fourth Mon 7:00
("We have probate records 1860s to 1960s, newspaper obituary index from 1910, birth and death records 1892–1905, marriage index 1864–1915, cemetery index, Neosho County, 1864–1976")
$3.00 per year membership

Chautauqua County, Kansas Historical and Genealogical Society
(see Historical Societies—Local and Regional, above)

Cherokee County Kansas Genealogical-Historical Society, Inc.
(100 South Tennessee—location)
PO Box 33 (mailing address)
Columbus, KS 66725-0033
(620) 429-2992
cckghs@columbus-ks.com
http://skyways.lib.ks.us/genweb/cherokee/society/cckghs.html
Marilyn Schmitt
Mon–Sat 1:00–5:00
Pub. *Relatively Seeking*, two times per year
(Cherokee County history and genealogy)
$15.00 per year membership

Cloud County Genealogical Society
(Frank Carlson Library, 702 Broadway—location)
PO Box 202 (mailing address)
Concordia, KS 66901-0202
cloudgen@care2.com
http://www.dustdevil.com/ccgs.htm
meetings at the Cloud County Courthouse meeting room, Ninth and Washington: third Tue (winter, except Dec) 7:00, (summer) 7:30
Pub. *Cloud County (KS) Genealogical Society Newsletter*, quarterly
(Cloud County and French-Canadian settlements in eastern Cloud County)
$5.00 per year membership; research: $5.00 per hour plus copies and postage

Coffey County Genealogical Society
712 Sanders Street
Burlington, KS 66939-1157
(620) 364-8795

Cowley County Genealogical Society
1518 East 12th Street
Winfield, KS 67156-3923
(620) 221-4591

Clarie Utt, Secretary-Treasurer
Cherokee Strip Living Museum, Arkansas City: May–Sept: Tue–Sat 10:00–5:00, Sun 1:00–5:00; Oct–Apr: Tue–Sun 1:00–4:00
$11.00 per year membership; research: $6.00 per hour plus copying costs and postage

Decatur County Genealogy Society
Decatur County Museum
258 South Penn Avenue
Oberlin, KS 67749-2245
(785) 475-2712 (Museum)
mad_genealogist@yahoo.com
http://skyways.lib.ks.us/genweb/decatur/genealogy_society_files/genealogical_society.htm
Marie Berls, Secretary-Treasurer; Ardie Grimes, Webmaster
10:00–5:00; meetings: first Thur 7:00
Pub. *Ancestree Kinnection*, quarterly
("The society's library collection is located in the basement of the Last Indian Raid Museum, 132 South Penn, Oberlin, KS 67749.")
$10.00 per year membership

Douglas County, Kansas, Genealogical Society
PO Box 3664
Lawrence, KS 66044-0664
dwvwiv@earthlink.net
http://skyways.lib.ks.us/genweb/douglas/dckgs.htm
Mary Burchill, President; Donald and Wilma Vaughn, Home Page Coordinators
Lawrence Public Library: Mon–Fri 9:30–9:00, Sat 9:30–6:00, Sun 2:00–5:00
Pub. *The Pioneer*, quarterly
$15.00 per year membership; research: $10.00

Family Researchers
(see Geary County Historical Society [Museum], Historical Societies—Local and Regional, above)

Finney County Genealogical Society
(Finney County Public Library, Genealogy Room—location)
PO Box 592 (mailing address)
Garden City, KS 67846-0592
(620) 272-3680
Patricia D. Smith, Research Query Chairman
Mon–Thur 9:00–8:30, Fri–Sat 9:00–6:00, Sun 1:00–6:00
Pub. *FCGS Newsletter*, quarterly, $10.00 per year subscription
research: $10.00 per hour

Flint Hills Genealogical Society
PO Box 555
Emporia, KS 66801-0555
editor@lyoncountyks.org (for queries to be printed in publication);
lyoncoks@bigfoot.com (for a list of publications offered for sale)
http://www.lyoncountyks.org
meetings at Emporia Public Library: second Thur 7:00
Pub. *Letters, Links & Legends*, quarterly
(Lyon County; indexed newspapers, marriage licenses and cemeteries for Lyon County)
$10.00 per year membership; research: $10.00 per hour

Fort Hays Kansas Genealogical Society
Fort Hays State University
Forsyth Library, Room 122
600 Park Street
Hays, KS 67601-4099
(785) 628-5901 (Library)

pnichola@fhsu.edu
http://www.fhsu.edu/forsyth_lib/arch.shtml
Patty Nicholas
Library: Mon–Thur 7:30–midnight, Fri
7:30–7:00, Sat 9:00–4:30, Sun
1:00–midnight; Archives: Mon–Fri
(including Jan intermission) 8:00–4:30,
Mon–Thur (summer) 7:30–5:00, Fri
(summer) 7:30–11:30 A.M.
$5.00 per year membership

Franklin County Genealogy Society, Inc.
PO Box 353
Ottawa, KS 66067-0353
(785) 242-5383
fcgs@swbell.net; reedlr@swbell.net
http://www.ukans.edu/heritage/chs/
franklin/indexes
meetings at the Conference Rooms of
Ransom Memorial Hospital, 13th and
Main, Ottawa: third Sun (except Dec)
2:00
Pub. *Quarterly* (online)
$12.00 per year membership

Genealogical Researchers
(see Dickinson County Historical Society,
Historical Societies—Local and Regional,
above)

Harper County Genealogical Society
Harper Public Library
1002 Oak Street
Harper, KS 67058-1233
peterson@kanokla.net
http://skyways.lib.ks.us/genweb/society/
harper
Carol (Burke) Peterson, Editor
meetings: third Tue (except Dec, see web site
for location and time)
Pub. *The Harper County Connections,*
quarterly
$7.50 per year membership

Heritage Genealogical Society
(see W. A. Rankin Memorial Library, City,
County and Regional Archives and Libraries,
above)

Hodgeman County Genealogical Society
PO Box 608
Jetmore, KS 67854-0608
(620) 357-8568
hcgs18m@hotmail.com
http://skyways.lib.ks.us/genweb/
hodgeman/hgplaces.html
Twila Smidt, President
$5.00 per year membership

**Jefferson County Genealogical Society,
Inc.**
(Old Jefferson Town, Highway
59—location)
PO Box 174 (mailing address)
Oskaloosa, KS 66066-0174
(785) 863-2070
JCGS1979@yahoo.com
http://skyways.lib.ks.us/kansas/genweb/
jefferso/jfcogen.html
Jim Sharkey, Corresponding Secretary
Jan–Dec: Sat 1:00–5:00; Apr–Nov: Sun
1:30–5:00
Pub. *Yesteryears: Jefferson County
Genealogical Society Newsletter,*
semiannually
$15.00 per year membership

**Johnson County Genealogical Society and
Library, Inc.**
(Johnson County Library—location)
PO Box 12666 (mailing address)
Shawnee Mission, KS 66282-2666

(913) 383-2368
queries@johnsoncountykansasgenealogy.org
(Corresponding Secretary); editor@
johnsoncountykansasgenealogy.org
http://www.johnsoncountykansas
genealogy.org
Bill Hawkins, President
Library: Mon–Thur 9:00–9:00, Fri
9:00–6:00, Sat 9:00–5:00, Sun 1:00–5:00
Pub. *The Johnson County Genealogist,*
quarterly (Mar, June, Sept, Dec)
$12.50 per year membership; queries: free to
members, $2.00 each for nonmembers

Labette Genealogical Society, Inc.
PO Box 544
Parsons, KS 67357-0544
cdshettler@terraworld.net
http://www.skyways.lib.ks.us/kansas/
genweb/society/parsons
Tina Rice, Correspondence Secretary; Alice
Schettler, Webmaster
research: $10.00 per hour plus SASE

**Linn County Historical and Genealogical
Society**
(see Historical Societies—Local and
Regional, above)

McPherson County Genealogical Society
PO Box 483
McPherson, KS 67460-0483
Norma Snell, President
Pub. *Leaves to Taproots,* ten times per year
(monthly, Sept–June)
("Collection moved to McPherson County
Old Mill Museum, Lindsborg.")
$10.00 per year membership

**Miami County Genealogy and Historical
Societies**
(Miami County Swan River Museum, 12
East Peoria, off the northeast corner of Park
Square—location)
PO Box 123 (mailing address)
Paola, KS 66071-0123
(913) 294-4940; (913) 533-2485 (Librarian)
mcsrm@micoks.net
http://www.micoks.net/~mcsrm
Fred Knoche, President; Betty Bendorf,
Librarian
Mon–Fri 11:00–3:00, Sat 10:00–4:00
Pub. *MICOGESOQU,* quarterly (Mar, June,
Sept, Dec)
$15.00 per year membership in both
societies; admission: donation

**Midwest Historical and Genealogical
Society**
(see Historical Societies—Local and
Regional, above)

Montgomery County Genealogical Society
(311 West 10th—location)
PO Box 444 (mailing address)
Coffeyville, KS 67337-0444
(620) 251-5265; (620) 251-0716
royd@hit.net (Webmaster)
http://www.rootsweb.com/~ksmontgo
Carol Duvall, President
Mon–Sat 9:00–5:00
Pub. *The Descender,* semiannually (May,
Nov)
$8.00 per year membership

Nemaha County Genealogical Society
113 North Sixth Street
Seneca, KS 66538-1748
(785) 336-2494
mcphilbrick@hotmail.com
http://www.ku.edu/kansas/seneca/gensoc/
gensoc.html

Marcia Philbrick, Editor
Seneca Free Public Library: Mon–Thur
10:00–8:00, Fri 10:00–5:00, Sat
10:00–2:00
Pub. *Nemaha County Genealogical Society
Newsletter,* quarterly
$10.00 per year membership; research:
hourly fee plus copying costs

**North Central Kansas Genealogical
Society**
(Hesperian Library, 802 Locust Street,
Second Floor of City Building—location)
PO Box 251 (mailing address)
Cawker City, KS 67430-0251
(785) 781-4925 (Hesperian Library, for
appointment only, no research over the
phone); (785) 781-4343 (Librarian,
weekdays); (785) 781-4303 (Ms. Reling)
gensoc@nckcn.com
http://skyways.lib.ks.us/kansas/towns/
Cawker/library.html#society
Celia Norton Kincheloe, North Central
Kansas Genealogical Society Librarian;
Dorothy Reling
Library: Mon, Thur & Sat 1:00–5:00, Tue
10:00–noon, Wed 1:00–7:00
Pub. *Waconda Roots and Branches,*
quarterly
$8.00 per year membership; research $5.00
and up, plus SASE, for records of Jewell
and Mitchell counties, principally, but can
refer to researchers of Cloud, Smith,
Osborne and Saline counties, Kansas

**Northwest Kansas Genealogical and
Historical Society**
Oakley Public Library
700 West Third Street
Oakley, KS 67748-1256
(785) 672-4389; (785) 672-4776 (Library)
Lillian Martin, President
Library: 10:00–5:00
(Logan County newspapers on film)

Norton County Genealogical Society
(1 Washington Square—location)
PO Box 446 (mailing address)
Norton, KS 67654-0446
(785) 877-2481
nortonpl@ruraltel.net
Fleta Hanlon, President
Mon–Thur 10:00–8:00, Fri–Sat closed early
Pub. *Norton County Tracer,* quarterly
(births, deaths, marriages, obituaries, old
papers, census records, area newspapers)
$8.00 per year membership

**Old Fort Genealogical Society of Southeast
Kansas, Inc.**
(502 South National Avenue, Fort Scott, KS
66701-1327—location)
PO Box 786 (mailing address)
Fort Scott, KS 66701-0786
(620) 223-3300
http://skyways.lib.ks.us/kansas/genweb/
society/ftscott
Virginia L. Brown, Librarian
Mon–Sat 1:00–4:00
Pub. *Old Fort Log,* three times per year
(southeastern Kansas; "local area
information")
$15.00 per year membership

**Osborne County Genealogical and
Historical Society**
307 West Main Street
Osborne, KS 67473-2425
(785) 346-9437
joehubbard@yahoo.com
Barbara Wilson, Research Associate
Mon–Fri 1:00–5:00, Sat 9:00–noon

Pub. *Leaves of Lineage*, quarterly; *Osborne County Genealogical Society Quarterly*
$10.00 per year membership

Phillips County Genealogical Society
(Phillipsburg City Library, 888 Fourth—location)
PO Box 114 (mailing address)
Phillipsburg, KS 67661-0114
(785) 543-5325 (Library); (785) 543-6550 (President); (785) 543-5680 (Research)
darrum@phillipsburg.net
http://skyways.lib.ks.us/kansas/genweb/phillips/plgensoc.html
Darlene Johnson, President; Katie Davis, Research
Genealogy Room: Mon–Fri 10:00–6:00, Sat 10:00–4:00
Pub. *Tree Tracker*, quarterly
$15.00 per year membership

Rawlins County Genealogical Society
(Atwood Public Library, 102 South Sixth—location)
PO Box 405 (mailing address)
Atwood, KS 67730-0405
(785) 626-3850
atwoodli@ruraltel.net
http://skyways.lib.ks.us/genweb/rawlins/rawgenesoc.html
Delores Luedke, Researcher
meetings at Atwood Public Library
Pub. *Rawlins County Chronicle*, quarterly
("family files, newspapers, obituaries, burial records, cemeteries, births, weddings, old tax and court records, scrapbooks, all indexed on database at Rawlins County Historical Society")
$5.00 per year membership; research: donation

Reno County Genealogical Society
PO Box 0005
Hutchinson, KS 67504-0005
(620) 663-2804
renocountyks@yahoo.com
http://renocountyks.homestead.com
Ruth Filbert, Editor
Hutchinson Public Library: Mon–Fri 9:00–9:00, Sat 9:00–6:00, Sun 1:00–5:00; meetings at Hutchinson Public Library: third Mon 7:00–9:00
Pub. *The Sunflower*, quarterly
$12.00 per year membership; research: $5.00 per hour plus expenses

Republic County Genealogical Society
(see Republic County Historical Society, Historical Societies—Local and Regional, above)

Riley County Genealogical Society and Public Library
2005 Claflin Road
Manhattan, KS 66502-3415
(785) 565-6495
rcgs03@cox.net
http://www.rileycgs.com
President
Tue, Thur & Sat 10:00–4:00, Wed 1:00–4:00 & 7:00–9:00, Sun 2:00–5:00
Pub. *Kansas Kin*, quarterly
("Our collection of over 7,000 volumes of books, microfilm, fiche, CD-ROMs covers most states and counties of Kansas. The society offers more than 100 publications for sale, which contain archival information for the five county area surrounding Riley County, Kansas.")
$20.00 per year membership; staff-conducted search available

Sherman County Historical and Genealogical Society
(see Historical Societies—Local and Regional, above)

Smoky Valley Genealogical Society and Library, Inc.
211 West Iron, Suite 205
Salina, KS 67401-2613
(785) 825-7573
Towneranch@aol.com
http://skyways.lib.ks.us/kansas/genweb/ottawa/smoky.html
Mary Jane McIntire, President
Mon–Sat noon–4:00
Pub. *Tree Climber*, quarterly
$20.00 per year membership

Southeast Kansas Genealogical Society
(Iola Public Library, 218 East Madison—location)
PO Box 393 (mailing address)
Iola, KS 66749-0393
Wanda Canfield, Corresponding Secretary
meetings at library: first Sat 1:00
Pub. *Treebark*, quarterly (Jan, Apr, July, Oct)
(state and federal census, 1855–1925; marriages of Allen County, 1856–1925; deaths from *Iola Reg.*, 1900–1996; births from Iola City Hall, 1895–1935; Marriage Book 1926–1956 of Allen County)
$15.00 per year membership; research: $7.00 per hour plus postage and copies at 15¢ each

Stafford County Historical and Genealogical Society
(see Historical Societies—Local and Regional, above)

Sumner County Historical and Genealogical Society
(see Historical Societies—Local and Regional, above)

Topeka Genealogical Society
(2717 S.E. Indiana—location)
PO Box 4048 (mailing address)
Topeka, KS 66604-0048
(785) 233-5762
library@tgstopeka.org
http://www.tgstopeka.org
Tom Muth, Corresponding Secretary
Wed–Thur & Sat 1:00–4:00, first & third Thur 5:30–8:30; meetings at the First Christian Church Fellowship Hall, 1880 S.W. Gage: fourth Wed (except month of annual conference & Nov–Dec) 7:30
Pub. *Topeka Genealogical Society Quarterly*; *News & Views*
$20.00 per year membership

Washington County Historical and Genealogical Society
(see Historical Societies—Local and Regional, above)

Wichita County Genealogical Society
(201 North Fourth Street—location)
PO Box 1561 (mailing address)
Leoti, KS 67861-1561
(620) 375-2316
genealogy@wichitacountymuseum.org
http://wichitacountymuseum.org/gensociety.htm
Jeanene French, Whichita County GenWeb Host
Tue 1:00–5:00; meetings: second Mon (Jan–May & Sept–Nov) 7:00

Wichita Genealogical Society
PO Box 3705

Wichita, KS 67201-3705
(316) 262-0611; (316) 687-5925
wichita.gen.soc@mail.com
http://skyways.lib.ks.us/orgs/wgs
Pub. *The Ark Valley Crossroads*, quarterly; *On the Trail* (current events, single-sheet newsletter), quarterly
(local and area cemeteries and mortuaries, obituaries and other newspaper extractions; a support group to the Genealogy Department of the Wichita Public Library)
$15.00 per year membership; research: $5.00 (one-hour maximum) plus copy costs, list of professional researchers available on request; queries published free for members, $2.00 each for nonmembers

Wilson County Historical Society and Genealogical Chapter
(see Historical Societies—Local and Regional, above)

Wyandotte County Genealogical Society
PO Box 4228
Kansas City, KS 66104-0228
http://kcgenealogy.com/wyandotte_county_genealogical_so.htm
Pub. *Bear Tracks*
$10.00 per year membership

Independent Publications and Miscellany

Center for Mennonite Brethren Studies
(see Religious Archives and Organizations—Mennonite, Part 3)

Dick Taylor's Ghostchaser
husker@sky.net
http://www.kancoll.org/chaser
Dick Taylor

The Dwight D. Eisenhower Library and Museum
200 Southeast Fourth Street
Abilene, KS 67410
(785) 263-4751; (877) RING-IKE; (785) 263-4218 FAX
Library@eisenhower.nara.gov
http://eisenhower.utexas.edu
Mon–Sun 9:00–4:45
("Records relate solely to Dwight D. Eisenhower")

Ellsworth County Independent/Reporter
202 North Douglas
Ellsworth, KS 67439
Garnell Hanson
Pub. *Kanhistique*, monthly, $24.00 per year subscription (history and antiques)

Fort Larned National Historic Site
Rural Route 3
Larned, KS 67550
(620) 285-6911
fols_superintendent@nps.gov
http://www.nps.gov/fols
George Elmore
8:00–5:00

Fort Wallace Memorial Association
Highway 40
Wallace, KS 67761
(785) 891-3564

Hamilton County Museum
(108 East Highway 50—location)
PO Box 923 (mailing address)
Syracuse, KS 67878
(620) 384-7496

Historic Old Mission Enthusiasts
6029 Larsen Lane
Shawnee Mission, KS 66203
(913) 631-8485

Kansas Department of Transportation
915 Harrison, Room 754
Docking State Office Building
Topeka, KS 66612-1568
(785) 296-3585
webmaster@ksdot.org
http://www.ink.org/public/kdot/maps/
    main.html (Maps)

Kansas Press Association
5423 S.W. Seventh
Topeka, KS 66606
(785) 271-5304
http://www.kspress.com
(directory of Kansas newspapers)

KsGenWeb
Part of The USGenWeb Project
tcward@columbus-ks.com
http://skyways.lib.ks.us/genweb/index.html
Tom and Carolyn Ward, Co-State
    Coordinators
(links to other Kansas resources)

Mountain Press
(see Tennessee, Part 2)

Wakefield Museum Association
(Sixth and Hickory—location)
PO Box 101 (mailing address)
Wakefield, KS 67487-0101

Kentucky

Archives and Libraries with Holdings in Genealogy

State Archives and Library

Kentucky State Archives
Kentucky Department for Libraries and
Archives
Public Records Division
Archives Research Room
(300 Coffee Tree Road—location)
PO Box 537 (mailing address)
Frankfort, KY 40602-0537
(502) 564-8300, ext 346/347; (502) 564-
    8704 (inquiries regarding research
    guidelines); (502) 564-5773 FAX
Jim.Prichard@ky.gov
http://www.kdla.ky.gov
James M. Prichard, Research Room
    Supervisor
Archives Research Room: Mon–Sat
    8:00–4:00; State Library Reference:
    Mon–Fri 8:00–4:30
Pub. *Friends of Public Archives, Inc.
    Newsletter*, quarterly
(collects Kentucky's public records: city,
    county and state, supplemented by
    Kentucky Genealogical Society Library)
research: $3.00 minimum plus copying costs
    for Kentucky residents, no prepayment
    required, $8.00 nonrefundable
    prepayment for out-of-state residents,
    covering thirty minutes of research time
    and three copies from microform originals
    or six copies from paper originals,
    additional copies to be billed

State Historical Societies

Historical Confederation of Kentucky
(Kentucky Historical Society—location)
PO Box 1792 (mailing address)
Frankfort, KY 40602-1792
(502) 564-3016; (502) 564-4701 FAX
Karla Nicholson
8:00–4:30
Pub. *Circuit Rider*, quarterly
$9.50 per year membership

Kentucky Historical Society Library
100 West Broadway
Frankfort, KY 40601
(502) 564-1792; (502) 564-4701 FAX
KHS@ky.gov
http://history.ky.gov
Anne McDonnell, Librarian; Tom
    Stephens, Editor
Thomas D. Clark Research Library: Tue–Sat
    8:00–4:00, Sun 1:00–5:00; Special
    Collections: Tue–Sat 8:00–4:00
Pub. *Kentucky Ancestors*, quarterly; *Register
    of the Kentucky Historical Society*,
    quarterly; *Bulletin of Kentucky Historical
    Society*, bimonthly
$25.00 per year membership (includes
    Bulletin and a choice of the *Register* or
    Kentucky Ancestors), $35.00 per year
    membership (includes all three
    periodicals)

City, County and Regional Archives and Libraries
(A more exhaustive list of public and
academic libraries can be found at http://
www.kdla.state.ky.us/libserv/publdir.htm or
http://www.kdla.net/intro/dir/2003-publibs.
pdf.)

Adair County Public Library

Kentucky History and Genealogy Section
307 Greensburg Street
Columbia, KY 42728-1488
(270) 384-2472; (270) 384-9446 FAX
eanj2@yahoo.com
http://www.geocities.com/adairlibrary
Attn: Lee Ann Jessee
Mon, Wed & Fri 8:00–4:30, Tue & Thur
    8:00–6:00, Sat 8:00–noon

Anchorage Civic Club Archives
City Hall
PO Box 23266
Anchorage, KY 40223
(502) 245-4654; (502) 245-5651 FAX
Peggy Revell, Director
Wed 10:00–noon, and by appointment
Pub. *Civic Club Newsletter*, quarterly
(little involving genealogy, but all city and
    school records, various organizations,
    maintains a file of names and where they
    can be found in document boxes)

Ballard/Carlisle/Livingston Public Library
Genealogy Section
(132 North Fourth Street, Wickliffe, KY
    42087—location)
PO Box 428 (mailing address)
Bardwell, KY 42023-0428
(270) 335-5059 voice & FAX
sonya_bclpl@yahoo.com
Sonya Mainord
Wed 3:00–6:00, Fri 9:00–4:00

Bath Memorial Library
(24 West Main Street—location)
PO Box 380 (mailing address)
Owingsville, KY 40360-0380
(606) 674-2531 voice & FAX
bcml@mail.state.ky.us
http://bathcountylibrary.tripod.com
Brenda Vance
Mon–Wed & Fri 9:00–5:00, Th8ur
    9:00–8:00, Sat 9:00–3:00

Behringer-Crawford Museum
(1600 Montague Road, Devou
    Park—location)
PO Box 67 (mailing address)
Covington, KY 41012
(859) 491-4003; (859) 491-4006 FAX
Laurie Risch, Executive Director
Tue–Fri 10:00–5:00, Sat–Sun 1:00–5:00 by
    appointment only
$10.00–$100.00 per year membership;
    museum admission: $3.00 for adults

Belcher History Center
(U.S. 460 East—location)
PO Box 10 (mailing address)
Belcher, KY 41513
(606) 754-8876
Fon R. Belcher, Ed.D., Director
Pub. *Belcher Bulletin*

Berea College
Hutchins Library
(Campus Drive—location)
CPO 2166 (mailing address)
Berea, KY 40404
(859) 986-9341, ext. 5260
Jim Gage, Editor
Mon–Fri 8:00–noon & 1:00–5:00
Pub. *Appalachian Heritage* (a literary
    magazine), quarterly, $18.00 per year
    subscription
(southern Appalachian region life and work)

Boone County Public Library
7425 U.S. 42
Florence, KY 41042-1994
(859) 371-6222; (859) 371-0037 FAX

info@bcpl.org
http://www.bcpl.org
Patricia Yannarella, Information Services
    Coordinator
Mon–Thur 9:00–9:00, Fri 9:00–6:00, Sat
    9:00–5:00; Sun 1:00–5:00
(Boone County history)

Boyd County Public Library
Minnie Winder Genealogy and Local History
Collection
1740 Central Avenue
Ashland, KY 41101-7653
(606) 329-0090
genealogy@thebookplace.org
http://www.thebookplace.org
Teresa Klaiber, Staff Genealogist
summer: Mon–Sat 10:00–8:00; winter:
    Mon–Sat 9:00–9:00, Sun 1:00–5:00
("Eastern Kentucky.")

Breathitt County Public Library
1024 College Avenue
Jackson, KY 41339-1016
(606) 666-5541; (606) 666-8166 FAX
http://www.breathittcountylibrary.com
Charles Riley, Genealogist
Nov–Feb: Mon & Wed–Thur 8:00–4:30, Tue
    & Fri 8:00–5:00, Sat 9:00–3:00

Breckinridge County Public Library
Special Collections
(112 South Main Street—location)
PO Box 248 (mailing address)
Hardinsburg, KY 40143-0248
(270) 756-2323; (270) 756-5634 FAX
debbie_drane@hotmail.com
Daniel Bays, Special Collections; Debbie
    Drane

Buchanan County Public Library
(see Virginia, Part 2)

Buffalo Trace/Fleming County Public
Library
303 South Main Cross Street
Flemingsburg, KY 41041-1298
(606) 845-7851; (606) 845-9571; (606) 845-
    7045 FAX
beverlyc@mail.state.ky.us
http://members.tripod.com/index-2.html
Beverly Cooper

Bullitt County Public Library
(127 North Walnut—location)
PO Box 146 (mailing address)
Shepherdsville, KY 40165-0146
(502) 543-7675; (502) 543-5487 FAX
rml@bcplib.org; bcpl@iglou.com
http://www.bcplib.org
Randall J. Matlow
Mon, Wed & Fri–Sat 9:00–5:00, Tue & Thur
    9:00–8:00, Sun 1:00–5:00

Campbell County Public Library
Fourth and Monmouth Streets
Newport, KY 41071-1695
(859) 291-4770; (859) 572-5035; (859) 572-
    5037 FAX
bbonney@cc-pl.org
Aileen Hurst, Reference; Barbara Bonney
Mon–Thur 10:00–8:00, Fri 10:00–6:00, Sat
    10:00–5:00

Casey County Public Library
Genealogical Research Center
238 Middleburg Street
Liberty, KY 42539-3002
(606) 787-9381; (606) 787-7720 FAX
janbanks@caseylibrary.org
http://www.caseylibrary.org
Jan J. Banks

(includes family files, books, maps, oral
    history tapes, microfilm of court records,
    and VCR tapes of guest speakers to the
    Bicentennial Heritage Corporation;
    includes publications on Maryland,
    Pennsylvania, Virginia, North and South
    Carolina, Georgia, Tennessee, Kentucky,
    Indiana, Missouri, Texas and all known
    early publications on Casey County and
    surrounding counties)

Henry M. Caudill Memorial Library
220 Main Street
Whitesburg, KY 41858-1137
(606) 633-7547; (606) 633-3407 FAX
hmclib@lcld.org
http://www.lcld.org/libraries/hmcl.html
Angelina R. Tidal, Director
Mon & Wed–Fri 9:00–5:00, Tue 9:00–7:00,
    Sat 9:00–4:00

Centre College
Special Collections
600 West Walnut Street
Danville, KY 40422
(859) 238-5272; (859) 236-7925
http://www.centre.edu/academic/library/
    archives/archives.html

Clark County Public Library
370 South Burns Avenue
Winchester, KY 40391-1876
(859) 744-5661; (859) 744-5993 FAX
Kelle Hoskins, Adult Services Librarian;
    Julie Maruskin
Mon–Thur 9:00–8:00, Fri 9:00–5:30, Sat
    9:00–5:00

George Coon Public Library
(114 South Harrison Street—location)
PO Box 230 (mailing address)
Princeton, KY 42445-0230
(270) 365-2884; (270) 365-2892 FAX
Judy Boaz, Director
Mon–Thur 9:00–6:00, Fri–Sat 9:00–5:00

Crittenden County Public Library
204 West Carlisle Street
Marion, KY 42064-1727
(270) 965-3354 voice & FAX
jfjpritchett@yahoo.com
Janice Pritchett

Cynthiana-Harrison County Public
Library
110 North Main Street
Cynthiana, KY 41031-1205
(859) 234-4881; (859) 234-0059 FAX
sellis@harrisonlibrary.org
http://harrisonlibrary.org
E. Susan Ellis

Eastern Kentucky University
Crabbe Library, Special Collections and
Archives
Library 126
Richmond, KY 40475-3121
(859) 622-1792; (859) 622-1174 FAX
http://www.library.eku.edu/sca/scahome.htm
Mrs. Jerry Parrish Dimitrov, Curator
Mon–Tue & Thur–Fri 8:00–5:00, Wed
    8:00–8:00
(Madison county, Kentucky, genealogy, early
    Boonesborough; limited staff research,
    local researchers list available)
copies: 20¢ each

Eastern Kentucky University
Jonathan Truman Dorris Museum
Richmond, KY 40475
(859) 622-5585

Eastern Kentucky University
Eastern Kentucky University Archives
521 Lancaster Avenue, Library 126
Richmond, KY 40475-3102
(859) 622-1792
http://www.library.eku.edu/sca
Mon–Fri 8:00–4:30, except school holidays

Elizabethtown Community College
Media Center/Microfilm
600 College Street
Elizabethtown, KY 42701

John Fox Jr. Genealogical Library
Duncan Tavern, DAR State Headquarters
and Historic Center
323 High Street
Paris, KY 40361
(859) 987-1788
Mrs. Kenney S. Roseberry, Volunteer
    Chairman
Tue–Sat 10:00–noon & 1:00–4:00
(DAR records, one-of-a-kind publications
    and manuscripts, "vertical family files,
    family biographies, Kentucky county
    records, Virginia, Maryland,
    Pennsylvania, etc., records")
$3.00 admission for all non-Kentucky DAR
    members; research: $5.00 for a simple
    query, 25¢ per sheet of copied
    information

Fulton County Public Library
312 Main Street
Fulton, KY 42041-1699
(270) 472-3439; (270) 472-6241 FAX
fultonpl@bellsouth.net
http://www.fultonlibrary.com
Elaine Allen, Director
Tue 10:30–5:00 & 6:00–8:00, Fri–Sat
    9:00–11:30 & 12:30–5:00
(Civil War collection, genealogical
    collection)

Gallatin County Public Library
(209 West Market Street—location)
PO Box 848 (mailing address)
Warsaw, KY 41095-0848
(859) 567-2786; (859) 567-4750 FAX
brendahawkins@gallatincountylibrary.org
http://gallatincountylibrary.org
Brenda Hawkins

Garrard County Public Library
101 Lexington Street
Lancaster, KY 40444-1155
(859) 792-3424; (859) 792-2366 FAX
garlib@hotmail.com
http://garrardpublib.state.ky.us
Joan Tussey, Director
Mon–Fri 9:00–5:00, Sat 9:00–3:00
("local genealogical holding")

Grayson County Public Library
130 East Market Street
Leitchfield, KY 42754-1439
(270) 259-5455; (270) 259-4552 FAX
gillespie@graysoncountylibrary.org
http://www.graysoncountylibrary.org
Karen Gillespie, Director
Mon & Thur 9:00–7:00, Tue–Wed & Fri–Sat
    9:00–5:00

Greenup County Public Library
614 Main Street
Greenup, KY 41144-1097
(606) 473-6514 voice & FAX
http://www.youseemore.com/greenup/
    default.asp
Dorothy K. Griffith, County Library Director
Mon–Tue & Thur–Fri 9:00–5:00, Wed
    9:00–8:00, Sat 9:00–2:00

(genealogy and local history collection)

Hacksma House Genealogy Library
(see Washington, Part 2)

Hancock County Archives
Old Court House, Third Floor
200 Court Square
Hawesville, KY 42348
(270) 927-8095
Mary Gibbs

Hardin County Public Library
North Branch
800 South Logsdon Parkway
Radcliff, KY 40160-1932
(270) 351-9999
hcpl@kvnet.org
http://www.hcpl.info
Vi Voge

Hardy Memorial Museum
296 South Main
Logan, KY 42276

Harvey Helm Memorial Library
301 Third Street
Stanford, KY 40484-1347
(606) 365-7513; (606) 365-3284 FAX
kay.peppard@mail.state.ky.us
Kay Peppard

Henderson County Public Library
101 South Main Street
Henderson, KY 42420-3599
(270) 826-3712; (270) 827-4226 FAX
nstallings@hcpl.org
http://www.hcpl.org
Niki Stallings, Local History/Genealogy
Services
Mon–Thur 9:00–8:00, Fri–Sat 9:00–5:00,
Sun 1:30–5:00

Hickman County Memorial Library
209 Mayfield Road
Clinton, KY 42031-1427
(270) 653-2225 voice & FAX
valerie@vci.net
Valerie Rushing

Historic Russellville
PO Box 116
Russellville, KY 42276
(270) 726-9501
jbasham@logantele.com
Pat Basham, Secretary
meetings at the Woman's Club Building, 145
East Fifth Street, Russellville: fourth Thur
5:00
Pub. *Newsletter*, annual
$10.00 per year membership

**Huntsville-Madison County Public
Library**
(see Alabama, Part 2)

Jackson County Public Library
(Courthouse Square—location)
PO Box 160 (mailing address)
McKee, KY 40447-0160
(606) 287-8113; (606) 287-7774 FAX
jcpl@prtcnet.org
Betty L. Bingham

Johnson County Public Library
444 Main Street
Paintsville, KY 41240-0788
(606) 789-4355; (606) 789-6758 FAX
jocol@foothills.net
http://mywebpage.netscape.com/
johnsoncolibrary
Karen Daniel

Mon, Wed & Fri 9:30–5:00, Tue & Thur
9:30–8:00, Sat 9:00–2:00

Kenton County Public Library
Fifth and Scott Streets
Covington, KY 41011-1530
(859) 491-7610; (859) 655-7956 FAX
dschroed@kenton.lib.ky.us
http://www.kenton.lib.ky.us
David E. Schroeder, Local History Librarian
Mon–Thur 10:00–9:00, Fri 10:00–6:00, Sat
10:00–5:00, Sun 1:00–5:00
(Kentucky history, emphasis on northern
Kentucky; online newspaper index
covering 1835–1930 and 1984 to the
present)

Kentucky Highlands Museum
PO Box 1494
Ashland, KY 41105
David R. Wilson, Executive Director
Pub. *Highlands Highlights*

Kentucky State University Archives
Blazer Library
Frankfort, KY 40601
(502) 227-6852
Jane A. Minder, Archives and Records
Manager

Laurel County Public Library
120 College Park Drive
London, KY 40741-1414
(606) 864-5759; (606) 864-9061 FAX
Library_Mail@laurellibrary.org
http://www.laurellibrary.org
Lori Acton

Lee County Public Library
(123 Center Street—location)
PO Box V (mailing address)
Beattyville, KY 41311-0013
(606) 464-8014; (606) 464-2052 FAX
lcpl01@tgtel.com
http://www.geocities.com/2942; http://www.
geocities.com/Athens/Olympus/2942
Sonya Spencer

Leslie County Public Library
(22065 Main Street—location)
PO Box 498 (mailing address)
Hyden, KY 41749-0498
(606) 672-2460; (606) 672-4213 FAX
leslib@tds.net
http://www.geocities.com/lesliepubliclibrary
Clifford Hamilton, Jr.
Mon–Fri 8:00–5:00, Sat 8:00–2:00

Lexington Public Library
Kentucky Room
140 East Main Street
Lexington, KY 40507-1376
(859) 231-5520
http://www.lpl.lib.ky.us/reference/
kyroom.html
Robin Rader, Assistant Manager, Reference
Department
Mon–Thur 9:00–9:00, Fri–Sat 9:00–5:00,
Sun 1:00–5:00
no costs

Logan County Public Library
201 West Sixth Street
Russellville, KY 42276-1411
(270) 726-6129; (270) 726-6127 FAX
lindak@loganlibrary.org
http://www.loganlibrary.org
Linda Kompanik

City of Louisville Archives
Memorial Auditorium
970 South Fourth Street

Louisville, KY 40203-3250
(502) 574-3244; (502) 574-4318 FAX
Sharon Receveur, Assistant Director, Office
of Information Services; Deborah Walker
9:00–5:00
(only City of Louisville government records,
also a records center for noncurrent,
nonpermanent records)
no research fee charged; copies: 25¢ each

Louisville Free Public Library
301 York Street
Louisville, KY 40203-2257
(502) 574-1600; (502) 574-1666 FAX
buthod@lfpl.org
http://lfpl.org
Craig Buthod
Mon–Thur 9:00–9:00, Fri–Sat 9:00–5:00
10¢ per copy from paper original, 20¢ per
copy from microfilm, plus handling
charges for mailing: $2.00 (1-10 pp.),
$3.00 (11-20 pp.), $4.00 (21-30 pp.),
$5.00 maximum

Lyon County Public Library
(261 Commerce Street—location)
PO Box 546 (mailing address)
Eddyville, KY 42038-0546
(270) 388-7720; (270) 388-7735 FAX
Vicki McIntosh
(has a genealogy section and family file for
researchers, but does not answer queries)

Marion County Free Public Library
201 East Main Street
Lebanon, KY 40033-1133
(270) 692-4698 voice & FAX
ehimes238@yahoo.com
Mary Parrott, Assistant Director
Mon, Wed & Fri 9:00–5:30, Tue & Thur
9:00–8:00
("We do not do extensive research.")

Marshall County Public Library
1003 Poplar Street
Benton, KY 42025-1315
(270) 527-9969; (270) 527-0506 FAX
mcpl@marshallcolibrary.org
http://www.marshallcolibrary.org
Barbara Serls, Director
Mon 9:00–8:00, Tue–Sat 9:00–5:00
(genealogical collection)

Martin County Public Library
(Main Street—location)
PO Box 1318 (mailing address)
Inez, KY 41224-1318
(606) 298-7766; (606) 298-0768 FAX
Patricia Crum

McCracken County Public Library
Special Collections Department
555 Washington Street
Paducah, KY 42003-1735
(270) 442-2510, ext. 24; (270) 442-2510
FAX
specialcol@mclib.net
http://www.mclib.net/specialcollections.htm
Vonnie Shelton, Special Collections Library
Assistant
Mon–Thur 9:00–8:45, Fri–Sat 9:00–5:45,
Sun 1:00–5:45

Menifee County Public Library
(140 Walnut Street—location)
PO Box 49 (mailing address)
Frenchburg, KY 40322-0049
(606) 768-2212; (606) 768-9676 FAX
Lillian Ebermann

Morehead State University
Camden-Carroll Library

Special Collections
Morehead, KY 40351
(606) 783-5107; (606) 783-2829
http://www.morehead-st.edu/units/
    library/special.html

Mount Sterling-Montgomery County Library
241 West Locust Street
Mount Sterling, KY 40353-1352
(859) 498-2404; (859) 498-7477 FAX
Hildreth Lyman

Muhlenberg County Public Libraries
Genealogy and Local History Annex
117 South Main Street
Greenville, KY 42345-1539
(270) 338-5388; (270) 338-9635 FAX
mcplgha@muhlon.com
http://www.mcplib.org
Sandra Galyen, Annex Outreach
Mon–Fri 9:00–5:00, Sat 9:00–1:00
("Collection includes Muhlenberg County
    genealogy materials, as well as other
    selected counties and states. Extensive
    collection relating to Muhlenberg County
    history and people.")

Murray State University
Forrest C. Pogue Library
Special Collections and Archives
1 Murray Street
Murray, KY 42071-3309
(270) 762-6152; (270) 762-4998
http://www.mursuky.edu/msml/Pogue.
    htm#special
Keith M. Heim, Ph.D., Head, Special
    Collections and Archives
Mon–Fri 8:00–4:30, Sat 10:00–3:00
    (schedule varies with school year)
(Kentucky and southeast U.S. genealogy and
    local history)

Murray State University
Wrather West Kentucky Museum
Murray, KY 42071-3308
(270) 762-4771

Israel T. Naamani Library
(see Jewish Genealogical Society of
Louisville, Ethnic Archives, Libraries, and
Societies, Part 3—Jewish)

Nelson County Public Library
90 Court Square
Bardstown, KY 40004-1584
(502) 348-3714; (502) 348-5578 FAX
nelsoncopublib@hotmail.com
http://www.nelsoncopublib.org
Irene Underwood

Nicholas County Memorial Library
223 North Broadway Street
Carlisle, KY 40311-1149
(859) 289-5595; (859) 289-4340 FAX
becky@nicholascountylibrary.com
http://www.nicholascountylibrary.com
Becky Reid

Northern Kentucky University
Christopher Gist Historical Society
Collection
Special Collections and Archives
Department
Library
Highland Heights, KY 41099-6101
(859) 572-6158; (859) 572-5390 FAX
http://www.nku.edu/~refdept/gist.html

Ohio County Public Library
413 Main Street
Hartford, KY 42347-1137

(270) 298-3790; (270) 298-4214 FAX
mjacquaviva@hotmail.com
Melissa J. Acquaviva

Owen County Public Library
118 North Main Street
Owenton, KY 40359-9201
(502) 484-3450 voice & FAX
bettina.somerville@mail.state.ky.us;
    owencopl@mis.net
http://www.owentonky.com/OCPL.html
Bettina Somerville

Owensboro-Daviess County Public Library
Kentucky Room: Local History and
Genealogy
450 Griffith Avenue
Owensboro, KY 42301-3699
(270) 684-0211, ext. 5; (270) 684-0218 FAX
kentucky@dcpl.lib.ky.us
http://www.dcpl.lib.ky.us
Shelia E. Heflin, Information Services
    Manager
Mon–Fri 9:00–9:00, Sat 9:00–6:00, Sun
    1:00–5:00
copies: 10¢–25¢ per page

Owsley County Public Library
(#2 Medical Plaza—location)
PO Box 280 (mailing address)
Booneville, KY 41314-0280
(606) 593-5700; (606) 593-5708 FAX
marcum1@prtcnet.org
Joyce Marcum

Pennyroyal Area Museum
217 East Ninth Street
Hopkinsville, KY 42240
(270) 887-4270

Perry County Public Library
(479 High Street—location)
PO Box 928 (mailing address)
Hazard, KY 41701-0928
(606) 436-2475; (606) 436-0191 FAX
pcpl479@gtemail.net
http://www.geocities.com/pcpl479

Pikeville Public Library
(119 College Street—location)
PO Box 471 (mailing address)
Pikeville, KY 41502-0471
(606) 432-1285; (606) 433-1616 FAX
pikeville@pikelibrary.org
http://www.pikelibrary.org
Delania Adkins

Portland Museum
2308 Portland Avenue
Louisville, KY 40212
(502) 776-7678
Nathalie Andrews, Executive Director
Pub. *Kicks*

Don F. Pratt Museum
G3/DPTM 101st ABN DIV (ASSLT) & Fort
Campbell
5702 Tennessee Avenue
Fort Campbell, KY 42223-5335
(270) 798-3215
Rex Boggs, Curator/Director
9:30–4:30 (guided tours upon request, 36
    hours notice)

Pulaski County Public Library
(107 North Main Street, Somerset, KY
42501—location)
PO Box 36 (mailing address)
Somerset, KY 42502-0036
(606) 679-8401; (606) 679-1779 FAX
pulaski.library@charterbn.com

http://www.youseemore.com/pulaski/
    default.asp
Judith Burdine

Rufus M. Reed Public Library
PO Box 359
Lovely, KY 41231-0359
(606) 395-5809 voice & FAX
Janet Copley

W. G. Rhea Public Library
(see Tennessee, Part 2)

Robertson County Public Library
(148 North Main Street—location)
PO Box 282 (mailing address)
Mount Olivet, KY 41064-0282
(606) 724-5746 voice & FAX
carol.mitchell@mail.state.ky.us
http://robertsonlibrary.com
Carol Mitchell
Mon–Tue & Thur–Fri 10:00–5:00, Wed
    10:00–7:00, Sat 9:00–noon

Rockcastle County Public Library
60 Ford Drive
Mount Vernon, KY 40456-0060
(606) 256-2388; (606) 256-5460 FAX
rcplib@mikrotec.com
http://www.rockcastlelibrary.com
Geraldine Robbin, Librarian
Mon–Wed & Fri 10:00–5:00, Thur
    noon–8:00, Sat 10:00–4:00

Rowan County Public Library
185 East First Street
Morehead, KY 40351-1631
(606) 784-7137; (606) 784-3917 FAX
helene.williams@mail.state.ky.us
http://rowancountypubliclibrary.state.ky.us
Helene Williams

Scott County Public Library
104 South Bradford Lane
Georgetown, KY 40324-2335
(502) 863-3566; (502) 863-9621 FAX
earlene.arnett@mail.state.ky.us
http://www.scottpublib.org
Earlene H. Arnett, Director
Mon–Thur 9:00–9:00, Fri–Sat 9:00–6:00,
    Sun 1:00–5:00; genealogist on duty in
    Local History Room: Thur 1:00–3:00
(local history collection)

John L. Street Library
244 Main Street
Cadiz, KY 42211-9153
(270) 522-6301; (270) 522-1107 FAX
tclibrary2001@yahoo.com
http://tclibrary.org
Pam Metts, Director; Ann McAtee,
    Volunteer
Library: Mon 9:00–8:00, Tue–Fri 9:00–5:30,
    Sat 9:00–noon; Volunteer: Tue
    12:30–5:30, Fri 12:30–5:00

Union County Public Library
126 South Morgan Street
Morganfield, KY 42437-1553
(270) 389-1696; (270) 389-3925 FAX
unionlib@dynasty.net
http://www.uclibrary.8m.com
Laura Wildey, Director
Mon–Tue & Thur–Fri 9:00–5:00, Wed
    9:00–6:00, Sat 9:00–2:00

University of Kentucky
Kentucky Humanities Council
Ligon House
Lexington, KY 40506-0442
(859) 257-5932

University of Kentucky
Margaret I. King Library
Department of Special Collections and
Archives
Lexington, KY 40506-0039
(859) 257-8611; (859) 257-8393
(Newspapers)
http://www.uky.edu/Libraries/Special
Ms. B. J. Gooch, Public Services
Coordinator
Mon–Fri 8:00–4:30, Wed (when university is
in session) 4:30–9:00, Sat 8:00–noon,
Sun (when university is in session)
2:00–5:00

University of Kentucky Libraries
Photographic Archives
111 Margaret I. King Library North
500 South Limestone Street
Lexington, KY 40506
(859) 257-8379
Bill Marshall, Director
Mon–Fri 8:00–5:00, Sat 8:00–noon

University of Louisville
University Archives and Records Center
Ekstrom Library Building
Louisville, KY 40292
(502) 852-6674; (502) 852-6673 FAX
archives@louisville.edu
http://www.louisville.edu/library/uarc
William J. Morison, Ph.D., Director

University of Louisville
Special Collections—Rare Books and
Photographic Archives
William F. Ekstrom Library
Belknap Campus
Louisville, KY 40292
(502) 852-6752; (502) 852-8734 FAX
http://www.louisville.edu/library
Delinda Stephens Buie, Curator; James C.
Anderson, Curator
Mon–Fri 10:00–4:00, Thur 4:00–8:00, and
by appointment

University of Louisville
University Photographic Archives
Louisville, KY 40292
(502) 588-6752

University of Mississippi
Center for the Study of Southern Culture
(see Mississippi, Part 2)

**Virginia Polytechnic Institute and State
University**
Appalachian history
(see Virginia, Part 2)

Washington County Public Library
210 East Main Street
Springfield, KY 40069-1125
(859) 336-7655; (859) 336-0256 FAX
lisak.jones@wcpl.ky.gov
http://www.wcpl.ky.gov
Lisa K. Jones, Library Director
Mon 10:00–8:00, Tue & Thur–Fri
10:00–5:00
no research assistance available

Wayne County Public Library
159 South Main Street
Monticello, KY 42633-1456
(606) 348-8565; (606) 348-3829 FAX
staff@waynepubliclibrary.net
http://www.waynepubliclibrary.net
Anne Garner
Mon–Tue & Thur–Fri 8:00–4:30, Wed & Sat
8:00–4:00

Mary Wood Weldon Memorial Public

Library
107 West College Street
Glasgow, KY 42141-2423
(270) 651-2824 voice & FAX
public_library@glasgow-ky.com
James Hyatt

Western Kentucky University
Kentucky Museum and Library
(1442 Kentucky Street—location)
1 Big Red Way (mailing address)
Bowling Green, KY 42101-3576
(270) 745-5083 (Reading Room, Second
Floor); (270) 745-6086 (Manuscripts/
Folklife Archives, Room E-216); (270)
745-2592 (Museum); (270) 745-6264
FAX
http://www.wku.edu/Library/dslc/ky-lib.htm
Constance A. Mills, Kentucky Library
Coordinator
Reading Room: Mon–Fri 8:00–4:30, Sat
9:30–4:00 (hours may vary during
holidays, semester breaks and summer
semester)
Pub. *The Fanlight*, irregularly
(Kentucky, with emphasis on south-central
region of the state and Shakers at South
Union, Kentucky)
requests for specific records only will be
considered and a list of professional
researchers is available upon request

Willard Library
(see Indiana, Part 2)

Historical Societies—Local and Regional

Allen County Historical Society
(301 North Fourth Street—location)
PO Box 393 (mailing address)
Scottsville, KY 42164-9757
(270) 237-3026
http://www.rootsweb.com/~kyallen/
Society.htm
Rosemary Harper, President
meetings: third Mon 7:00
$10.00 per year membership

Ancestral Trails Historical Society, Inc.
(Vine Grove Optimist Club, 127 West Main
Street—location)
PO Box 573 (mailing address)
Vine Grove, KY 40175
info@aths.com
http://www.aths.com
Paul W. Urbahns, President
Pub. *Ancestral News*, quarterly
(Breckinridge, Bullitt, Edmonson, Grayson,
Hardin, Hart, Jefferson, LaRue, Meade
and Nelson counties)
$10.00 per year membership

Anderson County Historical Society
PO Box 212
Lawrenceburg, KY 40342
(502) 839-3248
W. J. Smith

Auburn Historical Society
(433 West Main Street—location)
PO Box 114 (mailing address)
Auburn, KY 42206
(502) 542-4677
Eloise Hadden, President
meetings at the Auburn Museum: first Tue
(even-numbered months) 7:00 P.M.
Pub. *Newsletter*
(Logan County)
$5.00 per year membership

**Ballard-Carlisle Historical-Genealogical
Society**
(see Genealogical Societies—Local and
Regional, below)

Bell County Historical Society
PO Box 1344
Middlesboro, KY 40965
(606) 248-5304
bellhist_society@hotmail.com
Virginia T. Green, Corresponding Secretary
Mon–Thur 10:00–8:00, Fri 10:00–7:00, Sat
10:00–4:00 (closes one hour earlier in
summer)
Pub. *Gateway*, quarterly
$15.00 per year membership

Big Sandy Valley Historical Society
319 F.M. Stafford Avenue
Paintsville, KY 41240
Betty Hazelette, Secretary
meetings at Kenova, WV: second Sat of Apr;
at Breaks Interstate Park, second Sat of
Sept at Paintsville: second Sat of July; at
Louisa: second Sat of Nov
Pub. *Sandy Valley Heritage*, quarterly
$10.00 per year membership

Boyd County Historical Society
Boyd County Public Library
Minnie Winder Genealogy and Local History
Collection
1740 Central Avenue
Ashland, KY 41101
(specializes in Kentucky, Virginia, and
Pennsylvania)

Bracken County Historical Society
302 East Fourth
Augusta, KY 41002
(606) 756-2409
George Cummins, President
Pub. *Bracken County Historical Society*,
monthly
$7.50 per year membership

**The Breathitt County Historical and
Genealogical Society**
121 Turner Drive
Jackson, KY 41339
Nancy Herald
meetings in the Breathitt Public Library:
third Mon 7:00
Pub. *The Record*, quarterly
$7.00 per year membership

Breathitt County Historical Society
Quickaand, KY 41363

Breckinridge County Historical Society
c/o Breckinridge County Clerk
Courthouse Square
PO Box 498
Hardinsburg, KY 40143-0498
(270) 756-2246; (270) 756-5444 FAX
breckcohistsoc@geocities.com
Robert Moorman, President
meetings: fourth Mon
$10.00 per year membership

**Butler County Historical and Genealogical
Society, Inc.**
PO Box 435
Morgantown, KY 42261
(270) 526-4408
Carole J. Southerland, Secretary/Treasurer
Butler County Library: 9:00–4:00
Pub. *Kentucky Traces*, quarterly, $2.00 per
issue
$10.00 per year membership

Caldwell County Historical Society

PO Box 1
Princeton, KY 42445

**Campbell County Historical and
Genealogical Society**
19 East Main Street
Alexandria, KY 41001
(859) 635-6407
Campbellcohistorynews@juno.com
http://www.rootsweb.com/~kycchgs
Office: Tue 10:00–8:00, Sat 10:00–3:00;
    meetings: second Thur 7:30
Pub. *Campbell County History News*,
    quarterly
$10.00 per year membership

**Carter County Historical and
Genealogical Society**
PO Box 1128
Grayson, KY 41143

Christian County Historical Society
PO Box 890
Hopkinsville, KY 42240
(270) 886-3921
William T. Turner, Official City-County
    Historian
Mon–Fri 8:00–4:30
(social history, Edger Cayce, The Night
    Riders)

Clark County Historical Society
122 Belmont Avenue
Winchester, KY 40391

**Clay County Genealogical and Historical
Society**
(see Genealogical Societies—Local and
Regional, below)

Clinton County Historical Society
(103 North Cross Street, Granville Hotel
    Building—location)
PO Box 177 (mailing address)
Albany, KY 42602
(606) 387-6021 (work); (606) 387-5991
    (home); (606) 387-8092 FAX
Luther C. Conner, Jr., President
weekdays 8:00–5:00
$2.00 per year membership

Crittenden County Historical Society, Inc.
(West Carlisle Street—location)
PO Box 25 (mailing address)
Marion, KY 42064
(270) 965-9257

Danville-Boyle County Historical Society
PO Box 1122
Danville, KY 40422

**Estill County Historical and Genealogical
Society**
(133 Broadway, Irvine, KY
    40336—location)
PO Box 221 (mailing address)
Ravenna, KY 40472-0221
(606) 723-3806
Diane Rogers, President
Museum and Research Center: Sat
    10:00–4:00, and by appointment;
    meetings at Estill County Public Library,
    Irvine: first Tue 7:00 P.M.
Pub. *Estill County Historical and
    Genealogical Society*, six times per year
$15.00 per year membership

The Filson Historical Society
1310 South Third Street
Louisville, KY 40208
(502) 635-5083; (502) 635-5086 FAX
http://www.filsonhistorical.org

Mon–Fri 9:00–5:00; Library: Sat 9:00–noon
Pub. *The Filson History Quarterly*, $35.00
    per year subscription; *The Filson*,
    irregularly
(excellent research collections for Kentucky
    history and genealogy)
$50.00 per year membership; admission:
    $5.00 per day for members (under te
    $100.00 per year level), $10.00 for
    nonmembers

**Floyd County Historical and Genealogical
Society**
PO Box 982
Prestonsburg, KY 41653
meetings at Floyd County Library conference
    room: third Mon 7:00
$20.00 per year membership

Gallatin County Historical Society
Hawkins-Kirby House
PO Box 405
Warsaw, KY 41095
(859) 567-4591
Sue Bogardus, Vice President
Pub. *Year Book*, annually

Garrard County Historical Society
208 Danville Street
Lancaster, KY 40444
Pub. *Garrard County Historical Society
    Bulletin*, semiannually; *On the Garrard
    County Line*, semiannually
$5.00 per year membership

Grant County Historical Society, Inc.
PO Box 33
Mason, KY 41054
(859) 824-9202
BB15CHIPS@aol.com
Barbara Brown, Corresponding Secretary
Pub. *Grant County Historical Society
    Newsletter*, quarterly
$7.50 per year membership

Graves County Public Library
601 North 17th Street
Mayfield, KY 42066
(270) 247-2911; (270) 247-2990 FAX

Grayson County Historical Society
PO Box 84
Leitchfield, KY 42755
(270) 259-9645

Green County Historical Society
PO Box 276
Greensburg, KY 42743
William DeSpain, President
Pub. *Green County Review*, quarterly
$10.00 per year membership

Hancock County Historical Society
Old Court House
200 Court Square
Hawesville, KY 42348

Hardin County Historical Society
128 North Main Street
Elizabethtown, KY 42701
(270) 769-2301

Harrodsburg Historical Society
Genealogical Committee
(Morgan Row House, 220 South Chiles
    Street—location)
PO Box 316 (mailing address)
Harrodsburg, KY 40330
(859) 734-5985
http://www.rootsweb.com/~kymercer/hhs
summer: Tue 10:00–4:00, Tue–Sat
    1:00–4:00; Nov–Mar: Tue 10:00–4:00,

Wed–Sat 1:00–4:00
Pub. *Olde Towne Ledger*, bimonthly
(Mercer County and central Kentucky
    history)
$15.00 per year membership; admission:
    $5.00 for nonmembers; research: $10.00
    per hour

Hart County Historical Society
(109 Main Street—location)
PO Box 606 (mailing address)
Munfordville, KY 42765-0606
(270) 524-0101
http://www.battleforthebridge.org
Mary W. Branstetter, Clerk
Mon–Fri 9:00–4:00, Sat 10:00–4:00, no
    holidays
Pub. *Quarterly* (Jan, Apr, July, Oct)
("Family genealogy, family files, etc., also
    Civil War. Civil War Battlefield site,
    visitor's center under way.")
$20.00 per year membership

**Hatfield-McCoy Historical Society (Ky.-
W.Va.)**
PO Box 2676
South Williamson, KY 41503
(606) 237-4646
Tom Atkins
Pub. *Feud Country*, biannually
$20.00 per year membership

**Henderson County Genealogical and
Historical Society, Inc.**
(see Genealogical Societies—Local and
Regional, below)

Henry County Historical Society
PO Box 570
New Castle, KY 40050

Hickman County Historical Society
Route 1, Box 70
Clinton, KY 42031

Historical Society of Hopkins County
107 South Union Street
Madisonville, KY 42431
(270) 821-3986
J. Harold Utley, President
Mon–Fri 1:00–5:00
Pub. *Annual Yearbook*
$18.00 per year membership

**Jefferson County Genealogical and
Historical Society**
(see Genealogical Societies—Local and
Regional, below)

**Jeffersontown and Southeast Jefferson
County Historical Society**
2432 Merriwood Drive
Jeffersontown, KY 40299
(502) 267-1715

Jessamine Historical Society
501 South Third Street
Nicholasville, KY 40356-1811
Mr. Hager

Johnson County Historical Society
Johnson County Public Library
444 Main Street
Paintsville, KY 41240
(606) 789-4355; (606) 789-6758 FAX
Pat Patton, Corresponding Secretary
Library: Mon, Wed & Fri 9:30–5:00, Tue &
    Thur 9:30–8:00, Sat 9:00–2:00
Pub. *Highland Echo*, quarterly (Mar, June,
    Sept, Dec)
$10.00 per year membership

Kenton County Historical Society
PO Box 641
Covington, KY 41012
(859) 431-2666 (Editor); (859) 491-0490
(Secretary)
nkyheritage.kchs@juno.com (Editor);
jhboh@juno.com (Secretary)
Karl Lietzenmayer, Editor; John Boh,
Secretary
Pub. *Northern Kentucky Heritage*, two times
per year, $15.00 per year subscription for
nonmembers (award-winning "periodical
of regional history and genealogy");
Bulletin, monthly ("contains a monthly
meeting announcement and usually a
short article on local history")
(local history and genealogy, especially, but
not exclusively, for Boone, Campbell,
Carroll, Gallatin, Grant, Kenton, Owen,
and Pendleton counties of northern
Kentucky, also Bracken, Mason and other
associated counties; has index of Kenton
County federal censuses)
$22.00 per year membership (includes
subscription to *Northern Kentucky
Heritage*) $10.00 per year membership
(includes subscription to *Bulletin*)

Knott County Historical Society
PO Box 1023
Hindman, KY 41822
meetings at the Knott County Court House,
Hindman: last Thur evening
Pub. *Journal*, quarterly
$15.00 per year membership

Laurel County Historical Society
(Old City Hall Building, Broad
Street—location)
PO Box 816 (mailing address)
London, KY 40743-0816
(606) 864-0607
lchistsoc@alltel.net
http://www.laurelcountyhistoricalsociety.org
Shirley McCowan, Librarian
Wed–Sat 10:00–4:00; monthly meetings
second Thur 10:30
Pub. *Branches of Laurel*, quarterly
$15.00 per year membership; research:
$25.00 for initial search

**Lee County Historical and Genealogical
Society**
PO Box V
Beattyville, KY 41311

Leslie County Historical Society
Leslie County Public Library
PO Box 498
Hyden, KY 41749
(606) 672-2460 (Library)
Mason Collett, Library Director
Library: Mon–Fri 8:00–5:00, Sat 8:00–2:00

**Letcher County Historical and
Genealogical Society**
PO Box 312
Whitesburg, KY 41858
meetings at Harry M. Caudill Memorial
Library: second Tue 5:30
Pub. *Newsletter*
$12.00 per year membership

Lewis County Historical Society
(318 Lexington Avenue—location)
PO Box 212 (mailing address)
Vanceburg, KY 41179-0212
(606) 796-3778 (Corresponding Secretary)
Bettye B. Dillow, Corresponding Secretary
and Treasurer; Joan Godfrey, President
Fri–Sat 11:00–4:00
Pub. *Shakin' and Diggin'*, quarterly (Mar,

June, Sept, Dec)
$10.00 per year membership; research: $5.00
per hour, four-hour minimum

**Lewisburg/North Logan Historical
Commission**
PO Box 239
Lewisburg, KY 42256
(270) 755-4828
Mayor Gwyneth McKinney
meetings at the Dr. Sutton Building, Front
Street Lewisburg: second Thur 10:00

Lincoln County Historical Society
11475 Brodhead Road
Crab Orchard, KY 40419-9608
(606) 355-2204
Martha Scott

Logan County Genealogical Society, Inc.
(West Fourth Street in Archive
Building—location)
PO Box 853 (mailing address)
Russellville, KY 42276
(270) 726-8179
Judy Lyne, President; Connie Sitz, Office
Mon–Fri 8:30–3:00; meetings: Tue
send SASE with query

Lyon County Historical Society, Inc.
Lyon County Museum
PO Box 811
Eddyville, KY 42038
(270) 388-9986; (270) 388-7322
Odell Walker, Lyon County Historian
Museum: Wed–Sun (15 May–15 Oct)
1:00–4:00, and by appointment
$5.00 per year museum and society
membership; museum admission: $2.00
for nonmembers

Madison County Historical Society
PO Box 397
Richmond, KY 40476-0397
(859) 624-2760
http://www.iclub.org/kentucky/madison/
history
David C. Greene, Treasurer
Pub. *Heritage Highlights*, quarterly
(genealogical and historical society; queries
welcomed)
$15.00 per year membership

**Magoffin County Historical Society
Pioneer Village**
(191 South Church Street—location)
PO Box 222 (mailing address)
Salyersville, KY 41465
(606) 349-1607; (606) 349-1353 FAX
http://www.rootsweb.com/~kymhs
Connie A. Wireman, Director
Mon–Fri 10:00–4:00, and by appointment
Pub. *Magoffin County Historical Society
Journal*, quarterly
("We maintain a genealogy library, a
Magoffin County Kentucky Log Cabin
Pioneer Village, sponsor an annual
Founders Day Festival each Labor Day
weekend.")
$12.00 per year membership

**Marshall County Genealogical and
Historical Society**
(see Genealogical Societies—Local and
Regional, below)

**Martin County Historical and
Genealogical Society**
PO Box 501
Inez, KY 41224
lpreece@ameritech.net
http://www.rootsweb.com/~kymchgs/

MCHGS
Evelynn Cassady, President; Linda Preece
meetings at the Senior Citizens Building,
Inez, KY: first Thur 6:30
$15.00 per year membership

Mason County Historical Society
PO Box 13
Maysville, KY 41056
(606) 564-0900; (606) 564-7974 FAX
David Stumpf, President

Mason County Museum
215 Sutton Street
Maysville, KY 41056
(606) 564-5865; (606) 564-4372 FAX
museum@masoncountymuseum.org
http://www.masoncountymuseum.org
Sue Ellen Grannis, Curator
Apr–Dec: Mon–Fri 9:00–4:00, Sat
10:00–4:00; Jan–Mar: Tue–Fri 9:00–4:00,
Sat 10:00–4:00
Pub. *Mason County Museum Newsletter*,
quarterly
(extensive collection of family files)
$20.00 per year membership; admission:
$3.50 for nonmembers; research: $25.00
per hour

**McCracken County Genealogical-
Historical Society**
PO Box 7651
Paducah, KY 42002-7651
Roy F. Olson, Jr., Past President
meetings at McCracken County Public
Library: second Thur 1:30
Pub. *McCracken County, Ky. Genealogical-
Historical Journal*, two times per year
$12.00 per year membership; queries
accepted

Metcalfe County Historical Society
Route 1, Box 371
Summer Shade, KY 42166
(270) 428-3391
Kay Harbison

Montgomery County Historical Society
(30 East Main Street—location)
PO Box 861 (mailing address)
Montgomery, KY 40353
(270) 498-1413
Helene Perkins, President
Mon, Wed & Fri 11:00–3:00
$3.00 per year membership

Mount Washington Historical Society
PO Box 212
Mount Washington, KY 40047-0212
Mr. Smith
no research assistance, address genealogical
queries to Bullitt County Genealogical
Society

Northern Kentucky Heritage League
PO Box 104
Fort Mitchell, KY 41017

Ohio County Historical Society, Inc.
(415 Mulberry Street—location)
PO Box 44 (mailing address)
Hartford, KY 42347
(270) 298-3177; (270) 298-7452
Dorothy Gentry, President; Anna Laura
Duncan
Mon–Sun (Apr–Aug) 1:00–4:00
$10.00 per year membership

Owen County Historical Society
(Main Street—location)
PO Box 84 (mailing address)
Owenton, KY 40359

(502) 463-2633
Katie Gibson, President
meetings at Owen County Public Library:
third Mon 6:30 P.M.
Pub. *The Bulletin*, two times per year
$5.00 per year membership; research fees
vary, including postage and copies at 15¢
per page

**Pendleton County Historical and
Genealogical Society**
Route 5, Box 280
Falmouth, KY 41040
meetings at the Public Library, Falmouth:
third Sat 2:00
Pub. *Newsletter*, quarterly
$10.00 per year membership

**Perry County Genealogical and Historical
Society, Inc.**
(see Genealogical Societies—Local and
Regional, below)

**Pike County Society for Historical and
Genealogical Research**
PO Box 97
Pikeville, KY 41502
(606) 432-9371 (Library) (606) 432-4904
(Ms. Warrix's home)
Connie Maddox, President; Sharon D.
Warrix
Special Collections, Allara Library, Pikeville
College: Mon–Fri noon–4:00, and by
appointment
Pub. *Pike County Historical Review*,
quarterly
(Pike County genealogy and local history)
$20.00 per year membership; free queries for
members

Pulaski County Historical Society
(Pulaski County Public Library Building,
107 North Main Street, Somerset, KY
42501—location)
PO Box 36 (mailing address)
Somerset, KY 42502
Jerri Brown, President and Office Manager
Tue–Sat 1:00–4:00
Pub. *Newsletter*, semiannually (May, Nov)
$3.00 per year membership; research: $5.00
per surname

Red River Historical Society
(Main Street—location)
PO Box 195 (mailing address)
Clay City, KY 40312
(606) 663-2555
meetings at Red River History Museum,
Clay City: third Thur 7:00
(Powell County)

Rockcastle County Historical Society
Rockcastle County Public Library
PO Box 698
Mount Vernon, KY 40456
(606) 256-2397 (President's Home); (606)
256-2388 voice & FAX (Library)
Juanita Witt, President; Geraldine Robbin,
Librarian
Library: Mon–Wed & Fri 10:00–5:00, Thur
noon–8:00, Sat 10:00–4:00
Pub. *Rockcastle Reminiscence*, quarterly,
$5.00 per year subscription (includes
query)

Otto Rothert Historical Society
(Broad Street, Central City, KY
42330—location)
2727 State Route 189 South (mailing
address)
Greenville, KY 42345-4646
Alexander Cather

Rowan County Historical Society
PO Box 60
Morehead, KY 40351
(606) 784-9145 (President)
Lloyd Dean, President
meetings at public library: first Thur
Pub. *Past & Present*, monthly
$10.00 per year membership

The Russell County Historical Society
PO Box 544
Jamestown, KY 42629
(270) 866-7434
marynoel@duo-county.com
http://www.duo-county.com/~rcplib/
historicalsociety1.htm
Verlman York
meetings at the Russell County Public
Library: second Thur
Pub. *Newsletter*, quarterly
$10.00 per year membership

Shelby County Historical Society
PO Box 444
Shelbyville, KY 40066-0444
Pub. *Shelby County Historical Society
Newsletter*, approximately six times per
year
$15.00 per year membership

Simpson County Historical Society, Inc.
Simpson County Archives and Museum
206 North College Street
Franklin, KY 42134
(270) 586-4228; (270) 586-4429 FAX
oldjail@kih.net
Archives: Mon–Fri 9:00–4:00, Sat
10:00–2:00
Pub. *Jailhouse Journal*, quarterly (Jan, Apr,
July, Oct)
(repository for Simpson County court
records, genealogical library, some
Tennessee)
$10.00 per year membership; research: $5.00
plus SASE plus copying and postage

**South Central Kentucky
Historical/Genealogical Society**
PO Box 157
Glasgow, KY 42142-0157
http://www.rootsweb.com/~kybarren/
Resources/SCKHistGenSoc.htm
Martha P. Reneau, Editor
meetings at South Central Kentucky Cultural
Center, 200 West Water Street, Glasgow,
KY: fourth Thur (except Dec) 7:00 P.M.
Pub. *Traces*, quarterly
(historical, genealogical, Bible records, new
book reviews)
$12.00 per year membership

Southern Kentucky Past Finders
1095 Sportsman Club Road
Russellville, KY 42276
(270) 726-6604
David Guion
Meetings at Logan County Public Library:
third Tue (odd-numbered months)
(historical research, archeology, Civil War)
$10.00 per year membership

Taylor County Historical Social
(204 North Columbia—location)
PO Box 14 (mailing address)
Campbellsville, KY 42719
(270) 465-3400 (not at 204 North Columbia)
Gwynette Sullivan, Vice President
by appointment only
Pub. *Central Kentucky Researcher*, quarterly
$10.00 per year membership

Trimble County Historical Society

2926 Patton's Creek
Pendleton, KY 40055
MFallone@aol.com (withheld)
http://www.ole.net/~maggie/trimble/
histsoc.htm
Violet Jennings, President
monthly meeting third Sat (Apr–Nov) 1:30
Pub. *Trimble County Historical News*
(online)
$5.00 per year membership

Union County Historical Society/Museum
221 West McElroy
Morganfield, KY 42437
http://www.comsource.net/~kyseeker/
union/society.htm

Van Lear Historical Society
PO Box 12
Van Lear, KY 41265

**Wayne County Historical and
Genealogical Society**
PO Box 320
Monticello, KY 42633
Pub. *Overview*, quarterly
$15.00 per year membership

**Webster County Historical and
Genealogical Society**
(Webster County Courthouse—location)
PO Box 215 (mailing address)
Dixon, KY 42409
(270) 639-5439
lgc32738@apex.net
http://www.rootsweb.com/~kywebste/
wch_gs.htm
Lowell Gene Childress, President; Carolynn
H. Dunbar, Treasurer, Corresponding
Secretary
Wed–Fri 1:00–4:00
Pub. *Webster's Wagon Wheel*, quarterly
$15.00 per year membership

The Wise County Historical Society
The Appalachian Quarterly
(see Virginia, Part 2)

Woodford County Historical Society
121 Rose Hill
Versailles, KY 40383
(859) 873-6786
woodford@qx.net
http://www.woodfordkyhistory.org
Danna Estridge, Curator
Tue–Sat 10:00–4:00
Pub. *Woodford Heritage News*, quarterly
(Jan, Apr, July, Oct)
("Historical Society, Museum, Genealogy
Library")
$15.00+ per year membership; museum and
library admission: free; research: $15.00
per hour for members, $20.00 per hour for
nonmembers

Genealogical Societies

State Genealogical Society

Kentucky Genealogical Society, Inc.
PO Box 153
Frankfort, KY 40602-0153
(502) 875-4452
kygs@aol.com
http://www.kygs.org
Roberta Padgett, Corresponding Secretary
Research Room, Kentucky State Archives:
Tue–Sat (except Sat immediately
preceding or following state holidays)
8:00–4:00; meetings at Kentucky
Historical Center: second Thur 7:00;
annual seminar at Kentucky Historical

Center: first Sat in Aug
Pub. *Bluegrass Roots*, quarterly
(three million entries in Kentucky
　Genealogical Index)
$15.00 per year membership; research: no
　service, send SASE for list of researchers

Southern Society of Genealogists, Inc.
(see Alabama, Part 2)

Genealogical Societies—Local & Regional

Adair County Genealogical Society
(Adair County Public Library, 307
　Greensburg Street—location)
PO Box 613 (mailing address)
Columbia, KY 42728
(270) 384-2472
Beverly A. England, President
Library: Mon, Wed & Fri 8:00–4:30, Tue &
　Thur 8:00–6:00, Sat 8:00–noon
Pub. *Adair County Review*, quarterly (spring,
　summer, fall, winter)
(marriage bonds, cemetery records, family
　folders, census records)
$10.00 per year membership

**Ballard-Carlisle Historical-Genealogical
Society**
(Ballard-Carlisle-Livingston Public
　Library—location)
PO Box 279 (mailing address)
Wickliffe, KY 42087
(270) 628-3468
ccscotts@apex.net
http://www.ballardconet.com/bchgs
Bob Milner, President
Fri 9:00–4:00; meetings: second Sun (except
　Dec) 2:00
Pub. *The Root Diggers*, semiannually (Mar,
　Aug)
(Books, newspapers, microfilm, pictures, and
　private papers housed in the genealogy
　section of the Ballard-Carlisle-Livingston
　Public Library. "We have several
　publications of cemeteries, obits,
　marriages, Bible records, etc. Contact for
　publication list and costs.")
$10.00 per year membership; free queries to
　Lois M. Scott, Corresponding Secretary
　or via email

Bicentennial Heritage Corporation
148 Wolford Street
Liberty, KY 42539
(606) 787-6194; (606) 787-9381 (Library);
　(606) 787-7720 FAX (Library)
Gladys Cotham Thomas, President
Casey County Public Library: Mon–Thur &
　Fri 10:00–6:00, Sat 9:00–3:00; meetings:
　fourth Mon (Mar–June & Oct–Nov)
Pub. *Casey County, Ky. Kinfolk*, quarterly
$10.00 per year membership

Big Sandy Valley Genealogical Society
1215 Stafford Avenue
Paintsville, KY 41240
(606) 789-3416

Boyle County Genealogical Association
321 Springhill Drive
Danville, KY 40422
Kathryn Roller
Pub. *Danville Constitution*
$7.00 per year membership

Breathitt County Genealogical Society
Breathitt County Public Library
1024 College Avenue
Jackson, KY 41339
Pub. *Looking for Leads*, semiannually

**The Breathitt County Historical and
Genealogical Society**
(see Historical Societies—Local and
Regional, above)

Bullitt County Genealogical Society
(Ridgway Memorial Library on Walnut
Street, just south of the courthouse
annex—location)
PO Box 960 (mailing address)
Shepherdsville, KY 40165-9998
(502) 538-6428; (502) 538-8743
Doris C. Owen, President
Library: Mon–Sat 9:00–5:00, Tue 5:00–7:00;
　meetings third Thur 7:45
Pub. *Wilderness Road*, quarterly
(county records and family charts; "We are
　dedicated to preserving our history and
　helping others.")
$15.00 per year membership

**Butler County Historical and Genealogical
Society, Inc.**
(see Historical Societies—Local and
Regional, above)

**Campbell County Historical and
Genealogical Society**
(see Historical Societies—Local and
Regional, above)

**Carter County Historical and Genealogical
Society**
(see Historical Societies—Local and
Regional, above)

Christian County Genealogical Society
1101 Bethel Street
Hopkinsville, KY 42240
(270) 887-4262
http://www.kyseeker.com/christian/
　ccgsbks.htm
D. D. Cayce, President
11:00–8:00
Pub. *Tree Builders*, quarterly
$11.00 per year membership

**Clay County Genealogical and Historical
Society**
(115 Court Street—location)
PO Box 394 (mailing address)
Manchester, KY 40962
(606) 598-5507
James Welch, President
Mon–Tue 9:00–5:00, Thur–Fri 9:00–5:00
Pub. *Clay County Ancestral News*, two times
　per year
$18.00 per year membership

Corbin Genealogy Society
McBurney Building
(Barbourville Street—location)
PO Box 353 (mailing address)
Corbin, KY 40701
(606) 878-8074 (President)
Carol Pace, President
by appointment only
Pub. *Our Heritage*, quarterly
(Knox, Laurel and Whitley counties)
$15.00 per year membership

Crittenden County Genealogical Society
South Crittenden County Library
PO Box 61
Marion, KY 42064

Eastern Kentucky Genealogical Society
(Boyd County Public Library—location)
PO Box 1544 (mailing address)
Ashland, KY 41105-1544
James C. Powers, Corresponding Secretary
Pub. *Treeshaker*, quarterly

$10.00 per year membership

**Estill County Historical and Genealogical
Society**
(see Historical Societies—Local and
Regional, above)

Fayette County (KY) Genealogical Society
PO Box 8113
Lexington, KY 40533-8113
(859) 278-9966
mehurst@prodigy.net
Melvin E. Hurst, Editor
Pub. *The Fayette County (KY) Genealogical
　Society Quarterly* (Mar, June, Sept, Dec),
　$3.00 per issue
(includes area which was in Fayette County
　when it was formed in 1780 from
　Kentucky County, Virginia)
$12.00 per year membership; 50-word
　queries accepted from members only

**Floyd County Historical and Genealogical
Society**
(see Historical Societies—Local and
Regional, above)

Fulton County Genealogical Society
PO Box 1031
Fulton, KY 42041-1031
Elaine Allen, President
Fulton Public Library: Tue 10:30–5:00 &
　6:00–8:00, Fri–Sat 9:00–11:30 &
　12:30–5:00
Pub. *Fulton-Hickman County Journal*,
　semiannually
$10.00 per year membership

Graves County Genealogical Society
PO Box 245
Mayfield, KY 42006
Pub. *Journey into the Past*, semiannually
$10.00 per year membership

**Genealogical Society of Hancock County,
Kentucky**
(Old Court House, Third Floor—location)
PO Box 667 (mailing address)
Hawesville, KY 42348
(270) 927-8095
hcarchives@tds.net
George Gibbs, Editor and Vice President;
　Mary Gibbs, Archivist and Treasurer;
　Dorothy Watkins, President
Mon–Fri 8:00–4:00
Pub. *Forgotten Pathways*, quarterly
("Marriages, census, estates, wills,
　commonwealth, deeds.")marriage books
　of Hancock County)
$11.00 per year membership; research: $6.00
　per hour, half-hour minimum, plus copies
　at 15¢ each

Harlan Heritage Seekers
PO Box 853
Harlan, KY 40831
Pub. *Harlan Mountain Roots*, quarterly
$15.00 per year membership

**Henderson County Genealogical and
Historical Society, Inc.**
(1041 Fourth Street—location)
PO Box 303 (mailing address)
Henderson, KY 42420-0303
(270) 830-7514
netta1@bellsouth.net
http://www.rootsweb.com/~kyhchgs
Netta Mullin, First Vice President
meeting at Henderson County Public
　Library, Multi-Purpose Room: first Thur
　7:00
Pub. *The Legacy*, quarterly (Mar, June, Sept,

Dec), $3.00 per issue
$12.00 per year membership; research:
$15.00 per hour plus copies at 20¢ per
page

Henry County Genealogical Society
(see Tennessee, Part 2)

Hopkins County Genealogical Society, Inc.
(Madisonville-Hopkins County Public
Library—location)
PO Box 51 (mailing address)
Madisonville, KY 42431
Lanna Arnold, Corresponding Secretary
Mon–Wed & Fri 1:00–5:00, Fri 10:00–3:00
Pub. *Yesterday's Tuckaways*, quarterly
$15.00 per year membership

**Jefferson County Genealogical and
Historical Society**
PO Box 960
Shepherdsville, KY 40165-0960
Pub. *Jefferson County Genealogical and
Historical Society Quarterly* (July, Oct,
Jan, Apr)
$10.00 per year membership

Knox County Genealogical Society
2603 Aintree Way
Louisville, KY 40220
(502) 459-8718
Maxine Humfleet Jones, President
by appointment
Pub. *Knox County Kentucky Kinfolk*,
quarterly
$15.00 per year membership

KYOWVA Genealogical Society
(see West Virginia, Part 2)

**Lee County Historical and Genealogical
Society**
(see Historical Societies—Local and
Regional, above)

**Letcher County Historical and
Genealogical Society**
(see Historical Societies—Local and
Regional, above)

Louisville Genealogical Society
(The Church of Jesus Christ of Latter-day
Saints, Hurstbourne Lane and Linn Station
Road—location)
PO Box 5164 (mailing address)
Louisville, KY 40205-0164
(502) 245-4843
Helen H. Berger, Treasurer
second & fourth Tue 1:00, second Thur 7:30
P.M.
Pub. *Lines-and-By-Lines*, quarterly
$12.00 per year membership

**Marshall County Genealogical and
Historical Society**
(County Courthouse—location)
PO Box 373 (mailing address)
Benton, KY 42025
(270) 527-4749
marcoky@vci.net
Clara Creason, Secretary
County Archives: Mon & Wed–Thur
9:00–3:00
Pub. *Marshall County Genealogical and
Historical Society Newsletter*, quarterly,
no subscription without membership
("Our organization 'mans' the County
Archives.")
$12.00 per year membership

**Martin County Historical and
Genealogical Society**

(see Historical Societies—Local and
Regional, above)

Mason County Genealogical Society
(8031 Day Pike, Maysville, KY 41056-
9228—location)
PO Box 266 (mailing address)
Maysville, KY 41056
(606) 759-7257; (606) 759-5370 FAX
Edith Ryan, Corresponding Secretary
anytime; meetings at 8031 Day Pike,
Maysville, KY 41056: first Mon 7:00
Pub. *Mason County Genealogical Society
Newsletter*, quarterly
$10.00 per year membership

Muhlenberg County Genealogical Society
PO Box 758
Greenville, KY 42345
(270) 338-3713; (270) 338-5388 (Library)
Carol Brown, President
Muhlenberg County Public Libraries,
Genealogy and Local History Annex:
Mon 9:00–8:00, Tue–Fri 9:00–5:00, Sat
9:00–1:00
Pub. *The Heritage*, quarterly
$10.00 per year membership

Nelson County Genealogical Roundtable
(Nelson County Public Library, 90 Court
Square—location)
PO Box 409 (mailing address)
Bardstown, KY 40004-0409
(502) 348-3714 (Library)
Pub. *The Genealogist*, quarterly
$10.00 per year membership

**Pendleton County Historical and
Genealogical Society**
(see Historical Societies—Local and
Regional, above)

**Perry County Genealogical and Historical
Society, Inc.**
Perry County Public Library—upstairs
479 High Street
Hazard, KY 41701
(606) 436-5829
Helen P. Horne, Editor and Treasurer
Library: Mon–Fri 8:00–5:00, Sat 8:00–1:00
Pub. *Perry County Genealogical and
Historical Society Newsletter*, three times
per year (Apr, Aug, Dec)
$18.00 per year membership; research fees
from Tabatha L. Farler, PO Box 365,
Happy, KY 41746

**Pike County Society for Historical and
Genealogical Research**
(see Historical Societies—Local and
Regional, above)

Scott County Genealogical Society
Scott County Public Library
104 South Bradford Lane
Georgetown, KY 40324
(502) 863-3566 (Library)
jogt@aol.com; DBRscottky@aol.com
(President)
Doris B. Reed, President
Library: Mon–Thur 9:00–9:00, Fri–Sat
9:00–6:00, Sun 1:00–5:00; genealogist on
duty in Local History Room: Thur
1:00–3:00
Pub. *Scott County Genealogical Society
Newsletter*, quarterly
$10.00 per year membership

**South Central Kentucky
Historical/Genealogical Society**
(see Historical Societies—Local and
Regional, above)

South Kentucky Genealogical Society
Route 1, Box 3332
Franklin, KY 42134
Southern Kentucky Genealogical Society
PO Box 1782
Bowling Green, KY 42102-1782
Gail Jackson Miller, President
Pub. *The Longhunter*, quarterly
$20.00 per year membership

Tri-State Genealogical Society
(see Indiana, Part 2)

**Tug Valley Genealogical Society (Ky.-
W.Va.)**
PO Box 2676
South Williamson, KY 41503
(606) 237-4646
O. T. Atkins
Pub. *Tug Valley Heritage*, biannually
$20.00 per year membership

Washington County Genealogical Society
Washington County Public Library
210 East Main Street
Springfield, KY 40069
(859) 336-7655 (Library); (859) 336-0256
FAX (Library)
Lisa K. Jones, Library Director
Library: Mon 10:00–8:00, Tue & Thur–Fri
10:00–5:00

**Wayne County Historical and
Genealogical Society**
(see Historical Societies—Local and
Regional, above)

**Webster County Historical and
Genealogical Society**
(see Historical Societies—Local and
Regional, above)

**West-Central Kentucky Family Research
Association**
(3133 Commonwealth Court, Kentucky
Highway 54 East—Library-Workroom
location)
PO Box 1932 (mailing address)
Owensboro, KY 42302
(270) 683-4719
wckfra@yahoo.com
http://www.rootsweb.com/~kywckfra
Margaret Alford, *Bulletin* Editor; Dot
Smithson, *Kentucky Family Records*
Editor
Mon & Wed 9:00–2:00
Pub. *The Bulletin*, quarterly; *Kentucky
Family Records*, quarterly
$18.00 per year membership

Independent Publications and
Miscellany

**Alice Lloyd College Library—Special
Collections**
Appalachian Oral History Project
Pippa Passes, KY 41844
(606) 368-2101, ext. 7001
Tom Graham, Assistant Library Director
Mon–Fri 8:00–4:30, Sun 5:00–9:30
(Special Collections and Appalachian Oral
History Project mostly deal with the
history of the southeast Kentucky region)

Appalachian Roots
(see West Virginia, Part 2)

Steven A. Birchfield Publications
3201 Hardmoney Road
Paducah, KY 42003-1058
(270) 554-9579

Steven A. Birchfield
9:00–9:00
(specializes in McCracken County
    cemeteries and funeral home records)

Branches of the Bay Bookshop
(Whitley and McCreary counties)
(see Maryland, Part 2)

Byron Sistler and Associates, Inc.
(see Tennessee, Part 2)

Center for Appalachian Studies
(see North Carolina, Part 2)

The East Kentuckian
305 Albany Road
Lexington, KY 40503-2625
(859) 277-4569
Clayton R. Cox, Owner
Pub. *The East Kentuckian: A Journal of
    Genealogy and History*, quarterly (Mar,
    June, Sept, Dec), $10.00 per year
    subscription

Genealogical Institute
(see Independent Publications, Part 1)

**Hunting for Bears Genealogical and
Historical Society**
(see Alabama, Part 2)

Kentucky Biographies Project
http://www.starbase21.com/kybiog

**Kentucky Cabinet for Economic
Development**
Map Sales
500 Mero Street #23
Frankfort, KY 40601-1987
(502) 564-4715; (502) 564-4083 FAX
Jeff Rarden, Office Supervisor
Mon–Fri 8:00–4:00
Pub. *Kentucky Deskbook of Economic
    Statistics*, annually, $17.00 postpaid per
    issue
(source for state-made county and city maps,
    river charts, fishing maps, community
    profiles and brochures and geologic
    publications regarding minerals, coal,
    water and oil and gas and recreational
    type maps, as well as the Geological
    Quadrangle maps)

Kentucky Explorer
PO Box 227
Jackson, KY 41339
(606) 666-5060; (606) 666-7018
editor@kentuckyexplorer.com
http://www.kentuckyexplorer.comCharles
    Hayes, Editor
Pub. *Kentucky Explorer*, ten times per year,
    $21.00 per year subscription

Kentucky Geological Survey
Map and Publications Sale Office
University of Kentucky
228 Mining and Mineral Resources Building
Lexington, KY 40506-0107
(859) 257-5500; (877) 778-7827 (outside of
    Lexington)
http://www.uky.edu/KGS

Kentucky Oral History Commission
100 West Broadway
Frankfort, KY 40601
(502) 564-1792; (502) 564-4701 FAX
doug.boyd@mail.state.ky.us
Special Collections, Kentucky History
    Center
Mon–Fri 8:00–4:00
Pub. *Oral History in Kentucky*

The Kentucky Transportation Cabinet
501 High Street
Frankfort, KY 40622
(502) 564-4890; (502) 564-4809 FAX
http://www.kytc.state.ky.us

Kentucky Tree-Search
PO Box 22621
Lexington, KY 40522
Gwendolyn G. Tippie, Editor
Pub. *Kentucky Kinfolk*, quarterly, $17.00 per
    year subscription

Kentucky Vital Records Index
http://ukcc.uky.edu/~vitalrec

**Kin Hunters Genealogical Publications
and Research**
PO Box 151
Russellville, KY 42276-0151
Montgomery Vanderpool
Pub. *Kin Hunters*, quarterly (Jan, Apr, July,
    Oct), $16.00 for four-issue subscription,
    $30.00 for eight-issue subscription
(Logan, Todd, Simpson, Butler, Warren and
    Muhlenberg counties)
free queries

KyGenWeb
Part of The USGenWeb Project
http://www.kygenweb.net/index.html
Nancy Trice, State Coordinator; Bill
    Utterback, Assistant Coordinator
(links to other Kentucky resources)

Lexington Cemetery Company, Inc.
833 West Main Street
Lexington, KY 40508-2094
(859) 255-5522
Daniel R. Scalf, General Manager
Mon–Sat 8:00–4:00, Sun 1:00–4:00
(over 60,000 interments)
research fees depend on research time

Michiana History Publications
(see Indiana, Part 2)

*The Mountain Empire Genealogical
Quarterly*
(see Virginia, Part 2)

Mountain Press
(see Tennessee, Part 2)

Ohio River Valley Families
(see Ohio, Part 2)

Old News from Kentucky
PO Box 1164
Madisonville, KY 42431
Pub. *Old News from Kentucky*, quarterly

**Red River Meeting House and Cemetery
Association**
2459 Trimble Road
Adairville, KY 42202
(270) 539-6528
Richard Moore, President

Reppert Publications
Antique and Collectible News
(see Illinois, Part 2)

The Researchers
(8846 Maze Road, Indianapolis, IN 46259-
    9643—location)
PO Box 39063 (mailing address)
Indianapolis, IN 46239-0063
(317) 862-6133
Carley Gioe, Owner
Mon–Fri 9:00–5:00
(publisher of Kentucky wills and vital

records, including Kentucky county
    marriage records from the counties'
    formations to 1850, and some Virginia
    marriages)

Secretary of State Land Office
Room 80, Capitol Building
Frankfort, KY 40601
(502) 564-3490; (502) 564-6894 FAX
Kadkinson@mail.sos.state.ky.us
http://www.kysos.com
Kandie Adkinson, Administrative Supervisor
Mon–Fri 8:00–4:30
("Revolutionary War; land patents; digitized
    records")
copies: $1.00 per warrant, $1.00 per survey,
    $1.00 per grant, 50¢ for other pages

Silent Footsteps
306 Sequoia Drive
Leitchfield, KY 42754
Pub. *Silent Footsteps*, quarterly, $8.00 per
    year subscription

Simmons Historical Publications
(2015 SR 2192, near Metser, Boaz, KY
    42027—location)
PO Box 66 (mailing address)
Melber, KY 42069-0066
(270) 856-3552
Don Simmons, Owner
(publishes books on genealogical records,
    deeds, wills, marriage records, etc., from
    Kentucky, North Carolina, Tennessee and
    Virginia)

Southern Historical Press, Inc.
(see Publishers, Part 4)

Traveller Southern Families
(see Virginia, Part 2)

West Virginia University
Appalachian Studies Association
(see West Virginia, Part 2)

Louisiana

Archives and Libraries with Holdings in Genealogy

State Archives and Library

Le Comité des Archives de la Louisiane
PO Box 1547
Baton Rouge, LA 70821-1547
(225) 355-9906 (Publications Chairman);
(225) 387-4264 President); (225) 356-
4415 (Treasurer)
j.a.riffel@att.net
http://www.sos.louisiana.gov/archives/
archives/archives-comite.htm
Judy Riffel, Treasurer
Pub. *Le Raconteur*, four per year, $15.00 per
year (plus $3.50 after 1 Mar) subscription

**Louisiana Archives and Manuscripts
Association**
PO Box 51213
New Orleans, LA 70151-1213
http://nutrias.org/~nopl/lama/lama.htm
Pub. *Louisiana Archives and Manuscripts
Association Newsletter*, semiannually
(spring and fall)

Louisiana State Archives
Office of the Secretary of State
(3851 Essen Lane—location)
PO Box 94125 (mailing address)
Baton Rouge, LA 70804-9125
(225) 922-1000; (225) 922-1206 (Louisiana
Room); (225) 922-1184
(Genealogical/Vital Records); (225) 922-
1208 (Heritage Center)
archives@sos.louisiana.gov
http://www.sec.state.la.us/archives/
archives/archives-index.htm
Selena A. Baker, Archivist
Mon–Fri 8:00–4:30, Sat 9:00–5:00, Sun
1:00–5:00

State Library of Louisiana
(701 North Fourth Street—location)
PO Box 131 (mailing address)
Baton Rouge, LA 70821-0131
(225) 342-4923; (225) 219-4804 FAX
admin@state.lib.la.us
http://www.state.lib.la.us
Judith D. Smith, Head, Louisiana Section
Mon–Fri 8:00–4:30
Pub. *Searching for Your Ancestors . . . And
All That Jazz*, biannually (every two
years), free (available on homepage)
copies: 25¢ per page

State Historical Society

**Louisiana Genealogical and Historical
Society**
(see State Genealogical Society, below)

**City, County and Regional Archives and
Libraries**
(A more exhaustive list of public and
academic libraries can be found at
http://www.state.lib.la.us.)

Acadia Parish Library
Headquarters
(1125 North Parkerson Avenue—location)
PO Drawer 1509 (mailing address)
Crowley, LA 70526-1509
(337) 788-1880; (337) 788-3759 FAX
lylej@aol.com;
admin.b1ac@pelican.state.lib.la.us
http://www.acadia.lib.la.us
Lyle Johnson, Director

Allen Parish Library
(320 South Sixth Street—location)
PO Box 400 (mailing address)
Oberlin, LA 70655-0400
(337) 639-4315; (800) 960-3015; (337) 639-
2654 FAX
http://www.allen.lib.la.us
Dr. Wridley A. Fontenot, Assistant Director,
Archivist

L. W. Anderson Genealogical Library
(see Linebaugh Library, Tennessee, Part 2)

Ascension Parish Library
Donaldsonville Branch
500 Mississippi Street
Donaldsonville, LA 70346-2535
(225) 473-8052; (225) 473-9522 FAX
admin.c1ac@pelican.state.lib.la.us
Miss Angelle Deshautelles, Director

Ascension Parish Library
Gonzales Branch
708 South Irma Boulevard
Gonzales, LA 70737
(225) 647-8924; (225) 644-0063 FAX

Assumption Parish Library
293 Napoleon Avenue
Napoleonville, LA 70390-0786
(985) 369-7070; (985) 369-6019 FAX
apl1@pelican.state.lib.la.us;
admin.c1as@pelican.state.lib.la.us
Mary G. Judice, Librarian
Mon & Wed–Thur 8:30–5:30, Tue
8:30–7:00

Audubon Regional Library
West Feliciana Parish Branch
(11865 Ferdinand Street—location)
PO Box 3120 (mailing address)
Saint Francisville, LA 70775
(225) 635-3364; (225) 635-4986 FAX
slou3016@selu.edu
Connie Blakley, Branch Manager

Avoyelles Parish Library
104 North Washington Street
Marksville, LA 71351-2496
(318) 253-7559; (318) 253-6361 FAX
marksville.h1av@pelican.state.lib.la.us
http://wksta1.avoyelles.lib.la.us
Susan Guidry, Associate Librarian; Theresa
Thevenote, Director
Mon–Tue & Thur–Fri 8:00–5:00, Wed
9:00–6:00, Sat 9:00–1:00; 2/05
http://nutrias.org/~nopl/lama/guide/guide.
htm says 253-6561 FAX

**Bayou Lafourche Folklife and Heritage
Museum**
PO Box 416
Lockport, LA 70374
(504) 532-5609; (504) 532-3447
Marjorie Barker, Corresponding Secretary

Beauregard Parish Library
Genealogical Resources
205 South Washington Avenue
DeRidder, LA 70634
(337) 463-6217; (800) 524-6239; (337) 462-
5434 FAX
admin.w1bg@pelican.state.lib.la.us
http://www.beau.lib.la.us/index.html
Lilly Smith, Director

Bienville Parish Library
Headquarters
2768 Maple Street
Arcadia, LA 71001-3699
(318) 263-7410; (318) 263-7428 FAX
admin.g1bv@pelican.state.lib.la.us

http://www.bienville.lib.la.us
Peggy Wall, Director

Caldwell Parish Library
(Corner of Jackson & Pearl—location)
PO Box 1499 (mailing address)
Columbia, LA 71418-1499
(318) 649-2259
admin.t1cd@pelican.state.lib.la.us
Mary Poole, Director

Centenary College of Louisiana
Magale Library, Cline Room
(2911 Centenary Boulevard, Shreveport, LA
71104—location)
PO Box 41188 (mailing address)
Shreveport, LA 71134
(318) 869-5170; (318) 869-5094 FAX
http://www.centenary.edu/centenar/
campusrv/lib/library.html
Carolyn Garison, Collection Development

Le Cercle Historique
734 West Main Street
New Roads, LA 70760
(225) 638-7733
Olinde S. Haag
(Pointe Coupee Parish history and
genealogy)

DeSoto Parish Library
Headquarters
109 Crosby Street
Mansfield, LA 71052-2612
(318) 872-6100; (318) 872-6120 FAX
wberry@pelican.state.lib.la.us
Wanda A. Berry, Director

East Baton Rouge Parish Library
Bluebonnet Regional Branch
9200 Bluebonnet Boulevard
Baton Rouge, LA 70810
(225) 763-2283; (225) 231-3759 FAX
jmyers@CLSN3244.ebr.lib.la.us
Jeanell Strickland, Genealogy Librarian
Mon–Thur 9:00–9:00, Fri–Sat 9:00–6:00,
Sun 2:00–6:00
(covers all Southern states)

East Baton Rouge Parish Library
Headquarters
7711 Goodwood Boulevard
Baton Rouge, LA 70806-7625
(225) 231-3700; (225) 231-3759 FAX
cflint@ebr.lib.la.us;
admin.c1eb@pelican.state.lib.la.us
http://www.ebr.lib.la.us
Carolyn Flint, Head of Reference Services;
John B. Richard, Director

East Carroll Parish Library
109 Sparrow Street
Lake Providence, LA 71254-2645
(318) 559-2615 voice & FAX
admin.t1ec@pelican.state.lib.la.us
Ms. Reneè Whatley, Director

Evangeline Parish Library
(242 West Main Street—location)
PO Box 40 (mailing address)
Ville Platte, LA 70586
(337) 363-1369; (337) 363-2353
xxx1138@ucs.usl.edu
http://www.eplibrary.org
Sesley M. Saunders, Director

Franklin Parish Library
Headquarters
705 Prairie Street
Winnsboro, LA 71295-2795
(318) 435-4336; (318) 435-5946 FAX
FR_lib@alpha.nlu.edu

http://www.franklin.lib.la.us
Betty Coughran, Genealogy

Gallier House Museum
820 Saint Louis Street
New Orleans, LA 70112-3416
Pub. *Gallier House Museum Quarterly*

Foundation for Historical Louisiana
900 North Boulevard
Baton Rouge, LA 70802
Carolyn Bennett, Director

Huntsville-Madison County Public Library
(see Alabama, Part 2)

Iberia Parish Library
445 East Main Street
New Iberia, LA 70560-3710
(337) 373-0075; (337) 373-0086 FAX
admin.b1ib@pelican.state.lib.la.us
http://www.iberia.lib.la.us
Carla Hostetter, Director

Iberville Parish Library
(1501 J. Gerald Berret Boulevard—location)
PO Box 736 (mailing address)
Plaquemine, LA 70764-0736
(225) 687-4397; (225) 687-2520; (225) 344-6948; (225) 687-9719 FAX
ginger@pedio.iberville.lib.la.us
http://www.iberville.lib.la.us
Virginia Borron, Adult Services

Jackson Heritage Museum and Fine Arts Association
515 Cooper Avenue, South
Jonesboro, LA 71251
(318) 259-3119
Mrs. T. L. Colvin, Curator
(church records, parish history)

Jefferson Davis Parish Library
Headquarters
(118 West Plaquemine—location)
PO Box 356 (mailing address)
Jennings, LA 70546-0356
(337) 824-1210; (337) 824-5444 FAX
admin.b1jd@pelican.state.lib.la.us
http://www.beau.lib.la.us/jd.html
Linda LeBert, Director
(vorter registration rolls, newspapers, government records)

Jefferson Parish Library
(4747 West Napoleon Avenue—location)
PO Box 7490 (mailing address)
Metairie, LA 70001-7490
(504) 838-1100 voice & FAX
helpdesk@jefferson.lib.la.us
Dianne Bordelon, Reference Librarian
Mon–Fri 9:00–8:00, Sat 9:00–5:00

Jennings Carnegie Public Library
Attn: Emma Goodreau, Director
303 Cary Avenue
Jennings, LA 70546-5223
(337) 821-5517
egoodrea@pelican.state.lib.la.us;
    admin.b1jn@pelican.state.lib.la.us
(Jefferson Davis Parish)

Lafayette Public Library
(301 West Congress Street, Lafayette, LA 70501—location)
PO Box 3427 (mailing address)
Lafayette, LA 70502-3427
(337) 261-5787; (337) 261-5782 FAX
admin.b1lf@pelican.state.lib.la.us;
    gsmith@pelican.state.lib.la.us
Suzanne Pomerleau, Special Collections

Librarian; Gail Smith, Director
winter: Mon–Thur 9:00–9:00, Fri 9:00–6:00,
Sat 9:00–5:00; summer: Mon–Wed
9:00–7:00, Thur 9:00–9:00, Fri
9:00–6:00, Sat 9:00–5:00

Lafourche Parish Public Library
303 West Fifth Street
Thibodaux, LA 70301-3154
(985) 446-1163; (985) 446-3848 FAX
lpl1@pelican.state.lib.la.us
http://www.lafourche.lib.la.us
Cathy Richard, Library Associate; Paul
    Chiquet, Director
Mon–Fri 9:00–4:00

Lafourche Parish Public Library
Martha Sowell Utley Memorial
314 Saint Mary Street
Thibodaux, LA 70301-2620
(985) 447-4119; (985) 449-4128 FAX
http://www.lafourche.lib.la.us
Elizabeth Wise, Branch Librarian

Lasalle Parish Library
(3108 North First [Highway
127N]—location)
PO Box 3199 (mailing address)
Jena, LA 71342-3199
(318) 992-5675; (318) 992-7374 FAX
http://www.lasalle.lib.la.us
Frances McDonald, Library Director
8:00–5:00, Sat 9:00–1:00
(extensive genealogy, cemeteries, marriages,
    death notices [local paper], census, etc.)

LaSalle Museum Association
PO Box 1019
Jena, LA 71342
(318) 992-4475
Jane Baker, Director
(cemetery records, census, ephemera,
    photographs)

Lincoln Parish Library
509 West Alabama Avenue
Ruston, LA 71270-4231
(318) 251-5030; (318) 255-1920; (318) 251-5045 FAX
lnlib2@lincoln.lib.la.us
Marsha Clinton, Librarian
Mon–Fri 9:00–6:00

Livingston Parish Library
(Headquarters, 13986 Florida
Boulevard—location)
PO Drawer 397 (mailing address)
Livingston, LA 70754-0397
(225) 686-2436; (225) 686-3888 FAX
admin.c1lv@pelican.state.lib.la.us;
    livl@pelican.state.lib.la.us
http://www.livingston.lib.la.us
Allen Cunningham, Director; Iris Stilley,
    Assistant Librarian

Louisiana College
Norton Memorial Library
Pineville, LA 71359
(318) 487-7261; (318) 487-7191 FAX
martin@andria.lacollege.edu
http://www.lacollege.edu
W. Terry Martin, Director
(central Louisiana history, college archives,
    and Baptist Church)

Louisiana State Museum Historical Center
(Old U.S. Mint, 400 Esplanade
Avenue—location)
751 Chartres Street (mailing address)
New Orleans, LA 70176
(504) 568-8214; (800) 568-6968
kpage@crt.state.la.us

http://www.crt.state.la.us/crt/museum/
lsmnet3.htm
Kathryn Page, Curator of Maps and
    Manuscripts
Mon–Fri 9:00–5:00 by appointment only
(colonial Louisiana; special library,
    noncirculating)

Louisiana State University—Alexandria
James C. Bolton Library
8100 Highway 71 South
Alexandria, LA 71302-9121
(318) 473-6437; (318) 473-6556 FAX
aburns@pc01.lsua.edu
Dr. Anna Burns

Louisiana and Lower Mississippi Valley Collections
Special Collections, Hill Memorial Library
Louisiana State University
Baton Rouge, LA 70803-3300
(225) 388-6501; (225) 334-1695 FAX
http://www.lib.lsu.edu/special
Glenn L. McMullen, Curator
Mon–Fri 9:00–5:00, Sat 9:00–1:00
(Louisiana and the Lower Mississippi
    Valley, including Mississippi and
    Arkansas; French-language manuscript
    resources)
limited research, charges for copies

Louisiana State University—Baton Rouge
Middleton Library, Department of Archives
and Manuscripts
Room 202
Baton Rouge, LA 70803
(225) 388-2240

Louisiana State University—Eunice
Arnold LeDoux Library
PO Box 1129
Eunice, LA 70535
(337) 550-1380 (Office); (337) 550-1385
    (Reference)
Library Director
Mon–Wed 8:00–8:00, Thur–Fri 8:00–4:30,
    Sat (fall & spring) 9:00–noon, Sat
    (summer) 8:00–4:30, Sun (fall & spring)
    1:00–5:00
$10.00 Friends of the Library donation

Louisiana State University—Shreveport
Noel Memorial Library
Archives and Special Collections
1 University Place
Shreveport, LA 71115-2399
(318) 797-5378; (318) 797-5156 FAX
http://www.lsus.edu/library
Laura B. Conerly, Acting Archivist
Mon–Tue & Thur–Fri 8:00–4:30, Wed
    8:00–9:00
(Louisiana and Northwest Louisiana history

Louisiana State University—Shreveport
Pioneer Heritage Center
Bronson Hall 106
1 University Place
Shreveport, LA 71115-2399
(318) 797-5332; (318) 797-5237
mplummer@pilot.lsus.edu
http://www.lsus.edu/comm/social.htm
Marguerite R. Plummer, Director
by appointment
("A Regional History Museum; The Pioneer
    Heritage Center has transferred
    photographs and documents to Noel
    Memorial Library," Louisiana State
    University—Shreveport)

Louisiana State University—Shreveport
Red River Regional Studies Center
Bronson Hall 106

1 University Place
Shreveport, LA 71115-2399
(318) 797-5332; (318) 797-5237
mplummer@pilot.lsus.edu
Marguerite R. Plummer
Pub. *Red River Review*

Louisiana Tech University
Prescott Memorial Library
Special Collections, Manuscripts, and
Archives
300 Everett Street
Ruston, LA 71272
(318) 257-2935; (318) 257-2447 FAX
kathys@vm.cc.latech.edu
http://www.latech.edu/specialcollections
Michael A. DiCarlo, Assistant Director of
Public Serives
(north Louisiana history, university archives)

Loyola University of New Orleans
Loyola University Library
Special Collections and Archives
6363 Saint Charles Avenue
New Orleans, LA 70118
(504) 865-3186; (504) 865-3347 FAX
acarpntr@beta.loyno.edu
http://www.lib.loyno.edu
Art Carpenter, Archivist

Madison Parish Library
403 North Mulberry
Tallulah, LA 71282-3599
(318) 574-4308; (318) 574-4312 FAX
MA_LIB1@Alpha.nlu.edu
Gay Yerger, Director

McNeese State University
Archives and Special Collections
Frazar Memorial
PO Box 91445
Lake Charles, LA 70609-1445
(318) 475-5734; (318) 475-5719 FAX
bordelon@mail.mcneese.edu
http://www.mcneese.edu/depts/library/depts
Kathie Bordelon, Archivist/Special
Collections Librarian

Morgan City Archives
Young-Sanders Center
501 Federal Avenue
Morgan City, LA 70381
(504) 380-4650 voice & FAX
ysclee@iamerica.net
http://www.youngsanders.org
Patrick Hotard, Curator

Natchitoches Parish Library
431 Jefferson Street
Natchitoches, LA 71457
(318) 357-3280
admin.g1nt@pelican.state.lib.la.us
Beatrice Ponder, Parish Librarian

The Historic New Orleans Collection
Williams Research Center
410 Chartres Street
New Orleans, LA 70130
(504) 598-7171; (504) 598-7168 FAX
alfredl@hnoc.org
http://www.hnoc.org
Alfred E. Lemmon, Curator of Manuscripts
Tue–Sat 10:00–4:30
Pub. *The Historic New Orleans Collection
Quarterly*, no charge

The New Orleans Notarial Archives
Civil District Courts Building
421 Loyola Avenue
New Orleans, LA 70112
(504) 568-8577; (504) 568-8599
skrnona@gnofn.org

Sally K. Reeves, Archivist
Mon–Fri 9:00–4:00
(notarial acts, New Orleans and Louisiana
and the south, from 1731 to the present)

New Orleans Public Library
Louisiana Division
219 Loyola Avenue, Third Floor
New Orleans, LA 70112-2044
(504) 596-2614
http://nutrias.org
Collin B. Hamer, Jr., Head, Louisiana
Division
Mon–Thur 10:00–6:00, Fri–Sat 11:00–5:00
(All types of printed, manuscript, graphic,
and oral resources relating to the study of
Louisiana and its citizens; other areas of
interest include the Mississippi River, the
Gulf of Mexico, and the South; is the
official City Archives of New Orleans and
is also the official repository for the pre-
1928 records of the Civil Courts and the
pre-1932 records of the Criminal Courts
of Orleans Parish. "We also have census
microfilm through 1880 for southeast
U.S., including Texas, and through 1920
for Mississipi and Alabama.")
copies of exact references: $2.00 per page
(limit of five items) plus SASE; search
services: from $2.00 to $3.00 per name,
maximum of ten names per search

Nicholls State University Library
Ellender Memorial Library
Archives and Special Collections
PO Box 2028
Thibodaux, LA 70310
(504) 448-2621; (504) 448-4925 FAX
el-ca@nich-nsunet.nich.edu
Carol A. Mathias, Head

Northeast Louisiana University
Sandel Library
Archives and Special Collections
700 University Avenue
Monroe, LA 71209-0720
(318) 342-1054; (318) 342-1055; (318) 342-
1075 FAX
Glenn Jordan, Curator

Northwestern State University of
Louisiana
Eugene P. Watson Memorial Library
Cammie G. Henry Research Center
Natchitoches, LA 71497
(318) 357-4585; (318) 357-4468; (318) 357-
4470 FAX
Wernet@alpha.nsula.edu
http://www.nsula.edu/departments/
watson_library
Mary Linn Wernet, University Archivist

Nunez Community College
Archives
3700 LaFontaine Street
Chalmette, LA 70043
(504) 278-7440, ext. 244; (504) 278-7484
FAX
mcurtis@nunez.cc.la.us
http://www.nunez.cc.la.us
Meredith Curtis, Librarian
(books, institutional records, manuscript
collections, maps, newspapers, oral
history, photographs)

Opelousas-Eunice Public Library
Opelousas Public Library (Saint Landry
Parish)
(212 East Grolee Street—location)
PO Box 249 (mailing address)
Opelousas, LA 70570-0249
(337) 948-3693; (337) 948-5200

paopeul@unix1.sncc.lsu.edu
Walter O. Stubbs, Director

Ouachita Parish Public Library
1800 Stubbs Avenue
Monroe, LA 71201-2044
(318) 327-1490; (318) 327-1373 FAX
ou-libl@alpha.nlu.edu (Reference)
http://www.ouachita.lib.la.us
Miss Wheeler, Genealogy Department
Mon–Fri 9:00–5:30, Sat 9:00–5:00, Sun
2:00–5:00
(strong Southern states collection)

Plaquemines Parish Library
35572 Highway 11, South
Buras, LA 70041-1625
(504) 657-7121; (504) 657-7122; (504) 657-
6175 FAX
jcantwel@pelican.state.lib.la.us;
admin.s1pq@pelican.state.lib.la.us
Janet Cantwell, Director

Point Coupee Parish Library
201 Claiborne Street
New Roads, LA 70760-3403
(225) 638-7593; (225) 638-9841; (225) 638-
9847 FAX
admin.c1pc@pelican.state.lib.la.us
http://www.pointe-coupee.lib.la.us
Melissa K. Hymel, Director
Mon–Thur 8:30–8:30, Fri–Sat 8:30–5:00,
Sun 1:00–5:00

Rapides Parish Library
Main Branch
411 Washington Street
Alexandria, LA 71301-8338
(318) 442-1840; (318) 445-6436; (318) 445-
6478 FAX (Main Library); (318) 445-
6196 FAX (Administration)
admin.h1ra@pelican.state.lib.la.us
http://www.rpl.org
Wesley H. Saunders, Reference Coordinator;
Steve Rogge, Director
Mon–Sat 9:00–6:00
(specializes in Louisiana history and
genealogy)

Red River Parish Library
(2022 Alonzo Carroll—location)
PO Box 1367 (mailing address)
Coushatta, LA 71019-1367
(318) 932-5614; (318) 932-6747 FAX
mlewis@pelican.state.lib.la.us
Mr. Marvin W. Lewis, III, Director

Richland Parish Library
1410 Louisa Street
Rayville, LA 71269-3299
(318) 728-4806; (318) 728-6108 FAX
bdoran@pelican.state.lib.la.us
Brenda Doran, Director

Sabine Parish Library
Headquarters
705 Main Street
Many, LA 71449-3199
(318) 256-4150; (318) 256-4154 FAX
rmorris@pelican.state.lib.la.us
Rebecca Morris, Director

Saint Charles Parish Library
(Headquarters, 105 Lakewood
Drive—location)
PO Box 9494 (mailing address)
Luling, LA 70070-0975
(985) 785-8464; (985) 785-8499 FAX
mdesbord@stcharles.lib.la.us;
admin.s1ch@pelican.state.lib.la.us
Mary desBordes, Director; Christy Chandler,
Public Services Librarian

Saint James Parish Library
1879 West Main Street
Lutcher, LA 70071-9704
(985) 869-3618; (985) 869-8435 FAX
sjpl1@pelican.state.lib.la.us
http://www.stjames.lib.la.us
Sarah B. Byrd, Reference Librarian
Mon–Thur 8:30–6:00, Fri 8:30–5:00, Sat
    8:30–1:00

Saint John the Baptist Parish Library
1334 West Airline Highway
La Place, LA 70068-3721
(985) 652-6857; (985) 652-2144 FAX
rdesoto@stjohn.lib.la.us;
    admin.s1jb@pelican.state.lib.la.us
http://www.stjohn.lib.la.us
Michael Maurin, Reference; Randy A.
    DeSoto, Director
Mon–Thur 8:30–9:00, Fri–Sat 8:30–5:30

Saint Martin Parish Library
(201 Porter Street—location)
PO Box 79 (mailing address)
Saint Martinville, LA 70582-0079
(337) 394-2207; (337) 394-2248 FAX
http://www.stmartin.lib.la.us
Jeanne Essemier
Mon–Thur 8:00–8:00, Fri–Sat 8:00–5:00

Saint Tammany Parish Public Library
Covington Branch
310 West 21st Street
Covington, LA 70433-3100
(985) 893-6280; (985) 871-0124 (Electronic
    Resource Center)
http://www.sttammany.lib.la.us
Electronic Resource Center: Mon–Tue
    11:30–7:30, Wed–Fri 9:00–5:00

Shreve Memorial Library
(424 Texas Street, Shreveport, LA
71101—location)
PO Box 21523 (mailing address)
Shreveport, LA 71120-1523
(318) 226-5890; (318) 226-5871; (318) 226-
    4780 FAX
jgahagan@smlnet.sml.lib.la.us
http://www.shreve-lib.org
Faedra Wills, Genealogy Librarian; Julia
    Gahagan, Special Collections Librarian
Mon–Thur 9:00–7:00, Mon–Thur (Labor
    Day–Memorial Day) 9:00–9:00, Fri–Sat
    9:00–6:00, Sun 1:00–5:00
(emphasis is on the South, also a Louisiana
    Collection which is primarily history)

**Snyder Memorial Museum and Creative
Arts Center**
1620 East Madison Avenue
Bastrop, LA 71220
(318) 281-8760
Joni H. Noble, Director

Southeastern Lousiana University Library
Center for Regional Studies, Archives and
Special Collections
(Western Avenue—location)
SLU Station, Box 370 (mailing address)
Hammond, LA 70402
(985) 549-2151; (985) 549-3995 FAX
http://www.selu.edu
Samuel C. Hyde, Jr., Director

**Southwest Louisiana Genealogical and
Historical Library**
411 Pujo Street
Lake Charles, LA 70601-4254
(337) 437-3490; (337) 437-4198 FAX
gen@calcasieu.lib.la.us
http://www.calcasieu.lib.la.us
Shirley Burwell, Genealogist

Mon–Sat 9:30–5:30, Sun 1:30–5:30
("Part of the Calcasieu Parish Public Library
    System.")

Tangipahoa Parish Library
Genealogy Branch
200 East Mulberry Street
Amite, LA 70422
(504) 748-7559; (504) 748-2812 FAX
http://www.tangipahoa.lib.la.us
Lenore Johnson, Branch Manager
Mon–Fri 8:30–5:30, Sat 8:30–3:00

Terrebonne Parish Library
Main Branch
424 Roussell Street
Houma, LA 70360
(985) 876-5864
ter@pelican.state.lib.la.us
http://www.terrebonne.lib.la.us
Mon–Thur 9:00–8:00, Fri–Sat 9:00–5:00

Tulane University
Howard-Tilton Memorial Library
7001 Freret Street at Newcomb Place
New Orleans, LA 70118-5682
(504) 865-5685 (Manuscripts/Special
    Collections); (504) 865-5643 (Louisiana
    Collection); (504) 865-6773 (Louisiana
    Collection) FAX; (504) 865-5605
    (Reference); (504) 865-5681 (Latin
    American Archives)
meneray@mailhost.tcs.tulane.edu (Special
    Collections Division);
    lmiller@mailhost.tcs.tulane.edu
    (Manuscripts Department)
http://www.tulane.edu
Leon C. Miller, Manuscripts; Joan Caldwell,
    Louisiana Collection
General Library: Mon–Fri 8:30–12:45, Sat
    8:30–9:45, Sun 10:00–12:45 during
    school session; Manuscripts: Mon–Fri
    8:30–5:00, Sat 9:00–1:00; Louisiana
    Collection: Mon–Fri 8:30–5:00, Sat
    1:00–5:00

University of Louisiana, Lafayette
Jefferson Caffery Louisiana Room
Edith Garland Dupré Library
(302 East Saint Mary Boulevard, Lafayette,
LA 70503-2038—location)
PO Box 40199 (mailing address)
Lafayette, LA 70504-0199
(337) 482-6031; (337) 482-5841 FAX
jkiesel@louisiana.edu
http://library.louisiana.edu
Jean S. Kiesel, Louisiana Room Librarian
Mon–Tue 7:30 A.M.–9:00 P.M., Wed–Fri
    7:30–4:30, Sat 10:00–2:00
("We do not have the staff to do genealogical
    research for patrons.")

University of New Orleans
Earl K. Long Library/Louisiana and Special
Collections Department
Lakefront Campus
New Orleans, LA 70148
(504) 280-6543; (504) 280-7227 FAX
mewli@uno.edu
http://www.uno.edu/Welcome.shtml
Florence M. Jumonville, Head of Louisiana
    and Special Collections
Louisiana and Special Collections: Mon–Fri
    8:00–4:30, Sat (when classes are in
    session) 10:00–4:00 (some collections
    available by appointment only)
(specializes in Lutheran records, ethnic
    groups of New Orleans, preservation
    groups, Louisiana Supreme Court legal
    archives, business records, Orleans Parish
    School Board records, records of civic
    organizations)

University of Southern Alabama
Gulf Coast Historical Review
(see Alabama, Part 2)

Vermilion Parish Library
Abbeville Branch (Headquarters)
(200 North Magdalen Square, Abbeville, LA
70510—location)
PO Drawer 640 (mailing address)
Abbeville, LA 70511
(337) 893-2655 (Headquarters); (337) 893-
    2674; (337) 898-0526 FAX
jchoate@pelican.state.lib.la.us
Ms. Jackie Choate, Director

Vernon Parish Library
1401 Nolan Trace at Abe Allen Memorial
Drive
Leesville, LA 71446-4331
(337) 239-2027; (800) 737-2231; (337) 238-
    0666 FAX
hcoy@pelican.state.lib.la.us
http://www.beau.lib.la.us/vpl.html
Howard L. Coy, Jr., Director
Mon, Wed, Fri & Sat 8:00–5:30, Tue & Thur
    8:00–7:30
(participates in interlibrary loan, will only do
    simple search)

Washington Parish Library System
825 Free Street
Franklinton, LA 70438-1499
(985) 839-5336; (985) 839-7808 FAX
slou3012@selu.edu;
    admin.c1wa@pelican.state.lib.la.us;
    franklinton.c1wa@pelican.state.lib.la.us
Bonnie Dier, Genealogy Librarian
Mon–Fri 10:00–5:00, Sat 10:00–1:00

Washington Parish Library System
Bogalusa Branch
304 Avenue F
Bogalusa, LA 70427
(985) 735-1961
bogalusa.c1wa@pelican.state.lib.la.us
Alecia Applewhite, Branch Assistant
Mon 10:00–6:00, Tue–Fri 10:00–5:00, Sat
    10:00–3:00

Webster Parish Library
Headquarters
521 East and West Street
Minden, LA 71055
(318) 371-3080; 318-371-3075; (318) 371-
    3081 FAX
ehammont@pelican.state.lib.la.us
http://www.webster.lib.la.us
Ms. Eddie Hammontree, Director

West Baton Rouge Parish Library
830 North Alexander
Port Allen, LA 70767-2327
(225) 342-7920; (225) 342-7918 FAX
amarchia@pelican.state.lib.la.us;
    admin.c1we@pelican.state.lib.la.us;
    pawbr1@unix1.sncc.lsu.edu
Anna G. Marchiafava, Director
Mon, Wed & Fri 8:30–5:30, Tue & Thur
    8:30–8:00, Sat 9:00–5:00

Xavier University
Archives and Special Collections
7325 Palmetto Street
New Orleans, LA 70125
(504) 483-7655; (504) 486-2385 FAX
Lester Sullivan, University Archivist and
    Assistant Librarian for Special Collections

Historical Societies—Local and Regional

The Alexandria Historical and Genealogical Library and Museum
503 Washington Street
Alexandria, LA 71301
(318) 487-8556
Gic Kraushaar, President and Museum Director
Tue–Sat 10:00–4:00
$10.00 per year membership; free admission

Allen Genealogical and Historical Society
(see Genealogical Societies—Local and Regional, below)

American West Research Center and Historical Society, Inc.
(see Ohio, Part 2)

Attakapas Historical Association
University of Louisiana, Lafayette
PO Box 4-3010
Lafayette, LA 70504
(337) 231-6029
Glenn R. Conrad, Secretary-Treasurer
Pub. *Attakapas Gazette*, quarterly
$8.00 per year membership

Baton Rouge Genealogical and Historical Society
(see Genealogical Societies—Local and Regional, below)

Bernice Historical Society
Bernice Depot Museum and Captain Henderson Caboose
PO Box 186
Bernice, LA 71222
(318) 285-9071 (Town Hall)

Brimstone Historical Society and Museum
800 Picard Road
Sulphur, LA 70663
(337) 527-7142
Glenda L. Vincent, Museum Director
Mon–Fri 9:30–5:00
$10.00 per year membership

Caddo-Pine Island Oil and Historical Society
(207 Land Avenue—location)
PO Box 897 (mailing address)
Oil City, LA 70161
(318) 995-8645; (318) 995-6848 FAX
Coe Haygood, Director
(primarily historical, not genealogical; Caddo Indians, Kansas City Southern Railroad)

La Commission des Avoyelles, Inc.
PO Box 26
Hamburg, LA 71339
(318) 985-2791; (318) 985-2958 FAX
Carlos A. Mayeux, Jr.
Pub. *Annual Newsletter* (Aug)
("Historical organization. Publications for sale: history, genealogy, cookbooks.")

De Soto Historical and Genealogical Society
PO Box 523
Mansfield, LA 71052
(318) 872-1591
Raymond E. Powell, Past President and Board Member
Mon–Fri 8:00–4:00
Pub. *De Soto Plume*, quarterly
$10.00 per year membership

East Ascension Genealogical and Historical Society
(see Genealogical Societies—Local and Regional, below)

Evangeline Genealogical and Historical Society
(see Genealogical Societies—Local and Regional, below)

Franklin Parish Genealogical and Historical Society
(see Genealogical Societies—Local and Regional, below)

French Settlement Historical Society
(see Ethnic Archives, Libraries and Societies—French, Part 3)

Friends of Cabildo
701 Chartres Street
New Orleans, LA 70115
(504) 523-3939

German-Acadian Coast Historical and Genealogical Society
PO Box 517
Destrehan, LA 70047-0517
105101.1016@compuserve.com
Pub. *Les Voyageurs*, quarterly (Mar, June, Sept, Dec)
$15.00 per year membership

Gretna Historical Society
PO Box 115
Gretna, LA 70054
(504) 362-3854; (504) 363-1529 FAX
J. B. Borel, Archivist

Imperial/Saint Landry Genealogical and Historical Society
(see Genealogical Societies—Local and Regional, below)

Jackson Assembly, Inc.
PO Box 494
Jackson, LA 70748
(225) 634-7155

Le Musée de la Ville de Kaplan
Kaplan, LA
(318) 643-1528
kaplanmuseum@kaplantel.net
http://www.vrml.k12.la.us/vermilion
Mary V. Menard

LaFourche Heritage Society
PO Box 913
Thibodaux, LA 70302-0913
Dorothy Naquin

Lasalle Art Association and Genealogical Association
Route 1, Box 234
Trout, LA 71371
(318) 992-6210
Louise DeMars Windham, Past President

Edward Livingston Historical Association
PO Box 67
Livingston, LA 70754-0067
Warren B. Wall, President
Pub. *E.L.H.A. Gram*, quarterly

Louisiana Historical Association
Center for Louisiana Studies
University of Louisiana, Lafayette
PO Box 40831, USL
Lafayette, LA 70504
(337) 231-6029
Pub. *Louisiana History*, quarterly, $18.00 per year subscription; *Louisiana History Newsletter*, quarterly

Louisiana Roots
PO Box 383
Marksville, LA 71351

(318) 253-5413; (318) 253-7223 fax

Madison Parish Historical Society, Inc.
(400 North Mulberry Street—location)
PO Box 268 (mailing address)
Tallulah, LA 71284
(318) 574-3542
Glenn Booth, President
(genealogical records of Madison residents)
$15.00 per year membership

Mount Lebanon Historical Society
Stage Coach Trail Museum
Rt. 2, Box 50
Gibsland, LA 71028
(318) 843-6455; (318) 843-6255
P. J. Eaton, Corresponding Secretary

Natchitoches Genealogical and Historical Association
(see Genealogical Societies—Local and Regional, below)

Historical Society of North Caddo
PO Box 500
Vivian, LA 71082

North Louisiana Historical Association
PO Box 6701
Shreveport, LA 71136-6701
(318) 797-5355; (318) 797-5122 FAX
athompso@pilot.lsus.edu
Dr. Alan Thompson, Editor
Mon, Wed & Fri 10:00–11:00 & 1:00–3:00, Tue & Thur 9:00–noon & 1:00–3:00
Pub. *North Louisiana Historical Association Journal*, three times per year
$12.00 per year membership

Opelousas Historical Society
(Opelousas Museum and Interpretive Center, 329 North Main Street—location)
PO Box 712 (mailing address)
Opelousas, LA 70571-0712
(318) 948-2589; (318) 948-2534 FAX
Sue Deville, Director

Pointe de l'Eglise: Acadia Genealogical and Historical Society
(see Genealogical Societies—Local and Regional, below)

Red River Crossroads Historical and Cultural Association, Inc.
PO Box 322
Gilliam, LA 71029
(318) 296-4303; (318) 296-4233 FAX
Karen B. Logan, President, Board of Directors

River Road Historical Society
(9999 River Road—location)
PO Box 5 (mailing address)
Destrehan, LA 70047
(985) 764-9315; (985) 725-1929 FAX
destplan@aol.com
http://www.destrehanplantation.org
Irene Tastet, Administrator
9:30–4:00
Pub. *Le Communique*, quarterly

Saint Augustine Historical Society
PO Box 39
Melrose, LA 71456
(318) 357-0602
colsonj@cp-tel.net
http://members.tripod.com/creoles

Saint Charles Avenue Association
5801 Saint Charles Avenue
New Orleans, LA 70115

Saint Helena Historical Association
6370 Highway 43
Montpelier, LA 70422-8227
Inez B. Tate, President

Saint James Historical Society
PO Box 426
Gramercy, LA 70052
(504) 869-9752 voice & FAX

Saint Mary Genealogical and Historical Society
(see Genealogical Societies—Local and Regional, below)

Saint Tammany Historical Society, Inc.
Saint Tammany History Library
310 West 21st Street
Covington, LA 70433
(985) 893-6280; (985) 893-6281 FAX
John T. Hunley, Corresponding Secretary

Southeast Louisiana Historical Association
Southeastern Louisiana University
PO Box 789
Hammond, LA 70401-0789
Pub. *Southeast Louisiana Historical Association Papers*, annually
$5.00 per year membership

Southern Historical Association
Tulane University
New Orleans, LA 70118
(504) 865-6201

Southern Studies Institute
Northwestern State University of Louisiana
Natchitoches, LA 71497
(318) 357-5507
Dr. Maxine Taylor
Pub. *Southern Studies Journal*, quarterly, $20.00 per year subscription

Southwest Louisiana Historical Association
4201 Alma Lane
Lake Charles, LA 70605
(318) 478-5753
74434.3600@compuserve.com
Robert Benoit, President

Tangipahoa Parish Historical Society
200 East Mulberry Street
Amite, LA 70422-2524

Terrebonne Historical and Cultural Society, Inc.
(1208 Museum Drive, Houma, LA 70360—location)
PO Box 2095 (mailing address)
Houma, LA 70361
(985) 851-0154; (985) 868-1476 FAX
southdown@mobiletel.com
http://www.southdownmuseum.org
Stephen H. Braud, President
Tue–Sun 10:00–4:00
Pub. *THCS Newsletter*, quarterly
$10.00 per year membership

Vermilion Historic Foundation
(1600 Surrey Street—location)
PO Box 226 (mailing address)
Lafayette, LA 70502-2266
(337) 233-4077; (800) 99-BAYOU

Vermilion Historical Society
PO Box 877
Abbeville, LA 70511-0877
(318) 893-7142; (318) 893-4908 FAX
76462.1276@compuserve.com
Gary E. Theall, Secretary-Treasurer

Vernon Historical and Genealogical Society
3713 Highway 121
Leesville, LA 71446
(318) 238-2963
Doris H. Mayo, Editor

West Baton Rouge Historical Association
West Baton Rouge Museum
845 North Jefferson
Port Allen, LA 70767
(225) 336-2422; (225) 336-2448 FAX
Roddey Peebles, Jr., Curator
Mon 10:00–4:30 by appointment, Tue–Sat 10:00–4:30
Pub. *Ecoutez*, bimonthly

West Feliciana Historical Society
(Ferdinand Street—location)
PO Box 338 (mailing address)
Saint Francisville, LA 70775
(225) 635-6330
("We do not do any genealogical work and have no records.")

Winn Parish Genealogical and Historical Society
(see Genealogical Societies—Local and Regional, below)

Genealogical Societies

State Genealogical Society

Louisiana Genealogical and Historical Society
PO Box 82060
Baton Rouge, LA 70884-2060
Nell T. Boersma, Editor; Jane G. Aprill, President
Pub. *The Louisiana Genealogical Register*, quarterly
$25.00 per year membership

Southern Society of Genealogists, Inc.
(see Alabama, Part 2)

Genealogical Societies—Local & Regional

The Alexandria Historical and Genealogical Library and Museum
(see Historical Societies—Local and Regional, above)

Allen Genealogical and Historical Society
PO Box 789
Kinder, LA 70648

Ark-La-Tex Genealogical Association, Inc.
(see Arkansas, Part 2)

Baton Rouge Genealogical and Historical Society
PO Box 80565, S.E. Station
Baton Rouge, LA 70895-0565
(225) 765-7369
rcollins@intersurf.com
http://www.intersurf.com/~rcollins.brg.htm
Ruby Nell Collins, email and Web Page
meetings third Sat 1:30 at East Baton Rouge Parish Library, Bluebonnet Regional Branch
Pub. *le Baton Rouge*, quarterly
$20.00 per year membership

Central Louisiana Genealogical Society
PO Box 12206
Alexandria, LA 71315-2206
David Manning, President
meetings: first Sun 2:00–4:30
Pub. *Central Louisiana Genealogical Society Quarterly* (Jan, Apr, July, Oct)

(family charts, Bible records, original record abstracts)
$15.00 per year membership; queries: free 50-word queries for members, $2.50 for nonmembers

De Soto Historical and Genealogical Society
(see Historical Societies—Local and Regional, above)

East Ascension Genealogical and Historical Society
PO Box 1006
Gonzales, LA 70707-1006
(225) 644-4547; (225) 647-2987 FAX
James M. Templeton, Jr., President
Pub. *Journal of the East Ascension Genealogical and Historical Society*, quarterly
$10.00 per year membership

Evangeline Genealogical and Historical Society
PO Box 664
Ville Platte, LA 70586
(318) 599-2047
conway@century.inter.net
M. J. Conway, Treasurer
Mon–Fri 9:00–5:00, Sat 9:00–noon
Pub. *La Voix des Prairies*, quarterly
(emphasis on Louisiana and southwest genealogy)
$10.00 per year membership; free queries

Franklin Parish Genealogical and Historical Society
Route 4, Box 150
Winnsboro, LA 71295

Friends of Genealogy, Inc.
PO Box 17835
Shreveport, LA 71138-0835
(318) 424-7648; (318) 636-7798 voice & FAX
xhhu66a@prodigy.com
Laura H. Duffy, President; Janine J. Dunlap, Editor
8:00–8:00
Pub. *The Journal*, quarterly
$15.00 per year membership; free queries to members and nonmembers

German-Acadian Coast Historical and Genealogical Society
(see Historical Societies—Local and Regional, above)

Imperial/Saint Landry Genealogical and Historical Society
PO Box 108
Opelousas, LA 70571-0108
(337) 942-3332

Jefferson Genealogical Society
PO Box 961
Metairie, LA 70004-0961
jeffersongenealogicalsociety@yahoo.com
http://www.geocities.com/
jeffersongenealogicalsociety; http://www.freepages.genealogy.rootsweb.com/~saintdomingue (SIG)
Dwight Duplessis, President
Pub. *Jefferson Genealogical Society Newsletter*, bimonthly
("Also Saint-Domingue Special Interest Group: *Saint-Domingue Newsletter*, quarterly")
$10.00 per year membership; $8.00 per year membership in SIG; queries

Natchitoches Genealogical and Historical

Association
(Old Courthouse, Second and Church
Streets, Second Floor—location)
PO Box 1349 (mailing address)
Natchitoches, LA 71458-1349
(318) 357-2235
ngha@wnonline.net
http://www.rootsweb.com/~lanatchi/ngl.htm
Theophile Scott, President
Mon–Fri 9:00–4:00, Sat 10:00–4:00
Pub. *Natchitoches Genealogists*, two times
     per year, $6.00 per issue
$15.00 per year membership

**Genealogical Research Society of New
Orleans**
PO Box 51791
New Orleans, LA 70151-1791
(504) 488-1660
http://www.rootsweb.com/~lagrsno
Jack A. Belsom, President
Pub. *New Orleans Genesis*, quarterly (Jan,
     Apr, July, Oct)
("All books we receive are made a part of the
     collection at the New Orleans Public
     Library, Louisiana Division.")
$30.00 per year membership; free queries in
     quarterly; will "refer researchers to
     competent researchers or to the library
     that can handle their questions"

North Louisiana Genealogical Society
PO Box 324
Ruston, LA 71273-0324
Freida J. Hamilton, President
("The society is probably going to cease in
     the near future.")
$15.00 per year membership

**Plaquemines Deep Delta Genealogical
Society**
Plaquemines Parish Library
35572 Highway 11
Buras, LA 70041
(985) 657-7121 (Library)

**Pointe de l'Eglise: Acadia Genealogical
and Historical Society, Inc.**
PO Box 497
Crowle, LA 70527
thewayrichard@cox.net
http://www.rootsweb.com/~lapehgs/
     index.htm
Thelma Richard, Corresponding Secretary
Pub. *A la Pointe*, quarterly
("Other publications: *Cemetery Listings of
     Acadia Parish, Louisiana* [volumes 1–5],
     *World War I Acadia Parish Draft
     Registration* [6,900 records], *World War I
     Acadia Parish Veteran Discharge
     Records* [1,100], *Guidry Funeral Home
     Records* [3,072], *Savoie Family Book*,
     Acadia Parish Obituaries, [1870 to
     present]. Only lookups available at this
     time. Collection of articles of Acadia
     Parish history and genealogical data. The
     society was founded in 1989. We are a
     nonprofit organization with over 200
     members in 17 states. We support the
     Acadia Parish, Louisiana, Library
     system.")
$15.00 per year membership

**Saint Bernard Parish Genealogical
Society, Inc.**
PO Box 271
Chalmette, LA 70044-0271
(504) 271-0896
suewessing@cox.net
http://www.ccugpc.org/sbgs/sbgs.htm
Suzanne Wessing, President
Pub. *L'Heritage*, quarterly

$20.00 per year membership

**Saint Mary Genealogical and Historical
Society**
PO Box 662
Morgan City, LA 70381

Saint Tammany Genealogical Society
(310 West 21st Street, Covington, LA
70433—location)
PO Box 1904 (mailing address)
Covington, LA 70434-1904
(985) 892-6561
mdutsch@juno.com
http://www.StTammanyGS.org
Martha Dutsch, President
meetings: second Tue (Sept–May) 1:30
Pub. *St. Tammany Ancestral Roots*, quarterly
$15.00 per year membership; research: none
     available, but will list queries on its web
     site

**Southwest Louisiana Genealogical Society,
Inc.**
PO Box 5652
Lake Charles, LA 70606-5652
(337) 477-3087
phuffaker@xspedius.net
http://homepages.xspedius.net/mmoore/
     calcasie/swlgs.htm
Mrs. Pat Huffaker, President
Pub. *Kinfolks*, quarterly
$12.00 per year membership

Terrebonne Genealogical Society
PO Box 295, Station 2
Houma, LA 70360-5652
pchau@cajun.net
http://www.rootsweb.com/~laterreb/
     laterreb.htm
Phil Cauvin, President; Jess Bergeron,
     Corresponding Secretary
Terrebonne Parish Library: Mon–Thur
     9:00–7:00, Fri–Sat 9:00–5:00
Pub. *Terrebonne Life Lines*, monthly;
     *Terrebonne Genealogical Society
     Newsletter*, monthly
$20.00 per year membership

Vermilion Genealogical Society
(307 North Main Street—location)
PO Box 117 (mailing address)
Abbeville, LA 70511-0117
(337) 893-1363 (Secretary's office); (337)
     893-4965 (Secretary) FAX
Aline Meaux, President; Mary Broussard,
     Secretary
meetings bimonthly
Pub. *Echoes of the Past*, annually
$10.00 per year membership

**Vernon Historical and Genealogical
Society**
(see Historical Societies—Local and
Regional, above)

West Bank Genealogy Society
PO Box 872
Harvey, LA 70059-0872
(504) 364-3727; (504) 364-3723 FAX
m1c01@gnofn.org
http://www.challenger.net/local/users/
     lindas/jefferson/wbgs.html
Mary L. Cooper Pilgrim

West Baton Rouge Genealogical Society
PO Box 1126
Port Allen, LA 70767-1126
(225) 343-8417
Ann R. Newman, President
daily 9:00–4:00
Pub. *West Baton Rouge Genealogical

Society Newsletter, quarterly
$10.00 per year membership

**Winn Parish Genealogical and Historical
Society**
PO Box 652
Winnfield, LA 71483

Independent Publications and
Miscellany

Acadian House Publishing
PO Box 52247
Lafayette, LA 70505
(337) 235-7919; (337) 235-8851; (337) 235-
     9925 FAX
Trent Angers, Publisher
Mon–Fri 8:30–5:30
Pub. *Acadiana Profile, the Magazine of the
     Cajun Country*, bimonthly, $17.00 per
     six-issue subscription, $33.00 per twelve-
     issue subscription, $49.00 per eighteen-
     issue subscription, $65.00 per twenty-four
     issue subscription
(south Louisiana, "Cajun Country")
free catalog available on request

Action Cadienne (Cajun Action)
PO Box 60104
Lafayette, LA 70596-0104
info@actioncadienne.org
http://www.actioncadienne.org
Scott Long
$15.00 per year membership

Beau Fort Plantation
PO Box 2300
Natchitoches, LA 71457
(318) 352-9580; (318) 352-7280 FAX
Ann Brittain, Owner
(Natchitoches Parish genealogy)

Emy-Lou Biedenharn Foundation
2006 Riverside Drive
Monroe, LA 71201
(318) 387-5281; (318) 387-8253 FAX
Jim Bert, Executive Director
(house museum)

Cajun Clickers Computer Club
10120 Red Red Oak Drive
Baton Rouge, LA 70815
(225) 273-7113; (225) 273-7713 FAX
http://www.clickers.org
Art Nichols, President; Billy Danner,
     Membership Director
$42.00 per year membership

Comité Louisiane Française
2717 Massachusetts Avenue
Metairie, LA 70003
(504) 469-2555

Courier Publications
PO Box 1320
Winnfield, LA 71483-1320
Pub. *Louisiana State Courier*, quarterly,
     $20.00 per year subscription

**Department of Transportation and
Development**
maps@dotd.state.la.us
http://www.dotd.state.la.us/maps.shtml
(Maps)

**East Baton Rouge Park and Recreation
Commission**
Magnolia Mound
2161 Nicholson Drive
Baton Rouge, LA 70802
(225) 343-4955; (225) 343-6739 FAX

Gwen Edwards, Director

Eunice Museum
220 South C. C. Duson Drive
Eunice, LA 70535
(318) 457-6540
Erica Ledoux, Curator

F & M Enterprises
(see Mississippi, Part 2)

GENCOM PC User Group of Shreveport
9913 Dagger Point
Shreveport, LA 71115
hr50@softdisk.com
http://www.softdisk.com/comp/gencom

Genealogical Institute
(see Virginia, Part 2)

Genealogy Books and Consultation
(see Texas, Part 2)

Genealogy West, Inc.
West Bank of the Mississippi River
5644 Abby Drive
New Orleans, LA 70131-3808
(504) 393-8565
Marjorie H. Lessentine, Query Chairman and
    Founder
Pub. *Genealogy West Newsletter*, ten times
    per year (monthly, Sept–May & July)
$10.00 per year membership

Greater New Orleans Archivists
The Amistad Research Center
Tilton Memorial Hall, Tulane University
6823 Saint Charles Avenue
New Orleans, LA 70118-5698
(504) 865-5535
Rebecca Hankins, Newsletter Editor
Pub. *Greater New Orleans Archivists
    Newsletter*, three times per year
(activities of New Orleans Area professional
    archivists and their institutions, not open
    to nonprofessionals)

Grevenberg House Museum
Louisiana Landmarks Society, Saint Mary
Chapter
(407 Sterling Road—location)
PO Box 400 (mailing address)
Franklin, LA 70538
(318) 828-2092; (318) 828-2028 FAX
MLLuke@aol.com
Craig Landry, Tour Guide; Margie Luke,
    Treasurer

**Hunting for Bears Genealogical and
Historical Society**
(see Alabama, Part 2)

Imperial Calcasieu Museum
204 West Sallier Street
Lake Charles, LA 70601
(318) 439-3797; (318) 429-6040 FAX
Kathryn Bergstrom, Executive Director

J & W Publications
PO Box 19443
Shreveport, LA 71149-0443
(318) 686-5089
Wanda Head, Editor
Pub. *Claiborne Parish Trails* (north
    Louisiana), quarterly, $14.00 per year
    subscription

Kent Plantation House
Lousiana Department of Recreation and
Tourism
3601 Bayou Rapides Road
Alexandria, LA 71301

(318) 487-5998 voice & FAX
Billy King, Marketing Director
(maps, oral histories, photographs)

LaGenWeb
Part of The USGenweb Project
ACWomack@aol.com
http://www.lagenweb.org
Edward Hayden, State Coordinator; Annette
    Womack, Assistant Coordinator
(links to other Louisiana resources)

Louisiana Art and Folk Festival Museum
(Martin Place Lane—location)
PO Box 196 (mailing address)
Columbia, LA 71418
(318) 649-6722
Gay B. Phillips, Director

Louisiana Arts and Science Center
PO Box 3373
Baton Rouge, LA 70821
(225) 334-5272, ext. 14; (225) 344-9477
    FAX
Maria Jalenak, Museum Curator
(historical photographs)

**Louisiana Department of Culture,
Recreation and Tourism**
Louisiana Office of State Parks
1051 North Third Street
Baton Rouge, LA 70802
(225) 342-8111(225) 342-8107 FAX
Raymond Berthelot, Interpretive Program
    Developer
(manuscript collections, maps, oral histories,
    photographs, ephemera)

**Louisiana Department of Culture,
Recreation and Tourism**
Louisiana Division of Historical Preservation
PO Box 44247
Baton Rouge, LA 70804
(225) 342-8160; (225) 342-8173 FAX
hp@crt.state.la.us
http://www.crt.state.la.us/crt/ocd/hp/
    ocdhp.htm

Louisiana Folklore Society
University of Louisiana, Lafayette
Folklore Studies
PO Box 44691
Lafayette, LA 70504
(337) 482-5493
laudun@louisiana.edu
http://www.louisiana.edu/Academic/
    LiberalArts/ENGL/Folklore
John Laudun, Chair, Folklore Committee,
    Folklore Studies
Pub. *Louisiana Folklore Miscellany*,
    irregularly, $5.00 per year subscription

Miles-Hannah House Museum
PO Box 277
Delhi, LA 71232
(318) 878-3792 (City Hall)
Lynn Lewis, President

Mountain Press
(see Tennessee, Part 2)

Save Our Cemeteries, Inc.
2520 Prytania Street
New Orleans, LA 70130

Shreveport Exhibit Museum
3015 Greenwood Road
Shreveport, LA 71109
(318) 632-2020; (318) 632-2019
http://www.sec.state.la.us/shreve-1.htm

Southern Genealogical Institute

9418 Shartel Drive
Shreveport, LA 71118

**The Southern Genealogist's Exchange
Society, Inc.**
(see Florida, Part 2)

Southern Historical Press, Inc.
(see Publishers, Part 4)

**Southwest Mississippi and WF Parishes,
Louisiana**
School Library, 7024 Morgan Road
Greenwell Springs, LA 70739
Serena A. Haymon
(Publishes books on Mississippi and West
    Florida Parishes, Louisiana. "Now have
    database file and census and marriage
    search. Also have handwriting analysis
    from deed, will, etc.")
research: $15.00 plus copies at 5¢ per page
    for last-name search of database, $10.00
    per name for signature analysis

Texas State Historical Association
Southwestern Historical Quarterly
(see Texas, Part 2)

Traveller Southern Families
(see Virginia, Part 2)

U.S. District Court
Boggs Building, 500 Camp Street
New Orleans, LA 70130
(504) 589-4471

Zachary Historic Village
Mansfield McHugh House Museum
4524 Virginia Street
Zachary, LA 70791
(225) 654-1912; (504) 654-1916 FAX
Lois Hastings, Director

Maine

Archives and Libraries with Holdings in Genealogy

State Archives and Library

Maine State Archives
L.M.A. Building
State House Station, Number 84
Augusta, ME 04333-0084
(207) 287-5795; (207) 287-5739 FAX
anne.small@state.me.us
http://www.state.me.us/sos/arc
Jeffrey Brown, Archivist; Anne Small
Mon–Fri 8:00–11:30 & 12:30–4:00
(Maine state government records, county
    court records)

Maine State Library
L.M.A. Building
State House Station, Number 64
Augusta, ME 04333-0064
(207) 287-5600; (207) 287-5791
    (Newspapers); (207) 287-5615 FAX
janet.roberts@state.me.us (Newspapers)
http://www.maine.gov/msl
Susan McCarthy, Reference Librarian
Mon–Fri 9:00–5:00, Sat (during school year)
    noon–5:00
(New England, Atlantic Canada)

Maine State Museum
L.M.A. Building
State House Station, Number 83
Augusta, ME 04333-0083
(207) 289-2301; (207) 287-2301; (207) 287-
    6633 FAX
Paul E. Rivard, Director

State Historical Society

Maine Historical Society
489 Congress Street
Portland, ME 04101
(207) 774-1822; (207) 775-4301 FAX
rdesk@mainehistory.org (Research Library)
http://www.mainehistory.com
Nicholas Noyes, Librarian
Tue–Sat (except holiday weekends)
    10:00–4:00
Pub. *Maine History*, quarterly
(New England and Maritimes)
$30.00 per year membership; admission:
    $10.00 per day, $25.00 for a four-day
    pass

City, County and Regional Archives and Libraries
(A more exhaustive list of public and
academic libraries can be found at http://
www.state.me.us/msl/melibson.htm or
http://msl1.ursus.maine.edu/statsnew/
searchn.cfm.)

**Acadia National Park's William Otis
Sawtelle Collections and Research Center**
PO Box 177
Bar Harbor, ME 04609-0177
(207) 288-5463; (207) 288-5507
brooke_childrey@nps.gov
http://www.cr.nps.gov/csd/collections/
    acad.html
Brooke Childrey, Museum Curator
Tue–Fri 8:30–3:30, by appointment
("Cranberry Isles, Maine, New France,
    Acadia N.P., Saint Croix Island I.H.S.")
no research by mail; copies: 20¢ per side of
    page; photographic copying cost available
    upon request

Auburn Public Library
49 Spring Street (Court and Spring Streets)
Auburn, ME 04210-5981
(207) 782-3191
http://www.auburn.lib.me.us
Sarah Sabasteanski, Reference Librarian
winter: Mon & Thur 9:00–8:00, Tue–Wed &
    Fri 9:00–6:00, Sat 9:00–5:00; summer:
    Mon 9:00–8:00, Tue–Fri 9:00–6:00

Bangor Public Library
145 Harlow Street
Bangor, ME 04401-4900
(207) 947-8336
bplill@bpl.lib.me.us
http://www.bpl.lib.me.us
Barbara McDade, Director
winter: Mon–Thur 9:00–9:00, Fri–Sat
    9:00–5:00; summer: Mon–Thur
    9:00–7:00, Fri 9:00–5:00

Bennington Museum
(see Vermont, Part 2)

Bowdoin College
Hawthorne-Longfellow Library
Archives and Special Collections
3000 College Station
Brunswick, ME 04011-8421
(207) 725-3288
rlindema@bowdoin.edu
http://www.library.bowdoin.edu
Richard Lindemann, Director of Special
    Collections and Archives
Mon–Fri 8:30–5:00

Cary Library
Genealogy Room
107 Main Street
Houlton, ME 04730-2196
(207) 532-1302
bettyf@cary.lib.me.us
http://ece.wpi.edu/~baud/carylib/index.html
Betty Fraser, Director

Chebeague Island Library
247 South Road, Unit 3
Chebeague Island ME 04017-9999
(207) 846-4351
cheblib@hotmail.com
http://web.nlis.net/~bjohnson/library.html
Deborah A. Bowman, Director

Connecticut Valley Historical Museum
(see Massachusetts, Part 2)

John B. Curtis Free Public Library
187 Wilder Davis Road
Bradford, ME 04410-3428
(207) 327-2923
curtis.free.public.library@msln.net
Brenda S. Mowdy, Director

Curtis Memorial Library
23 Pleasant Street
Brunswick, ME 04011-2295
(207) 725-5242
refdesk@curtislibrary.com
http://www.curtislibrary.com
Larua Bean, Reference Librarian
Mon–Wed 9:30–8:00, Thur–Fri 9:30–6:00,
    Sat (winter) 9:30–5:00, Sat (summer)
    9:30–1:00
(two leaflets for SASE: *Information Sources
    on Genealogy at Curtis Memorial Library*
    and *Brunswick History: A Guide to Basic
    Sources*)

Dyer Library Association
371 Main Street
Saco, ME 04072-1582
(207) 283-3861

gmorin@dyer.lib.me.us
Caroline Pinkham, Administrative Assistant;
    Gerard Morin, Director
Library: Tue & Thur 10:00–8:00, Wed & Fri
    10:00–5:00; Historical Room: Tue
    1:00–3:00, Thur 10:00–noon &
    1:00–4:00, and by appointment
20¢ per photocopy, plus $2.50 shipping and
    handling

Ellsworth Public Library
20 State Street
Ellsworth, ME 04605-1924
(207) 667-6363; (207) 667-4901 FAX
charlene@ellsworth.lib.me.us
http://www.ellsworth.lib.me.us
Charlene Fox Clemons, Assistant Director
Mon–Tue & Fri 9:00–5:00, Wed & Thur
    9:00–8:00, Sat 9:00–2:00
("Home of The Alvin S. Whitmore Memorial
    Collection for Genealogical Research.
    Specializing in holdings on Hancock
    County, Maine, genealogy but with a
    variety of materials from other Maine,
    New England, and New Brunswick
    locations. Holdings include microfilms of
    the federal census for Hancock County,
    Maine, from 1790 to 1930, the complete
    run of The Cemetery Association series 1-
    3, various CD-ROM products and over
    600 books, both published and
    unpublished, pertaining to genealogical
    research.")
photocopies: 10¢ per page from paper
    originals, 25¢ per page from microfilm

Falmouth Memorial Library
5 Lunt Road
Falmouth, ME 04105-1292
(207) 781-2351; (207) 781-4094 FAX
library@falmouth.lib.me.us
http://www.falmouth.lib.me.us
Lynda Sudlow, Director

Farmington Public Library
117 Academy Street
Farmington, ME 04938-1996
(207) 778-4312
oplinger@farmington.lib.me.us
http://www.farmington.lib.me.us
Jean Oplinger, Director
Tue–Wed 10:00–8:00, Thur–Fri 10:00–6:00,
    Sat 10:00–2:00, Sat (July–Aug)
    10:00–noon
("We also have a notable collection of Maine
    authors, local and town history, and a
    genealogy reference library.")

Gardiner Public Library
Community Room
152 Water Street
Gardiner, ME 04345-2195
(207) 582-3312
annedavis@gpl.lib.me.us
http://www.gpl.lib.me.us/hist.htm
Anne Davis, Director
Tue 3:00–5:00, Thur 1:00–4:00

Kennebunk Free Library
112 Main Street
Kennebunk, ME 04043-1835
(207) 985-2173
Mon, Wed & Fri 1:00–8:00, Tue, Thur & Sat
    9:30–5:00
(has back copies of the local newspaper,
    York County Coast Star)

Lawrence Public Library
33 Lawrence Avenue
Fairfield, ME 04937-1298
(207) 453-6867
loubic@yahoo.com

http://www.lawrence.lib.me.us
Louella Bickford, Director

Lewiston Public Library
200 Lisbon Street
Lewiston, ME 04240-7117
(207) 784-0135; (207) 784-3011 FAX
http://www.LPLonline.org
Lizette R. Leveille, Reference Librarian
winter: Mon–Thur 9:00–8:00, Fri–Sat
   9:00–5:00; summer: Mon–Thur
   9:00–8:00, Fri 9:00–5:00, Sat 9:00–2:00
(Franklin Company Papers collection.
   "Libby Mill Papers. Gridley Barrows
   photograph and slide collection of
   Lewiston/Auburn architecture.")

McArthur Public Library
(270 Main Street—location)
PO Box 346 (mailing address)
Biddeford, ME 04005-0346
(207) 284-4181
reference@mcarthur.lib.me.us
http://www.mcarthur.lib.me.us
Robert Filgate, Director

Orono Public Library
Goodridge Drive
Orono, ME 04473-1493
(207) 866-5060
kmolloy@orono.lib.me.us
http://www.orono.lib.me.us
Katherine Whedon, Director

Patten Free Library in the Park
Sagadahoc History and Genealogy Room
33 Summer Street
Bath, ME 04530-2687
(207) 443-5141; (207) 443-3514 FAX
http://www.patten.lib.me.us
Elizabeth Hughes, Director
History and Genealogy Room: Sept–June:
   Tue–Sat noon–4:00, Sat 11:00–3:00;
   July–Aug: Mon–Fri noon–4:00

Penobscot Marine Museum
Stephen Phillips Memorial Library
(9 Church Street off U.S. Route 1—location)
PO Box 498 (mailing address)
Searsport, ME 04974-0498
(207) 548-2529; (207) 548-2520 FAX
http://www.penobscotmarinemuseum.org
John G. Arrison, Librarian/Archivist
June–Oct: Mon–Fri 9:00–4:00, Nov–May:
   Tue–Fri 9:00–4:00, second Sat
   10:00–3:00, and by appointment
Pub. *Bay Chronicle*, three times per year
   ("Maritime; Maine, Waldo County
   genealogy and local history")

Portland Public Library
5 Monument Square
Portland, ME 04101-4072
(207) 871-1700; (207) 871-1703 FAX
skaye@portland.lib.me.us
http://www.portlandlibrary.com/depts.html
Sheldon Kaye, Director

Sabbathday Lake Shaker Library
(see Religious Archives and Organizations,
Part 3)

Southern Maine Technical College
(see Portland Harbor Museum, Independent
Publications and Miscellany, below)

**The Mark and Emily Turner Memorial
Library**
39 Second Street
Presque Isle, ME 04769-2677
(207) 764-2571; (207) 768-5756 FAX
drasche@maine.rr.com

http://www.presqueisle.lib.me.us
Marilyn Clark, Librarian; Donna Rasche,
   Director
Mon–Thur 10:00–8:00, Fri 10:00–5:30, Sat
   (winter) 10:00–4:00
(Presque Isle newspapers from 1853)
nonresident borrowers card: $15.00

University of Maine at Fort Kent
Acadian Archives/Archives acadiennes
23 University Drive
Fort Kent, ME 04743
(207) 834-7535; (207) 834-7518 FAX
acadian@maine.maine.edu
http://www.umfk.maine.edu/infoserv/
   archives
Nicholas Hawes, Assistant Director
Mon–Thur 8:00–noon, Fri by appointment
(a regional archives of history and culture,
   focusing on the Upper Saint John Valley,
   an eighty-mile section of the border
   between Maine and New Brunswick, with
   a collection reflecting the predominantly
   French background nature of the
   population)

University of Maine
Special Collections Department
5729 Raymond H. Fogler Library
Orono, ME 04469-5729
(207) 581-1686; (207) 581-1653 FAX
spc@umit.maine.edu
http://www.library.umaine.edu/speccoll

University of Maine/Presque Isle
Library/Special Collections
181 Main Street
Presque Isle, ME 04769
(207) 768-9591
young@polaris.umpi.maine.edu
http://www.umpi.maine.edu/info/lib/
   specol.htm

Walker Memorial Library
800 Main Street
Westbrook, ME 04092-3421
(207) 854-0630
wmlx800@gwi.net
Carolyn Watkins, Director

Waterville Public Library
(address withheld upon request)

Wiscasset Public Library
Wiscasset Historical Committee of the
Wiscasset Public Library
(21 High Street—location)
PO Box 367 (mailing address)
Wiscasset, ME 04578-0367
(207) 882-7161; (207) 882-6698
wpl@wiscasset.lib.me.us
http://www.wiscasset.lib.me.us
Janet Morgan, Librarian
Tue & Thur–Fri 10:00–5:00, Wed
   10:00–7:00, Sat 10:00–3:00 (closed Sat in
   summers)

Historical Societies—Local and Regional

Albion Historical Society
PO Box 68
Albion, ME 04910
albionma@albionmaine.org
http://www.albionmaine.org

Alexander-Crawford Historical Society
216 Pokey Road
Alexander, ME 04694
(207) 454-7476
http://www.mainething.com/achs.htm

John Dudley, Archivist
by appointment
Pub. *A-CHS Newsletter*, quarterly
(Downeast Maine history and genealogy)
$7.50 per year membership

Allagash Historical Society
Route 161
Saint Francis, ME 04774
(207) 398-3335; (207) 398-3347; (207) 398-
   3159; (207) 398-3157
http://www.aroostook.me.us/allagash/
   historical.htm
Edith Kelly, President

Alna Historical Society
Old Alna Meeting House
Route 218
Alna, ME 04535
(207) 586-6928

Andover Historical Society
Andover, ME 04216

Androscoggin Historical Society
(County Building—location)
2 Turner Street (mailing address)
Auburn, ME 04210-5978
(207) 784-0586
itigapa@aol.com; androhs@verizon.net
http://www.rootsweb.com/~meandrhs
Michael Lord, Executive Secretary; David
   Young
Wed–Fri 9:00–noon & 1:00–5:00 (except Fri
   till 4:00 in winter)
Pub. *Androscoggin History*, three to four
   times per year
(genealogical resources)
$5.00 per year membership; research: $10.00
   per hour after the first hour, plus
   photocopies at 15¢ per page

Athens Historical Society
Academy Street
Athens, ME 04912

Bangor Historical Society
Penobscot Heritage Museum of Living
History
159 Union Street
Bangor, ME 04401
(207) 942-5766
info@bangorhistorical.org
http://www.bangorhistorical.org
Curator
Tours: Tue–Sat (June–Oct) 10:00–4:00
(history of Bangor and the Penobscot Valley
   Region; small library with books, city
   directories, as well as primary source
   material)
$25.00 per year membership; admission:
   donation; research: donation

Bar Harbor Historical Society
(Museum, 33 Ledgelawn Avenue—location)
34 Mount Desert Street (mailing address)
Bar Harbor, ME 04609
(207) 288-4245; (207) 288-3807
bhhistorical@acadia.net
http://www.barharborhistorical.org
Deborah M. Dyer, Curator
Mon–Sat 1:00–4:00 (15 June–1 Oct), after 1
   Oct by appointment
Pub. *Newsletter*, quarterly
$10.00 per year membership

Bath Historical Society
Patten Free Library in the Park
Sagadahoc History and Genealogy Room
33 Summer Street
Bath, ME 04530-2687
(207) 443-5141 (History and Genealogy

Room); (207) 443-3514 FAX (History
and Genealogy Room)
Denise R. Larson, Manager
History and Genealogy Room: Tue–Sat
noon–4:00, Sat (Oct–May) noon–4:00
Pub. *The Bath Historical Society Newsletter*,
bimonthly; *The Times of Bath*, three times
per year
$20.00 per year membership; research:
$10.00 per hour

Belfast Historical Society, Inc.
10 Market Street
Belfast, ME 04915

Berwick Historical Society, Inc.
PO Box 904
Berwick, ME 03901-0904

Bethel Historical Society, Inc.
(10-14 Broad Street—location)
PO Box 12 (mailing address)
Bethel, ME 04217-0012
(207) 824-2908; (800) 824-2910
info@bethelhistorical.org
http://www.bethelhistorical.org
Randall H. Bennett, Assistant
Director/Curator of Collections
Research Library: Tue–Fri (June–Oct)
1:00–4:00, Nov–May by appointment
Pub. *The Bethel Courier*, quarterly
("The Bethel Historical Society's research
collections contain a wide variety of
sources useful to genealogists and
historians. The collection includes several
thousand volumes, as well as an
impressive number of photographs, maps,
atlases, scrapbooks, newspapers, and
microforms. Strongly oriented to the
Bethel area, western Maine, and the
White Mountain area of New Hampshire,
these resources also include material
relating to other New England states,
eastern Canada, and various other parts of
the U.S.")
$10.00 per year membership; research:
prepaid, nonrefundable $10.00 per hour
(maximum $30.00 per request) for up to
ten photocopies per hour and searches in
printed sources but not manuscript or
unindexed materials; additional copies:
25¢ per page, reduced photocopy costs for
members

The Biddeford Historical Society
(McArthur Library—location)
PO Box 200 (mailing address)
Biddeford, ME 04005-0200
(207) 284-6841 (Library)
Charles L. Butler, Jr., Secretary and
Genealogist
Thur 11:00–noon
Pub. *Annual Report* (Apr)
(a secondary depository for Biddeford
records, 1653–1891)
$5.00 per year membership; research:
donation

Blue Hill Historical Society
Holt House
Water Street
Blue Hill, ME 04614

Boothbay Region Historical Society
(72 Oak Street—location)
PO Box 272 (mailing address)
Boothbay Harbor, ME 04538-0272
(207) 633-0820
brhs@gwi.net
http://www.boothbayhistorical.org
4 Jul–Labor Day: Wed & Fri–Sat
10:00–4:00; winter: Fri 10:00–noon, Sat

10:00–2:00
Pub. newsletter, semiannually (spring & fall)
$10.00 per year membership

Border Historical Society
Barracks Museum
(74 Washington Street—location)
1 Capen Avenue (mailing address)
Eastport, ME 04631
(207) 853-2328
Ruth McInnis, Board of Director
July–Aug: Tue–Sat 1:00–4:00
$5.00 per year membership

**Bradford Heritage: Museum and
Historical Society**
1163 Main Road
Bradford, ME 04410
(207) 327-1246 (President)
rspnh@juno.com
Muriel S. Parker, President and Librarian
Wed 9:00–10:00 & 5:00–7:00, Sat
10:00–3:00, and by appointment
(Bradford history scrapbook, tax records
from 1852, some vital records from 1860,
news clipping scrapbooks, miscellaneous
photos and documents)

Brewer Historical Society
Clewley Museum
199 Wilson Street
Brewer, ME 04412
(207) 989-7825

The Bridgton Historical Society
Gibbs Avenue Museum
PO Box 44
Bridgton, ME 04009-0044
(207) 647-3699
bhs@megalink.net
http://www.megalink.net/~bhs
July–Aug: Tue–Fri 10:00–4:00; Sept–June:
Tue & Thur 1:00–4:00, and by
appointment
Pub. *Bridgton Historical Society Newsletter*,
quarterly
(local history and genealogy; narrow gauge
Bridgton & Saco River Railroad)
$10.00 per year membership; research
$10.00 per hour

Brooksville Historical Society/Museum
Route 176
Brooksville, ME 04617
(207) 326-4900; (207) 326-4959; (207) 326-
4167

Brownfield Historical Society
RR 1, Box 560
Brownfield, ME 04010
http://www.conwayhistory.org/phl/
brownfield.html
Tue (Apr–Nov) 10:00–3:00; meetings: last
Wed (Apr–Oct)

Buckfield Historical Society
53 Young Lane
Buckfield, ME 04220

Bucksport Historical Society, Inc.
Main Street
Bucksport, ME 04416
(207) 469-2591

Bustins Island Historical Society
(Bustins Island, ME 04013—location)
PO Box 118 (mailing address)
South Freeport, ME 04078

Camden-Rockport Historical Society
Old Conway Complex and Museum
Rockport, ME 04856

Caribou Historical Society
PO Box 1058
Caribou, ME 04736

Chebeague Island Historical Society
Chebeague Island, ME 04017

**Cherryfield-Narraguagus Historical
Society**
(Main Street—location)
PO Box 96 (mailing address)
Cherryfield, ME 04622
(207) 546-7979
Margery Brown, President
Museum: July–Aug: Wed & Fri 1:00–4:00,
and by appointment
Pub. *Newsletter*, semiannually
$3.00 per year membership

China Historical Society
(Maine Street, China, ME 04330—location)
PO Box 587 (mailing address)
South China, ME 04358
(207) 445-3954
winterberry@pivot.net
Marc Johnson

Corinth Historical Society
PO Box 541
Corinth, ME 04427-0541
JamesRWilson2@hotmail.com
http://www.angelfire.com/me2/
corinthhistorical
Pub. newsletter, monthly
$10.00 per year membership

Cumberland Historical Society
(6 Blanchard Road—location)
PO Box 4A (mailing address)
Cumberland Center, ME 04021
(207) 829-5423
http://www.mainemuseums.org/htm/
museumdetail.php3?orgID=187
Wed 12:30–2:30

Cushing Historical Society/Museum
Hawthorne Point Road
Cushing, ME 04563
(207) 354-8262; (800) 261-1369

Dead River Area Historical Society
(172 Main Street—location)
PO Box 150 (mailing address)
Stratton, ME 04982
(207) 246-2271
Mary Henderson, President
Sat–Sun (Memorial Day–Labor Day)
11:00–3:00
Pub. *Calendar of Historical Pictures*,
annually
$8.00 per year membership

Deer Isle-Stonington Historical Society
(416 Sunset Road—location)
PO Box 652 (mailing address)
Deer Isle, ME 04627
(207) 348-2342
judyhill@acadia.net
Paul Stubing, President
July–Aug: Wed & Fri 1:00–4:00; Oct–May:
Mon & Thur
Pub. *Newsletter*, two times per year (spring,
fall)
("Museum, exhibits, archives")
$10.00 per year membership; research:
$15.00 per hour; per-page charge for
copies

Dexter Historical Society
Grist Mill Museum and Millers House
(Off Main Street, signs on Route
7—location)

The Genealogist's Address Book

PO Box 481 (mailing address)
Dexter, ME 04930
(207) 924-5721 (answering machine); (207) 924-3043 (Ms. Feurtado)
dexhist@panax.com
http://www.dextermaine.org/museum
Richard M. Whitney, Curator; Carol Feurtado
Mid-June to mid-Sept: Mon–Fri 10:00–4:00, Sat 1:00–4:00; all year by appointment for research
(much information on Dexter families)

Dixfield Historical Society/John L. Towle Antique Tool Museum
(63 Main Street—location)
PO Box 182
Dixfield, ME 04224-0182
(207) 562-7595
Donna Towle, President
Sat (summer) 1:00–3:00, and by appointment anytime
Pub. *Dixfield Star*, biannually
("Historical archives/local history")
$5.00 per year membership

Dover-Foxcroft Historical Society
Blacksmith Shop Museum
Chandler Road
Dover-Foxcroft, ME 04426
(207) 564-8618
Dave Lockwood, Curator
8:00–5:00

Dresden Historical Society
Dresden Brick School House
Route 128
Dresden, ME 04342
(207) 737-2839; (207) 737-8892

Durham Historical Society
27 Cyr Road
Durham, ME 04222-5323

East Machias Historical Society
PO Box 658
East Machias, ME 04654-0658

Easton Historical Society
PO Box 44
Easton, ME 04740-0044
(207) 488-6846; (207) 488-6652
Kevin Marquis

Eliot Historical Society
PO Box 3
Eliot, ME 03903

Ellsworth Historical Society
PO Box 355
Ellsworth, ME 04605

Fairfield Historical Society
42 Main Street
Fairfield, ME 04937

Falmouth Historical Society
PMB 367
202 U.S. Route One
Falmouth, ME 04104-1327
(207) 781-4727
mdevine1@maine.rr.com
http://www.falmouthmehistory.org
Marge Devine, President
Pub. *The Falmouth Gazette*

Fort Kent Historical Society
(10 Market Street—location)
PO Box 181 (mailing address)
Fort Kent, ME 04743
(207) 834-3933
Annette Daigle, President

1 July–16 Aug: Tue–Fri noon–4:00
Pub. *News Letter*, annually
$20.00 per year membership

Franklin Historical Society
Sullivan Road, Route 200
Franklin, ME 04634
(207) 565-3635; (207) 565-3323

Freeport Historical Society
Enoch Harrington House
45 Main Street
Freeport, ME 04032
(207) 865-3170
frphistory@aol.com
Randall Wade Thomas, Executive Director
Tue–Fri 10:00–2:00

Frenchboro Historical Society and Museum
Schoolhouse Hill
Frenchboro, ME 04635
(207) 334-2929
tgriski@aol.com (Toni Griski)
http://members.aol.com/frboro
Vivian Lunt, President
30 May–30 Sept: noon–7:00
Pub. *Newsletter*, semiannually
$5.00 per year membership

Fryeburg Historical Society/Museum
96 Main Street
Fryeburg, ME 04037-1126
(207) 935-4192 (Museum); (207) 697-3599 (Library)
museum@pivot.net; fhsresearch@adelphia.net
http://www.geocities.com/fryeburghs/index.htm
Nancy Ray, Director/Curator
Museum: Wed 9:00–noon, Thur 1:00–4:00; Genealogical Library: Wed–Sat 9:00–noon; Thur–Fri 1:00-4:00; meetings at American Legion Hall, Bradley Street: first Tue

Gorham Historical Society
28 School Street
Gorham, ME 04038
(207) 839-4313
http://www.cascofcu.com/ghs/home.html
Thur 10:00–1:00; meetings at Gorham Savings Bank operations center: second Mon (Sept–June) 7:30
Pub. George Watson, Archives newsletter

Gouldsboro Historical Society
Old Town House
Route 1
Gouldsboro, ME 04607
(207) 963-5530

Gray Historical Society
(Pennell Institute, Second Floor—location)
PO Box 544 (mailing address)
Gray, ME 04039
(207) 657-3339
cnlknapp@securespeed.net
http://www.graymaine.org/history.htm
Louise Knapp, President
meetings: Pennell Institute, conference room: second Wed 7:00
$3.00 per year membership

Greene Plantation Historical Society
(Greer's Corner—location)
169 Howard Road (mailing address)
Belmont, ME 04952
(207) 342-5208
Isabel Morse Maresh, Secretary
by appointment

(The society has a one-room schoolhouse at Greer's Corner, but because of vandalism, holdings—genealogies, Waldo County census records, etc.—can be seen only by appointment at the secretary's house.)
$5.00 per year membership

Guilford Historical Society
North Main Street
Guilford, ME 04443
(207) 876-2787

Hampden Historical Society
(Kinsley House Museum and Archives, 83 Main Road, South—location)
PO Box 456 (mailing address)
Hampden, ME 04444
(207) 862-2027
Geraldine Stanhope, President; Joan Recker, President
Apr–Oct: Tue 10:00–4:00, and by appointment
Pub. *Newsletter*, quarterly
$10.00 per year membership

Hancock Historical Society
Hancock Corner
Hancock, ME 04640
(207) 422-3080

Harpswell Historical Society
(Old Meeting House, Harpswell, ME 04079—location)
1334 Harpswell Island Road
Orr's Island, ME 04066
(207) 721-8950
gyork@clinic.net
Gerry York, Treasurer
Pub. newsletter, annually
$10.00 per year membership

Harrison Historical Society
121 Haskell Hill Road
Harrison, ME 04040
(207) 583-6225
Mary T. Carlson, Curator
by appointment; meetings: first Wed
("Cemetery records. Limited birth and death records. Maps.")
$5.00 per year membership; research: donation

Hawthorne Community Association
Hawthorne Road
Raymond, ME 04077

Hiram Historical Society
158 Sebago Road
Hiram, ME 04041
(207) 625-4663
rhammond@midmaine.com
http://www.rootsweb.com/~mechiram/contacts.htm
Donna Hammond

Island Falls Historical Society
Burley Street
Island Falls, ME 04037
(207) 463-2264

Islesboro Historical Society
(Old Town Hall/School, Main Road—location)
PO Box 301 (mailing address)
Islesboro, ME 04848
(207) 734-6733
Ms. Rowland Logan, Archivist
hours: various, summer only, by appointment
("We are a small volunteer organization . . . we do try to answer our mail—providing information if we can.")

Islesford Historical Society
(Islesford History Room, Islesford Library,
Moosewood Road—location)
Little Cranberry Island (mailing address)
Islesford, ME 04646
http://www.cranberryisles.com/little/
   hist_soc/index.html
Denise McCormick, Treasurer
$8.00 per year membership

Jackman-Moose River Historical Society
(574 Main Street—location)
PO Box 875 (mailing address)
Jackman, ME 04945
http://www.jackman.ws/historic.html
late May–Sept: Fri–Sat 1:00–4:00; meetings
   in the Jackman Public Library: second
   Wed 7:00
$4.00 per year membership

Jay Historical Society
Holmes-Crafts Homestead
Jay Hill
Jay, ME
(207) 645-2723

Kennebec Historical Society
(61 Winthrop Street—location)
PO Box 5582 (mailing address)
Augusta, ME 04332-5582
(207) 622-7718 voice & FAX
mail@kennebechistorical.org
http://www.kennebechistorical.org
Tue–Wed & Sat 10:00–2:00, Thur 6:00–8:00
$15.00 per year membership; research:
   $15.00

The Kennebunkport Historical Society
(The School House, 125 North Street, and
The Nott House, 8 Maine Street—location)
PO Box 1173 (mailing address)
Kennebunkport, ME 04046
(207) 967-2751; (207) 967-1205 FAX
KportHS@gwi.net
http://www.kporthistory.org
Ellen Driscoll Moy, Executive Director
The School House: Wed–Fri 10:00–4:00;
   The Nott House: mid-June to mid-Oct:
   Tue–Fri 1:00–4:00; Research: Thur–Fri
   afternoons, by appointment
Pub. *The Log*, quarterly
(Kennebunkport history, photograph
   collection)
$25.00 per year membership; admission to
   research facility: $2.00 for nonmembers;
   admission to The Nott House: $3.00;
   admisstion to The School House: free

**Kittery Historical Society and Naval
Museum**
(Rogers Road—location)
PO Box 453 (mailing address)
Kittery, ME 03904
(207) 439-3080

Knox Memorial Association
(High Street—location)
33 Knox Street (mailing address)
Thomaston, ME 04861
Mrs. L. French

Lee Historical Society/Museum
Main Street, Route 6
Lee, ME 04455
(207) 738-3533; (207) 738-4022

Leeds Historical Commission
PO Box 1
North Leeds, ME 04263
Constance Buckley

Lewiston Historical Commission

36 Oak Street
Lewiston, ME 04240

Liberty Historical Society
Old Octagonal Post Office
Main Street, Route 173
Liberty, ME 04949
(207) 589-4393

The Limerick Historical Society
(The Moore Building, corner of Main and
Cross Streets—location)
PO Box 83 (mailing address)
Limerick, ME 04048
info@limerickhistory.org
http://www.limerickhistory.org
June–Aug: Sat–Sun 10:00–2:00

Limington Historical Society
PO Box 84
Limington, ME 04049
http://www.limingtonhistory.org
Anne M. Dunbar, Secretary
$5.00 per year membership

**Lincoln County Cultural and Historical
Association**
(Federal Street—location)
PO Box 61 (mailing address)
Wiscasset, ME 04578
(207) 882-6817
LCHA@wiscasset.net
http://www.lincolncountyhistory.org

**Lincolnville Historical Society and School
House Museum**
(Route 173, Lincolnville Beach—location)
PO Box 211 (mailing address)
Lincolnville Center, ME 04850
(207) 789-5445 (School House Museum,
   seasonal); (207) 763-4332 (Treasurer)
loonmere@midcoast.com
http://www.lincolnvillehistory.org
Peggy S. Bochkay, Treasurer
June–Oct: Mon–Fri noon–3:00, Sat–Sun
   1:00–3:00
Pub. *L.H.S. Newsletter*, biannually
(very large photo collection of family
   members along with the genealogical
   background)
$5.00 per year membership; research: $10.00
   plus costs

Lisbon Historical Society
14 High Street
Lisbon, ME 04250

**Stewart M. Lord Memorial Historical
Society**
c/o Cummings Health Care
PO Box 367
Howland, ME 04448-0367

Lovell Historical Society
(Route 5—location)
PO Box 166 (mailing address)
Lovell, ME 04051
(207) 925-3234; (207) 925-2792 (President)
LovellHist@nh.adelphia.net
http://www.conwayhistory.org/phl/lovell.
   html
Roberta Chandler, President
Tue 1:00–4:00

Machiasport Historical Society
(Gates House, Route 92—location)
PO Box 301 (mailing address)
Machiasport, ME 04655-0301
(207) 255-8461; (207) 255-8557
Frank L. Foster, Treasurer
Mid-June to Labor Day: Tue–Sat 12:30–4:30
("Collection of genealogy of local families")

Madawaska Historical Society
Library Building
Main Street
Madawaska, ME 04756
(207) 738-4272

Milbridge Historical Society
Main Street
Milbridge, ME 04658

Milo Historical Society
12 High Street
Milo, ME 04463Milo, ME
(207) 943-2268
milohistorical@verizon.net
Dr. Ralph Monroe, President

Monmouth, Maine, Historical Society
(Monmouth Museum, 751 Main
Street—location)
PO Box 352 (mailing address
Monmouth, ME 04259-0352
(207) 933-2287; (207) 933-2752
agriffit@abacus.bates.edu
http://www.rootsweb.com/~mekenneb/
   monmouth/monhs.htm
Arthur M. Griffiths, President
meetings: fourth Mon (except July–Aug &
   Dec)

Moosehead Historical Society
(444 Pritham Avenue—location)
PO Box 1116 (mailing address)
Greenville, ME 04441-1116
(207) 695-2909; (207) 695-3163 FAX
history@midmaine.com
http://www.mooseheadhistory.org
Dr. Everett L. Parker, Executive Director
Mon–Fri 8:00–4:00; tours of Victorian
   mansion and Carriage House, etc.: mid-
   June–end of Sept: Wed–Fri 1:00–4:00
Pub. *Insight*, quarterly ("journal of news and
   history with scholarly articles on local
   history")
$5.00 per year membership

Morrill Historical Society
(Morrill, ME 04952—location)
Rural Route 1, Box 5845, Tufts Road
(mailing address)
Belfast, ME 04915
(207) 338-1405; (207) 338-5383 (President);
   (207) 338-1405 (Secretary)
F. Eleanor Warner, President; Josephine
   Grady, Secretary

**Mount Carmel Cultural and Historical
Center**
PO Box 155
L'Ille, ME 04749-0155

Mount Desert Island Historical Society
(Somesville Museum, 2 Oak Hill Road,
   Somesville, Mount Desert School House
   Museum, 373 Sound Drive, Route 198,
   Mount Desert—main research location)
PO Box 653 (mailing address)
Mount Desert, ME 04660
(207) 276-9323; (207) 276-4204 FAX
mdihistory@gwi.net
http://www.mdihistory.org
Jaylene Roths
Somesville Museum: 15 June–30 Sept:
   Tue–Sat 10:00–5:00; School House
   Museum: 1 June–15 Oct: Tue–Sat
   10:00–5:00 and by appointment in winter
Pub. *The History Journal*, $5.95
(primarily information on Somes family)
$10.00 per year membership

Naples Historical Society/Museum
Route 302, Village Green

Naples, ME 04055
(207) 693-6790

The New England Historic Genealogical Society
(see Massachusetts, Part 2)

New Gloucester Historical Society
(389 Intervale Road—location)
PO Box 531 (mailing address)
New Gloucester, ME 04260
Leonard L. Brooks, President
by appointment
Pub. *Footnotes*, quarterly
("archives and library")
$4.00 per year membership

New Sweden Historical Society
(Station Road—location)
PO Box 33 (mailing address)
New Sweden, ME 04762
(207) 896-3052
Carolyn Hildebrand, President
Wed–Sun (21 June–Labor Day) noon–4:00;
    Midsummer Festival, third weekend in
    June
Pub. *Newsletter*, four times per year
(Swedish heritage artifacts of New Sweden.
    "Museum/genealogy.")
$10.00 per year membership; admission:
    donation

Nobleboro Historical Society
198 Center Street, Old Route 1
Nobleboro, ME 04555
(207) 563-5874

Norridgewock Historical Society
11 Mercer Road
Norridgewock, ME 04957
(207) 634-5032
Lucille Greer, Curator
Wed 10:00–3:00, Sat (1 June–Labor Day)
    10:00–3:00
Pub. *Norridgewock Historical Society News*,
    four times per year, 50¢ to nonmembers

North Yarmouth Historical Society
10 Village Square Road
North Yarmouth, MD 04097
Archives: by appointment; monthly programs

Norway Historical Society
471 Main Street
Norway, ME 04268
(207) 743-7377
Charles Longley, Curator
Sat 9:00–noon, and by appointment
("Museum and genealogical area center.
    Books: *Norway in the 1840s* and *Geo.
    Whitman's Civil War Memories*")
$5.00 per year membership

Oakfield Historical Society
Oakfield Railroad Museum
PO Box 62
Oakfield, ME 04763
(207) 757-8575
oakfield.rr.museum@ainop.com
http://www.ainop.com/users/oakfield.rr/
    Oakfield-rr-museum.html

Old Berwick Historical Society/Counting House Museum
(Corner of Main and Liberty
Street—location)
PO Box 296 (mailing address)
South Berwick, ME 03908
(207) 384-0000
info@obhs.net
http://www.obhs.net
Wendy Pirsig, Archivist

July–Sept: Sat–Sun 1:00–4:00, and by
    appointment
(limited resource of local cemetery
    inventories and a few family histories, but
    not professionally oriented)
$15.00 per year membership; research:
    donation

Old Canada Road Historical Society
PO Box 742
Bingham, ME 04920
oldcanadaroad@yahoo.com;
    inghamite@yahoo.com
http://www.rootsweb.com/~meocrhs
("to research, publish, and preserve the
    history of Maine's Upper Kennebec
    Valley")

Old Carratunk Historical Society
PO Box 303
Bingham, ME 04920
Irene Foster, Chairman
("There is no museum or meeting place.")

Old Orchard Beach Historical Society
Harmon Museum
4 Portland Avenue
Old Orchard Beach, ME 04064
(207) 934-9319

Old York Historical Society
(207 York Street [Route 1A]—location)
PO Box 312 (mailing address)
York, ME 03909
(207) 363-4974
oyhs@oldyork.org
http://www.oldyork.org
Virginia S. Spiller, Librarian
Thur–Fri 9:00–5:00, Sat 10:00–4:00
(Local genealogies, manuscripts, 18th-
    century Maine history. includes museum
    buildings: Jefferds' Taver, The Old
    Schoolhouse, The Emerson-Wilcox
    House, Old Gaol (Jail), John Hancock
    Warehouse, George Marshall Store, The
    Elizabeth Perkins House, The Bragdon-
    Ramsdell House.)
$35.00 per year membership; admission:
    $5.00 for nonmembers; research: web site
    has downloadable application with a
    $15.00 fee

Orland Historical Society
Main Street, Route 175
Orland, ME 04472
(207) 469-2476

Otisfield Historical Society
(Otisfield Town Office Building, Route 121,
    Oxford Road—location)
202 Scribner Hill Road (mailing address)
Otisfield, ME 04270
(207) 539-2664; (207) 539-2521
http://www.rootsweb.com/~mecotisf/
    otis8.htm
David Hankins, President
$2.00 per year membership

Oxford Historical Society
683 Main Street
Oxford, ME 04270

Paris Cape Historical Society/Museum
(Route 26, north of Market
Square—location)
19 Park Street (mailing address)
South Paris, ME 04281
(207) 743-2462
http://www.rootsweb.com/~mecparis/
    pariscphs.html
Ben Conant, Curator
June–Dec: Thur & Sat 1:00-4:00

Parsonfield/Porter Historical Society
PO Box 92
Porter, ME 04068-0092
(207) 625-4667

Pejepscot Historical Society
159 Park Row
Brunswick, ME 04011
(207) 729-6606; (207) 729-6012 FAX
pejepscot@gwi.net
http://www.curtislibrary.com/pejepscot.htm
Jarrod Diels-Roll, Curator; Deborah Smith,
    Director
Research Room and Archives: Tue–Wed &
    Fri 9:00–5:00, Thur 9:00–8:00, Sat
    (June–Sept) 9:00–4:30, Sat (Oct–May)
    noon–4:00
Pub. *Cupola* (not genealogical), biannually
(historical information on the Brunswick,
    Topsham and Harpswell areas)
$15.00 per year membership; research
    service: free for members, $10.00 for
    nonmembers

Pemaquid Historical Association
23 Old Harrington Road
Pemaquid, ME 04558

Penobscot Nation Historical Society
(see Ethnic Archives, Libraries and
Societies—Native American, Part 3)

Pequawket Historical League
http://www.conwayhistory.org/phl.htm
meetings: second Tue (Feb, May, Aug &
    Nov)
("an association of historical societies and
    museums along the Maine and New
    Hampshire border")

Phillips Historical Society
PO Box 216
Phillips, ME 04966
(207) 639-3352; (207) 639-4001

Phippsburg Historical Society, Inc.
(Phippsburg Center—location)
PO Box 21 (mailing address)
Phippsburg, ME 04562
Ada M. Haggett
1:00–4:00

Pittsfield Historical Society
(Depot House Museum, 8 Central
Street—location)
PO Box 181 (mailing address)
Pittsfield, ME 04967
(207) 487-4926 (Secretary); (207) 487-3447
    (Museum)
jojfrost@midmaine.com
http://www.rootsweb.com/~mephs
Tom Brown, Acting Secretary

The Historical Society of Poland, Maine USA
Old SchoolHouse
1229 Main Street
Poland, ME 04015
(207) 998-2403
dunthur@pivot.net
http://www.polandhistoricalsociety.org
Sandra Dunlap, Secretary
$5.00 per year membership

Presque Isle Historical Society
16 Third Street
Presque Isle, ME 04769-2416
(207) 762-1151

Rangeley Lakes Region Historical Society
(2472 Main Street—location)
PO Box 521 (mailing address)
Rangeley, ME 04970-0521

(207) 864-5647
palmer@rangeley.org
Donald Palmer, President
July–Aug: Mon–Sat 10:00–noon
Pub. *Annual Newsletter*
$8.00 per year membership

Raymond-Casco Historical Society
10 McDermott Road
Rmond, ME 04071
rchs@raymondmaine.org
http://www.raymondmaine.org/
    historical_society/default.htm
Betty McDermott, Treasurer
meetings: May–Oct: third Mon
$5.00 per year membership

Readfield Historical Society
(Route 17—location)
PO Box 354 (mailing address)
Readfield, ME 04355-0354
(207) 685-3812
matt@pivot.net
http://www.rootsweb.com/~mecreadf/
    rdfldrhs.htm
Dale Porter Clark, President
summer: by appointment
Pub. *RHS Newsletter,* quarterly
$2.50 per year membership

Richmond Historical Society
7 Gardiner Street
Richmond, ME 04357
(207) 737-4166

Rumford Historical Society
Rumford Municipal Building
Congress Street
Rumford, ME 04276
(207) 364-8455
Myrtle McKenna, Historian
Thur 9:00–2:00
(histories of Rumford and surrounding
    towns, some genealogy)

Sagadahoc Preservation, Inc.
(804 Washington Street—location)
PO Box 322 (mailing address)
Bath, ME 04530

Sainte Agathe Historical Society
PO Box 237
Saint Agatha, ME 04772
(207) 543-6364
David Raymond, President
Mon (after Labor Day–15 June) 1:00–4:00,
    Tue–Sat 1:00–4:00
Pub. *Annual Newsletter*
(emphasis on local Saint John Valley, Maine,
    genealogy and history)
$2.50 per year membership

**Salmon Brook Historical Society of
Washburn**
Main Street
Washburn, ME 04786
(207) 455-8110; (207) 455-8279

Sanford Historical Committee
919 Main Street
Sanford, ME 04073
pauger@sanford.org
http://www.sanfordhistory.org

**The Scarborough, Maine Historical
Society and Museum**
(649 U.S. Route 1, Scarborough, ME
    04074—location)
 PO Box 156 (mailing address)
Scarborough, ME 04070
(207) 883-3539 (Becky Delaware)
Seasideinn@aol.com (Rodney Laughton);

hodgie@maine.rr.com
http://www.scarboroughmaine.com/historical
Becky Delaware; Rodney Laughton; Frank
    Hodgdon
Tue 9:00–noon; meetings: first Wed
    (Sept–May)
Pub. newsletter, monthly
$10.00 per year membership

Searsport Historical Society
Main Street, Route 1
Searsport, ME 04974
(207) 548-0245

Sebago Historical Society
PO Box 59
Sebago, ME
suemccabe@earthlink
http://www.rootsweb.com/~mecsebag/
    HistSoc.html
Sue McCabe, Recording Secretary

Sedgwick-Brooklin Historical Society
(Route 1, Box 4570—location)
PO Box 171 (mailing address)
Sedgwick, ME 04676
(207) 359-8977 (President)
R. M. Sargent, President
July–Aug: Sun 2:00–4:00
Pub. *Newsletter*, irregularly
(local history, library, some genealogy)

**South Portland-Cape Elizabeth Historical
Society**
(Braeburn Avenue—location)
PO Box 2623 (mailing address)
South Portland, ME 04106
(207) 799-1977
Lenora Bangert, President
Apr–Nov: Sat 1:00–4:00
$5.00 per year membership

Southern Aroostook Historical Society
Aroostook Historical and Art Museum
109 Main Street
Houlton, ME 04730
(207) 532-4216 (Museum)

Standish Historical Society
Old Red Church, Oak Hill Road
Standish, ME 04084
(207) 642-3216; (207) 642-4443; (207) 642-
    5170
Joline Webber, President; Myke Waite,
    Curator
summer: Tue & Thur 10:00–2:00

Stockholm Historical Society
(Lake and South Main Streets—location)
PO Box 37 (mailing address)
Stockholm, ME 04783
(207) 896-5731
Albertine Dufour, President

Stockton Springs Historical Society
PO Box 101
Stockton Springs, ME 04981
sshs@iname.com
http://www.bairnet.org/oganizations/sshs
meetings in the Masonic Hall of the Alice
    Ellis Memorial Library: first Sun
    (Feb–Nov) 2:00

Strong Historical Society
Vance and Dorothy Hammond Museum
Main Street
Strong, ME 04983
(207) 684-4137; (207) 684-3396

**The Sullivan and Sorrento Historical
Society**
(Sullivan Recreational Building, Route

1—location)
PO Box 44 (mailing address)
West Sullivan, ME 04689
(207) 422-6816(Curator)
hlm@downeast.net
http://ellsworthme.org/sshs
Barbara Potter, Curator
Tue 1:00–3:00

Sweden Historical Society
Blacksmith Shop Museum
RR 2
Harrison, ME 04040
(207) 647-5397 (President)
http://www.conwayhistory.org/phl/
    sweden.html
Tom Goodman, President

Thomaston Historical Society
PO Box 384
Thomaston, ME 04861
(207) 354-2295
katsmeow@adelphia.net
http://www.thomastonhistoricalsociety.com
Museum: June–Aug: Tue–Thur 2:00–4:00;
    meetings: first Thur (Apr–Nov) 7:30
$15.00 per year membership; admission:
    free; genealogical inquiries: Mrs.
    Margaret Hook, PO Box 156, South
    Thomaston, ME 04858

Trescott Historical Society
PO Box 1
Whiting, ME 04691
(207) 733-5548
http://www.trescotthistory.org
Bonnie E. Healy, Vice President

Union Historical Society
(343 Common Road—location)
PO Box 154 (mailing address)
Union, ME 04862
(207) 785-5444
ratracy@hotmail.com
http://www.midcoast.com/comespring
Dick Tracy
Robbins House (Union Common): Wed &
    Sat 9:30–noon
$5.00 per year membership

Unity Historical Society
PO Box 4
Unity, ME 04988
(207) 948-2798
history@UnityMaine.org
http://unitymaine.org/orgs/uhs/index.html

Vanceboro Historical Society
Water Street
Vanceboro, ME 04491
http://www.woolwichhistory.org

Vassalboro Historical Society
(Route 32—location)
PO Box 62 (mailing address)
East Vassalboro, ME 04935-0062
(207) 923-3505 (Museum); (207) 923-3533
    (Curator)
Betty Taylor, Secretary and Curator
hours: various

The Vinalhaven Historical Society
(High Street—location)
PO Box 339 (mailing address)
Vinalhaven, ME 04863
(207) 863-4410
vhhissoc@midcoast.com
http://www.midcoast.com/~vhhissoc
Roy Van N. Heisler, Secretary
Museum: 15 June–13 Sept: 11:00–3:00, and
    by appointment
$3.00–$25.00 per year membership;

research: $12.00 per hour after the first half-hour

Waldoboro Historical Society
(Route 220 South—location)
PO Box 110 (mailing address)
Waldoboro, ME 04572
William Travers, President
July–Labor Day: Mon–Sun 1:00–4:30
Pub. *WHS Newsletter*, one or two times per year
from $4.00 per year membership

Warren Historical Society
PO Box 11
Warren, ME 04864

Waterborough Historical Society
Route 5
East Waterboro, ME 04030
(207) 247-5878

Waterford Historical Society
(Mary Gage Rice Museum—Waterford Village, North Waterford, ME 04267—location)
PO Box 201 (mailing address)
Waterford, ME 04088
Norman Rust
Pub. *Waterford Echoes*, quarterly

Waterville Historical Society
Redington Museum
64 Silver Street
Waterville, ME 04901
(207) 872-9439

Wayne Historical Society
PO Box 243
Wayne, ME 04284
waynehs@gwi.net
http://www.cary-memorial.lib.me.us/historical
$10.00 per year membership

Weld Historical Society, Inc.
Wilton Road
Weld, ME 04285
Susan Stowell, President
Pub. *WHS Newsletter*

Historical Society of Wells and Ogunquit
Meetinghouse Museum
Genealogical and Historical Research Library
(Route 1, Post Road—location)
PO Box 801 (mailing address)
Wells, ME 04090
(207) 646-4775
wohistory@gwi.net
http://www.wellschamber.org/Historical/_Society.htm
Joan B. Adams, Chairperson of Board
Pub. *Waves & Furrows*

Westbrook Wilton Historical Society
Farm and Home Museum
Kineowatha Park
PO Box 33
Wilton, ME 04294

Whitefield Historical Society
(Townhouse Road—location)
PO Box 176 (mailing address)
Whitefield, ME 04353
(207) 549-5064

Windham Historical Society, Inc.
(234 Windham Center Road—location)
471 Falmouth Road (mailing address)
Windham, ME 04062
(207) 892-1433 (Mon 10:00–3:00); (207)

892-5381 (Historian)
Kay Soldier, Historian
Tue & Thur 10:00–3:00
Pub. *Windham Historical Society Newsletter*, six times per year
(Windham history and genealogy)
$5.00 per year membership; research: donation

Winslow Historical Society
(Lithgow Street—location)
16 Benton Avenue (mailing address)
Winslow, ME 04902

Winter Harbor Historical Society
(Main Street—location)
PO Box 400 (mailing address)
Winter Harbor, ME 04693
(207) 963-7461

Winterport Historical Association
PO Box 342
Winterport, ME 04496-0342
$3.00 per year membership

Winthrop Historical Society
PO Box 111
East Winthrop, ME 04343

Woodstock Historical Society/Museum
Route 26
Bryant Pond, ME 04219
(207) 665-2450

Woolwich Historical Society
(Nequasset Road—location)
PO Box 98 (mailing address)
Woolwich, ME 04579
(207) 443-4833
whs@gwi.net
http://www.woolwichhistory.org
July–Aug: Tue–Sat 10:30–2:30
$10.00 per year membership; admission: $3.00 for adults

Yarmouth Historical Society
(Third Floor, Merrill Memorial Library, 215 Main Street—location)
PO Box 107 (mailing address)
Yarmouth, ME 04096-0107
(207) 846-6259
Marilyn Hinkley, Director
Sept–June: Tue–Fri 1:00–5:00, Sat 10:00–5:00; July–Aug: Mon–Fri 1:00–5:00
Pub. *Yarmouth Historical Society Newsletter*, quarterly
$20.00 per year membership

Genealogical Societies

State Genealogical Society

Maine Genealogical Society
PO Box 221
Farmington, ME 04938-0221
Clayton Adams, President
Pub. *The Maine Genealogist*, quarterly
$20.00 per year membership; $5.00 new member fee; free queries for members

Genealogical Societies—Local & Regional

American-Canadian Genealogical Society
(see New Hampshire, Part 2)

The Hancock County Genealogical Society
PO Box 243
Bass Harbor, ME 04653
hanson@downeast.net
http://ellsworthme.org/hcgs
Wayne Patten, Treasurer; Patti Leland-

Hanson
meetings at Ellsworth Public Library: third Sat 2:30
(collection located in the Ellsworth Public Library, as part of the Alvin S. Whitmore Memorial Collection)
$10.00 per year membership

Le Club Calumet
Genealogical Section
PO Box 110
Augusta, ME 04330-0110

The New England Historic Genealogical Society
(see Massachusetts, Part 2)

Yankee Genealogical Society
Minnesota Genealogical Society
(see Massachusetts, Part 2)

York County Genealogical Society
(Wells, ME—library location)
PO Box 431 (mailing address)
Eliot, ME 03903-0431
(207) 439-4243
Thelma Remick, Treasurer
Library: Wed–Thur 10:00–4:00
Pub. *Journal*, quarterly
$15.00 per year membership; limited research will be done upon request

Independent Publications and Miscellany

L. C. Bates Museum of Good Will-Hinckley Homes
Hinckley Home-School-Farm
Route 201
Hinckley, ME 04944
(207) 238-4250 (Museum); (207) 238-4000 (School Office)
lcbates@gwh.org
http://gwh.org
Deborah Staber, Museum Staff
Wed–Sat 10:00–4:30, Sun 1:00–4:30, and by appointment
Pub. *Beaver Paw Press*, four times per year (publication of Museum); *Good Will-Record*, four times per year (publication of Good Will-Hinckley Home Association)
("Cultural and natural history museum with archives of Hinckley and Good Will-Hinckley homes")
$10.00 per year membership

Belfast Museum, Inc.
10 Market Street
Belfast, ME 04915
Andrew Kuby, President
Thur & Sun (summer) 1:00–4:00 by appointment
(Belfast history only)
donation

Broad Bay Family History Projects
(Waldoboro, ME 04572-0010—location)
6094 South Glen Oaks Drive (mailing address)
Murray, UT 84107
W. W. "Will" Whitaker, Editor
Pub. *Old Broad Bay Bund und Blatt*
(includes the 100+ families that established a German colony in Broad Bay [Waldoboro, Maine] in 1740-1753)

Burnham Tavern Museum
Hannah Weston Chapter, D.A.R.
(Main Street—location)
2 Free Street (mailing address)

Machias, ME 04654
(207) 255-4432
valdine@juno.com
Valdine C. Atwood, Chairman
Mon–Fri (June–Oct) 9:00–5:00, and by
    appointment
("Historic house, oldest building in eastern
Maine and only one with Revolutionary
War history.")
Washington County, Maine, genealogy
research

Castine Scientific Society
(Wilson Museum, John Perkins House, The
Blacksmith Shop, Hearse House, all on
Perkins Street—location)
PO Box 196 (mailing address)
Castine, ME 04421
(207) 326-8753
Patricia Hutchins
Wilson Museum: Tue–Sun 2:00–5:00 (27
    May–30 Sept); research by appointment
    only
Pub. *Wilson Museum Bulletin*, three times
    per year, $5.00 per year subscription

Center for Appalachian Studies
(see North Carolina, Part 2)

**Colonial Massachusetts and Maine
Genealogies**
(see Massachusetts, Part 2)

**Cumberland and Oxford Canal
Association**
36 Lester Drive
Portland, ME 04103
(207) 797-2745

Jonathan Fisher Memorial, Inc.
PO Box 537
Blue Hill, ME 04614
(207) 374-2780

The Fishermen's Museum
(Pemaquid Point—location)
3007 Bristol Road (mailing address)
New Harbor, ME 04554-4905
(207) 677-2494; (207) 677-2726
Mary Norton Orrick, Director
Memorial Day–Columbus Day: weekdays
    10:00–5:00, Sun 11:00–5:00
(artifacts, charts, old photographs, lighthouse
    memorabilia)

Friendship Museum, Inc.
(1 Martin Point Road—location)
PO Box 226 (mailing address)
Friendship, ME 04547
(207) 832-4221
case@midcoast.com
Lynn Case, President
Mon–Sat 1:00–4:00, Sun (1 July–Labor
    Day) 2:00–4:00
(memorabilia of the town)
$5.00 per year membership

Grand Banks Schooner Museum Trust
(100 Commercial Street, Boothbay Harbor,
ME 04538—location)
PO Box 123 (mailing address)
Boothbay, ME 04537
(207) 633-4727
Robert Ryan, Director

Historical Ink's Old Maps
(see New York, Part 2)

L'Heritage-Vivant—Living Heritage
(The Acadian Village, 5 miles north of Van
Buren—location)
PO Box 165 (mailing address)

Van Buren, ME 04785
(207) 868-2691; (207) 868-5042 (summer)
Anne L. Roy, President
15 June–15 Sept: noon–5:00
(sixteen buildings dating from 1800 to early
    1900)

Maine Department of Transportation
16 Statehouse Station
Augusta, ME 04333
(207) 287-2551
http://www.state.me.us/mdot

Maine Folklife Center
South Stevens Hall 5773
Orono, ME 04469-5773
(207) 581-1891; (207) 581-1823 FAX
folklife@maine.edu
http://www.umaine.edu/folklife
Edward D. Ives, Ph.D., President; Alicia
    Rouverol, Archives Manager
Mon–Fri 9:00–4:00
Pub. *Maine Folklife*
(Maine and the Maritime Provinces of
    Canada. "A collection of stories from the
    Maliseet [current preferred spelling] and
    Passamaquoddy Indians who occupied the
    border country between Maine and New
    Brunswick, Canada.")
$25.00 per year Basic membership

Maine Geological Survey
Maine Department of Conservation
22 State House Station
Augusta, ME 04333-0022
(207) 287-2801; (207) 287-2353
Christine.E.Sansouci@state.me.us
http://www.state.me.us/doc/nrimc/
    pubedinf/pubs/pubs.htm

**Maine League of Historical Societies and
Museums**
Stone House
Phippsburg, ME 04562
Dorris Isaacson, President

MeGenWeb
Part of The USGenWeb Project
PO Box 152
Danville, ME 04223
(207) 786-2129
mainegen@aol.com; tsvickery@adelphia.net
http://www.rootsweb.com/~megenweb
David C. Young, State Coordinator; Lee Ann
    Sharpe, Assistant Coordinator; Tina
    Vickery, Assistant Coordinator
(links to other Maine resources)

New England Connexion
(see Connecticut, Part 2)

**New England Old Newspaper Index
Project**
PO Box 152
Danville, ME 04223
(207) 786-2129; (207) 786-2129 FAX
NeonipME@aol.com
http://www.geocities.com/heartland/hills/
    1460
David Colby Young
(compiles and publishes vital records and
    genealogical and historical information
    from Maine newspapers, also supports
    microfilming of newspapers)
no costs, send resume with SASE to offer
    help

The New England Quarterly
(see Massachusetts, Part 2)

Nylander Museum
(393 Main Street—location)

PO Box 1062 (mailing address)
Caribou, ME 04736
(207) 493-4474; (207) 498-3098

Old Town Museum
(138 South Main Street—location)
PO Box 375 (mailing address)
Old Town, ME 04468
(207) 827-7256
William A. Osborne, Treasurer
1:00–5:00

Pioneer Publications
New England Queries and Reviews
(see Connecticut, Part 2)

Portland Harbor Museum
Fort Road-SMTC Campus
South Portland, ME 04106
(207) 799-6337
http://www.portlandharbormuseum.org
Martina Morrow, Museum Director
Apr–May & Oct–Nov: Fri–Sun; June–Sept:
    Mon–Sun 10:00–4:30

**Society for the Preservation of New
England Antiquities—Archives**
(see Massachusetts, Part 2)

Ruggles House Society
Columbia Falls, ME 04623
(207) 288-3597

Victoria Society of Maine
The Victoria Manson
109 Danforth Street
Portland, ME 04101
(207) 772-4841

**Visit Maine—Historical Sites and
Museums**
http://www.visitmaine.com/historic.html

York Institute Museum
375 Main Street
Saco, ME 04072
(207) 282-3031

Maryland

Archives and Libraries with Holdings in Genealogy

State Archives and Library

Maryland State Archives
Hall of Records Building
350 Rowe Boulevard
Annapolis, MD 21401-1686
(410) 260-6400; (800) 235-4045 (in
    Maryland); (410) 974-3895 FAX; (800)
    735-2258
archives@mdarchives.state.md.us
http://mdsa.net
Edward C. Papenfuse, Ph.D., State Archivist;
    Dr. R. J. Rockefeller, Reference Archivist
Public Search Room: Tue–Fri 8:00–4:30, Sat
    8:30–noon & 1:00–4:30
Pub. *The Bulldog*
("As the historical agency for Maryland, the
    State Archives is the central depository
    for government records of permanent
    value. Records date from the founding of
    the Maryland colony in 1634 through the
    1990s. They include colonial and state
    executive, legislative and judicial records;
    county probate, land and court records;
    business records; publications and reports
    of the state, county and municipal
    governments; records of religious bodies;
    and special collections of maps,
    newspapers, photographs, and private
    papers.")
research fee: $15.00 for mail reference;
    schedule of charges for photocopies

Maryland State Law Library
Court of Appeals Building, First Floor
361 Rowe Boulevard
Annapolis, MD 21401
(410) 974-3395; (410) 974-2063 FAX
mdlaw.library@courts.state.md.us
Mon, Wed & Fri 8:30–4:30, Tue–Thur
    8:30–9:00, Sat 9:00–4:00
(obituaries, history, genealogy, newspapers)

State Historical Society

Maryland Historical Society
201 West Monument Street
Baltimore, MD 21201-4674
(410) 685-3750, ext. 359 (Local and Family
    History); (410) 385-2105 FAX
library@mdhs.org
http://www.mdhs.org
Donna Williams, Acting Associate Director,
    Local and Family History Department
Library: Wed–Sat 10:00–4:30
Pub. *Maryland Historical Magazine*,
    quarterly; *News and Notes of MHS*, five
    times per year
(includes the genealogy collection of the
    George Peabody Library of The Johns
    Hopkins Library)
$40.00 per year membership; admission:
    $4.00 for nonmembers; research: fees
    vary for members and nonsubscribers,
    simple or complex research

City, County and Regional Archives and Libraries

(A more exhaustive list of public and
academic libraries can be found at
http://www.sailor.lib.md.us/MD_topics/lib.)

Allegany College of Maryland Library
Appalachian Collection
12401 Willowbrook Road, S.E.
Cumberland, MD 21502-2596

(301) 478-5294 (Coordinator)
http://www.ac.cc.md.us/library/
    genealog.shtml
Mary Huebner, Coordinator of Library
    Services
usually Mon–Thur 8:00–10:00, Fri
    8:00–4:30, Sat 10:00–2:00, Sun
    2:00–6:00 (hours may vary)
(Local history and genealogy for western
    Maryland and surrounding counties in
    West Virginia and Pennsylvania; more
    than 1,400 historical and genealogical
    books, about 300 oral history recordings,
    plus pamphlet and photograph file)
donation requested

Allegany County Library System
31 Washington Street
Cumberland, MD 21502-2981
(301) 777-1200 voice & FAX
lmckenney@allconet.org;
    mainpl@allconet.org
http://lib.allcnet.org
John Taube, Director
Mon–Thur 9:00–9:00, Fri–Sat 9:00–5:00,
    Sun 1:00–5:00

Anne Arundel County Public Library
Annapolis Area Branch
1410 West Street
Annapolis, MD 21401
(410) 222-1750
http://www.aacpl.net
Ellen Berkov, Annapolis Area Reference
    Librarian
Mon–Thur 9:00–9:00, Fri–Sat 9:00–5:00,
    Sun 1:00–5:00
(includes Maryland Gold Star Collection, a
    noncirculating collection of titles on
    Maryland history and genealogy)

C. Burr Artz Library
Maryland Room
110 East Patrick Street
Frederick, MD 21701
(301) 631-3757 (Maryland Room); (301)
    695-2905 FAX
fcplweb@fcpl.org
http://fcpl.org
James W. Lowry
Library: Mon–Thur 10:00–9:00, Fri–Sat
    10:00–5:00; Maryland Room: Mon–Wed
    1:00–4:00, Thur–Sat 10:00–1:00
(specializes in Frederick County history and
    genealogy)

Baltimore County Public Library
Catonsville Area Branch
1100 Frederick Road
Catonsville, MD 21228-5092
(410) 887-0951; (410) 788-8166 FAX
catonsvi@bcpl.net
http://www.bcplonline.org
Evangeline Benner, Branch Manager
Mon–Thur 10:00–9:00, Fri–Sat 10:00–5:30

Baltimore County Public Library
Reisterstown Branch
21 Cockeys Mill Road
Reisterstown, MD 21136
(410) 887-1165; (410) 833-8756 FAX
http://www.bcplonline.org
Grace Jonke, Branch Manager
Mon–Thur 10:00–9:00, Fri–Sat 9:00–5:30

Baltimore County Public Library
Towson Area Branch
320 York Road
Towson, MD 21204-5179
(410) 887-6166; (410) 887-3170 FAX
infoserv@bcpl.net
http://www.bcplonline.org

Jennifer Haire, Library Manager
Mon–Thur 10:00–9:00, Fri–Sat 10:00–5:30,
    Sun 1:00–5:00

Berlin Heritage Foundation, Inc.
(208 North Main Street—location)
PO Box 351 (mailing address)
Berlin, MD 21811
(410) 641-1019
Susan Taylor, Administrator
Memorial Day weekend–end of Oct: Mon,
    Wed & Fri–Sat 1:00–4:00
Pub. *BHF Newsletter*, three or more times
    per year
(operates a historic house museum of local
    history)
$10.00 per year museum membership

Bowie State University
Thurgood Marshall Library
Bowie, MD 20715-9465
(301) 464-7228; (301) 464-7843 FAX
http://www.bsu.umd.edu/library/bsu-
    libr.html

Caroline County Public Library
100 Market Street
Denton, MD 21629
(410) 479-1343 voice & FAX
preinhardt@caro.lib.md.us
http://www.caro.lib.md.us/library
Deborah Bennett, Assistant Administrator;
    Pat Reinhardt, Branch Manager
Mon & Fri 10:00–8:00, Tue–Thur & Sat
    10:00–5:30

Carroll County Public Library
50 East Main Street
Westminster, MD 21157
(410) 386-4490; (410) 386-4497 FAX
http://library.carr.org
Mon–Thur 9:30–8:45, Fri–Sat 9:30–5:00
(all genealogical services are now provided
    at this location by Carroll County
    Genealogical Society)

Cecil County Public Library
Information Services
301 Newark Avenue
Elkton, MD 21921-5441
(410) 996-5600; (410) 996-5604 FAX
ccplwebmaster@yahoo.com
http://www.ebranch.cecil.lib.md.us
Elona Rowland, Webmaster
Mon–Thur 10:00–9:00, Fri–Sat 10:00–5:00
no search services available

Charles County Public Library
2 Garrett Avenue
La Plata, MD 20646
(301) 934-9001; (301) 934-2297 FAX
http://www.ccplonline.org
Mon–Thur 9:00–8:00, Fri 1:00–5:00, Sat
    9:00–5:00, Sun (during the school year)
    1:00–5:00

City Hall Museum and Cultural Center
(110 West Church Street—location)
PO Box 884 (mailing address)
Salisbury, MD 21801
(410) 546-9007

Dorchester County Public Library
303 Gay Street
Cambridge, MD 21613
(410) 228-7331; (410) 228-6313 FAX
infodesk@dorchesterlibrary.org
http://www.dorchesterlibrary.org
Frances Cresswell, Adult Services
    Department Head
Mon, Wed & Fri 10:00–6:00, Tue & Thur
    10:00–8:00, Sat 9:00–5:00

Pub. *Gander* ("covers all library topics, not just the Maryland Room")

The Ruth Enlow Library of Garrett County
6 North Second Street
Oakland, MD 21550-1316
(301) 334-3996
info@relib.net
http://www.relib.net
Cathy Ashby, Director
Mon & Wed 9:15–8:00, Tue & Thur–Fri 9:15–5:30, Sat 9:00–4:00
no fees

John Fox Jr. Genealogical Library
(see Kentucky, Part 2)

Harford County Library
100 East Pennsylvania Avenue
Bel Air, MD 21014
(410) 638-3151; (410) 638-3155 FAX
http://www.harf.lib.md.us

Office of Historic Alexandria
5613 Belmont Avenue
Chevy Chase, MD 20815
Jean Taylor Federico

Johns Hopkins University
Milton S. Eisenhower Library
3400 North Charles Street
Baltimore, MD 21218
(410) 516-8348; (410) 516-7202 FAX
stimpert@jhu.edu; mburri@jhu.edu
http://archives.mse.jhu.edu
James Stimpert, Archives; Margaret Burri, Historical Manuscripts
Mon–Fri 8:30–5:00, Thur 8:30–8:00
("Holdings include official records of the Arts & Sciences, Engineering and part-time [i.e., nonmedical] divisions of the Johns Hopkins University [University Archives], and personal papers of many notable Hopkins faculty members [Historical Manuscripts]. Most holdings are directly related to the Johns Hopkins University"; early Americana collections, maps, and special collections)

Johns Hopkins University
Peabody Library
(see Maryland Historical Society, State Historical Society, above)

Huntsville-Madison County Public Library
(see Alabama, Part 2)

Kuethe Library
Historical and Genealogical Research Center
5 Craine Highway, S.E.
Glen Burnie, MD 21061
(410) 760-9679
barb@grempler.smart.net
http://www.aagensoc.org/kuethe.shtml
Barbara Grempler
Thur–Sat 10:00–4:00

Maryland Historical Trust Library
100 Community Place
Crownsville, MD 21032-2023
(410) 514-7655 (for appointments); (410) 987-4071 FAX
http://www2.ari.net/mdshpo
Mary Louise de Sarran, Librarian
by appointment only
Pub. *In Context*, online newsletter
(historical preservation, no genealogical research materials)

Menno Simons Historical Library

(see Virginia, Part 2)

Edward H. Nabb Research Center for Delmarva History and Culture
Salisbury University
Power Professional Building
1101 Camden Avenue
Salisbury, MD 21801
(410) 543-6312; (410) 677-5067
rcdhac@salisbury.edu
http://nabbhistory.salisbury.edu
Rebecca Miller, Executive Director
Mon 9:30–9:00, Tue–Fri 9:30–4:30, Sat 9:00–2:00
Pub. *ShoreLine*, monthly
("The Nabb Research Center has the largest genealogical collection of material on families of the Delmarva Peninsula, particularly the tri-county area of Worcester, Wicomico and Somerset [counties, Maryland], . . . Sussex County, Delaware, and Accomack and Northampton counties, Virginia . . . . We are the home of the Leslie P. Dryden Collection, a 250-volume collection covering some 1,800 surnames. We hold over 2,500 reels of microfilm containing the public records such as court records, probate records and land records for our eight-county regional area.")
$30.00 per year membership; admission: $5.00 per day

Ocean City Museum Society
Ocean City Life-Saving Station Museum
(813 South Boardwalk—location)
PO Box 603 (mailing address)
Ocean City, MD 21842
(410) 289-4991 (Museum)
Sandy@ocmuseum.org
http://www.ocmuseum.org
Sandra D. Hurley, Assistant Manager
June–Sept: daily 11:00–10:00; May–Oct: daily 11:00–4:00; winter: Sat–Sun 10:00–4:00
Pub. *Newsletter Scuttlebutt*, quarterly
(Ocean City history; some genealogy sources, contacts to other sources)
$5.00 per year membership; admission: $3.00 for adults

George Peabody Library of The Johns Hopkins University
(see Maryland Historical Society, State Historical Society, above)

Port Deposit Heritage Corporation-Paw Paw Museum
(98 North Main Street—location)
PO Box 101 (mailing address)
Port Deposit, MD 21904
(410) 378-3866; (410) 378-3533
Erika Quesenbery, Curator
second & fourth Sun (May–Oct) 1:00–5:00, and by appointment
("Maryland local history, Port Deposit family histories. Extensive collection of Civil War-era letters; USNTC Bainbridge History Repository.")

Enoch Pratt Free Library
Maryland Department
400 Cathedral Street
Baltimore, MD 21201-4484
(410) 396-5430 (Library); (410) 396-5468 (Maryland Department); (410) 396-9537 FAX
mdx@epfl.net
http://www.epfl.net/slrc/md
Jeffrey Korman; Mendy Gunter
Mon–Wed 10:00–8:00, Thur 10:00–5:30, Fri–Sat 10:00–5:00, Sun (Sept–May)

1:00–5:00
("Pratt's genealogical materials are located in the Maryland, Periodicals and Social Science and History Department. We do circulate some genealogy books")

Queen Anne's County Free Library
121 South Commerce Street
Centreville, MD 21617
(410) 758-0980; (410) 758-3719 FAX
http://www.quan.lib.md.us
Kimberly Baklarz, Assistant Administrator
Mon–Thur 10:00–8:00, Fri–Sat 9:00–5:00

Riversdale House Mansion
(4811 Riverdale Road—location)
6005 48th Avenue (mailing address)
Riverdale, MD 20737
(301) 864-0420; (301) 927-3498
http://www.lissa.net/riverdale/Riversdale.html
Edward Day, Director
Fri & Sun noon–4:00, and by appointment
(Calvert Mansion: "archives with local holdings")
costs for photocopies

Rockville Regional Library
Montgomery County Public Libraries
99 Maryland Avenue
Rockville, MD 20850
(301) 279-1953
http://www.montgomerylibrary.org
Patricia Burt
Mon–Thur 9:00–9:00, Fri–Sat 9:00–5:00, Sun (during school year) 1:00–5:00

Saint Mary's College of Maryland Library
Saint Mary's City, MD 20686
(301) 862-0264 (Circulation)
http://www.smcm.edu/library/index.htm
Deloris Bomarc, Head of Public Services
School semester: Mon–Thur 8:00 A.M.–midnight, Fri 8:00 A.M.–9:00 P.M., Sat 9:00–9:00, Sun noon–midnight

Saint Mary's County Memorial Library
Route 1, Box 9E
Leonardtown, MD 20650-9601
(301) 475-2846; (301) 475-4844 (Archives and Records Center); (301) 884-4415 FAX
webexpert@somd.lib.md.us
http://www.stmalib.org
Mary Wood, Director

Southern Maryland Studies Center
College of Southern Maryland
(8730 Mitchell Road—location)
PO Box 910 (mailing address)
La Plata, MD 20646-0910
(301) 934-2251, ext. 7110 (local); (301) 870-3008, ext. 7110 (Washington metro area); (301) 884-8131, ext. 7110 (Saint Mary's County)
smsc@csmd.edu
http://www.csmd.edu/library/SMSC/index.html
Sarah L. Barley, Coordinator
Reading Room: Mon–Thur 8:00 A.M.–10:00 P.M., Fri 8:00–4:00, Sat 9:00–4:00 (hours vary between college sessions); Documents Room: Mon–Fri 1:00–4:00

Maryland Room of the Talbot County Free Library
100 West Dover Street
Easton, MD 21601-2620
(410) 822-1626; (410) 820-8217 FAX
mdroom@talb.lib.md.us
http://www.talb.lib.md.us
Monique Gordy, Acting Custodian

Mon & Thur 9:00–9:00, Tue–Wed
9:00–6:00, Fri–Sat 9:00–5:00; summer:
Mon 9:00–9:00, Tue–Thur 9:00–6:00, Fri
9:00–5:00, Sat 9:00–1:00

University of Baltimore
Langsdale Library
1420 Maryland Avenue
Baltimore, MD 21201
(410) 837-4318; (410) 837-4330 FAX
swheeler@ubmail.ubalt.edu
http://www.ubalt.edu/www/langlib/index.
html

University of Maryland
Hornbake Library
Marylandia and Rare Book Department
Archives and Manuscript Department
College Park, MD 20742
(301) 405-9212; (301) 405-9058; (301) 314-
2709 FAX
dm185@umail.umd.edu
http://www.lib.umd.edu/mdrm
Doug McElrath, Curator
Mon–Fri 10:00–5:00, Sat noon–5:00 (check
web site for Sat openings)
("Although our resources are primarily not
genealogical in nature, we do have the
Federal Pupulation Census of Maryland
1790–1930, Baltimore City Directories
1794–1940, Maryland newspapers,
published genealogical source records
from Maryland, and Maryland
county/local history publications.")

University of Maryland, Baltimore County
Albin O. Kuhn Library
5401 Wilkens Avenue
Catonsville, MD 21228
(410) 455-2232
http://umbc7.umbc.edu/~curnoles/
aokweb.html
Simmona E. Simmons-Hodo
Mon–Thur 8:00 A.M.–11:00 P.M., Fri
8:00–6:00, Sat noon–6:00, Sun
noon–8:00

University of Mississippi
Center for the Study of Southern Culture
(see Mississippi, Part 2)

**Virginia Polytechnic Institute and State
University**
Appalachian history
(see Virginia, Part 2)

Washington College
Clifton M. Miller Library
300 Washington Avenue
Chestertown, MD 21620-1192
(410) 778-7292; (410) 778-7288 FAX
Judith I. Hymes, Director of Technical
Services
Mon–Thur 8:30–midnight, Fri 8:30–10:00,
Sat 10:00–10:00, Sun noon–midnight

Washington County Free Library
Western Maryland Room
100 South Potomac Street
Hagerstown, MD 21740
(301) 739-3250, ext. 158; (301) 739-5839
FAX
http://pilot.wash.lib.md.us/wcfl/index.html
John C. Frye, Director
Mon 2:00–9:00, Thur–Fri 9:00–5:00
(western Maryland and adjacent areas;
Hagerstown imprints; historical maps;
vertical file collecetion with index; family
files; 1870 federal census indexes for
Maryland, West Virginia, and Virginia;
1776 Maryland state census; Hagerstown
almanacs; obituary locator 1790–1968;

church records; high school yearbooks;
railroad materials; city directories and
telephone books; local histories;
naturalization and manumission records;
index to Hagerstown newspapers
1790–1844; extensive photograph
collection; cemetery records; Civil War
materials; Southern Historical Society
papers)
free room use, free parking

Wicomico County Free Library
(122-126 South Division Street—location)
PO Box 4148 (mailing address)
Salisbury, MD 21801
(410) 749-5171
http://www.co.wicomico.md.us/library.html
Joanne Doyle, Head of Reference
Mon–Thur 10:00–9:00, Fri–Sat 10:00–5:00

Worcester County Library
Worcester Room
307 North Washington Street
Snow Hill, MD 21863
(410) 632-2600; (410) 632-1159 FAX
worc@worc.lib.md.us
http://www.worc.lib.md.us/library/home.
html
Lisa Harrison, Coordinator of Community
Services
Mon & Wed 10:00–8:00, Tue & Thur–Fri
10:00–6:00, Sat 9:00–1:00
(local history and genealogy)

Historical Societies—Local and Regional

Allegany County Historical Society, Inc.
History House
218 Washington Street
Cumberland, MD 21502
(301) 777-8678
Jami Nealis, Administrative Assistant
Tue–Sat 10:00–4:00, Sun (June–Oct)
1:00–4:00
Pub. *Newsletter*, quarterly
("a small collection of local genealogy, most
of which is paper files")
$20.00 per year membership

The Allen Historical Society
PO Box 31
Allen, MD 21810
(410) 749-9064
jorge@dmv.com
George Shivers, President

Ann Arrundell County Historical Society
(Benson-Hammond House, Aviation
Boulevard and Andover Road—location)
PO Box 385 (mailing address)
Linthicum, MD 21090-0385
(410) 768-9518
Mark N. Schatz, Vice President Publications
Thur–Sat 11:00–3:00
Pub. *Anne Arrundel County History Notes*,
quarterly
$20.00 per year membership; tours: $2.00
donation from nonmembers

**Baltimore County Historical
Society—Library**
Agriculture Building
9811 Van Buren Lane
Cockeysville, MD 21030
(410) 666-1876 (Library); (410) 666-1878
(Museum)
bchistory@msn.com (Executive Director)
http://www.baltocohistsoc.org
Marjorie Shipley, Library Volunteer
Wed 1:00–4:00, Sat 10:00–3:00

Pub. *History Trails*, quarterly, $5.00
subscription (for libraries only)
(cemetery inscriptions, family histories,
newsletters, newspaper clippings,
obituaries)
$25.00 per year membership; research:
$15.00

Boyds-Clarksburg Historical Society, Inc.
(19510 White Ground Road—location)
PO Box 161 (mailing address)
Boyds, MD 20841-01061
(301) 972-0578

Brunswick History Commission
1 West Potomac Street
Brunswick, MD 21716
(301) 834-7500
Wendell Stewart, President
Wed 10:00–noon
("Our objective is to gather history of
Brunswick. One publication: *Brunswick
100 Years of Memories*, $17.00 ppd.")

Calvert County Historical Society, Inc.
Genealogy Section
(70 Church Street—location)
PO Box 358 (mailing address)
Prince Frederick, MD 20678
(410) 535-2452
inquiries@calverthistory.org
http://www.calverthistory.org
Susan Hance, Archivist
Tue–Thur 10:00–3:00
Pub. *News and Notes*, two times per year;
The Historian, annually
(includes Maryland and county history and
genealogy records)
$25.00 per year membership

Capital View Park Historical Society
10023 Menlo Avenue
Silver Spring, MD 20910-1055
(301) 588-4420

Caroline County Historical Society, Inc.
(The Courthouse Green—location)
PO Box 514 (mailing address)
Denton, MD 21629
(410) 482-8072
Jean L. Kelly, Secretary
by appointment
$10.00 per year membership

Historical Society of Carroll County, Inc.
210 East Main Street
Westminster, MD 21157-5225
(410) 848-6494
cchs@dcwi.com
http://www.carr.org/hscc
Jay A. Graybeal, Director
Tue–Fri 9:30–4:00, Sat 9:00–noon
Pub. *Carroll County History Journal*,
quarterly
(includes file cards, drawings, surveyors'
books and maps of early land patents and
settlement patterns in Western Maryland
[Baltimore, Carroll, Frederick and
Washington counties], journals, ledgers,
maps, scrapbooks, family papers,
photographs, files on the history of local
churches, and local newspapers: *The
Democratic Advocate* [1842–1972], *The
Carrolltonian* [1833–1844], *Union
Bridge Pilot* [1899–1972], *American
Sentinel* [1855–1928], and *Carroll
County Times* [1911–present])
$20.00 per year membership

Catoctin Furnace Historical Society
12320 Auburn Road
Thurmont, MD 21788

(301) 271-2306
Clement E. Gardiner, President

Catonsville Historical Society, Inc.
Catonsville Genealogical Section
(1824 Frederick Road—location)
PO Box 9311 (mailing address)
Catonsville, MD 21228
(410) 744-3034
chistory@catonsvillehistory.org
http://www.catonsvillehistory.org
Frank M. Wheltle, Chairman
meetings: first Wed (Feb–May & Sept–Dec)
$5.00 per year membership in Genealogical
    Section, plus compulsory membership in
    Catonsville Historical Society

The Historical Society of Cecil County
135 East Main Street
Elkton, MD 21921
(410) 398-1790
history@cchistory.org
http://cchistory.org
Michael Dixon, President
Mon noon–4:00, Tue 6:00–8:30, Thur
    10:00–4:00, fourth Sat 10:00–2:00
Pub. *The Bulletin of the Historical Society of
    Cecil County*, three times per year (Apr,
    Sept, Dec)
(Cecil County history)
$10.00 per year membership; research:
    donation

**The Historical Society of Charles County,
Inc.**
PO Box 2806
La Plata, MD 20646
(301) 934-2564
Mrs. George C. Dyson, Chair Genealogy and
    Research Committee
volunteer hours
Pub. *News and Notes from the Historical
    Society of Charles County*, quarterly;
    *Historical Society of Charles County
    Record*, quarterly
(Charles County history and genealogy)
$10.00 per year membership

Chevy Chase Historical Society
(address withheld upon request)

**Clear Spring District Historical
Association**
PO Box 211
Clear Spring, MD 21722
(301) 842-2342

Crisfield Heritage Foundation
3 Ninth Street
Crisfield, MD 21817-1028
(410) 968-2501
http://www.crisfield.org/
    Crisfieldheritage.htm

Darnestown Historical Society
14101 Berryville Road
Darnestown, MD 20874
(301) 869-8969

Dorchester County Historical Society
(Meredith House, 902 LaGrange
    Avenue—location)
PO Box 361 (mailing address)
Cambridge, MD 21613-2009
(410) 228-7953
dchs@fastol.com
http://www.bluecrab.org/dchs/index.html

Downs Park Historical Society
8311 John Downs Loop
Pasadena, MD 21122
(410) 222-6230

Rick Holt, Park Superintendent

Dundalk-Patapsco Neck Historical Society
(4 Center Place—location)
PO Box 21781 (mailing address)
Dundalk, MD 21222
(410) 284-2331
DUNHOST.SOC@aol.com
http://www.museumsusa.org/data/
    museums/MD/177468.htm
Eleanor Lukanich, President
Mon–Fri 10:00–5:00, Sat 1:00–5:00
Pub. *Society Newsletter*, monthly
(historical and genealogical information on
    Dundalk Patapsco Neck area)
$10.00 per year membership; research: copy
    fee only

Emmitsburg Historical Society
PO Box 463
Emmitsburg, MD 21727
J. R. Marsden, President
quarterly meetings: Mar, May, Sept, Nov
Pub. *Bits & Pieces*, quarterly
(Emmitsburg and central Maryland)
$10.00 per year membership

**Heritage Society of Essex and Middle
River, Inc.**
516 Eastern Boulevard
Essex, MD 21221-6701
(410) 574-6934
http://www.museumsusa.org/data/
    museums/MD/177519.htm
Paul Michael Blitz, Archivist
Museum: Sun 1:00–4:00, and weekdays by
    appointment for group tours; Archives: by
    appointment only
$5.00 per year membership; admission by
    donation

**The Historical Society of Frederick
County, Inc.**
24 East Church Street
Frederick, MD 21701
(301) 663-1188; (301) 663-0526 FAX
mhudson@hsfcinfo.org (Director);
    library@hsfcinfo.org
http://www.hsfcinfo.org/index.htm
Marie Washburn, Librarian; Barbara F.
    Johnson, Executive Director
Library: Tue–Sat 10:00–4:00; Museum:
    Mon–Sat 10:00–4:00, Sun 1:00–4:00
Pub. *Newsletter*, quarterly (members only);
    Journal, semiannually, $10.00
    subscription for two years or $5.00 per
    issue
(Frederick County history and genealogical
    research)
$20.00 per year membership; museum tours:
    $2.00; library admission: $2.00; research:
    $40.00

Garrett County Historical Society, Inc.
(123 Center Street—location)
111 East Oak Street (mailing address)
Oakland, MD 21550
(301) 334-3226; (301) 334-3403 (Curator)
http://www.deepcreektimes.com/gchs.html
Charlotte Friend, Curator
June–Aug: Mon–Fri 10:00–4:00
Pub. *Glades Star*, quarterly
$10.00 per year membership

Germantown Historical Society
PO Box 475
Germantown, MD 20875-0475
(301) 492-6282

Gibson Island Historical Society
Gibson Island, MD 21056
(410) 437-5270; (410) 255-5287

Greenbelt Historical Society
204 Lastner Lane
Greenbelt, MD 20770-1617
(301) 474-5156
Emory A. Harman, President
no set hours, always available

Hancock Historical Society
126 West High Street
Hancock, MD 21750-1138
http://www.hancockmd.com/org/historic/
    index.html

**The Historical Society of Harford County,
Inc.**
(143 North Main Street—location)
PO Box 366 (mailing address)
Bel Air, MD 21014-0366
(410) 838-7691; (410) 838-1213 (Hays
    House Museum); (410) 838-5257 FAX
harchis@msn.com
http://www.harfordhistory.net
Maryanna Skowronski, Administrator,
    Society Headquarters; Joan Betzold,
    Chairperson, Hays House Museum; Henry
    C. Peden, Genealogist, Research by Mail
Court Records Section: Tue 10:00–noon and
    1:00–2:30; Library and Family History:
    Thur 9:00–3:00, fourth Sat 10:00–2:00;
    Society Gift Shop: open on the days and
    times for the above sections; Hays House
    Museum, 324 South Kenmore Avenue,
    Bel Air: Sun 1:00–4:00, and by
    appointment
Pub. *Newsletter*, six times per year; *Harford
    Historical Bulletin*, quarterly
("The Historical Society of Harford County,
    Inc., was founded in 1885 and is the
    oldest county historical society in
    Maryland. Visit our web site to learn more
    about the society, its membership fees,
    research services by mail, user fees, and
    other information.")

Howard County Historical Society, Inc.
(8328 Court Avenue, Ellicott City, MD
    21043-4506—Museum location)
8324 Court Avenue—Library location)
PO Box 109 (mailing address)
Ellicott City, MD 21041
(410) 461-1050 (Museum); (410) 750-0370
    (Library)
Phyllis Knill, Museum Director; Mary K.
    Mannix, Library Director; Robin E.
    Emrich, Archivist
Museum: Tue & Sat 1:00–5:00, and by
    appointment; Library: Tue noon–8:00, Sat
    noon–5:00
Pub. *Legacy*, quarterly
(Howard County and Maryland history)
$15.00 per year membership

Kensington Historical Society
PO Box 453
Kensington, MD 20895-0453
(301) 942-8933

Historical Society of Kent County
(101 Church Alley—location)
PO Box 665 (mailing address)
Chestertown, MD 21620
(410) 778-3499; (410) 778-3747 FAX
hskcmd@friend.ly.net
http://www.hskcmd.com
Mary Kate O'Donnell, Executive Director
The Geddes-Piper House: Nov–Apr: Fri
    10:00–4:00; May–Oct: tours Sat–Sun
    1:00–4:00
Pub. *Old Kent*, quarterly
(local and Eastern Shore)
$25.00 per year membership; research:
    $10.00 per surname; copies: 25¢ per page

Laurel Historical Society
PO Box 774
Laurel, MD 20707
(301) 286-7031

Lincoln Park Historical Society
(111 West Montgomery Avenue—location)
PO Box 1884 (mailing address)
Rockville, MD 20849-1884
(301) 340-2974 (Library); (301) 762-1492
    (Museum)
info@montgomeryhistory.org
http://www.montgomeryhistory.org
Library: Tue–Sat 10:00–4:00, Sun
    1:00–4:00; Museum: Tue–Sun noon–
    4:00

Middletown Valley Historical Society
(305 West Main Street—location)
PO Box 294 (mailing address)
Middletown, MD 21769-0294
(301) 293-6816 (for appointments only);
    (301) 371-7582
http://www.museumsusa.org/data/
    museums/MD/178305.htm
Kathleen Rudesill, President
Library: June–Aug: Sun 2:00–5:00, and by
    appointment
(emphasis on Middletown Valley, Frederick
    County)
$10.00 per year membership

**Montgomery County (Maryland)
Historical Society**
(42 West Middle Lane—library location)
Beall-Dawson House
111 West Montgomery Avenue (mailing
address)
Rockville, MD 20850-4212
(301) 340-2974; (301) 762-1492
info@montgomeryhistory.org
http://www.montgomeryhistory.org
Jane C. Sween, Librarian
Tue–Sun noon–4:00
Pub. *News and Notes*, online newsletter
$35.00 per year basic membership

Mount Airy Historical Society
c/o Mount Airy Town Hall
(110 South Main Street—location)
PO Box 244 (mailing address)
Mount Airy, MD 21771-0244
(301) 829-0489
Sat noon–4:00

Prince George's County Historical Society
(Marietta, 5626 Bell Station Road, Glenn
Dale, MD—location)
PO Box 14 (mailing address)
Riverdale, MD 20737-0014
(301) 464-0590
http://www.pghistory.org
Sharon Sweeting, Librarian; Sarah Bourne,
    Assistant
Sat noon–4:00, and by appointment
Pub. *News and Notes*, ten times per year
$25.00 per year membership; no researchers
    available

Queen Anne's County Historical Society
(Tucker House, 124 South Commerce
Street—location)
PO Box 62 (mailing address)
Centreville, MD 21617-0062
(410) 758-3010
Mrs. Lee Brookes, President

Saint Mary's County Historical Society
(11 Court House Drive—location)
PO Box 212 (mailing address)
Leonardtown, MD 20650-0212
(301) 475-2467

smcha@erols.com
http://www.smchsonline.org
Bleecker S. Harrison, Executive Secretary
Tue–Sat 10:00–4:00
Pub. *Chronicles of Saint Mary's*, quarterly
$20.00 per year membership

Shady Side Rural Heritage Society, Inc.
(1418 E.W. Shady Side Road—location)
PO Box 89 (mailing address)
Shady Side, MD 20764-0089
(410) 867-4486
captainavery@prodigy.net
http://www.museumsusa.org/data/
    museums/MD/176838.htm
June Hall Chairman Board of Trustees; Janet
    Surrett, Museum Manager; Gail
    Schneider, Librarian
Mar–Dec: Sun 1:00–4:00, and by
    appointment
Pub. *SSRHS Newsletter*, quarterly
$15.00 per year membership

Silver Spring Historical Society
PO Box 1160
Silver Spring, MD 20910-1160
sshistory@yahoo.com
http://www.homestead.com/
    silverspringhistory

Smithsburg Historical Society, Inc.
Smithsburg, MD 21783
(301) 824-7234
leopards@erols.com
http://pilot.wash.lib.md.us/smithsburg/
    HIST.htm

Somerset County Historical Society
Treackle Mansion
PO Box 181
Princess Anne, MD 21853
(410) 651-2238

South Mountain Heritage Society
(3 East Main Street—location)
PO Box 509 (mailing address)
Burkittsville, MD 21718
(301) 834-7851

Takoma Park Historical Society
Municipal Building
7500 Maple Avenue
Takoma Park, MD 20012
(301) 585-3542

Historical Society of Talbot County, Inc.
(25 South Washington Street—location)
PO Box 964 (mailing address)
Easton, MD 21601
(410) 822-0773; (410) 322-7911 FAX
webmastr@hstc.org
http://www.hstc.org
Linda Prochaska
Tue–Sat 10:00–4:00; Library: by
    appointment

Thurmont Historical Society
(11 North Church Street—location)
PO Box 251 (mailing address)
Frederick, MD 21788-0251
(301) 271-1860
CISHIST@aol.com
Fri–Sat 9:00–1:00

Washington County Historical Society
Jamieson Memorial Library
The Miller House
(135 West Washington Street, Hagerstown,
MD 21740—location)
PO Box 1281 (mailing address)
Hagerstown, MD 21741-1281
(301) 797-8782

histsoc@earthlink.net
http://www.rootsweb.com/~mdwchs
Peggy Bledsoe, Library Consultant
Mon & Fri 9:00–4:00, Wed noon–4:00
(Washington and Frederick counties)
research: $15.00 per surname

Washington Grove Heritage Committee
PO Box 5
Washington Grove, MD 20880
(301) 926-4786
R. Carole Huberman, Chairman

**West Virginia and Regional History
Association**
(see West Virginia, Part 2)

Westside Historical Society
Mardela Springs, MD 21837
(410) 543-6502
http://www.museumsusa.org/data/
    museums/MD/180008.htm

Wicomico County Historical Society
(Pemberton Historical Park, Pemberton
Drive, Salisbury, MD 21801—location)
PO Box 573 (mailing address)
Salisbury, MD 21803-0573
(410) 860-0447
history@shore.intercom.net
http://skipjack.net/le_shore/whs

Woodsboro Historical Society, Inc.
PO Box 348
Woodsboro, MD 21798
(301) 624-4468
eyler93@msn.com

Worcester County Historical Society
PO Box 111
Snow Hill, MD 21863-0111
(410) 632-2600

Genealogical Societies

State Genealogical Society

Maryland Genealogical Society (MGS)
201 West Monument Street
Baltimore, MD 21201-4674
(410) 685-3750, ext. 360 (answering
    machine)
info@mdgensoc.org (General Information);
    bulletin@mdgensoc.org (*The Bulletin*);
    research@mdgensoc.org (Research
    Questions)
http://www.mdgensoc.org
Ella Rowe, Corresponding Secretary
Tue–Fri 10:00–4:30, Sat 9:00–4:30
Pub. *Maryland Genealogical Society
    Bulletin*, quarterly; *MGS Newsletter*,
    quarterly
$55.00 per year membership, which is now
    joint membership with the Maryland
    Historical Society and should be paid
    directly to them; research: $12.00 per
    hour in advance plus SASE

Southern Society of Genealogists, Inc.
(see Alabama, Part 2)

Genealogical Societies—Local & Regional

Allegany County Genealogical Society
(215 Bowen Street, Cumberland, MD
21502—location)
PO Box 3103 (mailing address)
La Vale, MD 21502
hmoorel@mindspring.com
Mon–Tue & Thur–Sat noon–8:00 (members
    only)
Pub. *Old Pike Post*, quarterly, $7.00 per year

subscription
$10.00 per year membership

Allegheny Regional Family History Society (ARFHS)
(see West Virginia, Part 2)

Anne Arundel Genealogical Society
(Kuethe Library, 3 Crain Highway, S.E., Glen Burnie—location)
PO Box 221 (mailing address)
Pasadena, MD 21123-0221
bdekeyser@juno.com
http://www.aagensoc.org
Jo Boroff, Corresponding Secretary; Betty deKeyser, Librarian
Library: Thur–Sat 10:00–4:00
Pub. *Anne Arundel Speaks*, quarterly
$15.00 per year membership; library admission: $2.00 donation for nonmembers

Baltimore County Genealogical Society, Inc.
(8601 Harford Road, Parkville, MD—location)
PO Box 10085 (mailing address)
Towson, MD 21285-0085
bcgs@mail.serve.com
http://www.serve.com/bcgs/bcgs.html
Elaine O. Zimmerman, President
Library: second Tuesday 5:00–9:00, second Thur & second Sat 10:00–2:00; meetings at library: fourth Sun (Sept–June) noon–4:30
Pub. *The Notebook*, quarterly
$15.00 per year membership

Calvert County Genealogy Society
PO Box 9
Sunderland, MD 20689
(410) 535-0839
Jerry and Mildred Bowen O'Brien, Editors
9:00–5:00
Pub. *Calvert County Genealogy Newsletter*, monthly
(includes southern Maryland's old families in Anne Arundel, Charles, Montgomery, Prince George's, and St. Mary's counties)
$15.00 per year membership

Carroll County Genealogical Society, Inc.
Carroll County Public Library
(50 East Main Street, Westminster, MD 21157—location)
PO Box 1752 (mailing address)
Westminster, MD 21158
http://www.carr.org/ccgs/ccgs.html
Maria Gilligan, President
Library: Mon–Thur 9:30–8:45, Fri–Sat 9:30–5:00
Pub. *Carrolltonian*, quarterly (Mar, June, Sept, Dec)
(includes Maryland history, local history, church and cemetery records)
$10.00 per year membership

Catonsville Historical Society, Inc.
Genealogical Section
(see Historical Societies—Local and Regional, above)

Genealogical Society of Cecil County, Inc.
(Colonial Charlestown, Inc., 343 Market Street—location)
PO Box 11 (mailing address)
Charlestown, MD 21914
(410) 287-8793
Joanne Daly, President
first Saturday of the month, and by appointment
Pub. *Genealogical Society of Cecil County*

Newsletter, quarterly
(includes surname files)
$8.00 per year membership

Frederick County Genealogical Society (FRECOGS)
(199 North Place, Frederick, MD 21701—book collection location
Non Profit Building and Supply, Corner of East and South Street—periodical location)
PO Box 234 (mailing address)
Monrovia, MD 21770
(301) 831-5781; (301) 834-9907
ckfpepper@aol.com
http://members.aol.com/frecogs/index.htm
Trudie Davis Long, Newsletter/Membership; Pepper Scotto
Book Collection: Tue 9:00–4:00, Wed 9:00–3:00, Thur 10:00–2:00, Sat 9:00–1:00, Tue–Fri 7:00 P.M.–9:00 P.M.; Periodical Collection: by appointment; meetings at Homewood at Crumland: second Sat 1:00
Pub. *Frecogs Newsletter*, bimonthly
(microfilm series of Holdcraft collection)
$20.00 per year membership

Harford County Genealogical Society
PO Box 15
Aberdeen, MD 21001
http://www.rtis.com/reg/md/org/hcgs
Harford County Historical Society Library: Thur 9:00–3:15; Genealogy Room: second & fourth Sat 10:00–2:00
Pub. *Newsletter*, bimonthly
$10.00 per year membership

Howard County Genealogical Society
PO Box 274
Columbia, MD 21045-0274
(410) 465-6696
apronstrings@erols.com
http://www.rootsweb.com/~mdhoward
Lorna Duane Smith, Vice President
Pub. *The Family Tree*, ten times per year
$10.00 per year membership

Lower Delmarva Genealogical Society (LDGS)
PO Box 3602
Salisbury, MD 21802-3602
(410) 742-3501 (Membership/Surname Chairman); (410) 546-0314 (Vice President)
Pegdl@intercom.net
http://www.rootsweb.com/~ldgs
Phyllis Cooper, President; Peg Lauridsen
Maryland Room of the Wicomico County Library: Thur 1:00–5:00
Pub. *More from the Shore*, semiannually (Mar, Sept)
("Maryland, eastern shore of Virginia and Maryland, state of Delaware")
$15.00 per year membership; queries free to members, short queries $5.00 for nonmembers; simple search (one date): $5.00 plus SASE, professional researchers available for longer inquiries

Genealogy Club of the Montgomery County (Maryland) Historical Society
(42 West Middle Lane—library location)
Beall-Dawson House
111 West Montgomery Avenue (mailing address)
Rockville, MD 20850-4212
(301) 340-2974; (301) 762-1492
info@montgomeryhistory.org
http://www.montgomeryhistory.org
Jane C. Sween, Librarian
Tue–Sun noon–4:00
Pub. *Line Upon Line*, ten times per year

$20.00 per year membership in Genealogy Club only, included in $35.00 per year basic membership in Historical Society

National Capital Buckeye Chapter (OGS)
(see Ohio, Part 2)

Prince George's County Genealogical Society
(12219 Tulip Grove Drive—location)
PO Box 819 (mailing address)
Bowie, MD 20718-0819
(301) 262-2063
http://www.rootsweb.com/~mdpgcgs
Wed 10:00–7:00, first Wed 10:00–1:00, last Sat 1:00–5:00
Pub. *Prince George's County Genealogical Society Bulletin*, five times per year (bimonthly, Sept–June), $4.00 per issue
("Research Center holdings include 4,000+ volumes, large periodical collection, registrar's files, family surname files, maps, Bible records, microforms, audio and video cassettes, CD collection, and manuscript material. Local and national in scope.")
$15.00 per year membership; admission: free; research: $10.00 per hour

Saint Mary's County Genealogical Society, Inc.
PO Box 1109
Leonardtown, MD 20650-1109
(301) 373-8458
ehayden@pastracks.com; smcgs@pastracks.com
http://www.smcgsi.org
Lorraine Bliss Wallace, President; Loranna Gray, Treasurer
Pub. *The Generator*, ten times per year
$10.00 per year membership

Upper Shore Genealogical Society of Maryland
(12156 Greensboro Road—location)
PO Box 275 (mailing address)
Easton, MD 21601
(410) 778-0584
http://www.chronography.com/usgs/index.html
Jane G. Whomsley, President
meetings: third Sun
Pub. *Chesapeake Cousins*, semiannually
(Eastern Shore of Maryland genealogy; published tombstone records of Caroline, Dorchester, Kent, Queen Anne, and Talbot counties)
$20.00 per year membership

Independent Publications and Miscellany

Historic Annapolis Foundation
Shiplap House
18 Pinkney Street
Annapolis, MD 21401-5553
(410) 267-7619; (800) 603-4020
riverar@annapolis.org
http://www.annapolis.org

Appalachian Roots
(see West Virginia, Part 2)

Branches of the Bay Bookshop
PO Box 736
Gambrills, MD 21054
tsurles@theauroragroup.com
http://brancesofthebay.com/index.htm
Trish Surles
(books on Maryland's Eastern Shore: Caroline, Kent, Queen Anne's and Talobt

counties; Whitley and McCreary counties, Kentucky)

Center for Appalachian Studies
(see North Carolina, Part 2)

Cindy's Genealogy on the Eastern Shore of Maryland, Delaware, and Virginia
bennetjh@shoreweb.com
http://www.shoreweb.com/cindy/index.html
Cindy Bennett

Colonial Charlestown, Inc.
(343 Market Street—location)
PO Box 11 (mailing address)
Charlestown, MD 21914
(410) 287-8793
Nelson H. McCall, President
by appointment
(Town of Charlestown records—Land, Minutes, Ledge and Death)

Colonial Roots
(see Delaware, Part 2)

Dorchester County Genealogical Magazine
1058 Taylors Island Road
Madison, MD 21648
(410) 228-5442
Debra S. Moxey, Editor
Pub. *Dorchester County Genealogical Magazine*, bimonthly, $14.00 per year subscription

Family Historians
c/o Civilian Welfare
9800 Savage Road
Fort George G. Meade, MD 20755-6000
Marvin D. Muhlhansen, President
Pub. *Rootbound*, bimonthly
$7.00 per year membership (activities and meetings, first Tue, not open to the public)

Genealogical Institute
(see Virginia, Part 2)

Genealogy and History of the Eastern Shore (GHOTES)
(see Virginia, Part 2)

GenLaw Resources
Box 9187
Gaithersburg, MD 20898-9187
genlaw@mindspring.com
Pat Andersen
Pub. *Western Maryland Genealogy*, quarterly
(includes western Maryland only)
$19.00 per year membership

Handley's Eastern Shore Maryland
Genealogy Project
shari@tyaskin.com
http://www.tyaskin.com/handley
Shari Handley

Historic Medley District, Inc.
PO Box 232
Poolesville, MD 20837
(301) 972-8588
Perry Kephart, President
John Poule Store and Seneca Schoolhouse in Poolesville, museums: Sun (Apr–Oct)
Pub. *HMD Newsletter*, occasionally
$10.00 per year membership

Hunting for Bears Genealogical and Historical Society
(see Alabama, Part 2)

John Brown Historical Foundation, Inc.

13701 Deakins Lane
Darnestown, MD 20874
(301) 963-3300; (301) 432-2666
Capt. South T. Lynn

MLH Research
3916 Bramble Road
Anniston, AL 36201
MariLee Beatty Hagness, Owner
Pub. *Maryland Connections Queries*, bimonthly, $17.00 per year subscription
(parish records, court records)
research: $10.00 per hour; queries

Maryland Roots and Branches
200 Weatherby Drive
Greenville, SC 29615-9731
Pub. *The Wye Oak Tree Newsletter*

MdGenWeb
Part of The USGenWeb Project
cyndiee@tampabay.rr.com
http://www.mdgenweb.org
Shari Handley, State Coordinator; Cyndie Enfinger, Assistant Coordinator
(links to other Maryland resources)

Mountain Press
(see Tennessee, Part 2)

Newtown Association, Inc.
PO Box 543
Salisbury, MD 21801
(410) 543-2111

Nixon Presidential Materials
National Archives at College Park
8601 Adelphi Road
College Park, MD 20740-6001
(301) 713-6950; (301) 713-6916
nixon@nara.gov
http://www.nara.gov/nixon

Pioneer Publications
Mid-Atlantic Queries & Reviews (DE-NJ-MD-PA)
(see Delaware, Part 2)

Preservation Association for Tudor Hall, Inc. (P.A.T.H., Inc.)
Tudor Hall
Bel Air, MD 21014
(410) 838-0466
Dorothy E. Fox, Secretary
Pub. *Pathways*, quarterly, $15.00 per year subscription
(genealogical services)

Preservation Society
812 South Ann Street
Baltimore, MD 21231
(410) 675-4776; (410) 675-6769

Records Management Division
(7275 Waterloo Road, Routes 175 and U.S. 1—location)
PO Box 275 (mailing address)
Jessup, MD 20794
(410) 799-1930
William E. Taylor, State Records Administrator
8:00–4:30
("RMD doesn't provide information to the general public.")

Rockville Historic Preservation, Ltd., Peerless
PO Box 4262
Rockville, MD 20849-4262
(301) 762-0096
http://www.peerlessrockville.org
(Primarily engaged in preservation, not

genealogy)

Society for the Preservation of Maryland Antiquities
2335 Marriottsville Road
Marriottsville, MD 21104
(410) 442-1772

Somerset County Historical Trust, Inc.
10380 Anderson Road
Princess Anne, MD 21853
(410) 651-0788
Mrs. Howard Yerges, Chairman
Mon–Fri 9:00–4:00
Pub. *Maryland Historical Trust Newsletter*
(genealogical services)
$15.00 per year membership; search requests turned over to Meredith Johnson, Princess Anne, $6.00 per hour

Historic Takoma Park
PO Box 5781
Takoma Park, MD 20913-5781
(301) 270-1700, ext. 662

University of Maryland
History Department
College Park, MD 20742
Pub. *Maryland Historian*, semiannually
$10.00 per year membership

West Virginia University
Appalachian Studies Association
(see West Virginia, Part 2)

Willow Bend Books, A Division of Heritage Books, Inc.
(see Booksellers, Part 4)

Massachusetts

Archives and Libraries with Holdings in Genealogy

State Archives and Library

Massachusetts Archives
Reference Desk
220 Morrissey Boulevard (Columbia Point)
Boston, MA 02125
(617) 727-2816; (617) 288-8429 FAX
archives@sec.state.ma.us
http://www.sec.state.ma.us/arc
Mon–Fri 9:00–5:00, Sat (except holiday
    weekends) 9:00–3:00

Supreme Judicial Court
Division of Archives and Records
Preservation
(Judicial Archives, Archives of the
    Commonwealth, 220 Morrissey Boulevard,
    Boston, MA 02125—location)
1300 New Court House (mailing address)
Boston, MA 02108
(617) 727-2816 (Judicial Archives); (617)
    557-1082 (Archivist); (617) 557-1088
    FAX
Elizabeth C. Bouvier, Head of Archives
Archives: Mon–Fri 9:00–5:00, Sat (except
    holiday weekends) 9:00–3:00
(locating and preserving inactive, historically
    important judicial records)

State Library of Massachusetts
George Fingold Library
State House, Room 341
Beacon Street
Boston, MA 02133
(617) 727-2590
Mon–Fri 9:00–5:00
("The State Library staff cannot undertake
    personal research projects. Researchers
    are welcome to visit and use the Library's
    collections; staff members are available to
    guide researchers. The Library is open to
    the public and charges no fees for use of
    the collections. Coin copiers are
    available.")

**Massachusetts Board of Library
Commissioners**
648 Beacon Street
Boston, MA 02215
(617) 267-9400; (800) 952-7403 (in
    Massachusetts); (617) 421-9833 FAX
info@mlin.lib.ma.us
http://mblc.state.ma.us/mblc/index.php

State Historical Society

Massachusetts Historical Society
1154 Boylston Street
Boston, MA 02215
(617) 536-1608
Virginia Smith, Reference Librarian
Library: Mon–Fri 9:00–4:45
Pub. *Proceedings*, annually
(manuscript repository, referring most
    genealogical queries to The New England
    Historic Genealogical Society)

City, County and Regional Archives and Libraries
(A more exhaustive list of public and
    academic libraries can be found at
    Massachusetts Library and Information
    Network, http://www.mlin.lib.ma.us/flash3.
    html [About Mass. Libraries].)

Abington Historical Commission

Town Hall
Abington, MA 02351
(781) 878-0009
Dr. George R. Horner, Chairperson
(not genealogical: historic sites)

Acton Historical Commission
377 Central Street
Acton, MA 01720
(978) 263-7081
Anita Dodson, Chairperson

Acton Memorial Library
486 Main Street
Acton, MA 01720-3999
(978) 264-9641; (978) 635-0073 FAX
http://www.actonmemoriallibrary.org
Susan J. Paju, Reference Librarian
Mon–Thur 9:00–9:00, Fri 9:00–5:00, Sat
    (fall–spring) 10:00–5:00, Sat (summer)
    9:00–1:00
Pub. *The Good Word*, quarterly
("Genealogy collection with emphasis on
    Massachusetts; also Civil War")

Acushnet Historical Commission
Town Hall
Acushnet, MA 02743
(508) 763-2488
Erwin Marks, Co-Chairperson
30 May–12 Oct: Sat–Sun & holidays
50¢ admission

Agawam Public Library
750 Cooper Street
Agawam, MA 01001-2177
(413) 789-1550; (314) 789-1552 FAX
http://www.agawam.ma.us/life/library
Judith Clini, Director
Mon–Thur 9:00–9:00, Fri 10:00–6:00, Sat
    (closed summers) 9:00–5:00

Amesbury Public Library
149 Main Street
Amesbury, MA 01913-2899
(978) 388-8148; (978) 388-2662
mam@mvlc.lib.ma.us
http://www.amesburylibrary.org
Mon–Thur 10:00–9:00, Fri–Sat 10:00–5:00,
    Sat (summer) 10:00–1:00

Amherst Historical Commission
Town Hall
Amherst, MA 01002
(413) 256-4032
Lynda Faye, Laison with Town; Don Frizzle,
    Chairperson
Mon–Fri 8:00–4:00
("We have records on all historic properties
    in Amherst.")

Aptucxet Trading Post Museum Complex
(see Bourne Historical Society, Inc.,
    Historical Societies—Local and Regional,
    below)

Arlington Historical Commission
Town Hall
Arlington, MA 02174
(781) 646-6694
Barbara Franco, Chairperson
(primarily historical, not genealogical; site
    preservation)

Atheneum Society of Wilbraham
450 Main Street
Wilbraham, MA 01095
(413) 596-4097
Martha D. Williams, President
hours: various
Pub. *The Peppercorn*, four times per year
$7.50 per year membership

Athol Historical Commission
584 Main Street
Athol, MA 01331
(978) 249-3208
Roderick McColl, Chairperson
(primarily historical, not genealogical: site
    preservation)

Attleboro Public Library
Reference Department
74 North Main Street
Attleboro, MA 02703-2280
(508) 222-0157; (508) 226-3326 FAX
http://www.sailsinc.org/Attleboro/apl.htm
Labor Day to mid-June: Mon–Thur
    8:30–8:30, Fri–Sat 8:30–4:30; summer:
    Mon & Wed–Fri 8:30–4:30
(local history)

Bacon Free Library
58 Eliot Street
South Natick, MA 01760-5542
(508) 653-6730
bfl@ma.ultranet.com
http://users.rcn.com/bfl
Tue 6:00 P.M.–8:30 P.M., Wed 2:00–4:30, Sat
    (16 Sept–14 June) 10:00–12:30

Barnstable Historical Commission
397 Main Street
Hyannis, MA 02601
(508) 771-7447
(primarily historical, not genealogical; site
    preservation, part of the town of
    Barnstable)

Barre Historical Commission
281 Old State Road
Barre, MA 01005
(978) 355-2327
Audrey Stevens, Chair

**Beardsley and Memorial Library of
Winsted**
(see Connecticut, Part 2)

Becket Historical Commission
Becket Town Hall
Main Street
Becket, MA 01223
(413) 623-8934 (Town Hall); (413) 623-
    5506 (Chair)
Constance Mulholland, Chair
meetings: every three months, second Wed
    7:00 P.M.

Bedford Free Public Library
7 Mudge Way
Bedford, MA 01730-2168
(781) 275-9440; (781) 275-6347 FAX
mmcculloch@mln.lib.ma.us
http://www.bedfordlibrary.net
Mon–Thur 9:00–9:00, Fri–Sat 9:00–5:00,
    Sun (Sept–May) 2:00–5:00

Lucius Beebe Memorial Library
345 Main Street
Wakefield, MA 01880-5093
(781) 246-6334; (781) 246-6385 FAX
wakefieldlibrary@noblenet.org
http://www.noblenet.org/wakefield
Charlotte Thompson
Mon–Thur 9:00–9:00, Fri 9:00–6:00, Sat
    9:00–5:00 (closed Sat in the summer)

Bellingham Historical Commission
Town Hall
Bellingham, MA 02019
(508) 966-1373
Florence McCracken, Chairperson
Pub. *Crimpville Comments*

Belmont Memorial Library
336 Concord Avenue
Belmont, MA 02478-0904
(781) 489-2000; (781) 489-5725
belmont@minlib.net
http://www.belmont.lib.ma.us
Duane Crabtree, Coordinator of Public
  Services
Mon–Thur 9:00–9:00, Fri–Sat 9:00–5:00,
  Sun (Oct–Apr) 1:00–5:00

Bennington Museum
(see Vermont, Part 2)

Bentley College
Solomon R. Baker Library Archives
17 South Forest Street
Waltham, MA 02154-4705
(781) 891-2308
John D. Cathcart

The Berkshire Athenaeum
Local History and Genealogy Department
1 Wendell Avenue
Pittsfield, MA 01201-6385
(413) 499-9486; (413) 499-9489 FAX
http://www.berkshire.net/PittsfieldLibrary
Katharine Westwood, Supervisor
winter (Sept to mid-June): Mon–Thur
    9:00–9:00, Fri 9:00–5:00, Sat
    10:00–5:00; summer (mid-June–Labor
    Day): Mon, Wed & Fri 9:00–5:00, Tue &
    Thur 9:00–9:00, Sat 10:00–1:00
(over 8,000 volumes in historical collections,
    vital records, church and cemetery
    records, census, newspapers, family
    history file, periodicals, indexes;
    Massachusetts local and New England
    regional historical and genealogical
    information)

Library of the Boston Athenaeum
10½ Beacon Street
Boston, MA 02108
(617) 227-0270; (617) 227-5266 FAX
Trevor J. Johnson, Reference Librarian
Mon–Fri 9:00–5:30, Sat (Oct–May)
    9:00–4:00
Pub. *Athenaeum Items*, quarterly
(New England state and local history and
    genealogy; researchers requested to call in
    advance for information)
$100.00 per year membership

Boston College
The John J. Burns Library
140 Commonwealth Avenue
Chestnut Hill, MA 02167
(617) 552-3282 (main number); (617) 552-
    8297
robert.oneill.1@bc.edu
Robert K. O'Neill, Ph.D., Burns Librarian
Mon–Fri 9:00–5:00
(local Boston history, West African and
    Caribbean history, the American Catholic
    Church and Jesuitana)

Boston Public Library
Social Sciences Department
(700 Boylston Street—location)
PO Box 286 (mailing address)
Boston, MA 02117
(617) 536-5400, ext. 261
info@bpl.org
http://www.bpl.org/electronic/genealogy.htm
    (Genealogy Resources)
Marta Pardee-King, Curator of Social
    Sciences
Mon–Thur 9:00–9:00, Fri–Sat 9:00–5:00,
    Sun (Oct–May) 1:00–5:00
(strong collections in New England
    genealogy and history)

The staff cannot undertake genealogical or
heraldic research; nor can it check our
holdings to determine if they contain
passages or sections of genealogies
pertinent to a particular family. The staff
cannot search shipping records, passenger
lists, or city directories unless a specific
year is given. Arrangements can be made
to photocopy pages of certain published
genealogies and armories, but only if
citations to author, title, and specific
pages are provided. The staff cannot
search the index to, nor provide abstracts
from the genealogical columns of the
Boston Evening Transcript. Inquirers
having specific citations to items in the
Transcript may request photocopies of
these items from the Library. Charges for
this service are available upon request.
Requests for photocopies must be made in
person or in writing

The Jonathan Bourne Historical Center
Bourne Archives
30 Keene Street
Bourne, MA 02532
(508) 759-6928
Patricia K. McAliece, Chairman
Tue 9:00–3:00
(responsible for custody, preservation and
    management of the permanently valuable,
    noncurrent records of the town; histories
    of town and its villages, Cape Cod Canal,
    genealogies, schools, industries,
    organizations, maps, pictures, etc.; center
    also houses the Bourne Historical Society,
    Inc., The Historic Commission, and The
    Society for Historic Preservation)
only charge is for copies

Jonathan Bourne Public Library
19 Sandwich Road
Bourne, MA 02532-3608
(508) 759-0644
http://www.bournelibrary.org
Diane W. Ranney, Assistant Director
Tue–Thur 9:00–8:00, Fri–Sat 9:00–5:30
("We do not specialize in genealogy due to
    the proximity of the Town Archives.")

Braintree Historical Commission
132 Middle Street
Braintree, MA 02184
(781) 843-5091
Ronald F. Frazier, Chairman
(operates out of The Braintree Historical
    Society, Inc.)

Brewster Historical Commission
Town Hall
Main Street
Brewster, MA 02631
(508) 896-3058
Marion H. Wylie, Chairperson
(primarily historical, not genealogical)

Bridgewater Public Library
15 South Street
Bridgewater, MA 02324-2593
(508) 697-3331; (508) 279-1467 FAX
bwpl@sailsinc.org
http://www.bridgewaterpubliclibrary.org
Elizabeth L. Gregg, Associate Director,
    Public Services
Library: Mon–Thur 9:00–8:00, Fri
    9:00–5:00, Sat (except summer)
    9:00–2:00; Historical Room: Tue
    2:00–4:00, Thur 2:00–4:00, and by
    appointment

Bridgewater State College
Clement C. Maxwell Library

Bridgewater, MA 02325
(508) 697-1756; (508) 531-1349 FAX
smbates@bridgew.edu
http://www.bridgew.edu/depts/maxwell/
    speccoll.htm
S. Mabell Bates, Archivist/Special
    Collections Librarian

Brockton Public Library
(155 West Elm Street, Brockton, MA 02301-
    5323—temporary location)
304 Main Street (mailing address)
Brockton, MA 02401
(508) 580-7890; (508) 580-7898 FAX
brockton@ocln.org
http://www.brocktonpubliclibrary.org
Lucia M. Shannon, Head of Adult Services
Mon–Tue noon–8:00, Wed–Sat 9:00–5:00

Brookline Historical Commission
Town Hall
2333 Washington Street
Brookline, MA 02146
(617) 232-9000, ext. 246
Judith Selwyn, Chairperson

Public Library of Brookline
361 Washington Street
Brookline, MA 02145-6864
(617) 730-2370; (617) 232-7146 FAX
cbattis@mln.lib.ma.us
http://www.town.brookline.ma.us/library
Cynthia Battis, Collection Development
    Librarian
Mon–Thur 10:00–9:00, Fri–Sat 10:00–5:00,
    Sun 1:00–5:00 (closed Sat–Sun mid-June
    to Labor Day)

Brooks Free Library
739 Main Street
Harwich, MA 02645-2752
(508) 430-7562; (508) 430-7564
Brooks@cape.com
http://www.vsg.cape.com/~brooks
Virginia Hewitt, Director

Burlington Historical Commission
Corner of Bedford and Cambridge Streets
Burlington, MA 01803
(781) 272-0606

Cambridge Historical Commission
831 Massachusetts Avenue
Cambridge, MA 02139
(617) 349-4683; (617) 349-3116 FAX
http://www.ci.cambridge.ma.us/~Historic
Charles M. Sullivan, Executive Director
Mon–Fri 9:00–5:00
("government agency/research library," about
    26,000 photographs and extensive local
    history collection)

Cambridge Public Library
449 Broadway
Cambridge, MA 02138-4191
(617) 349-4044; (617) 349-4026 FAX
Lib-Sugg@ci.cambridge.ma.us
http://www.ci.cambridge.ma.us/~CPL
Donald York, Assistant Director
Mon–Fri 9:00–9:00, Sat 9:00–5:00

Carlisle Historical Commission
(Carlisle Town Hall, 66 Westford
    Street—location)
PO Box 827 (mailing address)
Carlisle, MA 01741
(978) 369-6868; (978) 369-4521
FamariFaulkner@cs.com
Francene Amari-Faulkner, Clerk

Cary Memorial Library
1874 Massachusetts Avenue

Lexington, MA 02173
(781) 862-6288; (781) 862-7355 FAX
http://www.carylibrary.org
Julie Triessl, Curator
Mon–Thur 9:00–9:00, Fri–Sat 9:00–5:00,
    Sun (June–Aug) 1:00–5:00
(local history)

Chelmsford Historical Commission
281 Mill Road
Chelmsford, MA 01824
(978) 256-0436
John P. Richardson, Chairperson
(not genealogical)

Chelmsford Public Library
25 Boston Road
Chelmsford, MA 01824-3088
(978) 256-5521; (978) 256-2344
chelmsfordlib@netway.com;
    mcd@mvlc.lib.ma.us
http://www.chelmsfordlibrary.org
Linda Webb, Interlibrary Loan Department
Mon–Thur 9:00–9:00, Fri–Sat 9:00–5:30,
    Sun (Oct–May) 1:00–5:00

Chelsea Historical Archives
Chelsea Public Library
569 Broadway
Chelsea, MA 02150
(617) 884-0270; (617) 884-2335 (Library)
N. J. Minadakis, Director
Library: Mon–Fri 10:00–5:00

Chelsea Public Library
569 Broadway
Chelsea, MA 02150-2991
(617) 884-2335; (617) 889-8399; (617) 889-
    8397 (Director)
bcollins@mbln.lib.ma.us
http://chelsea_lib.tripod.com
Bob Collins, Director
Mon–Fri 10:00–5:00

Cheshire Historical Commission
(120 North Street—location)
PO Box 73 (mailing address)
Cheshire, MA 01225
(413) 743-2669 (Chairperson)
Eileen Nuttall, Chairperson

Chicopee Historical Commission
Office of Community Development
City Hall, Market Square
Chicopee, MA 01020
(413) 592-4942
Peter Derosier, Chairperson
(primarily historical, not genealogical)

Chilmark Historical Commission
(Route 1, South Road—location)
PO Box 438 (mailing address)
Chilmark, MA 02535
(508) 645-2500
Henry E. Scott, Jr., Chairperson
(primarily historical, not genealogical)

Cohasset Historical Commission
179 South Main Street
Cohasset, MA 02025
(781) 383-0234
Noel A. Ripley, Chairman

The Commonwealth Museum
220 Morrissey Boulevard (Columbia Point)
Boston, MA 02125
(617) 727-9268; (617) 825-3613 FAX
commonwealthmuseum@sec.state.ma.us
http://www.state.ma.us/sec/mus/musidx.htm
Stephen Kenney, Ph.D., Director
Mon–Fri 9:00–5:00, Sat 9:00–3:00 (closed
    some holiday weekends)

Concord Free Public Library
129 Main Street
Concord, MA 01742-2494
(978) 371-6242; (978) 371-6244 FAX
Leslie Nilson, Curator
Mon–Fri 9:00–1:00, Sat (Sept–June)
    9:00–1:00, and by appointment Tue–Thur
    1:00–5:00
(county history and literature, municipal
    records, genealogy)

Connecticut Valley Historical Museum
Research Library and Archives
(194 State Street—location)
220 State Street (mailing address)
Springfield, MA 01103
(413) 263-6800, ext. 230; (413) 263-6898
    FAX
cvhmgen@spfldlibmus.org
http://www.quadrangle.org/CVHM.htm
Margaret Humberston, Supervising Librarian
Wed–Fri noon–5:00, Sat–Sun noon–4:00
(history of greater Springfield area,
    Massachusetts and New England history,
    and New England genealogy)
$35.00 per year membership; admission:
    $3.00 (includes all museums); research:
    $20.00 per hour

Conway Historical Commission
PO Box 187
Conway, MA 01341
(413) 369-4654
Jack R. Ramey, Chairperson
meetings: second Wed

Dalton Historical Commission
462 Main Street
Dalton, MA 01226
Mary Ellen Shea, Chairperson
by appointment
(museum; records of local interest)

Danvers Historical Commission
c/o Town Hall
Sylvan Street
Danvers, MA 01923
(978) 777-2821
Toni E. Collins, Director
Mon–Fri 9:00–2:00

Dennis Memorial Library Association
1020 Old Bass River Road
Dennis, MA 02638-2523
(508) 385-2255; (508) 385-7322 FAX
nsymington@clamsnet.org
Nancy E. Symington, Director

**Historical Records of Dukes County,
Massachusetts**
Rural Route 2, Box 247
Vineyard, MA 02568
cbaer@vineyard.net
http://www.vineyard.net/vineyard/history

Duxbury Historical Commission
c/o Rockland Trust
2036 Washington Street, #FURNES
Hanover, MA 02339-1617
Jean Poindexter Colby, Chairman

Dyer Memorial Library
(28 Centre Avenue—location)
PO Box 2245 (mailing address)
Abington, MA 02351
(781) 878-8480
Marion Delaney, Curator and Librarian
Tue–Fri 1:00–5:00, second & fourth Sat
    noon–4:00
(private library, open to the public; town
    histories, vital records to 1850, some
    family histories)

East Bridgewater Historical Commission
418 Plymouth Street
East Bridgewater, MA 02333
(508) 378-7775

East Bridgewater Public Library
32 Union Street
East Bridgewater, MA 02333-1598
(508) 378-1616; (508) 378-1617 FAX
illeb@sailsinc.org
http://www.sailsinc.org/ebpl
Jane A. Finlay, Director of Library Services
Mon–Tue 9:00–8:00, Wed–Thur 9:00–5:00,
    Fri 1:00–5:00, Sat 9:00–1:00

East Longmeadow Historical Commission
Center Square
East Longmeadow, MA 01028
(413) 525-3305

Eastham Public Library
190 Samoset Road
Eastham, MA 02642-3109
(508) 240-5950; (508) 240-0786 FAX
magane@easthamlibrary.org;
    mail@easthamlibrary.org
http://www.easthamlibrary.org
Martha Magane, Director
Summer: Mon & Fri–Sat 10:00–4:00, Tue &
    Thur 10:00–8:00; winter: Wed & Fri–Sat
    10:00–4:00, Tue & Thur 10:00–8:00

Easthampton Historical Commission
Town Hall
Main Street
Easthampton, MA 01027
(413) 527-2211
Edward J. Dwyer, Chair
by appointment
(archives, various publications, general
    information)

Easton Historical Commission
Easton Town Office
Easton, MA 02356
(508) 238-9966
John J. Kent, Secretary

Egremont Historical Commission
PO Box 127
Egremont, MA 01252
(413) 528-5226
Ann M. Van Deusen, Member
Archives Room in Academy Building: first
    Sat 10:00–noon

Eldredge Public Library
The Edgar Francis Waterman Memorial
Genealogical Collection
564 Main Street
Chatham, MA 02633-2296
(508) 945-0274
igillies@clams.lib.ma.us
http://www.eldredgelibrary.org
Margery Corthell Campbell, Librarian
Tue, Thur & Sat 1:00–5:00
(holdings from Nova Scotia to Georgia)
no charge

Fairhaven Historical Commission
(address withheld upon request)
(Historical only. "The Historical
    Commission has never had records on
    genealogy.")

Falmouth Public Library
123 Katherine Lee Bates Road
Falmouth, MA 02540-2895
(508) 457-2555; (508) 457-2559 FAX
falmouthreference@falmouthpublic
    library.org
http://www.falmouthpubliclibrary.org

Fitchburg Historical Commission
City Hall, 718 Main Street
Fitchburg, MA 01420
(978) 345-9550
Stephen A. Svolis, Chairperson

Fitchburg Public Library
Willis Room
610 Main Street
Fitchburg, MA 01420-3146
(978) 345-9635; (978) 345-9631 FAX
mladd@cwmars.org
http://www.net1plus.com/users/fpl

J. V. Fletcher Library
50 Main Street
Westford, MA 01886-2599
(978) 692-5555; (978) 692-4418 FAX
mwf@mailserv.mvlc.lib.ma.us
http://www.westfordlibrary.org
Virginia Moore, Local History Librarian
Mon–Thur 10:00–9:00, Fri 1:00–5:00, Sat
    10:00–5:00
(Westford history and genealogy)
copies: 15¢ per page

Fobes Memorial Library
Historical Room
4 Maple Street
Oakham, MA 01068-9790
(508) 882-3372 voice & FAX
oakham@cwmars.org
Maude M. Stone, Director

Forbes Library
20 West Street
Northampton, MA 01060-3798
(413) 587-1012 (Reference); (413) 587-1015
    FAX
webmaster@forbeslibrary.org
http://www.forbeslibrary.org
Elise Bernier-Feeley, Reference Librarian
Wed 9:00–9:00, Thur 1:00–5:00, Fri–Sat
    9:00–5:00, and by appointment at the
    discretion of the librarian
("The 'Hampshire Room' [Genealogy and
    Local History Department] is a function
    of the Reference Department and is
    located on the second floor of the
    library.")

Forbush Memorial Library
118 Main Street
Westminster, MA 01473
(978) 874-7416
http://www.westminster-
    ma.org/library/index.htm
Betsy Hannula, Curator
Thur 3:00–5:00, and by appointment

Foxborough Historical Commission
Memorial Hall
Foxborough, MA 02035
(508) 543-5301

Framingham Historical Commission
Memorial Building
150 Concord Street
Framingham, MA 01701
(508) 877-4333
Stephen W. Herring, Chair

Franklin Historical Commission
(Washington Street at Colt Road—location)
PO Box 212 (mailing address)
Franklin, MA 02038
(508) 528-0646
delarn@aol.com
http://www.franklin.ma.us
Barbara Smith, Chairperson
Museum: Sun (May–Sept) 1:30–5:30

Gale Free Library
The Jane Wilson Local History Room
23 Highland Street
Holden, MA 01520-2599
(508) 829-0229
nrichard@cwmars.org
http://www.galefreelibrary.org/adult.html
Nancy Richards, Local History

**Gloucester Lyceum and Sawyer Free
Library**
(address withheld upon request)

Goodnow Library
21 Concord Road
Sudbury, MA 01776
(978) 443-1035; (978) 443-1047 FAX
goodnow@town.sudbury.ma.us
http://www.town.sudbury.ma.us/services/
    department_home.asp?dept=Library
Jennifer Root, Reference Librarian
Mon–Wed 10:00–8:30, Thur–Sat
    10:00–5:00, Sat (summer) 10:00–1:00,
    Sun (Oct–May) 2:00–5:00

Grafton Historical Commission
23 Keith Hill Road
Grafton, MA 01519
(508) 839-2245

Greenfield Historical Commission
Town Hall
14 Court Square
Greenfield, MA 01301
(413) 774-5363
Peter S. Miller, Chairman
evenings
("early vital records and general Greenfield
    history, knows where to find answers to
    Greenfield's history")

Greenfield Public Library
402 Main Street
Greenfield, MA 01301-3371
(413) 772-1545; (413) 772-1589 FAX
librarian@greenfieldpubliclibrary.org
http://www.greenfieldpubliclibrary.org
Pam Murray, Interlibrary Loan and Assistant
    Reference
Mon & Fri 10:00–5:00, Tue–Thur
    10:00–8:00
(local town histories, vital records to 1850,
    Town of Greenfield and Montague street
    listings 1891 to present, local newspaper
    microfilm 1792 to present)
research: copying costs plus postage, extra
    charge if search is lengthy

Hadley Historical Commission
hhc@hadleyma.org
http://www.ecommunityguide.com/
    hadley/attractions.shtml
("The Commission, which in Massachusetts
    is an appointed group in each city and
    town that oversees historical districts,
    writes grants for protection of historical
    sites, etc. We do not have a site that
    houses historical collections. Although
    members of the Commission do help
    people who send us email inquiries about
    genealogy, the Historical Society would
    be the appropriate listing.")

Halifax Historical Commission
Town Hall
Halifax, MA 02338
(781) 293-5761
Ernest Wilbur, Chairperson
(primarily historical, not genealogical)

Hamilton Wenham Public Library
14 Union Street

Hamilton, MA 01982
(978) 468-5577; (978) 468-5527; (978) 468-
    5535 FAX
http://www.hwlibrary.org
Mon–Thur 10:00–8:00, Fri–Sat 10:00–6:00
(former Wenham Public Library's local
    history and genealogy collection)

Harvard University
Baker Library, Historical Collection
    Department
(address withheld upon request)
("We are an academic library, and our
    collections are open only to scholars
    engaged in research for publication or
    other scholarly dissemination. Given the
    overwhelming number of requests we
    receive for access to our collections and
    the limited space available to us, we have
    had to limit ourselves to this constituency.
    We are not able to provide access to the
    genealogical community.")

Haverhill Public Library
99 Main Street
Haverhill, MA 01830-5092
(978) 373-1586; (978) 373-8466 FAX
mhv@mvlc.org
http://www.haverhillpl.org
Gregory H. Laing, Curator of Special
    Collections
Special Collections: Mon–Wed 10:00–1:00,
    2:00–5:00 & 6:00–9:00, Thur 10:00–1:00
    & 2:00–5:00, Sat 10:00–1:00 &
    2:00–5:00
(microfilm of Massachusetts vital records
    1841–1900, and the Massachusetts
    D.A.R. library materials, including 7,000
    volumes of Haverhill history, 8,250
    volumes in Pecker genealogy and local
    history collections, 500 volumes of
    military history, full runs of many
    periodicals)

Hawley Historical Commission
Middle Road
Hawley, MA 01339
(413) 339-5513
Harrison Parker, Chairman
(Hawley local history)

Hingham Public Library
66 Leavitt Street
Hingham, MA 02043-2997
(781) 741-1406; (617) 749-0956 FAX
hiref@ocln.org
http://www.hingham-
    ma.com/html/public_library.html
Walter T. Dziura, Director
Mon–Thur 10:00–9:00, Sat 9:00–5:00, Sun
    (winter only) 2:00–5:00

Hinsdale Historical Commission
PO Box 58
Hinsdale, MA 01235
(413) 655-2060
Peter White, Chairman
Library: Sat 10:00–noon & 2:00–4:00
    (Memorial Day–Labor Day)

Holyoke Public Library
335 Maple Street
Holyoke, MA 01040-4999
(413) 534-2211; (413) 532-4230 FAX
library@ci.holyoke.ma.us
Maria G. Pagán, Director; Paul Graves,
    History Room Assistant
Holyoke History Room: Tue 9:00–5:00, Thur
    9:00–5:00, Sat (after Labor Day to before
    Memorial Day weekend) 9:00–4:00

Hopedale Historical Commission

c/o Community House
43 Hope Street
Hopedale, MA 01747
(508) 473-0867
Olga Till, Chairman

Huntington Historical Commission
Worthington Road
Huntington, MA 01050
(413) 667-3003
Library: 1:00–4:00 (June–1 Sept, by
appointment)

Hyannis Public Library
401 Main Street
Hyannis, MA 02601-3903
(508) 775-2280
reference@hyannislibrary.org
http://www.hyannislibrary.org

Joshua Hyde Public Library
Local History Room
306 Main Street
Sturbridge, MA 01566-1242
(508) 347-2512; (508) 347-2872 FAX
library@town.sturbridge.ma.us;
    library@hey.net
http://www.hey.net/Sturbridge/library/
    index.html

The Jackson Homestead
527 Washington Street
Newton, MA 02458
(617) 552-7238; (617) 552-7228 FAX
http://www.ci.newton.ma.us/jackson
Susan D. Abele, Curator of Manuscripts and
    Photographs
Tue–Sat 11:00–5:00, Sun 2:00–5:00;
    research by appointment
Pub. *Jackson Homestead Newsletter*, four
    times per year
("Today the Homestead serves as a
    nationally accredited museum and center
    for Newton History." Local history and
    history of abolition activities.)
$20.00 per year membership

James Library
(24 West Street—location)
PO Box 164 (mailing address)
Norwell, MA 02061
(781) 659-7100
Caroline Chapin, Librarian
Mon & Wed–Fri 2:00–5:00, Tue
    10:00–1:00, Sat (Sept–June) 10:00–1:00

Jones Library
Local History and Genealogy Collection
43 Amity Street
Amherst, MA 01002-2285
(413) 256-4090; (413) 256-4096 FAX
http://www.joneslibrary.org
Tevis L. Kimball, Curator of Special
    Collections

Lancaster Historical Commission
Town Hall
Town Green
Lancaster, MA 01523
(978) 368-4355
Phyllis A. Farnsworth, Chairman
Tue 9:00–1:00

Lawrence Public Library
Information Services Coordinator
51 Lawrence Street
Lawrence, MA 01841-3805
(978) 794-5786; (978) 682-1727; (508) 688-
    3142 FAX
yiglesia@mailserv.mvlc.lib.ma.us
http://www.lawrencefreelibrary.org
Mon & Fri 10:00–5:00, Tue–Thur

10:00–8:00, Sat (Oct–May) 10:00–5:00

Lenox Historical Commission
Lenox Academy Building
75 Main Street
Lenox, MA 01240
(413) 637-1880
Marcia B. Brown, Chairman

Leominster Historical Commission
City Hall, 25 West Street, Room 13
Leominster, MA 01453
(978) 537-3684; (978) 534-7519
Evelyn B. Hachey

Lexington Historical Commission
(address withheld upon request)

(primarily historical, not genealogical)

Leyden Historical Commission
27 Eden Trail
Leyden, MA 01337
(413) 773-7336
Edith Fisher, Chairperson
(collection of artifacts, papers, clothing, etc.,
    held in town safe)

Lincoln Historical Commission
Town Offices
Lincoln, MA 01773
(781) 259-2610
Colin Smith, Chairman
(town archives)

Lynn Public Library
5 North Common Street
Lynn, MA 01902-4311
(781) 595-0567; (781) 592-5050 FAX
jreynold@noblenet.org
http://www.noblenet.org/lynn
Joan D. Reynolds, Chief Librarian; Nadine
    M. Mitchell, Head of Reference
Mon & Wed 1:00–9:00, Tue 9:00–9:00,
    Thur–Sat 9:00–5:00

Lynnfield Public Library
Local History/Genealogy Room
18 Summer Street
Lynnfield, MA 01940-1837
(781) 334-5411; (781) 334-2164 FAX
lfd@noblenet.org
http://www.noblenet.org/lynnfield
Nancy Ryan, Assistant Director/Head of
    Reference
Mon–Thur 9:00–9:00, Fri–Sat 9:00–5:00,
    closed Sat during the summer

Malden Historical Commission
200 Pleasant Street, Room 623
Malden, MA 02148
(781) 324-6600, ext. 210
Barbara L. Tolstrup, Chairperson

Malden Public Library
Malden, MA 02148-5208
(781) 324-0218; (781) 324-4467 FAX
sorn@maldenpubliclibrary.org
http://www.maldenpubliclibrary.org
Mon–Thur 9:00–9:00, Fri–Sat 9:00–6:00
    (closed Sat mid-June to mid-Sept)

Mansfield Historical Commission
265 Pratt Street
Mansfield, MA 02048
(508) 339-9492
Maureen Cooke, Chairperson

Marlborough Public Library
35 West Main Street
Marlborough, MA 01752-5510
(508) 624-6900; (508) 485-1494 FAX

wnoah@cwmars.org
http://www.marlborough.com/library.html
Wayne Noah, Reference Librarian
Mon–Thur 9:00–8:30, Fri noon–5:00, Sat
    9:00–5:00

Mashpee Historical Commission
(13 Great Neck Road, North—location)
Mashpee Town Hall, 16 Great Neck Road,
North (mailing address)
Mashpee, MA 02649
(508) 539-1438
Joanne M. Ferragamo, Chairperson
Mon, Thur & first Sat 9:00–1:00, and by
    appointment
(town history, Wampanoag history, Native
    Americans of the northeast)
free admission; research: donation plus copy
    costs

Medfield Historical Commission
Town Hall
Medfield, MA 02052
(508) 359-8505
Burgess P. Standley, Chairman

The Medford Public Library
Local History Resources
111 High Street
Medford, MA 02155-3870
(781) 395-7950
medford@minlib.net
http://www.medfordlibrary.orgBrian G.
    Boutilier, Director

Melrose Historical Commission
76 Linden Road
Melrose, MA 02176
(781) 665-5010
Arnold W. Williams, Chairman

Melrose Public Library
69 West Emerson Street
Melrose, MA 02176-3173
(781) 665-2313; (617) 662-4229 FAX
mel@noblenet.org
http://www.noblenet/melrose
Linda C. Walsh, Reference Librarian
Mon–Thur 9:00–9:00, Fri–Sat 9:00–5:00,
    Sun 1:00–5:00 (closed weekends
    July–Aug)

Memorial Hall Library
Elm Square
Andover, MA 01810-3656
(978) 623-8401, ext. 31
rdesk@mhl.org
http://www.mhl.org
Mon–Thur 9:00–9:00, Fri 9:00–5:30, Sat
    9:00–5:00, Sun 1:00–5:00; closed
    weekends during summer
(local history and genealogy)

The Memorial Libraries
(Memorial Street—location)
PO Box 53 (mailing address)
Deerfield, MA 01342
(413) 774-5581, ext. 125
David Bosse, Librarian
Mon–Fri 8:30–5:00
Pub. *Research at Deerfield*, infrequently
(Historic Deerfield Library: history, museum
    studies; Pocumtuck Valley Memorial
    Association Library: genealogy, local
    history, manuscripts, family papers,
    account books, town papers, diaries,
    church records, etc.)

Middlefield Historical Commission
Skyline Trail
Middlefield, MA 01243
(413) 623-8904

Marjorie Batorski, Chairperson

Milford Historical Commission
(Memorial Hall, School Street—location)
198 Purchase Street (mailing address)
Milford, MA 01757
(508) 473-7327
Marilyn Lovell, Secretary

Milford Town Library
80 Spruce Street
Milford, MA 01757-2031
(508) 473-2145; (508) 473-8651
http://www.infofind.com/library
Reference Librarian
Mon–Thur 9:00–9:00, Fri 9:00–6:00, Sat
   (Sept–June) 9:00–5:00

Millicent Library
(45 Center Street—location)
PO Box 30 (mailing address)
Fairhaven, MA 02719-0030
(508) 992-5342; (508) 993-7288 FAX
dcharpentier@sailsinc.org
http://www.millicentlibrary.org/archives.htm
Debbie Charpentier, Archivist

Milton Public Library
476 Canton Avenue
Milton, MA 02186-3299
(617) 698-5757
miref@ocln.org (East Milton Branch)
http://www.miltonlibrary.org
Daniel Haacker, Interim Director
Library: Mon–Thur 9:00–9:00, Fri
   1:00–5:30, Sat (Sept–June) 9:00–5:00;
   Historical Collection: Sat (Sept–June)
   9:00–noon
(Milton history/genealogy)

Morrill Memorial Library
(Walpole Street—location)
PO Box 220 (mailing address)
Norwood, MA 02062-0988
(781) 769-0200; (781) 769-6083 FAX
mphinney@minlib.net
http://www.ci.norwood.ma.us/library
Mary Phinney, Director
Mon–Fri 9:00–9:00, Sat 9:00–5:00, Sun
   1:00–5:00; closed Sat & Sun (4
   July–Labor Day)

Morse Institute Library
14 East Central Street
Natick, MA 01760
(508) 651-7300
http://www.morseinstitute.org/index.html
Carol Coverly, Reference; Paula Polk,
   Director
Mon–Thur 9:00–9:00, Fri–Sat 9:00–5:00
(Natick, Massachusetts, archives)
10¢ per page for copies

Mount Washington Historical Commission
(Town Hall—location)
Rural Delivery 3, Box 67A (mailing address)
Mount Washington, MA 01258
William D. Miles, Chairman

Needham Free Public Library
1139 Highland Avenue
Needham, MA 02194-3298
(781) 455-7559, ext. 2 (Reference Desk);
   (781) 455-7559, ext. 215 (Archives);
   (781) 455-7591 FAX
http://www.town.needham.ma.us/library
Sue A. Hoadley, Archivist
Library: Mon–Thur 10:00–9:00, Fri
   10:00–5:30, Sat 9:00–5:00, Sun
   (Sept–May) 1:00–5:00; Genealogy Room:
   open during regular library hours (check
   in at Reference Desk); Archives: by

appointment only
("The Reference Department has copies of
   Needham's local newspapers from 1874
   through the present on microfilm. The
   Genealogy Room has general genealogical
   publications; Massachusetts vital records
   and town histories; Needham town
   directories, annual town reports, high
   school yearbooks, and other items of local
   interest. The Archives is the repository for
   selected noncurrent town records, maps
   and publications, as well as collections of
   the records of civic organizations and
   individuals in Needham.")
photo copies: 10¢ per page ($2.00 minimum)

New Bedford Free Public Library
613 Pleasant Street
New Bedford, MA 02740-6203
(508) 991-6275, ext. 15; (508) 979-5825
   FAX
nbmref@sailsinc.org
http://www.ci.new-bedford.ma.us/
   SERVICES/LIBRARY/Library2.htm
Paul Cyr
Mon & Wed 9:00–9:00, Tue & Fri–Sat
   9:00–5:00

Newburyport Public Library
Hamilton Room
94 State Street
Newburyport, MA 01950-6619
(978) 465-4428; (978) 463-0394 FAX
msavage@mailserv.mvlc.lib.ma.us
http://www.newburyportpl.org
Dorothy LaFrance, Head Librarian
Library: Mon–Thur 9:00–9:00, Fri
   9:00–5:00, Sat (July–Aug) 9:00–1:00, Sat
   (Sept–June) 9:00–5:00, Sun (mid-Oct to
   mid-May) 1:00–5:00; Hamilton Room:
   call in advance
(Newbury/Newburyport family genealogies)

Newton Free Library
330 Homer Street
Newton, MA 02459-1415
(617) 552-7152
http://www.ci.newton.ma.us/library
Georgina J. Flannery, Newton Collection,
   Reference Department
Mon–Thur 9:00–9:00, Fri 9:00–6:00, Sat
   9:00–5:00, Sun (except summer)
   noon–5:00
Pub. *Newtoniana*, irregularly
(Newton archives; library does not do
   genealogical research)

Newton Historical Commission
213 East Court Street
Newton, MA 02159
(617) 552-7135
Mary E. Fortenberry, Chairman

North Adams State College
Freel Library, Special Collections
PO Box 9250
North Adams, MA 01247
(413) 662-5321; (413) 662-5286 FAX

**North Attleborough Historical
Commission**
Town Hall
43 South Washington Street
North Attleboro, MA 02760
(508) 699-0152
by appointment
("limited town records/maps")

Northampton Historical Commission
Planning and Development Office, City Hall
210 Main Street
Northampton, MA 01060

(413) 586-1266
Margaret Keller, Senior Planner
8:30–4:30

Northborough Free Library
34 Main Street
Northborough, MA 01532-1942
(508) 393-5025; (508) 393-5027 FAX
dfinnera@cwmarsmail.cwmars.org
http://www.town.northborough.ma.us/library
Daniel Finneran, Reference Librarian
Mon–Thur 9:30–8:30, Fri–Sat 9:30–5:00

Northfield Historical Museum
(Pine Street—location)
PO Box 159 (mailing address)
Northfield, MA 01360-0159
(413) 498-5565
Rosa S. Johnston, Registrar
July–Aug: 1:00–3:00
(local history and genealogy)

Norwell Public Library
64 South Street
Norwell, MA 02061-2433
(781) 659-2015; (781) 659-6755 FAX
Diane Gordon Kadanoff, Director

Ohoopee Regional Library
(see Georgia, Part 2)

Orleans Historical Commission
Town Hall
Orleans, MA 02653
(508) 255-2658
Charles H. Thomsen, Chairperson

Palmer Historical Commission
Town Administration Building
Main Street
Palmer, MA 01069
(413) 283-5061
Marion Lis
9:00–4:30

Peabody Essex Museum of Salem
(see Phillips Library, Peabody Essex
Museum, below)

Peabody Institute Library of Danvers
Danvers Archival Center
15 Sylvan Street
Danvers, MA 01923-2735
(978) 774-0554; (978) 762-0251 FAX
dan@noblenet.org
http://www.noblenet.org/danvers
Richard B. Trask, Town Archivist
Mon 1:00–7:30, Wed–Thur & first Sat
   9:00–noon & 1:00–5:00, second & fourth
   Fri 1:00–5:00, call or write before
   traveling
(emphasis on Danvers, Salem Village and
   colonial witchcraft; printed materials on
   local history and genealogy, 75,000
   manuscripts)

Phillips Library
Peabody Essex Museum
East India Square
Salem, MA 01970-3773
(978) 745-1876; (978) 744-0036 FAX; (978)
   744-6776 FAX
http://www.pem.org
William T. La Moy, James Duncan Phillips
   Librarian; Geraldine M. Ayers, Managing
   Editor, *American Neptune*; John Koza,
   Librarian/Archivist
call for hours
Pub. *Peabody Essex Museum Collections*,
   annually, $25.00 per year subscription
   within the U.S., $30.00 per year
   subscription outside the U.S.; *American*

Neptune, quarterly (winter, spring, summer, fall), $32.00 per year domestic subscription, $35.00 per year foreign subscription
(Massachusetts and New England history and culture; maritime history, not limited to Massachusetts area)
$40.00 per year membership

The Pilgrim Society
Pilgrim Hall Museum
75 Court Street (Route 3A)
Plymouth, MA 02360-3891
(508) 746-1620; (508) 747-4228 FAX
http://www.pilgrimhall.org
Peggy Baker, Director and Librarian
daily 9:30–4:30
(Not a lineage society. "Dedicated to preserving the artifacts and the legacy of the Pilgrims themselves; membership open to all interested parties." "The printed resources useful to a genealogist have been transferred on permanent loan to the library of the General Society of Mayflower Descendants.")

Plymouth Public Library
Plymouth Collection
132 South Street
Plymouth, MA 02360-2947
(508) 830-4250; (508) 830-4258 FAX
plreference@hotmail.com
http://www.gis.net/~ppl
Ms. Lee Regan, Head of Adult Services; Beverly Ness, History Room Assistant
Mon–Wed 10:00–9:00, Thur 10:00–6:00, Fri–Sat 10:00–5:30
Pub. *Plymouth Collection Newsletter*, irregularly (generally four times per year); *Genealogical and Local History Resources Available in Plymouth*, $6.00 plus shipping and handling
(over 1,200 items relating to local history, the descendants of the *Mayflower* Pilgrims and other immigrants who came to the Plymouth area in the 17th–20th centuries, including individual family histories, local town histories, genealogical journals, vital records of many Massachusetts communities, pamphlet collection, vertical file, and photographs)
mail and phone queries: 10¢ per page plus shipping and handling

Samuel S. Pollard Memorial Library
401 Merrimack Street
Lowell, MA 01852
(978) 970-4120; (978) 970-4117 FAX
mloref@mailserv.mvlc.lib.ma.us
http://www.pollardml.org
Peter Alexis, Local History
Mon 1:00–9:00, Tue–Wed & Fri 1:00–4:30, Thur 9:30–9:00

Princeton Public Library
2 Town Hall Drive
Princeton, MA 01541-1129
(978) 464-2115; (978) 464-2116 FAX
wpape@cwmars.org;
    library@town.princeton.ma.us
http://library.town.princeton.ma.us/
    services.html
Wendy F. Pape, Director

Provincetown Heritage Museum
Town Hall
356 Commercial Street
Provincetown, MA 02657
(508) 487-7098
Josephine DelDeo, Curator; David Colburn, Chairman

daily (14 June–12 Oct) 10:00–6:00

Quincy Historic Commission
City Hall, 1305 Hancock Street
Quincy, MA 02169
(781) 773-1380
Joyce Baker, Chairperson
(primarily historical, not genealogical)

Radcliffe College
Arthur and Elizabeth Schlesinger Library on the History of Women in America
(see Miscellaneous, Part 4)

Randall Library
19 Crescent Street
Stow, MA 01775-1150
(978) 897-8572; (978) 897-7379 FAX
swysk@minlib.net
Susan C. Wysk, Director

Randolph Historical Commission
54 South Street
Randolph, MA 02368
(781) 963-4385
Major Raymond P. MacGerrigle, Chairman
Ladies Library Association (Belcher House): by appointment

Reading Historical Commission
16 Lowell Street
Reading, MA 01867
(781) 942-0500
Sharon K. Ofenstein, Chairman

Reading Public Library
64 Middlesex Avenue
Reading, MA 01867-2550
(781) 944-0840; (781) 942-1021 FAX
readingpl@noblenet.org
http://www.readingpl.org
Sally McDonald, Reference Librarian
Mon–Thur 10:00–9:00, Fri–Sat 10:00–5:30, Sun 1:00–5:00
("Will answer brief questions regarding Reading history and vital records.")

Revere Historical Commission
City Hall, c/o Law Department
Revere, MA 02151
(781) 284-3600, ext. 140
Frederick Sannella, Chairman

Rochester Historical Commission
661 Walnut Plain Road
Rochester, MA 02770
(508) 763-8959
Naida Parker, Chairperson

Rockland Memorial Library
20 Belmont Street
Rockland, MA 02370-2232
(781) 878-1236; (781) 878-4013 FAX
http://rocklandmemoriallibrary.org
Mon–Thur 10:00–8:00, Fri–Sat 10:00–5:00
    (closed Sat in summer)
Pub. *Library News*, quarterly with occasional monthly updates (not genealogical)

Salem Public Library
370 Essex Street
Salem, MA 01970-3298
(978) 744-0860; (978) 745-8616 FAX
sal@noblenet.org
http://www.noblenet.org/libinfo/
    libinfo_sal.html
Elizabeth M. Armand, Reference Librarian
Mon–Thur 9:00–9:00, Fri–Sat 9:00–5:00

Salisbury Historical Commission
PO Box 5464
Salisbury, MA 01950

(978) 465-5546
Carol Sargent, Chairperson
three days per week during the summer, and by appointment

Salisbury Public Library
17 Elm Street
Salisbury, MA 01952-1935
(978) 465-5071
msa@mvlc.lib.ma.us
Gail Lyon, Director
Mon & Wed 10:00–5:00, Tue noon–8:00, Thur 10:00–8:00

Sandwich Historical Commission
Sandwich Archives and Historical Center
145 Main Street
Sandwich, MA 02563
(508) 888-4200
Barbara J. Walling, Chairperson

Savoy Historic Commission
720 Main Road
Savoy, MA 01256

Scituate Town Archives
Town Hall
600 Chief Justice Cushing Highway
Scituate, MA 02066-3297
(781) 545-8745; (781) 545-8704 FAX; (781)
    545-0043 (Home)
townclerk@town.scituate.ma.us
http://town.scituate.ma.us/gov_archives.htm
Elizabeth Foster, Town Archivist
Wed 9:00–4:00, and by appointment
(vital statistics, old Plymouth Colony and Massachusetts Bay Colony records from 1633, maps, church records, property records, assessors' records, genealogies and local histories, town meeting records, militia data, etc.)
research: $10.00; certified copies: $5.00

Scituate Town Library
85 Branch Street
Scituate, MA 02066-3297
(781) 545-8727
info@scituatetownlibrary.org
http://www.scituatetownlibrary.org
Mon–Wed 9:00–9:00, Thur 1:00–9:00, Sat 9:00–5:00, Sun (Oct–May) 1:00–5:00

Sharon Historical Commission
41 Bay Road
Sharon, MA 02067
(781) 784-5532
Chandler W. Jones, Chairman

Sharon Public Library
11 North Main Street
Sharon, MA 02067-1299
(781) 784-5974; (781) 784-4728 FAX
library@townofsharon.net
http://www.townofsharon.net/Public_
    Documents/SharonMA_Library/index
Tue–Thur 9:30–9:00, Fri–Sat 9:30–5:30

Sherborn Historical Commission
(Room in Town Offices Building, 19 Washington Street, Route 16—location)
PO Box 186 (mailing address)
Sherborn, MA 01770-0186
(508) 651-7850 (Selectmen's Office, for messages)
Elizabeth Johnson, Chairman
third Wed 7:30 at Town Offices, and by appointment

Shrewsbury Public Library
609 Main Street
Shrewsbury, MA 01545-5699
(508) 842-0081; (508) 841-8540 FAX

http://www.ci.shrewsbury.ma.us/library/
libtop.htm
George C. Brown, Assistant Director and
Head of Adult Services
Mon–Thur 9:00–9:00, Fri–Sat 9:00–5:00,
Sun 1:00–5:00
(history and biography)

Simmons College
Library
300 The Fenway
Boston, MA 02115
(617) 521-2440
http://www.simmons.edu
(archives, special collections, manuscripts)

**Henry E. Simonds Memorial Archives of
the Town of Winchester**
(see Winchester Historical Commission,
below)

Somerville Public Library
79 Highland Avenue
Somerville, MA 02143-1797
(617) 623-5000
http://www.ultranet.com/~somlib
Alix Minton Quan
Mon–Thur 9:00–9:00, Fri 9:00–6:00, Sat
(school year) 9:00–5:00

South Hadley Historical Commission
55½ North Main Street
South Hadley, MA 01075
(413) 532-1879
James B. Allen

Southampton Historical Commission
PO Box 59
Southampton, MA 01073-0059
Susan Kozub, Recording and Corresponding
Secretary

Southbridge Historical Commission
236 Main Street
Southbridge, MA 01550
(508) 764-8121
Helen E. Walkowiak, Secretary

Spencer Historical Commission
25 Pleasant Street
Spencer, MA 01562
(508) 885-3675
Anna Marie Hughes, Chairperson

Stockbridge Library Association
Historical Room
(Main Street—location)
PO Box 119 (mailing address)
Stockbridge, MA 01262-0119
(413) 298-5501 voice & FAX
Pauline D. Pierce, Curator
Tue–Fri 9:00–5:00, Sat 9:00–4:00

Richard Salter Storrs Library
The Hafer Local History and Genealogy
Room
693 Longmeadow Street
Longmeadow, MA 01106-2296
(413) 565-4181; (413) 565-4183 FAX
http://www.longmeadow.org/library/
overview.htm
Carl Sturgis, Director
Mon–Thur 10:00–8:00, Fri 10:00–5:00, Sat
10:00–4:00

Stow Historical Commission
Town Office Building
Stow, MA 01775
(978) 897-2787; (978) 897-2808
John Makey, Chair; Linda Hathaway-Smart,
Secretary

Sturbridge Historical Commission
Town Hall
Sturbridge, MA 01566
(508) 347-3000

The Sturgis Library
(3090 Main Street, Route 6A—location)
PO Box 606 (mailing address)
Barnstable, MA 02630-0606
(508) 362-6636; (508) 362-5467 FAX
sturgislib@attbi.com
http://www.capecod.net/sturgis
Susan R. Klein, Chief Librarian
Mon & Thur 10:00–2:00, Tue–Wed
1:00–9:00, Fri 1:00–5:00, Sat 10:00–4:00
(Cape Cod genealogy material)
genealogy room admission: $5.00 per day or
$25.00 per year for nonresidents of one of
seven communities within the town of
Barnstable

Sudbury Historical Commission
Town Hall
Sudbury, MA 01776
(978) 443-8205
Lyn MacLean, Chairman
Hosmer House: Memorial Day, 4 July,
Columbus Day & first weekend in Dec

Swampscott Historical Commission
Administration Building
Swampscott, MA 01907
(781) 596-8850; (781) 596-8870 FAX; (781)
596-8851 FAX
Louis A. Gallo, Chairman
(street listings, birth and death cards)

Swansea Free Public Library
69 Main Street
Swansea, MA 02777-4698
(508) 674-9609; (508) 675-5444 FAX
spl@ultranet.com
Kevin Lawton, Director
Mon–Thur & Sat 10:00–5:00, Mon–Tue &
Thur 6:30–8:30

Taft Public Library
(Main Street—location)
PO Box 35 (mailing address)
Mendon, MA 01756-0035
(508) 473-3259; (508) 473-7049 FAX
mendon@cwmars.org
http://www.lightband.com/~taft
Mon–Thur 9:00–8:00, Fri 9:00–5:00, Sat
9:00–2:00

Townsend Historic Commission
181 Fitchburg Road
Townsend, MA 01469
(978) 597-2668
Elsie Therrien

Tyringham Historical Commission
George Canon Road
Tyringham, MA 01264
(413) 243-0416
Clinton Elliot, Chairman
Library: Mon

University of Massachusetts at Amherst
W.E.B. DuBois Library
Special Collections
Amherst, MA 01003
(413) 545-0150
http://www.library.umass.edu/index.html

University of Massachusetts at Boston
Joseph P. Healy Library
Harbor Campus
100 Morrissey Boulevard
Dorchester, MA 02125-3393
(617) 287-5944

Elizabeth R. Mock, Archivist
Library: winter: Mon–Thur 8:00–10:00, Fri
8:00–6:00, Sat 9:00–5:00, Sun 1:00–8:00;
summer: Mon–Thur 8:00–6:00, Fri
8:00–5:00, Sat 9:00–5:00; Archives
Department: Mon–Fri 9:00–5:00

Uxbridge Historical Commission
Town Hall
South Main Street
Uxbridge, MA 01569
(508) 278-5544
J. Francis Cove, III, Chairman

Ventress Memorial Library
15 Library Plaza
Marshfield, MA 02050-4998
(781) 834-5535; (781) 837-8362 FAX
eriboldi@ocln.org
http://www.ventresslibrary.org
Bruce Brigell, Reference Librarian; Ellen
Riboldi, Director
Mon–Tue 10:00–9:00, Wed–Thur
10:00–5:30, Sat 9:30–5:30

The Vineyard Haven Library
200 Main Street
Vineyard Haven, MA 02568-9710
(508) 696-4211; (508) 696-7495 FAX
mconvery@clamsnet.org
http://www.vhlibrary.org
Marjorie P. Convery

Ware Historical Commission
PO Box 201
Middleborough, MA 02346
(508) 947-4433
George C. Decas, Chairperson

Watertown Free Public Library
123 Main Street
Watertown, MA 02172-4478
(617) 972-6431 (General); (617) 972-6436
(Reference); (617) 924-5471 FAX
LCOLE@ci.watertown.ma.us
http://watertownlib.org
Mon–Thur 9:00–9:00, Fri 9:00–5:00, Sat
(winter) 9:00–5:00, Sun (winter)
2:00–5:00
(local history/genealogy)
research: donation and SASE

Wayland Historical Commission
41 Cochituate Road
Wayland, MA 01778
Dorothy Walsh, Chairperson

Wayland Free Public Library
5 Concord Road
Wayland, MA 01778-1999
(508) 358-2311
wayland@mln.lib.ma.us
http://www.wayland.ma.us/library
Phoebe Homans
Mon–Thur 9:00–9:00, Fri 9:00–6:00, Sat
(Oct–May) 10:00–5:00, Sun (Oct–May)
2:00–5:00
Pub. *Wayland Free Public Library* (online)

Wendell Historic Commission
(45 Depot Road—location)
PO Box 112 (mailing address)
Wendell, MA 01379
(978) 544-7502
Jean S. Forward, Ph.D., Co-Chair
by appointment

Wenham Public Library
(see Hamilton-Wenham Public Library,
above)

West Springfield Historical Commission

200 Park Street
West Springfield, MA 01089
(413) 732-7230
fblally@k12s.phast.umass.edu
F. Bernard Lally, Chairperson

Westborough Public Library
55 West Main Street
Westborough, MA 01581-1989
(508) 366-3050; (508) 366-3049 FAX
http://www.westboroughlib.org
Mon–Thur 10:00–9:00, Fri 10:00–6:00, Sat
    10:00–5:00, Sun (Oct–May) 1:00–5:00
(Reed Collection)

Westfield Athenaeum
6 Elm Street
Westfield, MA 01085-2997
(413) 562-0716; (413) 568-7833 (Edwin
    Smith Historical Museum); (413) 568-
    0988 FAX
waref@cwmars.org (Reference Library)
http://www.westath.org
Joan B. Ackerman, Reference Librarian
Mon–Thur 8:30–8:00, Fri 8:30–5:00, Sat
    (fall–spring) 8:30–5:00
(local history and genealogy)
research: $5.00 minimum plus copies at 10¢
    per page

Weston Public Library
87 School Street
Weston, MA 02493-2541
(781) 893-3312; (781) 529-0174
Roberta Rothwell, Technical Services
    Librarian
Mon & Wed 9:00–9:00, Tue 1:00–9:00,
    Thur–Fri 9:00–6:00, Sat 9:00–5:00, Sun
    2:00–5:00

Whitman Historical Commission
Town Hall
Whitman, MA 02382
(781) 447-3267
Helen Clancy, Chairman
fourth Thur

Williams College
Williams College Archives and Special
Collections
Stetson Hall
Williamstown, MA 01267
(413) 597-2568; (413) 597-3931 FAX
archives@williams.edu
http://www.williams.edu/library/archives/
    index.html
Sylvia Kennick Brown, College
    Archivist/Special Collections Librarian
Archives and Special Collections: Mon–Fri
    9:00–noon & 1:00–4:30
(genealogy and biography of Williams
    alumni)

Williams College
Chapin Library
(Stetson Hall, Second Floor—location)
PO Box 426 (mailing address)
Williamstown, MA 01267
(413) 597-2462; (413) 597-2929 FAX
robert.l.volz@williams.edu
http://www.williams.edu/resources/chapin
Robert L. Volz, Custodian
Chapin Library: Mon–Fri 10:00–noon &
    1:00–5:00
(Important historical and literary collections,
    but little actual genealogical material,
    registers, diaries, etc.; "national and
    international holdings, late 8th to 21st
    centuries")
free, except costs of copying

Williamstown House of Local History

Milne Library Building, 1095 Main Street
Williamstown, MA 01267
(413) 458-2160
http://www.williamstown.net/hlh.htm
Nancy Burstein, Curator
by appointment
Pub. *Newsletter*, two times per year
(history of the town of Williamstown,
    Massachusetts, only)
$10.00 per year membership

Wilmington Historical Commission
Town Hall
Glen Road
Wilmington, MA 01887
(978) 658-3311
Winchester Historical Commission
Henry E. Simonds Memorial Archives of the
Town of Winchester
15 High Street
Winchester, MA 01890
(781) 721-7146
Susan Keats; Evelyn M. Hinde, Historical
    Services Coordinator
Library/Archives: Sept–June: Tue
    9:00–noon, Wed 11:00–6:00 &
    7:00–9:30; July: Mon & Wed 5:30–10:00
(Winchester, Massachusetts, history and
    genealogies)

Winchester Public Library
80 Washington Street
Winchester, MA 01890-2799
(781) 721-7171; (781) 721-7170 FAX
http://www.winpublib.org
Julie Kinchla, Head of Reference
Mon–Tue 9:30–9:00, Wed 1:30–9:00, Thur
    & Sat 9:30–5:30, Fri 1:30–5:30

Woburn Historical Commission
Woburn City Hall
10 Common Street
Woburn, MA 01801
John Ciriello, Chairman

Woburn Public Library
(45 Pleasant Street—location)
PO Box 298 (mailing address)
Woburn, MA 01801-0498
(781) 933-0148; (781) 938-7860 FAX
info@woburnpubliclibrary.org
http://www.woburnpubliclibrary.org
Sylvia C. Pope, Archivist
Mon–Thur 9:00–9:00, Fri–Sat 9:00–5:00

Woods Hole Library
Woods Hole Historical Collection and
Museum
(579 Woods Hole Road, Woods Hole, MA
    02543—location)
PO Box 185 (mailing address)
Woods Hole, MA 02543-0185
(508) 548-7270
woods_hole_historical@hotmail.com
http://woodsholemuseum.org
Jennifer Stone Gaines, Archivist
Archives: Tue & Thur 10:00–2:00; Exhibits:
    summer: Tue–Sat 10:00–4:00
Pub. *Spritsail*, biannually
(local history museum and archives with a
    little bit of genealogy included, also
    museum exhibits in the summer; Woods
    Hole is in the Town of Falmouth)
$25.00 per year minimum membership

Worcester Historical Museum
30 Elm Street
Worcester, MA 01609
(508) 753-8278
Library: Tue–Sat 10:00–4:00
Pub. *Worcester Historical Museum
    Newsletter*, semiannually

(Worcester and Worcester County)
$5.00 per year membership; museum
    admission: $2.00 suggested contribution
    for nonmembers

Worcester Public Library
3 Salem Square
Worcester, MA 01608-2074
(508) 799-1655
pchen@cwmars.org
http://www.worcpublib.org
Nancy E. Gaudette, Librarian, Worcester
    Collection; Jean W. Missud, Worcester
    Collection
Mon & Wed noon–9:00, Tue 10:00–9:00,
    Thur–Fri 10:00–5:30, Sat (Sept–June)
    10:00–5:30
("Call or write before coming; staff coverage
    limited.")

Wrentham Historical Commission
(677 South Street—location)
PO Box 841 (mailing address)
Wrentham, MA 02093-0006
(508) 384-2461
Earle T. Stewart, Chairman
by appointment
(Cemeteries, religious, military, schools,
    documents, vitals; "Always willing to
    help!")

Yarmouth Port Library
297 Main Street
Yarmouth Port, MA 02675
(508) 362-3717 voice & FAX
Virginia M. Gifford, Librarian
Tue–Thur 1:00–5:00, Wed 6:00–8:00, Sat
    10:00–1:00

Yesteryears Museum Association, Inc.
Main and River Streets
PO Box 609
Sandwich, MA 02563
(508) 888-1711
Diane Costa, Director
Mid-May–31 Oct: Mon–Sat 10:00–4:00
Pub. *Yesteryears Museum News*, annually
$15.00 per year membership

Historical Societies—Local and Regional

Acton Historical Society, Inc.
PO Box 2389
Acton, MA 01720
(978) 264-0690
Pub. *AHS Newsletter*

Adams Historical Society
McKinley Square
Adams, MA 01220
Eugene Michalenko
by appointment
Pub. *Adams Historical Society Newsletter*,
    eight times per year
("We don't have the staff to answer mail
    from researchers; we regret this and hope
    it will change in the future.")
$5.00 per year membership

American Antiquarian Society
185 Salisbury Street
Worcester, MA 01609-1634
(508) 755-5221, ext. 136; (508) 753-3311
    FAX
gopher://mark.mwa.org
Marie E. Lamoureux, Assistant Director of
    Reference Services
Mon–Fri 9:00–5:00 (closed stacks, readers
    need to complete an application and show
    two forms of identification)

Pub. *American Antiquarian Society Newsletter*, irregularly; *Proceedings of the American Antiquarian Society*, semiannually, $45.00 per year subscription
(American history and culture through 1876, strong collections of genealogies on early North American lines of descent, United States and Canadian local histories)
membership is by election

Amesbury History Committee
Lion's Mouth Road
Amesbury, MA 01913
(978) 388-1420
Margaret S. Rice, Director

Amherst Historical Society
Strong House Museum
67 Amity Street
Amherst, MA 01002
(413) 256-0678 (Museum); (413) 549-5438
Mary K. Steinway, President/Acting Director
Tue & Sat 1:00–4:00 (June–Sept), and by appointment

Andover Historical Society
97 Main Street
Andover, MA 01810
(978) 475-2236; (978) 470-2671 FAX
Barbara Thibault, Director
Tue–Fri 9:00–5:00, Sat (Sept–June) 9:00–5:00, Mon by appointment
Pub. *Andover Historical Society Newsletter*, quarterly
(emphasis on Andover history, genealogy and architecture; Charlotte Helen Abbot genealogies)
library admission: $4.00 for adults; research: $10.00 per hour; copies: 50¢ per page for mailed copies, 25¢ per page for in-house copies

Annawan Historical Society of Rehoboth
PO Box 71
Rehoboth, MA 02769
(508) 669-6464

The Arlington Historical Society and Smith Museum
7 Jason Street
Arlington, MA 02174
(781) 648-4300
Tina Dorr; Richard E. Erickson, President
Library: Tue–Sat 1:00–5:00 (Apr–Oct); Archives: Mon–Fri 9:00–4:30 by appointment

Ashburnham Historical Society, Inc.
PO Box 692
Ashburnham, MA 01430

The Ashfield Historical Society
(Main Street—location)
PO Box 277 (mailing address)
Ashfield, MA 01330
(413) 628-4541; (413) 628-3962 (Helen Hall, Howes Brothers collection)
July–Sept: Sun 2:00–5:00, and by appointment
Pub. *Newsletter*, quarterly
(archival photographic and genealogical material on Ashfield families; Howes Brothers photographic collection: 24,000 glass negatives, ca 1885–1907, of Connecticut River Valley area, viewable on microfilm at museum)
$15.00 per year membership

Ashland Historical Society
(2 Myrtle Street—location)
PO Box 145 (mailing address)

Ashland, MA 01721
Catherine Powers, Curator
Wed 7:00–9:00, Fri 10:00–4:00, Sat 9:00–noon
Pub. *Newsletter*, monthly
(Ashland history and genealogy)
$5.00 per year membership

Athol Historical Society
(1307 Main Street—location)
PO Box 21 (mailing address)
Athol, MA 01331
(978) 249-4890; (978) 249-6598 (Curator)
Dexter Gleason, Curator; Howard Wilson, President
June–July: Sun 2:00–4:00, and by appointment
(few genealogical files)
$5.00 per year membership

Barnstable Historical Society
Trayser Museum
PO Box 829
Barnstable, MA 02630
(508) 362-2092 (Trayser Museum); (508) 362-3658
http://www.barnstable-patriot.com/trayser
Samuel I. A. Anderson, Secretary
mid-June to mid-Oct: Tue–Sun 1:30–4:30
Pub. *Newsletter*, four times per year
$10.00 per year membership

The Barre Historical Society, Inc.
(18 Common Street—location)
PO Box 755 (mailing address)
Barre, MA 01005
(978) 355-4978; (978) 355-2810
Rita M. Robinson, President
June–Aug: Wed 2:00–4:00 & 7:00–9:00, and by appointment
$5.00 per year membership

Bay State Historical League
The Vale Lyman Estate
185 Lyman Street
Waltham, MA 02254-9998
(617) 899-3920; (617) 893-7832 FAX
Pub. *Bay State History*

Beacon Hill Civic Association
74 Joy Street
Boston, MA 02114
(617) 227-1922; (617) 227-7959 FAX
Tanya M. Holton, Executive Director; Kristine Glynn, Director of Public Relations and Marketing
9:00–5:00
Pub. *BHCA News*, monthly
$40.00 per year membership

Belchertown Historical Association
(20 Maple Street—location)
PO Box 1211 (mailing address)
Belchertown, MA 01007
(413) 323-6573
Caren Herrington, Curator
Library: about 15 May–15 Oct: Wed & Sat 2:00–5:00, and by appointment

Belmont Historical Society
Belmont Room (Local History Collection)
(336 Concord Avenue—location)
PO Box 125 (mailing address)
Belmont, MA 02178
(781) 489-2000
Madaline Marshall, Curator
Belmont Room: Mon, Wed & Fri 2:00–4:00, and by appointment
Pub. *Belmont Historical Society Newsletter*, quarterly

Berkley Historical Society

725 Berkley Street
Berkley, MA 02779
(508) 824-5367
Blanche E. Trzcinski, Curator

Berlin Art and Historical Society
(51 South Street—location)
PO Box 87 (mailing address)
Berlin, MA 01503-0087
(978) 838-2502
Barry Eager

Beverly Historical Society
117 Cabot Street
Beverly, MA 01915
(978) 922-1186
Daniel J. Hoisington, Director
Library at Cabot House: Wed–Sat 10:00–4:00, Sun (20 May–15 Oct) 1:00–4:00

Billerica Historical Society
(Clara Sexton House, 36 Concord Road—location)
PO Box 381 (mailing address)
Billerica, MA 01821
(978) 663-8769
Marion Potter, President

Blandford Historical Society
North Street
Blandford, MA 01008
(413) 848-2787
Hap Bush, President
by appointment only

Bolton Historical Society, Inc.
(676 Great Road, Route 117—location)
PO Box 211 (mailing address)
Bolton, MA 01740-0211
(978) 779-6392
last Thur 1:30–3:30, other times by appointment
$20.00 per year membership

The Bostonian Society
(15 State Street, Third Floor—location)
206 Washington Street (mailing address)
Boston, MA 02109-1773
(617) 720-1713 (Society); (617) 720-1713, ext. 12 (Library); (617) 720-3290 (Old State House Museum)
oldstatehouse@bostonhistory.org
http://www.bostonhistory.org
Nancy Richard, Director of the Library and Special Collections
Mon–Thur 9:30–4:30

Bourne Historical Society, Inc.
(Aptucxet Trading Post Museum Complex, 24 Aptucxet Road and Jonathan Bourne Historical Center—location)
PO Box 3095 (mailing address)
Bourne, MA 02532-0795
(508) 759-8167
info@bournehistoricalsoc.org
http://www.bournehistoricalsoc.org
Judith McAlister, Director
Aptucxet: Mon (July–Aug & holidays) 10:00–4:00, Tue–Sat (May–Oct) 10:00–4:00, Sun (May–Oct) 2:00–5:00
Pub. *Post Scripts*, quarterly (1 Mar, 1 June, 1 Sept, 1 Dec), not available by subscription
$20.00 per year membership

Boxford Historical Society
PO Box 281
Boxford, MA 01921
(978) 887-9545
Peter Loring, President

Boylston Historical Society, Inc.

(7 Central Street—location)
PO Box 459 (mailing address)
Boylston, MA 01505-0459
(508) 869-2720
Norman H. French, Curator
Tue 9:00–noon, and by appointment
(extensive real estate transactions
1730–1930, photo collection)
$10.00 per year membership; research:
$25.00 plus expenses

The Braintree Historical Society, Inc.
31 Tenney Road
Braintree, MA 02184-6512
(781) 848-1640
Marjorie Maxham, Librarian/Archivist
Tue–Wed 10:00–4:00 by appointment
(official custodian of the Penniman Family
Records)
$15.00 per year membership

Brewster Historical Society
PO Box 1146
Brewster, MA 02631
(508) 896-3058
Marion H. Wylie, President
Library: Wed–Fri 1:00–4:00 (summer)

Brighton-Allston Historical Society
30 Kenrick Street
Brighton, MA 02135
(617) 562-5348
mail@bahistory.org
William P. Marchione, Ph.D., President
by appointment only
(primarily Allston-Brighton communities
within Boston)
$10.00 per year membership; research: fee
by arrangement

Brockton Historical Society
216 North Pearl Street
Brockton, MA 02401
(508) 583-1039
gerryb@brocktonma.com
http://www.brocktonma.com
Gerald Beals, Acting Curator
Sun 2:00–4:00, and by appointment
Pub. *Brockton Historical Quarterly*
$10.00 per year membership

Brookline Historical Society
347 Harvard Street
Brookline, MA 02146
(617) 566-5747
Helen C. McIntosh, Curator
Pub. *Brookline Historical Society
Proceedings*

Buckland Historical Society
Upper Street
Buckland, MA 01338
(413) 625-6619
Helen Roberts, President

Burlington Historical Society, Inc.
Town Hall
Center Street
Burlington, MA 01803
(781) 272-4840
Pauline R. Keans, President

Cambridge Historical Society
159 Brattle Street
Cambridge, MA 02138-3300
(617) 547-4252; (617) 661-1623 FAX
Warren M. Little, Ed.D., Executive Director
Tue & Thur 2:00–5:00
Pub. *Proceedings*, infrequently, $10.00 per
issue

Canton Historical Society

1400 Washington Street
Canton, MA 02021
(781) 828-4962

Cape and Islands Historical Association
PO Box 50
Bourne, MA 02559-0050
(508) 888-3300, ext. 103

Cape Ann Historical Association
27 Pleasant Street
Gloucester, MA 01930
(978) 283-0455
Ellen Nelson, Librarian
Library: Wed & Sat 10:00–1:00, Thur
10:00–3:00, Fri 10:00–1:00 & 2:00–5:00;
Museum: Tue–Sat 10:00–5:00
Pub. *Cape Ann Historical Association
Newsletter*, quarterly
(fisheries/maritime, art history, Cape Ann
local history)
$20.00 per year membership

Cape Cod Maritime Historical Association
PO Box 176
Yarmouthport, MA 02675
(508) 362-1222

Centerville Historical Society
Centerville Historical Society Museum
(513 Main Street—location)
PO Box 491 (mailing address)
Centerville, MA 02632
(508) 775-0331
Nancy Lee Nelson, Director
Library: Wed–Sun (June to mid-Sept)
(part of the town of Barnstable)

Charlestown Historical Society
Bunker Hill Museum
43 Monument Square
Charlestown, MA 02129

Charlton Historical Society
PO Box 252
Charlton, MA 01507
(508) 248-3202
by appointment

The Chatham Historical Society, Inc.
(347 Stage Harbor Road—location)
PO Box 381 (mailing address)
Chatham, MA 02633
(508) 945-2493; (508) 945-1205 FAX
atwoodhouse@prodigy.net
http://www.chathamhistoricalsociety.org
Daniel L. Buckley, President
mid-June–Sept: Tue–Fri 1:00–4:00
(history or genealogical books pertaining to
Chatham)
$10.00 per year membership

Chelmsford Historical Society, Inc.
40 Byam Road
Chelmsford, MA 01824
(978) 256-2311
second & fourth Sun (June–Sept) 2:00–4:00
$10.00 per year membership; research: $5.00
plus postage

Chester Historical Society
(Old Jail, Route 20, Jacob's Ladder
Trail—location)
Town Hall, 15 Middlefield (mailing address)
Chester, MA 01011
Fay M. Piergiovanni, Chairperson
first Wed 9:00–1:00, or by appointment
Pub. *Chester Historical Society News*,
quarterly
$5.00 per year membership

Chesterfield Historical Society

Edwards Museum
North Street
Chesterfield, MA 01012
(413) 296-4759
Ruth Z. Temple, Museum Curator
Sat 2:00–4:00 (July–Aug)
(historical, not genealogical)

Clinton Historical Society
210 Church Street
Clinton, MA 01510
(978) 368-0084; (978) 365-4877

Cohasset Historical Society
(Pratt Building, 106 South Main
Street—location)
PO Box 627 (mailing address)
Cohasset, MA 02025
(781) 383-1434
David H. Wadsworth, Historian; Paula Kozol
or Kathleen O'Malley, Co-Presidents
by appointment
Pub. *Historical Highlights Newsletter*,
quarterly
admission: no charge

Colrain Historical Society
91 East Catamount Hill Road
Colrain, MA 01340-9514

Conway Historical Society
Conway, MA 01341
Museum: Sun (July–Aug) afternoons, and by
appointment
$18.00 per year membership

Danvers Historical Society
(13 Page Street—location)
PO Box 381 (mailing address)
Danvers, MA 01923
(978) 777-1666
Sarah E. Symmes, President
Pub. *Danvers Historical Collections*,
irregularly
$10.00 per year membership

Dedham Historical Society
(612 High Street—location)
PO Box 215 (mailing address)
Dedham, MA 02027-0215
(781) 326-1385
Ron@DedhamHistorical.org;
Genealogy@DedhamHistorical.org
http://www.DedhamHistorical.org
Ronald F. Frazier, Executive Director and
CEO
Tue–Fri 9:00–4:00, even-dated Sat
1:00–4:00
Pub. *Dedham Historical Society Newsletter*,
bimonthly
(an extensive genealogical and historical
library)
$25.00 per year membership; admission:
$5.00 for nonmembers; research: limited
research for a fee upon full completion of
research form on web site

Dennis Historical Society
(1736 Josiah Dennis Manse, Nobscusset and
Whig Street, Dennis, MA 02638 and 1801
Jericho-Trotting Park and Main, West
Dennis, MA 02670—location)
PO Box 607 (mailing address)
South Dennis, MA 02660
(508) 394-0017
Phyllis Horton, Curator
Jericho: July–Aug: Mon, Wed & Fri
2:00–4:00; DHS library at Josiah Dennis
Manse: July–Sept: Tue & Thur 2:00–4:00
Pub. *Dennis Historical Society Newsletter*,
monthly
(Dennis history)

$10.00 per year membership

Dighton Historical Society
Box 0693
Dighton, MA 02715
(508) 669-5514
Elaine Varley, Curator
by appointment
(history and documents of Dighton and
surrounding area)
$4.00 per year membership

Dorchester Historical Society
The William Clapp House
195 Boston Street
Dorchester, MA 02125
(617) 436-8367
Anthony M. Sammarco, Curator
by appointment
Pub. *Newsletter*, bimonthly
$6.00 per year membership

Douglas Historical Society, Inc.
(The E. N. Jenckes Store Museum, 283 Main
Street—location)
PO Box 176 (mailing address)
East Douglas, MA 01516-0176
(508) 476-3856
Jean Peterson, President
Apr–Nov: Sat–Sun 1:00–4:00

Dover Historical Society
(Sawin Museum, 80 Dedham Street and
Caryl House, 107 Dedham Street—location)
PO Box 534 (mailing address)
Dover, MA 02030
(508) 785-1832
Paul H. Tedesco, Ph.D., President; Shirley
McGill, Sawin Curator; Priscilla Pitt
Jones, Caryl House Curator; Elisha Lee,
Fisher Barn Curator
Sat (spring and fall) 1:00–4:00, and by
appointment
(history of Dover, Massachusetts, and its
citizens)
$15.00 per year membership; research: no
fee

Dracut Historical Society, Inc.
1660 Lakeview Avenue
Dracut, MA 01826
(978) 957-1701
Norma Taplin, President
Sun 1:00–3:00
$5.00 per year membership

**Duxbury Rural and Historical Society,
Inc.**
(685 Washington Street—location)
PO Box 2865 (mailing address)
Duxbury, MA 02331
(781) 934-6106
Marcia Solberg, Executive Director
Mon–Fri 9:00–5:00
Pub. *Newsletter*

Eastham Historical Society, Inc.
(Eastham Public Library—archives location)
PO Box 8 (mailing address)
Eastham, MA 02642
(508) 255-0773; (508) 255-8725
(Membership)
easthamarchives@easthamlibrary.org
http://www.easthamhistorical.org
Joan Sullivan, Public Relations Director
$10.00 per year membership

Easton Historical Society
(North Easton Railroad Station, 80 Mechanic
Street—location)
PO Box 3 (mailing address)
North Easton, MA 02356

(508) 238-7774
Dorothy Berry, Curator
second Sun 2:00–4:00, and by appointment
Pub. *Families—Chaffin's Early Easton
Families*
$7.00 per year membership

Elbow Plantation Historical Society
281 Chauncey Walker Street, Lot 53
Belchertown, MA 01007-9134
Frances T. Fulton, Secretary

Erving Historical Society
(Main Street, Erving, MA 01344—location)
9 Moore Street (mailing address)
Millers Falls, MA 01349

Essex County Historical Association
23 Bancroft Avenue
Beverly, MA 01915
(978) 927-0138

**Essex Historical Society and Shipbuilding
Museum**
(28 Main Street—location)
PO Box 277 (mailing address)
Essex, MA 01929
(978) 768-7541
Diana H. Stockton, Administrator
Thur–Sun (15 May–15 Oct) 10:00–4:00, and
year-round by appointment
("We have a wealth of papers from Essex
families, including Andrews, Burnham
and Story.")
50¢ per page for genealogical and headstone
transcription information

Everett Historical Society
Town Hall
Everett, MA 02149
(617) 387-7059
Ciro R. Yannaco

Fairhaven Historical Society
(address withheld upon request)
(primarily historical, not genealogical)

Fall River Historical Society
451 Rock Street
Fall River, MA 02720
(508) 679-1071; (508) 675-5754
Michael Martins, Curator
Tue–Fri (Apr–Dec) 9:00–4:30, Sat–Sun
(June–Sept) 1:00–5:00
Pub. *The Fall River Historical Society
Quarterly Report*
(history of Fall River, Massachusetts,
including Lizzie Borden)
$25.00 per year membership

Falmouth Historical Society
(55-65 Palmer Avenue, Falmouth, MA
02540—location)
PO Box 174 (mailing address)
Falmouth, MA 02541
(508) 548-4857; (508) 540-0968 FAX
fhs@cape.com; archives@cape.com;
JSPendery@msn.com;
cpowers@cape.com
http://www.falmouthhistoricalsociety.org
Joyce S. Pendery, CGRS, Genealogist;
Carolyn Powers, Executive Director
Archives and Office: Mon–Thur 9:00–1:00,
Fri 9:00–4:00, and by appointment;
Museum: 15 June–15 Sept: Wed–Sun
2:00–5:00
Pub. *Spritsail*, biannually; *Newsletter*,
irregularly
(Falmouth and related families)
$20.00 per year membership; museum
admission: $2.00 for nonmember adults

Fitchburg Historical Society
(50 Grove Street—location)
PO Box 953 (mailing address)
Fitchburg, MA 01420
(978) 345-1157; (978) 345-2229 FAX
Betsy Hannula, Executive Director
Museum: Mon–Tue & Thur 10:00–4:00,
Wed 10:00–6:00, first & second Sat
10:00–1:00
Pub. *Newsletter*, quarterly (no genealogical
information)
$20.00 per year membership; admission:
$10.00 for nonmembers

Foxborough Historical Society
PO Box 437
Foxborough, MA 02035

**Framingham Historical Society and
Museum**
(Corner of Vernon and Grove
Streets—location)
PO Box 2032 (mailing address)
Framingham, MA 01703-2032
(508) 872-3780 voice & FAX
research@framinghamhistory.org
http://www.framinghamhistory.org
Joan Mickelson Lukach, Ph.D.; Frederic
Wallace, Researcher
Wed–Thur 10:00–4:00, Sat 10:00–1:00
Pub. *Newsletter*, quarterly
(genealogies of local families)
$25.00 per year membership; admission: free
($2.00 donation suggested); research:
$8.00 per hour on site for nonmembers,
$10.00 by mail

Freetown Historical Society Museum
(1 Slab Bridge Road—location)
PO Box 253 (mailing address)
Assonet, MA 02702
(508) 644-5310 (Mondays)
Freetownhistorical@email.com
Curator
Mon 10:00–4:00, Sun (July–Aug) 1:00–4:00
(large local genealogical library,
computerized finding aid)

Georgetown Historical Society
Brocklebank House Museum
(108 East Main Street—location)
PO Box 376 (mailing address)
Georgetown, MA 01833
(978) 352-8372
Rosemary Morse, Curator
4 July–Columbus Day: Sun 2:00–5:00
$6.00 per year membership

Grafton Historical Society, Inc.
Grafton, MA 01519
(508) 839-2063
George Carroll, President

Historical Society of Greenfield
(43 Church Street—location)
PO Box 415 (mailing address)
Greenfield, MA 01302
(413) 772-6992
Tim Blagg, Curator
by appointment
$15.00 per year membership; research sub-
contracted to a professional

Groton Historical Society
172 Main Street
Groton, MA 01450
(978) 448-2046

Groveland Historical Society, Inc.
Uptack Road, Route 4
Groveland, MA 01834
(978) 372-6216

Mildred C. Esty, Secretary

Hadley Historical Society
(Hadley Historical Room, Goodwin
Memorial Library, Second Floor)
100 Middle Street (mailing address)
Hadley, MA 01035
(413) 586-0221; (413) 586-5661 FAX
Library room: weekends in some summer
months, and by appointment
("A private organization open to public
membership.")

Hamilton Historical Society
(Hamilton Town Hall, 577 Bay
Road—location)
PO Box 108 (mailing address)
Hamilton, MA 01936
Arthur H. Crosbie, Jr., President
Thur 1:00–4:00, and by appointment
$6.00 per year membership

**Historical Society of the Town of
Hampden, Inc.**
(616 Main Street—location)
PO Box 363 (mailing address)
Hampden, MA 01036
(413) 566-3466
Mrs. Gerald Doten, Curator
fourth Sun (May–Oct) 2:00–4:00, and by
appointment
(Hampden local history, some genealogy)
$5.00 per year membership

Hanover Historical Society
Stetson House
(514 Hanover Street—location)
PO Box 156 (mailing address)
Hanover, MA 02339
(781) 826-9575 (Wednesdays); (781) 826-
3736 (President)
Carol Franzosa, President
Wed 2:00–4:00, and by appointment; open
house: first weekend Dec
Pub. *The Hanover Historian*, four times per
year
(Hanover history, South Shore genealogy,
shipbuilding, North River)
$7.50 per year membership; research:
donation

Hardwick Historical Society
Hardwick Common
Hardwick, MA 01037
(413) 477-6635
Elizabeth Reilly, President

Harvard Historical Society
(215 Still River Road—location)
PO Box 542 (mailing address)
Harvard, MA 01451
(978) 456-8285
Camille Breeze, Curator
by appointment
Pub. *Harvard Historical Society*, two times
per year (spring and fall)
$15.00 per year membership

Harwich Historical Society
Brooks Academy Museum
80 Parallel Street
Harwich, MA 02645
(508) 432-8089
info@harwichhistoricalsociety.org
http://www.harwichhistoricalsociety.org
James Brown, Director
Wed & Fri–Sat 1:00–4:00, Thur 1:00–7:00
Pub. *Powder House Quarterly*
(vital records of Harwich, copies of *Harwich
Independent 1872–1948*, photographs,
several privately compiled genealogical
collections, etc.)

Hatfield Historical Society
(35 Main Street—location)
PO Box 168 (mailing address)
Hatfield, MA 01038
(413) 247-5545; (413) 247-9097 (Hatfield
Library)
Rita Prew, President
Fri 7:00 P.M.–9:00 P.M.
$5.00 per year membership

Haverhill Historical Society
Buttonwoods Museum
240 Water Street
Haverhill, MA 01830
(978) 374-4626

Heath Historical Society
Brunelle Road, Rural Free Delivery
Charlemont, MA 01339
William Thane, Curator

Holden Historical Society, Inc.
(Hendricks House, 1157 Main
Street—location)
PO Box 421 (mailing address)
Holden, MA 01520-0421
(508) 793-3448
Ross W. Beales, Jr., Membership Secretary
Sat 9:00–noon, and by appointment
Pub. *Newsletter*, three times per year
$6.00 per year membership

Hubbardston Historical Society
(Jonas Clark Buliding, Main
Street—location)
PO Box 119 (mailing address)
Hubbardston, MA 01452-0119
Joyce Green, Secretary
by appointment
$4.00 per year membership

Hyde Park Historical Society
Weld Hall-Hyde Park Branch, Boston Public
Library
30 Ayles Road
Hyde Park, MA 02136
(617) 361-4398
Nancy Hannan, President
by appointment
(archival material pertaining to Hyde Park
people and history)
$5.00 per year membership; research: $15.00
per hour; *Catalog of Genealogical
Materials*, $25.00

Ipswich Historical Society
Heard House Museum and Whipple House
54 South Main Street
Ipswich, MA 01938
(978) 356-2811
Stefanie J. Muscat, Director
Office: Mon–Fri 9:00–5:00; Houses have
seasonal hours (please call)

Jones River Village Historical Society
PO Box 22
Kingston, MA 02364
(781) 585-1664
Scot E. Lyall, President
$15.00 per year membership

**The Historical Society of Lawrence and Its
People**
Immigrant City Archives
(6 Essex Street—location)
PO Box 1638 (mailing address)
Lawrence, MA 01842
(978) 686-9230
Eartha Dengler, Executive Director
Mon–Fri 9:00–4:30 by appointment only
(local history, especially ethnic, labor, urban
planning, and history of immigrants to
New England; large collection of

photographs and oral history interviews)
$15.00 per year membership

The Lenox Historical Society
Lenox Academy Building
(65 Main Street—location)
PO Box 1856 (mailing address)
Lenox, MA 01240
(413) 637-1824
Nancy D. Marasco, Curator
Sat 11:00–2:00 and by appointment
Pub. *Lenox Historical Society Newsletter*,
quarterly
$12.00 per year membership

Leominster Historical Society
17 School Street
Leominster, MA 01453
(978) 537-5424
info@leominsterhistorical.org
http://www.leominsterhistorical.org
David Wilson, Trustee; Paul J. Benoit,
Trustee
Mon–Fri 9:00–2:00, Sat 9:00–noon
Pub. *Newsletter*, seven times per year
$15.00 per year membership

Leverett Historical Society
North Leverett Road
Leverett, MA 01054
(413) 367-2800

Lexington Historical Society
Munroe Tavern
(1332 Massachusetts Avenue—location)
PO Box 514 (mailing address)
Lexington, MA 02173-0005
(781) 862-1703
George Comtois, Executive Director
Library: Mon–Sat 10:00–5:00, Sun (19
Apr–31 Oct) 1:00–5:00; Archives: by
appointment; Administration: Mon–Fri
9:00–2:00

Lincoln Historical Society
Lincoln, MA 01773
(781) 259-8958

Littleton Historical Society
Houghton Memorial Building
(4 Rogers Street—location)
PO Box 721 (mailing address)
Littleton, MA 01460-2721
(978) 486-8202 (message recorder)
Nancy Bradbury, Curator
Wed 1:00–4:00, second Sun 2:00–4:00
(Littleton vital records and history)
$5.00 per year membership; research:
donation; copies: 10¢ per page

Longmeadow Historical Society
697 Longmeadow Street
Longmeadow, MA 01106
(413) 567-3600; (413) 567-5432
(appointments); (413) 567-5432 (Curator)
Mabel Crosmon Swanson, Curator
Library: Wed–Thur 9:00–noon, and by
appointment
(genealogical records)
$6.00 per year membership

Lowell Historical Society
Boott Cotton Mill Museum
(400 Foot of John Street, Lowell, MA
01852—location)
PO Box 1826 (mailing address)
Lowell, MA 01853
(978) 970-5180 (President); (978) 934-4998
(Librarian)
Louise Hunt, President; Martha Mayo,
Librarian
Tue–Wed 1:00–4:00

$10.00 per year membership

Lynn Museum
125 Green Street
Lynn, MA 01902
(781) 592-2465; (781) 592-0012 FAX
http://lynnmuseum.org
Diane Shepherd, Archivist/Librarian
Mon–Fri 9:00–noon & 1:00–4:00
(Lynn history, Lynn genealogy manuscripts,
    vital records for most of Massachusetts)
$20.00 per year membership; admission:
    $4.00; research: $10.00 per hour

Lynnfield Historical Society
PO Box 274
Lynnfield, MA 01940
(781) 334-4899; (781) 334-5411 (Library);
    (781) 334-3814 (President)
Shirley Northrup, President
Lynnfield Public Library: Mon–Thur
    9:00–9:00, Fri–Sat 9:00–5:00
Pub. *Historical Lynnfield*, quarterly
$3.00 per year membership

Malden Historical Society
Malden Public Library
36 Salem Street
Malden, MA 02148
(781) 338-9365; (781) 324-4467 FAX
    (Library)
President
by appointment
(Society not open to the public, publications
    available at the Malden Public Library)
$5.00 per year membership

Manchester Historical Society
10 Union Street
Manchester, MA 01944
(978) 526-7230
Lotte Calnek, Curator
July–Aug: Sat 10:00–4:00, Sun noon–4:00,
    and by appointment
Pub. *MHS Newsletter*, quarterly

Mansfield Historical Society, Inc.
(53 Rumford Avenue—location)
307 East Main Street (mailing address)
Norton, MA 02766
(508) 339-7398; (508) 285-4048
George Yelle, President
Mon 7:30–9:00; meetings Oct–Jan &
    Mar–May: second Monday 7:30
Pub. *The M.H.S. Newsletter*, seven times per
    year
$10.00 per year membership

Marblehead Historical Society
(170 Washington Street—location)
PO Box 1048 (mailing address)
Marblehead, MA 01945
(781) 631-1768
Karen MacInnis, Curator of Collections
Library: Tue–Fri 10:00–4:00
Pub. *MHS Newsletter*, three times per year
(Marblehead history and genealogy)
$25.00 per year membership; staff-done
    research: $15.00 per hour

Marlborough Historical Society
(377 Elm Street—location)
PO Box 513 (mailing address)
Marlborough, MA 01752
(508) 838-0479
Virginia H. Johnson, Curator
Archives: Mon 10:00–noon, and by
    appointment; Museum House: Sept–June:
    third Tue
Pub. *Newsletter*
$10.00 per year membership

Marshfield Historical Society
Webster and Careswell Streets
PO Box 1244
Marshfield, MA 02050
(781) 834-7236

Martha's Vineyard Historical Society
Vineyard Museum
(59 School Street—location)
PO Box 1310 (mailing address)
Edgartown, MA 02539-1310
(508) 627-4441; (508) 693-2725
    (Genealogist); (508) 627-4436 FAX
mvhist@vineyard.net
http://www.marthasvineyardhistory.org
Matthew Stackpole, Executive Director;
    Catherine Merwin Mayhew, Genealogist
mid-June to mid-Oct: Tue–Sat 10:00–5:00;
    mid-Dec to mid-Mar: Sat 10:00–4:00 and
    by appointment; mid-Mar to mid-June &
    mid-Oct to mid-Dec: Wed–Fri 1:00–4:00,
    Sat 10:00–5:00
Pub. *The Dukes County Intelligencer*,
    quarterly (Feb, May, Aug, Nov) (emphasis
    on Martha's Vineyard history); *Martha's
    Vineyard Historical Society Messenger*,
    quarterly (society news only)
$45.00 per year membership; admission:
    $7.00 summer, $6.00 winter, members
    free; research: $25.00 per hour

Mattapoisett Historical Society
Mattapoisett Museum and Carriage House
(5 Church Street—location)
PO Box 535 (mailing address)
Mattapoisett, MA 02739
(508) 758-2844
Bette A. Roberts, Curator
Sept–June: Tue–Wed & Fri 9:00–noon;
    July–Aug: Tue–Sat 1:00–4:30

Maynard Historical Society
Town Building, Main Street
Maynard, MA 01754
(978) 897-9696
Paul V. Boothroyd, Curator
daytime by appointment only
$5.00 per year membership

Medfield Historical Society
(6 Pleasant Street—location)
PO Box 233 (mailing address)
Medfield, MA 02052
Al Clark, President
Sat 9:00–1:00
Pub. *Bulletin*
$5.00 per year membership

Medford Historical Society
(10 Governors Avenue—location)
34 Summit Road (mailing address)
Medford, MA 02155
(781) 395-7863; (781) 391-8739
Michael F. Bradford, Curator; Dr. Joseph V.
    Valeriani, President
Sun 2:00–4:00, and by appointment
(emphasis on Massachusetts, Civil War, the
    slave trade, shipbuilding and rum
    distilling)
$8.00 per year membership

Melrose Historical Society, Inc.
(131 West Emerson Street—location)
PO Box 301 (mailing address)
Melrose, MA 02176
(781) 665-5010
Arnold W. Williams, Chairman

Mendon Historical Society
Mendon Historical Museum
(3 Main Street at Founders' Park—location)
PO Box 196 (mailing address)

Mendon, MA 01756
(508) 473-7672 (Curator's home)
Alice Pickering Palladini, Curator
30 May–Sept: Sat–Sun (two times per
    month) 2:00–4:00, Tue (once a month)
    6:30–8:00
(history and genealogy of Mendon and area
    towns)
$4.00 per year membership; museum
    admission: donation; research: postage
    plus copies at 20¢ per page

**Middleborough Historical Association,
Inc.**
(Jackson Street—location)
PO Box 304 (mailing address)
Middleborough, MA 02346
(508) 947-1969
Museum: July–Aug: Wed–Thur 1:00–3:00;
    Sept–Oct: second & fourth Sat 1:00–3:00;
    and by appointment
Pub. *The Middleborough Antiquarian*, three
    times per year
$10.00 per year membership

Middleton Historical Society
Lura Woodside Watkins Museum
Pleasant Street
Middleton, MA 01949
(978) 774-9301

Milton Historical Society
Suffolk Resolves House
1370 Canton Avenue
Milton, MA 02186
(617) 333-0644
MHS1904@aol.com
http://www.key-biz.com/ssn/
    Milton/hist_soc.html
Mr. and Mrs. Wesley J. Merritt, Curators
Library: by appointment; Archives in Milton
    Public Library

Monson Historical Society, Inc.
(1 Green Street—location)
PO Box 114 (mailing address)
Monson, MA 01057
(413) 267-4292
info@monsonhistoricalsociety.org
http://www.monsonhistoricalsociety.org
Dennis Swierad, Historian
by appointment

Montague Historical Society, Inc.
34 Central Street
Montague, MA 01351
(413) 367-2216

Monterey Historical Society
Monterey, MA 01245
(413) 528-3044
Mrs. John Fijux, President

**Nantucket Historical Association Research
Library**
(7 Fair Street—location)
PO Box 1016 (mailing address)
Nantucket, MA 02554
(508) 228-1655; (508) 325-7968 FAX
library@nha.org
http://www.nha.org
Georgen Gilliam, Curator of Library and
    Archives
Mon–Fri 10:00–4:00
Pub. *Historic Nantucket*, quarterly
("research library and archives, genealogical
    information for Nantucket")
$40.00 per year membership; admission:
    $5.00 nonmembers

Narragansett Historical Society
The Common

Templeton, MA 01468
(978) 939-8762

Natick Historical Society and Museum
Bacon Free Library Building Lower Floor
58 Eliot Street
South Natick, MA 01760
(508) 647-4841; (508) 653-5338
nathissoc@rcn.com
http://users.rcn.com/nathissoc
Anne K. Schaller, Director
Library: Tue 6:00 P.M.–8:30 P.M., Wed
   2:00–4:30, Sat (mid-June to mid-Sept)
   10:00–12:30, and by appointment
Pub. *The Arrow*, two or three times per year
   ("The Museum holds collections and
   memorabilia of many of Natick's
   distinguished people including Harriet
   Beecher Stowe, Henry Wilson, Vice
   President of the United States under U.S.
   Grant, and Horatio Alger, Jr. You will
   find our Mission on our web site.
   Reference library on local history, historic
   museum, and natural history museum.")
$15.00 per year membership; research:
   $20.00 per hour plus postage and copies
   at 20¢ per page; photographs may be
   purchased

Needham Historical Society, Inc.
53 Glendoon Road
Needham, MA 02192
(781) 444-3181
Henry Hicks, President

New Braintree Historical Society
PO Box 112
New Braintree, MA 1531

**The New England Historic Genealogical
Society (NEHGS)**
(see Genealogical Socieites—Local and
Regional, below)

North Andover Historical Society
153 Academy Road
North Andover, MA 01845
(978) 686-4035; (978) 686-6616
nahistory@juno.com
Carol Majahad, Executive Director
Tue–Fri 10:00–noon & 2:00–4:00, Mon by
   appointment
Pub. *North Andover Historical Society
   Newsletter*, three to four times per year
$20.00 per year membership; research:
   $15.00 for first hour, $10.00 for each
   additional full hour; admission: $7.00

**North Reading Historical and Antiquarian
Society, Inc.**
(Bow Street—location)
PO Box 354 (mailing address)
North Reading, MA 01864
(978) 664-1066
Thomas W. Parker, Curator
Spring & fall: Wed & Sun afternoons
Pub. *Newsletter*, irregularly
(historic house, artifacts, library)
$10.00 per year membership

Northampton Historical Society
(doing business as Historic Northampton)
46 Bridge Street
Northampton, MA 01060
(413) 584-6011
http://www.historic-northampton.org/601081
Kerry Buckley, Executive Director
Mar–Dec: Tue–Fri 10:00–4:00, Sat–Sun
   noon–4:00
Pub. *The Weathervane Newsletter*, quarterly
(Northampton, Massachusetts, history)
$40.00 per year membership

Northborough Historical Society, Inc.
(52 Main Street—location)
PO Box 661 (mailing address)
Northborough, MA 01532
(508) 393-6389
letusgothen@juno.com
http://www.northboroughhistsoc.org
Robert P. Ellis, Historian
by appointment: Museum: Sun (spring and
   fall) 2:00–4:00
Pub. *The Hourglass*, ten times per year
   (monthly, Sept–June, with local historical
   article in each issue)
$10.00 per year membership

Northbridge Historical Society
183 Cooper Road
Northbridge, MA 01534
(508) 234-5110
John Rogers, President

Norton Historical Society
(18 West Main Street, Route 123—location)
PO Box 1711 (mailing address)
Norton, MA 02766-0909
(508) 285-7070 (Wednesdays)
http://cs.wheatonma.edu/nhs
Ruth E. Goold, President
Wed–Thur 9:00–4:00, Wed 7:00–9:00;
   meetings: Sept–Nov & Jan–May: third
   Tue 8:00
Pub. *From the Schoolmarm's Desk*, eight
   times per year
$5.00 per year membership

Norwell Historical Society, Inc.
(Main Street—location)
PO Box 693 (mailing address)
Norwell, MA 02061
(781) 659-1888
Gertrude Daneau, President
hours: various
Pub. *Newsletter*, six times per year
$10.00 per year membership; limited
   research: donation, but will refer to
   professional researchers on request

Norwood Historical Society
93 Day Street
Norwood, MA 02062
(781) 762-9197
Barbara J. Rand, President
Library: by appointment

Historical Society of Old Abington
Dyer Memorial Library
(28 Centre Avenue—location)
PO Box 22 (mailing address)
Abington, MA 02351
(781) 878-8480 (Library)
Library: Tue–Fri 1:00–5:00, second & fourth
   Sat noon–4:00

Old Bridgewater Historical Society
Memorial Building
(162 Howard Street—location)
PO Box 17 (mailing address)
West Bridgewater, MA 02379
(508) 559-1510
Diana Lothrop, President
Wed 10:00–4:00, Sat 1:00–4:00 (Apr–Oct)
Pub. *Newsletter*, monthly
$12.00 per year membership

Old Colony Historical Society
66 Church Green
Taunton, MA 02780
(508) 822-1622
http://www.oldcolonyhistoricalsociety.org
Jane M. Hennedy, Director
Tue–Sat 10:00–4:00 (closed holidays and Sat
   before Mon holidays)

Pub. *Newsletter*, quarterly
(southeastern Massachusetts)
$30.00 per year membership; admission:
   $7.00 for genealogy research, $4.00 for
   other research; museum tours: $4.00 for
   adults; research: $15.00 per hour, plus
   copies at 25¢ each

Old Dartmouth Historical Society
Whaling Museum Library
18 Johnny Cake Hill
New Bedford, MA 02740
(508) 997-0046
Virginia M. Adams, Librarian
weekdays 10:00–noon & 1:00–4:00
Pub. *Bulletin from Johnny Cake Hill*, three
   times per year
(history of American whaling and of
   southeastern Massachusetts, particularly
   the New Bedford area)
$15.00 per year membership

Historical Society of Old Newbury
98 High Street
Newburyport, MA 01950
(978) 462-2681; (978) 462-0134 FAX
hson@greennet.net
Clifford Bonney, President
Library: Tue–Fri 10:00–4:00, Sat 11:00–2:00
(Newbury, Newburyport, and West Newbury
   families)
research: $10.00 per hour

Historical Society of Old Yarmouth
(11 Strawberry Lane—location)
PO Box 11 (mailing address)
Yarmouth Port, MA 02675
(508) 362-3021
info@hsoy.org
http://www.hsoy.org
Barbara Ryan, Director/Curator
Tue & Thur by appointment
Pub. *Beechcomber Newsletter*, three times
   per year
$15.00 per year membership

Orange Historical Society, Inc.
(41 North Main Street—location)
80 Fountain Street (mailing address)
Orange, MA 01364
Irene Ballou, President
Sun 2:00–4:00 (June–Aug), and by
   appointment
Pub. *Orange Historical Society, Inc.*

Orleans Historical Society
Margaret Stranger House
(3 River Road—location)
PO Box 353 (mailing address)
Orleans, MA 02653
(508) 240-1329
Jon Howard, Director
Mon & Fri 9:00–4:30; July–Aug: Mon–Fri
   noon–4:00
$5.00 per year membership

Osterville Historical Society and Museum
Parker and West Bay Roads
Osterville, MA 02655
(508) 428-5861; (508) 428-2241 FAX
welcom@osterville.org
http://www.osterville.org/OHSindex.htm
June–Sept: Thur–Sun 1:30–4:30

Peabody Historical Society and Museum
35 Washington Street
Peabody, MA 01960-5520
(978) 531-0805
Joseph M. Donlon, President
Office: Mon–Tue & Thur 9:00–4:00, Tue
   7:00 P.M.–9:00 P.M., Wed 1:00–4:00
$10.00 per year membership; research:

donation

Pelham Historical Society
(373 Amherst Road, Pelham, MA
01002—location)
40 South Valley Road (mailing address)
Amherst, MA 01002
(413) 253-3970 (President); (413) 253-7647
(Genealogist); (413) 253-2739
(Genealogy)
Elva Anderson, President; Robert Lord
Keyes, Genealogist
Museum: Sun (May–Sept) 1:30–4:30
Pub. *Newsletter*, annually
(Pelham and Prescott, Massachusetts; Shays'
Rebellion, 1786–1787)
$5.00 per year membership; queries free, but
would like to trade information if possible

Pembroke Historical Society, Inc.
Center Street
Pembroke, MA 02359
(781) 293-9083

Petersham Historical Society, Inc.
PO Box 364
Petersham, MA 01366-0364
James Baird, President
Library: by appointment
("We are involved in a major reorganization
and are open to the public only
occasionally. Completion aimed at
2004—the 250th anniversary of the
founder of the town." Daniel Shays; local
history and families.)
$10.00 per year membership

The Plainfield Historical Society, Inc.
344 Main Street
Plainfield, MA 01070
(413) 634-5417 (President)
Arvilla L. Dyer, President
Museum: by appointment

Princeton Historical Society
PO Box 199
Princeton, MA 01541-0199
Katherine L. Poor, President
(archival room at the Princeton Public
Library)

Quincy Historical Society
Adams Academy Building
8 Adams Street
Quincy, MA 02169
(617) 328-3480; (617) 472-4990 FAX
Edward Fitzgerald
Library: Mon & Wed 9:00–noon, Fri
1:00–4:00
Pub. *Quincy History*
$20.00 per year membership

Ramapogue Historical Society
(70 Park Street, West Springfield, MA
01089—location)
PO Box 826 (mailing address)
West Springfield, MA 01090
(413) 732-8049
Emily W. Delaney, Curator
Sat–Sun (mid-June to mid-Oct) 1:00–5:00

Reading Antiquarian Society
(Parker Tavern, 103 Washington
Street—location)
PO Box 842 (mailing address)
Reading, MA 01867
(781) 944-4030
Eleanor Dustin, President
Sun (May–Oct) 2:00–5:00
(local history)

Rehoboth Antiquarian Society

(Bay State Road—location)
PO Box 2 (mailing address)
Rehoboth, MA 02769

Roslindale Historical Society
PO Box 356
Boston, MA 02131
Sandra MacKinnon, President

Rowe Historical Society, Inc.
Kemp-McCarthy Memorial Museum
(282 Zoar Road, Rowe, MA 01367-
9774—location)
288 Zoar Road (mailing address)
Rowe, MA 01367-9774
(413) 339-4238
Alan W. Bjork, Museum Curator
Museum: first Sun of July until the third Sun
in Oct: 2:00–5:00; Oct–June: by
appointment
Pub. *The Bulletin*, three times per year; *Rowe
Massachusetts Yearbook*, annually
$5.00 per year membership

Rowley Historical Society
233 Main Street
Rowley, MA 01969
(978) 948-3381

Roxbury Historical Society, Inc.
Dillaway-Thomas House at Roxbury
Heritage State Park
(183 Roxbury Street, John Eliot
Square—location)
Dudley Station, PO Box 5 (mailing address)
Roxbury, MA 02119
(617) 445-3399; (617) 445-3397
Renita L. Martin, Program Coordinator
Wed–Fri 10:00–4:00, Sat–Sun noon–5:00
Pub. *The Roxbury Heritage News*

Royalston Historical Society
(The Common, Royalston, MA
01368—location)
Fernald Road (mailing address)
South Royalston, MA 01331
(978) 249-4964

**Village Improvement and Historical
Society of Royalston, Inc.**
Society Building
Royalston, MA 01368
(978) 249-2598; (978) 249-2018
Haines J. Kirkman, President; Patricia C.
Poor, Curator

Rumford Historical Association
90 Elm Street North
Woburn, MA 01801
(617) 933-0781

Sandisfield Historical Society
SR 66, Box 96
Sandisfield, MA 01255
second Sat 10:00

Sandwich Historical Society, Inc.
Sandwich Glass Museum
(129 Main Street—location)
PO Box 103 (mailing address)
Sandwich, MA 02563-0103
(508) 888-0251; (508) 888-4941 FAX
sgm@capecod.net
http://sandwichglassmuseum.org
Nezka Pfeifer, Curator
Feb–Mar: Wed–Sun 9:30–4:00; Apr–Dec:
Mon–Sun 9:30–5:00
Pub. *The Acorn*, annually (scholarly); *Cullet*,
two times per year
$20.00 per year membership; copies: 10¢ per
page

**Sandy Bay Historical Society and
Museums, Inc.**
(40 King Street—location)
PO Box 63 (mailing address)
Rockport, MA 01966
(978) 546-9533
Cynthia A. Peckham, Curator
Mon 9:00–1:00; mid-June to mid-Sept:
Tue–Sat 2:00–5:00, and by appointment
(local history and genealogy)
$10.00 per year membership; admission:
$3.00 for nonmembers; research by staff:
small fee

**Historical Society of Santuit and Cotuit,
Inc.**
(1148 Main Street—location)
PO Box 1484 (mailing address)
Cotuit, MA 02635-1484
(508) 428-3895; (508) 428-8008
William G. Morse, Jr., Treasurer
Thur & Sun 4:00–6:00 (last Sun in
June–Labor Day)
(part of town of Barnstable)

The Saugus Historical Society, Inc.
(59 Water Street, Saugus, MA
01906—location)
21 Lovell Road (mailing address)
Lynnfield, MA 01940
(781) 233-1191

Scituate Historical Society
PO Box 276
Scituate, MA 02066
(781) 545-1083
Pub. *Scituate Historical Society Bulletin*,
semiannually
$5.00 per year membership

Sharon Historical Society
30 Crest Road
Sharon, MA 02067
(781) 784-5137
Irving Post

Sheffield Historical Society
(161 Main Street—location)
PO Box 747 (mailing address)
Sheffield, MA 01257-0747
(413) 229-2694
mdrc@sheffieldhistory.org
http://www.sheffieldhistory.org
James Miller, Archivist
Mon & Fri 1:30–4:00, and by appointment
("History and genealogy for Sheffield and
surrounding towns in Berkshire County
and states of Connecticut and New York")
$20.00 per year membership; research:
donation for postage and copies

Shelburne Historical Society, Inc.
(33 Severance Street—location)
PO Box 86 (mailing address)
Shelburne, MA 01370
(413) 625-6150
Pub. *Mount Massaemet Shadows*, quarterly

Sherborn Historical Society
(Room in Town Offices Building, 19
Washington Street, Route 16—location)
PO Box 186 (mailing address)
Sherborn, MA 01770-0186
(508) 651-7850 (Selectmen's Office, for
messages)
Elizabeth Johnson, Curator; Faith Tiberio,
President
Mon 10:00–2:00, and by appointment
(Sherborn history, families, artifacts)
$7.50 per year membership; research:
donation plus copy costs

Shirley Historical Society
PO Box 217
Shirley, MA 01464
(978) 425-9328; (978) 425-4513
Meredith Marcinkewicz, Curator
Sat 10:00–1:00, and by appointment
(with special collections on MacKaye family
    and Shirley Shaker community)
$5.00 per year membership; copies: 25¢ per
    page

Shrewsbury Historical Society
Church Street
Shrewsbury, MA 01545

Sippicorn Historical Society
PO Box 541
Marion, MA 02738
Ellen Stone
Wed & Sat 11:30–5:00 (closed in the winter)
(local history)
$10.00 per year membership

Somerville Historical Society
Somerville Historical Museum
1 Westwood Road
Somerville, MA 02143
(617) 666-9810
Constance B. Fuller, Director, Museum
    Services

South Gardner Historical Society
55 Union Street
Gardner, MA 01440
(978) 632-5118
Warren M. Sinclair, President

Sterling Historical Society, Inc.
(7 Pine Street—location)
PO Box 356 (mailing address)
Sterling, MA 01564
Ruth M. Hopfmann, Curator
Tue 9:00–1:00, and by appointment with
    Curator
Pub. *SHS Newsletter*, quarterly
donation requested

Stoneham Historical Society, Inc.
36 William Street
Stoneham, MA 02180-3845
(781) 438-4185 or (781) 438-4542
Mary K. Marchant, Curator; Joanne B.
    Harriman, President
by appointment
Pub. *Stoneham Historical Society*, two times
    per year
research: voluntary contribution

Stoughton Historical Society
Lucius Clapp Memorial, Stoughton Center
(6 Park Street—location)
PO Box 542 (mailing address)
Stoughton, MA 02072
(781) 344-5456
Tue 2:00–4:00, Thur 7:00–9:00, and by
    appointment
Pub. *Stoughton Historical Society
    Newsletter*, five times per year
$10.00 per year membership

Stow Historical Society
PO Box 261
Stow, MA 01775
(978) 897-5996
Barbara P. Sipler, President
by appointment
(files on Gardner, Randall; local history)

Sudbury Historical Society
Loring Parsonage
(Old Sudbury Road—location)
PO Box 233 (mailing address)

Sudbury, MA 01776
(978) 443-6672
Hilda A. Whitney, Clerk

Sutton Historical Society, Inc.
4 Uxbridge Road
Sutton, MA 01590
(508) 865-2635
Janice Swindell, President
Pub. *Bulletin*

Swampscott Historical Society
99 Paradise Road
Swampscott, MA 01907
(781) 594-1297
Joseph J. Balsama, President
by appointment
$15.00 per year membership

Swansea Historical Society, Inc.
(Old Warren Road—location)
PO Box 723 (mailing address)
Swansea, MA 02777
(508) 379-0972
Carl Becker, President
Sun (July–Aug) 2:00–5:00

Swift River Valley Historical Society, Inc.
(40 Elm Street, North New Salem—location)
PO Box 22 (mailing address)
New Salem, MA 01355
(978) 544-6885; (978) 544-6207 (President)
Elizabeth L. Peirce, Curator-President
Museum: Wed (June–Aug) & Sun
    (June–Columbus Day) 1:00–4:00, and by
    appointment
Pub. untitled newsletter, three times per year
(museum created to remember the towns of
    Dana, Greenwich, Enfield, Prescott, and
    part of New Salem, which were destroyed
    to create Quabbin Reservoir)
$5.00 per year membership; research:
    donation appreciated

Topsfield Historical Society
(1 Howlett Street—location)
PO Box 323 (mailing address)
Topsfield, MA 01983-0523
(978) 887-3998
http://www.tiac.net/users/topshist/
    homepage.htm
Norman J. Isler, President
Wed, Fri & Sun (10 June–mid-Sept)
    afternoons
Pub. *Newsletter*, four times per year (with
    historical items of local interest)
(Old Topsfield families)
$15.00 per year membership

Truro Historical Society
Truro Historical Museum
(Lighthouse Road, North Truro, MA
    02652—museum location)
PO Box 486 (mailing address)
Truro, MA 02666
(508) 497-3397 (summer); (508) 349-2809
    (winter)
Elizabeth J. Allen, Curator
15 June–15 Sept: Mon–Sun 10:00–5:00
Pub. *News Letter*, annually
(materials on families Coan, Lombard, Rich,
    Snow, etc.)
$7.50 per year membership; museum or
    archives admission: $2.00

Upton Historical Society
PO Box 171
Upton, MA 01568
(508) 529-6200
Ashley Perkins, President; Carol Blomquist,
    House Committee Chairman
Building, Second Floor Rooms: Wed

9:00–noon; meetings: last Fri
Pub. *Newsletter*, monthly
$5.00 per year membership

Wakefield Historical Society
American Civic Center
467 Main Street
Wakefield, MA 01880
(781) 245-0549

Walpole Historical Society
(33 West Street—location)
PO Box 1724 (mailing address)
Walpole, MA 02081
(508) 668-0449 (Secretary)
Karl West, Secretary
by appointment
(some local histories and genealogies)
$5.00 per year membership

Waltham Historical Society
190 Moody Street
Waltham, MA 02453-5300
(617) 891-5815
http://www.walthamhistorical society.org
Joan Sheridan, President
by appointment only; meetings usually at
    Waltham Public Library or the Robert
    Treat Paine Estate or Gore Place: third
    Tue (Sept & May), third Sun (Nov &
    Mar)
$10.00 per year membership

Wareham Historical Society, Inc.
(8 Elm Street—location)
PO Box 211 (mailing address)
Wareham, MA 02571
(508) 295-3227
Betty Wright, Curator
July–Aug: Thur–Sun 1:00–4:00

Warwick Historical Society
(Morse Building, Athol Road, Warwick
    Center—location)
625 Winchester Road (mailing address)
Warwick, MA 01378
(413) 544-3461
Charles A. Phelps, President and
    Director/Curator)
by appointment

The Historical Society of Watertown
Edmund Fowle House
28 Marshall Street
Watertown, MA 02472
(617) 923-6067
Sigrid Reddy Watson, President
Mon–Fri 10:00–2:00
Pub. *The Town Crier*, quarterly, $6.00 per
    year subscription
$15.00 per year membership; searches by
    time spent

Wayland Historical Society
PO Box 56
Wayland, MA 01778
(508) 358-7959
John B. Wilson, President
Pub. *WHS Newsletter*

Webster Dudley Historical Society
(School Street—location)
43 Union Count Road (mailing address)
Webster, MA 01570
(508) 943-1965
Bertha A. Hart, President

Wellesley Historical Society
(229 Washington Street—location)
PO Box 81142 (mailing address)
Wellesley Hills, MA 02181
(781) 235-6690

Barbara Gorely Teller, Director/Curator
Library: Mon & Sat 2:00–4:30
Pub. *WHS Newsletter*
(Civil War books)
$15.00 per year membership

The Wellfleet Historical Society Museum
(Main Street—location)
PO Box 58 (mailing address)
Wellfleet, MA 02667
(508) 349-9157
Joan Hopkins Coughlin, Curator
Tue–Sat (late June–Aug) 2:00–5:00
Pub. *Beacon*, annually
$3.50 per year membership; $1.00 admission
   to museum (over 12 years of age)

**Wenham Historical Association and
Museum, Inc.**
132 Main Street
Wenham, MA 01984
(978) 468-2377; (978) 468-1763 FAX
thauck@wenhammuseum.org
http://www.wenhammuseum.org
Marilyn Corning, Librarian; Thomas Hauck,
   Development Director
Mon–Fri 10:00–4:00, Sat–Sun 1:00–4:00
Pub. *Wenham Museum Newsletter*,
   bimonthly; *Annual Report* (Apr/May)
(Wenham history, dolls, dolls' houses, model
   railroads; local genealogy in research
   library, papers on early Wenham, ice
   trade)
$30.00 per year membership

West Boylston Historical Society, Inc.
(65 Worcester Street—location)
PO Box 201 (mailing address)
West Boylston, MA 01583
(508) 835-6971
Gwen Soule, President and Curator
Mon & Thur 9:30–noon
Pub. *Old Stone News*, two times per year
   (Feb, Sept)
$10.00 per year membership

West Brookfield Historical Commission
Town Hall
Main Street
West Brookfield, MA 01585
(508) 867-2006; (508) 867-6011
(collection of manuscripts and unpublished
   genealogies, published histories, some
   church histories, First Precinct Parish
   Records from 1754 to 1826, many town
   reports and valuation and taxes books)

West Newbury Historical Association
PO Box 332
West Newbury, MA 01985
(978) 465-8046
Beatrice Downey, President

West Roxbury Historical Society
1961 Centre Street
Boston, MA 02132
(617) 325-3147
Daniel Cantwell
winter: Sat 9:00–5:00; summer: Mon & Thur
   noon–8:00, Tue, Wed & Fri 9:00–5:00

**Westborough Historical Society (and
Archives)**
(13 Parkman Street—location)
PO Box 149 (mailing address)
Westborough, MA 01581-1911
(508) 898-0975; (508) 366-2351 (Curator's
   home)
Kenneth Housman, President
third Thur
Pub. *Newsletter*, monthly
(maps, letters, wills, deeds, etc., of residents

and business/industry from 1717;
   birthplace of Eli Whitney)
$15.00 per year membership; research:
   hourly fee plus cost of copies to
   Jacqueline C. Tidman, Curator

Western Hampden Historical Society
Dewey House
PO Box 256
Westfield, MA 01086
(413) 562-3657
Barbara Bush, Chairperson, Board of
   Trustees

Westford Historical Society, Inc.
(2 Boston Road—location)
PO Box 411 (mailing address)
Westford, MA 01886
(978) 692-5550
http://www.westford.com/museum
Kenneth Tebbetts, President; Marilyn Day,
   Director
Office: Mon, Wed & Fri 9:00–1:00;
   Museum: Sun 2:00–4:00 (except major
   holiday weekends), and by appointment
Pub. *Museum Museings*, quarterly
("We publish an historic Westford calendar
   annually and have many publications
   available for sale in our store. We feature
   a collection of town artifacts, genealogies
   of early families, special exhibits.")
$25.00 per year membership

Westminster Historical Society
(Forbush Memorial Library, 110 Main
Street—museum location)
PO Box 177 (mailing address)
Westminster, MA 01473
(978) 874-5569
Liz Maillet, Administrator
Mon 7:00–9:00, Wed 6:00–8:00, Fri
   9:00–noon
Pub. *Newsletter*, four times per year
(artifacts and documents pertaining to the
   history of Westminster; General Nelson
   A. Miles)
$20.00 per year membership

Weston Historical Society
PO Box 343
Weston, MA 02193
(781) 237-1447 (Curator's home); (781)
   237-1471 (Curator's home) FAX; (781)
   891-4662 (President)
Dr. Vera Laska, Curator; William Martin,
   President
Wed 10:00–noon, and by appointment
Pub. *Bulletin*, two times per year (spring and
   fall)
$10.00 per year membership

Westport Historical Society, Inc.
(25 Drift Road—location)
PO Box 3031 (mailing address)
Westport, MA 02790-0700
(508) 636-6011
Lincoln S. Tripp, Director
Tue–Wed 9:00–noon & 1:00–4:00, and by
   appointment
Pub. *The Harbinger*, bimonthly
$10.00 per year membership; research:
   donation from nonmembers

Weymouth Historical Society
PO Box 56
Weymouth, MA 02190
Candace A. Wright, President

Winchendon Historical Society, Inc.
151 Front Street
Winchendon, MA 01475
(978) 297-0300 (Library)

Julia White, Co-curator
Tue evening (July–Aug)
$10.00 per year membership

Winchester Historical Society
PO Box 127
Winchester, MA 01890
(781) 721-7146
Mrs. Robert Bairnsfather, Chair of
   Genealogy Group
hours: various (call first)
Pub. *Black Horse Bulletin*, quarterly
$15.00 per year membership

Worthington Historical Society
(6 Williamsburg Road—location)
PO Box 12 (mailing address)
Worthington, MA 01098
(413) 238-5363
Edward Claydon, President
hours: various
$5.00 per year membership

Wrentham Historical Society
PO Box 300
Wrentham, MA 02093
(508) 384-7151
Jean Nall, President
Pub. *Newsletter*, about every five weeks
(vital statistics 1673–1930, with few
   exceptions)
$10.00 per year membership

Genealogical Societies

State Genealogical Societies

Massachusetts Genealogical Council
PO Box 5393
Cochituate, MA 01778
Gratia Mahony, Secretary
Pub. *MGC Newsletter*, quarterly
$7.50 per year membership

**The Massachusetts Society of
Genealogists, Inc. (M.S.O.G.)**
PO Box 215
Ashland, MA 01721-0215
(508) 792-5066
Katherine A. Gardner-Westcott, Librarian
Wed 11:00–3:00, Sat 10:00–4:00 (subject to
   change)
Pub. *MASSOG: A Genealogical Magazine
   for the Commonwealth of Massachusetts*,
   quarterly
$19.00 per year membership; queries free to
   members, $2.00 to nonmembers; research:
   $6.00 per hour (half-hour minimum) for
   members, $10.00 per hour for
   nonmembers, plus copies at 15-25¢ each,
   to be billed by Sylvia I. Bockstein,
   Research Coordinator, 172 Jackson Street,
   Jefferson, MA 01522-1469 or Research
   Committee, c/o MSOG Library

M.S.O.G. Chapters

Bristol County Chapter (M.S.O.G.)
(address withheld upon request)
all queries should be sent to the parent
   organization

Hampden Chapter (M.S.O.G.)
6 Ridgewood Road
Wilbraham, MA 01095
Roy Powers
Pub. *Hampden Chapter Newsletter*, monthly

Worcester Chapter (M.S.O.G.)
27 Brigham Hill Road
Grafton, MA 01519
Mary Ann Hall

Genealogical Societies—Local & Regional

Berkshire Family History Association
PO Box 1437
Pittsfield, MA 01201-1437
(413) 445-5521; (413) 623-5267
Donald L. Lutes, Jr., President
Berkshire Athenaeum: winter (Sept to June)
    Mon–Thur 9:00–9:00, Fri 9:00–5:00, Sat
    10:00–5:00; summer (July–Aug): Mon,
    Wed & Fri 9:00–5:00, Tue & Thur
    9:00–9:00, Sat 10:00–5:00
Pub. *Berkshire Genealogist*, quarterly
(western Massachusetts, Berkshire County
    and nearby)
$12.00 per year membership

Cape Cod Genealogical Society
PO Box 1394
Harwich, MA 01645
webmaster@capecodgensoc.org
http://www.capecodgensoc.org
meetings at the Brewster Ladies' Library
    Auditorium, 1822 Main Street, Brewster,
    MA; second Wed 10:00
Pub. *Cape Cod Genealogical Society
    Bulletin*, quarterly
(Cape Cod and Massachusetts genealogy)
$25.00 per year membership

**Central Massachusetts Genealogical
Society, Inc.**
(American Legion Post 129, Elm Street,
Gardner, MA 01440—location)
PO Box 811 (mailing address)
Westminster, MA 01473-0811
(978) 345-2459 (President)
president@cmgs-inc.org
http://cmgs-inc.org/index.html
Debra Esposito, President
fourth Tue (Jan–Nov) 7:00–9:00
Pub. *The Searchers*, bimonthly
$12.00 per year membership

Essex Society of Genealogists, Inc.
PO Box 313
Lynnfield, MA 01940-0313
(781) 664-9279
bobstone@tiac.net
http://www.esog.org
Virginia Basken, Secretary
Pub. *The Essex Genealogist* (*TEG*), quarterly
    (Feb, May, Aug, Nov), $4.50 per issue;
    The Newsletter of the ESOG, quarterly
    (Mar, June, Sept, Dec)
(Essex County, Massachusetts, also all
    eastern Massachusetts, New England, and
    the Maritime Provinces of Canada)
$22.00 per year membership (includes both
    publications)

Falmouth Genealogical Society
PO Box 2107
Teaticket, MA 02536
elizabeth65@verizon.net
http://www.falgen.org
Betty Dayton, Secretary
meetings at the Falmouth Public Library:
    second Sat 9:30
Pub. newsletter, bimonthly
$15.00 per year membership

Genealogical Roundtable
PO Box 654
Concord, MA 01742-0654
Connie T. Dearborn, President
meetings at Concord Free Public Library:
    fourth Mon (except June–Aug & Dec)
    1:00
Pub. *aROUNDtheTABLE*
(genealogy, history and literature)
$15.00 per year membership

Institute of Family History and Genealogy
99 Ash Street
New Bedford, MA 02740

**The New England Historic Genealogical
Society (NEHGS)**
101 Newbury Street
Boston, MA 02116-3007
(617) 536-5740; (888) 296-3447; (617) 536-
    7307 FAX
nehgs@nehgs.org
http://www.NewEnglandAncestors.org
Lynn Betlock, Marketing Director
Tue & Fri–Sat 9:00–5:00 (closed Sat before
    Mon holiday), Wed–Thur 9:00–9:00;
    check for winter schedule, Dec–Mar
Pub. *The New England Historical and
    Genealogical Register*, quarterly; *New
    England Ancestors*, five times per year;
    Great Migration Newsletter, quarterly,
    $10.00 per year online subscription for
    NEHGS members
("The country's oldest and largest
    genealogical society, NEHGS is a national
    center for local and family history. The
    primary focus is on New England and
    eastern Canadian genealogy and history,
    with an emphasis on countries and regions
    New Englanders migrated from and to.")
$60.00 per year membership (includes
    Register only); in-depth research: $40.00
    per hour for members, $60.00 per hour for
    nonmembers (maximum 5 hours per
    order); copies: $5.00 for members, $10.00
    for nonmembers, plus 35¢ per page and
    $3.50 s&h (maximum 35 copies per
    order); personal consultations: $50.00 per
    hour

**New York Genealogical and Biographical
Society Library**
(see New York, Part 2)

**Palm Beach County Genealogical Society,
Inc.**
(see Florida, Part 2)

Plymouth County Genealogists, Inc.
PO Box 7025
Brockton, MA 02301-7025
(508) 583-6106
nemens@comcast.net
http://www.rootsweb.com/~maplymou/
    pcgs/pcgsmain.htm
James E. Hoban, President; Nat Emens
first Sat (Sept–June) 1:00
Pub. *The Genealogical Inquirer*, ten times
    per year (monthly, except July–Aug)
(Plymouth County research only, not the
    entire state of Massachusetts)
$15.00 per year membership

The South Shore Genealogical Society
PO Box 396
Norwell, MA 02061-0396
John C. Murray, President
Mon–Sat 10:00–5:00; meetings: second Sat
    (Sept–June)
Pub. *Newsletter*, bimonthly
(research New England, the Midwest, Nova
    Scotia, maintains surname file)
$10.00 per year membership; accepts
    inquiries

**Western Massachusetts Genealogical
Society, Inc.**
PO Box 80206, Forest Park Station
Springfield, MA 01138-0206
roxie@map.com
http://www.rootsweb/~mawmgs
Dorothy Hauschild, President
meetings at Connecticut Valley Historical

Museum: first Wed (Sept–Nov &
    Mar–June) 5:00–9:00
Pub. *The American Elm*, quarterly
$15.00 per year membership

Yankee Genealogical Society
Minnesota Genealogical Society
5768 Olson Memorial Highway
Golden Valley, MN 55422
(763) 823-3412
mgsdec@mtn.org
http://www.mtn.org/mgs/yankee.html
Betty Schoon; Stephanie Martineau
Pub. *Newsletter*, quarterly
("to assist members in tracing their heritage
    in the states of Maine, New Hampshire,
    Vermont, Massachusetts, Connecticut,
    Rhode Island, New York, New Jersey,
    Pennsylvannia and Delaware")
$7.00 per year membership

Independent Publications and Miscellany

America's Homepage
http://pilgrims.net/plymouth
(genealogical and historical links)

**Ancient Free and Accepted Masons
Library**
Grand Lodge of Massachusetts
186 Tremont Street (corner of Boylston
    Street)
Boston, MA 02111
(617) 426-6040, ext. 131
Roberta A. Hankamer, Library Director
Mon–Fri 9:00–5:00; Sept–June: Thur
    9:00–7:00 also
(emphasis on freemasonry, especially in
    Massachusetts)

Archive Publishing
4 Mayfair Circle
Oxford, MA 01540-2722
(508) 987-0881
DeLene Holbrook, Owner
(New England original records, mostly on
    fiche, with current emphasis on
    Massachusetts, including original
    Massachusetts vital records, 1620–1905,
    for over 250 cities and towns; transcripts
    to 1850 for 179 towns)

Bartlett Museum
PO Box 692
Amesbury, MA 01913-0016
(978) 388-4528; (978) 388-1879
Evelyn Woodman, Secretary
Tue–Sun 1:00–5:00 (June–Oct)

Belmont Historic District Commission
Town Hall
Belmont, MA 02178
(781) 484-1084
Lynda P. Ogilby, Chairperson
(primarily historical, not genealogical)

The Berkshire Museum
39 South Street
Pittsfield, MA 01201
(413) 443-7171
Gary Burger, Director
Tue–Sat 10:00–5:00, Sun 1:00–5:00; Mon
    10:00–5:00 (July–Aug)

Blue Hill Adventure and Quarry Museum
29 Westwood Terrace
Westwood, MA 02090
(781) 326-0079 (B.H.A. 24-hour hot line
    information); (781) 326-2543
David P. Hodgdon, President, Executive

Director and Quarry Museum Curator activities on weekends and holidays, and by appointment
Pub. *Your Blue Hill Reservation*, $3.25 postpaid
(preservation of historical resources, "historic and recreation")

Colonial Massachusetts and Maine Genealogies
anderson207@earthlink.net
http://home.earthlink.net/~anderson207
G. Robert Anderson

Colonial Society of Massachusetts
87 Mount Vernon Street
Boston, MA 02108
(617) 227-2782
info@colonialsociety.org
http://www.colonialsociety.org
John W. Tyler, Editor of Publications
hours: various
Pub. *Publications of the Colonial Society of Massachusetts*, annually, priced from $35.00–$85.00 each
(promotes study of Massachusetts history and publishes documents and records, but maintains no library or collection, membership is by nomination)

Committee for a New England Bibliography, Inc.
233 Bay State Road
Boston, MA 02215
(617) 266-9706

Concord Antiquarian Museum
(200 Lexington Road—location)
PO Box 146 (mailing address)
Concord, MA 01742
(978) 369-9609
Dennis Fiori, Director
Mon–Sat 10:00–4:30, Sun 1:00–4:30

Fruitlands Museums, Inc.
Four Museums of American Art and History
102 Prospect Hill Road
Harvard, MA 01451
(978) 456-3924
Robert S. Farwell, Director; Michael Volmar, Curator
Library: Tue–Sun 10:00–5:00, and by appointment
Pub. *Mulberry Tree*, quarterly
(transcendentalism, Shaker, American Indian, 19th-century portraiture of the Hudson River School)
$40.00 per year membership

Hammond Castle Museum, Inc.
80 Hesperus Avenue
Gloucester, MA 01930
(978) 283-2080

Heritage Museums and Gardens
67 Grove Street
Sandwich, MA 02563
(508) 888-3300, ext. (History Museum)
info@heritagemuseums.org
http://www.heritagemuseumsandgardens.org

Historic Salem, Inc.
(Old Town Hall, Derby Square—location)
PO Box 865 (mailing address)
Salem, MA 01970
(978) 745-6470

Historical Ink's Old Maps
(see New York, Part 2)

Institute for Boston Studies
Boston College

140 Commonwealth Avenue
Chestnut Hill, MA 02167
(617) 552-8458
Sharlene Voogd Cochrane, Director
Resource Center: by appointment during school year

Institute for Massachusetts Studies
Westfield State College
Western Avenue
Westfield, MA 01086
(413) 572-5344
Martin Kaufman, Ph.D., Editorial Director
9:00–4:00
Pub. *Historical Journal of Massachusetts*, semiannually (winter & summer), $7.00 per year subscription
(history of Massachusetts)

John F. Kennedy National Historic Site
83 Beals Street
Brookline, MA 02146
(617) 566-7937; (617) 730-9884 FAX
http://www.nps.gov/jofi
Christine Arato, Supervisory Park Ranger; Janice Hodson, Senior Staff Curator
May–Oct: Wed–Sun 10:00–4:30
("Public house museum. Refer all research requests to Ms. Hodson.")

John Fitzgerald Kennedy Library and Museum
Columbia Point on Dorchester Bay
Boston, MA 02125-3398
(617) 929-4500; (877) 616-4599; (617) 929-4538 FAX
kennedy.library@nara.gov
http://www.jfklibrary.org
Frank Rigg
Library: Mon–Fri 9:00–5:00
(primarily historical, not genealogical)

Little Red Schoolhouse Association, Inc.
(Concord Avenue, Brockton, MA 02401—location)
PO Box 3036 (mailing address)
Brockton, MA 02404-3036
(508) 559-8871
Sal Madonna, Clerk
seasonal
Pub. *Newsletter*, quarterly
$5.00 per year membership

Longyear Museum
(see Religious Archives and Organizations—Christian Science, Part 3)

MaGenWeb
Part of The USGenweb Project
George@Waller.Org
http://www.rootsweb.com/~magenweb
George Waller, Coordinator
(links to other Massachusetts resources)

Massachusetts Geographic Information System (MassGIS)
251 Causeway Street, Suite 900
Boston, MA 02114
(617) 626-1057; (617) 626-1249 FAX
http://www.state.ma.us:80/mgis/order.htm

Massachusetts Historical Commission
Secretary of State's Office
220 Morrissey Boulevard (Columbia Point)
Boston, MA 02125-3314
(617) 727-8470; (617) 727-5128 FAX
mhc@sec.state.ma.us
http://www.state.ma.us/sec/mhc
Valerie A. Talmage, Executive Director
(primarily site preservation)

Microform Books

4 Mayfair Circle
Oxford, MA 01540-2722
(508) 987-0881
Jay M. Holbrook, Owner
(fiches of old printed records; Mayflower Descendant, Massachusetts vital records to 1850 for 210 towns)

Middlesex Canal Association
(Middlesex Canal Museum-Visitor Center, 71 Faulkner Street, North Billerica, MA 01862—location)
PO Box 333 (mailing address)
Billerica, MA 01821
(603) 672-7051 (New Hampshire); (978) 670-2740 (Museum)
Nolan Jones, President
Visitor Center: Apr–Sept: noon–4:00
Pub. *Towpath Topics*, biannually
(primarily historical, not genealogical)

New England Connexion
(see Connecticut, Part 2)
The New England Quarterly
Meserve Hall 243
Northeastern University
Boston, MA 02115
(617) 373-4445; (617) 373-2661 FAX
Professor William M. Fowler, Jr., Editor
Pub. *The New England Quarterly*, $25.00 per year subscription
(one of America's oldest scholarly journals, focuses on New England's history and literature)

Old South Meeting House
(address withheld upon request)
(limited amount of material on members of the Third Church [Congregational] in Boston, 1669–1870)

Pioneer Publications
New England Queries and Reviews
(see Connecticut, Part 2)

Society for the Preservation of New England Antiquities—Archives
Harrison Gray Otis House
141 Cambridge Street
Boston, MA 02114
(617) 227-3956
Ellie Reichlin; Lorne Condon
Tue–Fri 9:30–5:00 by appointment only
Pub. *SPNEA News*

Tales of Cape Cod, Inc.
(3046 Main Street—location)
PO Box 41 (mailing address)
Barnstable, MA 02630
Mrs. Gene D. Gardner, President
(produces historical publications, summer lecture series, weekly cable T.V. historic program; maintains pre-Revolutionary courthouse)
$15.00 per year membership

Wenham Historic District Commission
(Town Hall, Main Street—location)
PO Box 01984 (mailing address)
Wenham, MA 01984
(978) 468-4468
Harold W. Boothroyd, Chairman
(primarily historical, not genealogical)

Michigan

Archives and Libraries with Holdings in Genealogy

State Archives and Library
State Archives of Michigan
Michigan Historical Center
Department of History, Arts and Libraries
(702 West Kalamazoo Street—location)
PO Box 30740 (mailing address)
Lansing, MI 48909-8240
(517) 373-1408; (517) 241-1658 FAX
archives@michigan.gov
http://www.michiganhistory.org
Reference Desk
Mon–Fri 10:00–4:00

Library of Michigan
Michigan and Genealogy Special Collection
(717 West Allegan Street—location)
PO Box 30007 (mailing address)
Lansing, MI 48909-7507
(517) 373-1300
http://www.michigan.gov/hal
Mon–Fri 8:00–6:00, Sat 9:00–5:00, Sun
    1:00–5:00

State Historical Societies

Michigan Historical Commission
505 State Office Building
Lansing, MI 48913

Historical Society of Michigan
2117 Washtenaw Avenue
Ann Arbor, MI 48104
(734) 769-1828; (313) 769-4267 FAX
Thomas L. Jones, Executive Director
Mon–Fri 9:00–5:00
Pub. *Chronicle*, quarterly; *HSM Newsletter*,
    bimonthly; *Michigan Historical Review*,
    semiannually
("Center for teaching Michigan history;
    conferences, books, publications, no
    archives but small library for teachers.")
$25.00 per year membership

City, County and Regional Archives and Libraries
(A more exhaustive list of public and
academic libraries can be found at http://
mel.lib.mi.us/government/GOV-librarylist.
html, http://www.publiclibraries.com/
michigan.htm, or http://www.mla.lib.mi.us/
links/institmem.html.)

Adrian Public Library
143 East Maumee Street
Adrian, MI 49221
(517) 265-2265; (517) 265-8847 FAX
adrian@monroe.lib.mi.us
http://woodlands.lib.mi.us/adrian/adrian.htm
Jule J. Fosbender, Director
Mon–Tue & Thur 10:00–9:00, Wed & Fri
    10:00–5:30, Sat 9:30–5:30
(Adrian and Lenawee County)

Albion College Archives
(see The West Michigan Conference
Archives of the United Methodist Church,
Religious Archives and
Organizations—United Methodist, Part 3)

Albion Public Library
501 South Superior Street
Albion, MI 49224
(517) 629-3993; (517) 629-5354 FAX
albion@monroe.lib.mi.us
http://www.albionlibrary.org
Karen Sherrard, Director

Mon–Thur 10:00–7:00, Sat–Sun 1:00–5:00

Alpena County George N. Fletcher Public Library
211 North First Street
Alpena, MI 49707
(989) 356-6188; (989) 356-2765 FAX
http://www.alpenalib.org
Mon–Thur 9:30–9:00, Fri–Sat 9:30–5:00,
    Sun (except summer) 1:00–5:00

Ann Arbor District Library
343 South Fifth Avenue
Ann Arbor, MI 48104-2293
(734) 327-4200; (734) 327-8309 FAX
parkerj@aadl.org
http://www.aadl.org
Josie Parker, Director
Mon 10:00–9:00, Tue–Fri 9:00–9:00, Sat
    9:00–6:00, Sun 1:00–5:00

Armada Free Public Library
73930 Church Street
Armada, MI 48005
(586) 784-5921; (586) 784-8640 FAX
armedit@libcoop.net
http://armadalib.org
Margaret Smith, Director

Bacon Memorial District Library
45 Vinewood
Wyandotte, MI 48192
(734) 246-8357; (734) 282-1540 FAX
whayden@tln.lib.mi.us
http://www.wyandotte.lib.mi.us
Wallace Hayden, Local History Librarian
Mon–Thur 10:00–9:00, Fri–Sat 10:00–5:00
(Downriver area genealogy and local history,
    southern suburbs of Detroit)
research: up to a half-hour of research for
    $5.00, but no more detailed research

Baldwin Public Library
(300 West Merrill Street, Birmingham, MI
48009—location)
PO Box 3002 (mailing address)
Birmingham, MI 48012-3002
(248) 647-1700; (248) 647-6393; (248) 644-
    7297 FAX
http://baldwinlib.org
Sarah Ormond, Adult Services Department
    Head
Mon–Thur 9:30–9:00, Fri–Sat 9:30–5:30,
    Sun noon–5:00

Bay County Library System
Bay City Branch Library
708 Center Avenue
Bay City, MI 48708-5989
(989) 893-9566; (989) 893-9799 FAX
bclshq@baycountylibrary.org;
    t.birch@vlc.lib.mi.us (Tom Birch,
    Managing Librarian)
http://www.baycountylibrary.org
Mary McManman, Head of Reference
    Services
Mon–Thur 9:00–9:00, Fri–Sat 9:00–5:00,
    Sun (Sept–May) 1:00–5:00
(Michigan and Bay County genealogy
    holdings for entire library system,
    including Sage and South Side branches)
cost of photocopies plus mailing

Benton Harbor Public Library
213 East Wall Street
Benton Harbor, MI 49022
(269) 926-6139
bhlibrary@yahoo.com
http://www.geocities.com/bhlibrary

Boyne District Library
201 East Main Street

Boyne City, MI 49712
(231) 582-7861; (231) 582-2998 FAX
boynec1@northland.lib.mi.us
http://nlc.lib.mi.us/members/boyne_c.htm
Nancy Fulkerson, Assistant Librarian;
    Nannette Miller, Director

Branch District Library
Central Branch, Headquarters
10 East Chicago Street
Coldwater, MI 49036
(517) 278-2341; (517) 279-7134 FAX
Director@brnlibrary.org;
    automation@brnlibrary.org
http://www.brnlibrary.org
Shirley Pascal
Mon 10:00–8:00, Tue–Wed & Fri 9:00–5:00,
    Thur 9:00–8:00, Sat 9:00–4:00

Branch District Library
Union Township Library
221 North Broadway
Union City, MI 49094
(517) 741-5061 voice & FAX
union@brnlibrary.org
http://www.brnlibrary.org
Patricia Kaniewski, Branch Manager
Tue 9:30–5:00, Wed 11:30–7:00, Fri
    9:30–4:30, Sat 9:00–noon

Cadillac-Wexford County Public Library
411 South Lake Street
Cadillac, MI 49601-0700
(231) 775-6541
http://mmll.org/cadwex.html
Sept–May: Mon–Thur 8:30–8:30, Fri–Sat
    8:30–5:30; June–Aug: Mon & Wed
    8:30–8:30, Tue & Thur–Fri 8:30–5:30,
    Sat 8:30–12:30

Cass District Library
Local History Branch
(145 North Broadway—location)
319 M-62 N (mailing address)
Cassopolis, MI 49031-1099
(269) 445-3400; (269) 445-0412 (Branch);
    (269) 445-8795 FAX
cass@cass.lib.mi.us
http://cass.lib.mi.us/clh.html
Amy Druskovich, Local History Librarian
Mon–Thur 9:00–4:00, Sat 10:00–2:00
Pub. *Book Notes: The Newsletter of the Cass
    District Library* (online)
(county history, genealogies of families in
    county)
searches done on a donation basis,
    photocopy fees charged

Central Michigan University Library
Clarke Historical Library
Mount Pleasant, MI 48858
(989) 774-3352; (989) 774-2160 FAX
http://www.lib.cmich.edu/clarke
Mon–Fri 8:00–5:00
Pub. *Clarke Historical Library Newsletter*,
    semiannually
free

Cheboygan Public Library
107 South Ball Street
Cheboygan, MI 49721
(231) 627-2381; (231) 627-9172 FAX
cheboy1@northland.lib.mi.us
http://nlc.lib.mi.us/members/cheboyga.htm
Sue Ver Wys, Library Director
Mon–Thur 10:00–8:00, Fri 10:00–5:00, Sat
    10:00–3:00

Clawson Historical Museum
(41 Fisher Court—location)
425 North Main (mailing address)
Clawson, MI 48017

(248) 588-9169

Clements Library Associates
The University of Michigan-Ann Arbor
William L. Clements Library
909 South University Avenue
Ann Arbor, MI 48109-1190
(734) 764-2347; (734) 647-0716 FAX
clements.library@umich.edu
http://clements.umich.edu/associates.html
Pub. *American Magazine and Historical Chronicle*, semiannually
(a research library for primary materials in early American history, no strictly genealogical references)

Comstock Township Library
(6130 King Highway—location)
PO Box 25 (mailing address)
Comstock, MI 49041
(616) 345-0136; (616) 345-0138 FAX
http://www.comstocktownshiplib.org
Mark Crum, Reference Librarian
Mon–Thur 10:00–9:00, Fri 10:00–6:00, Sat 10:00–4:00
("Modest holdings in Comstock history")

Cranbrook Archives
(1221 North Woodward Avenue—location)
PO Box 801 (mailing address)
Bloomfield Hills, MI 48303-0801
(248) 645-3581; (248) 645-3029
http://www. cranbrook.edu
Mark Coir, Director
Mon–Fri 8:00–5:00

Marguerite DeAngeli Branch Library
921 West Nepessing Street
Lapeer, MI 48446
(810) 664-6971; (810) 664-5581 FAX
http://www.library.lapeer.org/deAngeli/mdeangeli.htm
June Mendel, Assistant Director
Mon–Thur 9:00–9:00, Fri 9:00–5:00, Sat (winter) 9:00–5:00, Sat (summer) 9:00–2:00, Sun (winter) noon–5:00

Detroit Public Library
Burton Historical Collection
5201 Woodward Avenue
Detroit, MI 48202-4093
(313) 833-1480; (313) 832-0877 FAX
dporemba@detroit.lib.mi.us
http://www.detroit.lib.mi.us/burton
David Poremba, Manager; Noel VanGorden, Chief of the Burton Collection
Tue–Wed noon–8:00, Thur–Sat 10:00–6:00

Dickinson County Public Library
401 Iron Mountain Street
Iron Mountain, MI 49801
(906) 774-1218; (906) 774-4079 FAX
dcl@dcl-lib.org
http://www.dcl-lib.org
winter: Mon–Fri 9:00–9:00, Sat 9:00–5:00, Sun 1:00–4:00; summer: Mon–Fri 9:00–8:00, Sat 9:00–1:00

Grace A. Dow Memorial Library
1710 West Saint Andrews Drive
Midland, MI 48640-2698
(989) 837-3449 (Library Reference Desk); (989) 837-3430 (Library Office); (989) 837-3468 FAX
gadml@midland-mi.org; mbarnard@midland-mi.org
http://www.midland-mi.org/gracedowlibrary
Melissa Barnard, Director
Mon–Fri 10:00–9:00, Sat 10:00–5:00, Sun (winter) 1:00–5:00
(houses collection of the Midland Genealogical Society)

Ecorse Public Library
4184 West Jefferson Avenue
Ecorse, MI 48229
(313) 389-2030; (313) 389-2032 FAX
http://www.ecorse.lib.mi.us
winter: Mon–Tue & Thur 10:00–6:00, Wed 10:00–8:00, Fri 10:00–4:00; summer: Mon–Tue & Thur 10:00–6:00, Wed 10:00–8:00, Sat 10:00–4:00

Flint Public Library
1026 East Kearsley Street
Flint, MI 48502-1994
(810) 232-7111, ext. 253; (810) 232-8360 FAX
gcoles@flint.lib.mi.us
http://www.flint.lib.mi.us/fpl.html
Angie Wesch, Librarian; Gloria Coles, Director
Mon–Thur 9:00–9:00, Fri–Sat 9:00–6:00

Fort Saint Joseph Museum
City of Niles History Department
508 East Main Street
Niles, MI 49120
(616) 683-4702
Carol Bainbridge, Director
Wed–Sat 10:00–4:00

Galesburg Memorial Library
188 East Michigan
Galesburg, MI 49053-9501
(269) 665-7839; (269) 665-7788 FAX

http://envoy.libofmich.lib.mi.us/isapi/4disapi.dll/directory/LibraryDetail.html?ID=116
Donna Kowalewski, Director
Tue & Thur–Fri 10:30–4:30, Wed noon–8:00, Sat 10:00–2:00

Grand Rapids/Kent County Community Archives and Research Center
223 Washington Street, S.E.
Grand Rapids, MI 49503
http://www.communityarchive.org
Marilyn Merdzinski; Bill Cunningham
not yet fully operational, will be by 2005
("All municipal and county records, plus museum collections. This will be managed by museum [Public Museum of Grand Rapids] but run collaboratively. 145,000 sq. ft. of storage of historical collections.")

Grand Rapids Public Library
Michigan and Family History Department
60 Library Plaza, N.E.
Grand Rapids, MI 49503-3093
(616) 456-3640
rraz@grpl.org
http://www.grpl.org
Robert Raz, Library Director
Mon–Wed 9:00–9:00, Thur–Sat 9:00–5:30
research: $10.00 per hour for all written inquiries

Hackley Public Library
316 West Webster Avenue
Muskegon, MI 49440
(231) 722-7276, ext. 233; (231) 726-5567 FAX
mferriby@hackleylibrary.org
http://www.hackleylibrary.org
Marty Ferriby, Director
Sept–May: Tue–Wed 9:00–8:00, Thur 9:00–6:00, Sat 9:00–5:00; summer hours vary

Hall-Fowler Memorial Library
126 East Main Street
Ionia, MI 48846

(616) 527-3680; (616) 527-6210 FAX
ionhn@lakeland.lib.mi.us
http://ionia.llcoop.org
Heidi Nagel, Director
Mon–Thur 10:00–8:00, Fri 10:00–6:00, Sat 10:00–5:00

Harrison Community Library
(105 West Main Street—location)
PO Box 380 (mailing address)
Harrison, MI 48625
(989) 539-6711; (989) 539-6301
http://www.geocities.com/Athens/Ithaca/4577
Anne Smith, Director
Mon 10:00–8:00, Tue–Fri 10:00–5:00, Sat 10:00–4:00

Henika District Library
149 South Main Street
Wayland, MI 49348
(269) 792-2891; (269) 792-0399 FAX
http://wayland.llcoop.org
Lynn Mandaville, Library Director
Mon, Wed & Fri 10:00–8:00, Tue & Thur 9:00–6:00, Sat 9:00–3:00

Herrick District Library
300 South River Avenue
Holland, MI 49423
(616) 355-1400
holrh@llcoop.org (Genealogy)
http://www.herrickdl.org
winter: Mon–Thur 9:00–9:00, Fri–Sat 9:00–6:00, Sun 2:00–5:00; summer: Mon–Thur 9:00–9:00, Fri 9:00–6:00, Sat 9:00–1:00
(specializes in Dutch genealogy, Holland, Michigan, genealogy)

Howell Area Archives
c/o Howell Carnegie District Library
314 West Grand River Avenue
Howell, MI 48843
(517) 546-0720, ext. 129 (voice mail)
archives@howelllibrary.org
Duane Zemper, Director
(houses most written material for all Livingston County; history and genealogy, "many obituaries")

Howell Carnegie District Library
314 West Grand River Avenue
Howell, MI 48843
(517) 546-0720; (517) 546-1494 FAX
zaenger@howelllibrary.org
http://howelllibrary.org
Diane McKee, Administrative Assistant; Kathleen Zaenger, Director
Mon–Thur 10:00–8:00, Fri noon–5:00, Sat 10:00–5:00

Hoyt Public Library
Eddy Historical Collection
505 Janes Avenue
Saginaw, MI 48607
(989) 755-0904; (989) 755-9828 FAX
saginaw@saginawlibrary.org
http://www.saginawlibrary.org
Anna Mae Maday, Eddy Room
Eddy Room: Mon–Thur 9:00–9:00, Fri–Sat 9:00–5:00, Sun (Oct–May) 1:00–5:00
(Saginaw and Michigan genealogy)
photocopy fee, staff research limited to indexed resources

Huron City Museum
(7930 Huron City Road, Port Austin, MI 48467—location)
17 Kercheval Avenue (mailing address)
Grosse Pointe, MI 48236
(989) 428-4123

Kathryn H. Parcells, President
July–Aug: Mon & Fri–Sun 10:00–4:00
("Historical museum village with library and archive.")

Iosco-Arenac District Library
120 West Westover Street
East Tawas, MI 48730-1239
(989) 362-2651; (989) 362-6056 FAX
director@ioscoarenaclibrary.org
http://www.ioscoarenaclibrary.org
Stephanie Mallak Olson, Director
Mon–Fri 8:00–4:30

Jackson District Library
Reference Department
244 West Michigan Avenue
Jackson, MI 49201
(517) 788-4316; (517) 788-4087, ext. 234 (Reference)
reference@jackson.lib.mi.us
http://www.jackson.lib.mi.us
Nancy Buckland; Elaine Piper
Sept–May: Mon–Thur 9:30–8:30, Fri 9:30–6:00, Sat 9:30–5:00; June–Aug: Mon–Thur 9:30–7:00, Fri 9:30–6:00, Sat 9:30–1:30

Kalamazoo Public Library
Clarence L. Miller Family Local History Room
315 South Rose Street
Kalamazoo, MI 49007
(616) 342-5745; (616) 342-9837, ext. 245; (616) 342-8342 FAX
Catherine@kpl.gov; Saul@kpl.gov (Saul Amdursky, Library Director)
http://www.kpl.gov/home.htm
Catherine A. Larson, Local History Specialist
Mon–Thur 9:00–9:00, Fri 9:00–6:00, Sat 9:00–5:00, Sun 1:00–5:00 during school year, closed Thur evening in summer
(emphasis on Kalamazoo County)
charge for copying and postage

Kalamazoo Valley Museum
(230 North Rose Street—location)
PO Box 4070 (mailing address)
Kalamazoo, MI 49003-4070
(616) 373-7984
Thomas Dietz, Curator of Research
Mon–Fri 9:00–5:00, by appointment; Mueum open weekends, but no research
Pub. *Museography*, three times per year (a family-oriented promotion)
(history/science museum, phono/photo collection, very limited genealogical information, "very limited archival collection")
no paid research

Lake Superior State University
Kenneth J. Shouldice Library
Sault Sainte Marie, MI 49783
(906) 635-2167
http://198.110.216.3/library
Mary M. June, Public Services Librarian
when classes are in session: Mon–Thur 7:30 A.M.–10:30 P.M., Fri 7:30–6:00, Sat 10:00–5:00, Sun 11:00–10:30; summer: Mon–Thur 7:30 A.M.–9:00 P.M., Fri 7:30–5:00, Sat 10:00–2:00
(specializes in Michigan history)

Lyon Township Public Library
(27005 Milford Road—location)
PO Box 326 (mailing address)
New Hudson, MI 48165
(248) 437-8800; (248) 437-4621
irish20@aol.com; lyonlibrary@yahoo.com
http://www.lyon.lib.mi.us

Cathrine Cottone, Genealogist/Clerk
Mon–Thur 10:00–9:00, Fri 10:00–5:00, Sat 10:00–3:00
("great collection of local history")
fee for copies

Mackinac Island Public Library
(Main Street—location)
Box C (mailing address)
Mackinac Island, MI 49757
(906) 847-3421; (906) 847-3368 FAX
PLIB@aol.com
http://cterwilliger.com/HTML/Mackinac/library.html
Stephanie McGreevy, Librarian

Mackinaw Public Library
(528 West Central Avenue—location)
PO Box 67 (mailing address)
Mackinaw City, MI 49701-0067
(231) 436-5451; (231) 436-7344 FAX
mackina1@northland.lib.mi.us
http://nlc.lib.mi.us/members/mackinaw.htm
Judy Ranville, Director

Mancelona Public Library
(202 West State Street—location)
PO Box 499 (mailing address)
Mancelona, MI 49659
(231) 587-9451
http://www.upnorthlife.com/mancelona/Library.asp

Manistee County Historical Museum
425 River Street
Manistee, MI 49660
(231) 723-5531
Steve Harold, Museum Director
Tue–Sat 10:00–5:00
(40,000 file cards on local residents)
$1.50 admission; no research by mail

Manistee County Library System
95 Maple Street
Manistee, MI 49660
(231) 723-2519; (231) 723-8270 FAX
admin@manisteelibrary.org
http://www.manisteelibrary.org
Pamela Spoor, Reference Librarian
winter: Tue–Wed 10:00–8:30, Thur–Fri 10:00–5:00, Sat 10:00–3:00; summer: Mon–Wed 10:00–8:30, Thur–Fri 10:00–5:00

Mason County Genealogical, Historical Resource Center
Rose Hawley Museum
White Pine Village
(see Mason County Historical Society, Historical Societies—Local and Regional, below)

McKay Memorial Library
(105 South Webster—location)
PO Box 308 (mailing address)
Augusta, MI 49012-0308
(616) 731-4000; (269) 731-5323 FAX
marlib@tdsnet.com
http://envoy.libofmich.lib.mi.us/isapi/4disapi.dll/directory/LibraryDetail.html?ID=16
Linda Mony, Director
Tue 9:00–5:00, Wed 10:00–7:00, Thur–Fri 10:00–5:00, Sat 10:00–2:00

Michigan State University
Archives and Historical Collections
101 Conrad Hall
East Lansing, MI 48824-1327
(517) 355-2330; (517) 353-9319 FAX
honhart@pilot.msu.edu
http://pilot.msu.edu/unit/msuarhc

Frederick L. Honhart, Ph.D., Director
Mon–Fri 8:00–noon & 1:00–5:00

Michigan State University Museum
Michigan State University
West Circle Drive
East Lansing, MI 48824-1045
(517) 355-2370; (517) 432-2846 FAX
C. Kurt Dewhurst, Ph.D., Director
Mon–Wed & Fri 9:00–5:00, Thur 9:00–9:00, Sat 10:00–5:00, Sun 1:00–5:00
Pub. *Michigan Folklife*, annually; *Associate*, quarterly
(archeology, folklife, AG history)

MTU Archives and Copper County Historical Collections
Michigan Technological University
1400 Townsend Drive
Houghton, MI 49931-1295
(906) 487-2505; (906) 487-2357 FAX
copper@mtu.edu
http://www.lib.mtu.edu/jrvp/index.htm
Mon–Fri 8:00–5:00
(U.S. and Michigan census, Polk directories, copper mining records; predominantly Houghton and Keweenaw counties, Michigan, but also Ontonagon, Baraga, Iron and Gogebic counties)

Milan Public Library
151 Wabash Street
Milan, MI 48160-1593
(734) 439-1240; (734) 439-1244 (Director); (734) 439-5625 FAX
gailhardenbergh@yahoo.com; milan@monroe.lib.mi.us
http://woodlands.lib.mi.us/milan
Gail Hardenbergh, Director

Milford Township Library
330 Family Drive
Milford, MI 48381
(248) 684-0845; (248) 684-2923 FAX
milford@tln.lib.mi.us
http://milford.lib.mi.us
Tina Hatch, Library Director
Mon–Thur 9:30–8:00, Fri–Sat 9:30–5:00, Sun 12:30–5:00

Monroe County Historical Museum
Monroe County Historical Commission Archives
126 South Monroe
Monroe, MI 48161
(734) 240-7780 voice & FAX (Museum); (734) 240-7787 (Archives)
Christine Kull, Archivist
Archives: Wed–Sat 10:00–1:00 & 1:30–5:00, and by appointment
(Monroe County history and genealogy)
June–Aug: $2.00 admission; research: first half-hour free, $11.00 per hour thereafter, plus photocopies at 25¢ per page

Monroe County Library System
Ellis Reference and Information Center
3700 South Custer Road
Monroe, MI 48161-9732
(734) 241-5277; (800) 462-2050; (734) 242-9037 FAX
njc@monroe.lib.mi.us
http://www.monroe.lib.mi.us
Carl Katafiasz, Head of Ellis Reference; Nancy Colpaert, Director
Mon–Thur 9:00–9:00, Fri 9:00–6:00, Sat 9:00–5:00
(southeast Michigan and northwest Ohio)

Montague Museum
(Church Street at Meade Street—location)
8679 Sheridan Street (mailing address)

Montague, MI 49437
(231) 893-4585; (231) 894-6813
John Leddick, Treasurer
Memorial Day–Labor Day: Sat–Sun
   1:00–5:00, and by appointment

Mount Clemens Public Library
150 Cass Avenue
Mount Clemens, MI 48043
(586) 469-6200
askmcpl@libcoop.net
http://www.libcoop.net/mountclemens
Deborah J. Mowat, Adult Services Librarian
Mon–Thur 9:30–9:00, Fri–Sat 9:30–5:30

Muskegon County Museum
430 West Clay Avenue
Muskegon, MI 49440-1002
(231) 722-0278; (231) 728-4119 FAX
Barbara L. Martin, Historian/Librarian
Mon–Fri 9:30–4:30
Pub. *The Muser*, quarterly
(specializes in "lumbering, shipping,
   Muskegon County history [cultural,
   industrial, natural]; over 10,000
   photographic images of people and places
   of Muskegon County")
$15.00 per year membership

Niles District Library
620 East Main Street
Niles, MI 49120
(269) 683-8545; (269) 683-0075 FAX
LH-gene@nileslibrary.com (Local History)
http://www.nileslibrary.com

Northville District Library
212 West Cady Street
Northville, MI 48167-1560
(248) 349-3020; (248) 349-8250 FAX
jherrin@tln.lib.mi.us
http://www.northville.lib.mi.us
Julie Herrin, Director

Northwestern Michigan College
Mark and Helen Osterlin Library
1701 East Front Street
Traverse City, MI 49684
(231) 922-1060
library@elmo.nmc.edu
http://www.nmc.edu/~library
Douglas Campbell, Public Services Librarian
academic term: Mon–Thur 8:00 A.M.–10:00
   P.M., Fri 8:00–5:00, Sat 11:00–5:00, Sun
   1:00–5:00; summer: Mon & Thur–Fri
   8:30–4:30, Tue–Wed 8:30 A.M.–9:30 P.M.

Novi Public Library
45245 West Ten Mile Road
Novi, MI 48375-3014
(248) 349-0720; (248) 349-6520 FAX
bjevans@tln.lib.mi.us
http://www.novi.lib.mi.us
Barbara Evans, Director
Mon–Thur 10:00–9:00, Fri–Sat 10:00–5:00

Ogemaw District Library
Main Branch
(107 West Main—location)
PO Box 427 (mailing address)
Rose City, MI 48654-0427
(989) 685-3300; (989) 685-3647 FAX
nathanj@kirtland.cc.mi.us
http://www.wplc.org/apps/lib_SearchAction-
   county.cfm
Jeanette Nathan, Director
Mon 10:00–8:00, Tue–Fri 10:00–5:00, Sat
   10:00–noon

Onaway Branch Library
(20774 State Street—location)
PO Box 742 (mailing address)

Onaway, MI 49765
(989) 733-6621; (989) 733-7842 FAX
onaway1@northland.lib.mi.us
http://nlc.lib.mi.us/members/presque.htm
Kathy Radzibon, Branch Clerk
Mon 10:00–5:00, Tue–Thur 2:00–7:00, Fri
   10:00–5:00

Ontonagon Township Library
311 North Steel Street
Ontonagon, MI 49953
(906) 884-4411; (906) 884-2829 FAX
morinbk@jamadots.com;
   ontlibrary@jamadots.com
http://www.mid-pen.lib.mi.us/Library/
   ontonagon/genealogy.htm
Barbara Morin, Library Director

Orion Township Public Library
825 Joslyn Road
Lake Orion, MI 48362
(248) 693-3000; (248) 693-3009 FAX
lsickles@tln.lib.mi.us
http://www.orion.lib.mi.us
Linda Sickles, Director
Mon–Thur 9:30–9:00, Fri–Sat 9:30–5:00;
   Sun (school year) 1:00–5:00

Parchment Community Library
401 South Riverview
Parchment, MI 49004
(616) 343-7747
parlib@hotmail.com
http://parlib.tripod.com
Mon–Thur 10:00–8:00, Fri 10:00–6:00, Sat
   10:00–4:00

Petoskey Public Library
451 East Mitchell Street
Petoskey, MI 49770
(231) 347-4211; (231) 347-3429 FAX
http://www.petoskeylibrary.org
Mon–Thur 10:00–8:00, Fri 10:00–5:00, Sat
   9:30–3:00

Plymouth Historical Museum
155 South Main Street
Plymouth, MI 48170
(734) 455-8940
Beth Stewart, Director
Wed–Thur & Sat 1:00–4:00, Sun 1:00–4:00
Pub. *Newsletter*
(Michigan history and genealogy, Civil War
   history)
$15.00 per year membership; research: $5.00
   on site, $10.00 from Internet

Portage Public Library
300 Library Lane
Portage, MI 49002-4399
(616) 329-4544; (616) 324-9222 FAX
answerline@pdl.lib.mi.us
http://www.pdl.lib.mi.us
Mon–Thur 9:00–9:00, Fri 9:00–6:00, Sat
   9:00–5:00, Sun (winter) 1:00–5:00

Presque Isle County Historical Museum
(176 West Michigan Avenue—location)
PO Box 175 (mailing address)
Rogers City, MI 49779
(989) 734-4121
Laural Maldonado Curator
1 June–31 Oct: Mon–Fri noon–4:00
(Presque Isle County *Advance* and Onaway,
   Michigan, *Outlook* newspapers on
   microfiche for the past 100 years)
$10.00 per year membership

Reed City Area Public Library
410 West Upton Avenue
Reed City, MI 49677
(231) 832-2131

http://www.multimag.com/reedcity/
   library.html
Mon & Wed noon–5:00, Tue & Thur
   noon–8:00; Fri 9:00–5:00, Sat 10:00–2:00

Richland Community Library
8951 Park Street
Richland, MI 49083-9630
(269) 629-9085; (269) 629-5330 FAX
http://www.richlandlibrary.org
Joan Split
Tue–Wed 10:00–7:00, Thur–Fri 10:00–5:00,
   Sat 9:00–4:00

**Rochester Hills Museum at Van Hoosen
Farm**
1005 Van Hoosen Road
Rochester Hills, MI 48306
(248) 656-4663; (248) 608-8198 FAX
rhmuseum@rochesterhills.org
http://www.rochesterhills.org/museum.htm
Patrick J. McKay, Supervisor of Interpretive
   Services
Wed–Sat 1:00–4:00
(local history, Stoney Creek Village, local
   archaeology)

Rochester Hills Public Library
500 Olde Towne Road
Rochester, MI 48307-2043
(248) 656-2900; (248) 650-7121 FAX
   (Administration); (248) 650-7130 FAX
   (Adult)
matscosa@rhpl.org
http://www.rhpl.org
Diane Burgeson; Sandra Matsco, Director
Mon–Thur 9:30–9:00, Fri 9:30–5:30, Sat
   9:30–5:00

Romulus Public Library
11121 Wayne Road
Romulus, MI 48174
(734) 942-7589; (734) 941-3575 FAX
dhazen@tln.lib.mi.us
http://www.romulus.lib.mi.us
Diane Hazen, Director
Mon–Thur 10:00–8:00, Fri (summer)
   noon–5:00; Sat (winter) noon–5:00

Rosa Public Library
401 South Capitol Avenue
Lansing, MI 48933-2037
(517) 325-6413; (517) 325-6423 FAX
johnsonk@cadl.org
http://www.cadl.org
Judy Forester, Head of Adult Services;
   Katharine Johnson, Librarian
Local History Room: Tue & Thur
   noon–3:00; Library: Mon & Wed
   9:30–8:30, Tue & Thur 9:30–5:30, Fri
   9:30–5:00, Sat 9:30–4:30 (if the Local
   History Room is closed, reference
   librarian will retrieve limited local history
   materials for patrons for in-library use)

Roseville Public Library
29777 Gratiot Avenue
Roseville, MI 48066
(586) 445-5407
http://www.libcoop.net/roseville
Mon–Thur 9:00–9:00, Fri–Sat (summer)
   9:00–5:00,Fri–Sat (winter) 9:00–5:00

Royal Oak Public Library
(222 East Eleven Mile Road, Royal Oak, MI
   48067—location)
PO Box 494 (mailing address)
Royal Oak, MI 48068-0494
(248) 246-3700; (248) 246-3701 FAX
avidal@tln.lib.mi.us
http://www.ci.royal-oak.mi.us/library
Anna Vidal, Head of Adult Services

Mon–Thur 10:00–9:00, Fri–Sat 10:00–6:00

Sage Branch Library
(see Bay County Library System, above)

Saint Clair County Library
210 McMorran Boulevard
Port Huron, MI 48060-4098
(810) 987-7323; (877) 987-7323; (810) 987-7874
jwarwick@sccl.lib.mi.us
http://www.sccl.lib.mi.us
Barbara King, Reference Librarian,
    Michigan Room; James Warwick,
    Director
Michigan Room: Mon 9:30–8:30, Tue–Thur
    9:00–4:30 by appointment; Library:
    Mon–Fri 9:00–9:00, Sat 9:00–5:30
(emphasis on Saint Clair County and Port
    Huron)
research: $7.50 minimum, $14.00 for
    searches of ½ hour or more; copies: $2.00
    for first copy, 25¢ for each additional
    copy, including mailing

Saint Clair Shores Public Library
22500 Eleven Mile Road
Saint Clair Shores, MI 48081-1399
(810) 771-9020; (810) 771-8935 FAX
orlandor@libcoop.net
http://www.libcoop.net/stclairshore
Cindy Bieniek, Archivist; Rosemary
    Orlando, Assistant Director
winter: Mon–Thur 9:00–9:00, Sat 9:00–5:00;
    summer: Mon–Thur 9:00–9:00, Fri
    9:00–5:00
(Great Lakes and Michigan historical
    collections)

Saint Joseph Public Library
Maud Preston Palenske Memorial Library
500 Market Street
Saint Joseph, MI 49085
(616) 983-7167; (616) 983-5804
http://www.youseemore.com/
    maudpreston/default.asp
Katherine W. Smith, Public
    Services/Reference Librarian
Mon–Thur 10:00–9:00, Fri–Sat 10:00–6:00,
    Sun (Oct–May) 1:00–5:00

**Sault Sainte Marie Foundation for Culture
and History**
(209 East Portage Avenue—location)
PO Box 627 (mailing address)
Sault Sainte Marie, MI 49783
(906) 632-1999
sues@sault.com
Dr. Susan Schacher
15 May–15 Oct: Mon–Sat 10:00–5:00, Sun
    noon–5:00

**Ella Sharp Museum Association of
Jackson**
3225 Fourth Street
Jackson, MI 49203
(517) 787-2320

Alfred P. Sloan Museum
1221 East Kearsley Street
Flint, MI 48503
(810) 760-1169
James Johnson, Interim Director
Pub. *Sloan News*
(genealogical services)

South Side Branch Library
(see Bay County Library System, above)

Southwest Michigan College Museum
58900 Cherry Grove Road
Dowagiac, MI 49047

(269) 782-1374
http://www.swmich.edu/museum
Director
Tue & Thur–Sat 10:00–5:00, Wed
    10:00–8:00
Pub. *SMC Museum News*, quarterly
$15.00 per year membership

Spies Public Library
940 First Street
Menominee, MI 49858
(906) 863-3911; (906) 863-2900 (Librarian);
    (906) 863-5000 FAX
cherylh@uproc.lib.mi.us
http://www.uproc.lib.mi.us/spies
Cheryl Hoffman, Director

**Sturgis Public Library and Information
Center**
(Corner of Nottawa and West
Streets—location)
255 North Street (mailing address)
Sturgis, MI 49091
(269) 659-7224; (269) 651-4534 FAX
sturgis@monroe.lib.mi.us
http://ci.sturgis.mi.us/library.htm
Karla A. Weidner, History Room Librarian
    winter: Mon–Wed 9:30–8:00, Thur–Fri
    9:30–5:30, Sat 9:30–2:00; summer: Mon
    & Thur 9:30–8:00, Tue–Wed & Fri
    9:30–5:30, Sat 9:30–12:30
("Specializing in Saint Joseph County
    history and genealogical information.")

Three Rivers Public Library
920 West Michigan Avenue
Three Rivers, MI 49093
(269) 273-8666; (269) 279-9654 FAX
scody@monroe.lib.mi.us;
    threer@monroe.lib.mi.us
http://threeriverslibrary.org
Shirley Cody, Director
Mon–Fri 10:00–7:00, Sat 11:00–3:00, Sun
    (School Year) 11:00–3:00

Traverse Area District Library
610 Woodmere Avenue
Traverse City, MI 49686
(231) 932-8500
libadmin@tadl.tcnet.org;
    webster@tadl.tcnet.org
http://www.tadl.tcnet.org
Michael McGuire, Library Director
Mon–Thur 9:00–9:00, Fri–Sat 9:00–6:00,
    Sun noon–5:00

Trenton Veterans Memorial Library
2790 Westfield
Trenton, MI 48183
(734) 676-9777 (Hours recording); (734)
    676-9773; (734) 676-9895 FAX
fsanak@tln.lib.mi.us
http://www.trenton.lib.mi.us
Francene Sanak, Director
Mon–Thur 10:00–9:00, Fri–Sat 10:00–6:00,
    Sun 1:00–5:00

Tri-Cities Historical Museum
1 North Harbor
Grand Haven, MI 49417
(616) 842-0700; (616) 842-3698 FAX
Elizabeth Kammeraad
Tue–Fri 10:00–5:00
Pub. *The Packet*
(local history)

Troy Public Library
510 West Big Beaver Road
Troy, MI 48084
(248) 524-3538; (248) 524-0112 FAX
rutledgm@libcoop.net
http://www.libcoop.net/troy

Marcia J. Rutledge, Head of Adult Services
Mon–Thur 10:00–9:00, Fri–Sat 10:00–6:00,
    Sun 1:00–6:00

The University of Michigan-Ann Arbor
Bentley Historical Library
Michigan Historical Collections
1150 Beal Avenue
Ann Arbor, MI 48109-2113
(734) 764-3482; (734) 936-1333 FAX
bentley.ref@umich.edu
http://www.umich.edu/~bhl/bhl/refhome/
    genie.htm (genealogical research)
Kathy Marquis, Reference Archivist
Mon–Fri 8:30–5:00; Sat (Sept–Apr)
    9:00–12:30

The University of Michigan-Dearborn
Mardigan Library
4901 Evergreen Road
Dearborn, MI 48128-1491
(313) 593-5598
rfraser@umich.edu;
    kmirwin@umd.umich.edu
http://www.umd.umich.edu

The University of Michigan-Flint
Flint Library
Genesee History Collection Center
Flint, MI 48502
(810) 762-3402

University of Michigan-Ann Arbor
(see Clements Library Associates, above)

Van Buren County Library
Webster Memorial Library
(200 North Phelps Street—location)
PO Box 143 (mailing address)
Decatur, MI 49045
(269) 423-4771; (269) 423-8373 FAX
dtate@vbdl.org; comments@vbdl.org
http://woodlands.lib.mi.us/van/vanburen.htm
Toni I. Benson, Librarian; David Tate,
    Director
Mon–Thur 9:00–8:00, Fri 9:00–5:00, Sat
    9:00–3:00

Vicksburg District Library
215 South Michigan
Vicksburg, MI 49097-1222
(616) 649-1648; (616) 649-3666 FAX
http://www.youseemore.com/vicksburg/
    directory.asp
Carolyn Sutter, Interim Director
Mon–Thur 10:00–8:30, Fri–Sat 10:00–5:00

Wayne State University
Walter P. Reuther Library
Archives of Labor History and Urban Affairs
5401 Cass Avenue
Detroit, MI 48202-1704
(313) 577-4024; (313) 577-4300 FAX
http://www.reuther.wayne.edu/
    collections.html
Philip P. Mason, Ph.D., Director
(primarily historical, not genealogical)

West Branch Public Library
119 North Fourth Street
West Branch, MI 48661-1217
(989) 345-2235; (989) 345-8735 FAX
m.boyd@vlc.lib.mi.us
http://www.vlc.lib.mi.us/WestBranch.html
Marsha Boyd, Director
Mon & Wed 10:00–6:00, Tue & Thur–Fri
    10:00–5:00, Sat 10:00–1:00

Western Michigan University
Archives and Regional History Collections
111 East Hall, East Campus
Kalamazoo, MI 49008-5307

(269) 387-8490; (269) 387-8484 FAX
arch_collect@wmich.edu
http://www.wmich.edu/library/depts/
    archives
Sharon Carlson, Director
fall/winter/spring: Tue–Fri 8:00–5:00, Sat
    9:00–4:00; July–Aug: Mon–Fri
    10:00–4:00
(Depository of the State Archives with local
    governmental records for twelve
    Michigan counties; houses Kalamazoo
    Valley Genealogical Society collection)

Peter White Public Library
217 North Front Street
Marquette, MI 49855
(906) 226-4311; (906) 226-1783 FAX
refdesk@uproc.lib.mi.us
http://www.uproc.lib.mi.us/pwpl
Caroline Jordan, Collection
    Development/Reference Librarian
Mon–Thur 9:00–9:00, Fri 9:00–6:00, Sat
    10:00–5:00

The Wilkinson Heritage Museum
15300 Red Arrow Highway
Union Pier, MI 49129
(616) 469-2090; (616) 469-6239 FAX
Nadra D. Kissman, President
Mon–Fri 9:00–5:00, Sat–Sun 11:00–5:00
donation accepted

Willard Library
7 West Van Buren Street
Battle Creek, MI 49017-3060
(616) 968-8166
rhulsey@willard.lib.mi.us
http://www.willard.lib.mi.us
Helen Jo Emerson, Reference Head
    Librarian; Marlene A. Steele; Richard
    Hulsey, Library Director
Mon–Thur 9:00–9:00, Fri–Sat 9:00–5:00

**The City of Wyoming Archives and
Historical Collections**
(Wyoming Public Library, 3350 Michael
    S.W.—location)
1155 28th Street S.W.
PO Box 905 (mailing address)
Wyoming, MI 49509-0905
(616) 251-3508 (appointments)
Robert Viol, Archivist
Mon & Wed 5:00–7:00, Tue 9:30–5:00, and
    by appointment
(Genealogical records, obituary files,
    cemeteries, census, churches, etc.
    Includes Wyoming Historical and
    Cultural Commission.)

Ypsilanti District Library
5577 Whittaker Road
Ypsilanti, MI 48197-9752
(734) 482-4110; (734) 482-0047 FAX
drummond@ypsilibrary.org
http://www.ypsilibrary.org
Paula Drummond, Reference Department
Mon 10:00–8:00, Tue–Thur 9:00–8:00,
    Fri–Sat 9:00–5:30

Historical Societies—Local and Regional

Albion Historical Society
The Gardner House Museum
500 South Eaton Street
Albion, MI 49224
(517) 629-5100
Apr–Oct: Sat–Sun 1:00–4:00, and by
    appointment
Pub. *Albion Historical Society Newsletter*,
    quarterly

(Transferred historical and genealogical
    archives to the Albion Public Library)
$5.00 per year membership

Alger County Historical Society
1496 Washington Street
Munising, MI 49862
(906) 387-4308; (906) 387-4188 FAX
Mary Jo Cook, President
10:00–5:00
Pub. *Alger Footprints*, quarterly
$10.00 per year membership

Allegan County Historical Society
(113 Walnut Street—location)
536½ Trowbridge Street (mailing address)
Allegan, MI 49010
(616) 673-8292 (Tuesdays); (616) 673-4853
Marguerite Miller, Museum Director

Arenac County Historical Society
(Michigan Avenue—location)
PO Box 272 (mailing address)
Au Gres, MI 48703
(989) 846-9967

Armada Area Historical Society
armedit@libcoop.net
meetings at Armada Free Public Library: first
    Wed
$10.00 per year membership

Arvon Township Historical Society
PO Box 151
Skanee, MI 49962
(906) 524-6934

**Au Sable-Oscoda Historical Society and
Museum**
(114 East River Road—location)
PO Box 679 (mailing address)
Oscoda, MI 48750
(989) 739-2782 voice & FAX
Fred Glass, President
Apr & Oct weekends: Sat 11:00–4:00, Sun
    noon–4:00; summer: Sat 10:00–5:00, Sun
    11:00–4:00
("Death records, cemetery records, many
    local history books, 1880 map. One new
    book title every 1½ years.")
$10.00 per year membership

Historical Society of Battle Creek
165 North Washington Avenue
Battle Creek, MI 49017
(616) 965-2613
T. Zoe Kimmel, Executive Director
Mon–Fri 9:00–noon
Pub. *Heritage Battle Creek*, two to four
    times per year, $7.00 to $9.00 per year
    subscription, with a 20% discount for
    members
from $20.00 per year membership

**Bay County Historical Society and
Historical Museum of Bay County**
321 South Washington Avenue
Bay City, MI 48708
(989) 893-5733
Gay McInerney, Director; Ron Bloomfield,
    Curator of Collections and Research
Mon–Sat 10:00–5:00, Sun 1:00–5:00

**Bay Mills-Brimley Historical Research
Society**
PO Box 273
Brimley, MI 49715
(906) 248-3665

Beaver Island Historical Society
(The Mormon Print Shop, 26250 Main
Street, corner of Forest and Main

Streets—location)
PO Box 263 (mailing address)
Beaver Island, MI 49782
(906) 448-2254; (906) 448-2106 FAX
Phyllis Gregg Moore, Director
Memorial Day–Labor Day: Mon–Sat
    11:00–5:00, Sun noon–3:00
Pub. *Journal of Beaver Island History*,
    irregularly
$10.00 per year membership; research:
    $10.00 per hour plus copying costs

Bellaire Area Historical Society
(202 North Bridge Street—location)
PO Box 646 (mailing address)
Bellaire, MI 49615
(231) 533-8631
Carol Boros
1 June–1 Sept: Mon–Fri 11:00–3:00, and by
    appointment
Pub. *News Letter*, annually
$5.00 per year membership

Bellevue Historical Society
212 North Main Street
Bellevue, MI 49021
(616) 763-9049 (Treasurer)
Bernard J. Geyer, Trustee; Joyce Miller,
    Treasurer
Mon–Fri 1:00–5:00
Pub. *BHS Newsletter*, quarterly (Jan, Apr,
    July, Oct)
("anniversaries, births, obituaries on file")
$5.00 per year membership

Benzie Area Historical Society
Benzie Area Historical Museum
(6941 Traverse Avenue—location)
PO Box 185 (mailing address)
Benzonia, MI 49616
(231) 882-5539 (Museum)
Debbra Kerby, Museum Manager
May–Dec: Mon–Sat 10:00–4:00
Pub. *Benzie Heritage*, quarterly
$25.00 per year membership; research:
    $10.00 per hour

Bernard Historical Society and Museum
7135 West Delton Road
Delton, MI 49046
(616) 623-5451

**Berrien County Historical Association,
Inc.**
1839 Courthouse Museum
(313 North Cass Street—location)
PO Box 261 (mailing address)
Berrien Springs, MI 49103
(616) 471-1202; (616) 471-7412 FAX
Bcha@berrienhistory.org (email queries
    welcome)
Robert Myers, Curator
Tue–Fri 9:00–4:00, Sat–Sun 1:00–5:00
    (appointment required for research)
Pub. *The Docket*, quarterly; *Berrien County
    Historical Association Annual Report*,
    annually
("indexes to Berrien County marriage
    records 1831–1929, death records
    1867–1929, probate court files
    1831–1930, naturalization applications
    1840–1894, and miscellaneous records")
$20.00 per year membership

Blissfield Historical Society
Blissfield Historic Depot Museum
7148 East Weston Road
Blissfield, MI 49228
Shelby Jean Raines, President
Sat–Sun noon–5:00, weekdays in the
    summer; meetings: third Tue; Victorsville
    School House, 424 Adrian Street: by

appointment only
$5.00 per year membership

Branch County Historical Society
(27 South Jefferson Street—location)
PO Box 107 (mailing address)
Coldwater, MI 49036
(517) 278-2871
Thomas Oxenham, Curator
Museum: Wed–Sun 1:00–5:00, and by
    appointment
Pub. *Newsletter*, monthly

Historical Society of Bridgeport
(6190 Dixie Highway—location)
PO Box 561 (mailing address)
Bridgeport, MI 48722
(517) 777-5230
Laura Frey, Museum Secretary and Curator
Tue–Sat 10:00–5:00
Pub. *Recollections*, about monthly
(Artifacts, family history. "Our genealogical
    research area will grow soon.")
$8.00 per year membership; research:
    donation plus postage and handling

Byron Center Historical Society
(2506 Prescott—location)
PO Box 20 (mailing address)
Byron Center, MI 49315-0020

Canton Historical Commission
46870 Cherry Hill
Canton, MI 48187
(734) 981-0087; (734) 495-0304
Melissa McCloc

Canton Historical Society and Museum
(Corner of Canton Center Road and Heritage
Park Drive—location)
PO Box 87362 (mailing address)
Canton, MI 48187
(734) 397-0088
Ronni Curtis, President
Tue & Sat 1:00–4:00
Pub. *Canton Historical Society News*,
    bimonthly
("Museum collection focuses mainly on
    Canton.")
$10.00 per year membership; museum
    admission: free; research: postage plus
    copies at 20¢ each

Cass City Area Historical Society
Rawson Memorial Library
6495 Pine Street
Cass City, MI 48726
(989) 872-2856; (989) 872-4073 FAX
http://rawson.lib.mi.us/casscityarea
    historicalsociety/index.htm
Pub. *Newsletter* (online)
$5.00 per year membership

Cass County Historical Commission
24010 Hospital Street, #105
Cassopolis, MI 49031-9690
(616) 445-9016
M. S. Federowski, Secretary
("Reprints of county histories, atlases.")
research: searches as time allows

**Historical Society of Cheboygan County,
Inc.**
(Corner Huron and Court—location)
PO Box 5005 (mailing address)
Cheboygan, MI 49721
(231) 627-5448
Quincy Leslie, President

Chelsea Historical Society
PO Box 117
Chelsea, MI 48118

(734) 475-7047

Chippewa County Historical Society, Inc.
(409 Ashmun Street—location)
PO Box 342 (mailing address)
Sault Sainte Marie, MI 49783
(906) 635-7082; (906) 635-9280 FAX
Susan James, Executive Secretary
Mon–Fri mornings, and by appointment
Pub. *River Soundings*, quarterly
$20.00 per year membership

Clarkston Historical Society
6085 South Main Street
Clarkston, MI 48016
Dennis Spande

Clinton County Historical Commission
8565 Grange
Portland, MI 48875
(517) 587-6839
Evelyn Weiland

Clinton County Historical Society
(Brook Road, Lansing, MI—Archives
location)
PO Box 174 (mailing address)
Saint Johns, MI 48879-1740
Mon–Tue 9:00–4:00
$6.00 per year membership (includes
    membership in The Genealogists of the
    Clinton County Historical Society)

**Community Historical Society and
Museum (Colon)**
(217 and 219 North Blackstone
Avenue—location)
PO Box 136 (mailing address)
Colon, MI 49040-0136
(616) 432-3804 (President); (616) 432-2462
    (Treasurer)
Joe Ganger, President; David J. Farrell,
    Treasurer
1 June–Labor Day: Tue, Thur & Sun
    2:00–4:30
$5.00 per year membership

**Commerce Township Area Historical
Society (CTAHS)**
(207 Liberty Street—location)
PO Box 264 (mailing address)
Walled Lake, MI 48390
(248) 624-2554; (248) 624-2309
Pub. *CTAHS Newsletter*, nine times per year
    (monthly, Sept–May)

Dearborn Historical Commission
Dearborn Historical Museum
915 South Brady
Dearborn, MI 48124
(313) 565-3000; (313) 565-4848 FAX
William K. McElhone, Curator of Research
Museum: Mon–Fri 9:00–5:00, Sat
    (May–Nov) 9:00–5:00, Sat (Nov–May)
    1:00–5:00
Pub. *Dearborn Historian*, quarterly

Detroit Historical Society
5401 Woodward Avenue
Detroit, MI 48202
(313) 833-7934
Michael W. R. Davis, Executive Director
Pub. *Detroit Historical Society Bulletin*

**Dexter Area Historical Society and
Museum**
3443 Inverness Street
Dexter, MI 48130
(734) 426-2519
dexmuseum@aol.com
http://www.hvcn.org/info/libdahs.html
Nancy J. Van Blaricum, Genealogist

May–Dec: Fri–Sat 1:00–3:00
Pub. *Dexter Area Historical Society
    Newsletter*, irregularly
("We have photocopies of early church
    records for most Dexter Protestant
    churches.")
$3.00 per year membership; research fees
    vary with requests

Drummond Island Historical Society
(Drummond Island Historical Museum, Old
Mill Drive—location)
PO Box 293 (mailing address)
Drummond Island, MI 49726
(906) 493-5746 (Museum); (906) 493-5224
Kathryne B. Lowe, Curator
daily (mid-May to 1 Oct) 1:00–5:00
Pub. *Chimney Chatter*, irregularly
("Early Island history, township records,
    scrapbooks and family albums.")

Elk Rapids Area Historical Society
Elk Rapids Historical Museum
(401 River Street—location)
PO Box 2 (mailing address)
Elk Rapids, MI 49629
(231) 264-5692
http://www.ole.net/~maggie/antrim/elk.htm
Glenn Newmann, Co-chairman
Museum: summer: Tue, Thur & Sat–Sun
    1:00–4:00; winter: Sat–Sun 2:00–4:00
("Four volumes of local history entitled *Bay
    Breezes*, 1870s–1885 for sale—from old
    newspapers.")

Elsie Historical Society
(145 West Main Street—location)
PO Box 125 (mailing address)
Elsie, MI 48831-0125
Elizabeth Hess
Historical Room: Wed 2:00–5:00
(local history and genealogy)

Farmington Hills Historical Commission
31555 Eleven Mile Road
Farmington Hills, MI 48336
(248) 701-8112
Brian Golden, Publications Chair
9:00–5:00
Pub. *Michigan History*, quarterly
$50.00 per year

Farmington Historical Commission
23600 Liberty Street
Farmington, MI 48335
(248) 474-4608
Kathryn Briggs, Chairman
8:30–4:30

Flat River Historical Society and Museum
(213 North Franklin Street—location)
PO Box 188 (mailing address)
Greenville, MI 48838
(231) 754-5296
by appointment

Flat Rock Historical Society
(Munger Lane, behind City Hall, corner of
Gibralter and Evergreen—location)
PO Box 337 (mailing address)
Flat Rock, MI 48134
(734) 782-5220; (734) 782-1269 (Secretary)
Lila Fedokovitz, Secretary
second Sun 1:00–4:00
Pub. *Newsletter*, quarterly
$5.00 per year membership

Flint Historic Commission
1101 South Saginaw Street
Flint, MI 48506
(810) 766-7426

The Flushing Area Historical Society
(431 West Main Street at Seymour
Road—location)
PO Box 87 (mailing address)
Flushing, MI 48433-0087
(810) 487-0814
http://www.flushinghistorical.org
Lois Bettesworth, Editor and Treasurer
Sun (Apr–Dec) 1:00–4:00
Pub. *Flushing Area Historical Society
    Newsletter*, monthly
("have published three volumes of Flushing
    history, including some family histories")
$3.00 per year membership; research: see
    web site for fees

Fort Miami Heritage Society of Michigan
708 Market Street
Saint Joseph, MI 49085
(269) 983-1191; (269) 983-1274 FAX
Kenneth R. Pott, Executive Director
Tue–Fri 9:00–5:00, by appointment

Franklin Historical Society
PO Box 7
Franklin Village, MI 48025

Fraser Historical Commission
16330 Fourteen Mile Road
Fraser, MI 48026
(810) 293-4036

Friends of Historic Meridian
(5151 Marsh Road, Okemos, MI
48864—location)
PO Box 155 (mailing address)
Okemos, MI 48805
(517) 349-1993
Elaine C. Davis, President
Pub. *The Toll-gate Keeper*

Friends of the Krause Memorial Library
Krause Memorial Library
140 East Bridge Street
Rockford, MI 49341
(616) 866-2352
Nancy Schellenberg, President
$10.00 per year membership

Garden City Historical Commission
6000 Middlebelt
Garden City, MI 48135
(734) 421-1262

**Grand Blanc Heritage Association and
Museum**
203 East Grand Blanc Road
Grand Blanc, MI 48439-1303
(810) 694-7274
Clare Hatten, Director
Wed 10:00–2:00, and by appointment
Pub. *Newsletter*, bimonthly
(local history and genealogy and artifacts;
    family histories, diaries, ledgers,
    obituaries, cemetery records)
$7.00 per year membership; museum
    admission: free; research: free
    genealogical help for Grand Blanc only

Grand Ledge Area Historical Society
(The Museum, 118 West Lincoln
Street—location)
PO Box 203 (mailing address)
Grand Ledge, MI 48837-0203
(517) 627-3149 (Museum); (517) 627-4949
    (Library); (517) 627-5170 (Library)
Neil Miller, President
Museum: Sun 2:00–4:00, and by
    appointment; Archival collection at the
    Grand Ledge Public Library, 131 East
    Jefferson, Grand Ledge, MI 48837
$10.00 per year membership

Grand Rapids Historical Society
Grand Rapids Public Library
Michigan and Family History Department
60 Library Plaza, N.E.
Grand Rapids, MI 49503-3093
(616) 456-3640 (Library)
http://www.iserv.net/grpl (Library)
David Wier, President
Library: Mon–Wed 9:00–9:00, Thur–Sat
    9:00–5:30
Pub. *Grand River Valley Review*

**Grandville Historical Commission and
Museum**
(3195 Wilson Avenue, S.W.—location)
PO Box 124 (mailing address)
Grandville, MI 49418
(616) 534-3871 (Chairman); (616) 531-3030
    (City Hall)
Bob Beauvais, Chairman
first Thur 1:00–4:00

Grass Lake Area Historical Society
PO Box 53
Grass Lake, MI 49240

**Gratiot County Historical and
Genealogical Society**
PO Box 73
Ithaca, MI 48847-1415
(989) 875-4974 (Museum); (989) 875-6232
    (Genealogy Library)
lsebring@nethawk.com
http://www.rootsweb.com/~migratio/
    gchgs.html
Lorna D. Sebring, Chair, Genealogical
    Group
Genealogy: Tue 1:00–5:00; Museum: Thur
    (June–Nov) 11:00–3:00
Pub. *Pages from the Past*, monthly
    (genealogical material four times per year)
(primarily Gratiot County research, but also
    some state and national)
$10.00 per year membership; research: $6.00
    per hour, $12.00 minimum, plus LSASE
    and 15¢ per page for copies

**Greater West Bloomfield Historical
Society**
PO Box 5024
Orchard Lake, MI 48033

Green Oak Township Historical Society
(Gage Museum, 6440 Kensington
Road—location)
PO Box 84 (mailing address)
Brighton, MI 48116
Cleo Moran, President
June–Aug: weekends 1:00–4:00, and by
    appointment
Pub. *Green Oak Historian*, four times per
    year
(early township families)
$7.00 per year membership; research:
    donation plus reproduction and mailing
    costs

Grosse Ile Historical Society
(East River Road and Parkway—location)
PO Box 131 (mailing address)
Grosse Ile, MI 48138
(734) 675-1250
Mar–Dec: Thur 10:00–noon, Sun 1:00–4:00
    (except holidays), and by appointment
Pub. *GIHS Newsletter*, quarterly
$10.00 per year membership

Hackley Heritage Association, Inc.
(484 West Webster Avenue, Muskegon, MI
49440—location)
PO Box 32 (mailing address)
Muskegon, MI 49443-0032

(231) 722-7578; (231) 759-2505

Heritage Hill Association
126 College Avenue, S.E.
Grand Rapids, MI 49503
(616) 459-8950

Holly Historical Society
306 South Saginaw
Holly, MI 48422
(248) 634-9233
Linda Smith, Genealogical Records
    Chairman; Sue Les, President
Tue–Thur 9:00–3:00, Sun 1:00–4:00
Pub. *Lantern Light*
$10.00 per year membership

Homer Historical Society
505 Grandview
Homer, MI 49245
(517) 568-3116
JoAnne Miller, Vice President
by appointment
Pub. *Homer Historical Society Newsletter*,
    two times per year

Houghton County Historical Society
(5500 Highway M-26—location)
PO Box 127 (mailing address)
Lake Linden, MI 49945
(906) 296-4121; (906) 296-9191 FAX
William Barkell, Secretary
seasonal museum
$10.00 per year membership

Houghton Lake Area Historical Society
(1625 West Houghton Lake Drive,
Prudenville, MI 48651—location)
PO Box 146 (mailing address)
Houghton Lake Heights, MI 48630
(989) 422-5074
R. W. Carman

Huron County Historical Society
Bad Axe Historical Society Chapter
223 Willis Street
Bad Axe, MI 48413
(989) 269-8165

Ionia County Historical Society
John C. Blanchard House
(253 East Main Street—location)
PO Box 1776 (mailing address)
Ionia, MI 48846
Ralph Bartlett, President of the Board
30 May–Labor Day: Sun noon–4:00
$10.00 per year membership

**Iosco County Historical Society and
Museum**
405 West Bay Street
East Tawas, MI 48730-1103
(989) 362-8911
Rosemary Klenow, President
Office: Wed–Sat 11:00–4:00; Museum:
    summer: Wed–Sat 1:00–4:00; fall–spring:
    Fri–Sat 1:00–4:00; and by appointment
Pub. untitled newsletter, quarterly

**Iron County Historical and Museum
Society**
PO Box 272
Caspian, MI 49915
(906) 265-2617; (906) 265-3942 (off-season)
Harold O. Bernhardt,
    President/Administrator
Pub. *Past Present Prints*

Ironwood Historical Society
PO Box 553
Ironwood, MI 49938
(906) 932-0287

Ray Maurin, Curator
Memorial Day–Labor Day: noon–4:00, and
by appointment

Kalamazoo County Historical Society
PO Box 1623
Kalamazoo, MI 49005
Jean Bright, President

Kalamo Township Historical Society
8889 Spore Highway
Vermontville, MI 49096
(517) 726-0408

Kalkaska County Historical Society
4360 Spencer Road, S.E.
Kalkaska, MI 49646-9621
(231) 258-8285
Geraldine Montgomery, Secretary
June–Aug: 1:00–4:00
donation accepted

Keweenaw County Historical Society
HC-1, Box 265L
Eagle Harbor, MI 49950
(906) 296-2561
Clarence J. Monette, Secretary
Pub. *Superior Signal*, quarterly, not available
by subscription
(no genealogical files, only local Keweenaw
County history)

Lake Odessa Area Historical Society
(Emerson Street—Depot Museum location)
Page Memorial Building
839 Fourth Avenue (mailing address)
Lake Odessa, MI 48849
(616) 374-8698
John Waite, President
meetings at the Emerson Manor, Lake
Odessa: second Thur 7:30
Pub. *Bonanza Bugle*, quarterly (Feb, May,
Aug, Nov)
(accumulated obituaries, microfilm of Ionia
County census 1870–1920, microfilm of
local newspapers 1891–1948)
$10.00 per year membership

Leelanau Historical Society, Inc.
(Leelanau Historical Museum, 203 East
Cedar Street—location)
PO Box 246 (mailing address)
Leland, MI 49654-0246
(231) 256-7475; (231) 256-7650 FAX
info@leelanauhistory.org
http://www.leelanauhistory.org
Laura J. Quackenbush, Curator
Archives: by appointment only
Pub. *LeeMuse*, quarterly
(local history collection)
$25.00 per year membership

Lenawee County Historical Society, Inc.
(Lenawee County Historical Museum, 110
East Church Street—location)
PO Box 511 (mailing address)
Adrian, MI 49221
(517) 265-6071
Doris Conklin Trowbridge, Archivist;
Charles N. Liquist, Ph.D., Curator
Pub. *From the Tower*, five times per year
$10.00 per year membership

**Les Cheneaux Historical Association:
Meridian Road**
Les Cheneaux Historical Museum and
Maritime Museum
PO Box 301
Cedarville, MI 49719
(906) 484-2821
Annegret Goehring, Curator
May & Oct: by appointment; June & Sept:

Tue–Sat 11:00–4:00; July–Aug: Mon–Fri
10:00–4:00, Sun 1:00–4:00

**Lincoln Park Historical Museum and
Society**
1335 Southfield Road
Lincoln Park, MI 48146
(313) 386-3137
kalkar@wyan.org (Webmaster)
http://www.rootsweb.com/~milphsm/
lphsm.htm
Tue–Thur 1:00–5:00; meetings: first Wed
(Oct–Dec & Feb–May) 7:30
Pub. *Historical Society Newsletter*, four
times per year
(genealogy library, collection of local
newspapers)
$5.00 per year membership

Little Traverse Regional Historical Society
Water Front Park
(100 Depot Court—location)
PO Box 162 (mailing address)
Petoskey, MI 49770
(231) 347-2620
http://www.freeway.net/community/civic/
historymuseum

Livonia Historical Society
Livonia Historic Preservation Commission
(Greenmead Historic Site, 38125 Eight Mile
Road, Livonia, MI 48152—location)
2050 Newburgh (mailing address)
Livonia, MI 48152
(734) 477-7375; (734) 477-6921 FAX
Marian Renaud
Mon–Fri 9:00–5:00
(300-volume library)

Luce County Historical Society
Luce County Historical Museum
110 East McMillan Avenue
Newberry, MI 49868-1555
(906) 293-5946
Lillian A. Waite

Mackinac Associates
PO Box 1800
Mackinac Island, MI 49757
(906) 847-3328 (summer); (517) 373-4296
(winter)
Carl R. Nold, Administrative Agent
9:00–5:00
Pub. *Curiosities*, quarterly
("Association to assist Mackinac State
Historic Parks with its educational
mission and help preserve Mackinac's
heritage.")
$40.00 per year membership

Macomb County Historical Society
Crocker House
15 Union
Mount Clemens, MI 48043
(586) 465-2488
Madeline Page, President
Mar–Dec: Tue–Fri 10:00–4:00, first Sun
1:00–4:00
Pub. *Newsletter, Macomb County Historical
Society*, monthly
(obituaries of former members of the society)
$20.00 per year membership

Maritime Heritage Alliance
322 Sixth Street
Traverse City, MI 49684-2414

**Marquette County Historical Society and
Museum**
J. M. Longyear Research Library
213 North Front Street
Marquette, MI 49855

(906) 226-3571
http://www.geocities.com/Marhistsoc.html
Linda K. Panian, Librarian; Frances Porter,
Executive Director; Meg Goodrich
Mon–Fri 10:00–noon & 1:00–5:00, third
Thur till 9:00
Pub. *Harlow's Wooden Man* (a journal of
general regional history, not genealogy),
quarterly
(has biographical card file, census
information, city directories, gazetteers,
pamphlets, vital records, cemetery
records, military records, photos, maps,
manuscripts, periodicals, local history
collection)
$20.00 per year membership; library
admission: $5.00 per project for
nonmembers, $2.00 per project for
university students; research: $15.00 per
hour, plus $3.50 minimum postage and
handling, plus copies at 25¢ each from
paper originals or 50¢ each from
microform originals

Marshall Historical Society, Inc.
PO Box 68
Marshall, MI 49068

Mason County Historical Society
(2 miles South, 1½ miles west of
Ludington—location)
1687 South Lake Shore Drive (mailing
address)
Ludington, MI 49431
(231) 843-4808; (231) 843-7089 FAX
info@historicwhitepinevillage.org
http://www.historicwhitepinevillage.org
Ronald M. Wood, Director
summer: Tue–Sun 11:00–4:30; spring & fall:
Tue–Fri 11:00–4:00
Pub. *History Happenings*, quarterly
(Same as Mason County Genealogical,
Historical Resource Center, Rose Hawley
Museum, White Pine Village.)
$35.00 per year membership; library
admission: $4.00 for nonmembers;
research: $10.00 per hour, $5.00 (half-
hour) minimum plus copies at 20¢ per
8½" x 11" page

Mason Historical Society
122 Walnut Court
Mason, MI 48854
(517) 676-2209
Virginia Schlichter, President

**Mayville Area Museum of History and
Genealogy**
(2124 Ohmer Road—location)
PO Box 242 (mailing address)
Mayville, MI 48744
(989) 843-7185
Jean McCrory, Genealogy Secretary
Memorial Day–Labor Day: Fri–Sat
10:00–4:00
Pub. *Newsletter*, annually (Oct)
(obituary file, family genealogies, births,
historical events)
$5.00 per year membership

Menominee County Historical Society
908 11th Avenue
Menominee, MI 49858
(906) 863-2797 (President)
Roger Seidl, President

Midland County Historical Society
Midland Center for the Arts
1801 West Saint Andrews Drive
Midland, MI 48640
(989) 835-7401
Gary F. Skory, Director

Mon–Fri 9:00–noon & 1:00–5:00
Pub. *The Midland Log*, annually, $5.00 per issue
$25.00 per year membership

Montrose Area Historical Society
Montrose Historical and Telephone Pioneer Museum
(144 East Hickory Street—location)
PO Box 577 (mailing address)
Montrose, MI 48457
(810) 639-6644
telemusm@gfn.org
http://www.gfn.org/telemusm
Barbara Hoskins, Secretary
Jan–Mar: Sun 1:00–5:00; Apr–Dec: Sat–Sun 1:00–5:00; tours by appointment; Office hours irregular (leave message on answering machine when personnel not available)
Pub. *Memory Lane Gazette*, quarterly (spring, summer, fall, winter), $6.00 per year subscription; *Montrose Historical and Pioneer Telephone Museum News*, quarterly, free
("Montrose, Michigan, history/artifacts; Telephone collection; genealogy")
$5.00 per year membership; admission: donation; tours: a small fee

New Baltimore Historical Society and Museum
51065 Washington
New Baltimore, MI 48047
(810) 725-4755; (810) 725-7987
Carmen Eggert, Curator; Ed Anne, President
Wed noon–2:00, Sat 11:00–1:00
Pub. *New Baltimore Historical Society Newsletter*, monthly
(genealogy and local history room)
$10.00 per year membership

Newaygo County Society of History and Genealogy
(1038 East Wilcox—location)
PO Box 68 (mailing address)
White Cloud, MI 49349
(231) 689-6631; (231) 689-6699
wclibrary@ncats.net
Allen Bradley, President
Evans Historical Collection: various
Pub. *NCSHG Newsletter*, bimonthly
$10.00 per year membership; research: specific documents found and mailed for $1.00 per copy, extensive searches referred to qualified area genealogists

North Berrien Historical Society
PO Box 207
Coloma, MI 49038
(616) 468-4228

Northville Historical Society
(Griswold Road—location)
PO Box 71 (mailing address)
Northville, MI 48167
(810) 348-1845
Diann Dupuis, Office Manager
Mon–Fri 9:00–1:00; Archives: Wed 9:00–11:00
Pub. *Mill Race Quarterly*
(includes information on early settlement, community history and some residents on microfilm)
from $10.00 per year membership

Oakland County Pioneer and Historical Society
(see Genealogical Societies—Local and Regional, below)

Oakland Township Historical Society

4393 Collins Road
Rochester, MI 48307
Delores Burkhart, Secretary-Treasurer
$6.00 per year membership

Oceana County Historical and Genealogical Society
114 Dryden Street
Hart, MI 49420
(231) 873-2600
Karen Urick, President
Wed 10:00–5:00
Pub. *Newsletter*, quarterly
(obituary files, cemetery census, old school records, maps, atlases, county newspaper microfilm, etc.)
$10.00 per year membership

Ogemaw Genealogical and Historical Society
(see Genealogical Societies—Local and Regional, below)

Ontonagon County Historical Society
422 River Street
Ontonagon, MI 49953-1614
(906) 884-6165
Ruth Ristola, Manager
Mon–Sat 9:00–5:00
("Ontonagon County history; we have quite a bit of genealogy and family trees on a computer that we have access to.")
$2.00 museum admission, copy fees only on materials

Pinckney Area Historical Society
PO Box 606
Pinckney, MI 48169

Pontiac Area Historical and Genealogical Society
(60 East Pike, Pontiac, MI 48342—location)
PO Box 430901 (mailing address)
Pontiac, MI 48343-0901
(248) 334-9929; (248) 334-3418
Joseph P. Lafnear, Sr., President
Pontiac Public Library, Lower Level: second Thur 7:30 P.M.
Pub. *Connections*

Rockwood Area Historical Society
PO Box 68
Rockwood, MI 48173

Romeo Historical Society
(132 Church Street—location)
PO Box 412 (mailing address)
Romeo, MI 48065
(810) 752-4111
Thelma Huet, Administrator
Wed 10:00–noon, and by appointment
$12.00 per year membership

Romulus Historical Society
c/o Romulus Public Library
11121 Wayne Road
Romulus, MI 48174
(734) 941-0775

Rose City Area Historical Society, Inc.
Ogemaw District Library
(107 West Main—location)
PO Box 427 (mailing address)
Rose City, MI 48654
(989) 685-3300
Roberta Willett, Corresponding Secretary
Library: Mon 10:00–8:00, Tue–Fri 10:00–5:00, Sat 10:00–noon
Pub. *Rose City Area Historical Society Newsletter*, three times per year
(Michigan and Ogemaw County history, Ogemaw County newspapers and

censuses on microfilm; "Our society is indexing the Ogemaw County newspapers.")
$5.00 per year membership

Roseville Historical and Genealogical Society
Roseville Public Library
29777 Gratiot Avenue
Roseville, MI 48066-2279
(586) 445-5407 (Library); (586) 445-2487 (President)
http://www.libcoop.net/roseville/rhgs.html
Patricia Chownyk, President
Pub. *RHGS "Newsletter,"* monthly
$10.00 per year membership

Saginaw County Historical Society
(County Castle Building, 500 Federal Avenue—location)
PO Box 390 (mailing address)
Saginaw, MI 48606
(989) 752-2861
Pub. *Saginaw County Historian*

Saint Clair Shores Historical Commission
Saint Clair Shores Public Library
22500 Eleven Mile Road
Saint Clair Shores, MI 48081-1399
(810) 771-9020 (Library); (810) 771-8935
Arthur Woodford, Director
Library: winter: Mon–Thur 9:00–9:00, Sat 9:00–5:00; summer: Mon–Thur 9:00–9:00, Fri 9:00–5:00
Pub. *Muskrat Tales*, two times per year, $3.00 per issue; *Newsletter*, six times per year, $3.00 per issue
(Great Lakes and Michigan historical collections)
$12.50 per year membership

Sanford Historical Society
(North Saginaw at Smith Street—location)
PO Box 243 (mailing address)
Sanford, MI 48657
(989) 687-2771

Sanilac County Historical Society
Sanilac Historical Museum
(228 South Ridge—location)
PO Box 158 (mailing address)
Port Sanilac, MI 48469
(810) 622-9946
Nancy Marvin, Administrator
Museum: June–Sept: Tue–Sun 10:00–4:30; Sept–June: Tue–Wed noon–4:00
(history of Sanilac County only, and some Marine)
$10.00 per year membership; research: $5.00 minimum

Saugatuck-Douglas Historical
Saugatuck-Douglas Museum
PO Box 617
Douglas, MI 49406
(269) 857-7900
http://www.accn.org/~sdhistory/Home.php
$25.00 per year membership

Schoolcraft Historical Society
16278 Prairie Rhonda
Schoolcraft, MI 49087
Earl Christiansen

Shepherd Area Historical Society
(314 Maple Street—location)
PO Box 505 (mailing address)
Shepherd, MI 48883
(989) 828-5881
Rose I. Cohoon, President
by appointment
$3.00 per year membership

Shiawassee County Historical Society
Shiawassee County Archives
PO Box 526
Owosso, MI 48867-0526
(989) 725-8549
couzynse@chartermi.net
Lucille Couzynse, Corresponding Secretary
by appointment
Pub. *Shiawassee Gazette*, three times per
    year
$12.00 per year membership

South Lyon Area Historical Society, Inc.
(300 Dorothy Street—location)
PO Box 263 (mailing address)
South Lyon, MI 48178

South Lyon Historical Commission
(214 West Lake Street—location)
PO Box 263 (mailing address)
South Lyon, MI 48178

**Sterling Heights Genealogical and
Historical Society**
(see Genealogical Societies—Local and
Regional, below)

**The Stockbridge Area
Genealogical/Historical Society**
(see Genealogical Societies—Local and
Regional, below)

Trenton Historical Commission
Trenton Historical Museum
(306 Saint Joseph—location)
2800 Third Street (mailing address)
Trenton, MI 48183
(734) 675-2130
Alfred Sidebottom, Chairman

Troy Historical Society
Troy Museum and Historical Village
(N.W. corner of Livernois and Wattles
Roads—location)
60 West Wattles Road (mailing address)
Troy, MI 48098
(248) 524-3570 (Museum)
museum@ci.troy.mi.us
Loraine Campbell, Manager
Tue–Sat 9:00–5:30, Sun 1:00–5:00
Pub. *Village Press*, quarterly
("City-owned museum with support from
    Troy Historical Society.")
$10.00 per year membership

Van Buren County Historical Society
(6215 East Red Arrow Highway,
East—location)
PO Box 452 (mailing address)
Hartford, MI 49057
(616) 621-2188
$10.00 per year membership; research:
    $10.00

Vicksburg Historical Society
7683 East YZ Avenue
Vicksburg, MI 49097-9714
(616) 649-2876; (616) 649-1733 (Museum,
    to leave a message)
Bonnie Holmes, President
Vicksburg Depot Museum, 300 North
    Richardson, Vicksburg, MI 49097: Sat
    1:00–4:00, and by appointment; meetings
    third Tue 7:30
Pub. *Depot Review*, semiannually
$5.00 per year membership

Washtenaw County Historical Society
Museum on Main Street: A Museum of
County Life
(500 North Main at Beakes Street, Ann
Arbor, MI 48104-location)

PO Box 3336 (mailing address)
Ann Arbor, MI 48106-3336
(734) 662-9092
http://www.washtenawhistory.org
Pub. *Washtenaw Impressions*, seven times
    per year
$15.00 per year membership

**Washtenaw County History District
Commission**
(c/o Washtenaw County Metropolitan
Planning Commission, 100 North Fourth
Avenue—location)
PO Box 8645 (mailing address)
Ann Arbor, MI 48107
(734) 994-2435
Ina Hanel, Staff Representative
meetings: first Thur; office: 8:30–5:00

Waterloo Area Historical Society
PO Box 37
Stockbridge, MI 49285
(517) 596-2254; (313) 769-2219 (Home)
Agnes Dikeman, Museum Director
summer: Tue–Sun 1:00–4:00; Sept: Sat–Sun
    1:00–4:00 (last tour 3:30)
Pub. *Quarterly Newsletter*
$5.00 per year membership

Wayne Historical Society
Wayne Historical Commission
1 Town Square
Wayne, MI 48184
(734) 722-0113

Wexford County Historical Society
(127 Beech Street—location)
PO Box 124 (mailing address)
Cadillac, MI 49601
(231) 775-1717
Linda Boyer, President
Wed–Fri (Memorial Day–Labor Day)
    noon–4:00, Sat noon–4:00, Sun (autumn)
    noon–4:00
$10.00 per year membership

White Lake Area Historical Society
7515 Highland Road
White Lake, MI 48383
http://www.whitelaketwp.com

Wyandotte Historical Society
Wyandotte Museum
2610 Biddle Avenue
Wyandotte, MI 48192
(734) 324-7297; (734) 324-7283 FAX
Marc M. Partin, Site Supervisor
Mon–Fri 9:00–5:00
Pub. *Wyandotte Historical Society
    Newsletter* (not genealogical), monthly
$10.00 per year membership

Ypsilanti Historical Society Museum
220 North Huron Street
Ypsilanti, MI 48197
(734) 482-4990; (734) 483-7481 FAX
http://www.hvcn.org/info/libyhma.html
Mrs. Billie Zolkosky, Archivist
9:00–noon
Pub. *Ypsilanti Gleanings*, quarterly
$5.00 per year membership

Zeeland Historical Society
37 East Main Avenue
Zeeland, MI 49464
(616) 772-4079
William S. Tuinstra, President
Dekker Huis Museum: mid-Mar to mid-Oct:
    Thur 10:00–4:00, Sat 10:00–1:00
Pub. *Timeline*, quarterly; *Year Book*,
    annually
(a few histories of local families for Holland-

Zeeland area)
from $10.00 per year membership

Genealogical Societies

State Genealogical Society

Michigan Genealogical Council
PO Box 80953
Lansing, MI 48908-0953
http://www.rootsweb.com/~mimgc
meetings at Library of Michigan: every other
    month
Pub. *Michigan Genealogical Council
    Newsletter*, four times per year
$10.00 per year membership

Genealogical Societies—Local & Regional

Armada Genealogical Society
http://www.armadalib.org

Bay County Genealogical Society
PO Box 1366
Bay City, MI 48706-0366
(989) 684-6819 (President's home)
theakergen@chartermi.net
http://community.mlive.com/cc/
    baygenealogy
Linda Theaker, President
Society library: by appointment; meetings at
    the Fremont Avenue United Methodist
    Church at the corner of Fremont Avenue
    and Wilson Street: second Wed (except
    July–Aug) 6:30
Pub. *The Clarion*, bimonthly
(Specializes in Bay County and Michigan.
    "Visit our web site for a list of available
    publications. An area resource booklet is
    being developed.")
$10.00 per year membership; research: fees
    and availability vary (done by volunteers)

Berrien County Genealogical Society
PO Box 8808
Benton Harbor, MI 49023-8808
bcgensoc@qtm.net
http://w3.qtm.net/bcgensoc
Brenda Sears, Corresponding Secretary;
    Harold Atwood, Librarian; Joyce Hudak,
    Research Director
Pub. *Pastfinder*, quarterly
(cemetery listings)
$18.00 per year membership; free queries
    with Berrien County connection

Branch County Genealogical Society
PO Box 443
Coldwater, MI 49036
nvance@cbpu.com
http://www.geocities.com/TheTropics/
    1050/Gensociety.html
Norman M. Vance
$5.00 per year membership; research in
    Branch County only: $6.00 for first hour,
    $5.00 for each hour thereafter

Calhoun County Genealogical Society
PO Box 777
Marshall, MI 49068
(616) 962-3498
THowell582@aol.com
Nancy Hibiske, President
meetings at VFW Hall: fourth Tue
    (Sept–June) 7:00
Pub. *Generations*, bimonthly
(cemetery transcriptions)
$12.00 per year membership

Cass River Genealogy Society
359 South Franklin Street
Frankenmuth, MI 48734

wickson@frankenmuthcity.com
http://www.frankenmuthcity.com/library/
genealogy.htm
Pub. *Newsletter*
$10.00 per year membership

Charlevoix County Genealogical Society
Boyne District Library
201 East Main Street
Boyne City, MI 49712
http://www.rootsweb.com/~micharle/cx-
03.htm
Nancy Fulkerson, President
meetings: first Thur 7:00
Pub. *Back-tracking Pa's Roots*, quarterly,
$5.00 per year subscription
(specializes in Charlevoix County only)
$10.00 per year membership; no search
services, but will send list of professional
researchers

Cheboygan County Genealogical Society
PO Box 51
Cheboygan, MI 49721
nhastie@voyager.net
http://www.rootsweb.com/~miccgs/
CCGSmainx.html
Nancy Hastie, President
meetings at Family House Restaurant:
second Wed 9:30 A.M.
Pub. *Cheboygan Rivertown Roots*, quarterly
$10.00 per year membership

**The Genealogists of the Clinton County
Historical Society**
(16101 Brook Road, Lansing, MI—Archives
location)
PO Box 23 (mailing address)
Saint Johns, MI 48879-0023
(517) 482-5117
Michael Pease, President
Mon–Tue 9:00–4:00, Thur–Fri 2:00–6:00
Pub. *Clinton County Trails*, quarterly
$10.00 per year membership (includes
membership in Clinton County Historical
Society); research: $6.00 per hour

Dearborn Genealogical Society
The McFadden-Ross House/Dearborn
Historical Museum
(915 South Brady, Dearborn, MI
48124—location)
PO Box 1112 (mailing address)
Dearborn, MI 48121-1112
(313) 565-3000 (Museum)
Dearbrown2@aol.com
http://www.rootsweb.com/~midgs/index.htm
Patricia Gee, President
Museum and Archives: Mon–Fri 1:00–4:00
Pub. *Dearborn Genealogical Society
Newsletter*, quarterly
$10.00 per year membership

Delta County Genealogical Society
314 North 20th Street
Escanaba, MI 49829
(906) 786-1893
Marguerite Larsen, Librarian
Pub. *Delta Pedigree Press*, quarterly
$7.00 per year membership

**The Detroit Society for Genealogical
Research, Inc.**
Detroit Public Library
Burton Historical Collection
5201 Woodward Avenue
Detroit, MI 48202-4093
(313) 833-1480 (Library); (313) 832-0877
FAX (Library)
umpadre@aol.com
http://www.fgs.org/~fgs/soc0042.htm
Rev. C. Corydon Randall II, President

Pub. *Detroit Society for Genealogical
Research Magazine*, quarterly; *Detroit
Society for Genealogical Research
Newsletter*, quarterly
$15.00 per year membership

Dickinson County Genealogical Society
Dickinson County Public Library
401 Iron Mountain Street
Iron Mountain, MI 49801
(906) 774-1218 (Library); (906) 774-4079
FAX (Library)
John Alquist, President
Library: winter: Mon–Fri 9:00–9:00, Sat
9:00–5:00, Sun 1:00–4:00; summer:
Mon–Fri 9:00–8:00, Sat 9:00–1:00
Pub. *Dickinson Diggins*, quarterly
$10.00 per year membership

Downriver Genealogical Society
(1335 Southfield Road—location)
PO Box 476 (mailing address)
Lincoln Park, MI 48146
(313) 382-3229 (President)
sherry@localonline.net
http://www.rootsweb.com/~midrgs/drgs.htm
Sherry Huntington, President
Tue–Thur & Sat 1:00–5:00; meetings at
Saint John's Church, Fourth and Chestnut
Streets, Wyandotte, MI: third Wed 7:30
P.M.
Pub. *Downriver Seeker*, quarterly
$10.00 per year membership

Eaton County Genealogical Society, Inc.
(100 West Lawrence Avenue, 1885
Historical Courthouse—location)
PO Box 337 (mailing address)
Charlotte, MI 48813
(517) 543-8792; (517) 543-6999 FAX
ecgsoc@juno.com
http://www.rootsweb.com/~miecgs/Index.
htm
Drouscella Halsey, Secretary
Mon–Thur 10:00–2:00, Mon 6:00–8:00
Pub. *Eaton County Quest*, $4.50 per issue
$15.00 per year membership; free queries for
members

Elkhart County Genealogical Society
(see Indiana, Part 2)

Farmington Genealogical Society
Farmington Community Library
Farmington Branch
23500 Liberty Street
Farmington, MI 48335-3570
(248) 474-7770
Myra Burger, Corresponding Secretary
Library: Mon–Thur 10:00–9:00, Fri–Sat
(during school year) 10:00–5:00
Pub. *Newsletter*, eight times per year
(monthly, except June–Aug & Dec)
$10.00 per year membership

Flint Genealogical Society
PO Box 1217
Flint, MI 48501-1217
Jack O. Briggs, Registrar
Mon–Fri 10:00–9:00
Pub. *Flint Genealogical Quarterly*, three
times per year; *Flint Genealogical Society
Newsletter*, monthly
(has Genesee County obituaries)
$15.00 per year membership

Ford Genealogy Club
Ford Motor Credit Company Building, Room
1491
Dearborn, MI 48126
mbrautig@yahoo.com;
miprofgenie@wwnet.net

http://www.wwnet.net/~krugman1/fgc
Michael Brautigan, Secretary; Karen
Krugman, President
Pub. *The Rear View Mirror* (by email or
USPS)
$12.00 per year membership (primarily Ford
and Visteon employees and spouses);
fifty-word queries: $1.00 for nonmembers

Four Flags Area Genealogical Society
(Niles Community Library Meeting
Room—location)
PO Box 414 (mailing address)
Niles, MI 49120
(616) 463-4696
Carole Kiernan, President
9:00–8:00
Pub. *Four Flags Tracer* (Berrien and Cass
counties), quarterly
$14.00 per year membership

**Friends of the Mitchell Public Library
Research Committee**
(address withheld upon request)

Gaylord Fact-Finders Genealogical Society
PO Box 1524
Gaylord, MI 49735-5534
(231) 584-2625
dmarz@avci.net
Donna M. Marrs, President
meetings: third Wed (Jan–June & Aug–Nov)
7:00–9:00
Pub. *The Keystone Newsletter*, quarterly
(Jan, Apr, July, Oct)
(Otsego County, Michigan, newspapers)
$10.00 per year membership; queries: $2.00
for nonmembers; research: $5.00 per hour
plus expenses

Genealogy Group
Benzie Area Historical Society
Benzie Area Historical Museum
(6941 Traverse Avenue—location)
PO Box 185 (mailing address)
Benzonia, MI 49616
(231) 882-5539 (Museum)
Florence Bixby, Curator

Grand Haven Genealogical Society
Loutit Library
407 Columbus
Grand Haven, MI 49417

**Grand Traverse Genealogical Society
(GTAGS)**
PO Box 2015
Traverse City, MI 49685-2015
(231) 995-9388
kayzins@aol.com
http://www.rootsweb.com/~migtags/gtag.
html
Jan Novak; Richard Hayes
Pub. *Kinship Tales*, quarterly (May, Aug,
Nov, Feb)
(includes the northern Michigan counties of
Antrim, Benzie, Kalkaska, Grand
Traverse, and Leelanau; census, cemetery
books; collection of books and film
housed at Traverse Area District Library)
$10.00 per year membership; research: $5.00
per hour plus expenses

**Gratiot County Historical and
Genealogical Society**
(see Historical Societies—Local and
Regional, above)

Harrison Area Genealogical Society
PO Box 796
Harrison, MI 48625
http://www.rootsweb.com/~miclare/

harrison.htm
Nancy Dunham, Corresponding Secretary
meetings at Harrison Community Library:
 first Wed
Pub. *Harrison Heritage Newsletter*, quarterly
$5.00 per hear membership

Holland Genealogical Society
Herrick Public Library
300 River Avenue
Holland, MI 49423
(616) 355-1400 (Library)
Don Johnson, President
Library: winter: Mon–Thur 9:00–9:00,
 Fri–Sat 9:00–6:00, Sun 2:00–5:00;
 summer: Mon–Thur 9:00–9:00, Fri
 9:00–6:00, Sat 9:00–1:00
Pub. *Family Ties*, three times per year
$15.00 per year membership

Huron County Genealogical Society
2843 Electric Avenue
Port Huron, MI 48060
Ford and Marilyn Hebner

Huron Shores Genealogical Society
1050 North Skeel Avenue
Oscoda, MI 48750
(989) 739-9581
Rosemary Klenow, President
Mon & Fri–Sat 9:00–5:00, Tue–Thur
 9:00–8:00
Pub. *Huron Shores Genealogical Society
 Newsletter*, monthly
$8.00 per year membership

Huron Valley Genealogical Society
Milford Township Library
1100 Atlantic Street
Milford, MI 48381
(248) 684-0845 (Library); (248) 684-2923
 FAX
milford@tln.lib.mi.us (Library)
http://milf.tln.lib.mi.us (Library)
Tina Hatch, Library Director

Ionia County Genealogical Society
13051 Ainsworth Road, Route 3
Lake Odessa, MI 48849-9406
(616) 374-3141; (616) 374-8424 FAX
pkswiler@voyager.net
http://www.rootsweb.com/~miionia/icgs.htm
Pamela K. Swiler, Founder
by appointment; meetings at the Lake Manor
 Apartments Community Room: second
 Sat (except Dec) 1:00
Pub. *Ionia County Genealogical Society
 Newsletter*, quarterly
$15.00 per year membership

Jackson County Genealogical Society
c/o Jackson District Library
244 West Michigan Avenue
Jackson, MI 49201
(517) 787-8105
Doris Littebrant, Research Coordinator
Library: Sept–May: Mon–Thur 9:30–8:30,
 Fri 9:30–6:00, Sat 9:30–5:00; June–Aug:
 Mon–Thur 9:30–7:00, Fri 9:30–6:00, Sat
 9:30–1:30
Pub. *Lexicon*, quarterly
$12.00 per year membership

Kalamazoo Valley Genealogical Society
(Western Michigan University, Archives and
 Regional History Collections—collection
 location)
PO Box 405 (mailing address)
Comstock, MI 49041
(616) 381-8445
mikvgs@hotmail.com; sanders@net-link.net
 (for membership application)

http://www.rootsweb.com/~mikvgs
Ruth H. Peterson, Editor
Archives: Fall/Winter/Spring: Tue–Fri
 8:00–5:00, Sat 9:00–4:00; July–Aug:
 Mon–Fri 10:00–4:00
Pub. *The Kalamazoo Valley Heritage*,
 monthly
(Kalamazoo County and southwestern
 Michigan)
$14.00 per year membership; research: $5.00
 per hour plus cost of copies

Kalkaska Genealogical Society
PO Box 353
Kalkaska, MI 49646

Lapeer County Genealogical Society
Marguerite DeAngeli Branch Library
921 West Nepessing Street
Lapeer, MI 48446
Corresponding Secretary
Library: Mon–Thur 9:00–9:00, Fri
 9:00–5:00, Sat (winter) 9:00–5:00, Sat
 (summer) 9:00–2:00, Sun (winter)
 noon–5:00
Pub. *Lapeer Legacy*, quarterly
$12.00 per year membership

Lenawee County Genealogical Committee
Lenawee County Historical Society, Inc.
(Lenawee County Historical Museum, 110
 East Church Street—location)
PO Box 511 (mailing address)
Adrian, MI 49221
(517) 265-6071
Doris Conklin Trowbridge, Archivist;
 Charles N. Liquist, Ph.D., Curator
Pub. *From the Tower*, five times per year
$10.00 per year membership

Livingston County Genealogical Society
PO Box 1073
Howell, MI 48844-1073
Cynthia Grostick, President
Pub. *Newsletter*, quarterly
$10.00 per year membership

Luce-Mackinac Genealogical Society
PO Box 113
Engadine, MI 49827-0113
wkuebler@portup.com; lakenyon@mich.com
http://www.rootsweb.com/~miluce/luce-
 mac.htm
Georgianna Kuebler, President; Lucille
 Kenyon, Secretary
Pub. newsletter
$6.50 per year membership

Lyon Township Genealogical Society
Lyon Township Public Library
(27005 Milford Road—location)
PO Box 326 (mailing address)
New Hudson, MI 48165
(248) 437-8800 (Library)
Mary Canfield, Library Director
Library: Mon & Fri 10:00–5:00, Tue & Thur
 10:00–9:00, Sat 10:00–3:00

Macomb County Genealogy Group
Mount Clemens Public Library
150 Cass Avenue
Mount Clemens, MI 48043
http://www.ole.net/~maggie/macomb/
 mcgroup.htm
Deborah J. Larsen, Assistant Library Director

Marquette County Genealogical Society
Peter White Public Library
217 North Front Street
Marquette, MI 49855
(906) 226-4311 (Library); (906) 226-1783
 FAX (Library)

SherryeW@aol.com
http://members.aol.com/MQTCGS/
 MCGS/mcgs.html
Sherrye Woodworth, Corresponding
 Secretary
Pub. *Lake Superior Roots*, three times per
 year
$12.00 per year membership

Mid-Michigan Genealogical Society
(Valley Court Community Center, 201
 Hillside Court, East Lansing, MI—location)
PO Box 16033 (mailing address)
Lansing, MI 48901-6033
Ruth Z. Lewis, C.G.R.S., Chairman,
 Research Committee
meetings fourth Wed (Jan–May &
 Sept–Nov) 7:15–9:00
Pub. *Newsletter*, three times per year
$10.00 per year membership; queries
 accepted from members only; research:
 $10.00 per hour

Midland Genealogical Society
Grace A. Dow Library
1710 West Saint Andrews Drive
Midland, MI 48640-2698
http://www.rootsweb.com/~mimgs
Bob Mass, President
meetings: third Wed (Sept–Nov & Jan–May)
 7:00
Pub. *Pioneer Record*, four times per year,
 $6.00 per year subscription
("Midland County research and publications:
 cemeteries, obituaries, marriages, church
 records, census; volunteers to help with
 library research and inquiries five
 afternoons per week." Issues Pioneer
 Certificate)
$14.00 per year membership; research: $5.00
 per hour ($3.00 minimum), plus cost of
 copies and postage

Genealogical Society of Monroe County, MI
(Society Archives, 126 South Monroe
 Street—location)
PO Box 1428 (mailing address)
Monroe, MI 48161
(734) 529-2216 (Archives)
flogen@dundee.net
http://www.tdi.net/havekost/gsmc.htm
Beulah Mens, President; Florence Wilson,
 Archives
Pub. *G.S.M.C. Record*, quarterly
$15.00 per year membership

Muskegon County Genealogical Society
Hackley Public Library
316 West Webster Avenue
Muskegon, MI 49440
http://MCGS1972@aol.com
Dawn M. Kelley, President
Pub. *Family Tree Talk*, quarterly
$15.00 per year membership; free queries for
 members and nonmembers; research: two
 hours research for nominal fee to cover
 postage and cost of copies

Newaygo County Society of History and Genealogy
(see Historical Societies—Local and
 Regional, above)

North Oakland Genealogical Society
Orion Room
Orion Township Public Library
825 Joslyn Road
Lake Orion, MI 48362
(248) 693-3001
Library: Mon–Thur 10:00–9:00, Fri–Sat
 10:00–5:00, Sun (fall–spring) 1:00–5:00,

closed holiday weekends; meetings: third
Thur (Feb–May & Sept–Nov) 7:00
Pub. *Heirlines*, monthly
$15.00 per year membership (to Ella Mae
Schultz, Membership Chairperson, 1440
Hemingway Road, Lake Orion, MI
48360)

Northeast Michigan Genealogical Society
Jesse Besser Museum
491 Johnson Street
Alpena, MI 49707
(989) 595-2384; (989) 354-8689; (989) 595-
2593 (President)
jr333@chartermi.net
http://www.rootsweb.com/~minemgs/
NEMGS_home_page.htm
Janet Romas, President
Museum: 10:00–5:00; meetings third Thur
6:30
Pub. *Roots and Branches*, quarterly
$10.00 per year membership; research: none
available by mail

Northville Genealogical Society
PO Box 932
Northville, MI 48167-0932
http://www.rootsweb.com/~mings
Pat Allen, Past President
meetings at Northville District Library:
second Sun (Sept–June)
Pub. *Northville Genealogy Society
Newsletter*, quarterly
$15.00 per year membership; research using
indexed materials only: first hour free,
$7.50 per hour thereafter

Northwest Territory Genealogical Society
(see Indiana, Part 2)

Oakland County Genealogical Society
(Baldwin Public Library, 300 West Merrill
Street, Birmingham, MI 48009—location)
PO Box 1094 (mailing address)
Birmingham, MI 48012
(248) 335-4061
John Beedle-Gee, President
meetings: first Tue (Oct–June) 7:00
Pub. *Quarterly, Acorns to Oaks*, quarterly
(Dec, Mar, June, Sept)
$10.00 per year membership

**Oakland County Pioneer and Historical
Society**
Pine Grove Historical Museum
Governor Moses Wisner Historic House
405 Oakland Avenue
Pontiac, MI 48342
(248) 338-6732; (248) 338-6731 FAX
ocphs@wwnet.net
http://wwnet.net/~ocphs/index.html
Administrative Director
Office and Library: Mon–Fri 9:00–4:00
Pub. *Oakland Gazette*, quarterly
(local, state, family histories, genealogy,
Civil War; Howlett Collection of local
history on specific families, Avery
Collection of marriages, births, deaths of
Oakland County families; 2,500 books,
1,500 bound periodical volumes, vertical
file of photographs. "Oldest county
historical society in Michigan [1874]")
admission: $5.00 for nonmembers; research:
see web site for fees by mail or email

**Oceana County Historical and
Genealogical Society**
(see Historical Societies—Local and
Regional, above)

**Ogemaw Genealogical and Historical
Society**

Ogemaw County Museum
PO Box 734
West Branch, MI 48661-0734

**Pontiac Area Historical and Genealogical
Society**
(see Historical Societies—Local and
Regional, above)

Presque Isle County Genealogical Society
Onaway Branch Library
PO Box 742
Onaway, MI 49765

Reed City Area Genealogical Society
(780 North Park Street—location)
PO Box 27 (mailing address)
Reed City, MI 49677
(231) 832-5431
Betsy Randall, President
1 May–1 Oct: Mon–Sun 1:00–4:00, and by
appointment
Pub. *RCAGS Reader*, semiannually
$7.00 per year membership

**Roseville Historical and Genealogical
Society**
(see Historical Societies—Local and
Regional, above)

Saginaw Genealogical Society, Inc.
Hoyt Public Library
Eddy Historical Collection
505 Janes Avenue
Saginaw, MI 48605
(989) 755-0904 (Eddy Room); (989) 755-
9828 FAX (Eddy Room)
Darlene A. Hudson, Corresponding Secretary
Eddy Room: Mon–Thur 9:00–9:00, Fri–Sat
9:00–5:00, Sun (Oct–May) 1:00–5:00;
meetings second Tue (Sept–Nov &
Jan–Apr) 6:30 in Auditorium
Pub. *Timbertown Log*, quarterly (fall, winter,
spring, summer); *Newsletter*, monthly
(collection devoted first to Saginaw, then
Michigan, but contains info for most of
the world; largest collection north of
Detroit)
$15.00 per year membership

Saint Clair Family History Group, Inc.
PO Box 611483
Port Huron, MI 48060-1483
(810) 982-0441 (President)
Jim Muir, President
Saint Clair County Library: meeting fourth
Wed
Pub. *Blue Water Family Backgrounds*,
quarterly
(genealogy and local history)
$10.00 per year membership; research:
$10.00 per name

The Searchers
14300 "V" Avenue
Vicksburg, MI 49097
(616) 778-3712
Lucille Pierson, President

Shiawassee County Genealogical Society
PO Box 841
Owosso, MI 48867
(989) 725-8549
couzynse@chartermi.net
Mrs. Robert Couzynse, Corresponding
Secretary
Mon–Thur 10:00–9:00, Fri–Sat 10:00–5:00
Pub. *Steppin' Stones*, three times per year
(Feb, June, Oct)
$15.00 per year membership

Southern Michigan Genealogical Society

PO Box 371
Litchfield, MI 49252

**Sterling Heights Genealogical and
Historical Society**
Sterling Heights Public Library
40255 Dodge Park Road
Sterling Heights, MI 48078-4496
(810) 977-6267
Julia Santini
Mon–Thur 9:30–8:30, Fri–Sat 9:30–5:00
(closed Sat in summer)
Pub. *Ancestral Tree*, quarterly
$8.00 per year membership

**The Stockbridge Area
Genealogical/Historical Society**
PO Box 966
Stockbridge, MI 49285
stockbridgeareaghs@hotmail.com
Cynthia Grostick, Secretary
Pub. *The Four Corners*, four times per year
$10.00 per year membership

Three Rivers Genealogy Club
13724 Spence Road
Three Rivers, MI 49093
Mrs. Robert Shingledecker

Tri-County Genealogical Society
21715 Brittany
Eastpointe, MI 48021-2503
(810) 774-7953
rfred27240@aol.com
Randy Ferrari
(serves Michigan and Ontario, Canada; also
conducting genealogy research in
Michigan)

Tri-State Genealogical Society
30874 U.S. #12
Sturgis, MI 49091

Tuscola County Genealogical Society
1658 West Gilford Road
Caro, MI 48723
Pub. *Tuscola County Genealogical Society
Newsletter*, bimonthly
$6.00 per year membership

Union City Genealogical Society
210 Charlotte Street
Union City, MI 49094
(517) 741-3597
Bradley C. Waite, Treasurer
by appointment
$6.00 per year membership

Van Buren Regional Genealogical Society
Van Buren County Library
Webster Memorial Library
(200 North Phelps Street—location)
PO Box 143 (mailing address)
Decatur, MI 49045
(616) 423-4771 (Library); (616) 423-8373
FAX (Library)
Toni I. Benson, Librarian
Library: Mon–Thur 9:00–8:00, Fri
9:00–5:00, Sat 9:00–3:00
Pub. *Van Buren Echoes*, quarterly
(local history, family history; "We also serve
Allegan, Berrien, Cass, and Kalamazoo
counties.")
$14.00 per year membership

**The Genealogical Society of Washtenaw
County, Michigan, Inc.**
PO Box 7155
Ann Arbor, MI 48107-7155
(734) 483-2799
wwwgswc@aol.com
http://www.hvcn.org/info/gswc

Marcia C. McCrary, President
Pub. *Family History Capers*, quarterly;
   *Genealogical Society of Washtenaw
   County Newsletter*, quarterly
$14.00 per year membership; research:
   $10.00 donation

Wayland Tree Tracers Genealogy Society
129 West Cedar Street
Wayland, MI 49348
(616) 792-2891
Donna L. Benedict, Corresponding Secretary
Wed 1:00–5:00
(specializes in eastern Allegan County)
donation accepted

Western Michigan Genealogical Society
Grand Rapids Public Library
Michigan and Family History Department
111 Library Street
Grand Rapids, MI 49503-3268
(616) 456-3640 (Library)
wmgs@wmgs.org
http://www.wmgs.org
Janet Jensen, Corresponding Secretary
Library: Mon–Wed 9:00–9:00, Thur–Sat
   9:00–5:30; meetings: first Sat (Sept–June)
Pub. *Michigana*, quarterly (Mar, June, Sept,
   Dec), $10.00 per year subscription;
   *Western Michigan Genealogical Society
   Newsletter*, irregularly
$16.00 per year membership; research:
   searches, c/o Search Committee: $10.00
   per hour ($5.00 minimum, $30.00
   maximum, includes up to five
   photocopies and postage in the U.S.)

**Western Wayne County Genealogical
Society**
PO Box 530063
Livonia, MI 48153-0063
(734) 425-8832
Pub. *The Society Page*, quarterly; *Messenger
   Newsletter*, four to five times per year
$10.00 per year membership; queries
   published in quarterly

Independent Publications and Miscellany

A.U.W. Genealogy Colloquium
1830 Washtenaw Avenue
Ann Arbor, MI 48104

Albion Historian
900 South Eaton Street
Albion, MI 49224
(517) 629-5402
albionfp@hotmail.com
Frank Passic
(books and articles, research, genealogy)

Ann Arbor Hands-On Museum
219 East Huron Street
Ann Arbor, MI 48104
(734) 995-5439

Ann Arbor Historical Foundation
312 South Division Street
Ann Arbor, MI 48104
(734) 996-3008

Con Foster Museum
(Grandview Parkway—location)
400 Boardman Avenue, PO Box 592
(mailing address)
Traverse City, MI 49685-0592
(231) 941-2332

Coppertown USA
(Red Jacket Road—location)

1197 Calumet Avenue (mailing address)
Calumet, MI 49913
(906) 337-4579

Gerald R. Ford Library
1000 Beal Avenue
Ann Arbor, MI 48109
(734) 741-2218; (734) 741-2341 FAX
ford.library@nara.gov
http://www.ford.utexas.edu
Mon–Fri 8:45–4:45
(historical, has only "a small and incomplete
   file on the ancestry of President Ford")

Public Museum of Grand Rapids
Van Andel Museum Center
272 Pearl Street, N.W.
Grand Rapids, MI 49504-5371
(616) 456-3977; (616) 456-3873
tchester@ci.grand-rapids.mi.us
http://www.grmuseum.org
Timothy J. Chester, Director
Mon–Fri 9:00–5:00, Sun noon–5:00 (361
   days per year)
Pub. *Museum Magazine*, quarterly;
   Discoveries, monthly
(specializes in Grand Rapids businesses,
   especially west Michigan furniture
   manufacturers)
$35.00 per year membership; research:
   $20.00 per hour

H-Michigan
H-Michigan-request@h-net.msu.edu
   (Editors)
http://www2.h-net.msu.edu/~michigan
(history discussion network)

Ingham County Commission on History
(Ingham County Courthouse—location)
PO Box 319 (mailing address)
Mason, MI 48854-0319
(517) 676-7213; (517) 676-7264 FAX
http://www.ingham.org
Becky Bennett, Secretary
Courthouse: Mon–Fri 8:00–5:00; tours by
   appointment
("Government facility, oldest County
   Historical Commission in the state; we do
   government research only, no public
   research is done except for informational
   services. *Ingham County Courthouse
   Walking Tour Book and History* by
   Thomas G. Clinton.")

**Kent County Council for Historic
Preservation**
115 College Avenue, S.E.
Grand Rapids, MI 49503
(616) 458-2422
Kinseeker Publications
(5697 Old Maple Trail—location)
PO Box 184 (mailing address)
Grawn, MI 49637
kinseeker6@aol.com
Vicki Wilson, Owner

Marine Historical Society of Detroit
29825 Joy Road
Westland, MI 48185
(734) 421-6130

Michiana History Publications
(see Indiana, Part 2)

**Michigan County Clerks Genealogical
Directory**
http://www.sos.state.mi.us/history/
   archive/archgene.html

Michigan Department of Transportation
State Transportation Building

425 West Ottawa Street
Lansing, MI 48933
(517) 322-1675
branklinf@mdot.state.mi.us
http://www.mdot.state.mi.us/mappub (Maps)

Michigan Historical Museum
717 West Allegan Street
Lansing, MI 48918
(517) 373-3559; (517) 373-1645 (magazine);
   (800) 366-3703 (museum and magazine)
http://www.sos.state.mi.us/history/
   museum/explore/explore.html
Basil Hedrick, Ph.D., Director, Division of
   Museums, Archaeology and Publications
Pub. *Michigan History Magazine*
(primarily historical, not a specific resource
   for genealogists)

Michigan Polonia
(see Ethnic Archives, Libraries and
Societies—Polish, Part 3)

MiGenWeb
Part of The USGenweb Project
slredmond@earthlink.net;
   brauschj@earthlink.net
http://www.rootsweb.com/~migenweb
Sandra Redmond, State Coordinator; Joan
   Brausch, Assistant Coordinator
(links to other Michigan resources)

Minnesota

Archives and Libraries with Holdings in Genealogy

State Archives and Library

Minnesota Historical Society Research Center
State Archives Department
345 Kellogg Boulevard, West
Saint Paul, MN 55102-1906
(651) 296-2143; (651) 297-7436 FAX
reference@mnhs.org
http://www.mnhs.org
Kathryn Otto, Head of Reference
Tue noon–9:00, Wed–Sat 9:00–5:00
Pub. *The Gazette*, quarterly, free
research: $12.00 per half-hour for Minnesota
    residents, $15.00 per half-hour for non-
    Minnesota residents, $11.00 per half-hour
    for members of the Minnesota Historical
    Society (see
    http://www.mnhs.org/library/about/servic
    es.html for more details and forms)

Minnesota Library Association
1619 Dayton Avenue, Suite 314
Saint Paul, MN 55104
(651) 641-0982; (612) 649-3169 FAX
alison@mnlibraryassociation.org
http://www.mnlibraryassociation.org

State Historical Societies

Minnesota Historical Society
345 Kellogg Boulevard, West
Saint Paul, MN 55102-1906
(651) 296-0332 (Membership); (888) 293-
    4440 (Membership)
membership@mnhs.org
http://www.mnhs.org/about/members/
    index.html
Rhonda Teich-Hickey, Membership Manager
Mon–Fri 8:30–5:00
Pub. *Minnesota History*, quarterly, $20.00
    per year subscription (free with
    membership); *Member News*, bimonthly
    (free with membership); *Roots*, quarterly,
    $5.00 per year subscription
$45.00 per year membership

Minnesota State Archaeologist's Office
Fort Snelling History Center
Saint Paul, MN 55111
Mark Dudzik, State Archaeologist
(listing of all cemetery sites older than 50
    years within the state)

Central Minnesota Historical Center
Saint Cloud State University
Learning Resources and Technology
Services
31 Centennial Hall
720 Fourth Avenue, South
Saint Cloud, MN 56301-4498
(320) 308-3254; (320) 255-2086; (320) 255-
    4778 FAX
pschenk@stcloudstate.edu
http://www.stcloudstate.edu/search/ contact.
    asp?contact=Central+Minnesota+Center
Pat Schenk, Archivist

Northeast Minnesota Historical Center
Library Annex 202, University of
Minnesota—Duluth
416 Library Drive
Duluth, MN 55812-3001
(218) 726-8526
pmaus@d.umn.edu
http://www.d.umn.edu/lib/collections/

nemn.html
Patricia Maus, Manager/Curator of
    Manuscripts
Mon–Fri 8:00–noon & 1:15–4:30
(archives for northeast Minnesota history: St.
    Louis, Lake, Cook and Carlton counties)
copies: 10¢ per page plus $1.50 postage

Northwest Minnesota Historical Center
Moorhead State University
Livingston Lord Library, Room 409
1104 Seventh Avenue, South
Moorhead, MN 56563
(218) 236-2346
archives@mnstate.edu
http://www.mnstate.edu/archives
Dr. Terry L. Shoptaugh
Mon–Fri 8:00–noon & 1:00–4:30
("Because other repositories in the region
    maintain well established genealogical
    collections, the Northwest Center does not
    actively collect genealogy materials. The
    Center does hold the family history
    collection of the Heritage Education
    Commission. Also, links to various
    genealogy web sites may be accessed
    here.")

Southwest Minnesota Historical Center
Southwest State University
Marshall, MN 56258
(507) 532-7373; (507) 537-6200 FAX
Jan Louwagie, Coordinator
afternoons, during academic calendar, by
    appointment

**University Archives and Southern
Minnesota Historical Center**
Mankato State University
Memorial Library
(Maywood and Ellis—location)
MSU #19, PO Box 8419 (mailing address)
Mankato, MN 56002
(507) 389-1029; (507) 389-5952; (507) 389-
    5953; (507) 389-5155 FAX
daardi.sizemore@mnsu.edu
http://www.lib.mnsu.edu/lib/archives/
    archives.html
Daardi Sizemore, Archives and Special
    Collections Librarian

West Central Minnesota Historical Center
University of Minnesota
Rodney A. Briggs Library
600 East Fourth Street
Morris, MN 56267
(320) 589-2211, ext. 6172
ummlib@morris.umn.edu
http://www.mrs.umn.edu/library
Professor John Quinn Imholte
20 hours per week
(Big Stone, Chippewa, Douglas, Grant, Pope,
    Stevens, Swift and Traverse counties
    records and manuscripts)

City, County and Regional Archives and Libraries
(A more exhaustive list of public and
academic libraries can be found at
http://www.mnlibs.org/dir/index.cfm.)

Anoka County Library
Northtown Central Library
711 Highway 10, N.E.
Blaine, MN 55434-2398
(612) 717-3267; (612) 717-3259 FAX
anoka@anoka.lib.mn.us;
    aclref@anoka.lib.mn.us
http://www.anoka.lib.mn.us

Austin Public Library
323 Fourth Avenue, N.E.

Austin, MN 55912-3370
(507) 433-2391; (507) 433-8787
aplref@selco.lib.mn.us
http://www.austin-
    mn.com/Library/libhome.htm
Linda Anderson, Reference Librarian
Mon–Thur 9:00–9:00, Fri–Sat 9:00–5:00,
    Sun (Labor Day to Memorial Day)
    1:00–5:00
("Maintain microfilm of Austin and Mower
    County newspapers, local cemetery index
    and obit. index.")

Bemidji State University
A. C. Clark Library
1500 Birchmont Drive, N.E.
Bemidji, MN 56601
(218) 755-3349; (218) 755-3342; (218) 755-
    2051 FAX
http://bsuweb.bemidji.msus.edu/~library
William Shaman, Librarian and University
    Archivist
by appointment only
(university archives only, no longer the
    North Central Minnesota Regional
    Historical Center)

Carleton College
Lawrence McKinley Gould Memorial
Library
Northfield, MN 55057
(507) 663-4266; (507) 663-4204 FAX
http://www.library/carleton.edu

Cleveland Historical Center
303 Broadway
Cleveland, MN 56017
(507) 931-2054; (507) 931-1510

Dakota County Library
1340 Wescott Road
Eagan, MN 55123-1099
(952) 688-1500; (952) 688-1515 FAX
askalibrarian@co.dakota.mn.us
http://www.co.dakota.mn.us/library
William G. Asp, Director

Duluth Public Library
520 West Superior Street
Duluth, MN 55802-1578
(218) 723-3802; (218) 723-3821; (218) 723-
    3815 FAX
webmail@duluth.lib.mn.us
http://www.duluth.lib.mn.us
David Ouse, Head, Reference; Don Johnson,
    Reference Librarian I
Mon–Thur 10:00–8:30, Fri noon–5:30, Sat
    (Oct–May) 10:00–4:00

The History Museum of East Otter Tail County
230 First Avenue North
Perham, MN 56573
(218) 346-7676
museum@eot.com
http://www.HistoryMuseumEOT.org
Lina Belar, Executive Director
Mon–Sat 10:00–5:00, Sun 1:00–4:00
("We maintain a searchable index of local
    historical records on the web. The site
    contains the East Otter Tail County
    History Books, Vol. I & II, an index to the
    Perham Enterprise-Bulletin newspapers
    since 1883, the register of births and
    deaths in Perham from 1880 to 1889, plus
    a database of historical photographs.")

1877 Peterson Station Museum
(228 Mill Street—location)
PO Box 233 (mailing address)
Peterson, MN 55962
(507) 895-2551

John Erickson, Curator
Sat–Sun (Memorial Day to Labor Day)
10:00–5:00

Freeborn County Historical Museum
1031 Bridge Avenue
Albert Lea, MN 56007
(507) 373-8003
fchm@smig.net
http://www.smig-net/fchm
Linda Evenson, Librarian
Museum and Library: Tue–Fri 10:00–5:00
Pub. *FCHM Newsletter*, quarterly
$20.00 per year membership; research:
$10.00 per hour

Hamline University
School of Law Library
1536 Hewitt Avenue
Saint Paul, MN 55104
(612) 641-2308; (612) 641-2435 FAX

Hay Lake School Museums
(Country Road 3 and Old Marine
Trail—location)
PO Box 123 (mailing address)
Scandia, MN 55073
Hazel Gronquist, Executive Director
Sat–Sun (May– 1 Nov) 1:30–4:30
Pub. *Historical Whisperings*, quarterly
(genealogical services)
$10.00 per year membership

Henderson Public Library
(110 South 6th Street—location)
PO Box 404 (mailing address)
Henderson, MN 56044-0404
(507) 248-3880 voice & FAX
libtsh@tds.lib.mn.us

Heritage-Hjemkomst Interpretive Center
202 First Avenue, North
Moorhead, MN 56560
(218) 233-5604; (218) 299-5511 (to
schedule a group tour)
http://www.hjemkomst-center.com
Rachel Asleson, Programs and Exhibits;
Charlotte Cox, Director
Mon & Wed–Sat 9:00–5:00, Tue
(June–Sept) 9:00–9:00, Sun noon–5:00
Pub. *Hjemkomst Interpretive Center*
(genealogical services)
$125.00 per year membership; admission:
$4.50 for adults

**Iron Range Research Center Library and
Archives**
A Division of the Iron Range Resources and
Rehabilitation Board
(Highway 169 West—location)
PO Box 392 (mailing address)
Chisholm, MN 55719
(218) 254-3325; (218) 254-4938 FAX
http://www.mtn.org/mgs/othersoc.html
Tom Sersha, Director
winter: Mon–Sat 9:00–4:00; summer:
Mon–Sun 10:00–7:00

**Lake Superior Marine Museum
Association**
(600 Canal Park Drive, Duluth, MN
55802—location)
PO Box 177 (mailing address)
Duluth, MN 55801
(218) 727-2497; (218) 720-5270 FAX
info@lsmma.com
http:/www.lsmma.com
Thomas R. Holden, Corresponding Secretary
spring & fall: Mon–Thur 10:00–4:30,
Fri–Sat 10:00–6:00; summer: Mon–Sat
10:00–9:00; winter: Fri–Sun 10:00–4:30;
appointments appreciated

Pub. *The Nor'Easter*, bimonthly (focus on
maritime industry and local and regional
history), $35.00 per year subscription
("Subject matter includes Corps of
Engineers, Duluth-Superior Harbor, Lake
Superior, and commercial shipping
history plus modern ports, connecting
channels, cargoes, and ships.")

**Minneapolis Public Library and
Information Center**
300 Nicollet Avenue
Minneapolis, MN 55401-1992
(612) 372-6547 (Humanities Department);
(612) 372-6648 (Special Collections,
Local History, no research by phone);
(612) 372-6623 FAX
http://www.mplib.org
Betsy Williams, Humanities Department
Head—Genealogy; Edward Kukla,
Special Collections Department
Head—Local History
Humanities Department: Mon–Thur
9:00–9:00, Fri 9:00–5:30, Sat 10:00–5:30
(genealogist on duty Wed 1:00–3:00);
Special Collections: Mon–Fri 9:00–5:30,
Sat 10:00–5:30
(Minneapolis local history)

Murphy's Landing
2187 East Highway 101
Shakopee, MN 55379
(952) 445-6900

**Nobles County Library and Information
Center**
407 12th Street
Worthington, MN 56187
(507) 372-2981; (507) 372-2982 FAX
rspillers@plumcreeklibrary.net;
mvaselaar@plumcreeklibrary.net
http://plumcreeklibrary.org/Adrian/
page11.html
Roger E. Spillers, Director
Mon–Tue & Thur 8:00–8:00, Wed & Fri
8:00–5:00, Sat 10:00–2:00

Olivia Historic Preservation Corporation
PO Box 148
Olivia, MN 56277
(320) 523-1322
Don Walser, President
(collects local historical documents)

Osakis Area Heritage Center
(Todd County Highway 46E or 801 E.
Nokomis—location)
PO Box 327 (mailing address)
Osakis, MN 56360
(320) 859-3777
osakis@midwestinfo.net
http://www.lakeOsakis.com
Jan Moore, Secretary; Jerry Leone, President
Mon–Fri 9:00–5:00
Pub. *Osakis Area Heritage Center
Newsletter*, quarterly
("Archive for local *Osakis Review*
newspaper, begun in 1891. Limited
research facility but files are available.
Office is shared with tourist and business
organizations.")
$6.00 per year membership; research: cost of
copies plus donation; admission: donation

Owatonna Public Library
(105 North Elm—location)
PO Box 387 (mailing address)
Owatonna, MN 55060
(507) 451-4660; (507) 444-2465 FAX
bonnie@selco.lib.mn.us
http://www.owatonna.mn.us
Bonnie Krueger, Reference Librarian

Mon–Thur 9:00–9:00, Fri–Sat 9:00–5:00,
Sun noon–4:00
research: nominal donation based on request

Ramsey County Library
Roseville Branch Library
2180 North Hamline Avenue
Roseville, MN 55113-4241
(651) 631-0494; (651) 631-0615 FAX
http://library.usask.ca/hytelnet/us4/us479.
html

Rochester Public Library
101 Second Street, S.E.
Rochester, MN 55904
(507) 285-8002
referenc@rochester.lib.mn.us
http://www.rochesterpubliclibrary.org
Greg Sauve, Reference Librarian
Mon–Thur 9:30–9:00, Fri–Sat 9:30–5:30,
Sat (summer) 9:30–1:30; Sun 1:30–5:30,
Sun (summer) closed

**Roseau County Historical Museum and
Interpretive Center**
110 Second Avenue, N.E.
Roseau, MN 56751
(218) 463-1918 (to arrange for group tours)
http://www.roseaucohistoricalsociety.org
Charleen Haugen, Director
1 May–31 Oct: Tue–Fri 9:00–5:00, Sat
9:00–4:00; 1 Nov–30 Apr: Tue–Sat
9:00–4:00
Pub. *Minnesota's Historic Northwest Annual
Newsletter*
("Research Center contains local and area
history archive. Included are vital records
index, census, cemetery, school records,
tax assessment records, court records,
immigration records, family, city, and
county indexes, family histories, atlases,
etc., for the researcher or family
historian.")
$10.00 per year membership; admission:
$2.00 for adults

Saint John's University
Alcuin Library
Collegeville, MN 56321
(320) 363-2122; (320) 363-2126 FAX
http://www.csbsju.edu/library/index.html

Saint Paul Public Library
90 West Fourth Street
Saint Paul, MN 55102-1668
(612) 292-6307 (Reference Room); (612)
292-6141 FAX
http://www.stpaul.lib.mn.us
Carol Martinson, Librarian II
Mon 11:30–8:00, Tue–Wed & Fri 9:00–5:30,
Thur 9:00–8:00, Sat 11:00–4:00
("Our main strength is newspaper clippings;
because of budget cuts we can only
provide a little assistance over the phone
or through the mail.")

Sandstone History and Art Center
(Fourth and Main—location)
PO Box 398 (mailing address)
Sandstone, MN 55072
(320) 245-2271
Muriel Ingseth
May–Oct: Thur 9:30–1:00, Fri noon–4:00,
Sat 10:00–2:00
admission: $1.00 for adults

South Saint Paul Public Library
106 Third Avenue, North
South Saint Paul, MN 55075-2098
(651) 554-3240; (651) 554-3241 FAX
http://www.southstpaul.org/departments/
Library

Carol Johnson, Director
Mon & Thur 9:00–8:00, Tue–Wed & Fri
　9:00–6:00, Sat (school year) 9:00–4:00

Southdale-Hennepin Area Library
Information Services
7001 York Avenue, South
Edina, MN 55435-4287
(952) 847-5900; (952) 830-4933; (952) 830-
　4976 FAX
http://www.hennepin.lib.mn.us
Mark Ranum, Coordinating Librarian
Mon–Thur 10:00–9:30, Fri–Sat 10:00–5:00,
　Sun (Oct–May) noon–5:00

Stillwater Public Library
Saint Croix Collection
223 North Fourth Street
Stillwater, MN 55082-4806
(651) 439-1675, ext. 16; (651) 439-0012
　FAX
http://www.ci.stillwater.mn.us/library
("Local history collection.")

University of Minnesota—Minneapolis
Law Library
229 19th Avenue, South
Minneapolis, MN 55455
(612) 625-4309; (612) 625-3478 FAX
http://www.umn.edu/law/library/
　welcome.htm

University of Minnesota—Saint Paul
Saint Paul Campus Central Library
1984 Buford Avenue
Saint Paul, MN 55108
(612) 624-1212 (Reference); (612) 624-3793
　FAX
http://www-stplib.umn.edu/stp

University of Saint Thomas
Archbishop Ireland Memorial Library
2260 Summit Avenue
Saint Paul, MN 55105
(612) 962-5453
j9malcheski@stthomas.edu

University of Saint Thomas
Department of Special Collections
O'Shaughnessy-Frey Library
(2115 Summit Avenue—location)
PO Box 5004 (mailing address)
Saint Paul, MN 55105-1096
(612) 962-5467
http://www.lib.stthomas.edu
Dr. John Davenport, Head of Special
　Collections
Mon–Fri 1:00–4:30, third Sat 10:00–noon &
　1:00–5:00, and by appointment
Pub. *Varia*, one or two times per year
(Luxembourg; Celtic nations: Ireland,
　Scotland, Wales; Isle of Man, Cornwall,
　and Brittany)
copies: 10¢ per page

Vermilion College
Vermilion Interpretive Center
(see Ely-Winton Historical Society,
Historical Societies—Local and Regional,
below)

Waseca-LeSueur Regional Library
(address withheld upon request)
("We have very few resources in genealogy,
　and generally refer patrons to the Waseca
　County Historical Society.")

Winona State University
Maxwell Library
Sanborn and Johnson Streets
Winona, MN 55987
(507) 457-5144; (507) 457-5586 FAX

http://www.winona.msus.edu/is-f/library-
　f/libhome.htm

Historical Societies—Local and Regional

Afton Historical Society
Museum
(3165 Saint Croix Trail—location)
PO Box 178 (mailing address)
Afton, MN 55001
(651) 436-3500
scriv@Pressenter.com
http://www.pressenter.com/~aftonhist
Sun (mid-May to mid-Oct) 1:00–4:00, Wed
　1:00–8:00, and by appointment
Pub. *Afton Historian*, two times per year
$10.00 per year membership

Aitkin County Historical Society
(20 Pacific Street, S.W.—location)
PO Box 215 (mailing address)
Aitkin, MN 56431
(218) 927-3348

Albany Heritage Society
PO Box 550
Albany, MN 56307-0550
(320) 845-2344
Bert Schunighamer, President
(genealogical services)

Albany Historical Society
PO Box 25
Albany, MN 56307
(320) 845-2982

**American West Research Center and
Historical Society, Inc.**
(see Ohio, Part 2)

Anoka County Historical Society
2135 Third Avenue North
Anoka, MN 55303-2285
(763) 421-0600; (763) 323-0218 FAX
achs@ac-hs.org
http://www.ac-hs.org/index
Bonnie McDonald, Executive Director
Tue–Sat 10:00–5:00
Pub. *History Center News*, six times per year
(Anoka County, Civil War)
$8.00 per year membership; research: $10.00
　per hour (requests by phone, email or
　FAX)

Atwater Area History Society
108 North Third Street
Atwater, MN 56209
(320) 974-8284

Barnesville Heritage Society
PO Box 126
Barnesville, MN 56514
(218) 354-2364

Bay Area Historical Society
(Outer Drive—location)
PO Box 33 (mailing address)
Silver Bay, MN 55614
(218) 226-4870
Ed Macki, Jr., Liaison
(early history of Lake County and
　commercial fishing)

**Becker County Historical Society and
Museum**
(Corner of Summit Avenue and West
Front—location)
PO Box 622 (mailing address)
Detroit Lakes, MN 56501
(218) 847-2938; (218) 847-5048 FAX

bolerud@tekstar.com
http://perham.eot.com/~bolerud/bchs.html
Harriet Davis, Director
Mon–Fri 8:00–4:30
Pub. *Newsletter*, quarterly
$10.00 per year membership

Belle Plaine Historical Society
(South Cedar Avenue—location)
PO Box 73 (mailing address)
Belle Plaine, MN 56011
(952) 873-6109

Beltrami County Historical Society
(130 Minnesota Avenue S.W., Bemidji, MN
56601—location)
PO Box 683 (mailing address)
Bemidji, MN 56619
(218) 444-DEPO (444-3376); (218) 444-
　3377
depot@paulbunyan.net
http://www.paulbunyan.net/users/depot/
　index.html
Wanda Hoyum, Director
Mon–Fri 9:00–4:00; Sat 10:00–4:00
Pub. *Depot Express*, quarterly
("We are now a full-service history center
　complete with a three-gallery museum,
　museum gift shop, research library and
　meeting room. We are located in the
　historic southern corridor of downtown
　Bermidji in the restored 1912 Great
　Northern Depot.")
$10.00–$24.00 per year membership;
　research: $10.00 per half-hour for
　nonmembers, free to members; admission:
　$3.00 for nonmember adults

Benton County Historical Society
PO Box 426
Sauk Rapids, MN 56379
(320) 253-9614
Dorothy Milnor, Executive Director
hours: various
Pub. *Benton Newsline*, quarterly
$25.00 per year membership; research: varies
　with each request

Bertha Historical Society, Inc.
Main Street and Second Avenue, West
Bertha, MN 56437
(218) 924-4095
Laura Foster, President
Pub. *Bertha Historical Society, Inc.*

Big Stone County Historical Society
985 U.S. Highway 12
Ortonville, MN 56278
(320) 839-3359
malum@info-link.net (withheld)
Ann Lundberg, Treasurer
Mon–Sat 10:00–5:00, Sun 1:00–4:00
("Process of updating and putting records on
　the computer; new exhibits")
costs: donation

Blue Earth County Historical Society
Heritage Center, 415 Cherry Street
Mankato, MN 56001
(507) 345-5566
bechs-research@juno.com
http://www.rootsweb.com/~mnbechs
Shelley Harrison, Archivist
Tue–Sat 10:00–4:00
Pub. *Newsletter*, bimonthly
$20.00 per year membership; research:
　$10.00 per hour plus 25¢ per copy;
　admission $2.00 for nonmembers

Brooklyn Historical Society
3824 58th Avenue, North
Brooklyn Center, MN 55429

(763) 537-2218
Barbara Sexton, Secretary
write for flyer

Brown County Historical Society
2 North Broadway
New Ulm, MN 56073
(507) 354-2016; (507) 354-1068 FAX
Darla Gebhard, Research Librarian
Research Library: Mon–Fri 10:00–5:00, Sat
    1:00–5:00
Pub. *News Notes*, quarterly
$20.00 per year membership; library
    admission: $2.00 for nonmembers;
    research: $10.00 per letter

Browns Valley Historical Society
514 Third Street, South
Browns Valley, MN 56219
(320) 695-2110

**Paul Bunyon Historical Society and
Museum**
Main Street
Akeley, MN 56433
(218) 652-2725 (President); (218) 652-2575
    (Curator)
Joyce Gunkel, President; Fran Lamb, Curator
summer months only, and by appointment
    with Curator
(emphasis on logging)

Cannon Falls Area Historical Society
PO Box 111
Cannon Falls, MN 55009
(507) 263-4080; (507) 263-4503

Canosia Historical Society
5762 North Pike Lake
Duluth, MN 55811
(218) 729-8963
Audrey Eaton, Director

Carlton County Historical Society
Carlton County History and Heritage Center
406 Cloquet Avenue
Cloquet, MN 55720
(218) 879-1938 voice & FAX
cchs@cpinternet.com;
    director@carltoncountyhs.org
http://www.carltoncountyhs.org
Marlene Wisuri, Director
Museum: Mon 9:00–8:00, Tue–Fri
    9:00–4:00
Pub. *Society News*, quarterly
$10.00 per year membership; research:
    $10.00 per hour for telephone or written
    requests

Cass County Museum/Historical Society
(201 Minnesota Avenue West—location)
PO Box 505 (mailing address)
Walker, MN 56484
(218) 547-7251
Renee Geving, Director
May–Sept: Mon–Sat 10:00–5:00, and by
    appointment during winter months
("County newspapers (1894–1991) on
    microfilm, numerous publications on
    county/family histories.")
$10.00 per year membership; research: $5.00
    plus copies

Center City Historical Society
PO Box 366
Center City, MN 55012
(651) 257-6818

Chaska Historical Society
City Hall
Chaska, MN 55318
(952) 448-4458

Chatfield Historical Society
314 South Main Street
Chatfield, MN 55923

Chippewa County Historical Society
(151 Pioneer Drive, Highways 7 and
59—location)
PO Box 303 (mailing address)
Montevideo, MN 56265
(320) 269-7636
cchs.june@juno.com
http://www.montechamber.com/cchs/cchshp
June Lynne, Executive Director
Mon–Fri 9:00–5:00
Pub. *Pioneer Crier*, monthly
$10.00 per year membership

Chisago County Historical Society
PO Box 146
Lindstrom, MN 55045
(651) 257-5310
Mon, Wed & Fri 10:00–3:00
Pub. *Chisago Heritage Newsletter*,
    bimonthly
$15.00 per year membership

Chisago County Historical Society
North Chapter
51245 Fairfield Avenue
Rush City, MN 55609
(320) 674-4122

Chisago County Historical Society
Taylors Falls Chapter
505 Folsom Street
Taylors Falls, MN 55084
(651) 465-3125

Christie Home Historical Society
110 Second Avenue, North
Long Prairie, MN 56347

Clarks Grove Area Heritage Society
PO Box 188
Clarks Grove, MN 56016

**Clay County Historical Society and
Museum**
(202 First Avenue, North—location)
PO Box 501 (mailing address)
Moorhead, MN 56560
(218) 299-5520; (218) 299-5525 FAX
mark.peihl@ci.moorhead.mn.us
http://www.info.co.clay.mn.us/History
Margaret Ristvedt, Office Manager
Mon–Sat 9:00–5:00, Thur 9:00–9:00, Sun
    noon–5:00
Pub. *Clay County Historical Society
    Newsletter*, bimonthly
(museum and archives)
$15.00 per year membership; admission: free
    to the public

Clearwater County Historical Society
(Highway 2 West, Shevlin, MN
56676—location)
PO Box 241 (mailing address)
Bagley, MN 56621
(218) 785-2000; (218) 78502440 FAX
cchshist@gvtel.com
Tamara Edevold, Executive Director
winter: Tue–Fri 10:00–4:00; summer:
    Tue–Sat 10:00–4:00
Pub. *Clearwater History News*, six times per
    year
$10.00 per year membership; research: $5.00
    initial cost

Cokato Historical Society
(94 West Fourth Street—location)
PO Box 269 (mailing address)
Cokato, MN 55321

(320) 286-2427; (320) 286-5876 FAX
cokatomuseum@cmgate.com
http://www.cokato.mn.us
Mike Worcester, Museum Director
Mon–Fri 9:00–4:30, Sat–Sun 1:00–4:00
Pub. *In the Midst*, quarterly
("Complete obituary index to local paper,
    Cokato Enterprise; state and federal
    census schedules for Wright County;
    other information indexed from local
    paper")
research: $10.00 per hour, copies 50¢ each

Comfrey Area Historical Society
PO Box 218
Comfrey, MN 56019

Community Historical Society
a.k.a. Alden Museum
115 North Broadway
Alden, MN 56009
(507) 874-3462 (Treasurer)
ruben@deskmedia.com
Ruben F. Schmidt, M.D., Treasurer
Memorial Day to Labor Day: Wed & Fri
    1:00–4:00, and by appointment
("limited genealogical resource material . . .
    but data about some local families")
$5.00 per year membership; admission:
    donation

Cook County Historical Society
(12 South Broadway—location)
PO Box 1293 (mailing address)
Grand Marais, MN 55604-1293
(218) 387-1678

Coon Rapids Historical Commission
1313 Coon Rapids Boulevard
Coon Rapids, MN 55433
(763) 755-2880
Gaylord Aldinger, Staff Liaison

Cottonwood Area Historical Society
PO Box 106
Cottonwood, MN 56229

Cottonwood County Historical Society
812 Fourth Avenue
Windom, MN 56101
(507) 831-1134; (507) 831-2665 FAX
http://www.mtn.org/mgs/othersoc/
    cottonwd.html
Linda Fransen, Director
Mon–Fri 8:00–4:00
Pub. *Newsletter*, quarterly
(computer database of county tax records,
    family history files, obituaries, etc.;
    comprehensive research library pertaining
    to Cottonwood County)
$15.00 per year membership; research:
    $10.00 per hour donation

Crosslake Historical Society Museum
PO Box 369
Crosslake, MN 56442
(218) 692-3731
Paul Fruth, Curator
Pub. *Crosslake Historical Society Museum*

Crow Wing County Historical Society
(320 Laurel Street—location)
PO Box 722 (mailing address)
Brainerd, MN 56401-0722
(218) 829-3268; (218) 828-4434 FAX
Mary Lou Moudry, Executive Director
Labor Day–Memorial Day: Mon–Fri
    1:00–5:00, Sat 10:00–2:00; Memorial
    Day–Labor Day: Mon–Fri 9:00–5:00, Sat
    10:00–2:00
Pub. *Historian*, quarterly
$15.00 per year membership; research:

donation plus charge for copies and postage

Cuyuna Range Historical Society
(101 First Avenue—location)
PO Box 128 (mailing address)
Crosby, MN 56441
(218) 546-6178 (summer); (218) 546-5435 (winter)
Elsi Mooers, President
Mon–Sat (June–Aug) 10:00–4:00
("Cuyuna Range iron ore history, early town and pioneer histories, artifacts, memorabilia, some genealogical information")
$5.00 per year membership

Dakota County Historical Society
Dakota County Historical Museum
130 Third Avenue, North
South Saint Paul, MN 55075
(651) 451-6260
Rebecca Snyder, Research Librarian
Tue–Wed & Fri 9:00–5:00, Thur 9:00–8:00, Sat 10:00–3:00
Pub. *Society Happenings*, quarterly; *Over the Years*, semiannually
$20.00 per year membership; research: $10.00 per hour; copies: 20¢ or 25¢ each

Dakota County Historical Society, Mendota-West Saint Paul Chapter
370 G Street
Mendota, MN 55150
Sharon Bruestle, Custodian
Pub. *The Little Historian*

Dodge County Historical Society
(615 North Main Street—location)
PO Box 433 (mailing address)
Mantorville, MN 55955-0433
(507) 635-5508
Idella M. Conwell, Director
1 May–15 Oct: Tue–Sun 1:00–4:00; 16 Oct–30 Apr: Thur–Sat 10:00–4:00
Pub. *Hilltop Chronicle*, quarterly
("Museum and research library.")
$10.00 per year membership; research: $8.00 per hour

Douglas County Historical Society
Knute Nelson Home
1219 Nokomis Street
Alexandria, MN 56308
(320) 762-0382; (320) 762-9062 FAX
Barbara Grover, Executive Director
Mon–Fri 8:00–5:00

Heritage Foundation of East Grand Forks
(218 N.W. Fourth Street—location)
PO Box 281 (mailing address)
East Grand Forks, MN 56721
(218) 773-7481

Eden Prairie Historical Society
Eden Prairie City Hall
8950 Eden Prairie Road
Eden Prairie, MN 55344
(952) 944-2486

Edina Historical Society and Museum
4711 West 70th Street
Edina, MN 55435
(952) 920-8952
Marian Hansen, Administrator
Thur 9:00–noon, Sat 10:00–noon
Pub. *Newsletter*, quarterly
$10.00 per year membership

Ellendale Area Historical Society
PO Box 334
Ellendale, MN 56026

Ely-Winton Historical Society
c/o Vermilion College
Vermilion Interpretive Center
1900 East Camp Street
Ely, MN 55731
(218) 365-3226 (Interpretive Center)
Judey Swenson, Manager
summer: 10:00–5:00; winter: by appointment

England Prairie Pioneer Club
Route 1, Box 36
Verndale, MN 56481
(218) 631-1770
Denny Richter, President

Esko Historical Society
(Highway 61 West—location)
PO Box 83 (mailing address)
Esko, MN 55733
(218) 879-4400

Evansville Historical Foundation
(304 South Gran Street—location)
PO Box 337 (mailing address)
Evansville, MN 56326
(218) 948-2010
ehf@gctel.com
http://www.evansvillemn.net
Pat Nitz
1 Apr–31 Oct: Mon–Fri 11:00–5:00, and by appointment
donation accepted

Excelsior-Lake Minnetonka Historical Society
(Village Hall, Third Street—location)
PO Box 305 (mailing address)
Excelsior, MN 55331
(952) 474-5880

Faribault County Historical Society
The Wakefield House
405 East Sixth Street
Blue Earth, MN 56013
(507) 526-5421
Constance Helgeson, President
Mon–Fri 9:00–2:00, and by appointment
Pub. *FCHS Newsletter*, three times per year
$3.00 per year membership; research: donation

Fillmore County Historical Society
Fillmore County History Center, Museum and Genealogy Library
202 County Road #8
Fountain, MN 55935
(507) 268-4449; (507) 268-4492 FAX
fillmorehistory@earthlink.net
Jerry Henke, Executive Director
Mon–Fri 9:00–4:00
Pub. *Rural Roots Newsletter* (not genealogical), quarterly
$10.00 per year membership

Finland Minnesota Historical Society
(5653 Little Marais Road—location)
PO Box 583 (mailing address)
Finland, MN 55603
(218) 353-7393
Nancy Mancini, President
weekends (June–Sept)
Pub. *FMHS Newsletter*, four times per year
(specializes in Finnish immigrants)
membership fees vary

Fridley Historical Society
(611 Mississippi Street, N.E.—location)
5273 N.E. Horizon Drive (mailing address)
Fridley, MN 55432
(763) 571-5041

Fulda Heritage Society

(Corner of Front Street and Saint Paul Avenue—location)
PO Box 275 (mailing address)
Fulda, MN 56131
(507) 425-2583
Howard E. Anderson, President
during Fulda Wood Duck Festival, last weekend of June, and by appointment
Pub. *Fulda Heritage Society*
$5.00 per year membership

Golden Valley Historical Society
7800 Golden Valley Road
Golden Valley, MN 55427
(763) 544-4547

Goodhue Area Historical Society
(address withheld upon request)
("We are organizing a local museum, but we do not have a building at this time. We do not have the staff or resources to answer patron inquiries at this time.")

Goodhue County Historical Society
1166 Oak Street
Red Wing, MN 55066
(651) 388-6024; (651) 388-3577
goodhuecountyhis@qwest.net
http://www.goodhuehistory.mus.mn.us
Char Henn, Director/CEO
Museum: Tue–Fri 10:00–5:00, Sat–Sun 1:00–5:00; Research library: Tue–Fri, and by appointment
Pub. *Goodhue County Historical News*, four times per year
$25.00 per year membership; research by mail or phone: free for the first 30 minutes, then $6.00 per half-hour, plus copy fees

Goodridge Area Historical Society, Inc.
Goodridge, MN 56725
(218) 378-4380; (218) 378-4280 FAX
Norma Hanson, President
Fri 1:00–5:00, Sat 11:00–4:00, Sun 1:00–4:00
$2.00 per year membership

Grant County Historical Society
(Highway 79 East—location)
PO Box 1002 (mailing address)
Elbow Lake, MN 56531
(218) 685-4864
gcmnhist@runestone.net
Patricia Benson, Curator
Mon–Fri 10:00–noon & 1:00–4:00, Sat (Memorial Day weekend–Sept) 10:00–noon & 1:00–4:00
(index to obituaries and marriages in local newspapers)
$5.00 per year membership; research: $5.00 per hour, plus copies at 10¢ or 25¢ per page

Hastings Historical Society
102½ Second Street, East
Hastings, MN 55033
Bertrand Goderstad

Hennepin History Museum
2303 Third Avenue, South
Minneapolis, MN 55404
(612) 870-1329; (612) 870-1320 FAX
http://www.hhmuseum.org
Jack A. Kabrud, Curator
Tue 10:00–2:00, Wed & Fri–Sun 1:00–5:00, Thur 1:00–8:00
Pub. *Hennepin History*, quarterly
("Hennepin County historical society and museum")
$30.00 per year membership

Heritage Huis
(downtown Hollandale—location)
PO Box 184 (mailing address)
Hollandale, MN 56045
(507) 889-4491
Doris Reynen, Chairman
by appointment
("small museum; Dutch-garbed guides;
Hollandale emphasis")
$25.00 life membership

Hesper/Mabel Area Historical Society
PO Box 56
Mabel, MN 55954
(507) 493-5018

Hibbing Historical Society
400 East 23rd Street
Hibbing, MN 55746
(218) 263-8522
hibbhist@uslink.net
Heather Jomaki, Manager
summer: Mon–Sat 9:00–4:00; winter:
Mon–Fri 10:00–3:00
Pub. *Frank's Place*, quarterly

Hill Farm Historical Society
28 Meadowlark Lane
North Oaks, MN 55127
(651) 484-1434

Historic Heartland Association, Inc.
PO Box 1
Brainerd, MN 56401
(218) 963-2218; (218) 277-7294

Hopkins Historical Society
(Hopkins Activities Center, 33 14th Avenue,
North—location)
1010 First Street, South (mailing address)
Hopkins, MN 55343-9475
(952) 979-0447
Dean Empanger, President
$10.00 per year membership

Houston County Historical Society
104 History Lane
Caledonia, MN 55921
(507) 724-3884
Shirley Johnson, President
Mon–Wed 10:00–4:00, Sat–Sun (June–Sept)
1:00–4:00, and by appointment
Pub. *Houston County Historical Society
Newsletter*, quarterly
("museum archives; maintains twelve
buildings")
$7.50 per year membership

Hubbard County Historical Society
(301 Court Avenue—location)
PO Box 327 (mailing address)
Park Rapids, MN 56470
(218) 732-5237
Johanna Verbrugghen,
Curator/Administrator
May–Sept: Tue–Sun 11:00–5:00
$5.00 per year membership; admission:
$1.00

Iron Range Historical Society
(Old Gilbert City Hall, 19 Soluth
Broadway—location)
PO Box 154 (mailing address)
Gilbert, MN 55741-0786
(218) 749-3150
Kathy Bergan, Secretary
Mon–Tue 9:00–2:00
Pub. *Range Reminiscing*, quarterly (Mar,
June, Sept, Dec)
(Eveleth, Minnesota, newspapers from 1902
to 1978, Gilbert newspapers from 1923,
family history)

$10.00 per year membership; research for
nonmembers: $5.00 per hour, plus copies
at 25¢ each and postage

Isabella Community Council
(9521 Kankinen Road—location)
Box 5 (mailing address)
Isabella, MN 55607
(218) 323-7644; (218) 323-7738
Patricia Thums, Secretary

Isanti County Historical Society
(1400 Highway 293—location)
PO Box 525 (mailing address)
Cambridge, MN 55008
(763) 689-4229
Valorie Arrowsmith, Director
Mon–Tue & Thur 9:00–3:30, and by
appointment
Pub. *Isanti Cuttings*, quarterly
$15.00 per year membership

Itasca County Historical Society
(Central School, 10 N.W. Fifth
Street—location)
PO Box 664 (mailing address)
Grand Rapids, MN 55744
(218) 326-6431
ichs@paulbunyan.net
Lilan Crowe, Executive Director
Mon–Fri 9:30–5:00, Sat 10:00–4:00
Pub. *Museum News*, quarterly
$20.00 per year membership

**Jackson County Historical Society and
Museum**
(307 North Highway 86—location)
PO Box 238 (mailing address)
Lakefield, MN 56150-0238
(507) 662-5505
Museum: Tue & Thur (Sept–Apr)
10:00–4:00; Mon–Fri (May–Aug)
10:00–4:00
Pub. *JCHS Jottings Newsletter*, three times
per year (Mar, July, Nov)
$20.00 life membership; research: $10.00 per
hour plus 25¢ per page copy charges,
including $5.00 nonrefundable deposit on
all requests (Jackson County only, include
SASE), members receive one hour free
per year

Jasper Historical Society
217 Second Street, S.E.
Jasper, MN 56144
(507) 348-9841

**Kanabec County Historical Society and
History Center**
(805 West Forest Avenue—location)
PO Box 113 (mailing address)
Mora, MN 55051
(320) 679-1665; (320) 679-1673 FAX
Edna Cole, Executive Director
Mon–Sat 10:00–4:30, Sun & holidays
12:30–4:30
Pub. *News*, quarterly
$20.00 per year membership; general
admission: $3.00 for nonmember adults;
research: $5.00 plus copies at 25¢ per
page

Kandiyohi County Historical Society
Lawson Memorial Research Center
610 N.E. Highway 71
Willmar, MN 56201
(320) 235-1881; (320) 235-1881 FAX
Kandhist@wecnet.com
http://freepages.genealogy.rootsweb.com/
~KCHS123
Mona Nelson-Balcer, Director
Mon–Fri 9:00–5:00

Pub. *Kandi Express*, quarterly
(local history and biography)
$10.00 per year membership

Kenyon Area Historical Society
(107 Gunderson Boulevard—location)
510 Fourth Street (mailing address)
Kenyon, MN 55946
(507) 789-5936
Lois Estrem, Secretary-Treasurer
tours every third weekend and by
appointment
("We are solely volunteers.")

**Kittson County History Center and
Museum**
(East Main Street—location)
PO Box 100 (mailing address)
Lake Bronson, MN 56734
(218) 754-4100
Cindy A. Adams, Museum Director
Mon–Fri 9:00–5:00, Sat & Sun (summer)
1:00–5:00
Pub. *Kittson County Historical Society
Newsletter*, two or three times per year
(microfilm newspapers from 1882, cemetery
records, census records, obituary files)
$5.00 per year membership; research:
donation

Koochiching County Historical Society
Koochiching County Historical Museum
214 Sixth Avenue
International Falls, MN 56649
(218) 283-4316
Sarah Williams, Executive Director
Museum: Mon–Fri 11:00–5:00, Sat–Sun &
holidays 1:00–5:00; Research Facilities
and Historical Society Office: Mon–Fri
(24 May–24 Sept) 9:00–5:00, Mon–Tue
(25 Sept–23 May) 9:00–4:00
Pub. *Koochiching Chronicle*, eight times per
year
$7.50 per year membership; museum
admission: $3.00 for nonmember adults

Lac qui Parle County Historical Society
250 Eighth Avenue, South
Madison, MN 56256
(320) 598-7678
Lorraine Connor, Curator
May–Sept
Pub. *Bulletin*, annually
("3,000 books and pamphlets, catalogued")
$5.00 per year membership

Lake Benton Historical Society
(110 South Street—location)
PO Box 205 (mailing address)
Lake Benton, MN 56149
(507) 368-9480
lbenton@itctel.com
http://itctel.com/lbenton
Heather Ulrich, Executive Director
yearly

Lake City Historical Society
City Hall
Lake City, MN 55041

**Lake County Historical Society and
Railroad Museum**
Railroad Depot Building
PO Box 128
Two Harbors, MN 55616
(218) 834-4898
Lakehist@lakenet.com
http://www.lakecountyhistoricalsociety.org
Rachelle King, Director
Pub. *Lake County Historical Society
Newsletter*, quarterly
(railroad history, lighthouse, 3M museum)

$15.00 per year membership

Lake of the Woods Historical Society
(Eighth Avenue, S.E.—location)
PO Box 808 (mailing address)
Baudette, MN 56623
(218) 634-1200; (218) 634-2075
Marlys Hirst, Curator
Tue–Sat (May–Sept) 10:00–4:00
Pub. *LOW County Newsletter*, annually

Lake Park Area Historical Society
PO Box 45
Lake Park, MN 56544-0045
(218) 238-5896
Carol Midthune, President
open only for special occasions

Lakeville Area Historical Society
City Hall
20195 Holyoke Avenue
Lakeville, MN 55044

Lamberton Area Historical Society
Community Building
110 Second Avenue, West
Lamberton, MN 56152
(507) 752-7063

**LeSueur County Historical Society,
Museum, and Genealogy Center**
(Fourth and Frank Streets—location)
PO Box 240 (mailing address)
Elysian, MN 56028
(507) 267-4620
David Wollin, Director-Museum; Shirley
    Zimprich, Coordinator-Genealogy Center
Memorial Day–Labor Day: Wed–Sun
    1:00–5:00; May: weekends only

LeSueur Historians
(709 North Second Street—location)
208 North Main Street (mailing address)
LeSueur, MN 56058
(507) 665-2050
Helen Meyer, President
Mon–Sun (June–Aug) 1:00–4:30, and by
    appointment
("We have a Genealogy Section.")
research: copying costs

Lincoln County Historical Society
Lincoln County Pioneer Museum
(610 West Elm—location)
4067 Brooks Street (mailing address)
Hendricks, MN 56136
(507) 275-3537
Mrs. Allen S. Johnson, Museum Director

Lindstrom Historical Society
PO Box 12
Lindstrom, MN 55045
(651) 257-2700

Little Canada Historical Society
515 East Little Canada Road
Little Canada, MN 55117
(651) 484-4783
Jean Donovan, President
Tue & Thur 9:00–1:00, Thur 6:00–8:00
Pub. *The Grist Mill*, quarterly, free to
    historical societies
("Our genealogical research is almost
    exclusively French-Canadian.")

Lyon County Historical Society
c/o Courthouse
607 West Main Street
Marshall, MN 56258
(507) 532-4694
Ellayne Conyers, Museum Director
12:30–4:30

(Lyon County and southwest Minnesota
    history)
$20.00 per year membership; copies: 50¢ per
    page

Madison Lake Area Historical Society
525 Main Street
Madison Lake, MN 56063

Mahnomen County Historical Society
Courthouse
PO Box 123
Mahnomen, MN 56557
(218) 935-5490
Grace Rock, Museum Aide
Mon & Wed 9:00–11:00 & noon–4:00, Fri
    8:00–11:00 & noon–4:00
Pub. *Mahnomen County Historical Society
    Newsletter*, semiannually

Marine Historical Society
Stone House Museum
Fifth and Oak Streets
Marine on Saint Croix, MN 55047

Marshall County Historical Society
(808 East Johnson Avenue—location)
PO Box 103 (mailing address)
Warren, MN 56762
(218) 745-4803
Ethel Thorlacius, Curator
May–Sept: Wed–Fri 9:00–5:00
admission: donation

Martin County Historical Society, Inc.
304 East Blue Earth Avenue
Fairmont, MN 56031
(507) 235-5178
Roy Levik, President
May–Sept: Mon 6:30 P.M.–8:30 P.M.,
    Tue–Sat 1:00–4:30
Pub. *Newsletter*, biannually
$10.00 life membership; research: $7.50 per
    hour plus postage, and copies at 25¢ each

McLeod County Historical Society
McLeod County Heritage and Cultural
Center
380 School Road, North
Hutchinson, MN 55350
(320) 587-2109
Patsy R. Prieve, Administrator
Pub. *MCHS Newsletter*

Meeker County Historical Society
GAR Hall—Meeker County Museum
308 Marshall Avenue, North
Litchfield, MN 55355
(320) 693-8911
garhall@willmar.net
http://+ccn.com/mn.tourism/exp/at1448.html
Paula Nelson, Director
Museum: Tue–Sun noon–4:00
Pub. *Meeker County Historical Society
    Newsletter*, quarterly
$10.00 per year membership

**Menahga Area Historical Society and
Museum**
(320 Helsinki Boulevard N.E.—location)
36959 Taylor's Beach Road (mailing
address)
Menahga, MN 56464
(218) 564-5063; (218) 564-4574 (President)
Elmer Bohjanen, President
Memorial Day–Labor Day: Tue–Sun
    1:00–4:00

**Milaca Area Historical Society and
Museum**
Milaca Community Library and Museum
145 Central Avenue South

Milaca, MN 56353
(320) 983-3677
Museum: Thur 1:00–4:00, Sat 10:00–1:00;
    archives during library hours: Tue–Wed
    & Fri 11:00–5:00, Thur 1:00–8:00, Sat
    10:00–1:00
(Milaca newspapers, Mille Lacs County
    census on microfilm, Mille Lacs County
    cemetery records)
$5.00 per year membership

Mille Lacs County Historical Society
(Depot Museum, 104 10th
Avenue—location)
101 10th Avenue, North (mailing address)
Princeton, MN 55371-1568
(763) 389-1296

Mille Lacs Lake Historical Society
(Main Street—location)
PO Box 42 (mailing address)
Isle, MN 56342

Minnesota Lake Area Historical Society
Kremer House Library and Museum
(317 Main—location)
PO Box 225 (mailing address)
Minnesota Lake, MN 56068
(507) 462-3420
Mary E. Herbst, President

Minnetonka Historical Society
13209 McGinty Road, East
Minnetonka, MN 55305
(952) 933-1611; (952) 938-0901 (President's
    home)
Maxine Dickson, President
phone inquiries only
Pub. *Minnetonka Mill Wheel Newsletter*,
    quarterly
(specializes in the city of Minnetonka)
$8.00 per year membership

Monongalia Historical Society
(220 Norwood Street S.W., one block west
of Millpond on Second Avenue, one block
south on Norwood Street—location)
18946 Highway 9 N.E. (mailing address)
New London, MN 56273
(320) 354-2557 (President)
Jean E. Kalevik, President
Memorial Day–Labor Day: Thur–Sun
    1:00–4:00

Moose Lake Area Historical Society
Village Hall Museum
Box 235
Moose Lake, MN 55707
(218) 485-4680
seasonal; meetings: quarterly
Pub. *MLAHS Newsletter*, two times per year
("Seasonal Soo Line Depot.")
$8.00 per year membership

Morrison County Historical Society
(The Charles A. Weyerhaeuser Memorial
Museum, 2151 South Lindbergh
Drive—location)
PO Box 239 (mailing address)
Little Falls, MN 56345-0239
(320) 632-4007
mchs@littlefalls.net
http://www.upstel.net/~johns/History/
    MorrisonCo.html
Jan Warner, Executive Director
Tue–Sat 10:00–5:00, Sun (Memorial
    Day–Labor Day) 1:00–5:00
Pub. *Morrison County Historical Society
    Newsletter*, quarterly
(emphasis on family history)
$20.00 per year membership; research: $5.00
    minimum (includes up to ten letter-size

copies and a half-hour of research time, $6.25 per fifteen minutes (after first half-hour)

Morristown Historical Society
PO Box 113
Morristown, MN 55052

Mower County Historical Society
(Mower County Fairgrounds, 1303 Sixth Avenue, S.W.—office location)
PO Box 804 (mailing address)
Austin, MN 55912
(507) 437-6082
http://fox.co.net/austin/arts/geneal.html
Monica Lonergan, Chairman
Genealogy Room: Sept–May: Mon–Fri 1:00–4:00; June–Aug: Tue–Sun 11:00–4:00; and by appointment
("Research library, especially Mower County")
$5.00 per year membership

Murray County Historical Society/Museum
(2480 29th Street—location)
PO Box 61 (mailing address)
Slayton, MN 56172
(507) 836-6533
society@frontiernet.net
Caryl Busman, Museum Director
summer: Tue–Sat 10:00–5:00, fall and spring: Mon–Fri 1:00–5:00, winter: Tue–Thur 1:00–5:00
(microfilm newspapers, naturalization records, census, family histories)
$5.00 per year membership; research: $20.00 per hour plus postage and copies

New Brighton Area Historical Society
PO Box 12062
New Brighton, MN 55112
Pub. *NBAHS Newsletter*

New Prague Historical Society
28438 141st Avenue
New Prague, MN 56071
(952) 758-2201

Nicollet County Historical Society and Museum
Treaty Site History Center
1851 North Minnesota Avenue
Saint Peter, MN 56082
(507) 931-2160; (507) 931-0172 FAX
nicolletco@aol.com; spchamb@mnic.net (Chamber of Commerce)
http://www.tourism.st-peter.mn.us/nicollet.php3
John W. Hans, Director
Mon–Sat 10:00–4:00, Sun 1:00–4:00
Pub. *The Crossing*, quarterly
(Nicollet County history; Treaty of Traverse des Sioux)
$20.00 per year membership

Nobles County Historical Society
Nobles County Library and Information Center
407 12th Street, Suite 2
Worthington, MN 56187
(507) 376-4431
Thomas Zishka, Museum Director
Mon–Fri 1:00–5:00
Pub. *Nobles County Historical Society Newsletter*, quarterly
$15.00 per year membership

North Saint Paul Historical Society
2666 East Seventh Avenue
North Saint Paul, MN 55109
(651) 779-6402

Priscilla Olson, Secretary; Betty Lyon, Museum Curator
Fri 1:00–4:00, Sat 10:00–1:00
$7.50 per year membership

Northfield Historical Society
408 Division Street
Northfield, MN 55057
(507) 645-9268
Susan Garwood, Executive Director
Tue–Sat 10:00–4:00, Sun 1:00–4:00
Pub. *Scriver Scribbler*, quarterly
("Minnesota history, Jesse James, Northfield history")
$25.00 per year membership

Olmsted County Historical Society
1195 County West Circle Drive S.W.
Rochester, MN 55902-6619
(507) 282-9447
http://www.millcomm.com/~gzimmer/ochs.html
Sherry Sweetman, Librarian/Archivist
Tue–Sat 9:00–5:00
Pub. *Olmsted Historian*
(printed county histories, plat maps, local newspapers, city directories, census, vertical files, books and periodicals, cemetery transcripts, probate records, guardianship records, grantor-grantee books, vital records)
$25.00 per year membership; admission: $2.00 for nonmembers; research by mail: $15.00 per hour (one-hour minimum), copies: 20¢ to 50¢ per page from paper originals, 40¢ per page from microform originals

Otter Tail County Historical Society
1110 West Lincoln Avenue
Fergus Falls, MN 56537
(218) 736-6038 (Museum)
otchs@prtel.com
LeAnn Neuleib, Office Manager; Kathy M. L. Evawold, Archivist
Library: Mon–Fri 9:00–5:00; Museum: Mon–Fri 9:00–5:00, Sat (Jan–Dec) 1:00–4:00, Sun (June–Sept) 1:00–4:00
Pub. *Otter Tail County Historical Society Newsletter*, bimonthly; *Otter Tail Record*, quarterly
$20.00 per year membership; research: $15.00 per hour

Ox Cart Trails Historical Society
(see North Dakota, Part 2)

Paynesville Historical Society
(543 River Street—location)
329 Washbune Ave (mailing address)
Paynesville, MN 56362
(320) 243-4433
Bertha Zniewski, Executive Secretary
$10.00 per year membership; admission: $1.00

Pennington County Historical Society
(Peder Engelstad Pioneer Village Oakland Park Road—location)
PO Box 127 (mailing address)
Thief River Falls, MN 56701
(218) 681-5767

Pine County Historical Society
Askov, MN 55704
(320) 838-3792
Elizabeth Espointour, President
Museum: Memorial Day–Labor Day: Tue–Sun 1:00–4:00
$10.00 per year membership

Pipestone County Historical Society and

Museum
113 South Hiawatha Avenue
Pipestone, MN 56164
(507) 825-2563
pipctymu@rconnect.com
http://www.pipestoneminnesota.com/museum
Chris Roelfsema-Hummel, Director of Museum
Mon–Sun 10:00–5:00 (9:00–8:00 during Hiawatha Pageant, last two weekends of July & first weekend of Aug)
Pub. *Newsletter*, quarterly
(local newspapers on microfilm from 1879, birth, marriage, obituary index, census records, plat maps, Close Brothers Land Sale Records [1800s–1900s], 2,000 Dr. Brown birth records, computer database index of many sources, glass negative collection [most identified, several thousand printable], photographic prints, Pipestone Indian School and Mdewakaton censuses, collection of printed family histories, family information files, other Pipestone County data)
$10.00 per year membership; admission $2.00; research: $5.00 plus 50¢ per copy

Plymouth Historical Society
(3605 Fernbrook Lane—location)
3400 Plymouth Boulevard (mailing address)
Plymouth, MN 55447
(763) 559-9201

Polk County Historical Society
(719 East Robert—location)
PO Box 214 (mailing address)
Crookston, MN 56716
(218) 281-1038
Ed Melby, President
20 May–15 Sept: noon–5:00
Pub. *Newsletter*, three times per year (Jan, May, Sept)
$5.00 per year membership

Pope County Historical Society
809 South Lakeshore Drive
Glenwood, MN 56334
(320) 634-3293
pcmuseum@runestone.net
Merlin Peterson, Curator
Tue–Sat 10:00–5:00
Pub. *PCHS Newsletter*, quarterly
("County historical artifacts and county genealogy; 40,000+ files on personal events, businesses, organizations, newspapers indexed from 1891")
$10.00 per year membership; admission: $3.00; research: $3.00 for nonmembers

Preston Historical Society
PO Box 63
Preston, MN 55965
(507) 765-4555
Richard Nelson

Ramsey County Historical Society
323 Landmark Center
75 West Fifth Street
Saint Paul, MN 55102
(612) 222-0701; (612) 223-8539
info@rchs.com
http://www.rchs.com
Business: Mon–Fri 9:00–5:00; Library: by appointment only
Pub. *Ramsey County History*, quarterly
(Ramsey County history; Saint Paul city directories, 1885–1959; Gibbs Museum of Pioneer and Dakotah Life)
$35.00 per year membership; research fees vary

Red Lake County Historical Society
Lake Pleasant School House
Route 1, Box 298
Red Lake Falls, MN 56750
(218) 253-2833

Red River Valley Heritage Society
(202 First Avenue, North—location)
PO Box 157 (mailing address)
Moorhead, MN 56561-0157
(218) 236-9140
Ramona Kooren, Executive Secretary
Pub. *Heritage Press*, bimonthly
(primarily historical, not genealogical)
$15.00 per year membership

Redwood County Historical Society
(507 Morten Drive—location)
Rural Route 2, Box 12 (mailing address)
Redwood Falls, MN 56283
(507) 637-3329

Renville County Historical Society
441 North Park Drive
Morton, MN 56270
(507) 697-6147
Lori Pickéll-Stangel, Director
Mon–Fri 10:00–4:00, Sun 1:00–4:00
("Renville County town newspapers 1870-2001")
$10.00 per year membership

Rice County Historical Society
1814 N.W. Second Avenue
Faribault, MN 55021
(507) 332-2121
Maynard Spitzock, Executive Director
fall, winter, spring: Mon–Fri 9:00–4:00;
    summer: Mon–Fri 9:00–4:00, Sat–Sun
    1:00–4:00
Pub. *The Rice County Historian*, quarterly
("Rice County burial records, 1882 & 1910
    history books, city directories, plat maps,
    family genealogies, newspaper records")
$20.00 per year membership; research by
    donation

Richfield Historical Society
Bartholomew House Museum
(6901 Lyndale Avenue, South—location)
PO Box 23304 (mailing address)
Richfield, MN 55423
(612) 798-6140
Ruthann Clay, Curator
May–Oct, by appointment
Pub. *Richfield Historical Society Newsletter*,
    six times per year
("Reference library, photos, family history,
    schools, churches")
$10.00 per year membership

Rock County Historical Society
(123 North Freeman Street—location)
PO Box 741 (mailing address)
Luverne, MN 56156
(507) 449-2115; (507) 283-9849
Betty Mann, President; Sr. Mariella Hinkley,
    Genealogist
Tue, Thur & Sat (1 June–Labor Day)
    2:00–4:00
("Hinkley House—a restored Victorian
    Home, 1892–1920, and the Rock County
    History Museum—collections from all the
    towns in Rock County, an obit file of
    citizens from 1890 to present.")
$15.00 per year membership; research: $5.00
    for an initial inquiry, $10.00 per hour for
    searches

Rockford Area Historical Society
Ames-Florida-Stork House
(8136 Bridge Street, on the Crow River, one

block north of Highway 55—location)
PO Box 186 (mailing address)
Rockford, MN 55373
(763) 477-5383
Wendy Biorn, Museum Coordinator
Memorial Day–8 Sept: Tue 11:00–2:00, Thur
    4:00–7:00, second Sun 1:00–2:45, closed
    4 July
Pub. *RAHS News*, monthly
$7.50 per year membership

Rosemount Area Historical Society
3130 145th Street, West
Rosemount, MN 55068

Roseville Historical Society
1910 West County Road B
Roseville, MN 55113
(651) 487-7773
mikewolf@attbi.com
http://mnrhs.tripod.com
Mike Wolf, President
Pub. *R.H.S. Memo*, quarterly
("Published books on the history of
    Roseville.")
$6.00 per year membership

Royalton Historical Society
(Center Street—location)
PO Box 196 (mailing address)
Royalton, MN 56373
(320) 584-5641; (320) 584-5417

Rushford Area Historical Organization
403 East North Street
Rushford, MN 55971
(507) 864-7223
Alton Morken, President

Sacred Heart Area Historical Society
77407 145th Street
Sacred Heart, MN 56285
(320) 765-2274

Saint Louis County Historical Society
506 West Michigan Street
Duluth, MN 55802
(218) 722-8011; (218) 727-8025 voice &
    FAX
CVB@Visit.Duluth.MN.us
http://www.visit.duluth.com/Depot/
    historic.html
Lawrence J. Sommer, Director
Pub. *Saint Louis County Historical Society
    Newsletter*, quarterly

Sauk Centre Area Historical Society
(Lower level of Bryant Public
    Library—museum location)
430 Main Street South (mailing address)
Sauk Centre, MN 56378
(320) 351-8777 voice & FAX
scahs@mainstreetcom.com
Joyce C. Lyng, Treasurer
Sept–May: Tue 2:00–4:30; June–Aug: by
    appointment
$7.00 per year membership; research: from
    $15.00

Schroeder Area Historical Society
(Cross River Heritage Center—temporarily
    closed location)
Schroeder, MN 55613

Scott County Historical Society
Stans Historical Center
235 South Fuller
Shakopee, MN 55379
(952) 445-0378 voice & FAX; (888) 325-
    2575
info@scottcountyhistory.org
http://www.scottcountyhistory.org

John Gutteter, Executive Director
Tue–Wed & Fri 9:00–4:00, Thur 9:00–8:00,
    Sat 10:00–3:00
Pub. *Newsletter*, quarterly
$15.00 per year membership; admission:
    $2.00 for nonmember adults

Sherburne County Historical Society
13122 First Street
Becker, MN 55308
(763) 261-4433
Kurt Kragness, Executive Director
8:00–5:00
Pub. *Historically Speaking*, quarterly

Sibley County Historical Society, Inc.
(Sibley County Historical Museum, 700
    Main Street—location)
PO Box 407 (mailing address)
Henderson, MN 56044-0407
(507) 248-3434; (507) 248-3687
Sharon Haggenmiller, Secretary
Memorial Day–Oct: Sun 2:00–5:00, and by
    appointment
Pub. *Sibley County Historical Society
    Newsletter*, quarterly
$6.00 per year membership; admission and
    research: donation

Sleepy Eye Historical Society
316 Walnut, S.E.
Sleepy Eye, MN 56085

South Saint Paul Historical Society
345 Seventh Avenue, South
South Saint Paul, MN 55075

**Spring Valley Community Historical
Society, Inc.**
(221 West Courtland—location)
Rural Route 2 Box 135 (mailing address)
Spring Valley, MN 55975
(507) 346-7659; (507) 346-2206
    (Genealogist)
Sharon Jahn, Genealogist
by appointment
("Complete genealogical research for Spring
    Valley area")
$8.00 per year membership

Stearns County Historical Society
Stearns County Heritage Center
(235 33rd Avenue, South—location)
PO Box 702 (mailing address)
Saint Cloud, MN 56302-0702
(320) 253-8424; (320) 253-2172 FAX
John Decker, Archivist
Mon–Sat 10:00–4:00, Sun noon–4:00
Pub. *Crossings*, bimonthly
$25.00 per year membership; admission:
    $4.00 minimum for adults; research:
    $4.00 minimum, $16.00 per hour plus 30¢
    per copy

Steele County Historical Society
1448 Austin Road
Owatonna, MN 55060-4018
(507) 451-1420
Marlene Knutson, Director/Curator
1 Oct–30 Apr: Mon–Fri 1:00–5:00; 1
    May–30 Sept: daily 1:00–5:00
("Steele County burial files and obituaries,
    history, Indian and military")
$10.00 per year membership; research: $5.00
    per hour

Stevens County Historical Society
Stevens County Genealogical Society
Nevada Avenue and Sixth Street
Morris, MN 56267
(320) 589-1719 (Historical Society); (320)
    589-2190 (President)

Dennis Warnes, President
Historical Society: Mon–Fri 9:00–noon &
1:00–5:00, Sun (summer only) 1:30–4:30
Pub. *Stevens County Genealogical Society
Newsletter*, quarterly (Feb, Apr, June,
Oct)
("funeral records, researching")
$10.00 per year membership (in both
Genealogical and Historical societies)

Swift County Historical Society
(On West Highway 12 in Benson—location)
2135 Minnesota Avenue, Building 02
(mailing address)
Benson, MN 56215-9304
(320) 843-4467
historical.society@co.swift.mn.us
Marlys Gallagher, Executive Director
Tue–Fri 10:00–4:30, Sat 10:00–3:00
Pub. *Echo*, six times per year
(obituary file for one-time residents of Swift
County, census files for Swift County,
county newspapers dating back to 1876)
$7.00 per year membership; research: $5.00
per hour for nonmembers ($5.00
minimum), plus charge for copies to both
members and nonmembers

Todd County Historical Society, Inc.
PO Box 146
Long Prairie, MN 56347-0146
Mon–Fri 10:00–noon & 1:00–4:00
Pub. *Todd County Historical Society, Inc.*

Tofte Historical Society, Inc.
North Shore Commercial Fishing Museum
(Highway 61—location)
PO Box 2312 (mailing address)
Tofte, MN 55615-2312
(218) 663-7150
http://www.boreal.org/nshistory
Mary Alice Hansen, Secretary
Mon–Sun 9:00–5:00
Pub. *North Shore Commercial Fishing
Journal*, four times per year
$15.00 per year membership; research: no
cost for search

Tower Soudan Historical Society
Train Coach
PO Box 413
Tower, MN 55790
(218) 753-3039

Traverse County Historical Society
(12th Street, North—location)
PO Box 868 (mailing address)
Wheaton, MN 56296-0868

Upsala Area Historical Society
(Main Street—location)
PO Box 35 (mailing address)
Upsala, MN 56384
(320) 573-4208
http://www.upstel.net/~johns/History/
History.html
Carol Gerads, President
summer holidays, and by appointment
Pub. *UAHS Newsletter*

Verndale Historical Society
112 North Farwell
Verndale, MN 56481
(218) 445-5745
Wilbur Desrocher, President
by appointment and special days
Pub. *Newsletter*, annually (Jan)
$3.00 per year membership

Virginia Area Historical Society
Heritage Center Museum
(800 Olcott Park, Ninth Avenue

North—location)
PO Box 736 (mailing address)
Virginia, MN 55792
(218) 741-1136
Melissa Sardnas, Secretary
1 May–30 Sept: Tue–Sat 11:00–4:00; 1
Oct–31 Dec: Thur–Sat 11:00–4:00
Pub. *Heritage News*, quarterly
$5.00 per year membership

Wabasha County Historical Society
3243 60th Avenue, S.W.
Rochester, MN 55902
daily 1:00–5:00

Wabasso County Historical Society
564 South Street
Wabasso, MN 56293

Wadena County Historical Society
603 North Jefferson
Wadena, MN 56482-2336
(218) 631-9079
wchs@lakesplus.com
Robert Zosel, Board Chairman
Tue–Fri 9:00–3:00
Pub. *WCHS Newsletter*, three times per year
$12.00 per year membership; research:
$15.00 basic fee; contributions welcome
to WCHS Foundation

Wanamingo Historical Society
Main Street
Wanamingo, MN 55983
(507) 824-2556
Mavis Kyllo, Vice President
Sun (summer) 1:00–4:00 by appointment
("Historic Log House on Main Street")
$2.50 per year membership

Warroad Historical Society
Warroad Heritage Center
(Main Street—location)
PO Box 688 (mailing address)
Warroad, MN 56763
(218) 386-1283
Mrs. Cal Marvin, Vice President; Ruth
Stukel, President
Mon–Sun 1:00–5:00
(files on local families and subjects,
computer scanner and printer, microform
reader-printer, county newspapers
1897–1990, Roseau County census
1895–1920)

Waseca County Historical Society
PO Box 314
Waseca, MN 56093
(507) 835-7700
http://www.historical.waseca.mn.us
Margaret Sinn, Executive Director
Mon–Fri 8:00–noon & 1:00–5:00, Sat
(Memorial Day–Labor Day) 1:00–5:00
Pub. *History Notes*, quarterly
("Our web site has over 10,000 photos, death
index, 10,000 names in newspaper index,
marriages, probates, etc.")
$20.00 per year membership

Washington County Historical Society
(602 North Main Street—location)
PO Box 167 (mailing address)
Stillwater, MN 55082
(651) 439-5956
Brent@wchsmn.org
http://www.wchsmn.org
Brent Peterson, Library Manager
Tue, Fri & Sun noon–5:00, Wed 3:00–9:00
Pub. *Historical Whisperings*, quarterly
("Washington County history, lumbering,
Civil War prison, business, rural
schools.")
$15.00 per year membership; admission for

on-site research: $3.00 for nonmembers;
research: $15.00 per hour

Watonwan County Historical Society
(423 Dill Avenue, S.W.—location)
PO Box 126 (mailing address)
Madelia, MN 56062
(507) 642-3247
Ruth Anderson, Museum Director
June–Sept: Mon–Thur 9:00–4:00, Sat–Sun
1:00–4:00; off season: Wed 1:00–3:00,
and by appointment

Wawina Area Historical Society
PO Box 102
Wawina, MN 55794
(218) 488-6588

Wayzata Historical Society
At the Depot
402 East Lake Street
Wayzata, MN 55391

Welcome Historical Society
109 Hulseman
Welcome, MN 56181
(507) 728-8806

West Concord Historical Society
PO Box 346
West Concord, MN 55985
(507) 527-2177

**Western Hennepin County Pioneer
Association, Inc.**
(1953 West Wayzata Boulevard—location)
PO Box 332 (mailing address)
Long Lake, MN 55356
(952) 473-6557
James R. Roehl, Archivist
Pub. *WHCPA Newsletter*

Westonka Historical Society
3740 Enchanted Lane
Mound, MN 55364

White Bear Lake Area Historical Society
2350 Joy Avenue
White Bear Lake, MN 55110
(651) 407-5327
WBLAHISTSOC@GoldenGate.net
http://www.wblareahostircalsociety.org
Sara Markoe Hanson
$15.00 per year membership

Wilkin County Historical Society
704 Nebraska Avenue
Breckenridge, MN 56520
(218) 643-1303
Ruth A. Poppel, Treasurer
Wed–Thur
$3.00 per year membership

**Wilkin County Historical Society
Genealogy Committee**
Wilkin-Richland Counties Genealogy Guild
RR 1, Box 116
Breckenridge, MN 56520
(218) 643-3166
John Boldingh

Winnebago Historical Society/Museum
(18 First Street, N.E.—location)
PO Box 218 (mailing address)
Winnebago, MN 56098
(507) 893-4660

Winona County Historical Society, Inc.
160 Johnson Street
Winona, MN 55987
(507) 454-2723; (507) 454-0006 FAX
archives@hbci.com

http://www.winona.msus.edu/
  historicalsociety
Mark F. Peterson, Executive Director
Museum: Mon–Fri 9:00–5:00, Sat–Sun
  noon–4:00; Archives: Mon–Fri
  10:00–noon & 1:00–5:00
Pub. *Argus*, bimonthly
$25.00 per year membership

Wright County Historical Society
2001 Highway 25 North
Buffalo, MN 55313
(763) 682-7323
Betty Dircks, Archivist
Oct–May: Mon–Fri 8:00–4:30; June–Sept:
  Tue–Sat 8:00–4:30
Pub. *Wright County Historical Society
  Newsletter*, quarterly
$10.00 per year membership; research: $7.50
  per half hour plus postage

**Yellow Medicine County Historical
Society and Museum**
(Junction Highways 23 and 67—location)
PO Box 145 (mailing address)
Granite Falls, MN 56241-0145
(320) 564-4478
Mildred Washburn, Curator
mid-May to mid-Oct: Tue & Fri 11:00–3:00,
  Sat–Sun noon–4:00
Pub. *Genealogy-history of Y.M. County
  News Letters*, quarterly
(has complete county burial register, plus
  obituary card file)
$5.00 per year membership; museum
  admission: free

Genealogical Societies

State Genealogical Societies

Minnesota Genealogical Society
5768 Olson Memorial Highway
Golden Valley, MN 55422
(763) 595-9347 (Library)
mgsdec@mtn.org
http://mngs.org
David E. Cross; Jean Jensen, Library
  Committee Chair
Wed–Thur & Sat 9:00–3:00, Tue & Thur
  6:30–9:30
Pub. *Minnesota Genealogist*, quarterly;
  *Minnesota Genealogical Society
  Newsletter*, quarterly
Branches: Computer Interest Group, Danish-
  American Genealogical Group, Douglas
  County Genealogical Society, Finnish
  Genealogy Group, Germanic Genealogy
  Society, Irish Genealogical Society,
  Northwest Territory Canadian and French
  Heritage Center, Norwegian-American
  Genealogy Association, Polish
  Genealogical Society of Minnesota,
  Swedish Genealogy Society of Minnesota,
  Yankee Genealogical Society (q.v.)
$28.00 per year membership

Genealogical Society of Minnesota
2642 University Avenue
Saint Paul, MN 55114
(612) 724-2101

Genealogical Societies—Local & Regional

Anoka County Genealogical Society
2135 Third Avenue North
Anoka, MN 55303-2285
(763) 421-0600; (763) 323-0218
acgsmn@yahoo.com
http://freepages.genealogy.rootsweb.com/
  ~relativememory
June Novak, President; Lucille Elrite, Vice

President; Marilyn Anderson, Webmaster
Tue–Sat 10:00–5:00
Pub. *The ACGS Time*
(research Anoka County pioneers)
$9.00 per year membership

Bemidji Genealogical Society
Bemidji Public Library
509 America Avenue N.W.
Bemidji, MN 56601

Genealogical Society of Carlton County
(Carlton County Historical Society, Carlton
County History and Heritage Center, 406
Cloquet Avenue—location)
PO Box 204 (mailing address)
Cloquet, MN 55720
(218) 389-6229 voice & FAX (Historical
  Society)
cchs@cpinternet.com (Historical Society)
http://www.carltoncountyhs.org (Historical
  Society)
Marlene Zalar
Museum: Mon 9:00–8:00, Tue–Fri
  9:00–4:00
Pub. *Genealogical Society of Carlton County
  Quarterly*
$10.00 per year membership

Chippewa County Genealogical Society
PO Box 303
Montevideo, MN 56265

Chisago County Genealogical Society
PO Box 146
Lindstrom, MN 55045-0146
(651) 257-5310
Mon, Wed & Fri 10:00-3:00
Pub. *CCHS Connection and Heritage*, six
  times per year
$15.00 per year membership

Cottonwood/Jackson Genealogy Group
c/o Jackson County Historical Society and
Museum
(307 North Highway 86—location)
PO Box 238 (mailing address)
Lakefield, MN 56150-0238
(507) 662-5505 (Historical Society)
jchs@rconnect.com (Historical Society)
1 May–Labor Day: Mon–Fri 10:00–4:00;
  Labor Day–30 Apr: Tue & Thur
  10:00–4:00
$5.00 per year membership for members of
  either Jackson County Historical Society
  or Cottonwood County Historical Society,
  otherwise $15.00 per year membership

Crow River Genealogical Society
380 School Road, North
Hutchinson, MN 55350
slee@hutchtel.net
Sandra Sandman, President

Crow Wing County Genealogical Society
(LDS Family History Center, 101 Buffalo
Hills Lane West—location)
2103 Graydon Avenue (mailing address)
Brainerd, MN 56401
(218) 829-9738
lkirk@brainerd.net (Home)
http://www.rootsweb.com/~mncwcghs
Lucille Kirkeby, Corresponding Secretary
Tue & Thur 9:00–5:30 (may be extended for
  the summer), Wed 6:30–8:30
Pub. *Heirmail*, quarterly
$10.00 per year membership; research: varies
  with individuals

Dakota County Genealogical Society
c/o Dakota County Historical Society
Dakota County Historical Museum

130 Third Avenue, North
South Saint Paul, MN 55075
(651) 455-7080
Vicki Young Albu, President
Library at Dakota County Historical Society
Pub. *The Dakota County Genealogist*,
  quarterly
$10.00 per year membership

Dodge County Genealogical Society
PO Box 683
Dodge Center, MN 55927
Pub. *Dodge County Genealogical Society
  Newsletter*
$10.00 per year membership

Douglas County Genealogical Society
Minnesota Genealogical Society
PO Box 505
Alexandria, MN 56308
(320) 763-3462 (Directions); (320) 763-3896
  voice & FAX
swartz@eot.com
http://www.rootsweb.com/~mndougla/
  dcgs.html
Ginny Swartz, President
meetings at 903 Park Street, N.E.,
  Alexandria: fourth Tue (except June–July)
Pub. *Relatively Speaking*, quarterly
$10.00 per year membership

Freeborn County Genealogical Society
1033 Bridge Avenue
Albert Lea, MN 56007-2205
(507) 373-9269
http://www.fcgs.org
Joanne Johnsrud, Secretary
Tue–Fri 1:00–5:00
Pub. *Freeborn County Tracer*, bimonthly
$15.00 per year membership

Heart O'Lakes Genealogical Society
(Becker County Museum, 714 Summit
Avenue—location)
PO Box 622 (mailing address)
Detroit Lakes, MN 56501-2824
(218) 847-2938
http://perham.eot.com/~bolerud/heart.html
Teresa Palmer, President; Julie M. Mastin,
  Corresponding Secretary
Mon–Tue & Thur–Fri 8:00–4:30, Wed 8:00
  A.M.–8:30 P.M.
Pub. *Heart O'Lakes Genealogical Society*,
  four times per year
(Becker County, Minnesota, information)
$5.00 per year membership

Hubbard County Genealogical Society
(Ira Benham Resource Center, in Hubbard
County Museum, 301 Court
Avenue—location)
PO Box 361 (mailing address)
Park Rapids, MN 56470
dhensel@eot.com
http://www.rootsweb.com/~mnhgs
Darryl Hensel, Researcher
May–Sept: Tue–Sun 11:00–5:00
$10.00 per year membership

Itasca County Genealogical Club
(Bovey Village Hall—library location)
PO Box 261 (mailing address)
Bovey, MN 55709
(218) 326-5342
Leona Litchke, President
Library: Mon & Thur 9:30–8:00, Tue–Wed
  noon–8:00, Fri 11:00–5:00
Pub. *Itasca Genealogy Club Newsletter*,
  quarterly
$7.00 per year membership; research:
  donation for work done by club members

Heritage Searchers of Kandiyohi County
PO Box 175
Willmar, MN 56201-0175
Pub. *Heritage HiLites*, bimonthly
("civil records, cemetery transcriptions for
all of county, county history, newspaper
indexes")
$10.00 per year membership; research:
donation

Martin County Genealogical Society, Inc.
222 East Blue Earth Avenue
Fairmont, MN 56031
(507) 235-3094; (507) 236-0996
jdparis@charter.net
http://www.rootsweb.com/~mnmartin
Dona Paris, Corresponding Secretary
Mon & Fri 9:30–4:00, Thur & Sat
9:30–11:30; meetings: third Sat 9:00
(Apr–Oct) & 10:00 (Nov–Mar)
Pub. *Tree Climber*, quarterly (Feb, May,
Aug, Nov)
("We have Martin County obituaries, city
directories, census, funeral home records,
cemeteries records, vital records,
newspapers/periodicals, histories, tax
records, county plat maps, county military
records.")
$15.00 per year membership; research: $5.00
per hour plus copies and postage for
members, $7.00 per hour plus copies and
postage for nonmembers

Meeker County Genealogical Society
GAR Hall—Meeker County Museum
308 Marshall Avenue, North
Litchfield, MN 55355

Minnkota Genealogical Society
PO Box 12744
Grand Forks, ND 58208-2744
fga49@myway.com
http://www.rootsweb.com/~minnkota
Rick G. Audette, President
meetings at the Campbell Library, 422
Fourth Street, N.W., East Grand Forks,
MN: second Tue 7:00
$10.00 per year membership

Mower County Genealogical Society
PO Box 145
Austin, MN 55912
(507) 437-6082
Library at Historical Center, Fairgrounds,
Austin: Mon–Fri 11:00–4:00
Pub. *Mower County Genealogical News*,
three times per year, $3.00 per year
subscription
(cemetery records)
$8.00 per year membership

Nobles County Genealogical Group
Nobles County Library and Information
Center
407 12th Street, Suite 2
Worthington, MN 56187
(507) 372-4431
http://www.wgtn.net/gp/
genealogicalgroup.htm
Dorothy Wagner
meetings: first Sat (Sept–June)
Pub. *Nobles County Genealogical Society
Newsletter*, quarterly
$5.00 per year membership; limited research
for members

Northwest Territory Genealogical Society
(see Indiana, Part 2)

Olmsted County Genealogical Society
(Olmsted County Historical Society, 1195
West Circle Drive S.W., Rochester, MN

55902-6619—location)
PO Box 6411 (mailing address)
Rochester, MN 55903
(507) 282-9447 (Olmsted County Historical
Society)
Sherry Sweetman, Librarian/Archivist,
Olmsted County Historical Society
Tue–Sat 9:00–5:00 (Olmsted County
Historical Society Library)
Pub. *Olmsted County Genealogical Society
Newsletter*, quarterly
("The Olmsted County Genealogical Society
is a support group for the Olmsted County
Historical Society Library. Their
dedicated members provide many hours of
volunteer time to the Olmsted County
Historical Society Library. The
partnership of these two organizations has
resulted in many new indexes and other
finding aids for genealogists.")
$10.00 per year membership

Otter Tail County Genealogical Society
1110 West Lincoln Avenue
Fergus Falls, MN 56537
(218) 736-6038 (Museum)
otchs@prtel.com
http://jsenterprises.com/ottertail/
genealogicalsociety.htm
Doloris Duncan
Library: Mon–Fri 9:00–5:00; Museum:
Mon–Fri 9:00–5:00, Sat (Jan–Dec)
1:00–4:00, Sun (June–Sept) 1:00–4:00;
meetings: third Mon 7:30
Pub. *Otter Tail County Genealogical
Newsletter*, quarterly
$10.00 per year membership; research:
$20.00 per surname

Pipestone County Genealogical Society
Pipestone County Historical Society and
Museum
113 South Hiawatha Avenue
Pipestone, MN 56164
(507) 825-2510 (President); (507) 825-2437
(Secretary/Treasurer)
Sheri Cox, President; Ruth Taylor,
Secretary/Treasurer
Museum: Mon–Sun 10:00–5:00; meetings
first Sat 2:00
Pub. *The Pipestem*, quarterly (spring,
summer, winter, fall)
$7.50 per year membership; museum
admission: $2.00; queries free to
members; research: charge to members,
plus LSASE and copies at 25¢ per page
from paper original and 50¢ per page from
microfilm original

Prairieland Genealogical Society
Southwest Minnesota Historical Center
Room 141-Social Science Building
Southwest State University
Marshall, MN 56258
(507) 537-7373
pgs@starpoint.net
http://freepages.genealogy.rootsweb.com/
~cmolitor
C. J. Molitor, Corresponding Secretary
9:00–noon & 1:00–4:00
Pub. *Prairieland Pioneer*, quarterly
$15.00 per year membership

Rainy River Valley Genealogical Society
PO Box 1032
International Falls, MN 56649

Range Genealogical Society
PO Box 388
Chisholm, MN 55719
Pub. *Northland Bulletin*, bimonthly; *Range
Genealogical Society Newsletter*,

quarterly

Red River Valley Genealogical Society
(see North Dakota, Part 2)

Renville County Genealogical Society
(221 North Main Street—location)
PO Box 331 (mailing address)
Renville, MN 56284
(320) 329-8193
Mary Lou Smith, Librarian
Mon–Fri noon–5:30, Mon 6:30–8:00, and by
appointment
Pub. *The Geneline—Renville County
Genealogical Society Newsletter*, quarterly
(Renville County data)
$10.00 per year membership

Rice County Genealogical Society
408 Division Street
Northfield, MN 55057
(507) 645-9268
njgilber@rconnect.com
Pub. *Rice Gleanings*, two times per year
$10.00 per year membership; research
available

Saint Cloud Area Genealogists, Inc.
PO Box 213
Saint Cloud, MN 56302-0213
pma@upstel.net; ralitke@stcloudstate.edu
http://www.rootsweb.com/~mnscag/SCAG
Pub. *PasTimes*, bimonthly
$12.00 per year membership; research: $7.50
per hour

Stevens County Genealogical Society
Morris Public Library
102 East Sixth Street
Morris, MN 56267
Joan Kopacek, Secretary/Treasurer
9:00–9:00
Pub. *Stevens County Genealogical Society
Newsletter*, quarterly (Feb, May, Aug,
Nov)
("Obituary Comm.-microfilm newspapers-
cemeteries")
$8.00 per year membership; research: $10.00
per hour plus copy costs

Traverse des Sioux Genealogical Society
1851 North Minnesota Avenue
Saint Peter, MN 56082-1727
Janet M. Larson, Correspondent
no membership fee

Twin Ports Genealogical Society
PO Box 16895
Duluth, MN 55816-0895
Pub. *Branching Out*, three times per year
(Sept, Dec, Mar)
(Duluth, Saint Louis County, Minnesota, and
Superior, Douglas County, Wisconsin)
$10.00 per year membership; research:
$10.00 per hour plus copies and postage

Waseca Area Genealogy Society (WAGS)
Waseca County Historical Society Museum
PO Box 314
Waseca, MN 56093
(507) 835-7700
director@historical.waseca.mn.us
http://www.historical.waseca.mn.us
Margaret Sinn, Executive Director of
Historical Society
Mon–Fri 8:00–noon & 1:00–5:00, Sat
(Memorial Day–Labor Day) 1:00–5:00
(a committee of the Waseca County Historical
Society, q.v.)
$20.00 per year membership; admission:
$5.00 for nonmembers

**Wilkin County Historical Society
Genealogy Committee**
Genealogy Guild of Wilkin County,
Minnesota, and Richland County, North
Dakota
(see Historical Societies—Local and
Regional, above)

Winona County Genealogy Roundtable
(160 Johnson Street—location)
PO Box 363 (mailing address)
Winona, MN 55987-0363
Pub. *Table Talk*, quarterly
$5.00 per year membership; research: $8.00
     per hour

Independent Publications and Miscellany

Carver-on-the-Minnesota, Inc.
PO Box 281
Carver, MN 55315
(952) 448-4580
Barbara Swanson
volunteer staff, no facility open

**Faribault Heritage Preservation
Commission**
208 N.W. First Avenue
Faribault, MN 55021
(507) 334-2222
Patricia Gustafson, Housing and
     Redevelopment Director
Mon–Fri 8:00–5:00
("videos, brochures, surveys, preservation,
     planning report, events, tours, elementary
     education curriculum development,
     educational presentations, workshops,
     etc., preservation of materials generated
     by the HPC")

**Lanesboro Historical Preservation
Association**
(105 Parkway, South—location)
PO Box 345 (mailing address)
Lanesboro, MN 55949
(507) 467-2177
June–Sept: 10:00–5:00
$3.00 per year membership

**Mayo Foundation Archives and Historical
Area**
200 First Street, S.W.
Rochester, MN 55901
(507) 282-2511, ext. 2585

**Minnesota Alliance of Local Historical
Museums**
c/o Stearns County Historical Society
Stearns County Heritage Center
(235 33rd Avenue, South—location)
PO Box 702 (mailing address)
Saint Cloud, MN 56302-0702

Minnesota Department of Transportation
395 John Ireland Boulevard
Saint Paul, MN 55155-1899
(800) 657-3774
info@dot.state.mn.us
http://www.dot.state.mn.us/mapsales (Maps)

Minnesota State Law Library
Room G25, Minnesota Judicial Center
25 Rev. Dr. Martin Luther King Jr.
Boulevard
Saint Paul, MN 55155
(651) 296-2775; (651) 296-6740 FAX
askalibrarian@courts.state.mn.us
http://www.lawlibrary.state.mn.us

William Mitchell College of Law

Warren E. Burger Law Library
871 Summit Avenue
Saint Paul, MN 55105
(612) 290-6424; (612) 290-6318 FAX
http://www.wmitchell.edu/library/index. html

MnGenWeb
Part of The USGenWeb Project
MNGenWeb@aol.com;
     RWFonkenMN@worldnet.att.net
http://www.rootsweb.com/~mngenweb
Jackie Hufschmid, State Coordinator;
     Michael Andrews, Assistant Coordinator;
     Terri Shipp, Assistant Coordinator
(links to other Minnesota resources)

Old Home Town Museum
(608 Fifth Street—location)
PO Box 593 (mailing address)
Stephen, MN 56757
(218) 478-3092

Park Genealogical Books
(1705 Marion Street North—office location)
PO Box 130968 (mailing address)
Roseville, MN 55113-0968
(651) 488-4416; (651) 488-2653
mbakeman@parkbooks.com
http://www.parkbooks.com
Mary Bakeman, Owner
Mon 10:00–3:00
Pub. *Minnesota Genealogical Journal*
     (covers Minnesota and prior territories,
     many manuscript transcriptions, not
     available elsewhere), semiannually (Mar,
     Sept), $23.00 per year subscription
     (foreign addresses add $5.00 per year),
     back issues for $12.00 plus postage ($4.00
     for first issue, 75¢ for each additional
     issue)

**Pig's Eye's Notepad—Historical
Encyclopedia of Saint Paul 1830–1850**
135 East Viking Drive #301
Little Canada, MN 55117
paul@lareau.org
http://www.lareau.org/pep.html
Paul J. Lareau

**Society for the Preservation of
Minnesota's Heritage**
PO Box 157
Minneota, MN 56264

**University of Minnesota, Department of
History**
269 A. B. Anderson Hall
Duluth, MN 55812
Roger A. Fischer, Chair
Pub. *Upper Midwest History*, annually

**Upsala Obituary, Marriage and Cemetery
Index**
johns@upstel.net
http://www.upstel.net/~johns/CemIndex/
     CemIndex.html

Winnebago Area Museum
36 North Main Street
Winnebago, MN 56098
(507) 893-3196

Mississippi

Archives and Libraries with Holdings in Genealogy

State Archives and Library

Archives and Library Division
Mississippi Department of Archives and
History
(200 North Street, Jackson, MS
39201—location)
PO Box 571 (mailing address)
Jackson, MS 39205-0571
(601) 576-6850; (601) 576-6975 FAX
refdesk@mdah.state.ms.us
http://www.mdah.state.ms.us
H. T. Holmes, Division Director
Search Room: Mon 9:00–5:00, Tue–Fri
     8:00–5:00, Sat 8:00–1:00 (closed state
     holidays)
(Mississippiana, including private man-
     uscripts and state government papers)
research: $15.00 per hour plus copy costs for
     out-of-state residents (subject to change)

Historic Jefferson College
Mississippi Department of Archives and
History
(U.S. Highway 61 North—location)
PO Box 700 (mailing address)
Washington, MS 39190-0700
(601) 442-2901
Anne Gray, Historian; Jim Barnett, Director
by appointment only

Mississippi Library Commission
(1221 Ellis Avenue—location)
PO Box 10700 (mailing address)
Jackson, MS 39289-0700
(601) 359-1036
mslib@mlc.lib.ms.us
http://www.mlc.lib.ms.us

Records Management Division
Mississippi Department of Archives and
History
929 High Street
Jackson, MS 39202
(601) 354-7688
William J. Hanna, Director

State Historical Society

**Historical and Genealogical Association of
Mississippi**
618 Avalon Road
Jackson, MS 39206
(601) 362-3079
Jackie Ratcliffe, Editor, Secretary-Treasurer
Pub. *Family Trails*

Mississippi Historical Society
PO Box 571
Jackson, MS 39205-0571
(601) 359-6850
Elbert R. Hilliard, Secretary-Treasurer
Pub. *Journal of Mississippi History*,
     quarterly; *Mississippi History Newsletter*,
     monthly
("The Mississippi Historical Society actually
     does not have an office as such, but merely
     a part-time secretary. Any queries sent to
     them are forwarded to the Department of
     Archives and History.")
$15.00 per year membership

**City, County and Regional Archives and
Libraries**
(A more exhaustive list of public and
academic libraries can be found at http://

www.mlc.lib.ms.us/directory/public/index.
cfm.)

L. W. Anderson Genealogical Library
(see Linebaugh Library, Tennessee, Part 2)

Judge George W. Armstrong Library
220 South Commerce Street
Natchez, MS 39120-3502
(601) 445-8862; (601) 446-7795 FAX
scassagne@homochitto.lib.ms.us
http://www.homochitto.lib.ms.us
Susan S. Cassagne, Director
Mon–Thur 9:00–6:00, Fri 9:00–5:00, Sat
9:00–1:00

Attala County Library
201 South Huntington Street
Kosciusko, MS 39090-9002
(662) 289-5141
attalagenealogy@midmissregional.lib.ms.us
http://www.mmrlsopac.lib.ms.us
Ann Fulghum, Genealogy Clerk
Mon–Fri 9:00–6:00, Sat 9:00–5:00

Batesville Public Library
206 Highway 51 North
Batesville, MS 38606
(662) 563-1038; (662) 563-6640 FAX
http://www.first.lib.ms.us
Mollie Gillespie, Head Librarian

Biloxi Public Library
139 Lameuse Street
Biloxi, MS 39530-4298
(228) 374-0330; (228) 374-0375 FAX
http://www.harrison.lib.ms.us
Murella Powell, Local History and
Genealogy Librarian
Mon–Thur 9:00–8:00, Fri–Sat 9:00–5:00

Birmingham Public Library
(see Alabama, Part 2)

Bolivar County Library
104 South Leflore Avenue
Cleveland, MS 38732
(662) 843-2774; (662) 843-4701 FAX
rwise@tecinfo.com
http://www.bolivar.lib.ms.us
Mr. Ronnie W. Wise, Director
Mon–Thur 9:00–8:00 (summer: 9:00–6:00),
Fri 9:00–5:00, Sat 9:00–5:00 (summer:
10:00–2:00)
(specializes in Bolivar County, Mississippi)

Carthage-Leake County Library
114 East Franklin Street
Carthage, MS 39051-3716
(601) 267-7821; (601) 267-5530 FAX
http://www.mmrlsopac.lib.ms.us
Mary Ellen Ellis, Librarian

**Carnegie Public Library of Clarksdale and
Coahoma County**
(114 Delta Avenue—location)
PO Box 280 (mailing address)
Clarksdale, MS 38614-0280
(662) 624-4461; (662) 627-4344 FAX
ref@cplclarksdale.lib.ms.us
http://www.cplclarksdale.lib.ms.us
Linda White, Reference Librarian
Mon 9:00–8:00, Tue–Thur 9:00–5:30, Fri
9:00–5:00, Sat 10:00–2:00

DeKalb Public Library
PO Box 710
DeKalb, MS 39328-0710
(601) 743-5981 voice & FAX
http://www.rootsweb.com/~mskemper/
library.html
Lynette Long, Librarian

Evans Memorial Library
105 North Long Street
Aberdeen, MS 39730
(662) 369-4601; (662) 369-2971 FAX
http://www.tombigbee.lib.ms.us
Barbara Blair, Genealogy Librarian
Mon–Fri 9:00–4:30, Sat 9:00–4:00

Forest Public Library
(210 South Raleigh—location)
PO Box 737 (mailing address)
Forest, MS 39074
(601) 469-1481; (601) 469-5903 FAX
forest@cmrls.lib.ms.us
http://www.cmrls.lib.ms.us
Shawna Alexander, Branch Manager

Greenwood-Leflore Public Library
Special Collections
405 West Washington
Greenwood, MS 38930-4297
(662) 453-3634; (662) 453-0683 FAX
http://www.mlc.lib.ms.us/directory/
public/system.cfm?adm_code=11
Susan Harris, Library Director
Mon–Wed 8:30–7:30, Thur–Sat 8:30–5:30
(Mississippi and southeastern U.S.
genealogy)
copies: 20¢ per page and "in some instances
there is a fee for postage"

Gulfport Public Library
(1300 21st Avenue—location)
PO Box 4018 (mailing address)
Gulfport, MS 39502-4018
(228) 863-6411; (228) 863-7433 FAX
m. powell@harrison.lib.ms.us
http://www.harrison.lib.ms.us
Murella Powell (Genealogy)
Mon–Thur 9:00–8:00, Fri–Sat 9:00–5:00

Hacksma House Genealogy Library
(see Washington, Part 2)

**The Library of Hattiesburg, Petal and
Forrest County**
329 Hardy Street
Hattiesburg, MS 39401-3824
(601) 582-4461; (601) 582-5338 FAX
http://www.hpfc.lib.ms.us Pamela J. Pridgen,
Director
Mon–Tue 9:00–8:30, Wed–Sat 9:00–5:30

**Huntsville-Madison County Public
Library**
(see Alabama, Part 2)

Iuka Public Library
204 North Main Street
Iuka, MS 38852
(662) 423-6300
freddas@nereg.lib.ms.us
http://www.nereg.lib.ms.us/Iuka.html
Fredda Sanderson, Librarian
Mon–Tue & Fri 10:00–6:00, Wed–Thur
10:00–7:00, Sat 10:00–4:00
(mostly local interest)

Jackson-George Regional Library System
3214 Pascagoula Street
Pascagoula, MS 39567-4217
(228) 762-3060; (228) 769-3146 FAX
pgstaff@jgrl.lib.ms.us
http://www.jgrl.lib.ms.us
Jean Strickland, Head, Genealogy and Local
History Department
Mon–Thur 9:00–8:00, Fri–Sat 9:00–5:00
(specializes in Mississippi and Alabama;
"large collection, excellent Genealogy
Department")

Jefferson County Library

218 South Main Street
Fayette, MS 39069
(601) 786-3982; (601) 786-9646 FAX
http://www.copjef.lib.ms.us
Marilyn Felton, Librarian

**Lauderdale County Department of
Archives and History**
(Courthouse Annex, Second Floor, 410
Constitution Avenue—location)
PO Box 5511 (mailing address)
Meridian, MS 39302-5511
(601) 482-9752; (601) 484-3994 FAX
archives@lauderdalecounty.org
http://lauderdalecounty.org/archives.html
Ward Calhoun, Records Manager
Mon–Fri 8:00–5:00
Pub. *Newsletter*, quarterly
("City and county public records,
approximately 200 publications
concerning people and events in east
Mississippi and west Alabama as well as
other genealogical works for research and
study.")
$10.00 per year membership

**Laurel-Jones County Library—Genealogy
Department**
530 Commerce Street
Laurel, MS 39440-3998
(601) 428-4313; (601) 428-4314 FAX
geneal@laurel.lib.ms.us
http://www.laurel.lib.ms.us
Susan Blakeney, Genealogist Librarian
Tue–Fri 1:00–5:00, Sat 10:00–2:00
(much county and southern history records)

Lee County Library
219 North Madison Street
Tupelo, MS 38804-3807
(662) 841-9029; (662) 841-9013 (Genealogy)
circulation@li.lib.ms.us
http://www.li.lib.ms.us
Louann Hurst, Director
Mon–Thur 9:30–8:30, Fri 9:00–5:00, Sat
9:00–5:00

Lincoln County Public Library
Local History and Genealogy Collection
(100 South Jackson Street—location)
PO Box 541 (mailing address)
Brookhaven, MS 39601-0541
(601) 833-3369; (601) 833-3381 FAX
6pll@llf.lib.ms.us
http://www.llf.lib.ms.us/Winnebago/
index.htm
Henry J. Ledet, Director
Mon & Wed 9:00–6:00, Tue & Thur
9:00–8:00, Fri–Sat 9:00–5:00
(local history and genealogy of Lincoln,
Lawrence and Franklin counties)

Lowndes County Library System
314 North Seventh Street
Columbus, MS 39701-4699
(662) 329-5304; (662) 329-5156 FAX
archives@lowndes.lib.ms.us
http://www.lowndes.lib.ms.us
Martha Sparrow, Archivist at Library
Library: Mon–Thur 9:00–6:00, Fri 9:00–5:00,
Sat 10:00–4:00; Archives: Mon–Fri
9:00–5:00, second Sat 10:00–4:00, fourth
Sat 11:00–3:00
("Library has genealogical materials for
Mississippi, Alabama, and all southern
states as well as information for other
areas.")

Marks-Quitman County Library
315 East Main
Marks, MS 38646-1320
(662) 326-7141; (662) 326-7369 FAX

Anne S. Kerr, Director

McCain Library and Archives
University of Southern Mississippi
Southern Station, Box 5148
Hattiesburg, MS 39406-5148
(601) 266-4345 (Reference desk)
http://www.lib.usm.edu/mccain.html
Mon–Thur 8:00–6:00, Fri 8:00–5:00, Sat
10:00–2:00
(emphasis on southern U.S.)

**Meridian-Lauderdale County Public
Library**
2517 Seventh Street
Meridian, MS 39301-4998
(601) 693-6771; (601) 486-2270 FAX
library@meridian.lib.ms.us
http://www.Meridian.Lib.MS.us
Carol James, Head of Genealogy Department
Mon–Fri 9:00–9:00, Sat 9:00–6:00

Millsaps College
(see J. B. Cain Archives of Mississippi
Methodism, Religious Archives and
Organizations—United Methodist, Part 3)

Mississippi College
Leland Speed Library
PO Box 51
Clinton, MS 39060-0051
(601) 925-3434
Rachel A. Pyron, Special Collections
Librarian
Mon–Fri 8:30–noon & 1:00–4:30 (except
college holidays)

Mississippi State Historical Museum
Mississippi Department of Archives and
History
Old Capitol Restoration
100 South State Street
Jackson, MS 39201
(601) 354-6222
Patti Carr Black, Museum Director

Mississippi University for Women
Fant Memorial Library
PO Box W-1625
Columbus, MS 39701
(662) 329-7332; (662) 329-7348 FAX
fdavison@MUW.edu
http://www.muw.edu
Freda M. Davison, Professor and Director of
Library Services
Mon–Fri 8:00–5:00 (extended hours during
semesters)
(University related historical archives
[alumni, etc.], Mississippi census and
newspapers on microfilm)
$10.00 per year for non-MUW affiliates

Mitchell Memorial Library
Reference, Special Collections
(Mississippi State University—location)
PO Box 9570 (mailing address)
Mississippi State, MS 39762
(662) 325-7679
lmueller@library.MsState.edu;
blove@library.MsState.edu
http://www.msstate.edu/library/sc
Lynne Mueller, Reference Librarian, Special
Collections
Mon–Fri 7:30–6:00, Sat 10:00–1:00 when
school is in session
(do not confuse with the L. W. Anderson
Genealogical Library)

Neshoba County Public Library
Genealogy/Mississippi Collection
230 Beacon Street
Philadelphia, MS 39350-3054

(601) 656-4911; (601) 656-6894 FAX
http://www.neshoba.lib.ms.us
Madonna J. Green, Director
Mon, Wed & Fri 9:00–5:00, Tue & Thur
9:00–7:00, Sat 9:00–noon

Northeast Regional Library
Corinth Public Library
1023 Fillmore Street
Corinth, MS 38834-4199
(662) 287-2441; (662) 287-7311; (662) 286-
8010 FAX
http://www.nereg.lib.ms.us
Mrs. Samuel Rea, Librarian
Mon–Thur 9:00–8:00, Fri–Sat 9:00–5:00

Noxubee County Library
103 East King Street
Macon, MS 39341-2832
(662) 726-5461 voice & FAX
bkoostra@noxubee.lib.ms.us
http://www.noxubee.lib.ms.us
Lucille Reeves
Mon–Tue & Thur–Fri 8:00–6:00

**Lafayette County and Oxford Public
Library**
401 Bramlett Boulevard
Oxford, MS 38655
(662) 234-5751; (662) 234-3155 FAX
http://www.first.lib.ms.us
Dorothy Fitts, Head Librarian
Mon–Thur 9:30–8:00, Fri–Sat 9:30–5:00,
Sun 2:00–5:00

Harriet Person Memorial Library
606 Main Street
Port Gibson, MS 39150-2433
(601) 437-5202; (601) 437-5787 FAX
http://www.mlc.lib.ms.us/directory/
public/system.cfm?adm_code=13
Nancy Batton-Butler, Director

Pike-Amite-Walthall Library System
1022 Virginia Avenue
McComb, MS 39648-3937
(601) 684-7034; (601) 250-1213 FAX
6ppa@pawls.lib.ms.us
http://www.pawls.lib.ms.us
Katherine M. Niemeyer, Special Services
Librarian
Mon & Wed 8:30–5:30, Tue & Thur
8:30–8:00, Fri–Sat 8:30–5:00

Ripley Public Library
308 North Commerce Street
Ripley, MS 38663-1721
(662) 837-7773 voice & FAX
http://www.nereg.lib.ms.us
Tommy Covington, Librarian
Mon, Wed & Fri–Sat 9:00–5:00, Tue & Thur
9:00–8:00

Jennie Stephens Smith Library
(219 King Street—location)
PO Box 846 (mailing address)
New Albany, MS 38652-846
(662) 534-4331; (662) 534-1991; (662) 534-
1937 FAX
tdj@union.lib.ms.us
http://www.mlc.lib.ms.us/directory/
public/system.cfm?adm_code=42
Tonja Johnson, Director
Mon, Wed & Fri 9:00–5:30, Tue & Thur
9:00–8:00, Sat 9:00–1:00

**Starkville-Oktibbeha County Public
Library**
(326 University Drive—location)
PO Box 1406 (mailing address)
Starkville, MS 39759
(662) 323-2766; (662) 323-9140 FAX

http://www.starkville.lib.ms.us
Virginia Holtcamp, Director
Mon–Thur 9:00–6:00, Fri–Sat 9:00–4:00
Sunflower County Library
201 Cypress Drive
Indianola, MS 38751-2415
(662) 887-1672; (662) 887-2641 FAX
ashands@sunflower.lib.ms.us
http://www.sunflower.lib.ms.us
Alice Shands, Director
Mon 9:00–8:00, Tue–Thur 9:00–6:00, Fri
9:00–5:00, Sat 9:00–4:00
(regional and Mississippi materials)

Union County Library
(see Jennie Stephens Smith Library, above)

Union Public Library
101 Peachtree Street
Union, MS 39365-2617
(601) 774-5096; (601) 774-8735 FAX
http://www.mlc.lib.ms.us/directory/
public/system.cfm?adm_code=19
Linda Hamm, Librarian
Mon–Fri 8:30–5:30

University of Mississippi
General Library
Archives and Special Collections
University, MS 38677
(662) 234-6091; (662) 234-6381 FAX
ullandi@sunset.backbone.olemiss.edu
(Mississippi Collection)
http://www.olemiss.edu

University of Mississippi
Center for the Study of Southern Culture
University, MS 38677
(662) 232-5993; (662) 232-5814 FAX
http://imp.cssc.olemiss.edu

University of Southern Alabama
Gulf Coast Historical Review
(see Alabama, Part 2)

Warren County-Vicksburg Public Library
Reference Department
700 Veto Street
Vicksburg, MS 39180-3568
(601) 636-6411; (601) 634-4809 FAX
http://www.warren.lib.ms.us
Rosemary Fairchild, Local History Librarian
Mon–Thur 9:00–8:00, Fri–Sat 9:00–5:00

Washington County Library System
William Alexander Percy Memorial Library
341 Main Street
Greenville, MS 38701-4066
(662) 335-2331; (662) 390-4758 FAX
kclanton@washington.lib.ms.us
http://www.washington.lib.ms.us
Ms. Kay Clanton, Director
Mon–Wed 9:00–8:00, Mon–Wed (summer)
9:00–7:00, Thur–Fri 9:00–6:00, Sat
1:00–5:00, Sun (except summer)
1:00–5:00

The Waynesboro Memorial Library
712 Wayne Street
Waynesboro, MS 39367
(662) 735-2268; (662) 735-6407 FAX
wlib@wwcls.lib.ms.us
http://www.wwcls.lib.ms.us
Patsy Brewer, Librarian
Mon, Wed & Fri 9:00–5:00, Tue & Thur
9:00–8:00, Sat 9:00–noon
(substantial genealogical holdings)

Historical Societies—Local and Regional

Amite County Foundation for Historic Preservation
Route 4, Box 226
Liberty, MS 39645
(601) 684-1281

Amite County Historical and Genealogical Society
Little Red School House Museum
PO Box 2
Liberty, MS 39645
(925) 254-1679
Sue Clark Severson, Secretary
$15.00 per year membership

Attala Historical Society
(The Mary Ricks Thornton Cultural Center, 200 North Huntington Street—location)
PO Box 127 (mailing address)
Kosciusko, MS 39090
(662) 289-5516
http://www.rootsweb.com/~msahs
Mrs. George Thornton, Director
Mon–Fri 1:00–4:00
$25.00 per year membership

Bolivar County Historical Society
1615 Terrace Road
Cleveland, MS 38732
(662) 843-8204
Pub. *Bolivar County Historical Society Publications*, irregularly

Brice's Crossroads Museum
(Intersection of Highways 45 and 370—location)
PO Box 100 (mailing address)
Baldwyn, MS 38824
(662) 365-2383; (662) 365-2274
Billy Roberson, Chairman, Brice's Crossroads Museum Commission

Calhoun County Historical and Genealogical Society, Inc.
PO Box 114
Pittsboro, MS 38951
http://personalpages.tds.net/~rosediamond/societymainpage.html
Bobby Inmon, Corresponding Secretary
meetings at the Calhoun County Courthouse: second Sun 2:00 (Jan, Mar, July, Sept, Nov)
Pub. *The Newsletter*, quaarterly
$14.00 per year membership

Chickasaw County Historical and Genealogical Society
PO Box 42
Houston, MS 38851
(662) 456-4512
tommyg@network-one.com
http://www.rootsweb.com/~mschchgs
Kay Y. Griffin, Editor
Pub. *Chickasaw Times Past*, quarterly
(genealogical and historical information of the original lands of Chickasaw County, including Chickasaw, Calhoun, Clay and Webster counties, Mississippi)
$20.00 per year membership

Choctaw County Historical and Genealogical Society
PO Box 1382
Ackerman, MS 39735
jgriffin@telepak.net

The Columbus and Lowndes County Historical Society
(316 Seventh Street—location)
916 College Street (mailing address)
Columbus, MS 39701
(662) 328-5437

Hancock County Historical Society
(108 Cue Street—location)
PO Box 312 (mailing address)
Bay Saint Louis, MS 39520
(228) 467-4090 voice & FAX
Charles Gray, President
Mon–Fri 8:00–4:00
Pub. *Historian of Hancock County*, monthly

Historic Natchez Foundation
(409 Franklin Street, Natchez, MS 39120—location)
PO Box 1761 (mailing address)
Natchez, MS 39121
(601) 442-2500
Ronald W. Miller, Executive Director
(primarily historical, not genealogical)

Itawamba County Historical Society
George Poteet History Center
(Church Street and Museum Drive—location)
PO Box 7G (mailing address)
Mantachie, MS 38855
(662) 282-7664 (History Center)
robfra@network-one.com
http://www.network-one/com/~ithissoc
Bob Frankes
by appointment in winter months
Pub. *Itawamba Settlers*, quarterly
$20.00 per year membership

Jackson County Historical Society
4602 Fort Drive
Pascagoula, MS 39567
(228) 769-1505

Marshall County Historical Society, Inc.
(220 East College Avenue—location)
PO Box 806 (mailing address)
Holly Springs, MS 38635
(662) 252-4437

Mississippi Coast Historical and Genealogical Society
(Biloxi Public Library—location)
PO Box 513 (mailing address)
Biloxi, MS 39533
(228) 374-0330 (Library)
Mary Louise Adkinson; Murella Powell, Local History and Genealogy Librarian
Pub. *Mississippi Coast Historical and Genealogical Journal*, annually
$15.00 per year membership

Mississippi Junior Historical Society
William Carey College
Hattiesburg, MS 39401
(601) 582-5051

Monroe County Historical Society, Inc.
30062 Sand Hill Road
Aberdeen, MS 39730
cjackson@entomology.msstate.edu;
jerryaharlow@aol.com
http://www.rootsweb.com/~msmonroe/histsoc.htm
Pub. *The Journal of Monroe County History of Mississippi*

Natchez Historical Society
(307 South Wall Street—location)
PO Box 49 (mailing address)
Natchez, MS 39120
Donna Jankey, Director of Library
Judge George W. Armstrong Library:
Mon–Thur 9:00–6:00, Fri 9:00–5:00, Sat 9:00–1:00

Northeast Mississippi Historical and Genealogical Society
(Lee County Library, 219 Madison Avenue,

Tupelo, MS 38804—location)
PO Box 434 (mailing address)
Tupelo, MS 38802-0434
(662) 841-9013
Martis D. Ramage, Jr., Editor
Mon–Thur 9:30–8:30, Fri–Sat 9:00–5:00
Pub. *Northeast Mississippi Historical and Genealogical Society Quarterly*
(Lee, Itawamba, Pontotoc, Monroe, Tippah, Prentiss, Alcorn, Tishomingo and Chickasaw counties)
$15.00 per year membership

Noxubee County Historical Society, Inc.
(411 South Jefferson Street—location)
PO Box 392 (mailing address)
Macon, MS 39341
(662) 726-5218
bkoostra@lib.ms.us
http://www.geocities.com/dennislr.geo/nchs.html
Lucille Reeves, President
meetings at the Noxubee County Library: first Wed 7:00
Pub. *NCHS Bulletin*
$10.00 per year membership

'Pan Gens,' Historical and Genealogical Society of Panola County, Mississippi
210 Kyle Street
Batesville, MS 38606
Norma Riser, Corresponding Secretary
Pub. *Panola Story*, quarterly
$10.00 per year membership

Pass Christian Historical Society, Inc.
(203 East Scenic Drive—location)
PO Box 58 (mailing address)
Pass Christian, MS 39571
W. C. Kidd, President
hours: various

Pearl River Historical Group
c/o Books and Things
120 Tate Street
Picayune, MS 39466
(601) 795-6773
vll@datasync.com
http://www.gulfcoastplus.com/histsoc/pearlriv.htm
Sweet Vickey Lang

Prentiss County Genealogical and Historical Society
(see Genealogical Societies—Local and Regional, below)

Rankin County Historical Society, Inc.
PO Box 841
Brandon, MS 39043
(601) 825-5937
Marjorie Steen, President
Museum: Sat–Sun 2:00–4:00 (Oct & May, approximately four or five weekends each), and by appointment
$5.00 per year membership; museum admission: free; research: simple searches done for cost of photocopies plus postage, extensive search for $20.00 per hour

Skipwith Historical and Genealogical Society, Inc.
(Lafayette County and Oxford Public Library—location)
PO Box 1382 (mailing address)
Oxford, MS 38655
(662) 234-6082
http://www.rootsweb.com/~mslafaye/books.htm
Dr. Willorod St. Amand, Vice President
Library: Mon–Thur 9:30–8:00, Fri–Sat 9:30–5:00, Sun 2:00–5:00

Pub. *Lafayette County Heritage News*,
quarterly (Oct, Jan, Apr, July)
$12.00 per year membership

Southern Studies Institute
(see Louisiana, Part 2)

Sunflower County Historical Society, Inc.
Sunflower County Library
201 Cypress Drive
Indianola, MS 38751-2415
(662) 887-2153 voice & FAX
(Headquarters); (662) 887-3758
(President)
Anice Powell, Treasurer; Sammy Ely,
President Director
(regional and Mississippi materials)
$5.00 per year membership

**Tate County Mississippi Genealogical and
Historical Society**
(see Genealogical Societies—Local and
Regional, below)

**Tippah County Historical and
Genealogical Society**
Ripley Public Library
308 North Commerce Street
Ripley, MS 38663
Tommy Covington, Librarian
Library: Mon, Wed & Fri–Sat 9:00–5:00,
Tue & Thur 9:00–8:00
Pub. *News & Journal*, irregularly
$12.00 per year membership

**Tishomingo County Historical and
Genealogical Society**
(203 East Quitman Street—location)
PO Box 273 (mailing address)
Iuka, MS 38852
(662) 423-3500
tcarchives@nadata.net
http://www.rootsweb.com/~mstchgs/
index.htm
Mon–Fri 10:00–4:00, Sat 10:00–2:00
Pub. *Chronicles and Epitaphs*, quarterly
("Tishomingo County research,
preservation")
$20.00 per year membership; admission:
$2.00 suggested donation

**Vicksburg and Warren County Historical
Society**
c/o Old Court House Museum
1008 Cherry Street
Vicksburg, MS 39180
(601) 636-0741
courthouse1860@aol.com
http://www.oldcourthouse.org
Gordon Cotton, Director; Blanche Terry,
Assistant Director
Mon–Sat 8:30–4:30 (CST) or 8:30–5:00
(CDST), Sun 1:00–4:30 (CST) or 1:00-
5:00 (CDST)
(holdings include Vicksburg and Warren
County marriage, funeral, census, etc.)
admission: 5.00 for adults

Webster County Historical Society
Route 3, Box 14
Eupora, MS 39744
(662) 258-6898

Wilkinson County Historical Society
c/o Wilkinson County Museum
Woodville Civic Club, Inc.
(203 Boston Row—location)
PO Box 1055 (mailing address)
Woodville, MS 39669
(601) 888-3998 (Museum)
Wilkmuseum@aol.com
Ernesto Caldeira, Museum Director

Museum: Mon–Fri 10:00–noon &
2:00–4:00, Sat 10:00–noon

**Winston County Historical and
Genealogical Society**
PO Box 428
Louisville, MS 39339

Yalobusha County Historical Society
PO Box 258
Coffeeville, MS 38922
Wade H. Johnson, Editor
Pub. *The Pioneer*, quarterly, $3.00 per issue
$15.00 per year membership; no research

Yazoo Historical Society
(332 North Main Street—location)
PO Box 575 (mailing address)
Yazoo City, MS 39194
(662) 746-2273

**Scott County Genealogical and Historical
Society**
(see Historical Societies—Local and
Regional, above)

Genealogical Societies

State Genealogical Societies

Mississippi Genealogical Society
PO Box 5301
Jackson, MS 39296-5301
James E. Griffith, President
$10.00 per year membership

**Historical and Genealogical Association of
Mississippi**
(see State Historical Society, above)

Southern Society of Genealogists, Inc.
(see Alabama, Part 2)

Genealogical Societies—Local & Regional

Genealogical Society of Adams County
PO Box 187
Washington, MS 39190
Mrs. V. L. Harker

Alcorn County Genealogical Society
PO Box 1808
Corinth, MS 38835
gran@tsixroads.com
http://www.avsia.com/acgs/index.html
Betty Robertson
Fri–Sat 10:00–4:00
Pub. *Cross City Connection*

**Amite County Historical and Genealogical
Society**
(see Historical Societies—Local and
Regional, above)

**Calhoun County Historical and
Genealogical Society**
(see Historical Societies—Local and
Regional, above)

Carroll County Genealogical Society
PO Box 282
Carrollton, MS 38917
Judy Stanford, President
meetings at the Carrollton-North Carrollton
Public Library: second Sun 2:00

**Chickasaw County Historical and
Genealogical Society**
(see Historical Societies—Local and
Regional, above)

**Choctaw County Historical and

Genealogical Society
(see Historical Societies—Local and
Regional, above)

**Claiborne/Jefferson County Genealogical
Society**
Harriet Person Memorial Library
(1005 College Street—location)
PO Box 1017 (mailing address)
Port Gibson, MS 39150

Columbus-Lowndes Genealogical Society
Lowndes County Library System
314 North Seventh Street
Columbus, MS 39701
Pub. *Historic Lowndes*, quarterly
$10.00 per year membership

Dancing Rabbit Genealogical Society
(Carthage Leake Library, 114 East Franklin
Street—meeting location)
PO Box 166 (mailing address)
Carthage, MS 39051
drgs@cdssoft.com
http://drgs.org
Wanda B. McHann, President
by appointment
Pub. *D.R.G.S. Newsletter*, monthly
("Published two books in 2003: *Cemeteries
of Leake County* and *Pedigrees of Leake
Countians*.")
$10.00 per year membership

**Genealogical Society of DeSoto County,
Mississippi**
(DeSoto County Courthouse—location)
PO Box 607 (mailing address)
Hernando, MS 38632-0607
(662) 429-1310
GSDCMS@hotmail.com
http://www.rootsweb.com/~msdesoto/
gsdcm.htm
Ozell D. Scott, President
Mon–Wed 10:00–4:00
Pub. *DeSoto Descendants*, quarterly
$15.00 per year membership

**The Family Research Association of
Central Mississippi**
PO Box 13334
Jackson, MS 39236-3334
Pub. *Newsletter*

Jackson County Genealogical Society
PO Box 984
Pascagoula, MS 39567
(228) 762-7777
Tommy Wixon, Editor
Pub. *Journal of Jackson County
Genealogical Society*, quarterly
$15.00 per year membership

Jones County Genealogical Organization
PO Box 2644
Laurel, MS 39442-2644
jcgho1@yahoo.com

Marshall County Genealogical Society
109 East Gholson Avenue
Holly Springs, MS 38635
Suzywa@aol.com
Suzy Stilwell, President

**Mississippi Coast Historical and
Genealogical Society**
(see Historical Societies—Local and
Regional, above)

Neshoba County Genealogy Group
(601) 656-4787
Doug McLain

Genealogical Society
(see Historical Societies—Local and
Regional, above)

Northeast Mississippi Historical and Genealogical Society
(see Historical Societies—Local and Regional, above)

Ocean Springs Genealogical Society
PO Box 1765
Ocean Springs, MS 39564-1765
dbkuhl@bellsouth; millron@iit.edu
http://www.rootsweb.com/~msogs
Dave Kuhl; Ron Miller
Pub. *Newsletter*, bimonthly
("Society combined ahnentafel, Jackson
County, Mississippi, 1912 school
census.")
$5.00 per year membership

'Pan Gens,' Historical and Genealogical Society of Panola County, Mississippi
(see Historical Societies—Local and Regional, above)

Prentiss County Genealogical and Historical Society
PO Box 491
Booneville, MS 38829
prentisscghs@yahoo.com
http://www.rootsweb.com/~mspcgs/
Index.html
Gloria Smith, Secretary/Treasurer
Pub. *Quarterly*
$20.00 per year membership

Scott County Genealogical and Historical Society
PO Box 128
Forest, MS 39074
scottcogensoc@yahoo.com
http://www.geocities.com/scottcogensoc
Dorothy Vance, Secretary
$12.00 per year membership

Skipwith Historical and Genealogical Society, Inc.
(see Historical Societies—Local and Regional, above)

Smith County Genealogical Society
PO Box 356
Raleigh, MS 39153
Lncwebb@direcway.com
Charlotte Webb, President
meetings at the Raleigh Public Library:
second Sat 10:00
$12.00 per year membership

South Mississippi Genealogical Society
PO Box 15271
Hattiesburg, MS 39404-5271
clarise@prodigy.net
http://members.tripod.com/smsghs
Elaine Bullock, President; Clarise Soper
monthly meetings
$20.00 per year membership

Tate County Mississippi Genealogical and Historical Society
(105 Court Street, Leroy Crockett
Building—location)
PO Box 974 (mailing address)
Senatobia, MS 38668
(662) 562-0390
Winnie H. Sykes, President
Thur–Fri 10:00–4:30
Pub. *Tate Trails*, quarterly
$15.00 per year membership

Tippah County Historical and Genealogical Society
(see Historical Societies—Local and Regional, above)

Tishomingo County Historical and Genealogical Society
(see Historical Societies—Local and Regional, above)

Vicksburg Genealogical Society
PO Box 1161
Vicksburg, MS 39181-1161
DARDEAUEA@aol.com
http://www.rootsweb.com/~msvgs/index.htm
E. A. (Tony) Dareau, Jr., Editor
meetings: 10:00 A.M. (even-numbered
months) & 6:30 P.M. (odd-numbered
months)
Pub. *Mississippi River Routes*, quarterly
("covers Mississippi counties and Louisiana
parishes along the Mississippi River from
Greenville, Mississippi, to Natchez,
Mississippi")
$20.00 per year membership; succinct and
focused queries welcome

The Wayne County Genealogical Organization
The Waynesboro Memorial Library
712 Wayne Street
Waynesboro, MS 39367
Betty Tiner, President
Pub. *Tracts and Trails*, quarterly

Winston County Historical and Genealogical Society
(see Historical Societies—Local and Regional, above)

Independent Publications and Miscellany

Center for Oral History and Cultural Heritage
(University of Southern Mississippi, College
Hall Room 112—location)
PO Box 5175 (mailing address)
Hattiesburg, MS 39406-5175
(601) 266-4575; (601) 266-6217 FAX
http://www-dept.usm.edu/~ocach;
http://www.usm.edu/msoralhistory
Dr. Curtis Austin and Dr. Charles Bolton,
Co-Directors

Courier Publications
PO Box 1320
Winnfield, LA 71483-1320
Pub. *Mississippi State Courier*, quarterly,
$15.00 per year subscription

F & M Enterprises
3058 Carmen Drive
Baton Rouge, LA 70709
(225) 927-0901; (800) 848-2463
Frances X. Westbrook, Owner
Mon–Fri 9:00–5:00
(southwest Mississippi, and the Mississippi
and Florida parishes of Louisiana)

Genealogical Institute
(see Virginia, Part 2)

Genealogy Books and Consultation
(see Texas, Part 2)

Hunting for Bears Genealogical and Historical Society
(see Alabama, Part 2)

The Magnolia Connection
PO Box 697
Ellisville, MS 39437
FSmith2015@aol.com
Flicka Smith
Pub. *The Magnolia Connection*, quarterly,

$16.00 per year subscription

Mississippi Department of Transportation
MDOT Administration Building
(401 North West Street, Jackson, MS
39201—location)
PO Box 1850 (mailing address)
Jackson, MS 39215-1850
(601) 359-7045 (Map Sales); (601) 359-7652
FAX (Map Sales)
paffairs@mdot.state.ms.us
http://www.gomdot.com/business/maps/
map_online.htm
Tom Thompson

Mississippi Memories
PO Box 18991
Shreveport, LA 71138-1991
(318) 686-3112
jsbridg@aol.com
Joyce Shannon Bridges, Co-editor
8:00–8:00
Pub. *Mississippi Memories*, quarterly (Feb,
May, Aug, Nov), $15.00 per year
subscription

Mountain Press
(see Tennessee, Part 2)

MsGenWeb
Part of The USGenweb Project
mccoybel@bellsouth.net
http://www.rootsweb.com/~msgenweb
Ellen Pack, State Coordinator; Melissa
McCoy-Bell, Assistant Coordinator
(links to other Mississippi resources)

Oktibbeha County Heritage Museum
203 Fellowship Road
Starkville, MS 39759
(662) 323-0211
Dr. George R. Lewis, Director
Tue–Thur 1:00–4:00, and by appointment
admission: donation

Pontotoc County Pioneers
207 North Main Street
Pontotoc, MS 38863
(662) 489-6748
Hazle Boss Neet, Editor

The Southern Genealogist's Exchange Society, Inc.
(see Florida, Part 2)

Southern Historical Press, Inc.
(see Publishers, Part 4)

Southwest Mississippi and WF Parishes, Louisiana
(see Louisiana, Part 2)

Traveller Southern Families
(see Virginia, Part 2)

Vicksburg Foundation for Historic Preservation
(1107 Washington Street, Vicksburg, MS
39183—location)
PO Box 254 (mailing address)
Vicksburg, MS 39181
(601) 636-5010
vburgfoundation@aol.com
http://preservevicksburg.com
Nancy H. Bell, Executive Director
Mon–Fri 8:00–5:00 by appointment
(primarily historical, not genealogical)

Wilkinson County Museum
Woodville Civic Club, Inc.
(203 Boston Row—location)
PO Box 1055 (mailing address)

Woodville, MS 39669
(601) 888-3998
Wilkmuseum@aol.com
Ernesto Caldeira, Director
Mon–Fri 10:00–noon & 2:00–4:00, Sat
    10:00–noon
Pub. *The Journal of Wilkinson County
    History*, approximately annually

Missouri

Archives and Libraries with Holdings in Genealogy

State Archives and Museum

Missouri State Museum
Capitol Building
Room B-2
Jefferson City, MO 65101
(573) 751-2854
L. T. Shelton, Curator of Collections
Mon–Fri 8:00–5:00, by appointment
(civic affairs and leaders; various ethnic
    groups; family and personal papers;
    government records; local history; the
    military, mining, and mineral industries;
    pioneer and frontier life; mainly physical
    artifacts with limited holdings of
    manuscripts, books and photographs)

Missouri State Archives
(600 West Main Street—location)
PO Box 1747 (mailing address)
Jefferson City, MO 65102
(573) 751-3280; (573) 526-7333 FAX
archref@sosmail.state.mo.us
http://www.sos.mo.gov/archives/Default.asp
Patricia Luebbert, Senior Archivist
Mon–Fri 8:00–5:00, Thur & Sat 8:30–3:30
("Currently have over 42,000 reels of county
    and local government records on
    microfilm, i.e. deed; marriages; circuit
    court records both civil and criminal;
    probate estate files including wills,
    inventories, settlements; county vital
    statistics, especially 1883–1893 and some
    others from before 1910. Records varying
    from county to county.)
no research fees; copies: 10¢ per page from
    paper originals, 25¢ per page from
    microform originals

Missouri State Library
(address withheld upon request)
("The major functions of the State Library
    are to provide direct library and
    information service in support of the
    executive and legislative branches of
    Missouri state government, to provide
    library service to blind and physically
    handicapped residents of Missouri and to
    promote the development and
    improvement of library services
    throughout the state"; for historical and
    genealogical sources see Missouri State
    Archives)

State Historical Societies

Missouri Historical Society
Library and Research Center
(225 South Skinker—location)
PO Box 11940 (mailing address)
Saint Louis, MO 63112-0040
(314) 746-4500; (314) 454-3100
    (Membership services); (314) 746-4599
    (General information)
library@mohistory.org
http://www.mohistory.org
Emily Jaycox, Librarian
Tue–Sat 10:00–5:00
Pub. *Gateway Heritage*, quarterly
(city and county directories; gazetteers;
    county, state and local histories; published
    transcripts and indexes to county records;
    family histories/genealogies; newspapers,
    maps, census, etc.; emphasis on St. Louis
    and regional history)
$55.00 per year membership; no research

service or members' queries

The State Historical Society of Missouri
Ellis Library Building
1020 Lowry Street
Columbia, MO 65201-7298
(573) 882-7083; (573) 884-4950 FAX
http://www.system.missouri.edu/shs
Mon–Fri 8:00–4:30, Sat 9:00–4:30 (closed
    holiday weekends)
Pub. *Missouri Historical Review*, quarterly
(resources include 456,000 volumes of
    monographs, serials, and state government
    publications; Missouri newspapers,
    1808–present; microfilm census records;
    maps; manuscript collections; photograph
    collection; art collection)
$10.00 per year membership

City, County and Regional Archives and Libraries

(A more exhaustive list of public and
    academic libraries can be found at http://
    www.sos.state.mo.us/library/libdir.asp.)

Adair County Public Library
1 Library Lane
Kirksville, MO 63501-2500
(660) 665-6038; (660) 627-0028 FAX
ahx001@mail.connect.more.net
http://adair.lib.mo.us
Glenda Davis, Director
Mon–Wed 9:00–8:00, Thur–Fri 9:00–6:00,
    Sat noon–4:00

Albany Carnegie Public Library
101 West Clay Street
Albany, MO 64402-1601
(660) 726-5615; (660) 726-4213 FAX
librarian@carnegie.lib.mo.us
http://carnegie.lib.mo.us/library.htm
Helen Henton, Librarian
Mon–Sat 11:00–5:00

Barry-Lawrence Regional Library
Cassville Branch
(301 West 17th Street—location)
PO Box D (mailing address)
Cassville, MO 65625-0904
(417) 847-2121; (417) 847-4679 FAX
wcm000@mail.connect.more.net
http://tlc.library.net/barry-
    lawrence/default.asp
Marion Stubblefield, Branch Manager
Mon–Thur 8:30–7:00, Fri–Sat 8:30–5:30

Battle of Lexington State Historic Site
(North 13th Street—location)
PO Box 6 (mailing address)
Lexington, MO 64067
(660) 259-4654; (660) 259-2378 FAX
http://mostateparks.com
Janae Fuller, Administrator
Mon–Tue (Mar–Oct) 10:00–4:00, Wed–Sat
    10:00–4:00, Sun (Labor Day–Memorial
    Day) noon–5:00, Sun (Memorial
    Day–Labor Day) noon–6:00
(emphasis on the Battle of Lexington during
    the Civil War, also family and local
    history)

Boonslick Regional Library
219 West Third Street
Sedalia, MO 65301-4596
(660) 826-6195; (660) 827-7111
huj001@mail.connect.more.net
http://204.185.183.77
Linda Allcorn, Director
(Benton, Cooper and Pettis counties)

Callaway County Public Library
Daniel Boone Regional Library

710 Court Street
Fulton, MO 65251-19926
(573) 642-7261; (573) 642-4439 FAX
dbrlpr@coin.org (Regional Library)
http://dbrl.org/branch/callaway/index.html
Nancy Belcher, Branch Manager
Mon–Thur 9:00–9:00, Fri–Sat 9:00–5:00

Cape Girardeau County Archive Center
112 East Washington
Jackson, MO 63755
(573) 204-2331; (573) 204-2334 FAX
archive@capecounty.us
http://www.showme.net/CapeCounty/
    archive/index.htm
Jane Randol, Director
Tue–Wed 9:00-5:00, Thur 9:00–7:00, Fri
    9:00–4:30, Sat 9:00–2:00

Cape Girardeau Public Library
Reference Department
711 North Clark
Cape Girardeau, MO 63701-4400
(573) 334-5279; (573) 334-8334 FAX
sct000@mail.connect.more.net
http://cgpl.clas.net/index.htm
Mon–Thur 9:00–9:00, Fri–Sat 9:00–5:00,
    Sun (Oct–Apr) noon–4:00
no staff available to answer research
    questions on particular families

Carrollton Public Library
206 West Washington
Carrollton, MO 64633-1261
(660) 542-0183 voice & FAX
hgn000@mail.connect.more.net
http://www.carolnet.com/library.htm
Charline Spangler, Librarian
Mon, Wed & Fri 10:00–5:00, Tue & Thur
    10:00–8:00, Sat 10:00–1:00, Sun
    1:00–5:00
(genealogy and local history)

Carthage Public Library
Genealogy Records
612 South Garrison
Carthage, MO 64836-1752
(417) 237-7040; (417) 237-7041 FAX
kzh015@mail.connect.more.net
http://carthage.lib.mo.us
Jennifer Richardson Seaton, Director
Mon–Wed 9:00–8:00, Thur–Fri 9:00–6:00,
    Sat 9:00–4:00

Cass County Library
400 East Mechanic
Harrisonville, MO 64701-2428
(816) 884-6223; (816) 884-2301 FAX
xrt003@mail.connect.more.net
http://www.casscolibrary.org
Sharon Willey, Director
Mon–Tue & Thur 8:30–8:30, Wed
    8:30–6:00, Fri–Sat 9:00–5:00
(southeastern U.S. and Missouri)

Clay County Archives and Historical Library, Inc.
(210 West Franklin—location)
PO Box 99 (mailing address)
Liberty, MO 64069-0099
(816) 781-3611
info@claycountyarchives.org
http://claycountyarchives.org
Kevin M. Fisher, Board President
Mon–Wed 10:00–4:00, first Wed 6:30–9:00,
    call in advance
Pub. *The Clay County Mosaic*, quarterly
(Collection includes birth records from
    1882–1884 and some later, early marriage
    returns, index to marriages in Clay
    County Recorder's Office, early
    naturalizations, death records from

1882–1884 and some later, cemetery
records, early court record books, funeral
home records and obituaries, closed
probate records 1822–1992, some family
Bible records, county census, early Circuit
Court records [civil] from 1822, slave
records and black marriages, early maps
and atlases, index to original Clay County
land grants, newspaper articles on Clay
County, early Clay County newspapers,
information on wars and veterans,
genealogical notes from the *Liberty
Tribune*, land abstracts, miscellaneous
deeds, etc., as well as the library of the
former Genealogical Society of Liberty)
$15.00 per year membership; research:
    $10.00 per surname for the first hour,
    additional research at $10.00 per hour
    must be authorized in advance; copies:
    $1.00 for original records, 15¢ per page
    from paper originals, 25¢ per page from
    microform originals

Columbia Public Library
Daniel Boone Regional Library
Reference Department
(100 West Broadway, Columbia, MO
65203—location)
PO Box 1267 (mailing address)
Columbia, MO 65205-1267
(573) 443-3161; (573) 499-0191 FAX
dbrlpr@coin.org
http://dbrl.org/branch/columbia/index.html
Mon–Thur 9:00–9:00, Fri 9:00–6:00, Sat
    9:00–5:00, Sun (Sept–May) 1:00–5:00

Dallas County Library
(219 West Main—location)
PO Box 1008 (mailing address)
Buffalo, MO 65622-1008
(417) 345-2647 voice & FAX
sgy000@mail.connect.more.net
Nancy Bradley, Director

Doniphan-Ripley County Library
207 Locust Street
Doniphan, MO 63935-1750
(573) 996-2616; (573) 996-4456 FAX
drclib@semo.net
Becky Wilcox, Director
Mon–Fri 9:00–8:00, Sat 9:00–noon

Dulany Memorial Library
501 South Broadway
Salisbury, MO 65281-1124
(660) 388-5712 voice & FAX
yie001@mail.connect.more.net
Cheryl Springer, Director
Mon–Fri noon–5:00, Sat 8:00–1:00
(material on Chariton County)

Dunklin County Library
209 North Main Street
Kennett, MO 63857
(573) 888-3561; (573) 888-6393 FAX
qjg003@mail.connect.more.net
http://dunklin-co.lib.mo.us/index.html

Farmington Public Library
108 West Harrison Street
Farmington, MO 63640-2508
(573) 756-5779; (573) 756-0614 FAX
http://www.ci.farmington.mo.us/library.htm
Lynn Crites, Director
Mon & Fri 10:00–5:30, Tue–Thur
    10:00–8:00, Sat 11:00–3:00
(large collection of miscellaneous obituaries,
    good history of local area and people)
no admission fee, copies 10¢ each, no staff to
    do extensive research by mail

Fayette Public Library

201 South Main
Fayette, MO 65248-1272
(660) 248-3348 voice & FAX
Cathey Monckton, Director
Mon–Fri 1:00–5:30, Sat 9:30–3:00
(limited genealogical materials)

Gentry County Library
304 North Park
Stanberry, MO 64489-1333
(660) 783-2335 voice & FAX
tgn002@mail.connect.more.net
http://www.gentrycountylibrary.org
Judy Beatty, Director
Mon–Fri 8:00–5:00, Sat 9:00–noon

Grundy County-Jewett Norris Library
1331 Main Street
Trenton, MO 64683-1824
(660) 359-3577; (660) 359-6220 FAX
DXC000@mail.connect.more.net
http://www.rootsweb.com/library.html
Catheryn Higdon
Mon–Fri 9:00–5:00, Sat 9:00–noon, and by
    appointment
(local history and genealogy)

Hacksma House Genealogy Library
(see Washington, Part 2)

Harry S. Truman Library
500 West U.S. Highway 24
Independence, MO 64050-1798
(816) 833-1400; (816) 833-4368 FAX
truman.library@nara.gov
http://www.trumanlibrary.org
Larry J. Hackman, Director
Mon–Fri 8:45–4:45, Sat by appointment
    8:45–12:45
(presidential library, an agency of the NARA;
    includes papers of administration officials,
    committees, commissions, or Truman's
    personal associates)

Henry County Public Library
123 East Franklin
Clinton, MO 64735-1462
(660) 885-2612; (660) 885-8953 FAX
lizell@tacnet.missouri.org
http://tacnet.missouri.org/index.html
Elizabeth A. Cashell, Director
Mon–Thur 8:00 A.M.–9:00 P.M., Sat
    8:00–5:00

The History Museum for Springfield-Greene County
830 Boonville, City Hall
Springfield, MO 65802
(417) 869-1976; (417) 864-2019 FAX
http://www.historymuseumsgc.org
Linda Green, Executive Director
Tue–Sat 10:30–4:30
Pub. *The History Museum Bulletin*,
    bimonthly
("Historical museum and archival library."
    Significant collections of historic regional
    photos, family collections, business
    collections from southwest Missouri)
$25.00–$100.00 per year museum
    membership; research: variable fees for
    searches and copying

Holden Public Library
101 West Third Street
Holden, MO 64040-1302
(816) 732-4545
http://www.go.holden.org/library.html
Vivian Ensley, Librarian
Tue–Wed & Fri 12:30–5:00, Thur 9:00–5:00,
    Sat 9:00–noon
(small local genealogical collection)

Jefferson County Library
3033 High Ridge Boulevard
High Ridge, MO 63049-2215
(636) 677-8186; (636) 677-8243 FAX
Northwest@jeffersoncountylibrary.org
http://jefcolib.lib.mo.us
Cindy Hayes, Manager
Mon–Thur 9:00–8:30, Fri 9:00–6:00, Sat
9:00–5:00

William Jewell College
Charles F. Curry Library
500 College Hill
Liberty, MO 64068-1896
http://www.jewell.edu
("There are a few things that researches can
use on a walk-in basis: *Liberty (Missouri)
Tribune* from 1846, post-Civil War voter
registration/loyalty oath records for Clay
County, and material on students and
faculty from 1849, but research help will
be limited as our first priority will be
curriculum support.")

Joplin Public Library
Genealogy Department
300 South Main Street
Joplin, MO 64801-2310
(417) 623-7953; (417) 624-5465 (Genealogy
Department); (417) 624-5217 FAX
ctrout@joplinpubliclibrary.org
http://www.joplinpubliclibrary.org
Genealogy Department: Tue–Wed & Fri–Sat
9:00–5:45, Sun 1:00–4:45

Kansas City Public Library
Missouri Valley Special Collections
311 East 12th Street
Kansas City, MO 64106-2454
(816) 701-3505
ask@kclibrary.org
http://www.kclibrary.org;
http://www.kcpl.lib.mo.us/sc/default.htm
(Special Collections)
Katherine Long, Department Manager
Mon–Thur 9:00–9:00, Fri–Sat 9:00–5:00,
Sun 1:00–5:00
(a large collection of census index books for
the years 1790–1870; also Kansas City,
Missouri, city directories from 1859 to the
present)

Keytesville Public Library
General Delivery
406 West Bridge Street
Keytesville, MO 65261-9999
(660) 288-3204
Joe Hickey, Librarian
Mon, Wed & Fri 2:00–4:30
(census lists, cemetery records, and some
other records)
research: limited to library holdings as time
permits for donation plus SASE; copies:
15¢ each plus SASE

Lebanon-Laclede County Library
Missouri Room
135 Harwood Avenue
Lebanon, MO 65536-3017
(417) 532-2148; (417) 532-7424 FAX
cdame@lebanon-laclede.lib.mo.us
http://lebanon.laclede.library.missouri.org
Cathy Dame, Director

The Linn Library
902 East Oak Street
Princeton, MO 64673
(660) 748-3905
Joe Dale Linn
by appointment

Little Dixie Regional Libraries

111 North Fourth Street
Moberly, MO 65270-1513
(660) 263-4426; (660) 263-4024 FAX
library@little-dixie.lib.mo.us
http://www.little-dixie.lib.mo.us
Karen Hayden, Reference and Adult Services
Librarian
Mon–Wed & Fri 9:00–6:00, Thur 9:00–8:00,
Sat 9:00–4:00
copies: 15¢ per page

Livingston County Library
450 Locust Street
Chillicothe, MO 64601-2597
(660) 646-0547; (660) 646-5504 FAX
ugy001@mail.connect.more.net
http://www.livcolibrary.org
Karen L. Hicklin, Director
Mon–Thur 9:00–7:00, Fri 9:00–5:00, Sat
9:00–4:00
(an extensive collection of digitized local
histories, which are indexed and
searchable)

Lohefener House Museum and Gifts
(710 Orange—location)
PO Box 33 (mailing address)
Concordia, MO 64020
(660) 463-7963
Lloyd and Nyla Shepard, Owners
Wed & Sat 10:00–4:00, and by appointment
(death notices 1870–1910 in German, 1880
census (within city limits only), some
family histories, written reminiscences
and centennial history book, lists of
confirmations, baptisms, marriages and
funerals, 1840–1990, local Lutheran
Church, United Church of Christ,
confirmation programs of church events
and history of Saint Paul's College
[Lutheran Church—Missouri Synod],
from 1883)

Marshall Public Library
214 North Lafayette
Marshall, MO 65340-1750
(660) 886-3391; (660) 886-2492 FAX
mplibrary@mid-mo.net
http://www.marshallpubliclibrary.com
Ms. Wicky Sleight, Library Director
Mon–Thur 9:00–9:00, Fri 9:00–6:00, Sat
9:00–5:00, Sun 1:00–5:00
(local history of Saline County and
genealogical material from Missouri and
eastern states from which Missouri settlers
came)

Maryville Public Library
509 North Main
Maryville, MO 64468-1610
(660) 582-5281; (660) 582-2411 FAX
ugb000@mail.connect.more.net
Margaret Kelley, Collection Coordinator
Mon–Wed 9:00–6:00, Thur 9:00–7:00,
Fri–Sat 9:00–6:00
(specializes in local history)

Mercer County Library
601 Grant
Princeton, MO 64673-1023
(660) 748-3725; (660) 748-3723 FAX
pii000@mail.connect.more.net
Mon–Fri 9:00–5:00; Sat 9:00–noon

Mexico-Audrain County Library
Mexico Headquarters
305 West Jackson Street
Mexico, MO 65265-2751
(573) 581-4939; (573) 581-7510 FAX
mexicoaudrain@netscape.net
http://members.socket.net/~macld/library.
html

Violet Lierheimer
Mon–Tue & Thur–Fri 9:00–4:00, Wed
2:00–8:00, Sat 2:00–4:00 (when
volunteers can staff the room)

Mid-Continent Public Library
Genealogy and Local History Branch
(317 West 24 Highway—location)
15616 East 24 Highway (mailing address)
Independence, MO 64050-2098
(816) 252-7228
ge_librarian@mcpl.lib.mo.us
http://www.mcpl.lib.mo.us/ge
Janice Schultz, Genealogy Librarian
Mon–Thur 9:00–9:00, Fri 9:00–6:00, Sat
9:00–5:00
(national in scope, includes circulating
collection)

Missouri Western State College Library
4525 Downs Drive
Saint Joseph, MO 64507
(816) 271-4573
Julia Schneider, Dean LRC
Mon–Thur 7:30 A.M.–11:00 P.M., Fri
7:30–4:30, Sat 10:00–5:00, Sun
2:00–11:00; between semesters: Mon–Fri
8:00–4:30; summer: Mon–Thur
7:30–7:00, Fri 7:30–4:30, Sun (while
school is in session) 1:00–6:00
(special collections on local history, personal
papers, university records, women's
materials)

Morgan County Library
102 North Fisher
Versailles, MO 65084-1202
(573) 378-5319
nea001@mail.connect.more.net
Glenn D. Housworth, Librarian
Mon–Fri 9:00–5:00, Sat 9:00–noon
(genealogy and local history)

Mound City Museum Association
104 East Seventh
Mound City, MO 64470
(660) 442-5635

**Museum of Evangel University of Arts and
Sciences**
1111 North Glenstone
Springfield, MO 65802
(417) 865-2815, ext. 8213
when university is open
(Ozark Indian artifacts and pioneer materials;
also Eskimo and Near Eastern objects)
free

Neosho-Newton County Library
201 West Spring Street
Neosho, MO 64850-1761
(417) 451-4231; (417) 451-6438 FAX
ymf001@mail.connect.more.net
http://www.neosholibrary.org
Shirley Gollhofer, Director
Mon–Thur 9:00–9:00, Fri–Sat 9:00–5:30

Nevada Public Library
(218 West Walnut—location)
PO Box B (mailing address)
Nevada, MO 64772-3026
(417) 448-2770; (417) 448-2771 FAX
rpr000@mail.connect.more.net
Susan McBeth, Director
Mon, Wed & Fri 10:00–6:00, Tue & Thur
10:00–8:00, Sat 10:00–2:00

Norborne Public Library
109 East Second Street
Norborne, MO 64668-1301
(660) 594-3514 voice & FAX
Doris S. Wightman, Librarian

Mon–Fri 8:00–noon & 1:00–5:00, Sat
8:00–noon
(local history)

Northeast Missouri University Archives
(see Truman State University, below)

Owens Library
Northwest Missouri State University
Maryville, MO 64468
(660) 562-1536
Vickey Baumli, Serials Technical Specialist
8:00–4:00
(census of Nodaway County, most Nodaway
county newspapers)
research: contact Vickey Baumli, 515 East
Fourth, Maryville, MO 64468, fees vary

Park University
Frances Fishburn Archives
McAfee Memorial Library
(8700 N.W. River Park Drive—location)
PO Box 61 (mailing address)
Parkville, MO 64152
(816) 741-2000, ext. 6285; (816) 741-4911
FAX
webmaster@mail.park.edu
http://www.park.edu
Carolyn Elwess, Assistant Archivist; Harold
Smith, Historian
Mon–Thur 8:00–9:30, Fri 8:00–4:30, Sat
10:00–4:00, Sun 4:00–9:30 during the
school semester (contact Historian before
visit)
(records limited to Park Alumni, former
students, faculty, Parkville and Platte
County history, but no general
genealogical information available)

Phelps County Archives
Phelps County Courthouse, Room 315
200 North Main
Rolla, MO 65401
(573) 364-1891

Powell Memorial Library
951 West College
Troy, MO 63379-1112
(636) 528-7853
Sharon Hasekamp, Librarian
Mon noon–7:00, Tue–Fri 8:00–7:00, Sat
9:00–1:00, except same holidays as
school district
not staffed to do research for people

Powers Museum
(1617 Oak Street—location)
PO Box 593 (mailing address)
Carthage, MO 64836
(417) 358-2667
http://www.powersmuseum.com
Michele Hansford, Director
mid-Mar to May & Nov to mid-Dec:
Tue–Sat 11:00–4:00; June–Oct: Tue–Sat
10:00–5:00, Sun 1:30–5:00; use of
archives and reference library by
appointment only
("Basically a local history resource, no
primary genealogical materials [census,
family books], etc.")

Pulaski County Library
(111 Camden Street—location)
PO Box 304 (mailing address)
Richland, MO 65556-0340
(573) 765-3642; (573) 765-5395 FAX
zfk000@mail.connect.more.net
http://www.pulaskicountylib.org
Osa Kays, Director
Tue 10:00–7:00, Wed–Thur 10:00–6:00,
Fri–Sat 10:00–5:00

Purvines Genealogical Library
(112 North Fourth Street—location)
614 Clark Street (mailing address)
Canton, MO 63435
(573) 288-5713
Jean Purvines, Librarian
Mon–Fri 9:00–4:30, Sat by appointment
(northeast Missouri genealogy)
$10.00 per year membership

Putnam County Library
(115 South 16th Street—location)
PO Box 305 (mailing address)
Unionville, MO 63565-0305
(660) 947-3192; (660) 947-7039 FAX
JNR000@mail.connect.more.net
http://putnamcountylibrary.lib.mo.us
Jami Livingston, Head Librarian
Mon–Fri 9:00–5:00, Sat 9:00–noon
donation accepted

Ray County Library
219 South College
Richmond, MO 64085-1614
(816) 470-3291; (816) 776-5794 FAX
raycopublibrary@yahoo.com
http://raycountylibrary.homestead.com/
raycountylibrary.html
Jason Alexander, Director
Mon–Thur 8:30–6:00, 8:30–5:00, Sat
9:00–noon
(A general collection)

River Bluffs Regional Library
Reference Service
927 Felix Street
Saint Joseph, MO 64501-2799
(816) 232-8151; (816) 232-7516 FAX
Mon–Thur 9:00–9:00, Fri–Sat 9:00–6:00,
Sun 1:00–5:00
(local and county history)
costs being revised, please phone

Riverside Regional Library
(204 South Union Avenue—location)
PO Box 389 (mailing address)
Jackson, MO 63755-0389
(573) 243-8141; (573) 243-8142 FAX
nhowland@showme.net
http://www.riversideregionallibrary.org
Nancy Howland, Director

Rolla Public Library
900 Pine Street
Rolla, MO 65401-3142
(573) 364-2604; (573) 341-5768 FAX
rollalib@rollanet.org
http://rollapubliclibrary.org
Cheryl A. Goltz, Director
Mon–Thur 9:00–9:00, Fri–Sat 9:00–5:00,
Sun 1:30–5:00

**Saint Charles City-County Library
District**
Kathryn Linnemann Branch Library
2323 Elm Street
Saint Charles, MO 63301-1493
(636) 946-6294; (636) 723-0232
aking01@mail.win.org
http://www.win.org/library/services/
lhgen/cinmenu.htm
Ann King; Judy Brown
Mon–Thur 9:00–9:00, Fri–Sat 9:00–6:00,
Sun 1:00–5:00

Saint Clair County Library
(115 Chestnut—location)
PO Box 575 (mailing address)
Osceola, MO 64776-0575
(417) 646-2214; (417) 646-8643 FAX
http://mostclair.lib.mo.us
Ruth Lewis, Director

Mon–Fri 8:00–5:00, Sat 8:00–noon
(local history and genealogy)
Saint Joseph Museum
(1100 Charles, Saint Joseph, MO
64501—location)
PO Box 128 (mailing address)
Saint Joseph, MO 64502-0128
(816) 232-8471; (816) 232-8482 FAX
sjm@stjosephmuseum.org
http://www.st.josephmuseum.org
Jackie Lewin, Head of Research
Mon–Fri 9:00–noon & 1:00–4:00
Pub. *The Happenings*, bimonthly
(includes St. Joseph and Missouri history,
Civil War, Pony Express, western
movement, Native American and natural
history)
copies: 10¢ per copy

Saint Louis County Library
Headquarters
1640 South Lindbergh Boulevard (at Clayton
Road)
Saint Louis, MO 63131-3598
(314) 994-3300 (Headquarters); (314) 994-
9411, ext. 215 (Supervisor of Reference);
(314) 994-9411, ext. 287 FAX
hreference@slcl.lib.mo.us
http://www.slcl.lib.mo.us
Barbara A. Mottin, Supervisor of Reference
Mon–Fri 8:30–9:00, Sat 8:30–5:00, Sun
(Sept–May) 1:00–5:00
(Saint Louis archdiocesan parish records on
microfilm and collection of the St. Louis
Genealogical Society: cemetery and
funeral home records, census and
Soundex, church records, city and county
directories, county histories, family
histories, immigration records, land
records, military records, newspapers,
periodicals, probate records, vital records)

Saint Louis Mercantile Library Association
(at the University of Missouri—Saint
Louis—location)
8001 Natural Bridge
Saint Louis, MO 63121
(314) 516-7240; (314) 516-7241
Bette Gorden, Curator

Saint Louis Public Library
History and Genealogy Department
1301 Olive Street
Saint Louis, MO 63103-2389
(314) 539-0386; (314) 539-0393 FAX
cmillar@slpl.lib.mo.us
http://www.slpl.lib.mo.us.
Cynthia Millar, Genealogy Librarian
Mon 10:00–9:00, Tue–Fri 10:00–6:00, Sat
9:00–5:00
Pub. *Gateway Family Historian*
copies: 15¢ each from paper originals, 25¢
each from microform originals, $1.00
postage and handling per order

Scenic Regional Library
New Haven Branch
901 Maupin
New Haven, MO 63068-1164
(573) 237-2189 voice & FAX
Carolyn Scheer, Reference Librarian
Tue & Thur–Fri 8:00–5:30, Wed 8:30–7:00,
Sat 8:30–1:00
(Franklin, Warren and Gasconade counties)

Sedalia Public Library
311 West Third Street
Sedalia, MO 65301-4399
(660) 826-1314; (660) 826-0396 FAX
uzx000@mail.connect.more.net
http://spl.lib.mo.us/index.asp
Donald G. Morton

Mon–Thur 9:00–9:00, Fri 9:00–6:00, Sat
    9:00–5:00, Sun 1:00–5:00
(local history; Sedalia newspapers on
    microfilm, 1870 to the present)
research: minimum $2.00, varies according to
    time spent searching, extensive research
    turned over to local researcher

Shelbina Carnegie Public Library
(102 North Center Street—location)
PO Box 247 (mailing address)
Shelbina, MO 63468
(573) 588-2271 voice & FAX
bonywood@yahoo.com
http://www.shelbinalibrary.org
Bonnie Wood, Assistant Librarian
Mon–Fri 11:00–5:30, Tue 5:30–8:00, Sat
    9:00–noon
(Shelby County histories, newspaper
    archives, cemetery records, censuses, etc.)
copies: 25¢ per page

Slater Public Library
311 North Main
Slater, MO 65349-1413
(660) 529-3100
library2@socket.net
Betty Jaeger
Mon–Fri 2:00–5:00
(genealogy and local history)

South Vernon Genealogical Library
Route 2, Box 10
Sheldon, MO 64784
(417) 884-2619
Wilma Lathrop, Historical Research and
    Librarian
Mon–Fri by appointment
research in Barton and Vernon counties:
    $10.00 per hour

Southeast Missouri State College
Kent Library
1 University Plaza
Cape Girardeau, MO 63701
(573) 651-2235; (573) 651-5103 FAX

Southwest Missouri Genealogical Library
(see Carthage Genealogical Society,
Genealogical Societies—Local and Regional,
below)

Southwest Missouri State University
Meyer Library
Lena Wills Collection
901 South National
Springfield, MO 65804
(417) 836-4535 (Reference/Information);
    (417) 836-6799 FAX
http://www.smsu.edu/contrib/library/
    library.html

Springfield-Greene County Library
Local History and Genealogy Department
(4653 South Campbell—location)
PO Box 760 (mailing address)
Springfield, MO 65801-0760
(417) 874-8112, ext. 138; (417) 874-8113
    FAX
http://www.thelibrary.springfield.
    missouri.org
Michael Glenn, Local History Librarian
Mon–Thur 8:30–9:00, Fri–Sat 8:30–9:00,
    Sun 1:00–5:00
(extensive newspaper indexing)
research (southwest Missouri or Greene
    County): copies at 50¢ each

Sullivan County Genealogy Library
Sullivan County Historical Society
North Water Street
Milan, MO 63556

(660) 265-3476
Mildred Baldridge
Tue (May–Oct) 9:00–noon & 1:00–4:00, and
    by appointment
(genealogy library and local memorabilia)
donation for research

Sullivan County Public Library
109 East Second Street
Milan, MO 63556-1331
(660) 265-3911 voice & FAX
dax001@mail.connect.more.net
Susan O'Connor, Director
Tue–Wed & Fri 9:00–5:00, Thur 9:00–9:00,
    Sat 9:00–3:00

Tree Trackers Library
(between Golden, MO, and Eagle Rock,
MO—location)
HCR-01, Box 1210 (mailing address)
Eagle Rock, MO 65641
(417) 271-3532
Phyllis Eldridge Friesner, Owner/Librarian
by appointment
("35-year collection open to the public as a
    'labor of love' in retirement; Books, film,
    fiche from all states and Norway, many
    family histories, lots of periodicals.")
research: donation for reimbursement of
    postage, copies, film rental

Truman State University
Special Collections, Pickler Memorial
Library
101 East Normal
Kirksville, MO 63501
(660) 785-4537; (660) 785-7368; (660) 785-
    4536 FAX
emdoak@truman.edu
http://library.truman.edu/departments/
    specialcollections.htm
Elaine Doak, Special Collections
    Librarian/Archivist
Mon–Fri 8:00–5:00, Sat (call first)
(Missouri history—state, county, local;
    University Archives, Central Wesleyan
    College Archives)

University City Public Library
6701 Delmar Boulevard
University City, MO 63130-3199
(314) 727-3150; (314) 727-6005 FAX
webmaster@ucpl.lib.mo.us
http://www.ucpl.lib.mo.us
Mon–Fri 9:00–9:00, Sat 9:00–5:00, Sun
    2:00–5:00
("Our [Historical Society of University City]
    archives are located in the University City
    Public Library. The library staff will take
    messages for us . . . , and the collection
    can be accessed during library hours. The
    Library has an extensive archival
    collection of their own.")

Washington Historical Museum
314 East Fourth Street
Washington, MO 63090
(636) 239-0280
(genealogy library)

Washington Public Library
415 Jefferson Street
Washington, MO 63090-2607
(636) 390-1070; (636) 390-0171 FAX
Mon–Wed 8:00–8:00, Thur–Fri 8:00–6:00,
    Sat 9:00–1:00
(very little genealogy information)

Waynesville-Kinderhook Library
(306 Historic 66 West—location)
PO 562 (mailing address)
Waynesville, MO 65583-2113

(573) 774-2965; (573) 774-6429 FAX
http://www.pulaskicountylib.org
Mon & Wed 10:00–6:00, Tue & Thur
    10:00–7:00, Fri–Sat 10:00–5:00

Webster County Library
(219 West Jackson Street—location)
PO Box 89 (mailing address)
Marshfield, MO 65706-0089
(417) 468-3335; (417) 468-2471 FAX
http://webstercounty.lib.mo.us
Elizabeth Sims, Library Director
Mon & Wed 9:00–6:00, Tue & Thur
    9:00–8:00, Fri–Sat 9:00–5:00

Webster University
Eden-Webster Library
475 East Lockwood Avenue
Saint Louis, MO 63119
(314) 961-3627; (314) 961-9063 FAX
edward@library2.websteruniv.edu
http://library2.websteruniv.edu/webdata/
    libhome.html

**Western Historical Manuscript
Collection—Columbia**
23 Ellis Library
University of Missouri
Columbia, MO 65201-5149
(573) 882-6028; (573) 884-0345; (573) 884-
    4950 FAX
Whmc@umsystem.edu
http://www.system.missouri.edu/whmc
David F. Moore, Associate Director
Mon & Wed–Fri 8:00–4:45, Tue 8:00
    A.M.–9:00 P.M., when university is in
    session
Pub. untitled newsletter
("WHMC has branches on all four campuses
    of the University of Missouri system, and
    loans its holdings among them.")

**Western Historical Manuscript
Collection—Kansas City**
University of Missouri
5100 Rockhill Road
302 Newcomb Hall
Kansas City, MO 64110-2499
(816) 235-1543; (816) 235-5500 FAX
whmckc@umkc.edu
http://www.umkc.edu/WHMCKC
David L. Boutros, Associate Director of
    Western Historical Manuscript Collection
Mon–Fri 8:00–5:00, evenings by appointment

**Western Historical Manuscript
Collection—Rolla**
(Room G-3, Curtis Laws Wilson Library
University of Missouri, Rolla (UMR)
Rolla, MO 65401-0249—location)
1870 Miner Circle (mailing address)
Rolla, MO 65409-0060
(573) 341-4874
whmcinfo@umr.edu
http://www.umr.edu/~whmcinfo
Mark C. Stauter, Ph.D., Associate Director
Mon–Fri 8:00–5:00
("General historical manuscript repository for
    southern Missouri; access to Western
    Historical Manuscript Collection statewide
    holdings.")

**Western Historical Manuscript
Collection—Saint Louis and State
Historical Society of Missouri Manuscripts
Joint Collection**
University of Missouri—Saint Louis
Thomas Jefferson Library, Room 222
8001 Natural Bridge
Saint Louis, MO 63121
(314) 553-5143; (314) 516-6034
    (Information); (314) 516-5060

(Reference); (314) 516-5853 FAX (mark all documents WHMC)
whmc@umsl.edu
http://www.umsl.edu/~whmc
Patricia L. Adams, Association Director
Mon & Wed–Fri 8:00–4:45, Tue until 8:00 A.M.–9:00 P.M.

Westminster College
Winston Churchill Memorial and Library at Westminster College
331 West Seventh Street
Fulton, MO 65251
(573) 592-5232
winings@jaynet.wcmo.edu
http://www.westminster-mo.edu
Jane Duncan Flink, Director of External Relations; Dr. Jerry D. Morelock, Executive Director

Westminster College
Reeves Library
501 Westminster Avenue
Fulton, MO 65251-1298
(573) 642-3361, ext. 247; (573) 642-6356 FAX
Lorna K. Mitchell, Head Librarian
Library: school year: Mon–Fri 8:00–5:00; summer and student break: Mon–Fri 8:00–11:00 A.M., Sat 1:00–5:00, Sun 1:00–11:00; Archives: Mon–Fri 8:00–5:00
(college archives and some materials on Fulton and Callaway counties)

Weston Historical Museum
601 Main Street
Weston, MO 64098
(816) 386-2977; (816) 386-2650 (President)
Mrs. John H. Gaskill, President
16 Mar–14 Dec: Sat 1:00–4:00, Sun 1:30–5:00, and by appointment

Wright County Library System
Courthouse
(Main Street—location)
PO Box 70 (mailing address)
Hartville, MO 65667-0070
(417) 741-7595
http://getgoin.net/info/orgs/wrightcolib
Mon, Wed & Fri 8:00–4:30, Tue & Thur 9:30–6:00, Sat 8:00–noon

Historical Societies—Local and Regional

Adair County Historical Society
211 South Elson
Kirksville, MO 63501-3466
peeve@cableone.net
http://www.artcom.com/museums/nv/af/ 63501-03.htm (Museum)
Mr. Pat Ellebracht, President
Wed–Fri 1:00–4:00
Pub. *The Adair County Historian*, quarterly (Jan, Apr, July, Oct)
$15.00 per year membership; research: $10.00 for a basic search, then $10.00 per hour

Affton Historical Society
(7801 Genesta—location)
PO Box 28855 (mailing address)
Saint Louis, MO 63123
(314) 352-5654; (314) 849-3859 FAX
Nancy Herndon, Conservator
third Sun (Mar–Nov), and by appointment
Pub. *Oakleaf*, quarterly
$10.00 per year membership

American West Research Center and Historical Society, Inc.
(see Ohio, Part 2)

Andrew County Museum and Historical Society
(202 East Duncan Drive—location)
PO Box 12 (mailing address)
Savannah, MO 64485-0012
(816) 324-4720; (816) 324-5271 FAX
andcomus@ccp.com
http://www.artcom.com/museums
Shirley Brown, Museum Administrator
Mon–Sat 10:00–4:00, Sun 1:00–4:00; Genealogy Department: Thur–Fri 10:00–4:00, and by appointment
Pub. *Diggin' History*, quarterly
(genealogy department in building)
$10.00 per year membership

Ash Grove Historical Society
606 West Boone
Ash Grove, MO 65604
(417) 672-2025

Atchison County Historical Society
Tarkio, MO 64491

Audrain County Historical Society
(501 South Musdrow Street—location)
PO Box 3 (mailing address)
Mexico, MO 65265
(573) 581-3910
Leta Hodge, Executive Director
Pub. *Graceland Gazette*

Augusta Historical Society
498 Schell Road
Augusta, MO 63332
(636) 228-4821

Barry County Genealogical and Historical Society
(see Genealogical Societies—Local and Regional, below)

Barton County Historical Society and Museum
(County Courthouse, West Basement—location)
PO Box 416 (mailing address)
Lamar, MO 64759
(417) 682-4141
Robert Douglas, President
Mon–Fri 1:00–4:00, closed all holidays
$6.00 per year membership; research: donation; museum admission: free

Bates County Historical Society
Museum of Pioneer History
100 West Fort Scot
Butler, MO 64730
May–Sept: 1:00–5:00

Belton Historical Society, Inc.
(512 Main Street—location)
PO Box 1144 (mailing address)
Belton, MO 64012
(816) 331-2321
Thomas H. Keeney
Mon, Wed & Fri–Sat 1:00–4:00, and by appointment
Pub. *BHS Newsletter*
requires donation for admission

Benton County Historical Society
(Warsaw, MO 65355—location)
1115 S.E. Z Highway (mailing address)
Deepwater, MO 64740
(660) 438-7590 (Historic Site and Archivist)
Robert L. Salley, Historic Site and Archivist of Benton County
$5.00 per year membership

Blue Springs Historical Society Archives
(Blue Springs City Hall—location)
1013 S.W. 21st (mailing address)
Blue Springs, MO 64015
(816) 229-1671
Karol R. Witthar, Archivist
by appointment
(local cemetery records, photos, family histories, etc.)
photocopy fees

Bollinger County Historical Society
PO Box 402
Marble Hill, MO 63764
(573) 238-4304
Cathy Thompson, Chair-Genealogy Committee
Pub. *Echo*, irregularly
$2.00 per year membership (to Norma Bohnsack, Rural Route 2, Box 1150, Marble Hill, MO 63764); research: for genealogical inquiries contact Cathy Thompson, 201 Mayfield Drive, Apartment 4, Marble Hill, MO 63764

Boone-Duden Historical Society
(3565 Mill Street—location)
PO Box 82 (mailing address)
New Melle, MO 63365
(636) 828-5887
http://www.norn.org/pub/other-orgs/bdhissoc
Lucille Wiechens, Historian
Sun 1:30–4:30
Pub. *Boone-Duden Historical Society Newsletter*, bimonthly
$10.00 per year membership

Boonslick Historical Society
PO Box 324
Boonville, MO 65233
(660) 882-5938
Adolph Hilden, Historian
Pub. *Boone's Lick Heritage*, quarterly
$10.00 per year membership; queries should include SASE

Butler County Historical Society, Inc.
(1016 North Main—museum location)
PO Box 1526 (mailing address)
Poplar Bluff, MO 63901
(573) 785-7558
Thelma Sanders, President and Museum Director
Sun 1:00–4:00, and by appointment
Pub. *Butler County Historical Society Newsletter*, quarterly
$10.00 per year membership; for research contact Betty Hanks, PO Box 416, Poplar Bluff, MO 63901, (573) 686-2211

Cabool History Society
PO Box 710
Cabool, MO 65689
(417) 962-4775

Caldwell County Historical Society
PO Box 32
Kingston, MO 64650
(816) 632-2320 (Treasurer)
David J. Reed, Treasurer
by appointment
(published *1876 Atlas, 1898 Atlas, Caldwell County History* Vol. I & II, *Peak in the Past*, Vol. I & II [Hist. Short Story], $35.00 ppd.)
$10.00 per year membership

Camden County Historical Society
(Highway V-Linn Creek—location)
PO Box 19 (mailing address)
Linn Creek, MO 65052
(573) 346-7191

Daphne Jeffries, President and Museum
Coordinator
Mon–Fri 10:00–4:00
Pub. *Camden County Historian*, irregularly
$10.00 per year membership

**Campbell Area Genealogical and Historical
Society**
(see Genealogical Societies—Local and
Regional, below)

Carondelet Historical Society
6303 Michigan Avenue
Saint Louis, MO 63111
(314) 481-6303
Lois Waninger, Museum Coordinator
Tue–Wed & Fri 9:30–noon, Sat 10:30–2:00
Pub. *Carondelet Historical Society
Newsletter*, twice per year
(emphasis on Carondelet area and Susan
Blow)
$10.00 per year membership

Cass County Historical Society, Inc.
Wade Archives
(400 East Mechanic—location)
PO Box 406 (mailing address)
Harrisonville, MO 64701-0406
(816) 887-2393
Irene Webster, Treasurer
Office: Mon–Fri 9:00–5:00
Pub. *Newsletter—Cass County Historical
Society*, quarterly
(County courthouse records, tax, probate, real
estate)
$10.00 per year membership; research: $5.00

Cedar County Historical Society
Jackson Street (Museum)
PO Box 111
Stockton, MO 65785
(417) 276-3622; (417) 276-5573
petern@microcore.net
Marie Heinemann, Board Member; Peter
Nichole, President
Museum: last Sat 10:00–noon & 1:00–4:00,
second Sat (June–Aug) 10:00–noon &
1:00–4:00
Pub. *Cedar County Historical Society News
Letter*, quarterly
$5.00 per year membership; research: "will
answer some family history requests and
questions on local history"

Centralia Historical Society, Inc.
319 East Sneed Street
Centralia, MO 65240
(573) 682-5711
Tue–Fri 9:00–noon & 1:00–3:00
(historical museum concentrating on local
history)

Chariton County Historical Society
115 East Second Street
Salisbury, MO 65281
(660) 388-5941
Martha Fellows, President
May–1 Oct: Sat–Sun 2:00–4:00 by
appointment
Pub. *Chariton County Newsletter*, quarterly
$5.00 per year membership

Clark County Historical Society, Inc.
(252 North Morgan—location)
PO Box 202 (mailing address)
Kahoka, MO 63445
(660) 727-1072
Fri 9:00–noon & 12:30–4:00, Sat 9:00–noon
(Missouri census, marriages, cemetery,
probate, obituaries)
$4.00 per year membership; research: $6.00
per hour plus copies at 25¢ each

**Clay County Museum and Historical
Society**
14 North Main Street
Liberty, MO 64068
(816) 792-1849
Ron Fuenfhausen, Curator
by appointment; Museum: Tue–Sat
1:00–4:00
Pub. *Our Clay Heritage*, quarterly
$8.00 per year membership; museum
admission; free to members

**Clinton County Historical Society and
Museum**
509 Broadway
Plattsburg, MO 64477
(816) 539-2992
Karma Kay, President
June–Aug: Sun 1:00–5:00, and by
appointment

Cole Camp Area Historical Society
(Cole Camp Branch of Boonslick Regional
Library, 104 East Main—location)
PO Box 206 (mailing address)
Cole Camp, MO 65325
(660) 668-3887
Patricia Beckman, Branch Supervisor
Tue 11:00–5:00, Wed noon–5:00, Thur
1:00–6:00, Fri 1:00–5:00, Sat 9:00–2:00
("Local newspapers since 1897 on microfilm,
Benton County census, local cemetery
records.")

Cole County Historical Society
Cole County Historical Museum
109 Madison Street
Jefferson City, MO 65101
(573) 635-1850
Guy P. Barrett, Director
Tue–Fri 9:30–4:00
$15.00 per year membership

Cooper County Historical Society
5236 Highway A
Bunceton, MO 65237

Crawford County Historical Society (MO)
308 North Smith Street
Cuba, MO 65453
(573) 885-6099
Bill Capehart, President; Bob Horsefield,
Vice President and Genealogy
2-4 days per week
Pub. *Crawford County Historical Society
Newsletter*, monthly
$5.00 per year membership

**Creve Coeur-Chesterfield Historical
Society**
11631 Olive Boulevard
Creve Coeur, MO 63141
(314) 434-5163

Crystal City Historical Society
130 Mississippi
Crystal City, MO 63019

Dade County Missouri Historical Society
207 McPherson
Greenfield, MO 65661
(417) 637-2744

Dallas County Historical Society
Dallas County Genealogical Society
HC 85, Box 291 B6
Buffalo, MO 65622-9805
(417) 345-7297
http://www.smsu.edu/contrib/bms/county/
dallas.htm#SOCIETY
Leni Howe, Secretary
by appointment

Pub. *News Bulletin* (published by Historical
Society only), semiannually
$5.00 per year membership

Daviess County Historical Society
c/o The Daviess County Library
306 West Grand Street
Gallatin, MO 64640
Jan Johnson, Librarian
Tue–Thur 9:00–6:00, Fri 9:00–5:00, Sat
9:00–1:00
all genealogy requests should be forwarded to
the library

DeKalb County Historical Society
PO Box 467
Maysville, MO 64469
Ruth Owen, President
Apr–Oct: Mon–Fri 9:00–3:30
Pub. *DeKalb County Heritage*, quarterly
(museum and genealogical library with
DeKalb County Records Center)
$7.50 per year

Dent County Historical Society
1202 Gertrude Street
Salem, MO 65560
(573) 729-5707
Ken Fiebelman
$5.00 per year membership

**Douglas County Historical and
Genealogical Society, Inc.**
(Wilson House, 401 East Washington, South
Side—location)
PO Box 986 (mailing address)
Ava, MO 65608
(417) 683-5799
http://www.goin.net/info/orgs
Guy H. Gettys, President
Sat 10:00–2:00, and by appointment
Pub. *Historical and Genealogical Society,
Inc Journal of Douglas County, MO*,
semiannually (summer and winter), $8.00
ppd. per issue
$16.00 per year membership; research: for a
small fee, depending on the amount of
time involved, by Pat Carmichael, Route 2,
Box 738, Ava, MO 65608, (417) 683-
6102; admission: $1.00

Excelsior Springs Historical Society
Excelsior Springs Historical Museum
101 East Broadway
Excelsior Springs, MO 64024
(816) 630-3712; (816) 630-8063 voice &
FAX
starmktg@epsi.net
Victoria A. Bates, President
Mon–Fri 9:00–4:00; viewing tours and
research by appointment
Pub. *The Phunn*, annually
$2.00 per year membership

Ferguson Historical Society
315 Darst Drive
Ferguson, MO 63135
(314) 521-0977

**Florissant Valley Historical and
Genealogical Society**
(No. 1, Traille de Noyer, Florissant, MO
63031—location)
PO Box 298 (mailing address)
Florissant, MO 63032
(314) 524-1100
Pub. *Florissant Valley Quarterly*
$6.00 per year membership

Foristell Area Historical Society
626 Ball Street
Wentzville, MO 63385

(636) 327-8234

Foundation for Restoration of Sainte Genevieve
70 South Third Street
Sainte Genevieve, MO 63670
(573) 883-2839

Gasconade County Historical Society
(315 Schiller, Hermann, MO 65041 and 105 South McFadden Street, Owensville, MO 65066—location)
PO Box 131 (mailing address)
Hermann, MO 65041
(573) 486-4028; (573) 437-5617
gchsarc@ktis.net
Herbert Lindroth, President
Archives: Tue–Thur 9:00–5:00, Sat 9:00–noon; Museum: Fri–Sat 11:00–3:00
Pub. *Gasconade County Historical Society Newsletter*, quarterly
$10.00 per year membership

Glasgow Area Historical and Preservation Society
100 Market
Glasgow, MO 65254
(660) 338-2377

Graham Historical Society
(see Nodaway County Genealogical Society, Genealogical Societies—Local and Regional, below)

Grand River Historical Society and Museum
(Forrest and Irvin—location)
PO Box 154 (mailing address)
Chillicothe, MO 64601
(660) 646-4323; (660) 646-4433
Dr. Frank E. Stark, President
Apr–Oct: Tue & Sun 1:00–4:00
Pub. *Herald*, quarterly
$2.00 per year membership

Historical Association of Greater Cape Girardeau, Inc.
325 South Spanish Street
Cape Girardeau, MO 63701
(573) 334-1177

Historical Association of Greater Saint Louis
3601 Lindell Boulevard
Saint Louis, MO 63108
(314) 658-2588

Greene County Historical Society
Box 3466 GSS
Springfield, MO 65808
(417) 881-6147
http://www.rootsweb.com/~gcmohs
Hayward Barnett, Executive Secretary
Mon–Sat 8:00–5:00
Pub. *Greene County Historical Society Bulletin*, three times per year
$10.00 per year membership; will respond to queries for SASE, research for a fee (request details)

Grundy County Historical Society
1100 Mabel Drive
Trenton, MO 64683
(660) 359-9297

Harrison County Historical Society
1604 Fuller Street
Bethany, MO 64424
(660) 425-8360

Henry County Historical Society
(203 West Franklin Street—location)

PO Box 65 (mailing address)
Clinton, MO 64735
(660) 885-8414
Marily Nold, Director; Mary Frances Abart, Genealogy Library
Apr–Dec: Tue–Sat 11:00–4:00
Pub. *The Informer*, quarterly
$8.00 per year membership

Hickory County Historical Society
(Wheatland, MO 65779—location)
PO Box 248 (mailing address)
Hermitage, MO 65668

Harvey J. Higgins Historical Society
1600 Main
Higginsville, MO 64037
(660) 584-3842
Don Smith, President
Mon–Fri 1:00–4:30, by appointment only (emphasis on Higginsville and its founder, Harvey J. Higgins)

Huntsville Historical Society
(107 North Main—location)
401 North Main (mailing address)
Huntsville, MO 65259
(660) 277-4486
Dora May Craven, First Vice President
Museum: Sat–Sun (Apr–Oct) 2:00–5:00, and by appointment
Pub. *Huntsville Historical Society Newsletter*, semiannually (Spring and Fall)
("We have a Museum and a Log Cabin [1823-Mayo Cabin].")
$10.00 per year membership

Iron County Historical Society
123 West Wayne Street
Ironton, MO 63650-1327
(573) 546-3513
Elizabeth Holloman, Museum Director
May–Oct: Sat–Sun 1:00–4:00
Pub. *Iron County Historical Society Newsletter*, quarterly
$3.00 per year membership

Jackson County Historical Society
(Archives and Research Library, 103 Independence Square Courthouse—location)
112 West Lexington, Room 103 (mailing address)
Independence, MO 64050
(816) 252-7454
Jane Flynn, President; Kathleen Halcro, Director
Mon–Wed & Fri 10:00–4:00, Sat 10:00–1:00
Pub. *Journal*, quarterly
("Strauss Peyton photographic collection, abstracts, personal diaries, business scrapbooks, and more)
$35.00 per year membership; fee admission; staff search: $10.00 per hour

Jasper County Historical Society
c/o Baker
3512 East Sunrise Drive
Joplin, MO 64801-8444
Eleanor Coffield

Jennings Historical Society
(8720 Jennings Road—location)
7028 Idlewild Avenue (mailing address)
Jennings, MO 63136
(314) 381-6650; (314) 381-7378 FAX
Linda Schmerber, President
by appointment
(Jennings history, Jennings/Fairview High Yearbooks, twenty years of *Jennings Progress* newspapers, genealogy of James Jennings and Ann Bradley Montague

Jennings of Cumberland County, Virginia)
$5.00 per year membership

Johnson County Historical Society, Inc.
Heritage Library
302 North Main Street
Warrensburg, MO 64093-1554
(660) 747-6480
Vivian Richardson, Curator
Library: Mon–Sat 1:00–4:00; Museum and Courthouse: Mon–Sat 1:00–4:00, Sun (June–Aug) 1:00–4:00
Pub. *Bulletin*, semiannually; *Johnson County Historical Society Journal*, semiannually; *Johnson County Historical Society Newsletter*
$5.00 per year membership

Joplin Historical Society
Schifferdecker Park
PO Box 555
Joplin, MO 64801
(417) 623-1180

Kimmswick Historical Society
(6000 Third Street—location)
PO Box 41 (mailing address)
Kimmswick, MO 63053
(636) 464-8676
Loretta Boemler, Museum Director; James Naes, President
Burgess-How House and Museum: Sun (Apr–Nov) 1:00–4:00
("Jefferson County history, photos, genealogy")
$10.00 per year membership; free admission to 1850s furnished log farmhouse

Kingdom of Callaway Historical Society
Westminster College
Winston Churchill Memorial and Library at Westminster College
331 West Seventh Street
Fulton, MO 65251
Barbara Huddleston, President; Rosemary Harris, Museum Director
Apr–30 Oct: Tue & Thur 1:00–4:00, and by appointment

Kirkwood Historical Society at Mudd's Grove
(302 West Argonne—location)
PO Box 200602 (mailing address)
Kirkwood, MO 63122
(314) 965-5151
bsnyder02@earthlink.net

http://www.kirkwoodarea.com/historic/main_frameset.htm
Mrs. Keith Williams, Museum Curator
Thur & Sun 1:00–4:00, and selected holidays
Pub. *Kirkwood Historical Review*, quarterly
(documents pertaining to history of Kirkwood; some history of St. Louis and state of Missouri documents, primarily as they relate to Kirkwood; books on history of Kirkwood to 1960, work in progress on history from 1960; works on Meremac Highlands resort area)
$25.00 per year membership

Laclede County Historical Society
PO Box 1341
Lebanon, MO 65536
(417) 588-1485; (417) 532-2725 Geneva Harris; (417) 532-4141 Charlene Hopkins; (417) 532-5758 Dorothy Calton
Geneva Harris, Charlene Hopkins or Dorothy Calton

Lawrence County Historical Society
PO Box 406

Mount Vernon, MO 65712
Pub. *Lawrence County Historical Society
   Bulletin*, quarterly, $10.00 per year
   subscription

Lee County Iowa Historical Society
(see Iowa, Part 2)

Lewis County Historical Society
Route 1, Box 72
Lewistown, MO 63452
(573) 497-2279

**Lexington Library and Historical
Association**
PO Box 121
Lexington, MO 64067
(660) 259-2023

Macon County Historical Society
120 Bennett Avenue
Macon, MO 63552
(660) 385-2826

The Historical Society of Maries County
PO Box 289
Vienna, MO 65582
(573) 422-3301
Mozelle Hutchison, Newsletter Editor
Research Room in the courthouse, Vienna:
   Wed 1:00–4:00, and by appointment
Pub. *The Maries Countian*, quarterly
$15.00 per year membership

Marion County Historical Society
5021 College
Hannibal, MO 63401
(573) 248-1884

Mercer County Historical Society, Inc.
310 West Main Street
Princeton, MO 64673

Mine Au Breton Historical Society
105 State Street
Potosi, MO 63664
(573) 438-4973
http://www.geocities.com/heartland/
   4386/mabhs.html
Catherine Polete, President; Marie Edgar,
   Secretary
daily 8-hour service
$3.00 per year membership; genealogy
   inquiries answered for donation to
   MABHS

Mississippi County Historical Society
(403 North Main—location)
PO Box 312 (mailing address)
Charleston, MO 63834
(573) 683-3837; (573) 683-4348
Benj. Bird Moore, Curator
usually Tue 1:30–3:30, and by appointment

**Moniteau County Missouri Historical
Society**
201 North High
California, MO 65018
(573) 796-3563 (during library hours only);
   (573) 796-2250 (Museum Chairman)
junebug1004@juno.com (Library/Genealogy
   Chairman)
Betty Williamson, Library/Genealogy
   Chairman; Alan Sparks, Web-site
   Specialist; Richard Schroeder, Museum
   Chairman
Thur–Sat (Apr–Oct) 1:00–5:00; Museum: by
   appointment
Pub. *Moniteau County Historical Society
   Newsletter*, quarterly
$5.00 per year membership; research: $5.00
   deposit plus SASE and cost of copies to be

billed, in-depth research at $10.00 per
   hour (plus postage and copies) upon
   receipt of a $30.00 deposit

Montgomery County Historical Society
112 West Second Street
Montgomery City, MO 63361
Marjorie M. Miller, Museum Director
by appointment
("Montgomery County memorabilia displays
   and genealogical research materials")
$5.00 per year membership

Morgan County Historical Society
118 North Monroe
Versailles, MO 65084
(573) 378-5530
wmwwms@laurie.net
William W. Williams (for cemetery and
   marriage records)
Tue–Fri noon–5:00, Sat 9:00–noon
(Morgan County cemetery listings indexed
   from 1830 to date, marriage records
   1833–1909)

Newton County Historical Society
(121 North Washington Street—location)
PO Box 675 (mailing address)
Neosho, MO 64850
(417) 451-4940
http://www.newtoncountyhistorical
   society.org
Suzie Crossno, Director
Wed–Sun 12:30–4:30
Pub. *Newton County Saga*, quarterly
$12.00 per year membership

Nodaway County Historical Society
(Mary H. Jackson Research Center, 110
North Walnut—location)
PO Box 324 (mailing address)
Maryville, MO 64468
(660) 582-8176
Margaret Kelley, Collection Coordinator
Feb–Nov: Tue–Fri 1:00–4:00, and by
   appointment
("Nodaway County Genealogical Society and
   Nodaway Chapter DAR collections are
   stored here, also." Some northwest
   Missouri local history; family
   information.)
free, open membership; research; donation
   for copies and postage

O'Fallon Historical Society
Civic Park Drive
O'Fallon, MO 63366

Old Mines Area Historical Society
(Fertile, Washington County, MO—location)
Rural Route 1, Box 1466 (mailing address)
Cadet, MO 63630-9801
(573) 586-5171
Alice L. Widmer, President
Tue by appointment
("French, ethnic and historical data; artifacts,
   publications; incorporated in 1978 to keep
   alive and make better-known the old
   French-American-Indian culture in this
   area and Catholic Parish three times the
   size of the city of Saint Louis; first mining
   settlement in Missouri.")
$5.00 per year membership; research:
   searches $10.00 each, $3.00 for each
   additional family sheet

Old Trails Historical Society
Bacon Log Cabin
(687 Henry Avenue—location)
PO Box 852 (mailing address)
Manchester, MO 63011
Irene Wirsing, President

by appointment and during special events
Pub. *Newsletter*, ten times per year
$10.00 per year membership

Osage County Historical Society
(402 East Main Street—location)
PO Box 402 (mailing address)
Linn, MO 65051
(573) 897-2932
Claudia Baker, Director
Wed 10:00–noon & 1:00–4:00, Sun
   (summer) 2:00–4:00
Pub. *OCHS Newsletter*, monthly
("Historic House [1895], recently placed on
   National Register of Historic Monuments."
   History of Osage County and surrounding
   counties; microfilm of county records.)
$15.00 per year membership; research:
   $10.00 per hour, minimum $25.00 for
   initial search; free library access for
   members

Overland Historical Society
9711 Lackland Road
Overland, MO 63114-3413
(314) 426-7027
LaVerne Dallas, President
by appointment
Pub. *Log House Gazette*, five times per year
   (Sept–June)
$10.00 per year membership; research:
   donation plus postage

Park University Historical Society
Park University
Frances Fishburn Archives
McAfee Memorial Library
(8700 N.W. River Park Drive—location)
PO Box 61 (mailing address)
Parkville, MO 64152
(816) 741-2000, ext. 6285; (816) 741-4911
   FAX
Carolyn Elwess, Assistant Archivist
by appointment (call during business hours,
   Mon–Fri 8:00–4:30)
Pub. *Dusty Shelf*, quarterly
$5.00 per year membership

Pemiscot County Historical Society
(Caruthersville Library—location)
PO Box 604 (mailing address)
Caruthersville, MO 63830
(573) 333-4326 (President)
Mary Belle Poteet, President
by appointment
Pub. *Pemiscot County Missouri Quarterly*
   (winter, spring, summer, fall)
("Primarily Pemiscot County, Missouri.")
$10.00 per year membership; research: cost of
   copies plus postage for members

Perry County Historical Society
(11 South Spring Street—location)
PO Box 97 (mailing address)
Perryville, MO 63775
http://perryvillemo.com (Link)
Trish Erzfeld, President
Apr–Sept: first & third Sat 10:00–2:00
Pub. *Heritage*, three times per year, $15.00
   per year subscription
$6.00 per year membership

Pettis County Historical Society
(Pettis County Courthouse—location)
Sedalia Public Library, 311 West Third Street
   (mailing address)
Sedalia, MO 65301-4399
(660) 826-1314
William B. Claycomb, President
Society: Mon–Fri 9:00–5:00; Library: winter:
   Mon–Thur 9:00–9:00, Fri 9:00–6:00, Sat
   9:00–5:00, Sun 1:00–5:00; summer: Mon

9:00–8:00, Tue–Fri 9:00–6:00, Sat
9:00–4:00, Sun 1:00–5:00
Pub. *Newsletter*, five times per year
  (bimonthly, Sept–May)
$3.00 per year membership; research: $10.00

Phelps County Historical Society
Dillon Log Cabin/Phelps County Museum
(302 Third Street—location)
PO Box 1535 (mailing address)
Rolla, MO 65402
(573) 364-5977
http://www.umr.edu/~whmcinfo/pchs
Pub. *PCHS Newsletter*

Platte County Historical Society and Museum
(220 Ferrel Drive—location)
PO Box 103 (mailing address)
Platte City, MO 64079-0103
(816) 431-5121 (Museum); (816) 858-3599
  (Office)
Betty Soper, Secretary
Mar–Oct: Tue & Sat 1:00–4:00, and by
  appointment
Pub. *Tri-mester*, three times per year
$12.00 per year membership

Pleasant Hill Historical Society, Inc.
PO Box 31
Pleasant Hill, MO 64080
(816) 987-3248 (President)
Mary Margaret Ledwidge, President
by appointment only
donation required for use of collection

Historical Society of Polk County, Missouri
(201 West Locust street—location)
PO Box 423 (mailing address)
Bolivar, MO 65613-0423
(417) 326-6850
polkcountymuseum@hotmail.com
http://www.rootsweb.com/~mohspcm/
  society.htm
Julie Wollard Trout, Webmaster
Mon–Sat 1:00–4:00; meetings: fourth Thur
  (Jan, Mar, May, July, Sept)
Pub. *Polk County Historama*, three times per
  year
$6.00 per year membership; admission: $2.00
  for adults

Ralls County Historical Society
PO Box 182
Center, MO 63436-0182
(573) 985-8211
Oliver N. Howard, President

Randolph County Historical Society
Historical Center
223 North Clark
Moberly, MO 65270
(660) 263-9396
rchs@missvalley.com
Karl and Cecy Rice, Co-Presidents
Museum/Library: Mon 10:00–noon, Thur
  1:00–3:00, Sat 9:00– noon
Pub. *Historical Report*, quarterly; *Old N'
  Newsletter*
$15.00 per year membership

Ray County Historical Society and Museum, Inc.
(901 West Royle Street—location)
PO Box 2 (mailing address)
Richmond, MO 64085-0002
(816) 776-2305
Roy Fehlman, Caretaker
Wed–Sat 10:00–5:00, and by appointment
Pub. *The Lookinglass*, quarterly
(museum and genealogical library)
$10.00 per year membership; research: $7.50

per hour plus copies at 15¢ each

Reynolds County Historical Society, Inc.
(Ellington Library, 110 South
  Main—location)
PO Box 281 (mailing address)
Ellington, MO 63638
(573) 663-2675 (Treasurer); (573) 663-7289
  (Library); (573) 663-3233 (Museum)
rcghs@mcmo.net
http://www.rootsweb.com/~moreynol
Lee Sylcox, Treasurer
Mon–Fri 9:00–5:00
Pub. *Kinfolks Search*, monthly
(formerly Reynolds County Genealogy and
  Historical Society)
$10.00 per year membership

Ripley County Historical Society
Current River Heritage Museum
101 Washington Street
Doniphan, MO 63935
(573) 996-5298; (573) 875-2180
Phoebe Braschler, Corresponding Secretary
Pub. *The Ripley County Heritage*, quarterly
$15.00 per year membership

Saint Charles County Historical Society
101 South Main Street
Saint Charles, MO 63301-2802
(636) 946-9828
SCCHS@mail.win.org
http://www.win.org/library/other/
  historical_society
Carol Wilkins, Archivist/Secretary
Mon, Wed, Fri and first & third Sat
  10:00–3:00
Pub. *Saint Charles Heritage*, quarterly (Jan,
  Apr, July, Oct); *Newsletter*, monthly
("Marriage, baptism, burial, census, land,
  probate, naturalization records/indexes for
  St. Charles County available for
  research.")
$20.00 per year membership; admission:
  $2.50 for nonmembers; research: $8.00
  per hour and 15¢ per photocopy from
  paper originals or 25¢ per photocopy from
  microform originals

Saint Clair County Historical Society
PO Box 376
Osceola, MO 64776
http://freepages.genealogy.rootsweb.com/
  ~cbell/historical
Wanda Alexander, Secretary
meetings at the Osceola County Health
  Department: second Tue (except Dec)
  7:00
$8.00 per year membership

Saint Francois County Historical Society
PO Box 575
Farmington, MO 63640
Ruth Womack, Corresponding Secretary
Pub. *Newsletter*, six times per year
$10.00 per year membership

Saline County Historical Society
PO Box 4028
Marshall, MO 65340
(660) 886-8013

The Scotland County Historical Society
Scotland County Museum
(311 South Main—location)
PO Box 263 (mailing address)
Memphis, MO 63555

Shelby County Historical Society
215 South Center
Shelbina, MO 63468
(573) 588-4480 (for tours)

Kathleen Wilham, President
Fri (June–Aug) 1:00–3:00; tours at any other
  time
$2.50 per year membership; search: $10.00
  per hour, four-hour minimum

South Howard County Historical Society
PO Box 201
New Franklin, MO 65274

Stoddard County Historical Society
(400 Center Street—location)
606 Guiling (mailing address)
Bloomfield, MO 63825
(573) 568-2163
Shannon J. Heilman, President
(cemetery book with index)
$5.00 per year membership

Stone County Historical Society
PO Box 63
Galena, MO 65656

Sullivan County Historical Society
North Water Street
Milan, MO 63556-1023
(660) 265-3476
http://www.rootsweb.com/~mosulliv/
  schistoricalsociety.html
Wayne Halter, President
by appointment
(genealogy library and local memorabilia)
$10.00 life membership

Texas County Genealogical and Historical Society
(see Genealogical Societies—Local and
Regional, below)

Tri-County Historical and Museum Society of King City, Inc.
508 North Grand Avenue and Junction
Highway 169
King City, MO 64463
(660) 535-4391
Danny Lewis, President
Memorial Day–Labor Day: weekends:
  1:00–4:00; Living History Day: third Sat
  of Sept
(genealogical records of local families
  available)
admission: donation

Union Cemetery Historical Society
227 East 28th Terrace
Kansas City, MO 64108-3277
(816) 472-4990
Wed 9:00–11:00, Fri 1:00–3:00
Pub. *Epitaph* (includes soldiers of all wars),
  quarterly, donation for subscription
("Dedicated to genealogy related to Union
  Cemetery only.")
$15.00 per year membership

Historical Society of University City
University City Public Library
6701 Delmar
University City, MO 63130
(314) 727-3150 (Library)
Library: Mon–Fri 9:00–9:00, Sat 9:00–5:00,
  Sun 2:00–5:00

Vernon County Historical Society (Bushwhacker Museum)
(231 North Main Street and 212 West
  Walnut—location)
231 North Main Street (mailing address)
Nevada, MO 64772
(417) 667-9602; (417) 667-5671 FAX
http://www.bushwhacker.org
Patrick Brophy, Curator
May–Oct: 10:00–4:00, and by appointment

Pub. *Bushwhacker Musings* (includes a genealogical section), quarterly ("Vernon County and region.")
$10.00 per year membership; basic fee for research: $15.00 for members, $25.00 for nonmembers

Walters-Boone County Historical Society
c/o Wilson-Wulff History and Genealogy Library
3801 Ponderosa Drive
Columbia, MO 65201
(573) 443-8936
http://www.coin.missouri.edu/community/genealogy/cent-mo/boco-mus.html
Tom Prater, Museum Curator, Harold C. Edwards, President
Apr–Oct: Tue–Fri noon–4:00, Sat–Sun 1:00–5:00, Nov–Mar: Wed & Fri noon–4:00, Sat–Sun 1:00–5:00
Pub. *BCHA Newsletter*

Warren County Historical Society
(Warren County Museum and Historical Library, Market and Walton Streets—location)
PO Box 12 (mailing address)
Warrenton, MO 63383
(636) 456-3820
Dona Bolton, Curator
third Sat of Apr–Oct: Sat 10:00–4:00, Sun 1:00–4:00
Pub. *Warren County Historical Society Newsletter*, three times per year
$3.00 per year membership; research: cost of copies

Washington Historical Society
(314 West Main Street—location)
PO Box 146 (mailing address)
Washington, MO 63090

Watkins Mill Association
Watkins Woolen Mill State Historic Site
26600 Park Road North
Lawson, MO 64062
(816) 296-3357
Ann M. Sligar, Site Administrator
Mon–Fri 8:00–4:00, and by appointment
(some local history)

Webster County Historical Society
(219 South Clay Street—location)
PO Box 13 (mailing address)
Marshfield, MO 65706
(417) 468-2284
dychepaulene@hotmail.com
Linda Blazer, Museum Director
Mon–Fri 10:00–4:00, Sun (May–15 Dec) 1:00–4:00, and by appointment
Pub. untitled newsletter, quarterly
$5.00 per year membership; research: minimal charges for county-wide research

Webster Groves Historical Society
1155 South Rock Hill Road
Webster Groves, MO 63119
(314) 968-1857
Charles F. Rehkopf, Archivist
Christopher Hawken House: weekends 1:00–4:00; Library and Archives: by appointment
Pub. *Webster Groves Historical Society Newsletter*, quarterly
("Kate Moody Papers, Laura Parker Papers, Esther Replogle programs and scrapbooks, records of the City of Webster Groves, local newspapers; probably one of the best collections of local history in Saint Louis County.")
$20.00 per year membership; research by

archivist: $10.00 per hour

Wentzville Community Historical Society/Archives
506 South Lynn Avenue
Wentzville, MO 63385

Westphalia Historical Society, Inc.
Westphalia, MO 65085
(573) 455-2337

Westport Historical Society
Harris Kearney House
4000 Baltimore
Kansas City, MO 64111
(816) 561-1821
Allin Phister, President
Mon–Fri 10:30–3:00, weekends by appointment
Pub. *The Westporter*
(Westport and early Kansas City history, and tours of the historic house and museum)
$15.00 per year membership

White River Valley Historical Society
PO Box 555
Point Lookout, MO 65726-0555
(417) 334-4807 (Secretary-Treasurer)
Ionamae Rebenstorf, Secretary-Treasurer
Pub. *White River Valley Historical Quarterly*
(southwest Missouri and northwest Arkansas)
$14.00 per year membership

Worth County Historical Society
Allendale, MO 64420
(660) 786-2318

Wright County Historical and Genealogical Society
PO Box 66
Hartville, MO 65667
(417) 741-6265

Genealogical Societies

State Genealogical Society

Missouri State Genealogical Association
PO Box 833
Columbia, MO 65205-0833
mosga@coin.org
http://mosga.missouri.org
Pub. *Missouri State Genealogical Journal*, quarterly; *Show Me State Genealogical News*, quarterly
$20.00 per year membership

Genealogical Societies—Local & Regional

Audrain County Area Genealogical Society
c/o Mexico-Audrain County Library
305 West Jackson Street
Mexico, MO 65265
Doris Pasley, President
meetings: third Sun (except July, Aug & Dec) 1:30
Pub. *Newsletter*, quarterly
(specializes in Audrain County, Missouri, genealogy, with some adjoining counties information; estimated 140,000 names in indexes)
$10.00 per year membership; research: $10.00 per name; search of indexes: $10.00 plus SASE and copies

Barry County Genealogical and Historical Society
PO Box 291
Cassville, MO 65625
http://www.rootsweb.com/~mobarry/

society.html
$10.00 per year membership

Genealogical Society of Butler County, Missouri, Inc.
PO Box 426
Poplar Bluff, MO 63901
(573) 686-8426
Mary Sue Beis, President
Pub. *Area Footprints*, semiannually (May, Nov), $17.00 for first year subscription, $12.00 per year subscription renewal
queries free to members, $1.00 for first 50 words, $2.00 for each additional 50 words for nonmembers

Campbell Area Genealogical and Historical Society
PO Box 401
Campbell, MO 63933-0401
Hal V. Miller, Secretary-Treasurer
(Currently inactive, may close its books soon.)

Cape Girardeau County Genealogical Society
Riverside Regional Library
(204 South Union Avenue—location)
PO Box 389 (mailing address)
Jackson, MO 63755
eddlemanw@sbcglobal.net
http://www.rootsweb.com/~mocgcgs
Dr. Bill Eddleman, President
Pub. *Collage of Cape County*, quarterly
(emphasis on southeast Missouri genealogy)
per year membership

Genealogical Society of Carter County
Route 1, Box 266
Ellsinore, MO 63937

Carthage Genealogical Society and Southwest Missouri Genealogical Library
611 Bellaire
Carthage, MO 64836
(417) 358-6494
Joan Kunkel, Genealogist and Librarian
by appointment
(Missouri and Arkansas research)

Genealogical Society of Central Missouri
(Wilson-Wulff History and Genealogy Library, 3801 Ponderosa, Columbia, MO 65203—location)
PO Box 26 (mailing address)
Columbia, MO 65205-0026
(573) 443-8964
djsapp1@mchsi.com
http://www.gscm.gen.mo.us
David Sapp, Past President
Apr–Oct: Tue–Fri noon–4:00, Sat–Sun 1:00–5:00, Nov–Mar: Wed & Fri noon–4:00, Sat–Sun 1:00–5:00
Pub. *The Reporter*, six times per year
(serving Boone County, Missouri, and surrounding counties)
$20.00 per year membership

Dade County Genealogical Society
PO Box 155
Greenfield, MO 65661

Dallas County Genealogical Society
(see Dallas County Historical Society, Historical Societies—Local and Regional, above)

Douglas County Historical and Genealogical Society, Inc.
(see Historical Societies—Local and Regional, above)

Dunklin County Genealogical Society
Dunklin County Library
209 North Main Street
Kennett, MO 63857
genealog@dunklin-co.lib.mo.us
Glenda Ford, President
8:30–5:30
Pub. *Semo Record*, quarterly
$10.00 per year membership

Florissant Valley Historical and Genealogical Society
(see Historical Societies—Local and Regional, above)

Four Rivers Genealogical Society
(314 West Main Street—location)
PO Box 146 (mailing address)
Washington, MO 63090

Genealogy Friends of The Library
(Neosho-Newton County Library, 201 West Spring—location)
PO Box 314 (mailing address)
Neosho, MO 64850-0314
(417) 451-4231 (Library)
Doris McCleary, President
Mon–Thur 9:00–9:00, Fri 9:00–5:30, Sat 9:00–5:00
Pub. *Newton County Roots*, quarterly
$9.00 per year membership

Gentry County Genealogical Society
Albany Public Library
101 West Clay
Albany, MO 64402
(660) 726-5615 (Library)
Helen Henton, Librarian
Library: Mon–Sat 11:00–5:00

Grundy County Genealogical Society
PO Box 223
Trenton, MO 64683
(660) 359-6512
Robert Greiner, President
Pub. *Grundy Gleanings*, quarterly, $2.50 per issue
$10.00 per year membership

Heritage Seekers
222 West Hamilton
Palmyra, MO 63461
(573) 769-3302
no genealogical research

Howard County Genealogical Society
206 North Linn Avenue, Route 1
Fayette, MO 65248
(660) 248-3247

Jackson County Genealogical Society
(Truman Depot, 111 West Pacific—location)
PO Box 2145 (mailing address)
Independence, MO 64055
(816) 252-8128
Dorothy J. Norris, President
Tue, Thur 10:00–4:00, Sat 9:00–5:00
Pub. *The Pioneer Wagon*, quarterly; *Pioneer Trails*, monthly (except June, July, Dec)
("We have obituaries from the *Kansas city Star*. Readings of cemeteries and marriage records and deeds.")
$15.00 per year membership; research: assistance by donation

Jefferson County MO Genealogical Society
PO Box 1342
High Ridge, MO 63049
(636) 892-2670
bdiehl@bsda-transit.org;
cosmergen@yahoo.com
http://www.rootsweb.com/~mojcgs/index.

html
Barb Diehl
Pub. *Newsletter*, quarterly
$12.00 per year membership

Joplin Genealogical Society
Joplin Public Library
300 South Main Street
Joplin, MO 64801-2310
Mon–Sat 9:00–6:00
$10.00 per year membership; search: $5.00 per name-per item (such as obituary)

Laclede County Genealogical Society
PO Box 350
Lebanon, MO 65536
Thomas C. Knight, President
Pub. *LCGS Newsletter*, quarterly
$10.00 per year membership

Genealogical Society of Liberty (Clay County, Missouri)
(see Clay County Archives and Historical Library, Inc., City, County and Regional Archives and Libraries, above)

Lincoln County Genealogical Society
PO Box 192
Hawk Point, MO 63349
(636) 338-4639
Robert Monroe
Pub. *Newsletter*, quarterly
$5.00 per year membership

Linn County, Missouri Genealogy Researchers
771 Tomahawk
Brookfield, MO 64628
Audrey Stigall

Livingston County Genealogical Society
Livingston County Library
450 Locust Street
Chillicothe, MO 64601-2597
(660) 646-0547 (Library); (660) 646-5504 FAX (Library)
travler1@aol.com (Editor)
http://livcolibrary.org (Library)
Robert Pigg, Newsletter Editor
Library: Mon–Thur 9:00–7:00, Fri 9:00–5:00, Sat 9:00–4:00
Pub. *Lifelines*, quarterly
("This address is a central collection point for all historical and genealogical information for the Livingston County and Grand River Basin area. Liaison with the county library, county historical museum, and various historical and preservation agencies in this one spot." Also publishes cemetery indexes, county atlases, miscellaneous historical information)
$15.00 per year membership

Mercer County Genealogical Society
c/o Mercer County Library
601 Grant
Princeton, MO 64673
(660) 748-3725 (Library)
Rosemary Beverage, Corresponding Secretary
Library: Mon–Fri 9:00–5:00, Sat 9:00–noon
Pub. *Pioneer Traces*, quarterly
$8.00 per year membership

Mid-Missouri Genealogical Society, Inc.
PO Box 715
Jefferson City, MO 65102
(573) 896-8117
Roger Baker, President
meetings at Missouri State Archives: first Thur 7:00–9:00

Pub. *Genealogia*, bimonthly
(Missouri regional and local genealogy; Civil War)
$15.00 per year membership

Mississippi County Genealogical Society
PO Box 5
Charleston, MO 63834
Nancy Raithel, Corresponding Secretary
Pub. *Muddy Roots*, quarterly
$15.00 per year membership; free queries for members

Nodaway County Genealogical Society
(Nodaway County Historical Society, 110 North Walnut—genealogical collection location)
PO Box 214 (mailing address)
Maryville, MO 64468
(660) 582-3254 (Treasurer)
mowry@msc-net.com
Joan Eitel, Publications Chairman, Treasurer; Letha Marie Mowry, Files Secretary
Mon–Fri & Sun 1:00–4:00
Pub. *Smoke Signals*, quarterly
(emphasis on northwest Missouri, includes over 100,000 cards of information now being placed on computer for speeding response time; these files are not open to the public and are available only through correspondence; houses the files of the disbanded Graham Historical Society)
$10.00 per year membership; Nodaway County files $1.00 and up (postage in loose stamps) plus SASE, depending on size of file

Northeast Missouri Genealogical Society
701 Madison
Canton, MO 63435
jyount@bigfoot.com
http://www.rootsweb.com/~monemgs
Jean Purvines, Secretary-Treasurer; Jim Yount, Webmaster
Pub. *Newsletter*
$10.00 per year membership

Northwest Missouri Genealogical Society
(412 Felix—location)
PO Box 382 (mailing address)
Saint Joseph, MO 64502
(816) 233-0524
jjhas27@ccp.com
http://www.rootsweb.com/~monwmgs
Juanita Haskins, Board Member
Tue 2:00–8:00, Wed–Fri 10:00–3:00, first & third Sat noon–4:00
Pub. *Northwest Missouri Genealogical Society Journal*, semiannually; *Newsletter*, quarterly
(serving Andrew, Atchison, Buchanan, Clinton, DeKalb, Gentry, Holt, Nodaway and Worth counties, as well as nearby counties in northeast Kansas)
$15.00 per year membership

Oregon County Genealogical Society
(In Public Library at #1 Court Square—location)
c/o Oregon County Courthouse
PO Box 324 (mailing address)
Alton, MO 65606
(417) 778-6414
Reva Baker, President
Mon–Fri 8:00–4:30
Pub. *Oregon County MO Newsletter*, quarterly
$5.00 per year membership

Ozarks Genealogical Society, Inc.
(534 West Catalpa Street—OGS Library location)

PO Box 3945 (mailing address)
Springfield, MO 65808
(417) 831-2773 (OGS Library); (417) 889-5677 (President)
ogsoc@sbcglobal.net
http://www.rootsweb.com/~ozarksgs
Luci Ortner, President
OGS Library: Tue (except third Tue) 6:00–8:30, third Tue 6:00–6:45, Wed 1:00–4:00, Sat 10:00–4:00; Springfield-Greene County Library: Mon–Thur 8:30–9:00, Fri–Sat 8:30–5:00, Sun (Sept–May) 1:00–5:00
Pub. *Ozar'kin: The People Who Settled the Missouri Ozarks* (covers southwest Missouri, south of the Osage River), quarterly, $15.00 per year subscription; *Newsletter*, ten times per year
$10.00 per year membership plus $10.00 initial registration

Phelps County Genealogical Society
PO Box 571
Rolla, MO 65402-0571
(573) 265-7401
pcgs@rollanet.org; mmrite@misn.com
http://www.rollanet.org/~pcgs
Mona Hale, Secretary
Saint James Memorial Library: Mon 10:00–8:00, Tue–Fri 10:00–5:00
Pub. *Phelps County Genealogical Society Quarterly* (Jan, Apr, July, Oct)
$18.00 per year membership

Pike County Genealogical Society
PO Box 364
Bowling Green, MO 63334
Pub. *Pike County Genealogical Society Quarterly*
$10.00 per year membership

Platte County Genealogical Society
(Platte County Historical Society and Museum, 220 Ferrell Drive—location)
PO Box 103 (mailing address)
Platte City, MO 64079-0103
(816) 431-5121 (Museum); (816) 858-3599 (Office)
Betty Soper, Historical Society Executive Secretary
Mar–Oct: Tue & Sat 1:00–4:00, and by appointment
$12.00 per year membership

Genealogy Society of Pulaski County Missouri
PO Box 226
Crocker, MO 65452
(573) 736-2391
Joanna Christian, Secretary; Edna Christian, Vice President
call in advance
Pub. *Newsletter*
$7.50 per year membership

Ray County Genealogical Association
901 West Royle Street
Richmond, MO 64085-1545
(816) 776-2053
Sue Alexander, President; Sandra McKemy, Corresponding Secretary
Wed–Sat 10:00–5:00
Pub. *Ray County Reflections*, quarterly
$15.00 per year membership

Reynolds County Genealogy and Historical Society, Inc.
(see Reynolds County Historical Society, Inc., Historical Societies—Local and Regional, above)

Saint Charles County Genealogical Society

(Historic Saint Charles County Courthouse, Second and Jefferson—location)
PO Box 715 (mailing address)
Saint Charles, MO 63302-0715
(636) 724-6668; (636) 946-0541
gennut62@yahoo.com
http://www.rootsweb.com/mosccgs
Marva Lee Roellig, President
Tue 9:00–2:00, last Tue 7:00–8:30 P.M.
Pub. *Tangled Roots*, quarterly
$15.00 per year membership; research: $5.00 per hour, $10.00 minimum

Saint Louis Genealogical Society
(4 Sunnen Drive, Suite 140—location)
PO Box 43010 (mailing address)
Saint Louis, MO 63143-0010
(314) 647-8547; (314) 647-8548 FAX
office@stlgs.org
http://stlgs.org/index.shtml
Ann Fleming, Research Director
Tue, Thur & Sat 9:00–noon
Pub. *S.L.G.S. Quarterly*; *News 'n' Notes*, monthly
(specializes in Saint Louis city and county)
$25.00 per year membership; research: fee schedule being revised

Santa Fe Trail Researchers Genealogical Society
3096 State Road J
Franklin, MO 65250
(660) 248-1826 FAX
Karen J. Boggs, Archivist

Shelbina Genealogical Society
Shelbina Carnegie Public Library
(102 North Center Street—location)
PO Box 247 (mailing address)
Shelbina, MO 63468
(573) 588-2271 voice & FAX (Library)
fgf001@mail.connect.more.net (Library Director); bonywood@yahoo.com (Library)
http://www.shelbinalibrary.org (Library)
Linda Kropf, Library Director; Bonnie Wood, Assistant Librarian
Library: Mon–Fri 11:00–5:30, Tue 5:30–8:00, Sat 9:00–noon

South Central Missouri Genealogical Society
(9 Court Square—library location)
939 Nichols Drive (mailing address)
West Plains, MO 65775
(417) 256-3769
Irene Kimberlin
Tue & Sat 9:00–noon
Pub. *Newsletter*, quarterly
("Howell County, Missouri, cemeteries, courthouse records.")
$8.00 per year membership

Texas County Genealogical and Historical Society
PO Box 12
Houston, MO 65483
(417) 967-2946; (417) 967-3484
Shirley "Herndon" Wenger, President
Tue 10:00–3:00
Pub. *Ozark Happenings*, quarterly; *Texas County Missouri Newsletter*
$10.00 per year membership

Thrailkill Genealogical Society
2018 Gentry Street North
Kansas City, MO 64116

Vernon County Genealogical Society
Nevada Public Library
225 West Austin
Nevada, MO 64772

(417) 667-2831
Madge P. Baze, President
Library: Mon–Wed & Fri 9:00–6:00, Thur noon–8:00, Sat 9:00–4:00

Webb City Area Genealogy Society
101 South Liberty
Webb City, MO 64870
(417) 673-4326; (417) 673-5703 FAX
Lucille Kent, President
Mon–Fri 1:00–4:30, Sat 11:30–3:30
Pub. *The Miner*, quarterly
(Jasper County cemeteries, newspapers, census)
$7.50 per year membership

West Central Missouri Genealogical Society and Library, Inc.
(125 North Holden—location)
PO Box 435 (mailing address)
Warrensburg, MO 64093
(660) 747-9664
Nadine Adams, Librarian
Sat 1:00–4:00
Pub. *The Prairie Gleaner*, quarterly
$10.00 per year membership

West Plains Genealogical Society
PO Box 138
West Plains, MO 65775
Larry Houf

Wright County Historical and Genealogical Society
(see Historical Societies—Local and Regional, above)

Independent Publications and Miscellany

Association of Saint Louis Area Archivists
Directory of Archives and Manuscripts
Index of Repositories in the St. Louis Area
c/o Daughters of Charity Archives
7800 Natural Bridge Road
Saint Louis, MO 63121
(314) 382-2800
http://library.wustl.edu/units/spec/archives/aslaa/directory/listing.html
Andrew Cooperman

Columbia Online Information Network (COIN)
PO Box 1693
Columbia, MO 65205-1693
http://www.coin.org/community/genealogy
Marilyn McLeod, Executive Director
(links for Howard, Boone and Callaway counties)

Family Publications
5628 60th Drive, N.E.
Marysville, WA 98270-9509
Rose Caudle Terry, Publisher
Pub. *Missouri Sources, Queries & Reviews*, two to four times per year, $8.95 per volume subscription, plus $1.50 postage per order

Family Tree Climbers
(D Hiway and Doniphan Street—location)
PO Box 422 (mailing address)
Lawson, MO 64062
Joyce Kindred, Secretary-Researcher
meetings: second Wed 9:00 A.M.
(mainly Ray County)
$3.00 per year membership

Frenchtown Museum
1400 North Second Street
Saint Charles, MO 63301

(636) 946-2865
http://home.stlnet.com/~tgodwin/vinson. html

Friends of Florida
PO Box 132
Stoutsville, MO 65283
(573) 672-3330
Grace Hilbert, Treasurer

Friends of Historic Boonville
(614 East Morgan—location)
PO Box 1776 (mailing address)
Boonville, MO 65233
(660) 882-7977
friendsart@mid-mo.net
http://www.mid-mo.net/friendsart
Dr. Maryelle H. McVicker, Administrator
Mon–Fri 9:00–5:00
Pub. *Friends Footnotes*, six times per year
(a growing library of past, recent genealogy
    requests; archives covers Cooper County
    and Boonville information)
$15.00 per year membership; research: basic
    $5.00 plus copies at 25¢ per page, $10.00
    additional for probate/deed/court records

Friends of Keytesville, Inc.
(412 West Bridge Street—location)
PO Box 40 (mailing address)
Keytesville, MO 65261
(660) 288-3425 (Home); (660) 288-3204
    (Museum)
Janet Weaver, Secretary
15 May–15 Oct: Mon–Fri 2:00–5:00

The Friends of Rocheport Museum
(First and Moniteau Streets—location)
120 North Clark (mailing address)
Rocheport, MO 65279
(573) 698-2835
JoAnn Moreau, President
Apr–Oct: Sat 2:00–4:00, Sun 1:00–5:00
admission: $1.00 donation

**Hunting for Bears Genealogical and
Historical Society**
(see Alabama, Part 2)

InfoTech Publications
PO Box 1705
Cottonwood, AZ 86326-1705
Marilyn H. or Everett Moore
8:00–5:00
Pub. *Catalog*
(98 titles on Missouri genealogy)

**Landmarks Commission of Kansas City
Missouri**
City Hall
414 East 12th Street
Kansas City, MO 64106
(816) 274-2555
Lisa Lassman Briscoe, Administrator
Mon–Fri 8:00–5:00
(building permits, inventories, assessment
    photos, etc.)

Mississippi Valley French Research
(see Illinois, Part 2)

Missouri Ancestors
1002 Arthur Street
Burkburnett, TX 76354
Pub. *Missouri Ancestors*, irregularly

**Missouri Department of Transportation
(MoDOT)**
General Services Division
Mapping and Graphics Section
(105 West Capitol Avenue—location)
PO Box 270 (mailing address)
Jefferson City, MO 65102

(573) 751-2551; (888) ASK-MODOT
    (within the state)
comments@mail.modot.state.mo.us
http://modot.state.mo.us/request_cntmap.
    htm

Missouri Pioneers
http://www.rootsweb.com/~mopionee
Julie Schossow
(a database of pioneers, not a lineage society)

Missouri Territorial Pioneers
3929 Milton Drive
Independence, MO 64055-4043
(816) 373-5309
Robert L. Grover, President

Missouri Town 1855
22807 Woods Chapel Road
Blue Springs, MO 64015
(816) 524-8770; (816) 795-8200 (Friends of
    Missouri Town 1855)

MoGenWeb
Part of The USGenweb Project
lflesher@fidnet.com
http://www.rootsweb.com/~mogenweb/
    mo.htm
Larry Flesher, State Coordinator
(links to other Missouri resources)

Mountain Press
(see Tennessee, Part 2)

Museum of Missouri River History
(see Nebraska, Part 2)

**Osage County Missouri Genealogy
Resources**
mgentges@mindspring.com
http://www.mindspring.com/~mgentges

Reppert Publications
Antique and Collectible News
(see Illinois, Part 2)

Saint Paul's College Historical Society
Concordia, MO 64020
(660) 463-2238
Richard Buesing
by appointment only
(collects materials documenting the history
    of St. Paul's College; materials
    concerning family and personal papers,
    local history and religion)

Seeking 'N Searching Ancestors
Route 1, Box 52
Saint Elizabeth, MO 65075
(573) 793-6998
Peggy Smith Hake, Editor
Pub. *Seeking 'N Searching Ancestors*
    (Miller, Maries, Pulaski, Camden and
    Cole counties), bimonthly, $7.00 per year

Southern Historical Press, Inc.
(see Publishers, Part 4)

Stauber Books
McDonald County Missouri
(see Oklahoma, Part 2)

Stephens Museum of Natural History
411 Central Methodist Square
Fayette, MO 65248
delliott@cmc.edu
Dr. Dan Elliott
Tue & Thur 1:00–5:00 during school year,
    and by appointment
(pioneer and frontier life, and religion)

Traveller Southern Families

(see Virginia, Part 2)

Harry S. Truman National Historic Site
223 North Main Street
Independence, MO 64050
(816) 254-2720; (816) 254-4491 FAX
Carol J. Dage, Museum Curator
daily 8:30–5:00; tours on Mon between
    Labor Day & Memorial Day

**Union Station Kansas City/Kansas City
Museum**
30 West Pershing Road
Kansas City, MO 64108
(816) 460-2052; (816) 460-2260 FAX
Denise Morrison, Archivist
Mon–Fri 8:30–5:00, by appointment only
(emphasis on Kansas City region from the
    1830s)
charges for photocopying and photo
    reproduction

Unterrified Democrat
(300 East Main Street—location)
PO Box 109 (mailing address)
Linn, MO 65051
(573) 897-3150
Jerry Voss, Publisher
Pub. *Unterrified Democrat*, weekly
    newspaper, $25.00 per year in-state
    subscription, $27.00 per year out-of-state
    subscription

Kansas City Possee—The Westerners
1250 West Gregory Boulevard
Kansas City, MO 64114
(816) 363-8174

Kathleen Wilham Research and Publishing
2 Sharon Drive
Shelbina, MO 63468-1562
(573) 588-4480
kwilham@missvalley.com
http://www.marktwain.net/~kwilham/
    index.html
Kathleen Wilham
Mon–Fri 8:00–5:00
(Publishes books on Adair, Audrain,
    Callaway, Knox, Lewis, Macon, Marion,
    Montgomery, Monroe, Ralls and Shelby
    counties. "Have a genealogical library in
    my home—Missouri, Kentucky, Virginia
    records.")
research: $10.00 per hour, four-hour
    minimum

Montana

Archives and Libraries with Holdings in Genealogy

State Archives and Library

Montana State Archives
Montana Historical Society
(Memorial Building, 225 North Roberts
Street, Helena, MT 59601—location)
PO Box 201201 (mailing address)
Helena, MT 59620
(406) 444-4774 (Archives)
Molly Miller, State Archivist
Mon–Fri 8:00–5:00

Records Management Bureau
Secretary of State
PO Box 202801
Helena, MT 59620-2801
(406) 444-2716; (406) 444-3976 FAX

Montana State Library
(1515 East Sixth Avenue—location)
PO Box 201800 (mailing address)
Helena, MT 59620-1800
(406) 444-3115; (406) 444-5374 (Reference);
(406) 444-5612 FAX
Mon–Fri 8:00–5:00
(not a genealogical library)

State Historical Society

Montana Historical Society
(Memorial Building, 225 North Roberts
Street, Helena, MT 59601—location)
PO Box 201201 (mailing address)
Helena, MT 59620-1201
(406) 444-2694; (406) 444-2696 FAX
mhslibrary@state.mt.us
http://www.his.state.mt.us
Angela Murray, Genealogical Reference
Library and Archives: Mon–Fri 9:00–noon &
1:00–5:00, Sat 9:00–1:00; Photograph
Archives: Mon–Fri 1:00–5:00, and by
appointment; Museum: Memorial Day to
Labor Day: Mon–Fri 8:00–6:00, weekends
& holidays 9:00–5:00; Museum: Labor
Day–Memorial Day: Mon–Fri 8:00–5:00,
Sat 9:00–5:00
Pub. *Montana, the Magazine of Western
History*, quarterly; *Montana Post*,
quarterly
$45.00 per year membership; admission:
$3.00 for adults

City, County and Regional Archives and Libraries
(A more exhaustive list of public and
academic libraries can be found at http://
montanalibraries.org, http://msl.state.mt.us/
mtLibraries.htm, or http://www.findthefun.
com/lists/vxMT13.htm.)

**Big Horn County Historical Museum and
Visitor Center**
Route 1, Box 1206A
Hardin, MT 59034
(406) 665-1671
Pub. *On the Big Horn*

Butte-Silver Bow Public Archives
(17 West Quartz, Butte, MT
59701—location)
PO Box 81 (mailing address)
Butte, MT 59703
(406) 723-8262
http://www.mtech.edu/silverbow/
archives.htm
Ellen Crain, Director

Mon–Fri 9:00–5:00
(newspaper index, cemetery index, obituary
file, death and birth records, city
directories, census, maps, books,
photographs; written requests welcome)
research: $15.00 per inquiry (please limit
search to three names at a time)

Butte-Silver Bow Public Library
226 West Broadway
Butte, MT 59701-9224
(406) 723-3361; (406) 782-1825 FAX
M. Andersen, Reference Librarian
Mon & Thur–Sat 10:00–5:00, Tue–Wed
10:00–8:00

Center for Great Plains Studies
(see Kansas, Part 2)

Center for Great Plains Study
(see Nebraska, Part 2)

Copper Village Museum and Art Center
Anaconda City Hall Cultural Center
401 East Commercial Street
Anaconda, MT 59711-2327
(406) 846-2422
http://www.mt-magda.org/cprvil.htm
Carol Jette, Director
(local history collection, genealogical
services)

Dawson County Library
(see Dawson County Tree Branches,
Genealogical Socieites—Local and Regional,
below)

Ekalaka Public Library
(Main Street—location)
PO Box 482 (mailing address)
Ekalaka, MT 59324-0482
(406) 775-6336
epl@midrivers.com
Jackie Dalzell, Library Director

Fallon County Library
(10 West Fallon Avenue—location)
PO Box 1037 (mailing address)
Baker, MT 59313-1037
(406) 778-2883; (406) 778-7160; (406) 778-
7116 FAX
jgunder@libmail.mtlib.org
Judy Gunderson

Glasgow City-County Library
408 Third Avenue, South
Glasgow, MT 59230-2498
(406) 228-2731; (406) 228-8193 FAX
gcclmt@hotmail.com
http://www.crystalpixels.com/town/
library.html

Great Falls Public Library
301 Second Avenue, North
Great Falls, MT 59401-2593
(406) 453-0349; (406) 453-0181 FAX
cchsa@mtlib.org
http://www.greatfallslibrary.org

Hardin Historical Museum
East of Hardin
Hardin, MT 59034
(406) 665-1671

Havre-Hill County Library
402 Third Street
Havre, MT 59501
(406) 265-2123; (406) 262-1091 FAX
bwilliam@mt.lib.org
http://www.mtha.mt.lib.org
Bonnie Williamson
Mon–Wed 10:00–9:00, Thur 10:00–5:00,

Fri–Sat noon–5:00

Headwaters Heritage Museum
(Corner of Main and Cedar Streets—location)
PO Box 116 (mailing address)
Three Forks, MT 59752
(406) 285-3644; (406) 285-4778 (Museum,
summer only)
Robin Cadby-Sorensen, Curator
Mon–Sat 9:00–5:00, Sun 1:00–5:00
Pub. *News*, biannually
(genealogical services; small library for this
area only)
$5.00 per year membership

Lewis and Clark Library
120 South Last Chance Gulch
Helena, MT 59601-4133
(406) 442-2380
librarians@mth.mtlib.org; web@mtlib.org (W
ebmaster)
http://www.lewisandclarklibrary.org
Deborah Schlesinger
Tue–Wed 10:00–8:00, Thur–Sat 10:00–5:00,
Sun 1:00–4:00

Lincoln County Library
Eureka Branch
(318 Dewey Avenue—location)
PO Box 401 (mailing address)
Eureka, MT 59917
(406) 296-2613 voice & FAX
ebrandt@libby.org
http://www.lincolcountylibraries.com/
eureka_library.html
Esther Brandt, Branch Librarian

Livingston-Park County Public Library
228 West Callender Street
Livingston, MT 59047-2618
(406) 222-0862; (406) 222-6522 FAX
mcummins@ycsi.net; lpcpublib@ycsi.net
http://library.ycsi.net
Milla L. Cummins, Director
Mon–Wed noon–8:00, Thur 10:00–8:00, Fri
10:00–6:00, Sat 10:00–5:00
(Home of the former Park County Genealogy
Society)

Miles City Public Library
(1 South 10th Street—location)
PO Box 711 (mailing address)
Miles City, MT 59301
(406) 232-1496; (406) 234-2095 FAX
mhamlett@midrivers.com
http://montanalibraries.org/Directory/
mldBdisplay.asp?LibraryID=850
Reference/Research Librarian
Tue & Thur 11:00–8:00, Wed 10:00–7:00,
Fri 10:00–6:30, Sat 9:00–5:30

Missoula Public Library
301 East Main
Missoula, MT 59802-4799
(406) 721-2665; (406) 728-5900 FAX
bammon@missoula.lib.mt.us;
mslaplib@missoula.lib.mt.us
http://www.missoula.lib.mt.us
Bette Ammon, Library Director; Paulette K.
Parpart
Mon–Thur 10:00–9:00, Fri 10:00–6:00, Sat
(after Labor Day–Memorial Day, subject
to change) 10:00–6:00

Montana State University—Billings
Library
1500 North 30th Street
Billings, MT 59101
(406) 657-1662 (Reference); (406) 657-1655
(Special Collections)
jlhowell@msubillings.edu;
library@msubillings.edu (Reference);

broberts@msubillings.edu (Special
Collections)
http://www.msubillings.edu/library
Jane Howell, Director

Montana State University—Bozeman
Merrill C. Burlingame Special Collections
and Archives
PO Box 17332
Bozeman, MT 59717-3320
(406) 994-4242; (406) 994-2851 FAX
http://www.lib.montana.edu/index.html

Montana State University—Northern
Vande Bogart Library
PO Box 7751
Havre, MT 59501
charrison@msun.edu
http://www.msun.edu/infotech/library

Montana Tech Library
1300 West Park Street
Butte, MT 59701-8997
(406) 496-4281; (406) 496-4133 FAX
astclair@mtech.edu
http://www.mtech.edu/library
Ann St. Clair, Director
Mon–Fri 7:30–4:00; Reference: Mon–Fri
10:00–noon & 1:00–4:00
(newspapers)

Museum of the Great Plains
(see Oklahoma, Part 2)

Musselshell Valley Historical Museum
524 First West
Roundup, MT 59072
(406) 323-1403
Ted Benes
Mon–Sun (May–Sept) 1:00–5:00

O'Fallon Historical Museum
(723 South Main—location)
PO Box 285 (mailing address)
Baker, MT 59313
(406) 778-3265
ofmuseum@midrivers.com
Lora Heyen, Curator
Mon–Fri 7 Sun 9:00–noon & 1:00–5:00
("From streetlight, seven blocks south on
Hwy. 7 & one block west.")
$15.00 per year membership

Old Trail Museum
Teton Trail Village
823 North Main Street
Choteau, MT 59422
(406) 466-5332
John W. Brandvold, Director
(local history collection)

Parmly Billings Library
510 North Broadway
Billings, MT 59101-1196
(406) 657-8258 (Reference Desk)
refdesk@billings.lib.mt.us
http://www.billings.lib.mt.us
Bill Cochran, Library Director
Tue–Thur 10:00–9:00, Fri–Sat 10:00–6:00,
Sun 1:00–5:00

Powell County Museum
1199 Main Street
Deer Lodge, MT 59722
(406) 846-3294 (summer); (406) 846-3111
(winter)
James Haas, Curator
June–Aug: Mon–Fri noon–5:00
Pub. *Museum Post*, annually
(old photo archives)

Rocky Mountain College

Paul M. Adams Memorial Library
1511 Poly Drive
Billings, MT 59102
(406) 657-1087; (406) 657-1085 FAX
ill@rocky.edu
http://library.rocky.edu
Janet Jelinek
Mon–Thur 7:30–10:00, Fri 7:30–4:30, Sun
1:00–10:00

Ronan City Library
203 Main Street, S.W.
Ronan, MT 59864-2706
(406) 676-3682; (406) 676-3683 FAX
ronanlib@ronan.net
http://www.ronan.net/~ronanlib
Marilyn Koester, Library Director
Thur–Fri 10:00–6:00, Sat 11:00–5:00

Sheridan County Library
100 West Laurel Avenue
Plentywood, MT 59254
(406) 765-2317; (406) 765-2129 FAX
slee@co.sheridan.mt.us
Sheila Lee, Library Director

The University of Montana
Mansfield Library
Missoula, MT 59812-1195
(406) 243-2053; (406) 243-4587
(Reference); (406) 243-2060 FAX
archives@selway.umt.edu (K. Ross Toole
Archives); mullin@selway.umt.edu
(Special Collections Department)
http://www.lib.umt.edu/dept/arch/arch.htm
Jodi Allison-Bunnell, Archivist
Archives and Special Collections Reading
Room: Mon–Fri 8:00–5:00

University of Utah Marriott Library
(see Utah, Part 2)

Yellowstone Western Heritage Center
2822 Montana Avenue
Billings, MT 59101
(406) 256-6809 ext. 25 (Archives); (406)
256-6809, ext. 27 (Historian); (406) 256-
6850 FAX
kevinkm@ywhc.org
http://www.ywhc.org
Lynda Bourgue Moss, Director; Kevin
Kooistra-Manning, Deputy Director,
Community Historian
Tue–Sat 10:00–5:00, Sun 1:00–5:00

Historical Societies—Local and Regional

**American Historical Association, Pacific
Coast Branch**
(see California, Part 2)

**American West Research Center and
Historical Society, Inc.**
(see Ohio, Part 2)

**Anaconda/Deer Lodge County Historical
Society**
401 East Commercial Street
Anaconda, MT 59711-2327
(406) 563-2220
Jerry Hansen, Historical Consultant
Tue–Sat 1:00–4:00, and by appointment
Pub. *Historical Review*, quarterly
$10.00 per year membership

Bitter Root Valley Historical Society
Ravalli County Museum
205 Bedford, Old Courthouse
Hamilton, MT 59840
(406) 363-3338 voice & FAX

rcmuseum@cybernet1.com
http://www.cybernet1.com/rcmuseum
Helen Ann Bibler, Director
mid-May to mid-Oct: Mon & Thur–Fri
10:00–4:00, Sat 9:00–2:00, Sun
1:00–4:00, with a program at 2:00 of
cultural or historical significance; mid-Oct
to mid-May: Sat 10:00–3:00
Pub. *The Newsletter*
(Has all newspapers published in Valley,
obits, etc., are catalogued. Published
Bitterroot Trails, three-volume history of
the early Bitterroot Valley, *The
Bitterrooter*, an historical novel, *Rocky
Mountain Spotted Fever: The Anatomy of
a Pestilence*)
$15.00 per year membership; research:
$10.00 base fee plus $10.00 per hour and
copies

Blaine County Historical Society
Blaine County Museum
(501 Indiana—location)
PO Box 927 (mailing address)
Chinook, MT 59523
(406) 357-2590
Madelein M. Marsonette, Museum Manager
summer: Tue–Sat 8:00–5:00, Sun 2:00–4:00;
winter: weekday afternoons

Butte Historical Society
(Butte-Silver Bow Public Archives, 17 West
Quartz—location)
PO Box 3913 (mailing address)
Butte, MT 59701
(406) 723-8262, ext. 306 (Archives)
Ellen Crain, Director of Archives
Mon–Fri 9:00–5:00
$10.00 per year membership; research: $7.50
per inquiry, plus copy costs

Carbon County Historical Society
(206 North Broadway—location)
PO Box 881 (mailing address)
Red Lodge, MT 59068
(406) 446-3667
Shirley Zupan, President
Mon–Fri 8:00–noon, and by appointment
Pub. *Cornerstones*, quarterly
$10.00 per year membership

Cascade County Historical Society
High Plains Heritage Center
422 Second Street South
Great Falls, MT 59405
(406) 452-3462
cchsa@mtlib.org
http://www.ohwy.com/mt/y/ycachimu.htm
Cindy Kittredge, Director
Tue–Fri 10:00–4:00, Tue–Fri (summer)
10:00–2:00, Sat 1:00–4:00
Pub. *Western Genesis*, quarterly
(Montana history; archives located on the
thrid floor of Great Falls Public Library)
$15.00 per year membership; $5.00 for each
request, $20.00 per hour for research

**Gallatin County Historical Society and
Pioneer Museum**
Old County Jail
317 West Main Street
Bozeman, MT 59715-4576
(406) 585-1311
Dennis Seibel, Executive Director
June–Sept: 10:00–4:30; Oct–May:
11:00–4:00, Sat 1:00–4:00
Pub. *Gallatin County Historical Society
Newsletter*, quarterly
(regional history)
$10.00 per year membership

Madison County History Association

207 Mill Street
Sheridan, MT 59749
(406) 842-5410

Meagher County Historical Society
PO Box 389
White Sulphur Springs, MT 59645
(406) 547-3965

Mineral County Museum and Historical Society
(Library Building, 301 East Second Avenue—location)
PO Box 533 (mailing address)
Superior, MT 59872
(406) 822-4516; (406) 822-4078 (Curator); (406) 822-4626 (Researcher)
Deb Davis, Curator; Cathryn Strombo, Researcher
Mon & Thur–Sun 4:00–8:00
Pub. *Mullan Chronicles*, quarterly
(specializes in John Mullan and Mullan Road; Civil War veterans who came to Montana)
$5.00 per year membership

MonDak Historical and Art Society/MonDak Heritage Center
(120 Third Avenue, S.E.—location)
PO Box 50 (mailing address)
Sidney, MT 59270
(406) 433-3500
mondakheritagecenter@hotmail.com
Melissa Lapham, Administrative Assistant
Summer: Tue–Fri 10:00–5:00, Sat–Sun 1:00–4:00; winter: Wed–Fri 10:00–4:00, Sat–Sun 1:00–4:00
("Research materials include area family history books, heritage record cards, some cemetery information, area newspapers from early 1900s and history files. We do not house specific homesteader information or records such as marriage, birth, death or census." Richland County, MonDak area history)
research: $5.00 per hour plus cost of copies and postage (by email available), $1.00 for each obituary look-up; visitors to the center may also use the library

Phillips County Historical Society/Museum
133 South First West
Malta, MT 59538
(406) 654-1037
http://icstech.com/~mteast/museum.html

Powder River Historical Society
(210 North Lincoln—location)
PO Box 575 (mailing address)
Broadus, MT 59317
(406) 436-2474
Jesse Barnhart, President

Richey Historical Society
(Main Street—location)
PO Box 218 (mailing address)
Richey, MT 59259
(406) 773-5656
Betty B. Whiteman, Secretary-Treasurer
Mon, Wed & Fri (Memorial Day–Labor Day) 2:00–5:00

Rosebud County Historical Society
Museum
(400 Woodrose—location)
PO Box 430 (mailing address)
Colstrip, MT 59323
Teresa Taylor, President
Pub. *RCHSM Newsletter*

Stumptown Historical Society
Central Avenue, Room 301

Whitefish, MT 59937
(406) 862-0067

Sun River Valley Historical Society
13847 Highway 200
Sun River, MT 59483
(406) 264-5572
Emma Toman, Agent
usually available
Pub. *SRVHS Newsletter*, annually (Mar)

Upper Blackfoot Valley Historical Society
PO Box 922
Lincoln, MT 59639
(406) 362-4099
http://shopsite.hicountry.com/page16.html

Upper Musselshell Historical Society/Museum
11 South Central Avenue
Harlowton, MT 59036
(406) 632-5519

Utica Museum and Historical Society
(100 Main Street, Utica, MT 59452—location)
HC 81, Box 560 (mailing address)
Hobson, MT 59452
(406) 423-5208
Barbara Twiford, Treasurer
Memorial Day–Labor Day: Sat–Sun 10:00–5:00, and by appointment
("Local histories and artifacts from homestead era. We do have two books with histories of local people.")
$3.00 per year membership

Wolf Point Area Historical Society
(200 Second Avenue, South—location)
PO Box 977 (mailing address)
Wolf Point, MT 59201-0977
(406) 653-1912 (June–Aug); (406) 653-1379 (Curator's home)
Alma Hall, Curator
June–Aug: 10:00–5:00

Genealogical Societies

State Genealogical Society

Montana State Genealogical Society
PO Box 989
Boulder, MT 59632-0989
nalley@aol.com; msgs@iname.com
http://www.rootsweb.com/~mtmsgs/ index.htm
Nancy Alley, Treasurer
Pub. *Grains of Research*
(issues First Families of Montana certificates to direct descendants of residents who arried prior to 8 Nov 1889)
$10.00 per year membership

Genealogical Societies—Local & Regional

BeaverHead Hunters Genealogical Society
Beaverhead County Museum
15 South Montana
Dillon, MT 59725
(406) 683-5027 (Museum)
RockHaven@3rivers.net; patdarl@hotmail.com; jinny@bmt.net (Jinny Greitl)
http://www.rootsweb.com/~mtmss/ soc_bhh.htm
Pat Darling, President
Pub. newsletter, quarterly
$11.00 per year membership; research: $5.00 "basic lookup," $5.00 per hour thereafter

Big Horn County Genealogical Society
PO Box 51

Hardin, MT 59034
http://www.rootsweb.com/~mtmsgs/ soc_bhcgs.htm
John Spomer, President
("We have about completed the updating of our obit file, going back to 1910. We have a listing of the Fairview Cemetery, and some church records")
$7.00 per year membership

Bitterroot Genealogical Society
(Ravalli County Museum, 205 Bedford, Old Courthouse, Hamilton, MT 59840—location)
PO Box 941 (mailing address)
Corvallis, MT 59828
(406) 961-4879
acosper@earthlink.net
http://www.rotsweb.com/~mtbgs/ bvgs_information.htm
Alan Cosper, President
meetings at Corvallis LDS Church, Eastside Highway: second Tue 1:00
$12.00 per year membership; research: $10.00 donation plus copying costs

Broken Mountains Genealogical Society (Liberty County)
Liberty County Library
PO Box 261
Chester, MT 59522
(406) 759-5445 (Library)
bubbles@ttc-cmc.net
http://www.rootsweb.com/~mtmsgs/ soc_bmgs.htm
Betty L. Marshall, Corresponding Secretary
Library: Mon, Wed & Fri 8:00–noon & 1:00–5:00, Tue & Thur 1:00–5:00 & 7:00–9:00
$10.00 per year membership

Butte Genealogical Society
1231 West Park Street
Butte, MT 59701
Vicki M. Miller
(Butte and southwest Montana)

Central Montana Genealogy Society, Inc.
Lewistown Public Library
701 West Main Street, Upper Floor
Lewistown, MT 59457
gen@lewistownlibrary.org
http://www.lewistownlibrary.org (click on Genealogy)
Mary Ann Quiring
Mon–Fri 1:00–4:00
(Fergus County, Montana, census 1900–1920, census indexes, cemetery records, school census 1900–1920, taxpayers 1920, county history, most area newspapers on microfilm; records before 1920 include Judith Basin and Petroleum counties. Formerly Lewistown Genealogy Society, Inc.)
$15.00 per year membership; research: $5.00 plus 15¢ per page for copies

Dawson County Tree Branches
(see The Tree Branches, below)

Fort Assiniboine Genealogical Society
PO Box 321
Havre, MT 59531
(406) 265-4409
http://www.rootsweb.com/~mtmsgs/ soc_fags.htm
Bonnie Whittemore, President
meetings: fourth Mon 7:00 (except Dec)
Pub. *Smoke Signals*, quarterly, $4.00 per year subscription
$5.00 per year membership

Gallatin Genealogy Society

PO Box 1783
Bozeman, MT 59771-1783
http://www.rootsweb.com/~mtmsgs/
    soc_ggs.htm
Kathleen Kracht; Eleanor Buzalsky
Tue & Thur 10:00–4:00 & 6:00–9:00;
    meetings at LDS Church, Third and
    Henderson: third Thur 7:30
Pub. *Gallatin Trails*, quarterly, $2.00 per
    issue
$9.50 per year membership

Glasgow Root Diggers
102 Bonnie Street
Glasgow, MT 59230
2clwilso@nemontel.com
http://www.rootsweb.com/~mtmsgs/
    soc_grd.htm
Charlotte Furhman; Dr. Charles Wilson
Pub. *Family History Newsletter*, quarterly
    (Glasgow local research)
$12.00 per year membership; research: will
    check local records for SASE and will
    make copies if payment is included

Great Falls Genealogical Society
High Plains Heritage Center
422 Second Street South
Great Falls, MT 59405
(406) 452-3462 (Heritage Center); (406) 727-
    3922
gfgs@mt.net
http://www.mcn.net/~gfgs
Larry D. Spicer, President
Museum: Tue–Fri 10:00–4:00, Tue–Fri
    (summer) 10:00–2:00, Sat 1:00–4:00
Pub. *Treasure State Lines*, quarterly; *The
    Falls Newsletter*, bimonthly
(Montana, Civil War, microform, CDs)
$20.00 per year membership

Jefferson County Genealogy Society
PO Box 1094
Boulder, MT 59632

Lewis and Clark Genealogical Society
(Mezzanine-Helena Public Library, 120
South Last Chance Gulch, Helena, MT
59601-4133—location)
PO Box 5313 (mailing address)
Helena, MT 59604
(406) 442-2380 (Library)
lcgen@mtlib.org; racfac@bigfoot.com
http://www.rootsweb.com/~mtlcgs/index. htm
Robert Cummings, President
Library: Tue–Thur 1:00–3:00 & 7:00–9:00,
    Sat 10:00–noon
Pub. *Faded Genes*, quarterly (Mar, June,
    Sept, Dec), $7.50 per year subscription
$12.00 per year membership

Lewistown Genealogy Society, Inc.
(see Central Montana Genealogy Society,
Inc., above)

Lincoln County Montana Genealogical Society
(406) 293-8343
ddeevy@libby.org
http://www.feldenzer.com/kootenai_
    county_genealogical_so_pg_1.htm
David Deevy, President
meetings at Lincoln County Annex Building,
    Lower Level: first Thur 7:00

Miles City Genealogical Society
Miles City Public Library
(1 South 10th Street—location)
PO Box 711 (mailing address)
Miles City, MT 59301
(406) 232-1496 (Library)
milescity@geocities.com

http://www.geocities.com/Heartland/
    Fields/6175
Reference/Research Librarian
Library: Tue & Thur 11:00–8:00, Wed
    10:00–7:00, Fri 10:00–6:30, Sat
    9:00–5:30
$10.00 per year membership

Milk River Genealogical Society
PO Box 1000
Chinook, MT 59523
7kjellum@3rivers.net; 7poppins@3rivers.net
http://www.rootsweb.com/~mtmsgs/
    soc_mrgs.htm
Karen Jellum; Mary Pyette
meetings at the Triple E Room of the
    Courthouse Annex: fourth Mon
    (Sept–May) 1:30

Phillips County Genealogical Society
PO Box 334
Malta, MT
http://www.rootsweb.com/~mtmsgs/
    soc_phcgs.htm
Delores Messerly

Powder River Genealogical Society
PO Box 394
Broadus, MT 59317
emmov@rangeweb.net
http://www.rangeweb.net/~emmov/prgs/
    prgs.html
Ann Emmons

Powell County Genealogical Society
912 Missouri Avenue
Deer Lodge, MT 59722
http://www.rootsweb.com/~mtmsgs/
    soc_pcgs.htm
Megan Thompson

Sheridan Daybreakers Genealogical Society
c/o Carrol Tronson
60 East Lake Highway
Medicine Lake, MT 59247
pchgrn&a@airtimeisp.net
http://www.rootsweb.com/~mtmsgs/
    soc_sdgs.htm
Carrol Tronson; Pamla Hendrickson
meetings in the Bicentennial Room of the
    courthouse: second Thur 10:00
vvvvvvv

Tangled Roots Genealogical Society
PO Box 1992
Cut Bank, MT 59427
roncamp@cut-bank.mt.us
http://www.rootsweb.com/~mtmsgs/
    soc_trgs.htm
Kathy Campbell
meetings at the LDS Family History Center:
    second Tue 7:00
Pub. *Tangled Roots*
$6.00 per year membership

The Tree Branches
PO Box 1275
Glendive, MT 59330-1275
(406) 365-4014
wyldrose@midrivers.com
http://www.cheyenneancestors.com/
    dawson/dwsgens.html
Betty Hagen, President
Pub. *The Tree Branch*, three times per year
    (annual current obituary index), $5.00 per
    year subscription
(maintains genealogy room at Glendive
    Public Library, 200 South Kendrick;
    published *Our Times Our Lives*, $30.00 +
    postage)
$6.00 per year membership; obituary search:
    $2.00

Tri-State Genealogical Society (SDGS)
(see South Dakota, Part 2)

Western Montana Genealogical Society
PO Box 2714
Missoula, MT 59806-2714
parpart@missoula.lib.mt.us
http://www.rootsweb.com/~mtwmgs
Paulette Parpart, Librarian
Pub. *WMGS Newsletter*, five times per year
    (Jan, Mar, May, Sept, Nov)
$11.00 per year membership; research: $5.00
    plus copies at 25¢ per page (billed)

Yellowstone Genealogy Forum
Parmly Billings Library
510 North Broadway
Billings, MT 59101
(406) 657-8258 (Reference Desk)
anitas2602@msn.com
http://www.rootsweb.com/~mtygf
Anita Smith, President
Library: Tue–Thur 10:00–9:00, Fri–Sat
    10:00–6:00, Sun 1:00–5:00
Pub. *The Gen-Bug News*, quarterly
$10.00 per year membership

Independent Publications and Miscellany

Daniels County Museum and Pioneer Town
(7 Country Road—location)
PO Box 133 (mailing address)
Scobey, MT 59263
(406) 487-5965; (406) 487-2224 FAX
papaegg@nemontel.net
http://www.scobey.org (museum listed on this
    site)
Mary Richardson, Archives
Memorial Day–Labor Day: 12:30–4:30;
    Winter: Tue 10:00–4:00
$15.00 per year membership

Dull Knife Community College
Northern Cheyenne Cultural Center
PO Box 98
Lame Deer, MT 59043
(406) 477-6215

Garfield County Museum
PO Box 145
Jordan, MT 59337
(406) 557-2589

The Last Leaf
1477 Highway 200 South
Glendive, MT 59330-9402
boobear@midrivers.com
Sylvia Mickelson, Trust, Publisher; Margaret
    Basta, Editor
Pub. *The Last Leaf, Dawson County
    Historical & Genealogical Newsletter*,
    quarterly, $5.00 per year subscription

Libby Heritage Museum
PO Box 628
Libby, MT 59923
(406) 293-7521
malyevac@libby.org; gruber@libby.org
http://www.folkways.org/Libby/museum.
    html
Bob Malyevac; Jeff Gruber

Liberty County Museum
(210 Second Street East—location)
PO Box 611 (mailing address)
Chester, MT 59522
(406) 759-5256
http://www.museumusa.org/data/
    museums/MT/66382.htm

Betty Frederickson, Treasurer
28 May–15 Sept: daily: 2:00–5:00 &
    7:00–9:00

Marias Museum of History and Art
206 12th Avenue, North
Shelby, MT 59474
(406) 434-2551

McCone County Museum
(1507 Avenue B, south end of town on U.S.
    200—location)
Box 127 (mailing address)
Circle, MT 59215
(406) 485-2414
Wendell Pawlowski, Chairman of Board
Mon–Fri 8:00–5:00
("I've had people stop in that were from New
    Jersey. And they said their neighbors told
    them, 'If you get to Circle, MT, don't miss
    the museum!!'")

Montana Department of Transportation
(2701 Prospect Avenue—location)
PO Box 201001 (mailing address)
Helena, MT 59620-1001
(406) 444-6200
http://www.mdt.state.mt.us/map (Maps)

Montana State University
Museum of the Rockies
South Seventh and Kagy Boulevard
Bozeman, MT 59717
(406) 994-2251

Montana Women's History Project
315 South Fourth Street, East
Missoula, MT 59801
(406) 728-3041

MtGenWeb
Part of The USGenweb Project
vicki@thauvin.net
http://rootsweb.com/~mtgenweb
Vicki Lindsay Thauvin, State Coordinator
(links to other Montana resources, including
    Native American)

Museum of the Yellowstone
(146 Yellowstone Avenue—location)
PO Box 411 (mailing address)
West Yellowstone, MT 59758
(406) 646-7814

Northwest Pioneer
(see Washington, Part 2)

Pioneer Memorial Museum
Highway 93, Council Park
Darby, MT 59829

Tobacco Valley Historical Village
PO Box 301
Eureka, MT 59917
Barbara Larson, Board of History Chairman

Valley County Pioneer Museum
816 U.S. Highway 2, West
Glasgow, MT 59230
(406) 228-8697

Victor Heritage Museum
Blake and Main
Victor, MT 59875
(406) 642-3997

Nebraska

Archives and Libraries with Holdings in Genealogy

State Archives and Library

State Archives Division
(see Nebraska State Historical Society,
Division of Library/Archives, State
Historical Societies, below)

Nebraska Library Commission
(address withheld upon request)
http://www.nlc.state.ne.us/docs/pilot/
    pilot.html (Nebraska State Government
    Publications, including "Guide to
    Genealogical Research" and "Historical
    Society Reference Information Guide")

Nebraska State Law Library
(Statehouse, Third Floor South—location)
PO Box 94926 (mailing address)
Lincoln, NE 68502
(402) 471-3189
("We do not have genealogy information in
    this Library. We are a legal library.")

State Historical Societies

Nebraska State Historical Society
John G. Neihardt Center
(Elm and Washington Street–location)
PO Box 344 (mailing address)
Bancroft, NE 68004
(402) 648-3388; (888) 777-4667
Neihardt@gpcom.net
http://www.neihardt.com/center
Ann E. Billesbach, Curator
(primarily historical, not genealogical)

Nebraska State Historical Society
Division of Library/Archives
(1500 R Street, Lincoln, NE
    68508—location)
PO Box 82554 (mailing address)
Lincoln, NE 68501-2554
(402) 471-4771; (402) 471-4772; (402) 471-
    4751; (402) 471-3600 FAX
aeb@nebraskahistory.org;
    bun@nebraskahistory.org
http://www.nebraskahistory.org/lib-
    arch/index.htm
Ann Billesbach, Head of Reference Services;
    Andrea I. Faling, Associate Director,
    Library/Archives
Mon–Fri 9:30–4:30, Sat 8:00–5:00, Sun
    1:30–5:00 (closed state holidays and
    Sundays prior to a Monday holiday)
Pub. *Nebraska History*, quarterly; *Historical
    Newsletter*, monthly; *Cornerstone*,
    quarterly
$25.00 per year membership

City, County and Regional Archives and Libraries
(A more exhaustive list of public and
academic libraries can be found at http://
www.nlc.state.ne.us/libraries or http://www.
nlc.state.ne.us/scripts/libdir/libdir.pl.)

Edith Abbott Memorial Library
(see Grand Island Public Library, below)

Alliance Knight Museum
(908 Yellowstone—location)
Drawer D (mailing address)
Alliance, NE 69301
(308) 762-2384
Becci Thomas, Curator

10:00–6:00
(compiling an extensive research library of
    area information)

Alliance Public Library
1750 Sweetwater Avenue, Suite 101
Alliance, NE 69301-4438
(308) 762-1387; (308) 762-4148 FAX
alibrary@panhandle.net
http://www.cityofalliance.net/id27.htm
Mavis McLean, Director
Sept–May: Mon–Thur 8:00–8:00, Fri–Sat
    10:00–5:00, Sun 2:00–5:00; June–Aug:
    Mon–Tue & Thur 8:00–6:00, Wed
    8:00–8:00, Fri–Sat 10:00–5:00

Baright Public Library
5555 South 77th Street
Ralston, NE 68127-2899
(402) 331-7636; (402) 331-1168 FAX
jgorman@cityofralston.com
Jan Gorman, Library Director
Mon–Thur 10:00–9:00, Fri–Sat 10:00–5:00
(houses the Nebraska Scottish Society's
    library of over 100 Scottish items and
    books on Scotland and Scottish history,
    available on interlibrary loan; very little on
    the history of Ralston, vertical file folders
    of clippings, archival documents and
    artifacts)

Bayard Public Library
(509 Avenue A—location)
Box B (mailing address)
Bayard, NE 69334-0676
(308) 586-1144; (308) 586-1061 FAX
bayardpbl@charter.net
Sharon Ulbrich, Director

Beatrice Public Library
100 North 16th Street
Beatrice, NE 68310-4100
(402) 223-3584; (402) 223-3913 FAX
lriedesel@beatrice.lib.ne.us
http://www..beatrice.lib.ne.us
Laureen Riedesel, Director
Mon–Thur 9:00–8:00, Fri–Sat 9:00–6:00,
    Sun 2:00–5:00
("Arrangements to borrow Nebraska State
    Genealogical Society books are negotiated
    with that organization.")
nonresident card: $25.00 per year

Beaver City Public Library
(408 10th Street—location)
PO Box 431 (mailing address)
Beaver City, NE 68926-0431
(308) 268-4115
bettyo@atcjet.net
http://www.bvrcity@swnebr.net
Betty Oliver, Director
Mon & Fri 1:00–5:00, Wed 9:00–noon &
    1:00–5:00, Thur 6:30–8:30, Sat 9:00–noon

Big Springs Public Library
(400 Pine Street—location)
PO Box 192 (mailing address)
Big Springs, NE 69122-5038
(308) 889-3482
http://www.findthefun.com/venues/
    v0034076.htm
Mary Beth Heidemann, Director

Blair Public Library
210 South 17th Street
Blair, NE 68008-2055
(402) 426-3617; (402) 426-4195 FAX (City
    Office)
library@huntel.net
http://www.Blairpubliclibrary.com
Ruth Peterson, Director
Mon–Tue 10:00–5:30, Thur–Fri 7:00–9:00

Bridgeport Public Library
(722 Main Street—location)
PO Box 940 (mailing address)
Bridgeport, NE 69336-0940
(308) 262-0326; (308) 262-1412 FAX
bplb26@hamilton.net
Donna Nelson, Director
Tue–Fri 1:30–5:30

Broadwater Public Library
(Highway 26 and Wehn Street—location)
Route 2, Box 64 (mailing address)
Broadwater, NE 69125-0064
(308) 489-0119
Emma (Curly) Abel, Director

Burt County Museum
(319 North 13th Street—location)
PO Box 125 (mailing address)
Tekamah, NE 68061-1415
(402) 374-1505
Bonnie Newell, Curator
Tue, Thur & Sat 1:00–5:00
Pub. *Burt County Museum Newsletter*,
    quarterly
("Our library includes cemetery listings and
    Tekamah newspapers 1800s–1900s.")
$6.00 per year membership; search: $10.00
    per hour

Center for Great Plains Studies
(see Kansas, Part 2)

Center for Great Plains Study
1214 Oldfather Hall
University of Nebraska
Lincoln, NE 68585
(402) 472-6058; (402) 472-0463
gpq@unlnotesorg.unl.edu
Mon–Fri 8:00–4:30
Pub. *Great Plains Quarterly*, $15.00 per year
    subscription, $38.00 for two-year
    subscription
(Kansas, Montana, Nebraska, North Dakota,
    Oklahoma, South Dakota and Texas)

Chadron Public Library
507 Bordeaux Street
Chadron, NE 69337-2696
(308) 432-0531; (308) 432-0534 FAX
deweycpl@echadron.net
Imogene Horse, Director

Chadron State College
Reta E. King Library
300 East 12th Street
Chadron, NE 69337
(308) 432-6271
http://www.csc.edu/library
Fall and Spring Academic Semester:
    Mon–Thur 7:00 A.M.–11:00 P.M., Fri
    7:00–6:00, Sat 9:00–6:00, Sun
    1:00–11:00; Vacation Period, Fall and
    Spring Academic Semester: Mon–Fri
    8:00–4:00; May–Aug: Mon–Thur
    7:00–7:00, Fri 7:00–5:00, June–July:
    Mon–Thur 7:00–9:00, Fri 7:00–5:00, Sun
    5:00–9:00

Chappell Memorial Library and Art Gallery
(289 Babcock Avenue—location)
PO Box 248 (mailing address)
Chappell, NE 69129-0248
(308) 874-2626
Dixie Riley, Director

W. Dale Clark Library
(see Omaha Public Library, below)

Columbus Public Library
2504 14th Street

Columbus, NE 68601-4988
(402) 564-7116; (800) 697-1037; (402) 563-
    3378 FAX
traut@columbusne.us
http://www.megavision.com/library
Robert Trautwein, Library Director
Mon–Thur 10:00–9:00, Fri 10:00–5:00,
    Sat–Sun 1:30–5:00
(electronic obituary index of local
    newspaper, *Columbus Telegram*, from
    1970)

Cravath Memorial Library
(243 North Main Street—location)
PO Box 309 (mailing address)
Hay Springs, NE 69347-0309
(308) 638-4541; (308) 638-4421
cravath@haysprings.net
Marianne Hanks, Director

Crawford Public Library
601 Second Street
Crawford, NE 69339-1151
(308) 665-1780; (308) 665-1780 FAX
crawlib@hotmail.com
Ellyn Renken, Director

Creighton University
Carl M. Reinert/Alumni Memorial Library
2500 California Plaza
Omaha, NE 68178
(402) 280-2227; (402) 280-2746 (Archives);
    (402) 280-2435 FAX
askus@creighton.edu
http://www.creighton.edu/RAL
hours: various, available on web site

Crete Public Library
(305 East 13th Street—location)
PO Box 156 (mailing address)
Crete, NE 68333-0156
(402) 826-3809; (402) 826-4199 FAX
lolivigni@crete-ne.com
Margaret Harding; Lisa Olivigni, Director
Mon, Wed & Fri–Sat 10:00–5:30, Tue &
    Thur 10:00–7:30, Sun (Sept–May)
    2:00–5:00
("We have many local records and work with
    the local genealogy group, but are not an
    'official' genealogy group.")

Dalton Public Library
Box 206
Dalton, NE 69131-0206
(308) 377-2413
Joan Panas, Director

Elkhorn Valley Museum and Research Center
515 Queen City Boulevard
Norfolk, NE 68701
(402) 371-3886
evmdirector@cableone.net;
    evmsec@cableone.net;
    evmresearch@cableone.net (Librarian)
http://www.elkhornvalleymuseum.org
David G. Klitz, Director; Lori Godel,
    Secretary; Nancy Zaruba, Librarian
Museum: Mon–Sat 10:00–4:00, Thur
    5:00–8:00, Sun 1:00–4:00; Research
    Center: Tue 5:00–8:00, by appointment a
    day or two in advance
("The Research Center houses the collections
    of the Madison County Genealogical
    Society, the Norfolk Nebraska Chapter of
    American Historical Society of Germans
    from Russia, the Christian photo
    collection as well as several hundred other
    photographs, and local family, city and
    business histories.")
$15.00 per year membership; museum
    admission: $4.00 for nonmember adults;

Research Center admission: free-will
donation plus fees for use of computers,
copiers and certain research completed by
the volunteers

Alice M. Farr Library
1603 L Street
Aurora, NE 68818-2132
(402) 694-2200; (402) 694-2272; (402) 694-
    2273 FAX
afl@hamilton.net
http://www.cityofaurora.org/library.html
Janette Thomsen, Director

Nancy Fawcett Memorial Library
(724 Oberfelder Street—location)
PO Box 318 (mailing address)
Lodgepole, NE 69149-0318
(308) 483-5714; (308) 483-5715 FAX
nafameli@daltontel.net
Norma Michelman, Director

Geneva Public Library
1043 G Street
Geneva, NE 68361-2024
(402) 759-3416 voice & FAX
dshearer@cheerful.com
http://www.ci.geneva.ne.us/General.htm#lib
Donna Shearer, Director
2:00–8:00

Gering Public Library
1055 P Street
Gering, NE 69341-2826
(308) 436-7443; (308) 436-6869 FAX
ndibacco@gering.org
http://www.gering.org/library
Nadine DiBacco, Director

Gibbon Heritage Center
(Court and Second—location)
PO Box 27 (mailing address)
Gibbon, NE 68840
(308) 468-5531
Avnelle Lauer, Secretary-Treasurer
by appointment; first Sun 2:00–4:00
(Gibbon and Buffalo counties)

Gordon City Library
101 West Fifth Street
Gordon, NE 69343-1260
(308) 282-1198; (308) 282-1431 FAX
gorcitli@gpcom.net
http://www.gordoncitylibrary.org
Maria Kling, Director
Mon–Thur 2:00–8:00, Sat noon–6:00

Gothenburg Public Library
1104 Lake Avenue
Gothenburg, NE 69138-1903
(308) 537-2591; (308) 537-3667 FAX
http://www.ci.gothenburg.ne.us/gov-
    serv.htm#library
Lisa Geiken, Director

Grand Island Public Library
Edith Abbott Memorial Library
Lue R. Spencer (DAR) and Ella Sprague
Genealogical Collections
211 North Washington
Grand Island, NE 68801-5855
(308) 385-5333; (308) 385-5339 FAX
sf@gi.lib.ne.us
http://www.gi.lib.ne.us
Steve Fosselman, Director
Mon–Thur 10:00–9:00, Fri–Sat 10:00–6:00,
    Sun 1:00–5:00
(Lue R. Spencer (DAR) and Ella Sprague
    Genealogical Collections)

Hemingford Public Library
(812 Box Butte—location)

PO Box 6 (mailing address)
Hemingford, NE 69348-0006
(308) 487-3454
hpl@bbc.net
http://angelfire.com/ne/hplibrary/index.html
Sheryl Roberts, Director

Holdrege Public Library
604 East Avenue
Holdrege, NE 68949-2399
(308) 995-6556; (800) 836-7323; (308) 995-
5732 FAX
hplb001@alltel.net
http://www.socentral.lib.ne.us/pls
Jeff Gilderson-Duwe, Director

Jensen Memorial Library
(443 North Kearney—location)
PO Box 264 (mailing address)
Minden, NE 68959-1767
(308) 832-2648; (308) 832-1642 FAX
minlib443@yahoo.com
Ellen Burchell, Director
Mon–Wed 11:00–8:00, Thur–Fri 11:00–5:30,
Sat 10:00–4:00

Kearney Public Library and Information Center
2020 First Avenue
Kearney, NE 68847-5306
(308) 233-3282; (308) 233-3291 FAX
http://www.kearneylib.org
Cindy Messenger, Reference Librarian
Mon–Thur 8:30–9:00, Fri–Sat 8:30–6:00

Keene Memorial Library
1030 North Broad Street
Fremont, NE 68025-4199
(402) 727-2694; (402) 727-2693 FAX
stephens@keene.lib.ne.us
http://keene.lib.ne.us
Ann Stephens, Director

Kilgore Memorial Library
521 Nebraska Avenue
York, NE 68467-3095
(402) 363-2620; (402) 362-3039; (402) 363-
2627 FAX
co51537@alltel.net
http://216.170.15.163
Stan Schulz, Director
Mon–Thur 10:00–9:00, Fri–Sat 10:00–5:00,
Sun 2:00–5:00

Kimball Public Library
208 South Walnut Street
Kimball, NE 69145-1238
(308) 235-4523; (308) 235-2971 FAX (city
hall)
kplib@megavision.com
http://www.kimball.ne.us/library.htm
Carolyn Brown, Director

Lewellen Public Library
(208 Main Street—location)
PO Box 104 (mailing address)
Lewellen, NE 69147-0104
(308) 778-5421
lp1022003@yahoo.com
Leone Wolfe, Director

Lexington Public Library
(103 East 10th Street—location)
PO Box 778 (mailing address)
Lexington, NE 68850-0778
(308) 324-2151; (308) 324-2140 FAX
http://library.cityoflex.com
Ruth Seward, Director; Elberta Brummet,
Assistant Director
Mon–Thur 10:00–9:00, Fri–Sat 10:00–5:00,
Sun 1:00–5:00

Lincoln City Libraries
Bennett Martin Public Library
136 South 14th Street
Lincoln, NE 68508-1899
(402) 441-8530; (402) 441-8500; (402) 441-
8586 FAX
r.shrader@mail.lcl.lib.ne.us
http://www.lcl.lib.ne.us
Rayma Shrader, Reference Department
Mon–Thur 9:00–9:00, Fri–Sat 9:00–6:00,
Sun 1:30–5:30
research: $1.00 plus 25¢ per page for copies

Lyman Public Library
(311 Jeffers Street—location)
PO Box 384 (mailing address)
Lyman, NE 69352-0384
(308) 787-1366; (308) 787-1420 FAX
vollibrary@actcom.net
Bonnie Youngquist, Director

Merrick County Historical Museum
(211 E Street—location)
1111 17th Avenue (mailing address)
Central City, NE 68826
(308) 946-2867
Nancy B. Johnson, Historian
by appointment

Minatare Public Library
(309 Main—location)
PO Box 483 (mailing address)
Minatare, NE 69356-0483
(308) 783-1414; (308) 783-2514
minatarepubliclibrary@hotmail.com
Lana D. Hatcher, Head Librarian
Mon 9:00–noon, Mon & Wed 1:30–4:30, Fri
noon–6:00
("*Minatar Lake* and *Minatare Free Press*
newspapers, along with books, magazines,
cassettes, VHS, filmstrips, information")

Mitchell Public Library
Quivey Memorial Building
1449 Center Avenue
Mitchell, NE 69357-1447
(308) 623-2222 voice & FAX
mipl@prairieweb.com
Maryruth Reed, Director

Morrill Public Library
(119 East Webster—location)
PO Box 402 (mailing address)
Morrill, NE 69358-0402
(308) 247-2611; (308) 247-2309 FAX
mpl@prairieweb.com
Judy Engebretsen, Director

Museum of the Great Plains
(see Oklahoma, Part 2)

Norfolk Public Library
308 Prospect Avenue
Norfolk, NE 68701-4138
(402) 644-8711; (402) 370-3260 FAX
tsmith@ci.norfolk.ne.us
http://www.ci.norfolk.ne.us/library
Ted Smith, Director
Mon–Thur 10:00–9:00, Fri–Sat 10:00–5:00,
Sun (except holidays) 1:30–4:30

North Platte Public Library
120 West Fourth Street
North Platte, NE 69101-3993
(308) 532-6560; (308) 535-8036; (308) 535-
8296 FAX
lawrencecc@ci.north-platte.ne.us
Cecelia Lawrence, Director
winter (Labor Day–Memorial Day):
Mon–Thur 9:00–9:00, Fri–Sat 9:00–6:00;
summer (Memorial Day–Labor Day):
Mon & Thur 9:00–9:00, Tue–Wed &

Fri–Sat 9:00–6:00

Omaha Public Library
W. Dale Clark Library
Genealogy Department
215 South 15th Street
Omaha, NE 68102-1629
(402) 444-4825; (402) 444-4507 FAX
heenan@omaha.lib.ne.us
http://www.omaha.lib.ne.us
Thomas Heenan, Head of History Department
Mon–Thur 9:00–9:00, Fri–Sat 9:00–5:30,
Sun 1:00–5:00
(7,000 books, 7,000 reels of federal
microfilm, genealogical periodicals, place
name directories and maps, Internet
access, specialized research in Nebraska
and states east of Nebraska)

Oshkosh Public Library
(305 West First Street—location)
PO Box 140 (mailing address)
Oshkosh, NE 69154-0140
(308) 772-4554; (308) 772-4492 FAX
oshpublib@lakemac.net
Carol Kyser, Director

Potter Public Library
(333 Chestnut—location)
PO Box 317 (mailing address)
Potter, NE 69156-0317
(308) 879-4345; (308) 879-4456 FAX
Donna Aurich, Librarian
Wed 9:00–noon & 1:00–5:00, Sat 9:00–noon

Quivey Memorial Library
(see Mitchell Public Library, above)

Reynolds Center
Stuhr Museum of the Prairie Pioneer
Box 1505
Grand Island, NE 68802-1505
(308) 385-5316; (308) 385-5028 FAX
Russ Czaplewski, Historian
Mon–Fri 9:00–5:00 (appointment preferred)
Pub. *Museum News*, monthly
(Hall County settlement, especially German
settlers)
research: $3.00 minimum

Rushville Public Library
(207 Sprague Street—location)
PO Box 473 (mailing address)
Rushville, NE 69360-0389
(308) 327-2740
Christine Plantz, Director

Scottsbluff Public Library
1809 Third Avenue
Scottsbluff, NE 69361-2417
(308) 630-6251; (308) 630-6250; (308) 630-
6293 FAX
brussell@scottsbluff.org
http://www.ci.scottsbluff.ne.us/
community/htm#library
Bev Russell, Director

Union College Library
3800 South 48th Street
Lincoln, NE 68506
(402) 486-2514

University of Kansas
Kansas Collection
Spencer Research Library
(see Kansas, Part 2)

University of Nebraska Kearney
Calvin T. Ryan Library
905 West 25th Street
Kearney, NE 68849
(308) 865-8535; (308) 865-8544

(Archives/Special Collections); (308) 865-8722 FAX
http://www.unk.edu/buildings/library

University of Nebraska
Archives and Special Collections Department
South Love Library
Rooms 310-311
Lincoln, NE 68588-0410
(402) 472-2531; (402) 472-3939
    (Newspapers)
mducey2@unl.edu
http://www.unl.edu/libr/libs/love/love.html
Mary Ellen Ducey
Mon–Thur 8:00–11:00, Fri 8:00–8:00, Sat
    9:00–5:00, Sun noon–11:00

University of Nebraska
University Archives
University Library
Omaha, NE 68182
(402) 554-2362; (402) 554-2661
    (Information); (402) 554-3202
    (Government Documents); (402) 554-2884
    (Special Collections)
http://revelation.unomaha.edu

Wayne Public Library
410 North Pearl Street
Wayne, NE 68787-1905
(402) 375-3135; (402) 375-5772 FAX
wpublib@cityofwayne.org
Lauran Lofgren, Director
Mon–Fri 12:30–8:30, Sat 10:00–6:00, Sun
    2:00–5:00
(has *Wayne Herald* weekly from 1884 to date
    with some exceptions; obituaries for
    persons buried in Wayne County)
search: $2.00 plus copying costs and SASE

Wilson Public Library
910 Meridian
Cozad, NE 69130-1755
(308) 784-2019; (308) 784-3509 FAX
wpublib@cozadtel.net
http://www.cozadnebraska.com/library.htm
Karen Hanson, Director
Mon–Thur (Sept–May) 10:00–8:00,
    Mon–Thur (June–Aug) 10:00–6:00, Fri
    10:00–5:00, Sat 10:00–3:00

Lydia Bruun Woods Memorial Library
120 East 18th Street
Falls City, NE 68355-2199
(402) 245-2913; (402) 245-3031 FAX
hschawang@hotmail.com
http://www.sentco/subscribers/fclib
Hope Schawang, Director
Mon–Thur noon–8:00, Fri noon–6:00, Sat
    11:00–4:00
no search fee, but most inquiries are directed
    to the Tri-State Corners Genealogical
    Society

Historical Societies—Local and Regional

Adams County Historical Society
Hastings Museum
(1330 North Burlington Avenue, Highway
    281 at 14th Street—location)
PO Box 102 (mailing address)
Hastings, NE 68902
(402) 463-5838
achs@inebraska.com
http://www.adamshistory.org/index.html
Catherine Renscher, Director
Tue–Fri 9:00–5:00, Sat 10:00–3:00
Pub. *Historical News*, bimonthly
$10.00 per year membership

American West Research Center and Historical Society, Inc.
(see Ohio, Part 2)

Antelope County Historical Society
(Highway 275—location)
305 K Street (mailing address)
Neligh, NE 68756
Alta DeCamp, President
Memorial Day–Labor Day: Fri–Sun
    1:30–4:30
Pub. *Antelope County Historical Society
    Newsletter*, four times per year
("We have cemetery records, county
    histories, and family genealogies.")
$10.00 per year membership

Arthur County Historical Society
PO Box 134
Arthur, NE 69121-0134

Banner County Historical Society
General Delivery
Harrisburg, NE 69345
W. Stoddard

Blaine County Historical Society
HC 64, Box 4A
Brewster, NE 68821
Alfred Schipporeit
research: "reasonable" fee

Boone County Historical Society
Route 1, Box 135
Albion, NE 68620
Mr. O'Brien

Brown County Historical Society
(corner of Fifth Street and Old Highway
    #7—location)
339 North Ash (mailing address)
Ainsworth, NE 69210
(402) 387-2427
http://www.rootsweb.com/~nebrown
Marilyn A. Calver, Member
by appointment
$10.00 per year membership; research: cost
    of photocopies plus postage

Brownville Historical Society
PO Box 1
Brownville, NE 68321
(402) 825-6001
Harold Davis, Vice President
May–Sept: 10:00–5:00
$8.00 per year membership

Buffalo County Historical Society
Trails and Rails Museum
710 West 11th Street
Kearney, NE 68845
(308) 234-3041
http://www.bchs.kearney.net
Sherrie Dux-Ideus
Mon–Fri
Pub. *Talse of Buffalo County*, six times per
    year
("We have cemetery records of the county,
    plus other records.")
$15.00 per year membership

Butler County Historical Society
Saint Joseph Villa
927 Seventh Street
David City, NE 68632
Mrs. C. Sargent

Cairo Roots Historical and Genealogical Society
PO Box 308
Cairo, NE 68804
Opal Schnet

hours: once a month

Cass County Historical Society
646 Main Street
Plattsmouth, NE 68048
(402) 296-4770
H. Margo Prentiss, Curator
Tue–Sat noon–4:00, Sun (Apr–Oct)
    noon–4:00
Pub. *Newsletter*, quarterly
from $10.00 to $500.00 membership

Cedar County Historical Society
405 Hoese Street
Hartington, NE 68739
Arnold Anderson, Director
by appointment

Chase County Historical Society
(Champion, NE—location)
73989 320 Avenue (mailing address)
Imperial, NE 69033
(308) 882-5774
http://freepages.genealogy.rootsweb.com/
    ~chasecountyne
Murlena Beard, President
Mother's Day to end of Aug: Sun 1:30–4:30
(Published twelve volumes of histories, from
    $1.50 to $5.00 each, $41.00 for the set)
$3.00 per year membership

Cherry County Historical Society
650 Essex Street
Valentine, NE 69201
(402) 376-2015
Marianne Beel, President

Cheyenne County Historical Association
Cheyenne County Museum
(Sixth and Jackson—location)
PO Box 596 (mailing address)
Sidney, NE 69162
(308) 254-2150
weekdays 1:00–4:00 (except 25 Dec–1 Jan)

Cheyenne County Historical Society
PO Box 802
Sidney, NE 69162
Cheyenne County Museum, Sixth and
    Jackson Streets, Sidney, NE 69162:
    weekdays 1:00–4:00 (except 25 Dec–1
    Jan)

Chimney Rock Historical Society
Bayard Chamber of Commerce
PO Box 626
Bayard, NE 69334

Clarkson Historical Society
(221 Pine—location)
412 West First (mailing address)
Clarkson, NE 68629-4015
(402) 892-3854
ljperin@megavision.com
Dee Perina, Treasurer, Lambert Perina,
    Trustee
Fri evening, Sat–Sun 11:00–10:00 by
    appointment, except the fourth weekend in
    June (Czech days in town)

Clay County Historical Society
Inland, NE 68954-0218
(402) 463-8198
George Woolsey

Cozad Historical Society
503 Lake Avenue
Gothenburg, NE 69138
(308) 537-7217

Crawford Historical Society
PO Box 165

Crawford, NE 69339-0165

Cuming County Historical Society
780 North Holbrook Road
Coupeville, WA 98239-3111
James Konopik, Jr.

Custer County Historical Society
(445 South Ninth Avenue—location)
PO Box 334 (mailing address)
Broken Bow, NE 68822
(308) 872-2203
http://www.rootsweb.com/~necuster
Mary Landkamer, Researcher
Mon–Fri 1:00–5:00
Pub. *Custer County Times*, semiannually
$20.00 per year membership

Dakota County Historical Society
PO Box 971
Dakota City, NE 68731
(402) 698-2288
Jean Culbertson, Secretary; Gary Sides,
	President
hours: various

Dawes County Historical Society Museum
(341 Country Club Road—location)
PO Box 1319 (mailing address)
Chadron, NE 69337
(308) 432-4999
Maggie Radcliffe, President; Belvadine
	Lecher, Curator
Mon–Sat 10:00–4:00, Sun & holidays
	1:00–5:00
Pub. *Dawes County Historical Society
	Newsletter*, quarterly
(Dawes County historical items; extensive
	genealogical and historical research
	library)
$5.00 per year membership; museum
	admission: donation; short queries for
	members

Dawson County Historical Society
Dawson County Museum
(805 North Taft Street—location)
PO Box 369 (mailing address)
Lexington, NE 68850-0369
(308) 324-5340
Bob Wallace, Museum Director
Mon–Sat 9:00–5:00, Sun 1:00–5:00
Pub. *The Dawson County Banner*, quarterly
$7.50 per year membership

Deuel County Historical Society
PO Box 324
Chappell, NE 69129
(308) 874-2865
Lester L. Becker, President

Dixon County Historical Society
PO Box 95
Allen, NE 68710-0095
Mrs. M. Greem

Dodge County Historical Society
(1643 North Nye Avenue—location)
PO Box 766 (mailing address)
Fremont, NE 68025-0766
(402) 721-4515; (402) 721-4515
Mary Hendrickson, Curator
Tue–Sun (Apr–Dec) 1:00–4:30
Pub. *Historical Society Newsletter*, bimonthly
(Fremont and Dodge County, Nebraska,
	history and information; Fremont City
	directories from 1891; Dodge County
	cemetery records)
$10.00 per year membership

Historical Society of Douglas County
(Library/Archives Center, Building 11A, Fort

Omaha Campus, Metro Community
	College—location)
PO Box 11398 (mailing address)
Omaha, NE 68111-0398
(402) 451-1013; (402) 451-1394 FAX
http://www.radiks.net/~hsdc-lac
Roger L. Reeves, Director
Tue–Fri 10:00–4:00
Pub. *The Banner*, quarterly
$15.00 per year membership; admission:
	$5.00 for research center; photocopies
	35¢ per page, photographs $16.00 per 8"
	x 10" b&w print, $25.00 per color print;
	research: $12.00 per hour; search of
	database: $1.50 per minute plus 65¢ per
	kilobyte of information and 5¢ per
	printout page

Fillmore County Historical Society
633 North 11th
Geneva, NE 68361
Mrs. S. Ashby, Secretary

Franklin County Historical Society
Route 1, Box 157
Franklin, NE 68939
(308) 425-3030
Mon–Fri
("museum, genealogy, historical")

Furnas County Historical Society
(401 Nebraska Avenue—location)
PO Box 303 (mailing address)
Arapahoe, NE 68922
(308) 962-5236
Weldon M. d'Allemand, Director
Sat (May–Sept) 2:00–5:00

Gage County Historical Society
(Second and Court Streets, 101 North
	Second—location)
PO Box 793 (mailing address)
Beatrice, NE 68310-0793
(402) 228-1679
http://Gagecountymuseum.Beatricene.com
Kent Wilson, Director
Tue–Fri 9:00–noon & 1:00–5:00, Sat
	(Memorial Day–Labor Day) 9:00–noon &
	1:00–5:00, Sun 1:30–5:00
Pub. *The Quarterly Express*, quarterly
$15.00 per year membership

Garfield County Historical Society
(737 H Street—location)
PO Box 517 (mailing address)
Burwell, NE 68823
(308) 346-5070
(primarily historical, not genealogical)

Genoa Historical Society
PO Box 425
Genoa, NE 68640-0425
A. Jarecke

Gothenburg Historical Society
(520 Ninth Street—location)
PO Box 153 (mailing address)
Gothenburg, NE 69138
Virginia Hilton, President
summer, and by appointment
(local history and Pony Express history)
$5.00 per year membership

Grant County Historical Society
Grant County Courthouse
Hyannis, NE 69350
(308) 458-2226

Hamilton County Historical Society
Plainsman Museum
210 16th Street
Aurora, NE 68818

(402) 694-6531
http://www.plainsmanmuseum.org
Sarah Polak, Director
Mon–Sat (1 Apr–31 Oct) 9:00–5:00,
	Mon–Sat (1 Nov–31 Mar) 1:00–5:00, Sun
	1:00–5:00
Pub. *Plainsman News*, four times per year
("Hamilton County history/genealogy; GAR;
	Royal Highlanders. Off-site county
	research also done, within county; plat
	books and other resources available.")
$10.00 per year membership; admission: free;
	research: $20.00 per request plus copies at
	10¢ each

Harlan County Historical Society
General Delivery
Orleans, NE 68966
Winnie Kuhl

Hay Springs Heritage Center
PO Box 236
Hay Springs, NE 69347

Hayes County Historical Society
General Delivery
Hayes Center, NE 69032
Lillian Fielding
SASE for information

High Plains Historical Society
423 Norris Avenue
McCook, NE 69001-2003
(308) 345-3661
Donna Kanowicz

Hitchcock County Historical Society
(313 East First Street—location)
PO Box 511 (mailing address)
Trenton, NE 69044
Angie Bowman, Director
Museum: Memorial Day weekend to Labor
	Day weekend: Thur & Sun 2:00–5:00
Pub. *Hitchcock County Historical Society
	Newsletter*, quarterly
$5.00 per year membership; genealogy
	research: $5.00 plus 20¢ per photocopy

Holt County Historical Society
401 East Douglas Street
O'Neill, NE 68763
(402) 336-2344
Donald L. Keyes, President; Carol Keyes,
	Curator
Feb–Dec: Mon–Thur 10:00–4:00
Pub. *Holt County Historical News Letter*,
	quarterly
(over 3,000 family histories on site)
$8.00 per year membership; research: $10.00
	per hour (on or off site) plus copies and
	postage

Hooker County Historical Society
General Delivery
Mullen, NE 69152
Mrs. Glen Tompkins

Johnson County Historical Society, Inc.
Third and Lincoln
Tecumseh, NE 68450
(402) 335-3292; (402) 335-5900; (402) 335-
	5900 FAX
http:/lasr.net (under Tecumseh, NE)
Boyd Mattox; Judy Coe
9:00–5:00
$10.00 per year membership; research: $5.00
	obituary fee

Keya Paha County Historical Society
Star Route 4
Springview, NE 68778
(402) 497-2162

Betty Witter, Secretary-Director

Lincoln County Historical Museum and Society
Western Heritage Center
(2403 North Buffalo—location)
201 Circle Drive (mailing address)
North Platte, NE 69101
(308) 534-5640
Memorial Day–Labor Day: Mon–Sat
9:00–6:00, Sun 1:00–5:00; and by
appointment
$10.00 per year membership

Lincoln/Lancaster Historical Society
Lincoln/Lancaster County Genealogical
Society
PO Box 30055
Lincoln, NE 68503-0055
Pub. *Newsletter*, monthly
$7.00 per year membership

Logan County Historical Society
PO Box 7
Stapleton, NE 69163-0007
(308) 636-2461
Wilma Salisbury, Member
("Published history of 100 years in 1884.")
research: for donation

Loup County Historical Society
(401 Murry Street—location)
PO Box 102 (mailing address)
Taylor, NE 68879-0102
(308) 942-3403; (308) 346-4772
http://www.rootsweb.com/~nelchs
Kevin Brown, President
summer weekends 1:00–5:00, and by
appointment; meetings at the Community
Center: first Mon (May–Oct) 7:30
$2.00 per year membership; research: $5.00
donation

Madison County Historical Society
(208 West Third Street—location)
PO Box 708 (mailing address)
Madison, NE 68748
(402) 454-3733
Carol Robertson, President
by appointment
(Madison County artifacts and history)
$3.00 per year membership

Mari Sandoz Heritage Society
The Mari Sandoz High Plains Heritage
Center
Chadron State College
300 East 12th Street
Chadron, NE 69337
(308) 432-6276
kkorte@csc.edu
http://www.csc.edu/alumni/sandoz.asp
Ken Korte, Director
8:00–4:30
Pub. *Mari Sandoz Heritage Society
Newsletter*, three times per year; *Annual
Distinguished Lecture* (monograph series)
(Western author, Mari "Sandoz interest,
Plains cattle industry, ranching, and other
localized topics")
$15.00 per year membership

Nance County Historical Society
(501 Broadway—location)
PO Box 333 (mailing address)
Fullerton, NE 68638
bmapes@hamilton.net
Betty J. Mapes, President
Sun 2:00–4:00
$2.50 per year membership

Naponee Historical Society

Naponee, NE 68960

http://www.4w.com/pages/psimpson/napo
neehist.html

Niobrara Historical Society
89054 519 Avenue
Niobrara, NE 68760
(402) 857-3794
Betty Swanson, Secretary
Seasonal, part time (call for appointment)
("We have a collection of local newspapers
from 1874 to present. Have large
collection [and growing] of files of family
history.")
donation appreciated

North Central Nebraska Historical Society
General Delivery
Stuart, NE 68780
Lawrence Hamik

North Platte Historical Association, Inc.
(11th and J Streets, Oregon Trail
Park—location)
PO Box 435 (mailing address)
Gering, NE 69341-0435
(308) 436-5411
Lillis E. Grassmick, Museum Director
Mon–Fri 8:30–5:00

Otoe County Historical Society
PO Box 175
Nebraska City, NE 68410
Sarah Whitten

Paradise Mills Historical Society
General Delivery
Waco, NE 68460
L. Murphy

Pawnee City Historical Society and Museum
(east edge on Highway 8—location)
1041 Fifth, Box 33 (mailing address)
Pawnee City, NE 68420
(402) 852-3131
http://www.pawneecountyhistory.com/pchsm
Yvonne Dalluge, Treasurer
Apr–Oct: Tue–Fri 9:00–2:00, Sat 9:00–4:00,
Sun 1:00–4:00; winter: Tue–Thur
9:00–4:00, and by appointment
(alumni information, funeral cards, pictures,
Nebraska and Pawnee County
information)
research: $5.00 or more

Perkins County Historical Society
PO Box 731
Grant, NE 69140
Ruth Schumacher

Peru Historical Foundation
(Fifth and California Street—location)
PO Box 195 (mailing address)
Peru, NE 68421
(402) 872-6875
Mary Ruth Wilson, President
Memorial Day–Labor Day: Sun 2:00–4:30
Pub. *Peru Historical Foundation News*,
semiannually (spring and fall)
(Gage County books, city directories,
cemetery lists)

Phelps County Historical Society
Nebraska Prairie Museum of the Phelps
County Historical Society
Holdrege Area Genealogy Club
(1 mile north of Holdrege on Highway
183—location)
PO Box 164 (mailing address)
Holdrege, NE 68949

(308) 995-5015 (Historical Society); (308)
995-6712 (President)
slater68949@rcom-ne.com
http://www.rootsweb.com/~nephelps/
phelpsgen.html
Sandra Slater, President of Genealogy Club
weekdays 10:00–5:00, Sun 1:00–5:00
Pub. *Phelps Helps*, quarterly
(specializes in Phelps County history and its
residents; Nebraska federal and state
censuses, Phelps County marriage records,
Camp Atlanta P.O.W. German Archives)
$10.00 per year membership; research: $5.00
per hour plus photocopy costs and postage

Plains Historical Society
Kimball Public Library
208 South Walnut
Kimball, NE 69145-0296
(308) 235-4523 (Library)
http://www.ci.kimball.ne.us/library.htm
(Library)
Betty Allen

Platte County Historical Society
PO Box 31
Columbus, NE 68601
Tim Terry, President

Polk County Museum Historical Society
Hawkeye Street
Osceola, NE 68651
(402) 747-7901
Ruth Lux, President and Director-Curator
Sun (1 June–1 Oct) 2:00–4:00, and by
appointment

Ponca Historical Society
(Adams House Museum, Third and
Court—location)
PO Box 403 (mailing address)
Ponca, NE 68770
(402) 755-2621; (402) 755-4165
Jackie King-Coughlin, President
Memorial Day–Labor Day: Sat–Sun
1:00–4:00
("Many scrapbooks on obituaries, weddings,
schools, ads, and Ponca in general."
"Naturalization records, cemetery records,
history of county.")
$10.00 per year membership

Ravenna Genealogical and Historical Society
(see Genealogical Societies—Local and
Regional, below)

Rock County Historical Society
PO Box 116
Bassett, NE 68714
(402) 684-3774
Clint Davis

Saline County, Nebraska, Historical Society, Inc.
1127 East Second Street
Friend, NE 68359-1113
(402) 947-2911
Norma Knoche, President
Sun 2:00–5:00, and by appointment
("Saline County and also Fillmore County for
genealogy purposes.")
$1.00 per year membership; search: suggested
donation with reply, depending on amount
of information, time and expenses

Sarpy County Historical Society
2402 Clay Street
Bellevue, NE 68005
(402) 292-1880

Saunders County Historical Society-

Museum
240 North Walnut
Wahoo, NE 68066-1858
(402) 443-3090 (Museum)
http://www.visitsaunderscounty.org/
  attractions/museum/index.htm
Erin Hauser, Curator
Museum: Nov–Mar: Tue–Fri 10:00–4:00;
  Apr–Oct: Tue–Sat 10:00–4:00, Sun
  1:30–4:30
Pub. *Saunders County Historical Society
  Newsletter*, four times per year
$10.00 per year membership

Seven Valleys Historical Society
General Delivery
Callaway, NE 68825
(308) 836-2728
Wayne Hoag

Sheridan County Historical Society
(East Highway 20—location)
PO Box 274 (mailing address)
Rushville, NE 69360
(308) 327-2961; (308) 327-2166 FAX
Robert W. Buchan, Curator
Memorial Day–Labor Day: Mon–Fri
  1:00–4:00

Sherman County Historical Society
(433 South Seventh—location)
PO Box 34 (mailing address)
Loup City, NE 68853
Dorothy Richardson, Secretary
Sun 2:00–4:00, and by appointment
$5.00 per year membership

Sioux County Historical Society
General Delivery
Harrison, NE 69346
summer

**Spalding Historical and Genealogical
Society**
Route 1, Box 13
Spalding, NE 68665
Mrs. L. J. Esch

Stanton County Historical Society
PO Box 149
Pilger, NE 68768-0146
Irene Wolverton

Table Rock Historical Society
PO Box 194
Table Rock, NE 68447
http://www.pawneecountyhistory.com/trhsm
Floyd Vrtiska, Society President

Thayer County Historical Society
Thayer County Museum
The Thayer County Historical and
Genealogical Library Room
PO Box 387
Belvidere, NE 68315
(402) 768-7313; (402) 768-6845
Jacqueline J. Williamson, Curator of Museum
May–Oct: Mon–Fri & Sun 1:00–4:00, and by
  appointment

Thurston County Historical Society
(500 Ivan Street—location)
PO Box 624 (mailing address)
Pender, NE 68047
(402) 385-3210
Helen Johnson, Curator
Tue, Thur & Sat 8:00–4:00
two- and ten-year memberships available

Tobias Community Historical Society
(Main Street—location)
Route 1, Box 9 (mailing address)

Tobias, NE 68453
(402) 243-2356
Judith K. Rada, Treasurer
by appointment
(specializes in Saline County history)

Valley Community Historical Society
Valley Historical Museum
(318 West Alexander—location)
PO Box 685 (mailing address)
Valley, NE 68064
(402) 359-2678 (Curator's home)
Mrs. Wayne Nielson, Curator and Librarian

Valley County Historical Society
117 South 16th Street
PO Box 101
Ord, NE 68862
(308) 728-5178
http://www.geocities.com/crdlibr/index.html
Patricia J. Turek, President
1 May–1 Oct: Mon–Fri 1:00–4:00; meetings
  third Tue 7:30
$10.00 per person

**Washington County Historical
Association/Museum**
(102 North 14th Street—location)
PO Box 25 (mailing address)
Fort Calhoun, NE 68023
(402) 468-5740
Agnes L. Smith, Curator
Mid-Mar to mid-Dec: Wed–Fri 8:30–4:30,
  Sat–Sun 1:30–4:30
Pub. *Washington County Historical
  Association Newsletter*, quarterly (spring,
  summer, fall, winter)
$5.00 per year membership

Wayne County Historical Society
(Seventh and Lincoln Streets—location)
PO Box 83 (mailing address)
Wayne, NE 68787
(402) 375-1278
Lois Shelton, President
Sun (May–Sept) 2:00–4:00

Webster County Historical Museum
(721 West Fourth Avenue—location)
PO Box 464 (mailing address)
Red Cloud, NE 68970-2221
(402) 746-2444
Helen Mathew, Director
Apr–Nov: daily 1:00–5:00; and year-round
  by appointment
small research fee, varies with category of
  need

Weeping Water Valley Historical Society
Weeping Water, NE 68463
(402) 267-5447

Genealogical Societies

State Genealogical Society

Nebraska State Genealogical Society
(Beatrice Public Library, 100 North 16th
Street, Beatrice, NE 68310—library location)
PO Box 5608 (mailing address)
Lincoln, NE 68505-0608
(402) 266-8881 (NSGS Librarian)
http://www.rootsweb.com/~nesgs
Rose Marie Hulse, NSGS Librarian
Library: Mon–Thur 9:00–8:00, Fri–Sat
  9:00–6:00, Sun 2:00–5:00
Pub. *Ancestree*, quarterly; *The New Brass
  Key Newsletter*, bimonthly
$20.00 per year membership

Genealogical Societies—Local & Regional

Adams County Genealogical Society
PO Box 424
Hastings, NE 68901
(402) 463-5838
acgs@inebraska.com
http://www.adamshistory.org/acgs.html
Tue–Fri 9:30–5:00, Sat 10:00–3:30
Pub. *Leafy Branches*, quarterly
$10.00 per year membership

Boone-Nance County Genealogical Society
PO Box 231
Belgrade, NE 68623
(308) 358-0836
http://www.rootsweb.com/~nenance/
  bngensoc.html
LaVerna Sauser, President
meetings at Boone County Courthouse,
  Albion, NE
Pub. *The Scout*, quarterly
$8.00 per year membership; research: $5.00
  initial fee, maximum $5.00 per hour plus
  50¢ each for photocopies, except $2.50 for
  a single marriage license copy or $5.00 for
  three

Cairo Roots (Hall County)
PO Box 326
Cairo, NE 68824

**Cairo Roots Historical and Genealogical
Society**
(see Historical Societies—Local and
Regional, above)

Cass County Genealogy Club
1116 Third Avenue
Plattsmouth, NE 68048

Chase County Genealogical Society
PO Box 303
Imperial, NE 69033-0303

Cheyenne County Genealogical Society
Cheyenne County Historical Society
PO Box 802
Sidney, NE 69162
Joyce Luce, President
Cheyenne County Museum, Sixth and
  Jackson Streets, Sidney, NE 69162: daily
  1:00–4:00 (except Dec 25-Jan 1)
Pub. *Cheyenne County Genealogical
  Newsletter*, semiannually
$10.00 per year membership; research: $5.00
  plus cost of copies

Cozad Genealogy Club
Wilson Public Library
Drawer C
Cozad, NE 69130
(308) 784-2879
Norma Beans

Custer County Genealogical Society
255 South 10th
Broken Bow, NE 68822

Dakota County Genealogical Society
PO Box 482
Dakota City, NE 68731
Jody K. Boyd, President

Eastern Nebraska Genealogical Society
PO Box 541
Fremont, NE 68025-0541
(402) 721-9553
http://www.connectfremont.org/club/
  engs.htm
Claire Mares, Editor
by appointment only; meetings at 1722 East
  19th: second Mon (Sept–May) 7:00
Pub. *Roots and Leaves*, quarterly; *Newsletter*,

monthly
$12.00 per year membership

Elkhorn Valley Genealogical Society
341 East Walnut
West Point, NE 68788
joelernesti@hotmail.com
http://www.rootsweb.com/~necuming/
evgs.html
Joel Ernesti
meetings at the John A. Stahl Library, 330
North Colfax, West Point, NE: third Mon
7:00
Connections, quarterly

Fillmore County Genealogical Society
307 Road T
Exeter, NE 68351
(402) 266-8881
Rose Marie Hulse, Secretary/Treasurer
$5.00 per year membership; "all queries
answered within reasonable time"

Flatwater Genealogical Society
PO Box 373
Gibbon, NE 68840
(308) 468-5656; (308) 468-6142
Evelyn Vohland

Fort Kearney Genealogical Society
PO Box 22
Kearney, NE 68847
(308) 234-6708
http://rootsweb.com/~nebuffal/fkgs.htm
Mary Garrison, President
Pub. *Buffalo Chip*, quarterly
$15.00 per year membership; research:
donation

Frontier County Genealogical Society
PO Box 242
Curtis, NE 69025

Furnas County Genealogical Society
PO Box 391
Beaver City, NE 68926-0391
(308) 268-2641
http://www.rootsweb.com/~nefurnas/
GenSocResources.html
Eula M. Brown, Librarian and Researcher
Pub. *Furnas County Genealogical Society
Newsletter*, quarterly
("Furnas County marriages, obituaries, family
histories)
$7.50 per year membership; research: $10.00
per hour plus copies

Greater Omaha Genealogical Society
PO Box 4011
Omaha, NE 68104-0011
GrOmahaGenSoc@aol.com
http://hometown.aol.com/gromahagensoc/
myhomepage/index.html
meetings at 900 North 90th, New Cassel:
third Wed 7:00, except July & Aug
Pub. *Westward Into Nebraska*, ten times per
year
$15.00 per year membership; research:
$10.00 per hour plus copy costs

Greater York Area Genealogical Society
Kilgore Memorial Library
521 Nebraska Avenue
York, NE 68467-3095
Ila Christensen, President
Pub. *Newsletter—Greater York Area
Genealogical Society*, semiannually
$2.00 per year membership; research: $5.00
per hour plus cost of copies

Holdrege Area Genealogy Club
(see Phelps County Historical Society,
Historical Societies—Local and Regional,

above)

Hooker County Genealogical Society
(Hooker County Library
basement—location)
PO Box 280 (mailing address)
Mullen, NE 69152
(308) 546-2458; (308) 546-2756
Betty Fletcher Brown, President; Virginia
Ericksen, Librarian
by appointment
Pub. *Hooker County Genealogical Quarterly*
("newspaper clippings from local newspapers
of birth, deaths and marriages;
alphabetical 3x5 card file of abstracts
taken from local newspaper giving
pertinent genealogical data")
$2.50 per year membership; research: $4.00
for original search, $4.00 per hour for
extended search, plus $1.00 per
photocopy

Jefferson County Genealogical Society
PO Box 163
Fairbury, NE 68352-0163
JCGS@neb.rr.com
http://www.rootsweb.com/~nejeffgs
Nancy Bettin, President
Pub. *The Pioneer Trail*, quarterly
$9.00 per year membership; queries

Lexington Genealogical Society
PO Box 778
Lexington, NE 68850-0778
ebrummet@atcjet.net
http://www.rootsweb.co/~nedawson/
lexsoc.html
Elberta Brummet, Research
meetings at the Lexington Public Library:
fourth Tue 7:30
Pub. *Dawson County Genealogical
Newsletter*, three times per year (winter,
summer and fall)
$10.00 per year membership

**Lincoln-Lancaster County Genealogical
Society**
Lincoln-Lancaster Historical Society
PO Box 30055
Lincoln, NE 68503-0055
ebachman1@unl.edu
http://www.rootsweb.com/~nellcgs
Pub. *Newsletter*, monthly
$12.00 per year membership

Madison County Genealogical Society
Elkhorn Valley Museum and Research
Center
PO Box 1031
Norfolk, NE 68702-1031
madisoncgs@cableone.net
President
Library: Thur 4:00–8:00, Fri 1:00–4:00;
meetings: third Tue 7:00
Pub. *Madison County Remembers*,
bimonthly
$10.00 per year membership; research:
$10.00 for limited search

Nemaha Valley Genealogy Society
PO Box 25
Auburn, NE 68305-0025
norvell@alltel.net
http://www.rootsweb.com/~nenemaha/
nvgs.html
Denny Norvel
meetings in the Library/ARchives Room of
the Nemaha Valley Museum, Auburn:
second Tue (except Aug & Dec) 7:30

**North Central Nebraska Genealogical
Society**

PO Box 376
O'Neill, NE 68763-0376

North Platte Genealogical Society
PO Box 1452
North Platte, NE 69101
North Platte Public Library
Pub. *Railroad Ties*, quarterly
$8.00 per year membership

**Northeastern Nebraska Genealogical
Society (NENGS)**
PO Box 249
Lyons, NE 68038-0249
Maxine Sandquist, Vice President
Pub. *NENGS Notes*, quarterly
(serves Burt County and also research queries
in regard to Cuming and Thurston
counties)
$10.00 per year membership

**Northern Antelope County Genealogical
Society**
PO Box 56
Orchard, NE 68764
(402) 893-4565
Dorothy Zimmerman, President
$5.00 per year membership

Northern Nebraska Genealogical Society
PO Box 362
O'Neill, NE 68763

Northwest Genealogical Society
PO Box 6
Alliance, NE 69301-0006
(308) 762-3677
Neva Lewis, Treasurer
Pub. *Wagoner Journal*, semiannually, $5.00
per issue
$12.50 per year membership

Nuckolls County Genealogy Society
PO Box 324
Superior, NE 68978
meetings at the Superior Public Library, 449
North Kansas: fourth Tue 7:30

Perkins County Genealogical Society
HC 80, Box 32
Grant, NE 69140-9516
Mrs. Glen Keller

Plains Genealogical Society
Kimball Public Library
208 South Walnut Street
Kimball, NE 69145-0296
Pub. *Newsletter of the Plains Genealogical
Society*
$5.00 per year membership

Platte Valley Kin Seekers
Columbus Area Genealogical Society
(Platte County Historical Museum, 2916 16th
Street—location)
PO Box 153 (mailing address)
Columbus, NE 68601
(402) 564-5829; (402) 564-0644; (402) 564-
3401
Frances Edwards, President; Kathirine Smith,
Treasurer
by appointment
Pub. *Quarterly*
$8.00 per year membership

Prairie Pioneer Genealogical Society, Inc.
PO Box 1122
Grand Island, NE 68802
(308) 384-3218
Ruth McClurkin, President
Pub. *Prairie Pioneer Genealogical Society*
(Hall County), quarterly

$12.00 per year membership

Ravenna Genealogical and Historical Society
(210 Grand Avenue—location)
PO Box 84 (mailing address)
Ravenna, NE 68869
http://www.rootsweb.com/~nebuffal/
ravenna.htm
Lois Johnsten
Fri 10:00–3:00
$5.00 per year membership; research: for
society cash donation

Saline County Genealogical Society
PO Box 24
Crete, NE 68333-0024
Pub. *County Lines*, quarterly, $2.50 per issue
$10.00 per year membership

Sarpy County Genealogical Society
2402 Sac Place
Bellevue, NE 68005-3932

Saunders County Genealogical Seekers
c/o Saunders County Historical Society-
Museum
240 North Walnut
Wahoo, NE 68066-1858
(402) 443-3090 (Museum)
Marlene McDonald, President
meetings third Tue (except summer) evenings
Pub. *Newsletter*, bimonthly
$5.00 per year membership; research:
donation to microfilm fund, plus copies
and postage

Seward County Genealogical Society
(616 Bradford, basement of the Seward Civic
Center—location)
PO Box 72 (mailing address)
Seward, NE 68434-1706
(402) 532-7635 (Editor)
pc00520@alltel.net
Alta Krasser, Editor
Tue 10:00–4:00; meetings at Seward Civic
Center: third Tue 10:30
Pub. *The Log*, quarterly (Jan, Apr, July, Sept)
$6.00 per year membership (includes *The
Log*, however requests an additional
donation of $2.50 for postage); research:
$5.00 per surname

**South Central Nebraska Genealogical
Society**
c/o Jensen Memorial Library
(443 North Kearney—location)
PO Box 264 (mailing address)
Minden, NE 68959-1767
(308) 832-2648 (Library); (308) 832-1642
FAX (Library)
Ms. Jerry M. Morris, Editor
Library: Mon–Wed 11:00–8:00, Thur–Fri
11:00–5:30, Sat 10:00–4:00
Pub. *Leaves From Our Family Tree*, quarterly
$7.50 per year membership

Southeast Nebraska Genealogical Society
c/o The Heritage Room
Beatrice Public Library
100 North 16th Street
Beatrice, NE 68310
Pub. *Homesteader*, quarterly
$10.00 per year membership

Southwest Nebraska Genealogical Society
(McCook Community College, 1205 East
Third, Tipton Hall, Room 2—location)
PO Box 156 (mailing address)
McCook, NE 69001
(308) 345-1738; (308) 345-4563
SWNGS@hotmail.com

http://www.rootsweb.com/~neswngs
by appointment
Pub. *Ancestors Unlimited*, quarterly
(specializes in Red Willow, Hitchcock,
Hayes, and Frontier counties)
$12.00 per year membership; free queries;
research: $5.00 per hour plus cost of
copies, SASE, and mileage if applicable

**Spalding Historical and Genealogical
Society**
(see Historical Societies—Local and
Regional, above)

Thayer County Genealogical Society
Thayer County Museum
The Thayer County Historical and
Genealogical Library Room
PO Box 387
Belvidere, NE 68315
(402) 768-7313; (402) 768-6845
Jacqueline J. Williamson, Curator of
Museum
May–Oct: Mon–Fri & Sun 1:00–4:00, and
by appointment
Pub. *Diggin for Roots*
$5.00 per year membership

Thayer Genealogical Society
345 Ninth Street
Hebron, NE 68370
Carol Burd

Thomas County Genealogical Society
PO Box 136
Thedford, NE 69166
Mrs. Calvin E. Jones

Tri-State Corners Genealogical Society
c/o Lydia Bruun Woods Library
120 East 18th Street
Falls City, NE 68355
(402) 245-5484
Dorothy Lewis
$5.00 per year membership

Valley County Genealogical Society
619 South 10th Street
Ord, NE 68862
(308) 728-3012
Patricia J. Tures, Researcher
Mon–Sat 1:00–5:30
(local families and history)

Washington County Genealogical Society
Blair Public Library
1665 Lincoln Street
Blair, NE 68008
meetings: first Tue (Jan–Nov)
research for contribution

Wayne County Genealogical Society
220 Sherman
Wayne, NE 68787
Nancy Sutton

Genealogical Society of Wayne, NE
1108 Walnut Street
Wayne, NE 68787
Steve Gross

Rebecca Winters Genealogical Society
PO Box 323
Scottsbluff, NE 69363-0323
http://www.rootsweb.com/~nerwgs
Harold L. Chapman
meetings in the Scottsbluff Public Library
Meeting Room: second Wed (except Aug
& Dec) 7:00
Pub. *Trail Seekers*, quarterly
(local records copied and indexed; Scotts
Bluff, Banner and Morrill counties)

$10.00 per year membership; research:
$10.00 for the first hour, $8.00 for each
additional hour or part thereof

Genealogical Society of York County
Route 1, Box 5
York, NE 68467
Carol McKenzie

Independent Publications and Miscellany

Museum of Missouri River History
Brownville State Recreation Area
PO Box 38
Brownville, NE 68321
(402) 825-3341
Clay W. Kennedy, Curator
Memorial Day–Labor Day: 10:00–5:00

Nebraska Department of Roads
Office Services Section, Room 11
(1500 Highway 2—location)
PO Box 9475 (mailing address)
Lincoln, NE 68509-4759
(402) 479-4503; (402) 479-3860 FAX
http://www.dor.state.ne.us/maps (Maps)

NeGenWeb
Part of The USGenweb Project
ne@usgenweb.org
http://www.rootsweb.com/~negenweb
("Sites for each Nebraska county can be
accessed through the main NeGenWeb
Project web site.")

Oldtime Nebraska
http://www.olden-times.com/
OldtimeNebraska
Dick Taylor

Pawnee County History
sitemgr@pawneecountyhistory.com
http://www.pawneecountyhistory.com
("Read interesting accounts of early-day
frontier experiences. Learn about the
pioneers who've given us a favorable
cultural legacy." Includes links.)

Verdigre Heritage Museum
Verdigre, NE 68783

Western Heritage Society
801 South 10th Street
Omaha, NE 68108
(402) 444-5071

Nevada

Archives and Libraries with Holdings in Genealogy

State Archives and Library

Nevada State Library and Archives
State Archives
100 North Stewart Street
Carson City, NV 89701-4285
(702) 684-3360 (Library); (702) 684-3310
   (Archives); (702) 684-3371 FAX
jmkintop@clan.lib.nv.us
http://dmla.clan.lib.nv.us/docs/nsla
Guy Louis Rocha, State Archives and
   Records Administrator; Jeffrey M. Kintop,
   State Archives Manager; Christopher G.
   Driggs, Archivist; Sesan E. Searcy,
   Archivist
Mon–Fri 8:00–5:00
research: $15.00 for Nevada residents, $20.00
   per hour for nonresidents, first hour free
   for state agencies; copies 30¢ each, except
   that the first ten copies are free to the
   general public and the first 50 pages are
   free to state agencies

State Historical Societies

Nevada Historical Society
1650 North Virginia Street
Reno, NV 89503
(775) 688-1190; (775) 688-2917 FAX
sksisco@clan.lib.nv.us;
   lmlibby@clan.lib.nv.us
http://dmla.clan.lib.nv.us/docs/museums/
   reno/his-soc.htm
Lee Mortensen, Librarian; Scott K. Sisco,
   Interim Director; Lynn Libby, Executive
   Assistant
Tue–Sat noon–4:00
Pub. *Nevada Historical Society Quarterly*
(Nevada and the Great Basin; "we are not a
   genealogical library, but we do have a lot
   of local history material.")
$25.00 per year membership

**Nevada State Museum and Historical
Society**
Department of Museums and History
700 Twin Lakes Drive
Las Vegas, NV 89107
(702) 486-5205; (702) 486-5172 FAX
damillma@clan.lib.nv.us
http://dmla.clan.lib.nv.us/docs/museums/
   lv/vegas.htm
David Millman, Curator
Mon–Fri 8:30–4:30
$25.00 per year membership

City, County and Regional Archives and Libraries
(A more exhaustive list of public and
academic libraries can be found at http://
www.clan.lib.nv.us/Polaris or http://dmla.
clan.lib.nv.us/docs/nsla/directory.)

Boulder City Library
701 Adams Boulevard
Boulder City, NV 89005
(702) 293-1281; (702) 293-0239 FAX
duncan@bclibrary.org
http://www.bclibrary.org
Duncan McCoy, Director

Churchill County Museum and Archives
1050 South Maine Street
Fallon, NV 89406
(775) 423-3677 (Museum); (775) 423-3662
   FAX

Jane Pieplow, Museum Director/Curator
Jan–Mar: Mon–Sat 10:00–4:00, Sun
   noon–4:00; Apr–Dec: Mon–Sat
   10:00–5:00, Sun noon–5:00
Pub. *In Focus*, annually

Douglas County Library
(1625 Library Lane—location)
PO Box 337 (mailing address)
Minden, NV 89423-0337
(775) 782-9841; (775) 782-5754 FAX
ldeacy@douglas.lib.nv.us
http://douglas.lib.nv.us
Linda Deacy, Library Director
Mon & Wed 9:00–8:00, Thur & Sat
   9:00–6:00

Humboldt County Library
85 East Fifth Street
Winnemucca, NV 89445-3095
(775) 623-6388; (775) 623-6438 FAX
jamarcin@clan.lib.nv.us
Sharon Allen, Library Director
Mon & Thur–Sat 9:00–5:00, Tue–Wed
   9:00–9:00

Las Vegas-Clark County Library District
Las Vegas Library
833 Las Vegas Boulevard, North
Las Vegas, NV 89101-2059
(702) 507-3500; (702) 507-3045 FAX
cabralesa@lvccld.org
http://post-office.lvccld.lib.nv.us/index.htm
Art Cabrales, Branch Manager

Mojave River Valley Museum Association
(see California, Part 2)

Northeastern Nevada Museum
(see Northeastern Nevada Historical Society,
Historical Societies—Local and Regional,
below)

**The Old Logandale School Historical
Museum and Cultural Arts Society**
(3011 Moapa Valley Boulevard—location)
PO Box 65 (mailing address)
Logandale, NV 89021
(702) 398-7272; (702) 398-7273
OLSHACSLYBRE@mvdsl.com
http://www.rootsweb.com/~nvolshcs
Virginia "Beezy" Tobiasson
Wed–Sat 10:00–4:00
("One of the best local collections of family
   histories, books, old photographs, poems,
   school annuals, school photos, and books
   written by local authors of the Moapa
   Valley and Southern Nevada.")
$25.00 per year membership

University of Nevada, Las Vegas (UNLV)
James R. Dickinson Library
Special Collections Department
4505 Maryland Parkway
Las Vegas, NV 89154-7010
(702) 895-3285; (702) 895-3850 FAX
michelp@nevada.edu
http://www.nscee.edu/unlv/libraries/
   services/speccol/sc.html

University of Nevada, Reno
Special Collections Department
University Library/322
Reno, NV 89557-0044
(775) 784-6538; (775) 784-6500, ext. 317
   (Newspapers)
blesse@admin.unr.edu (Newspapers)
http://www.unr.edu/~specoll/index.html
Mon–Fri 8:00–5:00, Sat (Sept to mid-Dec &
   Feb to mid-May) 1:00–5:00
("Nevada and the Great Basin history,
   includes books, photos, maps and

manuscripts; Great Basin Indians and
   women in the trans-Mississippi West")

University of Utah Marriott Library
(see Utah, Part 2)

**Washoe Archive and Cultural Resource
Center**
861 Crescent Drive
Carson City, NV 89701
(702) 888-0936

Washoe County Library System
(301 South Center Street, Reno, NV 89505-
2151—location)
PO Box 2151 (mailing address)
Reno, NV 89505-2151
(775) 785-4190; (775) 785-4692 FAX
ncumming@mail.co.washoe.nv.us
http://www.washoe.lib.nv.us
Nancy Cummings, Director

Western Heritage Center
(see Montana, Part 2)

Historical Societies—Local and Regional

**American Historical Association, Pacific
Coast Branch**
(see California, Part 2)

**American West Research Center and
Historical Society, Inc.**
(see Ohio, Part 2)

**Boulder City Museum and Historical
Association**
(444 Hotel Plaza—location)
PO Box 60516 (mailing address)
Boulder City, NV 89006
(702) 294-1988
bcmha@yahoo.com
Dennis McBride, Archivist
Museum: Mon–Sat 10:00–5:00, Sun
   noon–5:00; Archives: by appointment
Pub. *Newsletter*, bimonthly
$15.00 per year membership; admission:
   $2.00 for nonmembers

**Central Nevada Historical Society and
Museum**
(1900 Logan Field Road—location)
PO Box 326 (mailing address)
Tonopah, NV 89049
(775) 482-9676; (775) 482-5423 FAX
cnmuseum@citlink.net
http://www.tonopahnevada.com
Viola Whipperman, Assistant Curator
Apr–Sept: seven days 9:00–5:00; Oct–Mar:
   six days 11:00–5:00
Pub. *Central Nevada's Glorious Past*,
   semiannually (May, Nov)
(central Nevada history of Nye and Esmeralda
   counties)
$10.00 per year membership

Eureka County Historical Society
Eureka Sentinel Museum
PO Box 178
Eureka, NV 89316

Goldfield Historical Society
PO Box 225
Goldfield, NV 89013

Lake Tahoe Historical Society
(see California, Part 2)

North Central Nevada Historical Society
Humboldt County Museum

(Maple Avenue and Jungo Road—location)
PO Box 819 (mailing address)
Winnemucca, NV 89445
(775) 623-2912

Northeastern Nevada Historical Society
Northeastern Nevada Museum
1515 Idaho Street
Elko, NV 89801
(775) 738-3418
Pub. *Northeastern Nevada Historical Society
    Quarterly*
(Elko, Eureka, Humboldt, Lander, Pershing,
    and White Pine counties)
$20.00 per year membership

Washoe County Historical Society
629 Jones Street
Reno, NV 89503

Genealogical Societies

State Genealogical Society

Nevada State Genealogical Society
PO Box 20666
Reno, NV 89515
http://www.rootsweb.com/~nvsgs
Patty Wallace, President
meetings at the Family History Center, 4751
    Neil Road: third Tue (Sept–May) 7:15
Pub. *Nevada Desert*, nine times per year
    (monthly, Sept–May)
$15.00 per year membership

Genealogical Societies—Local & Regional

Carson City Genealogical Society
1509 Sharon Drive
Carson City, NV 89701
Michael Wittmuss

**Clark County Nevada Genealogical Society
(CCNGS)**
PO Box 1929
Las Vegas, NV 89125-1929
(702) 458-5540; (702) 225-5838 voice mail
Helen Smith, Editor
meetings: third Thur 7:00 P.M.–9:00 P.M.
Pub. *The Prospector*, quarterly (Jan, Apr,
    July, Oct), $11.00 per year subscription
$16.00 per year membership; three free
    queries per issue for members, $1.00 per
    query per issue for nonmembers; research:
    $10.00

Humboldt County Genealogical Society
Humboldt County Library
85 East Fifth Street
Winnemucca, NV 89445

Northeastern Nevada Genealogical Society
1515 Idaho Street
Elko, NV 89801
http://www.rootsweb.com/~nvnengs/
    index.html
Mrs. Primeaux, Archivist
Pub. *Chart and Quill*, quarterly

**Town of Round Mountain, Nevada
Genealogical Group**
PO Box 330
Round Mountain, NV 89045

Independent Publications and Miscellany

Clark County Heritage Museum
1830 South Boulder Highway
Henderson, NV 89015
(702) 455-7955; (702) 455-7948 FAX

http://www.co.clark.nv.us
Mark Ryzdynski, Museum Administrator
Mon–Sun 9:00–4:30
admission: $1.50 for adults

Lincoln County Museum
Pioche, NV 89043
(775) 962-5207

Lost City Museum
(721 South Moapa Valley
    Boulevard—location)
PO Box 807 (mailing address)
Overton, NV 89040
(702) 397-2193; (702) 397-8987 FAX
http://www.clan.lib.nv.us/docs/
    MUSEUMS/LOST/mus-lost.htm

Lyon County Museum
215 South Main
Yerington, NV 89447
(775) 463-2245
Rico Sacchini, Chairman
Thur–Sun 1:00–4:00, Sat (Apr–Oct)
    10:00–4:00
("Our resources are limited.")

Mineral County Museum
(10th and D Streets—location)
PO Box 1584 (mailing address)
Hawthorne, NV 89415
(775) 945-5142
Georgana Mayne, Director
Mon–Fri (summer) 11:00–5:00, Mon–Fri
    (winter) noon–4:00
("artifacts emphasis, not archival")

Nevada Department of Transportation
1263 South Stewart Street
Carson City, NV 89712
(775) 888-7627 (Maps); (775) 888-7115
    FAX
http://www.nevadadot.com/traveler/
    motorist_maps (Maps)

Nevada State Museum
Division of Museums and History
600 North Carson Street
Carson City, NV 89701
(775) 687-4810, ext. 239
Bob Nylen, Curator of History
8:30–4:30
Pub. *Nevada State Museum Newsletter*, six
    times per year
("History, geology, former U.S. mint, ghost
    town, mine replica.")
$25.00 per year membership

NVGenWeb
Part of The USGenWeb Project
(702) 397-2729
legacy@comnett.net
http://www.rootsweb.com/~nvgenweb
Patricia Scott, State Coordinator
hours: 24/7
("Nevada genealogical and research site
    which has links to all counties, vital
    records, census transcriptions, tax lists,
    surnames, newspapers, libraries, societies,
    places in Nevada, mines, articles, links to
    other Nevada sites.")

Sparks Heritage Foundation/Museum
820 Victorian Avenue
Sparks, NV 89431
(775) 355-1144

White Pine Public Museum
2000 Aultman Street
Ely, NV 89301
(775) 289-4710

New Hampshire

Archives and Libraries with Holdings in Genealogy

State Archives and Library

**New Hampshire Division of Records
Management and Archives**
Department of State
71 South Fruit Street
Concord, NH 03301-2410
(603) 271-2236; (603) 271-2272 FAX
fmevers@sos.state.nh.us
http://www.sos.nh.gov/archives
Frank C. Mevers, Ph.D., Director and State
    Archivist
Mon–Fri 8:00–4:30
(census records: 1732, 1744, 1767, 1776,
    1850–1880; court records: Inferior Court
    of Common Pleas to 1771, Rockingham
    County Court Records, 19th-century name
    change index; deed records: 224 volumes
    to about 1824; military records: French
    and Indian War papers, Revolutionary War
    rolls, Civil War, Spanish-American War;
    petitions to the Executive and Council and
    to the General Court; probate records to
    1771; town papers, court and probate
    records to ca 1900 for the counties of
    Grafton, Cheshire, Hillsborough,
    Merrimack, and Rockingham)

New Hampshire State Library
20 Park Street
Concord, NH 03301-6314
(603) 271-6823 (Genealogy Desk); (603)
    271-6826 FAX
tepare@library.state.nh.us
http://www.nh.gov/nhsl
Mon–Fri 8:00–4:30
Pub. *Genealogical Sources in New
    Hampshire*, irregularly (updated every two
    or three years), $1.00
(New Hampshire resources, including index
    to early town records, census indexes,
    town histories, family genealogies, etc.)

State Historical Societies

**Association of Historical Societies of New
Hampshire**
14 Ironwood Lane
Atkinson, NH 03811-2706
Mrs. P. M. Ilsley, Corresponding Secretary
meetings: fourth Sat 10:00–3:00
Pub. *The Associate*, four times per year (Apr,
    June, Aug, Oct)
(includes most of the historical societies in
    New Hampshire)
$5.00 per year membership

**New Hampshire Division of Historical
Resources**
PO Box 2043
Concord, NH 03301
(603) 271-3483
R. Stuart Wallace, Ph.D., Director/State
    Historic Preservation Officer
(not genealogical)

New Hampshire Historical Society
Tuck Library
30 Park Street
Concord, NH 03301-6384
(603) 228-6688; (603) 224-0463 FAX; (603)
    228-6308 (Museum)
jdesmarais@nhhistory.org
http://nhhistory.org;
    http://nhhistory.org/museum.html
(Museum of New Hampshire History, 6

Eagle Square, Concord, NH 03301-4923)
William Copeley, Librarian
Tue–Sat 9:30–5:00; Museum: Tue–Wed &
Fri–Sat 9:30–5:00, Thur 9:30–8:30, Sun
noon–5:00, Mon (1 July–15 Oct & Dec)
9:30–5:00
Pub. *New Hampshire Historical Society
Newsletter*, quarterly; *Historical New
Hampshire*, two times per year, no
subscription
("The largest collection of genealogical
sources in northern New England. Library
catalog of 50,000 items is part of web
site.")
$30.00 per year membership; admission:
$6.00 for nonmembers; museum
admission: charge for nonmembers

**City, County and Regional Archives and
Libraries**
(A more exhaustive list of public and
academic libraries can be found at http://
www.publiclibraries.com/newhampshire.
htm.)

Acworth Silsby Free Library
(Town Common, 1 Cold Pond
Road—location)
PO Box 179 (mailing address)
Acworth, NH 03601
(603) 835-2150
acworthl@sover.net
http://www.sover.net/~acworthl
Barbara Davis, Administrator
Tue, Thur & Sun 1:00–4:00
(local history and genealogy)

Barrington Public Library
Community Building, Star Route
39 Province Lane
Barrington, NH 03825
(603) 664-9715; (603) 664-5219 FAX
blibrary@metrocast.net
http://www.barringtonlibrary.com
Mon & Wed 10:00–4:30 & 7:00–9:00, Tue &
Thur–Fri 10:00–4:30, Sun 2:00–4:30

Bennington Museum
(see Vermont, Part 2)

George Holmes Bixby Memorial Library
(52 Main Street—location)
PO Box 69 (mailing address)
Francestown, NH 03043
(603) 547-2730

Bridge Memorial Library
Walpole Town Library
(48 Main Street—location)
PO Box 487 (mailing address)
Walpole, NH 03608-0487
(603) 756-9806; (603) 756-3308
(Librarian/Historian)
Virginia H. Putnam
Wed & Sat 2:00–4:00, Sun (June–Sept)
2:00–4:00, and by appointment

Canterbury Shaker Village
288 Shaker Road
Canterbury, NH 03224

Chichester Town Library
(161 Main Street, Chichester, NH
03258—location)
PO Box 582 (mailing address)
Chichester, NH 03263
(603) 798-5613; (603) 798-5439 FAX

Conant Public Library
(111 Main Street—location)
PO Box 6 (mailing address)
Winchester, NH 03470

(603) 239-4331
conantstaff@cheshire.net
http://adam.cheshire.net/~conantlibrary

Concord Public Library
45 Green Street
Concord, NH 03301
(603) 225-8670; (603) 230-3693 FAX
library@ci.concord.nh.us
http://www.onconcord.com/library
winter: Mon–Wed 9:30–8:30, Thur–Sat
9:30–5:30, Sun 1:00–5:00; summer:
Mon–Tue 9:30–8:30, Wed–Fri 9:30–5:30,
Sat 9:30–2:00
(Concord history collection)

Connecticut Valley Historical Museum
(see Massachusetts, Part 2)

Conway Public Library
The Nella Braddy Henney History Room
(15 Main Street—location)
PO Box 2100 (mailing address)
Conway, NH 03818
(603) 447-5552; (603) 447-6921 FAX
info@conway.lib.nh.us; conwaypl@ncla.net;
henneyhr@hotmail.com;
demerson@conway.lib.nh.us
http://www.conwayhistory.org/history_
room.html
David Emerson, Curator of Special
Collections
Library: Mon–Thur 10:30–8:30, Fri–Sat
10:30–5:30; History Room: Mon–Tue
10:00-5:00, Wed 5:30-8:30
(local history, town reports, family
genealogies of the area: Androscoggin
Valley, Brownfield, Gorham, Fryeburg,
Saco and Biddeford, Limington, Old
Kittery, and Parsonfield, Maine; Albany,
Antrim, Bethlehem, Carroll County,
Chester and Alburn, Concord, Coos
County, Conway, Dover, Dublin, Dun-
barton, Dunstable, Durham, Derry, Eaton,
Freedom, Jackson (Gilman's Location
only), Henniker, Jefferson, Keene,
Laconia, Lancaster, Londonderry,
Madison, Manchester, Orford, Pembroke,
Peterborough, Portsmouth, Randolf,
Stratham, Tamworth, Waterville Valley.)

Cook Memorial Library
(93 Main Street—location)
PO Box 249 (mailing address)
Tamworth, NH 03886
(603) 323-8510; (603) 323-2077 FAX
cooklib@ncia.net
http://www.Tamworth.lib.nh.us
Jay Rancourt, Library Director
Tue 10:00–8:00, Wed 1:00–8:00, Fri–Sat
10:00–4:00
copy costs

Dartmouth College
Baker Memorial Library
Hinman Box 6025
Hanover, NH 03755-3590
(603) 646-2704 (Reference); (603) 646-0931
(Reference); (603) 646-2037 (Special
Collections)
baker.library.reference@dartmouth.edu
http://www.dartmouth.edu
Robert D. Jaccaud, Genealogy Bibliographer;
Anne M. Ostendarp, Archivist
Reference: Mon–Thur 8:00 A.M.–10:00 P.M.,
Fri 8:00–6:00, Sat 9:00–6:00, Sun
1:00–10:00 (hours change); Special
Collections: Mon–Fri 8:00–4:30

Dover Public Library
73 Locust Street
Dover, NH 03820

(603) 516-6050; (603) 516-6053 FAX
http://www.dover.lib.nh.us
Carolyn Tremblay, Reference Librarian
Mon–Wed 9:00–8:30, Thur–Fri 9:00–5:30,
Sat (June–Aug) 9:00–1:00, Sat
(Sept–May) 9:00–5:00, Sun (Sept–Apr)
1:00–5:00
("We will attempt to answer date-specific
inquiries, but due to staffing limitations,
we cannot provide extensive research.")

Exeter Public Library
10 Chestnut Street
1 Founders Park
Exeter, NH 03833
(603) 772-3101
epl@exeterpl.org
http://www.exeterpl.org
Pamela Gjettum, Head Librarian; Nancy C.
Merrill, Reference Librarian
Mon–Thur 10:00–8:00, Fri–Sat 10:00–5:00

Fiske Free Library
108 Broad Street
Claremont, NH 03743
(603) 542-7017
csanborn@fiske.lib.nh.us
http://www.fiske.lib.nh.us
Colin Sanborn, Reference Historical
Librarian
Mon–Tue & Thur 9:00–7:00, Wed
9:00–5:00, Fri 11:00–5:00
Pub. *Genealogy and Local History at the
Fiske Free Library*, as required, $10.00
research: $25.00 per request for
genealogy/history

George Gamble Library
(Route 104—location)
PO Box 209 (mailing address)
Danbury, NH 03230-0209
(603) 768-9833
Janet McGonigle, Library Director/Librarian
Sat noon–4:00

Gay-Kimball Public Library
(10 South Main Street—location)
PO Box 837 (mailing address)
Troy, NH 03465
(603) 242-7743 voice & FAX
troylibrary@ptcnh.net
Darcy Doyle, Director
Tue–Thur 1:30–7:30, Sat 11:00–3:00

Gilsum Public Library
(Main Street—location)
PO Box 57 (mailing address)
Gilsum, NH 03448-0057
(603) 357-0320

Haynes Memorial Library
(33 Washburn Road—location)
567 Washburn Road (mailing address)
Alexandria, NH 03222
(603) 744-8987; (603) 744-6529
frannan@worldpath.net

Keene Public Library
Wright Room
60 Winter Street
Keene, NH 03431
(603) 352-0157; (603) 352-1101 FAX
bjwahl@ci.keene.nh.us
http://www.ci.keene.nh.us/library
David Howlett, Reference Librarian; B.J.
Wahl, Collection Development Librarian
Mon–Thur 9:00–9:00, Fri 9:00–6:00, Sat
(winter) 9:00–5:00, Sat (summer)
9:00–1:00
(emphasis on New Hampshire genealogy and
history; much of the Wright Room
collection has been moved to the

Historical Society of Cheshire County)

Keene State College
Mason Library
Preston Collection
Keene, NH 03431
(603) 352-1909, ext. 248
Robert J. Madden
hours: various, call ahead

Laconia Public Library
695 Main Street
Laconia, NH 03246
(603) 524-4775; (603) 527-1277 FAX
staff@worldpath.net
http://www.laconialibrary.org
Betty Derby

Lane Memorial Library
2 Academy Avenue
Hampton, NH 03842-2280
(603) 926-3368; (603) 926-1348 FAX
bteschek@hampton.lib.nh.us (Local History
    and Genealogy)
http://www.hampton.lib.nh.us

Leach Library
268 Mammoth Road
Londonderry, NH 03053
(603) 432-1132
leachlibrary@londonderry.org
http://www.londonderry.org
Research History Room: Mon–Fri 9:00–8:00,
    Sat 9:00–5:00

Manchester City Library
New Hampshire Room
Carpenter Memorial Building
405 Pine Street
Manchester, NH 03104-6199
(603) 624-6550, ext. 306
Coneil@ci.manchester.nh.us
http://www.manchester.lib.nh.us (under
    heading "New Hampshire Room")
Cynthia N. O'Neil
Labor Day to mid-June: Mon 8:30–12:30 &
    5:30–8:30, Tue–Thur 1:30–5:30, Fri
    8:30–5:30, Sat (Labor Day to mid-June)
    8:30–5:30
(emphasis on Manchester and New
    Hampshire local history and genealogy)
limited research by mail for a fee; no inter-
    library loans

Mansfield Public Library
(5 Main Street—location)
PO Box 210 (mailing address)
Temple, NH 03084
(603) 878-3100
mansfield@tellink.net
Priscilla Weston, Director
Mon, Wed & Fri 1:30–5:00, Tue 10:00–noon
    & 1:00–5:30, Wed 7:00–9:00, Sat
    2:00–5:00

Byron G. Merrill Library
(10 Buffalo Road—location)
PO Box 60 (mailing address)
Rumney, NH 03266
(603) 786-9520
rumneylibrary@adelphia.net
Tue & Thur 2:00–5:00 & 6:30–8:00, Sat
    10:00–noon

Moultonborough Public Library
(4 Holland Street—location)
PO Box 150 (mailing address)
Moultonborough, NH 03254
(603) 476-8895
Jane Rice, Assistant Librarian
Mon & Wed 1:00–8:00, Fri 10:00–6:00, Sat
    10:00–5:00; July–Aug: Tue & Sat

10:00–1:00
("We have some local history and genealogy
    information, which we are working to
    expand.")

Mount Caesar Union Library
628 Old Home Street
East Swanzey, NH 03446
(603) 357-0456
Ruth Palm, Director
Mon–Thur 1:00–5:00 & 6:30–9:00, Tue &
    Thur 9:30–11:30

Nashua Public Library
2 Court Street
Nashua, NH 03060-3475
(603) 594-3412; (603) 594-3457 FAX
http://www.gonashua.com
Mon–Fri 8:30 A.M.–9:00 P.M., Sat
    (Sept–June) 8:30–5:30, Sun (Sept–Apr)
    1:00–5:00

**Town of New Castle Archives and Records
Committee**
(Town Office, 49 Main Street—location)
PO Box 367 (mailing address)
New Castle, NH 03854
Eugene W. Morrill, Town Historian
by appointment only
(records dating from 1693, some incomplete;
    New Castle, formerly Great Island, was
    the early site of New Hampshire
    provincial government)
inquiries answered as time is available, must
    be accompanied by SASE

**New Durham Archives and Historical
Collections**
(Town Hall, Main Street, and New Durham
    Library, 2 Old Bay Road—location)
PO Box 207 (mailing address)
New Durham, NH 03855-0207
(603) 859-6881; (603) 859-2091 (Town
    Hall); (603) 859-2201 (Library)
Eloise Bickford, Town Historian
hours: various
("New Durham genealogy and New Durham
    history, photos, Civil War letters from
    New Durham residents; the collection is
    stored in both the Town Hall vault and the
    New Durham Library.")
research: $5.00, depending on scope and
    quantity

New Hampshire Farm Museum, Inc.
PO Box 644
Milton, NH 03851

New Hampshire Votech College
Library
2020 Riverside Drive
Berlin, NH 03570
(603) 752-1113

North Hampton Public Library
237A Atlantic Avenue
North Hampton, NH 03862-2313
(603) 964-6326; (603) 964-1107 FAX
nhpl@nhplib.org
http://www.nhplib.org
Pam Schwotzer, Director

Ohoopee Regional Library
(see Georgia, Part 2)

Old Store Museum Society of South Sutton
PO Box 462
South Sutton, NH 03273

Pelham Public Library
5 Main Street
Pelham, NH 03076

(603) 635-7581 voice & FAX
library@pelham-nh.com
http://www.pelham-nh-com/library

Pillsbury Free Library
18 East Main Street
Warner, NH 03278
(603) 456-2289; (603) 456-3177 FAX
info@warner.lib.nh.us
http://www.warner.lib.nh.us
Tue & Thur 9:00–noon & 1:00–8:00, Wed
    1:00–5:00, Sat 9:00–2:00

Portsmouth Athenaeum
(6-8 Market Square—public entrance
    location)
9 Market Square (mailing address)
Portsmouth, NH 03801
(603) 431-2538
Jane Porter, Keeper
Tue & Thur 1:00–4:00, Sat 10:00–4:00
(Piscataqua region history)

Portsmouth Public Library
8 Islington Street
Portsmouth, NH 03801
(603) 427-1540 (Main Desk); (603) 766-1720
    (Reference)
scpridham@lib.cityofportsmouth.com
http://cityofportsmouth.com/Library
Sherm Pridham, Director
Mon–Thur 9:00–9:00, Fri 9:00–5:30, Sat
    9:00–5:00

Philip Read Memorial Library
1088 Route 12A
Plainfield, NH 03781
(603) 675-6866
plfdlib@cyberportal.net
http://homepage.fcgnetworks.net/plfdlib
Nancy Norwalk, Librarian
Mon & Wed 7:00 P.M.–9:00 P.M., Mon, Wed
    & Fri 1:00–5:00, Sat 9:00–noon
(Plainfield genealogy and history; files on
    Maxfield Parrish and other Cornish Art
    Colony members)
copies: 15¢ per page

Richmond Archives
(Richmond Public Library, Route 119,
    Winchester Road—location)
c/o 480 Fitzwilliam Road (mailing address)
Richmond, NH 03470
(603) 239-4598
Norma Thibodeau
by appointment
("We have town histories and several books
    on the town available for purchase.
    Archives contains approximately 10,000
    pieces of documentation on the town of
    Richmond and its inhabitants.")

Olivia Rodham Memorial Library
(Nelson, NH—location)
Rural Free Deliver, Nelson (mailing address)
Marlborough, NH 03455
(603) 847-3214
http://top.monad.net/~oliviar/index.htm

Silsby Free Public Library
(226 Main Street—location)
PO Box 307 (mailing address)
Charlestown, NH 03603
(603) 826-7793
silsby@fmis.net
http://www.keenesentinel.com/communit/
    libraries/chastown.shtml

Strawbery Banke Museum
(454 Court Street—location)
PO Box 300 (mailing address)
Portsmouth, NH 03801-0300

(603) 422-7502; (603) 433-1115 FAX
http://wwwsc.library.unh.edu/specoll/
Sbanke/homepag.htm
Roberta L. Ransley, Librarian/Archivist
Tue 10:00–1:00, Thur 1:00–4:00, and by
appointment
(5,000 books, periodicals and microfilms,
emphasis on Portsmouth)

Sugar Hill Historical Museum
(Route 117—location)
PO Box 591 (mailing address)
Sugar Hill, NH 03585
(603) 823-5336; (603) 823-8431 FAX
http://Franconianoteh.org
Jane L. Vincent, Curator
15 June–15 Oct: Thur–Sat 1:00–4:00, and by
appointment
Pub. *Newsletter*, quarterly
(history of Sugar Hill and surrounding towns,
excellent library with genealogical
material relating to early families)
$25.00 per year membership

Tucker Free Library
Tucker Free Library
(11 Western Avenue—location)
PO Box 688 (mailing address)
Henniker, NH 03243
(603) 428-3471
tuckerfree@attbi.com
http://henniker.org

University of New Hampshire
Special Collections
The University Library
18 Library Way
Durham, NH 03824-3592
(603) 862-2714 (Special Collections); (603)
862-0277 (Archives); (603) 862-2637
FAX
archives@unh.edu
http://wwwsc.library.unh.edu/specoll/
izaak.htm
Bill Ross
Mon–Fri 8:00–4:30, Sat (during the semester)
1:00–5:00
(houses the Lamson Library of the Piscataqua
Pioneers)

Westmoreland Public Library
New England Collection
33 South Village Road
Westmoreland, NH 03467
(603) 399-7750
wpla@gis.net
http://www.keenesentinel.com/communit/
libraries/westmlnd.shtml

Wolfeboro Public Library
(259 South Main Street—location)
PO Box 710 (mailing address)
Wolfeboro, NH 03894
(603) 569-2428
wolfelib@metrocast.net
http://www.worldpath.net

Historical Societies—Local and Regional

Acworth Historical Society
Acworth Silsby Free Library
Town Common, 1 Cold Pond Road
Acworth, NH 03601
honeybrook@usaexpress.net
Pegi Kish, President
(local history and genealogy)

Albany NH Historical Society
1972 Route 16
Albany, NH 03818

efwnh@ncia.net
http://www.conwayhistory.org/phl/albany.
html
Elaine Wales, President
Museum: fourth Tue in June through first
Tue in Oct: first Tue 1:00–3:00, fourth
Tue 5:00–8:00; meetings: fourth Tue
(Mar, June, Sept, Nov)

Alton Historical Society
PO Box 536
Alton, NH 03809
by appointment; meetings at Gilman Library
$5.00 per year membership

Historical Society of Amherst, New Hampshire
PO Box 717
Amherst, NH 03031-0717
jmarshal@jlc.net
Jackie Marshall, Genealogy Committee
Town Museum: Sun (July–Aug) 1:30–4:00,
and for special events, and by
appointment
Pub. *Newsletter*, bimonthly
$15.00 per year membership; research:
donation

Andover Historical Society
PO Box 167
Andover, NH 03216

Antrim Historical Society
63 Pleasant Street
Antrim, NH 03440
Nina M. Harding

Ashland Historical Society
Whipple House Museum
(14 Pleasant Street—location)
PO Box 175 (mailing address)
Ashland, NH 03217

Atkinson Historical Society
10 Academy Avenue
Atkinson, NH 03811
(603) 362-4760
Una M. Collins, President
Wed 2:00–4:00, and by appointment
volunteer, free service

Auburn Historical Society
21 Deer Neck Road
Auburn, NH 03032
Joseph R. Higgins

Barrington Historical Society
49 Mallego Road
Barrington, NH 03825
(603) 664-9551
Andrea Calef Powell, Curator and Society
Genealogist
(Barrington/Strafford, New Hampshire,
families)
$5.00 per year membership

Bedford Historical Society
24 North Amherst Road
Bedford, NH 03110

Bennington Historical Society
PO Box 50
Bennington, NH 03442

Berlin and Coos County Historical Society
(119 High Street—location)
PO Box 52 (mailing address)
Berlin, NH 03570
leclerc1@ncia.net
http://www.conwayhistory.org/phl/
berlin.html
Odetta Leclerc, Curator; Renny Morneau,

President
Moffett House Museum: Tue–Sat noon–4:00,
Wed 6:00–8:00; meetings: second Mon

Boscawen Historical Society, Inc.
(King Street—location)
PO Box 3067 (mailing address)
Boscawen, NH 03303
Cynthia A. Houston, President
Sun 2:00–4:00
(history and local family genealogy;
published town histories with genealogy
section; maintains library archives)
$5.00 per year membership

Brentwood Historical Society
(Museum, 140 Crawley Falls Road,
Brentwood, NH 03833-6203—location)
Town Office, 1 Dalton Road (mailing
address)
Brentwood, NH 03833
(603) 642-8817 (Town Office); (603) 642-
5394 (Secretary)
Ruth H. Brown, Secretary
third Sat 10:00–2:00, and by appointment
only in winter months
$5.00 per year membership

Bridgewater Historical Society
Rural Free Delivery 2, Box 390
Plymouth, NH 03264

Brookline New Hampshire Historical Society
Meetinghouse Hall
10 Main Street
Brookline, NH 03033
(603) 673-0543; (603) 673-2243 FAX
brookliner@aol.com
Peter Cook

Campton Historical Society
Rural Route 1, Box 1046
Campton, NH 03223
David Dearborn

Canaan Historical Society and Museum
Canaan Street
Canaan, NH 03741
(603) 523-4202
Judge Dan W. Fleetham, Chairman
30 May–5 Oct: Sat 1:00–4:00

Candia Historical Society
PO Box 300
Candia, NH 03034

Canterbury Historical Society
(Old Tilton Road, Canterbury
Center—location)
PO Box 81 (mailing address)
Canterbury, NH 03224
(603) 783-9030 (President); (603) 783-4702
(Curator); (603) 783-9955 (Town offices)
ecsan426@aol.com (President);
canterbrk@aol.com (Curator)
Chuck Sanborn, President; Virginia Laplante,
Curator
last Sat in May–Columbus Day weekend:
10:00–noon, last Sat in July 10:00–4:00
Pub. *Newsletter*, three times per year
("Small museum, extensive archives
including family papers and early town
papers")
$10.00 per year membership

Center Harbor Historical Society
PO Box 98
Center Harbor, NH 03226

Charlestown Historical Society
PO Box 159

Charlestown, NH 03603
Marge Reed, Archive Chair
Tue 9:00–noon
("Archives are in Town Hall, Summer Street,
Charlestown.")

Chatham Historical Society
1209 Main Road
Chatham, NH 03813
(603) 694-2099
http://www.conwayhistory.org/phl/
chatham.html
Barbara Eastman, President and Curator
Wed 1:00–4:30; meetings: third Tue
(Apr–Oct)

Historical Society of Cheshire County
Archive Center
(246 Main Street—location)
PO Box 803 (mailing address)
Keene, NH 03431
(603) 352-1895
Alan F. Rumrill, Director
Mon–Tue & Thur–Fri 9:00–4:00, Wed
9:00–9:00, Sat 9:00–noon
Pub. *Newsletter of Historical Society of
Cheshire County*, five times per year
(New Hampshire and New England
genealogical research library)
$20.00 per year membership

Chester Historical Society
(115 Hanson Road—location)
PO Box 34 (mailing address)
Chester, NH 03036
(603) 887-5767
Charles H. Frederick, Sr., President

Chichester Historical Society
Chichester Library
(Main Street—location)
PO Box 582 (mailing address)
Chichester, NH 03263
(603) 798-5613 (Library)

Claremont Historical Society, Inc.
26 Mulberry Street
Claremont, NH 03743

Cohos Historical Society
(Marion Blodgett Museum, corner of Hollow
and Bog Roads—location)
PO Box 262 (mailing address)
North Stratford, NH 03590
president@cohoshistoricalsociety.org
Vicki DeLalla
meetings: third Wed 7:00 (EST) or 6:00
(EDST)

Colebrook Area Historical Society
(10 Bridge Street—museum location)
PO Box 32 (mailing address)
Colebrook, NH 03576
(603) 237-4470
agoodrum@ncia.net
Arnold Goodrum, President
Sat (July-Sept) 10:00–2:00); meetings:
second Thur (May–Nov) 7:00
("We do not have research files. We are only
an artifacts museum.")
admission: free

Conway Historical Society
(Eastman Lord House Museum, 100 Main
Street—location)
PO Box 1949 (mailing address)
Conway, NH 03818
(603) 447-5551; (603) 447-1991 FAX
info@conwayhistory.org;
director@conwayhistory.org
http://www.conwayhistory.orgDavid
Emerson, Director/Curator

Memorial Day–Labor Day: Tue & Thur
6:00–8:00, Wed 2:00–4:00; May &
Sept–Oct by appointment; meetings:
second Tue

Cornish Historical Society
Rural Route 2, Box 416
Cornish, NH 03745
(603) 675-6003
James B. Atkinson, President
$5.00 per year membership

Dalton Historical Society
220 Union Road
Dalton, NH 03598
(603) 837-9120
tbparks@earthlink.net
http://www.geocities.com/
daltonhistoricalsociety/index.html
Terri L. Parks
meetings at Town Hall: first Thur

Deerfield Heritage Commission
60 South Road
Deerfield, NH 03037-1709
(603) 463-7151 voice & FAX
Laura C. Guinan, Chairman

Deerfield Historical Society
141 Middle Road
Deerfield, NH 03037
Ruth Sanborn

Derring Historical Society
(Derring, NH—location)
Route 1, Box 69 (mailing address)
Hillsboro, NH 03244
(603) 529-2441
Thomas J. Copadis, Treasurer

Derry Historical Society and Museum
(Adams Memorial Building, 29 West
Broadway—location)
65 Birch Street (mailing address)
Derry, NH 03038-2733
(603) 432-3188 (Home)
Ralph S. Bonner, President
by appointment only
Pub. *Newsletter*, three times per year
$10.00 life membership; research: $20.00 per
hour for work that takes more than one
hour

Dublin Historical Society
(Main Street—location)
PO Box 415 (mailing address)
Dublin, NH 03444
(603) 563-8545
John Harris, Archivist; Nancy Campbell,
Assistant Archivist
usually five days per week 9:00–noon by
appointment
Pub. *DHS Newsletter*, quarterly
$20.00–$60.00 per year membership; send
donation plus copying and mailing costs
with information requests

Dummer Historical Society
1344 East Side River Road
Dummer, NH 03588
(603) 449-6628
dccrach@ncia.net
Rachel Jewett

Dunbarton Historical Society
31 Mansion Road
Dunbarton, NH 03045
M. Mann

Durham Historic Association, Inc.
(Corner of Route 108 at Main
Street—location)

PO Box 305 (mailing address)
Durham, NH 03824
(603) 868-5560 (Curator); (603) 868-5436
(Museum)
Mrs. John Hatch, Curator
June–Sept: Mon–Fri 2:00–5:00; Sept–June:
Tue & Thur 2:00–4:00, and by
appointment
Pub. *DHA Newsletter*, four to six times per
year
(genealogical material regarding Durham,
also history of Durham, 1900–1989)
research: cost of duplication plus mail

Effingham Historical Society
(Route 153, Effingham, NH—location)
PO Box 33 (mailing address)
South Effingham, NH 03882
effinghamhs@hotmail.com
http://www.conwayhistry.org/phl/
effingham.html
Wayne R. Dalpe, President

Enfield Historical Society
(Route 4-A—location)
Route 2, Box 397 (mailing address)
Enfield, NH 03748
(603) 632-7486

Epping Historical Society
PO Box 348
Epping, NH 03042

Errol Historical Society
PO Box 225
Errol, NH 03579
(603) 482-7771
Sharon Miller

Exeter Historical Society
(47 Front Street—location)
PO Box 924 (mailing address)
Exeter, NH 03833-0924
(603) 778-2335
exhissoc@aol.com
Barbara Rimkunas, Curator
Tue, Thur & Sat (Apr–Nov) 2:00–5:00, Tue,
Thur & Sat (Dec–Mar) 2:00–4:30; part-
time staff usually available Mon & Tue
A.M., Wed & Fri all day
Pub. *Exeter Historical Society Newsletter*,
three times per year
(maps, photographs, Exeter history)
copies: 25¢ per page

Farmington Historical Society
Webster Street
Farmington, NH 03835
Ann Place

Fitzwilliam Historical Society
Amos J. Blake House, On the Common
PO Box 76
Fitzwilliam, NH 03447
Barbara Crutchley, President
Memorial Day–Columbus Day: Sat
10:00–4:00, Sun 1:00–4:00, and by
appointment
$5.00 per year membership; search: $10.00
minimum or $25.00 per hour

**Francestown Improvement and Historical
Society**
G. H. Bixby Memorial Library
52 Main Street
Francestown, NH 03043
(603) 547-2730; (603) 547-2856
Ellen Neilley
$5.00 per year membership

Franconia Heritage Museum
(operated by Franconia Area Heritage

Council, 553 Main Street)
PO Box 169 (mailing address)
Franconia, NH 03580
(603) 823-5000; (603) 823-5951 (President)
Jewell Friedman, President/Curator
Thur & Sat 1:00–4:00, and by appointment
Pub. *Franconia Heritage News*, semiannually
("Franconia area of White Mountains. One-
room research library, second floor.")
admission: donation

Franklin Historical Society
PO Box 43
Franklin, NH 03235
Carlton C. Ham, Treasurer
$5.00 per year membership

Freedom Historical Society
(Allard House and Works Museum, Old
Portland Road—location)
PO Box 548 (mailing address)
Freedom, NH 03836-0548
stoneworkscarol@msn.com
http://www.conwayhistory.org/phl/
freedom.html
Carol Foord, President
July–Aug: Sat 10:00–noon, Sun 2:00–4:00;
meetings: first Tue (Except Jan–Feb &
Aug)

**Fremont, New Hampshire, Historical
Society**
225 South Road
Fremont, NH 03044
(603) 895-4032
Matthew E. Thomas, President
museum open by appointment

Gilmanton Historical Society
PO Box 236
Gilmanton, NH 03237

Gilsum Historical Society
PO Box 205
Gilsum, NH 03448
(603) 352-8542

Goffstown Historical Society
PO Box 284
Goffstown, NH 03045

Gorham Historical Society
25 Railroad Street
Gorham, NH 03581-1638
(603) 466-5570
deichl@ncia.net
http://www.conwayhistory.org/phl/
gorham.html
Dorothy Eichel, Secretary/Membership
Director
Rail Road Museum: daily 1:00–5:00

Goshen Historical Society, Inc.
Rural Free Delivery 2, Box 177
Newport, NH 03773
(603) 863-1509
D. W. Stephan

**Grafton County Historic and Genealogy
Society**
PO Box 1163
Ashland, NH 03217

Greenland Historical Society
459 Portsmouth Avenue
Greenland, NH 03840

Hampton Historians, Inc.
3 Thomsen Road
Hampton, NH 03842
(603) 926-2111

Hampton Historical Society/Tuck Museum
(40 Park Avenue—location)
PO Box 1601 (mailing address)
Hampton, NH 03843
(603) 929-0781
Betty Moore, Director
1 June–30 Sept: Wed, Fri & Sun 1:00–4:00;
1 Oct–31 May: Wed 9:00–noon & Sun
1:00–4:00
(Hampton history, early families)
$10.00 per year membership

Hancock Historical Society
(7 Main Street—location)
PO Box 138 (mailing address)
Hancock, NH 03449
(603) 525-9379
hanhistsoc@prexar.com
Eleanor H. Amidon, Museum Director
Business: Wed 9:00–11:00
research: $15.00 for basic search

Hanover Historical Society
Webster Cottage
(32 North Main Street—location)
PO Box 142 (mailing address)
Hanover, NH 03755
(603) 643-3074 (Curator)
Joanne Pomeroy, Curator
Memorial Day to Columbus Day: Wed &
Sat–Sun 2:30–4:30
(books and furnishings related to Daniel
Webster; all genealogical and most
historical requests are referred to Baker
Memorial Library, Dartmouth College)
$10.00 per year membership

Haverhill Historical Society
Court Street, Haverhill Corner
Haverhill, NH 03765
(603) 989-3337
Mrs. John Klitgord, Curator
by appointment

Hawke Historical Society
PO Box 402
Danville, NH 03819
(603) 642-8366
Peter S. Meigs, President
by appointment
Pub. *Reminiscences*, quarterly, subscription:
$8.00 for 4 issues
(oral history, house histories, genealogies,
maps, biographies of prominent citizens,
pictures, lists of veterans, vital statistics,
traditions, journals, descriptions of
archives acquisitions, etc.)

Henniker Historical Society
(5A Maple Street Academy Hall—location)
PO Box 674 (mailing address)
Henniker, NH 03242-0674
(603) 428-6267
Martha Taylor, Archives Chair
Thur & Sat 10:00–2:00, and by appointment
$5.00 per year membership

Hill Historical Society
(265 Murray Hill Road—location)
PO Box 193 (mailing address)
Hill, NH 03243
John P. Chandler, President

Hillsborough Historical Society, Inc.
(East Washington Road—location)
PO Box 896 (mailing address)
Hillsboro, NH 03244
(603) 478-3165; (603) 478-3913 (to arrange
for tour groups of Homestead)
Robert Charron, President
President Franklin Pierce Homestead (Routes
9 and 31): June: Sat–Sun; July–Aug:
Mon–Sat 10:00–4:00, Sun 1:00–4:00;

Sept–Columbus Day: Sat 10:00–4:00, Sun
1:00–4:00; open Memorial Day weekend,
4 July, and by appointment
$3.00 per year membership

Hinsdale Historical Society
(Town Hall, Main Street—location)
PO Box 122 (mailing address)
Hinsdale, NH 03451

Holderness Historical Society
PO Box 319
Holderness, NH 03245

Hollis Historical Society
PO Box 754
Hollis, NH 03049

Hudson Historical Society, Inc.
Route 4, Derry Road
Hudson, NH 03051
(603) 882-7474; (603) 882-9522
Arlene MacIntyre, Clerk/Treasurer

Jackson Historical Society
PO Box 8
Jackson, NH 03846
(603) 383-4060
info@jacksonNHhistory.org
http://www.conwayhistory.org/phl/
jackson.html
Ronald Hill, President
Museum: Memorial Day–Labor Day:
Sat–Sun 1:00-4:00; meetings at Christmas
Farm Inn: first Wed (except Jan–Feb)

Jaffrey Historical Society, Inc.
40 Main Street
Jaffrey Civic Center
Jaffrey, NH 03452
(603) 532-6527
Tue–Fri 1:30–5:00
Pub. *Newsletter*, bimonthly
(exhibits, archives at Civic Center)

Jefferson Historical Society
(900 Presidential Highway—location)
PO Box 143 (mailing address)
Jefferson, NH 03583
jcm@ncia.net
Joe Marshall, President
Tue, Thur & Sat (Memorial Day–Columbus
Day) 11:00–2:00
$10.00 per year membership

Kensington Historical Society
Kensington Social and Public Library
126 Amesbury Road
Kensington, NH 03833
(603) 772-5022 (Library)

**Kingston Improvement and Historical
Society, Inc.**
(Church on the Plains, Main
Street—location)
PO Box 663 (mailing address)
Kingston, NH 03848
(603) 642-5419
Joyce Davies, Secretary-Treasurer
by appointment
$5.00 per year membership; research:
donation

**Laconia Historical and Museum Society,
Inc.**
PO Box 1126
Laconia, NH 03247
Warren D. Huse, Curator
Pub. *The Laconia Historian*, nine times per
year
(general collection of photos and ephemera
pertaining to Laconia, Lakeport and The

Weirs (all part of City of Laconia); has very little genealogical material, per se; however can usually locate information on persons prominent in business or professional life via microfilm copies of local newspapers, especially if date of death is provided; "genealogical inquiries are best referred to the New Hampshire State Library and New Hampshire Historical Society")
$10.00 per year membership

Lancaster Historical Society
(Wilder Holton House Museum, 226 Main Street—location)
PO Box 473 (mailing address)
Lancaster, NH 03584
(603) 788-3004
femerson@ncia.net
Myra Emerson
meetings: second Wed 2:00 (Oct–Apr) or 7:00 (May–Sept)

Lebanon Historical Society, Inc.
40 Mascoma Street
Lebanon, NH 03766-2629
(603) 448-3118
http://www.lebanonnhhistory.org
Robert H. Leavitt, Curator and City Historian
meetings in the Marion J. Carter Homestead on Colburn Park: third Mon7:00
(published *Lebanon 1761–1994*, $42.00 postpaid)

Lee Historical Society
Lee Town Hall
7 Mast Road
Durham, NH 03824
hours: various
can't always answer inquiries

Lempster Historical Society
HCR 66, Box 875
Lempster, NH 03606
Emily Fairweather

Littleton Area Historical Society
Littleton Historical Museum
1 Cottage Street
Littleton, NH 03561
(603) 444-6435
Karen Tunney, Curator
Museum: Wed (Apr–Dec) & Thur (July–Oct) 1:30–4:30, and by appointment
("Local history—specifically Saranac Glove and Kilburn Stereoptican View Co., both local enterprises")

Londonderry Historical Society
PO Box 136
Londonderry, NH 03053
(603) 432-9619; (603) 432-1132 (Leach Library)
Junie Vickers; Melvin Watts, Town Historian
Research History Room at Leach Library: Mon–Fri 9:00–8:00, Sat 9:00–5:00
$10.00 per year membership

Lyme Historical Society
Lyme, NH 03678

Madbury Historical Society
13 Town Hall Road
Madbury, NH 03820

Madison Historical Society
(East Madison Road-Madison Corner—location)
PO Box 505 (mailing address)
Madison, NH 03849
http://ci.madison.nh.us
Mary Lucy

Museum: Memorial Day to Labor Day: Tue & Sun 2:00–4:00, and by appointment; meetings: third Thur (Apr–Oct) 7:00
$5.00 per year membership

Manchester Historic Association
129 Amherst Street
Manchester, NH 03101
(603) 622-7531; (603) 622-0822 FAX
history@manchesterhistoric.org
http://www.manchesterhistoric.org
Gail Nassell Colglazier, Director
Tue–Sat 10:00–4:00, Tue–Sat (summer) 10:00–4:00
$25.00 per year membership; research: $15.00 per hour

Marlborough Historical Society, Inc.
PO Box 202
Marlborough, NH 03455

Mason Historical Society
717 Greenville Road
Mason, NH 03048
(603) 878-2918

Meredith Historical Society
PO Box 920
Meredith, NH 03253
(603) 279-6136

Merrimack Historical Society
PO Box 1525
Merrimack, NH 03054
http://Merrimackonline.com (click onto historical society)
Rosemary Gagne, President
hours: various

Milford Historical Society
(6 Union Street—location)
PO Box 609 (mailing address)
Milford, NH 03055
Polly S. Cote, President
second Sat–Sun 2:00–4:00
Pub. *M. H. S. Newsletter*, four times per year

Moultonborough Historical Society
(Route 25—location)
PO Box 659 (mailing address)
Moultonboro, NH 03254
MHSociety@msn.com
http://moultonboroughhistory.org
Jane Rice, Corresponding Secretary
Wed (July–Aug) 1:00–3:00; meetings: second Mon
Pub. *Moultonboro Historical Society*, quarterly
("Most vital records and other written materials are available.")
$8.00 per year membership

Nashua Historical Society, Inc.
5 Abbott Street
Nashua, NH 03064
(603) 883-0015; (603) 889-8515 FAX
Jodi Lowery-Tilbury Research and Records Chair
Tue–Thur 10:00–4:00, Sat 1:00–4:00, and by appointment
Pub. *Nashua Historical Society Newsletter*, three times per year
("Our library contains great sources for genealogical research as well as historical research. In addition to Florence Speare Museum and Research Facility we also have an 1802-3 Abbot/Spalding House museum.")
$25.00 per year membership

The New England Historic Genealogical Society

(see Massachusetts, Part 2)

New Hampshire Antiquarian Society
(300 Main Street—location)
Route 3, Box 251 (mailing address)
Hopkinton, NH 03229
(603) 746-3825
Rosalind P. Hanson, President

New Hampton Historical Society
PO Box 422
New Hampton, NH 03256
(603) 744-6334; (603) 744-8600 FAX
fsjr@earthlink.net
http://www.rugreview.com/nhhs/nhhsind.htm
Frederick Smith, Jr., President
summer: limited hours
Pub. *Newsletter*, three times per year
("The Society has a small museum building that holds various artifacts and some genealogical information.")
$5.00 per year membership

New London Historical Society
(Little Sunapee Road—location)
PO Box 965 (mailing address)
New London, NH 03257
(603) 526-6564
Lynne Bell, President
free guided tours July–Aug: Wed 2:00–4:00; self-guided tours anytime

New Market Historical Society
Stone School Museum
(Granite Street—location)
51 North Main Street (mailing address)
Newmarket, NH 03857
(603) 659-7420
Sylvia Fitts Getchell, Curator
Memorial Day–Labor Day: Thur 2:00–4:00

Newbury Historical Society
PO Box 176
Newbury, NH 03255

Newfields Historical Society
PO Box 126
Newfields, NH 03856

Newington Historical Society
133 Fox Point Road
Newington, NH 03801
Dorothy M. Watson

Newport Historic District Commission
15 Sunapee Street
Newport, NH 03773
(603) 863-1877; (603) 863-8008 FAX
Sharon H. Christie

Newport Historical Society, Inc.
(Courthouse Square—location)
PO Box 492 (mailing address)
Newport, NH 03773
(603) 863-2079

Northam Colonists Historical Society
55 Applevale Drive
Dover, NH 03820
B. Hennessey

Northumberland Historical Society
2 State Street
Groveton, NH 03582
(603) 636-1450
paddyd@together.net
Priscilla Doherty, President
Museum in town office: mid-June–Labor Day: 9:00-4:00; meetings at St. Mark's Episcopal Church: second Tue 6:00

Northwood Pioneer Museum and

Historical Society
PO Box 379
Northwood, NH 03261
(701) 587-5421
Harriet Foss

Nottingham Historical Society
Van Dame Museum and Research
Center/Nottingham Square Schoolhouse
PO Box 241
Nottingham, NH 03290
(603) 868-2098
Nottinghamhs@aol.com
Lisa Kennard, Liaison
Nottingham Square Schoolhouse: by
  appointment
("Our town boasts four Revolutionary War
  generals: Bartlett, Butler, Cilley and
  Dearborn. We are creating our third
  museum: Patuccoway Grange Museum.")
$3.00 per year membership; free admission

Old Fort No. 4 Associates
PO Box 336
Charlestown, NH 03603

Old Meetinghouse Historical Association
PO Box 27
Sandown, NH 03873

Ossipee Historical Society
(52 Route 16B, Center Ossipee, NH
  03814—museum location)
PO Box 245 (mailing address)
Ossipee, NH 03864
(603) 539-2404
OssipeeHistoricalSociety@groups.msn.com
http://groups.msn.com/OssipeeHistorical
  Society/_homepage.msnw
Doris W. Ashton, President
Museum: July–Aug: Tue, Thur & Sat;
  meetings: Apr–Oct: third Tue
Pub. *Ossipee Almanac*, quarterly
$5.00 per year membership

Pelham Historical Society
8 Nashua Road
Pelham, NH 03076
Peterborough Historical Society
(19 Grove Street—location)
PO Box 58 (mailing address)
Peterborough, NH 03458
(603) 924-3235; (603) 924-3200
research@peterboroughhistory.org
http://www.peterboroughhistory.org
Michelle M. Stahl, Executive Director
Mon–Fri 10:00–4:00
(Peterborough, New Hampshire, history)

Piermont Historical Society
(High Street—location)
PO Box 273 (mailing address)
Piermont, NH 03779
Joe Medlicott, President
Pub. *Piermont Record*, occasionally
("Genealogical searches limited to Piermont
  Town sources.")
$3.00 per year membership

Pittsburg Historical Society
(Museum, Main Street—location)
PO Box 2 (mailing address)
Pittsburg, NH 03592
(603) 538-6342 (Curator); (603) 538-6681
  (President)
Earl Richards, Curator; Bill Bradley,
  President
Sat (July–Aug) 1:00-3:00; meetings: fourth
  Wed (May–Nov) 7:00
admission: free

Pittsfield Historical Society

Pittsfield, NH 03263
R. C. Van Horn

Plainfield Historical Society
(Route 12A—location)
PO Box 107 (mailing address)
Plainfield, NH 03781
Nancy Norwalk, Archivist
by appointment only
(Plainfield history)
$7.00 per year membership

Plaistow Historical Society
PO Box 434
Plaistow, NH 03865

Plymouth Historical Society
Rural Free Delivery 1, Box 2695
Plymouth, NH 03264
Mrs. William Batchelder

Portsmouth Historical Society
(State and Middle Streets—location)
PO Box 728 (mailing address)
Portsmouth, NH 03802-0728
(603) 436-8420 (Seasonal)
Carl W. Brage, Genealogical Coordinator
June–Oct: daily; Nov–May: periodic

Raymond Historical Society, Inc.
PO Box 94
Raymond, NH 03077

Rindge Historical Society
South Main Street
Rindge, NH 03461

Rochester Historical Society
PO Box 65
Rochester, NH 03867
(603) 332-4426
Florence Smith, Document Custodian
2:00–4:00 & 6:00–9:00
Pub. *Newsletter*, annually
$3.00 per year membership

Rye Historical Society
PO Box 583
Rye, NH 03870

Salem Historical Society
310 Main Street
Salem, NH 03079
(603) 890-2280
Beverly Glynn, President
Mon 2:00–5:00, and by appointment;
  monthly meetings: Mar–Nov

Salisbury Historical Society
Rural Free Delivery 1, Box 1487
Racoon Hill Road
Salisbury, NH 03268
C. E. Hughes

Sanbornton Historical Society
PO Box 2
Sanbornton, NH 03269
(603) 286-7227; (603) 286-8490 (President)
Evelyn Auger, President
by appointment only; meetings Apr–Oct: first
  Wed 7:30
(local history, limited early genealogy
  information)
$10.00 per year membership

Sandown Historical Society & Museum
PO Box 300
Sandown, NH 03873
(603) 887-6100 (Depot); (603) 877-4520
  (Curator)
http://www.sandownnh.com/history
Bertha Deveaw, Curator

Sat–Sun (May–Oct) 1:00–5:00

Sandwich Historical Society
(Elisha Marston House, 4 Maple
  Street—location)
PO Box 106 (mailing address)
Center Sandwich, NH 03227-0106
(603) 284-6269 voice & FAX
sandwichhistory@fcgnetworks.net
http://www.sandwichnh.com
Craig F. Evans, Director/Curator
June–Sept: Tue–Sat 11:00–5:00
Pub. *Sandwich Historical Society—Annual
  Excursion*, annually, $9.00 per issue
$20.00 per year membership

Historical Society of Seabrook
(Washington Street—location)
PO Box 414 (mailing address)
Seabrook, NH 03874
Eric M. Small, President
("Photos, local records, salt hay farming,
  shoemaking")
$10.00 per year membership

Shelburne Heritage Commission
74 Village Road
Shelburne, NH 03581
(603) 466-2621
danforth@ncia.net
Hildreth Danforth

Somersworth Historical Society
6 Drew Road
Somersworth, NH 03878

Stoddard Historical Society
PO Box 213
Stoddard, NH 03464

Strafford Historical Society
PO Box 33
Center Strafford, NH 03815

Stratham Historical Society, Inc.
(Route #33 and Winnicutt Road—location)
PO Box 39 (mailing address)
Stratham, NH 03885
stratham@ttlc.net
http://www.strathamhistoricalsociety.org
Barbara Mann, President
Tue 9:00–11:30, Thur 2:00–4:00, first Sun
  2:00–4:00
(archives, research library [genie] museum,
  "We have an excellent Wiggin genealogy
  reference.")
$5.00 per year membership

Sutton Historical Society
PO Box 503
South Sutton, NH 03273

Tamworth Historical Society
Genealogy and History Center of the Cook
  Memorial Library
PO Box 13 (mailing address)
Tamworth, NH 03886
(603) 383-8639
kurtzwhite@TTLE.net
http://www.conwayhistory.org/phl/
  tamworth.html
Jean Ulitz, Genealogy; Kristine Kurtz-White,
  President
Tue 2:00–4:00, Sat 10:00–noon; meetings at
  Remick Country Doctor Museum and
  Farm: third Wed (Apr–Oct)
$5.00 per year membership

Tilton Historical Society
PO Box 351
Tilton, NH 03276

Tuftonboro Historical Society
PO Box 372
Melvin Village, NH 03850

Twin Mountain-Bretton Woods Historical Society
PO Box 464
Twin Mountain, NH 03595
(603) 864-5573
John R. Gardiner
meetings: first Wed 7:00

Umbagog Area Heritage Committee
c/o Umbagog Area Chamber of Commerce
PO Box 113
Errol, NH 03579
(603) 482-3884
Debbie Freedman

Wakefield-Brookfield Historical Society
(Wakefield Road—location)
PO Box 795 (mailing address)
Brookfield, NH 03872
(603) 522-6415
candlchase@hotmail.com
http://www.conwayhistory.org/phl/
wakefield.html
Carolyn Chase
Little Red Schoolhouse Museum: May–Oct:
Tue 7:30 P.M.–9:00 P.M.; meetings: second
Tue (May–Oct)

The Walpole Historical Society
(Main Street—location)
PO Box 220 (mailing address)
Walpole, NH 03608
(603) 756-3449 (June–Sept); (603) 756-
3534; (603) 756-3308
(Librarian/Historian)
Mervin Stevens, President; Virginia Putnam,
Librarian/Historian
Wed & Sat 2:00–4:00, Sun (June–Sept)
2:00–4:00, and by appointment
Pub. *Walpole Historical Society Newsletter*,
two times per year
(excellent library/family histories made
available on request for out-of-town
visitors)
$10.00 per year membership

Warner Historical Society
PO Box 189
Warner, NH 03278
(603) 456-2437
Royal Latuch, President

Warren Historical Society
PO Box 114
Warren, NH 03279

Washington Historical Society
PO Box 90
Washington, NH 03280

Weare Historical Society
PO Box 33
Weare, NH 03281

Westmoreland Historical Society
PO Box 55
Westmoreland, NH 03467

Whitefield Historical Society
(Lower level, Fleet Bank Building, Kings
Square—location)
PO Box 21 (mailing address)
Whitefield, NH 03598
(603) 837-2386 (Secretary)
Eleanor Mason, Secretary
Thur 2:00–4:00, and by appointment;
meetings: second Wed (May–Oct)
Pub. *Annual Report*

(emphasis on Whitefield and the surrounding
areas; the White Mountain region)
$5.00 per year membership

Wilmot Historical Society, Inc.
Town Office Building
Wilmot Flat, NH 03287

Wilton Historical Society
PO Box 845
Wilton, NH 03086
Gail Proctor

Wolfeboro Historical Society
Pleasant Valley Schoolhouse
PO Box 1066
Wolfeboro, NH 03894
http://www.wolfeboro.com/histsoc.htm

Genealogical Societies

State Genealogical Society

**New Hampshire Society of Genealogists
(NHSOG)**
PO Box 2316
Concord, NH 03302-2316
(603) 225-3381
Pub. *New Hampshire Society of
Genealogists' Newsletter*, quarterly; *The
New Hampshire Genealogical Record*,
quarterly, $20.00 per year subscription
$20.00 per year membership

Genealogical Societies—Local & Regional

American-Canadian Genealogical Society
(4 South Elm Street—location)
PO Box 6478 (mailing address)
Manchester, NH 03108-6478
(603) 622-1554; (603) 626-9812 FAX
Perreault832@aol.com
http://www.acgs.org
Anne-Marie Perrault, President
Wed & Fri 9:00–9:00, Sat 9:00–4:00, and by
appointment
Pub. *American-Canadian Genealogist*,
quarterly
(an international organization; primarily
French-Canadian and Franco-American
resources, vital records from all New
England and New York)
Chapter: **Father Leo Begin Chapter**,
American-Canadian Genealogical Society,
PO Box 2125, Lewiston, ME 04240
$25.00 per year membership

**Grafton County Historic and Genealogy
Society**
(see Historical Societies—Local and
Regional, above)

Merrimack Valley Society of Genealogists
(44 Pleasant Street, Concord—location)
PO Box 173 (mailing address)
Contoocook, NH 03229-0173
Mrs. James W. Moreland, President
fourth Tue (Jan, Mar, May, Sept, Nov)
Pub. *Family Traces*, quarterly
$6.00 per year membership

**The New England Historic Genealogical
Society**
(see Massachusetts, Part 2)

North County Genealogical Society
PO Box 618
Littleton, NH 03561
(603) 444-2001
Elva M. Reeg, President

Piscataqua Pioneers

9 Lindy Avenue
Claremont, NH 03743-2926
(603) 542-6513
Alice C. Haubrich, Curator
(Lamson Library of the Piscataqua Pioneers is
housed at University of New Hampshire)

Rockingham Society of Genealogists
(Exeter Public Library—location)
PO Box 81 (mailing address)
Exeter, NH 03833-0081
(603) 436-5824
Carl W. Brage, Editor
Pub. *Kinship Kronicle*, quarterly (Mar, June,
Sept, Dec), $8.50 per year subscription
$15.00 per year membership

Strafford County Genealogical Society
PO Box 322
Dover, NH 03820
(603) 664-9090 (President's home)
Hal Inglis, President
Dover Public Library: Mon–Wed 9:00–8:30,
Thur–Fri 9:00–5:30, Sat (winter)
9:00–5:00, (summer) 9:00–1:00
Pub. *The Genealogical Record*, bimonthly
$12.00 per year membership

Yankee Genealogical Society
Minnesota Genealogical Society
(see Massachusetts, Part 2)

Independent Publications and Miscellany

Belknap Mill Society
Mill Plaza
Laconia, NH 03246
(603) 524-8813

Center for Appalachian Studies
(see North Carolina, Part 2)

Harold Gilman Historical Museum
PO Box 428
Alton, NH 03809
A. Haase

Historic Harrisville, Inc.
Church Hill
Harrisville, NH 03450
(603) 827-3722 (to leave message)
Mary Meath, Archives Director

Historical Ink's Old Maps
(see New York, Part 2)

New England Connexion
(see Connecticut, Part 2)

The New England Quarterly
(see Massachusetts, Part 2)

New Hampshire Legacy Magazine
(603) 883-3344
publisher@nh.com
http://www.nh.com/legacy/index.shtml
Pub. *New Hampshire Legacy Magazine*

**New Hampshire Old Graveyard
Association (NHOGA)**
8 Great Pond Road
Kingston, NH 03848-3747
(603) 642-5419
Joyce Davies, Corresponding Secretary
Pub. *Rubbings*, three times per year (May,
July, Sept)
(has name and date records from a few New
Hampshire towns, but can seldom assist
with genealogical queries, but does have a
good list of contacts in each town;

published *Graveyard Restoration Handbook*, $2.00 postpaid)
$5.00 per year membership

New Hampshire Department of Transportation
John O. Morton Building
1 Hazen Srive
Concord, NH 03302-0483
(603) 271-3734; (603) 271-3914 FAX
webmaster@dot.state.nh.us
http://webster.state.nh.us/dot/traveler/
 planning/travelplanning.htm (Trip
 Planning and Maps & Tools)

NHGenWeb
Part of The USGenweb Project
james@usroots.com; Mainegen@aol.com
http://www.rootsquest.com/~usgwnhus
James A. Streeter, State Coordinator; David
 Colby Young, Assistant Coordinator
(links to other New Hampshire resources)

The Old Man of the Mountains
Cannon Mountain
Franconia Notch, NH 03580
(603) 823-5563
http://mutha.com/oldmanmt.html
(historic photographs)

The Pierce Brigade
(14 Penacook Street—location)
PO Box 425 (mailing address)
Concord, NH 03302
(603) 224-7668 (House Chairman)
Anna Avery, House Chairman
15 June–Labor Day: 11:00–3:00, and by
 appointment
Pub. *Franklin Pierce Times*, quarterly,
 $11.50 per year subscription
(house museum, primarily historical not
 genealogical)
from $5.00 per year membership; admission:
 $2.00 for adults

Pioneer Publications
New England Queries and Reviews
(see Connecticut, Part 2)

Plymouth Historical Museum
Court Street
Plymouth, NH 03264
(603) 536-2337

Society for the Preservation of New England Antiquities—Archives
(see Massachusetts, Part 2)

Remick Country Doctor Museum and Farm
(58 Cleveland Hill Road—location)
Tamworth, NH 03886
(603) 323-7591
remick.foundation@rsc.net
http://www.remickmuseum.orgRobert C.
 Cottrell, Director
Mon–Fri 10:00–4:00, Sat (July–Aug)
 10:00–4:00, Wed–Sat (8 July–29 Aug)
 6:00–8:00

Woodman Institute
PO Box 146
Dover, NH 03821-0146
(603) 742-1038

Part 2. New Jersey

New Jersey

Archives and Libraries with Holdings in Genealogy

State Archives and Library

New Jersey State Archives
(225 West State Street, Level 2—location)
PO Box 307 (mailing address)
Trenton, NJ 08625-0307
(609) 292-6260; (609) 530-3200 (Records
 Center); (609) 396-2454 FAX
archives.reference@sos.state.nj.us
http://www.njarchives.org
Bette Epstein, Supervisor of Reference
 Service
Tue–Fri 8:30–4:30
transcripts of vital statistics, 1848–1878:
 $4.00 plus $1.00 per page for copies sent
 by mail

State Historical Societies

Association of New Jersey County Cultural and Heritage Agencies
c/o Camden County Cultural and Heritage
Commission
Hopkins House
250 South Park Drive
Haddon Township, NJ 08108
(856) 858-0040

League of Historical Societies of New Jersey
PO Box 909
Madison, NJ 07940
(201) 377-7023
bhunte@camden.lib.nj.us
http://www.lhsnj.org
Robert J. Hunter, President
(primarily historical, not genealogical)

New Jersey Historical Commission
(225 West State Street—location)
PO Box 305 (mailing address)
Trenton, NJ 08625-0305
(609) 292-6062; (609) 633-8168 FAX
NJHC@sos.state.nj.us
http://www.state.nj.us/state/history/
 hisidx.html
MarcMappen, Executive Director
8:30–4:30
Pub. *New Jersey Historical Commission
 Newsletter*, quarterly, $4.00 per year
 subscription
(ethnic history in New Jersey)

New Jersey Historical Society Library
52 Park Place
Newark, NJ 07102
(973) 596-8500, ext. 248 (Reference
 Librarian); (973) 596-8500, ext. 249
 (Reading Room); (973) 596-8500, ext.
 240 (Library Director); (973) 596-6957
 FAX
Info@jerseyhistory.org
http://www.jerseyhistory.org
Chad Leinaweaver, Library Director
Library: Tue–Sat noon–5:00
Pub. *New Jersey History*, two times per year
$25.00 per year membership (includes
 membership in Genealogy Club of the
 Library of the New Jersey Historical
 Society)

City, County and Regional Archives and Libraries
(A more exhaustive list of public and
academic libraries can be found at http://
www2.njstatelib.org/njlib/ref/njlibs.htm.)

Asbury Park Public Library
500 First Avenue
Asbury Park, NJ 07712
(732) 774-4221; (732) 988-6101 FAX
info@asburypark.lib.nj.us
http://www.asburypark.lib.nj.us
Mon–Wed 11:00–8:00, Thur 9:00–5:00,
 Fri–Sat noon–5:00

Atlantic City Free Public Library
(see Atlantic County Historical Society,
Historical Societies—Local and Regional,
below)

Atlantic County Library
Reference Center/New Jersey Collection
2 South Farragut Avenue
Mays Landing, NJ 08330
(609) 625-2776, ext. 310; (609) 626-8699;
 (609) 625-8143 FAX
wpaullin@acmail.aclink.org (William D.
 Paullin, Director);
 director@acmail.aclink.org
http://commlink.atlantic.county.lib.nj.us/
 aclsref.htm
Louisa C. Mazetis, Principal Librarian
Mon–Thur 9:00–9:00, Fri–Sat 9:00–5:00
(very limited collection)

Belleville Public Library and Information Center
221 Washington Avenue
Belleville, NJ 07109-3189
(973) 450-3434; (973) 450-9518 FAX
belleville_reference@nplhub.org
http://www.intac.com/~bplibn/hpfront.htm

Bloomfield Public Library
90 Broad Street
Bloomfield, NJ 07003
(973) 566-6200
BPLreference@yahoo.com
http://www.bloomfieldtwpnj.com/library.
 html
Mon–Wed 10:00–9:00, Thur–Fri 10:00–5:00,
 Sat (except summer) 9:00–1:00

Boonton Holmes Public Library
621 Main Street
Boonton, NJ 07005
(973) 334-2980; (973) 334-3917 FAX
boonton621library@hotmail.com
http://www.boonton.org/library/index.htm
Mon & Thur 10:00–9:00, Tue & Fri
 10:00–6:00, Wed 1:00–9:00, Sat
 10:00–3:00

Bradley Beach Library
511 Fourth Avenue
Bradley Beach, NJ 07720
(732) 776-2995; (732) 774-4591 FAX
kjklapperstuck@hotmail.com
http://www.bradleybeachlibrary.org
Karen J. Klapperstuck, Director
Mon noon–5:00, Mon (summer) 9:00–3:00,
 Tue & Thur noon–8:00; Wed & Fri
 9:00–5:00, Wed & Fri (summer)
 9:00–3:00, Sat 9:00–noon

Bridgeton Free Public Library
Woodruff Museum of Indian Artifacts
150 East Commerce Street
Bridgeton, NJ 08302
(856) 451-2620; (856) 455-1049 FAX
bpl@clueslibs.org
http://www.clueslibs.org/information/bpl/
 default.htm
Patricia W. McCulley, Director
Mon–Thur 10:00–9:00, Fri 10:00–5:00, Sat
 (Sept–May) 10:00–4:00, Sat (June–Aug)
 10:00–2:00
(20,000 artifacts from the Leni Lenape

Indians)

Brookdale Community College
Learning Resource Center
765 Newman Springs Road
Lincroft, NJ 07738
(732) 224-2706

Burlington County Library
5 Pioneer Boulevard
Westampton, NJ 08060
(609) 267-9660 (Reference Desk #2); (609)
   267-3971 FAX
http://www.burlco.lib.nj.us
Paula Marzella, Reference Librarian
Mon–Thur & Fri (Sept–June) 9:00–9:00, Fri
   (July–Aug) & Sat 9:00–5:00, Sun
   (Sept–June) 1:00–5:00

**Camden County Cultural and Heritage
Commission**
Hopkins House
250 South Park Drive
Haddon Township, NJ 08108
(856) 858-0040
maureen@camden.lib.nj.us
http://arts.camden.lib.nj.us
Gail Greenberg, Executive Director
Mon–Fri 9:00–4:00 (review of documents by
   appointment only, through Executive
   Director, index available)
(collection of original pioneer documents,
   Camden County history)

Camden County Library System
Echelon Urban Center
203 Laurel Road
Voorhees, NJ 08043
(856) 772-1636; (856) 772-6105 FAX
karen@camden.lib.nj.us
http://www.camden.lib.nj.us
Karen Avenick, Assistant Director
Mon–Fri 10:00–9:00, Sat 10:00–6:00, Sun
   1:00–5:00 (July–Aug: closed Sun)

Campbell Museum
Campbell Place
Camden, NJ 08103
(609) 342-6440

Cape May County Library
(30 West Mechanic Street—location)
4 Moore Road, DN 2030 (mailing address)
Cape May Court House, NJ 08210
(609) 463-6352; (609) 463-6313
lisab@Cape-may.County.lib.nj.us
http://www.Cape-may.County.lib.nj.us
Lisa Brownback, Librarian
Mon–Fri 8:30–9:00, Sat 9:00–4:30

Centenary College
Taylor Memorial Learning Resource Center
400 Jefferson Street
Hackettstown, NJ 07840-2100
(908) 852-1400, ext. 243
http://www.centenarycollege.edu/
   ce07000.html

Library of the Chathams
214 Main Street
Chatham, NJ 07928
(973) 635-0603
obrien@main.morris.org
http://www.chatham-
   nj.org/coin/chatlib/library.html
Diane O'Brien, Director
Mon–Thur 9:30–9:00, Fri 9:30–6:00, Sat
   9:30–5:00, Sun 2:00–5:00

Clark Public Library
303 Westfield Avenue
Clark, NJ 07066-1790
(908) 388-5999; (908) 388-7866 FAX

ref@clarklibrary.org
http://www.clarklibrary.org
Elaine Wade, Reference Librarian
winter: Mon & Wed–Thur 10:00–9:00, Tue
   & Fri 10:00–5:00, Sat 10:00–4:00;
   summer: Mon & Thur 10:00–9:00,
   Tue–Wed & Fri 10:00–5:00
$25.00 fee for nonresidents provides
   restricted borrowing privileges

Dennis Memorial Library
101 Main Street
Newton, NJ 07860
(973) 383-4810
bradshaw@hublib.lib.nj.us
http://www.sussexcountylibrary.org
Jennifer Bradshaw, Branch Librarian

East Brunswick Museum Corporation
(16 Maple Street—location)
PO Box 875 (mailing address)
East Brunswick, NJ 08816
(732) 257-1508
Mark Nonestied, President
Sat–Sun 1:30–4:00
("We welcome your inquiries!")
$15.00 per year membership; museum
   admission: free

East Orange Public Library
21 South Arlington Avenue
East Orange, NJ 07018
(973) 266-5613; (973) 674-1991 FAX
http://www.eopl.org
J. Robert Starkey
Mon–Tue & Thur 9:00–9:00, Wed
   9:00–6:00, Fri 10:00–6:00, Sat 9:00–5:00
(East Orange local history)

Easton Area Public Library
(see Pennsylvania, Part 2)

Edison Public Library
340 Plainfield Avenue
Edison, NJ 08817
(732) 287-2298; (908) 819-9134 FAX
jellmans@lmxac.org
http://www.lmxac.org/edisonlib/index.html
Judith Mansbach, Reference Librarian
winter: Mon–Thur 9:00–9:00, Fri–Sat
   9:00–5:00; summer: Mon–Wed
   9:00–9:00, Thur–Fri 9:00–5:00

Fairleigh Dickinson University
New Jersey Room
Messler Library
Madison, NJ 07940
(973) 443-8515 (Library); (973) 443-8500
   (Madison Campus)
Richard Goerner
Library: Mon–Thur 8:30 A.M.–10:00 P.M.,
   Fri 8:30–5:00, Sat 11:00–5:00, Sun
   1:00–9:00; New Jersey Room: Mon 8:30
   A.M.–9:00 P.M., Wed–Thur 8:30–6:00, Fri
   8:30–5:00

Hackettstown Free Public Library
110 Church Street
Hackettstown, NJ 07840
(908) 852-4936; (908) 852-7850 FAX
hfplinfo@goes.com
http://www.goes.com/hfplinfo
Mon–Thur 10:00–9:00, Fri 10:00–5:00, Sat
   9:00–noon
(local history)

Haddonfield Public Library
60 Haddon Avenue
Haddonfield, NJ 08033
(856) 429-1304; (856) 429-3760 FAX
dbr@camden.lib.nj.us
http://www.haddonfield.camden.lib.nj.us

Douglas B. Rauschenberger, Director
Mon–Fri 10:00–9:00, Sat 10:00–5:00, Sun
   1:00–5:00 (closed Fri evenings & Sun in
   July & Aug)

Hamilton Township Public Library
1 Municipal Drive
Trenton, NJ 08619
(609) 890-3460
Mon–Thur 9:00–8:30, Fri–Sat 9:00–5:00

Hunterdon County Library
314 State Route 12, Building 3
Flemington, NJ 08822
(908) 788-1444
http://www.hunterdon.lib.nj.us/branches/
   members.htm
Amanda Philipp, Reference Supervisor
Mon–Fri 8:30 A.M.–9:00 P.M., Sat 9:00–5:00
(Jerseyana collection has approximately 700
   volumes)

Irvington Public Library
Civic Square
Irvington, NJ 07111-2498
(973) 372-6400; (973) 372-6860; (973) 372-
   6054
Joan Weiss, Head of Reference
Mon–Tue & Thur 9:00–9:00, Wed & Fri
   9:00–5:30, Sat (mid-Sept to mid-June)
   9:00–5:00

Jersey City Public Library
New Jersey Room
472 Jersey Avenue
Jersey City, NJ 07302
(201) 547-4503; (201) 521-1669 FAX
http://www.jclibrary.org
Cynthia T. Harris, Librarian, Department
   Manager, New Jersey Room
Mon, Wed & Fri–Sat 9:00–5:00, Tue & Thur
   9:00–8:00
(city directories, New Jersey census records,
   local newspaper index, local and state
   history)

Johnson Free Public Library
275 Moore Street
Hackensack, NJ 07601
(201) 343-4169
taffe@bccls.org
http://www.bccls.org/hackensack
Val Clark, Head of Reference; Maureen
   Taffe, Director
Mon–Thur 9:00–8:45, Fri–Sat 9:00–4:45

Kearny Museum
318 Kearny Avenue
Kearny, NJ 07032
(201) 997-6911

Kinnelon Public Library
132 Kinnelon Road
Kinnelon, NJ 07405
(973) 838-1321; (973) 838-0741 FAX
vioreanu@main.morris.org
http://kinnelonlibrary.org
Judy Vioreanu
Mon 10:00–6:00, Tue–Thur 10:00–8:00, Fri
   10:00–5:00, sat 10:00–4:00

**Lebanon Township Museum at New
Hampton**
57 Musconetcong River Road
Hampton, NJ 08827
(908) 537-6464
Joan Lucas, Curator
Tue & Thur 9:30–5:00, Sat 1:00–5:00
Pub. *The Slate*, two times per year
(local genealogy)

Little Falls Public Library

8 Warren Street
Little Falls, NJ 07424
(973) 256-2784
dyan@palsplus.org (Webmaster)
http://www.palsplus.org/lfpl
Patricia Pelak, Acting Director
Mon–Thur 10:00–9:00, Fri 10:00–5:00, Fri
   (summer) 10:00–3:00, Sat (except
   summer) 10:00–3:00
(home of Little Falls Township Historical
   Society, but only limited genealogy
   resources)

Long Branch Free Public Library
Reference Department
328 Broadway
Long Branch, NJ 07740
(732) 222-3900
ibruck@lmxac.org
http://www.lmxac.org/longbranch/index. html
Muriel Scoles, Reference Department
Mon–Thur 10:00–8:00, Fri–Sat noon–5:00
(Monmouth County, New Jersey)

Long Branch Historical Museum
Saint James Episcopal Church
1260 Ocean Avenue
Long Branch, NJ 07740
(732) 229-0600; (732) 922-9879
Edgar N. Dinkelspiel, President
by appointment
free admission

Madison Public Library
39 Keep Street
Madison, NJ 07940
(973) 377-0722; (973) 377-3142 FAX
corletth@mpl.rosenet.org
http://www.rosenet.org/library
Helene Corlett, Local History Manager
Wed & Fri 9:00–6:00, Mon–Tue & Thur
   9:00–9:00, Sat 9:00–5:00, Sun
   (Sept–June) 2:00–5:00

Maplewood Memorial Library
Reference Department
51 Baker Street
Maplewood, NJ 07040-2618
(973) 762-1622; (973) 762-0762 FAX
reference@maplewoodlibrary.org
http://www.maplewoodlibrary.org
Mon–Thur 10:00–9:00, Fri–Sat 10:00–5:00,
   Sun 1:00–4:00, no weekend hours in
   summer
("Library makes no specific effort to build a
   genealogical collection, but has: local
   history clipping file; ninety years of
   microfilmed local weekly newspaper;
   Price & Lee Co. *Directory of the Oranges*,
   1892–1970 [final year of publication]")

Mercer County Public Library
2751 Brunswick Pike
Lawrenceville, NJ 08648
(609) 989-6918; (609) 989-6922 (Reference);
   (609) 538-1208 FAX
ebrown@mcl.org
http://www.mcl.org
Ellen O'Shea Brown, Library Director

The Metuchen Public Library
480 Middlesex Avenue
Metuchen, NJ 08840
(732) 632-8526; (732) 632-8535 FAX
http://www.metuchen.com/library.html

Middletown Township Public Library
55 New Monmouth Road
Middletown, NJ 07748
(732) 671-3700; (732) 671-5839 FAX
http://www.middletown.lib.nj.us
JoAnn B. Strano, Head of Reference

Mon–Thur 9:00–9:00, Fri 9:00–5:00, Sat
   9:00–5:00 (closed July & Aug)
(Middletown, Monmouth County, and New
   Jersey history sources; "library does not
   do mail-in research but will guide patrons
   in their research")

Midland Park Memorial Library
250 Godwin Avenue
Midland Park, NJ 07432
(201) 444-2390
http://www.bccls.org/members/mipk.shtml
Jean M. Scott, Director
Mon–Thur 10:00–9:00, Fri 10:00–5:00, Sat
   (Sept–June) 10:00–5:00, Sat (July–Aug)
   10:00–1:00, Sun (Oct–Apr) 1:00–5:00

Miller-Cory House Museum
(614 Mountain Avenue, Westfield, NJ
   07090—location)
PO Box 455 (mailing address)
Westfield, NJ 07091-0455
(908) 232-1776; (908) 232-1740 FAX
http://www.westfieldnj.com
Joan E. Barna, Services Coordinator
Sun (Sept–June) 2:00–5:00; Office:
   weekdays 9:00–noon
Pub. *The Broadside and The Beeline*, three
   times per year (Sept, Jan, Apr)
("An 18th-century living farm museum, out
   buildings, library")
$15.00 per year membership

Monmouth County Archives
125 Symmes Drive
Manalapan, NJ 07726
(732) 308-3772; (732) 409-4888 FAX
http://www.visitmonmouth.com/archives
Gary Saretzky, Archivist
Research on site: Mon–Wed 9:00–4:00;
   Office: Mon–Fri
("county government repository")
"no charge for quick lookups"; charge for
   copies

Monmouth University
Guggenheim Library
Special Collections
Cedar Avenue
West Long Branch, NJ 07764
(732) 571-3450; (732) 571-3636 FAX
http://www.monmouth.edu/irs/library/
   special.html

Morris County Library
The New Jersey Collection
30 East Hanover Avenue
Whippany, NJ 07981
(973) 285-6974
heagney@main.morris.org
http://www.gti.net/mocolib1/MCL.html
Marie Heagney, Principal Librarian
Mon–Thur 9:00–9:00, Fri–Sat 9:00–5:00,
   Sun (Sept–June) noon–5:00

Morris Genealogical Library
228 Elberon Avenue
Allenhurst, NJ 07711

**The Morristown and Morris Township
Library**
Local History Department
1 Miller Road
Morristown, NJ 07960
(973) 538-3473; (973) 267-4064 FAX
jochem@main.morris.org
http://www.morristownmorristwplibrary.info
Christine Jochem, Department Head
Mon–Thur 9:00–9:00, Fri 9:00–6:00, Sat
   (Sept–June) 9:30–5:00, Sat (July–Aug)
   10:00–2:00, Sun 1:00–5:00

New Brunswick Theological Seminary
Gardiner A. Sage Library
(address withheld upon request)
(emphasis on New York, New Jersey,
   Colonial Dutch, and Reformed Church in
   America. "We do not have original sources
   or information of value to a genealogist.")

New Jersey State Museum
Museums Council of New Jersey
(205 West State Street—location)
PO Box 530 (mailing address)
Trenton, NJ 08625-0530
(609) 292-6464 (Information); (609) 292-
   6308; (609) 599-4098 FAX
http://www.state.nj.us/state/museum
Leah P. Sloshberg, Director
Tue–Sat 9:00–4:45, Sun noon–4:45
Pub. *The Quarterly Calendar*
(collections and exhibitions and research in
   archaeology/ethnology, cultural history,
   etc.)
$40.00 per year membership

Newark Public Library
(5 Washington Street—location)
PO Box 630 (mailing address)
Newark, NJ 07101-0630
(973) 733-7776; (973) 733-7784
http://www.npl.org
Charles Cummings, Assistant Director,
   Special Collections/New Jersey
Tue, Thur & Sat 9:00–5:00, Wed 1:30–8:30,
   subject to change

Nutley Free Public Library
(address withheld upon request)

Ocean City Historical Museum
1735 Simpson Avenue
Ocean City, NJ 08226
(609) 399-1801; (609) 399-0544 FAX
http://www.ocnjmuseum.org
Linda A. Long, Business Administrator
May–Oct: Mon–Fri 10:00–4:00, Sat
   1:00–4:00; Oct–Apr: Mon–Sat 1:00–4:00
("Operated by Friends of the Ocean City
   Historical Museum")

Ocean County Library
Bishop Building
101 Washington Street
Toms River, NJ 08753
(732) 349-6200
hartmann_g@oceancounty.lib.nj.us (Grace
   Hartmann)
http://oceancountylibrary.org
Lois Jane Brown, Senior Librarian
Mon & Wed 1:00–9:00, Tue & Thur–Sat
   1:00–5:00
(New Jersey/Ocean County history and
   genealogy; all available federal censuses of
   New Jersey)

Township of Ocean Historical Museum
163 Monmouth Road
Oakhurst, NJ 07755
(732) 531-2136
Virginia Richmond, President
Tue 1:00–4:00
$10.00 per year membership

Paramus Public Library
East 116 Century Road
Paramus, NJ 07652
(201) 599-1305; (201) 599-0059
http://www.bccls.org/paramus
Sylvia Gaddi, Supervisor of Reference
   Services
Mon–Thur 9:30–9:00, Fri–Sat 9:30–5:00,
   Sun 1:00–5:00

Paterson Museum
2 Market Street
Paterson, NJ 07501
(973) 881-3874

Phillipsburg Free Public Library
200 Frost Avenue
Phillipsburg, NJ 08865
(908) 454-3712
lawson@hublib.lib.nj.us
http://www.pburglib.com
Pat Lawson, Director

Princeton Public Library
65 Witherspoon Street
Princeton, NJ 08542
(609) 924-9529; (609) 924-7937 FAX
http://www.princeton.lib.nj.us/info.html
Elba Barzelatto, Manager Information
   Services
Mon–Thur 9:00–9:00, Fri–Sat 9:00–5:30,
   Sun (Sept–June) 1:00–5:30
(emphasis on Princetoniana, very limited
   genealogical material)

Princeton University
Firestone Library
1 Washington Road
Princeton, NJ 08540
(609) 258-3184
http://infoshare1.princeton.edu:2003

Ramsey Free Public Library
30 Wyckoff Avenue
Ramsey, NJ 07446
(201) 327-1445
http://www.bccls.org/ramsey
Leona F. Schauble
Mon–Sat (summer: closed Sat)

Red Bank Public Library
84 West Front Street
Red Bank, NJ 07701
(732) 842-0690; (732) 842-4191 FAX
dsadel@lmxac.org (Director);
   rbref@lmxac.org
http://www.lmxac.org/redbank

Red Mill Museum Village
56 Main Street
Clinton, NJ 08809-1328
(908) 735-4101; (908) 735-0914 FAX
hhmredmill@yahoo.com
http://theredmill.org
Jean Daly, Collections Manager
Mon–Fri 9:00–5:00 by appointment
(Has Hunterdon County business ledgers and
   photographic archives)

Ruth L. Rockwood Memorial Library
10 Robert H. Harp Drive
Livingston, NJ 07039
(973) 992-4600; (973) 422-0150 FAX
sikora@bccls.org
http://www.bccls.org/livingston
Arlene Boland, Head of Reference
Mon & Thur 10:00–10:00, Tue & Wed
   10:00–9:00, Fri 10:00–6:00, Sat
   10:00–5:00, Sun 1:00–5:00
(local history information for the town of
   Livingston with some general New Jersey
   holdings for nearby areas)

Rowan University Library
Stewart Room, Campbell Library
201 Mullica Hill Road
Glassboro, NJ 08028-0701
(856) 256-4967; (856) 256-4924 FAX
William Garrabrant
Stewart Room: Mon–Fri 1:00–4:00; Main
   library: Mon–Thur 8:00 A.M.–midnight,
   Fri 8:00 A.M.–9:00 P.M., Sat 9:00–5:00,

Sun noon–10:00
(emphasis on New Jersey genealogy, Indians,
   Quakers, and college archives)

Roxbury Public Library
103 Main Street
Succasunna, NJ 07876
(973) 584-2400
romance@main.morris.org
http://roxburylibrary.org
Korin Rosenkrans, Reference; Marilyn
   Lukach, Adult Services
Mon–Thur 9:30–9:00, Fri 9:30–5:00, Sat
   (Sept–June) 9:30–3:00, Sat (July–Aug)
   9:30–1:00, Sun (Sept–June) 2:00–5:00

Rutgers University
Archibald Stevens Alexander Library
Special Collections and University Archives
169 College Avenue
New Brunswick, NJ 08901-1163
(732) 932-7510 (Reference); (732) 932-7012
   FAX
http://www.libraries.rutgers.edu/rul/libs/
   scua/scua.shtml
Bonita Craft Grant, New Jersey
   Bibliographer
Special Collections: during the school year:
   Mon–Fri 9:00–5:00, Sat 1:00–5:00;
   summer: Mon–Fri 9:00–5:00
(New Jersey history and genealogy, Rutgers
   University's archives and
   records/publications, rare books,
   manuscript materials; houses archives and
   records of the Genealogical Society of
   New Jersey and the DAR New Jersey
   Chapter)

Gardiner A. Sage Library
(see New Brunswick Theological Seminary,
above)

Sea Isle City Historical Museum
4416 Landis Avenue
Sea Isle City, NJ 08243
(609) 263-2992

Sparta Public Library
(address withheld upon request)

Richard Stockton College Library
Jim Leeds Road
Pomona, NJ 08240
(609) 652-4343
http://loki.stockton.edu/~millerr/libhome.
   htm

Sussex County Main Library
(Route 655, Frankford Township—location)
125 Morris Turnpike (mailing address)
Newton, NJ 07860
(973) 948-3660; (973) 948-2071 FAX
grohs@hublib.lib.nj.us
http://www.sussexcountylibrary.org
Therese Erskine, Reference Librarian
Mon–Thur 8:30–8:30, Fri 8:30–6:00, Sat
   9:00–5:00
no genealogical research services

Teaneck Public Library
840 Teaneck Road
Teaneck, NJ 07666
(201) 837-4171
mccue@bccls.org
http://www.teaneck.org
Michael McCue, Director
Mon–Thur 9:00–9:00, Fri 9:00–6:00, Sat
   9:00–5:00, Sun 12:30–5:30, Sun (Father's
   Day to mid-Sept) 1:00–4:00

Tenafly Public Library
401 Tenafly Road

Tenafly, NJ 07670
(201) 568-8680
wechtler@bccls.org
http://www.bccls.org/tenafly
Stephen Wechtler, Director
Mon–Tue & Thur 10:00–9:00, Wed
   10:00–6:00, Fri 10:00–5:00, Sat
   10:00–4:00

Trenton City Museum
Trenton Museum Society
Cadwalader Park
Trenton, NJ 08606
(609) 989-3632

Free Public Library of Trenton
Trentoniana Department
120 Academy Street
Trenton, NJ 08608
(609) 392-7188; (609) 392-7655 FAX
http://www.trentonlibrary.state.nj.us
Wendy M. Nardi, Historian and Curator
Mon & Wed–Thur 9:00–9:00, Tue & Fri–Sat
   9:00–5:00

**University of Medicine and Dentistry of
New Jersey**
Department of Special Collections
George F. Smith Library
30 12th Street
Newark, NJ 07103-2754
(973) 982-6293; (973) 982-7474
yzhang@umdnj.edu
http://www.umdnj.edu/librweb/about.htm
("Maintains collections in the history of
   medicine, university archives, and primary
   source materials. These collections include
   rare books, manuscripts, oral histories,
   photographs and illustrations, official
   UMDNJ records, and faculty papers.")

Warren County Library
Second and Hardwick Streets
Belvidere, NJ 07823
(908) 475-6322; (908) 475-5361; (908) 475-
   6359 FAX
Janet M. Davis, Reference Librarian
Mon–Thur 9:00–8:30, Fri 9:00–6:00, Sat
   10:00–3:00

Washington Free Public Library
20 West Carlton Avenue
Washington, NJ 07882
(908) 689-0201
wpldirec@hublib.lib.nj.us
http://www.goes.com/~wpl/wpl.htm
Carol McNeil, Senior Library Assistant
Mon–Fri 10:00–8:30, Sat 10:00–2:00
15¢ per photocopied page

Wayne Public Library
The Lockett Room
12 Nellis Drive
Wayne, NJ 07470
(973) 694-4272; (973) 692-0637 FAX
http://www.waynetownship.com/library

Westfield Memorial Library
550 East Broad Street
Westfield, NJ 07090
(908) 789-4090; (908) 789-0921 FAX
pisrael@wmlnj.org
http://www.wmlnj.org
Philip Israel, Library Director
Mon–Thur 10:00–9:00, Fri 10:00–5:00, Sat
   (Sept–June) 10:00–5:00, Sun (Sept–June)
   1:00–5:00

Willingboro Public Library
1 Salem Road
Willingboro, NJ 08046
(856) 877-6668; (609) 835-1699 FAX

cking@willingboro.org
http://www.willingboro.org/index.htm
Janet Cheeseman, Reference Librarian;
    Christine H. King, Library Director
Mon–Thur 9:00–9:00, Fri–Sat 9:00–5:00,
    Sun 1:00–5:00 (closed Sun in summer)
(Willingboro history and development)

Woodbridge Public Library
George Frederick Plaza
Woodbridge, NJ 07095
(732) 634-4450; (732) 634-1569 FAX
jhurley@lmxac.org
http://www.woodbridge.lib.nj.us
Wenda Rottweiler, Senior Librarian; John
    Hurley, Library Director
Mon–Thur 9:00–9:00, Fri–Sat 9:00–5:00,
    Sun (except summer) 1:00–5:00

Historical Societies—Local and Regional

Absecon Historical Society
618 Franklin Boulevard
Absecon, NJ 08201

Alexandria Township Historical Society
174 Warsaw Road
Frenchtown, NJ 08825
Mary Ellen Sodalvin, President

Allamuchy Township Historical Society
Rural Delivery 1, Box 111
Great Meadows, NJ 07838
Harold Drake, President

Allendale Historical Society, Inc.
PO Box 294
Allendale, NJ 07401
(201) 327-0605
Pat Wardell
Pub. *Allendale History and Heritage*,
    monthly
$8.00 per year membership

Allentown-Upper Freehold Historical Society
(76 North Main Street—location)
PO Box 328 (mailing address)
Allentown, NJ 08501
(609) 259-3171

Alpine Historical Society
PO Box 59
Alpine, NJ 07620
(201) 768-1360

Historical Society of Andover Boro
189 Main Street
Andover, NJ 07821
(973) 786-6829
Beatrice D. Rush, President

Atlantic County Historical Society
(907 Shore Road—location)
PO Box 301 (mailing address)
Somers Point, NJ 08244
(609) 927-5218
http://www.aclink.org/achs
Dale Lonkart, Librarian
Wed–Sat 10:00–3:30, first Thur 6:00–9:00
Pub. *Atlantic County Historical Society
    Annual*; *Atlantic Heritage*, quarterly
(emphasis on New Jersey history and
    genealogy; received collection of the
    Atlantic City Free Public Library)
$12.00 per year membership; research: fee
    quoted on request

Atlantic Highlands Historical Society
(22 Prospect Avenue—location)

PO Box 108 (mailing address)
Atlantic Highlands, NJ 07716
(732) 291-1861
Helen M. Marchette, President
June–Sept: Sun 1:00–4:00, and by
    appointment
Pub. *Portland Poynts*, bimonthly
$5.00 per year membership

Audubon Historical Society
238 Washington Terrace
Audubon, NJ 08106
(856) 547-0586
Jack H. Taylor, Alternate Delegate

Barnegat Historical Society
PO Box 381
Barnegat, NJ 08005
(609) 698-9586
Gary Brower, President

The Barnegat Light Historical Society
Barnegat Light Museum
(address withheld upon request)
Pub. *A Museum at the Shore*, as needed,
    $1.00 per issue
("There was limited record keeping in the
    early years of the BLM, and so what info
    we do have is sparse. We also don't have
    info on the people who lived in town
    during the early years [c. the 1870-80s] of
    Barnegat City [as it was known in those
    days].")

Barrington Historical Society
9 Beaver Drive
Barrington, NJ 08007
Mrs. Earl F. Shenk

Basking Ridge Historical Society
107 Dyckman Place
Basking Ridge, NJ 07920
(908) 766-3786

Batsto Citizens Committee
355 Mansion Avenue
Audubon, NJ 08106
(856) 547-6006
George C. Vail, Chairman

Battleground Historical Society
(Village Inn, 2 Water Street, Englishtown,
    NJ 07726—location)
PO Box 61 (mailing address)
Tennent, NJ 07763
(732) 446-2825
Mauriello Kieke, President
by appointment
Pub. *Matchaponix Journal*, bimonthly
(some genealogy of owners of Village Inn
    from 1726 and other associated
    information)
$20.00 per year membership

Bay Head Historical Society
PO Box 127
Bay Head, NJ 08742
(732) 892-0223
Evalyn Shippee, President

Bayonne Historical Society
PO Box 3034
Bayonne, NJ 07002
(201) 823-4840

Beavertown Historical Society
94 Beaver Brook Road
Lincoln Park, NJ 07035
(973) 694-0640
George Shanoian, President

Belleville Historical Society

Belleville Public Library and Information
Center
221 Washington Avenue
Belleville, NJ 07109
(973) 450-3434 (Library); (973) 450-9518
    FAX (Library)
http://www.intac.com/~bplibn/hpfront.htm
    (Library)

Bergen County Historical Society
194 Maplewood Avenue
Bogota, NJ 07603-1714
(201) 488-9463; (201) 343-4169 (Library)
http://maple.nis.net/~wardell/BCAssoc.htm
Amy C. Northrup, President; Val Clark, Head
    of Reference
Johnson Free Public Library: Mon–Thur
    9:00–8:45, Fri–Sat 9:00–4:45
Pub. *Bergen County History*, annually; *In
    Bergen's Attic*
$35.00 per year membership

Historical Society of Berkeley Heights
PO Box 237
Berkeley Heights, NJ 07922
(908) 464-0961
Helen Tyler, President

Berkeley Township Historical Society
759 U.S. Highway 9
Bayville, NJ 08721
(732) 269-9527

Berlin Long-A-Coming Historical Society
59 South White Horse Pike
Berlin, NJ 08009
(856) 767-6221
http://www.nextination.com/
    longacoming/index.shtml
Roy Schmidt, President
only occasionally; meetings nine months per
    year

Bethlehem Township Historical Society
PO Box 56
Asbury, NJ 08802

**Blackwells Mills Canal Historical
Association**
598 Elizabeth Street
Somerset, NJ 08873
(908) 873-2959
Eugene E. Howe

Historical Society of Bloomfield
Bloomfield Public Library
90 Broad Street
Bloomfield, NJ 07003
(973) 566-6220 voice & FAX
Bloomfhist@aol.com
Ina Campbell, President
Wed 2:00–4:30, Sat 10:00–12:30
Pub. *Newsletter: The New Town Crier*, four
    times per year, not available by
    subscription
("historical society with museum")
$7.00 per year membership; research:
    donation suggested

Blue Hills Historical Society
311 West End Avenue
North Plainfield, NJ 07060

Boonton Historical Society
619 Main Street
Boonton, NJ 07005
(973) 627-6205

Bordentown Historical Society
(13 Crosswicks Street—location)
PO Box 182 (mailing address)
Bordentown, NJ 08505

(609) 298-1740
http://bc.emanon.net/bhs
by appointment

Bradley Beach Historical Society
Bradley Beach Library
511 Fourth Avenue
Bradley Beach, NJ 07720
(732) 776-2995; (732) 988-8958 FAX
BBHS2000@Juno.com
Shirley Ayres, Historian for the Borough of
     Bradley Beach
meetings at the library: third Tue 7:00 P.M.
$15.00 per year membership

Brick Township Historical Society, Inc.
(The Havens Homestead, 521 Herbertsville
Road—proposed location)
PO Box 160 (mailing address)
Brick, NJ 08723
(732) 477-4513
Jane Fabach, President
$10.00 per year membership

Bridgeton Antiquarian League
353 Roadstown-Greenwich Road
Bridgeton, NJ 08302
(856) 455-4100
Joseph C. DeLuca, President

Brigantine Historical Society
470 West Shore Drive
Brigantine, NJ 08203

Burlington County Historical Society
Delia Biddle Pugh Library
(454 Lawrence Street—location)
457 High Street (mailing address)
Burlington, NJ 08016
(609) 386-4773; (609) 386-4828 FAX
Joan Lanphear, Librarian
Mon–Thur 1:00–4:00, Wed 10:00–noon, Sun
     2:00–4:00
Pub. *Burlington County Historical Society
     Newsletter*, quarterly
(New Jersey history, especially Burlington
     County; Burlington County genealogies)
$15.00 per year membership

City of Burlington Historical Society
City Hall
Burlington, NJ 08016
(609) 386-3993
http://bc.emanon.net/cgi-
     bin/burl/city_historical_society
Dr. Nicholas P. Kamaras

Byram Township Historical Society
3 Ghost Pony Road
Andover, NJ 07821
(973) 347-4585
Carl O. Johnson, President

Califon Historical Society
(The Old Stone Railroad Station, Route 512
and Railroad Avenue—location)
PO Box 424 (mailing address)
Califon, NJ 07830
(908) 832-2266
Donald E. Philhower Freibergs, President
first & third Sun (May–Dec) 1:00–3:00
(special collection of local history and
     artifacts pertaining to Califon and the
     surrounding area)
$15.00 per year membership

Camden County Historical Society
Park Boulevard and Euclid Avenue
Camden, NJ 08103-3697
(609) 964-3333

http://www.cyberenet.net/~gsteiner/njgen

web/camdenhs.html
Paul W. Schopp, Executive Director
Library: Tue & Thur 12:30–4:30, Sun
     1:00–5:00
Pub. *Communicator*, irregularly; *Camden
     County Historical Society Bulletin*,
     irregularly; *Camden County History
     Journal*, irregularly
$15.00 per year membership

**Campbell-Christie House Historical
Society**
530 James Street
New Milford, NJ 07646

**Cape May County Historical and
Genealogical Society**
John Holmes House
504 Route 9 North
Cape May Court House, NJ 08210-3070
(609) 465-3535; (609) 465-4274 FAX
museum@co.cape-may.nj.us
http://www.cmcmuseum.org
Ione E. Williams, Librarian
Library (call for appointment): Thur–Sat
     10:00–4:00; Museum (last ticket sold at
     3:00): Tue–Fri (Apr–Oct), Sat (year
     round) 9:00–4:00
Pub. *Cape May County Magazine of History
     and Genealogy*, annually; *The Cape May
     County Crier*, quarterly
$15.00 per year membership

Cedar Grove Historical Society
(903 Pompton Avenue—location)
PO Box 461 (mailing address)
Cedar Grove, NJ 07009
(973) 239-5414 (answering machine)
Mr. Christian Werndly, President

Chatham Historical Society
PO Box 682
Chatham, NJ 07928
Lester E. Lehman, Jr., President

Historical Society of Chatham Township
22 Papermill Road
Chatham, NJ 07928
(973) 635-1679
Robert D. Felch, President

Chester Historical Society
(245 West Main Street—location)
PO Box 376 (mailing address)
Chester, NJ 07930
(908) 879-2761
Leonard J. Taylor, Chester Township
     Historian; Matt Koppinger, President
Pub. *Newsletter*, bimonthly
(publishes local history)
$8.00 per year membership

Chesterfield Township Historical Society
PO Box 86
Crosswicks, NJ 08515

Clark Historical Society
430 Westfield Avenue
Room 18, Municipal Building
Clark, NJ 07066
(908) 381-3081
Constance W. Brewer, President

Coalition for New Jersey History
Allaire State Park, Allaire Road
Box 394A
Farmingdale, NJ 07727
(732) 938-2371
Patrick Clarke, Chair
(primarily historical, not genealogical)

Colts Neck Historical Society

(16 Crusius Place—location)
PO Box 101 (mailing address)
Colts Neck, NJ 07722
(732) 462-1378

**Cranbury Historical and Preservation
Society**
(Cranbury History Center, 6 South Main
Street—location)
PO Box 77 (mailing address)
Cranbury, NJ 08512
(609) 860-1889; (609) 655-3736; (609) 395-
     0420
historycenter@comcast.net
Roi Taylor, Co-Director
Mon & Thur 9:30–12:30, and by appointment
(genealogy collection of Cranbury and the
     surrounding communities)
research: donation plus cost of copies

Cranford Historical Society
Hanson House Annex
38 Springfield Avenue
Cranford, NJ 07016
(908) 276-0082
http://www.bobdevlin.com/crhissoc.html
Larry Fuhro, President
Pub. *Mill Wheel*, quarterly

Cumberland County Historical Society
Warren Lummis Library
(981 Ye Greate Street—location)
PO Box 16 (mailing address)
Greenwich, NJ 08323
(856) 455-8580
lummis2@juno.com
http://www.cchistsoc.org
Warren Q. Adams, Director
Mar–Nov: Wed 10:00–4:30, Fri–Sun
     1:30–4:30
Pub. *Cumberland Patriot*, quarterly
(history and genealogy of New Jersey and
     Cumberland County)
$8.00 per year membership

Denville Historical Society
Diamond Spring Road, Box 466
Denville, NJ 07834-0466
(973) 625-1165
Beverly Blanchard, President

Dover Area Historical Society
(Rockaway Boro Plaza—location)
PO Box 609 (mailing address)
Dover, NJ 07801
(973) 366-0786
George Lovrie, Museum Chair
meetings: last Wed
Pub. *Ye Old Tye News*, quarterly
$9.00 per year membership

Dunellen Historical Society
322 Whittier Avenue
Dunellen, NJ 08812

Eagleswood Historical Society
Route 9, Main Street
West Creek, NJ 08092
Helen Wisner

East Brunswick Historical Society
(43 Sullivan Way—location)
Box 12 (mailing address)
East Brunswick, NJ 08816
(732) 249-3522
Estelle Goldsmith, President
(published *East Brunswick—Monograph on
     E.B. History*; "also national scope")
$15.00 per year membership

East Hanover Historical Society
181 Mount Pleasant Avenue

East Hanover, NJ 07936
(973) 884-0038

Eatontown Historical Committee
(25 Cloverdale Avenue—location)
PO Box 109 (mailing address)
Eatontown, NJ 07724
(732) 542-5445
Patricia A. Collins, President

Edison Township Historical Society
328 Plainfield Avenue
Edison, NJ 08817
(732) 248-7310
David Sheehan

Egg Harbor City Historical Society
533 London Avenue
Egg Harbor City, NJ 08215
(609) 965-9073

Elizabethtown Heritage Society
500 North Broad Street
Elizabeth, NJ 07207
(908) 558-3044

Elizabethtown Historical Foundation
PO Box 1
Elizabeth, NJ 07207
Stewart B. Kean

Elmwood Park Historical Society
210 Lee Street
Elmwood Park, NJ 07407
(201) 797-2109
Geraldine Mola

Englewood Historical Society
500 Liberty Road
Englewood, NJ 07631-1411
(201) 568-0678; (201) 568-2567
Eleanor S. Harvey, President
monthly meeting in the Mackay Room of the
    Englewood Public Library
Pub. *Newsletter*, as needed
(gathers autobiographical sketches,
    documents and artifacts in a resource
    center in City Hall)
$10.00 per year membership

English Neighborhood Historical Society
656 Elm Street
Maywood, NJ 07607

Essex Fells Historical Society
96 Forest Way
Essex Fells, NJ 07021
Robert Holton

Evesham Historical Society
(65 North Locust Avenue—location)
PO Box 199 (mailing address)
Marlton, NJ 08053
(856) 983-0395
Sylvia W. Bakley, President

**Ewing Township Historic Preservation
Society**
27 Federal City Road
Ewing, NJ 08638
(609) 883-2455 voice & FAX
http://www.ethps.org
Mark Giallella, President
by appointment
$10.00 per year membership

Fair Haven Historical Society
(142 Lexington Avenue, Fairhaven, NJ
07704-3040—location)
PO Box 72 (mailing address)
Fair Haven, NJ 07704-0072
(732) 842-4453

Timothy J. McMahon, President/Historian
by appointment only
(Fair Haven and surrounding areas)
$5.00 per year membership

Fairfield Historic Committee
Fairfield Town Hall
230 Fairfield Road
Fairfield, NJ 07004
(973) 882-8399; (973) 882-0365 FAX
Charles Vanyo, Chair
8:30–4:30

Fairview Historic Society
3081 Fenwick Road
Camden, NJ 08104-2706
(856) 966-9899

Farmingdale Historical Society
2 Goodenough Road
Farmingdale, NJ 07727
(732) 938-2008
Mildred Megill, President

Ferromonte Historical Society
11 Hillside Avenue, Mine Hill
Dover, NJ 07801
(973) 361-8813
Sherry Lenox

Historical Society of Florham Park
PO Box 193
Florham Park, NJ 07932
(973) 377-6291

Fort Lee Historical Society
Borough Hall
309 Main Street
Fort Lee, NJ 07024
(201) 592-3580
Robert William

Fortescue Historical Society
Pier #1, Bayside
Fortescue, NJ 08321
Nicholas R. Beltrante, Esq.

Franklin Township Historical Society
84 Hillview Avenue
Franklin Park, NJ 08823
(908) 297-2641

**Frelinghuysen Township Historical
Society**
PO Box 411
Johnsonburg, NJ 07846
(908) 852-7362
Debra Natyzak-Osadca, President

Frenchtown Historical Association
Borough Hall
Second Street
Frenchtown, NJ 08825

Galloway Township Historical Society
366 Upland Avenue
Absecon, NJ 08201
(609) 652-3049
Robert Reid

Glen Ridge Historical Society
c/o Glen Ridge Congregational Church
PO Box 164
Glen Ridge, NJ 07028-0164
(973) 748-1784
Mrs. George Middleton, President

**Glen Rock Historical and Preservation
Society**
Municipal Building, Borough Hall
Glen Rock, NJ 07452
(201) 447-2414

William Maynard, President

Gloucester County Historical Society
17 Hunter Street
Woodbury, NJ 08096-4605
(856) 845-4771; (856) 845-0131 FAX
gchs@net-gate.com
http://www.rootsweb.com/~njglouce/gchs
Edith Hoelle, Librarian
Mon–Fri 1:00–4:00, Fri 6:00–9:30, first Sat
    10:00–4:00, last Sun 2:00–5:00
Pub. *Gloucester County Historical Society
    Bulletin*, quarterly
(New Jersey history, South Jersey genealogy)
$20.00 per year membership

Gouldtown Historical Society
372 Magnolia Street
Salem, NJ 08079
Donald Pierce

**Great Egg Harbour Township Historical
Society**
3515 Bargaintown Road
Egg Harbor Township, NJ 08234
June Sheridan, Local Historian
Pub. *Origins*, monthly

Greater Cape May Historical Society
(653½ Washington Street—location)
Box 495 (mailing address)
Cape May, NJ 08204
(609) 884-9100
http://www.capemayhistory.org
Jim Campbell, Historian
Colonial House Museum: 15 June–15 Sept:
    10:00–2:00, plus Victorian Week in Oct;
    Archives: by appointment only
Pub. *Homespun: Newsletter of the Greater
    Cape May Historical Society*, quarterly
("Colonial House Museum—permanent
    displays interpreting early Cape Island,
    plus annual historical exhibits.")
$10.00 per year membership; research:
    donation

Green Township Historical Society
PO Box 203
Tranquility, NJ 07879
(908) 383-5829; (908) 852-2186
Malcom Smith, President

Hackettstown Historical Society
106 Church Street
Hackettstown, NJ 07840
(908) 852-8797
Helen G. Montfort, Co-Archivist; Ruth
    Scarborough, Co-Archivist
Wed, Fri & Sun 2:00–4:00
$10.00 per year membership; research:
    minimum $15.00

Haddon Heights Historical Society
Haddon Heights Library
608 Station Avenue
Haddon Heights, NJ 08035
(856) 547-7132
Robert Hunter, President

Haddon Township Historical Society
224 Hazel Terrace
Westmont, NJ 08108

Historical Society of Haddonfield
Greenfield Hall
343 King's Highway, East
Haddonfield, NJ 08033
(856) 429-2462
http://www.haddonfield.com/history
Katherine Tossini, Librarian
Tue & Thur 9:30–11:30, first Sun 1:00–3:00,
    and by appointment

Pub. *HSH Newsletter*, quarterly
(Library has family papers of many early
    Haddonfield families.)
$20.00 per year membership

Township of Hamilton Historical Society
319 Clarktown Road
Mays Landing, NJ 08330
(609) 625-0805
Dottie Kinsey, President

Historical Society of Hamilton Township
9 Benson Lane
Trenton, NJ 08610
(609) 585-5435
Dr. James Federici, President

Hammonton Historical Society
767 Central Avenue
Hammonton, NJ 08037
(609) 561-2830
Jeanette Feeley
Pub. *HHS Newsletter*

Harding Township Historical Society
(Village and Millbrook Roads—location)
PO Box 1776 (mailing address)
New Vernon, NJ 07976
(973) 292-0161
Ellen Baumann, President

Hardyston Heritage Society
(North Woods Trail—location)
PO Box 434 (mailing address)
Stockholm, NJ 07460
(973) 697-8733
Barbara Lacatena, President

Harrington Park Historical Society
10 Herring Street
Harrington Park, NJ 07640
(201) 768-5675

Harrison Township Historical Society
(Routes 77 and 45—location)
PO Box 4 (mailing address)
Mullica Hill, NJ 08062
(856) 478-4949

Hazlet Township Historical Society
Municipal Offices
319 Middle Road
Hazlet, NJ 07730

Helmetta Historical Society
60 Main Street
Helmetta, NJ 08828
(732) 521-2402

Highland Park Historical Commission
PO Box 1330
Highland Park, NJ 08904
(732) 572-3400

Historical Society of Highlands
PO Box 13
Highlands, NJ 07732
(732) 291-4956
John Tomasulo, President

**Hightstown-East Windsor Historical
Society**
164 North Main Street
Hightstown, NJ 08520
(609) 371-9580
Richard S. Hutchinson, Editor, Genealogist
    by appointment
Pub. *Hightstown-East Windsor Historical
    Society News*, five times per year
(large local area manuscript collection,
    photos; Hightstown-East Windsor families
    and local history)

$15.00 per year membership

Hillsborough Historical Society
PO Box 720
Neshanic, NJ 08853
(908) 369-3659
Harry B. Smith

**Hillsborough Township Historic
Commission**
(Planning Board Office, Municipal Annex,
Neshanic, NJ 08853—location)
379 South Branch Road (mailing address)
Hillsborough, NJ 08844
(908) 369-4313

The Hillside Historical Society, Inc.
111 Conant Street
Hillside, NJ 07205
(908) 353-8828; (908) 352-9270
Arnold H. McClow, President
Tours of Woodruff House Historical
    Museum: third Sun 2:00–4:00, and by
    appointment
Pub. *The Core*, occasionally
$5.00 per year membership

Holmdel Historical Society
(Stilwell Road—location)
PO Box 282 (mailing address)
Holmdel, NJ 07733
(732) 946-8618
Gerald Ceres, President

Hope Historical Society
(High Street—location)
PO Box 52 (mailing address)
Hope, NJ 07844

Hopewell Valley Historical Society
PO Box 371
Pennington, NJ 08534-0371
hvhist@aol.com
http://www.rootsweb.com/~njhvhs
President
Pub. *Hopewell Valley Historical Society
    Newsletter*, four times per year
$15.00 per year membership

Howell Historical Society
407 Lakewood-Farmingdale Road
Howell, NJ 07731
(732) 938-5868 (732) 938-2212
Edith Smith, President

Hunterdon County Historical Society
Hiram E. Deats Memorial Library
114 Main Street
Flemington, NJ 08822
(908) 782-1091
Roxanne K. Carkhuff, Librarian
Thur 1:00–3:00 & 7:00–9:00, and by
    appointment
Pub. *Hunterdon Historical Newsletter*, three
    times per year
(emphasis on Hunterdon County genealogy
    and local history, plus manuscript
    collection)
$15.00 per year membership

Irvington Historical Society
34 Clinton Terrace
Irvington, NJ 07111-1417
(973) 374-7500
Harry Stevenson, President

Jamesburg Historical Association
203 Buckelew Avenue
Jamesburg, NJ 08831
(732) 521-0068
Nancy J. Luberecki, Acquisition Chairman
Sat 11:00–3:00; meeting first Wed 8:00 P.M.

Pub. *The House of Many Windows*,
    semiannually
$5.00 per year membership

Jefferson Township Historical Society
Dover-Milton Road
Oak Ridge, NJ 07438
(973) 697-8675; (973) 697-0258
Clifford Williams, President

Kearny Cottage Historical Association
Kearny Cottage
63 Catalpa Avenue
Perth Amboy, NJ 08861
(732) 826-1826; (732) 826-3928 (President)
Jack M. Dudas, Esq., President
Tue & Thur 1:00–4:00, Sun by appointment
(house museum)
$10.00 per year membership

Kenilworth Historical Society
567 Kenilworth Blvd.
Kenilworth, NJ 07033
(908) 276-8449
Robert Woods

Keyport Historical Society
(Steamboat Dock Museum, 2 Broad Street
[on the Bay]—location)
PO Box 312 (mailing address)
Keyport, NJ 07735
(732) 264-7822 (appointments); (732) 264-
    6119 (appointments); (732) 739-6390;
    (732) 264-1581
Angel Teandron, Curator
May–Sept: Mon 10:00–noon, Sun 1:00–4:00
Pub. *Steamboat Dock Museum Newsletter*,
    three or four times per year
(some genealogical information, birth,
    marriage and obituary index to *Matwen
    Journal* 1869–1928, some information on
    Green Grove Cemetery, Cedawood
    Cemetery, later called Raritan; a great deal
    of Keyport history)
$5.00 per year membership; museum
    admission: free

Kingwood Township Historical Society
Kingwood Township Municipal Building
PO Box 199
Baptistown, NJ 08803

Kinnelon Historical Commission
25 Kiel Avenue
Kinnelon, NJ 07405
(973) 838-0185

Lacey Township Historical Society
(Route 9—location)
PO Box 412 (mailing address)
Forked River, NJ 08731

Lake Hopatcong Historical Society
211 Park Heights Avenue
Dover, NJ 07801
(973) 366-2103
Martin Kane, President

Boro of Lakehurst Historical Society
505 Oak Street
Lakehurst, NJ 08733
(732) 657-8864
Mary Scilex

Lambertville Historical Society
(52 Bridge Street—location)
PO Box 2 (mailing address)
Lambertville, NJ 08530
(609) 397-0770

Lawnside Historical Society, Inc.
PO Box 608

Lawnside, NJ 08045
(856) 546-8850
lawn@juno.com
http://community.nj.com/cc/lawnsidehistory
Linda Waller, President
$15.00 per year membership

Lawrence Historical Society
(Port Mercer Canal House, 4274
Quakerbridge Road, Princeton, NJ
08540—location)
PO Box 6025 (mailing address)
Lawrenceville, NJ 08648
(609) 243-9108
David Kimzey, Caretaker
Open house: second Sun June, second
weekend Dec
Pub. *Newsletter*, semiannually (spring and
fall)

Leonia Historical Society
199 Christie Street
Leonia, NJ 07605
(201) 947-5647
Milton Ehrlich

Linwood Historical Society
1014 Maple Avenue
Linwood, NJ 08221
Michael Everett, President
Pub. *LHS Newsletter*

Little Falls Historical Society
(19 Warren Street—location)
PO Box 1083 (mailing address)
Little Falls, NJ 07424
(973) 256-3651 (President, evenings)
Clifford Swisher, President
generally Tue & Thur 1:00–4:00
Pub. *Little Falls Historical Newsletter*, five
times per year (15th of Jan, Mar, May,
Sept, Nov)
("Local history, Beattie Mill, Morris Canal,
Little Falls Laundry, local churches and
education. We have a collection of school
files from 1885 to 1985 which show
student name, address, age and parents'
address, as well as teachers and salaries.
Our organization was founded in 1968, but
this year is the first time that we have an
office and a central location for our files.
We are currently working to organize our
files, which we plan to put on discs with
copies for the local library and schools.")
$10.00 per year membership;; research: fees
to be determined

Little Falls Township Historical Society
Little Falls Library
8 Douglas Drive
Little Falls, NJ 07424
(973) 256-3651
Clifford Swisher, President

Little Silver Historical Society
Borough Hall
480 Prospect Avenue
Little Silver, NJ 07739
(732) 842-2400
David Griffith, President

Livingston Historical Society
(South Livingston Avenue—location)
PO Box 220 (mailing address)
Livingston, NJ 07039
Monte Caliman, President
Pub. *Livingston Historical Society
Newsletter*, seven times per year
$6.00 per year membership

Long Beach Island Historical Association
(Engleside and Beach Avenue—location)

PO Box 1222 (mailing address)
Beach Haven, NJ 08008
(609) 492-0700
archives@lbimuseum.org
http://lbimuseum.org
S. Mary T. Gruber, Genealogy Chairman
winter: Tue 1:00–4:00; summer: daily
2:00–4:00 & 7:00–9:00
Pub. *Museum Pieces*, quarterly
$10.00 per year membership

Long Hill Township Historical Society
1336 Valley Road
Stirling, NJ 07087
(908) 647-5762
Jennifer Lamson, President

Longport Historical Society
Borough Hall
2305 Atlantic Avenue
Longport, NJ 08403
(609) 823-1115

Lumberton Historical Society
PO Box 22
Lumberton, NJ 08048
(609) 247-4067
Doris Priest, President

Lyndhurst Historical Society
PO Box 135
Lyndhurst, NJ 07071
(201) 804-2513; (201) 939-7639
Marilyn Romano, President

Madison Historical Society
(Local History Center, Madison Public
Library, Keep Street—location)
PO Box 148 (mailing address)
Madison, NJ 07940
(973) 377-0722 (Library, ask for historical
society)
http://www.rosenet.org/mhs
Kate Malcolm, Custodian
Tue 9:30–3:00, and by appointment
("Madison history. *Madison Eagle*
newspaper index to 1882.")
donation accepted

Madison Township Historical Society
Thomas Warne Historical Museum and
Library
(Route 516, Old Bridge Township,
NJ—location)
150 Morristown Road (mailing address)
Matawan, NJ 07747
(732) 566-0348
Alvia D. Martin, Curator
Wed 9:30–noon, first Sun 1:00–4:00
Pub. *The Timepiece*, semiannually
(spring/summer and fall/winter)
$10.00 per year membership

Magnolia Historical Society
208 Brooke Avenue
Magnolia, NJ 08049
(856) 783-8585
Helen Bradley, President

Mahwah Historical Society
310 Forest Road
Mahwah, NJ 07430
(201) 891-9049
William Lamoreaux, President

Manchester Historical Society
18 Bowie Drive
Whiting, NJ 08759

Mansfield Township Historical Society
3121 Route 206
Columbus, NJ 08022-9530

(609) 298-4174

Mantua Historical Society
506 Buckingham Drive
Sewell, NJ 08080
Nancy Rotny

Maple Shade Historical Society
PO Box 368
Maple Shade, NJ 08052

Matawan Historical Society, Inc.
(94 Main Street—location)
PO Box 41 (mailing address)
Matawan, NJ 07747
(732) 566-3817
Sarah Ellison, President; Helen Henderson,
Director
Pub. *MHS Newsletter*

Maurice River Historical Society
PO Box 161
Mauricetown, NJ 08329
(no genealogical information)

Mauricetown Historical Society
(Front Street—location)
PO Box 1 (mailing address)
Mauricetown, NJ 08329
(856) 785-0457

Maywood Historical Committee
652 Grant Avenue
Maywood, NJ 07607
(201) 843-1130
Betty A. Fetzer, President

Medford Historical Society
PO Box 362
Medford, NJ 08055
(856) 835-2652

Merchantville Historical Society
1 West Maple Avenue
Merchantville, NJ 08109
(856) 665-1819
Edith Silberstein, President
by appointment
Pub. *Merchantville Historical Society
Newsletter*, annually
(collection of photographs)
$10.00 per year membership

**Metuchen-Edison Regional Historical
Society**
PO Box 61
Metuchen, NJ 08840
(732) 906-0529
$15.00 per year membership

Middletown Township Historical Society
(MacLeod-Rice House, Croydon Hall,
Leonardville Road, Leonardo, NJ
07737—location)
PO Box 180 (mailing address)
Middletown, NJ 07748
(732) 291-8739; (732) 671-2645 (President)
http://www.monmouth.com/~mcha3/
hsdir.html#middletown
Randall Gabrielan, President
Sun 1:00–4:00; meetings: third Mon (except
Dec) 8:00
Pub. *Newsletter of the MTHS*
(Refers genealogical queries to the
Monmouth County Historical Association
or the Shrewsbury Historical Society)
$5.00 per year membership

Millburn-Short Hills Historical Society
(1 Station Plaza [at the Short Hills train
station]—location)
PO Box 243 (mailing address)

Short Hills, NJ 07078
(973) 379-5032 voice & FAX
MSHHS2002@cs.com
http://community.nj.com/cc/millburn-shhistsoc
Lynne K. Ranieri, Vice President
Tue 5:30–7:30, Wed 3:30–5:30, first Sun 2:00–4:00
Pub. *The Thistle*, two times per year
$15.00 per year membership

Milltown Historical Society
PO Box 96
Milltown, NJ 08850
(732) 828-0249
D. Bruce Schwendeman, President

Historical Society of Millville
Second and Main Street
Millville, NJ 08332
(856) 825-0789; (856) 327-4944

Monmouth Beach Historical Society
23 Navesink Drive
Monmouth Beach, NJ 07750
(732) 222-2244
Mrs. Edwin L. Brower, President

Monmouth County Historical Association
70 Court Street
Freehold, NJ 07728-1795
(732) 462-1466; (732) 462-8346 FAX
mchalib@excite.com
http://www.monmouthhistory.org
Carla Z. Tobias, Librarian/Archivist
Library: Wed–Sat 10:00–4:00 (see web site for closings)
Pub. *Newsletter*, bimonthly
$35.00 per year membership; admission: $2.00 for nonmembers; research: $25.00 per hour, including postage and photocopies, payable in advance

Monmouth County Historical Commission
(address withheld upon request)
(Primarily historical, not genealogical. "We are a governmental body with no services to genealogists.")

Monroe Area Historical Society
(Dey Grove Road—location)
Rural Delivery 2, Box 60B (mailing address)
Englishtown, NJ 07726
Carol E. Dooley

Monroe Township Historical Society
(Main and Library Streets—location)
PO Box 474 (mailing address)
Williamstown, NJ 08094
(856) 728-0458

Montague Association for the Restoration of Community History (MARCH)
320 River Road
Montague, NJ 07827
(973) 293-3106 (Wednesday)
Gene Crawford, President; Alicia Batko, Historian
Wed 10:00–noon (volunteers on duty); meetings: last Thur 7:30, tours: July–Aug: Sun 1:00–4:00
Pub. *Notes, News, and Nostalgia*, quarterly
$5.00 per year membership; research: inquiries to Alicia Batko, Historian, SASE appreciated

Montclair Historical Society
Terhune Library
108-110 Orange Road
Montclair, NJ 07042-2133
(973) 744-1796; (973) 783-9149 FAX
http://interactive.net/~upper/crane.html

Karen Whitehaus, President
Office: 15 Sept–15 June: Mon–Fri 9:00–5:00; Crane House Museum: mid-Sept to mid-June: Sun 2:00–5:00; Terhune Library: by appointment
Pub. *Cranetown Crier*, ten times per year (monthly, Sept–June)
$25.00 per year membership

Montville Historical Society
(415 Boyd Street—location)
PO Box 497 (mailing address)
Boonton, NJ 07005
(973) 335-1970
Carol Catacchio, President

Historical Society of Moorestown
(Smith-Cadbury Mansion, 12 High Street—location)
PO Box 477 (mailing address)
Moorestown, NJ 08057
(856) 235-0353
http://www.moorestown.com/community/history
John Coles, President
Tue 1:00–3:00
(local history and local genealogy)
$15.00 per year membership

Morris County Heritage Commission
(300 Mendham Road—location)
Morris County Courthouse, PO Box 900 (mailing address)
Morristown, NJ 07960-0900
(973) 829-8117
heritage@co.morris.nj.us
http://www.co.morris.nj.us/Heritage/index.html
Peg Shultz, History Program Coordinator
Mon–Fri 8:00–5:00
Pub. *County Circular*, three times per year
research: depends on information requested

Morris County Historical Society
18 Jeffrie Trail
Whippany, NJ 07891
(973) 672-7278
Mrs. Terry Schlatter, President
Pub. *The Morris Gazette*

Mount Holly Historical Society
(307 High Street—location)
PO Box 4081 (mailing address)
Mount Holly, NJ 08060
(609) 267-8844

Mount Hope Historical Conservancy, Inc.
32 Mountain Avenue
Rockaway, NJ 07866
(973) 625-2508
Joanna Wheeler Peak, President

Mount Laurel Historical Society
314 Union Mill Road
Mount Laurel, NJ 08054
Rena W. Hallett

Mount Tabor Historical Society
PO Box 137
Mount Tabor, NJ 07878-0137
(973) 625-8742
Natalie Rowell, President

Mountainside Historical Society
Mountainside Free Public Library
Watchung Avenue
Mountainside, NJ 07092

Township of Neptune Historical Society
Neptune Township Historical Museum
(25 Neptune Boulevard—location)
PO Box 1125 (mailing address)

Neptune, NJ 07754-1125
(732) 775-8241, ext. 306; (908) 774-1132 FAX
http://www.monmouth.edu/irs/library/melon/neptune/library.htm
Evelyn Stryker Lewis, Curator/Vice President
Museum: Tue–Fri 1:00–5:00
Pub. *Township of Neptune Historical Society Newsletter*, quarterly
(museum has a reference library with a genealogy section; Monmouth County, New Jersey, history)

New Brunswick Historical Club
278 George Street
New Brunswick, NJ 08901
(732) 247-1695

New Egypt Historical Society
PO Box 295
New Egypt, NJ 08533
Carol Reed, President

New Providence Historical Society
(1350 Springfield Avenue—museum location)
Memorial Library, 377 Elkwood Avenue (mailing address)
New Providence, NJ 07974
(908) 665-1065
John Bale
Museum: first & third Sun, and by appointment: Mason Room, New Providence Memorial Library: Tue 10:00–noon, Thur 10:00–noon & 2:00–5:00
Pub. *Turkey Tracks*, quarterly
(New Providence genealogical and historical collection, photographs, maps, ledgers, etc.)
$10.00 per year membership

New Shrewsbury Historical Society
Wator Street
New Shrewsbury, NJ 07724
Mrs. Jack Branin

Newfield Historical Society
Newfield Borough Hall
107 N.E. Boulevard
Newfield, NJ 08344
(856) 697-3811; (856) 697-1100

North Arlington Historical Society
89 Canterbury Avenue
North Arlington, NJ 07032
(201) 998-6290

North Brunswick Historical Society
690 Cranbury Crossroad
North Brunswick, NJ 08902

North Caldwell Historical Society
120 Grandview Avenue
North Caldwell, NJ 07006
(973) 228-7257
Sue Schlesinger, Vice President

North Jersey Highlands Historical Society
8 Stoney Lane
West Milford, NJ 07480
(973) 208-0034
Nancy Gibbs, President
by appointment
Pub. *The Highlander*, annually, $6.00 per year subscription
(good library for North Jersey, especially ironworking, but relatively little on genealogy)
$15.00 per year membership

Nutley Historical Society

22 Newman Avenue
Nutley, NJ 07110
(973) 667-9121
Tracy Scheckel, President

Oak Summit School Historical Society
190 Oak Summit Road
Frenchtown, NJ 08825
(908) 996-4633
Irene Leon, Treasurer

Ocean County Historical Society
Strickler Research Library
Historical Research Department
(26 Hadley Avenue—location)
PO Box 2191 (mailing address)
Toms River, NJ 08754-2191
(732) 341-1880; (732) 341-4372 FAX
oceancounty.history@verizon.net
http://www.oceancountyhistory.org
Linda Kay, Librarian
Research: Tue–Thur 1:00–4:00, Sat
    10:00–2:00, first Fri 5:00-9:00, and by
    appointment
Pub. *The Scroll*, quarterly
("Collections include 8,000 volume research
    library, 7,800 photographs and maps,
    5,000 manuscripts and documents,
    newspapers and genealogy files for more
    than 600 families. OCHS also holds 300
    volumes and collections of public records
    on deposit from Ocean County.")
$30.00 per year membership; admission:
    $2.00 for nonmembers; limited research
    assistance: $15.00 per hour

Ocean Gate Historical Society
(Cape May and Asbury Avenues—location)
PO Box 895 (mailing address)
Ocean Gate, NJ 08740
(732) 269-3468
http://www.fieldtrip.com/nj/82693468.htm

Historical Society of Ocean Grove, N.J.
(50 Pitman Avenue—location)
PO Box 446 (mailing address)
Ocean Grove, NJ 07756
(732) 774-1869
Susan Roach, Administrative Assistant
Mon & Wed–Fri 10:00–4:00, Sat 10:00–5:00
Pub. *HSOG Newsletter*, two times per year
$20.00 per year membership

Township of Ocean Historical Society
342 Wells Avenue
Oakhurst, NJ 07755
(732) 531-0775
Kathleen Parrett, President

Oceanport Historical Society
20 Pemberton Avenue
Oceanport, NJ 07757
Helen Moffet

Ogdensburg Historical Society
15 Richards Street
Ogdensburg, NJ 07439
Wasco Hadowanetz

Old Bridge Historical Commission
1 Old Bridge Plaza
Old Bridge Township, NJ 08857
(732) 791-5600

Historical Society of Old Randolph
PO Box 1776
Ironia, NJ 07845
(973) 989-7095

Old Schralenburgh Historical Society
43 Overlook Road
Dumont, NJ 07628

Old Wall Historical Society
(Allgor-Barkalow Homestead Museum, 1701
New Bedford Road—location)
PO Box 1203 (mailing address)
Wall Township, NJ 07719
(732) 974-1430 (Sun); (732) 681-3806
    (President)
De Hearn, President
Sun 1:00–4:00, and by appointment
Pub. *Journal*, annually
(genealogy library, Wall Township and
    surrounding area)
$10.00 per year membership

Oldman Township Historical Society
(Railroad Avenue—location)
PO Box 158 (mailing address)
Pedricktown, NJ 08067
(856) 299-1743

Oxford Historical Society
(46 Kent Road—location)
PO Box 60 (mailing address)
Oxford, NJ 07863
(908) 453-3142
D. G. Cratch, President
$10.00 per year membership per mailing
    address; currently has no resources for
    organized searches, inquiries are
    forwarded to other agencies

**Paramus Historical and Preservation
Society**
27 Sullivan Drive
Emerson, NJ 07630
(201) 262-8711
http://maple.nis.net/~wardell/BCAssoc.htm
William Wassmann, President

Parsippany Historical Society
93 Intervale Road
Boonton, NJ 07005
(973) 334-2116
Roberta Chopko

Pascack Historical Society
(19 Ridge Avenue—location)
PO Box 285 (mailing address)
Park Ridge, NJ 07656
(201) 573-0307; (201) 664-4934
http://maple.nis.net/~wardell/BCAssoc.htm
Katherine P. Randall, President
Pub. *Relics*, quarterly
$10.00 per year membership; refers
    genealogical inquiries to the Bergen
    County Historical Society

Passaic County Historical Society
Passaic County Genealogy Club
Lambert Castle Museum and Library
3 Valley Road
Paterson, NJ 07509
(973) 247-0085; (973) 881-9434 FAX
http://www.geocities.com/pchsgs
Andrew F. Shick, Director
Museum: Wed–Sun 1:00–4:00; Library: Wed
    & Fri 1:00–4:00
Pub. *Castle Lite*, quarterly (Historical
    Society); *Castle Genie*, quarterly
    (Genealogy Club)
(Passaic County families, New Jersey
    families)
$20.00 per year membership; research:
    $30.00 for members, $50.00 for
    nonmembers

Pennsauken Historical Society
2506 Denby Avenue
Pennsauken, NJ 08109
(856) 663-1251
Robert Engelke, President

Pennsville Township Historical Society
273 Fort Mott Road
Salem, NJ 08079
(856) 935-6538
Grace Alliegro, President

Perth Amboy Historical Society
1 Lewis Street
Perth Amboy, NJ 08861

Phillipsburg Area Historical Society, Inc.
Municipal Building
675 Corliss Avenue
Phillipsburg, NJ 08865
(908) 454-5400, ext. 353; (908) 454-0816
Wayne Sherrer, President
by appointment only
Pub. *Newsletter*, five times per year (Mar,
    May, July, Sept, Nov), $10.00 per year
    institutional subscription
(local obituaries, weddings, births, etc.)
$10.00 per year membership; research:
    $12.00 per hour plus costs (copies, etc.)

Pilesgrove-Woodstown Historical Society
(42 North Main Street—location)
209 North Main Street (mailing address)
Woodstown, NJ 08098
(856) 769-4588
Ann W. Tatnall, President
Sat 10:00–1:00
("local genealogy-local history")

Piscataway Historical and Heritage Society
1001 Maple Avenue
Piscataway, NJ 08854
(732) 752-5252
Constance and John O'Grady, President

The Historical Society of Plainfield
Drake House
602 West Front Street
Plainfield, NJ 07060-1004
(908) 755-5831
Carol Davis, Genealogy Committee
    Chairperson
Sat 2:00–4:00
limited resources/search available: $5.00
    donation requested with response

Plainsboro Historical Society, Inc.
641 Plainsboro Road
Plainsboro, NJ 08536
(609) 799-0909
Phyllis DiFrancesco, President
Pub. *Reflections*

Point Pleasant Historical Society
PO Box 1273
Point Pleasant Beach, NJ 08742

Port Republic Historical Society
PO Box 215
Port Republic, NJ 08241
(609) 652-1352
Doris Mollock

Historical Society of Princeton
158 Nassau Street
Princeton, NJ 08542
(609) 921-6748; (609) 921-6939 FAX
http://www.princetonhistory.org
Gail F. Stern, Director
Tue–Sun noon–4:00 (winter hours vary)
Pub. *Princeton History*, annually, $5.00 per
    issue
$25.00 per year membership library
    admission: $3.00 for nonmembers;
    research: $10.00 for members, $15.00 for
    nonmembers

Rahway Historical Society, Inc.

(1632 Saint Georges Avenue—location)
PO Box 1842 (mailing address)
Rahway, NJ 07065
(732) 381-0441; (732) 388-0053
Linda McTeague, Director
(local history and genealogy)

John Ralston Historical Association
Box 301
Mendham, NJ 07945

Ramsey Historical Association
65 North Island Avenue
Ramsey, NJ 07446-2528
(201) 327-6467
http://maple.nis.net/~wardell/BCAssoc.htm
William Irwin, President

Riverfront Historical Society
1029 Cooper Street
Beverly, NJ 08010
William Moore, President
8:00–8:00
Pub. *R.H.S. Newsletter*, monthly
$20.00 per year membership

Riverside Township Historical Society
220 Heulings Avenue
Riverside, NJ 08075
J. Robert Espenschied

The Historical Society of Riverton, Inc.
405 Midway
Riverton, NJ 08077
(856) 829-6315
Betty B. Hahle, Historian
Pub. *Gaslight News*

Historical Society of the Rockaways
(Fraesch House, Mount Hope Road,
Rockaway, NJ 07866—location)
Box 100 (mailing address)
Hibernia, NJ 07842
(973) 366-6730
http://www.gti.net/rocktwp/commdir.
html#historical

The Rockingham Association
175 Hun Road
Princeton, NJ 08540
(609) 924-3625
Jack K. Rimalover, President

Roebling Historical Society
119 Second Avenue
Roebling, NJ 08554
(609) 499-2415; (609) 499-8868 FAX
Donna McElrea, President
meetings at Florence Township Library,
Roebling: third Mon 7:00
Pub. *Roebling Record*, quarterly
(Village of Roebling and John A. Roebling
and Sons, Co.)
$7.00 per year membership

Roseland Historical Society
36 Buttonwood Road
Essex Fells, NJ 07021
(973) 226-2708
Mary Lou Rowe, Delegate

The Roselle Historical Society, Inc.
116 East Fourth Avenue
Roselle, NJ 07203
(908) 245-9010
William Frolich, President
(Roselle and New Jersey history: "We try to
be cooperative with requests, but no
guarantee.")
$3.00 per year membership

Roselle Park Historical Society

9 West Grant Avenue
Roselle Park, NJ 07204
(908) 245-5422; (908) 245-9260
http://www.rosellepark.org/upclose/
history/museuminfo.htm
Patricia A. Pagnetti, Historian
Mon 7:00–9:00, Wed 10:00–2:00

Roxbury Township Historical Society
PO Box 18
Succasunna, NJ 07876

Rumson Historical Society
Wilson Circle
Rumson, NJ 07760
(732) 842-0338
Nora Archibald, President

Salem County Historical Society
Alexander Grant House
79-83 Market Street
Salem, NJ 08079
(856) 935-5004
http://www.cyberenet.net/~gsteiner/
njgenweb/salemnj.html
David W. Young, Director
Tue–Sat noon–4:00
Pub. *Newsletter*, four times per year
$20.00 per year membership

Sayreville Historical Society
(425 Main Street—location)
PO Box 18 (mailing address)
Sayreville, NJ 08872
(732) 257-0893
Helen Boehm, President

**Historical Society of Scotch Plains and
Fanwood**
(1840 Front Street—location)
PO Box 261 (mailing address)
Scotch Plains, NJ 07076
(908) 232-1199; (908) 232-2212 FAX
Richard A. Bousquet, President
first Sun 2:00–4:00
Pub. *Newsletter*, quarterly
("Local museum.")
$10.00 per year membership

Sewaren Historical Club
434 Cliff Street
Sewaren, NJ 07077

Shrewsbury Historical Society
(Museum, Education, and Research Center,
419 Sycamore Avenue—location)
PO Box 333 (mailing address)
Shrewsbury, NJ 07702
(732) 530-7974; (732) 741-9406 (President)
J. Louise Jost, President
Tue & Thur 1:00–3:00, Sat 10:00–4:00
$5.00 per year membership

Skylands Association
Box 302
Ringwood, NJ 07456
(973) 362-7527

Somers Point Historical Society
PO Box 517
Somers Point, NJ 08244

Somerset County Historical Society
Van Veghten Drive
Bridgewater, NJ 08807
(908) 218-1281
Dorothy Stratford, Corresponding Secretary
Tue noon–3:00 & 7:00–9:00
Pub. *Newsletter*, ten times per year
$10.00 per year membership

Historical Society of Somerset Hills

(15 West Oak Street—location)
PO Box 136 (mailing address)
Basking Ridge, NJ 07920
(908) 221-1770

Somerville Historical Society
16 East Summit Street
Somerville, NJ 08876

South Amboy Historical Society
109 Fletus Street
South Amboy, NJ 08879
Joseph Wojcieckowski

**South Orange Historical and Preservation
Society**
162 Irving Avenue
South Orange, NJ 07079
(973) 761-5508
Katherine Flaxman, Delegate

South Plainfield Historical Society
PO Box 11
South Plainfield, NJ 07080
(732) 754-3503
Mary Mazepa, President

South River Historical Society
(64-66 Main Street—location)
PO Box 545 (mailing address)
South River, NJ 08882
(732) 257-2200
http://www.rootsweb.com/~njsrhps
Marilyn Anastasio, President
first Sun 1:30–3:30, and by appointment
Pub. *South River Historical and Preservation
News*, five times per year
$5.00 per year membership

Southampton Historical Society
(17 Mill Street—location)
PO Box 2086 (mailing address)
Vincentown, NJ 08088
(609) 859-4042
Joseph Laufer, President
by appointment
Pub. *Hello Central*, quarterly
$5.00 per year membership

Historic Speedwell
333 Speedwell Avenue
Morristown, NJ 07960
(973) 540-0211
Sarah E. Henrich, Delegate

Spring Lake Historical Society, Inc.
(Municipal Building, Fifth and Warren
Avenue—location)
PO Box 703 (mailing address)
Spring Lake, NJ 07762
(732) 449-0772
Janice Sheehan, Vice President
Tue 10:00–noon, Sun 1:00–3:00
Pub. *Newsletter*, quarterly
(permanent museum and changing exhibit
gallery)
$15.00 per year membership

Springfield Historical Society
133 Short Hills Avenue
Springfield, NJ 07081
(973) 379-2634
Janice P. Bongiovanni, President

Squan Village Historical Society
(Main Street—location)
PO Box 262 (mailing address)
Manasquan, NJ 08736
(732) 223-6770

Stafford Township Historical Society
87 Stafford Avenue

Manahawkin, NJ 08050

Stillwater Township Historical Society
PO Box 23
Stillwater, NJ 07855
(973) 383-4822
Mrs. Augustus Roof

Stratford Historical Society
201 South Atlantic Avenue
Stratford, NJ 08084
(856) 435-5901
Walt Baxter, President

Summit Historical Society
(Carter House, 90 Butler Parkway—location)
PO Box 464 (mailing address)
Summit, NJ 07901
(908) 277-1747
Arthur Cotterell, President
Tue 9:30–noon, Wed 1:30–4:00
Pub. *The Historian*, four times per year
(local history: Summit organizations,
   individuals, schools, churches, businesses,
   etc.)
$10.00 per year membership

Sussex County Historical Society
(82 Main Street—location)
PO Box 913 (mailing address)
Newton, NJ 07860
(973) 383-6010
Robert Longcore, President
Fri 10:00–3:00, Sat 9:00–noon
Pub. *Old Sussex Almanack*, four times per
   year
$15.00 per year membership; admission:
   $5.00; research: $25.00

Swedesboro Historical Society
(Swedesboro-Paulsboro Road—location)
PO Box 219 (mailing address)
Swedesboro, NJ 08085
Elaine Roda, President

Tabernacle Historical Society
162 Carranza Road
Vincentown, NJ 08088
(609) 268-0473
Viola Sparagna, President
meetings at Town Hall: monthly evenings
(a small township historical society)

The Tewksberry Historical Society
6 Saw Mill Road
Lebanon, NJ 08833
(908) 832-2562
Stephanie V. R. Koven, President

Trenton Historical Society
PO Box 1112
Trenton, NJ 08606-1112
(609) 883-7368 (President)
Harold W. Thompson, Jr., President

Tuckerton Historical Society
PO Box 43
Tuckerton, NJ 08087

Union County Historical Society
116 East Fourth Avenue
Roselle, NJ 07203
(908) 245-9010
Ruth E. Frolich, Delegate
by appointment
$5.00 per year membership

Union Landing Historical Society
PO Box 473
Brielle, NJ 08730
(732) 528-5867
jbhistorian@usamailbox.com

John E. Belding, President
meetings: third Sun
("Last year restored Osborn family burial
   ground [21 graves].")
$10.00 per year membership

Union Township Historical Society
The Caldwell Parsonage Museum
909 Caldwell Avenue
Union, NJ 07083
(908) 964-9047
Michael Yesenko
by appointment
(publishes local history)

Upper Saddle River Historical Society
245 Lake Street
Upper Saddle River, NJ 07458
(201) 327-6470
http://maple.nis.net/~wardell/BCAssoc.htm
Bill Yeomans, President

Van Harlingen Historical Society
Ludlow Avenue
Belle Mead, NJ 08502
(908) 359-2415
Jessie Havens

Vernon Township Historical Society
5 Sleepy Hollow Road
Sussex, NJ 07461
(973) 875-9562
Joan Magura, President
Pub. *VTHS Newsletter*

Verona Historical Society
31 Thomas Street
Wayne, NJ 07470
(973) 694-5835
Arthur Smith, President

**Vineland Historical and Antiquarian
Society**
(108 South Seventh Street—location)
PO Box 35 (mailing address)
Vineland, NJ 08362
(856) 691-1111
Barbara Sheftall, President; Lana Emmanuel,
   Secretary
Tue–Sat 1:00–4:00 (closed July)
Pub. *Vineland Historical Magazine*,
   annually, $8.50 per year subscription
$15.00 per year membership

Voorhees Township Historical Society
820 Berlin Road
Voorhees, NJ 08043

Walpack Historical Society
PO Box 3
Walpack Center, NJ 07881
Leonard R. Peck, President
May–Oct
Pub. *Walpack Newsletter*, quarterly
$10.00 per year membership

**Warren County Historical and
Genealogical Society**
(313 Mansfield Street—museum and library
location)
PO Box 313 (mailing address)
Belvidere, NJ 07823-0313
(908) 475-2512; (908) 475-4246 (Museum
   recording machine); (908) 689-2993
   (President)
V. A. Brown, Curator; Hattie M. Seiwell,
   President
Sun 2:00–4:00
Pub. *Oak Leaves*, three to four times per year
$7.50 per year membership

Warren Township Historical Society

5 Wychwood Way
Warren Township, NJ 07059
(908) 469-2318
Alan A. Siegal, President
Pub. *Newsletter*, two times per year
$10.00 per year membership

Washington Township Historical Society
(6 Fairview Avenue—location)
PO Box 189 (mailing address)
Long Valley, NJ 07853
(908) 876-9696
Sun 2:00–4:00
(Morris County)
$8.00 per year membership

Watchung Hills Historical Society
102 Old Army Road
Bernardsville, NJ 07924
Mrs. Marion J. Kennedy

Watchung Historical Society
105 Turtle Road
Watchung, NJ 07060
President

Wayne Township Historical Commission
533 Berdan Avenue
Wayne, NJ 07470
(973) 694-7192

Wenonah Historical Society
206 South Princeton Avenue
Wenonah, NJ 08090
(856) 468-6594
Jean Ehlens

Historical Society of West Caldwell
(289 Westville Avenue—location)
PO Box 1701 (mailing address)
West Caldwell, NJ 07006
(973) 226-8976
Roxanne Douglas, President
$10.00 per year membership

West Long Branch Historical Society
PO Box 151
West Long Branch, NJ 07764
Thomas D. Bazley, President

West Paterson Historical Society
556 McBride Avenue
West Paterson, NJ 07424
(973) 345-1876
Alfred Baumann, President

West Portal Historical Society
PO Box 134
Asbury, NJ 08802

Historical Society of West Windsor
PO Box 38
Princeton Junction, NJ 08550
(609) 452-8598
Joan Parry

Westampton Township Historical Society
PO Box 132
Rancocas, NJ 08073-0132

Westfield Historical Society
(Town Hall, Second Floor, 425 East Broad
Street—location)
PO Box 613 (mailing address)
Westfield, NJ 07091
(908) 232-1776
history@westfieldnj.com
http://www.westfieldnj.com/history/
   index.htm
Ralph H. Jones, Curator
Mon–Fri 9:30–noon (except holidays)
Pub. *Westfield Historical Society Newsletter*,

quarterly
$10.00 per year membership

Wharton Historical Society
(10 North Main Street—location)
PO Box 424 (mailing address)
Wharton, NJ 07885

Wildwood Crest Historical Society
(Store #3, Crest Pier, 5800 Ocean Avenue,
Wildwood Crest, NY 08260—location)
2 Jefferson Avenue (mailing address)
Somers Point, NJ 08244-1524
(609) 729-4515
KirkHastings2@aol.com
http://www.cresthistory.org
Kirk Hastings, President
summer: Mon–Sun 7:00–9:00; winter: by
    appointment
("We also have a museum with many local
    photographs.")
$5.00 per year membership

Wildwood Historical Society, Inc.
George F. Boyer Historical Museum
Holly Beach Mall
3907 Pacific Avenue
Wildwood, NJ 08260
(609) 523-0277 (Museum); (609) 522-6285
    (President)
http://www.beachcomber.com/Ocean/
    Chamber/ocmuse.html
Larry M. Lillo, President
summer: Mon–Sun 9:30–2:30, winter:
    Thur–Sun 10:30–2:30
Pub. *News Letter*, semiannually (fall–winter,
    spring–summer)
(historical museum, research room, National
    Marbles Hall of Fame)
$10.00 per year membership

Willingboro Historical Society
Municipal Complex
Willingboro, NJ 08046

Wood-Ridge History Committee
c/o Wood-Ridge Memorial Library
231 Hackensack Street
Wood-Ridge, NJ 07075
(201) 438-2455
Ruth Stumm

Historical Association of Woodbridge
23 East Green Street
Woodbridge, NJ 07095
(732) 636-5874
John P. O'Connor, President

Wyckoff Historical Society
PO Box 73
Wyckoff, NJ 07481

Genealogical Societies

State Genealogical Societies

Genealogical Society of New Jersey
PO Box 1291
New Brunswick, NJ 08903
(732) 356-6920 (Corresponding Secretary)
Dorothy A. Stratford, Corresponding
    Secretary
Rutgers University, New Jersey Room,
    Alexander Library, Special Collections
    and Archives: Mon–Fri 9:00–5:00, Sat
    1:00–5:00
Pub. *The Genealogical Magazine of New
    Jersey*, three times per year; *Newsletter*,
    semiannually
(Bible records, gravestone inscriptions,
    surname data files, Revolutionary Soldier
    information files, abstracted records of

New Jersey churches, etc.)
$15.00 per year membership

Genealogical Societies—Local & Regional

**Genealogical Society of Bergen County,
N.J.**
(Ridgewood Public Library, 125 North
Maple Avenue, Ridgewood, NJ
07450—location)
PO Box 432 (mailing address)
Midland Park, NJ 07432
arnielang@worldnet.att.net
http://www.rootsweb.com/~njgsbc
Arnold Lang, President
meetings at Ridgewood Public Library:
    fourth Mon 7:00 P.M.
Pub. *The Archivist*, quarterly
$15.00 per year membership

**Cape May County Historical and
Genealogical Society**
(see Historical Societies—Local and
Regional, above)

Central Jersey Genealogy Club
PO Box 9903
Hamilton, NJ 08650

**Genealogy Club of the Metuchen-Edison
Regional Historical Society**
(see Historical Societies—Local and
Regional, above)

Monmouth County Genealogy Society
PO Box 5
Lincroft, NJ 07738-0005
(732) 462-1466; (732) 462-8346 FAX
kjshelly@infi.net
http://home.infi.net/~kjshelly/mcgs.html
Bea Denman Howley, President; Kevin
    Shelly, Webmaster
Library: Wed–Sat 10:00–4:00
Pub. *The Monmouth Connection*, bimonthly,
    $12.00 per year U.S. subscription
$15.00 per year membership

Morris Area Genealogy Society
PO Box 105, Convent Station
Convent Station, NJ 07961-0105
Linnea B. Foster, C.G.R.S.
Pub. *Morris Area Genealogy Society
    Newsletter*, quarterly (June, Sept, Dec,
    Mar)
(genealogical information pertaining to the
    Morris area)
$15.00 per year membership

**New York Genealogical and Biographical
Society Library**
(see New York, Part 2)

Ocean County Genealogical Society
376B Lighthouse Drive
Manhawkin, NJ 08050-2327
Barbara Jackson, President
Pub. *Newsletter*, semiannually (summer and
    winter)

Passaic County Genealogy Club
(see Passaic County Historical Society,
Historical Societies—Local and Regional,
above)

Genealogical Society of Salem County
PO Box 231
Woodstown, NJ 08098
http://www.rootsweb.com/~njsalem/
    gsscnj.html
meetings in the annex of the Woodstown
    Presbyterian Church: second Tue
    (Sept–June) 7:30

Pub. newsletter, quarterly
$10.00 per year membership

**Warren County Historical and
Genealogical Society**
(see Historical Societies—Local and
Regional, above)

Genealogical Society of the West Fields
c/o Westfield Memorial Library
550 East Broad Street
Westfield, NJ 07090
gswf@westfieldnj.com
http://westfieldnj.com/gswf
Richard C. Underhill, President
Pub. *Gleanings from the West Fields*,
    bimonthly (Feb, Apr, June, Aug, Oct, Dec)
(New Jersey local history and genealogy)
$10.00 per year membership; research:
    $10.00 for nonmembers

Yankee Genealogical Society
Minnesota Genealogical Society
(see Massachusetts, Part 2)

Independent Publications and Miscellany

**Atlantic County Cultural and Heritage
Commission**
40 Farragut Avenue
Mays Landing, NJ 08330
(609) 625-2776

**Barnegat Bay Decoy and Bayman's
Museum**
(137 West Main Street—location)
PO Box 52 (mailing address)
Tuckerton, NJ 08087
(609) 296-8868
charles@charlesjobesdecoys.com
http://www.charlesjobesdecoys.com/
    barnegat/museum.htm
Wed–Sun 10:00-4:30
admission: $2.00

**Belvidere Historic Preservation
Commission**
Town of Belvidere
691 Water Street
Belvidere, NJ 07823
(908) 475-5331; (908) 475-2512 (Secretary)
Jane W. Ott, Secretary
(Belvidere, Warren County, New Jersey)

**Bergen County Division of Cultural and
Historic Affairs**
Administration Building
Court Plaza South
21 Main Street
Hackensack, NJ 08601-7000
(201) 646-2786

Bergenfield Museum Society
PO Box 95
Bergenfield, NJ 07621
(201) 385-4599
Betty Schmelz, President

**Burlington County Cultural and Heritage
Commission**
(Smithville-Jacksonville Road, Eastampton,
NJ—location)
49 Rancocas Road (mailing address)
Mount Holly, NJ 08060
(609) 201-5068; (609) 265-5958
(primarily historical, not genealogical)

Camden Preservation Trust
811 Church Road
Cherry Hill, NJ 08002-1412

Edward Teitelman

Canal Society of New Jersey
(Waterloo Village, Stanhope—museum
location)
PO Box 737 (mailing address)
Morristown, NJ 07963-0737
(973) 722-9556
Robert H. Barth, President
Pub. *On the Level*, three times per year
(information on New Jersey's historic canals)
$20.00 per year membership

**Cape May County Department of Culture
and Heritage**
30 Mechanic Street
Cape May Court House, NJ 08210
(609) 463-6378; (609) 463-6335
http://cmcculture.org
Dr. Sue Jacobson, Executive Director
7:00–4:00

Historic District Commission (Cape May)
643 Washington Street
Cape May, NJ 08204
(609) 884-8411

**Essex County Department of Parks,
Recreation, Cultural and Historic Affairs**
160 Fairview Avenue
Cedar Grove, NJ 07009
(973) 484-6733

Fort Lee Historic Park
Hudson Terrace
Fort Lee, NJ 07024
(201) 461-1776
FLHP@INTAC.com
John Muller
Wed–Sun 10:00–5:00

The Gene Pool
(see Computer Interest, Part 4)

**Gloucester County Cultural and Heritage
Commission**
406 Swedesboro Road
Gibbstown, NJ 08027
(856) 423-0916

Haddonfield Preservation Society
(120 Warwick Road—location)
PO Box 196 (mailing address)
Haddonfield, NJ 08033
(856) 429-5486
Joan L. Aiken, Executive Director

Historic Paulus Hook Association, Inc.
66 Sussex Street
Jersey City, NJ 07302
Steven B. Sanders, President

Hopewell Museum
28 East Broad Street
Hopewell, NJ 08525
(609) 466-0103
http://www.fieldtrip.com/nj/94660103.htm
Beverly Weidl, Curator
Mon, Wed & Sat 2:00–5:00

The Horseneck Founders of New Jersey
genepool@attbi.com
http://www.rootsweb.com/~genepool/nj.htm
(History and links)

**Hudson County Division of Cultural and
Heritage Affairs**
Murdoch Hall
114 Clifton Place
Jersey City, NJ 07304
(201) 915-1212

**Hunterdon County Cultural and Heritage
Commission**
(3 Chorister Place—location)
PO Box 2900 (mailing address)
Flemington, NJ 08822-2900
(908) 788-1256; (908) 788-1259 FAX
cultural@co.hunterdon.nj.us
Donna Jenssen, Commission Secretary
Mon–Fri 8:30–4:30
("to promote interest and participation in and
understanding of local history, arts,
cultural values and goals of the
community and state by working directly
with arts and historical organizations,
schools, religious organizations, service
clubs, municipal governments and other
interested groups and individuals")

**Island Heights Cultural and Heritage
Association**
PO Box 670
Island Heights, NJ 08732
(732) 929-0695

Meadowlands Museum
(91 Crane Avenue—location)
PO Box 3 (mailing address)
Rutherford, NJ 07070
(201) 935-1175
meadowlandmuseum@aol.com
http://www.meadowlandsmuseum.org
Jackie Bunker-Lohrenz, Museum Director
call for hours, additional hours for school
vacations and summer

**Mercer County Cultural and Heritage
Commission**
640 South Broad Street
Trenton, NJ 08650
(609) 989-6701
(no genealogical records)

Millbrook Village Society, Inc.
Star Route/Fish Hill Road
Tannersville, PA 18372
(570) 629-0456
Bob Demarest, President
Memorial Day–the end of Oct: weekends
Pub. *Out of the Horse's Mouth*, semiannually
("Village located twelve miles north of Rt.
80 bridge over Delaware River in New
Jersey. Village not now inhabited.")
$2.00 per year membership

New Jersey Department of Transportation
Office of the Commissioner
(1035 Parkway Avenue—location)
PO Box 600 (mailing address)
Trenton, NJ 08625
(609) 530-2000; (800) VISIT-NJ
lorraine.plantone@doc.state.nj.us
http://www.state.nj.us/transportation/gis/
county_maps.htm (Maps)

**New Jersey Graveyard Preservation
Society**
PO Box 5
East Brunswick, NJ 08816

New Jersey History Online
macan@scils.rutgers.edu
http://scils.rutgers.edu/~macan/
nj.history.html

New Jersey State Police Museum
(River Road—location)
PO Box 7068 (mailing address)
West Trenton, NJ 08628
(609) 882-2000, ext. 6400

New Netherland Connections
(see New York, Part 2)

New Sweden Farmstead
Mayor Aitken Drive
Bridgeton City Park
Bridgeton, NJ 08302
(856) 455-9785
http://www.biderman.net/new.htm
Sat 11:00–5:00, Sun noon–5:00
admission: $3.00 for adults

NJGenWeb
Part of The USGenweb Project
cgcolo@juno.com; tcf@genealogist.net
http://www.rootsweb.com/~njgenweb/
index.html
Christine Goff, State Coordinator; Peggy
Tebbetts, State Coordinator
(links to other New Jersey resources)

**Ocean County Cultural and Heritage
Commission**
101 Hooper Avenue, Room 225
PO Box 2191
Toms River, NJ 08754-2191
(732) 929-4779

**Passaic County Cultural and Heritage
Council**
Passaic County College
College Boulevard
Paterson, NJ 07509
(973) 684-6555

Pioneer Publications
*Mid-Atlantic Queries & Reviews (DE-NJ-
MD-PA)*
(see Delaware, Part 2)

**Salem County Cultural and Heritage
Commission**
Salem Court House
92 Market Street
Salem, NJ 08079
(856) 935-7510, ext. 292

Sandy Hook Museum
Gateway N.R.A., Sandy Hook Unit
PO Box 437
Highlands, NJ 07732
(732) 872-0115

**Somerset County Cultural and Heritage
Commission**
Historic Court House
PO Box 3000
Somerville, NJ 08876
(908) 231-7110

Somerset County Genealogical Quarterly
PO Box 6493
Bridgewater, NJ 08807
Pub. *Somerset County Genealogical
Quarterly*, $15.00 per year subscription

South Jersey Magazine
(1226 West Main Street—location)
PO Box 847 (mailing address)
Millville, NJ 08332
(856) 825-1615
Shirley R. Bailey, Editor
Mon–Sat 8:00–5:00, or by chance
Pub. *South Jersey Magazine*, quarterly,
$10.00 per year second class subscription,
$19.00 per year first class subscription

Toms River Seaport Society
78 Water Street
Toms River, NJ 08753
(732) 349-9209

**Union County Division of Cultural and
Heritage Affairs**
633 Pearl Street

Elizabeth, NJ 07202
(908) 558-2550; (908) 352-3513 FAX
Susan P. Coen
8:30–5:00
("County government. Can provide
information and referral services to
genealogical questions concerning Union
County locations.")

**Historical Preservation Society of Upper
Township**
(859 South Shore Road—location)
PO Box 659 (mailing address)
Marmora, NJ 08223
(609) 628-3041

**Warren County Cultural and Heritage
Commission**
Shippen Manor
8 Belvidere Avenue
Oxford, NJ 07863
(908) 453-4381; (908) 453-4981 FAX
wcchc@nac.net
http://www.wcchc.org
George K. Warne, Chairman; Carol Cordes,
Secretary
Mon–Fri 8:30–5:00
Pub. *The Furnace*, quarterly, free

Warren County Morris Canal Commission
c/o Warren County Planning Board
Administration Building
Route 519
Belvidere, NJ 07823
(908) 475-8000, ext. 631
Dennis Bertland, Chair

**Woodstown Historical Preservation
Committee**
250 Howard Avenue
Woodstown, NJ 08098
Robert Nathan

New Mexico

Archives and Libraries with Holdings in Genealogy

State Archives and Library
New Mexico Records Center and Archives
1205 Camino Carlos Rey
Santa Fe, NM 87505
(505) 476-7951; (505) 827-7332; (505) 827-
7331 FAX; (505) 476-7909 FAX
sjarami@rain.state.nm.us
http://www.nmcpr.state.nm.us
Elaine Olah, State Records Administrator;
Sandra Jaramillo
Mon–Fri 8:00–5:00
Pub. *Quipu*, irregularly
(Spanish archives of New Mexico,
1621–1821)

New Mexico State Library
Southwest Room
1209 Camino Carlos Rey
Santa Fe, NM 87507
(505) 476-9700; (505) 476-9790 (Southwest
Room); (505) 476-9793 (Public
Services/Southwest Room); (505) 476-
9701 FAX
jjager@stlib.state.nm.us
http://www.stlib.state.nm.us
Jo Anne Jager, Public Services/Southwest
Room
Mon–Fri 9:00–5:00
Pub. *The Hitchhiker: State Library's Weekly
Newsletter*
(New Mexico history, New Mexico
newspapers; slowly building a New
Mexico genealogy section)

State Historical Societies

Historical Society of New Mexico
PO Box 1912
Santa Fe, NM 87504-1912
Pub. *La Cronica*, irregularly
$20.00 per year membership

Museum of New Mexico
The Palace of the Governors
(113 Lincoln Avenue—location)
PO Box 2087 (mailing address)
Santa Fe, NM 87504-2087
(505) 476-5059
jmarshall@mnm.state.nm.us
http://www.museumofnewmexico.org
Orlando Romero, History Librarian; Hazel
Romero, History Librarian; Thomas A.
Livesay, Director of Museum; Thomas E.
Chavez, Ph.D., Director of The Palace of
the Governors
Mon–Fri 1:00–5:00
Pub. *El Palacio*, quarterly
(a historical rather than a genealogical
resource; no staff to conduct genealogical
searches, and refers questions to the
Special Collections Branch at the
University of New Mexico)

**City, County and Regional Archives and
Libraries**
(A more exhaustive list of public and
academic libraries can be found at
http://www.stlib.state.nm.us/directory,
http://www.stlib.state.nm.us/publicservices
/libdirectory/links/links.html, or http://
www.publiclibraries.com/newmexico.htm.)

Alamogordo Public Library
920 Oregon Avenue
Alamogordo, NM 88310
(505) 439-4140 (Circulation); (505) 439-

4148 (Reference); (505) 439-4108 FAX
mschmitt@ci.alamogordo.nm.us
http://www.alamogordo.com/library/
index.html
Mary Leslie Schmitt, Reference Librarian
Mon–Thur 10:00–8:00, Fri–Sat 11:00–5:00,
Sun 1:00–5:00

**Albuquerque/Bernalillo County Library
System**
Special Collections Library
423 Central Avenue, N.E.
Albuquerque, NM 87102
(505) 848-1376; (505) 764-1574 FAX
SpecialCollections@cabq.gov
http://www.cabq.gov/library/specol.html
Gail Rasmussen, Genealogy Librarian
Tue–Sat 10:00–6:00
("Regional history, United States and New
Mexico genealogy.")

Artesia Historical Museum and Art Center
505 Richardson Avenue
Artesia, NM 88210
(505) 748-2390; (505) 746-3886 (Museum)
ahmac@putnetworks.net
http://www.vpa.org/museumsnm.html
Nancy Dunn, Director
Tue–Fri 9:00–noon & 1:00–5:00, Sat
1:00–5:00
(local and area history and family
information)
research: occasional copy fees only or cost

Artesia Public Library
306 West Richardson
Artesia, NM 88210
(505) 746-4252; (505) 746-3007 FAX
apublib@pvtnetworks.net
Tue–Thur 10:00–7:00, Fri–Sat 9:00–6:00

Aztec Museum Association
125 North Main
Aztec, NM 87410
(505) 334-9829; (505) 334-9707 FAX
http://www.nmculture.org/HTML/northw.
htm
Deah Folk, Curator
winter: 10:00–4:00; summer: 9:00–5:00
Pub. *Aztec Museum Association Newsletter*,
monthly
(area history, local genealogy, cemetery
records, oil and gas, forty years of
archives, local newspaper on microfilm
from 1914 to 1989, intermittent from
1890)
$20.00 per year membership; research:
$15.00 per hour

Thomas Branigan Memorial Library
200 East Picacho Avenue
Las Cruces, NM 88001
(505) 526-1047; (505) 647-9455 FAX
http://library.las-cruces.org
Marjory F. Day, Genealogy Librarian; Mark
Pendleton, Reference Librarian; Carol
Brey, Library Director
Mon–Thur 10:00–9:00, Fri–Sat 10:00–6:00,
Sun (Sept–May) 1:00–5:00

Carnegie Public Library
500 National Avenue
Las Vegas, NM 87701
(505) 454-1403; (505) 454-1401; (505) 425-
0193 FAX
joanncastillo21@hotmail.com
Joann Castillo

Kit Carson Historic Museums
(222 LeDoux Street—main office location)
PO Drawer CCC (mailing address)
Taos, NM 87571

(505) 758-0505; (505) 758-5440 (Archives); (505) 758-0062 (Archives); (505) 758-0330 FAX
http://www.nmculture.org (New Mexico Cultural Treasures)
Skip Miller, Co-Director; Karen S. Young, Co-Director; Joan Phillips, Registrar/Archivist; Nita Murphy, Librarian
Museum sites: daily 9:00–5:00; Archives: by appointment only
Pub. *Taos Lightnin'*, quarterly, $15.00 per year subscription
(archives focus on Spanish Colonial and American territorial history; Carson family, Lucien and Ferdinand Maxwell family, James White Leal family and Don Antonio Severino Martinez family genealogies)
$25.00 per year membership; research: $10.00 per hour, one-hour minimum; copies: 20¢ per page

Fray Angélico Chávez History Library and Photographic Archives
(110 Washington Avenue, Santa Fe, NM 87501—location)
PO Box 2087 (mailing address)
Santa Fe, NM 87504
(505) 827-6470; (505) 476-5092; (505) 476-5053 FAX
http://www.palaceofthegovernors.org/index.htm
Arthur L. Olivas

Clovis-Carver Public Library
701 Main Street
Clovis, NM 88101
(505) 769-7840; (505) 769-7842 FAX
http://www.andinfo.com/clovis/library

College of Santa Fe
Fogelson Library
1600 Saint Michaels Drive
Santa Fe, NM 87505-7615
(505) 473-6576; (505) 473-6577; (505) 473-6593 FAX
myers@csf.edu
R. David Myers

Eastern New Mexico University (ENMU)
Golden Library
Station 32
Portales, NM 88130
(505) 562-2624; (505) 562-2647 FAX
Melveta_Walker@enmu.edu
http://www.enmu.edu/academics/library/index.shtml
("Golden Library's special collections include the ENMU Archives, the New Mexico Collection, and New Mexico state government documents depository.")

Eastern New Mexico University (ENMU)
Roosevelt County Historical Museum
Station 30
Portales, NM 88130
(505) 562-2592; (505) 562-2578 FAX
http://www.nmculture.org/HTML/southe. htm

Farmington Museum
3041 East Main Street
Farmington, NM 87402
(505) 566-2290; (505) 326-7572 FAX
cdavis@fmtn.org
http://www.nmculture.org/HTML/northw.htm
Catherine Davis, Collection's Manager
Thur–Sat 8:00–5:00
Pub. *Footnotes*, bimonthly
(publication is not historical; collection on history of San Juan County, photo archives, family documents)

price list and policy available for photocopies and reprints of photographs

Fort Lewis College
(see Colorado, Part 2)

Lovington Public Library
115 South Main Street
Lovington, NM 88260
(505) 396-3144; (505) 396-7189 FAX
http://lovingtonpublib.leaco.net
Tueredia McBride, Director
Mon–Thur 9:30–7:30, Fri 9:30–5:30, Sat 9:30–1:30
(general genealogy collection, emphasizes southern and southwestern states)

Marshall Memorial Library
301 South Tin Avenue
Deming, NM 88030
(505) 546-8408; (505) 546-9202; (505) 546-9649 FAX
demingpl@zianet.com
http://www.zianet.com/demingpl
Margaret Becker, Director
Mon & Fri 9:00–5:00, Tue & Thur 9:00–8:00, Wed 9:00–6:00, Sat 9:00–1:00

Menaul Historical Library of the Southwest
Menaul School, 301 Menaul Boulevard, N.E.
Albuquerque, NM 87107
(505) 345-7727, ext. 25
Nona Browne, Secretary, Advisory Board
Mon–Fri 9:15–4:15
("We are basically an archival research library.")

Mesa Public Library
Los Alamos County Library System
2400 Central Avenue
Los Alamos, NM 87544-4014
(505) 662-8253; (505) 662-8245 FAX
Kathy Bjorklund, Reference
Mon–Thur 10:00–9:00, Fri 10:00–6:00, Sat 9:00–5:00, Sun 11:00–5:00, selected holidays 11:00–5:00
(New Mexico history, basic genealogy tools; no primary genealogical resources, but a selection of indexes, bibliographies and catalogs to help the genealogist locate information and resources)

Museum of the Great Plains
(see Oklahoma, Part 2)

New Mexico Highlands University (NMHU)
Thomas C. Donnelly Library
National Avenue
Las Vegas, NM 87701
(505) 425-7511 (University); (505) 454-3335 (Library); (505) 454-0026 FAX
rubenaragon@nmhu.edu
http://donnelly.nmhu.edu
Ruben F. Aragon, Library Director
Mon–Thur 7:30 A.M.–10:00 P.M., Fri 7:30–5:00, Sat 1:00–5:00, Sun 1:00–10:00, except spring break, spring recess, during finals and semester breaks (consult web site)

Portales Public Library
218 South Avenue B
Portales, NM 88130
(505) 356-3940; (505) 356-3964 FAX
ppl@yucca.net
http://www.portalesnm.org/library/home.htm
Denise Burnett, Library Director
Mon–Wed 10:00–6:00, Thur 10:00–7:00, Fri 10:00–5:00, Sat 10:00–2:00
(southwest materials and small genealogy

library)

Raton Museum
216 South First Street
Raton, NM 87740
(505) 445-8979
http://www.nmculture.org/HTML/northe. htm
Shannon Morrow, Director
winter: Wed–Sat 10:00–4:00; Memorial Day–Labor Day: Tue–Sat 9:00–5:00
(large photo archive and donated family histories/genealogies)

Rio Grande Historical Collections
New Mexico State University
Branson Library
PO Box 30006, Department 3475
Las Cruces, NM 88003-0006
(505) 646-4727; (505) 646-7477 FAX
archives@lib.nmsu.edu
http://lib.nmsu.edu
Austin Hoover, University Archivist
Mon–Fri 8:00–noon & 1:00–4:30, except university holidays
(specializes in New Mexico and the Spanish borderlands; microfilm of the Archivos Historicos del Arzobispado de Durango)

Roswell Public Library
301 North Pennsylvania Avenue
Roswell, NM 88201-4695
(505) 622-7101
http://www.RoswellpublicLibrary.org
Loretta Clark, Reference Librarian
Mon–Tue 9:00–9:00, Wed–Sat 9:00–6:00, Sun 2:00–6:00

San Juan County Museum Association
San Juan County Archaeological Research Center and Library
(6131 U.S. Highway 64, Farmington, NM 87401—location)
PO Box 125 (mailing address)
Bloomfield, NM 87413
(505) 632-2013; (505) 632-1707 FAX
http://www.nmculture.org/cgi-bin/instview.cgi?_recordnum=SJAR
Larry L. Baker, Executive Director
daily 9:00–5:00
Pub. *Newsletter of the San Juan County Museum Association*, quarterly
(collections specializing in regional archaeological and historical research)
$15.00 per year membership

City of Santa Fe Public Library
145 Washington Avenue
Santa Fe, NM 87501
(505) 984-6780 (Main Library); (505) 984-6676 FAX
library@ci.santa-fe.nm.us
http://sfweb.ci.santa-fe.nm.us/sfpl/index.html
Sandra Esquibel, Reference Coordinator
(primarily historical, "not a genealogical resource")

Silver City Museum
312 West Broadway
Silver City, NM 88061
(505) 538-5921; (505) 388-5721; (505) 388-1096 FAX
scmuseum@zianet.com
http://www.silvercitymuseum.org
Susan M. Berry, Museum Director
Tue–Fri 9:00–4:30, Sat–Sun 10:00–4:00
Pub. *The Mansardian*, quarterly (newsletter, not genealogical)
(local history information: newspaper indexes, biographical files, historic buildings, local records, photo archive)
$20.00 per year membership; photocopies: 25¢ per page

The Public Library
515 West College Avenue
Silver City, NM 88061
(505) 538-3672; (505) 388-3757 FAX
silvercitypl@yahoo.com
http://townofsilvercity.org/library/
    library_home.htm
Peter Crum, Reference Librarian
Mon & Thur 9:00–8:00, Tue–Wed
    9:00–6:00, Fri 9:00–5:00, Sat 9:00–1:00

Socorro Public Library
401 Park Street
Socorro, NM 87801
(505) 835-1114; (505) 835-1182 FAX
library@sdc.org
http://www.sdc.org/~library

Southern Methodist University
Clements Center for Southwest Studies
(see Texas, Part 2)

Truth or Consequences Public Library
325 Library Lane
Truth or Consequences, NM 87901-2375
(505) 894-3027; (505) 894-2068 FAX
torclibrary@zianet.com; torcpl@riolink.com
http://www.ci.truth-or-
    consequences.nm.us/library.htm
Ellanie Sampson, Librarian
Mon–Fri 9:00–7:00, Sat 9:00–noon

**University of New Mexico—General
Library**
Zimmerman Library
Albuquerque, NM 87131-1466
(505) 277-5761; (505) 277-7212 (Newspaper
    Project); (505) 277-6019 FAX
zimref@unm.edu; mfletch@unm.edu
    (Newspaper Project)
http://www.unm.edu
Marilyn Fletcher (Newspaper Project)
8:00–5:00
(has 457 newspaper titles from the 1840s on
    microfilm)

University of Utah Marriott Library
(see Utah, Part 2)

Western Heritage Center
(see Montana, Part 2)

Historical Societies—Local and Regional

Albuquerque Historical Society
PO Box 4552
Albuquerque, NM 87196
(505) 255-4595
Ann Johnson, Membership

**American Historical Association, Pacific
Coast Branch**
(see California, Part 2)

**American West Research Center and
Historical Society, Inc.**
(see Ohio, Part 2)

Artesia Historical and Genealogical Society
(Artesia Public Library—location)
PO Box 803 (mailing address)
Artesia, NM 88211-0803
(505) 746-4252 (Library); (505) 746-3101
    (Book Chairman)
Kay Peterson, Book Chairman
9:00–6:00; meetings: third Mon (Sept–May)
    9:30–11:00
Pub. *Newsletter*, three or four times per year
("Library staff does not do research.")
$10.00 per year membership

Cimarron Historical Society
c/o Old Mill Museum
NM 21
PO Box 58
Cimarron, NM 87714
(505) 376-2913
http://www.nmculture.ort/HTML/northe.htm

**Colonial New Mexico Historical
Foundation**
135 Camino Escondido
Santa Fe, NM 87501
(505) 982-5644

Columbus Historical Society, Inc.
(1902 Railroad Station Highway 9 &
    11—location)
PO Box 562 (mailing address)
Columbus, NM 88029
(505) 531-2620
http://www.nmculture.org
Marilyn B. Elliott, Curator
Sept–May: 11:00–4:00; summer: Mon–Thur
    10:00–1:00, Fri–Sun 10:00–4:00
$3.00 per year membership

Corrales Historical Society
PO Box 1051
Corrales, NM 87048
(505) 897-1150
Gay Betzer

El Paso County Historical Society
(see Texas, Part 2)

High Plains Historical Foundation, Inc.
313 Prairieview
Clovis, NM 88101
Harold A. Kilmer, President

Los Alamos County Historical Society
Los Alamos County Historical Museum
(1921 Juniper Street—location)
PO Box 43 (mailing address)
Los Alamos, NM 87544-0043
(505) 662-6272 (Office); (505) 662-4493
    (Museum); (505) 662-6312 FAX
historicalsociety@losalamos.com (General);
    museumshop@losalamos.com (Museum
    Shop)
http://www.losalamos.com/lahistory
Hedy M. Dunn, Museum Director
summer: Mon–Sat 9:30–4:30, Sun
    11:00–5:00; winter: Mon–Sat 10:00–4:00,
    Sun 1:00–4:00
Pub. *Newsletter*, quarterly
(Manhattan District history [WW II era], Los
    Alamos Ranch School [1918–1942]; no
    "real" genealogical database)
$35.00 per year membership; research:
    $20.00 per hour plus photo reproduction
    fees if necessary

Luna County Historical Society, Inc.
Deming Luna Mimbres Museum
301 South Silver Avenue
Deming, NM 88030
(505) 546-2382; (505) 546-2677 (Archives)
http://www.nmculture.org/HTML/
    southw.htm
Dolly Shannon, Archivist
Museum: daily 9:00–5:00; Archives: by
    appointment
("We operate chiefly as a museum,
    specializing in southern New Mexico and
    the Mimbres Indians; genealogy search as
    time permits.")
$3.00 per year membership; research:
    donation

Moriarty Historical Society and Museum
(777 Central Avenue, S.W.—location)

PO Box 1366 (mailing address)
Moriarty, NM 87035
(505) 832-4087
http://www.nmculture.org/HTML/central.
    htm
Susie McComb, Director
summer: Mon–Sat 10:00–5:00; winter:
    Mon–Fri 10:00–5:00, Sat 1:00–4:00
$10.00 for first-year membership, $7.00 per
    year renewal

Permian Historical Society
(see Texas, Part 2)

**Sacramento Mountains Historical Society,
Inc.**
(U.S. Highway 82—location)
PO Box 435 (mailing address)
Cloudcroft, NM 88317
(505) 682-2932
http://www.nmculture.org/HTML/southe. htm
Marie Wuersching, Museum Director
Tue–Sat 10:00–4:00

San Gabriel Historical Society
PO Box 1528
Santa Cruz, NM 87567
(505) 852-2112

Sandoval County Historical Society
PO Box 692
Bernalillo, NM 87004
(505) 867-2755
Martha Liebert

Sierra County Historical Society
211 Main
Truth or Consequences, NM 87901
(505) 894-6600
Ann Welborn, Director
Mon–Sat 9:00–5:00
$10.00 per year membership

Sociedad Historica de la Tierra Amarilla
PO Box 24
Los Ojos, NM 87551
(505) 345-5147

Socorro County Historical Society, Inc.
Hammel Museum
(Sixth Street—location)
PO Box 923 (mailing address)
Socorro, NM 87801
(505) 838-4141; (505) 835-3437 (Secretary)
http://www.rootsweb.com/~nmschs
Barbara DuBois, Secretary
Open house: first Sat 9:00–2:00
$20.00 per year membership

**Historical Center for Southeast New
Mexico, Inc.**
(formerly Chaves County Historical Society,
Inc.)
200 North Lea Avenue
Roswell, NM 88201
(505) 622-8333
http://roswell-usa.com/historic/index.html
David E. Orr, Administrator
Office: Mon–Fri 9:00–5:00; Archives: by
    appointment
("regional archival collections")

**Southeastern New Mexico Historical
Society**
101 South Halagueno
Carlsbad, NM 88220
(505) 885-6776

**Historical Society of Southwestern New
Mexico**
Western New Mexico University Museum
Silver City, NM 88061

(505) 538-6386

Taos County Historical Society
(121 C North Plaza, Old
Courthouse—location)
PO Box 2447 (mailing address)
Taos, NM 87571
Bob Romero
Mon, Wed & Fri 1:00–3:00
Pub. *Ayer y Hoy en Taos*, biannually, $3.00
    per issue
$15.00 per year membership

Tucumcari Historical Museum
416 South Adams Street
Tucumcari, NM 88401
(505) 461-4201
Bruce Nutt, Curator
1 June–31 Aug: 9:00–6:00; 1 Sept–30 May:
    9:00–5:00
("Historical displays at museum")

Tularosa Basin Historical Society
1301 North White Sands Boulevard
Alamogordo, NM 88310
(505) 434-4438
http://www.nmculture.org/HTML/southe.htm
Kathy Gren, Museum Director/Curator
Mon–Sat 10:00–4:00, Sun 1:00–4:00, closed
    all Federal holidays
$6.00 per year membership

Tularosa Village Historical Society
(608 Central Avenue—location)
30 Dusty Lane (mailing address)
Tularosa, NM 88352
(505) 585-9597 (Museum); (505) 585-2057
Norma E. Cinert, Secretary
Mon–Sat 1:00–4:00
$6.00 per year membership

Union County Historical Society
(Herzstein Memorial Museum, South Second
and Walnut—location)
PO Box 75 (mailing address)
Clayton, NM 88415-0075
(505) 374-2977
uchs@plateautel.net
http://www.herzsteinmuseum.org
D. Ray Blakeley, Director
1:00–5:00, and by appointment, closed Mon
Pub. *Union County Historical Society
    Review*, quarterly
$25.00 per year membership; research: "free
    to members, comp copy on request, no fee
    charged, donations accepted"

Valencia County Historical Society
Harvey House Museum
PO Box 166
Belen, NM 87002
(505) 861-0581
http://www.nmculture.org/HTML/central.
    htm

Western History Association
University of New Mexico
Albuquerque, NM 87131

Genealogical Societies

State Genealogical Society

New Mexico Genealogical Society
PO Box 8283
Albuquerque, NM 87198-8283
(505) 822-9067 (President); (505) 792-9696
    (Editor)
info@nmgs.org
http://www.nmgs.org
LeRoy Leopoldo Garcia, President; Karen
    Daniel, C.G., Editor

meetings at Albuquerque/Bernalillo County
    Library System, Special Collections
    Library; workshops and programs
    announced on the NMGS web site, at the
    library, and by mail to members
Pub. *New Mexico Genealogist*, quarterly
    (Mar, June, Sept, Dec)
$15.00 per year membership; research:
    $10.00 per hour (limit two hours paid in
    advance), plus copies at 25¢ per page,
    postage, and other expenses

Genealogical Societies—Local & Regional

Alamogordo Genealogical Society
PO Box 246
La Luz, NM 83337
(505) 434-1675
Joyce Taylor

The Genealogy Club of Albuquerque
11605 Hughes Avenue, N.E.
Albuquerque, NM 87112-1813
(505) 298-8018
Elizabeth Frost, President
meetings at Albuquerque/Bernalillo County
    Library System, Special Collections
    Library: second Wed 10:00
Pub. *Genealogy Club Quarterly* (Feb, May,
    Aug, Nov)
(promotes genealogy, provides educational
    aid, supports the library; The Genealogy
    Club consists primarily of members who
    are researching outside of New Mexico)
$10.00 per year membership

**Artesia Historical and Genealogical
Society**
(see Historical Societies—Local and
Regional, above)

Curry County Genealogy Society
c/o Clovis-Carver Public Library, Genealogy
Room
701 Main Street
Clovis, NM 88101
(505) 762-5408
Wanda Dunn, President
meetings in the Genealogy Room at Clovis-
    Carver Public Library: first Mon 7:00
    (except June–Sept & Dec), second Mon
    7:00 (Sept)
$10.00 per year membership

Eddy County Genealogical Society
Carlsbad Public Library
PO Box 461
Carlsbad, NM 88220
(505) 887-7167
Annette Price, President
Mon–Sat 10:00–8:00, Sun 2:00–5:00;
    meetings: second Sun 2:00
Pub. *Pecos Trails*, semiannually
$8.00 per year membership

Grant County Genealogical Society
PO Box 1581
Silver City, NM 88062
(505) 538-2329
barbarahrah@yahoo.com
Barbara Holley Rock
(society no longer active, but Mrs. Rock will
    assist with queries)

Las Vegas Genealogical Society
c/o Carnegie Public Library
500 National Avenue
Las Vegas, NM 87701-4399
(505) 454-1403 (Library); (505) 425-7175
Sue Parham
meetings: third Wed 7:00

Lea County Genealogical Society
Bill McKibben Senior Center
14 West Avenue F
Lovington, NM 88260
(505) 396-2608
Mrs. R. L. Binkley, President
meetings third Tue 1:30

Los Alamos Genealogical Association
PO Box 900
Los Alamos, NM 87544-0900
(505) 662-3381
jodiefrye@yahoo.com
Jodie C. Frye, Secretary
meetings at Mesa Public Library: second
    Thur 7:00 (except June–July)
Pub. *Los Alamos Genealogical Association
    Newsletter*, quarterly, $8.00 per year
    subscription

Roswell Genealogical Society
Roswell Adult Center
807 North Missouri
Roswell, NM 88201
(505) 622-6725
Clarence Rollins, President
$6.00 per year membership

Roswell New Mexico Genealogical Group
2604 North Kentucky
Roswell, NM 88201

Santa Fe Genealogical Society
140 West Coronado Road
Santa Fe, NM 87501
Cora Mae Stumpff

**Southeastern New Mexico Genealogical
Society**
(Agnes Kastner Head Center, Room 115, 200
East Park Street, Hobbs, NM
88240—location)
PO Box 5725 (mailing address)
Hobbs, NM 88241-5725
(505) 393-3658
Veta Blackburn, Assistant Librarian
Tue 2:00–4:00, Thur 6:00–9:00
Pub. *Newsletter*, monthly
$10.00 per year membership

Southern New Mexico Genealogical Society
Thomas Branigan Memorial Library
200 East Picacho Avenue
Las Cruces, NM 88001
(505) 526-1047 (Library)
wheelerwc@zianet.com
http://www.zianet.com/wheelerwc/
    GenSSNM
Marjory F. Day, Genealogy Librarian; Mark
    Pendleton, Reference Librarian; Carol
    Brey, Library Director
Mon–Thur 10:00–9:00, Fri–Sat 10:00–6:00,
    Sun (Sept–May) 1:00–5:00; meetings:
    fourth Thur
(New Mexico genealogy and resources)
$5.00 per year membership

Tatah Tracers Genealogical Society
(Salmon Ruins Library and Museum,
Bloomfield Highway, Farmington, NM
87401—location)
PO Box 125 (mailing address)
Bloomfield, NM 87413-0125
(505) 632-3668
Ken Gomez, President
meetings at the Civic Center in Farmington:
    second Tue (Sept–May) 7:30
Pub. *Tatah Tracer*, irregularly
$15.00 per year membership

Independent Publications and

Miscellany

Acoma Pueblo Museum
NM 23
PO Box 309
Acoma Pueblo, NM 87034
(505) 252-1139
http://www.nmculture.org/HTML/northw.
htm

Bandar Log, Inc.
(Main Street—location)
PO Box 86 (mailing address)
Magdalena, NM 87825
(505) 854-2715

Center for Southwest Research
University of New Mexico—General Library
Zimmerman Library
Albuquerque, NM 87131-1466
(505) 277-6451; (505) 272-2282 (Oral
History Program); (505) 277-6019 FAX
cswrref@unm.edu
http://www.unm.edu/~cswrref
Dave Baldwin, Interim Director; Carols
Vasquez, Oral History Program Director
8:00–5:00
(has *Diligencias Matrimoniales* 1678–1869
on microfilm, Dreesen extracts of
marriages from the 17th through 19th
century in the middle Rio Grande Valley,
and Olmsted translation and abstraction of
Spanish Enlistment Papers of New
Mexico, 1732–1820)

Comgenes
(see Computer Interest, Part 4)

**City of Las Vegas Museum and Rough
Riders Memorial Collection**
727 Grand Avenue
Las Vegas, NM 87701
(505) 454-1401, ext. 283; (505) 425-7335
FAX
http://nmculture.org (or through
http://moravalley.com)
Melanie LaBoruit, Museum Director
Mon–Fri 9:00–noon & 1:00–4:00, Sat
(May–Oct) 10:00–3:00, Sun (May–Oct)
noon–4:00
("We have many unidentified photographs
from San Miguel County and many Rough
Rider related correspondence files.")
research: currently no fee, "but limited staff
and volunteers, so time is sometimes
lapsed between request and response"

Million Dollar Museum
Carlsbad Caverns Highway
White's City, NM 88268
(505) 785-2291
http://www.caverns.com/~chamber/rec.htm

New Mexico Department of Tourism
(800) 733-6396, ext. 0643
webmaster@newmexico.org
http://www.newmexico.org/maps/index.html

The New Mexico Historical Review
Mesa Vista Hall 1013
University of New Mexico
Albuquerque, NM 87131-1186
(505) 277-5839; (505) 277-6023 FAX
nmhr@unm.edu
http://www.unm.edu/~nmhr
Elaine Carey, Managing Editor
Mon–Fri 9:00–3:00 (may vary)
Pub. *The New Mexico Historical Review*,
quarterly (Jan, Apr, July, Oct), $26.00 per
year subscription
(history of New Mexico and borderlands)

**New Mexico State Highway and
Transportation Department**
(1120 Cerrillos Road—location)
PO Box 1149 (mailing address)
Santa Fe, NM 87504-1149
(505) 827-5100
http://www.nmshtd.state.nm.us/maps/
default.asp (Maps)

NMGenWeb
Part of The USGenweb Project
(505) 299-7447
Capt.Pat@RootsQuest.com
http://www.rootsweb.com/~nmgenweb
Susan Bellomo, State Coordinator; Jo Fox,
Assistant Coordinator; Pat Smith,
Assistant Coordinator
(links to other New Mexico resources)

Santa Fe Trail Museum
(614 Maxwell Avenue—location)
PO Box 323 (mailing address)
Springer, NM 87747
(505) 483-2998
http://www.nmculture.org/HTML/northc.
htm
Michael W. Jones, Chairman of Museum
Committee
information: Mon–Fri 9:00–4:00; visiting:
Mon–Sat (June–Aug) 9:00–4:30
("no organized files of information")

Texas State Historical Association
Southwestern Historical Quarterly
(see Texas, Part 2)

Tome Parish Museum
(State Highway 47—location)
PO Box 397 (mailing address)
Tome, NM 87060
(505) 865-7497

University of Arizona Press
Journal of the Southwest
(see Arizona, Part 2)

**University of New Mexico—Map and
Geographic Information Center (MAGIC)**
Centennial Science and Engineering Library
Albuquerque, NM 87131-1466
(505) 277-4412

Western New Mexico University Museum
(1000 West College Avenue—location)
PO Box 680 (mailing address)
Silver City, NM 88061
(505) 538-6386; (505) 538-6178
http://www.nmculture.org/HTML/wnmu.htm

New York

Archives and Libraries with Holdings in Genealogy

State Archives and Libraries

New York State Archives
New York Department of Education
Cultural Education Center, Room 11D40
Albany, NY 12230
(518) 474-8955; (518) 473-7573 FAX
archref@mail.nysed.gov (Research
Assistance)
http://www.archives.nysed.gov
Mon–Fri 9:00–5:00
(archival records of New York State
government agencies, mostly
administrative and not of use to
genealogists)

New York State Library
Genealogy Section, Reference Services
Seventh Floor, Cultural Education Center
Empire State Plaza
Albany, NY 12230
(518) 474-5161
http://www.nysl.nysed.gov/gengen.htm
Henry Ilnicki, Senior Librarian
Mon–Fri 9:00–5:00 (coverage is by members
of the Capital District Genealogical
Society, "call genealogy desk if coming
long distance")
(New York State and Local History collection
contains materials depicting all periods
and aspects of New York State history
from colonial times to the present;
Genealogy Area includes an extensive
collection of printed histories on
individual families, national in scope with
an emphasis on New York, Pennsylvania,
New Jersey and New England), also DAR
and Loyalist records, census, periodicals,
probate, military, church and vital
records)

**New York State Library Newspaper
Project**
Sixth Floor, Cultural Education Center
Empire State Plaza
Albany, NY 12230
(518) 474-7491; (518) 474-5786 FAX
http://www.nysl.nysed.gov/nysnp

State Historical Societies

**Association of Public Historians of New
York State (APHNYS)**
http://www.tier.net/aphnys/cohistorians.html
Elizabeth Bartlow, Corresponding Secretary
("Working to promote the heritage and
history of New York State")

The New-York Historical Society
2 West 77th Street
New York, NY 10024-5194
(212) 873-3400
http://www.nyhistory.org
Tue–Sat 10:00–5:00 (Tue–Fri in summer)
free admission to library, fee for museum
galleries

New York State Historian
3097 Cultural Education Center
Empire State Plaza
Albany, NY 12230
(518) 474-5353
Dr. Kenneth Ames, State Historian

New York State Historical Association
(Fenimore House, Route 80, West Lake Road

[next to Fenimore Art Museum]—location)
PO Box 800 (mailing address)
Cooperstown, NY 13326-0800
(607) 547-1400 (Fenimore House Museum);
    (607) 547-1470 (Library); (607) 547-1405
    FAX (Library)
library@nysha.org
http://www.nysha.org
Wayne Wright, Associate Director of
    Research Library
Mon–Thur 10:00–6:00, Fri 10:00–5:00, Sat
    1:00–5:00; Special Collections: Mon–Fri
    1:00–5:00
Pub. *New York History*, quarterly, $35.00 per
    year subscription; *Heritage*, annually,
    $10.00 per year subscription
$45.00 per year membership (includes both
    periodicals); research: $35.00 per hour;
    admission: $5.00

Regional Council of Historical Agencies
Lake Road
Cooperstown, NY 13326
(607) 547-4131 (answering machine); (800)
    895-1648
Linda Norris, Projects Manager
Pub. *RCHA News*, quarterly
(serves Broome, Cayuga, Chemung,
    Chenango, Cortland, Delaware, Franklin,
    Hamilton, Herkimer, Jefferson, Lewis,
    Madison, Oneida, Onondaga, Ontario,
    Oswego, Otsego, Saint Lawrence,
    Schuyler, Seneca, Tioga, Tompkins and
    Wayne counties)
$25.00 per year membership; does not answer
    genealogical queries

**City, County and Regional Archives and
Libraries**
(A more exhaustive list of public and
    academic libraries can be found at http://
    www.nysl.nysed.gov/libdev/libs/publibs/ city.
    htm or http://www.nysl.nysed.gov/
    edocs/education/library/dir.)

Adams Center Free Library
18267 State Route 177, South Harbor Road
Adams Center, NY 13606
(315) 583-5501 voice & FAX
adclib@nnyln.net
http://www.nc3r.org/adc
Connie Holberg

Adams Free Library
Adams Municipal Building
2 North Main Street
Adams, NY 13605
(315) 232-2265
http://www.nc3r.org/admfl
Frances Sischo

Adirondack Museum Library
(Route 30—location)
PO Box 22 (mailing address)
Blue Mountain Lake, NY 12812-0099
(518) 352-7311; (518) 352-7653 FAX
jpepper@adkmuseum.org
http://www.adkmuseum.org
Jerold Pepper, Librarian
Mon–Fri 9:00–5:00

**Adriance Memorial Library/Greater
Poughkeepsie Library District**
93 Market Street
Poughkeepsie, NY 12601
(845) 485-3445; (800) 804-0092; (845) 485-
    3789 FAX
http://poklib.org/adriance.php
Myra Morales
by appointment only
(emphasis on Dutchess County and vicinity)

**Annie Porter Ainsworth Memorial
Library**
(6064 South Main Street—location)
PO Box 69 (mailing address)
Sandy Creek, NY 13145
(315) 387-3732; (315) 387-2005 FAX
scrlib@nnyln.net
http://www.nc3r.org/ncls/libs/scr.txt
Tue 1:00–6:00, Wed 1:00–4:00, Thur
    11:00–8:00, Fri 11:00–6:00, Sat
    10:00–1:00

Albany County Hall of Records
250 South Pearl Street
Albany, NY 12202
(518) 447-4500
http://nyslgti.gen.ny.us/achor
Mary F. Wallen, Executive Director
8:30–4:30

Albany Institute of History and Art
125 Washington Avenue
Albany, NY 12210
(518) 463-4478; (518) 463-5506
http://www.albanyinstitute.org
Jennifer Benedetto, Librarian
Library: by appointment only
(Albany and upper Hudson Valley region)
admission: $5.00; research: first hour free,
    $30.00 per hour thereafter

Albany Public Library
Pruyn Library
161 Washington Avenue
Albany, NY 12210
(518) 449-3380; (518) 449-3386 FAX
aplweb@uhls.lib.ny.us
http://www.albanypubliclibrary.org
Ellen K. Gamache, Local History Librarian
Mon–Thur 9:00–9:00, Fri 9:00–6:00, Sat
    9:00–5:00, Sun (except summer)
    1:00–5:00
(city and county of Albany)

Alfred University
Herrick Memorial Library
Special Collections
Saxon Drive
Alfred, NY 14802
(607) 871-2184; (607) 871-2385; (607) 871-
    2992 FAX
http://www.herr.alfred.edu/speccoll.htm

Allegany County Department of History
Courthouse
7 Court Street
Belmont, NY 14813
(716) 268-9293; (716) 268-9446 FAX
Craig R. Braack, County Historian
Mon–Fri 9:00–5:00

Allegany County Museum
11 Wells Street
Belmont, NY 14813
(716) 268-9293 (Museum); (716) 268-9446
    FAX
historian@alleganyco.com
Craig R. Braack, County Historian
Museum: winter: 9:00–noon & 1:00–5:00;
    June–Aug: 8:30–noon & 1:00–4:00
(census, land records, cemetery index)

Altamont Archives/Museum
Village Hall
115 Main Street
Altamont, NY 12009
(518) 861-8554

Andes Society for History and Culture
Main Street
Andes, NY 13731

Angelica Free Library
Colonial Rooms
(55 West Main Street—location)
PO Box 128 (mailing address)
Angelica, NY 14709-0128
(716) 466-7860 voice & FAX
http://www.stls.org/Angelica
Doris Feldbauer, Library Director

Ardsley Public Library
9 American Legion Drive
Ardsley, NY 10502
(914) 693-6636
agroth@wlsmail.org
http://www.wls.lib.ny.us/libs/ardsley
Angela Z. Groth, Director

Au Sable Forks Free Library
9 West Church Street
Au Sable Forks, NY 12912
(518) 647-5596
http://www.kvvi.net/~ausable

Babylon Public Library
24 South Carll Avenue
Babylon, NY 11702-3403
(631) 669-1624; (631) 669-7826 FAX
babllib@suffolk.lib.ny.us
http://www.suffolk.lib.ny.us/libraries/babl
Patricia LaWare, Reference and Adult
    Services Librarian
Mon–Thur 9:30–9:00, Fri–Sat 9:30–5:00,
    Sun 1:00–5:00

Baldwinsville Public Library
33 East Genesee Street
Baldwinsville, NY 13027
(315) 635-5631; (315) 635-6760 FAX
info@bville.lib.ny.us
http://www.bville.lib.ny.us
Margaret A. Van Patten, Head of
    Reference/Adult Services
Mon–Thur 10:00–9:00, Fri 10:00–5:00, Sat
    10:00–4:00, Sun (Sept–June) 1:00–5:00
(emphasis on Baldwinsville, New York)

Ballston Spa Public Library
21 Milton Avenue
Ballston Spa, NY 12020
(518) 885-5022 voice & FAX (with
    permission)
http://ballston.sals.edu
Virginia Humphrey, Director
mid-Sept to mid-June: Tue 10:00–8:00,
    Wed–Fri 10:00–7:00, Sat 10:00–4:00;
    mid-June to mid-Sept: Mon & Fri
    10:00–5:00, Tue–Thur 10:00–7:00, Sat
    10:00–1:00
(Saratoga County, New York; *Ballston
    Journal* partially indexed from 1847,
    various name indexes, Ballston Center
    Church records, other miscellaneous local
    history and genealogy sources)
limited searches for only very specific
    requests: $5.00 per hour

**Historical Museum of the Darwin R.
Barker Library**
(20 East Main Street—entrance to location)
7 Day Street (mailing address)
Fredonia, NY 14063
(716) 672-2114
Jutta Rawcliffe, Curator; Julia Fairbanks,
    Genealogist
Tue & Thur–Sat 2:30–4:30, Thur 7:00–9:00
Pub. *Member's Newsletter Quarterly*;
    Occasional Papers Series
(local historical and genealogical
    library/archives)
$10.00 per year membership; research:
    donation and copying costs, minimum
    $7.50

Frank J. Basloe Library
245 North Main Street
Herkimer, NY 13350-1918
(315) 866-1733 voice & FAX
http://www.midyork.org/herkimer
Heidi L. Moody, Library Director
Mon–Thur 9:00–8:00, Fri 9:00–5:00, Sat
    (Sept–June) 9:00–3:00

Bayville Free Library
34 School Street
Bayville, NY 11709
(516) 628-2765; (516) 628-2738 FAX
http://www.nassaulibrary.org/bayville/
    index.html
Regina Mascia, Director
Mon–Thur 10:00–9:00, Fri 10:00–5:00, Sat
    10:00–5:00 (Sat (summer) 10:00–1:00

Belden Noble Memorial Library
(Main Street, Route 22—location)
PO Box 339 (mailing address)
Essex, NY 12936
(518) 963-8079 voice & FAX
beldennoble@willex.com
http://www.cefls.org/essex.htm
Karen and Frank East, Directors

Bennington Museum
(see Vermont, Part 2)

The Berkshire Athenaeum
(see Massachusetts, Part 2)

Bethlehem Public Library
451 Delaware Avenue
Delmar, NY 12054
(518) 439-9314
bpl@uhls.lib.ny.us
http://www.uhls.org/bethlehem
Marie S. Carlson, Reference Librarian, Local
    History/Genealogy
winter: Mon–Fri 9:00–9:00, Sat 10:00–5:00,
    Sun (Sept–late June) 1:00–5:00
("Growing collection—emphasizes local
    genealogy, published records and
    passenger lists")

Binghamton University
Glenn G. Bartle Library
(Vestal Parkway East, Vestal, NY
    13850—location)
PO Box 6012 (mailing address)
Binghamton, NY 13902-6012
(607) 777-2345 (Main Reference Desk);
    (607) 777-4844 (Special Collections)
http://library.lib.binghamton.edu
Jeanne Eichelberger, Head, Special
    Collections; Ed Shephard,
    History/Genealogy Reference
Mon–Thur 8:00 A.M.–midnight, Fri 8:00
    A.M.–9:00 P.M., Sat noon–9:00, Sun
    noon–midnight; Special Collections:
    Mon–Fri 11:00–3:00 (summer hours vary)

Black River Free Library
(102-104 Maple Street—location)
Box 253 (mailing address)
Black River, NY 13612
(315) 773-5163
blrlib@nnyln.net
http://www.nc3r.org/ncls/libs/blr.txt
Sandra Lamb

Black Watch Memorial Library
195 Montcalm Street, East
Ticonderoga, NY 12883
(518) 585-7380; (518) 585-3209 FAX
http://www.cefls.org/ticonderoga.htm

Blauvelt Free Library
541 Western Highway

Blauvelt, NY 10913-1527
(845) 359-2811; (845) 398-0017 FAX
blv@rcls.org
http://www.rcls.org/blv
Mary Behringer, Director
Mon–Thur 10:00–9:00, Fri 10:00–5:00, Sat
    11:00–5:00 (summer 10:00–2:00), Sun
    2:00–5:00 (except summer)

Bodman Memorial Library
8 Aldrich Street
Philadelphia, NY 13673
(315) 642-3323
philib@nnyln.net
http://www.nc3r.org/ncls/libs/phi.txt
Barbara Digle
Wed–Thur 1:00–5:00, Wed 7:00–9:00, Sat
    9:00–1:00

Boston Historical Museum
Old Pioneer Church
(9410 Boston State Road—location)
PO Box 31 (mailing address)
Boston, NY 14025
(716) 941-3475
Research Library: Sun 2:00–4:00

Brentwood Public Library
Second Avenue and Fourth Street
Brentwood, NY 11717
(631) 273-7883
http://brentwood.suffolk.lib.ny.us
Carol Pomfrey
Mon–Tue & Thur–Fri 9:00–9:00, Wed & Sat
    9:00–5:00, Sun (Sept–May) noon–4:00

Brighton Memorial Library
2300 Elmwood Avenue
Rochester, NY 14618
(716) 473-5420
http://www.brightonlibrary.org

Brooklyn College
Museum of the Borough of Brooklyn at
    Brooklyn College
Bedford Avenue and Avenue H
Brooklyn, NY 11210
(718) 780-5152
http://www.brooklyn.cuny.edu/bc/fac/
    bclib.html
(received part of the collection of the former
    James A. Kelly Institute for Local
    Historical Studies)

Brooklyn Public Library
Brooklyn Collection
Central Library
Grand Army Plaza
Brooklyn, NY 11238
(718) 780-7794
http://www.brooklynpubliclibrary.org
Judith Walsh, Local History Librarian
Mon–Fri 11:00–1:00 & 3:00–5:00,
    Tue–Thur 6:00–7:30, Sat 10:00–1:00 &
    2:00–5:00, appointment advisable
(*Brooklyn Daily Eagle* morgue clippings ca
    1904–1955, but very few other
    genealogical materials)

**Brookside Museum-Saratoga County
History Center**
6 Charlton Street
Ballston Spa, NY 12020
(518) 885-4000 (Museum)
info@brooksidemuseum.org (Museum)
http://www.brooksidemuseum.org (Museum)
Tue–Fri 10:00–4:00, Sat noon–4:00

Broome County Public Library
185 Court Street
Binghamton, NY 13901
(607) 778-6400; (607) 778-1441 FAX

bcpl@co.broome.ny.us;
    gsmith@co.broome.ny.us
http://www.bclibrary.info
Gerald R. Smith, Library Assistant and
    County Historian
Mon–Thur 9:00–9:00, Fri–Sat 9:00–5:00
(Broome County, Binghamton, New York,
    history

Brownville-Glen Park Library
(216 Brown Boulevard—location)
PO Box 510 (mailing address)
Brownville, NY 13615
(315) 788-7889
brolib@nnyln.net
http://www.nc3r.org/ncls/bro.txt
Candace Wilde, Librarian
Tue–Wed & Fri noon–5:00 & 7:00–9:00, Sat
    10:00–2:00

**The Bryant Library Local History
Collection**
2 Paper Mill Road
Roslyn, NY 11576
(516) 621-2240
cmealing@bryantlibrary.org
http://www.nassaulibrary.org/bryant/
    index.html
Myrna L. Sloam, Archivist
by appointment
(history of Roslyn, New York, Long Island
    history; William C. Bryant, Christopher
    Morley Collections)

Buffalo and Erie County Public Library
1 Lafayette Square
Buffalo, NY 14203-1887
(716) 858-7103; (716) 858-7114 (Special
    Collections Room); (716) 858-6211 FAX
childsj@buffalolib.org
http://www.buffalolib.org/cl_collect
    details.html (Special Collections Room)
Robert M. Gurn, Head of Special Collections
Mon–Wed & Fri–Sat 8:30–6:00, Thur
    8:30–8:00, Sun (during the school year)
    1:00–5:00
(strong focus on Buffalo and Erie County
    history with some holdings for Allegany,
    Cattaraugus, Chautauqua, Genesee,
    Niagara, Orleans and Wyoming counties)

William H. Bush Memorial Library
PO Box 141
Martinsburg, NY 13404
(315) 376-7490
whbml@nc3r.org
http://www.nc3r.org/whbml
Dawn Manzer, Librarian
Mon, Wed & Fri 2:00–5:00 & 7:00–9:00, Sat
    11:00–2:00

Byron Historical Museum
East Main Street
Byron, NY 14422
(716) 548-2807; (716) 548-2252 (Town
    Historian)
Dora M. Jones, Town Historian
Sun (June–Sept): 2:00–4:30, by appointment

Canajoharie Library and Art Gallery
2 Erie Boulevard
Canajoharie, NY 13317
(518) 673-2314; (518) 673-5243 FAX
can_traha@sals.edu
http://www.clag.org
James Crawford, Curator
Mon–Fri 10:00–4:45, Thur 10:00–8:30, Sat
    10:00–1:30
(Montgomery County history and families)

Canisius College
Andrew Boushuis Library

Archives Department
Buffalo, NY 14208
(716) 888-2530
http://www.canisius.edu/canhp/canlib/
archives.html

Cape Vincent Historical Museum
(175 North James Street—location)
PO Box 376 (mailing address)
Cape Vincent, NY 13618
(315) 654-4400 (Office); (315) 654-3094
Jeanne Thompson, President of Board
1 July–Labor Day: 10:00–4:00
(only artifacts from local area)

Historical Room—Town of Caroline
(Town Hall, Slaterville Road—location)
PO Box 36 (mailing address)
Slaterville Springs, NY 14881
(607) 539-6464
Barbara B. M. Kone, Town Historian
Tue & Thur 6:30 P.M.–9:00 P.M., Fri
(May–Sept) 1:00–4:00, and by
appointment
(local family histories, early town records,
family files; includes hamlets of Caroline,
Caroline Center, Brooktondale, Slaterville
Springs and Speedsville)

Carthage Free Library
Heritage Room
412 Budd Street
Carthage, NY 13619
(315) 493-2620
carthage@northnet.org
http://www.nc3r.org/carlibrary
Jerold Anderson
Tue 6:00–8:00, Wed 2:00–4:00, and by
appointment

Catskill Public Library
1 Franklin Street
Catskill, NY 12414-1496
(518) 943-4230; (518) 943-1439 FAX
catskill@francomm.com
http://catskill.lib.ny.us

**Cattaraugus County Memorial and
Historical Museum**
Court Street
Little Valley, NY 14755
(716) 938-9111, ext. 440
Lorna Spencer, Curator/Director
Mon–Fri 9:00–4:30
(genealogy center, operated by County; local
census, Civil War rolls, cemeteries,
newspapers)
$10.00 per search

Cayuga Community College
Norman F. Bourke Memorial Library
Special Collections
197 Franklin Street
Auburn, NY 13021
(315) 255-1743, ext. 2296
cay_ref@cayuga-cc.edu
http://www.cayuga-cc.edu/library
Douglas O. Michael, Director
Mon–Thur 8:00 A.M.–9:30 P.M., Fri
8:00–4:30, Sun 1:00–7:30
no admission fee

Cazenovia Public Library
100 Albany Street
Cazenovia, NY 13035
(315) 655-9322
cazenovia@midyork.org;
cz_circ@midyork.lib.ny.us
http://www.midyork.org/Cazenovia
Betsy Horner, Archivist
Mon–Fri 9:00–9:00, Sat 10:00–6:00

Central Islip Public Library

33 Hawthorne Avenue
Central Islip, NY 11722
(631) 234-9333
cisplib@suffolk.lib.ny.us
http://www.suffolk.lib.ny.us/libraries/cisp
Mon–Fri 10:00–8:30, Sat 10:00–5:00, Sun
1:00–5:00 (closed Sun & Fri evening in
summer)

Central Square Library
(637 South Main—location)
PO Box 513 (mailing address)
Central Square, NY 13036
(315) 668-6104 voice & FAX
csqlib@nnyln.net
http://www.nc3r.org/ncls/libs/csq.txt
Mary Last, Librarian
Mon, Wed & Fri noon–8:00, Thur
9:00–12:30, Sat 10:00–1:00

Champlain Memorial Library
(148 Elm Street—location)
PO Box 279 (mailing address)
Champlain, NY 12919
(518) 298-8620 voice & FAX
champlib@primelink1.net
http://www.cefls.org/champlain.htm
Alison Mandeville, Director
Mon 1:00–7:00, Wed noon–5:00, Thur
4:00–8:00, Sat 9:00–2:00

Chapman Historical Museum
(see Glens Falls-Queensbury Historical
Association, Historical Societies—Local and
Regional, below)

Chateaugay Memorial Library
(191 East Main Street—location)
PO Box 10 (mailing address)
Chateaugay, NY 12920
(518) 497-6931; (518) 497-3126 FAX
chatmeml@northnet.org
http://www.cefls.org/chateaugay.htm
Eileen Clar, Director
Mon & Wed noon–8:00, Tue 9:00–noon, Sat
10:00–4:00

Chautauqua Institution
Smith Memorial Library/Archives
(21 Miller Avenue—location)
PO Box 1093 (mailing address)
Chautauqua, NY 14722
(716) 357-6332; (716) 357-6344 FAX
archives@chautauqua-inst.com
http://www.chautauqua-inst.org
John Schmitz, Archivist
June–Aug: Mon–Fri 9:30–5:00; Sept–May:
Mon, Wed & Fri 9:30–5:00

City History Center Library
Schenectady City Hall, Top Floor
105 Jay Street
Schenectady, NY 12305
(518) 377-7061
http://www.schist.org/cityhist.html
Mon, Wed & Fri 10:00–5:00
(not primarily genealogical)

Emma S. Clark Memorial Library
120 Main Street
Setauket, NY 11733
(631) 941-4080
emsclib@suffolk.lib.ny.us;
reference@emmaclark.org
http://emma.suffolk.lib.ny.us

Clermont State Historic Site
Route 1, Box 215
Germantown, NY 12526
(518) 537-4240
Bruce E. Naramore, Historic Site Manager
Tue–Sun 11:00–4:00

(genealogical services)

Cobblestone Society Museum
14393 Ridge Road
Albion, NY 14411
(716) 589-9013; (716) 589-9510

The Community Library
(Union Street—location)
PO Box 219 (mailing address)
Cobleskill, NY 12043-0219
(518) 234-7897; (518) 234-1163 FAX
coblib@telenet.net
http://www2.telenet.net/community/mvla/
cobl
Christine A. Dickerson, Director
Tue 10:30–8:00, Wed–Fri 10:30–6:00, Sat
10:00–1:00

Coburn Free Library
275 Main Street
Owego, NY 13827
(607) 687-3520; (607) 687-5628 FAX
cmburroug@clarityconnect.com
http://www.flls.org/memberpages/owego.
htm
Christine Burroughs
Mon–Tue & Thur 1:00–5:00 & 6:30–8:30,
Wed & Fri 10:00–5:00, Sat 1:00–5:00

Colonial Library
Historical Room
(61 Main Street—location)
PO Box B (mailing address)
Richburg, NY 14774
(716) 928-2694 voice & FAX
richburg@stls.org
http://www.stls.org/Richburg

Corinth Free Library
89 Main Street
Corinth, NY 12822
(518) 654-6913 voice & FAX
http://www.sals.edu/corinth.shtml
Rebecca Fasulo, Director
(local history)

Cornell University
John M. Olin Library
Ithaca, NY 14853
(607) 255-5258; (607) 255-9567
(Newspapers Department)
http://www.library.cornell.edu/okuref
(Genealogy Resources)

Cornell University
Croch Library
Ithaca, NY 14853-5302
(607) 255-3530

Crandall Public Library
Holden Room
(City Park—location)
251 Glen Street (mailing address)
Glens Falls, NY 12801-3539
(518) 792-6508; (518) 792-5251 FAX
info@crandalllibrary.org (General
Information); degarmo@crandalllibrary.
org
http://www.crandalllibrary.org
Todd De Gormo, Director Center for Folk
Life, History and Cultural Programs
winter: Mon–Tue & Thur–Fri 1:30–3:30,
Wed 4:00–8:00, Sat 1:00–4:00
(local history and genealogy, especially Glens
Falls, New York; the Town of
Queensbury, New York; nearby
communities; to some extent the rest of
northern New York State, Hudson River
Valley and other parts of New York State;
some New England)

Croghan Free Library
(Main Street—location)
PO Box 8 (mailing address)
Croghan, NY 13327
(315) 346-6521 voice & FAX
crolib@nnyln.net
http://www.nc3r.org/ncls/libs/cro.txt
Rose M. Buckingham, Librarian
Mon & Fri noon–5:00, Wed noon–8:00, Fri
    7:00–9:00

Crosby Public Library
(59 Main Street—location)
PO Box 120 (mailing address)
Antwerp, NY 13608
(315) 659-8564 voice & FAX
antlib@nnyln.net
http://www.nc3r.org/ncls/libs/ant.txt
Mrs. Charlee L. Cook

Crown Point State Historic Site
Rural Delivery 1, Box 219, Bridge Road
Crown Point, NY 12928
(518) 597-4666
William G. Farrar, Historic Site Manager
by appointment only
(documents, printed materials, and
    microfilm)

Mary Beatrice Cushing Memorial Library
(see Schoharie Free [Cushing Memorial]
Library, below)

Dansville Public Library
200 Main Street
Dansville, NY 14437-1316
(585) 335-6720; (585) 355-6133 FAX
director@dansville.lib.ny.us
http://dansville.lib.ny.us
Teresa A. Dearing, Director
Mon & Wed 10:00–8:30, Tue & Thur–Fri
    1:00–8:30, Sat (Sept to mid-June)
    noon–4:00

Charles Dawson History Center
Park Lane
West Harrison, NY 10604

Dexter Free Library
(120 East Kirby Street—location)
PO Box 544 (mailing address)
Dexter, NY 13634-0544
(315) 639-6785
dexlib@nnyln.net
http://www.nc34.org/dexterlib
Suzette Cummolletti, Director
Tue & Thur noon–5:00 & 6:00–8:00, Sat
    10:00–4:00

Diana Historical Museum
PO Box
Harrisville, NY 13648
(315) 543-2979
Ross Young, Curator and Diana Town
    Historian

Dodge Memorial Library
144 Lake Street
Rouses Point, NY 12979
(518) 297-6242; (518) 297-6943 FAX
http://www.cefls.org/rousespoint.htm

Dundee Woman's Study Club and Library
18 Water Street
Dundee, NY 14837
(607) 243-7047
Mon & Thur 2:00–8:00, Tue 2:00–6:00, Fri
    10:00–6:00, Sat 11:00–3:00

Dunkirk Historical Museum
513 Washington Avenue
Dunkirk, NY 14048

(716) 366-3797
http://c1web.com/local_info/artsed/dhm.html
Patricia Rosing, Secretary
Mon–Fri noon–4:00
research: for SASE

Durham Center Museum, Inc.
(Route 145—location)
HC 1, Box 28 (mailing address)
East Durham, NY 12423-9608
(518) 239-8461
Doug Thomsen, Curator
June–Aug: Wed–Thur & Sat–Sun 1:00–4:00,
    and by appointment
(genealogical library: cemetery records,
    Bible records, genealogies)
admission during off season: $2.00 per hour
    per person; research: donation for mailed
    requests

East Hampton Library
Pennypacker Long Island Collection
159 Main Street
East Hampton, NY 11937
(631) 324-0222; (631) 329-5947 FAX
ddayton@suffolk.lib.ny.us
http://www.peconic.net/easthampton/library
Diana Dayton, Librarian
Mon–Wed & Sat 1:00–4:30, and mornings
    by appointment, closed when librarian is
    on vacation, so confirmation call advised
(Long Island history and genealogy: local
    histories on over 280 place names, family
    histories on over 680 Long Island
    families, extensive collection of over 100
    Long Island newspapers, census returns,
    The Seversmith Collection, The Jeannette
    Edwards Rattray Collection, genealogical
    periodicals, and special indexes, etc.)

East Hounsfield Free Library
Arsenal Street Road
Watertown, NY 13601
(315) 788-0637; (315) 779-1499 FAX
eholib@nnyln.net
http://www.nc3r.org/ncls/libs/eho.txt
Mary Farrington, Librarian
Mon & Thur 5:00–8:00, Wed 3:30–6:30, Sat
    10:00–1:00

Edmeston Free Library/Museum
(6 West Street—library location; North
Street—museum location)
PO Box 167 (mailing address)
Edmeston, NY 13335-0167
(607) 965-8208 (Library)
ed_ill@4cty.org
http://lib.4cty.org/dialups/edmeston.html
Dorothy Blackman, Library Director
Tue 3:00–9:00, Wed–Thur 1:00–6:00, Sat
    9:00–1:00
("The town historian opens museum some
    Saturdays and by appointment. All
    genealogical material is there, none in the
    library.")

Edwards History Center
(8 First Street—location)
PO Box 100 (mailing address)
Edwards, NY 13635
(315) 562-3500
http://www.herd.org/edwards/museum
LaVerne H. Freeman, Town Historian
by appointment only

Elizabethtown Library Association
(River Street—location)
PO Box 7 (mailing address)
Elizabethtown, NY 12932
(518) 873-2670; (518) 873-2338 FAX
elizabethtownlibrary@charter.net
http://www.cefls.org/elizabethtown.htm

Amy Treffers, Director
Mon & Wed noon–6:00, Fri–Sat 10:00–2:00,
    special hours on holidays
(primarily historical, no genealogical
    records)

Ellenville Public Library and Museum
40 Center Street
Ellenville, NY 12428-1396
(845) 647-5530; (845) 647-3554 FAX
epl@rcls.org
http://www.rcls.org/epl
Pat Christian, Acting Director
Library: Mon & Thur–Fri 10:00–5:00;
    Museum: Apr–Dec: Wed & Fri–Sat
    noon–3:00
(local newspaper on microfilm from 1849,
    obituary file, books)

Ellisburg Free Library
(Eisenhower Road—location)
Box 115 (mailing address)
Ellisburg, NY 13636
(315) 846-5087 voice & FAX
elllib@nnyln.net
http://www.nc3r.org/ncls/libs/ell.txt
Sheila Bettinger

Elting Memorial Library
(see Haviland-Heidgerd Historical Collection,
below)

Erwin Library and Institute
Schuyler Street
Boonville, NY 13309
(315) 942-4834
http://www.midyork.org/LibraryList/
    LibraryInfo/Boonville.html
Lee Ann Riley and Donna Ripp, Directors
(northern Oneida County)

Erwin-Painted Post Museum
115 Water Street
Painted Post, NY 14870
9:00–4:00
(local history and Indian artifacts)
free admission

Evans Mills Public Library
(Noble Street—location)
PO Box 240 (mailing address)
Evans Mills, NY 13637
(315) 629-4483
evmlib@nnyln.net
http://www.nc3r.org/ncls/libs/evm.txt
Helen Tooley, Director
Mon–Tue & Thur 1:00–5:00, Mon
    6:30–8:30, Tue 7:00–9:00, Wed
    6:30–8:30, Sat 10:00–noon

Fayetteville Free Library
300 Orchard Street at the Historic Stickley
Factory
Fayetteville, NY 13066
(315) 637-6374; (315) 637-2306 FAX
sconsidine@fayettevillefreelibrary.org;
    faylib@ocpl.lib.ny.us;
    fayfree@ocpl.lib.ny.us
http://www.fayettevillefreelibrary.org
Susan Considine, Director

**Fenton History Center-Museum and
Library**
67 Washington Street
Jamestown, NY 14701
(716) 664-6256; (716) 483-7524 FAX
information@fentonhistorycenter.org
http://fentonhistorycenter.org
Karen E. Livsey, Librarian/Archivist; Carl
    Belknap, Genealogist/Researcher; Barbara
    Cessna, Genealogist/Researcher; Frances
    TeCulver, Genealogist/Researcher

Mon 10:00–9:00, Tue–Sat 10:00–4:00
Pub. *Fenton History Center-Museum and
Library Newsletter*, quarterly; *Annual
Report*
(collections concentrate on Jamestown and
southern Chautauqua County, but cover all
of the county and include family history
files, a card file for deaths and marriages
from 19th-century newspapers, printed
family genealogies, county census records
and indexes, Jamestown city directories,
plus manuscript and photograph
collections)
$30.00 per year membership; research:
$20.00; admission: $5.00

The Field Library
Peekskill Archives Collection
4 Nelson Avenue
Peekskill, NY 10566
(914) 737-1212; (914) 737-0714 FAX
scanaan@wlsmail.org (Sibyl Canaan, Library
Director)
http://www.peekskill.org
Barbara J. Zimmer, Archives Librarian
Mon–Tue & Thur–Fri 10:00–3:00, Wed
11:00–3:00, Sat (Oct–May) 10:00–5:00
(local history and genealogy)
out-of-state requests for research by mail:
$10.00 for first hour, $5.00 for each
additional hour

Floral Park Public Library
Tulip Avenue and Caroline Place
Floral Park, NY 110021
(718) 326-6330; (516) 437-6959 FAX
FloralPark@NassauLibrary.org;
floralpk@lilrc.org
http://www.nassaulibrary.org/fpark
Beverly DiGiulio, Reference Librarian
Mon–Tue & Thur 10:00–9:00, Wed & Fri
10:00–6:00, Sat 9:00–5:00

Roswell P. Flower Memorial Library
Genealogy Department
229 Washington Street
Watertown, NY 13601
(315) 788-2352
flower@northnet.org
http://www.flowermemoriallibrary.org/
genealogy.html
Mrs. Homer J. Perkins, Chairman
Mon–Tue & Thur 9:15–9:00, Wed
9:15–5:30, Fri–Sat 9:15–5:00; Genealogy
Department: Mon–Fri noon–4:00, Sat
9:30–11:30
copies: 20¢ each

**Fort Covington Reading Center and
Museum**
Chateaugay Street, Route 37
Fort Covington, NY 12937
(518) 358-4629; (518) 358-2025; (518) 358-
2511
info@cefls.org
http://www.cefls.org/fortcovington.htm
Jacqueline Harvey and Elizabeth Mount,
Town Historians
Library: Mon–Thur 10:00–2:00

Friends of the North Country, Inc.
1A Mill Street
Keeseville, NY 12944
(518) 834-9606
Ann Ruzow Holland, Executive Director
Mon–Fri 8:00–4:00 by appointment only

Friendship Free Library
Harold Reed Memorial History Room
(40 West Main Street—location)
PO Box 37 (mailing address)
Friendship, NY 14739-0037

(585) 973-7724 voice & FAX
Captice@shs.org
http://www.stls.org/Friendship
Norma Pizza, Town Historian
by appointment
research: for copy and mailing fees

Fryer Memorial Museum
(Corner of Route 46 and Williams
Road—location)
PO Box 177 (mailing address)
Munnsville, NY 13409
(315) 495-5395; (315) 495-6148
Olive S. Boylan, Museum Director and Town
and Village Historian
by appointment
(genealogy, local history, local Indian
history, etc.; not handicap accessible)
no membership fees; no costs

Fulton Public Library
160 South First Street
Fulton, NY 13069
(315) 592-5981; (315) 592-4504 FAX
fullib@nnyln.net; jhcook@northnet.org
http://www.nc3r.org/ncls/libs/ful.txt
Joyce H. Cook, Library Director
Mon, Fri & Sat 10:00–5:00, Tue–Thur
10:00–8:00

Garden City Public Library
60 Seventh Street
Garden City, NY 11530-2800
(516) 742-8405; (516) 294-6207 FAX
gcplref@lilrc.org
http://www.nassaulibrary.org/gardenc/
index.html
Vincent F. Seyfried, Village Historian
winter: Mon–Thur 9:30–9:00, Fri 9:30–5:30,
Sat 9:00–5:00; summer: Mon–Tue & Thur
9:30–9:00, Wed & Fri 9:30–5:30

Gates Public Library
1605 Buffalo Road
Rochester, NY 14624
(585) 247-6446 (Reference); (585) 426-5733
FAX
question@gateslibrary.org
http://www.gateslibrary.org
Judy MacKnight, Assistant Director
Mon–Fri 10:00–9:00, Sat 10:00–5:00
(small Rochester area local history
collection)

**Genesee County History Department and
Records Management**
3 West Main Street
Batavia, NY 14020
(716) 344-2550, ext. 2613

Genesee County Museum
PO Box 310
Mumford, NY 14511-0310

Genesis HealthCare Library
218 Stone Street
Watertown, NY 13601
(315) 782-7400, ext. 2152

Geneva Free Library
244 Main Street
Geneva, NY 14456
(315) 789-5303; (315) 789-9835 FAX
geneva@pls-net.org
http://www.geneva.pls-net.org

George and Margaret Gey Library
W. Alton Jones Cell Science Center
Old Barn Road
Lake Placid, NY 12946
(518) 523-2427

The Gilbertsville Free Library
Local History Collection
(19 Commercial Street—location)
PO Box 332 (mailing address)
Gilbertsville, NY 13776
(607) 783-2832
http://www.gilbertsville.com/library.htm
Leigh Eckmair, Historian/Archivist
Library: Mon–Wed & Fri 2:45–5:15, Wed
7:00 P.M.–8:30 P.M., Sat 9:00–1:00; Local
History Collection assistance available:
Sat 10:30–12:30 (call ahead before
visiting), and by appointment
(Village of Gilbertsville and Town of
Butternuts family and genealogy files,
village and township structural
inventories, cemetery records, school
records, tax records, voting records,
Otsego Journal on microfilm, atlases,
blueprints, maps, church records, census
records, photographs, vital statistics,
scrapbooks)
research: postage ($1.37 minimum) and
copies at 25¢ per page

Glen Cove Public Library
4 Glen Cove Avenue
Glen Cove, NY 11542-2885
(516) 676-2130; (516) 676-2788 FAX
glencove@lilrc.org
http://www.nassaulibrary.org/glencove
Jim Brown, Librarian
Mon–Fri 9:00–9:00, Sat (winter) 9:00–5:00,
Sat (summer) 9:00–1:00
(also Long Island history)

Great Neck Library
159 Bayview Avenue
Great Neck, NY 11023
(516) 466-8055; (516) 829-8297 FAX
gneck@nassaulibrary.org
http://www.nassaulibrary.org/gneck
Risha Rosner, Reference Librarian
Mon–Tue & Thur–Fri 9:00–9:00, Wed
10:00–9:00, Sat 1:00–6:00

Groton Public Library
112 East Cortland Street
Groton, NY 13073
(607) 898-5055 voice & FAX
groton@twcny.rr.com
http://www.flls.org/groton.htm
Susan Robey, Librarian

Guernsey Memorial Library
Otis A. Thompson Local History Room
3 Court Street
Norwich, NY 13815
(607) 334-4034
http://lib.4cty.org/otis.html
Katheryn L. Barton, Head Researcher
Mon–Fri 1:00–5:00, Sat 9:00–1:00, Sun
(Labor Day–Memorial Day) 1:00–4:00
(emphasis on central New York genealogy
and local history)
copies: 30¢ per page charge, $1.00 minimum

Hamilton College
College Hill
Clinton, NY 13323
(315) 859-4011
(microfilm of the *Clinton Courier*
newspaper)

Hamilton Public Library
13 Broad Street
Hamilton, NY 13346
(315) 824-3060
http://www.midyork.org/LibraryList/
LibraryInfo/Hamilton.html

The Hammond Library

(Main Street—location)
PO Box 245 (mailing address)
Crown Point, NY 12928
(518) 597-3616; (518) 597-3066
hlibrary@bluemoo.net; library@cptelco.net
http://www.hammondlibrary.com
Tue noon–6:00, Wed noon–5:00, Thur
    noon–4:00, Fri–Sat 9:00–2:00

Harborfields Public Library
(31 Broadway—location)
PO Box 354 (mailing address)
Greenlawn, NY 11740-1382
(516) 754-1180; (516) 757-4200; (516) 757-
    7216 FAX
pelsener@suffolk.lib.ny.us;
    harblib@suffolk.lib.ny.us
http://harb.suffolk.lib.ny.us
Paul Elsener, Library Director

The Museums at Hartwick
Hartwick College
Yager Hall
Oneonta, NY 13820
(607) 431-4480
Director
Mon–Sat 10:00–4:00, Sun 1:00–4:00
(teaches genealogy to college students and
    community special classes)

Haviland-Heidgerd Historical Collection
Elting Memorial Library
93 Main Street
New Paltz, NY 12561
(845) 255-5030; (845) 255-5818 FAX
Marion W. Ryan, Director
Mon–Tue & Thur 1:00–5:30, Wed & Fri
    10:00–5:30
(Ulster County history and genealogy, also
    Hudson Valley genealogy)
research fees on request

Hawn Memorial Library
220 John Street
Clayton, NY 13624
(315) 686-3762; (315) 686-6028 FAX
clalib@nnyln.net
http://www.nc3r.org/ncls/libs/cla.txt
Alice Barton, Senior Library Clerk; P.
    Tritton, Genealogy
Mon & Thur–Fri 10:00–5:00, Tue–Wed
    10:00–8:00, Sat 9:00–noon

Hay Memorial Library
(101 South Broad Street—location)
PO Box 288 (mailing address)
Sackets Harbor, NY 13685
(315) 646-2228 voice & FAX
sahlib@nnyln.net
http://www.nc3r.org/ncls/libs/sah.txt
Mrs. Toni Ellinger, Librarian

Hempstead Public Library
115 Nichols Court
Hempstead, NY 11550
(516) 481-6990; (516) 481-6719 FAX
hempstead@nassaulibrary.org
http://www.nassaulibrary.org/hempstd/
    index.html
Jean King, Head of Reference Department
Long Island Collection: by appointment only
("Emphasis on the Village of Hempstead.")

Henderson Free Library
(8939 State Route 178, Main
    Street—location)
PO Box 302 (mailing address)
Henderson, NY 13650
(315) 938-5032; (315) 938-7169; (315) 938-
    7038 FAX
henlib@nnyln.net
http://www.nc3r.org/ncls/libs/hen.txt

Cheryl Shutts
Mon & Wed 1:00–8:00, Tue 9:00–noon, Sat
    9:00–1:00

Henrietta Public Library
455 Calkins Road
Rochester, NY 14623
(716) 359-7092 (Reference); (716) 334-3401
    (Hours and Info)
jfunt@libraryweb.org
http://www.hpl.org
John Funt, Local History Librarian

Hepburn Library of Lisbon
PO Box 86
Lisbon, NY 13658
(315) 393-0111
lislib@nnyln.net
http://www.nc3r.org/ncls/libs/lis.txt
Sylvia Armstrong, Director
Mon 10:00–5:00, Tue & Thur 10:00–2:00 &
    7:00–9:00, Wed & Fri 2:00–5:00

Hermon Heritage Hall
(117 East Main Street—location)
PO Box 296 (mailing address)
Hermon, NY 13652-0296
(315) 347-3221
hheritgh@northnet.org;
    smallman@northnet.org
Mary H. Smallman, Chairperson
by appointment

Hinckley Foundation Museum
410 East Seneca Street
Ithaca, NY 14850
(607) 273-7053
Maeleah Carlisle, Director
Sat (Mar–Dec) 10:00–4:00, and by
    appointment
("small library and archives [ephemera], not
    much on specific families except for
    Henry Noble Hinckley"; Ithaca imprints)
$10.00–$500.00 per year membership

Historic Cherry Hill
523½ South Pearl Street
Albany, NY 12202
(518) 434-4791
Anne W. Ackerson, Director
(5,000 books, 30,000 manuscripts, 3,000
    photographs)

David A. Howe Public Library
151 North Main Street
Wellsville, NY 14895-1149
(585) 593-3410; (585) 593-4176 FAX
wellsville@stls.org
http://www.davidahowelibrary.org

**Huntington Free Library and Reading
Room**
9 Westchester Square
Bronx, NY 10461
(718) 829-7770; (718) 829-4875
Catherine McChesney, Librarian
Mon–Fri 10:00–4:30, by appointment
(serves as the library for the National
    Museum of the American Indian)

Huntington Memorial Library
New York Room
62 Chestnut Street
Oneonta, NY 13820-2498
(607) 432-1980; (607) 432-5623 FAX
http://www.4cls.org/webpages/members/
    Oneonta/hm12.htm
Marie Bruni, Director
Library: Mon–Thur 9:00–9:00, Fri
    9:00–5:30, Sat 9:00–4:00; New York
    Room: Mon–Fri 1:00–4:00, Tue–Wed &
    Fri 9:00–noon, Thur 6:00 P.M.–9:00 P.M.,

and by appointment
(Delaware and Otsego counties)

Huntington Public Library
Reference Department
338 Main Street
Huntington, NY 11743-6956
(631) 427-5165; (631) 673-3351 FAX
huntlib@suffolk.lib.ny.us
http://www.suffolk.lib.ny.us/libraries/hunt
Diana Navarro
Mon–Fri 9:00–9:00, Sat–Sun 9:00–5:00
(index to weekly *Long Islander*, published
    since 1838)

Ilion Free Public Library
78 West Street
Ilion, NY 13357-1797
(315) 894-5028; (315) 894-9980 FAX
Ilion@midyork.org
http://www.midyork.org/ilion
Bruce George, Director/Head Librarian; Joan
    Stalloch, Historical Room Clerk
Mon–Tue & Thur 9:00–9:00, Wed & Fri
    9:00–6:00, Sat (Sept–May) 9:00–1:00;
    Local History Collection: limited hours
(local history, local newspapers on microfilm,
    files, city directories, photos)

Irondequoit Public Library
Helen McGraw Branch
2180 East Ridge Road (between Culver Road
    and Route 590)
Rochester, NY 14622
(716) 336-6060
http://www.rochester.lib.ny.us/irondequoit

Jefferson Community College
Melvil Dewey Library
Outer Coffeen Street
Watertown, NY 13601
(315) 786-2224; (315) 786-2225
Ellen Childs; Teresa Blacklaw, Coordinator
    of Reference Services
Mon–Thur noon–4:00, Fri noon–2:00, and by
    appointment

Jericho Public Library
1 Merry Lane
Jericho, NY 11753-1792
(516) 935-6790; (516) 433-9581 FAX
bmurphy@jericholibrary.org
http://www.jericholibrary.org
Betsey Murphy, Local History Librarian
Library: Mon–Tue & Thur 9:00–9:00, Wed
    10:00–9:00, Fri 9:00–6:00, Sat 9:00–5:00,
    Sun (8 Sept–22 June) noon–5:00; Local
    History Librarian: Thur–Fri 1:00–5:00,
    alternate Sun noon–5:00
Pub. *Long Island Forum*
(focus on Jericho area history and Long
    Island history; small collection of Hicks,
    Seaman and Underhill families, oral
    history cassettes)
research: no private genealogical research,
    only minimal searches using in-house
    references

Jervis Public Library
613 North Washington Street
Rome, NY 13440-4203
(315) 336-4570
lchien@midyork.org
http://www.jervislibrary.org
Lori E. Chien, Local History/Genealogy
    Librarian
Mon–Thur 9:30–9:00, Fri 9:30–5:30, Sat
    9:30–5:00, Sun 1:00–5:00 (closed
    weekends in summer)
(Oneida County genealogy and local history;
    John B. Jervis papers by appointment
    only)

research: $25.00 per request, photocopies at 25¢ per page

Johnstown Public Library
38 South Market Street
Johnstown, NY 12095
(518) 762-8317; (518) 762-9776 FAX
dcallery@sals.edu
http://www.johnstown.com/city/library.html
Deborah J. Callery, Local History Researcher
Sept–May: Mon & Thur 1:00–8:00 Tue–Wed
   10:00–8:00, Fri 10:00–5:00, Sat
   10:00–1:00, Sun 1:00–4:00; June–Aug:
   Mon–Wed 10:00–8:00, Thur noon–8:00,
   Fri 10:00–5:00
(federal census from 1790, Elizabeth Cady
   Stanton and women's suffrage history and
   Mohawk Valley history beginning with Sir
   Wm. Johnson's arrival in mid-1700s;
   "This collection is primarily dedicated to
   the history of Johnstown, with other
   information, such as the development of
   the Valley as available.")

Keene Public Library
(HCR 1, Box 63A—location)
PO Box 206 (mailing address)
Keene, NY 12942
(518) 576-2200 voice & FAX
http://www.cefls.org/keene.htm

Keene Valley Library Association Archives
Loomis Room
(Main Street—location)
PO Box 86 (mailing address)
Keene Valley, NY 12943
(518) 576-4335 (Loomis Room); (518) 576-4693 FAX
library@kvvi.net
http://www.kvvi.net/~library
Patricia M. Galeski, Librarian for the
   Archives
Tue & Thur 9:00–noon
(news clippings, cemetery listings, photos,
   and genealogies)
charge varies according to materials

Keeseville Free Library
1721 Front Street
Keeseville, NY 12944
(518) 834-9054; (518) 834-9054 FAX
kesvlib@northnet.org
http://www.cefls.org/keeseville.htm
Winter: Mon & Fri 1:00–5:00, Wed & Sat
   10:00–noon & 1:00–5:00, Fri 7:00–9:00;
   Summer Mon–Thur 10:00–noon &
   1:00–5:00, Fri 7:00–9:00

Kingston Area Library
Local History Room
55 Franklin Street
Kingston NY 12401
(845) 331-0507 (Main); (845) 339-4260
   (Office); (845) 331-0988 (Reference);
   (845) 331-7981 FAX
kingstonlibrary@hvc.rr.com
http://www.kingstonlibrary.org

LaGuardia Community College
Fiorello H. LaGuardia and Wagner Archives
31-10 Thomson Avenue
Long Island City, NY 11101
(718) 626-5078; (718) 482-5065
http://www.laguardiawagneraarchive.
   lagcc.cuny.edu
Richard K. Lieberman, Ph.D., Director
(history of 20th-century New York City)

Lake Placid Public Library
67 Main Street
Lake Placid, NY 12946

(518) 523-3200
librarian@lakeplacidlibrary.org
http://www.lakeplacidlibrary.org
Therese K. Patnode, Director
Mon–Fri 10:00–5:30, Sat 10:00–4:00

The Landmark Society of Western New York
The Hoyt-Potter House
133 South Fitzhugh Street
Rochester, NY 14608
(716) 546-7029; (716) 546-4788 FAX; (716)
   546-7029, ext. 6 (24-hour info line)
http://www.landmarksociety.org/index.html
William Keeler, Curator/Librarian
Tue–Fri 9:00–5:00
Pub. *The Cornerstone*, monthly
(also houses the Wenrich Memorial Library)
$30.00 per year membership

Lehman College Library of the City University of New York
250 Bedford Park Boulevard, West
Bronx, NY 10468-1589
(718) 960-8577; (718) 960-7766
   (Information)
libref@lehman.cuny.edu
http://www.lehman.cuny.edu/library/
   library2.htm
Dr. Janet Butler Munch, Administrative
   Services Librarian
by appointment only
(Bronx research—Bronx Institute Archives)

Little Falls Public Library
10 Waverly Place
Little Falls, NY 13365
(315) 823-1542; (315) 823) 2995 FAX
http://www.midyork.org/LibraryList/
   LibraryInfo/LittleFalls.html
Jeffrey Singer, Director
Mon–Thur 10:00–8:00, Fri–Sat 10:00–5:00;
   July–Aug: closed Sat

Little Red Schoolhouse
Panama Rocks Road
Clymer Center, NY 14724
(716) 355-6391
http://c1web.com/local_info/artsed/lrs.html

Lockport Public Library
(23 East Avenue—location)
PO Box 475 (mailing address)
Lockport, NY 14095-0475
(716) 433-5935; (716) 439-0198 FAX
http://www.lockportlibrary.org

Locust Valley Library
170 Buckram Road
Locust Valley, NY 11560
(516) 671-1837; (516) 676-8164 FAX
lvlcontactus@hotmail.com (Adult Services)
http://www.nassaulibrary.org/locustv
Mon–Wed 9:15–9:00, Thur–Sat 9:15–5:00,
   Sun (mid-Sept–mid-June) 1:00–5:00

Long Island University
C. W. Post Campus
B. Davis Schwartz Memorial Library
Rare Book Room
700 Northern Boulevard
Brookville, NY 11548-1326
(516) 299-2880
http://www.cwpost.liunet.edu/cwis/cwp/
   library/sc/sc.htm
Conrad Schoeffling, Special Collections
   Librarian
Mon–Fri 9:00–5:00
Pub (houses part of the collection of The
   Cedar Swamp Historical Society)

Longwood Public Library

Thomas R. Bayles Local History Room
800 Middle Country Road
Middle Island, NY 11953
(631) 924-6400; (631) 924-7538 FAX
dclemens@suffolk.lib.ny.us
http://longwood.suffolk.lib.ny.us/
   bayleslist.html
David Clemens, Director

Lorenzo State Historic Site
17 Rippleton Road (NY Route 13)
Cazenovia, NY 13035
(315) 655-3200; (315) 655-4304 FAX
http://cazenovia.com/lorenzo/index.html
Sharon M. Cooney, Interpretive Programs
   Assistant
by appointment
(land records, cemetery and miscellaneous
   information; towns of Cazenovia,
   DeRuyter, Fenner, German, Lincklaen,
   Nelson, and Pitcher)
donation accepted

Lyme Free Library
(Main Street—location)
PO Box 369 (mailing address)
Chaumont, NY 13622
(315) 649-5454
chalib@nnyln.net
http://www.nc3r.org/ncls/libs/cha.txt
Nancy White

Lyme Heritage Center
28589 Empie Road
Three Mile Bay, NY 13693
(315) 649-5452
heritage@chaumontny.com
http://chaumontny.com/heritage.html
Julia Gosier, Town Historian
Tue–Wed & Fri–Sat 2:00–3:00, and by
   appointment
(family history, genealogy, local history)
donation accepted

MacSherry Library
112 Walton Street
Alexandria Bay, NY 13607
(315) 482-2241 (Business) voice & FAX
alblib@nnyln.net
http://www.nc3r.org/ncls/libs/alb.txt
Lil Purpura, Librarian
Tue–Thur 2:30–5:00 & 7:00–9:00, Fri
   2:30–5:00, Sat 10:00–noon & 1:00–4:00

Mamaroneck Free Library
136 Prospect Avenue
Mamaroneck, NY 10543
(914) 698-1250
http://www.wls.lib.ny.us/libs/mamaroneck

Mannsville Free Library
PO Box 156
Mannsville, NY 13661
(315) 465-4049; (315) 465-5515 FAX
mannsvl_library@nc3r.org
http://www.nc3r.org/mannsvl_library

Harris Memorial Library
(69 Main Street—location)
PO Box H (mailing address)
Otego, NY 13825-0552
(607) 988-6661
http://lib.4cty.org/dialups/OTEGO.HTML

Town of Massena Museum and Historian's Office
200 East Orvis Street
Massena, NY 13662
(315) 769-8571
Theresa Sharp, Town Historian
Mon–Fri 10:00–4:00 by appointment
(farming and lumbering community, turned

industrial with Alcoa in early nineteen
hundreds)
no charge for searches

Mather Homestead Museum
343 North Main Street
Wellsville, NY 14895
(585) 593-1636
(museum, library and memorial park, with an
1930s room; "history, local crafts, Sound
Adventures, an in-house music publishing
program, special attention to pleasures for
the blind and poorly sighted.")
free admission

Medaille College Library
18 Agassiz Circle
Buffalo, NY 14214
(716) 884-3281, ext. 283; (716) 884-9638
FAX

Middleburgh Library
7 Wells Avenue
Middleburgh, NY 12122-9662
(518) 827-5142 voice & FAX
midlib@telenet.net
http://www2.telenet.net/community/mvla/
midd
Mary France, Librarian
Mon 1:30–8:30, Tue 10:00–5:00 &
6:30–8:30, Wed 10:00–4:00, Thur
10:00–4:00 & 6:30–8:30, Sat 9:00–2:00

Mohawk Valley Museum
311 Main Street
Utica, NY 13501
(315) 724-2075

Montgomery Academy
Village Hall
133 Clinton Street
Maybrook, NY 12543
(845) 457-5135

**Montgomery County Department of
History and Archives**
Old Court House
(Railroad Street—location)
PO Box 1500 (mailing address)
Fonda, NY 12068-1500
(518) 853-8186; (518) 853-8392 FAX
http://co.montgomery.ny.us
Kelly A. Yacobucci Farquhar, Montgomery
County Historian/RMO (Records
Management Officer)
Sept–June: Mon–Fri 8:30–4:00; July–Aug:
Mon–Fri 9:00–4:00
(County-funded department; one of the
largest municipal genealogical and
historical research libraries and collections
in New York State; Mohawk Valley civil
and genealogy records.)
$12.00 ppd. for catalog of genealogical and
historical material, $9.00 ppd. for "Steeple
Chase" church history booklets; research:
$15.00 per hour plus 25¢ per photocopy,
$5.00 per certified copy

Montour Falls Memorial Library
(406 West Main Street—location)
PO Box 486 (mailing address)
Montour Falls, NY 14865-0486
(607) 535-7489 voice & FAX
mfl_dora@stls.org
http://www.stls.org/MontourFalls
Becky Smith, Library Director
Mon–Tue & Thur 2:00–6:00, Wed
2:00–8:00, Fri 2:00–5:00, Sat 10:00–2:00

Moore Memorial Library
59 Genesee Street
Greene, NY 13778

(607) 656-9349 voice & FAX
gr_mary@4cty.org
http://www.4cls.org/webpages/members/
Greene/Greene.html
Mary G. King, Librarian
Mon–Thur 9:30–8:00, Fri 9:30–5:00, Sat
9:30–3:30
(copies of *Chenango American* from 1855)

Morehouse Historical Museum
Route 8, Box 1
Hoffmeister, NY 13353
BearPath@ntcnet.com
http://www.rootsweb.com/~nyhamilt/
MoreMus/museum.html
Carol A. Ford, Town Historian
Memorial Day weekend–Labor Day
weekend: Sat–Sun 11:00–3:00

Mount Pleasant Public Library
350 Bedford Road
Pleasantville, NY 10570
(914) 769-0548; (914) 769-6149 FAX
mt.pleasant.lib@westchesterlibraries.org
http://www.mountpleasantlibrary.org

Mount Vernon Public Library
Local History Room
28 South First Avenue
Mount Vernon, NY 10550
(914) 668-1840, ext. 315; (914) 668-1018
FAX
http://www.wls.lib.ny.us/libs/mount_
vernon/mtv.html
Shannon E. Chandley, Curator
Mon–Fri 9:00–1:00, and by appointment

Goff Nelson Memorial Library
41 Lake Street
Tupper Lake, NY 12986
(518) 359-9421 voice & FAX
goffnelson@adelphia.net
http://www.cefls.org/tupperlake.htm
Mon–Thur 10:00–5:30 & 7:00–9:00, Fri
10:00–5:30

New City Library
The Rockland Room
220 North Main Street
New City, NY 10956
(845) 634-4997; (845) 634-4963; (845) 634-
0173 FAX
http://www.newcitylibrary.org
Sally Pellegrini, Local History Librarian
Mon–Fri 9:00–9:00, Sat 9:00–5:00 (summer:
10:00–5:00), Sun noon–8:00 (summer:
closed Sun)

**The City of New York Department of
Records and Information Services**
Municipal Reference and Research Center
(MRRC)
31 Chambers Street, Room 112
New York, NY 10007
(212) 788-8590; (212) 788-8589 FAX
http://www.ci.nyc.ny.us/html/doris/html/
dorisref.html
Joan Nichols, Acquisitions Librarian
Mon–Fri 10:00–4:00
(New York City government and history;
MRRC is a library, not an archives)

**The City of New York Department of
Records and Information Services**
Municipal Archives
31 Chambers Street, Room 103
New York, NY 10007
(212) 788-8580
http://www.nyc.gov/html/doris
Kenneth R. Cobb, Director
Archives: Mon–Thur 9:00–4:30, Fri
9:00–1:00

(includes New York City vital records [births
prior to 1910 and deaths prior to 1949,
marriages from 1847 to 1865, except
Brooklyn records] and other resources;
received part of the collection of the
former James A. Kelly Institute for Local
Historical Studies)

**New York Genealogical and Biographical
Society Library**
(see State Genealogical Societies, below)

The New York Public Library
Fordham Library Center Branch
2556 Bainbridge Avenue (near Fordham
Road)
Bronx, NY 10458
(718) 579-4244; (718) 579-4257 (Bronx
Reference Center); (718) 579-4222
(Fordham Center for Reading and
Writing)
http://www.nypl.org/branch

The New York Public Library
The Irma and Paul Milstein Division of
United States History, Local History and
Genealogy
Fifth Avenue and 42nd Street, Room 121
New York, NY 10018-2788
(212) 930-0828; (212) 930-0587 (Map
Division); (212) 930-0801 (Rare Books
and Manuscripts)
rcarr@nypl.org; ask@nypl.org
http://www.nypl.org/research/chss/lhg/
genea.html; http://www.nypl.org/
research/chss/subguides/milhist/home.
html (Military History Collection)
Ruth A. Carr, Division Chief
Mon & Thur–Sat 10:00–6:00, Tue–Wed
11:00–7:30

Newburgh Free Library
124 Grand Street
Newburgh, NY 12550
(845) 561-1985, ext. 24, 25, or 26; (845) 561-
2401 FAX
nflgref@rcls.org
http://www.neburghlibrary.org
Heather H. Georghiou, Librarian
Mon–Thur 9:00–9:00, Fri–Sat 9:00–5:00,
Sun 1:00–5:00

Newfield Public Library
(Main Street—location)
PO Box 154 (mailing address)
Newfield, NY 14867
(607) 564-3594 voice & FAX
http://www.flls.org/memberpages/
newfield.htm

**Niagara County Community College
Library**
Library Learning Center, Special Collections
3111 Saunders Settlement Road
Sanborn, NY 14132
(716) 731-3271, ext. 401; (716) 731-7118
FAX
http://www.sunyniagara.cc.ny.us/library/
special.html
(Native American Collection, including
reference books, biography, history, tribes,
mythology and periodicals, e.g. *Native
Peoples*, *Journal of Cherokee Studies*,
Northeast Indian Quarterly, *Akwekon
Journal*, *Turtle Quarterly* and *Southern
Indian Studies*)

Niagara Falls Public Library
Earl W. Brydges Library Building
1425 Main Street
Niagara Falls, NY 14305-2574
(716) 286-4899 (Local History); (716) 286-

4912 FAX
mfenni@nioga.org
http://www.niagarafallspubliclib.org/
local.htm
Reference Department
Local History Department, Niagara Room:
Mon–Fri 2:00–5:00
(Reference Department has all microfilm of
newspapers and census. Local History
Department has "an index to the *Niagara
Gazette* from 1854 to 1996. The index is
on our own database for 1996 to 2000. We
have our own in-house database for the
years 2001 and 2002. We also have an
index to vitals, covering the years 1854 to
1930, and 1980 to 2000.")

Town of Norfolk Historical Museum
(39 Main Street—location)
PO Box 643 (mailing address)
Norfolk, NY 13667
(315) 384-4575; (315) 384-3223
Tue–Thur 2:00–5:00 (also most Mon &
Wed)
(Norfolk history and genealogy)
no charge for research if done in museum, if
outside research is required, costs vary

**North Country Community College
Library**
(20 Winona Avenue—location)
PO Box 89 (mailing address)
Saranac Lake, NY 12983
(518) 891-2915
Patrick F. McIntyre, Director of Libraries
(materials on the Adirondack region)

North Merrick Public Library
1691 Meadowbrook Road
Merrick, NY 11566
(516) 378-7474; (516) 378-0876 FAX
http://www.nassaulibrary.org/nmerrick/
index.html
J. Jankolovits, Librarian
Mon–Thur 10:00–9:00, Fri 10:00–6:00, Sat
10:00–5:00, Sun 1:00–4:00
Pub. *Merrick Life*, weekly

North Rockland History Museum
20 Oak Street
Garnerville, NY 10923

North Tonawanda Public Library
505 Meadow Drive
North Tonawanda, NY 14120
(716) 693-4132; (716) 693-0719 FAX
jmckenna@ntonawanda.lib.ny.us
http://www.ntonawanda.lib.ny.us
Janet McKenna, Local History Librarian
Mon–Thur 9:30–9:00, Fri–Sat 9:30–5:00,
Sun (Sept–May) 1:00–5:00
(local history, Niagara County census, local
newspaper 1880+, city directory 1892+)
research: $3.00 per simple search, plus
copying and postage, fees on local topics
determined on individual basis

Ogden Farmers' Library
269 Ogden Center Road
Spencerport, NY 14559
(585) 352-2141
puttaro@mcls.rochester.lib.ny.us
http://www.ogdenny.com/Library
Patty Uttaro

Ogdensburg Public Library
312 Washington Street
Ogdensburg, NY 13669
(315) 393-4325; (315) 393-4344 FAX
franz@northnet.org
http://www.nc3R.org/ogdensburg
David A. Franz, Director

after Labor Day–4 July: Mon–Thur
9:00–9:00, Fri 10:00–6:00, Sat
10:00–5:00, Sun 1:00–5:00; 5 July–Labor
Day: Mon 9:00–6:00, Tue–Thur
9:00–9:00, Fri 10:00–6:00, Sat 9:00–1:00

Ohoopee Regional Library
(see Georgia, Part 2)

Old Merchants House of New York, Inc.
29 East Fourth Street
New York, NY 10003
(212) 777-1089

Old Stone Fort Museum/Library
(North Main Street—location)
Rural Delivery 2, Box 30A (mailing address)
Schoharie, NY 12157
(518) 295-7192
Christine Palmatier, Librarian/Archivist;
Martha Foland, Genealogy Volunteer
1 May–31 Oct: Museum: Tue–Sat
10:00–5:00, Sun noon–5:00; Library:
Tue–Sat 10:00–noon & 1:00–4:30, Sun
1:00–4:30

Oneida Public Library
220 Broad Street
Oneida, NY 13421
(315) 363-3050; (315) 363-4217 FAX
oneida@midyork.org
http://www.midyork.org/Oneida

Onondaga County Public Library
Local History/Special Collections
447 South Salina Street
Syracuse, NY 13202-2400
(315) 435-1800
anagle@mailbox.syr.edu
http://www.cny.com/OCPL
Mary Frances Smyth, Head of Information
Services
Mon & Thur–Sat 9:00–4:45, Tue–Wed
9:00–8:15

Town of Orleans Library
(Sunrise Avenue—location)
PO Box 139 (mailing address)
La Fargeville, NY 13656
(315) 658-2271
laflib@nnyln.net
http://www.nc3r.org/ncls/libs/laf.txt
Kelly J. Orvis, Director
Mon, Wed & Fri 9:00–noon & 1:00–5:00,
Tue 6:00–8:00, Sat 10:00–noon

Oswego School District Public Library
120 East Second Street
Oswego, NY 13126
(315) 341-5867; (315) 342-3206 FAX
oswegopl@northnet.org
http://www.nc3r.org/oswegocitylibrary
Carol Ferlito, Director
Mon–Fri 10:00–8:00, Sat–Sun noon–5:00

Paine Memorial Free Library
1 School Street
Willsboro, NY 12996-3727
(518) 963-4478; (518) 963-7778 FAX
http://www.willsborony.com/
PaineMemorialLibrary/default.html
Cheryl Blanchard, Director
Mon–Sat 9:00–5:00

Parish Public Library
(Corner of Main and Church
Streets—location)
PO Box 465 (mailing address)
Parish, NY 13131-0465
(315) 625-7130 voice & FAX
parishpl@northnet.org; parlib@nnyln.net
http://www.nc3r.org/ncls/libs/par.txt

Bridget Swartz, Town Historian and Library
Director
Mon 9:00–3:00, Mon & Thur 7:00–9:00,
Wed & Sat noon–5:00

Patchogue Medford Library
Local History Room
54-60 East Main Street
Patchogue, NY 11722
(631) 654-4700; (631) 289-3999 FAX
rgray@suffolk.lib.ny.us;
ptchlib@suffolk.lib.ny.us
http://pml.suffolk.lib.ny.us
Rosalind Gray

Patterson Library
40 South Portage Street
Westfield, NY 14787-1496
(716) 326-2154; (716) 326-2554 FAX
wlibrar2@cecomet.net;
plibrary@cecomet.net
http://www.cclslib.org/westfield/index.htm
winter: Mon–Tue & Thur 9:00–8:00, Wed &
Fri–Sat 9:00–5:00; summer: Mon &
Wed–Fri 9:00–5:00, Tue & Thur
9:00–8:00, Sat 9:00–1:00
(local history collection; no genealogical
services)
charge for copies and postage

Paul Smith's College
Paul Smith's College Historical Museum
Cubley Library
(Routes 86 & 30—location)
PO Box 256 (mailing address)
Paul Smiths, NY 12970
(518) 327-6313
Ted Mack, Librarian; Ruth Klein Hoyt,
College Archivist
Library: Mon–Fri 8:00–4:00; Museum: by
appointment

Pembroke History Room
Town Hall
1145 Main Road
Corfu, NY 14036
(716) 599-4892; (716) 762-8246 FAX
by appointment

Penfield Homestead Museum
(Historic Ironville—location)
703 Creek Road (mailing address)
Crown Point, NY 12928
(518) 597-3804; (518) 597-3229 FAX
penfield@cptelco.net
http://www.penfieldmuseum.org
Donna LaBounty, Museum Director
15 May–13 Oct: Wed–Sat 10:00–4:00, Sun
noon–4:00
(Crown Point and Essex County families,
local history)

Penfield Public Library
Penfield Local History Room
Division of Town Historian's Office
1985 Baird Road
Penfield, NY 14526
(716) 383-0500 (Library); (716) 383-0557
(Local History Room)
http://www.penfieldlibrary.org
Kathy Kanayer, Coordinator
Library: Mon–Thur 10:00–9:00, Fri–Sat
10:00–5:00, Sun (Sept–June) 2:00–5:00;
Local History Room: Mon–Tue & Thur
1:00–5:00, Mon–Tue 7:00–9:00, Sun
(Sept–June) 2:00–5:00, and by
appointment

Penn Yan Public Library
214 Main Street
Penn Yan NY 14527-1796
(315) 536-6114; (35) 536-0131 FAX

http://www.pypl.org
Mon–Fri 10:00–8:30, Sat (Sept–June)
10:00–3:00

Peru Free Library
(3024 Route 22, North Main
Street—location)
PO Box 96 (mailing address)
Peru, NY 12972
(518) 643-8618; (518) 643-8257 FAX
perulib@northnet.org
http://www.cefls.org/peru.htm

Philomathean Free Library
(8086 County Route 75—location)
PO Box 27 (mailing address)
Belleville, NY 13611
(315) 846-5103 voice & FAX; (315) 846-
5255 (Historian); (315) 846-5107 FAX
bellib@nnyln.net
http://www.nc34.org/ncls/libs/bel.txt
Lydia Miller, Librarian; Claude Poor,
Historian
Mon 7:00–9:00, Wed 1:00–5:00 &
7:00–9:00, Fri 5:00–9:00

Pickering-Beach Historical Museum
(West Main Street—location)
PO Box 204 (mailing address)
Sackets Harbor, NY 13685
(315) 646-2052; (315) 646-3868; (315) 646-
2815
John W. Deans, Chairperson

Piermont Public Library
153 Hudson Terrace
Piermont, NY 10968-1040
(845) 359-4595; (845) 365-1423 FAX
pmt@rcls.org
http://www.rcls.org/pmt
Grace Meyer, Director

Plainview-Old Bethpage Public Library
999 Old Country Road
Plainview, NY 11803
(516) 938-0077; (516) 938-8534 FAX
pobpl@hotmail.com
http://www.nassaulibrary.org/plainv
Mon–Fri 9:00–9:00, Sat 9:30–5:30, Sun
1:00–9:00

Plattsburgh Public Library
Local History Room
19 Oak Street
Plattsburgh, NY 12901
(518) 563-0921; (518) 563-7539 FAX
http://www.cefls.org/plattsburgh.htm
Colleen Pelletier, Head of Reference
Mon & Fri–Sat 9:00–5:00, Tue–Thur
9:00–8:00
("People coming from a long distance, who
wish staff assistance, should make an
appointment ahead of time.")

Port Chester Public Library
1 Haseco Avenue
Port Chester, NY 10573
(914) 939-6710; (914) 939-4735 FAX
http://www.portchesterlibrary.org
Mark Ross, Reference Librarian
Mon 9:00–9:00, Tue–Fri 9:00–5:00 Sat
(winter) 9:00–5:00

Port Jervis Free Library
138 Pike Street
Port Jervis, NY 12771-1879
(914) 856-7313; (914) 858-8710 FAX
ptj@rcls.org
http://www.rcls.org/ptj

Port Leyden Community Library
(3145 Canal Street—location)

PO Box 97 (mailing address)
Port Leyden, NY 13433
(315) 348-6077; (315) 348-4234 FAX
plylib@nnyln.net
http://www.nc3r.org/ncls/libs/ply.txt
Lyn Cyr, Librarian
Mon 9:00–1:00 & 6:00–9:00, Tue & Fri
1:00–5:00, Wed 6:00–9:00, Sat
10:00–noon

Port Washington Public Library
1 Library Drive
Port Washington, NY 11050
(516) 883-4400; (516) 883-7927 FAX
pwpl@lilrc.org
http://www.pwpl.org
Jerry McGee, Director; Priscilla Ciccariello,
Head of Information Services
Mon–Fri 9:00–9:00, Sat 9:00–5:00
Pub. *Port Washington Public Library
Newsletter*

Potsdam Public Museum
Civic Center, Park Street
Potsdam, NY 13676
(315) 265-6910
http://www.potsdam.ny.us/museum
Betsy L. Travis, Director
Tue–Thur & Sat 2:00–5:00, Fri 10:00–noon
& 2:00–5:00
Pub. untitled newsletter, quarterly, free
(local history museum, small local archives,
no library)
$15.00 per year membership in Friends of
the Potsdam Museum (to PO Box 161,
Potsdam, NY 13676)

James Prendergast Library Association
509 Cherry Street
Jamestown, NY 14701-5098
(716) 484-7135; (716) 487-1148
cway@cclslib.org
http://www.prendergastlibrary.org
Kim Morris, Reference Librarian; Catherine
A. Way, Assistant Director
Mon–Fri 9:00–9:00, Sat 9:00–5:00, Sun
(Nov–Apr) 1:00–4:00

Pulaski Public Library
Snow Memorial Building
4917 North Jefferson Street
Pulaski, NY 13142
(315) 298-2717 voice & FAX
pullib@nnyln.net
http://www.nc3r.org/ncls/libs/pul.txt
Margaret M. Weigel, Library Director
Mon–Fri 9:00–5:00, Tue & Thur 7:00–9:00,
Sat 9:30–12:30

Purchase Free Library
Purchase Street
Purchase, NY 10577
(914) 948-0550
http://www.wls.lib.ny.us/libs/purchase/
pur.html

Queens Borough Public Library
Long Island Collection
89-11 Merrick Boulevard
Jamaica, NY 11432
(718) 990-0770
http://www.queenslibrary.org/index.asp
Charles F. J. Young, Curator

**Louise Adelia Read Memorial
Library/Museum**
104 Read Street
Hancock, NY 13783-1147
(607) 637-2519; (607) 637-3377 FAX
ha_ill@4cty.org
http://www.4cls.org/webpages/members

Margaret Reaney Memorial Library
19 Kingsbury Avenue
Saint Johnsville, NY 13452
(518) 568-7822 voice & FAX
http://www2.telenet.net/community/mvla/
stjo
Marta Zimmerman, Assistant Library
Director
Mon–Wed & Fri 9:30–5:00, Mon & Fri
6:30–8:30, Thur 1:00–5:00, Sat
9:30–noon
(emphasis on Palatine Germans of the
Mohawk Valley)
research: $10.00 plus postage and copies at
25¢ per page

Rensselaer Falls Library
(Rensselaer Street—location)
PO Box 237 (mailing address)
Rensselaer Falls, NY 13680
(315) 344-7406
http://www.nc3r.org/fallslibrary
Tim Connolly, Library Manager
Mon 1:30–4:30 & 7:00–9:00, Wed
2:30–4:30, Fri 1:30–4:30

Rensselaer Public Library
810 Broadway
Rensselaer, NY 12144-2198
(518) 462-1193
http://www.uhls.org/uhls/members/
library.cfm?id=26
Kenneth A. Ryder, Director
(houses the collection of the City of
Rensselaer Historical Society)

Richmond Memorial Library
19 Ross Street
Batavia, NY 14020
(716) 343-9550; (716) 344-4651 FAX
btvweb@nioga.org
http://www.batavialibrary.org
Kathleen Facer, Adult Services Librarian
Mon–Tue & Thur 9:00–9:00, Wed
9:00–6:00, Fri–Sat 9:00–5:00 (closed Sat,
July–Aug)
(Genesee County, New York)

**City of Rochester Archives and Records
Center**
414 Andrews Street
Rochester, NY 14604
(716) 428-7331; (716) 428-6092 FAX
http://www.rochester.lib.ny.us/cityhall/
about_r/records/records.htm

Rochester Public Library
Local History Division
115 South Avenue
Rochester, NY 14604-1896
(716) 428-7338 (Local History and
Genealogy Department)
http://www.libraweb.org/central
Wayne K. Arnold, Head Librarian, Local
History Division
Mon & Thur 8:30–9:00, Tue & Fri
8:30–6:00, Sat 8:30–5:00
Pub. *Rochester History*, quarterly, $6.00 per
year subscription
(collection of printed genealogies, county and
town histories, census, Rochester
directories from 1827, suburban
directories from 1932, maps, newspapers
indexed 1818–1902, tombstone records,
scrapbooks, etc.

**Rochester Regional Research Library
Council**
Documentary Heritage Program
(390 Packett's Landing—location)
PO Box 66160 (mailing address)
Fairport, NY 14450

(585) 223-7570; (585) 223-7712 FAX

Rogers Memorial Library
9 Job's Lane
Southampton, NY 11968
(631) 283-0774; (631) 283-3717 FAX
dengelha@suffolk.lib.ny.us;
    rogmlib@suffolk.lib.ny.us
http://rogers.suffolk.lib.ny.us
Sue Ann Taylor, Reference Librarian
Mon–Thur 10:00–9:00, Fri–Sat 10:00–5:00
(Long Island, especially Southampton; "Staff
    is very limited and extended searches not
    possible")

Roxbury Library Association
Local History Room
(Main Street—location)
PO Box 186 (mailing address)
Roxbury, NY 12474
(607) 326-7901
ro_ill@4cty.org
http://www.4cls.org/webpages/members/
    Roxbury/Roxbury.html

Russell Public Library
(9 Prestle Street—location)
PO Box 510 (mailing address)
Russell, NY 13684
(315) 347-2115; (315) 562-3487
    (Appointments)
http://www.nc3r.org/russlib
Brenda L. Hale, Library Director
by apppointment

Gardner A. Sage Library
(see New Jersey, Part 2)

Saint Lawrence University
Owen D. Young Library
Special Collections
Canton, NY 13617
(315) 379-5476
dleonard@stlawu.edu
http://www.stlawu.edu/library/odyinfo.html
Darlene Leonard, Library Assistant, Special
    Collections; Mark McMurray, Special
    Collections Librarian and University
    Archivist
Mon–Fri 8:30–4:30
(northern New York)

Saint Mary's Hospital Library
89 Genesee Street
Rochester, NY 14611-3201

Samaritan Medical Center Library
830 Washington Street
Watertown, NY 13601
(315) 785-4191; (315) 779-5173 FAX
jgarvey@northnet.org
http://www.samaritanhealth.com/library.htm
Jeffrey M. Garvey, Director
Mon–Fri 8:00–5:00
(records from St. Joachims Hospital, Sisters
    Hospital, Mercy Hospital of Watertown,
    and School of Nursing from 1894)

William K. Sanford Town Library
629 Albany-Shaker Road
Loudonville, NY 12211-1196
(518) 458-9274; (518) 438-0988; (518) 482-
    5441 FAX
wkslibry@uhls.lib.ny.us
http://www.colonie.org/library
Mary Hoefgen, Head of Reference Services
Mon–Thur 9:00–9:00, Fri 9:00–6:00, Sat
    9:00–5:00, Sun (closed summer)
    1:00–5:00
(small collection of reference works, city
    directories, maps, oral history tapes,
    newspaper clipping file with an emphasis

on the Town of Colonie and surrounding
    localities, including some local church
    records and a few family histories)

Saranac Lake Free Library
Adirondack Collection
100 Main Street
Saranac Lake, NY 12983
(518) 891-4190 (Library); (518) 891-0807
    (Collection); (518) 891-5931 FAX
whitefie@northnet.org;
    saranac@northnet.org;
    mtucker@northnet.org
http://www.nc3r.org/slfl
Betsy Whitefield, Director; Michele Tucker,
    Collection Curator
Library: Mon–Sat 10:00–5:30, Thur
    (Sept–June) 10:00–8:00, Sat (July–Aug)
    10:00–1:00; Adirondack Collection:
    Mon–Fri 10:00–4:00

Saratoga County History Center
(see Brookside Museum-Saratoga History
Center, above)

Saratoga Springs Public Library
The Saratoga Room
49 Henry Street
Saratoga Springs, NY 12866-3271
(518) 584-7860, ext. 255
history@saratoga.lib.ny.us
http://www.library.saratoga.ny.us
Ellen deLalla, Local Historian
Mon & Thur 7:00 P.M.–9:00 P.M., Tue & Fri
    2:30–4:30, Wed 9:00–1:00, Sat
    noon–4:00
(collection concentrated on Saratoga
    Springs)

Saugerties Public Library
Washington Avenue
Saugerties, NY 12477
(845) 246-4317; (845) 246-0858 FAX
saugerts@seabridge.org
http://saugertiespubliclibrary.org
(all Saugerties newspapers on microfilm)

Scarsdale Public Library
54 Olmstead Road
Scarsdale, NY 10583
(914) 722-1300; (914) 722-1305 FAX
http://www.scarsdalelibrary.org
Florence Sinsheimer, Reference Librarian
Mon–Wed 10:00–9:00, Thur 10:00–6:00,
    Fri–Sat 9:00–5:00, Sun 1:00–5:00;
    summer hours differ slightly
(weekly newspaper *Scarsdale Inquirer* from
    1901 with index; local history collection,
    village reports from 1915, biographical
    clippings, organizations, phone books
    from 1931)

Schenectady County Public Library
99 Clinton Street
Schenectady, NY 12305-2083
(518) 382-4500; (518) 386-2241 FAX
scpl@scpl.org
http://www.scpl.org
Timothy McGowan, Head, Reference and
    Adult Services
Mon–Thur 9:00–9:00, Fri–Sat 9:00–5:00,
    Sun (Oct–Apr) 1:00–5:00

Schenectady Museum
Nott Terrace Heights
Schenectady, NY 12308
(518) 382-7890; (518) 382-7898 FAX

**Schoharie Free (Cushing Memorial)
Library**
(Bridge Street and Knower
    Avenue—location)

PO Box 519 (mailing address)
Schoharie, NY 12157-0519
(518) 295-7127 voice & FAX
sholib@midtel.net
http://www2.telenet.net/community/mvla/
    scho
Catherine Caiazzo, Director
Mon 9:00–noon, Tue 12:30–5:30, Thur
    1:00–5:00 & 7:00–9:00, Fri 12:30–6:00,
    Sat 9:00–12:30
copies: 20¢ per sheet

Schroon Lake Public Library
(South Avenue—location)
PO Box 398 (mailing address)
Schroon Lake, NY 12870
(518) 532-7737; (518) 532-9474 FAX
library@schroon.net
http://www.cefls.org/schroonlake.htm

Scottsville Free Library
(address withheld upon request)
("Our collection is small, covering only the
    Town of Wheatland and is staffed by a
    small group of volunteers. They are
    concerned that such wide-spread publicity
    would create too many requests for our
    volunteers to handle.")

Seymour Library
176-178 Genesee Street
Auburn, NY 13021
(315) 252-2571; (315) 252-7985 FAX
http://www.seymourlibrary.org
Mary Gilmore, History Room
History Room: Mon–Wed & Fri 2:00–5:00,
    Mon & Wed 6:00–9:00

Town of Shandaken Historical Museum
(26 Academy Street—location)
PO Box 678 (mailing address)
Pine Hill, NY 12465
(845) 254-4460 (Phoenicia library)
Evelyn Bennett, Director
Thur–Fri 11:00–4:00, Sat–Sun 1:00–4:00
("We are actually a museum with genealogy
    files and local history, artifacts, etc. for the
    town of Shandaken and about our
    township. The Town of Shandaken is
    comprised of twelve hamlets. We have a
    library in Pine Hill, called 'Morton
    Memorial Library.' Plus we have a library
    in Phoenicia.")
$5.00 per year membership

Sherman Free Library
20 Church Street
Port Henry, NY 12974
(518) 546-7461; (518) 546-3046 FAX
sherman@bluemoo.net
http://www.porthenry.com/phframes/
    library.htm
Nancy Tuffield, Librarian
Wed 9:00–2:00, Thur–Fri 2:00–7:00

Skemesborough Museum
PO Box 238
Whitehall, NY 12887
(518) 499-0225; (518) 499-0754

The Smithtown Library
Richard H. Handley Long Island History
Room
1 North Country Road
Smithtown, NY 11787
(631) 265-2072, ext. 38
http://www.smithlib.org
Richard B. Hawkins, Librarian
Wed 1:00–5:00 & 6:00–9:00, Tue &
    Thur–Fri 10:00–1:00 & 2:00–6:00, Sat
    9:00–1:00 & 2:00–5:00
(Smithtown Archives and Long Island

Special Collection)

South Central Research Library Council
Documentary Heritage Program
215 North Cayuga Street
Ithaca, NY 14850
(607) 273-9106; (607) 272-0740 FAX

Southold Free Library
Whitaker Historical Collection
(53705 Main Road—location)
PO Box 697 (mailing address)
Southold, NY 11971-0697
(631) 765-2077; (631) 765-2197 FAX
sohdlib@suffolk.lib.ny.us;
    whitaker@suffolk.lib.ny.us (Local History
    Questions)
http://sohd.suffolk.lib.ny.us
Melissa Andruski, Adult Services
Library: Mon, Wed & Fri 10:00–9:00, Tue,
    Thur & Sat 10:00–5:00, Sun (Sept–May)
    1:00–5:00; Whitaker Collection: Wed–Sat
    2:00–5:00

Southworth Library Association
(24 West Main Street—location)
PO Box 45 (mailing address)
Dryden, NY 13053
(607) 844-4782 voice & FAX
southwor@twcny.rr.com;
    drylib@clarityconnect.com
http://home.twcny.rr.com/southworth
Susan Rosenkoetter

Stamford Village Library
117 Main Street
Stamford, NY 12167-1029
(607) 652-5001
http://www.4cls.org/webpages/members/
    Stamford/Stamford.html

State University of New York at Albany
University Library B-3
Special Collections and Archives
1400 Washington Avenue
Albany, NY 12222
(518) 442-3544
http://www.albany.edu/library/oldlib/
    services/specoll.html

State University of New York at Brockport
Drake Memorial Library
College Archives, Special Collections
Brockport, NY 14420
(716) 395-5667; (716) 395-5651 FAX
http://cc.brockport.edu/~library1/
    archives.htm

State University of New York at Fredonia
Daniel E. Reed Library
Fredonia, NY 14063
(716) 673-3183; (716) 673-3185 FAX
Jack.Ericson@fredonia.edu
http://www.fredonia.edu/library
Jack T. Ericson, Archivist/Curator, Special
    Collections
winter: Mon–Fri 1:00–5:00; summer:
    Mon–Fri 1:00–4:00
(Chautauqua and Cattaraugus counties;
    Holland Land Company records on
    microfilm)
no research in response to written queries, but
    reference work for in-person patrons

**Penfield Library, State University of New
York at Oswego**
Oswego, NY 13126
(315) 341-3537; (315) 341-3567; (315) 341-
    3194 FAX
sturr@oswego.edu
http://www.oswego.edu/library
Nancy Osborne, Coordinator of Special

Collections; Ed Vermue, Assistant
    Coordinator
during the semester: Mon & Thur 1:30–4:30
(local history and college history)

Plattsburgh State University of New York
Special Collections
Room 132, Feinberg Library
2 Draper Avenue
Plattsburgh, NY 12901
(518) 564-5206
http://www2.plattsburgh.edu/acadvp/
    libinfo/library/speccoll.html
Wayne Miller, Special Collections Librarian
Tue 4:00–7:00, Wed 9:00–noon &
    1:00–4:00, Thur 9:00–12:30 & 1:00–4:00,
    Fri 10:00–12:30 & 1:00–4:00, Sat
    1:00–4:00
("Special Collections is an archive. Materials
    do not circulate. Certain restrictions
    apply, e.g., sign-in required, pencils only
    for note-taking.")

**State University of New York at Stony
Brook**
Long Island Archives Conference
Department of Special Collections
State University of New York Library
Stony Brook, NY 11794-3323
(631) 246-3615
http://www.sunysb.edu/libmap/nymaps.htm
    (The Map Collection)

SUNY College of Technology at Canton
Southworth Library
Cornell Drive
Canton, NY 13617
(315) 386-7058
Mary Bucher, Archivist/Librarian
Mon–Fri 9:00–5:00

**SUNY College of Agriculture and
Technonolgy at Cobleskill**
Library
Cobleskill, NY 12043
(Schoharie County history and genealogy)

SUNY Potsdam College
College Libraries
Special Collections
Potsdam, NY 13676
(315) 267-3326
subramjm@potsdam.edu
Jane Subramanian, College Archivist
Library: Mon–Thur 7:45 A.M.–11:00 P.M.,
    Sat 10:00–7:00, Sun noon–11:00, except
    during mid-terms, finals, holidays,
    intercessions, and summers); Special
    collections: by appointment
(northern New York and the Adirondack
    region)

Steele Memorial Library Association
101 East Church Street
Elmira, NY 14901-2799
(607) 733-8602; (607) 733-9176 FAX
ref@chstls.org
http://www.steele.lib.ny.us
Rita Dery, Librarian
Mon–Thur 9:00–9:00, Fri 9:00–5:00, Sat
    (except June–Sept) 9:00–5:00, Sun
    (except June–Sept) 1:00–5:00
research: $12.00 per hour plus copy costs

Strong Museum Library and Archives
1 Manhattan Square
Rochester, NY 14607
(716) 263-2700; (716) 263-2493 FAX
http://www.strongmuseum.org

Syosset Public Library
225 South Oyster Bay Road

Syosset, NY 11791-5897
(516) 921-7161
http://www.nassaulibrary.org/syosset
Isabel Goldenkoff
winter: Mon–Fri 9:00–9:00, Sat 9:00–5:00,
    Sun noon–5:00; summer: Mon–Fri
    9:00–9:00, Sat 9:00–1:00

Theresa Free Library
301 Main Street
Theresa, NY 13691
(315) 628-5972
crajner@northnet.org
http://www.northnet.org/theresalibrary
Christine Rajner, Director
Tue & Thur–Fri 1:30–5:00 & 7:00–9:00, Sat
    9:00–12:30

Didymus Thomas Memorial Library
(9639 Main Street—location)
PO Box 410 (mailing address)
Remsen, NY 13438
(315) 831-5651

    http://www.midyork.org/LibraryList/Librar
    yInfo/Remsen.html

Thousand Island Park Library
(42743 Saint Lawrence Avenue—location)
PO Box 1115 (mailing address)
Thousand Island Park, NY 13692
(315) 482-9098
tiplib@nnyln.net
http://www.nc3r.org/ncls/libs/tip.txt
Mabel Ann Heath, Librarian

Tompkins County Public Library
101 East Green Street
Ithaca, NY 14850
(607) 272-4555; (607) 272-8111 FAX
jsteiner@tcpl.org;
    jsteiner@mail.co.tompkins.ny.us
http://www.tcpl.org
Janet Steiner, Director

Town of Amherst Archives Center
5178 Main Street
Williamsville, NY 14221
(716) 631-7125

Trinity Museum
(Broadway and Wall Streets—location)
74 Trinity Place (mailing address)
New York, NY 10006
(212) 602-0872
David Jette, Verger
Mon–Fri 9:00–11:45 & 1:00–3:45, Sat
    10:00–3:45, Sun 1:00–3:45

Trocaire College Library
110 Red Jacket Parkway
Buffalo, NY 14220
(716) 826-1200; (716) 826-4704 FAX

Troy Public Library
100 Second Street
Troy, NY 12180
(518) 274-7071 (Reference); (518) 271-9154
    FAX
troyref@uhls.lib.ny.us
http://www.uhls.org/troy
Sarah K. Andrews, Reference, Local History
    and Genealogy Librarian
Mon–Tue 10:00–9:00, Wed–Sat 10:00–5:00,
    Sat (summer) 10:00–1:00
(local history and genealogy, Rensselaer
    County, City of Troy)
research: $25.00 for the first hour (including
    four copies and postage), $20.00 for each
    additional hour, 10¢ for each additional
    copy, plus additional postage if required
    (turnaround time about 2-3 months)

Ulysses Philomathic Library
(61 East Main Street—location)
PO Box 705 (mailing address)
Trumansburg, NY 14886
(607) 387-5623; (607) 387-3823 FAX
uphiloma@twcny.rr.com
http://www.ulysses.ny.us/library.html

Union College
Schaffer Library
807 Union Street
Schenectady, NY 12308
(518) 370-6620

University at Buffalo Science and Engineering Library
Map Collection
316 Capen Hall
Buffalo, NY 14260
(716) 645-2946; (716) 645-3710 FAX

University at Buffalo
Special Collection Reading Room
420 Capen Hall
Buffalo, NY 14260
(716) 645-2916; (716) 645-3714 FAX
Christopher Densmore, Acting Director
Mon–Fri 9:00–5:00
(University Archives serves as the official repository of historically significant university records of the University at Buffalo, documenting the history of the University and its students, alumni, faculty and administrators; also maintains a small local history collection and provides information about local sources available for research in the Buffalo area)

University of Rochester
Rare Books and Special Collections
Local History and Archives Room
Rush Rhees Library
Rochester, NY 14627
(716) 275-4477; (716) 273-1032 FAX
http://www.lib.rochester/edu/rhees
Mary M. Huth

Utica Public Library
303 Genesee Street
Utica, NY 13501
(315) 735-2279; (315) 735-2270; (315) 734-1034 FAX
uaref@midyork.org
http://www.uticapubliclibrary.org
Barbara Brookes, Reference Librarian
Mon–Wed 8:30–8:00, Thur–Fri 8:30–5:30, Sat (except summers) 8:30–5:00
research: $16.00 for inquiries from outside of the state, $10.00 for inquiries from outside of Mid-York Library System

Vestal Public Library
320 Vestal Parkway East
Vestal, NY 13850
(607) 754-4244 (Reference); (607) 754-7936 FAX
http://www.4cls.org/webpages/members/Vestal/Vestal.html

Voorheesville Public Library
51 School Road
Voorheesville, NY 12186
(518) 765-2791; (518) 765-3007 FAX
http://www.uhls.org/voorheesville

Wadhams Free Library
Route 22
Wadhams, NY 12990
(518) 962-8717 voice & FAX
wadh2@westelcom.com
http://www.cefls.org/wadhams.htm

Henry Waldinger Memorial Library
60 Verona Place
Valley Stream, NY 11582-3011
(516) 825-6422; (516) 825-6551 FAX
hwmlcontact@hotmail.com
http://www.nassaulibrary.org/valleyst/index.html
Mamie Eng
Mon–Tue & Thur–Fri 10:00–9:00, Wed 10:00–5:30, Sat 10:00–4:00

Warner Library
121 North Broadway
Tarrytown, NY 10591
(914) 631-2189
Jonathan Tee, Reference Librarian
Mon & Thur 1:00–9:00, Tue–Wed & Fri–Sat 10:00–5:00
(collection of materials, chiefly books, pertaining to Tarrytown and North Tarrytown)

Waterford Historical Museum and Cultural Center
2 Museum Lane
Waterford, NY 12188
(518) 238-0809 (answering machine)
Ida May Neary, President; Dennis Rivage, Town Historian, Merle Doud, Village Historian
Sat–Sun (spring–fall) 2:00–4:00, and by appointment
(no genealogy service)
$10.00 per year membership

The Wead Library
64 Elm Street
Malone, NY 12953-1594
(518) 483-5251; (518) 483-5225 FAX
http://www.cefls.org/malone.htm
David W. Minnich, Library Director
Mon–Wed & Fri noon–9:00, Tue & Thur 10:00–9:00, Sat noon–5:00; Summer: Mon–Fri 10:00–4:00 & 6:00–9:00

Wells Memorial Library
(Route 9N—location)
PO Box 57 (mailing address)
Upper Jay, NY 12987
(518) 946-2644 voice & FAX
UpperJayLibrary@Whiteface.net
http://www.wellsmemoriallibrary.homestead.com
Carde McDowell, Director
Library: Tue–Thur noon–5:00, Sat 11:00–4:00; Archives: by appointment

Wenrich Memorial Library
(see The Landmark Society of Western New York, above)

Western Monroe County Genealogical Society
Ogden Farmers' Library
269 Ogden Center Road
Spencerport, NY 14559

Westport Library Association
(Washington Street—location)
PO Box 436 (mailing address)
Westport, NY 12993-0436
(518) 962-8219; (518) 962-8964
wptlib@nc3r.org
http://www.nc3r.org/wptlib
Marilyn Trienens, Librarian
Tue 10:00–6:00, Thur 1:00–6:00, Sat 9:00–1:00; summer: Tue–Thur 10:00–6:00, Sat 9:00–1:00

City of White Plains City Archives
(100 Martine Avenue—location)
255 Main Street (mailing address)

White Plains, NY 10601-2409
(914) 422-1450
http://www.cityofwhiteplains.com
Elaine Massena, City Archivist
by appointment
(Government archives with additional "varied collections of photos, artifacts, scrapbooks, maps")

Woodgate Free Library
(11051 Woodgate Drive—location)
PO Box 52 (mailing address)
Woodgate, NY 13494
(315) 392-4814
http://www.midyork.org/LibraryList/LibraryInfo/Woodgate.html
John B. Isley, President
Mon 6:00–9:00, Wed 3:00–6:00, Sat 10:00–4:00

Pieter Claesen Wyckoff House Museum
(Clarendon Road at Ralph Avenue—location)
5816 Clarendon Road (mailing address)
Brooklyn, NY 11203-5444
Alan J. Lipsky, Administrator
Pub. *PCWHM Bulletin*
(genealogical services)

Yorktown Museum Record Center
c/o Town Hall
363 Underhill Avenue
Yorktown Heights, NY 10598
(914) 962-0341; (914) 962-7282
Doris P. Auser, Town Historian
Mon & Fri 9:00–12:30
(genealogical and local history collection, cemetery records, census and documents)

Historical Societies—Local and Regional
(Note that New York's network of official government historians are not genealogists and have been advised by the State Historian not to focus on genealogical research, but they may be able to direct the researcher to sources and persons who can help with genealogical questions.)

Adirondack Genealogical-Historical Society
(see Genealogical Societies—Local and Regional, below)

Alabama Historical Society
7079 Maple Street
Basom, NY 14013-9770
(716) 948-9886
Jean Richardson, Alabama Town Historian

Albany County Historian
Albany County Office Building
Office of the Albany County Historian
112 State Street, Room 800
Albany, NY 12207
(518) 447-5516
JTRAVIS@AlbanyCounty.com
John N. Travis
Mon–Fri 8:30–4:30

Municipal Historians

City of Albany
352 Second Avenue
Albany, NY 12209
(518) 434-5100
Virginia Bowers

Village of Altamont
27 Patricia Lane
Albany, NY 12203
(518) 356-1980

Alice Begley
(also historian of the Town of Guilderland)

Town of Berne
Town Hall
PO Box 34
Berne, NY 12023
(518) 872-0212 (Home)
Ralph11@AOL.com
http://Bernehistory.org/index.html
Ralph Miller

Town of Bethlehem
15 Heather Lane
Delmar, NY 12054
(518) 439-2041
Joseph A. Allgaier

Town of Coeymans
Route 143
Coeymans Hollow, NY 12046
(518) 756-8166
Marvin D. Wolfe

City of Cohoes
Waterford, NY 12188
William Horan

Town of Colonie
Memorial Town Hall
Newtonville, NY 12128
Jean Olton

Village of Colonie
14 Benjamin Lane
Albany, NY 12205
Linda Murphy

Town and Village of Green Island
Heatly School
171 Hudson Avenue
Green Island, NY 12183
Ginger Hewitt
(town and village are coextensive)

Town of Guilderland
Alice Begley (see Village of Altamont, above)

Town of Knox
PO Box 38
Knox, NY 12107
(518) 872-1585
Frieda Saddlemire
by appointment
("I live almost next door to the Knox [Historical Society] Museum, so I'm always available for tours, etc.")
no set fees

Village of Menands
Municipal Building
250 Broadway
Menands, NY 12204
Kevin Franklin

Town of New Scotland
82 Badgley Lane
Voorheesville, NY 12186
(518) 439-4889, ext. 5721
Robert Parmenter

Village of Ravena
171 Main Street
Ravena, NY 12143
Mary McCabe

Town of Rensselaerville
9 Fox Creek Road
Medusa, NY 12120
(518) 239-8483
Porter Wright

Village of Voorheesville
(14 Voorheesville Avenue—location)
Box 262 (mailing address)
Voorheesville, NY 12186
(518) 765-2468
Dennis Sullivan

City of Watervliet
c/o City Hall
Watervliet, NY 12189
(518) 447-4513
Craig Carlson

Town of Westerlo
350 County Route 402
Westerlo, NY 12193
(518) 797-3095
Dennis Fancher

Albany County Historical Association
Ten Broeck Mansion
9 Ten Broeck Place
Albany, NY 12210
(518) 436-9826

Albany South End Historical Society
20 Second Avenue
Albany, NY 12202
(518) 463-0249

Alden Historical Society
13213 Broadway
Alden, NY 14004
(716) 937-7606
by appointment

Alexandria Township Historical Society
Cornwall Brothers Building
Market Street
Alexandria Bay, NY 13607
(315) 482-4586
Doris Langlois, Vice President
(no genealogical department or services)

Alfred Historical Society
Terra Cotta Museum
PO Box 1137
Alfred, NY 14802
(607) 587-8886; (607) 587-4351 FAX
   (Hinkle Memorial Library, SUNY
   Alfred); (607) 587-8358 (President);
   (607) 587-4307 (Library Assistant)
Douglas Clarke, President; Galen Brooks,
   Library Assistant
Mon, Wed & Fri 11:00–4:00
(several genealogical books and collections
   of notes for Alfred area and Seventh Day
   Baptist families from Rhode Island west)

Allegany Area Historical Association
(25 North Second Street—location)
PO Box 162 (mailing address)
Allegany, NY 14706
(716) 372-2918
Mary Frances Potter, President
May–Oct: Wed 1:00–4:00
Pub. *Newsletter*, five times per year
$10.00 per year membership

Allegany County Historian's Office and County Museum
Courthouse
7 Court Street
Belmont, NY 14813
(716) 268-9293 (Museum); (716) 268-9446
   FAX
historian@alleganyco.com
Craig R. Braack, County Historian
Museum: winter: 9:00–noon & 1:00–5:00;
   June–Aug: 8:30–noon & 1:00–4:00

Municipal Historians

Town of Alfred
5146 Kenyon Road
Alfred Station, NY 14803
Jean Lang

Village of Alfred
Alfred, NY 14802
Peggy Rase

Town of Allen
Rural Delivery 1, Box 200
Angelica, NY 14709
Patricia Hopkins

Town of Alma
52 East Dyke Street, #1
Wellsville, NY 14895-1612
Norman Ives

Town of Almond
Almond, NY 14804
Richard Burdick

Village of Almond
post vacant

Town of Amity
Belmont, NY 14813
Jackie Manis

Town of Andover and Village of Andover
Harmon Street
Andover, NY 14806
Robert Baker

Town of Angelica and Village of Angelica
post vacant

Town of Belfast
70 West Hughes Street
Belfast, NY 14711
Dominic Curcio

Village of Belmont
post vacant

Town of Birdsall
(22 Meadowbrook Drive—location)
PO Box 15 (mailing address)
Canaseraga, NY 14822
(607) 545-6204
Faye Clancy
by appointment

Town of Bolivar and Village of Bolivar
Rural Delivery 1
Bolivar, NY 14715
Rose Feenaughty

Town of Burns
Canaseraga, NY 14822
Sherri Amers

Village of Canaseraga
post vacant

Town of Caneadea
Houghton, NY 14744
Larry Wilson

Town of Centerville
Centerville, NY 14029
Debbie Covert

Town of Clarksville
West Clarksville, NY 14786
Charlotte Gessel
10:00–5:00

Town of Cuba
44 South Street
Cuba, NY 14727

David Crowley

Village of Cuba
post vacant

Village of Fillmore
(Town of Hume Museum, 10842 Claybed
Road, Hume, NY 14745—location)
PO Box 302 (mailing address)
Fillmore, NY 14735
(585) 567-8399; (585) 567-4266 FAX
museum@humetown.org
http://www.Humetown.org
Mrs. Rondus Miller
Mon (Sept–June) 2:00–4:00, Mon
    (July–Aug) 9:00–noon & 1:00–4:00, Thur
    5:00–8:00, Sat 9:00–noon
("The Town of Hume Museum is the first
    town-owned museum in Allegany County.
    The museum was established in April of
    2000. Before that time our town
    historian's office was located in a private
    home. We are located in the northwest
    corner of Allegany County. The
    historian's office has over 3,000 index
    cards of obituaries, marriage and special
    events. Our genealogy records are
    growing.")
research: $15.00 for first search (name &
    date), $10.00 per additional search
    thereafter

Town of Friendship
c/o Friendship Library
Harold Reed Memorial History Room
(40 West Main Street—location)
PO Box 37 (mailing address)
Friendship, NY 14739
Norma Pizza

Town of Genesee
8474 Wells Road West
Little Genesee, NY 14754
millimanj@yahoo.com
Jean Milliman

Town of Granger
Rural Delivery 1
Fillmore, NY 14735
Loreen Bentley

Town of Grove
post vacant

Town of Hume
(10869 County Road 23, Hume, NY
14745—location)
PO Box 302 (mailing address)
Fillmore, NY 14735
(585) 567-8399; (585) 567-4266 FAX
museum@humetown.org
http://www.Humetown.org
Mrs. Rondus Miller

Town of Independence
Whitesville, NY 14897
Velma Westlake

Town of New Hudson
Black Creek, NY 14714
Neva Gross

Village of Richburg
post vacant

Town of Rushford
(Davies Room of Rushford
Library—location)
9004 Main Street (mailing address)
Rushford, NY 14777
Homer Norton
Tue & Thur 1:00–4:00, Wed 10:00–noon, by

appointment

Town of Scio
4054 McQueen Street
Scio, NY 14880
(585) 593-6375
mjcas@localnet.com
Cheryl Smith

Town of Ward
3015 Hogan Hill Road
Scio, NY 14880
(585) 268-5671
Rose Maine

Town of Wellsville
173 East State Street
Wellsville, NY 14895-1240
Diane Converso
(also historian of the village of Wellsville)

Village of Wellsville
Diane Converso (see Town of Wellsville,
    above)

Town of West Almond
Rural Delivery
Almond, NY 14804
Deborah Hoffman

Town of Willing
3052 Palmer Road
Wellsville, NY 14895-9746
Christina Case Wightman

Town of Wirt
Richburg, NY 14774
Betty Bartoo

Allegany County Historical Society
20 Willets Avenue
Belmont, NY 14813
(716) 268-7428
Bill Green, County Historian, Emeritus
(census and land records)
nominal research fees

Almond Historical Society
(7 Main Street—location)
376 Karr Valley Road (mailing address)
Almond, NY 14804
(607) 276-6465
http://www.rootsweb.com/~nyahs/
    AlmondHS.html
Charlotte K. Baker, President
Fri 2:00–4:00, plus open houses
Pub. *Almond Historical Society Newsletter*,
    four times per year
$6.00 per year membership; no search fee

Amagansett Historical Association
(Main Stree and Windmill Lane—location)
PO Box 7077 (mailing address)
Amagansett, NY 11930-7077
(631) 267-3020
Memorial Day–Labor Day: Fri–Sun
    10:00–4:00
("Genealogical inquiries should be made in
    writing. Long-distance phone calls are not
    returned." The association includes the
    Miss Amelia Cottage Museum and the
    Roy Lester Carriage Museum.)
$20.00 per year membership

Amenia Historical Society
(Main Street—location)
PO Box 22 (mailing address)
Amenia, NY 12501
(845) 373-9376; (845) 373-8867 FAX
AmeniaHistorical@aol.com
Ken Hoadley, Vice President
Mon–Fri 9:00–5:00

$10.00 per year membership

Amityville Historical Society
Lauder Museum
(170 Broadway—location)
PO Box 764 (mailing address)
Amityville, NY 11701
(631) 598-1486
Seth Purdy, Curator
Tue, Fri & Sun 2:00–4:00
Pub. *Dispatch*, quarterly
$20.00 per year membership

Anderson Falls Heritage Society
1790 Main Street
Keeseville, NY 12944
(518) 384-2839

Anderson Falls Historical Society
Community Center
1790 Main Street, Suite 3-4
Keeseville, NY 12944
Roby A. Scott, Treasurer
by appointment
$8.00 per year membership

**Anthropology Museum of the People of
New York**
3801 23rd Avenue
Astoria, NY 11105
(718) 626-0307

Arcade Historical Society
The Gibby House
(331 West Main Street—location)
PO Box 237 (mailing address)
Arcade, NY 14009
(716) 492-4466
Ann Drennan, Office Manager
Tue–Wed 10:00–4:00, and by appointment
Pub. *Arcade Historical Society News*, three
    times per year
$5.00 per year membership

Ardsley Historical Society
Ardsley Public Library
9 American Legion Drive
Ardsley, NY 10502
(914) 693-6027; (914) 693-6636 (Library)

Attica Historical Society
(130 Main Street—location)
PO Box 24 (mailing address)
Attica, NY 14011
(585) 591-2161 (answering machine)
Wed & Sat 1:00–4:00, and by appointment

Aurora Historical Society, Inc.
5 South Grove Street
East Aurora, NY 14052
(716) 652-7944
Donald H. Dayer, Town Historian
Wed 1:00–4:00

Austerlitz Historical Society
(Route 22—location)
PO Box 144 (mailing address)
Austerlitz, NY 12017
(518) 392-5933; (518) 392-5478 (President)
Phil Palladino, Director; Robert Herron,
    President
Pub. *Quarterly*
from $5.00 per year membership

Avoca Historical Society
4185 County Route 70
Avoca, NY 14809
(607) 566-2884
Grace S. Fox, Historian, Town of Avoca
by appointment
Pub. *Newsletter of Avoca Historical Society*,
    four times per year

$3.00 per year membership; research: $5.00
per hour for nonresidents

Avon Preservation and Historical Society
27 Genesee Street
Avon, NY 14414
Jean Batzing, Acting President

Baldwin Historical Society and Museum
(1980 Grand Avenue—location)
PO Box 762 (mailing address)
Baldwin, NY 11510
(516) 223-6900
Glenn F. Sitterly, Curator; Connie Grando,
    Secretary
by appointment
Pub. *Baldwin Historical Society Newsletter*,
    bimonthly
(Baldwin local history)

Barnes Historical Society
PO Box 300049, JFK Station
Jamaica, NY 11430-0049
(718) 528-5747
Albert Walker, Jr., Membership Chairman
(collects oral histories of African-American
    residents)

**Basket Historical Society of the Upper
Delaware Valley**
Route 11
Long Eddy, NY 12760
(845) 887-5417

Battle of Oriskany Historical Society
806 Utica Street
Oriskany, NY 13424
Robert H. Heeley, President

Bayside Historical Society
(Fort Totten—location)
PO Box 133 (mailing address)
Bayside, NY 11361
(718) 352-1548; (718) 352-3904 FAX
http://www.donohue.com/bayside
Geraldine Spinella, President
Sat 10:00–3:00, evening events
Pub. *Society News*, quarterly
$25.00 per year membership

Beacon Historical Society
The Howland Center
(477 Main Street—location)
PO Box 89 (mailing address)
Beacon, NY 12508
Joan Van Voorhis, City Historian
Thur 10:00–noon, Sat 1:00–3:00
Pub. *Newsletter*, monthly
(deals with Beacon and its antecedents,
    Fishkill Landing and Matteawan, and the
    immediate surroundings)
$10.00 per year membership; donation for
    search

Beauchamp Historical Club
828 Fairway Circle
Baldwinsville, NY 13027
Joseph P. Uirkler, President

Bedford Historical Society
(38 Village Green—location)
PO Box 491 (mailing address)
Bedford, NY 10506
(914) 234-9751; (914) 234-5461 FAX
bedhist@bestweb.net
http://bedfordhistoricalsociety.org
Lynne Ryan, Executive Director
Mon–Fri 9:00–2:30
("We have some genealogical information but
    most requests are handled by Bedford
    Town Historian.")
$35.00 per year membership

Historical Society of the Bellmores
(32 Stratford Court—location)
PO Box 912 (mailing address)
North Bellmore, NY 11710
(516) 221-4222
Ken Foreman, Curator
by appointment
(Long Island history)
$5.00 per year membership

Bellport-Brookhaven Historical Society
31 Bellport Lane
Bellport, NY 11713
(631) 286-9064
Richard Baldwin, Archivist
by appointment
$35.00 per year membership; research:
    $10.00 per year

**Egbert Benson Historical Society of Red
Hook**
PO Box 1813
Red Hook, NY 12571-0397

Bergen Historical Society
(7547 South Lake Road—location)
6833 Pocock Road (mailing address)
Bergen, NY 14416
(716) 494-1511; (716) 494-1456 (Historian)
by appointment with Town Historian

Town of Berne Historical Society
Historical Center
(Main Street—location)
PO Box 34 (mailing address)
Berne, NY 12023
(518) 872-0212 (home)
Ralph11@AOL.com
http://Bernehistory.org/index.html
Ralph Miller, Town Historian; Peg Lewis,
    President
Pub. *Newsletter*, two times per year
$2.00 per year membership

Town of Bethlehem Historical Association
Old Cedar Hill Schoolhouse
Route 144 at Clapper Road
Selkirk, NY 12158
(518) 767-9432

Big Flats Historical Society
(258 Hibbard Road—location)
PO Box 232 (mailing address)
Big Flats, NY 14814-0232
(607) 562-8773 (Curator); (607) 562-7460;
    (607) 562-3152
Glenn Bates, Curator
Tue 9:00–noon, Sun (July–Aug) 2:00–4:00
Pub. *Newsletter*, bimonthly
$10.00 per year membership

Big Springs Historical Society
Main Street
Caledonia, NY 14423
(716) 538-4473

Blenheim Bridge Historical Association
(Eastside Road—location
PO Box 833 (mailing address)
North Blenheim, NY 12131
Josephine Fuller, President and Town
    Historian
$3.00–$5.00 per year membership; research:
    donation

Bohemia Historical Society
(Bartunef House, Smithtown
Avenue/Museum Building, Locust
Avenue—location)
PO Box 67 (mailing address)
Bohemia, NY 11716
(631) 244-2707

Donna Schaefer, President
by appointment only
(publishes *The History of Bohemia*, $10.00)
$10.00 per year membership

**B.R.A.G. (Bolivar, Richburg, Allentown
and Genesee) Historical Society**
c/o Bolivar Free Library
390 Main Street
Bolivar, NY 14715
(716) 928-215; (Library); (716) 928-2659
    (B.R.A.G., Mon noon–9:00 only)
Jean Milliman, President
Library: Mon & Wed–Thur 6:00–9:00, Tue &
    Fri 12:30–4:30, Sat 12:30–3:30; President
    in attendance: Mon noon–9:00
Pub. *BRAG's Blast From the Past*, quarterly
$5.00 per year membership; search: $10.00
    plus cost of copies and postage

**Bowdoin Park Historical and Archeology
Association**
Bowdoin Park
85 Sheafe Road
Wappingers Falls, NY 12590
(845) 297-1224
E. Russell Lang, President
Pub. *BPHAA Newsletter*

Brentwood Historical Society
PO Box 465
Brentwood, NY 11717
(631) 273-2949
Frank J. Cannon, President

**Briarcliff Manor/Scarborough Historical
Society**
PO Box 11
Briarcliff Manor, NY 10510

Bridge Hampton Historical Society, Inc.
(2368 Montauk Highway [Corner of Montauk
and Corwith]—location)
PO Box 977 (mailing address)
Bridgehampton, NY 11932
(631) 537-1088; (631) 537-4225 FAX
bhhs@hamptons.com
http://www.hamptons.com/bhhs
Geoffrey Fleming, Director
1 Mar–30 May & 16 Sept–31 Dec: Mon–Fri
    11:00–4:00; 1 June–15 Sept: Tue–Sat
    11:00–4:00; year-round by appointment
Pub. *The Bridge*, annually
$50.00–$99.00 per year membership

Brighton Historical Society
52 Kimbark Road
Rochester, NY 14610
(716) 381-6202
Roberta Lachiusa, President

Broad Channel Historical Society
Broad Channel Branch Library
17 East 6 Road
Broad Channel, NY 11693
(718) 474-1127
tobytoborg@aol.com
Barbara Toborg
Pub. *Broad Channel Historical Calendar*,
    annually, $5.00

The Bronx County Historical Society
Theodore Kazimiroff Library
3309 Bainbridge Avenue
Bronx, NY 10467
(718) 881-8900; (718) 881-4827 FAX
http://www.bronxhistoricalsociety.org/
    index86.htm
Laura Tosi, Librarian
Mon–Fri 9:30–5:00
Pub. *The Bronx County Historical Society
    Journal*, semiannually; *The Bronx*

Historian Newsletter
$20.00 per year membership; research: minimum of two hours at $25.00 per hour, plus expenses, or five hours for genealogical searches

Official Bronx Historian
3309 Bainbridge Avenue
Bronx, NY 10467
Dr. Lloyd Ultan

Town of Brookfield Historical Society
(Main Street, next to Worden Press—location)
Box 143 (mailing address)
Brookfield, NY 13314
Gwendolyn Witter, President
Wed & Sat (May–Oct) 1:00–3:00, and by appointment
Pub. *Bailey's Corners Gazette*, six times per year
$5.00 per year membership; research: copy costs

Brooklyn Historian
(see Kings County Historian, below)

Brooklyn Historical Society
Genealogy Workshop
128 Pierpont Street, Corner Clinton Street
Brooklyn, NY 11201
(718) 624-0890; (718) 875-3869 FAX
http://www.brooklyn.story.org
Michell Hackwelder, Head Librarian

Broome County Historian
Broome County Public Library
185 Court Street
Binghamton, NY 13901-3503
(607) 778-2076
gsmith@co.broome.ny.us
Gerald R. Smith, Library Assistant and County Historian; Margaret Shiel, Deputy County Historian
Library: Thur 9:00–3:00 & 6:00–9:00
(Broome County, New York, history; Mr. Smith is also historian of the City of Binghamton)
out-of-state requests: $10.00 plus copies at 20¢ each

Municipal Historians

Town of Barker, Broome County, NY
(151 Hyde Street—location)
PO Box 66 (mailing address)
Castle Creek, NY 13744
(607) 648-4445
Tnclk@aol.com
Christine L. Gillett, Historian and Town Clerk
9:00–noon & 1:00–3:30

City of Binghamton
Gerald R. Smith (see Broome County Historian, above)

Town of Binghamton
1412 Hawleyton Road
Binghamton, NY 13903
Anne E. Lindsley

Town of Chenango
Schoolhouse Museum
c/o 1137 Front Street
Binghamton, NY 13905
Ajrfluff@aol.com
Alice Ruby

Town of Colesville
47 Flagg Road
Binghamton, NY 13904

Minerva D. Flagg

Town of Conklin
543 Pierce Creek Road
Binghamton, NY 13903
(607) 723-1737
Robert Barber

Village of Deposit
146 Front Street
Deposit, NY 13754
Mary Cable

Town of Dickinson
861 Chenango Street
Binghamton, NY 13901
Catherine McNally

Village of Endicott
Endicott Village Office
1009 East Main Street
Endicott, NY 13760
(607) 785-9427
TWENDICOTT@aol.com
R. Theodore (Ted) Warner

Village of Johnson City
Your Home Public Library
107 Main Street
Johnson City, NY 13790
Janet A. Ottman

Town of Kirkwood
1105 Old State Road
Binghamton, NY 13904
Robert Cleary

Town of Lisle and Village of Lisle
c/o Lisle Free Library
PO Box 202
Lisle, NY 13797-0202
Eleanor Ticknor

Town of Maine
2130 Bradley Creek Road
Johnson City, NY 13790
(607) 785-6488
annpagelewis@stny.rr.com
http://www.tier.net/mainehistory
Ann P. Lewis
by appointment

Town of Nanticoke
Nanticoke Town Hall
(755 Cherry Valley Hill Road, Maine, NY 13802—location)
PO Box 196 (mailing address)
Glen Aubrey, NY 13777
(607) 692-4041; (607) 692-3552 FAX
clowning88@aol.com
Joanne Costley, Town Clerk/Historian; Leroy Youngs, Co-historian

Village of Port Dickinson
786 Chenango Street
Binghamton, NY 13901
Catherine McNally

Town of Sanford
3 Lippencott
Deposit, NY 13754
Ann Parsons

Town of Triangle
3276 Route 206 NY
Whitney Point, NY 13862
Aleksandre Mesceda

Town of Union
3716 Maplehurst Drive
Endwell, NY 13760
Suzanne Meredith

Town of Vestal
Vestal Public Library
320 Vestal Parkway East
Vestal, NY 13850
Elizabeth Mae Bartlow

Village of Whitney Point
3124 Route 206 NY
Whitney Point, NY 13862
Juanita Aleba

Town of Windsor
140 Main Street
Windsor, NY 13865
(607) 655-2601
Helen B. Osborne

Village of Windsor
22 Chestnut Street
Windsor, NY 13865
Charles English

Broome County Historical Society
185 Court Street
Binghamton, NY 13901
(607) 785-3572
Charles J. Browne, Historian
Tue–Thur 10:00–8:00, Fri–Sat 10:00–4:00
Pub. *Broome County Historical Society Bulletin*, two times per year
(large manuscript and photograph collection, genealogy files, etc.)
$20.00 per year membership; $45.00 per year membership in both Roberson Center and the Historical Society; research: $10.00 prepaid for the first hour, $5.00 for each additional hour, plus copies at 25¢ per page

General Jacob Brown Historical Society
Bronn Mansion
216 Brown Boulevard
Brownsville, NY 13615
http://www.museumsusa.org/data/museums/NY/22965.htm

Brunswick Historical Society
(605 Brunswick Road, Eagle Mills, NY—location)
PO Box 1776 (mailing address)
Cropseyville, NY 12052
(518) 279-4024
Genealogy Chair
Wed noon–2:00, Sat 10:00–3:00
("Headquartered in an 1881 schoolhouse and is located 3 miles east of Troy. Published family genealogies, federal and state microfilmed census records.")
admission: free; copies: 25¢ per page; research: fee for mailed or emailed inquiries

Buffalo and Erie County Historical Society
Research Library
25 Nottingham Court
Buffalo, NY 14216
(716) 873-9644, ext. 306 (Reference Librarian); (716) 873-9612; (716) 873-8754 FAX
http://www.bechs.org/library/library-frm.html
Wed–Sat 1:00–5:00
(local history, i.e. Buffalo and Erie County; "We do not do research that consists of more than fifteen minutes of time to look in published directories or indexes.")
$30.00 per year membership; admission: $4.00 for nonmembers

Historical Association of the Town of Butternuts
Commercial Street and Marion Avenue

Gilbertsville, NY 13776
Winona Ferrara, Chair, Board of Trustees

Byron Historical Society
(Route 262—location)
PO Box 201 (mailing address)
Byron, NY 14422
Dora M. Jones, Town Historian
June–Aug: Sun 2:00–4:00
free admission

Cambria Historical Society
4159 Lower Mountain Road
Lockport, NY 14094
(716) 434-8937

Cambridge Historical Society
21 Broad Street
Cambridge, NY 12816
Audry Wallace, President
Museum: Sat 2:00–4:00 (July–Aug)

Town of Camillus Historical Society
(Sim's Store Museum, DeVoe Road,
Camillus, NY 13031—museum location)
4600 West Genesee Street (mailing address)
Syracuse, NY 13019
(315) 487-2326 (President); (315) 487-7386
(Society Historian); (315) 488-1234
(Town Clerk's Office, leave a message)
Judithann_705@Yahoo.com
Judy Fittipaldi, President; Ralph Sims,
Society Historian
Pub. *Camillus Chronicle*, monthly
(The society "is the historian for the entire
town.")
$5.00 per year membership

Cape Vincent Community Library
157 North Real
Cape Vincent, NY 13618
(315) 654-2132
Linda Voorhees

Town of Carmel Historical Society
(40 McAlpin Avenue—location)
PO Box 456 (mailing address)
Mahopac, NY 10541
(845) 628-0500 (recording, Dec–Apr)
LimaEb@aol.com; Carmelink@aol.com
http://www.putnamcountyny.com/
historian/carmel.htm
Lillian Eberhardt, President/Preservationist
Sun (Apr–Nov) 2:00–4:00, and by
appointment
("The society is a small [100 members]
volunteer manned organization. It
represents the Town of Carmel, covering
the hamlets of Carmel, Mahopac, and
Mahopac Falls.")
$5.00 per year membership

Castile Historical Society
17 Park Road
Castile, NY 14427
(716) 493-5370

Cattaraugus Area Historical Society
23 Main Street
Cattaraugus, NY 14719
(716) 257-9012

Cattaraugus County Historian
Historical Museum
303 Court Street
Little Valley, NY 14755
(716) 938-9111, ext. 440
http://www.rootsweb.com/~nycattar/
society.htm
Kenneth Kysor
Tue & Wed 9:00–4:30, and by appointment

Municipal Historians

Town of Allegany and Village of Allegany
2986 North Nine Mile Rd
Allegany, NY 14706
(716) 373-2072
Nancy Phearsdorf

Town of Ashford
9854 Route 240
West Valley, NY 14171
(716) 942-6669
B. Lynn Williams

Town of Carrollton
post vacant

Town of Coldspring
10292 Blood Road
Randolph, NY 14772
(716) 354-6505
Doris Van Sickle

Town of Conewango
Route 1, Cowen Road
Conewango Valley, NY 14726
Anna May Rhoades

Town of Dayton
(9561 Route 62—location)
PO Box 15 (mailing address)
Dayton, NY 14041
(716) 532-3758
Bennru00@yahoo.com
Ruth Bennett

Village of Delevan
PO Box 595
Delevan, NY 14042
nbbaker@aol.com
Naomi B. Baker
by appointment
(also historian of the town of Yorkshire)

Town of East Otto
(Main Street—location)
PO Box 152 (mailing address)
East Otto, NY 14729
(716) 257-3529
Jean Fleckenstein
by appointment only

Village of East Randolph
195 Main Street, ER
Randolph, NY 14772
(716) 358-6273
Dorothy Carnahan
(also historian of the town and village of
Randolph)

Town of Ellicottville
Box 617
Ellicottville, NY 14731
(716) 699-2162 (Home)
Mary Elizabeth Dunbar

Village of Ellicottville
Registrar of Vital Statistics
PO Box 475
Ellicottville, NY 14731
Paula Ayrhart

Town of Farmersville
1855 Rogers Road
Franklinville, NY 14737
(716) 676-9963
Alice Wright

**Town of Franklinville and Village of
Franklinville**
(2439 Lyndon—location)
PO Box 291 (mailing address)

Franklinville, NY 14737
(716) 676-5520
Joan C. Wilson

Town of Freedom
1931 Cheeseman Hill Road
Delevan, NY 14042
(716) 353-4604
Lorna Spencer

Village of Gowanda
Route 2, Box 66
Gowanda, NY 14070
Jean C. Hillis

Town of Great Valley
Back Kill Buck Road
Kill Buck, NY 14748
(716) 945-2281
Roberta Stone

Town of Hinsdale
McKinstry Road
Hinsdale, NY 14743
(716) 557-2437
Helen DeGolia

Town of Humphrey
3654 Bozard Hill Road
Great Valley, NY 14741
(716) 945-1319
Rosemary Hathaway

Town of Ischua
Main Street
Hinsdale, NY 14743
(716) 557-8809
Joyce Edwards

Town of Leon
Route 1, West Road
Conewango Valley, NY 14726
(716) 296-5217
Bertha Millspaw

Town of Little Valley
201 Third Street
Little Valley, NY 14755
Patrician Isaman
8:30–4:30
Pub. *Town Clerk*

Village of Little Valley
415 Court Street
Little Valley, NY 14755
(716) 938-6537
Shirley Stull
by appointment
("I index old records for county clerk under
Green Thumb, now Experiment Works.")

Town of Lyndon
6558 Snyder Road
Cuba, NY 14727
(716) 968-2057
sidk8zes@localnet.com
Sidney L. Emmons
by appointment
("51,000-person [and growing] gedcom on
local settlers, etc.")
free data exchange

Town of Machias
11114 Route 39
Machias, NY 14101
(716) 353-8846
Gail Watkins

Town of Mansfield
7619 Borroughs Road
Little Valley, NY 14755
(716) 257-3026

Gail M. Burroughs

Town of Napoli
131 Elm Creek Road
Randolph, NY 14772
(716) 358-3926
Annette Waite

City of Olean
302 Laurens Street
Olean, NY 14760
(716) 375-5642 (Office); (716) 373-1426
   (Home)
Anne Walsh
Tue & Fri 1:00–3:00

Town of Olean
1721 Goodrich Avenue
Olean, NY 14760
(716) 372-8450
Ruth Lowe

Town of Otto
9270 Ball Road
Cattaraugus, NY 14719
(716) 257-3030
Medora Ball

Town of Perrysburg
Route 2, Box 21
Gowanda, NY 14070
Lorraine Marvin

Village of Perrysburg
post vacant

Town of Persia
Route 2, Maltbie Road
Gowanda, NY 14070
(716) 532-2001
Jean C. Hillis

Town of Portville and Village of Portville
PO Box 253
Portville, NY 14770
(716) 933-8757
Jane G. Miller

Town of Randolph and Village of Randolph
Dorothy Carnahan (see Village of East
   Randolph Historian, above)

Town of Red House
2103 Baystate Road
Salamanca, NY 14779
(716) 945-5835
Jane S. France

City of Salamanca
81 Clinton Street
Salamanca, NY 14779
(716) 945-2312
Joan M. Formica

Town of Salamanca
8558 West Bucktooth Run
Little Valley, NY 14755
(716) 945-5074
William Goodman

Village of South Dayton
RVS
PO Box 9
South Dayton, NY 14138
Barbara Butcher

Town of South Valley
post vacant

Town of Yorkshire
Naomi B. Baker (see Village of Delevan,

above)

Cayuga County Historian
Historic Old Post Office Building
157 Genesee Street
Auburn, NY 13021-3490
(315) 253-1300
http://www.rootsweb.com/~nycayuga/
   cayhsltr.htm
Thomas G. Eldred
Mon–Fri 9:00–5:00
Pub. *Cayuga Gazette*, infrequently
$25.00 for all research

Municipal Historians

City of Auburn
post vacant

Town of Aurelius
6000 Route 90
Cayuga, NY 13034
M. Ruth Probst
(also historian of the village of Cayuga)

Village of Aurora
Sherwood Road
Aurora, NY 13026
Edward Kabelac

Town of Brutus
Old Brutus Historical Society, Inc.
(8943 North Seneca Street—location)
PO Box 516 (mailing address)
Weedsport, NY 13166
(315) 834-9342 (Historical Society)
mriley@thumpernet.com (Historical Society)
http://rootsweb.com/~nycayuga/obhs/
   index.html (Historical Society)
Jeanne Baker

Town of Cato
Cato Town Offices
11320 Short Cut Road
Cato, NY 13033
David Dudley

Village of Cato
Mechanic Street
Cato, NY 13033
Letha Kelly

Village of Cayuga
M. Ruth Probst (see Town of Aurelius,
   above)

Town of Conquest
10376 State Route 38
Port Byron, NY 13140
M. Joani Lincoln

Village of Fair Haven
Victory Street
Fair Haven, NY 13064
Erwin Fineout

Town of Fleming
5676 Silver Street Road
Auburn, NY 13021
Sheila S. Tucker

Town of Genoa
120 Fire Lane #1
King Ferry, NY 13081
Grayson Mitchell

Town of Ira
PO Box 239
Cato, NY 13033
Dorothy Southard
("I do NOT do genealogy work per se, but
   furnish information about families with

names folks are researching. They have to
sort out.")

Town of Ledyard
1099 Poplar Ridge Road
Aurora, NY 13026
Judy Furness

Town of Locke
Harris Hill Road
Locke, NY 13092
Esther Thornton

Town of Mentz
PO Box 302
Port Byron, NY 13140
mriley@thumpernet.com
Michael Riley

Village of Meridian
11194 Bonta Bridge Road
Cato, NY 13033-3330
Mrs. Marion Dudley

Town of Montezuma
Denman Road
Port Byron, NY 13140
Cheryl Longyear

Town of Moravia
18 Aurora Street
Moravia, NY 13118
Robert J. Scarry

Village of Moravia
PO Box 711
Moravia, NY 13118
Elsie Van Liew

Town of Niles
5870 New Hope Road
Moravia, NY 13118
Sue Stoyell

Town of Owasco
4912 Martin Road
Auburn, NY 13021
Laurel Auchampaugh

Village of Port Byron
Port Byron, NY 13140
Bruce Carter

Town of Scipio
2362 Koon Road
Auburn, NY 13021
Virginia Koon

Town of Sempronius
(address withheld upon request)

Town of Sennett
Sennett Town Office
6931 Cherry Street Road
Auburn, NY 13021
Angela Martino Gregory

Town of Springport
(address withheld upon request)
Jane Berry, Historian
("Our resources are small.")

Town of Sterling
832 State Route 104A
Sterling, NY 13156
Hallie A. Sweeting

Town of Summerhill
Route 4, Cutler School Road
Cortland, NY 13045
Gregory Reed

Town of Throop
7118 Negent Road
Auburn, NY 13021
Lauretta Graf

Village of Union Springs
post vacant

Town of Venice
2671 State Route 34
Aurora, NY 13026
Dorothy Wiggans

Town of Victory
12399 Upton Road
Red Creek, NY 13143
Katherine Bailey

Village of Weedsport
22 Bell Street
Weedsport, NY 13166
Howard Finley

Cayuga County Historical Society
Cayuga Museum of History and Art
203 Genesee Street
Auburn, NY 13021
(315) 253-8051; (315) 253-9829 FAX
cayugamuseum@adelphia.net
http://www.cayuganet.org/cayugamuseum
Eileen McHugh, Director
Museum: Tue–Fri 10:00–5:00, Sat–Sun
    noon–5:00; Office: Mon–Fri 9:00–5:00;
    Archives: by appointment

Cayuga-Owasco Lakes Historical Society
Luther Research Center and Archives
(14 West Cayuga Street—location)
PO Box 247 (mailing address)
Moravia, NY 13118
(315) 497-3206; (315) 497-3035 (evenings
    after 6:00)
sasto@localnet.com
http://www.rootsweb.com/~nycayuga/
    colhs:htm#LUTHER
Sue Stoyell, Vice President
by appointment
Pub. *Newsletter*, quarterly
(875 family files; preserving the history of
    the twelve towns south of Auburn:
    Fleming, Genoa, Ledyard, Locke,
    Moravia, Niles, Owasco, Scipio,
    Sempronious, Springport, Summerhill and
    Venice)
$6.00 per year membership; research: $10.00
    (local), $20.00 (extended)

Cedar Swamp Historical Society
(East of Hempstead Harbor, Long
Island—location)
Cedar Swamp Road (mailing address)
Glen Head, NY 11545
(516) 671-6156
John G. Peterkin, Founder
Mon–Fri 10:00–4:00; annual Revolutionary
    War Ceremony at East Hillside Cemetery:
    second Sun of Sept 1:45
Pub. *Cedar Swamp Historical Society
    Newsletter*, irregularly, before events
(Cedar Swamp region of North Shore of
    "Long Iland," east of Hempstead Harbor,
    primarily 1592–1815; collection of over
    1,100 books)
$15.00 per year membership

Central Park Historical Society
PO Box 178
Bethpage, NY 11714
(516) 933-1795
Ann Albertson, Vice President

Century House Historical Society

Route 213
Rosendale, NY 12472
rosendalebuff@aol.com
Dietrick Werner

Charleston Historical Society
741 Corbin Hill Road
Esperance, NY 12066
(518) 922-5867
Lorraine R. Whiting, Trustee, and Town
    Historian
May–Dec: weekends
Pub. *Charleston Historical Society
    Newsletter*, bimonthly
("The Society headquarters is the former
    First Baptist Church of Charleston. The
    present building dates from 1834 and is
    listed on the NYS Register of Historic
    Places.")
$5.00 per year membership (includes two
    free searches of the society's genealogical
    holdings)

Chautauqua County Historian
Chautauqua County Archives
(County Court House—location)
PO Box 170 (mailing address)
Mayville, NY 14757
(716) 753-4857
henrym@co.chautauqua.ny.us
Michelle Henry
June–Aug: Mon–Fri 8:30–4:30; Sept–May:
    Mon–Fri 9:00–5:00

Municipal Historians

Town of Arkwright
9030 Center Road
Fredonia, NY 14063-9766
(716) 673-1516 (Home)
Frances Cardot

Village of Bemus Point
80 Lakeside Drive
Bemus Point, NY 14712
Mary Jane Stahley

Village of Brocton
7970 Thayer Road
Portland, NY 14769
(716) 792-4368 (Home)
Edward T. Kurtz, Sr.

Town of Busti
post vacant
Town Hall
121 Chautauqua Avenue
Lakewood, NY 14750
(716) 763-8561; (716) 763-2953 FAX

Village of Cassadaga
239 Maple Avenue
Cassadaga, NY 14718-9725
(716) 595-3220
eKroon@netsync.net
Sheila B. Kroon

Village of Celoron
Celoron, NY 14720
Evelyn Adams

Town of Charlotte
(8 Parkway Drive—location)
PO Box 569 (mailing address)
Sinclairville, NY 14782
Donald L. Jordan
(also historian of the village of Sinclairville)

Chautauqua Institution
(see above)

Town of Chautauqua

5416 Meadows Road
Dewittville, NY 14728-9773
Gilbert T. Hayward

**Town of Cherry Creek and Village of
Cherry Creek**
(6409 South Route 83—location)
PO Box 78 (mailing address)
Cherry Creek, NY 14723
Joyce Chase

Town of Clymer
(356 Mohawk Street—location)
PO Box 114 (mailing address)
Clymer, NY 14724
(716) 355-9950
Suzanna Rhebergen

City of Dunkirk
720 Washington Avenue
Dunkirk, NY 14048
(716) 366-3797
Mrs. Robert Dew

Town of Dunkirk
post vacant
c/o Town Hall
(3737 Willow Road—location)
PO Box 850 (mailing address)
Dunkirk, NY 14048
(716) 366-3967

Town of Ellery
4826 Ellery-Centralia Road
Bemus Point, NY 14712
(716) 386-6321
Lorraine C. Smith

Town of Ellicott
(707 East Main Street—location)
PO Box 356 (mailing address)
Ellington, NY 14732
(716) 484-9202 (Home)
Candace Nickerson

Town of Ellington
914 West Main Street
Kennedy, NY 14747
(716) 287-3108
Laurene Rice

Village of Falconer
c/o Community Building
101 West Main Street
Falconer, NY 14733
Mrs. Jerry Lyon

Village of Forestville
10960 Denison Road
Forestville, NY 14062
Mildred Becker

Town of French Creek
c/o Arlene R. Bemis, Town Clerk
169 Route 426
Clymer, NY 14724
(716) 355-6374 (Home)

Town of Gerry
PO Box 111
Gerry, NY 14740
(716) 985-4492
Jean Bedient

Town of Hanover
Hanover Historical Center
68 Hanover Street
Silver Creek, NY 14136
(716) 934-0869
Vincent Martonis

Town of Harmony

3325 Carpenter Pringle Road
Ashville, NY 14710
(716) 789-5284 (Home)
Donna J. Johnson
(also historian of the village of Panama)

City of Jamestown
13 Lamont Street
Jamestown, NY 14701-2021
(716) 484-8289
B. Dolores Thompson
as needed

Town of Kiantone
531 Kiantone Road
Jamestown, NY 14701
(716) 569-5906
Jean Brustrom

Village of Lakewood
120 Chautauqua Avenue
Lakewood, NY 14750
Marie B. Burk

Institutions Lily Dale
11 Buffalo Street
Lily Dale, NY 14718
Ms. Paul Vogt

Village of Mayville
3343 Fluvanna Townline Road
Jamestown, NY 14701-9011
Dorothea Bertram

Town of Mina
PO Box 126
Findley Lake, NY 14736
(716) 769-7324 voice & FAX
sscarem@hotmail.com
Sharon Scarem

Town of North Harmony
PO Box 155
Stow, NY 14785
Robert Willsie

Village of Panama
PO Box 32
Panama, NY 14767
Irene Nagel

Town of Poland
3453 Route 62
Kennedy, NY 14747
(716) 267-3840
Roger Bish

Town of Pomfret
c/o Town Hall
9 Day Street
Fredonia, NY 14063
(716) 672-6888; (716) 672-7496

Town of Portland
PO Box 458
Brocton, NY 14716
(716) 792-4519
Jane Sinare

Town of Ripley
123 West Main Street
Ripley, NY 14775
Marie McCutcheon

Town of Sheridan
3578 East Main Road
Fredonia, NY 14063
(716) 672-4911
Frank Dorsett

Town of Sherman and Village of Sherman
(3091 Route 76—location)

PO Box 573 (mailing address)
Sherman, NY 14781
(716) 761-6049
Jean K. Hanson

Village of Silver Creek
Silver Creek Historical Society
172 Central Avenue
Silver Creek, NY 14136
(716) 934-3240 (Village Clerk)
Louis F. Pelletter

Village of Sinclairville
Donald Jordan (see Town of Charlotte,
above)

Town of Stockton
4513 East Railroad Avenue
Stockton, NY 14784
Helen Piersons

Town of Villenove
1129 Route 83
South Dayton, NY 14138
(716) 988-3616
Barbara J. Wise

Town of Westfield and Village of Westfield
42 Backman Avenue
Westfield, NY 14787
(716) 326-2154
Mary S. Dibble

Chautauqua County Historical Society
PO Box 7, Village Park
Westfield, NY 14787
(716) 326-2977
Nancy Brown, Director
Tue–Sat 10:00–5:00
Pub. *County History*, quarterly
$10.00 per year membership; research:
$10.00

Chautauqua Township Historical Society
Depot Museum on Route 394
Mayville, NY 14757
(716) 753-7535
Memorial Day–Labor Day: Fri–Sun
1:00–5:00

Cheektowaga Historical Association
Cheektowaga Historical Museum
(3329 Broadway—museum location)
Alexander Community Center (mailing
address)
Cheektowaga, NY 14227
(716) 684-6544 (Museum)
http://nyslgti.gen.ny.us/Cheektowaga/org.
htm#C10
Myra Gitter, Curator
Museum: first Sun 2:00–4:00; meetings at
275 Alexander Avenue, third Thur 7:00
Pub. *Cheektowaga Archival News*
(no records at museum location; local history
from 1850s)

Chemung County Historian
1011 Lincoln Street
Elmira, NY 14901
J. Arthur Kieffer

Municipal Historians

Town of Ashland
272 Main Street
Wellsburg, NY 14894
Miss Carol Doland
(also historian of the village of Wellsburg)

Town of Baldwin
2292 Wyncoop Creek Road
Lockwood, NY 14859

(607) 598-2698
Wendy Wolcott
9:00–5:00

Town of Big Flats
(12 Suburban Drive—location)
PO Box 95 (mailing address)
Big Flats, NY 14814
E. R. Van Etten

Town of Catlin
46 Smith Road
Beaver Dams, NY 14812
Eunice Smith

Town of Chemung
PO Box 113
Chemung, NY 14825
Joan B. Schafer

City of Elmira
1164 Hoffman Street
Elmira, NY 14905
Carl A. Morrell

Town of Elmira
415 East Water Street
Elmira, NY 14901
Thomas E. Byrne

Village of Elmira Heights
256 West 19th Street
Elmira Heights, NY 14903
Kenneth J. Erickson

Town of Erin
760 Marsh Road
Erin, NY 14838
Kathleen Schanbacher

Town of Horseheads
2227 Grand Central Avenue
Horseheads, NY 14845
Nadine Ferraioli

Village of Horseheads
post vacant

Village of Millport
post vacant

Village of Pine Valley
post vacant

Town of Southport
985 Sebring Avenue
Pine City, NY 14871
Nelda Holton

Town of Van Etten
151 Shoemaker Road
Van Etten, NY 14889
Sandy Gray

Village of Van Etten
(14 Hickory Grove Road—location)
PO Box 9 (mailing address)
Van Etten, NY 14889
(607) 589-4454; (607) 589-4925 FAX
William M. Gallow, Jr.
by appointment

Town of Veteran
104 Roemmelt Road
Horseheads, NY 14845
Robert Roemmelt

Village of Wellsburg
Miss Carol Dolan (see Town of Ashland,
above)

Chemung County Historical Society, Inc.

Mrs. Arthur W. Booth Memorial Library
415 East Water Street
Elmira, NY 14901
(607) 734-4167; (607) 734-4168; (607) 734-1565
http://www.rootsweb.com/~nychemun/cchsres.htm
Melissa Hollister, Registrar; Diane Janowski, Editor
Mon–Fri 9:00–5:00
Pub. *Chemung County Historical Society Newsletter*, bimonthly; *Chemung Historical Journal*, quarterly, $8.00 per year subscription
$15.00 per year membership; search $5.00 and $10.00

Chemung Valley Old Timers Association
(624 West Broad Street—location)
220 Sunnyfield Drive (mailing address)
Horseheads, NY 14845
(607) 739-1526

Chenango County Historian
Chenango County Historical Society Museum
Research Facility
45 Rexford Street
Norwich, NY 13815
(607) 337-1845
Dale C. Storms
Office: Mon–Fri 9:00–noon & 1:00–5:00
Pub. *Chenango County Historian's Newsletter*, two times per year (Apr, Oct)
search: $5.00 per name or $2.00 per last name per 50 pages for printout

Municipal Historians

Town of Afton and Village of Afton
335 State Highway 41
Afton, NY 13730
(607) 639-2720
Charles J. Decker
by appointment

Town of Bainbridge
99 North Main Street
Bainbridge, NY 13733
(607) 967-4833
Charles D. Lord

Village of Bainbridge
20 Bixby Street
Bainbridge, NY 13733
(607) 967-7435
Floyd L. Prouty

Town of Columbus
(40 Cushman Street—location)
PO Box 191 (mailing address)
New Berlin, NY 13411
(607) 847-6498
Barbara B. Avery
(also historian of the town of New Berlin)

Town of Coventry
820 Wylie-Horton Road
Harpursville, NY 13787
(607) 656-9517
Phyllis Lerwick

Town of Earlville
post vacant

Town of German
257 Maroney Road
McDonough, NY 13801
(607) 656-7580
Claudia C. White

Town of Greene and Village of Greene

(51 Genesee Street—location)
PO Box 129 (mailing address)
Greene, NY 13778
(607) 656-4191
Mildred Pixley

Town of Guilford
101 Furnace Hill Road
Guilford, NY 13780
(607) 895-6532
tgray@mkl.com
Tom Gray

Town of Lincklaen
(9774 Lincklaen Road—location)
PO Box 298 (mailing address)
DeRuyter, NY 13052
(315) 852-6081
Joy Lidell Barber

Town of McDonough
1144 County Road 5
McDonough, NY 13801
(607) 647-5607
Ruth Rounds

Town of New Berlin
Barbara B. Avery (see Town of Columbus, above)

Village of New Berlin
post vacant

Town of North Norwich
(183 Brookins Road—location)
PO Box 280 (mailing address)
North Norwich, NY 13814
(607) 336-7013
Janet Decker

City of Norwich
12 York Street, #2
Norwich, NY 13815
(607) 336-5867
Shirley Beckwith

Town of Otselic
(1518 County Road 16—location)
PO Box 141 (mailing address)
Plymouth, NY 13832
(607) 837-4631
Eloise Shuman
by appointment
copies: 10¢ each

Town of Oxford and Village of Oxford
(30 West State Street—location)
PO Box 663 (mailing address)
Oxford, NY 13830
(607) 843-9531
Charlotte Stafford

Town of Pharsalia
Rural Delivery 1
McDonough, NY 13801
(607) 863-3877
Joan Ortiz

Town of Pitcher
Springs Road
Pitcher, NY 13136
(607) 863-3511
Rita Stith

Town of Plymouth
Bates Road
HC 67, Box 188
South Plymouth, NY 13844
(607) 334-2083
Michael Meyers

Town of Preston

1310 County Road 4
Oxford, NY 13830
(607) 334-4848
V. Peter Mason

Town of Sherburne
3415 State Highway 80
Sherburne, NY 13460
(607) 674-4027
Rose Wellman

Village of Sherburne
c/o Kathleen M. Ellis, Village Clerk Treasurer
Municipal Building
15 West State Street
Sherburne, NY 13460
(607) 674-2300; (607) 674-4149 FAX

Town of Smithville
PO Box 217
Smithville Flats, NY 13841-0217
(607) 656-7969; (607) 656-8667
smithville@citlink.net
Alison Owens
Sept–June: Mon noon–6:00, Tue–Thur 9:00–1:00; July–Aug: Mon–Thur 8:00–noon
("Our collection includes the Town of Smithville cemeteries on searchable database; vital records on searchable database; other vital records and genealogical information on searchable database; donated family genealogies and family surname folders.")

Town of Smyrna and Village of Smyrna
(School Street—location)
PO Box 14 (mailing address)
Smyrna, NY 13464
(607) 627-6648
Cynthia Kumatz

Chenango County Historical Society Museum
Research Facility
45 Rexford Street
Norwich, NY 13815
(607) 337-1845; (607) 334-9227
http://www.chenangocounty.org/chencohistso
Mrs. Dale Green, Recording Secretary
Library: by appointment; Museum: winter: Wed 1:00–4:00, summer: Wed & Sat–Sun 1:00–4:00
Pub. *Newsletter*, semiannually (Apr, Oct) (local history information)
$15.00 per year membership

Cherry Valley Historical Association
(49 Main Street—location)
PO Box 115 (mailing address)
Cherry Valley, NY 13320
(607) 264-3098
Barbara Bell, Director
Mon–Sun (Memorial Day–15 Oct) 10:00–5:00, and by appointment
admission: $3.00 (ages 12-60), $2.50 (over 60), $1.00 each for groups of ten or more, under 11 free

Chili Historical Society
1365 Paul Road
Churchville, NY 14428
(716) 889-2823

Cincinnatus Area Heritage Society
PO Box 264
Cincinnatus, NY 13040
(607) 863-4251; (607) 863-4409

City Island Historical Society and Nautical

Museum
(190 Fordham Street—location)
PO Box 82 (mailing address)
Bronx, NY 10464
(718) 885-0008
http://www.cityislandmuseum.org
Thomas Nye, President; Edward Sadler, Vice
    President; Barbara Dolensek, Secretary;
    Carol Stewart, Treasurer
Sun 1:00–5:00
(nautical, marine, sailing, boatbuilding
    history and City Island families)
$20.00 per year membership

Clarence Historical Society
Clarence Historical Museum
(10465 Main Street—location)
PO Box 86 (mailing address)
Clarence, NY 14031
(716) 741-2281 (Society); (716) 759-8575
    (Museum); (716) 759-0997 (Genealogy
    Library)
Library: Wed 10:00–2:00

Clarkson University Archives
Educational Resources Center
Library-Archives
PO Box 5590
Potsdam, NY 13699-5590
(315) 268-2297
Iva Ramsdel, University Archivist
Mon–Fri 9:00–5:00 by appointment

Clay Historical Association
4591 Ver Plank Road
Clay, NY 13041
(315) 652-3288

**Clayton Thousand Islands Area Historical
Society**
(Thousand Islands Museum, 405 Riverside
Drive—location)
PO Box 28 (mailing address)
Clayton, NY 13624
(315) 686-5794; (315) 686-5323
Eva Rexford

Clinton County Historian
Clinton County Government Center, First
Floor
137 Margaret Street
Plattsburgh, NY 12901-2975
(518) 565-4749; (518) 565-1616 FAX
http://www.rootsweb.com/~nyclinto/
    historian.html
Addie L. Shields
9:00–4:00 by appointment
(also historian of the town of Beekmantown.
    "Local history as it fits into the greater
    scheme of settlement.")
small fee for photocopies

Municipal Historians

Town of Altona
(77 Station Street—location)
PO Box 197 (mailing address)
Altona, NY 12910
(518) 236-7420
Mrs. Walter Coolidge
by appointment

Town of Au Sable
71 Liberty Street
Keeseville, NY 12944
(518) 834-4614
Helen Eagle

Town of Beekmantown
Addie L. Shields (see ClintonCounty
    Historian, above)

Town of Black Brook
18 North Main Street
Au Sable Forks, NY 12912
(518) 647-5509
Doris Akey
by appointment

Town of Champlain
PO Box 3144
Champlain, NY 12919
(518) 298-8160
Rose Favreau
8:30–4:00 by appointment

Village of Champlain
35 Oak Street
Champlain, NY 12919
(518) 298-8169
Marie Bechard
8:30–5:00 by appointment

Town of Chazy
(456 Route 191 East—location)
PO Box 177 (mailing address)
Chazy, NY 12921
(518) 846-8395 (Office)
Marie Gennett
Mon–Fri 9:00–noon and by appointment

Town of Clintonville
1302 Route 9N
Clintonville, NY 12924
(518) 834-5267
Levi White

Village of Dannemora
PO Box 411
Dannemora, NY 12929
(518) 492-7000 (home)
Jarvis

Town of Ellenburg
Bohon Road
Churubusco, NY 12923
(518) 497-6055
Donna Bohon
Mon–Fri 9:00–4:00

Village of Keeseville
49 Liberty Street
Keeseville, NY 12944
(518) 834-7220
Jim Blaise

Town of Mooers and Village of Mooers
Mooers Town Office Complex
PO Box 242
Mooers, NY 12958
(518) 236-7927, ext. 105
Mrs. Carol Nedeau
Sept–June: 3:30–5:00, July–Aug: 9:00–noon,
    and by appointment

Town of Peru
Peru Town Hall
PO Box 596
Peru, NY 12972
(518) 643-9513 (Town Office)
John Roach

City of Plattsburgh
(Plattsburgh Public Library, Local History
Room—location)
62 Prospect Avenue (mailing address)
Plattsburgh, NY 12901
(518) 563-7178
baileyj@westelcom.com
James Bailey
Mon, Wed & Fri 4:00–5:30

Town of Plattsburgh
152 Banker Road

Plattsburgh, NY 12901
(518) 561-8101
Arnold Jubert
Tue & Thur 9:00–3:00

Village of Rouses Point
28 Pratt Street
Rouses Point, NY 12979
(518) 297-5502
Dawn O'Boyle
by appointment

Town of Saranac
83 Ganong Drive
Saranac, NY 12981
(518) 293-8251
Mrs. Jan Couture

Town of Schuyler Falls
135 Rabideau Street
Cadyville, NY 12918
(518) 293-8512
Michael Burgess

Clinton County Historical Association
48 Court Street
Plattsburgh, NY 12901
(518) 561-0340
John Tomkins, Director
Office: Mon–Fri 9:00–4:00 by appointment
    only; Museum: Tue–Fri noon–4:00, Sat
    1:00–4:00
Pub. *North Country Notes*, quarterly; *The
    Antiquarian*, annually (Oct or Nov;
    sponsors writing contest: McMasters
    Prize)
$15.00 per year membership; research:
    requests forwarded to county historian

Clinton Historical Society
(1 Fountain Street—location)
PO Box 42 (mailing address)
Clinton, NY 13323
(315) 859-1392
clintonhistoricalsociety@yahoo.com
http://clintonhistory.org
Richard Williams, President
Pub. *Newsletter*, ten to twelve times per year
    ("Society has Town of Kirkland and Village
    of Clinton families in the genealogy files;
    more are being solicited. The society has
    recently renovated the former Clinton
    Baptist Church [built 1832] for its
    quarters; the library is now being
    organized and is open for genealogists.")
$12.00 per year membership

Clovercroft Historical Society
Rural Delivery 2
Cobleskill, NY 12043
(518) 234-7134

Clymer Area Historical Society
(Clymer-Corry Road—location)
PO Box 114 (mailing address)
Clymer, NY 14724
(716) 355-9950
Suzanna Rhebergen, Town Historian
by appointment
$5.00 per year membership

Town of Cobleskill Historical Society
Cobleskill Public Library
Cobleskill, NY 12043

Cohocton Historical Society
(14 Maple Avenue—location)
PO Box 177 (mailing address)
Cohocton, NY 14826
(585) 534-5468 (President)
http://www.cohocton.bizland.com
Helen Francis, President

first Sat (May–Oct), and by appointment
Pub. *The Cohocton Journal*, bimonthly
(even-numbered months), $10.00 per year
subscription
("Cohocton history and current birth, death
and marriage, Cohocton newspapers
1894–1963.")

**Historical Society of the Town of Colonie,
Inc.**
Memorial Town Hall
207 Old Niskayuna Road, Box 212
Newtonville, NY 12128
(518) 783-2713

Colton Historical Society
(Main Street—location)
PO Box 223 (mailing address)
Colton, NY 13625
(315) 262-2524
Dennis E. Eickhoff, Director
June–Sept: 1:00–3:00, and by appointment
Pub. *CHS Newsletter*, four times per year,
$4.00 per year subscription
(history of Colton, New York)

Columbia County Historian
490 County Route 10
Germantown, NY 12526
(518) 828-3442; (518) 828-2969 FAX
Mary Howell
(history only, no genealogical research; also
historian of the town of Livingston)

Municipal Historians

Town of Ancram
PO Box 13
Ancram, NY 12502
(518) 329-0632
Clara Van Tassel

Town of Austerlitz
(11622 S.R. 22—location)
PO Box 17 (mailing address)
Austerlitz, NY 12017
(518) 392-4270; (518) 392-6028
slighthh@capital.net
Sarah B. (Sally) Light
("Historical and genealogical research and
writing, particularly houses. Have written
many articles for various publications.
The most recent is for *Early American
Life*. Primarily edit archeological reports.
Also edit for Hartgen Archeological
Associates, Inc., one of the largest
archeological firms in the northeast. Book
titles: *House Histories: A Guide to
Tracing the Genealogy of Your Home,
Canals and Crossroads, A
Sesquicentennial History of the Albany
Diocese*.")
research: $25.00 per hour plus 25¢ per mile,
copies, film processing, telephone calls,
etc.

Town of Canaan
(12913 Route 22—location)
PO Box 169 (mailing address)
Canaan, NY 12029
(518) 781-4801
Anna Mary Dunton

Town of Chatham
706 Route 13
Old Chatham, NY 12136-9705
(518) 794-7512
Kathryn Burgess
weekdays
("I have been historian 35 years. I do not do
extensive personal research. Just info from
my files. Those inquiring should ask for

limited information not lists.")

Village of Chatham
168 Hudson Avenue
Chatham, NY 12037
(518) 392-5377
Linda Conway

Town of Claverack
PO Box 320
Claverack, NY 12513
(518) 851-6834
Theodore Filli, Jr.

Town of Clermont
1 Buckwheat Road
Germantown, NY 12526
(518) 537-6604
Anne Poleschner

Town of Copake
Copake, NY 12516
(518) 325-5877
Gloria Lyons

Town of Gallatin
160 Church Road
Red Hook, NY 12571
(845) 756-2765
Katherine Tyler Brody

Town of Germantown
Germantown History Department
(Old Reformed Church Parsonage [1746],
Maple Avenue—location)
131 Northern Boulevard (mailing address)
Germantown, NY 12526
(518) 537-6309
Marguerite Riter
Sat 9:30–noon, and by appointment
("Have many books to help people in search
for their ancestors. Germantown [East
Camp] settled in 1710 by Palatines from
Germany.")
research: requested donation

Town of Ghent
Route 66
Ghent, NY 12075
(518) 392-2127
Calvin Pitcher

Town of Greenport
Town Hall Drive
Hudson, NY 12534
(518) 828-4656
David W. Hart

Town of Hillsdale
Collins Street
Hillsdale, NY 12529
Margaret Hunt

City of Hudson
25 Cross Street
Hudson, NY 12534
(518) 828-0034
Patricia Fenoff

**Town of Kinderhook and Village of
Kinderhook**
21 Albany Avenue
Kinderhook, NY 12106
(518) 758-7605
Ruth Piwonka

Town of Livingston
Mary Howell (see Columbia County
Historian, above)

Town of New Lebanon
New Lebanon, NY 12125

(518) 766-5071
Kevin Fuerst

Village of Philmont
Box 10
Philmont, NY 12565
(518) 672-7032
Charles Nichols

Town of Stockport
Box 124
Columbiaville, NY 12050
(518) 828-9172
Viola Williams

Town of Stuyvesant
30 Riverview Street
Stuyvesant, NY 12173
(518) 758-6752
Juanita Knott

Town of Taghkanic
Ancram, NY 12502
(518) 851-7349
Nancy Griffith

Village of Valatie
Marion Boulevard
Valatie, NY 12184
(518) 758-1656
Dominick Lizzi

Columbia County Historical Society
(5 Albany Avenue—location)
PO Box 311 (mailing address)
Kinderhook, NY 12106
(518) 758-9265; (518) 758-2499 FAX
Sharon Palmer, Executive Director
Mon, Wed & Fri 10:00–4:00, Tue & Thur
(May–Nov only) 10:00–4:00, Sat
1:00–4:00
$40.00 per year membership

Concord Historical Society
(98 East Main Street, Springville, NY
14141—location)
12102 Vaughn Street (mailing address)
East Concord, NY 14055
(716) 592-5546
Margaret Mayerat, Vice President-Historian;
Thomas A. Hawkins, Genealogy
Sun 2:00–4:00, and by appointment
Pub. *Concord Jottings*, three to four times per
year
$10.00 per year membership

Conesus Historical Society
Conesus Town Hall
Conesus, NY 14435
(716) 346-2201

Conklin Historical Society
(Town Hall, Conklin, NY—office location)
82 Pierce Creek Road (mailing address)
Binghamton, NY 13903
(607) 723-1737 (Historian)
Robert Barber, Conklin Town Historian
by appointment
$2.00 per year membership

Corning-Painted Post Historical Society
The Benjamin Patterson Inn Museum
59 West Pulteney Street
Corning, NY 14830
(607) 937-5281
Carrie Fellows, Educator/Curator
Mon–Fri 10:00–4:00
Pub. *CPPHS Newsletter*, monthly
("archives and collections of local history
material," "very little information for
genealogists other than Corning City
directories from the 1930s through the

1980s")

Cortland County Historian
Courthouse Building
46 Greenbush Street, Suite 1001
Cortland, NY 13045-3702
(607) 753-5360; (607) 758-5500 FAX
cbarber@cortland-co.org
http://www.cortlandny.com/community/
   history/historians
Cathy A. Barber
Mon–Fri 9:00–5:00
research: $10.00

Municipal Historians

Town of Cincinnatus
2816 Cincinnatus Road
Cincinnatus, NY 13040-9669
(607) 863-4391
Lorena Perkins

City of Cortland
Cortland County Historical Society
25 Homer Avenue
Cortland, NY 13045-2056
(607) 756-6071
Mary Ann Kane

Town of Cortlandville
3277 Terrace Road
Cortland, NY 13045
(607) 756-5725
Valerie Schmidt

Town of Cuyler
4721 Bennett Road
Cuyler, NY 13058-9621
(607) 842-6781
Ann Ludke

Town of Freetown
4288 Irish Hill Road
Marathon, NY 13803
(607) 849-6106
Susan Dellow

Town of Harford
(address withheld upon request)
("I am not yet up to speed in these
   [genealogical] matters. Any serious
   inquiries along this line should go to the
   Cortland County Historian.")

Town of Homer
22 Cherry Street
Homer, NY 13077-1537
(607) 749-3944
Josephine Brown

Village of Homer
7 King Street
Homer, NY 13077-1307
(607) 749-2573
Charles Jermy

Town of Lapeer
PO Box 533
Marathon, NY 13803-0533
(607) 849-6094
donbarber@worldnet.att.net
Donald Barber

Town of Marathon
1 South Street
Marathon, NY 13803
(607) 849-3661
Patricia McConnell

Village of Marathon
68 Cortland Street
Marathon, NY 13803-3712

(607) 849-6094
Marc Wheaton

Village of McGraw
PO Box 537
McGraw, NY 13101-0537
(607) 836-6738
Mary Kimberly

Town of Preble
2108 East Clark Road
Homer, NY 13077-9449
(607) 749-2044
Anne Henderson

Town of Scott
6936 NYS Route 41
Homer, NY 13077-9723
(607) 749-4461; (607) 749-7907 FAX
Marilyn Mowry

Town of Solon
3530 Stilwell Road
McGraw, NY 13101-9430
(607) 836-6638
Hazel Parsons

Town of Taylor
3845 Cheningo Solon Pond Road
Cincinnatus, NY 13040-9643
(607) 863-3556
Nancy Elwood

Town of Truxton
(3703 Main Street—location)
PO Box 98 (mailing address)
Truxton, NY 13158-0098
(607) 842-6684
Donald McCall

Town of Virgil
1189 West State Road
Cortland, NY 13045-9408
(607) 835-6321
Frances Bays

Town of Willet
PO Box 35
Willet, NY 13863
(607) 836-3344
Shirley Pember

Cortland County Historical Society, Inc.
(Suggett House Museum/Kellogg Memorial
   Research Library, Corner of Homer and
   Maple Avenues, entrance on Maple
   Avenue—location)
25 Homer Avenue (mailing address)
Cortland, NY 13045-2056
(607) 756-6071
http://www.rootsweb.com/~nycortla/
   chsfe.html
Mary Ann Kane, Director
Tue–Sat 1:00–5:00
Pub. *Roots & Branches*, irregularly;
   *Cortland County Historical Society
   Bulletin*; *News Notes from the Suggett
   House*, irregularly
(county cemeteries, federal and state
   censuses indexed for Cortland County)
$15.00 per year membership; museum
   admission: $2.00 for adult nonmembers;
   research library admission: $3.00 for the
   first hour and $1.00 for each additional
   hour for nonmembers; research: $10.00
   per hour plus copies, at 25¢ per copy, and
   postage

Covington Historical Society
(La Grange Road—location)
1088 Peoria Road (mailing address)
Pavilion, NY 14525

(716) 584-3254 (Historian)
Karen C. Milligan, Town Historian
by appointment

**The Cow Neck Peninsula Historical
Society**
Sands-Willets House
336 Port Washington Boulevard
Port Washington, NY 11050
(516) 365-9074
Mary Vahey, Curator
Sun 2:00–4:00, and by appointment
Pub. *CNPHS Journal*, annually
$25.00 per year membership; research:
   special requests honored at $5.00

Croton-on-Hudson Historical Society
1 Van Wyck Street
Croton-on-Hudson, NY 10520
(914) 271-4574
Joyce Finnerty, Village Historian
Mon 8:30–2:00 and by appointment
Pub. *Croton Historian*, four times per year
(Croton Dam and regional history, railroad,
   village history, some genealogy)
$8.00 per year membership

Cuba Historical Society
(16 Genesee Street—location)
PO Box 200 (mailing address)
Cuba, NY 14727
(716) 968-2633
David H. Crowley, Town/Village Historian
Fri 2:00–4:30, and by appointment
Pub. *Cuba Historical Society Newsletter*,
   quarterly
$10.00 per year membership

Cutchogue-New Suffolk Historical Council
(Village Green-Main Road—location)
PO Box 714 (mailing address)
Cutchogue, NY 11935
(631) 734-7122
srubenst@optonline.net
Stan Rubenstein, President
last weekend in June–Labor Day weekend:
   tours 1:00–4:00; June–Oct: groups by
   appointment

Dansville Area Historical Society
(4 Church Street—location)
PO Box 481 (mailing address)
Dansville, NY 14437-0481
(716) 335-8090
first & third Sat

Davenport Historical Society
Town Hall
Davenport, NY 13751
(607) 278-5600
Mary Beardsley, President

Town of Dayton Historical Society
(9561 Route 62—location)
PO Box 15 (mailing address)
Dayton, NY 14041
Bennru00@yahoo.com
Ruth Bennett, Secretary/Town Historian
Mon (summer) 12:30–2:30, third Wed
   (Mar–Nov) 7:30
$2.00 per year membership

Town of DeKalb Historical Association
(696 East DeKalb Road [intersection of U.S.
   Route 11 and East DeKalb Road]—location)
PO Box 111 (mailing address)
DeKalb Junction, NY 13630-0111
(315) 347-1900; (315) 347-3554
thompsbs@tds.net
http://www.herdcow.com/community/
   dhistory
Bryan Thompson, Chair

Wed 12:30–4:00, Thur 9:30–11:30
Pub. *Williamstown Gazette*, two times per year
("Archives for Township of DeKalb 1806 to present, includes cemetery records, scrapbooks, town meeting books, etc.")
$3.00 per year membership

Delaware County Historian
195 Main Street
Delhi, NY 13753
Clara H. Stewart

Municipal Historians

Town of Andes
Box 143
Andes, NY 13731
(845) 676-3212
Janis E. Reynolds

Village of Andes
post vacant

Town of Bovina
2299 County Highway #6
Bovina Center, NY 13740
(607) 832-4245; (607) 832-4446
Charles LaFever
all day

Town of Colchester
PO Box 336
Downsville, NY 13755
(607) 363-2212
Jane Flannery

Town of Davenport
c/o Margaret Bonney, Town Clerk
PO Box 88
Davenport Center, NY 13750
(607) 432-6749
Sally Beams

Town of Delhi
Rural Delivery 2
Delhi, NY 13753
(607) 746-2731
Billie Sturdevant

Village of Delhi
7 Division Street
Delhi, NY 13753
(607) 746-2857
Shirley Houck

Town of Deposit and Village of Deposit
2 Elm Street
Deposit, NY 13754
(607) 467-2719
Mary S. Cable

Village of Fleischmanns
post vacant

Town of Franklin
Rural Delivery 1
Franklin, NY 13775
(607) 829-5525
Ruth Sickler

Village of Franklin
PO Box 3
Franklin, NY 13775
(607) 829-8891
Donald E. Smith

Town of Hamden
PO Box 67
Hamden, NY 13782
(607) 746-6625
Gabrielle Buel

Town of Hancock
Hancock-Chehocton Historical Association
61 Wheeler Street
Hancock, NY 13783

Village of Hancock
post vacant

Town of Harpersfield
Harper Hill Road
Harpersfield, NY 13786
(607) 652-5152
Evangeline MacLaury

Village of Hobart
PO Box 177
Hobart, NY 13788
(607) 538-9279
Erma MacArthur

Town of Kortright
Roberts Road
Blommville, NY 13739
(607) 538-9227
Wilber Haynes

Village of Margaretville
c/o Betty DeSilva, Village Clerk
PO Box 228
Margaretville, NY 12455
(845) 586-4480
idme4549@catskill.net
Ira D. Lawrence

Town of Masonville
339 River Road
Mount Upton, NY 13809-2139
(607) 764-8440
geopolly@citlink.net
George & Polly Stafford
by appointment
("We are unpaid volunteers.")

Town of Meredith
HC 87, Box 341
Delhi, NY 13753-9311
(607) 746-2016
Bernice Telian

Town of Middletown, Delaware County
PO Box 373
Roxbury, NY 12474
(607) 588-6286
cvsnyder@usadatanet.net
Vesti Snyder
(information from 1880 to the present only, earlier records destroyed by a flood)

Town of Roxbury
Vega Mountain Road
Roxbury, NY 12474
(607) 326-3392
Peg O'Connell Flachs

Town of Sidney and Village of Sidney
Sidney Historical Society
(Sidney Civic Center, 21 Liberty Street, Second Floor, Room 218—location)
PO Box 2217 (mailing address)
Sidney, NY 13838

Town of Stamford and Village of Stamford
10 Beaver Street
Stamford, NY 12167
(607) 652-7839
Anne Willis

Town of Tompkins
1413 Mormon Hollow Road
Walton, NY 13856-3400
(607) 865-4069
Frances S. Webb

by appointment
research: "nominal fee, depending on how long it takes to find out and publish information requested"

Town of Walton
Walton Historical Society
Gardiner Place
Walton, NY 13856
(607) 865-6003
Maureen O'Connell, Secretary

Village of Walton
88 Townsend Street
Walton, NY 13856
(607) 865-4636
Frederica Cranston

Delaware County Historical Association
46549 State Highway 10
Delhi, NY 13753
(607) 746-3849; (607) 746-7326 FAX
dcha@delhi.net
http://www.rootsweb.com/~nydelaha
Helen Casey, Library Manager
Library: Mon–Tue 10:00–3:00
Pub. *Headwaters of History*, three times per year
$15.00 per year membership; research: $15.00 per hour

Depauville Library
Caroline Street
Depauville, NY 13632
(315) 686-3299
Connie Haver

The DeWitt Historical Society of Tompkins County and Tompkins County Museum
401 East State Street
Ithaca, NY 14850
(607) 273-8284; (607) 273-6107 FAX
http://www.lakenet.org/dewitt
Executive Director
Museum: Tue–Sat 11:00–5:00; Research: Tue, Thur & Sat 11:00–5:00
Pub. *Newsletter*, quarterly
(Tompkins County, history)
$25.00 per year membership; research: $11.50 per hour, two-hour minimum

Dobbs Ferry Historical Society
12 Elm
Dobbs Ferry, NY 10522
(914) 674-1007
Pub. *The Ferryman*

Douglaston and Little Neck Historical Society
328 Manor Road
Douglaston, NY 11363
(718) 225-4403
Julia Schoeck, Treasurer

Dryden Town Historical Society
History House
(36 West Main Street—location)
PO Box 69 (mailing address)
Dryden, NY 13053
(607) 844-9209
Sat 10:00–2:00, and by appointment
Pub. *Newsletter*, quarterly, not available by subscription
$10.00 per year membership; research: $10.00 donation

Dundee Area Historical Society
(26 Seneca Street—location)
PO Box 153 (mailing address)
Dundee, NY 14837
(607) 243-7047

Pamela M. Miller, Director
1 May–31 Oct: Tue–Fri 10:00–5:00, Sat
   8:30–12:30
("Historical society with an 1891 brick
   schoolhouse museum. Extensive
   genealogy files on families in southern
   Yates County and historical records of
   past businesses and events.")
$8.00 per year membership

Durham Center Museum
Route 145
East Durham, NY 12423
(518) 239-8461
Sancie Thomsen, Executive Director
May–Oct: Thur–Sun 1:00–4:00, Thur
   7:00–9:00
("local history")

Dutchess County Historian
c/o Dutchess County Historical Society
(549 Main Street—location)
PO Box 88 (mailing address)
Poughkeepsie, NY 12602

Municipal Historians

Town of Amenia
61 Powder House Road
Amenia, NY 12501
(845) 373-8069
Ken Hoadley

City of Beacon
Beacon Historical Society
The Howland Center
(477 Main Street—location)
PO Box 89 (mailing address)
Beacon, NY 12508
Joan Van Voorhis

Town of Beekman
Beekman Town Hall
Poughquag, NY 12570
Lee Eaton

Town of Clinton
(address withheld upon request)

Town of Dover
Dover Town Hall
Route 2, Box 132
East Duncan Hill Road
Dover Plains, NY 12522
Doris Dedrick

Town of East Fishkill
East Fishkill Town Hall
370 Route 376
Hopewell Junction, NY 12533
Everett Lee

Town of Fishkill
Fishkill Town Hall
401 Route 52
Fishkill, NY 12524
Willa Skinner

Village of Fishkill
40 Broad Street
Fishkill, NY 12524
Karen Hitt

Town of Hyde Park
13 Main Street
Hyde Park, NY 12538
Margaret Marquex

Town of LaGrange
LaGrange Town Hall
120 Stringham Road
LaGrangeville, NY 12540

Emily Johnson

Town of Milan
286 Milan Hollow Road
Rhinebeck, NY 12572
Patrick Higgins

Village of Millbrook
Millbrook Village Hall
Millbrook, NY 12548
David Greenwood

Village of Millerton
Simmons Street
Millerton, NY 12546
Chester Eisenhuth

Town of Northeast
North East Town Hall
Maple Avenue
Millerton, NY 12546
Chester Eisenhuth

Town of Pawling
Pawling Town Hall
160 Charles Colman Boulevard
Pawling, NY 12564
Myrna Hubert

Village of Pawling
post vacant

Town of Pine Plains
Pine Plains Town Hall
(South Main Street—location)
PO Box 320 (mailing address)
Pine Plains, NY 12567
Dyan Kilpatrick

Town of Pleasant Valley
(1554 Main Street—location)
Mill Building, Route 44 (mailing address)
Pleasant Valley, NY 12569
(845) 635-1148
Olive Doty
Mon 9:00–noon, and by appointment
Pub. *Voice Ledger*, weekly
("The town records were burned in 1914.
   [Have] what is available of the records of
   the Presbyterian Church from 1765, the
   St. Paul's Episcopal Church from
   1847–1956, and town clerk's records
   1824–1855 and 1896–1929.")

City of Poughkeepsie
Poughkeepsie City Hall
PO Box 300
Poughkeepsie, NY 12601
Herbert Saltford

Town of Poughkeepsie
Poughkeepsie Town Hall
Dutchess Turnpike
Poughkeepsie, NY 12603
Mona Vaeth

Town of Red Hook
PO Box 338
Red Hook, NY 12571-0338
J. Winthrop Aldrich

Village of Red Hook
Red Hook Village Hall
24 South Broadway
Red Hook, NY 12571
Rosemary E. Coons

Town of Rhinebeck
60 Cedar Heights Road
Rhinebeck, NY 12572
Nancy V. Kelly

Village of Rhinebeck
post vacant

Town of Stanford
Stanford Town Hall
Box 190, Route 82
Stanfordville, NY 12581
Mrs. Irving Burdick

Village of Tivoli
Tivoli Village Hall
48-A Broadway
Tivoli, NY 12585
Richard C. Wiles

Town of Unionvale
249 Duncan Road
Tymor Park
LaGrangeville, NY 12540
(845) 23-3817 (Home); (845) 724-5600
   (Office)
Joann Miracco
Tue 10:00–3:00

Town of Wappinger
Wappingers Town Hall
Box 324, Middlebush Road
Wappingers Falls, NY 12590
Brenda Von Burg

Village of Wappingers Falls
Wappingers Falls Village Hall
7 Spring Street
Wappingers Falls, NY 12590
Vicki Kolb

Town of Washington
Washington Town Hall
PO Box 667
Millbrook, NY 12545
Carmine DiArpino

Dutchess County Historical Society
(Clinton House State Historic Site, 549 Main
Street—location)
PO Box 88 (mailing address)
Poughkeepsie, NY 12602
(845) 471-1630; (845) 471-8777
Eileen M. Hayden, Director
Tue–Fri 10:00–3:00
Pub. *Yearbook*, annually, $10.00 per issue;
   Dutchess Historian, irregularly; *Dutchess
   County Historical Society Collections*,
   irregularly
$40.00 per year membership (includes
   Yearbook and *Dutchess Historian*);
   admission: $10.00 for nonmembers;
   research: $60.00 three-hour minimum

**Historical Society of the Town of East
Bloomfield Academy Museum**
(8 South Avenue—location)
PO Box 212 (mailing address)
East Bloomfield, NY 14443-0212
(585) 657-7244
EBHS1838@hotmail.com
http://www.rootsweb.com/~nyontari/
   ebhist.htm
C. Elsbree
Tue–Fri 9:30–3:30, Sat–Sun by appointment
Pub. *Academy Chronicles*, monthly
(local history, maps, articles on specific area
   families)
$10.00 per year membership; research: charge
   for searches

East Hampton Historical Society
101 Main Street
East Hampton, NY 11937
(631) 324-6850
Karen Hensel, Director

East Islip Historical Society
PO Box 389
Great River, NY 11739
Don Koch, President

East Quogue Historical Group
PO Box 144
East Quogue, NY 11942
Edna Jackson, President

East Springwater Historical Society
Springwater, NY 14560
(716) 383-1561

Eastchester Historical Society
(388 California Road, Bronxville, NY
    10708—location)
PO Box 37 (mailing address)
Eastchester, NY 10709
(914) 793-1900; (914) 337-1770 (Harriet
    Bianchi)
Harriet Bianchi
by appointment only
(resource for lower Westchester County;
    school house museum 1835; 19th-century
    collection of juvenile literature and
    textbooks; historical and genealogical
    reference library)
$20.00 per year membership; research:
    $10.00 for the first hour and $5.00 per
    hour thereafter

Eastville Community Historical Society
PO Box 2036
Sag Harbor, NY 11963
Marjorie Day, President

Eden Historical Society
8837 South Main Street
Eden, NY 14057
(716) 992-4165

R. T. Elethorp Historical Society
Hammond, NY 13646
Valera Bickelhaupt, Hammond Town
    Historian

Ellicottville Historical Society
Ellicottville Historical Museum
(2 Washington Street—location)
PO Box 485
Ellicottville, NY 14731
(716) 699-2162 (Town Historian)
Mary Elizabeth Dunbar, Ellicottville Town
    Historian
Sat–Sun (June–Sept) 1:00–4:00 (manned by
    volunteers), and by appointment with town
    historian

Elma Historical Society
(1910 Bowen Road—location)
PO Box 84 (mailing address)
Elma, NY 14059-0084
(716) 652-6310

Elmira Heights Historical Society, Inc.
(266 East 14th Street—location)
PO Box 2084 (mailing address)
Elmira Heights, NY 14903
(607) 732-5167
Kenneth J. Erickson, Village Historian
third Wed 4:00–7:00, and by appointment

**Endicott Historical and Preservation
Society**
PO Box 52
Endicott, NY 13760
(607) 783-8373

Enfield Historical Society
398 Harvey Hill Road
Trumansburg, NY 14886

(607) 273-5369 (Editor); (607) 272-5930
    (President)
Wilma Fisher, Editor; Doris Rothermich,
    President
Pub. *Newsletter*

Erie County Historian
Buffalo and Erie County Historical Society
25 Nottingham Terrace
Buffalo, NY 14216
(716) 873-9644; (716) 873-9612; (716) 873-
    8754 FAX
http://intotem.buffnet.net/bechs
Dr. William H. Siener, de facto Erie County
    Historian

Village of Akron
57 John Street
Akron, NY 14001
(716) 542-4573
John I. Eckerson
(also historian of the town of Newstead)

Town of Alden and Village of Alden
299 Exchange Street
Alden, NY 14006
Norma M. Sweet

Town of Amherst
3069 Tonawanda Creek Road
North Tonawanda, NY 14228
Dr. Andrea Shaw

Village of Angola
post vacant

Town of Aurora
Aurora Historical Society, Inc.
5 South Grove Street
East Aurora, NY 14052
(716) 652-3280; (716) 652-4286; (716) 652-
    8854 (East Aurora)
Donald H. Dayer
Wed 1:00–4:00
(also historian of the village of East Aurora)

Village of Blasdell
63 Pearl Street
Blasdell, NY 14219
Nina Brown

Town of Boston
9432 Boston State Road
Boston, NY 14025
James J. Jehle

Town of Brant
post vacant

City of Buffalo
post vacant

Town of Cheektowaga
Cheektowaga Town Hall
3223 Broadway
Cheektowaga, NY 14227
(716) 684-6544
Mary Holtz
first Sun 2:00–4:00

Town of Clarence
Clarence Town Hall
1 Town Place
Clarence, NY 14031
(716) 759-1118
Laura Grenzebach

Town of Colden
Heath Road
Colden, NY 14069
Julian Flackenstein

Town of Collins
Orchard Place
Collins, NY 14034
Mrs. Richard Gaffney

Town of Concord
13153 Morton's Corners Road
Springville, NY 14141
Lillian D. Geiger
(also historian of the village of Springville)

Village of East Aurora
Donald Dayer (see Town of Aurora, above)

Town of Eden
2795 East Church Street
Eden, NY 14057
(716) 992-3559
Norma Hardy Webb

Town of Elma
Elma Historical Society
(1910 Bowen Road—location)
PO Box 84 (mailing address)
Elma, NY 14059-0084
(716) 652-6310
Charlotte Yacabush

Town of Evans
South Creek Road
North Evans, NY 14112
Mrs. Annette M. Frost

Village of Farnham
PO Box 26
Farnham, NY 14061
Anna Martarana

Town of Grand Island
post vacant

Town of Hamburg
3697 Westview
Hamburg, NY 14075
James Baker

Village of Kenmore
info@community-history.org
C. George Carncross

Town of Lancaster
40 Clark Street
Lancaster, NY 14086
Dr. Harley E. Scott
Sun 3:00–5:00

Village of Lancaster
88 Church Street
Lancaster, NY 14086
Edward Mikula

Town of Marilla
South 2755 Three Rod Road
East Aurora, NY 14052-9535
Laura E. Neumann

Town of Newstead
John I. Eckerson (see Village of Akron,
    above)

Town of North Collins
2093 Shirley Road
North Collins, NY 14111
(716) 337-2702
ggbowman@msn.com
http://buffnet.net/~macdowel (for southern
    Erie County information)
Georgianne Bowman

**Town of Orchard Park and Village of
Orchard Park**
5800 Armor Duelles Road

Orchard Park, NY 14127
John N. Printy

Town of Sardinia
Town Hall
Savage Road
Sardinia, NY 14134
Florence Rupert

Village of Sloan
425 Reiman Street
Sloan, NY 14212

Village of Springville
Lillian D. Geiger (see Town of Concord,
above)

City of Tonawanda
post vacant

Town of Tonawanda
62 Devonshire Road
Tonawanda, NY 14223
John W. Percy
(history only, other queries receive reference
to professional genealogists)

Town of Wales
post vacant

Town of West Seneca
93 Carmelite Drive
West Seneca, NY 14224
Carole Taylor

Village of Williamsville
24 Garrison Road
Williamsville, NY 14221
Mary Jane Kibby

Esperance Historical Society and Museum
(Church Street—location)
PO Box 55 (mailing address)
Esperance, NY 12066
(518) 875-6854
Kenneth Jones, Esperance Town Historian
Memorial Day–Labor Day: weekends
1:00–5:00

Esquatak Historical Society
PO Box 151
Castleton-on-Hudson, NY 12033
(518) 732-2626

Essex County Historian
Brewster Memorial Library
Adirondack Center Museum
(Court Street—location)
PO Box 428 (mailing address)
Elizabethtown, NY 12932
(518) 873-6466
Reid Larson
by appointment
copies: 50¢ per page

Municipal Historians

Village of Bloomingdale
PO Box 16
Bloomingdale, NY 12913
Dorothy White

Town of Chesterfield
631 Highland Road
Keeseville, NY 12944-2314
(518) 834-7364
Grace Good

Town of Crown Point
c/o Penfield Foundation
Crown Point, NY 12928
Joan Hunsdon, President of the Penfield

Foundation

Town of Elizabethtown
Water Street
Elizabethtown, NY 12932
Conrad Hutchins

Town of Essex
Rural Route 1, Box 307
Essex, NY 12936
(518) 963-8782; (518) 963-7231
Shirley La Forest

Town of Jay
30 Glen Road
Jay, NY 12941
(518) 946-2597
Mary E. Wallace
Mon–Fri 10:00–4:00 by appointment

Town of Keene
PO Box 751
Keene, NY 12943
(518) 576-9550
Janet H. W. Hall

Village of Keeseville
1790 Main Street
Keeseville, NY 12944
(518) 834-9059; (518) 834-9050 FAX
Julie Latrell

Village of Lake Placid
Village Hall
Lake Placid, NY 12946
(518) 523-2597; (518) 523-1321 FAX
Eileen M. Valentine

Town of Lewis
PO Box 59
Lewis, NY 12950
(518) 873-6777; (518) 873-6838; (518) 873-
2372 FAX
James E. Pierce

Town of Minerva
1205 County Route 29
Olmstedville, NY 12857
(518) 251-2869; (518) 251-5136 FAX
Catherine Persons

Town of Moriah
41 West Street
Port Henry, NY 12974
(518) 546-7524 (Home)
http://www.porthenry.com (Town web site)
Joan Daby

Town of Newcomb
PO Box 477
Newcomb, NY 12852
Helen O'Donnell

Town of North Elba
301 Main Street
Lake Placid, NY 12946
(518) 523-2162; (518) 523-9569 FAX
Barbara S. Whitney

Town of North Hudson
North Hudson, NY 12855
(518) 532-9255
Patricia Schoch

Village of Port Henry
(25 South Main Street—location)
PO Box A (mailing address)
Port Henry, NY 12974
(518) 546-9933; (518) 546-8675 FAX
Suzanne Baker

Town of Saint Armand

Bloomingdale NY 12913
(518) 891-5573
Rita Gonyea

Village of Saranac Lake
Village Hall
Saranac Lake, NY 12983
(518) 891-4150
Marilyn Clement
(The village lies in both Essex and Franklin
counties)

Town of Schroon
Schroon Lake, NY 12870
(518) 532-0592
Alexander Vanlint

Town of Ticonderoga
349 Park Avenue
Ticonderoga, NY 12883
(518) 585-6354
Daniel Blanchette

Village of Ticonderoga
215 Champlain Avenue
Ticonderoga, NY 12883
Virginia R. Smith

Town of Westport and Village of Westport
Westport, NY 12993
(518) 962-8360
Helen Collins

Town of Willsboro
Mount View Road
Willsboro, NY 12996
(518) 963-4478
Janice Allen

Town of Wilmington
PO Box 180
Wilmington, NY 12997
(518) 946-7057
history@primelink1.net
Merri C. Peck
call or email for appointment or information

Essex County Historical Society
Brewster Memorial Library
Adirondack Center Museum
(Court Street—location)
PO Box 428 (mailing address)
Elizabethtown, NY 12932
(518) 873-6466
Pat Casselman; Gayle Meaker; Margaret
Gibbs, Director
Tue & Thur 9:00–3:00
Pub. *Reveille*

Town of Evans Historical Society
8351 Erie Road, Erie, County
Angola, NY 14006
Jack Ehmke, President
(local history)
$5.00 per year membership

Farmingdale-Bethpage Historical Society
PO Box 500
Farmingdale, NY 11735
(516) 249-0976
Barbara Post, President

Farmingville Historical Society
PO Box 311
Farmingville, NY 11738
(631) 698-0396
Dorothy Czenszak-McGowan, President

Fishkill Historical Society
Van Wyck Homestead Museum
(504 Route 9—location)
PO Box 133 (mailing address)

Fishkill, NY 12524
(845) 896-9560
Roy Jorgensen, President
Tue 7:00–9:00, Wed & Sat 10:00–noon,
weekends 1:00–4:00
Pub. *Van Wyck Dispatch*, monthly (quarterly
history issue)
("local southern Dutchess County, Putnam
County")
$9.00 per year membership

Dr. Asa Fitch Historical Society
http://www.sover.net/~salemny/histhl3.html

Fort Brewerton Historical Society
(9 U.S. Route 11—location)
PO Box 392 (mailing address)
Brewerton, NY 13029-0392
(315) 668-8801 voice & FAX
http://www.FortBrewerton.org
Peter Apgar, Executive Director
May–Oct: Fri & Sun 1:00–5:00, Sat
10:00–5:00; Archives: by appointment
Pub. *Newsletter*, quarterly
$25.00 per year membership

Fort Edward Historical Association
(22 & 29 Broadway—location)
PO Box 106 (mailing address)
Fort Edward, NY 12828-0106
(518) 747-9600
R. Paul McCarty, Director
genealogical queries: Wed 10:00–3:00
(genealogy and local history of Fort Edward
and Hudson Falls, Washington County,
New York)
from $10.00 per year membership; research
fees based on time and copy work

Fort Hamilton Historical Society
Fort Hamilton, NY 11252
(718) 630-4349
(primarily historical, no genealogical
materials)

Foundation Historical Association, Inc.
33 South Street
Auburn, NY 13021
(315) 252-1283

Four River Valleys Historical Society
PO Box 504
Carthage, NY 13619
(315) 773-5133
Nelson Eddy

Franklin County Historian
Franklin County Historical and Museum
Society
51 Milwaukee Street
Malone, NY 12953
(518) 483-2750
Virginia Anne Wolfe, Acting Contact Person
Sept–May: Sat 1:00–5:00; June–Aug:
Tue–Sat 1:00–4:00

Municipal Historians

Town of Altamont
130 Raquette River Drive
Tupper Lake, NY 12986
(518) 359-2532
William Frenette, Jr.
(also historian of the village of Tupper Lake)

Town of Bangor
Route 11B
Bangor, NY 12966
(518) 483-0939
Jess Chapin

Town of Bellmont

Banner House Inn
Chateaugay, NY 12920
(518) 425-6837
Muriel Chase

Town of Bombay
Rural Free Delivery 1
Bombay, NY 12914
(518) 358-2005
James Reardon

Village of Bombay
Bombay, NY 12914
Charles Reardon

Town of Brandon
Stevens Road
North Bangor, NY 12966
Beverly Hinkle

Town of Brighton
PO Box 107
Paul Smiths, NY 12970
(518) 327-3202
Elaine Sater

Village of Brushton
PO Box 441
Brushton, NY 12916
(518) 529-6069
Isabelle Dorey

Town of Burke
Rural Route 1, Box 147
Burke, NY 12917
(518) 483-4015
vonne Spinner

Village of Burke
Maple Street
Burke, NY 12917
Ruth Legacy

**Town of Chateaugay and Village of
Chateaugay**
65 East Main Street
Chateaugay, NY 12920
(518) 497-6333
Olin Cook

Town of Constable
PO Box 52
Constable, NY 12926
(518) 483-4124
Mary Ann Tallon

Town of Dickinson
PO Box 3
Dickinson Center, NY 12930-0003
(518) 856-9488
Betty Wood

Town of Duane
HCR 1, Box 126
Malone, NY 12953
(518) 483-4369
Gloria Gori

Town of Fort Covington
Foster Road
Fort Covington, NY 12937
(518) 358-2025
Jaqueline Harvey and Elizabeth Mount

Town of Franklin
Alder Brook
Star Route 1, Box 202
Au Sable Forks, NY 12912
(518) 891-1052
Teresa Eshelman

Town of Harrietstown

30 Main Street
Saranac Lake, NY 12983
(518) 891-1470 (c/o Town Clerk)
mbh@capital.net
Mary B. Hotaling
by appointment
("village development, camps, tuberculosis
treatment)

Town of Malone and Village of Malone
Franklin County Historical and Museum
Society
51 Milwaukee Street
Malone, NY 12953
(518) 483-2750
Marge Mahler

Town of Moira
PO Box 326
Brushton, NY 12916
Joyce M. Ranieri
by appointment only

Town of Santa Clara
PO Box 146
Saranac Lake, NY 12983
(518) 891-3237
Roy Resenbarker

Village of Saranac Lake
(see Essex County, above)

Village of Tupper Lake
William Frenette, Jr. (see Town of Altamont,
above)

Town of Waverly
Saint Regis Falls, NY 12980
(518) 856-9609; (518) 856-9720
Judy R. Weaver

Town of Westville
Rural Free Delivery 1, Box 166
Constable, NY 12926
Richard Avery

**Franklin County Historical and Museum
Society**
(51 Milwaukee Street—location)
PO Box 388 (mailing address)
Malone, NY 12953
(518) 483-2750
Virginia Anne Wolfe, Acting Contact Person
Sept–May: Sat 1:00–5:00; June–Aug:
Tue–Sat 1:00–4:00
Pub. *Franklin Historical Review*, annually
$15.00 per year membership

Franklin Square Historical Society
(Museum at John Street School, Nassau
Boulevard—location)
PO Box 45 (mailing address)
Franklin Square, NY 11010
Paul van Wie, President

French Creek Historical Society, Inc.
Route 2
Clymer, NY 14724
(716) 355-4101

Friends for Long Island's Heritage
1864 Muttontown Road
Muttontown, NY 11791-9652
(516) 571-7600; (516) 571-7623 FAX
info@fflih.org
http://www.fflih.org
Gerald S. Kessler, President
9:00–4:45
Pub. *Long Island Forum*, quarterly, $20.00
for two-year subscription for nonmembers,
$8.00 for two-year subscription for
members

Friends of the Nyacks, Inc.
PO Box 384
Nyack, NY 10960
(845) 358-2113
Betti Schlyer, Chairperson
9:00–5:00

Frontenac Historical Society
1 Foundry Street
Union Springs, NY 13160
(315) 889-7767

Fulton County Historian
187 Bleecker Street
Gloversville, NY 12078
(518) 725-3073
Lewis G. Decker

Municipal Historians

Town of Bleecker
184 County Highway 125
Gloversville, NY 12078
Eleanor Brooks

Town of Broadalbin and Village of Broadalbin
(Union Mills Road—location)
PO Box 548 (mailing address)
Broadalbin, NY 12025-0548
Gordon Cornell

Town of Caroga
(Route 10—location)
PO Box 344 (mailing address)
Caroga Lake, NY 12032
Inger McDaniel

Town of Ephratah
135 Church Street
Saint Johnsville, NY 13452
Evelyn Frasier

City of Gloversville
Historian's Office and City Archives
City Hall
95 Lincoln Street
Gloversville, NY 12078
tryonco@superior.net
James F. Morrison
Fri 6:00–9:00, and by appointment

Town of Johnstown
(Knoblauch Road—location)
PO Box 210 (mailing address)
Johnstown, NY 12095
Ruth Gros

Town of Mayfield and Village of Mayfield
33 West Main Street
Mayfield, NY 12117
Betty Tabor

Town of Northampton and Village of Northville
Northville, NY 12134
Gail Cramer

Town of Oppenheim
6845 State Highway 29
Dolgeville, NY 13329
Hector Allen

Town of Perth
(address withheld upon request)

Town of Stratford
1955 County Highway 119
Stratford, NY 13470
Carolyn Walker

Historical Society of Fulton, N.Y.

(177 South First Street—location)
PO Box 157 (mailing address)
Fulton, NY 13069
(315) 598-4616
http://www.artcom.com/museums/nv/gl/
13069.htm
Sandra Clarke, Director; Carrie Butler,
Coordinator
by appointment
$12.50 per year membership

Galen Historical Society
PO Box 43
Clyde, NY 14433

Genesee County Historian
"Old Enginehouse"
3 West Main Street
Batavia, NY 14020-2021
(716) 344-2550, ext. 2613; (716) 344-2442
history@co.genesee.ny.us;
sconklin@co.genesee.ny.us
Susan L. Conklin
Mon–Thur 9:00–4:30
fee for written requests

Municipal Historians

Town of Alabama
Alabama Town Hall
2218 Judge Road
Oakfield, NY 14125
(716) 948-9341 (Town); (585) 237-0104
(Home)
HistorianCindyA@netscape.net
http://www2.pcom.net/cinjod/historian
Cindy Amrhein
by appointment
(For inquires on birth, death, and marriage
records, please contact the Town Hall
directly [vital records are from 1882
forward]. For historical requests please
contact the historian by email or at her
home address: 10 Traver Place, Perry, NY
14530.)

Town of Alexander and Village of Alexander
10290 Goodman Road
Alexander, NY 14005-9737
(716) 591-1204
Katy Goodman

City of Batavia
41 Clinton Street
Batavia, NY 14020-2820
(716) 344-1633
Corinne Iwanicki
Mon–Fri 4:00–7:00 (by phone only)
("only within current city limits [no farms,
etc.]. I personally do *not* do genealogy
research but will direct to others and give
fees involved.")

Town of Batavia
(Town Hall, West Main Street
Road—location)
3484 South Main Street Road (mailing
address)
Batavia, NY 14020
pennyplant@yahoo.com;
BTCSDEPOT@aol.com
http://www.rootsweb.com/~nygenese/
batavia.htm
Gale M. Conn-Wright
(Batavia once covered all of Genesee
County, inquiries about localities outside
current Batavia boundaries should be
directed to historians of those present-day
towns)
charges for copies

Town of Bergen
7116 North Bergen Road
Bergen, NY 14416
(716) 494-1456
http://www.rootsweb.com/~nygenese/
bergen.htm
Vera (Peggy) Denton

Village of Bergen
(18 McKenzie Street—location)
PO Box 417 (mailing address)
Bergen, NY 14416-0417
(716) 494-1675
F. E. "Tally" Almquist

Town of Bethany
10122 Bethany Center Road
East Bethany, NY 14054-9706
(716) 343-0022
http://www.rootsweb.com/~nygenese/
bethany.htm
Helen Milroy

Town of Byron
6148 Bird Road
Byron, NY 14422-0201
(716) 548-2252
Dora M. Jones

Village of Corfu
PO Box 113
Corfu, NY 14036-0113
(716) 599-4840
Laura Fauth

Town of Darien
10709 Allegany Road
Darien Center, NY 14040
(716) 547-2294
Elmer Heiman

Town of Elba and Village of Elba
4494 North Byron Road
Elba, NY 14058
Scott D. Benz

Town of LeRoy
9306 Summit Street Road
LeRoy, NY 14482-8904
(716) 768-8376
Irene Walters

Village of LeRoy
LeRoy Historical Society
23 East Main Street
LeRoy, NY 14482-1209
(716) 768-7433
Lynne Belluscio
Historical Society: Tue–Fri 10:00–4:00, Sun
(Mar–Dec) 2:00–4:00, and by appointment

Town of Oakfield and Village of Oakfield
7483 South Pearl Street Road
Oakfield, NY 14125
(716) 948-9124
Gebruder@aol.com
http://www.rootsweb.com/~nygenese/
oakfield
Nancy Bow

Town of Pavilion
9901 Roanoke Road
Pavilion, NY 14525-9784
(716) 768-6095
Virginia Rigoni

Town of Pembroke
7905 Allegheny Road
Corfu, NY 14036-9724
(716) 762-8568
Lois Brockway

Town of Stafford
6684 Randall Road
LeRoy, NY 14482-9316
(716) 343-6699
Martha Heddon

Geneva Historical Society and Museum
Prouty Chew House
543 South Main Street
Geneva, NY 14456-3194
(315) 789-5151; (315) 789-0314 FAX
http://www.rootsweb.com/~nyontari/
   genhist.htm
Jennifer Walton, Archivist
Tue–Fri 1:30–4:30, and by appointment
(local and regional history)
$15.00 for initial search

Genoa Historical Society
Rural Life Museum
Route 34B
King Ferry, NY 13081
(315) 364-7550
Grayson Mitchell
Mon–Fri 9:30–3:00
Pub. *Southern Cayuga Tribune*, quarterly
$12.50 per year membership

Glen Haven Historical Society
(7325 Fairhaven Road—location)
PO Box 293 (mailing address)
Homer, NY 13077
(607) 749-7907
May–Sept: Sat 1:00–3:00 by appointment

**Glens Falls-Queensbury Historical
Association**
Chapman Historical Museum
348 Glen Street
Glens Falls, NY 12801
(518) 793-2826; (518) 793-2831 FAX
http://www.ChapmanMuseum.org
Rebecca Gereau Pelchar, Curator of
   Collections
Tue–Sat 10:00–5:00
Pub. *Bridging the Years*; *Shoulder Arms*
(a Regional History Center with a local
   history library/archives component relating
   to Glens Falls, the Town of Queensbury,
   and Warren, Washington and Saratoga
   counties)
$40.00 per year membership; admission:
   $2.00 for adults; fees for photocopies,
   photoreproduction and the use of any
   materials for publication

**Goshen Public Library and Historical
Society**
203 Main Street
Goshen, NY 10924
(845) 294-6606
Eulie Costello, Clerk, Historical and
   Genealogical Reference Room
Reference Room: Mon–Wed 10:00–6:00,
   Thur–Sat 10:00–2:00

Gouverneur Historical Association
30 Church Street
Gouverneur, NY 13642
(315) 287-0570

http://members.tripod.com/~gouvmuse/rea
   lpage.html
Joseph Laurenza, President
May–Oct: Wed & Sat 1:00–3:00

Gowanda Area Historical Society
(2 Chestnut Street, Corner of Chestnut
Street—location)
PO Box 372 (mailing address)
Gowanda, NY 14070
Philip Palen, Treasurer

Apr–Nov: first Sun, second Thur & fourth
   Sat 1:00–4:00
("Always ready to accommodate anyone at
   almost any time")

Grafton Historical Society
Grafton, NY 12082

Grand Island Historical Society
Beaver Island State Park
PO Box 135
Grand Island, NY 14072

The Gravesend Historical Society
PO Box 1643, Gravesend Station
Gravesend, NY 11223
(718) 375-6831; (718) 375-6831 FAX
Eric J. Ierardi, President
10:00–5:00
various memberships

Greater Astoria Historical Society
Quinn Memorial Building
35-20 Broadway
Long Island City, NY 11103-1193
(718) 278-2437
Debbie Van Cura, President

**The Historical Association of Greater
Liverpool**
Gleason House
Second Street
Liverpool, NY 13088

Greater Milford Historical Association
Milford, NY 13807

Greater Patchogue Historical Society
PO Box 102
Patchogue, NY 11772
Anne Swezey, Village Historian

**The Historical Society of Greater Port
Jefferson**
Mather House Museum
115 Prospect Street
Port Jefferson, NY 11777
(631) 473-2665
info@portjeffhistorical.org
http://www.portjeffhistorical.org
Sandra Swenk, Trustee
Memorial Day–Labor Day
("small archival collection")

Greater Ridgewood Historical Society
Queens Genealogy Workshop
Vander Ende-Onderdonk House
1820 Flushing Avenue
Ridgewood, NY 11385-1041
(718) 456-1776
htp://members.aol.com/ondrdnkhse/grhs.htm
George P. Miller, Archivist
by appointment; Workshop meetings: third
   Sat 1:30
Pub. *Newsletter*, quarterly
(emphasis on Long Island history and
   genealogy; extensive surname files; "All
   inquiries must be by correspondence
   only.")
$15.00 per year membership in Historical
   Society, additional $10.00 per year
   membership in Queens Genealogy
   Workshop; research: donation

Historical Society of Greece, N.Y.
(595 Long Pond Road, Rochester, NY
14612—location)
PO Box 16249 (mailing address)
Rochester, NY 14616
(716) 225-7221
http://www.greecechamber.org/
   town_of_greece_historical_society.htm

Lorraine Beane, President
Sun 2:00–4:30, and by appointment
Pub. *GHS Newsletter*, bimonthly
$5.00 per year membership

Greenbush Historical Society
PO Box 66
East Greenbush, NY 12061
Secretary
("We are small, mostly aging [aged], have no
   searchable genealogical data and no
   research capability; unlikely to produce
   any useful response to questions.")
$3.00 per year membership

Greene County Historian
138 Beecher Road
Coxsackie, NY 12051
(518) 731-1033; (518) 731-6822 (Home)
Dr. Raymond V. Beecher
Tue–Wed 10:00–2:00
(also historian of the town of Coxsackie)

Greene County Minority Historian
Box 76
Athens, NY 12015
(518) 943-7447
Charles B. Swain
("I do Civil War reenactments.")

Municipal Historians

Town of Ashland
760 North Settlement Road
Windham, NY 12496
(518) 734-3967
nyroots@aol.com
Joan Koster-Morales

Town of Athens
(16 Minerley Lane—location)
Rural Delivery 1, Box 16
Athens, NY 12015
(518) 945-1712
Edith S. Minerley
("I do not do genealogy. I am appointed by
   the Town of Athens, make reports to the
   Town Board and to the State of New York,
   and do articles for the Town Board and for
   the *Daily Mail*.")

Village of Athens
87 Second Street
Athens, NY 12015
(518) 945-1427
BJ4History@aol.com
Betty-Jean Poole

Town of Cairo
Route 4, Box 6
Cairo, NY 12413
(518) 622-2945
Robert Uzzilia

Town of Catskill
532 Cairo Junction Road
Catskill, NY 12414
(518) 943-2141
Betty D. Larsen

Village of Catskill
post vacant

Town of Coxsackie
Dr. Raymond V. Beecher (see Greene County
   Historian, above)

Village of Coxsackie
66 Mansion Street
Coxsackie, NY 12051
(518) 731-2718
Margaret A. Chaloner

Town of Durham
County Route 20
Cornwallville, NY 12418
Dan Clifton

Town of Greenville
Rural Delivery 1, Box 147
Freehold, NY 12431
(518) 634-2397
Donald B. Teator

Town of Halcott
post vacant

Town of Hunter
PO Box 129
Haines Falls, NY 12436
(518) 589-6150
Justine Hommel

Village of Hunter
post vacant

Town of Jewett
East Jewett, NY 12424
(518) 589-5228
Elwood Hitchcock

Town of Lexington
Lexington, NY 12452
(518) 989-6027
Karen Deeter

Town of New Baltimore
PO Box 137
New Baltimore, NY 12124-0137
(518) 756-9268
Dr. Clesson S. Bush

Town of Prattsville
(Washington Street—location)
PO Box 398 (mailing address)
Prattsville, NY 12468
(518) 299-3395
Muriel Pons
("Not technically a genealogist!")

Village of Tannersville
post vacant

Town of Windham
PO Box 116
Maplecrest, NY 12454-0116
(518) 734-3254
PMorrowJ@cs.com
Patricia Morrow

Greene County Historical Society
(Vedder Research Library, 90 County Route
42—location)
Rural Delivery (mailing address)
Coxsackie, NY 12051
(518) 731-1033 (Research Library); (518)
731-6490 (Bronck House Museum); (518)
731-6822
Raymond V. Beecher, Librarian
Tue–Wed 10:00–4:00, first Sat 9:00–noon
Pub. *Quarterly Journal*
(extensive genealogical holdings for Greene
County; now housing Surrogate Court
records)
$15.00 per year membership; research:
$25.00

**Greenlawn-Centerport Historical
Association and Museum**
Harborfields Public Library
(31 Broadway—location)
PO Box 354 (mailing address)
Greenlawn, NY 11740
(631) 754-1180 (Library)
GCHA-Info@usa.net

http://gcha.suffolk.lib.ny.us/links.htm
Michelle Chiarappa, Executive Director

Groton Historical Association
(168 Main Street—location)
PO Box 142 (mailing address)
Groton, NY 13073
(607) 898-5198; (607) 898-5787
Dr. Lucille S. Baker
Museum: Sat 10:00–2:00
Pub. *Newsletter*

Guilderland Historical Society
162 Main Street
Guilderland Center, NY 12085
(518) 861-8071

Guilford Historical Society
PO Box 201
Guilford, NY 13780
(607) 895-6532
tgray@mkl.com
http://www.mkl/guilford
Thomas Gray, Guilford Town Historian
by appointment only
$10.00 per year membership; research:
$30.00

The Half-Shire Historical Society
(North Main Street—location)
PO Box 73 (mailing address)
Richland, NY 13144
(315) 298-2986
George O. Widrig, President

Hamburg Historical Society
(address withheld upon request)
(museum only, no genealogical services)

Hamilton County Historian
County White House, Route 8
Lake Pleasant, NY 12108
(518) 548-5526
Paul Wilbur

Municipal Historians

Town of Arietta
Piseco Lake Historical Society
Old Piseco Road
Piseco, NY 12139
Julia Damkoehler

Town of Benson
PO Box 2078
Northville, NY 12134
(518) 863-6135
Daniel J. Meed
by appointment

Town of Hope
HC 1, Box 64
Northville, NY 12134-9543
(518) 924-2498
Clara Sue King
(records destroyed before 1900)

Town of Indian Lake
36 West Main Street
Indian Lake, NY 12842-1503
(518) 648-5377
bandb@telenet.net
http://members.tripod.com/b.zullo (A
History)
William Zullo
by appointment

Town of Inlet
(South Shore Road—location)
PO Box 298 (mailing address)
Inlet, NY 13360
Mrs. Peter Kallil

Town of Lake Pleasant
HC 1, Box 11
Lake Pleasant, NY 12108-9701
Ernest D. Virgil

Town of Long Lake
PO Box 187
Long Lake, NY 12847
(518) 624-3077
Jeanne F. Plumley
by appointment

Town of Morehouse
Route 8, Box 1
Hoffmeister, NY 13353
(315) 826-7109
BearPath@ntcnet.com
Carol A. Ford

Village of Speculator
post vacant

Town of Wells
PO Box 97
Wells, NY 12190
(518) 924-2535
Leona Aird
by appointment

Hamlin Historical Society
731 Walker-Lake Ontario Road
Hilton, NY 14468
(716) 964-2101 (Home)
Mary E. Smith, Town Historian

Hancock-Chehocton Historical Association
61 Wheeler Street
Hancock, NY 13783
Pat Green, President
Mon 1:00–3:00, and by appointment
Pub. *Point Mountain Press*, biannually
(limited to town of Hancock)
$5.00 per year membership; research:
donation, plus 15¢ per copy

Hannibal Historical Society
(Hannibal Community Center, 162 Oswego
Street—location)
PO Box 150 (mailing address)
Hannibal, NY 13074
(315) 564-5471; (315) 564-6232 (Home)
http://www.rootsweb.com/~nyoswego/
towns/hannibal (Town and Village
Historian, Lowell Newvine, as well as the
Hannibal Historical Society)
Virginia Davenport, Historian
by appointment; meetings: fourth Mon 7:00
$3.00 per year membership (to Lowell
Newvine, Vice President and Membership
Chairman)

Harmony Historical Society
(Blockville, NY 14710—location)
PO Box 127 (mailing address)
Ashville, NY 14710
(716) 782-3074
by appointment

Harrison Historical Society
(1 Park Lane, West Harrison, NY
10604—location)
PO Box 1696 (mailing address)
Harrison, NY 10528
(914) 948-2550
Barbara J. Specht, Assistant to Historian
Wed 9:00–3:30, and by appointment

Harrisville/Bonaparte History Association
8286 High Street
Harrisville, NY 13648
(315) 543-2987
Gladys Van Wyck, Harrisville Village

Historian

Hastings Historical Society
407 Broadway
Hastings-on-Hudson, NY 10706
(914) 478-2249
Mary Allison, Archivist
Mon 10:00–1:00, Thur 10:00–2:00
Pub. *Hastings Historian*, quarterly
$15.00 per year membership; unable to
supply genealogical research and doesn't
publish anything of a genealogical nature

Hempstead Village Historical Society
Hempstead Public Library
115 Nichols Court
Hempstead, NY 11550
(516) 481-6990 (Library)
hempstead@nassaulibrary.org
http://www.nassaulibrary.org/hempstd
Timothy Mulhearn

Henderson Historical Society
PO Box 322
Henderson, NY 13650
(315) 938-7163; (315) 938-7169 (Henderson
Free Library)
Eric Anderson
Mon & Wed 1:00–5:00 & 7:00–9:00, Sat
9:00–1:00

Herkimer County Historian
318 Margaret Street
Herkimer, NY 13350
James M. Greiner
(also historian of the town of Herkimer)

Municipal Historians

Village of Cold Brook
post vacant

Town of Columbia
597 Millers Mills
West Winfield, NY 13491
Doris Huxtable

Town of Danube
428 Dillenback Road
Little Falls, NY 13365
Linda Welden

Village of Dolgeville
post vacant

Town of Fairfield
PO Box 1
Middleville, NY 13406
JDieffenba@aol.com
Jane Dieffenbacher

Town of Frankfort
337 Second Avenue
Frankfort, NY 13340
Gina Bellino

Village of Frankfort
247 West Main Street
Frankfort, NY 13340
Vivian Sgroi

Town of Herkimer
James Greiner (see Herkimer County
Historian, above)

Village of Herkimer
post vacant

Village of Ilion
PO Box 360
Ilion, NY 13357-0360
George Hildebrant

Town of Litchfield
431 Albany Street
West Winfield, NY 13491
Elizabeth Ledda
("Historical programs for schools and
organizations.")

City of Little Falls
78 Moreland Street
Little Falls, NY 13365
Edwin J. Vogt

Town of Little Falls
211 Top Notch Road
Little Falls, NY 13365
Joan Cotton

Town of Manheim
18½ Howard Street
Dolgeville, NY 13329
(315) 429-3380
sperkins@dreamscape.com
Susan R. Perkins

Village of Middleville
post vacant

Village of Mohawk
6 Marshall Street
Mohawk, NY 13407
Lillian Gaherty

Town of Newport
Newport Historical Center
7435 Main Street
Newport, NY 13416
(315) 845-8434
Muriel Fenner; Patricia McKerrow
Mon, Wed & Fri 1:00–4:00

Village of Newport
PO Box 237
Newport, NY 13416
Margery Foss

Town of Norway
271 Snyder Road
Newport, NY 13416
Elizabeth Agne

Town of Ohio
HCR
Cold Brook, NY 13324
Marion Williams

Village of Poland
8916 Main Street
Poland, NY 13431
Paula Johnson
(also historian of the town of Russia)

Town of Russia
Paula Johnson (see Village of Poland, above)

Town of Salisbury
PO Box 241
Salisbury Center, NY 13454
Ann Schuyler

Town of Schuyler
Rural Delivery 3, McGowan Road
Frankfort, NY 13340
Betty Currier

Town of Stark
443 Hoke Road
Fort Plain, NY 13339
Chris Young

Town of Warren
929 Rock Hill Road
Mohawk, NY 13407

Garry Aney

Town of Webb
Town of Webb Historical Association
(Goodsell Museum, Corner of Gilbert and
Main Streets—location)
PO Box 513 (mailing address)
Old Forge, NY 13420
(315) 369-3838
historian@masterpieces.com;
director@webbhistory.org
http://www.webbhistory.org
Peg Masters, Historian; Gail Murray,
Director
Tue, Thur & Sat 10:00–2:00, and by
appointment
$10.00 per year membership

Town of Winfield
Rural Delivery 2, Route 20
West Winfield, NY 13491
Steven Davis

Herkimer County Historical Society
400 North Main Street
Herkimer, NY 13350
(315) 866-6413
herkimerhistory@yahoo.com
http://www.rootsweb.com/~nyhchs
Susan R. Perkins, Administrative Director
Pub. *Herkimer County Historical Crier*, six
times per year
$25.00 per year membership; admission:
$5.00 for nonmembers

Hicksville Historical Society
PO Box 443
Hicksville NY 11802
(516) 931-1417
Richard Evers, President

Town of Highlands Historical Society
Village Hall
303 Main Street
Highland Falls, NY 10928
(845) 446-0400 voice & FAX
sbailey@bestweb.net
http://highlandshistory.org
Stella Bailey, President
Mon–Fri 9:00–noon
Pub. *Newsletter*, two times per year, free
("Genealogy has become very popular in our
local community.")

Historical Society
33950 County Route 4
Clayton, NY 13624
(315) 686-5794
Norman Wagner

Town of Holland Historical Society
PO Box 95
Holland, NY 14080
(716) 537-2591

Holland Purchase Historical Society
Holland Land Office Museum
131 West Main Street
Batavia, NY 14020-2021
(716) 343-4727
info@hollandlandoffice.com

**Village of Honeoye Falls/Town of Mendon
Historical Society**
(1 Allen Park Drive—location)
50 East Street (mailing address)
Honeoye Falls, NY 14472
(716) 624-3810

Hoosick Township Historical Society
Louis Miller Museum
(166 Main Street—location)

PO Box 336 (mailing address)
Hoosick Falls, NY 12090
(518) 686-4682
Edith Beaumont, Museum Director; George
    Peer, HTHS President
Tue 1:00–4:00
(local history records; staffed completely by
    volunteers)

Hopkinton Historical Group
Hopkinton, NY 12965
(315) 328-4684
Margaret Zahler, President
Sun 1:00–3:00 and by appointment;
    July–Sept: afternoons

**Horseheads Cultural Center and Historical
Society, Inc.**
Zim Center
Horseheads, NY 14845
(607) 739-3938

**Horseheads Historical Society and
Museum**
Old Pennsy Railroad Depot
PO Box 194
Horseheads, NY 14845
(607) 739-3938
Nadine Myers Ferraioli, President
Mon–Fri 10:00–1:00
Pub. *HHSM Newsletter*, four times per year
(village history [formerly named Fairport and
    North Elmira], Chemung Canal history,
    Indian collection, and cartoonist Eugene
    "Zim" Zimmerman)
$3.00 per year membership; research:
    postage and donation for nonprofessional
    help

Hudson Mohawk Industrial Gateway
Foot of Polk Street
Troy, NY 12180

Huntington Historical Society
Resource Center and Archives
209 Main Street
Huntington, NY 11743
(631) 427-7064; (631) 427-7056 FAX
http://www.huntingtonli.org/hunthistorical
Irene Sniffin, Library Registrar
Tue–Fri 1:00–4:00 (subject to change)
Pub. *The New Portico*, monthly
(emphasis on Huntington and Long Island
    history and genealogy)
$25.00 per year membership

Hurley Heritage Society
(52 Main Street—location)
PO Box 1661 (mailing address)
Hurley, NY 12443
(845) 338-1661
http://www.HurleyHeritageSociety.org
Shirley Rifenburg, President
May–Nov: Sat 10:00–4:00, Sun 1:00–4:00
Pub. *Prologue*, five times per year
$10.00 per year membership

Hyde Park Historical Association
PO Box 235
Hyde Park, NY 12538
(845) 229-9115

Hyde Park Historical Society
Vanderbilt Mansion
(Route 9—location)
PO Box 182 (mailing address)
Hyde Park, NY 12538
(845) 229-8438

Interlaken Historical Society
(Main Street—location)
PO Box 270 (mailing address)

Interlaken, NY 14847
(607) 532-8505
http://www.museumsusa.org/data/
    museums/NY/23748.htm
Mary C. Willers, President
Tue–Thur 2:30–5:00 & 7:00–8:30, Sat
    10:00–1:00
Pub. *Between the Lakes*, quarterly
$5.00 per year membership

Irondequoit Historical Office and Museum
877 Helendale Road
Rochester, NY 14609
Robert Gustafson

Irvington Historical Society
(1 Bridge Street, Suite 97—location)
PO Box 23 (mailing address)
Irvington, NY 10533
(914) 591-0703
Peter Oley, Village Historian
by appointment
Pub. *The Roost*, three times per year
$10.00–$100.00 per year membership

Ischua Valley Historical Society
9 Pine Street
Franklinville, NY 14737
Gertrude H. Schnell, President (Miner's
    Cabin)
Memorial Day–Labor Day: Sun 2:00–5:00,
    and by appointment
Pub. *Newsletter*, quarterly
(local history, artifacts, genealogy)
$5.00 per year membership

Islip Hamlet Historical Society
PO Box 601
Islip, NY 11751
Susan Meringolo, Corresponding Secretary

Roeliff Jansen Historical Society
(Route 344—location)
PO Box 172 (mailing address)
Copake Falls, NY 12517
(518) 329-2376
Elinor Mettler, Museum Director
last weekend in June–first weekend in Sept
    or Columbus Day: Sat–Sun 2:00–4:00
("Do not have genealogist collection as such,
    but names in other archives.")

Jefferson County Historian
659 Bronson Street
Watertown, NY 13601
(315) 785-3144
Laura Lynne Scharer

Municipal Historians

Town of Adams
11911 U.S. Route 11
Adams Center, NY 13606
(315) 232-2232
Mrs. John Herse

Village of Adams
10 East Church Street
Adams, NY 13605
Charles Clark

**Town of Alexandria and Village of
Alexandria Bay**
46372 Goose Bay Road
Alexandria Bay, NY 13607
(315) 482-2907
Hazel S. McMane
8:30–noon & 1:30–4:00

Town of Antwerp
34542 County Route 22
Theresa, NY 13691

(315) 287-2293
Nancy Raymon
by appointment

Village of Antwerp
c/o Nora Geer, Village Clerk
Village Office
PO Box 292
Antwerp, NY 13608
(315) 659-8581
Mike Lamont

Village of Black River
112 Maple Street
Black River, NY 13612
(315) 773-5619
Joanne Russell

Town of Brownville
(16431 Star School House Road—location)
PO Box 89 (mailing address)
Dexter, NY 13634-3006
(315) 639-6266; (315) 639-3951
townbr@tds.net
June McCartin, Town Clerk
Mon–Fri noon–5:00

Village of Brownville
116 East Main Street
Brownville, NY 13615
(315) 782-4508
Gerald Hoard

Town of Cape Vincent
31564 Burnt Rock Road
Cape Vincent, NY 13618
(315) 654-2898
Peter Margray

Village of Cape Vincent
175 North James Street
Cape Vincent, NY 13618
(315) 654-4400
Jeanne Thompson

Village of Carthage
Carthage Free Library
Heritage Room
412 Budd Street
Carthage, NY 13619
(315) 493-2620; (315) 493-0406 (Home)
carthage@northnet.org
Laura Prievo
(also historian of the town of Wilna)

Town of Champion
10 North Broad Street
Carthage, NY 13619
(315) 493-3675
Suzanne Wiley
(also historian of the village of Deferiet)

Village of Chaumont
PO Box 367
Chaumont, NY 13622
Charles Dunham

Town of Clayton and Village of Clayton
405 Riverside Drive
Clayton, NY 13624
(315) 686-5794
Norman Wagner

Village of Deferiet
Suzanne Wiley (see Town of Champion,
    above)

Village of Dexter
(417 Liberty Street—location)
PO Box 145 (mailing address)
Dexter, NY 13634
(315) 639-6977

Pamela Kostyk

Town of Ellisburg and Village of Ellisburg
PO Box 82
Belleville, NY 13611
Marlene M. Hunter

Village of Evan Mills
post vacant

Village of Glen Park
post vacant

Town of Henderson
PO Box 40
Henderson, NY 13650
(315) 938-5183 (Home)
Eric Anderson

Village of Herrings
post vacant

Town of Hounsfield
310 General Smith Drive
Sackets Harbor, NY 13685
Mrs. G. Stanley Smith

Town of Leray
PO Box 321
Evans Mills, NY 13637
(315) 629-4914
John Burks
anytime

Town of Lorraine
(County Route 93—location)
PO Box 66 (mailing address)
Lorraine, NY 13659
(315) 232-2707
Arlene Moore

Town of Lyme
28589 Empie Road
Three Mile Bay, NY 13693
(315) 649-5452
Julia Gosier

Village of Mannsville
952 Douglas Street
Mannsville, NY 13661
F. H. Clark

Town of Orleans
Municipal Building
Sunrise Avenue
La Fargeville, NY 13656
(315) 658-4774
Bonita H. Shafer

Town of Pamelia
32272 County Route 15
Evans Mills, NY 13637
(315) 629-4635
Dori Kaleproth

Town of Philadelphia and Village of Philadelphia
(5 Aldrich Street—location)
PO Box 46 (mailing address)
Philadelphia, NY 13673
(315) 642-5502
Gwendolyn Acheson

Town of Rodman
Rodman, NY 13682
Dorothy Thomas

Town of Rutland
28411 State Route 126
Black River, NY 13612
(315) 788-3440
Gayle Reilly

Village of Rutland
post vacant

Village of Sackets Harbor
106 Hounsfield
Sackets Harbor, NY 13685
(315) 646-2155
Jean Derouin

Village of Stone Mills
Route 1, Box 240
Lafargeville, NY 13656
Rose Cullen

Town of Theresa and Village of Theresa
126 Morgan Street
Theresa, NY 13691
(315) 628-5429
Larry Honeywell

City of Watertown
Municipal Building, Room 101
Watertown, NY 13601
(315) 785-7769; 785-7780 (City Clerk's
    Office for appointment); (315) 785-7796
    FAX
ddutton@watertown-ny.com
http://citywatertown.org
Donna M. Dutton
1:00–4:00, and by appointment

Town of Watertown
post vacant

Village of West Carthage
West Carthage Village Archives
High Street
West Carthage, NY 13619
http://Sand-Tech.com
René LaPlante, RMO; Harold I. Sanderson,
    Historian/Archivist
informal, 4 hours per month, at the discretion
    of the historian
("Records are still being assessed and placed
    in the data base.")

Town of Wilna
Laura Prievo (see Village of Carthage,
    above)

Town of Worth
24530 Macklen Road
Lorraine, NY 13659-3150
(315) 232-4674
Bernard Macklen

Jefferson County Historical Society
228 Washington Street
Watertown, NY 13601
(315) 782-3491; (315) 782-2913 FAX
Elise D. Chan, Curator of Collections; Fred
    Rollins, Director
Tue–Fri 10:00–5:00, Sat (May–Nov)
    noon–5:00
Pub. *Bulletin of the Jefferson County
    Historical Society*, two times per year
$20.00 per year membership; no genealogical
    research services, all inquiries referred to
    the Genealogical Committee of Roswell P.
    Flower Memorial Library

Johnstown Historical Society
17 North William Street
Johnstown, NY 12095
(518) 762-7076

Jordan Historical Society and Museum
PO Box 622
Jordan, NY 13080

Kanestio Historical Society
21 Main Street

Canisteo, NY 14823
gdickey@infoblvd.net
George Dickey, Canisteo Town Historian

Kent Historical Society
PO Box 123
Carmel, NY 10512
(845) 225-4882
Joyce Morin, President
by appointment
(Kent census figures, Sybil Ludington File)
$10.00 per year membership

Kings County Historian
70 Remsen St. #6F
Brooklyn, NY 11204
http://webhost.brooklyn.lib.ny.us/world/
    manbeck.htm
John Manbeck
(Brooklyn Borough)

Kingsborough Historical Society
2001 Oriental Boulevard
Brooklyn, NY 11235
(718) 934-3122

Klyne-Esopus Historical Society/Museum
(Route 9W—location)
PO Box 180 (mailing address)
Ulster Park, NY 12487
(845) 338-8109
http://www.KlyneEsopus.org
Memorial Day weekend–30 June: Fri–Sun
    1:00–3:00; 1 July–7 Dec: Mon–Tue &
    Fri–Sun 1:00–4:00
Pub. *Newsletter*

Knickerbocker Historical Society, Inc.
(166 Knickerbocker Road—location)
PO Box 29 (mailing address)
Schaghticoke, NY 12154
(518) 677-3807
iseman7@aol.com
Stana Iseman, Project Director
12 July–24 Aug: Sun 11:00–3:00 and warm
    weather months by appointment
Pub. *Knickerbocker Mansion Newsletter*,
    quarterly; *The Knickerbocker*
    (genealogical newsletter), two times per
    year, $10.00 per year subscription
$10.00 per year membership (includes
    Knickerbocker Mansion Newsletter only)

Knox Historical Society
(Berne-Altamont Road, next to Fire
Department—location)
PO Box 11 (mailing address)
Knox, NY 12107-0011
(518) 872-2137; (518) 872-2551 (Town
    Hall)
Frieda Saddlemire, Town Historian; Virginia
    Quay, Treasurer
June–Sept: Sun 1:00–4:00, and by
    appointment
(ledgers, journals, church records, census
    information)
$2.00 per year membership; research:
    $5.00–$10.00 donation

Kuyahoora Valley Historical Society
Newport Historical Center
7435 Main Street
Newport, NY 13416
(315) 845-8434
Mary Ann Evans, Trustee; Muriel Fenner,
    Trustee; Patricia McKerrow
Mon, Wed & Fri 1:00–4:00
(Newport, Norway, Russia, Fairfield, and
    Ohio townships)
$5.00 per year membership

Lackawanna Area Historical Association

PO Box 64
Lackawanna, NY 14218

LaGrange Historical Society
PO Box 412
LaGrange, NY 12540

Lake George Historical Association
(Canada Street—location)
PO Box 472 (mailing address)
Lake George, NY 12845
(518) 668-5044
Margaret McClure, Administrator
by appointment
("LGHA is housed in and administers the Old
Court House Museum in Lake George."
Also bookstore.)

Lake Placid-North Elba Historical Society
Box 189
Lake Placid, NY 12946
(518) 523-1608
Laura Viscome
Museum: Tue–Sat (June–Sept) noon–4:00

**Lake Ronkonkoma Historical
Society/Museum**
(328 Hawking Avenue—location)
PO Box 716 (mailing address)
Lake Ronkonkoma, NY 11779
(631) 467-3152
Marjorie Raynor, President

Lancaster New York Historical Society
40 Clark Street
Lancaster, NY 14086
(716) 681-7719
http://intotem.buffnet.net/lancasterpast/
society
Ben Maryniak, President
Sun 2:00–5:00, and by appointment
Pub. *The Lancaster Legend*, monthly
$12.00 per year membership

Lansing Historical Association
PO Box 100
Lansing, NY 14882-0100
http://www.lightlink.com/dagra/lanhist/
join.htm
Pub. *Newsletter*

Lansingburgh Historical Society
(2 114th Street—location)
PO Box 219 (mailing address)
Lansingburgh, NY 12182
Alvin Thorne, Jr., President
by appointment only
(extensive manuscript collection)
$5.00 per year membership

Larchmont Historical Society
Mamaroneck Town Center
740 West Boston Post Road
Mamaroneck, NY 10543
(914) 381-2239
LHS@savvy.net
http://members.savvy.net/~lhs
Bruce R. Allen, Archivist
Mon & Thur 9:00–2:00, Tue 9:00–4:00
Pub. *Gazebo Gazette*, monthly
$10.00 per year membership

LeRoy Historical Society
23 East Main Street
LeRoy, NY 14482-1209
(716) 343-6699 (Appointments); (716) 768-
7433 (Village Historian)
Lynne Belluscio, Director/Curator and
Village Historian
Tue–Fri 10:00–4:00, Sun (Mar–Dec)
2:00–4:00, and by appointment

Levittown Historical Society
(Museum in School Building, Levittown
Education Center, Abbey Lane—location)
PO Box 57 (mailing address)
Levittown, NY 11756
(516) 735-9060
pollydwyer@aol.com
http://www.Levittownhistoricalsociety.org
Polly Dwyer, President
Wed 2:30–4:30, Fri 7:00–9:00
Pub. *Levittimes*, monthly
("We preserve Levitt and Sons, Levittown,
New York, house, memorabilia, and past
history.")
$7.00 per year membership

Lewis County Historian
(7552 South State Street—location)
PO Box 446 (mailing address)
Lowville, NY 13367
(315) 376-2825
lcho@northnet.org
http://web.northnet.org/lewiscountyhistorian
Lisa Becker
Wed (year round) & Tue–Fri (1 June–mid-
Oct) 10:00–3:00
25¢ per copy, no research charge

Municipal Historians

Village of Castorland
post vacant

Village of Constableville
3074 North Main Street
Constableville, NY 13325
(315) 397-2353
Ann M. McConnell
(also historian of the town of West Turin)

Village of Copenhagen
PO Box 201
Copenhagen, NY 13626
(315) 688-2973
Mary E. Boulio
Tue & Thur, or by appointment
(also historian of the town of Denmark)

Town of Croghan
(address withheld upon request)
(Primarily historical: "Genealogy is not part
of a local historian's job description.")

Town of Denmark
Mary E. Boulio (see Village of Copenhagen,
above)

Town of Diana
PO Box 216
Harrisville, NY 13648
(315) 543-2979
Ross Young

Town of Greig
PO Box 87
Greig, NY 13345
(315) 348-8016
Randy E. Kerr

Town of Harrisburg
Route 1, Box 65
Lowville, NY 13367
(315) 376-7095
Madeline Bernat

Village of Harrisville
8286 High Street
Harrisville, NY 13648
(315) 543-2987
Gladys Van Wyck

Town of Lewis

PO Box 123
West Leyden, NY 13489
(315) 942-4194
Rita Higby

Town of Leyden
PO Box 29
Port Leyden, NY 13433
(315) 348-6264
Sally Riley

Town of Lowville and Village of Lowville
7641 Collins Street
Lowville, NY 13367
(315) 376-2437
George R. Davis
by appointment

Village of Lyons Falls
7338 McAlpine Street
Lyons Falls, NY 13368
(315) 348-8216
Mary H. Teal
Mon–Sat

Town of Lyonsdale
Rural Delivery 1, Box 172
Port Leyden, NY 13433
(315) 942-4107
Dorothy O'Brien
by appointment

Town of Martinsburg
Rural Delivery 2, Box 135
Lowville, NY 13367
(315) 376-6805
Loretta M. Alexander
by appointment

Town of Montague
post vacant

Town of New Bremen
Rural Delivery 1, Box 86
Castorland, NY 13620
(315) 376-3356
Frederick J. Schneider
by appointment

Town of Osceola
Rural Route 3, Box 223
Camden, NY 13316
(315) 599-7396
Mary Munz
by appointment

Town of Pinckney
Rural Route 1, Box 118E1
Copenhagen, NY 13626
(315) 688-2957
Susan Townsend

Village of Port Leyden
(Port Leyden Museum, Lincoln and Main
Street—location)
c/o Sunset Nursing Home, 232 Academy
Street (mailing address)
Boonville, NY 13309-1397
(315) 348-6190
Alfred and Erna Ward
by appointment

Town of Turin
(Route 26, house # 4116, Village of Turin,
South State Street—location)
PO Box 147 (mailing address)
Turin, NY 13473
(315) 348-8507
Shirley Joslin
by appointment

Village of Turin

South State Street
Turin, NY 13473
(315) 348-8006
Mark Paczkowski

Town of Watson
PO Box 2
Lowville, NY 13367
(315) 376-3920
Charles Bunke

Town of West Turin
Ann M. McConnell (see Village of
    Constableville, above)

Lewis County Historical Society
(7552 South State Street—location)
PO Box 446 (mailing address)
Lowville, NY 13367
(315) 376-2825
lcho@northnet.org
Lisa Becker, Executive Director and Lewis
    County Historian
Mid-May to 15 Oct: 10:00–4:00
Pub. *Artifacts*, quarterly; *Lewis County
    Historical Society Journal*, annually
$5.00 per year membership

**Historical Association and Society of
Lewiston**
(Plain and Niagara Streets—location)
PO Box 43 (mailing address)
Lewiston, NY 14092
(716) 754-4214
Dorothy Cunningham, Acting Curator
Office: Wed 1:00–4:00; Museum: Wed–Sun
    (June–Aug) 1:00–4:00
Pub. *Historic Lewiston*, monthly
(Town and Village of Lewiston includes
    Sanborn, Dickersonville and part of Pekin)
$10.00 per year membership

Town of Lexington Historical Society
PO Box 247
Lexington, NY 12452
Karen Deeter, Town Historian

Lima Historical Society
(1850 Rochester Street—location)
PO Box 532 (mailing address)
Lima, NY 14485
(716) 263-2700; (716) 624-2595
Kathryn Grover, President

Lindenhurst Historical Society
Old Village Hall Museum
(215 South Wellwood Avenue—location)
PO Box 296 (mailing address)
Lindenhurst, NY 11757
(631) 957-4385
info@villageoflindenhurst.com
http://www.villageoflindenhurst.com/
    old_village_hall_museum.htm (village)
Evelyn Ellis, Village Historian
winter (1 Oct–31 May): Wed, Fri–Sat & first
    Sun 2:00–4:00; summer (1 June–30 Sept):
    Mon, Wed & Fri

Little Falls Historical Society Museum
319 South Ann Street
Little Falls, NY 13365-1362
(315) 823-0643; (315) 823-3381 (President)
http://littlefallsny.com/museum/museum.htm
Esther M. Brown, President
Tud, Thur & Sat, and by appointment
$10.00 per year membership

Little Nine Partners
The Historical Society
PO Box 243
Pine Plains, NY 12567

Little Red Schoolhouse Historical Society
PO Box 25
Coeymans Hollow, NY 12046
(518) 756-2562; (518) 756-8166
Alice Christiana, Historian
Sun (Sept–Oct) 2:00–5:00

Livingston County Historian
Historian's Office
5 Murray Hill Drive
Mount Morris, NY 14510
(585) 243-7955
historian@co.livingston.ny.us
Amie Alden
(primarily historical; "The purpose of this
    office is not genealogy.")

Municipal Historians

Town of Avon
71 Dooer Avenue
Avon, NY 14414
(716) 226-8559
Maureen Kingston

Village of Avon
post vacant

**Town of Caledonia and Village of
Caledonia**
Caledonia Town Hall
Main Street
Caledonia, NY 14423
Esther M. Hayward

Town of Conesus
PO Box 53
Conesus, NY 14435
(716) 346-2273
Joy Perovich

Town of Geneseo and Village of Geneseo
119 Main Street
Geneseo, NY 14454
David W. Parish
Mon–Fri 1:00–5:00
Pub. *Index to Geneseo Residents, 1821-
    2000*, irregularly
research: fee depending on time

Town of Groveland
6732 Groveland Hill Road
Groveland, NY 14462
Larry Turner

Village of Hemlock
bejim1@yahoo.com
B. J. Ebersold

Town of Leicester and Village of Leicester
PO Box 266
Leicester, NY 14481
(716) 382-3234
Tom Roffe

Town of Lima and Village of Lima
7411 College Street
Lima, NY 14485
(716) 624-4116
Joyce Rapp

Town of Livonia and Village of Livonia
3476 Pebble Beach Road
Lakeville, NY 14480
(716) 346-2370
Dorothy Meyer Wilkins

**Town of Mount Morris and Village of
Mount Morris**
55 Murray Street
Mount Morris, NY 14510
(716) 658-3665; (716) 658-3289

Historian@nscnet.net
Nick LoVerde

Town of North Dansville
14 Clara Barton Street
Dansville, NY 14437
(716) 335-2330; (716) 335-6587 (Home)
Quentin Masolotte
by appointment

Town of Nunda and Village of Nunda
Nunda Town Hall
Mill Street
Nunda, NY 14517-0699
Valerie Griffing

Town of Ossian
10731 Scott Hill Road
Dansville, NY 14437
Grover Keough

Town of Portage
1283 Thompson Road
Hunt, NY 14846
(716) 468-2627
Mary Ransom

Town of Sparta
(Route 256—location)
PO Box 378 (mailing address)
Dansville, NY 14437
(716) 335-6323
Lmarks3340@aol.com
Mary Jo Marks

Town of Springwater
PO Box 85
Springwater, NY 14560-0085
(716) 669-2127
Havilah Toland

Town of West Sparta
5093 Coffee Hill Road
Dansville, NY 14437
(716) 335-6305
David L. Palmer

Town of York
2246 Main Street
Piffard, NY 14533
(716) 243-3111
Margaret Copeland

Livingston County Historical Society
30 Center Street
Geneseo, NY 14454-1204
(716) 243-9147; (716) 243-2281 (to schedule
    tours)
morgandj@netacc.net
http://www.livingstoncountyhistorical
    society.org
Douglas Morgan, Webmaster
Tue (July–Aug) 2:00–5:00, Thur & Sun
    2:00–5:00
Pub. *Newsletter*, quarterly

**Livonia Area Preservation and Historical
Society**
(10 Commercial Street—location)
PO Box 155 (mailing address)
Livonia, NY 14487-0155
(585) 346-4579
laphs@localnet.com
http://www.lovoniahistory.org
Sarah Booher, President; Richard Brown,
    Vice President; Amy Hapeman, Curator
Fri–Sat 10:00–2:00
Pub. *Gazette News*, quarterly
("The records we do have are mainly from the
    Livonia Gazette, from 1875–1965 [other
    documents prior to that time are hard to
    come by, due to fires]; we also have books,

photographs, artifacts and maps of the Livonia area. People looking for marriage and death certificates and other genealogy records should contact Dorothy Meyer Wilkins, Town Historian.")
$10.00 per year membership; admission: donation

Lloyd Harbor Historical Society
Henry Lloyd House-Museum
Lloyd Harbor Road
Lloyd Harbor, NY 11743
(631) 424-6110; (631) 673-5476
Ceil Stepanian, Education Director

Lloyd Historical Society
38-A Bellevue Road
Highland, NY 12528
(845) 691-2145

Locke History Explorers
(Locke Town Hall—location)
4941 Harris Hill Road (mailing address)
Locke, NY 13092
(315) 497-0537
Esther Thornton, Historian
by appointment

Locust Valley Historical Society
Locust Valley Library
170 Buckram Road
Locust Valley, NY 11560
(516) 676-1837 (Library); (516) 676-8164 FAX (Library)
Helen Simons, President
Library: Mon–Thur 10:00–9:00, Fri–Sat 10:00–5:00
(local history)
$10.00 per year membership

Lodi Historical Society
(South Main Street, Route 414—location)
PO Box 279 (mailing address)
Lodi, NY 14860
(607) 582-6016
Harry H. Curtin, President
hours: various
$5.00 per year membership

Long Beach Historical Society
Long Beach City Hall
1 West Chester Street
Long Beach, NY 11561
(516) 432-1192
Alexandra Karafinas

Lower Hudson Conference of Historical Agencies and Museums
2199 Saw Mill River Road
Elmsford, NY 10523
(914) 592-6726; (914) 592-6946 FAX
Tema Harnik, Administrative Consultant
Mon–Fri 9:30–5:00
Pub. *Guide to Museums, Historical Organizations, Local Historians . . .*, irregularly; *Newsletter*, quarterly
(museum services organization)
$30.00 per year membership

Macedon Historical Society, Inc.
(1185 Macedon Center Road—location)
PO Box 303 (mailing address)
Macedon, NY 14502
(315) 986-4845
David Taber
by appointment
Pub. *Pioneers of Macedon*
$2.00 per year membership

Macomb Historical Association
(State Route 58, Brasie Corners, NY—location)

6726 State Highway 58 (mailing address)
Hammond, NY 13646
(315) 578-2349
Eloise Emrich, Historian
summer: Wed noon–5:00

Madison County Historian
County Building, Second Floor
North Court Street
Wampsville, NY 13163
(315) 366-2453
historian@co.madison.ny.us
Deborah Harmon

Municipal Historians

Town of Brookfield
Rural Delivery 1, Box 96
West Edmeston, NY 13485
(315) 899-3348
Mrs. Donald Witter

Village of Canastota
Municipal Building
205 South Peterboro Street
Canastota, NY 13032
(315) 697-6169; (315) 697-7559
davidsadler_13043@yahoo.com
David L. Sadler
by appointment
("History-genealogy; 17,000 name Canastota, N.Y., Obituary Index 1876–1999.")
photocopies of newspaper obituary notices: $1.00 each

Town of Cazenovia
7 Albany Street
Cazenovia, NY 13035
(315) 655-9213
Peggy Ladd
Mon–Fri 2:00–4:00
("We [the town historian and the archivist of Cazenovia Public Library] are individuals and we work with our historic materials.")

Village of Cazenovia
post vacant

Village of Chittenango
131 South Berkey Drive
Chittenango, NY 13037
(315) 687-9228
Richard F. Sullivan

Town of DeRuyter
715 Division Street
DeRuyter, NY 13052
(315) 852-6450
Duane Burdick

Village of Earlville
post vacant

Town of Eaton
PO Box 2
West Eaton, NY 13484
(315) 684-3527
Tom Ciarrocchi

Town of Fenner
3350 Wyss Road
Cazenovia, NY 13035
(315) 655-2192
Gerald Davies

Town of Georgetown
398 Route 80
Georgetown, NY 13072-9103
(315) 837-4727
paegeb@citlink.net
Phyllis Evans

Town of Hamilton
21 Milford Street
Hamilton, NY 13346
(315) 824-0836
Carl Peterson

Village of Hamilton
409 Savage Farm Drive
Ithaca, NY 14850-6506
Marion Blanchard

Town of Lebanon
Rural Delivery 2, Box 49E
Earlville, NY 13332
(315) 837-4220; (315) 691-2134
Dee Keller

Town of Lenox
146 West Center Street
Canastota, NY 13032
(315) 697-9385
Carol Weimer

Town of Lincoln
PO Box 35
Clockville, NY 13043
(315) 697-9324
Sharon Snell

Town of Madison
PO Box 117
Bouckville, NY 13310
(315) 893-1812
Helen Nower

Village of Madison
post vacant

Village of Morrisville
(3 Skyline Drive—location)
PO Box 157 (mailing address)
Morrisville, NY 13408
(315) 684-3355
William Helmer

Village of Munnsville
PO Box 177
Munnsville, NY 13409
(315) 495-5395; (315) 495-6148
Olive S. Boylan
by appointment
(also historian of the town of Stockbridge)

Town of Nelson
Tainter Road
Erieville, NY 13061
(315) 662-7787
James Tainter

City of Oneida
c/o Oneida Public Library
220 Broad Street
Oneida, NY 13421
(315) 363-3050 (Library); (315) 363-2117
David Alvord

Town of Smithfield
110 Crescent Drive
Kirkwood NY 13795
(607) 775-3103
dburdick@stny.rr.com
Donna Dorrance Burdick
(note that the Town of Smithfield is in Madison County, even though the historian lives in Broome County)

Town of Stockbridge
Olive S. Boylan (see Village of Munnsville, above)

Village of Wampsville
PO Box 51

Wampsville, NY 13163
(315) 363-3086
Douglas Loucks

Madison County Historical Society
Cottage Lawn House
435 Main Street
Oneida, NY 13421-2421
(315) 363-4136
Thomas Kernan, Director
Sept–May: Mon–Fri 9:00–4:00; June–Aug:
     Tue–Sat 9:00–4:00
Pub. *Heritage*, annually, $3.00 plus tax per
     volume
$15.00 per year membership; research: $2.00
     for nonmembers

Mamaroneck Historical Society
PO Box 776
Mamaroneck, NY 10543
http://www.westchesterlibraries.org/libs/
     mamaroneck/histsoc.htm
Gloria Pritts, Village Historian; Paula Lipsett,
     Town Historian
by appointment
Pub. *Newsletter*, monthly
$15.00 per year membership; research fees
     vary

Manhattan Borough Historian
Manhattan Borough Historian's Office
Municipal Building
1 Centre Street, 19th Floor
New York, New York 10007
(212) 669-8089; (212) 669-4900 FAX
Celedonia (Cal) Jones
Thur 9:00–4:00
(New York County)

Manlius Historical Society/Museum
(109 Pleasant Street—location)
PO Box 28 (mailing address)
Manlius, NY 13104-0028
(315) 682-6660; (315) 682-3252
http://www.manliushistory.org
Juliann Tasick, Director
Mon–Thur 2 hours A.M. & 2 hours P.M.
Pub. *The Seraph*, quarterly
(Town of Manlius history)
$3.00-30.00 per year membership

Historical Society of Mannsville/Ellisburg
Mannsville Museum
110 Lilac Park Drive
Mannsville, NY 13661
(315) 465-4049; (315) 465-6375 (Secretary's
     home)
Ellen B. Miller, President of Board of
     Trustees Library/Museum; Marjorie H.
     Joyner, Secretary/Treasurer
July–Sept: Thur–Fri 1:00–4:00
(genealogical services)

Manorville Historical Society
PO Box 4
Manorville, NY 11949
(631) 878-6672
Dorothy Magnani, President

Marcellus Historical Society
(6 Slocombe—location)
PO Box 165 (mailing address)
Marcellus, NY 13108-0165
(315) 673-1765
Peg Nolan, President and Town Historian
Tue 7:00–9:00, Sun 1:00–4:00, and by
     appointment
("We have lots of research records.")
$5.00 per year membership

Marilla Historical Society
(2 Rock Road—location)
PO Box 36 (mailing address)

Marilla, NY 14102
(716) 652-7370
Museum: third Sun 2:00–4:00

Marshall Historical Society
PO Box 232
Deansboro, NY 13328
(315) 841-4473; (315) 841-3589
Dorothy McConnell, Treasurer
Tue–Thur & Sat 10:00–3:00
Pub. *Marshall Historical Newsletter*,
     monthly
("Family histories of Town of Marshall")
$5.00 per year membership

Town of Maryland Historical Association
(disbanded, collection turned over to Town
     of Maryland Historian, Otsego County)

The Historical Society of the Massapequas
(4755 Merrick Road—location)
PO Box 211 (mailing address)
Massapequa, NY 11758
(516) 799-2023
most Sun (May–Sept) 2:00–4:00
Pub. *Newsletter*, bimonthly
(Long Island; Major Thomas Jones family)
$15.00 per year membership; research: free
     help

Mattituck Historical Society
(Main Road, Route 25—location)
PO Box 320 (mailing address)
Mattituck, NY 11952
(631) 298-8089
Gertrude Koop, Vice President

Mayfield Historical Society
33 West Main Street
Mayfield, NY 12117
(518) 661-5085

Medina Historical Society
406 West Avenue
Medina, NY 14103
(585) 798-3006
Marian Perry, President

Historical Society of the Merricks
2279 South Merrick Avenue
Merrick, NY 11566
(516) 379-3476
Louis Kruh, President
Pub. *Memories of the Merricks*

Mexico Historical Society
(South Jefferson Street—location)
PO Box 331 (mailing address)
Mexico, NY 13114
(315) 963-8542
http://www.easternlakeontario.com/
     mexico/history.htm
Bonnie Shumway, Town Historian
Tue 2:00–4:00, Sat 10:00–noon, by
     appointment

Middlebury Historical Society
c/o Middlebury Academy Museum
Academy Street
Wyoming, NY 14591
(716) 495-6582 (Curator); (716) 495-6692
Marsha Morey, President

Town of Middlefield Historical Association
PO Box 348
Cooperstown, NY 13326
Evelyn Blanco, President
July–Aug: Sat, and by appointment
Pub. *Newsletter*, annually (June or late May),
     free
(photographic collection)
$3.00 per year membership

Middlesex Heritage Group
Middlesex Town Hall
PO Box 147
Middlesex, NY 14707
Carol Francisco, President
Wed & Sat 9:00–noon
Pub. *Middlesex Heritage News*, quarterly
$7.00 per year membership; research: extra

**Historical Society of Middletown and
Wallkill Precinct, Inc.**
25 East Avenue
Middletown, NY 10940
(845) 343-6498
Charles L. Radzinsky, Curator
Wed 1:00–5:00, and by appointment
Pub. *Yearbook*, annually
$10.00 per year membership

**Miller Place-Mount Sinai Historical
Society**
(1720 William Miller House, 83 North
     Country Road—location)
PO Box 651 (mailing address)
Miller Place, NY 11764
(631) 331-4943
J. Thomas Clark, Corresponding Secretary
Sun (June–Oct) 1:30–4:30, and by
     appointment

Mineola Historical Society
(211 Westbury Avenue—location)
PO Box 423 (mailing address)
Mineola, NY 11501
(516) 742-0417 (President)
Neil Young, President/Historian
(local village history)
research: $10.00 if material found, no charge
     if search is negative

Minerva Historical Society
Minerva, NY 12851
(518) 251-2146
Pub. *Minerva Historical Society Quarterly*
$5.00 per year membership

Minisink Valley Historical Society
(138 Pike Street, Second Floor—Archives
     location
131 West Main Street—Museum location)
PO Box 659 (mailing address)
Port Jervis, NY 12771-0659
(845) 856-2375; (845) 856-1649
MVHS1889@magiccarpet.com;
     peter@minisink.org
http://www.minisink.org
Peter Osborne, III, Executive Director
Thur 1:00–4:00 & 6:00–8:00
Pub. *The Mennisenk*, quarterly
$15.00 per year membership

Office of the Monroe County Historian
Rundel Library
115 South Avenue
Rochester, NY 14604
(716) 428-7375; (716) 428-7313 FAX
http://www.rrlc.org/guide/arc25.shtml
Carolyn S. Vacca
Mon–Fri 9:00–1:00, and by appointment
(no genealogical work for nonresidents of the
     county)

Municipal Historians

Town of Brighton
PO Box 260
Paul Smiths, NY 12970-0260
Mary Jo Barone

Village of Brockport
c/o Brockport Village Hall
49 State Street

Brockport, NY 14420
wandrews@frontiernet.net
http://brockportny.org
William G. Andrews, Village Historian
    Emeritus

Town of Chili
(Town-o-Chili—location)
Chili Town Hall
3235 Chili Avenue (mailing address)
Rochester, NY 14624
(716) 889-4461
Jay Widener

Village of Churchville
9 Ridgefield Drive
Churchville, NY 14428
(716) 293-3756
Ronald Balczak
(also historian of the town of Riga)

Town of Clarkson
(Town Hall, 3710 Lake Road, Clarkson, NY
14430—location)
34 Oak Drive (mailing address)
Hamlin, NY 14464
Hazel Kleinbach
a couple of hours each week, and by
    appointment

**Town of East Rochester and Village of East
Rochester**
901 Main Street
East Rochester, NY 14445
Mary Conners

Village of Fairport
182 West Church Street
Fairport, NY 14450
Matson Ewell

Town of Gates
Gates Town Hall
1605 Buffalo Road
Rochester, NY 14624
(716) 247-6100
http://www.townofgates.org
Jack Hart
Mon, Wed & Fri 9:00–noon

Town of Greece
Historical Society of Greece, N.Y.
(595 Long Pond Road, Rochester, NY
14612—location)
PO Box 16249 (mailing address)
Rochester, NY 14616
(716) 225-7221 (Historical Society)
Lorraine Beane

Town of Hamlin
731 Walker-Lake Ontario Road
Hilton, NY 14468
(716) 964-2101 (Home); (716) 964-7385
    (Office)
Mary E. Smith

Town of Henrietta
(Henrietta Town Hall, 475 Calkins Row,
Henrietta, NY 14467—location)
98 Tall Oak Lane (mailing address)
Pittsford, NY 14534
(716) 334-3860 (Home)
Helen Elam
Office: Mon 2:00–8:00
research: $10.00 per hour

Village of Hilton
Hilton Community Center
59 Henry Street
Hilton, NY 14468
(716) 392-4144
historian@hiltonny.org

Mary P. Townsend
Sept–Apr: 1:30–4:45; May–Aug:
    12:30–4:00, and by special appointment

Village of Honeoye Falls
5 East Street
Honeoye Falls, NY 14472
(585) 624-1711; (585) 624-2588 FAX
Anne Bullock
Tue–Thur 9:30–noon

Town of Irondequoit
Irondequoit Town Hall
1280 Titus Avenue
Irondequoit, NY 14617
(585) 266-0456 (Home)
Patricia Wayne

Town of Mendon
179 Plains Road
Honeoye Falls, NY 14472
(585) 624-4709
dianeham@rochester.rr.com
Diane Ham
by appointment

Town of Ogden
388 Gillette Road
Spencerport, NY 14559
(716) 352-3672 (Home)
Shirley Nixon
(also historian of the village of Spencerport)

Town of Parma
Parma Town Hall
1300 Hilton Parma Road
Hilton, NY 14468
(716) 392-1915
Shirley Cox Husted
also Robert Gustafson, Town Genealogist,
    877 Helendale Road, Rochester, NY
    14609

Town of Perinton
Perinton Town Hall
1350 Turk Hill Road
Fairport, NY 14450
(585) 223-0770, ext. 125
jkeplinger@perinton.org
http://www.perinton.org
Jean Keplinger
Tue 9:00–1:00, and by appointment

Town of Pittsford and Village of Pittsford
11 South Main Street
Pittsford, NY 14534
(716) 248-6245 (Office); (716) 586-5608
    (Home)
Audrey M. Johnson
Thur 1:00–5:30

Town of Riga
Ronald Belczak (see Village of Churchville,
    above)

City of Rochester
Rundel Library
115 South Avenue
Rochester, NY 14604
(716) 428-7340; (716) 428-6383 FAX
rrosenbe@mcls.rochester.lib.ny.us
http://www.rochester.lib.ny.us/cityhall/
    about_r/history/history.htm
Ruth Rosenberg-Naparsteck

Town of Rush
Rush Town Hall
5977 East Henrietta Road
Rush, NY 14543
David Oliver

Village of Scottsville

post vacant

Village of Spencerport
Shirley Nixon (see Town of Ogden, above)

Town of Sweden
63 Park Avenue
Brockport, NY 14420
Kathleen Goetz

Town of Webster and Village of Webster
18 Lapham Park
Webster, NY 14580
(716) 265-3939 (Home); (716) 265-3308
    (Office)
Richard Batzing

Town of Wheatland
341 South Road
Scottsville, NY 14546-9506
(585) 889-3202
Florence Field
Mon–Fri 9:00–5:00
("local history and genealogy")

**Heritage and Genealogical Society of
Montgomery County**
Old Court House
(Railroad Street—location)
PO Box 1500 (mailing address)
Fonda, NY 12068-1500
(518) 853-8186 (Montgomery County
    Department of History and Archives);
    (518) 853-8392 FAX
histarch@capital.net
Stephen Helmin, President
Montgomery County Department of History
    and Archives: Sept–June: Mon–Fri
    8:30–4:00; July–Aug: Mon–Fri 9:00–4:00
(Reprinted *Beers' History of Montgomery &
    Fulton Counties*, 1878, $43.00 ppd.
    "Friends" society to Montgomery County
    Department of History and Archives, one
    of the largest municipal genealogical and
    historical research libraries and collections
    in New York State.)

Montgomery County Historian
Old Court House
(Railroad Street—location)
PO Box 1500 (mailing address)
Fonda, NY 12068-1500
(518) 853-8187; (518) 853-8186
    (Montgomery County Department of
    History and Archives); (518) 853-8392
    FAX
histarch@superior.net
http://co.montgomery.ny.us
Kelly A. Yacobucci Farquhar
Montgomery County Department of History
    and Archives: Sept–June: Mon–Fri
    8:30–4:00; July–Aug: Mon–Fri 9:00–4:00
research: $15.00 per hour; copies: 25¢ per
    page; catalog: $12.00 postpaid

Municipal Historians

Village of Ames
PO Box 644
Ames, NY 13317-0644
(518) 673-5793
Priscilla Smith

City of Amsterdam
Rural Delivery 4, Box 76A-81
Amsterdam, NY 12010
(518) 842-0583
Dorothea N. Cooper

Town of Amsterdam
Rural Delivery, Swart Hill Road
Amsterdam, NY 12010

(518) 843-2299; (518) 843-6136
Katherine Strobeck

Town of Canajoharie
24 Wheelock Street
Canajoharie, NY 13317
(518) 673-2379
Kathleen Hanford

Village of Canajoharie
Arkell Center, Apartment 109
2 Maple Avenue
Canajoharie, NY 13317
(518) 673-3351
Helena Glenar

Town of Charleston
741 Corbin Hill Road
Esperance, NY 12066
(518) 922-5867 (Home); (518) 475-0291
   (Work)
Lorraine Whiting

Town of Florida
110 Abraham Road
Amsterdam, NY 12010
(518) 842-0719
Tim Seivers

Village of Fonda
4 Montgomery Terrace Extension
Fonda, NY 12068
(518) 853-4354; (518) 853-3031
Volkert Veeder
(also historian for the town of Mohawk)

Village of Fort Johnson
7 Young Avenue
Fort Johnson, NY 12070
(518) 842-8806
Michael D. Mahoney

Village of Fort Plain
(15 Berthoud Street—location)
PO Box 278 (mailing address)
Nelliston, NY 13410
(518) 993-3805
Sandra Cronkhite
(also historian for the town of Palatine)

Village of Fultonville and Town of Glen
21 Willett Street
Fort Plain, NY 13339-1130
David Stone

Village of Hagaman
PO Box 226
Hagaman, NY 12086
Keith Schedlbauer

Town of Minden
19 High Street
Fort Plain, NY 13339-1314
(518) 993-3258 voice & FAX
davesues@telenet.net
David Manklow

Town of Mohawk
Volkert Veeder (see Village of Fonda,
   above)

Village of Nelliston
(73 East Main Street—location)
PO Box 307 (mailing address)
Nelliston, NY 13410
(518) 993-4674
Barbara Alkinburgh

Village of Palatine Bridge
(Staley Road—location)
PO Box 433 (mailing address)
Palatine Bridge, NY 13428

(518) 673-5324
Vernon Wagner

Town of Palatine
Sandra Cronkhite (see Village of Fort Plain,
   above)

Town of Root
493 State Highway 162
Sprakers, NY 12166
(518) 673-2630
Carol Soodsma

**Town of Saint Johnsville and Village of
Saint Johnsville**
7 Center Street
Saint Johnsville, NY 13452
(518) 568-2910; (518) 568-7904
Anita Smith

Town of Moriah Historical Society
34 Park Place/Iron Center
Port Henry, NY 12974
(518) 546-7524 (Home)
http://www.porthenry.com (Town web site)
Joan Daby, Historian
("The Iron Center is a museum of our iron
   ore and railroad industry.")

Moriches Bay Historical Society
Haven's House Museum
(Montauk Highway and Chet Sweezy
Road—location)
PO Box 31 (mailing address)
Center Moriches, NY 11934
(631) 878-1776
Christopher Berdan, President

Mount Gulian Society
145 Sterling Street
Beacon, NY 12508
(845) 831-8172

Mount Morris Historical Society
Mills Mansion
(14 Main Street—location)
PO Box 94 (mailing address)
Mount Morris, NY 14510
(716) 658-3292
Terry Mistretta, President

Mount Pleasant Historical Society
1 Town Hall Plaza
Valhalla, NY 10595
(914) 838-0402 FAX
kaspenwa@1st.net
Kathryn Aspenwall, Corresponding Secretary

**Landmark and Historical Society of
Mount Vernon**
Mount Vernon Public Library
Local History Room
28 South First Avenue
Mount Vernon, NY 10550
(914) 668-1840 (Library)
Shannon E. Chandley, Library Curator
Library: Mon–Fri 9:00–1:00, and by
   appointment

**Mountain Top Historical Society of
Greene County, Inc.**
Twilight Park
Box 263
Haines Falls, NY 12436
(518) 589-5357
info@mths.org
http://www.mths.org
Justine Hommel, President

Murray-Holley Historical Society Museum
(Geddes Street Extension—location)
PO Box 346 (mailing address)

Holley, NY 14470
(585) 638-7566
Mrs. Marshal DeFilipps, Museum Director
by appointment
(local history and genealogy)
$5.00 per year membership

Nanticoke Valley Historical Society
PO Box 75
Maine, NY 13802
(607) 862-3243
Janet B. Bothwell, Curator

Naples Historical Society
PO Box 489
Naples, NY 14512

Nassau County Historian
Nassau County Museum
1864 Muttontown Road
Syosset, NY 11791
(516) 571-7605
Edward J. Smits, Director
Mon–Fri 9:00–5:00

Municipal Historians

Village of Atlantic Beach
post vacant

Village of Baxter Estates
2 Harbor Road
Port Washington, NY 11050
Joyce C. Cailor

Village of Bayville
34 School Street
Bayville, NY 11709
Gladys Mack

Village of Bellerose
10 Massachusetts Boulevard
Bellerose Village, NY 11001
Carol Mylod

Village of Brookville
Cedar Swamp Road
Brookville, NY 11545
Rosemary Ahearn

Village of Cove Neck
PO Box 299
Oyster Bay, NY 11771-0299
Frances Roosevelt

Village of East Rockaway
376 Atlantic Avenue
East Rockaway, NY 11518
Mildred Roemer

Village of East Williston
29 Orchard Drive
East Williston, NY 11596
Kathy Meyer

Village of Farmingdale
42 Sherman Road
Farmingdale, NY 11735
(516) 249-3099
William J. Johnston

Village of Flower Hill
post vacant

Village of Freeport
Municipal Building
Freeport, NY 11520
Charles Zimmerman

Village of Garden City
163 Pine Street
Garden City, NY 11530

Vincent F. Seyfried

City of Glen Cove
44 Chestnut Street
Glen Cove, NY 11542
Daniel Russell

Village of Great Neck Estates
1 Deepdale Drive
Great Neck, NY 11021
Frieda Kessler

Village of Great Neck Plaza
PO Box 440, Gussack Plaza
Great Neck, NY 11021
Polly Whitehorn

Village of Great Neck
115 Hampshire Road
Great Neck, NY 11023
Jane Martino

Town of Hempstead
Town Hall Plaza
Main Street
Hempstead, NY 11550
Tom Saltzman

Village of Hempstead
99 Nichols Court
Hempstead, NY 11550
(516) 485-5737
Bruhah@aol.com
James York
Mon–Fri 8:30–4:15

Village of Hewlett Bay Park
post vacant

Village of Hewlett Harbor
449 Pepperidge Road
Hewlett Harbor, NY 11557
Mrs. Lee Kahan

Village of Hewlett Neck
30 Piermont Avenue
Hewlett, NY 11557
Bertram Kalisher

Village of Island Park
post vacant

Village of Kensington
post vacant

Village of Kings Point
275 Kings Point Road
Kings Point, NY 11024
F. John Handler

Village of Lake Success
post vacant

Village of Lattingtown
26 Wood Lane
Locust Valley, NY 11560
William Bales

Village of Laurel Hollow
44 Saint Charles Place
South Setauket, NY 11720-4703
Mrs. William S. Smoot

Village of Lawrence
240 Causeway
Lawrence, NY 11559
Mrs. Honor MacLean

City of Long Beach
260 West Walnut Street
Long Beach, NY 11561
Edward Graff

Village of Lynbrook
28 Hart Street
Lynbrook, NY 11563
Arthur Mattson

Village of Malverne
15 Wright Avenue
Malverne, NY 11565
Jerry Janeske

Village of Manorhaven
33 Manorhaven Boulevard
Port Washington, NY 11050
Alice Peckelis

Village of Massapequa Park
287 Illinois Avenue
Massapequa Park, NY 11762
Florence Michel

Village of Matinecock
PO Box 142
Locust Valley, NY 11560
Dorothy H. McGee

Village of Mill Neck
post vacant

Village of Mineola
post vacant

Village of Munsey Park
1777 Northern Boulevard
Manhasset, NY 11030
Eileen Brennan

Village of Muttontown
post vacant

Village of New Hyde Park
1420 Lincoln Avenue
New Hyde Park, NY 11040
Florence Lisanti

Town of North Hempstead
(220 Plandome Road—location)
PO Box 3000 (mailing address)
Manhasset, NY 11030
Joan Kent

Village of North Hill
post vacant

Village of Old Brookville
post vacant

Village of Old Westbury
1 Store Hill Road
Old Westbury, NY 11568
Richard Gachot

Village of Oyster Bay Cove
174 Cove Road
Oyster Bay, NY 11771
Paula Weir

Town of Oyster Bay
Town Hall
54 Audrey Avenue
Oyster Bay, NY 11771
Dorothy H. McGee

Village of Plandome Manor
(1526 North Plandome Road, Manhasset,
NY 11030—location)
PO Box 951 (mailing address)
Plandome, NY 11030
(516) 627-7067 FAX
Carlo Manganillo
Mon–Thur 9:00–4:00

Village of Plandome

2 Middle Drive
Plandome, NY 11030
Grace Jayne

Village of Port Washington North
1 Soundview Drive
Port Washington, NY 11050
George Williams

Village of Rockville Centre
9 Park Lane
Rockville Centre, NY 11570
(516) 764-7459
Frank E. Seipp
Sat–Sun 1:00–4:00, by appointment

Village of Roslyn Estates
3 Warner Avenue
Roslyn Heights, NY 11577
Ruth Hinrichs

Village of Roslyn
91 Remsen Avenue
Roslyn, NY 11576
Elizabeth H. Moger

Village of Russel Gardens
6 Melbourne Road
Great Neck, NY 11021
Dr. William S. Grauer

Village of Saddle Rock
post vacant

Village of Sands Point
c/o Village Hall
Sands Point, NY 11050
Irgigard Carras

Village of Sea Cliff
Sea Cliff Village Hall
Sea Cliff, NY 11579
Frank O. Braynard

Village of South Floral Park
post vacant

Village of Stewart Manor
181 Fernwood Terrace
Stewart Manor, NY 11530
John Ryan

Village of Thomaston
post vacant

Village of Upper Brookville
Wolver Hollow Road
Oyster Bay, NY 11771
Clarissa Watson

Village of Valley Stream
5 Horton Road
Valley Stream, NY 11580
Jack Sharkey

Village of Westbury
post vacant

Village of Williston Park
post vacant

Village of Woodsburgh
30 Piermont Avenue
Hewlett, NY 11557
Robert Kullman

Nassau County Historical Society
PO Box 207
Garden City, NY 11530
Denward W. Collins, Jr., President
Pub. *Nassau County Historical Society
Journal*, annually

(Long Island history)
$15.00 per year membership

National Temple Hill Association, Inc.
(1042 Route 94—location)
PO Box 315 (mailing address)
Vails Gate, NY 12584
(845) 561-5073
seasonal and by appointment; July–Sept: Sun
2:00–5:00
(The American Revolution; local history)
$15.00 per year membership

New Castle Historical Society
(Horace Greeley House, 100 King
Street—location)
PO Box 55 (mailing address)
Chappaqua, NY 10514
(914) 238-4666; (914) 238-1296 FAX
newcastlehs@aol.com
http://www.newcastlehistoricalsociety.org
Betsy Towl, Executive Director
Tue & Thur 1:00–4:00, Sat noon–4:00, and
by appointment
Pub. *Newsletter*, four times per year
("Town of New Castle. Special areas:
Quakers, Horace Greeley")
$25.00 per year membership

**The New England Historic Genealogical
Society**
(see Massachusetts, Part 2)

New Hartford Historical Society
(48 Genesee Street—location)
PO Box 238 (mailing address)
New Hartford, NY 13413
(315) 735-2332; (315) 737-8216
http://www.newhartfordpubliclibrary.org/
History.html
Barbara Munde, Secretary
Pub. *Tally-ho*, eight times per year
$8.00 per year membership

New Scotland Historical Association
(7 Old New Salem Road, New Scotland, NY
12127—location)
Box 541 (mailing address)
Voorheesville, NY 12186
(518) 756-9670
Joseph Hogan, President
Museum: Sun 2:00–4:00 (except Easter);
meetings: first Tue (Oct–Dec, Feb &
Apr–May), 1st Sun (Mar)
Pub. *Sentinel*, four times per year
(published book: *New Scotland Township*)
$10.00 per year membership

New Woodstock Historical Society
New Woodstock, NY 13122

New York City Boroughs' Historians
(see Official Bronx Historian, above; Kings
County Historian [Brooklyn], above;
Manhattan Borough Historian [New York
County], above; Queens County Historian,
below; Richmond County Historian [Staten
Island], below)

Newark Valley Historical Society
(Park Street, Municipal Building, Second
Floor—location)
PO Box 222 (mailing address)
Newark Valley, NY 13811
(607) 642-9516; (607) 687-1337 FAX
Harriet Miller, Executive Director
by appointment
Pub. *Newsletter*, six times per year, plus
annual report
(New York history)
$15.00 per year membership; library
admission to members only

**Historical Society of Newburgh Bay and
the Highlands**
189 Montgomery Street
Newburgh, NY 12550
(845) 561-2585

Town of Newfane Historical Society
Van Horn Mansion
2165 Lockport Olcott Road
Burt, NY 14028

Newfield Historical Society
541 Millard Hill Road
Newfield, NY 14867
(607) 564-3310
Florence Emery, President

Newstead Historical Society
PO Box 222
Akron, NY 14001
(716) 542-4369
Arlene Richardson, President
Pub. *Newstead Historical Society Newsletter*,
four times per year
$6.00 per year membership

Niagara County Historian
Niagara County Historian's Office
Civil Defense Building
139 Niagara Street
Lockport, NY 14094-2740
(716) 439-7324
Donna May Barnes, Deputy Historian
Tue–Thur 9:00–3:00
research: $25.00 plus copies at 25¢

Municipal Historians

Village of Barker
1116 Quaker Road
Barker, NY 14012
(716) 795-3575
Lorraine G. Wagner
(also historian for the town of Somerset)

Town of Cambria
4280 Church Road
Lockport, NY 14094
(716) 434-8937; (716) 433-8829
Vernette Genter

Town of Hartland
9035 Ridge Road
Gasport, NY 14067
(716) 735-7517; (716) 735-7179
Florence Arnold

Village of Lewiston
225 North Water Street
Lewiston, NY 14092
(716) 754-8814
Paul Brucato

City of Lockport
Lockport, NY 14094
(716) 439-6293

Town of Lockport
7122 North Ledge Drive
Lockport, NY 14094
(716) 434-0207
Mary L. Newhard

**Town of Middleport and Village of
Middleport**
8 Freeman Street
Middleport, NY 14105
(716) 735-9025 (Town); (716) 735-3303
(Village)
Anna Wallace

Town of Newfane

2538 Merritt Street
Newfane, NY 14108
(716) 778-8286
Judson Heck, Sr.

City of Niagara Falls
Niagara Falls Public Library
Local History Department, Niagara Room
Earl W. Brydges Library Building
1425 Main Street
Niagara Falls, NY 14305-2574
(716) 286-4899 (Library, Local History);
(716) 286-4912 FAX (Library)
Donald E. Loker

Town of Niagara
7530 Packard Road
Niagara Falls, NY 14304
(716) 297-6601; (716) 297-2150
Dorothy Rolling

Town of Pendleton
5201 North Tonawanda Creek Road
North Tonawanda, NY 14120
(716) 692-3257
Benny Sobczyk

Town of Porter
3452 East Avenue
Youngstown, NY 14174
(716) 745-7203
Cora Gushee

Town of Royalton
8700 Slayton Settlement Road
Gasport, NY 14067
(716) 772-2974
Donald Jerge

Town of Somerset
Lorraine G. Wagner (see Village of Barker,
above)

Town of Wheatfield
2552 Nicole Drive
Niagara Falls, NY 14304
(716) 731-2584
John Forcucci

Town of Wilson and Village of Wilson
PO Box 886
Wilson, NY 14172-0886

Village of Youngstown
162 Jackson Street
Youngstown, NY 14174
(716) 745-3423; (716) 745-7721
Donald Ames

Niagara Falls Historical Society, Inc.
Niagara Falls Public Library
Local History Department, Niagara Room
Earl W. Brydges Library Building
1425 Main Street
Niagara Falls, NY 14305-2574
(716) 286-4899 (Library, Local History);
(716) 286-4912 FAX (Library)
Donald E. Loker, President
Library: Mon 9:00–9:00, Tue–Fri 9:00–5:00,
second Sat (Sept–May) 9:00–1:00 &
2:00–5:00
Pub. *Out of the Mist*

North Castle Historical Society
Smith's Tavern
440 Bedford Road
Armonk, NY 10504
(914) 273-4510
http://nyslgti.gen.ny.us/northcastle/nchs.html
Sharon Tomback, Secretary
Pub. *North Castle History*, annually
$30.00 per year membership

North Collins Historical Society
PO Box 32
North Collins, NY 14111

Historical Society of the Town of North Hempstead
220 Plandome Road
Manhasset, NY 11030
(516) 627-0590

Northern New York Agricultural Historical Society
Northern New York Agricultural and History Museum
(Route 180, Stone Mills, 15 miles north of Watertown—location)
PO Box 108 (mailing address)
La Fargeville, NY 13656
(315) 658-2582; (315) 658-2353; (315) 658-4783
agstonemills@usadatanet.net
Marguerite Raineri, Director
Mon & Wed–Sun 9:00–4:00
(primarily historical, not genealogical)

Northport Historical Society/Museum
(215 Main Street—location)
PO Box 545 (mailing address)
Northport, NY 11768
(631) 757-9859
Barbra Wells Fitzgerald, Director

Norwood Historical Association and Museum
(39 North Main Street—location)
PO Box 163 (mailing address)
Norwood, NY 13668
(315) 353-2751; (315) 353-2537
Gerald Lacomb, Curator
Tue & Thur 2:00–4:00, and by appointment

Oakfield Historical Society
PO Box 74
Oakfield, NY 14125
Darlene Warner, President
Pub. *Newsletter*, monthly
$10.00 per year membership

Ocean Beach Historical Society
PO Box 701
Ocean Beach, NY 11770
(631) 583-8972
Shoshanna Cohen, Director

Ogden Historical Society, Inc.
PO Box 777
Adams Basin, NY 14410-0777

Ohio Historical Society
Rural Delivery
Cold Brook, NY 13324

Old Brutus Historical Society, Inc.
(8943 North Seneca Street—location)
PO Box 516 (mailing address)
Weedsport, NY 13166
(315) 834-9342; (315) 834-6779 (Howard J. Finley)
mriley@thumpernet.com
http://rootsweb.com/~nycayuga/obhs/index.html
Howard J. Finley
$5.00 per year membership

Old Onaquaga Historical Society
Saint Luke's Museum
PO Box 318
Harpursville, NY 13787
(607) 693-1298
(museum has very limited amount of research material and is not open regular hours)

Oneida County Historian
1608 Genessee Street
Utica, New York 13502
Kevin Marken

Municipal Historians

Town of Annsville
4061 Green Brook Lane
Taberg, NY 13471
James P. Armstrong

Town of Augusta
124 Madison Street
Oriskany Falls, NY 13425
Helen Alberding
(also historian of the village of Oriskany Falls)

Town of Ava
Rural Delivery 1
Ava, NY 13303
William Belewicki

Town of Barneveld
Parker Hollow Road
Barneveld, NY 13304
Elizabeth Alger

Town of Boonville
159 Schuyler Street
Boonville, NY 13309
(315) 942-2184
James S. Pitcher
by appointment

Village of Boonville
post vacant

Town of Bridgewater
PO Box 348
Bridgewater, NY 13318
Janice Jaquish

Village of Bridgewater
post vacant

Town of Camden
Dunbar Street
Camden, NY 13316
Mrs. Richard Scoville

Village of Camden
13 Watkins Avenue
Camden, NY 13316
Mrs. Elbert Peck

Village of Clayville
post vacant

Village of Clinton
1 Mulberry Street
Clinton, NY 13323
(315) 853-5018
Richard L. Williams
(also historian of the town of Kirkland)

Town of Deerfield
5418 Walker Road
Deerfield, NY 13502
Virginia Loin

Town of Florence
11899 Florence Road
Camden, NY 13316
(315) 245-0487
Sharron McNamara

Town of Floyd
Rural Delivery 4, Box 57, Camroden Road
Rome, NY 13440
Edwin C. Evans

Town of Forestport
PO Box 52
Woodgate, NY 13494
(315) 392-2142 FAX
John B. Isley

Village of Holland Patent
Steuben Street
Holland Patent, NY 13354
Mrs. Edward Christiana

Town of Kirkland
Richard L. Williams (see Village of Clinton, above)

Town of Lee
4855 Bowman Road
Taberg, NY 13471-3005
Virginia Ackerman

Town of Marcy
436 Morgan Road
Marcy, NY 13403
Raymond Ball

Town of Marshall
PO Box 233
Deansboro, NY 13328
(315) 853-4473
Dorothy McConnell

Town of New Hartford and Village of New Hartford
New Hartford Historical Society
(48 Genesee Street—location)
PO Box 238 (mailing address)
New Hartford, NY 13413
(315) 735-2332 (Historical Society)

Village of New York Mills
4 Clinton Street
New York Mills, NY 13417
Mildred Szarek

Village of Oneida Castle
PO Box 275
Oneida, NY 13421-0275
Mrs. Frederick Hill

Village of Oriskany Falls
Helen Alberding (see Town of Augusta, above)

Village of Oriskany
306 Miller Street
Oriskany, NY 13424
Geraldine Miller

Town of Paris
26 Church Road
Clayville, NY 13322
May Listovitch

Village of Prospect
Prospect, NY 13435
Audrey F. Worden

Town of Remsen
Starr Hill Road
Remsen, NY 13438
(315) 831-5443
Leonard Wynne
(also historian of the town of Steuben)

Village of Remsen
post vacant

City of Rome
c/o Kathleen Hynes-Bouska, Archivist and Educator
Rome Historical Society
200 Church Street

Rome, NY 13440
(315) 336-5870; (315) 336-5912 FAX

Town of Sangerfield
(125 White Street—location)
PO Box 505 (mailing address)
Waterville, NY 13480
Mrs. Martin Cleary
(also historian of the village of Waterville)

City of Sherrill
post vacant

Town of Steuben
Leonard Wynne (see Town of Remsen,
above)

Village of Sylvan Beach
PO Box 175
Brookfield, NY 13314
Jack Henke

Town of Trenton
c/o Town of Trenton Historical Department
PO Box 206
Barneveld, NY 13304
(315) 896-2664
http://www.town.trenton.ny.us
by appointment

City of Utica
Oneida County Historical Society
1608 Genesee Street
Utica, NY 13502-5425
(315) 735-3642 (Historical Society)
Joe Kelly

Town of Vernon and Village of Vernon
9 North Sconondoa Street
Vernon, NY 13476
Ellen Murphy

Town of Verona
(Town Office Building, 6600 Germany
Road—location)
5603 State Route 46 (mailing address)
Durhamville, NY 13054
Dorothy M. Cmaylo
by appointment

Town of Vienna
PO Box 250
North Bay, NY 13123
(315) 245-3308, ext. 26
Arlene F. Pifer

Village of Waterville
Mrs. Martin Cleary (see Town of Sangerfield,
above)

Town of Western
(9175 Main Street—location)
PO Box 42 (mailing address)
Westernville, NY 13486
Dr. Russell Marriott

Town of Westmoreland
5746 Shed Road
Rome, NY 13440
Nancy Prichard

Town of Whitestown
2324 Arnold Avenue
Yorkville, NY 13495
Marilyn Collea

Village of Yorkville
2 Coventry Avenue
Yorkville, NY 13495
Mrs. Robert Kohlbrenner

Oneida County Historical Society

1608 Genesee Street
Utica, NY 13502-5425
(315) 735-3642
ochs@borg.com
Kevin Marken, President
Tue–Fri 10:00–4:30, Sat 11:00–3:00
Pub. *Oniota*, quarterly
("Nonprofit historical society with research
and genealogical library. 250,000
documents, 50,000 photos, 20,000
objects. Founded 1876. Doubling library
space again in 2002.")
$25.00 per year membership; admission:
$5.00 for nonmembers; research: $15.00
minimum contribution

Onondaga County Historian
post vacant
c/o Judy Haven
Onondaga Historical Association
Research Center
311 Montgomery Street
Syracuse NY 13202
(315) 428-1862

Municipal Historians

Village of Baldwinsville
post vacant

Town of Camillus
(see Town of Camillus Historical Society,
above)

Village of Camillus
post vacant

Town of Cicero
573-1 West Seymour Street
Clay, NY 13041
Mrs. Kenneth Flynn

Town of Clay
4834 Grange Road
Clay, NY 13041
Ferdinand Lepinske

Delphi Falls
2043 Cardner Road
Cazenovia, NY 13035-9659
(315) 662-3668
Nancy Skeele Edwards

Town of DeWitt
c/o Assistant Headmaster
Manlius Pebble Hill School
5300 Jamesville Road
Dewitt, NY 13214
(315) 446-2452
Joseph O'Brien

Village of East Syracuse
post vacant

Town of Elbridge
Route 31
Jordan, NY 13080

Village of Elbridge
(822 Dumar Drive—location)
PO Box 1033 (mailing address)
Elbridge, NY 13060
Jean Schwartz

Town of Fabius
Box 115
Fabius, NY 13063
(315) 683-5506
Peter Schlicht

Village of Fabius
7753 Syr/Fab Road

Fabius, NY 13063
(315) 683-9446
Virginia Cameron

Town of Geddes
post vacant

Village of Jordan
c/o Jordan Historical Society
PO Box 622
Jordan, NY 13080
Mrs. Harvey Hudson, Historian

Town of LaFayette
Rural Delivery 1, Box 46
Tully, NY 13159
(315) 677-3678
Rev. Donald Moody
(also historian of the town of Manlius)

Village of Liverpool
314 Second Street
Liverpool, NY 13088
(315) 451-7091
dgutierr@twcny.rr.com
Dorianne Gutierrez
Thur 6:00–8:00, second & fourth Sat
noon–4:00

Town of Lysander
6 Lock Street
Baldwinsville, NY 13027
Luella Oakes

Town of Manlius
Mrs. Francis P. Rivette (see Village of
Fayetteville, above)

Village of Manlius
1301 Nottingham Road, Apartment C100
Jamesville, NY 13078-8782
Mary D. Shaw

Town of Marcellus
(6 Slocombe—location)
PO Box 165 (mailing address)
Marcellus, NY 13108-0165
(315) 673-1765
Peg Nolan

Village of Marcellus
post vacant

Village of Minoa
post vacant

Village of North Syracuse
Village Hall
600 South Bay Road
North Syracuse, NY 13212
Jane Kimpland

Town of Onondaga
4967 Carnarvon Road
Syracuse, NY 13215
L. Jane Tracy

Town of Otisco
3816 Oak Hill Road
Marietta, NY 13110
(315) 696-8454
Nancy L. Shelley

Town of Pompey
2327 Berry Road
Lafayette, NY 13084
(315) 677-3056
Sylvia Shoebridge

Town of Salina
200 Third Street
Liverpool, NY 13088

Mrs. Joseph Ostuni

Town of Skaneateles
c/o Town Hall
24 Jordan Street
Skaneateles, NY 13152
Beth Batele

Village of Skaneateles
28 Hannum Street
Skaneateles, NY 13152
Ms. Pat Blackler

Village of Solvay
315 Conklin Street
Syracuse, NY 13209-1248
Mrs. Andrew R. March

Town of Spafford
Historian
c/o Spafford Area Historical Society
(School House/Grange Building—location)
PO Box 250 (mailing address)
Marietta, NY 13110
(315) 636-8300; (315) 636-7782 FAX
E. C. (Lauri) Clark

City of Syracuse
post vacant

Town of Tully and Village of Tully
(22 State Street—location)
PO Box 201 (mailing address)
Tully, NY 13159-0201
(315) 696-5546; (315) 696-4693
Lynn M. Fisher

Town of Van Buren
post vacant

Onondaga Historical Association
Research Center
311 Montgomery Street
Syracuse, NY 13202-2098
(315) 428-1862
http://www.cnyhistory.org
Judy Haven, Research Coordinator
Tue–Fri 1:00–4:30, Fri 9:30–noon by
    appointment; Museum: Tue–Fri
    noon–4:00, Sat 11:00–4:00
Pub. *History Highlights* (newsletter, not
    genealogical), perhaps quarterly; *OHA
    Annual Report*, annually
    (Onondaga County history)
$30.00 per year membership; research:
    $20.00 minimum plus SASE, allow 8
    weeks for response

Ontario County Historian
3051 County Complex Drive
Canandaigua, NY 14424
(716) 396-4034; (716) 394-8523
PEP646@frontiernet.net
http://raims.com/historian/home.html
Dr. Preston E. Pierce
Tue & Thur 3:30–5:00
Pub. *Historian's Newsletter*, monthly, $7.00
    per year subscription

Municipal Historians

Town of Bristol
6740 County Road 32
Canandaigua, NY 14424
(716) 229-5420
Helen Fox

Town of Canadice
5949 County Road #37
Springwater, NY 14560
(716) 367-8052
Historian@Canadice.org

http://Canadice.org
Margaret Bott
by appointment
Pub. *Canadice Chronicle*, quarterly,
    donation for subscription
research fee schedule available from the
    historian

City of Canandaigua
113 Cliffside Road
Bristol Harbour
Canandaigua, NY 14424
(716) 394-8124
Dr. Marvin Rapp

Town of Canandaigua
55 North Main Street
Canandaigua, NY 14424
(716) 394-4975
Linda McIlveen

Village of Clifton Springs
52 West Main Street
Clifton Springs, NY 14432
(315) 462-9657
Frederick Gifford

Town of East Bloomfield
99 Main Street
East Bloomfield, NY 14443
(716) 657-6515
Diane Wade

Village of East Bloomfield
post vacant

Town of Farmington
140 County Road 8
Farmington, NY 14425
(716) 986-4796
Margaret Hartsough

City of Geneva
Prouty Chew House
543 South Main Street
Geneva, NY 14456-3194
(315) 789-5151
Stephen O'Malley

Town of Geneva
603 Reed Road
Geneva, NY 14456-9735
(315) 789-3922
Mabel S. Ansley

Town of Gorham
2655 Depew Road
Stanley, NY 14561
(716) 526-5389
Mary O. Melious

Village of Holcomb
post vacant

Town of Hopewell
3301 Algerine Street
Stanley NY 14561
(716) 526-6543
Leigh Rehner Jones

Town of Manchester
779 Field Street
Clifton Springs, NY 14432
(315) 462-3145
Richard Combs

Town of Naples
32 West Avenue
Naples, NY 14512
(716) 374-2560
William Vierhile

Village of Naples
post vacant

Town of Phelps
Phelps Community Historical Society
Museum
Phelps Historical Society
66 Main Street
Phelps, NY 14532
(315) 548-4940
histsoc@fltg.net
Don Tiffany
Thur–Fri 10:00–4:00

Village of Phelps
post vacant

Town of Richmond
(30 Church Street—location)
PO Box 369 (mailing address)
Honeoye, NY 14471
(716) 229-5641
Peggy Treble

Village of Rushville
post vacant

Town of Seneca
PO Box 39
Seneca Castle, NY 14547
(315) 526-5039
Jane Wolfe

Village of Shortsville
12 High Street
Shortsville, NY 14548
Ann Walker

Town of South Bristol
6500 Gannett Hill Road, West
Naples NY 14512
(716) 394-1505
Roger S. Brahm

Town of Victor
Town Hall
85 East Main Street
Victor, NY 14564
(716) 742-5085
Babette M. Huber

Village of Victor
post vacant

Town of West Bloomfield
(Wesley Road, Rural Delivery 2—location)
PO Box 34 (mailing address)
West Bloomfield, NY 14585
(716) 624-1888
Kurt Kleindienst

Ontario County Historical Society
55 North Main Street
Canandaigua, NY 14424
(716) 394-4975 voice & FAX
http://www.ochs.org
Linda McIlveen, Director of Research
Research Room: Tue–Sat 10:00–4:30, Wed
    10:00–9:00; Museum: Tue–Sat
    10:00–5:00
Pub. *Chronicle*, quarterly
(Ontario County history and local genealogy)
$20.00 per year membership; museum
    admission: $3.00; research room
    admission: $7.50 for nonmembers;
    research services: $15.00 plus copy costs

**Town of Ontario Historical and Landmark
Preservation Society**
(Heritage Square at Brick Church
    Corners—location)
PO Box 462 (mailing address)

Ontario, NY 14519
(315) 524-5356; (315) 524-0037
Thomas Treppa, President
six historic buildings: mid-May–Sept:
   Sat–Sun 1:30–5:00
Pub. *Newsletter*, bimonthly
$5.00–$150.00 per year membership; free
   admission

Orange County Historian
(1841 Court House—location)
101 Main Street (mailing address)
Goshen, NY 10924-1627
(845) 291-2386; (845) 291-2388
Theodore W. Sly, County Historian
Library Reference Room: Mon–Fri
   9:00–7:00, Sat 9:00–5:00

Municipal Historians

Town of Blooming Grove
Town Hall
PO Box 38
Blooming Grove, NY 10914
(845) 496-7230
Jean Versweyveld

Town of Chester
Town Hall
1786 Kings Highway
Chester, NY 10918
Clark J. Holbert

Village of Chester
Village Hall
47 Main Street
Chester, NY 10918
(845) 469-4405
Marjorie Nehrich

Village of Cornwall-on-Hudson
Village Hall
325 Hudson Street
Cornwall-on-Hudson, NY 12520
Colette Fulton

Town of Cornwall
Town Hall
183 Main Street
Cornwall, NY 12518
Janet Dempsey

Town of Crawford
c/o Town Hall
PO Box 109
Pine Bush, NY 12566
(845) 744-3946
Mary Smith

Town of Deerpark
(25 Old Grange Road—location)
PO Box A (mailing address)
Huguenot, NY 12746
(845) 856-2702; (845) 856-1558 FAX
Norma Schadt
Tue 10:00–4:00, and by appointment

Village of Florida
Village Hall
33 South Main Street
Florida, NY 10921
Gary Randall

Town of Goshen
Town Hall
41 Webster Avenue, Box 217
Goshen, NY 10924
Michelle P. Figliomeni, Ph.D.

Town of Greenville
Town Hall
65 County Route 55

Port Jervis, NY 12771
Peter Ewanciw

Village of Greenwood Lake
c/o Town Hall
(Church Street—location)
PO Box 7 (mailing address)
Greenwood Lake, NY 10925

Town of Hamptonburgh
Town Hall
Rural Delivery 3, Box 18, Bull Road
Campbell Hall, NY 10916
John Gramm

Village of Harriman
Village Hall
PO Box 337
Harriman, NY 10926
Evelyn McGarrah

Village of Highland Falls
Village Hall
303 Main Street
Highland Falls, NY 10928
Stella Bailey

Town of Highlands
Town Hall
213 Main Street
Highland Falls, NY 10928
Stella Bailey

Village of Maybrook
Village Hall
(109 Main Street—location)
PO Box 105 (mailing address)
Maybrook, NY 12543
Roberta Petzold

Town of Minisink
Town Hall
PO Box 349
Westtown, NY 10998
Edna Raymond

Town of Monroe
Town Hall
11-13 Stage Road
Monroe, NY 10950
James A. Nelson

Village of Monroe
Village Hall
7 Stage Road
Monroe, NY 10950
Charles J. King

Town of Montgomery
Town Government Center
110 Bracken Road
Montgomery, NY 12549-2627
(845) 475-2600; (845) 475-9098; (845) 457-
   2603 FAX
Rose Pennings
9:00–5:00
(published *Old Houses of Hanover* and
   *Historic Sites of the Town of
   Montgomery, Orange County, New York*,
   available from Town Clerk, $9.50 ppd.)

Village of Montgomery
Village Hall
133 Clinton Street
Montgomery, NY 12549
(845) 457-5135
Marion Wild

Town of Mount Hope
Town Hall
PO Box 471
Otisville, NY 10963

(845) 386-5214
Delores Hawkins

Town of New Windsor
555 Union Avenue
New Windsor, NY 12553
(845) 563-4609
historynw@aol.com
http://town.new-windsor.ny.us (Town)
Glenn Marshall

City of Newburgh
City Hall
83 Broadway
Newburgh, NY 12550
Kevin Barrett Bilali

Town of Newburgh
Town Hall
1496 Route 300
Newburgh, NY 12550
Les Cornell

Village of Otisville
Village Hall
(66 Highland Avenue—location)
PO Box 873 (mailing address)
Otisville, NY 10963
Vivian Ketcham

Village of Pine Island
Village Hall
140 Pulasky Highway
Pine Island, NY 10969
Frances Sodrick

City of Port Jervis
(14-20 Hammond Street—location)
PO Box 1002
Port Jervis, NY 12771
peter@minisink.org
Peter Osborne, III

Village of Prospect
post vacant

Village of Tuxedo Park
post vacant

Town of Tuxedo
(Temple Road—location)
PO Box 725 (mailing address)
Tuxedo, NY 10987
townclerk@tuxedogov.org;
   crsonne@netscape.net
Christian R. Sonne

Village of Tuxedo
post vacant

Village of Unionville
Village Hall
PO Box 542
Unionville, NY 10988
Donald O. Mavros

Village of Walden
Village Hall
8 Scofield Street
Walden, NY 12586
Marcus H. Millspaugh, Jr.

Town of Wallkill
Town Hall
(600 Route 211 East—location)
PO Box 398 (mailing address)
Middletown, NY 10940
Dorothy H. Ingrassia

Village of Warwick
Village Hall
(77 Main Street—location)

PO Box 369 (mailing address)
Warwick, NY 10990
Florence P. Tate

Village of Washingtonville
Village Hall
(29 West Main Street—location)
PO Box 140 (mailing address)
Washingtonville, NY 10992
Anthony Knipp

Town of Wawayanda
Town Hall
PO Box 106
Slate Hill, NY 10973
Emma Duvall; Margaret Myers; Elizabeth
  Kirby

Town of Woodbury
Town Hall
(470 Route 32—location)
PO Box 1004 (mailing address)
Highland Mills, NY 10930
Leslie Rose

Orange County Historical Society
(21 Clove Furnace Drive—location)
Box 55 (mailing address)
Arden, NY 10910
(845) 351-4696
Michelle P. Figliomeni, Ph.D., President
Mon–Fri 8:00–4:30
Pub. *O.C.H.S. Journal*, annually (scholarly
  journal)
$20.00 per year membership; research:
  $25.00 per hour

Orchard Park Historical Society
Johnson-Jolls House
(4287 South Buffalo Street—location)
5800 Armor Road (mailing address)
Orchard Park, NY 14127
(716) 667-2301
http://rin.buffalo.edu/c_erie/comm/cult/
  hist/_pres/agen/orch.html

Orleans County Historian
34 East Park Street
Albion, NY 14411
(716) 589-4174
C. Wilson Lattin
Mon, Wed & Fri 1:00–4:00

Municipal Historians

Town of Albion
Town Hall
3665 Clarendon Road
Albion, NY 14411
(716) 589-1998
coblstnfin@aol.com
http://www.rootsweb.com/~nyorlean
Cheryl Staines

Village of Albion
18 West Avenue
Albion, NY 14411
(716) 589-7714
Dr. Neil Johnson

Town of Barre
4510 Mathes Road
Holley, NY 14470
(585) 589-9960
Helen Mathes

Town of Carlton
926-12 Lakeside Bluff
Waterport, NY 14571
(585) 682-5775
Lysbeth Hoffman

Town of Clarendon
PO Box 145
Clarendon, NY 14429
Alan Isselhard

Town of Gaines
14407 Ridge Road
Albion, NY 14411
(716) 589-4355
deerob@mail.com
Delia Robinson

Village of Holley
19 North Main Street
Holley, NY 14470
(585) 638-8188
Marsha DeFilipps
(also historian of the town of Murray)

Town of Kendall
Town Hall
1873 Kendall Road
Kendall, NY 14476
(585) 659-2762; (585) 659-8203 FAX
M. Joette Knapp

Village of Lyndonville
76 West Avenue
Lyndonville, NY 14098
(585) 765-2333
Virginia Cooper
(also historian of the town of Yates)

Village of Medina
517 North Academy Street
Medina, NY 14103
(585) 798-2337
Shirley Nellist

Town of Murray and Village of Murray
Marsha DeFilipps (see Village of Holley,
  above)

Town of Ridgeway
517 North Academy Street
Medina, NY 14103
(585) 798-2337
rhn@eznet.net
Richard Nellist

Town of Shelby
10670 Maple Ridge Road
Medina, NY 14103
(585) 798-4632
Lou Fuller

Town of Yates
Virginia Cooper (see Village of Lyndonville,
  above)

Orleans County Historical Association
13979 Allen Road
Albion, NY 14411
(716) 589-4690

Ossining Historical Society Museum
196 Croton Avenue
Ossining, NY 10562
(914) 941-0001
info@ossininghistorical.org
http://www.ossininghistorical.org
Roberta Arminio, Town Historian
Mon, Wed & Sun 1:00–4:00, and by
  appointment
$20.00 per year membership; admission:
  free; research: $20.00 per hour

Oswego County Historian
384 East River Road
Oswego, NY 13126
(315) 349-8460; (315) 349-8458 FAX
bjdhistory@usadatanet.net

http://www.oswegocounty.com (research
  request forms)
Barbara J. Dix
Mon–Fri 9:00–5:00

Municipal Historians

Town of Albion and Village of Altmar
(312 County Route 52—location)
PO Box 394 (mailing address)
Altmar, NY 13302
(315) 298-5723
Florence Gardner
by appointment

Town of Amboy
2167 County Route 23
Williamstown, NY 13493
(315) 964-2415
Luceille Dunn
by appointment
("I am glad to do research and send out
  material on request.")

Town of Boylston
906 North Church Road
Lacona, NY 13083
(315) 387-5471
Rita Rombach

Village of Central Square
196 County Route 33
Central Square, NY 13036
(315) 668-2178
Irene Meyers
(also historian of the town of Hastings)

Village of Cleveland and Town of Constantia
Rural Route 1, Box 2821
Cleveland, NY 13042
(315) 675-8225
Joni Hinds
by appointment

City of Fulton
8 Riverview Drive
Fulton, NY 13069
(315) 593-7766
Mary Ellen Ross

Town of Granby
820 County Route 8
Fulton, NY 13069
(315) 598-6500
Elaine Woolridge

Town of Hannibal and Village of Hannibal
(1016 Auburn Street—location)
PO Box 325 (mailing address)
Hannibal, NY 13074
(315) 564-5650
lcnewvine@aol.com
http://www.rootsweb.com/~nyoswego/
  towns/hannibal (Town and Village
  Historian as well as the Hannibal
  Historical Society)
Lowell Newvine

Town of Hastings
Irene Meyers (see Village of Central Square,
  above)

Village of Lacona
297 VanAuken Road
Lacona, NY 13083
(315) 387-5350
Helen Potter

Town of Mexico and Village of Mexico
PO Box 357
Mexico, NY 13114

(315) 963-7034
Bonnie Shumway

Town of Minetto
PO Box 220
Minetto, NY 13115
(315) 343-2393
Charles Sweeting
by appointment

Town of New Haven
56 County Route 6A
Oswego, NY 13126
(315) 963-3159; (315) 963-3900
Aunt8@aol.com
Nancy Searles
by appointment

Town of Orwell
PO Box 23
Orwell, NY 13426
Robert G. Pratt
by appointment
("The Historical Collection is not at this time
    available for viewing nor access unless the
    Town Historian is present." *Orwell
    Remembered* and *Orwell Remembered,
    Volume Two* available.)
research (whether the historian does the
    research or the client meets with him at the
    Town Hall): $7.88 per hour plus copies at
    25¢ per double-sided copy and 15¢ per
    single-sided copy

City of Oswego
119 West Fourth Street
Oswego, NY 13126
(315) 343-1784
Rosemary Nesbitt

Town of Oswego
2320 County Route 7
Oswego, NY 13126
(315) 343-2586
Justin D. White

Town of Palermo
139 Island Road
Phoenix, NY 13135
(315) 593-6825
Beverly Beck

Town of Parish and Village of Parish
PO Box 145
Parish, NY 13131
(315) 625-7833
parishpl@northnet.org
Bridget Swartz

Town of Phoenix
post vacant

Village of Phoenix
455 Main Street
Phoenix, NY 13135
(315) 349-8460
bjdhistory@usadatanet.net
Barbara J. Dix
by appointment

Village of Pulaski
45 Lake Street
Pulaski, NY 13142
(315) 298-2622
Mary Parker

Town of Redfield
390 County Route 39
Williamstown, NY 13493
(315) 599-7737
Helen Anken

**Town of Sandy Creek and Village of
Sandy Creek**
(1992 Harwood Avenue—location)
PO Box 52 (mailing address)
Sandy Creek, NY 13145
(315) 387-5456, ext. 7; (315) 387-2702 FAX
Charlene Cole

Town of Schroeppel
Rural Route 3, Box 9A
Phoenix, NY 13135
(315) 668-3532
Peter Huntley
by appointment

Town of Volney
1445 County Route 6
Fulton, NY 13069
(315) 593-8288
George Wise
Tue and by appointment

Town of West Monroe
PO Box 25
West Monroe, NY 13167
(315) 668-2028
Lawrence Herbert

Town of Williamstown
(Route 17N—location)
PO Box 54 (mailing address)
Williamstown, NY 13493
(315) 964-2393
Glenna Gorski
by appointment

Oswego County Historical Society
Richardson-Bates House Museum
135 East Third Street
Oswego, NY 13126
(315) 343-1342
Terrence M. Prior, Director
Museum: Tue–Fri 10:00–5:00, Sat–Sun
    1:00–5:00; Library: Mon–Fri by
    appointment
(city and rural directories, obituary indexes
    and county cemetery indexes)
research: $22.50 by mail

Otego Historical Society
Harris Memorial Library
69 Main Street
Otego, NY 13825
(607) 988-6661 (Library); (607) 988-2225
    (Historical Society)
http://www.4cls.org/webpages/members/
    Otego/Otego.html

Otsego County Historian
Tuscan Road
Worcester, NY 12197
(607) 397-9705
Nancy Milavec

Municipal Historians

Town of Burlington
Star Route 51
Burlington Flats, NY 13315
Walton F. Dauchy

Town of Butternuts
Gilbertsville, NY 13776
Leigh Eckmair

**Town of Cherry Valley and Village of
Cherry Valley**
PO Box 464
Cherry Valley, NY 13320
Susan Miller

Village of Cooperstown

(22 Main Street—location)
PO Box 346 (mailing address)
Cooperstown, NY 13320
Marjorie Tillapaugh

Town of Decatur
County Route 38
Worcester, NY 12197
Mrs. Gene Schlierman

Town of Edmeston
59 South Street
Edmeston, NY 13335
(607) 965-8902 (Home)
Robert Nonenmacher
Edmeston Free Library/Museum: some Sat

Town of Exeter
Rural Delivery 3, Box 259
Richfield Springs, NY 13457
Dale Dyn

Village of Gilbertsville
Gilbertsville, NY 13776
Myrtie Webster Light

Town of Hartwick
2998 County Route 11
Hartwick, NY 13348
Anita Harrison

Town of Laurens
142 County Route 12
Laurens, NY 13796
Anna Elwin

Village of Laurens
Rural Delivery 3, Route 205
Oneonta, NY 13820
Richard Rose

Town of Maryland
(11 Division Street—location)
PO Box 231 (mailing address)
Schenevus, NY 12155
beech18@dmcom.net
Dorothy Parmerter

Town of Middlefield
573 Ricetown Road
Cooperstown, NY 13326
Francis E. Kubis

Town of Milford and Village of Milford
265 Eddie Martin Road
Milford, NY 13807
Sandra Bullard

Town of Morris
PO Box 242
Morris, NY 13808
(607) 263-5137 (Home)
Joyce R. Foote

Village of Morris
post vacant

Town of New Lisbon
1203 County Highway
Mount Vision, NY 13810
(607) 293-6170
Virginia A. Schoradt
by appointment

City of Oneonta
13 Taft Avenue
Oneonta, NY 13820-1913
Mark Simonson

Town of Oneonta
West Oneonta, NY 13861
Velma Green

Town of Otego
PO Box 128
Otego, NY 13825
Helen Groves

Town of Otsego
37 Nelson Avenue
Cooperstown, NY 13326
Marion Brophy

Town of Pittsfield
Rural Delivery 3, Box 47
New Berlin, NY 13411
Frances P. Chapin

Town of Plainfield
PO Box 79
West Winfield, NY 13491
Louise Isabell

Village of Richfield Springs
Box 51, Lake Street
Richfield Springs, NY 13439
Rose A. Agresti

Town of Richfield
PO Box 786
Richfield Springs, NY 13439
Monica Harris

Town of Roseboom
HCR 75, Box 24
Westford, NY 13488
Grace Thompson

Village of Schenevus
45 Main Street
Schenevus, NY 12155
Mildred Prager

Town of Springfield
Springfield Historical Society
PO Box 65
Springfield Center, NY 13468
Jeanette D. Smith

Town of Unadilla
PO Box 519
Unadilla, NY 13849
whbcphs@mkl.com
William H. Bauer
("Personally, my knowledge of genealogical
   research is very little. Often the best I can
   do is refer the party to another library or
   the county offices.")

Village of Unadilla
25 Main Street
Unadilla, NY 13849
Patricia Sheret

Town of Westford
PO Box 95
Worcester, NY 12197
Jane Huntington

Town of Worcester
PO Box 2
Worcester, NY 12197
Ldelongny@aol.com
Lawrence DeLong

Oxbow Historical Society
34542 County Route 22
Theresa, NY 13691
(315) 287-2293
Nancy Raymon, Antwerp Town Historian

Oyster Bay Historical Society
Earle-Wightman House
(20 Summit Street—location)
PO Box 297 (mailing address)

Oyster Bay, NY 11771-0297
(516) 922-5032; (516) 922-6892 FAX
obhistory@aol.com
http://members.aol.com/obhistory
Thomas A. Kuehhas, Director
Tue–Fri 10:00–2:00, Sat 9:00–1:00, Sun
   1:00–4:00
Pub. *The Freeholder*, quarterly
(documents, deeds, letters, manuscripts of
   residents of Town of Oyster Bay from
   1680 to the present, genealogies of local
   families; Theodore Roosevelt Collection)
$20.00 per year membership; research:
   $15.00 for members, $25.00 for
   nonmembers, includes five photocopies

Oysterponds Historical Society, Inc.
(Village Lane—location)
PO Box 70 (mailing address)
Orient, NY 11957
(631) 323-2480
Courtney Burns, Director
Summer: Sat–Sun 1:00–5:00, and all year by
   appointment
Pub. *OHS Newsletter*, quarterly
(east end of Long Island's North Fork;
   maritime and agricultural area, regional
   New York history, special exhibits and
   events)
$20.00 per year membership

Palatine Settlement Society
PO Box 183
Saint Johnsville, NY 13452
(518) 568-2346
Joyce Zbikowski, Secretary
by appointment
Pub. *Newsletter*, semiannually
(history of Mohawk Valley Palatines)
$10.00 per year membership

Parish Historical Society
(East Main Street—location)
PO Box 145 (mailing address)
Parish, NY 13131
(315) 625-4575
http://community.syracuse.com/cc/
   ParishHistoricalSociety
Mary Lou Miller Guindon
$5.00 per year membership

Parishville Historical Association
Parishville Museum
(Main Street—location)
PO Box 534 (mailing address)
Parishville, NY 13672
(315) 265-7619
Emma Remington, Town Historian and
   Curator
July–Aug: Tue & Thur 1:00–3:00, and by
   appointment
Pub. *Parishville Museum*

Pavilion Historical Society
11134 East Park Road
Pavilion, NY 14525

**Perinton Historical Society/Fairport
Historical Museum**
18 Perrin Street
Fairport, NY 14450
(585) 223-3989; (716) 377-8208 (Director);
   (716) 388-0078 (Curator)
http://www.angelfire.com/ny5/
   fairporthistmuseum
William Keeler, Curator
Tue & Sun 2:00–4:00, Thur 7:00 P.M.–9:00
   P.M.; summer: Tue -Fri & Sun 2:00–4:00,
   Tue & Thur 7:00–9:00, Sat 9:00–11:00
Pub. *Perinton Historigram*, eight times per
   year (Sept–May)
$10.00 per year membership

Town of Perth Historical Society
Route 6
Amsterdam, NY 12010
(518) 842-9497

Peterboro Area Historical Society
PO Box 42
Peterboro, NY 13134
(315) 684-9022
Beth Spokowsky, President
Museum: Sun (summer) 2:00–4:00 or by
   appointment
("We have information on residents in the
   Town of Smithfield and some information
   on the Smith family, the founders of the
   town. This especially refers to Gerrit
   Smith, the abolitionist and philathropist of
   Peterboro.")
$5.00 per year membership

Phelps Community Historical Society
Phelps Community Historical Society
   Museum
66 Main Street
Phelps, NY 14532
(315) 548-4940
histsoc@fltg.net
Don Tiffany, Town Historian
Thur–Fri 10:00–4:00
Pub. *Newsletter*, monthly

Piseco Lake Historical Society
Old Piseco Road
Piseco, NY 12139
Julia Damkoehler, Arietta Town Historian
July–Aug: Fri–Sun 1:00–4:00
("Small local museum.")

Pittstown Historical Society
(Pittstown, Rensselaer County—location)
PO Box 252
Valley Falls, NY 12185
Constance Kheel, President

Town of Pleasant Valley Historical Society
PO Box 766
Pleasant Valley, NY 12569

Poestenkill Historical Society
PO Box 140
Poestenkill, NY 12140-0140

Town of Pompey Historical Society
(Route 20 at intersection with Pompey Center
   Road—location)
2944 Michael Avenue, Pompey Hill (mailing
   address)
Jamesville, NY 13078
(315) 677-9416; (315) 677-0102 FAX
lmoffa@twcny.rr.com
Lisa Moffa, Museum Director
Museum: May–Sept: Sun 2:00–4:00, and by
   appointment; meetings: Apr–Oct
Pub. *PHS Newsletter*, three times per year
("includes Delphi Falls, Oran, Pompey
   Center, Pompey and Watervale")
$15.00 per year membership; research:
   queries to Sylvia Shoebridge, Town
   Historian, Maple Hill Farm, 2327 Berry
   Road, Lafayette, NY 13084, (315) 677-
   3056

Port Chester Historical Society
PO Box 1511
Port Chester, NY 10573
(914) 939-6040

Pound Ridge Historical Society
The Pound Ridge Museum
(Routes 137 and 172—location)
PO Box 51 (mailing address)
Pound Ridge, NY 10576

(914) 764-4333 (Museum)
Lise Mayers, President
Museum: Sat–Sun 2:00–4:00, and by
appointment (Mar–Dec)
Pub. *Pendulum*, four times per year
(history of Pound Ridge and its environs)
$25.00 per year membership

Princetown Historical Society
559 North Kelly Road
Schenectady, NY 12306
(518) 864-5218
Irma Mastrean, Princetown Historian
by appointment

Pulaski Historical Society
3428 Maple Avenue
Pulaski, NY 13142
(315) 298-4650; (315) 298-5235 (Tour
appointments)
Phspulaski@aol.com
http://community.syracuse.com/cc/
Pulaskihistorical
Mary Lou Morrow, Curator
Mar–May & Oct–Nov: Sat 10:00–1:00;
June–Sept: Thur 10:00–4:00, Sat
10:00–10:00; July–Aug: Thur
10:00–4:00, Fri 10:00–4:00, Sat
10:00–1:00
Pub. *Newsletter*
(newsletter doesn't contain genealogical
information)
$15.00 per year membership; genealogical
research at no charge, but requests
donation

Pultneyville Historical Society
PO Box 92
Pultneyville, NY 14538-0092
Ruth O. DeWitte, President
Pub. *Newsletter*, monthly

Putnam County Historian
Office of the County Historian and County
Archives
Records Center
68 Marvin Avenue
Brewster, NY 10509-1515
(845) 278-7209; (845) 278-4865 FAX
putpast@bestweb.net
http://www.putnamcountyny.com/historial
Richard A. Muscarella
Tue–Wed 10:00–4:00 (advance notice is
suggested), or by appointment
Pub. *Handbook for Putnam County History
and Genealogy*
(county government archives, historian's
collection)

Municipal Historians

Village of Brewster
Village Office
208 East Main Street
Brewster, NY 10509
(845) 279-3760
John Cesar

Town of Carmel
Carmel Town Hall
16 Fairview Road
Mahopac, NY 10541
(845) 628-5705
http://www.putnamcountyny.com/
historian/carmel.htm
Allan F. Warnecke

Village of Cold Spring
Village Office
87 Main Street
Cold Spring, NY 10516
(845) 265-3611; (845) 265-2756 (Home)

Donald H. MacDonald

Town of Kent
Kent Town Offices
Route 52
Carmel, NY 10512
(845) 225-2067; (845) 628-1825 (Home)
Joyce Morin

Village of Nelsonville
Village Office
258 Main Street
Nelsonville, NY 10516
(845) 265-2500

Town of Patterson
Patterson Town Hall
Routes 311 and 164
Patterson, NY 12563
(845) 878-6500; (845) 878-6897 (Home)
Edward Scrivani

Town of Philipstown
Philipstown Town Hall
238 Main Street
Cold Spring, NY 10516
(845) 265-3329; (845) 265-2756 (Home)
Donald H. MacDonald

Town of Putnam Valley
Putnam Valley Town Hall
265 Oscawana Lake Road
Putnam Valley, NY 10579
(845) 526-3280; (845) 528-4590 (Home)
Stephen L. Andersen

Town of Southeast
Southeast Town Hall
(1 Main Street—location)
PO Box O (mailing address)
Brewster, NY 10509
(914) 279-2196; (845) 279-8148 (Home)
John J. Dunford

**Putnam County Historical Society and
Foundry School Museum**
63 Chestnut Street
Cold Spring, NY 10516
(845) 265-4010; (845) 265-2884 FAX
Charlotte B. Eaton, Curator
Tue–Wed 10:00–4:00, Thur 1:00–4:00, Sun
2:00–5:00 (research library closed Sun)
Pub. *Newsletter*, semiannually
$25.00 per year membership

Putnam Valley Historical Society
(301 Peekskill Hollow Road—location)
PO Box 297 (mailing address)
Putnam Valley, NY 10579
(845) 528-1024
Barbara Doyle, Director
Tue–Wed 10:00–3:00, and other
unscheduled times
Pub. *Potpourri*, three times per year
(genealogies of local families, not verified;
local history)
$10.00 per year membership; admission:
donation

**Historical Society Quaker Hill and
Pawling, Inc.**
(East Main Street—location)
PO Box 99 (mailing address)
Pawling, NY 12564
(845) 855-5891; (845) 855-1248 (Programs
and Newsletter)
Betty Smith, Programs and Newsletter
Sat–Sun (May–Oct) 2:00–4:00
Pub. *Newsletter*, about four times per year
no cost

The Carriage House Museum of the Queen

Village Historical Society
(2 North Park Street—location)
PO Box 38 (mailing address)
Camden, NY 13316
(315) 245-4652 (answering machine)
historycamden@a-znet.com
Elaine H. Norton, President; Janet C.
Kuttruff, Vice President
1 May–30 Oct: Tue–Wed & Fri–Sat
1:00–4:00, and by appointment; special
exhibits May–Oct & Dec
(Camden area family histories and photos on
file, as well as histories of area churches,
schools, businesses, services, maps)
$5.00 per year membership; admission: no
fee; research: $5.00 to cover photocopies
and mailing

Queens County Historian
35-37 211th Street
Bayside, NY 11361
Stanley Cogan

Queens Historical Society (QHS)
(Kingsland Homestead, 143-35 37th Avenue,
Flushing, NY 11354—location)
35-37 211th Street (mailing address)
Bayside, NY 11361
(718) 224-9592; (718) 224-2771
http://www.preserve.org/queens
Stanley Cogan, County Historian; Mary
Cornell, Genealogy Research Analyst
County Historian: 9:00 A.M.–11:00 P.M.;
Office Assistance: Mon–Sat 9:30–5:00
Pub. *QHS Newsletter*, four times per year
$15.00 per year membership

Quogue Historical Society
PO Box 1207
Quogue, NY 11959
(631) 653-4111
Patricia Shuttleworth

Remsen-Steuben Historical Society
(Prospect Street—location)
PO Box 284 (mailing address)
Remsen, NY 13438
(315) 831-5443
Leonard Wynne, President

Rensselaer County Historian
post vacant
c/o Rensselaer County Historical Society
Hart-Cluett Mansion
59 Second Street
Troy, NY 12180
(518) 272-7232 (Museum Office); (518) 273-
1264 FAX
rchs@crisny.org
http://www.crisny.org/not-for-profit/rchs
Stacy Pomeroy Draper, Curator
Library: Tue–Fri 1:00–4:00, Sat 10:00–4:00;
Museum: Feb–Dec: Tue–Sat 1:00–4:00

Municipal Historians

Town of Berlin
(South Main Street—location)
PO Box 314 (mailing address)
Berlin, NY 12022-0314
(518) 658-2467; (518) 658-2266
Margaret Kinn

Town of Brunswick
Town Offices
308 Town Office Road
Troy, NY 12180
(518) 279-9714
Sharon Zankel
("not able to accept genealogical research
requests")

Village of Castleton-on-Hudson
99 South Main Street
Castleton-on-Hudson, NY 12033
(518) 732-4098
Ellen Allen

Town of East Greenbush
East Greenbush Town Hall
225 Columbia Turnpike
Rensselaer, NY 12144
(518) 477-4614
Beverly Kennedy

Town of Grafton
PO Box 133
Grafton, NY 12082
(518) 279-3205; (518) 279-3685
Irma Wagar

Village of Hoosick Falls
24 Munsell Street
Hoosick Falls, NY 12090
(518) 686-9015
George Peer

Town of Hoosick
156 Circular Street, Apartment 3
Saratoga Springs, NY 12866-2349
(518) 686-9008
Joseph Holloway

Village of Lansingburgh
(unincorporated village)
post vacant

Town of Nassau
29 Church Street
Nassau, NY 12123
(518) 766-4449; (518) 766-2343
Patricia Ann Davis

Village of Nassau
post vacant

Town of North Greenbush
27 Jordan Road
Troy, NY 12180
(518) 283-0534
Karen Hartgen Fisher

Town of Petersburg
296 Potter Hill Road
Petersburgh, NY 12138
(518) 658-2963; (518) 658-2475
Peter Schaapok

Town of Pittstown
35 Sherman Road
Valley Falls, NY 12185
(518) 663-5601; (518) 753-4222
Ellen L. Wiley

Town of Poestenkill
PO Box 210
Poestenkill, NY 12140
Florence Hill

Town of Sand Lake
Sand Lake Historian's Office
Town Hall
PO Box 273
Sand Lake, NY 12153
Petersburgh@aol.com
Judy Rowe
Tue 10:00–4:00

Town of Schaghticoke
111 Roe Road
Northline Drive
Melrose, NY 12121
(518) 235-5813
Christina Kelly

Village of Schaghticoke
77 Main Street
Schaghticoke, NY 12154
(518) 753-4721
Richard Lohnes

Town of Schodack
1771 Columbia Turnpike
Castleton-on-Hudson, NY 12033
(518) 477-5421; (518) 477-7983
Irene R. Saganich

Town of Stephentown
post vacant

City of Troy
(695 Fourth Avenue—location)
PO Box 124 (mailing address)
Lansingburgh, NY 12182
Frances Broderick, Unofficial Historian

Village of Valley Falls
State Street
Valley Falls, NY 12185
(518) 753-4936
Judy Hoag

Rensselaer County Historical Society
Hart-Cluett Mansion
59 Second Street
Troy, NY 12180
(518) 272-7232 (Museum Office); (518) 273-1264 FAX
rchs@crisny.org; research@rchsonline.org (research requests)
http://rchsonline.org/index.htm
Stacy Pomeroy Draper, Curator
Library: Tue–Fri 1:00–4:00, Sat 10:00–4:00; Museum: Feb–Dec: Tue–Sat 1:00–4:00
Pub. *Newsletter: Current History*, quarterly (family history and local history)
$35.00 per year membership; research: $20.00 per request

Rensselaer Falls Historical Association
PO Box 18
Rensselaer Falls, NY 13680
(315) 344-6681
Mimi Borr
by appointment

City of Rensselaer Historical Society
"The Agents House"
15 Forbes Avenue
Rensselaer, NY 12144

Rensselaerville Historical Society
(Grist Mill in hamlet of Rensselaerville, at the bridge—location)
PO Box 8 (mailing address)
Rensselaerville, NY 12147
(518) 797-3194
Edhase@aol.com
Janet Haseley, Research Chair
mid-May–mid-Oct: Wed 10:00–3:00; Memorial Day–Labor Day: Sat 2:00–4:00
Pub. *Rensselaerville Press*, quarterly
("The Historical Society has papers pertaining to the history of the township of Rensselaerville [which includes four other hamlets besides the hamlet of Rensselaerville], and genealogy information. Nothing is on computer, however; it is all handwritten. The hamlet of Rensselaerville has changed very little in 150 years, and the entire village is on the State and National Register of Historic Places.")
$5.00 per year membership; research: donation

Rhinebeck Historical Society

PO Box 291
Rhinebeck, NY 12572
$10.00 per year membership

Richmond County Historian
10 Richmond Terrace
Staten Island, NY 10301-1903
Richard B. Dickenson
(borough of Staten Island)

The Richmond Hill Historical Society
Chapter of The Queens Historical Society
86-20 115th Street
Richmond, Hills, NY 11418
http://www.richmondhillhistory.org
Pub. *Newsletter*, quarterly
$20.00 per year membership

Richville Historical Association
Rural Delivery 1, Box 171
Hermon, NY 13652
(315) 347-3221; (315) 287-0375
Stella Tamblin, President and Town Historian

Rochester Historical Society
Genealogy Section
485 East Avenue
Rochester, NY 14607
(716) 271-2705
Elizabeth G. Holahan, President; Meghan Lodge, Administrator
Reference: Mon–Fri 10:00–4:00; Archives: by appointment
Pub. *News and Notes*, periodically
(local history and genealogy of the pioneer families of Rochester)
$25.00 per year membership; admission: $2.00 for adults

Official Historian of Rockland County
12 Ashwood Lane
Garnerville, NY 10923
(845) 942-3383 (Office); (845) 947-1231 (Home)
Thomas F. X. Casey
(also historian of the town of Haverstraw)

Municipal Historians

Village of Airmont
Village Hall
(321 Route 59—location)
PO Box 578 (mailing address)
Airmont, NY 10982
(845) 357-8111; (845) 357-1611 (Home)
Robert A. Goetschius

Village of Chestnut Ridge
Village Hall
277 Old Nyack Turnpike
Spring Valley, NY 10977
(845) 425-2805
Dr. Eudice Charney

Town of Clarkstown
Town Hall
10 Maple Street
New City, NY 10956
(845) 639-2010; (845) 268-3012 (Home)
Robert Knight

Village of Grand View-on-Hudson
Village Hall
118 River Road
Grand View-on-Hudson NY 10960
(845) 429-0300; (845) 353-6710 (Home)
Carolla Dost

Town of Haverstraw
Thomas F. X. Casey (see Rockland County Historian, above)

Village of Haverstraw
Village Hall
40 New Main Street
Haverstraw, NY 10927
(845) 429-0300; (845) 429-7811 (Home)
Jack Berrian

Village of Hillburn
Village Hall
31 Mountain Avenue
Hillburn, NY 10931
(845) 357-2036
Chuck Stead

Village of Kasar
post vacant

Village of Montebello
Village Hall
1 Montebello Road
Suffern, NY 10901
(845) 357-2211; (845) 357-6383 (Home)
Craig H. Long
(also historian of the town of Ramapo)

Village of New Hempstead
Village Hall
108 Old School House Road
New City, NY 10956
(845) 354-8100; (845) 354-1122 (Home)
Stewart Schwartz

Village of New Square
Village Hall
766 North Main Street
New Square, NY 10977
(845) 354-5778

Village of Nyack
Village Hall
9 North Broadway
Nyack, NY 10960
(845) 358-0548; (914) 353-0851
Jean Pardo

Town of Orangetown
Town Hall
26 Orangeburg Road
Orangeburg, NY 10965
(845) 359-5100
Mary R. Cardenas

Village of Piermont
Village Hall
478 Piermont Avenue
Piermont, NY 10968
(845) 359-1258; (845) 359-4595 (Home)
Grace Meyer

Village of Pomona
c/o Village Hall
(50 Camp Hill Road—location)
PO Box 333 (mailing address)
Pomona, NY 10970
(845) 354-0545

Town of Ramapo
Town Hall
237 Route 59
Suffern, NY 10901
(845) 357-5100; (845) 357-6383 (Home)
Craig H. Long
(also historian of the Village of Montebello)

Village of Sloatsburg
Village Hall
96 Orange Turnpike
Sloatsburg, NY 10974
(845) 753-2727; (845) 753-5203 (Home)
Harrison Bush

Village of South Nyack

Village Hall
282 South Broadway
South Nyack, NY 10960
(845) 358-0287; (845) 358-2224 (Home)
Myra G. Starr

Village of Spring Valley
Village Hall
200 North Main Street
Spring Valley, NY 10977
(845) 352-1100; (845) 368-3468 (Home)
Robert F. Rubin

Town of Stony Point
Town Hall
74 East Main Street
Stony Point, NY 10980
(845) 786-3861
Stuart Gates

Village of Suffern
Village Hall
Suffern Village Museum
61 Washington Avenue
Suffern, NY 10901
(845) 357-2600 (Museum); (845) 357-3667
    (Home)
Gardner F. Watts

Village of Upper Nyack
Village Hall
328 North Broadway
Upper Nyack, NY 10960
(845) 358-0084
Winston Perry, Jr.

Village of Wesley Hills
Village Hall
432 Route 306
Wesley Hills, NY 10952
(845) 354-0400; (845) 354-9098 (H)
Alan Doberman

Village of West Haverstraw
1 Oldfield Court
Garnerville, NY 10923
(845) 947-2800; (845) 942-2773 (Home)
Cathy Grant

The Historical Society of Rockland County
20 Zukor Road
New City, NY 10956-4388
(845) 634-9629; (845) 634-9645; (845) 634-
    8690 FAX
HSRockland@aol.com;
    Marie_Koestler@juno.com
http://www.planet-rockland.org/histsoc
Marie Koestler, Genealogy Researcher
Offices: Tue–Fri 9:30–5:00; Museum:
    Tue–Sun 1:00–5:00; Library: Tue
    1:00–5:00
Pub. *Historical Society of Rockland County
    News*, quarterly; *South of the Mountains*,
    quarterly, $20.00 per year subscription
queries

Rockville Centre Historical Society
The Phillips House
(28 Hempstead Avenue—location)
PO Box 605 (mailing address)
Rockville Centre, NY 11570
Frank E. Seipp, President

Rocky Point Historical Society
PO Box 1720
Rocky Point, NY 11778
http://www.buoy.com/rphs/index.html
Suzanne Johnson, President
(published *The Noah Hallock Cemetery of
    Rocky Point*, $9.00 ppd.)

Thelma Rogers Genealogical and

Historical Society
(see Genealogical Societies—Local and
Regional, below)

Rome Historical Society
200 Church Street
Rome, NY 13440
(315) 336-5870; (315) 336-5912 FAX
Kathleen Hynes-Bouska, Archivist and
    Educator
Mon–Fri 9:00–4:00, and by appointment
Pub. *Annals and Recollections*, quarterly,
    $1.00 per issue
(Rome history, Erie Canal)
$10.00 per year membership; library
    admission: $5.00 for nonmembers

Roxbury Burrough's Club
Main Street
Roxbury, NY 12474

Rye Historical Society
1 Purchase Street
Rye, NY 10580-3002
(914) 967-7588 (Society); (914) 967-7595
    (Director); (914) 967-6253 FAX
http://www.ryehistoricalsociety.org/index.
    htm
Jan Kelsey, Interim Director
Office: Mon–Fri 9:00–4:00
research: $20.00 per hour (1 hour minimum)

Sackets Harbor Historical Society
Main Street
Sackets Harbor, NY 13685
(315) 646-3525; (315) 646-1708
Dave Alteri

Sag Harbor Historical Society
Umbrella House
PO Box 1709
Sag Harbor, NY 11963
(631) 725-5092
Joan Tripp, President

Saint Lawrence County Historian
Saint Lawrence County Historical
Association at the Silas Wright Museum
(3 East Main Street—location)
PO Box 8 (mailing address)
Canton, NY 13617-0008
(315) 386-8133 (Historical Association);
    (315) 386-8134 FAX (Historical
    Association)
slcha@northnet.org (Historical Association)
http://slcha.org (Historical Association)
Trent A. Trulock, Executive Director
Archives and Silas Wright House: Tue–Sat
    noon–4:00, Fri noon–8:00

Municipal Historians

Town of Brasher
(234 Dullea Road—location)
PO Box 132 (mailing address)
Brasher Falls, NY 13613
(315) 389-5717
Carl B. Goodrich
by appointment

Town of Canton and Village of Canton
c/o Municipal Building
Main Street
Canton, NY 13617
(315) 386-1633
Linda A. Casserly
Mon–Fri 8:00–9:00 & noon–5:00

Town of Clare
13 White Road
Russell, NY 13684
(315) 386-2201

Kathy Colton
by appointment

Town of Clifton
Clifton Community Center
(Route 3—location)
PO Box 640 (mailing address)
Cranberry Lake, NY 12927
(315) 848-2900
Jeanne Reynolds
by appointment

Town of Colton
PO Box 493
South Colton, NY 13687
(315) 262-2800
Dennis E. Eickoff

Town of DeKalb
(696 East DeKalb Road—location)
PO Box 111 (mailing address)
DeKalb Junction, NY 13630-0111
(315) 347-1900; (315) 347-3554
hist1900@tds.net
http://www.herdcow.com/community/
    dhistory
Virginia M. Flight Fischer
Wed 12:30–4:00, Thur 9:30–11:30
(includes DeKalb Junction, Old DeKalb
    [DeKalb Village], East DeKalb, Kendrew
    Corners, Osbornville, Bigelow, Stellaville,
    and Richville)

Town of Depeyster
363 East Road
Heuvelton, NY 13654
(315) 344-2360
Gloria Kimmel

Town of Edwards and Village of Edwards
(8 First Street—location)
PO Box 100 (mailing address)
Edwards, NY 13635
(315) 562-3500
LaVerne H. Freeman

Town of Fine
PO Box 238
Star Lake, NY 13690
(315) 848-3121; (315) 891-4538 (winter);
    (315) 848-3152 FAX
Jean Grimm
by appointment
("We have four small paperback books on the
    history of the town available for
    purchase.")

Town of Gouverneur
33 Pooler Street
Gouverneur, NY 13642
(315) 287-4684
Colin Graves

Village of Gouverneur
PO Box 48
Gouverneur, NY 13642
(315) 287-0934
Nelson B. Winters

**Town of Hammond and Village of
Hammond**
320 Lake Street
Hammond, NY 13646
(315) 324-5208
Valera Bickelhaupt

Town of Hermon
102 Germain Street
Hermon, NY 13652
(315) 347-2487
Carol Holly
by appointment

Village of Hermon
138 Church Street
Hermon, NY 13652-3189
(315) 347-3221
smallman@northnet.org
Mary H. Smallman
by appointment

Village of Heuvelton
5111 County Route 6
Ogdensburg, NY 13669
(315) 393-1538
Persis Y. Boyesen
(also historian of the city of Ogdensburg and
    the town of Oswegatchie)

Town of Hopkinton
290 Wilson Road
Saint Regis Falls, NY 12980
(518) 328-4456
Addie Miller

Town of Lawrence
PO Box 15
North Lawrence, NY 12967
(315) 389-4458
Elizabeth Winn
by appointment

Town of Lisbon
PO Box 216
Lisbon, NY 13658
(315) 393-7986
Mrs. Terry Fischer

Town of Louisville
611 County Route 39
Massena, NY 13662
(315) 769-0379
Paula Beattie

Town of Macomb
6726 State Highway 58
Hammond, NY 13646
(315) 578-2247
Eloise Emrich
by appointment

Town of Madrid
2273 State Highway 310
Madrid, NY 13660
(315) 322-4419
Marian Bouchard
by appointment

Town of Massena and Village of Massena
Town of Massena Museum and Historian's
Office
200 East Orvis Street
Massena, NY 13662
(315) 769-8571
Theresa Sharp
Mon–Fri 10:00–4:00

**Town of Morristown and Village of
Morristown**
518 River Road East
Ogdensburg, NY 13669
(315) 375-6390
Lorraine Bogardus

Town of Norfolk
Town of Norfolk Historical Museum
(39 Main Street—location)
PO Box 643 (mailing address)
Norfolk, NY 13667
(315) 384-3136; (315) 384-4575
http://www.northnet.org/norfolkny
Leon H. Burnap
Tue–Thur 2:00–5:00

Village of Norwood

38 Prospect Street
Norwood, NY 13668
(315) 353-4505
Susan Lyman
by appointment

Town of Parishville
PO Box 534
Parishville, NY 13672
(315) 265-7619
Emma Remington

Town of Piercefield
15 Circle Drive
Tupper Lake, NY 12986
(518) 359-9656
Stacy Gensel

Town of Pierrepont
5893 County Route 24
Canton, NY 13617
(315) 386-8311
Charlotte Regan

Town of Pitcairn
31 Edwards Road
Harrisville, NY 13648
(315) 543-2733
Pamela Conlin

Town of Potsdam
1218 County Route 35
Canton, NY 13617
Effa Sullivan

Village of Potsdam
Potsdam Public Museum
(Civic Center, Park Street—location)
PO Box 5168 (mailing address)
Potsdam, NY 13676
(315) 265-6910
Betsy Travis

Village of Rensselaer Falls
Rensselaer Falls Historical Association
PO Box 18
Rensselaer Falls, NY 13680
(315) 344-6681
Mimi Borr
by appointment

Village of Richville
PO Box 207
Richville, NY 13681
(315) 287-0182
Stella Tamblin

Town of Rossie
456 County Route 8
Hammond, NY 13646
(315) 324-5446
Sandra Wyman
Sat noon–4:00, by appointment only

Town of Russell
189 Belleville Road
Hermon, NY 13652
(315) 347-4661
Marie Rocca

Town of Stockholm
2295 County Route 47
Potsdam, NY 13676
(315) 353-4520
Mildred S. Jenkins

**Town of Waddington and Village of
Waddington**
Moore Museum
(79 Saint Lawrence Avenue—location)
PO Box 277 (mailing address)
Waddington, NY 13694

(315) 388-5967; (315) 388-5655
E. Jane Layo
May–Sept: Tue, Wed & Thur 10:00–2:00, Fri
10:00–noon, and by appointment:
Oct–Apr by appointment only
("I also have a great variety of reference
materials on genealogy from Canada. Also
have the listings of the cemeteries on the
U.S. side and the Canadian side that were
moved during the construction of the St.
Lawrence Seaway/Power Project. The
listings give the names of the people who
were buried in each of these cemeteries.
Will also do research on Canadian
cemetery records that I have. There is no
charge for families looking up their own
history, but there is a charge for those who
charge others to do this work.")

**The Saint Lawrence County Historical
Association at the Silas Wright Museum**
(3 East Main Street—location)
PO Box 8 (mailing address)
Canton, NY 13617-0008
(315) 386-8133; (315) 386-8134 FAX
slcha@northnet.org
http://slcha.org
Trent A. Trulock, Executive Director and
County Historian
Archives and Silas Wright House: Tue–Sat
noon–4:00, Fri noon–8:00
Pub. *The Quarterly*
$25.00 per year membership; museum
admission: free; archives admission: $5.00
for nonmembers

Salisbury Historical Society
Route 1
Dolgeville, NY 13329
(315) 429-3330
Dorothea S. Ives
Pub. *Salisbury Crier*

Sand Lake Historical Society
(Averill Park, NY 12018—location)
PO Box 492 (mailing address)
West Sand Lake, NY 12196
(518) 674-3127

Saratoga County Historian
Municipal Center
40 McMaster Street
Ballston Spa, NY 12020
(518) 884-4749; (518) 884-4170 FAX
Karen Ufford Campola
Tue–Thur 9:00–4:00
research: to $20.00

Municipal Historians

**Village of Ballston and Town of Ballston
Lake**
4 Edward Road
Ballston Lake, NY 12019
(518) 399-4436
Katherine Briaddy

Town of Ballston Spa
22 Hyde Boulevard
Ballston Spa, NY 12020
(518) 885-5809
Jean Puckhaber

Village of Ballston Spa
(see Brookside Museum-Saratoga County
History Center, City, County and Regional
Archives and Libraries, above)

Town of Charlton
2115 Route 67
Charlton, NY 12019
(518) 882-6866

Laura Lee Linder

Town of Clifton Park
1 Town Hall Plaza
Clifton Park, NY 12065
(518) 371-2691 (Home)
jscherer@mail.nysed.gov
John L. Scherer

Town of Corinth and Village of Corinth
22 Mallery Street
Corinth, NY 12822
(518) 654-6809
Arthur Eggleston

Town of Day
41 Shippes Road
Corinth, NY 12822
(518) 654-2209
Ruby Marcotte

Town of Edinburg
240 Tennantville Road
Edinburg, NY 12134
(518) 863-8337
Priscilla Edwards

Town of Galway and Village of Galway
6023 Crooked Street
Broadalbin, NY 12025
(518) 882-6765
Phyllis Keeler

Town of Greenfield
311 Daniels Road
Saratoga Springs, NY 12866
(518) 587-1927
Mary DeMarco

Town of Hadley
PO Box 323
Hadley, NY 12835
Carolyn Weiss

**Town of Halfmoon and Village of
Halfmoon**
151 Stone Quarry Road
Clifton Park, NY 12065
(518) 371-8602
Ellen Kennedy

Town of Malta
60 Round Lake Road
Ballston Lake, NY 12019
(518) 899-6765
Ruth W. Roerig

City of Mechanicville
607 Park Avenue
Mechanicville, NY 12118
(518) 664-7037
Paul Loatman

Town of Milton
503 Geyser Road
Ballston Spa, NY 12020
(518) 885-9220
Irene Wood
Mon–Fri 9:00–noon, and by appointment
("Inquiries must be received in writing.")

Town of Northumberland
9 Catherine Street
Gansevoort, NY 12831
(518) 793-2017
Georgia Ball

Town of Providence
7189 Barkersville Road, Route 1
Middle Grove, NY 12850
(518) 882-6550
Mary Packer

Village of Round Lake
PO Box 214
Round Lake, NY 12151
(518) 899-2800 (Home); (518) 899-2207
(Work)
Mary Hesson

City of Saratoga Springs
297 Broadway
Saratoga Springs, NY 12866
(518) 587-2358
Dr. Martha Stonequist
flexible
("Genealogical material is QUITE
LIMITED.")

Town of Saratoga
1104 Route 29
Schuylerville, NY 12871
(518) 695-6780 (evenings)
Thomas N. Wood, III
(also historian of the villages of Schuylerville
and Victory Mills)

Village of Schuylerville
Thomas N. Wood, III (see Town of Saratoga,
above)

Village of South Glens Falls
22 Washington Road
South Glens Falls, NY 12803
John Rafferty

**Town of Stillwater and Village of
Stillwater**
PO Box 700
Stillwater, NY 12170-0700
(518) 664-1847, ext. 11; (518) 664-4614
FAX
townhist@nycap.rr.com
Linda Saunders

Village of Victory
Thomas N. Wood, III (see Town of Saratoga,
above)

Town of Waterford
4 Third Avenue
Waterford, NY 12188
(518) 237-6733
Dennis Rivage

Village of Waterford
46 South Street
Waterford, NY 12188
(518) 237-1844
Ms. Merle Doud

Town of Wilton
PO Box 2175
Wilton, NY 12831
(518) 564-0429
Jean Woutersz

Saratoga County Historical Society
Brookside Museum
6 Charlton Street
Ballston Spa, NY 12020
(518) 885-4000 (Museum)
info@brooksidemuseum.org (Museum)
http://www.brooksidemuseum.org (Museum)
Susie Kilpatrick, Executive Director
Tue–Fri 10:00–4:00, Sat noon–4:00
Pub. *Columns*, bimonthly; *Grist Mill*,
annually
(Saratoga County history and genealogy;
genealogical research done by professional
genealogist)
from $15.00 per year membership; research
prices on request

Historical Society of Saratoga Springs

Casino Congress Park
PO Box 216
Saratoga Springs, NY 12866
(518) 584-6920

Sardinia Historical Society
Savage Road
Sardinia, NY 14134
(716) 496-8847

Saugerties Historical Society
Main Street
Saugerties, NY 12477
(845) 246-9529

Sayville Historical Society
Edwards Homestead
(39 Edwards Street—location)
PO Box 41 (mailing address)
Sayville, NY 11782
(631) 563-0186
Suzanne Rubilotta, President

Scarsdale Historical Society
937 Post Road
Scarsdale, NY 10583
(914) 723-1744

Schenectady County Historian
Schenectady County Office Building
620 State Street
Schenectady, NY 12305-2113
Larry W. Hart

Municipal Historians

Village of Delanson
16 Main Street
Delanson, NY 12053
(518) 895-8007
Jill Ammel

Town of Duanesburg
(5853 Western Turnpike, Duanesburg, NY
12056—location)
PO Box 101 (mailing address)
Quaker Street, NY 12141
(518) 895-8257
Arthur Willis
by appointment

Town of Glenville
88 Skyway Drive
Glenville, NY 12302-4518
Joan S. Szablewski

Town of Niskayuna
1 Niskayuna Circle
Schenectady, NY 12309
(518) 370-0693; (518) 386-4592
http://www.niskayuna.org/historia.htm
Linda Van Dyke

Town of Princetown
Rural Delivery 5, North Kelly Road
Schenectady, NY 12306
(518) 864-5218; (518) 864-5610
Irma Mastrean

Town of Rotterdam
58 Woodlawn Street
Schenectady, NY 12306
(518) 355-7820
John Papp, Jr.

City of Schenectady
Schenectady City Hall
Jay Street
Schenectady, NY 12305
(518) 388-4590
Larry W. Hart

Village of Scotia
Scotia History Center
Scotia Village Hall
4 North Ten Broeck Street
Scotia, NY 12302
(518) 374-1071
Michelle J. Norris

Schenectady County Historical Society
32 Washington Avenue
Schenectady, NY 12305
(518) 374-0263
http://www.scpl.org/schs.html
Virginia Bolen, Archivist/Librarian
Mon–Fri 1:00–5:00, Sat (Sept–June)
9:00–noon
Pub. *SCHS Newsletter*, bimonthly
(local history, genealogy, Dutch life)
from $25.00 per year membership; research:
$15.00 per hour, 20¢ per copy

Schoharie Colonial Heritage Association
PO Box 554
Schoharie, NY 12157
(518) 295-7505
Linda Feuz, President

Schoharie County Historian
PO Box 449
Middleburgh, NY 12122
Wallace C. Van Houten

Municipal Historians

Town of Blenheim
PO Box 863
North Blenheim, NY 12131
Josephine Fuller

Town of Broome
1186 Hauverville Road
Middleburgh, NY 12122
(518) 827-5092
Betty Chichester

Town of Carlisle
PO Box 46
Carlisle, NY 12031
(518) 234-7176
Carolyn Tillapaugh

**Town of Cobleskill and Village of
Cobleskill**
116 Hillside Avenue
Cobleskill, NY 12043
Robert Holt

Town of Conesville
1154 South Gilboa Road
Gilboa, NY 12076
(607) 588-9487
Beatrice Mattice

Town of Esperance
(Church Street—location)
PO Box 99 (mailing address)
Esperance, NY 12066
jonesk1@knick.net
http://www.townofesperance.org
Kenneth Jones

Town of Fulton
PO Box 34
Fultonham, NY 12071
Gladys Wayman

Town of Gilboa
Rural Delivery 1, Box 1-127
Gilboa, NY 12076
Richard Lewis

Town of Jefferson

PO Box 290
Jefferson, NY 12093
Walter Ruland

**Town of Middleburgh and Village of
Middleburgh**
(60 Prospect Street—location)
PO Box 983 (mailing address)
Middleburgh, NY 12122
Helene Farrell

Town of Richmondville
Rural Route 1, Box 255B, Winegard Road
Richmondville, NY 12149
Joseph Bernocco

Village of Richmondville
post vacant

Town of Schoharie
PO Box 711
Schoharie, NY 12157
Anne Hendrix
("I refer all genealogy to the Old Stone Fort,
Schoharie County Historical Society.")

Village of Schoharie
post vacant

Town of Seward
Rural Delivery 2, Clove Road
Cobleskill, NY 12043
William Gregory

Village of Sharon Springs
post vacant

Town of Sharon
PO Box 335
Sharon Springs, NY 13459
(518) 284-2177
Armandine Handy

Town of Summit
Baldwin Road
Summit, NY 12175
Howard Crapser

Town of Wright
Rural Delivery 2, Box 111
Schoharie, NY 12157
Ramona Tryon

Schoharie County Historical Society
145 Fort Road
Schoharie, NY 12157
(518) 295-7192
http://schohariehistory.net
Carla Kopecky, Director
1 May–1 Oct: Tue–Sun 10:00–5:00
Pub. *Schoharie County Historical Review*,
semiannually
(New York, Schoharie County history,
folklore)
$25.00 per year membership; museum
admission: $5.00 for adults; library
admission: free to members and county
residents, $6.00 for all others; research:
$10.00 per hour to Genealogy Volunteer

Schroeppel Historical Society
Corner Main and Volney Streets
Phoenix, NY 13135
Betty Thompson, President

**Schroon-North Hudson Historical Society,
Inc.**
PO Box 444
Schroon Lake, NY 12870
(518) 532-9194
Betty Osolin, President
July–Labor Day: Wed–Sun 12:30–4:30; after

Labor Day–Columbus Day weekend:
Sat–Sun 12:30–4:30
Pub. *SNHHS Newsletter*

Schuyler County Historian
3460 County Road 28
Watkins Glen, NY 14891
(607) 535-4577
Barbara H. Bell
(also historian of the town of Reading)

Municipal Historians

Village of Burdett
3927 Lake Street
Burdett, NY 14818
John Hunt

Town of Catharine
(Town Hall, 106 Grant Road, Odessa, NY
14869—location)
2351 Oak Hill Road (mailing address)
Alpine, NY 14805-9760
(607) 594-2062
quiltmtn@msn.com
Carol Fagnan
(The town of Catharine includes the village of
Odessa, and the hamlets of Catharine,
Alpine and Cayutaville)

Town of Cayuta
5985 State Route 13
Cayuta, NY 14824
Joyce Hill
(Cayuta includes the village of Cayuta and
part of Alpine)

Town of Dix
(304 Seventh Street—location)
2470 County Route 16 (mailing address)
Watkins Glen, NY 14891-9551
(607) 535-4730
Marian M. Boyce
hours: various
(Dix includes the village of Watkins Glen,
and the communities of Beaver Dams,
Townsend and Moreland)

Town of Hector
5588 Mark Taber Road
Trumansburg, NY 14886
Sandra Bradford
(Hector includes the villages of Burdett,
Valois, Mecklenburg, Trumansburg, etc.)

Village of Montour Falls
110 South Genesee
Montour Falls, NY 14865
Allen Sweet, Acting Historian

Town of Montour
1646 Fitzpatrick Hill Road
Montour Falls, NY 14865
Shirley Craver
(Montour includes the village of Montour
Falls, formerly called Havana)

Village of Odessa
317 Speedway Road
Odessa, NY 14869
Patti Lisk

Town of Orange
665 County Route 16
Painted Post, NY 14870
Joe Button
(Orange includes the village of Monterey)

Town of Reading
Barbara H. Bell (see Schuyler County
Historian, above)

Town of Tyrone
Tower Hill Road
Watkins Glen, NY 14891
Jesse Ellison

Village of Watkins Glen
303 North Franklin Street
Watkins Glen, NY 14891
Jean Kosty

Schuyler County Historical Society
(108 North Catharine Street—location)
PO Box 651 (mailing address)
Montour Falls, NY 14865
(607) 535-9741
Bonnie Dilts, Director
Mon–Thur 10:00–4:00, Sat noon–4:00
Pub. *Schuyler County Historical Society
Journal* (not genealogical), quarterly,
$1.50 per issue for nonmembers
(eleven exhibit rooms of local history, plus
research library)
$15.00 per year membership; museum
admission: donation; library admission:
$5.00 for nonmembers; research: $10.00
per hour, plus copies at 25¢ per page

Scotia History Center
Scotia Village Hall
4 North Ten Broeck
Scotia, NY 12302
Michelle J. Norris, Scotia Village Historian

Scriba Historical Society
PO Box 201
Lycoming, NY 13093-0201

Scriba Town Historical Association
Scriba Municipal Building
Rural Delivery 8
Oswego, NY 13126
(315) 342-6420

Seaford Historical Society
(Waverly Avenue—location)
2234 Jackson Avenue (mailing address)
Seaford, NY 11783
(516) 826-1150
Joshua Soren, President

Seneca County Historian
1 Di Pronio Drive
Waterloo, NY 13165
(315) 539-5655, ext. 2068
Charmoine Dinsmore
Mon & Wed 8:30–noon & 12:30–5:00, Thur
8:00–noon

Municipal Historians

Town of Covert
(3685 Clinton—location)
PO Box 35 (mailing address)
Interlaken, NY 14847
dbnelson@capital.net
Diane Bassette Nelson

Town of Fayette
3555 Route 89
Seneca Falls, NY 13148
(315) 549-7148
John Hoster

Village of Interlaken
PO Box 323
Interlaken, NY 14847
Maurice L. Patterson

Town of Junius
1589 Route 318
Waterloo, NY 13165
Anne White

Town of Lodi and Village of Lodi
(8479 Maple Street—location)
PO Box 180 (mailing address)
Lodi, NY 14860
Edith Brown

Town of Ovid and Village of Ovid
(2173 East Seneca Street—location)
PO Box 374 (mailing address)
Ovid, NY 14521
(607) 869-5222
ghsnyder@fltg.net
Gail H. Snyder

Town of Romulus
6969 East Lake Road
Ovid, NY 14521-9766
Sarah Dawley

Village of Seneca Falls
Auburn Road
Seneca Falls, NY 13148
Roberta Halden

Town of Varick
2385 Willers Road
Seneca Falls, NY 13148
Charmion Boyle Dinsmore

Town of Waterloo
20 West Clark Street
Waterloo, NY 13165
Betty Auten (see Seneca County Historian,
above)

Village of Waterloo
156 Virginia Street
Waterloo, NY 13165
(315) 539-0533 (Terwilliger Museum,
Waterloo Historical Society)
Beatrice Contant

Seneca Falls Historical Society
55 Cayuga Street
Seneca Falls, NY 13148
(315) 568-8412
Frances T. Barbieri, Associate
Director/Education Director
Mon–Fri 9:00–5:00, Sat noon–4:00, Sun
(June–Sept) noon–4:00
Pub. *S.F.H.S. Newsletter*, monthly
(local history, New York, women's rights)
from $15.00 to $5,000.00 per year
membership

Sharon Historical Society
Main Street, Route 10
Sharon Springs, NY 13459
(518) 284-2350
Omer Cousineau, President; Dorcas Comrie,
Curator
every day 1 July–Labor Day, and by
appointment; meetings: second Tue
(Apr–June & Sept–Dec)
(published *Reflections of Sharon* and
Nostalgia)
$5.00 per year membership; admission:
donation; research: no genealogical
research services, contact Armandine
Handy, Town Historian, Box 335, Sharon
Springs, NY 13459

Shelter Island Historical Society
Old Havens House
(16 South Ferry Road—location)
PO Box 847 (mailing address)
Shelter Island, NY 11964
(631) 749-0025; (631) 749-1825 FAX
sihissoc@optonline.net
Peggy Dickerson, Archive Committee
Chairperson
Mon–Fri 10:00–1:00, and by appointment

$25.00 per year membership

Sidney Historical Society
(Sidney Civic Center, 21 Liberty Street,
Second Floor, Room 218—location)
PO Box 2217 (mailing address)
Sidney, NY 13838
(607) 563-8787; (607) 563-1617 (President);
(607) 563-9527 (Curator)
webmaster@sidneyonline.com
http://www.sidneyonline.com
Neila C. Hayes, President
Tue 1:45–4:45, Thur 10:00–noon, and by
appointment
research: copies plus mailing costs

Silver Creek Historical Society
172 Central Avenue
Silver Creek, NY 14136
(716) 934-3240 (Village Clerk)
Louis F. Pelletter, Village Historian

Skaneateles Historical Society/Archives
The Creamery
28 Hannum Street
Skaneateles, NY 13152
http://www.skaneateles.com/genealogy.html

Smithtown Historical Society
Caleb Smith II House
5 North Country Road, Route 25A
Smithtown, NY 11787
(631) 265-6768
Louise Hall, Director; Bradley L. Harris,
President
Mon–Fri 9:00–4:00
(Smithtown history, Smith genealogy)

Snug Harbor Cultural Center
1000 Richmond Terrace
Staten Island, NY 10301
(718) 448-2500; (718) 442-8534 FAX
Celia Reilly, Director; Brian Rehr, Associate
PR/Marketing Department
Gallery: Wed–Sun noon–5:00
Pub. *Newsletter-Columns*, bimonthly
from $25.00 per year membership

Somers Historical Society
Elephant Hotel
PO Box 336
Somers, NY 10589
(914) 277-4977
Florence S. Oliver, Acting Archivist
by appointment

Historical Association of South Jefferson
(9 East Church Street—location)
PO Box 55 (mailing address)
Adams, NY 13605
(315) 232-2616; (315) 232-2178 FAX
hasjeff@imcnet.net
http://www.rootsweb.com/~nyjeffer/sjef.htm
Debbie Quick, Secretary
Mon–Tue & Thur 8:30–2:30, and by
appointment (subject to change)
costs for copies, membership not necessary to
do research on site

**Southampton Colonial Society and
Historical Museum**
(17 Meeting House Lane—location)
PO Box 303 (mailing address)
Southampton, NY 11969
(631) 283-1612; (631) 283-0605
Adele Cramer, Curator
12 June–15 Sept
(early Long Island history; Southampton
Historical Museum [PO Box 805,
Bridgehampton, NY 11932], Old Halsey
Homestead, Pelletreau Silversmith Shop,
Conscience Point)

Southold Historical Society
(54235 Main Street—location)
PO Box 1 (mailing address)
Southold, NY 11971
(631) 765-5500
Clara Bjerknes, Archives Chair
Archives: Mon, Wed & Fri 9:30–noon;
Office: Mon–Fri 9:30–2:30
$10.00 per year membership

Southport Historical Society
PO Box 146
Pine City, NY 14871

Spafford Area Historical Society
(School House/Grange Building—location)
PO Box 250 (mailing address)
Marietta, NY 13110
(315) 636-8300; (315) 636-7782 FAX
pbc@mailbox.shr.edu
E. C. (Lauri) Clark
Pub. *SAHS Newsletter*, monthly
$5.00 per year membership

Spencer Historical Society
Center Street
Spencer, NY 14883
Laura C. Uhl, Curator
June–Aug: Sun 2:00–5:00 and by
appointment
Pub. *Spencer Historical Society Newsletter*,
quarterly
(" We also have two cemetery booklets,
$3.00 each.")
$5.00 per year membership

Springfield Historical Society
PO Box 65
Springfield Center, NY 13468
Jeannette D. Smith, Town Historian

Springs Historical Society
Springs Library
Parsons-Anderson House
PO Box 1860
East Hampton, NY 11937
Heather Anderson, President

**Springwater-Websters Crossing Historical
Society**
PO Box 68
Springwater, NY 14560
Charles "Chuck" Julien, President

Stafford Historical Society
6684 Randall Road
LeRoy, NY 14482-9316
(716) 343-6699
Martha Heddon, Town Historian

Stanford Historical Society
Stanfordville, NY 12581

Staten Island Historical Society
411 Clarke Avenue
Staten Island, NY 10306-1198
(718) 351-9414 (Education Department);
(718) 351-1611 (Museum); (718) 351-
6057 FAX
Pub. *Richmondtown Restoration: Newsletter
of the Staten Island Historical Society*;
Staten Island Historian, quarterly, $9.00
per year subscription

Stephentown Historical Society
PO Box 11
Stephentown, NY 12168
(518) 733-6070; (518) 733-5235
Virginia Atwater, Genealogist
by appointment
research fees are voluntary

Sterling Historical Society
(104A at Sterling Center—location)
14412 Woods Road (mailing address)
Sterling, NY 13156
(315) 947-6461 (President)
Don H. Richardson, President
Museum: June–Oct: Sun 2:00–5:00
$3.00 per year membership; research: queries
to Hallie Sweeting, Genealogist and
Historian, 876 State Route 104A, Sterling,
NY 13156, (315) 947-5653

Steuben County Historian
(Historian's Office, corner of West Morris
Street and Cameron Park—location)
3 East Pulteney Square (mailing address)
Bath, NY 14810
(607) 776-9631, ext. 3411
http://nyslgti.gen.ny.us/Steuben/historian.
html
John C. Ormsby, Acting Historian
Mon–Fri 9:00–4:00

Municipal Historians

Village of Arkport
post vacant

Town of Avoca
4185 County Route 70
Avoca, NY 14809
(607) 566-2884
Grace S. Fox
by appointment

Village of Avoca
(3 Chase Street—location)
PO Box 462 (mailing address)
Avoca, NY 14809
Peter Gledhill

Town of Bath
16 Main Street
Savona, NY 14879
Richard Littell

Village of Bath
88 Geneva Street
Bath, NY 14810-9503
James E. Hope

Town of Bradford
PO Box 162
Bradford, NY 14815
Lottie Race

Town of Cameron
4848 County Route 10
Cameron, NY 14819
Julia Masti

Town of Canisteo
4150 County Route 30
Cameron, NY 14819
gdickey@infoblvd.net
George Dickey
Fri 1:00–3:00 at Kanestio Historical Society

Village of Canisteo
post vacant

**Town of Cohocton and Village of
Cohocton**
206 Point of Woods Drive
Albany, NY 12203
Dr. James Folts

City of Corning
70 East Third Street
Corning, NY 14830
Lois Janes

Town of Corning
20 Maple Street
Corning, NY 14830
Joyce Schreppell

Town of Dansville
9127 Strobel Road
Arkport, NY 14807
Sarah Gates

Town of Erwin
PO Box 52
Coopers Plains, NY 14827
Anna Sherwood

Town of Fremont
8098 State Route 21
Arkport, NY 14807-9441
Joann Spencer

Town of Greenwood
3870 County Route 61
Andover, NY 14806
Gerald Mullen

Village of Hammondsport
PO Box 11
Hammondsport, NY 14840
Terry Bretherton
(also historian of the town of Urbana)

Town of Hartsville
5084 Purdy Circle Road
Hornell, NY 14843
Betty Caple

Town of Hornby
185 South Place
Corning, NY 14830
Susan J. Moore

City of Hornell
58 Bennett Street
Hornell, NY 14843
Mrs. Robert Oakes

Town of Hornellsville
475 Cleveland Avenue
North Hornell, NY 14843-1022
Mary Ann Rutski
(also historian of the village of North
   Hornellsville)

Town of Howard
8030 County Route 70
Avoca, NY 14809
Sondra Lewis

Town of Jasper
3617 County Route 31
Canisteo, NY 14823
Twila J. O'Dell

Town of Lindley
Town Hall
535 State Road
Lindley, NY 14858
(607) 523-8851 (Home); (607) 523-8816
   (Town Hall)
piercecm@juno.com
Catherine M. Pierce
by appointment
("Since I do not have an office of my own at
   Town Hall, I encourage appointments.")

Village of North Hornell
Mary Ann Rutski (see Town of Hornellsville,
   above)

Village of Painted Post
post vacant

Town of Prattsburg
(Historian Office, Prattsburgh, NY
   14873—location)
30 Valley Brook Drive (mailing address)
Fairport, NY 14450
jpulver@rochester.rr.com
J. Douglas Pulver
Tue 10:00–3:00

Town of Pulteney
11150 County Road 78
Prattsburg, NY 14873
Emily Radigan

Town of Rathbone
6659 County Route 21
Addison, NY 14801
Isabelle Risley

Village of Riverside
post vacant

Village of Savona
(16 Main Street—location)
PO Box 674 (mailing address)
Savona, NY 14879
Richard Littell

Village of South Corning
20 South Maple Street
Corning, NY 14830
Joyce A. Schreppel

Town of Thurston
7494 Thurston Road
Campbell, NY 14821
Shirley Edsall

Town of Troupsburg
886 Main Street
Troupsburg, NY 14885
Sandra Szepansky

Town of Tuscarora
8338 Glendenning Creek Road
Lindley, NY 14858
(607) 523-8925
Vicki L. Jones
anytime by appointment

Town of Urbana
(see Village of Hammondsport, above)

Town of Wayland and Village of Wayland
14 Pine Street
Wayland, NY 14572
Marion Scott

Town of West Union
Route 2, Box 10
Rexville, NY 14877
Anna Cerrillo

Town of Wheeler
6167 Fritz Hill Road
Avoca, NY 14809
Melvin G. Partridge

Town of Woodhull
6298 Symonds Hill Road
Addison, NY 14801
norm@infoblvd.net
Norma B. Crane
5 days per week 9:00–noon

Village of Woodhull
1593 Mill Street
Woodhull, NY 14898
Kathryn Andrews

Steuben County Historical Society
(Magee House, Cameron Park—location)

PO Box 349 (mailing address)
Bath, NY 14810-0349
(607) 776-9930
Joseph E Paddock, President
Mon–Fri 10:00–3:00
Pub. *Steuben Echoes*, quarterly
$6.00 per year membership

Stirling Historical Society, Inc.
(Main Street—location)
PO Box 590 (mailing address)
Greenport, NY 11944
(631) 477-0099
Frank Coyle, President

Stockholm Historical Organization
Municipal Buiding
Winthrop, NY 13697
(315) 353-4520; (315) 384-4764
Mildred S. Jenkins, Stockholm Town
   Historian
June–Sept: Tue 1:00–3:00, and by
   appointment

Stony Brook Historical Society
PO Box 802
Stony Brook, NY 11790
Susan Jayne, President

Stony Creek Historical Association
Lanfear Road
Stony Creek, NY 12878
(518) 696-3488

Suffolk County Historian
Division of Cultural and Historical Services
Suffolk County Department of Parks
(Montauk Highway—location)
PO Box 144 (mailing address)
West Sayville, NY 11796
(631) 567-1487
J. Lance Mallamo

Municipal Historians

Village of Amityville
post vacant

Village of Asharoken
1 Asharoken Avenue
Northport, NY 11768
(631) 261-7098
Martin Richter
Pub. *Asharoken Newsletter*, monthly (free to
   residents)

Town of Babylon
151 Phelps Lane
North Babylon, NY 11703
(631) 957-7487
Robert Mills Smith

Village of Belle Terre
PO Box 112
Port Jefferson, NY 11777
Daniel Cornish

Village of Bellport
69 Country Club Road
Bellport, NY 11713
Malcolm Johnson

Village of Brightwaters
467 Lombardy Boulevard
Brightwaters, NY 11718
Rhoda Milligan

Town of Brookhaven
Town Hall
215 South Ocean Avenue
Patchogue, NY 11772
(631) 654-7897

MALLORYLEONIAK@NETSCAPE.NET
David Overton; Mallory Leoniak

Village of Dering Harbor
PO Box K
Shelter Island, NY 11964
Helen Loper

Town of East Hampton
PO Box 726
Amagansett, NY 11930
Carleton Kelsey

Village of East Hampton
4 Fireplace-Springs Road
East Hampton, NY 11937
N. Sherrill Foster

Village of Farmingdale
31 Lowell Drive
Farmingdale, NY 11735
Gary Hammond

Village of Freeport
post vacant

Village of Head of the Harbor
PO Box 416
Saint James, NY 11780
Barbara Van Liew

Village of Huntington Bay
230 Vineyard Road
Huntington, NY 11743
Mrs. G. David Gudebrod

Town of Huntington
228 Main Street
Huntington, NY 11743
(631) 351-3244
Rufus Langhans

Town of Islip
214 Tahlulah Lane
West Islip, NY 11795
Carl Starace

Village of Lindenhurst
72 Harrington Avenue
Lindenhurst, NY 11757
Evelyn Ellis

Village of Lloyd Harbor
32 Middle Hollow Road
Huntington, NY 11743
David C. Fuchs

Village of Nissequogue
1 Jefferson Ferry Drive, Apartment 8183
South Setauket, NY 11720-4735
Louise Hall

Village of North Haven
(335 Ferry Road—location)
PO Box 643 (mailing address)
Sag Harbor, NY 11963
Joseph Zaykowski

Village of Northport
180 Bayview Avenue
Northport, NY 11768
Dorothy Walker

Village of Ocean Beach
20 Ocean Road
Ocean Beach, NY 11770
Fred Charlton

Village of Old Field
105 Main Street
Port Jefferson Station, NY 11776-1001
Mildred Gillie

Village of Patchogue
Greater Patchogue Historical Society
PO Box 102
Patchogue, NY 11772
Anne Swezey

Village of Pine Valley
post vacant

Village of Poquott
post vacant

Village of Port Jefferson
post vacant

Village of Quogue
PO Box 1165
Quogue, NY 11959
Beatrice Marcks

Town of Riverhead
102 Sound Avenue
Riverhead, NY 11901
Justine Wells

Village of Saltaire
109 West 77th Street
New York, NY 10024
Elizabeth Starkey

Town of Shelter Island
Town Hall
Shelter Island, NY 11964
Louise Green

Village of Shoreham
post vacant

Town of Smithtown
Town Hall
Smithtown, NY 11787
Bradley Harris

Town of South Salem
post vacant

Town of Southampton
Town Hall
Southampton, NY 11968
Robert Keene

Town of Southold
(53095 Main Road—location)
PO Box 1179 (mailing address)
Southold, NY 11971
(631) 765-1981
Antonia Booth

Village of The Branch
post vacant

Village of Westhampton Beach
PO Box 991
Westhampton Beach, NY 11978
Theodore Conklin, Jr.
Suffolk County Historical Society
The Helen Raynor Hannah Memorial
Library, Genealogy Section
300 West Main Street
Riverhead, NY 11901
(631) 727-2881
http://www.liest.com/museum.html
Mr. Wally Broege, Director
Wed–Thur & Sat 12:30–4:30, by
appointment if coming from a distance
Pub. *Suffolk County Historical Society
Register*, quarterly
(local/regional history museum and library,
genealogical research library with both
published and unpublished materials:
wills, deeds, bills of sale, letters, account
books, ledgers, journals, diaries, maps,

atlases, photographs, scrapbooks, vertical
files arranged by towns, periodicals and
newspapers, photographic negatives,
members' ancestor charts, application
records of the disbanded Daughters of the
Revolution of 1776)
$25.00 per year membership; library
admission: $2.00 for nonmembers

Sullivan County Historian
PO Box 185
Barryville, NY 12719
(845) 557-6467
John Conway
(also historian of the town of Highland)

Municipal Historians

Town of Bethel
Drawer C
Kauneonga Lake, NY 12749
(845) 583-4300
Marion Vassmer

Village of Bloomingburg
PO Box 158
Bloomingburgh, NY 12721
(845) 733-1593
Loretta Franklin

Town of Cochecton
(Lake Huntington, NY 12752—location)
285 Tyler Road (mailing address)
Narrowsburg, NY 12764
(845) 252-7113
Salvatore B. Indelacato

Town of Delaware
Callicoon, NY 12723
(845) 887-5454
Mary Curtis

Town of Fallsburg
post vacant

Town of Forestburgh
44 Forestburgh Road
Forestburgh, NY 12777
(845) 794-8879
Margaret W. Abdoo

Town of Fremont
374 Friedernstein Road
Long Eddy, NY 12760
Thelma I. W. Herbert

Town of Highland
John Conway (see Sullivan County Historian,
above)

Village of Jeffersonville
post vacant
c/o Village Hall
(17 Center Street—location)
PO Box 155X (mailing address)
Jeffersonville, NY 12748
(845) 482-4275; (845) 482-5298 FAX

Town of Liberty and Village of Liberty
552 North Main Street
Liberty, NY 12754
(845) 292-8375
Delbert Van Etten

Town of Lumberland
PO Box 1
Glen Spey, NY 12737
(845) 856-6372; (845) 856-8600
Frank V. Schwarz

Town of Mamakating
Town Office

2948 Route 209
Wurtsboro, NY 12790
(845) 888-3000
Harold Lindsay or John Masten

Village of Monticello
post vacant

Town of Neversink
(273 Main Street—location)
PO Box 307 (mailing address)
Grahamsville, NY 12740
(845) 985-2452
Carol Smythe

Town of Rockland
Town Office
95 Main Street
Livingston Manor, NY 12758
(845) 498-4346
Wilmer E. Sipple

Town of Thompson
222 Gregory Road
Monticello, NY 12701
John Jurgens

Town of Tusten
380 Gables Road
Narrowsburgh, NY 12764
(845) 252-7575
Barbara Buckman

Village of Woodridge
PO Box 177
Woodridge, NY 12789
(845) 434-7030
James Slater

Village of Wurtsboro
post vacant

Sullivan County Historical Society
Sullivan County Museum
(265 Main Street—location)
PO Box 247 (mailing address)
Hurleyville, NY 12747-0247
(845) 434-8044
http://www.sullivancountyhistory.org
Charlotte Osterhout, Genealogist; Mr. F. Hill,
    President
Tue, and by appointment; Library: Tue &
    Thur 1:00–4:30, Museum: Wed–Sat
    10:00–4:30, Sun 1:00–4:30
Pub. *The Observer*, six issues per year
$15.00 per year membership

Taconic Valley Historical Society
(Hilltop Road—location)
PO Box 400 (mailing address)
Berlin, NY 12022-0400

Tappantown Historical Society
PO Box 71
Tappan, NY 10983
(845) 359-5490

Three Village Historical Society
(93 North Country Road—location)
PO Box 76 (mailing address)
East Setauket, NY 11733-0076
(631) 751-3730 voice & FAX
tvhistsoc@aol.com
http://members.aol.com/tvhs1
Michele M. Morrisson, Director
three days per week, and by appointment
Pub. *The Three Village Historian: Journal of
    the Three Village Historical Society*,
    annually, $7.00 per issue for nonmembers,
    $5.50 per issue for members
(villages of Setauket, Stony Brook, and Old
    Field, in Town of Brookhaven; Long

Island's North shore; ship building;
    Rhodes Collection/Historic Documents)
$20.00 per year membership

Ticonderoga Historical Society
The Hancock House
6 Moses Circle
Ticonderoga, NY 12883
(518) 585-7868; (518) 585-6367 FAX
ths2@capital.net
http://www.capital.net/~ths2/index.htm
Robin Trudeau, Staff Assistant; Karla Staudt,
    Staff Researcher
Wed–Sat 10:00–4:00
Pub. *"The Attic" Newsletter*
$25.00 per year membership

Tioga County Historian
(16 Court Street—location)
PO Box 307 (mailing address)
Owego, NY 13827
(607) 687-8646
esedore@usadatanet.net
Emma Sedore

Municipal Historians

Town of Berkshire
PO Box 5
Berkshire, NY 13736
(607) 657-4416
Nancy Hunt

Town of Candor and Village of Candor
90 Dry Brook Road
Willseyville, NY 13864
(607) 659-7661
Carole Henry

Town of Newark Valley
400 Shirley Road
Newark Valley, NY 13811
Shirley Callahan

Village of Newark Valley
post vacant

Town of Nichols and Village of Nichols
1058 East River Road
Nichols, NY 13812
(607) 699-3172
William Caloroso

Town of Owego
Lincolnshire Drive
Owego, NY 13827
(607) 687-1961
esedore@usadatanet.net
Emma Sedore

Village of Owego
post vacant

Town of Richford
PO Box 91
Richford, NY 13835
(607) 657-4497
Clarence Lacey

Town of Spencer and Village of Spencer
350 Van Etten Road
Spencer, NY 14883
(607) 589-6134
Jean Alve
by appointment
("large fill of clippings of local persons, from
    1886 to present. Have indexed numerous
    sources for information."
charges research fee

Town of Tioga
(Fifth Avenue—location)

50 Allyn Road (mailing address)
Tioga Center, NY 13845-0243
(607) 687-4732
Carole LaPlante
by appointment

Village of Waverly
Waverly Village Office
362 Broad Street
Waverly, NY 14892
Pauline Perry

Tioga County Historical Society
Museum and Genealogical Committee
110-112 Front Street
Owego, NY 13827
(607) 687-2460
http://www.tier.net/tiogahistory
Jean Winnie Neff, Executive Director
Tue–Fri 1:00–4:00, Sat 10:00–4:00

Tompkins County Historian
125 East Court Street
Ithaca, NY 14850
Carol Kammen

Municipal Historians

Town of Caroline
(Town Hall, 2670 Slaterville Road—location)
PO Box 136 (mailing address)
Slaterville Springs, NY 14881
(607) 539-6400; (607) 539-6464 (for
    appointments)
carolinehistorian@yahoo.com
Barbara B. M. Kone
31 May–30 Sept: Thur 7:00 P.M.–9:00 P.M.

Village of Cayuga Heights
post vacant

Town of Danby
134 Hornbrook Road
Ithaca, NY 14850
(607) 272-3287
Susan A. Hautala

Town of Dryden and Village of Dryden
PO Box 555
Dryden, NY 13053
Laurence "Beachy" Beach

Town of Enfield
487 Enfield Center Road
Ithaca, NY 14850
(607) 272-6412
sdt1@cornell.edu
Susan Thompson

Village of Freeville
Village Hall
Factory Street
Freeville, NY 13068
Joan Manning

Town of Groton
838 Buck Road
Groton, NY 13073
Juanita Griffin

Village of Groton
208 Cortland Street
Groton, NY 13073
(607) 898-3601
Lee Shurtleff

City of Ithaca
201 Worth Street
Ithaca, NY 14850
(607) 273-2133
Jane M. Dieckmann

Town of Ithaca
The DeWitt Historical Society of Tompkins
County
401 East State Street
Ithaca, NY 14850
(607) 273-3378; (607) 273-8284 (Society);
(607) 273-6107 FAX (Society)
dhs@lakenet.org (Society)
http://www.lakenet.org/dewitt (Society)
Geoffrey Morse

Town of Lansing
49 Myers Road
Lansing, NY 14882
(607) 533-4514
Louise Bement

Village of Lansing
post vacant

Town of Newfield
262 Van Kirk Road
Newfield, NY 14867
(607) 564-7778
Alan Chaffee

**Village of Trumansburg and Town of
Ulysses**
(Hector Street—location)
PO Box 49 (mailing address)
Trumansburg, NY 14886
(607) 387-5855
Esther Northrup

Tonawanda-Kenmore Historical Society
Saint Peter's Church
100 Knoche Road
Tonawanda, NY 14150
(716) 873-5774
millar@wzrd.com
http://freenet.buffalo.edu/~tot/htm/
o_hsoc.htm
Graham Millar, President
Sun (Apr–Oct) 2:00–5:00
(local "Town of Tonawanda" history)

Historical Society of the Tonawandas, Inc.
113 Main Street
Tonawanda, NY 14150-2129
(716) 694-7406
absgram@usa.net
Jane Penvose, Curator
Wed–Fri 10:00–4:30
Pub. *The Lumber Shover*, monthly
("Tonawanda and North Tonawanda, located
across the Erie Barge Canal from each
other in two separate counties, share a
common history." Research library has
census records and genealogical
information.)
$10.00 per year membership

Tully Area Historical Society
(24 State Street—location)
PO Box 22 (mailing address)
Tully, NY 13159-0022
(315) 696-4681
eleanor@dreamscape.com
http://www.tullyareahistorical.com
Eleanor L. Preston, President
Mon 9:00–5:00, Tue–Wed & Fri 9:00–1:00,
Sat 10:00–1:00
Pub. *TAHS Newsletter*, quarterly
$5.00 per year membership; research: $6.00
per hour

Tuxedo Historical Society
(Route 17—location)
PO Box 188 (mailing address)
Tuxedo, NY 10987
(845) 351-5611; (845) 351-4534
Talbot A. Love, President

Sat 2:00–4:00, Sun 2:00–5:00
Pub. *Inside/Out*, irregularly
("town and local news")
$7.00 per year

Ulster County Historian
11 Main Street
Saugerties, NY 12477
(845) 246-4754
karlynelia@aol.com
Karlyn Knaust Elia
(also historian of the town of Saugerties)

Municipal Historians

Town of Denning
2050 Denning Road
Claryville, NY 12725
(845) 985-2411
Jane Smith

Village of Ellenville
PO Box 6
Ellenville, NY 12428
(845) 647-3801
Paul Ross

Town of Esopus
PO Box 37
Rifton, NY 12471
prehnfm@juno.com
Florence Prehn

Town of Gardiner
2121 Route 4455
Gardiner NY 12525
carletonmabee@juno.com
Dr. Carleton Mabee

Town of Hardenbergh
HCR 3 Box 99
Margaretville, NY 12455
regalhill@catskill.net
Gail Hillriegel

Town of Hurley
c/o Town of Hurley Offices
569 Wamsley Place
Hurley, NY 12443
Hurleyhistory@cs.com
David Baker

City of Kingston
58 Valentine Avenue
Kingston, NY 12401
(845) 331-6535
Edwin Ford

Town of Kingston
906 Sawkill Road
Kingston, NY 12401
(845) 336-0339
http://NY.Town.kingston.us
Ernie Smith

Town of Lloyd
26 Maple Avenue
Highland, NY 12528
Dorothy Gruner
Town of Marbletown
405 Mohonk Road
High Falls, NY 12440
(845) 687-7031
Emily Stokes
("I am not a genealogist.")

Town of Marlborough
80 Gobblers Knob Road
Marlboro, NY 12542
(845) 236-7363
Marylou Mahon

Town of New Paltz
(10 Bruce Street—location)
PO Box 550 (mailing address)
New Paltz, NY 12561
(845) 255-0108 voice & FAX
Marksa@newpaltz.edu
Alfred H. Marks

Village of New Paltz
(10 Bruce Street—location)
PO Box 877 (mailing address)
New Paltz, NY 12561
(845) 255-0108 voice & FAX
Marksa@newpaltz.edu
Alfred H. Marks

Town of Olive
97 Drybrook Road
West Shokan, NY 12494
(845) 657-2565
Ruth Anne Muller

Village of Pine Hill
post vacant

Town of Plattekill
(Route HH/SS—location)
PO Box 45 (mailing address)
Modena, NY 12548
(845) 883-7331
Muriel Obermeyer
Thur–Fri 10:00–3:00

Town of Rochester
Rural Delivery 2
Accord, NY 12404
(845) 626-7103
Alice Schoonmaker

Town of Rosendale
Bloomington, NY 12411
(845) 338-7168
Ann Gilchrist

Village of Rosendale
post vacant

Town of Saugerties
Karlyn Elia (see County Historian)

Village of Saugerties
post vacant

Town of Shandaken
288 Route 214
Chichester, NY 12416
Charles Zimmermann

Town of Shawangunk
PO Box 336
Pine Bush, NY 12566
Shirley Orndorff

Town of Ulster
32 Lawrenceville Street
Kingston, NY 12401
(845) 331-3265
Bruce Burgher
by appointment

Town of Warwarsing
c/o Ed & Al's Barbershop
Canal Street
Ellenville, NY 12428
(845) 647-9684
John Unverzagt

Town of Woodstock
831 Zena Road
Woodstock, NY 12498
(845) 679-8036
http://www.woodstock-online.com/mini_

site/historicalsociety/historicalsociety.htm
Edgar C. Leaycraft

Ulster County Historical Society
(Route 209, Town of Marbletown—location)
PO Box 3752 (mailing address)
Kingston, NY 12402
(845) 338-5614
Amanda C. Jones, Executive Director
Wed–Sun (June–Sept) 1:00–5:00
Pub. *Ulster County Gazette*, three times per
    year
$10.00 per year membership

Ulysses Historical Society
(South Street, Trumansburg, NY
14886—location)
PO Box 445 (mailing address)
Trumansburg, NY 14886-0445
(607) 387-7833; (607) 387-7262 (President)
http://www.ulysses.ny.us/history
Marion Hoffmire, Genealogist; Ruth
    Wolverton, President
May–Sept: Thur–Sat 2:00–4:00
$8.00 per year membership; research: cost of
    materials plus donation

Unadilla Valley Historical Society
7-AA Main Street
Mount Upton, NY 13809
(607) 764-8492

Union Vale Historical Society
249 Duncan Road
Lagrangeville, NY 12540
(845) 724-5600
Mary Lou Deforest, President
meetings: first Mon
$5.00 per year membership

Upper Delaware Heritage Alliance
PO Box 143
Callicoon, NY 12723
(717) 685-4871 (Editor's residence in
    Pennsylvania)

Valley Historical Society
(Main at Lester Streets—location)
PO Box 1045 (mailing address)
Sinclairville, NY 14782
(716) 962-8520
http://clweb.com/local_info/artsed/vhs.html
Ruth I. Smith, President
summer: Sun 2:00–5:00, and by appointment
(cemetery, store, church, grange records to be
    examined in museum only)

Valley Stream Historical Society
PO Box 22
Valley Stream, NY 11582
(516) 872-4159 (516) 599-7069 FAX
VSHis@aol.com
http://www.nassaulibrary.org/valleyst/
    ushist.html
Carol McKenna, President
Sun 1:00–4:00
Pub. *Panorama*, ten times per year (monthly,
    except July–Aug)
$10.00 per year membership

Van Cortlandtville Historical Society
297 Locust Avenue
Peekskill, NY 10566-1308
(914) 737-7785
George Kummer, President
third Sat 2:00
Pub. *Historical Key*, quarterly
$10.00 per year membership

William K. Vanderbilt Historical Society
PO Box 433
Oakdale, NY 11769

(516) 567-2277

Vernon Historical Society
PO Box 786
Vernon, NY 13476
(315) 768-7091
Jon Landers, President
$2.00 per year membership

Victor Historical Society
PO Box 472
Victor, NY 14564-0472
(716) 924-2645

Virgil Historical Society
(East State Road, Route 90—location)
Route 2 (mailing address)
Cortland, NY 13045

Wading River Historical Society
PO Box 263
Wading River, NY 11792
(631) 929-1017
Peter Beyer, President

**Historical Society of Walden and the
Wallkill Valley**
PO Box 48
Walden, NY 12586
peisley@sunyorange.edu (withheld)
by appointment
Pub. *Newsletter*, two times per year
$7.50 per year membership; research:
    donation plus SASE

Walton Historical Society
Gardiner Place
Walton, NY 13856
(607) 865-6003
Maureen O'Connell, Secretary

Walworth Historical Society/Museum
(2257 Academy Street—location)
PO Box 142 (mailing address)
Walworth, NY 14568
(315) 524-9528

Warren County Historian
Warren County Municipal Center
1340 State Route 9
Lake George, NY 12845-9803
(518) 761-6544
Marjorie Swan
Tue & Thur 9:00–5:00

Municipal Historians

Town of Bolton
Bolton Town Hall
(Lakeshore Drive—location)
PO Box 698 (mailing address)
Bolton Landing, NY 12814
(518) 644-2444
Patricia Steele

Town of Chester
Historians Office
Municipal Center of the Town of Chester
PO Box 423
Chestertown, NY 12817
(518) 494-3044 (Home)
Phyllis Bogle
by appointment

City of Glens Falls
118 Crandall Street
Glens Falls, NY 12801
Dr. Robert King

Town of Hague
Hague, NY 12836
(518) 543-6620

Clifton West

Town of Horicon
PO Box 112
Brant Lake, NY 12815
(518) 494-4359
Colleen Murtagh

Town of Johnsburg
PO Box 126
Bakers Mills, NY 12811
(518) 251-2097
Doris H. Patton

Village of Lake George
72 Schuyler Street
Lake George, NY 12845
(518) 668-3043
Margaret A. Edwards

Town of Lake Luzerne
Lake Avenue
Lake Luzerne, NY 12846
(518) 696-2324
Beatrice Evans

Town of Queensbury
Queensbury Town Office Building
742 Bay Road
Queensbury, NY 12804-5902
(518) 761-8252; (518) 745-4474 FAX
historian@queensbury.net
http://www.queensbury.net
Dr. Marilyn J. Van Dyke
Wed 9:00–5:00
Pub. *Queensbury Town Report*, quarterly
    (community newsletter)

Town of Stony Creek
91 Waite Road
Stony Creek, NY 12878
(518) 696-2838
Cynthia Cameron

Town of Thurman
PO Box 29
Athol, NY 12810-0029
Robin D. Croissant

Town of Warrensburg
3847 Main Street
Warrensburg, NY 12885
(518) 623-5153
Mabel Tucker

Warren County Historical Society
(71 Lawrence Street, Glens Falls, NY
12804—location)
PO Box 769 (mailing address)
Lake George, NY 12845
(518) 743-0734
mail@warrencountyhistoricalsociety.org
http://www.warrencountyhistorical
    society.org
Dr. Marilyn J. Van Dyke, Executive Director
Tue 9:00–5:00, and by appointment
Pub. *Pasttimes*, quarterly
$15.00 per year membership; research:
    minimal copy fees

Town of Warren Historical Society
Main Street
Jordanville, NY 13407
(315) 858-1089

Warsaw Historical Society
PO Box 132
Warsaw, NY 14569
(716) 796-3422

Town of Warwick Historical Society
PO Box 353

Warwick, NY 10990
(845) 986-4833

Washington County Historian
Washington County Municipal Center
383 Broadway
Fort Edward, NY 12828
(518) 746-2178
wchist@co.washington.ny.us
Joseph Cutshall-King
Wed 8:30–noon & 1:00–4:30
Research: $10.00 per request; copies: $1.00
  per page

Municipal Historians

Town of Argyle and Village of Argyle
69 Brennan Road
Argyle, NY 12809
Sue Brennan

Town of Cambridge and Village of Cambridge
14 Gilmore Avenue
Cambridge, NY 12816
David Thornton

Town of Dresden
14057 State Route 22
Clemons, NY 12819-2301
Agnes Peterson
(prefers mail inquiries)

Town of Easton
Rural Delivery 1
Greenwich, NY 12834
Earline Houser

Town of Fort Ann and Village of Fort Ann
1133 County Route 16
Fort Ann, NY 12828
gnny1@localnet.com
Virginia Parrott
by appointment

Village of Fort Edward
85 Broadway
Fort Edward, NY 12828
R. Paul McCarty

Town of Greenwich
2 Academy Street
Greenwich, NY 12834
Cathy Sharp Barber

Town of Hampton
PO Box 11
Hampton, NY 12837
Carolyn McCullen

Town of Hartford
PO Box 35
Hartford, NY 12838
Sylvia Van Anden

Town of Hebron
1317 County Route 31
Granville, NY 12832
Drucille Craig

Village of Hudson Falls
(address withheld upon request)
(also historian of the town of Kingsbury)

Town of Jackson
Star Route
East Greenwich, NY 12826
Norma Skelly

Town of Kingsbury
Paul Loding, Historian (see Village of
  Hudson Falls, above)

Town of Salem and Village of Salem
(South Main Street—location)
PO Box 458 (mailing address)
Salem, NY 12865
William A. Cormier

Town of White Creek
(Mountain View Drive, Cambridge, NY
12816—location)
33 Quaker Hill Road (mailing address)
White Creek, NY 12057
mrobi47966@aol.com
Marilyn B. Robinson

Town of Whitehall and Village of Whitehall
99 Dodge Road
Whitehall, NY 12887-4015
Howard Bartholomew

Washington County Historical Society
Heritage Research Library
167 Broadway
Fort Edward, NY 12828
(518) 747-9108; (518) 746-1655 FAX
information@wchs-ny.org
http://www.wchs-ny.org
Wed & Fri noon–4:00, and by appointment
no charge for admission to library

Waterloo Library and Historical Society
Terwilliger Museum
(Memorial Day Museum, 35 East Main
Street—location)
31 East Williams Street (mailing address)
Waterloo, NY 13165
(315) 539-0533, (315) 539-7798 FAX
http://www.flls.org/waterloo/default.htm
James T. Hughes, Director of Museums
Terwilliger Museum: Tue–Fri 1:00–4:00;
  Memorial Day Museum: 15 May–15 Sept:
  Tue–Sat 1:00–4:00 and by appointment
(Terwilliger Museum: Waterloo and area
  history and historical records, local
  genealogical records. Memorial Day
  Museum: "Founding of Memorial Day,
  local veteran records, Civil War
  material.")
admission: donation; research: $20.00

Town of Watertown Historical Society
22867 County Route 67
Watertown, NY 13601
(315) 658-4774
Bonita H. Shafer, Town Historian

Watervliet Historical Society
PO Box 123
Watervliet, NY 12189
(518) 235-6699
EPBBELLMAN@aol.com
Eugene Burns, Treasurer

Wayne County Historian's Office
(9 Pearl Street—location)
PO Box 131 (mailing address)
Lyons, NY 14489
(315) 946-5470; (315) 946-5460 FAX
Deborah J. Ferrell, Historian
Mon–Fri 9:00–noon & 1:00–5:00
research: $14.00 per hour, $7.00 minimum,
  plus copies at 10¢ each from paper
  originals or 25¢ each from microfilm
  originals

Municipal Historians

Town of Arcadia
211 Moore Street
Newark, NY 14513
(315) 331-2707
Robert Hoeltzel

(also historian of the village of Newark)

Town of Butler
4455 Spring Lake Road
Wolcott, NY 14590
(315) 594-2510
Barbara Briscese

Village of Clyde and Town of Galen
134 Water Street
Clyde, NY 14433
(315) 923-4841
Hugh Miner

Town of Huron
11065 Ridge Road
Wolcott, NY 14590
(315) 594-1658
Carol Flint

Town of Lyons
3033 Middle Sodus Road
Lyons, NY 14489
(315) 946-4379
Carol Bailey

Village of Lyons
post vacant

Town of Macedon
411 Canal Drive, 2219 East
Macedon, NY 14502
(315) 986-5724
Helen Burgio

Village of Macedon
17 Lapham Street
Macedon, NY 14502
(315) 986-7733
Anita Crowley

Town of Marion
PO Box 22
Marion, NY 14505
(315) 926-4436
Carolyn Adriaansen

Village of Newark
Robert Hoeltzel (see Town of Arcadia,
  above)

Town of Ontario
1969 Lake Road
Ontario, NY 14519
(315) 524-9127
Mary Elizabeth Albright

Town of Palmyra
1180 Canandaigua Road
Palmyra, NY 14522
(315) 597-5521, ext. 112
historian@palmyrany.com
http://www.palmyrany.com
Beth Hoad

Village of Palmyra
post vacant

Village of Red Creek
6749 South Street
Red Creek, NY 13143
Grace Frost

Town of Rose
10612 Salter Road
North Rose, NY 14516
(315) 587-4532
James Ryan

Town of Savannah
High Street
Savannah, NY 13146

John Spellman

Town of Sodus
25 Smith Street
Sodus, NY 14551
(315) 483-9307
Richard Ransley

Village of Sodus
post vacant

Village of Sodus Point
post vacant

Town of Walworth
2219 Smith Hill Road
Walworth, NY 14568
(315) 524-9064
John M. Traas

Town of Williamson
PO Box 63
Pultneyville, NY 14538
(315) 589-8902
Chester Peters

Village of Wolcott
post vacant

Wayne County Historical Society
21 Butternut Street
Lyons, NY 14489
Mon–Fri 9:00–4:00

Town of Webb Historical Association
(Corner of Gilbert and Main
Streets—location)
PO Box 513 (mailing address)
Old Forge, NY 13420
(315) 369-3838
historian@masterpieces.com
http://www.masterpieces.com/history
Peg Masters, Director and Town Historian
Tue & Thur 9:00–2:00, Sat 9:00–1:00, Wed
    (July–Aug) 7:00–8:00

Webster Museum and Historical Society
1000 Ridge Road
Webster, NY 14580
(716) 872-1000

**Society for the Preservation of Weeksville
and Bedford-Stuyvesant History/The
Weeksville Society**
(1698 Bergen Street—location)
PO Box 120, Saint Johns Station (mailing
address)
Brooklyn, NY 11213
(718) 756-5250

West Monroe Historical Society
PO Box 25
West Monroe, NY 13167
(315) 676-7414 (Office); (315) 675-8408
    (Home)
Marion Hodges, Curator
May–Dec: Fri 10:00–4:00, Sun noon–4:00,
    and by appointment

**West Seneca Historical Museum and
Society**
(919 Mill Road—location)
PO Box 2 (mailing address)
West Seneca, NY 14224-3038
(716) 674-4283
Laura Dulinawka, Secretary/Treasurer
Tue 9:00–5:00
Pub. *Just for Old Times Sake*, $4.00 per issue
    plus postage

Historical Society of the Westburys
445 Jefferson Street

Westbury, NY 11590
(516) 333-0176
Jean Renison, Historical Coordinator

Westchester County Historian
Michaelian Office Building
Room 903
White Plains, NY 10601
(914) 285-2638
Susan Swanson
Mon–Thur 10:00–4:00

Municipal Historians

Village of Ardsley
Ardsley Village Hall
505 Ashford Avenue
Ardsley, NY 10502
(914) 693-1550
Daniel Kaufman

Town of Bedford
Town House
321 Bedford Road
Bedford Hills, NY 10507
(914) 666-4745
John Stockbridge
by appointment
("*Bedford Historical Records*, 9 volumes
    including Minutes of Town Meetings
    (1680–1841), Land Records (1680–1800),
    Soldiers of the Revolution, Town of
    Bedford Cemeteries (1681–1975),
    Bedford Genealogy, Descendants of the
    Original Proprietors. Copies of the above
    volumes are in all Bedford Public
    Libraries; some libraries also have
    genealogical sources, local histories.")

Village of Briarcliff
c/o Mayor
Municipal Building
111 Pleasantville Road
Briarcliff Manor, NY 10510
(914) 941-4800

Village of Bronxville
Village Hall
(200 Pondfield Road—location)
PO Box 7 (mailing address)
Bronxville, NY 10708
(914) 337-6500; (914) 793-6460 (Home)
Mary Huber

Village of Buchanan
Village Hall
236 Tate Avenue
Buchanan, NY 10511
(914) 737-1033
Anna Marie Burke

Town of Cortlandt
Town Hall
1 Heady Street
Cortlandt Manor, NY 10566
(914) 743-1024; (914) 271-1429 (Home)
Maureen M. Erickson

Village of Croton-on-Hudson
1 Van Wyck Street
Croton-on-Hudson, NY 10520
(914) 271-4781
Joyce Finnerty

Village of Dobbs Ferry
Village Hall
112 Main Street
Dobbs Ferry, NY 10522
(914) 693-2203; (914) 693-9319 (Home)
Judy Holzer

Town of Eastchester

Town Hall
40 Mill Road
Eastchester, NY 10709
(914) 771-3300; (914) 738-2087 (Home)
Richard Forliano

Village of Elmsfort
c/o 15 South Stone Avenue
Elmsford, NY 10523
(914) 592-6555

Town of Greenburgh
Town Hall
320 Tarrytown Road
Elmsford, NY 10523
(914) 993-1500
Jo-Anne Weinberg

Town of Harrison
Town Hall
Municipal Building
Harrison, NY 10528
(914) 825-2000; (914) 948-2550 (Home)
Michael R. Casarella

Village of Hastings-on-Hudson
Village Hall
7 Maple Avenue
Hastings-on-Hudson, NY 10706
(914) 478-3400; (914) 478-2935 (Home)
Mary Allison

Village of Irvington
Village Hall
85 Main Street
Irvington, NY 10533
(914) 591-7070; (914) 591-8137 (Home)
Peter Oley

Village of Larchmont
Village Hall
120 Larchmont Avenue
Larchmont, NY 10538
(914) 834-6230; (914) 834-5136 (Home)
Judith Spikes

Town of Lewisboro
Town Hall
11 Main Street
South Salem, NY 10590
(914) 763-3511
Maureen Koehl

Town of Mamaroneck
Town Hall
740 West Boston Post Road
Mamaroneck, NY 10543
(914) 381-7870; (914) 834-0254 (Home)
Paula Lipsett

Village of Mamaroneck
169 Mount Pleasant Avenue
Mamaroneck, NY 10543
(914) 777-7726; (914) 381-7815 (Home)
Gloria P. Pritts

Village of Mount Kisco
Village Hall
104 Main Street
Mount Kisco, NY 10549
(914) 241-0500; (914) 666-4604 (Home)
Oliver A. Knapp

Town of Mount Pleasant
Town Hall
1 Town Hall Plaza
Valhalla, NY 10595
(914) 742-2311; (914) 742-5213 (Home)
Wilfred V. Hurley

City of Mount Vernon
City Hall

1 Roosevelt Square
Mount Vernon, NY 10550
(914) 665-2351; (914) 668-3841 (Home)
Dr. Larry Spruill

Town of New Castle
Town Hall
200 South Greeley Avenue
Chappaqua, NY 10514
(914) 238-4771; (914) 238-6818 (Home)
Richard Neale

City of New Rochelle
City Hall
515 North Avenue
New Rochelle, NY 10801
(914) 654-2162; (914) 632-6119 (Home)
Thomas A. Hoctor

Town of North Castle
Town Hall
15 Bedford Road
Armonk, NY 10504
(914) 273-3321; (914) 234-7845 (Home)
Doris Finch Watson

Town of North Salem
Town Hall
266 Titicus Road
North Salem, NY 10560
(914) 669-5577; (914) 669-8459 (Home)
Richard Yakman

Town of Ossining
c/o Ossining Historical Society and Museum
196 Croton Avenue
Ossining, NY 10562
(914) 941-0001
Roberta Arminio

Village of Ossining
post vacant

City of Peekskill
c/o Peekskill Museum
PO Box 84
Peekskill, NY 10566
(914) 736-0473
John Curran

Town of Pelham
34 Fifth Avenue
Pelham, NY 10803
(914) 738-0777
Mimi Buckley & Susan Mutti

Village of Pelham
Village Hall
195 Sparks Avenue
Pelham, NY 10803
Kathleen Terkelsen

Village of Pelham Manor
post vacant

Village of Pleasantville
c/o Mount Pleasant Public Library
350 Bedford Road
Pleasantville, NY 10570
(914) 769-0548
Carsten Johnson

Village of Port Chester
c/o Port Chester Historical Society
PO Box 1511
Port Chester, NY 10573
(914) 939-6040 (Historical Society)

Town of Pound Ridge
179 Westchester Avenue
Pound Ridge, NY 10576
(914) 764-5511; (914) 764-5967 (Home)

Richard Major

Village of Rye Brook
c/o Mayor
90 South Ridge Street
Rye Brook, NY 10573

City of Rye
c/o Rye Historical Society
1 Purchase Street
Rye, NY 10580-3002
(914) 967-7588 (Society)
David Byrnes

Town of Rye
post vacant

Town of Scarsdale
post vacant

Village of Scarsdale
Village Hall
1001 Post Road
Scarsdale, NY 10583
(914) 722-1175
Irving Sloan

Village of Sleepy Hollow
Village Hall
28 Beekman Avenue
North Tarrytown, NY 10591
(914) 631-0533
Lucille & Theodore Hutchinson

Town of Somers
Town Hall
(Routes 100 and 202—location)
PO Box 245 (mailing address)
Somers, NY 10589
(914) 277-3323; (914) 277-3674 (Home)
Florence S. Oliver

Town of South Salem
post vacant

Village of Tarrytown
Village Hall
21 Wildey Street
Tarrytown, NY 10591
(914) 631-1652; (914) 631-5951 (Home)
Jerome Blood

Village of Tuckahoe
Village Hall
65 Main Street
Tuckahoe, NY 10707
(914) 961-3100; (914) 337-1771 (Home)
Ernest Zocctti

City of White Plains
City Hall
255 Main Street
White Plains, NY 10601
(914) 948-7183 (Home)
Renoda Hoffman

City of Yonkers
City Hall
40 South Broadway
Yonkers, NY 10701
(914) 377-6020; (914) 961-8985 (Home)
Jack Prill

Town of Yorktown
Town Hall
363 Underhill Avenue
Yorktown Heights, NY 10598
(914) 962-5722; (914) 962-2970 (Home)
Doris P. Auser

Westchester County Historical Society
Westchester County Archives

2199 Saw Mill River Road
Elmsford, NY 10523
(914) 592-4323; (914) 231-1515 FAX
info@westchesterhistory.com
http://www.westchesterhistory.com
Elizabeth Fuller, Librarian
Tue & Wed 9:00–4:00
Pub. *The Westchester Historian*, quarterly;
   Westchester Historical Happenings
$30.00 per year membership; research:
   $20.00–$30.00 per hour, depending on
   type of search

Western Monroe Historical Society
151 Main Street
Brockport, NY 14420
(716) 637-3645
Eunice Chesnut, Historian
Mon–Fri 9:00–noon; tours Sun (Apr–Nov)
   2:00–4:00
Pub. *Newsletter*, monthly
(file of newspaper clippings, etc.)
$25.00 per year membership

Westford Historical Society
(Town Hall—location)
PO Box 184 (mailing address)
Westford, NY 13488
(607) 638-9250
Richard Guthrie, President
by appointment
("Family records, business records,
   newspapers, education.")

Westhampton Beach Historical Society
(Mill Road—location)
PO Box 666 (mailing address)
Westhampton Beach, NY 11978
(631) 288-1139
Marion Van Tassel

Westport Historical Society
Barksdale Road
Westport, NY 12993
(518) 962-4809

Wheatland Historical Association
(Sage-Marlow House, 69 Main
Street—location)
PO Box 184 (mailing address)
Scottsville, NY 14546-0184
(716) 889-4574

Marcus Whitman Historical Society
PO Box 204
Gorham, NY 14461

Williamstown Historical Society
PO Box 218
Williamstown, NY 13493
(315) 964-1087
Daniel R. Althouse, President
by appointment

Wilson Historical Society
PO Box 830
Wilson, NY 14172-0830

**Woodhaven Cultural and Historical
Society**
93-34 91st Avenue
Woodhaven, NY 11421
(718) 846-1907
Leonora Lavan, President

Historical Society of Woodstock Museum
PO Box 841
Woodstock, NY 12498
(845) 679-6744
Edgar C. Leaycraft, Town Historian

Worcester Historical Society

(72 Main Street—location)
PO Box 186 (mailing address)
Worcester, NY 12197
Gynger O'Connor, President
June–Sept: Wed–Fri 1:00–3:00

Wyoming County Historian
Wyoming County Historian Office
26 Linwood Avenue
Warsaw, NY 14569
(716) 786-8818
Raymond G. Barber, Historian; Doris
   Bannister, Deputy Historian
Mon–Fri 9:00–4:00
Pub. *Historical Wyoming*, quarterly (July,
   Oct, Jan, Apr), $7.50 per year for mailed
   subscription, $2.00 per issue at office,
   $2.50 per mailed issue
(history of Wyoming County, New York,
   biographies, cemetery lists, soldiers, etc.)

Municipal Historians

Town of Arcade and Village of Arcade
7783 County Line Road
Arcade, NY 14009
(716) 492-4742
Jeffery C. Mason

Town of Attica
1680 Austin Road
Attica, NY 14011
(716) 591-0184
Lillian Merkle

Village of Attica
post vacant

Town of Bennington
1784 Burrough Road
Cowlesville, NY 14037
(716) 493-5370
Mrs. Alma Janish

Town of Castile
post vacant

Town of Covington
1088 Peoria Road
Pavilion, NY 14525
(716) 584-3254
Karen C. Milligan

Town of Eagle
(6591 Pearl Street—location)
PO Box 138 (mailing address)
Bliss, NY 14024
(716) 322-7337
Frank Noble

Town of Gainesville
4344 Gainesville Road
Silver Springs, NY 14550
(716) 786-5603
Stanley Rutherford

Village of Gainesville
post vacant

Town of Genesee Falls
6658 Church Road
Portageville, NY 14536
(716) 468-5296
Karen Quinn

Town of Java
4846 Michigan Road
Arcade, NY 14009
(585) 457-3079
Raymond Barber

Town of Middlebury

872 North Academy Street
Wyoming, NY 14591
(716) 495-6558
Doris Bannister

Town of Orangeville
3236 Buffalo Road
Varysburg, NY 14167
(716) 535-7543
haymaker@wycol.com
Richard Holbrook

Town of Perry
6496 Oatka Road
Perry, NY 14530
(716) 237-3581
Norma C. Spencer

Village of Perry
post vacant

Town of Pike and Village of Pike
6496 Hardys Road
Bliss, NY 14024
(716) 322-7228
Lunamae Flint

Town of Sheldon
2348 Route 98
Varysburg, NY 14167
(716) 535-7322
sheldonhistorian@aol.com
Barbara Durfee

Village of Silver Springs
post vacant

Town of Warsaw
5422 Keeney Road
Warsaw, NY 14569
(716) 786-8679
Michael Hyjek

Village of Warsaw
post vacant

Town of Wethersfield
3593 Route 78
Bliss, NY 14024
(716) 322-9094
Wilma Ikeler, Historian

Village of Wyoming
post vacant

Wyoming Historical Pioneer Association
18 East Main Street
Arcade, NY 14009

Wyoming Pioneer Historical Association
14 Covington Street
Perry, NY 14530
(716) 237-3458

Yaphank Historical Society
Hawkins-Jacobson House
(Yaphank Road—location)
PO Box 111 (mailing address)
Yaphank, NY 11980
(631) 924-3879; (631) 924-3743
Jack Rauh, President

**Yates County Genealogical and Historical
Society**
(see Genealogical Societies—Local and
Regional, below)

Yates County Historian
County Office Building, Suite 0032
417 Liberty Street
Penn Yan, NY 14527
(315) 536-5147; (315) 531-3226 FAX

history@yatescounty.org
http://www.linkny.com/~history
Frances Dumas, Historian
Office: Mon–Fri 8:00–4:30
(complete county records, well-indexed, town
   and village records on microfilm,
   newspapers on microfilm, database of
   county's cemeteries and burials)
research: $15.00 per hour

Municipal Historians

Town of Barrington
2751 Knapp Road
Dundee, NY 14837
Wilfred Knapp

Town of Benton
Flat Street
Penn Yan, NY 14527
Constance Murphy

Village of Dresden
57 Main Street
Dresden, NY 14441
Raymond Welker

Village of Dundee
40 Seneca Street
Dundee, NY 14837
Pamela Miller

Town of Jerusalem
Italy Hill Road
Branchport, NY 14418
Jane Davis

Town of Middlesex
Middlesex Town Hall
Middlesex, NY 14507
Stuart J. Mitchell

Town of Milo
26 Main Street
Penn Yan, NY 14527
Frances Dumas

Village of Penn Yan
3 Maiden Lane
Penn Yan, NY 14527
Frances Dumas

Town of Potter
Route 364
Middlesex, NY 14507
Wilson Simmons, Jr.

Village of Rushville
4606 Fergusons Cross Road
Rushville, NY 14544
Betty Clark

Town of Starkey
26 Seneca Street
Dundee, NY 14837
Pamela Miller

Town of Torrey
Dresden, NY 14441
Betty Smalley

Yonkers Historical Society
Grinton I. Will Library
(150 Central Park Avenue—location)
PO Box 190 (mailing address)
Yonkers, NY 10710
(914) 961-8940; (914) 961-8945 FAX
http://www.yonkershistory.org
Marianne Winstanley, Director
Tue & Thur 10:00–4:00
Pub. *The Yonkers Historical Society
   Newsletter*, quarterly

$20.00 per year membership

Genealogical Societies

State Genealogical Society

New York Genealogical and Biographical Society Library
122 East 58th Street
New York, NY 10022-1939
(212) 755-8532; (212) 754-4218 FAX
membership@nygbs.org; library@nygbs.org;
    publications@nygbs.org
http://www.nygbs.org
Joy Rich, Director of the Library; Lindsey
    Ottman, Director of Information Systems,
    Gayle Hathorne, Publications Coordinator
Library: Tue–Sat 9:30–5:00; Tech Center:
    Tue–Sat 9:30–5:00 (has additional access
    to computer databases for members);
    Office: Mon–Fri 9:30–5:00 (except legal
    holidays)
Pub. *The New York Genealogical and
    Biographical Record*, quarterly, $30.00
    per year subscription for libraries and
    nonmembers; *The NYG&B Newsletter*,
    quarterly (includes articles and news about
    the use of computer software and
    databases to enhance genealogical
    research; included in membership and
    library subscriptions)
("Publications focus on genealogy of New
    York State and City families and those of
    adjacent states. New York City and State
    sources and reference works, back issues
    of *The Record* and *The New York
    Gnealogical and Biographical Record* as
    listed in Publications Catalog online at
    www.nygbs.org. Library has more than
    120,000 titles including extensive
    collections of New York State and City
    primary sources, compiled genealogies,
    and local histories, and significant
    holdings for other eastern states.")
$60.00 per year membership (includes two
    periodicals as above; full access to library;
    access to members-only section of web
    site, which includes ProQuest's *New York
    Times* database 1851–1998; research and
    photocopying services by mail; free
    queries in *Newsletter* and web site; and
    discounts on occasional publications,
    conferences, lectures, and other
    educational programs. Some services and
    programs are available to nonmembers on a
    fee basis); admission to library's book
    collection: $10.00 donation for
    nonmembers

**New York State Council of Genealogical
Organizations**
PO Box 2593
Syracuse, NY 13220-2593
Joyce H. Cook, Editor
("We welcome members from outside New
    York State.")
Pub. *NYSCOGO Lifeline*, quarterly, $10.00
    per year subscription; *Naturalization
    Records of New York State*, $13.00
    postpaid, a county-by-county guide to
    records
$25.00 per year membership

Genealogical Societies—Local & Regional

**Adirondack Genealogical-Historical
Society**
Saranac Lake Free Library
100 Main Street
Saranac Lake, NY 12983
(518) 891-2236
peightal3@adelphia.com

http://freepages.genealogy.rootsweb.com/
    ~adkghs
Kathryn Peightal
Mon–Fri 10:00–5:00, Sat noon–5:00
$5.00 per year membership

American-Canadian Genealogical Society
(see New Hampshire, Part 2)

Amherst Museum Genealogy Society
c/o Amherst Museum
3755 Tonawanda Creek Road
Amherst, NY 14228
(716) 689-1440 (Museum); (716) 689-1409
    FAX (Museum)
amhmuseum@adelphia.net
http://www.amherstmuseum.org
Toniann Scime, Librarian, Assistant Curator
Mon–Fri 9:30–4:30 (call for appointment)
$20.00 per year membership in Amherst
    Museum Genealogy Society includes
    museum membership; admission: $5.00

Brooklyn Historical Society
Genealogy Workshop
(see Historical Societies—Local and
Regional, above)

Capital District Genealogical Society
PO Box 2175, Empire State Plaza Station
Albany, NY 12220-0175
http://www.familyhistory.com/societyhall/
    viewmember.asp?societyid=25
Volunteer Desk, New York State Library:
    Mon–Fri 9:00–5:00
Pub. *Capital District Genealogical Society
    Newsletter*, quarterly
(Albany, Columbia, Greene, Rensselaer,
    Schenectady and Schoharie counties)
$15.00 per year membership; queries: two
    free per year for members

Cattaraugus County Genealogical Society
PO Box 404
Salamanca, NY 14779
ccgs404@yahoo.com
Sharon Fellows, President
Pub. *Newsletter*

Central New York Genealogical Society
PO Box 104, Colvin Station
Syracuse, NY 13205
CNYGS@yahoo.com
http://www.rootsweb.com/~nycnygs
meetings at DeWitt Community Church,
    DeWitt, NY: (Mar–May & Sept–Nov)
Pub. *Tree Talks*, quarterly (Mar, June, Sept,
    Dec)
(includes Albany, Allegany, Broome,
    Cattaraugus, Cayuga, Chautauqua,
    Chemung, Chenango, Clinton, Columbia,
    Cortland, Delaware, Erie, Essex, Franklin,
    Fulton, Genesee, Greene, Hamilton,
    Herkimer, Jefferson, Lewis, Livingston,
    Madison, Monroe, Montgomery, Niagara,
    Oneida, Onondaga, Ontario, Orleans,
    Oswego, Otsego, Rensselaer, Saint
    Lawrence, Saratoga, Schenectady,
    Schoharie, Schuyler, Seneca, Steuben,
    Tioga, Tompkins, Warren, Washington,
    Wayne, Wyoming and Yates counties)
$30.00 per year membership

**Chautauqua County Genealogical Society
(C.C.G.S.)**
(D. R. Barker Museum, corner of Route 20
[Main Street] and Day Street—collection
location)
PO Box 404 (mailing address)
Fredonia, NY 14063
(716) 672-2114 (Museum)
barkermu@netsync.net

http://www.netsync.net/users/djyj/CCGS.
    htm
Walter Sedlmayer, President; Norwood J.
    Barris, Membership Chairman
Museum: Tue–Sat 1:00-5:00, Tue& Thur
    7:00–9:00
Pub. *Chautauqua County Genealogical
    Society Journal*, quarterly (Feb, May, Aug,
    Nov)
$11.00 per year membership; admission: free

Cortland County Genealogical Society
113 South Parkway
Groton, NY 13073
(607) 898-3381
Wayne Thurston, President
meetings: second Tue
$7.00 per year membership

The Dutch Settlers Society of Albany
23 Dresden Court
Albany, NY 12203
(518) 456-7202
John Wemple, President
Pub. *Yearbook of the Dutch Settlers Society
    of Albany*, every two to three years
$25.00 regular or Associate membership the
    first year, $12.00 per year thereafter

The Dutchess County Genealogical Society
(204 Spackenkill Road, Poughkeepsie, NY
12603—library location)
PO Box 708 (mailing address)
Poughkeepsie, NY 12602
(845) 462-2361 (President)
http://www.dcgs-gen.org
Linda Koehler, Librarian
Tue 9:00–2:00, Wed 5:00–9:00, Thur
    9:00–noon & 7:00–9:00
Pub. *The Dutchess*, quarterly
$20.00 per year membership; research:
    $10.00 for a surname search "only in our
    library"

Finger Lakes Genealogical Society
PO Box 47
Seneca Falls, NY 13148
J. E. Wood, President
Research Room, Mynderse Library: Mon–Fri
    2:00–5:00 & 7:00–9:00, Wed noon–4:00,
    Sat 2:00–5:00
Pub. *Pathways*, four times per year
$10.00 per year membership

Genesee Area Genealogists
c/o Richmond Memorial Library
19 Ross Street
Batavia, NY 14020
mjv21@eznet.netswleilani@yahoo.com
http://www.rootsweb.com/~nygags
Mary Van Alstyne, Editor; Joseph Welch,
    President; Kathleen Facer, Adult Services
    Librarian
Pub. *The Family Tree is Growing*, four times
    per year (Jan, Apr, July, Oct)
(emphasis on western New York)
$10.00 per year membership (to Leilani
    Spring, 3 Longs Lane, Corfu, NY 14036);
    research: copy costs and SASE

Heritage Hunters
PO Box 1389
Saratoga Springs, NY 12866-0884
(518) 587-5852
unlimitd1@juno.com
http://www.rootsweb.com/~nysarato
Ruth Ann Messick, Founder
meetings at Community Room of the new
    Saratoga Springs Public Library: noon on
    the third Sat (Feb–Nov)
Pub. *Newsletter*, bimonthly
(interested in genealogy and history,

especially in the preservation of genealogical and historical materials in and around Saratoga County)
$15.00 per year membership (includes spring edition of Surname List)

Huntington Historical Society Genealogy Workshop
(see Huntington Historical Society, Historical Societies—Local and Regional, above)

Jefferson County New York Genealogical Society (JCNYGS)
PO Box 6453
Watertown, NY 13601
jcnygs@imcnet.net
http://www.rootsweb.com/~nyjeffer/jeffsox.htm
meetings in the Dillenback Room of the Roswell P. Flower Memorial Library: second Mon 7:00
Pub. *The Informer*, six times per year
$15.00 per year membership

Kodak Genealogical Society
Kodak Park Activities Association
Eastman Kodak Company
Kodak Recreation Building 28
Rochester, NY 14652-3404

Livingston County Genealogical Society
5 Elizabeth Street
Dansville, NY 14437-1719
mslynbr@frontiernet.net
http://www.rootsweb.com/~nylcgs
Lynne Brill
meetings in the Conklin Room of the Dansville Public Library: first Tue 7:00
$3.00 per year membership

Genealogical Roundtable of Monroe County
35 Country Lane
Penfield, NY 14526-1028

Heritage and Genealogical Society of Montgomery County
(see Historical Societies—Local and Regional, above)

The New England Historic Genealogical Society
(see Massachusetts, Part 2)

New York Genealogical and Biographical Society Library
(see State Genealogical Societies, above)

Niagara County Genealogical Society
Niaragara County Historical Society Museum
215 Niagara Street, Second Floor
Lockport, NY 14094-2605
(716) 433-1033 (Library)
genealogy@niagaracounty.org
http://www.niagaracounty.org/genealogical_society_home.htm
Maureen Seifert, Corresponding Secretary
Thur–Sat 1:00–5:00 (call to ask if librarian is on duty)
Pub. *The Niagara County Genealogical Society Newsletter*, quarterly
(Niagara County, New York State, and the east)
$13.00 per year membership; queries: free to members only; research: no individualized research conducted

Northeastern New York Genealogical Society
(9 Lydia Street, South Glen Falls, NY 12803—location)

PO Box 4264 (mailing address)
Queensbury, NY 12804-1422
http://bfn.org/~ae487/nnygs.html
meetings at Glens Falls National Bank Community Room, Glens Falls: odd-numbered months
Pub. *The Patents*, bimonthly
(Warren, Washington, northern Saratoga, southern Essex, and parts of Hamilton counties)
$12.00 per year membership

Northern New York American-Canadian Genealogical Society
(Community Center, Old High School Building, Main Street, Keeseville, NY—location)
PO Box 1256 (mailing address)
Plattsburgh, NY 12901-1256
(518) 834-5401; (518) 236-7567
bobino1@northnet.org; grcp@juno.com
http://www.rootsweb.com/~nnyacgs
Barbara Seguin, Librarian and Vice President, Elizabeth Botten, President
Library: 1 Apr–30 Nov: Wed 1:00–6:00, Sat 11:00–4:00, also by appointment for members with two-weeks advance notice
Pub. *Lifelines*, two times per year
(southern Quebec, Northern New York, and Northern Vermont)
$20.00 per year membership

Nyando Roots Genealogical Society
180 River Drive
Massena, NY 13662-3181
(315) 769-9914 (Massena Library)
John Kormanyos, President
Mon & Fri 10:00–5:00, Tue–Thur 10:00–9:00
no charge for membership

Ontario County Genealogical Society
Ontario County Historical Society Museum/Archives
55 North Main Street
Canandaigua, NY 14424
http://www.ochs.org/Genealogy/Ocgs/index.html
Barbara V. Hill, Secretary
by appointment
(Ontario County manuscript collection, early records)
$8.00 per year membership

Orange County Genealogical Society
(1841 Court House—location)
101 Main Street (mailing address)
Goshen, NY 10924-1627
http://www.rootsweb.com/~nozell/ocgs
Robert Brennan, President
Mon & Fri 8:30–noon, first & third Tue 6:30–9:30, first & third Wed 8:30–4:00, first Sat noon–4:00, third Sat 9:00–4:00, by appointment by phoning (845) 294-5871 or (845) 294-9462; meetings: first Sat 9:00
Pub. *The Orange County Genealogical Society Quarterly*
$10.00 per year membership

Orleans County Genealogical Society
(Albion Town Hall, 3665 Clarendon Road—location)
PO Box 103 (mailing address)
Albion, NY 14411
ochomefront@yahoo.com
http://www.OrleansCountyGenealogical Society.org
Mark Rustay, Corresponding Secretary
meetings: second Sun 7:00
$15.00 per year membership

Oswego County Genealogy Society
Oswego County Records Center
384 East River Road
Oswego, NY 13126-5461
(315) 349-8460; (315) 349-8458 FAX
bdix@oswegocounty.com
Barbara J. Dix, County Historical Records Administrator/Historian
Mon–Fri 9:00–5:00
Pub. *Newsletter*, bimonthly

Painted Hills Genealogy Society
333 Hazzard Street
Jamestown, NY 14701
phillipswr@excite.com
http://www.paintedhills.org
Wendy Phillips, Treasurer
Pub. newsletter, quarterly
(Allegany, Cattaraugus, Chautauqua, and Steuben counties, New York; McKean and Potter counties, Pennsylvania)
$5.00 per year membership

Queens Genealogy Workshop
(see Greater Ridgewood Historical Society, Historical Societies—Local and Regional, above)

Rochester Genealogical Society
PO Box 10501
Rochester, NY 14610-0501
(716) 234-2584
jhall2@rochester.rr.com
http://www.vivanet.com/~halsey/rgs.html
Jim Hall, Membership Secretary
Pub. *Hear-Ye Hear-Ye*, three times per year
$15.00 per year membership

The Genealogical Society of Rockland County
PO Box 444
New City, NY 10956
protzy41@aol.com
http://www.rootsweb.com/~nyrockla/GSRC
Robert L. Protzmann, Membership Chairman and Treasurer
Pub. *Genealogical Society Newsletter*, quarterly
$15.00 per year membership; research of indexed records only

Thelma Rogers Genealogical and Historical Society
(118 East Dyke Street—location)
PO Box 1331 (mailing address)
Wellsville, NY 14895
(585) 593-1404 (Museum); (585) 593-3969 FAX (Museum)
Diane Converso, Town and Village Historian
Dyke Street Museum: Wed (Apr–Oct) 1:00–4:00, and by appointment
Pub. *Thelma Rogers Genealogical and Historical Society*, monthly

Saint Lawrence Valley Genealogical Society
PO Box 205
Canton, NY 13617-0205
eickhoff@aldus.northnet.org
Dennis E. Eickhoff, Editor
Tue–Sat 2:00–5:00
Pub. *SLVGS News*, bimonthly
(northern New York State, Ontario and Quebec)
$7.00 per year membership

Southern Tier Genealogical Society
PO Box 680
Vestal, NY 13851-0680
proski@stny.rr.com
http://www.rootsweb.com/~nybroome/stgs/stgs.htm

meetings at Vestal Public Library: first Thur (Mar–Nov) 7:00
Pub. *News Letter*, three to four times per year
$7.00 per year membership

Tri-Town Genealogical Society
323 Kreag Road
Pittsford, NY 14534
Mrs. Elbert Gerritz

Twin Tiers Genealogical Society, Inc.
PO Box 763
Elmira, NY 14902-0763
(607) 732-0443 (Editor); (607) 733-8602 (Librarian)
http://www.rootsweb.com/~nychemun/tths.htm
Virginia Erle, President/Editor; Rita Dery, Librarian
Steele Memorial Library: Mon–Thur 9:00–9:00, Fri 9:00–5:00, Sat (except June–Sept) 9:00–5:00, Sun (except June–Sept) 1:00–5:00
Pub. *Gemini*, quarterly
(Chemung, Schuyler, Steuben and Tompkins counties, New York, and Bradford and Tioga counties, Pennsylvania)
$7.00 per year membership; research: $10.00 per hour plus costs

Ulster County Genealogical Society
(Hurley Reformed Church, 17 Main Street—location)
PO Box 536 (mailing address)
Hurley, NY 12443
Joan C. Burridge, President
Jan–Nov: second Sat, third & fourth Mon 10:00–2:30, and by appointment
Pub. *The Genie*, quarterly
(Ulster County, New York)
$18.00 per year membership; research: by donation

Westchester County Genealogical Society
PO Box 518
White Plains, NY 10603-0518
(914) 941-9754 (Library)
http://www.rootsweb.com/~nywcgs
Philomena M. Dunn, President
Library, LDS Church, Route 134, Yorktown, NY: Tue–Thur 9:00–noon & 7:00–9:00; meetings at Aldersgate Methodist Church, Dobbs Ferry, NY: second Sat 10:00 A.M.
Pub. *Westchester County Genealogical Society Newsletter*, monthly; *Westchester Connections*, biannually (every other year); *Surname List*, biannually (every other year)
$20.00 per year membership

Western New York Genealogical Society, Inc.
(5859 South Park Avenue, Route 62—location)
PO Box 338 (mailing address)
Hamburg, NY 14075-0338
zgstag@yahoo.com
http://www.wnygs.org
Mrs. Kim Halas Grant, Corresponding Secretary
Pub. *Western New York Genealogical Society Journal*, quarterly (June, Sept, Dec, Mar)
(emphasis on eight western New York counties: Allegany, Cattaraugus, Chautauqua, Erie, Genesee, Niagara, Orleans and Wyoming; collection located in the Special Collections Department of Downtown branch of Buffalo and Erie County Public Library)
$20.00 first-year membership, $18.00 per subsequent-year membership; queries

accepted from members only; research: unable to do genealogical research

Yankee Genealogical Society
Minnesota Genealogical Society
(see Massachusetts, Part 2)

Yates County Genealogical and Historical Society
Oliver House Museum
200 Main Street
Penn Yan, NY 14527
(315) 536-7318; (315) 536-0976 FAX
ycghs@linkny.com
http://www.yatespast.com
Idelle Dillon, Executive Director
Mon–Fri 9:30–4:30, Sat by appointment
Pub. *Oliver House News*, monthly
$10.00 per year membership

Independent Publications and Miscellany

Amagansett Historical Association
PO Box 7077
Amagansett, NY 11930
Peter Garnham, President

Babylon Village Historical and Preservation Society
117 West Main Street
Babylon, NY 11702
(631) 669-1756
Alice Zaruka, President

Bath Historic Committee
(Cameron Street—location)
5 Ellis Avenue (mailing address)
Bath, NY 14810

Bayport Heritage Association
PO Box 4
Bayport, NY 11705
(631) 472-4625
Donald Weinhardt, President

Berkshire Conference of Women Historians
College of Staten Island (Cony)
Staten Island, NY 10301
(718) 390-7988

Anneke Jans and Everardus Bogardus Descendants Association
1121 Linhof Road
Wilmington, OH 45177-2917
(937) 382-3803
http://freepages.genealogy.rootsweb.com/~ghosthunter/Anneke/page0.htm
William Brower Bogardus, Family Representative
by appointment
Pub. *"Dear Cousin,"* unscheduled but usually at least twice per year, free
(extensive library permits research on virtually all Colonial families of early New York and New Jersey to about 1800)
no cost for newsletter or membership

The Bowne House Historical Society, Inc.
John Bowne House
37-01 Bowne Street
Flushing, NY 11354
(718) 359-0528; (718) 359-0873
Hank Ludder, Chairman
(primarily historical, not genealogical)

Brooklyn Museum/Wilbour Library and Archives
200 Eastern Parkway
Brooklyn, NY 11238-6052

(718) 638-5000; (718) 638-3731 FAX

Buffalo Fire Historical Society Museum
1850 William and North Ogden Streets
Buffalo, NY 14206
(716) 892-8400
http://www.ci.buffalo.ny.us/bfhs.htm
Records: Sat 10:00–4:00

Canaseraga Shawmut Station and Museum
193 Ames Nichols Road (Off Country Road 15A)
Canaseraga, NY 14822
(607) 545-6527
Harvey and Sue Lacy
by appointment

Center for Appalachian Studies
(see North Carolina, Part 2)

Central Queens Historical Association
PO Box N
Kew Gardens, NY 11415
(718) 544-1737
Jeff Gottlieb, President
(primarily historical and architectural, not genealogical)

Constable Hall Association, Inc.
Constable Hall, Box 36
Constableville, NY 13325
(315) 397-2323
Thomas Kelly, Director
Tue–Sat 10:00–4:00, Sun (28 May–15 Oct) 1:00–4:00

Cuba Museum
33 Genesee Street
Cuba, NY 14727
(716) 968-3679
Wed, and by appointment

Eagles Byte Historical Research
dminor@eznet.net (to subscribe to newsletter)
http://home.eznet.net/~dminor (concentrates on New York City and New York State)
David Minor
Pub. untitled newsletter, weekly, free via email (including the text of Mr. Minor's weekly radio segment which is heard on WXXI-FM, 91.5 and 90.3 FM, Rochester, approximately 11:00 A.M. every Saturday and available through streaming audio at http://www.wxxi.org)
("I do not do genealogical research as such, but I *do* research just about any historical subject, regardless of period or place.")
research: $10.00 per hour

Essex Community Heritage Organization, Inc.
(Station Road—location)
PO Box 250 (mailing address)
Essex, NY 12936-0250
(518) 963-7088
Robert J. Hammerslag, Executive Director
Mon–Fri 9:00–5:00
Pub. *ECHO Newsletter*; *ECHO Diary*, quarterly
(historic preservation, does not maintain genealogical files or data, focuses on architectural preservation)
$15.00 per year membership

The Family Tree
(3290 South Eagle Road, Eagle, ID 83616—location)
PO Box 4311 (mailing address)
Boise, ID 83711
(208) 939-7141

Anna Nasman, Office Manager
Pub. *New York Pedigrees*, monthly, $7.00 per issue postpaid; *Genealogical Journal of Jefferson County, New York*, annually (Apr), $17.50 per issue postpaid; *Genealogical Journal of Oneida County, New York*, annually (Aug), $17.50 per issue postpaid; *Genealogical Journal of Essex County, New York*, annually (Nov), $17.50 per issue postpaid

Federation of Historical Services
189 Second Street
Troy, NY 12180
(518) 273-3400
Cynthia A. Corbett, Executive Director
Pub. *Foundtable*
(service agency, not genealogical)

Fillmore House
24 Shearer Avenue
East Aurora, NY 14052

Franklin County Tombstone Transcriptions
http://freepages.genealogy.rootsweb.com/
~frgen/index.htm
Joyce M. Ranieri

Genealogical Institute
(see Independent Publications, Part 1)

Hampton Bays Historic and Preservation Society
PO Box 588
Hampton Bays, NY 11946
(631) 728-9325
Sandy Sullivan, President
(primarily historical, not genealogical)

Heritage North
PO Box 205
Colton, NY 13625
Dennis E. Eickhoff, Director
(publishes records of northern New York State, Ontario and Quebec)

Friends of Historic Kingston
PO Box 3763
Kingston NY 12402
(845) 339-0702

Historic Saranac Lake
(North Elba Town House, 132 River Street—location)
PO Box 1030 (mailing address)
Saranac Lake, NY 12983
(518) 891-0971
mbh@capital.net
http://www.HistoricSaranacLake.org
Mary B. Hotaling, Executive Director
Mon–Fri 9:00–1:00, and by appointment
Pub. *Historic Saranac Lake News*, two times per year
("New York historic preservation organization; scope includes historic buildings in village and surrounding area, especially relating to tuberculosis research and treatment.")

Historical Ink's Old Maps
335 Secret Lake Road
Athol, MA 01331-9579
sales@oldmapsne.com
http://www.oldmapsne.com (online catalog)
(Old maps of New York, Maine, Massachusetts, Rhode Island, New Hampshire, Vermont, and Connecticut cities, towns and villages, and gazetteer excerpts)
$2.00 for catalog or free with any order

Hofstra University
Long Island Studies Institute (LISI)
West Campus
Ninth Floor, Axinn Library
619 Fulton Avenue
Hempstead, NY 11550-1090
(516) 463-6409
Barbara M. Kelly, Ph.D., Curator
Mon–Fri 9:00–5:00
(New York State history)

Homeville Museum
49 Clinton Street, Route 41
Homer, NY 13077-1024
(607) 749-3105
Kenneth M. Eaton, Director
May–Oct: Thur 7:00 P.M.–9:00 P.M., second & fourth Sun 1:00–4:00, and by appointment
(model railroad and military museum)
admission: donation

Hudson Valley Network, Inc.
PO Box 67
Greenwood Lake, NY 10925
info@hvnet.com
http://www.hvnet.com
(Links to historic sites, books and publications)

The Indian Lake Museum
Corner of West Main Street and Crow Hill Road
Indian Lake, NY 12842
July–Oct: Tue & Thur 1:00–4:00, Fri 7:00–9:00

Kinship
305 Cedar Heights Road
Rhinebeck, NY 12572
(845) 876-4592 (Research/content information); (845) 876-4200 (Orders); (800) 249-1109 (Orders)
kinshipbooks@cs.com
http://www.kinshipny.com
Arthur C. M. Kelly, Editor
Mon–Sun 9:00–9:00
Pub. *The Capital* (Albany and Rensselaer counties), quarterly, $14.00 per year subscription; *The Columbia* (Columbia County), quarterly, $14.00 per year subscription; *The Mohawk* (Montgomery and Schenectady counties), quarterly, $14.00 per year subscription; *The Saratoga* (Saratoga County), quarterly, $14.00 per year subscription
(vital records, queries)
back issues of all titles available, also available in hardbound format

Lower East Side Tenement Museum
66 Allen Street
New York, NY 10002
(212) 431-0233; (212) 431-0402 FAX
http://www.wnet.org/tenement
Anita Jacobson, Curator
Mon–Sun 10:00–5:00
Pub. *Tenement Times*, biannually, $2.00 per issue
$30.00 per year membership

Lynbrook Historic and Preservation Society
28 Hart Street
Lynbrook, NY 11563
(516) 887-7673
Art Mattson, Co-chairman
(primarily to save Pearsall-Underhill House)

Malverne Historical and Preservation Society
Museum

PO Box 393
Malverne NY 11565
(516) 593-3806
Keith Rossein, President

Museum Association of New York (MANY)
265 River Street
Troy, NY 12180
(518) 273-3400; (518) 273-3416 FAX
Info@MANYonline.org
http://www.manyonline.org
("The Museum Association of New York is a service and advocacy organization for museums and historical organizations in New York State. As such, we generally do not deal directly with researchers.")

Nassau County Museum
Division of Museum Services
1864 Muttontown Road
Syosset, NY 11791
(516) 364-1050

New Netherland Connections
1232 Carlotte View Avenue
Berkeley, CA 94707-2707
(510) 524-5796
dkoenig@library.berkeley.edu
Dorothy A. Koenig, Editor
Pub. *New Netherland Connections*, quarterly (Feb, May, Aug, Nov), $15.00 per year subscription
(for those looking for Dutch Colonial ancestors and their descendants; New York/New Jersey area)

New Netherland Project
New York State Library
Cultural Education Center, Eighth Floor
Empire State Plaza
Albany, NY 12230
(518) 474-6067; (518) 486-4815 (Friends of the New Netherland Project); (518) 474-5786 FAX
http://nmp.nysed.gov

New York Family History
http://www.familyhistory.cc
Amy Larner Giroux, C.G.

New York History Net
http://www.nyhistory.com

New York State Bureau of Historic Sites
Office of Parks, Recreation, and Historic Preservation
Peebles Island
PO Box 219
Waterford, NY 12188
(518) 237-8643, ext. 200

New York State Museum
Division of History and Anthropology
3099 Cultural Education Center
Empire State Plaza
Albany, NY 12230
(518) 473-1299; (518) 474-2865
Martin Sullivan, Ph.D., Director and Assistant Commissioner
(objects only, not genealogical)

New York State Office for Technology
Center for Geographic Information
State Capitol, ESP
PO Box 2062
Albany, NY 12220-0062
(518) 443-2042; (518) 443-2787 FAX
sharon.oskam@oft.state.ny.us
http://www.nysgis.state.ny.us/index.html
Sharon Oskam
Mon–Fri 9:00–4:00 (Map sales and

Information)

New York State Queries
2206 West Borden Road
Spokane, WA 99224-9668
(509) 448-9263
http://www.cet.com/~weidnerc/newyork.html
Carolyn Wilson Weidner
Pub. *New York State Queries* (queries and
book reviews on New York State, and
every-name index), irregularly, $7.50
postpaid per issue

North Country Reference and Research Resources Council
6721 U.S. Highway 11
Potsdam, NY 13676-3132

NyGenWeb
Part of The USGenweb Project
hmwgenealogy@yahoo.com
http://www.rootsweb.com/~nygenweb
Lorraine Newsome, State Coordinator;
Martha Magill, Assistant Coordinator
(links to other New York resources)

Heritage Foundation of Oswego County
161 West First Street
Oswego, NY 13126
(315) 342-3354
Helen M. Breitbeck, Research Associate;
Patricia Levine, Director
Mon–Fri 10:00–3:00
(city directories, photographs, books,
architectural surveys; "our main focus is
historic preservation; we do not provide
genealogy services.")

Palatine House Museum
Spring House
PO Box 554
Schoharie, NY 12157-0554
(518) 295-7585

Pierrepont Museum
868 State Highway 68
Canton, NY 13617
http://www.museumsusa.org/data/
museums/NY/25827.htm
Charlotte Regan, Pierrepont Town Historian
second Wed & fourth Sat, and by
appointment

Zadock Pratt Museum
Main Street
Prattsville, NY 12468
(518) 299-3395
Muriel Pons, Director
Office: Mon–Fri 9:00–4:00
admission: donation

Franklin D. Roosevelt Library and Digital Archives
(address withheld upon request)
(primary historical, genealogical holdings are
on only the Roosevelt and Delano
families.)

Rushford Museum
Main Street
Rushford, NY 14777

Sagtikos Manor Historical Society
PO Box 5344
Bay Shore, NY 11706
(631) 661-8348
Nancy Donohue, President
10:00–4:00

Sea Cliff Village Museum
95 10th Street
Sea Cliff, NY 11579

(516) 671-0090

Senate House Museum
212 Fair Street
Kingston NY 12401

Southeastern New York Library Resources Council
(Route 299—location)
PO Box 879 (mailing address)
Highland, NY 12528
(845) 691-1258

Theodore Roosevelt Association
PO Box 719
Oyster Bay, NY 11771
(516) 921-6319
John A. Gable, Executive Director
Pub. *Journal*
(preserves Sagamore Hill and Theodore
Roosevelt's legacy)

Tri-Counties Genealogy and History
Joyce Tice@aol.com
http://www.rootsweb.com/~srgp/
welcome.htm#Joyce
Joyce Tice
(Chemung County, New York, and Bradford
and Tioga counties, Pennsylvania)

Upstate New York Genealogy
chris@andrle.com
http://www.andrle.com/newyork/ny.htm
Chris Andrle

West Hempstead Historical and Preservation Society
PO Box 61
West Hempstead 11552
(516) 538-6765
Marie Lebenberg, President

Western New York Association of Historical Agencies
131 West Main Street
Batavia, NY 14020-2021
(716) 345-0023
(service agency, not genealogical)

Western New York Heritage Press
495 Pine Ridge Road
Cheektowaga, NY 14225-2503
(716) 893-4011; (716) 893-4013 FAX
wnyheritage@buffalo.com
http://wnyheritagepress.org
Pub. *Western New York Heritage*, quarterly,
$24.00 per year subscription

Western New York Library Resources Council
Documentary Heritage Program
(4455 Genesee Street—location)
PO Box 400 (mailing address)
Buffalo, NY 14225-0400
(716) 633-0705; (716) 633-1736 FAX
hbamford@wnylrc.org
http://www.wnylrc.org
Heidi Bamford, Regional Archivist
Mon–Fri 9:00–5:00
(publishes a two-page section called "DHP
Diary" in the bimonthly WNYLRC
newsletter; maintains an extensive lending
library, list of titles available upon request
or online)

Yesteryears Magazine
3 Seymour Street
Auburn, NY 13021
Malcolm O. Goodelle, Owner
Pub. *Yesteryears Magazine, A Quarterly for
New York State Historical and
Genealogical Research*, quarterly

$9.00 per year membership

North Carolina

Archives and Libraries with Holdings in Genealogy

State Archives and Library
North Carolina State Archives
Department of Cultural Resources
Division of Archives and History
Archives and History—State Library
Building
(109 East Jones Street, Raleigh, NC 27601-2807—location)
4614 Mail Service Center (mailing address)
Raleigh, NC 27699-4610
(919) 807-7280; (919) 733-8807 FAX
archives@ncmail.net
http://www.ah.dcr.state.nc.us
Tue–Fri 8:00–5:30, Sat 9:00–noon & 1:00–5:00

State Library of North Carolina
Archives and History—State Library
Building
109 East Jones Street
Raleigh, NC 27601-2807
(919) 733-7222; (919) 733-5679 FAX
ktillotson@library.dcr.state.nc.us;
ptoms@library.dcr.state.nc.us
http://statelibrary.dcr.state.nc.us
Carolyn McConnell, Genealogy Assistant;
Kay Tillotson, Genealogy Information
Specialist; Pam Toms, Genealogical
Services Librarian
Mon–Fri 8:00–5:30, Sat 9:00–noon & 1:00–5:00

State Historical Society

Federation of North Carolina Historical Societies (FNCHS)
(109 East Jones Street, Raleigh, NC 27601—location)
4610 Mail Service Center (mailing address)
Raleigh, NC 27699-4610
(919) 733-7305
joann.williford@ncmail.net

http://www.ah.dcr.state.nc.us/affiliates/fnchs/fnchs.htm
Jo Ann Williford, Secretary-Treasurer
Mon–Fri 8:00–5:00
Pub. *Federation Bulletin*, quarterly
("This is a coalition of North Carolina
Historical Societies.")
$25.00 per year membership

North Carolina Society of Historians
PO Box 93
Sherrills Ford, NC 28673
Elizabeth Bray Sherrill, President

City, County and Regional Archives and Libraries
(A more exhaustive list of public and academic libraries can be found at http://statelibrary.dcr.state.nc.us/library/publib.htm.)

Alamance County Historical Museum
4777 South N.C. Highway 62
Burlington, NC 27215
(336) 225-8254
Dr. William M. Vincent
Tue–Fri 9:00–5:00, Sat 10:30–5:00, Sun 1:00–5:00
("The Museum houses archival materials and maintains a small genealogical reference library.")

Hampton B. Allen Library

120 South Greene Street
Wadesboro, NC 28170
(704) 694-5177
http://204.211.56.212
Barbara Briles, Genealogy Librarian
Mon, Wed & Fri 8:30–5:30, Tue & Thur 8:30–7:00, Sat 9:00–5:00, Sun 2:00–5:00

Asheboro Public Library
Randolph Room
201 Worth Street
Asheboro, NC 27203
(336) 318-6800 (Library); (336) 318-6815 (Randolph Room)
http://www.randolphlibrary.org/randolphroom.htm
Richard Wells, Director
Mon & Thur–Sat 9:00–5:00, Tue–Wed 9:00–9:00

Belhaven Memorial Museum, Inc.
(Main Street—location)
PO Box 220 (mailing address)
Belhaven, NC 27810
(252) 943-6817; (252) 943-2242; (252) 943-6197; (252) 943-2357 FAX
Peg McKnight, President
Mon–Tue & Thur–Sun 1:00–5:00, closed major holidays
free admission

Bladen County Public Library
(111 North Cypress Street—location)
PO Box 1419 (mailing address)
Elizabethtown, NC 28337
(910) 862-6990; (910) 862-8777 FAX
bcpl@bladenco.org
http://library.bladenco.org
Ms. Sherwin Rice, Library Director
Mon & Fri 8:30–5:30, Wed noon–5:30, Tue & Thur 8:30–5:30, Sat 8:30–3:30, Sun 2:00–4:30

Thomas Hackney Braswell Memorial Library
727 North Grace Street
Rocky Mount, NC 27804
(919) 442-1951; (252) 442-7366 FAX
director@braswell-library.org
http://www.braswell-library.org
Martha K. Turney, Director
Mon–Thur 9:00–9:00, Fri–Sat 9:00–5:00, Sun (Sept–May) 1:00–5:00

Buchanan County Public Library
(see Virginia, Part 2)

Burke County Public Library
204 South King Street
Morganton, NC 28655
(828) 437-5638; (828) 433-1914 FAX
webmaster@bcpls.org
http://www.bcpls.org
Gale Benfield, Curator, North Carolina Room
Mon & Thur 9:00–8:30, Tue–Wed & Fri 9:00–6:00, Sat 9:00–5:00

Cabarrus County Public Library
Charles A. Cannon Memorial Library
Local History Collection, Lore Room
27 Union Street, North
Concord, NC 28025-4793
(704) 920-2061; (704) 784-3822 FAX
kbridges@co.cabarrus.nc.us
http://www.cabarrus.lib.nc.us
Kathryn L. Bridges, Local History Librarian
Local History Collection: Mon–Thur 9:00–noon & 1:00–5:00 (subject to change), and by appointment (out-of-town patrons should call ahead to confirm staff availability)

("Cabarrus County, NC, genealogy and history, ca. 1750 to present")
research by mail: $5.00 per request, plus copies (limited availability); copies: 15¢ per page from paper originals, 25¢ per page from microform originals, some restrictions apply

Caldwell County Public Library
120 Hospital Avenue
Lenoir, NC 28645
(828) 757-1270; (828) 757-1413 FAX
http://www.co.caldwell.nc.us/depart/library/home.htm
Diaana Justice, Reference Librarian
Mon, Wed & Fri 8:30–5:30, Tue & Thur 8:30–8:30, Sat 9:00–4:00

Charles A. Cannon Memorial Library
(see Cabarrus County Public Library, above)

Catawba County Library
Rhodes Room: Local History and Genealogy
115 West "C" Street
Newton, NC 28658
(828) 464-2421; (828) 465-8293 FAX
cathyf@catawbacountync.gov
http://www.co.catawba.nc.us/library
Evelyn D. Rhodes, Genealogical Services Librarian; Karen Foss, Interim Director
Mon–Thur 8:00–8:30, Fri 8:00–5:00, Sat 8:30–5:00, Sun (Sept–Apr) 2:00–5:00

Public Library of Charlotte and Mecklenburg County
Robinson/Spangler Carolina Room
310 North Tryon Street
Charlotte, NC 28202-2176
(704) 336-2980; (704) 336-6236 FAX
ncr@plcmc.org
http://www.plcmc.org/carolinaroom
Christopher A. Bates, Curator and Manager
Mon–Thur 9:00–9:00, Fri–Sat 9:00–6:00, Sun 1:00–6:00

Charlotte Museum of History and Hezekiah Alexander Homesite
3500 Shamrock Drive
Charlotte, NC 28215
(704) 568-1774; (704) 566-1817 FAX
info@charlottemuseum.org
http://charlottemuseum.org
William P. Massey, President
Tue–Sat 10:00–5:00, Sun 1:00–5:00; call for appointment if you wish to use library or do genealogy research
(reference library [Lassiter Library]; genealogy listings, monographs and publications, focus on Alexander families of Piedmont Carolinas and other regional families)
$35.00 per year membership

Cherokee County Historical Museum, Inc.
87 Peachtree Street
Murphy, NC 28906
(828) 837-6792
cchm@webworkz.com
http://www.tib.com/cchm
Wanda Stalcup, Director
Mon–Fri 9:00-5:00
(artifacts, books, papers, photographs)

Cleveland County Memorial Library
(104 Howie Drive—location)
PO Box 1120 (mailing address)
Shelby, NC 28150-1120
(704) 487-9069; (704) 487-4856 FAX
cwilson@ccml.org; webmaster@ccml.org
http://www.ccml.org
Carol H. Wilson, Director
Mon–Thur 9:00–9:00, Fri 9:00–5:00, Sat

9:00–1:00
copies: 15¢ per page from paper originals,
25¢ per page from microform originals

Cumberland County Public Library
State and Local History Room
300 Maiden Lane
Fayetteville, NC 28301-5000
(910) 483-3745
ccplic@cumberland.lib.nc.us
http://www.cumberland.lib.nc.us/
hisroom.htm
James Britton, State and Local History
Librarian
Mon–Wed 9:00–9:00, Thur–Sat 9:00–6:00,
Sun (Sept–May) 2:00–6:00

Currituck County Library
Joseph Palmer Knapp Section
4261 Caratoke Highway
Barco, NC 27917-9707
(252) 453-8345 (no calls for genealogical
research); (252) 453-8717 FAX
http://www.earlibrary.org
Mon 9:00–8:00, Tue–Fri 9:00–6:00, Sat
10:00–4:00
SASE will be answered; copies: 15¢ per page
plus additional postage

Davidson County Historical Museum
(Old Courthouse on the Square—location)
2 South Main Street (mailing address)
Lexington, NC 27292
(336) 242-2035
Jeanette Wilson, Assistant

Davidson County Public Library
602 South Main Street
Lexington, NC 27292
(336) 242-2040; (336) 248-2141 FAX
jwilsonlex@yahoo.com
http://www.co.davidson.nc.us/library/
Default.htm
Jeanette B. Wilson, Genealogy Librarian
Mon–Thur 9:00–9:00, Fri–Sat 9:00–5:30

Davidson University
PO Box 1837
Davidson, NC 28036
(704) 892-2331; (704) 892-2625 FAX
http://www.davidson.edu/administrative/
library/little.htm

Duke University
William R. Perkins Library
Special Collections
PO Box 90185
Durham, NC 27708-0185
(919) 660-5822; (919) 684-2855 FAX
http://www.lib.duke.edu

Durham County Library
(300 North Roxboro Street—location)
PO Box 3809 (mailing address)
Durham, NC 27702
(919) 560-0171 (North Carolina Room);
(919) 560-0106 FAX
libraryreference@co.durham.nc.us
http://www.durhamcountylibrary.org
Lynn Richardson, North Carolina Reference
Librarian
Mon–Thur 9:00–9:00, Fri 9:00–6:00, Sat
9:30–6:00, Sun (except Memorial
Day–Labor Day) 2:00–6:00

Eden Public Library
North Carolina Collection
598 South Pierce Street
Eden, NC 27288
(336) 623-3168; (336) 623-1171 FAX
http://www.rcpl.org

Edgecombe Community College
Learning Resource Center
North Carolina and Local History Collection
2009 West Wilson Street
Tarboro, NC 27886
keenj@sco.ncdcc.cc.nc.us
http://www.edgecombe.cc.nc.us/LRC/
LRCWEB.HTM

Edgecombe County Memorial Library
Janie F. Allsbrook Local History Collection
909 Main Street
Tarboro, NC 27886
(252) 823-1141; (252) 823-7699 FAX
tthompson@edgecombelibrary.org
http://www.edgecombelibrary.org
Traci Thompson, Local History Librarian
Mon–Thur 9:00–9:00, Fri 9:00–6:00, Sat
9:00–5:00

Forsyth County Public Library
North Carolina Room/Genealogy
660 West Fifth Street
Winston-Salem, NC 27101
(336) 727-2152
carroljr@co.forsyth.nc.us
http://www.forsythlibrary.org/nc.html#1
Jerry R. Carroll, Head Librarian, North
Carolina Room
Mon–Thur 9:00–9:00, Fri 9:00–6:00, Sat
9:00–5:00, Sun (Sept–May) 1:00–5:00

Gaston-Lincoln Regional Library
1555 East Garrison Boulevard
Gastonia, NC 28054
(704) 868-2168; (704) 853-0609 FAX
refgcpl@hotmail.com
http://www.glrl.lib.nc.us
Brian C. Brown, Local History and
Genealogy Librarian
Mon–Thur 9:00–9:00, Fri–Sat 9:00–6:00,
Sun (Sept–May) 2:00–6:00
(North Carolina materials, especially Gaston
and Lincoln County family histories)

Greensboro Historical Museum
1309 Summit Avenue
Greensboro, NC 27401-3016
(336) 373-2043; (336) 373-2204 FAX
stephen.catlett@greensboro-nc.gov
http://www.greensborohistory.org
J. Stephen Catlett, Archivist
Pub. Tue-Fri 10:00-5:00 by appointment

Greensboro Historical Museum
130 Summit Avenue
Greensboro, NC 27401-3004
(704) 373-2043; (704) 373-2204 FAX
Stephen Catlett Archivist
Tue–Sat 10:00–5:00, Sun 2:00–5:00;
Archivist: Mon–Fri 9:00–5:00
Pub. *GHM Journal* (not genealogical)

Greensboro Public Library
(219 North Church Street, Greensboro, NC
27401—location)
PO Box 3178 (mailing address)
Greensboro, NC 27403-3178
(336) 373-2471 (main menu); (336) 335-
5430 (Information Services, including
NC/Genealogy Collection)
Arthur.Erickson@ci.greensboro.nc.us
http://www.greensborolibrary.org
Arthur Erickson, Genealogy Librarian
Mon–Fri 9:00–9:00, Sat 9:00–6:00, Sun
2:00–6:00; Librarian typically available
Mon–Fri 9:00–6:00
("In addition to an extensive collection of
Guilford County and North Carolina
family histories, abstracts, indexes,
newspapers, etc., we have the complete
North Carolina census on microfilm

(1790–1930), substantial South Carolina,
Tennessee and Virginia census holdings
and many Guilford County records on
microfilm from 1771 to roughly 1900.
Researchers can find and copy many
Guilford records in the library, without
going to the Register of Deeds or Clerk of
Court.")

Hacksma House Genealogy Library
(see Washington, Part 2)

Harnett County Library
Local History Room
(601 North Main Street—location)
PO Box 1149 (mailing address)
Lillington, NC 27546
(910) 893-3446; (910) 893-3001
bmaclean@harnett.org
http://www.harnett.org/library/hlochis.htm
Barbara MacLean, Reference Librarian
by appointment

Heritage Center
North Carolina Conference
Greensboro, NC 27411
(704) 379-7874

Heritage Place
Lenoir Community College
Learning Resources Center
(Highway 70 and 58 East—location)
PO Box 188 (mailing address)
Kinston, NC 28502
(252) 527-6223, ext. 508; (252) 527-6223,
ext. 501
Sue Rouse, Library Assistant
Mon–Thur 7:45–9:00, Fri 7:45–4:00 (varies
with college schedule)
(North Carolina local history museum)

Hertford County Library
(303 West Tryon Street—location)
PO Box 68 (mailing address)
Winton, NC 27986
(252) 358-7855; (252) 358-0368 FAX
luv2read27986@yahoo.com
http://www.albemarle-
regional.lib.nc.us/libraries/he.htm
Natalie Welker, Librarian; Jackie Ward,
Branch Manager
Mon & Wed–Fri 10:00–6:00, Tue noon–8:00,
Sat 9:00–noon

Hickory Public Library
375 Third Street, N.E.
Hickory, NC 28601
(828) 304-0500; (828) 304-0023 FAX
cjones@ci.hickory.nc.us
http://www.ci.hickory.nc.us/library
Jane L. Deal, R.G., Reference/Genealogy
Librarian; Corki Jones, Director
Mon–Thur 9:00–9:00, Fri–Sat 9:00–5:00,
Sun (Sept–May) 2:00–5:00
(local historians: Hahn/Heffner collections,
UDC & DAR; "For a library our size:
medium, we have a very good collection of
local history, genealogical, and state
resources, plus a very extensive vertical
file on all three areas.")
Catawba County residents free, out-of-county
$20.00 per year per family

High Point Public Library
North Carolina Room
(901 North Main Street—location)
PO Box 2530 (mailing address)
High Point, NC 27261-2530
(336) 883-3660 (Library); (336) 883-3637
(North Carolina Room); (336) 883-3657
FAX
jackie.hedstrom@ci.high-point.nc.us;

ncroom@ci.high-point.nc.us
http://www.high-point.net/dept/library
Jacquelyn Browning Hedstrom
Mon–Thur 8:00 A.M.–9:00 P.M., Fri
    8:00–6:00, Sat 9:00–noon & 1:00–6:00,
    Sun (Sept–May) 1:30–5:30 (call ahead to
    verify hours)
Pub. *Newsletter for the North Carolina
    Collection High Point Library*, quarterly,
    free
(North Carolina genealogy and local history,
    North Carolina census records, Civil War
    history)
no in-depth correspondence research; copies
    of very specific citations: $1.00 for the
    first page, 50¢ each for pages 2-10, 30¢ for
    each additional page

J. C. Holliday Memorial Library
Genealogy Department
217 Graham Street
Clinton, NC 28328
(910) 592-4153; (910) 590-3504 FAX
scpl@intrstar.net
http://www.sampsonnc.com/library.html
Robin Hollingsworth, Director

Huntsville-Madison County Public Library
(see Alabama, Part 2)

Iredell County Public Library
James Iredell History & Genealogy Room
(135 East Water Street—location)
PO Box 1810 (mailing address)
Statesville, NC 28677
(704) 878-3040; (704) 878-5449 FAX
http://www.iredell.lib.nc.us
Mardi J. Durham, Reference Librarian
Mon–Thur 9:00–9:00, Fri–Sat 9:00–6:00,
    Sun 2:00–6:00

Elbert Ivey Memorial Library
(see Hickory Public Library, above)

**Public Library of Johnston County and
Smithfield**
Johnston County Room
305 Market Street
Smithfield, NC 27577
(919) 934-8146; (919) 934-8084 FAX
http://www.geocities.com/Athens/
    Academy/1418
Mon–Tue & Thur 9:00–9:00, Wed & Fri
    9:00–5:30, Sat 9:00–5:00

Kannapolis Branch Library
The Kannapolis History Room
850 Mountain Street
Kannapolis, NC 28081
(704) 920-1180
kanhist@vnet.net
Larry Hayer, History Librarian
afternoons & Sat
(Cannon Mills Company archives, local
    history and local family history)

Lawrence Memorial Public Library
204 East Dundee Street
Windsor, NC 27983-1210
(252) 794-2244; (252) 794-1546 FAX
sanssouci204@yahoo.com
http://www.albemarle-
    regional.lib.nc.us/libraries/bertie.htm
Nancy B. Hughes, Branch Manager
Mon noon–8:00, Tue & Thur–Fri
    10:00–6:00, Wed 2:00–6:00, Sat
    9:00–noon
copies: 10¢ per page from paper original, 25¢
    per page from microform originals

Lincoln County Public Library
North Carolina Collection

306 West Main Street
Lincolnton, NC 28092-2616
(704) 732-9040; (704) 732-9042 FAX
Linc_Lib@yahoo.com (Local Historian)
http://www.gaston.net/glrl/glrlncc.htm
Lesley Levine
Mon–Tue & Thur 9:00–9:00, Wed & Fri–Sat
    9:00–6:00

Macon County Public Library
108 Wayah Street
Franklin, NC 28734
(704) 524-3600; (828) 524-9550 FAX
http://www.fontanalib.org
Nancy Van Hook; Karen Wallace, Librarian
Mon, Wed & Fri 11:00–5:30, Tue & Thur
    10:00–9:00, Sat 10:00–4:00

The Madison-Morgan Cultural Center
Museum Drive
Winston-Salem, NC 27105

Madison Public Library
Rockingham County Public Library
Genealogy Room
140 East Murphy Street
Madison, NC 27025
(336) 548-6553; (336) 548-2010 FAX
spell@library.rcpl.org;
    swilliams@library.rcpl.org (Sue Williams,
    Director)
http://www.rcpl.org/lib3.html
Sarah Pell, Branch Librarian
Mon 10:00–8:00, Tue & Fri 10:00–6:00,
    Wed 9:00–6:00, Thur noon–8:00, first,
    third and fifth Sat 9:00–4:00
(emphasis on Rockingham and Stokes
    counties)

Jacob S. Mauney Memorial Library
100 South Piedmont
Kings Mountain, NC 28086
(704) 739-2371; (704) 734-4499 FAX
Rose Turner, Director
Mon–Tue 9:00–8:00, Wed–Thur 9:00–6:00,
    Fri 9:00–5:00, Sat 9:00–1:00

May Memorial Library
Headquarters of Central North Carolina
    Regional Library
342 South Spring Street
Burlington, NC 27215
(336) 229-3588; (336) 229-3592 FAX
http://www.alamance-nc.com/library
Lisa Kobrin, Reference Librarian
Mon–Thur 9:00–9:00, Fri–Sat 9:00–6:00,
    Sun (Labor Day–Memorial Day)
    1:00–5:00, reference assistance not
    necessarily available at all times
(collection focuses on Alamance and Orange
    counties, with some information on
    surrounding counties)

McDowell County Public Library
90 West Court Street
Marion, NC 28752
(828) 652-3858; (828) 652-2098 FAX
http://www.main.nc.us/libraries/mcdowell
Elizabeth House, Assistant Librarian; Connie
    Curtis, Director
Mon, Wed & Fri–Sat 10:00–5:30, Tue &
    Thur 9:30–8:30
no research by staff, but will supply the
    names of area professionals

Murphy Public Library
101 Blumenthal Street
Murphy, NC 28906
(828) 837-2417; (828) 837-6416 FAX
http://www.webreadydesigns.net/nantahala
Becky Stiles, Library Director
Mon–Wed & Fri 9:00–6:00, Thur 9:00–9:00,

Sat 9:00–2:00

New Bern-Craven County Public Library
Kellenberger Room
400 Johnson Street
New Bern, NC 28560
(252) 638-7808
http://newbern.cpclib.org/nbccpl/cpcrl.html
Victor T. Jones, Jr., Local History and
    Genealogy Librarian
Mon–Thur 9:00–9:00, Fri–Sat 9:00–6:00,
    Sun 2:00–6:00
(eastern North Carolina, particularly Craven,
    Pamlico, and Carteret counties)
costs of copying and postage: minimum of
    $2.00

New Hanover Public Library
Local History and Genealogy
201 Chestnut Street
Wilmington, NC 28401-3942
(910) 341-4394; (910) 798-6305 (Local
    History Room); (910) 341-4388 FAX
http://www.co.new-
    hanover.nc.us/lib/localhis.htm
Beverly Tetterton, Special Collections
    Librarian
Mon–Wed 9:00–8:00, Thur–Sat 9:00–5:00,
    Sun 1:00–5:00
(vertical files, over 1,000 reels of microfilm
    of Wilmington newspapers from 1765,
    church records, African-American records,
    photographs, maps and books and
    pamphlets specializing in the local history
    and genealogy of southeastern North
    Carolina; special collection: Reaves
    Collection of Southeastern, North
    Carolina, families)

North Carolina Museum of History
(5 East Edenton Street, Raleigh, NC 27601-
    1011—location)
4650 Mail Service Center (mailing address)
Raleigh, NC 27699-4650
(919) 715-0200; (919) 733-8655 FAX
Betsy.Buford@ncmail.net;
    ncmoh@ncmail.net;
    jackson.marshall@ncmail.net
http://www.ncmuseumofhistory.org
Elizabeth F. Buford; Jackson Marshall,
    Researcher
Tue–Sat 9:00–5:00, Sun noon–5:00
Pub. *Tar Heel Junior Historian*,
    semiannually; *Cornerstone*, three times per
    year
free admission

Ohoopee Regional Library
(see Georgia, Part 2)

Onslow County Public Library
Tucker Littleton Room
58 Doris Avenue East
Jacksonville, NC 28540
(910) 455-7350; (910) 455-1661 FAX
http://www.onslow.com/library
Joan Brinson Dillemuth
Mon–Thur 9:00–9:00, Fri–Sat 9:00–6:00

Outer Banks History Center
(Roanoke Island Festival Park—location)
PO Box 250 (mailing address)
Manteo, NC 27954
(252) 473-2655; (252) 473-1483 FAX
Wynne C. Dough, Curator
Mon–Fri 9:00–5:00
Pub. *O.B.H.C. Associates Newsletter*,
    quarterly, $10.00 per year subscription
(a nonlending regional library and manuscript
    repository of the North Carolina
    Department of Cultural Resources,
    Division of Archives and History; houses

many types of genealogical resource materials, not entirely restricted to the coastal areas: more than 4,500 U.S. Life Saving Service and U.S. Coast Guard wreck documents, more than 3,000 photographs, more than 1,300 serials, more than 700 original maps and charts, and a variety of clippings, recordings, microforms, engravings, and ephemera) $15.00 per year membership; research: fees for copies

Pack Memorial Public Library
67 Haywood Street
Asheville, NC 28801
(704) 255-5203; (704) 255-5213 FAX
http://www.librarybuncombe.org/pack.htm
Mon–Thur 10:00–9:00, Fri–Sat 10:00–6:00, Sun (Sept–May) 2:00–6:00

Person County Public Library
North Carolina Room
319 South Main Street
Roxboro, NC 27573
(336) 597-7881
http://www.co.orange.nc.us/library/Hyconeechee.htm
Linda Howerton, Director
Mon–Thur 10:00–8:00, Fri 10:00–5:00, Sat 10:00–2:00

Olivia Raney Local History Library
4016 Carya Drive
Raleigh, NC 27610
(919) 250-1196
oliviaraney@co.wake.nc.us
http://www.co.wake.nc.us/library
Sue Zolkowski, Branch Supervisor
Mon & Thur 10:00–8:00, Tue–Wed 10:00–6:00, Sat 10:00–5:00

Reed Gold Mine Library
9621 Reed Mine Road
Stanfield, NC 28163

Reidsville Library
North Carolina Collection
204 West Morehead Street
Reidsville, NC 27320
(336) 349-8476; (336) 342-4824 FAX
http://www.rcpl.org

W. G. Rhea Public Library
(see Tennessee, Part 2)

Robersonville Public Library
(119 South Mail Street—location)
PO Box 1060 (mailing address)
Robersonville, NC 27871
(252) 795-3591; (252) 795-3359 FAX
http://www.bhmlib.org/bhm/default.asp
Madge R. Partin, Librarian
Mon–Fri 9:30–5:30, Sat 9:30–1:00

Robeson County Public Library
(101 North Chestnut Street—location)
PO Box 988 (mailing address)
Lumberton, NC 28358
(910) 738-4859; (910) 739-8321 FAX
ballchin@ncsl.dcr.state.nc.us
Barbara Allchin, Reference Librarian; Robert Fisher, Director
Mon, Wed & Fri–Sat 9:00–6:00, Tue & Thur 9:00–9:00
(local history and genealogy collection)

Rowan Public Library
Edith M. Clark History Room
(201 West Fisher Street, Salisbury, NC 28144—location)
PO Box 4039 (mailing address)
Salisbury, NC 28145-4039

(704) 638-3021; (704) 638-3013 FAX
RouseDH@co.rowan.nc.us
http://www.lib.co.rowan.nc.us/HistoryRoom/default.htm
Vanessa Sterling, Associate, Local History/Genealogy
Mon–Thur 9:00–9:00, Fri 9:00–5:00, Sat 9:00–5:00, Sun (Sept–May) 1:00–5:00
(emphasis on North Carolina genealogy with holdings covering the southeastern and mid-Atlantic states: Pennsylvania, Maryland, Virginia, North Carolina, South Carolina, Georgia, Tennessee and Kentucky)

Sandhill Regional Library
412 East Franklin Street
Rockingham, NC 28379
(910) 997-3388; (910) 997-2516
jbradsher@ncsl.dcr.state.nc.us
http://204.211.56.212
John Bradsher, Assistant Director

Scotland County Memorial Library
(312 West Church Street, Laurinburg, NC 28352—location)
PO Box 369 (mailing address)
Laurinburg, NC 28353
(910) 276-0563; (910) 276-4032 FAX
rbusko@scotlandcounty.org
Robert Busko, Director
Mon, Wed & Fri 10:00–6:00, Tue & Thur 10:00–8:00, Sat 9:00–5:00, Sun 2:00–6:00
copies: 20¢ per page, other fees depending on the request

Sheppard Memorial Library
Local History and Genealogy Room
530 Evans Street
Greenville, NC 27858
(252) 329-4580; (252) 329-4587 FAX
http://www.sheppardlibrary.org
Willie Nelms, Director

Stanly County Public Library
Margaret Johnston Heritage Room
133 East Main Street
Albemarle, NC 28001-4939
(704) 983-7329
scplweb@carolina.rr.com
http://www.stanlylib.org
Lu J. Koontz, Research Assistant; Penny Welling, Director
Mon–Thur 9:00–8:00, Fri 9:00–5:00, Sat (school year) 9:00–5:00, Sat (summer) 9:00–1:00
(North Carolina local history and genealogy)

Sullivan County Library
(see Tennessee, Part 2)

Richard H. Thornton Library
(210 Main Street—location)
PO Box 339 (mailing address)
Oxford, NC 27565
(919) 693-1121; (919) 693-2244 FAX
http://www.granville.lib.nc.us
Fann Montague, Library Associate
Library: Mon–Thur 10:00–8:00, Fri–Sat 10:00–5:00, Sun (Sept–May) 1:00–5:00; Genealogy Room Staff Person: Tue–Thur by appointment
search, copy and postage fee: $5.00 per request

Troy Public Library
(see Alabama, Part 2)

Union County Public Library
316 East Windsor Street
Monroe, NC 28110

(704) 283-8184; (704) 282-0657 FAX
http://www.union.lib.nc.us
Daniel S. MacNeill, Director
Mon, Wed & Fri 9:00–6:00, Tue & Thur 9:00–8:00, Sat 9:00–5:00, Sun (Sept–May) 2:00–5:00

University of Mississippi
Center for the Study of Southern Culture
(see Mississippi, Part 2)

University of North Carolina at Asheville
D. Hiden Ramsey Library
Special Collections
Southern Highlands Research Center
1 University Heights
Asheville, NC 28804
(704) 251-6336
hwykle@unca.edu
http://www.unca.edu/library/find.html

The University of North Carolina at Chapel Hill
North Carolina Collection
Louis Round Wilson Library
Campus Box 3930
Chapel Hill, NC 27599-3930
(919) 933-1172; (919) 962-4452 FAX
H. G. Jones, Ph.D., Curator
Pub. *Annual Reports of the North Caroliniana Society, Inc. and the North Carolina Collection*, annually

The University of North Carolina at Chapel Hill
Manuscripts Department
Campus Box 3926, Wilson Library
Chapel Hill, NC 27514-8890
(919) 962-1345; (919) 962-4452 FAX
mss@email.unc.edu
http://www.unc.edu/lib/mss
Head of Public Services
Mon–Fri 8:00–5:00, Sat 9:00–1:00
(North Carolina and the Southeast)
responds to reference requests

The University of North Carolina at Charlotte
Special Collections, J. Murrey Atkins Library
9201 University City Boulevard
Charlotte, NC 28223
(704) 547-2449
speccoll@email.uncc.edu
http://www.uncc.edu/lis/collections/special
Robin Brabham, Special Collections Librarian
(200+ manuscript collections, comprising approximately 1,000,000 items that document the social, political and architectural history of the greater Charlotte area; many of the collections contain material relevant to genealogical research)

Virginia Polytechnic Institute and State University
Appalachian history
(see Virginia, Part 2)

Wayne County Public Library
1001 East Ash Street
Goldsboro, NC 27530
(919) 735-1824; (919) 731-2889 FAX
wcpl@wcpl.org
http://www.wcpl.org
Rhonda Konig, Local History Librarian
Mon–Thur 9:00–9:00, Fri–Sat 9:00–5:30, Sun (during school year) 1:00–5:00
("We have a Local History Room.")

Wilkes County Public Library
Genealogy Research Room

215 10th Street
North Wilkesboro, NC 28659-1629
(336) 838-2818 (County Librarian); (336)
    667-2638
lgerhard@arlibrary.org
http://www.arlibrary.org/wilkes.htm
Louise Gerhard, County Librarian
Mon–Thur 8:00–8:30, Fri 8:00–5:00, Sat
    8:00–3:00

Wilson County Public Library
(249 West Nash Street—location)
PO Box 400 (mailing address)
Wilson, NC 27893-0400
(919) 237-5355; (252) 243-4311 FAX
pvalentine@wilson-co.com
http://www.wilson-co.com/library.html
Patrick Valentine, Director; Deborah Webb
Mon–Thur 9:00–9:00, Fri–Sat 9:00–6:00

Historical Societies—Local and Regional

Alleghany Historical-Genealogical Society, Inc.
(Alleghany County Courthouse—location)
PO Box 817 (mailing address)
Sparta, NC 28675
(336) 372-4214
Irene R. Wagner
Pub. *Alleghany Historical-Genealogical
    Society, Inc., Bulletin*, quarterly
$5.00 per year membership

Anson County Historical Society, Inc.
209 East Wade Street
Wadesboro, NC 28170-2229
(704) 694-6694; (704) 694-3763
ansonhistorical@alltel.net
http://home.alltel.net/ansonhistorical
Lynda Garibaldi, President
Mon–Fri 9:00–11:00 & noon–2:00
Pub. *Newsletter*, bimonthly
$15.00 per year membership

Apex Historical Society
PO Box 506
Apex, NC 27502
http://apexhisoc.freeservers.com
$15.00 per year membership

The Appalachian Consortium
University Hall
Boone, NC 28608
(828) 262-2064; (828) 262-6564
burlesonec@appstate.edu
http://www.uvawise.edu/appalcon
Mike Epley, Executive Director
8:00–4:30
(a nonprofit education dedicated to the
    preservation of the Appalachian region;
    publishes books about the region)
$50.00 per year membership

Ashe County Historical Society
c/o Ashe County Public Library
148 Library Drive
West Jefferson, NC 28694
http://www.ls.net/~newriver/nc/ashebook.
    htm

Avery County Historical Society
PO Box 266
Newland, NC 28657

Beaufort Historical Association
(100 Block Turner Street—location)
PO Box 363 (mailing address)
Beaufort, NC 28516-0363
(252) 728-5225; (252) 728-4966 FAX
bha@bmd.clis.com

http://www.historicbeaufort.com
Patricia Suggs, Executive Director
Apr–Oct: Mon–Sat 9:30–5:00 Nov–Mar:
    Mon–Sat 10:00–4:00
Pub. newsletter, quarterly
$25.00 per year membership

Black Creek Historical Society
PO Box 204
Black Creek, NC 27813

Bladen County Historical Society
(Harmony Hall Plantation, PO Box 297,
White Oak NC 28399—location)
PO Box 848 (mailing address)
Elizabethtown, NC 28337
(910) 866-4844; (910) 648-4340
sflewis@carolina.net; rlsmith@intrstar.net
http://www.rootsweb.com/~ncbladen/
    bchs.htm
Seth F. Lewis
$10.00 per year membership

Bladenboro Historical Society
Family History Room
818 South Main Street
Bladenboro, NC 28320
http://www.rootsweb.com/~ncbladen/
    bladenboro.htm
Sat–Sun 2:00–4:00

Brunswick County Historical Society
PO Box 874
Shallotte, NC 28459
(910) 754-8445
Gwen Causey, President
Pub. *BCHS Newsletter*

Burke County Historical Society
(The History Museum of Burke County, 201
West Meeting Street—location)
PO Box 151 (mailing address)
Morganton, NC 28655
(828) 437-3533; (828) 437-1777 (Museum)
thehistorymuseum@hci.net
http://www.thehistorymuseumofburke.org
Joe Avery, Treasurer
$25.00 per year membership

Caldwell County Historical Society
112 Vaiden Street, S.W.
Lenoir, NC 28645-5670
(704) 758-7121
http://caldwellheritagemuseum.org
Tue–Fri 10:00–4:30, Sat 10:00–3:00
$25.00 per year membership

Camden County Historical Society
Camden, NC 27921
(252) 336-2747

Carteret County Historical Society, Inc.
The History Place
1008 Arendell Street
Morehead City, NC 28557-4143
(252) 247-7533 voice & FAX
historyplace@starfishnet.com
http://www.thehistoryplace.org
Jack Spencer Goodwin, Director of Library
    Services; Leslie A. Ewen, President
    CCHS; Michelle Stokes, Director
    CCMHA
Tue–Sat 1:00–4:00
Pub. *The Researcher*, quarterly
(Carteret County history and genealogies)
$20.00 per year membership; charge for
    photocopies; accepts queries

Cary Historical Society
PO Box 134
Cary, NC 27512-0134
(919) 467-6989

Irene Kittinger, Treasurer
Pub. *CHS Newsletter*

Caswell County Historical Association, Inc.
(Richmond-Miles Museum, 15 Main Street
East—location)
PO Box 278 (mailing address)
Yanceyville, NC 27379
(336) 694-4965
Museum: Wed–Fri noon–4:00
Pub. *Newsletter of the Caswell County
    Historical Association, Inc.*, quarterly
    (Jan, Apr, July, Oct)
$20.00 per year membership; search fees are
    reasonable by member volunteers

Catawba County Historical Association, Inc.
(former Catawba County Courthouse, 15
North College Avenue—location)
PO Box 73 (mailing address)
Newton, NC 28658-0073
(828) 465-0383; (828) 465-0928 FAX
inquiry@catawbahistory.org
http://www.catawbahistory.org
Sidney Halma, Museum Director
Tue–Fri 9:00–4:00, Sat 10:00–4:00, Sun
    2:00–5:00
Pub. *Past Times*, quarterly
(primary sources)
$15.00 per year membership; free admission;
    research: $10.00 per hour

Chatham County Historical Association
PO Box 93
Pittsboro, NC 27312-0093
(919) 542-3603
http://www.chathamhistory.org (preferred
    way to communicate)
Pub. *Chatham Historical Journal*; *CCHA
    Newsletter*, occasionally (two to four per
    year)
$7.50 per year membership

Chicamacomico Historical Association
Chicamacomico Lifesaving Station
PO Box 5
Rodanthe, NC 27968
(252) 987-1552
Easter–Thanksgiving: Tue–Sat 9:00–5:00

Historical Society of China Grove
113 North Main Street
China Grove, NC 28023
(704) 857-1176

Cleveland County Historical Association and Museum
(Court Square—location)
PO Box 1335 (mailing address)
Shelby, NC 28150
(704) 482-8186
James D. Marler, Museum Director

Columbus County Historical Society
PO Box 339
Whiteville, NC 28472-0339

Cooleemee Historical Association and Mill Village Museum
(Old 14 Church Street—location)
PO Box 667 (Mailing address)
Cooleemee, NC 27014
(336) 284-6040; (336) 284-4983 FAX
blinky1@yadtel.net
http://www.members.tripod.com/ ~cooleemee
Lynn W. Rumley, Director
Wed–Sat 10:00–4:00, Sun 2:00–4:00
Pub. *Cooleemee History Loom*, quarterly
("We're building a network of cotton mill
    people across the south. Get in touch!")
$5.00 per year membership;

photoreproduction: $2.00 plus shipping and handling

Cumberland County Historical Society
525 Vista Drive
Fayetteville, NC 28305
kylewis@foto.infi.net
http://source.fayettevillenc.com/main.
  wsi?group_id=84
Kathryn Y. Lewis, Vice President
meetings at Heritage Place, 325 North Cool
  Spring Street:fourth Wed (Jan, Mar, June,
  Sept) noon
$5.00 per year membership

Currituck County Historical Society
PO Box 115
Poplar Branch, NC 27965
Pub. *Currituck County Historical Society*,
  irregularly
$12.50 per year membership

Davidson County Historical Association
1 South Main
Lexington, NC 27292
(336) 476-7213

Davie County Historical and Genealogical Society
371 North Main Street
Mocksville, NC 27028-2115
(336) 751-2023
Frances Beck, President; Doris B. Frye,
  Secretary
Library: Mon–Thur 9:00–8:30, Fri
  9:00–5:30, Sat 9:00–4:00, Sun 2:00–5:00
Pub. *The Davie Dossier*, quarterly
("The society houses its materials with that of
  the local public library.")
$5.00 per year membership

Duplin County Historical Society
Leora H. McEachern Library of Local History
(314 East Main Street—location)
PO Box 130 (mailing address)
Rose Hill, NC 28458-0130
(910) 289-2430 (Library, evenings only)
W. D. Herring, Librarian
7:00 P.M.–midnight, and other times by
  appointment
Pub. *Footnotes*, quarterly
(genealogical collection)
$10.00 per year membership

Eastern Cabarrus Historical Society and Museum
PO Box 1299
Mount Pleasant, NC 28124
(704) 436-6612
Resa Treadaway, President
May–Oct: Mon 10:00–4:00, first & third Sun
  2:00–5:00
("Site built as boys school 1852")
$25.00 per year membership

Edenton Historical Commission
The Barker House, 505 South Broad Street
Edenton, NC 27932-1937
(252) 482-7800
http://www.edenton.com/history/barker.htm
Mon–Sat 10:00-4:00, Sun 1:00-4:00

Edgecombe County Cultural Arts Council, Inc.
130 Bridgers Street
Tarboro, NC 27886
(252) 823-4159; (252) 823-6190 FAX
edgecombeArts@earthlink.net
http://www.edgecombeArts.org
Meade B. Horne, Director, Blount-Bridgers
  House
Mon–Fri 10:00–4:00, Sat–Sun 2:00–4:00

Pub. *Non Nulla*
(Blount, Bridgers families)
$25.00 per year membership; research: fees
  as agreed upon with client

Fair Bluff Historical Society
(339 Railroad Street—location)
PO Box 285 (mailing address)
Fair Bluff, NC 28439
(910) 649-7707

Gaston County Historical Society, Inc.
315 Union-New Hope Road
Gastonia, NC 28056
(704) 867-6712
confvet@aol.com (President)
Wilma Ratchford Craig, Editor; Bruce
  Cloninger, President
Pub. *Gaston County Historical Bulletin*

Gates County Historical Society
Old Gates County Courthouse
PO Box 98
Gates, NC 27937
(252) 357-1733
http://www.albemarled-nc.com/
  gates/history/courthse.htm
Edith Seiling, President
on request
Pub. *Gates County Historical Society
  Newsletter*, semiannually
$10.00 per year membership

Greater Fair Bluff Historical Society
PO Box 285
Fairbluff, NC 28439
Bettie Renfrow, President

Halifax County Historical Association
PO Box 12
Halifax, NC 27839
(252) 519-0700
eoverton@pure.net
http://www.halifax.com/historical
J. Rives Manning, Jr., Vice President
meetings: third Fri (Sept, Nov, Mar, May)
$8.00 per year membership

Hampstead Historical and Genealogical Society
PO Box 8
Hampstead, NC 28443

Henderson County Genealogical and Historical Society, Inc.
(see Genealogical Societies—Local and
Regional, below)

High Point Historical Society
High Point Museum
1859 East Lexington Avenue
High Point, NC 27262
(336) 885-1859; (336) 883-3284 FAX
http://www.highpointmuseum.org
Barbara Taylor, Executive Director
Tue–Sat 10:00–4:30, Sun 1:00–4:30
Pub. *Timepiece*, quarterly
("Gallery interpreting High Point history,
  gallery on High Point industries, one or
  two changing galleries—depending on
  size—of local exhibits.")
$15.00+ per year membership; free
  admission; research fee, depending on
  request

Alliance for Historic Hillsborough
150 East King Street
Hillsborough, NC 27278
(919) 732-7741; (919) 732-6322 FAX
alliance@historichillsborough.org
http://www.historichillsborough

Hillsborough Historical Society
(Corbin Street—location)
PO Box 871 (mailing address)
Hillsborough, NC 27278
(919) 732-8648
Clarence D. Jones, Office Manager
mornings only
Pub. *Newsletter*, quarterly
$10.00 per year membership

Hyde County Historical and Genealogical Society
7820 Piney Woods Road
Fairfield, NC 27826
(252) 926-4921; (252) 926-1955 (Library)
http://www.rootsweb.com/~nchyde/
  HCHGS.htm
Betty S. Mann, Treasurer
Library in the Mattamuskeet School, 20370
  U.S. 264, Swan Quarter, NC: Mon & Wed
  10:00–5:00, Tue & Thur 3:00–6:30, Fri
  10:00–3:30, Sat 9:00–1:00; summer: Mon
  & Wed 8:00–2:00 & 3:00–5:30, Tue &
  Thur 8:00–2:00 & 3:00–7:00, Fri
  8:00–2:00 & 3:00–4:00
Pub. *High Tides*, semiannually
(Hyde County and area history and
  genealogy)
$15.00 per year membership

Jackson County Historical Association
PO Box 173
Sylva, NC 28779

Jones County Historical Society
PO Box 401
Pollocksville, NC 28573-0401
(252) 224-8181; (252) 224-0178 FAX
James E. Carriker, President

Kannapolis History Associates
PO Box 21
Kannapolis, NC 28102-0021

Lee County Genealogical and Historical Society, Inc.
(see Genealogical Societies—Local and
Regional, below)

Lewisville Historical Society
PO Box 242
Lewisville, NC 27023

Lincoln County Historical Association, Inc.
403 East Main Street, Suite 302
Lincolnton, NC 28093
(704) 748-9090
Jason Harpe, Director
Pub. *Bits and Pieces*

Lower Cape Fear Historical Society
126 South Third Street
Wilmington, NC 28402
(910) 762-0492; (910) 763-5869 (Archives)
latimer@latimerhouse.org
http://www.latimerhouse.org
Jean S. Scott, Executive Director; Diane C.
  Cashman, Archivist
Society: Mon–Sat 10:00–4:00; Archives:
  Tue–Thur 10:00–12:30 and by
  appointment
Pub. *For the Record: Newsletter of the Lower
  Cape Fear Historical Society*; *Lower Cape
  Fear Historical Society Bulletin*, three
  times per year; *Lower Cape Fear
  Historical Society Journal*
(history of the Lower Cape Fear/southeastern
  North Carolina)
$20.00 per year membership (includes only
  For the Record and the *Bulletin*); research:
  copy costs, postage

Macon County Historical Society
36 West Main Street
Franklin, NC 28734
(828) 524-9758
historical@smnet.net
http://www.genealogybookstore.com/
publishing/macon/historical/
historicalsociety.htm
Barbara White, Executive Director
1 May–31 Oct: Tue–Fri 10:00–5:00, Sat
1:00–5:00, and by appointment; 1 Nov–30
Apr: Mon–Fri 10:00–4:00, and by
appointment; hours subject to change for
special events, etc.
Pub. *Macon County Echoes*, quarterly
(Macon County history and families)
$20.00 per year membership

Madison County Historical Society
PO Box 236
Marshall, NC 28753
(828) 689-1153

Malcolm Blue Historical Society
Malcolm Blue Farmstead and Museum
(609 Bethesda Road—location)
PO Box 603 (mailing address)
Aberdeen, NC 28315
(910) 944-7558; (910) 944-5967
malcolmblue@alltel.net
http://www.malcolmbluefarm.org
Pam Dannelley, Executive Director
Wed–Sat 1:00–4:00
Pub. *From out of the Blue*, quarterly
("Farmstead with 1825 farmhouse and farm
museum. Published *History of Aberdeen,
N.C.*, $36.80 ppd.")
$15.00 per year membership; no research
service

Martin County Historical Society
Francis M. Manning History Room
Martin County Community College Library
PO Box 468
Williamston, NC 27892-0121
(252) 792-1521, ext. 296 (Library); (252)
792-4425 FAX
http://www.visitmartincounty.com/
heritage_culture/resources.htm
Doris L. Wilson, Chairman
College Library hours
(local and regional historical and
genealogical materials)

Mecklenburg Historical Association
PO Box 35032
Charlotte, NC 28235
president@meckdec.org
http://www.meckdec.org
Chase Saunders, President
(has no staff or library and can only refer
users to libraries)

Mitchell County Historical Society
PO Box 651
Bakersville, NC 28705

Montgomery County Historical Society
PO Box 664
Troy, NC 27306

Moore County Historical Association
(Shaw House, Corner of Morganton and
Broad—location)
PO Box 324 (mailing address)
Southern Pines, NC 28388
(910) 692-2051 voice & FAX
moorehistory@connectnc.net
http://www.moorehistory.com
Janet Cunningham, Director
Mid-Jan to July & Sept to mid-Dec: Fri–Sat
1:00–4:00

(history of Moore county)
$15.00 per year membership; research:
donation for postage

Mordecai Square Historical Society
Capital Area Preservation (CAP)
Mordecai Historic Park
1 Mimosa Street
Raleigh, NC 27604
(919) 834-4844 (CAP)
Sally Poland, Executive Director
CAP Office: Mon–Fri 8:30–5:00
Pub. *Square Notes*; *Preservation Matters*,
quarterly
$25.00 per year membership

Murfreesboro Historical Association
(116 East Main Street—location)
PO Box 3 (mailing address)
Murfreesboro, NC 27855
(252) 398-5922; (252) 398-5871 FAX
histassn@albemarlenet.com
http://www.murfreesboronc.com

Nash County Historical Association, Inc.
100 Salem Court
Rocky Mount, NC 27804
(252) 443-6708
T. E. Ricks, President

New Bern Historical Society
(510 Pollock Street—location)
PO Box 119 (mailing address)
New Bern, NC 28563-0119
(252) 638-8558; (252) 638-5773 FAX
http://www.pamlico-
nc.com/historicnewbern/index.htm
Joanne Gwaltney, Executive Director
Mon–Fri 8:30–4:00
Pub. *Journal of the NBHS*, semiannually,
$5.00 per year subscription; *NBHS
Newsletter*

**Family Research Society of Northeastern
North Carolina**
(410 East Main Street, Suite 204—location)
PO Box 1425 (mailing address)
Elizabeth City, NC 27906-1425
(252) 333-1640
frsnnc3@hotmail.com
http://www.geocities.com/heartland/farm/
7890
Teresa Ferguson, Vice President
Tue, Thur & Sat 10:00–3:00
Pub. *Carolina Trees and Branches*, quarterly
plus yearly membership surname list
(covers Camden, Currituck, Chowan, Dare,
Gates, Pasquotank and Perquimans
counties, part of the original Albemarle
County)
$20.00 per year membership

Onslow County (NC) Historical Society
(Onslow County Museum, Richlands,
NC—location)
PO Box 5203 (mailing address)
Jacksonville, NC 28540
(910) 347-5287; (910) 324-5008 (Museum)
JoAnn Stidger Becker, Secretary
$10.00 per year membership

Pender County Historical Society
(100 West Bridger Street—location)
PO Box 1380 (mailing address)
Burgaw, NC 28425
(910) 259-8543
Carey E. Boney, Chairman
Sept–May: Thur–Sat 1:00-4:00; June–Aug:
Thur–Sat 2:00–5:00

Person County Historical Society, Inc.
PO Box 887

Roxboro, NC 27573
(336) 597-3134
pchs@esinc.net
http://www.rootsweb.com/~ncperson/
society.htm
meetings in the lower level of the Senior
Center on Depot Street: fourth Tue 7:00
$20.00 per year membership; research: for a
fee

Pitt County Historical Society
PO Box 1554
Greenville, NC 27835-1554
liz_sparrow@yahoo.com
http://www.pittcountyhistoricalsociety.com
Elizabeth Sparrow, Board Member

Randolph County Historical Society
(Asheboro Public Library, 201 Worth Street,
Asheboro, NC 27203—location)
PO Box 4355 (mailing address)
Asheboro, NC 27204
(336) 318-6815
L. McKay Whatley, President
Mon–Fri 9:00–5:00
$5.00 per year Associate membership

Richmond County Historical Society
PO Box 1763
Rockingham, NC 28380
secretary@rchs-nc.org; horace@peele.com
http://www.rchs-nc.org
J. Neal Cadieu, Secretary

**Society of Richmond County (North
Carolina) Descendants and Richmond
County Historical Collection**
PO Box 848
Rockingham, NC 28380-0848
(910) 997-6641
http://www.richmondcodescendants.org
Joe M. McLaurin, President
Pub. *The Richmond County Record*, three
times per year
$18.00 per year membership

Roanoke Island Historical Association
Fort Raleigh National Historic Site
PO Box 40
Manteo, NC 27954
(252) 473-2127
Robert Knowles, Ph.D., General Manager
(primarily historical, not genealogical)

Rockingham County Historical Society
PO Box 84
Wentworth, NC 27375
(336) 951-2595; (336) 342-5901 (Office)
Robert W. Carter, Jr., Editor
by appointment only
Pub. *Journal of Rockingham County History
and Genealogy*, semiannually; *Newsletter*,
quarterly
$12.00 per year membership

Rutherford County Historical Society
PO Box 1044
Rutherfordton, NC 28139

Sampson County Historical Society
PO Box 1084
Clinton, NC 28328
Helen Jean Faircloth, Treasurer
Pub. *Huckleberry Historian*, quarterly, $7.50
by mail or $5.00 online

**Southern Appalachian Historical
Association, Inc.**
PO Box 295
Boone, NC 28607
(828) 264-2120
William R. Winkler, III, Executive Producer

Southern Studies Institute
(see Louisiana, Part 2)

Southport Historical Society
PO Box 10014
Southport, NC 28461-0014
(910) 457-0579
shs@ec.rr.com
http://www.southporthistoricalsociety.com
only on special occasions and by appointment
Pub. *The Whittlers' Bench*, bimonthly
(includes a genealogy page)
$10.00 per year membership

Stokes County Historical Society
PO Box 250
Germanton, NC 27019
(336) 591-7969
StokesHistory@aol.com
http://www.piedmontcommunities.us/servlet/
go_procserv/dbpage=page&gid=01216001
150986273447978601
$10.00 per year membership

Surry County Historical Society
Edwards-Franklin House
125 Oakview Trail
Mount Airy, NC 27030

**Swain County Genealogical and Historical
Society**
(see Genealogical Societies—Local and
Regional, below)

Transylvania County Historical Society
Allison-Deaver House
PO Box 2061
Brevard, NC 18712
(828) 884-5137
Fri & Sun 1:00–4:00, Sat 10:00–4:00

**Tyrell County Genealogical and Historical
Society**
(see Genealogical Societies—Local and
Regional, below)

Vance County Historical Society
PO Box 2284
Henderson, NC 27536

Wachovia Historical Society
PO Box 20803
Winston-Salem, NC 27120-0803
starbuckrw@aol.com
http://www.wachoviatract.org
Richard Starbuck

Wake County Historical Society
PO Box 2
Raleigh, NC 27602

Warren County Historical Association
210 Plummer Street
Warrenton, NC 27589

Washington County Historical Society
PO Box 296
Plymouth, NC 27962

Watauga County Historical Society
East Mast, 253 Wm. Hardy Mast Road
Sugar Grove, NC 28679-9707

Wayne County Historical Association, Inc.
PO Box 665
Goldsboro, NC 27530-0665
(919) 736-5011
Emily Weil, Association President
Archives in the Local History Room at
Wayne County Public Library: Mon–Thur
9:00–9:00, Fri–Sat 9:00–5:30, Sun (during
school year) 1:00–5:00

Pub. *WCHA Reflections*, periodically
(Wayne County Historical Association is a
multifaceted umbrella organization
composed of: Old Dobbs County
Genealogical Society, Waynesborough
Commission, Wayne County Museum,
and Historical Association Revolving
Fund; central eastern North Carolina,
numerous publications about Wayne
County and the former Dobbs County;
owns and operates historic properties: the
1855 First Presbyterian Church, now
called Town Meeting Hall, and the 1927
Goldsboro Woman's Club building, now
the Wayne County Museum)
$10.00 per year membership in each
component or a total of $40.00 for
membership in all components

**Western North Carolina Historical
Association, Inc.**
Smioth-McDowell House Museum
283 Victoria Road
Asheville, NC 28801
(704) 253-9231; (828) 253-5518 FAX
smh@wnchistory.org
http://www.wnchistory.org
James C. McDonald, President
Pub. *WNCHA Newsletter*

The Wise County Historical Society
The Appalachian Quarterly
(see Virginia, Part 2)

**The Yadkin County Historical and
Genealogical Society, Inc.**
(The Tulbert House, 216 North Van Buren
Street—location)
PO Box 1250 (mailing address)
Yadkinville, NC 27055-1250
(336) 679-2982
Andrew L. Mackie, President
Thur 10:00–4:00, and by appointment
Pub. *The Yadkin County Historical and
Genealogical Society Journal*, quarterly
(Yadkin County, North Carolina, history,
genealogy, historic preservation of
properties, including abandoned
cemeteries)
$15.00 per year membership; queries
welcome

Yancey History Association
PO Box 1088
Burnsville, NC 28714

Genealogical Societies

State Genealogical Society

North Carolina Genealogical Society
PO Box 22
Greenville, NC 27835-0022
info@ncgenealogy.org
http://www.ncgenealogy.org
Crestena Oakley, Secretary
Pub. *North Carolina Genealogical Society
Journal*, quarterly; *NCGS News*, quarterly
$40.00 per year membership

Southern Society of Genealogists, Inc.
(see Alabama, Part 2)

Genealogical Societies—Local & Regional

Alamance County Genealogical Society
PO Box 3052
Burlington, NC 27215-3052
(336) 584-8381
alamancecogen@yahoo.com
http://www.rootsweb.com/~ncacgs
Corresponding Secretary

meetings at the Graham Civic Center, McGee
Street, Graham, NC: second Mon (except
June–Aug) 7:00
Pub. *Alamance Genealogist*, three times per
year (Jan, May, Sept)
(emphasis on Alamance County and early
Orange County)
$10.00 per year membership

Albemarle Genealogical Society
142 Waterlily Road
Coinjock, NC 27923
Lois Meekins, Corresponding Secretary
meetings at Currituck County Library: second
Tue (Jan, Apr, July, Oct) 7:30
Pub. *Albemarle Genealogical Society
Newsletter*, quarterly, $2.00 per issue
(primarily Currituck, Dare and Camden
counties)
$8.00 per year membership; queries free, but
members have priority as space permits

**Alexander County Ancestry Association,
Inc.**
PO Box 241
Hiddenite, NC 28636
(828) 635-0064
Evelina Miller, President
Tue & Thur 9:00–3:00
Pub. *Kinfolk and Connections of Alexander
County*, quarterly
$8.00 per year membership

**Alleghany Historical-Genealogical Society,
Inc.**
(see Historical Societies—Local and
Regional, above)

Anson County, NC Genealogical Society
300 Moores Lake Road
Wadesboro, NC 28170
staticchair28170@yahoo.com
Steve Bailey, President
Pub. *Anson County Genealogical Society
Newsletter*, four times per year
$15.00 per year membership

Beaufort County Genealogical Society
PO Box 1089
Washington, NC 27889-1089
(252) 946-4212
Louise M. Cowell, Treasurer; Ann Basnight,
President
meetings at Brown Library: first Tue
Pub. *Pamteco Tracings*, biannually, $6.00 per
issue or $12.00 per year for back issues
$10.00 per year membership

The Broad River Genealogical Society, Inc.
(1145 County Home Road—location)
PO Box 2261 (mailing address)
Shelby, NC 28151-2261
http://www.rootsweb.com/~ncbrgs/index. htm
archives: second & fourth Sat and second &
third Mon; meetings: second Sun (except
Nov) 3:00
Pub. *Eswau Huppeday (Line River in the
Cherokee Languages)*, quarterly
$20.00 per year membership

**Burke County Genealogical Society
(BCGS)**
(Burke County Public Library—location)
PO Box 661 (mailing address)
Morganton, NC 28655
http://www.rootsweb.com/~ncburke/
burkegs.htm
Gale Benfield, President
Pub. *Journal of Burke County Genealogical
Society*, quarterly
("The society supports and contributes to the
North Carolina Room at the Morganton

Branch of the Burke County Public Library.")
$15.00 per year membership; research: $2.00 plus copies at 25¢ per page mailed out

Cabarrus Genealogy Society
PO Box 2981
Concord, NC 28025-2981
Sheila Weaver, President
meetings at the Cabarrus Senior Center, 331 Corban Avenue, S.E., Concord, NC: second Tue 7:00 P.M.
Pub. *The Golden Nugget*, quarterly (Mar, June, Sept, Dec)
$15.00 per year membership

Caldwell County Genealogical Society
PO Box 2476
Lenoir, NC 28645-2476
(828) 758-1075; (828) 757-1272
Mon, Wed & Fri 8:30–5:30, Tue & Thur 8:30–8:00, Sat 8:30–1:00
Pub. *Caldwell County Genealogical Society Journal*, quarterly
$15.00 per year membership

Carolinas Genealogical Society
(Old Courthouse, on the Square—location)
PO Box 397 (mailing address)
Monroe, NC 28111
(704) 289-6737

http://www.rootsweb.com/~ncunion/Gene alogical_society.htm
Barbara Moore, President
Mon–Wed 10:00–3:00, Thur 1:00–4:00
Pub. *Bulletin of the Carolinas Genealogical Society*, quarterly; *Yearbook*, annually
(Piedmont section of North Carolina, upper-central South Carolina)
$18.00 per year membership

Catawba County Genealogical Society
PO Box 2406
Hickory, NC 28603-2406
Lucille Fulbright, President
meetings at Catawba County Library: fourth Tue (except Dec)
Pub. *Catawba Cousins*, quarterly
(Catawba County local and regional genealogy)
$10.00 per year membership

Coastal Genealogical Society
PO Box 1421
Swansboro, NC 28584
(252) 347-5287
JoAnn Stidger Becker, Secretary
Pub. *Coastal Genealogical Society*, quarterly
$10.00 per year membership

Craven County Genealogical Society
PO Box 1344
New Bern, NC 28562
(252) 633-5916
Robert D. Hennon, President
meetings: second Tue (except July–Aug)
Pub. *Trackers*, bimonthly
$15.00 per year membership

Cumberland County Genealogical Society
PO Box 53299
Fayetteville, NC 28305
(910) 484-5217
Mrs. W. D. Sherman, Corresponding Secretary
7:00 A.M.–9:00 A.M. & 6:00 P.M.–9:00 P.M.
Pub. *Newsletter*, eight times per year
(Cumberland, Bladen and Robeson counties)
$8.00 per year membership

Genealogical Society of Davidson County

PO Box 1665
Lexington, NC 27292
(336) 242-2040; (336) 248-4122 FAX
Jeanette Wilson, Librarian
Mon–Thur 9:00–9:00, Fri–Sat 9:00–5:30
Pub. *The Genealogical Journal*, quarterly; *Newsletter*, quarterly
$15.00 per year membership

Davie County Historical and Genealogical Society
(see Historical Societies—Local and Regional, above)

Durham-Orange Genealogical Society, Inc.
PO Box 4703
Chapel Hill, NC 27515-4703
Pub. *The Trading Path*, quarterly; *Newsletter*, eleven times per year (monthly, except June/July combined)
$15.00 per year membership; no charge for queries from members or nonmembers

Edgecombe County Genealogical Society
Edgecombe County Memorial Library
Janie F. Allsbrook Local History Collection
909 Main Street
Tarboro, NC 27886
(252) 827-4405 (President); (252) 823-1141 (Library); (252) 823-7699 FAX (Library)
tthompson@edgecombelibrary.org (Local History Librarian)

http://www.edgecombelibrary.org/history.htm
Betty Reason, President; Traci Thompson, Local History Librarian
Library: Mon–Thur 9:00–9:00, Fri 9:00–6:00, Sat 9:00–5:00; meetings at library: third Thur 7:00 (except July & Dec)
Pub. *Lines and Pathways of Edgecombe County*, monthly (except July & Dec)
$15.00 per year membership; research: $3.00 donation per inquiry plus copies

Family Finders Genealogical Society
410 Old Pollocksville Road
New Bern, NC 28562
(252) 633-4591
David Barteau, President
LDS Church: meetings second Tue 7:00 P.M.
Pub. *Family Finders*, bimonthly
$12.00 per year membership

Forsyth County Genealogical Society
(Forsyth County Public Library, 660 West Fifth Street, Winston-Salem, NC 27101—location)
PO Box 5715 (mailing address)
Winston-Salem, NC 27113-5715
(336) 724-0714
Cleo T. McBride, Treasurer
Pub. *Forsyth County Genealogical Society Journal*, quarterly; *Forsyth County Genealogical Society Newsletter*, monthly
(specializes in Forsyth, Stokes, Davie, Rowan and Surry counties)
$15.00 per year membership

Gaston-Lincoln Genealogical Society
1734 Rhyne-Carter Road
Gastonia, NC 28054
(704) 865-4737
jdglcg@carolina.rr.com
http://www.rootsweb.com/~ncglgs/Index.htm
Don Gladden, President

Granville County Genealogical Society, Inc.
PO Box 1746
Oxford, NC 27565

The Guilford County Genealogical Society
(First Friends Meeting, 2100 West Friendly Avenue—location)
PO Box 9693 (mailing address)
Greensboro, NC 27429-0693
maryab30@triad.rr.com
http://www.greensboro.com/gcgs
Thaxton Richardson, President
meetings: third Sat (Jan–May & Sept–Nov) 10:00 A.M.
Pub. *The Guilford Genealogist*, quarterly
$20.00 per year membership

Halifax County Genealogical Society
PO Box 447
Halifax, NC 27839
Pub. *Halifax County Genealogical Society Newsletter*

Hampstead Historical and Genealogical Society
(see Historical Societies—Local and Regional, above)

Harnett County (N.C.) Genealogical Society
(679 Leslie Campbell Avenue—location)
PO Box 219 (mailing address)
Buies Creek, NC 27506-0219
(910) 893-8786 FAX
ebrodin@intrstar.net
Professor Eric Brodin, Treasurer
Pub. *Heirs & Ancestors*, quarterly
$15.00 per year membership

Henderson County Genealogical and Historical Society, Inc.
(432 North Main Street—location)
PO Box 2616 (mailing address)
Hendersonville, NC 28793-2616
(828) 693-1531
hcgenhis@brinet.com
http://www.brinet.com/~hcgenhis
Evelyn Masden Jones
Mon–Fri 9:00–4:00, Sat 9:00–noon, and by appointment
Pub. *Henderson County North Carolina Genealogical and Historical Society Journal*, quarterly, $7.00 per issue
$20.00 per year membership

Huxford Genealogical Society, Inc.
(see Georgia, Part 2)

Hyde County Historical and Genealogical Society
(see Historical Societies—Local and Regional, above)

Genealogical Society of Iredell County
(Old Courthouse, Downtown, 200 South Center Street—location)
PO Box 946 (mailing address)
Statesville, NC 28677
(704) 878-5384
Nellie Gray Stimson, President
Tue & Fri 10:00–2:00
Pub. *Iredell County Tracks*, quarterly
(includes Homer Keever and Dr. P. F. Laugenour papers)
$10.00 per year membership; copies from files: 40¢ per page (plus $2.00 postage if over 50 pages)

Jackson County Genealogical Society, Inc.
(42 Asheville Highway, Suite 2, Sylva, NC 28779—location)
PO Box 2108 (mailing address)
Cullowhee, NC 28723
(828) 631-2646
jacksoncogen@aol.com
http://www.jcncgs.com

Mon–Thur 5:30–8:30, Sat 9:00–1:00
Pub. *Journeys Through Jackson*, bimonthly
$20.00 per year membership

Johnston County Genealogical Society
Public Library of Johnston County and
Smithfield
305 Market Street
Smithfield, NC 27577
(919) 934-8146
Dr. Luby F. Royall, President
Johnston County Room: Mon–Thur
9:00–9:00, Fri 9:00–5:30, Sat 9:00–5:00
Pub. *Johnston County Genealogical Society
Newsletter*, quarterly
$10.00 per year membership

**Lee County Genealogical and Historical
Society, Inc.**
PO Box 3216
Sanford, NC 27331-3216

Martin County Genealogical Society
PO Box 121
Williamston, NC 27892
(252) 792-5824
shepjr@coastalnet.com

McDowell Genealogical Society
Route 1, Box 796
Nebo, NC 28761
(828) 652-5377
Peggy Silvers

Moore County Genealogical Society, Inc.
PO Box 1183
Pinehurst, NC 28370-1183
Pub. *Moore County Genealogical Society
Newsletter*, quarterly
$12.00 per year membership

**Old Buncombe County Genealogical
Society, Inc.**
(#22 Innsbruck Mall, 85 Tunnel
Road—location)
PO Box 2122 (mailing address)
Asheville, NC 28802
(828) 253-1894
obcgs@buncombe.main.nc.us
http://www.obcgs.com
Zelma F. Smith, Office Manager
Mon 1:00–4:30 & 7:00–9:00, Tue–Fri
9:30–4:30, Sat 9:30–1:00
Pub. *A Lot of Bunkum*, quarterly
(Buncombe, Clay, Cherokee, Graham,
Haywood, Henderson, Jackson, Macon,
Madison, Transylvania, Swain and Yancey
counties, and the western areas of
McDowell, Rutherford and Polk counties)
$30.00 per year membership; research: $5.00
for members, $15.00 for nonmembers

Old Dobbs County Genealogical Society
PO Box 617
Goldsboro, NC 27533-0617
(919) 242-4772 (President)
Elizabeth Gordon Ellis, President
quarterly meetings at Western Sizzlin, Ash
and Berkely Boulevard, Goldsboro, NC:
fourth Sat (Jan, Apr, July, Oct)
Pub. *Old Dobbs Trail*, quarterly
(specializes in areas which were formerly Old
Dobbs County, now Wayne, Greene,
Lenoir and part of Wilson counties; vital
statistics, land records, Bible records, etc.;
limited research capability)
$10.00 per year membership; free queries for
members

Old New Hanover Genealogical Society
PO Box 2536
Wilmington, NC 28402-2536

(910) 452-9407
info@onhgs.org
http://www.onhgs.org
Sallie McClintock, Secretary
third Tue (Sept–May) in Room 105, Bear
Hall, University of North
Carolina—Wilmington
Pub. *Clarendon Courier*, quarterly
(areas of interest: New Hanover, Bladen,
Brunswick, Duplin, Onslow, Pender,
Columbus counties)
$15.00 per year membership

**The Genealogical Society of Old Tryon
County**
(2 West Main Street—location)
PO Box 938 (mailing address)
Forest City, NC 28043
(828) 248-4010
James O. Womack, President
Wed & Thur 9:30–2:00, Sat 1:30–4:30
Pub. *Bulletin of Old Tryon County, North
Carolina*, quarterly
$17.50 per year membership

Olde Mecklenburg Genealogical Society
PO Box 32453
Charlotte, NC 28232
OMGS1775@yahoo.com
http://www.rootsweb.com/~NCOMGS
Paul Buckly, Membership Secretary
Pub. *The Quarterly*; *Mecklenburg
Messenger*, monthly
$20.00 per year membership

Onslow County Genealogical Society
PO Box 1739
Jacksonville, NC 28541-1739
(910) 347-5287
JoAnn Stidger Becker, President
Onslow County Public Library: Sept–May:
first Tue
Pub. *Onslow County Genealogical Society
Newsletter*, quarterly
$10.00 per year membership

**Palm Beach County Genealogical Society,
Inc.**
(see Florida, Part 2)

Pitt County Family Researchers
PO Box 20339
Greenville, NC 27858-0339
(252) 355-6974
gregbullock-pcfr@cox.net
http://www.rootsweb.com/~ncpcfr
Greg Bullock, Secretary
Pub. *Pitt County Genealogical Quarterly*
(Feb, May, Aug, Nov), $30.00 per year
subscription

**Polk County North Carolina Genealogical
Society**
485 Hunting Country Road
Tryon, NC 28782
Frances N. Walker

Randolph County Genealogical Society
(Randolph County Historical Society, 201
Worth Street, Asheboro, NC
27203—location)
PO Box 4394 (mailing address)
Asheboro, NC 27204
(336) 318-6815
Ms. Jo Barrett, President
Mon–Fri 9:00–5:00, Sat staffed by
volunteers
Pub. *Randolph County Genealogical
Journal*, semiannually (Mar, Oct)
$10.00 per year membership (before 15 Feb,
$12.00 per year afterward)

**Genealogical Society of Rockingham and
Stokes Counties**
PO Box 152
Mayodan, NC 27027-0152
$15.00 per year membership

Genealogical Society of Rowan County
PO Box 4305
Salisbury, NC 28145-4305
jcwats@juno.com

http://www.lib.co.rowan.nc.us/HistoryRoo
m/html/gsrc.htm
June Clodfelter Watson, Editor
meetings at Rowan Public Library: third Tue
7:00
Pub. *Journal of the Genealogical Society of
Rowan County*, quarterly
(includes Old Rowan and present-day Rowan
County)
$15.00 per year membership

Scotland County Genealogical Society
PO Box 496
Laurel Hill, NC 28351

**Southeastern North Carolina Genealogical
Society**
Route 2, Box 291E
Whiteville, NC 28472

**Southwestern North Carolina Genealogical
Society**
Murphy Public Library
101 Blumenthal Street
Murphy, NC 28906
Pub. *Southwestern North Carolina
Genealogical Quarterly*, $3.00 per issue
(Cherokee, Clay and Graham counties)
$12.00 per year membership; no searching by
members available

Stanly County Genealogical Society
PO Box 31
Albemarle, NC 28002-0031
Lucille C. Curlee, Secretary
Pub. *The Stanly County Genealogical Society
Journal*, quarterly (Jan, Apr, July, Oct),
$2.00 per issue
(Stanly County and North Carolina
genealogical items)
$7.00 per year membership

Surry County Genealogical Association
(Surry Community College, Dobson, NC
27030—office location)
PO Box 997 (mailing address)
Dobson, NC 27017
(336) 786-7449
Judy Cardwell, President
anytime
Pub. *Surry County Genealogical Association
Quarterly* (Feb, May, Aug, Nov), $5.00
plus postage per issue
$15.00 per year membership; limited
research: free

**Swain County Genealogical and Historical
Society**
PO Box 267
Bryson City, NC 28713
E. Proctor
Pub. *Bone Rattler*, quarterly
$16.00 per year membership

**Tar River Connections Genealogical
Society**
PO Box 8764
Rocky Mount, NC 27804
Pub. *Connector*
(covers the eastern North Carolina area
known as the Tar River-Pamlico basin,

which includes those counties through which the Tar River and its major tributaries flow: Person, Granville, Vance, Franklin, Nash, Edgecombe, Pitt and Beaufort counties; database of surnames)
$10.00 per year membership; three free queries per year to members, queries $5.00 each to nonmembers

Toe Valley Genealogical Society
491 Beaver Creek Road
Spruce Pine, NC 28777

Tyrell County Genealogical and Historical Society
PO Box 686
Columbia, NC 27825
(252) 796-3791; (252) 797-4793
http://www.patriot.net/~cpbarnes/
   SOCIETY.HTM
meetings at the Senior Citizens Center, Bridge Street, Columbia: fourth Sun (Jan–Oct) 2:30
$20.00 per year membership

VA-NC-Piedmont Genealogical Society
(see Virginia, Part 2)

Wake County Genealogical Society
PO Box 17713
Raleigh, NC 27619
meetings fourth Tue
Pub. *Wake Treasures*, quarterly (spring, summer, fall, winter)
$20.00 per year membership

Washington County Genealogical Society
PO Box 567
Plymouth, NC 27962-0567
(252) 793-5236
ShirleyanBeacham Phelps, President
Pub. *WCGS News*, monthly
$15.00 per year membership; free queries for inclusion in newsletter; simple research requests and look-ups: free as time permits

Genealogical Society of Watauga County
PO Box 126 (DTS)
Boone, NC 28607

Wilkes Genealogical Society, Inc.
(Wilkes County Library, Genealogy Research Room, 10th Street—location)
PO Box 1629 (mailing address)
North Wilkesboro, NC 28659-1629
(336) 838-2818 (Library)
Wilma Jean Reynolds, President; Jason Duncan, Editor
Library: Mon–Thur 8:00–8:00, Fri 8:00–5:00, Sat 8:00–3:00
Pub. *Wilkes County Genealogical Society Bulletin*, quarterly
$15.00 per year membership

Wilson County Genealogical Society, Inc.
PO Box 802
Wilson, NC 27894-0802
(252) 243-1660
ancestor@wcgs.org
http://www.wcgs.org
Henry Powell, Treasurer
Wilson County Public Library: Mon–Thur 9:00–9:00, Fri–Sat 9:00–6:00
Pub. *Trees of Wilson: Wilson's Family Heritage*, ten times per year (monthly, except July & Dec)
("Publishes four volumes of Wilson County cemeteries and federal census of 1860 and 1870, sells copies of collected papers of the late Hugh B. Johnston [about 120 family files] under authority of his estate trustees. Publications catalog available by

request" and on web site.)
$20.00 per year membership

The Yadkin County Historical and Genealogical Society, Inc.
(see Historical Societies—Local and Regional, above)

Independent Publications and Miscellany

Anson County Heritage Book Committee
PO Box 417
Wadesboro, NC 28170
(published collection of family sketches)

Appalachian Roots
(see West Virginia, Part 2)

Argyll Colony Plus
6716 Meadow Haven
Fort Worth, TX 76132
Scott Buie, Editor
Pub. *Argyll Colony Plus* (Highland Scots of North Carolina), quarterly, $20.00 per year subscription

Byron Sistler and Associates, Inc.
(see Tennessee, Part 2)

Caldwell Heritage Museum
(112 Vaiden Street, behind the Davenport School—location)
901 College Avenue (mailing address)
Lenoir, NC 28645
(828) 758-4004
caldheritmus@aol.com
http://www.caldwellheritagemuseum.org/
   index.html
Bill Stronach, Director
Tue–Fri 10:00–4:30, Sat 10:00–3:00
$25.00 per year membership in Friends of the Museum

Cape Fear Museum of History and Science
814 Market Street
Wilmington, NC 28401
(910) 341-4350; (910) 341-4037 FAX
http://www.capefearmuseum.com
Mon (Memorial Day–Labor Day) 9:00–5:00, Tue–Sat 9:00–5:00, Sun 1:00–5:00
admission: $5.00 for adults

Center for Appalachian Studies
W. L. Eury Appalachian Collection
Carol Grotnes Berk Library, Second Floor
Appalachian State University
Boone, NC 28608
(828) 262-4072; (828) 262-2553 FAX
hayfj@appstate.edu
J. W. Williamson, Editor
Pub. *Appalachian Journal: A Regional Studies Review*, quarterly, $18.00 per year subscription
("We are a multi-disciplinary publication covering the entire Appalachian region": Alabama, Kentucky, Maine, Maryland, New Hampshire, New York, North Carolina, Pennsylvania, South Carolina, Tennessee, Vermont, Virginia, and West Virginia)

Central North Carolina Publications
PO Box 2681
Sanford, NC 27331-2681
James Vann Comer, Editor
Pub. *Central North Carolina Journal*, $7.50 per issue

Culbreth Associates
Route 2, Box 2987

Columbus, NC 28722
Pub. *For the Record: A Journal of Polk County History and Genealogy*, quarterly, $15.00 per year subscription

Friends of the Archives, Inc.
(109 East Jones Street, Raleigh, NC 27601-2807—location)
4614 Mail Service Center (mailing address)
Raleigh, NC 27699-4614
(919) 733-3952
http://www.ah.dcr.state.nc.us/affiliates/
   foa/foa.htm
$15.00 per year membership

Genealogical Institute
(see Virginia, Part 2)

Genealogical Research in Caldwell County, N.C.
(2724 Blowing Rock Boulevard—location)
PO Box 7 (mailing address)
Patterson, NC 28661-0007
(828) 758-8373
(publishes primary source records)
research: $5.00 per hour

Genealogy Books and Consultation
(see Texas, Part 2)

Headstones of Halifax
737 Franklin Street
Roanoke Rapids, NC 27870
(252) 519-0700
hfis@3rddoor.com
J. Rives Manning, Jr., Publisher
Pub. *Headstones of Halifax*, $17.00 ppd. per vol.

Historic Cabarrus, Inc.
(65 Union Street, South, Concord, NC 28025—location)
PO Box 966 (mailing address)
Concord, NC 28026
(704) 786-8515
Elizabeth Bennett, Executive Director
Mon–Fri 9:00–noon

Historic Flat Rock, Inc.
PO Box 295
Flat Rock, NC 28731
(828) 693-1638

Historic Hamilton Commission, Inc.
(Front Street, Hamilton, NC 27840—location)
508 Glenn Avenue (mailing address)
Rocky Mount, NC 27801
(252) 442-7941

Historic Jamestown Society, Inc.
PO Box 512
Jamestown, NC 27282
(336) 454-3819

Historic Robeson
PO Box 159
Lumberton, NC 28359

Historical Publications Section
Archives and History—State Library Building
(109 East Jones Street, Raleigh, NC 27601-2807—location)
4622 Mail Service Center (mailing address)
Raleigh, NC 27699-4622
(919) 733-7442; (919) 733-1439 FAX
annie.miller@ncmail.net
http://www.ah.dcr.state.nc.us/sections/hp/
   default.htm
Anne Miller, Editor (*North Carolina Historical Review*); Robert M. Topkins,

Editor (*Carolina Comments*); Jan-Michael Poff, Editor (The Colonia Records Project)
Pub. *North Carolina Historical Review*, quarterly (Jan, Apr, July, Oct), $25.00 per year subscription (including *Carolina Comments*); *Carolina Comments*, bimonthly; *The Colonial Records of North Carolina [Second Series]*, irregularly (individual volumes from $15.00–$75.00)

Hunting for Bears Genealogical and Historical Society
(see Alabama, Part 2)

The Mountain Empire Genealogical Quarterly
(see Virginia, Part 2)

Mountain Press
(see Tennessee, Part 2)

NCGenWeb
Part of The USGenweb Project
derickh@charter.net;
    PaulDBuckley@worldnet.att.net;
    carolinaroots@inmyattic.com
http://www.rootsweb.com/~ncgenweb
Derick Hartshorn, State Coordinator, Paul Buckley, Assistant Coordinator; Angie Rayfield, Assistant Coordinator
(links to other North Carolina resources)

North Carolina Department of Transportation
NC-DOT GIS Unit
1587 Mail Service Center
Raleigh, NC 27699-1587
(919) 250-4188; (919) 212-3103 FAX
jjeskiewicz@dot.state.nc.us
http://www.dot.state.nc.us/planning/
    statewide/gis/GIS_Mapping.html

North Carolina State Land Records Management Division
512 North Salisbury Street, Room 725
Raleigh, NC 27604
(919) 733-7006
http://www.secstate.state.nc.us/secstate/
    land.htm

Pioneer Publications
PO Box 1179
Tumtum, WA 99034-1179
(509) 276-1740
Shirley Penna-Oakes, Editor
Pub. *North/South Carolina Queries & Reviews*, $6.00 plus $1.75 postage per issue

Rockingham Society for Research and Preservation
PO Box 848
Rockingham, NC 28380-0848
(910) 997-6641

Rowan County Register
(403 Idlewood Drive—location)
PO Box 1948 (mailing address)
Salisbury, NC 28145-1948
(704) 633-3575
Jo White Linn, C.G., Editor
Pub. *Rowan County Register*, quarterly, $25.00 per year subscription
(twenty-six North Carolina counties and all of Tennessee formed from original Rowan County, North Carolina)

Sherrill Investigations
PO Box 5
Sherrills Ford, NC 28673-0005
(828) 478-2469; (828) 478-2469
Elizabeth Bray Sherrill, R.G.

Mon–Thur 9:00–3:00
Pub. *Stepping Back in Time* (eastern Catawba County—Mountain Creek, Catawba and Caldwell townships—Iredell and Lincoln counties), annually, $25.00 per year subscription
research: $25.00 per hour plus expenses

Simmons Historical Publications
(see Kentucky, Part 2)

Society of North Carolina Archivists
PO Box 20448
Raleigh, NC 27619-0448
sarah.koonts@ncmail.net
http://www.ncarchivists.org
Sarah Koonts, Secretary
(a professional organization of archivists representing 130 North Carolina public and private institutions and corporations; no research facilities, but publishes *Archival and Manuscript Repositories in North Carolina: A Directory*, $22.00 postpaid for nonmembers)

Somerset Place State Historic Site
(Route 1—location)
PO Box 215 (mailing address)
Creswell, NC 27928
(252) 797-4560
Leisa M. Brown, Site Manager
(genealogical services)

The Southern Genealogist's Exchange Society, Inc.
(see Florida, Part 2)

Southern Historical Press, Inc.
(see Publishers, Part 4)

Traveller Southern Families
(see Virginia, Part 2)

West Virginia University
Appalachian Studies Association
(see West Virginia, Part 2)

Families of Yancey County, North Carolina
PO Box 1035
North Highlands, CA 95660-1035
(916) 991-4165
ssnwms@hotmail.com
http://www.angelfire.com/wv2/sallysn-wms
Sally Seaman-Williams, Editor
Pub. *Families of Yancey County, North Carolina*, quarterly, $15.00 per year subscription
(publishes other books on Yancey County)

North Dakota

Archives and Libraries with Holdings in Genealogy

State Archives and Library

State Archives and Historical Research Library
(see State Historical Society, below)

North Dakota State Library
Liberty Memorial Building
Capital Grounds
604 East Boulevard Avenue, Depatment 250
Bismarck, ND 58505-0800
(701) 328-2492; (800) 472-2104; (701) 328-2040 FAX
tbodvig@state.nd.us
http://ndsl.lib.state.nd.us
Mon–Fri 8:00–5:00

State Historical Society

State Historical Society of North Dakota
State Archives and Historical Research Library
North Dakota Heritage Center
612 East Boulevard Avenue
Bismarck, ND 58505-0830
(701) 328-2668 (Division Office); (701) 328-2091 (Reference Desk); (701) 328-3710 FAX
gnewborg@state.nd.us
http://www.state.nd.us/hist
Gerald Newborg, Division Director; Dolores Vyzralek, Chief Librarian
Mon–Fri 8:00–5:00
Pub. *North Dakota History*, quarterly; *Plains Talk*, quarterly
(history of Dakota Territory, North Dakota, family history and genealogy; newspapers, census, naturalizations, index to deaths, marriages and divorces, index to naturalizations)
$30.00 per year membership; search fees: $5.00 per census, naturalization, obituary search, plus 25¢ per sheet for copies

City, County and Regional Archives and Libraries
(A more exhaustive list of public and academic libraries can be found at http://ndsl.lib.state.nd.us/Publications/Public Libraries.PDF or http://www.lib.ndsu.nodak.edu/govdocs/nddepdir.html.)

Bowdon Museum and Library
232 40th Avenue, N.E.
Bowdon, ND 58418
Rod Widicker

Buffalo Trails Museum
(Main Street—location)
PO Box 22 (mailing address)
Epping, ND 58843
(701) 859-4361
Mon (Labor-Day to Memorial Day) & Tue–Sat 10:00–4:00, Sun 1:00–5:00, and by appointment
(emphasis on regional history)
admission: $3.50 for adults

Carnegie Regional Library
49 West Seventh Street
Grafton, ND 58237-1409
(701) 352-2754; (701) 352-2757 FAX
crlmain@polarcomm.com
Garry Littlefield, Director
Mon–Thur 10:00–6:00, Fri–Sat 10:00–5:00
(regional collection, genealogical resources

limited)

Center for Great Plains Studies
(see Kansas, Part 2)

Center for Great Plains Study
(see Nebraska, Part 2)

Divide County Public Library
(204 First Street, N.E.—location)
PO Box 90 (mailing address)
Crosby, ND 58730
(701) 965-6305
divctylib@yahoo.com
Dorene E. Wenstad, Director
Mon–Fri 8:30–5:00
(books on local cemeteries, deaths and
indices of Divide County, also a few on
Williams and Burke counties, inventory
microfilms of most local newspapers,
dating back to the early 1900s)

Fargo Public Library
102 North Third Street
Fargo, ND 58102-4899
(701) 241-1491; (701) 241-1492
askreference@ci.fargo.nd.us
http://www.fargolibrary.org
Linda Clement-Sherman
Mon–Thur 9:00–9:00, Fri–Sat 9:00–6:00,
Sun (Sept–May) 1:00–5:00

Grand Forks Public Library
2110 Library Circle
Grand Forks, ND 58201-6324
(701) 772-8116; (701) 772-1379 FAX
gfplreference@hotmail.com
Mon–Thur 9:00–9:00, Fri–Sat 9:00–5:00,
Sun 1:00–5:00

Lake Region Heritage Center, Inc.
(502 Fourth Street—location)
PO Box 245 (mailing address)
Devils Lake, ND 58301
(701) 662-3701

Leach Public Library
417 Second Avenue, North
Wahpeton, ND 58075-4488
(701) 642-5732 voice & FAX
leachplib@702com.net
http://www.wahpeton.com/index.
    asp?Type=B_BASIC&SEC={859623EB-
    7500-4582-AC42-BD9530DB3647}
Bonnie R. MacIver, Director

Minot Public Library
516 Second Avenue, S.W.
Minot, ND 58701
(701) 852-1045; (701) 852-2595
jnarum@ndak.net
http://www.minotlibrary.org
Jeanne Narum, Reference Services
Mon–Thur 9:00–9:00, Fri 9:00–6:00, Sat
    10:00–4:00, Sun 1:00–5:00

Museum of the Great Plains
(see Oklahoma, Part 2)

North Dakota State University
North Dakota Institute for Regional Studies
North Dakota State University Libraries
(Corner of 12th Avenue and Albrecht
Boulevard—location)
PO Box 5599 (mailing address)
Fargo, ND 58105-5599
(701) 237-8914; (701) 231-7138 FAX
Michael.Miller@ndsu.nodak.edu
http://www.lib.ndsu.nodak.edu/ndirs
John E. Bye, Archivist
Mon–Fri (academic year) 8:00–5:00;
    Mon–Fri (summer) 7:30–5:00

("Collects printed and manuscript material
regarding North Dakota")

University of North Dakota
Elwyn B. Robinson Department of Special
Collections
Chester Fritz Library
PO Box 9000
Grand Forks, ND 58202-9000
(701) 777-4625 (Special Collections); (701)
    777-3319 FAX
sandy_slater@mail.und.nodak.edu
http://www.und.nodak.edu/dept/library/
    Collections/spk.html
Sandra J. Slater
Mon–Thur 8:00–5:00, Fri 8:00–4:30, Wed
    8:00–9:00, when classes are in session
Pub. *Guide to Norwegian Bygdeboker*,
    annually; *Guide to Family History
    Resources*, annually
(specializes in Norwegian ancestry, "955
    vols. bygdeboker" and North Dakota,
    South Dakota, Minnesota, and Ontario
    census records; North Dakota history:
    published and manuscript collections;
    research: $10.00 per hour plus 20¢ per page
    for photocopies

Historical Societies—Local and Regional

Almont Historical Society
PO Box 95
Almont, ND 58520
(701) 843-7032
Sig Peterson

**American Historical Association, Pacific
Coast Branch**
(see California, Part 2)

**American West Research Center and
Historical Society, Inc.**
(see Ohio, Part 2)

Barnes County Historical Society, Inc.
(315 North Central Avenue—location)
PO Box 661 (mailing address)
Valley City, ND 58072
(701) 845-0966; (701) 845-4282 FAX
bchistoricalsociety@hotmail.com
Wes Anderson, Museum Director
Mon–Sat 10:00–4:00, Sun by appointment
Pub. *Barnes County Quarterly*
(local organization histories, town and family
    histories)
$15.00 per year membership

**Billings County Historical Society
Museum**
PO Box 364
Medora, ND 58645
(701) 623-4829

**Bismarck-Mandan Historical and
Genealogical Society**
PO Box 485
Bismarck, ND 58502-0485
dearlsmith2019@msn.com;
    gzentz@bisman.com
http://www.rootsweb.com/~ndbmhgs
Don Smith, Treasurer; Gary Zentz, President
Pub. *The Dakota Homestead*, quarterly
$8.00 per year membership

Bottineau County Historical Society
1093 Highway 5 N.E.
Bottineau, ND 58318
(701) 228-2785
Twilla Glinz

Bowman County Historical Society

Pioneer Trails Regional Museum
(12 First Avenue N.E.—location)
PO Box 78 (mailing address)
Bowman, ND 58623
(701) 523-3600
ptrm@ptrm.org; gene@ptrm;
    history@ptrm.org
http://www.ptrm.org

Brenorsome Historical Society
PO Box 232
Tokio, ND 58379
(701) 294-3351
Louis Garcia, President
(Spirit Lake Dakota Nation, formerly Devils
    Lake Sioux Tribe; genealogy, history,
    customs, traditions; also local county
    history, etc.)

Buffalo Historical Society
(305 Fourth Street North—location)
PO Box 113 (mailing address)
Buffalo, ND 58011
(701) 633-5259
bankers@ictc.com
http://www.geocities.com/Athens/Forum/
    2253

**Burke County/White Earth Valley
Historical Society**
8334 Highway 50
Powers Lake, ND 58773
(701) 464-5771
Larry Tenjum, President
occasional, special dates
Pub. *Local*
$1.00 per year membership

Cass County Historical Society
(1351 West Main Avenue—location)
PO Box 719 (mailing address)
West Fargo, ND 58078
(701) 282-2822
info@bonanzaville.com
http://www.bonanzaville.com/main.php
Margo R. Lang, Administrative Manager
May: Mon–Fri 9:00-5:00; June–Sept:
    Mon–Sat 10:00-5:00, Sun noon–5:00; Oct:
    by appointment
Pub. *Bonanzaville Pioneer*, annually;
    Quarterly Newsletter
admission: 7:00

Casselton Historical Society
PO Box 86
Casselton, ND 58015
(701) 347-4163
Hank Weber

Cavalier County Historical Society
(Dresden, ND—museum location)
10123 95th Street, N.E.
Langdon, ND 58249
(701) 256-3342
Kathy Muhs
Library Day: first Sun (June–Sept) 2:00–5:00
Pub. *C.C. Museum Update*, semiannually
    (spring and fall)
donation accepted

Coteau Hills Historical Center, Inc.
PO Box 85
Forbes, ND 58439
(701) 357-8111
Iver Tveit

**Crosby Historical Society and Pioneer
Village**
West of City
Crosby, ND 58730
(701) 965-6705

Dakota Buttes Historical Society
HC 5, Box 615
Hettinger, ND 58639
(701) 567-2674
Maurice West

Dickey County Historical Society
207 Sixth Street North
Oakes, ND 58474
(701) 743-2843; (701) 783-4361 (Dickey
    County Historical Site)
mkunrath@drtel.net
http://www.rootsweb.com/~nddcnews
Sharalee Youngman

Divide County Historical Society
10350 110th Avenue N.W.
Noonan, ND 58765
(701) 965-6297
Perry Rosenquist

Dunn County Historical Society
153 Museum Trail
Dunn Center, ND 58626
(701) 548-8057
Maggie Piatz
hours: various
Pub. *Tales and Trails*, three times per year
$5.00 per year membership

**Eddy County Museum and Historical
Society**
325 First Avenue South
New Rockford, ND 58356-1707
(701) 947-2999
Naomi Allmoras

Edmore Historical Society
208 Adams Street
Edmore, ND 58330
(701) 644-2291
Paul Staffan

Ellendale Historical Society, Inc.
8836 92nd Street, S.E.
Ellendale, ND 58436
(701) 349-4329
Jeanette Robb-Ruenz

Emmons County Historical Society
612 North Broadway
Linton, ND 58552
(701) 254-4395
Kathryn Vetter
Pub. *ECHS Newsletter*

Enderlin Historical Society
PO Box 31
Enderlin, ND 58027

Fargo-Moorhead Heritage Society
PO Box 3161
Fargo, ND 58102
Deborah Frederickson, Treasurer

Flasher Historical Society
(Fifth Avenue, East—location)
PO Box 245 (mailing address)
Flasher, ND 58535
(701) 597-3721
Howard VandeVenter, President

Fort Pembina Historical Society
252 Montraille Street
Pembina, ND 58271
Mel Feldman
("Ours is a historical society with monthly
    meetings; no museum.")

Foster County Historical Society
7350 Ninth Street, N.E.
Carrington, ND 58421

(701) 674-3270
Henry Gussiaas, President

Geographical Center Historical Society
102 Highway 2 S.E.
Rugby, ND 58368-2444
(701) 776-6414
Pamela Schmitt, Curator
1 May–1 Oct: Mon–Sat 8:00–7:00, Sun
    1:00–7:00

Glen Ullin Historical Society
PO Box 681
Glen Ullin, ND 58631
(701) 348-3149
Alois Feser

Golden Valley County Historical Society
180 First Avenue, S.E.
Beach, ND 58621
(701) 872-3938

Grand Forks County Historical Society
Myra Museum, 2405 Belmont Road
Grand Forks, ND 58201-7505
(701) 775-2216
gfhistory@wiktel.com

Grant County Historical Society
6930 67th Avenue, S.W.
Elgin, ND 58533
Myron Theurer

Griggs County Historical Society
Route 2, Box 86
Cooperstown, ND 58425
(701) 797-2267
Orville Tranby, President

**Hatton-Eielson Museum and Historical
Association**
PO Box 278
Hatton, ND 58240-0278
(701) 543-3726
9:00–4:00

Hazelton Historical Society
PO Box 474
Hazelton, ND 58544

Hebron Historical and Art Society
PO Box 394
Hebron, ND 58638-0394
(701) 878-4326
Lambert Kastrow
holidays, and by appointment

Hettinger County Historical Society
Banot German Hungarian Museum
311 South Highway 22
Reeder, ND 58649-9435
(701) 853-2861
Theresa Bognor Montee-Nelson

Kidder County Historical Society
2535 39th Street, S.E.
Steele, ND 58482
(701) 475-2633
Audrey Quirt

**Lansford Threshers and Historical
Association, Inc.**
PO Box 26
Lansford, ND 58750
(701) 784-5897
Glen Carlson
Memorial Day–Labor Day: by appointment

**Larimore Community Museum and
Historical Society**
1865 39th Street, N.E.
Larimore, ND 58251

Gene Aanenson

Logan County Historical Society
708 Lake Avenue, West
Napoleon, ND 58561
(701) 754-2453

Manvel Historical Society
2890 Fiftheenth Street, N.E.
Manvel, ND 58256-9754
Annabel Montgomery

Marmarth Historical Society
PO Box 93
Marmarth, ND 58643
(701) 279-6996
Patti Perry
Pub. *Marmarth Historical Society*

McHenry County Historical Society
PO Box 179
Towner, ND 58788
(701) 537-5155
Nordis Wanberg

McIntosh County Historical Society
615 Center Avenue North
Ashley, ND 58413
Ron J. Meidinger, President

McKenzie County Heritage Association
PO Box 1260
Watford City, ND 58854-1260

**McKenzie County Museum and Historical
Society, Inc.**
PO Box 116
Grassy Butte, ND 58634-0116
Carla Fleck

**McLean County Historical Society
Museums**
(610 Main Avenue—location)
PO Box 124 (mailing address)
Garrison, ND 58540
(701) 462-3660; (701) 462-3744 (Curator)
vmerkel@westriv.com
http://www.wrtc.com/vmerkel/
    McLeanCountyMuseum
Vivian Merkel, Curator
Memorial Day—Labor Day: Tue–Sat
    2:00–5:00
admission: donation

Mercer County Historical Society
(Seventh Street and Central
    Avenue—location)
PO Box 1134 (mailing address)
Beulah, ND 58523-1134
Esther Scheidt, Secretary
summer: Sunday 1:00–4:00
Pub. *Bits and Pieces*, semiannually
$5.00 per year membership

Michigan Historical Society
PO Box 1883
Michigan, ND 58259
Patricia S. Danda

Minnewaukan Historical Society
PO Box 214
Minnewaukan, ND 58351
(701) 473-5488

Missouri Valley Historical Society
PO Box 941
Bismarck, ND 58502-0941
(701) 223-4838

MonDak Historical and Arts Society
(see Montana, Part 2)

Morton County Historical Society
4260 42nd Street
New Salem, ND 58563
(701) 843-7384
Condon Hartmann

Mountrail County Historical Society
PO Box 582
Stanley, ND 58784
(701) 628-2772
Gertrude Reep

Nelson County Historical Society
PO Box 428
Lakota, ND 58344
Terrence Devine

New Town Historical Society
PO Box 342
New Town, ND 58563-0342
(701) 627-3518
Mary Aubol

Niagara Community Historical Society
PO Box 26
Niagara, ND 58266
(701) 397-5201
Richard Hermann

Nome Historical Association
12128 59th Street, S.E.
Nome, ND 58062
(701) 924-8303
Richard Birklid

Northeastern North Dakota Heritage Association
Icelandic State Park
13571 Highway 5
Cavalier, ND 58220
(701) 265-4561

Oliver County Historical Society
1631 28th Street
Center, ND 58530
(701) 794-3342
Rodney Hickle

Ox Cart Trails Historical Society, Inc.
709 Dakota Court
Drayton, ND 58225
(701) 454-6103
secretary@oxcarttrails.com
http://www.oxcarttrails.com
Marlys Boll, Secretary
(history of northeastern North Dakota and
   northwestern Minnesota)
$10.00 per year membership

Pembina County Historical Society
PO Box 299
Cavalier, ND 58220
(701) 265-4614
hartje@sendit.nodak.edu
Earl Morrison

Pioneer Historical Society
1125 Tacoma Avenue, Apartment 213
Bismarck, ND 58504
(701) 223-3604
Roy Dockter

Pioneer Trails Historical Society
HC 1, Box 4
Grenora, ND 58845
(701) 694-3171
Sandra Rose

Ramsey County Historical Society
Gibbs Museum of Pioneer and Dakotah Life
(see Minnesota, Part 2)

Ransom County Historical Society
(101 Mill Road—location)
Box 5 (mailing address)
Fort Ransom, ND 58033-9740
(701) 973-4811; (701) 678-2045 voice &
   FAX
rbauer@northpro.net
http://members.tripod.com/rchsmuseum
Lyle Bjone, Caretaker
mid-May to end of Sept: daily 1:00–5:00
$10.00 per year membership

Renville County Historical Society
PO Box 213
Sherwood, ND 58782
(701) 459-2450
Oran Keith

Reynolds Historical Society
RR 1, Box 1G
Reynolds, ND 58275
Julie Monson

Richland County Historical Society
(Second Street and Seventh Avenue,
   Wahpeton, ND 58075—location)
PO Box 1292 (mailing address)
Wahpeton, ND 58075
(701) 642-3075
http://www.rootsweb.com/~ndrichla/
   hissoc.htm
Lois Berndt, Secretary-Treasurer
Tue, Thur & Sat–Sun 1:00–4:00, closed
   winters (30 Nov–30 Mar)
small charge for search, depending on time

Rolette County Historical Society
517 Second Street N.E.
Rolla, ND 58367-7226
(701) 477-6388
Gerald Fagerlund

Ryder Historical Society
20510 184th Street S.W.
Ryder, NH 58779
(701) 758-2527
Faye Karna

Sargent County Historical Society
9850 Highway 32
Havana, ND 58043
(701) 724-6388
Doris Gulsvig

Pioneer Historical Society for Sheridan County
1537 Garfield
Harvey, ND 58341
Monroe Raugust

Stark County Historical Society
PO Box 146
Dickinson, ND 58602
Viv Dinius

Steele County Historical Society
(Steele Avenue and Third Street—location)
PO Box 144 (mailing address)
Hope, ND 58046
(701) 945-2394
scmuseum@invisimax.com
Russell Ford-Dunker, Director
Tue–Fri 9:00–5:00, Sun (summer)
   2:00–5:00, and by appointment
("Archive Center-newspapers, family
   histories, records from 1883 on")
$5.00 per year membership; search fee:
   $10.00 per hour

Tioga Historical Society, Inc.
PO Box 671
Tioga, ND 58852

(701) 664-3602
John Thorburn

Towner County Historical Society
PO Box 189
Munich, ND 58352
Anita Barrett, President

Traill County Historical Society
(306 West Caledonia Avenue—location)
PO Box 173 (mailing address)
Hillsboro, ND 58045-0173
(701) 436-5959

Walsh County Historical Society
PO Box 263
Fessenden, ND 58438
Bobbie Weise, Secretary

Ward County Historical Society
Harmon House Archives and Research Center
PO Box 994
Minot, ND 58702
(701) 839-7330
wchs@minot.com; wchsvolunteers@srt.com
http://www.co.ward.nd.us/historical
by appointment only

Wells County Historical Society
(Wells County Fairgrounds—location)
PO Box 333 (mailing address)
Fessenden, ND 58438
(701) 547-3415
Lorraine Rau, President
May–Oct
Pub. *Wells County History*, monthly
$3.00 per year membership

Whitestone Historical Society
8692 98th Avenue, S.E.
Monanto, ND 58436
Dorene Brandenburger

Williams County Historical Society
519 11th Avenue West
Williston, ND 58801-4727
Jim Ryen

Genealogical Societies

Genealogical Societies—Local & Regional

Bismarck-Mandan Historical and Genealogical Society
(see Historical Societies—Local and Regional, above)

Bottineau Genealogical Society
614 West Pine Circle
Bottineau, ND 58318

Bowman County Genealogical Society
206 Ninth Avenue, N.W.
Bowman, ND 58623

Griggs County Genealogical Society
Giggs County Court House
PO Box 237
Cooperstown, ND 58425

James River Genealogical Society
651 Fourth Steet, North
Carrington, ND 58421

McLean County Genealogical Society
PO Box 157
Garrison, ND 58540
(701) 463-2091 (Treasurer); (701) 337-5559
   (Vice President)
dwhuettl@restel.net
Wanda G. Huettl, Treasurer; Betty Flath, Vice
   President

("We have cemetery records, obits, census for McLean County.")
$5.00 per year membership

Minnkota Genealogical Society
(see Minnesota, Part 2)

Mouse River Loop Genealogical Society
PO Box 1391
Minot, ND 58702-1391
agnes@srt.com
http://www.mrlgs-nd.org
Evelyn Zablotney, Board of Directors
meetings at Minot Public Library, South
Community Room: first Sat (except July)
1:00
Pub. *North Central North Dakota Genealogical Record*, quarterly
$15.00 per year membership

Red River Valley Genealogical Society Library
(112 North University Drive, Suite L-116—location)
PO Box 9284 (mailing address)
Fargo, ND 58106-9284
(701) 239-4129
RRVGS@Fargocity.com
http://www.fargocity.com\~rrvgs
Linda Zeutschel, Librarian
Library: Tue–Wed & Sat 11:00–3:00
Pub. *Red River Valley Genealogical Society Newsletter*, quarterly
$15.00 per year membership; admission:
$1.00 for nonmembers

South Western North Dakota Genealogical Society
HCR 01, Box 321
Regent, ND 58650

Genealogy Guild of Wilkin County, Minnesota, and Richland County, North Dakota
(see Wilkin County Historical Society
Genealogy Committee, Minnesota, Part 2)

Williams County Genealogical Society
(518 Broadway West—location)
PO Box 247 (mailing address)
Williston, ND 58801
(701) 572-3202 (evenings)
gjohnson@dia.net
Gloria Johnson, Chairman

Independent Publications and Miscellany

Alsen Museum
PO Box 124
Alsen, ND 58311
(701) 682-5301
Bernice Spenst

Buffalo Trails Museum
PO Box 22
Epping, ND 58843
(701) 859-4361
buffalotrails@epping.govoffice.com
http://www.epping.govoffice.com

Cape Hancock State Historic Site
101 West Main
Bismarck, ND 58501

Chateau de Mores State Historic Site
PO Box 106
Medora, ND 58645
(701) 623-4355; (701) 328-2666
drogness@state.nd.us
http://www.state.nd.us/hist/chateau/

chateau.htm
16 May–15 Sept: 8:30–6:30
admission: $6.00 for adults

Fort Totten State Historic Site
Pioneer Daughters Museum
PO Box 224
Fort Totten, ND 58335
(701) 766-4441; (800) 233-8048 (Devils
Lake Convention and Visitors Bureau)
jmattson@state.nd.us
http://www.state.nd.us/hist/TottenTotten
16 May–15 Sept: 8:00–5:00; 16 Sept–15
May: weekdays by appointment
admission: $4.00

Frontier Museum
Route 2, Box 9
Williston, ND 58801
(701) 572-5009

Lewis and Clark Trail Museum
Route 1, Box 73
Alexander, ND 58331
(701) 572-3535
Vince Rettig
Sun (Memorial Day–Labor Day) 1:00–5:00

Museum of Missouri River History
(see Nebraska, Part 2)

NDGenWeb
Part of The USGenweb Project
tstowell@chattanooga.net
http://www.rootsweb.com/~ndgenweb
Tim Stowell, State Coordinator; Joe
Zsedeny, Assistant Coordinator
(links to other North Dakota resources)

North Dakota Department of Transportation
608 East Boulevard Avenue
Bismarck, ND 58505-0700
(701) 328-2518 (Orders); (701) 328-4363
(Information)
dot@state.nd.us
http://www.state.nd.us/dot/gisinfo.html

Reynolds Community Museum
PO Box 14
Reynolds, ND 58275

Theodore Roosevelt Nature and History Association
PO Box 167
Medora, ND 58645
(701) 623-4466

Wimbledon Community Museum, Inc.
1306 Ninth Avenue, S.E.
Wimbledon, ND 58492
Les Koll, President

Ohio

Archives and Libraries with Holdings in Genealogy

State Archives and Library
Archives-Library Division
Ohio Historical Society
(Interstate Route 71 and 17th
Avenue—location)
1982 Velma Avenue (mailing address)
Columbus, OH 43211-2497
(614) 297-2510; 297-2340 (Local History
Office); (614) 297-2546 FAX
ohsref@ohiohistory.org
http://www.ohiohistory.org/resource/archlib
George Parkinson, Chief, Archives-Library
Division, and State Archivist; Gary J.
Arnold, Head of Reference Services;
Louise Jones, Head, Research Services
Tue–Sat 9:00–5:00
(member of the Ohio Network of American
History Research Centers, the designated
repository for local government records
and historical manuscript materials from
Delaware, Fairfield, Fayette, Franklin,
Knox, Licking, Madison, Marion,
Morrow, Pickaway and Union counties)
research: $20.00 per name in any one specific
type of indexed record or record group
during a time period that covers up to a
ten-year span (includes up to 4 pages of
copies); copies: $1.00 per prepaid request
(covers up to 4 pages), plus 25¢ for each
additional page, plus postage

State Library of Ohio
274 East First Avenue
Columbus, OH 43201
(614) 644-7061; (614) 644-6966 (Genealogy)
genhelp@sloma.state.oh.us
http://winslo.state.oh.us
Petta Khouw, Head, Genealogy Section
Mon–Thur 8:00–5:00, Fri 9:00–5:00
(includes Ohio, New England states, Virginia,
West Virginia and Kentucky)

State Historical Society

Ohio Association of Historical Societies and Museums (OAHSM)
1985 Velma Avenue
Columbus, OH 43211-2497
(614) 297-2340 (Ohio Historical Society
Local History Office)
jdbritton@ohiohistory.org
http://www.ohiohistory.org/resource/oahsm
J. D. Britton, Executive Secretary and
Manager of the OHS Local History Office
Pub. *The Local Historian*, bimonthly
$30.00 per year membership

Ohio Historical Society
Archives-Library Division
(Interstate Route 71 and 17th
Avenue—location)
1982 Velma Avenue (mailing address)
Columbus, OH 43211-2497
(614) 297-2300; (614) 297-2411 FAX
http://www.ohiohistory.org
Tue–Sat 9:00–5:00
Pub. *Echoes*, monthly, $5.00 per year
subscription; *Timeline*; *Ohio History*,
annually, $10.00 per year subscription;
research: $5.00 base fee for searching one
name in any one specific type of indexed
record or record group (covers up to four
pages of copies)

City, County and Regional Archives and Libraries

(A more exhaustive list of public and academic libraries can be found at http://winslo.state.oh.us/publib/libdir.html.)

Ada Public School District Library Historical Annex
320 North Main Street
Ada, OH 45810-1199
(419) 634-5246; (419) 634-9747 FAX
galvinro@oplin.org
http://www.ada.lib.oh.us
Patricia A. Kusner, Director
(collection of local historical books, newspapers, genealogical records, etc.)

Akron-Summit County Public Library
Special Collections Division
55 South Main Street
Akron, OH 44326-0001
(330) 643-9040; (330) 643-9084 FAX
http://www.ascpl.lib.oh.us
Judy James, Manager, Special Collections
Mon–Thur 9:00–9:00, Fri 9:00–6:00, Sat 9:00–5:00, Sun (school year) 1:00–5:00

Amos Memorial Public Library
230 East North Street
Sidney, OH 45365-2733
(937) 492-8354; (937) 492-9229 FAX
parsons@oplin.org
Scott Parsons, Director
Mon–Thur 10:00–9:00, Fri 10:00–6:00, Sat 10:00–5:00, Sun 1:00–5:00 (summer: closed Sun)

Ashland Public Library
224 Claremont Avenue
Ashland, OH 44805-3093
(419) 289-8188; (419) 281-8552 FAX
jordanpa@oplin.org
http://www.ashland.lib.oh.us
Pamela A. Jordan, Director
Mon–Thur 9:00–9:00, Fri–Sat 9:00–5:00; research help: first Tue 7:00–9:00, second Thur 1:00–3:00, third Sat 10:00–noon; meetings third Tue (Mar–Nov) 6:30–8:45

Aurora Memorial Branch Library
115 East Pioneer Trail
Aurora, OH 44202-7922
(330) 562-6502
http://www.portagecounty.lib.oh.us
Cheryl Chlysta, Librarian

Barberton Public Library
Local History Department
602 West Park Avenue
Barberton, OH 44203-2458
(330) 745-1194; (330) 745-8261 FAX
swartzel@oplin.org
http://www.barberton.lib.oh.us
Beth Swartz, Local History Librarian
winter (mid-Sept to early May): Mon–Thur 9:00–9:00, Fri–Sat 9:00–6:00, Sun 1:00–5:00; summer: Mon–Thur 9:00–9:00, Fri–Sat 9:00–6:00
Pub. *Keylines=Quarterly Newsletter for Barberton Public Library*
("Public library with archives and museum display of local interest. Berberton Public Library published two books on the history of Barberton. One is still available for purchase.")

Barnesville Hutton Memorial Library
308 East Main Street
Barnesville, OH 43713-1410
(740) 425-1651; (740) 425-3504 FAX
skaggsje@oplin.org
Jeff Scaggs, Director
summer: Mon–Wed 10:00–6:00, Thur–Sat 10:00–5:00, Fri 10:00–8:00; winter:

Mon–Thur 10:00–8:00, Fri 10:00–6:00, Sat 10:00–5:00
(Repository for holdings of Belmont County Chapter OGS)

Bellaire Public Library
Mellott Memorial Building
330 32nd Street
Bellaire, OH 43906
(740) 676-9421; (740) 676-7940 FAX
bellaire@oplin.org
http://www.bellaire.lib.oh.us
Mon–Fri 9:00–8:00, Sat 9:00–5:00, Sun 1:00–5:00

Bellbrook Historical Museum
42 North Main Street
Bellbrook, OH 45305
(937) 848-2415
Joanne Taylor Caffrey, Museum Trustee
Wed & Sun 1:00–3:00, Sat (Feb–Nov) 1:00–3:00
(a small local museum with some local records available for research: Bellbrook and Greene County)

Bellevue Public Library
224 East Main Street
Bellevue, OH 44811-1409
(419) 483-4769; (419) 483-0158 FAX
mcarver@bellevue.lib.oh.us
http://www.bellevue.lib.oh.us
Theodore R. Allison, Director
Mon–Thur 9:00–8:30, Fri–Sat 9:00–5:00

Belpre Public Library
2012 Washington Boulevard
Belpre, OH 45714
(740) 423-8381; (740) 423-8305 FAX
leslie@wcplib.lib.oh.us
http://www.wcplib.lib.oh.us
Leslie McKernan, Librarian
Mon–Wed & Fri–Sat 9:00–8:00

Bierce Library
The University of Akron
Archival Services
Buchtel Avenue
Akron, OH 44325-1702
(330) 972-7670; (330) 972-6383 FAX
jvmiller@uakron.edu
http://www.uakron.edu/archival/home.htm
John V. Miller, Jr., Director of Archival Services
Archives: Mon–Fri 8:00–5:00
(emphasis on northeastern Ohio; member of the Ohio Network of American History Research Centers, the designated repository for local government records and historical manuscript materials from Ashland, Coshocton, Holmes, Portage, Richland, Stark, Summit, Tuscarawas, and Wayne counties)

Birchard Public Library
(see Fort Stephenson Museum, below)

Bluffton-Richland Public Library
145 South Main Street
Bluffton, OH 45817-1265
(419) 358-5016; (419) 358-9653 FAX
schirmsh@oplin.org
http://library.norweld.lib.oh.us/Bluffton
Sheryl D. Schirmer, Director

Bowling Green State University
Center for Archival Collections
Fifth Floor, Jerome Library
Bowling Green, OH 43403-0175
(419) 372-2411; (419) 372-0155 FAX
scharte@bgnet.bgsu.edu
http://www.bgsu.edu/colleges/library/cac/

cac.html
Paul D. Yon, Director; Stephen Charter, Reference Archivist
Mon 8:30–8:00, Tue–Fri 8:30–4:30, Sun 4:00–8:00; summer: Mon–Thur 8:00–4:30, Fri 8:00–11:00
Pub. *Archival Chronicle*, three times per year, free subscription
(woman's history, labor history, Civil War, church history; member of the Ohio Network of American History Research Centers, the designated repository for local government records and historical manuscript materials from Allen, Crawford, Defiance, Erie, Fulton, Hancock, Hardin, Henry, Huron, Lucas, Ottawa, Paulding, Putnam, Sandusky, Seneca, Van Wert, Williams, Wood, and Wyandot counties)

Briggs Lawrence County Public Library
Local History and Genealogy Department
321 South Fourth Street (Second Floor)
Ironton, OH 45638
(740) 532-1124; (740) 867-3080; (740) 532-4948 FAX
genealogy@briggslibrary.com
http://www.briggslibrary.com/hamner/hamner.html
Martha J. Kounse, Local History and Genealogy Department's Manager
Thur 9:00–8:30, Fri–Sat 9:00–5:30; June–Aug: Sat 10:00–3:00 (call or email before traveling long distance)
("The staff doesn't accept genealogical requests by phone, letter or email. You can check our web site for a list of researchers and further information. The staff will continue to assist all persons who visit. We do not allow children under 18, and no food or drinks allowed. The Courthouse located in Ironton, Ohio [Probate Court] has microfilmed all births, deaths, marriages and wills. These documents are available at Briggs Library's Local History and Genealogy Department.")
copies: 10¢ each from paper originals, 25¢ each from microform originals (coin-operated machines, bring change or small currency)

Bryan Public Library
107 East High Street
Bryan, OH 43506-1702
(419) 636-6734; (419) 636-3970 FAX
yahrauje@oplin.org
http://www.williamsco.lib.oh.us
Jeff A. Yahraus, Circulation Supervisor
winter: Mon–Thur 10:00–8:30, Fri 10:00–8:00, Sat 10:00–5:00; summer: Mon–Fri 10:00–8:00, Sat 10:00–2:00

Burton Public Library
(14588 West Park—location)
PO Box 427 (mailing address)
Burton, OH 44021
(440) 834-4466; (440) 834-0128 FAX
http://burton.lib.oh.us
Pat Hauser, Adult Services Librarian
Mon–Thur 9:00–9:00, Fri–Sat 9:00–5:00, Sun (Sept–May) 1:00–5:00
(emphasis on Burton and Geauga County history)

Caldwell Public Library
(517 Spruce Street—location)
PO Box 230 (mailing address)
Caldwell, OH 43724-0230
(740) 732-4506; (740) 732-4795 FAX
http://www.caldwell.lib.oh.us
Marilyn S. Blaney, Director
Mon–Wed 9:00–8:00, Thur–Fri 9:00–5:00,

Sat 9:00–2:00
Pub. *Echoes*, bimonthly, free
(includes a room designated for genealogy
and local history with family search CD-
ROM)

Canal Fulton Public Library
154 Market Street, N.E.
Canal Fulton, OH 44614-1196
(330) 854-4148; (330) 854-9520 FAX
kindryje@canalfultonlibrary.org;
canful@oplin.org; canful@oplin.lib.oh.us
http://www.canal.lib.oh.us
Jean Kindry, Director
Mon–Sat 9:00–9:00
(emphasis on Ohio and Erie Canal local
history)

Carnegie Public Library
127 South North Street
Washington Court House, OH 43160-2283
(740) 335-2540; (740) 335-8409 FAX
http://www.cplwcho.org
Pam Waldrep, Adult Services
Mon–Thur 9:00–8:00, Fri–Sat 9:00–5:00;
summer (Memorial Day–Labor Day):
Mon–Wed 9:00–8:00, Thur–Fri 9:00–500,
Sat 9:00–noon

Carnegie Public Library
219 East Fourth Street
East Liverpool, OH 43920-3143
(330) 385-2048; (330) 385-2451 FAX
eastliv@oplin.org; refdept@oplin.org
http://www.carnegie.lib.oh.us
Reference Department
Mon–Thur 9:00–8:00, Fri–Sat 9:00–5:00,
Sun (Sept–May) 1:00–5:00

Champaign County Library
1060 Scioto Street
Urbana, OH 43078-2097
(937) 653-3811; (937) 653-5679 FAX
http://www.champaign.lib.oh.us
Linda M. Gieser, Circulation Supervisor
Mon–Thur 9:00–8:00, Fri–Sat 9:00–5:00,
Sun (during school year) 1:00–5:00
(mostly local and regional history)

Chardon Library
Anderson Allyn Room for Genealogical
Research
110 East Park Street
Chardon, OH 44024-1213
(440) 285-7601; (440) 285-3808 FAX
http://www.geauga.lib.oh.us
Sandy Malitz, Genealogy Specialist
Mon–Thur 9:00–9:00, Fri–Sat 9:00–5:00;
Sun (Labor Day–Memorial Day)
1:00–5:00
("Specialize in genealogy and local history
for Geauga County. Many Geauga County
indexes [birth and death (1867–1908),
marriage (1810–1919), census
(1900–1930), land ownership maps (1857,
1874, 1900), cemetery (through 2000)] are
available at http://www.usgenweb.com.
The records are available at the Chardon
Library.")

**Chillicothe and Ross County Public
Library**
(140-146 South Paint Street—location)
PO Box 185 (mailing address)
Chillicothe, OH 45601-3214
(740) 702-4145; (740) 702-4156 FAX
chillcot@oplin.org
http://www.chillicothe.lib.oh.us
Vicky Frey, Genealogy Researcher
Mon–Thur 9:00–9:00, Fri–Sat 9:00–5:30,
Sun (Labor Day–Memorial Day)
1:00–5:00

**Public Library of Cincinnati and Hamilton
County**
800 Vine Street
Cincinnati, OH 45202-2071
(513) 369-6905; (513) 369-6067 FAX
http://www.cincinnatilibrary.org
Patricia M. Van Skaik, Head, History and
Genealogy Department; Karen Beiser,
First Assistant
Mon–Fri 9:00–9:00, Sat 9:00–6:00, Sun
1:00–5:00
("One of the oldest and largest genealogy
collections west of the Allegheny
Mountains; nationwide collection of more
than 100,000 books, 50,000 reels of
microfilm and 250,000 microfiche,
including federal census records
1790–1930; ships passenger lists and
indexes; military pension application
indexes, Civil War regimental histories
and indexes to compiled service records,
local histories and land ownership maps
for most U.S. counties; city directories for
more than 1500 cities; subscriptions to
over 1500 genealogy periodicals, over
12,000 family histories with an online
index to surnames contained in each
book; and an extensive collection of
British, Irish, German and African-
American materials.")
free admission; fee for photocopies

Clark County Public Library
(201 South Fountain Avenue—location)
PO Box 1080 (mailing address)
Springfield, OH 45501-1080
(937) 328-6904; (937) 328-6908 FAX
http://www.ccpl.lib.oh.us
Mon–Fri 9:00–9:00, Sat 9:00–6:00, Sun
1:00–5:00

Clermont County Public Library
Doris Wood Branch
Genealogy Section
180 South Third Street
Batavia, OH 45103
(513) 732-2128
http://www.clermont.lib.oh.us
Mon–Thur 9:00–9:00, Fri–Sat 9:00–5:30
("CCPL houses the Clermont County
Genealogical Society's collection of
research materials. Many of the early, as
well as current, local newspapers are
available at CCPL on microfilm.")

The Cleveland Public Library
History and Geography Department
325 Superior Avenue
Cleveland, OH 44114-1271
(216) 623-2864 (History); (216) 623-2800
(Main library); (216) 902-4978 FAX
history@cpl.org
http://www.cpl.org
Mon–Sat 9:00–6:00, Sun 1:00–5:00

Columbus Metropolitan Library
Biography, History, Travel Division
96 South Grant Avenue
Columbus, OH 43215-4781
(614) 645-2710; (614) 645-2051 FAX
http://www.columbuslibrary.org
John Newman, Division Head
Mon–Thur 9:00–9:00, Fri–Sat 9:00–6:00,
Sun 1:00–5:00
(Houses Ohio materials such as county
histories and records of Ohio genealogy
and county historical societies and Ohio
census, but no family histories. "Access to
Internet resources.")
10¢ per photocopy

The Mary L. Cook Public Library

Mary K. Current Ohioana Room
381 Old Stage Road
Waynesville, OH 45068
(513) 897-4826; (513) 897-4856; (513) 897-
9215 FAX
swartzli@oplin.org
http://www.mlcook.lib.oh.us
Linda Crane Swartzel, Reference/Genealogy
Librarian
(a core collection of genealogy books for
states from which people living in this area
may have migrated, local Quaker records,
Ohio county histories, genealogical
information on local families, etc.; Warren
County)

Coshocton Public Library
Miriam C. Hunter Local History Room
Reference Department
655 Main Street
Coshocton, OH 43824-1697
(740) 622-0956; (740) 622-4331 FAX
coshpl@oplin.org
http://www.coshocton.lib.oh.us
Margaret Reveal, Genealogy/Local History
Mon–Thur 9:30–9:00, Fri 9:30–6:00, Sat
9:30–5:30, Sun (Jan–Mar) 1:00–5:00

Cuyahoga County Public Library
Fairview Park Regional Branch
21255 Lorain Road
Fairview Park, OH 44126
(440) 333-4700; (440) 333-0697 FAX
cwiggins@cuyahoga.lib.oh.us
http://www.cuyahogalibrary.org
Christy Wiggins, Regional Reference
Specialist, Genealogy
Mon–Thur 9:00–9:00, Fri–Sat 9:00–5:30,
Sun (Sept–May) 1:00–5:00
(regional library with genealogy specialty)

Cuyahoga County Public Library
Chagrin Falls Branch
100 East Orange Street
Chagrin Falls, OH 44022-2799
(440) 247-3556; (440) 247-0179 FAX
http://www.cuyahogalibrary.org

Cuyahoga County Public Library
Gates Mills Branch
(7580 Old Mill Road—location)
PO Box 249 (mailing address)
Gates Mills, OH 44040-0249
(440) 423-4808; (440) 423-1363 FAX
jmcpeak@cuyahoga.lib.oh.us
http://www.cuyahogalibrary.org
James McPeak, Librarian

**Dayton and Montgomery County Public
Library**
215 East Third Street
Dayton, OH 45402-2103
(937) 227-9500; (937) 227-9528 FAX
dayton@oplin.org
http://www.dayton.lib.oh.us
Carole Medlar, Genealogy Librarian
Mon–Fri 9:00–9:00, Sat 9:00–6:00, Sun
(fall–spring) 1:00–5:00
(Montgomery County and Miami Valley
records; strong southeast Pennsylvania and
New England collections)
research: $1.00 for out-of-state requests;
copies: 75¢ per page

Defiance Public Library
320 Fort Street
Defiance, OH 43512-2186
(419) 782-1456; (419) 782-6235 FAX
ohioandp@oplin.org
http://www.defiance.lib.oh.us/genealogy.asp
Beth Michel, Adult Services Supervisor
Mon–Thur 9:30–7:30, Fri 9:30–1:30, Sat

9:30–3:30, Sun (from Labor Day to
Memorial Day) 1:00–5:00
Pub. *Holding the Fort*, bimonthly, free
("Collection does not circulate.")

Deshler Edwin Wood Memorial Library
208 North East Avenue
Deshler, OH 43516
(419) 278-3616 voice & FAX
nageles@oplin.org
Esther Nagel, Director

Elmer's Genealogy Library
(see Florida, Part 2)

Euclid Public Library
631 East 222nd Street
Euclid, OH 44123-2091
(216) 261-5300; (216) 261-0628 FAX
dperdzock@euclidlibrary.org
http://euclidlibrary.org
Donna L. Perdzock, Director
Mon–Thur 9:00–9:00, Fri–Sat 9:00–5:00,
Sun (Sept–May) 1:00–5:00

Fairfield County District Library
219 North Broad Street
Lancaster, OH 43130-3098
(740) 653-2745
http://www.fairfield.lib.oh.us
Joyce Harvey, Coordinator of Adult Services
Mon–Thur 9:00–9:00, Fri–Sat 9:00–5:00,
Sun (Sept–May) 1:00–5:00

Findlay-Hancock County Public Library
206 Broadway
Findlay, OH 45840-3382
(419) 422-1712; (419) 422-1737; (419) 422-
0638 FAX
wooddi@oplin.org
http://www.findlay.lib.oh.us
Dianne Wood, Local and Family History
Librarian
Mon–Thur 9:30–8:30, Fri–Sat 9:30–5:00,
Sun 1:00–5:00
(a source of history and genealogy for Ohio
and the migration area into Ohio; Ohio
census 1820–1920, Hancock courthouse
records, newspaper collection from the
1850s, high school and college annuals for
the city and county, and city directories
from the 1890s)

Flesh Public Library
124 West Greene Street
Piqua, OH 45356-2399
(937) 773-6753; (937) 773-5981 FAX
odaja@oplin.org
James C. Oda, Archivist
Mon–Thur 9:00–8:30, Fri–Sat 9:00–5:30
Pub. *Historical Register*

Fort Stephenson Museum
Birchard Public Library
423 Croghan Street
Fremont, OH 43420
(419) 334-7101 (Museum)

Geneva Public Library
Platt R. Spencer (Memorial) Special
Collections and Archival Room
860 Sherman Street
Geneva, OH 44041-9101
(440) 466-4521, ext. 13; (440) 466-0162
FAX
genref@oplin.org
http://www.ashtabula.lib.oh.us
Louise Legeza, Archivist
Mon 10:30–noon & 12:30–8:00, Tue–Wed
10:30–8:00, Thur 10:30–5:00, Fri
11:00–4:00, Sat (except summer)
10:30–4:00

(specializes in Geneva, Ohio, area history
and Ashtabula County genealogy; Platt R.
Spencer family and business interests;
phonetic spelling movement books; old
and rare books: U.S. and foreign history,
Civil War, Mormon, medical, biography;
photos)
research: donation, but no extensive research
undertaken; copies: 20¢ each, minimum
$1.00

Grandview Heights Public Library
1685 West First Avenue
Columbus, OH 43212-3399
(614) 486-2951; (614) 481-7020 FAX
cpelz@ghpl.org
http://www.ghpl.org
Carol Pelz, Director
Mon–Fri 9:00–9:00, Sat 9:00–5:00; summer:
Mon–Fri 9:00–9:00, Sat 9:00–3:00

Granville Public Library
217 East Broadway
Granville, OH 43023-1398
(740) 587-0196; (740) 587-0197 FAX
http://www.granvillelibrary.org
Kay Bork, Head of Reference and
Information Services
Mon–Thur 9:00–9:00, Fri–Sat 9:00–6:00

Greene County Public Library
Greene County Room
(76 East Market Street—location)
PO Box 520 (mailing address)
Xenia, OH 45385
(937) 376-4952; (937) 372-4673 FAX
mkane@gcpl.lib.oh.us; gcr@gcpl.lib.oh.us
http://www.gcpl.lib.oh.us/services/
genealogy/genealogy.htm
Marianne Kane, Assistant
Mon–Thur 9:00–9:00, Fri–Sat 9:00–6:00,
Sun (during school year) 1:00–5:00
free admission

Greenville Public Library
Genealogy Department
520 Sycamore Street
Greenville, OH 45331-1438
(937) 548-3915; (937) 548-3837 FAX
gplibrary@wesnet.com
http://www.greenvillepublib.org
Jennifer J. Hart, Library Associate
Mon–Fri 9:00–7:30, Sat 9:00–4:30
fees: copy cost and postage

Guernsey County District Public Library
800 Steubenville Avenue
Cambridge, OH 43725-2385
(740) 432-5946; (740) 432-7142 FAX
http://www.gcdpl.lib.oh.us
Melissa L. Essex
Mon 11:30–8:00, Tue & Fri 9:00–5:30,
Wed–Thur 1:00–5:30, Sat 9:00–5:00
copies: 25¢ per page; research: "We
welcome brief and specific mail
inquiries."

Hamilton County Memorial Building
1225 Elm Street
Cincinnati, OH 45210
(513) 721-4506
(library includes local history and
architecture)

Hancock Historical Museum
422 West Sandusky Street
Findlay, OH 45840
(419) 423-4433
Doramae O'Kelley, Director/Curator
Wed–Fri & Sun 1:00–4:00
Pub. *Centerpieces*, quarterly
$15.00–$1,000.00 per year membership;

research: $15.00 per hour after the first
half-hour

Harris-Elmore Public Library
(328 Toledo Street—location)
PO Box 45 (mailing address)
Elmore, OH 43416
(419) 862-2482; (419) 862-2123 FAX
huizenge@oplin.org
http://library.norweld.lib.oh.us/Harris-Elmore
Georgiana Huizenga, Director
Mon–Thur 10:00–8:30, Fri–Sat 10:00–5:00
$18.00 per year membership

**Rutherford B. Hayes Presidential Center
Library**
Spiegel Grove
1337 Hayes Avenue
Fremont, OH 43420-2796
(419) 332-2081; (419) 332-4952
http://www.rbhayes.org
Rebecca Hill and Barbara Paff, Head
Librarians
Mon–Fri 9:00–5:00
(specializes in Ohio genealogy and local
history, Civil War, 19th-century history,
President R. B. Hayes and Hayes family)

Henderson Memorial Library Association
54 East Jefferson Street
Jefferson, OH 44047-1198
(440) 593-2515; (440) 576-3761; (440) 576-
8402 FAX
moyja@oplin.org
http://www.henderson.lib.oh.us
Janet Moy, Director

The Hudson Library and Historical Society
22 Aurora Street
Hudson, OH 44236-2947
(330) 653-6658; (330) 650-4693 FAX
elpolott@hudson.lib.oh.us
http://www.hudsonlibrary.org
James F. Caccamo, Archivist; E. Leslie
Polott, Director
Mon–Thur 9:00–9:00, Fri–Sat 9:00–5:00;
Archives: Mon–Sat 9:00–5:00
$7.50 per year membership

Huron County Historical Library
Administration Building (Basement)
180 Milan Avenue
Norwalk, OH 44857
(419) 668-4383
http://www.accnorwalk.com/~jkelble/
resources/library/hist.html

Jackson City Library
21 Broadway Street
Jackson, OH 45640-1695
(614) 286-2609; (740) 286-4111; (740) 286-
3438 FAX
cochrama@oplin.org
http://www.jacksoncity.lib.oh.us
Margaret Cochran, Director
Mon–Thur 9:00–8:00, Fri–Sat 9:00–5:00

**Mary Lou Johnson-Hardin County District
Library**
325 East Columbus Street
Kenton, OH 43326-1546
(419) 673-2278; (419) 674-4321 FAX
thaxtosa@oplin.org
http://library.norweld.lib.oh.us/kenton
Sandy Thaxton, Reference Librarian
Mon–Thur 9:00–8:00, Fri–Sat 9:00–5:00
("We hold Hardin County history books and
many other county histories. We also have
an obituary file, collection of marriage and
death records published by the Hardin
County Genealogical Society, cemetery
inscriptions for Kenton and Hardin County

townships," newspapers, census records, and Ohio soldiers' rosters.)
research: "genealogy lookups" but no in-depth staff-conducted research; copies: 20¢ per page

Johnson Memorial Library
116 West High Street
Hicksville, OH 43526
(419) 542-6200
durrema@oplin.org
http://www.defiance.lib.oh.us
Mary Lou Durre, Librarian
Mon & Wed 9:00–6:00, Tue & Thur 1:00–8:00, Fri 1:00–6:00, Sat 9:00–noon

Eleanor I. Jones Memorial Archives
1 Joy Lane
Camden, OH 45311
(937) 452-1238; (937) 452-3142
Linda J. Rhoden
second Tue 9:00–11:00, and by appointment (specializes in Camden, Ohio, history; Sherwood Anderson collection)

Junction City Branch Library
108 West Main Street
Junction City, OH 43748
(740) 987-7646; (740) 987-2238 FAX
pcdlpjc@oplin.org
Evelyn Angle Wolfe, District Manager
Mon & Wed 10:00–7:00, Fri 10:00–6:00, Sat 9:00–1:00

Kaubisch Memorial Public Library
Reference, Local History & Genealogy
205 Perry Street
Fostoria, OH 44830-2265
(419) 435-2813; (419) 435-5350 FAX
justicpe@oplin.org
http://fostoria.lib.oh.us/re.htm
Penny Justice
Mon–Thur 9:00–9:00, Fri–Sat 9:00–5:00

Kent Free Library
312 West Main Street
Kent, OH 44240-2493
(216) 673-4414; (330) 673-4893 FAX
http://www.kentfreelibrary.org
Carmen Z. Celigoj, Director
Mon–Fri 9:00–9:00, Sat 10:00–6:00, Sun (seasonally) 1:00–5:00

Kent State University Libraries
Department of Special Collections and Archives
1115 University Library, 12th Floor
Kent, OH 44242
(330) 672-2270
jsomers@lms.kent.edu
http://www.library.kent.edu/speccoll
Jeanne Somers, Acting Curator
Mon–Fri 1:00–5:00

Lakewood Public Library
15425 Detroit Avenue
Lakewood, OH 44107-3890
(216) 226-8275; (216) 521-4327 FAX
lpl@lkwdpl.org
http://www.lkwdpl.org
Kenneth Warren, Director
Mon–Fri 9:00–9:00, Sat 9:00–6:00, Sun 1:00–9:00

Lima Public Library
650 West Market Street
Lima, OH 45801
(419) 228-5113
http://www.limalibrary.com
Deborah Keenehan, Head of Reference Services
Mon–Thur 9:00–8:30, Fri–Sat 9:00–5:00, Sat

(Memorial Day–Labor Day) 9:00–noon
(emphasis on Allen County)
research: $7.50 per half-hour, limit $28.00

Logan County District Library
220 North Main
Bellefontaine, OH 43311-2288
(937) 599-4189; (937) 599-5503 FAX
kelleybi@oplin.org; lcdlref@oplin.org
http://www.loganco.lib.oh.us
Bianca E. V. Kelley, Genealogy/History
Mon–Thur 9:00–9:00, Fri 9:00–6:00, Sat (Sept–May) 9:00–6:00, Sat (June–Aug) 9:00–3:00, Sun (Jan–Apr) 1:00–4:00
(Logan County birth and death indexes 1909 to present)
copies: 20¢ per copy plus postage, obituary request $1.00

Lorain Public Library
351 Sixth Street
Lorain, OH 44052-1770
(440) 244-1192, ext. 253; (440) 244-1733 FAX
lor55@lorain.lib.oh.us
http://www.lorain.lib.oh.us
Joe Jeffries, Librarian
Mon–Thur 9:00–8:30, Fri–Sat 9:00–6:00, Sun (during school year) 1:00–5:00
Pub. *Adventures in Genealogy*, free online (microfilm of local newspaper from the late 1800s)

Loudonville Public Library
122 East Main Street
Loudonville, OH 44842-1267
(419) 994-5531; (419) 994-4321 FAX
burwelsu@oplin.org
http://www.loudonville.lib.oh.us
Thomas A. Szudy, Director
Mon–Fri 9:00–8:00, Wed & Sat 9:00–5:00, Sun (Oct–May) 1:00–4:00

Elizabeth M. MacDonell Memorial Library
620 West Market Street
Lima, OH 45801-4665
(419) 222-9426
http://www.worcnet.gen.oh.us/~acmuseum
Anna B. Selfridge, Curator, Archives and Manuscripts
Tue–Sat 1:00–5:00

Mansfield-Richland County Public Library
John Sherman Room
43 West Third Street
Mansfield, OH 44902-1295
(419) 521-3112 (Addlesperger); (419) 521-3115 (Furlong); (419) 525-4750 FAX
boyd_addlesperger@freenet.richland.oh.us; karen_furlong@freenet.richland.oh.us
http://www.mrcpl.lib.oh.us/shermrm
Boyd Addlesperger, Sherman Room Librarian; Karen Furlong, Sherman Room Assistant (Genealogy/Local History Collection)
Sherman Room: Mon–Thur 9:00–9:00, Fri–Sat 9:00–5:30, Sun (school year) 1:00–5:00

Marion Public Library
Ohio Room
445 East Church Street
Marion, OH 43302-4290
(740) 387-0992; (740) 382-3951
http://www.marion.lib.oh.us
Lynda Williams, Head, Reference
Mon–Fri 9:00–9:00, Sat 9:00–5:30, Sun (mid-Sept to mid-May) 1:00–5:00

Martins Ferry Public Library

(20 James Wright Place—location)
PO Box 130 (mailing address)
Martins Ferry, OH 43935-0130
(740) 633-0314; (740) 633-0935 FAX
myersyv@oplin.org
http://mfpl.org
Yvonne O. Myers, Director
Mon–Fri 9:00–8:00, Sat 10:00–5:00, Sun 1:00–5:00

Marysville Public Library
(231 South Plum Street, Marysville, OH 43040-1596—location)
PO Box 438 (mailing address)
Marysville, OH 43040-0438
(937) 642-1876; (937) 642-3457 FAX
sbanks@marysville.lib.oh.us
http://www.marysville.lib.oh.us
Mary Beth Merklin, President
Mon–Thur 10:00–8:00, Sat 10:00–5:00

McComb Public Library
Local History and Genealogy Department
(113 South Todd Street—location)
PO Box 637 (mailing address)
McComb, OH 45858
(419) 293-2425; (419) 293-2748 FAX
grosede@oplin.org
http://library.norweld.lib.oh.us/McComb
Debra Grose, Director
Fall–spring: Mon–Thur 9:30–8:00, Fri–Sat 9:30–5:00

McKinley Memorial Library
40 North Main Street
Niles, OH 44446-5082
(330) 652-1704; (330) 652-5788 FAX
mckinley@oplin.org
http://www.mckinley.lib.oh.us
Patrick E. Finan, Library Director
Mon–Thur 9:00–8:00, Fri–Sat 9:00–5:30, Sun (Sept–May) 1:00–5:00
(specializes in President William McKinley)
$10.00–$100.00 membership in Friends of the Library organization

McKinley Museum of History, Science and Industry
Ramsayer Research Library
800 McKinley Monument Drive, N.W.
Canton, OH 44708-4832
(330) 455-7043; (330) 455-1137 FAX
http://www.mckinleymuseum.org
W. J. Weber, Librarian
Library: Mon–Thur 9:30–1:00 & 2:00–4:30
Pub. *Museum Highlights* (specializes in McKinleyana), bimonthly
free admission to library

Medina County District Library
Medina Branch
Franklin Sylvester Genealogy Room
210 South Broadway
Medina, OH 44256
(330) 725-0588; (330) 725-2053 FAX
http://www.medina.info

Menno Simons Historical Library
(see Virginia, Part 2)

Mercer County Historical Museum
(130 East Market Street—location)
PO Box 512 (mailing address)
Celina, OH 45822-0512
(419) 586-6065
histalig@bright.net
Joyce L. Alig, Director
Wed–Fri 8:30–4:00
("We have printed a dozen local and Ohio history books.")
donation accepted

Middletown Public Library
125 South Broad Street
Middletown, OH 45044-4004
(513) 424-1251 (Information and Reference);
(513) 424-6585 FAX
http://www.middletownlibrary.org
Deirdre Root, Reference Librarian
Mon–Fri 9:00–9:00, Sat 9:00–5:00, Sun
(except in summer) 1:00–5:00

Milan-Berlin Township Public Library
(19 East Church Street—location)
PO Box 1550 (mailing address)
Milan, OH 44846
(419) 499-4117; (419) 499-4697 FAX
Linda Gattshall, Genealogy Coordinator
9:30–5:00; Sat 10:00–2:00

Milan Historical Museum
(10 Edison Drive—location)
PO Box 308 (mailing address)
Milan, OH 44846
(419) 499-2968; (419) 499-9004 FAX
Ellen E. Maurer, Administrator
Office: daily 9:00–5:00; Museum: Apr–Oct
Pub. *The New Milan Ledger*, two times per
year
(local Milan history, Western Reserve
history)

Minerva Public Library
677 Lynnwood Drive
Minerva, OH 44657-1200
(330) 868-4101; (330) 868-4267 FAX
martinbi@oplin.org
http://www.minerva.lib.oh.us
Bill Martino, Director

Monroe County District Library
96 Home Avenue
Woodsfield, OH 43793
(740) 472-1954; (740) 472-1110 FAX
Mon–Thur 10:00–8:00, Fri–Sat 10:00–5:00

Monroe County Library System
(see Michigan, Part 2)

Monroeville Public Library
(34 Monroe Street, Monroeville, OH 44847-
9722—location)
PO Box 276 (mailing address)
Monroeville, OH 44847-0276
(419) 465-2035; (419) 465-2812 FAX
santanja@oplin.org
http://www.accnorwalk.com/~jkelble/
resources/library/monpub.html
Janet Santana, Director

Morley Public Library
184 Phelps Street
Painesville, OH 44077-3926
(440) 352-3383; (440) 352-1069 FAX
mplgen@oplin.lib.oh.us
http://www.morleylibrary.org/genealogy.htm
Carl Engel, Local Historian; Sally Malone,
Genealogist
Mon–Thur 9:00–9:00, Fri 9:00–6:00, Sat
9:00–5:00, Sun (mid-Oct to Apr)
1:00–5:00; Genealogist available in the
Genealogy and Local History Room:
Mon–Wed 9:00–1:00, Thur 5:00–9:00,
alternate Fri & Sat 9:00–1:00 (please call
for specifics)
(emphasis on Lake County)

Mount Gilead Free Public Library
Genealogy Department
35 East High Street
Mount Gilead, OH 43338-1429
(419) 947-5866; (419) 947-9252 FAX
toddka@oplin.org (Kay Todd, Director)
http://mt-gilead.lib.oh.us

**Public Library of Mount Vernon and
Knox County**
201 North Mulberry Street
Mount Vernon, OH 43050-2413
(740) 392-2665; (740) 397-3866 FAX
jchidest@knox.net
http://www.knox.net/knox/library/
welcome.htm
John K. Chidester, Director
Mon–Fri 10:00–9:00, Sat 9:00–5:00

Muskingum County Library System
John McIntire Library
220 North Fifth Street
Zanesville, OH 43701
(740) 453-0391; (740) 455-6357 FAX
plymirso@oplin.org;
info@munskingumlibrary.org
http://www.muskingumlibrary.org/
libraryhome.htm
Jeffrey Eling (Local History/Genealogy),
Reference Librarian
Mon–Thur 9:00–8:00, Fri–Sat 9:00–5:30,
Sun (winter) 1:00–5:00

New London Public Library
67 South Main Street
New London, OH 44851-1194
(419) 929-3981; (419) 929-0007 FAX
nwlondon@oplin.org
http://www.newlondonohio.com/library.htm
Melissa Karnosh
Mon–Fri 9:00–5:00, Tue & Thur 7:00–8:30,
Sat 10:00–5:00

Norwalk Public Library
46 West Main Street
Norwalk, OH 44857-1449
(419) 668-6063; (419) 663-2190 FAX
norwalk@oplin.org

http://www.accnorwalk.com/~jkelble/reso
urces/library/norpub.html
Laureen Drapp, Director
Mon–Thur 10:00–8:30; Fri–Sat 10:00–5:00

Oberlin College Archives
(address withheld upon request)
("Due to budget cuts and staffing reductions,
we cannot handle any additional external
use.")

Ohio Genealogy Center
104 East Stafford Avenue
Worthington, OH 43085
(614) 436-8674

Ohio University
Vernon R. Alden Library
Archives and Special Collections
Park Place
Athens, OH 45701-2978
(740) 593-2710; (740) 593-0138 FAX
library@www.cats.ohiou.edu
http://www.library.ohiou.edu/libinfo/
depts/microforms/geneal.htm
(Genealogical Resources); http://www.
library.ohio.edu/libinfo/depts/archives/
index.htm (Special Collections)
George W. Bain, Head, Archives and Special
Collections
Archives: Mon–Fri 8:00–5:00, Sat
noon–4:00; Microforms Department open
evenings, weekends when university is in
session
(member of the Ohio Network of American
History Research Centers, the designated
repository for local government records and
historical manuscript materials from Athens,
Belmont, Gallia, Guernsey, Hocking,
Jackson, Lawrence, Meigs, Monroe, Morgan,
Muskingum, Noble, Perry, Pike, Ross,

Scioto, Vinton, and Washington counties)
research: $20.00 per hour (prorated to quarter
hours) plus 10¢ per page for copies

**Old Saint Mary's Historic Community
Center**
123 East 13th Street
Cincinnati, OH 45210
(513) 721-2298

Paulding County Carnegie Library
Genealogy Department
205 South Main Street
Paulding, OH 45879-1492
(419) 399-2032; (419) 399-2114 FAX
coydi@oplin.lib.oh.us
http://pauldingcountylibrary.org
Diana Coy, Assistant Director and Head of
Reference
Mon–Thur 9:00–8:00, Fri 9:00–5:30, Sat
(Sept–May) 9:00–3:00, Sat (June–Aug)
9:00–noon

Pemberville Public Library
(375 East Front Street—location)
PO Box 809 (mailing address)
Pemberville, OH 43450-9701
(419) 287-4012; (419) 287-4620 FAX
kingla@oplin.lib.oh.us
http://www.pembervillelibrary.org
Laura Zepernick King, Assistant Director,
Local and Family Historian
Mon & Tue 9:00–8:00, Wed 9:00–5:00, Thur
noon–8:00, Fri noon–5:00, Sat 10:00–1:00
(emphasis on Wood County and Freedom
Township, German research)
10¢ per page for photocopies

Peninsula Library and Historical Society
(6105 Riverview Road—location)
PO Box 236 (mailing address)
Peninsula, OH 44264-0236
(330) 657-BOOK
http://www.peninsulalibrary.org
Randolph S. Bergdorf, Archivist
Mon–Thur 9:00–8:00, Fri–Sat 9:00–5:00
Pub. *PLHS Newsletter*, bimonthly
(Peninsula, Boston Township, and Boston
Heights)
$2.00 per year membership in Friends of the
Library

Pike Heritage Foundation
110 South Market Street
Waverly, OH 45690
(740) 947-5281
Katherine Logan, Director
Sat–Sun 1:00–4:00

Portsmouth Public Library
Local History Department
1220 Gallia Street
Portsmouth, OH 45662-4185
(740) 354-5304; (740) 353-1249 FAX
localhistory@mail.portsmouth.lib.oh.us
http://www.portsmouth.lib.oh.us
Carolyn Cottrell, Local History Supervisor
Mon–Thur 9:00–8:00, Fri 9:00–6:00, Sat
9:00–5:30, Sun 1:00–5:00
("Collection includes Scioto County and
surrounding Southern Ohio and Northern
Kentucky information." County histories,
early marriages, census records,
newspapers, early court records, and
cemtery records, also surname and local
history files.)
copies: 10¢ per page from paper originals,
25¢ per page from microform originals;
research fee required outside of the county

Preble County District Library
Preble County Room

450 South Barron Street
Eaton, OH 45320-1705
(937) 456-4970; (937) 456-6092 FAX
pcroom@oplin.org
http://www.pcdl.lib.oh.us
Nancy J. Crowell, Librarian
Mon–Thur 9:00–8:00, Fri–Sat 9:00–5:00
research: $10.00 per hour pluse postage and
copies

Princeton Museum of Education
515 Greenwood Avenue
Cincinnati, OH 45246
(513) 771-3824
Peggy Shardelow, Director
by appointment
(archives of records and historical documents
pertaining to the Princeton City School
District, located thirteen miles north of
Cincinnati)

Puskarich Public Library
200 East Market Street
Cadiz, OH 43907-1185
(740) 942-2623; (740) 942-8047 FAX
http://www.harison.lib.oh.us
Linda Morgan, Genealogy Assistant
Mon–Thur 9:00–8:00, Fri 9:00–6:00, Sat
9:00–5:00
("County histories, census indexes and
microfilm, Harrison County newspapers
and legal records on microfilm, and
cemetery records")
copies: 15¢ per page from paper, 25¢ per
page from microfilm

Putnam County District Library
525 North Thomas Street
Ottawa, OH 45875-0308
(419) 523-3747; (419) 523-6477 FAX
http://www.putnam.co.lib.oh.us
Ruth Wilhelm, Local History Manager
Mon–Thur 9:00–8:00, Fri–Sat 9:00–5:00, Sat
(Memorial Day weekend–Labor Day
weekend) 9:00–1:00
(Putnam County and surrounding counties of
Northwest Ohio)
research: first ½ hour free, include SASE
with request; copies: 10¢ each, plus
postage

Reed Memorial Library
Reference Department
167 East Main Street
Ravenna, OH 44266-3197
(330) 296-2827
refreed@oplin.org
http://www.reed.lib.oh.us
Marjorie Smith, Reference Librarian
Mon–Fri 10:00–9:00, Sat 10:00 6:00
Pub. *Reed*, quarterly
(emphasis on Portage County history)

Robbins Hunter Museum
(221 East Broadway—location)
PO Box 183 (mailing address)
Granville, OH 43023
(740) 587-0430

Rodman Public Library
Reference Department
215 East Broadway Street
Alliance, OH 44601
(330) 821-2665; (330) 821-5053 FAX
departre@oplin.lib.oh.us
http://www.rodmanlibrary.com
Mon–Thur 9:00–9:00, Fri–Sat 9:00–5:30

Ida Rupp Public Library
Local History and Genealogy Department
310 Madison Street
Port Clinton, OH 43452-1921

(419) 732-3212; (419) 734-9867 FAX
idarupp@oplin.org
http://library.norweld.lib.oh.us/idarupp
Mon–Thur 9:30–8:30, Fri–Sat 9:30–5:30,
Sat (summer) 9:30–1:30, Sun (Jan–Mar)
1:00–4:00
copies: 15¢ or 25¢ per page from paper
originals, 25¢ per page from microform
originals

Saint Clairsville Public Library
(Across the street from the Belmont County
Courthouse on Main Street, U.S. Route
40—location)
108 West Main Street (mailing address)
Saint Clairsville, OH 43950-1225
(740) 695-2062; (740) 695-6420 FAX
perkinsh@oplin.org;
perkinsh@oplin.lib.oh.us
http://www.scpl.lib.oh.us
Mon–Wed & Fri 9:30–8:00, Thur 9:30–5:00,
Sat 9:00–5:00
(houses collection of Cumberland Trail
Genealogical Society)

Saint Paris Public Library
(127 East Main—location)
PO Box 740 (mailing address)
Saint Paris, OH 43072-0740
(937) 663-4349; (937) 663-0297 FAX
stparis@oplin.org
http://opac.st-paris.lib.oh.us
Nancy McAlpin, Director
Mon–Thur 10:00–8:00, Fri–Sat 9:00–5:00

Salem Public Library
Reference Department
821 East State Street
Salem, OH 44460-2298
(330) 332-0042; (330) 332-4488
library@salemohio.com
http://www.salemohio.com/library
Ann Grimes, Reference Librarian
Mon–Thur 10:00–9:00, Fri–Sat 10:00–6:00

Sandusky Library
114 West Adams Street
Sandusky, OH 44870
(419) 625-3834; (419) 625-4574 FAX
http://www.sandusky.lib.oh.us
Molly Carver, Assistant Director,
Community Relations
Labor Day–Memorial Day: Mon–Thur
9:00–8:30, Fri 9:00–6:00, Sat 9:00–5:00,
Sun (Oct–Apr) noon–5:00; Memorial
Day–Labor Day: Mon–Wed 9:00–8:30,
Thur–Sat 9:00–5:00
(Erie County history)

Sandusky Library Association
1154 West Adams Street
Sandusky, OH 44870
Julie Steinbrenner
Pub. *Follett House News*, quarterly

Sherwood Branch Library
117 Harrison
Sherwood, OH 43556
(419) 899-4343
hullca@oplin.org
http://www.defiance.lib.oh.us
Carol Hull, Librarian
Mon & Wed noon–8:00, Tue & Thur
9:00–6:00, Fri–Sat 9:00–noon

Kate Love Simpson Library
358 East Main Street
McConnelsville, OH 43756-1130
(740) 962-2533; (740) 962-3316 FAX
wagnerme@oplin.org;
wagnerme@oplin.lib.oh.us
http://www.morgan.lib.oh.us

Verna Trayer, Corresponding Secretary,
Morgan County Chapter OGS
Mon–Thur 10:00–8:00, Fri–Sat 10:00–5:00

**South Central Ohio Preservation Society,
Inc.**
178 Church Street
Chillicothe, OH 45601
(740) 774-3510
Mrs. Joseph VanMeter, Coordinator
(archives/manuscripts collection for southern
Ohio)

Stark County District Library
Genealogy Collection, Humanities
Department
715 Market Avenue, North
Canton, OH 44702-1080
(330) 452-0665, ext. 252; (330) 452-0403
FAX
scdl@starklibrary.org
http://www.starklibrary.org
Lauren K. Landis, Genealogist
Library: Mon–Thur 9:00–9:00, Fri–Sat
9:00–5:00
(collection includes vital records, probate
records, guardianships, naturalizations,
land records, common pleas court journals,
land tax records, military records, census,
county histories, atlases, cemetery records,
newspapers, city directories)

**Public Library of Steubenville and
Jefferson County**
Schiappa Branch Library
4141 Mall Drive
Steubenville, OH 43952
(740) 264-6166; (740) 264-7397 FAX
daysa@oplin.org
http://www.steubenville.lib.oh.us
Sandy Day, Local Historian/Genealogist
Mon–Fri 9:00–9:00, Sat 9:00–5:00, Sun
1:00–5:00
(Ohio local history and genealogy for Ohio
and a few other states; local newspaper on
microfilm from 1806)

Swanton Public Library
305 Chestnut Street
Swanton, OH 43558
(419) 826-2760; (419) 826-1020 FAX
hazelbsg@oplin.org
http://library.norweld.lib.oh.us/Swanton
S. Gayle Hazelbaker, Director

Taylor Memorial Public Library
2015 Third Street
Cuyahoga Falls, OH 44221-3205
(330) 928-2117; (330) 928-2535 FAX
http://www.taylor.lib.oh.us
Kathleen Fenning, Head, Reference
Department; Virginia Bloetscher
Mon–Thur 10:00–9:00, Fri 10:00–6:00, Sat
10:00–5:00, Sun (Oct–May) 1:00–5:00

Tiffin-Seneca Public Library
77 Jefferson Street
Tiffin, OH 44883
(419) 447-3751; (419) 447-3045 FAX
hillmepa@oplin.org (Patricia Hillmer,
Director)
http://tiffinsen.lib.oh.us
Margaret Baker, Reference Assistant
Mon–Thur 10:00–9:00, Fri–Sat 10:00–5:30,
Sun (during the school year) 2:00–5:00

Toledo-Lucas County Public Library
Local History and Genealogy Department
325 North Michigan Street
Toledo, OH 43624-1614
(419) 259-5233; (419) 255-1334 FAX
http://www.toledolibrary.org

James C. Marshall, Manager
Mon–Thur 9:00–9:00, Fri–Sat 9:00–5:30,
Sun (Sept–May) 1:00–5:30
(Collections include local history of Toledo
and Lucas County, Ohio, and genealogical
materials covering all of Ohio, plus the
adjacent states and the original thirteen
states.)

Trenton Library
21 East State Street
Trenton, OH 45067
(513) 988-9050
jgirton@mail.mpl.lib.oh.us
http://www.middletownlibrary.org
Judi Girton, Librarian
Mon–Thur 1:00–8:00, Sat 9:00–4:00

Troy-Miami County Public Library
Historical Collection
Hayner Cultural Center
301 West Main Street
Troy, OH 45373
(937) 339-0457
Juda Moyer, Librarian
Tue–Sat 10:00–4:00, Tue–Wed 7:00
    P.M.–9:00 P.M., Sun 1:30–4:30

Troy-Miami County Public Library
(see Troy Historical Society, Historical
Societies—Local and Regional, below)

Union Township Library
7900 Cox Road
West Chester, OH 45069
(513) 777-3131
smayhugh@mail.mpl.lib.oh.us
http://www.middletownlibrary.org
Steve Mayhugh, Librarian
Mon–Fri 10:00–8:30, Sat 10:00–5:00

University of Akron
(see Bierce Library, above)

University of Cincinnati
University Libraries
Archives and Rare Books Department
PO Box 210113
Cincinnati, OH 45221-0113
(513) 556-1959; (513) 556-1955 (German-
    Americana Collection); (513) 556-2113
    FAX
don.tolzmann@uc.edu
http://www.libraries.uc.edu/libinfo/arb.html
Dr. Don Heinrich Tolzmann, Curator,
    German-Americana Collection
Mon–Fri 8:00–5:00 (advance correspondence
    recommended for access to holdings,
    closed University holidays); German-
    Americana Collection: Mon, Wed & Fri
    8:00–noon
(member of the Ohio Network of American
    History Research Centers, the designated
    repository for local government records
    and historical manuscript materials from
    Adams, Brown, Butler, Clermont, Clinton,
    Hamilton, Highland, and Warren counties)
copies by mail: $5.00 minimum

University of Toledo
Ward M. Canaday Center
2801 West Bancroft Street
Toledo, OH 43606
(419) 537-2443
Richard Oram, Director

Upper Sandusky Community Library
Heritage Room
301 North Sandusky Avenue
Upper Sandusky, OH 43351-1139
(419) 294-1345; (419) 294-4499 FAX
hullka@oplin.org

http://www.upper-sandusky.lib.oh.us
Katherine Hull, Director
Mon–Fri 9:00–9:00, Sat 9:00–1:00
(holdings include Wyandot County
    information, census and indexed booklets,
    family histories, county histories,
    newspapers on microfilm, etc.)

Warren-Trumbull County Public Library
Local History and Genealogy Center
444 Mahoning Avenue, N.W.
Warren, OH 44483-4692
(330) 399-8807, ext. 120; (330) 399-3988
    FAX
http://www.wtcpl.lib.oh.us/LH&G.htm
Carol Willsey Bell, Genealogist
Local History and Genealogy Center: Mon &
    Thur–Fri 9:00–5:00, Tue–Wed 9:00–8:45
    (7:45 in summer), Sat 9:00–noon &
    12:30–5:00
(emphasis on Trumbull County and Warren,
    not Warren County; Pennsylvania church
    records; special collections: Ohio census
    1820–1930, Ohio death certificates
    1908–1944)
research: copy costs only

Washington County (Ohio) Public Library
Local History and Genealogy Department
418 Washington Street
Marietta, OH 45750-1922
(740) 376-2172; (740) 376-2175 FAX
ernie@wcplib.lib.oh.us
http://www.wcplib.lib.oh.us
Ernest Thode, Manager, Local History and
    Genealogy
Mon–Thur 9:00–8:30, Fri–Sat 9:00–5:00

Way Public Library
101 East Indiana Avenue
Perrysburg, OH 43551-2295
(419) 874-3135 voice; (419) 874-6129 FAX
calderte@oplin.lib.oh.us
http://www.way.lib.oh.us
Teresa Calderone, Local History Librarian
Mon–Thur 9:00–8:30, Fri–Sat 9:00–5:30,
    Sun (seasonal) 1:00–5:00
(specializes in Perrysburg and northwest
    Ohio)

Wayne County Public Library
Genealogy Department
304 North Market Street
Wooster, OH 44691-3593
(330) 262-0916, ext. 225; (330) 262-7313
    FAX
getit@wayne.lib.oh.us
http://www.wayne.lib.oh.us
Deborah Keener, Head of Genealogy and
    Local History
Mon–Fri 8:30 A.M.–9:00 P.M., Sat 9:00–6:00,
    Sun (during the school year) 1:00–5:00
("We have a large collection, for a county
    library, and have specialized in the path of
    immigration from Pennsylvania, Maryland
    and New Jersey into our section of Ohio;
    we are strong on the lower third of
    Pennsylvania; we also are strong on
    Wayne and surrounding counties.")
minor research by mail for cost of copies
    with SASE; names of local researchers
    supplied on request

Wayne Public Library
Local History Room
(137 East Main Street—location)
PO Box 489 (mailing address)
Wayne, OH 43466
(419) 288-2708; (419) 288-3766 FAX
barnhate@oplin.org
http://library.norweld.lib.oh.us/Wayne
Teresa Barnhart, Director

**Mary H. Weir Public Library (Jefferson
County, Ohio)**
(see West Virginia, Part 2)

Westerville Public Library
Ohio Room
126 South State Street
Westerville, OH 43081-2095
(614) 882-7277; (614) 882-5369 FAX
barlowd@westervillelibrary.org
http://www.westervillelibrary.org
Don W. Barlow, Director

Westlake-Porter Public Library
27333 Center Ridge Road
Westlake, OH 44145-3925
(440) 871-2600; (440) 871-6969 FAX
porter@oplin.org
http://www.westlakelibrary.org
Cynthia A. Hall, Assistant Coordinator of
    Reference Services
Mon–Thur 9:00–9:00, Fri–Sat 9:00–5:00,
    Sun (after Labor Day to before Memorial
    Day) 1:00–5:00
(for Westlake, Dover, Ohio; general
    genealogy reference and circulating
    collection; microfilm of local newspaper,
    Westlife, from 1955)

Weston Public Library
Grand Rapids Branch
(17620 Bridge Street—location)
PO Box 245 (mailing address)
Grand Rapids, OH 43522
(419) 832-5231; (419) 832-8104 FAX
http://library.norweld.lib.oh.us/weston/br.
    htm

Willard Memorial Library
6 West Emerald Street
Willard, OH 44890-1498
(419) 933-8564; (419) 933-4783 FAX
http://library.norweld.lib.oh.us/willard
Beverly Brandt, Reference Assistant
Mon–Thur 10:00–8:30, Fri–Sat 10:00–5:00;
    Summer: Mon–Tue & Thur 10:00–8:30,
    Wed 10:00–noon, Fri 10:00–5:00, Sat
    10:00–2:00

**Wilmington Public Library of Clinton
County**
268 North South Street
Wilmington, OH 45177-1696
(937) 382-2417; (937) 382-1692 FAX
meyersju@oplin.org
http://www.wilmington.lib.oh.us
Judith K. Meyers, Director
Mon–Thur 10:00–8:00, Fri–Sat 10:00–5:00

Wood County District Public Library
Local History Department
251 North Main Street
Bowling Green, OH 43402-2477
(419) 352-5104; (419) 354-1134 FAX
zenglema@oplin.org
http://wcdpl.lib.oh.us
Marian L. Zengel, Local History Librarian
Mon–Thur 9:00–8:30, Fri–Sat 9:00–5:00

Wright Memorial Public Library
1776 Far Hills Avenue
Dayton, OH 45419-2598
(937) 294-7171; (937) 294-8572; (937) 294-
    8578 FAX
walderan@oplin.org
http://www.wright.lib.oh.us
Antoinette Walder, Director
Mon–Fri 9:00–9:00, Sat 9:00–5:00, Sun
    1:00–5:00

Wright State University
Paul Laurence Dunbar Library

Special Collections and Archives
Dayton, OH 45435-0001
(937) 873-2092; (937) 873-2356 FAX
http://130.108.121.217/staff/dunbar/arch/
   schome.htm
Dawne Dewey, Archivist
Mon–Fri 8:30–5:00, Tue & Wed (academic
   quarter only) 7:00 P.M.–10:00 P.M., Sun
   (academic quarter only) 2:00–5:00
(member of the Ohio Network of American
   History Research Centers, the designated
   repository for local government records
   and historical manuscript materials from
   Auglaize, Champaign, Clark, Darke,
   Greene, Logan, Mercer, Miami,
   Montgomery, Preble, and Shelby counties;
   also houses a variety of family histories,
   local newspapers on microfilm and
   genealogical journals as well as a special
   collection of over 2,000 published
   volumes pertaining to the local and
   regional history of southwestern Ohio)
research: $1.00 plus postage and cost of
   copies at 10¢ each from paper originals,
   20¢ each from microform originals

**Public Library of Youngstown and
Mahoning County**
Information Services Department
305 Wick Avenue
Youngstown, OH 44503-1003
(330) 744-8636, ext. 151; (330) 744-8636,
   ext. 152; (330) 744-3355 FAX
reference@libraryVisit.org
http://www.libraryVisit.org
Diane Vicarel, Supervisor; Ollie McCurdy,
   Librarian
Mon–Thur 9:00–9:00, Fri–Sat 9:00–5:30
Pub. *Bibliofiles*, quarterly, free
copies: 10¢ per page plus $5.00 via U.S. Mail
   or $10.00 via FAX outside area code 330

**Youngstown Historical Center of Industry
and Labor**
(151 West Wood Street—location)
PO Box 533 (mailing address)
Youngstown, OH 44501-0533
(330) 743-5934; (330) 743-2999
http://winslo.ohio.gov/ohswww/youngst/
   arch_lib.html
Randall S. Gooden, Head, Archives-Library
Tue–Sat 9:00–5:00
(member of the Ohio Network of American
   History Research Centers, the designated
   repository for local government records
   and historical manuscript materials from
   Carroll, Columbiana, Harrison, Jefferson,
   Mahoning, and Trumbull counties)

Youngstown State University
Maag Library
Wick Avenue
Youngstown, OH 44503

Historical Societies—Local and Regional

Adams County Historical Society
Adams County Heritage Center
(State Route 247 North—location)
PO Box 306 (mailing address)
West Union, OH 45693
(937) 544-8522
Stephen Kelley, President
Thur & Sat noon–4:00
Pub. *The Centinel of the North-western
   Territory*, bimonthly
$5.00 per year membership

**Alexander Local Genealogical and
Historical Society**
(see Genealogical Societies—Local and
Regional, below)

Alexandria Community Historical Society
23 West Main Street
Alexandria, OH 43001
Betty Duke, President
Sun 2:00–4:00

Allen County Historical Society
Elizabeth M. MacDonell Memorial Library
620 West Market Street
Lima, OH 45801-4665
(419) 222-9426
http://www.worcnet.gen.oh.us/~acmuseum
Anna B. Selfridge, Curator, Archives and
   Manuscripts; Ray Schuck, Director
Library: Tue–Sat 1:00–5:00
Pub. *Allen County Historical Society
   Newsletter*, bimonthly; *Allen County
   Reporter*, three times per year
$10.00 per year membership

Alpine Hills Historical Museum
(106 West Main Street—location)
PO Box 293 (mailing address)
Sugarcreek, OH 44681
(330) 852-2223; (330) 852-4113
Les Raser, Curator
Apr–Nov: Mon–Sat 10:00–4:30

Amalthea Historical Society
(975 South Sunbury Road—location)
483 Dempsey Road (mailing address)
Westerville, OH 43081
(614) 891-6363
Tim Milligan, Secretary
Pub. *Amalthea Chimes*, three times per year
$3.00 per year membership

Amelia Historical Society
44 West Main Street
Amelia, OH 45102
(513) 753-4747
meetings at the Morse House, 44 Oak Street:
   fourth Mon 7:30

**American West Research Center and
Historical Society, Inc.**
Park Chester Building
10605 Chester Avenue
Cleveland, OH 44106-2240
(216) 721-9594
(states west of the Mississippi: Arizona,
   Arkansas, California, Colorado, Idaho,
   Illinois, Iowa, Kansas, Louisiana,
   Minnesota, Missouri, Montana, Nebraska,
   Nevada, New Mexico, North Dakota,
   Oklahoma, Oregon, South Dakota, Texas,
   Utah, Washington, Wisconsin, Wyoming)

Amherst Historical Society
(Quigley Museum, Corner of South Lake and
Milan Avenue—location)
PO Box 272 (mailing address)
Amherst, OH 44001-1311
(440) 988-7255
Valerie Jenkins, Museum Curator
Wed 9:00–3:00, and special weekends
Pub. *AHS Newsletter*, three times per year;
   Quigley Quest, three times per year
(genealogy section; specializes in Sandstone
   area history)
$10.00 per year membership

Anderson Township Historical Society
6550 Clough Pike
Cincinnati, OH 45230
(513) 231-2114
Albert Wettstein, President
Pub. *Surveyor*

Ashland County Historical Society

Ashland County Historical Museum
(414 Center Street—location)
PO Box 484 (mailing address)
Ashland, OH 44805
(419) 289-3111
Marybelle H. Landrum, Secretary/Manager
Wed, Fri & Sun (Apr–Dec) 1:00–4:00, Sun
   (Jan–Mar) 1:00–4:00
Pub. *County Crier*, three times per year
$7.50 per year membership

Ashville Area Heritage Society
281 Randolph Street
Ashville, OH 43103
(740) 983-3166

**Athens County Historical Society and
Museum**
65 North Court Street
Athens, OH 45701-2506
(740) 592-2280
achsm@athenshistory.org
http://www.athenshistory.org/index.html
Joanne D. Prisley, Director
Mon–Fri 10:00–4:00, and by appointment
Pub. *Athens Historical Society and Museum
   Bulletin*, bimonthly
(Athens County history and genealogy;
   genealogical and history research library)
$10.00 per year membership; research:
   $10.00 per hour plus copies

Auglaize County Historical Society
223 South Main Street
Saint Marys, OH 45885-2208
(419) 394-7069 (answering machine when
   museum is closed); (419) 394-5243
   (President)
George Neargarder, President
by appointment
Pub. *Auglaize County Historical
   Society—Newsletter*, bimonthly
("We opened a second museum: The
   Wapakoneta Historical Museum, 206 West
   Main Street, Wapakoneta, OH.")
$10.00 per year membership

Aurora Historical Society
PO Box 241
Aurora, OH 44202
Wallace Martel, Museum Director
Tue & Thur 1:00–4:00
Pub. *The Aurora Pioneer*, quarterly

Avon Historical Society
2940 Stoney Ridge Road
Avon, OH 44011
(440) 934-6106
Jean A. Fischer, President
by appointment

Bainbridge Historical Society, Inc.
(Dr. John Harris Dental Museum, 208 West
Main Street—location)
PO Box 424 (mailing address)
Bainbridge, OH 45612-0424
(740) 634-2881; (740) 634-2246 (President)
http://www.bainbridgedentalmuseum.com
Cherry D. Miller, President
June–Aug: Tue–Sat noon–4:00, Sun
   1:00–4:00; Apr–May & Sept–Oct:
   Sat–Sun noon–4:00, and by appointment

Barberton Historical Society
PO Box 666
Barberton, OH 44203
(330) 745-9383

Bath Township Historical Society
4655 Medina Road
Akron, OH 44321
Mrs. E. S. Stein

Bedford Historical Society, Inc.
(30 South Park Street—location)
PO Box 46282 (mailing address)
Bedford, OH 44146
(440) 232-0796
ace@aceverdad.com
http://www.bedfordohio.com/history
Richard J. Squire, Director of Museum
Bedford Museum: Mon & Wed 7:30
P.M.–10:00 P.M., Thur 10:00–4:00, second
Sun 2:00–5:00
Pub. *The Bedford Bee*, bimonthly
(local and area genealogy resources, archives,
reference library)
$7.50 per year membership

Bellevue Area Historical Commission
PO Box 304
Bellevue, OH 44811

Bellville Historical Society
Box 4511, Rule Road
Bellville, OH 44813
(419) 886-3680
http://www.angelfire.com/oh/bellville

Belmont County Historical Society, Inc.
(532 North Chestnut Street—location)
PO Box 434 (mailing address)
Barnesville, OH 43713
(740) 425-2926
Howard LeMasters, Treasurer
1 May–1 Oct: Thur–Sun 1:00–4:30, and all
year by appointment
$15.00 per year membership

Belpre Historical Society
(509 Ridge Street—location)
PO Box 731 (mailing address)
Belpre, OH 45714-0731
(740) 423-7382; (740) 423-7388
Nancy M. Sams, President
Sat (July–Aug) 1:00–4:00, by appointment
Pub. *Farmers Castle Journal*, quarterly
("Southeastern Ohio Underground Railroad
special exhibit. Volunteer operated,
community supported.")
$7.50 per year membership

Berea Area Historical Society
Mahler Museum and History Center
(118 East Bridge Street—location)
PO Box 173 (mailing address)
Berea, OH 44017
(440) 243-2541
http://members.aol.com/bereahist/index.html
meetings: fourth Wed (Sept–May)
(history of Berea and Middleburg Township)
$15.00 per year membership

Bethel Historical Association and Museum
(Grant Memorial Building, Corner of Main
[SR 125] and Plane Street—location)
100 South Main
Bethel, OH 45106
(513) 734-7049; (513) 734-4357 FAX
Museum: first Sat 1:00–4:00, and by
appointment; meetings: third Tue 7:30

Bexley Historical Society
Bexley Historical Commission
2242 East Main Street
Bexley, OH 43209
(614) 235-8694
Betty Gearhart, Secretary
Pub. *Historical Herald*

Black River Historical Society
309 West Fifth Street
Lorain, OH 44052
(440) 245-2563; (440) 245-3591 FAX
brhsmoore@centurytel.net

http://www.lorainecityhistory.org
Frank Sipkovsky, President
Wed & Sun 1:00–4:00, Fri 10:00–1:00
Pub. *Moore Memos*, quarterly
(museum has "some info on Lorain, Ohio,
residents from 1890s to the present.")
$10.00 per year membership

Botkins Historical Society
(Shelby House Hotel Museum, West State
Street—location)
PO Box 256 (mailing address)
Botkins, OH 45306
BotkinsHS@aol.com
http://members.aol.com/BotkinsHS/
history/bhshome/html
Brad Reed, President
first & third Sun, and by appointment;
meetings: first Thur
Pub. *Whistle Stop Newsletter*

Brecksville Historical Association
History Center and Archives
Blossom Hill Complex
Brecksville, OH 44141
(440) 526-7165

**Brewster-Sugar Creek Township
Historical Society**
45 South Wabash Avenue
Brewster, OH 44613
(330) 767-0045
Robert E. Lockring, President
Mon–Sun 8:00–2:00 (except holidays)
Pub. *News Letter*, quarterly
("Railroad documents and museum, local
including villages in Sugar Creek
Township area.")
$15.00 per year membership; research:
$25.00 per hour

Brooklyn Historical Society, Inc.
4442 Ridge Road
Brooklyn, OH 44144-3353
(216) 749-2804
Barbara Stepic, President
Tue 10:00–2:00, Sun (Apr–Dec) 2:00–5:00,
closed holiday weekends
(small library)
$4.00 per year membership

Brookville Historical Society
(14 Market Street—location)
PO Box 82 (mailing address)
Brookville, OH 45309
(937) 833-3470

Brown County Historical Society
(Corner of Apple and Cherry Street, Old
County Jail—location)
PO Box 238 (mailing address)
Georgetown, OH 45121
(937) 444-3521
Dorothy Helton
Thur & Sat noon–5:00
Pub. *Bits of Our Heritage*, quarterly (Apr,
July, Oct, Dec)
$3.00 per year membership

Bucyrus Historical Society
(202 South Walnut Street—location)
PO Box 493 (mailing address)
Bucyrus, OH 44820
(419) 562-6386
Linda Blicke, Curator
Mon (Mar–Dec) 1:00–4:00, Sun 2:00–4:00
Pub. *Scrogg's House News*, quarterly
(Crawford County News)

**Butler-Clear Fork Valley Historical
Society**
(43 Elm Street—location)

PO Box 186 (mailing address)
Butler, OH 44822
Tina Welty, Volunteer Curator
twenty hours per month
Pub. *The Clear Fork Grist*, quarterly, free

**Butler County Historical Society and
Museum**
327 North Second Street
Hamilton, OH 45011
(513) 896-9930
bcomuseum@fuse.net
http://home.fuse.net/butlercountymuseum
Marjorie Brown, Director
Tue–Sun 1:00–4:00
Pub. *Newsletter—Butler County Historical
Society*, six times per year
(Butler County history and surrounding area;
genealogy room: many resource materials)
$10.00 per year membership; admission:
$1.00 for nonmembers; research: postage
plus copies at 25¢ per page

Canal Fulton Heritage Society
Heritage House and Old Canal Days Museum
116 South Canal Street
Canal Fulton, OH 44614-1044
(330) 854-3808
Ann A. McLaughlin, President
by appointment only
Pub. *The Canaler*, monthly

Carlisle Area Historical Society
453 Park Drive
Carlisle, OH 45005
by appointment
Pub. *Carlisle Area Historical Gazette*;
Newsletter, three times per year
$10.00 per year membership

Carroll County Historical Society
PO Box 174
Carrollton, OH 44615
(330) 735-2839

Centerville Historical Society
Centerville Historical Commission
Walton House
89 West Franklin Street
Centerville, OH 45459-4735
(937) 433-0123
Lynn E. Russell, Administrator
Thur 1:00–4:00, and by appointment
Pub. *Newsletter*
$10.00 per year membership

Chagrin Falls Historical Society
Shute Memorial Building
21 Walnut
Chagrin Falls, OH 44022-3125
(440) 247-4695
Mrs. Pat Zalba, Curator; Mrs. D. Pauly,
Librarian
Thur 2:00–4:00, and by appointment
charge for postage and copying

Champaign County Historical Society
(809 East Lawn—location)
PO Box 65 (mailing address)
Urbana, OH 43078-0065
(937) 653-6721

Chesterland Historical Foundation
PO Box 513
Chesterland, OH 44026-0513
(440) 729-1830

Cheviot Historical Society
3814 Harrison Avenue
Cheviot, Ohio 45211
(513) 481-9468
http://www.cheviot.org

Elizabeth Nelson
(history of the city of Cheviot)
$5.00 per year membership

The Cincinnati Historical Society
The Cincinnati Historical Society Library and
Museum Center
1301 Western Avenue
Cincinnati, OH 45203-1129
(513) 287-7097; (513) 287-7095 FAX
http://www.cincymuseum.org
Laura L. Chace, Director
Mon–Fri noon–5:00, Sat 9:00–5:00
Pub. *Queen City Heritage*, quarterly
(the Old Northwest Territory, southwestern
    Ohio and metropolitan Cincinnati)
free admission; research rates: 15¢ per
    exposure for photocopies, $5.00 minimum
    postage and handling, plus $25.00 per
    hour for nonmembers, $15.00 per hour (no
    charge for the first hour) for members and
    nonprofit organizations, $35.00 per hour
    for commercial groups; copies: 15¢ per
    page plus service charge for orders of
    $25.00 or more, $5.00 minimum postage
    and handling

Clark County Historical Society
Heritage Center of Clark County
(117 South Fountain Avenue—location)
PO Box 2157 (mailing address)
Springfield, OH 45501
(937) 324-0657
Virginia Weygandt, Curator
Archives/Library: Tue–Wed & Sat 9:00–5:00,
    Museum: Tue–Sat 9:00–5:00
Pub. *Champion City*, quarterly
$35.00 per year membership

The Clermont County Historical Society
(Harmony Hill Association and Museum, 299
South Third Street, Williamsburg, OH
45176—location)
PO Box 14 (mailing address)
Batavia, OH 45103-0014
(513) 724-6222
Richard Crawford, Conservator
Clermont County Historical Society:
    meetings and programs at Clermont
    College: monthly (except Jan, July, Dec)
Pub. *The Clermont Historian*, ten times per
    year (monthly, except Jan & Dec)
$10.00 per year membership

**Cleveland Police Historical Society
Museum**
1300 Ontario Street
Cleveland, OH 44113
(216) 623-5055; (216) 623-5145 FAX
museum@stratos.net
http://www.clevelandpolicemuseum.org
David C. Holcombe, Executive Director
Mon–Fri 10:00–4:00; call for summer Sat
    hours
Pub. *The Hot Sheet*, quarterly
(primarily historical, not genealogical)
$26.00 per year membership; research:
    $10.00 donation form general, Non-Police

The Clinton County Historical Society
(149 East Locust Street—location)
PO Box 529 (mailing address)
Wilmington, OH 45177-0529
(937) 382-4684; (937) 382-5634 FAX
info@clintoncountyhistory.org
http://www.clintoncountyhistory.org
Joyce Thackston, Director
Mar–Dec: Wed–Sat 1:00–4:30; Jan–Feb:
    Thur & Sat 1:00–4:30
Pub. *Rombach Place*, four times per year
$15.00 per year membership

Clyde Heritage League, Inc.
PO Box 97
Clyde, OH 43410
Donald H. Hemminger, President
Pub. *CHL News*

Coalton Historical Society
552 Keystone Station Road
Jackson, OH 45640
Robert Ervin

Coleraine Historical Society
PO Box 53726
Colerain Township, OH 45253
http://www.rootsweb.com/~ohcths
Bailey Rogers, Historian
active research by appointment
Pub. *The Pageant*, quarterly
(Coleraine Township and greater Cincinnati
    area history)
$8.00 per year membership

College Hill Historical Society
5907 Belmont Avenue
Cincinnati, OH 45229
(513) 681-2470

Columbia Historical Society
PO Box 983
Columbia Station, OH 44028

**Historical Society of Columbiana and
Fairfield Township**
10 East Park Avenue
Columbiana, OH 44408
(330) 482-4896 (Himes)
Ada Wilhelm and Deborah Himes, Co-
    Chairmen of Genealogy Committee
Tue 9:00–11:00, weekends in summer
Pub. *Quarterly Newsletter*
("Columbiana Village and Fairfield
    Township—all volunteer help.")
$7.00 per year membership; research: $5.00
    per hour plus any additional costs for
    copying for initial computer search

Crestline Historical Society
(211 Thoman Street—location)
PO Box 456 (mailing address)
Crestline, OH 44827
(419) 683-3410
Ray Holland, President
by appointment, summer weekends
$6.00 per year membership

Dalton Community Historical Society
766 Mount Eaton Road
Dalton, OH 44618
Mrs. D. Rudy

Darke County Historical Society, Inc.
Garst Museum
205 North Broadway
Greenville, OH 45331-2222
(937) 548-5250
Judy Logan, Director
Garst Museum Library: Tue–Sat 11:00–5:00,
    Sun 1:00–5:00

**Defiance County Historical Society-Au
Glaize Village**
(12296 Krouse Road—location)
PO Box 801 (mailing address)
Defiance, OH 43512
(419) 393-2662
Judy Butler, Public Relations
Event weekends, June–Aug: 10:00–5:00
(19th-century recreated rural village and farm
    museum)
$5.00 per year membership; admission:
    $3.00 for adults

Delaware County Historical Society
(157 East William Street—location)
PO Box 317 (mailing address)
Delaware, OH 43015
(740) 369-3831
dchsdcgs@midohio.net
http://206.31.169.201/dchsdcgs
Marilyn M. Cryder
Sat 2:00–4:30, Thur 9:30–noon & 1:00–4:30
Pub. *Quarterly*
$10.00 per year membership

Delhi Township Historical Society
468 Anderson Ferry Road
Cincinnati, OH 45238
(513) 451-4313; (513) 251-1390
http://www.delhihistoricalsociety.org
Feb–Nov: Tue, Thur & Sun noon–3:00, and
    by appointment
Pub. *Footprints*, quarterly
(family history files with more than 14,000
    listings, census records, family
    genealogies, some probate records)
$20.00 per year membership; research: copies
    at 5¢ per page

Delphos Historical Association
PO Box 294
Delphos, OH 45833
Ron Leonhart

Dover Historical Society
J. E. Reeves Victorian Home, Carriage House
Museum, and Heirloom Gardens
325 East Iron Avenue
Dover, OH 44622-2105
(330) 343-7040; (800) 815-2794; (330) 343-
    6290 FAX
reeves@tusco.net
http://doverhistory.org
Chris Nixon, Director; James D. Nixon,
    Assistant Director
Office: Mon–Fri 10:00–4:00; Museum:
    seasonal
Pub. *News Letter*, quarterly
museum admission: $5.00 per person

Dublin Historical Society, Inc.
(6669 Coffman Road—location)
PO Box 2 (mailing address)
Dublin, OH 43017
(614) 764-9906
Elizabeth Myers, President

East Liverpool Historical Society
PO Box 476
East Liverpool, OH 43920
(330) 386-5964
Timothy R. Brookes, President
hours: various
Pub. *The City of Hills and Kilns*, quarterly
$10.00 per year membership

East Palestine Historical Society
555 Bacon Avenue
East Palestine, OH 44413-1530

**Otto E. Ehrhart-Paulding County
Historical Society**
City Hall
North Main Street
Antwerp, OH 45813
(419) 258-8161
James S. Temple, President
(genealogical services)

Enon Community Historical Society, Inc.
Genealogical Committee
(45 Indian Drive—location)
PO Box 442 (mailing address)
Enon, OH 45323
(937) 864-7080

Tue & Wed 1:00–4:00, Wed 6:00–8:00, Sat 10:00–2:00
Pub. *Images*, quarterly
(some census CDs, marriage CDs, microfiche, etc.)
$7.00 per year membership; research: actual cost of research, copies, etc.

The Euclid Historical Society
21129 North Street
Euclid, OH 44117
(216) 383-8299
Roy R. Larick, Jr., President
Pub. *The Scroll*

Fairfield Heritage Association, Inc.
105 East Wheeling Street
Lancaster, OH 43130-3706
(740) 654-9923; (740) 654-9890 FAX
Mary Lou McCandlish, Executive Secretary
Tue–Fri 9:00–4:00
Pub. *Fairfield Heritage Quarterly*, $1.00 per issue
(area historical information but limited genealogical information)
$10.00 per year membership

Fairport Harbor Historical Society
Fairport Marine Museum
129 Second Street
Fairport Harbor, OH 44077
(440) 354-4825
Helen Kasari, Historian
Memorial Day–Labor Day weekend: Wed & Sat–Sun 1:00–6:00
Pub. *Through the Porthole*, quarterly
(Great Lakes shipping, Fairport history)
$5.00–$100.00 per year membership

Fairview Park Historical Society
21779 Seabury
Fairview Park, OH 44126
(440) 734-2067

Farmersville Historical Society, Inc.
PO Box 198
Farmersville, OH 45325
Mary P. Gisewite, President
Pub. *Farmersville Historical Society Newsletter*, quarterly

Fayette County Historical Society
Fayette County Museum
517 Columbus Avenue
Washington Court House, OH 43160-1427
(740) 335-2953
http://www.washingtonch.com/faytrav/museum.htm (Museum)
Carol Carey, Curator
Museum: Sat–Sun (May–Oct), and by appointment
no admission charge; $5.00 per year membership

Firelands Historical Society Research Center
Laning-Young Research Center
(9 Case Avenue—location)
PO Box 572 (mailing address)
Norwalk, OH 44857-0572
(419) 668-6038
http://www.accnorwalk.com/credits/norwalk/firelands/index.html
Henry R. Timman, Trustee
Apr–May & Sept–Nov: Sat–Sun noon–4:00;
June–Aug: Tue–Sun noon–5:00
Pub. *Firelands Pioneer*, biannually (every other year), $17.00 per issue, $16.00 per year subscription to members
(Firelands and Ohio history and genealogy)
$12.00 per year membership (does not include periodical)

Forest Area Historical Society
6081 Dublinshire Drive
Dublin, OH 43017-3419
Jean March

Fort Loramie Historical Association
(Main and Elm Street—location)
PO Box 276 (mailing address)
Fort Loramie, OH 45845
(937) 295-3855
June–Sept: Sun 1:00–4:00

Fostoria Area Historical Society and Museum
(123 West North Street—location)
PO Box 142 (mailing address)
Fostoria, OH 44830
George A. Gray, President/Curator
Apr & Oct–Nov: Sat 1:30–4:30
Pub. *Monthly News Letter* with "Society Programe Monthly"
("A very eclectic collection of area related objects. 1941 Seagraves Ladder-Pumper Firetruck & 1918 Allen Automobile.")
$15.00 per year membership

Franklin Area Historical Society
Harding Museum
302 Park Avenue
Franklin, OH 45005
(513) 746-8295; (513) 746-4466
Ann Squier, Manager
Sun (Apr–Nov) 2:00–5:00, and year-round by appointment
Pub. *Franklin Area Historical Society Newsletter*, five times per year
$15.00 per year membership

Franklin County Genealogical and Historical Society
(see Franklin County Chapter, OGS, State Genealogical Society, OGS Chapters, below)

Franklin Township Historical Society
PO Box 653
Felicity, OH 45120-0653
(513) 876-2077
meetings at the Felicity Community Building, Main Street: first Thur 7:00

Fulton County Historical Society
657 Meadow Lane
Wauseon, OH 43567

Gahanna Historical Society
101 South High Street
Gahanna, OH 43230
(614) 475-3342
Mrs. LaRoux Mentz, Genealogist
by appointment
(has a continually growing file of early Gahanna settlers)

Galion Historical Society, Inc.
(132 South Union Street—location)
PO Box 125 (mailing address)
Galion, OH 44833
(419) 468-9338
Jerry A. Lantz, President
Sun (June–Oct); tours at 1:30, 2:15 & 3:00
Pub. *The Historian*, four times per year
$10.00 per year membership

Gallia County Historical/Genealogical Society
Gallia County Chapter OGS
412 Second Avenue
Gallipolis, OH 45631
(740) 446-7200
histsoc@zoomnet.net
http://www.zoomnet.net/~histsoc
Henrietta Evans, Corresponding Secretary

Mon–Fri 10:00–4:00, Sat 10:00–1:00
Pub. *The Glade*, quarterly
(First Families of Gallia County files, growing library collection; Revolutionary Soldiers Who Lived in Gallia County files)
$15.00 per year membership

Gates Mills Historical Society
PO Box 191
Gates Mills, OH 44040-0191

Geauga County Historical Society
(14653 East Park Street—location)
PO Box 153 (mailing address)
Burton, OH 44021
(440) 834-4012
Marlene Collins, Office Manager
by appointment
Pub. *The Quarterly*
$15.00 per year membership

The Historical Society of Germantown
(47 West Center Street—location)
PO Box 144 (mailing address)
Germantown, OH 45327-0144
(937) 855-7951 voice & FAX
barbwachter@earthlink.net
http://www.home.earthlink.net/~barbwachter/histsocgermantown
Barbara C. Wachter, Administrator
Office: Mon–Wed 8:00–noon; Museum: May–Dec: Sat 10:00–12:30, Sun 1:00–3:00
Pub. *Newsletter*, bimonthly
$10.00 per year membership

Girard Historical Society
307 Churchhill Road
Girard, OH 44420
(330) 545-3893
Jane Harris

Gnadenhutten Historical Society
(352 South Cherry Street—location)
PO Box 396 (mailing address)
Gnadenhutten, OH 44629-0396
(740) 254-4143; (740) 254-4992 FAX
gnadmuse@tusco.net
http://www.tusco.net/gnaden
Barbara McKeown, Secretary/Treasurer
June–Aug: Mon–Sat 10:00–5:00, Sun noon–5:00; Sept–Oct: weekends noon–5:00, and by appointment
(history only, no genealogy records)

Goshen Township Historical Society and The Anchorage
(1843 SR 28, near intersection of SR 28 and SR 132—location)
Box 671 (mailing address)
Goshen, OH 45122
(513) 575-1027; (513) 722-3830
http://angelfire.com/oh4/Anchorage
Museum: Tue 10:00–3:00, Museum Day in Apr, special events, and by appointment
admission: free

Historical Society of Grand Rapids
PO Box 124
Grand Rapids, OH 43522
Ann Taskey, Treasurer
$2.00 per year membership

Granger Library and Historical Society
1261 Granger Road
Medina, OH 44256-7337
(330) 239-1523
RWHPJH@aol.com
Robert W. Hummel, President
Sat (Apr–Oct) 1:00–3:00

Granville, Ohio, Historical Society

(115 East Broadway—location)
PO Box 129 (mailing address)
Granville, OH 43023
(740) 587-3951
granvillehistorical@juno.com
Sat–Sun (Apr–Oct) 1:00–4:00
Pub. *The Historical Times*, quarterly
$10.00 per year membership

Grassy Run Historical Arts Committee
3551 Inez Avenue
Bethel, OH 45106
(513) 734-1119
meetings at the Hartman Log Cabin, U.S. 50
    and Aber Road: third Tue 7:00
(participates in local historical events, holds
    an annual Time Line Heritage Rendezvous
    at Harmony Hill, Williamsburg, in April)

**Greater Loveland Historical Society
Museum**
201 Riverside Avenue
Loveland, OH 45140
(513) 683-5692 voice & FAX
glhsm@fuse.net
http://home.fuse.net/lovelandmuseum
Jo Ann Richardson, Director
Fri–Sun 1:00–4:30, and by appointment;
    meetings: selected third Wed
Pub. *Reflections....then and now*, bimonthly
$10.00 per year membership

**Greater Milford Area Historical Society
and Promont Museum**
906 Main Street
Milford, OH 45150-1767
(513) 248-0324; (513) 831-0815
Steven C. Kottsy, Director
Museum: Fri & Sun 1:30–4:30, and by
    appointment for groups; meetings at the
    American Legion Annex: first Thur 6:30

The Greene County Historical Society
74 West Church Street
Xenia, OH 45385
(937) 372-4606; (937) 372-5660 FAX
GCHSXO@aol.com
Joan Baxter, Executive Secretary
Tue–Fri 9:00–noon & 1:00–3:30, Sat
    (June–Aug) 1:30–4:00
Pub. *Our Heritage*, monthly
$15.00 per year membership

Guernsey County Historical Society
(218 North Eighth Street—location)
PO Box 741 (mailing address)
Cambridge, OH 43725
(740) 439-4686

Harmony Hill Association and Museum
229 South Third Street
3907 SR 133
Williamsburg, OH 45176
(513) 724-7790; (513) 724-7824
second Mon 10:00

Harrison County Historical Society
Baker Institute for Local Studies
168 East Market Street
Cadiz, OH 43907
(740) 942-3900
Mon–Fri noon–3:00

The Heritage Commission Corporation
(Depot Office, 147 West Mound Street—first
location
Opera House, 37 South Chillicothe
Street—second location)
PO Box 457 (mailing address)
South Charleston, OH 45368
(937) 462-7236 (President's home)
George H. Berkhofer, President and

Executive Director
Depot (museum and archives): second Sun
    1:00–5:00, and by appointment
Pub. *Newsletter*, bimonthly
(print, manuscript and photographic
    collection; local history and genealogy)
$5.00 per year membership; research: $5.00

Highland County Historical Society
Highland House Museum
151 East Main Street
Hillsboro, OH 45133
(937) 393-3392
Margaret Van Frank, Director
Fri 1:00–5:00, Sun 1:00–4:00, and by
    appointment
Pub. *Museum Muses*, three to four times per
    year
("historical society displays items relating to
    Highland County")
$8.00 per year membership

Hiram Township Historical Society, Inc.
(Century House Museum, Garfield
Road—location)
PO Box 1775 (mailing address)
Hiram, OH 44234
Monica W. Fratus, President
Hiram College Archives: Mon–Fri 9:00–5:00
Pub. *Newsletter*, quarterly
(specializes in Ohio, Connecticut Western
    Reserve, Disciples of Christ, Hiram
    College)
$10.00 per year membership

Historic Lyme Village Association
(5001 State Route 4—location)
PO Box 342 (mailing address)
Bellevue, OH 44811
(419) 483-4949
http://www.lymevillage.com
Alvina Schaeffer, Village Curator/Co-
    ordinator
Tue–Sun (June–Aug) 1:00–5:00, Sun (May
    & Sept) 1:00–5:00
Pub. *Lyme Lines*, monthly
$20.00 per year membership; admission:
    $7.00 for adults

Hocking County Historical Society
PO Box 262
Logan, OH 43138

Holmes County Historical Society
(232 North Washington Street—location)
PO Box 126 (mailing address)
Millersburg, OH 44654
(330) 674-0022

Hudson Heritage Association
(34 North Main Street—location)
PO Box 2218 (mailing address)
Hudson, OH 44236
(330) 653-5024
Warren Wickes, President
Mon–Tue & Thur–Fri 11:00–1:00
Pub. *Hudson Heritage Newsletter*, monthly

**The Hudson Library and Historical
Society**
(see City, County and Regional Archives and
Libraries, above)

Indian Hill Historical Society
Indian Hill Historical Museum Association
(8650 Camargo Road—office and library
location)
8100 Given Road (mailing address)
Cincinnati, OH 45243-1520
(513) 891-1873 voice & FAX
ihhist@one.net
http://www.indianhill.org

Julie Brumleve, Administrator
Mon–Fri 10:00–5:00
Pub. *The Sampler*, monthly
(focus on local history)
$40.00 per year membership

Jackson Center Historical Society
General Delivery
Jackson Center, OH 45334
Bernadine Heintz

Jackson Township Historical Society
(Massillon, OH 44646—location)
PO Box 35171 (mailing address)
Canton, OH 44735

Jefferson County Historical Association
Jefferson County Historical Museum and
Genealogical Library
(Corner of North Fifth Street and Franklin
Avenue—location)
PO Box 4268 (mailing address)
Steubenville, OH 43952
(740) 283-1133
Mary Hanlin, Volunteer Librarian; Marge
    Harris, Museum Director
Library: 10:00–3:00; Museum: by
    appointment only
Pub. *Newsletter Jefferson County Historical
    Association*, bimonthly
$10.00 per year membership; $2.00 museum
    admission

Kent Historical Society
(Birkner Tower, 5792 Glad
Boulevard—location)
PO Box 663 (mailing address)
Kent, OH 44240
(330) 678-2712
Stephen Paschen, Director
Wed & Fri 12:30–4:30
Pub. *Newsletter*, quarterly
$10.00 per year membership

**Kettering-Moraine Museum and Historical
Society**
35 Moraine Circle South
Kettering, OH 45439

Kettlersville Historical Society
General Delivery
Kettlersville, OH 45336

Kidron Community Historical Society
Kidron-Sonnenberg Heritage Center
(13153 Emerson Road—location)
PO Box 234 (mailing address)
Kidron, OH 44636-0234
(330) 857-9111; (330) 857-1475 (Director)
http://www.bright.net/~swisstea
Bruce Detweiler Breckbill, Director
summer: Tue, Thur & Sat noon–4:00; winter:
    Thur & Sat noon–4:00
Pub. *Bit o' Vit*, quarterly
(access to over 500,000 names in different
    databases plus many books, primarily
    Swiss Mennonite, German/Russian
    Mennonite, and Amish in origin)
$10.00 per year membership; research:
    donation for search time plus $1.00 per
    page for printout

Lake County Historical Society
8610 King Memorial Road
Mentor, OH 44060-7959
(440) 255-8979; (440) 255-8980 FAX
information@lakehistory.org
http://www.lakehistory.org
Joan Kapsch, Executive Director
Tue–Fri 10:00–5:00
Pub. *Lake County History Review*, three times
    per year

$25.00 per year membership; research fees based on time

Lake Erie Islands Historical Society
Put-in-Bay, OH 43456
(419) 285-2804
http://www.leihs.org

Lakeside Heritage Society, Inc.
Heritage Hall Museum and Archives
238 Maple Avenue
Lakeside, OH 43440
(419) 798-5719
Neil L. Allen, President
Memorial Day–Labor Day
Pub. *Lakeside Manifest-Newsletter*, quarterly
("Collections—memorabilia of Lakeside and the Marblehead Peninsula, Johnson Island artifacts, and Indian artifacts.")
$5.00 per year membership

Lakewood Historical Society
14710 Lake Avenue
Lakewood, OH 44107
(216) 221-7343
http://www.lkwdpl.org/histsoc
Sandra L. Koozer, Curator
Wed 1:00–4:00, Sun 2:00–5:00
Pub. *LHS Newsletter*

Lawrence County Historical Society
(The Lawrence County Museum, 506 South Sixth Street—location)
PO Box 73 (mailing address)
Ironton, OH 45638
(740) 532-1222
Sharon Kouns, President
Museum: Fri–Sun (1 Apr–15 Dec) 1:00–5:00
Pub. *The Lawrence Countian*, six times per year
$10.00 per year membership

Leetonia Historical Society
Public Library
38027 Old 344
Leetonia, OH 44431
John C. Simonds

Lenox Historical Society, Inc.
3424 Lenox and New Lyme Road
Jefferson, OH 44047
(440) 294-2640

LeRoy Heritage Association
(Route 86, Brakeman Road—location)
12941 Girdled Road (mailing address)
Painesville, OH 44077
(440) 254-4955

Licking County Historical Society
(Sixth [Veterans] Park, Newark, OH 43055—location)
PO Box 785 (mailing address)
Newark, OH 43058-0785
(614) 345-4898
Karen Dickman, Office Manager and Librarian
Tue–Fri 1:00–4:30
Pub. *The Licking County Historical Society Quarterly*, $10.00 per year subscription
("Museum and library containing information about people, industry and businesses of Licking County.")
$15.00 per year membership

Limaville Historical Society, Inc.
PO Box 13
Limaville, OH 44640

Lisbon Historical Society
(100 East Washington Street—location)
PO Box 191 (mailing address)

Lisbon, OH 44432
(330) 424-1861
Jewyl Hina, Museum Curator
1 June–15 Sept: Tue 10:00–3:00, Sun 1:00–4:00
Pub. *Preface*, quarterly
$10.00 per year membership

Liverpool Township Historical Society
(Center Road—location)
PO Box 399 (mailing address)
Valley City, OH 44280
(330) 483-3994

The Logan County Historical Society and Museum
(521 East Columbus Avenue—location)
PO Box 296 (mailing address)
Bellefontaine, OH 43311
(937) 593-7557
Corinne M. Dixon, Archives Library
May–Oct: Wed–Sun 1:00–5:00; 1 Nov–1 May: 1:00–4:00
Pub. *Logan County Historical Society Newsletter*, bimonthly
(large museum with an Archives Library, also a Genealogical Library)
$10.00 per year membership; research: $7.00 per hour (limit two hours, unless directed otherwise); copies: 20¢ per page

Lorain County Historical Society
Hicks Memorial Library
509 Washington Avenue
Elyria, OH 44035
(440) 322-3341; (440) 322-2817 FAX
lchsdirector@alltel.net; hickslib@alltel.net
William Bird, Director
Office LCHS: Tue–Fri 10:00–5:00; Library: 11:00–4:00
Pub. *Hickory Leaves*, quarterly
$25.00 per year membership; admission: $3.50 for adult nonmembers; research: $10.00 per hour for mail and email requests

Louisville Area Historical-Preservation Society
523 East Main Street
Louisville, OH 44641
(330) 875-4180

Lower Muskingum Historical Society
Main and Park Street
Beverly, OH 45715
(740) 984-2489; (740) 984-2141
weekends (June–Aug) 2:00–4:00
Pub. *Reflections Along the Muskingum*, quarterly
$3.00 per year membership

Lucasville Area Historical Society
PO Box 761
Lucasville, OH 45648
(740) 259-4392
Alice Moulton Barker
by appointment
$1.00 per year membership

Madison County Historical Society
(260 East High Street—location)
PO Box 124 (mailing address)
London, OH 43140
(740) 852-2977
Gretchen Green, Director
first full weekend of each month 1:00–4:00, Wed 1:00–4:00
Pub. *Log Cabin Sentinel*, quarterly
$10.00 per year membership

The Madison Historical Society
(13 West Main Street—location)

PO Box 91 (mailing address)
Madison, OH 44057
Louanna M. Billington, Curator
Wed–Sat 11:00–4:00
Pub. *The Times*, monthly
$10.00 per year membership

The Mahoning Valley Historical Society
The Arms Family Museum of Local History
648 Wick Avenue
Youngstown, OH 44502-1289
(330) 743-2589; (330) 743-7210 FAX
archives@mahoninghistory.org
H. William Lawson, Director; Pamela L. Pletcher, Archivist
Archives: Tue–Fri 9:00–4:00, Sat 1:00–5:00
Pub. *Historical Happenings*, bimonthly
(history and genealogy of Mahoning Valley watershed: Mahoning, Columbiana, Portage and Stark counties, Ohio, and Mercer and Lawrence counties, Pennsylvania, region; the Arms family; original probate files and civil court files, 1846–1900, for Mahoning County)
$20.00 per year membership; research: fees available upon request, members pay only for copies and postage and have free admission to archives

Maple Heights Historical Society
(5810 Dunham Road—location)
PO Box 37103 (mailing address)
Maple Heights, OH 44137
Frank Baloga, President; John Straka, Treasurer
Mon & Wed (summer) 7:00–9:00, second Sun (June & Sept) 1:00–4:00
$5.00 per year membership

Marion County Historical Society
Heritage Hall
169 East Church Street
Marion, OH 43302
(740) 387-4255
http://www.genealogy.org/~smore/marion
Dr. John D. Telfer, Executive Director
Reading Room (entrance on State Street): Mon–Fri 9:00–1:00; Research Library: by appointment; Museum: summer: Wed–Sun 1:00–4:00, winter: Sat–Sun 1:00–4:00
Pub. *Hallmarks*, quarterly
(emphasis on Marion County, Ohio; Heritage Hall also includes "Wyandot Popcorn Museum," Harding Presidential Collections, and Marion County Hall of Fame)
$7.50 per year membership

Marlboro Historical Society, Inc.
7344 Edison Street
Hartville, OH 44632
(330) 935-2830 (Secretary); (330) 935-2229; (330) 935-2441 FAX
dmayes@cannet.com (Denise Mayes)
Mary E. Devies, Treasurer
History room open on request; meetings: third Tue 7:00
("*Heritage Handbook* for sale, $10.00. New *Heritage Handbook* is being compiled for Ohio Bicentennial, 2003.")
$5.00 per year membership

Martins Ferry Area Historical Society
Sedgwick Historical Museum
(627 Hanover Street—location)
PO Box 422 (mailing address)
Martins Ferry, OH 43935
(740) 633-3134 (President)
Kay Ziegler, President
Tue–Sat (May–Oct) noon–4:00, and by appointment
Pub. *Ferry Landing Newsletter*, three times

per year
(Martins Ferry City and Area Museum;
Imperial glass collection; Martins Ferry is
part of Northwest Territory called "Seven
Ranges.")
$5.00 per year membership; research: by
request, no standard fee

Mason Historical Society
(Alverta Green Museum, 207 Church
Street—location)
PO Box 82 (mailing address)
Mason, OH 45040
(513) 398-6750 (Museum); (513) 398-6583
http://ww2.eos.net/edsale/cities/Mason/
museum/html
Lucy Gorsuch
Thur–Fri 1:00–4:00

Matamoras Area Historical Society, Inc.
(200 Main Street—location)
PO Box 1846 (mailing address)
New Matamoras, OH 45767-1846
(740) 865-2171
vincentb@1st.net
http://www.matamorashistory.org
Blanche Y. Brown; Diana Weeter McMahan,
Membership Secretary
Fri & Sat, and by appointment
Pub. *Newsletter*, quarterly
(maintains a museum of local history)
$10.00 per year membership; research: free,
"We are happy to share our manuscripts
and genealogy materials"

Maumee Valley Historical Society
1031 River Road
Maumee, OH 43537
(419) 893-9602; (419) 893-3108 FAX
Marilyn Wendler, Curator
Pub. *Ohio Cues*, eight times per year, $8.00
per year subscription; *Northwest Ohio
Quarterly*, semiannually (in two double
issues)
$29.00 per year membership

**Mayfield Township Historical Society and
Library**
606 Som Center Road
Mayfield Village, OH 44143-2311
(440) 461-0055
Jeanne Thompson Clough, Librarian
Mon & Sat 10:00–2:00
Pub. *Mayfield Township Historical Society
Newsletter*, quarterly
("Restored historical house; museum;
quilters; and historical and genealogical
library")
$5.00 per year membership; research: fees
vary

Medina County Historical Society
(206 North Elmwood—location)
PO Box 306 (mailing address)
Medina, OH 44258
(330) 722-1341
Thomas D. Hilberg, Curator
Tue & Thur 9:30–5:50; meetings: second
Mon 7:00; open house: first Sun
1:00–4:00
Pub. *Smart Talk*, monthly
("We operate out of the John Smart House
Museum and Research Center.")
$15.00 per year membership

**Meigs County Pioneer and Historical
Society, Inc.**
(see Genealogical Societies—Local and
Regional, below)

**Miami County Historical and Genealogical
Society, Chapter OGS**

PO Box 305
Troy, OH 45373-0305
Virginia L. Brown, Corresponding Secretary
meetings: third Tue (except July–Aug)
Pub. *Miami Meanderings*, quarterly
$10.00 per year membership; research: fees
set by individuals

**Miami Valley Council on Genealogy and
History**
(see Genealogical Societies—Local and
Regional, below)

Miamisburg Historical Society
(Miamisburg, OH 45342—location)
PO Box 774 (mailing address)
Miamisburg, OH 45343-0774
Connie Kline, Genealogist
(operates the Daniel Gebhart Tavern
Museum; "Genealogy records are
available through the local branch of the
Montgomery County Library.")

Middlefield Historical Society
PO Box 1100
Middlefield, OH 44062
(440) 632-0400

Middletown Historical Society
(Titus Avenue at Veriety Parkway—location)
PO Box 312 (mailing address)
Middletown, OH 45042
(513) 422-4781
Everett W. Sherron, President
Sun (Apr–Oct) 2:00–4:00, and by
appointment
Pub. *News Letter*, eight times per year
(Middletown history and Miami Erie Canal
History)
$5.00 per year membership

Minerva Area Historical Society
(128 North Market—location)
103 Murray Avenue (mailing address)
Minerva, OH 44657
(330) 868-4287
Mon–Wed 9:00 A.M.–11:30 A.M.
(Minerva area history)

Minster Historical Society
PO Box 58
Minster, OH 45865

Mohican Historical Society
Celo Redd Fisher Museum
203 East Main Street
Loudonville, OH 44842-1214
(419) 994-4050
James Sharp, Curator
Sat–Sun (Memorial Day–Labor Day)

Monroe County Historical Society
(217 Eastern Avenue—museum location
118 Home Avenue—office location)
PO Box 538 (mailing address)
Woodsfield, OH 43793
(740) 472-1933; (740) 9131 FAX
mchs2000@1st.net
http://www.monreohistoricalsociety.com
Robert Indermuhle, President; Barbara Ann
Gatten, Secreatary/Treasurer
Museum: June–Oct: Mon–Fri 10:00–4:00,
Sun 2:00–5:00; Office: Mon–Fri
9:00–4:00, Sun 2:00–5:00 and Fair Week
Pub. *Monroe County Heritage*, three times
per year, free subscription
$10.00 per year membership

**The Montgomery County Historical
Society**
Old Court House Museum
7 North Main Street

Dayton, OH 45402-1903
(937) 228-6271
Sarah J. Sessions, Curator of History and
Collections
Museum: Tue–Fri 10:00–4:30, Sat noon–4:00
Pub. *Columns*, bimonthly
(specializes in Miami Valley, Montgomery
County, Dayton local history (not
genealogy); inventors: Wright Brothers,
Patterson family of NCR)
research: $5.00 per hour for members, $7.50
per hour for nonmembers; photocopies:
10¢ each for letter size and 20¢ each for
legal size for members, 25¢ and 30¢ each
for nonmembers

Morgan County Historical Society
(126 East Main Street—location)
PO Box 524 (mailing address)
McConnelsville, OH 43756
(740) 962-4785
Betty White, Treasurer
Mon–Fri (summer) 1:00–3:00, Sat
10:00–noon
Pub. *Elk Eye*, quarterly
$5.00 per year membership

The Morrow County Historical Society
PO Box 21
Mount Gilead, OH 43338
(419) 946-7264 (evenings)
James D. Miller, President
Sun 2:00–5:00, and by appointment
Pub. *Newsletter*, quarterly
$7.50 per year subscription

Mount Healthy Historical Society
1544 McMakin Avenue
Mount Healthy, OH 45231
(513) 522-3939
Marian Blum, Curator
Tue, Thur & Sat 9:00–noon
$5.00 per year membership; pictures: $5.00
service fee plus cost of copy

**Historical Society of Mount Pleasant, Ohio,
Inc.**
Union Street
Mount Pleasant, OH 43939
(740) 769-2893; (800) 752-2631
http://users.1stnet.gudzent
Sherry Sawchuk, President
by appointment
Pub. *The Town Crier*, four times per year
(Quakers, Anti-slavery underground railroad,
early Ohio)
$10.00 per year membership; research for
hourly rate plus copy charge and postage

Munroe Falls Historical Society
(83 Munroe Falls Avenue—museum location)
43 Munroe Falls Avenue (mailing address)
Munroe Falls, OH 44262
(330) 688-5878 (Curator)
lown96@aol.com
Marilyn Lown, Curator
third Sun (except Jan & July–Aug), and by
appointment
Pub. *Olde Heritage*, eight times per year
(museum of area artifacts, local history
library)
$7.50 per year membership

**Pioneer and Historical Society of
Muskingum County**
(see Genealogical Societies—Local and
Regional, below)

Muskingum Valley Archeological Survey
24 South Sixth Street
Zanesville, OH 43701
Pub. *Muskingum Annals*, irregularly

$10.00 per year membership

Navarre-Bethlehem Township Historical Society
(123 North High Street—location)
PO Box 291 (mailing address)
Navarre, OH 44662
(330) 879-5938
Don Cooke, President
Wed 9:00–11:30 A.M.

New Albany-Plain Township Historical Society
(4659 Reynoldsburg-New Albany Road—location)
PO Box 219 (mailing address)
New Albany, OH 43054
(614) 855-9809
Emily Eby, Editor
Pub. *New Albany Plain Township Historical Society Newsletter*, about nine times per year
("Most of our information is limited to New Albany and Plain Township, located in Franklin County, Ohio.")
from $2.50 to $35.00 per year membership

New Bremen Historic Association
Genealogy Department
(120 North Main Street—location)
PO Box 73 (mailing address)
New Bremen, OH 45869
Sun (June–Aug) 2:00–4:00 (initial inquiries by mail only)
Pub. *The Towpath*, quarterly
$5.00 per year membership; research: initial fee of $10.00 absolutely required for reply

Newcomerstown Historical Society
Old Temperance House Tavern Museum
(221 West Canal Street—location)
PO Box 443 (mailing address)
Newcomerstown, OH 43832
Barbara Scott, President
Memorial Day–Labor Day: Tue–Sun 10:00–4:00

Niles Historical Society
(503 Brown Street—location)
PO Box 368 (mailing address)
Niles, OH 44446
(330) 544-2143
Meredith Elliott, Administrative Assistant
Office: Mon & Wed 9:00–1:00; meetings: first Sun 2:00–5:00
Pub. *The Niles Register*, monthly
("We are not strong in the genealogical area.")
$10.00 per year membership

Noble County Historical Society
PO Box 128
Caldwell, OH 43724
http://www.geocities.com/Heartland/ 6854/noble.html
Sigrid Merry
$8.00 per year membership

North Royalton Historical Society
11398 Royalton Road
North Royalton, OH 44133

Northampton Historical Society
783 West Bath Road
Cuyahoga Falls, OH 44223
Carrie Swain

Northwest Franklin County Historical Society
(Adjacent to Franklin County Fairgrounds—location)
PO Box 413 (mailing address)

Hilliard, OH 43026-0413
(614) 777-4852; (614) 876-2155 (Home)
Patricia L. Garbrandt, President
by appointment only
Pub. *The Northwest Chronicle*, five times per year (Feb, Apr, June, Sept, Nov)
("Have a collection of births, deaths, marriages and area history.")
$10.00 per year membership; admission: $1.00; research: fees vary

Oakwood Historical Society
1947 Far Hills Avenue
Dayton, OH 45419-2536
(937) 299-3793
Kathy Ellis, Genealogy Chairman
by appointment
Pub. *Newsletter*, eleven times per year (monthly, Jan–Nov)
("1867 farm house with summer kitchen attached 1920. Arts & crafts residence.")
$20.00 per year membership; library use: free to members, $1.00 per month for nonmembers

Old Bethel Historical Society and Methodist Church
(East Fork Lake Area—location)
3196 SR 133 (mailing address)
Bethel, OH 45106
(513) 734-4696 (President)
Marty Robinson, President
by appointment

Historical Society of Old Northfield
(9390 Olde Eight Road, Northfield Center, OH 44067—location)
PO Box 99 (mailing address)
Northfield, OH 44067
Mildred A. McCarty, President
Palmer House Museum: second & fourth Sun (Apr–Dec) 3:00–5:00
Pub. *Historical Society of Olde Northfield*, three times per year
$5.00 per year membership

Old Northwest Historical Society
c/o Victoria Retirement Center
1500 Sherman Avenue
Cincinnati, OH 45212
rrowan@fuse.net
meetings: second Sun 2:30
Pub. *The Old Northwest Historical Society "Trading Post"*
(The Tecumseh Club is a support organization to benefit the Loyal Shawnee Tribe of Oklahoma)

Oregon Jerusalem Historical Society of Ohio, Inc.
(3320 Starr Avenue—location)
3464 Starr Avenue (mailing address)
Oregon, OH 43616
(419) 691-7193

Ottawa County Historical Society
(4392 East Ledge Avenue—location)
PO Box 385 (mailing address)
Port Clinton, OH 43452
$5.00 per year membership

Owensville Historical Society
c/o Village Hall
115 West Main
Owensville, OH 45160
(513) 732-0566
meetings: third Sun

Parma Area Historical Society
(6975 Ridge Road—location)
PO Box 29002 (mailing address)
Parma, OH 44129

(440) 845-9770

Historical Society of Parma Heights
Town Hall
6281 Pearl Road
Parma Heights, OH 44130

John Paulding Historical Society Museum
(102 Fairground Drive—location)
James Sponsellar's Office
200 North Williams Street (mailing address)
Paulding, OH 45879
Lesli Wiedenhamer, President
Tue 10:00–4:00
Pub. *Newsletter*, four times per year
$3.00 per year membership; admission: free

Pemberville-Freedom Area Historical Society
PO Box 802
Pemberville, OH 43450
(419) 287-4305
http://www.hcnet.org/organizations/p/ pemhistsoc.html
Todd Sheets

Peninsula Library and Historical Society
(see City, County and Regional Archives and Libraries, above)

Historical Society of Perry County
(105 South Columbus Street—location)
PO Box 746 (mailing address)
Somerset, OH 43783-0746
(740) 743-2591
pchs@netpluscom.com
http://www.netpluscom.com/~pchs

Pickaway County Historical Society Chapter OGS
Genealogical Library
(Moore House, 304 South Court Street—location)
PO Box 85 (mailing address)
Circleville, OH 43113
(740) 474-9144
pkwyhist@bright.net
http://www.rootsweb.com~ohpickaw/gen. html
Darlene Weaver, Library Director
Tue–Fri 1:00–4:00
Pub. *Pickaway Quarterly*
(Pickaway County obituaries 1826–1996)
$25.00 per year membership; research: $8.00 per surname

Plymouth Area Historical Society
7 East Main Street
Plymouth, OH 44865-1201
(419) 687-5411

Portage County Historical Society, Inc.
6549 North Chestnut Street
Ravenna, OH 44266
(330) 296-3523
history@config.com
http://history.portage.oh.us
Raymond E. Wilson, President; Betty O'Neil, Researcher
Tue, Thur & Sun 2:00–4:00
Pub. *News/Views Portage County Historical Society*, quarterly
$7.00 per year membership

Preble County Historical Society
7693 Swartzel Road
Eaton, OH 45320
(937) 787-4256; (937) 787-9662 FAX
http://pchs.preblecounty.com
Jane Lightner, Executive Director
Library: Mon–Fri 9:00–8:00, Sat 9:00–5:00, Sun 1:00–5:00

Pub. *Telltales*, quarterly
$10.00 per year membership; research:
    donation

Putnam County Historical Society
(201 East Main Street—location)
PO Box 264 (mailing address)
Kalida, OH 45853
(419) 532-3008 (Office and Museum)
Ettie M. Rieman, Secretary
Wed 9:00–noon, Sun 1:00–4:00, except
    holidays
Pub. *Putnam County Heritage*, quarterly
$8.00 per year membership

Ragersville Historical Society, Inc.
(Sugarcreek, OH 44681—location)
1924 Dover Avenue (mailing address)
Dover, OH 44622

Reynoldsburg Truro Historical Society
1399½ Lancaster Avenue
Reynoldsburg, OH 43068
(614) 863-6969

Rocky River Historical Society
1600 Hampton Road
Rocky River, OH 44116
(440) 333-7610

Ross County Historical Society
45 West Fifth Street
Chillicothe, OH 45601
(740) 772-1936
Brian Hackett, Director
Pub. *Recorder*

Salem Historical Society and Museum
208 South Broadway
Salem, OH 44460
(330) 337-8514
Josephine Rupe, Director
by appointment
Pub. *The Bugle*, bimonthly
$8.00 per year membership

Sandusky County Historical Society
1337 Hayes Avenue
Fremont, OH 43420-2796

Scioto Society, Inc.
(215 West Second Street—location)
PO Box 73 (mailing address)
Chillicothe, OH 45601
(740) 775-4100

Seneca County Historical Society
Seneca County Museum
28 Clay Street
Tiffin, OH 44883-2231
(419) 447-5955
Rosalie Adams, Director

Sharon Township Heritage Society
PO Box 154
Sharon Center, OH 44274
(330) 336-3832
Robert J. Remark, President
$6.00 per year membership

Shelby County Historical Society
PO Box 376
Sidney, Ohio 45365-0376
http://www.shelbycountyhistory.org
Sherrie Casad-Lodge, Web Site Manager
$20.00 per year membership

Smithfield Historical Society
PO Box 484
Smithfield, OH 43948

Solon Historical Society

Solon Historical Museum
33975 Bainbridge Road
Solon, OH 44139
(440) 248-6419
Patricia W. Baumann, President
hours: one hour prior to scheduled 8:00 P.M.
    meetings, second Wed 1:00–4:00, and by
    appointment

South Euclid Historical Society
5147 Cheltenham Boulevard
Lyndhurst, OH 44124
Ester Eich, Curator
Sat 1:00–4:00

Southern Lorain County Historical Society
Spirit of '76 Museum
(201 North Main Street—location)
PO Box 76 (mailing address)
Wellington, OH 44090
(440) 647-4367; (440) 647-4576 (President)
Charles Oney, President
Apr–Oct: Sat–Sun 2:30–5:00
$10.00 per year membership

Stark County Historical Society
McKinley Museum of History, Science and
    Industry
Ramsayer Research Library
800 McKinley Monument Drive, N.W.
Canton, OH 44708
(330) 455-7043
W. J. Weber, Librarian
Library: Tue–Wed & Fri 12:30–4:30
research: postage plus copies at 25¢ each for
    8½" x 11" paper, 50¢ each for 11" x 17"
    paper

Stow Historical Society
(Young Road—location)
PO Box 1425 (mailing address)
Stow, OH 44224
(330) 688-1718
Catherine Flower, President
Sun 1:00–4:00, and by appointment
Pub. *Heritage Reserve News*, monthly
$5.00 per year membership

Strongsville Historical Society
13305 Pearl Road
Strongsville, OH 44136
(440) 572-0057
Carole L. Maatz, President
Apr–Nov: Wed & Sat–Sun 1:00–4:00, and
    by appointment
Pub. *Strongsville Historical Society
    Newsletter*, bimonthly
$15.00 per year membership

Summit County Historical Society
550 Copley Road
Akron, OH 44320
(330) 535-1120; (330) 535-0250 FAX
schs@summithistory.org
http://www.summithistory.org
Paula G. Moran, Executive Director
Perkins Stone Mansion, Corner of South
    Portage Path and Copley Roads: Tue–Fri
    9:00–4:00
Pub. *Old Portage Trail Review*, bimonthly
$20.00 per year membership; museum
    admission: $5.00 for adults

Swiss Community Historical Society
(see Ethnic Archives, Libraries and
    Societies—Swiss, Part 3)

Tallmadge Historical Society
PO Box 25
Tallmadge, OH 44278
(330) 630-9760
Richard L. Smith, President; Steve Brunot,

Vice President
open on request
Pub. *Bulletin*, eight times per year (monthly,
    Oct–May)

Three Rivers Historical Society
(Cleves and North Bend, Miami Township,
    Hamilton County—location)
3289 Triplecrown Drive (mailing address)
North Bend, OH 45052
Marjorie Burress, Local Historian
inquiries by mail only

Toronto Historical Society
326 Vollmer Street
Toronto, OH 43964

Trenton Historical Society
17-A East State Street
Trenton, OH 45067
(513) 988-9634; (513) 424-0740
Doris L. Page and JoAnn Howell, Curators
first Sat (May–Aug) 1:00–4:00; tours by
    appointment
$5.00 per year membership

Troy Historical Society
PO Box 401
Troy, OH 45373-0401
gmeeker5@woh.rr.comhttp://www.tdn-
    net.com/genealogy
Pub. *The Troy Times*, nine times per year
    (monthly, Oct–June)
("Local history—Miami County and
    surrounding counties. Research
    Room—Troy Miami County Public
    Library [419 West Main Street] and Troy
    Historical Society combined. No inter-
    library loans."
$7.00 per year membership; research: LSASE
    a must, $5.00–$10.00, depending upon
    how much time is needed to complete the
    request, and those requiring a lot of time
    will be turned over to a professional
    researcher

Trumbull County Historical Society
(John Stark Edwards House and Museum,
    303 Monroe Street, N.W., Warren,
    OH—location)
PO Box 1907 (mailing address)
Warren, OH 44482-1907
(330) 394-4653
sites@trumbullcountyhistory.org;
    membership@trumbullcountyhistory.org
http://www.trumbullcountyhistory.org/
    preservationHarding.htm

Tuscarawas County Historical Society
(629 Wabash Avenue, N.W.—location)
PO Box 462 (mailing address)
New Philadelphia, OH 44663
(330) 364-5577

Twinsburg Historical Society
(8996 Darrow Road—location)
PO Box 7 (mailing address)
Twinsburg, OH 44087
(330) 487-5565
Lea M. Bissell, Secretary
last Sun (Feb–Dec) 2:00–5:00, and special
    scheduled tours and open house dates
Pub. *Twinsburg Historical Society
    Newsletter*, monthly
$6.00 per year membership; research: cost of
    copies made

Union County Historical Society
PO Box 303
Marysville, OH 43040

Union Township Historical Museum

Quaker Heritage Center
47 North Miami Street
West Milton, OH 45383-1831
(937) 698-3820

Van Wert County Historical Society
(602 North Washington Street—location)
PO Box 621 (mailing address)
Van Wert, OH 45891-0621
(419) 238-5297
Sun 2:00–4:30, and tours on request
Pub. *Historical Happenings*, quarterly
(Van Wert County artifacts)
$10.00 per year membership; research:
    $14.00 per hour plus copying costs

The Village Historical Society, Inc. of Harrison, Ohio
(10580 Marvin Road—location)
c/o 6590 Kilby Road (mailing address)
Harrison, OH 45030-8914
(513) 367-4984; (513) 367-4984
E. B. Woelfel, Vice-President/Restoration
    Chair; Mary Lou Smith, President
third Sun (May–Oct) 1:30–4:00
Pub. *Looker Chronicles*, semiannually
("Preservation of historic site: Home of
    Ohio's fifth governor [1814], Orhniel
    Looker, Revolutionary soldier, first
    Governor of Ohio from Hamilton
    County.")
$7.50 per year membership

The Vinton County Historical & Genealogical Society, Inc.
(207 South Sugar Street, McArthur,
    OH—location)
PO Box 306 (mailing address)
Hamden, OH 45634-0306
(740) 596-0253; (614) 384-2467 (President)
cweese@raex.com
http://www.rootsweb.com/vinton/ogschapt.htm
Lawrence McWhorter, President
Wed–Fri 11:00–2:00, and by appointment
    (please call before coming, as hours may
    change at any time)
Pub. *Vinton County Heritage*, quarterly
$10.00 per year membership

Warren County Historical Society
105 South Broadway
Lebanon, OH 45036
(513) 932-1817; (513) 932-8560 FAX
wchs@go-concepts.com
http://www.wchmuseum.com
Mary Payne, Director
Tue–Sat 9:00–4:00, Sun noon–4:00
Pub. *Historicalog*, quarterly with updates
(Warren County genealogy, Shaker, Quaker,
    Western Star on microfilm)
$20.00 per year membership

Historical Society of Warren Township
211 Main Street
Tiltonsville, OH 43963
Robert Richardson

Washington County Historical Society Library
417 Second Street—Rear
Marietta, OH 45750
(740) 373-1788
Fran Kigans, Director
Mon–Fri 10:00–4:00, weekends and evenings
    by appointment
Pub. *Tallow Light*, quarterly
(Washington County quadrennial
    enumerations from 1807–1911; over
    10,000 court records between 1789 and
    1804)
$20.00 per year membership

Washington Township Historical Society
711 Bolender Road
Moscow, OH 45153
(513) 876-2971

Waterville Historical Society
10243 Rue de Lac Road
Whitehouse, OH 43571-9522
Sara C. Holliker

Wellsville Historical Society
(River Museum, 1003 Riverside—location)
PO Box 13 (mailing address)
Wellsville, OH 43968-0013
(330) 532-1018; (330) 532-1176
    (Genealogist)
Mary Clark, Genealogist
Museum: Sun (June–Sept) 1:00–5:00
(research in Columbiana and Jefferson
    counties)
$5.00 per year membership; research: $1.00
    per page

West Carrollton Historical Society
323 East Central Avenue
Dayton, OH 45449
(937) 859-5912

Western Columbiana County Historical Society
(4355 Homeworth Road—location)
3530 Bandy Road (mailing address)
Homeworth, OH 44634
(330) 525-7804 (Treasurer)
Rosanna J. McGee, Treasurer
Pub. *Middle Sandy Flintstone*, quarterly
$6.00 per year membership

Western Lake Erie Historical Society
(2319 Torrey Hill Drive, Toledo, OH
    43606—location)
PO Box 5311 (mailing address)
Toledo, OH 43611-0311
(419) 473-9534
Harry Archer, Historian
by appointment
Pub. *Marine History Lines*, approximately
    quarterly
$15.00, $25.00, $50.00, $500.00 per year
    membership; research fees negotiable

The Western Reserve Historical Society Library
Case Western Reserve University
10825 East Boulevard
Cleveland, OH 44106-1777
(216) 721-5722; (216) 721-5702 FAX
webmaster@wrhs.org
http://www.wrhs.org
Kermit J. Pike, Library Director
Library: Tue & Thur–Sat 9:00–5:00, Wed
    9:00–9:00, Sun noon–5:00
Pub. *The Western Reserve Historical Society
    Genealogical Committee Bulletin*,
    quarterly, $5.00 per year subscription
(235,000 books, 25,000 volumes of
    newspapers, 30,500 rolls of microfilm,
    1,000,000 prints and photographs, and
    more than 3,000 collections of
    manuscripts and archives which comprise
    more than six million items from New
    England to Georgia and west to the
    Mississippi River; also regional African
    American and ethnic archives, Ohio Labor
    history and urban archives; member of the
    Ohio Network of American History
    Research Centers, the designated
    repository for local government records
    and historical manuscript materials from
    Ashtabula, Cuyahoga, Geauga, Lake,
    Lorain and Medina counties)
$40.00 per year membership; admission:

$7.50 for adults; research: $30.00 per hour
    (half-hour minimum), includes up to ten
    copies, $10.00 for each additional ten
    copies, plus postage and handling

Whitehouse Historical Society
PO Box 2571
Whitehouse, OH 43571

Williams County Historical Society
(Williams County Fairgrounds, State Route
    107—location)
PO Box 415 (mailing address)
Montpelier, OH 43543
(419) 485-8200
Carol Eschhofen, Director of Education and
    Development
second & fourth Sun (May–Oct) 2:00–4:00
Pub. *Northwest Historian*, quarterly
$7.50 per year membership

Willoughby Historical Society
Willoughby-Eastlake Public Library
The Collection Room
30 Public Square
Willoughby, Ohio 44094
(440) 942-3200
webmaster@wepl.lib.oh.us
http://www.wepl.lib.oh.us
fourth Tue 6:00 P.M.–8:00 P.M., second Wed
    1:00–3:00
(manuscripts, scrapbooks, maps, roster of
    Ohio soldiers, history books, pioneer
    history, photographs, school histories,
    directories, diaries, school annuals and
    microfilm of Willoughby newspapers from
    1879)
$5.00 per year membership

Wood County Historical Society
Wood County Historical Museum
13660 County Home Road
Bowling Green, OH 43402
(419) 352-0967
http://www-
    wbgu.bgsu.edu/nwoetf/ode/historical_soci
    ety.htm
Sandra Fouty, Director; Andrew S. Kalmar,
    President
Tue–Fri 9:30–4:30, Sat–Sun 1:00–4:00
Pub. *The Black Swamp Chanticleer*,
    bimonthly
$7.50 per year membership

Woodville Historical Society
107 East Main Street
Woodville, OH 43469
Kermit Hoesman, President
Museum: Wed–Fri (except Jan–Feb)
    2:00–4:00
$2.00 per year membership

Worthington Historical Society Library
50 West New England Avenue
Worthington, OH 43085
(614) 885-1247
Lillian Skeele, Librarian
Wed 10:00–3:00, and by appointment
Pub. *The Intelligencer*, ten times per year
(Worthington history, art history, lace,
    interior design)
$7.00 per year membership

Wyandot County Historical Society
(130 South Seventh Street—location)
PO Box 372 (mailing address)
Upper Sandusky, OH 43351
(419) 294-3857
David Barth, Treasurer
Thur–Sun (1 May–31 Oct) 1:00–4:30
Pub. *News Letter*, five times per year
$10.00 per year membership

Yellow Springs Historical Society
(405 Corry Street—location)
PO Box 501 (mailing address)
Yellow Springs, OH 45387
(937) 767-7375

Genealogical Societies

State Genealogical Society

The Ohio Genealogical Society (OGS)
Library
(34 Sturges Avenue—location)
PO Box 2625 (mailing address)
Mansfield, OH 44906-0625
(419) 522-9077; (419) 522-0224 FAX
ogs@freenet.richland.oh.us
http://www.ogs.org
Thomas Stephen Neel, Office Manager;
    Elizabeth S. Glasgow, Librarian
summer (1 June–1 Sept): Tue–Sat 9:00–5:00;
    winter (1 Sept–1 June): Tue & Thur
    1:00–5:00, Wed 9:00–1:00, Fri–Sat
    9:00–5:00
Pub. *The Report*, quarterly; *The Ohio
    Genealogical Society Newsletter*, monthly;
    Ohio Records and Pioneer Families,
    quarterly, $18.00 per year subscription;
    Ohio Civil War Genealogy Journal,
    quarterly, $18.00 per year subscription
(sponsors First Families of Ohio, a lineage
    society for members with pre-Dec 31,
    1821 Ohio ancestors; The Society of Civil
    War Families of Ohio, a lineage society for
    members with Ohio ancestors who served
    in the Civil War)
$27.00 per year membership (includes *The
    Report* and *The Ohio Genealogical Society
    Newsletter*)

OGS Chapters (local affiliates)

Allen County Ohio Genealogy Society
PO Box 1104
Lima, OH 45802
paufff@nwoss.com
http://allencogenealogysociety.homestead.
    com/main.html
Fran Pauff
meetings at the Elizabeth M. MacDonell
    Memorial Library: third Sun (except
    June–Aug & Dec) 1:45
Pub. *The Newsletter*, bimonthly
$10.00 per year membership

The Alliance Genealogical Society (TAGS)
PO Box 3630
Alliance, OH 44601-7630
tags_ogs@hotmail.com
http://www.rootsweb.com/~ohags
Carolyn Miller, President; Alice Bidlack,
    Secretary
Alliance Rodman Public Library: Mon–Thur
    9:00–9:00, Fri–Sat 9:00–5:30
Pub. *TAGS—The Alliance Genealogy Society*,
    ten times per year (monthly, except July &
    Dec)
$10.00 per year membership

Ashland County, Ohio Genealogy Society
PO Box 681
Ashland, OH 44805-0681
http://www.rootsweb.com/~ohacogs
Rita Kopp, Librarian
Library research help: first Tue 7:00–9:00,
    second Thur 1:00–3:00, third Sat
    10:00–noon; meetings at Ashland Public
    Library: third Tue (Mar–Nov) 6:30
Pub. *Pastfinder*, quarterly
$10.00 per year membership

Ashtabula County Genealogical Society,

Inc.
Geneva Public Library
Platt R. Spencer (Memorial) Special
Collections and Archival Room
860 Sherman Street
Geneva, OH 44041-9101
(440) 466-4521, ext. 13 (Library); (216) 466-
    0162 FAX (Library)
acgs@ashtabulagen.org
http://www.ashtabulagen.org
Library: Mon 10:30–noon & 12:30–8:00,
    Tue–Wed 10:30–8:00, Thur 10:30–5:00,
    Fri 11:00–4:00, Sat (except summer)
    10:30–4:00; meetings: fourth Wed 1:00
    (except June–Aug & Dec), fourth Wed
    7:00 (June–Aug)
Pub. *Ancestor Hunt*, quarterly (Feb, May,
    Aug, Nov)
$10.00 per year membership; queries: free
    for members; research: $10.00 per hour
    from May Colling, retainer recommended

Athens County Chapter OGS
Athens County Historical Society and
Museum
65 North Court Street
Athens, OH 45701-2506
(740) 592-2280
genealogy@athenshistory.org
http://www.athenshistory.org/genealogy
Joanne D. Prisley, Director ACHS&M
Mon–Fri 1:00–4:00, and by appointment;
    meetings: third Mon (except July & Aug)
Pub. *The Bulletin*, bimonthly
$10.00 per year membership (includes
    membership in The Athens County
    Historical Society and Museum);
    research: $10.00 per hour, plus copies

Auglaize County Genealogical Society
PO Box 2021
Wapakoneta, OH 45895-0521

    http://www.rootsweb.com/~ohaugogs/ind
    ex.html
Richard Bowersock, President
meetings in the basement meeting room of
    the Auglaize County Public District
    Library, 203 South Perry Street: first Sat
    (Sept–May) 1:30
Pub. *Fallen Timbers Ances-Tree*, quarterly
$10.00 per year membership

Belmont County Chapter OGS
(125 East Main Street—location)
PO Box 285 (mailing address)
Barnesville, OH 43713-0285
BCCOGS@hotmail.com
http://www.rootsweb.com\~ohbelogs\
Peggy J. Hatcher, President
meetings at Barnesville Hutton Memorial
    Library: second Sun(except Dec) 7:00
Pub. *Belmont County Genealogy News*,
    quarterly (Mar, June, Sept, Dec)
$10.00 per year membership; queries: free
    newsletter queries to nonmembers, $1.00
    each for nonmembers

Brown County Chapter OGS
("Old County Jail" corner of Apple and
Cherry Streets—location)
PO Box 83 (mailing address)
Georgetown, OH 45121-0083
(937) 444-3521 (Vice President)
Dorothy Helton, Vice President
Thur–Sat noon–5:00; meetings: third Thur
    8:00
Pub. *On the Trail*, quarterly
("We are always glad to help and will do
    research from the library, which has most
    of the county records, cemeteries.")
$7.00 per year membership; research from

library: copy and postage fee

Butler County Chapter OGS
PO Box 2011
Middletown, OH 45044-2011
(513) 422-1490
da120757@cinci.rr.com
http://da120757.tripod.com/bcogs
Ellen Essig, Corresponding Secretary
meetings at the Middletown Public Library:
    second Sat
Pub. *Pathways*, quarterly
$10.00 per year membership

Carroll County, Ohio Genealogical Society
(24 Second Street, N.E.—location)
PO Box 36 (mailing address)
Carrollton, OH 44615
(330) 627-9411; (330) 627-2570
    (Corresponding Secretary); (330) 627-
    2094 (Temporary Librarian)
loishemming@eohio.net
Helen Rankin, Corresponding Secretary; Lois
    Hemming, Temporary Librarian
Mon–Wed 9:00–noon, Thur–Fri 1:00–4:00,
    Sat 10:00–2:00, drop-ins welcome,
    appointments accepted
Pub. *Carroll Cousins*, four times per year
$10.00 per year membership; research: $5.00
    per hour

Champaign County Genealogical Society
PO Box 682
Urbana, OH 43078-0682
(937) 652-3673
nleasure@foryou.net
http://www.rootsweb.com/~ohchampa/
    society.htm
Pat Stickley, Corresponding Secretary
meetings at the Champaign County Historical
    Society: second Mon (Sept–June) 7:00
Pub. *Champaign County Genealogical
    Society Newsletter*, quarterly
$10.00 per year membership; queries: free;
    research in library and courthouse: $5.00
    per hour plus copies

Clark County Genealogical Society
(third floor of the Heritage Center, 117 South
Fountain Avenue—location)
PO Box 2524 (mailing address)
Springfield, OH 45501-2524
(937) 324-0657, ext. 235
FHulsizer@aol.com
http://www.rootsweb.com/~ohcccogs
Robert E. Hulsizer, President
Tue & Thur 1:00–4:00; meetings in the
    Discovery Room: second Sat 11:00
    (except July–Aug & Dec)
Pub. *Clark County Kin*, quarterly
(specializes in Clark County and Ohio)
$12.00 per year membership; research: $5.00
    for members, $7.00 for nonmembers

Clermont County Genealogical Society
PO Box 394
Batavia, OH 45103-0394
(513) 723-3423 (voice mail)
CCGSmail@aol.com
http://www.rootsweb.com/~ohclecgs
Debra Geesner, President; Donald Johnson
meetings in the Clermont County Public
    Library, Doris Wood Branch: first Thur
    7:30
Pub. *Clermont County Genealogical Society
    Newsletter*, quarterly
(collection housed at the Clermont County
    Public Library)
$10.00 per year membership

Clinton County Genealogical Society
(149 East Locust Street—location)

PO Box 529 (mailing address)
Wilmington, OH 45177-0529
(937) 382-4684
cmmiller@erinet.com
Maxine Miller, Genealogist and Volunteer
    Coordinator
Mar–Dec: Wed–Sat 1:00–4:30; Jan–Feb:
    Thur & Sat 1:00–4:30; meetings at Clinton
    County Historical Society: fourth Mon
    (except Dec) 7:30
Pub. *Clinton Chronicle*, quarterly
$8.00 per year membership

Columbiana County Chapter OGS
PO Box 861
Salem, OH 44460-0861
(330) 332-5263 (Mr. Lewis)
mcreatore02@msn.com
http://www.rootsweb.com/~ohcolumb
Scott Lewis
Mon–Thur 10:00–9:00, Fri–Sat 10:00–5:00;
    meetings in the Salem Historical Society:
    second Wed 7:00
Pub. *Columbiana County Connection*,
    monthly
$12.00 per year membership

Coshocton County Chapter OGS
PO Box 128
Coshocton, OH 43812-0128
(740) 622-4706
Glenn Kinkade, Editor
meetings at the Coshocton Public Library:
    third Tue 7:30
Pub. *The Kinsman Courier*, quarterly
$10.00 per year membership

Crawford County Chapter OGS, Inc.
PO Box 92
Galion, OH 44833-0092
(419) 562-5420
ccgs_oh@yahoo.com
http://www.rootsweb.com/~ohcgs
Mary Fox, President
meetings: third Thur (except Feb, July–Aug,
    Dec) 7:30
Pub. *Tracking in Crawford County, Ohio*,
    nine times per year
$8.00 per year membership

East Cuyahoga Chapter OGS
PO Box 24182
Lyndhurst, OH 44124-0182
MorgaBD@msn.com
Regis Campbell, President
Pub. *Speaking Relatively*, quarterly
$15.00 per year membership

Southwest Cuyahoga Chapter OGS
(18825 Royalton Road—location)
13305 Pearl Road (mailing address)
Strongsville, OH 44136-3403
(440) 238-6370
cngwilli@nls.net
http://members.aol.com/gmtjaden
Grace A. Williams, Vice President
Pub. *Newsletter of the Southwest Cuyahoga
    Chapter of OGS*, three times per year
$10.00 per year membership

Cuyahoga Valley Chapter OGS
PO Box 41414
Brecksville, OH 44141-0414
chsutton11@aol.com
by appointment (mail requests only)
Pub. *Footsteps to the Past*, quarterly
(emphasis on Brecksville and Independence
    area)
$10.00 per year membership

Cuyahoga West Chapter OGS
PO Box 26196

Fairview Park, OH 44126-0196
CuyahogaWest@att.net
Jeanne B. Workman, President
Pub. *Tracer*, quarterly
$15.00 per year membership

Darke County Genealogical Society
PO Box 908
Greenville, OH 45331-0908
(937) 526-3953 (President); (937) 548-8174
    (Treasurer)
ahuffman@wesnet.com
http://www.calweb.com/~wally/darke/
    society.htm
Alice Huffman, President; Doris Aultman,
    Treasurer
Pub. *The Kindling*, quarterly
(maintains a library at Garst Museum in
    Greenville, including several file cabinets
    of family files and many family histories;
    also publishes books of local interest)
$14.00 per year membership

**Defiance County County, Ohio
Genealogical Society**
PO Box 7006
Defiance, OH 43512-7006
defiancegenealogy2002@yahoo.com
http://www.rootsweb.com/~ohdcgs/
    defiancecountygensoc.html
Mrs. Pat Little, Department Head, Ohioana
    Room, Defiance Public Library
Defiance Public Library, Ohioana Room:
    Mon–Fri 9:00–5:00, "evenings—on your
    own to 8:00 P.M."; Library: Mon–Thur
    9:00–8:00, Fri–Sat 9:00–5:30 (summer:
    Sat 9:00–noon)
Pub. *Yesteryears Trails*, quarterly
$7.00 per year membership

**Delaware County Genealogical Society,
Inc.**
(157 East William Street—location)
PO Box 1126 (mailing address)
Delaware, OH 43015-8126
(740) 369-3831
mdbarnhart@earthlink.net
http://www.midohio.net/dchs/dcgs
Crystal Kohler, President
Mar to mid-Nov: Wed & Sat–Sun 2:00–4:30,
    Thur 10:00–11:45 & 1:00–4:30; mid-Nov
    to Mar: Sun only 2:00–4:30
Pub. *Delaware Genealogist's*, quarterly
$10.00 per year membership

Erie County Chapter OGS
PO Box 1301
Sandusky, OH 44871-1301
http://www.rootsweb.com/~oheccogs
Elizabeth N. Proudfoot, President
Pub. *Erie County Connection*, six times per
    year (Mar, Apr, May, Sept, Oct, Nov)
$10.00 per year membership

Fairfield County Chapter OGS
PO Box 1470
Lancaster, OH 43130-0570
(740) 653-2745, ext. 109 (please leave a
    voice mail message)
chapter@fairfieldgenealogy.org
http://www.fairfieldgenealogy.org
Karen S. Smith
meetings at Fairfield County District Library:
    third Thur 7:00 (except July & Dec)
Pub. *Fairfield Trace*, quarterly
$10.00 per year membership

Fayette County Genealogical Society
PO Box 342
Washington Court House, OH 43160-0342
(740) 335-6060 (President); (740) 636-9703
    (Ms. Moore)

db9620@dragonbbs.com
http://www.geocities.com/db9620
Bettie Kerr Gray, President; Helen R. Moore
meetings at Carnegie Library, Genealogical
    Room or Meeting Room
Pub. *The Fayette Connection*, quarterly
$10.00 per year membership; research: $5.00
    and $10.00

Franklin County Chapter OGS
Franklin County Genealogical and Historical
    Society
PO Box 44309
Columbus, OH 43204-0309
FCGHS@yahoo.com; BrRatekin@aol.com
http://www.rootsweb.com/~ohfcghs
Bruce Ratekin, Webmaster
Mon, Wed & Fri 10:00–3:00, Sun 1:00–5:00
Pub. *The Franklintonian*, six times per year,
    the last issue of the year being an index of
    all of the issues
$15.00 per year membership; research:
    $15.00 per hour

Fulton County Chapter OGS
PO Box 337
Swanton, OH 43558-0337
ronnan@voyager.net
http://www.rootsweb.com/~ohfulton
Jana Broglin, President
Pub. *Fulton Footprints*, quarterly
(collection deposited with Swanton Public
    Library)
$12.00 per year membership

**Gallia County Historical/Genealogical
Society**
(see Historical Societies—Local and
Regional, above)

Geauga County Chapter OGS
Geauga County Genealogical Society
Chardon Library
Anderson Allyn Room for Genealogical
    Research
110 East Park Street
Chardon, OH 44024-1213
Pub. *Raconteur*, quarterly
(specializes in Geauga County)
$7.50 per year membership

**Greater Cleveland Genealogical
Society—Cuyahoga County**
PO Box 40254
Cleveland, OH 44140-0254
mjfc99@core.com
http://www.rootsweb.com/~ohgcgg
Marilyn Carlson, President
meetings at Fairview Park Regional Library
Pub. *The Certified Copy*, quarterly
$15.00 per year membership; "queries
    submitted for free"

Greene County Chapter OGS
(Greene County Room, Greene County
District Library—location)
PO Box 706 (mailing address)
Xenia, OH 45385-0706
(937) 376-2995
Blin4012@aol.com
http://www.rootsweb.com/~ohgccogs
Pub. *Leaves of Greene*, bimonthly
$10.00 per year membership

Guernsey County Genealogical Society
(125 North Seventh Street—location)
PO Box 661 (mailing address)
Cambridge, OH 43725-0661
(740) 432-9249
gccogs@earthlink.net
Kurt Tostenson, President
Tue & Thur 1:00–4:00

Pub. *Guernsey Roots and Branches*, quarterly (Guernsey County information)
$10.00 per year membership; copies: 20¢ each from paper originals, 25¢ each from microform originals

Hamilton County Chapter OGS
PO Box 15865
Cincinnati, OH 45215-0865
(513) 956-7078
egan@fuse.net
http://members.aol.com/ogshc
Kenny R. Burck, President
Pub. *The Tracer*, quarterly; *The Gazette*, quarterly
("All holdings are located at the Public Library of Cincinnati and Hamilton County, Main Branch. Special Interest Groups: African American, Computer, Irish and German. The Chapter has published 33 volumes for Hamilton County Researchers, including 14 volumes in the Hamilton County, Ohio Cemetery Services.")
$15.00 per year membership; research of chapter publications and surname card file: $5.00 for one hour for members, $10.00 for nonmembers

Hancock County Chapter OGS
PO Box 672
Findlay, OH 45840-0672
(419) 422-1737 (Reference Department)
hancock_ogs@hotmail.com
http://www.rootsweb.com/~ohhccogs
Margaret Kelley, Corresponding Secretary
winter: Mon–Thur 9:30–8:30, Fri–Sat 9:30–5:00; summer: Mon–Sat 9:30–5:00
Pub. *Hancock Heritage*, quarterly
$10.00 per year membership

Hardin County Genealogical Society
(211 West Franklin Street—location)
PO Box 520 (mailing address)
Kenton, OH 43326-0520
(419) 673-1335
HCGS@HardinCountyConnections.com
http://www.hardincountyconnections.com
Charles R. Kelley, President
Pub. *Track and Trace*, quarterly
$7.50 per year membership; research SASE and cost of copies

Harrison County Genealogical Society
First Families of Harrison County
45507 Unionvale Road
Cadiz, OH 43907-9723
bjackson@1st.net;
    harrisonheritage@yahoo.com
http://www.rootsweb.com/~ohharris/hcgs.htm
Dorothy Greer, Corresponding Secretary
Tue & Thur 11:00–4:00, and by appointment
Pub. *Our Harrison Heritage*, quarterly (winter, spring, summer, fall)
(members of First Families of Harrison County must have an ancestor who was in Harrison County by Dec 31, 1830)
$10.00 per year membership

Henry County Genealogical Society
PO Box 231
Deshler, OH 43516
information@henrycountyohiogenealogy.org
http://www.henrycountyohiogenealogy.org/index.html
Phyllis LaRue, Corresponding Secretary
meetings at Edwin Wood Memorial Library: third Mon (except Dec) 7:00
Pub. *Henry County Genealogical Society*, bimonthly
$7.00 per year membership

Hocking County Chapter OGS
PO Box 115
Rockbridge, OH 43149-0115
(740) 385-6512 (Treasurer)
Robert E. Redd, Treasurer and Corresponding Secretary
meetings at Logan-Hocking Public Library, 230 East Main Street: fourth Thur 7:30
Pub. *The Hocking Sentinel*, quarterly
$10.00 per year membership

Holmes County Chapter OGS
PO Box 136
Millersburg, OH 44654-0136
Dená Crider, President
meetings at the Holmes County Library, 3102 Glen Drive: fourth Thur 7:30
Pub. *Holmes County Heirs*, bimonthly (probate and circuit court records, 1824–1900)
$10.00 per year membership

Hudson Genealogical Study Group
The Hudson Library and Historical Society
22 Aurora Street, #G
Hudson, OH 44236
hgsg@bigfoot.com
http://www.rootsweb.com/~ohhudogs/hudson.htm
Pub. *The Hudson Green*, quarterly (Mar, June, Sept, Dec)
$7.50 per year membership

Huron County Chapter OGS
PO Box 923
Norwalk, OH 44857-0923
jkelble@accnorwalk.com
http://www.rootsweb.com/~ohhuron
fourth Mon (except Dec) 7:30
Pub. *The Kinologist*, four times per year
$10.00 per year membership

Jackson County Chapter OGS
PO Box 807
Jackson, OH 45640-0807
JCOGS@Scioto.org
http://www.scioto.org
Karen Davis, President
meetings at Jackson City Library: third Mon 7:30
Pub. *Poplar Row*, quarterly
$10.00 per year membership

Jefferson County Chapter OGS
PO Box 2367
Wintersville, OH 43953
VERSTRATEN@Prodigy.net
http://www.jeffcochapter.com
Flora L. Ver Straten, President
meetings at Public Library of Steubenville and Jefferson County, Schiappa Branch Library: first Tue 7:00
Pub. *Jefferson County Lines (Quarterly) Newsletter*
$10.00 per year membership; research: donation

Knox County Chapter OGS
PO Box 1098
Mount Vernon, OH 43050-1098
(740) 392-7716
Public Library of Mount Vernon and Knox County: Mon–Fri 10:00–9:00, Sat 9:00–5:00
Pub. *Tree Climbers*, quarterly
$6.00 per year membership

Lake County Genealogical Society
Morley Public Library
184 Phelps Street
Painesville, OH 44077-3927
(440) 352-3383
LCGSOhio@juno.com
http://www.morleylibrary.org/genealogy_lcgs.htm
meetings: last Thur 10:00 A.M. (except Aug & Dec)
Pub. *Lake Lines*, quarterly
(specializes in Lake County)
$5.00 per year membership

Lawrence County Genealogical Society
PO Box 1035
Ironton, OH 45639-1035
lawcoloreman@aol.com
http://www.lawrencecountyohio.com/gensoc/gensoc.htm
Pub. *LawCo Lore*, quarterly; *The Lawrence Register—Southern Ohio's Genealogical and Historical Website, Lawrence County*, online magazine
$7.00 per year membership

Licking County Genealogical Society
101 West Main Street
Newark, OH 43058
(614) 345-3571; (614) 344-6777 (Librarian's home)
lcgs@npls.org
http://lcgs.npls.org/index.html
Betty Rose, Head Librarian
Tue–Thur & Sat 1:00–4:00, Wed (Mar–Nov) 6:30 P.M.–9:00 P.M.
Pub. *Licking Lantern*, quarterly (plus index issue)
$12.00 per year membership

Logan County Genealogical Society
(521 East Columbus Avenue—location)
PO Box 36 (mailing address)
Bellefontaine, OH 43311-0036
(937) 592-6191 (President of Society, no phone on premises)
logangs@loganrec.com; efeads@logan.net
http://www.co.logan.oh.us/museum/Genealogy/genealogy.html
Edith Eads
May–Oct: Wed & Fri 1:00–5:00, Sun 2:00–5:00; Nov–Apr: Fri 1:00–4:00
Pub. *Branches and Twigs*, quarterly
$12.00 per year membership; research: $7.00 per hour plus copies and postage

Lorain County Chapter OGS
PO Box 865
Elyria, OH 44036-0865
margral5@aol.com
http://www.centuryinter.net/lorgen
Margaret Cheney, President
Pub. *Lorain County Researcher*, quarterly
(specializes in genealogy and history of Lorain and neighboring counties in the Western Reserve)
$5.00 per year membership

Lucas County Chapter OGS
Toledo-Lucas County Public Library
Local History and Genealogy Department
325 North Michigan Street
Toledo, OH 43624-1614
rmchenry@sev.org
http://www.utoledo.edu/gried/lcogs.htm
D. R. McHenry, Corresponding Secretary
Pub. *Fort Industry Reflections*, quarterly
(Lucas County, Ohio, and state of Ohio genealogy; "sponsors First Families of Lucas County with membership limited to those who can prove descent from an early resident of Lucas County, Ohio.")
$8.00 per year membership; research: $7.00 per hour, plus photocopies at 15¢ per page and postage without SASE

Madison County Chapter OGS

PO Box 102
London, OH 43140-0102
Pub. *Madison County Chapter OGS Newsletter*
$7.00 per year membership

Mahoning County Chapter OGS
PO Box 9333
Boardman, OH 44513-9333
MCCOGS@zoominternet.net
http://www.mahoningcountychapterogs.org/chapter_website_001.htm
Judy J. Bishara, Treasurer
Pub. *Mahoning Meanderings*, nine times per year
$13.00 per year membership

Marion Area Genealogical Society
(169 East Church Street—location)
PO Box 844 (mailing address)
Marion, OH 43301-0844
rcarlcar@gte.net
http://www.rootsweb.com/~ohmags
Jane Ratterman, President
meetings: first Sat 10:00 (Mar–Dec)
Pub. *Marion Memories*, quarterly (Feb, May, Aug, Nov)
$8.00 per year membership; queries: one free query in newsletter for nonmembers, no charge for members; research: $10.00 per surname, copies: 15¢ each

Medina County Genealogical Society
PO Box 804
Medina, OH 44256-0804
ffmccoordinator@zoominternet.net
http://www.rootsweb.com/~ohmedina/index.htm/#mcgs
Pub. *Medina County Story*, quarterly
$10.00 per year membership

Meigs County Genealogical Society
Meigs County, Ohio, Chapter OGS
PO Box 346
Pomeroy, OH 45769-0346
Keith Ashley, President
Pub. *The Megaphone*, quarterly
$7.00 per year membership

Mercer County Chapter OGS
PO Box 437
Celina, OH 45822-0437
dgrace@bright.net
http://mccogs.ohgenweb.net
Dwane Grace, President
Pub. *Mercer County Monitor*, quarterly
$10.00 per year membership

Miami County Historical and Genealogical Society
(see Historical Societies—Local and Regional, above)

Monroe County Chapter OGS
PO Box 641
Woodsfield, OH 43793-0641
(740) 483-1481 (Home)
neiswong@1st.net
http://www.rootsweb.com/~ohmccogs
Karen Romick
Pub. *The Navigator*, quarterly (Jan, Apr, July, Oct)
$7.00 per year membership

Montgomery County Genealogical Society
PO Box 1584
Dayton, OH 45401-1584
(937) 274-3502; (937) 236-4617 (President)
carolynjburns@woh.rr.com
http://www.rootsweb.com/~ohmontgs
Donna Tusty, Corresponding Secretary
meetings at Dayton and Montgomery County

Public Library: second Sat 1:30–4:00
Pub. *Family Tree*, monthly
$12.00 per year membership

Morgan County Chapter OGS
PO Box 418
McConnelsville, OH 43756-0418
creed_22@hotmail.com
Verna Trayer, Corresponding Secretary
Kate Love Simpson Library: Mon–Thur 10:00–8:00, Fri–Sat 10:00–5:00
Pub. *Morgan Link*, quarterly
$8.00 per year membership; queries: free for members, $1.00 each for nonmembers; research: $10.00 donation for limited research for nonmembers, no charge for members

Morrow County Genealogical Society
PO Box 401
Mount Gilead, OH 43338-0401
patron@bright.net; b.j.gameier@juno.com
http://www.rootsweb.com/~ohmorrow
Betty Meier
Pub. *The Monument*, quarterly
$5.00 per year membership

Muskingum County Chapter OGS
(Muskingum County Library System, John McIntire Library—location)
PO Box 2427 (mailing address)
Zanesville, OH 43702-2427
BETW@prodigy.net
http://www.rootsweb.com/~ohmuskin/mccogs
Hilda E. Yinger, Librarian
Library: Mon–Tue & Thur–Sat 9:00–5:00, Wed 9:00–8:00, Sun (except summer, after Memorial Day) 1:00–5:00
Pub. *The Muskingum*, ten times per year
$10.00 per year membership

Noble County Chapter OGS
(Caldwell Public Library, Genealogy Room—library collection location)
PO Box 174 (mailing address)
Caldwell, OH 43724-0174
(740) 732-2093 (Secretary)
Susan K. Radcliff, Secretary
Caldwell Public Library: Mon–Wed 9:00–8:00, Thur–Fri 9:00–5:00, Sat 9:00–2:00; meetings at Caldwell City Hall, 215 West Street: fourth Sun (Mar, June, Sept, Oct)
Pub. *Noble County Newsletter*, quarterly
$8.00 per year membership; copies: 10¢ per page

Ottawa County Chapter OGS
PO Box 193
Port Clinton, OH 43452-0193
(419) 734-7396
kolinko@cros.net; ocgs@cros.net
http://www.rootsweb.com/~ohoccgs
Linda Kolinko, Editor; Carol Kessler, Editor
meetings: third Tue 7:00
Pub. *Marshland to Heartland*, quarterly
(Ottawa County records of genealogical interest)
$10.00 per year membership

Paulding County Genealogical Society
Paulding County Carnegie Library
Genealogy Department
205 South Main Street
Paulding, OH 45879-1492
(419) 399-4663 (evening)
Marilyn J. Smith, Corresponding Secretary
Library: Mon–Thur 9:00–8:00, Fri 9:00–5:30, Sat (Sept–May) 9:00–3:00, Sat (June–Aug) 9:00–noon; meetings: second Wed 6:30 (except July–Aug & Dec)

Pub. *Paulding Pathways*, quarterly
$10.00 per year membership; research: (in library and at courthouse) for cost of copies at 10¢ per page from paper originals, 15¢ per page from microform originals

Perry County Chapter OGS
PO Box 275
Junction City, OH 43748-0275
(740) 987-7646 (Library, for general information only)
susays@ohiohills.com
Evelyn Angle Wolfe, District Manager at Junction City Branch Library; Sue Saylor, Chapter Librarian and Corresponding Secretary
Junction City Branch Library: Mon & Wed 10:00–7:00, Fri 10:00–6:00, Sat 10:00–3:00; McGahan Historical and Genealogical Room, Perry County Public Library, 117 South Jackson Street, New Lexington 43764: Mon–Thur 9:00–8:00, Fri 9:00–6:00, Sat 10:00–3:00
Pub. *Perry County Heirlines*, quarterly (cemetery, marriage, death and census publications)
$10.00 per year membership; research: $10.00 per surname

Pickaway County Historical Society
(see Historical Societies—Local and Regional, above)

Pike County Genealogical Society
PO Box 224
Waverly, OH 45690-0224
pikeogs@hotmail.com; janiec444@yahoo.com
http://www.rootsweb.com/~ohpcgs
Janie Conklin, Treasurer
Pub. *Pike Speaks*, quarterly
$10.00 per year membership

Portage County Chapter OGS
PO Box 821
Ravenna, OH 44266-0821
http://history.portage.oh.us/genealogy_society.html
Barb Petroski, Librarian, PCHS
meetings at Portage County Historical Society: third Sat (except July–Aug & Dec)
Pub. *Portage Path to Genealogy*, eight times per year (Jan, Feb, Mar, Apr, May, Sept, Oct, Nov)
("Have genealogical library material at Reed Memorial Library and Portage County Historical Society.")
$10.00 per year membership

Preble County Genealogical Society
Preble County District Library
Preble County Room
450 South Barron Street
Eaton, OH 45320-1705
(937) 456-4331
http://www.pcdl.lib.oh.us/pcgs.htm
Susan H. Kendall, Library Director/Newsletter Editor
Mon–Fri 9:00–8:00, Sat 9:00–5:00, Sun 1:00–5:00
Pub. *Preble's Pride* (emphasis on southwest Ohio), quarterly
$15.00 per year membership

Putnam County Genealogy Society
PO Box 403
Ottawa, OH 45875-0403
(419) 523-3747
lhermill@oplin.org; lhermill@oplin.lib.oh.us
http://www.putnamgenealogy.com

Linda Hermiller, Corresponding Secretary
Heritage Room, Putnam County District
    Library: Mon–Thur 9:00–8:00, Fri–Sat
    9:00–5:00, Sat (Memorial Day
    weekend–Labor Day weekend) 9:00–1:00
Pub. *Putnam Pastfinder*, quarterly (Feb, May,
    Aug, Nov, plus an index in Dec)
    (cemetery books)
$10.00 per year membership; research: no
    fees for general index search, charge for
    postage and copies

Richland County Chapter OGS
PO Box 3823
Mansfield, OH 44907-3823
sunda@prodigy.net
http://www.rootsweb.com/~ohrichgs
Pub. *The Pastfinder*, quarterly
    ("We do not have an open library. Copies of
    all our material is given to the Ohio
    Genealogical Society's library, as we are
    in the same town.")
$10.00 per year membership

Ross County Chapter OGS
(444 Douglas Avenue—location)
PO Box 6352 (mailing address)
Chillicothe, OH 45601-6352
(740) 773-2715
rcgs@bright.net
Caroline Whitten, President; Grace Baer,
    Librarian
Mon, Wed & Fri 1:00–4:00, Thur 6:00–9:00,
    Sat 9:00–noon
Pub. *Ross County Genealogical Society
    Newsletter*, quarterly
$12.00 per year membership; research:
    $10.00 donation for search of indexes of
    material in library

Sandusky County Kin Hunters
Spiegel Grove
Fremont, OH 43420-2796
info@kinhunters.org
http://www.kinhunters.org
Pub. *Kith 'n Kin*, bimonthly
$10.00 per year membership

Scioto County Chapter OGS
PO Box 812
Portsmouth, OH 45662-0812
(740) 259-4649
information@sccogs.com
http://www.sccogs.com
Patricia Russell, Corresponding Secretary
Portsmouth Public Library: Mon–Fri
    9:00–8:00, Sat 9:00–5:30, Sun 1:00–5:00;
    meetings: second Sat of odd-numbered
    months
Pub. *Scioto County Chapter Ohio
    Genealogical Society Newsletter*,
    bimonthly
$10.00 per year membership; research $10.50
    per hour (two hour retainer); research:
    minimal research for members

Seneca County Genealogical Society
PO Box 157
Tiffin, OH 44883-0157
seneca09@senecasearchers.org
http://www.senecasearchers.org
Ruth Brill, Co-editor
Mon–Thur 10:00–9:00, Fri–Sat 10:00–5:00
Pub. *Seneca Searchers*, bimonthly
    (specializes in Seneca County, Ohio,
    genealogy)
$10.00 per year membership

Shelby Genealogical Society
Richland County-Shelby Chapter OGS
PO Box 766
Shelby, OH 44875-0766

clabaugh@richnet.net
http://www.rootsweb.com/~ohscogs
Ruby Bonecutter, Newsletter Editor
meetings at the Church of God, 3616 State
    Route 39S: first Thur (except July & Aug)
    7:00
Pub. *Shelby Spirits*, ten times per year
$10.00 per year membership

Southern Ohio Chapter OGS
Southern Ohio Genealogical Society
PO Box 414
Hillsboro, OH 45133
Pub. *Roots & Shoots*, quarterly
$9.00 per year membership

Stark County Chapter OGS
7300 Woodcrest, N.E.
North Canton, OH 44721-1949
(330) 494-9574
starkquery@yahoo.com
http://www.stark.lib.oh.us/ohiogen/Sccgs.
    html
Stark County District Library, Canton:
    second Thur 6:30
Pub. *Tree Climber*, monthly
    (books on Stark County, Ohio)
$10.00 per year membership

Summit County Chapter OGS
PO Box 2232
Akron, OH 44309-2232
(330) 699-4511
SummitOGS@ald.net
http://www.acorn.net/gen
Marilyn Kirn Kovatch, Editor
Pub. *The Highpoint*, ten times per year
    ("Primarily Summit County genealogical
    material")
$7.00 per year membership; queries: free

Trumbull County Genealogical Society
PO Box 309
Warren, OH 44482-0309
http://www.rootsweb.com/~ohtcgs
Pub. *Ancestry Trails*, monthly
$10.00 per year membership

**Tuscarawas County Genealogical Society
Library and Archives**
(307 Center Street, Dennison—location)
PO Box 141 (mailing address)
New Philadelphia, OH 44663-0141
(330) 269-2602
tcgs1@aol.com
http://web.tusco.net/tuscgen/society.htm
Keith A. Schaar, President
Apr–Setp: Tue–Sat 11:00–3:00; Oct–Mar:
    Tue, Thur & Sat 11:00–3:00
Pub. *Tuscarawas County Pioneer
    Footprints*, quarterly (Feb, May, Aug,
    Nov)
(Tuscarawas County and surrounding
    counties; Moravian history and ancestry)
$12.00 per year membership; admission:
    $2.00 for nonmembers over 18

Union County Genealogical Society
(Marysville Public Library, 231 South Court
Street—location)
PO Box 438 (mailing address)
Marysville, OH 43040-0438
(937) 642-4694; (937) 642-6147 (Secretary);
    (937) 642-1876
dgresh@urec.net
http://www.rootsweb.com/~ohuniogs
Dorothy McKitrick, Corresponding
    Secretary; Mary Seslar, Secretary
meetings: third Tue (except Dec) 7:00
Pub. *Union Echoes*, bimonthly
$8.00 per year membership; unlimited
    queries free for members, one free query

for nonmembers; research: limited to
    Union County only, $10.00 deposit

Van Wert County Chapter OGS
PO Box 485
Van Wert, OH 45891-0485
http://www.rootsweb.com/~ohvanwer
Carol Thomas, President
Brumback Library, Second floor: Mon–Thur
    9:00–8:00, Fri–Sat 9:00–5:00
Pub. *The Van Wert Connection*, quarterly
    (spring, summer, fall, winter)
$10.00 per year membership

**The Vinton County Historical &
Genealogical Society, Inc.**
Chapter OGS
(see Historical Societies—Local and
Regional, above)

Warren County Genealogical Society
406 Justice Drive
Lebanon, OH 45036
(513) 695-1144
wcgs@co.warren.oh.us
http://www.co.warren.oh.us/genealogy/
    index.htm
Diana Linkous, President
Resource Center/Library in the Warren
    County Administration Building: Mon–Fri
    9:00–4:00
Pub. *Heir-Lines*, quarterly, $3.00 per issue
    ("We have a large collection of Warren
    County records, easily accessible by
    indexes: birth, marriages, cemeteries,
    deaths, obits, census, will and estate,
    guardianship, microfilms, CDs, etc. Our
    collection extends to other Ohio counties
    and other states. We also have biographies,
    vertical files, and family folders on many
    surnames.")
$10.00 per year membership; queries: three
    free queries for members, $3.00 per query
    for nonmembers; research: available

Washington County Chapter OGS
PO Box 2174
Marietta, OH 45750-2174
(740) 373-1641
Sharon Cory Gardner, Newsletter Editor
Washington County Public Library:
    Mon–Thur 9:00–8:30, Fri–Sat 9:00–5:00
Pub. *Washington*, quarterly
$8.00 per year membership

Wayne County Genealogical Society
PO Box 856
Wooster, OH 44691-0856
(330) 264-3413
http://www.rootsweb.com/~ohwayne/
    wcgs.htm
Robert Gates, President
meetings at Wayne County Public Library:
    first Sat (except Dec) 2:00
Pub. *Wayne Ancestors*, quarterly (spring,
    summer, fall, winter)
$12.00 per year membership; $10.00
    application for Pioneer Families

Williams County Genealogical Society
PO Box 293
Bryan, OH 43506-0293
(419) 636-4151
webmaster@wcgs-ogs.com
http://www.wcgs-ogs.com
Alice Shaffer, President
meetings in the Community Room, East End
    Pool, East High Street, Bryan, OH: second
    Mon 7:30 P.M.
Pub. *Ohio's Last Frontier*, quarterly; *Monthly
    Messenger*
    ("The society maintains a surname file in

addition to pedigree charts submitted by WCGS members; this file is maintained at the Bryan Public Library; has set up a First Families of Williams County, open to WCGS members who can provide documentation proving a direct line ancestor residing in what was known as Williams County, Ohio, as of 1860.")
$12.00 per year membership

Wood County Chapter OGS
Wood County Genealogical Society
(Local and Family History Center, Office Building, Courthouse Square—location)
PO Box 722 (mailing address)
Bowling Green, OH 43402-0722
wcogs@wcnet.org
http://www.rootsweb.com/~ohwccogs
Chloe Genson, Editor
Mon–Fri 9:00–noon
Pub. *Newsletter of Wood County Genealogical Society*, bimonthly, back issues $5.00 per year plus $2.50 postage and handling
("Any member of the Wood County Chapter of the Ohio Genealogical Society is eligible for membership in First Families of Wood County provided the member can prove that one or more direct ancestors lived in Wood County on or before December 31, 1855.")
$10.00 per year membership, $15.00 for application in FFWC

Wyandot Tracers: Wyandot County Genealogical Society
PO Box 414
Upper Sandusky, OH 43351-0414
http://www.udata.com/users/hsbaker/tracers.htm
Jean Moon, President
Upper Sandusky Community Library:
Mon–Fri 9:00–9:00, Sat 9:00–1:00
Pub. *Newsletter*, bimonthly
$8.00 per year membership

Out-of State OGS Chapters

Florida Chapter OGS
PO Box 466
Melrose, FL 32666-0466
betdaclwho@aol.com
http://www.rootsweb.com/~flfcogs
Damon Hostetler, President
meetings: third weekend in Feb
Pub. *The Quest*, bimonthly (Jan, Mar, May, July, Sept, Nov)
$10.00 per year membership; no research services; copies: 20¢ per page from paper originals, 25¢ per page from microform originals

Genealogical Societies—Local & Regional

The Adams County Genealogical Society
(Adams County Heritage Center, State Route 247 North and Heritage Way—location)
PO Box 231 (mailing address)
West Union, OH 45693
(937) 544-8522
acgs@bright.net
http://www.bright.net/~acgs
Thur & Sat noon–4:00
Pub. *Our Heritage*, quarterly
$10.00 per year membership

Alexander Local Genealogical and Historical Society
2565 Pleasant Hill Road
Athens, OH 45701
M. L. Bowman

Crawford County Genealogical Society
(see Crawford County Chapter OGS, State Genealogical Society, OGS Chapters, above)

Cumberland Trail Genealogical Society
(Saint Clairsville Public Library—collection location)
PO Box 576 (mailing address)
Saint Clairsville, OH 43950
(740) 695-2062 (Library); (740) 676-4132 (Rick Sowinski); (740) 695-1355 (Kim Conley)
Rick Sowinski and Kim Conley, Co-Presidents
meetings: second Mon 6:30
Pub. *Trail Blazer*
(primarily interested in Belmont County, but also the surrounding counties of Monroe, Noble, Guernsey, Harrison and Jefferson; county histories, family genealogies, local census, local newspapers, Ohio Civil War Veterans, cemetery records, obituary file, surname file, etc.)
$10.00 per year membership

Fostoria Lineage Research Society
Kaubisch Library
205 Perry Street
Fostoria, OH 44830-2265
http://www.fostoria.org/history/Genealogy
Jan Herbert, Vice President
meetings: third Mon (except through the summer)
$5.00 per year membership; will answer queries for cost of postage and photocopies

Friends of the Library Genealogical Research Group
1268 Kenwood Avenue
Springfield, OH 45505-3253
(937) 323-2905
SylviaROlson@juno.com
http://www.rootsweb.com/~ohflgrg
Sylvia Ridenour Olson
(Many publications listed on web site.)
$3.00 per year membership

KYOWVA Genealogical Society
(see West Virginia, Part 2)

Meigs County Pioneer and Historical Society, Inc.
Meigs County Museum
144 Butternut Avenue
Pomeroy, OH 45769
(740) 992-3810
Margaret Parker, President
Tue–Fri 1:00–4:30
Pub. *Meigs County Historian*, quarterly
$10.00 per year membership; museum admission: $1.00 donation

Miami Valley Council on Genealogy and History
4290 Honeybrook Avenue
Dayton, OH 45415
(937) 290-2811
Wright State University, Special Collections and Archives: Mon–Fri 8:30–5:00, Tue & Wed (academic quarter only) 7:00 P.M.–10:00 P.M., Sun (academic quarter only) 2:00–5:00
Pub. *The History Tree*, quarterly
$10.00 per year membership

Pioneer and Historical Society of Muskingum County
(304 Woodlawn Avenue—location)
PO Box 2201 (mailing address)
Zanesville, OH 43701-4940
(740) 454-9500

Wendell Litt, Director
Pub. *Quarterly*
$7.50 per year membership

Northwest Territory Genealogical Society
(see Indiana, Part 2)

Northwestern Ohio Genealogical Society (NWOGS)
(see Toledo Area Genealogical Society, below)

Shelby County Genealogical Society
c/o 17755 State Route 47
Sidney, OH 45365-9242
(937) 492-0071 (Editor)
Betty Bevans, Editor
Pub. *Shelbyana*, quarterly (Jan, Apr, July, Oct)
(specializes in Shelby County, Ohio)
$10.00 per year membership (1 or 2 people at same address); research: Barbara Adams, Researcher, 21674 Dingman-Slagle Road, Sidney, OH 45365-9140, (937) 492-2742

South Central Ohio Genealogical Society
PO Box 6352
Chillicothe, OH 45601

Southwest Butler County Genealogical Society
c/o Soldiers, Sailors and Pioneers Monument
3 South Monument Avenue
Hamilton, OH 45011

Toledo Area Genealogical Society
PO Box 352258
Toledo, OH 43635-2258
dianepatton@att.net
http://www.tagsohio.org
Diane Patton, Corresponding Secretary
meetings in the Common Space I on Reynolds Road between Dorr and Bancroft Streets: second Mon (Sept–May) 7:00
Pub. *Newsletter—Northwestern Ohio Genealogical Society Newsletter*, quarterly
(Formerly the Northwestern Ohio Genealogical Society.)
$10.00 per year membership

Tri-State Genealogical Society
(see West Virginia, Part 2)

Wayne County, Indiana, Genealogical Society
(see Indiana, Part 2)

Wellington Genealogy Group
PO Box 224
Wellington, OH 44090
Linda Navarre, President
meetings at Wellington Town Hall: first Wed
$10.00 per year membership

Independent Publications and Miscellany

Canal Society of Ohio
Summit County Historical Society
550 Copley Road
Akron, OH 44320
Pub. *Towpaths*, quarterly, $10.00 per year library subscription
$18.00 per year membership

Council of Historic Institutions and Preservation Societies (CHIPS) (Summit and Portage Counties)
The Hudson Library and Historical Society
22 Aurora Street
Hudson, OH 44236

(330) 653-6658 (Library); (330) 650-4693
FAX (Library)
James F. Caccamo, Director and Library
Archivist
Library: Mon–Thur 9:00–9:00, Fri–Sat
9:00–5:00; Archives: Mon–Sat 9:00–5:00

Darke County Ohio Genealogical Researchers
jetorres@indiana.edu
http://php.ucs.indiana.edu/~jetorres/dco.html
Jane Barr Torres

Direct Line Software
Land Record Reference
(see Miscellaneous, Part 4)

East Fork Valley Consortium
Box 500
Williamsburg, OH 45176
meetings at Bank One: second Thur 6:30
(made of the Harmony Hill Association,
Clermont County Historical Society,
Grassy Run Historical Arts Committee,
and June in Olde Williamsburg [q.v.])

Electronic Oberlin Group Website
Oberlin Organization and Their Histories
(address withheld upon request)
Gary.Kornblith@oberlin.edu
http://www.oberlin.edu/EOG
Gary J. Kornblith, Professor of History and
Webmaster
(pictures and short biographies of people in
Oberlin's history; images of buildings and
landmarks in Oberlin, past and present;
short histories of local organizations,
including churches; records from
Oberlin's past, including census data; links
to other web sites relevant to Oberlin;
Oberlin History Timeline through 1900)

French Ancestors
2923 Tara Trail
Beavercreek, OH 45434-6252
(937) 429-2979
doylemr@aol.com
Marianne R. Doyle
Pub. *French Ancestors*, bimonthly, $8.00 per
year subscription
("This is a small newsletter which deals with
the French ancestors of families who
settled in western Ohio in the mid-1800s,
includes extracts from original French
records and cultural, historical, and
genealogical information of general
interest.")

Genealogical Research and Consultation
(12 Residence Drive—location)
PO Box 119 (mailing address)
Washington Court House, OH 43160-0119
(740) 335-0266; (740) 333-3530 FAX
Ms. Sandy Fackler, Editor and Publisher
Pub. *The Fayette County Journal of
Genealogy and History*, quarterly, $20.00
per year subscription

Governor's Office of Veterans' Affairs
65 South Front Street, Suite 426
Columbus, OH 43215
(614) 728-0155
Frank Mechem, Administrative Assistant
8:00–4:30
(maintains wartime discharge papers and
form DD-214; Civil War records, etc.)

H-Ohio
History and Culture of the State of Ohio
H-Ohio-request@h-net.msu.edu
http://www2.h-net.msu.edu/~ohio
H-Ohio Editors
(history discussion network)

Historic New Richmond
(Ross-Gowdy House, 125 George
Street—location)
PO Box 2 (mailing address)
New Richmond, OH 45147
(513) 553-9770
Nrohist@aol.com
http://www.historicnewrichmond.org
Hazel Davis, Curator
Sun 1:00–5:00, and by appointment;
meetings: fourth Thur

Historic Perrysburg, Inc.
(420 East Front Street—location)
PO Box 703 (mailing address)
Perrysburg, OH 43551
(419) 874-2815

**Historic Preservation Guild of Hancock
County**
(315 East Crawford—location)
PO Box 621 (mailing address)
Findlay, OH 45840
Rev. James H. Nye, President and Curator
second & fourth Sat & Sun 1:00–4:00
Pub. *Patchworks of History*
(owns and operates the 1840 DeWald-Funk
House Museum)
$10.00 per year membership; museum
admission: $3.00 for adults

Historic Southwest Ohio, Inc.
The John Hauck House Museum
812 Dayton Street
Cincinnati, OH 45214
(513) 721-3570
Janet H. Hauck, Manager of Hauck House
Fri–Sun 1:00–5:00, and by appointment
(a house museum in the 19th-century
townhouse of German brewer John
Hauck)
$20.00 per year membership

**Hunting for Bears Genealogical and
Historical Society**
(see Alabama, Part 2)

Miami Valley Genealogical Index
Computerized Heritage Association
Joe.boss@voyager.net
http://www.pcdl.lib.oh.us/miami/miami.htm
Joe Bosserman

Michiana History Publications
(see Indiana, Part 2)

Muskingum County Footprints
2740 Adamsville Road
Zanesville, OH 43701-8461
(740) 453-8231
hyinger@msmisp.com
Hilda E. Yinger, Co-Author
Pub. *Muskingum County Footprints*
(Muskingum County records and
miscellaneous information, church, school
and newspaper extracts), semiannually,
costs vary with size of publication

OhGenWeb
Part of The USGenweb Project
sciototrails@iname.com;
jkelble@accnorwalk.com
http://www.scioto.org/OHGenWeb
Allen Richmond, State Coordinator; Judy
Kelble, Assistant Coordinator
(links to other Ohio resources)

Ohio Department of Transportation
1980 West Broad Street
Columbus, OH 43223
(614) 466-7170; (614) 844-8662
http://www.dot.state.oh.us/dist1/

planning/ohio_maps.htm (Maps)

Ohio River Valley Families
daved@orvf.com
http://orvf.com
A. David Distler
("companion web site includes a searchable
genealogy database of over 97,000
individuals focused on early settlers of the
Ohio Valley," families that at any time
lived within fifty miles of the Ohio River,
which runs through or borders on
Pennsylvania, West Virginia, Ohio,
Kentucky, Indiana, Illinois)

Ohio State Land Office
88 East Broad Street
Columbus, OH 43266-0040
Auditor

Ohioana Library Association
274 East First Avenue
Columbus, OH 43201
(614) 466-3831; (614) 728-6974 FAX
ohioana@sloma.state.oh.us
http://www.oplin.lib.oh.us/OHIOANA
Barbara Meister, Librarian
Mon–Fri 8:30–4:30
Pub. *Ohioana Quarterly* (not genealogical,
contains reviews of books written by
Ohioans or about Ohio), quarterly (Mar,
June, Sept, Dec), $20.00 per year
subscription
(archive for works by and about
Ohio/Ohioans, with biographies of over
10,000 Ohio writers, also music, William
Dean Howells, and family histories)

Pioneer Publications
PO Box 1179
Tumtum, WA 99034-1179
(509) 276-1740
Shirley Penna-Oakes, Editor
Pub. *Ohio Queries*, $6.00 plus $1.75 postage
per issue; *OH-IN-IA Queries & Reviews*,
$6.00 plus $1.75 postage per issue

Ridgewood Preservation, Inc.
256 21st Street, N.W.
Canton, OH 44709
(330) 454-8471

Tiffin Historic Trust
(172 Jefferson Street—location)
PO Box 333 (mailing address)
Tiffin, OH 44883
(419) 447-4789
Mary Lewis, Treasurer
by appointment
(local preservation)

Ulysses S. Grant Birthplace
1591 SR 232
Point Pleasant, OH 45153
(513) 553-4911
Nrohist@aol.com
http://www.historicnewrichmond.org/
grantsbirghplace.html
Apr–Oct: Wed–Sat 9:30–5:30, Sun
noon–5:00
(primarily historical: artifacts, furniture and
photographs, not genealogical)

Van Wert and Surrounding Counties, Ohio
19133 Plum Street
Venedocia, OH 45894
(419) 667-3151
Lois Bassett, Editor and Owner
Pub. *Van Wert and Surrounding Counties,
Ohio* (early county records of genealogical
interest, every-name index), annually,
$14.50 per year issue

Anadarko Community Library
215 West Broadway
Anadarko, OK 73005-2841
(405) 247-7351; (405) 247-2024 FAX
library@netride.net
Christina Owen, Director

Oklahoma

Archives and Libraries with Holdings in Genealogy

State Archives and Library

Oklahoma State Archives and Records Management
The Oklahoma Department of Libraries
200 N.E. 18th Street
Oklahoma City, OK 73105-3298
(405) 521-2502 (Department of Libraries);
(405) 521-2502 (Archives and Records);
(800) 522-8116; (405) 525-7804 FAX
http://www.odl.state.ok.us/oar/index2.htm
Gary Harrington, Head, Archives Division
Mon–Fri 8:00–5:00

State Historical Society

Oklahoma Heritage Association
Oklahoma Heritage Center
(201 N.W. 14th Street—location)
1500 North Robinson (mailing address)
Oklahoma City, OK 73103
(405) 235-4458; (888) 501-2059; (405) 235-2714 FAX
oha@oklahomaheritage.com
http://www.oklahomaheritage.com
Paul Lambert, Ph.D., Executive Director
Pub. *Oklahoma Heritage News*

Oklahoma State Historical Society and Museum
Wiley Post Historical Building
2100 North Lincoln Boulevard
Oklahoma City, OK 73105-4997
(405) 521-2491; (405) 521-2492 FAX
libohs@ok-history.mus.ok.us
http://www.ok-history.mus.ok.us
Laura Martin, Library Staff
Mon 9:00–7:45, Tue–Sat 9:00–4:45
Pub. *Mistletoe Leaves*, monthly; *The Chronicles of Oklahoma*, quarterly
(family histories, Oklahoma history—including local and county histories; Native Americans of Oklahoma)
$20.00 per year membership; research: $15.00 for all out-of-state letters, plus photocopies and shipping (to be invoiced)

City, County and Regional Archives and Libraries
(A more exhaustive list of public and academic libraries can be found at http://www.odl.state.ok.us/go/pl.asp.)

Altus Public Library
Southern Prairie Library System
421 North Hudson Street
Altus, OK 73521
(580) 477-2890; (580) 477-3626 FAX
spls@spls.lib.ok.us
http://www.spls.lib.ok.us
Tammy Davis (Genealogy/Reference)
Mon & Fri–Sat 10:00–6:00, Tue & Thur 10:00–9:00
("Concentrating collecting information on 'Old Greer County, Oklahoma,' including current counties of Jackson, Greer, Harmon, and Beckham.")

Alva Public Library
(504 Seventh Street—location)
PO Box 234 (mailing address)
Alva, OK 73717
(580) 327-1833; (580) 327-5329 FAX
alvalib@alvaok.net
http://www.alvaok.net/alvalib
Larry Thorne, Library Director

Mon 10:00–9:00, Tue–Sat 10:00–5:30

Ardmore Public Library
320 E Street, N.W.
Ardmore, OK 73401
(580) 223-8290; (580) 223-2033 FAX
cfranks@ardmorepublic.lib.ok.us
http://www.ardmorepublic.lib.ok.us
Carolyn Franks, Director
Mon–Thur 10:00–8:30, Fri–Sat 10:00–4:00
(home of Mac McGalliard Historical Collection of local history)

Ataloa Lodge Museum
(On the campus of Bacone College—location)
2299 Old Bacone Road (mailing address)
Muskogee, OK 74403
(918) 683-4581, ext. 283; (918) 687-5913 FAX
Thomas R. McKinney, Museum Director
Mon–Fri 10:00–4:00
(Dawes Commission papers)

Atoka County Library
215 East A Street
Atoka, OK 74525
(405) 889-3555; (580) 889-8860 FAX
crlsato@oltn.odl.state.ok.us
http://www.regional-sys.lib.ok.us
Alice Withrow, Director

Bartlesville Area History Museum
401 South Jonnstone
Bartlesville, OK 74003
(918) 338-4290; (918) 337-5336; (918) 337-5338 FAX
http://www.bartlesvillehistory.com/home.html
Karen Smith Woods, Director/Curator; Mary Campbell, Collections Coordinator
Tue–Sat 10:00–4:00
Pub. *Newsletter*

Bartlesville Public Library
600 South Johnstone
Bartlesville, OK 74003
(918) 337-5333 (Local and Family History Area); (918) 337-5353; (918) 337-5338 FAX
genealogy@bartlesville.lib.ok.us
http://www.bartlesville.lib.ok.us
Joan Singleton, Library Director
Mon–Thur 9:00–9:00, Fri–Sat 9:00–5:30
(Cherokee and Delaware Rolls, local newspaper from 1895, Indiana Territory and Oklahoma Territory census, federal census indices for all states and all years as available.)

Buckley Public Library
Genealogy Department
408 Dewey Avenue
Poteau, OK 74953
(918) 647-3833; (918) 647-8910 FAX
neff@sepl.lib.ok.us
http://www.sepl.lib.ok.us
Elizabeth Neff, Librarian
Mon–Fri 9:00–6:00, Sat 9:00–3:00

Center for Great Plains Studies
(see Kansas, Part 2)

Center for Great Plains Study
(see Nebraska, Part 2)

Chandler-Watts Memorial Library
History-Genealogy Department
(321 North Oak—location)
PO Box 696 (mailing address)
Stratford, OK 74872
Kay Sumner, Director

9:00–6:00, Tue 9:00–8:00

Cherokee City-County Public Library
602 South Grand Avenue
Cherokee, OK 73728
(580) 596-2366; (580) 596-2968 FAX
cherlb_2000@yahoo.com
Mary Berry
Mon–Fri 1:00–6:00, Sat 9:00–noon

Chickasha Public Library
527 West Iowa Avenue
Chickasha, OK 73018
(405) 222-6075; (405) 222-6072 FAX
cathcook@chickasha.lib.ok.us
Catharine Cook, Director

Choctaw County Library
208 East Jefferson
Hugo, OK 74743
(405) 326-5591; (580) 326-7388 FAX
braddock@sepl.lib.ok.us
http://www.sepl.lib.ok.us
Sharyl Braddock, Librarian

Coal County Historical and Mining Museum, Inc.
212 South Broadway
Coalgate, OK 74538-2612
(580) 927-2360; (580) 927-2060 (Board Chairman)
ginna@mmind.net (Board Chairman)
Geraldine Vance, Tour Director; Virginia Townsend, Board Chairman
Tue–Fri 10:00–4:00
("Have many Coal County courthouse records, naturalization records, Indian Territory marriage records; WPA census, cemetery records.")

Cushing Public Library
(215 North Steele—location)
PO Box 551 (mailing address)
Cushing, OK 74203
(918) 225-4188; (918) 225-6201 FAX
ruthannjohnson2002@yahoo.com
Ruth Ann Johnson, Director

El Reno Carnegie Library
Archives Room
215 East Wade
El Reno, OK 73036
(405) 262-2409; (405) 422-2136 FAX
ercl215@netscape.net
Dianne Costin, Director
Mon–Fri 9:00–5:00, Sat 9:00–1:00

Elk City Carnegie Library
221 West Broadway
Elk City, OK 73644
(580) 225-0136; (580) 225-1051 FAX
elkcity_lib@itlnet.net
Pat Sprowls, Director

Public Library of Enid and Garfield County
(120 West Maine, Enid, OK 73701—location)
PO Box 8002 (mailing address)
Enid, OK 73702-8002
(580) 234-6313; (580) 233-2948 FAX
wlarrison@enid.lib.ok.us
http://www.enid.org/library.htm
Wilita Larrison, Director
Mon–Thur 9:00–9:00, Fri–Sat 9:00–6:00, Sun 1:00–6:00

Fairview City Library
(115 South Sixth Street—location)
PO Box 419 (mailing address)
Fairview, OK 73737
(580) 227-2190; (580) 227-2187 FAX

fairviewlibrary@yahoo.com
http://www.fairview.org

Fort Sill Museum
Department of Army
437 Quanah Road
Fort Sill, OK 73503-5100
(580) 442-5123
Towana D. Spivey, Director/Chief Curator
7:30–4:30
Pub. *Fort Sill Museum*
(specializes in Native Americans and frontier military)
free

Gateway to the Panhandle
PO Box 27
Gate, OK 73844
(580) 934-3133
Florence Whisenhurt, Curator
Mon–Sat 1:00–6:00

Thomas Gilcrease Institute of American History and Art
1400 Gilcrease Museum Road
Tulsa, OK 74127-2100
(918) 596-2700 voice & FAX
Sarah Erwin, Curator of Archival Collections
Tue–Sat 9:00–5:00, Sun & federal holidays 11:00–5:00
Pub. *Gilcrease Journal*, two times per year
(historical archives, documents and maps)
$30.00 per year out-of-state membership

Grove Public Library
1140 NEO Loop
Grove, OK 74344
(918) 786-2945; (888) 291-8150 (free from within 918 area code); (918) 786-5233 FAX
grovepl@eodls.lib.ok.us
http://www.eodls.lib.ok.us/grove.html
Marcia Austin, Librarian
Mon, Wed & Fri 8:30–5:00, Tue & Thur 8:30–9:00, Sat 8:00–noon
(Member Eastern Oklahoma District Library System. Delaware and adjoining counties, Cherokee records, all Oklahoma censuses, Soundex for 1900 Indian Territory and Oklahoma Territory, excellent general collection.)

John F. Henderson Memorial Library
(116 North Williams—location)
PO Box 580 (mailing address)
Westville, OK 74965-0580
(918) 723-5002; (888) 291-8147; (918) 723-3400 FAX
jfhenderson@eodls.lib.ok.us
http://www.eodls.lib.ok.us
Sue Ann Ghormley, Branch Manager

Idabel Public Library
(2 Southeast Avenue D—location)
PO Box 778 (mailing address)
Idabel, OK 74745
(580) 286-6406; (580) 286-3708 FAX
potts@sepl.lib.ok.us
http://www.sepl.lib.ok.us
Linda Potts, Librarian
9:00–6:00

Montfort and Allie B. Jones Memorial Library
111 West Seventh Avenue
Bristow, OK 74010-2401
(918) 367-6562; (918) 367-1156 FAX
dlawrence@bristow.lib.ok.us
http://www.bristow.lib.ok.us
Donna Lawrence, Director
(census and newspapers)

Kennedy Library of Konawa
Route 1, Box 3
Konawa, OK 74849
(580) 925-3662; (580) 925-3882 FAX
http://www.konawa.k12.ok.us
Karla Davis, Director
Mon–Fri (during school year) 8:00–3:30, Mon–Tue (summer) 8:00–3:30, Thur 6:00–8:00

Lawton Public Library
Family History Research Room
110 S.W. Fourth Street
Lawton, OK 73501
(580) 581-3450; (580) 248-0243 FAX
http://www.cityof.lawton.ok.us/library
Paul Follett, Genealogy Librarian
Mon–Thur 10:00–9:00, Fri 10:00–6:00, Sat 10:00–5:00, Sun (Sept–May) 1:00–5:00
(emphasis on Oklahoma, the south, and Native Americans—houses the Kowa, Comanche, and Apache (KCA) Research Collection; has little on other tribes)

Layland Museum
(see Texas, Part 2)

Mangum Civic Center and Public Library
Margaret Carder Library
203 West Lincoln
Mangum, OK 73554
(580) 782-3185; (580) 782-5308 FAX
mangumlib@mangum.lib.ok.us
http://www.rootsweb.com/~okgcghs/mcl.html
Pub. Mon–Fri 10:00–noon & 1:00–5:00, Sat 9:00–noon

Martin East Regional Library
2601 South Garnett Road
Tulsa, OK 74129
(918) 669-6340; (918) 669-6344 FAX
cchilto@tulsalibrary.org
http://www.tulsalibrary.org
Christy Chilton, Director

McAlester Public Library
401 North Second Street
McAlester, OK 74501
(918) 426-0930; (918) 423-5731
whanway@sepl.lib.ok.us;
sauro@sepl.lib.ok.us
http://www.mcalester.lib.ok.us
Wayne Hanaway, Executive Director; Christine Sauro, Librarian
Mon–Tue & Thur 9:00–8:00, Wed & Fri 9:00–5:00, Sat 9:00–1:00

Metropolitan Library System
Downtown Library
Charles E. France Room, Oklahoma Collection
131 Dean A. McGee Avenue
Oklahoma City, OK 73102
(405) 231-8650; (405) 232-5493 FAX
http://www.mls.lib.ok.us
Kay Bauman, Library Manager
Mon & Wed–Thur 9:00–6:00, Tue 9:00–9:00, Fri & Sat 9:00–5:00
(limited genealogical use, *Daily Oklahoman* on microfilm but no index)
copies: 25¢ per page plus postage

Metropolitan Library System
Ralph Ellison Library
2000 N.E. 23rd
Oklahoma City, OK 73111
(405) 424-1437; (405) 424-1443 FAX
Ralphellison@mls.lib.ok.us
http://www.mls.lib.ok.us/Library/re.htm
Darcus D. Smith, Director
Mon–Thur 9:00–8:00, Fri 9:00–6:00, Sat

9:00–5:00

Miami Public Library
200 North Main
Miami, OK 74354
(918) 541-2292; (918) 542-3064; (918) 542-9363 FAX
mjohnson@miami.lib.ok.us
http://www.miami.lib.ok.us
Marcia Johnson, Director
Mon & Wed–Thur 9:00–8:00, Tue & Fri–Sat 9:00–5:00, Sun 1:00–5:00

Muldrow Public Library
(City Hall Building, 100 South Main Street—location)
PO Box 449 (mailing address)
Muldrow, OK 74948-0449
(918) 427-6703; (888) 291-8153; (918) 427-7315 FAX
bethiaowens@eodls.lib.ok.us
http://www.eodls.lib.ok.us
Bethia Owens, Branch Manager

Museum of the Great Plains
(601 Ferris—location)
PO Box 68 (mailing address)
Lawton, OK 73502
(580) 581-3460; (580) 581-3458 FAX
Steve Wilson, Director (History)
Mon–Fri 8:00–5:00
Pub. *Great Plains Journal*, annually;
   Museum of the Great Plains Newsletter,
   $15.00 per year subscription
(specializes in ten-state Great Plains region:
   Colorado, Kansas, Montana, North
   Dakota, Nebraska, New Mexico,
   Oklahoma, South Dakota, Texas, and
   Wyoming)
$30.00 per year membership

Museum of the Western Prairie
(1100 North Hightower—location)
PO Box 574 (mailing address)
Altus, OK 73521
(580) 482-1044

Muskogee Public Library
801 West Okmulgee
Muskogee, OK 74401
(918) 682-6657, ext. 257
history@eok.lib.ok.us
http://www.eok.lib.ok.us
Wally Waits, Head of Genealogy and Local History
Mon–Thur 9:00–9:00, Fri 9:00–6:00, Sat 9:00–4:00

Norman Public Library
225 North Webster
Norman, OK 73070
(405) 321-1481; (405) 360-7007 FAX
http://www.pioneer.lib.ok.us
Tue–Thur 1:00–5:00, Sat 9:00–3:00

Northeastern State University
John Vaughan Library/Learning Resources Center
(see Ethnic Archives, Libraries and Societies—Native American, Part 3)

Oklahoma City University
Archives and Special Collections
Dulaney-Browne Library
2501 North Blackwelder
Oklahoma City, OK 73106
(405) 521-5067
cwolf@okcu.edu
http://www.okcu.edu/library/ar.htm
Christina Wolf, Archivist
Mon–Fri 8:30–5:00 by appointment only
("The Archives and Special Collections

department includes the Archives of the Oklahoma Conference of the United Methodist Church, University Archives, and the George Shirk Oklahoma History Center.")

Oklahoma State Museum
Wiley Post Historical Building
2100 North Lincoln Boulevard
Oklahoma City, OK 73105
(405) 521-2491

Oklahoma State University
OSU Library, Special Collections
Stillwater, OK 74078
(405) 744-6311
Heather Lloyd

Oklahoma Territorial Museum
406 East Oklahoma Avenue
Guthrie, OK 73044-3317
(405) 282-1889
Wayne A. Ward, Museum Supervisor
(genealogical services)

Old Greer County Museum and Hall of Fame, Inc.
222 West Jefferson
Mangum, OK 73554-4022
(580) 782-2851
Shirley Stark, Co-Curator
Tue–Fri 9:00–noon
(genealogical services)
$25.00 per year membership; donation accepted for searches

Perry Carnegie Library
302 North Seventh Street
Perry, OK 73077
(405) 336-4721; (580) 336-5497 FAX
staff@perry.lib.ok.us
Karen Bigbee, Head Librarian
Mon 1:00–6:00, Tue–Fri 9:00–6:00, Sat 9:00–noon

Pioneer Museum and Art Center
2009 Williams Avenue
Woodward, OK 73801-5717
(580) 256-6136
http://www.museumstuff.com/details/org_20020201_16165.html
Kathy Smith, Assistant Curator; Joyce Read, Tourism
10:00–5:00
(family history books 1915–1994, 1910 plat book)

Ponca City Cultural Center and Indian Museum
1000 East Grand Avenue
Ponca City, OK 74601
(580) 762-6123
Delia F. Castor, Curator

Ponca City Library
515 East Grand Avenue
Ponca City, OK 74601
(580) 767-0345; (580) 767-0377 FAX
Loyd M. Bishop, Genealogy Librarian
Mon–Thur 9:00–9:00, Fri 9:00–6:00, Sat 9:00–5:00, Sun (during school year) 2:00–5:00
("Library with local history and genealogy. 3,500 volumes of books, 6,000 microfilm.")

Prague Historical Museum
(1008 North Jim Thorpe Boulevard—location)
N.B.U. 8601 (mailing address)
Prague, OK 74864
(405) 567-4750

Diane Kinzey, President
Mon, Wed & Fri 1:00–4:00
Pub. *Newsletter*, biannually
("The museum has the area cemetery records. Our history book is a one-time publication done this year as our city celebrates its Centennial. *Prague, the First One-hundred Years*.")
$10.00 per year membership

Sapulpa Public Library
27 West Dewey
Sapulpa, OK 74066-3909
(918) 248-5979 (Genealogy); (918) 224-3546 FAX
sapulpalibrary@yahoo.com
Barbara Carter, Genealogy Librarian
Genealogy: Mon & Thur noon–8:00, Tue noon–7:00, Wed noon–6:00, Fri 10:00–5:00, Sat 9:00–1:00
copies: 25¢ each plus SASE

Schusterman Benson Library
Tulsa City County Library System
3333 East 32nd Place
Tulsa, OK 74135
(918) 746-5027; (918) 746-5026 FAX
khuber@tulsalibrary.org
http://www.tulsalibrary.org
Kathy Huber, Genealogy Librarian
Mon–Thur 10:00–8:00, Fri–Sat 10:00–5:00, Sun (Sept–May) 1:00–5:00
(emphasis on five civilized tribes, eastern and southern states)

Southern Methodist University
Clements Center for Southwest Studies
(see Texas, Part 2)

Stephens County Historical Museum
PO Box 1294
Duncan, OK 73534
(580) 252-0717
Don Stevens, Director
(genealogical services)

Stillwater Public Library
1107 South Duck
Stillwater, OK 74074
(405) 372-3633; (405) 624-0552 FAX
libdirector@stillwater.org
http://www.stillwater.lib.ok.us
Lynda Reynolds, Director
Mon–Thur 9:00–9:00, Fri–Sat 9:00–6:00, Sun 1:00–5:00

The Talbot Library and Museum
(406 South Colcord Avenue—location)
PO Box 349 (mailing address)
Colcord, OK 74338-0349
(918) 326-4532
Donna Clark, Secretary
Tue–Fri 9:00–5:00, Sat 1:00–5:00
Pub. *T.L.& M. Genealogy Magazine*,
   bimonthly, $15.00 per year subscription;
   Goingsnake Messenger, quarterly, $15.00 per year subscription
("We are a research library, specializing in N.E. Oklahoma, N.W. Arkansas and Cherokee area genealogy and history. We also have a museum of local history and artifacts.")
details of membership program upon request; no admission fee

Stanley Tubbs Memorial Library
101 East Cherokee
Sallisaw, OK 74955-4621
(918) 775-4481 voice & FAX
http://www.eodls.lib.ok.us

University of Oklahoma

Western History Collections
630 Parrington Oval, Room 452
Norman, OK 73069
(405) 325-3641; (405) 325-6069 FAX
http://www.lib.uoknor.edu/depts/west/
    index.htm
Bradford Koplowitz, Assistant Curator
Mon–Fri 8:00–5:00, Sat 8:00–noon (during
    school year)

University of Tulsa
McFarlin Library
2933 East Sixth Street
Tulsa, OK 74104-3123
(918) 631-2880; (918) 631-3791 FAX
http://www.utulsa.edu
(Cherokee, Choctaw and Creek manuscripts,
    Oklahoma history and special collections)

University of Utah Marriott Library
(see Utah, Part 2)

Vinita Public Library
Maurice Haynes Memorial Building
215 West Illinois Avenue
Vinita, OK 74301
(918) 256-2115; (918) 256-2309 FAX
staff@vinita.lib.ok.us
http://www.vinitapl.okpls.org
Susan Ryals, Director
Mon & Thur 10:00–8:00, Tue–Wed & Fri
    noon–6:00, Sat 10:00–4:00

Watonga Public Library
301 North Prouty Avenue
Watonga, OK 73772
(580) 623-7748; (580) 623-7747 FAX
bookwoman@watonga.lib.ok.us
http://www.watonga.com/library

Waynoka Public Library
113 East Cecil
Waynoka, OK 73860
(580) 824-6181
waynokalibrary@hotmail.com
Mae Converse, Librarian
Mon–Fri 10:00–noon & 1:00–5:30
("complete microfilm copies of Waynoka
    newspapers from the 1890s, also area
    towns' newspapers: Quinlan, Alva, Avard,
    Dacoma, Freedom, and others")

Weatherford Public Library
(address withheld upon request)

(houses the collection of the Western Plains-
    Weatherford Genealogy Society)

Western Heritage Center
(see Montana, Part 2)

Woodward Public Library
Genealogy Department
1500 Main Avenue
Woodward, OK 73801
(580) 254-8544; (580) 254-8546 FAX
cterry@woodward.lib.ok.us
Connie Terry, Director
Mon–Sat

Historical Societies—Local and Regional

Adair County Historical and Genealogical Association
Adair County History Commission
Rural Route 6, Box 1775
Stilwell, OK 74960-8716
(918) 696-2749
http://www.rootsweb.com/~okadair/
    achga.html

Virgie Starr, Treasurer
daily 8:00–10:00
(specializes in history of Adair County,
    Cherokee history, genealogy; publication
    sold out)

Alfalfa County Historical Society Museum
(119 West Main—location)
PO Box 201 (mailing address)
Cherokee, OK 73728
(580) 596-2513
Nancy Harmon, President
Tue & Thur–Fri 10:00–5:00
Pub. *Alfalfa County Historical Society
    Newsletter*, quarterly
$10.00 per year membership

American West Research Center and Historical Society, Inc.
(see Ohio, Part 2)

Apache Historical Society
(100 West Evans—location)
PO Box 101 (mailing address)
Apache, OK 73006
(405) 588-3392
Mary Joyce Swanda, Secretary-Treasurer
Mon–Fri 1:00–5:00
(very little research material)
$10.00 per year membership

Arbuckle Historical Society of Murray County
402 West Muskogee Street
Sulphur, OK 73086
(580) 622-5593
Roland Earsom, Grant Chairman
Thur 11:00–4:00, Fri & Sat 10:00–4:30, Sun
    1:00–4:00

Arkansas River Historical Society Museum
5350 Cimarron Road
Catoosa, OK 74015
(918) 266-2291; (918) 266-7678 FAX
museum@tulsaport.com
http://www.tulsaweb.com/port
Allan Avery, Curator
Mon–Fri 8:00–4:30
Pub. *Reflections*, two times per year, free on
    request
(covers Oklahoma, Arkansas, Kansas and
    Colorado region)

Atoka County Historical Society
(Confederate Memorial Museum, Highway
    69 North—location)
PO Box 245 (mailing address)
Atoka, OK 74525
(580) 889-7192
okcoatoka@usgennet.org
http://www.usgennet.org/usa/ok/county/
    atoka/ConfMuseum.html
Gwen Walker, Site Manager; Ruth Atteberry
    Adams, Webmaster
Mon–Sat 9:00–4:00, Sun noon–4:00
Pub. *Confederate Memorial Museum
    Newsletter*, quarterly
$5.00 per year membership; research:
    $20.00, includes search of local funeral
    home records, cemetery inventory,
    marriage records and newspaper files for
    obituaries if a death date is supplied, and
    copies if appropriate

Beaver County Historical Society, Inc.
Beaver County Fairgrounds
PO Box 457
Beaver, OK 73932
(580) 625-4439
Jean Long, Curator
Wed–Sat 1:30–5:30, Sun 1:30–4:30

$10.00 per year membership

Beaver River Genealogical and Historical Society
(see Genealogical Societies—Local and
    Regional, below)

Bixby Historical Society
PO Box 1046
Bixby, OK 74008
bixby.okhs@cox.net
http://www.rootsweb.com/~okbhs
Loueen Morgan, First Vice President
Pub. *The Review*
$10.00 per year membership

Broken Arrow Historical Society and Museum
1800 South Main Street
Broken Arrow, OK 74012-6503
(918) 258-2616
http://www.brokenarrowok.gov/our-
    citizens/quality_life/city_partners_historic
    al.htm.htm
Tue–Fri noon–4:00 Sat 10:00–2:00
$10.00 per year membership

Bryan County Heritage Association, Inc.
(203 North McKinley—location)
PO Box 153 (mailing address)
Calera, OK 74730
(580) 434-5848
wellis@redriverok.com
http://www.rootsweb.com/~okbcha
Wanda Shelton, Treasurer
Mon–Fri 10:00–4:00
Pub. *Bryan County Heritage Quarterly* (May,
    Aug, Nov, Feb)
$12.50 per year membership

Canadian County Historical Society
600 West Wade
El Reno, OK 73036
(405) 262-5121
Pub. *Canadian County Historical Society*,
    monthly
$10.00 per year membership

Canadian Rivers Historical Society
R.P. 1, Box 135
Geary, OK 73040

Cherokee Dixieland Historical Society/Museum
Webbers Falls Historical Society/Museum
Commercial and Main Streets
Webbers Falls, OK 74470
(918) 464-2728

Choctaw Historical Society/Choctaw Caboose Museum
(Corner of N.E. 23rd and Henney
    Road—location)
2701 North Triple XXX Road (mailing
    address)
Choctaw, OK 73020-8402
(405) 390-2771
Grady A. O'Connor, Custodian of Museum
Memorial Day–Labor Day: Sat 10:00–4:00,
    Sun 2:00–5:00, and by appointment

Coal County Historical and Genealogical Society
PO Box 436
Coalgate, OK 74538
(580) 927-3103
rheawat@mmind.net
http://www.rootsweb.com/~okcoalgs
Doris Breger, Vice President
Tue & Thur–Fri 4:00–6:30; meetings second
    Mon 7:00 P.M.
Pub. *Coal County News Letter*, bimonthly

$10.00 per year membership

Cotton County Historical Society
Walters Museum
116 North Broadway
Walters, OK 73572
(580) 875-3335
Byrleta Holt, President

Delaware County (Oklahoma) Historical Society
(538 Krause Street—museum location)
PO Box 567 (mailing address)
Jay, OK 74346
(918) 253-4345
Wynona S. Nelson, Curator
Mon, Wed & Fri 1:00–4:00
Pub. *Heritage of the Hills*, two times per year (spring and fall)
$15.00 per year

Dewey County Historical Society
Route 1, Box 53
Camargo, OK 73835
(580) 328-5623

Drummond Historical Society
402 South Main
Drummond, OK 73735
dkaupke@enid.com
Dovie A. Kaupke

Drumright Historical Society, Inc.
Drumright Community Historical Museum
301 East Broadway Street
Drumright, OK 74030
(918) 352-3002
info@drumrighthistoricalsociety.org
http://www.drumrighthistoricalsociety.org
Wed–Fri noon–4:00, Sat 9:00–5:00
$7.00 per year membership

Eastern Oklahoma Historical Society and Carl Albert State College
Robert S. Kerr Museum
Route 1, Box 1060
Poteau, OK 74953
(918) 647-9579
Carol A. Spindle, Director
Mon–Fri 9:00–5:00, Sat–Sun 1:00–5:00 (groups by appointment)
("Contains Senator Robert S. Kerr memorabilia, two Viking rune stones, Spiro Mounds artifacts, pioneer items." Covers seven counties. Cherokee and Choctaw Indians.)
donation accepted

Edmond Historical Society and Museum
431 South Boulevard
Edmond, OK 73034
(405) 340-0078; (405) 340-2771 FAX
http://www.edmondhistory.org
Claudia Miller, President; Brenda Granger, Executive Director
Tue–Fri 10:00–4:00, Sat 1:00–4:00
Pub. *The Society Report*, three times per year (genealogy computer center)
$25.00 per year membership

The Ellis County Historical Society
Route 2, Box 92
Arnett, OK 73832
(580) 885-7705 (after 9:00 P.M.)
echslfox@pldi.net
http://www.usgennet.org/usa/ok/county/ ellis/elgensoc.html
Linda Fox, President
online until 9:00 P.M.
$3.00 per year membership; research: by donation

Fairfax Area Historical Society

332 South Fourth
Fairfax, OK 74637
(918) 642-3834
Mary L. Clement, Treasurer

Fort Gibson Genealogical and Historical Society
(see Genealogical Societies—Local and Regional, below)

Garfield County Historical Society
PO Box 3337
Enid, OK 73702

Goingsnake District Heritage Association
John F. Henderson Memorial Library
PO Box 180
Westville, OK 74965
(918) 326-4532 (Editor at The Talbot Library and Museum)
Virgil Talbot, Editor and Historian
Pub. *The Goingsnake Messenger*, quarterly, $4.25 per issue
$10.00 per year membership

Grady County Historical Society
(415 West Chickasha Avenue, Chickasha, OK 73018—location)
PO Box 495 (mailing address)
Chickasha, OK 73023
Ms. Adrian M. Drew, Secretary
Tue–Sat 10:00–4:00
$20.00 per year membership

Grant County Historical Society and Museum
(Cherokee and Main—location)
PO Box 31 (mailing address)
Medford, OK 73759-0031
(580) 395-2888; (580) 395-2822; (580) 395-2343 FAX
Wed 2:00–5:00
$5.00 per year membership; $5.00 for research

Haskell County Historical and Genealogical Society
(Haskell County Historical Museum, 204 East Main Street—location)
PO Box 481 (mailing address)
Stigler, OK 74462
(918) 967-8681
http://www.rootsweb.com/~okhaskel/ hasksoc.htm
Vivian Hickman, Treasurer
Mon–Wed 10:00–2:00; meetings: last Thur every other month
$5.00 per year membership

Haskell County Historical Society
204 East Main Street
Stigler, OK 74462
http://www.rootsweb.com/~okhaskel/ hasksoc.htm

Hughes County Historical Society
114 North Creek Street
Holdenville, OK 74848
(405) 379-6723

Johnston County Genealogical and Historical Society
(see Genealogical Societies—Local and Regional, below)

Latimer County Genealogical and Historical Society
(see Genealogical Societies—Local and Regional, below)

Lincoln County Historical Society
Museum of Pioneer History

717-719 Manvel on Route 66
Chandler, OK 74834-2842
(405) 258-2425
lchs@brightok.net
http://www.rootsweb.com/~okgenweb/ helplinks/lincoln.html
Jeanette Haley, Curator
Mon–Fri 9:30–4:00, Sat (Apr–Dec) 9:30–2:00
Pub. *Lincoln County Historical Society Newsletter*, quarterly
(artifacts in museum, cemetery records of Lincoln County, census, newspapers on microfilm, family and town history)
$15.00 per year membership; admission: donation; research: $10.00

Logan County Historical Society
(107 East Oklahoma Avenue—location)
119 South Broad (mailing address)
Guthrie, OK 73044
(405) 282-3706

Love County Historical Society, Inc.
Pioneer Museum
(101 S.W. Front—location)
PO Box 134 (mailing address)
Marietta, OK 73448
(580) 276-2869
Laquitta Ladner, President and Newsletter Editor
closed for repairs
Pub. *LCHS Newsletter*, quarterly ("Oklahoma history, area history, genealogy")
$10.00 per year membership

Major County Historical Society
Fairview, OK 73737
(580) 227-2265

Mayes County Historical Society, Inc.
Coo-Y-Yah County Museum
(Eighth Street and South 69 Highway—location)
PO Box 969 (mailing address)
Pryor, OK 74362
(918) 825-2222
http://www.pryorwebdesign.com/pryor/ pryor.html
Mrs. William M. Thomas, President
Tue–Wed & Sat–Sun 1:00–4:00
Pub. *NewsLetter*, quarterly, free

McClain County Historical and Genealogical Society
203 Washington Street
Purcell, OK 73080-4227
(405) 527-5894
http://www.rootsweb.com/~okmchgs/ mchgs.htm
Joyce A. Rex, Curator and County Historian
McClain County Museum: Mon–Fri noon–4:00, and by reservation (five days in advance)
Pub. *McClain County, Oklahoma Historical and Genealogical Society Quarterly* (Feb, May, Aug, Nov)
(Old Pontotoc County, Chickasaw Nation, Indian Territory; obituary abstraction in progress, microfilm of territorial records and family histories. Published *1890 Census and 1878 Annuity Rolls of Chicawaw Nation, Indian Territory*; *History and Heritage of McClain County, OK*; *McClain Co., OK, Marriages, 1863–1895, Plus Matrimonial Miscellany (formerly Old Pontotoc Co., Chick Na., Ind. Terr.*; and *McClain Co., OK, Death Records, 1880–1984.*)
$8.00 per year membership

Mounds Historical Society, Inc.

PO Box 274
Mounds, OK 74047
History@Mounds.org
http://www.mounds.org/history
meetings at Mounds Christian Church: first
Thur 7:00
$10.00 per year membership

Newkirk Community Historical Society
(101 South Maple Street—location)
500 West Eighth (mailing address)
Newkirk, OK 74647
(580) 362-3330
Karen Dye, Project Director
Sun 2:00–4:00
$4.00 per year membership

No Man's Land Historical Society and Museum
(207 West Sewell Street—location)
PO Box 278 (mailing address)
Goodwell, OK 73939
(580) 349-2670
Dr. Kenneth R. Turner, Director
Tue–Sat 9:00–noon & 1:00–5:00
Pub. *Vox Nemenis*, quarterly
("Area newspapers, archives, some civil
records, photographs related to Oklahoma
Panhandle.")
$15.00 per year membership

North Central Oklahoma Historical Association
(417) East Grand Avenue—location)
PO Box 2811, Department DP (mailing
address)
Ponca City, OK 74602
(580) 765-4600; (580) 765-7169
http://www.brigadoon.com/~famfox/
ncohafrt.htm

Nowata County Historical Society
121 South Pine Street
Nowata, OK 74048-3413
(918) 272-1191
Maudie Randall, Curator
Pub. *NCHS Newsletter*

Okfuskee County Historical Society
407 West Broadway Street
Okemah, OK 74859-2401
(918) 623-2027

Oklahoma County Historical Society
Museum of the Unassigned Lands
4300 North Sewell
Oklahoma City, OK 73118
(405) 521-1889
Margaret R. Woods, Curator
Mon, Wed & Fri 10:00–3:00, Tue & Thur by
appointment for groups
Pub. *Oklahoma County Historical Society
Newsletter*, quarterly
("The Museum of the Unassigned Lands tells
the story of the Oklahoma land run of
1889.")
$10.00 per year membership

Osage County Historical Society
(700 North Lynn Avenue—location)
PO Box 267 (mailing address)
Pawhuska, OK 74056
(918) 287-9924; (918) 287-9119 (Museum)
ochm@husky-net.net
http://www.osagecohistoricalmuseum.com
Betty W. Smith, Director
Mon–Fri 9:00–5:00

Owasso Historical Society
PO Box 1481
Owasso, OK 74055
OwassoOklahoma@yahoo.com

http://www.rootsweb.com/~okohs
Laura Goumaz Flebbe
$5.00 per year membership

Pawnee County Historical Society
(605 Fifth Street—location)
PO Box 472 (mailing address)
Pawnee, OK 74058
(918) 762-3881
Dana Hicks, President
Wed 10:00–4:00, and by appointment

Payne County Historical Society
PO Box 2262
Stillwater, OK 74076
customfinancialgroup@juno.com
http://www.cowboy.net/non-
profit/pchs/pchs.htm
Pub. *Payne County Historical Review*,
semiannually
$12.00 per year membership

Perkins Historical Society, Inc.
PO Box 788
Perkins, OK 74059-0788
perkinshis@aol.com
http://members.aol.com/perkinshis

Pioneer Historical Society
1127 South Seventh Street
Ponca City, OK 74601-6712

**Pittsburg County Genealogical and
Historical Society**
(see Genealogical Societies—Local and
Regional, below)

**Plains Indians and Pioneers Historical
Foundation**
Plains Indians and Pioneers Museum
2009 Williams Avenue
Woodward, OK 73801-5717
(580) 256-6136; (580) 256-2577 FAX
pipm@swbell.net
http://www.lasr.net/leisure/oklahoma/
woodward/woodward/att1.html
Frankie A. Herzer, Director
Tue–Sat 10:00–5:00, Sun 1:00–4:00
(Southern Cheyenne and Arapaho Indians
and European settlers)
admission: donation

**Pontotoc County Historical and
Genealogical Society**
Mattie Logsdon Memorial Library
221 West 16th Street
Ada, OK 74820
PeggySAtwood@aol.com
http://www.rootsweb.com/~okpontgs
Peggy Dean-Atwood
Mon–Wed 12:30–4:00, second Sat
9:00–2:00; meetings: third Mon 10:00
Pub. *Pontotoc County Quarterly*
$15.00 per year membership; admission: 50¢
for members, $2.00 for nonmembers

Historical Society of Pottawatomie County
1301 East Farrall
Shawnee, OK 74801
(405) 273-5062

Pushmataha County Historical Society
(125 West Main Street—location)
PO Box 285 (mailing address)
Antlers, OK 74523
(580) 587-2304 (President)
Myrtle Edmond, President
Tue 9:00–noon
$10.00 per year membership; research: $5.00
donation to research library

Red River Valley Historical Association

Southeastern Oklahoma State University
PO Box 4014
Durant, OK 74701
(580) 924-0121, ext. 203

Rogers County Historical Society
PO Box 774
Claremore, OK 74018
jcary3@aol.com
http://www.rchs1.org
$10.00 per year membership

Sapulpa Historical Society, Inc.
(100 East Lee Street, Sapulpa, OK
74066—location)
PO Box 278 (mailing address)
Sapulpa, OK 74067
(918) 224-4871; (918) 224-7765 FAX
saphistsoc@juno.com
Doris R. Yocham, President
Mon–Thur 10:00–3:00
Pub. *Our Heritage*, bimonthly

Sayre Historical Society
Shortgrass Country Historical
Society/Museum
106 East Poplar Avenue
Sayre, OK 73662
(580) 928-5757

Sod House Museum and Historical Society
Rural Route 1
Aline, OK 73716
(580) 463-2441

Southwestern Oklahoma Historical Society
PO Box 3693
Lawton, OK 73502-3693
http://www.sirinet.net/~lgarris/swogs
Alicia Abbott, Corresponding Secretary
Pub. *Prairie Lore*, semiannually (Apr, Oct)
(covers Beckham, Caddo, Comanche, Cotton,
Grady, Greer, Harmon, Jackson, Jefferson,
Kiowa, Stephens, Tillman, and Washita
counties)
$10.00 per year membership

**Tillman County Historical and Educational
Society**
(Tillman County Historical Museum, 201
North Ninth Street—location)
PO Box 833 (mailing address)
Frederick, OK 73542
(580) 335-5844; (580) 335-2805 (President);
(580) 335-7541 (Musuem)
bradbenson@pldi.net
http://www.frisco.org/msw/mswtil.htm
Frances Goodknight, President; Bradford Lee
Benson
Wed & Sat–Sun 2:00–4:00, and by
appointment
Pub. *TCHES Newsletter*, annually
$5.00 per year membership; no research
services

**Tonkawa Historical Society and McCarter
Museum of Tonkawa History**
(220 East Grand Avenue—location)
PO Box 27 (mailing address)
Tonkawa, OK 74653
(580) 628-2895
marilee@kskc.net
Marilee Helton, President
Mon–Sat 1:00–3:00
$10.00 per year membership

Top of Oklahoma Historical Society
303 South Main
Blackwell, OK 74631-3347
(580) 363-0209
Ocie Anderson, Director

Tulsa County Historical Society
2445 South Peoria
Tulsa, OK 74114
(918) 712-9484; (918) 712-1939 FAX
ths@tulsahistory.org
http://www.tulsahistory.org
$25.00 per year membership

Turley Historical Society
6540 North Peoria Avenue
Tulsa, OK 74126
(918) 425-8429

Washington County Historical Society, Inc.
PO Box 255
Bartlesville, OK 74003
(918) 333-0073

Washita County Historical Society
(115 East First Street—location)
PO Box 153 (mailing address)
Cordell, OK 73632
(580) 343-2554
Wayne Boothe, President
Fri, and by appointment
Pub. *Annual Report* (Jan)
("10,000 items of Washita County history.")
$5.00 per year membership

Waynoka Historical Society
(202 South Cleveland—location)
PO Box 193 (mailing address)
Waynoka, OK 73860
(580) 824-1886; (580) 824-5871
waynokahs@hotmail.com
http://www.pldi.net/~harpo
Sandra Olson, President
Thur–Sat 6:00–8:00, and by appointment
("historical society, air and rail museum")
$25.00 per year membership

Webbers Falls Historical Society/Museum
(see Cherokee Dixieland Historical
Society/Museum, above)

Western Trail Historical and Genealogical Society
Museum of the Western Prairie
(1100 North Hightower—location)
PO Box 574 (mailing address)
Altus, OK 73521
(580) 482-1044 (Museum)

Western Trails Museum
2229 Gray Freeway
Clinton, OK 73601
(580) 323-1020

Wynnewood Historical Society
Route 1, Box 189
Wynnewood, OK 73098

Genealogical Societies

State Genealogical Societies

Genealogical Institute of Oklahoma
3813 Cashion Place
Oklahoma City, OK 73112
Pub. *Dusty Trails*, quarterly

Federation of Oklahoma Genealogical Societies (FOGS)
PO Box 26151
Oklahoma City, OK 73126-0151
Pub. *Newsletter*, quarterly; *Directory of Oklahoma Sources*, annually

Oklahoma Genealogical Society
(Wiley Post Historical Building, 2100 North
Lincoln Boulevard, Oklahoma City, OK
73105—meetings location)

PO Box 12986 (mailing address)
Oklahoma City, OK 73157-2986
(405) 528-7460 (Officer's home)
okgensoc@aol.com; RondaRed@aol.com
(Webmaster for inquiries concerning web
site)
http://www.rootsweb.com/~okgs
Billie Fogarty, President; Rhonda Redden,
Webmaster
meetings in the auditorium: first Mon 6:00
Pub. *Oklahoma Genealogical Society
Quarterly*
$15.00 per year membership; research:
$15.00 per hour plus copies (send
payment for first hour and SASE)

Genealogical Societies—Local & Regional

Adair County Historical and Genealogical Association
(see Historical Societies—Local and
Regional, above)

Apache Area Genealogical Society
(224 East Evans Avenue—location)
PO Box 999 (mailing address)
Apache, OK 73006
ryoung9583@aol.com
Roy B. Young, President
by appointment
("Research library. Published *Centennial
History Book*.")
$10.00 per year membership

Atoka County Genealogical Society
PO Box 245
Atoka, OK 74525

Bartlesville Genealogical Society
Bartlesville Public Library
600 South Johnstone
Bartlesville, OK 74003
Pub. *Bartlesville Genealogical Society
Newsletter*, monthly
$9.00 per year membership

Beaver River Genealogical and Historical Society
Route 1, Box 79
Hooker, OK 73945
(580) 652-2716; (580) 652-2766 FAX
jdjok@ptsi.net
Dallas Mayer, Founder
Mon–Sun 9:00–10:00
Pub. *Beaver River News*, bimonthly
$10.00 per year membership; research: $5.00
plus copy cost

Bristow Genealogical Society
418 East Second
Bristow, OK 74010
(918) 367-6633
Leatha Morton, Secretary
volunteer
("Our club very seldom meets but I still
answer requests as secretary.")
$10.00 per year membership

Broken Arrow Genealogical Society
(The Main Place, 1800 South Main Street,
Broken Arrow, OK 74012-6503—location)
PO Box 1244 (mailing address)
Broken Arrow, OK 74013-1244
(918) 251-8155 (Librarian); (918) 455-8619
(Editor)
http://www.rootsweb.com/~okbags
Rosemary Paul, Librarian; Marmie Apsley,
Editor
Tue, Thur & Sat noon–4:00
Pub. *The Green Country Quarterly*
$10.00 per year membership

Caddo County Genealogical Society
Anadarko Community Library
215 West Broadway
Anadarko, OK 73005-2841
ccgs73005@yahoo.com
http://www.rootsweb.com/~okcadcgs

Canadian County Genealogical Society
PO Box 866
El Reno, OK 73036
(405) 262-2409; (405) 262-1551
CANCOGEN@aol.com
http://www.rootsweb.com/~okccgs
Joann Nitzel, President
Archives Room, Carnegie Library: Mon–Fri
9:00–5:00, Sat 9:00–1:00
(information on Fort Reno and Fort Reno
Cemetery; over 400 microfilm rolls of
county newspapers, probate records and
marriages, also census 1890–1920, county
history book and county family history
book)
$10.00 per year membership; research: $6.00
per hour plus cost of copies and postage

Choctaw County Genealogical Society
703 East Jackson
Hugo, OK 74743
jimblankenship43@sbcglobal.net
http://www.rootsweb.com/~okccgs2
Jim Blankenship, President
Pub. *Drum Beats Newsletter*, quarterly
$15.00 per year membership

Cleveland County Genealogical Society/Library
(Park Plaza II Building, 1005 North Flood,
Suite 136, Norman, OK 73069—location)
PO Box 6176 (mailing address)
Norman, OK 73070
(405) 329-9180; (405) 329-4481 (Library)
ccgs@coxinet.net
http://www.rootsweb.com/~okccogs
Olier Valliere, Library Director; Alan
Montgomery, President
Tue, Thur & Sat 1:00–5:00, closed football
Saturdays
Pub. *Cleveland County Genealogical Society
Newsletter*, quarterly
$15.00 per year membership

Coal County Historical and Genealogical Society
(see Historical Societies—Local and
Regional, above)

Cotton County Genealogy Society
202 North Broadway
Walters, OK 73572
mmlmw711@cs.com; leew@ionet.net

Craig County Oklahoma Genealogical Society
(Vinita Public Library, 215 West
Illinois—location)
PO Box 484 (mailing address)
Vinita, OK 74301
(918) 256-2115 (no research); (918) 256-
2309 FAX
kavolscof@junct.com
Connie Schofield, President
Mon & Thur noon–8:00, Tue–Wed & Fri
noon–6:00, Sat noon–4:00
Pub. *Craig County Genealogical Society
Newsletter*, two times per year
(specializes in Cherokee Indians and
Cherokee Nation records and local history)
$3.00 per year membership; research: $5.00
plus SASE for one hour, $7.50 per hour
thereafter

Creek County Genealogy Society

DMcda6708@aol.com
Diann McDaniel

Cushing Genealogical Society
c/o Cushing Public Library
PO Box 551
Cushing, OK 74203
pattib@brightok.net
http://www.rootsweb.com/~okcgs
Patti Brandle
meetings in the basement of the Cushing
    Public Library: first Mon 7:00
Pub. newsletter, quarterly
$15.00 per year membership

Delaware County Genealogical Society
Grove (Oklahoma) Public Library
1140 NEO Loop
Grove, OK 74344
dcgsinc@hotmail.com
("Volunteers are available at times. Inquire
    ahead.")
Pub. *Delaware Family Trail*, quarterly
$7.50 per year membership; research: send
    queries by mail or email ("Volunteers will
    reply.")

Edmond Genealogical Society
Edmond Historical Society and Museum
431 South Boulevard
Edmond, OK 73034
Gb4886@aol.com
http://www.rootsweb.com/~okegs/index.htm
Gene Burleson
meetings: second Mon (Sept, Nov, Jan, Mar,
    May)

**Elk City Genealogical Society of Western
Oklahoma**
1119 Crestview Drive
Elk City, OK 73644

Fairfax Genealogical Society
432 South Fifth Street
Fairfax, OK 74637

Family Finders Genealogy Club
PO Box 738
Nowata, OK 74048

**Fort Gibson Genealogical and Historical
Society**
PO Box 804
Fort Gibson, OK 74434
Pub. *Newsletter of the Fort Gibson
    Genealogical and Historical Society*,
    quarterly
$5.00 per year membership

Frontier Researchers Genealogical Society
(see Arkansas, Part 2)

Garfield County Genealogical Society
PO Box 1106
Enid, OK 73702-1106
loburd59@hotmail.com
Lois Burdick; Teresa Yoho Ballard, Editor
Pub. *Roots and Branches*, quarterly (May,
    Aug, Nov, Feb)
$15.00 per year membership

Grady County Genealogical Society
PO Box 767
Chickasha, OK 73023-0767
(405) 224-7482
Jean Moore, Treasurer; Janell Looney, Editor
9:00–5:30, Mon & Thur 9:00–8:00
Pub. *Grady County Genealogical Society
    Newsletter*, quarterly (spring, summer, fall,
    winter)
$12.00 per year membership

**Greer County Genealogical and Historical
Society**
Mangum Civic Center and Public Library
Margaret Carder Library
203 West Lincoln
Mangum, OK 73554
http://www.rootsweb.com/~okgcghs
Hettie Day, Member; Mary Beth Jones,
    President
meetings: third Tue (Sept–May6:00
Pub. *Greer Frontier*, semiannually
$10.00 per year membership; research:
    $10.00 for census or newspapers

Harmon County Genealogical Society
102 West Broadway Street
Hollis, OK 73550-4202
(580) 688-9545; (580) 688-2622 FAX

**Haskell County Historical and
Genealogical Society**
(see Historical Societies—Local and
Regional, above)

**Johnston County Genealogical and
Historical Society**
PO Box 705
Tishomingo, OK 73460
(580) 371-3351

**Kingfisher-Blaine Counties Genealogical
Society**
kbcgs73750@yahoo.com
meetings at Chisholm Trail Historical
    Museum (see Miscellaneous, Part 4): first
    Thur (except Apr, July & Oct) 6:00;
    meetings at Watonga Library: first Thur
    6:00
$15.00 per year membership; research:
    $10.00 per hourplus copies and postage

Kiowa County Genealogical Society
PO Box 191
Hobart, OK 73651-0191
kcgenealogy@itlnet.net
Donnie Young, President

Konawa Genealogy Society
(Kennedy Library of Konawa, at Konawa
Public Schools, 700 West South
Street—location)
Route 1, Box 3 (mailing address)
Konawa, OK 74849
konawa_genealogy@yahoo.com
http://marti.rootsweb.com/Konawa
June Neal, Secretary; Anita Ranells,
    Treasurer
meetings: second Thur 7:00
Pub. *String of Beads*, quarterly
("Working on Seminole County abstracting
    cemeteries, marriages, school districts,
    etc.; trying to preserve Seminole County
    records")
$10.00 per year membership; research: free
    to members, fee according to work needed
    for nonmembers

**Latimer County Genealogical and
Historical Society**
PO Box 1
Wilburton, OK 74578
lcghs@eosc.edu; lcghs@eosc.cc.ok.us
Hoyt Duncan

LeFlore County Genealogist
(Route 2, Box 55—location)
1003 Highland (mailing address)
Wister, OK 74966
(918) 655-3126
Gloryann Hankins Young
(eastern Oklahoma and western Arkansas
    research books)

catalog for SASE

Logan County Genealogical Society, Inc.
(Oklahoma Territorial Museum, 406 East
Oklahoma Avenue—location)
PO Box 1419 (mailing address)
Guthrie, OK 73044-1419
shranch@aol.com
http://www.rootsweb.com/~oklcgs
Lola Price, Secretary
Research library may be used by
    appointment; library is unstaffed, but
    available same hours as Museum; closed
    Mondays and federal holidays
Pub. *LCGS Quarterly*
$15.00 per year membership

Major County Genealogical Society
PO Box 74
Fairview, OK 73737
MajorCoOK@yahoo.com
http://www.rootsweb.com/~okmajor/
    mcgs.htm
meetings in the Fairview City Library: first
    Tue 7:00
$10.00 per year membership; research: $5.00
    per hour plus copies

Mayes County Genealogical Society
PO Box 924
Chouteau, OK 74337
meetings at the Pryor Public Library, 505
    East Graham, Pryor, OK: second Mon
    7:00
Pub. *TreeSearchers*, quarterly
$10.00 per year membership

**McClain County Historical and
Genealogical Society**
(see Historical Societies—Local and
Regional, above)

McCurtain County Genealogy Society
PO Box 1832
Idabel, OK 74745
(580) 286-6406
mcgs@oio.net
http://www.rootsweb.com/~okmcgs/
    index.html
Idabel Public Library: 9:00–6:00
Pub. *Intikba*, quarterly
$10.00 per year membership

McCurtain Genealogical Society
dfsumner@crosstel.net
http://members.tripod.com/mccurtain_2/
    index.htm
(Haskell County, Oklahoma)

**The McIntosh County Lake Eufaula Area
Genealogical Society**
PO Box 1035
Eufaula, OK 74432
Loy Sunday, President
Pub. *McIntosh County Lake Eufaula Area
    Genealogical Society Newsletter*, quarterly

Muldrow Genealogical Society
(Muldrow Public Library—location)
PO Box 349 (mailing address)
Muldrow, OK 74948-0349
Pub. *Newsletter*, quarterly (Mar, June, Sept,
    Dec)
$5.00 per year membership

Muskogee County Genealogical Society
Muskogee Public Library
801 West Okmulgee
Muskogee, OK 74401
mucogeso@yahoo.com
http://www.rootsweb.com/~okmuscgs
Cleo Shamblin, Vice President

Pub. *Muskogee County Genealogical Society Quarterly*, $8.00 per year subscription
$10.00 per year membership

Noble County Genealogical Society
601 12th Street
Perry, OK 73077

Noble County Genealogy Society
1409 Country Club Drive
Perry, OK 73077
Dr. Charles Martin

North Caddo Genealogical Society
PO Box 425
Hinton, OK 73047
Geneyag@hintonet.net

Northwest Oklahoma Genealogical Society
(Woodward Public Library, 1500 Main Avenue, Woodward, OK 73801—location)
PO Box 834 (mailing address)
Woodward, OK 73802
echslfox@pldi.net (Editor)
http://www.usgennet.org/usa/ok/county/
    dewey (Dewey County); http://www.
    usgennet.org/usa/ok/county/ellis (Ellis
    County); http://www.usgennet.org/usa/
    ok/county/harper (Harper County); http://
    www.rootsweb.com/~okmajor/major.htm
    (Major County); http://www.usgennet.
    org/usa/ok/county/woodward (Woodward
    County)
Christy Siemsen, Vice President; Linda Fox,
    Keyfinder Editor; Donna Dryer,
    Webmaster
meetings at Woodward Public Library: third
    Tue 6:00
Pub. *Key Finder*, four times per year (spring,
    summer, fall, winter), $3.00 per issue
    subscription (exchange program available)
("Covers four northwest counties in
    Oklahoma [Woodward, Ellis, Dewey,
    Harper]. We have a genealogical room at
    the [Woodward] Public Library that has all
    the material for this society.")
$15.00 per year membership; 50-word
    queries free to members, $2.00 for
    nonmembers; research: fees vary
    depending on type of request (newspaper,
    microfilm, courthouse, travel, etc.), plus
    copy costs

Okmulgee County Genealogical Society
PO Box 805
Okmulgee, OK 74447
Johnny Johnson, President
Pub. *Newsletter*, semiannually
$8.00 per year membership

Osage County Genealogical Society
301 East Sixth Street
Pawhuska, OK 74056
Juanita Neighbors, Secretary-Treasurer
Mon–Fri 8:00–6:00, Sat 8:00–4:00
(Osage Indian research, Osage County
    research)
$7.00 per year membership

Ottawa County Genealogical Society
PO Box 1383
Miami, OK 74354
meetings third Mon 7:00 in the Nine Tribes
    Towers Dining Room
Pub. *Smoke Signals*, quarterly
(specializes in Oklahoma and American
    Indian genealogy)
$10.00 per year membership; research: $8.00
    per hour

Payne County Genealogical Society
PO Box 2708

Stillwater, OK 74076
PCGSOK@yahoo.com
http://www.pcgsok.org
Mary Alice Foster, Secretary
Pub. *The Recorder*, three times per year
$15.00 per year membership; research:
    $10.00 per hour

Pioneer Genealogical Society
(Ponca City Library, 515 East
    Grand—location)
PO Box 1965 (mailing address)
Ponca City, OK 74602-1965
JnMilStafford@cableone.net
http://www.kaycounty.info/pgs/frtpage.html
Jay Stafford, Project Chairman
Pub. *Pioneer Genealogical Society
    Newsletter*, quarterly, $5.00 per year
    subscription
(Cherokee Strip Land Run, computer users'
    group)
$8.00 per year membership

**Pittsburg County Genealogical and
Historical Society**
113 East Carl Albert Parkway
McAlester, OK 74501
(918) 426-0388
tobucksy@osu-ext.pittsburg.ok.us
http://www.osu-
    ext.pittsburg.ok.us/tobucksy/history.htm
Mon–Fri 9:00–3:00, Sat 10:00–4:00
Pub. *Tobucksy News*, three times per year,
    $3.50 per issue
(also Indian genealogical resource)
$15.00 per year membership; research: free
    except for copies and postage

**Pontotoc County Historical and
Genealogical Society**
(see Historical Societies—Local and
Regional, above)

Poteau Valley Genealogical Society
(Buckley Public Library, 408
Dewey—location)
PO Box 1031 (mailing address)
Poteau, OK 74953-1031
dbrown@clnk.com
http://www.rootsweb.com/~okleflor/pvgs.
    htm
Arlene LeMaster, President
Pub. *The LeFlore County Heritage*, four
    times per year
(publishes books of LeFlore County
    genealogical and historical information)
$10.00 per year membership; research:
    research: $7.50 per hour plus copies; free
    queries for members

Pottawatomie County Genealogy Club
(241 Masonic Building, Ninth and Bell,
Shawnee, OK 74801—location)
PO Box 3256 (mailing address)
Shawnee, OK 74802
(405) 273-5695
Laquita Hackett, President
Wed–Fri 10:00–1:00
Pub. *Pottawatomie County Genealogy Club
    Newsletter*, quarterly
(index of marriages and deeds, cemetery
    books, probate records)
$15.00 per year membership

Rogers County Genealogical Society
(Belvedere Mansion, Fourth and
Chickasaw—location)
PO Box 2493 (mailing address)
Claremore, OK 74018
Mon–Sat 10:00–4:00

Sequoyah Genealogical Society

PO Box 1112
Sallisaw, OK 74955

**Southwest Oklahoma Genealogical Society
(SWOGS)**
PO Box 148
Lawton, OK 73502-0148
lgarris@sirinet.net
http://www.sirinet.net/~lgarris/swogs
Aulena Scearce Gibson, Corresponding
    Secretary
Pub. *Tree Tracers*, quarterly
$15.00 per year membership

Spencer Genealogical Society
PO Box 394
Spencer, OK 73084

Stephens County Genealogical Society
Stephens County Genealogical Research
Library
301 North Eighth
Duncan, OK 73533

Stratford Roots
c/o Chandler-Watts Library
History-Genealogy Department
(321 North Oak—location)
PO Box 696 (mailing address)
Stratford, OK 74872
(580) 759-2684
Lorene Donehew, Corresponding Secretary
Library: 9:00–6:00, Tue 9:00–8:00
Pub. *Stratford Oklahoma Roots*, quarterly
(includes area within 10- to 12-mile radius
    around Stratford, in Garvin, Ponotoc and
    McClain counties, including Old McGee
    Indian Territory)
$10.00 per year membership

Tecumseh Genealogy Club
1307 North Rangeline
Tecumseh, OK 74873

TX-OK Panhandle Genealogical Society
(see Texas, Part 2)

Three Forks Genealogical Society
102 South State Street
Wagoner, OK 74467
(918) 485-2741
threeforksgen@hotmail.com
Bonni Bunting, President
Tue–Thur 9:00–noon
Pub. *Three Forks Genealogy*, quarterly
$12.00 per year membership; research: $5.00
    plus copies

Tulsa Genealogical Society Library
(9072 East 31st Street—location)
PO Box 585 (mailing address)
Tulsa, OK 74101-0585
(918) 627-4224
LLCGRAMMIE@aol.com
http://www.tulsagenealogy.org
Janice Meredith, Librarian
Mon & Sat 9:00–5:00, Wed 1:00–5:00
Pub. *Tulsa Annals*, three times per year
$20.00 per year membership; research:
    donation to TGS

**Western Plains-Weatherford Genealogy
Society**
(219 East Franklin—location)
PO Box 1672 (mailing address)
Weatherford, OK 73096
kim1@hintonet.net
http://www.rootsweb.com/~okcuster/
    wpwgs.htm
Kim Ralston Dresser, President and Editor
meetings at the city hall: third Mon
    (Feb–June & Sept–Nov)

Pub. *Western Plainsman*, four times per year
$18.00 per year membership

Western Trail Historical and Genealogical Society
(see Historical Societies—Local and Regional, above)

Western Trails Genealogical Society
(Jackson County, Oklahoma, Southern Prairie Library, Altus, TX—location)
PO Box 70 (mailing address)
Altus, OK 73522
(580) 266-3358
jdmartin@intellisys.net
http://www.rootsweb.com/~okjackso/
    wtgsweb/wtgshome.htm
Jodean McGuffin Martin, Librarian
Pub. *Western Trail Newsletter*, quarterly
("We are a depository for old Greer County, Texas, from 1880–1907; at statehood we became Greer, Harmon, Beckham, and Jackson counties, Oklahoma.")
$10.00 per year membership; $25.00 per family name (three hours)

Independent Publications and Miscellany

BJ's Place—Genealogy Home Page
bjsbytes@enid.com
http://www.harvestcomm.net/personal/
    bjsbytes
Betty Jo Scott
(links and surname database)

Blaine County People and Place History, Inc.
PO Box 30
Watonga, OK 73772
(580) 623-4922
W. Dale Reynolds, President
research: normally no fee, donation accepted

Bristow Historic Museum
1 Railroad Place
Bristow, OK 74010
(918) 367-5151

Center for Southwest Research
(see New Mexico, Part 2)

Cherokee Strip Museum
2617 West Fir
Perry, OK 73077
(580) 336-2405
Kaye Bond, Curator
Tue–Fri 9:00–5:00, Sat 10:00–4:00

Cherokee Strip Museum of Alva
901 14th Street
Alva, OK 73717
(580) 327-2030

Elk River Current
(see Missouri, Part 2)

Mountain Press
(see Tennessee, Part 2)

OkGenWeb
Part of The USGenweb Project
okgenweb@cox.net
http://www.rootsweb.com/~okgenweb;
    http://www.rootsweb.com/~itgenweb
    (Oklahoma/Indiana Territory)
Marti Graham, State Coordinator
(links to other Oklahoma resources)

Oklahoma Military Department
3501 Military Circle

Oklahoma City, OK 73111-4398
(405) 425-8000
Col. William Francis, PIO
Mon–Fri 7:00–4:30

Oklahoma Yesterday Publications
8745 East Ninth Street
Tulsa, OK 74112
Dorothy J. Mauldin, Editor
Pub. *Oklahoma Yesterday*, quarterly

Sons and Daughters of the Cherokee Strip Pioneers
Journal of the Cherokee Strip
(see Lineage, Hereditary and Patriotic Societies, Part 3)

Stauber Books
62753 East 313 Road
Grove, OK 74344-5716
(918) 786-3569
rstauber7@hotmail.com
http://www.gregathcompany.com/
    stauberbooks.html
Rose Stauber
("Publisher of genealogical books for Delaware County, Oklahoma; northeast Oklahoma; McDonald County, Missouri.")

Texas State Historical Association
Southwestern Historical Quarterly
(see Texas, Part 2)

University of Arizona Press
Journal of the Southwest
(see Arizona, Part 2)

Oregon

Archives and Libraries with Holdings in Genealogy

State Archives and Library
Archives Division
Secretary of State
800 Summer Street, N.E.
Salem, OR 97310
(503) 373-0701; (503) 373-0953 FAX
reference.archives@state.or.us
http://arcweb.sos.state.or.us;
    http://arcweb.sos.state.or.us/databases/sear
    chgeneal.html (Genealogical Name Database Search);
    http://arcweb.sos.state.or.us/geneal.html
    (Records of Interest to Genealogists)
Roy C. Turnbaugh, State Archivist; Layne Sawyer, Supervising Reference Archivist
Mon–Fri 8:00–5:00

Oregon State Library
State Library Building
25 Winter, N.E.
Salem, OR 97310-0641
(503) 378-4277; (503) 588-7119 FAX
http://www.osl.state.or.us/home
Craig Smith, Reference Supervisor
Mon–Fri 10:00–5:00, second Sat 10:00–4:00

State Historical Society

Oregon Historical Society
Oregon Historical Records Advisory Board
1200 S.W. Park Avenue
Portland, OR 97205
(503) 222-1741; (503) 306-5240 (Reference Department)
orhist@ohs.org
http://www.ohs.org
Bob Kingston, Reference Librarian
Wed & Fri–Sat 11:30–5:00, Thur 11:30–8:00
Pub. *OHS Spectator*, quarterly
("photograph collection with reproduction services")
$40.00 per year membership; complex admission: $6.00 for nonmember adulst; research: $35.00 per hour, $20.00 minimum for ½ hour, plus $3.00 postage; photocopies: 20¢ per page from paper originals ($1.00 minimum), $1.00 each from microform originals (noncommercial use) plus $1.00 surcharge for each multiple of 10

City, County and Regional Archives and Libraries
(A more exhaustive list of public and academic libraries can be found at http://www.osl.state.or.us/home/libdev/pldirp.pdf or http://www.osl.state.or.us/home/libdev/pldir.htm.)

Albany Public Library
1390 Waverly Drive, S.E.
Albany, OR 97321-6945
(541) 917-7581; (541) 917-7586 FAX
http://www.ci.albany.or.us
Kimberly Kuhn, Library Assistant II; Diane White
Mon 10:00–8:00, Tue–Fri 10:00–6:00, Sat 10:00–5:00, Sun 1:00–5:00
("Albany, Linn County, and Oregon archives; Oregon history collection, genealogy library")
"ready reference" searches free, in-depth searches $7.50 per hour

Astoria Public Library
450 10th Street

Astoria, OR 97103-4699
(503) 325-READ; (503) 325-2017 FAX
Judy Dugan, Library Director
Mon–Thur 10:00–8:00, Fri–Sat 10:00–6:00,
    Sun (except summer) 2:00–5:00
(local newspaper index card file, 1873–1957,
    plus some recent years)

Baker County Public Library
2400 Resort Street
Baker City, OR 97814-2798
(541) 523-6419; (541) 523-9088 FAX
alethab@oregontrail.net
Aletha Bonebrake

Lavola Bakken Memorial Library
Douglas County Museum of History and
Natural History
(123 Museum Drive—location)
PO Box 1550 (mailing address)
Roseburg, OR 97470
(541) 957-7007; (541) 440-4506 FAX
Fred R. Reenstjerna, Research Librarian
Library: Mon–Fri noon–4:30
(22,000 photos, 1,000 books and 300+
    manuscripts, 5,000 documentary artifacts;
    collection documenting Douglas County
    history and natural history)
no charge for brief inquiries, extensive
    research at $25.00 per hour (one-hour
    minimum), plus cost of copies; museum
    admission: $3.50 per person

Benton County History Center
110 N.W. Third Street
Corvallis, OR 97330-4701
http://www.peak.org/lewish/histcent.htm

Mary Jane Brookfield Library
PO Box 34
Brookings, OR 97415

Coos Bay Public Library
525 West Anderson Avenue
Coos Bay, OR 97420-1678
(541) 269-1101; (541) 269-7567 FAX
cventgen@coosnet.com
http://www.coosnet.com/library
Carol Ventgen
Mon–Wed 10:00–8:00, Thur–Fri 11:00–5:30,
    Sat 11:00–5:00

Corvallis-Benton County Public Library
Reference
645 N.W. Monroe Avenue
Corvallis, OR 97330-4798
(541) 757-6793; (541) 766-6726 FAX
carolyn.rawles-heiser@ci.corvallis.or.us
http://www.thebestlibrary.com
Carolyn Rawles-Heiser
Mon–Fri 9:00–9:00, Sat 9:00–6:00, Sun
    noon–6:00
(Oregon and Benton County history, Oregon
    census microfilm, Corvallis newspaper on
    microfilm)

Dallas Public Library
Oregon Collection
950 Main Street
Dallas, OR 97338-2802
(503) 623-2633; (503) 623-7357 FAX
donna@ccrls.org
http://www.ci.dallas.or.us/library/library.
    html
Donna Zehner

The Dalles-Wasco County Public Library
722 Court Street
The Dalles, OR 97058-2270
(541) 296-2815; (541) 296-4179 FAX
http://www.ci.the-dalles.or.us
Lorna Elliott, Library Clerk (Genealogy)

Tue–Wed 11:00–8:30, Thur–Fri 10:00–6:00,
    Sat 10:00–3:00

**Discovery Center and Wasco County
Historical Museum, Library**
5000 Discovery Drive
The Dalles, OR 97058
(541) 296-8600, ext. 219
library@gorgediscovery.org
Joanne Ward
Mon, Wed & Fri 11:00–3:00
("Our library has some Wasco County
    genealogical information [mainly
    newspaper clippings and books].")

Douglas County Library System
1409 N.E. Diamon Lake Boulevard
Roseburg, OR 97470-3361
(541) 440-4311; (541) 440-4315 FAX
mtleek@co.douglas.or.us
http://www.co.douglas.or.us/library
Max Leek
Mon noon–8:00, Tue–Wed 10:00–8:00, Thur
    10:00–6:00, Fri–Sat 10:00–4:00
("Local newspapers back to 1867 on
    microfilm. No index.")
photocopy costs

Eastern Oregon State College
Walter M. Pierce Library
Eighth and K
La Grande, OR 97850
(541) 963-1540
http://lib.www.eosc.osshe.edu
Douglas Oleson, Director
Mon–Thur 7:30–11:00, Fri 7:30–4:30, Sat
    1:00–5:00, Sun 5:00–11:00; vacation
    periods: Mon–Fri 7:30–4:30

Elgin Public Library
(260 North 10th—location)
PO Box 67 (mailing address)
Elgin, OR 97827-0067
(541) 437-2860; (541) 437-2253 FAX
Theresa Chandler

Eugene Public Library
100 West 10th Avenue
Eugene, OR 97401-3035
(541) 682-5450; (541) 682-5898 FAX
connie.j.bennett@ci.eugene.or.us
http: www.ci.eugene.or.us/library
Connie Bennett

Grant County Historical Museum
(101 South Canyon City Boulevard,
Highway 395—location)
PO Box 464 (mailing address)
Canyon City, OR 97820
(541) 575-0362; (541) 575-0666 (Co-
    chairman); (541) 575-1578 (Mr. Round)
Grace K. Williams, Co-chairman; Louis
    Round
1 June–30 Sept: Mon–Sat 9:00–4:30, Sun
    1:00–5:00
(pictures and records of families and people
    in Grant County)

Hermiston Public Library/Archives
235 East Gladys Avenue
Hermiston, OR 97838-1827
(541) 567-2882; (541) 667-5055 FAX
mwilliams@hermiston.or.us
http://www.hermiston.or.us/library
MLou Williams

Hillsboro Public Library
Shute Park Branch
775 S.E. 10th Avenue
Hillsboro, OR 97123-4798
(503) 615-6500; (503) 615-6501 FAX
http://www.ci.hillsboro.or.us/library/

default.asp
(local obituary index)

Hood River County Museum
Port Marine Park
PO Box 781
Hood River, OR 97031
(541) 386-6772
Earlene A. Hinrich, Secretary
Wed–Sun (Apr–Oct) 10:00–4:00
(historical and biographical resources)

Independence Public Library
Local History
311 South Monmouth Steet
Independence, OR 97351-1998
(503) 838-1811; (503) 838-4486 FAX
robinp@ccrls.org
http://www.ccls.org/independence
Robin Puccetti

**Jackson County Public Library/Main
Branch**
413 West Main Street
Medford, OR 97501-2730
(541) 774-8673; (541) 774-6748 FAX
budgerl@jacksoncounty.org; info@jcls.org
http://www.jcls.org
Ronnie Lee Budge

Josephine County Library System
Main Branch
200 N.W. "C" Street
Grants Pass, OR 97526-2094
(541) 474-5482; (541) 474-5485 FAX
sluce@co.josephine.or.us
http://www.josephine.or.us/library/index.
    html
Sue Luce

Klamath County Library
126 South Third Street
Klamath Falls, OR 97601-6394
(541) 882-8894; (541) 882-8895; (541) 882-
    6166 FAX
aswanson@co.klamath.or.us
http://www.lib.co.Klamath.or.us
Helen Morehouse, Branch Coordinator;
    Leonard Swanson
winter: Tue 11:30–8:00, Wed–Sat 9:30–6:00;
    summer: Mon 11:30–8:00, Tue–Fri
    9:30–6:00

La Grande Public Library
1006 Penn Avenue
La Grande, OR 97850-2496
(541) 962-1339; (541) 962-1338 FAX
http://www.ci.la-
    grande.or.us/dept_library.cfm
Joanne Cowling, Director
Mon–Fri 10:00–6:00

Lake Oswego Public Library
706 Fourth Street
Lake Oswego, OR 97034-2399
(503) 636-7628; (503) 635-4171 FAX
dainslie@ci.oswego.or.us;
    jrose@ci.oswego.or.us
http://www.ci.oswego.or.us/library
Donna Ainslie

Lane County Museum
740 West 13th Avenue
Eugene, OR 97402
(541) 687-4239
lchm@efn.org
http://www.lchmuseum.org
Everad Stelfox, Museum Director
Research Library: by appointment only
research: fees charged on an individual basis

Lebanon Public Library

626 Second Street
Lebanon, OR 97355-3329
(541) 451-7461; (541) 258-2080 FAX
dlee@ci.lebanon.or.us
Denice Lee, Interim Director
Mon–Thur 11:00–7:00, Fri–Sat 11:00–4:00

Lewis and Clark College
Aubrey R. Watzek Library
615 S.W. Palatine Hill Road
Portland, OR 97219
(503) 768-7270
refdesk@lclark.edu
http://www.lclark.edu/~refdesk

**Linn County Historical Museum and
Moyer House**
(101 Park Avenue—location)
PO Box 607 (mailing address)
Brownsville, OR 97327
(541) 466-3390
http://linnhistory.peak.org/bhistories.html
Charlene Scott, Museum Manager; Richard
    R. Milligan, Historian
Mon–Sat 11:00–4:00, Sun 1:00–5:00
Pub. *Friends Newsletter*, semiannually,
    $15.00 per year subscription

McMinnville Public Library
225 North Adams
McMinnville, OR 97128-5425
(503) 435-5555; (503) 472-5247; (503) 472-
    1429 FAX; (503) 435-5560 FAX
http://www.maclibrary.org
Marcia Blevins, Reference Supervisor; Anne
    VanSickle
Tue–Thur 9:00–9:00, Fri–Sat 9:00–5:00, Sun
    (Sept–May) 1:00–5:00

Monmouth Public Library
(168 South Ecols Street—location)
PO Box 10 (mailing address)
Monmouth, OR 97361-0010
(503) 838-1932; (503) 838-3899 FAX
http://www.ccrls.org/monmouth
Ron Baker

Morrow County Museum
Genealogical Research Center
PO Box 1153
Heppner, OR 97836
(541) 676-5524
krebs_2506@hotmail.com
http://www.mcmuseum.org
Robin Krebs
Mar–Oct: Tue–Fri 1:00–5:00
$15.00 per year membership (to Larry Mills,
    PO Box 515, Heppner, OR 97836)

Multnomah County Public Library
Humanities Department
801 S.W. 10th Avenue
Portland, OR 97205-2597
(503) 988-5123
cindyg@multcolib.org
http://www.multcolib.org
Joan Zornman
Tue–Thur 9:00–9:00, Fri–Sat 9:00–6:00, Sun
    1:00–5:00

Oregon City Public Library
362 Warner Milne Road
Oregon City, OR 97045-4020
(503) 657-8269; (503) 657-3702 FAX
http://www.oregoncity.lib.or.us
Sue Adams, Reference Librarian; Dee Craig
Mon–Thur 10:00–8:00, Fri–Sat 10:00–6:00,
    Sun (Oct–May) 1:00–5:00
(Oregon history, Oregon indexes, local
    newspapers)
no research or genealogical librarians on
    location

Oregon Institute of Technology
3201 Campus Drive
Klamath Falls, OR 97601
Pub. *Shaw Historical Library Journal*,
    semiannually, $18.00 per year
    subscription

Oregon State University
Archives
94 Kerr Administration Building
Corvallis, OR 97331-2103
(541) 737-2165; (541) 737-2400
http://www.orst.edu/Dept/archives
    (Archives); http://www.orst.edu/Dept/
    Special_Collections (Special Collections)

Oregon State University
Valley Library
Corvallis, OR 97331-4501
(541) 737-2971 (Map Room); (541) 737-
    2075 (Special Collections)
http://www.orst.edu/dept/library

Pacific University Archives and Museum
Pacific University
2043 College Way
Forest Grove, OR 97116
(503) 359-2117; (503) 359-2236 FAX
Richard T. Read, University
    Archivist/Museum Curator
Archives: Mon–Fri 9:00–5:00; Museum:
    Tue–Fri 1:00–4:30
(university publications from 1863, papers
    and manuscripts, Congregational Church
    publications and documents to about
    1925, historical monographs, "Pacificana
    Collection" and photographs

**City of Portland Stanley Parr Archives
and Records Center**
9360 North Columbia Boulevard
Portland, OR 97203
(503) 823-4631
Josephine Dwyer, Records Management
    Officer; Marcus Robbins, Archivist
8:00–5:00

Silverton Public Library
410 South Water Street
Silverton, OR 97381-2198
(503) 873-5173; (503) 873-6227 FAX
marlyss@ccrls.org
http://www.open.org/silverpl
Marlys Swalboski

Siuslaw Pioneer Museum
(Highway 101 at Milepost 192—location)
PO Box 2637 (mailing address)
Florence, OR 97439
(541) 997-7884
museum@winfinity.com
Perla Campbell, Library Manager
Tue–Sun noon–4:00 (closed Dec)
("Siuslaw River Valley family histories;
    regional history, vintage photographs;
    maps, charts and plats. Cemetery
    records.")
research, nominal charges plus reproduction
    and mailing

Siuslaw Public Library
(1460 9th Street—location)
PO Box A (mailing address)
Florence, OR 97439-0022
(541) 997-3132; (541) 997-4007 FAX
skidmore@siuslaw.lib.or.us
Stephen Skidmore

Southern Oregon State College Library
1250 Siskiyou Boulevard
Ashland, OR 97520-5076
(541) 552-6839; (541) 552-6429 FAX

Spokane Public Library
(see Washington, Part 2)

Springfield Public Library
225 North Fifth Street
Springfield, OR 97477-4697
(541) 726-3766; (541) 726-3747 FAX
library@ci.springfield.or.us
http://www.ci.springfield.or.us/library
Jenny Peterson, Adult Services Division
    Manager
Mon–Tue 10:00–7:00, Wed 10:00–5:00,
    Thur–Sat noon–5:00

Tigard Public Library
13125 S.W. Hall Boulevard
Tigard, OR 97223-8192
(503) 684-6537; (503) 598-7515 FAX
http://www.ci.tgard.or.us
Kate Miller, Adult Services Librarian
Mon–Fri 9:30–9:00, Sat 9:30–5:00, Sun
    1:00–5:00

Tillamook County Library
210 Ivy Street
Tillamook, OR 97141-2298
(503) 842-4792; (503) 842-1120 FAX
scharlton@mail.crsn.lib.or.us
http://www.co.tillamook.or.us/gov/
    Library/default.html
Sara Charlton
Mon–Thur 9:00–9:00, Fri–Sat 9:00–5:30

Tillamook County Pioneer Museum
2106 Second Street
Tillamook, OR 97141-2306
(503) 842-4553; (503) 842-2592 FAX
Wayne Jensen, Director
Research Library: Mon–Fri 8:00–5:00
(local genealogical information)
research: $5.00 minimum plus 20¢ per page

Toledo Public Library
173 N.W. Seventh Street
Toledo, OR 97391-1217
(541) 336-3132; (541) 336-3428 FAX
librarydirector@cityoftoledo.org
http://www.cityoftoledo.org/library.htm
Peter Rayment
Mon–Fri 1:00–9:00, Sat 10:00–5:00, Sun
    1:00–5:00
(has *Lincoln County Leader* newspaper; "no
    searching, limited staff")

University of Oregon
Knight Library, Special Collections
Eugene, OR 97403-1299
(541) 346-3068; (541) 346-1818 (Reference)
mrwatson@oregon.uoregon.edu
    (Newspapers)
http://libweb.uoregon.edu
Fraser Cocks, Curator, Special Collections
Mon–Fri 8:30–4:30
(emphasis on Oregon history)

University of Utah Marriott Library
(see Utah, Part 2)

University of Washington Libraries
(see Washington, Part 2)

Western Heritage Center
(see Montana, Part 2)

Western Oregon State College Library
345 North Monmouth Avenue
Monmouth, OR 97361
(503) 838-8890; (503) 838-8474 FAX

Historical Societies—Local and Regional

ALSI Historical and Genealogical Society, Inc.
(320 Grant—location)
PO Box 822 (mailing address)
Waldport, OR 97394
(541) 563-7092
Fri noon–4:00, Sat–Sun 10:00–4:00
(local scope, plus census CDs for the U.S.)
$3.00 per year membership

American Historical Association, Pacific Coast Branch
(see California, Part 2)

American West Research Center and Historical Society, Inc.
(see Ohio, Part 2)

The Aurora Colony Historical Society
15008 Second Street
Aurora, OR 97002
(503) 678-5754
Daniel E. McElhinny, Executive Director
Feb–Dec: Tue–Sat 10:00–4:00, Sun noon–4:00
Pub. *ACHS Newsletter*

Bandon Historical Society/Coquille River Museum
(270 Fillmore Street, Highway 101 and Fillmore—location)
PO Box 737 (mailing address)
Bandon, OR 97411
(541) 347-2164
Judith Knox, Assistant Curator
Mon–Sat 10:00–4:00, Sun (spring & summer) noon–3:00
("not set up for research at present")
$15.00 per year membership

Benton County Historical Society and Museum
(1101 Main Street—location)
PO Box 47 (mailing address)
Philomath, OR 97370-0047
(541) 929-6230
http://www.peak.org/~lewisb/Museum.html
William Lewis, Director
Tue 12:30–3:00
Pub. *The Society Record*

Big Butte Historical Society
432 Pine Street
Butte Falls, OR 97522
(541) 865-3332

Brooks Historical Society
3995 Brooklake Road, N.E.
Salem, OR 97303-9728
(503) 390-0690

Cannon Beach Historical Society
(1387 South Spruce—location)
Box 1005 (mailing address)
Cannon Beach, OR 97110
(503) 436-9301; (503) 436-0490 FAX
cbhs@seasurf.net
http://www.cannon-beach.net/cbhs
Sharon M. Stewart, Coordinator
$15.00 per year membership

Chetco Valley Historical Society/Museum
PO Box 2126
Harbor, OR 97415-0304

Clackamas County Historical Society
Museum of the Oregon Territory
211 Tumwater Drive
Oregon City, OR 97045
(503) 655-5574; (503) 655-0035
museum@orcity.com
http://www.orcity.com/museum

Patrick Harris, Executive Director
Mon–Fri 10:00–4:00, Sat–Sun 1:00–5:00
Pub. *Clackamas County Historical Society Update*, monthly
("Research library within museum. Library is run by Clackamas County Family History Society, a separate organization.")
$20.00 per year membership; admission: donation

Clatsop County Historical Society
(714 Exhange Street—location)
PO Box 88 (mailing address)
Astoria, OR 97103-0088
(503) 325-2203; (503) 325-7727 FAX
cchs@seasurf.net
http://www.clatsophistoricalsociety.org
Lisa Penner, Curator of Collections
Office: 9:00–4:00; Museum: (Oct–May) 11:00–4:00, (May–Oct) 10:00–5:00; Archives and Research Library (in Heritage Museum): Tue–Fri 9:00–noon & 1:00–4:00
Pub. *CUMTUX, Clatsop County Historical Society Quarterly*; *Clatsop County Historical Society Newsletter*, bimonthly
(county, regional, and state history)
$30.00–$49.00 per year membership

Columbia County Historical Society
(Old County Courthouse—location)
PO Box 837 (mailing address)
Saint Helens, OR 97051
(503) 397-3868
cchsb@columbia-center.org
R. J. "Bob" Brown, President
Fri & Sun 1:00–4:00
Pub. *Newsletter*, monthly; *Columbia County Histories*, $5.00 each or 22 volumes plus index for $100.00
(marriages 1850–1900, cemetery records from 1850, of the entire county)
$12.00 per year membership

Coos County Historical Society Museum
1220 Sherman Avenue
North Bend, OR 97459-3615
(541) 756-6320
museum@uci.net
http://cooshistory.org
Ann Koppy, Director
Tue–Sat 10:00–4:00
Pub. *Newsletter*, three times per year
$10.00 per year membership

Crook County Historical Society
A. R. Bowman Museum
246 North Main Street
Prineville, OR 97754-1852
(541) 447-3715
bowmuse@netscape.net
http://www.bowmanmuseum.org/m
Gordon Gillespie, Director
Mon–Fri 10:00–5:00, Sat 11:00–4:00, Sun 11:00–5:00
Pub. *Crook County Historical Society Newsletter*, quarterly
$10.00 per year membership; admission: free

Curry County Historical Society
Curry County Museum
PO Box 1598
Gold Beach, OR 97444-1598
(541) 247-6113
http://goldbeach.org/history/gbhistory9.html (Museum)
Mildred Walker, Curator; Walt Schroeder, President
30 May–30 Sept: Tue–Sat noon–4:00; 1 Oct–29 May: Sat noon–4:00
Pub. *Curry County Echoes*, monthly
(Curry history, genealogy)

$10.00 per year membership

Deschutes County Historical Society, Genealogical Committee
(Idaho and Wall Street—location)
PO Box 5252 (mailing address)
Bend, OR 97708
(541) 389-1813
Roland Anderson, Manager
Tue–Sat 10:00–4:30
Pub. *Newsletter*, monthly
(specializes in central Oregon history, Deschutes and Crook counties)
$10.00 per year membership

Deschutes Pioneers Association
2861 N.W. Polarstar Avenue
Bend, OR 97701-8664
(541) 382-3456
Barbara Buxton, Membership Chair
Pub. *Deschutes Pioneers' Gazette*, annually
$5.00 per year membership

Fairview-Rockwood-Wilkes Historical Society
(60 Main Street—location)
PO Box 946 (mailing address)
Fairview, OR 97024
(503) 261-8078
frwinfo@frwhs.org
http://www.frwhs.org
Nancy Hoover, Membership Coordinator
$15.00 per year membership

Gilliam County Historical Society Museum Complex
(Highway 19, adjacent to Burns Park and the fairgrounds—location)
PO Box 377 (mailing address)
Condon, OR 97823
(541) 384-4233
Karen Wilde, Secretary
1 May–31 Oct: Wed–Sun 1:00–5:00
$10.00 per year membership; admission: $2.50 suggested donation for adults

Gold Hill Historical Society
PO Box 26
Gold Hill, OR 97525

Gresham Historical Society
(Museum, Main Street—location)
PO Box 65
Gresham, OR 97030
(503) 661-0347
ghs@gresham.org
http://www.gdda.org/ghs.htm
Tue & Thur 10:00–4:00, Sat noon–4:00; meetings: fourth Tue 7:00

Harney County Historical Society
Harney County Historical Museum
(18 W Street—location)
PO Box 388 (mailing address)
Burns, OR 97720-1226
(541) 573-5618; (541) 573-2636 (Museum)
Dorothea Purdy, President
9:00–5:00
Pub. *Harney County Historical Highlights*, bimonthly
$10.00 per year

Josephine County Historical Society
Schmidt House Museum
512 S.W. Fifth Street
Grants Pass, OR 97526-2804
(541) 479-7827
josephinehistorical@charter.net
http://www.webtrail.com/jchs/index.html
Rose M. Scott, Executive Director
Tue–Fri 1:00–4:00
Pub. *The Oldtimer Newsletter*, quarterly

(specializes in southern Oregon)
$15.00 per year membership

Junction City Historical Society
(Lee House, 655 Holly Street
Pitney House Museum, 289 West
Fourth—location)
655 Holly Street (mailing address)
Junction City, OR 97448
(541) 998-3657
http://www.junctionCity/history.com
Kitty Goodin, Curator
last Sun 1:00–4:00
Pub. *Newsletter*, annually
("History museum, local Junction City.")
$5.00 per year membership

Klamath County Historical Society
Klamath County Museum
1451 Main Street
Klamath Falls, OR 97601
(541) 883-4208
Museum: Tue–Sat 9:00–5:00
Pub. *Klamath Echoes*, annually

Lake County Historical Society
PO Box 48
Lakeview, OR 97630
Edward A. Henry, President
meetings at the Lake County Courthouse:
third Wed
Pub. *Lake County*
$15.00 per year membership

Lane County Historical Society
(740 West 13th Avenue, Eugene, OR 97402-
4010—location)
PO Box 11532 (mailing address)
Eugene, OR 97440-3732
Pub. *Lane County Historian*, three times per
year, no subscriptions; *Lane County
Historical Society Newsletter*, five times
per year, no subscriptions
$10.00 per year membership

Lincoln County Historical Society
Burrows House Museum
545 S.W. Ninth
Newport, OR 97365-4726
(541) 265-7509
http://www.newportnet.com/newport/
library/LCHS.htm
Loretta Harrison, Executive Director
summer: Tue–Sun 10:00–5:00; winter:
Tue–Sun 11:00–4:00
Pub. *The Quarterly*
("maritime history focus, central Oregon
coast")
$10.00 per year membership

Linn County Historical Society
1132 30th Place, S.W.
Albany, OR 97321-3419
(541) 926-4680; (541) 791-4707 FAX
harrison@cmug.com
http://www.linnhistorical.com
Glenn Harrison, President and Newsletter
Editor
Pub. *Linn County Historical Society
Newsletter*, 4 times per year (Jan, Mar,
May, Oct)
$15.00 per year membership (to Karen Engel,
730 Washington Street, S.W., Albany, OR
97321)

Malheur County Historical Society
1186 S.W. Sixth Avenue
Ontario, OR 97914-3310
(541) 889-5073
Hugh R. Lackey, Treasurer
meetings second Thur
Pub. *Malheur County Review*, bimonthly

$8.00 per year membership

Marion County Historical Society
(N.W. corner, Mission Mill
Village—location)
260 12th Street, S.E. (mailing address)
Salem, OR 97301
(503) 364-2128; (503) 391-5356 FAX
mchs@open.org
http://www.open.org/mchs
Kyle Jansson, Executive Director
Mon–Sat 9:30–4:30
Pub. *Historic Marion*, quarterly; *Marion
County History*, intermittently
(a nonprofit, educational society with
museum, research library and archives for
the preservation of Marion County
history)
$20.00 per year membership; general
admission: $1.00

Milton-Freewater Area Historical Society
Frazier Farmstead Museum
1403 Chestnut Street
Milton-Freewater, OR 97862
(541) 938-4636; (541) 928-3480
museum@bmi.net
http://museum.bmi.net
Thur–Sat 11:00–4:00

Morrow County Historical Society
PO Box 1153
Heppner, OR 97856
Ruth McCabe, Secretary

North Bend Public Library
1800 Sherman Avenue
North Bend, OR 97459
(541) 756-0400; (541) 756-1073 FAX

North Santiam Historical Society
143 Wall, N.E.
Mill City, OR 97360
(503) 897-4088

Oakland Museum Historical Society
4999 Nonpareil Road
Sutherlin, OR 97479-9709

Pacific Northwest Historians Guild
(see Washington, Part 2)

Polk County Historical Society
(560 Pacific Highway West, Rickreall, OR
97371—location)
PO Box 67 (mailing address)
Monmouth, OR 97361
(503) 623-6251
pchs@open.org
http://www.open.org/~pchs (includes
publication sales)
Pat Smith, President, Nita Wilson, Archivist
Mon, Wed & Fri–Sun 1:00–5:00
Pub. *The Polk Poker*, quarterly; *Historically
Speaking*, every two years (booklet of
historical stories)
(depository for the now disbanded Polk
County Genealogical Society; museum
has historical artifacts, archives, research
library)
$10.00 per year membership; research:
$10.00 per hour plus copying costs

The Saint Paul Mission Historical Society
(see Religious Archives and
Organizations—Roman Catholic, Part 3)

Santiam Historical Society
(260 North Second Avenue—location)
PO Box 574 (mailing address)
Stayton, OR 97383-1710
(503) 769-1406; (503) 769-5299

Carol Zolkoske
Fri–Sat 1:00–4:00

Scotts Mills Area Historical Society
Second and Grandview
Scotts Mills, OR 97375

Seaside Museum and Historical Society
(570 Necanicum Drive—location)
PO Box 1024 (mailing address)
Seaside, OR 97138-1024
(503) 738-7065; (503) 738-0671
smhs@seasurf.net
http://www.seasidemuseum.org
Phyllis Hamlin, Office Staff
Office: 10:00–2:00; Museum: Mon–Sun
(summer) 10:30–4:00, Mon–Sun (winter)
noon–3:00
Pub. *Making History Together*, quarterly
(collecting and interpreting materials
illustrative of the history of Seaside and
the surrounding area; emphasis on Lewis
and Clark Saltmakers)
$10.00 per year membership; museum
admission: $2.00 for adults; research: free
to members, except 10¢ per copy

Sherman County Historical Society
(200 Dewey Street—location)
PO Box 173 (mailing address)
Moro, OR 97039
(541) 565-3232; (541) 565-3080 FAX
info@shermanmuseum.org
http://www.shermanmuseum.org
Joe Weber, President
Museum: May–Oct: 1:00–5:00
Pub. *Sherman County: For the Record*,
semiannually, $5.00 per issue
(publishes historical anthology)
$17.50 per year membership

South Umpqua Historical Society
(Pioneer/Indian Museum, 421 West Fifth
Street—location)
PO Box 1112 (mailing address)
Canyonville, OR 97417
(541) 839-4845
gynn@mcsi.net
Gynn O. Deaton, Treasurer
Wed–Sun 1:00–5:00
Pub. *Pioneer Days in the South Umpqua
Valley*, annually, $5.00 per year
subscription
$15.00 per year membership

Southern Oregon Historical Society
Research Library
106 North Central Avenue
Medford, OR 97501
(541) 773-6536; (541) 776-7994 FAX
library1@sohs.org
http://www.sohs.org
Carol Samuelson, Librarian
Tue–Sat 1:00–5:00
Pub. *Southern Oregon Heritage*, quarterly,
$29.00 per year subscription
from $15.00 per year membership; research
library search fee: first half-hour free,
$10.00 per half-hour thereafter, plus $5.00
user fee

**Tillamook County Historical Society
Genealogy Study Group**
PO Box 123
Tillamook, OR 97141
wrberry@wcn.net
Willard R. Berry, Chair

Troutdale Historical Society
104 S.E. Kibling Street
Troutdale, OR 97060
http://www.stateoforegon.com/troutdale/

historical_society
$8.00 per year membership

Umatilla County Historical Society
(108 S.W. Frazer—location)
PO Box 253 (mailing address)
Pendleton, OR 97801
(541) 276-0012; (541) 276-7989
uchs@oregontrail.net
http://www.umatillahistory.org/history.htm
Julie Reese, Executive Director
Tue–Sat 10:00–4:00
Pub. *Pioneer Trails*, three times per year
$12.00 per year membership

Wasco County Historical Society
(address withheld upon request)
("The Historical Society does not have files
   or information.")

Washington County Historical Society
17677 N.W. Springville Road
Portland, OR 97229
(503) 645-5353; (503) 645-5650
Winifred Herrschaft, Research Assistant;
   Mark E. Granlund, Executive Director
Mon–Sat 10:00–4:00
Pub. *The Express*, quarterly
$20.00 per year membership

Yamhill County Historical Society
(Corner of Sixth and Market
   Streets—location)
PO Box 484 (mailing address)
Lafayette, OR 97127
(503) 472-7328 (President)
Shirley Venhaus, President
1 Sept–31 May: Sat–Sun 1:00–4:00; 1
   June–31 Aug: Wed–Sun 1:00–4:00
Pub. *The Westside*, 9 times per year (monthly,
   Sept–May)
$7.50 per year membership

Genealogical Societies

State Genealogical Societies

Genealogical Council of Oregon
PO Box 237
Crawfordsville, OR 97336-0237
mjc@proaxis.com
http://www.rootsweb.com/~orgco/Index.htm
Mary Jean Crawford, Treasurer
$10.00 per year membership

Genealogical Forum of Oregon, Inc.
Headquarters and Library
(1505 S.E. Gideon Street—location)
PO Box 42567 (mailing address)
Portland, OR 97242-0567
(503) 963-1932; (561) 325-7676 FAX
info@gfo.org; research@gfo.org
http://gfo.org
Mary Lou Stroup, Library Director; Eileen
   Chamberlin, President
Mon, Wed & Sat 9:30–3:00 (except second
   Sat 9:30–1:00 & 2:30–5:00), Tue & Thur
   9:30–9:00, Sun noon–5:00
Pub. *Bulletin—Genealogical Forum of
   Oregon*, quarterly (Sept, Dec, Mar, June);
   The Forum Insider Newsletter, eight times
   per year; *Genealogical Forum of Oregon,
   Inc.* (membership directory), annually
$30.00 per year membership

Oregon Genealogical Society
(955 Oak Alley, Eugene, OR 97401-
3108—location)
PO Box 2306 (mailing address)
Eugene, OR 97440-2306
(541) 345-0399
http://www.rootsweb.com/~orlncogs/

ogsinfo.htm
Linda Van Orden, Treasurer and
   Membership Chair
Mon & Wed 10:00–2:00, Fri 10:00–5:00, Sat
   (except fourth Sat) 10:00–4:00, Sun
   noon–4:00
Pub. *The Quarterly* (Jan, Apr, July, Oct),
   $3.00 per issue; *Oregon Genealogical
   Society Newsletter*, bimonthly
(Oregon history and research; issues Oregon
   Pioneer Certificates, $10.00 [write for
   application].)
$25.00 per year membership; research:
   $10.00 per hour plus costs

Genealogical Societies—Local & Regional

**ALSI Historical and Genealogical Society,
Inc.**
(see Historical Societies—Local and
Regional, above)

Baker County Genealogy Club
c/o Baker County Public Library
2400 Resort Street
Baker City, OR 97814
(541) 523-6419 (Library); (541) 523-9088
   FAX (Library)

Bend Genealogical Society
PO Box 8254
Bend, Oregon 97708
http://www.rootsweb.com/~ordeschu/
   bend-gs
Adele Loudermilk
Library: first & third Tue noon–4:00, second
   & fourth Tue 10:00–4:00
Pub. *Distant Voices*, monthly
$15.00 per year membership

Benton County Genealogical Society
PO Box 1511
Corvallis, OR 97330
(541) 757-2316
rootsfinder@pioneer.net
http://www.rootsweb.com/~orbentgs
Gene Kelsey, President
Benton County Historical Society and
   Museum Annex: Tue 12:30–3:00;
   meetings: second Sat (Sept–June)
   10:00–3:00
Pub. *Newsletter*, monthly
(library covers all fields of genealogy)
$10.00 per year membership; admission: first
   time library use free to nonmembers

Blue Mountain Genealogical Society
PO Box 1801
Pendleton, OR 97801
(541) 276-6000
bopp@oregontrail.net; sandral@ucinet.com
http://www.uci.net/~sandral
Rosemary Farley, Researcher; Karen Bopp,
   President
(Umatilla County cemetery records)
$7.50 per year membership; research: $7.50
   per hour

Clackamas County Family History Society
(211 Tumwater Drive—location)
PO Box 995 (mailing address)
Oregon City, OR 97045-2900
(503) 655-5574
http://ccfhs.1extreme.net
Sandy McGuire, President
Tue–Wed 10:00–4:00, first & third Sat
   1:00–5:00; meetings at West Linn Public
   Library, 1595 Burns Street, West Linn,
   OR: fourth Mon 7:00
Pub. *Clackamas Legacy*, quarterly;
   Newsletter, quarterly
(Library, located in the building of the

Clackamas County Historical Society,
   includes census 1842–1900, 1910
   Soundex, cemetery records, donation land
   claims, family histories, first jail book,
   Grand Army of the Republic members
   pedigree charts, marriage records
   1848–1925, probate from 1854,
   provisional land claim records, taxes from
   1865.)
$15.00 per year membership

Clatsop County Genealogical Society
Astoria Public Library
450 10th Street
Astoria, OR 97103
shargrov@pacifier.com
http://www.pacifier.com/~karenl
Pub. *The Forebears*, quarterly
$15.00 per year membership

Columbia Gorge Genealogical Society
The Dalles-Wasco County Public Library
722 Court Street
The Dalles, OR 97058
vhambv@hotmail.com
http://community.gorge.net/genealogy/
   index.html
Earline Wasser, Editor
Pub. *Tales and Trails—Newsletter*, quarterly
$15.00 per year membership

Cottage Grove Genealogical Society
(Cottage Grove Community Building, 207
North H Street—location)
PO Box 388 (mailing address)
Cottage Grove, OR 97424-0015
(541) 942-3068 (Phyllis Pruitt,
   Corresponding Secretary and Researcher);
   (541) 942-2502 (to schedule
   appointments)
jane.a.myers@att.net
http://www.rootsweb.com/~orlane/links/
   cggs.htm
Jane Myers, Librarian; Joanne Skelton,
   Secretary, Dorothy Gertsner, Editor,
   Carole Chapman, President
Library: Wed–Sat 1:00–4:00, Wed 6:30–9:00
   and by appointment
Pub. *Trees from the Grove*, quarterly (Feb,
   May, Aug, Nov)
("We have over 5,000 volumes, 200 CD-
   ROMs in our library, growing manuscript
   file [three four-drawer file cabinets, 36 feet
   shelf space], and a fast-growing film and
   fiche collection that covers entire U.S. and
   a fairly well known vertical file; special
   collection: Cottage Grove, Oregon, area.")
$15.00 per year membership; queries free for
   members, $1.00 for nonmembers for two
   queries per issue for $1.00; research: $7.50
   per hour

Crook County Genealogical Society
A. R. Bowman Museum
246 North Main Street
Prineville, OR 97754-1852
(541) 447-3715
bowlib@crestviewcable.com
http://www.bowmanmuseum.org/
   genealogical.htm
Vivian Zimmerlee, Librarian
meetings at Presbyterian Church, 1771 N.W.
   Madras Highway, Prineville, OR: third
   Wed 7:30
Pub. *Crook County Genealogical Society
   Newsletter*, quarterly
("Crook County census, courthouse and
   cemetery records, most all Crook County
   newspapers from 1887.")
$10.00 per year membership; small charge for
   copies

Deschutes County Historical Society, Genealogical Committee
(see Historical Societies—Local and Regional, above)

Digger O'Dells Restaurant Genealogical Society
2211 Spring Street
Medford, OR 97504-6377
Susan Geear

Genealogical Society of Douglas County
Douglas County Courthouse
1036 S.E. Douglas Avenue, Room 111
Roseburg, OR 97470-3301
(541) 673-6940 (Librarian); (541) 440-6178
gsdc@co.douglas.org.us
http://www.rootsweb.com/~orgsdc
Eileen Talburt, Librarian
Tue–Fri 1:00–4:00
Pub. *Douglas County Pioneer*, quarterly
$10.00 per year membership

Emerald Empire Genealogical Workshop
2540 Barnett Street
Bremerton, WA 98310-5202
Lorraine Cowles Sencevicky

End of the Trail Researchers (EOTR)
145 24th Avenue, S.E.
Salem, OR 97301
Chapter: **Central Oregon Chapter**, c/o
    Clark, 6060 Coyote, Redmond, OR 97465

Grant County Genealogical Society
(Grant County—location)
PO Box 418 (mailing address)
Canyon City, OR 97820
(541) 575-2757 (President); (541) 575-0545
    (Secretary)
lgcook1@oregontrail.net (President);
    gmabetty@oregontrail.net (Secretary)
Linda Cook, President; Betty Elliott,
    Secretary
Pub. *Grant County Genealogical Society
    Newsletter*, quarterly
(published *Cemetery Book I* [Dayville and
    Mt. Vernon areas], *Cemetery Book II*
    [Canyon City Cemetery], *Cemetery Book
    III* [Restlawn & St. Andrews, John Day &
    Canyon City], *Yesteryears in Grant
    County*, and *Marriage Book*)
$10.00 per year membership; research: $7.50
    per hour plus cost of copies at 25¢ per
    page

Grants Pass Genealogical Society
(Barn of Josephine County Historical Society,
    512 S.W. "K" Street—location)
PO Box 1834 (mailing address)
Grants Pass, OR 97528
dlthomas@terragon.com
Don Thomas, President
meetings: second Tue & fourth Wed
$7.50 per year membership

Harney County Genealogy Society
c/o 426 East Jefferson
Burns, OR 97720

Juniper Branch of Family Finders, Inc.
21 S.E. "D" Street
Madras, OR 97741-1605
(541) 475-9745
jbff@madras.net
http://www.jbff.org
Mon–Thur 10:00–4:00, Fri 10:00–3:00;
    business meetings: second (Sept–May)
    Tue 7:30, research: fourth Tue (Sept–May)
    7:00
Pub. *Newsletter*, eight times per year
    (monthly, Jan–May & Sept–Nov)

$15.00 per year membership; research:
    $10.00 per hour plus copy and postage
    costs

Klamath Basin Genealogical Society
PO Box 366
Klamath Falls, OR 97601
George Norman, President
meetings at Klamath County Library
$10.00 per year membership

La Pine Genealogical Society
(La Pine Branch Deschutes County
    Library—location)
PO Box 1081 (mailing address)
La Pine, OR 97739
$5.00 per year membership

Lebanon Genealogical Society
Lebanon Public Library
626 Second Street
Lebanon, OR 97355
linnhistory@hotmail.com
http://www.usgennet.org/usa/or/town/
    lebanon
Jane Hutchings, Secretary; Jan Phillips,
    Webmaster
meetings: first Fri 7:00 P.M.
(specializes in Oregon, Linn County,
    Lebanon)
$10.00 per year membership; search fee:
    donation plus cost of copies and postage

Linn Genealogical Society
(Linn County Courthouse, 300 West Third
    Avenue, S.W.—location)
PO Box 1222 (mailing address)
Albany, OR 97321-0537
byronbray@cmug.com
http://www.rootsweb.com/~orlinngs
Byron Bray, Webmaster
Mon–Fri 10:00–4:00; meetings at Albany
    Public Library: first Sat 1:00
Pub. *The Heritage Newsletter*, monthly
$15.00 per year membership

Madras Genealogical Society
671 Southwest Fairgrounds
Madras, OR 97741
Pauline Chain

Milton-Freewater Genealogical Club
127 S.E. Sixth Street
Milton-Freewater, OR 97862
Carmen Buff

Mount Hood Genealogical Forum
(950 South End Road—location)
PO Box 744 (mailing address)
Oregon City, OR 97045
(503) 656-6021
Theoda Burns, Librarian
Tue 10:00–8:00
$8.00 per year membership

Pocahontas Trails Genealogical Society
Oregon Regional Chapter
406 Casa De Loma
Sutherlin, OR 97479

Polk County Genealogical Society
(see Polk County Historical Society,
    Historical Societies—Local and Regional,
    above)

Port Orford Genealogical Society
Port Orford Public Library
555 West 20th Street
Port Orford, OR 97465

Rogue Valley Genealogical Society, Inc.
(95 Houston Road—location)

PO Box 1468 (mailing address
Phoenix, OR 97535-1468
(541) 512-2340
info@rvgslibrary.org
http://www.rvgslibrary.org
Emillee Brazill, Library Director
Mon–Sat 10:00–3:00
Pub. *Rogue Digger*, quarterly; *Between Us
    Diggers*
(Largest genealogical library in southern
    Oregon, with over 3,000 volumes.)
$25.00 per year membership; library
    admission: free to members, $3.00 for
    nonmembers

Siuslaw Genealogical Society
PO Box 1540
Florence, OR 97439
Eleanor Duree, President
meetings at Siuslaw Public Library: third
    Wed (Sept–June)
Pub. *GEN-TREE*, quarterly (Sept, Dec, Mar,
    June)
$12.00 per year membership

Sweet Home Genealogical Society
Sweet Home Library
PO Box 279
Sweet Home, OR 97386
(541) 367-5007
Rosella Burns, President
Library: Mon–Tue & Thur 11:00–8:00,
    Fri–Sat 11:00–5:00
Pub. *Distant Trails*, quarterly (Dec, Mar,
    June, Sept)
(Collection, housed in the city library,
    includes death, marriage and divorce
    indexes, Oregon donation land claims,
    census records.)
$5.00 per year membership

Tillamook County Historical Society Genealogy Study Group
(see Historical Societies—Local and
Regional, above)

Washington County Family History Society
wcfhs@ancestraltracks.com
http://www.rootsweb.com/~orwcfhs
meetings: second Thur
Pub. *GeneaLog*, quarterly

Willamette Valley Genealogical Society
Oregon State Library
Genealogy Room
PO Box 2083
Salem, OR 97308
http://www.osl.state.or.us/home/gen/
    wvgs.html
Mon–Fri 10:00–4:00; meetings at library:
    second Sat 10:00–4:00
Pub. *Willamette Valley Genealogical Society
    Newsletter*, monthly; *Beaver Briefs*,
    quarterly
(Marion County, Oregon and Oregon
    research)
$15.00 per year membership

Woodburn Genealogical Club
1015 McKinley
Woodburn, OR 97071
Lynn Faulk
("Work in conjunction with Woodlawn
    Public Library; sponsor continual field
    trips; on-going class; we do help with
    queries on local research when we can.")
$10.00 per year membership

Yamhill County Genealogical Society
(McMinnville Public Library, 225 North
    Adams Street—location)
PO Box 568 (mailing address)

McMinnville, OR 97128
johnny6_28_66@yahoo.com
http://www.geocities.com/ycgsociety/
    index.html
Barbara Koch, Editor
Library: Mon–Thur 10:00–9:00, Fri–Sat
    10:00–6:00 (volunteers available most
    Weds 1:30–3:30); meetings first Sat
    9:30–12:30
Pub. *Timber Trails*, quarterly (Jan, Apr, July,
    Oct)
(specializes in family reunions, family
    newsletters, queries; Yamhill County
    marriages, deaths, cemetery records)
$15.00 per year membership

Yaquina Genealogical Society
c/o Toledo Public Library
173 N.W. Seventh Street
Toledo, OR 97391
(541) 336-3132
cmoody@newportnet.com
http://www.rootsweb.com/~orygs
Chuck Moody
Pub. *The Searchlight*, quarterly, $5.00 per
    year subscription

Independent Publications and Miscellany

Boston Mill Society
1132 30th Place S.W.
Albany, OR 97321-3419
mthomp9689@aol.com
http://www.bostonmill.org
("To interpret the agricultural, commercial,
    industrial and social life of Oregon's
    Willamette Valley.")

Eastern Oregon Museum
PO Box 182
Haines, OR 97833
(541) 856-3233
juliehan@eoni.com
http://hainesoregon.com/eomuseum.html
Viola Perkins, President
Mon–Sun (May–Labor Day): 9:00–5:00

Family Publications
5628 60th Drive, N.E.
Marysville, WA 98270-9509
Rose Caudle Terry, Publisher
Pub. *Oregon Trail Sources, Queries &*
    Reviews, two to four times per year, $8.95
    per volume subscription, plus $1.50
    postage per order

The Gene Pool
(see Computer Interest, Part 4)

The Heritage
35145 Balboa Place, S.E.
Albany, OR 97321
Richard R. Milligan, Co-publisher
Pub. *The Heritage*, monthly, $12.00 per year
    subscription

Historic Preservation League of Oregon
3534 S.E. Main Street
Portland, OR 97214-4263

Hutson Museum
4967 Baseline Drive
Mount Hood Parkdale, OR 97041-9727
(541) 352-6808

Multnomah County School District No. 1
Portland Public Schools
Records Management Office
Child Services Center
531 S.E. 14th Avenue

Portland, OR 97214-2485
(503) 916-5840, ext. 273; (503) 916-2727
    FAX (attention: Records Management)
Mon–Fri 8:00–5:00
(public school records from 1856)
no search or copy fee for most records, no
    patron direct access to records

Northwest Pioneer
(see Washington, Part 2)

Oregon-California Trails Association
(see Miscellaneous, Part 4)

Oregon Department of Transportation
Geographic Information Services Unit
555 13th Street, N.E., Suite 2
Salem, OR 97301-4178
odot.maps@odot.state.or.us
http://www.odt.state.or.us/tdmappingpublic
    (Maps)

Oregon Geographic Names Board
1230 S.W. Park Avenue
Portland, OR 97205
(503) 222-1741
Tom McAllister, Chair

Oregon Historic Cemeteries Association
PO Box 802
Boring, OR 97009
(503) 658-4522; (503) 658-3111 FAX
ohca@oregoncemeteries.org
http://www.oregoncemeteries.org
Jeanne Robinson, Executive Director
by appointment
Pub. *OHCA Ledger*, triannually
(long-term goal to create an all-name
    database of Oregon burials)
voluntary membership: from $15.00 to
    $1,000.00 per year

Oregon Pioneers
mransom@peak.org
http://www.peak.org/~mransom/pioneers.
    html
Mike Ransom

Oregon/Washington Queries
(419 West Third—location)
PO Box 117 (mailing address)
Everson, WA 98247
Pub. *Oregon/Washington Queries*

OrGenWeb
Part of The USGenweb Project
linnhistory@hotmail.com;
    johnhenrymccoy@hotmail.com
http://www.rootsweb.com/~orgenweb
Jan Phillips, State Coordinator; Janine
    Borks, Assistant Coordinator; John
    McCoy, Assistant Coordinator
(links to other Oregon resources)

Schminck Memorial Museum
128 South E Street
Lakeview, OR 97630-1721
(541) 947-3134
jenglenn@centurytel.net
Sherrain Colenn, Curator
Tue–Sat 1:00–4:00
(early newspapers, books, obituaries,
    marriages)

Springfield Historical Commission
Springfield Public Library
225 Fifth Street
Springfield, OR 97477
(541) 726-3775
Diane Debex, Historical Coordinator
(primarily historical, not genealogical)

University of California Press
Pacific Historical Review
(see California, Part 2)

Wallowa County Museum
PO Box 430
Joseph, OR 97845
(541) 432-1794
Callol Coppin, Director; Grace Bartlett,
    Curator
end of May to end of Sept: 10:00–5:00

Pennsylvania

Archives and Libraries with Holdings in Genealogy

State Archives and Library

Pennsylvania State Archives
Reference Section
(Third and Forster Streets—location)
PO Box 1026 (mailing address)
Harrisburg, PA 17108-1026
(717) 783-3281
http://www.phmc.state.pa.us/bah/dam/
overview.htm
Tue–Fri 9:00–4:00, Sat (microfilm only)
9:00–noon & 1:00–4:00, audio and video
collections by appointment only
(collection features military records,
immigration and naturalization records,
vital statistics, prison records, census and
land records, etc., plus special collections
of maps and photographs)
research: $10.00 per name per item in
indexed records only, including copying
up to 10 pages

State Library of Pennsylvania
Forum Building
(Walnut Street and Commonwealth
Avenue—location)
PO Box 1601 (mailing address)
Harrisburg, PA 17105-1601
(717) 787-4440 (Information); (717) 783-
5950 (Reference); (717) 783-5968
(Newspapers); (717) 783-2070 FAX
jtownsend@state.pa.us
http://www.statelibrary.state.pa.us/libraries
Judith TownsendAssistant Director
Mon & Wed–Sat 9:30–4:30, Tue 9:30–8:30
(Pennsylvania local history and genealogy
collection is "available on self-service
basis; there is no staff assigned, and no
service by mail from the collection.")

State Historical Societies

Heritage Society of Pennsylvania
PO Box 146
Laughlintown, PA 15655

**The Pennsylvania Federation of Museums
and Historical Organizations**
(Third and Forster Streets, Harrisburg, PA
17120—location)
PO Box 1026 (mailing address)
Harrisburg, PA 17108-1026
(717) 787-3253; (717) 787-4822 FAX
Jean H. Cutler, Executive Director
8:30–4:30
Pub. *Tapestry*, quarterly; *Directory of
Museums and Historical Organizations in
Pennsylvania*, $5.95
(a professional association of Pennsylvania
museums and historical organizations; not
a genealogical society)
$30.00 per year membership

Pennsylvania Heritage Society
(Third and North Streets—location)
PO Box 11466 (mailing address)
Harrisburg, PA 17108-1466
(717) 787-2407; (717) 783-9924 FAX
Marcia B. Gobrecht, Executive Secretary
10:00–4:30
Pub. *Pennsylvania Heritage Quarterly
Newsletter*; *Pennsylvania Heritage
Magazine*, quarterly, $20.00 per year
subscription
(a nonprofit support organization of the
Pennsylvania Historical and Museum

Commission)
$35.00 per year membership

**Pennsylvania Historical and Museum
Commission**
(Third and North Streets—location)
PO Box 1026 (mailing address)
Harrisburg, PA 17108-1026
(717) 787-3362
http://www.phmc.state.pa.us
Pub. *Pennsylvania Heritage*, quarterly,
$15.00 per year subscription, $5.00 per
issue

The Pennsylvania Historical Association
Penn State—Harrisburg
Swatara Building
777 West Harrisburg Pike
Middletown, PA 17057-4898
(717) 774-4829
LeRoy W. Toddes, Business Secretary
Wed 9:30–noon
Pub. *Pennsylvania History: A Journal of
Mid-Atlantic Studies* (not genealogical),
quarterly
$25.00 per year membership

Historical Society of Pennsylvania
1300 Locust Street
Philadelphia, PA 19107-5699
(215) 732-6200; (215) 732-2680 FAX
webmaster@hsp.org
http://www.hsp.org
David Moltke-Hansen, President and CEO;
Lee Arnold, Director of the Library and
Collections; Rachel Onuf, Director of
Archives; Laura E. Beardsley, Head of
Graphics; Amy L. Rojek, Cataloger; Max
E. Moeller, Director of Public Services;
Daniel Rolph, Head of Reference Services
Library: Tue & Thur–Fri 9:30–4:45, Wed
1:00–8:45, Sat 10:00–4:45
Pub. *The Pennsylvania Magazine of History
and Biography*, quarterly; *Pennsylvania
Legacies*, semiannually
(genealogical library for eastern United
States)
$45.00 per year membership; research:
$30.00 for the first hour and $25.00 for
each additional hour for members, $40.00
for the first hour and $30.00 for each
additional hour for nonmembers, plus
photocopies at 50¢ per page and possibly
$5.00 shipping

City, County and Regional Archives and
Libraries
(A more exhaustive list of public and
academic libraries can be found at http://
www.statelibrary.state.pa.us/libraries/cwp/vie
w.asp? a=11&Q=79040&LibrariesNav=|
1222|1237.)

**Aaronsburg Historical Museum
Association**
(116 West Plum Street—location)
PO Box 80 (mailing address)
Aaronsburg, PA 16820
(814) 349-8276
Bruce Teeple, Curator
Wed 7:00 P.M.–9:00 P.M., Sat 1:00–4:00, and
by appointment
$5.00 per year membership; research: no
fees, but would appreciate copies of work

Albion Area Public Library
History Room
111 East Pearl Street
Albion, PA 16401-1202
(814) 756-5400 voice & FAX
albion@erie.net
http://www.erie.net/~albion

Jan Petrus, Librarian
Mon–Wed 9:00–7:00, Sat 9:00–3:00

Allegany College of Maryland Library
Appalachian Collection
(see Maryland, Part 2)

**The Community Library of Allegheny
Valley**
Local History Department
400 Lock Street
Tarentum, PA 15084
(724) 226-0770
http://www.einpgh.org/ein/alvalley/local.
html
David Kupas
Mon noon–8:00, Tue–Wed 10:00–6:00, Fri
10:00–4:00, Sat 10:00–2:00
("Holdings include records pertaining to
Allegheny, Armstrong, Butler, and
Westmoreland counties. Particular
emphasis is given to the Allegheny-Kiski
River Valley.")
research: "Please refer to research policy on
library's web site."

Allentown Public Library
1210 West Hamilton Street
Allentown, PA 18102-4371
(610) 820-2400
http://www.allentownpl.org

Altoona Area Public Library
The Pennsylvania Room
1600 Fifth Avenue
Altoona, PA 16602-3693
(814) 946-0417, ext. 131; (814) 946-3230
FAX
gkuhn@altoonalibrary.org
http://www.altoonalibrary.org
Georgia Kuhn, Reference Librarian
Mon–Tue & Thur 8:30–9:00, Wed & Fri
8:30–5:00, Sat 9:00–5:00, Sun 1:00–4:00
(primarily Blair County; Altoona and Blair
County histories, obituary index from
1967; searchable *Altoona Mirror* obituary
index online)
research: $1.00 per page for mailed
photocopies; staff cannot do genealogy
searches

Apollo Memorial Library
219 North Pennsylvania Avenue
Apollo, PA 15613-1397
(724) 478-4214
apollolibrary@hotmail.com
http://home.kiski.net/~alibrary
Vicki Held, Technician
Tue–Thur 11:00–7:00, Fri–Sat 9:00–4:00
research: $10.00 donation

Beaver Area Historical Museum
(1 River Road Extension—location)
PO Box 147 (mailing address)
Beaver, PA 15009
(724) 775-7174
Joanna Ashburn, Director
Mar–Dec: Wed & Sat 10:00–4:00, Sun
1:00–4:00
Pub. *Foundations*, periodically (at least
annually)
(primarily historical; no genealogical
resources or personnel trained in that field)
$10.00 per year membership

Bedford County Library
(see Pioneer Historical Society of Bedford
County, Historical Societies—Local and
Regional, below)

Benson Memorial Library
213 North Franklin Street

Titusville, PA 16354-1788
(814) 827-2913
http://ccfls.org/benson
Mon–Thur 10:00–8:00; Fri–Sat 10:00–5:00

Bloomsburg Public Library
225 Market Street
Bloomsburg, PA 17815-1726
(570) 784-0883; (570) 784-8541 FAX
http://townhall.bafn.org/library/bloom.htm
Mon–Fri 9:00–8:00, Sat 9:00–1:00

Bloomsburg University
Harvey A. Andruss Library
400 East Second Street
Bloomsburg, PA 17815
(570) 389-4204; (570) 389-3895 FAX
http://www.bloomu.edu/library/pages/
    library.html

Eva K. Bowlby Public Library
311 North West Street
Waynesburg, PA 15370-1238
(724) 627-9776; (724) 852-1900 FAX
http://www.greenepa.net/~bowlby
Mon–Fri 1:00–4:00, Sat 10:00–4:00

James V. Brown Library
19 East Fourth Street
Williamsport, PA 17701-6390
(570) 326-0536, ext. 24 or ext. 13; (570) 323-
    6938 FAX
ask@jvbrown.edu
http://www.jvbrown.edu
Rhonda Fisher, Reference Librarian
Mon–Thur 9:00–9:00, Fri 9:00–6:00, Sat
    9:00–5:00, Sun 1:00–5:00
(Lycoming County history and genealogy;
    does not answer genealogical questions by
    phone or FAX)
research: $10.00 plus copies and postage for
    out-of-state inquiries

Buhl-Henderson Community Library
(see Shenango Valley Community Library,
below)

Butler Area Public Library
Weir Genealogy Room
218 North McKean Street
Butler, PA 16001-4911
(724) 283-5026; (724) 285-5090 FAX
http://butler.library-online.org
Luanne Eisler, Genealogist
winter: Mon–Thur 8:30–9:00, Fri–Sat
    9:00–5:00; summer: Mon–Thur
    9:00–9:00, Fri–Sat 9:00–5:00
research: copying fees and donation to build
    and maintain genealogy collection; copies:
    25¢ per page

Cambria County Library
248 Main Street
Johnstown, PA 15901-1677
(814) 536-5131, ext. 211; (814) 536-6905
    FAX
http://www.cclib.lib.pa.us
Mr. Lou Pocchiari, Reference Librarian
Mon–Thur 8:30–9:00, Fri 8:30–5:00, Sat
    9:00–4:00, Sun (from after Labor Day to
    before Memorial Day) 1:00–4:00
("Public library with genealogy department
    and local history archives. Index to the
    obituaries from *Johnstown Tribune
    Democrat* 1853–present. Local history
    collection, the Johnstown floods.")
research: $5.00 per name

Carnegie Free Library
Resource and Research Center for Beaver
County and Local History
1301 Seventh Avenue

Beaver Falls, PA 15010-4219
(724) 846-4340, ext. 5; (724) 846-0370 FAX
CFL2000@mailcity.com
http://www.co.beaver.pa.us/Library/main.
    html
Bill Irions
Mon 3:00–8:00, Tue–Thur 10:00–4:00,
    Fri–Sat 10:00–3:00
Pub. *Milestones*, quarterly, $5.00 per year
    subscription

The Carnegie Library of Pittsburgh
Pennsylvania Department
4400 Forbes Avenue
Pittsburgh, PA 15213-4080
(412) 622-3114; (412) 622-3154
trru@carnegielibrary.org
http://www.carnegielibrary.org
Marilyn Holt, Department Head
Mon–Thur 9:00–9:00, Fri–Sat 9:00–5:30,
    Sun 1:00–5:00

**Centre County Library and Historical
Museum**
203 North Allegheny Street
Bellefonte, PA 16823-1601
(814) 355-1516
Paroom@centrecountylibrary.org
http://www.centrecountylibrary.org
Joyce Adgate, Pennsylvania Room Assistant
    and Museum Caretaker
Mon–Fri 9:00–5:00, Sat 9:00–noon &
    1:00–5:00
(Pennsylvania history and genealogy:
    Spangler genealogical papers, J. Marvin
    Lee genealogical collection, newspapers,
    census, county histories, over 500 family
    histories, general reference sources and
    indexes)
limited research to answer one or two
    specific questions, copy fees and postage

**Chester County Archives and Records
Service**
Government Services Center, Suite 080
601 Westtown Road
West Chester, PA 19382-4527
(610) 344-6760
http://www.chesco.com/~cchs/
    chesco_archives.html
Jeffrey D. Rollison, Director of Archives
Mon–Fri 9:00–4:00

Coyle Free Library
102 North Main Street
Chambersburg, PA 17201-1676
(717) 263-1054; (717) 263-2248 FAX
fcls_ref@hotmail.com
http://fclspa.org/coyle/coyle.htm
Paula Schechter, Reference Librarian
summer: Mon–Thur 9:00–8:30, Fri
    9:00–5:00, Sat (June–Aug) 9:00–noon
(Franklin County local history and
    genealogy)
copies: 15¢ per page plus postage

Darby Free Library
History Room
(1001 Main Street—location)
PO Box 164 (mailing address)
Darby, PA 19023-0164
(610) 586-7310; (610) 586-2781 FAX
darby@delco.lib.pa.us
http://www.darbylibrary.org
Library: Mon & Fri 10:00–5:00, Tue
    10:00–7:00, Wed 10:00–6:00, Thur
    noon–7:00, Sat 9:00–4:00; History Room:
    Mon noo–4:00, and by appointment

**Dayton and Montgomery County Public
Library**
(see Ohio, Part 2)

Easton Area Public Library
Marx History Room
515 Church Street
Easton, PA 18042-3587
(610) 258-2917, ext. 115
webmaster@eastonpl.org
http://www.eastonpl.org
Sharon Gothard, Library Assistant; Barbara
    Bailey Bauer, Curator of Special
    Collections
History Room: Mon–Fri 10:00–noon &
    1:00–4:00, Sat 9:00–noon & 1:00–5:00
(more than 18,000 volumes of local and
    family history, abstracts of Northampton
    County wills 1752–1840 and every-name
    index, union index to local religious
    records, newspaper abstracts of marriages
    and deaths 1799–1902, some obituary
    indexing from 1909–1945, obituary
    indexes 1946 to date, Northampton
    County cemetery project, newspaper item
    file from 1799, family history files,
    historical vertical files, picture file)
queries should be accompanied by SASE,
    donation appreciated; copies: 10¢ each
    from paper originals, $1.00 each from
    microform originals, plus postage: $1.50
    for up to a maximum of 10 pages

Erie County Library System
160 East Front Street
Erie, PA 16507-1554
(814) 451-6900; (814) 451-6927 (Heritage
    Room); (814) 451-6907 FAX
reference@erielibrary.org
http://www.ecls.lib.pa.us
Cindy Kerchoff, Head of Reference
Mon–Tue 9:00–9:00, Wed–Fri 9:00–8:00,
    Sat 9:00–5:00

Everett Free Library
137 East Main Street
Everett, PA 15537-1259
(814) 652-5922; (814) 652-5425 FAX
info@everettlibrary.org
http://www.everettlibrary.org
Diana L. Megdad, Library Director
Mon–Tue & Thur 1:00–8:00, Wed
    10:00–5:00, Fri 10:00–8:00, Sat 9:00–4:00
(census, *Bedford County Press* on microfilm
    from 1868–1892 and 1894–1982, except
    1905, 1918, 1928, 1930)

Ford City Public Library
1136 Fourth Avenue
Ford City, PA 16226-1202
(724) 763-3591
http://www.nb.net/~fcpl
Joanne Germy, Library Director
winter: Mon–Wed noon–7:00, Thur–Fri
    10:00–5:00, Sat 9:00–4:00; summer:
    Mon–Tue & Thur–Fri 9:00–4:00, Wed
    9:00–7:00, Sat 9:00–1:00
$12.00 per year membership

John Fox Jr. Genealogical Library
(see Kentucky, Part 2)

Franklin and Marshall College
Shadek-Fackenthal Library
Archives and Special Collection Division
(College Avenue and James Street—location)
PO Box 3003 (mailing address)
Lancaster, PA 17604-3003
(717) 291-4225
Ann Kenne, College Archivist and Special
    Collections Librarian
Mon–Fri 9:00–noon & 1:00–5:00
("Not interested in the genealogical aspect,"
    collection includes information about
    people who were associated with college
    from 1787; "Archives no longer has

microfilm of church and pastoral records of the Evangelical and Reformed Churches.")

Franklin Public Library
Pennsylvania Room
421 12th Street
Franklin, PA 16323-1205
(814) 432-5062; (814) 432-8998 FAX
http://www.madbbs.com/~franklinpl
Sylvia M. Coast, Pennsylvania Room Clerk
Library: Mon–Fri 9:00–8:00, Sat 9:00–5:00;
Pennsylvania Room: Mon & Fri–Sat 9:00–5:00, Tue 9:00–8:00
(Emphasis on Venango County, not Franklin County. "We have about 130,000 obituaries on index cards and 233 rolls of census microfilm for Western Pennsylvania.")
mail research: $20.00 for a family search

Amelia S. Givin Free Library
114 North Baltimore Avenue
Mount Holly Springs, PA 17065-1201
(717) 486-3688
amelia@ccpa.net
http://www.ccpa.net/ls/MHShome.html
Cynthia Stratton Thompson, Director
Mon–Thur 10:00–9:00, Fri 10:00–6:00, Sat 9:00–4:00

Greater Canonsburg Public Library
68 East Pike Street
Canonsburg, PA 15317-1312
(724) 745-1308; (724) 745-4958 FAX
gcplgenealogy@attglobal.net
http://www.cbgpublib.org
Mon–Thur 11:00–8:00, Fri 11:00–5:00, Sat 10:00–5:00

Green Free Library
Pennsylvania Room
134 Main Street
Wellsboro, PA 16901-1489
(570) 724-4876; (570) 724-7605 FAX
http://home.epix.net/~greenlib
Cassandra Grant
Sept–May: Mon–Fri 10:00–8:00, Sat 10:00–5:00; June–Aug: Mon–Fri 10:00–8:00, Sat 10:00–2:00
(local history)

Greensburg Hempfield Area Library
237 South Pennsylvania Avenue
Greensburg, PA 15601-3086
(724) 837-5620 (Main); (724) 837-8441 (Reference)
http://www.ghal.org
Cesare J. Muccari, Library Director
winter: Mon–Thur 10:00–7:50, Fri–Sat 10:00–4:50; summer: Mon & Thur 10:00–7:50, Tue–Wed & Fri–Sat 10:00–4:50

Haverford College
Magill Library
370 Lancaster Avenue
Haverford, PA 19041-1392
(610) 896-1274
elapsans@haverford.edu
http://www.haverford.edu/library/sc/sc.html
(Special Collections)

Heritage Center of Lancaster County, Inc.
13 West King Street
Lancaster, PA 17603
(717) 299-6440
http://www.lancasterheritage.com

Jane I. and Annetta M. Herr Memorial Library
Pennsylvania Room
500 Market Street
Mifflinburg, PA 17844
(570) 966-0831
herr@herrlibrary.org
http://www.herrlibrary.org
Mon–Fri 7:00 P.M.–9:00 P.M., Tue–Thur 11:00–5:00, Sat 10:00–5:00

Historic Schaefferstown, Inc.
Thomas R. Brendle Memorial Library and Museum
PO Box 307
Schaefferstown, PA 17088
(717) 949-2626
John T. Hickernell, Committee Chairman
weekends (June–Oct) noon–4:00

Historic Yellow Springs, Inc.
(Art School Road—location)
PO Box 62 (mailing address)
Chester Springs, PA 19425
(610) 827-7414; (610) 827-1336 FAX
http://www.yellowsprings.org
Caroline M. Stuckert, Ph.D., Executive Director
Mon–Fri 9:00–4:00; grounds always open
(historical site with a historic archives and library "to enhance our heritage and provide a center for research")
membership fee

Jenkintown Library
Pennsylvania Collection
460 Old York Road
Jenkintown, PA 19046-2829
(215) 884-0593; (215) 884-2243 FAX
http://www.jenkintown.com/library
Bonnie Miller

Johnsonburg Public Library
520 Market Street
Johnsonburg, PA 15845-0240
(814) 965-4110; (84) 965-3320 FAX
jburglib@ncentral.com
http://www.johnsonburglibrary.ncentral.com
Marie Biel, Genealogy Consultant
Mon & Fri 10:00–5:00, Tue–Thur 10:00–8:00, Sat 9:00–4:00

Lackawanna County Library System
Albright Memorial Library
520 Vine Street
Scranton, PA 18510-3298
(570) 348-3000; (570) 348-3020 FAX
refdept@albright.org
http://www.albright.org
Mon–Thur 9:00–9:00, Fri 9:00–5:30, Sat 9:00–5:00, Sun 2:00–5:00

Lancaster County Library
125 North Duke Street
Lancaster, PA 17602
(717) 394-2651; (717) 394-3083 FAX
lanpublib@shrsys.hslc.org
http://www.lancaster.lib.pa.us
Gerald Bruce, Reference Librarian
Mon–Thur 9:00–9:00, Fri–Sat 9:00–5:30 (no staff available to do research)
copies: 25¢ or 32¢

Lebanon Community Library
125 North Seventh Street
Lebanon, PA 17042-5000
(717) 273-7624; (717) 273-2719 FAX
tremaine@lebanoncountylibraries.org
http://www.lebanoncountylibraries.org/lebanon/index.htm
Jayne Tremaine, Executive Director
Mon–Thur 9:00–8:00, Fri–Sat 9:00–5:00

Martinsburg Community Library—Liebegott Collection
201 South Walnut Street
Martinsburg, PA 16662-1129
(814) 793-3335; (814) 793-9755 FAX
jpaden@atlanticbbn.net
http://nbcsd.k12.pa.us/mar_lib.htm
Joyce A. Paden, Head Librarian
Mon–Sat 1:00–4:30, Mon–Thur 6:30–8:30, Sun 2:00–4:30 (summer hours may vary)
(collection of family histories)

McKeesport Heritage Center
1832 Arboretum Drive
McKeesport, PA 15132
(412) 678-1832

Meadowcroft Museum of Rural Life
401 Meadowcroft Road
Avella, PA 15312
(724) 587-3412; (724) 587-3414 FAX
mcroft@cobweb.net
http://www.meadowcroftmuseum.org
("Meadowcroft has a small research library with local history information and a collection of historic photographs. This library is open by appointment only.")

Media-Upper Providence Free Library
The Media Borough Historic Archives
Front and Jackson Streets
Media, PA 19063
(610) 566-1918; (610) 566-9056 FAX
media@delco.lib.pa.us
http://www.medialibrary.org
Orion Jurkowski, Library Director
Mon 10:00–8:00, Tue–Thur 10:00–9:00, Fri 10:00–6:00, Sat 10:00–4:00, Sun 1:00–4:00
("It contains more than 1,300 old photographs, newspapers and newspaper clippings, some dating back into the early 1800s. There is also a large collection of local post cards, pamphlets, old deeds and legal papers, including a complete history of the Borough of Media and the Police and Water departments. The collection also houses photos and historic documents of Upper Providence and Nether Providence townships.")

Menno Simons Historical Library
(see Virginia, Part 2)

Mennonite Historians of Eastern Pennsylvania
Mennonite Heritage Center
565 Yoder Road, Box 82
Harleysville, PA 19438
(215) 256-3020; (215) 256-3023 FAX
http://www.mhep.org
Joel D. Alderfer, Librarian
Tue–Fri 10:00–5:00, Thur 7:00 P.M.–10:00 P.M.
Pub. *MHEP Quarterly*
(local Mennonite history, Pennsylvania-German studies, genealogy and local history of Bucks and Montgomery counties, Pennsylvania)
$25.00 per year membership; admission: $3.00 per day for nonmembers; research: 10% discount for members

Mercer Area Library
145 North Pitt Street
Mercer, PA 16137-1206
(724) 662-4233; (724) 662-8893 FAX
mercerarealib@htol.net
http://206.180.110.12/mercer
Connie Jewell, Library Director
Mon–Thur 9:30–8:00, Fri 9:30–6:00, Sat 8:00–3:00, Sat (summer) 8:00–noon

Monroe County Public Library, Inc.

a.k.a. Eastern Monroe Public Library
1002 North Ninth Street
Stroudsburg, PA 18360
(570) 421-0800; (570) 421-0212 FAX
monroepl@epix.net
http://www.monroepl.org
Barbara Reiser, Adult Services Librarian
Mon–Thur 9:00–9:00, Fri 9:00–6:00, Sat
9:00–5:00; Sun 1:00–5:00
photocopies: 15¢ per page, plus postage

Montgomery County Archives
1880 Markley Street
Norristown, PA 19401
(610) 278-3441

**Montgomery County-Norristown Public
Library**
1001 Powell Street
Norristown, PA 19401-3817
(610) 278-5100
http://mnl.mclinc.org
Loretta Righter, Head, Reference Department
winter: Mon–Wed 9:00–9:00, Thur
9:00–6:00, Fri–Sat 9:00–5:00, Sun
1:00–5:00; summer: Mon–Wed 9:00–8:00,
Thur 9:00–6:00, Fri 9:00–5:00

Montgomery Area Public Library
1 South Main Street
Montgomery, PA 17754
(570) 547-6212; (570) 547-0648 FAX
mapl@lycoming.org
http://www.ncldistrict.org/montgomery
Susan Thomas, Librarian
Mon–Wed & Fri noon–8:00, Sat 9:00–4:00

**Morgantown Public Library (southwestern
Pennsylvania)**
(see West Virginia, Part 2)

Mount Lebanon Public Library
(address withheld upon request)
("We do not have staff or funds to answer
questions by mail")

Myerstown Community Library
(199 North College Street—location)
PO Box 246 (mailing address)
Myerstown, PA 17067-0246
(717) 866-2800; (717) 866-5898 FAX
llm@lebanoncountylibraries.org
http://www.lebanoncountylibraries.org/
myerstown/index.htm
Linda Manwiller, Director
Mon & Wed–Thur noon–8:00, Tue
noon–6:00, Fri 10:00–6:00, Sat
(Sept–May) 9:00–4:00, Sat (June–Aug)
9:00–1:00
("Pennsylvania German/local area holdings.")

New Castle Public Library
207 East North Street
New Castle, PA 16101-3691
(724) 658-6659, ext. 112; (724) 658-9012
FAX
History@newcastle.lib.pa.us
http://www.newcastle.lib.pa.us
Betty Pallerino, Periodicals/Genealogy; Chris
Fabian; Kate Minteer; Bev Zona
Mon–Thur 8:30–8:30, Fri–Sat 8:30–5:30
(Pennsylvania county histories, census
1790–1930, Soundex (before 1930), DAR
repository, DAC collection,
marriage/obituary index for *New Castle
News* 1849 to date)

Northland Public Library
300 Cumberland Road
Pittsburgh, PA 15237-5455
(412) 366-8100
northland@einetwork.net

http://www.einetwork.net/ein/northalnd/
index.html
Mon–Fri 9:00–9:00, Sat 9:00–5:00, Sun
1:00–5:00

Ohoopee Regional Library
(see Georgia, Part 2)

Oil City Library
Heritage Room
2 Central Avenue
Oil City, PA 16301
(814) 677-4057; (814) 678-3072; (814) 676-
8028 FAX
ocensle@csonline.net
http://www.csonline.net/oclibrary
Heritage Room Staff
Tue & Sat 1:00–5:00

Old Mill Village Museum Association, Inc.
(Pennsylvania Route 848, Harford Road, 1
mile south of New Milford—location)
PO Box 434 (mailing address)
New Milford, PA 18834
(570) 465-9508
Col. Daw Lee, Vice President
summer: noon–6:00
Pub. *Museum-Archives-Historical Library*,
bimonthly
(history and genealogy, 1620–1890)
$15.00 per year membership

Osterhout Free Public Library
71 South Franklin Street
Wilkes-Barre, PA 18701-1287
(570) 823-0156, ext. 11
dsuffren@osterhout.lib.pa.us (General
Information);
reference@osterhout.lib.pa.us (Reference)
http://www.osterhout.lib.pa.us
Dianne Suffren
Sept–June: Mon–Thur 9:00–9:00, Fri
9:00–6:00, Sat 9:00–5:00; June–Sept:
Mon & Thur 9:00–9:00, Tue–Wed
9:00–6:00, Fri 9:00–5:00
(some local history books)
copies: 10¢ each from paper originals, 25¢
each from microform originals

Pennsylvania State University
W313 Pattee Library
Historical Collection and Labor Archives
University Park, PA 16802
(814) 863-2505
http://www.libraries.psu.edu/crsweb/
speccol/spcoll.htm

City of Philadelphia
Department of Records
Philadelphia, PA 19107-3209
(215) 686-2263
David Miller, Editor
8:15–4:45
Pub. *The Philadelphia Record*, biannually,
free
(records management, archival and general
information)

Free Library of Philadelphia
1901 Vine Street
Philadelphia, PA 19103-1189
(215) 686-5396
http://www.library.phila.gov/central/ssh/
waltgen/geneal/1.htm (Genealogy
Pathfinder)
Walter D. Stock, Library Supervisor I
Mon–Wed 9:00–9:00, Thur–Fri 9:00–6:00,
Sat 9:00–5:00, Sun (during school year)
1:00–5:00

The Library Company of Philadelphia
1314 Locust Street

Philadelphia, PA 19107
(215) 546-3181
nscalessa@librarycompany.org (Website
Coordinator)
http://www.librarycompany.org
John C. Van Horne, Ph.D., Librarian

The Athenaeum of Philadelphia
219 South Sixth Street
Philadelphia, PA 19106-3794
(215) 925-2688; (215) 925-3755 FAX
athena@libertynet.org
http://www.libertynet.org/~athena
Roger W. Moss, Ph.D., Executive Director
Mon–Fri 9:00–5:00 by appointment only
(research library specializing in American
architecture and interior decoration,
1790–1945, also biographies of architects;
extensive holdings of rare books,
drawings, manuscripts)
no research for hire available

**Pittsburgh History and Landmarks
Foundation**
James D. Van Trump Library
1 Station Square, Suite 450
Pittsburgh, PA 15219-1134
(412) 471-5808; (412) 471-1633 FAX
Albert M. Tannler, Historical Collections
Director
Mon–Fri 9:00–5:00 by appointment only
(houses books, manuscripts, periodicals,
historic site survey data, photographs and
other visual documentation, maps and plat
books, renderings and blueprints, and
other materials pertaining to architecture
and preservation; not genealogical)

Pottsville Free Public Library
16 North Third Street
Pottsville, PA 17901-2905
(570) 622-8880; (570) 622-2157 FAX
potpublib@iu29.org;
pot@iu29.schiu.k12.pa.us
http://www.pottsville.com/library/genie.htm
John Walker, Head Reference Librarian
Mon–Thur 8:30–8:30, Fri–Sat 8:30–5:00
(Schuylkill County with particular emphasis
on county seat, Pottsville; Molly
Maguires)

Priestly-Forsythe Library
(address withheld upon request)

Reading Public Library
100 South Fifth Street
Reading, PA 19602-1602
(610) 655-6355 (Reference); (610) 655-6609
FAX
rplref@reading.lib.pa.us
http://www.reading.lib.pa.us
Donna Geib, Head of Reference Services
Mon–Wed 8:15–9:00, Thur–Fri 8:15–5:30,
Sat 8:45–5:00; Pennsylvania Room:
Mon–Tue & Thur–Fri 10:30–4:00, Wed
10:30–3:30, Sat 11:00–3:00
(Pennsylvania-German culture; "We don't
have enough staff to undertake open
searches.")
$8.00 per year membership in Friends of the
Reading-Berks Public Library; research:
$2.00 plus cost of photocopies at 10¢ each

Annie Halenbake Ross Library
Pennsylvania Room
232 West Main Street
Lock Haven, PA 17745-1241
(570) 748-3321; (570) 748-1050 FAX
ross@rosslibrary.org
http://www.rosslibrary.org
Audrey Miller-Bongar
Mon & Thur 9:00–8:00, Tue–Wed & Fri–Sat

9:00–5:00

Christian C. Sanderson Museum
(Route 100, north of Route 1—location)
PO Box 153 (mailing address)
Chadds Ford, PA 19317
(610) 388-6545
T. R. Thompson
(very little genealogical information)

Saxton Community Library
(315 Front Street—location)
PO Box 34 (mailing address)
Saxton, PA 16678
(814) 635-3533; (814) 635-3001
saxlib@nb.net
http://www.saxtonlibrary.org
Judy L. Williams, Librarian
Mon & Wed 10:30–8:00, Tue & Thur
2:30–8:00, Sat 9:00–4:00
("We are a public library and don't have the
staff to do searches. Items in the
Pennsylvania collection do not leave the
library."
copies: 15¢ each, plus tax

Schwenkfelder Library, Inc.
(see Religious Archives and Organizations,
Part 3)

Sewickley Public Library
500 Thorn Street
Sewickley, PA 15143-1533
(412) 741-6920; (412) 741-6099
schneiderl@einetwork.net;
sewickley@einetwork.net
http://www.einetwork.net/ein/sewickley
Lynne Schneider, Public Services Librarian
winter: Mon–Fri 9:30–9:00, Sat 9:00–5:00,
Sun 1:00–5:00; summer: Mon–Fri
9:30–8:00, Sat 9:30–5:00

Shenango Valley Community Library
11 North Sharpsville Avenue
Sharon, PA 16146-2107
(724) 981-4360
Fessel_m@hotmail.com
Loretta Barker DeSantis, Librarian
Tue–Thur 10:00–8:00, Fri–Sat 10:00–5:00

Joseph T. Simpson Public Library
16 North Walnut Street
Mechanicsburg, PA 17055-3362
(717) 766-0171; (717) 766-0152 FAX
mechanicsburg@ccpa.net
http://www.ccpa.net/ls/MCHhome.html
Sue Erdman, Library Director
Mon–Thur 10:00–9:00, Fri–Sat 10:00–5:00,
Sat (July–Aug) 10:00–2:00, Sun
(Sept–June) 1:00–5:00

**Susquehanna County Historical Society
and Free Library Association**
(see Historical Societies—Local and
Regional, below)

Bayard Taylor Memorial Library
(216 East State Street—location)
PO Box 730 (mailing address)
Kennett Square, PA 19348-3112
(610) 444-2702; (610) 444-1752 FAX
jlordi@ccls.org
http://www.bayardtaylor.org
Joseph A. Lordi, Library Director
Mon–Thur 9:00–8:00, Fri 9:00–5:00, Sat
9:00–4:00

Temple University
Paley Library
Special Collections
13th Street and Berks Mall
Philadelphia, PA 19122

(215) 204-8230; (215) 204-5201 FAX
whitetm@astro.ocis.temple.edu
http://www.temple.edu

Union City Area Historical Museum
PO Box 321
Union City, PA 16438
(814) 438-7573
Thomas Schiewe, President

University of Pennsylvania
Van Pelt-Dietrich Library Center
3420 Walnut Street
Philadelphia, PA 19104-6206
(215) 898-7555; (215) 898-7556 (Reference
Department); (215) 985-1445 (PACSCL);
(215) 985-1446 FAX
http://www.libertynet.org:80/~pacscl
hours: various
(Philadelphia Area Consortium of Special
Collections Libraries [PACSCL] has no
holdings of its own and cannot direct
inquiries)

University of Pittsburgh
Archives Service Center
363 Hillman Library
Pittsburgh, PA 15260
(412) 648-7977
Dr. Ruth C. Carter, Head, Archives Service
Center
Mon–Fri 9:00–5:00
("multi sources for genealogy and family
history research")

University of Pittsburgh Library System
(Darlington Memorial Library, 601 Cathedral
of Learning—location)
363 Hillman Library (mailing address)
Pittsburgh, PA 15260
(412) 624-4491
http://www.pitt.edu/~hilmlib
Charles E. Aston, Jr., Head, Special
Collections Department
Mon–Fri 1:00–5:00

Upper Darby Free Public Library
Sellers Memorial Free Library
76 South State Road
Upper Darby, PA 19082-1999
(610) 789-4440; (610) 789-5319 FAX
upperdarby@delco.lib.pa.us
http://www.delco.lib.pa.us/liblist/ud.html
Thomas Roy Smith, Sellers Archivist
Special Collections-Local History Section:
Mon–Tue 10:00–4:00
(Darby Watershed historical background,
1200 Upper Darby Township photographs
1840–1940; Upper Darby Township is
situated at the interior limits of the state's
first permanent European settlement)

**Virginia Polytechnic Institute and State
University**
Appalachian history
(see Virginia, Part 2)

Warren Public Library
205 Market Street
Warren, PA 16365-2305
(814) 723-4650; (814) 723-4521 FAX
pwolboldt@warrenlibrary.org
http://www.warrenlibrary.org
Penelope Wolboldt, Head of Reference
Mon–Fri 9:00–9:00, Sat 9:00–1:00, Sun
1:00–5:00
(Emphasis on Warren County and petroleum
history)
copies: 20¢ per page

Citizens Library, Washington
Special Reference Room

55 South College Street
Washington, PA 15301
(724) 222-2400; (724) 225-7303 FAX
citlib@citlib.org
http://www.citlib.org
Rama Karamcheti, Reference Librarian
Mon–Fri 9:30–9:00, Sat 9:30–5, Sun
(Sept–May) 2:00–5:00
research: $5.00 per name, includes postage
and up to five copies plus search of
newspaper obituaries, marriage and birth
announcements (as long as the complete
dates are provided) and search of the card
catalog, pedigree charts, surname files, and
indexed county histories and biographies;
additional copies: 50¢ each

Mary H. Weir Public Library
(see West Virginia, Part 2)

West Chester University
Frances Harvey Green Library
University Avenue and High Street
West Chester, PA 19380
(610) 436-3383
http://www.wcupa.edu/library.fhg

West Overton Museum
West Overton Village
Scottdale, PA 15683-1168
(724) 887-7910
Rodney A. Sturtz, Executive Director
1 May–31 Oct: Tue–Sat 10:00–4:00, Sun
1:00–5:00
Pub. *The Village Progress*, bimonthly
(archival resources available focusing on
Overholt family, West Overton Village,
and limited local history; "no family
genealogical info except for Overholt-
Frict-Nash family")
$15.00 per year membership; research: $1.00
per hour archival fee

Whitehall Township Public Library
Local History Collection
3700 Mechanicsville Road
Whitehall, PA 18052-3399
(610) 432-4339
schwartzl@cliu.org
http://whitehall.lib.pa.us/toc.htm#info
Linda Matula Schwartz, Webmaster
Labor Day to Memorial Day: Mon–Thur
10:00–9:00, Fri 10:00–6:00; Memorial
Day to Labor Day: Mon–Thur 10:00–8:00,
Fri 10:00–6:00
(emphasis on Whitehall local history)

Wilkinsburg Public Library
Wilkinsburg Borough Building
605 Ross Avenue
Pittsburgh, PA 15221-2195
(412) 244-2940
http://www.einetwork.net/ein/wlksbrg

Historical Societies—Local and Regional

Adams County Historical Society
(111 Seminary Ridge—location)
PO Box 4325 (mailing address)
Gettysburg, PA 17325
(717) 334-4723; (717) 334-0722
Russell M. Swody, Executive Director
Tue–Wed & Sat 9:00–noon & 1:00–4:00,
Thur 6:00–9:00; tours: Wed & Sat
10:00–2:00
Pub. *Adams County History*, annually; *ACHS
Newsletter*, nine times per year
$25.00 per year membership; admission:
$5.00 for nonmembers; tours: $3.00;
research: $25.00 per hour, $50.00

minimum

Allegheny Foothills Historical Society
Boyce Park Administration Building
675 Old Frankstown Road
Pittsburgh, PA 15239
(412) 327-0338 (Boyce Park Business Office)
Sun (June–Sept) 1:00–4:00
no genealogical research at this time

Allegheny-Kiski Valley Historical Society, Inc.
224 East Seventh Avenue
Tarentum, PA 15084-1513
(724) 224-7666
(no genealogy department)

Apollo Area Historical Society
Apollo Memorial Library
219 North Pennsylvania Avenue
Apollo, PA 15613-1334
(724) 478-4214 (Library)
apollolibrary@hotmail.com (Library)

Armstrong County Historical Society
Lankerd Thomas Genealogical Library
(300 North McKean Street—location)
PO Box 735 (mailing address)
Kittanning, PA 16201
(724) 548-5707
Connie Mateer, Research
Tue–Thur noon–4:00, and by appointment
Pub. *Newsletter*, quarterly
(Armstrong County records)
$8.00 per year membership

Avonmore Area Historical Society
209 Fifth Street
Avonmore, PA 15618
(724) 697-4963
Charles Sharek, President
Pub. *AAHS Newsletter*

Beaver County Historical Research and Landmarks Foundation
1216 L. Fourth Street
Beaver, PA 15009

Beaver Falls Historical Society and Museum
Carnegie Free Library
Resource and Research Center for Beaver
County and Local History
1301 Seventh Avenue
Beaver Falls, PA 15010
(724) 843-6930; (724) 846-0370 FAX
Ken Britten
Mon–Wed & Fri 10:00–3:00
Pub. *The "Beaver Countian,"* quarterly
donation accepted

Bedford County Heritage Commission, Inc.
137 East Pitt Street
Bedford, PA 15522
(814) 623-1771

Bedford County Historical Commission
Pioneer Library
242 East John Street
Bedford, PA 15522-1750

Pioneer Historical Society of Bedford County
Pioneer Library
242 East John Street
Bedford, PA 15522-1750
(814) 623-2011
http://www.rootsweb.com/~pabedfor/plibrary.html
William Clark, President; Kay Williams, Librarian
Mon–Fri 9:00–4:00, first Tue & Thur

7:30–9:30, Sat 9:00–noon
Pub. *The Pioneer*, quarterly
(history and genealogy, includes former
collection belonging to Bedford County
Library)
$15.00 per year membership

Bell Township Historic Preservation Society
(Saint James Church Road—location)
PO Box 286 (mailing address)
Salina, PA 15680
(724) 349-3825
A. William Wolford, President
Pub. *Meetinghouse News*

Historical Society of Berks County
940 Centre Avenue
Reading, PA 19605
(610) 375-4375; (610) 375-4376
society.library@verizon.net
http://www.histsoc@berksweb.com
Barbara A. Brophy, Director of the Library
and Archives
Tue–Sat 9:00–4:00
Pub. *Historical Society Review*, quarterly
(Pennsylvania-German materials)
$25.00 per year membership

Berlin Area Historical Society
400 Vine Street
Berlin, PA 15530-0011
(814) 267-5987
http://www.berlinpa.com
Bill Buratty, Researcher; Paul E. Pritts,
Curator
Mon 1:00–4:00, Wed & Sat 9:00–3:00
Pub. *Memos*, quarterly
$10.00 per year membership

Berwick Historical Society
102 East Second Street
Berwick, PA 18603
(570) 759-8020
http://www.berwickhistoricalsociety.org
William Golder, Curator
Tue–Wed 1:00–4:30, Sat 1:00–4:00
Pub. *Historical Gems*, three times per year
$10.00 per year membership; no search fees

Blair County Historical Society
(Baker Mansion Museum, 3500 Baker
Boulevard—visitor's entrance at 3415 Oak
Lane, rear of building, location)
PO Box 1083 (mailing address)
Altoona, PA 16603
(814) 942-3916
Timothy C. Van Scoyoc, Curator
summer: Tue–Sun 1:00–4:30; winter: Tue &
Fri 9:30–4:30
Pub. *The Mansion*, quarterly
(Blair County newspapers, marriage records,
some Civil War histories)
$12.00 per year membership; $3.00 library
admission for nonmembers; surname
research: $10.00

Historical Society of the Blairsville Area
116 East Campbell Street
Blairsville, PA 15717
(724) 459-0580

Bloomingrove Historical Society
Dunkard Church Road
Cogan Station, PA 17728
(570) 435-2997

Boyd County Historical Society
(see Kentucky, Part 2)

Boyertown Area Historical Society
43 South Chestnut Street

Boyertown, PA 19512-1508
(610) 367-5255

Braddock's Field Historical Society, Inc.
419 Library Street
Pittsburgh, PA 15104-1609
(412) 351-5356
http://www.einetwork.net/ein/braddock/membership.html
Pub. untitled newsletter, bimonthly
$15.00 per year membership

Bradford County Historical Society
109 Pine Street
Towanda, PA 18848
(570) 265-2240
bchs@cyber-quest.com
Henry G. Farley, Presidents
Wed–Fri 10:00–4:00, Sat 10:00–noon
Pub. *The Settler*, quarterly (Feb, May, Sept, Nov)
$25.00 per year membership; admission: free
to members; research: $30.00 per surname

Bristol Cultural and Historical Foundation
321 Cedar Street
Bristol, PA 19007-5001
(215) 781-9895

Brownsville Historical Society
PO Box 24
Brownsville, PA 15417

Bucks County Historical Society
Spruance Library
84 South Pine Street
Doylestown, PA 18901-4999
(215) 345-0210; (215) 230-0823 FAX
mmlib@mercermuseum.org
http://www.mercermuseum.org
Beth Lander, Director of Library Services
Tue 1:00–9:00, Wed–Sat 10:00–5:00
Pub. *Penny Lots*, quarterly
$35.00 per year membership; research:
$40.00

Butler County Historical Society
(National City Bank Building, 106 North
Main Street, Seventh Floor—location)
PO Box 414 (mailing address)
Butler, PA 16001
(724) 283-8116; (724) 283-2505 FAX
http://www.butlercounty.com/local/historical
Office: Mon–Fri 9:00–1:00 (closed
government holidays)
Pub. *Butler County Historian*, bimonthly
(Butler County history)
$15.00 per year membership; research:
$15.00 plus copies and postage

California Area Historical Society
(429 Wood Street, California, PA 15419-
1139—location)
PO Box 624 (mailing address)
California, PA 15419-0624
(724) 938-3250
Mary Beth Graf, President
Tue–Thur 9:00–4:00
Pub. *California Crier*, quarterly
$12.00 per year membership

Cambria County Historical Society
(615 North Center Street, Ebensburg, PA
15931-1122—location)
PO Box 278 (mailing address)
Ebensburg, PA 15931
(814) 472-6674
Kathy Jones, Curator
Tue–Fri 10:00–4:00, Sat 9:00–1:00
Pub. *The Cambria County Heritage*, quarterly
$10.00 per year membership

Cameron County Historical Society, Inc.
102 West Fourth Street
Emporium, PA 15834
Sandra R. Hornung, Genealogist
anytime by appointment
(Cameron County, Pennsylvania, only)
research: $25.00 per family name

Carbondale Historical Society and Museum, Inc.
(Carbondale City Hall and Courthouse—location)
PO Box 151 (mailing address)
Carbondale, PA 18407-2356
(570) 282-0385
S. Robert Powell, President
Mon–Fri 9:00–1:00
Pub. *Newsletter*, quarterly
(emphasis on Carbondale, anthracite mining and the Delaware and Hudson Railroad)
$25.00 per year membership

Carnegie Historical Society
140 East Mall Plaza
Carnegie, PA 15106
(412) 276-7447

Centre County Historical Society
Centre Furnace Mansion
1001 East College Avenue
State College, PA 16801
(814) 234-4779
Jacqueline J. Melander, President
Mon, Wed, Fri & Sun 1:00–4:00
Pub. *Centre County Heritage*
(not the county's source for most genealogical records)

Chadds Ford Historical Society
(Route 100, ¼ mile north of Route 1—location)
PO Box 27 (mailing address)
Chadds Ford, PA 19317
(610) 388-7376; (610) 388-7480 FAX
cfhs@voicenet.com
http://www.de.psu.edu/cfhs
Elizabeth Y. Rump, Administrator
Mon, Wed & Fri 9:00–2:00, and by appointment
Pub. *Chadds Ford Historical Society Newsletter*, quarterly
(research library contains primarily references for the Chadds Ford area, limited collection of genealogy of local families)
$20.00 per year membership

Chester County Historical Society
225 North High Street
West Chester, PA 19380-2691
(610) 692-4800; (610) 692-4357
Roland H. Woodward, Executive Director
Tue & Thur–Sat 10:00–4:00, Wed 1:00–8:00
Pub. *Chester County Historical Society Newsletter*, quarterly
$30.00 per year membership; research: $20.00 per name

Chestnut Hill Historical Society
8708 Germantown Avenue
Philadelphia, PA 19118
(215) 248-9744; (215) 247-9329 FAX
ljarvis@CHHIST.org
Liz Jarvis, Curator
Curator: Tue & Fri 9:30–2:30

Clarion County Historical Society
17 South Fifth Avenue
Clarion, PA 16214-1501
(814) 226-4450; (814) 226-7106 FAXFAX
Lindsley A. Dunn, Director-Curator
Museum: Thur–Sat 1:00–4:00; Library: Tue–Sat 10:00–5:00

Pub. *The Iron County Chronicle*, quarterly
(genealogy and local history of western Pennsylvania counties)
$10.00 per year membership; research: $15.00

Clearfield County Historical Society
104 East Pine Street
Clearfield, PA 16830-2517
(814) 765-6125

Clinton County Historical Society
Heisey Museum
362 East Water Street
Lock Haven, PA 17745
David Winton, Executive Director
Tue–Fri 10:00–4:00
Pub. *Newsletter*, quarterly
$10.00 per year membership

The Historical Society of the Cocalico Valley
(249 West Main Street—location)
PO Box 193 (mailing address)
Ephrata, PA 17522
(717) 733-1616
Cynthia Marquet, Librarian
Mon & Wed–Thur 9:30–6:00, Sat 8:30–5:00
Pub. *Journal of the Historical Society of the Cocalico Valley*, annually
(emphasis on northern Lancaster County)
$18.00 per year membership; library admission: $3.00; research: $25.00 flat mail fee

Cochranton Heritage Society
PO Box 598
Cochranton, PA 16314

Colonial Philadelphia Historical Association
The Independence Hall Association
Carpenter's Hall
320 Chestnut Street
Philadelphia, PA 19106
(215) 925-7887

Columbia County Historical and Genealogical Society
(225 Market Street—location)
PO Box 360 (mailing address)
Bloomsburg, PA 17815-0360
(570) 784-1600
bdmfarv@ptd.net
http://www.colcohist-gensoc.org (includes form for research questions)
Tue & Fri 9:00–3:00, Thur 9:00–7:30, Sat 9:00–12:30
("In 1999, the [former Columbia County] Historical Society and [the former] Central Susquehanna Valley Genealogy Society merged.")
$18.00 per year membership; research for nonmembers: $2.00 per hour per person, plus copies at 30¢ each

Conemaugh Township Historical Society
100 South Main Street
Davidsville, PA 15928
http://www.ctcnet.net/ConemaughTwp/history.htm

Conneaut Valley Area Historical Society (CVAHS)
PO Box 266
Conneautville, PA 16406
http://www.toolcity.net/~cvahs
Betty Kovac, President
Sat noon–2:00
Pub. *Newsletter*, two times per year

Connellsville Area Historical Society

299 South Pittsburgh Street
Connellsville, PA 15425-3580
(724) 628-5640; (724) 628-5636 FAX
chs@cvzoom.net
Barbara Lowry, Secretary
Mon–Fri 10:00–3:00
Pub. *Connellsville Area Historical Society Newsletter*, quarterly
(census records, local newspapers, obituaries, printed histories)
$10.00 per year membership; research: $5.00 per research unit

Corry Area Historical Society
(935 Mead Avenue—location)
PO Box 107 (mailing address)
Corry, PA 16407-1247
(814) 664-4749

Crawford County Historical Society
Meadville Public Library, Second Floor
848 North Main Street
Meadville, PA 16335-2673
(814) 724-6080
cchs@ccfls.org
http://ccfls.org/historical
Mon–Tue & Thur–Fri 1:00–5:00, Sat 9:00–noon

Crescent-Shousetown Area Historical Association
PO Box 253
Glenwillard, PA 15046

Cumberland County Historical Society and The Hamilton Library Association
(21 North Pitt Street—location)
PO Box 626 (mailing address)
Carlisle, PA 17013-0626
(717) 249-7610; (717) 258-9332 FAX
info@historicalsociety.com
http://www.historicalsociety.com
Linda F. Witmer, Executive Director; Christa Bassett Hess, Librarian
Mon 7:00 P.M.–9:00 P.M., Tue–Fri 10:00–4:00, Sat 10:00–1:00
Pub. *Cumberland County History*, semiannually; *Newsletter*, quarterly; County Heritage Series (seven volumes to date)
$30.00 per year membership; research: $50.00 for nonmembers, $40.00 for members

The Historical Society of Dauphin County
John Harris/Simon Cameron Mansion
219 South Front Street
Harrisburg, PA 17104
(717) 233-3462; (717) 233-6059 FAX
Warren W. Wirebach, Librarian
Alexander Family History Library: Mon–Thur 1:00–4:00; Photograph and Manuscript Archives: by appointment
Pub. *Oracle* (not genealogical, "merely an events schedule"), quarterly
(Dauphin county family history)
$25.00 per year membership; research: fees vary

The Delaware County Historical Society
(Room 208 of the Delaware County Community College, Malin Road Center—location)
85 North Malin Road (mailing address)
Broomall, PA 19008-1928
(610) 359-1148
http://www.delcohistory.org
Trudy Carroll, Administrator
Tue 1:00–8:00, Wed 9:00–4:00
Pub. *The Bulletin*, quarterly
(Chester F. Baker Notebooks, Dr. Anna Broomall Collection, books, periodicals,

county newspapers, atlases, census, genealogies, directories, photographs, church and cemetery records, vital records, etc.)

$20.00 per year membership; admission $3.00 for nonmembers; research: $25.00 per hour

Depreciation Lands Association
Depreciation Lands Museum
(Hampton Historical Commission, 4743 South Pioneer Road, Hampton, PA—location)
PO Box 174 (mailing address)
Allison Park, PA 15101
(412) 486-0563 (Office); (412) 486-2187 (Home)
Elizabeth M. Hunter, Chairman, Hampton Historical Commission
Sat 10:00–2:00, Sun 1:00–4:00; Annual Fall Festive, first Sat in Oct: 11:00–4:00
Pub. *The Newydd*, quarterly
(genealogical services)
$10.00 per year membership

Derry Area Historical Society
PO Box 64
New Derry, PA 15671
(724) 694-9564
nquirer@juno.com
http://www.derryhistory.org

Derry Township Historical Society
(50 North Linden Road—location)
PO Box 316 (mailing address)
Hershey, PA 17033
(717) 520-0748; (717) 835-0331 FAX
dths@hersheyhistory.com
http://www.herseyhistory.com
Kathy Lewis, President; Lee Weist, Librarian
Mon 9:00–4:30, Wed noon–4:30, Sat 9:00–noon
Pub. *Reflection*, bimonthly
("historical and genealogical library—primarily local")
$15.00 per year membership; admission: free; research: fees depend on time needed

Donora Historical Society
510 Meldon Avenue
Donora, PA 15033-1333
(724) 379-7014; (412) 379-8809 FAX
http://www.westol.com/~shawley/dhs

Downington Historical Commission
Borough of Downington
4 West Lancaster Avenue
Downingtown, PA 19335
(610) 269-0344

Downingtown Historical Society
PO Box 9
Downingtown, PA 19335
(610) 269-6009
Leonard Sideman, President

DuBois Area Historical Society
(30 West Long Avenue—location)
PO Box 401 (mailing address)
DuBois, PA 15801-0401
(814) 371-9006
Audrey Lott, President
Apr–Dec: Tue & Fri 2:00–4:00, Wed 10:00–4:00
$10.00 per year membership

Elizabeth Township Historical Society
5811 Smithfield Street
Boston, PA 15135-1136
(412) 754-2030; (412) 754-2036
eths@icubed.com
http://www.15122.com/eths

Ronald F. Morgenstern, Executive Director
Tue–Thur 9:30–4:00, Fri 7:00 P.M.–10:00 P.M.
Pub. *Between Two Rivers*, bimonthly
$15.00 per year membership; research: $10.00 per hour per surname plus $2.00 to cover postage and copies ("All requests must be in writing with a retainer in the form of a check or money order made out to the society. Anything additional will be billed.")

Elk County Historical Society
(109 Center Street—location)
PO Box 361 (mailing address)
Ridgway, PA 15853
(814) 776-1032
Iva A. Fay, Archivist
Tue–Thur 1:30–4:00, and by appointment
Pub. *The Elk Horn*, three times per year at irregular intervals, $8.00 per year subscription
$5.00 per year membership; research fees charged by genealogist, who is away Jan–Mar, and vary with amount of time or money spent

Erie County Historical Society and Museum
Erie County History Center
(417-421 State Street—location)
419 State Street (mailing address)
Erie, PA 16501
(814) 454-1813
echs@eriecountyhistory.org
http://www.eriecountyhistory.org
Annita Andrick, Director, Library and Archives
Tue–Sat 10:00–5:00; reduced morning hours in fall and winter, call to confirm; Genealogy volunteers available Thur mornings and Sat 11:30–2:00
Pub. *Journal of Erie Studies*, two times per year (also online)
("There are many genealogy-related resources and research materials available on site at the History Center. The ECHS&M also includes the Watson-Curtze Mansion and Battles Museums of Rural Life sites, with exhibits and programming." History of northwestern Pennsylvania, particularly Erie County.)
$35.00 per year membership; museum admission at the Headquarters Building: $4.00 for adults; library and archives admission: free; research: all genealogy requests are referred to Erie Society for Genealogical Research

Evans City Historical Society
220 Wahl Avenue
Evans City, PA 16033
(724) 538-3629

Fairview Area Historical Society
(Sturgeon House, 4302 Avonia Road—location)
PO Box 553 (mailing address)
Fairview, PA 16415
(814) 474-5855
jmink@velocity.net
Joan Mink, Genealogical Queries
Sturgeon House: Sun (June–Aug) 1:00–4:00, Sun before Memorial Day: 1:00–4:00, Memorial Day: 10:00–4:00, Sat of first weekend in Dec: 10:00–4:00, Sun of first weekend in Dec: noon–4:00; Chapel in cemetery: Memorial Day: 10:00–noon; meetings: third Wed (Sept–May) 7:30
Pub. *Newsletter*, quarterly
("The Sturgeon House was listed on the Pennsylvania Inventory of Historical Sites

and was accepted for placement on the National register of Historical Places. It is now used as a museum, a depository of local historical data and a meeting place.")
$10.00 per year membership

Fallowfield Historical Society
660 Buck Run Road
Coatesville, PA 19320-4240
(215) 383-1591
http://www.museumsusa.org/data/museums/PA/30309.htm
Margaret S. Young, President
fourth Mon (except June–Aug & Dec)
$2.00 per year membership

Fayette County Historical Society
Route 40W
Uniontown, PA 15401
(724) 439-4422

Forest County Historical Society
PO Box 546
Tionesta, PA 16353

Fort Le Boeuf Historical Society
(Judson House—location)
PO Box 622 (mailing address)
Waterford, PA 16441
(814) 796-6030
Dorris A. Proctor, J.H. Coordinator
Wed (Apr–Oct) 9:30–3:00
$5.00 per year membership; research: donation accepted by volunteers

Fort Loudon Historical Society
(1720 Brooklyn Road—location)
PO Box 181 (mailing address)
Fort Loudon, PA 17224-0181
(717) 369-3473

Fort Manson Historical Society
548 North Main Street
Masontown, PA 15461
(724) 583-9944

Fort Shirley Heritage Association
Rural Delivery 1
Shirleysburg, PA 17260
Barbara McMath

Fort Vance Historical Society
2 Kerr Street
Burgettstown, PA 15021

Historical Society of Fort Washington
473 Bethlehem Pike
Fort Washington, PA 19034
(215) 646-6065
buck0858@aol.com
Betty Sadler, Librarian
Wed 2:00–4:00, first & third Sun 2:00–4:00 (closed July–Aug)
Pub. *The Bulletin*, ten times per year (monthly, Sept–June)
(local history, newspapers, archival library)
$15.00 per year membership; research: donation

Historical Society of Frankford
1507 Orthodox Street
Philadelphia, PA 19124
(215) 743-6030
http://libertynet.org/~gencap/frankford.html

Friendship Hill Association
PO Box 24
New Geneva, PA 15467
(724) 725-9190
Guy Clegg, President
Pub. *Echoes*

Fulton County Historical Society, Inc.
(110 Lincoln Way, East—location)
PO Box 115 (mailing address)
McConnellsburg, PA 17233
(717) 485-3207 (Secretary); (717) 485-3134
(Librarian)
Glenn Cordell, Secretary; Hazel Harr,
Librarian
Thur 1:00–4:00 & 7:00–9:00
Pub. *Local History or Genealogical Resource
Booklet*, annually, $4.00 per issue
$5.00 per year membership

Germantown Historical Society
5501 Germantown Avenue
Philadelphia, PA 19144-2291
(215) 844-0514; (215) 844-2831 FAX
ghs@libertynet.org
http://libertynet.org/ghs
Marion Rosenbaum, Librarian
Tue & Thur 9:00–5:00, Sun 1:00–5:00
Pub. *Germantown Crier*, two times per year
$30.00 per year membership; one-time
admission: $7.50 for adults; research:
$50.00 for two hours

Goschenhoppen Historians, Inc.
(116-118 Gravel Pike—location)
PO Box 476 (mailing address)
Green Lane, PA 18054
(215) 234-8953
"Abe" Roan, First Vice President
Museum: Sun (Apr–Nov) 1:30–4:00; Library:
by appointment
(Pennsylvania-German history and folk
culture, local and regional history of
Goschenhoppen Folk Region)

Gratz Historical Society
(8 West Market Street—location)
PO Box 507 (mailing address)
Gratz, PA 17030
(717) 365-3342
Lois E. Schoffstall, Director
Wed noon–5:00
Pub. *Die Tseiding*, quarterly
(Information on Dauphin, Schuylkill and
Northumberland counties. "We also have a
twelve-room museum, plus other exhibit
buildings and barn.")
$10.00 per year membership; library
admission: $3.00; tours May–Nov $3.00

Great Arrow Historical Association
968 Chapel Road
Monaca, PA 15061
(724) 744-8129

Greater Hazleton Historical Society
55 North Wyoming Street
Hazleton, PA 18201
(570) 455-8576

The Historical Society of Green Tree
10 West Manilla Avenue
Pittsburgh, PA 15220
(412) 921-2319
Marilyn Albitz, President
Tue 9:00–noon and 7:00–9:00, and by
appointment
Pub. *Green Tree Lore*, quarterly
(Green Tree area history, southwest
Allegheny County census)
$10.00 per year membership

Greene County Historical Society
Rural Route 2
PO Box 127
Waynesburg, PA 15370
(724) 627-3204
http://www.greenepa.net/~museum
Elizabeth Glass, Director

$5.00 per year membership

Greenville Area Historical Society
(946 College Avenue—location)
PO Box 25 (mailing address)
Greenville, PA 16125
(724) 588-5736
Gwinn Linegar

Hanover Area Historical Society
(105 High Street—location)
PO Box 305 (mailing address)
Hanover, PA 17331
(717) 632-3207; (717) 632-5199 FAX
Carolyn S. Stauffer, Executive Director
Mon–Fri 9:00–2:00
Pub. *HAHS News*, bimonthly
$15.00 per year membership; research:
$10.00

Haverford Township Historical Society
(Karokung Drive, Powder Mill Valley
Park—location)
PO Box 825 (mailing address)
Havertown, PA 19083
(610) 446-7988
Mary Courtney, President
Tue 10:00–noon (first weekend May–Oct,
weekends in Dec), and by appointment

Hay Creek Valley Historical Association
(Joanna Furnace—location)
PO Box 36 (mailing address)
Geigertown, PA 19523
(610) 286-0388
Mark Zerr, President
Pub. *The Journal*, quarterly
("We are a nonprofit group working with
volunteer time and labor to restore
historic Joanna Furnace, an early
American iron-making community.")
$3.00 per year membership

Hellertown Historical Society
150 West Walnut Street
Hellertown, PA 18055
(610) 838-1770

The Highlands Historical Society
Highlands Mansion
7001 Sheaff Lane
Fort Washington, PA 19034
(215) 641-2687
Catherine G. Hoffman-Lynch, Director
(primarily historical, not genealogical)

Historic Langhorne Association
160 West Maple Avenue
Langhorne, PA 19047
(215) 757-1888
Romaine Boyer Macht, President
Wed noon–1:00
Pub. *HLA Newsletter*, monthly
(research library)
$15.00 per year membership

**Homestead Pennsylvania Historical
Society**
1110 Silvan Avenue
Homestead, PA 15120

Hulmeville Historical Society, Inc.
(114 Trenton Avenue—location)
PO Box 7002 (mailing address)
Penndel, PA 19047
Donald L. Haefner, Archivist
Pub. *Town Crier*, four times per year, free

The Hummelstown Area Historical Society
(North Rosanna Street and North
Alley—location)
PO Box 252 (mailing address)

Hummelstown, PA 17036
(717) 566-8447
Joseph M. Brightbill, President
winter: third Sun 2:00–4:00, and by
appointment; summer: Sun 2:00–4:00
Pub. *Newsletter*, quarterly
(emphasis on central Pennsylvania
[Hummelstown area], family genealogies
and cemetery records)
$5.00 per year membership

Huntingdon County Historical Society
(106 Fourth Street—location)
PO Box 305 (mailing address)
Huntingdon, PA 16652
(814) 643-5449
Joanne Dolnikowski, Genealogist
mid-Mar to mid-Nov: Tue–Wed 9:00–4:00; 1
Jan–15 Mar: Wed only and by special
advance appointment
Pub. *Newsletter* (not genealogical), four to
five times per year, no regular schedule
$10.00 per year membership

**Historical and Genealogical Society of
Indiana County**
200 South Sixth Street
Indiana, PA 15701-2999
(724) 463-9600; (724) 463-9899 FAX
Alice K. Lackner, Executive Director
Mon–Fri 9:00–4:00, Sat 10:00–3:00
Pub. *Clark House Newsletter*, monthly;
Indiana County Heritage, irregularly, free
with membership or $4.95 per issue; *Clark
House Quarterly*, free with membership or
$1.00 per issue
$15.00 per year membership; admission:
$3.00 for nonmembers

Indiana University of Pennsylvania
IUP Library
Special Collections
Indiana, PA 15705-1096
(724) 357-3039
Dr. Larry Krorh, Director of Libraries
Mon–Fri 9:00–4:30

Jacobsburg Historical Society
PO Box 345
Nazareth, PA 18064
(610) 759-9029
A. James Shedlauskas, President
Pub. *Jacobsburg Record*, bimonthly
$7.50 per year membership

Jamestown Area Historical Society
405 Summit Street
Jamestown, PA 16134
(724) 932-5997

**Jefferson County Historical and
Genealogical Society**
(232 Jefferson Street, across from police
station, behind courthouse—location)
PO Box 51 (mailing address)
Brookville, PA 15825
(814) 849-0077
Bruce McMurray, Secretary; Carole Briggs,
Curator
Tue–Sun 2:00–5:00 (winter hours may vary,
closed major holidays)
Pub. *The Jeffersonian*, quarterly
(library contains all authoritative histories of
Jefferson County, directories, genealogical
reference volumes, newspaper collection,
periodicals; archives contains surname,
topical and ephemera files, family
genealogies, manuscripts [Bibles, diaries,
scrapbooks, account books, personal and
family papers, etc.], maps, photographs,
census microfilms, plus records from civic,
fraternal and professional organizations,

churches and cemeteries, schools, business
and industry)
$10.00 per year membership; research:
$15.00 per hour

Jefferson County Historical Society
100 Franklin Avenue, #B
Brookville, PA 15825-1166
Mr. Altman

Jersey Shore Historical Society
200 South Main Street
Jersey Shore, PA 17740
(570) 398-1973

Juniata County Historical Society
498 Jefferson Street, Suite B
Mifflintown, PA 17059
(717) 436-5152

Kittochtinny Historical Society, Inc.
"The Old Jail"
(175 East King Street—location)
PO Box 733 (mailing address)
Chambersburg, PA 17201
(717) 264-1667
Lillian Colletta, President
Library: winter (29 Nov–30 Apr): Tue
5:00–8:00, Wed–Thur noon–4:00; summer
(1 May–30 Aug): Tue 5:00–8:00,
Wed–Sat 9:30–4:00; fall (1 Sept– 28 Nov)
Tue 5:00–8:00, Thur–Sat 9:30–4:00;
Museum: Apr–Dec: Thur–Sat 9:30–4:00
Pub. *Newsletter*, eight times per year
(monthly, Apr–Dec)
(publishes Franklin County research
materials; library is a
historical/genealogical resource center)
$15.00 per year membership; research: 20¢
per page for copies

Kutztown Area Historical Society
(Normal Avenue and Whiteoak
Street—location)
PO Box 307 (mailing address)
Kutztown, PA 19530
(610) 683-7697
Ms. P. Allison duPont, President
first Sun 2:00–4:00, and by appointment;
monthly programs third Tue
Pub. *Along the Saucony*, quarterly;
Newsletter, monthly
(library specializing in local history; no
genealogical records)
$15.00 per year membership

The Lackawanna Historical Society
The Catlin House
232 Monroe Avenue
Scranton, PA 18510
(570) 344-3841; (570) 344-3851 FAX
lhs@albright.org
Mary Ann Moran, Executive Director
Tue–Fri 10:00–5:00, Sat noon–3:00
Pub. *The Lackawanna Historical Society
Journal* (emphasis on scholarly articles, no
queries), quarterly
(collection pertaining to the history of
Lackawanna County and northeastern
Pennsylvania from the 1700s: books,
photographs, manuscripts, etc.)
$22.00 per year membership; research: $5.00
for members, $10.00 for nonmembers

Lakemont Historical Park Museum, Inc.
411 Fourth Street, Lakemont
Altoona, PA 16602
(814) 943-1761; (814) 943-7449
Robert Leidy

Lancaster County Historical Society
230 North President Avenue

Lancaster, PA 17603-3125
(717) 392-4633; (717) 293-2739 FAX
lchs@ptd.net
http://lanclio.org
Mary Virginia Shelley, Librarian; Thomas
Ryan, Director
Tue & Thur 9:30–9:30, Wed & Fri–Sat
9:30–4:30
Pub. *Journal of the Lancaster County
Historical Society*, quarterly (John W. W.
Loose, Editor); *The Historian*, quarterly
(Marjorie R. Bardeen, Editor)
(Genealogical and historical research library
and archive; history and biography of
Lancaster County, Pennsylvania; Jasper
Yeates Colonial Law Library)
$30.00 per year membership; admission:
$5.00

Lansdale Historical Society
137 Jenkins Avenue
Lansdale, PA 19446
(215) 855-1872

Latrobe Area Historical Society
(1501 Ligonier Street—location)
PO Box 266 (mailing address)
Latrobe, PA 15650
(724) 539-8889
Kit Snyder, Treasurer
Tue 9:00–noon, Fri 9:00–3:00
small fee charged

Lawrence County Historical Society
(408 North Jefferson Street, New Castle, PA
16101—location)
PO Box 1745 (mailing address)
New Castle, PA 16103
(724) 658-4022 voice & FAX
Robert A. Presnar, Executive Director
Tue–Sat 9:00–5:00
research: $20.00 plus copying costs

Lebanon County Historical Society
Hauck Memorial Library
924 Cumberland Street
Lebanon, PA 17042
(717) 272-1473
Christine L. Mason, Librarian/Assistant
Coordinator
Mon–Fri & Sun 1:00–4:30, Mon 7:00–9:00
Pub. *Seeds of History*, bimonthly
(Lebanon County genealogy; Coleman
Collection; Bethlehem Steel Collection)
$20.00 per year membership; research:
$10.00 per hour, copies: 40¢ per page

Lehigh County Historical Society
(Old Courthouse, Hamilton at
Fifth—location)
PO Box 1548 (mailing address)
Allentown, PA 18105
(610) 435-4664; (610) 435-9812
http://www/geocities.com/Heartland/
plains/3955/LCHS.htm
Carol Herrity, Assistant Librarian
Mon–Sat 10:00–4:00
Pub. *Proceedings*, biannually (even years);
Town Crier, four times per year
(a large collection of church records of
Lehigh and surrounding counties; census;
published genealogies; city and county
directories)
$25.00 per year membership; admission
$4.00 for nonmembers; research: $15.00
per hour plus $5.00 postage and handling
and copy costs at 25¢ each

Levittown Historical Society
(7200 New Falls Road—location)
PO Box 1641 (mailing address)
Levittown, PA 19058

Ligonier Valley Historical Society
(Route 30, East Laughlintown—location)
PO Box 167 (mailing address)
Laughlintown, PA 15655-0167
(724) 238-6818
Tue–Fri 10:00–4:00
Pub. *Newsletter*, quarterly
(Ligonier Valley history; limited library of
photos, letters; other documents, which
have not been indexed or copied, are not
available for public research)
$15.00 per year membership; admission: free

Limerick Township Historical Society
545 West Ridge Pike
Limerick, PA 19468
(610) 495-5229
Dorothy L. Jones, President
Wed 9:00–4:00
Pub. *Limerick Township Historical Society
(newsletter)*, quarterly
("On National Historic Register. *Journey
Through Time*, a local history book
available.")
research: fee individually determined

Linesville Historical Society
PO Box 785
Linesville, PA 16424
(814) 683-4035

Lititz Historical Foundation, Inc.
(137-139 East Main Street—location)
PO Box 65 (mailing address)
Lititz, PA 17543
(717) 627-4636
Charles Steffy
May–Oct: Mon–Sat 10:00–4:00; Nov–Dec:
limited hours
Pub. *Historic Journal*, four times per year
$10.00 per year membership

Little Beaver Historical Society, Inc.
(710 Market Street—location)
PO Box 304 (mailing address)
Darlington, PA 16115
(724) 827-8841
Allen Ferguson

**Lower Macungie Township Historical
Society**
PO Box 3722
Wescosville, PA 18106
http://www.geocities.com/Heartland/
3955/LMTHS.htm

Lower Merion Historical Society, Inc.
(Ashbridge House, Rosemont, PA—location)
PO Box 51 (mailing address)
Ardmore, PA 19003-0051
(610) 525-5831
Thur 1:00–4:00 (except holidays)
Pub. *Newsletter*, quarterly
(library and museum, emphasizing lower
Merion Township)

Luzerne County Historical Society
Bishop Memorial Library
49 South Franklin Street
Wilkes-Barre, PA 18701
(570) 823-6244; (570) 823-9011 FAX
executivedirector@luzernecountyhistory.com
http://www.luzernecountyhistory.com
Patti Golubieski, Librarian/Archivist
Library: Tue–Fri noon–4:00, Sat 10:00–4:00
Pub. *Forecast*, quarterly
$25.00 per year membership; admission:
$5.00 for nonmembers

Lycoming County Historical Society
The Thomas T. Taber Museum of The
Lycoming County Historical Society

858 West Fourth Street
Williamsport, PA 17701-5824
(570) 326-3326; (570) 326-3689 FAX
Sandra B. Rife, Director
Museum: Tue–Fri 9:30–4:00, Sat
    11:00–4:00, Sun (May–Oct) 1:00–4:00;
Library: Tue–Thur noon–4:00, and by
    appointment
Pub. *Society News*, bimonthly; *Lycoming
    County Historical Society Annual Journal*
(Lycoming County local history and
    genealogy)
$35.00 per year membership; research:
    $15.00 per hour

Mahonoy Valley Historical Society
312 Hobart Street
Gordon, PA 17936
(570) 875-3347
Virginia Yarnell

Manheim Historical Society
210 South Charlotte Street
Manheim, PA 17545
(717) 664-3486

Marple Newtown Historical Society
PO Box 755
Broomall, PA 19008
(610) 353-4967
mnhistsoc@juno.com
A. Richard Paul, President
$5.00 per year membership

Masontown Historical Society
PO Box 769
Masontown, PA 15461

Mauch Chunk Historical Society
14 West Broadway
Jim Thorpe, PA 18229
(570) 325-4439
(Carbon County)

McKean County Historical Society
(Old County Jail Museum, 500 King
    Street—location)
Courthouse, Main Street, PO Box 202
(mailing address)
Smethport, PA 16749
(814) 887-5142; (814) 887-5571
    (Courthouse)
George E. Berkwater, President
Tue & Thur 1:00–4:00; summer: Mon–Fri
    1:00–4:00
Pub. *Bucktail—Newsletter*, quarterly
("outstanding county museum in old jail
    setting"; genealogical services)
$10.00 per year membership; research: starts
    at $5.00

Mercer County Historical Society
119 South Pitt Street
Mercer, PA 16137
(724) 662-3490
http://www.mchs.pathway.net
Robert B. Fuhrman, Executive Director
Tue–Fri 10:00–4:30, Sat 10:00–3:00
Pub. *Mercer County Heritage*, quarterly
$15.00 per year membership; research:
    $10.00 initial fee

Middletown Historical Association
2651 Langhorne Yardley Road
Langhorne, PA 19047
(215) 968-5119

Mifflin County Historical Society
(17 North Main Street, Lewistown, PA
    17044-2128—museum location)
1 West Market Street, Suite 1 (research
library location and mailing address)

Lewistown, PA 17044-2128
(717) 242-1022
mchistory@acsworld.net
http://www.mccoyhouse.com
Karen L. Aurand, Library Secretary
Tue & Wed 10:00–4:00, first & third Sat
    10:00–3:00
Pub. *Mifflin County Historical News*,
    quarterly
$10.00 per year membership

Mill Creek Valley Historical Association
Baker-Dungan Museum
Pennsylvania State University
(Beaver Campus, Monaca, PA
15061—location)
1334 Midland Beaver Road (mailing
address)
Industry, PA 15052
(724) 643-8969
Clude Piquet

**The Millbrook Society/Amy B. Yerkes
Museum**
(32 North York Road, second
floor—location)
PO Box 506 (mailing address)
Hatboro, PA 19040
(215) 957-1877
milbrook@voicenet.com
David T. Shannon, Jr., Executive Director
Tue 7:00–9:00, and by appointment
Pub. *Grist: The Millbrook Society Journal*,
    four times per year
(historical archives for the Hatboro-Horsham
    area)
$15.00 per year membership

**Historical Society of Millersburg and
Upper Paxton Township**
(330 Center Street—location)
PO Box 171 (mailing address)
Millersburg, PA 17061
(717) 692-4084; (717) 692-4933
Harry S. Mayhew, Genealogy Committee
    Chairman
Tue–Fri 9:00–11:00, and by appointment
Pub. *The Herald*, quarterly
$7.00 per year membership

Milton Historical Society
River Road
Milton, PA 17847
(570) 742-7057

Monongahela Area Historical Society
(717 West Main Street—location)
PO Box 152 (mailing address)
Monongahela, PA 15063
(724) 258-7148

Monroe County Historical Association
(900 Main Street—location)
537 Ann Street (mailing address)
Stroudsburg, PA 18360
(570) 421-7703; (570) 421-9199 FAX
Janet Mishkin, Executive Director
Tue–Fri 10:00–4:00; Sun 1:00–4:00
Pub. *The Fanlight*, quarterly
(Monroe County genealogy and local
    history)
$20.00 per year membership; research:
    $10.00 per hour

Monroeville Historical Society
2700 Monroeville Boulevard
Monroeville, PA 15146
(412) 372-9133

**The Historical Society of Montgomery
County**
1654 DeKalb Street

Norristown, PA 19401
(610) 272-0297; (610) 272-2609 FAX
http://libertynet.org/~gencap/montcopa.html
Vivian Taylor, Genealogist
Mon & Wed–Fri 10:00–4:00, Tue 1:00–9:00
Pub. *The Historical Society of Montgomery
    County Bulletin*, semiannually
$25.00 per year membership; admission:
    $4.00 for nonmembers; research: $25.00
    per hour prepaid

Montour County Historical Society
(1 Bloom Street—location)
PO Box 8 (mailing address)
Danville, PA 17821

Mount Union Historical Society
(27 East Market Street—location)
PO Box 1976 (mailing address)
Mount Union, PA 17066
(814) 542-2974

**Muncy Historical Society and Museum of
History**
(44 North Main Street—location)
PO Box 11 (mailing address)
Muncy, PA 17756
(570) 546-3431
http://members.aol.com/LCGSgen/muncy.
    htm
Pub. *Now and Then*, three times per year
$10.00 per year membership

New Berlin Heritage Association
Market and Vine Street
New Berlin, PA 17855
(570) 966-0065

New Hope Historical Society
(Main and Ferry Streets—location)
PO Box 41 (mailing address)
New Hope, PA 18938-0041
(215) 862-5652 (A.M.); (215) 794-8932
    (information/appointment)
Faith W. Crown, Archivist
tours: end of Apr–beginning of Dec: Fri–Sun
    1:00–5:00
Pub. *Newsletter*, irregularly (usually three to
    four times per year)
(some genealogies, local periodicals, New
    Hope Impressionist School; Parry family)
inquiries for donation

Newcomen Society of the United States
412 Newcomen Road
Exton, PA 19341
(610) 363-6600

Newtown Historic Association, Inc.
(Court and Centre Avenue—location)
PO Box 303 (mailing address)
Newtown, PA 18940
(215) 968-4004
Carrie Wetherby
Tue 9:00–2:00, Thur 7:00 P.M.–9:00 P.M.
Pub. *Half Moon*, bimonthly
(local history library, genealogy and property
    searches)
$10.00 per year membership

Newville Historical Society
Dougherty-Welch House
69 South High Street
Newville, PA 17241
(717) 776-6210
jbrehm@epix.net
http://www1.trib.com/CUMBERLINK/
    cumb/hist.groups.html
Joan L. Brehm, Librarian
Mon–Fri 9:30 A.M.–11:30 A.M., Fri 6:30
    P.M.–8:30 P.M., and by appointment
(local history)

$10.00 per year membership; research: no fee; copies: 10¢ per page plus postage

North-Central Pennsylvania Historical Association
311 North Front Street
Milton, PA 17847
(570) 742-9323

Northampton County Historical and Genealogical Society
Mary Illick Memorial Library
107 South Fourth Street
Easton, PA 18042
(610) 253-1222
Paul A. Goudy, Executive Director
Thur & Fri 1:00–4:00
Pub. *Northampton Notes* (no queries), quarterly
(3,000 family files, 5,000 books, 500 maps, 2,000 photos of places, 120,000 photos of people)
$25.00 per year membership; research: $25.00 for the first hour

Northumberland County Historical Society
The Hunter House
1150 North Front Street
Sunbury, PA 17801
(570) 286-4083
Jack L. Pensyl, Librarian
Charlotte Darrah Walter Genealogical and Historical Library: Mon, Wed & Fri 1:00–4:00, first Sat (Apr–Oct) 1:00–4:00; Museum: Mon, Wed & Fri–Sat 1:00–4:00
Pub. *NCHS Newsletter*, irregularly
(surname files, published family histories, vital records, cemetery records, church records, tax records, Orphans Court docket, W.P.A. files for a five-county area, city directories, 19th-century newspapers and personnel rosters from the French and Indian War, Revolutionary War and Civil War)
$12.00 per year membership; library admission: $3.00 for nonmembers; research: $10.00 for one name only; copies: 25¢ each

Octarara Area Historical Society
440 Strasburg Avenue
Parkesburg, PA 19365
(610) 857-3830

Oil City Heritage Society
PO Box 962, Oil Creek Station
Oil City, PA 16301

Old York Road Historical Society
Jenkintown Library
460 Old York Road
Jenkintown, PA 19046-2303
(215) 886-8590
http://www.oyrhs.org
Mon 7:00–9:00, Tue 11:00–2:00, Wed 10:30–3:00
Pub. *Old York Road Historical Society Bulletin*, annually on an irregular basis
$20.00 per year membership; research: details posted on web site under "collections"

Oswayo Valley Historical Society
PO Box 639
Shinglehouse, PA 16748
(814) 697-6964

Historical Society of Perry County
Headquarters and Museum
PO Box 81
Newport, PA 17074
(717) 567-3079 (Secretary)
Carl Tressler, President; Resta Tressler,

Secretary
Museum, Blue Ball Tavern, Little Buffalo State Park, Newport, PA: Sun (Memorial Day–Labor Day) 2:00–4:30, and by appointment
(no genealogical research services provided by staff)
$10.00 per year membership

The Perry Historians
(Route 34 between Newport and New Bloomfield—location)
PO Box 73 (mailing address)
Newport, PA 17074
(717) 582-4896
Wed 3:00–9:00, daytime hours posted in Mar each year
Pub. *The Perry Review*, annually; *The Airy Review*, bimonthly
$20.00 per year membership

Perryopolis Area Historical Society, Inc.
PO Box 303
Perryopolis, PA 15473

Historical Society of Phoenixville Area
Main and Church
Phoenixville, PA 19453
(610) 935-7646

Pike County Historical Society
c/o Milford Community House
(608 Broad Street—location)
PO Box 915 (mailing address)
Milford, PA 18337
(717) 296-8126

Pine Grove Historical Society
240 South Tultehocken Street
Pine Grove, PA 17963
(570) 345-6559

Plymouth Historical Society
115 Gaylord Avenue
Plymouth, PA 18651
(570) 779-5840

Plymouth Meeting Historical Society
(2130 Sierra Road—location)
PO Box 167 (mailing address)
Plymouth Meeting, PA 19462
(610) 828-8111
Suzanne Marinell, Administrative Assistant
Tue & Fri 10:00–4:00
Pub. *PMHS Newsletter*
$10.00 per year membership; research: $10.00 per hour

Potter County Historical Society
(308 North Main Street—location)
PO Box 605 (mailing address)
Coudersport, PA 16915
(814) 274-4410
pottercohist@adelphia.net
http://www.pottercountypa.net
Robert K. Currin, Curator; Leon B. Reed, Sr., President
Mon & Fri 1:00–4:00
Pub. *Potter County Historical Society Quarterly Bulletin*, $5.00 per year subscription
(county history)

Pottstown Historical Society
PO Box 120
Pottstown, PA 19464
(610) 323-8500
George Wausnock

Punxsutawney Area Historical and Genealogical Society, Inc.
Bennis House Museum

(401 West Mahoning Street—location)
PO Box 286 (mailing address)
Punxsutawney, PA 15767
(814) 938-2555; (814) 938-4434 (Genealogy Chairman)
mweimer@penn.com
http://users.penn.com/~mweimer/historcl.html
Vivian Waite, Genealogy Chairman
Tue 10:00–4:00, Fri–Sun (1 June–31 Aug) 2:00–4:00
Pub. *Histo-Report*, irregularly
$5.00 per year membership; research: $10.00; copies: 25¢ each for nonmembers, 10¢ each for members

Quakertown Historical Society, Inc.
(126 North Main Street—location)
PO Box 846 (mailing address)
Quakertown, PA 18951-1114
(215) 536-3298
Glenn Bosworth, President
by appointment
$10.00 per year membership

Radnor Historical Society
Finley House
113 West Beechtree Lane
Wayne, PA 19087-3212
(610) 688-2668
Pub. *Radnor Historical Society Bulletin*, annually
$3.00 per year membership

Red Lion Area Historical Society
PO Box 94
Red Lion, PA 17356
(717) 244-2501
Bruce F. Knisley, President
Pub. *Newsletter*, monthly
(baptismal and marriage records by parish to 1920; "Information provided through the mail, no visits by the public.")
$20.00 per hour for research

Ross Township Historical Society
102 Evergreen Hamlet
Pittsburgh, PA 15209
(412) 821-8888

Roxborough-Manayunk-Wissahickon Historical Society
6245 Ridge Avenue
Philadelphia, PA 19128
(215) 508-3928
gojohnny59@aol.com
http://www.philanet.com/Philadelphia
John M. Johnstone, President
by appointment for archives; monthly meetings
Pub. *Society Newsletter*, monthly
$10.00 per year membership

Historical Society of Saint Mary's and Benzinger Township
Genealogy Department
99 Erie Avenue
Saint Mary's, PA 15857-1408
(814) 834-6525
Melna Simbeck, Secretary
Tue 10:00–4:00, Thur 1:00–4:00 & 6:00–8:00
$6.00 per year membership; research: $5.00

Saltsburg Area Branch Historical Society, Inc.
PO Box 12
Saltsburg, PA 15681
(724) 639-3692
Rebecca B. Hadden, President

The Historical Society of Schuylkill County

(305 North Centre Street—location)
PO Box 1356 (mailing address)
Pottsville, PA 17901-7356
(570) 622-7540; (570) 628-2012 FAX
llward@voicenet.net
Dr. Peter Yasenchak, Director
Wed 1:30–7:00, Fri 10:00–4:00, Sat
    9:00–1:00
$20.00 per year membership; admission:
    $3.00; research: $25.00 per hour

Sewickley Valley Historical Society
200 Broad Street
Sewickley, PA 15143
(412) 741-5315; (412) 741-3458 (Archivist);
    (412) 741-8806 FAX
Betty G. Y. Shields, Executive Director
Tue–Fri 10:00–2:00, and by appointment
Pub. *Signals*, eight to ten times per year
    (extensive collection of obituary notices)
$20.00 per year membership; $10.00 per year
    out-of-state membership

Shippensburg Historical Society
(52 West King Street—location)
PO Box 539 (mailing address)
Shippensburg, PA 17257
(717) 532-6727
Myrtle Yohe, Genealogy Chairman
Wed 1:00–4:00, Sat 1:00–4:00
$10.00 per year membership

Skippack Historical Society
PO Box 389
Eagleville, PA 19408
(610) 539-6224
G. Keith Funk, President
8:00–5:00

Slippery Rock Heritage Association
PO Box 511
Slippery Rock, PA 16057
(724) 794-8600
Pub. *Slippery Rock Heritage Association,
    Inc., Newsletter*, quarterly
$10.00 per year membership

Snyder County Historical Society
(30 East Market Street—location)
PO Box 276 (mailing address)
Middleburg, PA 17842
(570) 837-6191; (570) 837-4282 FAX
Lee E. Knepp, Secretary
Thur & Fri 10:00–3:00
Pub. *Annual Bulletin*
(local history and genealogy)
$15.00 per year membership

Solebury Township Historical Society
PO Box 223
Solebury, PA 18963
(215) 297-8771

**Historical and Genealogical Society of
Somerset County, Inc.**
10649 Somerset Pike
Somerset, PA 15501
(814) 445-6077; (814) 443-6621 FAX
Susan Seese, Librarian
Tue–Sat 9:00–5:00, Sun noon–5:00
Pub. *The Laurel Messenger*, quarterly (Feb,
    May, Aug, Nov)
$20.00 per year membership; research for one
    name: $20.00 for the first hour and $15.00
    for each additional hour for nonmembers,
    $15.00 for the first hour and $10.00 for
    each additional hour for members; specific
    copy requests: $2.00 each, plus postage
    and copy fee of 25¢ per page from paper
    originals or 50¢ each from microfilm
    originals

South Bethlehem Historical Society
479 Brighton Street
Bethlehem, PA 18015
(610) 758-8790

Springford Area Historical Society
1 Reading Railroad Plaza
Royersford, PA 19468
(610) 948-7127

**Springs Historical Society/Casselman
Valley**
PO Box 62
Springs, PA 15562
(814) 662-2625
Eileen Mort, Curator
Museum: Wed–Sat (24 May to mid-Oct)
    1:00–5:00
Pub. *Chronicle*, annually
$10.00 per year membership; museum
    admission: $1.50 for nonmember adults

State Belt Historical Society
PO Box 58
Mount Bethel, PA 18343
(570) 897-6521
Diane Temples, President
(State Belt region of Northampton County)

**Stoneboro Community and Historical
Society**
Lake Street
Stoneboro, PA 16153

Strongstown Historical Society
(Route 422, Strongstown, PA
15956—location)
PO Box 75 (mailing address)
Strongstown, PA 15957
(814) 749-0722

**Sullivan County Historical Society and
Museum**
Courthouse Square
LaPorte, PA 18626
(570) 924-3549
Louise Woodhead, President
June–Sept: Wed & Sat

**Susquehanna County Historical Society
and Free Library Association**
2 Monument Square
Montrose, PA 18801-1115
(570) 278-1881; (570) 278-9336 FAX
suspulib@epix.net; sctylibrary@stny.rr.com
http://www.susqcolibrary.org/main.htm
Elizabeth A. Smith, Curator; Debra
    Adleman, Assistant Curator
May–Oct: Mon–Fri 9:00–5:00; Nov–Apr:
    Mon & Thur–Fri 9:00–5:00, Tue–Wed
    noon–5:00
Pub. *Susquehanna County Historical Society
    Journal of Genealogy and Local History*,
    biannually
$15.00 per year membership; reference room
    admission: $2.00 for nonmembers;
    research: $30.00 plus postage and copying
    costs

Susquehanna Depot Historical Society
PO Box 161
Susquehanna, PA 18847

Tamaqua Historical Society
118 West Broad Street
Tamaqua, PA 18252
(570) 668-5722

Tioga County Historical Society
Robinson House Museum
A. William and Rhoda E. Ladd Genealogical
Library

Office of County Historian
(120 Main Street—location)
PO Box 724 (mailing address)
Wellsboro, PA 16901
(570) 724-6116
tiogachs@epix.net
http://www.rootsweb.com/~patioga/tchs.htm
Scott P. Gitchell, Executive Director
Mon–Fri noon–4:00
Pub. *Tioga Chronicles*, three times per year;
    Tioga County Historical Review, annualy
$15.00 per year membership

Titusville Historical Society
Benson Memorial Library
213 North Franklin Street
Titusville, PA 16354-1788
(814) 827-2913 (Library)
http://ccfls.org/benson (Library)

Trappe Historical Society
201 Main Street
Trappe, PA 19426
(610) 489-8883

Tri County Heritage Society
PO Box 352
Morgantown, PA 19543
(610) 286-7477

Tulpehocken Settlement Historical Society
(116 North Front Street—location)
PO Box 53 (mailing address)
Womelsdorf, PA 19567
(610) 589-2527
Earl W. Ibach, Director
Apr–Oct: Mon–Tue & Thur–Sun 1:00–4:00;
    Nov–Mar: Mon–Tue, Thur–Fri & Sun
    1:00–4:00
Pub. *Tulpehocken Tattler*, quarterly, $2.00
    per issue; *Die Shilgrut fun der Tulpehock*,
    annually
(genealogical library and rotating historical
    exhibits in museum)
$15.00 per year membership

Tuscarora Township Historical Society
Bradford County
Rural Delivery 2, Box 105-C
Laceyville, PA 18623
(570) 869-2184
Hedy Chaffee, Presiding Director
Mon 9:00–5:00, and anytime upon request
Pub. *Once Upon a Time*, monthly
(genealogy and local history of Susquehanna,
    Bradford and Wyoming counties)
$15.00 per year membership; research:
    $10.00 per hour

Tyrone Area Historical Society
5 Oak Hill Lane
Tyrone, PA 16686
(814) 684-3248
Suzanne Sickler Ohl
by appointment
Pub. *Society Newsletter*, three times per year;
    Annual Report, annually
(Tyrone area history: people, places, events)
$10.00 per year membership

Union County Historical Society
Union County Courthouse
102 South Second and Saint Louis Streets
Lewisburg, PA 17837
(570) 524-8666; (570) 524-8738
historical@ptd.net
http://www.rootsweb.com/~paunion/
    society.html
Carol Manbeck, Office Manager
Mon–Fri 8:30–noon & 1:00–4:30
Pub. *Union County Heritage*, biannually (in
    even numbered years), $15.00 per issue

$25.00 per year membership

Uniontown Area Historical Society
PO Box 193
Uniontown, PA 15401
(724) 439-8571

The Valley Forge Historical Society
PO Box 122
Valley Forge, PA 19481-0122
(610) 783-0535; (610) 783-0448 FAX
http://www.libertynet.org/lha/valleyforge
Ms. Stacey A. Swigart, Museum and
    Collections Director
currently not open to the public
(very little genealogical resources;
    information pertains to history of Valley
    Forge and the American War for
    Independence; emphasis on the collection
    of artifacts)
$20.00 per year membership

Venango County Historical Society
(301 South Park Street—location)
PO Box 101 (mailing address)
Franklin, PA 16323
(814) 437-2275
Rainy Linn, President
Jan–Apr: Sat 10:00–2:00; May–Dec:
    Tue–Thur & Sat 10:00–2:00 (call before
    out-of-town visit)
Pub. *The Venango Intelligencer*, quarterly
$15.00 per year membership

**Victorian Vandergrift Museum and
Historical Society**
151 Lincoln Avenue
Vandergrift, PA 15690
(724) 568-1990

Warren County Historical Society
(210 Fourth Avenue—office location)
PO Box 427 (mailing address)
Warren, PA 16365-0427
(814) 723-1795
Michelle Gray, Office Manager
Mon–Fri 8:30–4:30, Sat (Apr–Nov)
    9:00–noon
Pub. *Stepping Stones* (not genealogical),
    three times per year
$20.00 per year membership; research: $7.50
    per hour, $25.00 minimum

**Warrior Run Fort Freeland Heritage
Society**
PO Box 26
Turbotville, PA 17772
(570) 538-1417

Washington County Historical Society
LeMoyne House
49 East Maiden Street
Washington, PA 15301
(724) 225-6740
Melissa Metz, Administrative Assistant
Tue–Fri 11:00–4:00
Pub. *Focus*, bimonthly
(history of Washington County, also
    regimental histories from Washington
    County regiments)
$15.00 per year membership; research:
    $15.00 per hour, discounted to members

Wattsburg Area Historical Society
(14438 Main Street—location)
PO Box 240 (mailing address)
Wattsburg, PA 16442-0240
(814) 739-2952
Thomas Coatoam, Secretary
second and fourth Sat–Sun 1:00–4:00, and by
    appointment
Pub. *Wattsburgh Occasional*, quarterly

(Wattsburg Borough and Amity and
    Venango townships
$5.00 per year membership

Wayne County Historical Society
(810 Main Street—location)
PO Box 446 (mailing address)
Honesdale, PA 18431
(570) 253-3240
Gloria McCullough, Research Librarian
Museum: Jan–Feb: Sat 10:00–4:00;
    Mar–May: Wed–Fri 1:00–4:00, Sat
    10:00–4:00; June–Sept: Mon & Wed–Sat
    10:00–4:00, Sun (except first three Sun in
    June & first Sun in July) noon–5:00;
    Oct–Dec: Mon & Wed–Fri 1:00–4:00, Sat
    10:00–4:00, first & second Sun in Oct
    noon–5:00; Library: same as museum,
    except closed Sun
Pub. *Wayne County Historical Society
    Newsletter*, four times per year
(Wayne County history and genealogy)
$15.00 per year membership; research library
    admission: free for members, $3.00 for
    nonmembers; research: $30.00 for initial
    two-hour search, $15.00 for each
    additional hour; copies: $3.00 minimum

Waynesboro Historical Society
138 West Main Street
Waynesboro, PA 17268
(717) 762-1747
Kathryn Hoffman, President; Julia Wells,
    Genealogy Volunteer
Wed 1:00–5:00, Thur & Sat 10:00–4:00, Fri
    10:00–1:00
$20.00 per year membership; research:
    donation

**West Virginia and Regional History
Association**
(see West Virginia, Part 2)

**West Whiteland Township Historical
Commission**
Whiteland Towne Center
Exton, PA 19341
(610) 363-8091

**Historical Society of Western
Pennsylvania**
Pittsburgh Regional History Center
1212 Smallman Street
Pittsburgh, PA 15222-4208
(412) 454-6000
Sharon Watson-Mauro, Librarian
Tue–Sat 9:30–4:30
Pub. *Jots from the Point*, nine times per year;
    Pittsburgh History, quarterly
$25.00 per year membership

Westmoreland County Historical Society
951 Old Salem Road
Greensburg, PA 15601
(724) 836-1800; (724) 836-2702 FAX
history@starofthewest.org
James V. Steeley, Executive Director
Tue–Fri 10:00–5:00, Sat 10:00–1:00
Pub. *The Westmoreland Chronicle*,
    bimonthly; *Westmoreland History*, three
    times per year
$25.00 per year membership; research:
    volunteer genealogist answers genealogy
    correspondence

Whitehall Historical Preservation Society
Mickley and Lenhart Roads
Whitehall, PA 18052
(610) 776-7166

Wilkinsburg Historical Society
Wilkinsburg Public Library

605 Ross Avenue
Pittsburgh, PA 15221-2195
(412) 244-2940; (412) 243-6943 FAX
Joel D. Minnigh
10:00–5:00
Pub. *The Archives*, nine times per year
    (monthly, except Dec–Feb)
$15.00 per year membership

Wissahickon Valley Historic Society
1400 Blue Bell Road
Blue Bell, PA 19422
(215) 646-6541

Governor Wolf Historical Society
(6600 Jacksonville Road—location)
PO Box 134 (mailing address)
Bath, PA 18014
(610) 837-9015

Wyoming County Historical Society
(Corner of Bridge and Harrison
    Streets—location)
PO Box 309 (mailing address)
Tunkhannock, PA 18657-0309
(570) 836-5303
Paula Radwanski, Secretary
Wed, Tue (15 Apr–15 Oct) & first & third Sat
    10:00–4:00, and by appointment
Pub. *Lest We Forget—Wyoming County
    Pioneers*, semiannually (Feb, Sept)
(genealogical library and museum; "The
    collection includes numerous books on
    New England ancestry, newspapers dating
    back to 1796 and census records for
    Wyoming and surrounding counties; also
    on file are records for over 90 area
    cemeteries as well as various other
    information about local history.")
$15.00 per year membership; queries: 15¢ per
    word (first 30 words free to members);
    research: $20.00 initial research plus
    copies

Wyoming Historical and Geological Society
(see Luzerne County Historical Society,
    above)

Yardley Historical Association, Inc.
(46 West Afton Avenue—location)
PO Box 212 (mailing address)
Yardley, PA 19067
(215) 493-9883

**York County Heritage Trust (Historical
Society of York County Library/Archives)**
250 East Market Street
York, PA 17403-2013
(717) 848-1587; (717) 812-1204 FAX
library@yorkheritage.org
http://www.yorkheritage.org
June Lloyd, Librarian/Archivist
Tue–Sat 9:00–5:00
(local history and genealogy)

Zelienople Historical Society
(243 South Main Street—location)
PO Box 45 (mailing address)
Zelienople, PA 16063-0045
(724) 452-9457
zeliehistory@fyi.net
http://www.fyi.net/~zhs
Joyce M. Bessor, Administrator
Mon–Fri 9:00–4:00
Pub. *ZHS Newsletter*, quarterly
(concentration on southwest Butler County
    and northwest Beaver County families,
    history of local area; specialty: Passavant
    and Buhl and Ziegler/Zeigler family
    histories. "Library has about 1,000 books
    and numerous files dealing with genealogy
    for numerous local families, and books

dealing with local, state, national and world history.")
$15.00 per year membership; research: $5.00 per hour (maximum $25.00 per day), fees vary, based on complexity

Genealogical Societies

State Genealogical Society

The Genealogical Society of Pennsylvania
215 South Broad Street, Seventh Floor
Philadelphia, PA 19107-5325
(215) 545-0391; (215) 545-0936 FAX
gsppa@aol.com
http://libertynet.org/gspa
Jane Adams Clarke, Executive Director
Mon–Wed & Sat 10:00–4:00, Sat by appointment only
Pub. *The Pennsylvania Genealogical Magazine*, semiannually, $15.00 per year subscription; *Penn in Hand*, quarterly
$45.00 per year membership; research: $20.00 per hour; admission: $5.00 for nonmembers

Genealogical Societies—Local & Regional

Allegheny Regional Family History Society
(see West Virginia, Part 2)

Beaver County Genealogical Society
Resource and Research Center for Beaver County and Local History
c/o Nancy Y. Lindemann
3225 Dutch Ridge Road
Beaver, PA 15009
W. Martin Ruckert, President; William E. Irion, Resource and Research Center Director
Resource and Research Center: Mon 5:00–8:00, Tue–Thur 11:00–5:00, Fri 11:00–3:00
Pub. *Gleanings*, quarterly
$10.00 per year membership

Berks County Genealogical Society
3618 Kutztown Road
Laureldale, PA 19605
(610) 921-4970
Berksgenes@yahoo.com
http://www.berksgenes.org
C. E. Cole Muhlenberg Center/Arts Building: Mon & Wed–Sat 1:00–5:00
Pub. *Journal*, quarterly; *Branches of Berks*, eight times per year
(Berks County and bordering counties)
$15.00 per year membership; admission: $5.00 for nonmembers

Blair County Genealogical Society, Inc.
(2012 12th Avenue—location)
PO Box 855 (mailing address)
Altoona, PA 16603
(814) 942-3681 (Library)
Helen Danemark, Librarian; Jennie Amrhein, Corresponding Secretary
Mon 6:30 P.M.–9:30 P.M., Wed 10:00–3:30 & 6:30–9:30, Thur 10:00–3:30
Pub. *Blair County Genealogical Society Newsletter*, quarterly
$15.00 per year membership; library admission: free

Bradford County Genealogical Society
21 Main Street
Towanda, PA 18848

Bucks County Genealogical Society
PO Box 1092
Doylestown, PA 18901
(215) 230-9410

Audrey J. Wolfinger, President
Wed–Fri 1:00–5:00
Pub. *The Newsletter*, three times per year; *The Journal*, annually (Fall)
(sponsors an annual two-day conference)
$20.00 per year membership; research: $5.00

Cameron County Genealogical Society
102 West Fourth Street
Emporium, PA 15834
(814) 486-2162

Capital Area Genealogical Society
PO Box 4502
Harrisburg, PA 17111-0502
(717) 5435-2622
Robert Viguers, Jr.
second Sun 2:00–2:30
Pub. *Keystone Seekers*, quarterly
(Dauphin and Cumberland counties; capital area cemeteries; no library or research facility)
$13.00 per year membership

Central Pennsylvania Genealogical Pioneers
120 Catawissa Avenue
Sunbury, PA 17801
Mrs. Strive

Central Susquehanna Valley Genealogy Society
(see Columbia County Historical and Genealogical Society, Historical Societies—Local and Regional, above)

Centre County Genealogical Society
PO Box 1135
State College, PA 16804
(814) 238-4060
http://www.rootsweb.com/~paccgs
Elizabeth A. Dutton, Corresponding Secretary
meetings: first Thur (Sept–May, except Dec)
Pub. *Centre County Roots*, quarterly
("We are transcribing and publishing all Centre County tombstone inscriptions.")
$12.00 per year membership

Columbia County Historical and Genealogical Society
(see Historical Societies—Local and Regional, above)

Cornerstone Genealogical Society
(Eva K. Bowlby Public Library, 311 North West Street—location)
PO Box 547 (mailing address)
Waynesburg, PA 15370
(724) 627-5653
http://www.vicoa.com/cornerstone
Laurine Williams, President
Pub. *Cornerstone Clues*, quarterly
$15.00/$20.00/$50.00 per year membership

Crawford County Genealogical Society
848 North Main Street
Meadville, PA 16335-2673
(814) 724-6080
Annette Lynch, Corresponding Secretary
Pub. *Crawford County Genealogy*, semiannually
(inquiries welcome)
$15.00 per year membership

Elk County Genealogical Society
Rural Route 2, Box 64
Johnsonburg, PA 15845

Erie Society for Genealogical Research
PO Box 1403
Erie, PA 16512-1403

(814) 454-1813 (Erie County Historical Society)
http://www.pa-roots.com/~erie
Linda Waha, President
Tue–Sat 10:00–5:00
Pub. *Keystone Kuzzins*, quarterly
$15.00 per year membership; mail requests for research accepted

Fayette County Genealogical Society
24 Jefferson Street
Uniontown, PA 15401-3699
fcgs_mail@yahoo.com
Pub. *Fayette Families*

Historical and Genealogical Society of Indiana County
(see Historical Societies—Local and Regional, above)

Jefferson County Historical and Genealogical Society
(see Historical Societies—Local and Regional, above)

Lycoming County Genealogical Society
(Lycoming County Historical Museum, 858 West Fourth Street—location)
PO Box 3625 (mailing address)
Williamsport, PA 17701-3625
LCGSgen@aol.com
http://members.aol.com/LCGSgen/lcgs.htm
Robin Leidhecker, President
Tue–Thur 1:00–4:00 by appointment only
Pub. *Lycoming Lineage*, bimonthly
(county-wide tax records 1850–1950, family files, church and cemetery records)
$10.00 per year membership; research: $12.00 per hour

McKean County Genealogical Society
PO Box 207A
Derrick City, PA 16727

Mercer County Genealogical Society
(Shenango Valley Community Library—location)
PO Box 812 (mailing address)
Sharon, PA 16146-0812
(724) 346-5117
Toni Sheehan, Secretary
Tue 10:00–4:00
Pub. *Past Times*, eight times per year, $10.00 per year subscription; *Mercer County Genealogical Society Newsletter*
(emphasis on Mercer and adjoining counties; cemetery books, history books, vertical files, census)
$10.00 per year membership; research: $7.50 per hour

Montgomery Area Genealogical Society
Montgomery Public Library
1 South Main Street
Montgomery, PA 17751
(570) 547-6212 (Library)

Montgomery County Genealogical Club
(see The Historical Society of Montgomery County, Historical Societies—Local and Regional, above)

New York Genealogical and Biographical Society Library
(see New York, Part 2)

North Hills Genealogists
c/o Northland Public Library
300 Cumberland Road
Pittsburgh, PA 15237-5455
(412) 931-5406; (412) 366-8100
Pub. *The Newsletter*, ten times per year

(monthly, except July & Dec)
(publishes cemetery listings by township)
no research, queries free in newsletter

Northampton County Historical and Genealogical Society
(see Historical Societies—Local and Regional, above)

Northeast Pennsylvania Genealogical Society (NEPGS)
(156 North Main Street—location)
PO Box 1776 (mailing address)
Shavertown, PA 18708-0776
(570) 674-7648
fjoyce@epix.net
http://www.rootsweb.com/~panepgs
Marge Sawyer, Corresponding Secretary
Thur & Sat by appointment
Pub. *The Heritage*, quarterly
$15.00 per year membership

Genealogical Research Society of Northeastern Pennsylvania, Inc. (GRSNP)
(210 Grant Street—Research Center location)
PO Box 1 (mailing address)
Olyphant, PA 18447-0001
(570) 383-7661; (570) 383-7466 FAX
genealogy@usnetway.com
http://www.cfrobbins.com/grsnp
Joseph J. Bryer, Research Coordinator
Mon, Wed & Sat 10:00–2:00, Wed 6:00–9:00; meetings in The Lackawanna Heritage Apartments Community Room, 211 Susquehanna Avenue: third Wed (execpt Dec) 7:00–9:00
Pub. *The Searcher*, quarterly
(Lackawanna, Luzerne, Wayne, Pike, Monroe and Susquehanna counties)
$25.00 per year membership; research: $10.00 for a simple search (date of the event is known), $35.00 for informational research, all search results include photocopying and postage up to $1.00

Old York Road Genealogical Society
1030 Old York Road
Abington, PA 19001
(215) 887-7683
Kenneth F. Hayes, President
second Tue 7:00
Pub. *Old York Road Genealogical Society Quarterly Newsletter*
(emphasis on education for local family genealogists)
$10.00 per year membership

Painted Hills Genealogy Society
(see New York, Part 2)

Palm Beach County Genealogical Society, Inc.
(see Florida, Part 2)

Punxsutawney Area Historical and Genealogical Society, Inc.
(see Historical Societies—Local and Regional, above)

Historical and Genealogical Society of Somerset County, Inc.
(see Historical Societies—Local and Regional, above)

South Central Pennsylvania Genealogical Society, Inc.
PO Box 1824
York, PA 17405-1824
(717) 843-6169 (Director)
Secretary@SCPGS.org
http://SCPGS.org
Mrs. Pat Gross, Director of Operations

meetings: first Sun (Sept–Nov & Jan–June) 2:15
Pub. *Special Publications*, once or twice per year; *Our Name's the Game*, ten times per year (monthly, except July/Aug & Nov/Dec combined issues)
(emphasis on York and Adams counties; maintains file of surnames being researched by members)
$20.00 per year membership; queries: free to members; research: $15.00 donation from members, $30.00 fee from nonmembers

Genealogical Society of Southwestern Pennsylvania
(Citizens Library, Special Reference Room—collection location)
PO Box 894 (mailing address)
Washington, PA 15301-0984
Mary B. Chadwick, President
Library: Mon–Fri 10:00–9:00, Sat 10:00–5:00, Sun 2:00–5:00; summer: Mon–Thur 10:00–9:00, Fri 10:00–6:00, Sat 10:00–5:00
Pub. *Keyhole*, quarterly
(southwestern Pennsylvania)
$10.00 per year membership if paid by 15 Jan, $12.00 thereafter, $14.00 per year foreign membership

Tarentum Genealogical Society
(The Community Library of Allegheny Valley, 315 East Sixth Avenue—location)
PO Box 66 (mailing address)
Tarentum, PA 15084-0066
74bug@nauticom.net
http://www.rootsweb.com./~patgs/index.html
Editor
meetings: third Mon 8:00
Pub. *Newsletter*, bimonthly
$10.00 per year membership; research: limited to holdings at Community Library of Allegheny Valley, please send SASE with query

Tri-State Genealogical Society
(see West Virginia, Part 2)

Twin Tier Genealogical Society, Inc. (Bradford and Tioga counties, PA)
(see New York, Part 2)

Venango County Genealogical Club
Oil City Library
Heritage Room
2 Central Avenue
Oil City, PA 16301
(814) 677-4057 (Library); (814) 678-3077
vengen@csonline.net
http://www.csonline.net/vengen
Gary Edwards, President
Heritage Room: Tue & Sat 1:00–5:00
Pub. *V.C.G.C. Newsletter*, quarterly
(Venango County and northwest Pennsylvania genealogy and history)
$10.00 per year membership

Warren County Genealogical Society
50 Second Street
Youngsville, PA 16371
(814) 563-9696
Virginia Roberts, Treasurer
$5.00 per year membership

Western Pennsylvania Genealogical Society
4400 Forbes Avenue
Pittsburgh, PA 15213-4080
(412) 687-6811
Pub. *The Quarterly*; *JOTS*, ten times per year
(sponsors Computer, English-Welsh,

German, Irish, New England and Scottish interest groups)
$20.00 per year membership; two free queries per quarter

Yankee Genealogical Society
Minnesota Genealogical Society
(see Massachusetts, Part 2)

Independent Publications and Miscellany

Appalachian Roots
(see West Virginia, Part 2)

Armstrong-Kittaning Trail Society of Pennsylvania
514 Penn Street
Hollidaysburg, PA 16648
(814) 695-0777
Sylva L. Emerson, Secretary-Treasurer
(Huntingdon, Blair, Cambria, Indiana and Armstrong counties)

Atwater Kent Museum
15 South Seventh Street
Philadelphia, PA 19106
(215) 922-3031

Dale E. Berger
1301 Bradford Road
Oreland, PA 19075-2414
(215) 836-4727
daleb@voicenet.com
Dale E. Berger, Publisher
Mon–Fri 10:00–4:00
(publishes histories of the Albright, Altemose, Cooper, Laubach, Meckes, and Wint families, and *Guide to Cemeteries and Burial Grounds of Monroe County, Pennsylvania*)

The Bradford Landmark Society
45 East Corydon Avenue
Bradford, PA 16701
(814) 362-3906
bradland@penn.com
Larry Richmond, Director of Genealogy
Mon, Wed & Fri 11:00–2:00, and by appointment
("Bradford history, obits, cemetery records")
$10.00 per year membership; research: $3.00 per lookup

Brandywine Crucible, Inc.
800 Franklin Drive
San Marcos, TX 78666
(512) 392-2092; (512) 392-1428
jandhcox@thrifty.net
http://homepages.rootsweb.com/~brandywi
Joe Burton Cox, President
Pub. *Newsletter*
(a nonprofit heritage society dealing with families—Cox, Hussey, Wierman, Day, Dixon, Carr, and others—who pioneered in the Brandywine Valley of Pennsylvania, and their descendants)

Canal Museum
(Hugh Moore Park, 200 South Delaware Drive—location)
PO Box 877 (mailing address)
Easton, PA 18044
(610) 258-7155

Center for Appalachian Studies
(see North Carolina, Part 2)

Direct Line Software
Land Record Reference
(see Miscellaneous, Part 4)

Erie Yesterday, Inc.
417 State Street
Erie, PA 16501-1106
(814) 454-1813
echs@velocity.net
http://www.goerie.com/erieyesterday
Terrance Cavanaugh, President
(an association of historical agencies)

Gilman Museum
(East Durham Street—location)
PO Box M (mailing address)
Hellertown, PA 18055
(610) 838-8767
Robert Gilman, Jr., Co-owner

Historic Catasauqua Preservation Association
8 Race Street
Catasauqua, PA 18032-1909
(610) 266-2948
meetings at Catasauqua Public Library, Third
    and Bridge Streets, PO Box 127: third Tue
    (Sept–May)

Historical Center
PO Box 81
Richfield, PA 17086
(717) 694-3211; (717) 694-3543
Noah L. Zimmerman; J. Lloyd Gingrich
Tue 7:00 P.M.–9:00 P.M., Sat 9:00–4:30
Pub. *Historical Center Echoes*, quarterly
$15.00 per year membership (includes
    Echoes) or $20.00 per year membership
    (includes *Pennsylvania Mennonite
    Heritage*, published by Lancaster
    Mennonite Historical Society, and *Echoes*)

Hoenstine Rental Library
(see Lending Libraries, Part 4)

Annie S. Kemerer Museum
427 North New Street
Bethlehem, PA 18018
(610) 868-6868
Gerald Robert Bastoni, Director
(primarily historical, not genealogical)

Lancaster County Connections
PO Box 207
Hershey, PA 17033-0207
(717) 533-5662
Gary T. Hawbaker, Owner/Editor
Pub. *Lancaster County Connections*,
    quarterly, $17.50 per year subscription

Lancaster County Heritage
PO Box 7773
Lancaster, PA 17604-7773
Peggy Sheets Manning, C.G., Editor
Pub. *Lancaster County Heritage*, quarterly,
    $15.00 per year subscription

Mechanicsburg Museum Association
3 West Allen Street
Mechanicsburg, PA 17055
(717) 697-6088
Fern Oram, Acquisitions
Tue–Thur 9:00–noon

Ohio River Valley Families
(see Ohio, Part 2)

PaGenWeb
Part of The USGenWeb Project
chepburn@cox.net; Bakergen@aol.com
http://www.pagenweb.org
Nathan Zipfel, State Coordinator; Carol
    Hepburn, Assistant Coordinator; Bob
    Baker, Assistant Coordinator
(links to other Pennsylvania resources)

Pennsylvania Dutch Folk Culture Society
Baver Memorial Library
Folklife Museum
Main and Willow Streets
Lenhartsville, PA 19534
(610) 562-4803
Florence Bauer, President
Apr–May & Sept–Oct: Sat 10:00–4:00, Sun
    1:00–4:00; summer: Mon–Sun
    10:00–5:00
Pub. *Pennsylvania Dutch News and Views*,
    semiannually
(Berks and neighboring counties;
    Pennsylvania German folklife and
    genealogy library)
$10.00 per year membership

Pioneer Publications
*Mid-Atlantic Queries & Reviews (DE-NJ-
MD-PA)*
(see Delaware, Part 2)

Reading Public Museum and Art Gallery
500 Museum Road
Reading, PA 19611
(610) 371-5850

The Rosenbach Museum and Library
2010 DeLancey Place
Philadelphia, PA 19103
(215) 732-1600
Ellen S. Dunlap, Director

Rough and Tumble Engineers Historical Association, Inc.
(U.S. Route 30, halfway between Coatesville
and Lancaster, PA—location)
PO Box 9 (mailing address)
Kinzers, PA 17535
(717) 442-4249
Dale Young, President
Memorial Day–Labor Day: Fri–Sat
    10:00–3:00
Pub. *The Whistle*, quarterly
$15.00 per year membership

Southwest Pennsylvania Genealogical Services
PO Box 253
Laughlintown, PA 15655
(724) 238-3176
William L. Iscrupe, Editor/Publisher
Pub. *Saint Clair's Bedford: The History and
    Genealogy of Bedford County, PA*,
    quarterly, $14.00 per year subscription;
    Pennsylvania Genealogist and Historian,
    quarterly, $16.00 per year subscription;
    *La Fayette: The History and Genealogy of
    Fayette County, PA*, quarterly, $17.00 per
    year subscription; *Old Westmoreland: The
    History and Genealogy of Westmoreland
    County, PA*, quarterly, $17.00 per year
    subscription; *Somerset Past: The History
    and Genealogy of Somerset County, PA*,
    quarterly, $14.00 per year subscription

Swigart Museum
PO Box 214, Museum Park
Huntingdon, PA 16652
(814) 643-0885

The Tombstone Hopper, Jefferson County, PA
10 Cherry Street
Brookville, PA 15825
harrypat@alltel.net
http://www.tombstonehopper.com
Patricia Steele
(publishes books on Jefferson County)
research: $10.00 per hour plus copies and
    postage

Tri-Counties Genealogy and History
(see New York, Part 2)

Warrior Trail Association, Inc.
Route 1, Box 35
Spraggs, PA 15362
Lucille Phillips

West Virginia University
Appalachian Studies Association
(see West Virginia, Part 2)

Rhode Island

Archives and Libraries with Holdings in Genealogy

State Archives and Library

State Archives and Public Records Administration
337 Westminster Street
Providence, RI 02903
(401) 222-2353; (401) 222-3199 FAX
reference@archives.state.ri.us
http://www.state.ri.us/archives
Mon–Sat 8:30–4:30
(state government records)
limited research performed by Archives staff, but written requests can contain no more than two names per request; charge for photocopies

Rhode Island Department of Library Services
(401) 222-2726; (401) 222-4195 FAX
http://www.lori.state.ri.us

Rhode Island State Library
Office of the Secretary of State
State House, Room 208
337 Westminster Street
Providence, RI 02903
(401) 222-2473; (401) 222-3034 FAX
tevans@sec.state.ri.us;
   statelibrary@sec.state.ri.us
http://www.state.ri.us/library/web.htm
Thomas Evans, State Librarian
Mon–Sat 8:30–4:30
("We are the state legislative library. We do not have a genealogical collection.")

State Historical Society

Heritage Foundation of Rhode Island
Rhode Island Hospital Trust National Bank
1 Hospital Trust Plaza
Providence, RI 02903
(401) 278-8353

Rhode Island Historical Preservation and Heritage Commission
150 Benefit Street
Providence, RI 02903
(401) 222-2678; (401) 222-2968 FAX
http://www.rihphc.state.ri.us

Rhode Island Historical Society
(121 Hope Street at the corner of Power—Library location)
110 Benevolent Street (mailing address)
Providence, RI 02906
(401) 273-8107; (401) 273-8111
   (Manuscripts); (401) 273-8112 (Graphics);
   (401) 751-7931 FAX
http://www.rihs.org
Meredith Sorozam, Associate Librarian-Director/Reference Librarian
Tue–Sat 9:00–5:00, third Wed 11:00–5:00; Manuscripts and Graphics: by appointment
Pub. *Rhode Island History*, quarterly, back issues $5.00 each
("Rhode Island history and genealogy. Reading Room open to the public." Copies of statewide marriage and death indexes, 1853–1900.)
admission: $5.00 for out-of-state nonmembers

City, County and Regional Archives and Libraries
(A more exhaustive list of public and academic libraries can be found at http://www.lori.ri.gov/lori/default.php.)

Barrington Public Library
281 Country Road
Barrington, RI 02806
(401) 247-1920; (401) 247-3763; FAX
director@barringtonlibrary.org
http://www.barringtonlibrary.org
Deborah Barchi, Director

Bennington Museum
(see Vermont, Part 2)

The John Nicholas Brown Center for the Study of American Civilization
(357 Benefit Street—location)
PO Box 1880, Brown University (mailing address)
Providence, RI 02912
(401) 272-0357; (401) 272-1930 FAX
Joyce M. Botelho, Director
Mon–Fri 8:30–5:00; Memorial Day–Labor Day: Mon–Fri 8:00–4:00; research by appointment only
("Our archival collections focus on the Brown family of Providence, Rhode Island.")

Brown University
John Carter Brown Library
20 Prospect Street
Providence, RI 02912
(401) 863-2725

   http://www.brown.edu/Facilities/John_Carter_Brown_Library

Brown University
The John Hay Library
(20 Prospect Street—location)
PO Box A (mailing address)
Providence, RI 02912
(401) 863-2146; (401) 863-2093
rock@brown.edu (Reference)
http://www.brown.edu/facilities/
   University_Library/general/libraries/hay.html
Jean Rainwater, Coordinator of Reader Services
Mon–Fri 9:00–5:00
Pub. *Books at Brown*, annually, $10.00 per issue
("We do not collect with genealogy in mind or offer services geared to the needs of genealogists.")

Connecticut Valley Historical Museum
(see Massachusetts, Part 2)

Coventry Public Library
1672 Flat River Road
Coventry, RI 02816
(401) 822-9100; (401) 822-9105
   (Reference); (401) 822-9133 FAX
askreference@coventrylibrary.org;
   debbi@seq.clan.lib.ri.us
http://www.coventrylibrary.org
Lynn Blanchette, Library Director
Mon–Thur 9:00–9:00, Fri–Sat 9:00–5:00, Sun 1:00–4:00; summer: Mon–Thur 9:00–8:00, Fri 9:00–5:00, Sat 9:00–1:00

East Greenwich Free Library
82 Peirce Street
East Greenwich, RI 02818
(401) 884-9510; (401) 844-3790 FAX
karentr@seq.clan.lib.ri.us
http://www.eastgreenwichlibrary.org
Robert Balliot, Information Services Librarian; Karen A. Taylor, Librarian
Mon–Thur 10:00–8:00, Fri–Sat 10:00–4:00

(extensive Rhode Island genealogy and history sources)

Jamestown Philomenian Library
Local History Collection
26 North Main Road
Jamestown, RI 02835
(401) 423-7280; (401) 423-7281 FAX
Library@jamestownri.com
http://www.jamestownri.com/library

Langworthy Public Library
Historical Archives
(24 Spring Street—location)
Box 478 (mailing address)
Hope Valley, RI 02832
(401) 539-2851
http://www.langworthy.org/archives.htm
David Panciera, Director
Library: Mon–Tue & Thur 6:00–9:00, Wed 10:00–5:00, Fri 2:00–5:00, Mon (winter) 2:00–5:00, Sat (winter) 10:00–5:00, Sat (summer) 9:00–noon; Archives: Wed 1:00–3:00, and by appointment
(The Gladys Palmer Collection containing local information about genealogy, land evidence, wills, and local buildings. Bernard Kenyon Collection of genealogy. Gladys Segar photograph collection.)

Lincoln Public Library
145 Old River Road
Lincoln, RI 02865
(401) 333-2421; (401) 333-2422; (401) 333-4154 FAX
http://www.lincolnlibrary.com
Becky A. Boragine, Director
Mon–Thur 9:00–8:00, Fri–Sat 9:00–5:00, closed Sat in July & Aug

Newport Public Library
Aquidneck Park
(300 Spring Street—location)
Box 8 (mailing address)
Newport, RI 02840
(401) 847-8720; (401) 847-8756; (401) 842-0841 FAX
nptref@lori.state.ri.us
http://138.16.137.5/nptlib
Regina Slezak, Director
Mon 12:30–9:00, Tue–Thur 9:30–9:00, Fri–Sat 9:30–6:00, Sun 1:00–5:00; summer: Mon 11:00–8:00, Tue–Thur 9:00–8:00, Fri–Sat 9:00–6:00

The Providence Athenaeum
251 Benefit Street
Providence, RI 02903
(401) 421-6970; (401) 421-2860 FAX
Lee Tererow, Assistant Director
Mon–Fri 8:30–5:30, staff assistance by appointment
$135.00 per year membership; no admission charge for nonmembers

Providence College
Phillips Memorial Library
River Avenue at Eaton Street
Providence, RI 02918
(401) 865-2242
http://www.providence.edu/library

Providence Public Library
225 Washington Street
Providence, RI 02903
(401) 455-8000; (401) 455-8005 (Reference); (401) 455-8013 FAX
pplref@provlib.org
http://www.provlib.org
Mon–Thur 9:00–8:00, Fri–Sat 9:00–5:30, Sun (Oct–May) 1:00–5:00

South County Museum, Inc.
Quaker Lane, Route 2
North Kingston, RI 02852
(401) 295-0498

University of Rhode Island
University Libraries
Special Collections
15 Lippitt Road
Kingston, RI 02881
(401) 874-2594; (401) 874-4608 FAX
dcm@uri.edu; archives@etal.uri.edu
http://www.uri.edu/library/
    special_collections/index.html
David C. Maslyn, Head, Special Collections
Mon–Fri 8:30–4:30
(Rare Books, Rhode Island Book Collection,
    Archives, Manuscripts and Personal
    Papers, Rhode Island Episcopal Church
    Records, Rhode Island Political Papers,
    Oral Histories)

Warwick Public Library
Greene Collection
600 Sandy Lane
Warwick, RI 02886
(401) 739-5440; (401) 732-2055 FAX
warwickpl@ids.net; wpleref@lori.state.ri.us
http://wpl.lib.ri.us
Douglas Pearce, Director
Mon–Thur 9:00–9:00, Fri–Sat 9:00–5:00,
    Sun (Sept–May) 1:00–5:00

West Warwick Public Library
1043 Main Street
West Warwick, RI 02893
(401) 828-3750; (401) 828-8493 FAX
wwaref@wwlibrary.org
http://www.wwlibrary.org
Maureen Delovio, Head of Reference
Mon–Wed 9:00–9:00, Thur–Fri 9:00–5:00,
    Sat (Oct–May) 9:00–5:00, Sat (June–Aug)
    10:00–2:00, Sun (Oct–May) noon–4:00
("Small local genealogical collection.
    Pawtuxet Valley Daily Times 1892- and
    Pawtuxet Valley Gleaner 1876–1906 on
    microfilm. There is a name index for the
    Pawtuxet Valley Daily Times 1892–1895
    available on our website.")

Westerly Public Library
(38 Broad Street—location)
PO Box 356 (mailing address)
Westerly, RI 02891
(401) 596-2878; (401) 596-2877; (401) 596-
    5600 FAX
http://www.clan.lib.ri.us/wes/index.php
Margaret Victoria, Head of Reference; J.
    Michael Barber, Reference Assistant
Mon–Wed 8:00 A.M.–9:00 P.M., Thur–Fri
    8:00–5:00, Sat (except summer) 8:00–3:00

Historical Societies—Local and Regional

Barrington Preservation Society
(Barrington Public Library, 281 Country
    Road—location)
PO Box 178 (mailing address)
Barrington, RI 02806
(401) 247-3770
Burton_Edwards@brown.edu
Van Edwards, President
Tue & Sat 10:00–2:00
(genealogical services)
$15.00 per year membership

Blackstone Valley Historical Society
1873 Old Louisquisset Pike
Lincoln, RI 02865
(401) 725-BVHS

third Sun (Sept–June) 1:30, and by
    appointment
Pub. *The Landmark*, ten times per year
    (monthly, Sept–June)
$15.00 per year membership

Block Island Historical Society
(Corner of Old Town Road and Ocean
Avenue—location)
PO Box 79 (mailing address)
Block Island, RI 02807
(401) 466-2481 (July–Aug); (401) 466-5009
    (all year, off season)
Robert B. Willis, Treasurer and Genealogist
July–Aug: daily 10:00–4:00; June &
    Sept–Oct: weekends
$10.00 per year membership; research:
    donation

Bristol Historical and Preservation Society
48 Court Street
Bristol, RI 02809
(401) 253-5705; (401) 253-8825

**Burrillville Historical and Preservation
Society**
PO Box 93
Pascoag, RI 02859
(401) 569-5451

Charlestown Historical Society
PO Box 100
Charlestown, RI 02813-0100
(401) 364-7507
http://www.charlestown.com/ri/
    historicalsociety/index.htm

Coventry Historical Society
(Route 117—location)
PO Box 401 (mailing address)
Coventry, RI 02816
Lillian Thurston, President
fourth Thur 7:00 P.M.–9:00 P.M.
$5.00 per year membership

Cranston Historical Society
Governor Sprague Mansion
1351 Cranston Street
Cranston, RI 02920
(401) 944-9226
RCarosi@aol.com
http://www.geocities.com/Heartland/
    4678/Sprague.html

Glocester Heritage Society
(1181 Main Street—location)
PO Box 269 (mailing address)
Chepachet, RI 02814
(401) 568-1866
Joanne S. Anderton, Archivist
Sat 11:00–3:00, and by appointment
$15.00 per year membership

Hopkinton Historical Association
Town House Road
Hopkinton, RI 02833

Jamestown Historical Society
(92 Narragansett Avenue—location)
PO Box 156 (mailing address)
Jamestown, RI 02835
(401) 423-0784
Mary Miner, Archivist
Museum: late June–Aug: Tue–Sat 1:00–4:00
$10.00 per year membership

Little Compton Historical Society
Wilbor House
(548 West Main Road—location)
PO Box 577 (mailing address)
Little Compton, RI 02837
(401) 635-4035

Sheila Mackintosh, President
Mid-June to mid-Sept: Mon & Thur–Sun
    2:00–5:00

Main Street Association of Wickford
68 Main Street
Wickford, RI 02852
(401) 294-6479

Massasoit Historical Association
PO Box 203
Warren, RI 02885

Middletown Historical Society, Inc.
(Corner Prospect and Paradise Avenues,
Middletown, RI 02840—location)
PO Box 4196 (mailing address)
Middletown, RI 02842
(401) 849-1870
Stanley Grossman, President
Pub. *MHS Newsletter*, quarterly
(New England heritage)

**The New England Historic Genealogical
Society**
(see Massachusetts, Part 2)

Newport Historical Society
82 Touro Street
Newport, RI 02840
(401) 846-0813; (401) 846-1853
Bertram Lippincott, III, C.G., Librarian
Tue–Fri 9:30–4:30, Sat 9:30–noon
Pub. *Newport History*, quarterly; *Newport
    Historical Society Newsletter*
(second largest genealogical collection in
    Rhode Island)
$30.00 per year membership

North Smithfield Heritage Association
PO Box 413
Slatersville, RI 02876

The Pettaquamscatt Historical Society
2636 Kingstown Road
Kingston, RI 02881
(401) 783-1328
Christopher Bickford, Director
Tue, Thur & Sat 1:00–4:00
(History of Washington County. "Will answer
    genealogical queries.")
$10.00 per year membership

Scituate Preservation Society, Inc.
(706 Hartford Pike—location)
PO Box 551 (mailing address)
North Scituate, RI 02857
(401) 647-5010
Fred T. Faria, President
(genealogical services)
$15.00 per year membership

Tiverton Historical Society
3908 Main Road
Tiverton, RI 02878
(401) 624-8881
John L. Berg, President
Pub. *Patchwork History of Tiverton*

The Warwick Historical Society
25 Roger Williams Circle
Warren, RI 02888
(401) 737-8160; (401) 467-7647
    (Wednesdays)
Mildred Longo, Librarian
Wed 9:00–1:00
(history and genealogy research center for
    Warwick only)
$10.00 per year membership

Westerly Historical Society
PO Box 91

Westerly, RI 02891
(401) 377-2602
http://www.watchhill.com/
   historicalsociety/index.html
Dwight Brown, First Vice President
$5.00–$25.00 per year membership; search
   fees: $5.00 for first half-hour, $10.00 for
   each additional hour

Western Rhode Island Civic Historical Society
1 Station Street
Coventry, RI 02816
(401) 397-5135
Paula Rossi, Curator
June–Sept: Sat 1:00–4:00

The Woonsocket Historical and Preservation Society
42 South Main Street
Woonsocket, RI 02895
(401) 356-0067
Phyllis H. Thomas, Director
Tue 10:00–3:00, Fri–Sat 11:00–3:00

Genealogical Societies

State Genealogical Society

Rhode Island Genealogical Society
49 Farm Street
Dover, MA 02030
Robert Carter Arnold
Pub. *Rhode Island Roots*, quarterly (Mar,
   June, Sept, Dec)
$10.00 per year membership

Genealogical Societies—Local & Regional

American-Canadian Genealogical Society
(see New Hampshire, Part 2)

The New England Historic Genealogical Society
(see Massachusetts, Part 2)

Newport Genealogical Society
160 Bristol Ferry Road
Portsmouth, RI 02871
(401) 847-1576

Yankee Genealogical Society
Minnesota Genealogical Society
(see Massachusetts, Part 2)

Independent Publications and Miscellany

Company of the Gloucester Light Infantry
(Dorr Drive, Chepachet, RI 02814—location)
212 Farnum Pike (mailing address)
Smithfield, RI 02917
(401) 568-0034
Ens. Sheri L. Vieira, R.I.M., Secretary
(Rhode Island Historical Commands
   Member; "We are an original charter
   group, 1774 Rhode Island Militia.")

Foster Preservation Society
PO Box 51
Foster, RI 02825

Historical Ink's Old Maps
(see New York, Part 2)

The League of Rhode Island Historical Societies
39 Forsythia Lane
Cranston, RI 02920
(401) 942-3015
Robert Drew, President

New England Connexion
(see Connecticut, Part 2)

The New England Quarterly
(see Massachusetts, Part 2)

The Preservation Society of Newport County
(address withheld upon request)
Pub. *Newport Gazette*, quarterly;
   *Preservation Society of Newport County
   Annual Report*
(operates a collection of house museums,
   does not maintain a research facility or
   library)

Pioneer Publications
New England Queries and Reviews
(see Connecticut, Part 2)

Society for the Preservation of New England Antiquities—Archives
(see Massachusetts, Part 2)

Providence Preservation Society
24 Meeting Street
Providence, RI 02903
(401) 831-7440

Rhode Island Cemeteries Database
http://members.tripod.com/~debyns/
   cemetery.html

Rhode Island Department of Transportation
2 Capitol Hill
Providence, RI 02903-1124
(401) 222-1362
Webmaster@dot.state.ri.us
http://www.dot.state.ri.us/WebMaps (Maps)

Rhode Island Families Association
PO Box 1414
Ashburn, VA 20146-1414
rigr@pop.erols.com
http://www.erols.com/rigr
Nellie Beaman, Editor
Pub. *Rhode Island Genealogical Register*
   (volumes 1–20) (index to all the wills in
   Rhode Island from 1636–1850, volume 16
   RIGR); *Rhode Island Vital Records*, New
   Series (volumes 3–13)
$35.00 per year membership; copies of will
   abstracts: $15.00 for one or $25.00 for
   two

Rhode Island Genealogy Page
http://users.ids.net/~jcraig/ri_gen.htm

RIGenWeb
Part of The USGenweb Project
ri@usgenweb.com
http://www.rootsweb.com/~rigenweb
(links to other Rhode Island resources)

South Carolina

Archives and Libraries with Holdings in Genealogy

State Archives

South Carolina Department of Archives and History
8301 Parklane Road
Columbia, SC 29223
(803) 896-6104; (803) 896-6198 FAX
tuttle@scdah.state.sc.us
http://www.state.sc.us/scdah
Steven D. Tuttle, Supervisor of Reference
   Service
Mon–Fri 8:45–4:45
("Permanently valuable public records of
   South Carolina 1671–ca 1950.")

South Carolina State Library
(address withheld upon request)
(materials relating to South Carolina history
   only, not a genealogy library, defers to
   South Carolina Department of Archives
   and History and to the University of South
   Carolina's South Caroliniana Library)

State Historical Societies

South Carolina Historical Association
Francis Marion College
Florence, SC 29501
Pub. *South Carolina Historical Association
   Proceedings*, annually

South Carolina Historical Society
100 Meeting Street, Fireproof Building
Charleston, SC 29414
(843) 723-3225; (843) 723-8584 FAX
info@SCHistory.org
http://www.SCHistory.org
Jackie McCall, Research Consultant
Tue–Fri 9:00–4:00, Sat 9:00–2:00 (call in
   advance in case of schedule change)
Pub. *The South Carolina Historical
   Magazine*, quarterly; *Carologue*, quarterly
("Historical Society maintains the most
   extensive private collection of South
   Carolina genealogical material; also
   material on other states.")
$55.00 per year membership; library
   admission: $5.00 for nonmembers;
   research from Research Consultant:
   $15.00 per half hour, $75.00 for up to four
   hours of unrestricted search of all
   materials

City, County and Regional Archives and Libraries
(A more exhaustive list of public and
   academic libraries can be found at
   http://www.state.sc.us/scsl/colibs1.html.)

Abbeville-Greenwood Regional Library
Greenwood County Library
106 North Main Street
Greenwood, SC 29646-2240
(864) 223-4515; (864) 941-4650; (864) 941-
   4651 FAX
http://www.greenwoodcountylibrary.org
Mon–Tue & Thur 9:00–9:00, Wed & Fri
   9:00–5:30, Sat 10:30–5:00, Sun 2:00–5:00
(houses collection of the Old Ninety Six
   District Chapter [SCGS] and the DAR, but
   has no staff to handle correspondence)

Aiken County Historical Museum
433 Newberry Street, S.W.
Aiken, SC 29801
(803) 642-2015

http://www.scescape.com/
aikenhistoricalmuseum
Nana Farris, Museum Director
Pub. *MuseNews*
(research facility)

Beaufort County Library
South Carolina Room
311 Scott Street
Beaufort, SC 29902-5591
(843) 525-4000; (843) 525-4055 FAX
http://www.co.beaufort.sc.us/bftlib/
default.htm
Julie Zachowski, Director

Calhoun County Museum
Archives Library
303 Butler Street
Saint Matthews, SC 29135
(803) 874-3964; (803) 874-1242 FAX
Debbie U. Roland, Director
9:00–4:00 by appointment only

Camden Archives and Museum
1314 Broad Street
Camden, SC 29020-3535
(803) 425-6050; (803) 424-4053 FAX
http://www.camden-sc.org/Museum.asp
Agnes B. Corbett, Director
Mon–Fri 8:00–5:00, first & third Sun
1:00–5:00
("Museum with local artifacts and research
library operated by City of Camden;
general history and genealogy, SCDAR
Library located here.")
free in-house research, $10.00 per hour for
requests by mail (subject to change)

Charleston City Archives and Records
701 East Bay Street
Charleston, SC 29402
(843) 724-7301; (843) 720-3897 FAX
Jane Boyd, Archivist
Mon–Fri 8:30–5:00
("Primarily a records storage
facility/warehouse for modern municipal
records; there are no records stored here
which would be of much assistance to
researchers.")

Charleston County Public Library
South Carolina Room
68 Calhoun Street
Charleston, SC 29403
(843) 805-6956
http://www.ccpl.org/opener.html
Mon–Thur 9:00–9:00, Fri–Sat 9:00–6:00,
Sun 2:00–5:00
(Charleston and the Low Country)

Charleston Library Society
164 King Street
Charleston, SC 29401
(843) 723-9912
Catherine Sadler, Librarian
Mon–Fri 9:30–5:30, Sat 9:30–2:00
Pub. *Newsletter*, four times per year annual
report; *The Charleston Reader*, quarterly
(no genealogy)
("Subscription library since 1748 continues
today." A full-service library and
archives—limited genealogical materials
are available: early South Carolina
newspapers, census, city directories of
Charleston from 1782.)
$35.00 per year membership; admission:
$3.00 per day

Cherokee County Public Library
300 East Rutledge Avenue
Gaffney, SC 29340-2299
(864) 487-2711; (864) 487-2752 FAX

http://andy.appnet.org/cherokee/index.htm
Anne Moseley, Director
Mon–Tue 10:00–8:00, Wed–Fri 10:00–6:00,
Sat 10:00–4:00
(small library of genealogical books,
microfilms of newspapers and Draper
Papers)

The Citadel
The Citadel Archives and Museum
171 Moultrie Street
Charleston, SC 29409
(843) 953-6846
Jane Yates, Director
Archives: Mon–Fri 8:30–5:00 by
appointment; Museum Mon–Fri & Sun
2:00–5:00, Sat noon–5:00, closed for
college, religious, and national holidays
(specializes in The Citadel, history of The
Military College of South Carolina)

Darlington County Library
204 North Main Street
Darlington, SC 29532-3108
(843) 398-4940; (843) 398-4942 FAX
http://darlington-lib.org
Sue Rainey, Director
Mon & Wed 9:00–9:00, Tue & Thur–Fri
9:00–6:00, Sat 10:00–2:00, Sun
2:00–5:00

Fairfield County Museum
Fairfield Genealogy Room
(231 South Congress Street—location)
PO Box 6 (mailing address)
Winnsboro, SC 29180
(803) 635-9811
Mrs. Marion E. Stevenson
Wed 10:30–4:30

Francis Marion University
James A. Rogers Library
Arundel Room
Florence, SC 29501-0547
(843) 661-1300
http://vax.fmarion.edu/marion

**The Genealogical and Historical Research
Center**
(see Sumter County Genealogical Society,
Genealogical Societies—Local and Regional,
below)

Greenville County Library
Stow South Carolina Historical Collection
300 College Street
Greenville, SC 29601
(864) 242-5000, ext. 269; (864) 235-8375
FAX
http://www.greenvillelibrary.org
Joyce Borders, Head, Local Information and
History Section
Mon–Fri 9:00–9:00, Sat 9:00–6:00, Sun
2:00–6:00
(emphasis on South Carolina and
southeastern U.S.)

Horry County Memorial Library
1008 Fifth Avenue
Conway, SC 29526-4354
(843) 248-1543; (843) 248-1548 FAX
http://www.horry.lib.sc.us
John R. Gaumer, Director
Mon–Thur 9:00–9:00, Fri–Sat 9:00–6:00

**Huntsville-Madison County Public
Library**
(see Alabama, Part 2)

Kershaw County Library
1304 Broad Street
Camden, SC 29020-3595

(803) 425-1508; (803) 425-7180 FAX
http://www.kershaw.lib.sc.us
Penny Harvey, Director
Mon–Thur 9:00–9:00, Fri 9:00–6:00, Sat
9:00–1:00, Sun 2:00–5:00

Lancaster County Library
313 South White Street
Lancaster, SC 29720-2506
(803) 285-1502; (803) 285-6004 FAX
lanclib@infoave.net
http://www.lanclib.org
Gary Harris, Reference Assistant
Mon–Thur 9:00–8:00, Fri 9:00–5:30, Sat
9:00–5:00

Laurens County Library
1017 West Main Street
Laurens, SC 29360-2640
(864) 984-0596; (864) 984-0598 FAX
http://www.lcpl.org
Elaine Martin
Mon & Thur 9:00–9:30, Tue–Wed
9:00–6:00, Fri 9:00–5:00, Sat 9:00–1:00

Marion County Library
101 East Court Street
Marion, SC 29571-3699
(843) 423-8300; (843) 423-8302 FAX
http://www.marioncountylibrary.org
Mon & Wed 9:30–8:30, Tue & Thur
9:30–6:00, Fri 9:30–5:30, Sat 9:30–1:00

Newberry County Library
1300 Friend Street
Newberry, SC 29108-3400
(803) 276-0854; (803) 276-7476 FAX
Tucker Neel Taylor, Library Director
Mon & Wed–Fri 9:00–6:00, Tue 9:00–8:00,
Sat 9:00–4:00

Oconee County Library
501 West South Broad Street
Walhalla, SC 29691-2105
(864) 638-4133; (864) 638-4132 FAX
http://ocplibrary.org
Mon–Tue 9:00–9:00, Wed–Fri 9:00–6:00,
Sat 9:00–1:00

Ohoopee Regional Library
(see Georgia, Part 2)

Orangeburg County Library
(510 Louis Street, N.E.—location)
PO Box 1367 (mailing address)
Orangeburg, SC 29116-1367
(803) 533-5864 (Reference Office); (803)
533-5860 FAX
cbull@orangeburgcounty.org
http://www.orangeburgcounty.org/library/
default.html
Capers B. Bull, Jr.
Mon–Tue 10:00–9:00, Wed–Fri 10:00–6:00,
Sat 9:00–5:00
photocopies: 10¢ per page plus $2.50
handling fee

**Pendleton District Historical, Recreational
and Tourism Commission**
(125 East Queen Street—location)
PO Box 565 (mailing address)
Pendleton, SC 29670
(864) 646-3782; (800) 862-1795; (864) 646-
2506 FAX
pendtour@innova.net
http://www.pendleton-district.org
Donna Roper, Assistant Director
Mon–Fri 9:00–4:30
Pub. *Friends of the Pendleton District
Commission Newsletter*, three times per
year
("We are a three-county government agency;

our work includes maintaining a local history/genealogy archives and support library, as well as tourism promotion, festivals, etc.")
$25.00–$250.00 per year membership; responds to inquiries of limited scope (expect delay due to staff limitations)

Pickens County Library
110 West First Avenue
Easley, SC 29640-2998
(864) 850-7077; (864) 859-9679; (864) 850-7088 FAX
http://www.pickens.lib.sc.us
Kay Pettit
Mon–Thur 9:00–9:00, Fri 9:00–6:00, Sat 9:00–4:00, Sun 2:30–5:30

W. G. Rhea Public Library
(see Tennessee, Part 2)

Richland County Public Library
Local History Room
1431 Assembly Street, #8
Columbia, SC 29201-3101
(803) 799-7084; (803) 929-3438 FAX
http://www.richland.lib.sc.us/index.html

Spartanburg County Public Libraries
Chesnee Branch Library
716 South Alabama Street
Chesnee, SC 29323
(864) 461-2423
http://www.spt.lib.sc.us
Mary Mills, Genealogical Advisor; Lynn Goen, Staff Genealogist; Mike Seagle, Head Librarian
Mon, Wed & Fri noon–6:00, Tue & Thur 10:00–8:00, Sat 10:00–4:00
(the bulk of the genealogical collection has been moved to Spartanburg County, Public Libraries, Spartanburg, except for vertical files of families and some abstracts)

Spartanburg County Public Libraries
Kennedy Room of Local History
151 South Church Street
Spartanburg, SC 29306-3241
(864) 596-3508; (864) 596-3518 FAX
http://www.spt.lib.sc.us
Debra Hutchins, Local History Librarian
Mon–Fri 9:00–9:00, Sat 9:00–6:00, Sun 1:30–6:00
(specializes in South Carolina; recently acquired Mary Mills collection from Chesnee Branch Library)

Troy Public Library
(see Alabama, Part 2)

University of Mississippi
Center for the Study of Southern Culture
(see Mississippi, Part 2)

University of South Carolina
Institute for Southern Studies
(address withheld upon request)
(803) 777-2340
Walter B. Edgar, Ph.D., Director
Pub. *South by Southeast*
("We offer no research or genealogical assistance")

University of South Carolina
University South Caroliniana Society
The South Caroliniana Library
(located on the University Horseshoe)
Columbia, SC 29208
(803) 777-3131; (803) 777-3132; (803) 777-5183 (Manuscripts)
rcopp@tcl.sc.edu; cuthrellb@tcl.sc.edu

http://www.sc.edu/library/socar
Roberta VH. Copp, Head, Book Division
Library: Mon, Wed & Fri 8:30–5:00, Tue & Thur 8:30–8:00, Sat 9:00–1:00; schedule varies during intersession periods; Manuscripts: Mon–Fri 8:30–5:00, Sat 9:00–1:00
copies: 35¢ per page in house, 50¢ per page plus $5.00 postage and handling by mail

Virginia Polytechnic Institute and State University
Appalachian history
(see Virginia, Part 2)

Williamsburgh Historical Museum
135 Hampton Avenue
Kingstree, SC 29556
(843) 355-3306
History1@FTC-i.net
Joanne Brown, Director
Tue–Wed 10:00–3:00, Thur 1:00–5:00

Historical Center of York County
212 East Jefferson Street
York, SC 29745
(803) 684-7262; (803) 684-0230 FAX
http://www.yorkcounty.org
Nancy Sambets, Archivist
Mon–Fri 10:00–4:00
research: $5.00 for non-York County residents

York County Library
Local History Collection
(138 East Black Street—location)
PO Box 10032 (mailing address)
Rock Hill, SC 29731-0032
(803) 324-3055
http://www.yclibrary.org
Mary Mallaney
Mon–Thur 9:00–9:00, Fri–Sat 9:00–6:00
("Will only search within the library's collection. Delay can be several weeks.")
research: $25.00 per hour; copies: 25¢ each from paper originals, 50¢ each from microform originals

Historical Societies—Local and Regional

Abbeville County Historical Society
432 College Avenue
Abbeville, SC 29620
(864) 459-2466

Abbeville District Historical Association
PO Box 578
McCormick, SC 29835
(864) 465-2347

Aiken County Historical Society
PO Box 1775
Aiken, SC 29802
(803) 649-9653
Edward Cushman, President
Pub. *Journal of the ACHS*

Allendale County Historical Society
University of South Carolina, Salkehatchie
Allendale, SC 29810
(803) 584-3446

Anderson County Historical Society
PO Drawer 785
Anderson, SC 29622
(864) 646-3782 (information)
Donna Roper, Curator
Pub. *New Highland Sentinel*, semiannually (Apr, Oct)
$6.00 per year membership

Bamberg County Historical and Genealogical Society
604 East Railroad Avenue
Bamberg, SC 29003
(803) 245-2901

Barnwell County Historical Society
Route 2, Box 166
Blackville, SC 29817
Mrs. D. Ross

Beaufort County Historical Society
PO Box 55
Beaufort, SC 29901-0055

Calhoun County Historical Society
Calhoun County Museum/Cultural Center
(303 Butler Street, Saint Matthews, SC 29135—location)
PO Box 367 (mailing address)
Cameron, SC 29030
(803) 874-3964 (Museum); (803) 874-1242 FAX
Debbie U. Roland, Director
by appointment only
Pub. *Calhoun County Historical Society Monthly*

Central Heritage Society
416 Church Street
Central, SC 29630
(864) 639-2156

Cherokee Historical Society
Cherokee Historic and Preservation Society, Inc.
Winnie Davis Hall of History
Limestone College
PO Box 998
Gaffney, SC 29340
(864) 489-4172
Sarah Blanton

Chester County Historical Society Museum
107 McAlily Street
Chester, SC 29706-1741
(803) 385-2330
Gary Roberts, Museum Director
Pub. *CCHSM Quarterly Newsletter*

Chesterfield Historical Society
209 Green Street
Cheraw, SC 29520
Mrs. J. H. Wannamaker

Clarendon County Historical Society
3509 Lake Avenue, Apartment 1213
Columbia, SC 29206-5185
Mrs. W. H. Threatt

Coker College
Pee Dee Heritage Center
(address withheld upon request)

Darlington County Historical Commission
204 Hewitt Street
Darlington, SC 29532
(843) 398-4710; (843) 398-4742 FAX
DCHC1968@aol.com
Horace F. Rudisill, Director
Mon–Fri 9:00–5:00
(Darlington County records prior to 1900, courthouse records, newspapers, family name records)

Dillon County Historical Society
PO Box 187
Lake View, SC 29563
(843) 759-2773

Edgefield County Historical Society
(320 Norris Street—location)

PO Box 174 (mailing address)
Edgefield, SC 29824
(803) 637-5306
Joanne T. Rainsford, President
Mon–Fri 9:00–5:00; tours by appointment
$2.00 donation

Fairfield County Historical Commission
Fairfield County Museum
231 South Congress Street
Winnsboro, SC 29180
(803) 635-9811

Florence Heritage Foundation, Inc.
(1159 Brunwood, Florence, SC
29501—location)
PO Box 1909 (mailing address)
Florence, SC 29503
(843) 662-3258

**Georgetown County Historical
Commission**
(Front and Screven Streets—location)
PO Box 902 (mailing address)
Georgetown, SC 29440
(843) 546-7423
Carter Elliott, Chairman; James A. Fitch,
Director

Georgetown County Historical Society
719 Prince Street
Georgetown, SC 29440
Leta Stearns

Greenville County Historical Society
201 Crescent Avenue
Greenville, SC 29602
Nancy Hassold
Pub. *Greenville County Historical Society
Proceedings and Papers*, irregularly

Greenwood County Historical Society
Abbeville-Greenwood Regional Library
Greenwood County Library
106 North Main Street
Greenwood, SC 29646-2240
Library: Mon–Tue & Thur 9:00–9:00, Wed &
Fri 9:00–5:30, Sat 10:00–5:00, Sun
2:00–5:00

**Hampton County Historical Society
Museum**
104 Mulberry Street
Hampton, SC 29924
(803) 943-5484
Mildred B. Rivers, Director/Curator
Thur 10:00–noon & 4:00–7:00, by
appointment
(published book on Hampton County: *Both
Sides of the Swamp*, $25.00)

Hilton Head Island Historical Society
8 Moon Shell Road
Hilton Head Island, SC 29938
Thomas McCammon

Historic Camden Revolutionary War Site
(222 Broad Street—location)
PO Box 710 (mailing address)
Camden, SC 29020-0710
(803) 432-9841; (803) 432-3815 FAX
Joanna B. Craig, Director
Mon–Sat 10:00–5:00, Sun 1:00–5:00; Self-
guided tours: daily 10:00–4:45; guided
tours: Tue–Fri 10:30, 1:30, 3:00, Sat
10:30–4:00, Sun 1:30–4:00
Pub. *Historic Camden Newsletter*, annually
(a museum offering help with genealogical
research; "American Revolution, Southern
Campaign, national/international scope")
$30.00 per year membership

Horry County Historical Society
(606 Main Street—location)
PO Box 2025 (mailing address)
Conway, SC 29526-4340
(843) 488-1966
http://www.webgroup.com/~hchs
Executive Director
no set hours
Pub. *Independent Republic Quarterly*
$30.00 per year membership

Jasper County Historical Society
PO Box 1267
Ridgeland, SC 29936
(843) 726-8126
Zenie Ingram

Kershaw County Historical Society
(Bonds Conway House, 811 South Fair
Street—location)
PO Box 501 (mailing address)
Camden, SC 29020
(803) 425-1123
kchistory@mindspring.com
http://www.mindspring.com/~kchistory
Kathleen P. Stahl, Executive Secretary
Thur 1:00–5:00
Pub. *Update—Newsletter of the Kershaw
County Historical Society*, quarterly
("We publish books on county history; we do
not do genealogical research.")
$25.00 per year membership

Laurens County Historical Society
PO Box 292
Laurens, SC 29360
Mrs. Fred Irwin

Lexington County Historical Society
231 Devin Drive
Lexington, SC 29070
Laura S. McMahan, President

Lynches River Historical Society
(College Street—location)
PO Box 26 (mailing address)
Bethune, SC 29009

Marion County Historical Society
PO Box 188
Marion, SC 29571
(843) 464-8685 (President)
Reginald McDaniel, President
Pub. *Newsletter*, irregularly
$5.00 per year membership

Marlborough Historical Society Archives
121 South Marlboro Street
Bennettsville, SC 29512
(843) 479-5624
Susan Turpin, Director
by appointment only
Pub. *Marlborough Historical Society
Newsletter*, quarterly
(history of Marlboro County and Pee Dee
area)
$10.00 per year membership; research: fees
vary

**McCormick County Historical
Commission**
PO Box 578
McCormick, SC 29835
(864) 465-2347

McCormick County Historical Society
PO Box 230
Mount Carmel, SC 29840
(864) 391-2131
Wes McAllister
8:00–5:00
("We are an educational type organization

meeting semiannually, fall and spring)

Newberry County Historical Society
PO Box 393
Newberry, SC 29108
Mrs. Sudie Crump Wicker

North Augusta Historical Society
107 West Pine Grove Avenue
North Augusta, SC 29841
(803) 279-2951
Lark W. Jones, President

**Orangeburg County Historical
Commission**
Courthouse
PO Box 219
Orangeburg, SC 29115
(803) 534-5176

**The Orangeburg County Historical
Society, Inc.**
(Bull and Middleton Streets—location)
PO Box 1881 (mailing address)
Orangeburg, SC 29116-1881
Alfred S. Gramling, Director, A. S. Salley
Archives
by appointment only
Pub. *OCHS, Inc. Newsletter*, two or three
times per year as needed

**Orangeburg Historical and Genealogical
Society, Inc.**
467 Palmetto Parkway, N.E.
Orangeburg, SC 29115
(803) 536-1305
Lawrence C. Bryant, Ph.D., President
Pub. *Orangeburg Historical and
Genealogical Record*

Pickens County Historical Society
(104 North Lewis Street—location)
PO Box 775 (mailing address)
Pickens, SC 29671
(864) 878-7847
Anne Poulos, President
Pub. *Pickens County Historical Museum*

Piedmont Historical Society
(Spartanburg County Public Libraries,
Kenedy Room of Local History—location)
PO Box 8096
Spartanburg, SC 29305
(864) 585-8125; (864) 585-0308
Joseph R. Gainey, President
Pub. *Upper South Carolina Genealogy and
History*, quarterly (Feb, May, Aug, Nov)
("Genealogy and history of upstate families of
South Carolina")
$20.00 per year membership

Saluda County Historical Society
(Law Range—location)
PO Box 22 (mailing address)
Saluda, SC 29138
(864) 445-8550
Mary B. Parkman, President
Pub. *SCHS Newsletter*

Southern Studies Institute
(see Louisiana, Part 2)

Spartanburg County Historical Association
(501 Otis Boulevard in Regional
Museum—location)
PO Box 887 (mailing address)
Spartanburg, SC 29304-0887
(864) 596-3501 voice & FAX
http://www.spartanarts.org/history/index.
html
Carolyn Creal, Curator
Mon–Fri 9:00–5:00

Pub. *The Drover' Post*, quarterly
$15.00 per year membership; no genealogical research services, but provides referrals

Sumter County Historical Commission
Sumter County Cultural Center
155 Haynsworth Street, Room 142
Patriot Hall
Sumter, SC 29151-0306
(803) 436-2257
Wed & Thur 1:00–4:00
(historical preservation, publications of a historical orientation, erecting of historical markers, and research into items of interest to Sumter County, including genealogical studies: special project: Afro-American Sumter County, South Carolina genealogies)
society no longer does any research

Three Rivers Historical Society
(Main Street—location)
PO Box 811 (mailing address)
Hemingway, SC 29554
(843) 558-2355
Nell G. Morris, Registrar and Publications Chairman
usually 9:00–5:00, call for appointment
Pub. *The Three Rivers Chronicle*, quarterly
$12.00 per year membership

Union County Historical Foundation
(Corner East Main and South Church Streets—location)
PO Drawer 220 (mailing address)
Union, SC 29379
(864) 427-3134
Thomas E. Bishop, Curator
by appointment, except summer and Nov–Dec; Museum: first Sat & Sun (Feb–Nov) 3:00–5:00, and by appointment; meetings: fourth Tue (Feb, May, Aug, Nov)
Pub. *Historical Newsletter*, semiannually
from $5.00 per year membership

York County Historical Society
PO Box 3061
Rock Hill, SC 29730
Dr. Lucille Delano

Genealogical Societies

State Genealogical Society

South Carolina Genealogical Society (SCGS)
(114 South Fourth Street, in the Hartsvillle Train Depot—location)
PO Box 492 (mailing address)
Greenville, SC 29602
scgen@peoplepc.com
http://scgen.org/index.htm
John L. Andrews, Jr., Archivist
Mon & Fri 1:00–5:00, Sat 9:00–3:00, Sun 2:00–5:00
Pub. *The Carolina Herald*, semiannually; *South Carolina Genealogical Newsletter*, quarterly
membership is through the affiliated chapters

SCGS Chapters

Anderson County Chapter (SCGS)
PO Box 74
Anderson, SC 29622-0074
http://www.rootsweb.com/~scanders/andgensoc.html
Phillip M. Cheney, President
$13.00 per year membership

Beaufort Chapter (SCGS)
PO Box 1070
Saint Helena Island, SC 29920
Linda Hoffman and Nancy Chesnutt, President
$20.00 per year membership

Catawba-Wateree Chapter (SCGS)
Camden Archives and Museum
1314 Broad Street
Camden, SC 29020-3535
CatawbaWatereeGS@aol.com; SCSunset@aol.com
http://www.mindspring.com/~graysky1/page3.html
Larry Booher, Editor
Pub. *Catawba-Wateree Messenger*, monthly (covering Kershaw and Lancaster counties, South Carolina)
$20.00 per year membership

Charleston Chapter (SCGS)
PO Box 20266
Charleston, SC 29413-0266
http://www.scgen.org/charlestonmain.htm
Carolyn Garrett, Membership Chairman
Pub. *Low Country Courier*, ten times per year
$18.00 per year membership; queries accepted

Chesterfield District Chapter (SCGS)
(Chesterfield Genealogical Research Library, 115 Green Street—location)
PO Box 167 (mailing address)
Chesterfield, SC 29709
(843) 623-2244; (843) 623-2278 FAX
cdcscgs@yahoo.com
http://www.chesterfielddistrictchapter.org/chesterfieldsc
Sharon F. Corey, President, Corresponding Secretary, Editor
Mon & Fri 1:00–4:00, Tue–Thur 10:00–4:00, Sat by appointment
Pub. *Chesterfield District Chronicle*, quarterly, $4.00 per issue
$20.00 per year membership (must be a full member of another S.C.G.S. chapter); no research service

Columbia Chapter (SCGS)
PO Box 11353
Columbia, SC 29211-1353
ozzie_29223@yahoo.com (Webmaster)
http://www.rootsweb.com/~scccscgs
Sylvia Castles, Archivist; Gene Osburn, Webmaster
by appointment
Pub. *The Columbia Journal*, irregularly
$20.00 per year membership

Dutch Fork Chapter (SCGS)
PO Box 481
Chapin, SC 29036
(803) 279-0322
DutchForkGenSoc@aol.com
http://www.dutchforkchapter.homestead.com
William B. Rauch, President; Marlene K. Walker, Web Administrator
meetings: third Wed 10:00 A.M.–11:00 A.M.
Pub. *Dutch Fork Digest*, quarterly
(dedicated to research of families with origins in the Dutch Fork section of South Carolina; family name queries, family histories)
$20.00 per year membership

Fairfield Chapter (SCGS)
PO Box 93
Winnsboro, SC 29180
(803) 781-2679
FairfieldBill1@aol.com
http://www.rootsweb.com/~scfairfi/

gensoc.html
William Wall, President
$20.00 per year membership

Greenville Chapter (SCGS)
PO Box 16236
Greenville, SC 29606
info@greenvillegenealogy.org
http://www.greenvillegenealogy.org
Terrald Knorr, President
Pub. *Greenville Chapter Newsletter-South Carolina Genealogical Society*, monthly
$20.00 per year membership

Hilton Head Island Chapter (SCGS)
Hilton Head Island Genealogical Society
PO Box 5492
Hilton Head Island, SC 29938-5492
John Griffin, President
(includes north central upstate area: Chester, York, Lancaster, Union and Fairfield counties)
$20.00 per year membership

Laurens District Chapter (SCGS)
PO Box 1217
Laurens, SC 29360-1217
John Griffin, President
$15.00 per year membership

Old Darlington District Chapter (SCGS)
PO Box 175
Hartsville, SC 29551-0175
(843) 857-0300
jandr45985@aol.com
http://www.geocities.com/Heartland/Estates/7212
John L. Andrews, Jr., First Vice President
Pub. *Old Darlington District Flag*, quarterly
$20.00 per year membership

Old Edgefield District Chapter (SCGS)
Old Edgefield District Genealogical Society
(Tompkins Library, 104 Courthouse Square—location)
PO Box 546 (mailing address)
Edgefield, SC 29824-0546
(803) 637-4010
tompkinslibrary@jetbn.net
http://oedgs.com
Carol Hardy Bryan, Editor
Mon–Fri 9:00–4:00, and weekends by appointment
Pub. *Quill*, bimonthly
("Emphasis on families and history of Edgefield District.")
$25.00 per year membership; admission: one free visit, then $5.00 for nonmembers

Old Newberry District Chapter (SCGS)
406 East Florida Street
Clinton, SC 29325-2430
(864) 833-2239
d03_9957_@bellsouth.net
http://www.rootsweb.com/~scondc
Elizabeth S. Pitts
monthly meeting
Pub. *Old Newberry District Quarterly*
$20.00 per year membership

Old Ninety Six Chapter (SCGS)
(Highway 34 Fire Department—location)
PO Box 3468 (mailing address)
Greenwood, SC 29648
(864) 223-5151 voice & FAX
hwash@emeraldis.com
http://www.scgen.org/oldninetysix.htm
Josephine M. Wash, Editor
Abbeville-Greenwood Regional Library:
Mon–Tue & Thur 9:00–9:00, Wed & Fri 9:00–5:30, Sat 10:00–5:00, Sun 2:00–5:00; meetings third Sun except

June–Aug & Dec
Pub. *Genealogical Roots and Branches (GRAB)*, quarterly, free newsletter exchange
(western South Carolina: Old Abbeville District, Old 96 District)
$15.00 per year membership

Old Pendleton District Chapter (SCGS)
228 Ivydale Drive
Greenville, SC 29609-1927
(864) 859-2392
cmurphree@hisxmark.com (Webmaster)
http://www.oldpendleton.homestead.com
Margarette B. Swank, Editor and Treasurer; Charles Murphree, Webmaster
Pub. *Old Pendleton District Chapter Newsletter*, nine times per year (monthly, except July–Aug & Dec) (contains information on Pickens, Anderson and Oconee counties, South Carolina, formerly Old Pendleton District and Pickens District)
$20.00 per year membership

Old Saint Bartholomew Chapter (SCGS)
104 Wade Hampton Avenue
Walterboro, SC 29488-9261
(843) 549-5757
osbcscgs@yahoo.com
http://www.rootsweb.com/~scosbc
John E. Turbeville, President
$12.00 per year membership

Pee Dee Chapter (SCGS)
(101 North Main Street—location)
PO Box 1428 (mailing address)
Marion, SC 29571
(843) 431-5024
hhend85@aol.com
http://scgen.org/peedee.htm
Maxcy Foxworth, Archivist; Hal Hendrix, Treasurer
Mon–Thur 1:00–5:00
Pub. *Pee Dee Queue*, bimonthly
$15.00 per year membership

Pinckney District Chapter (SCGS)
(385 South Spring Street, Spartanburg, SC 29301—location)
PO Box 5281 (mailing address)
Spartanburg, SC 29304
http://scgen.org/pinckneymain.htm
Mike Becknell, Vice President
Pub. *Bulletin*, quarterly (Mar, June, Sept, Dec)
(emphasis on Spartanburg, Cherokee and Union counties)
$25.00 per year membership

Sumter County Genealogical Society (SCGS)
The Genealogical and Historical Research Center
(Old Carnegie Library Building, 219 Liberty Street, Sumter, SC 29150—location)
PO Box 2543 (mailing address)
Sumter, SC 29151-2543
(803) 773-9144
cgibbs@sc.rr.com
http://www.rootsweb.com/~scscgs
Chuck S. Gibbs, President; Lauren Decker, Museum Archivist
Mon–Sat 9:00–5:00
Pub. *The Sumter Black River Watchman*, nine times per year (monthly, except June–Aug)
(has U.D.C. applications and the Janie Revill files; specializing in Old Sumter District area history and genealogy)
$20.00 per year membership (includes membership in and publications of South Carolina Genealogical Society);

admission: $5.00 for nonmembers; research: "volunteers will try to answer written or phoned requests for information as we have time to do so"

Southern Society of Genealogists, Inc.
(see Alabama, Part 2)

Genealogical Societies—Local & Regional

Aiken-Barnwell Genealogical Society
PO Box 415
Aiken, SC 29801-0415
(803) 648-3898
Albert H. Peters, III, President
Mon, Wed & Fri 10:00–5:00, Tue & Thur noon–9:00, Sat 9:00–1:00; meetings at Aiken Library: third Sun 3:00 (except June–Aug)
Pub. *ABGS News and Journal*, quarterly
$20.00 per year membership

Bamberg County Historical and Genealogical Society
(see Historical Societies—Local and Regional, above)

Carolinas Genealogical Society (Upper-Central South Carolina)
(see North Carolina, Part 2)

Chester District Genealogical Society
PO Box 336
Richburg, SC 29729-0336
Jean Nichols, Editor
by appointment
Pub. *The Bulletin*, quarterly
(serves the upper central part of South Carolina: Chester, Lancaster, York, Fairfield, and Union counties; has surname book listing members and up to ten surnames they're searching, $5.00)
$20.00 per year membership

Huxford Genealogical Society, Inc.
(see Georgia, Part 2)

Lexington County Genealogical Association
PO Box 1442
Lexington, SC 29072
Pub. *Lexington Genealogical Exchange*, quarterly, $5.00 per issue
$20.00 per year membership

Orangeburg Historical and Genealogical Society, Inc.
(see Historical Societies—Local and Regional, above)

Independent Publications and Miscellany

Aiken County Historical Commission
Aiken County Historical Museum
433 Newberry Street, S.W.
Aiken, SC 29801
(803) 649-4658; (803) 642-2015 (Museum)
http://www.scescape.com/aikenhistoricalmuseum (Museum)

Anderson County Museum
(202 East Greenville Street, Anderson, SC 29621—location)
PO Box 8002 (mailing address)
Anderson, SC 29622
(864) 260-4737; (864) 260-4044
acm@andersoncountysc.org
http://www.andersoncountysc.org/museum.htm
Paula Reel, Director

Mon–Fri 10:00–4:00
$35.00+ per year membership; free admission

Appalachian Roots
(see West Virginia, Part 2)

The Bluffton Historical Preservation Society, Inc.
PO Box 742
Bluffton, SC 29910
(843) 757-3650 (Mrs. Caldwell); (843) 757-6604 FAX
Mrs. Arthur B. Elliott, Secretary; Mrs. B. M. Caldwell
Pub. *Newsletter*, annually
$10.00 per year membership

Center for Appalachian Studies
(see North Carolina, Part 2)

Edisto Island Historic Preservation Society
8123 Chisolm Plantation Road
Edisto Island, SC 29438-6618
(843) 869-1954

The Florence Museum
558 Spruce Street
Florence, SC 29501
(843) 662-3351
Dana Parker, Executive Director
Tue–Sat 10:00–5:00, Sun 2:00–5:00

Fort Jackson Museum
Fort Jackson, SC 29207
(803) 751-7419

Genealogical Institute
(see Virginia, Part 2)

Genealogy Books and Consultation
(see Texas, Part 2)

Historic Brattonsville
1444 Brattonsville Road
McConnells, SC 29726
(803) 684-2327

Hunting for Bears Genealogical and Historical Society
(see Alabama, Part 2)

Lancaster County Society for Historical Preservation
PO Box 1132
Lancaster, SC 29721
(803) 285-9455
D. Lindsay Pettus, President
Pub. *Newsletter*, quarterly
$20.00 per year membership

Marion County Museum
(101 Willcox Avenue—location)
PO Box 220 (mailing address)
Marion, SC 29571
(843) 423-8299
W. Thomas Lett, Director
Tue–Fri 9:00–noon & 1:00–5:00

Mountain Press
(see Tennessee, Part 2)

Pioneer Publications
North/South Carolina Queries & Reviews
(see North Carolina, Part 2)

Rice Museum
(Front and Screven Streets—location)
PO Box 902 (mailing address)
Georgetown, SC 29440
(843) 546-7423
James A. Fitch, Director

Richland County Historic Preservation Commission
1616 Blanding Street
Columbia, SC 29201
(803) 252-1770

Roots and Branches—Genealogy from the Carolinas
carolinaroots@inmyattic.com
http://www.inmyattic.com/roots
Angie

SCGenWeb
Part of The USGenweb Project
vproc@ix.netcom.com
http://www.geocities.com/Heartland/
    Hills/3837
Victoria Proctor, State Coordinator
(links to other South Carolina resources)

South Carolina Department of Transportation
SCDOT Map Sales Office
955 Park Street
Columbia, SC 29202-0191
(803) 737-1501
http://www.dot.state.sc.us/getting/maps.html
    (Maps)

South Carolina Genealogy Search Engine
http://scgenealogy.virtualave.net/search.htm
Avery J. Parker

South Carolina Information Highway (SCIway)
http://www.sciway.net/hist/genealogy
(links to resources)

The South Carolina Magazine of Ancestral Research (SCMAR)
PO Box 21766
Columbia, SC 29221-1766
(803) 772-6919
Brent H. Holcomb, Editor
Pub. *The South Carolina Magazine of Ancestral Research*, quarterly, $30.00 per year subscription

South Carolina State Museum
South Carolina Museum Commission
301 Gervais Street
Columbia, SC 29201
(803) 737-4921
Overton G. Ganong, Director

The Southern Genealogist's Exchange Society, Inc.
(see Florida, Part 2)

Southern Historical Press, Inc.
(see Publishers, Part 4)

The Summerville Preservation Society
(201 West Caroline Avenue—location)
PO Box 511 (mailing address)
Summerville, SC 29484
Heyward G. Hutson, President
no regular hours

Traveller Southern Families
(see Virginia, Part 2)

Vereen Historical Gardens
(Little River, SC—location)
706 15th Avenue, South (mailing address)
North Myrtle Beach, SC 29582
(843) 272-6303
CBurginBerry@aol.com
C. B. Berry, Chairman

West Virginia University
Appalachian Studies Association

(see West Virginia, Part 2)

South Dakota

Archives and Libraries with Holdings in Genealogy

State Archives and Library

American Family Records Association (AFRA)
Alexander Mitchell Public Library
Genealogy Circulation Collection
519 South Kline Street
Aberdeen, SD 57401-2596
(605) 626-7097 (Library)
Shirley Arment, Reference and Genealogy
    Librarian
Library: Mon–Thur 9:00–9:00, Fri 9:00–6:00,
    Sat 1:00–5:00, Sun (Sept–June) 1:00–5:00
(about 600 titles in circulating collection)

South Dakota State Archives
Cultural Heritage Center
900 Governors Drive
Pierre, SD 57501-2217
(605) 773-3804; (605) 773-6041 FAX
Archref@state.sd.us
http://www.sdhistory.org/arc/archives.htm
Reference Desk
Mon–Fri 9:00–4:30, except legal holidays
(A-V materials, government records, Indian
    Archives, library, manuscripts, maps,
    microfilm, newspapers, photographs)

South Dakota State Library
Mercedes MacKay Memorial Building
Branch
800 Governors Drive
Pierre, SD 57501-2294
(605) 773-3131; (605) 773-4369; (800) 423-
    6665; (605) 773-4950 FAX
library@state.sd.us
http://www.sdstatelibrary.com
Dayton W. Canaday, History; Laura Glum,
    Genealogy
Mon–Fri 8:00–5:00

State Historical Society

Archives of the South Dakota State Historical Society
Cultural Heritage Center
900 Governors Drive
Pierre, SD 57501-2217
(605) 773-3804; (605) 773-6041 FAX
Archref@state.sd.us
http://www.sdhistory.org
Ken R. Stewart, Research Room
    Administrator
Mon–Fri & first Sat 9:00–4:30
Pub. *South Dakota History*, quarterly; *History
    Notes*, biannually
$35.00 per year membership; research: fee
    charged

City, County and Regional Archives and Libraries
(A more exhaustive list of public and
academic libraries can be found at http://
www.sdstatelibrary.com/forlibrarians/
directories.)

Adams Museum
(54 Sherman—location)
PO Box 252 (mailing address)
Deadwood, SD 57732-1364
(605) 578-1714
http://www.blackhills.com/museum/
    index.html
Carolee Smith-Rogers, Curator
1 Oct–30 Apr: Tue–Sat 10:00–4:00, Sun
    noon–4:00; 1 May–30 Sept: Mon–Sat

9:00–6:00, Sun 9:00–5:00
(museum archives)
research: $50.00 per hour

Augustana College
The Center for Western Studies
(2201 South Summit Avenue—location)
PO Box 727 (mailing address)
Sioux Falls, SD 57197
(605) 336-4007; (800) 727-2844, ext. 4007;
(605) 274-4999 FAX; (605) 274-5447
FAX
huseboe@augie.edu
http://www.augie.edu/CWS
Arthur R. Huseboe, Executive Director
Mon–Fri 8:00–noon & 1:00–5:00

Grace Balloch Memorial Library
Spearfish Municpal Service Center
South Dakota History Room
625 Fifth Street
Spearfish, SD 57783-2311
(605) 642-1330
kfollett@sdln.net
http://www.sdln.net/libs/spf
Kathy Follette, Reference
Mon–Thur 10:00–8:00, Fri 10:00–5:00, Sat
9:00–5:00; summer: Mon–Thur
9:00–7:00, Fri 9:00–5:00, Sat 9:00–2:00
("We have Queen City Mail and Black Hills
Pioneer on microfilm. We will send these
to a requesting library for $5.00 per roll.
We have a South Dakota history collection
that we circulate and some rare materials
that we do not circulate.")
research: $20.00 per hour

Belle Fourche Public Library
905 Fifth Avenue
Belle Fourche, SD 57717-1702
(605) 892-4407
Pat Engebretson, Librarian
Mon–Thur 10:00–7:00, Fri–Sat 10:00–5:00

Brookings Public Library
515 Third Street
Brookings, SD 57006
(605) 692-9407; (605) 692-9386 FAX
elandau@sdln.net
http://www.brookings.com/library
Elvita Landau, Director
Mon–Thur 10:00–9:00, Fri 10:00–5:00, Sat
9:00–5:00, Sun (except Aug) 2:00–5:00

Leland D. Case Library for Western Historical Studies
E. Y. Berry Library Learning Center
Black Hills State University
University Station, Box 9548
Spearfish, SD 57799
(605) 642-6361
Colleen Kirby, Special Collections Librarian
Mon–Fri (when school is in session)
8:00–noon & 2:00–5:00

Center for Great Plains Studies
(see Kansas, Part 2)

Center for Great Plains Study
(see Nebraska, Part 2)

Dacotah Prairie Museum
(21 South Main Street—location)
PO Box 395 (mailing address)
Aberdeen, SD 57402-0395
(605) 622-7117
Sue Gates, Director
Office: Mon–Fri 8:00–5:00; Galleries:
Tue–Fri 9:00–5:00, Sat–Sun 1:00–4:00
Pub. *Dacotah Prairie Times*, quarterly
(Brown County, SD, history, oral history
tapes, family history files, newspapers, city

directories)
$25.00 per year membership; search: $5.00
per hour plus copies at 15¢ per page

Deadwood Public Library
435 Williams Street
Deadwood, SD 57732-1113
(605) 578-2821; (605) 578-2170 FAX

http://www.sdln.net/libs/dwd/Text/WebPages/WebHome.htm
Terri Davis, Director
Mon–Wed 10:00–8:00, Thur–Sat noon–4:00
(primarily Deadwood family information,
limited information for remainder of
Lawrence County, index to newspapers
from 1876)
archival research: $5.00 minimum, plus
postage and copies at 20¢ per page

Huron Public Library
521 Dakota Avenue, South
Huron, SD 57350
(605) 353-8530; (605) 353-8531 FAX
csmith@sdln.net
http://hpllib.sdln.net
Colleen Smith, Library Director
Mon–Thur 10:00–8:00, Fri 10:00–6:00, Sat
(school year) 10:00–5:00, Sat (summer)
10:00–1:00

Mitchell Public Library
221 North Duff Street
Mitchell, SD 57301-2596
(605) 995-8480; (605) 995-8482 FAX
http://mitlib.sdln.net
Sandra Spanos, Assistant Librarian
winter: Mon–Thur 10:00–8:00, Fri–Sat
10:00–6:00, Sun 2:00–5:00; summer:
Mon–Sat 10:00–6:00
(genealogical material available through
Online Computer Library Center [OCLC]
member libraries)

Alexander Mitchell Public Library
Genealogy Circulation Collection
519 South Kline Street
Aberdeen, SD 57401-2596
(605) 626-7097
ampl@sdln.net
http://ampl.sdln.net
Shirley Arment, Reference and Genealogy
Librarian
Mon–Thur 9:00–9:00, Fri 9:00–6:00, Sat
9:00–5:00
(about 600 titles in circulating collection)

Alexander Mitchell Public Library
Genealogy Circulation Collection
(see South Dakota, Part 2)

Museum of the Great Plains
(see Oklahoma, Part 2)

Rapid City Public Library
610 Quincy Street
Rapid City, SD 57701
(605) 394-4171
http://www.sdln.net/libs/rcp
Eka M. Parkison
Mon–Thur 9:00–9:00, Fri–Sat 9:00–5:30,
Sun (Sept–May) 1:00–5:00

Rawlins Municipal Library
1000 East Church Street
Pierre, SD 57501
(605) 773-7421; (605) 773-7423 FAX
http://www.dakotariver.com/rawlins/
index.htm

Siouxland Libraries
201 North Main Avenue

Sioux Falls, SD 57104
(605) 367-7082
http://www.siouxland.lib.sd.us
Doug Murdock, Reference Department Head
Mon–Thur 9:30–9:00, Fri 9:30–6:00, Sat
9:30–5:00, Sun (Sept–May) 1:00–5:00

South Dakota State University Archives
BL 241/Box 2115
Brookings, SD 57007
(605) 688-5106; (605) 688-6133 FAX
http://lib.sdstate.edu/archives/index.html
Stephen Van Buren, University Archivist and
Head of Special Collections
Mon–Fri 8:00–3:00, by appointment

University of South Dakota
I. D. Weeks Library
Vermillion, SD 57069
(605) 677-5305; (605) 677-5450 (Special
Collections); (605) 677-5629 (Government
Documents)
http://www.usd.edu/library

Vermillion Public Library
18 Church Street
Vermillion, SD 57069
(605) 624-2741
http://www.usd.edu/vpl
Jane Larson, Director
Mon–Thur 10:00–9:00, Fri 10:00–6:00,
Sat–Sun 10:00–5:00 (summer closed Sun)

Historical Societies—Local and Regional

Aberdeen Area Genealogical Society (AAGS)
PO Box 493
Aberdeen, SD 57401-0493
(605) 225-4111
T. J. Bud Schaffer, President
meetings second Sat 2:00
Pub. *The Tree Climber*, quarterly
$12.00 per year membership; research: $2.00
per name

American Historical Association, Pacific Coast Branch
(see California, Part 2)

American West Research Center and Historical Society, Inc.
(see Ohio, Part 2)

Bennett County Historical Society
HWC 1, Box 5
Martin, SD 57551
Diana Nelson

Bowdle Historical Society
North of Main Street
Bowdle, SD 57428
Erma Maier, President

Brookings County Historical Society/Museum
(215 Samara Avenue—location)
PO Box 608 (mailing address)
Volga, SD 57071
(605) 627-9149
Howard Lee, Treasurer
Mon–Sun (Memorial Day–Labor Day)
2:00–5:00
Pub. *The Window*, quarterly
$10.00 per year membership

Brule County Historical Society
PO Box 47
Kimball, SD 57355

Butte County Historical Society, Inc.
PO Box 2
Newell, SD 57760
(605) 456-2938
Tim Velder, President
$3.00 per year membership

Charles Mix County Historical Society
(East Highway 46/50—location)
PO Box 444 (mailing address)
Wagner, SD 57380
(605) 384-3716 (President); (605) 384-3118
(Vice President)
Ed Staudenmier, President; Dick Kafka, Vice
President
weekends (such as Memorial Day & Labor
Day weekend)
("Artifacts, memorabilia, items of farms early
1900s. We have six buildings with items
of the 1900s–1940s, plus two large display
buildings. We have some local family
histories, government records, etc., but no
actual census records.")
$25.00 membership

Clark County Historical Society
Beauvais Heritage Museum
HiWay 212 and Dakota Street
Clark, SD 57225
(605) 532-3922; (605) 532-5216
Ailene Luckhurst, President
1 June–1 Sept: Wed–Fri 1:00–4:00 by
appointment
Pub. *Newsletter*, annually
$3.00 per year membership

Codington County Historical Society, Inc.
Kampeska Heritage Museum
27 First Avenue, S.E.
Watertown, SD 57201
(605) 886-7335
Joanita Kant Monteith, Executive Director
Tue–Sat 1:00–5:00, mornings by appointment
Pub. *CCHS Newsletter*, bimonthly
(Codington County history)
$10.00 per year membership

Custer County Historical Society
PO Box 826
Custer, SD 57730

Dalesburg-Hub City Historical Society
30493 464th Avenue
Centerville, SD 57014-6403

Deuel County Historical Society, Inc.
PO Box 676
Clear Lake, SD 57226-0676
E. Gieser

Douglas County Historical Society
(Courthouse Grounds—location)
PO Box 638 (mailing address)
Armour, SD 57313
(605) 724-2129
Sharon Wiese, President
by appointment
(family histories on file)
research: SASE

Dunham Historical Society
(Jerauld County Pioneer Museum, consisting
of Heritage Center, Dean Annex, Rural Shop,
Country School—location)
PO Box 473 (mailing address)
Wessington Springs, SD 57382
(605) 539-1852
Arlein Fransen, Museum Director
Thur 9:30–11:30 & 1:00–3:30, Fri 1:30–3:30
("We have files on former and present county
residents available for genealogists.")

Fall River County Historical Society
Route 1, Box 180
Hot Springs, SD 57747
(605) 745-4725
Mabel M. Gillis, President
first Mon in June–after Labor Day:
9:00–5:00
donation accepted

Faulk County Historical Society
PO Box 584
Faulkton, SD 57438
(605) 598-4285
Bonnie Wuger, President; Beverly Brewer,
Secretary
Pickler Mansion Museum: 1 May–Labor
Day: daily 1:00–5:00
$5.00 per year membership

Garretson Area Historical Society
609 Main Avenue
Garretson, SD 57030
(605) 594-6694

Gary Historical Association
Gary, SD 57237
(605) 272-5553; (605) 272-5267

Grant County Historical Society
Third Avenue and Third Street
Milbank, SD 57252
Alfred Pay, President
Pub. *GCHS Newsletter*

Gregory County Historical Society, Inc.
PO Box 322
Burke, SD 57523
(605) 775-2641
Jack Broome

Hurley Historical Society
PO Box 302
Hurley, SD 57036
(605) 238-5725

**Hyde County Historical and Genealogical
Society (SDGS)**
(113 Iowa South—location)
PO Box 392 (mailing address)
Highmore, SD 57345
(605) 852-3103
Sue Grable, President
by appointment
Pub. *Tumbleweeds*, quarterly, $1.00 per issue
$7.00 per year membership

James Valley Historical Society
(South Dakota State Fairgrounds—location)
38459 211th Street (mailing address)
Wolsey, SD 57384-8605
Louella Barrows, President
Fair week: 9:00–7:00; and by appointment

Keystone Area Historical Society
(410 Third Street—location)
PO Box 177 (mailing address)
Keystone, SD 57751
(605) 666-4494
Mon–Sat (June–Aug) 10:00–3:00
Pub. *Holy Terror Tattler*, annually
("Museum is located in Victorian School
House, built in 1899 for 300 students at a
cost of $10,000.00.")
$5.00 per year membership

Lake County Historical Society
Smith-Zimmerman Heritage Museum
Dakota State University Campus
221 N.E. Eighth Street
Madison, SD 57042
(605) 256-5308; (605) 256-5643 FAX
smith.zimmermann@dsu.edu

http://www.smith-zimmermann.dsu.edu
Lori Norby, President; Dr. Clyde Brashier,
Editor
Thur–Sun 1:00–4:30, and by appointment
Pub. *The Heritage Herald*, quarterly
$5.00 per year membership

Lennox Area Historical Society
(Main Street—location)
PO Box 337 (mailing address)
Lennox, SD 57039
(605) 647-2287

**Lyman County Historical Society and
Museum**
(209 West Highway 16—location)
PO Box 231 (mailing address)
Presho, SD 57568-0231
(605) 895-9446
Beverly Kenobbie, Curator
Memorial Day–Labor Day: daily 2:00–8:00
Pub. *Newsletter*, four or five times per year
$15.00 life membership

**McCook County Museum and Historical
Society**
(120 West Norton—location)
PO Box 176 (mailing address)
Salem, SD 57058
(605) 425-3181
Lois Melton, President
Apr–Nov: Mon 1:30–5:00

Mellette County Historical Society
(Corner Main and State Street—location)
DWR 4 (mailing address)
White River, SD 57579-0712
(605) 259-3347 voice & FAX (President);
(605) 259-3346 (Treasurer)
Devota Hutchinson, President; Barbetta
Krogman, Treasurer
weekdays, and by appointment
Pub. *Newsletter*, periodically
("South Dakota and Mellette County history
[towns: White River, Wood, Norris,
Mosher]. We are regrouping with an
emphasis on genealogy records.")

Menno Historical Society
Menno Heritage Museum
150 Poplar
Menno, SD 57045
(605) 387-2867
Dorothy Harnisch, President

Minnehaha County Historical Society
Siouxland Heritage Old Courthouse Museum
200 West Sixth Street
Sioux Falls, SD 57104-6001
(605) 334-7762 (Museum); (605) 373-0723
FAX (Museum)
jbbsodak@aol.com
http://www.sdhistory.org/Hist_Orgs/
minnehahaco.htm
Bruce Blake, Director
Museum: Wed 1:00–5:00 and by
appointment; meetings: third Thur
(Sept–May) 7:00
Pub. *Newsletter*, nine times per year
(monthly, Sept–May)
$15.00 per year membership

**Crooks Council of the Minnehaha County
Historical Society**
Route 11, Box 339
Crooks, SD 57020
(605) 543-5232

MonDak Historical and Arts Society
(see Montana, Part 2)

Moody County Historical Society

East Park Road
Flandreau, SD 57028
(605) 997-2198

Oelrichs Historical Society
PO Box 104
Oelrichs, SD 57763
(605) 535-6375
Violet S. Biever, President
(Published *In the Shadow of the Butte
Oelrichs*, 1984, $30.00 plus postage.)

Old Stanley County Historical Society
(410 West Main—location)
PO Box 698 (mailing address)
Fort Pierre, SD 57532
(605) 223-2757

Oldham Library and Historical Association
PO Box 243
Oldham, SD 57051
(605) 482-8178; (605) 482-8158
Shirley Gruenhagen, President; JoAnn
Nelson, Librarian
Museum: Sun in the summer; Library: limited
hours

Perkins County Historical Society
HCR-69
PO Box 417C
Bison, SD 57620
(605) 244-5416
Dorothy Haugen, Secretary

Potter County Historical Association
PO Box 1
Gettysburg, SD 57442
(605) 765-5691

Prairie Historical Society, Inc.
(Prairie Village, two miles west of Madison
on Highway 34—location)
PO Box 256 (mailing address)
Madison, SD 57042
(800) 693-3644
Karen Becker, Village Manager; Sue Janssen,
Administrator
1 May–1 Oct: 9:00–6:00

Scotland Historical Society
331 Fourth Street
Scotland, SD 57059
(605) 583-2978
Viola L. Bauder, President
Memorial Day–Labor Day: Sun 1:30–5:00

Spink County Historical Society
(Redfield, SD—location)
Frankfort, SD 57440 (mailing address)
(605) 472-0758

Springfield Historical Society
PO Box 333
Springfield, SD 57062
(605) 369-2498

Timber Lake and Area Historical Society
(Cheyenne River Sioux
Reservation—location)
PO Box 181 (mailing address)
Timber Lake, SD 57656
(605) 865-3546
Jim Nelson, Board Member
Mon–Tue 9:00–5:00
Pub. *Timber Lake and Area Historical
Society Newsletter*, quarterly
("Reservation and homesteading history of
northwestern South Dakota; museum and
photo archives")
$10.00 per year membership

Tripp County Historical Society

801 West Fifth Street
Winner, SD 57580-1416
(605) 842-0704

**Union County Historical Society and
Museum**
(124 East Main Street—location)
PO Box 552 (mailing address)
Elk Point, SD 57025-0552
(712) 568-3100 (Iowa)
http://www.acsnet.com/~jkjar
Sherri McKee, President
Sat–Sun 1:00–4:00, and by appointment
Pub. *Sands of Time*, quarterly
("Lewis and Clark's First Election site,
Union County history, genealogy,
artifacts, diorama.")
$15.00 per year membership

Wakonda Historical Society
Wakonda, SD 57073
(605) 267-2847
Dolores Haver, President

Yankton County Historical Society, Inc.
Dakota Territorial Museum
(Westside Park, 610 Summit—location)
PO Box 1033 (mailing address)
Yankton, SD 57078
(605) 665-3898
Fred Binder, President
Pub. *Museum Chronicle*, semiannually

Genealogical Societies

State Genealogical Society

South Dakota Genealogical Society
PO Box 1101
Pierre, SD 57501
(605) 224-2670
http://www.rootsweb.com/~sdgenweb/
gensoc/sdgensoc.html
Laura Glum, Corresponding Secretary
Pub. *SDGS Quarterly*, quarterly; *South
Dakota Genealogical Society Newsletter*
$20.00 per year membership

SDGS Affiliates

Aberdeen Area Genealogical Society
Box 493
Aberdeen, SD 57402-0493

**Bennett County Genealogical Society
(SDGS)**
PO Box 483
Allen, SD 57714

**Brookings Area Genealogical Society
(SDGS)**
524 Fourth Street
Brookings, SD 57006
Pub. *Brookings Area Genealogical Society*,
bimonthly
$6.00 per year membership

Family Tree Society (SDGS)
PO Box 202
Winner, SD 57580

Heritage Club-Platte (SDGS)
507 East Third, #10
Platte, SD 57369

**Hyde County Historical and Genealogical
Society (SDGS)**
(see Historical Societies—Local and
Regional, above)

Kingsbury Genealogical Society
PO Box 330

DeSmet, SD 57231-0330

Lyman-Brule Genealogical Society (SDGS)
110 East Lawler
Chamberlain, SD 57325
mnesladek@hotmail.com
http://www.geocities.com/lbgs2/index
meetings at Cozard Memorial Library,
Chamberlain: third Mon 6:00
$12.00 per year membership

Mitchell Area Genealogical Society (SDGS)
c/o Mitchell Public Library
221 North Duff Street
Mitchell, SD 57301
(605) 996-6321 (Chairperson)
Marilyn Roth, Chairperson
$5.00 per year membership

**Moody County Genealogical Society
(SDGS)**
501 West First Avenue
Flandreau, SD 57028-1003
Anna Duncan, President
Pub. *Moody County Pioneer*, quarterly
("Any info for Moody County. We have
many indexes at our fingertips; six file
drawers of family histories.")
$5.00 per year membership; research: $10.00
per hour

Murdo Genealogical Society (SDGS)
PO Box 441
Murdo, SD 57559

**North Central South Dakota Genealogical
Society (SDGS)**
178 Southshore Drive
Mina, SD 57462-3000
mkrueger@iw.net
http://www.rootsweb.com/~sdgenweb/
gensoc/ncgensoc.html
Morrie Krueger

**Pierre-Fort Pierre Genealogical Society
(SDGS)**
PO Box 925
Pierre, SD 57501
(605) 223-9773
Tina Manning, President
Mon–Fri 9:00–9:00, Sat–Sun 1:00–5:00
Pub. *Pierre-Fort Pierre Genealogical Society
Newsletter*, quarterly
$10.00 per year membership

**Rapid City Society for Genealogical
Research, Inc. (SDGS)**
PO Box 1495
Rapid City, SD 57709
rapidcitygenealogy02@yahoo.com
http://www.rootsweb.com/~sdrcsgr/
rapid_city_society.htm
Glenda Neal, Editor
meetings in the Canyon Lake Senior Citizens
Center, 2900 Canyon Lake Drive: third Fri
7:30
Pub. *Black Hills Nuggets*, quarterly
$15.00 per year membership

Sioux Valley Genealogical Society (SDGS)
(Siouxland Heritage Old Courthouse
Museum—library location)
200 West Sixth Street (mailing address)
Sioux Falls, SD 57104-6001
(605) 334-7762 (Museum); (605) 367-6004
FAX (Museum)
lisa53john@sio.midco.net
http://www.rootsweb.com/~sdsvgs
Jeannette Allard-Fiskum, Library Committee
Mon–Sat 1:00–5:00
Pub. *The Pioneer Pathfinder*, quarterly
(Pioneer Certificates are available to the

descendants of those who lived in Dakota Territory prior to statehood on 2 November 1889.)
$12.00 per year membership

Tri-State Genealogical Society (SDGS)
c/o Belle Fourche Public Library
905 Fifth Avenue
Belle Fourche, SD 57717-1702
Pat Engebretson, President
Pub. *Wymon Dak Messenger*, quarterly (emphasis on western South Dakota, also neighboring Wyoming and Montana)
$5.00 per year membership

Watertown Regional Genealogical Society (SDGS)
611 N.E. "B" Avenue
Watertown, SD 57201
(605) 882-6220
$8.00 per year membership; research (able to research local records): $10.00 per hour (minimum 1 hour)

Genealogical Societies—Local & Regional

Black Hills Genealogy Club
PO Box 372
Rapid City, SD 57701
Pub. *Dakota Territory*, quarterly

Lake County Genealogical Society
Dakota State University
Karl Mundt Library
Madison, SD 57042

Independent Publications and Miscellany

Black Hills Mining Museum
(323 West Main—location)
PO Box 694 (mailing address)
Lead, SD 57754-1604
(605) 584-1605
bhminmus@mato.com
http://www.mining-museum.blackhills.com
Donald D. Toms, Curator
May–Oct: Mon–Sun 9:00–5:00
Pub. *BHMM Newsletter*
("Black Hills mining history, Lead historical and genealogical information)
$5.00 per year membership

Brookings Historic Preservation Commission
(311 Third Avenue—location)
Box 270, City Hall (mailing address)
Brookings, SD 57006
http://www.sdstate.edu/~wbhp/http/historic.html

Chamberlain Area Historical Preservation Association, Inc. (CAHPA)
115 West Lawler
Chamberlain, SD 57325
(605) 734-6542 voice & FAX
http://www.geocities.com/Heartland/Hills/5089

Dakotaland Museum
(Third Street and South Dakota State Fairgrounds—location)
Box 1254 (mailing address)
Huron, SD 57350
(605) 352-2646 (Museum); (605) 352-2633 (Home)
Ruby Johannsen, Director
Memorial Day–Labor Day: 9:30–11:30, 1:00–4:00 & 6:30–8:30

Eureka Pioneer Museum of McPherson

County, Inc.
(Highway #10—location)
1210 North Lake Drive (mailing address)
Eureka, SD 57437
(605) 284-2711; (605) 284-2987 (Home)
Edmund Opp, Curator
Wed–Fri 9:00–5:00, Sat–Sun 2:00–5:00
Pub. *Eureka Pioneer Museum of McPherson County, Inc.*, as needed, free subscription
$5.00 per year membership; admission: free

High Plains Heritage Center Museum
(825 Heritage Drive—location)
PO Box 542 (mailing address)
Spearfish, SD 57783
(605) 642-9378; (605) 642-8463 FAX
http://www.state.sd.us/state/executive/tourism/adds/highpla.htm
Leo E. Giacometto, Executive Director
Mon–Sun 9:00–5:00
$200.00 life membership

Homestead Records
gkrell@aol.com
http://members.aol.com/gkrell/homestead/home.html
Gary E. Krell
(information on homestead and other land patent records for South Dakota)

Klein Foundation, Inc.
1820 West Grand Crossing
Mobridge, SD 57601
(605) 845-7243
Diane Kindt, Director
Mon & Wed–Fri 9:00–noon & 1:00–5:00, Sat–Sun 1:00–5:00
(collection of pioneer and Native American artifacts from the Dakota Plains)

Charles Mix Historical Restoration Society
Geddes Historic District Museum Complex (Fourth and Main Street—location)
PO Box 97 (mailing address)
Geddes, SD 57342
(605) 337-2501
Ron Dufek, Secretary
May–Sept: 7:00–7:00
(local fur trade)
donation

Museum of Missouri River History
(see Nebraska, Part 2)

W. H. Over State Museum
South Dakota State Historical Society, USD
414 East Clark Street
Vermillion, SD 57069
(605) 677-5228
Julia Vidicka, Museum Director

Pioneer Club of Western South Dakota
HCR 61, Box 3
Midland, SD 57552
(605) 843-2150
Elaine Koehler, President
(genealogical services)

Prayer Rock Museum
(Main Street—location)
PO Box 201 (mailing address)
Britton, SD 57430
http://www.brittonsd.com/~prayer-rock
Marie Myklegard, President
Mon–Sat (June–Aug) 11:00–4:00

Robinson State Museum
Association of South Dakota Museums
(Memorial Building, 500 East Capitol, Pierre, SD 57102—location)
200 West Sixth Street (mailing address)

Sioux Falls, SD 57104-6001
(605) 773-3797

Scotland Heritage Chapel and Museum
811 Sixth Street
Scotland, SD 57059
(605) 583-2344
Marvin Thum, Curator
Memorial Day to Labor Day: Sun 2:00–4:00, and by appointment
("We have three buildings containing artifacts and histories.")
$2.00 per year membership

SDGenWeb
Part of The USGenweb Project
jfisher@ucla.edu; kheidel@tri.net
http://www.rootsweb.com/~sdgenweb
Joy Fisher, State Coordinator; Kathy Welch Heidel, Assistant Coordinator; Fred Dethlefsen
(links to other South Dakota resources)

South Dakota Department of Tourism
711 East Wells Avenue
Pierre, SD 57501-3369
(605) 773-3301; (800) SDAKOTA (travel info); (605) 773-3256 FAX
sdinfo@state.sd.us
http://www.travelsd.com
8:00–5:00
(free highway map and vacation guide)

State of South Dakota Department of Transportation
Map Sales, Internal Services
700 East Broadway Avenue
Pierre, SD 57501-2586
(605) 773-3249
http://www.sddot.com/pe/data/map_price.asp
Don Skinner

South Dakota State Agricultural Heritage Museum
South Dakota State University
PO Box 2207C
Brookings, SD 57007-0999
(605) 688-6226; (605) 688-6303 FAX
http://www.sdstate.edu/~wahm

Westerners International, Dakotah Corral
1905 South Sixth Avenue
Sioux Falls, SD 57105
(605) 332-4188

Tennessee

Archives and Libraries with Holdings in Genealogy

State Archives and Library

Tennessee State Library and Archives
State Library and Archives Building
403 Seventh Avenue, North
Nashville, TN 37243-0312
(615) 741-2764; (615) 741-6471 FAX
reference@state.tn.us
http://www.state.tn.us/sos/statelib/
tslahome.htm
Charles Sherrill, Director, Public Services
Mon–Sat 8:00–6:00

State Historical Societies
Tennessee Historical Commission
Department of Environment and
Conservation
Clover Bottom Mansion
2941 Lebanon Road
Nashville, TN 37243-0442
(615) 532-1550; (615) 532-1549 FAX
Herbert.Harper@state.tn.us
http://www.tennessee.gov/environment/hist
Herbert L. Harper, Executive Director
Mon–Fri 8:00–4:30
Pub. *The Courier* (not genealogical, deals
with preservation of historic buildings),
three times per year, free; *The Tennessee
Conservationist*, $10.00 per year
subscription

Tennessee Historical Society
Ground Floor, War Memorial Building
300 Capital Boulevard
Nashville, TN 37243-0084
(615) 741-8934; (615) 741-8937 FAX
tnhissoc@tennesseehistory.org
http://www.tennesseehistory.org
("The collections of the Tennessee Historical
Society are held at the Tennessee State
Library and Archives and the Tennessee
State Museum.")
Pub. *Tennessee Historical Quarterly*, $35.00
per year subscription

City, County and Regional Archives and Libraries
(A more exhaustive list of public and
academic libraries can be found at
http://www.state.tn.us/sos/statelib/publib.)

Archives of Appalachia
Sherrod Library
East Tennessee State University (ETSU)
PO Box 70665, ETSU
Johnson City, TN 37614
(423) 439-4338; (423) 439-4126 FAX
myersn@etsu.edu
http://cass.etsu.edu/archives
Norma Myers, Curator
Mon–Fri 8:00–4:30
Pub. *Archives of Appalachia Newsletter*,
semiannually, free

Art Circle Public Library
154 East First Street
Crossville, TN 38555-4696
(931) 484-6790; (931) 484-2350 FAX
dkkokes@crossville.com
http://www.artcircle.crossville.com
Debra K. Kokes, Director
Mon–Tue & Thur–Fri 8:00–7:00, Wed & Sat
8:00–4:00

Birmingham Public Library
(see Alabama, Part 2)

Bledsoe County Public Library
(102 East Cumberland Avenue—location)
PO Box 465 (mailing address)
Pikeville, TN 37367-0465
(423) 447-2817; (423) 447-3002 FAX
Carolyne L. Knight, Director
Mon–Wed & Fri 10:00–4:00, Sat 10:00–2:00
cost of copying and postage

Blount County Public Library
508 North Cusick Street
Maryville, TN 37804
(423) 982-0981; (865) 977-1142 FAX
http://www.korrnet.org/bcpl
Kathryn E. Pagles, Director
Mon–Thur 9:00–8:00, Fri–Sat 9:00–5:30,
Sun 1:00–5:00
(emphasis on Blount County and
surrounding area)
research: $10.00 minimum

Blount County Records Management
337 Court Street
Maryville, TN 37804
(865) 273-5796; (865) 273-5799 FAX
Jackie Glenn, Records Manager
Mon–Fri 8:00–4:30, by appointment

Carroll County Library
625 High Street
Huntingdon, TN 38344-3903
(502) 732-7020; (502) 732-6753 FAX
karen.pierce@state.tn.us
http://www.users.kih.net/~carrolllib/
index.html
Karen Pierce, Director
Mon 12:30–8:00, Tue–Wed & Fri–Sat
9:30–5:00, Thur 9:30–8:00
(a small genealogy room)

**Chattanooga-Hamilton County
Bicentennial Library**
Local History and Genealogy Department
1001 Broad Street
Chattanooga, TN 37402-2652
(423) 757-5317; (423) 757-4994 FAX
library@lib.chattanooga.gov
http://www.lib.chattanooga.gov
Mary M. Helms, Head, Local History and
Genealogy
Mon–Thur 9:00–9:00, Fri–Sat 9:00–6:00,
Sun (Sunday after Labor Day–Sunday
before Memorial Day) 2:00–6:00
(southeast U.S. genealogy, local and state
history)

Chattanooga Regional History Museum
400 Chestnut Street
Chattanooga, TN 37402
(423) 265-3247
David Estabrook, Executive Director
(primarily historical, not genealogical)

Cheatham County Public Library
188 County Services Drive, Suite 200
Ashland City, TN 37015
(615) 792-4828; (615) 792-2054 FAX
gjacoway@bellsouth.Net
http://bellsouthpwp.net/library
Glenda Jacoway, Director
Mon & Thur–Fri 9:00–5:00, Tue 9:00–8:00,
Wed noon–5:00, Sat 9:00–1:30

Chester County Library
119 East Main Street
Henderson, TN 38340-0323
(731) 989-4673 voice & FAX
nancy.canada@state.tn.us
Nancy Canada, Director
Mon–Fri 9:30–5:00, Sat 9:30–12:30

Clarksville-Montgomery County Public

Library
350 Pageant Lane, #501
Clarksville, TN 37040-0005
(931) 648-8824; (931) 648-8831 FAX
director@clarksville.org
http://www.clarksville.org
Tim Pulley, Reference Assistant; Stephen
Lesnak, Director
Mon, Wed & Fri–Sat 9:00–6:00, Tue & Thur
9:00–8:00
research fees vary with information requested

Clay County Public Library
116 Guffey Street
Celina, TN 38551-9802
(931) 243-3442; (931) 243-4876 FAX
Judith.Cutright@state.tn.us
http://www.dalehollowlake.org/library
Judith Cutright, Director
Mon–Tue & Thur–Fri 8:30–4:30, Wed
3:00–8:00, Sat 9:00–1:00

Cleveland Public Library-History Branch
833 North Ocoee Street
Cleveland, TN 37311-2240
(423) 479-8367 voice & FAX
http://www.clevelandlibrary.org
Barbara Fagen, CRGS, History Branch
Manager
Mon & Fri–Sat 9:00–2:00, Tue & Wed
9:00–noon & 1:00–5:00, Thur 1:00–5:00
& 6:00–9:00
(emphasis on Bradley County and
surrounding areas, local family history)

Clinton Public Library
118 South Hicks Street
Clinton, TN 37716-2826
(865) 457-5400
jgiles@usit.net
Jane A. Giles, Director
Mon & Thur 10:00–8:00, Tue–Wed &
Fri–Sat 10:00–5:00

Cocke County Records Commission
111 Court Avenue, Room 101
Newport, TN 37821
(423) 623-6176; (423) 623-6178 FAX
Janice A. Butler, County Clerk

Coffee County Archives
Coffee County Administrative Plaza
1327 McArthur Drive
Manchester, TN 37355
Betty M. Majors, Archivist
Tue 8:30–1:30

Coffee County Lannom Memorial Library
312 North Collins Street
Tullahoma, TN 37388-3229
(931) 455-2460; (931) 454-2300 FAX
director@lannom.org
http://www.lannom.org
Susan Stovall, Director
Mon–Tue & Thur 9:00–9:00, Wed & Fri
9:00–5:00, Sat 9:00–4:00

Columbia State Community College
John W. Finney Memorial Library
1665 Hampshire Pike
Columbia, TN 38401
(931) 540-2560; (931) 540-2565 FAX
Briscoe_M@coscc.cc.tn.us
http://www.coscc.cc.tn.us/lrc
Martha Briscoe, Library Assistant
Summer: Mon–Thur 7:45–6:00, Fri
7:45–4:15; Spring/Fall: Mon–Thur
7:45–9:00, Fri 7:45–4:15

Cumberland University
Vise Library, Stockton Archives
1 Cumberland Square

Lebanon, TN 37087
(615) 444-2562, ext. 1174; (615) 444-2569
  FAX
mnoel@cumberland.edu
Dr. Frank Burns
by appointment only (part time)
research: $25.00 basic fee

**Customs House Museum and Cultural
Center**
(200 South Second Street, Clarksville, TN
  37040—location)
PO Box 383 (mailing address)
Clarksville, TN 37041-0383
(931) 648-5780; (931) 533-5179 FAX
amy@customshousemuseum.org
http://www.customshousemuseum.org
Amy Andersen-Rude, Registrar
Museum: Tue–Sat 10:00–5:00, Sun
  1:00–5:00; Archives: by appointment only
  ("Access to archives is very limited.")
Pub. *Art 'N Facts*, bimonthly
(local archives)
see web site for admission and membership
  fees; research and reproduction fees vary

Dandridge Memorial Library
(1235 Circle Drive—location)
PO Box 339 (mailing address)
Dandridge, TN 37725-0339
(865) 397-9758; (865) 397-0950 FAX
dand@charter.net
Jean Chambers, Director
Mon & Wed–Fri 7:30–5:30

Dickson County Archives
(Charlotte Courthouse, 4 Court
Square—location)
PO Box 155 (mailing address)
Charlotte, TN 37036
(615) 789-4171, ext. 307; (615) 789-6005
Linda J. Parker, Archivist
Mon–Fri 8:00–4:00

**Fayetteville-Lincoln County Public
Library**
400 Rocky Knob Lane
Fayetteville, TN 37334-2558
(931) 433-3286; (931) 433-0063 FAX
cheri.lopeman@state.tn.us
Cheri Lopeman, Director; Judy Pitts; Nancy
  Hillis
Mon–Sat 9:00–5:00, Tue 9:00–8:00

Mildred G. Fields Memorial Library
1075A East Van Hook Street
Milan, TN 38358-2898
(731) 686-8268; (731) 686-3207 FAX
http://www.cityofmilantn.com/library.htm
Dorothy Bruce, Director
Mon–Tue 9:00–6:00, Wed–Fri 9:00–5:00,
  Sat 9:00–noon
(genealogy and history)

E. G. Fisher Public Library
(1289 Ingleside Avenue, Athens, TN 37371-
3319—location)
PO Box 1815 (mailing address)
Athens, TN 37371-1815
(423) 745-7782; (423) 745-1763 FAX
bamercer@bellsouth.net
Beth Allen Mercer, Director
Mon–Tue & Thur 9:30–8:00, Wed & Fri
  9:30–5:30, Sat 10:00–5:00

Fort Loudoun Regional Library Center
718 George Street, N.W.
Athens, TN 37303-2214
(423) 745-5194; (800) 624-1982; (423) 745-
  8086 FAX
lynette.sloan@state.tn.us
http://www.state.tn.us/fortloudoun

Lynette Sloan, Director
Mon–Fri 8:00–4:30

Franklin County Archives
Project Preservation
304 First Avenue, N.W.
Winchester, TN 37398-1447
(931) 962-1474; (931) 967-7802 FAX
jbigger@edge.net
Jeanne Ridgway Bigger, Director
Project Preservation: Wed 9:00–3:00;
  Archives: Mon–Fri 8:00–4:00
("We [Project Preservation] have over
  70,000 names drawn from the loose
  papers from 1811–1870. We are trying to
  get the 1870s ready for publication as we
  have already published the 1811–1860
  [out of print]. The record center is in two
  rooms at the court house in Franklin
  County, Tennessee, and the deed books
  and chancery and county court books are
  available all week. We still have the tax
  and circuit court minute books at the
  Archives.")
research: for SASE

Giles County Old Records Department
Giles County Courthouse
PO Box 678
Pulaski, TN 38478
(931) 363-8434
Clara M. Parker, Director
Mon–Fri 8:00–4:00

Giles County Public Library
122 South Second Street
Pulaski, TN 38478-3285
(931) 363-2720 (ask for Genealogy Room);
  (931) 424-7032 FAX
glibrary@bellsouth.net
Alice Trimble, Director
Giles County Public Library: Mon–Tue
  10:00–8:00, Wed & Fri 10:00–5:00, Sat
  10:00–4:00, Sun 2:00–4:00

Greenville-Greene County Public Library
T. Elmer Cox Historical and Genealogical
Collection
229 North Main Street
Greeneville, TN 37745-3816
(423) 638-9866; (423) 638-3841 FAX
dmiller@ggcpl.org
http://www.ggcpl.org
Madge Walker, Library Director; Don
  Miller, Director, Cox Collection
Tue–Wed & Fri 10:00–5:00, Thur
  11:00–8:00, Sat 10:00–2:00

Hardin County Library
1100 Pickwick Street South
Savannah, TN 38372-3502
(731) 925-4314; (731) 925-7132 FAX
jeanette.k.smith@state.tn.us
http://www.hardinhistory.com/history/
  library.htm
Janell Russell, Reference Librarian; Jeanette
  K. Smith, Director
Mon–Tue & Thur 9:00–8:00, Wed
  9:00–noon, Fri 9:00–5:00, Sat 9:00–1:00
research: only questions that don't require
  extensive research

Henry County Archives
55 Jones Bend Extension Road
Paris, TN 38242
(731) 642-1222
Paul L. Russell, Chairman, Archival Records
  Committee
Tue 9:00–noon

Highland Rim Regional Library Center
2118 East Main Street

Murfreesboro, TN 37130-4009
(615) 893-3380; (800) 257-7323 (in
  Tennessee); (615) 895-6727 FAX
Melanie.Estal@state.tn.us
http://www.state.tn.us/sos/statelib/p&d/
  highrim
Melanie Estal, Technical Coordinator
(Serves Bedford, Cannon, Coffee, Franklin,
  Lincoln, Moore, Rutherford, Trousdale
  and Wilson counties.)

Elmer Hinton Memorial Library
301 Portland Boulevard
Portland, TN 37148-1229
(615) 325-2279; (615) 325-7061 FAX
brusell@bellsouth.net
http://www.portlandtn.com/library.html
Barbara Russell, Director; Wanda Hawkins,
  Researcher
Tue & Thur 10:00–8:00, Wed & Fri
  10:00–6:00, Sat 10:00–2:00

Charles Ralph Holland Memorial Library
(205 West Hull Avenue—location)
PO Box 647 (mailing address)
Gainesboro, TN 38562-0647
(931) 268-9190; (931) 268-5706 FAX
dale.stapp@state.tn.us
Dale Stapp, Director
Mon–Fri 11:00–5:30, Sat 10:00–3:00

Humphreys County Public Library
201 Pavo Avenue
Waverly, TN 37185-1529
(931) 296-2142; (931) 296-2143; (931) 296-
  6520 FAX
Ethel M. Carmical, Director
Summer: Mon–Fri 10:00–5:00; winter: Mon
  & Wed–Sat 10:00–5:00, Tue 10:00–6:00

Huntsville-Madison County Public Library
(see Alabama, Part 2)

Jackson/Madison County Library
433 East Lafayette Street
Jackson, TN 38301-6386
(731) 425-8600; (731) 425-8609 FAX
tnroom@aeneas.net
http://www.jmcl.tn.org
Jack D. Wood, Tennessee Room Librarian
Mon, Wed & Fri–Sat 9:00–5:00, Tue & Thur
  9:00–8:00
("Public library with genealogy and local
  history research collection.")
limited searches only, minimum $3.00
  (includes first four copies) plus additional
  copies at 25¢ per page

Jefferson County Museum and Archives
(County Courthouse, 202 West Main
Street—location)
PO Box 1193 (mailing address)
Dandridge, TN 37725
(865) 397-4904
Lura B. Hinchey, Director
Mon–Fri 9:00–4:00; archives by appointment

Johnson City Public Library
100 West Millard Street
Johnson City, TN 37604-4731
(423) 434-4450; (423) 434-4469 FAX
info@jcpl.net
http://www.jcpl.net
Linda Blanton, Technical Services Librarian;
  John Hart, Adult Reference Librarian
Mon–Wed 9:00–8:00, Thur–Sat 9:00–6:00,
  Sun 1:00–6:00
(emphasis on Upper East Tennessee,
  southwest Virginia and western North
  Carolina)

Jonesborough-Washington County History

Museum
Jonesborough Civic Trust
(117 Boone Street—location)
PO Box 375 (mailing address)
Jonesborough, TN 37659
(423) 753-5961 (Visitors Center); (423) 753-9775 (Museum); (423) 753-1010
Randy Sanders, Director
Mon–Fri 8:00–5:00, Sat–Sun 10:00–5:00
research fees vary according to information desired

King College
(see Religious Archives and Organizations—Presbyterian, Part 3)

Kingsport Public Library and Archives
400 Broad Steet
Kingsport, TN 37660-4292
(423) 229-9489; (423) 224-2539 (Reference)
hwhittaker@wrlibrary.org
http://kingsportarchives.org
Helen F. Hamilton, Senior Library Assistant; Helen Whittaker, Director
Mon–Thur 9:00–8:00, Fri–Sat 9:00–5:15
(Tennessee history and local history and genealogy)

Kingston Public Library
1001 Bradford Way, #3
Kingston, TN 37763-3100
(423) 376-9905; (865) 376-2301 FAX
Directorkpl@bellsouth.net
Susan Ladd, Librarian; Steve Jacks, Director
Mon & Thur 10:00–7:30, Tue–Wed & Fri 10:00–5:30, Sat 10:00–2:00

Knox County Archives
(East Tennessee Historical Center, 314 West Clinch Avenue, Second Floor, Knoxville, TN 37902-2203—location)
500 West Church Avenue (mailing address)
Knoxville, TN 37902-2505
(865) 215-8800; (865) 215-8804, (865) 215-8836 FAX
archives@knoxlib.org
http://www.knoxlib.org/archives.htm
Doris Rivers Martinson, CA, Manager and Archivist
Mon–Fri 9:00–5:30

Lawrence County Archives
218 North Military Avenue, Suite B-1
Lawrenceburg, TN 38464
(931) 766-1576
lcarchives@lorettotel.net
http://web.infoave.net/~lcarchives/archives.htm
Kathy Niedergeses, Director
Mon–Fri 8:00–4:30
("The Archives is a local government archives housing all the old records of the county plus census, cemetery, etc. records. We also have a very large selection of local history books, plus census, cemetery, family books, and much more for sale. We are actually nearly a one stop research facility open to the public and also offer research services for off-site researchers.")

Lincoln County Archives
1000-B West Washington Street
Fayetteville, TN 37334
(931) 732-4214
Peggy G. Bevels, Chair, County Archives/County Commissioner
Thur 9:00–3:00

Linebaugh Public Library
Historical Research Room
105 West Vine Street
Murfreesboro, TN 37130-3673

(615) 893-4131; (615) 890-4858 FAX
djordon@linebaugh.org
http://www.linebaugh.org/hr.htm
Donna Jordon
(Includes The L. W. Anderson Genealogical Collection,)

Linebaugh Public Library
Historical Research Room
105 West Vine Street
Murfreesboro, TN 37130
(615) 893-4131, ext. 23; (615) 848-5038 FAX
http://www.linebaugh.org
Donna S. Jordon, Reference Clerk
Mon–Thur 9:00–9:00, Fri–Sat 9:00–5:00, Sun 1:00–6:00

Gorham MacBane Public Library
405 White Street
Springfield, TN 37172-2340
(615) 384-5123; (615) 384-0106 FAX
gorhampl@bellsouth.net
Betty Dailey, Director
Mon, Wed & Fri–Sat 9:00–5:00, Tue & Thur 9:00–8:00, Sun 2:30–5:00

Macon County Public Library
(311 Church Street—location)
PO Box 231 (mailing address)
Lafayette, TN 37083-1607
(615) 666-4340; (615) 666-8932 FAX
julia.marshall@state.tn.us
http://www.rootsweb.com/~tnmchs
Tina Short, Secretary; Julia Marshall, Director
Mon–Fri 8:00–4:45, Sat 8:00–1:45
Pub. *Quarterly*
("County history and genealogy")
$12.50 per year

Madison County Government
100 East Main Street, Suite 302
Jackson, TN 38301
(731) 423-6020; (731) 988-3820 FAX
Anissa Gaines, Archivist
Mon–Fri 9:00–5:00
(county archives, from 1821)

Madisonville Public Library
305 College Street
Madisonville, TN 37354-0099
(423) 442-6617; (423) 442-8142 FAX
http://www.madisonvillelibrary.org
Kim Hicks, Director
Tue–Sat 10:00–4:00

Wm. H. & Edgar Magness Community House and Library
118 West Main Street
McMinnville, TN 37110-2516
(931) 473-2428; (931) 473-6778 FAX
william.e.magness@state.tn.us
Mary Robbins, Director; Brad Walker, Staff Genealogist
Mon 8:00–8:00, Tue 9:00–8:00, Wed & Fri 9:00–5:00, Sat 8:00–2:00

Maury County Archives
201 East Sixth Street
Columbia, TN 38401
(931) 381-1565; (931) 381-6370 FAX
Bob Duncan, Director
Mon & Thur 8:00–8:00, Tue–Wed & Fri 8:00–4:00
Pub. *Historic Maury Quarterly*

Maury County Public Library
211 West Eighth Street
Columbia, TN 38401-3282
(931) 388-6332; (931) 388-6371 FAX
epotts@maryco.org

http://www.maurycountylibrary.org
Elizabeth Potts, Director
Mon–Wed 9:00–8:00, Thur–Sat 9:00–5:00

Maury County Public Library
Mount Pleasant Branch Library
(200 Hay Long Avenue—location)
PO Box 71 (mailing address)
Mount Pleasant, TN 38474-0071
(931) 379-3752; (931) 379-3774 FAX
mtpleasantlibrary@yahoo.com
http://www.maurycountylibrary.org
Janice Jones, Director
Mon & Wed 10:00–9:00, Tue & Thur–Sat 10:00–5:00

Calvin M. McClung Historical Collection
Knox County Public Library System
(East Tennessee Historical Center, 314 West Clinch Avenue, Knoxville, TN 37902-2203—location)
500 West Church Avenue (mailing address)
Knoxville, TN 37902-2505
(865) 215-8801; (865) 215-8836 FAX
kcplmccl@korrnet.org
http://www.knoxlib.org
J. Stephen Cotham, Manager
Mon–Tue 9:00–8:30, Wed–Fri 9:00–5:30, Sat 9:00–5:00, Sun 1:00–5:00
(Specializes in East Tennessee; "Holdings include papers of over forty regional genealogists: books, maps, manuscripts, newspapers, photographs, clippings files, architectural plans and drawings, microfilm.")

McNairy County Records Commission
(Courthouse, 170 West Court, Suite B3—location)
PO Box 764 (mailing address)
Selmer, TN 38375
(731) 645-6432; (731) 645-9124 FAX
Nancy Kennedy, Director
Mon–Tue & Thur–Fri 9:00–1:00

McWherter Library
Special Collections/Mississippi Valley Collection
Campus Box 52-6500
Memphis State University
Memphis, TN 38152
(901) 678-2210; (901) 678-8218 FAX
efrank@memphis.edu
http://www.lib.memphis.edu
Ed Frank, Curator
Mon–Fri 8:00–4:30, Sun 1:00–5:00 during semesters
(Tennessee and mid-south materials; "Genealogy collection supports our historical materials, genealogy is not the main focus of the collection.")

Belle Meade Plantation
5025 Harding Road
Nashville, TN 37205
(615) 356-0501, ext. 33; (800) 270-3991; (615) 356-2336 FAX
Historian@BelleMeadePlantation.com; information@BelleMeadePlantation.com
http://www.bellemeadeplantation.com
Sharon Maguire, Assistant Curator of Research and Collections
Tours: Mon–Sat 9:00–5:00, Thur–Sat 6:00–8:00, Sun 11:00–5:00
$40.00 per year membership; tours: $10.00 for adult nonmembers

Memphis/Shelby County Public Library and Information Center
Central Library
History Genealogy Travel and Social Sciences Department

The Genealogist's Address Book

3030 Poplar Avenue
Memphis, TN 38111-3527
(901) 415-2700 (Central Library); (901) 415-2742 (Genealogy)
hisref@memphis.lib.tn.us
http://www.memphislibrary.lib.tn.us/history/index.html
Correspondence Librarian
Mon–Fri 10:00–5:00
("The Memphis & Shelby County Room holds a wide variety of material providing information about the development of the city and county. The local history collection includes books, photographs, maps, newspaper clippings and pamphlets, Memphis periodicals, manuscript collections, and oral history tapes. Genealogy materials in microform and print enable one to research family history, tracing the movements of relatives, especially in the southeastern United States. The collection includes more than 20,000 genealogy books as well as magazines and other kinds of material.")
reference service: $15.00 minimum for up to one half hour service, payable in advance, $15.00 for each additional half hour, $15.00 additional for same-day or next-day service; copies: 20¢ per page, $4.00 minimum handling for 1-5 copies, $15.00 per hour additional charge for more than 5 copies (not applicable to libraries)

Metropolitan Archives of Nashville and Davidson County
3801 Green Hills Village Drive
Nashville, TN 37215
(615) 862-5880; (615) 862-5883 FAX
metroarchives@yahoo.com (Friends of Metropolitan Archives)
http://www.geocities.com/metroarchives (Friends of Metropolitan Archives)
C. Kenneth Fieth, Director
Mon–Thur 9:30–5:30, Sat 9:00–5:00
(Nashville/Davidson County archives, congressional papers also)
$10.00 per year membership to Friends of Metropolitan Archives

Middle Tennessee State University
Center for Historic Preservation
PO Box 80
Murfreesboro, TN 37132
(615) 898-2947
James K. Huhta, Ph.D., Director
(not genealogical)

Middle Tennessee State University
Albert Gore, Sr., Research Center
PO Box 193
Murfreesboro, TN 37132
(615) 898-2632; (615) 898-5059 FAX
lpruitt@mtsu.edu
http://janus.mtsu.edu
Lisa J. Pruitt, Ph.D., Director
Mon–Fri 8:00–4:00
(includes Civil War materials)

Middle Tennessee State University
Todd Library
Murfreesboro, TN 37132
(615) 898-2549
kmiddlet@frank.mtsu.edu
http://frank.mtsu.edu/~kmiddlet/history/women.html

Monroe County Archives
105 College Street
Madisonville, TN 37354
(423) 442-3981
Lynn McConkey, County Genealogist
Tue–Fri 9:00–11:00

research within archives: cost of copies; research outside archives: $10.00 per hour

Morristown-Hamblen Library
Meta Turley Goodson Historical Room
417 West Main Street
Morristown, TN 37814-4686
(423) 586-6410; (423) 587-6226 FAX
library@lcs.net
Ann C. Steffen, Library Director
Mon, Wed & Fri–Sat 9:00–5:30, Tue & Thur 9:00–8:00
(more than 1,500 books as well as microfilm copies of census records and the local newspapers)
limited research and information on fees: Sandra Menders, 5642 Long Creek Road, Morristown, TN 37813

Mount Juliet-Wilson County Library
Madelon Wright Smith Memorial Archives
(2765 North Mount Juliet Road—location)
PO Box 319 (mailing address)
Mount Juliet, TN 37122-0319
(615) 758-7051; (615) 754-2439 FAX
mt.julietlibrary@comcast.net
http://www.mtjulietlibrary.net
Cyndie Todd, Genealogist
Mon–Tue & Thur 9:00–8:00, Wed & Fri–Sat 9:00–5:00; genealogist on site Mon, Wed & Sat 9:00–noon

The Public Library of Nashville and Davidson County
The Ben West Library
Nashville Room
615 Church Street
Nashville, TN 37203-2314
(615) 862-5842; (615) 862-5838 FAX
ereference@nashville.gov
http://www.library.nashville.org/Library/Depts/Nashroom.html (Nashville Room)
Dr. Sue Loper, Special Collections Division Manager; Mary Glenn Hearne, Nashville Room Manager
Mon–Sat 9:00–5:00, Sun (Oct–May) 2:00–5:00
(emphasis on middle Tennessee history and genealogy)

Oak Ridge Public Library
Civic Center
1401 Oak Ridge Turnpike
Oak Ridge, TN 37830-6206
(865) 482-8455; (865) 482-8459
mlux@ci.oak-ridge.tn.us
http://orserv01.ci.oak-ridge.tnh.us/orlib.htm
Martha W. Lux, Head of Reference
Mon–Thur 10:00–9:00, Fri 10:00–6:00, Sat 9:00–6:00, Sun 2:00–6:00

Obion County Museum
1004 Edwards Street
Union City, TN 38261
(731) 885-6774
Mary Ann Overman, Corresponding Secretary
Sat–Sun 1:00–4:00, and by appointment
("The museum has a small room for genealogical research.")
admission: free

Ohoopee Regional Library
(see Georgia, Part 2)

Overton County Archives
317 University Street
Livingston, TN 38570
(931) 823-8864
reda@twlakes.net
Reda Bilbrey, County Archivist
by appointment

("We are beginning to type in the data base but think it will take a long time. We lost many of the old records when the courthouse was remodeled in the 1970s.")

Overton County Public Library
225 East Main Street
Livingston, TN 38570-1959
(931) 823-1888 voice & FAX
director@overtoncolibrary.com
http://www.overtoncolibrary.com
Janet W. Gann, Director
Mon & Wed–Fri 9:00–5:00, Tue 9:00–7:00, Sat 9:00–2:00
("Approximately 500 books in the genealogy section—many on specific families—and will assist people [on-site] with their research. Although we aren't sufficiently staffed to do 'look-ups' for people, we forward requests to Overton County Historical Society.")

Paris-Henry County Heritage Center
(614 North Poplar Street—location)
PO Box 822 (mailing address)
Paris, TN 38242
(731) 642-1030; (731) 642-1096 FAX
heritage@aeneas.net
William W. Harle, Curator
Mon–Fri 9:00–5:00
("We are a local history museum with some of the Henry County Historical Society's files located here.")
$25.00 per year membership; admission: free

Perry County Public Library
Route 10, Box 3A, College Avenue
Linden, TN 37096-0369
(931) 589-5011; (931) 589-6210 FAX
Dorothy Pevahouse, Director
Mon–Tue & Thur–Fri 9:00–5:00, Wed 9:00–noon

Anna Porter Public Library
Smoky Mountain Collection
207 Cherokee Orchard Road
Gatlinburg, TN 37738-3417
(865) 436-5588 voice & FAX
kt@annaporterpl.org
http://www.annaporterpl.org
Kenton Temple, Director
Mon & Wed–Fri 10:00–5:00, Tue 10:00–8:00, Sat 10:00–1:00

Putnam County Library
50 East Broad Street
Cookeville, TN 38501-3210
(931) 526-2416; (931) 372-8517 FAX
dianed@pclibrary.org
http://www.pclibrary.org
Diane Duncan, Director
Mon 9:00–8:00, Tue–Fri 9:00–6:00, Sat 9:00–5:00, Sun 1:00–5:00

W. G. Rhea Public Library
Genealogy Department
400 West Washington Street
Paris, TN 38242-3903
(731) 642-1702; (731) 642-1777 FAX
woinman@hotmail.com
http://www.angelfire.com/tn2/woinman
Linda Dunlap
Mon, Wed & Fri–Sat 9:00–5:00, Tue & Thur 9:00–7:00
("Genealogical resources: books, maps, microfilm, microfiche covering research for Tennessee, Western Kentucky, early Virginia, North and South Carolina, etc., online catalog of materials with volunteer look-up assistance available.")

Robertson County Archives

504 South Willow Street
Springfield, TN 37172
(615) 382-6928
archives@kytnresearch.com
Yolanda Reid, County Historian
Mon–Fri 8:00–4:00
research: $5.00 plus copy costs for one
surname, one type of record, for a ten-year
time period

Elma Ross Public Library
1011 East Main Street
Brownsville, TN 38012-2652
(731) 772-9534; (731) 772-5416 FAX
Ramona.Stevenson@state.tn.us
http://www.pchnet.com/library/default.htm
Reese J. Moses, Volunteer; Ramona
Stevenson, Director
Mon 10:00–8:00, Tue–Fri 10:00–5:00, Sat
1:00–5:00

Rutherford County Archives
Rutherford County Courthouse, Suite 301
Murfreesboro, TN 37130
(615) 897-4609
http://www.rutherfordcounty.org/archives
Mon–Fri 8:00–3:30

Sevier County Library
321 Court Avenue
Sevierville, TN 37862-3412
(865) 453-3532; (865) 908-6108 FAX
kcwm@sevierlibrary.org
http://www.sevierlibrary.org
K.C. Williams, Director
Mon & Thur 10:30–8:00, Tue–Wed & Fri
10:30–6:00, Sat 10:30–4:00

Shelby County Archives
150 Washington Avenue, Second Floor
Memphis, TN 38103
(901) 545-4356; (901) 545-4311 FAX
archives@co.shelby.tn.us
http://www.archives.co.shelby.tn.us (under
construction)
John Dougan, Shelby County Archivist;
Vincent L. Clark, Public Service Manager
Mon–Fri 8:00–4:30
(County Mayor's Papers 1976–2002, County
Commission Minutes 1830–1995, County
Commission Records 1820–1865, Death
Certificates 1848–1951, Marriage Records
1820–2002, Probate Files 1820–1900,
Probate Minutes 1820–2001, Will Books
1820–2001, Naturalization Records
1856–1906, Deed Records 1820–2002,
Subdivision Plats 1820–2002, Aerial
Photos 1837–1990, Military Discharges
1928–2002, Tax Assessment Books
1868–1992, Property Assessment Cards
1939–1976, Building Permits 1964–1999,
Circuit Court Minutes 1828–1988, Circuit
Court Cases 1851–1964, Chancery Court
Minutes 1849–1998, Chancery Court
Cases 1849–1975, Criminal Court Minutes
1848–1985, Criminal Court Cases
1911–1971, Prison Registers 1913–1990,
Memphis City Council Records
1850–1989)

Smith County Public Library
215 Main Street, North
Carthage, TN 37030-1539
(615) 735-1326; (615) 735-2317 FAX
Pat.Bush@state.tn.us
http://smithlib.org
Patricia K. Bush, Director
Mon–Fri 8:30–4:00, Sat 9:00–noon
Pub. *Smith County Historical and Genealogy
Quarterly*, $12.50 per year subscription
from PO Box 112, Carthage, TN 37030

Smyrna Public Library
400 Enon Springs Road West
Smyrna, TN 37137-3214
(615) 459-4884; (615) 459-2370 FAX
ckersey@linebaugh.org
http://www.linebaugh.org/smyrna/home.htm
Lynda Duke, Reference Clerk; Carol Kersey,
Director
Mon–Thur 9:00–8:00, Fri–Sat 9:00–5:00

Southern Adventist University
McKee Library
(4881 Taylor Circle—location)
PO Box 629 (mailing address)
Collegedale, TN 37315
(423) 238-2790; (423) 238-3009 FAX
lgrace@southern.edu
http://www.library.southern.edu
Loranne Grace, Director, Technical Services
Tue 9:00–4:00, by appointment
(newspapers, manuscripts)

H. B. Stamps Memorial Library
407 East Main Street
Rogersville, TN 37857-3315
(615) 272-8710; (423) 272-9261 FAX
hbslib@chartertn.net
Jeannie Davis, Director and Hawkins County
Coordinator
Mon, Wed & Fri 9:30–5:00, Tue & Thur
9:30–8:00, Sat (Sept–May) 9:30–5:00

Stokely Memorial Library
383 East Broadway
Newport, TN 37821-3105
(423) 623-3832 voice & FAX
meschelyn@charter.net
http://stokelylibrary.d2g.com
Meschelyn Barrett, Director; Karen Travis,
Webmaster
Mon–Sat 10:00–5:00

Sullivan County Library
(1655 B_lountville Boulevard—location)
PO Box 510 (mailing address)
Blountville, TN 37617-0510
(423) 279-2714; (423) 279-2836 FAX
khamrick@wrlibrary.org
http://www.wrlibrary.org/index.htm
Kay P. Hamrick, Director
Mon, Wed & Fri–Sat 9:00–5:00, Tue & Thur
9:00–6:30
(specializes in eastern Tennessee,
northwestern North Carolina, and
southwestern Virginia)

Sumner County Archives
155 East Main Street
Gallatin, TN 37066
(615) 452-0037; (615) 452-1442 FAX
http://www.sumnertn.org/archives
Shirley Wilson, Director
Mon–Fri 8:00–4:30, occasional Sat by
appointment
(library collection and court records, middle
Tennessee genealogy with emphasis on
Sumner County)
research: $5.00 plus SASE

Sweetwater Public Library
210 Mayes Avenue
Sweetwater, TN 37874-2620
(423) 337-5274; (423) 337-0552 FAX
swepltn@compfxnet.com
Beverly Bollenbacher, Director
Mon–Wed & Fri 10:00–6:00, Thur
10:00–8:00

Tennessee Technological University
Box 5066
Cookeville, TN 38505
(931) 372-3470

http://www2.tntech.edu/library/
departments/archives/html
Christine S. Jones, Regional History
Librarian
Mon–Fri 8:00–4:30
(primarily historical)

University of Memphis
(see McWherter Library, above)

University of Mississippi
Center for the Study of Southern Culture
(see Mississippi, Part 2)

The University of Tennessee, Knoxville
The James D. Hoskins Special Collections
Library
1041 Cumberland Avenue
Knoxville, TN 37996-4000
(865) 974-4480; (865) 974-0560 FAX
special@aztec.lib.utk.edu
http://www.lib.utk.edu/spcoll
Mon–Fri 9:00–5:30
(contains university archives)

The University of Tennessee, Knoxville
The Frank H. McClung Museum
1327 Circle Park Drive
Knoxville, TN 37996-3200
(865) 974-2144; (865) 974-3827 FAX
museum@utk.edu
http://mcclungmuseum.utk.edu
Jefferson Chapman, Ph.D., Director
Museum: Mon–Sat 9:00–5:00, Sun 1:00–5:00
(historical museum; do not confuse with
Calvin McClung Historical Collection of
the Knox County Public Library System or
with the University Library's James D.
Hoskins Special Collections Library)
$30.00 per year membership; admission: free

University of Tennessee at Martin
Corbitt Special Collections and Archives
Paul Meek Library
Martin, TN 38238
(731) 587-7094; (731) 587-7074 FAX
speccoll@utm.edu
http://www.utm.edu/departments/
acadpro/library/speccoll.htm
Richard Saunders, Curator
Mon–Fri 8:00–5:00, and by appointment
("The focus is on the genealogy and local
history of northwest Tennessee, Tennessee
at large, and the state's historical
antecedents [North Carolina, specifically].
Other states are included. There are
approximately 3,000 volumes and 800
reels of microfilm.")

University of the South Archives
Jessie Ball DuPont Library
735 University Avenue
Sewanee, TN 37375-4005
(931) 598-3212; (931) 598-1702
aarmour@sewanee.edu
http://www.library.sewanee.edu/dept/
archives/home.html
Anne Armour, Head of Archives, Rare
Books, and Preservation
Mon–Fri 9:00–noon & 1:00–4:00

Van Buren County Archives
County Administrative Building
Spencer, TN 38585
(931) 946-7486
BillJ3370@Blomand.net
Agnes C. Jones, Archivist
by appointment

Vanderbilt University
Jean and Alexander Heard Library
Special Collections and University Archives

419 21st Avenue, South
Nashville, TN 37240
(615) 322-2807
smith@library.vanderbilt.edu
http://www.library.vanderbilt.edu/
 speccol/schome.html
Juanita Murray, Head of Special Collections
 and University Archivist
Mon–Fri 9:00–4:00

Virginia Polytechnic Institute and State University
Appalachian history
(see Virginia, Part 2)

Wartburg Public Library
(514 Spring Street—location)
PO Box 366 (mailing address)
Wartburg, TN 37887-0366
(423) 346-2479 voice & FAX
kathy.byrd@state.tn.us
http://members.tripod.com/waratburglibrary
Kathleen Byrd, Director
Mon & Fri 11:00–5:30, Tue–Thur
 11:00–5:00

Washington County-Jonesborough Library
200 Sabin Drive
Jonesborough, TN 37659-1306
(423) 753-1800; (423) 753-1802 FAX
http://www.wrlibrary.org/washco.htm
Emily Eddy, Director
Mon & Thur 9:00–8:00, Tue–Wed & Fri
 9:00–6:00, Sat 9:00–2:00
(emphasis on east Tennessee and Washington
 County)
searching done as volunteers have the time;
 copies: 15¢ per page

Wayne County Public Library
(Highway 64 East—location)
PO Box 630 (mailing address)
Waynesboro, TN 38485-0630
(931) 722-5537 voice & FAX
katherine.morris@state.tn.us;
 kmorris@mail.state.tn.us
Katherine Morris, Director
Mon–Tue & Thur–Fri 10:00–6:00, Wed &
 Sat 10:00–2:00

Ned R. McWherter Weakley County Library
341 Linden Street
Dresden, TN 38225-1400
(731) 364-2678; (731) 364-2599 FAX
Candy McAdams, Director
Mon–Thur 9:00–5:00, Fri 9:00–5:30, Sat
 9:00–noon

White County Public Library
144 South Main Street
Sparta, TN 38583-2299
(931) 836-3613; (931) 836-2570 FAX
Cathymt@charter.net
http://www.wtclibrary.org
Cathy Taylor, Director
Mon & Wed–Sat 8:00–5:00, Tue 8:00–8:00

White Pine Public Library
(1708 Main Street—location)
PO Box 430 (mailing address)
White Pine, TN 37890-0430
(865) 674-6313; (865) 674-8511 FAX
wppl@charter.net
Betty Jo Moore, Director
Mon & Wed–Thur 9:00–5:30, Fri 9:00–3:00

Williamson County Archives
PO Box 1006
Franklin, TN 37065-1006
(615) 790-5462
Louise G. Lynch, Archivist/Director

Mon–Fri 8:00–noon & 1:00–4:25

Williamson County Public Library
Genealogy Library
(Old Post Office Building, 510 Columbia
 Avenue—location)
611 West Main Street (mailing address)
Franklin, TN 37064-2723
(615) 595-1246; (615) 494-9247 FAX
ddouglass@lib.williamson-tn.org
http://lib.williamson-tn.org
Dorris Douglass, Genealogy Librarian
Tue–Sat 8:30–5:00
(houses the Edythe Rucker Whitley
 Collection)
research: minimum $6.50 including postage
 and up to ten photocopies; additional
 copies: 25¢ each from paper originals,
 50¢ from microform originals

Wilson County Archives
111 South College Street
Lebanon, TN 37087
(615) 443-1993; (615) 443-1576 FAX
http://www.wilsoncounty.com
Linda Granstaff; Thomas Partlow, Director
Mon–Fri 9:00–3:00

Wynnewood
Route 1, Box 5
Castalian Springs, TN 37031
(615) 452-5463

Historical Societies—Local and Regional

Anderson County Historian
Anderson County Tennessee Archives
100 South Main, Room 204 Vault
Clinton, TN 37716
(865) 457-6242
S080332@aol.com
Mary S. Harris
Mon–Fri 8:30–4:30

Association for the Preservation of Tennessee Antiquities (APTA)
Belle Meade Mansion
110 Leake Avenue
Nashville, TN 37205
(615) 352-8247
http://www.mtsu.edu/~histpres/APTA
Cherrie H. Hall, Executive Director
Mon–Thur
Pub. *Intercom*, biannually
$10.00 per year membership

Bedford County Historian
912 Shelbyview Drive
Shelbyville, TN 37160
Tim and Helen Marsh
Courthouse Archives: Bedford County
 Courthouse: Wed 8:00–noon

Bedford County Historical Society
705 South Cannon
Shelbyville, TN 37160
(931) 685-4898
rebelace@cafes.net
Roy Bartlette, President
Pub. *Bedford County Historical Quarterly*
 (Mar, June, Sept, Dec), $3.25 per issue
$12.50 per year membership; no research
 service available

Benton County Historian
Benton County Library
121 South Forrest Avenue
Camden, TN 38320-1712
(731) 584-0778; (731) 584-1098 FAX
Virginia L. Whitworth

Bledsoe County Historian
Route 1
Pikeville, TN 37367
Elizabeth Robnett

Blount County Genealogical and Historical Society
(see Genealogical Societies—Local and
 Regional, below)

Blount County Historian
1308 Brannon Drive
Maryville, TN 37801
Inez Burns

Bradley County Historian
3765 Hillsdale Drive, N.E.
Cleveland, TN 37312
Dr. Bill Snell

Bradley County Historical Society
Lee College
Cleveland, TN 37311
(423) 479-8367
Dr. William Snell
Cleveland Public Library—History Branch:
 Tue–Wed 9:00–noon & 1:00–4:00, Thur
 1:00–5:00 & 6:00–9:00, Fri–Sat 9:00–2:00
(emphasis on Bradley County and
 surrounding areas, local family history)

Brentwood Historical and Genealogical Society
Middle Tennessee Society of Professional
 Genealogists
Brentwood, TN 37024
TTVLittle@aol.com
T. Vance Little, City Historian
Mon–Fri 9:00–4:00
Pub. *Tennessee Genealogical Review
 Quarterly*, $25.00 per year subscription
("Maintain computerized bibliography of
 original and secondary sources for each
 county and state available from leading
 archives and record repositories.")
quotations offered on specific research needs

Bristol Historical Association, Inc.
PO Box 204
Bristol, TN 37621

Campbell County Historian
PO Box 1193
LaFollette, TN 37766
Judge Greg Miller

Campbell County Historical Society
103 South Sixth Street
LaFollette, TN 37766
(423) 566-5381
Trulene H. Nash, Vice President,
 Publications
Mon–Fri 9:00–2:00, Sat (May–Aug)
 9:00–2:00
Pub. *The Campbell Countian*, quarterly
$10.00 per year membership

Caney Fork River Historical Association, Inc.
(Luttrell Avenue—location)
PO Box 153 (mailing address)
Smithville, TN 37166
(615) 597-4646

Cannon County Historian
Adams Memorial Library
212 College Street
Woodbury, TN 37190
(615) 563-5861; (615) 563-2140 FAX
adammem@mail.state.tn.us
Kathryn Bensinger, Director
Mon, Wed & Fri–Sat 9:00–4:00, Tue & Thur

9:00–8:00
("Local History Room")
research: no search but "will copy and send
   specific information"

Carroll County Historian
640 Main Street
McKenzie, TN 37201
Patricia Clark

Carroll County Historical Society
Gordon Browning Museum and Genealogical
Library
640 North Main Street
McKenzie, TN 38201
(731) 352-3510; (731) 352-3456 FAX
gbmuseum@aeneas.net
http://gbmuseum.tn.org
Jere R. Cox, Director, Curator
Mon–Tue & Thur–Fri 9:00–4:00
Pub. *Newsletter*, occasionally
(general research for Carroll and adjacent
   counties)
$5.00 per year membership; research:
   donation and postage plus copies at 20¢
   each

Carter County Historian
(post vacant)

Cheatham County Historian
106 Smith Street
Ashland City, TN 37015
James B. Hallums

Chester County Historian
241 Crook Avenue
Henderson, TN 38340
Mr. Bobby Barnes

Chester County Historical Society
PO Box 721
Henderson, TN 38340-0721
http://erc.jscc.cc.tn.us/jfn/libjmc/Chester.
   html

Claiborne County Historian
PO Box 6
Tazewell, TN 37879
John J. Kivette

Claiborne County Historical Society
PO Box 32
Tazewell, TN 37879
(423) 626-7261
Brenda Burchfield, Treasurer
Pub. *Reflections*, quarterly, $5.00 per issue
$10.00 per year membership

Clay County Historian
PO Box 447
Celina, TN 38551-0447
Mrs. W. B. Upton

Cocke County Historian
532 Fourth Street
Newport, TN 37821
Edward R. Walker, III

Coffee County Historian
7614 Maple Springs Road
Manchester, TN 37355
Mr. Jess Lewis, Jr.

Coffee County Historical Society, Inc.
Coffee County Courthouse
101 West Fort Street
Manchester, TN 37355
(931) 728-0145
http://www.cafes.net/jlewis/pubs.htm
Pub. *Coffee County Historical Quarterly*

Crockett County Historian

Route 1
Humboldt, TN 38343
Mrs. Charles C. James

Cumberland County Historian
East First Street
Crossville, TN 38555
(931) 484-6397
Donald Brookhart

Davidson County Historian
4204 Hood Avenue
Nashville, TN 37215
John L. Connelly

Sam Davis Memorial Association
Sam Davis Road
Smyrna, TN 37167
(615) 459-2341

Decatur County Historian
59 East Fourth Street
Parsons, TN 38363
A. W. Primm

Deer Lodge Historical Society
(302 Old Deer Lodge Pike—location)
PO Box 5 (mailing address)
Deer Lodge, TN 37726
(423) 965-2525; (423) 965-3472; (423) 965-
   3575; (423) 965-2000 FAX
Susie Kries, Chairman
hours: various
(The Weidemann Hotel [under
   reconstruction] will house D.L.H.S."
   Published *Deer LodgeCentennial
   1886–1986, United We Cook 2002*,
   $13.50 ppd.)
$5.00 per year membership

Dekalb County Historian
835 South College Street
Smithville, TN 37166
Thomas G. Webb

Dickson County Historian
206 Bellwood Circle
Dickson, TN 37055
George Jackson

Dickson County Historical Society
PO Box 611
Charlotte, TN 37036
George E. Jackson
by appointment

Dyer County Historian
360 Greenway Street, Apartment #1
Dyersburg, TN 38024-2459
Wallace Milan

East Tennessee Historical Society
(600 Market Street—location)
PO Box 1629 (mailing address)
Knoxville, TN 37901-1629
(865) 215-8824
http://www.east-tennessee-history.org
Kent Whitworth, Executive Director; Cherel
   Henderson, Associate Director
Calvin McClung Historical Collection:
   Mon–Tue 9:00–8:30, Wed–Fri 9:00–5:30,
   Sun 1:00–5:00; Office: Mon–Fri
   9:00–5:00; Museum: Tue–Sat
   10:00–4:00, Sun 1:00–5:00
Pub. *Journal of East Tennessee History*,
   annually; *Tennessee Ancestors*, three
   times per year; *Newsline*, quarterly
Affiliates: **First Families of Tennessee; The
   East Tennessee Society for the
   Preservation of Friends (Quaker)
   History; Grainger County Historical
   Society; The Overmountain Victory**

Trail Association, Inc.
$35.00 per year membership

Fayette County Historian
PO Box 127
Moscow, TN 38057
Mrs. J. R. Morton

Fayette County Historical Society
PO Box 304
Somerville, TN 38068
Anne H. Thompson, President
Pub. *The Fayette County Historical Society
   Bulletin*

Fentress County Historian
Route 2, Box 150
Jamestown, TN 38556
Lorraine Cargile

Fentress County Historical Society
PO Box 178
Jamestown, TN 38556
(931) 879-7512
Christene Barton, Librarian
Mon–Tue & Thur–Sat 9:00–11:00 &
   noon–5:00
Pub. *Fentress County (TN) Historical Society
   Newsletter*, quarterly, $5.00 per year
   subscription
$8.00 per year membership

**The Heritage Foundation of Franklin and
Williamson County**
(510 Fifth Avenue—location)
PO Box 723 (mailing address)
Franklin, TN 37065-0723
(615) 591-8500; (615) 591-8502 FAX
Mary Pearce, Executive Director
9:00–4:00
Pub. *The Sentinel*, quarterly
$35.00 per year membership

Franklin County Historian
720 Long Point Lane
Belvidere, TN 37306
Howard M. Hannah

Franklin County Historical Society
PO Box 130
Winchester, TN 37398-0130
(931) 962-1476
Travis Hitt, President
11:30–4:30
Pub. *Franklin County Historical Review*,
   annually; *Historical Tidings*, quarterly
$25.00 per year membership

Gibson County Historian
101 South Court Square
Trenton, TN
(731) 855-1142
Frederick M. Culp

Giles County Historian
307 Longmeadow Circle
Pulaski, TN 38478
Pauline Cross

Giles County Historical Society
(122 South Second Street—location)
PO Box 693 (mailing address)
Pulaski, TN 38478
(931) 363-2720 (ask for Genealogy Room)
George Newman, President
Giles County Public Library: Mon–Tue
   10:00–8:00, Wed & Fri 10:00–5:00, Sat
   10:00–4:00, Sun 2:00–4:00
Pub. *Giles County Historical Society Bulletin*,
   quarterly
$8.00 per year membership

Grainger County Historian
Route 2
Rutledge, TN 37861
Jack McGoldrick

Grainger County Historical Society
An Affiliate of the East Tennessee Historical
Society
PO Box 215
Rutledge, TN 37861
gpoingerhist@cs.com
Kevin Cowins, President
$10.00 per year membership

**Greenbrier Historical Society Museum and
Library**
(205 West College Street—location)
PO Box 695 (mailing address)
Greenbrier, TN 37073
(615) 643-8461
Shelia Watts, President
Wed–Fri 10:00–4:00, Sat 10:00–1:00

Greene County Chapter
East Tennessee Historical Society
PO Box 1202
Greeneville, TN 37743

Greene County Heritage Trust
PO Box 1630
Greeneville, TN 37744
(423) 638-6303

Greene County Historian
PO Box 1202
Greeneville, TN 37744
Marie Harmon

Grundy County Historian
Grundy County History Museum
3066 Browns Hollow Road
Tracy City, TN 37387
(931) 592-6557
William Ray Turner
by appointment
(Collection of 20,000 photos, thousands of
local papers. Published *The Mountain
Goad: Story of the Local Railroad from
Cowan, TN, to Palmer, TN*, $15.25 ppd.)

Grundy County Historical Society
(The Tracy City Public Library—location)
Box 1422 (mailing address)
Tracy City, TN 37387
(931) 592-9714; (931) 592-9715 FAX
cflury@blomand.net
Leslie Coppinger, Tracy City Librarian;
Catherine Flury, President
Mon, Wed & Fri 10:00–4:30
Pub. *Pathfinder*, quarterly
("We welcome all contributions [historical
and family genealogy material].")
$15.00 per year membership; research:
$10.00 ($5.00 is returned if nothing is
found), plus postage and copies at 25¢ per
page

Hamblen County Historian
1960 Silver City Road
Russellville, TN 37860
Mrs. Berwin Haun

Hamilton County Historian
2815 Military Road
Chattanooga, TN 37409
John Wilson

Hancock County Historian
PO Box 277
Sneedville, TN 37869
Scott Collins

**Hancock County Historical and
Genealogical Society**
PO Box 277
Sneedville, TN 37869
(423) 733-4524; (423) 733-2762 FAX
Scott F. Collins, Clerk and Master
daily 8:00–4:00, Wed 8:00–noon
Pub. *Our Mountain Heritage*, quarterly
$5.00 per year membership

Hardeman County Historian
618 Clifft Street
Bolivar, TN 38008
Faye Tennyson Davidson

Hardin County Historian
c/o **Hardin County Historical Society**
PO Box 1012
Savannah, TN 38372
Mary Elizabeth Hitchcock

Hardin County Historical Society
PO Box 1012
Savannah, TN 38372
(731) 925-3106
http://www.hardinhistory.com/history/
member.htm
Henry Williams, Treasurer; Ronney R.
Brewington, Editor; Mary Elizabeth
Hitchcock, President
Mon–Fri 8:00–4:00
Pub. *Hardin County Historical Quarterly*
$12.00 per year membership; free queries

**Hawkins County Genealogical and
Historical Society**
(see Genealogical Societies—Local and
Regional, below)

Hawkins County Historian
426 West Main
Rogersville, TN 37857
Henry R. Price

Haywood County Historian
(Haywood County Historical Committee)
PO Box 207
Brownsville, TN 38012
Mr. Lynn Shaw

**Haywood County Historical
Society/Museum**
127 North Grand Avenue
Brownsville, TN 38012
http://erc.jscc.cc.tn.us/jfn/libjmc/
Haywood.html

Henderson County Historian
45 State Route 100
Reagan, TN 38368-6226
Randy Hart

Henderson County Historical Society
PO Box 128
Wildersville, TN 38388

Henry County Historian
511 North Poplar
Paris, TN 38242
Mary Ashley Morris

Hickman County Historian
Route 1, Box 64
Nunnelly, TN 37061
Edward Dotson

Highland Rim Historical Society
PO Box 411
Portland, TN 37148
(615) 325-6029
Vivian Russell, President

Houston County Historian
Route 1, Box 135
Erin, TN 37061
Nina Finley

Humphreys County Historian
107 Carroll Avenue
Waverly, TN 37185
John H. Whitfield

Humphreys County Historical Society
105½ Carroll Avenue
Waverly, TN 37185
John H. Whitfield, President

Jackson County Historian
PO Box 177
Gainesboro, TN 38562
Mr. Ronnie West

James County Historical Society
(4366 Prospect Church Road, Ooltewah, TN
37363—location)
PO Box 32 (mailing address)
Hixson, TN 37343-0032
(423) 396-2438
David Knisley, Vice President
("County officers, post offices, schools,
marriage records, service records collected
by members." *James County History*,
$30.00 plus postage. Reprint of 1916
edition of *James County Times* newspaper,
$5.00 plus postage.)

Jefferson County Historian
PO Box 886
Dandridge, TN 37725
Jean Patterson Bible, Former Historian

Jefferson County Historical Society
PO Box 325
Dandridge, TN 37725

Johnson County Historian
508 Hospital Road
Mountain City, TN 37683
Thomas W. Gentry

Knox County Historian
1216 Weisgarber Road
Knoxville, TN 37919
Mrs. Park Niceley

Lake County Historian
303 Lake Street
Ridgely, TN 38080
Abigail Hyde

Lauderdale County Historian
957 Doctor Hall Road
Halls, TN 38040-8727
Bettie B. Davis

Lawrence County Historian
Lawrence County Archives
218 North Military Avenue, Suite B-1
Lawrenceburg, TN 38464
(931) 766-1576; (931) 766-1558 FAX
lcarchives@lorettotel.net
http://web.infoave.net/lcarchives/lcgenso. htm
Kathy Niedergeses, Director of Archives
Archives: Mon–Fri 8:00–4:30

Lawrence County Historical Society
(Waterloo Street—museum location)
1106 Hickory Street (mailing address)
Lawrenceburg, TN 38464
Bobby Alford, Chairman

Lewis County Historian
205 West Main Street
Hohenwald, TN 38462

Marjorie B. Graves

Lincoln County Historical Society
202 East Washington Street
Fayetteville, TN 37334
Pub. *The Volunteer*
$7.50 per year membership

Loudon County Heritage Association
PO Box 466
Loudon, TN 37774

Loudon County Historian
309 Elkmont Road
Knoxville, TN 37922
Joe Spence

Macon County Historian
Route 4, Box 53
Lafayette, TN 37083
Harold Blankenship

Macon County Historical Society
PO Box 231
Lafayette, TN 37083
(615) 666-6030
Randy G. East, President
Pub. *Macon County Historical Society
    Newsletter*, quarterly
(Macon County and surrounding area history
    and genealogy)
$12.50 per year membership; queries

Madison County Historian
1723 North Highland
Jackson, TN 38301
Harbert Alexander

**Marion County Genealogical and
Historical Group**
(see Genealogical Societies—Local and
Regional, below)

Marion County Historian
618 Holly Avenue
South Pittsburg, TN 37380
Patsy Beene

Marshall County Historian
310 Farmington Road
Lewisburg, TN 37091
Charlene Nicholas

Marshall County Historical Society
224 Third Avenue, North
Lewisburg, TN 37091
(931) 359-2383
Mrs. Knox Bigham, Secretary
Pub. *Quarterly*
$10.00 per year membership

Maury County Historian
609 West Seventh Street
Columbia, TN 38401
Bob Duncan

Maury County Historical Society
PO Box 147
Columbia, TN 38401
Columbia Public Library: Mon–Fri 9:00–5:00
Pub. *Historic Maury*, quarterly; *Newsletter*,
    monthly
$10.00 per year membership

McMinn County Historian
Route 1
Riceville, TN 37370
Bill Akins

McNairy County Historian
PO Box 317
Adamsville, TN 38310

Bill Wagoner

Meigs County Historian
River Road
Decatur, TN 37322
Shirley Jennings

**Historical Commission of Metropolitan
Nashville-Davidson County**
701 Broadway, B-20
Nashville, TN 37203
(615) 259-5027

Monroe County Historian
508 West North Street
Sweetwater, TN 37874
(423) 337-7844
jrwbl@msn.com
Walter Lumsden, Jr.

Monroe County Historical Society
A Chapter of the East Tennessee Historical
Society
bobjulian@tellico.net
Bob Julian

Montgomery County Historian
PO Box 3533
Clarksville, TN 37043
Eleanor Williams

Montgomery County Historical Society
PO Box 262
Clarksville, TN 37041

Moore County Historian
Route 3, Box 3164
Tullahoma, TN 37388
Joyce Neal

**Morgan County Genealogical and
Historical Society**
(see Genealogical Societies—Local and
Regional, below)

Morgan County Historian
PO Box 336
Wartburg, TN 37887
Donald Todd

**Morristown-Hamblen Historical and
Bicentennial Commission**
(Rose Center, 432 West Second Street,
North—location)
PO Box 1976 (mailing address)
Morristown, TN 37814
(423) 581-4330; (423) 581-4307 FAX
rosecent@usit.net
http://www.rosecenter.org
Bill Kornrich, Director
Mon–Fri 9:00–5:00

**Mount Juliet-West Wilson County
Historical Society**
(Mount Juliet Senior Center—location)
PO Box 337 (mailing address)
Mount Juliet, TN 37122
(615) 754-2418
dgferrell@aol.com
http://www.members.aol.com/genny1/
    mtjuliet.html
Donna Graves Ferrell, President
meetings at the Mount Juliet Senior Center:
    second Sun 2:00
Pub. *The Chronicle*, quarterly
(collects family histories of Mount Juliet-
    West Wilson people; archives housed in
    the Mount Juliet Public Library)
$10.00 per year membership; queries
    accepted

Obion County Historical Society

PO Box 241
Union City, TN 38281
(731) 885-2322 (Secretary)
Martha Clendenin, Corresponding Secretary
hours: various
Pub. *Obion Origins*, quarterly
$10.00 per year membership; research Obion
    County records: $5.00 per hour plus cost
    of copies and postage

Oliver Springs Historical Society
(Oliver Springs Southern Railway Depot, 610
    Walker Avenue—location)
Internet Inquiry Service
Union Planters Building
727 Main Street (mailing address)
Oliver Springs, TN 37840
(423) 435-1711
http://www.public.usit.net/nwcs
Sue St. John, Director
Mon–Fri 9:00–5:00

Overton County Historical Society
(The Old Jail Building—location)
PO Box 753 (mailing address)
Livingston, TN 38570

**Pellissippi Genealogical and Historical
Society**
(see Genealogical Societies—Local and
Regional, below)

Perry County Historian
Box 105
Linden, TN 37096
Gus A. Steele

Perry County Historical Society
Perry County Public Library
Route 10, Box 3A
Linden, TN 37096
(931) 593-3373 (Editor)
http://www.Tngenweb.ususit.com/perry
Mary Bowen, Editor
Mon–Tue & Thur–Fri 9:00–5:00, Wed & Sat
    9:00–noon
Pub. *Perry County Historical Society
    Quarterly*
$5.00 per year membership; free answer to
    queries regarding Perry County genealogy

Pickett County Historian
Route 1, Box 160
Byrdstown, TN 38549
Richard W. Pierce

**Pleasant Hill Historical Society of the
Cumberlands, Inc.**
(Main Street—location)
PO Box 264 (mailing address)
Pleasant Hill, TN 38578
(931) 277-3193

Polk County Historian
(Corner of Commerce and Poplar—location)
PO Box 636 (mailing address)
Benton, TN 37307
(423) 338-1005
Marian Bailey Presswood

**Polk County Historical and Genealogical
Society**
PO Box 636
Benton, TN 37307
presswood@wingnet.net
http://www.Tngenweb.ususit.com/polk
Marian Bailey Presswood, President and Polk
    County Historian
Pub. *PCHGS Quarterly-Newsletter* (Feb,
    May, Aug, Nov)
("We have a small genealogy library at the
    office.")

$15.00 per year membership

Putnam County Historian
1009 West Cemetery Road
Cookeville, TN 38501
Ms. Pat Franklin

Rhea County Historian
3433 Knollwood Hills Drive
Chattanooga, TN 37415
Betty Broyles

Rhea County Historical Society
PO Box 31
Dayton, TN 37321

Roane County Heritage Commission, Inc.
(Roane County Archives, 119 Court
Street—location)
PO Box 738 (mailing address)
Kingston, TN 37763
(865) 376-9211
http://www.roanetnheritage.com
Robert L. Bailey, Director
Tue–Fri 9:00–4:00
Pub. *Heritage Newsletter*, quarterly
$25.00 per year membership

Roane County Historian
PO Box 493
Kingston, TN 37763
Robert L. Bailey

Robertson County Historian
3512 Pleasant Grove Road
White House, TN 37188
Yolanda Reid

Robertson County Historical Society
Robertson County History Museum
(509 West Court Square—location)
PO Box 1022 (mailing address)
Springfield, TN 37172
(615) 382-7173
Maxine Elliott, President
Fri 10:00–4:00, and by appointment; meets
first Mon
$10.00 per year membership

Rocky Mount Historical Association
Rocky Mount Living History Museum
(200 Hyder Hill Road—location)
PO Box 160 (mailing address)
Piney Flats, TN 37686
(423) 538-7396; (888) 538-1791; (423) 538-
5983 FAX
rmm@preferred.com
http://pages.preferred.com/~rmm
Deborah Montanti, Director
Mon–Sat 10:00–3:00; Living History tours:
Wed–Sat 10:00–3:00, call for winter hours
(Jan–Feb)
Pub. *Rocky Mount Gazette*, bimonthly
(tours and educational programs and special
events throughout the year)
$25.00 per year membership

Rutherford County Historian
7931 West Jefferson Pike
Smyrna, TN 37167
Ernest K. Johns

Rutherford County Historical Society, Inc.
PO Box 906
Murfreesboro, TN 37133-0906
Pub. *Frow Chips*, eleven times per year;
*Rutherford County Historical Society
Publications*, semiannually
$10.00 per year membership

Scott County Historian
Scott County Historical Society

PO Box 7
Huntsville, TN 37756
Irene B. Baker

Scott County Historical Society
PO Box 7
Huntsville, TN 37756
(423) 663-2316; (423) 663-2753 FAX
proy@highland.net
Irene B. Baker, President and County
Historian
9:00–noon
Pub. *SCHS Newsletter*, quarterly
(publishes over 70 books)
$20.00 per year membership

Sequatchie County Historian
Route 1, Box 3
Dunlap, TN 37327
Henry Camp

Sevier County Historian
220 Dollywood Lane
Pigeon Forge, TN 37863
Beulah D. Linn

Shelby County Historian
PO Box 241813
Memphis, TN 38124-1813
Edward F. Williams, III

Smith County Historian
1117 Main Street
Carthage, TN 37030
Sue W. Maggart-Petty
by appointment

**Smith County Historical and Genealogical
Society**
PO Box 112
Carthage, TN 37030
(615) 735-0200
swpetty@mwsi.net
Sue W. Maggart-Petty, County Historian
by appointment

Smoky Mountain Historical Society
(Sevier County Heritage Museum, 167 East
Bruce Street—location)
PO Box 5078 (mailing address)
Sevierville, TN 37864
(865) 453-4058 (Museum)
smhsquery@smokykin.com
http://www.smokykin.com/smhs
Roy Glenn Cardwell; Patsy Bradford,
Museum Director
Museum: Mon–Tue & Thur–Fri noon–5:00,
Sat noon–3:00; meetings: Jan, Mar, May,
July, Sept, Nov
Pub. *The Smoky Mountain Historical Society
Journal*, quarterly (spring, summer, fall,
winter), $4.00 per issue
(Tennessee regional and local history)
$10.00 per year membership

Southern Studies Institute
(see Louisiana, Part 2)

Stewart County Historian
607 Jackson Avenue
Carthage, TN 37030
Nelda Saunders

Sullivan County Historian
320 Highridge Road
Kingsport, TN 37660
Dr. Elery A. Lay

Sullivan County Historical Society
PO Box 60
Blountville, TN 37617
Elizabeth Hockman, Corresponding

Secretary

Sumner County Historian
332 East Main Street
Gallatin, TN 37066
John Garrott

Sumner County Historical Society
PO Box 1871
Gallatin, TN 37066
(615) 452-2701 (Secretary)
Shirley Wilson, President

Tipton-Haynes Historical Association
PO Box 225
Johnson City, TN 37605-0225

Trousdale County Historian
165 Averitt Ferry Lane
Lebanon, TN 37087
Walter L. Buckingham

Unicoi County Historian
453 Ash Street
Erwin, TN 37650
Walter B. Garland

Unicoi County Historical Society
c/o Hilda Padgett
405 Ohio Avenue
Erwin, TN 37650
James Stevens, President
Erwin Utilities Building: fourth Mon
$5.00 per year membership; nonmembers
may use the society's library

Union County Historian
Union County Historian
3212 Curtis Lane
Knoxville, TN 37918-4003
(865) 687-3842
Bonnie Heiskell Peters
(published *Union County Schoolday
Memories*, $5.00 ppd., *Our Union County
Families*, $56.00 ppd., *Union County
Faces of War*, $40.00 ppd.)

Union County Historical Society, Inc.
PO Box 95
Maynardville, TN 37807
(865) 687-2137
William G. Tharpe, President
Roy Acuff Union Museum and Library,
Maynardville: Mon–Tue 10:00–4:00, Sun
1:00–5:00
Pub. *Pathways: History and Genealogical
Journal*, quarterly, $4.00 per issue (for
back issues)
$12.00 per year membership

Van Buren County Historian
HC 69, Box 688
Spencer, TN 38585
Agnes C. Jones

Van Buren County Historical Society
(Burritt Memorial Building, Highway
30—location)
HC 69, Box 688 (mailing address)
Spencer, TN 38585
(931) 946-7486
BillJ3370@Blomand.net
Agnes C. Jones, President
by appointment
Pub. *Van Buren County Historical Journal*,
annually, $12.00 per issue postpaid; *Van
Buren County Historical Society
Newsletter*, two times per year
("We have journals, census of county, and
county marriage books for sale.")
$12.50 per year membership

Warren County Historian
PO Box 563
McMinnville, TN 37110
(931) 668-8766
James A. Dillon, Jr.

Washington County Historian
241 Brethren Church Drive
Jonesborough, TN 37659-6288
Ruth Broyles

Washington County Historical Association
PO Box 205
Jonesborough, TN 37659
Mrs. Ray Stahl

Wayne County Historian
(Room 305, Wayne County
Courthouse—location)
PO Box 476 (mailing address)
Waynesboro, TN 38485-0476
(931) 722-5016
J. Charles Hardin

Wayne County Historical Society
PO Box 866
Waynesboro, TN 38485
Pub. *Wayne County Historian*, quarterly
$5.00 per year membership

Weakley County Historian
204 Poplar Street
Martin, TN 38238-3120
Virginia C. Vaughan

West Tennessee Historical Society
PO Box 111046
Memphis, TN 38111
(901) 372-7495
Douglas W. Cupples, Ph.D., President
Pub. *West Tennessee Historical Society
Papers*, annually
$15.00 per year membership

White County Historian
PO Box 15
Doyle, TN 38559
Mary West Holland

Williamson County Historian
1135 Lewisburg Pike
Franklin, TN 37064
Joe Bowman

Williamson County Historical Society
PO Box 72
Franklin, TN 37064
Pub. *Williamson County Historical Society
Journal*, irregularly
$10.00 per year membership

Wilson County Historian
112 South College Street
Lebanon, TN 37087-3623
William "Vincent" Simms

The Wise County Historical Society
The Appalachian Quarterly
(see Virginia, Part 2)

Genealogical Societies

State Genealogical Society

Southern Society of Genealogists, Inc.
(see Alabama, Part 2)

The Tennessee Genealogical Society
(9114 Davies Plantation Road—library
location)
PO Box 247 (mailing address)
Brunswick, TN 38014-0247

(901) 381-1447
tngensociety@yahoo.com
http://www.tngs.org
Jim Bobo, President
Tue, Thur & Sat 10:00–2:00
Pub. *'Ansearchin' News*, quarterly (Mar,
June, Sept, Dec), $20.00 per year
subscription
(emphasis on the state of Tennessee)
$25.00 per year membership; one fifty-word
query per year free to subscribers;
research: send SASE

Genealogical Societies—Local & Regional

**Blount County Genealogical and
Historical Society**
Blount County Public Library
(301 McGhee Street, Maryville, TN
37801—location)
PO Box 4986 (mailing address)
Maryville, TN 37802-4986
(865) 982-0981 (Library)
Jane Kizer Thomas, President
Library: Mon–Thur 9:00–8:00, Fri
9:00–5:30, Sat 9:00–5:30, Sun 1:00–5:00
Pub. *The Blount Journal*, semiannually
(spring and fall)
$10.00 per year membership; queries free for
members only; research: $5.00 minimum

**Brentwood Historical and Genealogical
Society**
(see Historical Societies—Local and
Regional, above)

**Delta Genealogical Society (southeast
Tennessee)**
(see Georgia, Part 2)

Greene County Genealogical Society
(Tennessee Room, Greeneville Public
Library—location)
229 North Main Street (mailing address)
Greeneville, TN 37745-3842
Jan Maddux, Vice President; Wesley Lott,
Vice President
meetings:; first Thur 7:00 P.M.
Pub. *The Greene County Pioneer*,
semiannually (May, Nov)
(upper east Tennessee)
$15.00 per year membership

Hamblen County Genealogical Society
(Morristown-Hamblen Library, 417 West
Main Street, Morristown, TN
37814—location)
PO Box 1213 (mailing address)
Morristown, TN 37816-1213
(423) 586-6410
Mrs. Billie H. Inman, President
meetings at Morristown-Hamblen Library:
first Thur 1:00 (except summer)
Pub. *Hamblen Heritage*, quarterly
(specializes in Hamblen County, formed
1870 from Jefferson, Grainger and part of
Hawkins counties)
$10.00 per year membership; free queries
and surname listings; research: members
try to answer all letters accompanied by
SASE

**Hancock County Historical and
Genealogical Society**
(see Historical Societies—Local and
Regional, above)

**Hawkins County Genealogical and
Historical Society**
PO Box 429
Rogersville, TN 37857-0429
hcghs@hotmail.com

http://www.rootsweb.com/~tnhcghs
George Webb, President
Pub. *Distant Crossroads*, quarterly
$15.00 per year membership

Henry County Genealogical Society
PO Box 1411
Paris, TN 38242
(731) 642-4178; (731) 593-5592 FAX
hcgs2@hotmail.com
http://www.angelfire.com/tn2/
henrycogensociety
Linda Dunlap
meetings each quarter
Pub. *The Newsletter*
("Genealogical Society working to promote
and assist with research in Henry and
surrounding counties of Tennessee as well
as western Kentucky.")
$15.00 per year membership; one free look-
up per quarter for information contained in
resources at our local public library;
submission of one free query per
newsletter, additional queries at $1.00
each

Holston Territory Genealogical Society
(see Virginia, Part 2)

Jonesborough Genealogical Society
Washington County-Jonesborough Library
200 Sabin Drive
Jonesborough, TN 37659
(423) 753-1800 (Library); (423) 753-1802
(Library)
Anne Shaw, Library Services
Library: Mon & Thur 9:00–8:00, Tue–Wed &
Fri 9:00–6:00, Sat 9:00–2:00
Pub. *The Jonesborough Record*, quarterly
$15.00 per year membership; limited
research: 25¢ per copy plus postage and
mailing costs

Lawrence County Genealogical Society
218 North Military Avenue, Suite B-1
Lawrenceburg, TN 38464
(931) 766-1576
lcarchives@lorettotel.net
http://web.infoave.net/~lcarchives/lcgs.htm
Kathy Niedergeses
Pub. *Journal*, quarterly
(First Families of Lawrence County program
issues certificates for $10.00 fee and proof
of descent)
$10.00 per year membership

Lincoln County Genealogical Society
1508 West Washington Street
Fayetteville, TN 37334
Jack Towry, President
Sat–Sun 1:00–5:00
Pub. *Lincoln Lineage*, semiannually
("Large collection of family files.")
$10.00 per year membership, $13.00 per year
membership plus independently published
periodical, *Lincoln County Tennessee
Pioneers*, semiannually (Jan, July); queries
free to members or subscribers; research in
society library: free for members

**Marion County Genealogical and
Historical Group**
6611 Old Dunlap Road
Whitwell, TN 37397
(423) 658-5770
lat1@aol.com
http://www.rootsweb.com/~tnmarion/
genealogical_group.htm
Lloyd Tate, President
meetings at the Whitwell Library: second Sat
2:00
Pub. *Searcher*, quarterly

$15.00 per year membership

McNairy County Genealogical Society
PO Box 1023
Selmer, TN 38375

Mid-West Tennessee Genealogical Society
PO Box 3343
Jackson, TN 38303-0343
skelly@usit.net
http://www.jmcl.tn.org/Mid-West_Tn.html
Dr. Pam Dennis, President
Pub. *Family Findings*, quarterly
("Information is available at the Tennessee
Room of the Jackson/Madison County
Library.")
$15.00 per year membership

**Morgan County Genealogical and
Historical Society**
(Wartburg Public Library—location)
PO Box 684 (mailing address)
Wartburg, TN 37887
(423) 346-3137; (423) 346-2479 FAX
Ms. Sammy Ruth McPeters, President
Mon–Fri 11:00–5:00, Sat 10:00–1:00
Pub. *The Morgan County Messenger*,
quarterly (spring, summer, fall, winter)
$15.00 per year membership; research: $4.00
plus copies of courthouse records at $1.00
per page

Paris Area Genealogical Society
PO Box 636
Paris, TN 38242

**Pellissippi Genealogical and Historical
Society**
(Courthouse, 100 South Main, Room 204
Vault, Clinton, TN 37716—location)
932 Offutt Road (mailing address)
Clinton, TN 37716
(865) 457-6242
S080332@aol.com
Mary S. Harris, County Historian
Mon–Fri 8:30–4:30
Pub. *Pellissippi Genealogical and Historical
Society*, quarterly
(emphasis on Anderson County)
$16.00 per year membership

**Polk County Historical and Genealogical
Society**
(see Historical Societies—Local and
Regional, above)

Roane County Genealogical Society
(Kingston Public Library, 1001 Bradford
Way, #3, Kingston, TN 37763—location)
323 West Ridgecrest Drive (mailing address)
Kingston, TN 37763-3223
Marjory M. Watts, Corresponding Secretary
Library: Mon & Thur 10:00–7:30, Tue–Wed
& Fri 10:00–5:30, Sat 10:00–2:00
Pub. *Roane Ramblings*, quarterly
(John M. McMurray Collection includes
"printed materials, vertical family files,
Researcher's Crossfile, every record
available on microfilm for Roane and
adjacent counties.")
$15.00 per year membership; research of
indexed materials: $4.00 per hour plus
postage and copying

Signal Mountain Genealogical Society
103 Florida Avenue
Signal Mountain, TN 37373
James L. Douthat, President
Pub. *Genealogical Signals*, monthly
$5.00 per year membership

**Smith County Historical and Genealogical
Society**
(see Historical Societies—Local and
Regional, above)

Sullivan County Genealogy Club
(Sullivan County Library, 1655 State Route
37—location)
PO Box 568 (mailing address)
Blountville, TN 37617
(423) 279-2714 (Library)
Kay P. Hamrick, Library Director
Library: Mon, Wed & Fri–Sat 9:00–5:00,
Tue & Thur 9:00–6:30; meeting: third
Thur 7:00
$15.00 per year membership

**Upper Cumberland Genealogical
Association**
(Putnam County Library, 48 East Broad
Street—location)
PO Box 575 (mailing address)
Cookeville, TN 38503-0575
clark@blomand.net
http://www.jagunet.com/~mbar/ucga.htm
Maurine Patton, Treasurer
Pub. *The Upper Cumberland Researcher*,
quarterly
$10.00 per year membership; queries free to
members

**Warren County Genealogical Association,
Inc.**
(Wm. H. & Edgar Magness Community
House and Library, 118 West Main
Street—location)
PO Box 411 (mailing address)
McMinnville, TN 37110-0411
(931) 473-2428; (931) 473-6778 FAX
scurtis@mail.state.tn.us
http://www.mcminnville2000.com
Susan Curtis, Director
Mon 8:30–9:30, Tue–Wed & Fri–Sat
10:00–4:30; meetings at the McMinnville
Electric service building on Morford
Street: fourth Sat 2:00, except Dec
Pub. *Warren County Tennessee
Genealogical Bulletin*, quarterly
$10.00 per year membership

**Watauga Association of
Genealogists—Upper East Tennessee**
PO Box 117
Johnson City, TN 37605-0117
(423) 753-3116 (Secretary)
Mary Sue Going, Corresponding Secretary
Johnson City Public Library: monthly
meeting
Pub. *Watauga Association of Genealogists
Bulletin*, semiannually (May, Oct)
$12.00 per year membership; no research
services, but referrals provided

Weakley County Genealogical Society
PO Box 894
Martin, TN 38237
Pansy N. Baker, President
Pub. *Forget Me Not*, quarterly
$7.50 per year membership

Independent Publications and
Miscellany

Appalachian Roots
(see West Virginia, Part 2)

Bailey Publishing and Research Associates
(630 Old Poplar Springs Road—location)
PO Box 493 (mailing address)
Kingston, TN 37763
jameym@roanetnheritage.com (Web Master)
http://www.roanetnheritage.com/bailey (The

Roane County Heritage Commission Web
Site)
Robert L. Bailey, Owner; Jamey McLoughlin,
Web Master
Pub. *Roane Roots*, quarterly, $12.00 per year
subscription
(publishes books on Roane and Morgan
counties, Tennessee and performs
genealogical research for all east
Tennessee counties)
research: $13.00 per hour (includes up to 10
copies), single document retrieval: $5.00
(includes one copy), 25¢ per page for each
additional copy

Beech Grove Confederate Cemetery
206 Greenfield Avenue
Tullahoma, TN 37388
Carl Monin

Byron Sistler and Associates, Inc.
(1712 Natchez Trace—location)
PO Box 120934 (mailing address)
Nashville, TN 37212
(615) 297-3085; (615) 298-2807 FAX; (800)
578-9475 (orders only)
including nights and weekends
(emphasis on Tennessee censuses, marriages,
church records; dealer in Tennessee, North
Carolina, Kentucky and Virginia
genealogical books)

Historic Carnton Plantation
1345 Carnton Lane
Franklin, TN 37069
(615) 794-0903; (615) 794-6563 FAX
carnton@mindspring.com
http://www.carnton.org
Angela Calhoun, Executive Director
(house museum)

Center for Appalachian Studies
(see North Carolina, Part 2)

Direct Line Software
Land Record Reference
(see Miscellaneous, Part 4)

Duck's Old Time Journal
3351 Oak Ridge Road
Palmyra, TN 37142-2339
(931) 326-5389
Robert Donald "Duck" Davidson
8:00–8:00
Pub. *Duck's Old Time Journal*, monthly,
$6.00 per year subscription; *South of the
River* (yearbook with index), annually,
$6.00 each (fourteen published so far)
("Old time news of happenings 'South of the
River,' Montgomery County, Tennessee,
includes some family history, but mostly
weddings, school, church, accidents,
murders, etc., everything at least fifty years
old." Also publised *Palmyra Then to Now*,
$6.00, *Southside Then to Now*, $6.00, and
three volumes of *Northwest Territory*,
$6.00 each)
research available

East Tennessee Heritage Foundation, Inc.
1345 Oak Ridge Turnpike #318
Oak Ridge, TN 37830
(865) 691-8760
http://www.EastTennRoots.com
Paula Gammell, Editor
Pub. *East Tennessee Roots
Genealogical/Historical Quarterly*, $30.00
per year subscription

Genealogical Institute
(see Virginia, Part 2)

Genealogy Books and Consultation
(see Texas, Part 2)

Genealogy Friends: Partyline
PO Box 863
Hendersonville, TN 37077
(615) 824-2317
Nancy P. Goodman, Editor and Publisher
Pub. *Genealogy Friends: Partyline* (emphasis
on Middle Tennessee), bimonthly, $10.00
per year subscription, $1.00 plus SASE for
sample copy

The Hermitage
Home of President Andrew Jackson
Ladies Hermitage Association
4580 Rachel's Lane
Hermitage, TN 37076
(615) 889-2941; (615) 889-9289 FAX
museumservices@thehermitage.com
http://www.thehermitage.com
Martha Mullin, Curator
Mon–Fri 9:00–5:00 by appointment only
Pub. *The Hermitage*, quarterly
("The Hermitage maintains limited
information on the Jackson descendants,
the family of Rachel Donelson Jackson
[descendants of Captain John Donelson],
and the Hermitage slave community. We
prefer initial contact in writing [email or
letter] rather than phone call.")
$35.00 per year membership

Historic Rugby, Inc.
Rugby Restoration Association
(Highway 52—location)
PO Box 8 (mailing address)
Rugby, TN 37733
(423) 628-2441
Office: Mon–Fri 9:00–5:00
Pub. *Rugbeian*, quarterly, $15.00 per year
subscription

**Hunting for Bears Genealogical and
Historical Society**
(see Alabama, Part 2)

**President Andrew Johnson Museum and
Library**
Tusculum College
PO Box 5025, Tusculum College
Greeneville, TN 37743
(423) 636-7348; (423) 638-7166 FAX
gcollins@tusculum.edu
http://www.tusculum.edu/museum/johnson
George Collins, Director
Mon–Fri 9:00–5:00

**Knob Creek Museum and Pioneer
Homestead**
243 Denny Mill Road
Johnson City, TN 37604
(423) 282-1165
George and Margaret Holley, Owners
15 Apr–1 Nov: by appointment
("Relics and history of Knob Creek
community.")
admission: donation

Lenoir Museum
Norris Dam State Park
Norris, TN 37828
(865) 494-9688; (865) 494-0488

Lincoln County Tennessee Pioneers
238 Point Clear
Conroe, TX 77304-1276
(936) 856-5624
Jane Warren Waller
9:00–5:00
Pub. *Lincoln County Tennessee Pioneers*,
semiannually, $8.00 per year subscription

**The Abraham Lincoln Library and
Museum**
Cumberland Gap Parkway
Harrogate, TN 37752-2006
(423) 869-6235; (423) 869-6350 FAX
museum@lmunet.edu
http://www.lmunet.edu/museum/index.html
Charles Hubbard, Dean of Lincolniana
(Lincoln and the Civil War)

Lovelady Publications
280 Maple Street
Erin, TN 37061
(931) 289-3751
Charles Lovelady, Publisher, Joyce
Lovelady, Editor
noon–9:00
Pub. *Hornberger Journal* (includes Stewart,
Houston, Humphries, Dickson,
Montgomery, Robertson, Hickman
counties and the old Tennessee County;
history, genealogy articles, queries for
Tennessee and adjoining states),
bimonthly, $17.00 per year subscription

McMinn County Living Heritage Museum
(522 West Madison Avenue—location)
PO Box 889 (mailing address)
Athens, TN 37371-0889
(423) 745-0329 voice & FAX
http://www.usit.com/livher
Ann S. Davis, Executive Director
Tue–Fri 10:00–5:00, Sat 10:00–5:00
(primarily historical, not genealogical;
newspapers, photographs, maps)

Middle Tennessee State University
Tennessee Folklore Society
PO Box 70
Murfreesboro, TN 37132
(615) 898-2576; (615) 898-5098 FAX
Dr. Charles Wolfe, Editor; Karen Bourcy,
Secretary
8:00–4:00
Pub. *Quarterly*
$15.00 per year membership

*The Mountain Empire Genealogical
Quarterly*
(see Virginia, Part 2)

Mountain Press
(4503 Anderson Pike—location)
PO Box 400 (mailing address)
Signal Mountain, TN 37377-0400
(423) 886-6369 (Office); (423) 886-5312
FAX
James L. Douthat, Owner
daily 9:00–5:00
Pub. *Southern Genealogical Index*
(seventeen southern states: Alabama,
Arkansas, Florida, Georgia, Kansas,
Kentucky, Louisiana, Maryland,
Mississippi, Missouri, North Carolina,
Oklahoma, South Carolina, Tennessee,
Texas, Virginia, West Virginia), annually,
$10.00 per issue; *Appalachian Families*
(migration of families through the
Appalachian region of the mid-Atlantic
states), quarterly, $15.00 per year
subscription; *TN Genealogy & History*,
three times per year, $20.00 per year
subscription

Museum of Appalachia
2819 Andersonville Highway
Clinton, TN 37716
(865) 494-7680
John Rice Irwin

Oaklands Association
(900 North Maney Avenue, Murfreesboro,

TN 37130—location)
PO Box 432 (mailing address)
Murfreesboro, TN 37133
(615) 893-0022; (615) 893-0513 FAX
James W. Manning, Jr., Director
Mon by appointment, Tue–Sat 10:00–4:00,
Sun 1:00–4:00
Pub. *Oaklands Minitor*, occasionally

**The Overmountain Victory Trail
Association, Inc.**
Sycamore Shoals State Park
1651 West Elk Avenue
Elizabethton, TN 37643
$8.00 per year membership

Buford Pusser Home and Museum
(342 Pusser Street—location)
PO Box 301 (mailing address)
Adamsville, TN 38310
(731) 632-1401
Terry Thrasher, City Administrator
1 May–31 Oct: 9:00–5:00; 1 Nov–30 Apr:
10:00–4:00

Carroll Reece Museum
East Tennessee State University
PO Box 70660, ETSU
Johnson City, TN 37614-0660
(423) 929-4392
Helen Roseberry, Director
Museum: Mon–Sat 9:00–4:00, Sun
1:00–4:00; Office: Mon–Fri 9:00–5:00
Pub. *Newsletter*, three times per year
("We are a collecting and exhibiting
museum.")
$10.00 per year membership

Reppert Publications
Antique and Collectible News
(see Illinois, Part 2)

Restore Our County, Inc.
PO Box 325
Dandridge, TN 37725
(865) 397-9392; (865) 397-2373

Rowan County Register
(see North Carolina, Part 2)

Serviceberry Press
A Subsidiary of New South Architectural
Press
5632 Meadowcrest Lane
Nashville, TN 37209
(615) 356-3136
Ilene Jones-Cornwell, General Editor
(devoted to genealogy and southern/local
history)

Simmons Historical Publications
(see Kentucky, Part 2)

Smoky Mountain Ancestral Quest
http://www.smokykin.com

**The Southern Genealogist's Exchange
Society, Inc.**
(see Florida, Part 2)

Southern Historical Press, Inc.
(see Publishers, Part 4)

Tennessee Department of Transportation
James K. Polk Building
505 Deaderick Street, Suite 700
Nashville, TN 37243-1120
(615) 741-2848
TDOT.Commissioner@state.tn.us
http://www.tdot.state.tn.us/maps.htm (Maps)
Commissioner J. Bruce Saltsman, Sr.

The Tennessee State Museum
James K. Polk Center
505 Deaderick Street
Nashville, TN 37243-1120
(615) 741-2692
Tue–Sat 10:00–5:00, Sun 1:00–5:00
(a history museum)

Tennessee Valley Authority
400 West Summit Hill Drive
Knoxville, TN 37902
(865) 632-3466

Tipton-Haynes State Historic Site
(2620 South Roan Street—location)
PO Box 225 (mailing address)
Johnson City, TN 37605
(423) 926-3631
zoe@wireco.net
http://tipton-haynes.org
Penny McLaughlin, Executive Director
Apr to mid-Dec: 10:00–4:00; mid-Dec to
    Mar: call for winter hours

TnGenWeb
Part of The USGenweb Project
ncole@coffey.com; assttnsc@tngenweb.org
http://www.rootsweb.com/~tngenweb
Nancy Cole, State Coordinator; Cathy Hall,
    Assistant Coordinator
(links to other Tennessee resources)

Traveller Southern Families
(see Virginia, Part 2)

**Mary Walker Historical and Educational
Foundation**
3031 Wilcox Boulevard
Chattanooga, TN 37411
(423) 622-3217

West Virginia University
Appalachian Studies Association
(see West Virginia, Part 2)

Texas

Archives and Libraries with Holdings in Genealogy

State Archives and Library

**Texas State Library and Archives
Commission**
(1201 Brazos Street, Austin, TX
78701—location)
PO Box 12927 (mailing address)
Austin, TX 78711-2927
(512) 463-5463 (Genealogy); (512) 463-
    5455 (Reference/Documents); (512) 463-
    5480 (State Archives); (512) 463-5436
    FAX
geninfo@tsl.state.tx.us (Genealogy);
    archinfo@tsl.state.tx.us (Archives)
http://www.tsl.state.tx.us/arc/genfirst.html
Diana Houston, Assistant Director,
    Information Services
Genealogy: Tue–Sat 8:00–5:00; Archives
    and Reference/Documents: Mon–Fri
    8:00–5:00

Texas General Land Office
Archives and Records Division
Stephen F. Austin Building
1700 North Congress, Room 800
Austin, TX 78701-1495
(512) 463-5277
archives@glo.state.tx.us
http://www.glo.state.tx.us
Susan Dorsey, Director
Mon–Fri 8:00–5:00
("Original land grants issued by the Crown
    of Spain, the Republic of Mexico, the
    Republic of Texas, and the State of
    Texas")

Texas Historical Commission
(1511 Colorado, Austin, TX
78701—location)
PO Box 12276 (mailing address)
Austin, TX 78711-2276
(512) 463-6100; (512) 475-4872 FAX
Curtis Tunnell, Executive Director and State
    Historic Preservation Officer
(not genealogical: site preservation)

State Historical Society

Texas State Historical Association
2.306 SRH, University Station
Austin, TX 78712
(512) 471-1525; (512) 471-1551 FAX
rtyler@mail.utexas.edu
http://www.tsha.utexas.edu
Ron Tyler, Ph.D., Director
Mon–Fri 8:00–5:00
Pub. *Texas Historian*, quarterly, $7.00 per
    year subscription; *Riding Line*, quarterly;
    Southwestern Historical Quarterly
(no reference departments, no genealogical
    searches)
$35.00 per year membership

Texian Heritage Association
15742 Fitzhugh Road
Austin, TX 78736
(512) 264-2355
ths@nabi.net
http://www.texianlegacy.com
Charlie Yates, Executive Director

City, County and Regional Archives and Libraries
(A more exhaustive list of public and
academic libraries can be found at http://
castor.tsl.state.tx.us/ld/pubs/pls/index.html.)

Abilene Public Library
202 Cedar Street
Abilene, TX 79601-5793
(915) 677-2474, ext. 115
http://www.abilenetx.com/apl
Susan Tipton, Genealogy Department
Mon–Tue & Thur 9:00–9:00, Wed & Fri–Sat
    9:00–6:00
(houses the Scarborough Library of
    Genealogy, History and Biography of the
    South and Southwest, formerly at
    McMurry College Library)

Amarillo Public Library
(413 East Fourth Street, Amarillo, TX 79101-
1523—location)
PO Box 2171 (mailing address)
Amarillo, TX 79189-2171
(806) 378-4211 (Special Collections
    Department)
Reference@amarillolibrary.org
http://www.amarillolibrary.org
Rob Groman, Head of Special Collections
    Department
Mon–Thur 9:00–9:00, Fri–Sat 9:00–6:00,
    Sun 2:00–6:00

American Cotton Museum
(600 East Interstate 30—location)
PO Box 347 (mailing address)
Greenville, TX 75403
(903) 454-1990
Carol Taylor, Executive Director
Tue–Sat 10:00–5:30, Sun 1:00–5:00
Pub. *The History Hunter*, quarterly
(Hunt County, northeast Texas, cotton
    production)
$10.00–$100.00 per year membership;
    research: $5.00 per hour

Angelo State University
Porter Henderson Library
West Texas Collection
(Houston Harte University Center—location)
PO Box 11013 (mailing address)
San Angelo, TX 76909
(915) 942-2164
Suzanne.Campbell@angelo.edu
http://www.angelo.edu/admn/library/
    westtx/westtx.htm
Suzanne Campbell
Mon–Wed 10-noon & 1:00–6:00, Thur
    1:00–9:00, Fri 1:00–5:00
(regional and state as well as local holdings)

Aransas County Library
701 East Mimosa
Rockport, TX 78382-4150
(361) 790-0153; (361) 790-0150 FAX
admin@acplibrary.org
http://www.acplibrary.org
Mary Ragsdale, Librarian
Mon–Fri 9:00–6:00, Sat 10:00–2:00
volunteers do research

Archer County Museum
(201 North Sycamore—location)
PO Box 102 (mailing address)
Archer City, TX 76351
(940) 423-6426
Jack Loftin, Chairman
Sat 9:00–5:00, Sun 1:00–5:00
(complete grave census of 70,000 in the 70
    mile by 80 mile north Texas area, Archer,
    Clay, Jack and Young counties)

Arlington Public Library
101 East Abram Street
Arlington, TX 76010-1183
(817) 459-6900; (817) 459-6902 FAX
rsmith@pub-lib.ci.arlington.tx.us;
    webmail@pub-lib.ci.arlington.tx.us

http://www.pub-lib.ci.arlington.tx.us
Rick Smith
Mon–Thur 9:00–9:00, Fri–Sat 9:00–6:00

Atlanta Public Library
Genealogy Section
101 West Hiram Street
Atlanta, TX 75551-2509
(903) 796-2112; (903) 796-3434; (903) 799-
4067 FAX
aplib@swbell.net
Lee Hamilton

Austin Public Library
Austin History Center
(810 Guadalupe, Austin, TX 78701-
2314—location)
PO Box 2287 (mailing address)
Austin, TX 78768-2287
(512) 499-7480; (512) 974-7483 FAX
ahc_reference@ci.austin.tx.us
http://www.ci.austin.tx.us/library/lbahc.htm
Biruta Celmins Kearl, Administrator
Mon–Thur 10:00–9:00, Fri–Sat 10:00–6:00,
Sun noon–6:00
(Travis County, Texas)

Stephen F. Austin State University
The Center for East Texas Studies
(Ferguson Building 340—location)
PO Box 6134, Stephen F. Austin Station
(mailing address)
Nacogdoches, TX 75962
(936) 468-1392; (936) 468-2190 FAX
CETS@sfasu.edu
http://www.sfasu.edu

Stephen F. Austin State University
Steen Library
East Texas Research Center
PO Box 13055, Stephen F. Austin Station
Nacogdoches, TX 75962-3055
(936) 468-4100
AskETRC@sfalib.sfasu.edu
http://libweb.sfasu.edu/etrc/default.htm
Linda Cheves Nicklas, Director
Mon–Fri 8:00–5:00, Sat 10:00–6:00

Stephen F. Austin State University
Texas Folklore Society
(108 Rusk Building—location)
PO Box 13007, Stephen F. Austin Station
(mailing address)
Nacogdoches, TX 75962-3007
(936) 468-4407; (936) 468-1028 FAX
fabernethy@sfasu.edu
http://jacobi.sfasu.edu/tfs
F. E. Abernethy, Secretary-Editor
Mon–Fri 8:00–5:00
Pub. *Publications of the Texas Folklore
Society*, annually
$15.00 per year membership

Bastrop Public Library
(1100 Church Street, Bastrop, TX 78602-
3207—location)
PO Box 670 (mailing address)
Bastrop, TX 78602-0670
(512) 321-5441; (512) 321-3163 FAX
mickey@bastroplibrary.org
http://www.bastroplibrary.org
Mickey DuVall

Bay City Public Library
1100 Seventh Street
Bay City, TX 77414-4915
(979) 245-6931; (979) 245-2614 FAX
adirector@baycitytxlib.org
Rosanne Burgess, Director
Mon–Thur 9:00–8:00, Fri 11:00–6:00, Sat
9:00–6:00

Baylor County Historical Museum
c/o STOUT
(200 West McLain Street—location)
803 Stout Road (mailing address)
Seymour, TX 76380-8916

Belton City Library
301 East First Avenue
Belton, TX 76513-3168
(254) 933-5830
library@ci.belton.tx.us; blibrary@vvm.com
http://www.cityofbelton.org
Lena Armstrong, Director
Mon–Fri noon–5:00, Sat 9:00–1:00
(Belton and Bell County history and
genealogy)
no search service, will supply names of
professional researchers

Museum and Archives of the Big Bend
PO Box C-210
Alpine, TX 79832
(915) 837-8143
Tue–Sat 9:00–5:00, Sun 1:00–5:00

Blanco Library
James A. and Evelyn Williams Memorial
Library
Texanna Collection
1118 North Main Street
Blanco, TX 78606-4838
(210) 833-4280 voice & FAX
blanlib@moment.net; blancoso@moment.net
http://www.blancolib.org
Gwen Michal, Librarian
Mon–Fri 9:00–noon, Mon & Thur
6:00–8:00, Wed & Fri 2:00–8:00, Sat
9:00–3:00

Bonham Public Library
305 East Fifth Street
Bonham, TX 75418-4002
(903) 583-3128; (903) 583-8030 FAX
dmccutcheon@netexas.net;
bonhamlibrary@texoma.net
Barbara McCutcheon

Brazoria Branch Genealogical Library
620 South Brooks Street
Brazoria, TX 77422-9022
(979) 798-2372; (979) 798-4013 FAX
Jerry Measells

Brazoria County Historical Museum
100 East Cedar
Angleton, TX 77515
(979) 864-1208
research@bchm.org
http://www.bchm.org
Jamie Murray, Information Resources
Coordinator; Jackqueline Haynes,
Director
Tue–Fri 9:00–5:00, Sat 9:00–3:00
Pub. *The Window Pane*, quarterly
("Old 300" genealogy database on web site,
Brazoria County family biography file,
oral history audio tape collection,
historical photograph collection, cemetery
database for Brazoria County; includes
Brazoria County, Austin's Colony, and
Texas history)
$25.00 per year membership

Herman Brown Free Library
Burnet County Library System
J. Frank Dobie Room
100 East Washington Street
Burnet, TX 78611-3114
(512) 756-2328; (512) 756-2610 FAX
hbfl@moment.net
Paula L. Harris
Mon–Fri 10:00–6:00

Brownwood Public Library
600 Carnegie Boulevard
Brownwood, TX 76801-7097
(915) 646-0155; (915) 646-6503 FAX
dir@bwdpublib.org; staff@bwdpublib.org
http://bwdpublib.org
Mat McConnell

Bryan Public Library
201 East 26th Street
Bryan, TX 77803-5356
(979) 779-1736 (Reference)
cmounce@ci.bryan.tx.us
http://www.bcslibrary.org
Nancy McCraw Ross, Senior Reference
Librarian; Clara B. Mounce
Mon–Tue & Thur 9:00–9:00, Wed & Fri–Sat
9:00–5:00
(genealogical and local history collections
with emphasis on Brazos County history)

Tom Burnett Memorial Library
400 West Alameda Street
Iowa Park, TX 76367-1616
(940) 592-4981; (940) 592-4664 FAX
suem@wf.net
Susan Maness

Cameron Public Library
304 East Third Street
Cameron, TX 76520-3350
(254) 697-2401 voice & FAX
camlib7@hotmail.com
Kay King, Director
Mon noon–7:00, Tue–Fri 9:00–5:00

Carnegie History Center
125 South College Avenue
Tyler, TX 75702
(903) 593-7989
Geoffrey Willbanks, Executive Director

Carrollton Public Library
4220 North Josey Lane
Carrollton, TX 75010-4600
(972) 466-3353; (972) 466-3360; (972) 466-
3394 FAX; (972) 466-4722 FAX
lucile.dade@cityofcarrollton.com
http://www.cityofcarrollton.com/library
Lucile Dade

Center for Great Plains Studies
(see Kansas, Part 2)

Center for Great Plains Study
(see Nebraska, Part 2)

Chambers County Library
(202 Cummings Street—location)
PO Box 520 (mailing address)
Anahuac, TX 77514-0520
(409) 267-8261; (409) 267-8263; (409) 267-
3783 FAX
lparsons@chambers.lib.tx.us
http://www.chambers.lib.tx.us
Ann Weaver; A. Lynette Parsons
Mon–Tue 8:00–6:00, Wed–Fri 8:00–5:00,
Sat 9:00–1:00

Childress Heritage Museum
210 Third Street, N.W.
Childress, TX 79201
(940) 937-2261
Jenny Lou Taylor, Executive Director
Mon–Fri 9:00–5:00
(Childress County exhibits and history)

**Clayton Library, Center for Genealogical
Research**
A unit of the Houston Public Library
5300 Caroline
Houston, TX 77004-6896

(832) 393-2600; (713) 527-9447 FAX
Marje.Harris@cityofhouston.net
http://www.hpl.lib.tx.us/hpl/branches/
cla_home.html
Margaret J. Harris, Manager
Mon–Wed 9:00–9:00, Thur–Sat 9:00–5:00
("A nationwide genealogical collection with some foreign materials, including Index to Eng/Welsh vital records 1837–1930, Deutsche Geshlecter Buch. All federal census and Soundex through 1920 and about 1/3 of the 1830 census and Soundex. A collection of 19th and 20th century passenger lists and indexes for particularly east and gulf coast ports. Indexes to federal military service and pensions from Revolutionary War through Spanish American War; WWI draft registration cards for several states and index to soldiers who died in WWII. State and county records and compiled sources representing all 50 states along with special collections such as Draper Manuscripts, McCubbin Collection, COM index for South Carolina. American Indian, African American, Hispanic and other ethnic compiled sources and original records. Lineage material from many patriotic societies, family histories, vertical files, periodicals, maps, finding aids.")

Cleburne Public Library
(302 West Henderson Street, Cleburne, TX 76033-5494—location)
PO Box 657 (mailing address)
Cleburne, TX 76033-0657
(817) 645-0936; (817) 645-0934; (817) 556-8816 FAX
Lanad@cleburne.net
http://www.cleburne.ci.tx.us
Lana Dibble

Comanche County Historical Museum
(100 Moorman Drive—location)
PO Box 22 (mailing address)
Comanche, TX 76442
Fain McDaniel, President
Sat–Sun 2:00–4:00
(collection of artifacts and memorabilia)

Corpus Christi Public Library
Local History/Genealogy Department
805 Comanche Street
Corpus Christi, TX 78401-2798
(361) 880-7030 (Local History); (361) 880-7000 (Library); (361) 880-7005 FAX
library@ccpl.ci.corpus-christi.tx.us
http://www.library.ci.corpus-christi.tx.us
Margaret Rose, Librarian
Mon–Thur 9:00–9:00, Fri–Sat 9:00–6:00, Sun 2:00–6:00

Corsicana Public Library
Genealogy Room
100 North 12th Street
Corsicana, TX 75110-5205
(903) 872-3071; (903) 654-4814 FAX
http://www.ci.corsicana.tx.us/library.html
Greg Hill, Library Director
Mon–Tue 10:00–8:00, Wed–Fri 10:00–6:00, Sat 10:00–4:00
volunteer research only

Coryell Museum and Historical Center
718 East Main Street
Gatesville, TX 76528
(254) 865-5007
info@coryellmuseum.org
http://www.coryellmuseum.org
Tue–Sat 10:00–3:00

Crosby County Pioneer Memorial

101 West Main
Crosbyton, TX 79322
(806) 675-2331
Verna Anne Wheeler, Executive Director
Tue–Sat 9:00–noon & 1:00–5:00
("Material available that relates to Crosby County: histories and obituaries.")

Dallas Public Library, Genealogy Section
J. Erik Jonsson Branch
History and Social Sciences, Genealogy Section
1515 Young Street, Eighth Floor
Dallas, TX 75201-5499
(214) 670-1424; (972) 670-7839 FAX
director@dallaslibrary.org
http://www.dallaslibrary.org
Lloyd DeWitt Bockstruck, F.N.G.S., Supervisor, Genealogy Section
Mon–Thur 9:00–9:00, Fri–Sat 9:00–5:00, Sun 1:00–5:00

Dallas Public Library, Texas-Dallas History and Archives Division
J. Erik Jonsson Branch
1515 Young Street, Seventh Floor
Dallas, TX 75201-5499
(972) 670-1435
http://www.dallaslibrary.org
Marvin H. Stone, Division Manager
Mon–Thur 9:00–9:00, Fri–Sat 9:00–5:00, Sun 1:00–5:00
(specializes in historic photographs, maps, newspapers, JFK assassination collection)

The Daughters of the Republic of Texas Library
(300 Alamo Plaza at Crockett Street—location)
PO Box 1401 (mailing address)
San Antonio, TX 78295-1401
(210) 225-1071; (210) 225-8155; (210) 212-8514 FAX
drtl@drtl.org
http://www.drtl.org
Cathy Herpich, Director
Mon–Sat 9:00–5:00
(Texas history and early Texas genealogy)

Deaf Smith County Museum
(400 Sampson—location)
PO Box 1007 (mailing address)
Hereford, TX 79045
(806) 364-4338
Paula Edwards, Executive Director
Mon–Sat 10:00–5:00
Pub. *Deaf Smith County Historical Society Newsletter*, three times per year
(primarily historical, not genealogical)

Deer Park Independent School District Historical Museum
204 Ivy
Deer Park, TX 77536
(281) 479-2831

Deer Park Public Library
3009 Center Street
Deer Park, TX 77536-5099
(281) 479-5276
csuessmuth@deerparktx.org
Katie Hill, Assistant Library Director; Charles Suessmuth
Mon & Wed 9:00–6:00, Tue & Thur 9:00–9:00, Fri–Sat 9:00–5:00
(history, but "no genealogy research materials")

Denton Public Library System-Emily Fowler Central Library
502 Oakland Street
Denton, TX 76201-3102

(940) 349-8561; (940) 349-8569; (940) 349-8260 FAX
library@cityofdenton.com
http://www.dentonlibrary.com
Linda Touraine, Coordinator of Adult Services
Mon, Wed & Fri–Sat 9:00–6:00, Tue & Thur 9:00–9:00, Sun 1:00–5:00
("In addition to local Denton history collection, have a Texas collection; genealogy covers all states with emphasis on the southern states.")
limited research: $5.00 minimum (includes 10 copies), additional charges for photocopies over 10

Duncanville Public Library
201 James Collins Boulevard
Duncanville, TX 75116-4818
(972) 780-5050; (972) 780-4958 FAX
cbryan@ci.duncanville.tx.us
http://www.ci.duncanville.tx.us/library.htm
Carla W. Bryan

Ector County Library
321 West Fifth Street
Odessa, TX 79761-5024
(915) 332-0633; (432) 337-6502 FAX
http://www.ector.lib.tx.us
Doris Baker, Head, Southwest History/Genealogy Department
Genealogy Department: Mon–Thur 8:30–8:30, Fri–Sat 9:30–6:00, Sat 9:00–noon & 1:00–6:00

El Campo Museum of Art, History and Natural Science
(2350 North Mechanic—location)
PO Box 23 (mailing address)
El Campo, TX 77437-0023
(979) 541-5092
Denise Prochazka, Curator

El Paso Museum of History
12901 Gateway West
El Paso, TX 79927
(915) 858-1928
Barbara J. Ardus, Curator

El Paso Public Library
501 North Oregon Street
El Paso, TX 79901-1193
(915) 543-5474 (Government Documents/Genealogy); (915) 543-5440 (Southwest Collection); (915) 543-5410 FAX
breycx@ci.el-paso.tx.us
http://www.ci.el-paso.tx.us/library.htm
Mon–Thur 8:30–8:30, Fri–Sat 8:30–5:30; Sun 1:00–5:00

El Progreso Memorial Library
129 West Nopal Street
Uvalde, TX 78801-5284
(830) 278-2017; (830) 278-4940 FAX
lsmanderson@hotmail.com
http://www.elprogreso.org
Susan Anderson, Director
Mon–Wed & Fri 9:00–6:00, Thur 9:00–8:00, Sat 9:00–1:00

Euless Public Library
201 North Ector Drive
Euless, TX 76039-3595
(817) 685-1489; (817) 267-1979 FAX
http://www.euless.org/library/library.html
Vicki Stone, Public Services Librarian
Mon–Tue & Thur 10:00–9:00, Wed 10:00–6:00, Fri–Sat 10:00–5:00, Sun 1:00–5:00
("The Euless Public Library's Genealogy section has a reader printer, a computer

with access to ancestry.com, Family Tree Maker™, the 1880 United States Census and National Index on CD, and a printer. Our collection includes the census index for most states (late 1700s to early 1900s], periodicals, newsletters, reference materials, and circulating materials. If a patron cannot find an item, we can do Interlibrary Loan or find a location in the Dallas/Fort Worth metroplex that does have it.")

Fannin County Museum of History
1 Main Street
Bonham, TX 75418
(903) 583-8042
Tom Scott, President/Director
Tue–Thur 10:00–4:00
(Some basic area history available, but all genealogical material has been donated to Bonham Public Library. "We no longer accept telephone calls concerning genealogical material.")
$20.00–$500.00 per year membership

Fayette Heritage Museum and Archives
855 South Jefferson
La Grange, TX 78945
(979) 968-6418; (979) 968-5357 FAX
library@fais.net
Margaret Huenefeld, Curator/Archivist
Tue 10:00–6:30, Wed–Fri 10:00–5:00, Sat 10:00–1:00, Sun 1:00–5:00
(Fayette County, Texas)

Floyd County Historical Museum
(105 East Missouri Street—location)
PO Box 304 (mailing address)
Floydada, TX 79235-0304
(806) 983-2415
Nancy Marble
Mon–Fri 1:00–5:00
Pub. *MuseBriefs*, annually
(genealogical library specializing in local history and genealogy)
no cost; no fee for research inquiries

Fort Belknap Archives (Young County)
Route 1, Box 27
Newcastle, TX 76372
B. A. Ledbetter, Archivist
Sat–Sun 9:00–5:00
$5.00 per year membership

Fort Bend Museum Association
(500 Houston Street, Richmond, TX 77469—location)
PO Drawer 460 (mailing address)
Richmond, TX 77406-0460
(281) 342-6478; (281) 342-1256 (Executive Director)
http://www.fortbendmuseum.org
Michael Rugeley Moore, Executive Director
Tue–Fri 9:00–5:00, Sat 10:00–5:00, Sun 1:00–5:00
Pub. *Texian Gazette*, bimonthly, $20.00 per year nonmembers subscription
("Focus of Austin's Colony, early Texas settlement, and local history.")
$50.00–$100.00 per year membership

Fort Concho National Historic Landmark
630 South Oakes
San Angelo, TX 76903
(915) 657-4441
http://www.fortconcho.com
Evelyn Lemons, Historian/Archivist
by appointment
Pub. *Fort Concho Guidon*, quarterly
(Indian Wars military history 1866–1891, west Texas history 1866–1920, local history, Texas history)

$25.00 per year membership

Fort Worth Museum of Science and History
1501 Montgomery
Fort Worth, TX 76107
(817) 732-1631
T. Lindsay Baker, Curator of History; Karen Turner, Manager of Volunteer Services and Public Relations

Fort Worth Public Library
Genealogy and Local History Department
500 West Third Street
Fort Worth, TX 76102-7309
(817) 871-7740 (Genealogy)
genlhst@fortworthlibrary.org
http://www.fortworthlibrary.org
Ken Hopkins, Supervisor and Municipal Archivist
Mon–Thur 9:00–9:00, Fri–Sat 10:00–6:00, Sun noon–6:00
("Specializes in Texas, Southern and Midwestern states; Fort Worth and Tarrant County history; City archives")

Frankston Depot Library and Museum, Inc.
(Town Square, South—location)
PO Box 639 (mailing address)
Frankston, TX 75763-0639
(903) 876-4463; (903) 876-3226 FAX
depotlibrary@msn.net
Patricia Montrose, Library Director
Tue & Sat 9:00–5:00, Thur noon–7:00
out-of-county user fee: $15.00 per year

Freestone County Historical Museum
(302 East Main Street—location)
PO Box 524 (mailing address)
Fairfield, TX 75840
fcmuseum@airmail.net
Molly Fryer
Wed & Fri–Sat 9:00–4:00
("Specializing in Freestone County history in conjunction with Freestone County Genealogical Society")

Galveston County Historical Museum
2219 Market Street
Galveston, TX 77550
(409) 766-2340; (409) 795-2157 FAX
christy.carl@galvestonhistory.org
http://www.galvestonhistory.org
Christine S. Carl, Director
Mon–Sat 10:00–4:00, Sun noon–4:00

Gatesville Public Library
811 East Main Street
Gatesville, TX 76528-1432
(254) 865-5367; (254) 248-0986 FAX
faye.nichols@ci.gatesville.tx.us
http://www.gatesvillecitylibrary.org
Faye Nichols
Mon, Wed & Fri 9:00–5:00, Tue & Thur noon–8:00, Sat 9:00–3:30

George Memorial Library
Genealogy Department
Fort Bend County Libraries
1001 Golfview Drive
Richmond, TX 77469-5141
(281) 342-4455; (281) 341-2608
dfojtik@fortbend.lib.tx.us
http://www.fortbend.lib.tx.us/gm.html
W. M. Von Maszewski, Department Manager
Mon–Thur 9:00–9:00, Fri–Sat 9:00–5:00, Sun (except summer) 1:00–5:00
("genealogical materials pertain primarily to the southeastern U.S.; Civil War [Confederacy] microfilm collection")

Gibbs Memorial Library
305 East Rusk Street
Mexia, TX 76667-2398
(254) 562-3231; (254) 562-0828 FAX
ref@gibbslibrary.com
http://www.gibbslibrary.com
John West, Genealogist
Wed 10:00–6:00
research: $10.00, includes research time and six photocopies; additional copies: 15¢ each

Grand Prairie Public Library System
901 Conover Drive
Grand Prairie, TX 75051-1521
(972) 237-5700; (972) 237-5750 FAX
hours: various

Grand Saline Public Library
201 East Pacific Avenue
Grand Saline, TX 75140-1934
(903) 962-5516; (903) 962-6866 FAX
catj@lcii.net
Helen Hale

Grapevine Public Library
1201 Municipal Way
Grapevine, TX 76051-5545
(817) 410-3400 (Library); (817) 410-3429 (Genealogy Librarian); (817) 410-3084 FAX
nmaxwell@grapevine.lib.tx.us
http://www.grapevine.lib.tx.us
Nancy Maxwell, Genealogy Librarian
Mon–Thur 9:00–9:00, Fri–Sat 9:00–6:00, Sun 2:00–6:00

Gregg County Historical Museum
(214 North Fredonia Street, Longview, TX 75601—location)
PO Box 3342 (mailing address)
Longview, TX 75606
(903) 753-5840
Ellie Caston, Ph.D., Museum Director
Tue–Sat 10:00–4:00
Pub. *Museumemo*, semiannually (spring and fall)
("We provide information about our local history, but offer very little genealogical information.")
from $25.00 to $1,000.00 per year membership

Hacksma House Genealogy Library
(see Washington, Part 2)

Z. I. Hale Museum
242 West Dole Street
Winters, TX 79567
(historical museum)

Nita Stewart Haley Memorial Library and History Center
1805 West Indiana
Midland, TX 79701
(915) 682-5785
Robin L. McWilliams, Curator

Harlingen Public Library
410 76 Drive
Harlingen, TX 78550-5072
(956) 430-6650; (956) 430-6633 FAX
rendon@harlingen.lib.tx.us;
    admin@harlingen.lib.tx.us
http://www.harlingen.lib.tx.us
Ruben Rendon
Mon–Thur 10:00–9:00, Fri 1:00–5:00

Gladys L. Harrington Public Library
(see Plano Public Library System, below)

Harrison County Historical Museum

Peter Whetstone Square
Marshall, TX 75670
(903) 938-2680

http://www.rootsweb.com/~txharris/hcmuseum.htm
Mildred Hooper, Office Manager
Mon–Sat 10:00–5:00, Sun 1:30–5:00
Pub. *Harrison County Historical Museum Monthly Newsletter*
$25.00 per year membership

W. Walworth Harrison Public Library
Genealogy Room
1 Lou Finney Lane
Greenville, TX 75401-5988
(903) 457-2992; (903) 457-2961 FAX
ctaylor@ci.greenville.tx.us
http://www.greenville.lib.tx.us
Carol Taylor, Librarian for Genealogy/Local History
Mon–Thur 9:30–8:30, Fri–Sat 9:30–5:30
(specializes in Texas, southern states, and Hunt County, Texas)

Heritage Farmstead Museum
1900 West 15th Street
Plano, TX 75075
(972) 881-0140
museum@airmail.net
http://www.heritagefarmstead.org
Ted Peters, Director
Mon–Fri 9:00–5:00, Sat–Sun 1:00–5:00
Pub. *Heritage Today*, quarterly
free

Hickman Library and Museum
(609 Main Street—location)
PO Box 66 (mailing address)
Big Lake, TX 76932
(915) 884-2082
Ann Schneemann, Chairman Reagan County Historical Association
Wed afternoons and special events
no costs

Hidalgo County Historical Museum
121 East McIntyre
Edinburg, TX 78539
(956) 383-6911; (956) 381-8518 FAX
hchm@hiline.net
David J. Mycue, Curator of Archives and Collections
Museum archives and library: Tue–Fri 9:00–5:00
Pub. *Borderlines*, quarterly
("HCHM archives specializes in Spanish-surnamed genealogical collections and early Rio Grande Valley settlers and pioneers.")
$25.00 per year membership; research: $12.00 per hour, plus copies at 10¢ each

Hill College History Complex
(see Confederate Research Center, Miscellaneous, Part 4)

Hillsboro City Library
118 South Waco Street
Hillsboro, TX 76645-7708
(254) 582-7385; (254) 582-7765 FAX
hillsboro.library@glade.net
http://library.ci.hillsboro.tx.us
Susan S. Mann

Hood County Public Library
222 North Travis
Granbury, TX 76048-2164
(817) 573-3569 voice & FAX
hoodcoli@itexas.net
Jeanell Morris, Librarian
Mon 10:00–7:00, Tue 10:00–9:00, Wed–Sat

10:00–6:00

Houston County Visitors Center/Museum, Inc.
(303 South First Street—location)
PO Box 449 (mailing address)
Crockett, TX 75835
(936) 544-9520
Mary A. Lowe, President
Wed 2:00–4:00, and by appointment
("diaries, photos, Houston County history segments, exhibits")
$10.00 per year membership

Sam Houston Regional Library and Research Center (Southeast Texas)
(650 FM 1011—location)
PO Box 310 (mailing address)
Liberty, TX 77575-0310
(936) 336-8821
SamHoustonCenter@tsl.state.tx.us
http://www.tsl.state.tx.us
Robert L. Schaadt, Director-Archivist
Mon–Fri 8:00–5:00, Sat 9:00–4:00
(part of the Archives and Information Services Division of the Texas State Library, serves as the Regional Historical Resource Depository for Southeast Texas: Chambers, Hardin, Jasper, Jefferson, Liberty, Newton, Orange, Polk, San Jacinto and Tyler counties)

Huntsville Public Library
1216 14th Street
Huntsville, TX 77340-4507
(936) 291-5470; (936) 291-5472; (936) 291-5418 FAX
linda.dodson@ci.huntsville.tx.us
http://www.huntsville.lib.tx.us
Judy Hunter, Librarian; Linda Dodson
Mon–Thur 9:00–7:00, Fri–Sat 10:00–5:00
(Texana Collection, family Bible records, Civil War and World War II collections)

Hutchinson County Historical Museum
618 North Main
Borger, TX 79007
(806) 273-0130
Ed Benz, Director
Mon–Fri 9:00–5:00, Sat 11:00–4:30, Sun (Labor Day–Memorial Day) 2:00–5:00
Pub. *Quarterly Newsletter*, free
(county families up to 1979, limited research resources)

Irving Public Library
(801 West Irving Boulevard, Irving, TX 75060-2898—location)
PO Box 152288 (mailing address)
Irving, TX 75015-2288
(972) 721-2628; (972) 721-2606; (972) 259-1171 FAX; (972) 721-2463 FAX
planders@irvinglibrary.org;
reference@irvinglibrary.org
http://www.irving.lib.tx.us
P. Landers

Jacksonville Public Library
502 South Jackson Street
Jacksonville, TX 75766-2415
(903) 586-7664; (903) 586-3397 FAX
director@jacksonvillelibrary.com;
webmaster@jacksonvillelibrary.com
http://www.jacksonvillelibrary.com
Barbara Crossman

Key Genealogical Library
2200 North Yarbrough Drive, #B-281
El Paso, TX 79925-6333
Tue–Wed 10:00–4:00, Sat 10:00–2:00, Tue 6:00 P.M.–9:00 P.M.

Kurth Memorial Library
Ora McMullen Room, Genealogy, Local and State History
706 South Raguet Street
Lufkin, TX 75904-3922
(936) 699-4126; (936) 639-2487 FAX
http://www.kurthmemoriallibrary.com
Cindy McMullen, Head of Ora McMullen Room
Mon–Thur 9:00–8:00, Fri 9:00–5:30, Sat 9:00–1:00
("All Texas census 1850–1930. Genealogical information in print on 247 Texas counties.")

Lamar University
(Highway 69 at University Drive—location)
PO Box 1007 (mailing address)
Beaumont, TX 77710
(409) 835-0823; (409) 838-9107 FAX
Christy Marino, Curator
Tue–Sun 1:00–5:00
costs vary

Laredo Public Library
Bruni Plaza Branch Library
1120 San Bernardo Avenue
Laredo, TX 78040-4489
(956) 795-3035; (956) 795-3039 FAX
http://www.laredolibrary.org
Sandra L. Chamberlain, Librarian
Tue–Thur 9:00–9:00, Fri–Sat 9:00–6:00

Layland Museum
201 North Caddo
Cleburne, TX 76031
(817) 645-0940; (817) 641-4161 FAX
Julie P. Baker, Curator
(research libraries on local history, Native Americans)

Longview Public Library
222 West Cotton Street
Longview, TX 75601-6348
(903) 237-1350; (903) 237-1327 FAX
manager@longview.lib.tx.us
http://www.longview.lib.tx.us
Pauline Cox
Mon, Wed–Fri 9:00–noon & 1:00–6:00

Lubbock City-County Library
1306 Ninth Street
Lubbock, TX 79401-2798
(806) 767-2836; (806) 767-2830 FAX
jclausen@mail.ci.lubbock.tx.us
http://library.ci.lubbock.tx.us
Jane Clausen, Public Services Director
Mon–Thur 9:00–9:00, Fri–Sat 9:00–6:00, Sun 1:00–5:00
(has genealogy department)

Luling Public Library
215 South Pecan Avenue
Luling, TX 78648-2607
(830) 875-2813
lullib78648@yahoo.com
Nancy M. Gilchrist

Martin County Historical Museum
(207 Broadway—location)
PO Box 929 (mailing address)
Stanton, TX 79782
(915) 756-2722
Tue–Sat 9:00–4:00

Matagorda County Museum
2100 Avenue F
Bay City, TX 77414
(979) 245-7502
Mary Belle Ingram, Archives Chair
Tue–Fri 10:00–4:00, Sat–Sun 1:00–4:00
(Matagorda County history and genealogy;

"We have an early newspaper collection of Matagorda County.")

McKinney Memorial Public Library
101 East Hunt Street
McKinney, TX 75069-3807
(972) 547-7323; (972) 542-0868 FAX
bwright@mckinneytexas.org
Beth Scudder

McMurry College Library
Scarborough Library of Genealogy, History and Biography of the South and Southwest
(see Abilene Public Library, above)

Medallion Home/Pioneer Park Association
c/o Chamber of Commerce
School Street
Kermit, TX 79745
(915) 586-2507
first Sun 3:00–5:00

Mesquite Public Library
300 Grubb Drive
Mesquite, TX 75149-3492
(972) 216-6229 (Genealogy); (972) 216-6220; (972) 216-6740 FAX
mainbr@library.mesquite.tx.us
http://www.cityofmesquite.com/library
Marjorie Bays
Mon–Thur 9:00–9:00, Fri–Sat 9:00–6:00

Midland County Historical Museum
301 West Missouri
Midland, TX 79701
(915) 688-8947
Nancy R. McKinley, Director
Mon–Wed & Fri–Sat 2:00–5:00
(archival material)

Midland County Public Library
The John and Rosalind Redfern Genealogical Research Center
301 West Missouri
Midland, TX 79701-5108
(915) 688-8991 (Main Number); (915) 683-2708; (915) 688-8996 FAX
denise_johnson@co.midland.tx.us
http://www.co.midland.tx.us/library; http://www.rootsweb.com/~txmidlan/mcl.htm (Genealogical Research Center)
Denise Johnson, Librarian; Becky Britton, Special Collections
Sept–May: Mon–Thur 9:00–9:00, Fri–Sat 9:00–6:00; June–Aug: Mon 9:00–9:00, Tue–Sat 9:00–6:00

Montgomery County Memorial Library
Central Library
(104 I-45 North—location)
PO Box 867 (mailing address)
Conroe, TX 77301
(936) 788-8363 (Genealogy); (936) 539-7814; (936) 788-8324 FAX
http://www.countylibrary.org/gen.htm
Barbara Hawkins Franz, Genealogy Librarian
Mon & Fri–Sat 9:00–5:00, Tue–Thur 9:00–9:00
(Texas and the southern states, including Arkansas, Missouri and Oklahoma)

Moody Texas Ranger Library
PO Box 2570
Waco, TX 76702
(254) 750-5986; (254) 750-8629

Moore Memorial Public Library
1701 Ninth Avenue, North
Texas City, TX 77590-5496
(409) 643-5979; (409) 948-1106 FAX
http://www.texascity-library.org
Susie Moncla

Mon–Wed 9:00–9:00, Thur–Fri 9:00–6:00, Sat 10:00–4:00

Mount Pleasant Public Library
213 North Madison
Mount Pleasant, TX 75455-3944
(903) 575-4180; (903) 577-8000 FAX
library@mpcity.org
http://www.ci.mount-pleasant.tx.us/library/library.htm
Lori Rigney, Head Librarian
Mon–Fri 9:00–6:00, Sat 9:00–1:00

Clint W. Murchison Memorial Library
121 South Prairieville Street
Athens, TX 75751-2595
(903) 677-7295; (903) 677-7275 FAX
library@hendersoncotx.com
http://www.hendersoncountylibrary.org
Sara Brown
Mon–Fri 10:00–6:00, Sat 9:00–1:00

Museum of the Great Plains
(see Oklahoma, Part 2)

New Boston Public Library
127 North Ellis Street
New Boston, TX 75570-2905
(903) 628-5414 voice & FAX
library@valornet.com
Julie A. Woodrow, Librarian
Mon 10:00–6:30, Tue 10:00–8:00, Wed–Fri 10:00–5:00, Sat 9:00–1:00

Nicholson Memorial Library
625 Austin Street
Garland, TX 75040-6365
(972) 205-2503; (972) 205-2523 FAX
cbausch1@earthlink.net
http://www.nmls.lib.tx.us
Terry Tule, Genealogical Librarian; Claire Bausch
Mon–Thur 10:00–9:00, Fri–Sat 10:00–6:00
Pub. *Garland Genealogical Society Newsletter*, monthly
$15.00 per year membership

Old Spanish Missions Historical Research Collection and Texana Collection
2002 Sueltenfuss Library
Our Lady of the Lake University
411 S.W. 24th Street
San Antonio, TX 78207
(210) 434-6711, ext. 321
garza@lake.ollusa.edu
http://lib.ollusa.edu/libinfo/info/collections.htm
Vicky Marlette, Special Collections Librarian; Antoinette Garza
Mon–Fri by appointment

Palestine Public Library
Special Collections
1101 North Cedar
Palestine, TX 75801-7607
(903) 729-4121; (903) 729-4062 FAX
genlib@palestine.lib.tx.us
http://www.palestine.lib.tx.us
Beth Perry
Mon & Thur noon–8:00, Tue 10:00–8:00, Wed & Fri 10:00–6:00, Sat 10:00–4:00

Panhandle-Plains Historical Museum
(2503 Fourth Avenue, Unit 60967, Canyon, TX 79015—location)
WT Box 60967, WTAMU (mailing address)
Canyon, TX 79016
(806) 651-2274; (806) 651-2250 FAX
bbustos@wtpphmfs.wtamu.edu
http://www.wtamu.edu/museum/home.html
Betty L. Bustos, Assistant Archivist
Mon–Fri 9:00–noon & 1:00–5:00

Paris Junior College
A. M. and Welma Aikin, Jr., Regional Archives
2400 Clarksville Street
Paris, TX 75460-6298
(903) 784-9411
http://gen.1starnet.com/lamargen.htm
Daisy Harvill, Director
(northeast Texas)

Paris Junior College
Mike Rheudasil Learning Center
2400 Clarksville Street
Paris, TX 75460-6298

Paris Public Library
326 South Main Street
Paris, TX 75460-5825
(903) 785-8531; (903) 784-6325 FAX
blandon@1starnet.com
http://www.paristexaslibrary.com
Betty Landon
(has city directories from 1940)

Lucy Hill Patterson Memorial Library
201 Ackerman Street
Rockdale, TX 76567-201
(512) 446-3410; (512) 446-5597 FAX
pattersonlib@rockdalecityhall.com; mtodd@rockdalecityhall.com
http://www.main.org/patlib/patlib.htm
Melanie Todd, Head Librarian
Tue–Wed & Fri 10:00–5:00, Thur 1:00–8:00, Sat 10:00–2:00

Perry Memorial Library
22 S.E. Fifth Avenue
Perryton, TX 79070-3112
(806) 435-5801; (806) 435-4266 FAX
persan@usa.com
http://www.hlc-org/perryton
Sandra Sears
Mon 10:00–8:00, Tue–Fri 10:00–5:30, Sat 10:00–1:00

Pilot Point Community Library
(324 South Washington Street, Pilot Point, TX 76258-8906—location)
PO Box 969 (mailing address)
Pilot Point, TX 76258-0969
(940) 686-5004; (940) 686-2833 FAX
pilotpoint.library@verizon.net
Phyllis Tillery

Pioneer City/County Museum
610 East Third
Sweetwater, TX 79556
(915) 235-8547
H. E. Pepper, Manager
(manuscript collection)

Pioneer, Trail Driver and Former Texas Rangers Association, Inc.
3805 Broadway
San Antonio, TX 78209
(210) 822-9011
Pat Halpin, Secretary-Treasurer
Tue–Sun (1 May–1 Sept) 10:00–5:00, Wed–Sun (1 Sept–1 May) 11:00–4:00
(Texas history)

Plano Public Library System
Gladys Harrington Library
Genealogy/Texana Department
1501 18th Street
Plano, TX 75074-6001
(972) 941-7175; (972) 941-7292 FAX
lynnd@plano.com
http://www.planolibrary.org
Lynn Day, Senior Public Services Librarian
Mon–Thur 10:00–9:00, Fri–Sat 10:00–6:00, Sun 1:00–5:00

("Library with local, state, national and international holdings.")

Port Arthur Public Library
4615 9th Avenue
Port Arthur, TX 77642-5799
(409) 985-8838; (409) 985-5969 FAX
rcline@gtbizclass.com
http://www.pap.lib.tx.us
Jill Stockinger, Chief Librarian and Reference Department Head; Ray Cline
Mon–Thur 10:00–9:00, Fri 10:00–6:00, Sat 10:00–5:00, Sunday (except summer) 2:00–5:00

Quitman Public Library
(202 East Goode Street, Quitman, TX 75783-2533—location)
PO Box 1677 (mailing address)
Quitman, TX 75783-1677
(903) 763-4191; (903) 763-2532 FAX
directd@quitmanlibrary.org
http://www.quitmanlibrary.org
Dorothy Demontigny, Library Director; Darlene DelaRosa
Mon & Thur 9:00–9:00, Tue & Fri 9:00–5:00

Ralls Historical Museum
(801 Main Street—location)
PO Box 384 (mailing address)
Ralls, TX 79357
(806) 253-2425
Pauline Watkins, Executive Director

Rankin Museum
(Fifth and Main Streets—location)
PO Box 82 (mailing address)
Rankin, TX 79778
(915) 693-2371
Helen Hurst
Thur–Sat afternoons
(archives focus on Upton County; obituaries, newspapers)

Red River Historical Museum of Sherman
301 South Walnut
Sherman, TX 75090
(903) 893-7623
rrhms@texoma.net
Kelli L. Pickard, Director
Tue–Fri 10:00–noon & 1:00–4:30, Sat 2:00–5:00
Pub. *Red River Historical Museum Sentinel*, bimonthly
("We have limited information on specific families of the county; we mostly have general history of the area.")
$25.00 per year membership; research: $10.00 per hour plus copy costs

Rice University
Woodson Research Center
Fondren Library
(6100 South Main Street—location)
PO Box 1892 (mailing address)
Houston, TX 77251-1892
(713) 527-8101, ext. 2586; (713) 285-5207 FAX
boothe@rice.edu; jsh@rice.edu (*Journal*)
Pub. *Journal of Southern History*

Richardson Public Library
900 Civic Center Drive
Richardson, TX 75080-5298
(972) 238-4000; (972) 744-4350; (972) 744-5806 FAX; (972) 952-0870 FAX
jane.merz@cor.gov
http://www.cor.net/library
Jane Shelton-Merz

Riviera Historical Museum
Seventh and North Boulevard

Riviera, TX 78379
(361) 296-3676

Rosenberg Library
2310 Sealy Avenue
Galveston, TX 77550-2296
(409) 763-8854; (409) 763-0275 FAX
jaugelli@rosenberg-library.org
http://www.rosenberg-library.org
Casey Edward Greene, Head of Special Collections; John Augelli
Tue–Sat 9:00–5:00

Round Rock Public Library System
211 East Main
Round Rock, TX 78664-5245
(512) 218-7000; (512) 218-7061 FAX
ejohnston@round-rock.tx.us
http://www.ci.round-rock.tx.us/library/library.html
Elizabeth Johnston, Genealogy & Local History Librarian
Mon–Thur 9:00–9:00, Fri–Sat 9:00–6:00, Sun 1:00–6:00
(Houses collection of the Williamson County Genealogical Society, "general genealogical titles and census, census indexes, etc., from many states")

San Antonio Public Library
Texana and Genealogy Area
600 Soledad Street
San Antonio, TX 78205-1200
(210) 207-2500; (210) 207-2603 FAX; (210) 207-2558 FAX
rsparks@sanantonio.gov; libwebadmin@sanantonio.gov
http://www.sanantonio.gov/library
Jo Myler, Librarian III
Mon–Thur 9:00–9:00, Fri–Sat 9:00–5:00, Sun 11:00–5:00
Pub. *The Explorer*, quarterly
(San Antonio and Texas; U.S.; Mexico)

San Augustine Public Library
413 East Columbia Street
San Augustine, TX 75972-2111
(936) 275-5367; (936) 275-5049 FAX
sauglib@yahoo.com
Mrs. Pat Snider, Director
Mon–Fri 9:00–5:00, Sat 9:00–2:00
(local history and genealogy; "carefully compiled cataloging of cemeteries of San Augustine County.")

San Jacinto Museum of History Association
3800 Park Road, 1836
La Porte, TX 77571
(281) 479-2421

Schleicher County Public Library
(201 South Main Street—location)
PO Box 611 (mailing address)
Eldorado, TX 76936-0611
(915) 853-3767; (915) 853-2963 FAX
jeri.whitten@netxv.net; sepl@wcc.net
Jeri Whitten
10:00–5:00

Scurry County Library
1916 23rd Street
Snyder, TX 79549-1910
(915) 573-5572; (915) 573-1060 FAX
scurrycl@snydertex.com
http://snydertex.com/sclibrary
Noreen E. Taylor, Librarian; L. Jane Romine
Mon, Wed & Fri–Sat 10:00–6:00, Tue & Thur 10:00–9:00

Seguin/Guadalupe County Public Library
707 East College Street
Seguin, TX 78155-3299

(830) 401-2422; (830) 401-2477 FAX
jacki@seguin.lib.tx.us; library@seguin.lib.tx.us
http://www.seguin.lib.tx.us
Mark Gretchen
Mon–Thur 10:00–9:00, Fri–Sat 9:00–5:00

Sherman Public Library
Local History and Genealogy Department
421 North Travis Street
Sherman, TX 75090-5975
(903) 892-7240; (903) 892-7101 FAX
jbanfield@grayson.edu
http://www.barr.org/sherman.htm
Jacqueline Banfield, Assistant Library Director
Mon, Wed & Fri 9:00–6:00, Tue & Thur 9:00–9:00, Sat 9:00–5:00

Singletary Memorial Library
207 East Sixth Street
Rusk, TX 75785-1103
(903) 683-5916; (903) 683-5964 FAX
mtl@hotmail.com
Ruth Mather

Genealogical Research Center and Library of Southeast Texas
Route 1, Box 40S
Kountze, TX 77625
Pub. *International Genealogical Exchange*, monthly, $12.00 per year subscription

Southern Methodist University
Clements Center for Southwest Studies
(356 Dallas Hall—location)
PO Box 750176 (mailing address)
Dallas, TX 75275-0176
(972) 768-3684; (972) 768-4129 FAX
swcenter@mail.smu.edu
http://www.smu.edu/~swcenter
(Arizona, New Mexico, Oklahoma, Texas, and southern California)

Southmost College
Arnulfo L. Oliveira Memorial Library
Hunter Room
83 Fort Brown
Brownsville, TX 78520
(956) 544-8221
Yolanda Gonzalez
Mon–Thur 7:30–10:00, Fri 7:30–5:00, Sat 10:30–4:00, Sun 2:00–9:00

Southwestern University
A. Frank Smith, Jr., Library Center
Special Collections Department
PO Box 770
Georgetown, TX 78627-0770
(512) 863-1568
stallark@southwestern.edu
http://www.southwestern.edu/library/special-collections.html

Sterling Municipal Library
Mary Elizabeth Wilbanks Avenue
Baytown, TX 77520-4258
(281) 427-7331; (281) 420-5347 FAX
dfischer@hpl.lib.tx.us; smlib@hpl.lib.tx.us
http://www.sml.lib.tx.us
Denise Fischer
Mon–Thur 10:00–9:00, Fri–Sat 10:00–6:00

Swenson Memorial Museum Research Library
(116 West Walker—location)
PO Box 350 (mailing address)
Breckenridge, TX 76424
(254) 559-8471
http://www.ohwy.com/tx/s/swmemuoa.htm
Freda Mitchell, Museum Director
Tue–Sat 10:00–noon & 1:00–5:00

research: $5.00 plus copy expenses

Tarrant County Historical Commission Archives
(Room B100 [Basement], Civil Courts Building, 100 North Houston Street—location)
100 East Weatherford Street (mailing address)
Fort Worth, TX 76196
(817) 884-3272
Susan Pritchett, Archivist
Mon–Fri 9:00–5:00
("Records of Tarrant County, Texas, including land records predating burning of courthouse in 1876; early marriage certificates, school information, business and commercial records. Not a primary genealogy resource, but some holdings may be useful.")

Temple Public Library
100 West Adams Avenue
Temple, TX 76501-7658
(254) 298-5556; (254) 298-5328 FAX
jduer@ci.temple.tx.us
http://library.ci.temple.tx.us
Beverly Snow, Reference Librarian; Judith A. Duer
Mon, Wed & Fri 10:00–6:00, Tue & Thur 10:00–9:00, Sat 10:00–5:00

Texarkana Museums System
(219 State Line Avenue, Texarkana, TX 75501—location)
PO Box 2343 (mailing address)
Texarkana, TX 75504
(903) 793-4831; (903) 793-7108 FAX
http://www.texarkanamuseums.org
Sammy Wacasey, Research Librarian
by appointment only
Pub. *Artifacts*, quarterly
("Regional research library and archives with statewide holdings.")

Texarkana Public Library
600 West Third Street
Texarkana, TX 75501-5054
(903) 794-2149; (903) 794-2139 FAX
acoleman@cableone.net;
sholmes@cableone.net
http://www.txar-publib.org
Alice Coleman
Mon–Wed 9:00–9:00, Thur–Sat 9:00–6:00

Texas A & I University
South Texas Archives
821 West Santa Gertrudis Avenue
Kingsville, TX 78363
(361) 595-2819
Toni Nagel, Archivist

Texas A & M University—Corpus Christi
University Library
6300 Ocean Drive
Corpus Christi, TX 78412
(361) 994-2301
Dr. Thomas H. Kreneck, Special Collections Librarian/Archivist
Mon–Fri 8:00–5:00
(special emphasis on history of south Texas and northern Mexico)

Texas Seaport Museum
Pier 21, Number 8
Galveston, TX 77550
(409) 763-1877; (409) 763-3037 FAX
elissa@galvestonhistory.org
http://www.tsm-elissa.org
Christine Hayes, Education Coordinator
daily 10:00–5:00
(Includes online immigration database,

mostly Germans and Eastern Europeans, entering through the Port of Galveston 1840–1950.)
admission: $5.00 for adults, includes use of immigration database; research: $10.00 per person by mail

Texas State Museum of History
1616 West Abram Street
Arlington, TX 76013
(817) 460-4001; (817) 460-4017 FAX
Dr. R. Peter Mooz, Executive Director
Wed–Fri 10:00–4:00, Sat–Sun 1:30–4:30
Pub. *TSMH Universe and Fielder World*, quarterly
from $35.00 per year membership; admission charge for nonmembers

Texas Woman's University
Blagg-Huey Library
Box 425528
Denton, TX 76204-5528
(940) 898-3701; (940) 898-3808 FAX
ref@twu.edu; jhepner@twu.edu
(Reference/Documents Librarian)
http://www.twu.edu/library
John C. Hepner, Reference/Documents Librarian
Mon–Thur 7:30 A.M.–midnight, Fri 7:30 A.M.–9:00 P.M., Sat 9:00–6:00, Sun (school year) 2:00–midnight, Sun (winter) 2:00–10:00
(a university library, which generally does not assist with genealogical research nor actively collect in this subject area, but has a "Genealogy" Ready Reference web page to assist users in locating Internet resources)

Tyler Public Library
Genealogy/Local History Room
201 South College Avenue
Tyler, TX 75702-7381
(903) 531-1316; (903) 593-7323; (903) 531-1329 FAX
citylibn@tylertexas.com;
library@tylertexas.com
http://www.tylerlibrary.com
Chris Albertson
Mon–Thur 10:00–8:00, Fri–Sat 10:00–5:00, Sun 1:00–5:00
(emphasis on Tyler and Smith County)

Tyrell Historical Library
Beaumont Public Library System
(695 Pearl Street, Beaumont, TX 77701-3524—location)
PO Box 3827 (mailing address)
Beaumont, TX 77704-3827
(409) 833-2759; (409) 833-5828 FAX
http://www.rootsweb.com/~txjeffer/library.htm
David E. Montgomery, Library Manager
Tue–Sat 8:30–5:30

Unger Memorial Library
Local History and Genealogy Section
825 Austin Street
Plainview, TX 79072-7235
(806) 296-1148; (806) 291-1245 FAX
http://www.texasonline.net/unger
John Sigwald, Librarian
six days per week (summer five days per week)
Pub. *Unger Ululations* (not genealogical)

University of Mississippi
Center for the Study of Southern Culture
(see Mississippi, Part 2)

University of North Texas Archives
PO Box 5188, NT Station

Denton, TX 76203
(940) 565-2766
Richard L. Himmel, Archives Librarian
(emphasis on north central Texas)

University of Southern Alabama
Gulf Coast Historical Review
(see Alabama, Part 2)

University of Texas at Arlington
Special Collections
University Library
PO Box 19497
Arlington, TX 76019-0497
(817) 272-3393; (817) 272-3360 FAX
http://www.uta.edu/library/SpCo/
special_collections.html
Dr. Gerald D. Saxon, Assistant Director for Special Collections
Mon–Fri 8:00–5:00, Sat 10:00–5:00
Pub. *The Compass Rose*, semiannually, free

The University of Texas at Austin
Eugene C. Barker Texas History Center
The Center for American History
Sid Richardson Hall 2.101
Austin, TX 78712
(512) 495-4515; (512) 495-4542 FAX
http://www.lib.utexas.edu/Libs/CAH/cah.html
Dr. Don E. Carleton, Director; Reference Librarian
Mon–Sat 9:00–5:00
Pub. *Center for American History Newsletter*, irregularly
(a national collection with emphasis on Texas, southern and southwestern U.S., and the Rocky Mountain west)
charge for photocopying and photographs and other duplication of materials

The University of Texas at Austin
Perry Castaneda Library
Austin, TX 78712
(512) 495-4250
http://www.lib.utexas.edu

The University of Texas at Austin
Center for Studies in Texas History
Austin, TX 78712
rtyler@mail.utexas.edu
http://www.dla.utexas.edu/texhist

The University of Texas at Austin
Mirabeau B. Lamar Library
Austin, TX 78712

The University of Texas at Austin
Winedale Historical Center
PO Box 11 (FM 2714)
Round Top, TX 78954
(979) 278-3530
Gloria Jaster, Administrator
weekdays 9:00–5:00
Pub. *The Ouid Nuch*, quarterly

University of Texas at El Paso (UTEP)
C. L. Sonnichsen Special Collections Department
El Paso, TX 79968
(915) 747-5683; (915) 747-5345 FAX
http://www.utep.edu/~library

University of Texas at San Antonio
Institute of Texan Cultures
801 South Bowie Street
San Antonio, TX 78205-3296
(210) 458-2228; (800) 776-7651; (210) 458-2218
http://www.utsa.edu/itc/libsvc1.htm
(includes Hispanic research)

University of Texas at San Antonio
Library, Special Collections Department
6900 North Loop 1604 West
San Antonio, TX 78249-0651
(210) 458-5505; (210) 458-4571
dguerra@lonestar.utsa.edu
http://www.lib.utsa.edu/
Special_Collections/lib.

The University of Texas-Pan American Library
Special Collections/Lower Rio Grande Valley
Historical Collection
1201 West University Drive
Edinburg, TX 78539-2999
(956) 381-2726
ggause@panam.edu
http://www.lib.panam.edu
George R. Gause, Jr., Special Collections
Librarian
Mon–Thur 8:00–9:00, Fri 8:00–5:00, Sat
11:00–7:00
(comprehensive coverage of geographical
area from Laredo to Corpus Christi to
Brownsville, Texas, and the Mexican
states of Tamaulipas, Nuevo Leon, and
Coahuila, Mexico)

University of Utah Marriott Library
(see Utah, Part 2)

Valley Mills History Museum
(Fifth Street and Avenue E—location)
PO Box 168 (mailing address)
Valley Mills, TX 76689
(254) 932-5277

Van Alstyne Public Library
(117 North Waco Street—location)
PO Box 629 (mailing address)
Van Alstyne, TX 75495-0629
(903) 482-5991; (903) 482-1316 FAX
vanalstynepl@texoma.net
http://www.vanalstynepl.lib.tx.us
Juanita Hazelton

Waco-McLennan County Library System
1717 Austin Avenue
Waco, TX 76701-1794
(254) 750-5945 (Genealogy Librarian); (254)
750-5954 (Volunteer Desk); (254) 750-
5946 (Library); (254) 750-5940 FAX
(Library)
bbuckner@ci.waco.tx.us
http://www.waco-
texas.com/city_depts/libraryservices/librar
yservices.htm
Terri Hugo, Librarian, Special Collections;
Bill Buckner, Manager of the
Periodicals/Genealogy Division
Mon–Thur 10:00–9:00, Fri–Sat 10:00–6:00,
Sun 1:00–5:00
(specializes in Texas and genealogy)

Waller County Historical Museum
(4026 Fifth Street—location)
PO Box 235 (mailing address)
Brookshire, TX 77423
(281) 934-2826

**Wallisville Heritage Park Library
(Chambers County)**
(Exit 807 on Interstate 10 East, Wallisville
exit—location)
PO Box 16 (mailing address)
Wallisville, TX 77597-0016
(409) 389-2252; (409) 389-2342 FAX
wallishp@aol.com
Kevin R. Ladd, Director
Mon–Sat 8:00–5:00
Pub. *The Age*, monthly, $20.00 per year
subscription

("This is a private-funded library and
museum which maintains files on some
700 Chambers County families and some
600 historical topics relative to the
county's history. They also have some
2,000 books in their library.")
$20.00 per year membership; search: cost of
photocopies

Wayland Baptist University
Hale County Historical Commission
Museum of the Llano Estacado
1900 West Seventh Street
Plainview, TX 79072
(806) 296-5521
Eddie Guffee, Museum Director

Weatherford Public Library
1014 Charles Street
Weatherford, TX 76086-5098
(817) 598-4150; (817) 598-4161 FAX
ckendrick@ci.weatherford.tx.us
http://www.weatherford.lib.tx.us
Evlyn Broumley, Librarian; C. Kendrick
Mon, Wed & Fri–Sat 10:00–6:00, Tue &
Thur 1:00–9:00

Weslaco Public Library
525 South Kansas Avenue
Weslaco, TX 78596-6215
(956) 968-4533; (956) 969-4069 FAX
Reference@weslaco.lib.tx.us
http://www.weslaco.lib.tx.us
Michael Fisher, Acting Director
Mon–Thur 9:00–9:00, Fri–Sat 9:00–6:00,
Sun 1:00–6:00
("Very limited genealogy collection.")

Western Heritage Center
(see Montana, Part 2)

Western Texas College
Scurry County Museum
6200 College Avenue
Snyder, TX 79549-6105

Wharton County Historical Museum
(3615 North Richmond Road—location)
PO Box 349 (mailing address)
Wharton, TX 77488
(979) 532-2600
Sylvia B. Ellis, Executive Director
Tue–Fri 9:30–noon & 1:00–4:30, Sat
1:00–4:00
(genealogical services)
$25.00 per year membership

Whitesboro Public Library
308 West Main Street
Whitesboro, TX 76273-1639
(903) 564-5432; (903) 564-6105 FAX; (903)
564-6886 FAX
whlibrary@yahoo.com
Priscella Thetford, Library Director
Mon–Fri 9:00–5:30

Wichita County Archives
600 Scott Street, Room 305
Wichita Falls, TX 76301
(940) 766-8137
Lita Watson, Archivist
Tue–Wed 9:00–11:30 & 1:00–4:00
(Wichita County history: people, businesses,
events)
charge for copying and postage

Wichita Falls Public Library
600 11th Street
Wichita Falls, TX 76301-4604
(940) 761-8800; (940) 767-0868, ext. 251;
(940) 767-1058 FAX
pgrc@wfpl.net

http://www.wfpl.net
Andrew C. Jelen, Genealogy Librarian
Tue 11:00–8:00, Wed–Thur 9:00–5:00, Sat
1:00–5:00

Witte Museum
3801 Broadway
San Antonio, TX 78209
(210) 357-1900; (210) 357-1850
(Membership)
witte@wittemuseum.org
http://www.wittemuseum.org
Irma Guerrero, Director of Public Relations
Mon & Wed–Sat 10:00–5:00, Tue
10:00–9:00, Sun noon–5:00
("If genealogists and/or historians, or other
researchers are interested in doing research
in any of the Witte collections or archives,
they may contact us directly. The Witte
Museum has a well-known San Antonio
and South Texas regional collection,
including art, Native American, textiles,
history, photo, and newspaper archives.")
$35.00 per year membership

John H. Wootters Crockett Public Library
(708 East Goliad Avenue, Crockett, TX
75835-2121—location)
PO Box 1226 (mailing address)
Crockett, TX 75835-1226
(936) 544-3089; (936) 544-4139 FAX
shofflib@crockettlibrary.com
http://www.crockettlibrary.com
Marsha Edmiston, Director; Sharlene
Hoffmaster
Tue 9:00–8:00, Wed 9:00–5:00, Thur
9:00–1:00
Pub. *Newsletter*, monthly
research: donation plus $1.00 per page for
copies

Historical Societies—Local and Regional

**American West Research Center and
Historical Society, Inc.**
(see Ohio, Part 2)

**Atascosito Historical Society (Liberty
County)**
PO Box 4003
Liberty, TX 77575-4003
Sandra J. Pickett, President
(Acts as Friends of the Sam Houston
Regional Library and Research Center;
"has no holdings and does not perform
research.")
$5.00 per year membership

Austin County Historical Commission
206 South Masonic Street
Bellville, TX 77418

Heritage Society of Austin, Inc.
(1711 Rio Grande—location)
PO Box 2113 (mailing address)
Austin, TX 78768
(512) 474-5198; (512) 474-2125 FAX
http://www.heritagesocietyaustin.org
Karyn Schroeder, Administrative Assistant
Mon–Fri 8:30–5:30

Bastrop County Historical Society
(702) Main Street—location)
PO Box 279 (mailing address)
Bastrop, TX 78602
(512) 321-6177

**Beaumont Heritage Society (Jefferson
County)**
2985 French Road

Beaumont, TX 77706
(409) 898-0348
Becki Stedman
Tue–Sat 10:00–1:00, Sun 1:00–4:00
Pub. *We're Making History*, quarterly

Bellville Historical Society (Austin County)
PO Box 67
Bellville, TX 77418

Bexar County Historical Commission
233 North Pecos La Trinidad, Suite 420
San Antonio, TX 78207
(210) 270-6581; (210) 270-6713 FAX
Virginia S. Nicholas, Chair
(considers requests for historical markers)

Big Thicket Association
FM-770
PO Box 198
Saratoga, TX 77585
(936) 274-5000

Boerne Area Historical Preservation Society (Kendall County)
(402 Blanco Street—location)
PO Box 178 (mailing address)
Boerne, TX 78006
(830) 249-2030
Betty Thomas, President
Boerne Public Library

Borden County Historical Commission
PO Box 23
Gail, TX 79738

Bosque County Collection
Research Center for Local History
Bosque County Historical Commission
(101 North Main—location)
PO Box 534 (mailing address)
Meridian, TX 76665
(254) 435-6182; (254) 435-2272 FAX
bosquecountycollection@htcomp.net
http://www.htcomp.net/bcc
Elizabeth Torrence, Chair BCHC, Director of Collection
Mon–Tue & Thur 10:00–4:00, Sat 10:00–3:00
Pub. *Bosque Letter*, two times per year
$25.00 per year membership; research: $10.00 per hour, plus $1.00 per page for copies

Bosque Valley Heritage Society
PO Box 168
Valley Mills, TX 76689

Historical Commission (Bracketteville)
PO Box 1791
Brackettville, TX 78832

Brewster County Historical Commission
PO Box 1620
Alpine, TX 79831

Brooks County Historical Commission
604 West Blucher
Falfurrias, TX 78355
Florence Schuetz

Brown County Historical Society
(109 Azalea Drive, Brownwood, TX 76801—location)
PO Box 146 (mailing address)
Brownwood, TX 76804-0146
(915) 646-8208
Pauline G. Hochhalter, Treasurer
(publishes historical books on Brown County)
$4.00 per year membership

Brownsville Historical Association
Stillman House Museum
(1305 East Washington Street—location)
PO Box 846 (mailing address)
Brownsville, TX 78520
(956) 542-3929; (956) 541-5560
Rita Krausse, Acting Executive Director
Museum: Mon–Fri 10:00–noon & 2:00–5:00, Sun 3:00–5:00
Pub. *BHA Newsletter*, bimonthly
(Pierce Collection contains birth, marriage and death records for Mexican towns of Matamoros, Reynosa, Mier and Camargo, 1800–1900)
$12.00 per year membership

Burnet County Heritage Society
(Fort Croghan Grounds and Museum, 703 Buchanan Drive, Highway 29 West—location)
PO Box 74 (mailing address)
Burnet, TX 78611
(512) 756-8281
Thur–Sat 10:00–4:00
$5.00 per year membership

Genealogical and Historical Society of Caldwell County
(see Genealogical Societies—Local and Regional, below)

Calhoun County Historical Commission
(202 South Ann Street—location)
PO Box 988 (mailing address)
Port Lavaca, TX 77979
(361) 553-6342; (361) 553-4689 (Museum); (361) 553-7070 FAX
George Fred Rhodes, Chairman and Curator
Mon–Fri 9:00–5:00; Calhoun County Museum, 301 South Ann Street, Port Lavaca, TX 77979: Tue–Fri 1:30–4:30, Sat 10:00–2:00
free admission to museum

Carson County Historical Commission
PO Box 310
Panhandle, TX 79068
(806) 537-5237
Mrs. J. B. McCray, Chairman

Carson County Historical Survey Committee
Carson County Square House Museum
(Fifth and Elsie Streets—location)
PO Box 276 (mailing address)
Panhandle, TX 79068-0276
(806) 537-3118 (Committee); (806) 537-3524 (Museum)
Don L. Markham, Museum Director

Carza County Historical Museum
111 North Avenue, North
Post, TX 79356
(806) 495-2782
Maxine Earl, Secretary
10:00–noon & 1:00–3:00
("C.W. Post, cereal king, planned our town 1907.")

The Castro Colonies Heritage Association
PO Box 636
Castroville, TX 78009
(210) 931-2564
http://www.rootsweb.com/~txmedina/ccha.htm
(the culture and history of the Castro Colonies of Castroville, Quihi, Vandenburg, and D'Hanis established in Medina County, 1844–1847)
$10.00 per year membership

Chambers County Heritage Society

PO Box 870
Mont Belvieu, TX 77580
(281) 576-2594
Harry Daves, President
(Chambers County history and genealogy)
$5.00 per year membership

Cherokee County Historical Commission
(Wells Fargo Bank Building, Suite 300—location)
PO Box 1128 (mailing address)
Jacksonville, TX 75766
(903) 586-4057
John Allen Templeton, Chairman
Mon, Wed & Fri 10:00–noon & 2:00–4:00
(a unit of the Texas Historical Commission, not involved in genealogy)

Coke County Historical Commission
PO Box 33
Robert Lee, TX 76945
(915) 453-2641
Fran Lomas, Commission Chairman

Collin County Historical Commission
Court House
McKinney, TX 75069
Herb Yoehle, Chairman

Collin County Historical Society, Inc.
Old Post Office Museum
Chestnut at Virginia Streets
McKinney, TX 75069
(972) 542-9457; (972) 377-2949
Elisabeth R. Pink, Director
Tue (May–Sept) 1:00–5:00, first Sat

Collin County Oral History Association
Route 4, Box 149-C
McKinney, TX 75070
(972) 548-4793
L. Gene Richardson, Ph.D., President
(primarily historical, not genealogical)

Collingsworth County Historical Commission
(1307 Bowie—location)
PO Box 169 (mailing address)
Wellington, TX 79095
(806) 447-5496

Comfort Heritage Foundation, Inc.
(Old Comfort Bank Building, High and Seventh Street—archives location)
PO Box 433 (mailing address)
Comfort, TX 78013
(830) 995-3264 (Archivist); (830) 995-5018 (President)
Margaret Morries, Archivist; Don Breithaupt, President
Tue 9:00–noon, and by appointment
("Following restoration of our building we will expand our hours of operation.")
(Historic photographs, documents, etc.; just beginning a genealogy department)
$20.00 per year membership

Cooke County Heritage Society
(210 South Dixon—location)
PO Box 150 (mailing address)
Gainesville, TX 76241
(940) 668-8900
Shana Powell, Curator
Tue–Fri 10:00–5:00

Crockett County Historical, Scientific and Museum Society
(404 11th Street—location)
PO Box 1444 (mailing address)
Ozona, TX 76943
(915) 392-2837
Geniece Childress, Director of Museum
Mon–Fri 9:00–5:00, some Sat 10:00–4:00

The Genealogist's Address Book

research fees vary

Cypress Basin Genealogical and Historical Society (Titus County)
(see Genealogical Socieites—Local and Regional, below)

Dallam-Hartley Counties Historical Association, Inc.
Dallam-Hartley Counties XIT Museum
(108 East Fifth Street—location)
PO Box 710 (mailing address)
Dalhart, TX 79022
(806) 249-5390
Dessie M. Hanburg, Director
Mon–Sat 9:00–5:00

Dallas County Heritage Society, Inc.
Old City Park
1717 Gano Street
Dallas, TX 75215
(972) 653-6238; (972) 421-5141
Thomas H. Smith, Ph.D., Executive Director
Pub. *Legacies*

Dallas County Historical Commission
634 Records Building
Dallas, TX 75202-3504
(972) 653-6714
8:00–4:30
Pub. *County Chronicle*, bimonthly

Dallas Historical Society
(3939 Grand Avenue, Hall of State, Fair Park, Dallas, TX 75210—location)
G. B. Dealey Library
PO Box 150038 (mailing address)
Dallas, TX 75315-0038
(972) 421-4500, ext. 105 (C.O.O.); (972) 421-7500 FAX
frank@dallashistory.org
http://www.dallashistory.org
Frank Wilson, Chief Operating Officer
Pub. *The Register*

Denison Historical Society
530 West Hanna Street
Denison, TX 75020
(903) 465-1075

Denison Library Historical and Genealogical Society
(300 West Gandy, Denison, TX 75020-3153—location)
Route 1, Box 237C (mailing address)
Denison, TX 75021
(903) 465-9447
Vicki E. Hempkins, President
(film and books available)

Denison Public Library
300 West Gandy Street
Denison, TX 75020-3153
(903) 465-1797; (903) 465-1130 FAX
arbailey@texoma.net
http://www.barr.org/denison.htm
Alvin R. Bailey
Mon, Wed & Fri 9:00–6:00, Tue & Thur (school days) 9:00–9:00, Tue & Thur (Memorial Day–Labor Day) 9:00–7:00 Sat 9:00–1:00, Sun 1:00–5:00

Denton County Historical Commission
Courthouse-on-the-Square Museum, Inc.
(First Floor, Historic 1896 Restored Courthouse on the Square, 110 West Hickory, Denton, TX 76201—location)
PO Box 2800 (mailing address)
Denton, TX 76202
(940) 565-8697; (800) 346-3189; (940) 565-8693 FAX
Norma Lynn Gamble, Museum Director

Research facilities and Office: Mon–Fri 8:00–5:00; Exhibit Rooms: Tue–Sat 10:30–4:30
(early newspapers on microfilm, *Pilot Point Post Signal* pre-1925; extensive photograph collection from the 1800s through the 1950s; family histories; cemetery surveys for Denton County)

Historical Society of Denton County
PO Box 50503
Denton, TX 76206-0503
(940) 387-8948
http://www.dentonhistory.org/HSDCPage.html
Mike Cochran, Editor
Pub. *The Denton Review*, occasionally; *The Denton History Page*
$20.00 per year membership

Dimmit County Historical Society
Faren Road
Carrizo Springs, TX 78834
Mr. Bradshaw

Dumas Genealogical and Historical Society
(see Genealogical Societies—Local and Regional, below)

Duncanville Historical Commission, Inc.
(100 East Center—location)
PO Box 280 (mailing address)
Duncanville, TX 75116
(972) 296-1401

East End Historical Association (Galveston County)
PO Box 2424
Galveston, TX 77550

East Texas Historical Association
Department of History
Stephen F. Austin State University
PO Box 6223, Stephen F. Austin Station
Nacogdoches, TX 75962
(936) 468-2407; (936) 468-2190 FAX
AMcDonald@sfasu.edu
http://leonardo.sfasu.edu/etha
Archie P. McDonald, Ph.D., Executive Director and Editor
Mon–Fri 8:00–5:00
Pub. *East Texas Historical Journal*, two times per year (spring and fall)
$25.00 per year membership

El Paso County Historical Commission
PO Box 701
El Paso, TX 79945-9998
(915) 581-1111 (Chairperson's work); (915) 751-3631 (Chairperson's home)
Prestene M. Dehrkoop, Chairperson
meetings second Mon

El Paso County Historical Society
(207 Maricopa Drive—location)
PO Box 28 (mailing address)
El Paso, TX 79940
Lillian Collingwood, Editor
Pub. *Password*, quarterly
(emphasis on west Texas, New Mexico, northern Mexico and eastern Arizona)
$25.00 per year membership

Ennis Heritage Society
PO Box 189
Ennis, TX 75120
Louise McCall, President
Pub. *EHS Newsletter*

Donna Hooks Fletcher Historical Museum
331 South Main Street
Donna, TX 78537

(956) 464-3285

Forney Heritage Society (Kaufman County)
98 FM 2757
PO Box 1292
Forney, TX 75126
(972) 552-3681
Linda F. Harwell, President
Pub. *The Timekeeper*, quarterly
$7.50 per year membership

Fort Clark Historical Society (Kinney County)
PO Box 1061
Brackettville, TX 78832
(830) 563-2709 (Curator)
Sat–Sun 1:00–4:00, and by appointment
(emphasis on U.S. Cavalry, southwestern Texas frontier)

Fort Stockton Historical Society
Riggs Museum
301 South Main
Fort Stockton, TX 79735
(915) 336-2167
ViCindy Riggs, Director/Curator
Mon–Sat 10:00–5:00, Sun 1:30–5:00, Sun (summer) 1:30–8:00
Pub. *Fort Stockton Historical Society Newsletter*, quarterly

Galveston Historical Foundation
502 20th Street
Galveston, TX 77550-2014
(409) 765-7834; (409) 765-7851 FAX
foundation@galvestonhistory.org; marsh.davis@galvestonhistory.org
http://www.galvestonhistory.org
J. Marshall Davis, Executive Director
Pub. *Membership Update*
$40.00 per year membership

Gillespie County Historical Society
312 West San Antonio Street
Fredericksburg, TX 78624
(830) 997-2835
Paul Camfield, Museum Director
Mon–Sat 10:00–5:00, Sun 1:00–5:00
Pub. *GCHS De Trompetour*, quarterly
(no in-depth genealogical archive, holdings are more general in nature)

Gonzales Historical Society
Archives and Records Center
PO Box 77
Gonzales, TX 78629
(830) 672-7970
gonzalesco@gvec.net; leehuff@gvtc.com
http://www.gvec.net/gonzalesco
Aurale Huff
Mon–Fri 9:00–5:00

Grand Prairie Historical Commission
PO Box 534045
Grand Prairie, TX 75051
(972) 264-9536

Grayson County Historical Commission
Room 5, Grayson County Courthouse
Sherman, TX 75090
Clyde L. Hall, Ph.D., Chairman

Gregg County Historical Commission
417 Mobberly Avenue
Longview, TX 75602
(903) 753-5337
Norman W. Black, D.D.S., Chairman

Gregg County Historical Society
PO Box 542
Longview, TX 75606

Grimes County Heritage Association
1215 East Washington Avenue
Navasota, TX 77868

Grimes County Historical Commission
Route 2, Box 3494
Navasota, TX 77868
(936) 894-2520

Hamilton County Historical Society
(113 West Henry—location)
PO Box 106 (mailing address)
Hamilton, TX 76531
(254) 386-3088 (Society President); (254)
386-5631 (Museum President); (254) 386-
4534 (Museum Vice President)
Wesley Jones, President of Historical Society;
Frances Gardner, President of Museum;
Agatha Wiedebusch, Vice President of
Museum
Fri 1:00–4:00, Sat 10:00–noon & 1:00–4:00

Hansford County Historical Commission
(Station Master's House Museum, 30 South
Townsend, Spearman, TX 79081—location)
Box 130 (mailing address)
Gruver, TX 79040
(806) 659-3008; (806) 733-2551
Joel Lee Lackey

Harris County Heritage Society
1100 Bagby
Houston, TX 77002
(713) 655-1912
Jane N. Cable, Director
Pub. *Panorama*

**Hemphill County Historical and
Genealogical Society**
Route 2
Canadian, TX 79014
Mr. and Mrs. John Ramp

Henderson County Historical Commission
(Old Henderson Jail, 201 East Larkin
Street—location)
PO Box 1412 (mailing address)
Athens, TX 75751
(903) 677-7269; (903) 675-6199
http://rootsweb.com/~txhchc/main.htm
Office: Mon–Tue 8:00–4:00, Fri 8:00–noon
Pub. *Henderson County Historical
Commission Newsletter*, monthly (online)
(genealogical records and county records of
Henderson County only; handles referrals
of genealogical research from the
Henderson County Clerk's Office)

Henderson County Historical Society
(217 North Prairieville Street—location)
PO Box 943 (mailing address)
Athens, TX 75751
(903) 677-7269

Hidalgo County Historical Commission
313 Vermont Street
McAllen, TX 78501
(956) 687-4736

Hidalgo County Historical Society
PO Box 81
Edinburg, TX 78540-0081

Hillsboro Heritage League (Hill County)
PO Box 2
Hillsboro, TX 76645

Historic Waco Foundation
407 Columbus Avenue
Waco, TX 76701

Houston County Historical Commission

Courthouse, First Floor
629 North Fourth Street
Crockett, TX 75835
(936) 544-3255, ext. 238; (936) 544-8053
FAX
http://www.io.com/~dwhite/hcbooks.html
Eliza H. Bishop, Researcher
Mon–Fri 10:00–4:00
$10.00 per year membership

**Ingleside-On-The-Bay Historical
Society/Museum**
(475 Starlight at the corner of Ebony at IOB
City Hall—location)
PO Box 514 (mailing address)
Ingleside, TX 78362
(361) 776-2658
Chris Mircovich, Vice President
Mon–Fri 10:00–1:00, second Sun 2:00–5:00
("Partial cemetery records for San Patricio,
Bee, Live Oak, Aransas, Goliad, Nueces,
McMullen and Karnes counties.")
$10.00 per year membership

Jefferson County Historical Commission
(1149 Pearl Street, Beaumont, TX
77701—location)
PO Box 4025 (mailing address)
Beaumont, TX 77704
(409) 835-8701
Susan C. Arceneaux, Coordinator
Mon–Thur 8:00–3:00
Pub. *Jefferson County History News*, four
times per year (not necessarily quarterly)
(Jefferson County history and general Texas
history)
membership is by appointment, but anyone
may be on our mailing list

Jefferson Historical Society and Museum
223 Austin Street
Jefferson, TX 75657
Mrs. E. P. Starie

**Jollyville-Pond Springs Historical
Association**
7203 South Ute Trail
Austin, TX 78729
(512) 258-5688 (Home); (512) 460-1639
(Work); (512) 258-7116 FAX
Gravelady@austin.rr.com
Karen R. Thompson, Author/Historian
(specializes in the history of the Republic of
Texas, 1821–1846)

Karnes County Historical Society
Karnes County Museum at Old Helena
(Highway 81, Courthouse Square—location)
PO Box 162 (mailing address)
Karnes City, TX 78118
(830) 780-3210
Letha McClure, Manager/Curator
Tue–Sat 9:00–5:00
Pub. *Yearly Newsletter*, annually (Oct)
$3.00 per year membership

**Kent County Genealogical and Historical
Society**
(see Genealogical Societies—Local and
Regional, below)

Knox County Historical Commission
(Second Floor of Courthouse—location)
PO Box 124 (mailing address)
Benjamin, TX 79505
(940) 454-2229 voice & FAX
Mary Jane Young, Chairperson
Tue–Fri 8:00–5:00
(family history file, county cemetery survey;
books on Gilliland, Munday, Rhineland
and Truscott communities)
research: $5.00

**Lake Jackson Historical Association
(Brazoria County)**
(249 Circle Way—location)
PO Box 242 (mailing address)
Lake Jackson, TX 77566
(979) 297-1570; (979) 285-0043 FAX
http://lakejacksonmuseum.org
Marla Sweetin Laughlin, Museum Director
Tue–Sat 10:00–4:00, Sun 1:00–5:00
$20.00 per year membership

Leon County Historical Commission
(417 Post Street—location)
PO Box 400 (mailing address)
Centerville, TX 75855
(903) 545-2283
Ruby Johnson, Chairman (History-
Genealogy)

Liberty County Historical Commission
(1710 Sam Houston—library location)
PO Box 334 (mailing address)
Hardin, TX 77561
(936) 298-9202
Kevin R. Ladd, Chairman
no research fees

Lipscomb County Historical Commission
(see Wolf Creek Heritage Museum, below)

**Lower Gulf Coast Genealogical and
Historical Society**
(see Genealogical Societies—Local and
Regional, below)

Lubbock Heritage Society
PO Box 5443
Lubbock, TX 79417

Mason County Historical Society
Mason County Historical Museum
(303 Moody—location)
PO Box 303 (mailing address)
Mason, TX 76856
Mrs. Hilton Moneyhon, Museum Director

Menard County Historical Society
(Menard Museum, Frisco Railroad Depot on
U.S. Highway 83—location)
PO Box 663 (mailing address)
Menard, TX 76859
(325) 396-3074; (325) 396-2245; (325) 396-
2619
http://www.rootsweb.com/~txmenard/
hist/histsoc.htm
$7.50 per year membership

**Mesquite Historical and Genealogical
Society**
Mesquite Public Library
(300 Grubb Drive—location
PO Box 850165 (mailing address)
Mesquite, TX 75185-0165
(972) 216-6229
DStuart101@aol.com
http://www.rootsweb.com/~txmhgs/
page1.htm
Marjorie Bays, Librarian
Mon–Tue & Thur 9:00–9:00, Wed & Fri–Sat
9:00–6:00; meetings: second Thur
(Oct–June) 7:00 P.M.–9:00 P.M.
Pub. *The Mesquite Tree*, quarterly (Mar,
June, Sept, Dec); *Mesquite Historical and
Genealogical Society Newsletter*, monthly
$15.00 per year membership; queries to
Deborah Stuart, Editor, email:
DStuart101@aol.com; research register:
$3.00

Midland County Historical Society
Midland County Historical Commission
2102 Community Lane

Midland, TX 79701
Nancy R. McKinley, President and Chair of
Commission
Midland County Historical Museum:
Mon–Wed, Fri–Sat 2:00–5:00
$10.00+ per year membership; search: $20.00
per hour

Mineral Wells Heritage Association
(201 N.W. Fifth Avenue—location)
400 N.W. Seventh Street (mailing address)
Mineral Wells, TX 76067
Effie Birdwell, Museum Curator
by appointment
("We are a preservation group of the history
of our city.")
$10.00 per year membership

Mission Trail—Los Pueblos Association
453 West Burt
El Paso, TX 79927
(915) 859-6956

Mitchell County Historical Commission
1100 East 10th, #6, Quail Run Apartments
Colorado City, TX 79512
(915) 728-8269
Steve Manning

Monte Vista Historical Association
PO Box 12386
San Antonio, TX 78212
(210) 735-5533

**Montgomery County Genealogical and
Historical Society, Inc.**
(see Genealogical Societies—Local and
Regional, below)

Navarro County Historical Society
912 West Park Avenue
Corsicana, TX 75110
(903) 654-4846
http://www.rootsweb.com/~txnavarr/
historical_society/index.htm

Nederland Historical Society
1903 Atlanta
Nederland, TX 77627
Wanda Weatherford, President

New Braunfels Conservation Society
PO Box 310933
New Braunfels, TX 78130-0933
(830) 625-5593

**Newton County, Texas, Historical
Commission**
(½ block east of Courthouse—location)
PO Box 1383 (mailing address)
Newton, TX 75966
(409) 379-2109
newton@jas.net (subject line: Genealogy)
http://www.jas.net/~newton/links.htm
Pauline Hines; Bonnie Smith, Chairperson
Mon–Fri 9:00–5:00
("Historical Newsletter," a weekly column in
Newton County News)

North Fort Worth Historical Society
131 East Exchange, Suite 110
Fort Worth, TX 76106
(817) 625-5082; (817) 625-5083 FAX
Sue McCafferty, President
Museum, Suite 113: Mon–Fri 10:00–5:00,
Sun 12:30–4:30; Office, Suite 110:
Mon–Fri 10:00–5:00
(operates the Stockyards Museum)

The North Texas Historian
2627 Loftin Road
Windthorst, TX 76389-4641

(940) 423-6426
Jack Loftin
7:00–noon

Old Mageetie Association
(700 Alan Bean—location)
PO Box 189 (mailing address)
Wheeler, TX 79096
(806) 826-3289

**Old Mobeetie Association of Mobeetie Jail
Museum**
Old Town
Mobeetie, TX 79061
(806) 845-3401
Dale Corcoran, President
(Early Panhandle family histories and
museum; archives also includes records of
Czech Poban community)
$5.00 per year membership

Orange County Historical Commission
1301 Park Avenue
Orange, TX 77630
(409) 886-1312; (409) 886-0450 FAX
Howard C. Williams, M.D., P.A., Chairman
Pub. *Las Sabinas*, four times per year
(large collection of Orange County photos
and historical material, WW II ship
building, many DDs & DEs)
$15.00 per year membership

Orange County Historical Society
PO Box 1345
Orange, TX 77630-1345
(409) 883-2925
Juanita Toronjo, Treasurer
Pub. *Las Sabinas*, quarterly, $6.00 per issue
$20.00 per year membership

Palacios Area Historical Association
(401 Commerce Street—location)
PO Box 11 (mailing address)
Palacios, TX 77465
(361) 972-1148; (361) 972-2270; (361) 972-
3960
Colleen Claybourn, Chair
Museum: Fri 2:00–5:00, and by appointment
Pub. *Newsletter*, quarterly
("We have begun genealogy files at the
museum: clippings, photos, letters, etc.";
"local military, LaSalle's 'LaBelle' site,
commercial fishing.")
$10.00 per year membership; search fees:
very economical—usually free

Palo Pinto County Historical Association
(two blocks south Highway 180, N.E.
Courthouse corner—location)
PO Box 105 (mailing address)
Mineral Wells, TX 76067-4226
(940) 653-2555
Ann Reagan, Secretary
June–Aug: Sat–Sun 2:00–4:00, tours by
appointment only; meetings in County 4-
H Building
$5.00 per year membership

**Panhandle-Plains Historical Society
(Randall County)**
Panhandle-Plains Historical Museum
(2503 Fourth Avenue—location)
PO Box 6067, W. T. Station (mailing
address)
Canyon, TX 79016
(806) 651-2274; (806) 656-2250 FAX
museum@wtamu.edu
http://www.wtamu.edu/museum
Betty L. Bustos, Assistant Archivist
Museum: Mon–Fri 9:00–noon & 1:00–5:00
Pub. *Panhandle-Plains Historical Review*
(northwest Texas), annually (Feb), $20.00

per copy, back issues available
$20.00 per year membership

Panola County Historic Foundation, Inc.
100 East Sabine
Carthage, TX 75633
(903) 693-8689
Corcy Bankhead, President
Mon–Fri 8:00–5:00
Pub. *Heritage Gazette*, annually; *Texas Tea
Room Tidbits*, weekly (not included in
membership)

Permian Historical Society
University of Texas of the Permian Basin
4901 West University
Odessa, TX 79762-0001
(915) 552-2381
Bobbie Jean Klepper, Archivist
Mon, Wed & Fri 8:00–noon & 1:00–5:00,
Thur 8:00–noon & 1:00–10:00, shortened
hours between semesters, closed weekends
and all university holidays
Pub. *Permian Historical Annual*
(Permian Basin includes Andrews, Crane,
Crockett, Culberson, Ector, Gaines,
Glasscock, Howard, Loving, Martin,
Midland, Mitchell, Pecos, Reagan, Reeves,
Upton, Ward, and Winker counties, Texas,
and Lea County, New Mexico; archival
collection, housed in the UTPB library,
contains "records, documents,
photographs, biographical data and other
historical material and books to benefit the
student researcher, scholar, genealogist,
and history buff.")
$10.00 per year membership

Peters Colony Historical Society
PO Box 110846
Carrollton, TX 75011
John England, President
Pub. *Elm Fork Echoes*, semiannually, $6.36
per issue postpaid, including tax
(specializes in northwest quadrant of Dallas
County, Texas)

Polk County Heritage Society
120 Mockingbird Lane
Livingston, TX 77351
(936) 327-5945

Reagan County Historical Association
Hickman Library and Museum
(609 Main Street—location)
PO Box 66 (mailing address)
Big Lake, TX 76932
(915) 884-2082
Ann Schneemann, Chairman
Wed afternoons and special events

Refugio County Historical Society
Refugio County Museum
102 West Street
Refugio, TX 78377
(361) 526-5555
Maxine Reilly, Director
Tue–Fri 9:00–5:00, Sat 1:00–5:00
$10.00 per year membership

Roberts County Historical Commission
Roberts County Museum
(Highway 60—location)
PO Box 306 (mailing address)
Miami, TX 79059
(806) 868-3291
Tue–Fri 10:00–5:00, Sun 2:00–5:00
(specialty: "THS-TAM-NWTMA")

Roscoe Historical Society
PO Box 421
Roscoe, TX 79545

Billy Joe Jay

Rusk County Historical Foundation
(514 North High Street—location)
PO Box 1773 (mailing address)
Henderson, TX 75652
(903) 657-2261
William Ashby, President
Mon–Fri 1:00–5:00
(emphasis on Texas, Georgia and other states)
no fee

Salado Historical Society (Bell County)
PO Box 251
Salado, TX 76571
Patricia L. Barton, President
(not a genealogical group)

San Angelo Genealogical and Historical Society, Inc.
(see Genealogical Societies—Local and Regional, below)

San Antonio Conservation Society
107 King William Street
San Antonio, TX 78204-1399
(210) 224-6163; (210) 224-6163 FAX
conserve@saconservation.org
Bruce MacDougal, Executive Director

San Antonio Genealogical and Historical Society
(see Genealogical Societies—Local and Regional, below)

San Jacinto County Historical Commission and Heritage Society
PO Box 505
Coldspring, TX 77331
(936) 653-2009

The Heritage Association of San Marcos, Inc.
(308 East Hopkins Street—location)
PO Box 1806 (mailing address)
San Marcos, TX 78667-1806
(512) 392-9997; (512) 393-3735 FAX
http://www.centuryinter.net/smheritage
Frances E. Stovall, Coordinator Heritage Tourism
Pub. *Heritage Highlites*, quarterly
(maintains a house museum)
$25.00 per year membership

Santa Fe Area Historical Foundation, Inc.
(11225 Texas Highway 6—location)
PO Box 275 (mailing address)
Santa Fe, TX 77517
(409) 925-3009
third Sun 2:00–5:00, special events, and by appointment
("The Depot Museum of the Towns Along the Santa Fe; extensive pictorial files of West Galveston County, 1890–ca 1950")

Schleicher County Historical Society
PO Box 473
Eldorado, TX 76936

Sherman County Historical Society
(17 North Main—location)
PO Box 1248 (mailing address)
Stratford, TX 79084
(806) 396-2582
annpwells@yahoo.com
Mon–Fri 8:00–noon & 2:00–4:00, and by appointment

Smith County Historical Society, Inc.
Carnegie History Center
125 South College Avenue
Tyler, TX 75702

(903) 592-5993; (972) 593-7989 (History Center)
Jack Pollard, President
Wed & first Sat 1:00–4:30
Pub. *Chronicles of Smith County, Texas*, semiannually
$15.00 per year membership or subscription

Smithville Heritage Society
602 Main Street
Smithville, TX 78957
(512) 237-4545

The Sophienburg-New Braunfels Archives and Museum of History
401 West Coll Street
New Braunfels, TX 78130
(830) 629-1572 (Museum); (830) 629-1900 (Archives); (830) 629-3906 FAX (Museum); (830) 608-0825 FAX (Archives)
http://www.nbtx.com/sophienburg
Michelle Oatman, Executive Director; Becky Lombardo, Manager of Archives
Archives: Mon–Fri 10:00–4:00, Museum: Mon–Sat 10:00–5:00, Sun 1:00–5:00
(holds collection of the Comal County Genealogy Society)
$15.00 per year membership; admission: $5.00 for adults; research or translation services: $10.00 per hour; photographic reproduction: prices vary

Southeast Texas Genealogical and Historical Society
(see Genealogical Societies—Local and Regional, below)

Southern Studies Institute
(see Louisiana, Part 2)

Starr County Historical Society
601 East Main
Rio Grande City, TX 78582
(956) 487-4839
Dr. Bruno M. Trevino
8:00–6:00

State Association of Texas Pioneers
(3805 Broadway—location)
137 West Mayfield (mailing address)
San Antonio, TX 78221-1202
(210) 822-9011

Stephens County Historical Association
201 North Harding
Breckenridge, TX 76024

The Sugar Land Heritage Society
302 Oyster Creek
Sugar Land, TX 77478
(281) 494-3485
Mrs. Walter S. McMeans, President
(emphasis on Sugar Land and Fort Bend County)
$3.00 per year membership

Tarrant County Historical Society
3724 Cresthaven Terrace
Fort Worth, TX 76107
(817) 625-1881

Taylor Conservation and Heritage Society (Williamson County)
PO Box 385
Taylor, TX 76574

Terrell County Historical Commission
PO Box 7
Sanderson, TX 79848
(915) 345-2648 (President); (915) 345-2285 (Corresponding Secretary); (915) 345-

2177 (Staff Person)
http://www.abilene.com/taylorhist
Patty Phillips, President; Margaret Farley, Corresponding Secretary; Carolyn Hutto, Staff Person
Mon–Fri 1:00–5:00, Sat–Sun 3:00–5:00

Texana Heritage Society
Texana Presbyterian Church
501 Apollo Drive
Edna, TX 77957
(361) 782-3400

Texas City Heritage Association
PO Box 2091
Texas City, TX 77590
(409) 948-3411

Texas Gulf Coast Historical Association
Department of History
University of Houston
Houston, TX 77004
(713) 749-4680

Texas Gulf Historical Society
Goodhue Building
PO Box 1621
Beaumont, TX 77704
(409) 833-0817
W. S. Shepherd, Secretary and Treasurer
Pub. *Texas Gulf Historical and Biographical Record*, annually (Dec), $10.00 per issue
$15.00 per year membership

Texas Old Missions and Forts Association
7617 Woodthrush Drive
Dallas, TX 75230-4860

Texas Wendish Heritage Society
(see Ethnic Archives, Libraries and Societies—German, Part 3)

Tom Green County Historical Preservation League
PO Box 1625
San Angelo, TX 76902

Tom Green County Historical Society
PO Box 5602
San Angelo, TX 76902-5602
(915) 942-2164
Barbara Barton, President
meetings at Fort Concho NHS, Officers Quarter #8: third Mon (Jan–Oct)
$10.00 per year membership

Trinity County Historical Commission
PO Box 386
Trinity, TX 75862

Truscott Historical Preservation Association
Truscott, TX 79260
(940) 474-3339
Margaret Daniel, Chairman
Pub. *Between the Wichitas*

Tyler County Heritage Society/Whitmeyer Genealogy Library
Heritage Village Museum
(Highway 190 West—location)
PO Box 888 (mailing address)
Woodville, TX 75979
(409) 283-2272; (409) 283-2194 FAX
Ofeira A. Gazzaway, Director
Tue, Thur & Sat 10:00–2:00
(published *Sketches of Tyler County, Gravestone Inscriptions, Tyler County Census*, and more)
$20.00 per year membership

Uvalde County Historical Commission

141 Bluebonnet, South
Uvalde, TX 78801
(830) 278-2193

Van Alstyne Historical Society Museum
(216 East Jefferson—location)
PO Box 1552 (mailing address)
Van Alstyne, TX 75495-1552
(903) 482-5877
http://www.vanalstynepl.lib.tx.us/
historical_society.htm
Ruth-Lee Cason, Secretary
May–Sept: Tue & Thur 2:00–4:00, Sat
noon–2:00, and by appointment
$6.00 per year membership

Victoria County Historical Commission
210 East Forrest
Victoria, TX 77901
(361) 575-5210
Charles Spurliz, Chairman

Waller County Historical Commission
PO Box 1099
Waller, TX 77484
(936) 826-3617 (Chairman)
lynpete@earthlink.net
http://home.earthlink.net/~lynpete/wchc. html
Richard L. Senasac, Chairman; Lynwood
Peterson, Webmaster
(operates museum and has an extensive list of
publications, many of which would be of
genealogical interest)

Waller County Historical Society, Inc.
PO Box 971
Waller, TX 77484
(936) 826-3617 (President)
Richard L. Senasac, President
(financial arm of Waller County Historical
Commission; no museum or publishing
program, concentrates on research and
restoration)

Webb County Heritage Foundation
(500 Flores Avenue—location)
PO Box 446 (mailing address)
Laredo, TX 78042-0446
(956) 727-0977
Margarita Araiza, Interim Director
8:30–5:00
Pub. *The Heritage Register*, quarterly
$25.00 per year membership

Weimar Heritage Society/Museum
125 East Main Street
Weimar, TX 78962
(979) 725-8203

West Texas Historical Association
Hardin-Simmons University
PO Box 16172
Abilene, TX 79698
(915) 677-8351
Dr. B. W. Aston, Executive Director
Mon–Fri 8:00–5:00
Pub. *WTHA Year Book*, annually (Nov)
$15.00 per year membership

White Settlement Historical Society
214 Meadow Park Road
White Settlement, TX 76108
(817) 246-4971

Whiteface Historical Society
(Second and Taylor—location)
403 Fillmore (mailing address)
Whiteface, TX 79379
(806) 287-1318
Ken Darnell, Secretary/Treasurer
by appointment
("General museum.")
$5.00 per year membership

Wichita County Heritage Society
900 Bluff
Wichita Falls, TX 76301
(940) 723-0623

Wise County Historical Society, Inc.
(Wise County Heritage Museum, 1602 South
Trinity—location)
PO Box 427 (mailing address)
Decatur, TX 76234
(940) 627-5586; (940) 627-3732
wisemuseum@ntws.net
Rosalie Gregg, Director
Mon–Sat 9:00–4:00, Sun 1:30–5:00
Pub. *Wise County Historical Commission
and Wise County Historical Society
Newsletter*, ten times per year (monthly,
except Aug & Dec)
(collection of research material: census
records, newspapers, county histories,
birth, marriage and death records, books
on Lost Battalion)
$10.00 per year membership; admission: free
for members; research: $1.00 for first
hour, 50¢ for each additional hour;
copies: 25¢ each

**Wolf Creek Heritage Museum/Lipscomb
County Historical Commission**
(Highway 305 and Main Street—location)
PO Box 5
Lipscomb, TX 79056
(806) 852-2123
Mildred Becker, Director
Mon, Wed & Fri 10:00–4:00, Sun 2:00–4:00
("*Lipscomb County History, German Family,
Cemetery Register, Military Memorials,
Historical Society Reprints [1967-83]*,
$24.50 ppd. 1800 newspaper on
microfiche.")
research: $5.00 per hour

Yoakum County Historical Commission
PO Box 960
Plains, TX 79355

**Yorktown Historical Society (De Witt
County)**
Yorktown Historical Museum
(Main and Eckhardt Streets—location)
Route 2, Box 123-C-1 (mailing address)
Yorktown, TX 78164
(361) 564-2174 (President)
Mrs. Kurt Hartmann, President
Thur & Sun 2:30–4:30
(artifacts, books, antiques, etc., depicting
local history; published book, *Yorktown,
Its History, 1848–1989*)

Zapata County Historical Commission
La Paz Museum
A. L. Benavides Elementary School
PO Box 219
San Ygnacio, TX 78067
(956) 765-5611

Genealogical Societies

State Genealogical Society

Southern Society of Genealogists, Inc.
(see Alabama, Part 2)

Texas State Genealogical Society (TSGS)
2505 Beluche Drive
Galveston 77551-1503
(409) 744-4359 (President)
Bdunquez@aol.com;
tlbowers@orbitworld.net
http://www.rootsweb.com/~txsgs
Betty Hendricks Dunquez, President
10:00–5:00

Pub. *Stirpes*, quarterly; *Texas State
Genealogical Society Newsletter*
(Sponsors Texas First Families Certificate)
$20.00 per year membership

Genealogical Societies—Local & Regional

Amarillo Genealogical Society
Amarillo Public Library
(413 East Fourth Street, Amarillo, TX
79101—location)
PO Box 2171 (mailing address)
Amarillo, TX 79189-2171
(806) 378-4211 (Special Collections
Department)
Rob Groman, Head of Special Collections
Department
Library: Mon–Thur 9:00–9:00, Fri–Sat
9:00–6:00, Sun 2:00–6:00
Pub. *The Reflector*, quarterly
$10.00 per year membership

Ancestor Club
PO Box 228
Winnie, TX 77665-0228
Mr. Silva

Anderson County Genealogical Society
PO Box 2045
Palestine, TX 75802-2045
bonniew@e-tex.com
$15.00 per year membership

Angelina County Genealogical Society
PO Box 150631
Lufkin, TX 75915-0631
Delbert Richardson, President
Pub. *Echoes Through the Pines*
$7.50 per year membership

Ark-La-Tex Genealogical Association, Inc.
(see Arkansas, Part 2)

**Arlington Genealogical Society (Tarrant
County)**
Arlington Public Library
101 East Abram Street
Arlington, TX 76010-1183
njdnord@flash.net
http://www.rootsweb.com/~txags/ags.htm
Dale Nordstrom, Secretary
meetings: second Tue 6:30
Pub. *Newsletter*, monthly
$15.00 per year membership

**Atascosa County Genealogical Society
Library**
(Aigner-Mummee Memorial Building, Fourth
and H Avenue—location)
PO Box 93 (mailing address)
Poteet, TX 78065
(830) 276-4684
acgsl@hillcountry.net; acgsli@aol.com
http://members.aol.com/poteetlib/gen/
index.html

Athens Genealogical Organization
c/o C. W. M. Memorial Library
121 South Prairieville Street
Athens, TX 75751
(903) 675-2694
Mary Lee Barnes, Editor
Library: Mon–Fri 10:00–6:00, Sat 9:00–1:00
Pub. *Texas AGO*, two times per year
(Henderson County, Texas, records)
$12.00 per year membership for nonresidents;
research: $10.00 per hour

Austin Genealogical Society
PO Box 10010
Austin, TX 78766-1010
president@austintxgensoc.org

http://www.austintxgensoc.org
meetings at Covenant Presbyterian Church,
3003 Northland Drive, Austin, TX 78731:
fourth Tue (Jan–July & Sept–Oct) & third
Tue (Nov) 7:30
Pub. *Austin Genealogical Society Quarterly*;
Austin Genealogical Society Newsletter,
irregularly
$16.00 per year membership

Bay Area Genealogical Society
PO Box 891447
Houston, TX 77289-1447
president@TxBayAreaGen.org
http://www.rootsweb.com/~txbags/
baygen.html
Ron Cox, President
Pub. *Quarterly*
(Harris and Galveston counties)

Baytown Genealogical Society
PO Box 2486
Baytown, TX 77522
(281) 479-3244
Victoria L. Klehn, President
Sterling Municipal Library: Mon–Thur
10:00–9:00, Fri–Sat 10:00–6:00
Pub. *Baytown Genealogical Society
Newsletter*, monthly
$10.00 per year membership

Big Bend Genealogical Society
PO Box 1251
Alpine, TX 79831
reprevin@hotmail.com
http://www.rootsweb.com/~txbcgs
Suzy Ervin, President

Genealogical Society of the Big Spring
Howard County Library
Fourth and Scurry Streets
Big Spring, TX 79720
Pub. *Signal Peak*, monthly

Brazos Genealogical Association
PO Box 5493
Bryan, TX 77805-5493
holt@cy-net.net
http://users.txcyber.com/~bga/index.html
Trey Holt, Vice President
Pub. *Brazos Genealogist*, quarterly
$20.00 per year membership

Brazosport Genealogical Society
Brazosport College Library
PO Box 813
Lake Jackson, TX 77566
dpugh@brazosport.cc.tx.us
http://www.brazosport.cc.tx.us/~gensoc
Dr. Don Pugh, President
(some publication of local records)
$12.00 per year membership

Burkburnett Genealogical Society
Burkburnett Library
215 East Fourth Street
Burkburnett, TX 76354-3446
(940) 569-2991
G. Thomas Fairclough, Librarian
Tue–Fri 11:30–6:00, Sat 10:00–2:00

Burnet County Genealogical Society
c/o Herman Brown Free Library
Burnet County Library System
J. Frank Dobie Room
100 East Washington Street
Burnet, TX 78611
(512) 756-2328
genealogy@281.com
http://www.rootsweb.com/~txburnet/
announce.htm#GenSoc
Edna Hood Cheatham, Editor

Library: Mon–Fri 10:00–6:00; meetings:
third Thur 10:15
Pub. *Burnet County Genealogical Society
Newsletter*, quarterly
$8.00 per year membership

**Genealogical and Historical Society of
Caldwell County**
Luling Public Library
215 South Pecan Avenue
Luling, TX 78648
(830) 875-9466
ccg&hsoc@bcsnet.net
http://www.rootsweb.com/~txcaldwe/
socpage.htm
Eva Wilson, Editor
Pub. *Plum Creek Almanac*, semiannually
(May, Nov), $9.00 for the current issue,
$8.00 for back issues
$18.00 per year membership

Calhoun County Genealogical Society
PO Box 299
Port Lavaca, TX 77979-0299
(361) 552-2588
Pub. *Karankawa Kountry*, semiannually
$10.00 per year membership

Camp County Genealogical Society
(102 Quitman Street, Garrett/Shelby
Building—location)
PO Box 1083 (mailing address)
Pittsburg, TX 75686
(903) 856-2062
Kinard75@cs.com
http://www.rootsweb.com/~txccgs/
members.htm
Glenda Kinard, President
meetings: fourth Tue 7:00 P.M.
Pub. *Rear View Notes*, quarterly
$15.00 per year membership; free queries in
periodical

Cass County Genealogical Society
PO Box 880
Atlanta, TX 75551-0880
(903) 796-2107
cass_tx_gen_soc@yahoo.com
http://homepages.rootsweb.com/
~danasite/CCGS
Patsy R. Livingston, President
Mon–Fri 10:00–5:30, Sat 10:00–2:00
Pub. *Cass County Connections*, four times
per year (Mar, June, Oct, Dec)
(county cemetery books, county records)
$12.00 per year membership

Central Texas Genealogical Society
Waco-McLennan County Library System
1717 Austin Avenue
Waco, TX 76701
pasd@mindspring.com
http://www.rootsweb.com/~txmclenn/
ctgs.htm
meetings: fourth Mon 7:00 P.M.
Pub. *Heart of Texas Records*, four times per
year (Apr, June, Sept, Jan)
$15.00 per year membership

**Chaparral Genealogical Society and
Library**
(310 North Live Oak, Tomball, TX
77375—location)
PO Box 606 (mailing address)
Tomball, TX 77377
(281) 255-9081
society@chaparraltx.org
Janis Duhe, Trustee
Mon–Wed & Sat 10:00–3:00

Cherokee County Genealogical Society
PO Box 1332

Jacksonville, TX 75766
(903) 586-0135 (Editor); (903) 743-5443
(President)
ccgs@tyler.net
http://www.tyler.net/ccgs/default.html
Gordon Bennett, Editor; Williams H. Hermes,
President
Pub. *Tree Talk*, quarterly
(publishes genealogical or historical material
from Cherokee County)
$12.00 per year membership; limited
research: may be available for a nominal
fee

Childress County Genealogical Society
117 Avenue B, N.E.
Childress, TX 79201
(940) 937-8421 voice & FAX
Cecil Mills, Assistant Librarian
Mon–Fri 12:30–5:30

Clayton Library Friends
PO Box 271078
Houston, TX 77277-1078
erootrot@usa.net
http://www.hpl.lib.tx.us/clayton/CLF.html
Elizabeth Nitschke Hicks, Angel Chair; Don
Pusch, Treasurer
Pub. *CLF (Clayton Library Friends)
Newsletter*, quarterly (Feb, May, Aug,
Nov)
("largest genealogical group in Texas—five
years in a row")
$10.00 per year membership

Coastal Bend Genealogical Society
PO Box 2826
Corpus Christi, TX 78480
acostell@stx.rr.com
http://www.rootsweb.com/~txcbgs/cbgs.htm
Katie Costello, Corresponding Secretary
meetings at the Corpus Christi Science and
History Museum, 1900 North Chaparral
(under the bridge next to the shipping
channel): second Sat (odd-numbered
months) 2:00
Pub. *Reflections*, quarterly
$15.00 per year membership

Collin County Genealogical Society
PO Box 865052
Plano, TX 75086-5052
(972) 596-3567
ccgs_nl_editor@hotmail.com
http://www.rootsweb.com/~txcolcgs
Aurora Chancy, Editor
meetings in Plano Public Library System,
Gladys L. Harrington Public Library:
second Wed (Aug–May) 7:30; Collin
County Genealogical Society Computer
User's Group meetings: fourth Wed 7:30
Pub. *Collin Chronicles*, quarterly; *Collin
County Genealogical Society Newsletter*,
bimonthly
$18.00 per year membership

Comal County Genealogy Society
(Sophienburg Museum and Archives,
Research Room—location)
PO Box 310160 (mailing address)
New Braunfels, TX 78131-0160
(830) 629-1572 (Sophienburg Museum and
Archives)
Alton Rahe, President
Archives: Mon–Fri 10:00–4:00
Pub. *Family Footsteps*, three times per year
(Mar, July, Nov)
(German/Texas research Comal County and
other German settlements in Texas)
$15.00 per year membership; research: $5.00
minimum

Coryell County Genealogical Society
Gatesville Public Library
811 Main Street
Gatesville, TX 76528
http://www.rootsweb.com/~txcoryel
Faye McCracken
Pub. *Coryell Kin*, quarterly
$12.50 per year membership

Cottle County Genealogical Society
PO Box 1005
Paducah, TX 79248

Cross Timbers Genealogical Society
PO Box 197
Gainesville, TX 76241
Wanda Fleitman, President
meetings at Cooke County Library: first Mon
    (Feb–June, Aug & Oct–Dec), first Tue
    (Sept)
Pub. *Cross Timbers' Post*, quarterly (Mar,
    June, Sept, Dec)
(Cooke County, Texas, and some surrounding
    counties)
$10.00 per year membership; queries: free

**Cypress Basin Genealogical and Historical
Society (Titus County)**
PO Box 403
Mount Pleasant, TX 75455
Billy F. Walker, President
meetings second Thur
Pub. *Cypress Basin Genealogical and
    Historical Society Reporter*, three times
    per year
$10.00 per year membership

Dallas County East Genealogical Society
7637 Mary Dan Drive
Dallas, TX 75217-4603
Pub. *Texas Kin*, three times per year
$10.00 per year membership

Dallas Genealogical Society
PO Box 12446
Dallas, TX 75225-0446
(469) 948-1106
info@dallasgenealogy.org
http://www.dallasgenealogy.org
meetings in the auditorium of the J. Erik
    Jonsson Library, 1515 Young Street
Pub. *The Dallas Quarterly*; *Dallas
    Genealogical Society Newsletter*,
    bimonthly
(sponsors African American Network Group,
    Latin-American Interest Group, Computer
    Interest Group and Professional Interest
    Group)
$18.00 per year membership

Deaf Smith County Genealogical Society
Deaf Smith County Library
211 East Fourth Street
Hereford, TX 79045

**Denison Library Historical and
Genealogical Society**
(see Historical Societies—Local and
Regional, above)

Denton County Genealogical Society
PO Box 424707
Denton, TX 76204
(940) 387-4741
Diana White; Holly Hervey
Denton Public Library
$10.00 per year membership; research:
    $30.00 for two hours

Donley County Genealogical Society
PO Box 116
Clarendon, TX 79226

Dumas Genealogical and Historical Society
127 Oak Avenue
Dumas, TX 79029

East Bell County Genealogical Society
3219 Meadow Oaks Drive
Temple, TX 76502-1752
(254) 778-2073 (President)
http://www.rootsweb.com/~txebcgs
Wanda Donaldson, President
meetings at Temple Public Library: third Tue
(Texas State Genealogical Society, Partner
    Society Member)
$12.00 per year membership

East Texas Genealogical Society
PO Box 6967
Tyler, TX 75711-6967
(903) 592-6576 (President's work); (903)
    592-6782 FAX (President)
scottfitzgerald@tyler.net (President);
    marylove@tyler.net (Webmaster)
http://www.rootsweb.com/~txetgs
Scott Fitzgerald, President; Sunshine
    Knowles, Corresponding Secretary; Mary
    Love Berryman, Webmaster
Mon–Fri 8:00–5:00
Pub. *East Texas Family Records* (*EFTR*),
    quarterly; *Newsletter: The Bulletin*,
    monthly
(publishes books on East Texas family
    records covering six counties: Anderson,
    Gregg, Henderson, Panola, Rusk and
    Smith counties)
$12.00 per year membership; queries: free

El Paso Genealogical Society
El Paso Public Library
501 North Oregon Street
El Paso, TX 79901-1193
dot@whc.nt
http://www.rootsweb.com/~txepgs
meetings at All Saints Episcopal Church
    Parish Hall, 3500 McRae: second Thur
    7:00
Pub. *Rio Grande Researcher*, quarterly
(emphasis on southwest genealogy: Arizona,
    southern California, New Mexico, Texas)
$12.00 per year membership

Ellis County Genealogical Society
PO Box 479
Waxahachie, TX 75168-0479
sylsmith@azmail.net
http://www.rootsweb.com/~txellis/esoc.htm
Sylvia Smith, President
meetings at the Ellis County Woman's
    Building, 407 West Jefferson Street: first
    Mon 7:00
Pub. *Searchers and Researchers*, quarterly
    (Mar, June, Sept, Dec), $3.00 per issue
$16.00 per year membership; research: no
    research but will send list of local
    professionals

Erath County Genealogical Society
c/o Dublin Public Library
206 West Blackjack Street
Dublin, TX 76446
janice@htcomp.net
http://www.rootsweb.com/~txerath/
    gene_soc_temp.htm
meetings at the First American Bank, 2207
    West Washington, Stephenville, TX:
    second Thur 6:30
Pub. *The Cross Timbers Historian*
$15.00 per year membership

Fannin County Genealogical Society
605 Agnew
Bonham, TX 75418
Pub. *Fannin County Genealogical Quarterly*

Five Hills Genealogical Society
PO Box 1723
Copperas Cove, TX 76522
gballentine@hot.rr.com
http://www.rootsweb.com/~txfhgs
George H. Ballentine, Newsletter Editor
meetings in the Grace United Methodist
    Church, 101 West Avenue F, Copperas
    Cove: third Thur 6:30

Fort Belknap Genealogical Association
Murray Route
Graham, TX 76046
Barbara Ledbetter
Pub. *Fort Belknap Genealogical Association
    Bulletin*, semiannually

Fort Brown Genealogical Society
608 East Adams
Brownsville, TX 78520
(956) 542-4824

Fort Worth Genealogical Society (FWGS)
PO Box 9767
Fort Worth, TX 76147-0767
(817) 457-3330
khopkins@fortworthlibrary.org
http://www.rootsweb.com/~txfwgs
Kenneth Hopkins, Librarian
Pub. *Footprints*, quarterly (Feb, May, Aug,
    Nov); untitled newsletter, eleven times per
    year (monthly, except Dec)
("Source material-Tarrant County and
    surrounding counties, including Bible
    records, court records, misc. genealogical
    materials"; sponsors Computer Users
    Group)
$23.00 per year membership; queries; free
    with Texas connection

Franklin County Genealogical Society
(Genealogical Research Room, 110 East
Main Street on the Square—location)
PO Box 1563 (mailing address)
Mount Vernon, TX 75457
(903) 537-3931
fcgensoc@mt-vernon.com
http://www. mt-
    Vernon.com/~skelly/pages/gensoc.htm
Mon–Fri 10:00–4:00, Sat 10:00–2:00;
    meetings: second Mon 7:00
$15.00 per year membership

The Fredericksburg Genealogical Society
108 North Edison Street
Fredericksburg, TX 78624-0164
(830) 990-4045
thesociety@fbgtxgensoc.org
http://www.fbgtxgensoc.org

Freestone County Genealogical Society
(East side of Square—location)
PO Box 14 (mailing address)
Fairfield, TX 75840
(903) 389-2292
http://www.rootsweb.com/~txfreest/fcgs/
    index.htm
Lena Bonner, Vice President
by appointment; meetings at City Hall:
    second Mon
Pub. *Freestone Frontiers*, quarterly (Feb,
    May, Aug, Nov), $3.50 per issue (for back
    issues)
$12.50 per year membership

Galveston County Genealogical Society
PO Box 1141
Galveston, TX 77553
(409) 744-4359 (First Vice-President)
bdunquez@aol.com
http://www.rootsweb.com/~txgalves/gcgs.
    htm

Betty Hendricks Dunquez, First Vice-
President
meetings at the Rosenberg Library: first Thur
7:00
$7.00 per year membership

Garland Genealogical Society
PO Box 461882
Garland, TX 75046-1882
ljdolby@prodigy.net
http://www.geocities.com/TheTropics/
1926/society.html
Linda-Jeanne Dolby
(disbanded 2001, but web site still active)

German-Texan Heritage Society
(507 East 10th Street—location)
PO Box 684171 (mailing address)
Austin, TX 78768-4171
(512) 482-0927
info@GermanTexans.org
http://www.gths.net
Teresa Chavez, Director; Theresa G. Gold,
Genealogy Editor
Mon–Fri 8:00–4:30
Pub. *Journal*, three times per year;
Newsletter, three times per year
("Preservation of German heritage in Texas;
German-Texan family histories; we are in
the process of building a library for
historians and genealogists.")
$10.00 per year membership; research: free
for members, $10.00 for nonmembers

Gilmer Genealogical Society
West Pine Street
Gilmer, TX 75644

Grand Prairie Genealogical Society
PO Box 532026
Grand Prairie, TX 75053-2026
meetings at St. Andrews Episcopal Church,
Seventh and Hill Streets: first Thur 6:30

Grapevine Name-Droppers
Grapevine Public Library
1201 South Main
Grapevine, TX 76051-5545
(817) 267-1645 (Coordinator); (817) 481-
0424 FAX
Frances P. Malcolm, Coordinator
meetings: second Mon 10:00–12:30

Grayson County Genealogical Society
Sherman Public Library
Local History and Genealogy Department
421 North Travis
Sherman, TX 75090-5975
Pub. *Bulletin*, irregularly
$10.00 per year membership

Gregg County Genealogy Society
(Longview Public Library, 222 West Cotton,
Longview, TX 75601—location)
PO Box 2985 (mailing address)
Longview, TX 75606-2985
(903) 237-1350
http://www.chrysalis.org/DallasGen.So/
gcgs.htm
Library: Mon, Wed & Thur–Fri 9:00–noon &
1:00–6:00
Pub. *Gregg County Genealogy Society*,
monthly
$15.00 per year membership

Guadalupe County Genealogical Society
Seguin/Guadalupe County Public Library
707 East College Street
Seguin, TX 78155
(830) 379-1531; (830) 488-2337 (Treasurer)
Al Hagedorn, Treasurer
Library: Mon–Thur 10:00–9:00, Fri–Sat

9:00–5:00
Pub. *Journal*, quarterly (Feb, May, Aug,
Nov)
$15.00 per year membership

**Hamilton County Genealogy Society and
Central Texas Research Center**
209 West Henry
Hamilton, TX 76531
(254) 386-4566; (800) 460-2847
hcgs@htcomp.net; carlian@why.net
http://websites.hamiltontexas.com/
hamiltongenealogylibrary
Carlian Massingaill Pittman, President;
Nancy Hengst, Secretary/Treasurer
Mon–Sat 9:00–5:00; meetings: fourth Thur
7:00
Pub. *Family Circle Journal*, three times per
year (Apr, Aug, Dec)
$15.00 per year membership

Harris County Genealogical Society
PO Box 391
Pasadena, TX 77501
dmcanally@pdq.net
http://www.hcgs.org
Mel McAnally, Librarian
Pub. *The Living Tree News*, semiannually
$15.00 per year membership

Harrison County Genealogical Society
PO Box 597
Marshall, TX 75671
(903) 938-2680
Museum@shreve.net
http://www.rootsweb.com/~txharris/
hcgensoc.htm
Ruth Briggs, Secretary/Treasurer
Tue–Sat 10:00–4:00
Pub. *Ancestor Issues*, quarterly
$10.00 per year membership

Haskell County Genealogical Society
300 North Avenue, East
Haskell, TX 79521

Heart of Texas Genealogical Society
PO Box 133
Rochelle, TX 76872

**Hemphill County Historical and
Genealogical Society**
(see Historical Societies—Local and
Regional, above)

Hi-Plains Genealogical Society
c/o Unger Memorial Library
825 Austin Street
Plainview, TX 79072-7235
(806) 296-1148 (Library); (806) 291-1245
FAX (Library)
johnsigwald@texasonline.net (Library)
http://www.texasonline.net/unger (Library
John Sigwald, Library Liaison
Library: six days per week (summer five days
per week)
(marriage records to 1941, burials for Hale
County from the late 1800s to the present)
$10.00 per year membership

Hill Country Genealogical Society
HC 07, Box 52
Llano, TX 78643
Evelyn Wade
Pub. *Hill Country Genealogical Society
Quarterly*
$7.00 per year membership

Hill County Genealogical Society
PO Box 636
Hillsboro, TX 76645-0636
Mollie Stinson, President; Anita Adler,

Editor
meetings at 201 East Franklin Street: first of
month 6:30
Pub. *Hill County Crossroads*, quarterly,
$2.50 per issue
$15.00 per year membership

Hood County Genealogical Society
Restored Granbury Depot
PO Box 1623
Granbury, TX 76048-8623
(817) 573-2557 (Depot); (817) 573-8810
(President)
ancestor@hcnews.com;
granbury@emcee.com
http://www.granburydepot.org/home/
HCGShomePage.htm
Syvilla Lemons, Chairman of the Depot
Preservation Committee; Roy E. Malone,
Editor
Tue–Thur noon–4:00, Sat 10:00–3:00
Pub. *Hood County Genealogical Society
Quarterly* (May, Aug, Nov, Feb)
$10.00 per year membership; in-depth
research: $5.00 per hour

Hopkins County Genealogical Society
(312½ North Davis Street—location)
PO Box 624 (mailing address)
Sulphur Springs, TX 75483-0624
(903) 885-8523
Danna E. Elliott, President
Research Center: Mon–Fri 9:00–5:00, Sat
9:00–noon
Pub. *Hopkins County Heritage*, quarterly
$12.00 per year membership

Houston Genealogical Forum
PO Box 271466
Houston, TX 77277-1466
(713) 827-4440 (message line)
info@hgftx.org
http://www.hgftx.org
Pat Metcalfe, Librarian
meetings at Bayland Park Community Center:
first Sat (Sept–May) 10:00 A.M.–11:00
A.M.
Pub. *The Bulletin*, nine times per year
(monthly, Sept–May); *The Genealogical
Record*, quarterly (Mar, June, Sept, Dec)
$18.00 per year membership

The Humble Area Genealogical Society
PO Box 2723
Humble, TX 77347-2723
(281) 358-3062
http://www.rootsweb.com/~txthags
Bernard Balser, President
meetings: second Mon (Sept–May) 7:15;
collection housed at Kingwood College,
Kingwood, TX 77339
Pub. *The Humble Genealogist*, quarterly
$10.00 per year membership

The Hunt County Genealogical Society
PO Box 398
Greenville, TX 75403-0398
June Nichols, Corresponding Secretary
(publishes books of marriages, funeral home
records, census, school warrant and
depository records, chattel mortgages, etc.)
$7.50 per year membership; research: brief
responses to questions will be answered
and more detailed research for $7.50 per
hour plus costs

Hutchinson County Genealogical Society
(Hutchinson County Library, 625 Weatherly
Street, Borger, TX 79007—location)
PO Box 5356 (mailing address)
Borger, TX 79008-5356
(806) 273-0126; (806) 273-0128 FAX

Cleo Morrison
Mon–Tue & Thur 10:00–8:00, Wed & Fri
    10:00–6:00, Sat 1:00–5:00
$7.50 per year membership

Irving Genealogical Society
PO Box 170881
Irving, TX 75017-0881
irfinggensociety@yahoo.com
http://www.rootsweb.com/~txigs/index.html
Elizabeth Goode, Secretary
$18.00 per year membership

Johnson County Genealogical Society
PO Box 1256
Cleburne, TX 76033-1256
(817) 645-3104 (Publicity); (817) 558-3210
    (Secretary)
http://www.htcomp.net/jcgs/soc/soc.htm
Sandra Osborne, President, Dee Eltzroth,
    Publicity; Lois Howard, Program
    Chairman and Secretary
meetings: second Thur
Pub. *Finders Keepers*, semiannually (spring,
    fall)
$15.00 per year membership; research:
    usually $20.00 plus SASE

Kaufman County Genealogical Society
PO Box 337
Terrell, TX 75160-0337
Barbara Sloan, President
Terrell Public Library: Mon–Tue 10:00–8:00,
    Wed–Thur 10:00–6:00, Fri noon–5:00, Sat
    10:00–4:00
Pub. *Kaufman Kounty Konnections*, quarterly
    (Mar, June, Sept, Dec)
(specializes in genealogy, family history,
    cemeteries, and census records of the area,
    obituaries from county newspapers,
    microfilmed church records)
$15.00 per year membership; limited free
    research for members only

Genealogical Society of Kendall County
PO Box 623
Boerne, TX 78006
Boerne Public Library
Pub. *Keys to the Past*, quarterly
(some local family histories, but expanded
    collection covers a great deal of the rest of
    the U.S. in different time periods, and
    some foreign material)
$15.00 per year membership

**Kent County Genealogical and Historical
Society**
PO Box 6
Jayton, TX 79528

Kerrville Genealogical Society, Inc.
Kerr Regional History Center and Archives
425 Water Street
Kerrville, TX 78028
http://www.ktc.net/kgs
Judith A. Trolinger, Volunteer KGS Librarian
Mon–Sat 10:00–4:00; meetings at Butt-
    Holdsworth Memorial Library, 505 Water
    Street: third Wed (Jan–May & Sept–Nov)
Pub. *Kerr Trails*, quarterly
(library collection of several thousand
    volumes, strong on local area)
$10.00 per year membership

Kingsland Genealogical Society
PO Box 952
Kingsland, TX 78639
nannie4@juno.com
http://www.rootsweb.com/~txkinggs
Sara Holland
meetings at the Kingsland Community
    Center: second Tue 2:00

$12.00 per year membership

The Lamar County Genealogical Society
1125 Bonham Street
Paris, TX 75460
(903) 784-5020
betsym@stargate.1starnet.com
http://gen.1starnet.com/lamargen.htm
meetings: third Thur 6:30
Pub. *Lamar County History and Genealogy*,
    annually
$25.00 per year membership

Lamesa Area Genealogical Society
(511 North Third Street—location)
PO Box 1264 (mailing address)
Lamesa, TX 79331
Martha Stewart, President
Mon–Fri 9:30–5:30
Pub. *Threads of Life*, semiannually
    (genealogical and local source material)
$10.00 per year membership

Lancaster Genealogical Society
sylsmith@azmailnet
http://pages.prodigy.net/procyon/
    lancaster/lgslstn.htm
Sylvia Stanford Smith

Lee County Genealogical Society
177 South Mason
Giddings, TX 78942

Leon County Genealogical Society
(Old Courthouse—location)
PO Box 400 (mailing address)
Centerville, TX 75833
(903) 322-2710
http://www.rootsweb.com/~txleon
Fae Boutotte, Corresponding Secretary
Mon–Fri 1:00–4:00
Pub. *Leon Hunters Dispatch (Quarterly)*,
    quarterly
$15.00 per year membership

Los Bexareños Genealogical Society
PO Box 1935
San Antonio, TX 78297
(210) 822-1526
Dan Gomez, Editor
Pub. *Los Bexareños Genealogical Register*,
    quarterly (Mar, June, Sept, Dec)
$25.00 per year membership

**Lower Gulf Coast Genealogical and
Historical Society**
http://www.phoenix.net/~dsk/genealogy.
    html

Madison County Genealogical Society
PO Box 26
Madisonville, TX 77864

**Mansfield Historical and Genealgoical
Society and Museum**
(101 East Broad Street—location)
PO Box 304 (mailing address)
Mansfield, TX 76063
mhs@mansfieldhistory.org
http://www.mansfieldhistory.org

Marion County Genealogical Society
PO Box 224
Jefferson, TX 75657-0224
http://www.rootsweb.com/~txmarion/
    resources/MCGS.html
meetings at the First United Methodist
    Church, 305 Henderson Street: first Sat
    10:00
Pub. untitled quarterly
$10.00 per year membership

Matagorda County Genealogical Society
PO Box 264
Bay City, TX 77404-0264
Carol Sue Gibbs
Pub. *Oak Leaves*, semiannually, $12.50 per
    issue
$20.00 per year membership

McAllen Genealogical Society
PO Box 4714
McAllen, TX 78502-4714
(956) 686-5669 (Librarian's home)
librarian@mcallen.lib.tx.us
http://www.mcallen.lib.tx.us/orgs/
    genealog/mcgensoc.htm
Janette Josserand, Genealogical Librarian
Mon–Wed 9:00–9:00, Thur–Fri 9:00–5:00,
    Sat–Sun 1:00–5:00; meetings at McAllen
    Memorial Library, 601 North Main Street:
    fourth Mon (Sept–Nove & Jan–April)
    2:00, second Mon (Dec) 2:00
Pub. *Palm Breezes Newsletter*, quarterly
    (complete *New England Historical and
    Genealogical Register*, *The America
    Genealogist*, *Arkansas Family Historian*,
    Connecticut Nutmegger, *The Georgia
    Genealogical Magazine*, *Hawkeye
    Heritage* (Iowa), *"Ansearchin'" News*
    (Tennessee), *The Virginia Genealogist*,
    Confederate Veteran, *Periodical Source
    Index* (PERSI); 4,500 volumes in an all-
    around collection, except the West)
$15.00 per year membership

Menard Genealogical Society
PO Box 714
Menard, TX 76859

**Mesquite Historical and Genealogical
Society**
(see Historical Societies—Local and
Regional, above)
Mid-Cities Genealogical Society
PO Box 407
Bedford, TX 76095-0407
(817) 283-3422
mwpasley@attbi.com
http://www.geocities.com/mcgstx
Martha Pasley, Newsletter Editor
meetings at Euless Public Library: first Thur
    7:00
Pub. *Mid-Cities Genealogical Society
    Newsletter*, monthly
$15.00 per year membership

Midland Genealogical Society
Midland County Public Library
The John and Rosalind Redfern Genealogical
Research Center
301 West Missouri
Midland, TX 79701
adgmz@yahoo.com
http://www.rootsweb.com/~txmidlan/mgs.htm
David G. Miller, Webmaster
Pub. *Midland Genealogical Newsletter*; *The
    Thorny Trail*, biannually, $12.00 per year
    subscription
(microfilm copies of all Midland unprotected
    birth and death records)
$12.00 per year membership

Milam County Genealogical Society
Lucy Hill Patterson Memorial Library
201 Ackerman Street
Rockdale, TX 76567
lhprml@excite.com
http://www.geocities.com/milamco/
    milam-002.htm
meetings at the NBC Bank Community Room
    across the street from the Library, at the
    corner of Ackerman and Cameron Streets,
    Rockdale, TX: first Thur 7:00

Pub. *The Legacy*, monthly
$15.00 per year membership

Montgomery County Genealogical and Historical Society, Inc.
(221 North Thompson—location)
PO Box 867 (mailing address)
Conroe, TX 77305-0867
(936) 788-8363
http://www.rootsweb.com/~txmcghs/
mcghs.htm
Charles Hereford, President
Montgomery County Library, Conroe, TX:
Mon & Fri 10:00–5:00, Tue–Thur
10:00–8:00, Sat 9:00–5:00; Office: Mon &
Wed 10:00–3:00
Pub. *The Herald*, quarterly
$25.00 per year membership

Nacogdoches Genealogical Society
(First United Methodist Church—location)
PO Box 4634, Stephen F. Austin Station
(mailing address)
Nacogdoches, TX 75962
(936) 564-5544
genealogy@etxquest.com
http://www.rootsweb.com/~txngs
Debbie Parker Wayne, Secretary
Steen Library, Special Collections
Department: 10:00–5:00
Pub. *Yesterday*, annually
$15.00 per year membership

Navarro County Genealogical Society
(Corsicana Public Library, Genealogy Room,
100 North 12th Street, Corsicana, TX
75110—location)
PO Box 2278 (mailing address)
Corsicana, TX 75151-2278
(903) 654-4846; (903) 654-4810; (903) 654-4812

http://www.rootsweb.com/~txnavarr/genea
logical_society/index.htm
David Franklin, President; Verna Bonner,
Vice President
Pub. *Navarro Leaves and Branches*, quarterly
$10.00 per year membership; volunteer
research only

New Boston Genealogical Society
(New Boston Public Library, 127 North
Ellis—location)
PO Box 104 (mailing address)
New Boston, TX 75570
(903) 628-2418
John Inman, President
Mon–Fri 10:00–5:00
Pub. *The New Bostonian*, quarterly
$10.00 per year membership

North Collin County Genealogical Society
McKinney Memorial Public Library
220 North Kentucky Street
McKinney, TX 75069
(972) 542-4461 (Library); (972) 542-1344
FAX (Library)
Kenneth Cole, Webmaster
meetings in the Dulaney Room of the
McKinney Memorial Library: on the first
Sat 10:15 A.M.

North Texas Genealogical Association
PO Box 4602
Wichita Falls, TX 76308
(940) 692-2583
beckywyatt@aol.com
http://ntxga.com
Beverly Wyatt, Library Chairman
Wichita Falls Public Library, Genealogy
Room: Tue 11:00–8:00, Wed–Fri
9:00–5:00, Sat 1:00–5:00

Pub. *North Texas Trail Tracers*, quarterly;
Newsletter, monthly
$10.00 per year membership

Pacer-Hunt County Genealogical Society
PO Box 2306
Quinlan, TX 75474
$14.00 per year membership

Parker County Genealogical Society
Weatherford Public Library
1214 Charles Street
Weatherford, TX 76086
(817) 594-2767 (Library)
Evlyn Broumley, Librarian
Mon, Wed & Fri–Sat 10:00–6:00, Tue &
Thur 1:00–9:00
Pub. *Trails West*, quarterly
$10.00 per year membership

Pecan Valley Genealogical Society (Brown County)
Brownwood Public Library
600 Carnegie Boulevard
Brownwood, TX 76801-7038
(915) 646-0155 (Library)

Permian Basin Genealogical Society
Ector County Library
321 West Fifth Street
Odessa, TX 79761
(915) 332-0633 (Library)
Doris Baker, Head, Southwest
History/Genealogy Department
Genealogy Department: Mon–Thur
8:30–8:30, Fri–Sat 9:30–6:00, Sat
9:00–noon & 1:00–6:00
Pub. *Treeshaker*, semiannually
$15.00 per year membership

Piney Woods Pioneer Genealogical Society
Genealogical Research Center and Library of
Southeast Texas
Route 1, Box 40S
Kountze, TX 77625

Porciones Genealogical Society
PO Box 392
Edinburg, TX 78540-0392
Pub. *Porciones Genealogical Society
Journal*, semiannually

Randolph Area Genealogical Society
PO Box 2134
Universal City, TX 78148
(210) 659-7881 (President)
Trudy Messick, Secretary/Treasurer
meetings third Wed (Jan–Nov) 7:00
("Society family names in search; presently
performing cemetery research with
published indexes soon to be printed of
Guadalupe County, Texas.")
$12.00 per year membership

Red River County Texas Genealogical Society
(Red River County Public Library, Locust
Street—location)
PO Box 516 (mailing address)
Clarksville, TX 75426
(903) 427-3991 (Library); (903) 784-4975
(President)
Zoe Farmer, President
meetings second Mon 7:30
Pub. *Red River County Texas Genealogical
Society Newsletter*, quarterly
$10.00 per year membership

Rockwall County Genealogical Society
(815 East Washington—location)
PO Box 471 (mailing address)
Rockwall, TX 75087

(972) 771-9018
http://www.rockwallroots.org/rcgs
Mary Williams, President
meetings at Rockwall Center, 801 East
Washington: third Tue 7:30
Pub. *RockwallCoGenSoc Quarterly*
$15.00 per year membership

Root Seekers Genealogical Society
Tri County Library
PO Box 1770
Mabank, TX 75147-1770
(903) 451-2213

Rusk County Genealogical Society
(203 North Van Buren, Henderson, TX
75652—location)
PO Box 1314 (mailing address)
Henderson, TX 75653-1314

San Angelo Genealogical and Historical Society, Inc.
(Church of Christ Fellowship Hall, 902 North
Main Street—location)
PO Box 3453 (mailing address)
San Angelo, TX 76902-3453
(915) 949-3223
hamnutibud@cs.com
http://www.rootsweb.com/saghs
Jerry Hambright, President
meetings first Tue (Sept–May) 7:30
Pub. *Stalkin' Kin*, quarterly (Aug, Nov, Feb,
May)
(Coke, Concho, Crockett, Glasscock, Irion,
Kimble, Menard, Reagan, Runnels,
Schleicher, Sterling, Sutton, and Tom
Green counties; Bible records, members'
ancestor charts, court records, cemeteries,
etc.)
$15.00 per year membership; free queries to
members first and to others as space
allows

San Antonio Genealogical and Historical Society
(401 Isom Road, Suite 540, San Antonio, TX
78216—location)
PO Box 17461 (mailing address)
San Antonio, TX 78217-0461
(210) 342-5242; (210) 342-0386 FAX
saghs@texas.net
http://saghs.home.texas.net
Nancy Brennan, President
Mon & Sun 10:00–4:00, Wed 10:00–9:00,
Sun 1:00–5:00; meetings third Sat
(Jan–May & Sept–Oct)
Pub. *Our Heritage*, two times per year (Jan
and July), $25.00 per year subscription for
libraries and societies; *Newsletter*
$35.00 per year membership; research: $7.00
per hour

San Marcos/Hays County Genealogy Society
PO Box 503
San Marcos, TX 78667
(512) 353-5823
Pat Young, President
$12.00 per year membership

Scurry County Genealogical Society
(Scurry County Library, 1916 23rd Street,
Snyder, TX 79549—location)
PO Box 195 (mailing address)
Snyder, TX 79550
Library: Mon, Wed & Fri–Sat 10:00–6:00,
Tue & Thur 10:00–9:00
Pub. *White Buffalo Tales*, semiannually (Apr,
Oct)
(courthouse records)
$12.50 per year membership; research:
donation

Scurry County Museum Genealogical Group
Western Texas College
Scurry County Museum
6200 College Avenue
Snyder, TX 79549-6105

South Plains Genealogical Society
PO Box 6607
Lubbock, TX 79493-6607
(806) 747-1319
palowrie@dtnspeed.net
http://members.door.net/spgs
Yvonne S. Perkins, President
Mahon Public Library: Mon–Thur 9:00–9:00,
 Fri–Sat 9:00–6:00, Sun 1:00–5:00
Pub. *SPGS Newsletter*, monthly, $7.50 per
 year subscription
$10.00 per year membership; quick research:
 $10.00

South Texas Genealogical Society, Inc.
(Bee County Public Library—location)
PO Box 754 (mailing address)
Beeville, TX 78104-0754
(361) 358-8757
STGS@beeville.net
http://www.beeville.net/STGS/Index.htm
Kay Mix, Corresponding Secretary
meetings third Tue 7:00
Pub. *South Texas Genealogical Society, Inc.,
 Quarterly*, $10.00 per year subscription
(Bee, Live Oak, Goliad, Refugio, Karnes and
 San Patricio counties)
$15.00 per year membership

**Southeast Texas Genealogical and
Historical Society**
Tyrrell Historical Library
Beaumont Public Library System
(695 Pearl Street—location)
PO Box 3827 (mailing address)
Beaumont, TX 77704
fhallen@swbell.net
http://www.rootsweb.com/~txsetghs
Fred Allen
Pub. *Tyrrell Historical Library Association
 Newsletter*, various; *Southeast Texas
 Genealogical and Historical
 Society—Yellowed Pages*, quarterly,
 $14.00 per year subscription
$15.00 per year membership

Southwest Genealogical Society
San Antonio College Library
1300 San Pedro Avenue
San Antonio, TX 78212

Southwest Texas Genealogical Society
PO Box 295
Uvalde, TX 78802
Scottie Molloy, Editor/Publisher
El Progreso Memorial Library: Mon–Wed &
 Fri 9:00–6:00, Thur 9:00–8:00, Sat
 9:00–1:00
Pub. *Branches and Acorns*, quarterly, $10.00
 per year subscription
(Dimmit, Edwards, Frio, Kinney, Medina,
 Real, Uvalde and Zavala counties)
$15.00 per year membership

Stephens County Genealogical Society
Swenson Memorial Museum Research
Library
(116 West Walker—location)
PO Box 350 (mailing address)
Breckenridge, TX 76424
(254) 559-8471
kshort@kroo.com
http://www.rootsweb.com/~txscgs
Freda Mitchell, Corresponding Secretary;
 Ken Short, Webmaster

Library: Tue–Sat 10:00–noon & 1:00–5:00

Texarkana U.S.A. Genealogy Society
PO Box 2323
Texarkana, TX 75504-2323
Pub. *Texarkana U.S.A. Quarterly*
$10.00 per year membership

Texas City Ancestry Searchers
(Moore Memorial Library, 1701 Ninth
Avenue, North, Texas City, TX
77590—location)
PO Box 3301 (mailing address)
Texas City, TX 77592-3301
(409) 935-5343
Zora A. Evans, Editor and Newspaper
 Column Chairman
8:00–4:00 or evenings
Pub. *Through the Spyglass*, quarterly, $12.00
 per year subscription
(local history, copies of local records)
$7.00 per year membership

TX-OK Panhandle Genealogical Society
c/o Perry Memorial Library
Fifth and Ash
Perryton, TX 79070
(806) 435-5801 (Library)
Library: Mon 10:00–8:00, Tue–Fri
 10:00–5:30, Sat 10:00–1:00
Pub. *The TX-OK Panhandler*, quarterly
$10.00 per year membership

Texas Research Ramblers
740 Garden Acres
Bryan, TX 77802-4005
(979) 846-8278
Mary Collie Cooper, President
Pub. *Newsletter*

**Timpson Area Genealogical and Heritage
Society of Shelby County, Texas**
(Town Square, 191 Bremond
Street—location)
PO Box 726 (mailing address)
Timpson, TX 75975
(936) 254-3344; (936) 254-3500 (Library)
timpsgen@loblolly.org
Burk Moreland, President
Mon–Fri 10:00–4:00; meetings at the library:
 third Wed 2:00
Pub. *The Tap Root*, quarterly
$15.00 per year membership; queries: two
 free queries per year for members;
 research: very reasonable fees

Tip-O-Texas Genealogical Society
Harlingen Public Library
410 76 Drive
Harlingen, TX 78550-5072
(956) 423-1941 (President)
Carolyn McCarley, President
meetings: third Thur (except Dec) 10:00
Pub. *The Tips*, quarterly
(volumes in every category of research,
 planned to complement the McAllen and
 Brownsville, Texas, genealogical
 collections and includes local material as
 well)
$15.00 per year membership

**Tri-County Genealogical Society and
Library**
(Corner of Connett and Thomas Streets in
the historic First Presbyterian
Church—location)
PO Box 107 (mailing address)
Leonard, TX 75452-0107
(903) 587-2246
Louise Karr, President
Library: by appointment; meeting first Tue
 7:00

Pub. *Tri-County Newsletter*, quarterly
("Our area of interest has grown from the
 original three counties of Collin, Fannin,
 and Hunt, to include all of the north Texas
 area.")
$15.00 per year membership

Upton County Genealogical Society
PO Box 6
Rankin, TX 79778

Van Alstyne Genealogical Society
Van Alstyne Public Library
(117 North Waco—location)
PO Box 629 (mailing address)
Van Alstyne, TX 75495-0629
http://www.vanalstynepl.lib.tx.us/
 GeneologyHome.htm
meetings: third Mon (Mar, July, Oct) 7:00

Van Zandt County Genealogical Society
(Van Zandt County Courthouse Annex
Building, Corner of Highway 19 and Terrell
Street—location)
PO Box 716 (mailing address)
Canton, TX 75103-0716
(903) 567-5012
suegen@vzinet.com
http://www.rootsweb.com/~txvzcgs/vzgs. htm
Sue Wilkinson, Editor
Mon–Fri 9:00–4:00, Sat 9:00–1:00
Pub. *Our Heritage*, quarterly (Feb, May, Aug,
 Nov)
$10.00 per year membership; queries; free;
 research: limited amount done by members

Victoria County Genealogical Society
(302 North Main Street, Victoria, TX
77901—location)
PO Box 413 (mailing address)
Victoria, TX 77902
rvinc@cox-internet.com
http://www.viptx.net/vcgs/vcgs.html
Martha Jones, President Elect; Bob Vincent,
 Membership
meetings at the First Christian Church,
 Colorado and Ben Jordan, Victoria, in the
 Fellowship Hall: second Mon 7:00
Pub. *Victoria—Crossroads of South Texas*,
 quarterly
$20.00 per year membership

Walker County Genealogical Society
PO Box 1295
Huntsville, TX 77342-1295
betwil@aol.com
http://www.dickensonresearch.com/
 wcgen.htm
Mrs. Johnnie Jo Dickenson, President; Beth
 Williamson, Editor
Pub. *Walker County Genealogical Society
 Newsletter*, nine times per year (monthly,
 except June–July & Dec)

Ward County Genealogical Society
400 East Fourth Street
Monahans, TX 79756
(915) 943-6312
Nancy Tucker Jordan, Librarian
Mon–Fri 10:00–5:15
Pub. *Ward County Heritage*, semiannually
 (Apr, Oct)
(local newspaper on microfilm, 1931 to date;
 poll tax transcribed, 1913–1961; funeral
 homes records and cemetery lists)
$15.00 per year membership; search: $5.00
 per hour plus copies at 10¢ per page

West Bell Genealogical Society
PO Box 851
Killeen, TX 76540
(254) 699-2143

schoenem@vvm.com
http://www.rootsweb.com/~txwbgs
Mark Schoenermann, President
meetings at Killeen Public Library, 205 East
    Church Street: first Thur 6:30
Pub. *Bell County Genealogist*, quarterly
$12.00 per year membership

West Texas Genealogical Society
PO Box 2307
Abilene, TX 79604
Abilene Public Library: Mon–Tue & Thur
    9:00–9:00, Wed & Fri–Sat 9:00–6:00
Pub. *West Texas Genealogical Society
    Bulletin*, quarterly
$10.00 per year membership

Western Trails Genealogical Society
(see Oklahoma, Part 2)

Williamson County Genealogical Society
PO Box 585
Round Rock, TX 78680-0585
http://www.rootsweb.com/~txwcgs/
    WCGS.html
meetings at the Georgetown Public Library,
    800 Martin Luther King, Georgetown, TX:
    second Tue (Jan–July, Sept–Nov) 7:30
Pub. *The Chisholm Trail*, quarterly, $4.00
    each
(sponsors annual seminar; issues a Pioneer
    Families of Williamson County certificate
    to descendants of any person living in
    Williamson County before the end of
    1880; collection housed at Round Rock
    Public Library)
$15.00 per year membership

Wood County Genealogical Society
PO Box 832
Quitman, TX 75783
Woodco@Cox-internet.com
http://www.rootsweb.com/~txwood/wcgs.
    htm
Corresponding Secretary
meetings: monthly (except June–Aug & Dec)
Pub. *Wood County Genealogical Society
    Newsletter*, eight times per year (monthly,
    except June–Aug & Dec)
$10.00 per year membership

Independent Publications and Miscellany

Bigfoot Wallace Museum
Big Foot, TX 78005

The George Bush Presidential Library and Museum
1000 George Bush Drive West
College Station, TX 77845
(979) 260-9552; (979) 260-9557 FAX
library@bush.nara.gov
http://bushlibrary.tamu.edu
Warren Finch, Deputy Director
Mon–Sat 9:30–5:00, Sun noon–5:00
(primarily historical, very few genealogical
    records, mostly secondary sources on the
    George H. W. Bush core family)
admission: $5.00

Cactus Park and Museum
PO Drawer F
George West, TX 78022
(361) 449-1556

Center for Southwest Research
(see New Mexico, Part 2)

Collie-Cooper Enterprises
740 Garden Acres

Bryan, TX 77802-4005
(979) 846-8278
Mary Collie Cooper
(book publications on Brazon, Madison and
    Robertson counties)
no periodical

Coryell County Museum Foundation, Inc.
(110 Eighth Street—location)
PO Box 24 (mailing address)
Gatesville, TX 76528
(254) 865-5421
Helen Swift, Board Chairperson
Fri–Sat 9:00–5:00, Sun 1:00–5:00

Cowboy Country Museum
113 Wetherbee
Stamford, TX 79553
(915) 773-2411

Denver City Museum
505 North Avenue C
Denver City, TX 79323
(806) 592-2897
Carl Johnson, President
Tue–Thur 1:00–4:00, and by appointment
$10.00 per year membership

Ellis County Museum, Inc.
(201 South College Street, Waxahachie, TX
    75165—location)
PO Box 706 (mailing address)
Waxahachie, TX 75168
(972) 937-0681
ecmuseum@cnbcom.net
http://www.rootsweb.com/~txecm
Shannon Simpson, Curator
Mon–Sat 10:00–5:00, Sun noon–4:00

Foard County Museum/McAdams Ranch
PO Box 609
Crowell, TX 79227
(254) 655-3395

Frontier Times Museum
(510 13th Street—location)
PO Box 1918 (mailing address)
Bandera, TX 78003-1918
(830) 796-3864
Pat D'Spain, President
Mon–Sat 10:00–4:30, Sun 1:00–4:30
Pub. untitled membership letter, annually
("We have artifacts from around the world.")
$10.00 per year membership

Great 1900 Galveston Storm Website
http://freepages.genealogy.rootsweb.com/
    ~barnette
Mic Barnette
("Between 6,000 and 10,000 people are
    reputed to have died in this terrible storm.
    The web site contains the names of all
    known victims who perished and is
    dedicated to discovering more about those
    named people and to learning the names
    of those not known.")

Genealogical Institute
(see Virginia, Part 2)

Genealogy Books and Consultation
1217 Oakdale Street
Houston, TX 77004-5813
(713) 522-7444
Norma Chudleigh, Ph.D., A.G., Owner
Mon–Wed & Fri 1:00–6:00, Sat 10:00–5:00
(specializes in The South)

H-Texas
H-Texas-request@h-net.msu.edu (Editors)
http://www2.h-net.msu.edu/~texas
(history discussion network)

Heritage House of Orange County Association, Inc.
905 West Division Street
Orange, TX 77630
(409) 886-5385; (409) 886-0917 FAX
http://heritagehouseoforange.org
Dan T. Ryder, Administrator
Office: Mon–Fri 8:00–5:00; Tours: Tue–Fri
    10:00–4:00
Pub. *Heritage Gazette*

Historical Projects Houston County, Texas, Inc.
629 North Fourth Street
Crockett, TX 75835
(936) 544-3269
Eliza H. Bishop, Director
24-hours per day
(specializes in Houston County; "supports
    and guides Houston County historical
    work.")
$10.00 per year membership

Hunting for Bears Genealogical and Historical Society
(see Alabama, Part 2)

Lyndon Baines Johnson Library and Museum
2313 Red River Street
Austin, TX 78705
(512) 916-5137
webmaster@lbjlib.utexas.edu
http://www.lbjlib.utexas.edu
Reading Room: Mon–Fri 9:00–5:00

Lamesa-Dawson County Museum
(South Second Street and Avenue
    M—location)
404 21st Place (mailing address)
Lamesa, TX 79331

The Laredo Children's Museum
West End, Washington Street
Laredo, TX 78040
(956) 721-5321
Irma Peña, Executive Director
Office: Mon–Fri 8:00–5:00; Museum:
    Thur–Sat 10:00–5:00, Sun 1:00–5:00
$35.00 per year membership; admission:
    $2.00 for adults

Lone Star Junction
http://www.lsjunction.com/index.htm

Mendoza Trail Museum
PO Box 782
McCamey, TX 79752-0782
(915) 652-3192
Sandra Vickers, Curator

Moody Museum
(114 West Ninth Street—location)
PO Box 765 (mailing address)
Taylor, TX 76574

Morton Museum of Cooke County
210 South Dixon
Gainesville, TX 76240
(940) 668-8900
Shana Powell, Curator
Pub. *Heritage Highlights*

Mountain Press
(see Tennessee, Part 2)

Museum for East Texas Culture
400 Micheaux Avenue
Palestine, TX 75801-3628
(903) 723-1914
Drew Franklin, Director

The Museum of East Texas
503 North Second Street
Lufkin, TX 75901
(936) 639-4434
Mark A. Tullos, Jr., Executive Director

Old Rock House
(Highway 84—location)
PO Box 335 (mailing address)
Santa Anna, TX 76878
(915) 348-3283

Our Family Times
PO Box 387
Port Neches, TX 77651
Pub. *Our Family Times*, quarterly, $15.00 per
  year subscription

Pioneer Town
333 Wayside Drive
Wimberley, TX 78676
(512) 847-2517

Presidio La Bahia
(U.S. Highway 183 and 77-A—location)
PO Box 57 (mailing address)
Goliad, TX 77963
(361) 645-3752

Red River Valley Museum
(4600 College Drive, West—location)
PO Box 2004 (mailing address)
Vernon, TX 76384
(940) 553-1848
Ann G. Huskinson, Executive Director

Rio Grande Valley Museum
Boxwood at Raintree
Harlingen, TX 78550
(956) 430-8500; (956) 430-8502 FAX
rgvmuse@hiline.net
http://www.hiline.net/rgvmuse
Linn R. S. Keller, Museum Director
Wed–Sat 10:00–4:00, Sun 1:00–4:00

River Valley Pioneer Museum
(118 North Second—location)
PO Box 1201 (mailing address)
Canadian, TX 79014
(806) 323-6548; (806) 323-8993
Sharon Wright, Director
Tue–Fri 9:00–noon & 1:00–4:00, Sun
  2:00–4:00
(Hemphill County, Texas)

Robertson County Homepage
http://www.geocities.com/Heartland/
  Plains/3451
Shari Simonds

Slaton Museum Association
(155 North Eighth—location)
PO Box 555 (mailing address)
Slaton, TX 79364
Almarine Childers, President
Tue–Fri 1:00–5:00
$10.00 per year membership; admission: free

Society of Southwest Archivists
Texas Tech University
PO Box 4090
Lubbock, TX 79409

Southern Historical Press, Inc.
(see Publishers, Part 4)

Star of the Republic Museum
Washington-on-the-Brazos State Historical
Park
PO Box 317
Washington, TX 77880
(936) 878-2461

Houston McGaugh, Director
daily 10:00–5:00

Tejas Publications and Research
2507 Tannehill Drive
Houston, TX 77008-3052
(713) 864-6862 (8:00–5:00); (713) 864-3540
  FAX
treviawbeverly@aol.com (8:00–5:00)
Trevia Wooster Beverly,
  Researcher/Genealogy
  Instructor/Speaker/Author/Editor/Book
  Reviewer/Cemetery Preservationist
("I have prepared and published several
  county cemetery directories, written
  articles for the *CLF Newsletter* [Clayton
  Library Friends] and *The Genealogical
  Record* [Houston Genealogical Forum]. I
  serve on the staff of the Angelina College
  Summer genealogy Conference, Lufkin,
  Texas. 2003 will be our seventh year.")
research fees vary

**Texas Historical and Ancestry
Researchers**
(see Ethnic Archives, Libraries and
Societies—African, Part 3)

Texas Oral History Association
Carroll Library, Baylor University
PO Box 97271
Waco, TX 76798-7271
(254) 710-3437; (254) 710-1571 FAX
lois_myers@baylor.edu
http://www3.baylor.edu/TOHA
Lois E. Myers, Secretary-Treasurer
Pub. *TOHA Newsletter*, three to four times
  per year; *The Sound Historian*, annually,
  $5.00 per issue
$10.00 per year membership

Texas State Cemetery
901 Novasota Street
Austin, TX 78702
(512) 463-0605; (512) 463-8811 FAX
statecemetery@tbpc.state.tx.us
http://www.cemetery.state.tx.us
Clint Lynch, Director of Research
Visitors Center: Mon–Fri 8:00–5:00,
  Grounds: Mon–Sun 8:00–5:00

Toa Mo Ga Memorial Museum
PO Box 455
Plains, TX 79355
(806) 456-4823

Traveller Southern Families
(see Virginia, Part 2)

TxGenWeb
Part of The USGenweb Project
http://www.rootsweb.com/~txgenweb
Trey Holt, State Coordinator
(links to other Texas resources)

University of Arizona Press
Journal of the Southwest
(see Arizona, Part 2)

Victoria Regional Museum Association
502 North Liberty
Victoria, TX 77901
(361) 575-8227
Clara Kilgore, Executive Director
Pub. *VRMA News*
(primarily historical, not genealogical,
  operates McNamara House Museum and
  the Nave Museum)

West of the Pecos Museum
(First and Cedar Streets [U.S. Highway
285]—location)

PO Box 1784
Pecos, TX 79772
(915) 445-5076; (915) 445-3149 FAX
Dorinda Millan, Curator
Memorial Day–Labor Day: Mon–Sat
  9:00–5:00, Sun 1:00–4:00; Labor
  Day–Memorial Day: Tue–Sat 9:00–5:00
("Western history museum.")
$25.00 per year membership

Wichita Falls Museum and Art Center
2 Eureka Circle
Wichita Falls, TX 76308
(940) 696-5358
Carole Bonaman, Executive Director
Tue–Sat 10:00–5:00

Williamson County Homepage
http://www.flash.net/~hmwalden/
  willcoun.htm
Harry Walden
free queries

Edwin Wolters Museum
(306 South Avenue I—location)
Route 1, Box 16 (mailing address)
Shiner, TX 77984
(361) 594-3566
Bernard J. Siegel, Jr., Curator
Mon–Fri 8:00–5:00, second & fourth Sun
  2:00–5:00

Yoakum Heritage Museum
(312 Simpson—location)
PO Box 2 (mailing address)
Yoakum, TX 77995
(361) 293-7022
Dennis Rowan, Executive Director
Mon–Sat 1:00–5:00, Sun 3:00–5:00
Pub. *The Newsletter*, annually

Utah

Archives and Libraries with Holdings in Genealogy

State Archives and Library

State Archives and Record Services
Archives Building
State Capitol
PO Box 141021
Salt Lake City, UT 84114-1021
(801) 538-3013; (801) 538-3354 FAX
research@state.ut.us
http://www.archives.state.ut.us
Jeffery O. Johnson, State Archivist
Mon–Fri 8:00–5:00
(statewide births and deaths 1898–1905)

Utah State Library
2150 South 300 West
Salt Lake City, UT 84115
(801) 466-5888
cward@slcpl.lib.ut.us
http://library.utah.gov
Chip Ward, Librarian
Mon–Fri 8:00–5:00
Pub. *Directions for Utah Libraries*, monthly

State Historical Society

Association of Utah Historians
1845 South 1800 East
Salt Lake City, UT 84108
(801) 533-7037
Craig Fuller, Executive Secretary

Utah State Historical Society
300 Rio Grande
Salt Lake City, UT 84101-1182
(801) 533-3500; (801) 533-3501
(Information); (801) 533-3504 FAX
cergushs@utah.gov
http://history.utah.gov
Alan Barnett
Mon–Fri 10:00–5:00, Sat 10:00–2:00
Pub. *Utah Historical Quarterly*, $20.00 per
year subscription; *Beehive History*,
annually; *Utah State Historical Society
Newsletter*, bimonthly
(50,000 volumes plus manuscripts,
photographs, microform, maps and
architectural drawings)
$20.00 per year membership

City, County and Regional Archives and Libraries
(A more exhaustive list of public and
academic libraries can be found at
http://library.utah.gov/directories.html.)

Brigham Carnegie Library
26 East Forest
Brigham City, UT 84302-2198
(435) 723-5891; (435) 723-5850; (435) 723-2813 FAX
susan@peachy.bcpl.lib.ut.us
http://bcpl.lib.ut.us
Susan Hill, Director

Brigham Young University
2250 Harold B. Lee Library
Microforms/Genealogy Department
Provo, UT 84602
(801) 422-8770
diane_parkinson@byu.edu
http://www.lib.byu.edu/hbll
Diane R. Parkinson, Microforms Librarian
Mon–Sat 8:00 A.M.–9:45 P.M., second &
fourth Sun 9:00–6:45

Cedar City Public Library
136 West Center Street
Cedar City, UT 84720-2560
(435) 586-6661
http://www.cedarcitylibrary.org

Fairview Museum of History and Art
(85 North 100 East—location)
PO Box 157 (mailing address)
Fairview, UT 84629
(435) 427-9216
Betty N. Jorgensen, President
10:00–6:00

**Family History Library of The Church of
Jesus Christ of Latter-day Saints**
Genealogical Society of Utah
35 North West Temple
Salt Lake City, UT 84150-3400
(801) 240-2331; (800) 453-3860, ext. 22331;
(800) 346-6044 (from the U.S. or Canada
for the location of local FHCs); (801)
240-1584 FAX
fhl@ldschurch.org
http://www.familysearch.org
Jimmy B. Parker, Manager
Mon 7:30 A.M.–6:00 P.M., Tue–Sat 7:30
A.M.–10:00 P.M.
(The Genealogical Society of Utah is the
acquisitions arm of the Family History
Library. Membership is limited to
employees of the Church's corporation.
No research services are provided by the
Society, but it accredits professional
genealogists, and the Library provides
personal, on-site assistance. At the
present, Church policy opposes
commercial publication of the names and
mailing addresses of the more than 3,500
branch Family History Centers in some
eighty countries. Call for the location of
the nearest FHC, where microfilm copies
of most of the Family History Library's
holdings are available.)

Fort Lewis College
(see Colorado, Part 2)

**Helper Western Mining and Railroad
Museum**
(296 South Main—location)
PO Box 221 (mailing address)
Helper, UT 84526
(435) 472-3009
http://www.wmrrm.org
Lori Perez, Archivist
Museum: winter: 11:00–4:00, summer:
10:00–6:00; Archives: by appointment
("Coal mining, railroad history, immigrant
history, local history, mining records,
historic photo collection, archives.")
admission: donation

Hyrum City Museum
(3 South Center—location)
42 West Third South (mailing address)
Hyrum, UT 84319
(435) 245-6850

Logan Library
Archives
255 North Main
Logan, UT 84321
(435) 750-9870; (435) 753-5026
rjenkins@loganutah.org
http://www.logan.lib.ut.us
Ronald Jenkins, Director
Mon–Thur 10:00–9:00, Fri–Sat 10:00–6:00
(not primarily genealogical)

Manti City Library
2 South Main Street

Manti, UT 84642-1349
(435) 835-2201
http://library.utah.gov/manti.html

**Mountain West Center for Regional
Studies**
University Hill
Logan, UT 84322-0735
(435) 750-3630
F. Ross Peterson, Ph.D., Director

Orem Public Library
58 North State Street
Orem, UT 84057-5596
(801) 229-7047; (801) 224-7050
lgwallace@ci.orem.ut.us
http://www.oremlibrary.org
Louise G. Wallace, Director

Provo Public Library
550 North University Avenue
Provo, UT 84601-1618
(801) 852-6663
genen@provo.lib.ut.us
http://www.provo.lib.ut.us

Salt Lake City Public Library
210 East 400 South
Salt Lake City, UT 84111-2804
(801) 524-8200
ntessman@mail.slcpl.lib.ut.us
http://www.slcpl.lib.ut.us
Nancy Tessman, Director
Mon–Thur 9:00–9:00, Fri–Sat 9:00–6:00

Southern Utah University Library
Special Collections
351 West Center Street, Garden Level
Cedar City, UT 84720
(435) 586-7933; (435) 586-7945 (Special
Collections); (435) 865-8152 FAX
nickerson@suu.edu
http://www.li.suu.edu/library/lispcoll.htm
(Special Collections)
Jackie F. Robinson
Mon–Fri 8:00–5:00

Springville Public Library
50 South Main
Springville, UT 84663-1358
(801) 489-2720; (801) 489-2721
lcatherall@springville.org
http://library.utah.gov/springville.html
Lynette Catherall, Director
Mon–Thur 10:00–9:00, Fri 10:00–6:00, Sat
10:00–4:00

Uintah County Library
Regional History Center
155 East Main Street
Vernal, UT 84078-2695
(435) 789-0091
ebaker@easilink.com (Evan L. Baker,
Director)
http://www.uintah.lib.ut.us
Doris Burton
Mon 8:00–noon, Tue–Thur 2:00–8:00,
Fri–Sat 2:00–6:00
Pub. *Outlas Trail History Journal*, two times
per year
$15.00 per year membership; search fee:
$5.00 per hour

University of Utah Marriott Library
Special Collections, Fifth Floor
1400 East 200 South
Salt Lake City, UT 84112
(801) 581-8864 (Manuscripts); (801) 581-8863 (Western Americana)
http://www.lib.utah.edu/spc/spc.html
Dr. Gregory Thompson, Curator; Nancy
Young, Head, Manuscripts; Walter Jones,

Head, Western Americana
(manuscripts, books, periodicals, etc., on
Utah, the Mormons and the West:
Arizona, California, Colorado, Idaho,
Montana, New Mexico, Nevada,
Oklahoma, Oregon, Texas, Washington
and Wyoming)

Utah State University
Merrill Library
Special Collections and Archives, First Floor
Logan, UT 84322
(435) 797-2663
http://www.usu.edu/~specol/index.html
Pub. *Western Historical Quarterly*

Utah Valley State College (UVSC)
Library
Sparks Special Collection Room
800 West University Parkway
Orem, UT 84058-0001
(801) 222-8265; (801) 222-8173
http://www.uvsc.edu/studsvc/library

Weber County Library
Nonfiction Department
Special Collection Room
2464 Jefferson Avenue
Ogden, UT 84401-2488
(801) 627-6920; (801) 399-8519 FAX
http://www.weberpl.lib.ut.us
Mon–Thur 10:00–9:00, Fri–Sat 10:00–6:00
(emphasis on Utah history, Mormonism,
railroad history)

Western Heritage Center
(see Montana, Part 2)

Historical Societies—Local and Regional

Alta Historical Society
PO Box 8016
Alta, UT 84092
(801) 742-3522
by appointment
("Very informal collection of Alta
memorabilia")

American Historical Association, Pacific Coast Branch
(see California, Part 2)

American West Research Center and Historical Society, Inc.
(see Ohio, Part 2)

Brigham Young University
Charles Redd Center for Western Studies
Provo, UT 84602
(801) 378-4048
Thomas G. Alexander, Ph.D., Director

Cache Valley Historical Society
290 West Center Street
Logan, UT 84321
(435) 752-2169; (435) 752-5797

Carbon County Historical Society
PO Box 1708
Price, UT 84501
(435) 637-6126
http://www.lofthouse.com/USA/Utah/
carbon/cchs.html
Pub. *Carbon County Journal*, annually, $5.00
each
$5.00 per year membership

Centerville Historical Society
511 East 400 South
Centerville, UT 84014

(801) 295-2742

Daggett County Historical Society
PO Box 428
Dutch John, UT 84023

Draper Historical Society
12441 South 900 East
Draper, UT 84020

Emery County Historical Society
PO Box 741
Castle Dale, UT 84513-0741
(435) 381-2428

Historic Willard Society
156 North 200 West
Willard, UT 84340

Iron County Historical Society
c/o Southern Utah State University Library
Special Collections
351 West Center Street, Garden Level
Cedar City, UT 84720
(435) 586-7933 (Library); (435) 586-7945
(Special Collections); (435) 865-8152
FAX (Library)
nickerson@suu.edu (Library)
http://www.li.suu.edu/library/lispcoll.htm
(Special Collections)
York Jones, President
Library: Mon–Fri 8:00–5:00

Old Court House Museum
PO Box 165
Beaver, UT 84713

Park City Historical Society
PO Box 668
Park City, UT 84060

Utah Heritage Foundation
355 Quince Street
Salt Lake City, UT 84103
(801) 533-0858

Genealogical Societies

State Genealogical Society

Utah Genealogical Association
PO Box 1144
Salt Lake City, UT 84110-1144
(888) INFO-UGA (463-6842)
southwickn@cableone.net
http://www.infouga.org
Neal Southwick, President
Pub. *UGA Newsletter*, quarterly (Mar, June,
Sept, Jan); *Utah Genealogical Journal*
(treats Utah, U.S., and International
genealogical and local history topics),
quarterly (Mar, June, Sept, Jan), $5.00
postpaid per issue
Chapters: **Computer Chapter**, Randall
Hamilton, President, 1552 North 1725
West, Layton, UT 84041, (801) 544-0821;
Irish Chapter, Josie Bullock, President,
1590 Treeview Drive, Salt Lake City, UT
84124, (801) 227-9057; **Great Salt Lake
Chapter**, Vaughn Simon, President, PO
Box 11193, Salt Lake City, UT 84147,
(801) 596-9881; **Northern Idaho
Chapter**, Ellie Grover, President, PO Box
685, Bonners Ferry, ID 83805, (208) 267-
7939; **Utah Valley Chapter**, John
Whitaker, President; **Morgan Valley
Chapter**, Holly Hansen, President, 1950
North 6900 East, Croydon, UT 84018-
9707, (801) 829-3295; **Tooele Chapter**,
John Peck, President, 206 East Vine
Street, Tooele, UT 84074, (435) 882-3648
$25.00 per year membership

Genealogical Society of Utah
(see Family History Library of The Church of
Jesus Christ of Latter-day Saints, City,
County and Regional Archives and Libraries,
above)

Independent Publications and Miscellany

Conference of Intermountain Archives
The Church of Jesus Christ of Latter-day
Saints
50 East North Temple
Salt Lake City, UT 84150
(801) 240-3644
Wayne Harper, Secretary

Emery County Museum
PO Box 1088
Castle Dale, UT 84513-1088
(435) 748-2444

Moab Museum
118 East Center Street
Moab, UT 84532
(435) 259-7430

Mormon Pioneer Trail Home Page
http://www.omahafreenet.org/ofn/trails

Temple Area Genealogical Library
Manti, UT 84642

Tracing Mormon Pioneers
(see Religious Archives and
Organizations—Latter-Day Saints [Mormon],
Part 3)

Utah History Encyclopedia
http://media.utah.edu/medsol/UCME/
UHEindex.html

UtGenWeb
Part of The USGenweb Project
http://www.rootsweb.com/~utgenweb/
index.html
Andy E. Wold, State Coordinator
(links to other Utah resources)

Vermont

Archives and Libraries with Holdings in Genealogy

State Archives and Library

Public Records Division
General Services Department
(U.S. Route 2, Middlesex—location)
PO Drawer 33 (mailing address)
Montpelier, VT 05633-7601
(802) 828-3700; (802) 828-3710 FAX
A. John Yacauum, Director Public
　　Records/General Services
Mon–Fri 8:00–4:00

Vermont State Archives
Office of the Secretary of State
26 Terrace Street, Drawer 09
Montpelier, VT 05609-1103
(802) 828-2308; (802) 828-1135 FAX
kwatters@sec.state.vt.us
http://vermont-archives.org
Kathy White, Staff Assistant
Mon–Fri 7:45–4:30
(governor's records, election records,
　　legislative records, surveyors-general
　　records, Manuscript Vermont State Papers,
　　municipal charters and charter
　　amendments, deeds and leases, Stevens
　　Collection and miscellaneous records)
copies: 4¢ per page; research: free first half-
　　hour, 23¢ per minute thereafter

Vermont Department of Libraries
Reference and Law Services
109 State Street
Montpelier, VT 05609-0601
(802) 828-3268; (802) 828-2199 FAX
marj.zunder@dol.state.vt.us
http://dol.state.vt.us
Marjorie D. Zunder, Division Director
Mon–Fri 7:45–4:30

State Historical Society

Vermont Historical Society
Vermont History Center
60 Washington Street
Barre, VT 05641-4209
(802) 479-8500; (802) 479-8510 FAX
Vhs@vhs.state.vt.us;
　　vt_hist_soc@vals.state.vt.us
http://www.vermonthistory.org
Paul A. Carnahan, Librarian
Tue–Fri 9:00–4:00
Pub. *Vermont History*, irregularly
$40.00 per year membership

City, County and Regional Archives and Libraries
(A more exhaustive list of public and
academic libraries can be found at
http://dol.state.vt.us/gopher_root5/libraries/
dir/vt_lib_dir_1999.txt.)

Aldrich Public Library
(see Archives of Barre History, below)

Archives of Barre History
Aldrich Public Library
6 Washington Street
Barre, VT 05641-4227
(802) 476-7550
http://www.aldrich.lib.vt.us
Karen Lane, Library Director
Archives: by appointment; Library:
　　Mon–Wed noon–8:00, Thur 10:00–6:00,
　　Fri noon–6:00, Sat 10:00–4:00
("Collection covers Barre City and Barre

Town, Vermont, only.")
research: no charge for the first 15 minutes,
　　$10.00 for each half-hour thereafter

Bennington Museum
Genealogy and History Library
75 West Main Street
Bennington, VT 05201
(802) 447-1571; (802) 442-8305 FAX
genealogylibrary@benningtonmuseum.com
http://www.bennington.lib.vt.us/index.html
Tyler Resch, Librarian
June–Oct: Mon–Sat 11:00–5:00; Nov–May:
　　Thur–Sat 11:00–5:00
("Library devoted to Vermont history and
　　New England genealogy)
$30.00 per year membership (includes
　　unlimited admission); admission:
　　$5.00/$6.00 to museum gives use of
　　library; copies: 10¢ per image; limited
　　staff research for a donation to cover cost
　　of copies and postage

The Berkshire Athenaeum
(see Massachusetts, Part 2)

Bixby Memorial Free Library
285 Main Street
Vergennes, VT 05491
(802) 877-2211
Bixby-Verg@dol.state.vt.us
http://www.vergennes.org/bixby
Lois C. Noonan, Librarian
daily afternoons, Wed & Sat morning
("Material in process of being organized")

The Brooks Memorial Library
Vermontiana Collection
224 Main Street
Brattleboro, VT 05301
(802) 254-5290; (802) 257-2309 FAX
Brattlib@brooks.lib.vt.us
http://www.brooks.lib.vt.us/library.htm
Jerry Carbone, Library Director
Mon–Wed 9:00–9:00, Thur–Fri 9:00–6:00,
　　Sat (Labor Day–Memorial Day)
　　9:00–5:00, Sat (summer) 9:00–noon
(collection includes Brattleboro and
　　Windham County)

Castleton State College
Calvin Coolidge Library
Seminary Street
Castleton, VT 05735
(802) 468-5611, ext. 257; (802) 468-1475
　　FAX; (802) 468-2421 FAX
sandy.duling@castleton.edu
http://www.csc.vsc.edu
Sandy Duling, Library Director

Connecticut Valley Historical Museum
(see Massachusetts, Part 2)

Craftsbury Public Library
(1376 North Craftsbury Road—location)
PO Box 74 (mailing address)
Craftsbury Common, VT 05827
(802) 586-9683
Linda J. Wells, Librarian

Fletcher Free Library
235 College Street
Burlington, VT 05401
(802) 863-3403 (Library); (802) 865-7217
　　(Reference Desk); (802) 865-7227 FAX
http://www.fletcherfree.org
Anita Danigelis, Reference Librarian
Mon–Tue & Thur–Fri 8:30–6:00, Wed 8:30
　　A.M.–9:00 P.M., Sat 9:00–5:30, Sun
　　noon–6:00
fees for obituary searches and for faxing
　　materials

Goodrich Memorial Library
202 Main Street
Newport, VT 05855
(802) 334-7902
Newport@vals.state.vt.us
http://www.newport.lib.vt.us
Cindy Karasinski, Librarian
Mon–Fri 9:30–5:00, Sat 9:30–3:00

Haskell Free Library and Opera House
(93 Caswell Avenue—location)
PO Box 337 (mailing address)
Derby Line, VT 05830
(802) 873-3022
haskellm@sower.net
Kim Prangley, Executive Director
Tue–Wed & Fri–Sat 10:00–5:00, Thur
　　10:00–8:00
("Also information for Stanstead County and
　　surrounding area. Our library straddles the
　　U.S. Canadian border, and we serve both
　　communities/countries.")

Hitchcock Memorial Library and Museum
(1275 Route 100—location)
PO Box 87 (mailing address)
Westfield, VT 05847
(802) 744-6621; (802) 744-2440
HMLWestfield@vals.state.vt.us
http://vmga.org/essex/hitchcock.html
Mary Alice Brenner, Librarian
Thur 1:00–4:00 & 7:00–8:00, and by
　　appointment in the summer

Ilsley Public Library
75 Main Street
Middlebury, VT 05753-1486
(802) 388-4095 (Adult Services); (802) 388-
　　4367 FAX
iplill@myriad.middlebury.edu
http://www.ilsleypubliclibrary.org
Mon, Wed & Fri 10:00–6:00, Tue & Thur
　　10:00–8:00, Sat 10:00–4:00, Sun
　　(Oct–Apr) 1:00–4:00

Lyndon State College
Samuel Read Hall Library
(Northeast Kingdom Road—location)
PO Box 919 (mailing address)
Lyndonville, VT 05851
(802) 626-9371, ext. 147; (802) 626-6366;
　　(802) 626-6448 (ILL); (802) 626-9576
　　FAX
garet.nelson@lyndonstate.edu
http://www.lyndonstate.edu/library
Garet Nelson, Director

Middlebury College
Egbert Starr Library
Meredith Wing, Level 4
Vermont Collection
Middlebury, VT 05753
(802) 388-3711; (802) 388-3467 FAX
raum@myriad.middlebury.edu
http://www.middlebury.edu/library/
　　genealogy.html

Proctor Free Library
4 Main Street
Proctor, VT 05765
(802) 459-3539
proctorfree@dol.state.vt.us
Mary Brough, Librarian
Mon–Thur 9:00–11:00 & 2:00–8:00, Fri
　　9:00–noon & 1:00–5:00, Sat 9:00–noon

Rockingham Free Public Library
65 Westminster Street
Bellows Falls, VT 05101
(802) 463-4270
http://www.vmga.org/windham/
　　rockingham.html

Becky Hollis, Librarian
Mon & Thur 1:00–8:00, Tue 9:00–8:00, Wed
(except summer) 1:00–8:00, Fri
9:00–5:00, Sat 9:00–noon
$15.00 nonresident's fee

Rokeby Museum
4334 Route 7
Ferrisburg, VT 05456
(802) 877-3406
rokeby@globalnetisp.net
http://www.rokeby.org
Jane Williamson, Director
by appointment
Pub. *Messenger*, quarterly
(Quakerism, abolition, agricultural history,
and Robinson family)
$20.00 per year membership

Russell Collection of Vermontiana
Martha Canfield Memorial Free Library
(Main Street, Route 7A—location)
PO Box 267 (mailing address)
Arlington, VT 05250
(802) 375-6153
http://www.vermonttowns.com/Arlington/
educational/lib/lib.html
J. H. Kennedy, Curator
Tue 9:00–5:00, and by appointment

Rutland Free Library
10 Court Street
Rutland, VT 05701-4058
(802) 773-1860; (802) 773-1861; (802) 773-
1825 FAX
paulajb@rutlandfree.org
http://www.rutlandfree.org
Paula J. Baker, Director
Mon–Wed 9:00–9:00, Thur–Fri 9:00–5:30,
Sat 9:00–5:00

Saint Albans Free Library
Vermont Room
11 Maiden Lane
Saint Albans, VT 05478
(802) 524-1507; (802) 524-1514 FAX
StAlbans@vals.state.vt.us
http://www.state.vt.us/s2
MaryPat Larrabee, Librarian

Saint Johnsbury Athenaeum
1171 Main Street
Saint Johnsbury, VT 05819-2289
(802) 748-8291
inform@helicon.net
http://www.stjathenaeum.org
Mon & Wed 10:00–8:00, Tue & Thur–Fri
10:00–5:30, Sat 9:30–4:00

John Woodruff Simpson Library
(East Craftsbury, VT—location)
Rural Route 1, Box 1035 (mailing address)
Craftsbury Common, VT 05826
(802) 586-9692
http://www.vmga.org/essex/woodruff.html
Sherry Urie, Librarian
Wed & Sat 9:00–noon, 2:00–5:00 &
7:00–9:30, Sun after Sunday school

Springfield Town Library
43 Main Street
Springfield, VT 05156
(802) 885-3108; (802) 885-4906 FAX
springfieldlibrary@hotmail.com
Russell S. Moore, Director
Mon–Thur 10:00–9:00, Fri 10:00–5:00, Sat
10:00–3:00
(Vermont genealogies, family and town
histories, with emphasis on Springfield
and Windsor County, some New
Hampshire and Massachusetts records)
$25.00 per year fee for nonresident

borrowers; in-house use of materials at no
charge

University of Vermont
Special Collections
Bailey/Howe Memorial Library
Burlington, VT 05405
(802) 656-2138; (802) 656-4038 FAX
edow@zoo.uvm.edu;
cgallagh@uvmvm.uvm.edu (Newspapers)
http://moose.uvm.edu
Reference Specialist
Mon–Thur 10:00–9:00, Fri 10:00–5:00, Sat
10:00–1:00, Sun 1:00–4:00; call for
intersession hours
(Vermont history; "Our primary clientele is
the University of Vermont academic
community and researchers of Vermont
history.")
charge for photocopying and other
reproductions

University of Vermont Library
Wilbur Collection of Vermontiana
Burlington, VT 05405-0036
(802) 656-2631
J. Kevin Graffagnino, Curator
Pub. *Liber*

Alice M. Ward Memorial Library
(Village Green, 27 Park Street—location)
PO Box 134 (mailing address)
Canaan, VT 05903
(802) 266-7135; (802) 266-7766; (802) 266-
7867 FAX
http://www.vmga.org/essex/ward.html
Jennifer Muse, Librarian
Library: Mon–Fri 1:00–6:00, Sat
11:00–1:00; Museum: by appointment
(a local heritage museum on the second floor
of the library, developed by the Canaan
Historical Society)

Norman Williams Public Library
10 South Park Street
Woodstock, VT 05091
(802) 457-2295
Woodstock@vals.state.vt.us
http://www.uvm.edu/~histpres/vtiana/
nwilliams.html
Katherine Ludwig, Librarian
Mon–Fri 10:00–5:00, Tue–Wed 7:00
A.M.–9:00 P.M., Sat 10:00–4:00

Historical Societies—Local and Regional

Addison Town Historical Society
Rural Delivery 1, Box 1348
Vergennes, VT 05491
(802) 759-2406
Thomas Johnson, President

Barnard Historical Society Museum
Charles Danforth Public Library
Barnard, VT 05031
(802) 234-9183
Eleanor Tatro
Fri 2:00–4:00, Sat 10:00–noon, and by
appointment

Barnet Historical Society
(Goodwillie House, 26 Goodwillie Road,
Barnet Center—location)
97 Old West Road (mailing address)
Barnet, VT 05821
(802) 633-2563 (Treasurer); (603) 633-4373
(President)
Florence E. Grahek, Treasurer; Rae McBride,
President
by appointment

(maintains 1791 Goodwillie House, artifacts,
pictures, products of local industry)
$5.00 per year membership

The Bellows Falls Historical Society
(Adams Grist Mill Museum, Mill
Street—location)
7 Atkinson Street (mailing address)
Bellows Falls, VT 05101
(802) 463-3374 (President); (802) 463-3092
(Secretary)
facades@sover.net (President);
ourtown@sover.net (Secretary)
Dennis Ladd, President; Cathy Bergmann,
Secretary
July–Aug: Sat–Sun 1:00–4:00, and by
appointment

Berlin Historical Society, Inc.
Rural Route 4, Box 2210
Montpelier, VT 05602
(802) 223-1203
Norbert Rhinerson, President

Bethel Historical Society, Inc.
Bethel Historical Society Museum
Church Street
Bethel, VT 05032
(802) 234-9413
Clara Abbott and Richard Edmunds, Curators
July–Aug: Sun 2:00–5:00

Black River Historical Society
(14 High Street—location)
PO Box 73 (mailing address)
Ludlow, VT 05149
(802) 228-5050
Georgia L. Brehm, Museum Director
Tue–Sat noon–4:00
(published local history)
$10.00 per year membership

Bradford Historical Society
(Bradford Academy—location)
PO Box 301 (mailing address)
Bradford, VT 05033
(802) 222-9026; (802) 222-4727 (Town Hall)
Phyllis Lavelle, Curator
Fri 2:00–4:00
(Bradford history)

Braintree Historical Society
33 Old Bass Road
Randolph, VT 05060
(802) 728-5272
phawley@sover.net
Phyllis N. Hawley, Secretary
by appointment
Pub. *Braintree Historical Society Newsletter*,
annually
("local history, preservation and maintainance
of Braintree Hill Meeting House and
environs; collecting artifacts and archives
[including genealogies] pertaining to
Braintree")
$5.00 per year membership

Brattleboro Historical Society
(230 Main Street, Brattleboro, VT
05301—location)
PO Box 6392 (mailing address)
Brattleboro, VT 05302
(802) 254-5037
histsoc@sover.net
http://Brattleborohistoricalsociety.org
Wayne Carhart, President
Thur 1:00–4:00, Sat 9:00–noon
Pub. *Newsletter*, two times per year
(Brattleboro history)
$5.00–$100.00 per year membership;
research: $10.00 per hour

Bridport Historical Society Museum
(Route 22-A—location)
Rural Route 1, Box 656 (mailing address)
Bridport, VT 05734
(802) 758-2654
Margaret Sunderland, Curator
Father's Day, and by appointment

Bristol Historical Society Museum
Howden Hall Community Center
Main Street
Bristol, VT 05443
(802) 453-6029
Evelyn Dike, President
summer: Mon–Sun 10:00–4:00; Mar–Oct:
Thur 7:30–9:30, and by appointment

Brookfield Historical Society
Marvin Newton House
447 Ridge Road
Brookfield, VT 05036
(802) 276-3036
E. Gray, Researcher
search fee: $10.00 per hour

Cabot Historical Society, Inc.
(Main Street, Cabot, VT 05647—location)
Rural Free Delivery, Lower Cabot (mailing
address)
Marshfield, VT 05658
(802) 563-2558
Leonard Spencer, President
4 July, Old Home Week, Fall Foliage
Festival, and by appointment

Canaan Historical Society
(Alice M. Ward Memorial Library,
upstairs—location)
PO Box 371 (mailing address)
Canaan, VT 05903
(802) 266-8845
Joan L. Cowan, Curator
when library is open or by appointment
admission: free

Castleton Historical Society Museum
(Main Street—location)
PO Box 219 (mailing address)
Castleton, VT 05735
(802) 468-5523
Mary Williamson
summer and fall: Sun 1:00–4:00

Cavendish Historical Society
(Main Street—location)
PO Box 110 (mailing address)
Cavendish, VT 05142
(802) 484-7498
Linda.M.Welch@Dartmouth.edu
http://www.web-home.com/vt-
genealogy/cavendish.htm
Mr. Carmine Guica, Genealogist and
Historian
June–Oct: Sun 2:00–4:00, and by
appointment
$5.00 per year membership

Chelsea Historical Society, Inc.
(Main Street—location)
PO Box 206 (mailing address)
Chelsea, VT 05038
(802) 685-4860
W. S. Gilman, Vice President

Chester Historical Society
(Main Street on the Green—location)
PO Box 118 (mailing address)
Chester, VT 05143
(802) 875-6211
Chris Curran, President
Sat (July–Oct) 2:00–4:00
$10.00 per year membership; research:

donation plus copy and mailing costs

Chittenden County Historical Society
PO Box 1576
Burlington, VT 05402-1576
(802) 864-4716
LFLEURY@Prodigy.net
Pub. *Chittenden County Historical Society
Bulletin*, quarterly
$20.00 per year membership; research: none

Concord Historical Society Museum
(Concord Town Hall, Main Street, Concord,
VT—location)
PO Box 195 (mailing address)
Concord, VT 05824
(802) 695-3330
Kathleen Fisher, President
last weekend in Sept, and by appointment

Crystal Lake Falls Historical Association
(The Pierce House, Water Street—location)
PO Box 253 (mailing address)
Barton, VT 05822
(802) 525-6251
Avis Harper, President
Mid-June to mid-Sept: Tue & Thur
10:00–noon & 2:00–4:00, Wed
2:00–4:00, Sat 10:00–noon
$5.00 per year membership; "no charge for
museum"

Danville Historical Archives
(Pope Memorial Library, The
Green—location)
PO Box 260 (mailing address)
Danville, VT 05828
(802) 684-2256
Jean Ashley, Librarian
Mon & Wed 9:00–7:00, Fri 9:00–6:00, Sat
9:00–noon

Derby Historical Society
(Main Street—location)
PO Box 357 (mailing address)
Derby, VT 05829
(802) 766-5324
gardyne@together.net
Bill Gardyne, President
by appointment

Dorset Historical Society
(Main Street—location)
PO Box 52 (mailing address)
Dorset, VT 05251
(802) 867-0331
Patricia Carmichael, President
winter: Fri–Sat 10:00–noon; summer: Fri
10:00–noon, Sat 10:00–2:00
$7.00 per year membership

Enosburgh Historical Society
(Freight Depot, Railroad Street—location)
PO Box 98 (mailing address)
Enosburgh Falls, VT 05450
(802) 933-2102
janiceellen@vtlink.net
John Whiting, President; Barbara Hayes,
Secretary; Janice Geraw, Curator
June–Aug: Sat 1:00–4:00
Pub. *Historical Digest*, four times per year
$5.00 per year membership

Essex Community Historical Society
(Routes 15 and 128—location)
3 Browns River Road (mailing address)
Essex Junction, VT 05452
(802) 878-6486

Fairfax Historical Society
(1181 Main Street, Route 104—location)
PO Box 145 (mailing address)

Fairfax, VT 05454
(802) 849-6638 (President)
http://www.geocities.com/Heartland/
Farm/9445/index.html
Michael R. Cain, President
Sun 2:00–4:00 (July, Aug, first two Sun in
Sept & first two Sun in Oct), and by
appointment
$2.00 per year membership

Fairfield Historical Society
c/o Fairfield Town Clerk
Fairfield, VT 05455
(802) 827-6160; (802) 827-3261
Julie Wolcott, President; Patty Esden, Vice
President

Fairlee Historical Society
Fairlee Town Hall
PO Box 95
Fairlee, VT 05045
(802) 333-9729; (802) 333-4363
Hester Gardner, Curator
as needed
(local genealogical research)
$2.00 per year membership

Ferrisburg Historical Society
PO Box 181
North Ferrisburg, VT 05473-0181
(802) 425-3380
Silas Towler, President
Pub. *Ferrisburg Memoirs*

Georgia Historical Society
Genealogy Committee
Box 2072
Georgia, VT 05468
(802) 524-4539
Peter Mallett
4 July–Labor Day: Mon, Wed & Sat
2:00–4:00
Pub. *Georgia Town History*, annually (Mar),
$10.00 plus postage (genealogy chapter
within book)

Glover Historical Society
Municipal Building, Second Floor
Glover, VT 05839
(802) 525-6227 (Town Clerk)
Wayne H. Alexander, President
June–Aug: Wed P.M., and by appointment

Grafton Historical Society, Inc.
(Main Street—location)
PO Box 202 (mailing address)
Grafton, VT 05146
(802) 843-2489
http://www.graftonhistory.org
Rosalys B. Wilson, Registrar
Pub. *Newsletter*, two times per year
(published history of Grafton)
$5.00/$10.00/$25.00 per year membership;
research: $25.00 per hour

Greensboro Historical Society
PO Box 151
Greensboro, VT 05841
Jenny Stoner, President
Tue–Thur 10:00–1:00, Sat 10:00–noon
Pub. *Hazen Road Dispatch*, one time per
year, $4.50 postpaid per issue
$6.00 per year membership

Groton Historical Society
(Route 302, Main Street—location)
PO Box 89 (mailing address)
Groton, VT 05046
(802) 584-3417
Richard Brooks, President
Sun (July–Aug) 2:00–5:00, all day on Fall
Foliage Day

Guilford Historical Society
(Guilford Center Road—location)
236 School Road (mailing address)
Guilford, VT 05301
Addie Minott, President
Memorial Day–Columbus Day: Tue & Sat
10:00–2:00
Pub. *The Guilford Slate*, three to four times
per year
("Historical society and museum; local
history; some local genealogy; changing
exhibit each summer.")
$5.00 per year membership

Halifax Historical Society Museum
(West Halifax, VT—location)
Rural Route 4, Box 531 (mailing address)
Brattleboro, VT 05301
(802) 368-7490
Susan Rusten and Edith Bickle, Curators
open periodically throughout the summer and
by request

Hartford Historical Society
(c/o Town of Hartford, 171 Bridge Street,
White River Junction, VT 05001—location)
PO Box 547 (mailing address)
Hartford, VT 05047
(802) 295-3077; (802) 295-6382 FAX
pstark@hartford-vt.org
Pat Stark, Archivist
Mon–Fri 9:00–4:00, and by appointment
send SASE with any requests

Hartland Historical Society
Hartland, VT 05048
(802) 436-2444 (Town Clerk)
Lee Motschman, President
Mon 2:00–4:00; meetings: second Wed
Pub. *Newsletter of Hartland Historical
Society*, semiannually
$5.00 per year membership; genealogical
research for donation

The Highgate Historical Society
PO Box 71
Highgate Center, VT 05459
Evangeline A. Malaney, Secretary

Holland Historical Society, Inc.
(Gore Road—location)
591 Page Hill Road, Holland (mailing
address)
Derby Line, VT 05830
(802) 895-2917
Penelope Tice, President
by appointment
Pub. *Newsletter*, annually
("Historical society and museum, local
artifacts and photos.")
$3.00 per year membership

Huntington Historical Society
Lower Village
PO Box 147
Huntington, VT 05462
(802) 434-4350

Island Pond Historical Society, Inc.
(Canadian National Railway
Station—location)
PO Box 408 (mailing address)
Island Pond, VT 05846
(802) 482-3923
C. F. Biron, President
by appointment

Isle La Motte Historical Society
1830 Schoolhouse
Isle La Motte, VT 05463
(802) 928-3422
Howard or Harriot Schwenker

July–Aug: Sat 1:00–4:00

Jericho Historical Society
(Old Mill, Route 15—location)
PO Box 35 (mailing address)
Jericho, VT 05465
(802) 899-3225
http://www.vermontcrafts.com/members/
JericSoc322.html
Ray Miglionico, Archivist
Mon 2:30–4:00, Thur 6:30–7:30
Pub. *The Jericho Reporter*, quarterly
(local history)

Lincoln Historical Society
(Quaker Street—location)
c/o Town Clerk (mailing address)
Lincoln, VT 05443
(802) 453-3628 voice & FAX
Steve Harris, President
Memorial Day–12 Oct: Sun noon–4:00, and
by appointment

Londonderry Historical Society
(Custer Sharp House, Middletown
Road—location)
PO Box 398 (mailing address)
Londonderry, VT 05148
(802) 824-4406
Robert McCabe, M.D., President; Kathleen
Wright, Corresponding Secretary
summer: Sat 10:00–2:00
$15.00 per year membership

Town of Lunenburg Historical Society
Route 1, Box 29A
Lunenburg, VT 05906
(802) 892-5317
Evan Hammond, President; Judith C. Young,
Secretary
Pub. *Echoes*, occasionally
$3.00 per year membership

Lyndon Historical Society
PO Box 85
Lyndon Center, VT 05850
(802) 626-8746
boerad@sover.net
http://www.sover.net/~boerad/historical
Virginia C. Downs, Co-Editor and Co-
President
meetings at the Cobleigh Library,
Lyndonville at least four times a year
Pub. *Lyndon Legacy*, quarterly
$5.00 per year membership

Manchester Historical Society
(Mark Skinner Library—museum location)
PO Box 363 (mailing address)
Manchester, VT 05254
(802) 362-3747
Mary Bort, Curator
by appointment; monthly meetings
(local history and genealogy)

Historical Society of Marlboro
PO Box 131
Marlboro, VT 05344
(802) 254-9152
L. Bourne, President; Tom Huenik, Secretary
July–Aug: Sat 2:00–5:00

Middlesex Historical Society
84 McCullough Hill Road
Middlesex, VT 05602
pattyw@sover.net
Patricia Wiley, President

**Middletown Springs Historical Society,
Inc.**
(The Green—location)
PO Box 1126 (mailing address)

Middletown Springs, VT 05757
(802) 235-2376
David P. Wright, Trustee
Sun (30 May–30 Oct) 2:00–4:00
Pub. *Middletown Springs Historical Society
Newsletter*, three to four times per year
$8.00 per year membership; research:
donation

Milton Historical Society
Milton Museum
(Main Street—location)
PO Box 2 (mailing address)
Milton, VT 05468
(802) 893-2267 (Ms. Brown); (802) 893-
2340 (Curator)
Gwen Brown; Jane FitzGerald, Curator

Missisquoi Valley Historical Society
(Main Street—location)
PO Box 237 (mailing address)
North Troy, VT 05859
(802) 988-2677
Maurice Phillips, President
June–Aug: Sat–Sun 2:00–5:00

Montgomery Historical Society Museum
(Montgomery Village—location)
PO Box 47 (mailing address)
Montgomery, VT 05470
(802) 326-4404
Sally Newton, Secretary
Sat (July–Aug) noon–3:00, and by
appointment

Montpelier Heritage Group, Inc.
PO Box 671
Montpelier, VT 05601-0671
Pub. *Montpelier Heritage Group Newsletter*,
quarterly
(historical society and historic preservation
group)
$10.00 per year membership

Morristown Historical Society
(Noyes House Museum, Main
Street—location)
PO Box 1299 (mailing address)
Morrisville, VT 05661-1299
(802) 888-7617; (802) 888-5605
Dawn K. Andrews, President
July–Aug: Wed–Sat 1:00–4:00
Pub. *Morristown Two Times*

**The New England Historic Genealogical
Society**
(see Massachusetts, Part 2)

Northfield Historical Society
(South Main Street—location)
PO Box 88 (mailing address)
Northfield, VT 05663
(802) 485-8081
Alan H. Weiss, President
Pub. *Dog River Crier*, three times per year
$5.00–$25.00 per year membership

Norwich Historical Society
(37 Church Street—location)
PO Box 341 (mailing address)
Norwich, VT 05055
(802) 649-0124; (802) 649-1071
NHS@tpk.net
William M. Aldrich, President; Martha
Nelson, Treasurer
Wed 2:30–4:30, and by appointment
$15.00 per year membership

Orleans County Historical Society, Inc.
Old Stone House Museum
Brownington Village
Rural Route 1, Box 500

Orleans, VT 05860
(802) 754-2022
http://homepages.together.net/~osh
Tracy N. Martin, Museum Director
Museum: July–Aug: Mon–Sun 11:00–5:00;
    15 May–30 June & 1 Sept–15 Oct:
    Mon–Tue & Fri–Sun 11:00–5:00;
    Archives: by appointment only
Pub. *The Old Stone House Museum Bulletin*,
    three times per year, $10.00 per year
    subscription, free on request to nonprofit
    institutions
(Orleans County, Vermont)
    admission: $5.00 general admission, $4.00
    for Orleans County residents, $2.00 for
    students under 12

Pawlett Historical Society
Pawlet, VT 05761

Peacham Historical Association
Church Street
Peacham, VT 05862
(802) 592-3571
Lorna Quimby, Curator and President
by appointment
Pub. *Peacham Patriot*, irregularly
$5.00 per year membership; research: $5.00
    per hour

Pittsfield Historical Society
(Town Hall—location)
PO Box 808 (mailing address)
Pittsfield, VT 05762
(802) 746-8147
L. Fifield, Secretary/Treasurer
Apr–Nov: 1:00–3:00, and by appointment

Pittsford Historical Society
(Eaton Hall, Route 7—location)
PO Box 423 (mailing address)
Pittsford, VT 05763
(802) 483-6623
Jean Davies, Curator
Tue (Mar–Nov) 9:00–4:00, Sat (July–Aug)
    9:00–4:00

Poultney Historical Society
Rural Free Delivery 1, Box 177
Poultney, VT 05764
(802) 287-5268
Ruth Czar, President
Sun (June–Aug) 1:00–5:00, and by
    appointment

Proctor Historical Society
Proctor Free Library
4 Main Street
Proctor, VT 05765
Nancy Kennedy, Researcher

Putney Historical Society
(Main Street, Town Hall—location)
PO Box 233 (mailing address)
Putney, VT 05346
(802) 387-5862
Laura Heller
Wed 2:00–4:00, and by appointment

Randolph Historical Society, Inc.
(Salisbury Street, Randolph—location)
PO Box 15 (mailing address)
Randolph Center, VT 05061
(802) 728-5398
Wes Herwig, Curator
by appointment
fee for research

Reading Historical Society Museum
Reading, VT 05062
(802) 484-7271
Walter Mendoza

Thur (mid-June to mid-Sept) 2:00–4:00

Readsboro Historical Society
(Route 100 across from the Post
Office—location)
Rural Route 1, Box 277 (mailing address)
Readsboro, VT 05350
(802) 423-5394
Mrs. Melvin H. Coe, President
by appointment
$3.00 per year membership

Rochester Historical Society
Town Library
Rochester, VT 05767
(802) 767-4453
Charles Woolley, President
Memorial Day to mid-Oct: Tue 1:00–7:00,
    Thur 1:00–5:00, Sat 9:00–1:00

Rockingham Meeting House Association
(Rockingham, VT—location)
29 Oak Hill Terrace (mailing address)
Bellows Falls, VT 05101
(802) 463-3941
John A. Leppman, President
July–Aug: daily 10:00–5:00
("Our services to genealogists are rather
    slight.")

Royalton Historical Society
Rural Route 1, Box 89D
Royalton, VT 05068
(802) 763-8567
John P. Dumville, President
by appointment
(small local historical society with
    collections focused on town)
$5.00 per year membership

Rutland Historical Society
96 Center Street
Rutland, VT 05701-4023
(802) 775-2006; (820) 773-7525 (President)
Helen Davidson, President
Mon 6:00 P.M.–9:00 P.M., Sat 1:00–4:00, and
    by appointment
Pub. *Rutland Historical Society Quarterly*;
    News from Nickwackett, quarterly
(a volunteer, nonprofit organization,
    specializing in Proctor, Rutland Town,
    West Rutland and Rutland City history)
$10.00 per year membership; admission:
    free; research: first hour free, reasonable
    fees for additional research; copy facilities
    available

Saint Albans Historical Society
Saint Albans Historical Museum
(Corner of Bishop and Church
Street—location)
PO Box 722 (mailing address)
Saint Albans, VT 05478
(802) 527-7933
Donald J. Miner, Director
June–Sept: Mon–Sat 1:00–4:00
Pub. *St. Albans Historical Society
    Newsletter*, three times per year
(a historical museum specializing in local
    history)
$15.00 per year membership; no genealogical
    search services

Saxtons River Historical Society
PO Box 18
Saxtons River, VT 05154
(802) 869-2566
Luring@vermontel.net
Louise Luring
Summer: Sat & Sun 2:00–4:30, and by
    appointment
Pub. *SRHS Newsletter*, two to three times per

year
$5.00 per year membership

Shaftsbury Historical Society
(Baptist Meeting House, Route 7-A, Center
Shaftsbury, VT—location)
PO Box 401 (mailing address)
Shaftsbury, VT 05262
(802) 447-7488
Robert J. Williams, Curator
Tue–Sun (15 June–15 Oct) 2:00–4:00
$5.00 per year membership; research: no fee

Sherburn Historians
1879 River Road
Killington, VT 05751
Mowle4@aol.com
Margaret Mowle, President

Shoreham Historical Society
Route 22-A
Shoreham, VT 05770
(802) 897-2600
Sue MacIntire, Curator
year-round by appointment

Shrewsbury Historical Society, Inc.
Museum
(5419 Route 103—location)
925 Keiffer Road (mailing address)
Cuttingsville, VT 05738
(802) 492-3378 (Genealogist)
Anne F. Spencer, Genealogist
Sat–Sun (summer) 1:00–3:00, and by
    appointment
(Shrewsbury history: account books, diaries,
    business records, school records, town
    reports, photographs; Shrewsbury
    genealogies, etc.)
$10.00 per year membership

Springfield Art and Historical Society
(Miller Art Center, 9 Elm Street—location)
PO Box 313 (mailing address)
Springfield, VT 05156
Fred Richardson, Treasurer and Researcher
Tue–Fri 10:00–4:00, Sat 1:00–4:00
Pub. *News & Reviews*, quarterly
(Springfield history from 1750)
$15.00 per year membership; research:
    donation or exchange

Stannard Historical Society
9 Willey Road
Greensboro Bend, VT 05842
(802) 533-2561
Ann Lawless, Chairperson
(no genealogical material, maintains church
    building)

Stowe Historical Society
Akeley Memorial Building, Stowe History
Room, Town Hall
(Main Street—location)
PO Box 224 (mailing address)
Stowe, VT 05672
(802) 253-6133
http://www.vmga.org/lamoille/stowehs.html
by appointment

Strafford Historical Society
PO Box 100
Strafford, VT 05072-0100
(802) 765-4321
gwenda.smith@valley.net
Gwenda Smith, Historian-Curator
by appointment only
Pub. *Membership Newsletter*, annually
("local history and families of Strafford
    only")
research fees vary

Thetford Historical Society
(Bicentennial Building, 16 Library
Road—location)
PO Box 33 (mailing address)
Thetford, VT 05074
(802) 785-2068
Charles Latham, Librarian
Mon & Thur 2:00–4:00, Tue 10:00–noon
Pub. *Newsletter*, irregularly
("Genealogical files on Thetford families;
manuscript collections; some biographies
and family histories.")
membership for donation; research: no
service available

**Tinmouth Historical and Genealogical
Society**
(Town Clerk's Office, 9 Mountain View
Road—location)
515 North End Road (mailing address)
Tinmouth, VT 05773
(802) 446-2498 voice & FAX
tinmouth@tax.state.vt.us
Gail Fallar, Town Clerk
Mon & Wed 8:00–noon & 1:00–5:00, Fri
8:00–noon
Pub. *Tinmouth Channel*, four times per year
(very small)
$12.00 per year membership

Vernon Historians, Inc.
(Route 142 and Pond Road—location)
Rural Route 1, Box 196, Pond Road (mailing
address)
Vernon, VT 05354
(802) 254-8015
Robert Johnson, President
Sun (early June–late Aug) 2:00–4:00, closed
4 July weekend

Walden Historical Committee
PO Box 54
West Danville, VT 05873
(802) 563-2472
Elizabeth P. Hatch, Chairman
Pub. *Walden 200*, two times per year (spring
and fall), $8.00 per year subscription
(Walden folk history)
research: $10.00 per year

Wallingford Historical Society
(Second Floor of the Town Hall—museum
location)
PO Box 327 (mailing address)
Wallingford, VT 05773
(802) 446-2336
demery@vermontel.net
Joyce Barbieri

Waterbury Historical Society Museum
28 North Main Street
Waterbury, VT 05676
(802) 244-7036
Linda Kaiser, Secretary
Mon–Wed 10:00–8:00, Fri 10:00–5:00, Sat
9:00–noon
Pub. *Waterbury Historical Society
Newsletter*, four times per year
$5.00 per year membership

Weathersfield Historical Society
(The Reverend Dan Foster House,
Weathersfield Center Road, Weathersfield,
VT—location)
PO Box 126 (mailing address)
Perkinsville, VT 05151-0126
(802) 263-3055 (Dan Foster House); (802)
263-8753 (leave your phone number)
rwdbry@sover.net (Rebecca W. Tucker,
Archivist and Genealogist)
http://www.weathersfield.org (Town of
Weathersfield, Vermont, web site)

Alison Roth, Treasurer
15 June–1 Oct: Mon & Thur–Sun 2:00–5:00,
and by appointment
Pub. *Newsletter*, three times per year
$7.50 per year membership

Wells Historical Society
Rural Route 1, Box 37
Wells, VT 05774
(802) 645-0435
Barbara J. Goodspeed, President

West Haven Historical Society
2919 Main Road
West Haven, VT 05743
(802) 265-3675; (802) 265-2177; (802) 265-
4576
kellis@rrmc.org
Kerry Ellis, Secretary

West Windsor Historical Society
(Route 44, Brownsville, VT—location)
PO Box 12 (mailing address)
West Windsor, VT 05037
(802) 484-7474
Mary B. Fenn, Chairman of Historic Records
Committee
Thur 9:00 A.M.–11:00 A.M., and by
appointment
Pub. *West Windsor Historical Society
Newsletter*, quarterly
$5.00 per year membership

Westminster Historical Society
(Town Hall, Route 5, Westminster,
VT—location)
Route 3, Box 634 (mailing address)
Putney, VT 05346
(802) 387-5778
Patricia Haas
Sun (summer) 2:00–4:00
research: will look up information in their
collection and in the town records on
request

The Weston Historical Society
Farrar-Mansur House Museum
(On The Green—location)
PO Box 247 (mailing address)
Weston, VT 05161
(802) 824-6781
Museum: May–Oct
Pub. *Times of Weston*
(provides genealogical services)

Whitingham Historical Society
(Whitingham, VT—location)
PO Box 125 (mailing address)
Jacksonville, VT 05342
Stella Stevens, President
Sun (June–Oct) 2:00–4:00
("History and artifacts of our town")

Williamstown Historical Society
(2476 Vermont Route 14 [Main
Street]—location)
PO Box 338
Williamstown, VT 05679
(802) 433-1283 (President)
Adam Boyce, President and Curator
May–Oct: various times and by appointment
("One of the largest collections on display in
central Vermont, featuring items of
Williamstown's social, industrial,
religious and political past from 1790 to
the present.")
$5.00 per year membership

Williston Historical Society
PO Box 995
Williston, VT 05495
Rick Brownell, President

Pub. *Williston Historical Society Bulleton*,
quarterly
from $4.00 per year membership

Historical Society of Windham County
(Route 30—location)
PO Box 246 (mailing address)
Newfane, VT 05345
(802) 365-4148
Joan Marr, Curator
Late May–mid-Oct: Wed–Sun 2:00–5:00
Pub. *News & Views*, three times per year
(county history and genealogy)
$7.00 per year membership; copies: 25¢ each

Winooski Historical Society
(73 East Allen Street—location)
21 Park Street (mailing address)
Winooski, VT 05404
(802) 655-3561

Woodstock Historical Society, Inc.
26 Elm Street
Woodstock, VT 05091
(802) 457-1822
http://www.uvm.edu/~histpres/vtiana/
woodstockhs.html
Marie McAndrew-Taylor, Archivist
Mon–Fri 10:00–5:00 by appointment
(emphasis on central Windsor County, special
publications on specific topics)
copying fees and shipping and handling fees

Genealogical Societies

State Genealogical Society

Genealogical Society of Vermont
PO Box 1553
Saint Albans, VT 05478-1006
jtyler@sover.net
http://www.rootsweb.com/~vtgsv
by appointment
Pub. *Vermont Genealogy*, quarterly, *The GSV
Newsletter*, quarterly
$20.00 per year membership

Genealogical Societies—Local & Regional

American-Canadian Genealogical Society
(see New Hampshire, Part 2)

**The New England Historic Genealogical
Society**
(see Massachusetts, Part 2)

**New York Genealogical and Biographical
Society Library**
(see New York, Part 2)

**Tinmouth Historical and Genealogical
Society**
(see Historical Societies—Local and
Regional, above)

Yankee Genealogical Society
Minnesota Genealogical Society
(see Massachusetts, Part 2)

Independent Publications and
Miscellany

Billings Farm and Museum
(River Road—location)
PO Box 489 (mailing address)
Woodstock, VT 05091-0489
(802) 457-2355; (802) 457-4663 FAX
David A. Donath, Director; Esther Munroe
Swift, Librarian/Archivist
Museum: daily (1 May–31 Oct) 10:00–5:00
(history and 19th-century agricultural history)

Center for Appalachian Studies
(see North Carolina, Part 2)

Claudette's
3962 Xenwood Avenue South
Saint Louis Park, MN 55416-2842
Claudette Atwood Maerz
Pub. *Across the Border* (includes northern
Vermont counties of Essex, Lamoille,
Chittenden, Caledonia, Grand Isle,
Franklin, Washington and Orleans, and
Quebec's eastern townships), quarterly,
$14.00 per year subscription in the U.S.,
$16.00 per year subscription in Canada;
Current Genealogical Publications,
annually

Discovery Museum
51 Park Street
Essex Junction, VT 05452
(802) 878-8687
Lynnette Donahue, President Board of
Directors
Sept–June: Tue–Wed 11:00–4:00, Thur–Sat
10:00–5:00, Sun 1:00–5:00; July–Aug:
Tue–Sat 10:00–5:00, Sun 1:00–5:00
(children's museum)

Historical Ink's Old Maps
(see New York, Part 2)

New England Connexion
(see Connecticut, Part 2)

The New England Quarterly
(see Massachusetts, Part 2)

Pioneer Publications
New England Queries and Reviews
(see Connecticut, Part 2)

**Society for the Preservation of New
England Antiquities—Archives**
(see Massachusetts, Part 2)

Sheldon Museum
1 Park Street
Middlebury, VT 05753
(802) 388-2117
sheldon_mus@myriad.middlebury.edu
http://www.vtweb.com/vermont
weathervane/96.8august/history.html
Nancy Rucker
Tue–Fri 1:00–5:00
Pub. *Sheldon Museum News & Notes*,
quarterly
from $20.00 per year membership

Shores Memorial Museum
(Center Street—location)
PO Box 35 (mailing address)
Lyndon Center, VT 05850
(802) 626-5742; (802) 626-8574 (Curator)
Ruth McCarty, Curator
Sat–Sun (Memorial Day–Labor Day)
2:00–4:00, and by appointment

**Vermont Agency of Transportation
(VTrans)**
(1 National Life Drive—location)
Drawer 33 (mailing address)
Montpelier, VT 05633-0001
(802) 828-0180
Shawn.Nailor@state.vt.us
http://aot.state.vt.us/omc/default.htm
Shaw G. Nailor

Vermont Folklife Center
(2 Court Street—location)
PO Box 442 (mailing address)
Middlebury, VT 05753
(802) 388-4964; (802) 388-1844 FAX

http://www.uvm.edu/~histpres/vtiana/
vtfolk.html
Mon–Fri 9:00–5:00 by appointment

Vermont Old Cemetery Association
PO Box 132
Townshend, VT 05353
(802) 365-7937
http://sageunix.uvm.edu/~rresnik/doc/
voc.htm
Charles Marchant, Secretary
Pub. *VOCA Newsletter*, quarterly, $5.00 per
year subscription, $20.00 for five years

VtGenWeb
Part of The USGenWeb Project
1717 Edgewater Avenue
Fort Wayne, IN 46805
(260) 426-3729
Mensch-Family@worldnet.att.net
http://home.att.net/~Local_History/
VT_History.htm
Ann McRoden Mensch, State Coordinator
and Professional Historical Genealogist
(links to other Vermont resources)

Virginia

Archives and Libraries with
Holdings in Genealogy

State Archives and Library

The Library of Virginia
800 East Broad Street
Richmond, VA 23219-8000
(804) 692-3500; (804) 692-3777 (Library
Reference); (804) 692-3888 (Archives
Reference); (804) 692-3556 FAX
refdesk@lva.lib.va.us (Library Reference
Services); archdesk@lva.lib.va.us
(Archives Research Services)
http://www.lva.lib.va.us
Conley L. Edwards, State Archivist;
Catherine Mishler, Reference Services
Director; Alexandra Gressitt, Archives
Research Services Director
Mon–Sat 9:00–5:00 (except legal holidays)
Pub. *Virginia Cavalcade*, quarterly, $3.95 for
single copy, $10.00 per year subscription
research: fees listed on web site

Virtual Library of Virginia (VIVA)
gailmac@vt.edu
http://web.viva.lib.va.us/viva/libraryviva.cfm

State Historical Society

Virginia Historical Society
(428 North Boulevard, Richmond, VA
23220—location)
PO Box 7311 (mailing address)
Richmond, VA 23211-0311
(804) 358-4901 (Main); (804) 342-9677
(Library); (804) 342-9649 (Genealogy
Information); (804) 355-2399 FAX
fpollard@vahistorical.org
http://www.vahistorical.org
Frances S. Pollard, Director of Library
Services
Mon–Sat 10:00–5:00
Pub. *Virginia Magazine of History and
Biography*, quarterly
(magazine does not publish genealogical
material)
$35.00 per year membership

**City, County and Regional Archives and
Libraries**
(A more exhaustive list of public and
academic libraries can be found at
http://www.lva.lib.va.us/whoweare/
directories/valib/webah.asp.)

**City of Alexandria Archives and Records
Center**
(801 South Payne Street—location)
Box 178, City Hall (mailing address)
Alexandria, VA 22313
(703) 519-3326
Tod Chernikoff, Records Administrator and
Archivist
Mon–Fri 8:00–4:00
(Records of the City of Alexandria, 1920 to
the present; local government archives
only)
copy fee

Alexandria Public Library
Local History Special Collections
717 Queen Street
Alexandria, VA 22314-2420
(703) 838-4555; (703) 838-4577, ext. 213
(Local History Special Collections); (703)
706-3912 FAX
http://www.alexandria.lib.va.us
Joyce A. McMullin, Branch Librarian

Mon–Thur 9:00–9:00, Fri 9:00–6:00, Sat
9:00–5:00
Pub. *The Doorway*, quarterly, free

Amherst County Historical Museum
(154 South Main Steet—location)
PO Box 741 (mailing address)
Amherst, VA 24521
(434) 946-9068
achmuseum@aol.com
http://members.aol.com/achmuseum/
achmhis.htm
Michael N. Morell, County Museums
Coordinator
Tue–Sat 9:00–4:30
Pub. *Muse*, quarterly
(general county history and genealogy)
$15.00 per year membership; research:
$15.00 for one name, $25.00 for three
names

Amherst County Public Library
(382 South Main Street—location)
PO Box 370 (mailing address)
Amherst, VA 24521
(804) 946-9388; (804) 946-9348 FAX
feedback@acpl.us
http://www.acpl.us
Carl Merat, Director
Mon–Wed & Fri–Sat 9:00–5:30, Thur
9:00–8:00

Arlington County Public Library
Virginia Room
1015 North Quincy Street
Arlington, VA 22201-4603
(703) 358-5966
libraries@co.arlington.va.us
http://www.co.arlington.va.us/lib
Judith Knudsen
Mon–Tue, Thur & Sat 10:00–5:00, Wed
1:00–9:00
("Historical, genealogical, and current
information about Virginia and Arlington
County")

Augusta County Library
1759 Jefferson Highway
Fishersville, VA 22939
(540) 949-6354; (540) 885-3961
http://www.lib.co.augusta.va.us
Barbara Olsen, Reference Librarian
Mon–Thur 9:00–9:00, Fri–Sat 9:00–5:00

Thomas Balch Library
208 West Market Street
Leesburg, VA 22075
(703) 737-7195; (703) 737-7150 FAX
balchlib@leesburgva.org
http://www.leesburgva.org/
town_services/thomas_balch.cfm
Jane Sullivan, Library Manager
Mon & Thur–Fri 10:00–5:00, Tue
10:00–8:00, Wed 2:00–8:00, Sat
11:00–4:00, Sun 1:00–5:00
(Loudoun County collection: genealogies,
family files, obituaries, marriage records,
census, wills, deeds, newspapers, tax rolls,
cemetery records, etc.)

Bassett Historical Center
Genealogy Room
3964 Fairystone Park Highway
Bassett, VA 24055-5547
(540) 629-9191; (540) 629-9840 FAX
baslib@hotmail.com
http://www.brrl.lib.va.us
Patricia C. Ross, Head of Genealogy Services
Mon, Wed & Thur 10:00–6:00, Tue
noon–8:00, Fri–Sat 10:00–2:00
(Henry County and the surrounding area)
copies: 10¢

Bedford City/County Museum
201 East Main Street
Bedford, VA 24523
(540) 586-4520
Ellen A. Wandrei, Managing Director
Mon–Sat
Pub. *Museum Newsletter*, quarterly, $5.00
donation for subscription
(small genealogical library and research
room)
$1.00 admission to museum and/or research
library

Bridgewater College
Alexander Mack Memorial Library
East College Street
Bridgewater, VA 22812
(540) 828-5410; (540) 828-5482 FAX
rgreenaw@bridgewater.edu
http://www.bridgewater.edu/departments/
library/library.html
Ruth Greenawalt, Library Director
Mon–Fri 8:00–5:00

Bristol Public Library
701 Goode Street
Bristol, VA 24201-4199
(276) 645-8780
judbarry@bristol-Library.org
http://www.bristol-library.org
Jud Barry, Director; Susan Whitt, Assistant
Director
Mon–Thur 9:00–8:00, Fri–Sat 9:00–5:00
(Bristol, Virginia and Tennessee history, area
family files, area cemetery records)
research: $25.00 per hour for searches over
30 minutes, plus copies at 25¢ per page

Buchanan County Public Library
(Poe Town Road—location)
Route 2, Box 3 (mailing address)
Grundy, VA 24614
(540) 935-6581; (540) 935-6292 FAX
angela@bcplnet.org
http://www.bcplnet.org
Pat Hatfield, Director
Mon 1:00–8:00, Tue–Wed & Fri–Sat
8:30–5:00, Thur 8:30–8:00
(southwest Virginia history and genealogy,
also collects eastern Kentucky and some
western North Carolina records)

Campbell County Public Library
(684 Village Highway—location)
PO Box 310 (mailing address)
Rustburg, VA 24588
(434) 332-9560; (434) 332-9697 FAX
http://tlc.library.net/campbell
Wilma Dotson, Public Services Librarian
Mon, Wed & Fri–Sat 9:00–5:30, Tue & Thur
9:00–9:00

Central Rappahannock Regional Library
1201 Caroline Street
Fredericksburg, VA 22401
(540) 372-1144; (540) 371-7965 FAX
http://www.LibraryPoint.org
Mon–Thur 9:00–9:00, Fri–Sat 9:00–5:30,
Sun 1:00–5:30
copies: 15¢ each

Chesapeake Public Library
William McGhee Wallace Memorial Room
298 Cedar Road
Chesapeake, VA 23320-5598
(757) 382-6461; (757) 436-8301 FAX
stillman@chesapeake.lib.va.us
http://www.chesapeake.lib.va.us
Margaret P. Stillman, Director
Mon–Thur 9:00–9:00, Fri–Sat 9:00–5:00,
Sun 1:00–5:00

Chesterfield County Library
(9501 Lori Road—location)
PO Box 297 (mailing address)
Chesterfield, VA 23832-0297
(804) 784-1603; (804) 748-1601; (804) 751-
4679 FAX
http://library.co.chesterfield.va.us
Barbara A. Lattimer, Librarian
Mon–Thur 10:00–9:00, Fri–Sat 10:00–5:30

College of William and Mary
Omohundro Institute of Early American
History and Culture
Earl Gregg Swem Library Building
PO Box 8781
Williamsburg, VA 23187-8781
(757) 221-1126 (*Quarterly*); (757) 221-3508
(Reference and Information Department,
Swem Library); (757) 221-1110
(Omohundro Institute); (757) 221-1047
FAX (Omohundro Institute)
pvhigg@facstaff.wm.edu;
ieahc1@facstaff.wm.edu (Omohundro
Institute)
http://swem.wm.edu
Pat Higgs, Office Manager; Beverly Smith,
Secretary to the Director
Mon–Fri 8:30–5:30
Pub. *The William and Mary Quarterly: A
Magazine of Early American History and
Culture*, 3rd series (emphasis is no longer
on Virginia history or genealogy),
quarterly, $30.00 per year subscription;
Uncommon Sense, two times per year, not
available by subscription
(not a historical society but maintains a small
library and is devoted to the publication of
scholarly articles and books in the field of
early American studies from discovery to
approximately 1815)
$50.00 per year membership

Culpeper County Library
271 Southgate Shopping Center
Culpeper, VA 22701
(540) 825-8691; (540) 825-7486 FAX
culpepercl@summit.net
http://tlc.library.net/culpeper
Susan J. Keller, Director
Mon–Thur 10:00–9:00, Fri–Sat 10:00–5:00,
Sun (Sept–May) 1:30–5:00

The Danville Public Library
511 Patton Street
Danville, VA 24541
(434) 799-5195; (434) 799-5221 FAX
stephjc@ci.danville.va.us
http://www.ci.danville.va.us/library/info.html
Jay Stephens, Library Director
Mon & Thur 9:00–9:00, Tue–Wed & Fri
9:00–5:00, Sat 9:00–1:00

**Research Center for Delmarva History and
Culture**
(see Maryland, Part 2)

Eastern Shore of Virginia Public Library
(23610 Front Street—location)
PO Box 360 (mailing address)
Accomac, VA 23301
(757) 787-3400; (757) 787-2241 FAX
rkeeney@espl.lib.va.us
http://www.espl.org
W. Robert Keeney, Director

Essex Public Library
117 North Church Lane
Tappahannock, VA 22560
(804) 443-4945; (804) 443-6444 FAX
http://www.essexlibrary.org
Bess Haile, Director

Fairfax County Public Library
Fairfax City Regional Library
Virginia Room
3915 Chain Bridge Road
Fairfax, VA 22030
(703) 246-2123; (703) 385-1911 FAX
va_room@fairfaxcounty.gov
http://www.fairfaxcounty.gov/library/
branches/vr
Suzanne Sheldon Levy, Virginia Room
Librarian
Mon–Thur 10:00–9:00, Fri 10:00–6:00, Sat
10:00–5:00, Sun noon–6:00
("We have a good basic genealogical/local
history collection, also basic U.S. and
international sources and a great deal on
the states Virginians came directly from
and went directly to.")
copies: 15¢ each

Fluvanna County Library
(Highway 15 South at Carysbrook—location)
PO Box 548 (mailing address)
Fork Union, VA 23055
(804) 842-2230 voice & FAX
http://www.fcplva.org
Marcia Drane, Director
Mon–Tue 9:00–6:00, Wed–Thur noon–8:00,
Fri 9:00–5:00, Sat 9:00–3:00

John Fox Jr. Genealogical Library
(see Kentucky, Part 2)

Franklin County Public Library
120 East Court Street
Rocky Mount, VA 24151
(540) 483-3098; (540) 483-1568 FAX
cstanley@franklincountyva.org
http://www.franklincountyva.org/library/
index.htm
Dorothy Hodges, Technical Services
Librarian
Mon–Tue & Thur 8:30–8:00, Wed & Fri–Sat
8:30–5:00
(genealogy materials are noncirculating; "Due
to limited staff, extensive searches are not
available; lists of amateur genealogists
available for specific searches.")
copies: 10¢ per page, up to 10 pages, plus
postage

**Fredericksburg Regional Genealogical
Society**
c/o Fredericksburg Methodist Church
308 Hanover Street
Fredericksburg, VA 22404
(540) 373-7114

Galax-Carroll Regional Library
608 West Stuart Drive
Galax, VA 24333
(540) 236-2042; (276) 236-5153 FAX
lbryant@galaxcarroll.lib.va.us
http://galaxcarroll.lib.va.us
Laura A. Bryant, Director
Mon, Wed & Fri 9:00–5:00, Tue & Thur
9:00–7:00, Sat 10:00–2:00

George Mason University
Special Collections Department
Fenwick Library-2C
Fairfax, VA 22030-4444
(703) 993-2220; (703) 993-2229 FAX
speccoll@gmu.edu
http://www.gmu.edu/library/
specialcollections

Hacksma House Genealogy Library
(see Washington, Part 2)

**Hampton Center for the Arts and
Humanities**

Hampton Recreation Department
22 Wine Street
Hampton, VA 23669

Hampton Public Library
Virginiana Room
4207 Victoria Boulevard
Hampton, VA 23669-3596
(757) 727-1314
http://www.hamptonpubliclibrary.org
Elizabeth A. Wilson, Senior Library
Assistant
Mon–Thur 9:00–9:00, Fri–Sat 9:00–5:00,
Sun 1:00–5:00
(a special collection of materials on Virginia
history and genealogy, focusing primarily
on the local area; housing over 7,000
titles, which include published materials,
microform, maps, vertical files, and
photos)

Handley Regional Library
Archives Room
(100 West Piccadilly Street, Corner of
Braddock Street—location)
PO Box 58 (mailing address)
Winchester, VA 22604
(540) 662-9041; (540) 722-4769 FAX
reference@hrl.lib.state.va.us
http://www.hrl.lib.state.va.us/handley/
default.asp
Tue–Wed 1:00–9:00, Thur–Sat 10:00–5:00
(manuscripts, maps, photographs, published
books and ephemera; "Our collection
focus is the lower Shenandoah Valley; the
Archives is jointly operated by The
Handley Library and the Winchester-
Frederick County Historical Society.")

Heritage Public Library
(9001 Boulevard Road—location)
PO Box 8 (mailing address)
Providence Forge, VA 23140
(804) 966-2480; (804) 966-5982 FAX
http://heritagelibrary.org
Alah M. Bernstein, Director
Mon–Tue & Thur 9:00–8:00, Wed & Fri
9:00–5:30, Sat 9:00–2:00
("We are the public library for the Virginia
counties of Charles City and New Kent.")

**Huntsville-Madison County Public
Library**
(see Alabama, Part 2)

Information Center (Petersburg, Virginia)
(400 East Washington Street—location)
PO Box 2107 (mailing address)
Petersburg, VA 23803
(804) 861-8080

J. Robert Jamerson Memorial Library
(106 Main Street—location)
PO Box 789 (mailing address)
Appomattox, VA 24522
(434) 352-5340; (434) 352-0933 FAX
http://65.169.41.33/Jamerson/default.asp
Megan Gibbs, Director

Jefferson-Madison Regional Library
201 East Market Street
Charlottesville, VA 22902
(434) 979-7151; (434) 971-7035 FAX
halliday@avenue.org
http://jmrl.org/main/main.htm
John Halliday, Director

Jones Memorial Library
Lynchburg Public Library
2311 Memorial Avenue
Lynchburg, VA 24501
(434) 846-0501; (804) 846-1572 FAX

webmaster@jmlibrary.org
http://www.jmlibrary.org
Edward Gibson, Librarian
Tue & Thur 1:00–9:00, Wed & Fri
1:00–5:00, Sat 9:00–5:00
Pub. *JML Notes*, semiannually
(Virginia genealogy, Lynchburg-area history)
interlibrary loans and OCLC $10.00 each,
copies by mail $5.00, in-house copies 25¢
each

**The Charles Pinckney Jones Memorial
Library, Inc.**
406 West Riverside Street
Covington, VA 24426
(540) 962-3321; (540) 962-8447 FAX
janis01@ntelos.net
http://www.cpjones.org
Thurman Pugh, Director; Diana Hawkins,
Assistant Director
Mon, Wed & Fri 9:30–5:30, Tue & Thur
9:30–8:30, Sat (school year) 9:30–2:30,
Sat (summer) 9:30–12:30
(genealogy and local history collection
including Alleghany County, City of
Covington, Clifton Forge, and some other
Virginia counties' history)

Kenmore Association Library
1201 Washington Avenue
Fredericksburg, VA 22401
(540) 373-3381; (540) 371-6066 FAX

Kirn Memorial Library
Sargeant Memorial Room
Norfolk Public Library
301 East City Hall Avenue
Norfolk, VA 23510-1703
(757) 664-7323, ext 3736; (757) 664-7321
FAX
yhillia@city.norfolk.va.us
http://www.npl.lib.va.us
Peggy A. Haile, Librarian
Mon & Sat 10:00–5:00, Tue, Thur & Sun
1:00–5:00, Wed 1:00–9:00
(collects and maintains a historical collection
of Norfolkiana, Virginiana and genealogy,
now more than 16,000 books, 3,700
microforms and 20,000 photographs)
no research fee; charge for copies and mailing
only

Loudoun Museum, Inc.
16 Loudoun Street, S.W.
Leesburg, VA 20175
(703) 777-7427; (703) 737-3861 FAX
http://loudounmuseum.org
Douglas Foard, Executive Director
Feb–Dec: Mon–Sat 10:00–5:00, Sun
1:00–5:00
Pub. *Heritage Review*, quarterly
("The museum contains 6,000 items and
artifacts of Loudoun history." History
museum for Loudoun County and
Leesburg; a good historical resource with
limited genealogical information.)
$30.00 per year membership

**The Lyceum—Alexandria's History
Museum**
George Washington Bicentennial Center
201 South Washington Street
Alexandria, VA 22314
(703) 838-4994; (703) 838-4997 FAX
lyceum@ci.alexandria.va.us
http://oha.ci.alexandria.va.us/lyceum
James C. Mackay, Director
Mon–Sat 10:00–5:00, Sun 1:00–5:00
Pub. *The Alexandria Observer*, quarterly
(includes Virginia history and local history)

Lynchburg Museum System

(901 Court Street, Lynchburg, VA
24504—location)
PO Box 60 (mailing address)
Lynchburg, VA 24505
(434) 847-1459
Adam E. Scher, Curator of Collections
Mon–Fri 8:00–4:30
Pub. *Signpost*, quarterly, free to volunteers
and donors
(manuscript and photographic collections
related to Lynchburg, Virginia; Museum
System operates Lynchburg Museum,
Point of Honor and the Miller-Claytor
House)

Madison County Library
(402 North Main Street—location)
PO Box 243 (mailing address)
Madison, VA 22727
(540) 948-4720; (540) 948-4919 FAX
http://www.lva.lib.va.us/whoweare/
directories/valib/webip.asp
Bonnie Utz, Director

James Madison University
Carrier Library
Special Collection Department
Harrisonburg, VA 22807
(540) 568-3612; (540) 568-3405 FAX
bolgiace@jmu.edu
http://www.jmu.edu/libliaison/sc/aboutsc.
htm
(central Shenandoah Valley: Page,
Rockingham, Shenandoah, and Augusta
counties; little genealogical data)

Massanutten Regional Library
Main Library, 174 South Main Street
Harrisonburg, VA 22801
(540) 434-4475; (540) 434-4382 FAX
mrl@mrlib.org
http://www.mrlib.org/mainlibrary.htm
Phillip T. Hearne, Director
Mon & Fri 9:00–6:00, Tue–Thur 9:00–9:00,
Sat 9:00–5:00

Menno Simons Historical Library
Eastern Mennonite University
(see Religious Archives and
Organizations—Mennonite, Part 3)

Monroe Museum and Memorial Library
908 Charles Street
Fredericksburg, VA 22401
(540) 899-4559

Montgomery-Floyd Regional Library
125 Sheltman Street
Christiansburg, VA 24073
(540) 382-6965; (540) 382-6964 FAX
feedback@mfrl.org
http://www.montgomery-floyd.lib.va.us
Marsha Hertel, Director
Mon–Thur 10:30–8:30, Sat 10:30–5:30, Sun
2:00–5:30

Museum of American Frontier Culture
(1250 Richmond Road, Staunton, VA
24401—location)
PO Box 810 (mailing address)
Staunton, VA 24402-0810
(540) 332-7850; (540) 332-9989 FAX
Katharine L. Brown, Ph.D., Director of
Research and Collections
Museum: Mon–Sun 9:00–5:00; Library:
Mon–Fri 10:00–4:00 by appointment only
Pub. *Newsletter*, quarterly
(library and research center; 17th & 18th
century English, Irish, Scotch-Irish,
German, Valley of Virginia)
$35.00 per year membership (includes
museum admission and ship discount);

staff cannot undertake searches

Newport News Public Library System
Martha Woodroof Hiden Virginiana Room
Main Street Library
1100 Main Street
Newport News, VA 23601-4105
(757) 591-4858; (757) 591-4860 FAX
http://www.nngov.com/library/virgrm/
virgana.htm
Sue Baldwin, Supervising Librarian
Mon–Thur 9:00–9:00, Fri–Sat 9:00–6:00,
Sun 1:00–5:00
(includes Old Dominion Land Company
records: company developed city of
Newport News—497 deeds and abstracts,
775 maps and company records,
1829–1948)
queries: $1.00 mailing fee; copies: 15¢ per
page

Nottoway County Library
400 Tyler Street
Crewe, VA 23930
(804) 645-9310; (804) 645-8513 FAX
npierce@nottlib.org
http://www.nottlib.org/nottoway/default.asp
Nancy S. Pierce, Director

Ohoopee Regional Library
(see Georgia, Part 2)

Old Dominion University
The Perry Library Special Collections
Norfolk, VA 23529-0256
(757) 683-4483; (757) 683-5954 FAX
special@libstaff.lib.odu.edu
http://netserv.lib.odu.edu
Mon–Fri 9:00–4:30, and by appointment
("diaries, letters, legal and campaign files,
photographs, and maps that document
such subjects as the Civil War, Virginia
politics, military history, African-
American history, Norfolk urban
redevelopment, women's history, and
local history")

Page Public Library
(100 Zerkel Street—location)
PO Box 734 (mailing address)
Luray, VA 22835
(540) 743-6867; (540) 743-7661 FAX
http://www.mrlib.org/pagepublic.htm
Mon, Wed & Fri–Sat 10:00–5:00, Tue
10:00–6:00, Thur 10:00–9:00

Pamunkey Regional Library
(7527 Library Drive—location)
PO Box 119 (mailing address)
Hanover, VA 23069
(804) 537-6091; (804) 537-6210; (804) 537-
6211; (804) 537-6212; (804) 537-6389
FAX
http://www.pamunkeylibrary.org
Fran Freimarck, Director
Mon–Wed 9:00–9:00, Tue & Fri 9:00–6:00,
Sat 9:00–2:00

Pearisburg Public Library
209 Fort Branch Road
Pearisburg, VA 24134
(540) 921-2556; (540) 921-1708 FAX
sjvroberts@yahoo.com
Sandra V. Robertson, Librarian
Mon noon–8:00, Tue noon–5:00, Wed & Fri
9:00–5:00, Thur 9:00–8:00, Sat 9:00–1:00

Petersburg Public Library
William R. McKenney Branch Building
Reference Department
137 South Sycamore Street
Petersburg, VA 23803

(804) 733-2387; (804) 733-7972 FAX
webmaster@ppls.org
http://www.ppls.org
Pat Ward, Public Services Librarian
Mon & Wed 9:00–9:00, Tue & Thur–Sat
9:00–5:30
(Civil War and Virginia interest)

Portsmouth Public Library
601 Court Street
Portsmouth, VA 23704
(757) 393-8365; (757) 393-8501; (757) 393-
8973 (Reference); (757) 393-5107 FAX
http://www.ci.portsmouth.va.us/ppl/
index.html
Mary E. Goodman, Manager Main Library
Mon–Fri 9:00–9:00, Sat 9:00–5:00
(includes records of Norfolk County, of
which Portsmouth was the county seat
until 1858 when it became an independent
city)

Prince William Public Library System
RELIC (Ruth Emmons Lloyd Information
Center for Genealogy and Local History)
Bull Run Regional Library
8051 Ashton Avenue
Manassas, VA 20109-2892
(703) 792-4540; (703) 792-4520 FAX
pwlibrary@pwcgov.org (use RELIC in
subject line)
http://www.pwcgov.org/library/relic
Donald L. Wilson, Virginiana Librarian
Mon–Thur 10:00–9:00, Fri–Sat 10:00–5:00,
Sun (mid-Sept to early June) noon–5:00
Pub. *Prince William Reliquary*, quarterly
(electronic journal, free at web site)
("Virginia statewide local history and
genealogy, with a focus on Prince William
County. An emphasis on Civil War and
Revolutionary War history. Selection of
genealogy materials for nearby states and
immigrant origins. Pathfinders available at
our web site: *Climbing Your Family Tree*,
Chasing the Civil War, *Roots in Prince
William*. Offers genealogy programs and
workshops.")
free admission; photocopies: 15¢ per page

Radford Public Library
30 First Street
Radford, VA 24141
(540) 731-3621; (540) 731-4857 FAX
afisher@radford.va.us
http://www.radford.va.us/library/index.html
Ann H. Fisher, Library Director
Mon–Wed 10:00–8:30, Thur–Fri 10:00–5:30,
Sat 10:00–4:30, Sun (winter) 2:00–5:00
(mostly southwestern Virginia material;
Internet access available for public use)

Walter Cecil Rawls Library and Museum
(22511 Main Street—location)
PO Box 310 (mailing address)
Courtland, VA 23837
(757) 653-2821; (757) 653-9374 FAX
webmaster@blackwaterlib.org
http://www.blackwaterlib.org
Beverly Worsham, Assistant Director
Mon & Wed–Thur 9:00–8:30, Tue & Fri
9:00–5:00, Sat 9:00–3:00

W. G. Rhea Public Library
(see Tennessee, Part 2)

Richmond Public Library
101 East Main Street
Richmond, VA 23219
(804) 780-4672; (804) 646-4550; (804) 646-
7685 FAX
litandhisdept@ci.richmond.va.us (Cyber
Librarian);

artandmusicdept@ci.richmond.va.us;
bstdept@ci.richmond.va.us (Business,
Science, and Technology)
http://www.richmondpubliclibrary.org
Ellen Parnell, Senior Librarian, Literature and
History Department
Sept–May: Mon–Thur 9:00–9:00, Fri
9:00–6:00, Sat 9:00–5:00; June–Aug:
Mon–Thur 9:00–9:00, Fri 9:00–6:00, Sat
9:00–1:00
("does not acquire genealogical material"; has
Richmond city directories 1819 to the
present)

Roanoke City Public Library
Virginia Room
706 South Jefferson Street
Roanoke, VA 24016
(540) 981-2073; (540) 981-1781 FAX
http://www.roanokegov.com/library/
index.html
Alice Carol Tuckwiller
Mon–Sat 9:00–5:00

Samuels Public Library
538 Villa Avenue
Front Royal, VA 22630
(540) 635-3153; (540) 635-7229 FAX
reference@spl.state.va.us
http://www.shentel.net/library/samuels
Barbara Ecton, Director
Mon–Thur 10:00–9:00, Fri–Sat 10:00–5:00,
Sun 1:00–5:00
copies: 20¢ per page

Shenandoah County Library
300 Stoney Creek Boulevard
Edinburg, VA 22824
(540) 984-8200; (540) 984-8207 FAX
jmm_scl@shentel.net
http://www.shenandoah.co.lib.va.us
Robert L. Pasco, Director; Jean M. Martin,
Archivist
Mon, Wed & Fri 10:00–6:00, Tue & Thur
10:00–8:00, Sat 10:00–4:00

Southside Regional Library
(316 Washington Street—location)
PO Box 10 (mailing address)
Boydton, VA 23917
(434) 738-6580; (434) 738-6070 FAX
http://www.srlib.org

Anne Spencer Memorial Foundation
(1313 Pierce Street—location)
1306 Pierce Street (mailing address)
Lynchburg, VA 24501
(434) 845-1313

Staunton Public Library
1 Churchville Avenue
Staunton, VA 24401
(540) 332-3902; (540) 332-3906 FAX
library@ci.staunton.va.us
http://www.staunton.va.us/library/
spinlibr.htm
Ruth Arnold, Director
Mon–Thur 9:00–9:00, Fri–Sat 9:00–5:00, Sat
(June–Aug) 9:00–1:00)

Suffolk Public Library System
Morgan Memorial Library
443 Washington Street
Suffolk, VA 23434
(757) 934-7686; (757) 539-7155 FAX
ref@suffolk.lib.va.us
http://www.suffolk.lib.va.us
Elliott A. Drew, Director
Mon–Tue 9:00–8:00; Wed–Sat 9:00–5:30

Sullivan County Library
(see Tennessee, Part 2)

Tazewell County Public Library
Genealogy Department
(310 East Main Street—location)
PO Box 929 (mailing address)
Tazewell, VA 24651
(540) 988-2541; (540) 988-5980
http://www.tcplweb.org
Nora W. Lockett, Reference Librarian
Mon–Wed & Fri–Sat 9:00–5:30, Thur
9:00–8:30, Sun 2:00–6:00
copies: first ten pages free, 10¢ per page for
each additional page, plus postage

Troy Public Library
(see Alabama, Part 2)

University of Mississippi
Center for the Study of Southern Culture
(see Mississippi, Part 2)

University of Virginia
Special Collections Department
Alderman Library
Charlottesville, VA 22903-2498
(434) 924-3021 (Reference Department);
(434) 924-3243
mssbks@virginia.edu
http://www.virginia.edu/speccol
hours: various; call (804) 924-7911

University of Virginia
Mary Washington College
Simpson Library
1801 College Avenue
Fredericksburg, VA 22401-4664
(540) 654-1125; (540) 654-1147
http://library.mwc.edu

Valentine Museum
Reference Services
1015 East Clay Street
Richmond, VA 23219
(804) 649-0711
Reference Services: Wed & Fri 9:00–noon &
1:00–4:00
Pub. *VM News*

Virginia Beach Public Library
Central Library
Local History Genealogy Collection
4100 Virginia Beach Boulevard
Virginia Beach, VA 23452-1767
(757) 431-3001 (Telephone Reference);
(757) 431-3072 (Central Librarian); (757)
431-3018 FAX
eref@vbgov.com (reference questions
pertaining to Virginia Beach and/or
Princess Anne County);
cbarkley@vbgov.com
http://VBgov.com/libraries
Carolyn L. Barkley, Central Librarian
Mon–Thur 10:00–9:00, Fri–Sat 10:00–5:00,
Sun (Oct–May) 1:00–5:00
Pub. *The Beach* (monograph $7.95 plus
4.5% tax for Virginia residents)

Virginia Commonwealth University
James Branch Cabell Library
Special Collections Department
(901 Park Avenue—location)
PO Box 842033 (mailing address)
Richmond, VA 23284-2033
(804) 828-1108; (804) 828-0151 FAX
ulsjbcsca@hsc.vcu.edu
http://www.library.vcu.edu/jbc/speccoll/
speccoll.html
Curtis Lyons, Head
Mon–Fri 9:00–noon & 1:00–6:00, and by
appointment

Virginia Commonwealth University
Tompkins-McCaw Library

(509 North 12th Street—location)
PO Box 980582 (mailing address)
Richmond, VA 23298-0582
(804) 828-9898; (804) 828-6089 FAX
jkoste@gems.vcu.edu
http://exlibris.uls.vcu.edu/library/tml/
speccoll/hmpge.html

Virginia Military Institute
VMI Archives
Preston Library
Lexington, VA 24450
(540) 464-7566; (540) 464-7089 FAX
archives@vmi.edu
http://www.vmi.edu/archives
Diane B. Jacob, Archivist
Mon–Fri 8:00–4:30, appointment strongly
recommended

**Virginia Polytechnic Institute and State
University**
Newman Library-Special Collections and
Manuscripts
PO Box 90001
Blacksburg, VA 24062-9001
(540) 231-6308; (540) 231-9263; (540) 231-
3694 FAX
gailmac@vt.edu
http://www.lib.vt.edu
(Appalachian history [Appalacian Mountain
areas: Kentucky, Maryland, North
Carolina, Pennsylvania, South Carolina,
Tennessee, Virginia, and West Virginia];
Civil War; maps, oral history,
photographs, special collections)

Washington and Lee University
James G. Leyburn Library
Special Collections
Lexington, VA 24450
(540) 463-8663; (540) 463-8649; (540) 463-
8640; (540) 463-8640 FAX
bbrown@wlu.edu
http://www.wlu.edu/~library/leyburn/
index.html
C. Vaughan Stanley, Special Collections
Librarian
Mon–Fri 9:00–5:00, when university is in
session; summer: Mon–Fri various, please
call
(specializing in Rockbridge County, Virginia,
genealogy)
copies: 15¢ per page plus $2.00 service
charge

Washington County Public Library
Local History and Genealogy Room
205 Oak Hill Street
Abingdon, VA 24210
(276) 676-6298; (276) 676-6235 FAX
refdesk@wcpl.net
http://www.wcpl.net
John J. Cromer, Reference Librarian; Joan
Boone, Reference Speicalist
Mon–Thur 9:00–9:00, Fri–Sat 9:00–5:00,
Sun (Sept–May) 2:00–5:00
("Predominantly published resources about
Washington County, Virginia, and
Southwest Virginia counties and some
Virginia materials in general. Resources
are not available for Interlibrary Loan.")
research: staff does not conduct genealogy
research; copies: 10¢ per page plus
postage

Mary Ball Washington Museum
(8346 Mary Ball Road—location)
PO Box 97 (mailing address)
Lancaster, VA 22503-0097
(804) 462-7280; (804) 462-6107
Christine C. Townley, Executive Director
Tue by appointment, Wed–Fri 10:00–5:00,

Sat 10:00–3:00
Pub. *Mary Ball Washington Museum Journal,* quarterly; *Post Rider Quarterly* (in planning)
(genealogical research center, Virginia history research library; various genealogical research services, workshops, classes, seminars and group research trips)

Waynesboro Public Library
600 South Wayne Avenue
Waynesboro, VA 22980
(540) 949-6173; (540) 942-6753 FAX
devoydh@ci.waynesboro.va.us (Reference)
http://www.waynesboro.va.us/library.html
Dorothy Anne Reinbold, Library Director
Mon–Fri 9:00–9:00, Sat 9:00–5:00
Research: queries must be mailed

Westmoreland County Museum and Library
43 Court Square
Montross, VA 22520
(804) 493-8440
Mon–Sat (1 Nov–31 Mar) 10:00–4:00,
Mon–Sat (1 Apr–31 Oct) 10:00–5:00
(houses the collection of the Northern Neck of Virginia Historical Society)

Wythe-Grayson Regional Library
Grayson County Public Library
(147 South Independence Avenue—location)
PO Box 159 (mailing address)
Independence, VA 24348
(276) 773-3018; (276) 773-3289 FAX
kdanner@wythegrayson.lib.va.us
http://wythegrayson.lib.va.us
Katie Danner, Genealogy Contact
Mon, Wed & Fri 9:00–5:30, Tue & Thur 9:00–7:00, Sat 10:00–2:00

Wytheville Community College Library
1000 East Main Street
Wytheville, VA 24382
(276) 223-4742; (800) 468-1195 (toll free in Virginia only); (276) 223-4778 FAX
wcrobea@wc.cc.va.us
http://www.wcc.vccs.edu
Anna Ray Roberts, Coordinator of Library Services
Mon–Fri 8:00–5:00 during regular school sessions, call ahead if possible
(southwest Virginia local history and genealogy)

York County Public Library
8500 George Washington Highway
Yorktown, VA 23692
(757) 890-5107 (Reference); (757) 890-5127 FAX
http://www.yorkcounty.gov/library/index.html
Lucinda Munger-Kress, Director
Mon–Thur 10:00–9:00, Fri 10:00–6:00, Sat 10:00–5:00, Sun 1:00–5:00

Historical Societies—Local and Regional

Albemarle County Historical Society
The McIntire Building
200 Second Street, N.E.
Charlottesville, VA 22902-5245
(434) 296-1492 (Director); (434) 296-7294 (Librarian)
http://monticello.avenue.gen.va.us/community/agencies/achs
Lynne C. Heetderks, Executive Director; Margaret M. O'Bryant, Librarian
Charlottesville-Albemarle Historical Collection: Mon–Fri 9:00–5:00, Sat

10:00–1:00
Pub. *Magazine of Albemarle County History,* annually; *Bulletin of the Albemarle County Historical Society,* quarterly
$30.00 per year membership

Alexandria Historical Society, Inc.
The Lyceum
George Washington Bicentennial Center
201 South Washington Street
Alexandria, VA 22314
(703) 548-1776 (Society); (703) 838-4994 (Lyceum); (703) 838-4997 FAX (Lyceum)
James C. Mackay, Lyceum Director
Lyceum: Mon–Sat 10:00–5:00, Sun 1:00–5:00

Amelia County Historical Society/Library
PO Box 113
Amelia, VA 23002
(804) 561-3180

Amelia Historical Society
Church Street
Amelia, VA 23002

Arlington Historical Society, Inc.
(1805 South Arlington Ridge Road, Arlington, VA 22202—location)
PO Box 402 (mailing address)
Arlington, VA 22210
(703) 892-4204
Dr. Harold Handerson
Fri–Sat 11:00–3:00, Sun 2:00–5:00
Pub. *Arlington Historical Magazine,* annually, $9.50 per year subscription

Augusta County Historical Society
PO Box 686
Staunton, VA 24402-0686
(540) 886-1479 (Editor)
Pub. *Augusta Historical Bulletin,* semiannually (May, Nov)
$10.00 per year membership; research: $8.00 per hour plus cost of copies and postage over 32¢

Avoca Museums and Historical Society
1514 Main Street
Altavista, VA 24517-1132
(434) 369-1076

Bath County Historical Society, Inc.
PO Box 212
Warm Springs, VA 24484
(540) 839-2543; (540) 839-2566 FAX
bathcountyhistory@tds.net
Margo Oxendine, Executive Director
Tue–Sat 9:00–4:00
Pub. *Newsletter,* quarterly
("Publishes 20± genealogical reference books.")
$15.00 per year membership; research: $20.00 per hour ($20.00 minimum)

Bedford Historical Society, Inc.
(315 North Bridge Street—location)
PO Box 602 (mailing address)
Bedford, VA 24523
http://members.aol.com/bedfordhs
President

Botetourt County Historical Society, Inc.
Courthouse Square
PO Box 468
Fincastle, VA 24090
(540) 473-3713
ehonts@aol.com
http://truth.idbsu.edu/bhs/bhs.html

Boyd County Historical Society

(see Kentucky, Part 2)

Campbell County Historical Society
PO Box 560
Rustburg, VA 24588

Carroll County Historical Society
PO Box 937
Hillsville, VA 24343
(540) 728-2125 Secretary (daytime)
Shelby Inscore Puckett, Editor
Mon–Fri 8:00–3:30
Pub. *Carroll County Chronicles,* quarterly
$12.00 per year membership

Chesterfield Historical Society of Virginia
(10011 Iron Bridge Road—location)
PO Box 40 (mailing address)
Chesterfield, VA 23832
(804) 748-1026; (804) 748-3032 FAX
Nancy Carter Crump, Executive Director
Mon–Fri 10:00–4:00
Pub. *The Messenger,* quarterly; *The Journal of the Chesterfield Historical Society,* annually
$12.00 per year membership

Clarke County Historical Association
(32 East Main Street—location)
PO Box 306 (mailing address)
Berryville, VA 22611
(540) 955-2600; (540) 955-0285 FAX
archives@visuallink.com
http://visuallink.net/ccha
Mary T. Morris, Archivist
by appointment
Pub. *Clarke County Proceedings,* annually
$20.00 per year membership; research: call for rates

Craig County Historical Society
(223 Main Street—location)
PO Box 206 (mailing address)
New Castle, VA 24127-0206
(540) 864-5220
L. Clayton Abbott, Chairman
mornings only
Pub. *Our Proud Heritage,* semiannually
$3.00 per year membership

Culpeper Historical Society, Inc.
PO Box 785
Culpeper, VA 22701

Cumberland County Historical Society
PO Box 188
Cumberland, VA 23040-0188
(804) 492-4533
Sue C. Seawell, Secretary
Pub. *Cumberland County, Virginia, Historical Bulletin,* annually (Oct), $6.50 per year subscription
$10.00 per year membership

Eastern Shore of Virginia Historical Society
(Kerr Place, 69 Market Street—location)
PO Box 193 (mailing address)
Onancock, VA 23417
(757) 787-8012
John H. Verrill, Executive Director; Lacy Dick, Archivist
Library: Wed 1:00–4:00; Museum: Tue–Sat 10:00–4:00
(library with many local sources)
$3.00 admission

Essex County Historical Society
278 West Gwynn Field Road
Tappahannock, VA 22560
http://www.iocc.com/~swright/esxsoc.html
Mike Marshall, President

Pub. *Bulletin*, semiannually
$10.00 per year membership

Historical Society of Fairfax County, VA
PO Box 415
Fairfax, VA 22030
(703) 246-2123
Susan Leigh, Secretary; Suzanne Sheldon
Levy, Virginia Room Librarian
Fairfax City Regional Library, Virginia
Room: Mon–Thur 9:00–9:00, Fri
9:00–6:00, Sat 9:00–5:00, Sun noon–8:00
Pub. *Historical Society of Fairfax County,
VA Yearbook*, biannually, $7.50 per issue
$15.00 per year membership

Falls Church Historical Commission
City Clerk
300 Park Avenue
Falls Church, VA 22046
(703) 241-5014
8:00–5:00
("We are just beginning to inventory births,
marriages, burials, wills.")

**The Fauquier Heritage and Preservation
Society**
(4110 Windhester Road—location)
PO Box 594 (mailing address)
Marshall, VA 20116
(540) 364-3440
http://www.fhs.org/Dig/page19.htm
Robert L. Sinclair, President
Tue–Thur 10:00–4:00, other days by
appointment
Pub. *The Fauquier Heritage Society News*,
quarterly
(Virginia local history and genealogy; houses
entire collection of John K. Gott, local
author and historian, who is on site on
Wednesdays; plus other publications,
family histories and genealogies)
$10.00 per year membership; queries
answered by mail or published in
newsletter

Fauquier Historical Society, Inc.
The Old Jail Museum
(Court House Square and Ashby Street,
Warrenton, VA 20186—location)
PO Box 675 (mailing address)
Warrenton, VA 20188
(540) 347-5525 (Museum); (540) 347-0607
(Museum Director)
Mrs. Jackie Lee, Museum Director
Museum: Tue–Sun 10:00–4:00
Pub. *Fauquier Historical Society "News &
Notes,"* biannually
("Mostly northern Virginia
history—emphasis on county history";
especially history of Fauquier County and
Warrenton: names, places, events; museum
exhibits covering pre-Revolutionary to
20th century; resource material for county
sites)
$15.00 per year membership; research: fees
by genealogist, Phyllis Scott, (703) 347-
2054

Flowerdew Hundred Foundation
1617 Flowerdew Hundred Road
Hopewell, VA 23860
(804) 541-8897
flowerdew@firstsaga.com
http://www.flowerdew.org
Dennis Pickeral
by appointment
$25.00 per year membership

Fluvanna County Historical Society
Old Stone Jail Museum
PO Box 132

Palmyra, VA 22963
(434) 842-3557
Josephine Snead, President
May–Sept: Sat & Sun afternoons
Pub. *Fluvanna County Historical Society
Bulletin*, semiannually
$10.00 per year membership

Giles County Historical Society
(200 North Main Street—location)
PO Box 404 (mailing address)
Pearisburg, VA 24134
(540) 921-1050
gileschs@i-plus.net
http://personal.picusnet.com/gileschs
Barbara Rowlette, Curator
Museum: Wed–Fri noon–5:00, Sat–Sun
2:00–5:00; Research: Thur noon–5:00
Pub. *Newsletter*, quarterly
$10.00 per year membership; research by
donation fees

Gloucester Historical Commission
PO Box 1176
Gloucester, VA 23061

Goochland County Historical Society
(2875 River Road West—location)
PO Box 602 (mailing address)
Goochland, VA 23063
(804) 556-3966 voice & FAX
http://www.goochlandhistory.org
Phyllis B. Silber, Administrator
summer: Tue–Fri 10:00–3:00; winter:
Wed–Fri 10:00–3:00
Pub. *GCHS Magazine*, annually, $10.00 per
issue; *GCHS Newsletter*, three times per
year
(includes research library with central
Virginia and James River records)
$25.00 per year membership; research:
$15.00 per half-hour, $30.00 per hour

Grayson County Historical Society, Inc.
PO Box 529
Independence, VA 24348
Pub. *Glimpses of Grayson*
$5.00 per year membership

Great Falls Historical Society
PO Box 56
Great Falls, VA 22066
(703) 759-5803
Susan Cochran, President
Pub. *Reflections*, biennually, costs vary

Greene County Historical Society
PO Box 185
Stanardsville, VA 22973
Pub. *Greene County Magazine*, annually
$5.00 per year membership

Gum Springs Historical Society
8100 Fordson Road
Alexandria, VA 22306
(703) 799-1198
http://www.lke-comply.com/fcmn/htm/
gshs/gshs.htm

Hanover County Historical Society, Inc.
(Old Jail-Hanover County Courthouse, Route
301—location)
PO Box 91 (mailing address)
Hanover, VA 23069
(804) 537-6262 (Office); (804) 746-2377
(President)
Anne Geddy Cross, President
Pub. *Hanover County Historical Society
Bulletin*, semiannually (June, Nov);
Highlights, about three times per year
$10.00 per year membership; research:
services not available

**Harrisonburg-Rockingham Historical
Society**
Shenandoah Valley Folk Art and Heritage
Center
(382 High Street—location)
PO Box 716 (mailing address)
Dayton, VA 22821
(540) 434-4032 (President's work); (540)
828-4858 (President's home); (540) 879-
2681 voice & FAX (Museum)
http://www.marketplace.staunton.va.us/
valyhst/hrhs.html
Larry Bowers, President
Mon & Wed–Sat 10:00–4:00
Pub. *Harrisonburg-Rockingham Historical
Society Newsletter*, quarterly; *Rockingham
Recorder*, irregularly
(genealogical library which also holds history
and Civil War information related
primarily to Rockingham County; a
bookstore in Dayton which carries a wide
range of genealogical books; museum in
Harrisonburg; Stonewall Jackson Valley
Campaign Electric Map at 301 South
Main, Harrisonburg)
$25.00 per year membership; library
admission: $5.00 for nonmembers

King and Queen Historical Society
(King and Queen Court House, Green
Historical District—location)
PO Box 129 (mailing address)
King and Queen Court House, VA 23085
(804) 769-3355 (Treasurer); (804) 785-9558
(Museum answering machine)
Robert T. Ryland, Jr., Treasurer
Museum: Sat 10:00–4:00, Sun 1:00–5:00;
Access to records: by appointment
Pub. *Bulletin of King and Queen Historical
Society*, semiannually (Jan, July), $3.00
per issue ppd.
("In our archives we have a few early records
given by individuals; most of county's
records burned by Yankees 1863.")
$10.00 per year membership; research: no
capability for significant searches

King George County Historical Society
PO Box 424
King George, VA 22485

**Lee County Historical and Genealogical
Society**
Po Box 231
Jonesville, VA 24263

Louisa County Historical Society
(Museum in the old jail adjacent to the Louisa
County Courthouse—location)
PO Box 1172 (mailing address)
Louisa, VA 23093
http://monticello.avenue.gen.va.us/
Library/JMRL/Louisa/historical.html
Sat–Sun 2:00–4:00
Pub. *Louisa County Historical Magazine*,
semiannually; *Louisa County Historical
Society Newsletter*
(archives not yet open to researchers, hence
no genealogical services)
$15.00 per year membership

Lynchburg Historical Foundation, Inc.
(325 12th Street, Lynchburg, VA
24504—location)
PO Box 248 (mailing address)
Lynchburg, VA 24505
(434) 528-5353
Nancy Jamerson Weiland, Office Manager
Tue–Thur 8:30 A.M.–12:30 P.M.
Pub. *Lynch's Ferry Magazine*, semiannually,
$4.18 per year subscription; *View From
the Terrace*, quarterly, free

$20.00 per year membership

Martinsville-Henry County Historical Society
PO Drawer 432
Martinsville, VA 24114

Mathews County Historical Society, Inc.
PO Box 855
Mathews, VA 23109

New River Historical Society
Wilderness Road Regional Museum
(5240 Wilderness Road—location)
PO Box 373 (mailing address)
Newbern, VA 24126
(540) 674-4835
wrrm@psknet.com
Ann S. Bailey
Mon–Sat 10:30–4:30; Museum: Mon–Sat 10:30–4:30, Sun 1:30–4:30
Pub. *NRHS Journal*, annually, $2.50 per issue for nonmembers; *Benchmarks*, quarterly
(local history of Floyd, Giles, Montgomery and Pulaski counties, and the city of Radford)
$15.00 per year membership; museum admission: $2.00 for adults

Norfolk County Historical Society of Chesapeake, VA
Chesapeake Public Library
William McGhee Wallace Memorial Room
298 Cedar Road
Chesapeake, VA 23320
(757) 382-6591; (757) 382-6461 (Library); (757) 436-8301 FAX (Library)
Joe Law, President
Library: Mon–Thur 9:00–9:00, Fri–Sat 9:00–5:00, Sun 1:00–5:00
("Neither the library nor the historical society do genealogical research for patrons; list of researchers for hire available on request.")
$7.50 per year membership

Norfolk Historical Society
PO Box 6367
Norfolk, VA 23508-0367
(757) 423-0989
webmaster@norfolkhistorical.org
http://www.norfolkhistorical.org
Pub. *Courier*, quarterly
$25.00 per year membership

Northern Neck of Virginia Historical Society
PO Box 716
Montross, VA 22520
Mrs. George Mason, III, Executive Secretary
Pub. *The Northern Neck of Virginia Historical Magazine*, annually, $14.00 per year subscription
(The "combined research collections of Northern Neck of Virginia Historical Society and Westmoreland County Museum & Library . . . totaling about 1,000 volumes, are inter-shelved on the second floor of the Westmoreland County Museum)
$20.00 per year membership

Northumberland County Historical Society
(86 Back Street—location)
PO Box 221 (mailing address)
Heathsville, VA 22473
(804) 580-8581
Virginia Burgess, Executive Secretary
Tue–Thur 9:00–4:00
Pub. *The Bulletin*, annually
$15.00 per year membership; research: $5.00,

includes five photocopies, additional copies at 5¢ each

Orange County Historical Society, Inc.
130 Caroline Street
Orange, VA 22960-1533
(540) 672-5366
http://www.orangecohist.org
Kenneth M. Clark, Administrator
Mon–Fri 1:00–5:00
Pub. *Orange County Historical Society Newsletter*, bimonthly
("The Society's library contains more than 2,000 volumes, and there are over 1,000 files with information on local families, historic buildings and sites, plus a map collection. Information is available not only on Orange County, but also on our neighboring counties, such as Madison, Culpeper and Greene; there is also data on the early settlement of the Virginia Piedmont, historic homes, Civil War history, and many other fields of interest.")
$12.50 per year membership

Patrick County Historical Society, Inc.
(116 West Blue Ridge Street—location)
PO Box 1045 (mailing address)
Stuart, VA 24171
(276) 694-2840
Virginia Collins, Museum Staff Genealogist; Barbara C. Baughan, Volunteer
Tue–Sat 10:00–2:00
(local family files and others related to this area of Virginia, deed index, cemeteries, etc.)
$10.00 per year membership; search in society holdings for postage and copy costs only

Pittsylvania Historical Society
PO Box 1206
Chatham, VA 24531
(434) 432-5031
Preston B. Moses, President
hours: various
Pub. *The Packet*, quarterly (Feb May, Aug, Nov)
("Pittsylvania-Virginia genealogical-historical events, etc.")
$10.00 per year membership

Portsmouth Historical Association
221 North Street
Portsmouth, VA 23704
(757) 393-0241
Alice C. Hanes, President

Prestwould Foundation
(Route 15-N, Rural Free Delivery 2—location)
PO Box 872 (mailing address)
Clarksville, VA 23927
(434) 374-8672
Julian D. Hudson, Director
Apr–Oct: 12:30–4:30
(house museum, primarily historical, not genealogical)
admission: $4.50 for adults

Princess Anne County/Virginia Beach Historical Society
2040 Potters Road
Virginia Beach, VA 23454
http://virginiabeachhistory.org
Sid Vaughn, President
Historic Home: Wed (July–Aug) noon–5:00
Pub. *PAC Newsletter*

Rappahannock Historical Society/Library
PO Box 261

Washington, VA 22747-0261
(540) 675-1163

Roanoke Valley Historical Society
(1 Market Square, Center-in-the-Square, Roanoke, VA 24011—location)
PO Box 1904 (mailing address)
Roanoke, VA 24008
(540) 342-5770; (540) 224-1238 FAX
Clare White, Librarian
weekdays 10:00–5:00, Sun 1:00–5:00
Pub. *Newsletter*, monthly; *Journal*, annually

Rockbridge Historical Society
(101 East Washington Street—location)
PO Box 514 (mailing address)
Lexington, VA 24450
(540) 464-1058; (540) 463-8663 (Washington and Lee University Library Special Collections Department)
Alice Williams, Curator
Campbell House: summer: Tue–Fri 10:00–3:00, Sat 10:00–1:00; winter: Tue–Sat 10:00–1:00
Pub. *News Notes*; *Proceedings of the Rockbridge Historical Society*
$7.50 per year membership (includes *News Notes*)

Salem Historical Society
(801 East Main Street—location)
PO Box 201 (mailing address)
Salem, VA 24153
(540) 389-6760

Seneca Road Historical Society
(625 Seneca Road—location)
PO Box 32 (mailing address)
Great Falls, VA 22066

Shenandoah County Historical Society
c/o Shenandoah County Library
300 Stoney Creek Boulevard
Edinburg, VA 22824
(540) 984-8200; (540) 984-8207 FAX
scl@shentel.net
David L. Steinberg, Director of the Library
Library: Mon–Tue & Thur 10:00–8:00, Wed & Fri 10:00–6:00, Sat 10:00–4:00
Pub. *Shenando News* (emphasis on Shenandoah County and Valley of Virginia), quarterly
$10.00 per year membership

Smyth County Historical and Museum Society, Inc.
(Stadium Road—location)
PO Box 788 (mailing address)
Marion, VA 24354-0788
(540) 783-2745 (Curator)
Mrs. H. B. Eller, Curator
Sun (1 June to 1 Sept) 2:00–5:00, special openings for students from grade and high schools
$5.00 per year membership

Southern Studies Institute
(see Louisiana, Part 2)

The Historical Society of Southwest Virginia
PO Box 3877
Wise, VA 24293
Rhonda Robertson, Secretary
Pub. *Historical Sketches of Southwest Virginia*, annually
$7.00 per year membership

Spotsylvania Historical Association, Inc.
PO Box 64
Spotsylvania, VA 22553
(540) 582-5672

Staunton River Historical Society
Willie Hodges Booth Museum
(Main Street—location)
PO Box 270 (mailing address)
Brookneal, VA 24528

Suffolk-Nansemond Historical Society
PO Box 1255
Suffolk, VA 23439-1255
(757) 562-4403
Mrs. Carl R. Saunders, Chair, Genealogy
    Committee

Tazewell County Historical Society, Inc.
(100 Fincastle Turnpike—location)
PO Box 916 (mailing address)
Tazewell, VA 24651-0916
(276) 988-4069; (276) 988-3581 (Mrs.
    Surface)
http://www.cc.utah.edu/~pdp7277/taze-
    soc.html
Patricia W. Surface
Wed 11:00–1:00, and by appointment;
    meetings first Sun 2:30
Pub. *Tazewell County Historical Society
    Newsletter*, quarterly (Mar, June, Sept,
    Dec)
(five published volumes of photo albums,
    mostly before 1925)
$12.00 per year membership

Warren Heritage Society
101 Chester Street
Front Royal, VA 22630
(540) 636-1446
Ben Weddle, President
Mon–Fri 10:00–4:00
Pub. *WHS Newsletter*, quarterly
$15.00 per year membership

**Historic Society of Washington County,
Virginia, Inc.**
(306 Depot Square [Old Train
Station]—location)
PO Box 484 (mailing address)
Abingdon, VA 24212-0484
(276) 623-8337
Kitty M. Henninger, President; Nancy
    Leasure, Library Director
Mon–Fri 10:00–4:00
Pub. *News Letter*, five times per year; *Annual
    Bulletin*
(computer database with over 240,000
    entries; list of publications for sale)
$25.00 per year membership; research: $5.00
    limited search for nonmembers, research
    policy available upon request; copies: 20¢
    each plus postage, send SASE for
    information

Waterford Foundation, Inc.
PO Box 142
Waterford, VA 20197
(540) 882-3018; (540) 882-3921 FAX
Martha Baine, Archivist; Bronwen Souders,
    Genealogical Researcher and Historian
by appointment
(Waterford families and history, especially
    history and genealogies of the black
    families in Waterford)
$35.00 per year foundation membership, from
    $50.00 Friends of Waterford membership

**West Virginia and Regional History
Association**
(see West Virginia, Part 2)

Williamsburg Area Historical Society
285 Neck-O-Land Road
Williamsburg, VA 23185
(757) 229-2158
Ed Belvin, Former Vice President

(presently inactive but still answers inquiries;
    deals only with local history from 1800,
    not genealogy)

**Winchester-Frederick County Historical
Society**
1340 South Pleasant Valley Road
Winchester, VA 22601-4447
(540) 662-6550; (540) 662-6991 FAX
wfchs@shentel.net
Cissy Shull, Executive Director
Mon–Fri 9:00–5:00
Pub. *Winchester-Frederick County
    Historical Society Journal*; *Newsletter*,
    quarterly
$15.00 per year membership

The Wise County Historical Society
(Wise County Courthouse, Main
Street—archives and office location)
PO Box 368 (mailing address)
Wise, VA 24293
(540) 328-6451
Rhonda Robertson, Secretary
9:00–4:30 by appointment (office manned by
    volunteers)
Pub. *The Appalachian Quarterly* (Mar, June,
    Sept, Dec), $10.00 per year subscription
(quarterly covers the southern Appalachians:
    Kentucky, Tennessee, North Carolina,
    Virginia and West Virginia)
$10.00 per year membership; research:
    inquiries answered if accompanied by
    SASE

Wythe County Historical Society Library
205 Tazewell Street
Wytheville, VA 24382-2313
(276) 223-3331
Cathy Carlson Reynolds, Archivist
Wed–Fri 10:00–4:00, Sat noon–4:00
Pub. *Wythe County Historical Review*, two
    times per year
$15.00 per year membership; research:
    $15.00 per hour off-site research fee;
    admission free

Genealogical Societies

State Genealogical Societies

**Genealogical Research Institute of
Virginia "GRIVA"**
PO Box 29178
Richmond, VA 23242-0178
griva_mail@yahoo.com
http://www.rootsweb.com/~vagriv
Jean B. Robinson, Past President
Pub. *GRIVA News & Notes*, quarterly (Sept,
    Dec, Mar, June), $15.00 per year
    subscription
$15.00 per year membership; no research by
    mail

Southern Society of Genealogists, Inc.
(see Alabama, Part 2)

Virginia Genealogical Society
5001 West Broad Street, Suite 115
Richmond, VA 23230-3023
(804) 285-8954; (804) 285-0394 FAX
mail@vgs.org
http://www.vgs.org
Emily Rusk, Executive Director
Tue–Wed 7:30–2:30
Pub. *Magazine of Virginia Genealogy*,
    quarterly; *The Virginia Genealogical
    Society Newsletter*, bimonthly (Feb, Apr,
    June, Aug, Oct, Dec)
$26.00 per year membership

Genealogical Societies—Local & Regional

Alleghany Highlands Genealogical Society
1011 North Rockbridge Avenue, Suite 102
Covington, VA 24426-1136
(540) 962-1501
InnaMcAlli@aol.com; yorkylvr@intelos.net
http://www.rootsweb.com/~vaallegh/AHGS
Inna Henderson, First Vice President
meetings: second Thur 7:00
Pub. *Newsletter*
$15.00 per year membership

**Allegheny Regional Family History Society
(ARFHS)**
(see West Virginia, Part 2)

Caroline County Genealogical Society
PO Box 9
Bowling Green, VA 22427

**Central Virginia Genealogical Association,
Inc. (CVGA)**
PO Box 5583
Charlottesville, VA 22905-5583
SDuBar@aol.com
http://www.avenue.org/cvga
Susan DuBar, Corresponding Secretary
Pub. *Central Virginia Heritage*, quarterly
(includes central Virginia counties of present-
    day Albemarle, Amherst, Appomattox,
    Augusta, Bedford, Buckingham,
    Campbell, Culpeper, Cumberland,
    Fluvanna, Greene, Goochland, Louisa,
    Madison, Nelson, Orange, Page,
    Rockbridge, Rockingham and Shenandoah
    counties; library housed at the Albemarle
    County Historical Society)
$15.00 per year membership

Culpeper Genealogical Society
PO Box 1326
Culpeper, VA 22701
momdsb@summit.net
http://www.rootsweb.com/~vacgs
Donna S. Boyd
Pub. *Culpeper Connections*, quarterly
$15.00 per year membership

Fairfax Genealogical Society
PO Box 2290
Merrifield, VA 22116-2290
(703) 536-6205; (888) 828-4121
Fairfax City Regional Library, Virginia
    Room: Mon–Thur 9:00–9:00, Fri
    9:00–6:00, Sat 9:00–5:00, Sun noon–8:00
Pub. *Newsletter*, five times per year
    (Sept–May)
(published five volumes of Fairfax County
    gravestones)
$10.00 per year membership; research: list of
    local researchers available

**The Memorial Foundation of the
Germanna Colonies in Virginia, Inc.**
PO Box 279
Locust Grove, VA 22508-0279
(540) 423-1700; (540) 423-1747 FAX
office@germanna.org
http://www.germanna.org
Rose Marie Martin, Office Administrator
Germanna Community College Library:
    Tue–Sat 1:00–5:00
Pub. *Germanna*, quarterly; *The Germanna
    Record*, occasionally
(extensive collection of genealogy, history
    and biography pertaining to the pioneer
    settlers composing the Germanna Colonies
    in Virginia, 1714 and 1717, later arrivals
    and their descendants)
$10.00 per year membership

**Harrisonburg-Rockingham Genealogical
Society**

5058 Cross Keys Road
Mount Crawford, VA 22841
Elizabeth Keagy, Past Secretary
(society currently inactive, but the past
    secretary will answer queries with SASE
    and will do some research for a fee)

Holston Territory Genealogical Society
PO Box 433
Bristol, VA 24203-0433
(423) 968-4815
Mrs. Vandy Mauk, Corresponding Secretary
Pub. *The Holston Pastfinder*, quarterly (Sept,
    Dec, Mar, June)
(emphasis on southwest Virginia and
    northeast Tennessee genealogy and
    history)
$18.00 per year membership

**Lee County Historical and Genealogical
Society**
(see Historical Societies—Local and
Regional, above)

Loudoun Genealogy Society
PO Box 254
Leesburg, VA 20178
(703) 779-1328 (Thomas Balch Library)
Karen Titus, President
meeting first Wed 7:00
Pub. *Loudoun: The 1757 Legacy*, quarterly
$10.00 per year membership

Lower Delmarva Genealogical Society
(see Maryland, Part 2)

Mount Vernon Genealogical Society
Hollin Hall Senior Center
1500 Shenandoah Road
Alexandria, VA 22308
Ed Schott, Coordinator
Library: Tuesday 10:00–2:00; meetings:
    second Wed 1:00
Pub. *Mt. Vernon Genealogical Society
    Newsletter*, monthly
$10.00 per year membership

**Genealogical Society of Page County,
Virginia**
(Page Public Library, 100 Zerkel
Street—location)
PO Box 734 (mailing address)
Luray, VA 22835
takelley@erols.com
http://www.rootsweb.com/~vagspc/pcgs.htm
Teresa Kelley, President
Pub. *Mountain Memories*, quarterly
(preserves Page County's past for
    genealogical researchers)
$15.00 per year membership

**Palm Beach County Genealogical Society,
Inc.**
(see Florida, Part 2)

Portsmouth Genealogical Society
Portsmouth Public Library
(601 Court Street, Portsmouth, VA
23704—location)
3908 Turnpike Road (mailing address)
Portsmouth, VA 23701
(757) 393-1205; (757)
Bettie Jo Matthews, President
meetings: fourth Sat 2:00
Pub. *Portsmouth Genealogical Society
    Newsletter*, quarterly
(extensive information on Norfolk County,
    including every tombstone in the area,
    births, deaths, obituaries)
$12.00 per year membership; research: $7.50
    per hour, five-hour minimum

**Prince William County Genealogical
Society**
PO Box 2019
Manassas, VA 22110-0812
(703) 754-2234
hcpusey@ix.netcom.com
Sallie C. Pusey, Registrar
Pub. *Kindred Spirits (The Newsletter of the
    Prince William County Genealogical
    Society)*, monthly
$10.00 per year membership

**Rockbridge Area Genealogical Society
(RAGS)**
PO Box 92
Rockbridge Baths, VA 24473
(540) 464-1058
http://www.rockbridgegenie.org
Darcy McCabe, Treasurer
Pub. *Newsletter*, quarterly
$15.00 per year membership

**South Central Virginia Genealogical
Society, Inc.**
Route 1, Box 66-G
Pamplin, VA 23958
scvgs@prodigy.net
http://www.rootsweb.com/~vascvgs
Wanda Brooks, Secretary
Sat 9:00–1:00, and by appointment; meetings
    at the Pamplin United Methodist Church,
    Pamplin, VA: second Sat 1:30
Pub. *Familiy Ties*, bimonthly
("serves the following counties: Amelia,
    Appomattox, Brunswick, Buckingham,
    Campbell, Charlotte, Cumberland,
    Halifax, Lunenburg, Mecklenburg,
    Nottoway, Pittsylvania, and Prince
    Edward"
$15.00 per year membership

**Southwestern Virginia Genealogical
Society, Inc.**
PO Box 12485
Roanoke, VA 24026-2485
Pub. *Virginia Appalachian Notes (VAN)*,
    quarterly (Feb, May, Aug, Nov)
(includes southwestern Virginia and
    Roanoke Valley)
$20.00 per year membership

**The Hugh S. Watson, Jr., Genealogical
Society of Tidewater Virginia**
(d.b.a. Tidewater Genealogical Society)
14415 Old Courthouse Way
Newport News, VA 23608-3728
VATGS@verizon.net
http://www.rootsweb.com/~vatgs
William Lester, President
Pub. *Virginia Tidewater Genealogy*,
    quarterly
$15.00 per year membership; research: no
    individual research but will answer
    queries with SASE

Virginia Beach Genealogical Society
PO Box 62901
Virginia Beach, VA 23466-2901
joanored@aol.com
http://www.rootsweb.com/~vavbgs
Joan Wright, Membership
meetings: second Thur
Pub. *First Landing*, quarterly (Feb, May,
    Aug, Nov)
$12.00 per year membership; queries $1.00
    for nonmembers

VA-NC-Piedmont Genealogical Society
PO Box 2272
Danville, VA 24541-0272
(434) 799-5195
vancsoc@gamewood.net

http://www.rootsweb.com/~vancpgs/
    Index.htm
Marilyn Halstead, Corresponding Secretary
Search Room: Tue 2:00–5:00, Thur
    6:00–9:00 (first Thur 3:00–6:00), Fri
    10:00–5:00, Sat 10:00–1:00
Pub. *Piedmont Lineages*, quarterly, $15.00
    per year for back issues, $3.75 per issue
$15.00 per year membership; queries: free to
    members, $1.00 for first 50 words and
    $2.00 for anything over 50 words to
    nonmembers

Independent Publications and
Miscellany

Appalachian Roots
(see West Virginia, Part 2)

**Association for the Preservation of Virginia
Antiquities**
204 West Franklin Street
Richmond, VA 23220
(804) 648-1889
apva@apva.org
http://www.apva.org

Beyond Germanna
PO Box 120
Chadds Ford, PA 19317
(610) 388-1305
johblank@pipeline.com
http://www.germanna.com
John Blankenbaker, Publisher
Pub. *Beyond Germanna, A
    Newsletter/Journal for Virginia Piedmont
    Germans*, six times per year, $16.00 per
    year subscription
(specializes in early 18th century, interested
    in settlers' origins, history, genealogies,
    associated families, and dispersion to other
    areas; "The word 'Germanna' refers to the
    location in Virginia where Lt. Gov.
    Alexander Spotswood settled a small
    group of Germans in 1714; today
    Germanna is located in Orange County in
    a horseshoe bend of the Rapidan River
    where Virginia State Highway 3 crosses
    the Rapidan.")

Blue Ridge Institute
State Route 40
Ferrum, VA 24088
(540) 365-4415
J. Roderick Moore, Director
Pub. *BRI Records*

Bridgewater College
Reuel B. Pritchett Museum of Bridgewater
College
(Basement Cole Hall, East College
Street—location)
College Box 147 (mailing address)
Bridgewater, VA 22812
(540) 828-2501, ext. 647
Byron J. Wampler, Director
Tue–Thur 2:00–4:00, College special events,
    and by appointment
Pub. *Newsletter*, semiannually
(historical artifacts, but no library of
    genealogical significance)

Byron Sistler and Associates, Inc.
(see Tennessee, Part 2)

Center for Appalachian Studies
(see North Carolina, Part 2)

**Cindy's Genealogy on the Eastern Shore of
Maryland, Delaware, and Virginia**
(see Maryland, Part 2)

Colonial Roots
(see Delaware, Part 2)

The Colonial Williamsburg Foundation
John D. Rockefeller, Jr. Library
(313 First Street—location)
PO Box 1776 (mailing address)
Williamsburg, VA 23187-1776
(757) 565-8510 (Reference Desk)
http://www.history.org
Juleigh Muirhead Clark, Public Services
  Librarian
Reference: Mon–Fri 11:00–4:00; Special
  Collections: Mon–Fri 10:00–3:00
Pub. *Colonial Williamsburg Journal*,
  quarterly, $35.00 per year donation
(Williamsburg, Virginia—18th-century; "Our
  focus is Williamsburg residents.")

Cox/Phillips
PO Box 186
Southmont, NC 27351
(336) 798-2401
Elza B. Cox, Editor
Pub. *Cox/Phillips Newsletter*, quarterly,
  $10.00 per year subscription
(emphasis on southwest Virginia)

Direct Line Software
Land Record Reference
(see Miscellaneous, Part 4)

Fairfax County Publications Center
12000 Government Center Parkway, Suite
156
Fairfax, VA 22035
(703) 324-2974
(distributes books published by the Fairfax
  County Office of Comprehensive
  Planning, by the Fairfax County History
  Commission, and by other county
  governmental organizations)

Genealogical Institute
(Independent Publications, Part 1)

**Genealogy and History of the Eastern
Shore (GHOTES)**
bgcox@ix.netcom.com
http://www.esva.net/ghotes

Genealogy Books and Consultation
(see Texas, Part 2)

Gunston Hall Plantation
Library and Archives
10709 Gunston Road
Mason Neck, VA 22079-3901
(703) 550-9220; (703) 550-9480 FAX
Historic@GunstonHall.org
http://www.gunstonhall.org
Kevin Shupe, Library, Internet & Technology
  Manager
Mon–Fri 9:30–4:30 by appointment only
(primarily historical, not genealogical)
admission: $7.00 for adults

**Historic Crab Orchard Museum and
Pioneer Park, Inc.**
(Route 19-460 at Crab Orchard
  Road—location)
Route 1, Box 194 (mailing address)
Tazewell, VA 24651
(276) 988-6755; (276) 988-9400 FAX
histcrab@netscope.net
http://histcrab.netscope.net
Ross Weeks, Jr., Director
Mon–Sat 9:00–5:00, Sun (May–Sept)
  2:00–5:00
Pub. *Pisgah Pathfinder*, quarterly
$25.00 per year membership; research; none
  done by staff

Historic Dumfries, Virginia, Inc.
Weems-Botts Museum
(3944 Cameron Street, corner of Duke and
Cameron Streets—location)
PO Box 26 (mailing address)
Dumfries, VA 22026
(703) 221-2218 voice & FAX
weemsbotts@msn.com
http://www.geocities.com/hdvinc
Kimberly D. Ward, Administrative Director
Tue–Sat 10:00–4:00
Pub. *Ye Olde Town Crier*, bimonthly
(includes books, periodicals, articles, etc.,
  concerning the heritage of the people and
  places of historic Dumfries; issues
  certificates of ancestry to descendants of
  pioneers who came to Dumfries or the
  surrounding area by 1850)
$15.00 per year membership; $15.00 for
  Pioneers of Dumfries, Virginia,
  Certificate of Ancestry; admission: $3.00
  for adults; research: $10.00 per hour, plus
  copies at 25¢ per page, and $3.00
  shipping/handling

Historic Fincastle, Inc.
(James Early Cabin, 121 East Murray
Street—location)
PO Box 19 (mailing address)
Fincastle, VA 24090
(540) 473-2022
Mrs. Harry Kessler, Chairman, Archives
by appointment only
(Fincastle Rifles, Civil War Unit, G. N.
  Fulton-Potter, Lewis and Clark, cemetery
  records before 1900, Fincastle and
  Botetourt counties history; "We offer
  limited genealogy research.")
$5.00 per year membership

Historic Occoquan, Inc.
(423 Mill Street—location)
PO Box 65 (mailing address)
Occoquan, VA 22125
(703) 491-752

Historic Vienna, Inc.
PO Box 53
Vienna, VA 22180
(703) 938-5187

**Hunting for Bears Genealogical and
Historical Society**
(see Alabama, Part 2)

Lee Hall Depot Foundation
(Elmhurst and Warwick
Boulevard—location)
163 Yorktown Road (mailing address)
Newport News, VA 23603
(757) 888-3371; (757) 888-3373 FAX
Jennifer Williams, Development Coordinator
to be announced
$20.00 per year membership

Lineage Search Associates
6419 Colts Neck Road
Mechanicsville, VA 23111-4233
(804) 730-7414 voice & FAX; (800) 728-
  1935
Michael E. Pollock, President
Mon–Sat 8:00 A.M.–10:00 P.M.
Pub. *Frederick Findings*, quarterly, $25.00
  per year subscription
(the Shenandoah Valley and eastern
  panhandle of West Virginia: Clarke,
  Frederick, Page, Shenandoah and Warren
  counties, Virginia, and Berkeley, Grant,
  Hampshire, Hardy, Jefferson, Mineral and
  Morgan counties, West Virginia)
queries: three free queries per issue for
  members, $8.00 for nonsubscribers,

includes issue in which the query appears

Lineages, Inc.
Department A-F
PO Box 417
Salt Lake City, UT 84110
(800) 338-5114
Johni Cerny, President
Pub. *Before Germanna* (monograph series),
  $10.00 per issue

Mariner's Museum
100 Museum Drive
Newport News, VA 23606-3759
(757) 591-7782
library@mariner.org
http://www.mariner.org/library.html
research: $25.00 in advance

Jeff Matthews Memorial Museum
606 West Stuart Drive
Galax, VA 24333

**Montgomery Museum and Lewis Miller
Regional Art Center**
300 South Pepper Street
Christiansburg, VA 24073
(540) 382-5644

**The Mountain Empire Genealogical
Quarterly**
PO Box 628
Pound, VA 24279
(540) 796-5233
Joan S. Vanover, Executive Secretary
Pub. *The Mountain Empire Genealogical
  Quarterly* (Kentucky, North Carolina,
  Tennessee, Virginia and West Virginia),
  quarterly, $20.00 per year subscription

Mountain Press
(see Tennessee, Part 2)

**Museum in Memory of Virginia E.
Randolph**
2200 Mountain Road
Glen Allen, VA 23060
(804) 262-3363

**Newport News Warwick Historical
Preservation Association**
(Warwick Court House, Old Courthouse
Way, Newport News, VA 23608—location)
PO Box 1812 (mailing address)
Newport News, VA 23601
http://www.rootsweb.com/~vannwhpa
John V. Quarstein, Administrator, Historic
  Services
to be announced
Pub. *NNWHPA Newsletter*, monthly
(local history)
$15.00 per year membership

Newsome House Foundation
2803 Oak Avenue
Newport News, VA 23607
(757) 247-2380; (757) 928-6754 FAX
Katrina Boston, Site Coordinator
Mon–Sat 10:00–4:00
Pub. *Newsome Star*, annually
(local history)
$10.00 per year membership

**Northern Virginia Association of
Historians**
George Mason University, History
Department
Fairfax, VA 22030
(703) 323-2242

Northern Virginia Genealogy
39475 Tollhouse Road

Lovettsville, VA 20180-9703
martyhiatt@starpower.net
Ms. Marty Hiatt, CGRS, Publisher
Pub. *Northern Virginia Genealogy*, annually,
    $22.00 per year subscription
("Information from the area of Old Prince
    William, Virginia. That includes the
    counties of Fairfax, Fauquier, Loudoun,
    Prince William, Arlington and
    Alexandria.")
free queries to subscribers

The Petersburg Museums
15 West Bank Street
Petersburg, VA 23803
(804) 733-2404
Suzanne Savery, Director
Trapezium House: Mon–Sun (1 Apr–31 Oct)
    10:00–5:00; Farmer's Bank: Mon &
    Fri–Sun (1 Apr–31 Oct) 10:00–5:00;
    Seige Museum, Centre Hill Mansion,
    Visitor's Center, Blandford Church:
    Mon–Sun 10:00–5:00

The Portsmouth Museums
420 High Street
Portsmouth, VA 23704
(757) 393-8983

The Researchers
(see Kentucky, Part 2)

Simmons Historical Publications
(see Kentucky, Part 2)

**The Southern Genealogist's Exchange
Society, Inc.**
(see Florida, Part 2)

Southern Historical Press, Inc.
(see Publishers, Part 4)

The Southside Virginian
2236 Cedar Crest Road
Richmond, VA 23235
(804) 272-4875
Kathryn Hooper, Managing Editor
Pub. *The Southside Virginian: A Journal of
    Genealogy and History*, quarterly (Jan,
    Apr, July, Oct)
$20.00 per year membership

Southwest Virginia Ancestors Quarterly
Route 2, Box 307
Clintwood, VA 24228
(540) 926-6837
Betty R. Mullins, Editor
Mon–Fri 8:00–5:00
Pub. *Southwest Virginia Ancestors Quarterly*
    (spring, summer, fall, winter)
$20.00 per year membership

Southwest Virginian
1046 Spruce Street
Norton, VA 24273
Rhonda S. Roberson, Editor
Pub. *Southwest Virginian, Journal of
    Genealogy and History Covering Virginia
    This Side of the Blue Ridge*, bimonthly,
    $14.00 per year subscription

Surname Searchers Quarterly
1231 Quicksburg Road
Quicksburg, VA 22847
Pub. *Surname Searchers Quarterly*

Tidewater Virginia Families
316 Littletown Quarter
Williamsburg, VA 23185-5519
(757) 220-4888; (757) 220-0975 FAX
http://www.tidewatervirginiafamilies
Virginia Lee Hutcheson Davis,

Editor/Publisher
Mon–Fri 10:00–8:00
Pub. *Tidewater Virginia Families: A
    Magazine of History and Genealogy*
    (Tidewater history and genealogy,
    including Caroline, Charles City,
    Elizabeth City, Essex, Gloucester,
    Hanover, Henrico, James City, King and
    Queen, King George, King William,
    Lancaster, Mathews, Middlesex, New
    Kent, Richmond, Northumberland,
    Warwick, Westmoreland, and York
    counties; "unpublished county, church,
    Bible records, and family histories"),
    quarterly (Feb/Mar, May/June, Aug/Sept,
    Nov/Dec), $28.00 per year U.S.
    subscription; CD every-name index, vols.
    1-10, $25.00

Topp of the Line
1304 West Cliffwood Court
Spokane, WA 99218-2917
(509) 467-2299
Bette Butcher Topp
Pub. *Virginia/West Virginia Queries*,
    irregularly, $7.75 postpaid, standing order
    option

Traveller Southern Families
http://misc.traveller.com/genealogy/
    index.html
(Includes Alabama, Arkansas, Florida,
    Georgia, Kentucky, Louisiana,
    Mississippi, Missouri, North Carolina,
    South Carolina, Tennessee, Texas,
    Virginia, and West Virginia, but not
    Maryland—links, resources and query
    posts.)

VaGenWeb
Part of The USGenweb Project
fspradlin@earthlink.net
http://www.rootsweb.com/~vagenweb
Freddie Spradlin, State Coordinator; Linda
    Lewis, Assistant Coordinator
("The VAGenWeb is a loosly organized
    project made up entirely of volunteers
    hosting web pages for each county and
    independent city in Virginia.")

Virginia Department of Transportation
VDOT Central Office
1221 East Broad Street
Richmond, VA 23219
(804) 786-2801
vamaps@virginiadot.org
http://virginiadot.org/infoservice/faq-
    brochures.asp (Maps)
("The Official State Transportation Map is a
    biennial publication; the county and
    scenic roads maps are not produced on a
    regular schedule.")

The Virginia Genealogist
PO Box 5860
Falmouth, VA 22403-5860
John Frederick Dorman, Editor
Pub. *The Virginia Genealogist*, quarterly,
    $25.00 per year subscription
(includes Virginia and West Virginia)

Virginia Genealogy Webring
aricka7565@aol.com
http://members.tripod.com/
    ~AlanCheshire/vagenring.html
Alan Rickards, Ringmaster

Virginia Living Museum
524 J. Clyde Morris Boulevard
Newport News, VA 23601-1999
Robert P. Sullivan

Virginia Military Institute
Virginia History and Museums Federation
Jackson Memorial Hall
Lexington, VA 24450
(540) 463-6232

Virginia War Museum
9285 Warwick Boulevard
Newport News, VA 23607
(757) 247-8523; (757) 247-8627
http://www.warmuseum.org
John V. Quarstein, Administrator, Historic
    Services
Mon–Sat 9:00–5:00, Sun 1:00–5:00
Pub. *The Correspondent*, quarterly
(Virginia and U.S. military history)
$20.00 per year membership; admission:
    $2.00 for adults

West Virginia University
Appalachian Studies Association
(see West Virginia, Part 2)

Washington

Archives and Libraries with Holdings in Genealogy

State Archives and Library

Washington State Archives
(1129 Washington St., S.E.—location)
PO Box 40238 (mailing address)
Olympia, WA 98504-0238
(360) 586-1492
research@secstate.wa.gov
http://www.secstate.wa.gov/archives
David Hastings, Chief, State Government
    Archives
Mon–Fri 8:00–4:30

Washington State Archives, Central Regional Branch
Bledsoe-Washington Archives Building
Central Washington University-MS 7547
Ellensburg, WA 98926-7547
(509) 963-2136; (509) 963-1753 FAX
Mon–Fri 8:30–4:30
(Benton, Chelan, Douglas, Franklin, Grant,
    Kittitas, Klickitat, Okanogan, and Yakima
    counties)

Washington State Archives, Eastern Regional Branch
Eastern Washington University
960 Washington Street
Cheney, WA 99004
(509) 235-1519; (509) 359-6286 FAX
era@mail.ewu.edu
http://www.secstate.wa.gov/archives/
    archives_eastern.aspx
Sherry Bays, Archivist
8:00-4:30
(Adams, Asotin, Columbia, Ferry, Garfield,
    Lincoln, Pend Oreille, Spokane, Stevens,
    Walla Walla, and Whitman counties;
    records of local government agencies and
    state agencies with local offices)
free admission; research: $25.00 per hour,
    $12.50 minimum

Washington State Archives, Northwest Region
Western Washington University
Bellingham, WA 98225-9123
(360) 650-3125; (360) 650-3323
state.archives@wwu.edu
http://www.secstate.wa.gov/archives/
    archives_northwest.aspx
Diana L. Shenk, Regional Archivist; Susan
    Fahey, Assistant Archivist
Mon–Fri 8:30–noon & 1:30–4:30
(Clallam, Island, Jefferson, San Juan, Skagit,
    Snohomis, and Whatcom counties;
    original public records generated by
    counties, cities, local schools, and other
    districts)

Washington State Archives, Southwest Regional Branch
(1120 Washington Street, S.E.—location)
PO Box 40238 (mailing address)
Olympia, WA 98504-0238
(360) 753-1684; (360) 586-4898; (360) 664-
    2803 FAX
lweaver@secstate.wa.gov
http://www.secstate.wa.gov/archives/
    archives_southwest.aspx
Lanny Weaver, Assistant Southwest Regional
    Archivist
(Clark, Cowlitz, Grays Harbor, Lewis,
    Mason, Pacific, Skamania, Thurston, and
    Wahkiakum counties)

Washington State Library
Washington/Northwest Collection
PO Box 2475
Olympia, WA 98504-2475
(360) 753-4024; (360) 753-2475 FAX; (360)
    753-7575 FAX
askalibrarian@secstate.wa.gov
http://www.secstate.wa.gov/library
Gayle Palmer, Senior Librarian
Mon–Fri 10:00–5:00
(participates in inter-library loan service;
    genealogical holdings relate to
    Washington state only)

State Historical Society

Washington State Historical Society
Heritage Resource Center
211 West 21st Avenue
Olympia, WA 98501
(360) 586-0219
jpeterson@wshs.wa.gov
http://www.washingtonhistory.org/wshs/hrc
Jean Peterson, Editor
Pub. *Washington Heritage Bulletin*,
    periodically by email
$10.00 per year membership

Washington State Historical Society
Special Collections Division
1911 Pacific Avenue
Tacoma, WA 98402
(253) 272-3500; (253) 272-9747
    (Information Line); (888) 238-4373;
    (253) 798-5900 FAX
jmartin@wshs.wa.gov (Membership)
http://www.washingtonhistory.org/wshs/
    index.htm
E. K. C. Nolan, Curator
Tue–Thur 12:30–4:30, by appointment only
Pub. *Columbia: Magazine of Northwest
    History*, quarterly
("We do not gather genealogical materials,
    nor do we do genealogical research; we
    have transferred most of our genealogical
    material to the Tacoma Public Library,
    which does specialize in genealogy; we
    don't maintain death indexes, obituary
    collections, photographs, ephemera, etc.")
$45.00 per year membership

City, County and Regional Archives and Libraries
(A more exhaustive list of public and
academic libraries can be found at http://
wlo.statelib.wa.gov/services/index.htm.)

Adam East Museum and Art Center
(122 West Third—location)
PO Box 1579 (mailing address)
Moses Lake, WA 98837
(509) 766-9395
Chris Fiala Erlich, Director
Tue–Sat noon–5:00
Pub. *Membership Letter—MAC Happenings*,
    quarterly
("Historical and archives, scholastic or
    public; have started an education program
    and local history project")
$15.00 per year Booster membership

Auburn Public Library
1102 Auburn Way South
Auburn, WA 98002-6298
(253) 931-3018; (253) 931-5105 FAX
http://wlo.statelib.wa.gov/
    detail.cfm?LibraryID=712
Fran Wendtland, Manager
Mon–Thur 10:00–9:00, Fri 10:00–6:00, Sat
    10:00–5:00, Sun 1:00–5:00

Bellingham Public Library

Research Desk
(210 Central Street—location)
PO Box 1197 (mailing address)
Bellingham, WA 98225
(360) 676-6860; (360) 676-7795 FAX
jcarterson@cob.org
http://www.city-
    govt.ci.bellingham.wa.us//bplhome.htm
Julie Carterson, Director
Mon–Thur 10:00–9:00, Fri–Sat 10:00–6:00,
    Sun (Sept–May) noon–5:00; volunteer
    research help: Wed 10:00–2:00
(genealogy collection of about 1,200 titles,
    broad coverage; collection of journals
    from about 140 genealogical societies,
    many dating 1975–1995)

Bellvue Regional Library
Special Collections
1111 110 Avenue, N.E.
Bellevue, WA 98004
(425) 450-1760
http://www.kcls.org
Mon–Thur 10:00–9:00, Fri 10:00–6:00, Sat
    10:00–5:00, Sun 1:00–9:00

Bleyhl Community Library
311 Division Street
Grandview, WA 98930
(509) 882-9217
ldunham@grandview.wa.us
http://wlo.statelib.wa.gov/
    detail.cfm?LibraryID=15
Linda G. Dunham, Librarian
Mon–Thur 1:30–9:00, Tue & Thur
    10:00–noon, Fri–Sat 1:30–5:30
("Grandview history; some early birth,
    marriage and death records for Yakima
    County 1869–1903; Grandview cemetery
    records to 1972; many high school annuals
    1913 to the present; Grandview history
    [some photos] chronological, not
    indexed")
research: postage and copies at 50¢ per page

Burlington Public Library
900 East Fairhaven Street
Burlington, WA 98233-1998
(360) 755-0760; (360) 755-0717 FAX
cperkins@burlington.lib.wa.us
http://www.sos.net/home/burlpl/bplib.htm
Christine Perkins, Director
Mon–Thur 11:00–8:00, Fri–Sat 11:00–5:00

Colville Public Library
195 South Oak
Colville, WA 99114
(509) 684-6620; (509) 684-3911 FAX
amanda@scrld.org
http://www.scrld.org
Amanda McKeraghan, Director
Mon–Wed 11:00–8:00, Thur–Fri 11:00–6:00,
    Sat 11:00–5:00

Cowlitz County Historical Museum
405 Allen Street
Kelso, WA 98626
(360) 577-3119
David W. Freece, Museum Director
Mon–Sat 9:00–5:00 by appointment
Pub. *Cowlitz Historical Quarterly* (emphasis
    on Cowlitz County and southwest
    Washington), $15.00 per year subscription

Du Pont Historical Museum
207 Brandywine Avenue
Du Pont, WA 98327
(253) 964-8895

Ellensburg Public Library
209 North Ruby Street
Ellensburg, WA 98926-3338

(509) 962-7250; (509) 962-7295 FAX
klinec@epl.eburg.com
http://epl.eburg.com
Milton Wagy, Local History Associate;
    Celeste M. Kline, Director
Mon–Thur 10:00–8:00, Fri 10:00–6:00,
    Sat–Sun 1:00–5:00
("local history collection of books, archival
    local club materials, extensive local
    history photographs, oral history audio-
    cassette collection; pamphlets, newspapers
    on microfilm")
charges for copies and postage

Ephrata Public Library
45 Alder Street, N.W.
Ephrata, WA 98823-1663
(509) 754-3971 voice & FAX
http://www.ncrl.org/index.html
Caroline Hedges, Librarian
Mon–Thur 10:00–8:00, Fri 10:00–4:00, Sat
    11:00–4:00

Everett Public Library
Northwest Room
2702 Hoyt Avenue
Everett, WA 98201-3556
(425) 259-8020; (425) 257-8005 (Northwest
    Room); (425) 257-8017 FAX
libnw@ci.everett.wa.us
http://www.epls.org/nw

The Fiske Genealogical Foundation
Fiske Genealogical Library
1644 43rd Avenue East
Seattle, WA 98112-3222
(206) 328-2716
http://www.fiskelibrary.org
Mary C. Stevenson, Librarian
Mon & Sat 10:00–3:00, Wed noon–8:00,
    Thur 3:00–8:00, Sun 1:00–4:00
Pub. *Newsletter*, quarterly
(over 7,500 volumes concentrating on the
    thirteen original states plus Tennessee,
    Kentucky, Ohio and Indiana; also a unique
    collection of card files
library admission: $5.00 per day or $40.00
    per year

Forks Memorial Library
(171 North Forks Avenue—location)
PO Box 1817 (mailing address)
Forks, WA 98331
(360) 374-6402; (360) 374-6499 FAX
http://www.nols.org
Frances Henneke, Branch Manager
Mon–Wed noon–8:00, Thur–Sat 10:00–5:00

Fort Vancouver Regional Library
1007 East Mill Plain Boulevard
Vancouver, WA 98663-3599
(360) 695-1566; (360) 693-2681 FAX
bziegman@fvrl.org
http://www.fvrl.org
Bruce Ziegman, Director
Mon–Thur 10:00–9:00, Fri–Sat 10:00–6:00,
    Sun 1:00–9:00
(Clark County history)

Grant County Historical Museum
(742 Basin Street, N.W.—location)
PO Box 1119 (mailing address)
Orting, WA 98360
(360) 754-3334

Hacksma House Genealogy Library
1815 Grant Road
East Wenatchee, WA 98802
(509) 884-7662
Nellie Bruton Hacksma
by appointment only
(primarily Eastern and Southern emphasis:

Alabama, Arkansas, Georgia, Illinois,
    Indiana, Iowa, Kentucky, Mississippi,
    Missouri, North Carolina, Tennessee,
    Texas, and Virginia)

**Heritage Quest Research Library and
Bookstore**
909 Main Street, Suite 5
Sumner, WA 98390
(253) 863-1806; (253) 863-0577 FAX
http://www.hqrl.com
Susan Hudgens, Director
Mon–Tue & Thur–Sun 11:00–4:00, Wed
    9:00–9:00
("HQRL is a nonprofit genealogy library,
    managed and staffed entirely by
    volunteers. HQRL's collection includes
    books, microfiche, and microfilm, with an
    emphasis on census films. We have one of
    the largest microfilm collections in the
    Pacific Northwest. HQRL also houses a
    bookstore where you can purchase books,
    forms, and supplies.")
$30.00 per year membership; admission: first
    visit free, then $4.00 per day for
    nonmembers; research: $15.00 per hour

Highline Community College
Genealogy Collection
(2400 South 240th Street—location)
PO Box 98000 (mailing address)
Des Moines, WA 98198
(206) 878-3710, ext. 3230
http://flightline.highline.edu
Reference Librarians

King County Law Library
W621 King County Courthouse
516 Third Avenue
Seattle, WA 98104
(206) 296-0940; (206) 205-0513 FAX
http://www.nwlaw.com/kcll

Kitsap Regional Library
Poulsbo Branch
700 N.E. Lincoln Road
Poulsbo, WA 98370
(360) 779-2915; (360) 779-1051 FAX
slavin@krl.org
http://www.krl.org
Susan Lavin, Branch Manager

**Klondike Gold Rush National Historical
Park—Seattle Unit**
117 South Main Street
Seattle, WA 98104
(206) 553-7220; (206) 553-0614 FAX
Willie Russell, Superintendent
9:00–5:00
(research library; Klondike Gold Rush 1896-
    98, emphasis on Seattle)

Longview Public Library
Genealogy Room
1600 Louisiana Street
Longview, WA 98632-2993
(360) 442-5300; (360) 422-5954 FAX
chris.skaugset@ci.longview.wa.us
http://www.longviewlibrary.org
Chris Skaugset, Adult Services
Mon–Thur 10:00–9:00, Fri–Sat 10:00–5:00,
    Sun noon–5:00; Genealogy Room
    Volunteers: Wed 1:00–3:00

Mid-Columbia Library
405 South Dayton
Kennewick, WA 99336
(509) 582-4745; (509) 734-7446 FAX
http://mcl-lib.org
Thomas Moak, Senior Librarian
Mon–Wed 9:00–9:00, Thur–Sat 9:00–5:00

Mount Vernon City Library
315 Snoqualmie Street
Mount Vernon, WA 98273-4226
(360) 336-6209; (360) 336-6259 FAX
http://www.ci.mount-
    vernon.wa.us/department.asp_Q_pagenum
    ber_E_65
Ann Grimm, Director
Mon–Thur 10:00–8:00; Fri 10:00–5:00, Sat
    10:00–5:00, Sun 1:00–5:00

Neill Public Library
North 210 Grand Avenue
Pullman, WA 99163-2693
(509) 334-4555 (Weekdays); (509) 334-3595
    (Evenings and Weekends); (509) 334-
    6051 FAX
mikep@neill-lib.org; library@neill-lib.org
http://www.neill-lib.org
Mike Pollastro, Director
Tue–Wed 10:00–8:00, Thur–Fri 10:00–6:00,
    Sat 1:00–5:00

North Central Washington Museum
127 South Mission
Wenatchee, WA 98801
(509) 664-5989
Mary L. Thomsen, Editor; Mark Behler,
    Archivist
Mon–Fri 8:00–5:00
Pub. *The Confluence*, quarterly, $2.00 per
    issue
("We do have an archival library with
    extensive holdings; in addition, we house
    the Genealogical Society of North Central
    Washington's library; they are an affiliate
    organization.")

North Olympic Library System
2210 South Peabody Street
Port Angeles, WA 98362-6598
(360) 417-8500; (360) 457-2581 FAX
stratton@nols.org
http://www.nols.org
George Stratton, Director
Mon & Fri–Sat 10:00–5:00, Tue–Thur
    10:00–8:00

Old Molson and Schoolhouse Museums
(Main Street, Molson, WA—location)
915 Nine Mile-Molson Road (mailing
    address)
Oroville, WA 98844
(509) 485-3292 voice & FAX
Mary Louise Loe, Museum Director
Old Molson: Apr–Nov: daylight hours;
    Schoolhouse Museum: Memorial Day
    weekend–Labor Day: 10:00–5:00
(Okanogan Highlands history and artifacts
    from the early 1900s)

Olympia Timberland Library
313 Eighth Avenue SE
Olympia, WA 98501-9300
(360) 352-0595; (360) 586-3207 FAX
cheywood@timberland.lib.wa.us
http://timber20.timberland.lib.wa.us/
    trlinfo.htm
Cheryl Heywood, Community Librarian III
Mon–Tue 10:00–9:00, Wed–Thur
    11:00–9:00, Fri–Sat 10:00–5:00, Sun
    (Oct–May) 1:00–5:00

Orcas Island Historical Museum
PO Box 134
Eastsound, WA 98245
(360) 376-4849

Puget Sound Regional Archives
Pritchard-Fleming Building
3000 Landerholm Circle S.E., MS-N100
Bellevue, WA 98007-6484

(425) 564-3940
archives@bcc.ctc.edu
Mon–Fri 8:30–4:30

Richland Genealogical Library
1314 Goethals Avenue
Richland, WA 99354
http://www.rootsweb.com/~wargl/index. html
Mon & Sat 9:00–5:00, Tue–Fri 9:00–9:00

Richland Public Library
955 Northgate Drive
Richland, WA 99352-3539
(509) 942-7450; (509) 943-7455; (509) 943-7457; (509) 942-7447 FAX
emokler@richland.lib.wa.us
http://www.richland.lib.wa.us
Judy McMakin, Reference Librarian; Earlene Mokler, Auto Systems Coordinator
summer: Mon–Thur 10:30–9:00, Fri–Sat 10:30–5:30; Sept–May: Mon–Fri 10:30–9:00, Sat 10:30–5:30, Sun 1:00–5:00

Seattle Pacific University Library
3307 Third Avenue, West
Seattle, WA 98119-1997
(206) 281-2982
http://www.spu.edu/depts/library

Seattle Public Library
Genealogy Section
History, Travel, Maps Department
1000 Fourth Avenue
Seattle, WA 98104
(206) 386-4625 (History and Genealogy)
infospl@spl.lib.wa.us
http://www.spl.org
Darlene E. Hamilton, Senior Librarian; Heather McLeland-Wieser
Mon–Thur 9:00–9:00, Fri 10:30–6:00, Sat 9:00–6:00, Sun 1:00–5:00
(Genealogy Collection covers U.S., with some regions stronger than others; library also has a separate Northwest History Collection)

Seattle Public Schools Archives and Records Management Center
Frank B. Cooper Elementary School, Room 20
5950 Delridge Way, S.W., AB-345
Seattle, WA 98106
(206) 281-6564; (206) 281-6466 FAX
http://sea.css.ssd.k12.wa.us/archives/welcome.htm

Seattle University
Lemieux Library
900 Broadway
Seattle, WA 98122
(206) 296-6228 (Hours); (206) 296-6230 (Reference)
libref@seattleu.edu
http://www.seattleu.edu/lemlib/llhomepg. htm

Library and Historical Museum (Shaw Island)
PO Box 844
Shaw Island, WA 98286
Frances Hilen, Curator

Shoreline Historical Museum
(749 North 175th Street—location)
PO Box 7171 (mailing address)
Seattle, WA 98133
(206) 542-7111
Victoria Stiles, Director
Archives: Wed 10:00–1, and by appointment
Pub. *Shoreline Historical Museum Newsletter*, quarterly
$10.00 per year membership

Spokane Public Library
906 West Main
Spokane, WA 99210-0976
(509) 626-5300 (Switchboard); (509) 444-5336 (Reference); (509) 444-5357 (Genealogy room, when volunteers on duty)
telref@spokanelibrary.org
http://www.spokanelibrary.org
Jan Sanders, Director
Library: Mon–Tue noon–8:00, Wed–Sat 10:00–6:00; Genealogy volunteers: Tue noon–8:00, Thur 10:00–6:00, Sat 10:00–2:00
(two different collections, one for genealogy and one on the Pacific Northwest)

Stanwood Library
(9701 271st Street, N.W.—location)
PO Box 247 (mailing address)
Stanwood, WA 98292
(360) 629-3132; (360) 629-3516 FAX
http://wlo.statelib.wa.gov/detail.cfm?LibraryID=372
Icle Crow, Managing Librarian
Mon–Thur 10:00–9:00, Fri–Sat 10:00–5:00

Steilacoom Historical Museum Association
(122 Main Street—location)
PO Box 88016 (mailing address)
Steilacoom, WA 98388
(253) 584-4133
http://www.steilacoom.org/museum
Dave Welch
Nov–Dec & Feb: Fri–Sun 1:00–4:00; Mar–Oct: Tue–Sun 1:00–4:00
Pub. *Steilacoom Historical Museum Quarterly*
(some local genealogy materials)
$20.00 per year membership; admission: free

Tacoma Public Library
Northwest Room
1102 Tacoma Avenue South
Tacoma, WA 98402-2098
(253) 591-5622; (253) 627-1693 FAX
webfoot@tpl.lib.wa.us
http://www.tpl.lib.wa.us/nwr/nwdata.htm
Gary Fuller Reese, Managing Librarian
Mon–Thur 9:00–9:00, Fri–Sat 9:00–6:00
("We have half of the fiche provided by UMI. We have much of what the Index to American Genealogy has indexed and two years ago spent about twenty thousand dollars on getting the indexed items in our collections. We maintain an obituary index which is online and have about 400,000 entries. Our place names Internet file is on a statewide level. We have 15,600 full text biographies of Washington state people ranging from one page to, in the case of Chief Seattle, 130 pages. We are building local files of pioneer deaths, pioneer births, local businesses, etc.")

University of Puget Sound
Collins Memorial Library/Archives
1500 North Warner
Tacoma, WA 98416
(253) 756-3100; (253) 756-3500 FAX
http://www.ups.edu/library/services/archives/intro.htm

University of Utah Marriott Library
(see Utah, Part 2)

University of Washington Libraries
Manuscripts, Special Collections, University Archives Division
Box 352900
Seattle, WA 98195-2900

(206) 543-1929
speccoll@u.washington.edu
http://www.lib.washington.edu/specialcoll
Carla Rickerson, Pacific Northwest Librarian
Mon–Tue & Thur–Fri 10:00–5:00, Wed 10:00–8:00, Sat 1:00–5:00 (Manuscripts and University Archives Collections are not available for use on Saturdays), Mon–Fri 1:00–5:00 between quarters when school is not in session
("Emphasis on local history rather than genealogy. Not staffed to provide genealogical research but can suggest professional research assistance. Print collection emphasis on Pacific Northwest history. Manuscript collections emphasis on ethnic Jewish, ethnic Japanese-American, and ethnic Scandinavian-American in Washington.")

Walla Walla Public Library
238 East Alder
Walla Walla, WA 99362-1967
(509) 527-4550; (509) 527-3748 FAX
mvanpelt@ci.walla-walla.wa.us
http://wlo.statelib.wa.gov/detail.cfm?LibraryID=433
Stephen C. Towery
Mon–Tue noon–8:00, Wed 10:00–8:00, Thur–Sat 10:00–5:00

Washington State University
Holland Library
Manuscripts, Archives, and Special Collections
Pullman, WA 99164-5610
(509) 335-MASC
8:00–11:45
("no genealogy collection, just research materials")

Western Heritage Center
(see Montana, Part 2)

Whatcom Museum Archives
Syre Education Center
(201 Prospect Street—location)
121 Prospect Street (mailing address)
Bellingham, WA 98226
(360) 676-6981; (360) 738-7397; (360) 738-7409 FAX
http://www.city-govt.ci.bellingham.wa.us/cobweb/museum/welcome.htm

Whitman County Library System
South 102 Main Street
Colfax, WA 99111-1892
(509) 397-4366; (509) 397-6156 FAX
kirkpatr@colfax.com; info@whitco.lib.wa.us
http://wlo.statelib.wa.gov/detail.cfm?LibraryID=446
Steve Kenworthy, Director; Kristie Kirkpatrick, Director of Public Services
Mon–Thur 9:00–8:00, Fri 9:00–6:00, Sat 9:00–5:00

Wilson Library
Western Washington University
Bellingham, WA 98225
(360) 650-3193
Virginia Beck, Special Collections Manager
Mon–Fri 8:00–5:00
("We have biographical information for some faculty and area residents.")

Historical Societies—Local and Regional

Adams County Historical Society Museum
Phillips Building

PO Box 188
Lind, WA 99341
(509) 677-3219; (509) 677-3393

American Historical Association, Pacific Coast Branch
(see California, Part 2)

American West Research Center and Historical Society, Inc.
(see Ohio, Part 2)

Anderson Island Historical Society
9306 Otso Point Road
Anderson Island, WA 98303
(253) 884-2135
Ray Walberg, President
Memorial Day weekend to Labor Day weekend: noon–4:00

Asotin County Historical Society
(215 Filmore Street—location)
PO Box 367 (mailing address)
Asotin, WA 99402-0367
(509) 243-4659; (509) 243-1331
jomiller@clarkston.com
MoAnne Miller, President; Daisy Roberts, Attendant
Tue–Sat 1:00–5:00
Pub. *ACHS Newsletter*, quarterly
("We do a lot of research of families as we have all the old newspapers starting late 1800s.")

Bainbridge Island Historical Society
Bainbridge Island Historical Museum
Strawberry Hill Park
7650 N.E. High School Road
Bainbridge Island, WA 98110
(206) 842-2773
bihs@nwinet.com
http://www.bicomnet.com/bihs
Joan Piper, Executive Director
Museum: Tue, Thur & Sun 1:00–4:00, Sat (1 May–30 Sept) 1:00–4:00
Pub. *Members Newsletter*, three times per year
$20.00–$29.00 per year membership; research: $25.00 per hour thereafter

Benton County Museum and Historical Society, Inc.
(Seventh Street and Paterson Road—location)
PO Box 591 (mailing address)
Prosser, WA 99350
(509) 786-3842

Black Diamond Historical Society
(32627 Railroad and Baker Streets—location)
PO Box 232 (mailing address)
Black Diamond, WA 98010-9762
(360) 886-2142; (360) 886-1168
Robert Eaton, President
Sat–Sun noon–3:00, Thur 9:00–4:00
Pub. *Newsletter*, quarterly
$5.00 per year membership

Camas-Washougal Historical Society
Two Rivers Heritage Museum
(1 16th Street—location)
PO Box 204 (mailing address)
Washougal, WA 98671
(360) 835-8742
Curtis Hughey, Society President; Betty Ramsey, Museum Director
Tue–Sat 11:00–3:00
("families, businesses, land, etc., 500+ family histories, 5,000+ photos, many artifacts including Native American")
$12.00 per year membership; admission: $3.00 for adults

Chehalis Valley Historical Society
(703 West Pioneer, Montesano, WA 98563—location)
268 Oak Meadows Lane (mailing address)
Oakville, WA 98568
(360) 273-8044 (Librarian); (360) 249-5800 (Museum answering machine)
Mrs. Kelle A. Davis, Genealogical Librarian
Museum: Sat–Sun 1:00–4:00
Pub. *The Chehalis Valley Historian*, quarterly
("Chehalis [pre-1913] and Grays Harbor County [after 1913] information from Montesano to eastern county line: towns of Elma, Malone, Porter, Oakville and Montesano; this is not connected with the Town of Chehalis, Washington, nor the county (Lewis) it is located in; our county's name was changed from Chehalis County to Grays Harbor County in 1913.")
$10.00 per year membership

Chelan County Historical Society
(600 Cottage Avenue—location)
PO Box 22 (mailing address)
Cashmere, WA 98815-1602
(509) 782-3230
Jim Wilson, President; Geri Inabnit, Museum Coordinator
Mon–Sat 10:00–4:30, Sun 1:00–4:30
$10.00 per year membership

Clallam County Historical Society
Clallam County Museum
223 East Fourth Street
Port Angeles, WA 98362-3098
(360) 417-2364
Kathy Monds, Museum Manager
Sept–May: Mon–Fri 10:00–4:00; June–Aug: Mon–Sat 10:00–4:00
(Clallam County history)
$15.00 per year membership

Cle Elum Historical Society
(Carpenter House Museum, 320 West Third—location)
413 East Second Street (mailing address)
Cle Elum, WA 98922-1205
(509) 674-2268; (509) 674-5702
Cecelie Maybo, President
15 May–15 Sept
("We do not have much written history at this time."; also Telephone Museum, 221 East First, PO Box 11, Cle Elum, WA 98922)

Columbia County Genealogical and Historical Society
(see Genealogical Societies—Local and Regional, below)

Des Moines Historical Society
(728 225th South, Upstairs—location)
PO Box 98055 (mailing address)
Des Moines, WA 98198
(206) 824-5226
Carol Davis, Secretary
Sat (June–Sept) 1:00–4:00; tours by appointment throughout the year
(formerly known as Greater Des Moines-Zenith Historical Association and Museum; refurbished museum; catalogue of over 2,000 photos from pioneer days to the present)
$10.00 per year membership

Duvall Historical Society
PO Box 385
Duvall, WA 98019
Tove Burhen, President
Pub. *Wagon Wheel Newsletter*, ten times per

year (monthly, Sept–June), $5.00 per year subscription
$5.00 per year membership

East Benton County Historical Society
(205 Keewaydin Drive—location)
PO Box 6964 (mailing address)
Kennewick, WA 99336
(509) 582-7704
http://www.owt.com/ebchs/ebchs
Vickie Bergum, Director
Tue–Sat noon–4:00
Pub. *The Courier*, quarterly
(large local listing of alphabetized obituaries, research with reference materials and files which may be used on site)
$15.00 per year membership

Eastern Lewis County Historical Society
Old Settlers Museum
Gust Backstrom Park
PO Box 777
Morton, WA 98356
(360) 496-5602 (Treasurer); (360) 496-3348 (President)
Alma Chamberlain, President
Fri–Sun (June–Aug) 1:00–4:00, and alternated with 5:00–8:00

Eastern Washington State Historical Society
(see Northwest Museum of Arts and Culture, below)

Eatonville Historical Society
42310 Lynch Creek Road
Eatonville, WA 98328
(253) 832-6096

Edmonds South Snohomish County Historical Society and Museum
(118 Fifth Avenue, North—location)
PO Box 52 (mailing address)
Edmonds, WA 98020
(425) 774-0900
http://www.historicedmonds.org
Joni Sein, Museum Director
Wed–Sun 1:00–4:00
Pub. *Museum Light*, quarterly
(local history of Edmonds and South Snohomish County)
$20.00 per year membership

Fort Vancouver Historical Society of Clark County, Inc.
Clark County Historical Museum
1511 Main Street
Vancouver, WA 98668
(360) 695-4681 (Museum)
Gus Norwood, Museum Director; Bill Hidden, President
Tue–Sat 1:00–5:00
Pub. *Clark County History*, annually
$6.50 per year membership

Fox Island Historical Society
PO Box 242
Fox Island, WA 98333-0242
(253) 549-2461; (253) 549-2239

Franklin County Historical Society
305 North Fourth Avenue
Pasco, WA 99301-5324
(509) 547-3714; (509) 545-2168 FAX
Gabriele Sperling, Director
Tue–Sat noon–4:00
Pub. *The Franklin Flyer*, quarterly, $2.25 per issue; *Newsletter*
$15.00 per year membership; free admission

Gig Harbor Peninsula Historical Society
(3510 Rosedale Street—location)

PO Box 744 (mailing address)
Gig Harbor, WA 98335
Chris Fiala Erlich, M.A.
Office: Mon & Wed 9:00–noon; Museum:
    Wed–Sat 1:00–4:00
Pub. untitled newsletter, quarterly
$15.00 per year membership

Granite Falls Historical Society
(Corner Wabash and Indiana
Street—location)
PO Box 135 (mailing address)
Granite Falls, WA 98252
(360) 691-7640

Greater Des Moines-Zenith Historical Association and Museum
(see Des Moines Historical Society, above)

Ilwaco Heritage Foundation Research Library
(117 S.E. Lake Street—location)
PO Box 153 (mailing address)
Ilwaco, WA 98624
(360) 665-3446; (360) 642-4615
Joan Mann, Librarian
Museum: Mon–Sat 10:00–4:00; Library:
    Mon & Fri 10:00–noon & 1:00–3:00

Index Historical Society-Pickett Museum
(505 Avenue A—location)
PO Box 107 (mailing address)
Index, WA 98256
(360) 793-1534
Louise Lindgren, Director
Sun (Memorial Day weekend–Labor Day
    weekend) noon–3:00
Pub. *Newsletter*, quarterly
(names from town records, extensive photo
    collection; mining, logging and quarry
    history, local floods, and general history of
    the Index area)
$10.00 per year membership; museum
    admission: free

Island County Historical Society
(908 N.W. Alexander Street—location)
PO Box 305 (mailing address)
Coupeville, WA 98239
(360) 678-3310
Sandra Plush, Museum Manager
winter: Mon & Fri–Sun 11:00–4:00; summer:
    Mon–Sun 10:00–5:00
Pub. *Island Heritage*, quarterly

Issaquah Historical Society
(165 S.E. Andrews Street—location)
PO Box 695 (mailing address)
Issaquah, WA 98027
(425) 392-3500
info@issaquahhistory.org
http://www.issaquahhistory.org
Erica S. Maniez, Director
Thur–Sat 11:00–3:00, and by appointment
Pub. *Past Times*, quarterly
some research/copy fees may apply

Jefferson County Historical Society and Museum
McCurdy Research Library
540 Water Street
Port Townsend, WA 98368
(360) 385-1003
jchsmuseum@olympus.net
http://www.jchsmuseum.org
Dr. Nicki R. Clark, Director
Mon–Sat 11:00–4:00, Sun 1:00–4:00
Pub. *JCHS Newsletter*, quarterly
(Jefferson County history)
$15.00 per year membership; research:
    $10.00 per hour

Association of King County Historical Organization
PO Box 3257
Seattle, WA 98114
Dick Wagner, President
meetings: last Tue (except July & Dec)
Pub. *AKCHO Member Roster*, biannually
    (even years)
$10.00 per year membership

Kitsap County Historical Society
9945 N.E. West Kingston Road
Kingston, WA 98346
Suzanne Arness Halcyon
Tue–Sat 10:00–5:00
(Kitsap County history)

Lake Chelan Historical Society
(204 East Woodin Avenue—location)
PO Box 1948 (mailing address)
Chelan, WA 98816
(509) 682-5644
David H. Davis, President
Mon–Sun (June–Sept) 1:00–4:00, and by
    appointment
Pub. *Lake Chelan History Notes*, irregularly
$5.00 per year membership

Lewis County Historical Society
Lewis County Historical Museum
Genealogical Committee
599 N.W. Front Street
Chehalis, WA 98532
(360) 748-0831
Brenda A. O'Connor, Museum Director
Tue–Sat 9:00–5:00, Sun 1:00–5:00
Pub. *Lewis County Log*, quarterly
("approximately 30,000 obituary files
    1966–1993, many earlier, but not
    consecutive; photograph file, 12,000
    catalogued, varied subjects; local history
    files and family files")
$15.00 per year membership

Lincoln County Historical Society
(Park and Sixth Street—location)
PO Box 585 (mailing address)
Davenport, WA 99122
(509) 725-6711; (509) 726-0561 (Treasurer)
Verna Johns, Treasurer
Museum: daily (May–Sept) 9:00–5:00
Pub. *Lincoln County Historical Society
    Newsletter*, semiannually
$10.00 per year membership

Lopez Island Historical Society and Museum
PO Box 163
Lopez Island, WA 98261
(360) 468-2049; (360) 468-3447 (Curator's
    home)
Nancy McCoy, Curator
July–Aug: Wed–Sun noon–4:00; May–June
    & Sept: Fri–Sun noon–4:00
$5.00 per year membership

Maple Valley Historical Society
(23015 S.E. 216th Way—location)
PO Box 123 (mailing address)
Maple Valley, WA 98038
(425) 432-3470
Dan Nicholas, President
Museum: first & third Sat 11:00–3:00
Pub. *Maple Valley Bugle*, quarterly; small
    local history booklet, annually
$10.00 per year membership

Mason County Historical Society Museum
(427 Railroad Avenue—location)
PO Box 1366 (mailing address)
Shelton, WA 98584
(360) 426-1020

Michael Fredson, President; Billie L.
    Howard, Museum Director
Tue–Fri noon–5:00, Sat noon–4:00
Pub. *Mason County Historical Society
    Newsletter*, ten times per year (monthly,
    Mar–Dec)
$12.00 per year membership

Mukilteo Historical Society
304 Lincoln Avenue
Mukilteo, WA 98275
(425) 355-2144

Newcastle Historical Society
14553 S.E. 55th Street
Bellevue, WA 98006
(425) 746-2482

Northwest Museum of Arts and Culture/Eastern Washington State Historical Society
2516 West First Avenue
Spokane, WA 99204
(509) 363-5313
Rayette Wilder, Archives Librarian
Tue–Fri 11:00–5:00, Wed 11:00–8:00, Sat
    11:00–5:00 by appointment
Pub. *Museum Notes*, quarterly

Okanogan County Historical Society and Museum
(1410 Second Avenue North—location)
PO Box 1129 (mailing address)
Okanogan, WA 98840
(509) 422-4272
ochs@ncidata.com
Marilynn Moses, Coordinator; Gero
    Mitschelen, President
Museum: May–Sept: 11:00–4:00; Research
    Center: 8:00–noon
Pub. *The Okanogan County Heritage*,
    quarterly
(Research Center houses library, photo
    collections, historical documents,
    interviews, maps, etc.)
$25.00 per year membership

Pacific County Historical Society and Museum Foundation
(1008 West Robert Bush Drive, South Bend,
    WA 98588—location)
PO Box P (mailing address)
South Bend, WA 98586
(360) 875-5224
Museum@Willapabay.org
http://Pacificohistory.org
Bruce Weilepp, Museum Director
Mon–Sun 11:00–4:00
Pub. *The Sou'wester*, quarterly
(Washington history, local history; proper
    name index to local newspapers)
$20.00 per year membership

Pend Oreille County Historical Society
(402 South Washington Avenue—location)
PO Box 1409 (mailing address)
Newport, WA 99156
(509) 447-5388; (509) 447-2770 (President)
Evelyn Reed, President
Mid-May to end of Sept: Mon–Sun
    10:00–4:00, and the rest of the year by
    appointment; Research library: by
    appointment
Pub. *The Big Smoke* (stories written by
    former or present residents), annually,
    $7.00 per issue
(some family histories and area histories,
    large photo collection and local weekly
    back to 1900)
$5.00 per year membership (does not include
    periodical); research: donation

Polson Park and Museum Historical Society
PO Box 432
Hoquiam, WA 98550
(360) 533-5862
Toni Gwin, Curator-Manager

Renton Historical Society and Museum
235 Mill Avenue, South
Renton, WA 98055
(425) 255-2330
saanderson@ci.renton.wa.us
Steve Anderson, Museum Director
Tue–Sat noon–4:00
Pub. *Renton Historical Society Quarterly*
$10.00 per year membership; research: 30 minutes free, $25.00 per hour thereafter

Roslyn Historical Museum Society
PO Box 281
Roslyn, WA 98941
(509) 649-2776 (Curator)
Mary Andler, Curator
1:00–4:00, and by appointment

San Juan Historical Society
(405 Price Street—location)
PO Box 441 (mailing address)
Friday Harbor, WA 98250
(360) 378-3949
Jennifer Fleming, Director
Apr–Sept: Wed–Sat 1:00–4:00; Oct–Mar: Tue & Thur 10:00–2:00
Pub. *SJHS Newsletter*, quarterly
$10.00 per year membership

Historical Society of Seattle and King County
(d.b.a. Museum of History and Industry)
(address withheld upon request)
$15.00 per year membership

Skagit County Historical Society
Skagit County Historical Museum
(501 South Fourth Street—location)
PO Box 818 (mailing address)
La Conner, WA 98257
(360) 466-3365
museum@co.skagit.wa.us
http://www.skagitcounty.net/museum
Karen Marshall, Museum Director
Exhibition Gallery: Tue–Sun 11:00–5:00; Archives/Library: by appointment only
Pub. *Skagit County Historical Society Quarterly Newsletter*
$25.00–$250.00 per year museum membership

Skamania County Historical Society
PO Box 396
Stevenson, WA 98648
(509) 427-5141, ext. 235
Sharon Tiffany, Director
Pub. *Skamania County Heritage*, quarterly
$7.00 per year membership

Snohomish County Historical Association
Heritage Center, Museum and Library
(2817 Rockefeller Avenue—location)
PO Box 5203 (mailing address)
Everett, WA 98206
(425) 259-2022

Snohomish Historical Society
(118 Avenue B—location)
PO Box 174 (mailing address)
Snohomish, WA 98291-0174
(360) 568-5235
Victor Harrington, Archivist
Mon–Tue 10:00–noon, Fri–Sun noon–4:00
(maintains Blackman Museum and Old Snohomish Village; focus on city of Snohomish)
$10.00 per year membership

South Thurston County Historical Society
(Tenino Depot Museum, Park Street—location)
PO Box 339 (mailing address)
Tenino, WA 98589
(360) 264-4321; (360) 264-4637
Jean Montgomery, President
18 Apr–15 Oct: Fri–Sun noon–4:00
$5.00 per year membership; research fees vary, including cost for copies

Genealogical Society of South Whidbey Island
PO Box 976
Langley, WA 98260
lroetci@aol.com
http://www.rootsweb.com/~wagsswi
Laura Roetcisoender, President
$15.00 per year membership

Southeastern Lincoln County Historical Society
General Delivery
Sprague, WA 99032

Southwest Seattle Historical Society
c/o South Seattle Community College
6000 16th Avenue, S.W.
Seattle, WA 98106
(206) 764-5357; (206) 764-5371
Mon–Fri 8:00–4:30
Pub. *Footprints*, quarterly
(history/artifacts of West Seattle and White Center)
$10.00 per year membership

Stanwood Area Historical Society
(D. O. Pearson House, 27112 102nd Avenue, N.W.—location)
PO Box 69 (mailing address)
Stanwood, WA 98292
(360) 629-6110
kprasse@camano.net
http://www.sahs-fncc.org/SAHSbib.html

Stevens County Historical Society, Inc.
(700 North Wynne Street—location)
PO Box 25 (mailing address)
Colville, WA 99114
(509) 684-5968
William E. Winn, Jr., Curator/Administrator
Pub. *In-Review*
$10.00 per year membership

Sumner Historical Society
(Sumner Ryan House Museum, 1228 Main Street—location)
PO Box 517 (mailing address)
Sumner, WA 98390
(253) 863-8936
Dorothy Peterkin, Curator
Apr–Oct & Dec: Wed & Sat–Sun 1:00–4:00, and by appointment
Pub. *Quarterly Newsletter*
("research of pioneer family history and early history of the area")
$7.50 per year membership

Sunnyside Museum and Historical Association
(Fourth and Grant Street—location)
PO Box 782 (mailing address)
Sunnyside, WA 98944
(509) 837-6010

Tacoma Historical Society
(3712 South Cedar Street, #101—location)
PO Box 1865 (mailing address)
Tacoma, WA 98401

(253) 472-3738
http://www.powerscourt.com/ths
Pub. *City of Destiny Newsletter*
$15.00 per year membership

Tumwater Historical Association
PO Box 4315
Olympia, WA 98501-0315
Sandi Gray, President
(The Tumwater Association publishes *The History of Tumwater*, a set of four volumes describing the settling and early years of Tumwater, Washington, which is the first American community north of the Columbia River. The books are available at the above address for $25.00 per set, or priced individually.")
$10.00 per year membership

Vashon Maury Island Heritage Association
PO Box 723
Vashon, WA 98070
(206) 567-4663

Wahkiakum County Historical Society/Museum
(65 River Street—location)
PO Box 541 (mailing address)
Cathlamet, WA 98612
(360) 795-3954

Waitsburg Historical Society
(Fourth and Main Street—location)
PO Box 442 (mailing address)
Waitsburg, WA 99361
(509) 337-6582
Jan

Walla Walla Valley Pioneer and Historical Society
Fort Walla Walla Museum Complex
Myra Road
Walla Walla, WA 99362
(509) 525-6966 (Museum); (509) 525-7703 (Society)
C. William Burk, Museum Director

Whatcom County Historical Society
PO Box 2116
Bellingham, WA 98227
(360) 676-0582
editor@whatcomhistory.net
http://www.whatcomhistory.net
Neill D. Mullen, Sales
Pub. *Newsletter*, five to six times per year, not available by subscription
$10.00 per year membership

White River Valley Museum
918 H Street, S.E.
Auburn, WA 98002
(253) 939-2783 (information); (253) 939-4523 (staff); (253) 931-5105 FAX
Patricia Cosgrove, Museum Director
Museum: Thur–Sun 1:30–4:30, and by appointment
Pub. *Newsletter*, quarterly
(reference library with collection of area newspapers, photographs, documents and school annuals)
$15.00 per year membership

Whitman County Historical Society
(623 North Perkins Avenue—location)
PO Box 67 (mailing address)
Colfax, WA 99111
(509) 332-5752; (509) 332-1029
http://www.wsu.edu:8080/~kemeyer/wchs.html
Larry R. Stark, Editor
Wed morning
Pub. *Bunchgrass Historian*, quarterly

$10.00 per year membership

Genealogical Societies

State Genealogical Society

Washington State Genealogical Society
PO Box 1422
Olympia, WA 98507-1422
(360) 352-0595
geniebug@comcast.net
http://www.rootsweb.com/~wasgs
Roger H. Newman, Corresponding Secretary
Pub. *Washington State Genealogical Society Newsletter*, bimonthly
$10.00 per year membership

Genealogical Societies—Local & Regional

Anacortes Genealogical Discussion Group
Anacortes Senior Center
1601 22nd Street
Anacortes, WA 98221

Belfair Genealogical Society of Mason County Washington
c/o Puget Sound Genealogical Society
PO Box 1931 (mailing address)
Port Orchard, WA 98366-0805
jfhort@aol.com
http://www.rootsweb.com/~wabgs
Madi Cataldo and Estelle Foster, Co-presidents
meetings at the Belfair Community Baptist Church: first Tue (Feb–Nov); 12:30

Camwood Genealogical Workshop
D. O. Pearson House Museum
27112 102nd Avenue
Stanwood, WA 98292

Chelan Valley Genealogical Society
PO Box Y
Chelan, WA 98816
(509) 682-5131 (Library)
lmart@crcwnet.com
http://www.rootsweb.com/~wachelan/cvgs.html
Linda Martinson
meetings at Chelan City (Public) Library: third Tue 4:00
Pub. *The Apple Orchard*, bimonthly
("We are collecting Chelan County records")
$10.00 per year membership; research: send SASE for fees

Clallam County Genealogical Society
PO Box 1327
Port Angeles, WA 98362
(360) 417-5000
ccgs@olypen.com
http://www.olypen.com/ccgs
Ron Foss, President
Mon–Fri 10:00–4:00
Pub. *CCGS Bulletin*, quarterly
(general genealogical research, specializing in Clallam County)
$20.00 per year membership (includes membership in Clallam County Historical Society); research: $5.00 per hour plus copies, $5.00 minimum

Clark County Genealogical Society
(717 Grand Boulevard, Vancouver, WA 98661—location)
PO Box 5249 (mailing address)
Vancouver, WA 98668-5249
(360) 750-5688
ccgswa@pacifier.com
http://www.ccgs-wa.org
Pub. *"Trail Breakers"—Clark County Genealogical Society*, quarterly;

Newsletter
$25.00 per year membership

Columbia County Genealogical and Historical Society
627 Harlem Road
Dayton, WA 99328

Eastern Washington Genealogical Society
PO Box 1826
Spokane, WA 99210-1826
(509) 444-5357 (Spokane Public Library Genealogy Room, Tue, Thur & Sat only)
charles_hansen@prodigy.net
http://www.rootsweb.com/~waewgs
Charles Hansen
Tue noon–8:00, Thur 10:00–6:00, Sat 10:00–2:00
Pub. *The Bulletin*, quarterly
$20.00 per year membership

Eastern Washington Genealogical Society, Metis Genealogical Society Chapter
North 6206 Washington
Spokane, WA 99208
Pub. *Newsletter of Genealogical Research of the North American Indian*, quarterly
$3.50 per year membership

Eastside Genealogical Society
PO Box 374
Bellevue, WA 98024-0374
gyoung@seanet.com
http://www.rootsweb.com/~wakcegs/index.htm
meetings at Bellevue Regional Library: second Thur (except Dec) 7:00
Pub. *The Bulletin Board*, eleven times per year
$10.00 per year membership

Forks Genealogical Society
Forks Memorial Library
(171 Forks Avenue South—location)
PO Box 1817 (mailing address)
Forks, WA 98331

Grant County Genealogical Society
Ephrata Public Library
45 Alder Street, N.W.
Ephrata, WA 98823-1663
meetings: third Mon 7:30
Pub. *Big Bend Register*, quarterly
$20.00 per year membership; research: by donation to library

Grays Harbor Genealogical Society
PO Box 867
Cosmopolis, WA 98537-0867
(360) 249-4632
ghgs@mail.techline.com
http://users.techline.com/ghgs
meetings at Hoquiam Library, Courtesy Room: second Sat 10:00
Pub. *The Family Tree-Searcher*, bimonthly
$15.00 per year membership; research: fee negotiable

Jefferson County Genealogical Society
PO Box 627
Port Townsend, WA 98368-0627
(360) 385-9495
wajcgs@olympus.net
http://www.rootsweb.com/~wajcgs
Joan Buhler, Corresponding Secretary
Mon–Sat 11:00–4:00, Sun 1:00–4:00
Pub. *Jefferson County Genealogical Society Newsletter*, quarterly
$15.00 per year membership

Kittitas County Genealogical Society
(413 North Main, Suite D—location)

PO Box 1342 (mailing address)
Ellensburg, WA 98926-1342
(509) 925-5951
Margorie E. Boles, Librarian; Virginia C. Hanks, Librarian
Mon–Fri 10:00–4:00
Pub. *Kittitas Kinfolk*, quarterly
("Good local records; also more records of other areas.")
$10.00 per year membership

Lewis County Genealogical Society
PO Box 782
Chehalis, WA 98532
http://www.rootsweb.com/~walcgs
Pub. newsletter, bimonthly
$12.00 per year membership

Lewis County Historical Society
Genealogical Committee
(see Historical Societies—Local and Regional, above)

Lower Columbia Genealogical Society
(Longview Public Library—location)
PO Box 472 (mailing address)
Longview, WA 98632-0472
locoges472@yahoo.com
http://ci.longview.wa.us/library/genindex/htm
Terry Mattison, President
Pub. *The Key*, quarterly
$15.00 per year membership; $5.00 per hour, one-hour minimum, plus LSASE, and copies extra

North Beach Genealogical Society
PO Box 2007
Ocean Shores, WA 98569

North Pend Oreille Genealogical Society
PO Box 311
Ione, WA 99139-0311
meetings at Senior Center: last Mon

Northeast Washington Genealogical Society
c/o Colville Public Library
195 South Oak
Colville, WA 99114
(509) 935-4039 (President)
bljones@theofficenet.com
http://news.ole
Doris Winskie, Quarterly Editor; Linda Jones, President
meetings: third Wed (except Dec) 1:30
Pub. *Pioneer Branches*, quarterly (Oct, Jan, Apr, July)
$15.00 per year membership; research: $15.00

Northern Kittitas County Genealogical Society
McMurdie
362 Peavine Road
Ellensburg, WA 98926-8984

Okanogan County Genealogical Society
(Okanogan County Historical and Genealogical Research Center, 1410 Second, North, Okanogan, WA 98840—location)
263 Old Riverside Highway (mailing address)
Okanogan, WA 98841
(509) 826-1686
Lola Power, Librarian
Mon–Fri 9:00–noon, afternoons by appointment; meetings: first Thur 7:00
$15.00 per year membership; research: variable

Olympia Genealogical Society
PO Box 1313

Olympia, WA 98507-1313
OlympiaGenSoc@bigfoot.com
http://www.rootsweb.com/~waogs
Roger H. Newman, Research Chairman
Pub. *Olympia Genealogical Society
    Quarterly*
(Thurston County, Washington, records)
$15.00 per year membership; research fee
    quotation for SASE

Pacific County Genealogical Society
PO Box 843
Ocean Park, WA 98640-0843
(360) 665-6293
Joy G. Taylor, Editor
daytime
Pub. *Clan Digger*, monthly
(emphasis on southwest Washington
    genealogy)
$10.00 per year membership

Puget Sound Genealogical Society
(The Research Library, Suite A102, 2501
S.E. Mile Hill Drive, Port Orchard,
WA—location)
PO Box 1931 (mailing address)
Port Orchard, WA 98366-0805
(360) 874-8813
wmbrich@aol.com
http://www.rootsweb.com/~wapsgs/
    homepage.htm
Bill Richardson, Education
fourth Tue (Mar–Oct) 7:00, (Nov–Dec) 1:00
Pub. *Family Backtracking*, quarterly
$12.00 per year membership; queries as space
    allows

Seattle Genealogical Society
(6200 Sand Point Way, N.E.,
#101—location)
PO Box 15329 (mailing address)
Seattle, WA 98115-0329
(206) 522-8658
seagen@foxinternetcom
http://www.rootsweb.com/~waseags
Tue–Sat 10:00–3:00
Pub. *Seattle Genealogical Society Newsletter*,
    monthly; *Seattle Genealogical Society
    Bulletin*, quarterly
(specializes in Washington and Scandinavia)
$20.00 per year membership; research: $8.00

Skagit Valley Genealogical Society
PO Box 715
Conway, WA 98238-0715
h. rasar2@verizon.net
http://www.rootsweb.com/~wasvgs
Hazel Rasar, President
meetings at Mount Vernon Presbyterian
    Church, 1511 East Broadway: fourth Tue
    7:00
Pub. *Skagit Valley Genealogical Society
    Newsletter*, quarterly
(publishes local death records)
research: $10.00 donation

Sno-Isle Genealogical Society
(Martha Lake Community Club, Alderwood
Manor, WA—location)
PO Box 63 (mailing address)
Edmonds, WA 98020-0063
(425) 776-1938
mvreid@eskimo.com
http://rootsweb.com/~wasigs
Judith Thompson, President
meetings first Wed 7:30
Pub. *The Sounder*, quarterly
$15.00 per year membership; queries free to
    members

South King County Genealogical Society
(Auburn Public Library, 808 Ninth Street

S.E., Auburn, WA 98002—collection
    location)
PO Box 3174 (mailing address)
Kent, WA 98032-0203
johnnger2000@yahoo.com
http://rootsweb.com/~waskcgs
Gerry Bechen, Secretary
Pub. *The So King Newsletter*, bimonthly
$10.00 per year membership

Steilacoom Genealogy Organization
c/o Steilacoom Historical Museum
Association
(122 Main Street—location)
PO Box 88016 (mailing address)
Steilacoom, WA 98388
(253) 588-2585
Cy Happy

**Stillaguamish Valley Genealogical Society
and Library**
(135 North Olympic—location)
PO Box 34 (mailing address)
Arlington, WA 98223-0034
(360) 435-4838 (Library)
cornynyblod@juno.com
http://www.rootsweb.com/~wastvgs
Marilou Cory Nyblod, President
Tue noon–4:00, Thur 10:00–2:00
Pub. *Stillaguamish Star*, bimonthly
(Civil War collection, including War of the
    Rebellion series; info from Snohomish
    County cemeteries and *Everett Herald*
    obituaries; local papers: *Arlington Times*,
    Granite Falls Record, and *Stanwood
    News*)
$15.00 per year membership

Sumner Genealogical Group
Sumner Public Library
1116 Fryar Avenue
Sumner, WA 98390
(253) 863-0441

**Tacoma-Pierce County Genealogical
Society**
PO Box 1952
Tacoma, WA 98401
(253) 572-6650 (Message)
MAlexan206@aol.com
http://www.rootsweb.com/~watpcgs/
    tpcgs.htm
Maxine Alexander
Tacoma Public Library: Mon–Thur
    9:00–9:00, Fri–Sat 9:00–6:00
Pub. *The Researcher*, quarterly
$18.00 per year membership

Tri-City Genealogical Society
PO Box 1410
Richland, WA 99352-1410
(509) 545-5534 (Editor's home)
tcgresearch@hotmail.com
http://www.cbvcp.com/tcgs
Lee Smith, Editor
Pub. *Tri-City Genealogical Society Bulletin*,
    three times per year (Mar, July, Nov)
(northwest genealogy)
$13.00 per year membership; research:
    $10.00 minimum

Walla Walla Valley Genealogical Society
PO Box 115
Walla Walla, WA 99362-0115
Gwen Wall, President
Pub. *Blue Mountain Heritage*, quarterly
$10.00 per year membership

Wenatchee Area Genealogical Society
(133 South Mission—library location)
PO Box 5280 (mailing address)
Wenatchee, WA 98807-5280
(509) 664-3346

info@wags-web.org
http://www.wagsweb.org
Louis Guizzetti President
Wenatchee Valley Museum Annex Building:
    Tue–Thur & Sat 1:00–4:00
Pub. *Appleland Bulletin*, quarterly
("Records for North Central Washington,
    including Chelan and Douglas counties")
$20.00 per year membership

Whatcom Genealogical Society
PO Box 1493
Bellingham, WA 98227-1493
(360) 734-9835
http://www.rootsweb.com/~wawhatco
Merrily Lawson, Editor
meetings at Bellingham Public Library:
    second Mon (Sept–June) 7:00
Pub. *The Bulletin*, quarterly
(emphasis on northwestern Washington
    genealogy, Whatcom, San Juan and Skagit
    counties)
$12.00 per year membership; research:
    $10.00 per hour donation plus cost of
    copies and postage; free queries for
    nonmembers

**Whidbey Island Genealogical Searchers
(WIGS)**
PO Box 627
Oak Harbor, WA 98277-0627
Ruth Hancock, Secretary
meetings at the Heller Road Fire Station, Oak
    Harbor: second Tue 1:00
$7.00 per year membership

Whitman County Genealogical Society
(WCGS Library, Gladish Community Center,
115 S.W. State Street—location)
PO Box 393 (mailing address)
Pullman, WA 99163-0393
(509) 334-9583 (President)
http://www.rootsweb.com/~wawcgs
Jean Innerarity, President
Neill Public Library: Wed 9:00–noon, and by
    appointment; meetings: second Thur
Pub. *Whitman County Genealogical Society
    News Letter*, ten times per year (monthly,
    except Aug & Dec)
$20.00 per year membership; research:
    $10.00 per hour

Willapa Harbor Genealogical Society
Raymond Public Library
507 Duryea Street
Raymond, WA 98577

Yakima Valley Genealogical Society
(2609 River Road—location)
PO Box 445 (mailing address)
Yakima, WA 98907-0445
(509) 248-1328
fl635@nwinfo.net
http://www.rootsweb.com/~wayvgs
Ellen Brzoska, Librarian
Mon–Fri 10:00–4:00, Sat (Oct–May)
    10:00–4:00
Pub. *Yakima Valley Genealogical Society
    Bulletin*, quarterly
(Washington area and nationwide
    bibliographies, indexes and society
    bulletins; obituary index kept to date of
    Yakima County deaths, coordinates
    cemeteries, sexton's records and mortuary
    records; "list is available at web site and is
    updated twice a year")
$15.00 per year membership

Independent Publications and
Miscellany

Anacortes Museum
Research Library
1305 Eighth Street
Anacortes, WA 98221-1833
(360) 293-1915; (360) 293-1929 FAX
museum@cityofanacortes.com;
    sarvisw@cityofanacortes.org
Terry Slotemaker, Educator; Will Sarvis,
    Curator of Collections and Interpretation
Mon & Thur–Fri 1:00–5:00

Forks Timber Museum
1421 South Forks Avenue
Forks, WA 98331
(360) 374-9663

Kittitas County Museum
114 East Third Avenue
Ellensburg, WA 98926
(509) 925-3778

Longmire Museum
General Delivery
Longmire, WA 98397
(360) 569-2211

Marymoor Museum
(6046 West Lake Sammamish
    Parkway—location)
PO Box 162 (mailing address)
Redmond, WA 98073-0162
(425) 885-3684
Kimberly Haas, Director
Tue–Thur 11:00–4:00, Sun 1:00–5:00
Pub. *Marymoor Musings*, quarterly
$15.00 per year membership

Museum and Arts Center
(544 North Sequim Avenue—location)
175 West Cedar Street (mailing address)
Sequim, WA 98382
(360) 681-2257, (360) 681-2325
Dr. Deborah Rambo, Executive Director
Museum: Tue–Sat 9:00–4:00, Sun (summer)
    1:00–4:00; Administration Building:
    Tue–Fri 9:00–3:00
$20.00 per year membership

Northwest Pioneer
East 13124 Nixon
Spokane, WA 99216
Joanne M. Elliott
Pub. *Northwest Pioneer (Oregon,
    Washington, Idaho, and Montana)*, $6.00
    per volume

**Northwest Seaport Maritime Heritage
Center**
1002 Valley Street
Seattle, WA 98109-4332
(206) 447-9800

Oregon/Washington Queries
(see Oregon, Part 2)

Othello Community Museum
(Third and Lurch—location)
PO Box 121 (mailing address)
Othello, WA 99344
(509) 488-2268

Sidney Museum and Arts Association
202 Sidney Avenue
Port Orchard, WA 98366
(360) 876-3693

Stillaguamish Valley Pioneer Museum
20722 67th Avenue, N.E.
Arlington, WA 98223
(360) 435-7289
http://www.ohwy.com/wa/s/stillvpm.htm

Toppenish Museum
1 South Elm
Toppenish, WA 98948
(509) 865-4510
Tue–Sat 1:30–4:30, and by appointment

University of California Press
Pacific Historical Review
(see California, Part 2)

WaGenWeb
Part of The USGenweb Project
sweeney2@wolfenet.com
http://www.rootsweb.com/~wagenweb
Mike Sweeney, State Coordinator
(links to other Washington resources)

**Washington State Department of
Transportation**
Transportation Building
(310 Maple Park Avenue, S.E.—location)
PO Box 47300 (mailing address)
Olympia, WA 98504-7300
(360) 705-7000
info@wsdot.wa.gov
http://www.wsdot.wa.gov/mapsdata.htm
    (Maps)
Mon–Fri 8:00–5:00

Western Frontier Museum
2301 23rd Avenue, S.E.
Puyallup, WA 98372
(253) 845-4402

Women's Heritage Center
5226 17th, N.E.
Seattle, WA 98105
(206) 784-6569
Lela Hilton, President

Yakima Valley Museum
2105 Tieton Drive
Yakima, WA 98902
(509) 248-0747; (509) 453-4890 FAX
info@yakimavalleymuseum.org
Michael Siebol, Curator of Collections
Tue–Sun 10:00–5:00
$30.00 per year membership

West Virginia

Archives and Libraries with Holdings in Genealogy

State Archives and Library

**West Virginia Division of Culture and
History**
Archives and History Section
The Cultural Center
Archives and History Library
State Capitol Complex, Building 9
1900 Kanawha Boulevard, East
Charleston, WV 25305-0300
(304) 558-0230, ext. 168
http://www.wvculture.org/history
Fredrick H. Armstrong, Director
Mon–Thur 9:00–8:00, Fri–Sat 9:00–6:00
Pub. *West Virginia History*, annually, $15.00
    per issue; *Goldenseal*, quarterly, $15.00
    per year subscription

State Historical Society

Mining Your History Foundation
PO Box 6923
Charleston, WV 25362-0923
(304) 525-5720
wescochran@juno.com
http://www.rootsweb.com/~myhf
Wes Cochran, President
("a statewide genealogy and local history
    society networking among similar
    organizations throughout the state;
    dissemi-nation of information about West
    Virginia groups on a national level,
    support of the State Archives with
    donations and volunteer hours")
$15.00 per year membership

West Virginia Historical Society
PO Box 5220
Charleston, WV 25361
(304) 348-2277; (304) 348-0230; (304) 558-
    2779 FAX
http://www.wvhistorical.com
Rodney A. Pyles, Director
Mon–Thur 9:00–9:00, Fri 9:00–5:00, Sat
    1:00–5:00
Pub. *West Virginia Historical Society
    Quarterly*
$10.00 per year membership

**City, County and Regional Archives and
Libraries**
(A more exhaustive list of public and
academic libraries can be found at
http://librarycommission.lib.wv.us.)

Alderson-Broaddus College
Pickett Library
College Hill
Philippi, WV 26416
(304) 457-1700, ext. 306; (304) 457-6229;
    (304) 457-6239 FAX
http://ab.edu/ab/catalog/facilities.html
Edward Gibson, Head Librarian

Allegany College of Maryland Library
Appalachian Collection
(see Maryland, Part 2)

Bethany College
T. W. Phillips Library
Alexander Campbell Archives
Bethany, WV 26032
(304) 829-7325; (304) 829-7333 FAX
http://info.bethany.wvnet.edu/Resources/
    Library/*Index.html

Boone-Madison Public Library
375 Main Street
Madison, WV 25130
(304) 369-7842; (304) 369-2950 FAX
http://boone.lib.wv.us
Mary Horn, Director
Mon–Sat 9:00–5:00
("genealogy room")

Brooke County Public Library
945 Main Street
Wellsburg, WV 26070
(304) 757-1551; (304) 737-1010 FAX
http://129.71.94.5/htdocs/brooke/wells/
    welllib.html
Mary Kay Wallace, Director
Mon–Thur 11:00–8:00, Fri–Sat 9:00–5:00;
    summer: Mon–Thur 10:00–7:00, Fri–Sat
    9:00–5:00

Burnsville Public Library
Kanawha Street
Burnsville, WV 26335
(304) 853-2338 voice & FAX
Mary S. Black

Cabell County Public Library
Huntington Public Library
455 Ninth Street Plaza
Huntington, WV 25701
(304) 523-9451; (304) 522-4721 FAX
jrule@cabell.lib.wv.us;
    library@cabell.lib.wv.us
http://cabell.lib.wv.us
Sarah Gibbs, Head of Reference; Judy K.
    Rule, Director
Mon–Wed 9:00–9:00, Thur–Sat 9:00–5:00;
    summer hours vary

Calhoun County Public Library
Genealogy Collection
(Mill Street North—location)
PO Box 918 (mailing address)
Grantsville, WV 26147
(304) 354-6300 voice & FAX
http://calhoun.lib.wv.us
Glada M. Stump, Librarian
Mon–Fri 10:00–5:00

Clarksburg-Harrison Public Library
West Virginia Collection
404 West Pike Street
Clarksburg, WV 26301
(304) 624-6512, ext. 21
houchin@clark.lib.wv.us
http://clarksburglibrary.info
David Houchin, Genealogy and History
West Virginia Room: Mon–Fri 9:00–noon &
    1:00–5:00, Sat 9:00–noon

Davis and Elkins College
Booth Library
100 Campus Drive
Elkins, WV 26241-3996
(304) 636-1900; (304) 637-1232; (304) 636-
    0650 FAX
http://www.dne.wvnet.edu/PROGS/
    LIBRARY.HTM
Kathy Doig

Doddridge County Public Library
117 Court Street
West Union, WV 26456
(304) 873-1941 voice & FAX
ashcathy@hp9k.clark.lib.wv.us
http://dodd.clark.lib.wv.us
Cathy Jo Ash, Librarian
Mon 8:30–7:00, Tue & Thur–Fri 8:30–5:00;
    Sat 9:30–noon

Elkins-Randolph County Public Library
416 Davis Avenue

Elkins, WV 26241
(304) 637-0287; (304) 637-0288 FAX
taylora@hp9k.clark.lib.wv.us
Audrey Taylor, Director

Fairmont State College
Ruth Ann Musick Library
Fairmont, WV 26554-2491
(304) 367-4123; (304) 366-4870 FAX
http://129.71.46.56

Family Research Library and Archives
805 State Street
Gassaway, WV 26624
Wilma Myers

Gassaway Public Library
536 Elk Street
Gassaway, WV 26624
(304) 364-8292 voice & FAX
gsb01007@mail.wvnet.edu
Brenda Hickman, Director

Gilmer County Public Library
214 Walnut Street
Glenville, WV 26351
(304) 462-5620 voice & FAX
galenzal@hp9k.clark.lib.wv.us
Louise Galenza

Hamlin-Lincoln County Public Library
Genealogical Research Room
7999 Lyne Avenue
Hamlin, WV 25523
(304) 824-5481 voice & FAX
msmith@cabell.lib.wv.us
Margaret Smith

Hampshire County Public Library
153 West Main Street
Romney, WV 26757
(304) 822-3185; (304) 822-3955 FAX
riffle_b@martin.lib.wv.us
http://HampshireCoPublicLib.com
Brenda Carol Riffle, Director
Mon & Fri 10:00–8:00, Tue–Thur
    10:00–6:00, Sat 10:00–4:00
copies: 50¢ plus SASE; will do limited
    research

Hardy County Public Library
102 North Main Street
Moorefield, WV 26836
(304) 538-6560; (304) 538-2639 FAX
zirk_m@martin.lib.wv.us
http://hardycounty.martin.lib.wv.us
Marjorie Zirk, Librarian
Mon–Sat 9:00–4:30
(census & newspapers on microfilm, family
    histories, maps, books)
20¢ per page for copying, plus state tax

Jackson County Public Library
208 North Church Street
Ripley, WV 25271
(304) 372-5343; (304) 372-5344 FAX
ripleypl@hp9k.park.lib.wv.us;
    pauleyl@hp9k.park.lib.wv.us
http://jackson.park.lib.wv.us
Lynn Pauley, Circulation/ILL
Mon & Fri 10:00–5:00, Tue–Thur
    10:00–8:00, Sat 10:00–3:00; last week in
    May–first week in Sept: Mon–Wed & Fri
    10:00–5:00, Thur 10:00–8:00, Sat
    10:00–3:00
research: requests are handed over to a
    volunteer and can take some time

Kanawha County Public Library
123 Capitol Street
Charleston, WV 25301-2686
(304) 343-4646; (304) 348-6530

david.schau@kanawha.lib.wv.us
http://kanawha.lib.wv.us
David Schau, Reference
Mon–Fri 9:00–9:00, Sat 9:00–5:00, Sun
    (Sept–Apr) 1:00–5:00
(West Virginia local history only, no
    genealogy)

Marion County Library
Genealogy Room
321 Monroe Street
Fairmont, WV 26554
(304) 287-2411
dottsj@clark.lib.wv.us
http://129.71.94.65/special_collections.htm
Jill Dotts, Librarian
Mon–Fri 9:00–6:00, Sat 9:00–4:00;
    Genealogy Department: Mon 10:00–6:00,
    Tue–Fri 10:00–2:00

Marshall University
James E. Morrow Library
Special Collections Department
1 John Marshall Drive
Huntington, WV 25755
(304) 696-2343; (304) 696-2361 FAX
speccoll@marshall.edu
http://www.marshall.edu; http://marshall.
    edu/speccoll/rg-title.html (Historical
    Resources Guide)
Lisle G. Brown
University Sessions: Mon–Wed 8:00–8:00,
    Thur–Fri 8:00–5:00, Sun 1:00–6:00
(local history and genealogy)

**Martinsburg-Berkeley County Public
Library**
Public Square
101 West King Street
Martinsburg, WV 25401
(304) 267-8933; (304) 267-9720 FAX
hammersl@martin.lib.wv.us
http://tlc.library.net/martin/default.asp
Keith E. Hammersla, Reference Librarian
Mon–Fri 9:00–9:00, Sat 9:00–5:00, Sun
    1:00–5:00

Mason City Public Library
(8 Brown Street—location)
PO Box 609 (mailing address)
Mason City, WV 25260
(304) 773-5580 voice & FAX
thompsnp@hp9k.park.lib.ww.us
Pamela Thompson

Mason County Public Library
Sixth and Viand Street
Point Pleasant, WV 25550
(304) 675-2913; (304) 675-2943 FAX
dhopson@citynet.net
Debbie Hopson

McClintic Public Library
The West Virginia and Appalachian
Collection
500 Eighth Avenue
Marlinton, WV 24954-1227
(304) 799-4165; (304) 799-6000; (304) 799-
    3988 FAX
director@pocahontaslibrary.org
http://pocahontaslibrary.org/marlinton/
    appalachian_collection.htm
Allen Johnson, Librarian
Mon–Thur 9:00–8:00, Fri 9:00–6:00, Sat
    10:00–2:00

Menno Simons Historical Library
(see Virginia, Part 2)

Miracle Valley City-County Public Library
700 Fifth Street
Moundsville, WV 26041-1034

(304) 845-6911; (304) 845-6912 FAX
feryokc@weirton.lib.wv.us
http://129.71.94.5/htdocs/marshall/
  mound/moundlib.html
Catherine Feryok
Mon–Wed 10:00–8:00, Thur–Sat 10:00–6:00

Monroe County Public Library
(103 South Street, Route 219—location)
PO Box 558 (mailing address)
Union, WV 24983
(304) 772-3038; (304) 772-4052 FAX
mccurdy@raleigh.lib.wv.us
http://monroe.lib.wv.us
Doris McCurdy, Library Director
Mon–Wed & Fri 9:00–6:00, Sat 9:00 noon

Moomau Public Library
18 Mount View Street
Petersburg, WV 26847
(304) 257-4122 voice & FAX
carrbara@martin.lib.wv.us
Barbara S. Carr, Director

Morgantown Public Library
West Virginia Collection and Archives
373 Spruce Street
Morgantown, WV 26505
(304) 291-7425; (304) 291-7437 FAX
hathaway@hp9k.clark.lib.wv.us
http://clark.lib.wv.us/morg/morg.html
Donna Rae Houatter, Reference Specialist;
  Ellen Hathaway
Mon–Thur 9:00–8:00, Fri–Sat 9:00–5:00
(a small collection specializing in West
  Virginia history and Monongalia County
  genealogy; "Invites completed searches
  [genealogical] pertinent to the northern
  West Virginia or southwestern
  Pennsylvania area.")
research: $10.00 per search (includes staff
  time, postage, and up to ten pages of
  photocopying)

Ohio County Public Library
52 16th Street
Wheeling, WV 26003
(304) 232-0244; (304) 232-6848 FAX
ocplweb@weirton.lib.wv.us
http://wheeling.weirton.lib.wv.us

Old Charles Town Library
200 East Washington Street
Charles Town, WV 25414
(304) 725-5801; (304) 725-6618
Marcia Lance, Director
Mon 9:00–9:00, Tue–Fri 9:00–5:30, Sat
  9:00–1:00
(emphasis on Shenandoah Valley genealogy,
  West Virginia history, and Civil War
  history)
$5.00 per year membership (must be a
  Jefferson County resident to check out
  materials)

**Parkersburg and Wood County Public
Library**
3100 Emerson Avenue
Parkersburg, WV 26104-2414
(304) 420-2587; (304) 420-4589 FAX
library@hp9k.park.lib.wv.us (Reference)
http://parkersburg.lib.wv.us
Lindsay Roseberry, Reference Librarian
Mon–Thur 9:00–9:00, Fri–Sat 9:00–5:00,
  Sun (Labor Day–Memorial Day)
  1:00–5:00
(local and statewide collection; "One of the
  best genealogical libraries in northern
  West Virginia.")
$1.00 for research, 10¢ per copy plus postage
  or SASE

Pendleton County Public Library
(504 North Main Street—location)
PO Box 519 (mailing address)
Franklin, WV 26807
(304) 358-7038 voice & FAX
bates_v@martin.lib.wv.us
http://pendleton.lib.wv.us
Mon 1:00–5:00, Tue–Fri 9:00–5:00, Sat
  9:30–noon

Philippi Public Library
102 South Main Street
Philippi, WV 26416
(304) 457-3495 voice & FAX
weekleym@hp9k.clark.lib.wv.us
Mary Ellen Weekley, Library Director
Mon–Fri 9:00–8:00, Sat 10:00–1:00

Pleasants County Public Library
101 Lafayette Street
Saint Marys, WV 26170-1025
(304) 684-7494 voice & FAX
polinge@park.lib.wv.us;
  polinge@hp9k.park.lib.wv.us
http://pleasants.lib.wv.us
Eleanor Poling, Director
Mon–Wed 10:00–8:00, Thur 5:00–8:00, Fri
  10:00–5:00, Sat 10:00–3:00, Sun
  2:00–5:00

Putnam County Library
4219 State Route 34
Hurricane, WV 25526
(304) 757-7308; (304) 757-7307 FAX
putnam@cabell.lib.wv.us
http://cabell.lib.wv.us/putnam
Peggy Sue Bias

Ritchie County Public Library
130 North Court Street
Harrisville, WV 26362
(304) 643-2717 voice & FAX
seesee@hp9k.park.lib.wv.us
http://ritchie.lib.wv.us
Emilee Seesee, County Director
Mon & Thur 9:00–8:00, Tue & Fri
  9:00–5:30, Wed 9:00–noon, Sat
  9:00–2:00

Roane County Public Library
110 Parking Plaza
Spencer, WV 25276
(304) 927-1130; (304) 927-1196 FAX
boggessa@wirefire.com
http://roanecountylibrary.org
Arlene Boggess, Genealogy
Mon–Fri 9:00–5:00, Sat 9:00–noon

Shepherdstown Public Library
(German and King Streets—location)
PO Box 278 (mailing address)
Shepherdstown, WV 25443
(304) 876-2783; (304) 876-6213 FAX
info@lib.shepherdstown.wv.us
http://www.lib.shepherdstown.wv.us
Margaret W. Didden, Adult Services
Mon–Thur 10:00–7:00, Sat 9:00–1:00

**General Adam Stephen Memorial
Association, Inc.**
(309 East John Street—location)
PO Box 1496 (mailing address)
Martinsburg, WV 25402-1496
(304) 267-4434
1 May–31 Oct: Sat–Sun 2:00–5:00

Summers County Public Library
201 Temple Street
Hinton, WV 25951
(304) 466-4490; (304) 466-5260 FAX
zieglerm@raleigh.lib.wv.us
http://summers.lib.wv.us

Myra Ziegler
Mon, Wed & Fri 9:00–5:00, Tue & Thur
  9:00–9:00, Sat 9:00–3:00

Sutton Public Library
Fourth Street
Sutton, WV 26601
(304) 765-7224 voice & FAX
long_pat@hp9k.clark.lib.wv.us
Patricia Long

Taylor County Public Library
200 Beech Street
Grafton, WV 26354
(304) 265-6121; (304) 265-6122 FAX
reed@westvirginia.net
http://taylor.clark.lib.wv.us
Erika Reed

University of Mississippi
Center for the Study of Southern Culture
(see Mississippi, Part 2)

Upshur County Public Library
Rural Route 6, Box 480
Tennerton Road
Buckhannon, WV 26201
(304) 473-4219; (304) 473-4221 FAX; (304)
  473-4222 FAX
tolliver@clark.lib.wv.us
http://upshurcounty.lib.wv.us

**Virginia Polytechnic Institute and State
University**
(see Virginia, Part 2)

Mary H. Weir Public Library
3442 Main Street
Weirton, WV 26062-4590
(304) 797-8510; (304) 797-8526 FAX
fundisl@weirton.lib.wv.us
http://wheeling.weirton.lib.wv.us
Lois Aleta Fundis, Reference Librarian
Mon & Fri–Sat 10:00–5:00, Tue–Thur
  10:00–8:00 (reference services may not be
  available until noon)
(emphasis on Weirton, along with Hancock
  and Brooke counties and adjacent areas in
  Pennsylvania and Ohio; census microfilm
  for Hancock and Brooke counties,
  microfilm of newspapers)
searches by mail will be charged cost of
  postage, photocopies and WV sales tax
  (can now e-mail "photocopies" from
  microfilm); will also send list of local
  genealogists and genealogy organizations

Williamson Public Library
(Memorial Building, corner of First Avenue
and Logan Street, in courthouse
Square—location)
Court House Annex (mailing address)
Williamson, WV 25661
(304) 235-6029 voice & FAX
william@cabell.lib.wv.us

Dora B. Woodyard Memorial Library
(Mulberry Street—location)
Box 340 (mailing address)
Elizabeth, WV 26143
(304) 275-4295 voice & FAX
http://dorabwoodyard.lib.wv.us
Karen Ancrile, Librarian
Mon & Thur 8:00–7:00, Tue–Wed & Fri
  8:00–5:00; summer: Mon 9:00–8:00,
  Tue–Fri 1:00–5:00

Wyoming County Public Library
(Castle Rock Avenue—location)
PO Box 130 (mailing address)
Pineville, WV 24874-0130
(304) 732-6228; (304) 732-6899 FAX

http://wyoming.lib.wv.us
Melissa Rena Conley, Branch Manager
Mon & Thur–Fri 10:00–6:00, Tue
    10:00–7:00, Sat 10:00–5:00

Historical Societies—Local and Regional

Barbour County Historical Society
Main and Depot
Philippi, WV 26416
(304) 457-4846; (304) 457-3349
    (appointments)
Virginia Smith, President
1 May–1 Nov: 11:00–4:00; winter: by
    appointment only
Pub. *Barbour County Historical Society
    Letter*, quarterly
(specialty: Civil War information—first land
    battle, 3 June 1861, and other information)
$5.00 per year membership (c/o Eliz.
    Ramsey, 225 Garnett Street, Philippi, WV
    26416)

The Berkeley County Historical Society
(The Belle Boyd House, 126 East Race
    Street—location)
PO Box 1624 (mailing address)
Martinsburg, WV 25401
(304) 267-4713
bchs15@earthlink.net
http://www.bchs.org
Don C. Wood, President
Archives Division: Wed–Thur 9:00–4:00,
    Wed 6:30 P.M.–9:00 P.M.; Headquarters,
    The Belle Boyd House: Mon–Sat
    10:00–4:00, closed Christmas–New Year's
    Day
Pub. *The Berkeley Journal*, annually, $7.50
    postpaid per issue; *Berkeley County
    Historical Society Newsletter*, quarterly
(national register and landmarks on Berkeley
    County, genealogy files on Berkeley,
    Jefferson and Morgan counties, also wills,
    deeds, and vital records)
$20.00 per year membership (includes both
    publications); admission: no entrance fee

The Braxton Historical Society
226 Birch Street
Gassaway, WV 26624-1104
(304) 364-5552
gse02006@mail.wvnet.edu
Helen L. Traugh, President
three meetings per year
Pub. *Journal of the Braxton Historical
    Society*, quarterly (Mar, June, Sept, Dec)
$5.00 per year membership

Buffalo Historical Society
PO Box 144
Buffalo, WV 25033
(304) 937-2241

**Calhoun County Historical and
Genealogical Society**
(Board of Education Plaza, High
    Street—location)
PO Box 242 (mailing address)
Grantsville, WV 26147
(304) 354-7614
Mary Ann Barrows, Secretary
Pub. *Lines and Links*, three times per year
$5.00 per year membership

**Clay County Landmarks Commission and
Historical Society**
PO Box 523
Clay, WV 25043

Elk-Blue Creek Historical Society, Inc.

(14/16 Maple Lane—location)
PO Box 649 (mailing address)
Elkview, WV 25071
(304) 965-5016
Edith Brewer, Consultant and Board Member
monthly meetings
Pub. *Elk River Communities*, about once
    every five years
no membership fee

Fayette County Historical Society
PO Box 463
Ansted, WV 25812-0463
(304) 469-9505

Gilmer County Historical Society
(302 East Main Street—location)
PO Box 235 (mailing address)
Glenville, WV 26351
(304) 462-4295
history@itol.net
Margaret Moss, Secretary
Mon–Sat 10:00–1:00
Pub. *Gilmer County Historical Society
    Newsletter*, quarterly (Apr, July, Oct, Jan)
$15.00 per year membership; genealogical
    queries to Kyle Emerson, 82 Grand Teton
    Drive, Saint Peters, MO 63376

**Grant County Genealogical-Historical
Society**
(see Genealogical Societies—Local and
Regional, below)

Grant County Historical Society, Inc.
PO Box 665
Petersburg, WV 26847
(304) 257-1444

Greenbrier Historical Society
North House Museum
301 West Washington Street
Lewisburg, WV 24901
(304) 645-3398; (304) 645-5201 FAX
archives@greenbrierhistorical.org;
    info@greenbrierhistorical.org
http://www.greenbrierhistorical.org/ghs.html
Frances Swope, Archivist
Thur & Sat 1:00–4:00
Pub. *Journal*, annually, $16.50 per issue for
    in-state nonmembers, $16.25 per issue for
    out-of-state nonmembers; *Appalachian
    Springs*, quarterly, $2.50 per issue for in-
    state nonmembers, $2.25 per issue for
    out-of-state nonmembers
(history, persons, places, events pertaining to
    the Greenbrier Valley area of West
    Virginia)
$15.00 per year membership

Hampshire County Historical Society
170 East Birch Lane
Romney, WV 26757
(no research by staff personnel)

**Harpers Ferry Historical Association and
Bookshop**
Harpers Ferry National Historical Park
(Shenandoah Street—location)
PO Box 197 (mailing address)
Harpers Ferry, WV 25425
(304) 535-6881; (800) 821-5206
hfha@earthlink.net
http://www.harpersferryhistory.org
Debbie Piscitelli, Executive Director
Mon–Sun 9:00–5:00
Pub. *Newsletter*
(a cooperating association with the National
    Park Service; publishes and operates a
    bookstore with Tombstone Inscription
    books for Jefferson County, West
    Virginia, and Virginia Civil War

regimental series, along with about 3,000
    other titles on Harpers Ferry, the Civil
    War, and African-American history)

Harrison County Historical Society
Stealy Goff Vance House
(123 West Main Street, Clarksburg, WV
    26301—location)
PO Box 2074 (mailing address)
Clarksburg, WV 26302-2074
(304) 842-3073
Madge McDaniel, Treasurer
Fri (May–Sept) 2:00–4:00
Pub. *Harrison County Historical Society
    Newsletter*, semiannually
$5.00 per year membership

**Hatfield-McCoy Historical Society (Ky.-
W.Va.)**
(see Kentucky, Part 2)

Historical Society of Helvetia
General Delivery
Helvetia, WV 26224

**Historic Shepherdstown Commission and
Museum**
(129 East German Street, Entler Hotel, Room
    200—location)
PO Box 1786 (mailing address)
Shepherdstown, WV 25443
(304) 876-0910
Cynthia S. Cook, Administrator
Museum: Apr–Oct: Sat 11:00–5:00, Sun
    1:00–4:00; Archives: by appointment
Pub. *Newsletter*, quarterly
$10.00 per year membership

Jackson County Historical Society
(City Building or Library—location)
PO Box 22 (mailing address)
Ripley, WV 25271
(304) 372-2541 (Treasurer)
Vera S. Crum, Treasurer
Pub. *Jackson County History*, quarterly (Jan,
    Apr, July, Oct), $10.00 per year
    subscription
$14.00 per year membership with periodical,
    $4.00 per year membership without
    periodical

Jefferson County Historical Society
PO Box 485
Charles Town, WV 25414
Dr. John E. Stealey, III, President
Pub. *Magazine of the Jefferson County
    Historical Society*, annually
$5.00 per year membership

Marion County Historical Society
PO Box 1636
Fairmont, WV 26555-1636

Marshall County Historical Society
PO Box 267
Moundsville, WV 26041

Mason City Historical Society
(6 Brown Street—location)
5 Pomeroy Street (mailing address)
Mason, WV 25260
(304) 773-5557

Mason Historical Society
PO Box 125
Hartford, WV 25247

McDowell Historical Society
PO Box 369
War, WV 24892
(304) 875-2841

Mercer County Historical Society, Inc.
PO Box 5012
Princeton, WV 24740-5012
(304) 425-4990
commander@inetone.net
Glenn Belcher, President
daily 10:00–2:00
Pub. *Mercer Dateline*, monthly
$10.00 per year membership

Mineral County Genealogical-Historical Society
(see Genealogical Societies—Local and Regional, below)

Mingo County Historical Society
PO Box 2581
Williamson, WV 25661
(604) 237-4646
Oscar Atkins
meetings at Williamson Public Library

Monongalia County Historical Society
PO Box 127
Morgantown, WV 26505
Joseph Costello, President
Pub. *Monongalia Chronicle*

Monroe County Historical Society
PO Box 465
Union, WV 24983
Jay Banks, Corresponding Secretary
Museum: Mon–Sat 10:00–4:00, Sun 1:00–4:00 (30 May to mid-Oct)
Pub. *Monroe County Historical Society Newsletter*, quarterly (Mar, June, Sept, Dec)
$10.00 per year membership

Morgan County Historical and Genealogical Society
(Morgan County Public Library—location)
PO Box 52 (mailing address)
Berkeley Springs, WV 25411
Paul Mellott, President
$5.00 per year membership

Nicholas County Historical and Genealogical Society
PO Box 443
Summersville, WV 26651
(304) 872-1696; (304) 872-2478

Pendleton County Genealogical-Historical Society
(see Genealogical Societies—Local and Regional, below)

Pendleton County Historical Society, Inc.
(Main Street—location)
PO Box 383 (mailing address)
Franklin, WV 26807
(304) 358-7366
Richard Ruddle, Jr., President
$3.00 per year membership

Pleasants County Historical Society
(Jim Spence Community Building, Pleasants County Park, 605 Cherry Street—location)
PO Box 335 (mailing address)
Saint Marys, WV 26170
(304) 684-7621
Walter S. Carpenter, President
by appointment; meetings: third Thur 7:30
(Pleasants County and West Virginia history)
$3.00 per year membership

Pocahontas County Historical Society, Inc.
810 Second Avenue
Marlinton, WV 24954
(304) 799-6659 (Summer); (304) 799-4973 (Year Round)

William P. McNeel, Historian
Pub. *Pocahontas County Newsletter*, annually

Preston County Historical Society
(109 East Washington Street—location)
102 Aurora Street (mailing address)
Terra Alta, WV 26764
http://www.hhs.net/sss/preston/pchs.htm
Charles A. Thomas, Jr., Curator (to visit the museum at History House); Janice Cale Sisler, President (other)
May–Sept: Sun 1:30–4:30
Pub. *NOW . . . And Long Ago*, semiannually
("Our three-story, thirteen-room museum has miscellaneous books, papers and photographs, unorganized, but does not have genealogy reference library.")
$5.00 per year membership (to PO Box 113, Bruceton Mills, WV 26525-0113)

Raleigh County Historical Society
Wildwood House
(Beckley, WV—location)
PO Box 897 (mailing address)
Skelton, WV 25919-0897

Randolph County Historical Society
PO Box 1164
Elkins, WV 26241
(304) 636-0841; (304) 636-1958; (304) 636-1959
Randolph Allan, President; Madeline Crickard, Librarian
Pub. *Magazine of History and Biography*

Ritchie County Historical Society
310 Myles Avenue
Pennsboro, WV 26415
(304) 643-2738
debrular@charter.net
David M. Scott, President
Old Stone House Museum, Pennsboro, WV: by appointment
Pub. *Ritchie County Historical Society Newsletter*, quarterly
$10.00 per year membership

Roane County Historical Society
PO Box 161
Spencer, WV 25276

Saint Albans Historical Society
2745 Lincoln Avenue
Saint Albans, WV 25177
(304) 727-5972
Jack Cook, President
Pub. *Coalsmouth Journal*
$7.00 per year membership

Summers County Historical Society
PO Box 295
Hinton, WV 25951-0295

Taylor County Historical and Genealogical Society, Inc.
(Taylor County Library—location)
PO Box 522 (mailing address)
Grafton, WV 26354
http://www.rootsweb.com/~wvtaylor/tchgs.htm
Tom Dadisman
Library: Wed 9:15–noon (only), and some help on other days
Pub. *Taylor County Profile*, four times per year
(over 1,000 books and papers; assorted genealogical and historical subjects of Taylor County, West Virginia, wills, deeds, obits, pedigrees, etc.)
$12.00 per year membership; queries free to members, $5.00 each for nonmembers;

research fees by arrangement

Tucker County Historical Society, Inc.
(Tucker County Board of Education Annex Building—location)
PO Box 13 (mailing address)
Hambleton, WV 26269
(304) 478-3074
James D. Phillips, President
Memorial Day weekend & Sun (summer) 2:00–4:00
Pub. *News Letter*, annually
(history of Tucker County)
$10.00 per year membership; search fees: $10.00

Tyler County Heritage and Historical Society
PO Box 317
Middlebourne, WV 26149
(304) 758-4288
E. G. Moore
Pub. *Heritage Windows*, quarterly
$9.00 per year membership

Upper Vandalia Historical Society
224 Beechwood Estates
Scott Depot, WV 25560
(304) 760-2121 voice & FAX; (304) 755-4677 (Treasurer)
clw2121@msn.com
http://freepages.history.rootsweb.com/~vandalia
Cheryl Wintz Withrow, President
meetings at the Poca Public Library: last Sun (Jan, Apr, July, Oct) 2:00
Pub. *Upper Vandalia Journal*, quarterly (Jan, Apr, July, Oct)
$10.00 per year membership

The Upshur County Historical Society
History Center
(81 West Main Street—museum location; 29 West Main Street—document repository location)
PO Box 2082 (mailing address)
Buckhannon, WV 26201
noelwtenney@yahoo.com
http://www.msys.net/uchs
Noel W. Tenney, Ph.D., Director of Special Projects
Upshur County Historical Society Document Repository: Tue 6:00–8:00; Museum: Sun (June–Sept) 1:00–4:00
Pub. *UCHS Newsletter*, occasionally
$10.00 per year membership

Webster County Historical Society
PO Box 1012
Summersville, WV 26651

West Augusta Historical and Genealogical Society
2515 10th Avenue
Parkersburg, WV 26101-5829
Pub. *Newsletter, West Augusta Historical and Genealogical Society*, bimonthly
$4.00 per year membership

West Virginia and Regional History Association
West Virginia and Regional History Collection
West Virginia University
(Sixth Level, Downtown Campus Library—location)
PO Box 6069 (mailing address)
Morgantown, WV 26506-6069
(304) 293-3536; (304) 293-3981 FAX
http://www.libraries.wvu.edu/wvcollection
Dr. John A. Cuthbert, Curator
Mon–Sat 9:00–4:45, closed Sat when

university classes are not in session
Pub. *West Virginia and Regional History
Collection Newsletter*, two times per year
("We are a research library and archives,
holding books, newspapers, archives,
manuscripts, photographs and prints,
sound recordings, and other historical
resources concerning West Virginia, the
central Appalachian Region, and the
Upper Ohio Valley. Our genealogical
holdings for this region are extensive.")
$10.00 per year membership; copying fee for
nonresidents: $10.00 for up to 50 copies

Wheeling Area Historical Society
PO Box 283
Wheeling, WV 26003
(304) 277-2241
Margaret A. Brennen, President
Pub. *Upper Ohio Valley Historical Review*,
irregularly

The Wise County Historical Society
The Appalachian Quarterly
(see Virginia, Part 2)

**Wood County Historical and Preservation
Society, Inc.**
1212 Washington Avenue
Parkersburg, WV 26101
Jeff Little, President

Genealogical Societies

State Genealogical Society

**West Virginia Genealogical Society, Inc.,
and Library**
(5153 Route 119 North—location)
PO Box 249 (mailing address)
Elkview, WV 25071
(304) 965-1179
ebw104@juno.com
http://www.rootsweb.com/~wvgs
Esther Warner, Treasurer
Mon & Wed 10:00–7:00, Sat 10:00–2:00
Pub. *L.O.G.* (Ledger of Genealogy), quarterly
("genealogical data, library volunteer eager to
help, correspondence and library
committee to answer short
questions—over 700 volumes to date, 40
out-of-state journals")
$15.00 per year membership; queries $3.00
for nonmembers; search fee: postage and
copying fee, plus donation

Genealogical Societies—Local & Regional

**Allegheny Regional Family History Society
(ARFHS)**
(Beverly, WV—library location)
PO Box 1804 (mailing address)
Elkins, WV 26241
(304) 636-1650
lferguson@meer.net
http://www.swcp.com/~dhickman/arfhs.html
Madeline W. Crickard, Librarian
Wed 1:00–4:00, Sat 10:00–2:00; meetings at
Randolph County Historical Society
Museum: first Tue 7:00
Pub. *Allegheny Regional Ancestors Journal*,
four times per year (spring, summer, fall,
winter), $5.00 plus tax per copy for
nonmembers
$20.00 per year membership; research:
$25.00 for first five hours; search: $25.00
for the first five hours

**Berkeley County Genealogical-Historical
Society**
PO Box 679
Martinsburg, WV 25401

Boone County Genealogical Society
PO Box 306
Madison, WV 25130
yvonnebooz@hotmail.com
http://www.rootsweb.com/~wvbcgs
Yvonne (Bell) Booz, Director
Boone Genealogical Quarterly; *Kith and Kin
of Boone County, West Virginia*, annually,
$13.00 per issue
(Boone County, West Virginia, history)
Pub. $8.00 per year membership (includes
only quarterly)

Braxton County Genealogical Society
Elk River Route, Box 32
Gassaway, WV 26624

Brooke County Genealogy
(Brooke County Public Library—location)
PO Box 144 (mailing address)
Beech Bottom, WV 26030-0144
momhubbard@worldnet.att.net
http://www.brookecountywvgenealogy.org
Wed & Sat 2:00–4:00; meetings at Brooke
County Public Library third Sat 1:00
Pub. *Brooke Crossing*, quarterly
$12.00 per year membership

**Calhoun County Historical and
Genealogical Society**
(see Historical Societies—Local and
Regional, above)

**Genealogical Society: Fayette and Raleigh
Counties, Inc.**
PO Box 68
Oak Hill, WV 25901-0068
312026Winetone.net
http://www.geocities.com/suefoxus/
countryside.html
Gloria Friedrichs, President
Pub. *Newsnotes*, quarterly
$10.00 per year membership

**Grant County Genealogical-Historical
Society**
Lahmansville, WV 26731
Gail Snyder

Harrison County Genealogical Society
PO Box 387
Clarksburg, WV 26301
Pub. *Harrison County Genealogical Society
Newsletter*, quarterly
$10.00 donation per year membership; free
queries for members

KYOWVA Genealogical Society
Keenan House
(232 Main Street, Huntington, WV
25702—library location)
PO Box 1254 (mailing address)
Huntington, WV 25714-1254
(304) 525-1367; (304) 525-4367
Ernestine Hippert, President; Sheri Pettit
Mon 6:00 P.M.–9:00 P.M., Wed 10:00–3:00,
Sat 10:00–4:00
Pub. *KYOWVA Genealogical Society*,
quarterly
(workshops, book fairs, computer groups,
research help, library assistance, books of
the area for sale)
$12.00 per year membership

Kanawha Valley Genealogical Society, Inc.
(Nitro Community Center, Nitro, WV
25143—location)
PO Box 8555 (mailing address)
South Charleston, WV 25303
Donald E. Peterson, President
first & third Wed 10:00–4:00, Tue preceding
first and third Wed 6:00 P.M.–9:00 P.M.

Pub. *The Journal*, quarterly
(computer programs and CD-ROM disks
available; computer interest group active)
$15.00 per year membership

Lincoln County Genealogical Society
7999 Lyne Avenue
Hamlin, WV 25523
(304) 524-7326
ccmcwv@hotmail.com;
esmith@cabell.lib.wv.us
http://freepages.genealogy.rootsweb.com/
~lincolncowvgensoc
Elwanda Smith, President; Lula Yeager,
Secretary
Mon & Wed–Fri 9:00–5:00, Tue 9:00–8:00,
Sat 9:00–2:00; meetings at Hamlin
Lincoln County Public Library: second
Tue
Pub. *Lincoln Lineage*, three times per year
$10.00 per year membership

Logan County Genealogical Society
(Southern West Virginia Community College
Library—location)
PO Box 1959 (mailing address)
Logan, WV 25601
(304) 792-7098 (for library hours)
Hester Ann Hodges, Treasurer
meetings at The Southern Library: second
Mon (except June) 6:00 P.M., picnic in
June
Pub. *Logan County Ancestree*, quarterly
$15.00 per year membership; library open to
members only

Marion County Genealogy Club
(Marion County Library, Genealogy Room,
321 Monroe Street, Fairmont, WV
26554—location)
1700 Ritchie Avenue (mailing address)
Fairmont, WV 26554-4539
(304) 366-1210, ext. 12
http://www.rootsweb.com/~marion/
genealogyclub.html
Eleanor Carter
Pub. *Genealogy Gleanings*, quarterly (Mar,
June, Sept, Dec)
$7.00 per year membership

**Mineral County Genealogical-Historical
Society**
107 Orchard Street
Keyser, WV 26726
Rev. W. W. Harvey

Mingo County Genealogical Society
PO Box 2581
Williamson, WV 25661
(604) 237-4646
http://www.rootsweb.com/~wvmingo/
mingogs.htm
Tom Atkins, Treasurer and Co-Editor
meetings at Williamson Public Library: third
Tue 7:00
Pub. *Heritage of Mingo*, biannually, $7.50
per issue
$10.00 per year membership

**Morgan County Historical and
Genealogical Society**
(see Historical Societies—Local and
Regional, above)

**Nicholas County Historical and
Genealogical Society**
(see Historical Societies—Local and
Regional, above)

**Pendleton County Genealogical-Historical
Society**
Upper Tract, WV 26886

Donna Kimble

Taylor County Historical and Genealogical Society, Inc.
(see Historical Societies—Local and Regional, above)

Tri-State Genealogical Society
PO Box 454
Newell, WV 26050
(304) 387-1788; (412) 573-9367; (216) 523-3587
Catherine Elliot, President, Rosemarie Snyder Davis, Secretary
meets at former Wells School on Washington Street, Route 2, Newell
Pub. *TSGS Quarterly Newsletter*
(Ohio, Pennsylvania and West Virginia)
$7.00 per year membership

Tug Valley Genealogical Society (Ky.-W.Va.)
(see Kentucky, Part 2)

West Augusta Historical and Genealogical Society
(see Historical Societies—Local and Regional, above)

Wetzel County Genealogical Society, Inc.
PO Box 464
New Martinsville, WV 26155-0464
Carol Hassig, President
New Martinsville Public Library: Mon–Wed & Fri–Sat 10:00–5:00
Pub. *W.C.G.S. Newsletter*, quarterly
(Wetzel County, West Virginia, and surrounding areas)
$10.00 per year membership

Wheeling Area Genealogical Society
PO Box 6450
Wheeling, WV 26003-6450
MStaley206@aol.com
http://www.rootsweb.com/~wvwags
Mary Staley
$10.00 per year membership

Wyoming County Genealogical Society
PO Box 1186
Pineville, WV 24874-1186
(304) 732-8394; (304) 294-6108; (304) 732-9472
http://www.rootsweb.com/~wvwyomin/gensocity.htm
newsletter, quarterly
Pub. meetings at Wyoming County Public Library, Pineville: first Mon 6:00 (EST) or 7:00 (EDST)
$10.00 per year membership

Independent Publications and Miscellany

Americana Museum
401 Aurora Avenue
Terra Alta, WV 26764
(304) 789-2361; (304) 789-2418 FAX
Ruth E. Teets, Owner
summer: by appointment only
admission: $2.00 for adults

Appalachian Roots
PO Box 165
Davisville, WV 26142
Mary Jo Brown, Editor and Publisher
Pub. *Appalachian Roots*, monthly, $18.00 per year subscription
(includes entire Appalachian Mountain area of the following states: Kentucky, Maryland, North Carolina, Pennsylvania, South Carolina, Tennessee, Virginia, West Virginia)
free queries

Beckley Exhibition Coal Mine
Drawer AJ
Beckley, WV 25802

Center for Appalachian Studies
(see North Carolina, Part 2)

Doddridge County Publications
11965 Cameo Place
Granada Hills, CA 91344
(publishes books on Doddridge County)

Families of Wyoming County, West Virginia
PO Box 1035
North Highlands, CA 95660-1035
(916) 991-4165
Sally Williams, Editor
Pub. *Families of Wyoming County, West Virginia*, irregularly, $15.00 per four-issue volume
(publishes other books on Wyoming County)

Family Tree Exchange
(see Virginia, Part 2)

Genealogical Institute
(see Virginia, Part 2)

Henderson Hall
(address withheld upon request)
("We are not a resource open to the public in the area of genealogy.")

Lee Cabin Museum
Lost River State Park
Route 2, Box 24
Mathias, WV 26812

Lineage Search Associates
Frederick Findings
(see Virginia, Part 2)

The Mountain Empire Genealogical Quarterly
(see Virginia, Part 2)

Mountain Press
(see Tennessee, Part 2)

Ohio River Valley Families
(see Ohio, Part 2)

Salem Teikyo University
Fort New Salem
Salem, WV 26426
(304) 782-8245; (304) 782-5323
http://stulib.salem-teikyo.wvnet.edu/www/fort_menu_3796.html

Stories About Gilbert, West Virginia, and Surrounding Communities
Route 4, Box 7-C (Needmore Road)
Cameron, NC 28326-8904
(919) 245-7461 FAX
gilbert@pinehurst.net
http://home.pinehurst.net/gilbert
Col. Darrell G. Brumfield (Ret)

Sunrise Museums
746 Myrtle Road
Charleston, WV 25314
(304) 344-8035

Topp of the Line
Virginia/West Virginia Queries
(see Virginia, Part 2)

Traveller Southern Families
(see Virginia, Part 2)

The Virginia Genealogist
(see Virginia, Part 2)

Weirton Historical Landmarks Commission
3632 Collins Way
Weirton, WV 26062
(304) 723-5117; (304) 748-5826 (Home)
Shari Pepper, Chairman

West Virginia Department of Transportation
Parkways, Economic Development and Tourism Authority
3310 Piedmont Road
Charleston, WV 25311
(304) 926-1900; (304) 926-1909 FAX
info@dot.state.wv.us
http://www.wvdot.com/7_tourists/7d_maps&touristinfo.htm (Maps)

West Virginia Hillbilly
407 Jackson Street
Minerva, OH 44657-1319
Sandy McCauley, Owner-Publisher
Mon–Fri 8:00–5:00
Pub. *West Virginia Hillbilly*, biweekly, $30.00 per year subscription
(history-education)

West Virginia Histories Homepage
http://www.clearlight.com/~wvhh
(In association with amazon.com, includes a bibliography, bookstore and some online material.)

West Virginia State Farm Museum
Route 1, Box 479
Point Pleasant, WV 25550
(304) 675-5737

West Virginia University
Appalachian Studies Association
Regional Research Institute
Morgantown, WV 26506
(304) 558-0220, ext. 35
(Kentucky, Maryland, North Carolina, Pennsylvania, South Carolina, Tennessee, Virginia, and West Virginia)

WVGenWeb
Part of The USGenWeb Project
wvgenweb@citynet.net
http://www.rootsweb.com/~wvgenweb
Les Shockey, State Coordinator; Valerie F. Crook, Assistant Coordinator
(links to other West Virginia resources)

Wisconsin

Archives and Libraries with Holdings in Genealogy

State Archives and Libraries

Area Research Centers

Northland College
Dexter Library
1411 Ellis Avenue
Ashland, WI 54806
(715) 682-1311
Dr. J. Paul O'Keefe
Mon 1:00–3:00, Tue 11:30–2:00 &
  3:30–10:00, Wed 1:00–3:00 & 5:30–9:00,
  Thur noon–2:00 & 4:00–10:00, Fri
  9:00–11:00
(Area Research Center for Ashland, Bayfield,
  and Iron counties)

Superior Area Research Center
Superior Public Library
1530 Tower Avenue
Superior, WI 54880-2532
(715) 394-8860; (715) 394-8870 FAX
JenningsJ@ci.superior.wi.us
http://www.wisconsinhistory.org/
  libraryarchives/arcnet/superior.asp
Barry Singer, Archives Director; Janet
  Jennings, Library Director
Research Center: Mon & Wed 9:30–noon &
  1:00–5:00; Library: Mon–Thur 9:30–8:30,
  Fri 9:00–5:30, Sat (Labor Day–the Fri
  before Memorial Day) 1:00–4:30
(Area Research Center for Douglas County)

University of Wisconsin—Eau Claire
William D. McIntyre Library, Special
  Collections
Eau Claire, WI 54702-4004
(715) 836-2739; (715) 836-2949 FAX
library.archives@uwec.edu
http://www.uwec.edu/muirha/index.htm
Heather A. Muir, Head of Special Collections
  and University Archivist
Mon–Fri 8:00–5:00
(emphasis on Chippewa Valley history and
  genealogy; university archives; Area
  Research Center for Buffalo, Chippewa,
  Clark, Eau Claire, Rusk, and Taylor
  counties with manuscripts and public
  records)

University of Wisconsin—Green Bay
Cofrin Library
Special Collections/Area Research Center
2420 Nicolet Drive
Green Bay, WI 54311-7001
(920) 465-2539
speccoll@uwgb.edu
http://www.wisconsinhistory.org/
  libraryarchives/arcnet/greenbay.asp
Debra Anderson, Special Collections and
  Area Research Center Coordinator
Mon–Tue & Thur–Fri 12:30–4:30, Wed
  12:30–5:00 & 6:00–9:00
(Area Research Center for Brown, Calumet,
  Door, Florence, Kewaunee, Manitowoc,
  Marinette, Menominee, Oconto,
  Outagamie, and Shawano counties;
  holdings include original records for the
  listed counties; document types include
  citizenship, probate, vital records, land
  records, censuses and maps)

Special Collections/Area Research Center
Eugene W. Murphy Library
University of Wisconsin—La Crosse
1631 Pine Street

La Crosse, WI 54601
(608) 785-8511; (608) 785-8639 FAX
specoll@uwlax.edu
http://www.wisconsinhistory.org/
  libraryarchives/arcnet/lacrosse.asp
Paul Beck, Special Collections Librarian
Mon–Fri 10:00–5:00, Wed 7:00–9:00, Sat
  1:00–4:00; summer: Mon–Thur
  noon–3:30
(Area Research Center for Jackson, La
  Crosse, Monroe, Trempealeau, and
  Vernon counties)
research: $10.00 per hour

Archives/Area Research Center
University of Wisconsin—Milwaukee
Golda Meir Library, Room W250
(2311 East Hartford Avenue—location)
PO Box 604 (mailing address)
Milwaukee, WI 53201-0604
(414) 229-5402; (414) 229-3605 FAX
archives@gml.lib.uwm.edu
http://www.wisconsinhistory.org/
  libraryarchives/arcnet/milwauke.asp
Christel Maass, Archivist (withheld)
spring and fall semesters: Mon–Tue & Fri
  8:00–4:30; Wed–Thur 8:00–8:00; summer
  and other times: Mon–Fri 8:00–4:30
(Area Research Center for Milwaukee,
  Ozaukee, Sheboygan, Washington, and
  Waukesha counties; bibliographic data is
  available through the Golda Meir
  Library's PantherCat online catalog
  system on the web at
  http://library.uwm.edu, OCLC, or
  WISCAT)
specific research: $7.50 per one-page record,
  $5.00 for 2-20 additional pages, 25¢ for
  each additional page, $7.50 per tax roll
  searched; general research: $25.00
  minimum (up to one hour), $12.50 per
  half-hour, $4.00 for 2-20 additional
  pages, 25¢ for each additional page

University of Wisconsin—Oshkosh
Area Research Center, Forrest R. Polk
  Library
800 Algoma Boulevard
Oshkosh, WI 54901
(920) 424-3347; (920) 424-2175 FAX
archives@uwosh.edu
http://www.uwosh.edu/archives
Gerald J. Krueger, Documents Librarian
Mon–Fri 9:00–noon & 1:00–4:00
(Area Research Center for Dodge, Fond du
  Lac, Green Lake, Marquette, and
  Winnebago counties; marriages, births
  and deaths, pre-1907 cannot be
  photocopied)

University of Wisconsin—Parkside
Parkside Library
(D2 Level of the Library, 900 Wood
  Road—location)
PO Box 2000 (mailing address)
Kenosha, WI 53141-2000
(262) 595-2411
http://www.wisconsinhistory.org/
  libraryarchives/arcnet/parkside.asp
Ellen J. Pedraza, Archivist/Librarian
Mon–Tue & Thur–Fri 8:00–noon, Wed
  5:00–9:00
(emphasis on local history and genealogy;
  Area Research Center for Kenosha and
  Racine counties)

The University of Wisconsin—Platteville
Southwest Wisconsin Room—Elton S.
  Karrmann Library
1 University Plaza
Platteville, WI 53818-3099
(608) 342-1719; (608) 342-1645 FAX
http://www.wisconsinhistory.org/

  libraryarchives/arcnet/plattvil.asp
James Hibbard, Archivist
SW Wisconsin Room, when school is in
  session: Mon–Fri 1:00–5:00 (closes at
  4:00 on Fri during summer session), Tue
  & Thur 5:00–9:00
(Area Research Center for Crawford, Grant,
  Green, Iowa, Lafayette, and Richland
  counties; collection emphasis on southwest
  Wisconsin and upper Mississippi,
  including Jo Daviess County, Illinois, and
  Dubuque; lead-zinc mining district of
  southwest Wisconsin, northeast Iowa and
  northwest Illinois)

**University of Wisconsin—River Falls Area
Research Center and University Archives**
Chalmer Davee Library
410 South Third Street
River Falls, WI 54022
(715) 425-3567
http://www.wisconsinhistory.org/
  libraryarchives/arcnet/riverfls.asp
During school semesters: Mon–Wed & Fri
  8:00–4:30, Thur 8:00–8:00, Sat
  1:00–4:00; summer & university holidays:
  Mon–Fri 10:00–4:30
(Area Research Center for Burnett, Pierce,
  Polk, and Saint Croix counties)
limited research conducted by staff

University of Wisconsin—Stevens Point
University Library
Nelis R. Kampenga University Archives and
  Area Research Center
900 Reserve Street
Stevens Point, WI 54481
(715) 346-2586
archives@uwsp.edu
http://library.uwsp.edu/depts/archives/
  archives.htm
Bill Paul, University Archivist
Mon, Wed & Fri 8:00–noon & 1:15–4:30,
  Tue & Thur 8:00–noon (hours may vary,
  call ahead for verification)
(Area Research Center for Adams, Juneau,
  Langlade, Lincoln, Marathon, Portage,
  Waupaca, Waushara, and Wood counties)

University of Wisconsin—Stout
Robert L. Pierce Library
Menomonie, WI 54751-0790
(715) 232-2300
http://www.wisconsinhistory.org/
  libraryarchives/arcnet/stout.asp
Gayle Martinson, University and Area
  Archivist
Mon–Fri 8:00–5:00, Mon–Wed 7:00–9:00,
  Sat noon–3:00 (hours vary during
  university recesses, please call)
(Area Research Center for Barron and Dunn
  counties)

University of Wisconsin—Whitewater
(2210 Harold Anderson Library, 800 West
  Main Street—location)
PO Box 900 (mailing address)
Whitewater, WI 53190
(262) 472-5520; (262) 472-5727
westonk@uwwvax.uww.edu
http://www.wisconsinhistory.org/
  libraryarchives/arcnet/whitewtr.asp
Karen Weston, Area Research Center Curator
Mon–Fri noon–4:00
(Area Research Center for Jefferson, Rock,
  and Walworth counties)
copies: 10¢ each

Wisconsin Historical Society
Area Research Center
(see State Historical Society, below)

Wisconsin Department of Public Instruction
Division of Library Services
Bureau for Interlibrary Loan and Resource Sharing
2109 South Stoughton Road
Madison, WI 53716
(608) 224-6167
Mon–Fri 7:45–4:30

State Historical Society

Wisconsin Council for Local History
816 State Street
Madison, WI 53706
(608) 262-2316

Wisconsin Historical Society
816 State Street
Madison, WI 53706-1488
(608) 264-6535 (Reference Librarian); (608) 264-6460 (Reference Archivist); (608) 264-6598 (Newspapers)
http://www.wisconsinhistory.org
James L. Hansen, Reference Librarian
when University of Wisconsin is in session: Mon–Thur 8:00–9:00, Fri–Sat 8:00–5:00; when university is not in session: Mon–Sat 8:00–5:00; Archives: Mon–Fri 8:00–5:00, Sat 9:00–4:00
Pub. *Wisconsin Magazine of History*, quarterly; *Columns—Newsletter of the State Historical Society of Wisconsin*, bimonthly
(library has a strong collection with emphasis on North American genealogy; archives serves as Area Research Center for Columbia, Dane and Sauk counties)
$40.00 per year membership

City, County and Regional Archives and Libraries
(A more exhaustive list of public and academic libraries can be found at http://www.dpi.state.wi.us/dpi/dlcl/pld/wis_lib.html.)

Appleton Public Library
225 North Oneida Street
Appleton, WI 54911-4780
(920) 832-6173; (920) 832-5907 FAX
refquest@apl.org
http://www.apl.org
Wisconsin Collection Librarian
Mon–Thur 9:00–9:00, Fri 9:00–6:00, Sat 1:00–5:00

Aram Public Library
404 East Walworth Avenue
Delavan, WI 53115-1208
(262) 728-3111 voice & FAX
jbalazs@delavan.lib.wi.us
http://www.lakeshores.lib.wi.us/Dynamic Site/script_modules/mlib/mlib.pl?id=24
Joe Balazs, Director

Beaver Dam Community Library
311 North Spring Street
Beaver Dam, WI 53916-2043
(920) 887-4631; (920) 887-4633 FAX
mevis@mwfls.org; bdref@mwfls.org
http://www.beaverdam.lib.wi.us
Mark Arend, Assistant Librarian; Susan Mevis, Director
Mon–Fri 9:00–8:30, Sat 9:00–5:00
copies: 15¢ each from paper originals, 25¢ each from microfilm originals

Beloit Public Library
409 Pleasant Street
Beloit, WI 53511-6272
(608) 364-2905; (608) 364-2907 FAX
http://als.lib.wi.us/BPL

Peg Bredeson, Director
Mon–Thur 9:30–8:45, Fri–Sat 9:30–5:15

Bonduel Community Archives
(108 South First Street—location
PO Box 205 (mailing adress)
Bonduel, WI 54107

Brown County Library
Local History and Genealogy Department
515 Pine Street
Green Bay, WI 54301-5194
(920) 448-4394
http://www.dct.com/org/bcl
Mary Jane Herber
winter: Mon–Sat 1:00–5:00, Wed 6:00–9:00; summer: Mon–Fri 1:00–5:00, Wed 6:00–8:00
copies: 25¢ per page, $3.00 minimum

Burlington Public Library
Wisconsin Territory's territorial papers
(see Iowa, Part 2)

Chippewa Falls Public Library
105 West Central Street
Chippewa Falls, WI 54729-2397
(715) 723-1146; (715) 720-6922 FAX
cflib@ifls.lib.wi.us
http://www.chippewafallslibrary.org
Jan Adams, Reference Librarian
winter: Mon–Thur 9:00–8:00, Fri 9:00–6:00, Sat 10:00–5:00, Sun 1:00–5:00; summer: Mon & Thur 9:00–8:00, Tue–Wed & Fri 9:00–6:00, Sat 10:00–1:00

Chippewa Valley Museum
(Carson Park—location)
PO Box 1204 (mailing address)
Eau Claire, WI 54702
(715) 834-7871; (715) 834-6624 FAX
info@cvmuseum.com
http://www.cvmuseum.com
Museum: Memorial Day–Labor Day: daily 10:00–5:00; Museum: school year: Tue–Sun 1:00–5:00; Library: Mon–Fri
("The Chippewa Valley Museum is a regional history museum. Our nationally recognized exhibits tell the varied and intertwining stories of the Chippewa Valley, from its earliest inhabitants to the present. Museum Library serves as a regional archive with 14,000 historic images and more than 25,000 documents, manuscripts and other sources available for research.")
admission: $3.00 for adults

Cottage Grove Area Historical Society
(Flynn Hall—location)
2323 Cottage Grove Road (mailing address)
Cottage Grove, WI 53527
(608) 839-4624
smsteele@facstaff.wisc.edu
http://www.cottagegroveonline.com/community/cgahs
Sara Steele, Archives and "Look Ups"
by appointment; meetings: third Tue 7:00 (summer), 2:00 (winter)
Pub. newsletter, monthly

The Cudahy Family Library
3500 East Library Drive
Cudahy, WI 53110
(414) 769-2244; (414) 769-2252 FAX
rebecca.roepke@mcfls.org
http://www.mcfls.org/cpl
Rebecca Roepke, Director
Mon–Thur 10:00–9:00, Fri–Sat 9:00–5:00, Sun noon–4:00

Door County Library

Door County History Room
107 South Fourth Avenue
Sturgeon Bay, WI 54235-2203
(920) 743-6578; (920) 743-6697 FAX
rberger@mail.nfls.lib.wi.us
Rebecca N. Berger, Director; Nancy Emery, Adult Services Librarian
Mon–Thur 9:00–9:00, Fri 9:00–6:00, Sat 9:00–5:00

Fond du Lac Public Library
32 Sheboygan Street
Fond du Lac, WI 54935-4271
(920) 929-7086; (920) 929-7082 FAX
http://www.fdlpl.org
Kay Conrad, Reference Librarian
Mon–Thur 9:00–9:00, Fri 9:00–6:00, Sat (winter) 9:00–5:00, Sat (summer) 9:00–noon, Sun (winter) 1:00–4:00
charges for photocopies

Fox Lake Historical Museum, Inc.
(211 Cordelia Street—location)
W9369 County Trunk C (mailing address)
Fox Lake, WI 53933
(920) 929-2376
Norma R. Heuer, Curator
Memorial Day–first week in Oct: first & third Sun 1:00–4:00, and by appointment
Pub. *Newsletter*, annually
(local history and large collection of Indian artifacts)
$3.00 per year membership

Hartford Public Library
115 North Main
Hartford, WI 53027-1596
(262) 673-8240; (262) 673-8300 FAX
http://www.hnet.net/~hpl
Shirley Hess, History Room Coordinator
Hartford History Room: first & third Thur (Jan–Nov) 10:00–8:00, second, fourth and fifth Thur (all year) 10:00–4:00, remaining Thur 9:00–3:00, and by appointment
("Research—family, business, building, etc.")

Hartland Public Library
110 East Park Avenue
Hartland, WI 53029-2130
(262) 367-3350; (262) 367-2251 FAX
hplinfo@hartland.lib.wi.us
http://www.hartlandlibrary.org
Nancy Massnick, Library Director
Mon–Thur 9:00–8:30, Fri 9:00–5:00, Sat 9:00–4:00, Sat (summer) 10:00–noon

Hedberg Public Library
Reference Department
316 South Main Street
Janesville, WI 53545-3971
(608) 758-6581 (Reference Department); (608) 758-6615 FAX
hplweb@als.lib.wi.us
http://hedbergpubliclibrary.org
Karen Krueger, Director
Mon–Fri 9:00–9:00, Sat 9:00–5:30, Sun (Sept–May) 9:00–1:00
(primarily Janesville, some Rock County records)
research, limited genealogy requests by mail only: SASE plus copies at 15¢ per page from paper originals, 20¢ per page from microform originals

Hoard Historical Museum
407 Merchants Avenue
Fort Atkinson, WI 53538
(920) 563-7769; (920) 568-3203 FAX
hartwick@hoardmuseum.org
http://www.hoardmuseum.org
Sue Hartwick, Director
winter: Tue–Sat 9:30–3:30; summer: Tue–Sat

9:30–4:30, Sun 11:00–3:00
(cemetery records of Jefferson County, local
family records, platt maps, church and
school records, local business records)

Holly History and Genealogy Center
(see Waupaca Historical Society, Historical
Societies—Local and Regional, below)

Johnson Public Library
131 East Catherine Street
Darlington, WI 53530-1359
(608) 776-4171; (608) 776-3365 FAX
http://www.swls.org/darlingtonlibrary/
index.html
Marion Howard, Head Librarian
Mon & Wed–Thur 1:30–8:30, Tue
1:30–5:30, Fri 10:00–5:00, Sat
8:30–12:30; Historical Library Room: Tue
2:00–4:00
(Lafayette County historical and genealogical
research materials)

Karl Junginger Memorial Library
625 North Monroe Street
Waterloo, WI 53594-1183
(920) 478-3344; (920) 478-2351 FAX
kjml@mwfls.org (Reference);
taylorc@mwfls.org
http://www.waterloo.lib.wi.us
Joel Zibell, Librarian; Cynthia Taylor,
Director
Labor Day–Memorial Day: Mon–Thur
10:00–8:00, Fri 1:00–6:00, Sat
10:00–2:00; Memorial Day–Labor Day:
Mon–Thur 10:00–7:00, Fri 10:00–5:00,
Sat 10:00–2:00

Kenosha Public Library
Reference Department
Gilbert M. Simmons Library
(711 59th Place—location)
PO Box 1414 (mailing address)
Kenosha, WI 53141-1414
(262) 942-3700
http://www.kenosha.lib.wi.us
Tracy Blaschka, Head of Reference and
Electronic Services
Mon–Thur 9:00–8:00, Fri 9:00–6:00, Sat
9:00–5:00
Pub. *Genealogy: Resources and Services,
Kenosha Public Library*, irregularly, $5.00
postpaid per issue
(During the library's expansion and
renovation, the collection has been moved
to 8207 22nd Avenue.)
photocopy and postage charges

La Crosse Public Library
Archives and Local History Department
800 Main Street
La Crosse, WI 54601-4122
(608) 789-7136; (608) 789-7106 FAX
archives@lacrosse.lib.wi.us
http://lacrosselibrary.org/archives.htm;
http://lacrosselibrary.org/genealogy
(Genealogy databases online)
Anita Taylor Doering, Archivist
Mon–Thur 9:00–9:00, Fri–Sat 9:00–5:00,
Sun 1:00–5:00
("Depository of the La Crosse Area
Genealogical Society materials; also
federal and state census for Wisconsin;
area newspapers, city directories, local
newspaper indexes to genealogical events,
etc.")
in-depth research by staff: $10.00 per half-
hour ($10.00 minimum), plus SASE;
copies: 25¢ per page from microform
originals, 10¢–20¢ per page from paper
originals, depending on size

Lower Wisconsin River Genealogical and

Historical Research Center
PO Box 202
Wauzeka, WI 53826-0202
(608) 326-2739; (608) 875-5806 (Editor)
Carol Higgins, Secretary-Treasurer
Pub. *Looking for Yesterday*, quarterly
(Crawford, northern Grant, southern
Richland, and northwestern Iowa
counties, Wisconsin)
$5.00 per year membership

McMillan Memorial Library
490 East Grand Avenue
Wisconsin Rapids, WI 54494-4898
(715) 423-1040; (715) 423-2665 FAX
http://www.scls.lib.wi.us/mcm/local/
local_genealogy
Ronald McCabe, Director
Mon–Thur 9:00–9:00, Fri 9:00–6:00, Sat
9:00–5:00, Sun 1:00–5:00; hours vary
during summer
(emphasis on Wood County)

Madeline Island Historical Museum
PO Box 9
La Pointe, WI 54850
(715) 747-2415
http://www.wisc.edu/shs-
archives/arcnet/madislan.html
(Ashland, Bayfield, and Iron counties)

Madison Public Library
201 West Mifflin Street
Madison, WI 53703-2597
(608) 266-6300; (608) 266-6363; (608) 266-
4338 FAX
madtech@scls.lib.wi.us (Webmaster)
http://www.scls.lib.wi.us/madison/index.
html
Barbara L. Dimick, Director
Mon–Wed 8:30–9:00, Thur–Fri 8:30–5:30,
Sat 9:00–5:30

Manitowoc Public Library
707 Quay Street
Manitowoc, WI 54220-4539
(920) 683-4862; (920) 683-4863; (920) 683-
4873 FAX
alanempl@mcls.lib.wi.us
http://www.manitowoc.lib.wi.us
Joyce Peterson, Librarian; Alan Engelbert,
Director
school year: Mon–Thur 9:00–9:00, Fri
9:00–6:00, Sat 9:00–5:00, Sun
noon–4:00; summer: Mon–Thur
9:00–7:00, Fri 9:00–6:00, Sat 9:00–1:00
(Manitowoc newspaper articles and
obituaries, church records, published local
histories, and photograph collection)
limited research in the library's collection:
$15.00 per hour, $15.00 deposit

Marathon County Public Library
300 North First Street
Wausau, WI 54403-5405
(715) 261-7200; (715) 261-7210 FAX
mjbethke@mcpl.lib.wi.us
http://www.mcpl.lib.wi.us
Gary Gisselman, Head, Adult Services
Division
Mon–Thur 9:00–8:30, Fri–Sat 9:00–5:00,
Sun (Sept–May) 1:00–5:00

Mead Public Library
Information Services
710 North Eighth Street
Sheboygan, WI 53081-4563
(920) 459-3400; (920) 459-4336 FAX
meadweb@esls.lib.wi.us
http://www.sheboygan.lib.wi.us
Susan Mathews, Coordinator of Information
Services

Sept–May: Mon–Thur 9:00–9:00, Fri–Sat
9:00–5:00; Oct–Apr: Sun 1:00–5:00;
summer: Mon & Wed 9:00–9:00, Tue &
Thur–Fri 9:00–5:00, Sat 9:00–1:00

Milwaukee Public Library
814 West Wisconsin Avenue
Milwaukee, WI 53233-2385
(414) 286-3000; (414) 286-2794 FAX
http://www.mpl.org/File/branch_central.htm
Kathleen M. Huston, Director; Virginia
Schwartz, Coordinator of Humanities
Mon–Thur 9:00–8:30, Fri–Sat 9:00–5:30
(collection of city directories as far back as
1847)

The Minocqua Museum, Inc.
(416 Chicago Avenue—location)
PO Box 1007 (mailing address)
Minocqua, WI 54548
(715) 356-7666
Daniel D. Scrobell, President
Mon–Fri (June–Aug) 10:00–4:00
("historical museum")
$15.00 per year membership

**Monroe County Local History Room and
Museum**
200 West Main Street
Sparta, WI 54656
(608) 269-8680; (608) 269-8921 FAX
mclhr@centurytel.net
Jarrod M. Roll, County Historian
Mon–Wed & Fri 9:00–4:30, Thur 9:00–9:00,
Sat 10:00–4:30

Neenah Public Library
(240 East Wisconsin Avenue—location)
PO Box 569 (mailing address)
Neenah, WI 54957-0569
(920) 751-4722; (920) 751-4931 FAX
thomas@neenahlibrary.org
http://www.neenahlibrary.org/geneal.htm
Mike Thomas, Adult Services Librarian
school year: Mon–Thur 9:00–9:00, Fri
9:00–6:00, Sat 9:00–5:00, Sun 1:00–5:00;
summer: Mon–Thur 9:00–9:00, Fri
9:00–6:00, Sat 9:00–1:00

Neville Public Museum
210 Museum Place
Green Bay, WI 54303
(920) 448-4460
Ann L. Koski, Director
Archives and Library by appointment
(local history collection)
research: $25.00 per hour

Oconomowoc Public Library
200 South Street
Oconomowoc, WI 53066-5299
(262) 569-2193; (262) 569-2176 FAX
http://www.wcfls.lib.wi.us
Charles R. McKenna, Director
Mon–Thur 10:00–9:00, Fri 10:00–5:00, Sat
9:00–5:00; summer hours vary

Oshkosh Public Library
106 Washington Avenue
Oshkosh, WI 54901-4985
(920) 236-5226 (Genealogy and Local
History); (920) 236-5200; (920) 236-5228
FAX
nichols@mail.winnefox.org
http://www.oshkoshpubliclibrary.org
John V. Nichols, Director
Sept–May: Mon–Fri 9:00–9:00, Sat
9:00–5:00, Sun 1:00–5:00; June–Aug:
Mon–Fri 9:00–9:00, Sat 9:00–1:00

Oshkosh Public Museum
1331 Algoma Boulevard

Oshkosh, WI 54901
(920) 424-4731; (920) 424-4732; (920) 424-
4738 FAX
info@publicmuseum.oshkosh.net
http://publicmuseum.oshkosh.net
Scott Cross, Archivist
Tue–Sat 9:00–5:00, Sun 1:00–5:00

Plymouth Public Library
(address withheld upon request)
("We have no staff available for assistance, so
it would be best not to publicize our
resources.")

Portage County Public Library
Charles M. White Library Building
1001 Main Street
Stevens Point, WI 54481-2860
(715) 346-1544; (715) 346-1548; (715) 346-
1239 FAX
bstack@uwsp.edu
http://library.uwsp.edu/pcl
Robert J. Stack, Director
Mon–Thur 9:30–9:00, Fri 9:30–6:00, Sat
9:30–5:00, Sun 1:00–5:00; summer: Mon
& Thur 9:30–8:00, Tue–Wed & Fri
9:30–5:00, Sat 9:00–noon

Racine Heritage Museum
Research Center
701 South Main Street
Racine, WI 53403-1211
(262) 636-3926; (262) 636-3940 FAX
http://www.spiritofinnovation.org
Dick Ammann, Archivist
Tue & Sat 1:00–4:00, Thur 5:00–7:45
("We are a county-wide repository for
institutional, manufacturing, and
genealogical information.")
research: $20.00 for the first hour, including
return postage and photocopying, $15.00
for each additional hour, $50.00 per hour
rush fee (one week), one-source look-up
for $10.00, payment must accompany
mailed request

Racine Public Library
Reference and Local History Librarian
75 Seventh Street
Racine, WI 53403-1200
(262) 636-9217; (262) 636-9260 FAX
macphail@racinelib.lib.wi.us
http://www.racinelib.lib.wi.us
Jessica MacPhail, Director
Mon–Thur 9:00–9:00, Fri–Sat 9:00–5:30, Sat
(June–Aug) 9:00–1:00, Sun (Oct–Apr)
2:00–5:00
(Racine and Racine County history)
research: $16.00 per hour

Rhinelander District Library
106 North Stevens Street
Rhinelander, WI 54501-3193
(715) 365-1070; (715) 365-1076 FAX
kwendt@wvls.lib.wi.us
http://wvls.lib.wi.us/
RhinelanderDistrictLibrary
Kris Adams Wendt, Director
Mon–Wed 8:00–8:00, Tue–Wed (summer)
8:00–5:00; Thur–Fri 8:00–5:00, Sat
9:00–1:00

Maude Shunk Public Library
W156 N8446 Pilgrim Road
Menomonee Falls, WI 53051-3140
(262) 532-8900; (262) 532-8949 FAX
http://www.mf.lib.wi.us
Anne Reid, Adult Services Librarian
Mon–Fri 9:00–9:00, Sat 9:00–5:00

Spillman Library
719 Wisconsin Avenue

North Fond du Lac, WI 54937-1335
(920) 929-3771; (920) 929-3669 FAX
director@northfonddulaclibrary.org
http://www.northfonddulaclibrary.org
Lois Potratz, Director
Mon & Thur noon–8:00, Tue noon–5:00,
Wed & Fri 10:00–5:00, Sat (Labor
Day–Memorial Day) 10:00–1:00

Superior Public Library
(see Superior Area Research Center, State
Archives and Libraries, Area Research
Centers, above)

University of Wisconsin—Superior
Jim Dan Hill Library
(19th and Weeks Avenue—location)
1800 Grand (mailing address)
Superior, WI 54880
(715) 394-8512; (715) 394-8462 FAX
http://www.uwsuper.edu
Ella Cross, Reference and Government
Documents Librarian
Mon–Fri 8:00–4:30 by appointment
(University of Superior history and archives)

University of Wisconsin—Wausau
University of Wisconsin Center—Marathon
County
518 South Seventh Avenue
Wausau, WI 54401
(715) 845-9602
George Newtown, Ph.D., Dean

Vaughn Public Library
502 West Main Street
Ashland, WI 54806-1584
(715) 682-7060; (715) 682-7185 FAX
http://www.ci.ashland.wi.us/dept/library/
index.html
James Trojanowski, Director

Vernon County Historical Museum
(410 South Center Street—location)
PO Box 444 (mailing address)
Viroqua, WI 54665
(608) 637-7396
vcmuseum@frontiernet.net
Judy Mathison, Curator
15 May–15 Sept: Tue–Sun noon–4:00, and
by appointment; winter: Tue–Thur
noon–4:00
Pub. *Newsletter*, quarterly
(local genealogy; local history of Vernon
County)
$10.00 per year membership

Waukesha County Museum
Research Center
101 West Main Street
Waukesha, WI 53186
(262) 548-7186
Terry Becker, Librarian
Tue–Sat 9:00–4:30 (except holiday
weekends)
(Waukesha County family and local history)
$2.50 per day on-site user fee; research by
mail: $5.00 per year

Waukesha Public Library
321 Wisconsin Avenue
Waukesha, WI 53186-4786
(262) 524-3682; (262) 524-3677 FAX
refemail@waukesha.lib.wi.us
http://www.waukesha.lib.wi.us
Shirley Chilson, Head of Information
Services
Mon–Fri 9:00–9:00, Sat 9:00–5:00, Sat
(summer) 9:00–1:00, Sun (Oct–Apr)
noon–5:00

Wauwatosa Public Library

7635 West North Avenue
Wauwatosa, WI 53213-1778
(414) 471-8484 voice & FAX
tosa.mail@mcfls.org
http://tpublib.fp.execpc.com
Mary Mulroy, Director

West Bend Community Memorial Library
630 Poplar Street
West Bend, WI 53095-3246
(262) 335-5151; (262) 335-5150 FAX
libref@hnet.net
http://www.hnet.net/~wbcml
Michael Tyree, Director

Whitefish Bay Public Library
5420 North Marlborough Drive
Whitefish Bay, WI 53217-5347
(414) 964-4380; (414) 964-5733 FAX
tracyb@wfblibrary.org
http://www.wfblibrary.org
Tracy Blaschka, Director

Historical Societies—Local and Regional

Adams County Historical Society
(507 Main Street—location)
PO Box 264 (mailing address)
Friendship, WI 53934
(608) 339-7732
adamschs@palacenet.net
http://www.adamshistory.com

Alma Historical Society and Museum
505 South Second Street
Alma, WI 54610

**American West Research Center and
Historical Society, Inc.**
(see Ohio, Part 2)

Ashland County Historical Society
Ashland Historical Museum
509 West Main Street
Ashland, WI 54806
(715) 682-4911
ashlandhistory@centurytel.net
http://www.ashlandhistory.com
Mon–Fri 10:00–4:00

Badger Historical Society
PO Box 186
Shullsburg, WI 53586
(608) 965-3474

Barron County Historical Society
1870 13½ Avenue
Cameron, WI 54822
(715) 458-2842 (Home); (715) 458-2080
(Office)
museum1@chibardun.net
http://www.barroncountymuseum.com

Bay View Historical Society
PO Box 07614
Milwaukee, WI 53207
(414) 769-0110
Eric Western, President
Pub. *Bay View Historian*

Bayfield County Historical Society
Bayfield County Courthouse
Washburn, WI 54891
(715) 373-5345
Ruth Harnois, Secretary
by appointment
Pub. *Historical Happenings*, two or three
times per year
("Bayfield County Historical Society has five
sub-chapters, but inquiries could be

The Genealogist's Address Book

directed to proper organization.")
$3.00 per year membership; research: $5.00 minimum

Bayfield Heritage Association
117 South First
Bayfield, WI 54814
(715) 779-5958

Belleville Area Historical Society
PO Box 478
Belleville, WI 53508

Beloit Historical Society
845 Hackett Street
Beloit, WI 53511
(608) 365-7835; (608) 365-5999 FAX
beloiths@ticon.net
http://www.ticon.net/~beloiths
Paul K. Kerr, Director; Loretta Hatch,
  Volunteer Coordinator
Mon–Fri 9:00–4:00
Pub. *"Confluence" Past Meets Present*,
  quarterly
$15.00 per year membership

Berlin Historical Society
(111 South Adams Avenue—location)
PO Box 21 (mailing address)
Berlin, WI 54923
(920) 361-4343; (920) 361-0807 (President's
  home)
John Wahlers, President
by appointment
(local history)
$4.00 per year membership

Black Earth Historical Society
PO Box 214
Black Earth, WI 53515

Bloomer Historical Society
1104 Vine Street
Bloomer, WI 54724
(715) 568-2011

Brandon Historical Society
(Museum, 102 East Main Street—location)
125 North State Street (mailing address)
Brandon, WI 53919
tdeboer@centurytel.net
http://www.wlhn.org/fond-du-lac/
  communities/brandon/
  brandon_historical_society.htm
Carrie Schmidt, President; Twilah DeBoer,
  Secretary
meetings: third Mon 6:30
$5.00 per year membership

Brodhead Historical Society
1101 East Sixth Avenue
Brodhead, WI 53520
(608) 897-8048
Secretary

Brown County Historical Society
(1008 South Monroe Avenue, Green Bay, WI
  54301—location)
PO Box 1411 (mailing address)
Green Bay, WI 54305-1411
(920) 435-4922; (920) 455-4518
bchs@netnet.net
http://www.browncohistoricalsoc.org
Wendy Barszcz, Executive Director
Mon–Fri 8:30–3:30
Pub. *Voyageur: Northeast Wisconsin's
  Historical Review*, semiannually, $10.00
  per issue; *The Historical Bulletin*, five
  times per year
("Our society does not keep vital statistics.
  We are basically a building preservation-
  oriented society. Our publications contain
  articles and information which might be of
general interest to genealogists. For vital
statistics for Brown County, contact
Brown County Library.")
$20.00 per year membership

Brown Deer Historical Society, Inc.
(4800 West Green Brook Drive—location)
8035 North Grandview Drive (mailing
  address)
Brown Deer, WI 53223
(414) 354-4116
Dorothy Kittleson, President
Open Houses held in the 1884 School in
  May & July–Aug
Pub. *Brown Deer Historical Society, Inc.
  NEWSLETTER*, four times per year (Jan,
  Apr, June, Oct)
$15.00 per year professional or business
  membership

Buffalo County Historical Society
(407 South Second Street, Alma, WI 54610-
  0087—location)
PO Box 394 (mailing address)
Alma, WI 54610
(608) 685-6290; (608) 685-6290 FAX
historical@buffalocounty.com;
  gschloss@nelson-tel.net
http://www.bchsonline.com
Gary Schlosstein, President and County
  Historian
Mon–Fri 8:00–4:30
$10.00 per year membership; research:
  $10.00 per hour for members, $15.00 per
  hour for nonmembers, plus copies

Burlington Historical Society
232 North Perkins Boulevard
Burlington, WI 53105
(262) 767-2884; (262) 767-2844 FAX
burlingtonhistory@core.com
http://burlingtonhistory.org
Doug Lind, President
Museum: Sun 1:00–4:00; Pioneer Log
  Cabin, located in Wehmhoff Square:
  Sat–Sun (May–Oct) 1:00–4:00; Whitman
  School, an 1840s schoolhouse: by
  appointment
Pub. *Burlington Historian*, quarterly
$5.00 per year membership; research: fees
  variable

The Burnett County Historical Society
(8500 County Road U—location)
PO Box 153 (mailing address)
Danbury, WI 54830-0159
(715) 866-8890
fahp@centurytel.net
Kevin Klucas
25 May–1 Sept: Wed–Sun; Sept–May:
  Mon–Fri
Pub. *Burnett County Historical Society
  Newsletter*, four times per year
("Operates Burnett County History Research
  Library. Operates Forts Folle Audine
  Historical Park.")
$20.00 per year membership

Cadott Area Historical Society Museum
(630 North Highway 27—location)
PO Box 1 (mailing address)
Cadott, WI 54727Cadott, WI 54727
(715) 289-3867
Mon 9:00–4:00

Chippewa County Historical Society
123 Allen Street
Chippewa Falls, WI 54729
(715) 723-4399

Clark County Historical Society, Inc.
PO Box 41
Neillsville, WI 54456

Clinton Community Historical Society
PO Box 606
Clinton, WI 53525
(608) 676-4940

Clintonville Area Historical Society
(32 11th Street—location)
Beggs Furniture, 210 Fairway Drive (mailing
  address)
Clintonville, WI 54929-1063
Richard K. Beggs, President
Memorial Day–Labor Day: Sun & holidays
  1:00–4:00
(minimal capability for genealogist's type
  work)
$5.00 per year membership

Columbia County Historical Society
(112 Main Street, Pardeeville, WI
  53954—location)
Route 1, W 3988 Highway 33 (mailing
  address)
Cambria, WI 53923
(920) 348-5516
Tue–Sat (June–Aug) 1:00–4:00
$5.00 per year membership

Crawford County Historical Society
505 South State Street
Prairie Du Chien, WI 53821
(608) 326-6330

Crivitz-Stephenson Historical Society
Crivitz Area Museum
Crivitz, WI 54114

Cross Plains-Berry Historical Society
9260 Far View Road
Mazomanie, WI 53528

Cudahy Historical Society
PO Box 332
Cudahy, WI 53110
jmhchs@yahoo.com
http://www.ci.cudahy.wi.us/
  Historical_Society/index.htm
John Hundseder, President
$7.00 per year membership

Dane County Historical Society
PO Box 5003
Madison, WI 53705
dchs@danenet.wicip.org
http://danenet.wicip.org/dchs
Michael Boure, President; Donna Hartshorne,
  Archivist
by appointment
Pub. *DCHS Newsletter*, quarterly
$8.00 per year membership

Dartford Historical Society
(501 Mill Street—location)
PO Box 638 (mailing address)
Green Lake, WI 54941
(920) 294-6194
http://www.wlhn.org/green_lake/
  dartford_historical_society.htm
Lawrence Behlen, President
Fri 10:00–4:00, Sat (Apr–Sept) 10:00–noon
Pub. *Dartford News*, six times per year
(local history archives)
$10.00 per year membership

DeForest Area Historical Society
(119 East Elm Street—location)
PO Box 124 (mailing address)
DeForest, WI 53532
(608) 846-5519 (President)
John Englesby, President
second Sun (June–Dec) 1:00–4:00

Pub. *News and Notes*, semiannually (spring
and fall)
(history of DeForest area)
$10.00 per year membership

Dells County Historical Society
(600 Broadway—location)
PO Box 177 (mailing address)
Wisconsin Dells, WI 53965
(608) 254-8321
Bud Gussel, President
noon–3:00
(published book, *Others Before You*)
$5.00 per year membership

De Pere Historical Society
White Pillars Museum
403 North Broadway
De Pere, WI 54115
(920) 336-3877
Laurel Towns, Curator
Mon–Fri noon–4:00, Sat by appointment
Pub. *Historical Society Newsletter*, three
times per year
(De Pere, Wisconsin history)
$10.00–$24.00 membership; research: $5.00
per hour

**Dodge County Historical Society and
Museum**
105 Park Avenue
Beaver Dam, WI 53916
(920) 887-1266
dchs@powercom.net
http://www2.powercom.net/~dchs/Index.htm
Joanne L. Wells, Museum Director
Tue 10:00–1:00, Wed–Sat 2:00–5:00

Door County Historical Society
Door County Museum
18 North Fourth Avenue
Sturgeon Bay, WI 54235
(920) 743-5809
1 May–31 Oct: daily 10:00–4:30

Douglas County Historical Society
1101 John Avenue
Superior, WI 54880
(715) 392-8449; (715) 395-5639 FAX
dchs@douglashistory.org
http://www.douglashistory.org
winter: Wed–Fri 10:00–2:00; summer (after
Memorial Day): Tue–Sat 10:00–2:00

Drummond Historical Society
c/o Drummond Public Library
(14990 Superior Street—location)
PO Box 23 (mailing address)
Drummond, WI 54832-0023

Dunn County Historical Society
1820 Wakanda Street
Menomonie, WI 54751
(715) 232-8685
dchs@discover-net.net
http://discover-net.net/~dchs

Eagle River Historical Society
(519 East Sheridan Street—location)
PO Box 2011 (mailing address)
Eagle River, WI 54521
(715) 479-2396
Lenore Farrell, Secretary
Tue–Fri 10:00–3:00
(Published *Loggers and Trappers Were the
First Settlers of Eagle River*. "History of
Eagle River dating back to 1850.")
$5.00 per year membership; no research
services available

East Troy Area Historical Society
PO Box 722

East Troy, WI 53120
(262) 642-5936 (days); (262) 642-5281
(nights)
Alfred Gruling, President
Pub. *Walk Around the Square*

Elmbrook Historical Society
PO Box 292
Brookfield, WI 53008-0292
(262) 782-4057
jwintersberger@wi.rr.com
http://www.elmbrookhistoricalsociety.org
Elizabeth "Betty" Hoffmann, President

Evansville Grove Society
PO Box 234
Evansville, WI 53536
(608) 882-6939

Fairwater Historical Society
PO Box 151
Fairwater, WI 53931
rmschust@facstaff.wisc.edu
http://www.wlhn.org/fairwater_histsoc/
index.html
Bob Schuster, Curator-Historian

Fitchburg Historical Society
Fitchburg City Hall
5520 Lacy Road
Fitchburg, WI 53711

Fond du Lac County Historical Society
Adams House Family Heritage Center
PO Box 1284
Fond du Lac, WI 54936-1284
(920) 922-1166; (920) 922-0991 FAX
fdlhistorical@dotnet.com;
adamsrc@dotnet.com
http://www.fdl.com/history
John J. Ebert, Director, Adams House; Sally
Albertz, Chair, Family Heritage Center
Mon & Thur 9:00–11:00 A.M., Wed
1:00–7:00, Sat 10:00–2:00, and by
appointment
Pub. *Fond du Lac County Historical Society
Newsletter*, quarterly
$7.00 per year membership; resource center
admission: $3.00 for nonmembers

**Forest County Historical and Genealogical
Society/Museum**
(105 West Jackson Street—location)
PO Box 432 (mailing address)
Crandon, WI 54520
(715) 478-5900

Fort Atkinson Historical Society
Hoard Historical Museum
407 Merchants Avenue
Fort Atkinson, WI 53538
(920) 563-7769; (920) 568-3203 FAX
info@hoardmuseum.org
http://www.hoardmuseum.org
Sue Hartwick, Director
Memorial Day–Labor Day: Tue–Sat
9:30–4:30, Sun 11:00–3:00; Labor
Day–Memorial Day: Tue–Sat 9:30–3:30
Pub. newsletter, quarterly
admission: donation

Genesee Heritage Society
PO Box 52
Genesee Depot, WI 53127
(262) 968-3166

Germantown Historical Society, Inc.
PO Box 31
Germantown, WI 53022
(262) 251-6378
Irene M. Blau, President
Pub. *Newsletter*

Gordon-Wascott Historical Society
PO Box 173
Gordon, WI 54838

Grant County Historical Society
129 East Maple Street
Lancaster, WI 53813
(608) 723-4925 (Museum)
Albert D. Weber, Director Cunningham
hours: various
Pub. *Here & There in Grant County*, four
times per year, $1.50 per issue

Grantsburg Area Historical Society
PO Box 35
Grantsburg, WI 54840

Green County Historical Society, Inc.
(1617 Ninth Street—museum location)
2109 20th Avenue (mailing address)
Monroe, WI 53566
(608) 325-2609
http://www.fgs.org/~fgs/soc0203.htm
Mrs. John M. Irvin, Treasurer and Museum
Chairman
Sat–Sun (June to mid-Sept) 2:00–5:00
(local history museum, no research facility,
no staff to do research, does not operate a
library)
$5.00 per year membership; $1.00 museum
admission

Greendale Historical Society
5321 Morningside Drive
Greendale, WI 53129
(414) 421-8163
http://www.greendale.org

Greenfield Historical Society
W208 S6833 High Bluff Drive
Muskego, WI 53150

Hales Corners Historical Society
5885 South 116th Street
Hales Corners, WI 53130
(414) 529-6150 (Hales Corners Library,
inquiries will be forwarded to the
Historical Society)
mkochis@execpc.com
http://www.historichalescorners.org
Kathleen O'Brien, President; Nancy Kochis,
Webmaster
by appointment
Pub. *Newsletter*, quarterly (for members, not
genealogy)
(History of Hales Corners and southwestern
Milwaukee County. "We are a totally
volunteer organization, with no paid
staff.")
$5.00 per year membership

Hartland Historical Society
PO Box 54
Hartland, WI 53029

Hawks Inn Historical Society, Inc.
(426 Wells Street—location)
PO Box 180104 (mailing address)
Delafield, WI 53018
(262) 646-8540
http://www.hawksinn.org
Shirley Seltzer, Archives
May–Oct: tours Sat 1:00–4:00
Pub. *Hawks Inn Newsletter*, quarterly, free
(emphasis on Wisconsin history and
stagecoach inn restoration; "early
settlement and pioneers Delafield area;
Hawks family, Cushing family, Delafield
family, among others")
$15.00 per year membership; research for a
fee

High Cliff Historical Society

(N7526 Lower Cliff Road, Sherwood, WI
54169-9703—location)
Box #1 (mailing address)
Sherwood, WI 54169
(920) 989-1636
Russ J. Bishop, President
May–Sept: Sat–Sun 1:00–5:00
$5.00 per year membership

Hillsboro Area Historical Society, Inc.
(Museum in City Park—location)
PO Box 9 (mailing address)
Hillsboro, WI 54634
(608) 489-3192
Betty Havlik, President
Sun (summer) 1:00–4:00, and by
    appointment
$5.00 per year membership

Historic Blooming Grove Historical Society
(Dean House, 4718 Monona Drive—location)
PO Box 6740 (mailing address)
Monona, WI 53716
(608) 249-7920
annwide@email.msn.com
http://www.wlhn.org/daneco/hbg
Ann Waidelich, Curator
second Sun 1:00–4:00, most Mon mornings
Pub. *Blooming Grove Courier*, three times
    per year
("Covers historic township of Blooming
    Grove, some of which is now in the cities
    of Madison and Monona, Wisconsin.")
$10.00 per year membership

Historic Madison, Inc.
Box 2721
Madison, WI 53701
(608) 233-9394
mlgajewski@aol.com
http://danenet.wicip.org/hmi
Mark Gajewski
Pub. *Journal of the Four Lake Region*
$15.00 per year membership

Horicon Historical Society
(322 Winter Street—location)
PO Box 65 (mailing address)
Horicon, WI 53032
Margaret Bartelt, Secretary

Hustisford Historical Society
(134 North Ridge Street—location)
PO Box 44 (mailing address)
Hustisford, WI 53034
(920) 349-3377
Cheryl Danis, President
June–Sept: second & fourth Sun 1:00–3:00,
    and by appointment
Pub. *The Spinning Wheel*, quarterly
$5.00 per year membership

Iola Historical Society
(Depot Street—location)
Box 111 (mailing address)
Iola, WI 54945
(715) 445-3445
Gloria Briquelet, Archives Historian
by appointment
Pub. *Iola Historical Society—Remembering
    the Past . . .* , three to four times per year
$5.00 per year membership

Iowa County Historical Society
PO Box 38
Dodgeville, WI 53533

Iron County Historical Society
(303 Iron Street—location)
PO Box 4 (mailing address)
Hurley, WI 54534
(715) 561-2244

W. Hoepner, President
Mon, Wed & Fri–Sat 10:00–2:00
$1.00 per hour to use microfilm reader,
    $1.00 per year Iron County newspapers

Jackson County Historical Society
(13 South First Street—location)
223 North Fourth Street (mailing address)
Black River Falls, WI 54615
(715) 284-4659

Jackson Historical Society
2860 Division Road
Jackson, WI 53037
(262) 677-4825
rdausman@execpc.com
http://villageofjackson.com/history.htm
Ray Dausman
occasionally by appointment; meetings at
    Mill Road Museum: second Mon 6:30
Pub. *The Church Mouse*
(history of town and village of Jackson,
    Washington County)

Jefferson Historical Society
305 South Main Street
Jefferson, WI 53549

Jump River Valley Historical Society, Inc.
(W9224 U.S. Highway 8—location)
PO Box 104 (mailing address)
Catawba, WI 54515
(715) 339-2642
Anna Timmers, Secretary; Agnes Wudel,
    Chairperson
first & third Sat (June–Sept) 9:00–3:00
("We have not been organized long—have
    lots to do yet.")

Juneau County Historical Society
(211 North Union Street—location)
PO Box 321 (mailing address)
Mauston, WI 53948
Nancy McCullick, President
Memorial Day weekend–Labor Day
    weekend: Sat–Sun 1:00–4:00; Christmas
    open house: 29–30 Nov & 6–7 Dec:
    1:00–8:00, and by appointment
Pub. *Juneau County Historical Society
    Quarterly Bulletin*
$3.00 per year membership

**Kenosha County Historical Society
Museum Library**
Kenosha History Center
220 51st Place
Kenosha, WI 53140-2909
(262) 654-5770; (262) 654-1730 FAX
Cynthia Nelson, Curator of Collections
Tue–Fri 10:00–4:30, Sat 10:00–4:00, Sun
    noon–4:00; Archives: Wed–Fri 2:00–4:30
    and by appointment
Pub. *Southport Newsletter*, quarterly
$20.00 per year membership

Kewaskum Historical Society, Inc.
1202 Park View Drive
Kewaskum, WI 53040

Kewaunee County Historical Society
Kewaunee County Historical Museum
(Court House Square, 613 Dodge Street,
    Kewaunee, WI 54216—location)
N9307 Abitz Lane (mailing address)
Luxemburg, WI 54217
(920) 866-2719; (920) 487-2374 (Research
    Center)
gabitz@netnet.net
Gerald V. Abitz, President; George Miller,
    Research Center
Mon–Sun (Memorial Day weekend–Labor
    Day) 10:30–4:30, and by appointment;

Research Center, 207 Steele Street,
    Algoma: Thur–Sat noon–4:00 and by
    appointment
Pub. *KCHS Newsletter*, semiannually (spring
    and fall)
(Kewaunee County history, artifacts, and
    genealogy; supplies
    http://www.rootsweb.com/~wikewaun/ind
    ex.htm with information)
museum admission: $2.00

Kiel Historical Society
227 Fremont Street
Kiel, WI 53042

Knox Creek Heritage Center, Inc.
(N4517 West Knox Road—location)
N4233 West Knox Road (mailing address)
Brantwood, WI 54513
(715) 564-2525
mbraski@hotmail.com
Marcella Braski, President
by appointment
Pub. *Knox Times*, semiannually
$5.00 per year membership

Koshkonong Prairie Historical Society
PO Box 190
Cambridge, WI 53523
webmaster@koshkonong.org
http://koshkonong.org
$10.00 per year membership (to Larry
    Gunnelson, Treasurer, W9352 Highway C,
    Cambridge, WI 53523)

La Crosse County Historical Society
Swarthout and Riverside Museum
(112 South Ninth Street—location)
PO Box 1272 (mailing address)
La Crosse, WI 54602
(608) 782-1980; (608) 793-1359
lchs@centurytel.net
http://www.lchsonline.org
Brenda R. Jordan, Curator/Registrar
Mon–Fri 9:00–5:00
Pub. *Past, Present & Future*, bimonthly
(local history, Upper Mississippi River
    valley)
$25.00 per year membership

Lafayette County Historical Society
525 Main Street
Darlington, WI 53530-0312
(608) 776-8340
Marion Howard, Curator Archives; Fran
    Fink, Museum
Mon–Sun 1:00–4:00
Pub. *Looking Backwards*, quarterly
$10.00 per year membership

Lake Mills-Aztalan Historical Society
Route 2
Jefferson, WI 53549

Langlade County Historical Society
(404 Superior Street—location)
PO Box 219 (mailing address)
Antigo, WI 54409
(715) 627-4464
Barbara MacPhail, Curator
Mon & Wed–Fri 9:30–3:30, Sat–Sun
    10:00–3:00
$10.00 per year membership

Linden Historical Society
2073 Sunny Slope Road
Mineral Point, WI 53565
Jim Jewell

Luther Valley Historical Society, Inc.
(158 Depot Street—location)
PO Box 253 (mailing address)

Footville, WI 53537-0253
(608) 876-6892
http://www.madison.com/communities/
    luthervalleyhisotircalsociety/index.php
meetings: second Thur (Mar–Nov) 7:00
$5.00 per year membership

Manitowoc County Historical Society
1701 Michigan Avenue
Manitowoc, WI 54220
(920) 684-4445; (920) 684-0573 FAX
mchistscoc@lakefield.net
http://www.mchistsoc.org
Sarah Johnson, Executive Director
Mon–Fri 9:00–4:00
Pub. *Pinecrest Spirit Newsletter*, quarterly;
    *Manitowoc County Historical Society
    Monographs*, annually
$15.00 per year membership

Marathon County Historical Society
Marathon County Historical Museum
410 McIndoe Street
Wausau, WI 54403
(715) 848-6143; (715) 848-0378 (Library);
    (715) 848-0576 FAX
research@marathoncountyhistory.org
http://www.marathoncountyhistory.com
Mary Jane Hettinga, Librarian/Archivist
Tue–Thur 9:00–3:30
(logging, native American, regional and local
    history)

Marinette County Historical Society
Marinette Historical Museum
(Highway 41 Stephenson Island, Marinette,
WI—location)
PO Box 262 (mailing address)
Marinette, WI 54143
(715) 732-0831
Walter Stepniak, Curator
10:00–4:30
Pub. *The Historian*, quarterly
$10.00 per year membership

Marion Area Historical Society
PO Box 321
Marion, WI 54950

Markesan Historical Society
Grand River Valley Museum and Depot
214 East John Street
Markesan, WI 54946
(920) 398-3554
http://www.wlhn.org/green_lake/
    communities/markesan/markesan.htm

Marquette County Historical Society
(125 Lawrence Street—location)
PO Box 172 (mailing address)
Westfield, WI 53964
mchs@co.marquette.wi.us
http://mailserver.co.marquette.wi.us/MCHS
Fran Sprain, Curator; Esther Brancel,
    President
June–Aug: Wed & Sat 1:00–4:00
Pub. *Imprints on the Sands of Marquette
    County*, three or four times per year
(growing file of genealogies)
$10.00 per year membership; research within
    MCHS collection: $10.00 per hour

Marshall Area Historical Society
5470 Ridge Road
Marshall, WI 53559

Mayville Historical Society, Inc.
(Corner of North German and Bridge
Streets—location)
PO Box 82 (mailing address)
Mayville, WI 53050
(920) 387-2420 (Museum); (920) 387-5233

(President's home)
Ann Guse, President
second & fourth Sun (May–Oct) 1:30–4:30
Pub. *Wagon Wheels*, quarterly
$5.00 per year membership; no genealogical
    research service of any kind

Mazomanie Historical Society
(Research Center, 102 Broadhead
Street—location)
PO Box 248 (mailing address)
Mazomanie, WI 53560
(608) 795-2104; (608) 795-2992 (Museum)
vmatz@tds.net
http://www.rootsweb.com/~wimhs
Virgil Matz, Research Historian
Mon & Thur 9:00–noon & 2:00–8:00, Tue
    2:00–8:00, Fri 1:00–6:00, Sat 10:00–1:00
(Mazomanie records and newspapers, etc;
    limited Black Earth records)
$6.00 per year membership: research: no
    charge

McFarland Historical Society
(5814 Main Street—location)
PO Box 94 (mailing address)
McFarland, WI 53558
(608) 838-3992
bluebee@madtown.net
http://www.madison.com/communities/
    mhs/index.php
Memorial Day–Sept: Sun 1:00–4:00, and by
    appointment
admission: free

Mellen Area Historical Society
(City Hall, corner of Main and Bennett
Streets—location)
PO Box 522 (mailing address)
Mellen, WI 54546
(715) 274-3931
Vyola Turney, President
Mon–Fri 9:00–noon
$8.00 per year membership

Menasha Historical Society
636 Walbrun Street
Menasha, WI 54952

Menomonee Falls Historical Society
Old Falls Village Museum
N96 W15791 County Line Road
Menomonee Falls, WI 53051
(262) 255-8346
jsteliga@wi.rr.com
http://www.shoppingthevillage.com/
    history.htm
Carol Prestin, President
admission: $3.00 for adults

Mequon Historical Society
6100 West Mequon Road
Mequon, WI 53092
(262) 242-3290; (262) 242-3107

Mercer Historical Society
PO Box 638
Mercer, WI 54547
(715) 476-9191

Merrill Historical Society, Inc.
Merrill Historical Museum
804 East Third Street
Merrill, WI 54452-2425
(715) 536-5652
MerrillHS@aol.com
Beverly King, Research Director
Mon–Fri 1:00–4:00
Pub. *Northwoods Historian*, bimonthly
$15.00 per year membership; research:
    donation plus copying and mailing costs

Middleton Historical Society
7410 Hubbard Avenue
Middleton, WI 53562
(608) 836-7614

Milton Historical Society
(742 East Madison—winter office location
18 South Janesville—summer office location)
PO Box 245 (mailing address)
Milton, WI 53563
(608) 868-7772
miltonhouse@miltonhouse.org
http://www.miltonhouse.org
Judy Scheehle, Director
Museum: Mon–Fri (Memorial Day–Labor
    Day) 10:00–4:00; research by appointment
Pub. *The Herlad*, quarterly
research by staff: $10.00 per hour, $10.00
    minimum deposit, copies: 25¢ each

Milwaukee County Historical Society
910 North Old World Third Street
Milwaukee, WI 53203
(414) 273-8288
mchs@prodigy.net
http://www.milwaukeecountyhistsoc.org
Judith A. Simonsen, Curator of Research
    Collections
Mon–Fri 9:30–noon & 1:00–4:30, Sat
    10:00–noon & 1:00–4:30 (call ahead to
    verify Saturday hours)
Pub. *Magazine*, quarterly; *Newsletter*,
    monthly
("Naturalization papers, court cases,
    coroner's inquests, biographical indexes,
    census, city directories, maps,
    photographs")
$20.00 per year membership; research: $6.00
    for general search

Mineral Point Historical Society
Davis Street
Mineral Point, WI 53565

Monroe County Historical Society, Inc.
1488 Aqua Road
Black River Falls, WI 54615-7609
(608) 269-8680
mclhr@centurytel.net
Pub. *Monroe County Historical Society
    Newsletter*, bimonthly; *Portals of Time*
(all genealogical inquiries referred to County
    Historian at Monroe County, Wisconsin,
    Local History Room and Research
    Library)
$35.00 per year membership

Monticello Area Historical Society
PO Box 463
Monticello, WI 53570
http://www.monticellowi.com/mahs.htm

Mount Horeb Area Historical Society
(138 East Main Street—archives location)
408 Lake Street (mailing address)
Mount Horeb, WI 53572
http://www.mounthoreb.org
second & fourth Wed: 12:30–3:30
$15.00 per year membership; museum
    admission: donation

Mountain Historical Society
PO Box 198
Mountain, WI 54149
debclerk@ez-net.com
http://www.rootsweb.com/~wioconto/
    MHSPage.htm
$10.00 per year membership

Muskego Historical Society
(Old Town Hall, W180-S7732 Pioneer
Drive—location)

PO Box 137 (mailing address)
Muskego, WI 53150
(262) 679-5667
Ron Peters, President
Pub. *MHS Newsletter*

Neenah Historical Society
(336 Main Street—location)
PO Box 343 (mailing address)
Neenah, WI 54956
(920) 729-0244
Mrs. Nathan Wauda, President
$8.00 per year membership

Neosho Historical Society
Neosho Village Museum, Highway 67, south
of bridge—location)
PO Box 105 (mailing address)
Neosho, WI 53059
(920) 625-3632
Michael A. Weynand, President
second (year-round) & fourth (Apr–Oct) Sun
1:00–4:00, and by appointment
Pub. *Neosho Museum Researcher*, quarterly
("developing an excellent regional county
research library")

New Berlin Historical Society
(19765 West National Avenue, New Berlin,
WI 53146—location)
5575 South Maberry Lane (mailing address)
New Berlin, WI 53151
(262) 679-1783
dchermann@aol.com
Jackie Hermann, President
by appointment, and three special open
houses (various dates)
Pub. *New Berlin Almanack*, irregularly
$10.00 per year membership

New Glarus Historical Society
Swiss Historical Village
(612 Seventh Avenue—location)
PO Box 745 (mailing address)
New Glarus, WI 53574-0745
(608) 527-2317
Gail Beal, Correspondence Secretary
1 May–31 Oct: Mon–Fri 9:00–4:30

New Holstein Historical Society
(2025 Randolph Avenue—location)
PO Box 144 (mailing address)
New Holstein, WI 53061
(920) 898-5358
Michael Cramer, President
Sun (Memorial Day–Labor Day) 1:00–4:00,
and by appointment
Pub. *New Holstein Historical Society Annual
Newsletter*
$3.00 per year membership

**North Wood County Historical Society,
Inc.**
(212 West Third Street—location)
PO Box 142 (mailing address)
Marshfield, WI 54449
(715) 387-3322
Kathie Haynes, Coordinator
Mon–Thur 1:00–4:00, Sun 1:30–4:00
$5.00 per year membership; research:
donation

Northland Historical Society
PO Box 325
Lake Tomahawk, WI 54539
(715) 277-2788

Norway Historical Society
Col. Heg Memorial Park
6300 Heg Park Road
Wind Lake, WI 53185

Oak Creek Historical Society
PO Box 243
Oak Creek, WI 53154
applenancy@milwpc.com
http://ochistorical.freeservers.com
Nancy Honadel
Sun 2:00–4:00

The Oconomowoc Historical Society
(103 West Jefferson Street—museum
location)
PO Box 969 (mailing address)
Oconomowoc, WI 53066
(262) 569-0740
oconomowochistsociety@juno.com
http://www.oconomowoc.org/Library/
Outreach.htm
Kathi Klann, Administrator; Frank
Anderson, President
May–Dec: Fri–Sun 1:00–5:00, and by
appointment
Pub. *Coo-No-Mo-Wauk*, quarterly
$15.00 per year membership

Oconto County Historical Society
PO Box 272
Oconto, WI 54153
(920) 834-6206
Amélia Canilho Burke, President
7 June–Labor Day: Mon–Sat 10:00–4:00,
Sun noon–4:00
Pub. *News from the Northwoods*, quarterly
$10.00 per year membership; historical
research: $10.00 per hour

Omro Area Historical Society
(114 Main Street and 160 Main
Street—location)
PO Box 133 (mailing address)
Omro, WI 54963
Gordon Moran, Secretary-Treasurer
summer weekends 1:00–4:00, and by
appointment
$5.00 per year membership

Onalaska Area Historical Society
741 Oak Avenue South, Museum Suite
Onalaska, WI 54650

Oregon Area Historical Society
PO Box 262
Oregon, WI 53757

Outagamie County Historical Society, Inc.
330 East College Avenue
Appleton, WI 54911
(920) 733-8445
ochs@foxvalleyhistory.org
http://www.foxvalleyhistory.org
Matthew Carpenter, Curator of Collections
Mon (June–Aug) 10:00–5:00, Tue–Sat
10:00–5:00, Sun noon–5:00
Pub. *History Today*, bimonthly
("history of lower Fox River Valley; Charles
A. Grignon family")
$15.00 per year membership

**Ozaukee County Historical Society
Archives**
(West 63 North 643 Washington
Avenue—location)
PO Box 206 (mailing address)
Cedarburg, WI 53012
(262) 377-4510 (Office); (262) 377-4510
FAX (Press send/start on your machine)
rrenz47043@aol.com
http://www.co.ozaukee.wi.us/ochs
Ruth Renz, Archivist
Tue 9:00–3:00
Pub. *Newsletter*, quarterly
$10.00 per year membership; research or
user fee: $2.00

Palmyra Historical Society
(226 West Main Street—location)
PO Box 265 (mailing address)
Palmyra, WI 53156
hours: various
Pub. *NewsLetter*, quarterly
$10.00 per year membership

Pepin County Historical Society
Washington Square, Box 74
Durand, WI 54736

Peshtigo Historical Society
(400 Oconto Avenue—location)
1100 French Street (mailing address)
Peshtigo, WI 54157
(715) 582-4987
Don Hansen, President
9:00–4:30
Pub. *Peshtigo Fire Museum*

Pewaukee Area Historical Society
The Clark House Museum
(206 East Wisconsin Avenue—location)
PO box 105 (mailing address)
Pewaukee, WI 53072
(262) 691-0233
pahs53072@hotmail.com
http://clarkhousemuseum.lakecountrybusiness
.com/ihtml/public/mainframe.ihtmlSandi
Smith
$15.00 per year membership

Pierce County Historical Association
414 West Main
Ellsworth, WI 54011
(715) 273-6611
Reta Sanford, Archivist
weekday afternoons
Pub. *Pierce County's Heritage*, irregularly
$8.00 per year membership

Polk County Historical Society
Polk County Museum
(Rt. 1, Box 208—location)
PO Box 41 (mailing address)
Balsam Lake, WI 54810-0041
(715) 485-3136
RonH@co.polk.wi.us
http://www.co.polk.wi.us/history
Ron Hedberg
Mon–Sun noon–4:00; meetings at the Polk
County Center Building: fourt Tue
admission: $3.00 for adults

Port Washington Historical Society
PO Box 491
Port Washington, WI 53074
(262) 376-3190 (Research Center)
pwhsrc@yahoo.com
http://www.portwashingtonhistorical
society.org
$20.00 per year membership

Portage County Historical Society
PO Box 672
Stevens Point, WI 54481
(715) 344-7607
jerryrohlinger@yahoo.com
http://www.pchswi.org
Tim Siebert, President
Pub. *Portage County Historical Society
Newsletter*, semiannually
$15.00 per year membership; search: $5.00
per hour plus costs

Poynette Area Historical Society
(116 North Main Street—location)
PO Box 162 (mailing address)
Poynette, WI 53955
(608) 635-2600; (608) 635-2970
Ruth Dunn, President

Wed 1:00–3:00, Sat 10:00–2:00; meetings at
the Poynette Village Hall: fourth Mon
7:00
(artifacts, genealogies, photographs, maps
and abstracts, cemetery records, diaries,
church and school records, veteran
records, etc.)
$5.00 per year membership

Price County Historical Society
(Old Town Hall Museum, W7213
Pine—location)
PO Box 156 (mailing address)
Fifield, WI 54524-0156
(715) 762-4571 (Curator)
Patricia Schroeder, Curator
June–Labor Day: Fri & Sun 1:00–5:00, and
by appointment
Pub. *Price County Historical Society
Newsletter*, three to four times per year
$5.00 per year membership; research: $5.00
for one name, reasonable date, in
courthouse or newspaper

Princeton Historical Society, Inc.
(632 West Water Street and 1009 West Main
Street—location)
321 Harvard Street (mailing address)
Princeton, WI 54968
(920) 295-4949
Gary Wick, President
West Main: Thur 1:00–4:00 by appointment
Pub. *Princeton Historical Society News*,
quarterly
$5.00 per year membership; research:
donation

**Racine County Historical Society and
Museum, Inc.**
Archives
701 South Main Street
Racine, WI 53403-1211
(262) 636-3926; (262) 636-3940 FAX
Archives: Tue & Sat 1:00–4:00, Thur
5:00–7:45; Museum: Tue–Fri 9:00–5:00,
Sat–Sun 1:00–5:00
Pub. *Focus*, quarterly
(both historical and genealogical; local
industrial and cultural history)
$20.00 per year membership; research:
$10.00 per hour minimum, $25.00 per
hour for rush processing; copies: 25¢ each
plus LSASE

Reedsburg Area Historical Society, Inc.
(3 miles east of Reedsburg on Highway
33—location)
PO Box 405 (mailing address)
Reedsburg, WI 53959
(608) 727-2922 (President); (608) 524-2545
(Mr. Steinweg)
http://www.reedsburg.com/rahs.htm
Lavern Kruse, President; Conrad Steinweg
Sat–Sun (Memorial Day weekend–Sept)
1:00–4:00
Pub. *Newsletter*, annually
("In the library we have collections of various
books and scrapbooks.")
$3.00 per year membership

Ripon Historical Society
(508 Watson Street—location)
PO Box 274 (mailing address)
Ripon, WI 54971-0274
(920) 748-5354
woolley611@yahoo.com
http://my.core.com/~riponhistsoc
Bill Woolley, President; Harry Heileman,
Treasurer
$10.00 per year membership

Rochester Area Historical Society

2441 Beck Drive
Waterford, WI 53185-5101
Joan Beck, President

Rock County Historical Society
(10 South High Street—location)
PO Box 8096 (mailing address)
Janesville, WI 53545
(608) 752-5891
rchs@rchs.us
http://www.rchs.us
Maurice J. Montgomery, Curator/Archivist
Archives, Wilson King Stone House, 931
Mineral Point Road: Wed–Thur
9:00–3:00 by appointment
Pub. *Rock County Recorder*, quarterly
(Rock County history and genealogy;
Wisconsin history)
$25.00 per year membership

Rusk County Historical Society
(Rusk County Fairgrounds—location)
700 College Avenue West, Apartment 247
(mailing address)
Ladysmith, WI 54848-2165
(715) 532-6450

Saint Croix County Historical Society
Octagon House
1004 Third Street
Hudson, WI 54016
(715) 386-2654
Dorothy Wilson, President
Tue–Sat 10:00–11:30 & 2:00–4:30, Sun
2:00–4:30
Pub. *The Bulletin*, semiannually
$5.00 per year membership

Saint Francis Historical Society
Saint Francis City Hall
4234 South Nicholson Avenue
Saint Francis, WI 53207

Saint Nazianz Area Historical Society
PO Box 9
Saint Nazianz, WI 54232

**Sauk County Historical Society and
Museum**
(431 Fourth Avenue—location)
PO Box 651 (mailing address)
Baraboo, WI 53913
(608) 356-1001
http://www.saukcounty.com/schs.htm
Kathy Waddell, Curator; Mona Larsen,
President
Tue–Sun (May–Sept) 2:00–5:00, and by
appointment
Pub. *Sauk Trails*, quarterly
(Sauk County history and genealogy)
$15.00 per year membership; museum
admission: $2.00 for nonmembers;
research: $15.00 per hour for
nonmembers, $10.00 per hour for
members, plus cost of copies and postage

Sauk-Prairie Historical Society, Inc.
922 Water Street
Sauk City, WI 53583

Saukville Area Historical Society
(Headquarters [Old Firehouse], 200 North
Mill Street—location)
PO Box 80015 (mailing address)
Saukville, WI 53080
sahs@artin.org
http://come.to/sahs
meetings: third Mon 7:30
Pub. newsletter
$10.00 per year membership

Sawyer County Historical Society and

Museum
(Route 6, County Trunk "B"—location)
PO Box 384 (mailing address)
Hayward, WI 54843
(715) 634-8053
info@SawyerCountyhist.org;
histbuff@SawyerCountyHist.org
http://www.sawyercountyhist.org
Mon–Wed & Sat–Sun noon–4:00
$10.00 per year membership; admission: free

Shawano County Historical Society
(524 North Franklin—location)
1003 South Main Street (mailing address)
Shawano, WI 54166
(715) 524-4744
Mrs. William Bayer, President
June–Aug: Wed & Sat–Sun 1:30–4:00
$2.00 per year membership

**Sheboygan County Historical Research
Center, Inc.**
518 Water Street
Sheboygan Falls, WI 53085
(920) 467-4667, (920) 467-1395 FAX
schrc@execpc.com
http://www.schrc.org
Rose M. Rumpff, Executive Director; Janice
Hildebrand, Librarian
Tue–Sat 9:00–4:00
Pub. *Quarterly*
(Sheboygan County history and genealogy)
$10.00 per year membership

Shorewood Historical Society
3930 North Murray Avenue
Shorewood, WI 53211

Solon Spring Historical Society
PO Box 198
Solon Spring, WI 54873

South Milwaukee Historical Society
(717 Milwaukee Avenue—location)
3516 18th Avenue (mailing address)
South Milwaukee, WI 53172
(414) 762-7605; (414) 768-8790
http://www.southmilwaukee.org/
historical_society/historic.htm
Dean Marlowe, Jr., President
summer: Sun
Pub. *Newsletter*, quarterly
$8.00 per year membership

**South Wood County Historical
Corporation**
540 Third Street
Wisconsin Rapids, WI 54494
(715) 423-1580
Dave Engel, Director
Pub. *River City Memoirs*

Stanley Area Historical Society
(228 Helgerson Street, Corner of Church
Street—location)
403 Franklin Street (mailing address)
Stanley, WI 54768
(715) 644-5492 (ask for Betty)
http://timbertrails.com/sahsm1.htm
David Jankoski, President
Sat–Sun (June–Sept) 1:00–4:00
Pub. *Stanley Historical Society Newsletter*,
semiannually (May Nov)
("family information, photos, vital
information")
$5.00 per year membership; research:
donation

Stockbridge Community Historical Society
Box 68, 315 Lake Street
Stockbridge, WI 53088
(920) 439-1853 voice & FAX

George L. Ecker, Director
("1890 Blacksmith
Museum—new—Sturgeon Center of The
World—Village located on Lake
Winnebago.")

Stoughton Historical Society
901 Highway 51
Stoughton, WI 53589
SHS@expressiveimage.com
http://www.expressiveimage.com/
hstorical.html
$15.00 per year membership

Sun Prairie Historical Society
Sun Prairie Historical Library and Museum,
Inc.
(115 East Main Street—location)
240 Jones Street (mailing address)
Sun Prairie, WI 53590
(608) 837-2915; (608) 825-6879 FAX
pklein@cityofsunprairie.com
http://www.sunprairie.com/docs/
department_home.php?department_id=
18&main_id=504
Peter Kline, Curator
Archives: by appointment

Taylor County Historical Society, Inc.
(845A East Broadway—location)
224 South Second Street (mailing address)
Medford, WI 54451
(715) 748-3808
Elaine Mravik, Curator
Museum: Thur–Fri 11:00–4:00, except
holidays
Pub. *Log Cabin News*, four times per year
(prior to membership meetings)
$5.00 per year membership

Three Lakes Historical Society Museum
(1798 Huron Street—location)
PO Box 58 (mailing address)
Three Lakes, WI 54562
(715) 546-2295
http://www.nnex.net/~robwack/museum.htm
Walt Goldsworthy, Administrator
May–Sept: 10:00–4:00
Pub. *Echo*
(general and family histories, many pictures,
maps, etc.)

Trempealeau Community Heritage Society
PO Box 109
Trempealeau, WI 54661
(608) 534-6555
Carol Bagley

Trempealeau County Historical Society
(N33015 Square Bluff Road, Whitehall, WI
54773—location)
Bank of Galesville (mailing address)
Galesville, WI 54630
(608) 985-3310
Nancy Bergman, Board Member
$5.00 per year membership; research: $6.00
per hour

Two Rivers Historical Society, Inc.
Washington House Museum and Visitor
Center
1622 Jefferson Street
Two Rivers, WI 54241
(920) 793-2490
http://lhinn.com/history.html
Walter L. Vogl, President
Mon–Sun 9:00 A.M.–9:00 P.M.
Pub. *Two Rivers Historical Society
Newsletter*, quarterly
$5.00 per year membership; admission: free

Historical Society of the Upper Baraboo

Valley
(Valton, WI—location)
E 940 Painted Forest Drive (mailing address)
Wonewoc, WI 53968
(608) 983-2854
Lorene Simons, President

Vernon County Historical Society
(410 South Center Street—location)
PO Box 444 (mailing adress)
Viroqua, WI 54665
(608) 637-7396

Walworth County Historical Society
(9 East Rockwell Street—location)
PO Box 273 (mailing address)
Elkhorn, WI 53121
(262) 723-4248
walcohistory@elket.net
http://www.geocities.com/walcohistory
Walter Dunn, President
Wed–Sun 1:00–5:00
(Walworth County history)
$15.00 per year membership; research fees
vary

**Washburn County Historical Society and
Museum**
PO Box 366
Shell Lake, WI 54871
(715) 468-2982; (715) 468-7615
Lucille Miller, Historical Museum Secretary

**Washington County Historical Society,
Inc.**
Research Center, Old Courthouse Square
Museum
340 South Fifth Avenue
West Bend, WI 53095
(262) 335-4678
research@historyisfun.com
http://www.historyisfun.com
Mary Ann Parlow, Museum Administrator
Tours and gift shop: Tue–Thur 10:00–4:00,
Sun 1:00–4:00; research: by appointment
Pub. *The Court Reporter*, quarterly; exhibit
catalogs
(information on Washington County dating
back to 1840; Old Jailhouse at 340 South
Fifth Avenue)
$8.00 per year membership

Waterloo Area Historical Society
PO Box 52
Waterloo, WI 53594

Watertown Historical Society
919 Charles Street
Watertown, WI 53094
(920) 261-2796
whs@watertownhistory.org
http://www.watertownhistory.org
Bill Jannke, III,
President/Historian/Archivist
Memorial Day–Labor Day: 10:00–4:00; after
Labor Day–before Memorial Day:
11:00–3:00; open 7 days a week 1 May to
31 Oct
Pub. *The Historical Review*, quarterly
$10.00 per year membership; research:
$20.00 initial search

Waukesha County Historical Society
Waukesha County Museum, Research Center
101 West Main Street
Waukesha, WI 53186
(262) 521-2859
Susan K. Baker, Executive Director
Tue–Sat 10:30–4:30
Pub. *WCHS News*, quarterly; *Landmark*,
quarterly
$17.00 per year membership

Waupaca County Historical Society
823 Depot Street
Manawa, WI 54949
(920) 596-3467

Waupaca Historical Society
Holly History and Genealogy Center
321 South Main Street
Waupaca, WI 54981
(715) 258-5958
wauphistsoc@waupacaonline
http://www.waupacahistory.org
Hutchison House Museum, South Park:
Memorial Day–Labor Day: Sat–Sun &
holidays: 1:00–4:00; Holly History and
Genealogy Center: Wed & Fri noon–3:00
(Sep5–May) or noon–4:00 (June–Aug),
Sat 9:00–noon

Waupun Historical Society
(Waupun Heritage Museum, 22 South
Madison—location)
314 Beaver Dam Street (mailing address)
Waupun, WI 53963
(920) 324-3878
James Laird, President
first & third Sun 1:30–4:00, and by
appointment

Waushara County Historical Society, Inc.
(Waushara County Jail, 221 South Sainte
Marie Street—location)
PO Box 616 (mailing address)
Wautoma, WI 54982-0616
(920) 787-7584 (during open hours only)
http://www.rootsweb.com/~wiwausha/
histsoc.html
Bruce B. Runnels, President; Michael
Bednarek, Genealogist
Wed 1:00–3:00 & Sat (Memorial Day–Labor
Day) 1:00–4:00, and group tours by
appointment
Pub. *Waushara County Historical Society
Newsletter*, one or two times per year
$5.00 per year membership; research: $10.00
per hour (all inquiries should be submitted
in writing via U.S. mail); copies:
25¢–$1.00 each

Wauwatosa Historical Society
Kneeland-Walker House and Gardens
7406 Hillcrest Drive
Wauwatosa, WI 53213-2226
(414) 774-8672; (414) 774-3064 FAX
webinfo@wauwatosahistoricalsociety.org
http://www.wauwatosahistoricalsociety.org
Kathleen Ehley, President
Mon–Thur 9:00–1:00 (call to confirm)
Pub. *Historic Wauwatosa*, bimonthly
(19th-century school house program for
children, adult education programs, special
events)
$15.00 per year membership

West Allis Historical Society
8405 West National Avenue
West Allis, WI 53227
(414) 541-6970
John R. Clow, Jr., President
Museum: Tue 7:00 P.M.–9:00 P.M., Sun
2:00–4:00
Pub. *Buzz*, bimonthly
$8.00 per year membership per year

West Milwaukee Historical Society
4826 West Beloit Road
West Milwaukee, WI 53214
(414) 384-3522

West Salem Historical Society
360 North Leonard
West Salem, WI 54669

(608) 786-1399 (Memorial Day–Labor Day);
(608) 786-1675 (President)
Errol Kindschy, President
10:00–4:30
("West Salem area; only getting started in this field; have old scrapbooks, books, information on families of area")

Whitefish Bay Historical Society
1144 East Henry Clay Street
Whitefish Bay, WI 53217

Whitewater Historical Society and Museum
Whitewater Street
Whitewater, WI 53190

Wild Rose Historical Society
(Main Street—location)
PO Box 63 (mailing address)
Wild Rose, WI 54984
(920) 622-3575
Rodney Radloff
15 June–1 Sept

The Winnebago County Historical and Archaeological Society
Morgan House
234 Church Street
Oshkosh, WI 54901
(920) 235-3091; (920) 232-0200
info@morganhouse.org
http://www.morganhouse.org

Winneconne Historical Society, Inc.
(611 West Main Street—location)
PO Box 262 (mailing address)
Winneconne, WI 54986
(920) 582-4132
chamber@winneconne.org
http://www.winneconne.org/historical1.htm
Loren J. Driscoll, President
Museum, Marble Park: Sun (Memorial Day–Labor Day) 1:30–4:30

Wittenberg Area Historical Society
(500 West Summit Street—location)
PO Box 224 (mailing address)
Wittenberg, WI 54499
(715) 454-6535; (715) 252-2715
mtmev@yahoo.com
Mario Meverden, Secretary/Treasurer
Museum: Sun (Memorial Day–Labor Day) 1:30–4:00
("Hope this winter to establish early 1900s law office and archives of early printed matter of the local village government." Photographs, recreated country store, original village plat map, artifacts.)
$5.00 per year membership

Genealogical Societies

State Genealogical Societies

Wisconsin Genealogical Council, Inc.
109 Summer Street
Schofield, WI 54476-1282
Pat Kell, Newsletter Editor
Pub. *WGC Newsletter*, quarterly
$7.00 per year membership

Wisconsin State Genealogical Society, Inc. (WSGS)
PO Box 5106
Madison, WI 53705-0106
wsgs@chorus.net
http://www.wsgs.org
Mike Moffatt, Administrative Assistant
Pub. *WSGS Newsletter*, quarterly (June, Sept, Jan, Apr)
(Wisconsin source material)

$18.00 per year membership

Genealogical Societies—Local & Regional

Ashland-Bayfield Counties Tree Climbers
52890 Penokee Lane
Mason, WI 54856
(715) 765-4597
genealogy@cheqnet.net
Carol Jones Wilson
(Ashland and Bayfield County research and area surname connections)
organization not formally in existence but still holding meetings; research: $10.00 per hour

Bay Area Genealogical Society, Inc.
PO Box 283
Green Bay, WI 54305-0283
(920) 494-9286
Myra Michaletz, Editor
Pub. *Gems of Genealogy*, six times per year
(all Brown County cemeteries, some adjacent counties)
$10.00 per year membership; research fees vary

Burlington Genealogical Society
PO Box 593
Burlington, WI 53105
louannc@mia.net
http://www.rootsweb.com/~wiburlgs
meetings at Burlington Historical Society Museum: third Wed 7:00

Chippewa County Genealogical Society
123 Allen Street
Chippewa Falls, WI 54729
(715) 723-4399
Mary Klawiter, President
Tue 9:00–4:00; meetings: fourth Mon (except June–July & Dec)
Pub. *The Newsletter*, five times per year
(all county records; county-wide cemetery index; a highly praised library of research materials)
$10.00 per year membership

Coulee Region Family Research Society at Norskedalen
c/o Norskedalen Nature and Heritage Center, Inc.
PO Box 235
Coon Valley, WI 54623-0235
(608) 452-3424; (608) 452-3157 FAX
info@norskedalen.org
http://www.norskedalen.org
Sharon Twinde, President
Thrune Visitors' Center, Exhibits, Library, Gift Shop, Arboretum and Trails: Mon–Fri (15 Apr–31 Oct) 9:00–4:00, Mon–Fri (1 Nov–14 Apr) 10:00–4:00, Sat (15 Apr–31 Oct) 10:00–4:00, Sun (all year) noon–4:00; Skumsrud Heritage Farm: 1 June–31 Aug: Mon–Fri 11:00–4:00, Sat 10:00–4:00, Sun noon–4:00
(small library; "Norwegian emigration to Coon Valley, Wisconsin")
admission (both centers on the same day): $4.00 for adults

Dane County Genealogical Society
PO Box 5652
Madison, WI 53705-0652
robert.gibbons1@charter.net
http://www.rootsweb.com/~wiscwsgs
Robert Gibbons, President
Pub. newsletter
(serves Columbia, Dane, Dodge, Green, Jefferson and Rock counties)
$15.00 per year membership

Dodge-Jefferson Counties Genealogical Society
(504 South Fourth Street—location)
PO Box 91 (mailing address)
Watertown, WI 53094-0091
(920) 262-2362
djcgs@dodgejeffgen.com
http://www.dodgejeffgen.com
Bill Jannke, President
meetings at Heritage Hall, 504 South Fourth Street, Watertown: second Mon 7:15; Library: Tue 9:00–noon, Thur 1:00–4:00 (except last Thur), last Thur 6:00–9:00
Pub. *Out on a Limb*, quarterly
(holdings housed at Heritage Hall include area church and cemetery records, obituaries and marriages from area newspapers, directories, family histories, county histories, census, passenger lists, vital records, surname card index, etc.)
$12.00 per year membership

Dubuque County-Key City Genealogical Society Chapter (IGS)
(see Iowa, Part 2)

Dunn County Genealogical Society
PO Box 633
Menomonie, WI 54751

Genealogical Research Society of Eau Claire
c/o Chippewa Valley Museum
PO Box 1204
Eau Claire, WI 54702
grsec@cvmuseum.com
http://www.rootsweb.com/~wigrsec
meetings at the Chippewa Valley Museum: second Sat (Sept–May) 9:30 A.M.
Pub. *Sawdust City Roots*, five times per year (Sept/Oct, Nov/Dec, Jan/Feb, Mar/Apr, May)
$10.00 per year membership

Fond du Lac County Genealogical Society
PO Box 1264
Fond du Lac, WI 54936-1264
(920) 921-2193
dodowenr@dotnet.com
http://www.rootsweb.com/~wifonddu/resources/organizations/fdlgensoc.htm
Dorothy F. Wiener, Secretary
meetings at Fond du Lac Public Library: first Mon 7:00 (6:30 during the summer)
Pub. *Newsletter*, quarterly (May, Aug, Nov, Feb)
(There are 21 townships with 102 known cemeteries, of which 80 have been indexed.)
$15.00 per year membership; search of index of names: $1.00 for nonmembers

Forest County Historical and Genealogical Society/Museum
(see Historical Societies—Local and Regional, above)

Fox Valley Genealogical Society
(425 West Park Ridge Avenue—location)
PO Box 1592 (mailing address)
Appleton, WI 54913-1592
(920) 733-5358
Mr. Jerry T. Long, Query Editor
Wed 10:00–9:00, Fri–Sat 9:00–4:00
Pub. *Genealogical Gems*, quarterly
(northeast Wisconsin: Outagamie, Calumet, and Waupaca counties)
$8.00 per year membership; research: SASE

Grant County Genealogical Society
PO Box 281
Dickeyville, WI 53808-0281

(608) 568-3124
reese@mwci.net
http://www.rootsweb.com/~wigrant/
gcgensoc.htm
Karen Reese, President
by appointment
Pub. *Grant County Heritage*, quarterly
$5.00 per year membership; cemetery
surname search: $3.00

Green County Genealogical Society
PO Box 313
Monroe, WI 53566
pgleigh@sbcglobal.net
http://www.rootsweb.com/~wigreen/gcgs.
html
Peggy Rockwell Gleich, Vice President
$10.00 per year membership

Hartford Area Genealogy Society
c/o Hartford Public Library
115 North Main
Hartford, WI 53027
Shirley Hess, President
meetings in the Hartford Public Library,
Hartford History Room: fourth Mon
(Jan–Apr & June–Nov) 1:30
$3.00 per year membership

Heart O' Wisconsin Genealogical Society
PO Box 516
Wisconsin Rapids, WI 54495-0516
maktranscriber@yahoo.com
http://www.rootsweb.com/~wiwood/
HeartOWi/h-master.htm
Don Litzer, 2001-02 Vice-Chair and
McMillan Memorial Library Head of
Adult Services
Pub. *Heart O' Wisconsin Genealogical
Society Newsletter*, quarterly
(emphasis on Wood County; local cemetery
and newspaper indexes)
$12.00 per year membership

Iowa County Genealogical Society
PO Box 321
Dodgeville, WI 53533-0321
ecgs@friendsnfamily.net
http://www.wiiowagensoc.org
Cheryl Schmidt, President

Kenosha County Genealogy Society
4902 52nd Street
Kenosha, WI 53144
(262) 652-2410
Lois Roepke Stein, Founding Member and
Past President
Pub. *Southport Echo*, bimonthly
$8.00 per year membership; free queries in
newsletter; research: donation

La Crosse Area Genealogical Society
PO Box 1782
La Crosse, WI 54602-1782
rmunns@uwalumni.com
http://www.rootsweb.com/~wilacgs
Roxanne Munns
meetings at the La Cross Public Library: 7:00
Pub. *La Crosse Area Genealogical Society
Quarterly*
$15.00 per year membership

Lafayette County Genealogical Society
PO Box 443
Shullsburg, WI 53586
janiceronnerud@hotmail.com
http://www.rootsweb.com/~wilafcgs
Janice Ronnerud, Chair
Pub. *Ancestral Diggins of Lafayette County*,
quarterly
$7.00 per year membership

Langlade County Genealogical Society
PO Box 307
Antigo, WI 54409
genealogist@verizon.net
http://www.rootsweb.com/~wilcgs
Pub. *Trees*, quarterly (Jan, Apr, July, Oct)
$10.00 per year membership; research:
donation

Manitowoc County Genealogical Society
PO Box 1745
Manitowoc, WI 54221-1745
(920) 682-1046
macoppens@milwpc.com
Mary Ann President
first Tue 7:00–9:00 (site may vary)
Pub. *Family Vines*, quarterly (Apr, July, Oct,
Jan)
$5.00 per year membership; research: $10.00
per hour

Marathon County Genealogical Society
PO Box 1512
Wausau, WI 54402-1512
http://www.geocities.com/mcgsociety
Dan Sharpee, Chairman, Pat Kell, Editor
Pub. *Pinery Pedigree*, bimonthly
$10.00 per year membership

Marshfield Area Genealogy Group
PO Box 337
Marshfield, WI 54449
(715) 387-4044
schnitz@wctc.net
http://marshfieldgenealogy.homestead.
com/indexmagg~hs4.html
Vickie Schnitzler, President
meetings: fourth Thur (except Aug, Nov &
Dec)
Pub. *Kith N Kin*, bimonthly
("Covers areas of Clark County, western
Marathon County and northern Wood
County)
$12.00 per year membership

**Milwaukee County Genealogical Society,
Inc.**
PO Box 27326
Milwaukee, WI 53227-0326
mcgs_website@ameritech.net
http://www.Milwaukeegenealogy.org
Betty Jane Larson, Treasurer
Pub. *M.C.G.S. Reporter*, quarterly
$12.00 per year membership; research: $5.00
per name per source

**Monroe, Juneau, Jackson County
Genealogy Workshop, Inc. (Wisconsin)**
PO Box 363
Sparta, WI 54656
(608) 269-5203
Carolyn Hendersin, President
Pub. *MJJCGW Newsletter*, quarterly
(tri-county genealogical society)
$7.00 per year membership

Northern Wisconsin Genealogists
(Corner of Zingler and Evergreen—location)
1188 East Ridlington Avenue (mailing
address)
Shawano, WI 54116-3724
(715) 526-2946
Kathleen Z. Hoffman
Tue–Thur & Sat 9:00–4:00
$5.00 per year membership

Northwest Territory Genealogical Society
(see Indiana, Part 2)

Northwoods Genealogical Society
(see Oneida County Genealogical Society,
below)

**Oconomowoc Genealogical Club of
Waukesha County**
733 East Sherman Avenue
Oconomowoc, WI 53066
(262) 567-3197
Mrs. R. L. Palmer, President
10:00–9:00

Oconto County Genealogical Society
PO Box 114
Suring, WI 54174
ocgs@ez-net.com
http://www.rootsweb.com/~wiocgs
meetings in the Suring High School Library:
third Mon 7:00
$5.00 per year membership

Oneida County Genealogical Society
Northwoods Genealogical Society
Rhinelander District Library
106 North Stevens Street
Rhinelander, WI 54501

Price County Genealogical Club
W6298 County Road D
Phillips, WI 54555
(715) 339-3667
Linda Loula

Rhinelander Historical Society/Museum
9 South Pelham Street
Rhinelander, WI 54501
(715) 369-3833

Rock County Genealogical Society, Inc.
(Rock County Historical Society, 10 South
High Street, Second Floor, Janesville, WI
53545—library location)
PO Box 711 (mailing address)
Janesville, WI 53547-0711
(608) 756-4509 (Library); (608) 752-2688
(Information)
rock_wi_genealogy@yahoo.com
http://www.rootsweb.com/~wircgs
David Bradford
Tue–Thur 9:00–3:00, appointment helpful
Pub. *The Rock County Genealogical Society,
Inc. Member News*, five times per year
(Sept, Nov, Jan, Mar, May)
$8.00 per year membership; queries free for
members, $1.00 for nonmembers

Saint Croix Valley Genealogical Society
PO Box 396
River Falls, WI 54022
http://www.pressenter.com/~scvgs
meetings in Room 104 of the Chalmer Davee
Library, University of Wisconsin—River
Falls: third Thur (Sept–May) 7:30
Pub. *Pipost*, quarterly
$15.00 per year membership

Sheboygan County Genealogical Society
518 Water Street
Sheboygan Falls, WI 53085
(920) 467-4667
Wayne G. Koene, President
Tue–Sat 9:00–4:00
Pub. *Sheboygan County Genealogist*,
quarterly
(family histories of Sheboygan County
families)
$7.00 per year membership

Stevens Point Area Genealogical Society
Portage County Library
1001 Main Street
Stevens Point, WI 54481-2860
(715) 346-1548 (Library)
Ruth Steffen, President
Library: Mon–Fri 9:30–9:00, Sat 9:30–5:00,
reduced summer hours

Pub. *Pedigree Pointers*, quarterly
(serves Portage County)
$10.00 per year membership

Taylor County Genealogical Society
224 South Second Street
Medford, WI 54451-1899
taylorcogensociety@yahoo.com
http://www.rootsweb.com/~witcgs
meetings at the Frances L. Simek Memorial
    Library, 400 North Main Street, Medford:
    second Thur (except June–Aug): second
    Thur
$8.00 per year membership

Three Lakes Genealogical Society
PO Box 760
Three Lakes, WI 54562
tlgswi@aol.com
http://www.rootsweb.com/~witlgs/tlgs.
    index.htm
meetings at Edward U. Demmer Memorial
    Library, Three Lakes: fourth Mon 1:00
$15.00 per year membership

Twin Ports Genealogical Society
(see Minnesota, Part 2)

Walworth County Genealogical Society
PO Box 159
Delavan, WI 53115-0159
(262) 728-3719 (Treasurer)
wcgs2000@hotmail.com
http://www.walworthcgs.com/index.html
Pegy Rockwell Gleich, President
meetings at United Methodist Church, 213
    South Second Street, Delavan, WI 53115:
    first Tue 7:00; Library in basement of the
    Aram Public Library: Tue 10:00–2:00,
    second Sat 11:00–2:00
Pub. *Walworth County Genealogical Society
    Newsletter*, bimonthly
$10.00 per year membership

Washburn County Genealogical Society
(102 West Second Avenue—location)
PO Box 366 (mailing address)
Shell Lake, WI 54871
(715) 468-2982
Bonnie Brandt, President
Memorial Day–Labor Day: Wed–Sat
    10:00–4:00
Pub. *Roots in Washburn County*, quarterly
$7.00 per year membership; research fees
    vary

Waukesha County Genealogical Society
PO Box 1541
Waukesha, WI 53187-1541
Pub. *WCGS Newsletter*, three times per year
("Waukesha County only; we are private
    citizens who work on our own family
    trees; we have no office and no
    government funding; send an SASE if you
    want a reply.")
$10.00 per year membership; SASE for list of
    researchers who require minimum of three
    hours with payment in advance for
    research in Waukesha County and
    Milwaukee only

Waupaca Area Genealogical Society
PO Box 42
King, WI 54946
WaupacaAreaGenSoc@hotmail.com
http://www.rootsweb.com/~wiwaupac/
    WAGS/WAGS.htm
meetings at the Holly History and Genealogy
    Center: second Thur 6:30
$10.00 per year membership

White Pine Genealogical Society

Marinette Chamber
601 Marinette Avenue
Marinette, WI 54143-1633

Winnebagoland Genealogical Society
Oshkosh Public Library
106 Washington Avenue
Oshkosh, WI 54901-4985
Pub. *Winnebagoland Roots*, quarterly
$7.00 per year membership

Independent Publications and Miscellany

Camp Five Museum Foundation, Inc.
5480 Connor Farm Road
Laona, WI 54541
(715) 674-3414; (715) 674-7400 FAX
Catherine C. Dellin, President
trains: Mon–Sat (mid-June to late Aug)
    11:00, noon, 1:00, 2:00
(historical logging museum with active
    blacksmith shop)

Chalet of the Golden Fleece
618 Second Street
New Glarus, WI 53574
(608) 527-2614

Friends of Beckman Mill
(1019 North 17th Street—location)
PO Box 1986 (mailing address)
Manitowoc, WI 54221-1986
(920) 682-6229
stude14@sbcglobal.net
http://www.beckmanmill.org
Harold (Buzz) Beckman
(preservation society with link to Beckman
    family genealogy on web site)
$15.00 per year membership

Jackson County, WI, Genealogy
W11770 County Road P
Black River Falls, WI 54615-5926
http://discover-net.net/~sdeddy
Sue Eddy

**Madeline Island Historical Preservation
Association**
PO Box 250
La Pointe, WI 54850

Madison Trust for Historic Preservation
PO Box 296
Madison, WI 53701-0296
thetrust@madisontrust.org
http://www.madisontrust.org

New Richmond Preservation Society
New Richmond Heritage Center
1100 Heritage Drive
New Richmond, WI 54017
(715) 246-3276; (888) 320-3276; (715) 246-
    7215 FAX
nrpsinc@pressenter.com
http://www.pressenter.com/~nrpsinc
Mon–Fri 10:00–4:00
Pub. newsletter
$5.00 per year membership

WiGenWeb
Part of The USGenweb Project
tsvickery@adelphia.net;
    makkuehl@yahoo.com
http://www.rootsweb.com/~wigenweb
Tina Vickery, State Coordinator; Marcia Ann
    Kuehl, Assistant Coordinator
(links to other Wisconsin resources)

Wisconsin Department of Transportation
Map and Publications Sales

DOT Map Sales
(3617 Pierstorff Street [Truax
    Field]—location)
PO Box 7713 (mailing address)
Madison, WI 53707
(608) 246-3265
kenneth.cowan@dot.state.wi.us;
    william.schloemen@dot.state.wi.us
http://www.dot.state.wi.us/dtid/bhd/
    maps.html
Ken Cowan; Bill Schloemer

Wisconsin Land Records
http://searches.rootsweb.com/cgi-
    bin/wisconsin/wisconsin.pl

Wisconsin State Old Cemetery Society
(6100 West Mequon Road, Mequon, WI
    53092—location)
8724 West Magnolia Street (mailing address)
Milwaukee, WI 53224-4024
(414) 771-7781
Robert J. Felber
by appointment with president
Pub. *Inscriptions: Newsletter of the
    Wisconsin State Old Cemetery Society*,
    four or five times per year
("cemetery stone inscriptions" and
    preservation interests)
$8.00 per year membership

Wyoming

Archives and Libraries with Holdings in Genealogy

State Archives and Library

Wyoming State Archives
Archives and Historical Research
Barrett State Office Building
2301 Central Avenue
Cheyenne, WY 82002
(307) 777-7826; (307) 777-7044 FAX
wyarchive@state.wy.us
http://wyoarchives.state.wy.us (includes many
    items posted online)
Curtis Greubel, Supervisor
Research Room: Mon–Fri 8:00–4:45
Pub. *Wyoming History News*, bimonthly;
    *"Old News": Wyoming State Archives
    Newsletter* (online)
("This unit collects and manages public
    records from Wyoming state and local
    governments that have long-term
    administrative, legal, and historical value.
    These records document the activities of
    government in Wyoming and the history
    of the state and area available for research.
    Archives and Historical Research also
    collects nongovernmental records of
    historical value concerning Wyoming and
    the western United States. This group of
    records includes: Western books and
    periodicals, Wyoming newspapers,
    manuscript collections, Wyoming and
    western maps, military records, Wyoming
    business records, historical photographs,
    and biographies.")

Wyoming State Library
Supreme Court Building
2301 Capitol Avenue
Cheyenne, WY 82002-0060
(307) 777-7281; (307) 777-6289 FAX
http://www-wsl.state.wy.us
Mon–Fri 8:00–5:00
(no longer houses Wyoming State Genealogy
    Collection; see Laramie County Library
    System)

State Historical Society

Wyoming State Historical Society
1740 H184 Dell Range Boulevard
Cheyenne, WY 82002
(307) 635-4881
membership@wyshs.org
http://wyshs.org
Judy West, Membership Coordinator
Pub. *Annals of Wyoming: The Wyoming
    History Journal*, quarterly
(no archives or other collection)
$20.00 per year membership

City, County and Regional Archives and Libraries
(A more exhaustive list of public and
academic libraries can be found at
http://www-wsl.state.wy.us/libraries or
http://cowgirl.state.wy.us/directory.)

Albany County Public Library
310 South Eighth Street
Laramie, WY 82070-3969
(307) 721-2580, ext. 16
http://acpl.lib.wy.us
Boyd A. Broughton, Adult Services
Mon–Thur 10:00–8:00, Fri–Sat 1:00–5:00

Buffalo Bill Historical Center
Harold McCracken Research Library

720 Sheridan Avenue
Cody, WY 82414
(307) 587-4771
http://www.truewest.com/BBHC/index.htm

Casper College
Goodstein Foundation Library
Special Collections Department
125 College Drive
Casper, WY 82601
(307) 268-2680; (307) 268-2682 FAX
cspcbibman@wyld.state.wy.us
http://www.cc.whecn.edu/library/sc.htm

Goshen County Library
2001 East A Street
Torrington, WY 82240
(307) 532-3411
ihoy@will.state.wy.us
http://www-
    wsl.state.wy.us/goshen/index.html
Isabel Hoy, Director
Mon 8:00–8:00, Tue–Fri 10:00–6:00, Sat
    10:00–3:00

**Hot Springs County Museum and Cultural
Center**
700 Broadway
Thermopolis, WY 82443
(307) 864-5183
history@trib.com
http://w3.trib.com/~history
Dr. Alexandra F. Service, Director
summer: Mon–Sat 9:00–7:00, Sun
    1:00–5:00; winter: Mon–Sat 9:00–5:00
("Museum with historical and photographic
    archives, extensive information on
    families in Hot Springs County, WY.")
research: $10.00 per hour; photo prints:
    $4.00 per photo

Johnson County Library
171 North Adams
Buffalo, WY 82834
(307) 684-5546; (800) 661-7071; (307) 684-
    7888 FAX
njenning@will.state.wy.us
http://www-wsl.state.wy.us/johnson
Nancy L. Jennings, Genealogy and Local
    History
Mon–Thur 10:00–8:00, Fri–Sat 10:00–5:00
(specializes in homesteaders, Indian wars,
    Bozeman Trail, forts, oral histories, cattle
    war, all on local level, and area
    genealogy)
copy and postage charges

Laramie County Library System
Central Library
Genealogy Collection
2800 Central Avenue
Cheyenne, WY 82001-2799
(307) 634-3561, ext. 132; (307) 634-2082
    FAX
sseniawski@larm.lib.wy.us
http://www.lclsonline.org
Sue Seniawski, Genealogy Specialist; Lucie
    Osborn, Director
Mon–Thur 10:00–9:00, Fri–Sat 10:00–6:00,
    Sun (Sept–May) 1:00–5:00
(western history; houses Laramie County
    Library System Genealogy Collection,
    over 10,000 volumes covering the U.S.
    and some foreign countries and other
    local historical and genealogical
    collections)

Museum of the Great Plains
(see Oklahoma, Part 2)

Park County Library System
Cody Library

1057 Sheridan Avenue
Cody, WY 82414
(307) 527-8820; (307) 527-8823 FAX
parkill@will.state.wy.us
http://www-wsl.state.wy.us/park
Mary Robinson
Mon & Thur noon–5:30 & 7:00–9:00,
    Tue–Wed & Fri 10:00–5:30, Sat
    10:00–1:00

Platte County Public Library
Wyoming Room
904 Ninth Street
Wheatland, WY 82201
(307) 322-2689; (307) 322-2783 (Wyoming
    Room); (800) 841-0964; (307) 322-3540
    FAX
jhenion@will.state.wy.us
http://www-wsl.state.wy.us/platte/index.html
Julie Henion, Director

Riverton Branch Library
1330 West Park Avenue
Riverton, WY 82501
(307) 856-3556; (307) 857-3722 FAX
riverton@will.state.wy.us
http://www.fremontcountylibraries.org
Mon–Tue & Thur noon–9:00, Wed
    9:00–9:00, Fri 9:00–1:00

Riverton Museum/Research Library
700 East Park Avenue
Riverton, WY 82501
(307) 856-2665
lokejo@bresnan.net
http://www.wyoming.com/~rivmus

Sheridan County Fulmer Library
Wyoming Room
335 West Alger Street
Sheridan, WY 82801
(307) 674-8585, ext. 7 (Wyoming Room);
    (307) 674-7374 FAX
sherwyo@will.state.wy.us
http://www.sheridanwyolibrary.org
Karen Woinoski, Wyoming Room Supervisor
Wyoming Room: Mon–Thur 9:00–9:00,
    Fri–Sat 9:00–5:00

Sweetwater County Historical Museum
3 East Flaming Gorge Way
Green River, WY 82935
(307) 872-6435; (307) 872-3234 FAX
http://www.sweetwatermuseum.org
Ruth Lauritzen, Director
Apr–Dec: Mon–Sat 10:00–6:00; Jan–Mar:
    Mon–Fri 9:00–5:00
Pub. *Overland & Underground*, quarterly
minimal copy and photo reproduction fees;
    research: "inquiries accepted by mail, e-
    mail & telephone—small projects only"

Teton County Historical Research Center
c/o County Clerk's Office
(105 Mercill Avenue—location)
PO Box 1727 (mailing address)
Jackson, WY 83001-1727

Teton County Library
Western Americana, Special Collections
(125 Virginian Lane—location)
PO Box 1629 (mailing address)
Jackson, WY 83001
(307) 733-2164; (307) 733-4568 FAX
tetnref@will.state.wy.us
http://tclib.org/information/indexJH.html
Mon–Thur 10:00–9:00, Fri 10:00–5:30, Sat
    10:00–5:00, Sun 1:00–5:00

Uinta County Library System
Reference Services
701 Main Street

Evanston, WY 82930
(307) 789-1328; (307) 789-0128 FAX
dcollum@will.state.wy.us
http://www-wsl.state.wy.us/uinta
Dale Collum, County Library Director
Mon–Thur 9:00–7:00, Fri–Sat 9:00–5:00
(local cemetery listings, local newspapers on
  microfilm)

University of Utah Marriott Library
(see Utah, Part 2)

University of Wyoming
(American Heritage Center, Centennial
  Complex, 13th and Ivinson—location)
PO Box 3924 (mailing address)
Laramie, WY 82071-3924
(307) 766-4114; (307) 766-5511 FAX
AHCRef@UWyo.edu
http://www.uwyo.edu/ahc/geninfo.htm
Rick Ewig, Assistant Director; Lori Olson,
  Reference Archivist
winter: Mon–Fri 8:00–5:00, Sat 11:00–5:00;
  summer: Mon–Fri 7:30–4:30, Sat
  11:00–5:00
Pub. *Heritage Highlights*, biannually
no charge

University of Wyoming Library
(13th and Ivinson Streets—location)
PO Box 3334, University Station (mailing
  address)
Laramie, WY 82071-3334
(307) 766-3224; (307) 766-2070 (Coe
  Reference)
CoeRef@uwyo.edu
http://www-lib.uwyo.edu

Western Heritage Center
(see Montana, Part 2)

**Western Wyoming Community College
Library**
2500 College Drive
Rock Springs, WY 82902-0428
(307) 382-1700; (307) 382-7665 FAX
http://www.wwcc.cc.wy.us/college/library

Weston County Museum District
Anna Miller Museum
(401 Delaware—location)
PO Box 698 (mailing address)
Newcastle, WY 82701
(307) 746-4188; (307) 746-4629 FAX
annamm@mail1.trib.com
Bobbie Jo Tysdal, Director
Mon–Fri 9:00–5:00
("*Newcastle Newsletter Journal* 1890–1949,
  court dockets, Cambria records, photo
  archives")

Historical Societies—Local and Regional

Albany County Historical Society
1409 Downey Street
Laramie, WY 82070
(307) 742-5988
http://www.uwyo.edu/ahc/achs/index.html

**American Historical Association, Pacific
Coast Branch**
(see California, Part 2)

**American West Research Center and
Historical Society, Inc.**
(see Ohio, Part 2)

**Centennial Valley Historical
Association—Nici Self Museum**
(2734 Highway 130—location)

PO Box 200 (mailing address)
Centennial, WY 82055
(307) 742-7158
haemavrick@aol.com
Jane H. Houston, Secretary
Mon & Fri–Sun 1:00–4:00; special tours can
  be arranged as requested
("Historical museum—much is Wyoming,
  ranching, lumbering, mining and
  railroading.")
$5.00 per year membership

Fort Bridger Historical Association, Inc.
Fort Bridger State Historic Site
(37000 Business Loop I-80—location)
PO Box 112 (mailing address)
Fort Bridger, WY 82933
(307) 782-3842; (307) 782-7181 FAX
ftbridger@bvea.net
Tisa L. Cheney, Administrative Assistant
Winter: 9:00–5:00; Summer: 8:00–6:30
("Chapter of the Wyoming State Historical
  Society, operates the Museum sales desk
  with many historical books and historical
  items.")
$9.00 per year membership, plus $20.00 per
  year membership in the Wyoming State
  Historical Society

Fort Laramie Historical Association
(3½ miles southwest of the Town of Fort
  Laramie on Highway 160—location)
HC 72, Box 389 (mailing address)
Fort Laramie, WY 82212
(307) 837-2662; (800) 321-5456
Pat Fullmer, Business Manager
Mon–Sun 8:00–4:30 (except Christmas,
  Thanksgiving, and New Year)
Pub. *Mail Order Catalog*, annually
("We have one of the best western book
  stores to choose titles from including
  westward expansion, overland migration,
  Native Americans, western military
  history, and Fort Laramie specific.")
$10.00 per year membership

**Fort Phil Kearney/Bozeman Trail
Association**
PO Box 5013
Sheridan, WY 82801
Patty Myers, Secretary
Pub. *Lookout*, three times per year (Nov,
  Mar, July)
("Historic sites at Fort Phil Kearney and
  along the Bozeman Trail; focus on Indian
  Wars related history, 1864–1868.")
$10.00 per year membership

Lincoln County Historical Society
Kemmerer, WY 83101

Niobara County Historical Society
Stagecoach Museum
(322 South Main—location)
PO Box 367 (mailing address)
Lusk, WY 82225
(307) 334-3444 (Museum)
Mon–Sat 10:00–5:00 (if staff is available)
$10.00 per year membership; research: $5.00
  per hour

Park County Historical Society Archives
1002 Sheridan Avenue
Cody, WY 82414
(307) 527-8530
Jeanie Cook
Mon–Fri 9:00–noon & 1:00–4:00
(a small local history archive center; Park
  County and Big Horn Basin)
$3.50 per year membership

**Saratoga Historical and Cultural
Association**
Saratoga Museum
(104 Constitution Avenue—location)
PO Box 1131 (mailing address)
Saratoga, WY 82331
(307) 326-5511
Pat Bensen, Museum Director
Memorial Day weekend–Labor Day: daily
  1:00–5:00
$10.00 per year membership

Star Valley Historical Society
PO Box 1212
Afton, WY 83110

Sublette County Historical Society, Inc.
Museum of the Mountain Man
(700 East Hennick—location)
PO Box 909 (mailing address)
Pinedale, WY 82941
(307) 367-4101; (307) 367-6768 FAX
Laurie M. Latta, Executive Director
1 May–1 Oct: Mon–Sun 10:00–6:00; winter:
  by appointment
Pub. *Beaver Plew*, three times per year, not
  available by subscription
(mountain men, local history, western
  settlement)
$25.00 per year membership

Genealogical Societies

Genealogical Societies—Local & Regional

Albany County Genealogical Society
PO Box 1902
Laramie, WY 82073-1902

Casper Amateur Genealogists
Casper College
Administration Building, Room 298
125 College Drive
Casper, WY 82601
Pam Martin, Genealogy Teacher
forwards queries to the Natrona County
  Genealogical Society

Cheyenne Genealogical Society
Laramie County Library System
Genealogy Collection
2800 Central Avenue
Cheyenne, WY 82001
(307) 632-6676 (Book Chairman)
SLassField@aol.com
Sharon Lass Field, Book Chairman
(over 10,000 volumes covering the U.S. and
  some foreign countries)
research: ½ hour search for specific data for
  SASE

Fremont County Genealogical Society
Riverton Branch Library
1330 West Park Avenue
Riverton, WY 82501
(307) 856-5310; (307) 856-3556 (Library)
Marlys Bias, Editor
Library: Mon–Tue & Thur noon–9:00, Wed
  9:00–9:00, Fri 9:00–1:00
Pub. *Nostalgia News*, quarterly
$10.00 per year or $3.00 per copy

**Laramie Peekers Genealogy Society of
Platte County, Wyoming**
1108 21st Street
Wheatland, WY 82201
Cindy Anderson

Natrona County Genealogical Society
PO Box 9244
Casper, WY 82609
(307) 265-0206
Pam Martin, President

$3.50 per year membership

Park County Genealogy Society
PO Box 3056
Cody, WY 82414

Powell Valley Genealogical Club
(830 North Day—location)
PO Box 184 (mailing address)
Powell, WY 82435

Sheridan Genealogical Society, Inc.
Wyoming Room, Sheridan County Fulmer
Library
335 West Alger Street
Sheridan, WY 82801
(307) 674-8585, ext. 7 (Wyoming Room)
Wyoming Room: Mon–Thur 9:00–9:00,
   Fri–Sat 9:00–5:00
Pub. *Dusty Trails*, quarterly
(county obituary, marriage, naturalization,
   homestead records)
$10.00 per year membership; queries: $1.00

Sublette County Genealogy Society
PO Box 1186
Pinedale, WY 82941

Tri-State Genealogical Society (SDGS)
(see South Dakota, Part 2)

Independent Publications and Miscellany

El'n Al Enterprises
PO Box 62
Kaycee, WY 82639-0062
http://www.buffalo.com/JohnsonCounty/
   jchist/jchistmn.htm#mainmenu
(history of Johnson County)

Historic Milwaukee, Inc.
828 North Broadway, Suite 110
Milwaukee, WI 53202
histmilw@execpc.com
http://www.historicmilwaukee.org
Sandy Ackerman, Executive Director
(primarily historical and preservationist, not
   genealogical)

Laramie Plains Museum
603 Ivinson Avenue
Laramie, WY 82070
(307) 742-4448

Rock River Museum
131 Avenue C
Rock River, WY 82058
(307) 2386

State Historic Preservation Office
6101 Yellowstone Road, Second Floor
Cheyenne, WY 82002
(307) 777-7697; (307) 777-6421 FAX
http://commerce.state.wy.us/cr/SHPO

Trail End State Historic Site
400 Clarendon Avenue
Sheridan, WY 82801
(307) 674-4589; (307) 672-1729 FAX
cgeorg@missc.state.wy.us
http://wave.sheridan.wy.us/~trailend.
   index/html
Cynde Georgen, Site Superintendent
June–Aug: 9:00–6:00; spring/fall: 1:00–4:00;
   closed 15 Dec–31 Mar

WyGenWeb
Part of The USGenweb Project
sleonard@wyoming.com
http://www.rootsweb.com/~wygenweb

Carol Haagensen, State Coordinator;
   Suzanne Leonard, Assistant Coordinator
(links to other Wyoming resources)

Wyoming Department of Transportation
5300 Bishop Boulevard
Cheyenne, WY 82009-3340
(307) 777-4375 (Information)
http://wydotweb.state.wy.us

**Wyoming Geographic Information
Advisory Council (WGIAC)**
(address withheld upon request)

Wyoming Pioneer Memorial Museum
(400 West Center Street—location)
PO Box 911 (mailing address)
Douglas, WY 82633
(307) 358-9288; (307) 358-9293 FAX
Arlene Ekland-Earnst, Curator
summer: Mon–Fri 8:00–5:00, Sat 1:00–5:00;
   winter: Mon–Fri 8:00–5:00

Yellowstone National Park Museum
PO Box 168
Yellowstone National Park, WY 82190
(307) 344-2262
http://www.cr.nps.gov/csd/collections/
   yell.html

Trust Territories

American Samoa

Archives and Libraries with Holdings in Genealogy

Office of Archives and Records
American Samoa Government
Pago Pago, AS 96799
(684) 699-6848; (684) 699-6849 FAX
asgoarm@blueskynet.as
James B. Himphill, Territorial Archivist
Mon–Fri 7:30–4:00
(U.S. Naval Station records 1900–1951;
   Department of Interior records
   1951–1977; and American Samoa
   government records from 1977; microfilm
   collections start from the 1840s; bilingual
   Samoan-English services)
$5.00 research/certification fee for village
   censuses or certified statements

Historical Societies—Local and Regional

**American Historical Association, Pacific
Coast Branch**
(see California, Part 2)

Guam

Archives and Libraries with Holdings in Genealogy

**City, County and Regional Archives and
Libraries**

**Richard Flores Taitano Micronesian Area
Research Center**
University of Guam
UOG Station
Mangilao, GU 96913
(671) 735-2160; (671) 734-7403 FAX
http://www.uog.edu/mard
Omaira Brunal-Perry, Head Librarian
Mon–Fri 9:00–5:00
("Research library—Guam and Micronesia.")
contact librarian for fees

Historical Societies—Local and Regional

**American Historical Association, Pacific
Coast Branch**
(see California, Part 2)

Mariana Islands

Historical Societies—Local and Regional

**American Historical Association, Pacific
Coast Branch**
(see California, Part 2)

Independent Publications and Miscellany

**Commonwealth Council for Arts and
Culture**
(Capitol Hill, Saipan—location)
PO Box 553 CHRB (mailing address)
Saipan, MP 96950
(670) 322-9982; (670) 322-9983; (670) 322-

9028 FAX
Genevieve S. Cabrera, Executive Director
Mon–Fri 7:30–4:30
Pub. *Fina'tinas Marianas*, annually, free
  public service publication

Puerto Rico

Archives and Libraries with Holdings in Genealogy

City, County and Regional Archives and Libraries

Conservation Trust of Puerto Rico
PO Box 4747
San Juan, PR 00905
(787) 722-5834

Genealogical Societies

Genealogical Societies—Local & Regional

Hispanic Genealogical Society of New York
(see Ethnic Archives, Libraries and
Societies—Spanish, Part 3)

**Puerto Rican/Hispanic Genealogical
Society**
25 Ralph Avenue
Brentwood, NY 11717-2424
(631) 834-2511
(list of Hispanic genealogical resources by
  country)

Virgin Islands

Archives and Libraries with Holdings in Genealogy

Territorial Archives and Library

**Virgin Islands Department of Conservation
and Cultural Affairs**
Enid M. Baa Library and Archives
Division of Libraries, Museums and
Archeological Services
(20 Dronningens Gade, Saint Thomas, VI
08802—location)
PO Box 390 (mailing address)
Charlotte Amalie
Saint Thomas, VI 00801
(340) 774-0630
June A. V. Lindqvist, Librarian, Von
  Scholten Collection
Mon–Fri 9:00–5:00, Sat 9:00–3:00

Saint Croix Landmarks Society
Library and Archives
52 Estate Whim
Frederiksted
Saint Croix, VI 00840
(340) 772-0593
sxlslib@viaccess.net
Carol Wakefield, Librarian; Barbara Hagan-
  Smith, Archivist
Tue–Fri 1:00–5:00, Sat 10:00–4:00
Pub. *Postkassen* (not genealogy oriented),
  quarterly
$35.00 per year membership; research: fees
  private ("There is, at present, insufficient
  staff to do research")

Part 3. Ethnic and Religious Organizations and Research Centers

Ethnic Archives, Libraries and Societies

General

Balch Institute for Ethnic Studies of The Historical Society of Pennsylvania
Center for Immigration Research
18 South Seventh Street
Philadelphia, PA 19106-3794
(215) 925-8090
library@hsp.org (Research Inquiries)
http://www.balchinstitute.org
Dr. John Tenhula
Mon–Sat 9:00–5:00
Pub. *New Dimensions*

California Ethnic and Multicultural Archives (CEMA)
University of California
Davidson Library
Santa Barbara, CA 93106
(805) 893-8563; (805) 893-3062; (805) 893-4676
http://www.library.ucsb.edu//speccoll/cemabro.html

Center for Ethnic Studies
Kent State University
University Library
Room 318
Kent, OH 44242
Lubomyr R. Wynar, Editor
Pub. *Ethnic Forum*

Ethnic Cultural Center of Minnesota
400 Third Avenue, South
South Saint Paul, MN 55075
(651) 455-4449

Ethnic Heritage Council of the Pacific Northwest
305 Harrison Street, Suite 322
Seattle, WA 98109-4645
(206) 443-1410
Jennifer Kulik, Director
9:30–5:30
Pub. *Calendar: Monthly Guide to Northwest Ethnic Events*, $15.00 per year subscription; *Contact: Directory of Ethnic Organizations in Washington*, biannually, $12.00 per issue; *Fortelling*, quarterly
$30.00 per year membership

Ethnic Research Archives
229 Montclair Avenue
Newark, NJ 07104
(973) 482-2297
Dr. Charles Allan Baretski, Executive Director and Archivist
(not open to the public)

Genealogical Institute
(Independent Publications, Part 1)

Harvard University
Peabody Museum of Archaeology and Ethnology
11 Divinity Avenue
Cambridge, MA 02138
(617) 495-2254; (617) 495-2248 (General Information)
C. C. Lamberg-Karlovsky, Director
Mon–Sat 9:00–4:30, Sun 1:00–4:30

International Museum of Cultures
7500 West Camp Wisdom Road
Dallas, TX 75236
(972) 298-9446

Maryland Ethnic Heritage Commission
Department of Housing and Community Development
100 Community Place
Crownsville, MD 21032-2023
(410) 514-7000; (800) 756-0119 (in Maryland)
customerservice@dhcd.state.md.us
http://www.dhcd.state.md.us
Pub. *Tapestry*; *Directory of Ethnic Organizations, Associations, Clubs and Societies*

National Association for Ethnic Studies, Inc.
Department of English
Arizona State University
Box 870302
Tempe, AZ 85287-0302
(480) 965-2197
Susan L. Rockwell, Director
Pub. *Ethnic Studies Review*, three times per year; *Explorations in Sights and Sounds*, annually; *The Ethnic Reporter*, semiannually
$45.00 per year membership

New York State Association of European Historians
27 Maple Avenue
Highland, NY 12528
(845) 691-8062

UCLA Fowler Museum of Cultural History
405 Hilgard Avenue
Los Angeles, CA 90024-1549
(310) 825-4361
Betsy Escandor, Administrative Assistant
Administrative Offices: Mon–Fri 8:00–noon & 1:00–5:00; Galleries: Wed–Sun noon–5:00, Thur noon–8:00
(non-Western material culture, not genealogical)

The University of Texas at El Paso
Centennial Museum
Wiggins and University
El Paso, TX 79968-0533
(915) 747-5565
Pat Mora, Director
(collections in ethnology)

The WorldGenWeb Project
jarvis@arizona.edu
http://www.worldgenweb.org
Mike Jarvis, North America Board Member
(Links to sites for individual countries)

Acadian
(see French)

African-American
(see also Melungeon)

African American Cultural Alliance
(1819 Charlotte Avenue, Nashville, TN 37203—location)
PO Box 22173 (mailing address)
Nashville, TN 37202
(615) 299-0412; (615) 254-0970

Kwame Lillard, President
Office: 4:00–8:00
("We perform historical events, African American Civil War tributes.")

African American Cultural and Genealogical Society
(314 North Main—location)
PO Box 25251 (mailing address)
Decatur, IL 62523
(217) 429-7458
AACGS@springnetl.com
http://www.milikin.edu/academics/UniversityWidePrograms/africanamericansociety.html
Jean Tohill, Executive/Program Director

African-American Cultural Center
350 Masten Avenue
Buffalo, NY 14209
(716) 884-2013; (716) 885-2590 FAX
Agnes M. Bain, Executive Director; Alicia Banner, Assistant Director
Mon–Fri 10:00–9:00, Sat 10:00–6:00
$5.00 per year membership

African American Cultural Heritage Center and Museum
3434 South R.L. Thornton Freeway
Dallas, TX 75224
(972) 375-7530

African American Genealogical Association/Trans-Catawba
Office of Historical Coordinator
211 West Water Street
Lincolnton, NC 28092
(704) 736-8442

African-American Genealogy Group (AAGG)
PO Box 27356
Philadelphia, PA 19118-0356
(215) 572-6063; (215) 885-7244 FAX
info@aagg.org
http://www.aagg.org/index.html

African American Museum
1765 Crawford Road
Cleveland, OH 44106
(216) 791-1700
Linda Cross, Executive Director
Mon–Tue & Thur–Fri 10:00–5:00, Sat–Sun 11:00–3:00
$20.00 per year membership (includes free general admission)

African American Museum and Library at Oakland
PO Box 71043
Oakland, CA 94612-7143
(510) 597-5053; (510) 597-5030
E. Hope Hayes, Administrative Director
Tue 11:30–7:00, Wed–Thur & Sat 10:00–5:30, Fri noon–5:30
Pub. *From the Archives*, quarterly
(specializes in African Americans in California)
$20.00 per year membership

African American Museum and Research Center
The Walker Foundation
705 West Van Buren Avenue
Las Vegas, NV 89106
(702) 647-2242

African American National Capital Area Historical and Genealogical Society
PO Box 34683
Washington, DC 20043

African Americans in Southeastern Ohio (AFROAMSEO)
mperdrea@oucsace.cs.ohiou.edu
http://www.seorf.ohiou.edu/~xx057
Michel S. Perdreau, Executive Director

Africana Studies Research Center Library
Cornell University
310 Triphammer Road
Ithaca, NY 14850
(607) 255-3822; (607) 256-5229; (607) 255-0784 FAX
afrlib-mailbox@cornell.edu
http://www.library.cornell.edu/africana
James E. Turner, Director

AfriGeneas: African Ancestored Genealogy
PO Box 4906
Blue Mountain, AL 36204
(256) 820-8794; (256) 820-8339 FAX
feedback@afrigeneas.com;
    webguru@afrigeneas.com
http://www.afrigeneas.com
B. J. Smothers, Website Coordinator)

Center for Afroamerican and African Studies
(200 West Hall—location)
University of Michigan
550 East University Street (mailing address)
Ann Arbor, MI 48109
(734) 764-5518 (Main Office); (734) 764-5518 (Library); (734) 763-0543 FAX
Professor Sharon F. Patton, Director of Center; Elizabeth James, Librarian
Mon–Thur 10:00–5:00, Sun 1:00–5:00
(reference/resource center with print and nonprint materials, limited resources on genealogy)

Afro-American Communities Project
Constitution Avenue between 12th and 14th Streets
Room C-340, National Museum of American History
Smithsonian Institution
Washington, DC 20560
(202) 357-3182
James O. Horton, Ph.D., Director

Afro-American Cultural and Historical Society
8716 Harkness Road
Cleveland, OH 44106
(216) 795-3121
Icabod Flewellen, Curator and Historian
by special permission

Afro-American Heritage Association
PO Box 451
Rome, NY 13440
(315) 337-5018
Mrs. Jessie Thorpe, Librarian/Museum Chairperson

Afro-American Historical and Cultural Museum
67 West Sharpnack Street
Philadelphia, PA 19119-2722
(215) 574-0380
http://www.fieldtrip.com/pa/55740380.htm
Nannette A. Clark, Executive Director
Tue–Sat 10:00–5:00, Sun noon–6:00
Pub. *Insight—Quarterly Newsletter*
(African American history and art of Philadelphia, Delaware valley, and Pennsylvania, national and internationally focused exhibition occasionally)

Afro-American Historical and Genealogical Society, Inc.
PO Box 73067
Washington, DC 20056-3067
(202) 234-5356; (202) 829-8970; (202) 829-9280 FAX
http://www.aahgs.org
Barbara Dodson Walker
Pub. *AAHGS News*, bimonthly; *Afro-American Historical and Genealogical Society Journal*, two times per year
$35.00 per year membership

Afro-American Historical and Genealogical Society
North Alabama
109 Gorham Drive
Huntsville, AL 35811

Afro-American Historical and Genealogical Society
Tucson
2501 North Goyette
Tucson, AZ 85712
emilyricketts@webtv.net
http://aztucson.com/nonprofit/aahgs-tucson
membership in the national organization is a prerequisite for membership in the local chapter

Afro-American Historical and Genealogical Society
Arkansas Chapter
PO Box 4294
Little Rock, AR 72214
(501) 225-2029 FAX
ttenplewis@aol.com
http://arkansas.aahgs.org
Tamela Tenpenny-Lewis, President
Pub. *AAHGS Arkansas "NEWS"*
$50.00 per year chapter dues plus membership in the national organization

Afro-American Historical and Genealogical Society
James Dent Walker Chapter
PO Box 60632
Washington, DC 20039-0632
(202) 722-0408
cah_howard@msn.com
http://www.rootsweb.com/~mdaahgs
Charles A. Howard

Afro-American Historical and Genealogical Society Central Florida
Central Florida Chapter
PO Box 1347
Orlando, FL 32802-1347
(407) 836-8332 (7:30–4:15)
kom222@yahoo.com
http://www.rootsweb.com/~flcfaahg
K. O. Mitchell, President
Pub. *Chapter Newsletter*, monthly (online)

Afro-American Historical and Genealogical Society
Metro Atlanta Chapter
PO Box 54063
Atlanta, GA 30308
notrub18@bellsouth.net
Carolyn Corpening Row, President

Afro-American Historical and Genealogical Society
Little Egypt
207 Lendview Drive
Carbondale, IL 62901
membership in the national organization is a prerequisite for membership in the local chapter

Afro-American Historical and Genealogical Society
PO Box 438652
Chicago, IL 60643
membership in the national organization is a prerequisite for membership in the local chapter

Afro-American Historical and Genealogical Society
Baltimore
PO Box 9366
Baltimore, MD 21229-3125
membership in the national organization is a prerequisite for membership in the local chapter

Afro-American Historical and Genealogical Society
Central Maryland
PO Box 648
Columbia, MD 21045
JGourdin@comcast.net
membership in the national organization is a prerequisite for membership in the local chapter

Afro-American Historical and Genealogical Society
Prince George's County Maryland Chapter
PO Box 44252
Fort Washington, MD 20744-4252
(301) 292-2751
quinns12@att.net
http://pgcm.aahgs.org
William Q. O. Shelton, President
meetings at Saint Ignatius of Loyola Catholic Church, 2315 Brinkley Road, Oxon Hill, MD 20745: third Sat (Sept, Nov, Jan, Mar, May)
$10.00 per year chapter dues plus membership in the national organization

Afro-American Historical and Genealogical Society
New England
42 Laurelwood Drive
Stoughton, MA 02072
membership in the national organization is a prerequisite for membership in the local chapter

Afro-American Historical and Genealogical Society
Landon Creek
3934 Monsols Drive
Florissant, MO 63034
margaret.j.durham@niduscenter.com
membership in the national organization is a prerequisite for membership in the local chapter

Afro-American Historical and Genealogical Society
145 Van Nostrand Avenue
Jersey City, NJ 07305
0b104216m1121p@cs.com
membership in the national organization is a prerequisite for membership in the local chapter

Afro-American Historical and Genealogical Society
Chapter 2000
55 West 68th Street
New York, NY 10023
(212) 799-0322
AMartin219@aol.com
Antonia Cottrell Martin
meetings: quarterly

membership in the national organization is a
prerequisite for membership in the local
chapter

**Afro-American Historical and
Genealogical Society**
Jean Sampson Scott Chapter-Greater New
York
PO Box 022340
Brooklyn, NY 11201-0049
(212) 330-7882 (Answering service)
wilk112@msn.com
http://www.aahgsny.org
membership in the national organization is a
prerequisite for membership in the local
chapter

**Afro-American Historical and
Genealogical Society**
North Carolina/Piedmont-Triad
PO Box 36254
Greensboro, NC 27416
northampto@aol.com
http://www.people-places.com/aahgs
Larnar DeLoatch, President
membership in the national organization is a
prerequisite for membership in the local
chapter

**Afro-American Historical and
Genealogical Society**
Pittsburgh
PO Box 5707
Pittsburgh, PA 15208
aahgspgh08@aol.com
http://www.rootsweb.com/~mdaahgs/
pittsburgh to http://pittsburgh.aahsg.org
membership in the national organization is a
prerequisite for membership in the local
chapter

**Afro-American Historical and
Genealogical Society**
H-Town Chapter
Texas Southern University Law Library
3100 Cleburne
Houston, TX 77004
aahgs-htown@sbcglobal.net
http://htown.aahgs.org
Karim T. Aldridge-Rand, President
membership in the national organization is a
prerequisite for membership in the local
chapter

**Afro-American Historical and
Genealogical Society**
Hampton Roads
PO Box 2448
Newport News, VA 23609-2448
selinva@aol.com
membership in the national organization is a
prerequisite for membership in the local
chapter

**Afro American Historical and
Genealogical Society of Delaware**
512 East Fourth Street
Wilmington, DE 19801
(302) 571-9300 voice & FAX

**Afro-American Historical Association of
Fauquier County**
(4249 Loudoun Avenue—location)
PO Box 340 (mailing address)
The Plains, VA 20198
(540) 253-7488
aaha@infi.net

**Afro-American Historical Association of
the Niagara Frontier**
PO Box 1663
Buffalo, NY 14216

(716) 883-4418
Monroe Fordham, President
Pub. *Afro-Americans in New York Life and
History: An Inter-disciplinary Journal*,
semiannually

Afro-Gen
PO Box 17684
Nashville, TN 37217
(615) 399-7064
Dr. Tammie M. Young, Director
(Black family genealogy/history; school's
history)

Alexandria Black History Resource Center
638 North Alfred Street
Alexandria, VA 22314-1823
(703) 838-4356, (703) 706-3999 FAX
http://ci.alexandria.va.us/
libraries_museums/bhrc.html
Audrey Davis, Assistant Director
Tue–Sat 10:00–4:00
("The Watson Reading Room, a
noncirculating research repository
focusing on issues of African-American
history and culture . . . provides more
information on history than specifically on
genealogy. Nevertheless, the Watson
Reading Room currently has over 2,000
holdings documenting the history of
African Americans.")

The Amistad Research Center
Tilton Memorial Hall, Tulane University
6823 Saint Charles Avenue
New Orleans, LA 70118-5698
(504) 865-5535; (504) 862-3222; (504) 865-
5580 FAX
arc@mailhost.tcs.tulane.edu
http://www.arc.tulane.edu/~amistad
Donald DeVore, Executive Director
Mon–Sat 9:00–4:30
Pub. *Amistad Reports*, quarterly
(African-Americans, Native Americans,
Hispanics, Asian-Americans; houses
American Home Missionary Society
Collection; "Genealogical reference books
only.")

**The Association for the Study of Afro-
American Life and History, Inc.**
1407 14th Street, N.W.
Washington, DC 20005-3705
(202) 667-2822; (202) 387-9802 FAX
asalh@earthlink.net
Irena T. Webster, Executive Director
Mon–Fri 9:00–5:00
Pub. *Negro History Bulletin*, quarterly,
$30.00 per year subscription; *Journal of
Negro History*, quarterly, $25.00 per year
subscription
$40.00 per year membership

**Avery Research Center for African
American History and Culture**
College of Charleston
125 Bull Street
Charleston, SC 29424
(843) 727-2007; (843) 727-2017 FAX
http://www.cofc.edu/library/avery/avery.html
Dr. W. Marvin Dulaney, Executive Director;
Dr. Karen Chandler, Director
Mon–Sat noon–5:00
(African-American history and culture in
South Carolina, very little material on
genealogy)

Beck Cultural Exchange Center, Inc.
1927 Dandridge Avenue
Knoxville, TN 37915
(865) 524-8461
Robert J. Booker, Executive Director

Tue–Sat 10:00–6:00
(local Black history, photographs,
biographies, books of oral histories)
free admission to galleries

Bethune Museum and Archives, Inc.
National Historic Site
1318 Vermont Avenue, N.W.
Washington, DC 20005
(202) 332-9201
Bettye Collien-Thomas, Ph.D., Executive
Director
Pub. *Legacy*
(Afro-American women's history)

Black Archives History Foundation
5400 N.W. 22nd Avenue
Miami, FL 33142
(305) 636-2390; (305) 636-2391 FAX

Black Archives of Mid-America
2033 Vine
Kansas City, MO 64108
(816) 483-1300

Black Catholic History Project
Office of Black Catholics
Archdiocese of Washington (District of
Columbia)
(5001 Eastern Avenue—location)
PO Box 29260 (mailing address)
Washington, DC 20017-0260
(301) 853-4579; (301) 853-7671 FAX
obc@adw.org
Jacqueline E. Wilson, Executive Director
9:00–5:00
Pub. *Newsletter: To Give Light*, bimonthly
(Black Catholics, African-Americans,
racism, Archdiocese of Washington
[Prince George's, Montgomery, St.
Mary's, Charles and Calvert counties,
Maryland, and Washington, DC]; some
Baltimore and national information)

Black Family History Society
PO Box 1515
Gilbert, AZ 85299-1515

Black Genealogy Research Group
c/o Giles
3745 S.W. Monroe Street
Seattle, WA 98126-3462
meetings at Douglass-Truth Library, 23rd
and Yesler, Seattle: first Sat 10:00

Black Genealogy Search Group
PO Box 40674
Denver, CO 80204-0674

Black Heritage Council
The Alabama Historical Commission
468 South Perry Street
Montgomery, AL 36130-0900
(334) 230-2661 (BHC); (334) 242-3184
(Commission); (334) 240-3477 FAX
(Commission)
http://www.preserveala.org/intro1.htm
Ardeania W. Ward, Black Heritage
Coordinator

Black Heritage Museum of West Alabama
Stillman College
PO Box 1430
Tuscaloosa, AL 35403
(205) 349-4240

Black Historical Society
4230 East 25th North
Wichita, KS 67220
(316) 683-1247

Black Historical Society of Santa Clara

468 North 11th Street
San Jose, CA 95112
(408) 295-9183

Black Resources Information Coordinating Services
614 Howard Avenue
Suite 125-9
Tallahassee, FL 32301
(850) 576-7522
Emily A. Copeland, President

Blockson Afro-American Collection
Temple University
Sullivan Hall, First Floor
12th Street and Berks Mall
Philadelphia, PA 19122
(215) 204-6632; (215) 204-5197
aberhanu@thunder.ocis.temple.edu
http://www.temple.edu/blockson

The Ollie L. Brown Afro-American Heritage Collection
Alabama State University
Montgomery, AL 36101
(334) 262-3581
Marcia Martin

Buffalo Genealogical Society of the African Diaspora
PO Box 2534
Buffalo, NY 14240-2534
(716) 878-8010; (716) 836-0126

California African-American Genealogical Society
PO Box 8442
Los Angeles, CA 90008-0442

California Afro-American Museum
600 State Drive, Exposition Park
Los Angeles, CA 90037

Census Schedules and Black Genealogical Research: One Family's Experience
deborah.hollis@colorado.edu
http://www.colorado.edu/libraries/
    govpubs/debbie/cover.htm
Deborah R. Hollis

Chattanooga African-American Heritage Museum
(200 East Martin L. King
Boulevard—location)
PO Box 11493 (mailing address)
Chattanooga, TN 37416
(423) 266-8658; (423) 267-1076 FAX
http://www.anet
Vilma Scruggs Fields, Director
Mon–Fri 10:00–5:00, Sat noon–4:00
Pub. *The Heritage*, quarterly
admisstion: $1.00 for adults

Christine's Genealogy Website
http://ccharity.com
(Africa, African American genealogy, Black
    history, slavery, and genealogy news and
    resources)

Public Library of Cincinnati and Hamilton County
(see Ohio, Part 2)

Clayton Library, Center for Genealogical Research
(see Texas, Part 2)

Compton Public Library
240 West Compton Boulevard
Compton, CA 90220
(310) 637-0202; (310) 537-1141 FAX
Sharon M. Johnson, Community Library

Manager
Tue–Thur 10:00–8:00, Fri 10:00–6:00, Sat
    10:00–5:00
("Our library is no longer the site of the
    Black Resource Center, a.k.a. Afro-
    American Resource Center. We still carry
    a substantial amount of Black titles,
    however they are general interest and not
    necessarily for scholarly research.")

Oliver Cromwell Black History Society
c/o Afri-Mail Institue
348 High Street
Burlington, NJ 08016
(609) 387-8133; (609) 877-1449; (609) 387-
    8144 FAX
http://bc.emanon.net/cgi-bin/burl/
    oliver_cromwell_society

Digging It Up African-American Research and Consulting Firm
70 Fairlie Street, Suite 330
Atlanta, GA 30303
(404) 688-6509
Herman "Skip" Mason, Jr., President
9:00–5:30
(professional research, speakers bureau,
    photo archives, tours, appraisals of Black
    memorabilia)
hourly fees and package fee

The DuSable Museum of African American History, Inc.
(57th East Cottage Grove Avenue—location)
740 East 56th Place (mailing address)
Chicago, IL 60637-1495
(773) 947-0600; (773) 947-0677 FAX
Gwendolyn Keita Robinson, Ph.D.,
    Executive Director
Museum: spring–fall: Mon–Wed & Fri–Sat
    10:00–5:00, Thur 10:00–6:00, Sun
    noon–5:00, winter: Mon–Sat 10:00–4:00,
    Sun noon–4:00; Museum Archives:
    Mon–Fri 9:00–5:00, Sat–Sun noon–5:00
$25.00 per year membership

First African Baptist Church Museum
(see Religious Archives and
Organizations—Baptist, Part 4)

First National Black Historical Society of Kansas
(601 North Water—location)
PO Box 2695 (mailing address)
Wichita, KS 67201
(316) 262-7651

Florida A & M University
Black Archives
Research Center and Museum
Tallahassee, FL 32307
(850) 599-3020
http://www.famu.edu/dev/
    Dblackarchives.html
James N. Eaton, Archivist/Curator

The Hollis Burke Frissell Library
Tuskegee Institute
Tuskegee, AL 36088
(334) 727-8888
Daniel T. Williams, Archivist
Mon–Thur 8:00–10:00 P.M., Fri 8:00–4:30

Great Plains Black Museum Archives and Int. Center
2213 Lake Street
Omaha, NE 68110
(402) 345-2212; (402) 345-6817
Bertha Calloway, Director

Hampton University
University Museum (Huntington Building)

Hampton, VA 23668
(757) 727-5374
Ramona Austin, Director; Donzella Maupin,
    Archives Assistant
Archives: Mon–Fri 8:00–5:00
(African and Native American)

Harrison Museum of African American Culture
523 Harrison Avenue, N.W., Ground Floor
Roanoke, VA 24016
(540) 345-4818; (540) 345-4831 FAX
Melody S. Stovall, Executive Director
Mon–Fri 10:00–5:00, Sat–Sun 1:00–5:00
Pub. *Brochure*, biannually; *Annual Report*
(local archives, museum store)

Indiana Historical Society
450 West Ohio Street
Indianapolis, IN 46202-3269
(317) 234-0049
wgibbs@indianahistory.org
http://www.indianahistory.org
Wilma Gibbs, Program Archivist
Library: Tue–Sat 10:00–5:00
Pub. *Black History News and Notes*,
    quarterly
$35.00 per year membership

Leavenworth Afro-American Historical Society
PO Box 3151
Fort Leavenworth, KS 66027
(913) 651-4584

Lincoln University
Inman E. Page Library
Jefferson City, MO 65101
(573) 681-5501
Elizabeth Wilson, Director
Mon–Thur 8:00–10:00, Fri 8:00–5:00, Sat
    10:00–4:00, Sun 3:00–10:00
(African-American history and culture)

Maryland Commission on Afro-American History and Culture
Banneker-Douglass Museum of Afro-
American Life and History
Mount Moriah A.M.E. Church
84 Franklin Street
Annapolis, MD 21401
(410) 269-2893
http://www.marylandhistoricaltrust.net/
    bdm.html
Steven C. Newsome, Executive Director
Museum: Tue–Fri 10:00–3:00, Sat
    noon–4:00

Middletown African-American Historical Society
4521 Poppy Drive
Middletown, OH 45044-5228
(513) 424-1791

Moorland-Spingarn Research Center
Howard University
500 Howard Place, N.W.
Washington, DC 20059
(202) 806-7239
Dr. Thomas C. Battle, Director
Mon–Thur 9:00–4:45, Fri 9:00–4:30
(African and African-American)
fee schedule for photoduplication services

Morgan County African-American Museum
(156 Academy Street-location)
PO Box 482 (mailing address)
Madison, GA 30650
(706) 342-9191; (706) 342-9197 FAX

Historical Society of Mount Pleasant,

Ohio, Inc.
(underground railroad, see Ohio, Part 2)

Museum of Afro-American History
Abiel Smith School
46 Joy Street
Boston, MA 02114
(617) 742-1854
http://www.boston.com/arts/museums/
    musafam.htm

**National Afro-American Museum and
Cultural Center**
1985 Velma Avenue
Columbus, OH 43211
(614) 466-1500
**The New York Public Library, Schomburg
Center for Research in Black Culture**
515 Malcolm X Boulevard
New York, NY 10037-1801
(212) 491-2200
http://www.nypl.org/research/sc/sc.html
Howard Dodson, Director
June–Sept: Mon & Wed noon–8:00, Tue &
    Thur–Fri 10:00–6:00; Oct–May:
    Mon–Wed noon–8:00, Thur–Sat
    10:00–6:00 (Archives closes at 5:00, art
    collection by appointment only)
Pub. *Journal of the Schomburg Center*,
    quarterly, $35.00 per year for subscription
    and notices of events
("Librarians at the Center are *not*
    genealogists and have only a rudimentary
    knowledge of genealogy; our specialty is
    Black history.")

**North Carolina Afro-American Heritage
Society**
PO Box 26334
Raleigh, NC 27611

**Ouachita African-American Historical
Society**
Northeast Louisiana Delta African American
Heritage Museum
PO Box 168
Monroe, LA 71210
(318) 323-1167 voice & FAX
Nancy T. Johnson, Director

**Parting Ways—The Museum of Afro-
American Ethnohistory, Inc.**
(130 Court Street, Plymouth, MA—location)
PO Box 541 (mailing address)
Marion, MA 02738
(508) 746-6028

**Pendleton Foundation for Black History
and Culture**
(address withheld upon request)

Penn Center, Inc.
York W. Bailey Museum
PO Box 126, Martin Luther King Boulevard
Saint Helena Island, SC 29920
(843) 8838-2432 Main Office; (843) 838-
    2474
info@penncenter.com
http://www.penncenter.com
Annette Teasdell, Acting Director of
    History/Culture
Mon–Sat 11:00–4:00, by appointment
Pub. *Penn Pals Newsletter*
("Los country African American history.
    Holdings are historical more than
    genealogical.")
admission: $4.00 for adults; research: $25.00

Persistence of the Spirit
http://www.aristotle.net/persistence
("an interpretive study of the people and
    events that contributed to the Black

experience in Arkansas")

Plantation Society in the Americas
(see Miscellaneous, Part 4)

Mattye Reed African Heritage Center
2711 McConnell Road
Greensboro, NC 27401

Rhode Island Black Heritage Society
46 Aborn Street
Providence, RI 02903

**River Road African American Museum
and Gallery**
PO Box 1357
Gonzales, LA 70707-1357
(225) 562-7703; (225) 647-5711 FAX
Kathe Hambrick, Museum Director

Saint Joseph's Historic Foundation, Inc.
804 Old Fayetteville Street
Durham, NC 27702
(919) 683-1709
Walter J. Norflett, Executive Director
(African American culture and history)

**San Diego African-American Genealogy
Research Group (SDAAGRG)**
(9026 Three Seasons Road, San Diego, CA
92126—location)
PO Box 740240 (mailing address)
San Diego, CA 92174-0240
(619) 262-5810
IBeMarti@aol.com
Margaret Lewis
meetings at the Malcolm-X Branch Library,
    Market & Euclid Streets: second Sat
    (Jan–Feb, Apr–May, July–Aug, Oct–Nov)
    10:00–1:00; meetings at the San Diego
    FHC: second Sat (Mar, June, Sept., Dec)
    10:00–1:00

**San Francisco African American
Historical and Cultural Society**
Fort Mason Center, Building C, Room 165
San Francisco, CA 94123
(415) 441-0640

Staten Island Institute of Arts and Sciences
75 Stuyvesant Place
Staten Island, NY 10301
Patricia Gordon Michael, Executive Director
Pub. *Proceedings of the SIIAS*
(history of the Black community)

Taps Quarterly
13509 Pendleton Street
Oxon Hill, MD 20022
Shannon Bridget Murphy
Pub. *Taps Quarterly*

**Tarrant County Black Historical and
Genealogical Society, Inc.**
PO Box 50432
Fort Worth, TX 76105-0432
Lenora Rolla, Executive Director; Gayle W.
    Hanson, Editor
Mon–Fri 11:00–5:00; meetings at Town
    Center Mall: first Mon 10:00
Pub. *Tarrant County Black Historical and
    Genealogical Society Newsletter*,
    bimonthly, $6.00 per year subscription
(Blacks of the southwest; early Black settlers
    of Tarrant County, Texas, especially the
    Fort Worth area)
$12.00 per year membership

Texas Historical and Ancestry Researchers
(1009 Eric Avenue, Arlington, TX 76012-
3205—location)
PO Box 122058 (mailing address)

Arlington, TX 76012-8058
(817) 276-1640
http://www.geocities.com/sunchief3
Gayle W. Hanson
Pub. *The Chronicle*, quarterly, $15.00 per
    year subscription
(specializes in Texas and African-American
    history and ancestry, research, publishes
    record abstracts)

Fred Hart Williams Genealogical Society
Detroit Public Library
Burton Historical Collection
5201 Woodward Avenue
Detroit, MI 48202-4093
(313) 438-3233; (313) 833-1480 (Library);
    (313) 832-0877 FAX (Library)
Roy L. Roulhac, President
Library: Tue & Thur–Sat 9:30–5:30, Wed
    1:00–9:00
Pub. *Quarterly Newsletter*

**Miriam B. Wilson Foundation/Old Slave
Mart Museum and Library**
6 Chalmers Street
Charleston, SC 29401
(843) 883-3797

Wisconsin Black Historical Society
2620 West Center Street
Milwaukee, WI 53206
(414) 372-7677

Albanian
(see also Eastern European, Italian)

American Indian
(see Native American)

Arab
(see Religious Archives and
Organizations—Islamic)

Armenian
(see also Religious Archives and
Organizations—Armenian)

Armenian Genealogical Society
PO Box 1383
Provo, UT 84603-1383
(801) 298-5358, ext. 570 (Ted Powell,
    Trustee)
audrey_megerian@byu.edu;
    Megerian@fhs.byu.edu
http://feefhs.org/am/frg-amgs.html
Audrey Megerian, President
Pub. *Armenian Records*
(filmed records from Australia, Austria,
    Bangladesh, Burma, Cyprus, Egypt,
    England, Greece, Hungary, India,
    Indonesia, Israel, Italy, Jordan, Lebanon,
    The Netherlands, Poland, Singapore,
    Switzerland, Turkey, U.S.A., the former
    U.S.S.R., and Yugoslavia)

Armenian General Benevolent Union
Alex Manoogian School Library
22001 Northwestern Highway
Southfield, MI 48075
(248) 569-2988
Linda Houhanisin, Media Specialist

**Armenian Library and Museum of
America (ALMA)**
65 Main Street
Watertown, MA 02172
(781) 926-2562; (781) 926-0175 FAX
Gary Lind-Sinanian, Curator
Mon & Sun 1:00–5:00, Tue 1:00–5:00 &
    7:00–9:00
Pub. *Armenian Library and Museum of*

America Newsletter, three times per year; *Alma Matters*, quarterly
(14,000 volumes in library, but very limited genealogical materials)
$35.00 per year membership

Armenian Research Center
University of Michigan-Dearborn
4901 Evergreen Road
Dearborn, MI 48128-1491
(313) 593-5181
gottenbr@umich.edu
http://www.umd.umich.edu/dept/armenian
Dennis R. Papazian, Director
Mon–Fri 9:30–6:30, and by appointment on weekends
("We receive 35 different periodicals, journals, and newspapers on a regular basis.")

National Association for Armenian Studies and Research, Inc. (NAASR)
6 Divinity Avenue
Cambridge, MA 02138
Pub. *Report*, quarterly; *Bulletin for Advancement of Armenian Studies*, semiannually

Asian
(see also Filipino)

The Amistad Research Center
(see African-American, above)

The Asia Society
725 Park Avenue
New York, NY 10021
(212) 288-6400

Association for Asian Studies
(address withheld upon request)
Pub. *Journal of Asian Studies*, quarterly; *Journal of Asian Business*, quarterly; *Newsletter*, five times per year
(not a resource for genealogical information)

China Institute in America
125 East 65th Street
New York, NY 10021
(212) 744-8181
F. Richard Hsu, President

Chinese American Cultural Association
1768 Sweetwood Drive
Daly City, CA 94015-2011
Nissi S. Wang

Chinese American Librarians Association (CALA)
University of California Irvine (UCI) Libraries
Irvine, CA 92623
http://www.lib.siu.edu/swen/cala/calachap.htm (chapters)
Sally Tseng, CALA Executive Director

Chinese Culture Center of San Francisco
750 Kearny Street, Third Floor
San Francisco, CA 94108
(415) 986-1822; (415) 986-2825 FAX
http://www.c-c-c.org
Manni Liu, Curator
Tue–Sun 10:00–4:00
Pub. *Chinese Culture Center Newsletter*, quarterly
(rotating art exhibitions, classes, lectures, genealogy research program)
$25.00 per year membership

Chinese Historical Society of America (CHSA)
965 Clay Street

San Francisco, CA 94108-1527
(415) 391-1188; (415) 391-1150
info@chsa.org
http://www.chsa.org
Melissa M. Szeto, Executive Director
Tue–Fri 11:00–4:00, Sat–Sun noon–4:00
Pub. *The Bulletin*, monthly; *Chinese America: History and Perspectives*, annually, $15.00
("Chinese American history, culture and art. CHSA Museum and Learning Center houses artifacts, photographs, and hosts programs, workshops and lectures on Chinese American history.")
$50.00 per year membership

Chinese Historical Society of Southern California
(415 Bernard Street, Los Angeles, CA 90012—location)
PO Box 862647 (mailing address)
Los Angeles, CA 90086-2647
(323) 222-0856; (323) 221-4162 FAX
chssc@chssc.org
http://www.chssc.org
Linda Chong
9:00–6:00
Pub. *News 'n Notes*, monthly and online, *Gum Saan Journal*, bi-annually

Council on East Asian Libraries
c/o East Asian Library
1100 East 57th Street
Chicago, IL 60637-1502
(773) 702-8436; (773) 702-6623 FAX
felsing@oregon.uoregon.edu
http://darkwing.uoregon.edu/~felsing/ceal/welcome.html

Gardena Library
Los Angeles County Public Library
1731 West Gardena Boulevard
Gardena, CA 90247
(310) 323-6363
Marjorie Delida, Senior Librarian
(Japanese-American)

Hawaii Chinese History Center
111 North King Street, Room 410
Honolulu, HI 96817
(808) 521-5948
Roger K. S. Liu, President
Mon, Wed & Fri 10:00–noon
Pub. *HCHC Newsletter*, quarterly, $10.00 per year subscription

Japanese American History Archives
1840 Sutter Street
San Francisco, CA 94115
(415) 776-0661
http://www.e-media.com/fillmore/museum/jt/jaha/jaha.html
(photo archives)

The Morikami Museum and Japanese Gardens
4000 Morikami Park Road
Delray Beach, FL 33446
(561) 495-0233; (561) 499-2557 FAX
Larry Rosensweig, Director
Tue–Sun 10:00–5:00
Pub. *The Morikami Newsletter/Calendar*, quarterly
(Japanese colony, Yawato, FL)
$35.00 per year membership

The New York Public Library, Asian and Middle Eastern Division
Fifth Avenue and 42nd Street, Room 219
New York, NY 10018-2788
(212) 930-0716

asiaref@nypl.org
http://www.nypl.org/research/chss/ort/ort.html
John M. Lundquist, Ph.D., The Susan and Douglas Dillon Chief Librarian

Pacific Asia Museum
46 North Los Robles Avenue
Pasadena, CA 91101
(626) 449-2742; (626) 449-2754 FAX
Paulitte Pang, Communications Coordinator
Wed–Sun 10:00–5:00
Pub. *Pacific Asia Museum Newsletter*, bimonthly
(Asian and Pacific Islands art and culture)
$37.00 per year membership

San Jose Historical Museum Archives
Chinese Historical and Cultural Project
1600 Senter Road
San Jose, CA 95112-2599
(408) 277-4017; (408) 287-2290 (Archives); (408) 277-3890 FAX (Archives)
http://www.dnai.com/~rutledge/CHCP_museum.html
Leslie Masunaga, Archivist
Archives: Mon–Fri by appointment, Wed 1:00–4:00
(San Jose, Santa Clara Valley, New Almaden Mines)
museum admission: $4.00 for adults; copies: 15¢ per page

University of Washington Libraries
(see Washington, Part 2)

Vietnam Foundation
6713 Lumsden Street
McLean, VA 22101

Wing Luke Asian Museum
407 Seventh Avenue, South
Seattle, WA 98104
(206) 623-5124 (Education Express); (206) 623-5190
Peter Moy, President, Board of Trustees; Ron Chew, Director, Museum; Charlene Mano, Education Coordinator
Museum: Tue–Fri 11:00–4:30, Sat–Sun noon–4:00
Pub. *Newsletter*, quarterly
(specializes in Asian Americans)
$30.00 per year membership

Assyrian
(see Religious Archives and Organizations—Islamic)

Australian

Australian Family History Compendium
Australian Institute of Genealogical Studies
coherent@cohsoft.com.au
http://www.cohsoft.com.au/afhc/aigs.html
Pub. *Genealogist*, quarterly, $25.00 per year

National Archives of Australia
http://www.naa.gov.au/Publications/memento/memento.html (*Memento*)
Linda Macfarlane, Access Services
Canberra Reading Room: Mon–Sat 9:00–5:00, Tue 9:00–9:00
Pub. *Memento*, three times per year (also available online)

Western Australia Genealogical Society, Inc.
PO Box 4327
Davis, California 95617-4327
webmaster@wags.org.au
http://www.wags.org.au

John D. Movius, Alternate U.S. FEEFHS
Representative
Pub. *Quarterly Western Ancestor Newsletter*
$12.00 initiation fee, $36.00 per year
membership

Austrian
(see also Banat, Eastern European, Galician,
German, Hungarian, and Slovenian)

**American Committee to Promote Studies
of the History of the Habsburg Monarchy**
c/o Department of History
Louisiana State University
Baton Rouge, LA 70803
(225) 388-4471
Karl A. Roider, Jr., Ph.D., Executive
Secretary
Pub. *Newsletter for Habsburg and Austrian
History*

Baltic
(see Eastern European, Estonian, and
Lithuanian)

Banat

Banat Genealogy Mailing List
PO Box 262
Lapeer, Michigan 48446-0262
BANAT-admin@rootsweb.com
http://feefhs.org/banat/frgbanat.html
Chris J. Lamesfield, Moderator; Bob Madler,
President
(devoted primarily to the German settlers in
the Banat area, which comprised the
Hungarian counties of Torontal, Temes
and Krasso-Szereny, which lie north of
the Danube, east of the Tisza/Tisa and
south of the Maros Rivers, formerly part
of the Austrian Empire and divided after
WW II among Romania, Yugoslavia and
Hungary; also research interests in the
neighboring area of Batschka, formerly
the Hungarian county of Bacs-Bodrog,
which was between the Tisza/Tisa and
Danube Rivers)

Bangladesh
(see Asian)

Basque
(see also Spanish)

Basque Museum and Cultural Center
611 Grove Street
Boise, ID 83702
(208) 343-2671; (208) 336-4801 FAX
http://www.basquemuseum.com
Patty A. Miller, Executive Director
Tue–Fri 10:00–4:00, Sat 11:00–3:00

Basque Studies Program
(address withheld upon request)
(cannot respond to genealogical questions)

Buber's Basque Page
http://weber.u.washington.edu/~buber/
basque.html

Belarusian

Zhurtavannie Bialaruskaj Shliachty
(Association of the Belarusian Nobility)
2050 Spring Valley Road
Lansdale, PA 19446-5114
(215) 584-4742; (215) 688-0273 FAX
tarnowg@war.wyeth.com
http://feefhs.org/by/frg-zbs.html
George Tarnowski, FEEFHS Representative

(US)
Pub. *Hodnasc* (*Dignity*), irregularly; *Klejnot*,
at least three times per year
membership restricted to individuals of noble
descent

Belgian

The Belgian Researchers, Inc.
Belgian American Heritage Association
(BAHA)
62073 Fruitdale Lane
La Grande, OR 97850-5312
(541) 963-6697; (541) 962-7604 FAX
Pierre L. Inghels, President
Pub. *Belgian Laces*, quarterly
("specializes in history-genealogy-heraldry,
doing research for Belgians in the states
and for Belgian-Americans in Belgium")
$12.00 per year membership

**Center for Belgian Culture of Western
Illinois**
712 18th Avenue
Moline, IL 61265
(309) 762-0167
Joan Loete, Librarian/Genealogist
Wed & Saturday afternoons, and by
appointment
Pub. *Newsletter*, monthly
$15.00 per year membership

**Genealogical Society of Flemish-
Americans**
18740 Thirteen Mile Road
Roseville, MI 48066
(810) 776-9579 (Secretary)
Margaret Roets, Corresponding Secretary
Library: 10:00–2:30, and by appointment;
meetings: Sept–June: second & fourth Sat
Pub. *Flemish-American Heritage*,
semiannually (Feb, Aug); *Genealogical
Society of Flemish-Americans Newsletter*,
semiannually
$10.00 per year membership

Genealogie in België
Sylvain.Devriendt@advalvas.be,
Auteur/Commentaar
http://users.skynet.be/sky60754/genealbe

Peninsula Belgian American Club
1255 North 12th Place
Sturgeon Bay, WI 54235-1159
(920) 743-4973
kmpd@charter.net
http://www.rootsweb.com/~wipbac
Kim Potier Davis, Secretary/Treasurer

Rock Island County Historical Society
(see Illinois, Part 2)

University of Wisconsin—Green Bay
Cofrin Library
(see Wisconsin, Part 2)

Bohemian
(see Czech and German)

BosNet
webwiz@bosnet.org
http://www.bosnet.org
(Bosnian Ingathering Manuscript Program)

Bosnian
(see also Eastern European)

Breton
(see French and Irish)

British
(see also Cornish, English, Irish, Scottish
and Welsh)

British Data Archive, Ltd.
100064.737@compuserve.com
http://BritishDataArchive.com
Nigel Bayley
24 hour information and ordering
(publishes UK census material on CD-ROM
and DVD, containing original images of
census records, indexed by street and
area; free catalog)

**Public Library of Cincinnati and Hamilton
County**
(see Ohio, Part 2)

Bukovinian

Bukovina Society of the Americas
(722 Washington—location)
PO Box 81 (mailing address)
Ellis, KS 67637-0081
(785) 625-9492; (785) 726-4568
windholz@bukovinasociety.org;
LJensen@aol.com
http://www.bukovinasociety.org
Oren Windholz, President; Larry R. Jensen,
Webmaster
Pub. *Bukovina Society of the Americas
Newsletter*, quarterly
(Bukovina: From 1775 to 1918, the
easternmost crown land of the Austrian
Empire; now divided between Romania
and Ukraine; Bukowina or Buchenland in
German, Bukowina in Polish, Bucovina in
Romanian, and Bukovyna in Ukrainian)
$10.00 per year membership

Bulgarian
(see also Eastern European)

Byelorussian
(see also Eastern European and Russian)

Cajun
(see French)

Canadian
(see also French)

Association Canado-Américaine
PO Box 989
Manchester, NH 03105-0989
(800) 222-8577
http://www.acafraternal.org/~aca

Heritage North
(see New York, Part 2)

**National Archives of Canada/Archives
nationales du Canada**
(613) 995-5138 (General
Inquiries/Renseignements généraux);
(613) 992-3884 (Reference
Services/Services à la reférénce); (613)
996-7458 (Genealogy Services,
Renseignements généaolgiques); (613)
943-0837 (Personnel Records/Dossiers
personnels); (866) 578-7777 (toll free
number/Numéro sans frais); (613) 995-
6274 FAX; (613) 947-8456 (Personnel
Records)
http://www.archives.ca
Reference Room (where the Reference and
Genealogy Desks are located) Mon–Fri
(except statutory holidays) 8:30–5:00;
Reading Room: (Mon–Fri (and statutory
holidays) 8:00–6:00

**The National Library of Canada
(NLC)/Bibliothèque Nationale du Canada**
http://www.nlc-bnc.ca

**The New England Historic Genealogical
Society**
(see Massachusetts, Part 2)

**Northern New York American-Canadian
Genealogical Society**
(see New York, Part 2)

**Saint Lawrence Valley Genealogical
Society**
(see New York, Part 2)

Carpatho-Russian
(or Ruthenian, see also Slovak, below, and
Religious Archives and
Organizations—Orthodox)

Carpatho-Rusyn Knowledge Base
PO Box 339
Davisburg, MI 48350-0339
(248) 620-0234 FAX
http://www.carpatho-rusyn.org
Gregory A. Gressa, Director; Megan A.
Smolenyak, Assistant Director

Carpatho-Rusyn Research Center
PO Box 131B
Orwell, VT 05760
Pub. *The Carpatho-Rusyn American*,
quarterly, $12.00 per year subscription

The Carpatho-Rusyn Society
125 Westland Drive
Pittsburgh, PA 15217-2538
http://www.carpatho-rusyn.org
Richard D. Custer, Editor
Pub. *New Rusyn Times*, six times a year
$20.00 per year membership

Lemko Association
(555 Provinceline Road—location)
PO Box 156 (mailing address)
Allentown, NJ 08501-0156
(609) 758-1115; (609) 758-7301 FAX
Alexander Hezenchak, President
9:00–5:00
Pub. *Karpatska Rus*, twenty-three times per
year
(Carpatho-Rusyn)
$20.00 per year membership

Osturna Descendants
119 Belvedere Street
Nazareth, PA 18064-2112
(610) 759-2740; (610) 882-8836, FAX
http://feefhs.org/rusyn/frg-od.html
Mike Smolenyak, Co-editor
Pub. *Osturna Descendants*, quarterly, $8.00
per year subscription
(Osturna was originally the most western
outpost of the Carpathian-Rusyn ethnic
region and is now in the Republic of
Slovakia, on the border with Poland)

The Rusin Association of Minnesota
1817 121st Avenue, N.E.
Blaine, MN 55449
(763) 754-7463
Rusinmn@aol.com
http://feefhs.org/rusyn/frg-ramn.html
Karen Varian, President
Pub. *Trembita*, quarterly
("Rusin [Carpatho-Rusin]")
$10.00 per year membership

Celtic
(see also Irish, Scottish and Welsh)

Celtic Studies Publications, Inc.
PO Box 639
Andover, MA 01810-0011
(978) 474-9193; (978) 474-0592 FAX
CelticSP@aol.com

Channel Islandish
(see English)

Chicano
(see Spanish)

Chinese
(see Asian)

Cornish
(see also English and Irish)

The Cornish American Heritage Society
5 Hampton Court
Neptune, NJ 07753-5672
http://www.cousinjack.org
Nancy Oster Heydt, President
biannual "Gathering of Cornish Cousins"
Pub. *Tam Kernewek*, quarterly
(Cornish genealogy)
$10.00 per year membership

**Pennsylvania Cornwall
Association—Penkernewek**
301 West Pennsylvania Avenue
Pen Argyl, PA 18072
(610) 863-9537
hfbray@epix.net
http://www.pacornish.org
Harry Bray, Treasurer
Pub. *Newsletter*, quarterly
$15.00 per year membership

Creole
(see also French and Spanish)

Plantation Society in the Americas
(see Miscellaneous, Part 4)

Croatian
(see also Eastern European and Hungarian)

**The Association for Croatian Studies
(ACS)**
Department of History
John Carroll University
Cleveland, OH 44118
(216) 397-4758
George J. Prpic

Croatia Genealogy Home Page
PO Box 4327
Davis, CA 95617-4327
http://dcn.davis.ca.us/~feefhs/cro/frg-hr.html

Croatian Ethnic Institute, Inc.
4851 South Drexel Boulevard
Chicago, IL 60615
(773) 373-4670; (773) 373-4746 FAX
croetljubo@aol.com
http://www.croatian-institute.org
Ljubo Krasić, Director
Mon–Sat 9:00–noon & 2:00–5:00
Pub. *Croatian Almanac-Hrvatski Kalendar*,
annually, $15.00 subscription
admission: free

Croatian Fraternal Union
100 Delaney Street
Pittsburgh, PA 15235
(412) 351-3909
Pub. *Zajednicar*, weekly
$45.00 per year Associate membership

**Croatian Genealogical and Heraldic
Society**
2527 San Carlos Avenue
San Carlos, CA 94070-1747
(650) 592-1190
croatians@aol.com
http://www.croatians.com
Adam S. Eterovich, Founder
by appointment

Croatian Heritage Museum and Library
34900 Lake Shore Boulevard
Willoughby, OH 44095-2043
(440) 946-2044

Croatian Information Service
PO Box 660546
Arcadia, CA 91006

Croatian National Association
1608 South Fremont
Alhambra, CA 91803

Croatian Roots
PO Box 462
Salisbury, CT 06068
fritz@croatianroots.com
http://www.croatianroots.com
Fritz Frigan

Cuban
(see also Spanish)

Circulo Guinerode Los Angeles
434 South Alvarado Street
Los Angeles, CA 90057
(213) 483-9126
Efren Besanilla, President
(Cuban)

Cuban Genealogical Resources
http://www.cubagenweb.org
Ed Elizondo, Webmaster

Cuban Genealogical Society
PO Box 2650
Salt Lake City, UT 84110-2650
(801) 968-7312
http://www.rootsweb.com/~utcubangs
Mayra F. Sanchez-Johnson, President
5:00–9:00
Pub. *Revista*, three times per year
$20.00 per year membership

University of Miami
Archives and Special Collections
Department
(see Florida, Part 2)

Czech
(see also Eastern European, Slovak, and
Polish)

**Archives of the Czechs and Slovaks
Abroad**
The University of Chicago Library
c/o June Pachuta Farris, Curator
1100 East 57th Street
Chicago, IL 60637-1502
(773) 753-2856 (Dr. Hruban)
http://www.lib.uchicago.edu:80/libinfo/
sourcesbysubject/slavic/acasa.html
Dr. Zdenek Hruban, Contact Person
by appointment only
(primarily a research collection, not
organized for genealogical searching;
specializes in Czechs, Slovaks and
Moravians, general and local history of
Czech and Slovak emigration)

California Czech and Slovak Club

PO Box 20542
Castro Valley, CA 94546-8542
(510) 581-9986; (510) 581-0213 FAX
http://www.rahul.net/njs/ccsc/index.html
Ilonka Martinka-Torres, President
Pub. *Noviny* (*News*), four times per year
(Mar, June, Sept, Dec)
(maps, dictionaries, novelty items, books;
translation services available; Czech,
Slovak, Moravian, Ruthenian, and
Silesian history, language, culture,
heritage and customs; Czech and Slovak
genealogy, heritage, culture and customs)
$15.00 per year membership

Czech and Slovak American Genealogy Society of Illinois
PO Box 313
Sugar Grove, IL 60554-0313
Jzel@aol.com
http://members.aol.com/chrismik/csagsi.htm
Joe Hartzel, President; Paul S. Valasek,
D.D.S., Editor
Pub. *Koreny* (*Roots*), quarterly
(interested in Bohemia, Slovakia, Moravia,
Silesia, Ruthenia, etc.)
$15.00 per year membership

Czech and Slovak Genealogical Society of Arizona (CSGSA)
4921 East Exeter Boulevard
Phoenix, AZ 85018-2942
djanca@worldnet.att.net
http://www.rootsweb.com~azcsgsa
Dorothy Janca, President
Pub. *Vcera a dnes Journal*
$20.00 per year membership

Czech and Slovak Search Group
209 South Ogden
Denver, CO 80209-2321

The Czech, Bohemian, and Moravian Genealogical Research Page
(314) 831-9482
Czeching@iarelative.com
http://iarelative.com/czech
Greg Kopchak

Czech Cultural Club
(13th and Martha Streets—location)
2234 South 13th Street (mailing address)
Omaha, NE 68103
Lorraine Duggin, Secretary
Pub. *Sokol Omaha News*, about ten times per
year
$10.00 per year membership

Czech Heritage Preservation Society, Inc.
PO Box 3
Tabor, SD 57063
(605) 589-3494
Vlasta Miller, Secretary
Pub. *CHPS Annual Newsletter*, annually
(Oct)
$3.00 per year membership

Czech Heritage Society of Texas
4810 Spellman
Houston, TX 77035
(713) 726-0282
Anna Kprec, State President
Pub. *Cesky Hlas*, quarterly
(specializes in history of Czechs in Texas,
and genealogy)
$8.00 per year membership

Czechoslovak Genealogical Society International
(1650 Carroll Avenue, Saint Paul, MN
55104—location)
PO Box 16225 (mailing address)

Saint Paul, MN 55116-0225
(612) 645-4585
cgsi@aol.com
http://members.aol.com/cgsi
Mark Vasko-Bigaouette
Pub. *Nase Rodina (Our Family) Quarterly
Publication*, quarterly; *Rocenka*, bi-yearly
(every other year)
(Bohemian, German, Hungarian, Jewish,
Moravian, Russian, Ruthenian, Silesian
and Slovak ancestry)
$20.00 per year membership

Czechoslovak Heritage Museum, Library and Archives
CSA Fraternal Life
122 West 22nd Street
Oak Brook, IL 60521
(630) 795-5800
Pub. *CSA Journal (Journal
Czechoslovenskych Spolku V Americe)*,
monthly
(Czech, Moravian, and Slovak)
$12.00 per year subscription

National Czech and Slovak Museum and Library
30 16th Avenue S.W.
Cedar Rapids, IA 52404-5904

Oklahoma Czechs, Inc.
(Fifth and Cedar, Yukon, OK
73099—location)
PO Box 850211 (mailing address)
Yukon, OK 73085
(405) 354-7573
Al Zajic, President
meetings: last Mon 7:30

Old Homestead Publishing Company
PO Box 45
Hallettsville, TX 77964
Doug Kubicek, Editor
Pub. *Nase Dejiny, The Magazine of Czech
Genealogy*, bimonthly

Old Mobeetie Association of Mobeetie Jail Museum
(see Texas, Part 2)

Radio Prague History Online
http://www.radio.cz/history

Society for the History of Czechoslovak Jews, Inc.
(see Jewish, below)

Sokol Detroit
23600 West Warren Avenue
Dearborn Heights, MI 48127
(313) 278-2558
Mr. G. Durkin
Pub. *Sokol Detroit News*, monthly, $5.00 per
year subscription

Wilber Czech Museum
(102 West Third Street—location)
PO Box 253 (mailing address)
Wilber, NE 68465
(402) 821-2183

Danish
(see also Swedish and Norwegian)

C. A. Dana—Life Library
(see Religious Archives and
Organizations—Lutheran, Part 3)

Danish American Fellowship
4200 Cedar Avenue, South
Minneapolis, MN 55407
(612) 729-3800

Danish-American Genealogical Group
Minnesota Genealogical Society
5768 Olson Memorial Highway
Golden Valley, MN 55422
(763) 595-9347 (Library)
wcholm@aol.com
http://www.wolfbors.com/~danish
Bill Holmquist
fourth Mon (except Aug & Dec) in the
Danish-American Fellowship Center
$12.00 per year membership

Danish American Heritage Society
4105 Stone Brooke Road
Ames, IA 50010
(515) 232-7479
James D. Iversen, President
Pub. *The Bridge*, semiannually; *Newsletter*,
semiannually
("The DAHS is a historical association
interested in recording the contributions
of Danish immigrants to American culture
and society.")
$30.00 per year membership to DAHS, c/o
Grand View College, Third Floor West
Old Main, 1200 Grandview Avenue, Des
Moines, IA 50316-1599

Danish Emigration Archives
http://www.cybercity.dk/users/ccc13656

The Danish Immigrant Museum
Family History and Genealogy Center
(4210 Main Street—location)
PO Box 249
Elk Horn, IA 51531-0249
(712) 764-7008; (877) 764-7008; (712) 764-
7010 FAX
genealogy@danishmuseum.org;
librarian@danishmuseum.org
http://www.danishmuseum.org/genealogy
Michele McNabb, Librarian/Manager
Nov–Apr: Tue–Wed & Fri 10:00–4:00;
May–Oct: Tue–Wed, Fri, and first & third
Sat 9:00–5:00
Pub. *America Letter* (not genealogical,
except for an article from the Family
History and Genealogy Center), three
times per year
admission: $5.00 for adults, $2.00 for 8–17
year olds; $20.00+ per year membership;
search fees vary

University of Washington Libraries
(Scandinavian, see Washington, Part 2)

Dutch
(see also Belgian; for "Pennsylvania Dutch"
see German)

Albany Museum: Ancestry Research-Genealogy
W.Jervois@ru.ac.za
http://www.ru.ac.za/departments/am/
geneal.html
William Jervois, Resident Genealogist
Mon–Fri 8:00–12:45 and most afternoons

Amherst Museum Genealogy Society
Amherst Museum
Nederlander Research Library and Archives
(see New York, Part 2)

Datatrace Systems
(see Miscellaneous, Part 4)

Dutch Family Heritage Society
2463 Ledgewood Drive
West Jordan, UT 84084-5738
(801) 967-8400; (801) 963-4604 FAX
Mary Lynn Spijkerman Parker, President and
Editor

Pub. *Dutch Family Heritage Society Quarterly*
(specializes in Dutch in America, Dutch culture, and genealogical research in America and The Netherlands, includes book reviews, immigrant databases)
$20.00 per year membership

The Dutch Settlers Society of Albany
Rural Delivery 2, Box 313
Altamont, NY 12009
Joan Burns, President
Pub. *Yearbook of the Dutch Settlers Society of Albany*, every two to three years
$25.00 regular or Associate membership the first year, $12.00 per year thereafter

The Frisian Roundtable
2885 Roosevelt Avenue
Bronx, NY 10465
Roy C. Ketlsen, Editor
Pub. *The Frisian Roundtable*

Greater Sioux County Genealogical Society Chapter (IGS)
(see Iowa, Part 2)

Heritage Hall-Calvin College and Calvin Theological Seminary Archives
3207 Burton Street, S.E.
Grand Rapids, MI 49546
(616) 957-6313; (616) 957-6146 FAX
http://www.calvin.edu/hh
Wendy Blankespoor
Mon–Fri 8:00–4:30
Pub. *Origins—Historical Magazine of the Archives*, semiannually, $10.00 per year subscription
(obituaries, anniversary announcements in *Banner* and *De Wachter* from 1868, shipping records 1835–1896, 1900–1940)
research: $15.00 per hour

Herrick Public Library
(see Michigan, Part 2)

Hillsboro Historical Society and Museum
(see Kansas, Part 2)

Holland Library
Market Street
Alexandria Bay, NY 13607
(315) 482-2241

The Holland Page
http://ourworld.compuserve.com/
     homepages/paulvanv/homepage.htm

Holland Society of New York Library
(see Lineage, Hereditary and Patriotic Societies, Part 4)

The Joint Archives of Holland
History Research Center
Hope College
PO Box 9000
Holland, MI 49422-9000
(616) 395-7798; (616) 395-7197
archives@hope.edu
Larry J. Wagenaar, Director
Mon–Fri 9:00–5:00 (call for holiday hours)
(houses "the collections of The Holland Historical Trust (Holland Museum) Hope College and Western Theological Seminary")
Pub. *The Joint Archives Quarterly*

Mennonite Historical Library
(see Indiana, Part 2)

New York Genealogical and Biographical Society Library

(see New York, Part 2)

Northwestern College
Ramaker Library
Dutch Heritage Room
101 Seventh Street
Orange City, IA 51041
(712) 707-7311; (712) 707-7247
jhilbe@nwciowa.edu
Judy Hilbelink, Curator
Mon–Thur 7:30–midnight, Fri 7:30
    A.M.–10:00 P.M., Sat 8:30 A.M.–5:00 P.M.,
    Sun 2:30 P.M.–midnight (closes at 4:30 weekdays and closed Sat & Sun during school holidays)

Historical Society Reformed Church of America
(see Religious Archives and Organizations—Reformed, Part 3)

TCI Genealogical Resources
(see Spanish, below)

Yvette's Dutch Genealogy Homepage
genealogy@twente.nl
http://www.twente.nl/~genealogy

Eastern European
(see also Balkan and Russian)

Federation of Eastern European Family History Societies (FEEFHS)
PO Box 4327
Davis, CA 95617-4327
(530) 753-3206
http://feefhs.org
John D. Movius, Second Vice President
Pub. *FEEFHS Newsletter*, quarterly (Jan, Apr, July, Oct), $10.00 per year subscription (does not include query privileges); *FEEFHS Addressbook & Resource Guide*, biannually, $4.00 postpaid (available in hard copy or on diskette in DOS 6.2)
(embraces the political boundaries of Albania, Austria [including Italy's Friuli and Tyrol], Belarus, Bosnia and Herzegovina, Bulgaria, Croatia, former Czechoslovakia [Czech and Slovak republics], Estonia, Germany [all, but emphasizing former East Germany], Greece, Hungary, Latvia, Lithuania, Macedonia, Moldova, Poland, Romania, Russia [including Siberia], Slovenia, Ukraine, Yugoslavia [both Serbia and Montenegro], and virtually all of the areas settled or once controlled by Germany [except Alsace-Lorraine], including East and West Prussia, the Baltic states, Polish Pomerania, Posen and Silesia, Galicia, the Banat, Rusin, Volhynia and all German-Russian colonies; maintains Internet lists of professional genealogists, translators, authors and lecturers)
$15.00 per year membership; free queries for members

The New York Public Library, Slavic and Baltic Division
Fifth Avenue and 42nd Street, Room 216-217
New York, NY 10018
(212) 930-0714 (General Reference); (212) 930-0935; (212) 930-0940 FAX; (212) 930-0693 FAX
slavicref@nypl.org
http://www.nypl.org/research/chss/slv/
    slav.balt.html
Wojciech Siemaszkiewicz
Mon & Thur–Sat 10:00–5:45, Tue–Wed
    11:00–7:15

("The Division has a number of checklists and published articles to materials pertaining to genealogy. Particular strengths include monographic and periodical works produced by the various immigrant communities in New York.")

Egyptian
(see also Religious Archives and Organizations—Islamic)

American Coptic Association
PO Box 9119
Jersey City, NJ 07304

English
(see also Cornish and Irish)

British Family Historical Society of Los Angeles
22941 Felbar Avenue
Torrance, CA 90505

British Heritage Society
4177 Garrick Avenue
Warren, MI 48091
(810) 757-4177
Anton_The_Lord_Hartforth@msn.com

British Interest Group of Wisconsin and Illinois (BIGWILL)
PO Box 192
Richmond, IL 60071-0192
(815) 455-7150; (608) 752-8816
bigwill@yahoo.com
http://www.rootsweb.com/~willbig
Ann Wells, President; Peggy Rockwell Gleich, Vice President
Grace Lutheran Church, 6000 Broadway Street, Richmond, IL: third Saturday of every other month (Jan, Mar, May, July, Sept, Nov)
Pub. *BIGWILL Newsletter*, six times per year (English, Irish, Scottish, and Welsh)
$15.00 per year membership

British Isles Family History Society-USA
(10741 Santa Monica Boulevard, West Los Angeles, CA 90025—library location)
2531 Sawtelle Boulevard, #134 (mailing address)
Los Angeles, CA 90064-3163
(310) 398-3924
Annie Lloyd, Editor
Mon & Fri–Sat 9:00–5:00, Tue–Wed & Thur 9:00–9:00; special British Isles research help: Wed 10:00–8:00; meetings: second Wed (except Aug & Dec) 7:00; classes on British and Irish genealogical subjects: second Wed (except Aug & Dec) 3:00
Pub. *Newsletter*, bimonthly; *British Isles Family History Society-USA, Journal*, quarterly (spring, summer, fall and winter); *Y Ddraig Goch* (The Red Dragon); quarterly
(English, Irish, Scottish, and Welsh)
$20.00 per year membership, plus $5.00 to join the Irish and the Welsh Interest Groups

British Isles Genealogical Research Association
PO Box 19775
San Diego, CA 92159-0775
(619) 469-1677 (England/Wales); (858) 453-9053 (Ireland); (858) 748-6589 (Scotland)
Klund@grossmont.k12.ca.us
Kathleen Lund, England/Wales Interest Group; Mary Russell, Ireland Interest Group; Tom Clark, Scotland Interest

Group
meetings at the Joyce Beers Community
Center: third Wed (Jan, Mar, May, July,
Sept, Nov), fourth Sat (Feb, Apr, June,
Aug, Oct)
Pub. *Newsletter*, quarterly
$15.00 per year membership

Channel Islands Genealogy
johnf14246@aol.com
http://www.rootsweb.com/~jfuller/ci.html
John Fuller

Colorado Cornish Cousins
7945 South Gaylord Way
Littleton, CO 80122

Cowles Magazines
6405 Flank Drive
Harrisburg, PA 17105
(717) 657-9555
Ed Holm, Editor
Pub. *British Heritage*, bimonthly, $19.95 per
year subscription

English Genealogical Society
Minnesota Genealogical Society, English
Branch
5768 Olson Memorial Highway
Golden Valley, MN 55422
(952) 881-6755
http://www.mngs.org/branches.html
Nancy Jensen
Tue & Thur 6:30–9:30, Wed–Thur & Sat
10:00–4:00
Pub. *Newsletter*, three times per year, $7.50
per year subscription

GENUKI Family History News
http://www.genuki.org.uk/news
Rob Thompson, Editor
Pub. *GENUKI Family History News* (e-zine)
(Included on GENUKI site, which also
features research guidance and searchable
database)

**International Society for British
Genealogy and Family History**
PO Box 3115
Salt Lake City, UT 84110-3115
http://www.genealogysourcecatalog.com/
ISBGFH.htm
Hazel M. Tibbitts, Corresponding Secretary
Pub. *International Society for British
Genealogy and Family History
Newsletter*, quarterly
$15.00 per year membership

Jersey Archives Service
http://www.jersey.gov.uk/heritage/
archives/jasweb.html

Krans-Buckland Family Association, Inc.
PO Box 1025
North Highlands, CA 95660-1025
(916) 332-4359; (916) 339-1633 FAX
jkbfa@worldnet.att.net
Joyce Buckland, Editor/President
by appointment only
Pub. *The English Researcher*, temporarily
discontinued
("In addition to our library of British
reference material, we also have a
considerable amount of history on the
early settlers of the Rio Linda, Elverta,
Reigo and Antelope areas of northern
Sacramento County.")

Museum of American Frontier Culture
(see Virginia, Part 2)

Public Record Office

http://www.open.gov.uk/pro/prohome.htm

Saint George's Society of New York
175 Ninth Avenue
New York, NY 10011-4977
(212) 924-1434; (212) 727-1566 FAX
info@stgeorgessociety.org
http://www.stgeorgessociety.org
$85.00 per year membership (limited to
"subjects, or descendants of subjects, of
England, the United Kingdom, the
Commonwealth, those who serve in
His/Her Britannic Majesty's Armed
Forces or husbands of members of the
Daughters of the British Empire, and
wives of Society members")

Society of Genealogists
http://www.cs.ncl.ac.uk/genuki/SoG
Pub. *Genealogists' Magazine*, quarterly
$20.00 per year membership

The Watkinson Library
Trinity College
300 Summit Street
Hartford, CT 06106
(860) 297-2268
Jeffrey H. Kaimowitz, Ph.D., Head Librarian
When college is in session: Mon–Fri
9:30–4:30, call for Sat & summer hours
(British history, topography, genealogy, and
heraldry)
no research services available

**Western Pennsylvania Genealogical
Society**
(see Pennsylvania, Part 2)

Eskimo
(see Native American)

Estonian
(see also Eastern European)

Estonian American National Council
Estonian House
243 East 34th Street
New York, NY 10016
(212) 684-0336
Jaan Ulesoo, President

Estonian Educational Society of Detroit
PO Box 344
Trenton, MI 48183
(734) 676-8783
Thomas Ruben, President

European
(see also Balkan, Eastern European, and
German)

**Genealogical Association of English
Speaking Researchers in Europe**
CMR 420, Box 142
APO, AE 09063
011-49-06227-51942; 011-49-06227-54008
FAX
Lou Hays Whitworth

Immigration History Research Center
University of Minnesota
(see Minnesota, Part 2)

Filipino

**Filipino American Historical Society of
Chicago**
5462 South Dorchester Avenue
Chicago, IL 60615-5309
(773) 752-2156; (773) 955-3635 FAX

Finnish
(see also Norwegian and Swedish)

Cokato-Finnish American Society
10783 County Road 3, S.W.
Cokato, MN 55321
(320) 286-2833

Family History Finland
545 Wildwind Drive, S.E.
Salem, OR 97302
(503) 315-8209
rumcd@open.org;
christopher.rumbaugh@ci.corvallis.or.us
http://www.open.org/~rumcd/genweb/
finn.html
Christopher D. Rumbaugh

Family Sleuths
PO Box 526163
Salt Lake City, UT 84152-6163
(801) 467-4201 voice & FAX
sleuths@sisna.com
http://feefhs.org/fi/frg-fs.html
Timothy Laitila Vincent, A.G.
(links to other sites; Finnish, Swedish,
Norwegian)

Genealogical Society of Finland
Finnish Genealogical Links
http://www.genealogia.fi/finnlinks
Mon 1:00–6:00, Tue 10:00–4:00, Thur
10:00–6:00, some Sat (check web site)
and by appointment

Finland Historical Society
(see Minnesota, Part 2)

Finn Creek Museum
Minnesota Finnish-American Historical
Society, Chapter 38
(four miles south of New York Mills on
County Road #135—location)
PO Box 134 (mailing address)
New York Mills, MN 56567
(218) 385-2200 (Chairperson); (218) 385-
2233 (Museum)
Reuben Anderson, Chairperson
Memorial Day–Labor Day: noon–5:00, and
by appointment
(preserving Finnish heritage)

**Finnish American Heritage Society of
Maine**
PO Box 249
West Paris, ME 04289
(207) 674-3094
Barbara Payne, Treasurer
Sept–June: third Sun
Pub. *The Maine Finn*, quarterly, $3.00 per
year subscription
$5.00 per year membership, restricted to
persons of Finnish descent, and their
spouses

Finnish-American Historical Archives
Finnish-American Heritage Center
Suomi College
601 Quincy Street
Hancock, MI 49930
(906) 487-7273; (906) 487-7347; (906) 487-
7367 (Heritage Center); (906) 487-7387
FAX (Heritage Center)
http://www.suomi.edu/lnk/FHC.html
(Heritage Center)
E. Olaf Rankinen, Archivist; Lorraine
Richards, Archives Assistant
Mon–Fri 9:00–4:00
$30.00 per year membership; research: fees
lower

Minnesota Finnish-American Historical

Society
Chapter 38
Route 3, Box 312
Sebeka, MN 56477
Fred Siirila, President
$7.00 per year membership

Finnish American Historical Society of Michigan, Inc.
19885 Melrose
Southfield, MI 48075
(248) 354-1994
Felix V. Jackonen, President

Finnish American Historical Society of North Dakota
HCR 2, Box 24
Lakota, ND 58344
(701) 259-2127
Ben Varnson

Finnish-American Historical Society of the West
PO Box 5522
Portland, OR 97228-5522
(503) 654-0448
http://www.teleport.com/~finamhsw
Gene A. Knapp, Editor/State Corp Agent
Mon–Fri 10:00–5:00
Pub. *Finnam Newsletter* (not genealogical), quarterly
(not able to respond to genealogical requests; documents immigrant culture using manuscrupts, oral histories, photographs and maps)
$10.00 per year membership

Finnish American League for Democracy
147 Elm Street
Fitchburg, MA 01420

Finnish Genealogy Group
Minnesota Genealogical Society
5768 Olson Memorial Highway
Golden Valley, MN 55422
(763) 595-9347 (Library)
http://feefhs.org/misc/frgfinmn.html
Joan Newman
Pub. *Newsletter*
$10.00 per year membership

Finnish Pioneer Crafts Guild
Superior Restorations, Inc.
PO Box 31
Greenbush, WI 53026
(920) 526-3433

Minnesota Historical Society
(see Minnesota, Part 2)

New York Mills/Finnish American Society
PO Box 316
New York Mills, MN 56567
(218) 385-2075; (218) 385-2085

Pasadena Historical Museum and Finnish Folk Art Exhibit
Pasadena Historical Society Research Library
470 West Walnut Street
Pasadena, CA 91103
(626) 577-1660
Tim Gregory, Archivist
Thur–Sun 1:00–4:00

Sampo Publishing, Inc.
PO Box 120804
New Brighton, MN 55112
(651) 636-6348
Mike Karni, Editor and Publisher
Mon–Fri 9:00–5:00
Pub. *Finnish Americana*, annually, $6.00 per issue, plus $1.00 postage and handling ("Finnish immigration to North America, its history and culture")

Sisu Heritage, Inc.
PO Box 127
Embarrass, MN 55732
(218) 984-2552
awj@cpinternet.com
Virginia Johnson, Treasurer
Pub. *Sisu Heritage Newsletter*, biannually ("Finnish organization to promote our heritage. We maintain and restore old log structures, craft shop.")
$10.00 per year membership

Suomi Conference of the Lutheran Church in America
516 Villa Verde
Rio Rancho, NM 87124
(505) 898-6673
E. Olaf Rankinen, Archivist

Flemish
(see Belgian)

French
(see also Canadian, Creole, and Irish; Louisiana, Part 2; and Lineage, Hereditary and Patriotic Societies—Huguenot, Part 4)

The Acadian Cultural Exchange of Northern Maine
(U.S. #1—location)
776 Main (mailing address)
Madawaska, ME 04756
(207) 738-4272
Géraldine Pelletier Chassé, Chairman
8:00–5:00, and evenings by appointment
(covers The Saint John Valley, formerly known as the Madawaska Territory, home of a people divided by an international boundary: Allagash, Daigle, Eagle Lake, Fort Kent, Frenchville, Grand Isle, Hamlin, Keegan, Lille, Madawaska, Saint David, Saint Francis, Saint John, Sainte Agathe, Sinclair, Soldier Pond, Van Buren and Wallagrass)

Acadian Cultural Society
PO Box 2304
Fitchburg, MA 01420
(978) 342-7173
ronfrazier@hotmail.com
http://www.AcadianCultural.org
Ronald F. Frazier, President; Dennis Boudreau, Editor
by appointment
Pub. *Le Reveil Acadien: The Acadian Awakening*, quarterly
(cultural issues of French-speaking Canadians who migrated as far south as Louisiana. "Our library has been put on permanent loan to the Fitchburg Public Library.")
$20.00 per year membership (U.S.), $25.00 (American) per year membership (outside the U.S.)

Acadian Genealogy Exchange
3265 Wayman Branch Road
Covington, KY 41015
(859) 356-9825 voice & FAX
janjehn@aol.com
http://acadiangenex.com
Janet B. Jehn, Editor
by appointment
Pub. *Acadian Genealogy Exchange*, quarterly, $17.00 per year subscription, including annual every-name index in Oct issue, $20.00 per year subscription outside

U.S
(French-Canadian, Acadian and Cajun genealogy and history)

Acadian Genealogy Homepage
cajun@acadian.org
http://www.acadian.org/mad-soc.html

Acadian Heritage Society
159 East Andover Road
Rumford, ME 04276
(207) 364-8651
Marie Thérèse Martin, President
seasonal
(Acadian genealogy)

Acadian House Publishing
(see Louisiana, Part 2)

Les Acadiens Du Texas
La Maison Beausoleil
(Port Neches, TX—location)
2015 Kingsley (mailing address)
Beaumont, TX 77705
(409) 832-6733
Clyde Vincent, President

American-Canadian Genealogical Society (ACGS)
(4 Elm Street—location)
PO Box 6478 (mailing address)
Manchester, NH 03108-6478
(603) 622-1554 (to confirm hours of operation before visiting after 6:00 P.M.)
ACGS@acgs.org; editor@acgs.org
http://www.acgs.org
Pauline Cusson, President
Wed & Fri 9:00-9:00 (call to confirm hours of operation before visiting after 6:00 P.M., Sat 9:00-4:00
Pub. *American-Canadian Genealogist*, quarterly

American-Canadian Genealogical Society
(see New Hampshire, Part 2)

American-French Genealogical Society
(First Universalist Church, 78 Earle Street, Woonsocket, RI 02895—location)
PO Box 2113 (mailing address)
Pawtucket, RI 02861-2113
(401) 765-6141 voice & FAX
http://users.ids.net/~afgs/afgshome.html
Roger Beaudry, President
Tue noon–10:00 P.M., first Sat 10:00–4:00
Pub. *Je Me Souviens*, semiannually (fall and spring)
(French/Canadian descent; large collection of books, 3,600 rolls of microfilm originally from the Drouin Institute in Montreal, and microfiche)
$30.00 per year membership

Association Canado-Américaine
(Genealogy turned over to the American-Canadian Genealogical Society)

Jacques Timothé Boucher de Montbrun Heritage Society
2156 Valley View Road
Joelton, TN 37080
T. Weldon DeMunbrun, President
Pub. *Le Journal*, quarterly
(French colonial history and family genealogy; specific interest in the French colonial history of the Greater Mississippi Valley, computer data on 6,000 de Montbruns)
$15.00 per year membership

Bourbonnais Grove Historical Society
(see Illinois, Part 2)

La Société de Cajuns
Les Memoirs du Bayou Lafourche
(121 West 111 Street, Cutoff, LA
70345—location)
PO Box 581 (mailing address)
Golden Meadow, LA 70357
(504) 475-5757
morgeron@cajunnet.com
Myrtle Orgeron; Audrey Hubert

Le Cercle de La Fleur de Lis
PO Box 2756
Gary, IN 46403
(219) 938-7403; (219) 882-2655

Claudette's
(see Vermont, Part 2)

Cloud County Genealogical Society
(see Kansas, Part 2)

Le Comité des Archives de la Louisiane
(see Louisiana, Part 2)

Comité Louisiane Française
2717 Massachusetts Avenue
Metairie, LA 70003
(504) 469-2555

Commission des Avoyelles, Inc.
(see Louisiana, Part 2)

La Société Historique Franco-Américaine
PO Box F
Woonsocket, RI 02895-0989
(401) 769-0520

Franco-American Centre
(52 Concord Street, Manchester, NH
03101—location)
PO Box 994 (mailing address)
Manchester, NH 03105
(603) 669-4045
iciyvonne@aol.com
http://www.francoamericancentrenh.com
Yvonne Cyr Bresnahan, Executive Director

Franco-American Genealogical Society of York County
(McArthur Library—location)
PO Box 472 (mailing address)
Biddeford, ME 04005
(207) 284-4167 (Secretary)
Camille L. Bolduc, Secretary
Pub. *Maine's Franco-American Heritage*,
    annually (Oct)
$15.00 per year membership; queries free to
    members

Le Centre D'Heritage Franco American
81 Ash Street
Lewiston, ME 04240
(207) 783-9248
Lucille Dulee

French Ancestors
(see Ohio, Part 2)

French Azilum, Inc.
Route 2, Box 266
Towanda, PA 18848
(570) 265-3376
Pat Zalinski, Site Manager
1 May–15 Oct: 11:00–4:30 (last tour 4:00)
(site of colony for refugees from the French
    Revolution and from the Haitian
    Revolution)
admission: $4.50 for adults

French Canadian/Acadian Genealogists of Wisconsin
PO Box 414

Hales Corners, WI 53130
kdupuis@wi.rr.com
http://www.fcgw.org
Kateri T. Dupuis, President
by appointment
Pub. *French Canadian/Acadian
    Genealogists of Wisconsin Quarterly*
$20.00 per year membership

French-Canadian Genealogical Society of Connecticut, Inc.
(53 Tolland Green—location)
PO Box 928 (mailing address)
Tolland, CT 06084-0928
(860) 872-2597
http://www.fcgsc.org
Germaine A. Hoffman, Library Director
Mon & Wed 1:00–8:00, Sat 9:00–4:00, Sun
    1:00–4:00
Pub. *Connecticut Maple Leaf*, semiannually
("Major resources for French-Canadian and
    Acadian genealogy research.")
$25.00 per year membership; admission:
    $5.00

French Institute/Alliance Française
Library
22 East 60th Street
New York, NY 10022-1077
(212) 355-6100, ext. 216; (212) 935-4119
    FAX
reference@fiaf.org
http://www.fiaf.org
Katharine Branning, Library Director
Library: Mon–Thur 11:30–8:00
will provide brief information and referrals,
    but will not undertake detailed
    genealogical research

The French Library and Cultural Center
53 Marlborough Street
Boston, MA 02116
(617) 266-4351
library@frenchlib.org
http://www.frenchlib.org
Jane M. Stahl, Librarian
Library: Labor Day–July: Tue–Thur
    10:00–8:00, Fri–Sat 10:00–5:00
Pub. *Les Nouvelles*, five times per year
(French and Francophone studies, all French-
    speaking peoples, regardless of country of
    origin, i.e. Haiti, Algeria, Quebec; no
    genealogical material)
from $25.00 per year membership

French Settlement Historical Society
PO Box 365
French Settlement, LA 70733
(225) 698-9886
Mercy Lobell, President
Creole House Museum: Apr–Aug: Sun
    (except Mother's Day) 1:00–4:00;
    Sept–Mar: second Sun 1:00–4:00
Pub. *Newsletter*, quarterly; *Newsletter*,
    quarterly; *French Settlement Historical
    Register*, annually
$5.00 per year membership; free admission
    to museum

Heritage North
PO Box 205
Colton, NY 13625
Dennis E. Eickhoff, Director
(publishes records of northern New York
    State, Ontario and Quebec)

Center for Icarian Studies
Western Illinois University Library
1 University Circle
Macomb, IL 61455-1391
(309) 298-1575; (309) 298-2767
http://www.wiu.edu/library/units/

archives/online/index.htm#icarian
Mon–Fri 8:00–4:30
Pub. *Newsletter*
(Utopian groups, established by mostly
    French-born immigrants, near Dallas,
    Texas, Nauvoo, Illinois, Corning, Iowa,
    Saint Louis, Missouri, and San Francisco,
    California. "Collections include
    manuscripts, microfilm, rare books,
    journal articles on the Icarians,
    photographs, and historical monographs.
    A descriptive inventory and finding aid
    for the collection is on file in the Western
    Illinois University Library Archives.")

Jefferson Genealogical Society
Saint-Domingue Special Interest Group
(see Louisiana, Part 2)

Little Canada Historical Society
(see Minnesota, Part 2)

Madawaska Historical Society
(see Maine, Part 2)

Mallet Library at Union Saint-Jean-Baptiste
A Division of Catholic Family Life
Insurance
(68 Cumberland Street—location)
PO Box F (mailing address)
Woonsocket, RI 02895-0989
(800) 225-8752, ext. 143; (401) 766-3014
    FAX
Dr. Charles Emile, Librarian
Wed 9:00–noon, Thur–Fri 9:00–3:00
(Franco-American history, genealogy, parish
    records, out-of-circulation French
    newspapers, photographs)

Mississippi Valley French Research
PO Box 502
Cambria, IL 62915-0502
(618) 985-6857
MVFR@onemain.com
Eugene Beckett, Genealogist
after 5:30 P.M.
Pub. *Hello Cousins*, monthly, $22.00 per
    year subscription
(Includes Missouri and Illinois, "as most
    Mississippi Valley French were in these
    states.")

Northwest Territory, Canadian and French Heritage Center (NWTC&FHC)
Minnesota Genealogical Society
5768 Olson Memorial Highway
Golden Valley, MN 55422
(763) 595-9347 (Wed 9:00–3:00); (612)
    832-9923 (Ms. Chandler, before 9:00
    P.M.)
patdot831@aol.com
http://www.mtn.org/mgs/nw.html
Dorothy Chandler
Pub. *Cousins et Cousines*, quarterly
$15.00 per year membership

Saint Lawrence Valley Genealogical Society
(see New York, Part 2)

1699 Historical Committee
PO Box 713
Ocean Springs, MS 39564
(228) 875-0664
(first French Colony)

TCI Genealogical Resources
(see Spanish, below)

University of Maine at Fort Kent
Acadian Archives/Archives acadiennes

(see Maine, Part 2)

Vermont French-Canadian Genealogical Society
(Saint John's Club, 9 Central Avenue—library locatio)
PO Box 65128 (mailing address)
Burlington, VT 05406-5128
http://members.aol.com/vtfcgs/genealogy/
  index.html

Museum of Waldensian Heritage
(see Religious Archives and Organizations—Waldensian, Part 3)

French-Canadian
(see French)

Galician

Along the Galician Grapevine
(see Religious Organizations and Archives—Mennonite, Part 3)

Genealogy of Halychyna/Eastern Galicia
bielawam@optonline.net
http://www.halgal.com
Matthew Bielawa

Galizien German Descendants (GGD)
2035 Dorsch Road
Walnut Creek, CA 94598-1126
(925) 944-9875
wraybet@pacbell.net
http://www.galiziengermandescendants.org
Betty Wray, Editor
Pub. *Galizien German Descendants Newsletter*, quarterly
("from the German-speaking settlers of the Austro-Hungarian province of Galizien [in English, Galicia]")

German
(see also Banat, Czech, Eastern European, Galician, Jewish, Polish, and Swiss)

American Historical Society of Germans from Russia (AHSGR)
631 D Street
Lincoln, NE 68502-1199
(402) 474-3363; (402) 474-7229 FAX
ahsgr@ahsgr.org
http://www.ahsgr.org;
  http://www.ahsgr.org/soar.htm (Saving Our Ancestral Records [SOAR])
JoAnn Kuhr, Research Director; Jan Tracy Roth, Executive Director
Mon–Fri 9:00–4:00, Sat 9:00–1:00
Pub. *Clues*, quarterly; *Journal*, quarterly; *Newsletter*, quarterly
$50.00 per year membership through individual chapters; $4.50 for individual copies plus $2.50 postage and handling for the first item, 75¢ for each additional item

American Historical Society of Germans from Russia
Arizona Sun Chapter
(address withheld upon request)

American Historical Society of Germans from Russia
Central California Chapter
Genealogy Research Library and Museum
3233 North West Avenue
Fresno, CA 93705-3402
(559) 229-8287 (Library); (559) 229-6078 FAX
ahsgrfr@mindspring.com
http://www.ahsgr.org/cacentra.html

Mon–Fri noon–4:00, Sat 9:30–noon
Pub. *Monthly Chapter Newsletter*
$10.00 per year membership in local chapter; admission to Library and Museum: free

American Historical Society of Germans from Russia
Golden Gate Chapter
2725 Belmont Canyon Road
Belmont, CA 94002-1204
(650) 591-5143
Robert Shouse

American Historical Society of Germans from Russia
Lodi, California Chapter
Helen Bernice Madden
3525 Veneman Avenue North
Modesto, CA 95356-2435
(209) 524-6330
blauweg@aol.com

American Historical Society of Germans from Russia
Mount Diablo Chapter
11 Wandel Drive
Moraga, CA 94556-1829
(925) 376-3002; (510) 642-6108 FAX
siebert@are.berkeley.edu
Jerry Siebert

American Historical Society of Germans from Russia
Sacramento Valley Chapter
624 Shangri Lane
Sacramento, CA 95825-5505
(916) 925-5054
Robert Benson

American Historical Society of Germans from Russia
Southern California Chapter
15619 Ogram Avenue
Gardena, CA 90249-4445
(310) 675-2745
whbonner@aol.com
http://feefhs.org/frgahssc.html
Wayne H. Bonner, President
Pub. *AHSGR Southern California Chapter Newsletter*, quarterly
(includes Los Angeles, San Diego, Riverside, San Bernardino and Orange counties)
$5.00 per year chapter membership, in addition to membership in the parent organization

American Historical Society of Germans from Russia
Colorado Springs Chapter
3330 Templeton Gap Road, Unit 78
Colorado Springs, CO 80907-5747
(719) 282-9364
Cleora J. Nelsons

American Historical Society of Germans from Russia
Denver Metro Chapter
13245 Grove Way
Broomfield, CO 80020
(303) 469-5705
rsandm@aol.com
http://www.teleport.com/nonprofit/ahsgr/
  codenver.html
Richard E. Sandmeier

American Historical Society of Germans from Russia
Melon Valley Chapter
708 South 13th Street
Rocky Ford, CO 81067-2132
(719) 254-3819
Josephine Geringer

American Historical Society of Germans from Russia
Northern Colorado Chapter
1104 West Magnolia
Fort Collins, CO 80521
(970) 484-9771
ronfarm15@aol.com
http://www.teleport.com/nonprofit/ahsgr/
  conorthe.html
Ron Greenwald
no dues separate from parent society

American Historical Society of Germans from Russia
Nation's Capital Area Chapter
11816 Selfridge Road
Silver Spring, MD 20906-4736
(301) 949-4880 (answering machine)
Rita Simmersbach Scheirer
$7.00 per year membership in local chapter; no research per se, but will help find answers to questions (for research fees regarding the German Captured Records at the National Archives, most often in the well-known EWZ Files, send to "Attention: ROOTSearch")

American Historical Society of Germans from Russia
Florida Suncoast Chapter
9705 Fox Hearst Road
Tampa, FL 33647
(813) 973-2512
jpfab2tam@aol.com
Lee J. (Jim) Fabricius

American Historical Society of Germans from Russia
Northern Illinois Chapter
208 Cold Spring Court
Palatine, IL 60067
(847) 397-7604
Cgorr@aol.com
http://www.teleport.com/nonprofit/ahsgr/
  ilnorthe.html
Carolyn Gorr, President

American Historical Society of Germans from Russia
Golden Wheat Chapter
2029 University
Wichita, KS 67213-3375
(316) 283-3129
edrif@msn.com
Carol J. Riffel

American Historical Society of Germans from Russia
Heart of America Chapter
117 East Minneapolis Street
Salina, KS 67401-6024
(785) 827-0782
Melvina Gack

American Historical Society of Germans from Russia
Heritage Seekers of Southwest Kansas Chapter
511 Baughman
Ulysses, KS 67880
(620) 356-2228
D. B. Schwartzkopf

American Historical Society of Germans from Russia
Kansas City Area Chapter
4441 West 52nd Terrace
Roeland Park, KS 66205
(913) 362-7635
Richard Ubert

American Historical Society of Germans from Russia

Northeast Kansas Chapter
4625 N.W. Geronimo Trail
Topeka, KS 66618
(785) 246-2821
Frank Jacobs

American Historical Society of Germans from Russia
Post Rock Chapter
18350 Homer Road
Russell, KS 67665
(785) 483-3976
Frederick Boxberger

American Historical Society of Germans from Russia
Sunflower Chapter
874 Samara, Munjor
Hays, KS 67601
(785) 625-6411
Betty Pfannenstiel

American Historical Society of Germans from Russia
Flint Michigan Chapter
4167 West Four Lakes Drive
Linden, MI 48451
(810) 629-8710
Robert G. Ringler

American Historical Society of Germans from Russia
Saginaw Valley Chapter
6910 Trowbridge Circle
Saginaw, MI 48603
(989) 799-4266
clniederusa@netscape.net
Carol L. Niederquell
meetings: fourth Tue (Feb, Apr, Aug, Oct) &
    a Sun in Dec

American Historical Society of Germans from Russia
Southwest Michigan Chapter
1468 Saint Joseph Circle
Saint Joseph, MI 49085-9707
pkoe662885@aol.com
Paul Koehler

American Historical Society of Germans from Russia
North Star of Minnesota Chapter
PO Box 583642
Minneapolis, MN 55458-3642
http://www.ahsgr.org/ahsgrchp.
    html#Minnesota
Pub. *Chapter Newsletter*

American Historical Society of Germans from Russia
Yellowstone Valley Chapter
715 West Fifth Street
Laurel, MT 59044
(406) 628-6795
Howard Guenther

American Historical Society of Germans from Russia
Lincoln Nebraska Chapter
3300 Serenity Circle, #10
Lincoln, NE 68506
(402) 423-4345
Ruth White
(collection housed at Elkhorn Valley
    Museum and Research Center, Lincoln)

American Historical Society of Germans from Russia
Midlands Chapter
9373 Maplewood Boulevard
Omaha, NE 68134-4663
(402) 572-8871

Dr. Michel Mallenby

American Historical Society of Germans from Russia
Nebraska Panhandle Chapter
2430 Avenue C
Scottsbluff, NE 69361
(308) 632-2459
Shirley Flack

American Historical Society of Germans from Russia
Northeast Nebraska Chapter
314 South 13th Place
Norfolk, NE 68701-1214
(402) 371-0693
ruthelaine@uswest.net (Jan–Apr)
http://www.teleport.com/nonprofit/ahsgr/
    nenorthe.thml
Ruthie Galitz

American Historical Society of Germans from Russia
Central Oklahoma Chapter
Eleanor Barnes
1106 West Brooks Street
Norman, OK 73069-4539
(405) 321-7835
http://www.teleport.com/nonprofit/ahsgr/
    okcentra.html

American Historical Society of Germans from Russia
Golden Spread Chapter
Rural Route 2, Box 88
Shattuck, OK 73858
Marilyn Schoenhals, Secretary

American Historical Society of Germans from Russia
Oregon Chapter
8618 S.E. 36th Avenue
Portland, OR 97222-5522
(503) 659-8248
rahaas@haasfamily.us
Roger Haas
Pub. *Newsletter*, bimonthly

American Historical Society of Germans from Russia
Center of the Nation Chapter
7 Swan Lane
Spearfish, SD 57783
(605) 642-1149
jhi@rushmore.com
James H. Ingenthorn

American Historical Society of Germans from Russia
Homestead Chapter
PO Box 98
Freeman, SD 57029-0098
(605) 925-7834
Bernie Koller

American Historical Society of Germans from Russia
Golden Spread Chapter
PO Box 207
Darrouzett, TX 79024
(806) 624-2217
Esther Miller

American Historical Society of Germans from Russia
Utah Chapter
259 East 500 North
Lehi, UT 84043-1638
(801) 731-3054
Phillip E. Boltz

American Historical Society of Germans

from Russia
Big Bend Chapter
202 West Second
Ritzville, WA 99169-1704
(509) 659-1537
tjspreng@ritzcom.net
Thelma Sprenger

American Historical Society of Germans from Russia
Blue Mountain Chapter
(address withheld upon request)

American Historical Society of Germans from Russia
Central Washington Chapter
306 North Alder
Toppenish, WA 98948
(509) 865-2059
huscoord@wolfenet.com
Louise Potter

American Historical Society of Germans from Russia
Columbia Basin Chapter
1820 West Part Street
Pasco, WA 99301
(509) 545-9423
Martha Yates

American Historical Society of Germans from Russia
Greater Seattle Chapter
7010 17th Avenue N.E.
Seattle, WA 98115
(206) 523-4136
Richard Meyer

American Historical Society of Germans from Russia
Greater Spokane Chapter
2936 Grandview Avenue
Spokane, WA 99224-5525
(509) 624-6947
smickrf@foxinternet.net
Robert Smick

American Historical Society of Germans from Russia
Olympic Peninsula Chapter
30 Raccoon Road
Sequim, WA 98382
(360) 683-1765
marva@olypen.com
Marva McKenzie, Past President

American Historical Society of Germans from Russia
Ranier Chapter
1007 North Meridian
Puyallup, WA. 98371
(253) 845-0136
Ella Reese

American Historical Society of Germans from Russia
Fox Valley of Wisconsin Chapter
945 Anchorage Court
Oshkosh, WI 54901-2056
(920) 235-7231
Don Kutchera
("Volga Germans")

American Historical Society of Germans from Russia
Southeastern Wisconsin Chapter
3121 Pioneer Road
Mequon, WI 53097-1620
lustyal@aol.com
Raymond L. Lusty, Sr.

American Historical Society of Germans

from Russia
Land of Goshen Chapter
100 East 23rd Avenue
Torrington, WY 82240
(307) 532-2534
John Reichert

American Historical Society of Germans from Russia
Southeastern Wyoming Chapter
2415 Van Lennen
Cheyenne, WY 82001
(307) 634-0309
dennisguil@aol.com
Barbara Jo Guilford

American/Schleswig-Holstein Heritage Society
PO Box 313
Davenport, IA 52805-0313
(563) 324-7326 voice & FAX
Scharlott Goetsch Blevins, Genealogy
    Director and Librarian
by appointment only
Pub. *American/Schleswig-Holstein Heritage
    Society Newsletter*, bimonthly
$12.00 per year membership

Archives in Germany
Internet Sources of German Genealogy
hanacek@abacus.s.bawue.de
http://www.bawue.de/~hanacek/info/
    earchive.htm
Andreas Hanacek

Association of German Nobility in North America
3571 East Eighth Street
Los Angeles, CA 90023

Leo Baeck Institute
(see Jewish, below)

Beyond Germanna
(see Virginia, Part 2)

Broad Bay Family History Projects
(see Maine, Part 2)

Bush-Meeting Dutch
(see Religious Archives and
Organizations—United Methodist, Part 3)

Center for Mennonite Brethren Studies
(see Religious Archives and
Organizations—Mennonite, Part 3)

Public Library of Cincinnati and Hamilton County
(see Ohio, Part 2)

Comal County Genealogy Society
(see Texas, Part 2)

Die Pommerschen Leute
PO Box 7309
Burbank, CA 91510-7369
tperrone@cwia.com
http://feefhs.org/dpl/frg-dpl.html;
    http://feefhs.org/dpl/dv/dv-intro.html (Die
    Vorfahren Web Database Index of
    Individual Names)
Pub. *Die Pommerschen Leute* (*The
    Pomeranian People*Pomeranians
    1839–1899), quarterly, $10.00 per year
    subscription

Ellis County Historical Society
Volga and Bokovina Germans
(see Kansas, Part 2)

The Emsland Society

4325 Saint Lawrence Avenue
Cincinnati, OH 45205-1539
(513) 921-0629
alberto@worldnet.att.net
http://geocities.com/heartland/4018
Albert Olthaus, President
(covers Landkreis Emsland in the former
    Prussian province of Hannover, including
    the towns of Andervenne, Bawinkle,
    Beesten, Bockhorst, Börger, Breddenberg,
    Dersum, Dörpen, Dohren, Emsbüren,
    Esterwegen, Freren-Stadt, Fresenburg,
    Geeste, Gersten, Groß Berßen, Handrup,
    Haren Stadt, Haselünne-Stadt, Heede,
    Herzlake, Hilkenbrook, Hüven, Klein
    Berßen, Kluse, Lähden, Lahn, Langen,
    Lathen, Lehe, Lengenreich, Lingen (Ems)-
    Stadt, Lorup, Lünne, Meppen-Stadt,
    Messingen, Neubörger, Neulehe,
    Neiderlangen, Oberlangen, Papenburg-
    Stadt, Rastdorf, Renkenberge, Rhede,
    Salzbergen, Schapen, Sögel,
    Spahnharrenstätte, Spelle, Stavern,
    Surwold, Sustrum, Thuine, Twist, Vrees,
    Walchum, Werlte, Werpeloh, Wettrup,
    and Wippingen; northwest German
    genealogy and history)
free exchange of information

Frankenmuth Historical Association
613 South Main
Frankenmuth, MI 48734
(989) 652-9701; (989) 652-9390 FAX
Mary Nuechterlein, Collections Manager
Mon–Fri 9:00–5:00, and some weekends by
    appointment
Pub. *FHA Newsletter*, three times per year
("Library covers only descendants of
    communities of Frankenmuth,
    Frankentrost, Frankenlust and
    Richville/Frankenhilf.")
$40.00 per year membership; research:
    $10.00 per hour

genealogy.net
webmaster@genealogy.net
http://www.genealogienetz.de/genealogy.
    html
("the number one source in German
    genealogy"; includes mailing list and
    newsgroup)

The Georgia Salzburger Society
(see Georgia, Part 2)

German-American Family Society of Akron, Inc.
3871 Ranfield Road
Brimfield, OH 44240
(330) 678-8229
Pub. *Newsletter (Rundschreiben)*, irregularly
(no genealogy functions, only a
    social/cultural organization)

German-American Genealogical Association Europe
HQ USAREUR
CMR 420, Box 502
APO, AE 09063
011-49-6227-51942; 011-49-6227-54008
    FAX
Lu Hays Whitworth, President
Pub. *Family Finder Newsletter*

German-American Genealogical Club
86th CSG/RSSRR, Box 24
APO New York, NY 09012
Terryl M. Allen, President

German American Heritage Association of Oklahoma (GAHA)
Modern Language Department
Oklahoma City University

2501 North Blackwelder
Oklahoma City, OK 73106
Christiane Faris, President
$10.00 per year membership

The German-American Heritage Institute
7824 West Madison
Forest Park, IL 60130-1485
(708) 366-0017
Gary Neusbieser

German-Bohemian Heritage Society
(800 West Idaho Avenue, Saint Paul, MN
    55117—location)
PO Box 822 (mailing address)
New Ulm, MN 56073-0822
(507) 488-0405
Lalghbs@newulmtel.net;
    rpaulgb@skypoint.com
http://www.rootsweb.com/~gbhs
Robert J. Paulson, Founder

German Genealogical Digest
(245 North Vine Street, Suite 106, Salt Lake
    City, UT 84103—location)
PO Box 112054 (mailing address)
Salt Lake City, UT 84147
editor@german-digest.com
http://feefhs.org/pub/frg-ggdp.html
Laraine Ferguson, Editor; Gay Kowallis,
    Editor
Pub. *German Genealogical Digest*,
    quarterly, $28.00 per year subscription or
    $9.00 per issue in the U.S., $32.00 per
    year subscription or $12.00 per issue in
    Canada, $41.00 per year subscription or
    $12.00 per issue elsewhere
list of published articles for SASE

German Genealogical Index
PO Box 582155
Minneapolis, MN 55458-2155

German Genealogical Society of America (GGSA)
(2125 Wright Avenue, Suite C-9, La Verne,
    CA 91750—location)
PO Box 291818 (mailing address)
Los Angeles, CA 90029
(909) 593-0509
Ken Michel, Research Director; William
    Toeppe, Librarian
Wed & Sat 1:00–5:00, and by appointment
Pub. *Newsletter*, ten times per year
("CD-ROM lists; international phone books,
    current from German-speaking nations")
$20.00 per year membership; admission:
    $3.00 for nonmembers; research: $16.00
    per hour

Society of German Genealogists for Eastern Europe
contact@sggee.org
http://www.sggee.org
John Marsch
Pub. *SGGEE Journal*
$30.00 per year membership

German Genealogy Group
5 Eden Drive
Smithtown, NY 11787
(631) 979-6241
hschrade@suffolk.lib.ny.us
Hans W. Schrader, President
Pub. *Newsletter*, ten times per year
(lending library, translation service,
    GEDCOM indexes, proposed mentoring
    service)
$15.00 per year membership

German Genealogy Group of Long Island
PO Box 1004

Kings Park, NY 11754
(631) 265-0621
deckerle@optonline.net
http://www.germangenealogygroup.com
Don Eckerle
meetings at the Family History Center,
  Plainview: first Thur (Sept–June) 7:30
Pub. *Der Ahnenforscher*, ten times per year
  (Sept–June)
$15.00 per year membership

German Interest Group-Wisconsin
PO Box 2185
Janesville, WI 53547-2185
GIG_WI@hotmail.com
http://www.rootsweb.com/~wigig/index.
  html
meetings at Alliant Energy, 3730 Kennedy
  Road, Janesville
Pub. *German Interest Group-Wisconsin
  Newsletter*, quarterly
$7.50 per year membership; no research by
  mail

German Research Association (GRA)
PO Box 711600
San Diego, CA 92171-1600
(619) 420-4557 (President)
donaritchi@aol.com
http://www.feefhs.org/gra/frg-gra.html
Dona Ritchie, President
8:00–5:00; meetings: first Sat 9:30–noon
Pub. *The German Connection*, quarterly
$18.00 per year membership

German Society of Pennsylvania
611 Spring Garden Street
Philadelphia, PA 19123
(215) 627-2332; (215) 627-5297 FAX
contact@germansociety.org
http://www.german-society.org
Ms. Jackie Schmenger, Business Manager
Library: Tue, Thur & Sun 10:00–4:00
  (archives are in storage at present)
Pub. *Die neue Pennsylvanische Staatsbote*,
  monthly (except summer)
$40.00 per year membership

German-Texan Heritage Society
(see Texas, Part 2)

Germanic Genealogy Society
Minnesota Genealogical Society
(Buenger Memorial Library, Concordia
College, 275 North Syndicate Street, Saint
Paul, MN 55104-5494—library location)
PO Box 16312 (mailing address)
Saint Paul, MN 55116-0312
(763) 595-9347 (Library); (763) 641-8240
  (for Library hours); (763) 777-6463;
  (763) 920-8118 (Kent Cutkomp)
msmedia@gte.net; kermit.e.frye@cdev.com
  (Mr. Frye); ggsqueries@hotmail.com
http://feefhs.org/ger/frg-ggs.html
Michael Haase, President; Kermit E. Frye
Pub. *Germanic Genealogy Journal*,
  quarterly; *GGS Connect*, four or five
  times per year (prior to meetings in Feb,
  May, Sept & Nov)
$12.00 per year membership; research: $2.00
  per surname or specific question for
  members, $7.00 for nonmembers

Germans from Russia Heritage Society
1125 West Turnpike Avenue
Bismarck, ND 58501-8115
(701) 223-6167
rachel@grhs.org
http://www.grhs.com
Rachel Schmidt, Office Manager
Mon–Fri 8:00–4:30
Pub. *Heritage Review*, quarterly

("The GRHS Library contains family
  histories, local histories, obituaries,
  pedigree charts, and passenger lists as
  well as other reference materials." Web
  site lists regional interest groups: Beresan,
  Bessarabia, Crimea, Grossliebental.)
$25.00 per year membership; research:
  $10.00 per hour

Germans from Russia Oregon & SW Washington (GROW)
8618 S.E. 36th Avenue
Portland, OR 97222-5522
(503) 659-8248
rahaas@haasfamily.us
Roger Haas
Pub. *Newsletter*, bimonthly

Germantown Historical Society
(see Pennsylvania, Part 2)

Glückstal Colonies Research Association
611 Esplanade
Redondo Beach, CA 90277-4130
(310) 540-1872
gcra31@aol.com
http://www.raile.com/gluckstal
Margaret Freeman, Executive Director
by appointment
Pub. *GRCA Newsletter*, semiannually
(specializes in inhabitants of the Glückstal
  colonies in South Russia; "goal: list all of
  inhabitants of the colony group from
  founding, 1803–1809, to demise during
  World War II")
$15.00 per year membership

Goethe Institute Inter Nationes
170 Beacon Street
Boston, MA 02116
(617) 262-6050
http://www.Goethe.dc/boston
Hans-Ulrich Kaup, Librarian
Sept–Aug: Mon–Fri 9:00–6:00
("Current German newspapers and
  magazines. Reading room only. We do not
  loan out books.")

Goschenhoppen Historians, Inc.
(see Pennsylvania, Part 2)

Gottscheer Heritage and Genealogy Association (GHGA)
PO Box 725
Louisville, CO 80027-0725
anthro@privatei.com
http://www.gottschee.org
Elizabeth A. Nick, President
8:00–5:00
Pub. *The Gottschee Tree*, quarterly; *The
  Gottscheer Connection*; *Membership
  Roster*, annually
("Purpose of the GHGA is to preserve the
  ancestral heritage, culture, history, and
  genealogical records of the Gottscheers,
  descendants of the people who lived in the
  German-speaking district of Gottschee in
  the Austrian Duchy of Carniola [Krain],
  which was part of the Austro-Hungarian
  Empire until 1918. From 1918 until 1991,
  Gottschee was part of the northernmost
  Yugoslav Republic of Slovenia. Since
  1991, Gottschee is a city [Kocevje] and
  district [Kocevska] in Slovenia")
$22.00 per year membership

Harmonie Associates, Inc.
(see Religious Archives and
Organizations—Harmonist, Part 3)

The Sidney Heitman Germans from Russia Collection

Colorado State University
University Archives, Morgan Library
Fort Collins, CO 80523-1019
(970) 491-1844; (970) 491-1195 FAX
pvandeve@manta.colostate.edu
Patricia Van Deventer, Library Technician
  II, University Archives Staff Supervisor;
  John Newman, Archivist, Special
  Collections Department, Colorado State
  University Libraries

Hettinger County Historical Society
Banot German Hungarian Museum
(see North Dakota, Part 2)

Hillsboro Historical Society and Museum
(see Kansas, Part 2)

Historic Bethel German Colony
PO Box 127
Bethel, MO 63434
(660) 284-6200
Elizabeth Fakazis, Executive Director
("Bethel was established as a communal
  colony in the mid-1800s; many of the
  original structures, and descendants of the
  founders, are still here.")

Historic Harmony/Harmony Museum
(218 Mercer Street—location)
PO Box 524 (mailing address)
Harmony, PA 16037
(724) 452-7341; (888) 821-4822
hmuseum@fyi.net
http://harmonymuseum.org
Kathy Luck, Administrator
Tue–Sun 1:00–4:00
Pub. *Historic Harmony Newsletter*, monthly
("Local history museum, some genealogical
  information." Emphasis on Germans,
  Harmony Society, Mennonites. "Harmony
  was first home (1804–1814) of communal
  Harmony Society of German immigrants,
  subsequently was a Mennonite
  community for much of the 19th
  century.")
$20.00 per year membership; research:
  charges fees plus photocopies

Immigrant Genealogical Society
(see Immigration Research Centers, Part 4)

Indiana German Heritage Society, Inc.
401 East Michigan Avenue
Indianapolis, IN 46204
(317) 464-9004 (Office); (812) 988-2866
  (Home); (317) 630-0035 FAX
reichman@indiana.edu
http://www.ulib.iupui.edu/kade
Ruth Reichmann, Ph.D., President
weekdays through Foundation Office
Pub. *The Indiana German Heritage Society
  Newsletter*, quarterly
$20.00 per year membership

Jensen Publications
PO Box 441
Pleasant Grove, UT 84062-0441
http://feefhs.org/frg-jp.html
Larry R. Jensen, Author, Self-Publisher and
  Lecturer
(publishes books on German research)

Kutschurgan Village Project
724 S.W. Hayter Street
Dallas, OR 97338-1845
(503) 623-5529
rpschuh@teleport.com
http://www.teleport.com/nonprofit/grhs/
  pugetsnd.html
Bob Schuh, Project Coordinator

**Landsmannschaft der
Bessarabiendeutschen**
Heimatmuseum der Deutschen aus
Bessarabien
c/o North Dakota State University Libraries
(Corner of 12th Avenue and Albrecht
Boulevard—location)
PO Box 5599 (mailing address)
Fargo, ND 58105-5599
(701) 231-8416; (701) 231-7138 FAX
Michael.Miller@ndsu.nodak.edu
http://www.lib.ndsu.nodak.edu/grhc
Professor Michael M. Miller, Germans from
   Russia Bibliographer
Mon–Fri (academic year) 8:00–5:00;
   Mon–Fri (summer) 7:30–5:00
Pub. *Mitteilungsblat*, monthly

**Landsmannschaft der Deutschen aus
Russland**
c/o Germans from Russia Heritage Collection
North Dakota State University Libraries
(Corner of 12th Avenue and Albrecht
Boulevard—location)
PO Box 5599 (mailing address)
Fargo, ND 58105-5599
(701) 231-8416
Michael.Miller@ndsu.nodak.edu
http://www.lib.ndsu.nodak.edu/grhc/info/
   introduction/landsmann.html
Professor Michael M. Miller, Germans from
   Russia Bibliographer
Mon–Fri (academic year) 8:00–5:00;
   Mon–Fri (summer) 7:30–5:00
Pub. *Volk auf dem Weg*, monthly, 54.00 DM
   per year subscription
(Black Sea Germans, Crimean Germans,
   Caucasus Germans, Mennonite Germans,
   Volga Germans)

The Linden Tree
(see Publishers, Part 4)

Lineages, Inc.
Before Germanna
(see Virginia, Part 2)

Links Genealogy Publications
8125 Arroyo Vista Drive
Sacramento, CA 95823-5935
(916) 628-3381
ijones@accessbee.com
Iris Carter Jones, Owner
Mon–Fri 9:00–5:00
Pub. *Krefeld Immigrants and Their
   Descendants* (for descendants of the 1683
   immigrants who settled Germantown in
   Philadelphia, semiannually, $17.00 per
   year subscription (subscribers receive free
   queries)

**The Memorial Foundation of the
Germanna Colonies in Virginia, Inc.**
(see Virginia, Part 2)

**Mennonite Historians of Eastern
Pennsylvania**
(see Pennsylvania, Part 2)

The Mid-Atlantic Germanic Society
PO Box 2642
Kensington, MD 20895-2642
http://www.rootsweb.com/~usmags
Patricia Cramer, Corresponding Secretary
Pub. *Der Kurier*, quarterly
("Germans who settled in the mid-Atlantic
   area.")
$10.00 per year membership

Museum of American Frontier Culture
(see Virginia, Part 2)

North Dakota State University
Germans from Russia Heritage Collection
North Dakota State University Libraries
North Dakota State Institute for Regional Studies
(Corner of 12th Avenue and Albrecht
Boulevard—location)
PO Box 5599 (mailing address)
Fargo, ND 58105-5599
(701) 237-8914; (701) 231-8416 (to confirm
   library hours); (701) 293-5564
   (Bibliographer); (701) 231-7138 FAX
Michael.Miller@ndsu.nodak.edu
http://www.lib.ndsu.nodak.edu/grhc
   (Collection)
Professor Michael M. Miller, Bibliographer
Mon–Fri (academic year) 8:00–5:00;
   Mon–Fri (summer) 7:30–5:00
(emphasis on Bessarabian, Black Sea, and
   Crimean Germans history and culture)

ODESSA
http://pixel.cs.vt.edu/library/odessa.html
(a German-Russian genealogical library)

**Orangeburg German-Swiss Genealogical
Society**
3415 Pine Belt Road
Columbia, SC 29204
(803) 577-5898
http://www.netside.com/~genealogy/
   orangeburgh.htm
Louis U. Ulmer
Pub. *Orangeburg German-Swiss Newsletter*,
   bimonthly
$10.00 per year membership, c/o Bill R.
   Linder, 6129 Leesburg Pike, No. 820,
   Falls Church, VA 22041

Ostfriesen Ancestral Research Association
143 Virginia Avenue
Bethalto, IL 62010
Rev. Kenneth DeWall

**Ostfriesen Genealogical Society of
America**
(168 North Lake Street, Forest Lake, MN
55025—location)
PO Box 474 (mailing address)
Wyoming, MN 55092
lstrong@cornernet.com
http://www.rootsweb.com/~mnogsm
Dale Carlson
Pub. newsletter, quarterly
research: $15.00 per hour

Ostfriesian Genealogical Society
(address withheld upon request)
Pub. *Ostfriesen Genealogical Society
   Newsletter*, monthly
(local meetings only, does not respond to
   queries)
$25.00 per year membership

**Palatine and Pennsylvania-Dutch
Genealogy**
http://www.geocities.com/Heartland/3955
Kraig Ruckel

Palatines to America
611 East Weber Road
Columbus, OH 43211-1097
pal-am@juno.com
http://PalAm.org
Office Manager or Librarian
Wed 12:30–4:00, first Sat 10:00–2:00, third
   Fri 9:00–4:00, weekends by chance or by
   appointment; annual conference in June;
   spring & fall chapter conferences
Pub. *Palatine Patter*; *The Palatine
   Immigrant*, quarterly
("A national genealogical society of those
   seeking the origin of their German-

speaking ancestors")
$20.00 per year membership (includes
   membership in one state chapter, $5.00
   per year membership in each additional
   chapter); research and queries for
   members only, library open to all

Palatines to America, Colorado Chapter
7079 South Marshall Street
Littleton, CO 80123-4607
(303) 979-5968
http://www.dcn.davis.ca.us/~feefhs/
   frgpalco.html
Pub. *CO-PAL-AM*
$20.00 per year membership in national
   society includes membership in one state
   chapter

Palatines to America, Illinois Chapter
PO Box 9638
Peoria, IL 61612-9638
(309) 691-0292
ralphkroehler@prodigy.net
Marjorie Kroehler, Secretary
Pub. *Illinois Chapter Newsletter*, six times
   per year
$28.00 per year membership in the national
   society and one state chapter

Palatines to America, Indiana Chapter
PO Box 40435
Indianapolis, IN 46240-0435
(317) 875-7210
Pub. *Indiana Chapter Newsletter*, quarterly
$20.00 per year membership in national
   society includes membership in one state
   chapter

Palatines to America, New York Chapter
119 Myers Road
Howes Cave, NY 12092-9801
Pub. *Yorker Palatine*
$20.00 per year membership in national
   society includes membership in one state
   chapter

Palatines to America, Ohio Chapter
Capital University, Box 101
Columbus, OH 43209-2394
(614) 875-1933
Pub. *Palatine Heritage*, quarterly
$20.00 per year membership in national
   society includes membership in one state
   chapter

**Palatines to America, Pennsylvania
Chapter**
PO Box 280
Strasburg, PA 17579-0280
(717) 244-7358
http://genealogy.org/~palam
Lois C. Byrem, Membership Registrar
Pub. *Penn Pal*, quarterly
$20.00 per year membership in national
   society includes membership in one state
   chapter

Palatines to America, Virginia Chapter
3249 Cambridge Court
Fairfax, VA 22030-1942
(703) 591-3656
toedick@aol.com
Monika E. Edick, President
Pub. *That Wagon Road*, quarterly
$20.00 per year membership in national
   society includes membership in one state
   chapter

**Palatines to America, West Virginia
Chapter**
572 Plymouth Avenue
Morgantown, WV 26505-2142

(304) 599-1672
Antialee M. Garletts, President
Pub. *Pal-Am Mountaineer*, three or four
times per year
$20.00 per year membership in national
society includes membership in one state
chapter

Pennsylvania Dutch Folk Culture Society
(see Pennsylvania, Part 2)

**Pennsylvania German Cultural Heritage
Center**
Kutztown University
Weisenberger Alumni Center
Kutztown, PA 19530
(610) 683-1330
pgchc@kutztown.edu
http://www.kutztown.edu/community/pgchc

**The Pennsylvania German Research
Society**
Route 1, Box 478
Sugarloaf, PA 18249
(570) 788-5133
Carolyn Boyer-Dryfoos, President
Pub. *Der Überblick*, quarterly
(Pennsylvania-Germanic research, German
emigrant searches; annual genealogical
research tour to Germany, Austria, and
Switzerland)
$20.00 per year membership

Pommerscher Verein—Central Wisconsin
PO Box 358
Wausau, WI 54402-0358
(715) 359-0024
donz@gitllc.com
Donald D. Zamzow, Newsletter Editor; Bob
Gruling, Query Responder
Pub. *Dat Pommerscher Blatt*, quarterly
("This is an organization devoted to the
promotion and preservation of the
heritage and language of the Pomeranian
German immigrants to Wisconsin. A
major component of our club also
included genealogy research."
$15.00 per year membership, plus $5.00
initiation fee

Die Pommerscher Verein—Freistadt
(Lindenwood School, 12351 North Granville
Road, Mequon, WI—location)
PO Box 204 (mailing address)
Germantown, WI 53022-0204
(262) 353-8949
pommern@execpc.com;
nschroed@execpc.com
http://feefhs.org/GER/pvf/frg-pvf.html
Norman Schroeder, Chairman Computer and
Website Committee
second Thur 10:00–4:00, second Fri 7:00
P.M.–10:00 P.M.
Pub. *Rundschreiben-Pom. Ver. Freistadt*,
quarterly
(Pomeranian history and genealogy, books,
maps, also studies and collects items on
customs and trachts or period dress)
$15.00 per year membership

Sacramento German Genealogy Society
PO Box 660061
Sacramento, CA 95866-0061
(916) 753-3206; (916) 421-8032 FAX
pres@sacgergensoc.org
http://www.sacgergensoc.org
Chuck Knuthson, President
meetings at Northminster Presbyterian
Church, 3235 Pope Avenue (near Watt
Avenue, south of I-80), Sacramento:
fourth Tue (Jan–Oct) 1:00
Pub. *Der Blumenbaum*, quarterly (Jan, Apr,

July, Oct)
$15.00 per year membership

**Society for German American Studies
(SGAS)**
German Department
Saint Olaf College
Northfield, MN 55057-1098
(507) 645-8562 (*Newsletter* Editor); (913)
864-4803 (*Yearbook* Editor) (507) 646-
3732 FAX
rippley@stolaf.edu
http://feefhs.org/frg-sgas.html
Professor LaVern Rippley, Newsletter Editor
Pub. *Society for German-American Studies
Newsletter*, quarterly; *Yearbook of
German-American Studies*, annually,
$20.00 per issue, c/o William Keel,
German Department, University of
Kansas, 2080 Wescoe Hall, Lawrence, KS
66045
$20.00 per year membership

**Society for the History of Germans in
Maryland**
(107 East Chase Street—location)
PO Box 22585 (mailing address)
Baltimore, MD 21203
(410) 685-0450
Gerard Wm. Wittstadt, President
Pub. *The Report: A Journal of German-
American History*, every year or two
("The Society does not provide a genealogy
service, nor does it maintain a research
library."
$15.00 per year membership

Texas Seaport Museum
(see Texas, Part 2)

Texas Wendish Heritage Society
Texas Wendish Heritage Museum
1011 County Road 212
Giddings, TX 78942
(979) 366-2441; (979) 366-2805 FAX
wendish@bluebon.net
http://wendish.concordia.edu
Barbara P. Hielscher, Museum Director;
Georgie B. Boyce, President
Mon–Fri & Sun 1:00–5:00, Sat (Easter-
Labor Day) 1:00–5:00
(Wends: a Slavic people of eastern Germany)
$12.50 per year membership

**Transylvania Saxon Genealogy and
Heritage Society, Inc.**
PO Box 3319
Youngstown, OH 44513-3319
(330) 783-1947
pkreutzerj@aol.com
http://www.feefhs.org/ah/hu/frgtsghs.html
Pau Kreutzer, Jr., Executive Director
Pub. *Transylvania Saxon Tapestry*, quarterly
(area is variously named Transilvania,
Ardeal, Siebenbürgen or Siebenbuergen,
and Erdély)
$15.00 per year membership

Tulpehocken Settlement Historical Society
(see Pennsylvania, Part 2)

University of Cincinnati
German-Americana Collection
(see Ohio, Part 2)

The University of Texas at Austin
The Ouid Nuch
(see Texas, Part 2)

Weld Library District
Centennial Park Branch Library
(see Colorado, Part 2)

**Western Pennsylvania Genealogical
Society**
(see Pennsylvania, Part 2)

Zichydorf Village Association
(306) 789-4481
gschwartz@accesscomm.ca
http://feefhs.org/zva/frg-zva.html
Glenn Schwartz, ZVA Coordinator
Pub. *ZVA Newsletter*, semiannually
("Purpose is to gather, share, and preserve
information about Zichydorf and the
immediately surrounding area and the
families whose history is associated.
Zichydorf was a German village in the
Austro-Hungarian empire that currently
lies in Serbia near the Romanian border.
The surrounding area includes the nearby
village of Geroghausen. These two
German villages were also known by the
Hungarian and Serbian names of
Zichyfalva, Mariolana, and Plandiste in
the case of Zichydorf and Györyhaza, and
Velika Greda in the case of
Georghausen."
$10.00 per year membership, plus a one-time
library contribution of $25.00

Greek
(see also Eastern European)

Chian Federation
44-01 Broadway
New York, NY 11103

Evrytanian Association
121 Greenwich Road
Charlotte, NC 28211
(704) 366-6571
Olga Kleto
Pub. *Velouchi Bulletin*, quarterly
("founded as a philanthropic organization in
1944 by Evrytanians (from the state of
Evrytania, central Greece) emigrating to
the U.S."

Hellenic Museum and Cultural Center
168 North Michigan Avenue, Fourth Floor
Chicago, IL 60601-7509
(312) 726-1234; (312) 726-8539 FAX
Themi Vasils
Wed–Fri 11:00–3:00
(Greek immigrant experience)

**Saint Photios Greek Orthodox National
Shrine**
(41 Saint George Street—location)
PO Box AF (mailing address)
Saint Augustine, FL 32085
(904) 829-8205
(New Smyrna Colony of Greeks in America)

Guatemalan
(see Spanish)

Haitian
(see French)

Hispanic
(see Spanish)

Hungarian
(see also Banat, Czech, Eastern European,
Polish, and Slovenian)

Alex Glendinning's Hungarian Pages
glen@itl.net
http://user.itl.net/~glen/Hungarianintro.html
Alex Glendinning
(links to other eastern European resources, as

well as Hungarian)

American Hungarian Federation
1450 Grace Avenue
Cleveland, OH 44107

American Hungarian Library and Historical Society
215 East 82nd Street
New York, NY 10028
(212) 744-5298
Dr. Leslie E. Acsay
Pub. *Hungarian Digest*, quarterly

Hettinger County Historical Society
Banot German Hungarian Museum
(see North Dakota, Part 2)

Hungarian/American Friendship Society
1035 Starbrook Drive
Galt, CA 95632
(209) 744-8099
doug@dholmes.com
http://www.dholmes.com
Douglas Holmes, Director
Pub. *Régi Magyarország "Old Hungary"*
(the newsletter of the Hungarian/American Friendship Society of Sacramento), quarterly, $3.00 per issue
(covers modern Hungary, Slovakia, and parts of Romania—Transylvania "Erdély" and the Banat; part of far-western Ukraine; and parts of Croatia, Slovenia and Serbia; books and maps of Hungary, Slovakia, Ukraine, Transylvania, Banat)
$10.00 per year membership (includes free advice during research); Hungarian, German, Romanian and Slovak translation services for members only

Hungarian Genealogical Society
415 Bridgeview Drive
Perrysburg, OH 43551-1958
Pub. *Newsletter*, quarterly

Hungarian Genealogy Newsletter
PO Box 13548
Saint Louis, MO 63138
Maryann Schicker
Pub. *Hungarian Genealogy Newsletter*
(primarily Baldman, Friez, Horvath, Siklost, Staub, Tinya, Toth and Weisz families)

Hungarian Heritage Center
300 Somerset Street
New Brunswick, NJ 08903
(732) 846-5777

Hungarian-Jewish Special Interest Group
(see Jewish, below)

Dr. Andrew T. Udvardy Reference Library
66 Plum Street
New Brunswick, NJ 08902

University of Chicago Library
Louis Szathmary Family Collection
1100 East 57th Street
Chicago, IL 60637-1502
(773) 702-0691
Barbara Van Deventer, Assistant Director for Collection
development items from the collection that are not cataloged may be paged from special collections Mon–Fri 9:00–5:00
(A large collection of books and serials in broad subjects, not primarily genealogy-related; "The Hungarian works have not been cataloged, but brief records for over 2,000 of them are in our online catalog.")

Icarian
(see French)

Icelandic
(see Swedish)

Indian
(see Asian or Native American)

Irish
(see also English and Scottish)

All-Ireland Heritage, Inc.
PO Box 7
Dunn Loring, VA 22027
(703) 560-4496
Donna Reid Hotaling, President
Pub. *All-Ireland Heritage*, quarterly, $24.00 per year subscription

American Committee for Irish Studies
Department of English
University of Wisconsin
Milwaukee, WI 53201
(414) 963-4508
John R. Moore, President

American Irish Historical Society (AIHS)
Library
991 Fifth Avenue
New York, NY 10028
(212) 288-2263; (212) 628-7927
http://www.aihs.org
William Cobert, Director
Mon–Fri 10:30–5:30
Pub. *Recorder*, semiannually, $22.50 per year subscription
("Our library has only a very small and selective genealogical collection; we do not undertake genealogical research on behalf of interested parties.")
$100.00 per year membership

Ancient Order of Hibernians in America
National Secretary's Office
31 Logan Street
Auburn, NY 13021-3925
(315) 904-8777 (National Editor); (315) 904-0005 FAX (National Editor)
http://www.aoh.com
Frank Feighery, National Editor
The National Hibernian Digest (a tabloid newspaper, the official organ of the AOH), six times per year, $8.00 per year subscription from National Editor, 530 Ellsworth Avenue, A1, Bronx, NY 10465-1751
("The Ancient Order of Hibernians is a fraternal order, founded in New York City in 1836, and open to Catholic men of Irish birth or descent. Our sister organization is the Ladies Ancient Order of Hibernians.")

Belgrave Publications
(distributed by Irish Books and Media, Inc.)
1433 Franklin Avenue, East
Minneapolis, MN 55404-2135
(612) 871-3505; (612) 871-3358
irishbook@aol.com
Ethna McKiernan, President
Mon–Fri 8:30–5:00
Pub. *Irish Roots*, quarterly, $18.00 per year subscription

Buffalo Irish Genealogical Society
GAAA Library Buffalo Irish Center
245 Abbott Road
Buffalo, NY 14220
(716) 662-1164
Dmshine@aol.com
http://www.buffalonet.org/army/bigs.htm

Donna M. Shine, Treasurer
Oct–June: third Tue 6:00–9:00, first & second Sat 10:00–2:00; July–Sept: by appointment

Public Library of Cincinnati and Hamilton County
(see Ohio, Part 2)

Dome Shadow Press
(see Publishers, Part 4)

Eibhlin's Genealogy Pages
Irish in 19th-Century Portsmouth, New Hampshire
http://www.fortunecity.com/bally/limerick/123/gen/dir.htm
Eibhlin MacIntosh
(online book with other Irish links)

The Society of the Friendly Sons of Saint Patrick of Philadelphia
PO Box 969
Dublin, PA 18917-0969
(215) 249-9337; (215) 249-9331 FAX
info@friendlysons.com
http://www.friendlysons.com
(links of interest)

Irish America Magazine/Irish Voice Newspaper
(432 Park Avenue South, Suite 1503, New York, NY 10016—office location)
PO Box 1277 (mailing address)
Bellmawr, NJ 08099-5277
(212) 725-2993 (New York); (800) 582-6642 (Subscription requests); (212) 779-1198 FAX (New York)
http://www.irishamerica.com
Christine Rein, Marketing and Events Coordinator
9:30–5:30
Pub. *Irish America Magazine*, bimonthly, $21.95 per year subscription; *Irish Voice Newspaper*, weekly, $30.00 per year subscription
(magazine includes "Irish Roots," genealogy column)

The Irish American Cultural Institute (IACI)
University of Saint Thomas
(2115 Summit Avenue—location)
Mail #5026 (mailing address)
Saint Paul, MN 55105-1096
(612) 962-6040
Pub. *Journal of Irish Studies, Éire-Ireland*, quarterly, $35.00 per year subscription

Irish American Heritage Center
4626 North Knox Avenue
Chicago, IL 60630-4030
(773) 282-7035; (773) 282-7045; (773) 282-0380 FAX
Frank Kilker
Office: Mon–Fri 9:00–5:00, Sat 9:00–2:00; Museum: Wed–Sat by appointment
(culture and community life)

TIARA (The Irish Ancestral Research Association)
PO Box 619
Sudbury, MA 01776-0619
(978) 894-0062
ahern@world.std.com
http://world.std.com/~ahern/TIARA.html
meetings in Lecture Room 307, Higgins Hall, Boston College, Commonwealth Avenue, Chestnut Hill, MA: second Fri (Sept–June) 7:30
Pub. *TIARA*, quarterly; *Meeting Notice*, monthly

(Irish, Irish-American, Irish-Canadian;
publishes *Helpful Suggestions for Irish
Research*, $6.00 postpaid)
$10.00 per year membership

Irish Cultural Center Library
2700 45th Street
San Francisco, CA 94116-2696
(415) 661-2700

The Irish Family History Forum, Inc.
PO Box 67
Plainview, NY 11803-0067
CorresSecy@ifhf.org
http://www.ifhf.org
Meg Assip, Corresponding Secretary
Pub. *News Letter of the Irish Family History
Forum, Inc.*, ten times per year (monthly,
Sept–June)
(metropolitan New York area and U.S.;
member surname search list)
$15.00 per year membership

Irish Family History Foundation
http://www.irishroots.net
("The Irish Family History Foundation is the
co-ordinating body for a network of
government-approved genealogical
research centres in the Republic of Ireland
[Eire] and in Northern Ireland which have
computerised tens of millions of Irish
ancestral records of different types." The
web site includes links to centers.)
research: $70.00 initial search for centers
providing full service, $230.00 for
comprehensive family history report,
single-record searches also available from
several centres

The Irish Genealogical Foundation
PO Box 7575
Kansas City, MO 64116
(816) 454-2410 voice & FAX
http://www.irishroots.com (free newsletter on
home page)
Michael C. O'Laughlin, Proprietor and
Editor
Pub. *Journal of Irish Families*, monthly;
quarterly email newsletter available free
on home page
(1,000 volume lending library for Irish
research; database of 62,000 surname
listings; publisher of Irish family works in
America; seller of new and used books of
Irish interest)
$54.00 per year membership (includes six
issues of journal per year), $104.00 per
year gold membership (includes twelve
issues of journal per year); free catalog on
request

**Irish Genealogical Society, International
(IGSI)**
Minnesota Genealogical Society
(5768 Olson Memorial Highway, Golden
Valley, MN 55422—library location)
PO Box 16585 (mailing address)
Saint Paul, MN 55116-0585
(763) 595-9347 (Library); (952) 595-9437
(Ms. Lund); (952) 574-1436 (Ms.
Mullinax)
miscmute@aol.com (Ms. Lund)
http://www.rootsweb.com/~irish
Kathy Lund; Beth Mullinax
Library: Wed–Thur & Sat 9:00–3:00, Tue &
Thur 6:30–9:30; Irish Days: second Sat
Pub. *The Septs*, quarterly (Jan, Apr, July,
Oct)
(Irish and Ireland, including the Scots-Irish)
$15.00 per year membership; research: free
advice to members

Irish Genealogical Society of Wisconsin
PO Box 13766
Wauwatosa, WI 53213-1220
(414) 251-5564 FAX
jmcnamee@wi.rr.com
http://my.execpc.com/~igsw
meetings at The Shorewood Library
Community Center, 2030 East Shorewood
Boulevard, Shorewood, WI: usually on a
Mon 7:00
Pub. *The Irish Genealogical Quarterly*
(Irish family research, Irish-American and
Irish history)
$15.00 per year membership

Irish Interest Group of Portland
PO Box 42567
Portland, OR 97242-0567
(503) 287-9672
Mary Griffin, Chairperson

County Mayo Chronicles
PO Box 535
Farmington, MI 48332
http://genealogy.org/~ajmorris/ireland/
ireemg1.htm (Irish Emigrants);
http://genealogy.org/~ajmorris/ireland/
ireland.htm (Irish Genealogy)
Andrew J. Morris
Pub. *County Mayo Chronicles*, quarterly,
$14.00 per year subscription

Museum of American Frontier Culture
(see Virginia, Part 2)

National Archives of Ireland
http://www.kst.dit.ie/nat-arch

Pioneer Publications
PO Box 1179
Tumtum, WA 99034-1179
(509) 276-1740
Shirley Penna-Oakes, Editor
Pub. *Irish Queries*, $6.00 plus $1.75 postage
per issue

University of Saint Thomas
Luxembourg; Celtic nations: Ireland,
Scotland, Wales; Isle of Man, Cornwall, and
Brittany
(see Minnesota, Part 2)

Utah Genealogical Association
Irish Chapter
(see Utah, Part 2)

**Western Pennsylvania Genealogical
Society**
(see Pennsylvania, Part 2)

Italian
(see also Eastern European)

American-Italian Historical Association
169 Country Club Road
Chicago Heights, IL 60411
(708) 756-5359 (day); (708) 756-7168
(evening); (708) 756-5320 FAX
d-candeloro@govst.edu
http://www.mobilito.com/aiha
Dominic Candeloro, AIHA Executive
Director
$35.00 per year membership

American Italian Renaissance Foundation
(537 South Peters Street—location)
PO Box 2392 (mailing address)
New Orleans, LA 70130
(504) 522-7294; (504) 522-1657 FAX
http://www.airf.org
Bette Cadwell
Wed–Sat 10:00–3:00

Pub. *Italian American Digest*, quarterly,
$10.00 per year subscription
("Houses The Maselli Museum and Research
Library.")

**Buffalo and Western New York Italian
Genealogy Society**
238 Fairways Boulevard
Tonawanda, NY 14150-4601
(716) 833-2792; (716) 695-2923

**The John D. Calandra Italian American
Institute**
The City University of New York
Graduate Center
25 West 43rd Street
New York, NY 10036
(212) 642-2094; (212) 642-2030 FAX
Dr. Joseph V. Scelsa; Maria Fosco
Pub. *Quarterly*, free

Enrico Fermi Cultural Center
610 East 186th Street
Bronx, NY 10458
(718) 933-6410

**Genealogical and Heraldic Institute of
America**
American Italian Congress
Italian Historical Society of America
111 Columbia Heights
Brooklyn, NY 11201
(718) 852-2929

Italian American Cultural Society
28111 Imperial
Warren, MI 48063

Italian Cultural Center
1621 North 39th Avenue
Stone Park, IL 60165-1105
(708) 345-3842
Mon–Fri 10:00–5:00

Italian Cultural Society
(Twenty-fourth Street and Fourth
Avenue—location)
PO Box 189427 (mailing address)
Sacramento, CA 95818
(916) 482-5900 or ITALY-00; (916) 482-
5909 or ITALY-09 FAX
italy@lanset.com
http://italiancenter.net
Bill Cerruti, Executive Director
Mon–Sun 10:30–9:30
Pub. *Altre Voci*, bimonthly
$25.00 per year membership

Italian Genealogical Group
PO Box 626
Bethpage, NY 11714
http://italiangen.org
June DeLalio
meetings: second Sat (Sept–June)
Pub. *Newsletter*, 10 times per year (monthly,
Sept–June); *Surname Database*, annually
$20.00 per year membership

The Italian Genealogy Homepage
Italian Surname Database
ItalianGenealogy@tardio.com
http://italiangenealogy.tardio.com
(articles, links, chat and tips)

Italian Genealogy Interest Group
POINTers In Person, Chapter No. 16
PO Box 2544
Vista, CA 92085-2544
(760) 734-1920
pointsd@yahoo.com
http://www.geocities.com/pointsd
quarterly meetings

Italian Genealogy Society of America
PO Box 3572
Peabody, MA 01961-3572
mdmelnyk@attbi.com
http:/64.252.159.163/igsa/Default.htm
Marcia Iannizzi Melnyk
Pub. *Lo Specchio*, quarterly
$15.00 per year membership

Italo-Albanian Home Page
Stradiotti@aol.com
http://members.aol.com/itaalbi/web/
     arberesh/htm
John D. Cusimano
(descendants of Western Balkan people who
     migrated to Italy in the 15th and 16th
     centuries because of the Ottoman Turkish
     invasions of their ancestral homelands)

**Order of Italian Sons and Daughters of
America**
Weirtonian Lodge No. 183
351 Fairview Drive
Weirton, WV 26062-2408
(304) 797-7680; (304) 797-1349 FAX
Chester P. Grossi, President
Unione, two times per month

**Order of Italian Sons and Daughters of
America**
419 Wood Street
Pittsburgh, PA 15222
(a fraternal association)

Order of Sons of Italy in America
Garibaldi-Meucci Museum
420 Tompkins Avenue
Staten Island, NY 10305
(718) 442-1608; (718) 442-8635
http://community.silive.com/cc/
     GaribaldiMeucci
Emily T. Gear, Curator/Director
Tue–Sun 1:00–5:00
(library and research facility)
$25.00 per year membership; Italian
     language classes: $140.00 for 15 weeks

Order of the Sons of Italy
219 E Street, N.E.
Washington, DC 20002

**POINT/POINTers (Pursuing Our Italian
Names Together)**
PO Box 14966
Las Vegas, NV 89114-4966
(702) 257-6628
POINTERSEDITOR@aol.com
Thomas E. Militello, M.D., Founder
http://www.point-pointers.net
Pub. *POINTers*, quarterly; *Directory* (lists all
     surnames in the POINT surname
     database), annually
(atabase of 22,000 surnames from 4,700
     members)
$40.00 per year membership (submissions to
     database are free)

Society for Italian American History
Boston College
140 Commonwealth Avenue
Chestnut Hill, MA 02167

Japanese
(see Asian)

Jewish
(see also Czech and Polish)

American Jewish Archives
Hebrew Union College
Jewish Institute of Religion

3101 Clifton Avenue
Cincinnati, OH 45220-2488
(513) 221-1875, ext. 403; (513) 221-7812
     FAX
http://home.fuse.net/aja
Kevin Proffitt, Archivist
Mon–Fri 8:30–5:00
Pub. *American Jewish Archives*,
     semiannually
admission: donation

American Jewish Committee
165 East 56th Street
New York, NY 10022
http://www.ajc.org

American Jewish Historical Society
Friedman Memorial Library
2 Thornton Road
Waltham, MA 02154
(781) 891-8110; (781) 899-9208 FAX
http://www.ajhs.org
Mon–Fri 8:30–5:00; Reading Room:
     Mon–Fri 9:00–4:30 by appointment
Pub. *American Jewish History*, quarterly;
     Heritage, semiannually
from $50.00 per year membership; research
     and photocopying fees

Annenberg Research Institute
420 Walnut Street
Philadelphia, PA 19106
(215) 238-1290; (215) 238-1540 FAX
http://libertynet.org/~gencap/ari.html

**Archives of the Jewish Federation of
Nashville and Middle Tennessee**
801 Percy Warner Boulevard
Nashville, TN 37205
(615) 356-3242, ext. 255; (615) 352-0056
     FAX
library@jewishnashville.org
Lee Haas, Director of Libraries and Archives
Mon–Fri 8:30–5:00

Arizona Jewish Historical Society
4710 North 16th Street, Suite 201
Phoenix, AZ 85013
(602) 241-7870; (602) 264-9773 FAX
azjhs@aol.com
http://aspin.asu.edu/azjhs
Risa Mallin, Executive Director
Mon–Fri 9:00–1:00
Pub. *Heritage*, semiannually
("Genealogy is not our primary mission; it is
     a committee.")
$25.00–$500.00 per year membership

**Arizona Jewish Historical
Society—Historical Committee**
720 West Edgewood Avenue
Mesa, AZ 85210

**Arizona Jewish Historical Society of
Southern Arizona, Inc.**
Committee on Genealogy
4181 East Pontatoc Canyon Drive
Tucson, AZ 85718
(520) 299-4486; (520) 615-4672 FAX
Lipseya@prodigy.net
Alfred E. Lipsey, Chair
8:00–5:00
Pub. *The Chronicle*, three times per year
$25.00 per year membership

Avotaynu, Inc.
155 North Washington Avenue
Bergenfield, NJ 07621
(201) 387-7200; (201) 387-2855 FAX
garymokotoff@avotaynu.com
http://www.avotaynu.com
Gary Mokotoff, Publisher

9:00–5:00
Pub. *Avotaynu, The International Review of
     Jewish Genealogy*, quarterly, $32.00 per
     year subscription in the U.S. or Canada,
     $61.00 for two years, $83.00 for three
     years, add $8.00 for each year's
     subscription outside the U.S. or Canada
(Jewish and central and eastern European)

Leo Baeck Institute
15 West 16th Street
New York, NY 10011
(212) 744-6400; (212) 988-1305 FAX
lbaeck@lbi.cjh.org
http://www.lbi.org
Carol Kahn Strauss, Executive Director;
     Karen S. Franklin, *Stammbaum*
Reading Room: Mon–Thur 9:30–4:30
Pub. *Stammbaum: The Newsletter of
     German-Jewish Genealogical Research*,
     two times per year, $20.00 per year
     subscription in the U.S., Canada and
     Mexico, $28.00 per year subscription in
     all other countries (magazine devoted to
     genealogical research in German-speaking
     countries: Germany, Austria, Switzerland,
     Alsace, Bohemia); *LBI News*,
     semiannually; *LBI Memorial Lecture*;
     Publications List; *LBI Yearbook*,
     annually; *Bulletin des LBI* (in German),
     quarterly
("The Leo Baeck Institute is devoted to
     studying the history of German-speaking
     Jewry from its origins to its tragic
     destruction by the Nazis and to preserving
     its culture.")
$100.00 per year membership (does not
     include *Stammbaum*)

Belarus SIG
davefox73@earthlink.net
http://www.jewishgen.org/Belarus
David Fox, Coordinator
("The purpose of the Belarus SIG is to
     combine our resources of time, expertise
     and money to aid Jewish genealogy
     researchers with an interes in the *gubernii*
     (provinces) of Grodno, Minsk, Mogilev
     and Vitebsk, as well as in the Lida and
     Vileika *uyezds* (districts) of the Vilna
     gubernia." Includes many links to
     resources)

**The Leona G. and David A. Bloom
Southwest Jewish Archives**
The University of Arizona Library
Special Collections
(1510 East University—location)
PO Box 2100055 (mailing address)
Tucson, AZ 85721-0055
(520) 621-6423 (Reading Room); (520) 621-
     9733 FAX
davisj@u.library.arizona.edu
http://www.library.arizona.edu/images/
     swja/swjalist.html
Jan Davis, Library Specialist
Fall and spring semesters: Mon–Thur
     9:00–6:00, Fri 9:00–5:00, Sat noon–4:00;
     Summer session: Mon–Fri 10:00–5:00;
     Intersession: Mon–Fri 11:00–5:00
(includes West Texas, New Mexico, Arizona
     and Southern California)

**B'nai B'rith Klutznick National Jewish
Museum**
1640 Rhode Island Avenue, N.W.
Washington, DC 20036
(202) 857-6583; (202) 857-6609
Ori Z. Soltes, Director
Mon–Fri & Sun 10:00–5:00
Pub. *Museum Newsletter*, semiannually;
     exhibit catalogues

(holdings also include archaeology and contemporary art, not only ritual and folk art)
from $36.00 per year membership

Bohemia-Moravia SIG
http://www.jewishgen.org/BohMor
("A site dedicated to the study of Jewish genealogy in the regions of Bohemia, Moravia and Austria.")

William Breman Jewish Heritage Museum
Ida Pearle and Joseph Cuba Jewish Archives and Genealogical Center
1440 Spring Street
Atlanta, GA 30309
(404) 873-1661; (404) 874-7043 FAX

Chicago Jewish Historical Society
Spertus Museum of Judaica
618 South Michigan Avenue
Chicago, IL 60605
(312) 663-5634 (answering machine)
Walter Roth, President; Clare Greenberg, Secretary
Pub. *Chicago Jewish History*, quarterly, $1.50 postpaid per issue
("The Society seeks out, collects and preserves appropriate written, spoken and photographic records; publishes historical information; holds public meetings at which various aspects of Chicago Jewish history are treated; mounts appropriate exhibits; and offers tours of Jewish historical sites.")
$25.00 per year membership

Columbus Jewish Historical Society
1175 College Avenue
Columbus, OH 43209
(614) 237-7686
Barbara R. Schehr, Executive Director
Mon–Thur 9:00–3:00
Pub. *Reflections*, three times per year
$25.00 per year membership

Computer Center for Jewish Genealogy
654 Westfield Avenue
Elizabeth, NJ 07208
(908) 353-5575; (908) 353-6080 FAX
Dr. Neil Rosenstein
by appointment
(Jewish and rabbinical genealogy; Chassidic dynasties)

Congregation Beth Ahabah Museum and Archives Trust
1109 West Franklin Street
Richmond, VA 23220
(804) 353-2668
Cynthia N. Krumbein, Director/Archivist
Mon & Sun 10:00–3:00, Tue–Wed 10:00–4:00, Thur 10:00–2:00
Pub. *Generations*, three times per year
$25.00 per year membership; research: $25.00 minimum; museum admission: $2.00 per person suggested donation

Congregation Bina
600 West End Avenue, Apartment 1-C
New York, NY 10024-1643
(212) 873-4261
Samuel M. Daniel, Editor
9:00–5:00
Pub. *Kol Bina*, occasionally, free
(concerning the Jews of India in the U.S.)

Congregation Mickve Israel
PO Box 816
Savannah, GA 31402-0816

Dallas Jewish Historical Society

Genealogy Division
7900 Northaven Road
Dallas, TX 75230
(214) 369-8373
info@djhs.com
http://www.djhs.org/index.php?menu=1
Debbie Tobias, Director
Mon–Tue & Thur 10:00–3:00
Pub. *Journal of Dallas Jewish Historical Society*, quarterly
(dealing specifically with Dallas Jewish history and genealogy, although has some U.S. and foreign historical and genealogical publications and newsletters on site)
$50.00 per year membership

Denmark SIG
elsebeth@paikin.dk
http://www.jewishgen.org/Denmark
("The purpose of the Denmark SIG is to gather, present and preserve genealogical and historical information about the Jewish communities primarily in Denmark. The mobility between the Scandinavian countries has always been significant; it must therefore be tantamount that the Denmark SIG does not strictly confine itself to Denmark—but if possible and when necessary try to encompass information from the other Scandinavian countries.")

Early American SIG
http://www.jewishgen.org/EarlyAmerican
Rachel Unkefer, Coordinator
("A resource for genealogists researching Jewish families who came to the United States before the larger immigration waves of the 1880s and later.")

El Paso Jewish Historical Society
Temple Mount Sinai
4408 North Stanton
El Paso, TX 79902
(915) 532-5959

EugeneGen
The Eugene Oregon Jewish Genealogy Study Group
815 Park Terrace
Eugene, OR 97404-3081
charlesf@booksandwriters.com
http://www.nwfam.com/eugenegen.html
Charles Fleishman

Isaac Franck Jewish Public Library
Board of Jewish Education
11710 Hunters Lane
Rockville, MD 20852-2363

French SIG
http://www.jewishgen.org/French
Pierre Hahn, Coordinator; Rosanne Leeson, Coordinator
("Information about researching in the French-speaking countries of France, Belgium, Luxembourg and the Suisse Romande.")

Genealogy and Family History Committee of the New Mexico Jewish Historical Society
1428 Miracerros Loop, South
Santa Fe, NM 87501-4024
(505) 988-5751
sgitomer@aol.com
http://www.nmculture.org/HTML/northc.htm
Steven J. Gitomer
Pub. *Newsletter*, quarterly
$24.00 per year membership

The Genealogy Council of the Jewish Museum of Maryland
3200 Pinkney Road
Baltimore, MD 21215
Elizabeth Carus

German Jewish Special Interest Group (GerSIG)
Leo Baeck Institute
15 West 16th Street
New York, NY 10011
(212) 744-6400 (Karen Franklin), (212) 988-1305 FAX (Karen Franklin)
wlfrank@pacbell.net;
KFranklin@lbi.cjh.org;
JPL25@cornell.edu (Lowens);
obermayer@alum.mit.edu
http://www.jewishgen.org/GerSIG
Werner Frank, Karen Franklin, John Lowens, and Arthur Obermayer, Coordinators
("Our purpose is to present and preserve genealogical information about the Jewish communities in German-speaking regions and to trace our ancestors and better understand the lives they led. Our coverage includes other German-speaking areas such as Austria, parts of Switzerland, Alsace, Lorraine, Bohemia and Moravia.")

Gesher Galicia
c/o 549 Cypress Lane
Severna Park, MD 21146
geshergalicia@comcast.net
http://www.jewishgen.org/galicia
Shelley Kellerman Pollero, Coordinator
Pub. *The Galitzianer*, quarterly; *Gesher Galicia Family Finder*, annually, subscriptions available to organizations and libraries
("Gesher Galicia is a membership organization for those interested in researching their *Jewish* roots in the former Austrian province of Galicia, now part of southern Poland and part of western Ukraine.")
$30.00 per year membership (information and Membership Form on web site; send to Membership Chair, Leon Gold, PO Box 31093, Santa Barbara, CA 93130-1093, LJG218@worldnet.att.net)

Greater Houston Jewish Genealogical Society
3446 Quail Meadow
Missouri City, TX 77459
gses3446@hal-pc.org
http://www.texsys.com/ghjgs
Evan Snyder
$18.00 per year membership

Holocaust Library and Research Center
(see Miscellaneous, Part 4)

Holocaust Memorial and Resource Center of Central Florida
(see Miscellaneous, Part 4)

Holocaust Center of Greater Pittsburgh
(see Miscellaneous, Part 4)

Hungarian Special Interest Group (H-SIG)
http://www.jewishgen.org/Hungary
Vivian Kahn, Moderator
by appointment only
("JewishGen Hungarian Special Interest Group [H-SIG] is for those with Jewish roots in the area known as 'greater Hungary' or pre-Trianon Hungary and includes areas that at one time were

predominantly Hungarian speaking. This includes the whole of or parts of present-day Slovakia, Poland, Ukraine, Czech Republic, Hungary, Austria, Croatia, Serbia, and Romania.")
$10.00 per year membership

Illiana Jewish Genealogical Society
404 Douglas Street
Park Forest, IL 60466
(708) 748-5962
Henry Landauer, President
Pub. *Illiana Jewish Genealogical Society*, quarterly
$20.00 per year membership

International Association of Jewish Genealogical Societies (IAJGS)
PO Box 1094
Agoura Hills, CA 91376
(818) 991-5864
HBookbinder@mednet.ucla.edu
http://www.iajgs.org
Hal Bookbinder, President
(an organization of organizations, "to provide a common voice for issues of significance to its members, to advance our genealogical avocation, and to coordinate items such as the annual Jewish Genealogy Conference")

The Jewish Family Name File
c/o *The National Jewish Post and Opinion*
238 South Meridian Street, Room 502
Indianapolis, IN 46225-1024
Jpost@jewishpostopinion.com
http://www.jewishpostopinion.com
David L. Gold
(mail inquiries only, no telephone or personal inquiries)
75¢ plus SASE for information on services and other publications

Jewish Genealogical Society, Inc.
PO Box 6398
New York, NY 10128
(212) 294-8326
jgsny@aol.com
http://www.jgsny.org
Alex E. Friedlander, President
monthly meetings: Sept–June
Pub. *Dorot*, quarterly
$25.00 per year membership in New York area, $20.00 per year membership if more than 100 miles from New York

Jewish Genealogical Society of Arizona
720 West Edgewood Avenue
Mesa, AZ 85210
(480) 969-1201
Carlton Brooks

Jewish Genealogical Society, Los Angeles
PO Box 55443
Sherman Oaks, CA 91413-5544
(818) 991-5864
soniahoff1@aol.com
http://www.jgsla.org
Sonia Hoffman, President
meetings: third Mon (except July)
Pub. *Roots-Key*, quarterly
$25.00 per year membership

Jewish Genealogical Society of Sacramento
2351 Wyda Way
Sacramento, CA 95825-1160
(916) 485-7258
Judith Persin
meetings: third Mon (Sept–July)

Jewish Genealogical Society of Colorado

1982 South Oneida Street
Denver, CO 80224

Jewish Genealogical Society of Connecticut, Inc.
17 Salem Walk
Milford, CT 06430
(203) 874-4572
Howard Siegel
Kol Havarim, Glastonbury Congregation, or Shalom, Orange Congregation: third Sun 1:30
Pub. *Quest*, quarterly
$24.00 per year membership

Jewish Genealogical Society of Broward County
PO Box 17251
Fort Lauderdale, FL 33318
(954) 472-5455; (954) 791-1467 FAX
Bob Koltnow, President
meetings: last Wed 7:00 (Sept–June)
Pub. *Family Gatherings*, monthly
$20.00 per year membership

Jewish Genealogical Society of Greater Miami
18441 N.E. 20th Court
North Miami Beach, FL 33179
(305) 932-1725
Anita R. Drexler, Historian/Librarian
monthly Sun morning

Jewish Genealogical Society of Greater Orlando
PO Box 941332
Maitland, FL 32794
(407) 862-0043
Jay Schleichkorn, President
second Tues (except July–Aug)
Pub. *Etz Chaim* (*Tree of Life*), quarterly, $5.00 per copy
$25.00 per year membership

Jewish Genealogical Society of Palm Beach County (JGSPBCI)
(South County Civic Center, 16700 Jog Road, Delray Beach—location)
PO Box 7796 (mailing address)
Delray Beach, FL 33484
(561) 734-7946
jakies51@aol.com
Dr. Marvin Hamburg, President
meetings: Oct–May: second Wed 1:00–4:00
Pub. *Scattered Seeds*, four times per year, $3.50 per issue for back issues
$18.00 per year membership

Jewish Genealogical Society of Georgia
2700 Claridge Court
Atlanta, GA 30360
(770) 458-6664
Gary Palgon, President
Pub. *Yichus Y'all*, quarterly
$25.00 per year membership

Jewish Genealogical Society of Illinois
PO Box 515
Northbrook, IL 60065-0515
(312) 666-0100
jrfraz@comcast.net
http://www.jewishgen.org/jgsi
Judith R. Frazin, President
Pub. *Morasha*, quarterly
("We are an organization which helps people who are doing family history research. We have no files or records, but we can give help on how to do research.")
$25.00 per year membership; Hebrew, Yiddish, German and Polish translation services for members

Jewish Genealogical Society of Louisville
Israel T. Naamani Library
3600 Dutchmans Lane
Louisville, KY 40205
(502) 459-0798
Milton Z. Russman, Special Librarian
Mon & Wed 9:00–5:00, Tue 9:00–7:00, Thur 9:00–6:00, Fri 1:00–3:00, Sun 1:00–5:00
Pub. *Toledoth—These Are the Generations*, free

Jewish Genealogical Society of Greater Washington
PO Box 31122
Bethesda, MD 20824-1122
http://www.jewishgen.org/jgsgw
Faith Nachman Klein, President
most Sundays 10:00–noon
Pub. *Mishpacha*, quarterly, $10.00 per year subscription
$20.00 per year membership

Jewish Genealogical Society of Greater Boston
PO Box 610366
Newton Highlands, MA 02161-0366
(617) 796-8522 (answering machine)
info@jgsgb.org; president@jgsgb.org
http://www.jgsgb.org
Fred Davis, President
Pub. *Mass-Pocha*, quarterly, $12.00 per year nonmember or out-of-area subscription
$25.00 per year membership; admission to meetings: $5.00 for nonmembers

Jewish Genealogical Society of Michigan
PO Box 251693
West Bloomfield, MI 48325-1693
Plutsk@aol.com; jgsprograms@aol.com
http://www.jgsmi.org
Steve Gold
Pub. *Generations*, irregularly
$36.00 per year membership

Jewish Genealogical Society of Saint Louis (JGSSTL)
United Hebrew Congregation
1 Gudder Campus
13788 Conway Road
Creve Coeur, MO 63141
letvak@aol.com
http://www.stlcyberjew.com/jgs-stl

Jewish Genealogical Society of Southern Nevada
PO Box 29342
Las Vegas, NV 89126
carmont7@juno.com
Carole Montello, President
meetings: third Sun
Pub. *Family Legacies*
$20.00 per year membership

Jewish Genealogical Society of North Jersey
YM-YWHA of North Jersey
Charles and Bessie Goldman Library
1 Pike Drive
Wayne, NJ 07470
(973) 595-0100, ext. 36
http://community.nj.com/cc/jgsnorthjersey
Ms. Evan Stollbach
third Thur 7:00 P.M.
Pub. *Yichus*
$20.00 per year membership

Jewish Genealogical Society of Greater Buffalo
174 Peppertree Drive, #7
Amherst, NY 14228
(716) 691-4828

Muriel Selling

Jewish Genealogical Society of Rochester
265 Viennawood Drive
Rochester, NY 14618
(716) 271-2118, (716) 477-5789 FAX
bkahn@frontiernet.net
http://www.memo.com/jcc/jgsr
Dr. Bruce Kahn, President

Jewish Genealogical Society of Dayton
PO Box 60338
Dayton, OH 45406
(937) 277-3995
Dr. Leonard Spialter, President
Pub. *HA-GESHER* (*The Bridge*), monthly
(computerized database on past and current
Jewish community of Dayton)
$15.00 per year membership

Jewish Genealogical Society of Oregon
PO Box 19736
Portland, OR 97280
sgshapiro@comcast.net
http://www.rootsweb.com/~orjgs
Sandra Shapiro, President
meetings: bimonthly (Sept–May)
Pub. *Shalshelet*, quarterly
$23.00 per year membership

**Jewish Genealogical Society of Greater
Philadelphia**
1279 June Road
Huntingdon Valley, PA 19006-8405
priluki@voicenet.com
http://www.jewishgen.org/jgsp
Leonard Markowitz
meetings at Gratz College: second Mon
(except Jan, Feb, July, Aug) 7:45 P.M.
Pub. *Chronicles*, quarterly; *Bulletin*, monthly
("comprehensive genealogical library [over
400 titles] in a dedicated area within the
Tuttleman Library at Gratz College")
$20.00 per year membership: queries: $6.00
for first 25 words, 25¢ for each additional
word, free name, address and phone
number

Jewish Genealogical Society of Pittsburgh
2131 Fifth Avenue
Pittsburgh, PA 15219
(412) 471-0772; (412) 471-1004 FAX
JulFalk@aol.com
http://www.jewishgen.org/jgs-pittsburgh
Julian Falk, Chairman
Pub. *Z'chor/Remember*, semiannually, $2.50
per issue for nonmembers
$20.00 per year membership

**Jewish Genealogical Society of Salt Lake
City**
3510 Fleetwood Drive
Salt Lake City, UT 84109
Thomas W. Noy

**Jewish Genealogical Society of Tidewater
Virginia**
Jewish Community Center
7300 Newport Avenue
Norfolk, VA 23505
(757) 489-1371
meetings: fourth Sun (Sept–June)

**Jewish Genealogical Society of
Washington State**
c/o 23208 N.E. 126th Street
Redmond, WA 98053
maven@jgsws.org
http://www.jgws.org
meetings at Stroum Jewish Community
Center, 3801 East Mercer Way, Mercer
Island: second Mon 7:00

Jewish Genealogical Society of Montreal
(514) 484-0100; (514) 484-7306
President@jgs-montreal.org
http://www.jgs-montreal.org
Stanley Diamond, President

**Jewish Genealogy Society of Orange
County**
2370-1D Via Mariposa, West
Laguna Hills, CA 92653-2150
(949) 855-4692
Dorothy Kohanski, Membership
meetings: second Sun 2:00–4:00
Pub. *Shorashim*, three times per year, $8.00
per year subscription
$18.00 per year membership

Jewish Genealogy Society of New Orleans
PO Box 7811
Metairie, LA 70010-7811
(504) 888-3817
vkarno@kozberg.com
Vicki Karno, Vice President
meetings: Sun afternoon (six times per year,
Sept, Oct, Nov, Mar, Apr, May)
Pub. *Bayou Branches*, one or two times per
year
$25.00 per year membership

**Jewish Genealogy Society of Long Island,
Inc.**
37 Westcliff Drive
Dix Hills, NY 11746
(631) 549-9532
JGSLI@suffolk.lib.ny.us
http://www.jewishgen.org/jgsli
Renée Steinig, Community Liaison
Library housed at the Plainview-Old
Bethpage Public Library, 999 Old
Country Road, Plainview, NY 11803:
Mon–Fri 9:00–9:00, Sat 9:30–5:30, Sun
1:00–9:00; meetings at the Mid-Island
JCC, 45 Manetto Hill Road, Plainview:
fourth Sun (Sept–June)
Pub. *Lineage*, quarterly
$20.00 per year membership

**Jewish Genealogy Society of Cleveland,
Inc.**
996 Eastlawn Drive
Highland Heights, OH 44143-3126
(216) 449-2326; (216) 621-7560 FAX
Arlene Blank Rich, President
Volunteer Group: 9:00–9:00
Pub. *The Cleveland Kol*, quarterly, $6.50 per
issue
("We strongly emphasize networking and
help out-of-towners locate their family
roots.")
$25.00 per year membership

**Jewish Historical Society of Greater
Hartford**
Simons Family Suite
335 Bloomfield Avenue
West Hartford, CT 06117-1542
(860) 236-4571, ext. 341; (860) 233-0802
FAX
Marsha Lotstein, Director
by appointment
Pub. *Connecticut Jewish History*, irregularly,
$13.00 postpaid per volume to
nonmembers, $6.00 postpaid per volume
for members
(library and archival material relating to
greater Hartford)
$25.00 per year membership

**Jewish Historical Society of Greater New
Haven, Inc.**
SCSU, Wintergreen Building
501 Crescent Street

New Haven, CT 06515-1355
(203) 392-6125
Marian Ottaviano, Administrator
Mon–Fri 8:30–12:30
Pub. *Jews in New Haven*, approximately
every two years
("Our holdings consist of archival
information and memorabilia
documenting the history of the Jewish
community of the New Haven area.")
$15.00 per year membership; research:
$20.00 for the first hour, $9.00 for each
additional half-hour

**Jewish Historical Society of Greater
Stamford**
(1035 Newfield Avenue—location)
PO Box 3326 (mailing address)
Stamford, CT 06905
(203) 321-1373, ext. 150; (203) 322-6081
FAX
Irwin J. Miller, Historian
archives open by appointment only
Pub. *Heritage*, two times per year
(Colonial Jewish families in Connecticut;
Greater Stamford includes Greenwich,
New Canaan, Darien and Pound Ridge)
$15.00 per year membership; no research fee

Jewish Historical Society of Delaware
c/o Historical Society of Delaware
505 North Market Street
Wilmington, DE 19801-3091
(302) 655-7161; (302) 655-6232 (Archives);
(302) 655-7844 FAX
http://www.hsd.org/jhsd.htm
Historical Society of Delaware: Mon
1:00–9:00, Tue–Fri 9:00–5:00
$20.00 per year membership

**Jewish Historical Society of Michigan,
Genealogical Branch**
Jewish Genealogical Society of Detroit
3345 Buckingham Trail
West Bloomfield, MI 48033
Janice Goldstein

Jewish Historical Society of Michigan
(163 Madison Avenue, Detroit, MI
48226—location)
24680 Rensselaer (mailing address)
Oak Park, MI 48237
Pub. *Michigan Jewish History*, irregularly
$15.00 per year membership

**Jewish Historical Society of the Upper
Midwest**
Hamline University
1536 Hewitt Avenue
Saint Paul, MN 55104
(612) 641-2407; (612) 641-2956 FAX (to
Jewish Historical Society)
Linda Schloff, Ph.D., Director
Mon & Wed 9:00–5:00, Thur 9:00–noon
Pub. *The Legend*, three to four times per year
$25.00 per year membership; research: first
15 minutes free, will offer list of searchers
for hire

Jewish Historical Society of Central Jersey
228 Livingston Avenue
New Brunswick, NJ 08901
(732) 249-4894; (732) 821-8129 (President);
(732) 828-7415 (Genealogy Chair); (732)
940-1253 FAX (President)
jhscj@cs.com; reiss@rci.rutgers.edu
http://jewishgen.org/jhscj
Alvin Rockoff, President; Nathan Reiss,
Genealogy Chair
Mon–Thur 10:00–2:00, Fri (winter)
9:00–noon, Fri (summer) 10:00–1:00
Pub. *JHSCJ Newsletter*, four to six times per

year
("Dedicated to the preservation of the Jewish history of Central New Jersey, the JHSCJ serves Middlesex, Union, Somerset, Warren, and Hunterton counties. The main functions are to promote, research, and publish when possible all facets of Central New Jersey's Jewish experience. We maintain an Archival Collection of over 130 linear feet of material, which is available to researchers. Our reference library has over 800 volumes. We promote educational programs and exhibits for both the Jewish and general communities.")
$25.00 per year membership

Jewish Historical Society of Metro West
901 Route 10 East
Whippany, NJ 07981
(973) 884-4800, ext. 565; (973) 428-420 FAX
jfien@aol.com
http://www.fiengroup.com/jhs/jhs.htm

The Jewish Historical Society of North Jersey
PO Box 708
West Paterson, NJ 07424-0708
(973) 785-9119
Jerry Nathans, President
Pub. *Newsletter*, semiannually
(local Jewish history; "We do not have personnel or facilities to allow access to our collection.")
$10.00 per year membership

Jewish Historical Society of Trenton
865 Lower Ferry Road
Trenton, NJ 08628
(609) 883-2228

Jewish Historical Society of New York, Inc.
(address withheld upon request)
Pub. *JHS Newsletter*
("The JHSNY does not maintain a library or archives. It's strictly a program-sponsoring organization.")

Jewish Historical Society of South Carolina
College of Charleston
66 George Street
Charleston, SC 29424-0001
(803) 953-7625
perlmutterm@cofc.edu
Martin Perlmutter

Jewish Historical Society of Memphis
163 Beale Street
Memphis, TN 38103
(901) 682-3023
Harriet W. Stern, President
Pub. *JHSM Newsletter*

Jewish Museum of Maryland
15 Lloyd Street
Baltimore, MD 21202
(410) 732-6400; (410) 732-6451 FAX
http://www.jewishmuseumMD.org
Robin Waldman, Archivist
Library and Archives: Mon–Fri 9:30–4:30 by appointment with Archivist; Museum and tours: Tue–Thur & Sun noon–4:00
Pub. *Generations*, annually, $6.00 per issue; *Museum Matters*, quarterly
(Archives of some synagogues, histories, midwife records, rabbi marriage records, personal papers of some outstanding Jewish leaders of Baltimore, businesses; "Genealogies of Maryland Jewish families

are indexed and actively sought.")
$25.00 per year membership; research: $15.00 per surname within facility, $20.00 per surname outside

Jewish Reconstructionist Federation
78 Montgomery Avenue, Suite 9
Elkins Park, PA 19027
http://www.jrf.org

Jewish Resources on the Internet
http://www.opus1.com/emol/tucson/directory/jewish.html

Jewish Theological Seminary of America
Library, Archives and Rare Book Room
3080 Broadway
New York, NY 10027
(212) 678-8080
Mon–Fri 8:30–5:00

JewishGen: The Home of Jewish Genealogy
http://www.jewishgen.org
("JewishGen®, Inc. is the primary Internet source connecting researchers of Jewish genealogy worldwide. Its most popular components are the JewishGen Discussion Group, the *JewishGen Family Finder* (a database of 300,000 surnames and towns), the comprehensive directory of InfoFiles, *ShtetLinks* for over 200 communities, and a variety of databases such as the *ShtetlSeeker* and *Jewish Records Indexing-Poland*. JewishGen's online *Family Tree of the Jewish People* contains data on over two million people.")

K.A.M. Isaiah Israel Congregation
Morton B. Weiss Museum of Judaica
1100 Hyde Park Boulevard
Chicago, IL 60615-2899
(773) 924-1234; (773) 924-1238 FAX
Vicki Goldwyn, Administrator; Rabbi Arnold Jacob Wolf
Mon–Thur 8:30–5:00, Fri 8:30–4:00
(research library)

Kielce-Radom Special Interest Group
Gracie Station, PO Box 127
New York, NY 10027
wblatt@jewishgen.org
http://www.jewishgen.org/KRSIG
Warren Blatt, Editor; Debra Braverman, Membership
Pub. *Kielce-Radom SIG Journal*, quarterly, $26.00 per year subscription in the U.S., $30.00 per year in Canada, $37.00 per year elsewhere
("The Kielce-Radom SIG is for those who are tracing their Jewish roots in Kielce and Radom gubernias [provinces] of the Russian Kingdom of Poland. We have published complete extracts of over 35,000 19th-century Jewish birth, marriage and death records for this region.")

Latin American SIG
http://www.jewishgen.org/infofiles/latamsig.txt
Rob Weisskirch and Carol Skydell, Coordinators
("The Latin American SIG is dedicated to serving as clearinghouse of Jewish genealogical information about present and past communities throughout Latin America. We work cooperatively and reciprocally with individual Jews, Jewish organizations, and Jewish genealogical societies, especially those in Latin America.")

Latvian Jewish Genealogy Special Interest Group
5450 Whitley Park Terrace, Apartment 901
Bethesda, MD 20814-2061
mgetz@erols.com
http://www.jewishgen.org/latvia
Mike Getz, Project Chairman and Treasurer
Pub. *Latvia SIG*, quarterly
(focuses on Jewish genealogical research in Latvia; "to provide research tools to assist members with their own research but we do not have resources to do research on individual families for our members")
$20.00 per year membership

Lithuanian Special Interest Group, Inc. (LitvakSIG)
Department 77-9253
Chicago, IL 60678-9253
litvaks@aol.com
http://www.jewishgen.org/litvak
Pub. *LitvakSIG Digest*, daily (email discussion group)
("LitvakSIG is the primary Internet source connecting researchers of Lithuanian-Jewish genealogy worldwide. Our purpose is to discover, present, and preserve information about our ancestors' lives in Lithuania, and to better understand the lives they led, before the destruction of 95% of Lithuanian Jews in the Shoah.")
$36.00 per year membership

A Living Memorial to the Holocaust-Museum of Jewish Heritage
(see Miscellaneous, Part 4)

Michiana Jewish Historical Society
PO Box 11074
South Bend, IN 46634-0074
(219) 233-9553

National Museum of American Jewish History
55 North Fifth Street, Independence Mall East
Philadelphia, PA 19106-3794
(215) 923-3811
Sallie M. Gross, Associate Director

National Museum of American Jewish Military History
1811 R Street, N.W.
Washington, DC 20009
(202) 265-6280; (202) 462-3192 FAX
Larry J. Richardson, Administrator
Mon–Fri 9:00–5:00; Museum: Sun 1:00–5:00
Pub. *Museum News*, quarterly
(Jewish military; museum, archives, library)
$18.00 per year membership

Nebraska Jewish Historical Society
333 South 132nd Street
Omaha, NE 68154
(402) 334-6442; (402) 334-6441
Barbara Morrison-Bresler, Archivist/Historian
Mon–Thur 9:00–5:30, Fri 9:30–4:00
("We do not specialize in genealogy but have some limited genealogical information in our files.")
$15.00 per year membership

The New York Public Library, Dorot Jewish Division
Fifth Avenue and 42nd Street, Room 84
New York, NY 10018-2788
(212) 930-0601; (212) 642-0141 FAX
freidus@nypl.org
http://www.nypl.org/research/chss/jsw/

jewish.html
Mon & Thur–Sat 10:00–6:00, Tue–Wed
11:00–7:30

Peninsula Jewish Historical Society
2700 Spring Road
Newport News, VA 23606
(757) 930-1422; (757) 435-0737 (President)
Sue Anne Bangel, President
("Small collection of photographs and
memorabilia with oral history tapes and
transcripts of 100, telling the story of
Peninsula Jewry.")
$15.00 per year membership

Philadelphia Jewish Archives Center at the Balch Institute
The Balch Institute for Ethnic Studies
Center for Immigration Research
18 South Seventh Street
Philadelphia, PA 19106-3794
(215) 925-8090, ext. 228
http://www.libertynet.org/~balch
Lily G. Schwartz, Archivist
Mon–Fri 9:00–5:00 (closed Jewish holidays)
Pub. *Philadelphia Jewish Archives Center
News*, semiannually
(The greater Philadelphia Jewish community)
fee scale for staff search of records

Sylvia Plotkin Judaica Museum
10460 North 56th Street
Scottsdale, AZ 85253
Pamela Levin, Director
Tue–Thur 10:00–3:00, Sun noon–3:00
admission: $2.00; Friends Membership
program

Rabbinic Genealogy Special Interest Group (Rav-SIG)
seflaum@aol.com
http://www.jewishgen.org/Rabbinic
Shirley Rotbein Flaum, Coordinator
Pub. *Online Journal*
("a central clearinghouse for researchers of
rabbinic ancestry and rabbinic
genealogies")

Rhode Island Jewish Historical Association
130 Sessions Street
Providence, RI 02906
(401) 728-5067
Eleanor F. Horvitz, Librarian/Archivist
Mon–Fri 9:00–1:30
Pub. *Rhode Island Jewish Historical
Association Newsletter*, quarterly; *Rhode
Island Jewish Historical Notes*, annually,
$20.00 per issue for nonmembers
(city directories, archives on individual
Jewish families and organizations to
which they belonged, synagogue and
cemetery records)
$25.00 per year membership; research: no
standard fee, copying on acid-free paper:
25¢ per sheet

Rocky Mountain Jewish Historical Society and Beck Archives
Penrose Library
University of Denver
2199 South University Boulevard
Denver, CO 80208
(303) 871-3020
Jeanne Abrams, Ph.D., Executive Director
by appointment
Pub. *Rocky Mountain Jewish Historical
Notes*, irregularly
(collection includes records of the National
Jewish Hospital and the Jewish
Consumptives Relief Society (JCRS))
$30.00 per year membership

Romanian Jewish Genealogy Special Interest Group
(303) 451-6080 (Publisher)
http://www.jewishgen.org/romsig
(exchanging information about their
genealogical research for Jewish ancestors
from Romania—past and present
boundaries, including Bessarabia and
Bukovina; searchers for non-Jewish
ancestors are welcome to join, but
emphasis is on finding old censuses, vital
statistics, synagogue, school, and burial
society records specifically identified as
Jewish)
$20.00 per year membership; translation of
Romanian, Hebrew and/or Yiddish texts
for members only

Routes to Roots
136 Sandpiper Key
Secaucus, NJ 07094-2210
(201) 866-4075; (201) 864-9222 FAX
http://www.routestoroots.com
Miriam Weiner, C.G., President
(Authored *Jewish Roots in Poland* and
Jewish Roots in Ukraine and Moldova.
Offers "archive research in Poland,
Ukraine, Moldova and Belarus,
customized tours for individuals and
families to Ukraine, Moldova and Belarus,
and 'Town Visits' on your behalf to towns
in Ukraine, Moldova and Belarus.")

Russian-Baltic Information Center—Blitz
(see Russian, below)

The San Diego Jewish Genealogical Society
PO Box 927089
San Diego, CA 92192-7089
(619) 280-2913 (Vice President)
wsmarcus@cox.net
http://www.sdjgs.org
Wayne Marcus, President; Jeff Doerner, Vice
President
meetings at the Lawrence Family Jewish
Community Center, 4126 Executive
Drive, La Jolla (near UTC): second Sun
(except May and Jewish holidays)
1:00–4:00
Pub. *Discovery*, four times per year
(Extensive private library)
$25.00 per year membership; meeting
admission: $3.00 for nonmembers

San Francisco Bay Area Jewish Genealogical Society
PO Box 471616
San Francicso, CA 94147-1616
jfrankel@lmi.net
http://www.jewishgen.org/sfbajgs
Jeremy Frankel, President
meetings: third Sun (odd-numbered months
in San Francisco) 1:00, third Mon (even-
numbered months in Los Altos Hills) 7:30
Pub. *Zichron Note: San Francisco Bay Area
Jewish Genealogical Society*, $5.00 per
issue to nonmembers
$20.00 per year membership

Savannah Jewish Archives
c/o Georgia Historical Society
501 Whittaker Street
Savannah, GA 31499

SefardSIG
malkajef@orthohelp.com
http://www.jewishgen.org/SefardSIG
Jeff Malka, Webmaster
("for researchers of Sephardic genealogy:
Jews who are descendants of the former
Jews of Spain and Portugal.")

Society for the History of Czechoslovak Jews, Inc.
87-08 Santiago Street
Holliswood, NY 11423
(718) 468-6844
Lewis Weiner and Gertrude Hirschler,
Editors
Pub. *Review of the Society for the History of
Czechoslovak Jews*, annually, $9.00 per
issue for nonmembers, $8.00 per issue for
members
$15.00 per year membership (does not
include periodical)

South Africa Jewish Genealogy Special Interest Group (SA-SIG)
saul@swico.demon.co.uk; mgetz@erols.com
http://www.jewishgen.org/SAfrica
Dr. Saul Issroff, Editor-in-Chief; Beryl
Baleson, Editor; Mike Getz, Subscription
Pub. *The SA-SIG Newsletter*
("SA-SIG provides information of interest to
those researching Jewish family history in
the communities of South Africa, Lesotho
[Basutoland], Botswana [Bechuanaland],
Zimbabwe [Southern Rhodesia], Zambia
[Northern Rhodesia], Swaziland,
Moçambique and the former Belgian
Congo.")

Southern Jewish Historical Society
History Department
Valdosta State College
PO Box 179
Valdosta, GA 31698
(229) 333-5947

Suwalk-Lomza Interest Group
3701 Connecticut Avenue, N.W., Apartment
#228
Washington, DC 20008-4556
http://feefhs.org/jsig/frgslsig.html
Marlene Silverman, Ph.D., Chairman and
Editor
Pub. *Landsman*, quarterly
(for Jewish genealogy; focus on the former
Polish provinces of Suwalki and Lomza as
constituted in 1866–1914, today's southern
Lithuania and northeastern Poland)
$22.00 per year membership

Temple Israel Library
Longwood Avenue and Plymouth Street
Boston, MA 02215
(617) 566-3960
Ann Abrams, Librarian
Sept–May: Mon 3:00–9:00, Tue 1:00–6:00,
Wed 11:00–3:00, Thur 9:00–6:00, Sun
9:00–1:00; June–Aug: Mon–Thur
9:00–5:00

Ukraine SIG
haflo@shaw.ca
http://www.jewishgen.org/Ukraine
Florence Elman, Coordinator
("To facilitate access to records of former
Russian Empire Gubernias now in
Ukraine: Podolia, Volhynia, Kiev,
Poltava, Chernigov, Kharkov, Kherson,
Taurida and Ekaterinoslav.")

Union of American Hebrew Congregations
838 Fifth Avenue
New York, NY 10021
http://www.uahc.org

Union of Orthodox Jewish Congregations of America
333 Seventh Avenue
New York, NY 10001
http://www.ou.org

United States Holocaust Memorial Museum
(see Miscellaneous, Part 4)

United Synagogues of Conservative Judaism
155 Fifth Avenue
New York, NY 10010
http://www.uscju.org

University of Judaism
Department of Jewish History
Los Angeles, CA 90077
Joel Rembaum, Chair

University of Washington Libraries
(see Washington, Part 2)

Western Jewish History Center Commission for the Preservation of Pioneer Jewish Cemeteries and Landmarks
Judah L. Magnes Memorial Museum/Blumenthal Library
2911 Russell Street
Berkeley, CA 94705
(510) 549-6932; (510) 549-6956; (510) 849-2710 (Commission); (510) 549-6950 (Commission)
Ruth Kelson Rafael, Head Archivist
Mon–Thur 10:00–4:00 by appointment
(primarily northern California, but also includes material from thirteen western states)
research: $15.00 per hour if noncommercial, $25.00 if commercial; the first ½ hour of research is free

Western States Jewish History Association
3111 Kelton
Los Angeles, CA 90034
(310) 475-1415
Rabbi William Kramer
Pub. *Western States Jewish History*, quarterly, $25.00 per year subscription from Subscription Office, 22711 Cass Avenue, Woodland Hills, CA 91364

Wisconsin Jewish Genealogical Society
9280 North Fairway Drive
Milwaukee, WI 53217
(414) 351-2190
pdeshur@wi.rr.com
Penny Deshur, President
Pub. *Family Finding*, quarterly
$25.00 per year membership

World Jewish Genealogy Organization/Yochson Institute
PO Box 190420
Brooklyn, NY 11219-0009
(718) 435-4400; (718) 633-7050 FAX
Rabbi N. Halberstam
by appointment only
(computer database of names, not online; published 640-volume *Avoth Ubinim* and encyclopedia of Jewish genealogy, also available on CD in Hebrew and English)
catalog available on request

YIVO Institute for Jewish Research
15 West 16th Street
New York, NY 10011
http://spanky.osc.cuny.edu/~rich/yivo
Pub. *YIVO Annual*, annually; *News of the YIVO*, semiannually
(Eastern European Jewish history and culture; Yiddish language and literature; Jewish immigration to the U.S.; anti-Semitism; holocaust)
$50.00 per year membership

Kashubian
(see Polish)

Korean
(see Asian)

Latin American
(see Spanish)

Latvian
(see also Eastern European and Jewish)

American Latvian Association
400 Hurley Avenue
Rockville, MD 20850
(301) 340-1914
Anita Terauds, Secretary General
9:00–5:00
Pub. *Latvian Dimensions*, quarterly
$25.00 per year membership

Latvia Research List
Route 2, Box 1619A
McAllen, TX 78504-9802
texprice97@aol.com
http://feefhs.org/baltic/lv/lvrl.html
Bonnie Price
Latvian Society of Iowa
(1372 East 12th, Des Moines, IA 50316—location)
2653 Grandview Avenue (mailing address)
Des Moines, IA 50317
(515) 262-7707
Imants Kalnins, President

Lithuanian
(see also Eastern European, and Polish)

American Lithuanian Roman Catholic Women
8 Hartford Road
Worcester, MA 01606

Baltech Publishing
PO Box 225
Lemont, IL 60439-0225
(630) 257-7546; (630) 257-7547 FAX
editor@lithuanianheritage.com
http://www.lithuanianheritage.com
Val Ramonis, Publisher/Editor
Pub. *Lithuanian Heritage Magazine*, bimonthly, $29.95 per year subscription (includes column, "Our Lithuanian Roots"), $55.00 for two years

The Balzekas Museum of Lithuanian Culture
Immigration History and Lithuanian American Genealogy Society
6500 South Pulaski Road
Chicago, IL 60629-5136
(773) 582-6500; (773-582-5133 FAX
editor@lithuanianmuseum.org
http://www.lithaz.org/museums/balzekas
Mrs. Jessie Daraska, Director
Reference Library: by appointment; Museum: Mon–Sun 10:00–4:00
Pub. *Genealogija: The Lithuanian-American Genealogy Newsletter*, quarterly, $10.00 donation for subscription; admission: $3.00 for nonmembers

Lietuvos Bajoru Karaliskoji Sajunga (LBKS)
Royal Lithuanian Nobility Association
lbks@tinklapis.lt
http://lbks.tinklapis.lt/en
Mrs. Undine Nasvytyte

Lithuanian Research List
webmaster@feefhs.org
http://feefhs.org/baltic/lt/ltrl.html

Tegan Gillette
(A site with query posts and links to resources)

World Lithuanian Archives
5620 South Claremont Avenue
Chicago, IL 60636
(773) 434-4545
(archives primarily of societies, etc.; no interest in genealogy, refers queries to The Balzekas Museum of Lithuanian Culture)

Luxembourgian
(see Belgian and Irish)

Macedonian
(see Eastern European)

Manx
(see English and Irish)

Melungeon
(see also African and Native American)

Melungeon Ancestry Research and Information Page
http://www.geocities.com/alhnmelungeon
(The American Local History Network)
(links to other resources)

Mexican
(see also Spanish)

The University of Texas-Pan American Library
(see Texas, Part 2)

Middle Eastern
(see Asian)

Moldavian
(see Eastern European)

Montenegrin
(see Eastern European)

Moravian
(see Czech, above, and Religious Archives and Organizations—Moravian)

Native American
(see also Government Departments and Agencies and Melungeon)

Accohannock Tribe
PO Box 404
Marion, MD 21838
(410) 623-2660
http://skipjack.net/le_shore/heritage/nativam

Adair County Historical and Genealogical Association
Cherokee history
(see Oklahoma, Part 2)

Akwesasne Library and Culture Center, Inc.
Akwesasne Museum
(address withheld upon request)
(Native American resources, no extensive genealogical data, queries referred to a professional genealogist)

Alaska Indian Arts, Inc.
(Building 13, Fort Seward Drive—location)
PO Box 271 (mailing address)
Haines, AK 99827
(907) 766-2160

(not primarily genealogical)

Am-Toola Publications
East 4516 Sixth Avenue
Spokane, WA 99212
Pub. *American Indian Family Lines*, $20.00
  per year subscription, $7.00 per issue

American Indian Culture Research Center
Blue Cloud Abbey
PO Box 98
Marvin, SD 57251-0098
(605) 432-5528; (605) 432-4754 FAX
http://www.daknet.com/~indian/dakota.html
Rev. Stanislaus Maudlin, O.S.B., Director
8:00–4:30

American Indian Studies Center
3220 Campbell Hall, Box 951548
UCLA
Los Angeles, CA 90095-1548
(310) 825-7315; (310) 206-7060
aisc@ucla.edu
http://www.sscnet.ucla.edu/indian
Pamela Grieman, Managing Editor
Mon–Fri 8:00–5:00
Pub. *American Indian Culture and Research
  Journal*, quarterly, $7.00 per issue
$25.00 per year membership

American Society for Ethnohistory
Duke University Press
(6697 College Station—location)
Box 906660 (mailing address)
Durham, NC 27708-0660
(919) 687-3602; (888) 387-5687
http://ethnohistory.org
Pub. *Ethnohistory*
("Founded in 1954 to promote the
  interdisciplinary investigation of the
  histories of the Native Peoples of the
  Americas.")
$35.00 per year membership

The Amerind Foundation, Inc.
(Triangle T. Road—location)
PO Box 248 (mailing address)
Dragoon, AZ 85609
(520) 586-3666
Anne I. Woosley, Ph.D., Director
(research library)

The Amistad Research Center
(see African-American, above)

Anchorage Museum of History and Art
121 West Seventh Avenue
Anchorage, AK 99501
(907) 343-6189 (Archives); (907) 343-6149
  FAX

  http://www.ci.anchorage.ak.us/Services/D
  epartments/Culture/Museum/index.html
  (Museum)
M. Diane Brenner, Museum Archivist
Mon–Fri 10:00–noon, afternoons by chance
  or appointment
("The museum does not specialize in
  genealogy. The only holdings that may
  relate are historical photographs. We are
  not equipped to do genealogical research
  for others but can respond to specific
  questions. The museum holds all the
  material of the Cook Inlet Historical
  Society.")

Blackfoot Cultural Program
PO Box 850
Browning, MT 59417
(406) 338-7406

Branch of Tribal Operations

Bureau of Indian Affairs
101 North Fifth Street
Muskogee, OK 74401-6206
(918) 687-2313
Karen J. Ketcher, Tribal Operations Officer
Mon–Fri 7:15–4:30
(verifying and researching roll numbers for
  the Five Civilized Tribes of northeastern
  Oklahoma: Cherokee, Choctaw, Creek,
  Chickasaw, and Seminole; tribes do their
  own ancestral research)

Brenorsome Historical Society
(see North Dakota, Part 2)

Bridgeton Free Public Library
Woodruff Museum of Indian Artifacts
(see New Jersey, Part 2)

Buechel Memorial Lakota Museum
Saint Francis Mission
(address withheld upon request)

California State Indian Museum
2618 K Street
Sacramento, CA 95816
(916) 324-0971
Ranger Jon Bergasser
10:00–5:00
(primarily historical, no genealogical
  information available at or from the
  museum or its staff)

Catoosa County Historical Society
(see Georgia, Part 2)

**Cherokee Heritage and Museum
Association**
Route 7, Box 297
Cherokee, CA 95965
(530) 533-1849

Cherokee Historical Association
PO Box 398
Cherokee, NC 28719
(828) 497-2111; (828) 497-6987
Barry Hipps, General Manager; Margie
  Douthit, Marketing Director
("The Cherokee Historical Association has
  no access to any tribal enrollment or other
  records, as its function on the Cherokee
  Reservation is to produce the outdoor
  drama, "Unto These Hills," and present
  other attractions such as Oconaluftee
  Indian Village, with a goal to preserve and
  perpetuate the history and tradition of the
  Cherokee Indian.")

Cherokee History
admin@cherokeehistory.com
http://cherokeehistory.com
Ken Martin

**Cherokee Indian Descendants
Genealogical, Cultural and Research
Organization**
1300 North Hatchery Road
Morgan, UT 84050
(801) 829-6758
Lanora M. Grondel

Museum of Cherokee Indian
PO Box 1599
Cherokee, NC 28719
(828) 497-3481
Joan Greene, Archivist
Tue–Thur 9:00–3:30
Pub. *Journal of Cherokee Studies*, annually,
  $5.00 per issue

Cherokee Museum Association
4227 Cherokee Road

Oroville, CA 95965
(530) 533-1849

Cherokee Nation of Oklahoma
PO Box 948
Tahlequah, OK 74465
(918) 456-6485
(northeastern Oklahoma counties of Adair,
  Cherokee, Craig, Delaware, Mayes,
  McIntosh [part], Nowata, Ottawa [part],
  Rogers, Sequoyah, Tulsa [part], Wagoner,
  Muskogee [part], and Washington)

Cherokee National Historical Society, Inc.
Cherokee Heritage Center
PO Box 515
Tahlequah, OK 74465-0515
(918) 456-6007; (918) 456-6165 FAX
info@cherokeeheritage.org;
  archives@cherokeeheritage.org;
  genealogy@cherokeeheritage.org
http://www.cherokeeheritage.org
Mary Ellen Meredith, President and
  Executive Director
Mon–Sat 10:00–5:00, Sun noon–5:00
Pub. *The Columns*, quarterly
$30.00 per year membership

**Cheyenne and Arapaho Tribal Museum
and Archives**
Route 1, Box 138
Watonga, OK 73772
(580) 886-3479
George F. Sutton, Director

Cheyenne Genealogy Research
webmaster@cheyenneancestors.com
http://www.cheyenneancestors.com
Timothy D. Cook

The Chickasaw Nation Headquarters
(Chickasaw Cultural Center, 520 East
  Arlington at Mississippi—location)
PO Box 1548 (mailing address)
Ada, OK 74820
(580) 436-2603, ext. 7324; (580) 310-6406
  FAX
Glenda A. Galvan, Manager
Tue 9:00–5:00
Pub. *Chickasaw Times*, monthly, free;
  Journal of Chickasaw History, $20.00 per
  year subscription
(Chickasaw history, genealogy, biographies)

Chieftains Museum
(800 Riverside Parkway—location)
PO Box 373 (mailing address)
Rome, GA 30162
(706) 291-9494 voice & FAX
http://www.romegeorgia.com/chiefmus.html

Choctaw Nation of Oklahoma
(16th and Locust—location)
PO Drawer 1210 (mailing address)
Durant, OK 74701
(580) 924-8280; (580) 924-4529 FAX
Brenda Hampton, Director Tribal
  Membership
Mon–Fri 8:00–4:30
("Choctaw or Mississippi Indians living in
  Indian Territory [Oklahoma] 1899–1906
  and who may have enrolled in the final
  Dawes Commission Rolls.")
research: "No cost for research if your
  ancestors were of Choctaw descent.
  Research is only done if we have a
  completed research paper," available
  upon request

**Clayton Library, Center for Genealogical
Research**
(see Texas, Part 2)

Collier County Museum
(see Florida, Part 2)

Colorado River Indian Tribes Museum/Library
Route 1, Box 23-B
Parker, AZ 85344
(928) 669-9211
Mike Flores, Librarian

Comanche Tribe of Oklahoma
Enrollment Office
PO Box 908
Lawton, OK 73502
(580) 492-3775; (580) 492-4981 FAX
Zenia Anderson, Enrollment Director
8:00–5:00

Commission on Indian Affairs
Department of Housing and Community Development
100 Community Place
Crownsville, MD 21032-2025
http://www.dhcd.state.md.us/mcia/index.cfm
Amos Goodfox, Chairman
Pub. *MCIA Newsletter*, online newsletter

Community Memorial Museum of Sutter County
(1333 Butte House Road, Yuba City, CA 95993—location)
PO Box 1555 (mailing address)
Yuba City, CA 95992
(530) 822-7141; (530) 822-7291 FAX
Julie Stark, Director/Curator
Tue–Fri 9:00–5:00, Sat–Sun noon–4:00
Pub. *Muse News, Sutter County Historical Society Bulletin*, quarterly
(collection includes Maidu Indian artifacts)
$15.00 per year membership

Cortez Center
25 North Market Street
Cortez, CO 81321
(970) 565-1151
http://www.swcolo.org/Tourism/IndianCulture.html

Craig County Oklahoma Genealogical Society
(see Oklahoma, Part 2)

Crow Tribal Council
PO Box 159
Crow Agency, MT 59022
(406) 638-2601

Custer Battlefield Historical and Museum Association
Custer Battlefield National Monument
PO Box 36
Crow Agency, MT 59022
(406) 638-2382

Datatrace Systems
(see Miscellaneous, Part 4)

Denver Public Library
(see Colorado, Part 2)

Eastern Band of Cherokee Office Headquarters
Cherokee Enrollment Office
(Highway 441N, approximately 3/4 mile from town—location)
PO Box 455 (mailing address)
Cherokee, NC 28719
(828) 497-4072; (828) 497-2952 FAX
8:00–4:30
(tribal rolls, 1835–1924, begin with those who were living on the reserved land established in western North Carolina,

cover areas of North Carolina, Georgia, Tennessee, Alabama)
research: $100.00 (allow 10-12 weeks)

Eastern Oklahoma Historical Society and Carl Albert State College
Robert S. Kerr Museum
Cherokee and Choctaw Indians
(see Oklahoma, Part 2)

Eastern Shawnee Tribe of Oklahoma
PO Box 350
Seneca, MO 64865
(417) 666-2435; (918) 666-3325 FAX

Eastern Washington Genealogical Society, Metis Genealogical Society Chapter
Newsletter of Genealogical Research of the North American Indian
(see Washington, Part 2)

Family Tree Resource Network, Inc.
(see Illinois, Part 2)

Five Civilized Tribes Museum
Agency Hill, Honor Heights Drive
Muskogee, OK 74401
(918) 683-1701; (918) 683-3070 FAX
Clara Beekie, Executive Director; Mikel Parkes, Administrative Assistant
Mon–Sat 10:00–5:00, Sun 1:00–5:00
(Cherokee, Choctaw, Creek, Chickasaw and Seminole)

Flathead Culture Committee
Confederated Salish and Kootenai Tribes
(address withheld upon request)
(no genealogical services)

Forsyth County Heritage Foundation
County Government Building
PO Box 762
Cummings, GA 30130
(770) 887-1626
Don L. Shadburn, County Historian and Director
by appointment only
(historical/genealogical materials on pioneer families and Cherokee mixed-blood families of Forsyth County)

Fort Lewis College
Center of Southwest Studies
(see Colorado, Part 2)

Fort Ticonderoga
(see Miscellaneous—Military, Part 4)

Fox Lake Historical Museum, Inc.
(see Wisconsin, Part 2)

Samuel K. Fox Museum
PO Box 273
Dillingham, AK 99576
(907) 842-2322
Lynn Fox, Museum Director
Mon–Thur noon–5:00, Sat noon–4:00
(not primarily genealogical, emphasis on art, especially Yupik Eskimo)

Friends of the Middle Border Museum of American Indian and Pioneer Life
(1311 South Duff Street—location)
PO Box 1071 (mailing address)
Mitchell, SD 57301
(605) 996-2122; (605) 996-0323 FAX
Chris Hanson Executive Director
June–Aug: Mon–Sat 8:00–6:00; May & Sept: Mon–Fri 9:00–5:00, Sat–Sun 1:00–5:00; Oct–Apr: by appointment
Pub. *Middle Border Bulletin*, quarterly
$15.00 per year membership

Fulton County Historical Society, Inc.
(see Indiana, Part 2)

Genealogical Institute
(see Independent Publications, Part 1)

The Grand Village of the Natchez Indians
400 Jefferson Davis Boulevard
Natchez, MS 39120
(601) 446-6502
Jim Barnett, Director

William S. Hart Museum
24151 San Fernando Road
Newhall, CA 91321
(661) 254-4584; (661) 254-4585
Katherine H. Child, Collections Manager
(primarily collection of Western art, including native artifacts)

Ned A. Hatathli Museum
Navajo Community College
Tsaile, AZ 86556
(928) 724-3311, ext. 206
Harry Walters
Mon–Fri 8:00–5:00

Hauberg Indian Museum
Black Hawk State Park
1510 46th Avenue
Rock Island, IL 61201
(309) 788-9536

Historical Archive Collection of Nez Perce People
http://www.nezperce.com/archive2.html

Hoonah Indian Association
PO Box 144
Hoonah, AK 99829
(907) 945-3600
Wanda Culp, Tribal Administrator

Huntington Free Library and Reading Room
(see New York, Part 2)

Collis P. Huntington Memorial Library
(see African-American, above)

Index of Native American Resources on the Internet
(see Indian Pueblo Cultural Center, Inc., below)

The Indian and Colonial Research Center, Inc.
The Eva Butler Library
(Main Street, Route 27—location)
PO Box 525 (mailing address)
Old Mystic, CT 06372
(860) 536-9771
http://www.geocities.com/icrc06372
Michael Spellmon, Librarian
Apr–Nov: Tue, Thur & Sat 2:00–4:00
Pub. *Newletter*, quarterly
("Extensive collection of Native American history and artifacts
$10.00 per year membership; admission: free; in-house genealogy research: $10.00 per surname plus 25¢ per copy

Indian City U.S.A., Inc.
(2½ miles south on State Highway 8—location)
PO Box 695 (mailing address)
Anadarko, OK 73005
(405) 247-5661; (405) 247-2467 FAX
George F. Moran, General Manager
Mon–Sun 9:00–5:00

Indian Heritage Museum

PO Box 225
Rancocas, NJ 08073
(856) 261-4747

Indian Museum of the Carolinas, Inc.
607 Turnpike Road
Laurinburg, NC 28352
(910) 276-5880
Margaret Houston, Ph.D., Director

Indian Pueblo Cultural Center, Inc.
2401 12th Street, N.W.
Albuquerque, NM 87102
(505) 843-7270; (800) 766-4406; (505) 842-6959 FAX
http://hanksville.phast.umass.edu/defs/
independent/PCC/PCC.html; http://
hanksville.phast.umass.edu/misc/
NAresources.html (Index of Native
American Resources on the Internet)
Pat Reck, Museum Curator
Museum: daily 9:00–5:00

Indian Temple Mound Museum
(139 Miracle Strip Parkway, Fort Walton
Beach, FL 32548—location)
PO Box 4009 (mailing address)
Fort Walton Beach, FL 32549
(850) 243-6521
Steven Tuthill, Curator

Indian Territory Genealogical Society
c/o University Archives
Northeastern Oklahoma State University
Tahlequah, OK 74465
Mr. Lee, Registrar of Cherokee Nations

Indian Village Association
2177 Burns
Detroit, MI 48214
(313) 821-9165

The Institute for American Indian Studies
(38 Curtis Road—location)
PO Box 1260 (mailing address)
Washington, CT 06783
(860) 868-0518; (860) 868-1649 FAX
Alberto C. Meloni, Executive Director
Mon–Sat 10:00–5:00, Sun noon–5:00
Pub. *NETOP*, four times per year

Iroquois Indian Museum
(Caverns Road—location)
PO Box 7 (mailing address)
Howes Cave, NY 12092-0007
(518) 296-8949; (518) 296-8955 FAX
info@iroquoismuseum.org
http://www.IroquoisMuseum.org
Genealogist
Museum: 1 Apr–30 June & Labor Day–31
Dec: Tue–Sat 10:00–5:00, Sun
noon–5:00; 1 July–Labor Day weekend:
Mon–Sat 10:00–6:00, Sun noon–6:00;
Library: by appointment only
Pub. *Museum Notes*, quarterly
(specializes in the Iroquois—Mohawk,
Oneida, Onondaga, Cayuga, Seneca,
Tuscarora)
$25.00 per year membership; research:
donation for nonmembers

Kake Tribal Heritage Foundation
(93009 Glacier Highway—location)
PO Box 263 (mailing address)
Juneau, AK 99801
(907) 790-2214 (Juneau); (907) 785-3221
(Kake); (907) 785-67407 FAX

Kansas City Public Library
(Wyandotte, see Kansas)

Kenitzee Indian Tribe

(2255 Ames Street—location)
PO Box 988 (mailing address)
Kenai, AK 99611
(907) 283-3633; (907) 283-3052 FAX

Kialegee Tribal Town
(108 North Main—location)
PO Box 332 (mailing address)
Wetumka, OK 74883
(405) 452-3262; (405) 452-3413 FAX
http://www.Kialegee.org
Yvette Powell, Enrollment Clerk
Mon–Fri 9:00–5:00

Kootenai Cultural Center
PO Box 1452
Elmo, MT 59917
(406) 849-5541

Koshare Indian Museum, Inc.
(115 West 18th Street—location)
PO Box 580 (mailing address)
La Junta, CO 81050-0580
(719) 384-4411
Michael J. Menard, Museum Director
summer: 10:00–5:00; winter Tue–Sun
12:30–4:30
Pub. *Koshare News*, semiannually
copy fee

Lawton Public Library
(see Oklahoma, Part 2)

Layland Museum
(see Texas, Part 2)

**Lenni Lenape Historical Society/Museum
of Indian Culture**
2825 Fish Hatchery Road
Allentown, PA 18103-9801
(610) 797-2121; (610) 797-2801 FAX
lenape@lenape.org
http://www.lenape.org
Carla Messinger, Executive Director
general visitors: Fri–Sun noon–3:00; groups
and individuals: Tue–Sun by appointment
only
Pub. *Lenape Olam*, four to six times per year
(for members only)

William Pryor Letchworth Museum
Letchworth State Park
Castile, NY 14427
(716) 493-3617; (716) 493-5272 FAX
Brian Scriven, Historic Site Manager
daily (mid-May–Oct) 10:00–5:00
(archives and private library of W. P.
Letchworth with Native American
material)

Lower Muskogee Creek Tribe
Tama Tribal Town
107 Long Pine Drive
Whigham, GA 31797
(229) 762-3165 voice & FAX

Luna County Historical Society, Inc.
(see New Mexico, Part 2)

Makah Cultural and Research Center
PO Box 160
Neah Bay, WA 98357
(360) 645-2711
(a subdivision of the Nootka)

Malki Museum
Morongo Indian Reservation
(11-795 Fields Road—location)
PO Box 578 (mailing address)
Banning, CA 92220
(909) 849-7289
Hazel Duro, Secretary/Receptionist

10:00–4:00
Pub. *Journal of California and Great Basin
Anthropology*, two times per year, $15.00
per book

Marin Museum of the American Indian
2200 Novato Boulevard
Novato, CA 94948
(415) 897-4064

**Marquette Mission Park and Museum of
Ojibwa Culture**
500-566 North State Street
Saint Ignace, MI 49781
(906) 643-9161 (Museum and Director's
Office)
Molly M. Perry, Museum Director
Memorial Day weekend to late June:
Mon–Sun 11:00–5:00, late June–Labor
Day: Mon–Sun 10:00–8:00, Sun
noon–8:00; Labor Day–early Oct:
Mon–Sun 11:00–6:00
Pub. *The Bridge: Bridging Culture and
History*, about three times per year
("We do not have genealogical information
in our collections, but one of our staff
members provides her services on a free-
lance basis, especially for Native
American genealogy.")
$2.00 museum admission for adults

Mashpee Historical Commission
(see Massachusetts, Part 2)

**Mashpee Wampanoag Indian Tribal
Council, Inc.**
(483 Great Neck Road, South—location)
PO Box 1048 (mailing address)
Mashpee, MA 02649
(508) 477-0208; (508) 477-1218
mashpwamp@aol.com
Patricia A. Oakley, Historian/Genealogist

Carrie M. McLain Memorial Museum
Bering Strait Eskimos
(see Alaska, Part 2)

Mesa Southwest Museum
53 North Macdonald
Mesa, AZ 85201-7325
(480) 644-2169
Tray C. Mead, Museum Administrator
(features native cultures)

Mescalero Apache Cultural Center
PO Box 176
Mescalero, NM 88340
(505) 671-4494

Miami Tribe of Oklahoma
PO Box 1326
Miami, OK 74355
(918) 542-1445; (918) 542-7260 FAX

Mid-America All Indian Center Museum
650 North Seneca
Wichita, KS 67203
(316) 262-5221
Carl Ponce, Museum Director
Pub. *M.A.A.I.C. Newsletter*, monthly;
Museum Notes, quarterly

**Minneapolis Regional Native American
Center**
1530 East Franklin Avenue
Minneapolis, MN 55404
(612) 348-5600

**Mitchell Indian Museum at Kendall
College**
2408 Orrington Avenue
Evanston, IL 60201-2899

(847) 866-1395

Modoc Tribe of Oklahoma
515 G Southeast
Miami, OK 74354-8224
(918) 542-1190; (918) 542-5415 FAX

MtGenWeb
(see Montana, Part 2)

Muscogee (Creek) Nation
PO Box 580
Okmulgee, OK 74447
(918) 756-2911

Museum Evangel College of Arts and Sciences
(Ozark and Eskimo, see Missouri)

Museum of Northern Arizona
(see Arizona, Part 2)

Museum of the Cherokee Strip
507 South Fourth Street
Enid, OK 73701-5835
(580) 237-1907
Glen McIntyre, Site Attendant
Tue–Fri 9:00–5:00, Sat 2:00–5:00
(Cherokee and Cheyenne)

NANA Museum of the Arctic
(Corner Second and Third Streets—location)
PO Box 49 (mailing address)
Kotzebue, AK 99752
(907) 442-3304; (907) 442-2866 FAX
Kari Westlund, Program Consultant
(not primarily genealogical, emphasis on Inupiat Eskimo culture)

Nanticoke Indian Association, Inc.
(Route 24, 7 miles east of Millsboro—location)
Route 4, Box 107-A (mailing address)
Millsboro, DE 19966
(302) 945-3400 (Tribal Office); (302) 945-7022 (Museum)
Odette Wright, Curator
Museum: winter: Tue–Thur 9:00–4:00, Sat noon–4:00; summer: Tue–Thur 9:00–4:00, Sat 10:00–4:00, Sun noon–4:00
admission: $1.00 for adults

National Museum of the American Indian
George Gustav Heye Center
1 Bowling Green
New York, NY 10004
(212) 668-6624 (recorded message)
Museum: Tue–Sat 10:00–5:00, Sun 1:00–5:00; Archives: by appointment
Pub. *Native Peoples*; *Smithsonian Runner*
(the archives contains the primary documentation of the museum; the photography archives contains approximately 100,000 images; the resource center makes available to the public a variety of information concerning the native peoples of the Americas)
$20.00 per year membership (*Native Peoples* only), $35.00 per year membership (includes both periodicals); admission: $5.00 for nonmember adults

Native America-South Dakota GenWeb Project
http://www.geocities.com/Heartland/Plains/8430/index.htm

Native American Genealogy
http://members.aol.com/bbbenge/front.html

Native American Genealogical Research

and Publishing Company with Oklahoma Yesterday Publications
(see Publishers, Part 4)

Native American Heritage Commission
Office of the Governor
915 Capitol Mall, Room 364
Sacramento, CA 95814
(916) 653-4082
Larry Myers, Executive Secretary

Native American Heritage Museum at Highland Mission
(Route 1—location)
1737 Elgin Road (mailing address)
Highland, KS 66035
(785) 442-3304
http://kuhttp.cc.ukans.edu/heritage/kshs/places/highland.htm

Native American Resource Center
University of North Carolina at Pembroke
PO Box 1510
Pembroke, NC 28372-1510
(910) 521-6282
Stanley Knick, Ph.D., Director/Curator
Mon–Fri 8:00–5:00
Pub. *Spirit*, quarterly

Native American Resources
http://cowboy.net/native/indian.links.html

Native American Who's Hot
http://www.cris.com/~misterg/award/whoshot.shtml

Native Genealogy
http://www.edwards1.com/rose/genealogy/native-gen/native-gen.htm

NativeWeb
http://web.maxwell.syr.edu/nativeweb/index.html

Navajo Page
webmaster@navajopage.com
http://www.navajopage.com/index.php
(includes "Clan Finder")

Newberry Library
(see Illinois, Part 2)

Nez Perce National Historical Park
(U.S. Highway 95 South, ½ mile south of Highway 12 Junction—location)
Route 1, Box 100 (mailing address)
Spalding, ID 83540
(208) 843-2261; (208) 843-2201 FAX
Franklin C. Walker, Superintendent
Mon–Fri 8:00–4:30
(specializes in history of Nez Perce Indians; does not have genealogical records)

Northwest Museum of Arts and Culture/Eastern Washington State Historical Society
(see Washington, Part 2)

Oklahoma Tribes and Officials
http://www.fed.us/tribes.html

Old Northwest Historical Society
(see Ohio, Part 2)

Oneida Tribe of Indians of Wisconsin
Norbert Hill Center, South Building
(7210 Seminary Road—location)
PO Box 365 (mailing address)
Oneida, WI 54155
(920) 869-2130 (Records Management System); (920) 869-2194 FAX
Charlene E. Cornelius, Records

Manager/Archivist
Mon–Fri 8:00–4:30
Pub. *Kalihwisaks* (local tribal news), monthly, $24.00 per year subscription (genealogy for tribal enrolled members only)
fee: $15.00 (provided by enrollment office)

Oregon Province Archives of the Society of Jesus
Gonzaga University
Spokane, WA 99258
(509) 328-4220, ext. 3144
Fr. Neill R. Meany, S.J., Archivist
9:00–4:30
(northwest U.S. and Alaska)

Osage Nation of Oklahoma
Osage Tribal Museum, Library and Archives
c/o Osage Tribal Council
PO Box 779
Pawhuska, OK 74056; (918) 287-1060 FAX
(918) 287-5441 (Museum); (918) 287-5432; (918) 287-2257 FAX
http://www.osagetribe.com
Kathryn RedCorn, Director

Ottawa County Genealogical Society
(see Oklahoma, Part 2)

Ottawa Tribe of Oklahoma
PO Box 110
Miami, OK 74355
(918) 540-1536; (918) 542-3214 FAX

Owasco Stockaded Indian Village
Cayuga Museum of History and Art
(Emerson Park—location)
203 Genesee Street (mailing address)
Auburn, NY 13021
(315) 253-8051
Professor Long or Ms. Logan

Pawnee Historical and Cultural Museum
657 Harrison Street
Pawnee, OK 74058-2520
(918) 762-3706

Penobscot Nation Historical Society
Penobscot Nation Museum
5 Downstreet Street
Indian Island, ME 04468
firekpr@hotmail.com
http://www.penobscotnation.org/museum/index.htm
James Neptune
Mon, Wed–Thur & Sat–Sun 10:00–3:00

Peoria Tribe of Indians of Oklahoma
PO Box 1527
Miami, OK 74354
(918) 540-2535; (918) 540-2538 FAX

Pharaoh Indian Museum
Third House Museum
Theodore Roosevelt County Park
Montauk Highway
Montauk, NY 11954
(631) 852-7878
Robert Pharaoh
(Montaukett artifacts)

Plains and Emigrant Tribes of Kansas
http://history.cc.ukans.edu/heritage/old_west/indian.html

Plains Indians and Pioneers Historical Foundation
(see Oklahoma, Part 2)

Ponca City Cultural Center and Indian Museum
(see Oklahoma, Part 2)

Poppenhusen Institute
114-04 14th Road
College Point, NY 11356
(718) 358-0067
Susan K. Brustman, Executive Director
(Matinecock Indian exhibit, educational
    programs)

Potawatomi Tribal Museum
1901 South Gordon Cooper Drive
Shawnee, OK 74801-8604
(405) 275-3119

**Society for Preservation of Indiana
Heritage**
PO Box 23
Thorntown, IN 46071
(765) 436-2202

Quapaw Tribal Business Committee
PO Box 765
Quapaw, OK 74363
(918) 542-1853; (918) 542-4694 FAX

Quechan Indian Museum
Fort Yuma Indian Hill
PO Box 1899
Yuma, AZ 85366
(928) 572-0661
Pauline Jose, Manager
Mon–Fri 8:00–5:00, Sat 10:00–4:00
("Museum also has military and Spanish era
    history.")

Red Clay State Historic Park
1140 Red Clay Park Road, S.W.
Cleveland, TN 37311
(423) 478-0339; (423) 9614-7251 FAX
Lois I. Osborne, Park Manager
Visitors' Center and Library: 1 Mar–30 Nov:
    Mon–Sat 8:00–4:30 Sun 1:00–4:30; 1
    Dec–21 Dec & 2 Jan–29 Feb: Mon–Fri
    8:00–4:15, Sat–Sun 1:00–4:15
("Native American and Cherokee holdings in
    our library but all genealogical works are
    Cherokee.")
copies: 10¢ each

Saint Joseph Museum
(see Missouri, Part 2)

San Gabriel Historical Association
Gabrielino Indians
(see California, Part 2)

Schiele Museum
Southeastern Native American Studies
Program
1500 East Garrison Boulevard
Gastonia, NC 28054
(704) 866-6900
Steven M. Watts, Program Director

**Schingoethe Center for Native American
Cultures**
(Dunham Hall, corner of Marseillaise and
    Randolph—location)
347 South Gladstone (mailing address)
Aurora, IL 60506-4892
(630) 844-4892; (630) 844-5512; (630) 844-
    7830 FAX
Dr. Michael J. Riley, Director
Mon–Tue & Thur–Fri 10:00–4:30, Sun
    1:00–4:00

Schusterman Benson Library
(see Oklahoma, Part 2)

Seminole Nation Historical Society
(524 South Wewoka—location)
PO Box 1532 (mailing address)
Wewoka, OK 74884

(405) 257-5580
Tue–Sun 1:00–5:00

Seminole Nation of Oklahoma
PO Box 1498
Wewoka, OK 74884
(405) 257-5017 FAX

Seminole Tribe of Florida
http://www.gate.net/~semtribe/library/
    library.html

Seneca-Cayuga Tribe of Oklahoma
PO Box 1283
Miami, OK 74355
(918) 542-6609; (918) 542-3684 FAX

Seneca-Iroquois National Museum
(794-814 Broad Street—location)
PO Box 442 (mailing address)
Salmanca, NY 14779
(716) 945-1738; (716) 945-1760 FAX
Judith Greene, Director
1 Apr–30 Sept: Mon–Sun 9:00–5:00;
    Oct–Mar: Mon–Fri 9:00–5:00
no genealogical research, refers inquiries to
    Seneca Nation of Indians, Clerk's Office

Seneca Nation of Indians
Tribal Clerk's Office
1490 Route 438
Irving, NY 14081
(716) 532-4900
Mon–Fri 8:00–4:30
(tribal enrollment records for Seneca Nation
    of the Iroquois Confederacy only)
$50.00 fee

Shawnee Mission Indian Historical Society
4833 Black Swan
Shawnee Mission, KS 66202
(913) 631-9990

**Sheldon Jackson Museum, Division of
Alaska State Museums**
104 College Drive
Sitka, AK 99835
(907) 747-8981; (907) 747-3004 FAX
Peter L. Corey, Curator of Collections
winter: Mon–Fri 8:00–5:00, Sat 9:00–4:00;
    summer (approximately 15 May–15 Sept):
    Mon–Sun 8:00–5:00
(Tingit, Haida, Tsimshian, Aleut, Athabaskan
    and Eskimo ethnographic materials; no
    archives other than what applies to the
    history of the institution and collections,
    no genealogical records)

Sheldon Museum and Cultural Center
(see Alaska, Part 2)

Shoshone-Bannock Indian Tribes
PO Box 306
Fort Hall, ID 83203
(208) 238-3700; (208) 237-9791; (208) 237-
    0797 FAX
http://www.eerc.und.nodak.edu/cert/
    shosh.htm

Siouxland Valley Genealogical Society
(see South Dakota, Part 2)

Six Nations Indian Museum
HCR 01, Box 10
Onchiota, NY 12989
(518) 891-2299
redmaple@northnet.org
http://www.thebeadsite.com/MUS-F4.htm
John Fadden, Curator
July–Aug: Tue–Sun 10:00–5:00, and by
    appointment to groups June & Sept
(particularly the Haudenosaunee; informa-

tional charts on Six Iroquois Nations
    Confederacy: Cayuga, Mohawk, Oneida,
    Onondaga, Seneca and Tuscarora)
admission charge

Southeastern Cherokee Confederacy
PO Box 367
Ochlockee, GA 31733
(229) 547-5497; (229) 365-6017 FAX

Southern Ute Community Library
(330 Burns Avenue—location)
PO Box 989 (mailing address)
Ignacio, CO 81137-0348
(970) 563-0235; (970) 563-0396 FAX

Southern Ute Indian Cultural Center
(Highway 172—location)
PO Box 737 (mailing address)
Ignacio, CO 81137
(970) 563-4531
Helen Hoskins, Director
Pub. *Ute Legacy*

**Stockbridge-Munsee Historical
Library/Museum**
Route 1
Bowler, WI 54416
(715) 793-4270
Bernice Miller, Research Historian
Mon–Fri 8:00–4:30, Sat by appointment

Teysen's Woodland Indian Museum
(416 South Huron Avenue—location)
PO Box 399 (mailing address)
Mackinaw City, MI 49701
(231) 436-7011

Thlopthlocco Tribal Town
PO Box 188
Okemah, OK 74859
(918) 623-2620; (918) 623-0419 FAX (call
    before faxing)

Three Affiliated Tribes Museum
(Hiway 23, 4 miles west of New
    Town—location)
PO Box 147 (mailing address)
New Town, ND 58763-0147
(701) 627-4477
info@mhanation.com
http://www.mhanation.com
Marilyn Hudson, Administrator
daily 10:00–6:00
(Fort Berthold Reservation; Mandan,
    Hidatsa, Arikara)

Tongass Historical Museum
Totem Heritage Center
(601 Deermount—location)
629 Dock Street (mailing address)
Ketchikan, AK 99901
(907) 225-5900; (907) 225-5602 FAX
Roxana Adams, Museum Director
(not genealogical—native site and art
    preservation)

**Turtle Mountain Chippewa Historical
Society**
Chippewa Heritage Center
PO Box 257
Belcourt, ND 58316
(701) 477-6451

**United Keetoowah Band of Cherokee
Indians**
PO Box 746
Tahlequah, OK 74465-0746
(918) 456-9601 FAX

University of Nebraska Press
PO Box 880484

Lincoln, NE 68588
Kirt Card
Pub. *American Indian Quarterly*, $40.00 per
    year subscription

University of Nevada, Reno
Special Collections Department
(see Nevada, Part 2)

University of Oklahoma
Western History Collections
(see Oklahoma, Part 2)

University of Tulsa
McFarlin Library
(Cherokee, Choctaw and Creek manuscripts;
see Oklahoma, Part 2)

**Ute Mountain Ute Tribal Research
Archives Library**
Tribal Compound
Boix CC
Towaoc, CO 81334
(970) 565-3751, ext. 257; (970) 565-7412
    FAX
http://www.swcol.org/Tourism/
    IndianCulture.html

**John Vaughan Library/Learning
Resources Center**
Special Collections Department, Room 221
Northeastern Oklahoma State University
Tahlequah, OK 74464, ext. 3252
(918) 456-5511
library@cherokee.nsuok.edu
http://www.nsuok.edu/jvl/jvlspc.html
Helen Wheat, Special Collections Librarian

**Waponahki Resource Center and Sipayik
Museum**
Route 190
Perry, ME 04667
(207) 853-4001

West Florida Regional Library System
(see Florida, Part 2)

**Wheelwright Museum of the American
Indian**
(704 Camino Lejo, Santa Fe, NM
87501—location)
PO Box 5153 (mailing address)
Santa Fe, NM 87502
(505) 982-4636; (800) 607-4636; (505) 989-
    7386 FAX
Yvonne Bond, Public Relations
Mon–Sat 10:00–5:00, Sun 1:00–5:00
Pub. *The Messenger*, annually; *Wheelwright
News Calendar*, bimonthly
(library and archives emphasis on Navajo
    tribe)
$25.00 per year membership

Willow Creek-China Flat Museum
(see California, Part 2)

Wyandotte Nation of Oklahoma
PO Box 250
Wyandotte, OK 74370
(918) 678-2297; (918) 678-2944 FAX
Juanita McQuistion
Mon–Tue 8:00–2:00
Pub. *Historian*

Yakima National Museum
(Highway 97—location)
PO Box 151 (mailing address)
Toppenish, WA 98948
(509) 865-2800
http://www.yakima.net/yakima/tourist/
    indian.htm

**Chickasaw Council House Research
Center**
(205 North Fisher Street—location)
PO Box 717 (mailing addres)
Tishomingo, OK 73460

Maine Folklife Center
(see Maine, Part 2)

Norse
(see Norwegian, Swedish and Scottish)

Norwegian
(see also Finnish and Swedish)

Coulee Region Family Research Society
(see Wisconsin, Part 2)

Little Norway, Inc.
3576 Highway JG-N
Blue Mounds, WI 53517
(608) 437-8211

**Norwegian American Bygdelagenes
Fellesraad**
10129 Goodrich Circle
Bloomington, MN 55437
(952) 831-4409
http://www.lexiaintl.org/sylte/bygdelag.html
Marilyn Somdahl, President

**Norwegian American Genealogy
Association**
Minnesota Genealogical Society
1046 19th Avenue, S.E.
Minneapolis, MN 55414
(763) 434-5074
jerijon@aol.com
http://www.mtn.org/mgs/naga/nagindx.htm
Susan Lee

**Norwegian-American Historical
Association (NAHA)**
Rolvaag Memorial Library
Saint Olaf College
1510 Saint Olaf Avenue
Northfield, MN 55057-1097
(507) 646-3221; (507) 646-3734 FAX
naha@stolaf.edu
http://www.stolaf.edu/stolaf/other/naha/
    naha.html
Ruth Hanold Crane, Assistant Secretary
Archives: Mon–Fri 8:00–noon & 1:00–4:00
(Houses manuscripts, diaries, periodicals,
    newspapers, family histories,
    organizational records, etc.; main
    emphasis is the history of Norwegian
    emigration, settlement and development
    of Norwegian America; has several
    genealogical resources, but genealogy is
    not primary work; publishes about one
    historical title per year)
$25.00 per year membership; research:
    $20.00 for nonmembers

**The Norwegian Emigrant Museum and
Research Center**
http://museumsnett.no/emigrantmuseum
Pub. *Brev Hjemmefra* (for members of the
    museum's "Friends" organization)

Norwegian Emigration Center
http://home.sn.no/home/henningh/
    utvasent.htm

Norwegian Historical Data Centre
http://isv.uit.no/seksjon/rhd

Sons of Norway

1455 West Lake Street, Second Floor
Minneapolis, MN 55408
(612) 827-3611; (800) 945-8851; (612) 827-
    0658 FAX
fraternal@sofn.com
http://www.sonsofnorway.com
LaDonn M. Jonsen, Culture and Special
    Events Coordinator
Reference Only Library: Mon–Thur
    8:00–4:00
Pub. *Viking*, monthly, $25.00 per year
    nonmember subscription (query column,
    "The Lost Branch," is printed as space is
    available and is a membership benefit)
("Sons of Norway Reference Library is a
    self-service, nonlending library that
    contains one of the larger collections of
    Norwegian/Norwegian-American books
    on immigration to America; some
    bygdeboker [history of Norwegian
    communities and farms, including the
    families that lived there], and many other
    Norwegian/Norwegian-American
    selections. Sons of Norway does NOT do
    genealogical research. Materials are only
    for on-site research. Our library has
    Internet connection for visitors, also self-
    service. Topographical maps with current
    Norwegian farm names are available by
    special order at [800] 945-8851. Other
    Norwegian maps are also available.
    Online ordering from our website is also
    available.")
$35.00 per year membership

Sons of Norway Lodge
Norwegian Genealogy Group
2006 East Vista Way
Vista, CA 92084-3321

Tree Trackers Library
(see Missouri, Part 2)

University of North Dakota
(see North Dakota, Part 2)

Valdres Samband Lag
1522 North Greenwood Court
Eagan, MN 55122
bettylou@spacestar.net
http://www.valdressamband.org
Betty Rockswold, Contact Person and
    Genealogist
Stevne (Convention): late June in one of the
    upper midwest states
Pub. *Budstikken*, semiannually (May, Dec)
("dedicated to the preservation and culture of
    Valdres, Oppland County, Norway";
    organized 1899)
$10.00 per year membership (to Diane
    Lerohl, Secretary, 13400 Pepperwood
    Circle, Minnetonka, MN 55305); free
    genealogy help for members

**Vesterheim Genealogical Center and
Naeseth Library**
415 West Main Street
Madison, WI 53703-3116
(608) 255-2224; (608) 255-6842 FAX
http://fjordinfo.vestdata.no/offentleg/
    sffarkiv/sffutvgc.htm
Blane Hedberg, Director
Tue–Fri 1:00–5:00 by appointment only
Pub. *Norwegian Tracks*, quarterly
(the genealogical division of the Norwegian-
    American Museum)
$35.00 per year museum and center
    membership

Carl B. Ylvisaker Library
Concordia College
Moorhead, MN 56562

(218) 299-4640; (218) 299-4253 FAX
library@cord.edu
http://home.cord.edu/dept/library
School year: Mon–Thur 7:45–midnight, Fri
7:45–5:00, Sat 10:00–10:00, Sun
noon–midnight; summer: Mon–Fri
8:00–4:30 (school vacations may vary),
call ahead for appointment
(emphasis on Norway and Sweden)

Palatine
(see Galician and German)

Polish
(see also Eastern European)

Alliance College Library
Polish National Alliance of the U.S. of North
America
(see University of Pittsburgh, Slavic
Department, below)

Alliance of Poles of America
6966 Broadway Avenue
Cleveland, OH 44105
(216) 883-3131
Ewa Trzeciak, Librarian; Barbara
VonBenken, Recording Secretary of
Alliance and Chair of Library Committee
Wed evening, Sun afternoon
Pub. *Alliancer (Zwiazkowiec)*, monthly

The Central Archives of Polonia
The Orchard Lake Schools
3535 Indian Trail
Orchard Lake, MI 48324
(248) 683-0412; (248) 683-0409
Carol Pettey Baerman, Vice Director
Mon–Thur 9:00–noon & 1:00–4:00
(appointment suggested)
reading room admission: free; research: no
service

Connecticut Polish American Archive
Ellen Burritt Library
Central Connecticut State University
New Britain, CT 06050
(860) 832-2086; (860) 832-2085; (860) 832-
2118 FAX; (860) 832-3409
http://library.ccsu.ctstateu.edu/
~wolynska/home.htm

Freistadt Historical Society
(see Religious Archives and
Organizations—Lutheran, Part 3)

**Kashubian Association of North
America—KANA**
PO Box 27732
Minneapolis, MN 55427-0732
(763) 545-7107
info@KA-NA.org; bkrbechek@att.net
http://www.KA-NA.org
Blanche Krbechek
Pub. *Przyjaciel ludu Kaszubskiego (Friend
of the Kashubian
People)*, quarterly (spring, summer, fall and
winter)
("The Kaszubs are an ancient Slavic tribe.
Today the Kashubian region
approximately includes Gdansk [Danzig]
and an egg-shaped region north, south and
west of Gdansk, covering part of the
present-day Polish provinces of
Bydgoszcz, Gdansk, and Slupsk.")
$15.00 per year membership

Michigan Polonia
cjensen@mipolonia.net
http://mipolonia.net
Ceil Jensen

Józef Pilsudski Institute of America
180 Second Avenue
New York, NY 10003-5778
(212) 505-9077; (212) 505-9052 FAX
Jacek Galazka
Mon–Wed 10:00–5:00
Pub. *Niepodleglosc (Independence)*,
annually, $15.00 plus postage per issue;
Bulletin, annually
(history of modern Poland from 1863)
membership includes only *Bulletin*

Polish American Cultural Center
308 Walnut Street
Philadelphia, PA 19106
(215) 922-1700

**Polish American Cultural Institute of
Minnesota**
4935 Abbott Avenue, North
Minneapolis, MN 55429

Polish American Historical Association
Saint Mary's College of Ave Maria
University
3535 Indian Trail
Orchard Lake, MI
(248) 683-1743
PAHAStM@aol.com
http://www.pahaol.com
Dr. Karen Majewski, Executive Secretary
and Newsletter Editor
Pub. *PAHA Newsletter*, semiannually (Mar,
Oct); *Polish American Studies*,
semiannually
$20.00 per year membership

Polish American Museum
16 Bellview Avenue
Port Washington, NY 11050
(516) 883-6542
http://www.liglobal.com/t_i/attractions/
museums/polish

**The Polish Genealogical Society of
America, Inc.**
984 North Milwaukee Avenue
Chicago, IL 60622-4101
(773) 384-3352
pgsamerica@aol.com
http://www.pgsa.org
Rosalie Lindberg, President
Library: 10:00–4:00 (volunteers work at
different times—library closed Thur)
Pub. *PGSA Journal*, quarterly; *Rodziny*
(researching all lands and people who are or
were under Polish rule and sovereignty)
$15.00 per year membership

Polish Genealogical Society of California
PO Box 713
Midway City, CA 92655-0713
paul.lipinski@acm.org;
information@pgsca.org;
president@pgsca.org
http://www.pgsca.org
Paul R. Lipinski, President
Pub. *Bulletin*, quarterly
$20.00 per year membership

**The Polish Genealogical Society of Greater
Cleveland**
906 College Avenue
Cleveland, OH 44113
(216) 459-0209
edjmendyka@aol.com; pulaskipro@aol.com
http://feefhs.org/pol/frgpgsgc.html
Edward J. Mendyka; John Szuch, President
Pub. *Our Polish Ancestors*, quarterly
("Genealogical interest generally; Polish
genealogy specifically.")
$20.00 per year membership

**Polish Genealogical Society of
Massachusetts**
PO Box 381
Northampton, MA 01061-0381
(413) 586-1827 FAX
jskibiski@aol.com
http://feefhs.org/pol/frgpgsma.html
John F. Skibiski, Jr., President
three program meetings per year
Pub. *Biuletyn Korzenie (Roots Newsletter)*,
two times per year (Mar, Oct)
$15.00 per year membership

Polish Genealogical Society of Michigan
Detroit Public Library
Burton Historical Collection
5201 Woodward Avenue
Detroit, MI 48202-4007
(313) 833-1480 (Library); (313) 833-1485
robertp@bignet.net
http://www.pgsm.org
Robert Postula, President
Library: Tue & Thur–Sat 9:30–5:30, Wed
1:00–9:00
Pub. *The Eaglet*, three times per year
$15.00 per year membership

Polish Genealogical Society of Minnesota
Minnesota Genealogical Society, Polish
Branch
5768 Olson Memorial Highway
Golden Valley, MN 55422
(763) 595-9347 (Library)
http://www.rootsweb.com/~mnpolgs/pgs-
mn.html
W. Kornel Kondy, President and Editor
Pub. *Polish Genealogical Society of
Minnesota Newsletter*, quarterly
("Membership is open to anyone with
ancestry or interest in Poland or in
historical Polish lands. This would
include: Poles, Germans, Ukrainians,
Russians, Jews, Ruthenians, Rusins,
Silesians, and others.")
$15.00 per year membership

**Polish Genealogical Society of New York
State (PGSNYS)**
c/o 12645 Route 78
East Aurora, NY 14052-9511
(716) 826-9482
president@pgsnys.org
http://www.pgsnys.org
David Newman, President
meetings at Villa Maria College, Pine Ridge
Road, Cheektowaga: second Thur
(Aug–June) 7:00–9:00 (research hours
Jan, Mar, Apr, June, Sept, Oct)
Pub. *Searchers*, triannually (Mar, July, Nov)
$15.00 per year membership; exchanged
newsletters with sister societies

**Polish Genealogical Society of the
Northeast**
8 Lyle Road
New Britain, CT 06053-2104
(860) 229-8873; (860) 223-5596
pgsctne@yahoo.com
http://www.pgsctne.org
Jonathan D. Shea, President/Archivist
Mon 10:00–2:30, and by appointment (call
first for use of most materials, which are
stored off-site)
Pub. *Pathways and Passages*, semiannually,
$15.00 per year subscription, $27.00 for
two-year subscription
professional translators and researchers
available on a fee basis: Polish, Russian,
German, Latin, Spanish

Polish Genealogical Society of Wisconsin
PO Box 342341

Milwaukee, WI 53234-2341
(414) 628-3742
christon@execpc.com
http://feefhs.org/pol/frgpgswi.html
Josephine Christon, Recording Secretary;
    Raymond Supercynski, President
Pub. *Korzenie* (*Roots*), quarterly
$10.00 per year membership

Polish Historical Commission
Central Council of Polish Organizations
4219 Stanton Avenue
Pittsburgh, PA 15201-2252
(412) 782-2166
Joseph A. Borkowski, Chairman
University of Pittsburgh, Hillman Library:
    Mon–Fri 10:00–3:00
Pub. *Polish Day Annual Program*, $2.50 per
    issue
inquiries must be accompanied by SASE

The Polish Museum of America Library
984 North Milwaukee Avenue
Chicago, IL 60622-4101
(773) 384-3352
rkujawa@prcuofa.org; JLorys@aol.com
http://www.prcuofa.org/pma
Mr. Jan M. Lorys, Director of Museum
Library: Mon–Tue & Fri–Sat 10:00–4:00,
    Wed 1:00–7:00; Museum: Mon–Wed &
    Fri–Sun 11:00–4:00
Pub. *The Polish Museum of America
    Newsletter*, quarterly
(Polish literature and Polonica)
$25.00 per year museum membership,
    $15.00 per year library fee

Polish National Alliance
6100 North Cicero
Chicago, IL 60646

Polish Nobility Association Foundation
Villa Anneslie
529 Dunkirk Road
Baltimore, MD 21212-2014
(410) 377-4352 (718) 383-0594; (718) 383-
    0594 FAX (Heraldry); (410) 377-4352
    FAX (Headquarters)
Maggie973@aol.com (Webmaster);
    len218a@mindspring.com (Headquarters)
http://www.angelfire.com/mn3/pnaf/
    index.html
Leonard J. Suligowski, Director of Heraldry;
    Pani Margaret Odrowaz-Sypniewski,
    BFA, PNAF, Webmaster
Pub. *White Eagle: Journal of the Polish
    Nobility Association Foundation*,
    semiannually
(Polish-Lithuanian)
$15.00 per year membership; research:
    $25.00 per name

**Polishville Cemetery and Grotto
Association and Esther Johanna Peck
Museum**
(1345 Tamarack Avenue—location)
1157 Raspberry Avenue (mailing address)
Brighton, IA 52540-8553
(319) 694-3495; (319) 694-3580
William E. Peck, President
by appointment
Pub. *Newsletter*, usually four times per year
(Polish heritage, operating on a very small
    scale)

University of Pittsburgh
Slavic Department
Pittsburgh, PA 15260
(houses collection of the former Polish
    National Alliance of the U.S. of North
    America)

Pomeranian
(see Eastern European, German and Polish)

Portuguese
(see also Spanish)

**The American-Portuguese Genealogical
and Historical Society, Inc.**
PO Box 644
Taunton, MA 02780-0644
Cecilia M. Rose, Executive Secretary
Pub. *Bulletinboard*, quarterly
$10.00 per year membership

Hawaii Council on Portuguese Heritage
810 North Vineyard Boulevard, Room 7
Honolulu, HI 96817
(808) 845-1616; (808) 841-0066

**Portuguese Genealogical Society of Hawaii
(PGSH)**
810 North Vineyard Boulevard, Room 11
Honolulu, HI 96817
(808) 841-5044
Mon, Wed & Fri–Sat 10:00–3:00
Pub. *A Nossa Herança* (Our Portuguese
    Heritage), quarterly
(whalers and families before 1878, 20,000
    family names of emigrants from Portugal
    to Hawaii, 1878 to 1913)
$10.00 per year membership; research:
    donation

Portuguese Historical and Cultural Society
1035 Starbrook Drive
Galt, CA 95632
(209) 744-8099
doug@dholmes.com
http://www.dholmes.com
Doug da Rocha Holmes, Board Member,
    Professional Genealogist
meetings: first Tue 7:00 in Saint Elizabeth
    Church Hall, 12th and S Streets,
    Sacramento
Pub. *O Progresso*, quarterly (Mar, June,
    Sept, Dec), (covers Sacramento region
    Portuguese cultural information, events,
    genealogy article by Doug da Rocha
    Holmes)
$12.00 per year membership

**Sociedade Portuguesa Raintta Santa Isabel
(S.P.R.S.I.)**
3031 Telegraph Avenue
Oakland, CA 94609
(510) 658-0983; (510) 658-6517 FAX
Silvia Ponte, Business Manager
8:00–4:30
Pub. *Buletim*, quarterly
(a benefit fraternal society)
$6.00 per year membership

Prussian
(see Eastern European, German)

Romanian
(see also Banat, Eastern European)

Romania Research List
http://feefhs.org/ro/rorl/rorl.html
Barbara Foosaner

The Romania (Rumania) Homepage
SNiculescu@aol.com
http://feefhs.org/ro/frg-ro.html

Susan Niculescu

Romanian American Heritage Center
2540 Grey Tower Road
Jackson, MI 49201-2208
(517) 522-8260; (517) 522-8236 FAX
http://feefhs.org//ro/frg-rahc.html
Eugene S. Raica, President and Editor
Pub. *Information Bulletin*, bimonthly
(has Andrica collection, from discontinued
    American Romanian Review;
    Romanian/Eastern Orthodox, Byzantine
    Rite Catholic)

Romanian Folk Art Museum
2526 Ridgeway
Evanston, IL 60201-1160
(847) 328-9099

**Romanian Jewish Genealogical Special
Interest Group**
(see Jewish, above)

Romanian Library
200 East 38th Street
New York, NY 10016
(212) 687-0181
Emilia Gheorghe, Acting Director
Pub. *Romanian Bulletin*, monthly

Society Farsarotul
593 Clinton Avenue
Bridgeport, CT 06605

United Romanian Society
14512 Royal Drive
Sterling Heights, MI 48312-4368
http://feefhs.org/ro/urs/frg-urs.html
Eugene S. Raica, Cultural Activities Director

Rusin
(see also Russian, Polish, and Slovak)

Russian
(see also Czech, Eastern European, German, Polish, and Slovak)

American Russian History Society
1272 47th Avenue
San Francisco, CA 94107

Blitz Information Center
907 Mission Avenue
San Rafael, CA 94901
(415) 453-3579; (415) 453-0343 FAX
enute@igc.org
http://feefhs.org/blitz/frgblitz.html
W. Edward Nute, Coordinator
Mon–Fri 8:00–5:00
(search of the records of Russian Archives,
    publishes historic and archival reference
    books; Russian Empire, Russian, Jewish,
    German, Baltic, Ukrainian)
$50.00 for preliminary search

Facts OnLine
812 Vista Drive
Camano Island, WA 98292
(360) 387-8901
Julia Petrakis, Owner
9:00–6:00
(maintains an office in Moscow, providing
    access to records in Russian archives)
research: $10.00 per hour, plus $1.00 per
    photocopy, plus travel, archive and
    shipping fees from Russia

Mennonite Historical Library
(see Indiana, Part 2)

Museum of Russian Culture, Inc.
2450 Sutter Street
San Francisco, CA 94115
(415) 751-1572; (415) 911-4082
Nicholas A. Slobedehikoff, Director

Russian-American Genealogical Archival Source (RAGAS)
(Moscow, Russia—location)
1929 18th Street, N.W. (mailing address)
Washington, DC 20009-1710
(301) 229-3819 (Editor)
http://feefhs.org/ragas/frgragas.html
Vladislav Y. Soshnikov, Historian/Archivist, Director, RAGAS/Moscow; Patricia A. Eames, Editor
Pub. *RAGAS Resources*, quarterly (spring, summer, fall, winter), $15.00 per year subscription from PO Box 236, Glen Echo, MD 20812-0236
(includes pre-revolution, 1917, archival records in Byelarus, Ukraine, Russia)
$25.00 nonrefundable fee for information, $50.00 deposit for more involved research

Russian Heraldry
http://sunsite.cs.msu.su/heraldry

Russian Heritage Society
PO Box 364
Agoura Hills, CA 91376-0364
(818) 991-0242; (818) 991-6752 FAX
http://feefhs.org/frg-rhs.html
H. Diane Connolly, U. S. Representative

Russian Nobility Association
971 First Avenue
New York, NY 10022
(212) 755-7528
Prince Alexes Scherbatan, President

Soviet-American Genealogical Archival Service
National Archives and Records Administration
Office of Public Programs
Seventh Street and Pennsylvania Avenue, N.W.
Washington, DC 20408
Pat Eames, Volunteer Coordinator

Ruthenian
(see also Czech and Polish)

Scandinavian
(see Danish, Finnish, Norwegian, Swedish and Scottish)

Scottish
(see also English and Irish)

Argyll Colony Plus
(see North Carolina, Part 2)

Caledonian Society of Cincinnati
6910 Bridgetown Road
Cincinnati, OH 45248
(513) 574-2969
ArchKSW2@aol.com
http://orbweb.com/caledonian
Arch Ott; Jesse Andrews, Secretary
(devoted to preserving and promoting Scottish culture and heritage. Links to other resources, including magazines and newspapers)
$10.00 per year membership, plus a $5.00 processing fee (membership restricted to adult male Scottish nationals or males of Scottish decent)

Council of Scottish Clan Associations

PO Box 27268
Houston, TX 77227

Council of Scottish Clans and Associations, Inc.
PO Box 2828
Moultrie, GA 31776-2828
(229) 985-6540
Beth Gay, DCTJ, FSA Scot, National Executive Secretary
Annual General Meeting held each July at Grandfather Mountain Highland Games

Electric Scotland
http://www.electricscotland.com
Alastair McIntyre
24/7
Pub. *Family Tree Newspaper*, bimonthly (online); *Newsletter*, weekly (online)
("Get your Scottish web site listed free at http://www.scotsearch.org," Scotland's Search Engine)

Institute of Scottish Studies
Old Dominion University
Department of History
College of Arts and Letters
Norfolk, VA 23529-0336
(757) 683-3949; (757) 683-5644 FAX
William S. Rodner, Ph.D., Editor
Pub. *Scotia: Interdisciplinary Journal of Scottish Studies*, annually, $10.00 per year subscription

Link O Mania Scotland on the Web
http://link-o-mania.com/scotgen.htm

Minnesota Coalition of Scottish Clans
1940 Inglehart Avenue, #31
Saint Paul, MN 55104
(612) 645-7413
Judith Lynn Finley, Toiseach (President)
("Only clan societies are members, but we are pleased to help inquirers find a clan connection and to help new clan societies become organized; we offer diverse historic and genealogical services through our membership; resource for all clans in Minnesota, especially for Macalester Fair and other Celtic celebrations.")

Museum of American Frontier Culture
(see Virginia, Part 2)

National Library of Scotland
http://www.nls.uk

Ellen Payne Odom Genealogy Library
(see Georgia, Part 2)

Ralston Public Library
(see Nebraska, Part 2)

The Saint Andrew's Society of Philadelphia
http://www.standrewsociety.org

The Scotch-Irish Foundation
PO Box 181
Bryn Mawr, PA 19010
(609) 429-5747 (President, New Jersey); (609) 354-0848 FAX; (215) 925-8090 (Custodian of the Records)
http://www.scotch-irishcentral.org/Scotch-Irish_Foundation.html
Barton E. Harrison, President
The Balch Institute for Ethnic Studies: Mon–Sat 9:00–5:00
Pub. *Library and Archives Catalogue*, irregularly, $10.00 per issue
(organized by The Scotch-Irish Society of the United States of America to collect

material on Ulster Plantation, Scotch-Irish settlements in America, and colonies' influence in building the U.S., also family registrations and related documents; "We do not provide a genealogical service; all of our books, family records are available to the public free of charge at The Balch Institute for Ethnic Studies, Philadelphia.")

The Scotch-Irish Society of the United States of America
PO Box 181
Bryn Mawr, PA 19010
(609) 429-5747 (President, New Jersey); (609) 354-0848 FAX
http://www.rootsweb.com/~sisusa
Barton E. Harrison, President
(no genealogical services; exists for "the preservation of Scotch-Irish history, the keeping alive the esprit de corps of the race, and the promotion of social intercourse and fraternal feeling among its members now and hereafter"; in 1949 established The Scotch-Irish Foundation, whose collection is deposited at The Balch Institute for Ethnic Studies, Philadelphia)
$15.00 application fee, $20.00 per year membership; research: contact Mrs. D. J. Pontarelli, 449 West Montgomery Avenue, Apartment 209, Haverford, PA 19041, (610) 649-4772 or Stewart Yost, 1530 Locust Street, Suite K, Philadelphia, PA 19602, (215) 985-0583

Scotland Genealogy: Tracing Your Scottish Ancestery
http://www.geo.edu.ac.uk/home/Scotland/genealogy.html

Scottish Genealogy Society
http://www.taynet.co.uk/users/scotgensoc

Scottish Historic and Research Society of the Delaware Valley, Inc.
102 Saint Paul's Road
Ardmore, PA 19003-2811
(610) 649-4144
Blair C. Stonier, President
evenings and weekends by appointment
Pub. *The Rampant Lion*, eleven times per year
$15.00 per year membership

Scottish Reference Information (Database)
http://www.ktb.net/~dwills/13300-scottishreference.htm

Scottish Society of Northern Colorado
3200 Silverthorn Drive
Fort Collins, CO 80526

Scottish Tartans Museum/Heritage Center
33 East Main Street
Franklin, NC 28734-3025
(828) 524-7472

Unicorn Limited, Inc.
(Scottish, Celtic and Norse, see Antiquarian Book Dealers, Part 4)

Western Pennsylvania Genealogical Society
(see Pennsylvania, Part 2)

Serbian
(see Croatian, Eastern European, and Hungarian)

Siberian

(see also Eastern European)

"Conversations with the Elders"
(see Catholic Apostolic Administration of
Asian Russia, Religious Archives and
Organizations—Roman Catholic, Part 3)

Silesian
(see also Czech, Eastern European, and Polish)

Silesia Research List
1910 East 5685 South
Salt Lake City, UT 84121-1343
goldcontac@aol.com
http://feefhs.org/de/sil/silrl/silrl.html
Joseph L. (Joe) Reimann

Slavic
(see also Eastern European)

Center for Slavic Culture
Illinois Benedictine College
Lisle, IL 60532
(630) 968-7270
Bert A. Thompson, Director of Library
   Service
("The Czech Heritage Collection has been
   put in closed storage and is not available
   for use.")

East Europe Connection
(formerly The Slavic Connection)
1711 Corwin Drive
Silver Spring, MD 20910-1533
(301) 585-0117
http://feefhs.org/frg-eec.html
Lawrence Krupnak

Slavic Research Institute
17907 Kuykendahl Suite 202
Spring, TX 77379
(281) 251-7690; (281) 251-7691 FAX
thrncirik@aol.com
http://Czechusa.com
Thomas Hrncinik, A.G., President

Soc.Genealogy.Slavic
http://feefhs.org/socslav/frg-slav.html
Stephen Kymlicka
(newsgroup, help and links to other
   resources)

Texas Wendish Heritage Society
(see German, above)

Slovak
(see also Carpatho-Russian, Czech, Eastern European, Hungarian, and Slavic)

**The Eastern Slovakia, Slovak and
Carpatho-Rusyn Genealogical Research
Page**
2233 Keeven Lane
Florissant, MO 63031
(314) 831-9482
Greg@iarelative.com
http://www.iarelative.com/slovakia.html
Greg Kopchak
(offers online tools, resources, and
   information to help you search your
   Slovak or Carpatho-Rusyn family history
   and ancestry; links to other sites)

Jankola Library and Slovak Archives
Danville, PA 17821
(570) 275-3581; (570) 275-5606
Sister M. Martina Tybor, Director and
   Archivist
by arrangement ("We prefer exploring our

reserves for data on a given topic and
forwarding relevant material prepared on
our copier; our books do not circulate.")

Saint Leo's Genealogy Group
16253 Glendale Avenue
Strongsville, Ohio 44136
(440) 572-0139
Lkoboyle@aol.com
http://feefhs.org/slovak/frg-slgg.html
Louise K. O'Boyle, Secretary/Treasurer
meetings at St. Leo's Parish Community
   Center, 4940 Broadview Road, Cleveland:
   third Thur 7:30
$10.00 per year membership

Slavic Roots Genealogy Services
6780 North Applegate Road
Grants Pass, OR 97527
oregonjohn@peoplepc.com
http://www.slavicroots.com
John A. Hudick
("Slovak and Rusyn Roots" guide for
   research in the Slovak and Czech
   republics, links to Internet sources and
   newsgroups; published *Finding Your
   Ancestral Village . . . in the Former
   Austro-Hungarian Empire*)

Slovak Genealogical Research Center
6862 Palmer Court
Chino, CA 91710-7343
(909) 627-2897
rplutko@aol.com
http://feefhs.org/SLOVAK/frg-sgrc.html
Ray Plutko, Director
Pub. *Slovak Genealogy Kit*
("Private Research Center/Collection. Slovak
   genealogy kit and individual village
   histories.")

**Slovak Heritage and Folklore Society
International**
151 Colebrook Drive
Rochester, NY 14617-2215
(585) 342-9383; (585) 342-0443 FAX
helenezx@aol.com
http://feefhs.org/slovak/frgshfsi.html;
   http://www.helenezx.homestead.com
   (includes database, "Slovak Pride," listing
   over 19,000 surnames and villages)
Helene Cincebeaux, Director and Editor
Pub. *Slovakia*, quarterly (features history,
   culture and genealogy)
("The Society published a book, *Slovak
   Pride*, with 23,000 listings of surnames
   and the villages they came from and
   genealogical tips for searching in
   Slovakia.")
$12.00 per year membership

Slovak Institute
2900 East Boulevard
Cleveland, OH 44104
Andrew Pier, Director

**Library and Museum of Slovak Language,
History, Literature, and Culture**
Slovak Cultural, Educational and Literary
Center
775 West Drahner Road
Oxford, MI 48371
(248) 628-2872
Sister Gabrielle Woytko, O.P., Librarian-
   Curator
by appointment

The Slovak Museum and Archives
(Jednota Press, Rosedale Avenue and
Jednota Lane—location)
PO Box 750 (mailing address)
Middletown, PA 17057

(717) 944-2403
http://feefhs.org/slovak/frg-sgrc.html
Anna Chladek Sutherland, Curator and
   Archivist
Mon–Fri 8:30–4:00
Pub. *Jednota*, two times per month, $25.00
   per year subscription in the U.S., $50.00
   per year subscription abroad

Slovak-World Home Page
gecovic@fris.sk
http://www.fris.sk/Slovak-World
Miroslav Gecovic
7:00 A.M.–8:00 P.M.

Slovakia Home Page
http://www.tuzvo.sk/homepage.html

**Slovakia—Surname Location Reference
Project (SLRP)**
PO Box 31831
Cleveland, OH 44131-0831
no phone calls for initial contact
jhornack@rampant.com
http://feefhs.org/frg-slrp.html
Joseph J. Hornack, Founder/Director
("offers query and information service,
   published series by county, in English, to
   Slovak/American periodicals; database of
   submitted surnames and their location of
   roots in Slovakia, free access to those
   added contributors and with email
   researching contacts living abroad; open
   to all with roots in the geographic area of
   the Slovak Republic and the former
   Slovakia)
fee: submission of a pedigree chart starting
   from the submitter

Wisconsin Slovak Historical Society
PO Box 164
Cudahy, WI 53110-0164
(414) 681-1692
Laura Thompson, Research Director
hours: various
Pub. *Wisconsin Slovak*, four times per year
$10.00 per year membership

Slovenian
(see also Croatian, Eastern European, German, and Hungarian)

Pokrajinski Arhiv Maribor
Slovenian Regional Archives at Maribor
miro@parmb.pokarh-mb.si
http://feefhs.org/slovenia/si/frg-msra.html
Miroslav Novak, Ph.D.

Slovene National Benevolent Society
247 West Allegheny Road
Imperial, PA 15126-9786

**Slovenian Genealogical Society
International, Inc.**
52 Old Farm Road
Camp Hill, PA 17011-2604
(717) 731-8804 (5:00 P.M.–7:00 P.M. only)
apeterlin@panetwork.com
http://sloveniangenealogy.org
Al Peterlin, President
Pub. *Newsletter*, quarterly
(Slovenia once was the northernmost
   republic of Yogoslavia; it was once part
   of Austria-Hungary; it is now an
   independent country)
$10.00 per year membership

**Slovenian Genealogical Society
International, Inc.**
Colorado Chapter
8950 3-R Road
Beulah, CO 81023

gexe@aculink.net
http://sloveniangenealogy.org/chapters/
    Colorado.htm
Shirley Sturtevant, President

Slovenian Genealogical Society International, Inc.
Metropolitan Washington DC Chapter
JohnLipold@cs.com
http://sloveniangenealogy.org/chapters/
    MetroWashDC.htm
Pub. *Newsletter*, semi-annually

Slovenian Genealogical Society International, Inc.
Florida Chapter
7605 Harvey Street
Pensacola, FL 32506-5022
Rleskov@aol.com
http://sloveniangenealogy.org/chapters/
    Florida.htm
Raymond F. Leskovec, President

Slovenian Genealogical Society International, Inc.
Illinois Chapter
1436 Gardner Road
Westchester, IL 60154
Demeter209@aol.com
http://sloveniangenealogy.org/chapters/
    Illinois.htm
Mary Anne Aguilar, President

Slovenian Genealogical Society International, Inc.
Indiana Chapter
PO Box 59
Westfield, IN 46074-0059
clipper66@webtv.net
Sharon Shoemaker, President

Slovenian Genealogical Society International, Inc.
Mid Continental States Chapter
200 East Fifth Street
Valley Center, KS 67147-2602
http://sloveniangenealogy.org/chapters/
    MidContinental_.htm
Christie R. Supancic Johnson, President

Slovenian Genealogical Society International, Inc.
Michigan Upper Peninsula Chapter
(347 Rock Street—location)
PO Box 550 (mailing address)
Marquette, MI 49855
edelene@dioceseofmarquette.org
Elizabeth Delene

Slovenian Genealogical Society International, Inc.
Minnesota Chapter
417 N.W. Ninth Street
Chisholm, MN 55719-1542
(218) 254-5801
trupar@uslink.net
http://sloveniangenealogy.org/chapters/
    Minnesota.htm
Terry Rupar, President

Slovenian Genealogical Society International, Inc.
Ohio Chapter
12185 Pheasant Run Circle
North Royalton, OH 44133-5678
http://sloveniangenealogy.org/chapters/
    Ohio.htm
Rose Marie Jisa, President
East Side Group meets at the Euclid Public
    Library; West Side Group meets at the
    Parma Regional Library (Jan, Apr, July,
    Oct)

Slovenian Genealogical Society International, Inc.
Pennsylvania Chapter
1350 Peiffers Lane
Steelton, PA 17113
Jacquelyn@sloveniangenealogy.org
http://sloveniangenealogy.org/chapters/
    Pennsylvania.htm
Jacquelyn Zulli, President

Slovenian Genealogical Society International, Inc.
Texas Chapter
340 Treeline Park, Apartment 315
San Antonio, TX 78209
http://sloveniangenealogy.org/chapters/
    Texas.htm
Mike Fox, President

Slovenian Genealogical Society International, Inc.
Western States Chapter
9863 Countrywood Drive
Sandy, UT 84092
heatherQ@planet-soft.com
http://sloveniangenealogy.org/chapters/
    Western_States.htm
Heather W. Quinton
(includes the states of Arizona, California,
    Idaho, Montana, Nevada, New Mexico,
    Utah, and Wyoming)

Slovenian Genealogical Society International, Inc.
Pacific Northwest Chapter
3536 Ashworth Avenue North
Seattle, WA 98103-8934
gorsha@juno.com
http://sloveniangenealogy.org/chapters/
    Pacific_Northwest.htm
(includes the states of Alaska, Oregon and
    Washington

Slovenian Genealogical Society International, Inc.
Wisconsin Chapter
69820 West Long Lake Road
Iron River, WI 54847
http://sloveniangenealogy.org/chapters/
    Wisconsin.htm
Mary Lou Deyak Voelk, President

Slovenian Genealogical Society International, Inc.
Australia Chapter
fergeusw@bigpond.com
Helen S. Oppelli

Slovenian Genealogical Society International, Inc.
Brazil Chapter
vida@brasmail.com.br
http://sloveniangenealogy.org/chapters/
    Brazil.htm
Lucy Petroucic

Slovenian Genealogical Society International, Inc.
Canada Chapter
momcat52@hotmail.com
http://sloveniangenealogy.org/chapters/
    BritColumbia.htm
Linda Lenassi Tomlin, President

Slovenian Genealogical Society International, Inc.
Ontario Chapter
frank_pinter@dofasco.ca;
    fmajzelj@cogeco.ca
http://sloveniangenealogy.org/chapters/
    Ontario.htm
Frank Pinter, Jr. and Frank Majzelj, Co-

Presidents

Slovenian Genealogical Society International, Inc.
Republic of Slovenia Chapter
walshslov@hotmail.com
http://sloveniangenealogy.org/chapters/
    Slovenia.htm
Patricia Walsh

Slovenian Genealogy Center
Saint Mary's Church
211 East Mesa
Pueblo, CO 81006
Robert Blazich

Slovenian Women's Union of America
Slovenian Heritage Museum
431 North Chicago Street
Joliet, IL 60432
(815) 727-1926
Jonita Ruth, Heritage Director
Mon–Thur 10:00–2:00, weekends by
    appointment
Pub. *Zarja—The Dawn*, six times per year
$15.00 per year membership

South African
(see Dutch)

Spanish
(see also Basque and Creole)

The Amistad Research Center
(see African-American, above)

Centro de Studios Chicanos Research Center
San Diego State University
San Diego, CA 92182
(619) 286-5145
Juan D. Tapia, Coordinator

Chicano Reference Library
590S The Nitery
Stanford University
Stanford, CA 94305
(650) 497-2798
Juanita Villalobos, Director
Green Library
Pub. *Chicano Reference Library
    Bibliography*, annually

Chicano Research Collection
Department of Archives and Manuscripts
Hayden Library
Arizona State University
Tempe, AZ 85287-1006
(480) 965-3145
Christine Marin, Curator
Mon 11:00–7:00, Tue–Wed 8:00–7:00,
    Thur–Fri 8:00–5:00, Sat 1:00–5:00
(Mexican-American history; Mexican-
    Americans in the U.S.)

Chicano Studies Library
University of California
3408 Dwinelle Hall
Berkeley, CA 94720
(510) 642-3859
Oscar Trevino, Serials Librarian

Clayton Library, Center for Genealogical Research
(see Texas, Part 2)

Denver Public Library
(see Colorado, Part 2)

Duke University Press
(6697 College Station—location)

PO Box 90660 (mailing address)
Durham, NC 27708-0660
(919) 687-3600; (888) 651-0122 (Book
Orders); (888) 387-5765 (Journal
Subscriptions); (919) 688-4574 FAX
orders@dukeupress.edu
Pub. *Hispanic American Historical Review*,
quarterly, $40.00 per year subscription

El Paso County Historical Society
(see Texas, Part 2)

Mel Fisher Maritime Heritage Society
(200 Greene Street, Key West, FL
33040—location)
PO Box 511 (mailing address)
Key West, FL 33041
(305) 294-2633
Dr. Madeleine Burnside, Executive Director
Mon–Sun 9:00–5:00
Pub. *Astrolabe*, annually; *Navigator*,
monthly
(Spanish colonial era)
$20.00 per year membership

FLSV Genealogy Record
7747 Wildwood Road
Findlay, OH 45840-9538
(419) 424-1199
Alicia Dapore
8:00–5:00
Pub. *FLSV Genealogy Record
(Fabela/Lozano/Solis/Villanueva)*,
quarterly, $10.00 per year subscription
(Mexican)
free searches

Heráldica y Genealogía
webmaster@heraldry-and-genealogy.com
http://www.ctv.es/artes/home.htm/home.
html

***La Herencia Del Norte—Hispanic Heritage
Magazine***
http://www.herencia.com
*La Herencia Del Norte—Hispanic Heritage
Magazine*

Hidalgo County Historical Museum
(see Texas, Part 2)

Genealogical Society of Hispanic America
PO Box 9606
Denver, CO 80209-0606
Donie Nelson, Membership Chair
Pub. *Nuestras Raices*, quarterly
("Hispanic genealogy.")
$20.00 per year membership

Genealogical Society of Hispanic America
Southern California Branch (GSHA-SC)
PO Box 2472
Santa Fe Springs, CA 90670-0472
http://home.earthlink.net/~ririgoyen

Hispanic Family History Society
3607 South Kenneth Place
Tempe, AZ 85282

**Hispanic Genealogical Research Center of
New Mexico**
1331 Juan Tabo, N.E., Suite P, #18
Albuquerque, NM 87112
(505) 836-5438
HGRC@HGRC-NM.org
http://www.hgrc-nm.org
Ron Miera, President
meetings at Albuquerque Public Library,
Special Collections Library: first Sat
10:00
Pub. *Herencia*, quarterly
$20.00 per year membership

Hispanic Genealogical Society
PO Box 231271
Houston, TX 77223-1271
joguerra@hispanicgs.com
http://www.hispanicgs.com
Jose O. Guerra, Jr., President
Pub. *Hispanic Genealogical Journal*,
semiannually
$15.00 per year membership

**Hispanic Genealogical Society of New
York**
Murray Hill Station, PO Box 818
New York, NY 10156-0602
(212) 532-3662
webjefe@hispanicgenealogy.com
http://www.hispanicgenealogy.com
Charles Fourquet-Batiz, Vice President and
Co-Founder
Pub. *Nuestra Herencia*
(helping Hispanics/Latinos to find their
family origins, specializing in Puerto
Rican genealogy)
free membership

Hispanic Genealogy
http://home.att.net/~Alsosa
Alfred Sosa
Pub. *Enlaces* (online)
(Sponsors an online forum: Hispanic
Genealogy Forum)

**Society of Hispanic Historical and
Ancestral Research**
PO Box 490
Midway City, CA 92655-0490
(714) 894-8161
mimilozano@aol.com
http://members.aol.com/shhar;
http://www.somosprimos.com (*Somos
Primos*)
Mimi Lozano
8:00–5:00
Pub. *Somos Primos*, monthly (free e-zine
online)
("helping Hispanics, world-wide, in
researching their family genealogy";
Hispanic/Latino heritage, Mexican-
American, indigenous and Black
connections, international ethnic Spanish
historical connections)
free membership

Hispanic History and Ancestry Research
9511 Rockpoint Drive
Huntington Beach, CA 92646

Hispanic Institute of Columbia University
(Casa Hispánica, Room 405—location)
612 West 116th Street (mailing address)
New York, NY 10027
(212) 854-5610; (212) 854-5322 FAX
Dr. Elzbieta Szoka, Editor
Mon–Fri 9:00–5:00
Pub. *Revista Hispánica Moderna*,
semiannually (June, Dec), $25.00 per year
subscription
("Our archives—very well-known among
scholars—have an extensive bibliography
and numerous clippings dealing with the
literature and culture of the Spanish- and
Portuguese-speaking countries; although
the archives have been closed since 1969,
they are valuable and are open to all
students and members of the Hispanic
Institute.")

The Hispanic Society of America
613 West 155th Street
New York, NY 10032
(212) 926-2234
Gerald J. MacDonald, Curator, Modern

Library
Museum: Tue–Sat 10:00–4:30, Sun
1:00–3:00; Library: Tue–Sat 10:00–4:15
(Spanish [including Basque and Catalan],
Portuguese, and Hispanic-American)
membership by election only

**Jesuit Historical Institute, American
Division**
(see Religious Archives and
Organizations—Roman Catholic, Part 3)

Los Bexareños Genealogical Society
(see Texas, Part 2)

**Los Californianos, Hispanic Ancestors of
Alta California**
4530 LaCrosse Avenue
San Diego, CA 92117
(619) 273-2260
Alice Thomson, Membership Chairman
quarterly meetings at various locations: Sat
& Sun
Pub. *Antepasados*, annually; *Noticias*,
quarterly
(descendants of Hispanics in Alta California
before February 1848)
regular membership subject to approval of
Genealogy Committee, spouses also
eligible, historians and libraries
(corresponding) eligible with approval of
board

Los Descendientes del Presidio de Tucson
(1711 North Painted Hills Road, Tucson, AZ
85745-1535—location)
PO Box 50871 (mailing address)
Tucson, AZ 85703
(520) 743-8233
Theresa G. Montaño, President
8:00–5:00
Pub. *Newsletter*, quarterly
about $300.00

**Los Fundadores, The Founders and
Friends of Santa Clara County**
(see California, Part 2)

Los Pobladores 200
(see California, Part 2)

**Mexican American Cultural Heritage
Center**
2940 Singleton Boulevard
Dallas, TX 75212
(972) 630-1680

Museum of New Mexico
(see New Mexico, Part 2)

New Mexico Records Center and Archives
404 Montezuma Street
Santa Fe, NM 87501
(505) 827-7332; (505) 827-7331 FAX
http://www.state.nm.us
Elaine Olah, State Records Administrator
Mon–Fri 8:00–5:00
Pub. *Quipu*, irregularly
(Spanish archives of New Mexico,
1621–1821)

**Puerto Rican/Hispanic Genealogical
Society**
(see Puerto Rico, Part 2)

Saint Augustine Historical Society
(see Florida, Part 2)

Santa Barbara Historical Society
(see California, Part 2)

Society for Spanish and Portuguese

History
Boston College
140 Commonwealth Avenue
Chestnut Hill, MA 02167

Southmost College
Arnulfo L. Oliveira Memorial Library
(see Texas, Part 2)

**Spanish American Genealogical
Association**
PO Box 5407
Corpus Christi, TX 78405

University of Texas at Austin
Benson Latin American Collection
PO Box P
Austin, TX 78713-8916
(512) 495-4520; (512) 495-4568
blac@lib.utexas.edu
http://www.lib.utexas.edu/Libs/Benson/
benson.html

University of Texas at San Antonio
Institute of Texan Cultures
(see Texas, Part 2)

Swedish
(see also Finish and Norwegian)

**American Friends of the Swedish
Emigrant Institute of Sweden, Inc.**
3452 Fourth Street
East Moline, IL 61244
(309) 755-2858
Lennart Setterdahl
("As of now we are only working with direct
research 'out in the field.' The result will
be handled by Svenska Emigrantinstitutet,
Växjö, Sweden. Our office will not
answer any inquiries from the public.")

American Swedish Historical Museum
1900 Pattison Avenue
Philadelphia, PA 19145-5901
(215) 389-1776; (215) 389-7701 FAX
ashm@libertynet.org
http://www.americanswedish.org
Margaretha Talerman, Curator
Tue–Fri 10:00–4:00, Sat–Sun noon–4:00,
and by appointment
Pub. *Newsletter*, quarterly
$35.00 per year membership

The American Swedish Institute
2600 Park Avenue
Minneapolis, MN 55407
(612) 871-4907; (612) 871-4908; (612) 871-
8682 FAX
Jan McElfish, Editor/Publicist; Marita
Karlisch, Archives and Library
Tue & Thur–Sat noon–4:00, Wed
noon–8:00, Sun 1:00–5:00; Archives and
Library: by appointment only Tue &
Thur–Fri noon–4:00, Wed noon–8:00,
third Sat noon–4:00
Pub. *ASI Posten*, eleven times per year
(monthly)
$33.00 per year membership

Bishop Hill Heritage Association
(see Illinois, Part 2)

Independent Order of Svithiod
5518 West Lawrence Avenue
Chicago, IL 60630
(773) 736-1191
iosvithiod@juno.com
Betty Jane Clausen, Secretary-Treasurer
9:00–5:00
Pub. *Svithiod Journal*, monthly
("Swedish, Norwegian, Danish, Finnish, and

Icelandic")
$1.00 per year membership

Lewes Historical Society
119 West Third
Lewes, DE 19958
(302) 645-7640
Dr. James E. Marvil, President

Maine's Swedish Colony
PO Box 50
New Sweden, ME 04762
(207) 896-3199; (207) 896-3120 FAX; (207)
896-5624 FAX
http://www.state.me.us/sos/arc/external/
otherins.htm

**National Council of the Swedish Cultural
Society in America**
PO Box 8042
Saint Paul, MN 55108-8042
(612) 645-8578 voice & FAX
L. Christina Sjostedt, National President
Pub. *Swedish Heritage*, quarterly
$5.00 per year membership

New Sweden, Iowa, Descendants
(see Iowa, Part 2)

Nordic Heritage Museum
3014 N.W. 67th
Seattle, WA 98117
(206) 789-5707; (206) 789-3271 FAX
http://www.ohwy.com/wa/n/nordichm.htm
Marianne Forssblad, Ph.D., Director
Tue–Sat 10:00–4:00, Sun noon–4:00
Pub. *Nordic News*, bimonthly
(Nordic-Scandinavian: Denmark, Finland,
Iceland, Norway, Sweden; genealogical
information with largest holdings in
Norwegian "Bygdevøker")
$30.00 per year membership

Old Swedes Foundation
Holy Trinity (Old Swedes') Church
Foundation, Inc.
Hendrickson House Museum and Old
Swedes' Church
606 Church Street
Wilmington, DE 19801-4421
(302) 652-5629; (302) 652-8615 FAX
oldswedes@aol.com
http://www.oldswedes.org
Jo Thompson, Curator/Business Manager
(Tue–Fri), Ray Nichols, Archivist (Mon &
Wed)
Mon–Sat 10:00–4:00
Pub. *Old Swedes' Foundation Newsletter*,
annually
(Old Swedes vital records, births/baptisms,
marriages and burials, available from
1713 to the present [mostly]; excellent
library concentrating on colonies/states in
the Mid-Atlantic area"; Swedish/Finnish)
$25.00 per year membership; research for
baptism, marriage or burial of one
individual: $10.00 (includes photocopies
of the event from printed copies of the
church records, but a letter attesting to the
information is $5.00 extra), determining if
and when members of a certain family
were buried in the church yard: $10.00
(includes a photocopy of records, where
possible, and a letter attesting to the
information), researching records on some
of the early Swedish families for a specific
name and making photocopies: $10.00
plus 20¢ per page

Pacific Lutheran University
Robert A. L. Mortvedt Library
(see Religious Archives and

Organizations—Lutheran, Part 3)

Scandinavian Heritage Association
1412 Debbie Drive
Minot, ND 58701
George Officer

Scandinavian Queries
Route 2, Box 671
Grangeville, ID 83530-9635
(208) 983-0515
Anne Long
Pub. *Scandinavian Queries* (Denmark,
Finland, Norway, Sweden, Iceland),
irregularly, $6.50 per year subscription
(Idaho residents add 5% sales tax)

Seattle Genealogical Society
(Scandinavia; see Washington, Part 2)

Swedish American Historical Society
North Park College
5125 North Spaulding Avenue
Chicago, IL 60625-4816
(773) 583-5722; (773) 583-2700, ext. 5267
(Library)
http://www.northpark.edu/library/swedish-
american_history/index.html
Karna Anderson, Office Manager
9:00–noon
Pub. *Swedish American Historical Quarterly*
$25.00 per year basic membership

Swedish American Museum
5211 North Clark Street
Chicago, IL 60640-2101
(773) 728-8111; (773) 728-8870 FAX
Kerstin Lane, Executive Director
Tue–Fri 10:00–4:00, Sat–Sun 10:00–3:00
Pub. *FLAGGAN*, quarterly
$25.00 per year membership

**The Swedish Ancestry Research
Association (SARA)**
PO Box 70603
Worcester, MA 01607-0603
SARAMembership@Netscape.net
http://sarassociation.tripod.com
meetings: Sept–June
Pub. *Newsletter*, ten times per year
(Sept–June); *Journal*, annually (featuring
a province of Sweden)
$20.00 per year membership

Swedish Colonial Society
916 Swanson Street
Philadelphia, PA 19147
(215) 389-1513
http://libertynet.org/~gencap/scs.html
Rev. David Rivers, Secretary
Pub. *Swedish Colonial Society Newsletter*,
semiannually
("New Sweden period, 1638–1786")
$20.00 per year membership

The Delaware Swedish Colonial Society
606 Church Street
Wilmington, DE 19801
Al Ostrand, President
Pub. *Smörgåsnews*
(ethnic and colonial Swedish)
$10.00 per year

The Swedish Finn Historical Society
6512 23rd Avenue, N.W., #301
Seattle, WA 98117-5728
(206) 706-0738; (206) 782-5813 FAX
Bonnie Olson, Secretary
Mon 9:30–12:30, Thur 9:30–12:30, and by
appointment
Pub. *The Swedish Finn Historical Society
Newsletter*, quarterly

(specializes in Finland's Swedes)
$12.50 per year membership; research:
donation

Swedish Genealogy Club of the American Swedish Historical Museum
2700 Pattison Avenue
Philadelphia, PA 19145
(215) 389-1776
William Fagerstrom, President
meetings: third Thur (Jan, Mar, May, Sept, Nov) 7:00 P.M.–9:00 P.M.
$10.00 per year membership

Swedish Genealogy Pages
http://algonet.se/~floyd/scandgen

Swedish Genealogy Society of Minnesota
Minnesota Genealogical Society
5768 Olson Memorial Highway
Golden Valley, MN 55422
(763) 429-7377
pjsveria@mtn.org
http://www.mtn.org/mgs/sweden
Phyllis Pladsen
Pub. *Tidningen*, quarterly

Swedish Historical Society
404 South Third Street
Rockford, IL 61104-2013
(815) 963-5559
Rev. Ragnar Moline, President
by appointment
Pub. *Swedish Heritage*, annually, $3.00 per year subscription
$8.00 per year membership

Swedish Information Services
Consulate General of Sweden
http://www.webcom.com/sis/order.html
(publishes "Tracing Your Swedish Ancestry" and other informative publications)

Swenson Swedish Immigration Research Center
Augustana College
639 38th Street
Rock Island, IL 61201-2296
(309) 794-7204; (309) 794-7443 FAX
sag@augustana.edu
http://www.augustana.edu/ administration/swenson
Jill A. Seaholm, Researcher; Christina Johansson, Archives/Library; Anne Jenner, Researcher/Cataloger; Dr. Dag Blanck, Director
Tue–Fri by appointment (except during holidays and school vacation)
Pub. *Swenson Center News*, annually; *Swedish American Genealogist*, quarterly
(Augustana Lutheran Church [Swedish], Evangelical Covenant Church, Swedish Baptist Conference, Swedish Methodist Church, Evangelical Free Church and Swedish Episcopal)
$25.00 per year membership

Vasa Order of America National Archives, Inc.
(109 South Main—location)
PO Box 101 (mailing address)
Bishop Hill, IL 61419
(309) 927-3898 voice & FAX
Richard W. Horngren, Archivist
1 Apr–20 Dec: Mon–Sat 10:00–3:00, Sun noon–4:00, and other times by appointment
Pub. *The Vasa Star* (published by VOA Grand Lodge), six times per year
(specializes in Swedish-American, Swedish, Scandinavian material, not primarily a genealogical resource, but "happy to give

basic information on Swedish genealogy and the Swedish language, geography, etc.")
$10.00 per year membership; research: generally free to members, negotiated for others

Dalesburg Scandinavian Association
30595 University Road
Vermillion, SD 57069-6507

Swiss
(see also Galician and German)

Immigrant Genealogical Society
(see Immigration Research Centers, Part 4)

New Glarus Historical Society
(see Wisconsin, Part 2)

Swiss American Historical Society
(Washington, DC—location)
6440 North Bosworth Avenue (mailing address)
Chicago, IL 60626
(773) 262-8336
Professor Erdmann Schmocker, President
Pub. *Swiss American Historical Society Review*, three times per year
(promotes research involving Swiss immigrants)
$30.00 per year membership

Swiss Community Historical Society
9255 Lugabell Road
Bluffton, OH 45817
Herman Hilty

The Swiss Connection
2845 North 72nd Street
Milwaukee, WI 53210
(414) 778-1224; (414) 778-2109 FAX
Maralyn A. Wellauer, Editor
Mon–Sat noon–8:00
Pub. *The Swiss Connection*, quarterly, $12.00 per year subscription (Sept–June), $20.00 per year overseas subscription
research: $45.00–$65.00 per hour

Swiss Genealogy
http://www.mindspring.com/~philipp/che.html

Swiss Genealogy on the Internet
http://www.kssg.ch/chgene/welcome-e.htm

Swiss Heritage Society
1200 Swiss Way
Berne, IN 46711
(219) 589-8007 (summer months only)
Gretchen Lehman, Secretary
Mon–Sat 10:00–4:00
Pub. *Swiss Echoes*, semiannually (spring and fall), donation
(specializes in Swiss culture)

Swiss Historical Society of Gruetli, Tennessee
(address withheld upon request)

Swiss Mennonite Cultural and Historical Association
109 East Hirschler
Moundridge, KS 67107
(620) 345-2844

Swiss Society of Genealogy Studies
http://www.3dplus.ch/~nickj/Engl_SSEG.html

Taiwanese
(see Asian)

Ukrainian
(see also Eastern European, German, Hungarian, Polish, and Russian)

Saint Basil's College
195 Glenbrook Road
Stamford, CT 06902

Ukrainian Fraternal Association
1327 Wyoming Avenue
Scranton, PA 18509-2849
(570) 347-5649
Ivan Oleksyn, President
8:00–4:30
Pub. *Forum, Ukrainian Review*, quarterly, $12.00 per year subscription; *Narodna Volya* (newspaper), weekly, $10.00 per year subscription

Ukrainian Genealogical and Heraldic Society
573 N.E. 102nd Street
Miami Shores, FL 33138

The Ukrainian Museum
203 Second Avenue
New York, NY 10003
(212) 228-0110; (212) 228-1947 FAX
Lydia Hajduczok
Wed–Sun 1:00–5:00

Ukrainian Museum-Archives, Inc.
1202 Kenilworth Avenue
Cleveland, OH 44113-4417
(216) 741-4537

United Ukrainian American Relief Committee
1206 Cootman Avenue
Philadelphia, PA 19111
(215) 728-1630; (215) 728-1631 FAX
Stepan Hawrysz, Executive Director
Mon–Fri 9:00–4:00

Vietnamese
(see Asian)

Welsh
(see also English, Irish, and Scottish)

Bryn Mawr Club of Akron
1860 Second Street, Apartment 663
Cuyahoga Falls, OH 44221
Judith Hedges

Cambrian Heritage Society
200 Lakewood Boulevard
Madison, WI 53704
Shirley Levine

San Diego Cambrian Society
1694 Via Elisa
El Cajon, CA 92021
Karen R. Mueller

Cambrian Society of the Delaware Valley
96 Charlotte Drive
Philadelphia, PA 18966
Joan Brown

Nanticoke Cambrian Society
247 State Street
Nanticoke, PA 18634
Catherine Jonathon

Plymouth Cambrian Society
464 Beaumont Street
Warrior Run, PA 18706

Cambrian Society of Portland

13508 278th Street East
Graham, WA 98338-8757
Richard J. Davies

Celtic Cultural Coalition
One West 69th Street
Kansas City, MO 64113
Ann McFerrin

Celtic Photos and Crafts
10 Hemingway Road
North Haven, CT 06473-3737
(800) IM-WELSH voice & FAX (8:00
A.M.–9:00 P.M.)
celticpandc@mindspring.com
http://www.celticpandc.com
Earl T. Williams, Jr., B.A.M.,
Director/Owner
Pub. *Catalog*, annually, free
(books, recordings, Welsh learning materials,
etc.; mail-order Welsh imports)

**Celtic (Welsh, Irish, Scottish) Society of
the Ozarks**
2214 East Cherryvale
Springfield, MO 65804-4524
(417) 883-8396
Dr. J. C. Holsinger, Secretary
quarterly public meetings
Pub. *The Dragon, The Thistle, and The
Harp*, quarterly
(an interest group that meets for lectures and
singing of Celtic music; no genealogical
research)
$5.00 per year membership

Cymdeithas Cymreig Yr Idaho
6700 McGlochin Road
Boise, ID 83709
David Lyle Perry

Cymdeithas Madog
Welsh Language Institute of North America
2160 Roblyn
Saint Paul, MN 55104
John Kudlaty, President

Cymrodorion Society of Greater Boston
411 Dudham Avenue
Needham, MA 02492
(781) 444-6140
Mair Lustig

Dr. Edwards Memorial Church
Edwardsville, Pa.
428 North Maple Street
Kingston, PA 18704
Donna Morgan

Green Mountain College
(see Religious Archives and
Organizations—United Methodist, Part 3)

National Welsh-American Foundation
(Sefydliad Cenedlaethol Cymru-America)
PO Box 1827
Shavertown, PA 18708-0827
(570) 696-NWAF
http://www.wales-usa.org
Bette Handley, Office Manager
Tue–Fri noon–5:00
Pub. *The Eagle and the Dragon* (*Yr Eryr A'r
Ddraig*), quarterly (Jan, Apr, July, Oct)
(dedicated to the preservation of Welsh
culture, also has a book search project
which saves books, pamphlets,
manuscripts, and other printed
memorabilia of historical value to
libraries)
$15.00 per year membership

Ninnau Publications, Inc.

11 Post Terrace
Basking Ridge, NJ 07920
(908) 766-6736; (908) 221-0744 FAX
Arturo Roberts, President
8:00 A.M.–10:00 P.M.
Pub. *Ninnau—The North American Welsh
Newspaper*, monthly, $15.00 per year
subscription in the U.S., $18.00 per year
subscription in Canada, £10.00 per year
subscription in Britain
(Welsh news and features of interest to
Welsh Americans, including genealogy,
English language)

The Owain Glendower Society
2144 Elmwood
Tulsa, OK 74106
Stafford Davis

Puget Sound Welsh Association
PO Box 19344
Seattle, WA 98109-0344
http://www.scn.org/people/welsh
Jackie Cedarholm, President

Radnor Heritage Society
5767 Hadley Road
Radnor, OH 43066
Mary Anne Thomas, President

Rehoboth Capel Cymraeg, Delta, Pa.
809 Kellog Road
Lutherville, MD 21093
Richard Price Baskwill, Pastor

Remsen-Steuben Historical Society
(see New York, Part 2)

Sacramento Cylch Cymraeg
4916 Palm Avenue
Sacramento, CA 95841
(916) 332-4550
Patricia Hillman, President

Saint David's Society of Connecticut, Inc.
PO Box 193
North Haven, CT 06473
(203) 239-5455
http://www.celticpandc.com/
cpc8a.html#st.davids
Earl T. Williams, Jr.
Pub. *Newsletter*, quarterly
$12.00 per year membership

**Saint David's Society of the Capital
District**
PO Box 3768
Albany, NY 12203-0768
(518) 377-7970; (518) 453-6312 FAX
welsh@dragonflower.com
http://timesunion.memlink.com/
communities/welsh
Robert Jones, President
by appointment
Pub. *Newsletter*
$10.00 per year membership

**Gulf Coast Saint David's Welsh Society of
Sarasota, Florida**
1528 Vermeer Drive
Nokomis, FL 34275
(941) 488-5793 (President); (941) 349-5558
(Secretary)
Russell Williams, President; Mrs. Rhianon
Hardy, Corresponding Secretary (Welsh-
speaking)

**Saint David's Welsh Society of Saint
Petersburg and the Suncoast**
1020 Lake Avoca Drive
Tarpon Springs, FL 34689
(727) 446-1431

Rhys Moore, President
Wesleyan Church, Largo, FL: third Tue
(Oct–May)
$5.00 per year membership

Saint David's Society of Georgia
3484 River Heights Crossing, S.E.
Marietta, GA 30067-4502
Sally Evans Funderburk

**The Saint David's Society of the State of
Kansas**
(Emporia, KS—location)
PO Box 11 (mailing address)
Lebo, KS 66856-0011
(620) 256-6687
Paula or Buddy Evans, Members
24-hours

Saint David's Society of Emporia
1019 Eln Street
Emporia, KS 66801
Claudia Mayes

**The Saint David's Welsh Society of
Greater Kansas City**
12716 Baltimore Court
Kansas City, MO 64145-1257
pottssh@cs.com
http://home.swbell.net/celizwh/sdws.htm
Sharon Potts, Recording Secretary
Pub. *The Red Dragon*, bimonthly
(specializes in Welsh culture)
$5.00 per year membership

Saint David's Society of Lyon County
Rural Route 4
Emporia, KS 66801
Marylin Hoy

Saint David's Society
804 Philadelphia Avenue
Silver Spring, MD 20910
A. Desroith

Saint David's Society of Minnesota
4908 Marigold Avenue North
Brooklyn Park, MN 55443-1769
Ann St. Martin

**Saint David's Society of Greater Saint
Louis**
3563 Lost Meadow Court
Saint Louis, MO 63129
Ida Mae Williams Arnold

Saint David's Welsh Society of Nebraska
8310 Elizabeth Drive
Lincoln, NE 68505
(402) 483-7237
Gweneth Colgrove, President; Dr. Orvid
Owens, Editor
Pub. *Saint David's Welsh Society of
Nebraska Newsletter*, two times per year,
$4.00 per year subscription

Saint David's Society of Nebraska
324 West Koenig
Grand Island, NE 68801
Bonnie Owens

Saint David's Society of New York
The Salmagundi Club
47 Fifth Avenue
New York, NY 10003
(212) 989-5159
Pub. *Our Welsh Heritage*

**Saint David's Society of Greater Buffalo,
N.Y.**
552 East River Road
Grand Island, NY 14072

Tom Edwards, President

Saint David's Society of Rochester and Genesee Region
91 Valley Circle
Rochester, NY 14622
William Carr

Saint David's Society of Utica, Inc.
2311 West Highland Avenue
Yorkville, NY 13495
(315) 797-3247
Patricia C. Divers, Membership Chair
$5.00 per year membership

Heights Saint David's Society
434 Academy Street
Wilkes-Barre, PA 18702
Scot Powell

Saint David's Society of Lackawanna County
2 Gladiola Drive
Clarks Summit, PA 18411
Robert Doble

Saint David's Society of Pittsburgh
(412) 851-9212 (Home)
canrichdavies@aol.com
http://www.stdavidssociety.homestead.com
Richard W. Davies, Secretary
Pub. *St. David's Newsletter* (online)
$15.00 per year membership

Saint David's Society of Schuylkill and Carbon Counties
139 South Mill Street
Saint Clair, PA 17901
Ron Davenport

Saint David's Welsh Society of the Slate Belt, Bangor, Pennsylvania
PO Box 174
Wind Gap, PA 18091-0174
http://www.yourpastconnections.com/sdws
Bronwen Pritchard
meetings at the Washington Township Elementary School on Route 191: fourth Tue (Feb–June & Sept–Nov) 7:00

Saint David's Society of Wyoming Valley
158 Courtdale Avenue
Courtdale, PA 18704-1121
(570) 283-0417
David Martin, Secretary

Saint David's Society of Youngstown
411 Tamplin Street
Sharon, PA 16146
(724) 981-3071; (724) 983-2944; (724) 983-2820 FAX
http://www.rio.edu/madog/Directory/records.asp?ID=15
Dr. John Tamplin

Saint David's Society of South Carolina
PO Drawer 150
Florence, SC 29503

Saint David's Society of Texas
5836 Preston Havan Drive
Dallas, TX 75230
Marilyn Williams

Saint David's Society of Poultney
60 Norton Avenue
Poultney, VT 50764-1029

Saint David's Society of the Inland Empire
3503 North Calispel
Spokane, WA 99215
Mrs. Robert Valentine

Welsh Saint David's Society of Spokane
West 624 Providence
Spokane, WA 99205

Saint David's Society of Oshkosh, Wisconsin and Winnebago County, Welsh Settlement
504 Russell Drive, Apartment 27
Ripon, WI 54971-1058
(920) 748-6237
Mrs. Olwen Morgan Welk, President; Mr. Lee E. Morgan, Vice President; Eleanor Jones, Secretary; Miss Ilah E. Morgan, Treasurer
annual meetings at Algoma Boulevard United Methodist Church, 1174 Algoma Boulevard, Oshkosh, WI 54901: Sun afternoon near 1 Mar, Saint David's Day
(Welsh heritage and social organization)

Saint David's Society of Racine
1106 Sheraton Drive
Racine, WI 53402

Saint David's Society of Waukesha County
(Waukesha, WI—location)
110 North Fairview Avenue (mailing address)
North Prairie, WI 53153
(262) 392-2717
Alice Whitmore
annual meetings: first week in Mar

Saint David's Welsh-American Society of Washington, DC
1420 Madison Court
Hyattsville, MD 20782
(202) 234-6162; (301) 439-5265
Cheryl Mitchell, President

Sons and Daughters of Wales
PO Box 352
Ipswich, SD 57451
Beth Pond, President

The Welsh-American Family History Association (W.A.F.H.A.)
4202 Clark Street
Kansas City, MO 64111
Judith Brougham

Welsh-American Genealogical Society (WAGS)
13 Norton Avenue
Poultney, VT 05764-1011
wagsjan@sover.net
http://britannia.com/wales/wags.html
Janice B. Edwards, Vice President/Secretary
Pub. *Newsletter*, quarterly
$10.00 per year membership

Welsh-American Heritage Museum
412 East Main Street
Oak Hill, OH 45656
(740) 682-7172
Mildred Bangert, Curator
Mon, Wed & Fri 8:00–noon, Tue & Thur 8:00–5:00, weekends by chance
(Family histories, old S.S. books of area; "We have a limited genealogy section but hope to add to it.")
$5.00 per year membership

Welsh American Heritage Museum
Cambria Women's Welsh Club of Niles, Ohio
1525 Stewart Circle, N.W.
Warren, OH 44484
Irene Brooks

Welsh American Society of Dallas
1447 Vanderbilt

Plano, TX 75023
Chris Grooms

Welsh American Society of Northern California
3199 Lucas Drive
Lafayette, CA 94549-5560
(925) 283-0912
president@wasnc.org
http://www.wasnc.org
Idris Evans, President
$20.00 per year membership

Welsh American Society of Southern California
1933 Temple Avenue
Signal Hill, CA 90804
Donald Davies

Welsh Harp Society of Kansas City
4204 Clark Street
Kansas City, MO 64111
Judith Brougham

The Welsh National Gymanfa Ganu Association, Inc.
Gustavus Adolphus College Box B47
800 West College Avenue
Saint Peter, MN 56082-1498
(507) 933-7540; (507) 933-6228; (877) 831-0563; (507) 933-6284 FAX
ellis@gustavus.edu
http://www.wngga.org
Dr. Ellis J. Jones, Executive Director
Mon–Fri 8:00–5:00
Pub. *HWYL*, quarterly
(to preserve, develop and promote our Welsh religious and cultural heritage and our religious and cultural traditions, including but not limited to the Gymanfa Ganu, and to do all things necessary and proper to accomplish and enhance the same)
$10.00 per year membership

The Arizona Welsh Society, Sun City Chapter
4901 West Sandra Terrace
Glendale, AZ 85306
Beth Herbet
1:30–4:00

Welsh Society of the Monterey Peninsula
565 Hillcrest Avenue
Pacific Grove, CA 93950
Joan Heebner

Colorado Welsh Society
Greeley, CO
plightse@info2000.net
Paul Lightsey, President

Welsh Society of Delaware
953 Devon Drive
Newark, DE 19711
(302) 368-4927; (302) 368-2318
sianfrick@compuserve.com
Siân Frick, Secretary
research: "We do not undertake genealogical research, although some of our members do have some interest in it."

Iowa Welsh Society-Cymdeithas Gymreig Iowa
408 East Salem
Indianola, IA 50125
(515) 961-3201
hallross@aol.com
Ruth Hall, President
Pub. *Iowa Welsh Society-Cymdeithas Gymreig Iowa Newsletter*, usually four times per year
$7.50 per year membership; translation

services available by some members

Lawrence Area Welsh Society
1722 Tennessee Avenue
Lawrence, KS 66044
Caroline Abels

Welsh Society of Greater Boston
99 Mount Auburn Street
Cambridge, MA 02138
Allan Davifon

Welsh Society of Detroit
10 Dorothea
Mount Clemens, MI 48043
John O. Morgans

Welsh Society of Grand Rapids
8222 Thornapple River Drive
Caledonia, MI 49316
Alan Jones

Nebraska Welsh Society
5446 Locust Street
Lincoln, NE 68516
Morgan Bevan, President

Welsh Society of Central New Jersey
24 Essex Road
Scotch Plains, NJ 07076
Dr. Phillip Davies

Welsh Society of New Mexico
513 Barlane N.W.
Albuquerque, NM 87107
Rhianwen Roberts Gerard, President

Welsh Society of Richville
6689 River Road
Gouverneur, NY 13642
(315) 287-0375; (315) 287-1187
Richard Moore
by appointment only

Welsh Society of the Southern Tier
19 Riverview Road
Binghamton, NY 13901
(607) 722-7062
Jack Watkins
meetings at East Side Congregational
    Church, Robinson Street, Binghamton,
    NY
(southern New York and northern
    Pennsylvania)

Welsh Society of the Carolinas
PO Box 1416
Davidson, NC 28036
(704) 655-0754
http://www.welshcarolina.org
Robery Glyn Maier

Welsh Society of Central Ohio
PO Box 12023
Columbus, OH 43212
(614) 470-4999
http://www.Ligtel.com/~WALES
Bob Penry, Genealogist
$10.00 per year membership

Welsh Society of Cincinnati
3306 Eastside Avenue
Cincinnati, OH 45208
Robert Meredith

Cleveland Welsh Society
4988 Farnhurst Road
Lyndhurst, OH 44124
Alcwyn Isaac

Welsh Society of Columbus
2121 Arlington Avenue, No. 8

Columbus, OH 43221
Lillian Brownfield

Gomer Welsh Society
Allen County Museum
620 West Market Street
Lima, OH 45801

Welsh Society of Greater Cincinnati
6327 Parkman Place
Cincinnati, OH 45213
David Taliesin Richards, Interim President

Northwestern Ohio Welsh Society
3837 Pioneer Road
Elida, OH 45807
Alice Davis Bushong

Pottsville Welsh Society
1750 Brownstone Boulevard, Apartment K
Toledo, OH 43614-1369
Karen Saylor

Welsh Society of Berks County
Rural Delivery 6, Box 53
Sinking Spring, PA 19608
David W. Davies, Jr.

Welsh Society of Greater Harrisburg, Pa.
130 Conodoguinet Avenue
Camp Hill, PA 17011
(717) 761-0639
Betty Lindermann, President
9:00–5:00
Pub. *The Dragon Speaks*, monthly
$7.00 per year membership

Maen Hir Welsh Society
3554 Cold Springs Road
Huntingdon, PA 16652

The Welsh Society of Philadelphia
(450 Broadway, Camden, NJ
08103—location)
PO Box 7287 (mailing address)
Saint Davids, PA 19087-7287
(609) 964-0891 (New Jersey)
Dalex@macconnect.com (withheld)
http://www.welsh-society-phila.org
Dave "Dalex" Walker, Jr., Corresponding
    Secretary
Pub. *The Newsletter of the Welsh Society of
    Philadelphia*, three times per year
(deals mainly with ethnic social functions)
$25.00 per year voting membership (open to
    those of Welsh descent), $25.00 per year
    nonvoting Associate membership (open to
    those interested in the Welsh Society,
    Welsh Culture, and history)

Welsh Society
211 Washington Street
Port Carbon, PA 17965

**Red Dragon Welsh Society of Greater
Hazelton**
431 Sixth Street
Weatherly, PA 18201
(717) 455-4518
Louise Patterson

Knoxville (Tennessee) Welsh Society
520 Roth Road
Sevierville, TN 37862

North Texas Welsh Society
PO Box 832222
Richardson, TX 75083-2222
(972) 394-6574
Sallie Huffman

Welsh Society of Fredericksburg, VA

Box 723
Fredericksburg, VA 22404
(540) 659-1879
Ruth Esaeas

North West Welsh Society
2801 S.W. 172nd Street
Seattle, WA 98166-3245
D. Williams

Welsh Society of West Virginia
Fifth Avenue at 10th Street
Huntington, WV 25706

Welsh Society of Madison
421 Bryce Canyon Crescent
Madison, WI 53705
Barbara Hughes

**Western Pennsylvania Genealogical
Society**
(see Pennsylvania, Part 2)

**WISE Search Group (Wales, Ireland,
Scotland, England)**
1840 South Wolcott Court
Denver, CO 80219-4309

Y Drych
Box 8337
Utica, NY 13505
(315) 841-4105; (315) 841-4104
Patricia Louise, Publisher/Owner
Pub. *Y Drych* (*The Mirror*), monthly, $20.00
    per year U.S. subscription, $35.00 for
    two-year U.S. subscription, $30.00 per
    year Canadian subscription, $50.00 for
    two-year Canadian subscription
(includes news of Wales, news of Welsh
    North American people and events, Welsh
    language lessons, Welsh recipes, features
    on Welsh culture and history)

Yugoslavian
(see also Banat, Croatian, Eastern European,
    German, Slavic, and Slovenian)

Cultural Society of South Slavs (CSSS)
3510 Xylon Avenue North
New Hope, MN 55427
(763) 544-6433
http://feefhs.org/frg-csss.html
James J. Smrekar
Pub. *Adria*, six times per year
(covers Bosnia, Bulgaria, Croatia,
    Macedonia, Serbia and Slovenia, all
    persons with ancestral links to any region
    in former Yugoslavia)
$20.00 per year membership; research
    services for members only, including
    some translation of Slovenian and
    Croation

Religious Archives and Organizations

General

Atlanta University Center
Theological Services
Robert W. Woodruff Library
111 James P. Brawley Drive, S.W.
Atlanta, GA 30314
(404) 522-8980, ext. 1216
jtroutma@auctr.edu
http://www.auctr.edu
Joseph E. Troutman, Head, Theology
Department

Indiana Religious History Association
PO Box 88267
Indianapolis, IN 46208
James J. Divita, Ph.D., President
Pub. *IRHA Newsletter*, quarterly
$10.00 per year membership

International Council of Community Churches
21116 Washington Parkway
Frankfort, IL 60423-3112
http://www.akcache.com/community/iccc.html

University of Chicago
Joseph Regenstein Library
(see Illinois, Part 2)

Yale Divinity School Library
409 Prospect Street
New Haven, CT 06511
(203) 432-6374
http://www.library.yale.edu/div
Martha Smalley, Research Services Librarian

Advent Christian

Merged in 1964 with Life and Advent Union, which was founded in 1848.

Advent Christian Church
(14601 Albemarle Road—location)
PO Box 23152 (mailing address)
Charlotte, NC 28227
http://www.adventchristian.org

Charles B. Phillips Library
Aurora University
Aurora, IL 60506-4892
(630) 844-5438; (630) 844-3848 FAX
Susan L. Craig, Director of the Library
(Advent Christian Church, founded 1860)

Adventist
(see also Advent Christian and Seventh Day Adventist, which are the two largest denominations stemming from the work of William Miller and his "American Millerite Association")

Church of God General Conference
PO Box 100,000
Morrow, GA 30260
http://abc-coggc.org
(formed from a union in 1921 of several older adventist groups, including Church of Christ in Christ Jesus, Church of God of the Abrahamic Faith, etc.)

Church of God (Seventh Day)
(330 West 152nd Avenue-location)
PO Box 33677 (mailing address)
Denver, CO 80233
Offices@cog7.org

http://www.cog7.org
(founded in 1863 from groups that split in 1858 from the Seventh Day Adventists and from Iowa and Michigan congregations; before 1884 was called Church of Christ or Church of Jesus Christ, and added "Seventh Day" to its name in 1923; site lists individual congregations)

Church of Jesus Christ
PO Box 1414
Cleveland, TN 37311

African Methodist Episcopal Church (A.M.E.)
(see also United Methodist)

African Methodist Episcopal Church (A.M.E.)
1134 11th Street, N.W.
Washington, DC 20001
http://www.amecnet.org

African Methodist Episcopal Church (A.M.E.)
Office of the Historiographer
PO Box 301
Williamstown, MA 02167
(413) 597-2484
http://www.amecnet.org
Dr. Dennis Dickerson, Historiographer

African Methodist Episcopal Zion Church
(see also United Methodist)

African Methodist Episcopal Zion Church
PO Box 32843
Charlotte, NC 28323
http://www.amezion.org

African Orthodox Church
(see Orthodox)

Albanian Orthodox Archdiocese in America
(see Orthodox)

Alexandrian Catholic
(see Orthodox)

Amended Christadelphians
(see Christadelphians)

American Association of Free Lutheran Churches
(see Lutheran)

American Baptist Association
(see Baptist)

American Baptist Churches in the U.S.A.
(see Baptist)

American Bible Society

American Bible Society Library and Archives
1865 Broadway
New York, NY 10023-9980
(212) 408-1258
http://www.americanbible.org

American Carpatho-Russian

Orthodox
(see Orthodox)

American Catholic Church
(see Roman Catholic)

American Episcopal Church
(see Episcopal)

American Evangelical Christian Churches

American Evangelical Christian Churches
PO Box 47312
Indianapolis, IN 46277
http://www.aeccministries.com

American Lutheran Church
(see Lutheran)

The American Millennial Association
(see Adventist)

American Rescue Workers
(see Christian Church of North America)

Amish
(see Mennonite)

Anabaptist
(see Hutterite, Moravian, Schwenkfelder and Church of God in Christ, Mennonite)

Anglican
(see Episcopal)

Anglican Catholic Church
(see Episcopal)

The Anglican Rite Archdiocese of the Americas
(see Episcopal)

Antiochene Catholic
(see Orthodox)

Antiochian Orthodox
(see Orthodox)

Apostolic Catholic Assyrian Church of the East, North American Dioceses
(see Orthodox)

Apostolic Christian Church of America
(Samuel Froehlich founded the Apostolic Christian Church of America in the early 1830s. It is related to the Apostolic Christian Church [Nazarene].)

Apostolic Christian Church (Nazarene)
1135 Sholey Road
Richmond, VA 23231

Apostolic Christian Church of America
c/o Apostolic Christian Publishing Company
(805 West Cruger Road—location)
PO Box 52 (mailing address)
Eureka, IL 61530
http://www.bibleviews.com/AC.html

Apostolic Christian Church of America
3420 North Sheridan Road

Peoria, IL 61604
http://www.apostolicchristian.org

Apostolic Episcopal Church
(see Episcopal)

Apostolic Faith Mission Church of God

Apostolic Faith Mission Church of God
6615 S.E. Duke Street
Portland, OR 97206
http://www.apostolicfaith.org

Apostolic Lutheran Church of America
(see Lutheran)

Apostolic Orthodox Catholic Church (North American Old Catholic)
(see Old Catholic)

Apostolic Overcoming Holy Catholic Church of God, Inc.

Apostolic Overcoming Holy Catholic Church of God, Inc.
1120 North 24th Street
Birmingham, AL 35234
http://prairienet.org/staoh
(originally called the Ethiopian Overcoming Holy Church of God)

Armenian Apostolic Church of America
(see Orthodox)

Armenian Catholic
(see Orthodox)

Assemblies of the Church of Jesus Christ
(see Assemblies of the Lord Jesus Christ)

Assemblies of God International
(see also Independent Assemblies of God, International)

Assemblies of God International Fellowship
PO Box 22410
San Diego, CA 92192-2410
(858) 677-9701; (858) 677-0038 FAX
info@agifellowship.org
http://www.agifellowship.org

Flower Pentecostal Heritage Center
1445 North Boonville Avenue
Springfield, MO 65802
(417) 862-1447; (417) 862-4400; (417) 862-6203
http://www.agheritage.org
Joyce Lee, Archivist
Mon–Fri 8:00–4:30
Pub. *The Assemblies of God Heritage*, quarterly, $15.00 per year subscription
("Our holdings focus on the history of the Assemblies of God, but they also include materials of the Pentecostal, charismatic, and evangelical traditions as they relate to our Fellowship.")

Assemblies of the Lord Jesus Christ

(formed by a merger of the Assemblies of the Church of Jesus Christ, Jesus Only Apostolic Church of God and the Church of the Lord Jesus Christ; see also Bible Way Church of Our Lord Jesus Christ, World Wide, Inc.)

Assemblies of the Lord Jesus Christ
875 North White Station Road
Memphis, TN 38122
http://www.aljc.org

Associate Presbyterian Church
(see Presbyterian)

Associate Reformed Presbyterian Church
(see Presbyterian)

Association of Evangelical Lutheran Churches
(see Lutheran)

Bahá'i

Bahá'i
866 UN Plaza, Suite 1202
New York, NY 10017
http://www.bahai.org
(founded in 1863, established in the U.S. in 1912)

National Bahá'í Archives
Bahá'í House of Worship, 100 Linden Avenue, Wilmette, IL 60091—location)
1233 Central Street (mailing address)
Evanston, IL 60201-1611
(847) 869-9039
archives@usbnc.org
Roger M. Dahl, Archivist
Mon–Fri 10:00–5:00, closed holidays and Bahá'í Holy Days

Baptist
(see also Lutheran, United Church of Christ)

American Baptist Association
4605 North State Line Avenue
Texarkana, TX 75503
http://www.abaptist.org

American Baptist Churches in the U.S.A.
American Baptist Archives Center
PO Box 851
Valley Forge, PA 19482-0851
(610) 768-2374
http://www.abc-usa.org/abhs

American Baptist Historical Society
The American Baptist—Samuel Colgate Historical Library
1106 South Goodman Street
Rochester, NY 14620-2532
(716) 473-1740
Dana Martin, Acting Director of the Library
Mon–Fri 9:00–5:00
Pub. *American Baptist Quarterly*, $21.00 per year subscription
("Persons join Baptist churches as adults. Baptismal records do not include birth dates, birthplaces, or names of parents. Marriage records have been considered the private property of the officiating minister and are not kept with church records. There is normally no place in Baptist church records where birth dates, birthplaces, names of parents or names of other family members can be found. To search for information in Baptist congregational records, the inquirer must identify the name of the congregation, its

location, and which of the 50+ different Baptist denominations it is affiliated with before he or she can begin to determine which library might hold such a record—in the unlikely event it has not been destroyed. There is no indexing of church records by member; it is useless to ask for the 'Smith family church records.' The only record of membership in a Baptist church is the record kept by the local church. Whether that record will be preserved when the church is disbanded is the separate decision of each individual congregation.")

Archives of the Mexican Baptist Convention of Texas
8019 Panama Expressway, South
San Antonio, TX 78224
(210) 924-4338

Arkansas Baptist State Convention Collection
Ouachita Baptist University
Riley-Hickingbotham Library
(410 Ouachita—location)
OBU Box 3729 (mailing address)
Arkadelphia, AR 71923
(870) 245-5332
richterw@obu.edu
http://www.obu.edu/library/baptistrecords.htm
Wendy Richter, Archivist
Mon–Fri 8:00–4:00

Baptist Bible Fellowship International
PO Box 191
Springfield, MO 65801
http://www.bbfi.org

Baptist General Conference
2002 South Arlington Heights Road
Arlington Heights, IL 60005
http://bgc.bethel.edu

Baptist Missionary Association of America
PO Box 193920
Little Rock, AR 72219-3920
http://www.bmaa-missions.com

Bethel Seminary
Carl H. Lundquist Library
3949 Bethel Drive
Saint Paul, MN 55112
(612) 638-6184
s-oslund@bethel.edu
http://bethel.edu/seminary_academics/semilibrary/home.htm
Sandra Oslund, Librarian
Mon–Tue & Thur 8:00–1:30, Wed 8:00–8:00, Fri 8:00–6:00, Sat 10:00–6:00

Carson-Newman College
Stephens-Burnett Library
Mildred L. Iddins Special Collections
1634 Russell Avenue
Jefferson City, TN 37760
(865) 471-3542; (865) 471-3450 FAX
alang@cn.edu
http://library.cn.edu:8686
Albert L. Lang, Technical Services Librarian
Mon & Wed–Fri 8:30–4:00, Tue 8:30–noon

Conservative Baptist Association of America (CB America)
1501 West Mineral Avenue, Suite B
Littleton, CO 80120-5612
http://www.cbamerica.org

Cooperative Baptist Fellowship (CBF)
PO Box 450329
Atlanta, GA 31145-0329

http://www.cbfonline.org

Ethel Taylor Crittenden Collection in Baptist History
Z. Smith Reynolds Library, Room 600
Wake Forest University
PO Box 7777
Winston-Salem, NC 27109
(336) 758-3978; (336) 758-8831 FAX
http://www.wfu.edu/library/baptist
Sharon E. Snow, Director
Mon–Fri 8:30–5:00

Eastern Baptist Theological Seminary
The Library
6 Lancaster Avenue
Wynnewood, PA 19096
(610) 645-9318
Melody Mazuk, Director
Mon–Thur 8:30–10:00, Fri 8:30–4:30, Sat
    9:00–4:30
$5.00 per photocopy request ("We require
    ALA form")

First African Baptist Church Museum
Franklin Square
23 Montgomery Street
Savannah, GA 31401
(912) 233-2244; (912) 234-7950 FAX
Thurmond Tillman

Florida Baptist Historical Society
Stetson University
Campus PO Box 8353
DeLand, FL 32720-3757
(386) 822-7186
E. Earl Joiner, Th.D., Curator
hours: various
Pub. *Newsletter*, annually, $2.00 per issue

Franklin College Library
(see Indiana, Part 2)

Free Will Baptist Historical Collection
Moye Library
Mount Olive College
634 Henderson Street
Mount Olive, NC 28365
(919) 658-7168; (919) 658-8934 FAX
gbarefoot@moc.edu
http://www.moc.edu
Gary Fenton Barefoot, Curator
Mon–Thur 8:00 A.M.–10:00 P.M., Fri
    8:00–5:00, Sat–Sun by appointment only
(Free Will Baptists, especially in north and
    southeast North Carolina concentration)
limited searching free, photocopy charges for
    information supplied

National Association of Free Will Baptists
PO Box 5002
Antioch, TN 37011-5002
http://www.nafwb.org

General Association of Regular Baptist Churches
1300 North Meacham Road
Schaumburg, IL 60173
http://www.garbc.org

General Association of General Baptist Churches
100 Stinson Drive
Poplar Bluff, MO 63901
http://www.angelfire.com

Georgia Baptist History Depository
Special Collections
Mercer University Main Library
1300 Edgewood Avenue
Macon, GA 31207-0001
(478) 752-2968; (478) 752-2111 FAX

http://tarver.mercer.edu/
    special_collections/GBHD.htm
Susan G. Broome, Special Collections
    Librarian
Mon–Fri 9:00–noon & 1:00–5:00

Kentucky Baptist Convention Archives
(10701 Shelbyville Road—location)
PO Box 43433 (mailing address)
Louisville, KY 40253-0433
(502) 245-4101, ext. 324
Cheryl Doty, Archivist
(nothing in the way of genealogy, archives of
    the state Baptist organization, nor of the
    churches)

Linfield College Library
McMinnville, OR 97158

Louisiana Baptist Convention
Mae Lee Memorial Library and Archives
PO Box 311
Alexandria, LA 71309-0311
(318) 448-3402; (318) 445-0055 FAX
LBC_Karon@linknet.net
Karon Smith, Archivist

Midwestern Baptist Seminary Library
5001 North Oak Street Trafficway
Kansas City, MO 64118
(816) 453-4600
Craig Kubic, Director
school year: Mon–Fri 7:45–10:00, Sat
    9:00–4:00; summer: Mon–Fri 8:00–5:00;
    closed holidays
(records and publications of the seminary and
    Baptist Church)

Mississippi Baptist Historical Commission
Mississippi College
Leland Speed Library
PO Box 51
Clinton, MS 39060-0051
(601) 925-3434 (Library)
Rachel A. Pyron, Special Collections
    Librarian
Library: Mon–Fri 8:30–noon & 1:00–4:30
    (except college holidays)
(history of Mississippi Baptists)

Missouri Baptist Historical Society
Partee Center for Baptist Historical Studies
William Jewell College Library
Liberty, MO 64068
(816) 781-7700, ext. 5490; (816) 415-5047
    FAX
parteecenter@william.jewell.edu
Angela N. Stiffler, Director
Mon–Fri 9:00–4:00 by appointment
Pub. *'Show Me' Baptist History*, annually
(focuses on Baptist life in Missouri since
    1805)
$10.00 per year membership

National Baptist Convention of America
777 South R.L. Thornton Freeway, Suite 205
Dallas, TX 75203
http://members.aol.com/nbyc1/nbca.html

National Baptist Convention, U.S.A., Inc.
1700 Baptist World Center Drive
Nashville, TN 37207

National Missionary Baptist Convention of America
PO Box 512096
Los Angeles, CA 90051-0096
http://www.natl-missionarybaptist.com

New Orleans Baptist Theological Seminary
John T. Christian Library

4110 Seminary Place
New Orleans, LA 70126
(504) 286-3618; (504) 286-8429 FAX
kysylvest@nobts.edu
http://www.nobts.edu
Kathy Sylvest, Archivist/Extension Center
    Librarian

North American Baptist General Conference
1 South 210 Summit Avenue
Oakbrook Terrace, IL 60181
http://www.nabconference.org

North American Baptist Heritage Commission
1525 South Grange Avenue
Sioux Falls, SD 57105
(605) 335-9071; (605) 335-9078; (605) 335-
    9090 FAX
NABArchives@nabs.edu
Berneice Westerman, Associate Archivist;
    George W. Lang, Director
Mon–Fri 1:00–4:00
Pub. *Heritage Horizons*, three times per year
("Auxiliary of the North American Baptist
    Conference. Archival materials of
    Conference Office as well as of local
    churches and Conference Organizations;
    rare and historical books; museum
    holdings.")
$25.00 per year membership; research:
    $10.00 per hour, $15.00 for obituary
    search

Ottawa University
Myers Library
1001 South Cedar Street
Ottawa, KS 66067-3399
(785) 242-5200, ext. 5444; (785) 242-7429
    FAX
Jane Ann Westrum, Library Director
Mon–Thur 7:45–10:30, Fri 7:45–4:30, Sat
    noon–5:00, Sun 2:00–10:30; summer
    hours vary
(university and Baptist history)

National Primitive Baptist Convention U.S.A.
6433 Hidden Forrest Drive
Charlotte, NC 28213
http://www.pb.org (The Primitive Baptist
    Web Station)

Progressive National Baptist Convention, Inc.
601 50th Street, N.E.
Washington, DC 20019
http://www.pnbc.org

Separate Baptists in Christ
10102 North Hickory Lane
Columbus, IN 47203
http://www.separatebaptist.org

Seventh Day Baptist Historical Society
(3120 Kennedy Road—location)
PO Box 1678 (mailing address)
Janesville, WI 53547-1678
(608) 752-5055
http://www.seventhdaybaptist.org
Rev. Don A. Sanford, Historian
Pub. *SDBHS Annual Report*, annually

South Carolina Baptist Historical Society
South Carolina Baptist Historical Collection
James B. Duke Library
Furman University
3300 Poinsett Highway
Greenville, SC 29613-4100
(864) 294-2194
glen.clayton@furman.edu

http://library.furman.edu
J. Glen Clayton, Curator
Mon–Fri 8:30–4:30, except school holidays,
    please call before coming
Pub. *Journal of the South Carolina Baptist
    Historical Society*, annually

**Southern Baptist Historical Library and
Archives**
Southern Baptist Convention Building
901 Commerce Street, Suite 400
Nashville, TN 37203-3630
(615) 244-0344
http://www.sbhla.org
Bill Sumners, Director of Library and
    Archives
Mon–Fri 9:00–4:00
Pub. *Baptist History and Heritage* (Baptist
    historical materials, especially Southern
    Baptist), quarterly, $10.95 per year
    subscription

Tennessee Baptist Historical Society
PO Box 347
Brentwood, TN 37027
(615) 373-2255

Texas Baptist Historical Center-Museum
10405 FM 50
Brenham, TX 77833
(979) 836-5117
Paul Sevar, Director
Wed–Sat 10:00–4:00
free

Texas Baptist Historical Society
Texas Baptist Historical Collection
Southwestern Baptist Theological Seminary
A. Webb Roberts Library
(2001 West Seminary Drive—location)
PO Box 22000 (mailing address)
Fort Worth, TX 76122-2490
(817) 923-1921, ext. 3330
Dr. Alan J. Lefever, Archivist/Special
    Collections Librarian
Mon–Fri 8:00–noon & 1:00–5:00
Pub. *Texas Baptist History*, annually
    ("We major in historical research, primarily
    Texas Baptist church history, but do
    answer some genealogical questions,
    whenever we can, from our resources.")
$10.00 per year membership; no research fee
    except cost of materials

Virginia Baptist Historical Society
University of Richmond
PO Box 34
Richmond, VA 23173
(804) 289-8434
Darlene Slater, Research Assistant
weekdays 9:00–noon & 1:00–4:00 by
    appointment only
Pub. *Virginia Baptist Register*, annually,
    $6.00 per year subscription
$15.00 per year membership; research by
    mail, $22.00 per hour

**West Virginia Baptist Historical Society,
Inc.**
Parchment Valley Conference Center
Route 2, Box 304
Ripley, WV 25271
(304) 346-2036
Roscoe C. Keeney, Jr., Archivist
weekdays by appointment
Pub. *West Virginia Baptist Historical Society
    News Letter*, semiannually
(depository for West Virginia Baptist history:
    organizational, churches, clergy, laity and
    youth; individual files and church files, as
    well as annual reports, clippings, and
    library available)

$5.00 per year membership

Baptist Bible Fellowship
International
(see Baptist)

Baptist Brethren
(see Baptist and Brethren)

Baptist General Conference
(see Baptist)

Baptist Missionary Association
of America
(see Baptist)

Beachy Amish Mennonite
Churches
(see Church of God in Christ, Mennonite)

Berean Fundamental Church

Berean Fundamental Church
PO Box 6103
Lincoln, NE 68506

Bible Fellowship Church

Bible Fellowship Church
3000 Fellowship Drive
Whitehall, PA 18052
http://www.bfc.org
(of Mennonite origin, originally called the
    Evangelical Conference)

Bible Presbyterian Church
(see Presbyterian)

Bible Way Church of Our Lord
Jesus Christ, World Wide, Inc.
(an offshoot of Assemblies of the Lord Jesus
    Christ)

**Bible Way Church of Our Lord Jesus
Christ, World Wide, Inc.**
4949 Two-Notch Road
Columbia, SC 29204
http://www.biblewaychurch.org

Brethren

The Brethren and Pietist movements in
Germany fathered the Evangelical United
Brethren (EUB), which merged with others
in 1968 to form the present-day United
Methodist Church.
    The EUB was formed in 1946 by the
merger of the majority "Liberal" or "New
Constitution" branch of the Church of the
United Brethren in Christ, formed in 1889,
and the former Evangelical Church. The
group of ministers and their followers known
as the United Brethren since 1767, added the
words "in Christ" to the denomination's
name when it was officially organized in
1800, so they would not be confused with the
Moravians who also had been known as the
"United Brethren" or "Unitas Fratrum" since
1727. In the late 1860s the Hoffmanites left
the United Brethren in Christ and in 1878
officially organized themselves as today's
United Christian Church. The minority
"Radical" or "Old Constitution" United
Brethren in Christ have preserved their
original name since the 1889 schism: Church
of the United Brethren in Christ [Old
Constitution].

German Baptists who immigrated to the
U.S. became known as German Baptist
Brethren, "Dunkards," or "Dunkers" from
the German *tunker*. In 1908 they were
renamed the Church of the Brethren. In 1881
the Old German Baptist Brethren [Old Order
Dunkers] broke with the Church of the
Brethren.
    The Brethren Church (Ashland), formerly
called the Progressive Convention of the
Tunker Church in Ashland, Ohio, resulted
from an 1882 schism with the Church of the
Brethren. The Fellowship of Grace Brethren
Church is an offshoot of The Brethren
Church (Ashland).
    Czech immigrants formed a confederation
of congregations called the Evangelical
Unity of the Czech-Moravian Brethren in
Northern America, and later Unity of the
Brethren.
    The Evangelical Covenant Church has
roots in the Pietist tradition.
    The Brethren in Christ Church was
originally called the River Brethren,
separating from the Mennonites.
    The Church of God (Anderson, Indiana)
has origins in the Pietest movement and the
Brethren churches.
    Christian Brethren or Plymouth Brethren
have their roots in the British Isles and not in
the Brethren or Pietist movements.
    Hutterian Brethren or Hutterites stem
from the Anabaptist movement.

Brethren Church (Ashland)
(see also Brethren)

Brethren Church (Ashland)
524 College Avenue
Ashland, OH 44805
http://www.brethrenchurch.org

Brethren in Christ Church
(see also Brethren)

Brethren in Christ Church
PO Box A
Grantham, PA 17207-0901
http://www.bic-church.org/index.htm

**Brethren in Christ Historical Library and
Archives**
Archives of Messiah College
(1 College Avenue—location)
PO Box 3002 (mailing address)
Grantham, PA 17027
(717) 691-6048; (717) 691-6042 FAX
archives@messiah.edu
Dori I. Steckbeck, Director
Mon–Fri 9:00–5:00 (call before visiting)
Pub. *Brethren in Christ History and Life*,
    three times per year, $10.00 per year
    subscription
(obituaries, marriages and births from 1885
    of people associated with the Brethren in
    Christ Church; genealogies of Brethren in
    Christ and some Mennonite families)

Brothers of Christ
(see Christadelphians)

Bruderhof Communities
(see Mennonite)

Buddhist

Buddhist Churches of America
1710 Octavia Street
San Francisco, CA 94109
(415) 771-6293; (415) 776-5600

bcahq@pacbell.net
http://www.fogbank.com/bca
(Site lists temples of the Buddhist Churches of America.)

Byzantine Catholic
(see Orthodox)

Campbellites
(see Disciples of Christ)

Catholic
(see Roman Catholic, Orthodox)

Chaldean Catholic
(see Orthodox)

Christadelphians
(Otherwise known as the Brothers of Christ, with Amended Schism)

Christadelphians
1000 Mohawk Drive
Elgin, IL 60120-3148
http://www.christadelphia.org

Christian and Missionary Alliance

Christian and Missionary Alliance
PO Box 35000
Colorado Springs, CO 80935-3500
http://www.cmalliance.org

Christian Brethren
(see also Brethren)

Christian Brethren
327 Prairie Avenue
Wheaton, IL 60187-3408

Christian Catholic Church

Christian Catholic Church
Dowie Memorial Drive
Zion, IL 60099

Christian Church of North America, General Council

American Rescue Workers
643 Elmira Street
Williamsport, PA 17701
http://www.arwus.com
(the charitable branch of the Christian Church)

Christian Church of North America, General Council
1294 Rutledge Road
Transfer, PA 16154-9005
(724) 962-3501; (724) 962-1766 FAX
http://www.ccna.org

Christian Churches
(see also Advent Christian, Apostolic Christian Church, Church of Christ, Disciples of Christ and United Church of Christ)

Christian Churches and Churches of Christ
(4210 Bridgetown Road—location)
PO Box 11326 (mailing address)
Cincinnati, OH 45211
http://www.cwv.net/christ'n

Reese Resource Center
Central Christian College of the Bible

911 East Urbandale Drive
Moberly, MO 65270-1997
(660) 263-3933; (660) 263-3533 FAX
pagee@cccb.edu
http://www.cccb.edu
Patty Agee, Librarian
During school year: Mon–Wed 8:00 A.M.–10:00 P.M., Thur 8:00 A.M.–9:00 P.M., Fri 8:00–8:00, Sat 9:00–5:00; summer: Mon–Fri 8:00–5:00
Pub. *The Sentinel*, semiannually
("A four-year private religious college, affiliated with Christian Churches-Churches of Christ"; 120 linear feet of papers, including the Walter C. Coble-Mission Files of worldwide mission newsletters from 1930s to present for Christian Churches/Churches of Christ)

Christian Churches and Churches of Christ
(Each congregation is largely autonomous. See also Disciples of Christ and Churches of Christ)

Christian Congregation, Inc.

Christian Congregation, Inc.
804 West Hemlock Street
LaFollette, TN 37766

Christian Methodist Episcopal Church
(see also United Methodist Church)

Christian Methodist Episcopal Church
4466 Elvis Presley Boulevard
Memphis, TN 38116
http://www.c-m-e.org

Christian Reformed Church in North America
(see Reformed)

Christian Science

The First Church of Christ, Scientist
Church History, A221
175 Huntington Avenue
Boston, MA 02115
(617) 450-3503
http://www.tfccs.com
Yvonne C. Fettweis, Manager, Church History
8:00–4:15
(very little vital statistics information)
research: $30.00

Longyear Museum
1125 Boylston Street
Chestnut Hill, MA 02487
http://www.longyear.org/about.html
Pub. *Quarterly News*
("To advance the understanding of the life and work of Mary Baker Eddy, the Discoverer, Founder and Leader of Christian Science.")

Church of Christ
(see Adventist)

Church of Christ (Holiness) U.S.A.

Church of Christ (Holiness) U.S.A.
(329 East Monument Street—location)
PO Box 3622 (mailing address)
Jackson, MS 39207

http://www.cochusa.com/main.htm

Church of Christ in Christ Jesus
(see Adventist)

Church of Christ, Scientist
(see Christian Science)

Church of Christ (Temple Lot)

Church of Christ (Temple Lot)
(20 South River Boulevard—location)
PO Box 472 (mailing address)
Independence, MO 64501-0472
http://www.church-of-christ.com

Church of England
(see Episcopal)

Church of God and Saints of Christ
(also known as "Christian Israelites.")

Church of God and Saints of Christ
3825 Central Avenue
Cleveland, OH 44115
http://www.churchofgod1896.org

Church of God (Anderson, Indiana)
(see also Brethren)

Church of God (Anderson, Indiana)
PO Box 2420
Anderson, IN 46018-2420
http://www.chog.org

Church of God by Faith, Inc.

Chruch of God by Faith, Inc.
1315 South Lane Avenue, Suite 6
Jacksonville, FL 32206
http://www.cogbf.org

Church of God (Cleveland, Tennessee)

Church of God (Cleveland, Tennessee)
(2490 Keith Street—location)
PO Box 2430 (mailing address)
Cleveland, TN 37320-2430
(423) 472-3361; (423) 478-7066
http://www.churchofgod.cc

Church of God (General Conference)
(see Adventist)

Church of God (Holiness)

Church of God (Holiness)
(7407 Metcalf—location)
PO Box 4711 (mailing address)
Overland Park, KS 66204
http://www.kccbs.edu/cogh

Church of God in Christ

Church of God in Christ
272 South Main Street
Memphis, TN 38101

Church of God in Christ, International

Church of God in Christ, International
170 Adelphi Street
Brooklyn, NY 11205

Church of God in Christ, Mennonite

(see also Bible Fellowship Church, Brethren,
Conservative Mennonite Conference,
Evangelical Mennonite Church, Fellowship
of Evangelical Bible Churches, General
Conference of Mennonite Brethren
Churches, Hutterite Brethren and Missionary
Church)

Along the Galician Grapevine
PO Box 194
Butterfield, MN 56120-0194
(507) 956-5815
gvtl@rconnect.com
http://feefhs.org/gal/aga/frg-aga.htm
Glen Linscheid, Editor
8:00 A.M.–10:00 P.M.
Pub. *Along the Galician Grapevine*, annually
(Dec), no subscriptions available,
examination copy for LSASE
(lists births, deaths, marriages, and family
reunions for the dispersed descendants of
the 1880s Mennonite emigrants to North
America from the Austrian Crownland of
Galicia, at times referred to as Kleinpolen
in the German; 17,000-entry database on
the surnames Bachmann, Bergthold,
Brubacher, Ewy, Forrer Hubin, Jotter,
Kintzi, Klein, Linscheid, Merk, Miller,
Rupp, Schmidt and Stauffer)

Beachy Amish Mennonite Churches
3015 Partridge Road—location)
PO Box 73 (mailing address)
Partridge, KS 67566
http://www.mhsc.ca

Bluffton College
Mennonite Historical Library
Bluffton, OH 45817-1195
(419) 358-3365
Ann Hilty, Librarian
Mon–Fri 1:00–5:00 (call before traveling to
the library)

Center for Mennonite Brethren Studies
1717 South Chestnut Avenue
Fresno, CA 93702
(559) 453-2225; (559) 453-2124 FAX
kennsrem@fresno.edu
http://www.mbconf.ca/mbstudies/index.
en.html
Kevin Enns-Rempel, Archivist
Mon–Fri 8:00–noon & 1:00–5:00
$25.00 per year membership

Center for Mennonite Brethren Studies
Tabor College
400 South Jefferson
Hillsboro, KS 67063
(620) 947-3121, ext. 342; (620) 947-3121,
ext. 318
Peggy Goertzen, Director
Mon–Fri 9:00–noon & 1:30–4:00, and by
appointment
Pub. *Newsletter*, annually
("Mennonite Brethren historical records:
congregational, conference, photographs,
manuscripts, as well as materials on
Mennonites in general and Germans from
Russia, also strong collection of Marion
County, Kansas records.")

Centre For Mennonite Brethren Studies
(204) 669-6575
http://www.mbconf.ca/mbstudies

Abe Dueck, Director
8:30–4:30
Pub. *Mennonite Historian*, quarterly,
published jointly with the Mennonite
Historical Centre, $9.00 (Canadian) per
year subscription in the Canada, $8.00
(U.S.) per year subscription in the U.S.

Church of God in Christ, Mennonite
PO Box 230
Moundridge, KS 67107
http://www.bibleviews.com

Germantown Mennonite Historic Trust
6133 Germantown Avenue
Philadelphia, PA 19144
(215) 843-0943; (215) 843-6263
Mr. Galen Horst-Martz, Executive Director
Tue–Fri 9:00–3:00 by appointment only
Pub. *Friends of Germantown* (primarily
relating to those families connected with
the Germantown Mennonite
congregation), three times per year
$25.00 per year membership

Historic Harmony/Harmony Museum
(see Ethnic Archives, Libraries and
Societies—German, Part 3)

Historical Center
(see Pennsylvania, Part 2)

**Historical Committee and Archives of the
Mennonite Church**
1700 South Main Street
Goshen, IN 46526
(219) 535-7477; (219) 535-7293 FAX
http://www.goshen.edu/mcarchives
John E. Sharp, Director; Dennis Stoesz,
Archivist
Mon–Fri 8:00–noon & 1:00–5:00
Pub. *Mennonite Historical Bulletin*,
quarterly, $25.00 per year subscription

**Illinois Mennonite Historical and
Genealogical Society**
(State Route 116—location)
PO Box 1007 (mailing address)
Metamora, IL 61548-0819
(309) 367-2551; (309) 392-2518 FAX
http://www.rootsweb.com/~ilmhgs
Carolyn Nafziger, President
Apr–Oct: Fri & Sat 10:00–4:00, Sun
1:30–4:30
Pub. *Mennonite Heritage*, quarterly; *Illinois
Mennonite Heritage Newsletter*,
semiannually
$25.00 per year membership

Kidron Community Historical Society
(primarily Swiss Mennonite, German/
Russian Mennonite, and Amish; see Ohio,
Part 2)

Lancaster Mennonite Historical Society
2215 Millstream Road
Lancaster, PA 17602-1499
(717) 393-9745
http://www.lmhs.org
David J. Rempel Smucker, Genealogist;
Lloyd Zeager, Librarian
Tue–Sat 8:30–4:30
Pub. *Pennsylvania Mennonite Heritage*
(illustrated journal), quarterly; *Mirror*
(newsletter), bimonthly
("Our library is a local history resource on all
religious groups but with an emphasis on
Mennonites and Amish.")
$25.00 per year membership

Masthof Press and Bookstore
Route 1, Box 20, Mill Road

Morgantown, PA 19543-9701
(610) 286-0258; (610) 286-6860 FAX
masthof@ptd.net; mefamhis@ptd.net
http://feefhs.org/men/frg-mfh.html
Lois Ann Mast, Publisher
Mon–Sat 9:00–5:00
Pub. *Mennonite Family History* (Mennonite,
Anabaptism, Amish, and Brethren
genealogy and family history), quarterly,
$18.00 per year subscription

Mennonite Heritage Centre
MHC Library and Archives
(204) 888-6781; (204) 831-5675 FAX
aredekopp@mennonitechurch.ca
http://www.mennonitechurch.ca/
programs/archives
Alf Redekopp, Director
Mon–Fri 8:30–4:30, Sat (Gallery only)
noon–5:00
Pub. *Mennonite Historian*, quarterly,
published jointly with the Centre for
Mennonite Brethren Studies, $8.00
(Canadian) per year subscription in
Canada, $8.00 (U.S.) per year
subscription in the U.S.

Mennonite Heritage Museum
(200 North Poplar—location)
PO Box 231 (mailing address)
Goessel, KS 67053
(620) 367-8200
Kristine Schmucker, Director/Curator
May–Sept: Tue–Fri 10:00–5:00, Sat–Sun
1:00–5:00; Oct–Dec & Mar–Apr:
Tue–Sun 1:00–4:00
Pub. *The Heritage Newsletter*, semiannually
$10.00 per year membership; admission:
$2.50 for adults

**Mennonite Historians of Eastern
Pennsylvania**
(see Pennsylvania, Part 2)

Mennonite Historical Library
(also Hutterite Brethren resources, see
Indiana, Part 2)

Mennonite Historical Society of Iowa
Mennonite Historical Museum
(411 Ninth Street—location)
PO Box 576 (mailing address)
Kalona, IA 52247
(319) 656-3271
Frank Yoder, President
Apr–Oct: 10:00–4:00; Nov: 11:00–3:00
Pub. *Iowa Mennonite Historical Reflections*,
quarterly
$10.00 per year membership

Mennonite Library and Archives
Bethel College
300 East 27th
North Newton, KS 67117-9989
(316) 284-5304
http://www.bethelks.edu/services/mla
John D. Thiesen, Archivist
Mon–Fri 10:00–noon & 1:00–5:00
Pub. *Mennonite Life*, quarterly, $18.00 per
year subscription, $27.00 for two-year
subscription

Molotschna Villager
2002 West Sunnyside Drive, Apartment
3105
Phoenix, AZ 85029-3555
http://feefhs.org/men/frg-mv.html
Hildegard Wasnick, Village Coordinator
Pub. *Mennonite German-Russian Newsletter*

Menno Simons Historical Library
Eastern Mennonite University

Harrisonburg, VA 22802
(540) 432-4178; (540) 432-4977 FAX
bowmanlb@emu.edu; huberhe@emu.edu
http://www.emu.edu/units/library/histlib. htm
Lois B. Bowman, Librarian
Mon–Fri 8:00–noon & 1:00–5:00
(including Anabaptist, Mennonite, Amish
and local Virginia materials; Mennonite
and local Germanic genealogy; local
Lutheran and Reformed Church records;
material on Pennsylvania, Maryland, West
Virginia and Ohio)
donation accepted

Swiss Mennonite Cultural and Historical Association
(see Ethnic Archives, Libraries and
Organizations—Swiss, Part 3)

Church of God, Mountain Assembly, Inc.

Church of God, Mountain Assembly, Inc.
(256 North Florence Avenue—location)
PO Box 157 (mailing address)
Jellico, TN 37762
(888) 423-CGMA; (423) 784-3258 fAX
cgmahdq@jellico.com
http://www.cgmahdq.org

Church of God of Prophecy Worldwide
(grew out of the principles of the Church of
God [Cleveland, Tennessee])

Church of God of Prophecy Worldwide
(3720 North Keith Street—location)
PO Box 2910 (mailing address)
Cleveland, TN 37320-2910
webservant@cogop.org
http://www.cogop.org

Church of God of the Abrahamic Faith
(see Adventist)

Church of God (Seventh Day)
(see Adventist)

Church of Jesus Christ
(see Adventist)

Church of Jesus Christ (Bickertonites)

Church of Jesus Christ (Bickertonites)
2007 Cutter Drive
McKees Rocks, PA 15136

The Church of Jesus Christ of Latter-day Saints
(see also The Community of Christ [formerly
called The Reorganized Church of Jesus
Christ of Latter Day Saints, which
incorporated the "New Organization" in
1860], Church of Christ [Temple Lot],
Church of Jesus Christ [Bickertonites] and
Strangites)

Brigham Young University, Hawaii Campus
Joseph F. Smith Library
(see Hawaii, Part 2)

Early Mormon Research Institute
PO Box 2650
Salt Lake City, UT 84110-2650
Pub. *The Nauvoo Journal*, quarterly, $18.00

per year subscription

Family History Library of The Church of Jesus Christ of Latter-day Saints
(see Utah, Part 2)

Historical Department, The Church of Jesus Christ of Latter-day Saints
50 East North Temple Street, East Wing
Salt Lake City, UT 84150
(801) 240-2745 (Library—Archives
Division)
http://www.lds.org
Christine Cox, Director, Library Division
Mon–Fri 8:00–4:30
(*historical*, not genealogical focus; do not
confuse with the Family History Library)

Mormon Historical Association
(123 Joseph Smith Building—location)
Brigham Young University
PO Box 7010, University Station (mailing
address)
Provo, UT 84602
Pub. *Journal of Mormon History*, annually

Mormon History Association
2470 North 1000 West
Layton, UT 84041
(801) 773-4620; (801) 779-1348 FAX

Pioneer Genealogy Society
(see Miscellaneous, Part 4)

Tracing Mormon Pioneers
http://www.vii.com/~nelsonb/pioneer.htm
(emigration card index, handcart companies,
Mormon emigrant ships, pioneer
companies, etc.)

University of Utah Marriott Library
(see Utah, Part 2)

Church of Laestadius
(see Lutheran)

Church of Our Lord Jesus Christ of the Apostolic Faith, Inc.

Church of Our Lord Jesus Christ of the Apostolic Faith, Inc.
444 West Penn Street
Philadelphia, PA 19144
http://www.apostolic-faith.org

Church of the Brethren
(see also Brethren)

The Church of the Brethren General Board
Brethren Historical Library and Archives
1451 Dundee Avenue
Elgin, IL 60120-1694
(847) 742-5100, ext. 294; (847) 742-6103
FAX
http://www.brethren.org/genbd/bhla
Kenneth M. Shaffer, Jr., Director
Mon–Fri 9:00–noon & 1:00–4:00
(formerly The German Baptist Brethren; for
Brethren who trace their origins to
Schwarzenau, Germany, in 1708)
genealogical research: $25.00 per hour

Fellowship of Brethren Genealogists
Indiana Section
Timbercrest Home
North Manchester, IN 46962
(219) 982-4732
Keith E. Ross

Fellowship of Brethren Genealogists (Church of the Brethren)
1451 Dundee Avenue
Elgin, IL 60120-1694
(847) 742-5100
mcadamsr@hotmail.com
http://www.bretren.org/genbd/bhla/
FoBG.html
Gwendolyn F. Bobb, Executive Director;
Ron McAdams
Brethren Historical Library and Archives:
Mon–Fri 9:00–noon & 1:00–4:00
Pub. *Newsletter, Fellowship of Brethren
Genealogists*, quarterly
("Brethren related to the group founded
1708, Schwarzenau, Germany; there are
many other Brethren groups that are not
in our purview, such as the United
Brethren, about which we often receive
inquiries.")
$10.00 per year membership

United Brethren Historical Center
RichLyn Library
Huntington College
Huntington, IN 46750
(219) 359-4064, (219) 358-3698 FAX
Jane E. Mason, Archivist
Mon–Thur 9:00–5:00 by appointment only
to ensure access
(Archives of Huntington College and the
Church of the United Brethren in Christ;
does not include the "Liberal" or "New
Constitution" branch of the United
Brethren in Christ which broke away in
1889 and merged in 1946 with the
Evangelical Church to form the
Evangelical United Brethren Church; no
birth or baptismal records)
$15.00 for genealogical research done by
staff; copies: 25¢ per page

Church of the Living God, Christian Workers for Fellowship
(see Pentecostal)

Church of the Living God (The Pillar and Ground of the Truth, Inc.)
(see Pentecostal)

Church of the Lord Jesus Christ
(see Assemblies of the Lord Jesus Christ)

Church of the Lutheran Brethren of America
(see Lutheran)

Church of the Lutheran Confession
(see Lutheran)

Church of the Nazarene

Church of the Nazarene Archives
6401 The Paseo
Kansas City, MO 64131
(816) 333-7000; (816) 361-4983 FAX
singersol@nazarene.org
http://www.nazarene.org/hoo/archives.html
Stan Ingersol, Ph.D., Denominational
Archivist
Mon–Fri 8:00–4:30
("Information on all ordained clergy in the
U.S. and Canada; information only on
those laity who were prominent in district

and general church affairs, but not those who were simply church members")

Nazarene College of Rochester
Lorette Wilmot Library
4245 East Avenue
Rochester, NY 14610
(716) 586-2525, ext. 450; (716) 248-8766 FAX
http://www.naz.edu/dept/library/index.html

Church of the United Brethren in Christ
(see also Brethren, United Methodist)

Church of the United Brethren in Christ
302 Lake Street
Huntington, IN 46750
http://www.ub.org

Churches of Christ
(Each congregation is largely autonomous. See also Christian Churches and Churches of Christ, and Disciples of Christ)

Center for Restoration Studies
Brown Library
Abilene Christian University
ACU Station Box 29208
Abilene, TX 79699-9208
(915) 674-2347
churchillc@nicanor.acu.edu
http://bible.acu.edu/crs
Craig Churchill
hours: various
("Churches of Christ; Restorationism/Restitutionism; files on preachers, churches, missions, etc.")

Churches of Christ
PO Box 726
Kosciusko, MS 39090
http://www.church-of-christ.org

The Gospel Advocate Archives and Library
The Gospel Advocate Company
1006 Elm Hill Park
Nashville, TN 37210
(615) 254-8781
by appointment
Pub. *The Gospel Advocate*, monthly, $14.95 per year subscription
(Restoration Movement/Churches of Christ)

David Lipscomb University
Beaman Library
3901 Granny White Pike
Nashville, TN 37204-3951
(615) 269-1793; (615) 269-1807 FAX
marie.byers@lipscomb.edu
Marie Byers, Reference Librarian
Mon–Fri 1:00–4:00

Churches of Christ in Christian Union

The Reformed Methodist Church merged with the Churches of Christ in Christian Union in September 1952.

Churches of Christ in Christian Union
1426 Lancaster Pike—location)
Box 30 (mailing address)
Circleville, OH 43113
http://www.bright.net/~ccuhq

Reformed Methodist Union Episcopal Church
1136 Brody Avenue

Charleston, SC 29407

Churches of God

Churches of God, General Conference (CGGC)
(700 Melrose Avenue—location)
PO Box 926 (mailing address)
Findlay, OH 45839
(419) 424-1961; (419) 424-3433 FAX
director@cggc.org
http://www.cggc.org
Wayne Boyer, Executive Director

The Community of Christ

The Community of Christ
Archives
1001 West Walnut
Independence, MO 64050-3562
(816) 833-1000, ext. 2457; (816) 521-3089 FAX
bbernauer@cofChrist.org
http://www.cofChrist.org
Barbara Bernauer, Assistant Archivist
Mon–Fri 8:00–5:00
(specializes in RLDS/Community of Christ history, RLDS membership and branch records)

John Whitmer Historical Association
427 West 70th Street
Kansas City, MO 64113-2022
(816) 333-5315; (816) 361-6960
http://JWHA.info
Norman L. Bernauer, Executive Sectretary
Pub. *John Whitmer Historical Association Journal*, annually (Oct); *Newsletter*, irregularly
(Community of Christ and Mormon historical research.)
$20.00 per year membership

Congregational
(see also United Church of Christ)

Congregational Christian Church (National Association)
PO Box 1620
Oak Creek, WI 53154
http://www.naccc.org

Conservative Congregational Christian Conference
7582 Currell Boulevard, Suite 108
Saint Paul, MN 55125
http://www.ccccusa.org

Congregational Holiness Church

Congregational Holiness Church
3888 Fayetteville Highway
Griffin, GA 30223
http://www.ch.church.com

Congregational Methodist Church
(withdrew from the Methodist Episcopal Church, South, but later a part split and joined the Congregational Church; see also United Methodist Church)

Congregational Methodist Church
PO Box 9
Florence, MS 39073

Conservative Baptist Association of America (CB

America)
(see Baptist)

Conservative Mennonite Conference (CMC)
(see also Church of God in Christ, Mennonite)

Formerly Conservative Mennonite Amish Conference.

Conservative Mennonite Conference
9910 Rosedale-Milford Center Road
Irwin, OH 43029
http://www.cmcrosedale.org

Cooperative Baptist Fellowship (CBF)
(see Baptist)

Coptic Orthodox Church
(see Orthodox)

Covenant

Covenant Archives and Historical Library
North Park College
5125 North Spaulding Avenue
Chicago, IL 60625-4816
(773) 244-6224; (773) 267-2362
Tim Johnson, Archivist
by appointment
(Evangelical Covenant Church of America, founded by Swedish immigrants of Pietist tradition)

Evangelical Covenant Church
5101 North Francisco Avenue
Chicago, IL 60625
http://www.covchurch.org

Cumberland Presbyterian Church
(see Presbyterian)

Cumberland Presbyterian Church in America
(see Presbyterian)

Defenseless Mennonite Church
(see Evangelical Mennonite Church)

Disciples of Christ
(ee also Christian Churches and Churches of Christ)

Barton Stone's "Stoneites," along with Abner Jones's First Christian Church at Lyndon, Vermont, and a group led by James O'Kelly's merged and called themselves "Christians." In 1832 they merged with the "Campbellites," followers of Thomas Campbell and his son, Alexander, calling themselves the Christian Church or the Disciples of Christ, and otherwise labeled "restorationists" or belonging to the Restoration Movement. The Christian Churches and Churches of Christ later split away. Congregations are mostly autonomous.

Brite Divinity School Collection
Mary Couts Burnett Library
Texas Christian University
PO Box 298400
Fort Worth, TX 76129
(817) 921-7668; (817) 921-7282 FAX
http://www.library.tcu.edu

Robert A. Olsen, Librarian
(specialty: "Christian Church [Disciples of
Christ]")

Christian Church (Disciples of Christ)
(130 East Washington Street—location)
PO Box 1986 (mailing address)
Indianapolis, IN 46206
http://www.disciples.org

Disciples of Christ Historical Society
1101 19th Avenue, South
Nashville, TN 37212-2196
(615) 327-1444
dishistsoc@aol.com
http://www.dishistsoc.org
May Reed, Assistant to the Director of
Library and Archives
Mon–Fri 8:00–4:30
Pub. *Discipliana*, quarterly
("We are primarily a church archives but
have a large amount of congregational
information." "Stone-Campbell
Restoration Movement.")
$15.00 per year membership

Emmanuel School of Religion
1 Walker Drive
Johnson City, TN 37601
(423) 461-1541; (423) 926-6198 FAX
library@esr.edu
http://www.esr.edu
Thomas E. Stokes, Librarian
Mon–Fri
(Restoration Movement, the Stone-Campbell
movement, Christian Church [Disciples of
Christ], Christian Churches/Churches of
Christ)

Hiram Township Historical Society, Inc.
(see Ohio, Part 2)

Johnson Bible College
Glass Memorial Library
7900 Johnson Drive
Knoxville, TN 37998
(865) 251-2277; (865) 251-2278 FAX
library@jbc.edu
http://www.jbc.edu/library
Carolyn Lowe, Librarian
by appointment
(Restoration or Stone-Campbell Movement)

Divine Science

Divine Science Federation International
2025 35th Street, N.W.
Washington, DC 20007
http://www.divinescience.org

Dunkers
(see Brethren)

Eastern Orthodox
(see Orthodox)

Eastern Rite Catholic Churches
(see Orthodox)

Elim Fellowship

Elim Fellowship
1703 Dalton Road
Lima, NY 14485
http://www.elim.edu

Episcopal

Diocesan sites may list an archive for
records of the diocese and discontinued

parishes, a historigrapher, and/or contacts for
individual congregations. A complete list of
dioceses and congregations is at
http://www.episcopalchurch.org/webpages or
http://www.theredbook.org. Schism groups,
which may have records of their parent
Protestant Episcopal [now simply Episcopal]
parishes, include the the National
Organization of the New Apostolic Church
of North America, the Reformed Episcopal
Church, the Southern Episcopal Church, the
Episcopal Orthodox Christian Archdiocese
of America, The International Communion of
the Charismatic Episcopal Church, The
Province of Christ the King, the Anglican
Catholic Church, and the American
Episcopal Church. These latter two groups
formed the Anglican Rite Jurisdiction of the
Americas.

Anglican Catholic Church
107 West Broadway
Gettysburg, PA 17325
http://www.anglicancatholic.org

**The Anglican Rite Archdiocese of the
Americas**
Saint Andrew's Anglican Church
1524 Sam Bass Road
Round Rock, TX 78681
(512) 255-2986 (Archbishop); (512) 244-
2909 (Saint Andrew's)
anglicanarchdiocese@yahoo.com
http://www.anglicanrite.org
Archbishop Arlen Jones

Anglicans Online
http://www.anglicansonline.org/usa/
index.html
(links to dioceses and individual parishes)

**Apostolic Episcopal Church—Order of
Corporate Reunion**
PO Box 2401
Apple Valley, CA 92307
http://www.celticsynod.org/aec.htm

**The Archives of the Episcopal Church
USA**
Research Office
(606 Rathervue Place—location)
PO Box 2247 (mailing address)
Austin, TX 78768
(512) 472-6816; (512) 480-0437 FAX
Research@episcopalarchives.org
http://episcopalarchives.com
Mark J. Duffy, Canonical Archivist and
Director of Archives
9:00–5:00
Pub. *Etcetera*
(The web site lists Episcopal holdings in
other repositories, includes links to other
Episcopal organizations, and has a short
article on research in church records.)

Church Historical Society
Archives of the Episcopal Church, USA
General Convention of the Episcopal Church
(606 Ratherview Place—location)
PO Box 2247 (mailing address)
Austin, TX 78768-2247
(512) 472-6816
V. Nelle Bellamy, Ph.D., Archivist
Pub. *Anglican and Episcopal History*
(houses records of the Domestic and Foreign
Missionary Society)

**Dalcho Historical Society of the Protestant
Episcopal Church in South Carolina**
(1020 King Street—location)
PO Box 2127 (mailing address)
Charleston, SC 29403

(843) 722-4075

Diocesan Archives

The Episcopal Diocese of Alabama
Carpenter House
521 North 20th Street
Birmingham, AL 35203-2611
(205) 715-2060 (Office); (205) 715-2066
FAX
dservant@dioala.org
http://www.dioala.org
Denise Servant, Staff Secretary Receptionist
Mon–Thur 8:00–4:30, Fri 8:00–noon

Episcopal Diocese of Alaska
1205 Denali Way
Fairbanks, AK 99701
(907) 452-3040; (907) 456-6552 FAX
http://home.gci.net/~episcopalak
Virginia MacDonald, Historiographer,
Archives

The Episcopal Diocese of Arizona
114 West Roosevelt Street
Phoenix, AZ 85003-1406
(602) 254-0976
ofcmgraz@qwest.net
http://www.episcopal-az.org
Julia Forrest, Office Manager/Convention
Secretary/Archives
Office: Mon–Thur 8:30–5:00, Fri 8:30–4:00

The Episcopal Diocese of Arkansas
(301 West 17th Street—location)
PO Box 164668 (mailing address)
Little Rock, AR 72216-4668
(501) 372-2168; (501) 372-2147 FAX
http://www.arkansas.anglican.org
Michael McNeely, Historiographer; Ms.
Tommie Mitchell, Secretary

Episcopal Diocese of California
1055 Taylor Street
San Francisco, CA 94108
(415) 673-5015; (415) 673-9268
marybethb@diocal.org (General
Information), info@diocal.org
http://www.diocal.org
Elizabeth Lee Abbott, Archivist; Mary Beth
Brown, Office Manager
by appointment

The Diocese of El Camino Real
Mission House
(1092 Noche Buena Street, Seaside,
CA—location)
PO Box 1903 (mailing address)
Monterey, CA 93942
(831) 394-4466; (831) 394-7133 FAX
http://www.ecrweb.org/page/page/
201839.htm
Janis Higginbotham, Director of
Communications

The Episcopal Diocese of Los Angeles
The Cathedral center of Saint Paul
(840 Echo Park Avenue, Los Angeles, CA
90026—location)
PO Box 512164 (mailing address)
Los Angeles, CA 90051-0164
(213) 482-2040, ext. 265; (213) 482-5304
FAX
archivist@ladiocese.org
http://www.ladiocese.org
Larson (Canon) Earleen, Archivist

**The Episcopal Diocese of Northern
California**
The Diocesan Office
(1318 27th Street—location)
PO Box 161268 (mailing address)

Sacramento, CA 95816-5902
(916) 442-6918; (916) 442-6927 FAX
Diocese_NCalif@dncweb.org
http://www.dncweb.org

The Episcopal Diocese of San Diego
2728 Sixth avenue
San Diego, CA 92103
(619) 291-5947
EDSD-web@EDSD.org; edsd-web@n2.net
http://www.edsd.org
Rebecca Williamson, Communications
Manager

The Episcopal Diocese of San Joaquin
4159 East Dakota Avenue
Fresno, CA 93726-5227
(559) 244-4828
sjoaquin@sjoaquin.net
http://sanjoaquin.anglican.org

The Diocese of Colorado
1300 Washington Street
Denver, CO 80203-2008
(303) 837-1173; (303) 837-1311 FAX
http://www.coloradodiocese.org

**Archives of the Episcopal Diocese of
Connecticut**
1335 Asylum Avenue
Hartford, CT 06105-2295
(860) 521-8975; (860) 523-1410
http://www.ctdiocese.org/diocese/
r_archives.htm
The Rev. Dr. Robert G. Carroon, Archivist
Mon–Fri 8:30–4:30 by appointment
(Episcopal church records from Colonial
period to mid-20th century)
copies: 25¢ per page

The Episcopal Diocese of Delaware
Archives of the Diocese of Delaware
(Episcopal)
Oberod Conference Center, 400 Burnt Mill
Road
Centerville, DE 19807
(302) 654-4148; (302) 654-7615 FAX
http://www.dioceseofdelaware.net

Episcopal Diocese of Washington Archives
Washington National Cathedral
Mount Saint Albans
Massachusetts and Wisconsin Avenues,
N.W.
Washington, DC 20016-5098
(202) 537-6881; (202) 364-6600 FAX
rhewlett@cathedral.org
http://www.loc.gov/rr/mail/religion/epa3.
html
Richard G. Hewlett, Historiographer
(a few 20th-century parish registers for
parishes that are no longer in existence,
no staff research services are provided)

The Episcopal Diocese of Florida
325 Market Street
Jacksonville, FL 32202
(904) 356-1328; (888) 763-2602
diocese@diocesefl.org; virginiabb@aol.com
http://www.diocesefl.org
Virginia Barker

The Episcopal Diocese of Central Florida
1017 East Robinson Street
Orlando, FL 32801
(407) 423-3567, ext. 308; (800) 299-3567;
(407) 872-0006 FAX
history@episcopalfamily.com
http://www.cfdiocese.org
Beatrice Wilder, Historiographer

Diocese of Central Gulf Coast

(201 North Baylen Street, Pensacola, FL
32502—location)
PO Box 13330 (mailing address)
Pensacola, FL 32591-3330
(251) 626-0053 (Historiographer); (850)
434-8577 FAX
staff@diocgc.org
http://www.diocgc.org
Kit Caffey, Registrar-Historiographer

Episcopal Diocese of Southeast Florida
525 N.E. 15th Street
Miami, FL 33132
(305) 373-0881; (305) 375-8054 FAX
info@diosef.org
http://diosef.org

**The Episcopal Diocese of Southwest
Florida**
(8411 25th Street, East, Parrish, FL
34219—location)
PO Box 763 (mailing address)
Ellenton, FL 34222
(941) 776-1018; (941) 776-9811 FAX
bpersson@dioceseswfla.org
http://www.diocesewfla.org
Beverly Persson, Office Manager (Clergy
and Lay Records, Parochial Reports)

The Diocese of Georgia
Diocesan House
611 East Bay Street
Savannah, GA 31401-1296
(912) 236-4279, ext. 813; (912) 236-2007
FAX
vicschuster@att.net
http://www.georgia.anglican.org
Vicki Schuster, Staff Support Secretary

The Episcopal Diocese of Atlanta
Episcopal Center
2744 Peachtree Road
Atlanta, GA 30305
(404) 601-5320; (404) 601-5330 FAX
dcampbell@episcopalatlanta.org
http://www.episcopalatlanta.org
Denise Campbell, Receptionist/Office
Assistant

Episcopal Church, Diocesan Archives
229 Queen Emma Square
Honolulu, HI 96813-2304
(808) 536-7776; (808) 538-7194 FAX
http://www.episcopalhawaii.org
Marie Elesarke, Administrative Assistant

Episcopal Diocese of Idaho
(510 West Washington, Boise, ID
83702—location)
PO Box 936 (mailing address)
Boise, ID 83701
(208) 345-4440; (208) 345-9735 FAX
carrolk@idahodiocese.org
http://idahodiocese.org
Carrol Keller, Administrative Assistant
(for the Archives of the Episcopal Diocese of
Idaho, see Boise State University,
Albertsons Library, Part 2)

Episcopal Diocese of Chicago
Archives and Historical Collections
Saint James Cathedral
65 East Huron Street
Chicago, IL 60611
(312) 787-6410; (312) 751-4200 (Episcopal
Church Center); (312) 787-4534 FAX
jruby@epischicago.org
http://www.epischicago.org
Juleigh Ruby, Administrative Assistant

Episcopal Diocese of Quincy
3601 North North Street

Peoria, IL 61604-1599
(309) 688-8221; (309) 688-8229 FAX
DOQ@ocslink.com
http://www.quincy.anglican.org

**The Episcopal Church in the Diocese of
Springfield**
Diocesan Center
821 South Second Street
Springfield, IL 62704
(217) 525-1876; (217) 525-1877 FAX
http://www.episcopalspringfield.org

**Archives of the Episcopal Diocese of
Indianapolis**
Episcopal Diocese of Indianapolis
1100 West 42nd Street
Indianapolis, IN 46208
(317) 926-5454; (317) 926-5456 FAX
penceshartom@aol.com
http://www.indydiocese.org/public.htm

**The Episcopal Diocese of Northern
Indiana**
117 North Lafayette Boulevard
South Bend, IN 46601
(574) 233-6489; (574) 287-7914 FAX
jbeatty@acpl.lib.in.us
http://www.ednin.org
John Beatty, Archivist/Historiographer

Episcopal Diocese of Iowa
225 37th Street
Des Moines, IA 50312
(515) 277-6165; (515) 277-0273 FAX
diocese@iowaepiscopal.org;
nmorton@iowaepiscopal.org
http://www.iowaepiscopal.org
Nancy Morton, Webmaster

The Episcopal Diocese of Kansas
835 S.W. Polk
Topeka, KS 66612
(785) 267-8663 (Chubb); (316) 684-7797
(Pott)
http://www.episcopal-ks.org
Deacon Donald A. Chubb and Katie Pott,
Co-historiographers

The Episcopal Diocese of Western Kansas
(138 South Eighth Street—location)
PO Box 2507 (mailing address)
Salina, KS 67402-2507
(785) 825-1626; (785) 825-0974 FAX
http://www.westernkansas.org

The Episcopal Diocese of Kentucky
6 Eastover Court
Louisville, KY 40206
(502) 893-2632
http://www.episcopalky.org
Sharon Receveur, Historiographer
by appointment
(Diocesan records since 1895, office records,
diocesan reports, some church records)

The Episcopal Diocese of Lexington
(204 East Fourth Street—location)
PO Box 610 (mailing address)
Lexington, KY 40588-0610
(859) 252-6527; (859) 231-9077 FAX
Diocese@diolex.org
http://www.diolex.org

The Episcopal Diocese of Lousiana
1623 Seventh Street
New Orleans, LA 70115
(504) 895-6634
hmurrell@edola.org
http://www.edola.org
Harriet Murrell, Director, School for
Ministry and Diocesan Archivist

The Diocese of Western Louisiana
(335 Main Street, Pineville, LA
71360—location)
PO Box 2031 (mailing address)
Alexandria, LA 71309-2031
(318) 442-1304; (318) 442-8712 FAX
LadyDiWhi@aol.com
http://www.diocesewla.org
Dianne White, Registrar of the Diocese

Archives of the Episcopal Diocese of Maine
143 State House
Portland, ME 04101
(207) 772-1953 (Diocesan Office); (800)
244-6062, ext. 37 (Mon); (207) 773-0095
emaule@diomaine.org
http://www.diomaine.org/dioarchives.htm
Elizabeth S. Maule, Archivist

Episcopal Diocese of Maryland
Maryland Diocesan Archives
Diocesan Center
4 East University Parkway
Baltimore, MD 21218
(410) 467-1399; (800) 443-1399; (410) 584-
7788 FAX
http://www.ang-md.org/diocese/
archives.html
Kingsley Smith

**The Episcopal Church Diocese of Easton
in Eastern Maryland**
314 North Street
Easton, MD 21601-3684
(410) 822-1919, ext. 113; (410) 763-8259
FAX
reese@dioceseofeaston.org
http://www.dioceseofeaston.org
Deacon Reese S. Rickards

Episcopal Diocese of Massachusetts
The Diocesan Library and Archives
138 Tremont Street, Third Floor
Boston, MA 02111
(617) 482-4826, ext. 504; (800) 696-6079,
ext. 504 (in Massachusetts); (617) 482-
8431 FAX
http://www.diomass.org/Archives.htm
Sandra Sudak, Diocesan Archivist
winter: Mon–Fri 8:30–4:30; summer:
Mon–Fri 8:30–3:30; call for appointment
donation suggested for reference services

**The Episcopal Diocese of Western
Massachusetts**
37 Chestnut Street
Springfield, MA 01103
(413) 737-4786; (413) 746-9873 FAX
wcoyne@diocesewma.org
http://www.diocesewma.org
William H. Coyne, Archdeacon

**The Episcopal Church Center of the
Diocese of Michigan**
4800 Woodward Avenue
Detroit, MI 48201-1399
(313) 832-4400; (313) 831-0259 FAX
kbota@edomi.org
http://www.edomi.org
Karen D. Bota, Diocesan Communication
Coordinator

Episcopal Diocese of Eastern Michigan
924 North Niagara Street
Saginaw, MI 48602
(989) 752-6020; (989) 752-6120 FAX
http://www.eastmich.org

**The Episcopal Diocese of Northern
Michigan**
131 East Ridge
Marquette, MI 49855

(906) 228-7160; (906) 228-7171 FAX
diocese@dionomi.org
http://www.dionomi.org

Diocese of Western Michigan
2600 Vincent Avenue
Portage, MI 49024-5653
(616) 381-2710; (616) 381-7067 FAX

Episcopal Diocese of Minnesota
The Episcopal Center
1730 Clifton Place, Suite 201
Minneapolis, MN 55403-3242
(612) 871-5311; (612) 871-0552 FAX
gordon.t@episcopalmn.org
http://www.episcopalmn.org
Thomas Gordon, Director of
Communications

Episcopal Diocese of Mississippi
Allin Diocesan House
(118 North Congress Street, Jackson, MS
39201—location)
PO Box 23107 (mailing address)
Jackson, MS 39225-3107
(601) 948-5954; (601) 354-3401 FAX
vapatterson38@aol.com
http://www.dioms.org
Mrs. V. A. Patterson, Archivist

Diocese of Missouri
The Episcopal Church in Eastern Missouri
1210 Locust Street
Saint Louis, MO 63103
(314) 231-1220; (314) 231-3373
suerehkopf@cs.com
http://www.missouri.anglican.org
Sue Rehkopf, Diocesan Archivist

**Archives of the Diocese of West Missouri
(Episcopal)**
(420 West 14th Street—location)
PO Box 413227 (mailing address)
Kansas City, MO 64141
(816) 471-6161
http://www.diowestmo.org (Diocese)
Doris M. Anderson, Historiographer

The Episcopal Diocese of Montana
515 North Park Avenue
Helena, MT 59601
(406) 442-2230; (406) 442-2238 FAX
mtdiocese@aol.com
http://mtepiscopal.homestead.com

The Episcopal Diocese of Nebraska
109 North 18th Street
Omaha, NE 68102
(402) 341-5373; (402) 341-8683 FAX
diocese@episcopal-ne.org
http://www.episcopal-ne.org/index.shtml

Episcopal Diocese of Nevada
6135 Harrison Drive, Suite 1
Las Vegas, NV 89120-4076
(702) 737-9190; (702) 737-6488 FAX
http://episcopaldiocesenevada.org

Diocese of New Hampshire
63 Green Street
Concord, NH 03301-4243
(603) 224-1914; (603) 225-7884 FAX
http://www.nhepiscopal.org
Margaret "Peg" Aldrich, Registrar/Archivist

**The Episcopal Church Diocese of New
Jersey**
808 West State Street
Trenton, NJ 08618-5326
(609) 394-5281, ext. 15; (609) 394-9546
FAX
lfish@newjersey.anglican.org

http://www.newjersey.anglican.org
The Rev. Laurence D. Fish, Sr.,
Historiographer and Registrar

The Diocese of Newark
31 Mulberry Street
Newark, NJ 07102
(973) 622-4306; (973) 430-9900; (973) 622-
3503 FAX
http://www.dioceseofnewark.org
Margaret Giammarino,
Receptionist/Registrar

The Diocese of the Rio Grande
4304 Carlisle Boulevard, N.E.
Albuquerque, NM 87107-4811
(505) 881-0636; (505) 883-9048 FAX
http://riogrande.Ocatach.com/main.html
Dr. C. Evan Davies, Archivist

Episcopal Diocese of New York
1047 Amsterdam Avenue
New York, NY 10025
(212) 316-7400; (212) 316-7405 FAX
info@dioceseny.org
http://www.dioceseny.org/index.cfm

Episcopal Diocese of Albany, New York
68 South Swan Street
Albany, NY 12210
(518) 465-4737
diocese@albanydiocese.org
http://www.albanyepiscopaldiocese.org

The Diocese of Central New York
310 Montgomery Street, Suite 200
Syracuse, NY 13202-2093
(315) 747-6596; (315) 478-1632 FAX
office@cny.anglican.org
http://www.cny.anglican.org

The Episcopal Diocese of Long Island
35 Cathedral Avenue
Garden City, NY 11530
(516) 248-8000
info@dioceselongisland.org
http://www.dioceselongisland.org/index.
shtml

Episcopal Diocese of Rochester Archives
935 East Avenue
Rochester, NY 14607
(716) 473-7780; (716) 473-3195 FAX
DavidS@Rochesterepiscopaldiocese.com
http://www.rochesterepiscopaldiocese.
org/archives.html
David Sisson

**The Episcopal Diocese of Western New
York**
1114 Delaware Avenue
Buffalo, NY 14209
(716) 881-0660
archives@EpiscopalWNY.org;
swampcrone@prodigy.net
http://buffalolore.buffalonet.org/
episcopal/episcopalarchives.htm
Nancy Piatkowski, Diocesan Archivist

**Archives of the Episcopal Diocese of North
Carolina**
(201 Saint Alban's Drive—location)
PO Box 17025 (mailing address)
Raleigh, NC 27619
(919) 787-6313, ext. 229; (919) 787-0156
FAX
http://www.episdionc.com
Michelle A. Francis, Archivist; The Rev.
Canon Ted Malone, Director of
Communications and Historiographer

The Episcopal Diocese of East Carolina

(705 Doctors Drive—location)
PO Box 1336 (mailing address)
Kinston, NC 28503
(252) 522-0885, ext. 118; (252) 523-5272
    FAX
snunn@diocese-eastcarolina.org
http://www.diocese-eastcarolina.org
Mr. H. Mack Bell, Historiographer; Scott
    Nunn, Web Editor

Episcopal Church in the Diocese of Western North Carolina
900 B CenterPark Drive
Asheville, NC 28805
(828) 225-6656; (828) 225-6657 FAX
bishop@diocesewnc.org (Diocesan Office)
http://www.diocesewnc.org

The Episcopal Diocese of North Dakota
(3600 South 25th Street—location)
PO Box 10337 (mailing address)
Fargo, ND 58106-0037
(701) 235-6688; (701) 232-3077 FAX
starkw@polar.polarcomm.com (Webmaster)
http://www.geocities.com/Heartland/
    Plains/1981/diocofnd.htm

The Episcopal Church in the Diocese of Ohio
Trinity Commons
2230 Euclid Avenue
Cleveland, OH 44115
(216) 771-4815; (216) 623-0735 FAX
bdonahue@dohio.org
http://www.dohio.org
Brenda Donahue, Secretary

The Episcopal Church in Southern Ohio
412 Sycamore Street
Cincinnati, OH 45202-4179
(513) 287-7089; (513) 421-0315 FAX
llchace@one.net
http://www.episcopal-dso.org
The Rev. Dcn. Laura L. Chase,
    Historian/Archivist

Episcopal Diocese of Oklahoma
924 North Robinson
Oklahoma City, OK 73102
(405) 232-4820; (405) 232-4912 FAX
supchurch@episcopaloklahoma.org
http://episcopaloklahoma.org
The Rev. Stan Upchurch, Diocesan Archivist

Diocese of Oregon
The Episcopal Church in Western Oregon
11800 S.W. Military Lane
Portland, OR 97219-8436
(503) 636-5613; (503) 636-5616 FAX
http://www.diocese-oregon.org
Kyle Wiseley, General Services
    Administrator and Information System
    Manager

Diocese of Eastern Oregon
PO Box 1548
The Dalles, OR 97058
(541) 298-4477; (541) 298-7578; (541) 296-
    0939 FAX
http://theredbook.org/redbook/directories/
    diocese_3.asp?organization_id=
    68&from=province (Unofficial)
Rt. Rev. William Otis Gregg, Bishop

Episcopal Diocese of Pennsylvania
240 South Fourth Street
Philadelphia, PA 19106
(215) 627-6434; (215) 627-7550 FAX
gerriew@diopa.org
http://www.diopa.org/diopa
Gerrie Wilson, Receptionist

The Episcopal Diocese of Bethlehem
333 Wyandotte Street
Bethlehem, PA 18015
(610) 691-5655; (800) 358-5655 (PA only)
webmaster@diobeth.org
http://www.diobeth.org

Episcopal Diocese of Central Pennsylvania
(101 Pine Street—location)
PO Box 11937 (mailing address)
Harrisburg, PA 17108
(717) 236-5959; (717) 236-6448
mgebhart@diocesecpa.org
http://www.diocesecpa.org
Maureen Gebhart, Diocesan Staff Secretary

Diocese of Northwestern Pennsylvania
145 West Sixth Street
Erie, PA 16501
(814) 456-4203
http://www.dionwpa.org

The Episcopal Diocese of Pittsburgh
535 Smithfield Street, 900 Oliver Building
Pittsburgh, PA 15222
(412) 281-6131, ext. 138; (412) 471-5591
    FAX
wohleber@pgh.anglican.org
http://www.pgh.anglican.org
Lynne Wohleber, Diocesan Archivist

The Episcopal Diocese of Rhode Island
Diocesan House and Resource Center
275 North Main Street
Providence, RI 02903-1298
(401) 274-4500; (401) 331-9430 FAX
Diocese@episcopalri.org
http://www.episcopalri.org/conv_main.cfm
("Records from antiquity and from some
    closed parishes are stored in the Special
    Collections Department of the University
    of Rhode Island Library. Additional
    diocesan records are kept there as well as
    in a vault in Diocesan House." The
    diocesan web site lists the location of the
    records of closed parishes as well as the
    changes in names of churches.)

The Episcopal Diocese of South Carolina
Diocesan House
(126 Coming Street, Charleston, SC
    29403—location)
PO Box 20127 (mailing address)
Charleston, SC 29413
(843) 722-4075; (843) 723-7628 FAX
office@dioceseofsc.org (Archive
    Information)
http://www.dioceseofsc.org

The Episcopal Diocese of Upper South Carolina
1115 Marion Street
Columbia, SC 29201
(803) 771-7800
diocese@edusc.org
http://www.edusc.org
Peggy Hill, Director of Communications

Diocese of South Dakota
500 South Main Avenue
Sioux Falls, SD 57104-6814
(605) 338-9751; (605) 336-6243 FAX
dosdakota@qwest.net
http://www.diocesesd.org
Mary Armin, Administrative Assistant

Episcopal Diocese of Tennessee
50 Vantage Way, Suite 107
Nashville, TN 37228
(615) 251-3322; (615) 251-8010 FAX
info@episcopaldiocese-tn.org
http://episcopaldiocese-tn.org

The Episcopal Diocese of East Tennessee
814 Episcopal School Way
Knoxville, TN 37932
(865) 966-2110; (865) 966-2536 FAX
rdavenport@etdiocese.net
http://www.etdiocese.net
Rosemary Davenport, Staff Executive
    Assistant

The Diocese of West Tennessee
692 Poplar Avenue
Memphis, TN 38105
(901) 526-0023; (901) 526-1555 FAX
info@episwtn.org
http://www.episwtn.org

The Episcopal Diocese of Texas
3203 West Alabama
Houston, TX 77098
(713) 520-6444; (713) 520-5723 FAX
cbarnwell@epicenter.org
http://www.epicenter.org
Carol Barnwell, Communications
    Coordinator

The Episcopal Diocese of Dallas
1630 North Garrett Avenue
Dallas, TX 75206
(214) 826-8310; (214) 826-5968 FAX
mridenour@episcopal-dallas.org
http://www.episcopal-dallas.org
Mary Alice Ridenour, Receptionist

The Episcopal Diocese of Fort Worth
2900 Alemeda Street
Fort Worth, TX 76116
(817) 244-2885; (817) 244-3363 FAX
diocese@fwepiscopal.org
http://www.fwepiscopal.org/index1.html

The Episcopal Diocese of Northwest Texas
1802 Broadway
Lubbock, TX 79401
(806) 763-1370, ext. 201; (806) 472-0641
    FAX
diocese@nwt.org
http://www.nwt.org
Edna Chambers, Business Manager

The Episcopal Diocese of West Texas
111 Torcido
San Antonio, TX 78209
(210) 824-5387; (210) 822-8779 FAX
General.Mail@dwtx.org
http://www.westtexasonline.org

Episcopal Diocese of Utah-Resource Center
(80 South 300 East—location)
PO Box 3090 (mailing address)
Salt Lake City, UT 84110-3090
(801) 322-4131; (801) 322-5096 FAX
http://www.episcopal-ut.org
Paula C. Madsen, Coordinator
Mon–Fri 8:30–5:00

The Episcopal Diocese of Vermont
Diocesan Center
5 Rock Point Road
Burlington, VT 05401
(802) 877-3895 (Historiographer's Home);
    (802) 860-1562 FAX
eallison@dioceseofvermont.org
http://www.dioceseofvermont.org
Elizabeth E. Allison, Historigrapher
8:30–4:30
(archives contain some "parish registers from
    a few, small churches which are no longer
    in existence," also "microfilm of old
    parish registers from active churches
    around the diocese," copies of which are
    available through the Family History

Library of The Church of Jesus Christ of Latter-day Saints; "with some books of bishops' official acts 1854 to the present, records of SPG, papers and testimonials relating to clergy")
search fees vary

The Episcopal Diocese of Virginia
May House, 110 West Franklin Street
Richmond, VA 23220
(804) 643-8451
ksmith@thediocese.net
http://www.thediocese.net
Karen Smith, Receptionist and
  Administrative Assistant

Episcopal Church in the Diocese of Southern Virginia
600 Talbot Hall Road
Norfolk, VA 23505
(757) 423-8287 (Office); (800) 582-8292;
  (757) 440-5354 FAX
fjacobson@tcc.vccs.edu
http://www.southernvirginia.anglican.org/
  index.html
Mrs. Fran Jacobson, Historiographer

The Episcopal Diocese of Southwestern Virginia
(1002 First Street, S.W., Roanoke, VA
  24016—location)
PO Box 2279 (mailing address)
Roanoke, VA 24009-2279
(540) 342-6797; (540) 343-9114 FAX
info@dioswva.org
http://www.dioswva.org

Diocese of Olympia Archives
The Episcopal Church in Western
  Washington
(1551 10th East, Seattle, WA 98102-
  4298—location)
PO Box 12126 (mailing address)
Seattle, WA 98102-0126
(206) 325-4200; (206) 325-4631 FAX
info@ecww.org
http://www.olympia.anglican.org
Diane Wells, Archivist/Records Manager
Archives: Tue–Thur 9:00–5:00; Office:
  Mon–Fri 9:00–5:00
(Journals, sacramental records, official
  records of the diocese; "genealogical
  requests as time allows")
research: by the hour plus costs of copying

Episcopal Diocese of Spokane
245 East 13th Avenue
Spokane, WA 99202
(509) 624-3191
elainef@spokanediocese.org
http://www.spokanediocese.org
Ruth Farnham, Historiographer; Elaine
  Foerster, Executive Secretary

Episcopal Diocese of West Virginia
(1608 Virginia Street East, Charleston, WV
  25311—location)
PO Box 5400 (mailing address)
Charleston, WV 25361
(304) 344-3597 (Office); (304) 343-3295
  FAX
mbailey@wvdiocese.org
http://www.wvdiocese.org
Mollie Bailey, Secretary/Receptionist

Episcopal Diocese of Eau Claire
510 South Farwell Street
Eau Claire, WI 54701
(616) 835-3331
http://www.dioceseofeauclaire.org
Joan Smalstig, Secretary

The Episcopal Diocese of Fond du Lac, Wisconsin
(39 North Sophia Street, Fond du Lac, WI
  54935-3343—location)
PO Box 149 (mailing address)
Fond du Lac, WI 54936-0149
(920) 921-8866; (920) 921-8761 FAX
http://www.episcopalfonddulac.org

The Episcopal Diocese of Milwaukee
804 East Juneau Avenue
Milwaukee, WI 53202-2798
(414) 272-3028; (414) 272-7790 FAX
info@diomil.org
http://www.episcopalmilwaukee.org

Episcopal Diocese of Wyoming
104 South Fourth Street
Laramie, WY 82070
(307) 742-6606; (307) 742-2888 FAX
norm@wydiocese.org
http://www.wydiocese.org
Norm Peterson, Communications Officer

Navaholand Area Mission
PO Box 720
Farmington, NM 87499-0720
(505) 327-7549; (505) 327-6904 FAX
http://www.theredbook.org/redbook/
  directories/diocese_3.asp?organization_
  id=114

Diocese of Puerto Rico
(Carretera 848 Km 1.0, Sain Just, Trujillo
  Alto, PR 00976—location)
Apartadó 902 (mailing address)
Saint Just, PR 00978
(787) 761-9800; (787) 761-0320 FAX
http://www.iepanglicom.org
Illmo. y Rvdmo. David Andrés Álvarez

Diocese of the Virgin Islands
PO Box 10437
Saint Thomas, VI 00801
(340) 776-1797; (340) 777-8485 FAX
tad931@worldnet.att.net

Episcopal Church Home Archives
505 Mount Hope Avenue
Rochester, NY 14620
(716) 546-8400; (716) 325-6553 FAX

The Episcopal Church in the United States of America (ECUSA)
Episcopal Church Center
815 Second Avenue
New York, NY 10017
(212) 716-6000; (800) 334-7626
dengland@episcopalchurch.org (Director of
  the Office of Communication)
http://ecusa.anglican.org

The Episcopal Missionary Church
600 Oak Hollow Lane
Fort Worth, TX 76112
info@emchome.org
http://www.emchome.org

The International Communion of the Charismatic Episcopal Church
46797 Trailwood Place
Potomac Falls, VA 20165
http://www.diochi.org

National Organization of the New Apostolic Church of North America
3753 North Troy Street
Chicago, IL 60618
http://www.nak.org

Reformed Episcopal Church

826 Second Avenue
Blue Bell, PA 19422-1257
http://www.recus.org

Saint Anne's Episcopal Church Historical Commission
8 Kirk Street
Lowell, MA 01852
(978) 452-2150
Louise K. Hunt, Chairperson
Library: Wed 9:00–noon, and by
  appointment
research: $10.00 per hour

Southern Episcopal Church
234 Willow Lane
Nashville, TN 37211-4945
http://www.angelfire.com/biz/Southern

Episcopal Orthodox Christian Archdiocese of America
(see Episcopal)

Evangelical
(see also Lutheran, Protestant, United
Church of Christ, United Methodist)

The Evangelical Church established its independence from the United Methodist Church in 1968 with congregations from both the Methodist Church and the Evangelical United Brethren. The Holiness Methodist Church merged with it in 1982.

The Evangelical Church
Denominational Office
9421 West River Road
Minneapolis, MN 55444-1141
(763) 424-2589; (763) 424-9230 FAX
ecdenom@usfamily.net
http://theevangelicalchurch.com
Dr. Bill Vermillion, General Superintendent

Evangelical and Reformed
(see United Church of Christ)

Evangelical Congregational Church
(see also United Methodist)

Evangelical Congregational Church
100 West Park Avenue
Myerstown, PA 17067
http://eccenter.com

Evangelical Covenant
(see Covenant and Lutheran)

Evangelical Free Church of America
(see also Lutheran)

Evangelical Free Church of America
901 East 78th Street
Minneapolis, MN 55420-1300
http://efca.org
(formed in 1950; parent groups formerly
  known as Swedish Ansgarii Synod,
  Mission Synod, Swedish Evangelical Free
  Mission, Swedish Evangelical Free
  Church, and Norwegian-Danish
  Evangelical Free Church Association)

Evangelical Friends International—North American Region
(see Religious Society of Friends [Quakers])

Evangelical Lutheran Church in America
(see Lutheran)

Evangelical Lutheran Joint Synod of Wisconsin and Other States
(see Lutheran)

Evangelical Mennonite Brethren
(see Fellowship of Evangelical Bible Churches)

Evangelical Mennonite Church
(see also Church of God in Christ, Mennonite)

Formerly the Defenseless Mennonite Church

Evangelical Mennonite Church
1420 Kerrway Court
Fort Wayne, IN 46805
http://www.brookside.org

Evangelical Methodist Church
(see also United Methodist Church)

Evangelical Methodist Church
PO Box 17070
Indianapolis, IN 46217
http://www.emchurch.org

Evangelical Presbyterian Church (EPC)
(see Presbyterian)

Evangelical Protestant
(see United Church of Christ)

Evangelical Synod of North America
(see United Church of Christ)

Evangelical United Brethren
(see United Methodist)

Fellowship of Evangelical Bible Churches
(formerly the Evangelical Mennonite Brethren, see also Church of God in Christ, Mennonite)

Fellowship of Evangelical Bible Churches
5800 South 14th Street
Omaha, NE 68107

Fellowship of Grace Brethren Churches
(see also Brethren)

Fellowship of Grace Brethren Churches
PO Box 386
Winona Lake, IN 46590
http://www.fgbc.org

Finnish Apostolic Lutheran Church of America
(see Lutheran)

Free Magyar Reformed Church in America
(see Reformed)

Free Methodist Church of North America
(see also United Methodist)

Marston Memorial Historical Center and Archives
Marston Historical Center and Free Methodist Archives
Free Methodist World Ministries Center
(770 North Highschool Road—location)
PO Box 535002 (mailing address)
Indianapolis, IN 46235-5002
(317) 244-3660, ext. 281; (317) 244-1247 FAX
History@fmcna.org
http://www.freemethodistchurch.org/ ~marston/archives.htm
Cathy Fortner, Director
Mon–Fri 8:30–4:30
(Free Methodist Church)

Free Will Baptists
(see Baptist and Pentecostal Free Will Baptist Church)

French Protestant
(see Lineage, Hereditary and Patriotic Societies—Huguenot, Part 4)

Friends
(see Religious Society of Friends [Quakers])

Full Gospel Assemblies International

Full Gospel Assemblies International
PO Box 1230
Coatesville, PA 19320

Full Gospel Fellowship of Churches and Ministers International

Full Gospel Fellowship of Churches and Ministers International
4325 West Ledbetter Drive
Dallas, TX 75233
http://www.fgcmi.org

General Association of General Baptist Churches
(see Baptist)

General Association of Regular Baptist Churches
(see Baptist)

General Conference of Mennonite Brethren Churches
(merged in 2001 with the Mennonite Church; see also Church of God in Christ, Mennonite)

General Conference of Mennonite Brethren Churches
4824 Butler Avenue
Fresno, CA 93727-5097
http://www.mbconf.org

General Convention of the New Jerusalem in the U.S.A.
(see Swedenborgian Societies)

General Council
(see Lutheran)

General Synod
(see Lutheran)

German Baptist Brethren
(see Brethren)

German Evangelical Lutheran Synod of Wisconsin
(see Lutheran)

German Reformed
(see United Church of Christ)

Grace Gospel Fellowship

Grace Gospel Fellowship
(2125 Martindale, S.W.—location)
PO Box 9432 (mailing address)
Grand Rapids, MI 49509
http://www.ggfusa.org

Greek Orthodox Archdiocese of America
(see Orthodox)

Harmonist

Harmonie Associates, Inc.
Old Economy Village
14th and Church Streets
Ambridge, PA 15003
(724) 266-1803
Raymond V. Shepherd, Jr., Director
(Harmonists, a German, Christian communal society, 1785–1905)

Historic Harmony/Harmony Museum
(see Ethnic Archives, Libraries and Societies—German, Part 3)

Hasidic Judaism
(see Ethnic Archives, Libraries and Societies—Jewish, Part 3)

Hoffmanite
(see United Christian Church)

Holiness
(see Apostolic Overcoming Holy Catholic Church of God, Church of Christ [Holiness] U.S.A., Church of God [Holiness], Church of the Nazarene, Wesleyan Church)

Holiness Methodist Church
(see Evangelical)

Holy Eastern Orthodox and Apostolic Church in North America, Inc.
(see Orthodox)

Huguenot
(see Lineage, Patriotic and Hereditary Societies, Part 4)

Hungarian Reformed Church in America
(see Reformed)

The Hutterite Brethren Church
(see also Brethren and Church of God in Christ, Mennonite)

The Hutterite Genealogy Initiative

http://feefhs.org/hut/frg-hut.html
(Hutterian Brethren, 1755–1879; links to
other sites)

Independent Assemblies of God, International
(see also Assemblies of God)

Independent Assemblies of God, International
Head Office
(Santa Ana, CA—location)
PO Box 2130 (mailing address)
Laguna Hills, CA 92654-2130
(949) 859-6946; (949) 859-0683 FAX
http://www.iaogi.org
Gary Dull

Independent Fundamental Churches of America (IFCA International, Inc.)

Independent Fundamental Churches of America (IFCA International, Inc.)
(3250 Fairlanes—location)
PO Box 810
Grandville, MI 49468
http://www.ifca.org

International Church of the Foursquare Gospel

International Church of the Foursquare Gospel
(1910 West Sunset Boulevard, Suite 210—location)
PO Box 26902 (mailing address)
Los Angeles, CA 90026-0176
http://www.foursquare.org

The International Communion of the Charismatic Episcopal Church
(see Episcopal)

International Pentecostal Church of Christ

International Pentecostal Church of Christ
(2245 State Route 42 S.W.—location)
PO Box 439 (mailing address)
London, OH 43140
http://members.aol.com/hqipcc

International Pentecostal Holiness Church

International Pentecostal Holiness Church
PO Box 12609
Oklahoma City, OK 73157
http://www.iphc.org

Islam

Islamic Center of New York
Mosque of New York
1711 Third Avenue
New York, NY 10029
Pub. *Bulletin*, quarterly, contribution
(not ethnic, not racial)

Islamic Center of North America
PO Box 38
Plainfield, IN 46168
http://www.isna.net

Islamic Center of Washington

2551 Massachusetts Avenue, N.W.
Washington, DC 2008

Muslim American Society
W. Deen Muhammed
PO Box 1944
Calumet City, IL 60409

Jehovah's Witnesses

Jehovah's Witnesses
25 Columbia Heights
Brooklyn, NY 11201-2483
http://www.watchtower.org

Jesus Only Apostolic Church of God
(see Assemblies of the Lord Jesus Christ)

Jewish Reconstructionist Federation
(see Ethnic Archives, Libraries and Societies—Jewish, Part 3)

Judaism
(including Hasidic Judaism, Union of American Hebrew Congregations [Reform], Union of Orthodox Jewish Congregations of America, The United Synagogue of Conservative Judaism, Jewish Reconstructionist Federation; see Ethnic Archives, Libraries and Societies—Jewish, Part 3)

Korean-American Presbyterian Church
(see Presbyterian)

Latter-day Saint (Mormon)
(see The Church of Jesus Christ of Latter-day Saints)

Latvian Evangelical Lutheran Church in America
(see Lutheran)

Liberal Catholic

The Liberal Catholic Church broke with the Old Catholic Church in 1916, and later became the Liberal Catholic Church International (LCCI) and the Liberal Catholic Church, Province of the U.S. (LCC).

Liberal Catholic Church International
1206 Ayers Avenue
Ojai, CA 93023
http://www.thelcc.org

The Liberal Catholic Church—Province of the U.S.A.
http://members.tripod.com/~LiberalCatholic
(The site has a list of churches and locations.)

Lutheran
(see also Church of God in Christ, Mennonite)

Individual Lutheran congregations may have been part of associations that formed, split, and reunited or changed affiliation. Associations formed in the 20th century but with roots in the past include American Association of Free Lutheran Churches, Church of the Lutheran Brethren of America, Church of the Lutheran Confession, Evangelical Luthern Church in America, and Wisconsin Evangelical Lutheran Synod.

Other groups include the Apostolic Lutheran Church of America (Church of Laestadius, formerly Finnish Apostolic Lutheran Church of America), the Latvian Evangelical Lutheran Church in America, the Lutheran Church—Missouri Synod, the Norwegian Lutheran Church of America, and the United Lutheran Church (including the former General Synod [consisting of several synods], the General Council [formed when several synods and the Pennsylvania Ministerium withdrew from the General Synod], and the United Synod of the South.)

American Association of Free Lutheran Churches
3110 East Medicine Lake Boulevard
Minneapolis, MN 55441
http://www.aflc.org

American Association of Lutheran Churches
801 West 106th Street, #203
Minneapolis, MN 55420
http://www.taalc.org

Apostolic Lutheran Church of America
332 Mount Washington Way
Clayton, CA 94517-1546
http://www.apostolic-lutheran.org

Archives, North Carolina Synod
Evangelical Lutheran Church in America (ELCA)
1988 Lutheran Synod Drive
Salisbury, NC 28144-5700
(704) 633-4861
Pastor Karl M. Park
Tue & Thur 9:30–noon, and by appointment
(Lutheran congregation records, North Carolina and Tennessee synod records, all records filed by church categories rather than family names)
research: initially free, detailed at $15.00 per hour; copies: 25¢ per page

Church of the Lutheran Brethren of America
PO Box 655
Fergus Falls, MN 56538
http://www.clba.org

Church of the Lutheran Confession
501 Grover Road
Eau Claire, WI 54701
http://www.clclutheran.org

Concordia Historical Institute
The Lutheran Church—Missouri Synod
801 DeMun Avenue
Saint Louis, MO 63105-3199
(314) 505-7900; (314) 505-7901 FAX
http://www.chi.lcms.org
Rev. Daniel Preus, Director
Mon–Fri 8:30–4:30
Pub. *Concordia Historical Institute Quarterly*
(emphasis on Lutheran and German-American records; "We can help people determine the best places to check for church records, family history, Lutheran related.")
$25.00 per year membership; admission free for members, $10.00 for nonmembers; loan of materials by mail: $20.00; research: first half-hour free for members and nonmembers, second half-hour free for members and $10.00 for nonmembers, each additional hour $20.00 for members and $30.00 for nonmembers; photocopies: 15¢ per page for members and 20¢ for nonmembers, up to 149 pages, 30¢ per

page thereafter for members and 40¢ for nonmembers

C. A. Dana—Life Library
(address withheld upon request)
(resource for the United Evangelical Lutheran Church and the Danish immigrant archive; not a genealogical resource for the general public and does not encourage unsolicited requests)

Evangelical Lutheran Church in America
(321 Bonnie Lane, Elk Grove Village, IL 60007—location)
8765 West Higgins Road (mailing address)
Chicago, IL 60631-4198
(847) 690-9410; (847) 690-9502 FAX
archives@elca.org
http://www.elca.org/os/archives/intro.html
Elisabeth Wittman, Director for Archives; Joel Thoreson, Assistant Archivist for Reference
Mon–Fri 8:30–5:00 (advance appointment advised)
Pub. *ELCA Archives Network News*, two times per year (Mar, Sept), available on request
(Church formed 1 Jan 1988 by the merger of the Lutheran Church in America, the American Lutheran Church and the Association of Evangelical Lutheran Churches; specialty: religion, immigration, and ethnic history; microfilm loan of congregational records)
reading room open to the general public; photocopy services available; research for a fee available

Evangelical Lutheran Synod Historical Society
6 Browns Court
Mankato, MN 56001-6121
(507) 388-5969
http://www.evluthsyn.org
Professor Norman Holte, President and Archivist
Mon & Wed–Thur 9:00–11:00 A.M.
Pub. *Oak Leaves*, quarterly
$15.00 per year membership

Folke Bernadette Memorial Library
Gustavus Adolphus College
Saint Peter, MN 56082
(507) 933-7572; (507) 933-7569; (507) 933-6292
folke@gac.edu
http://www.gac.edu/Academics/Resources/Library
8:00 A.M.–midnight
(includes church records of five earlier conferences of the Lutheran Church, basically those based in Minnesota)

Freistadt Historical Society
Trinity Lutheran Church
10729 West Freistadt Road
Mequon, WI 53092
(262) 242-0653
Leroy Boehlke, Vice President
by appointment
(Lutheran and Pomeranian genealogy)

The Georgia Salzburger Society
(see Georgia, Part 2)

Luther College Archives
Preus Library
Decorah, IA 52101
(563) 387-1805
Shan Thomas, Archivist
Mon–Fri 1:30–5:00, and by appointment
(specializes in Luther College and

Norwegian Synod Records)

Luther Seminary
Gullixson Hall
Region 3 Archives, Third Floor
2481 Como Avenue
Saint Paul, MN 55108
(612) 641-3205

Lutheran Archives Center at Philadelphia
Krauth Memorial Library
Lutheran Theological Seminary
7301 Germantown Avenue
Philadelphia, PA 19119-1794
(215) 248-6383 (long distance calls cannot be returned); (215) 248-6327 FAX
mtairyarchives@ltsp.edu
http://www.ltsp.edu/krauth/archives.html
John E. Peterson, Curator; Robyn A. Kulp, Research Services
by appointment (office hours generally are Tue & Fri 1:30–5:00)
Pub. *Archives Advocate* (a nongenealogical newsletter), occasionally, $10.00 donation for subscription
("Northeast Regional Archives for the Evangelical Lutheran Church in America [New England, Upstate New York, New Jersey, and roughly the eastern third of Pennsylvania—ELCA Region Seven), housing records from closed congregations or those few congregations which have chosen to deposit them in the center.")
admission: $5.00; research: $20.00 for the first hour, $15.00 for each additional hour (three hours maximum)

Lutheran Church Archives of Metropolitan New York
Wagner College Library
Staten Island, NY 10301
(718) 271-2466

Lutheran Church—Missouri Synod
1333 South Kirkwood Road
Saint Louis, MO 63122-7295
http://www.lcms.org

Lutheran Historical Society
61 Seminary Ridge
Gettysburg, PA 17325
C. H. Glatfelter, Director Emeritus (contact withheld)
(no archives and no library)

The Lutheran Historical Society of Eastern Pennsylvania
(Krauth Memorial Library, Lutheran Archives Center at Philadelphia—corporate location)
7301 Germantown Avenue (mailing address)
Philadelphia, PA 19119-1794
(215) 248-6383; (215) 248-6327 FAX
John E. Peterson, Society Curator
Tue & Fri 1:30–5:00
Pub. *The Periodical*, semiannually (Apr, Oct)
("The Society holds no church records and does not provide genealogical services. Contact the Lutheran Archives Center at Philadelphia for further information.")
$7.50 per year membership

Lutheran Theological Seminary
A. R. Wentz Library
Gettysburg, PA 17325
Sara Mummert
(some data about Lutheran records in central Pennsylvania; library not open to genealogists; microfilm copies of the records are available through the Family

History Library of The Church of Jesus Christ of Latter-day Saints)

Lutherans Online
Genealogy Exchange
http://www.lutheransonline.com/lutheransonline/genealogy

Pacific Lutheran University
Robert A. L. Mortvedt Library
Tacoma, WA 98447
(253) 535-7586
http://www.plu.edu/libr/services.html;
http://www.plu.edu/libr.siec.html
(Scandinavian Immigrant Experience Collection); http://www.plu.edu/libr/archives (Archives)

Perry County Lutheran Historical Society of Altenburg, Inc.
PO Box 53
Altenburg, MO 63732
(573) 824-5542
Leonard A. Kuehnert, President
by appointment
("Lutheran Church, Missouri Synod has its roots in the Saxon Immigration to Perry County in 1839. Altenburg has the first Lutheran seminary building [now a museum] west of the Mississippi River. We have books for sale about the history of our 1839 settlements as these were centered in the Lutheran Church.")

Saint Peter Lutheran Church Museum
208 East Schaumburg Road
Schaumburg, IL 60194
(847) 843-0799

Swenson Swedish Immigration Research Center
(Augustana Lutheran Church [Swedish], Evangelical Covenant Church, Swedish Baptist Conference, Swedish Methodist Church, Evangelical Free Church, and Swedish Episcopal; see Ethnic Archives, Libraries and Societies—Swedish, Part 3)

University of New Orleans
Earl K. Long Library/Louisiana and Special Collections
(see Louisiana, Part 2)

Wartburg Theological Seminary
Archives
333 Wartburg Place
Dubuque, IA 52003
(563) 589-0320; (563) 589-0333 FAX
bwiederaenders@wartburgseminary.edu
Robert C. Wiederaenders, Archivist
morning only
("My expertise is Lutheran Church in America records. We have records of over 200 congregations here and access to 5,000 congregations on microfilm. I serve both Wartburg Seminary and Region 5 of the ELCA [twelve synods in Iowa, Illinois, Wisconsin and Upper Michigan].")
research: first half-hour is free

Wisconsin Evangelical Lutheran Synod (WELS) Historical Institute
2929 North Mayfair Road
Milwaukee, WI 53222
(414) 256-3201
http://www.wels.net
Dr. James G. Kiecker
by appointment
Pub. *Wels Historical Institute Journal*, two times per year

Lutheran Church in America
(see Lutheran)

Lutheran Church—Missouri Synod
(see Lutheran)

Malankara Orthodox Syrian Church
(see Orthodox)

Mariavite
(see Old Catholic)

Maronite Catholic
(see Orthodox)

Mar Thoma Orthodox Syrian Church (Indian Orthodox)
(see Orthodox)

Mennonite
(see Church of God in Christ, Mennonite)

Mennonite Brethren in Christ
(see Missionary Church)

Methodist
(see also Lutheran, Free Methodist and United Methodist)

World Methodist Council
(575 Lakeshore Drive—location)
PO Box 518 (mailing address)
Lake Junaluska, NC 28745
(828) 456-9432
georgefreeman@mindspring.com
Dr. George H. Freeman, General Secretary
Pub. *World Parish*, quarterly

Methodist Episcopal
(see United Methodist)

Methodist Protestant
(see United Methodist)

Millerites
(see Adventist)

Mission Synod
(see Evangelical Free Church of America)

Missionary Baptist Convention of America
(see Baptist)

Missionary Church
(see also Church of God in Christ, Mennonite)

Formed with the merger of the Missionary Church Association and the United Missionary Church, which was formerly known as the Mennonite Brethren in Christ.

Missionary Church
(3811 Vanguard Drive—location)
PO Box 9127 (mailing address)
Fort Wayne, IN 46899-9127
http://www.mcusa.org

Moravian
(see also Ethnic Archives, Libraries and Societies—Czech, Part 3)

Morava Krasna
151 Colebrook Drive
Rochester, NY 14617-2215
(585) 342-9383; (585) 342-0443 FAX
helenezx@aol.com
Helene Cincebeaux, Editor
Pub. *Morava Krasna*
(Database of some 5,000 listings of epople with Moravian heritage.)

Moravian Archives, Southern Province
(457 South Church Street, Winston-Salem, NC 27101—location)
PO Box L (mailing address)
Winston Salem, NC 27108-0377
(910) 722-1742
nblum@mcsp.org
http://moravianarchives.org
Rev. Dr. C. Daniel Crews, Archivist
Mon–Fri 9:30–noon & 1:30–4:30
Pub. *Annotations*, semiannually, distributed to Friends who have given to the Archives
("We are not a lending library; we do not photocopy our records.")
research: $15.00 per hour

The Moravian Archives
West Locust Street
Bethlehem, PA 18018-2757
(610) 866-3255
Vernon H. Nelson, Archivist; Albert H. Frank, Assistant Archivist
Mon–Fri 8:00–noon & 1:00–4:00, by appointment only, call ahead
("We do not have a large enough staff to do research for a fee.")

Moravian Church (Unitas Fratrumj)
(1021 Center Street—location)
PO Box 1245 (mailing address)
Bethlehem, PA 18016-1245
http://www.moravian.org

The Moravian Heritage Society
17907 Kuykendahl Suite 202
Spring, TX 77379
(281) 251-7690; (281) 251-7691 FAX
thrncirik@aol.com
http://Czechusa.com
Thomas Hrncinik, A.G., and Helene Cincebeaux, Co-directors
Pub. *Morava Krasna*, quarterly
$10.00 per year membership

Moravian Historical Society
Whitefield House
214 East Center Street
Nazareth, PA 18064
(610) 759-5070; (610) 759-2461 FAX
http://www.moravianhistoricalsociety.org
Susan M. Dreydoppel, Executive Director
Moravian Historical Museum: Mon–Sun 1:00–4:00, and by appointment
Pub. *Transactions of the Moravian Historical Society*, biennially (Oct of even years); *Moravian Historian*, quarterly
$25.00 per year membership

Moravian Museums and Tours
66 West Church Street
Bethlehem, PA 18018
(610) 867-0173; (610) 694-0960 FAX
Rebecca Hordis, Collections Manager
Mon–Fri 9:00–5:00
Pub. *Moravian Museum of Bethlehem News*, quarterly

Tuscarawas County Chapter OGS
Tuscarawas County Genealogical Society, Inc.
(see Ohio, Part 2)

Mormon
(see The Church of Jesus Christ of Latter-day Saints)

Muslim
(see Islam)

National Association of Free Will Baptists
(see Baptist)

National Baptist Convention, U.S.A., Inc.
(see Baptist)

National Missionary Baptist Convention of America
(see Baptist)

National Organization of the New Apostolic Church of North America
(see Episcopal)

Nation of Islam
(see Islam)

Nazarene
(see Church of the Nazarene)

Netherlands Reformed Congregations in North America
(see Reformed)

New Organization
(see The Church of Jesus Christ of Latter-day Saints)

NNew Apostolic Church of North America
(see Episcopal)

Non-Chalcedonian Churches
(see Orthodox)

North American Baptist Conference
(see Baptist)

North American Old [Roman] Catholic
(see Old Catholic)

Norwegian-Danish Evangelical Free Church Association
(see Evangelical Free Church of America)

Norwegian Lutheran Church of America
(see Lutheran)

Old Catholic

The Old Catholic Church broke with the Roman Catholic Church in the late 19th century. It subsequently split into the Old Catholic Church of America, the Old Roman Catholic Church of North America, the North American Old Catholic Church, the North American Old Roman Catholic Church, the Old Roman Catholic Church

(English Rite), the Polish National Catholic Church of America, the Apostolic Catholic Orthodox Church and the Mariavite Old Catholic Church, Province of North America.

Apostolic Orthodox Catholic Church (North American Old Catholic)
(7100 Regency Square, Suite 210
Houston, TX 77036-3202
(713) 977-2855; (713) 266-2456; (713) 266-0845 FAX
http://www.apostoliccatholic.org

Old Catholic Church of America
409 North Lexington Parkway
DeForest, WI 53532
http://www.oldcatholic.org

Old Roman Catholic Church of North America
1207 Potomac Place
Louisville, KY 40214
http://www.orccna.org

Polish National Catholic Church Commission on History and Archives
1031 Cedar Avenue
Scranton, PA 18505
http://www.pgsa.org/pncc.htm

Polish National Catholic Church of America
1006 Pittston Avenue
Scranton, PA 18505
http://www.pncc.org

Old German Baptist Brethren
(see also Brethren)

Old German Baptist Brethren
6952 North Montgomery County Line Road
Englewood, OH 45322-9748
http://www.cob-net.org/docs/groups.htm

Old Order Amish Churches
(see Church of God in Christ, Mennonite)

Old Order (Wisler) Mennonite Church
(see Church of God in Christ, Mennonite)

Old Roman Catholic
(see Old Catholic)

Open Bible Standard Churches

Open Bible Standard Churches
2020 Bell Avenue
Des Moines, IA 50315
http://www.openbible.org

Oriental Orthodox Churches
(see Orthodox)

Orthodox

Churches in communion with the Roman Catholic Church are called Eastern Rite Catholic or Uniate Churches: Patriarchate of Alexandria, the Patriarchate of Antioch, the Patriarchate of Constantinople, the Patriarchate of Jerusalem, and the Orthodox Churches of Albania, Bulgaria, the Czech and Slovak Republics, Cyprus, Georgia, Greece, Poland, Romania, Russia, Serbia and some from Syria. Non-Chalcedonian or Oriental Orthodox Churches include the Alexandrian (Copts and Ethiopians), Antiochene (Maronites, Syrians,

Malankarese), Armenian, Chaldean (Chaldean and Malabarese) and Byzantine (Hungarian, Yugoslav, Melkites, Ukranian). Other churches trace their roots to the Orthodox bodies, such as the African Orthodox Church, the Holy Eastern Orthodox and Apostolic Church in North America.

African Orthodox Church
137 Alston Street, N.W.
Cambridge, MA 02139

Albanian Orthodox Archdiocese of America
523 East Broadway
South Boston, MA 02127
http://www.oca.org/oca/al
Pub. *The True Light*, monthly

American Carpatho-Russian Orthodox Greek Catholic Church
312 Garfield Street
Johnstown, PA 15906
(814) 536-4207
http://www.goarch.org
Msgr. John Yurisin, Diocesan Vicar
9:00–5:00
Pub. *The Church Messenger*, biweekly, $12.00 per year subscription

Antiochian Orthodox Christian Archdiocese of North America
(358 Mountain Road—location)
PO Box 5238 (mailing address)
Englewood, NJ 07631-5238
(201) 871-1355; (201) 871-7954 FAX
archdiocese@antiochian.org
http://www.antiochian.org
The Very Reverend George S. Corey, Vicar General
9:00–5:30
Pub. *The Word*, ten times per year (monthly, except July–Aug), $3.00 per issue, $20.00 per year subscription in the U.S. and Canada, $26.00 per year foreign subscription

Holy Apostolic Catholic Assyrian Church of the East, North American Dioceses
Patriarchate
7201 North Ashland
Chicago, IL 60626
(773) 465-4777; (847) 966-0012 FAX
http://www.cired.org/aceov.html

Armenian Apostolic Church of America
138 East 39th Street
New York, NY 10016-4885
http://www.armprelacy.org

Armenian Church of North America, Western Diocese
1201 North Vine Street
Hollywood, CA 90038
(323) 466-5265
Archbishop Vatche Hovsepian

Bulgarian Eastern Orthodox Church
550-A West 50th Street
New York, NY 10019

Byzantine Catholic Seminary Library
3605 Perrysville Avenue
Pittsburgh, PA 15214
(412) 321-8383
Rev. John S. Custer, S.T.D., Librarian
by appointment

Byzantine Rite Eparchy of Parma
1900 Carlton Road
Cleveland, OH 44134-3129

Mr. Pataki

Coptic Orthodox Church
PO Box 384
Cedar Grove, NJ 07009
http://www.nacopticchurch.org

Diocese of Saint Nicholas
2245 West Rice Street
Chicago, IL 60622

Diocese of the Armenian Church of America
630 Second Avenue
New York, NY 10016
(212) 686-0710; (212) 686-0245 FAX
info@armenianchurch.org
http://www.armenianchurch.org
Very Reverend Father Krikor Maksoudian
Mon–Fri 9:00–5:00
Pub. *The Armenian Church (Hagastanyants Yegeghestsi)*, monthly

Eparchy of Van Nuys
5335 Sepulveda Boulevard
Van Nuys, CA 91411

Greek Orthodox Archdiocese, North and South America
8-10 East 79th Street
New York, NY 10021
(212) 628-2500
http://www.goarch.org
Miss Niki Calle, Archivist
Pub. *Orthodox Observer*, biweekly

Holy Cross Romanian Orthodox Church
950 Maple Street
Hermitage, PA 16146
(724) 346-3151
Rev. Fr. Nathaniel Popp, Pastor

Holy Eastern Orthodox and Apostolic Church in North America, Inc.
HC 74, Box 419-2
Mountain View, AR 72560
http://www.theocacna.org

Malankara Orthodox Syrian Church
80-34 Commonwealth Boulevard
Bellerose, NY 11426
http://www.marlankara.org/american.html

Mar Thoma Orthodox Syrian Church (Indian Orthodox)
2320 South Merrick Avenue
Merrick, NY 11566
http://www.marthomachurch.org

Metropolitan Archdiocese of Pittsburgh, Byzantine
Byzantine Catholic World
66 Riverview Avenue
Pittsburgh, PA 15214-2253

Orthodox Church in America
(6850 Northern Boulevard, Route 25A, Oyster Bay Cove—location)
PO Box 675 (mailing address)
Syosset, NY 11791
(516) 922-0550
Alexis Liberovsky, Archivist
Mon–Fri 9:00–5:00 by appointment
("We have in our repository the records of the central administration of the Orthodox Church in America dating back to 1840, as well as about thirty collections of personal papers of various bishops, clergy and other active churchmen. Also included in our collection are the records of a few church related organizations as well as periodicals, books and video

tapes. However, genealogical material in our collection is limited since metrical books (church records, baptisms, funerals, weddings), with a few exceptions, are usually kept and maintained by the local parishes. We are, however, able to provide genealogical data on our clergy. I would be able also to refer researchers to the appropriate parish.")

Orthodox Church in America (Russian Orthodox)
PO Box 675
Syosset, NY 11791-0675
http://www.oca.org

Romanian American Heritage Center
(see Ethnic Archives, Libraries and Societies—Romanian, Part 3)

Romanian Orthodox Episcopate of America
2535 Grey Tower Road
Jackson, MI 49201-9120
http://www.roeg.org

Russian Orthodox Church Outside of Russia
75 East 93rd Street
New York, NY 10128
http://www.rocor.org

Saint Ephrem Educational Center
1555 South Meridian Road
Youngstown, OH 44511
(330) 792-1532
Helen Catherman, Librarian
Pub. *Saint Ephrem Quarterly*
(Maronite Catholic)

Saint Josaphat's Ukrainian Catholic Seminary
201 Taylor Street, N.E.
Washington, DC 20017-1097
(202) 529-1177
Msgr. John Bura, Rector
9:00–5:00

Saint Mary Protectress
1745 Washington Avenue
Bronx, NY 10457

Saint Peter's Armenian Church
110 Troy-Schenectady Road
Watervliet, NY 12189
(518) 274-3673

Serbian Eastern Orthodox Church in the U.S.A and Canada
Office of External Affairs
2311 M Street, N.W., Suite 402
Washington, DC 20037
http://oea.serbian-church.net

Syrian (Syriac) Orthodox Church of Antioch
Archdiocese of the Eastern United States
260 Elm Avenue
Teaneck, NJ 07661
http://www.syrianorthodoxchurch.org

Ukrainian Catholic Diocese
161 Glenbrook Road
Stamford, CT 06902

Ukrainian Catholic Eparchy of Philadelphia
815 North Franklin Street
Philadelphia, PA 19123

Ukrainian Orthodox Church of the U.S.A.
135 Davidson Avenue

Somerset, NJ 08873
http://www.ucofusa.org

Orthodox Church in America (Russian Orthodox)
(see Orthodox)

Orthodox Presbyterian Church
(see Presbyterian)

Patriarchal Parishes of the Russian Orthodox Church in the USA
(see Orthodox)

Pennsylvania Ministerium
(see Lutheran)

Pentecostal
(see Assemblies of God; Assemblies of the Lord Jesus Christ; Bible Way Church of Our Lord Jesus Christ; Christian Catholic Church; Christian Church of North America; Church of God [Cleveland, Tennessee]; Church of God in Christ; Church of Our Lord Jesus Christ of the Apostolic Faith; Church of the Living God [Christian Workers for Fellowship]; Church of the Living God [The Pillar and Ground of the Truth, Inc.]; Congregational Holiness Church; Elim Fellowship; Full Gospel Fellowship of Churches and Ministers; Independent Assemblies of God, International; International Church of the Foursquare Gospel; International Pentecostal Church of Christ; International Pentecostal Holiness Church; Open Bible Standard Churches; Pentecostal Assemblies of the World; Pentecostal Church of God; Pentecostal Free Will Baptist Church; United Holy Church of America; United Pentecostal Church International; and Vineyard Churches)

Church of the Living God (The Pillar and Ground of the Truth, Inc.)
4520 Ashland City Highway
Nashville, TN 37208
http://www.clgpgt.org

Church of the Living God (Christian Workers for Fellowship)
430 Forest Avenue
Cincinnati, OH 45229

House of God, Which is the Church of the Living God, the Pillar and Ground of the Truth
866 Georgetown Street
Lexington, KY 40508
webmaster@houseofgod.org
http://www.houseofgod.org

Pentecostal Assemblies of the World, Inc.

Pentecostal Assemblies of the World, Inc.
3939 Meadows Drive
Indianapolis, IN 46205
http://members.tripod.com/paw_inc/index.html

Pentecostal Church of God

Pentecostal Church of God
(4901 Pennsylvania—location)
PO Box 850 (mailing address)
Joplin, MO 64802
http://www.pcg.org

Pentecostal Free Will Baptist Church

Pentecostal Free Will Baptist Church, Inc.
(1200 Bud Hawkins Road, Dunn, NC 28334—location)
PO Box 1568 (mailing address)
Dunn, NC 28335
(910) 892-4161; (888) 668-9362; (910) 892-6876 FAX
pholmes@intrstar.net
http://www.pfwb.org
Paula Holmes, Administrative Assistant
Mon–Fri 9:00–5:00
(Site includes a "church locater.")

Pentecostal Union
(see Pillar of Fire)

Pietist
(see Brethren and Covenant)

Pilgrim Holiness Church
(see Wesleyan Church)

Pillar of Fire
(formerly Pentecostal Union; see also United Methodist)

Pillar of Fire
PO Box 9159
Zarephath, NJ 08890
http://www.gospelcom.net/pof

Plymouth Brethren
(see Brethren)

Polish National Catholic Church of America
(see Old Catholic)

Presbyterian

In 1810 some Presbyterians withdrew from the Church in Tennessee to form the Cumberland Presbyterians. In 1837 another schism took place between "New School" and "Old School." Four "New School" synods were expelled and coalesced into a separate General Assembly. The remainder became the Presbyterian Church in the U.S.A. (PCUSA). An 1858 merger between the Associate Presbyterian Church and much of the Associate Reformed Presbyterian Church formed the United Presbyterian Church of North America (UPCNA). During the Civil War Southern "New School" Presbyterians formed the United Synod of the Presbyterian Church, and "Old School" advocates formed the Presbyterian Church in the Confederate States of America. After the war, New and Old School reunited to form the Presbyterian Church in the United States (PCUS), whose offices were centralized under the General Assembly Mission Board. In the North, the two schools had been holding separate general assemblies during the war, but they joined together in 1870 as the Presbyterian Church in the U.S.A. (PCUSA), assuming some of the Cumberland Presbyterians, and later admitting both the Welsh Calvinist Methodists and the United Presbyterian Church of North America (UPCNA) to become the United Presbyterian Church in the U.S.A. (UPCUSA). In 1983 the northern UPCUSA merged with the southern PCUS to form the Presbyterian Church (U.S.A), the largest Presbyterian group. Other

Presbyterian groups exist outside the mainstream, including the Associate Reformed Presbyterian Church, the Cumberland Presbyterian Church, the Cumberland Presbyterian Church in America, the Evangelical Presbyterian Church (EPC), the Korean-American Presbyterian Church, the Orthodox Presbyterian Church, the Presbyterian Church in America and the Reformed Presbyterian Church of North America. It's essential to determine what modern denomination incorporates a given historical congregation. The Presbyterian Church of America was an independently formed fundamentalist church, which divided into the Orthodox Presbyterian Church and the Bible Presbyterian Church. The latter was a principal in the American Council of Christian Churches.

The Amistad Research Center
American Home Missionary Society Collection
(see Ethnic Archives, Libraries and Societies—African-American, Part 3)

Associate Reformed Presbyterian Church
3132 Grace Hill Road
Columbia, SC 29204
http://www.arpsynod.org

Bible Presbyterian Church
webmaster@bpc.org
http://www.bpc.org
(Site lists individual congregations.)

Columbia Theological Seminary
John Bulow Campbell Library
701 Columbia Drive
Decatur, GA 30030
(404) 378-8821
Mon–Thur 8:30–10:00, Fri 8:30–6:00, Sat 9:00–5:00
(Southern Presbyterianism; "We have almost nothing to help with genealogical research; our collection is for ministerial training.")

Cumberland Presbyterian Church
78 Union Avenue
Memphis, TN 38104
http://www.cumberland.org

Cumberland Presbyterian Church in America
226 Church Street
Huntsville, AL 35801
http://www.cumberland.org/cpca

Evangelical Presbyterian Church (EPC)
29140 Buckingham Avenue, Suite 5
Livonia, MI 48154
http://www.epc.org

Hanover College
Duggan Library
PO Box 287
Hanover, IN 47243-0287
(812) 866-7164; (812) 866-7172 FAX
Dennis K. Kovener, Assistant Librarian
Mon–Thur 7:45 A.M.–11:00 P.M., Fri 7:45 A.M.–10:00 P.M., Sat 10:00 A.M.–10:00 P.M., Sun 1:00 P.M.–11:00 P.M.
(records of the Presbyterian Church in Indiana)

Historical Foundation of the Cumberland Presbyterian Church and the Cumberland Presbyterian Church in America
1978 Union Avenue
Memphis, TN 38104-4134

(901) 276-8602; (901) 272-3913 FAX
archives@cumberland.org
http://www.cumberland.org/hfcpc
Susan Knight Gore, Director
by appointment
(Cumberland Presbyterian, 1810 to the present)

King College
E. W. King Library
1350 King College Road
Bristol, TN 37620
(423) 652-4790; (423) 652-4871 FAX
library@king.edu
http://www.king.edu/library
Matthew S. Peltier, Library Director
Mon–Sun
(local presbytery records)

Korean American Presbyterian Church
2853 West Seventh Street
Los Angeles, CA 90005
(213) 389-9133; (213) 389-6133 FAX
http://www.kapc.org

Korean Presbyterian Church in America
(280 Fairfield Place—location)
PO Box 457 (mailing address)
Morganville, NJ 07951
(714) 816-1100; (908) 591-2260 FAX
("This body was founded in 1976 with the union of three presbyteries of Korean immigrant churches affiliated with the Presbyterian Church of Korea [TongHap] before deciding to become an independent national body. The church cooperates closely in mission with the Korean Christian Church in Japan and the Presbyterian Church [USA].")

North Carolina Presbyterian Historical Society
Trinity Presbyterian Church
607 Hospital Road
Starkville, MS 39759-2119
(601) 323-9340
Dr. James D. MacLeod, Jr.
Pub. *Sketches of North Carolina*

Orthodox Presbyterian Church
(607 North Easton Road, Building E—location)
Box P (mailing address)
Willow Grove, PA 19090-0920

Presbyterian Church Archives
Union Theological Seminary in Virginia
3401 Brook Road
Richmond, VA 23227
(804) 355-0671; (804) 378-4375 FAX
http://leo.vsla.edu/reposit/sites/uts.html
Mon–Fri 8:30 A.M.–11:00 P.M., Sat 8:30–5:00 (when school is in session, except closed for Thanksgiving, Christmas and Easter vacations); summer: Mon–Fri 8:30–5:00, Sat 8:30–1:00
(Microfilm records of local Presbyterian churches in Virginia, as of 1985. "We no longer provide any family history services.")

Presbyterian Church in America
1852 Century Place
Atlanta, GA 30345-4305
http: www.pcanet.org

Presbyterian Church (U.S.A.)
100 Witherspoon Street
Louisville, KY 40202
http://www.pcusa.org

Presbyterian Historical Church, Montreat

Office
(318 Georgia Terrace [at Assembly Drive]—location)
PO Box 849 (mailing address)
Montreat, NC 28757
(828) 669-7061
wbynum@history.pcusa.org
http://www.history.pcusa.org
William B. Bynum, Assistant Director for Reference
Mon–Fri 8:30–4:30, except holidays
(specializes in Presbyterian Church records from southern states; organization formerly known as Historical Foundation of the Presbyterian and Reformed Churches)
$40.00 per year membership; admission: $5.00 for nonmembers

Presbyterian Historical Society
Reference Services
425 Lombard Street
Philadelphia, PA 19147-1516
(215) 627-1852; (215) 627-0509 FAX
refdesk@history.pcusa.org
http://www.history.pcusa.org
Mon–Fri 8:30–4:30 by appointment (except holidays)
Pub. *American Presbyterians, Journal of Presbyterian History*, quarterly
$15.00 per year membership; research: no service, but will refer inquiries to professionals

Princeton Theological Seminary Libraries
(Library Place and Mercer Street—location)
PO Box 111 (mailing address)
Princeton, NJ 08542-0803
(609) 497-7950
http://www.ptsem.edu/grow/library/index.htm

Reformed Presbyterian Church of North America
7408 Penn Avenue
Pittsburgh, PA 15208
http://www.reformedpresbyterian.org

San Francisco Theological Seminary
Library
105 Seminary Road
San Anselmo, CA 94960

Presbyterian Church in America
(see Presbyterian)

Presbyterian Church in the Confederate States of America
(see Presbyterian)

Presbyterian Church in the U.S.A. (PCUSA)
(see Presbyterian)

Presbyterian Church in the United States (PCUS)
(see Presbyterian)

Presbyterian Church of America
(see Presbyterian)

Presbyterian Church (U.S.A)
(see Presbyterian)

Primitive Baptist
(see Baptist)

Primitive Methodist Church in the U.S.A.
(formerly Society of the Primitive Methodists; see also United Methodist)

Primitive Methodist Church in the U.S.A.
1045 Laurel Run Road
Wilkes-Barre, PA 18702
http://www.primitivemethodistchurch.org

Progressive Convention of the Tunker Church
(see Brethren)

Progressive National Baptist Convention
(see Baptist)

Protestant

Almost all trinitarian denominations, except the Orthodox and Roman Catholic, are considered Protestant.

Protestant Reformed Churches in America
(see Reformed)

Billy Graham Center
Wheaton College
500 College Avenue
Wheaton, IL 60187-5593
(630) 752-5910 (The Archives)
bgcarc@wheaton.edu
http://www.wheaton.edu/bgc/archives/
archhpl.html
Wayne D. Weber, Reference Archivist
Mon–Fri 10:00–5:00, Sat 10:00–2:00
Pub. *Centerline* (general); *Witness* (The Archives), three times per year online; *Resource Notes* (Library)
("The Archives focus on the history of nondenominational Protestant missions and evangelism. Personnel files of missionary organizations.")
Archives admission: free

Protestant Episcopal
(see Episcopal)

The Province of Christ the King
(see Episcopal)

Quaker
(see Religious Society of Friends [Quakers])

Radio Church of God
(see Worldwide Church of God)

Reformed
(see also Church of God in Christ, Mennonite, Evangelical, Presbyterian and United Church of Christ)

The Reformed Church in America is of Dutch origin. The Christian Reformed Church in North America (CRC) broke with the parent organization in 1850. The Protestant Reformed Churches in America was formed from the CRC, and still later, the Netherlands Reformed Congregations in North America also broke with the CRC. The Reformed Church in Hungary became the Reformed Church in the United States and its autonomous branch, the Free Magyar Reformed Church in America, which became

the Hungarian Reformed Church in America. Most of the Reformed Church in the United States merged with the Evangelical and Reformed Church, which later joined with the Congregational Christian Churches to form the United Church of Christ. Part, however, survived the merger.

Calvin College
Christian Reformed Church
3201 Burton, S.E.
Grand Rapids, MI 49506
(616) 957-6000
(Dutch-American settlement in western Michigan, church history)

Christian Reformed Church in North America (CRC)
2850 Kalamazoo Avenue, S.E.
Grand Rapids, MI 49560
http://www.crcna.org

Hungarian Reformed Church in America
13 Grove Street
Poughkeepsie, NY 12601
http://www.calvinsynod.org

Netherlands Reformed Congregations in North America
1261 Beckwith, N.E.
Grand Rapids, MI 49505
http://home.earthlink.net/~vogelaar/nrc/
church.htm

Protestant Reformed Churches in America
4949 Ivanrest Avenue
Grandville, MI 49418
http://www.prca.org

Reformed Church in America
Office of the General Secretary
475 Riverside Drive, 18th Floor
New York, NY 10115
http://www.rca.org

Reformed Church in the United States
6121 Pine Vista Way
Elk Grove, CA 95758
http://www.rcus.org

Historical Society Reformed Church of America
21 Seminary Place
New Brunswick, NJ 08901
(732) 246-1779 (Archives)
rgasero@aol.com
http://www.rca.org/resource/archives
Russell L. Gasero, Archivist
by appointment only
research: $25.00 per hour

Reformed Church in America
(see Reformed)

Reformed Church in North America
(see Reformed)

Reformed Church in the United States
(see Reformed and United Church of Christ)

Reformed Episcopal Church
(see Episcopal)

Reformed Methodist Union Episcopal Church
(see Churches of Christ in Christian Union)

Reformed Presbyterian Church of North America
(see Presbyterian)

Religious Society of Friends (Quakers)

Groups with various numbers of yearly meetings, monthly meetings and regional associations are Friends General Conference, Friends United Meeting, Religious Society of Friends (Conservative) or Wilburites, Evangelical Friends Alliance, and, most recently, the Evangelical Friends International—North American Region.

Archives of the New England Yearly Meeting of Friends
Rhode Island Historical Society
121 Hope Street
Providence, RI 02906
(401) 331-8575; (401) 751-7930 FAX
neym@rihs.org
Marnie Miller-Gutsell, NEYM Archivist
Tue–Sat 9:00–5:00; appointments required to view original records
(Most records available on microfilm in the Rhode Island Historical Society Library)
free admission; research: $35.00 for the first hour and $30.00 for each additional hour for members of the Rhode Island Historical Society, $45.00/$40.00 for nonmembers

Baltimore Yearly Meeting of the Religious Society of Friends
Baltimore Monthly Meeting of Friends, Stony Run
5116 North Charles Street
Baltimore, MD 21210
(410) 435-3773; (410) 435-3779 FAX
Ronald Mattson, Executive Secretary; Mary Dunlap, Archivist
9:00–3:00

National Society, Descendants of Early Quakers
(see Lineage, Hereditary and Patriotic Societies, Part 4)

Earlham College
Friends Collection
Lilly Library
801 National Road West
Richmond, IN 47374
(765) 983-1511
tomh@earlham.edu
http://www.earlham.edu/www/library/
files/tour/about.htm
Thomas D. Hamm, Archivist and Curator
Mon–Fri 9:00–noon & 1:00–4:00, some evenings and weekends
(specializes in Friends of Wayne County, Indiana; Quakers in the Midwest; and Quaker genealogy)

The East Tennessee Society for the Preservation of Friends (Quaker) History
An Affiliate of the East Tennessee Historical Society
2429 Brook Road
Greenback, TN 37742
Scott Knight, Secretary
$5.00 per year membership

Evangelical Friends International—North American Region
1975 Raisin Center Highway
Adrian, MI 49221
http://www.evangelical-friends.org

George Fox College
Quaker Collection
Shambaugh Library
Newberg, OR 97132

Friends General Conference (FGC)
Religious Society of Friends
1216 Arch Street, 2B
Philadelphia, PA 19107
(215) 561-1700
http://www.fgcquaker.org
Jennifer Stromsten, Development Secretary
Pub. *Friends Journal*, twenty times per year
(does not keep historical records or archives,
but has a bookstore for people to learn
about Quaker history and heritage)

Friends United Meeting
101 Quaker Hill Drive
Richmond, IN 47374-1980
http://www.fum.org

Friends University
Edmund Stanley Library
Quaker Collection
2100 West University Avenue
Wichita, KS 67213-3397
(316) 261-5880
pappas@friends.edu
http://www.friends.edu/Library/
     SpecialCollections/histori_photos.asp
Avis German, Acting Curator; David Pappas,
     Director
Mon, Wed & Fri 8:00–4:00

The Gene Pool
(see Computer Interest, Part 4)

Genealogical Society of Pennsylvania
(see Pennsylvania, Part 2)

Guilford College
Hege Library
Friends Historical Collection
5800 West Friendly Avenue
Greensboro, NC 27410-4175
(336) 316-2264
hegefhc@guilford.edu
http://www.guilford.edu/library/fhc
Gwen Erickson, Librarian and College
     Archivist
Tue–Fri 9:00–noon & 2:00–5:00
Pub. *The Southern Friend: Journal of the
     North Carolina Friends Historical
     Society*, semiannually
$10.00 suggested donation

Haverford College
Friends Historical Association
Haverford College Library
370 Lancaster Avenue
Haverford, PA 19041-1392
(610) 896-1161; (610) 896-1102 FAX
fha@haverford.edu
Joelle Bertolet, Office Manager
Mon–Fri 9:00–12:30 & 1:30–4:30 (holidays
     and summer until 4:00)
Pub. *Quaker History*, semiannually (spring
     and fall)
(Religious Society of Friends-Quakers)
$15.00 per year membership

Haverford College
The Quaker Collection
Haverford College Library
370 Lancaster Avenue
Haverford, PA 19041-1392
(610) 896-1161; (610) 896-1102 FAX
genalog@haverford.edu
http://www.haverford.edu/library/sc
Joelle Bertolet, Executive Assistant
Mon–Fri 9:00–12:30 & 1:30–4:30 (holidays

     & summer until 4:00)
(Religious Society of Friends-Quakers
     resources)
research: a half-hour free

New York Yearly Meeting
(see Swarthmore College, Friends Historical
Library of Swarthmore College, below)

**Historical Committee of the Yearly
Meeting**
Route 2
Barnesville, OH 43713

Historical Society of Pennsylvania
(see Pennsylvania, Part 2)

Honey Creek Church Preservation Group
(see Iowa, Part 2)

Indiana Historical Society
(see Indiana, Part 2)

Indiana University
Library
Bloomington, IN 47401

Malone College
Quaker Collection
Everett L. Cattell Library
515 25th Street, N.W.
Canton, OH 44709
(330) 471-8317; (330) 454-6977 FAX
Stanford Terhune, Director
Mon–Thur 8:00 A.M.–11:30 P.M., Fri
     8:00–10:00, Sat 10:00–10:00, Sun
     2:00–10:00
(Ohio Yearly Meeting, Evangelical Friends
     Church—Eastern Region)

Maryland State Archives
(see Maryland, Part 2)

**Historical Society of Mount Pleasant,
Ohio, Inc.**
(see Ohio, Part 2)

New Castle Historical Society
(see New York, Part 2)

Newport Historical Society
(see Rhode Island, Part 2)

North Carolina Friends Historical Society
PO Box 8502
Greensboro, NC 27419
ncfhs@ncfhs.org
http://www.ncfhs.org
Pub. *The Southern Friend: Journal of the
     NCFHS*, semiannually; *Newsletter*
$20.00 per year membership

Ohio Historical Society
(see Ohio, Part 2)

Pendle Hill Library
Pendle Hill
Wallingford, PA 19086

William Penn College
Quaker Collection
Wilcox Library
North Market Street
201 Trueblood Avenue
Oskaloosa, IA 52577
(641) 673-1096
Mon–Thur 8:00–10:00, Fri 8:00–5:00, Sat
     9:00–5:00, Sun noon–10:00

State Library of Pennsylvania
(see Pennsylvania, Part 2)

Quaker Corner
http://www.rootsweb.com/~quakers

Quaker Queries
(323 Cedarcrest Court, East—location)
PO Box 779 (mailing address)
Napavine, WA 98565-0779
(360) 262-3300
http://www.localaccess.com/rubym
Ruby Simonson McNeill
Pub. *Quaker Queries*, irregularly, $7.75
     postpaid per issue

Quaker Yeomen
2421 S.E. 54th Court
Hillsboro, OR 97123-8151
Patti Smith Lamb, Editor and Publisher
Pub. *Quaker Yeomen*, quarterly, $18.00 per
     year U.S. subscription, $24.00 per year
     foreign subscription

The Religious Society of Friends
http://quaker.org
(links and subscription mailing lists)

Rokeby Museum
(see Vermont, Part 2)

Swarthmore College
Friends Historical Library of Swarthmore
College
500 College Avenue
Swarthmore, PA 19081-1399
(610) 328-8496; (610) 328-7329 FAX
friends@swarthmore.edu
http://www.swarthmore.edu/library/friends
Mary Ellen Chijioke, Curator
Mon–Fri 8:30–4:30, Sat (when the college is
     in session) 9:00–noon (closed 1 Jan, 4
     July, Thanksgiving weekend & Christmas
     week)
Pub. *Guide to Manuscript Collections*
(Quaker history and genealogy, houses the
     collection of minutes and membership
     records and constituent meetings formerly
     held by the Haviland Records Room, New
     York Yearly Meeting)
SASE with inquiries

Union Township Historical Museum
Quaker Heritage Center
(see Ohio, Part 2)

University of Illinois
(see Illinois, Part 2)

Whittier College
Quaker Collection
Wardman Library
Whittier, CA 90608
(562) 907-4247
8:00–4:30

**Wrightsboro Quaker Community
Foundation, Inc.**
633 Hemlock Drive
Thomson, GA 30824
(706) 595-5584

Reorganized Church of Jesus Christ of Latter Day Saints
(see Community of Christ)

Republican Methodist
(formed in 1792 by Methodist followers of
James O'Kelly; see United Methodist)

Restorationists
(see Disciples of Christ)

River Brethren
(see Brethren)

Roman Catholic

(Roman Catholic church records useful to genealogical searchers of baptisms, marriages, and funerals are generally kept in the parishes or centralized in the chancery office of the appropriate diocese or archdiocese; see also Old Catholic and Orthodox.)

American Catholic Historical Association
(address withheld upon request)
(a society of professional historians, and a few amateurs; "This association does not provide genealogical research services of any kind.")

American Catholic Historical Society
PO Box 84
Philadelphia, PA 19105
(215) 925-5752
Philadelphia Archdiocesan Historical Research Center: Mon–Fri 9:00–4:00
Pub. *American Catholic Historical Society Records*, quarterly

Associated Archives
5400 Roland Avenue
Baltimore, MD 21210
(410) 864-7074
archives@stmarys.edu
Tricia Pyne, Director
Mon–Fri 8:30–4:30, by appointment only
("The Archives of the Archdiocese of Baltimore are now housed with the Archives of the Sulpician Priests and the Archives of Saint Mary's Seminary under the general title of Associated Archives. Original sacramental records of the Roman Catholic Archdiocese of Baltimore are kept in each individual parish rather than in our central archives. Microfilms of such records of about 75 parishes are available to the public at the Maryland State Archives. The records of closed Catholic parishes are usually available at the next nearest Catholic church. A few have been transferred to our central archives, but, due to their historical value, they can generally be viewed only on microfilm at the Maryland State Archives.")

Association of Catholic Diocesan Archivists
1100 Chartres Street
New Orleans, LA 70116-2596
(504) 529-2651; (504) 529-3075 FAX
archives@archdiocese-no.org
Dr. Charles E. Nolan, President
Pub. *ACDA Bulletin*, quarterly, $15.00 per year subscription

The Augustinians
Province of Our Mother of Good Counsel
20300 Governors Highway
Olympia Fields, IL 60461
(708) 748-9500
Province Secretary

Boston College
The John J. Burns Library
(see Massachusetts, Part 2)

Catholic Apostolic Administration of Asian Russia
1701 Hall Street
Hays, KS 67601-3199
(785) 625-6577 (school hours); (785) 625-

4483 (other hours); (785) 625-3912 FAX
tmpbb@fhsuvm.fhsu.edu
http://feefhs.org/fg/frg-lfs.html
Father Blaine Burkey of the Capuchin-Franciscan Order (O.F.M. Cap), Editor
Pub. *a letter from SIBERIA*, irregularly, archives online
(Siberia and the Russian Far East, and the Roman Catholic Church under the leadership of Bishop Joseph Werth, S.J., which serves several hundred thousand Germans, Poles, Ukrainians, Lithuanians, and other ethnic groups, most of whom were displaced from other parts of the then Commonwealth of Independent States [C.I.S.] during the Stalinist era)

Catholic Record Society—Diocese of Columbus
197 East Gay Street
Columbus, OH 43215
(614) 241-2571
http://www.colsdisc.org (under "offices")
Donald M. Schlegel, Vice Chairman/Secretary
Wed mornings
Pub. *Barquilla de la Santa Maria*, monthly, $25.00 per year institutional subscription
(Ohio east of a line drawn from Kenton to Portsmouth)
$15.00 per year membership; research by volunteers

The Catholic University of America
Department of Archives, Manuscripts and Museum Collections
5 Mullen Library
Washington, DC 20064
(202) 319-5065; (202) 319-4735 FAX
meagher@cua.edu
http://www.libraries.cua.edu/archives.html
Dr. Timothy Meagher, Archivist
Mon–Fri 9:00–5:00
(not a repository for records of baptism, marriage or burial, which are generally kept in the parishes or centralized in the chancery offices of the appropriate diocese or archdiocese; includes official depository for such organizations as the National Catholic Educational Association, the National Conference of Catholic Charities (now Catholic Charities USA), the National Councils of Catholic Women and Men, and the United States Catholic Conference & National Conference of Catholic Bishops, as well as Catholic University)

Cushwa Center for the Study of American Catholicism
Room 614, Hesburgh Library
University of Notre Dame
Notre Dame, IN 46556
(219) 631-5441; (219) 631-8471 FAX
cushwa.1@nd.edu
Barbara Lockwood, Assistant to the Director
8:00–5:00
Pub. *American Catholic Studies Newsletter*, semiannually (spring and fall), $12.00 for two-year subscription
(no archives, but passes everything on to the University of Notre Dame archives)

Diocesan Archives

Archdiocese for the Military Services
PO Box 4469
Washington, DC 20017-0469
(202) 269-9100; (202) 269-9022 FAX
info@milarch.org
http://www.milarch.org
Mr. Frank Calandra, Sacramental Records

Diocese of Birmingham
PO Box 12047
Birmingham, AL 35202-2047
Most Rev. David E. Foley, Bishop of Birmingham

The Archdiocese of Mobile Archives
(400 Government Street—location)
PO Box 1966 (mailing address)
Mobile, AL 36633
(334) 434-1583
Shirley Zieman, Archival Secretary
Mon & Wed 9:00–4:00
("Archival records of baptisms, marriages, and burials begin in 1704 and end in 1860 except for a few burial records which end in 1880; there are gaps in the records due to fires, hurricanes, war and itinerant missionaries, some of whom kept sketchy records or no records.")
$7.50 per hour research; $5.00 per copy of record

Diocese of Anchorage
225 Cordova Street
Anchorage, AK 99501
(907) 258-7898; (907) 279-3885 FAX
Brother Charles McBride, CSC, Archives Director
by appointment only
(history of archdiocese since 1966, Alaska since 1900)

Diocese of Fairbanks
1316 Peger Road
Fairbanks, AK 99709
(907) 474-0753; (907) 474-8009 FAX
Sr. Marilyn Marx, SNJM, Chancellor
Mon–Fri 8:30–4:30
research: $5.00

The Diocese of Phoenix
400 East Monroe
Phoenix, AZ 85004
(602) 257-0030
Mon–Fri 8:00–4:30

The Archives, Diocese of Tucson
8800 East 22nd Street
Tucson, AZ 85710
(520) 886-5201
Dan Brosnan, Archivist, Historian, Records Manager, and Museum Director
Tue–Thur 8:00–2:00

Diocese of Little Rock
(2415 North Tyler Street—location)
PO Box 7239 (mailing address)
Little Rock, AR 72217-7239
(501) 664-0340, ext. 366; (501) 664-9186 FAX
Sister Catherine Markey, Archivist
by appointment only

The Diocese of Los Angeles
Archival Center
15151 San Fernando Mission Boulevard
Mission Hills, CA 91345
(818) 365-1501; (818) 365-3276 FAX
Kevin Feeney, Adjunct Archivist and Records Manager
Mon–Fri 8:30–4:30

The Diocese of Monterey Archives
PO Box 2048
Monterey, CA 93942
(831) 373-2127, ext. 327; (831) 373-1175 FAX; (831) 373-3534 FAX
archives@dioceseofmonterey.org
by appointment only (please request family history form with which to make your request)

(sacramental registers: baptisms, confirmations, marriages, deaths for Old California missions: Carmel Mission, Carmel; San Antonio Mission, Jolon; San Juan Bautista Mission, San Juan Bautista; San Carlos Cathedral, Monterey; Mission Soledad, Soledad; San Luis Obispo Mission, San Luis Obispo; San Miguel Mission, San Miguel; Santa Cruz Mission, Santa Cruz)
$20.00 per search ("We do not have facilities for the public to do genealogical research. We ask interested parties to submit their request on a standard form which we provide free upon request. Results are mailed.")

Roman Catholic Diocese of Oakland Archives
3014 Lakeshore Avenue
Oakland, CA 94610-3615
(510) 893-4711; (510) 273-4946 FAX
Mary C. Batiza, Archivist
Tue 8:45–4:45
Pub. *The Catholic Voice* (Diocesan newspaper), biweekly
("All our sacramental records are kept at the parishes, not the archives.")

Diocese of Orange
990 Temple Terrace
Laguna Beach, CA 92651
(949) 494-9701
Rev. William Krekelberg, Archivist

Historical Archives of the Diocese of Sacramento
2110 Broadway
Sacramento, CA 95818-2541
(916) 733-0299 (no inquiries by phone, send letter with SASE)
Rev. William Breault, S.I., Archivist
by appointment
("Archives are parish and diocese-centered, 1850–1930, as contained in newspapers, baptismal, marriage, confirmation registers journals from the beginning of the diocese—and earlier; some original diaries and journals, information on early priests and bishops—and histories of the diocese.")
research: $50.00 and up for detailed search for names (includes photocopy, translation, sources)

Diocese of San Bernardino
1201 East Highland Avenue
San Bernardino, CA 92404-4641
(909) 384-8207
http://www.sbdiocese.org
Dr. R. Bruce Harley, Archivist
Tue & Thur 10:00–4:00
(established 1978, contact parent areas for older records)

The Diocese of San Diego
Mission San Diego de Alcala—Archive-Library
Mission San Diego Historical Society
10818 Mission San Diego Road
San Diego, CA 92108
(619) 283-6338; (619) 490-8200 (Diocesan Archives)
Sister Catherine Louise La Coste, C.S.J., Archivist-Librarian
Tue & Thur 10:00–noon; Diocesan Archives is not staffed and is closed to research except by appointment (PO Box 85728, San Diego, CA 92186)
Pub. *Newsletter—Mission San Diego Historical Society Quarterly*
(not only religious, lots of California history

and original documents, also Spanish, Mexican and American history, San Diego history from 1769 onward, and lots of Indian history for California and the California missions)
$10.00 per year membership; copies: 5¢ per page

Diocese of San Francisco
320 Middlefield Road
Menlo Park, CA 94025
(650) 328-6502
Dr. Jeffrey Burns, Archivist
Mon–Fri 10:00–4:00

Diocese of San Jose
Archives and Records
900 Lafayette Street, Suite 4
Santa Clara, CA 95126
(408) 292-7128
bentley@dsj.org
http://www.dsj.org
Bayne Bentley

Diocese of Santa Rosa
(547 B Street—location)
PO Box 1297 (mailing address)
Santa Rosa, CA 95402
(707) 545-7610
Msgr. James Pulskamp, Archivist

Diocese of Colorado Springs
29 West Kiowa Street
Colorado Springs, CO 80903
(719) 636-2345; (719) 636-1216
Sister J. Jacobsen, O.S.B., Archivist
Mon–Fri 1:00–4:00

Archives of the Archdiocese of Denver
Catholic Pastoral Center
1300 South Steele Street
Denver, CO 80210
(303) 722-4687; (303) 715-2037 FAX
libraryl@archden.org;
    greg.kail@archden.org
http://www.archden.org

Diocese of Pueblo
Catholic Pastoral Center
1001 North Grand Avenue
Pueblo, CO 81003
(719) 544-9861; (719) 544-5202 FAX
Lorraine Guerin, Archivist
8:00–noon & 1:00–5:00
research: $7.00 per hour

Diocese of Bridgeport
The Catholic Center
238 Jewett Avenue
Bridgeport, CT 06606-2892
(203) 372-4301
Rev. John Horgan, Archivist

Archdiocese of Hartford Archives
134 Farmington Avenue
Hartford, CT 06105
(860) 541-6491; (860) 541-6309 FAX
archives@aohct.org
Maria Medina, MS, Archivist
Mon–Fri 10:00–4:30 by appointment only
("An archives with information relative to the development of the Archdiocese of Hartford, its bishops, parishes, and priests. Sacramental records available on microfilm, originals kept in the local parishes. Access restrictions may apply to any collection.")
charge for photocopying

The Diocese of Norwich
(201 Broadway—location)
PO Box 587 (mailing address)

Norwich, CT 06360
(860) 887-9294
Rev. Msgr. Thomas R. Bride, V.G.
9:00–5:00
Pub. *Four County Catholic*, free

The Diocese of Wilmington Archives
(8 Old Church Road [at Route 100], Greenville, DE—location)
PO Box 2030 (mailing address)
Greenville, DE 19899
(302) 655-0597 (Tue only)
donndevine@aol.com
http://www.magpage.com/~tdoherty/ dioceswm.html (for list of film numbers); http://www.lalley.com (searchable database of pre-1870 register entries)
Donn Devine, Archivist
Tue 10:00–3:00, and by appointment (advance reservation for microfilm reader suggested)
(Roman Catholic records of Delmarva Peninsula; holds microfilms of parish records through 1960, which are also available at other local area research libraries and through the Family History Library of The Church of Jesus Christ of Latter-day Saints)

The Archdiocese of Washington (District of Columbia)
(5001 Eastern Avenue—location)
PO Box 29260 (mailing address)
Washington, DC 20017-0260
(301) 853-3800; (301) 853-3246
http://www.adw.org/home.html
Deac. Bernard Bernier, Archivist
Mon–Fri 8:30–5:30

The Archdiocese of Miami
9401 Biscayne Boulevard
Miami Shores, FL 33138
(305) 757-6241

Catholic Diocese of Orlando
(421 East Robinson—location)
PO Box 1800 (mailing address)
Orlando, FL 32802
(407) 246-4845; (407) 246-4942 FAX
http://www.orlandodiocese.org
Karen Jackson, Archivist
Mon–Fri 8:00–4:00

Diocese of Palm Beach
PO Box 109650
Palm Beach Gardens, FL 33410-9650
(561) 775-9507; (561) 775-9556 FAX
Mary Lou Hughes, Archivist and Records Manager

Diocese of Pensacola-Tallahassee
PO Drawer 17329
Pensacola, FL 32522
(850) 432-1515; (850) 436-6424 FAX

Diocese of Saint Augustine
PO Box 24000
Jacksonville, FL 32241
(904) 262-3200; (904) 262-0698
Rev. Philip Gagan, Archivist
Mon–Thur 10:00–3:00
(microfilm of the Diocesan records available at the Saint Augustine Historical Society, Saint Augustine, FL)

Diocese of Saint Petersburg
6363 Ninth Avenue, North
Saint Petersburg, FL 33743
(813) 344-1611; (813) 345-2145
Lisa B. Mobley, Archivist
Mon–Fri 8:30–5:00

The Archdiocese of Atlanta
680 West Peachtree Street, N.W.
Atlanta, GA 30308-1984
(404) 885-7253; (404) 885-7494 FAX
http://www.archatl.com/archatl.htm
Anthony R. Dees, Archivist
Mon–Thur 8:00–4:00 by appointment only
(very little genealogical material, as the
sacramental registers are at the parishes)

Catholic Diocese of Savannah
Catholic Pastoral Center
601 East Liberty Street
Savannah, GA 31401-5196
(912) 238-2320; (912) 238-2335 FAX
http://www.interpath.net/~mdoyle/
svhhom.html
Sister Mary Faith McKean, RSM, Vice
Chancellor
Mon–Fri 9:00–4:00 by appointment only
Pub. *The Southern Cross Newspaper*,
weekly, $15.00 per year subscription

**Roman Catholic Church in the State of
Hawai'i**
Diocese of Honolulu
Chancery Office
1184 Bishop Street
Honolulu, HI 96813
(808) 533-1791; (808) 521-8428 FAX
Rev. Msgr. Raymond J. Nishigaya
9:00–3:00

Roman Catholic Diocese of Boise
Chancery Office
303 Federal Way
Boise, ID 83705
(208) 342-1311; (208) 342-0224 FAX
Deacon Gerald Pera, Chancellor/Archivist
9:00–5:00
research fees based on information requested

Diocese of Belleville
222 South Third Street
Belleville, IL 62220
(618) 234-3157; (618) 277-0387 FAX
Sister Mary Kenan Wolff, SSNO, Archivist
Mon & Thur 8:15–4:15, by appointment only
(archives not open to the public)

Archdiocese of Chicago
Joseph Cardinal Bernardin Archives and
Records Center
711 West Monroe Street
Chicago, IL 60661
(773) 736-5150; (773) 736-0488 FAX
Nancy Sandleback, Assistant Archivist
by appointment only, genealogical research
through the mail

Diocese of Joliet
425 Summit Street
Joliet, IL 60435
(815) 722-6606; (815) 722-6602
Sister Judith Davies, O.S.F., Chancellor
by appointment only

Diocese of Rockford
1245 North Court Street
Rockford, IL 61103
(815) 962-3709; (815) 968-2824 FAX
Rev. Charles McNamee, Chancellor and
Archivist
by appointment only

Diocese of Evansville
Catholic Center
PO Box 4169
Evansville, IN 47724-0169
(812) 424-5536
Judy Neff, Chancellor
Archives: by appointment; Brute Library:

Memorial Day to Labor Day: 12:30–4:00

Archdiocese of Indianapolis
(address withheld upon request)
(Parish histories, priests' biographies, etc.;
"Sacramental records are kept in each
individual parish.")

Diocese of Lafayette-in-Indiana
The Bishop's Office
PO Box 260
Lafayette, IN 47902-0260
(765) 742-0275
Rev. Robert Leo Sell, Vicar General and
Moderator of the Curia
Mon–Fri 7:30–4:30

Diocese of Davenport
Saint Vincent Center
2706 North Gaines
Davenport, IA 52804
(563) 324-1912, ext. 231 (Work); (563) 386-
8132 (Home)
Arnold Wieser, Archivist
Mon–Fri 8:00–3:00 by appointment
searches: voluntary contributions

The Diocese of Des Moines
Archives
c/o Saint Ambrose Cathedral
607 High Street
Des Moines, IA 50309

**The Archives of the Archdiocese of
Dubuque**
(1229 Mount Loretta Avenue, Dubuque, IA
52003—location)
PO Box 479 (mailing address)
Dubuque, IA 52004-0479
(563) 556-2580; (563) 556-5464 FAX
http://www.arch.pvt.k12.ia.us
Rev. Loras C. Otting, Director of the
Archives
Mon–Fri 9:00–4:30
(original correspondence of Bishop Loras
and of Bishop Cretin)

The Diocese of Sioux City
(1821 Jackson Street, Sioux City, IA
51105—location)
PO Box 3379 (mailing address)
Sioux City, IA 51102-3379
(712) 255-7933; (712) 233-7525; (712) 233-
7598 FAX
http://www.scdiocese.org/dioceseindex.html
(click on archives)
Mon–Fri 8:30–noon & 1:00–4:30
Pub. *The Globe* (not genealogical), weekly
(50 times per year), $18.00 per year
subscription within the diocese, $20.00
elsewhere in the U.S.
("Basically we have corporate records of the
diocese, sketchy until 1940s; we are not
computerized; although we have
transcripts of extant sacramental and
burial records from parishes of the diocese
from approximately 1918, and for many of
the earlier ones, we have many still
missing; we can sometimes tell which
parish should be consulted by dates of
first resident pastor; for social security,
the person must make the request, or the
Social Security Office; post 1920 personal
information released only to the
individual or to one that person has
authorized to receive it—authorization
proven.")
research: fees depend on the service given

Diocese of Dodge City
(910 Central—location)
PO Box 137 (mailing address)

Dodge City, KS 67801
(620) 227-2500; (620) 227-1570 FAX
Timothy Wenzl, Archivist
Mon–Fri by appointment

The Archdiocese of Kansas City in Kansas
Chancery Office
12615 Parallel Avenue
Kansas City, KS 66107
(913) 721-1570; (913) 721-1577 FAX
Rev. Leo Cooper, Archivist and Assistant
Chancellor
Mon–Fri 8:30–noon & 1:00–5:00

Diocese of Salina
(103 North Ninth Street—location)
PO Box 980 (mailing address)
Salina, KS 67402-0980
(785) 827-8746; (785) 827-6133 FAX
Msgr. James E. Hake, Chancellor and
Archivist
by appointment only

The Diocese of Covington
1140 Madison Avenue
Covington, KY 41011

Diocese of Lexington
1310 Leestown Road
Lexington, KY 40582
(859) 253-1993; (859) 254-6284 FAX
Sister Mary K. Seibert, Chancellor
by appointment only
("Catholic Diocese of Lexington was
established in 1988 from counties
formerly part of the Diocese of Covington
and the Archdiocese of Louisville; older
records are not always available at this
office.")

Roman Catholic Archdiocese of Louisville
PO Box 1073
Louisville, KY 40203
(502) 585-3291
The Rev. Robert Dale Cieslik, Chancellor-
Archivist
Mon–Fri 8:30–4:30 by appointment only
all requests must be made in writing

Roman Catholic Diocese of Owensboro
Catholic Pastoral Center
600 Locust Street
Owensboro, KY 42301-2130
(270) 683-1545, ext. 133; (270) 683-6883
FAX
http://www.catholic-chur/archivist.html
Sister Emma Cecilia Busam, O.S.U.,
Archivist and Records Manager
Tue–Wed 8:00–4:00, and by appointment
Pub. *Western Kentucky Catholic* (not an
archival publication but diocesan), ten
times per year (monthly, Aug–May),
$10.00 per year subscription
(seeks to promote understanding of the
origins, aims and goals of the diocese;
collects, preserves and makes available
records of individuals and organizations
engaged in work which reflects that of the
Catholic Church in the diocese to
researchers in pursuit of historical and
genealogical research)

The Diocese of Alexandria
(4400 Coliseum Boulevard, Alexandria, LA
71303—location)
PO Box 7417 (mailing address)
Alexandria, LA 71306
(318) 445-2401; (318) 448-6121
Msgr. Joseph Susi, Chancellor/Archivist
8:00–4:30
("We only do baptismal searches as we do
not have all the records for our Diocese.")

research: $10.00 for the first hour, $2.00 for each additional hour, plus $4.00 per certificate

The Diocese of Baton Rouge
Department of the Archives
(1800 South Acadian Thruway—location)
PO Box 2028 (mailing address)
Baton Rouge, LA 70821-2028
(225) 387-0561 (for information only); (225) 387-0561, ext. 220
archives@diobr.org
Lee Leumas, Genealogy Researcher
Mon–Fri 9:00–2:00, by appointment only
(repository of the sacramental records of the Catholic churches within the civil parishes of Ascension, Assumption, East Baton Rouge, East Feliciana, Iberville, Livingston, Pointe Coupee, Saint Helena, Saint James, Tangipahoa, West Baton Rouge and West Feliciana, generally prior to 1900; annually published nineteen volumes of sacramental records from the Acadian records of St. Charles-aux-Mines, Grand Pré in Acadia [1707–1748] and St. Francis of Point Coupée [1728–1769], through the Colonial period [1770–1803], and up to 1894)
research: $15.00 per hour; microfilm copies: $10.00; certified certificates: $5.00 each; books: $30.00 each

Diocese of Houma-Thibodaux
Historical Research Center
205 Audubon Avenue
Thibodoux, LA 70301
(985) 446-2383; (985) 449-0574 FAX
Msgr. R. Boudreaux, Archivist
Mon–Tue & Thur 8:00–4:00

Catholic Diocese of Lafayette
Archives
1408 Carmel Drive
Lafayette, LA 70501-5298
(318) 261-5639; (318) 261-5635 FAX
Anna Jane Marks, Archivist

The Archdiocese of New Orleans
Archdiocesan Historical Archives
1100 Chartres Street
New Orleans, LA 70116-2596
(504) 529-2651; (504) 529-2001 FAX
archives@archdiocese-no.org
http://www.catholic.org/neworleans/archives
Dr. Charles E. Nolan, Archivist
Mon–Fri 9:00–5:00 by appointment for historical research (all genealogical requests handled by mail)
(Comprised eight civil parishes: Jefferson, Orleans, Plaquemines, Saint Bernard, Saint Charles, Saint John the Baptist, Saint Tammany, and Washington; baptisms, marriages and funerals records 1718–1806; archives also houses early records from four New Orleans cemeteries: Saint Louis, Saint Patrick, Saint Joseph, and Saint Roch; has published eleven volumes of sacramental records, 1718–1815)
$12.00 plus SASE per family history record requested, plus an additional $8.00 for a photocopy (if possible) in addition to the English certificate (no more than four requests at a time), c/o Department of Sacramental Registers

Diocese of Shreveport (Louisiana)
Archives
3500 Fairfield Avenue
Shreveport, LA 71104
(318) 868-4441; (318) 868-4605 FAX
http://www.dioshpt.org

Christine D. Rivers, Vice Chancellor for Archives and Records
Mon–Fri 8:00–4:00 by appointment only
Pub. *The Catholic Connection*, monthly (contains column, "Historical Perspectives")
("This repository holds copies of sacramental records of baptism, marriage and death from 1866–1929 for the sixteen northern parishes (counties) of the State of Louisiana, i.e., Bienville, Bossier, Caddo, Claiborne, DeSoto, East Carroll, Jackson, Lincoln, Morehouse, Ouachita, Red River, Richland, Sabine, Union, Webster and West Carroll.")
charge for photocopies

The Chancery of the Diocese of Portland
(510 Ocean Avenue, Portland, ME 04103—location)
PO Box 11559 (mailing address)
Portland, ME 04104-7559
(207) 773-6471; (207) 773-0182 FAX
Sister Therese Pelletier, Archivist
Tue & Thur 9:00–4:30
(does not hold materials for genealogy at the chancery)

Archives of the Archdiocese of Baltimore
(see Associated Archives, above)

Archdiocese of Boston
2121 Commonwealth Avenue
Brighton, MA 02135
(617) 746-5795; (617) 746-5797
http://www.rcab.org/archives/welcome.htm
Robert Johnson-Lally, Archivist/Records Manager
Tue–Thur 10:00–4:00 by appointment (closed holidays and holy days)
20¢ per photocopy from paper, 50¢ photocopy from microfilm, $25.00 per hour for research by staff

Diocese of Fall River
Box 2577 Fall River
Fall River, MA 02722-2577
(508) 675-1311
Msgr. John J. Oliviera, Chancellor and Archivist

Diocese of Worcester
49 Elm Street
Worcester, MA 01609
(508) 791-7171; (508) 753-7180 FAX
Rev. F. Stephen Pedone, Judicial Vicar
(religious; canon law archives and library)

The Archdiocese of Detroit
Archives
1234 Washington Boulevard
Detroit, MI 48226-1875
(313) 237-5846; (313) 237-5791 FAX
Roman P. Godzak, Archivist/Records Manager
Mon–Fri 8:30–4:30

Diocese of Gaylord (Roman Catholic)
611 North Street
Gaylord, MI 49735
(989) 732-5147; (989) 705-3589 FAX
mdickers@dioceseofgaylord.org
http://www.dioceseofgaylord.org/dioceseindex.html
Rev. Gerald F. Micketti, Archivist; Mary Dickerson, Archival Liaison
Mon–Fri 8:00–4:30

Diocesan Archives, Diocese of Grand Rapids
660 Burton Street, S.E.
Grand Rapids, MI 49507-3290

(616) 243-0491; (616) 243-4910 FAX
Fr. Dennis W. Morrow, Archivist
by appointment
research: $10.00 per hour; copies: $5.00 per record found

Catholic Diocese of Lansing
Archives
1500 East Saginaw Street, Suite 2
Lansing, MI 48906-5550
(517) 485-9902; (517) 484-8880 FAX
Rev. George C. Michalek, Archivist
Tue 9:00–4:00
(focuses on the history of Catholicism in Clinton, Eaton, Genesee, Hillsdale, Ingham, Jackson, Lenawee, Livingston, Shiawassee and Washtenaw counties of south central Michigan)

The Diocese of Marquette
(444 South Fourth Street—location)
PO Box 550 (mailing address)
Marquette, MI 49855
(906) 225-1141; (906) 225-0437
Rev. Peter Oberto, Chancellor and Judicial Vicar; Rev. Howard Brown, Archivist; Ms. Regis Walling, U.P. Historical Society
Mon–Fri 8:00–noon & 1:00–4:00
Pub. *U. P. Catholic Diocesan Newspaper*, semimonthly, $18.00 per year subscription

Diocese of Newton
8525 Cole
Warren, MI 48093-5239
(810) 558-0143
Bishop Nicholas Samra, Auxiliary Bishop, Diocese of Newton (Melkite)

The Diocese of Saginaw
5800 Weiss Street
Saginaw, MI 48603

The Diocese of Duluth
2830 East Fourth Street
Duluth, MN 55812
(218) 724-9111; (218) 724-1056 FAX
Rev. Patrick Moran, Archivist
daily 8:30–4:30

The Diocese of New Ulm
1400 Sixth North Street
New Ulm, MN 56073
(507) 359-2966
Rev. Dennis Labat, Chancellor

Archives—Diocese of Saint Cloud
214 Third Avenue South
Saint Cloud, MN 56301
(320) 251-2340; (320) 251-0470 FAX
Louise Theisen, Archivist
daily 8:00–noon

The Archdiocese of Saint Paul and Minneapolis
226 Summit Avenue
Saint Paul, MN 55102
(612) 291-4429; (612) 290-1629 FAX
Patrick Anzelc, Assistant Archivist
Mon–Fri 9:00–5:00, researchers Tue & Wed
(parish records available on microfilm, small charge for copies)
admission: $8.00; research: $8.00 per hour

The Diocese of Winona
(55 West Sanborn—location)
PO Box 588 (mailing address)
Winona, MN 55987
(507) 452-7692; (507) 454-8106
Rev. Edward McGrath, Chancellor
Mon–Fri 8:00–4:30

Catholic Diocese of Biloxi
(120 Reynoir Street—location)
PO Box 1189 (mailing address)
Biloxi, MS 39533
(228) 374-0222
Msgr. Andrew Murray, Vicar General and
Chancellor
8:30–5:00

Catholic Diocese of Jackson
(237 East Amite Street—location)
PO Box 2248 (mailing address)
Jackson, MS 39225-2248
(601) 969-1880; (601) 960-8455 FAX
Jo Ann Haien, Archivist
Tue 1:00–4:00, Wed 10:00–4:00 by
appointment
no research by mail, but all sacramental
requests are honored and research through
the archives' microfilm or referral to the
original parish is facilitated

Diocese of Jefferson City
PO Box 417
Jefferson City, MO 65102
(573) 635-9127; (573) 635-2286 FAX
Sister M. Johanning, Chancellor
Mon–Fri 8:00–5:00

**Catholic Diocese of Kansas City-Saint
Joseph**
(300 East 36th Street, Kansas City, MO
64111—location)
PO Box 419037 (mailing address)
Kansas City, MO 64141-6037
(816) 756-1850, ext. 211; (816) 756-0878
FAX
coleman@diocesekcsj.org
http://www.diocese-kcsj.org
Rev. Michael Coleman, Archivist
Mon–Thur 9:00–5:00, by appointment only,
consideration given to research after hours
and on Saturday
("Records of baptism, marriage [most likely
complete, if they survived fires and
floods], deaths, first communions,
confirmations [not complete everywhere],
Catholic cemetery records [not complete
everywhere], histories of parishes,
institutions and organizations. Local
records begin in 1834. There is access to
records going back to 1822, copied from
Jesuit Archives in St. Louis. The diocese
comprises 23 counties in west and
northwest Missouri, from the Iowa state
line to Vernon County inclusive, and from
the Kansas state line to Johnson and
Livingston counties on the east.")
SASE appreciated for mailed records

Archives of the Archdiocese of Saint Louis
20 Archbishop May Drive
Saint Louis, MO 63119
(314) 792-7022
anewcomer@archstl.org
http://www.archstl.org/archives
Audrey P. Newcomer, Director/Archivist
Mon–Fri 8:30–4:00
research: $5.00 per record, donation
appreciated for search

**Archives of the Diocese of Great Falls-
Billings**
(121 23rd Street, South—location)
PO Box 1399 (mailing address)
Great Falls, MT 59403
(406) 727-6683; (406) 454-3480 FAX
Rev. Dale McFarlane, Diocesan Archivist
Mon–Fri 8:00–5:00 preferably by
appointment

The Diocese of Helena

(515 North Ewing—location)
PO Box 1729 (mailing address)
Helena, MT 59624-1729
(406) 442-5820; (406) 442-5191 FAX
dbrinkel@diocesehelena.org
http://www.diocesehelena.org
Sr. Dolores Brinkel, SCL, Archivist
not open to the public for genealogical
research; submit written request
("Our genealogical information is confined
to records of baptism and marriage, and
some burials in western Montana. When
submitting request, include approximate
date, place [and parish if at all possible]
and parents' names.")

Diocese of Lincoln
3400 Sheridan Boulevard
Lincoln, NE 68506
(402) 488-0921
Sister Loretta Gosen, Archivist
Mon–Fri 8:30–4:30

The Archdiocese of Omaha
Chancery Office
100 North 62nd Street
Omaha, NE 68132
(402) 558-3100; (402) 551-4212 FAX
Fr. Michael F. Gutgsell, Chancellor
Mon–Fri 8:30–5:00

The Diocese of Reno-Las Vegas
(Chancery Office, 515 Court
Street—location)
PO Box 1211 (mailing address)
Reno, NV 89504
(775) 329-9274, ext. 19; (775) 329-6581
FAX
Carmen Goday, Office Manager
8:30–noon & 1:00–4:30
(some baptismal records from 1800 to early
1900s for state of Nevada; most
sacramental records were destroyed
during some of the fires in a couple of
churches in Virginia City and Gold Hill)
$5.00 per copy for certificates

The Diocese of Manchester
Chancery Office
(153 Ash Street—location)
PO Box 310 (mailing address)
Manchester, NH 03105

Archdiocese of Newark
Seton Hall University
University Archives
Duffy Hall
400 South Orange Avenue
South Orange, NJ 07079-2696
(973) 761-9476; (973) 761-9550 FAX
Msgr. William Noe Field, Archivist and
Records Manager
Mon–Fri 8:30–5:00

Diocese of Paterson
777 Valley Road
Clifton, NJ 07013
(973) 777-8818; (973) 777-8976 FAX
Rev. Raymond Kupke, Archivist
by appointment only

Diocese of Trenton
701 Lawrenceville Road
Trenton, NJ 08648
(609) 882-7125; (908) 350-5001
Msgr. Joseph Shenrock, Archivist
by appointment only

The Diocese of Gallup
(711 South Puerco Drive, Gallup, NM
87301—location)
PO Box 1338 (mailing address)

Gallup, NM 87305
(505) 863-4406
Brother Duane Torisky, Chancellor and
Archivist

The Diocese of Las Cruces
1280 Med Park Drive
Las Cruces, NM 88005
(505) 523-7577; (505) 524-3874
Rev. John Tickle, Archivist; Dolores Diaz,
Librarian
Mon–Fri 8:00–5:00

The Archdiocese of Santa Fe
213 Cathedral Place
Santa Fe, NM 87501
(505) 983-3811; (505) 982-5619
Marina Ochoa
by appointment

**Roman Catholic Diocese of Albany
Archives**
40 North Main Avenue
Albany, NY 12203
(518) 453-6600; (518) 453-6793 FAX
Nola.Brunner@rcda.org
Sister Nola Brunner, Archivist
Mon–Fri 8:30–4:30

Roman Catholic Diocese of Brooklyn
Office of the Archivist
310 Prospect Park West
Brooklyn, NY 11215
(718) 965-7300, ext. 1001; (718) 965-7302
FAX
archives@dioceseofbrooklyn.org
http://www.dioceseofbrooklyn.org
Joseph W. Coen, C.A., Archivist; Patrick J.
McNamara, Ph.D., Assistant Archivist
Mon–Wed & Thur–Fri 9:30–4:00 by
appointment
Pub. *The Tablet*, newspaper
(sacramental registers not centralized, except
closed parishes/hospitals; closed Catholic
school records, except schools run by
religious communities; see *Priests &
Parishes of the Diocese of Brooklyn
1853–1990*, 2 vols., $15.00 each, and
*Chronological List of Churches in the
Diocese of Brooklyn*, Brooklyn Parishes
$2.00, Queens Parishes $2.00)
research: $25.00 per genealogical request;
$10.00 per student record

The Catholic Center (Buffalo)
795 Main Street, Fourth Floor
Buffalo, NY 14203
(716) 847-5561
http://www.buffalodiocese.org
Msgr. Walter Kern, Archivist
Mon–Fri 9:00–4:00 by appointment
("We do not have personnel to do research;
many of our sacramental records also
contain confidential information.")

Archdiocese of New York
(address withheld upon request)
("I do not do genealogical research.")

Diocese of Ogdensburg
Chancery Office
(622 Washington Street—location)
PO Box 369 (mailing address)
Ogdensburg, NY 13669
(315) 292-2920
Rev. Terry LaValley, Chancellor; Rev.
Lawrence Cotter, Archivist
Mon–Fri 9:00–noon & 1:00–4:00

Archives, Diocese of Rochester
1150 Buffalo Road
Rochester, NY 14624

(716) 328-3210
Rev. William Graf, Associate Archivist
9:00–4:00 by appointment only
(will direct calls and requests to proper
church for marriage, baptism and burial
records from 1914)

Diocese of Syracuse
(240 East Onondaga Street, Syracuse, NY
13202-2608—location)
PO Box 511 (mailing address)
Syracuse, NY 13201
(315) 470-1493
Carl H. Roesch, Archivist
Mon–Tue & Thur–Fri 9:00–noon

Catholic Diocese of Charlotte
1123 South Church Street
Charlotte, NC 28203-4003
(704) 370-6299
cbarnes@CharlotteDiocese.org
Johanna Mims, Archivist
Tue & Thur 9:00–3:00

The Diocese of Raleigh Archives
(300 Cardinal Gibbons Drive—location)
715 Nazareth Street (mailing address)
Raleigh, NC 27606
(919) 821-9709
Bradley K. Blake, Archivist
Mon, Wed & Fri 8:30–5:00

The Diocese of Bismarck Archives
(520 North Washington Street, Bismarck,
ND 58501—location)
PO Box 1137 (mailing address)
Bismarck, ND 58502-1137
(701) 222-3035
Marge Grosz, Librarian
Mon–Fri 8:00–5:00

The Diocese of Fargo Archives
(1310 Broadway—location)
PO Box 1750 (mailing address)
Fargo, ND 58107
(701) 235-6429
Sister M. James Merrick, Archivist

Archdiocese of Cincinnati
Historical Archives of the Chancery
Mount Saint Mary's Seminary
6616 Beechmont Avenue
Cincinnati, OH 45230-5900
(513) 231-0810; (513) 231-3254 FAX
Don H. Buske, Archivist
Mon–Wed 8:30–4:30
(sacramental records for the nineteen-county
area of southwestern Ohio; all
genealogical research done by mail)
research: $25.00 fee, check or money order
to the Historical Archives of the chancery,
submit full name, type of record,
approximate date (within five years),
exact parish

Archives, Diocese of Cleveland
Chancery Building
1027 Superior Avenue
Cleveland, OH 44114
(216) 696-6525, ext. 345
Christine L. Krosel, Director of Archives
Mon–Fri 9:00–5:00 by appointment only
(northern Ohio, eight-county area:
Cuyahoga, Geauga, Lake, Lorain, Medina,
Summit, Ashland and Wayne counties)
$6.50 per hour for research, rates subject to
change

The Diocese of Columbus
Saint Charles Prep School, Archives
2010 East Broad Street
Columbus, OH 43209

(614) 252-1225
Rev. Thomas Bennett, Archivist
by appointment only

The Diocese of Steubenville
(422 Washington Street—location)
PO Box 969 (mailing address)
Steubenville, OH 43952
(740) 282-3631
Linda Nichols, Chancellor
9:00–noon & 1:00–4:00
Pub. *Domina* (Diocesan Directory),
biannually (every two years), $7.00 per
issue
(specializes in "parishes, institutions,
departments, priests, religious of
diocese.")

Archives, Diocese of Toledo
Catholic Center
1933 Spielbusch
Toledo, OH 43624-1371
Sister Mary Lourde Beauregard, Records
Manager
Wed & Fri 9:00–5:00
Pub. *ACOA Bulletin*
(has some parishes' sacramental books on
microfilm)
no search service unless provided with name,
year, and specific parish church

The Diocese of Youngstown
Chancery Office
144 West Wood Street
Youngstown, OH 44503
(330) 744-8451; (330) 742-6448 FAX
Nancy L. Yuhasz, Chancellor
Mon–Fri by appointment only

Diocese of Tulsa
(820 South Boulder, Tulsa, OK
74119—location)
PO Box 2009 (mailing address)
Tulsa, OK 74101
(918) 587-3115; (918) 587-6692 FAX
Rita Burns, Archivist
Mon–Fri 9:00–5:00

Diocese of Portland
2838 East Burnside Street
Portland, OR 97214-1895
(503) 233-8334
Mary A. Grant, Archivist

Diocese of Erie
Saint Mark's Center
PO Box 10397
Erie, PA 16514
(814) 824-1138
Chris Prehoda, Secretary
Mon–Fri 9:30–noon & 2:00–4:30
(published two volumes of the history of the
diocese)

Diocese of Greensburg
723 East Pittsburgh Street
Greensburg, PA 15601
(724) 837-0901; (724) 837-0857
Bina Guerrieri, Secretary to the Archives
Mon–Fri 9:00–5:00

**Archives, Roman Catholic Diocese of
Harrisburg**
(4800 Union Deposit Road—location)
PO Box 2153 (mailing address)
Harrisburg, PA 17105-2153
(717) 657-4804, ext. 214; (717) 657-7673
FAX
Kathleen Signor, Assistant Chancellor for
Archives/Archivist
Mon–Fri 8:30–4:30
Pub. *Catholic Witness*, bimonthly
(sacramental records; parish histories for

Catholic Diocese of Harrisburg)
genealogical research: $25.00 per hour

**Philadelphia Archdiocesan Historical
Research Center**
Archives and Historical Collections
1000 East Wynnewood Road
Overbrook, PA 19096-3001
(215) 667-2125
http://www.archdiocese-
phl.org/ch/archives.html;
http://libertynet.org/~gencap/borromeo.ht
ml (Saint Charles Borromeo Seminary,
Ryan Memorial Library)
Joseph J. Casino, Archivist
Mon–Fri 9:00–4:00
(holds baptismal and marriage records prior
to 1900 for parishes presently within the
Archdiocese of Philadelphia)
genealogical research: $15.00 for first hour,
$10.00 for each additional hour

Archives and Record Center (Pittsburgh)
125 North Craig
Pittsburgh, PA 15213
(412) 621-6217; (412) 621-5237 FAX
archives@diopitt.org
Kenneth White, Director; Rev. E.
McSweeney, Archivist
Mon–Fri 8:30–4:30
(files of deceased clergy of the Catholic
Diocese of Pittsburgh; publishes parish
sacramental records, which have been
centralized in the archives if over seventy
years old)
search: $15.00 for the first hour and $10.00
for each additional hour

Diocese of Scranton
300 Wyoming Avenue
Scranton, PA 18503-1279
(570) 346-8910
Msgr. Neil J. Van Loon, Chancellor
by appointment only

The Diocese of Providence
(address withheld upon request)
(collects documentation on the acts, the
agencies, and the institutions of the
diocese, does not collect personal
histories or sacramental records, which
are kept by individual parishes)

Diocese of Charleston Archives
(114 Broad Street [Rear]—location)
PO Box 818 (mailing address)
Charleston, SC 29402
(843) 724-8372
http://www.catholic-doc.org
Mary Giles, C.A., Archivist
by appointment

The Diocese of Rapid City
Chancery Office
606 Cathedral Drive
Rapid City, SD 57701
(605) 343-3541; (605) 343-7985 FAX
Sister Celine Erk, Archivist
Mon–Tue 8:00–5:00

The Diocese of Sioux Falls Archives
Catholic Chancery Office
523 North Duluth Avenue
Sioux Falls, SD 57104
(605) 334-9861
webpage@sfcatholic.org
http://www.diocese-of-sioux-falls.org
Mon–Fri 9:00–5:00

Diocese of Memphis
1325 Jefferson Avenue
Memphis, TN 38104

(901) 722-4700; (901) 722-4769
Mrs. V. Dominioni, Administrative
Assistant, Office of the Bishop

Catholic Historical Society of the Diocese of Amarillo
(2200 North Spring Street—location)
PO Box 5664 (mailing address)
Amarillo, TX 79117-5644
(806) 381-9866; (806) 383-8452 FAX
Margret Ference, Curator
Tue & Thur 10:00–2:00, and by appointment
$10.00 per year membership

Catholic Archives of Texas (Diocese of Austin)
(1600 North Congress Avenue, Austin, TX 78701—location)
PO Box 13124, Capitol Station (mailing address)
Austin, TX 78711-3124
(512) 476-6296; (512) 476-3715 FAX
cat@onr.com
http://www.onr.com/user/cat
Kinga Perzynska, Archivist
Mon–Fri 9:00–5:00
(Catholic sacramental records on microfilm to be viewed at the archives)
search: $10.00 per hour plus copies at 25¢ per page from paper originals or 50¢ per page from microfilm originals

Diocese of Beaumont
PO Box 3948
Beaumont, TX 77704-3948
(409) 838-0451; (409) 838-4511
Rev. Bennie Patillo, Chancellor, Vicar-General, and Archivist
Mon–Fri 8:30–4:30

Diocese of Brownsville
PO Box 2279
Brownsville, TX 78522
(956) 542-2501
Sister Esther Dunegan, Archivist

Diocese of Corpus Christi
(address withheld upon request)

Diocese of Dallas
3725 Blackburn
Dallas, TX 75219
(972) 528-2240; (972) 526-1743
Estelle Metzger, Archivist
Mon–Wed 9:00–5:00
("We do not profess to do genealogy; on rare occasion we do issue a baptismal certificate; we have to know the name and birth date and the family connection to even consider this type of inquiry; and since some information is really confidential and sacred, we do not participate in this type of exercise.")
research: $25.00 for the first hour

Historical Archives, Catholic Diocese of El Paso
499 Saint Matthew's Street
El Paso, TX 79907
(915) 595-5008
Very Rev. Edward Roden-Lucero, Chancellor

Diocese of Fort Worth
800 West Loop, 820 South
Fort Worth, TX 76108
(817) 560-3300; (817) 244-8839 FAX
Carol Watson, Records Manager
Mon–Fri 8:00–5:00

Archives, Diocese of Galveston-Houston
(1700 San Jacinto—location)

PO Box 907 (mailing address)
Houston, TX 77001-0907
(713) 659-5461; (713) 759-9151 FAX
lmay@diogh.org
http://www.diogh.org
Lisa May, Archivist
Mon–Fri 8:30–noon & 1:00–4:30; research by appointment
(sacramental records after 1930 are closed to genealogical research)

Diocese of San Angelo
804 Ford
San Angelo, TX 76905
(915) 651-7500; (915) 651-6688 FAX
Mary Sue Brewer, Secretary to the Bishop and Archivist
Mon–Fri 9:00–5:00

Catholic Archives at San Antonio
(2718 West Woodlawn—location)
PO Box 24810 (mailing address)
San Antonio, TX 78228-0410
(210) 734-2620, ext. 103
eloch@archdiosa.org
Brother Edward Loch, S.M., Archivist
Mon–Tue & Thur–Fri 9:00–noon & 1:00–4:00, Wed 9:00–11:30 & 1:00–4:00, by appointment only
Pub. *Guide to Catholic Archives at San Antonio*, occasionally
("Records span 1703 to present [closed 1930 to present]. Covers all Catholic churches in 32 counties in south-central Texas.")
use of microfilm: $3.00 per hour or any part of an hour; archival assistance: $5.00 per hour; research by staff, when available: $10.00 per hour, $20.00 minimum; copies: 20¢ per page from paper originals, $1.00 per page from microform originals

Archives, Diocese of Salt Lake City
Pastoral Center
27 C Street
Salt Lake City, UT 84103-2397
(801) 328-8641, ext. 346; (801) 328-9680 FAX
Gary Topping, Archivist
Tue–Thur 1:30–5:00

Archives of the Roman Catholic Diocese of Burlington
Bishop Brady Center
351 North Avenue
Burlington, VT 05401
(802) 658-6110
William W. Goss, Archivist
by appointment

Diocese of Arlington
(200 North Glebe Road, Suite 608—location)
80 North Glebe Road (mailing address)
Arlington, VA 22203
(703) 524-2124
Sister Mary Arthur, Archivist

Diocese of Richmond
811 Cathedral Place
Richmond, VA 23220
(804) 359-5661; (804) 358-9159
by appointment only

Archives of the Archdiocese of Seattle
The Chancery
910 Marion Street
Seattle, WA 98104
(206) 654-4655
Christine Taylor, Archivist
Mon–Fri 9:00–5:00 by appointment only
(Roman Catholic sacramental records)
research: starting at $5.00

Diocese of Spokane
Diocesan Archives
1023 West Riverside Avenue—location)
PO Box 1453 (mailing address)
Spokane, WA 99210
(509) 358-7349
Rev. Ted Bradley, Archivist-Records Manager
hours: various

The Diocese of Wheeling-Charleston
(1300 Bryan Street—location)
PO Box 230 (mailing address)
Wheeling, WV 26003
(304) 233-0880
Rev. Robert C. Nash, Archivist

The Diocese of Green Bay
Archives
(1825 Riverside Drive—location)
PO Box 23825 (mailing address)
Green Bay, WI 54305-3825
(920) 272-8186; (920) 272-8187
kmatthies@gbdioc.org
http://gbdioc.thinksite.com/pg/resourcesArchives.tpl
Tue (except first Tue) 9:00–noon & 1:00–4:00, and by appintment
("We have microfiche copies of sacramental records for entire diocese—sixteen counties of northeastern Wisconsin; some records begin in 1830s.")
admission: $5.00 for a half-day, $10.00 for full day; research: $20.00 per hour plus copies and postage

The Diocese of La Crosse Archives
(3710 East Avenue, South—location)
PO Box 4004 (mailing address)
La Crosse, WI 54602-4004
(608) 788-7700; (608) 788-8413
Rev. Michael Gorman, Chancellor/Archivist
Mon–Fri 8:00–4:30

The Diocese of Madison
The Bishop O'Connor Catholic Pastoral Center
702 South High Point Road
Madison, WI 53719-4999
(608) 821-3140
http://www.madisondiocese.org
Rev. John G. Stillmank, S.T.L.

The Archdiocese of Milwaukee
PO Box 07912
Milwaukee, WI 53207-0912
(414) 769-3407; (414) 769-3408 FAX
Timothy Cary, Archivist and Records Manager
by appointment only
(microfilms of pre-1921 sacramental records available from the Family History Library of The Church of Jesus Christ of Latter-day Saints)

The Diocese of Superior
(1201 Hughitt Avenue—location)
PO Box 969 (mailing address)
Superior, WI 54880
(715) 392-2937; (715) 392-2015 FAX
Rev. James Tobalski, Chancellor and Archivist
Mon–Fri 8:30–5:00

The Diocese of Cheyenne
PO Box 426
Cheyenne, WY 82003

Daughters of Charity Archives—Albany
96 Menands Road
Albany, NY 12204-1499

(518) 462-5593
Elaine Wheeler, Provincial Archivist
Mon–Fri 8:30–4:30, weekends by
    appointment
(Roman Catholic records, also history of care
    of orphans in many cities, but does not
    have children's records; records of
    hospitals from 1848)

**Franciscan Friars of the Atonement
Archives**
(Graymoor, Route 9—location)
PO Box 300 (mailing address)
Garrison, NY 10524
(845) 424-2120
wgagne@atonementfriars.org
Fr. Walter Gagne, SA, Director, Archives
    and Record Center
9:30–4:00

Gonzaga University
Special Collections Department
Foley Center Library
Spokane, WA 99258
(509) 328-4220, ext. 3814; (509) 324-5904
    FAX
http://www.gonzaga.edu/foley/speccoll.html
(Jesuit Oregon Province Archives)

Grace and Holy Trinity Cathedral
(415 West 13th Street—location)
PO Box 23218 (mailing address)
Kansas City, MO 64141
(816) 474-8260

Indiana Province Archives Center
Congregation of Holy Cross
(Douglas Road between 933 and Juniper
Road—location)
PO Box 568 (mailing address)
Notre Dame, IN 46556
(574) 631-5371
ipac.1@nd.edu
William G. Blum, Assistant Archivist
Mon–Fri 8:30–noon
(Archival collection of Indiana Province of
    Priests of the Congregation of Holy
    Cross)
research: $15.00 per hour, photocopies: 25¢
    per sheet, photographs: cost of lab

**Jesuit Historical Institute, American
Division**
University of Arizona
Arizona State Museum
Building 26
Tucson, AZ 85721
(520) 621-6278; (520) 621-9188 FAX
Charles Polzer, Sr., Curator and Director
8:00–5:00
(holdings on Spanish colonial New Spain
    [Mexico])

Marquette University
Department of Special Collections and
Archives
PO Box 3141
Milwaukee, WI 93201-3141
(414) 288-7256
http://www.marquette.edu/library/
    collections/archives/index.html

Maryland Catholics on the Frontier
http://www.pastracks.com/~ehayden/mcf/
    welcom.html

Monastic Heritage Museum
Sisters of the Order of Saint Benedict
104 Chapel Lane
Saint Joseph, MN 56374
(320) 363-7100

Nazareth Archival Center
PO Box 3000
Nazareth, KY 40048-3000
(502) 348-1500
8:30 A.M.–11:30 A.M., and by appointment
(Catholic church in Kentucky since 1812;
    genealogies of some families of members
    of SCN congregation)

**New Jersey Catholic Historical Records
Commission**
(238 East Blancke Street—location)
PO Box 1246 (mailing address)
Linden, NJ 07036
(908) 486-1022

The Old Bohemia Historical Society, Inc.
(Bohemia Church Road—location)
PO Box 61 (mailing address)
Warwick, MD 21912
(302) 378-5800 (in Delaware)
Rev. Thomas A. Flowers, President and
    Pastor
by appointment
(Maryland ecclesiastical history, Catholic
    Diocese of Wilmington history, no
    sacramental records, which have been
    taken to the The Diocese of Wilmington
    Archives, Greenville, DE; "Old Bohemia"
    is the popular name given to the first
    permanent Catholic site on the Delmarva
    Peninsula, established in 1704 and has no
    particular connection to Bohemia in
    Europe or to those of Czech or Slovak
    ancestry)
$15.00 per year membership; $40.00 for
    three years membership

Roman Catholic Church Council
3211 Fourth Street
Washington, DC 20017
http://www.vatican.va

Archives of Saint Mary's Seminary
(see Associated Archives, above)

The Saint Paul Mission Historical Society
(4225 Mission Avenue, N.E.—location)
PO Box 158 (mailing address)
Saint Paul, OR 97137-0158
(503) 633-2501
http://www.rootsweb.com/~orspmhs/
    stpaulindex.html
Joe McKay, President
by appointment
("Collects and preserves the culture of the
    first settlers in Oregon"; Catholic Church
    records of the Pacific Northwest)

Seton Hall University
Msgr. William Noé Field Archives and
Special Collections Center
Walsh Library
400 South Orange Avenue
South Orange, NJ 07079-2696
http://library.shu.edu/SpecColl.htm
Alan Delozier, University Archivist; Kate
    Dodds, Archival Associate/Genealogist
Mon–Fri 9:30–4:30 (appointments
    recommended)
Pub. *New Jersey Catholic Records
    Commission Newsletter*
("New Jersey Roman Catholic history,
    Archdiocese of Newark history
    [1853–present], Seton Hall University
    history [1856–present], sacramental
    records [1850–1925 approx., depends
    upon the parish and dates of closure for
    various churches], and various manuscript
    collections.")

Archives of the Sulpician Priests
(see Associated Archives, above)

The Texas Catholic Historical Society
c/o Texas Catholic Conference
1625 Rutherford Lane
Austin, TX 78754-5105
(512) 339-9882; (512) 339-8670
jd10@swt.edu
http://www.onr.com/user/cat/TCHS.htm;
    http://www.history.swt.edu/Catholic_Sout
    hwest.htm (journal)
Secretary
Pub. *The Texas Catholic Historical Society
    Newsletter*, free; *Catholic Southwest: A
    Journal of History and Culture*, annually
$15.00 per year membership

**The United States Catholic Historical
Society**
The Catholic Center
1011 First Avenue
New York, NY 10022
(800) 225-7999
http://www.uschs.com

University of Notre Dame Archives
Room 607, Hesburgh Library
Notre Dame, IN 46556
(219) 631-6448; (219) 631-7980 FAX
archives.1@nd.edu
http://www.nd.edu/~archives
Sharon Sumpter, Assistant Archivist
Mon–Fri 8:00–5:00
("We hold few genealogical records. Please
    note that each diocese is responsible for
    keeping the records of the parishes within
    its borders. Contact the Chancery Office
    of each diocese for their records. We do
    hold genealogical records for the local
    area here, i.e. South Bend-Niles,
    Kentucky, and colonial Louisiana, among
    others.")

Ursuline Sisters Archives
Mount Saint Joseph
8001 Cummings Road
Maple Mount, KY 42356-9999
(270) 229-4103, ext. 302; (502) 299-4127
    FAX
archives@maplemount.org
http://www.ursulinesmsj.org
Sister Vickie Cravens, O.S.U. Archivist
Mon–Fri 8:30–4:30
Pub. *The Community Newsletter*, bimonthly,
    voluntary offering
(archives set up in 1983; files and folders on
    Sisters, employees and others, and a
    genealogy section in our Research Room)
research: fees vary according to request type,
    please inquire in advance

Wadhams Hall Seminary
6866 State Highway 37
Ogdensburg, NY 13669
(315) 393-4231; (315) 393-4249 FAX
Father Robert Jollett, Director
Mon–Fri 8:00–4:00, summer by appointment
(diocese of Ogdensburg)

Romanian Orthodox Episcopate of America
(see Orthodox)

Russian Orthodox Church Outside of Russia
(see Orthodox)

Salvation Army

**Salvation Army Archives and Research
Center**
615 Slaters Lane

Alexandria, VA 22313
(703) 684-5500
http://www.salvationarmy.org

The Salvation Army Southern Historical Center
1032 Stewart Avenue, S.W.
Atlanta, GA 30310
(404) 752-7578; (404) 753-4166
John G. Merritt, Director

The Salvation Army Western Territorial Museum
30840 Hawthorne Boulevard
Rancho Palos Verdes, CA 90275
(310) 534-6097; (310) 534-7157 FAX
Frances C. Dingman
museum temporarily closed, only historical services
(collection restricted to Salvation Army officers in the thirteen western states, cannot help with people who just attended the army at some time)

Schwenkfelder

The Schwenkfelder Library and Heritage Center
105 Seminary Street
Pennsburg, PA 18073
(215) 679-3103
http://www.schwenkfelder.org
David W. Luz, Director; Hunt Schenkel, Archivist
Tue–Wed & Fri 9:00–4:00, Thur 9:00–8:00, Sat 10:00–3:00, Sun 10:00–3:00
(radical reformation, Schwenkfelders, local history, and Pennsylvania German culture; "Library is known for genealogy research of the area.")

Separate Baptists in Christ
(see Baptist)

Serbian Eastern Orthodox Church
(see Orthodox)

Seventh Day Adventist

General Conference of Seventh Day Adventists
12501 Old Columbia Pike
Silver Spring, MD 20904-6600
(301) 680-6000
http://northamerica.adventist.org
F. Donald Yost, Director of Archives and Statistics

Seventh Day Baptist General Conference
(see Baptist)

Shaker

Sabbathday Lake Shaker Library
(Route 26—location)
707 Shaker Road (mailing address)
New Gloucester, ME 04260
(207) 926-4597
brooks1@shaker.lib.me.us
http://www.shaker.lib.me.us
Tina S. Agren, Librarian
Tue–Thur 8:30–4:30, by appointment only
Pub. *The Shaker Quarterly*, annually, $20.00 for annual issue
(Shakers and other radical Christian groups; Shaker manuscript collection; Index Nominum of over 15,000 names with

biographical data; library collection brochure available on request.)

Shaker Heritage Society
1848 Shaker Meeting House
Albany-Shaker Road
Albany, NY 12211
(518) 456-7890
Ned Pratt, Director
Mon (1 Nov–21 Dec) 9:30–4:00, Tue–Sat 9:30–4:00
Pub. *Watervliet Shaker Journal*, quarterly
$20.00 per year membership

Shaker Historical Society
16740 South Park Boulevard
Shaker Heights, OH 44120
(216) 921-1201
http://www.cwru.edu/orgs/shakhist/shaker.htm
Catherine R. Winans, Director
Tue–Fri & Sun 2:00–5:00
Pub. *The Journal*, quarterly
(Nord Library: Shaker societies; North Union Shakers; local history)
$20.00 per year membership; students may borrow books with a $20.00 returnable deposit

Shi'ism
(see Islam)

Society of Friends
(see Religious Society of Friends [Quakers])

Society of the Primitive Methodists
(see Primitive Methodist Church in the U.S.A.

Southern Baptist Convention
(see Baptist)

Southern Episcopal Church
(see Episcopal)

Spiritualist

National Spiritual Alliance of the U.S.A.
67 Mine Road
Winchester, NH 03470

National Spiritualist Association of Churches
PO Box 217
Lily Dale, NY 14752
http://www.nsac.org

Theosophical Society in America
PO Box 270
Wheaton, IL 60189
http://www.theosophical.org

Stoneites
(see Disciples of Christ)

Strangites

Church of Jesus Christ of Latter Day Saints
(Mormon Road and Highway 11—location)
PO Box 491 (mailing address)
Burlington, WI 53105-0491
Elders@Strangite.org
http://www.strangite.org

Sufism
(see Islam)

Sunnism
(see Islam)

Swedenborgian Societies
(Although Emmanuel Swedenborg never founded a church, his followers established Swedenborg Societies or a Swedenborgian Church.)

The New Church (Church of the New Jerusalem)
PO Box 743
Bryn Athyn, PA 19009
(877) 411-HOPE
http://www.newchurch.org

Swedenborgian Church of North America
The General Convention of the New Jerusalem in the U.S.A.
11 Highland Avenue
Newtonville, MA 02460
(617) 969-4240; (617) 964-3258 FAX
manager@swedenborg.org
http://www.swedenborg.org

Swedish Ansgarii Synod
(see Evangelical Free Church of America)

Swedish Baptist
(see Lutheran)

Swedish Episcopal
(see Lutheran)

Swedish Evangelical Free Church
(see Evangelical Free Church of America)

Swedish Evangelical Free Mission
(see Evangelical Free Church of America)

Swedish Methodist
(see Lutheran)

Syrian Orthodox Church of Antioch
(see Orthodox)

Theosophical Society in America
(see Spiritualist)

Triumph the Church and Kingdom of God in Christ, International

Triumph the Church and Kingdom of God in Christ, International
213 Farrington Avenue, S.E.
Atlanta, GA 30315

Tunker Church
(see Brethren)

Ukrainian Catholic
(see Orthodox)

Uniate Churches
(see Orthodox)

Union American Methodist Episcopal Church
(see United Methodist)

Union Church of Africans
(see United Methodist)

Union of American Hebrew Congregations (Reform)
(see Ethnic Archives, Libraries and Societies—Jewish, Part 3)

Union of Orthodox Jewish Congregations of America
(see Ethnic Archives, Libraries and Societies—Jewish, Part 3)

Unitarian Universalist Association of Congregations

The association was formed from a blend of the American Unitarianism of the early Congregational Church's Liberal Christian movement and the Universalist movement.

Andover Harvard Theological Library
Harvard Divinity School
Manuscripts and Archives
45 Francis Avenue
Cambridge, MA 02138
(617) 496-5153; (617) 496-4111 FAX
frances_odonnell@harvard.edu
http://www.hds.harvard.edu/library
Frances O'Donnell, Curator of Manuscripts and Archives
Mon–Fri 9:00–5:00
(manuscript church records)

First Unitarian Universalist Society of Albany
405 Washington Avenue
Albany, NY 12206
(518) 463-7135

Unitarian Universalist Association of Congregations Archives
25 Beacon Street
Boston, MA 02108
(617) 742-2100
http://www.uua.org
Deborah Weiner, Director of Public Information
winter: Mon–Fri 9:00–5:00; summer: Mon–Fri 9:00–4:00

Unitarian Universalist Historical Society
Membership Office
(c/o Unitarian Universalist Association, 25 Beacon Street, Boston, MA 02108—location)
PO Box 2776 (mailing address)
Duxbury, MA 02331
revebs@aol.com; cwdev@att.net
http://www.uua.org/uuhs
Fred Stevens, Membership Clerk
Pub. *Proceedings of the UU Historical Society*
$25.00 per year membership

United Brethren in Christ
(see Brethren, Church of the United Brethren in Christ, United Christian Church and United Methodist)

United Christian Church

Formerly known as Hoffmanites, the early founders left the United Brethren in Christ and in 1878 officially organized as today's United Christian Church.

United Christian Church Archives
2080 White Oak Street

Lebanon, PA 17042
Elder David W. Heagy, General Conference Secretary
(formerly part of the Church of the United Brethren in Christ)

United Church of Christ
(see also Congregational Methodist Church)

The Evangelical Protestant Church of North America joined with the National Council of Congregational Churches to form the Evangelical Protestant Conference of Congregational Churches. The group merged with the Christian Church in 1931 to form the Congregational Christian Churches. In the 1957 the bulk of that group merged with the Evangelical and Reformed Church (the product of a merger between the Evangelical Synod of North America and the Reformed Church in the United States) and became the United Church of Christ.

Andover Newton Theological School
Franklin Trask Library
169 Herrick Road
Newton Centre, MA 02459
(617) 964-1100, ext. 252
http://www.ants.edu
(Baptist, Congregational and Church of Christ)

Congregational Christian Historical Society, Inc.
14 Beacon Street
Boston, MA 02108
(617) 523-0470; (617) 523-0491
http://www.14beacon.org
Harold F. Worthley, Th.D., Executive Secretary/Archivist
Mon–Fri 8:30–4:30
Pub. *News from the Congregational Christian Historical Society*, semiannually
(United Church of Christ and Congregational Christian Churches)
$25.00 per year membership

Archives of the Evangelical Synod of North America at Eden Theological Seminary (One of the Precursor Denominations of the United Church of Christ) and Deaconess Archives
475 East Lockwood
Saint Louis, MO 63119-3192
(314) 918-2515; (877) 627-5650 FAX
http://www.eden.edu
Valerie Detjen, Assistant Archivist
Mon & Wed–Thur 8:30–4:30, summer hours vary
(Evangelical Synod of North America church and pastoral records, especially German Evangelical churches and agencies. "The Archives are housed on the lower level of the Eden-Webster (Luhr) Library.")
admission: contribution

Evangelical and Reformed Historical Society
Lancaster Theological Seminary
Phillip Schaff Library
555 West James Street
Lancaster, PA 17603
(717) 290-8711; (717) 290-8704
http://www.erhs.info
Mon–Thur 9:00–4:00
(includes German Reformed as well as Evangelical and Reformed records in Pennsylvania, most holdings available on microfilm from LDS Family History Centers)
$25.00 per year membership; admission: $5.00

Hammond Library
Chicago Theological Seminary
5757 University Avenue
Chicago, IL 60637
(773) 752-5757, ext. 225
Rev. Neil Gerdes
("Records from Chicago area Congregational Churches that closed in the 1930s; no staff to service records, requests handled on a time available basis.")
$3.00 for searches within our parameters

Hawaiian Mission Children's Society Library
(see Hawaii, Part 2)

United Church of Christ
700 Prospect Avenue
Cleveland, OH 02108
(216) 736-2106; (216) 736-2203 FAX
kellyb@ucc.org
http://www.ucc.org
Bridgette A. Kelly, Archivist

United Evangelical Lutheran Synod
(see Lutheran)

United Holy Church of America, Inc.

United Holy Church of America, Inc.
312 Umstead Street
Durham, NC 27702
http://members.aol.com/newpent/nphca

United Lutheran Church
(see Lutheran)

United Methodist Church
(see also Brethren and Lutheran)

The United Methodist Church includes the former Methodist Church and the former Evangelical United Brethren Church (itself a union of the Evangelical Church [formerly the Evangelical Association, some of whose members withdrew to join the Evangelical United Brethren Church and some to form the United Evangelical Church which reunited in part in 1922, but some declined unification and formed the Evangelical Congregational Church) and the Evangelical United Brethren Church [EUB]). Other United Methodist predecessors, splinter groups and former splinter groups include African Methodist Episcopal Church (A.M.E.), African Methodist Episcopal Zion Church, Christian Methodist Episcopal Church, Congregational Methodist Church, Methodist Protestant, Evangelical Church of North America, Evangelical Congregational Church, Evangelical Methodist Church, Free Methodist Church of North America, Methodist Episcopal Church, and Methodist Episcopal Church, South, Pillar of Fire, Primitive Methodist Church in the U.S.A., Southern Methodist Church, Union American Methodist Episcopal Church (formerly the Union Church of Africans), and the Wesleyan Church.

Baker University
United Methodist Historical Library
606 Eighth Street
Baldwin City, KS 66006
(785) 594-6451, ext. 380
Harvey Kreutziger
Mon–Fri 8:00–noon, and by appointment

Banneker-Douglas Museum
(see Ethnic Archives, Libraries and Societies—African, Part 3)

Bush-Meeting Dutch
Illinois College
Jacksonville, IL 62650
(217) 245-3460
Dr. David Koss, Professor of Religion, Editor
Pub. *The Bush-Meeting Dutch: A Quarterly Newsletter of Local History and Genealogy of the Former Evangelical United Brethren Church, Its Predecessors, and Sister Churches*, $5.00 per year subscription
(German-American churches)
$2.00 per obituary search

J. B. Cain Archives of Mississippi Methodism
Millsaps-Wilson Library
Millsaps College
Jackson, MS 39210
(601) 974-1077; (601) 974-1082 FAX
mcintdw@millsaps.edu
http://library.millsaps.edu/library
Debra McIntosh, College Archivist
weekdays 8:30 A.M.–12:30 A.M. (when the college is in session)
("Methodist church history in Mississippi; genealogy is not a focus of this collection.")
research: $10.00 per name

Centenary College of Louisiana
Sam Peters Research Center
(address withheld upon request)
("Methodist and Centenary materials were transferred to our new archival facility; the rest of the collection includes census reports, some land records, and a good number of family histories; most are specific to this part of the state")

Centenary United Methodist Church (Missouri East)
(16th and Pine Streets—location)
55 Plaza Square (mailing address)
Saint Louis, MO 63103
(314) 421-3136
Paula Price, Membership Secretary
Mon–Fri 9:00–4:00

Center for the Evangelical United Brethren Heritage
United Theological Seminary
1810 Harvard Boulevard
Dayton, OH 45406
(937) 278-5817, ext. 2220; (937) 278-5701 FAX
http://www.united.edu/eubcenter
James D. Nelson; Gail M. Stevens Shourds, Archivist
Mon–Fri 8:00–4:00, and by appointment
Pub. *The Telescope-Messenger*, semiannually
(Archival respository of Evangelical United Brethren Church [1946–1968], Church of the United Brethren in Christ [1800–1946], Evangelical Association/ Evangelical Church [1800–1946], United Evangelical Church [1889–1922].)
$10.00+ membership

Archives of DePauw University and Indiana United Methodism
(see DePauw University, Roy O. West Library, Indiana, Part 2)

B. L. Fisher Library
Asbury Theological Seminary

North Lexington Avenue
Wilmore, KY 40390
(859) 858-3581, ext. 235
Sylvia U. Brown, Special Collections Librarian
8:00–noon & 1:00–4:30

McKendree College
Lebanon, IL 62254

Methodist Historical Society
PO Box 127
Madison, NJ 07940
(973) 408-3189
http://www.gcah.org
Pub. *The Historian's Digest*, quarterly

Methodist Historical Society
(address withheld upon request)

The Missouri Methodist Historical Society
The Missouri United Methodist Archives
Smiley Memorial Library
411 Central Methodist Square
Fayette, MO 65248
(816) 415-0480 (Editor)
jogooch@aol.com
http://www.cmc.edu/library/Archives/ Historical_society.html
John O. Gooch, Editor
Pub. *Towards the Setting Sun*
$12.00 per year membership or subscription

North Georgia Methodist Historical Society
1015 Ruckersville Road
Elberton, GA 30635
(706) 283-8426
Rev. Ann Nell Fletcher, Chair
$10.00 per year membership

Roberts Wesleyan College
Kenneth B. Keating Library
Archives and Chesbrough-Roberts Historical Center
2301 Westside Drive
Rochester, NY 14624
(716) 594-6016

Charles Andrew Rush Library
Birmingham-Southern College
Arkadelphia Road
Birmingham, AL 35254
(205) 226-4740
Mon–Thur 8:00–midnight, Fri 8:00–5:00, Sat 9:00–5:00, Sun 2:00–noon

Saint Paul School of Theology
5123 Truman Road
Kansas City, MO 64127-2499
(816) 483-9600
William S. Sparks, Director of Library and Information Services
by appointment
(annual conference journals from the 1850s, clergy biographies, printed histories)

Southeastern Jurisdictional Administrative Council
The United Methodist Church
Commission on Archives and History
The SEJ Heritage Center
PO Box 1165
Lake Junaluska, NC 28745
(828) 452-2881, ext. 781
Mrs. Gerry Reiff, SEJ Director of Archives and History
Tue–Fri 9:30–4:00; longer hours during summer season
Pub. *SEJ/HS Notes: The Newsletter of the Southeastern Jurisdictional Historical Society, The United Methodist Church,*

quarterly, $7.00 per year subscription to Rev. Lawrence Lugar, 334 Grape Arbor Drive, Fayetteville, NC 28301)
(history of Methodism in the southeast and the history of the Lake Junaluska Assembly, but limited genealogical resources, only on United Methodist clergy of the southeast; all local church membership rolls and other records of local churches go to the annual conference depository when no longer needed by the local church)

Southern Methodist Church
PO Box 39
Orangeburg, SC 29116-0039
http://www.southernmethodistchurch.org

Southern Methodist University
DeGloyer Library of Special Collections
Dallas, TX 75275
(972) 768-2012; (972) 768-1565 FAX
http://www.smu.edu/~cul/degolyer/index. html

Southwestern College
Memorial Library
100 College Street
Winfield, KS 67156

United Methodist Church
(810 12th Avenue, South—location)
PO Box 320 (mailing address)
Nashville, TN 37202-0320
http://www.umc.org

United Methodist Church
Fountain Square
PO Box 505
Contoocook, NH 03229

United Methodist Conference Archives

North Alabama Conference Archives
Birgmingham-Southern College Library
Birmingham, AL 35254
(205) 226-4752
ghubbs@bsc.edu
http://www.gcah.org/Directory/CommAH. htm
Guy Hubbs
Mon–Fri 9:00–4:00

Methodist Archives
Houghton Memorial Library
Archives and Special Collections
Huntingdon College
1500 East Fairview Avenue
Montgomery, AL 36106-2148
(334) 833-4413; (334) 263-4465
mpickard@huntingdon.edu
http://www.gcah.org/Conference/umac/ awf.htm
Mary Ann Pickard, Archivist
Mon–Fri 9:00–4:00 by appointment
(Genealogical data limited to Methodist ministers in Alabama and West Florida, and college alumni: Methodist Episcopal Church 1808–1938, Methodist Protestant Church 1829–1938, Methodist Episcopal Church, South 1846–1938, The Methodist Church 1939–1967, United Methodist Church from 1968. Alabama/ West Florida Conference, Depository of Archives and Historical Materials)

Alaska Missionary Conference
Commission on Archives and History
(3402 Wesleyan Drive, Anchorage, AK 99508-4866—location)
12585 Glacier Highway (mailing address)
Juneau, AK 99801-8630

(907) 279-4862 (Archives); (907) 333-5050
(Archivist); (907) 279-4862 FAX (with
prior notice); (907) 333-2304 FAX
http://gcah.org/Conference/umac/ak.htm
Bea Shepard, Archivist
by appointment

Desert Southwest Conference
1550 East Meadowbrook Drive
Phoenix, AZ 85040-4040
(602) 258-8048
marlenenn@msn.com;
conference@desertsw.org
http://www.gcah.org/Conference/umac/
dsw.htm
Marlene Northup, Archivist
by appointment

Arkansas Area United Methodist Archives
Olin C. Bailey Library
Hendrix College
1600 Washington Street
Conway, AR 72032
(501) 336-9321; (501) 336-9001 FAX
http://www.gcah.org/Conference/umac/
arc.htm
Mauzel Beal, Archivist
Thur 10:00–2:00, Sat 1:00–4:00, and by
appointment
(Arkansas area Methodist clergy only, SASE
required. Little Rock and North Arkansas
conferences)

**California-Nevada United Methodist
Archives**
Graduate Theological Union
2400 Ridge Road
Berkeley, CA 94709
(650) 952-5177
seyale@earthlink.net
http://www.gtu.edu/library/archives
Dr. Stephen E. Yale
by appointment
Pub. *Newsletter*, semiannually
(second depository at J.A.B. Fry Library,
University of the Pacific)
$5.00 per year membership in Methodist
Historical Society (address withheld);
genealogical research: $25.00 per hour

California-Pacific Conference Archives
Claremont School of Theology
1325 North College Avenue
Claremont, CA 91711-3199
(909) 626-3521
ellisbigbear@earthlink.net
Betty Clements, Archivist; Lyman B. Ellis,
Secretary

The Iliff School of Theology Archives
Margaret E. Scheve Archives
Ira J. Taylor Library
2201 South University Boulevard
Denver, CO 80210
(303) 765-3179; (303) 777-0164 FAX
meidson@iliff.edu
http://www.iliff.edu/taylor_library/
special.htm; http://discuss.iliff.edu/
meidson/archives
Paul Millette, Archivist; Marshall Eidson,
Curator of Archives/Special Collections
Mon–Thur 12:30–4:00 by appointment
(United Methodist Church, Rocky Mountain
Conference, including church membership
and baptism records)

Peninsula-Delaware Conference Archives
Barratt's Chapel and Museum
(U.S. Route 113 or State Route
12—location)
6362 Bay Road (mailing address)
Frederica, DE 19946

(302) 335-5544; (302) 335-5750 FAX
barratts@aol.com
http://users.aol.col/barratts/home.html
Lynn Hobbs, Curator
Sat–Sun 1:30–4:30
(The oldest house of worship still extant in
the U.S. built solely for and by a
Methodist Society)

Florida Conference Archives
(E. T. Roux Library, Florida Southern
College—location)
PO Box 3767 (mailing address)
Lakeland, FL 33802
(863) 688-9276
http://www.gcah.org/Directory/
CommAH.htm
Nell Thrift, Archivist
hours: various
$10.00 donation requested for genealogical
research

Emory University
Pitts Theology Library
Chandler School of Theology
Archives and Manuscripts
505 Kilgo Circle
Atlanta, GA 30322
(404) 727-4166; (404) 727-1222 (Clemens);
(404) 727-1223 (Graham); (404) 727-
1219 FAX
jscleme@emory.edu; rawrigh@emory.edu
http://www.pitts.emory.edu/Archives/
Organization.html
Joan Clemens; Anne Graham
("We have very little information that is of
use to genealogists, and we do not
conduct research for genealogists." North
Georgia United Methodist Conference
files.)

The Methodist Museum
Epworth By The Sea
South Georgia Methodist Conference Center
PO Box 20407
Saint Simons Island, GA 31522
(912) 638-4050 (Museum)
http://www.gcah.org/Directory/CommAH.
htm
Mary McCook, Museum Director; Mary
Vice, Archivist
Tue–Sat 9:00–4:00
Pub. *Historical Highlights*, biannually by the
South Georgia Conference Historical
Society
$10.00 per year membership

Illinois Great Rivers Conference
United Methodist Church
Historical Society and Conference Archives
(1211 North Park Street—location)
PO Box 515 (mailing address)
Bloomington, IL 61702-0515
(309) 828-5092; (309) 829-8369 FAX
http://www.gch.org/Conference/umac/
igrc.htm
Richard A. Chrisman, Conference Historian
weekdays 8:00–noon
Pub. *Historical Messenger*, quarterly
$10.00 per year membership; research:
$10.00 per hour plus copy costs, must
send SASE

**Illinois Great Rivers (Southern)
Conference Archives**
Holman Library
McKendree College
701 College Road
Lebanon, IL 62254
(618) 632-1115
haroldisbl@aol.com
http://www.gcah.org/Conference/umac/

igrs.htm
Linda Isabell, Archivist
by appointment

**Northern Illinois Conference of the United
Methodist Church**
Garrett-Evangelical Theological Seminary
The United Library
2121 Sheridan Road
Evanston, IL 60201
(708) 866-3902
http://www.gcah.org/Directory/CommAH.
htm
Kevin B. Leonard, Archivist
by appointment only, written inquiries
welcome
(United Methodist and antecedent
denominations in approximately the
northern third of Illinois: Methodist
Church, Methodist Episcopal Church,
Evangelical United Brethren, United
Brethren in Christ, Evangelical Church,
Evangelical Association; also some
records of Scandinavian Methodist
Churches and organizations from other
regions of the United States)

**Southern Illinois Conference of the United
Methodist Church**
Commission on Archives and History
1919 West Broadway
Mount Vernon, IL 62864
(618) 242-4070; (618) 242-9227 FAX
Rev. Eugene Black, Chairperson
9:00–4:00

North Indiana Conference Archives
(see DePauw University, Roy O. West
Library, Indiana, Part 2)

South Indiana Conference Archives
(see DePauw University, Roy O. West
Library, Indiana, Part 2)

**Archives of the Iowa Conference of the
United Methodist Church**
Chadwick Library
Iowa Wesleyan College
601 North Main
Mount Pleasant, IA 52641
(319) 385-6321
archives@iaumc.org
http://www.iaumc.org
Esther Wonderlich, Archivist
Mon–Fri 1:00–3:00 (prefer written requests)
(Iowa Methodist pastors and Iowa churches)
$10.00 per name per search

**Kansas East Conference of the United
Methodist Church Archives**
Baker University
Collins Library
(Eighth and Fremont, Terrace
Level—location)
PO Box 65 (mailing address)
Baldwin, KS 66006
(785) 594-8380
Brenda.Day@bakeru.edu;
day@harvey.bakeru.edu
http://www.bakeru.edu/library/archives/
BakerArchives.htm
Brenda Day, Archivist
Mon–Fri 10:00–noon & 1:00–3:00, and by
appointment
research: $20.00 per hour ($10.00
minimum), plus copies at 15¢ per page;
admission: free

**Kansas West Conference Archives of the
United Methodist Church**
9440 East Boston, Suite 198
Wichita, KS 67207-3600

(316) 684-0266
lbechtel@kswestumc.org
http://www.gcah.org/Directory/CommAH.
htm
Leda Bechtel, Archivist
by appointment
("Emphasis on United Methodist and
predecessor denominational history in
western two-thirds of Kansas, as well as
local churches in that geographic area,
and former clergy.")
research: $8.00 per hour by archivist, no
charge for local church information

Red Bird Missionary Conference Archives
6 Queendale Center
Beverly, KY 40913
(606) 598-3189 (Home); (606) 598-5915;
(606) 598-6405 FAX
redbirdco@kih.net
http://www.gbgm-umc.org/redbirdconference
Eldon Shickell, Chair, Commission on
History and Archives

Kentucky Conference Archives
B. L. Fisher Library
Asbury Theological Seminary
Wilmore, KY 40390
(859) 858-2235
bill_kostlevy@asburyseminary.edu
http://www.gcah.org/Directory/
CommAH.htm
William Kostlevy
by appointment only

Archives and History
The Louisiana Conference of The United
Methodist Church
(Magale Library—location)
PO Box 41188
Shreveport, LA 71134-1188
timhebert@earthlink.net
http://www.iscuo.org
Kyle Labor, Archivist; Tim Hebert,
Chairperson, Commission on Archives
and History
("A smaller amount of material is located at
the university library of Dillard University
in New Orleans,"
http://www.iscuo.org/dillard.htm)

Commission on Archives and History
35 Highland Avenue
Gardiner, ME 04345
Elizabeth Bachelder, Chairman
(Handles historical operations of the New
England Conference [formerly the Maine
Conference, the New Hampshire
Conference, and the Southern New
England Conference] of the United
Methodist Church. The collection pertains
primarily but not exclusively to Methodist
clergy. For New Hampshire matters,
contact Charles W. Kern, Conference
Historian, 4192-09 Northgate Drive, KK9,
Kissimmee, FL 34746-6444, (407) 933-
0412)

United Methodist Historical Society, Inc.
Lovely Lane Museum
2200 Saint Paul Street
Baltimore, MD 21218
(410) 889-4458; (410) 889-1501 FAX
http://www.bwconf.org/archivehistory/
index.htm
Suni Johnson, Director of Archives and
History, Baltimore-Washington
Conference, UMC; Rev. Edwin Schell,
Executive Secretary
Mon & Fri 10:00–4:00, and by appointment
Pub. *Third Century Methodism*, two to four
times per year

("Our archives holds church records only
from churches within the boundaries of
the Baltimore-Washington Conference
and only of churches that have closed.
Churches that are still in operation or have
merged with other congregations are
responsible for maintaining their own
records. We can refer researchers to the
proper UMC archives if necessary."
Includes United Methodist and
predecessor organizations: Methodist
Protestant, Methodist Episcopal,
Methodist Episcopal Church North and
South, United Brethren in Christ and
Evangelical United Brethren)
$10.00 per year membership; admission:
$2.00 for nonmembers; research: $10.00
minimum, plus 15¢ per copy and postage

**United Methodist Church, New England
Conference, Commission on Archives and
History**
745 Commonwealth Avenue
Boston, MA 02215
(617) 353-1323; (617) 358-0699 FAX
neccah@bu.edu
Stephen Pentek, Archives Coordinator
Mon–Fri 9:00–3:00 (mail inquiries on
Methodist Episcopal, Methodist, or
United Methodist Church in New
England; appointments suggested before
on-site visit)

**Detroit Conference United Methodist
Archives**
Shipman Library
Adrian College
111 South Madison
Adrian, MI 49221
(517) 265-5161, ext. 4429
jsimmons@adrian.edu
Rev. James G. Simmons, Archivist
usually Mon–Thur 8:00–noon
Pub. *The Historical Messenger*, quarterly
(archives for Detroit Conference Methodist
Episcopal, Methodist Protestant,
Methodist, and United Methodist
churches and clergy)
$6.00 per year membership in The Friends of
the Archives

**The West Michigan Conference Archives
of the United Methodist Church**
Special Collections of the Stockwell-Mudd
Libraries
Albion College
611 East Porter Street
Albion, MI 49224
(517) 629-0487; (517) 629-0504 FAX
archives@albion.edu
http://www.albion.edu/library/
specialcollections/metharch.asp
Jennifer Thomas, Archivist
by appointment only
("This is also the Archives for Albion
College.")
research: first 30 minutes free, $10.00 per
hour thereafter

**Minnesota Conference Archives, United
Methodist Church**
122 West Franklin Avenue, Room 400
Minneapolis, MN 55404
(612) 870-0058, ext. 249; (612) 870-1260
FAX
thelma.boeder@mnumc.org
http://www.gcah.org/Directory/CommAH.
htm
Thelma Boeder, Archivist
weekdays only, hours and days vary

Mississippi Conference Archives

(see J. B. Cain Archives of Mississippi
Methodism, Millsaps-Wilson Library, above)

The Missouri United Methodist Archives
Smiley Memorial Library
411 Central Methodist Square
Fayette, MO 65248
(660) 248-6271
muma@cmc.edu
http://www.cmc.edu/library/Archives/
ARCHIVES.html
Joy Dodson, Archives Technician
Mon–Fri 8:00–5:00
(Missouri Methodism from the 1800s:
United Methodist, United Brethren,
Evangelical, Methodist Episcopal,
Methodist Episcopal South, German
Methodist, Methodist Protestant)
research: $5.00 per hour

Missouri East Conference Archives
(see Western Historical Manuscript
Collection, Missouri, Part 2)

**United Methodist Archives—Yellowstone
Conference**
(Paul M. Adams Memorial Library, Rocky
Mountain College, 1511 Poly Drive,
Billings, MT 59102—location)
PO Box 2012 (mailing address)
Billings, MT 59103-2012
(406) 259-7956
bfumc@mcn.net
http://www.gcah.org/Directory/CommAH.
htm
Joyce Jensen, Archivist; Cathie Pasco,
Committee Chair
by appointment when Adams Library is open
("Yellowstone Conference, particularly
Montana portion")
donation accepted

**Historical Center of the Nebraska
Conference of the United Methodist
Church**
(Cochrane-Woods Library, Lower Level,
Nebraska Wesleyan University—location)
PO Box 4553 (mailing address)
Lincoln, NE 68504-0553
(402) 465-2175
nebrumchc@yahoo.com
http://www.umcneb.org (Conference web
site)
Erin Nellessen, Curator
Tue–Thur 8:30–4:30
research: $30.00 per hour, personal research

**General Commission on Archives and
History**
The United Methodist Church
Drew University Campus
(36 Madison Avenue—location)
PO Box 127
Madison, NJ 07940
(973) 408-3189; (973) 408-3909 FAX
dapatterson@gcah.org
http://www.gcah.org
Dawn Patterson
Mon–Fri 9:00–5:00
Pub. *Methodist History*, quarterly, $20.00
per year subscription; *The Historian's
Digest*
("The center undertakes limited genealogical
research. Our work is usually limited to
obituaries of ordained clergy, though
sometimes we can find information on
missionaries. The fee is $25.00,
nonrefundable. It must be noted that
churches are not required to give their
records to a conference archive. We also
undertake limited general research on
subjects pertaining to Methodism. . . . The

Greater New Jersey Conference is a result of the August 1999 merger of the former Southern New Jersey and Northern New Jersey conferences.")

New Mexico Conference Archives
2210 Silver Avenue, S.E.
Albuquerque, NM 87106
(505) 232-8710; (505) 265-6184 FAX
http://www.gcah.org/Directory/CommAL.
htm
Elizabeth Collins, Archivist
Mon–Tue 9:00–3:00 by appointment

C. Wesley Christman Archives
New York Annual Conference Center
20 Soundview Avenue
White Plains, NY 10606
(914) 997-1570; (888) 696-6922
archives@nyac.com
http://www.gcah.org/Directory/CommAH.
htm
Bette Johnson Sohm, Archivist

North Central New York Conference Archives
(8422 North Main Street—location)
PO Box 1515 (mailing address)
Cicero, NY 13039-1515
(315) 699-3042; (315) 699-8774 FAX
ncnysharon@aol.com;
gtstremain@earthlink.net
http://www.ncnyumc.org/archiveshistory/
research
Sharon Markowski; Gilbert Smith, Archivist
Mon–Fri 9:00–4:00 by appointment

Troy Conference Center
Attn: Archives
PO Box 560
Saratoga Springs, NY 12866
(518) 474-5963 (Home)
http://www.gcah.org/Directory/
CommAH.htm
Jim Dorsaro, Archivist; Erica Burke,
Archives Assistant

Green Mountain College
(Griswold Library, Poultney, VT 05764-1199—location)
Clover Street, Box 113 (mailing address)
Ocean Park, ME 04063
(802) 287-9313 (Vermont)
Charles Schwartz, Curator
academic year 8:00 A.M.–10:30 P.M., summer
8:00–4:00 (closed weekends)
(Troy Conference United Methodist and
Welsh ethnic materials; no research in this
collection is done by on-site library staff.)

Western New York Conference Archives
Central Park United Methodist Church
216 Beard Avenue
Buffalo, NY 14214
(716) 833-3193
marillaumc@juno.com
http://www.www.gcah.org/Directory/
CommAH.htm
Matthew Stengel, Commission on Archives
and History Chair; Robert Leaqch,
Archivist; Duane W. Priset, Historian; G.
Calvin Sheasley, Research Requests

Wyoming Annual Conference of the United Methodist Church: Archives Center
(1700 Monroe Street, Endicott, NY 13760-5599—location)
PO Box 58 (mailing address)
Endicott, NY 13761-0058
(607) 757-0608; (607) 757-0752 FAX
history@epix.net;

rmschlock@wyomingconference.org
http://www.wyomingconference.org
Ken Bitler, Archivist
Thur 10:00–3:00 by appointment only
("Our conference has been in existence since
1852. It has United Methodist Churches
in Northeastern Pennsylvania and the
Southern Tier of New York. Counties
include NY: Broome, Tioga, Chenango,
Otsego, Delaware; PA: Bradford,
Susquehanna, Wyoming, Lackawanna,
Luzerne.")

North Carolina Conference Archives
North Carolina Archives Room
(1307 Glenwood Avenue—location)
PO Box 10955 (mailing address)
Raleigh, NC 27605
(919) 832-9560; (919) 834-7989 FAX
archives-history@nccumc.org;
engrill@pinehurst.net
http://www.gcah.org/Directory/CommAH.
htm
Laura Bailey; C. Franklin Grill, Historian
Mon–Fri 9:00–1:00 by appointment

Western North Carolina United Methodist Commission on Archives and History
(3400 Shamrock Drive, Charlotte, NC 28215—location)
PO Box 18005 (mailing address)
Charlotte, NC 28218-0005
(704) 535-2260, ext. 168
archives@wnccumc.org
Dr. Nancy Anderson, Archivist; Nancy
Spaine, Assistant Archivist
Tue–Wed 9:00–4:00 (appointment
requested)
(Western North Carolina Conference of the
United Methodist Church)
research: $10.00 per hour over one hour;
copies: 25¢ per page

Archives of Ohio United Methodism
Beeghly Library
Ohio Wesleyan University
43 Rowland Avenue
Delaware, OH 43015
(740) 368-3285
aoum@owu.edu
http://cc.owu.edu/~librweb/spuma.htm
Carol Holliger, Acting Curator
Mon–Fri 9:00–2:30
("Jointly sponsored and supported by the
University and the East and West Ohio
Conferences of the United Methodist
Church.")

Oklahoma Conference Archives
(see Oklahoma City University, Oklahoma,
Part 2)

Oklahoma Indian Missionary Conference Archives
HC 30, Box 2450
Lawton, OK 73501
dwoimc@aol.com
http://www.gbgm-umc.org/oimc
Charles Quoetone, Chair; Louvina Frank,
Secretary

UM Archives, Oregon Idaho Conference
680 State Street, Suite B-60
Salem, OR 97301
(503) 371-3901
djk1508@aol.com; smkmikie@aol.com;
lila25@juno.com
http://www.gcah.org/Directory/CommAH.
htm
Don and Shirley Knepp, Co-archivists
(Oregon); Lila Hill, Archivist (Idaho)
by appointment

Western Pennsylvania Conference Archives
Smeltzer-Bell Research Center
Pelletier Library
Allegheny College
Meadville, PA 16335
(814) 337-5007
uma@alleg.edu
http://www.umchurch.org
William L. Waybright, Archivist

United Methodist Archives
Central Pennsylvania Conference of the
United Methodist Church
Lycoming College Library
Williamsport, PA 17701
(570) 321-4088
loyer@lycoming.edu
http://www.lycoming.edu/dept/umarch
Mon 9:00–8:00
("Each congregation is responsible for
maintaining its own records of
membership, baptisms, marriages, etc.
The archives does not attempt to gather
information of this nature from individual
congregations. The archives will,
however, attempt to put individuals
seeking such information in contact with
the proper local congregation.")

Methodist Historical Center
c/o Historic Saint George's Church
(235 North Fourth Street, above Benjamin
Franklin Bridge—location)
326 New Street (mailing address)
Philadelphia, PA 19106
(215) 925-7788
Brian McCloskey, Administrator
10:00–3:00
(Methodist library and archives for eastern
Pennsylvania Conference—United
Methodist Church only; "America's
oldest continuously used United
Methodist edifice")

South Carolina United Methodist Collection
Sandor Teszler Library
Wofford College
429 North Church Street
Spartanburg, SC 29303-3663
(864) 597-4309; (864) 597-4329 FAX
stonerp@wofford.edu
http://www.wofford.edu
Phillip Stone, Archivist
Mon–Fri 9:30–noon & 1:00–4:00, by
appointment
(South Carolina Conference)

Dakotas Conference of the United Methodist Church
Archives and History Library
(1331 West University—location)
Box 460 (mailing address)
Mitchell, SD 57301-0460
(605) 996-6552 (voice mail available); (605)
996-1766 FAX
pat.breidenbach@dakotasumc.org
http://www.dakotasumc.org
Patricia A. Bridenbach, Archivist
Tue–Thur 9:00–noon & 1:00–4:00 by
appointment

Tennessee Conference Archives
520 Commerce Street, Suite 205
Nashville, TN 37203-3714
(615) 263-0518
vunruh@comcast.net
http://www.gcah.org/Directory/CommAH.
htm
Von W. Unruh, Commision on Archives and
History Chair

Thur 1:00–4:30
Pub. *Methodism in the Tennessee Conference*, quarterly, $12.00 per year subscription
$20.00 per year membership

Holston Conference Archives
Kelly Library of Emory and Henry College
Archives and Special Collections
PO Box 948
Emory, VA 24327-0948
(276) 944-6208
rjvejnar@ehc.edu
http://www.library.ehc.edu/archives.html
Mon–Fri 8:30–4:30

Memphis Conference United Methodist Archives
Luther L. Gobbel Library
Lambuth University
705 Lambuth Boulevard
Jackson, TN 38301
(731) 425-3327
wood-j@lambuth.edu
http://www.lambuth.edu/academics/library/MemphisConferenceArchives.html
Jackie Wood, Archivist
Mon–Fri 8:30–4:30, and by appointment
(United Methodist religious archives of extreme West Tennessee and Kentucky only: obituaries of ministers who died in the immediate area, no information on individual church members; depository of the administrative business records, not of individual church records; "We have no paid staff and can do minimal genealogy requests on a 'when we have time' basis, must have SASE.")
copy and postage charges

Texas Conference Archives
Doornbos Library
Lon Morris College
Jacksonville, TX 75766
http://www.gcah.org/Directory/CommAH.htm
Bill B. Hedges, Historian
Tue–Wed 9:00–3:00 and by appointment

Central Texas Conference
Texas Wesleyan University
West Library
1201 Wesleyan Street
Fort Worth, TX 76105-1536
(817) 531-6550
roszellc@txwes.edu
http://www.gcah.org/Conference/umac/ctx.htm
Carol Roszell, Archivist
Mon–Fri 8:00–3:30; research visits by appointment
research: fee required for extended work, all or email for fees

North Texas Conference Archives
Center for Methodist Studies at Bridwell Library
Southern Methodist University
Perkins School of Theology
(address withheld upon request)
Mon–Fri by appointment (withheld)
("We . . . do not have the staff to do genealogical research. We archive only the official records of the North Texas Conference, and do not maintain membership, death/birth records. We refer all related questions to the General Commission on Archives and History of the United Methodist Church, which only have clergy records." The library houses the archives of the South Central

Jurisdiction of the United Methodist Church, including the Rio Grande Conference.)

Archives of Northwest Texas Conference
McMurry Station, Box 218
Abilene, TX 79697
(915) 793-4696
http://www.gcah.org/Directory/CommAH.htm
Pat Williamson, Archivist

Rio Grande Conference Archives
2108 Robin Street
McAllen, TX 78504
http://www.gcah.org/Directory/CommAH.htm
Jose Glindo, Chair; Minerva Garza, Secretary
(depository at Southern Methodist University, Bridwell Library)

Southwest Texas Conference Archives
United Methodist Center
16400 Huebner Road
San Antonio, TX 78248
(210) 408-4500
http://www.gcah.org/Directory/CommAH.htm
Douglas Cannon, Research Requests
9:00–4:00

Virginia Conference Archives
Methodist Conference and District Records
Randolph-Macon College Library
Special Collections
PO Box 5005
Ashland, VA 23005-5505
(804) 752-7200
http://www.rmc.edu/directory/offices/library/specialcollections/confer.asp

Pacific Northwest Conference Archives
5323 97th Avenue Court West
University Place, WA 98467
(253) 564-3757 voice & FAX
http://www.gcah.org/Directory/CommAH.htm
Richard A. Seiber, Archivist
by appointment only
(Archive East at Central United Protestant, (CUP) Richland, WA, Archives West at Wesley Homes (Wesley Terrace), Des Moines, WA 98198. "The East Side houses the old Columbia River Conference material, and the West Side houses the old Puget Sound Conference material. These two conferences were merged in 1928 to be the Pacific Northwest Conference. The main archives are at the University of Puget Sound, Tacoma." [see Washington, Part 2])

West Virginia Conference Methodist Collection
West Virginia Wesleyan College Library
59 College Avenue
Buckhannon, WV 26201
(304) 473-8456; (304) 493-6532 (for appointment, not research requests)
tolliver_t@academ.wvwc.edu
Patricia Prout Tolliver, Researcher
by appointment only (please call first, because the college staff is not able to help visitors to this collection)
(West Virginia Conference United Methodist and predecessors; "This is the depository for the West Virginia Conference under the Commission on Archives and History for that conference.")
research: written queries only, no fee required, but donation requested, copies 10¢ per page

Historical Library and Archives
Wisconsin United Methodist Conference Center
(750 Windsor Street—location)
PO Box 620 (mailing address)
Sun Prairie, WI 53590-0620
(608) 837-7328, ext. 243
archives@wisconsinmc.org
http://www.wisconsinmc.org/archives
Mary Schroeder, Archivist and Historical Librarian
Mon–Tue & Thur 8:00–noon
Pub. *Wisconsin Annual Conference Yearbook and Journal*, annually
research fee requested

United Theological Seminary
Memorial Library
1810 Harvard Boulevard
Dayton, OH 45406-4599
(937) 278-5817; (937) 275-5701 FAX
library@united.edu
http://library.united.edu/library.asp
Sarah D. Brooks Blair; Gail M. Stevens Shourds, Archivist
Mon–Fri (varies with academic terms)
(Archival respository of United Theological Seminary and the Center for the Evangelical United Brethren Heritage [predecessor denomination in the United Methodist Church])

Virginia United Methodist Historical Society
(address withheld upon request)
no staff resources to genealogical research

United Missionary Church
(see Missionary Church)

United Pentecostal Church International

United Pentecostal Church International
8855 Dunn Road
Hazelwood, MO 63042
http://www.upci.org

United Presbyterian Church in the U.S.A. (UPCUSA)
(see Presbyterian)

United Presbyterian Church of North America (UPCNA)
(see Presbyterian)

The United Synagogue of Conservative Judaism
(see Ethnic Archives, Libraries and Societies—Jewish, Part 3)

United Synod of the Presbyterian Church
(see Presbyterian)

United Synod of the South
(see Lutheran)

Unity Movement

Association of Unity Churches
PO Box 610
Lee's Summit, MO 64063
http://www.unity.org

Unity School of Christianity
Unity Archives

1901 N.W. Blue Parkway
Unity Village, MO 64065-0001
(816) 524-3550, ext. 2370 (Library); (816)
    524-3550, ext. 2020 (Unity Archives);
    (816) 251-3555 FAX
archives@unityworldhq.org
Carolyn Stewart, Archivist
Mon–Thur 7:30–5:00
Pub. *Unity Magazine*, monthly, $19.95 per
    year subscription in the U.S., $34.95 per
    year subscription in Canada; *Daily Word*,
    monthly, $12.95 per year subscription in
    the U.S.
(materials on the Unity Movement which
    began in 1889 in Kansas City, Missouri)

Unity of the Brethren
(see also Brethren)

Unity of the Brethren
Board of Christian Education
9063 Bell Meadows Boulevard
Belton, TX 76513
(254) 947-0295; (254) 947-0195 FAX
ronwinsman@hotmail.com
http://www.unityofthebrethren.org
Dee Winsman, Chairman

Universalist
(see Unitarian Universalist)

Vineyard Churches

VineyardUSA
PO Box 2089
Stafford, TX 77497-8464
(281) 331-8463; (281) 313- 8464 FAX
info@vineyardusa.org
http://vineyardusa.org
Bert Waggoner, National Director

Volunteers of America, Inc.

Volunteers of America, Inc.
1660 Duke Street
Alexandria, VA 22314-3421
http://www.voa.org

Waldensian

Museum of Waldensian Heritage
Rodoret Street
Valdese, NC 28690
(828) 874-2531
(Waldenses, French Christian followers of
    Pierre Waldo)

Welsh Calvinist Methodists
(see Presbyterian)

Wesleyan Church
(see also United Methodist)

Founded by Methodists, the church was
formerly known as the Wesleyan Methodist
Connection and as the Wesleyan Methodist
Church of America before merging with the
Pilgrim Holiness Church.

**Wesleyan Church Archives and Local
History Library**
PO Box 50434
Indianapolis, IN 46250
(317) 774-7996
clarkb@wesleyan.org
http://www.wesleyan.org/gensec/archives
William C. Clark, Archives Director

Wisconsin Evangelical

Lutheran Synod
(see Lutheran)

Worldwide Church of God
(formerly Radio Church of God)

Worldwide Church of God
300 West Green Street
Pasadena, CA 091123
http://www.wcg.org

Part 4. Special Resources

Lineage, Hereditary and Patriotic Societies

Conference of Patriotic and Historical Societies
122 East 58th Street
New York, NY 10022-1939

Colonial

Society of Americans of Colonial Descent
4207 64th Street
Woodside, NY 11377-5046
Roger M. L. Schmitt

Ancient and Honorable Artillery Company of Massachusetts
(Fourth Floor of Faneuil Hall—location)
Armory, Faneuil Hall (mailing address)
Boston, MA 02109
(617) 227-1638; (617) 227-7221 FAX
Dr. John F. McCaulay, Curator
Military Museum and Library: Mon–Fri
   10:00–4:00
Pub. *The Ancients*
(oldest chartered military organization in the
   western hemisphere, and the third oldest
   in the world)

The Order of Descendants of the Ancient and Honorable Artillery Company
Committee on Lineages
253 Tremont Street
Melrose, MA 02176-1835
(781) 662-8034
Dr. Roswell Levi Atwood, Chairman,
   Committee on Lineages
9:00–3:00
Pub. *The Ancients*, annually
("male having descent from member of The
   Ancient and Honorable Artillery
   Company 1637–1774, descent from
   minister who preached The Election
   Sermon, General Court member, present
   Company member 'by right of descent'")
$100.00 life membership

National Society, Women Descendants of the Ancient and Honorable Artillery Company
1234 South Cumberland Avenue
Park Ridge, IL 60068-5238
(847) 823-0502
Adeline Potter Beier, Honorary President
   National

The Society of the Ark and the Dove
c/o Maryland Historical Society
201 West Monument Street
Baltimore, MD 21201-4674
http://www.thearkandthedove.com
Charles B. Calvert, Governor
Pub. *Chronicles of the Society of the Ark and
   the Dove*, semiannually or as needed
(membership restricted to those who are
   "lineally descended from Sir George
   Calvert, or an ancestor, as the propositus,
   who came over either on the *Ark* or the
   Dove, bearing the first Maryland
   Colonists under the command of
   Governor Leonard Calvert, which sailed
   from Cowes, Isle of Wight, England, on
   St. Cecilia's Day the 22nd of November
   1633, and who settled the Province of
   Maryland")

membership applications to Mrs. Barrett L.
   McKown, 3580 Spouth River Terrace,
   Edgewater, MD 21037-3245

National Society, Children of the American Colonists
(see National Society, Daughters of
American Colonists, below)

The National Society of The Colonial Dames of America
Dumbarton House
2715 Que Street, N.W.
Washington, DC 20007-3071
(202) 337-2288
http://www.nscda.org
Registrar
Mon–Fri 9:00–5:00; Museum: Tue–Sat
   10:00–1:00

The National Society of the Colonial Dames, Colorado
McAllister House Museum
423 North Cascade Avenue
Colorado Springs, CO 80903
(719) 635-7925
Patric Fox, Co-Curator; Barbara Gately, Co-
   Curator
May–Aug: Wed–Sat 10:00–4:00, Sun
   noon–4:00; Sept–Apr: Thur–Sat
   10:00–4:00
admission: $5.00 for adults

The National Society of the Colonial Dames of America in the State of Connecticut
The Webb-Deane-Stevens Museum
211 Main Street
Wethersfield, CT 06109
(860) 529-0612
Robert A. Guffin, Jr., Director/Curator

The National Society of the Colonial Dames of America, Georgia
329 Abercorn Street
Savannah, GA 31401
(912) 233-6854; (912) 338-1828 FAX
Shelby Myrick, Jr.

The National Society of the Colonial Dames of America, Maine
(Tate House, 1270 Westbrook
Street—location)
PO Box 31 (mailing address)
Portland, ME 04112-0031
(207) 772-2023

The National Society of the Colonial Dames of America in the State of New Jersey
Buris Road
Mount Holly, NJ 08060
(609) 267-1054

The National Society of Colonial Dames of America in the State of New York
Library
215 East 71st Street
New York, NY 10021
(212) 744-3572
Margaret Warner, Executive Secretary
by appointment

The National Society of the Colonial Dames of America in the State of South Carolina
79 Cumberland Street

Charleston, SC 29401
(843) 722-3767

The National Society of the Colonial Dames of America in Tennessee
Travellers' Rest Historic House Museum
636 Farrell Parkway
Nashville, TN 37220
(615) 832-8197
Mrs. Fletch Coke, Archivist

The National Society of the Colonial Dames of America, Wisconsin
4529 West Bonnie Court
Mequon, WI 53092
(262) 242-4529
Mrs. Samuel E. Greeley, Registrar

Georgia Society, Colonial Dames, XVII Century
PO Box 249
Eastman, GA 31023-0249
John H. Goddard

South Carolina Society, Colonial Dames, XVII Century
124 Dunbarton Circle
Aiken, SC 29801
(803) 648-8516

Colonial Order of the Acorn
122 East 58th Street
New York, NY 10022-1939

The Society of Colonial Wars in the State of New York
122 East 58th Street
New York, NY 10022-1939
(212) 755-7082

National Society of the Dames of the Court of Honor
2165 Leafmore Drive
Decatur, GA 30033
Harvey Cromwell

National Society of the Dames of the Court of Honor
Oklahoma Society
1111 Ridge Road
Stillwater, OK 74074
Mrs. Pete Pappas, President

National Society, Daughters of American Colonists
National Society, Children of the American
Colonists
2205 Massachusetts Avenue, N.W.
Washington, DC 20008-2813
(202) 667-3076
Mrs. Charles W. Miles, III, Editor
Tue–Thur 9:00–4:00
Pub. *The Colonial Courier*, three times per
   year (spring, fall and winter), $5.00 per
   year subscription
invitational membership fees vary by state;
   no search fees, contact National Librarian;
   queries to be printed in the magazine,
   contact National Chairman of
   Genealogical Department

Oklahoma Society, National Society, Daughters of American Colonists
11805 Camelot Drive
Oklahoma City, OK 73120-6715
(405) 755-4428
Mrs. Earl J. Hampton, Oklahoma State

Regent

National Society, Daughters of the 17th Century
(address withheld upon request)

Order of Descendants of Colonial Physicians and Chirurgeons
9317 Bent Tree Circle
Wichita, KS 67226
(316) 634-1930
Mrs. Richard C. McGehee, President General
$100.00 life membership

National Society, Descendants of Early Quakers
111 Webster Park Avenue
Columbus, OH 43214
Pub. *Plain Language*, semiannually, $15.00
    per year subscription
(genealogy, history, and records of early
    Quakers; membership open to men,
    women and children who can establish
    descent, lineal or collateral, from an early
    member of the Society of Friends
    throughout the world)
$25.00 nonrefundable application fee,
    $100.00 life membership

National Society of Descendants of Lords of Maryland Manors
3721 Alton Place, N.W.
Washington, DC 20016

The Society of Descendants of the Colonial Clergy
255 Madison Street
Dedham, MA 02026
Mrs. Frederick Johnson

The Georgia Salzburger Society
(see Georgia, Part 2)

Holland Society of New York Library
122 East 58th Street
New York, NY 10022-1939
(212) 758-1675; (212) 758-2232 FAX
hollsoc@aol.com
http://hollandsociety.com/contact.html
Delia Nelson, Genealogist for Library; Dr.
    David Voorhees, Historian and Editor
Fri 11:00–4:00 (closed Aug)
Pub. *de Halve Maen (Half Moon)*, quarterly,
    $28.50 postpaid per year subscription
(membership restricted to "descendants in
    the direct male line from those who lived
    in the colonies under Dutch rule in
    America before or during 1675")

Huguenots
(see Lineage, Hereditary and Patriotic
Societies—Huguenot, below)

Jamestowne Society
PO Box 17426
Richmond, VA 23226-7426
(804) 673-6006
Judith N. Hart, Executive Director
Pub. *The Jamestown Society Register of
    Qualifying Seventeenth Century
    Ancestors*, $10.00
$300.00 life membership

Jamestowne Society, First Georgia Company
494 Hickory Hills Trail
Stone Mountain, GA 30083-4372
(770) 469-5224
http://www.jamestowne.org/company/gal.
    htm

General Society of Mayflower

Descendants
National Headquarters
(4 Winslow Street, Plymouth, MA
02360—location)
PO Box 3297 (mailing address)
Plymouth, MA 02361-2397
(508) 746-3188
http://www.mayflower.org
Caroline Lewis Kardell, Historian General
10:00–3:30
Pub. *The Mayflower Quarterly*, $10.00 per
    year subscription for nonmembers
(membership is through the individual state
    societies)

Society of Mayflower Descendants
Alabama Society
77 Fairway Drive
Birmingham, AL 35213-4240
Mrs. James Porter, Historian

Society of Mayflower Descendants
Alaska Society
jsseitz@alaska.com
Janet S. Seitz

Society of Mayflower Descendants
Arizona Society
Dawn Hines, Historian

Society of Mayflower Descendants
Arkansas Society
PO Box 1477
Rogers, AR 72757
(501) 925-1638 (daytime); (501) 925-3100
    (evenings and weekends)
Kathlyn Brown

California Mayflower Society
(405 14th Terrace Level, Oakland, CA
94612-2704—location)
PO Box 20417 (mailing address)
Oakland, CA 94620-0417
(510) 451-9599
Dr. Oliver S. Hayward, Librarian
Mon 8:00–4:00

Society of Mayflower Descendants in the State of Colorado
1069 South Garfield Street
Denver, CO 80209-5007
(303) 759-5989
Virginia Kracaw, Deputy Governor and
    Editor; Helen M. Clark, Secretary
Pub. *The Pilgrim Times*, two times per year
$20.00 per year membership, plus $30.00
    initiation fee

The Society of Mayflower Descendants in the State of Connecticut
MHurtuk@aol.com
http://www.ctmayflower.org
Marjorie Hurtuk, Historian
Pub. *(Connecticut) Nutmeg Gratings*, three
    times per year
(Individuals going to this web site can enter a
    Mayflower lineage for an initial review of
    the earliest generations)

Society of Mayflower Descendants in the State of Delaware
111 Norris Road, Alapocas
Wilmington, DE 19803
(302) 655-8066
raselhague@aol.com
Mrs. Ellsworth K. Holden, Governor; Ruth
    Holden, Historian
Pub. *Mayflower Lynes*, semiannually

Society of Mayflower Descendants
District of Columbia Society
1202 Saugus Court

Great Falls, VA 22066-2016
Barbara Hensley Carpenter

Society of Mayflower Descendants
Florida Society
605 Via Tunis Drive
Punta Gorda, FL 33950-6620
(941) 505-8408
flash1620@comcast.net
http://www.geocities.com/flmayflower
Muriel Curtis Cushing, State Historian
Pub. *The Florida Pilgrim*, semi-annually

Georgia Society of Mayflower Descendants
359 Whitlock Avenue, S.W.
Marietta, GA 30064
(770) 428-4706
Virginia Hargis, Corresponding Secretary;
    Jennifer Harrison
Pub. *Mayflower News of Georgia*,
    semiannually (usually Mar, Oct)

State Society of Mayflower Descendants in Hawaii
225 Kaiulani Avenue, #1005
Honolulu, HI 96815-3044
mayflower@emailhawaii.net;
    robert.townsend5@gte.net
http://www.geocities.com/hawaii1620
Robert Townsend, Historian
Pub. *Ka Pupu Nihoniho*, semi-annually
$15.00 per year membership

The Society of Mayflower Descendants in Idaho
327 Hillview Drive
Boise, ID 83712-8115
Bethel L. Marshall
("We have no central office, officers serve
    for three years.")

Society of Mayflower Descendants
Illinois Society
703 South Bodin
Hinsdale, IL 60521
Membership@IllinoisMayflower.org
Mrs. William van Cleve, Membership
    Secretary

Society of Mayflower Descendants
Indiana Society
Marhphillips@aol.com
Marilyn Phillips, Historian

Iowa Society of Mayflower Descendants
Iowa Society
9107 Tanglewood Drive
Des Moines, IA 50322-7422
(515) 252-0929
Maureen Wilson, Editor
Pub. *Hawkeye Newsletter*, semiannually
    (Apr, Oct), $1.00 per issue to
    nonmembers

Society of Mayflower Descendants—Kansas
lmytinger@aol.com
Laura D. Mytinger, Corresponding Secretary

Kentucky Society of Mayflower Descendants
Carol Woo

Society of Mayflower Descendants
Maine Society
PO Box 622
Yarmouth, ME 04096
JCI4822@juno.com
Judith Elfring, Maine State Historian
hours: various
$35.00 initiation fee and $20.00 per year

membership

Society of Mayflower Descendants in the State of Maryland
5215 Saint Alban's Way
Baltimore, MD 21212-3323
(410) 433-4992
Claire A. Richardson, State Historian
Pub. *The Maryland Mayflower Log*,
    irregularly
$50.00 filing fee, $25.00 initiation fee,
    $25.00 per year membership (Mayflower
    descendants only)

Massachusetts Society of Mayflower Descendants
100 Boylston Street, Suite 750
Boston, MA 02116
(617) 266-1624; (617) 749-5747 (Editor)
http://www.tiac.net/users/msmd
Alicia Crane Williams, Editor
Mon–Fri 9:00–4:00, open to members and
    applicants only
Pub. *The Mayflower Descendant, A
    Magazine of Pilgrim Genealogy and
    History*, semiannually (c/o 18 Martin's
    Cove Road, Hingham, MA 02043; vols.
    1–34 published 1899–1937, revived in
    1985 with vol. 35)
$18.00 per year membership

Society of Mayflower Descendants
Michigan Society
umpadre@aol.com
Rev. C. Corydon Randall II, Historian

Society of Mayflower Descendants in the State of Minnesota
1735 19th Terrace, N.W.
New Brighton, MN 55112-5441
(651) 633-5759
decoursey@earthlink.net
William Leslie DeCoursey, Historian
noon–5:00
Pub. *Minnesota Pilgrim News*, quarterly,
    $5.00 per year subscription

Society of Mayflower Descendants in the State of Mississippi
PO Box 12428
Jackson, MS 39236-2428
Helen DeForce Buford
Pub. *Mississippi Mayflower Messenger*,
    semiannually (spring and fall)
$15.00 per year membership

The Society of Mayflower Descendants in the State of Missouri
5583 Wieland Drive
Saint Louis, MO 63128-3932
(314) 391-1603
marylossos@yahoo.com
http://www.rootsweb.com/~mosmd/missouri
Mary Lossos, Corresponding Secretary
Pub. *The Compact*, two to three times per
    year
$20.00 per year membership

Society of Mayflower Descendants
Montana Society
PO Box 366
Manhattan, MT 59741
duddy@in-tch.com
Mrs. John S. West, Secretary; Mrs. Dorothy
    M. Duddy, Historian

Nevada Society of Mayflower Descendants
98 Cabernet Parkway
Reno, NV 89512-4720
NV-Mayflower@excite.com
Deborha Sugden, Secretary; Timothy Trissel,
    Historian

Society of Mayflower Descendants
New Hampshire Society
314 High Street
Hampton, NH 03842-4004
Ann T. Morton
Pub. *The Shallop*, semiannually

Society of Mayflower Descendants in the State of New Jersey
142 North Chestnut Street
Westfield, NJ 07090
(908) 233-7410
Pmahansen@aol.com
Mrs. Carl B. Hansen, Historian
Pub. *New Jersey Newsletter*, semiannually

New Mexico Society of Mayflower Descendants
6716 McCallum Boulevard
Dallas, TX 75252-5931
Mrs. Charles Runyan, Corresponding
    Secretary; Justine H. Laquer

Society of Mayflower Descendants in the State of New York
122 East 58th Street
New York, NY 10022-1946
(212) 759-1620
questions@mayflowernewyork.org
Sarah C. Morse, Executive Secretary
Sept–June: 9:00–4:30
Pub. *New York Newsletter*, semiannually
$75.00 application fee, $75.00 per year
    membership

Society of Mayflower Descendants in the State of North Carolina
219 Woodhaven Road
Greenville, NC 27834-6919
Sylvia Corey, Membership Chairman; Rick
    Barr

Society of Mayflower Descendants
North Dakota Society
1245 11th Street, North
Fargo, ND 58102
Vivian W. Broberg, Secretary

Society of Mayflower Descendants in Ohio
12145 Thames Place
Cincinnati, OH 45241-6019
(513) 761-6513
dkcscamp@raex.com
Nancy Foster, Corresponding Secretary

Society of Mayflower Descendants
Oklahoma Society
Lois Mae Copley

Society of Mayflower Descendants in Oregon
1208 Leland Drive
Medford, OR 97501-3995
(541) 779-0348
Neil Watson
Pub. *Oregon Pilgrim*, semiannually
$35.00 application to General Society,
    $15.00 per year membership

Society of Mayflower Descendants in the Commonwealth of Pennsylvania
280 Upper Gulph Road
Wayne, PA 19087-2416
(877) SAIL-1620 (toll free); (610) 526-9162
    FAX
membership@sail1620.org (Membership
    information)
http://www.libertynet.org/~maflower
Janet Springer, Secretary
Pub. *Pennsylvania Mayflower Quarterly*
$40.00 + $15.00 to join, $20.00 per year
    membership

Rhode Island Mayflower Descendants
http://www.mayflower-ri.org
Priscilla G. Usher, Governor

The Society of Mayflower Descendants in the State of South Carolina
8 Castle Hall Court
Columbia, SC 29209-0807
(803) 790-6688 (Corresponding Secretary);
    (864) 963-4706 (Governor)
Brewster210@aol.com
Sarah L. Clingman, Corresponding
    Secretary; Joseph Edgar Sherman, Jr.,
    Governor
9:00–5:30
Pub. *Palmetto Log*

Society of Mayflower Descendants in South Dakota
PO Box 517
Platte, SD 57369-0517
sdmf@midstatesd.net
Margaret Bobertz

Society of Mayflower Descendants
Tennessee Society
PO Box 393
Hixson, TN 37343-0393
Charles Ward, Historian

Society of Mayflower Descendants in Texas
7923 Woodway
Houston, TX 77063
(713) 974-2766
Mrs. Jack L. Vandagriff; Hallie Price Garner
Pub. *Quarterly*
$14.00 per year membership; $35.00
    admission fee

Society of Mayflower Descendants, State of Utah
1871 Condie Drive
Salt Lake City, UT 84119-5501
Lynne S. Turner, Historian

Society of Mayflower Descendants
Vermont Society
6126 Bennett's Corner Road
Memphis, NY 13112
(315) 672-5882
SAMatyas@aol.com
http://members.aol.com/samatyas
Sharon A. Matyas, Historian

Society of Mayflower Descendants
Virginia Society
http://www.mayflower.org (General Society)
David J. Chapin

Society of Mayflower Descendants in Washington State
PO Box 30691
Seattle, WA 98103-4726
(206) 783-7674
WEGard@aol.com
Margaret Hyre, Corresponding Secretary
9:00–5:00
Pub. *Evergreen Log*, three times per year

Society of Mayflower Descendants
West Virginia Society
301 Woodbridge Drive
Charleston, WV 25311
Denise L. Gould

Society of Mayflower Descendants
Wisconsin Society
352 River Drive
Appleton, WI 54915
martell135@aol.com
http://www.mayflowerwi.org

Mary C. Howden, Secretary; Joan Pekowsky, Historian

Society of Mayflower Descendants
Wyoming Society
2222 Montana Avenue
Sun Prairie, WY 53590
Elwood M. Porter II

National Society of New England Women
24 Elizabeth Drive
Bella Vista, AR 72714-2452
Ruth M. Oberhelman, President General
Pub. *The Clipper*, quarterly, $3.00 per year subscription

National Society of Old Plymouth Colony Descendants
24 Pilgrim Drive
Winchester, MA 01890-3371
Mrs. Francis Harding Huron, President General
$75.00 life membership

The Order of Colonial Lords of Manors in America
122 East 58th Street
New York, NY 10022-1939

Pilgrim Society
(see Massachusetts, Part 2)

The Pilgrims of the United States
122 East 58th Street
New York, NY 10022-1939

Pioneer Genealogy Society
(see Miscellaneous, Part 4)

The Saint Andrew's Society
(see Ethnic Archives, Libraries and Societies—Welsh, Part 3)

Saint George's Society of New York
(see Ethnic Archives, Libraries and Societies—Welsh, Part 3)

Saint Nicholas Society of the City of New York
122 East 58th Street
New York, NY 10022-1939
(212) 753-7175
Pub. *Weathercock*, quarterly

Sons and Daughters of the Pilgrims, National Society
3917 Heritage Hills Drive, #104
Bloomington, MN 55437-2633
(952) 893-9747 (evenings); (952) 885-9776 (days)
Arthur Louis Finnell, Registrar General
Pub. *The Pilgrim News-Letter*, two times per year

National Society Sons of American Colonists
9033 Lyndale Avenue, South, Suite 108
Bloomington, MN 55420-3535
(952) 893-9747 (evenings); (952) 885-9776 (days)
Arthur Louis Finnell, Registrar General
by appointment
Pub. *The Colonial Son*, one or two times per year

The Welcome Society of Pennsylvania
415 South Croskey Street
Philadelphia, PA 19146
(215) 732-2322
Sara L. March, Secretary
Mon–Fri 9:00–5:00

(descendants of those who arrived in Pennsylvania with William Penn between December 1681 and December 1682)
$20.00 per year membership

The Welsh Society of Philadelphia
(see Ethnic Archives, Libraries and Societies—Welsh, Part 3)

Revolutionary War

National Society, Children of the American Revolution (D.A.R.)
1776 D Street, N.W., Room 224
Washington, DC 20006-5392
(202) 638-3153; (202) 737-3162 FAX
hq@nscar.org
http://www.nscar.org
Mon–Fri 8:30–4:00
(a separate organization from the D.A.R.)

Continental Ladies
57 Peirce Street
East Greenwich, RI 02818
(401) 884-4110

National Society, Daughters of the American Revolution (D.A.R.)
Library
1776 D Street, N.W.
Washington, DC 20006-5303
(202) 879-3229 (Library); (202) 628-1776; (724) 443-6893 (Membership)
http://www.dar.org
Eric G. Grundset, Library Director; Karin Lund, Membership Chairman
Mon–Fri 8:45–4:00, Sun 1:00–5:00 (closed Sun before holiday, and closed to the public in mid-Apr)
Pub. *Daughters of the American Revolution Magazine*, ten times per year, $12.00 per year subscription; *Continental Columns*, quarterly (reprinted in *DAR Magazine*)
(collection includes "all periods of U.S. history and records for the entire country"; nearly 3,000 chapters worldwide)
entrance fee to nonmembers

DAR State Societies

Alabama Society Daughters of the American Revolution (ASDAR)
ltorbb@gulftel.com
http://www.gulftel.com/asdar
Mary Collins, Corresponding Secretary

Alaska Society Daughters of the American Revolution
Debora Refior, State Corresponding Secretary

Arizona Society Daughters of the American Revolution (ASDAR)
(address withheld upon request)

Arkansas Society Daughters of the American Revolution (ASDAR)
http://www.baxtercountyonline.com/arkdar

California State Society Daughters of the American Revolution (CSSDAR)
201 West Bennett Avenue
Glendora, CA 91741-2535
(626) 963-1776
CSSDAR@aol.com
http://www.californiadar.org

Colorado Society Daughters of the American Revolution
titus@sopris.net
http://members.aol.com/coloradodar

Suzi Titus, Corresponding Secretary

Delaware Society Daughters of the American Revolution
gingtrader@aol.com
http://members.aol.com/DEAncestor/dechaps.htm
State Registrar

District of Columbia Daughters of the American Revolution
dardc@starpower.net
http://www.dcdar.org

Florida Society Daughters of the American Revolution
http://fldar.org

Georgia Society Daughters of the American Revolution
http://geocities.com/Heartland/Ridge/4935

D.A.R. Memorial Library
(see Hawaii, Part 2)

Idaho Society Daughters of the American Revolution
http://www.geocities.com/idahodar

Illinois Society Daughters of the American Revolution
hootowl422@aol.com
http://members.aol.com/hootowl422/joyce
Anita Velloff, Webmaster

Daughters of the American Revolution, Francis Vigo Chapter DAR Genealogical Library
3 West Scott Street
Vincennes, IN 47592
(812) 882-2096
http://ipfw.edu/ipfwhist/historgs/indar.htm (State Society)
Jane Prather Niehaus, Librarian
Thur 10:00–4:00
(early Knox County, Indiana, genealogy and history)
copies: 10¢ each

Iowa Society Daughters of the American Revolution
http://angelfire.com/ia2/iowastatedar
Christie A. Noble, State Regent

Kansas Society Daughters of the American Revolution
http://www.geocities.com/Kansasdar

Kentucky Society Daughters of the American Revolution
Duncan Tavern Historic Center
Paris, KY 40361
sunshine@kycom.net
http://www.kentuckydar.org
Lynda Williams Closson, Regent; Constance Combs Kincer, Corresponding Secretary

Louisiana Society Daughters of the American Revolution
http://geocities.com/darla1776/index.html
Mrs. E. Newton Dodd

Maine Society Daughters of the American Revolution
29 White Street
Augusta, ME 04330
(207) 622-3632
sharon.ap@verizon.net
http://www.geocities.com/Heartland/Ridge/9336
Sharon Ann Paradis, Chairman, Genealogical Records Committee

Maryland Society Daughters of the American Revolution
http://pws.prserv.net/usinet.jsutton/
   MDSTATE.htm

Massachusetts Society Daughters of the American Revolution
massdar@aol.com
http://members.aol.com/massdar/
   Massachusetts_DAR/mdar.htm

Michigan Society Daughters of the American Revolution
DARofMichigan@aol.com
http://www.geocities.com/Heartland/
   Meadows/6543

Minnesota Society Daughters of the American Revolution
http://www.rootsweb.com/~mnmsdar/
   Minnesota.html

Mississippi State Society Daughters of the American Revolution (MSSDAR)
(MSSDAR Genealogical Library, On Grounds of "Rosalie"—location)
PO Box 485 (mailing address)
Hazlehurst, MS 39083
http://users.telapex.com/~dar/mssdar.htm
Wendy D. Cartwright, Library Chairman
Mon–Sat 10:00–4:00
$10.00 per year membership; admission:
   $3.00 for nonmembers

Missouri Society Daughters of the American Revolution
Roslyn Heights
Boonville, MO 65233
(660) 882-5320 (State Curator)
spfdgood@aol.com
http://www.mssdar.org
Sally Bueno, Missouri Vice-Regent

Nebraska Society Daughters of the American Revolution
Library
202 West Fourth Street
Alliance, NE 69301
http://www.geocities.com/Heartland/
   Plains/8019/index.html
Dawn Feldkamp

Nevada Society Daughters of the American Revolution
DixieLeeNV@aol.com
http://www.rootsweb.com/~nvnsdar/
   index.html
Dixie Judge, Registrar

New Hampshire Society Daughters of the American Revolution
nhsodar@hotmail.com
http://www.rivier.edu/staff/ebean/web/
   index.htm

New Jersey Society Daughters of the American Revolution
Beth109@comcast.net
http://njdar.org/njdar/default.htm
Miss Mary T. Bannan, State Regent

New Mexico Society Daughters of the American Revolution
http://rootsweb.com/~nmsodar/nmso/
   index.html

Daughters of the American Revolution
New York State Chapter
http://www.nydar.org

National Society, Daughters of the American Revolution

Hendrick Hudson Chapter
Robert Jenkins House and Museum
113 Warren Street
Hudson, NY 12534
(518) 851-9049
Marion F. Berntson, Curator
(genealogy library)

Daughters of the American Revolution
Irondequoit Chapter
11 Livingston Park
Rochester, NY 14608
(716) 232-4509

North Carolina Society Daughters of the American Revolution
http://www.northcarolinasocietydar.org
Mrs. Richard A. Boyd, State Regent

North Dakota Society Daughters of the American Revolution
nengle@bis.midco.net
http://www.cuttington.org/NDDAR/state.
   htm
Nancy Englerth, Webmaster

Daughters of the American Revolution, Ohio
1887 Northcliff Drive
Columbus, OH 43229-5332
osdar@aol.com
http://www.members.aol.com/osdar/
   index.html

Oklahoma State D.A.R. Library
c/o Oklahoma Historical Society
Library Resources Division
Wiley Post Historical Building
2100 North Lincoln Boulevard
Oklahoma City, OK 73105-4997
(405) 521-2491 (Oklahoma Historical
   Society)
jlevans@sstelco.com (State Society)
http://okdar.org (State Society)
Janice Evans
Library Resources Division: Mon 9:00–8:00,
   Tue–Sat 9:00–5:00

Oregon State Society of Daughters of the American Revolution
(3190 Chandler Egan Drive, Medford, OR 97504-7787—location)
PO Box 1033 (mailing address)
Scappoose, OR 97056-1033
(503) 678-5537 (Robert Newell House);
   (503) 633-2237 (Pioneer Mothers'
   Memorial Cabin)
http://www.rootsweb.com/~orossdar
Virginia Gloyd Berg
Museums: Fri–Sun & holidays (Mar–Oct)
   1:00–5:00
("Two Museums, 8089 Champoeg Road
   N.E., Saint Paul, OR 97137: Restored
   house of Robert E. Newell, early settler,
   politician, entrepreneur, originally built in
   1852 and houses inaugural gowns worn
   by Oregon Governors' wives, along with
   quilts, basketry, period furnishings, etc.
   (Old Butteville jail and one-room
   schoolhouse and teacherage also on the
   museum grounds). Pioneer Mothers'
   Memorial Cabin located within
   Champoeg Park, a greatly enlarged log
   cabin built of peeled hand-hewn logs,
   built in 1930 for a museum by the DAR
   and furnished much like a pioneer home
   on French Prairie in 1850s and 60s.")

Pennsylvania Society Daughters of the American Revolution
andgail@yahoo.com
http://www.geocities.com/Heartland/

Farm/1548
Ms. Andrea G. Hajducko, Pennsylvania State
   Volunteer Information Specialists
   Chairman

Rhode Island Society Daughters of the American Revolution
(401) 822-1737
ford8@cox.net
http://members.cox.net/ford8/ridar
Lorraine Hilton, State Registrar

South Carolina State Society Daughters of the American Revolution
ESTGen@aol.com
http://home.att.net./~scs.dar/index.html
Betty Thompson, State Registrar

Tennessee Society Daughters of the American Revolution
(901) 754-6383 (but better to contact via
   email)
ChrisEyeC@aol.com
http://members.aol.com/chucalissa/
   tnsdar/tnsdar.htm
C. E. Clapsadle, Site Content Editor
24/7 on the web

Texas Society Daughters of the American Revolution
http://tsdar.org
Mrs. L. Winston Morris, Corresponding
   Secretary

Utah Society Daughters of the American Revolution
(Society Records [1899–1975] are deposited
   with University of Utah, Marriott
   Library.)

Vermont Society Daughters of the American Revolution
marthelstj@hotmail.com
http://www.northshirecomputer.com/
   VTDAR/index.html
Marjorie Brown, Membership Information

Virginia Society Daughters of the American Revolution
peggy@marshallhall.org
http://www.vadar.org
Peggy Marshall, State Volunteer Information
   Specialists Chairman

Washington State Society Daughters of the American Revolution
http://home.attbi.com/~jmccoy/wssdar

West Virginia Society Daughters of the American Revolution
http://www.wvdar.org
Mrs. Robert Frankenberry, Corresponding
   Secretary

Daughters of the American Revolution
Wisconsin State Society
nainnits@coredcs.com
http://runegraphics.com/wsdar

Wyoming Society Daughters of the American Revolution
http://w3.trib.com/~wydar/index.html
State Regent

Daughters of the Cincinnati
122 East 58th Street
New York, NY 10022-1939
(212) 319-6915
http://fdncenter.org/grantmaker/cincinnati
Mrs. Robert G. Shaw, Registrar

Descendants of the Signers of the Declaration of Independence
c/o Historical Society of Pennsylvania
1300 Locust Street
Philadelphia, PA 19107-5699

Society of the Descendants of Washington's Army at Valley Forge
PO Box 915
Valley Forge, PA 19482-0915
(610) 666-5464
Betty Brown Miller, Commander-in-Chief
Pub. *The Encampment*, quarterly

Society of the Cincinnati Library
2118 Massachusetts Avenue, N.W.
Washington, DC 20008
(202) 785-2040
emclark@societyofthecincinnati.org
Ellen McCallister Clark, Library Director
Mon–Fri 10:00–4:00 by appointment
(not a genealogical library, but for
    Revolutionary War research)

Society of the Founders of Norwich, Connecticut
(see Lineage, Hereditary and Patriotic
    Societies—Regional, below)

National Society, Sons of the American Revolution
National Headquarters
1000 South Fourth Street
Louisville, KY 40203
(502) 589-1776; (502) 589-1671
execdin@sar.org
http://www.sar.org
Wayne R. Wiedman, Executive Director;
    Michael A. Christian, Librarian
9:30–4:30
Pub. *SAR Magazine*, quarterly, $10.00 per
    year nonmembers subscription
$12.00 per year membership (costs vary with
    membership in state societies)

SAR Chapters

Alabama Society, Sons of the American Revolution
PO Box 516
Lacey's Spring, AL 35754-0516
(256) 498-5127
kc4ykz@mindspring.com
http://www.sar.org/alssar
Edson A. Worden, Secretary

Alaska Society, Sons of the American Revolution
PO Box 873823
Wasilla, AK 99687
(907) 376-5566
http://www.sar.org/akssar
Joe A. Clapp, Secretary/Treasurer
Mon–Fri 8:00 A.M.–9:00 P.M.
$20.00 per year state dues

Arizona Society, Sons of the American Revolution
212 West Country Gables Drive
Phoenix, AZ 85023-5250
(602) 863-2520
jjones3549@aol.com
http://www.sar.org/azssar/azssar.htm
Mike Jones, President
8:00–6:00

Arkansas Society, Sons of the American Revolution
5097 Brewster Street
Springdale, AR 72764
(501) 750-3946 (Secretary)
gordonhale@alltel.net (Genealogist)

http://www.geocities.com/Heartland/
    Hollow/8048
Walter E. Smith, Secretary; Gordon D. Hale,
    Genealogist

California Society, Sons of the American Revolution
PO Box 60
Atwood, CA 92811-0060
(714) 524-7788
http://www.sar.org/cassar
Floyd J. Shadwick, Secretary
Pub. *Drumbeat*

Colorado Society, Sons of the American Revolution
1860 South Holly Street
Denver, CO 80222-3929
(303) 756-5793
http://www.cossar.org
David L. Van Wormer

Connecticut Society, Sons of the American Revolution (CTSSAR)
PO Box 411
East Haddam, CT 06423
(860) 873-3399
info@ctssar.org
http://www.ctssar.org
Stephen P. Shaw, Registrar
Pub. *Connecticut Line Newsletter*, online at
    http://www.ctssar.org/articles/
    connecticut_line.htm, Stephen P. Shaw,
    Editor, stephen@paysonllc.com

Delaware Society, Sons of the American Revolution
204 Prospect Avenue
Wilmington DE 19803
(302) 478-1651
DEPatriot@aol.com (Website Manager)
http://www.sar.org/dessar/default.htm
Lyman Brenner, Secretary

District of Columbia Society, Sons of the American Revolution
725 15th Street, N.W., Suite 607
Washington, DC 20005
(202) 638-6444; (202) 638-6333 FAX
http://www.sar.org/dcssar

Florida Society, Sons of the American Revolution
1316 East Ridge Village Drive
Miami, FL 33157
http://www.flssar.org
J. Alan Cross, Sr., President; Richard Q.
    Fowler, Sitemaster

Georgia Society, Sons of the American Revolution
452 River Forest Run
Cleveland, GA 30528-2578
(706) 865-3345
kopugh@hemc.net
http://www.sar.org/gassarl
Kline O. Pugh, Secretary

Hawaii Society, Sons of the American Revolution
luigi@hawaii.rr.com (President)
http://communities.msn.com/HawaiiSociety
    SonsoftheAmericanRevolution
Bill Settle, Secretary; Louis Torraca,
    President

Idaho Society, Sons of the American Revolution
1224 East Hays Street
Boise, ID 83712-7414
(208) 343-4059
http://www.sar.org/idssar/idahopage.htm

H. Norris Lynch, Secretary/Treasurer

Illinois Society, Sons of the American Revolution
5 Woodland Drive
Effingham, IL 62401
(217) 342-4442
Csener@aol.com
Charles Sener, President; Duane R. Neet,
    Secretary

Indiana Society, Sons of the American Revolution
1598 Constitution Row
Crawfordsville, IN 47933-7605
burtonre@aol.com
http://www.geocities.com/inssar-south
William R. Hawley, Editor; Robert E.
    Burton, Secretary
Pub. *Hoosier Patriot*, quarterly

Iowa Society, Sons of the American Revolution
931 32nd Street
West Des Moines, IA 50265
(515) 282-6095; (515) 282-2084 FAX
davisjc@ecity.net
http://www.sar.org/iassar/iowapage.htm
James C. Davis, Secretary

Kansas Society, Sons of the American Revolution
113 15 Applewood Drive
Kansas City, MO 64134
(816) 761-7453
TEPeter100@aol.com
http://www.ksssar.org
Timothy E. Peterman, Membership Secretary
Pub. *Liberty Bell*
(Membership applications are housed in the
    Kansas State Historical Society; address is
    for membership inquiries only.)

Kentucky Society, Sons of the American Revolution
375 Polley Drive
Madisonville, KY 42431
(270) 825-0585
James Harold Utley

International District, Sons of the American Revolution
(address withheld upon request)

Louisiana Society, Sons of the American Revolution
5535 Berkshire Avenue
Baton Rouge, LA 70806-8036
(225) 767-0847 (Martin)
Bobcraigsr@aol.com (Craig)
http://gnofn.org/~lassar
Michael H. Martin, Secretary; Robert B.
    Craig, Secretary

Maine Society, Sons of the American Revolution
91 Thing's Corner Road
PO Box 67
Limerick, ME 04048-0067
(207) 793-8041; (207) 793-3577 FAX
Cmdr. Harry W. Kinsley, Jr., USN (Ret),
    Secretary
Pub. *Newsletter*, approximately six times per
    year
cost as dictated by National Society and State
    Society ("members are invited and elected
    to membership if qualified")

Maryland Society, Sons of the American Revolution
PO Box 82
Woodstock, MD 21163-0082

(410) 750-9315
mdsar@juno.com
http://www.sar.org
Kenneth E. Zimmerman, Membership
Secretary

Massachusetts Society, Sons of the American Revolution
10 Old Colony Way
Scituate, MA 02066
(781) 545-6909
jmanning@massar.org
http://www.massar.org
John T. Manning, First Vice President
by appointment
Pub. *MASSAR Bulletin* (members only)

Michigan Society, Sons of the American Revolution
168 Shore Brook Lane
Commerce Township, MI 48390-4508
(248) 960-7635
rasteele@ameritech.net (President)
http://www.sar.org (national society)
Richard A. Steele, State President
Pub. irregular periodical materials

Minnesota Society, Sons of the American Revolution
2700 East Minnehaha
Minneapolis, MN 55406
(612) 721-4275
sjernest@hotmail.com
http://www.sar.org/mnssar
John Hallberg Jones, Secretary

Mississippi Society, Sons of the American Revolution
2418 South Shore Drive
Biloxi, MS 39532-3028
(228) 388-3071
Oddville50@aol.com
http://www.sar.org/mssar
Douglas A. Harper, Secretary

Missouri Society, Sons of the American Revolution
(3929 Milton Drive, Independence, MO 64055-4043—location)
PO Box 1369 (mailing address)
Jefferson City, MO 65102
GroverSAR@aol.com
http://www..liming.org/sar
Robert L. Grover, Membership
Pub. *Missouri Compatriot*, three times per year
("The objects of our Society are declared to be patriotic, historical, and educational, and shall include those intended or designed to perpetuate the memory of these patriots who, by their services or sacrifices during the war of the American Revolution, achieved the independence of the American people; to unite and promote fellowship among their descendants. Programs are available.")

Montana Society, Sons of the American Revolution
http://www.sar.org/mtssar
Thomas C. Howard, Secretary; Richard L. Thoroughman, Webmanager

Nebraska Society, Sons of the American Revolution
4438 Sherman Street
Lincoln, NE 68506-6433
mrudebusch@juno.com
http://www.geocities.com/Heartland/Oaks/4173/NESSAR.html
Merle Rudebusch, Secretary-Treasurer

Nevada Society, Sons of the American Revolution
4522 Laguna Vista Street
Las Vegas, NV 89147-6097
NVSSAR@excite.com (Registrar)
http://sar.annetta.com
Ben Allen, Secretary; Charles Recker, Registrar

New Hampshire Society, Sons of the American Revolution
PO Box 6131
Concord, NH 03303-6131
TFKNH@aol.com
http://www.sar.org/nhssar
Thomas F. Kehr, President
$20.00 per year

New Jersey Society, Sons of the American Revolution
105 Cranford Avenue
Cranford, NJ 07016-2407
http://aerialbear.com/NJSSAR
Paul W. Cook, Secretary

New Mexico Society, Sons of the American Revolution
PO Box 525
Placitas, NM 87043
(505) 867-4831
sngwrand@arriba.nm.org
http://www.sar.org/states/statchap.html
George Randle, Secretary

Empire State Society (NY), Sons of the American Revolution
96 Old Mill Pond Road
Nassau, NY 12123-2633
(518) 766-2142
jgoebel16@juno.com
http://www.sar.org/essar
Jonathan E. Goebel, Secretary

North Carolina Society, Sons of the American Revolution
114 Ridge Creek Road
Salisbury, NC 28147
(704) 639-7502; (704) 639-9845
fgradyhall@msn.com
http://www.csb.uncwil.edu/people/gowari/projects/ncssar
Frank Grady Hall, III

National Society, Sons of the American Revolution
18660 State Route 550
Amesville, OH 45711-9417
(740) 448-7269
jhlochary@cs.com
http://www.sar.org/ohssar/ohssar.html
James H. Lochary, Secretary

Oklahoma Society, Sons of the American Revolution
2832 East 87th Street
Tulsa, OK 74137
(918) 298-1514
JoeWest99@aol.com
http://www.geocities.com/heartland/park/8391/Okssar.htm
Arnold Joe West, Secretary/Treasurer
("not a source for genealogical information for the general public; all such records are maintained at the national level")

Oregon Society, Sons of the American Revolution
9525 S.W. Cecelia Terrace
Portland, OR 97223-7232
(503) 246-5828
cba@teleport.com
http://www.sar.org/orssar

Rola A. Cook

Pennsylvania Society, Sons of the American Revolution
(81 South Main Street—location)
PO Box 805 (mailing address)
Biglerville, PA 17307
(717) 677-4611
http://www.sar.org/passar
J. Fenwick Shugrue, Third Vice President/Secretary

Rhode Island Society, Sons of the American Revolution
40 Cedar Pound Drive #5
Warwick, RI 02886-0879
(401) 884-3856
http://www.sar.org/states/statchap.html
Norris G. Abbott, III, Secretary

The Dakota Society, Sons of the American Revolution
2436 Canyon Lake Drive
Rapid City, SD 57702-2402
(605) 343-0596
ktjohn@rapidnet.com
http://www.sar.org/dkssar
Dr. Keith T. Johnson, D.V.M., Secretary
(includes both North and South Dakota)
$62.00 membership for the first year, which includes year's dues of $23.00; $28.00 for the first year for a son, grandson, nephew or grand nephew of an SAR or DAR member if they are under 25 years of age

South Carolina Society, Sons of the American Revolution
PO Box 1378
Camden, SC 29020-1378
FKBabbitt@aol.com
http://www.duesouth.net/~cook/scssar.htm
Col. (Ret.) Frank K. Babbitt, Jr., Secretary-Treasurer

Tennessee Society, Sons of the American Revolution
48 Redthorn Cove
Cordova, TN 38018-7244
raclapsadl@aol.com
http://www.sar.org/tnssar/tnssar.htm
Raymond A. Clapsadle, Secretary
Pub. *Tennessee Rifleman*

Texas Society, Sons of the American Revolution
2014 Forest Trail
Temple, TX 76502-2616
http://www.txssar.org
James G. Robertson, President

Utah Society, Sons of the American Revolution
3844 South Danbury Circle
Magna, UT 84044-2223
(801) 250-7733
http://www.sar.org/utssar
Eric Dan Richhart, Secretary/Treasurer

Vermont Society, Sons of the American Revolution
PO Box 7
Peru, VT 05152
(802) 864-3740
Stewart W. Read, Secretary

Virginia Society, Sons of the American Revolution
15762 Edgewood Drive
Montclair, VA 22026-1728
(703) 897-4875; (703) 670-9474 FAX
vassaroffice@comcast.net
http://www.sar.org/vassar

Mrs. B. J. Simpson, Office Manager

Washington Society, Sons of the American Revolution
PO Box 142
Port Orchard, WA 98366
(360) 754-6203
Framsey@attbi.com
http://www.sar.org/wassar/index.htm
Frederic R. Ramsey, Secretary/Registrar
$135.00 membership

West Virginia Society, Sons of the American Revolution
2837 Spring Valley Drive
Huntington, WV 25704
http://www.sar.org/states/statchap.html
Lyle D. McCullough, Secretary

Wisconsin Society, Sons of the American Revolution
13625 West Burleigh Road, #7
Brookfield, WI 53005-3096
(262) 821-2916
wispres@wissar.org
http://www.wissar.org
Crofton "Pete" Thorp, President

Wyoming Society, Sons of the American Revolution
2932 Ridgecrest Drive
Casper WY 82604-4620
(307) 265-2289
http://www.sar.org/wyssar
Darrell D. Jackson, Secretary

Sons of the Revolution
Sons of the Revolution Building
600 South Central Avenue
Glendale, CA 91204
(818) 240-1775
Edwin W. Coles, Library Director
Wed noon–8:00; Thur–Sat 10:00–4:00

Sons of the Revolution in the State of Michigan
411 Bartlett Street
Lansing, MI 48915
James T. Lyons

Varnum Continentals
6 Main Street
PO Box 14
East Greenwich, RI 02818
(401) 884-4110

War of 1812

Society of the Descendants of the Alamo
PO Box 4641
Honolulu, HI 96812
Charles Edward Phebus, President General
Pub. *Alamo Descendants Newsletter*
membership open to any person twenty-one
years of age or older who can prove their
legal, lineal, or collateral descent from
one of the heroes of the Alamo who died
in its defense

National Society, United States Daughters of 1812
1461 Rhode Island Avenue, N.W.
Washington, DC 20005
(202) 745-1812
by appointment
Pub. *National Society United States Daughters of 1812 Newsletter*, quarterly

United States Daughters of 1812
Georgia State Society
PO Box 160

Kingston, GA 30145-0160

Oklahoma Society, National Society United States Daughters of 1812
9015 East 28th Street
Tulsa, OK 74129-6801
(918) 627-1431
Mrs. George F. Williams, State President

United States Daughters of 1812
Alexander Daugherty Chapter
901 Storey
Midland, TX 79701
(915) 683-2015

Veteran Corps of Artillery, State of New York
Constituting the Military Society of the War of 1812
Seventh Regiment Armory
643 Park Avenue
New York, NY 10021
(212) 249-3919
http://www.vca1790.org
Major General John E. Connelly, III, Commanding
Tue 5:30–10:00
Pub. *Roster*, biannually
("Restricted and limited to the proper
descendants of Commissioned Officers,
Aides-de-Camp, Officers and seamen of
private armed vessels, and Revenue
Cutters in actual service; enlisted men of
the Army, Navy, Marine Corps of the
United States, during the War of 1812; to
the proper descendants of original and
Hereditary members heretofore elected.")

General Society of the War of 1812
PO Box 106
Mendenhall, PA 19357
Dr. Forrest R. Schäeffer
membership fees from state societies;
research: $10.00 per name

Society of the War of 1812 in the State of Ohio
34465 Crew Road
Pomeroy, OH 45769
(740) 992-7874
Keith D. Ashley, Secretary-Treasurer
Pub. *Lake Erie Ledger*, semiannually
$21.00 per year membership

Mexican War

Aztec Club of 1847
The Military Society of the Mexican War
1846–1848
9101 MacMahon Drive
Burke, VA 22015
C. Lansdown Hunt
(descendants of participants in the war with Mexico)

Descendants of Mexican War Veterans, DMWV
National Office
PO Box 830482
Richardson, TX 75083-0482
dmwv@aol.com
http://members.aol.com/dmwv/home.htm
Steven R. Butler, President
Pub. *Mexican War Journal*, quarterly,
$25.00 per year subscription for
nonmembers; *The American Eagle, A
Newsletter of the Descendants of Mexican
War Veterans*, quarterly, $15.00 per year
subscription for nonmembers
$10.00 adult initiation fee, $5.00 junior
initiation fee, $25.00 per year adult
membership; no search fees

Civil War

Children of the Confederacy
Memorial Building
328 North Boulevard
Richmond, VA 23220-4057
(804) 355-1636; (804) 353-1396 FAX
http://www.hqudc.org/CofC/index.html
Mon–Fri 9:00–4:30
Pub. *The Courier*, quarterly, $8.00 per issue

Civil War Descendants Society
Confederate Descendants Society
PO Box 233
Athens, AL 35611

Civil War Plymouth Pilgrims Descendants Society
113 Briarwood Lane
Summerville, SC 29483
(843) 875-9013
http://members.aol.com/CWPPDS/
homepage.html
Edward Boots, President
Pub. *Voices From Plymouth*
(membership open to descendants of and
anyone interested in the Union soldiers,
dubbed "The Plymouth Pilgrims," who
participated in the Battle of Plymouth,
North Carolina, in April of 1864: 101st
and 103rd Pennsylvania, 16th
Connecticut, 85th New York and Second
North Carolina regiments; not to be
confused with the Plymouth Pilgrims of
Massachusetts)
$15.00 per year membership (c/o Scott
Holmes, 4910 Grape Tree Lane, Roanoke,
VA 24018)

Dames of the Loyal Legion of the United States
(see Military Order of the Loyal Legion of
the United States, below)

Daughters of the Union, 1861–1865, Inc.
11396 Grand Oak Drive
Grand Blanc, MI 48439
(810) 694-6879
Mrs. Robert Hatten

Daughters of Union Veterans of the Civil War, 1861–1865
National Headquarters, D.U.V. Registrar's
Office
503 South Walnut Street
Springfield, IL 62704-1932
(217) 544-0616
duvcw@comp.net; dlvgen@proaxis.com
http://www.duvcw.org
Anna Kinnison, National Treasurer; Donna
Vaughn, National Membership
Chairperson
Mon–Fri 9:00–4:00, Sat–Sun by
appointment
(membership limited to descendants of Civil
War Union veterans)
visitations free

Daughters of Union Veterans of the Civil War, 1861–1865
California and Nevada Department
(address withheld upon request)

Daughters of Union Veterans of the Civil War, 1861–1865
Colorado and Wyoming Department
311 South Walnut Street
Kimball, NE 69145-1431
(308) 638-8819
Ellenor Larsen, PNP

Daughters of Union Veterans of the Civil

War, 1861–1865
District of Columbia Department
6721 Amlong Avenue
Alexandria, VA 22306
(703) 768-2648
Patricia Kottemann; Roena Baes, PNP
Pub. *General Orders*, semiannually

Daughters of Union Veterans of the Civil War, 1861–1865
Idaho Department
1815 West Honeysuckle
Hayden, ID 83835-9511
(208) 772-5778 voice & FAX
Lelah Lough Achey, Secretary

Daughters of Union Veterans of the Civil War, 1861–1865
Illinois Department

Daughters of Union Veterans of the Civil War, 1861–1865
Indiana Department
0202 County Road 36
Avilla, IN 46710
(260) 357-4216
Vickie Day, Department Chief of Staff
("Membership in our organization is only with direct lineage to a Civil War Veteran.")

Daughters of Union Veterans of the Civil War, 1861–1865
Iowa Department
413 23rd S.W.
Mason City, IA 50401-6401
(641) 423-9450
megadam51@hotmail.com
Megan Adams

Daughters of Union Veterans of the Civil War, 1861–1865
Kansas Department
1508 West 17th
Hutchinson, KS 67501-2607
(620) 662-5906
Doris Phillips

Daughters of Union Veterans of the Civil War, 1861–1865
Maine Department
Slide Inn Road
Stoneham, ME 04231
(207) 928-2611
slideinn@pivot.net
Lesley Gouin Dean, President

Daughters of Union Veterans of the Civil War, 1861–1865
Massachusetts Department
Box 1196
Lawrence, MA 01840
(603) 870-0043
CYNAUXSUV@aol.com
Cynthia W. Brown

Daughters of Union Veterans of the Civil War, 1861–1865
Michigan Department
1504 Longfellow
Detroit, MI 48206-2000
(313) 866-8630; (313) 869-0568 FAX
cholduv@ameritech.net
Celestine Hollings

Daughters of Union Veterans of the Civil War, 1861–1865
Minnesota Department
325 South Maple
LeCenter, MN 56057
(507) 357-4488
Helen Meyer, Board Member

Pub. *General Orders*, three times per year

Daughters of Union Veterans of the Civil War, 1861–1865
Missouri Department
332 North Market
Memphis, MO 63555

Daughters of Union Veterans of the Civil War, 1861–1865
Nebraska Department
1845 F Street, Apartment 12
Lincoln, NE 68508-3458
(402) 474-3803
b.dunekacke@juno.com
Barbara (Bobbi) Dunekacke

Daughters of Union Veterans of the Civil War, 1861–1865
New York Department
11077 Hoxie Road
West Edmeston, NY 13485-9669
(315) 855-4184
Dorothy Prentice, PDP

Daughters of Union Veterans of the Civil War, 1861–1865
Ohio Department
4000 Carmont Avenue S.W.
Navarre, OH 44662
(330) 879-5243
price@sssnet.com
Rochelle Price

Daughters of Union Veterans of the Civil War, 1861–1865
Oklahoma Department
1202 Barkley Avenue
Norman, OK 73071-4814
(405) 364-2967
Judith Mahan, Secretary

Daughters of Union Veterans of the Civil War, 1861–1865
Oregon Department
5050 Columbus Street, S.E., #64
Albany, OR 97321-8017
(541) 926-9240
dlvgen@proaxis.com
Donna Vaughan, President

Daughters of Union Veterans of the Civil War, 1861–1865
Pennsylvania Department
1795 Verdan Drive, South
York, PA 17403
(717) 846-1036
apd@nfdc.net
Alfreda P. Davidson
research: $18.00 in York County, $25.00 per hour in Harrisburg (plus travel expenses), other areas by arrangement

Daughters of Union Veterans of the Civil War, 1861–1865
Washington and Alaska Department
15407 East Springfield Avenue
Veradale, WA 99037-9537
(509) 928-2566
Irbutons@aol.com
Irene R. Berg, PNP and Registered Parliamentarian

Daughters of Union Veterans of the Civil War, 1861–1865
Latha Jane Boyd Tent #1
425 Evergreen Drive
Hurst, TX 76054-2013
(817) 577-0645
rebeltrumpet@sbcglobal.net
http://www.geocities.com/Pentagon/Quarters/7706/DUV.html

Kathy Wells, President Tent #1, Texas
meetings: fourth Sat 11:00
(a patriotic and historical organization)
$17.25 per year membership

Ladies of the Grand Army of the Republic, Inc.
279 Homewood Avenue
Tonawanda, NY 14217-1162
JMCLGAR@aol.com
http://suvcwl.org/lgar.htm
Evelyn Petch Krantz, National Registrar
Pub. *Bugle Call*, quarterly, $4.00 per year subscription
(open to all female blood-relatives, ten years of age or older, of honorably discharged Union soldiers, sailors and marines of the Civil War, and also ex-army nurses of that war, 20,000 records of eligibility on file; oldest of the Allied Orders that require direct lineage with a Union Civil War Veteran)
research: donation plus SASE

G.A.R. Memorial and Veterans' Military Museum
(23 East Downer Place—location)
PO Box 1865 (mailing address)
Aurora, IL 60507-1865
(630) 897-7221
Art Stiegleiter, Director
Mon, Wed & Fri noon–4:00, and by appointment
(local history, genealogy, military)

Grand Army of the Republic (G.A.R.)
Grand Army of the Republic Memorial Museum
78 East Washington Street
Chicago, IL 60602
(312) 269-2926
http://suvcw.org/gar.htm
Laura Linard, Curator

Grand Army of the Republic War Museum
Ruan House Library
4278 Griscom Street
Philadelphia, PA 19124-3954
(215) 289-6484
garmuslib@aol.com
http://suvcw.org/garmus.htm

Women's Relief Corps National Headquarters, G.A.R.
Grand Army of the Republic Museum
629 South Seventh Street
Springfield, IL 62703-1636
(217) 522-4373
streeterla@cbpu.com
Bonita Wiggins
Wed–Sat 10:00–4:00, and by appointment

Hood's Texas Brigade Association
(see Confederate Research Center, Misscellaneous, Part 4)

Military Order of the Loyal Legion of the United States
Dames of the Loyal Legion of the United States
Civil War Library and Museum
1805 Pine Street
Philadelphia, PA 19103
(215) 546-2425; (215) 735-8196 (Library)
http://www.libertynet.org/~cwlm (Library)
William A. Hamann, III, Recorder-in-Chief
Mon–Sat 10:00–4:00
Pub. *Historical Journal Quarterly*
(membership for descendants of Union officers or their siblings)

Military Order of the Stars and Bars
Sons of Confederate Veterans
Georgia Division
PO Box 763
Kennesaw, GA 30144
(770) 436-9600; (770) 436-0607 FAX
http://scv.org

Military Order of the Stars and Bars
New Mexico Sons of Confederate Veterans
3021 Espanola, N.E.
Albuquerque, NM 87111

Indian Territory Society—Military Order of the Stars and Bars
3500 Wagonwheel Road
Edmond, OK 73083
(405) 348-4462
rebeljag@aol.com
Jeff Massey, Division Adjutant
$30.00 per year membership (open to all male descendants of Confederate officers and civil officials of the Confederate states and Confederate government)

Military Order of the Stars and Bars
Sons of Confederate Veterans-Camp
McIntosh (Tulsa)
PO Box 35851
Tulsa, OK 74153-0851
(918) 252-2890; (918) 492-1054 (Commander)
Carl Fallen, Commander
meetings at Promonade Meeting Room: third Thur 6:15
Pub. *Confederate Veteran*, bimonthly
(Oklahoma Confederate Veteran Grave Location Project: "The Camp is searching for Confederate Veterans buried in Oklahoma only; the public is requested to send any known information concerning the burial locations of Confederate Veterans nationally"; history, genealogy, southern heritage)
$14.00 per year membership

Military Order of the Stars and Bars
Sons of Confederate Veterans, Inc.
(740 Mooresville Road, Columbia, TN 38401—location)
PO Box 59 (mailing address)
Columbia, TN 38402-0059
(931) 380-1844; (800) MY-DIXIE; (931) 381-6712 FAX
scvihq@scv.org
http://www.scv.org
Ben C. Sewell III, Executive Director; Jason Goodrich, Membership Coordinator
Mon–Fri 8:00–5:00, Sat 11:00–4:00
Pub. *Confederate Veteran*, bimonthly,
   $16.00 per year subscription in the U.S.,
   $26.00 per year subscription elsewhere
$20.00 per year membership

Military Order of the Stars and Bars
Sons of Confederate Veterans
West Virginia Division
Rural Route 9, Box 67
Princeton, WV 24740
(304) 487-0829
commander@inetone.net
Glenn Belcher, Division Commander
daily 10:00–5:00
Pub. *Mountain Rebel*, quarterly
$3.00 per year full membership

Military Order of the Stars and Bars
Sons of Confederate Veterans
Flat Top Copperheads Camp 1694
PO Box 1846
Princeton, WV 24740
(304) 425-4990

commander@inetone.net
Glenn Belcher, Commander
Pub. *Copperhead Courier*, monthly
$34.00 per year membership

Sons of Confederate Veterans
(see also Military Order of the Stars and Bars, above)

Oklahoma Division—Sons of Confederate Veterans
3500 Wagonwheel Road
Edmond, OK 73083
(405) 348-4462
rebeljag@aol.com
Jeff Massey, Division Adjutant
Pub. *The Rebel Yell*, monthly, $20.00 per year subscriptions
(open to all male descendants of War Between the States Confederate veterans)

Sons of Sherman's March to the Sea
(see Civil War Sons, Miscellaneous, Part 4)

Sons of Union Veterans of the Civil War
411 Bartlett Street
Lansing, MI 48915
SUVWEBMSTR@aol.com
http://suvcw.org
James T. Lyons, National Secretary; Keith G. Harrison, Past Commander-in-Chief and National SUVCW Webmaster

Auxiliary to the Sons of Union Veterans of the Civil War
MarAuxSuv@aol.com

Sons of Union Veterans of the Civil War
Department of California and Pacific (includes Nevada and Hawaii)
http://home.inreach.com/tadcamp/deptca.html
Daniel R. Earl

Sons of Union Veterans of the Civil War
Colorado/Wyoming Department (includes Montana and Utah)
3844 South Danbury Circle
Magna, UT 84044-2223
(801) 773-4620
refoals@msn.com
http://suvcw.org/co/deptco.htm
Eric Dan Richhart, Secretary/Treasurer

Sons of Union Veterans of the Civil War
Department of Connecticut
PO Box 153
Rockville, CT 06066
(860) 648-1202
henrycu@aol.com
http://suvcw.org/deptct.htm;
   http://pages.cthome.net/ne.civilwar.mus (New England Civil War Museum)
Henry T. Cullinane, Secretary-Treasurer

Sons of Union Veterans of the Civil War
Department of Florida
9624 N.W. 41st Street
Sunrise, FL 33351-7675
(954) 742-9841
http://suvcw.org/deptfl.htm
Jerry L. Lippincott, Secretary-Treasurer

Sons of Union Veterans of the Civil War
Department of Illinois
1005 Hillcrest Drive
Sparta, IL 62286
(618) 443-3542
winemake@egyptian.net
http://www.execpc.com/~sril/ilsuvcw.html
Charles Willman, Secretary/Treasurer

Sons of Union Veterans of the Civil War
Department of Indiana
natalie@in-motion.net
http://suvcw.org/in/DEPTIN.html
Shawn Clements, Secretary-Treasurer

Sons of Union Veterans of the Civil War
Department of Iowa
1731 Red Oak Drive
Coralville, IA 52241
(319) 338-7713
http://showcase.netins.net/web/rittel/suvcw/iowa/deptio.html
Dr. Les E. Weber

Sons of Union Veterans of the Civil War
Department of Kansas
600 North Hersey Avenue
Beloit, KS 67420-2321
http://suvcwks.tripod.com
Dean K. Speaks, PDC, Secretary/Treasurer

Sons of Union Veterans of the Civil War
Department of Kentucky
253 Tando Way
Covington, KY 41017
(937) 612-2228
http://www.geocities.com/Pentagon/Bunker/1827
Bernie O'Bryan, Secretary

Sons of Union Veterans of the Civil War
Department of Maine
1239 State Highway 150
Parkman, ME 04443
(207) 277-3947
boothroy@somtel.com
http://www.powerlink.net/mcgill/page45.html
Eric J. Boothroyd, Commander

Sons of Union Veterans of the Civil War
Department of Maryland (includes Virginia, West Virginia, Delaware and the District of Colubmia)
42 Half Penny Lane
Catonsville, MD 21228
(410) 288-3727
BHorganPA@aol.com
http://suvcw.org/md/deptmd.htm
Brian W. Horgan, Secretary/Treasurer

Sons of Union Veterans of the Civil War
Department of Massachusetts
PO Box 11
Winchester, MA 01890-0011
(781) 729-3311
secretary@suvmass.org
http://www.suvmass.org
William T. Ryerson, Sr., P.D.C., Secretary

Sons of Union Veterans of the Civil War
Department of Michigan
1111 South Kern Road
Fowlerville, MI 48836-9257
jrmsuvcw@aol.com
http://suvcw.org/mi/deptmi.htm
Richard F. Lee, Secretary, John Mann, Editor
Pub. *Michigan's Messenger*

Sons of Union Veterans of the Civil War
Department of Missouri
4729 Mehl Avenue
Saint Louis, MO 63129
(314) 892-2158
RPETRO7776@aol.com
http://www.geocities.com/Pentagon/Barracks/2683
Bob Petrovic, P.D.C., Secretary/Treasurer

Sons of Union Veterans of the Civil War
Department of Nebraska

mrudebusch@juno.com
http://www.geocities.com/Heartland/
 Oaks/4173/nedsuvcw.htm
Merle A. Rudebusch

Sons of Union Veterans of the Civil War
Department of New Hampshire
PO Box 853
Sunapee, NH 03782
(603) 863-1674; (603) 763-6067
esurat@yahoo.com
http://nhsuv.iwarp.com/Deptnh.htm
Richard Woodbury, Secretary

Sons of Union Veterans of the Civil War
Department of New Jersey
147 Canterbury Court
Hightstown, NJ 08520
(609) 448-6355
Dmartin@Peddie.org
http://ftp.genlyon.addr.com/index.html
Dr. David G. Martin
(has over 60,000 burial sites of New Jersey
 Civil War veterans)

Sons of Union Veterans of the Civil War
Department of New York
452 West 22nd Street, Apartment 5A
New York, NY 10011
(212) 989-6642
douglasmharding@juno.com
http://suvcw.org/ny/deptny.htm
Douglas M. Harding
Pub. *The Volunteer*, five times per year,
 $4.00 per year subscription
membership open to direct descendants or
 collateral relatives, plus Associate
 membership available

Sons of Union Veterans of the Civil War
Department of Ohio
2449 Center Avenue
Alliance, OH 44601
(330) 823-6919
http://suvcw.org/oh/deptoh.htm
Richard L. Greenwalt, Past Commander-in-
 Chief, Ohio Department Secretary
Pub. *Lineage Society*
(tracing Ohio Civil War veterans, no in-
 depth genealogy)

Sons of Union Veterans of the Civil War
Department of Oklahoma
PO Box 1892
Stillwater, OK 74076
greenpheon@cox.net
http://bronzestar.tripod.com/oklahoma
 departmentsonsofunionveteransofthecivil
 war
Walt Cross, Secretary
Pub. *Newsletter*

Sons of Union Veterans of the Civil War
Department of Pennsylvania
7 Hallack Drive
East Berlin, PA 17316
(717) 259-7971
http://schooloftime.101main.com/sons/
 Padept/opening.html
Pub. *Banner*, quarterly

Sons of Union Veterans of the Civil War
Department of Rhode Island
PO Box 40488
Providence, RI 02940-0488
hdviking@aol.com
http://www.geocities.com/Pentagon/3614
Leo F. Kennedy, Commander

Sons of Union Veterans of the Civil War
Department of Tennessee (includes
Alabama)

106 Sunnyfield Drive
Madison, AL 35758-6816
spearce@knology.net
http://suvcw.org/tn/depttn.html
Steve Pearce, Secretary/Treasurer

Sons of Union Veterans of the Civil War
Department of Vermont
H.E.K. Hall Camp #28
95 Corinth Road
Chelsea, VT 05038
http://www.calcaminedesign.com/suvcw
Floyd Blodgett, Commander
$25.00 per year membership

Sons of Union Veterans of the Civil War
Department of Wisconsin (includes
Minnesota)
secretary@suvcw-wi.org
http://www.suvcw-wi.org
Ronald M. Aronis, Secretary

United Daughters of the Confederacy
UDC Memorial Building
328 North Boulevard
Richmond, VA 23220-4057
(804) 355-1636; (804) 353-1396 FAX
hqudc@rcn.com
http://www.hqudc.org
Mon–Fri 9:00–4:30
Pub. *United Daughters of the Confederacy*,
 eleven times per year (monthly, except
 June/July combined), $12.00 per year
 subscription, includes queries
genealogical research is not available from
 the UDC business office

United Daughters of the Confederacy
Alabama Division
403 Sunset Avenue
Albertville, AL 35950
(256) 878-2920

United Daughters of the Confederacy
Joseph E. Johnston Chapter #198
261 Anderson Drive
Eufaula, AL 36027-6020
Mrs. Curtis A. Hicks, President

United Daughters of the Confederacy
Georgia Division
1604 Executive Park Lane, N.E.
Atlanta, GA 30329-3115
(404) 634-9866 voice & FAX

A & I Van Nostrand Woman's Relief
Corps #169
(Town of Granger, Allegany
County—location)
5507 County Road 4 (mailing address)
Fillmore, NY 14735
(585) 567-8718
Delores B. Curry, President, Corps #169
meetings: second Mon 7:00
$2.00 membership

Wisconsin Veterans Museum Research
Center
30 West Mifflin Street
Madison, WI 53707
(608) 267-1790; (608) 264-7615 FAX
http://badger.state.wi.us/agencies/dva/
 museum/wvmmain.html
Tue–Fri 9:30–4:30
("Computerized listing of Wisconsin Civil
 War soldiers")

The Society of Civil War Families of Ohio
The Ohio Genealogical Society (OGS)
Library
(34 Sturges Avenue—location)
PO Box 2625 (mailing address)

Mansfield, OH 44906-0625
(419) 522-9077; (419) 522-0224 FAX
http://www.ogs.org
Thomas Stephen Neel, Office Manager;
 Elizabeth S. Glasgow, Librarian
summer (1 June–1 Sept): Tue–Sat 9:00–5:00;
 winter (1 Sept–1 June): Tue & Thur
 1:00–5:00, Wed 9:00–1:00, Fri–Sat
 9:00–5:00
Pub. *The Report*, quarterly; *The Ohio
 Genealogical Society Newsletter*,
 monthly; *Ohio Records and Pioneer
 Families*, quarterly, $18.00 per year
 subscription; *Ohio Civil War Genealogy
 Journal*, quarterly, $18.00 per year
 subscription
(sponsors First Families of Ohio, a lineage
 society for members with pre-Dec 31,
 1821 Ohio ancestors; The Society of Civil
 War Families of Ohio, a lineage society
 for members with Ohio ancestors who
 served in the Civil War)
$27.00 per year membership (includes *The
 Report* and *The Ohio Genealogical
 Society Newsletter*)

Indian Wars

Continental Society Sons of Indian Wars
3917 Heritage Hills Drive, #104
Bloomington, MN 55437-2633
(952) 893-9747 (evenings); (952) 885-9776
 (days)
Arthur Louis Finnell, Registrar General
Pub. *Peace Pipe*, two times per year

Spanish-American War

National Fort Daughters of '98
Junior Organization of United Spanish War
Veterans
7101 Hope Avenue
Cleveland, OH 44102
Mrs. Marion E. Gross, National Adjutant
Mon–Fri 9:00–5:00
Pub. *Daughters of '98 Bulletin*, quarterly
$2.00 per year membership

Sons of the Spanish-American War
Veterans
2755 Curlew Road, #31
Palm Harbor, FL 34684
Ronald C. Pratt, National Treasurer
(membership open to sons, grandsons, great-
 grandsons, nephews, grand nephews,
 great-grand nephews of veterans of the
 Spanish-American War; no information
 on veterans available from Secretary)
$3.00 per year membership

National Auxiliary United Spanish War
Veterans
414½ East Avenue
North Augusta, SC 29841-3837
(803) 442-9321
Marie C. Cruise, National Secretary-
 Treasurer
Mon–Fri 9:00–5:00
Pub. *General Orders*, semiannually; special
 notices as needed
(primarily interested in Veterans)
$3.00 per year membership, special mailing
 list $3.00 per year

Miscellaneous Military

Military Order of Foreign Wars of the
United States 1894–1994
(122 East 58th Street, New York, NY 10022-
1939—location)
147 Jefferson Court (mailing address)

Norristown, PA 19401
(610) 275-7582 (Pennsylvania); (212) 751-5168 (New York)
josephmartinezjr@aol.com
http://foxfall.com/mofw.htm
1st Lieutenant Joseph A. Martinez, Jr.
("Membership is bestowed upon officers and former officers of the Armed Forces of the United States, and its allies, who meet certain requirements. So too lineal descendants of officers who served in foreign wars of the United States from The War of the Revolution to The Persian Gulf Conflict are welcome to inquire as to eligibility. It is well to keep in mind that membership is by invitation only. Candidates must be sponsored and seconded by men and women on the active membership roster.")

Regional

Native Daughters of the Golden West
555 Baker Street
San Francisco, CA 94117-1405
(415) 921-2664
Reference Room: first Tue 10:00–2:00 and by appointment
(includes over 33,000 entries in *Roster of California Pioneers*, people who entered the state or were born in the state prior to 1870)

Grand Parlor, Native Sons of the Golden West
414 Mason Street, Suite 300
San Francisco, CA 94102
(415) 392-1223; (415) 392-1224 FAX
Ronald W. Koepen, Grand Secretary
7:00–3:00
Pub. *The Native Son*, six times per year
$15.00 per year membership

The New England Society in the City of New York
122 East 58th Street
New York, NY 10022-1939
(212) 752-1938

California Pioneer Project
wjb@lightspeed.net
http://www.cagenweb.com/cpl
Steve Williams, Moderator

Los Fundadores, The Founders and Friends of Santa Clara County
(see California, Part 2)

Los Californianos, Hispanic Ancestors of Alta California
(see Ethnic Archives, Libraries and Societies—Spanish, Part 3)

Society of California Pioneers
PO Box 191850
San Francisco, CA 94119-1850
Pub. *The Pioneer*, semiannually
(membership open only to qualified applicants)

Pioneer Association/Pioneer Women
Donath Lake Farm
8420 South County Road 13
Fort Collins, CO 80525

Descendants of the Founders of Ancient Windsor
33 Hillcrest Road
Windsor, CT 06095
(860) 688-6822
Donna H. Siemiatkoski, Editor
Windsor Historical Society: 1 Apr–31 Oct:

Tue–Sat 10:00–4:00; 1 Nov–31 Mar: Mon–Fri 10:00–4:00
Pub. *Newsletter: Descendants of the Founders of Ancient Windsor*, quarterly
$5.00 per year membership, plus $15.00 (one time) registration fee

Saybrook Colony Founders Association, Inc.
PO Box 1635
Old Saybrook, CT 06475-1000
(860) 388-2234; (860) 395-3123
Elaine F. Staplins, President
Pub. *Hear-Saye*, quarterly
(genealogical services; social history of Saybrook Colony)
$12.00 per year membership

Society of the Descendants of the Founders of Hartford
PO Box 215
West Hartford, CT 06107
Allen R. Yale, Genealogist
$25.00 initial membership, $10.00 per year thereafter

Society of the Founders of Norwich, Connecticut
(348 Washington Street—location)
PO Box 13 (mailing address)
Norwich, CT 06360
(860) 889-9440; (860) 887-2417 (President's Home)
Ann Cannon, President
May–Oct: 2:00–5:00, and by appointment
("The Society owns and operates the Leffingwell Inn Museum. The original home was built in 1675 and later sold to Thomas Leffingwell. In 1701 Thomas Leffingwell converted the home into an Inn. The Inn was purchased by the Society and currently houses artifacts from the Revolutionary period. The Museum is open to the public.")
$15.00 per year membership; research: $20.00, limited to those who are identified with the original Founders of Norwich

Sons and Daughters of the Province and Republic of West Florida 1763–1810
PO Box 82672
Baton Rouge, LA 70884-2672

First Families of Georgia, 1733–1797
15 Watson Drive
Newnan, GA 30263

Daughters of Hawaii
(address withheld upon request)
("records on Hulihee Palace Museum in Kailua-Kona, the Queen Emma Summer Palace in Honolulu, and the Daughters of Hawaii; institution and collection founded in 1903; fifteen linear feet of holdings," primarily a museum, does not give out its members' genealogy)

The Idaho Genealogical Society, Inc.
Oregon Trail Project
(see Idaho, Part 2)

Decatur Genealogical Society
Macon County Pioneer Certificates
(see Illinois, Part 2)

Society of Indiana Pioneers
450 West Ohio Street
Indianapolis, IN 46202-3269
(317) 233-6588
rdorrel@indianahistory.org
http://www.indianapioneers.com
Ruth Dorrel, Genealogist and Office

Manager
by appointment
Pub. *Yearbook*, annually
$20.00 per year membership

Kansas Council of Genealogical Societies, Inc.
(certificate program for descendants of pioneers, see Kansas, Part 2)

Kansas Pioneers Project
http://history.cc.ukans.edu/heritage/pioneers/pion_main.html

Native Sons of Kansas City
(4200 West 54th Street, Shawnee Mission, KS 66205—location)
PO Box 1111 (mailing address)
Shawnee Mission, KS 66222
(913) 432-9231

Society of Kentucky Pioneers
(address withheld upon request)
Pub. *Kentucky Pioneer Genealogy and Records*

Louisiana Colonials
1911 Octavia Street
New Orleans, LA 70115

Piscataqua Pioneers
210 Lowell Street
Wilmington, MA 01887
William Frost
(descendants of original settlers on the Piscataqua River in Maine and New Hampshire prior to 1776)

The Hereditary Order of the First Families of Massachusetts
The Committee on Admissions
253 Tremont Street
Melrose, MA 02176-1835
(781) 662-8034
Dr. Roswell Levi Atwood, Chairman, Committee on Admissions
9:00–3:00
Pub. *Puritan Chronicle*, annually
(descendants of settlers in the Massachusetts Bay Colony before 1650)
$65.00 entrance fee, $20.00 per year membership

National Society of Old Plymouth Colony Descendants
(see Lineage, Hereditary and Patriotic Societies—Colonial, above)

The Plymouth Hereditary Society
The Secretary General
253 Tremont Street
Melrose, MA 02176-1835
(781) 662-8034
Dr. Roswell Levi Atwood, Secretary General
9:00–3:00
Pub. *Plymouth Annals*, annually
("An applicant must be a member of one of the following: The General Society Sons of the Revolution, The National Society Sons of the American Revolution, The National Society of the Daughters of the American Revolution. There must be proven descent from ancestors who resided in Plymouth Colony previous to the year 1692.")
$100.00 life membership

Sons and Daughters of the First Settlers of Newbury, Massachusetts
(76 State Street—location)
PO Box 444 (mailing address)
Newburyport, MA 01950

Noreen Pramberg, Executive
Secretary/Editor
by appointment
Pub. *Descend-O-Gram*, quarterly
$25.00 membership application, $10.00 per
year membership

**Descendants of the First Families of
Minnesota**
3917 Heritage Hills Drive, #104
Bloomington, MN 55437-2633
(952) 893-9747 (evenings); (952) 885-9776
(days)
Arthur Louis Finnell, Registrar General
by appointment

Territorial Pioneers
1395 McKinley
Saint Paul, MN 55108

Daughters of Old Westport
8124 Pennsylvania Lane
Kansas City, MO 64114

**Descendants of the Founders of New
Jersey**
222 Elm Street
Westville, NJ 08093
(856) 456-1098
Richard M. Burr, Registrar General
Pub. *Founders of New Jersey—Brief
Biographies by Descendants*, irregularly

**Society of Richmond County (North
Carolina) Descendants and Richmond
County Historical Collection**
(see North Carolina, Part 2)

Pioneer Daughters
Pembina County Chapter
Neche, ND 58265
(701) 886-7619

First Families of Guernsey County
65664 North 77 Drive
Cambridge, OH 43725
Mary Kappes
(membership open to descendants of
residents of Guernsey County before
1830)

The First Families of Ohio
(see The Society of Civil War Families of
Ohio, Lineage, Hereditary and Patriotic
Societies—Civil War, above)

**Harrison County Genealogical Society,
Chapter OGS**
First Families of Harrison County
(see Ohio, Part 2)

Lucas County Chapter OGS
First Families of Lucas County
(see Ohio, Part 2)

Williams County Chapter OGS
First Families of Williams County
(see Ohio, Part 2)

Wood County Chapter OGS
First Families of Wood County
(see Ohio, Part 2)

1889'er Society
3621 N.W. 43rd Street
Oklahoma City, OK 73112-6359

**First Families of the Twin Territories
(FFTT)**
(A committee of the Oklahoma Genealogical
Society)
PO Box 12986

Oklahoma City, OK 73157-2986
(405) 946-7714 (Chairman's home)
okgensoc@aol.com
http://www.rootsweb.com/~okgs/fftt.htm
June C. Stone
meets annually
Pub. *Newsletter*, annually
(membership available upon proof of direct
lineage from an original pioneer of
Oklahoma who was here before statehood,
16 November 1907)
$25.00 life membership

**Sons and Daughters of the Cherokee Strip
Pioneers**
PO Box 465
Enid, OK 73701
Pub. *Journal of the Cherokee Strip*, annually,
$5.00 per issue
$5.00 per year membership

Oregon Genealogical Society
Oregon Pioneer Certificates
(see Oregon, Part 2)

Sons and Daughters of Oregon Pioneers
PO Box 6685
Portland, OR 97228
(503) 222-5014
Frances Caskey, Membership and Former
President
Pub. *Newsletter*, occasionally
(membership is open to anyone whose family
came to Oregon before 14 Feb 1859)
$10.00 per year membership, plus one-time
$10.00 fee for a membership certificate

**The Society of First Families of South
Carolina, 1670–1700**
PO Box 21328
Charleston, SC 29413-1328
(843) 577-4324
William E. Craver, Jr., President
9:00–5:00

Sioux Valley Genealogical Society
Pioneer Certificates
(see South Dakota, Part 2)

Society of Black Hills Pioneers
c/o Adams Museum
(54 Sherman—location)
PO Box 252 (mailing address)
Deadwood, SD 57732-1364
(605) 578-1714 (Museum)
http://www.blackhills.com/museum/
index.html (Museum)
Carolee Smith-Rogers, Museum Curator
Museum: 1 Oct–30 Apr: Tue–Sat
10:00–4:00, Sun noon–4:00; 1 May–30
Sept: Mon–Sat 9:00–6:00, Sun 9:00–5:00
(museum archives)
research: $50.00 per hour

First Families of Tennessee
Affiliate of the East Tennessee Historical
Society
(600 Market Street—location)
PO Box 1629 (mailing address)
Knoxville, TN 37901-1629
(865) 544-5732; (865) 544-4319 FAX
Kent Whitworth, Executive Director; Cherel
Henderson, Associate Director
Calvin McClung Historical Collection:
Mon–Tue 9:00–8:30, Wed–Fri 9:00–5:30,
Sun 1:00–5:00; Office: Mon–Fri
9:00–5:00; Museum: Tue–Sat
10:00–4:00, Sun 1:00–5:00
(descendants of persons living in Tennessee
prior to its admission into the union in
1796)

First Families of the State of Franklin
2007 Sherwood Drive, #D
Johnson City, TN 37601-3236
Mrs. Ray Stahl
(descendants of pioneers who lived in the
area that was the state of Franklin in 1788
or before)

Daughters of the Republic of Texas
French Legation Museum
802 San Marcos Street
Austin, TX 78702-2647
(512) 472-8180; (512) 472-9457 FAX
Director
Tue–Sun 1:00–5:00

**The Daughters of the Republic of Texas
Library**
(see Texas, Part 2)

San Jacinto Descendants
1718 Searcy
San Antonio, TX 78232
(210) 494-7278
Carl S. Mauthe, President General

**International Society, Daughters of Utah
Pioneers**
300 North Main Street
Salt Lake City, UT 84103-1699
(801) 538-1050; (801) 538-1119
dupmuseum@juno.com
http://eddy.media.utah.edu/medsol/
UCME/d/DAUGHTERSUTPIO.html
Mary A. Johnson, President
Museum: Mon–Sat 9:00–5:00, Sun
(June–Aug) 9:00–5:00
Pub. *Pioneer Pathways*, annually, $16.00

Daughters of Utah Pioneers Relic Hall
(420 Clay Street—location)
Old Mill Road (mailing address)
Montpelier, ID 83254
(208) 847-1069

**Rhoades Valley Camp, Daughters of Utah
Pioneers**
PO Box 311
Kamas, UT 84036

**South Box Elder, Daughters of Utah
Pioneers**
566 North First Street East
Brigham City, UT 84302
(435) 723-3819

Pioneer Utah's Online Electronic Library
http://pioneer.uen.org

National Society, Sons of Utah Pioneers
3301 East 2820 South
Salt Lake City, UT 84109-4260
(801) 484-4441; (801) 328-8200 (*Pioneer*);
(801) 328-8249 FAX (*Pioneer*)
http://uvol.com/sup
Florence C. Youngberg, Director; Martin
Lewis, Vice President Sales and
Marketing
Tue 9:00–4:00, Wed & Thur 9:00–9:00
Pub. *Pioneer*, bimonthly, $2.95 per issue
from 180 North Wright Brothers Drive,
Building 6, Salt Lake City, UT 84116
$12.50 per year membership

Historic Dumfries, Virginia, Inc.
Pioneers of Dumfries, Virginia
(see Virginia, Part 2)

Jamestowne Society
(see Lineage, Hereditary and Patriotic
Societies—Colonial, above)

Descendants of the French Creek Pioneers
c/o Rural Route 2, Box 69
French Creek, WV 26218
(304) 924-6374
Virginia Bly Hoover, Secretary
Pub. *The Pioneer*, biannually (Aug of even-
numbered years), $12.00 postpaid for
back issues
(responds only to descendants of pioneer or
village present and former inhabitants; no
information furnished to professional
genealogists)
$12.00 per year membership; research: "no
information furnished to professional
genealogists, respond only to village
inhabitants (past or present) or
descendants of village pioneers"

Hacker's Creek Pioneer Descendants, Inc.
Central West Virginia Genealogy and
History Library
(Jackson's Mill Road, about two miles from
Route 19, Jane Lew, WV 26378—location)
45 Abbotts Run Road (mailing address)
Horner, WV 26372
(304) 269-7091; (304) 269-4430 FAX
hcpd@hackerscreek.com
http://www.hackerscreek.com
Joy Stalnaker, Executive Director
Library: Mon & Thur 10:00–8:00, Tue–Wed
& Fri 10:00–3:00, Sat 10:00–2:00
Pub. *Up the Creek*, quarterly
(includes central West Virginia, with special
emphasis on Lewis, Harrison, Upshur,
Gilmer, Barbour, Randolph, Doddridge
and Braxton counties)
$25.00 per year membership

Royal and Noble

Colonial Order of the Crown
PO Box 27023
Philadelphia, PA 19118

**National Society, Daughters of the Barons
of Runnymeade**
(address withheld upon request)

**International Society of the Descendants of
Charlemagne**
Office of the Governor General
(3960 Barcelona Street—location)
PO Box 5259 (mailing address)
Titusville, FL 32783-5259
(321) 267-0351; (321) 267-0263 FAX
Most Rev. Lowell A. Barker, Governor
General
by appointment only
Pub. *News Letter*, occasionally
(Royal and noble lineages)
$50.00 life membership; computer search: 5¢
per page

Descendants of Edward I
(916) 344-7579
Virgil Obert

**Society of Descendants of Knights of the
Most Noble Order of the Garter**
PO Box 4944
Philadelphia, PA 19119

The Ermine Society
PO Box 71839
Tuscaloosa, AL 35407
info@erminesociety.org
http://www.erminesociety.org/main.html
(Membership is open to persons with
legitimate titles of nobility but also to
several other categories, including officers
in the military and professors in
recognized colleges and universities, etc.)

$100.00 admission fee, no annual dues

National Society of Magna Carta Dames
PO Box 4222
Philadelphia, PA 19144

**Order of the Crown of Charlemagne in the
United States of America**
2449 South Bolton Avenue
Indianapolis, IN 46203-5643
William Prosser Nottingham, President
General

Plantagenet Society
PO Box 27165
Philadelphia, PA 19118

**Sovereign Colonial Society, Americans of
Royal Descent**
PO Box 27112
Philadelphia, PA 19118

**Niadh Nask (The Military Order of the
Golden Chain)**
PO Box 11084
Tuscaloosa, AL 35486-0025
Dr. David Pittman Johnson
hours: various
Pub. *The International Journal of the Niadh
Nask*, two times per year, $25.00 per year
subscription
(The Niadh Nask is an order of knighthood
established in Ireland in the pre-Christian
era; The Hereditary Head is The
MacCarthy Mór, Prince of Desmond and
Head of the ancient Irish Royal House of
Munster)

Huguenot

Huguenot Heritage
35 Sutton Place, Suite 6-E
New York, NY 10022-2464
(212) 759-6222
Karen McGarry
10:00–5:00 by appointment only
Pub. *Huguenot Heritage*, three times per year
("Nonprofit educational organization
concentrating on the cultural history of
the Huguenots and their descendants.
Huguenot Heritage does not provide any
genealogical service.")

The Huguenot Historical Society
PO Box 339
New Paltz, NY 12561-0339
(845) 255-1660; (845) 255-0376 FAX
hhsoffice@hhs-newpaltz.org
http://home.earthlink.net/~rctwig/hhs1.htm
Timothy F. Harley, Director
30 May–31 Oct: Wed–Sat 10:00–4:00;
Nov–30 May: by appointment
Pub. *The Messenger*, three times per year
(is supported in part by its member family
associations: The Bevier-Elting Family,
The Crispell Family, The Deyo Family,
The Freer-Low Family, The Gerow
Family, The LeFevre Family, the Magny
Family, The Schoonmaker Family and
The Terwilliger Family associations)
$15.00 per year membership (includes
membership in one family association)

The Huguenot Society of America
Library
122 East 58th Street
New York, NY 10022-1939
(212) 755-0592
http://huguenotsocietyofamerica.org
Dorothy F. Kimball, Executive Secretary
Tue–Wed 10:00–4:00

The Huguenot Society of South Carolina
138 Logan Street
Charleston, SC 29401-1941
(843) 723-3235; (843) 853-8476 FAX
archivist@cchat.com; huguenot@cchat.com
http://www.huguenotsociety.org
Harriott Cheves Leland,
Archivist/Researcher
Mon–Fri 9:00–2:00
Pub. *Transactions of Huguenot Society of
South Carolina*, annually, overruns
available for sale
$15.00 per year membership

Huguenot Society of Texas
10002 Ella Lee Lane
Houston, TX 77042-2912

**The Huguenot Society of the Founders of
Manakin in the Colony of Virginia**
6515 Martin Mill Pike
Knoxville, TN 37920
Rick Ford
by appointment
Pub. *The Huguenot*, biannually (every two
years), $10.00 per issue

**The Huguenot Society of the Founders of
Manakin in the Colony of Virginia**
Georgia Branch
206 Bolling Road, N.E.
Atlanta, GA 30305-3107
(404) 233-1920 voice & FAX

Huguenot Society of Wisconsin
8920 North Lake Drive
Bayside, WI 53217-1940
(414) 351-0644
Cchew@execpc.com
http://my.execpc.com/~drg/wihs.html
Carol Chew, President

National Huguenot Society
9033 Lyndale Avenue, South, Suite 108
Bloomington, MN 55420-3535
(952) 893-9747 (evenings); (952) 885-9776
(days)
http://huguenot.netnation.com/general
Arthur Louis Finnell, Executive Director
Mon–Fri 1:00–5:00
Pub. *The Cross of Languedoc*, two times per
year

Miscellaneous

Daughters of American Pioneers
Centennial Chapter
2334 Broad Street
Parkersburg, WV 26101

Descendants of Whaling Masters, Inc.
28 Fort Street
Fairhaven, MA 02719
weekdays 10:00–noon & 1:00–4:00
$5.00 per year membership

Order of Descendants of Ancient Planters
http://tyner.simplenet.com/planters/htm

Sons and Daughters of Pioneer Rivermen
(see Miscellaneous—Transportation, Part 4)

Surname Registries

Ancestors Unlimited
10853 Danube Avenue
Granada Hills, CA 91344

Association of One-Name Studies
(see Independent Publications, Part 1)

Double Check Research
Box 126
Higgins, TX 79046

Ed Nugent's Family Tree
nugent_tree@geocities.com
http://www.geocities.com/Heartland/
Plains/8622
Ed Nugent
(free surname search of over 100,000
records)

Family History Network
(see Publishers, Part 4)

Family Registry™
(see Ancestral File Operations, Computer
Interest, Part 4)

Family Services
East 12502 Frideger
Elk, WA 99009
(data available on 3½" disks in GEDCOM
format, uploaded to Compuserve)
free submission and notification of all
matches of your ancestors when you submit
to database, free electronic catalog; family
disk or family group sheets: $15.00 per
surname ($25.00 for common surname in
FGS format, $2.00 for index)

G-Tree
1021 Market Street
Sainte Genevieve, MO 63670

German Genealogical Index
(see Ethnic Archives, Libraries and
Societies—German, Part 3)

Heritage Genealogical Society
2552 Snow Mountain Drive
Sandy, UT 84092

International Genealogical Directory
International Society for British Genealogy
and Family History
PO Box 3115
Salt Lake City, UT 84110-3115

**The Irish Family Group Sheet Exchange
(IFGSX)**
PO Box 535
Farmington, MI 48332
Andrew J. Morris
free registration; access: up to 20 sheets on
one surname (and variants) for $4.00 (add
$1.00 for postage outside the U.S.)
database: 600 surnames

Online Genealogical Database Index
(see Computer Interest, Part 4)

Personalized Computer Service
5818 Handel Court
Huber Heights, OH 45424
free registration (prefers group sheets or full
data of each surname: last name, first,
middle, event, year, city or county and
state or country); access: $1.00 per
surname; database: over 500,000
(surnames continually added); established
1979

Researchers Surname Index
468 South Street, Apartment G
Lockport, NY 14094-3940
Faith G. Haungs
free registration; access: $1.00 per surname,
plus SASE (full refund if nothing found);
database: 29,000 surnames from around
the world; established 1981

Surname Databank
3227 Travelers Palm Drive
Edgewater, FL 32141
G. & B. Morgan
free registration; access: $1.00 per surname

Surname Exchange
152-18 Union Turnpike, #5E
Flushing, NY 11367
Leonard Jacobs
(includes Ackerman, Baker, Brown, Carroll,
Carson, Cisneros, Clark, Cobb, Crane,
Donovan, Elliott, Faucett, Fox, Gallagher,
Hoffman, Jacobs, James, Kelly, Lang,
McLaughlin, Martin, Moore, O'Neill,
Phillips, Peters, Sanders, Schmidt,
Shepard, Singer, Thompson, Walsh,
Winter)
registration: $1.00 per surname, $7.00 for all
surnames, free registration for researchers;
access: $1.00 per surname, $7.00 for all
surnames

Surname Heritage
3569 Ledyard Way
Aptos, CA 95003

United Ancestries
PO Box 2408
Park City, UT 84060-2408

Western Heraldry Organization
General Surname Index
10195 West 17th Place
Lakewood, CO 80215-2805
Florence N. Young, President
free registration; access: $1.00 per surname,
plus SASE; established 1973

Yates Publishing
Family Group Sheet Exchange
PO Box 67
Stevensville, MT 59870
(406) 777-3797
Bill Yates, Editor
Mon–Fri 8:30–4:30
(U.S. before 1900)
registration: free with order; access: copies of
files vary; database: over 120,000 records
(sheets); established 1981

Adoption Registries, Search Groups and Information Centers

Aborn
Jeep@Aborn.org; Taap@aborn.org (online
newsletter)
http://www.Aborn.org
Gen Goad and JDG, Co-founders
Pub. *The Adoption Activism Press*, online at
http://www.aborn.org/Taap
("Aborn is a grassroots organization working
to open sealed adoption records
nationwide.")

Adopted Child
PO Box 9362
Moscow, ID 83843
(208) 882-1794

Adoptee/Birthfamily Registry
PO Box 803
Carmichael, CA 95608
(916) 485-4119; (916) 944-7312
Trudy Helmlinger, Ph.D.
Mon–Fri 8:00–5:00
Pub. *Adoptee/Birthfamily Registry*, annually,
$25.00 per issue
free listing

Adoptee/Birthparent Connections
8820 Kennedy Lane
San Miguel, CA 93451
Tina Peddie, Adoption Search Consultant
(includes Brynberg)

Adoptee Identity Doorway
PO Box 361
South Bend, IN 46624
(219) 272-3520

**Adoptees Adult Liberation Movement
Triad**
1725 Atascadero Drive
Columbia, SC 29206
(803) 787-3778; (803) 787-4192
Mildred Szakacsi, Founder
Pub. *Search-Support and Birth Registry*,
three times per year
(serves South Carolina)
$35.00 per year membership

Adoptees and Birthparents in Search
PO Box 6426B
Greenville, SC 29606

**Adoptees and Natural Parents
Organization**
949 Lacon Drive
Newport News, VA 23608
(757) 764-9091 (no calls after 10:00 P.M.
eastern time)
Billie Quigley, President
(a support group for adoptees, birthparents;
search assistance limited to some areas of
Virginia)

Adoptees', Birthparents' Association
2027 Finch Court
Simi Valley, CA 93063-3720

Adoptees in Search (AIS)
PO Box 41016
Bethesda, MD 20824
(301) 656-8555; (301) 652-2106 FAX
ais20824@aol.com
Joanne W. Small, MSW., Director
Mon–Fri 9:00–5:00, plus 24-hour answering
service
Pub. *AIS Newsnotes*, bimonthly
(adoptee/birth relative searches)
$75.00 (tax-deductible) membership plus
benefits (search registry); search fee:
hourly rate, with retainer (non-tax-
deductible)

Adoptees Information Service, Inc.
19 Marion Avenue
Mount Vernon, NY 10552

**Adoptees Liberty Movement Association
(ALMA)**
San Francisco Bay Area Chapter
PO Box 21554
Concord, CA 94521-0554
(925) 686-2469; (510) 763-1218
Pub. *The Alma Searchlight*, quarterly
Chapters: **Alaska**: Northwest Regional
Office, PO Box 372, Glennallen, AK
99588; **California**: Emily Carter, PO Box
2341, Alameda, CA 94501; Henrietta
Buchanan, PO Box 9425, Canoga Park,

CA 91309-0425; Gary & Carol McDowell, PO Box 8081, Sacramento, CA 95818; Bridie Kelly, PO Box 880335, San Diego, CA 92108; Mary Anna DeParcq, PO Box 1233, Simi Valley, CA 93062; Leila Higgs, PO Box 271, Vina, CA 96092; **Michigan**: Deborah Smith, Michigan Coordinator, PO Box 1804, Royal Oak, MI 48068-1804, (313) 542-2930
$55.00 registration fee

Adoptees Search Connection
1203 Hill Street
Suffield, CT 06078
(860) 668-1042
Nancy Sitterly
(serves western Massachusetts and Connecticut)

Adoptee's Search for Knowledge
PO Box 762
East Lansing, MI 48826-0762
(517) 321-7291; (517) 321-3331 FAX
Jeanette Abronowitz, Executive Director, Searcher
10:00–3:00
(Adoption searches [siblings, relatives, biological parents and others separated by adoption]; certified confidential court intermediary; adoptee must be 18 years old. Ingham, Easton, Clinton counties, Lansing)
search and confidential intermediary fee: $250.00 total ("fee set by state covers total, is flat with no promises of reunion")

Adoption Advisory Council, Inc.
2448 Stuart Street
Brooklyn, NY 11229
Dr. Irene Ganelli

Adoption Alliance of Vermont
17 Hopkins Street
Rutland, VT 05701
(802) 773-7078
Maureen S. Vincent
(serves Vermont and the surrounding area)

Adoption and Family Reunion Center
PO Box 239
Moore, SC 29369
(864) 574-0681
Liz White
(serves South Carolina)

Adoption and Family Search
898 Jeri Lane
Boulder City, NV 89005-2220
(702) 293-6863; (702) 293-0844 FAX
Michael Paris, Consultant
by appointment

Adoption and Medical Information Registry
New York State Department of Health
Corning Tower
Empire State Plaza
Albany, NY 12237-0023
(518) 474-9600
Peter M. Carucci, Director of Vital Records
8:30–4:30
("Provides general, nonidentifying information to adoptees who are 18 years of age or older and who were born and adopted in New York State. Also provides current names and address upon registration of adoptee and biological parents. Files certified medical information updates from birth parents anytime after the adoption, and updates are available upon request by adoptee on

adoptive parents, if adoptee is under eighteen years of age.")
$75.00 for adoptees, $20.00 for birth parents (waived if currently receiving public assistance)

Adoption Answers Support Kinship (AASK)
8 Homestead Drive
South Glastonbury, CT 06073-2804
(860) 657-4005 voice & FAX
Judy Taylor, Director
10:00–10:00; meetings: third Sun 2:00–5:00
("Search assistance is offered on the phone.")
$5.00 meeting fee

Adoption Connection
842 Country Stone Drive
Saint Louis, MO 63021

Adoption Connection Exchange
Family and Children's Services
4623 Falls Road
Baltimore, MD 21209-4900

Adoption Connection, Inc.
O'Shea Building
11 Peabody Square, Number 6
Peabody, MA 01960
(978) 532-1261; (978) 532-0427
Susan Darke
9:00–4:00
Pub. *Happenings*, quarterly
(serves New England; reunites adoptees, birthparents and adoptive families)
fees: from $50.00 to $400.00

Adoption Connection of Louisiana
PO Box 6921
Metairie, LA 70009
(504) 277-0030; (504) 887-7198
Dianne Sercovich

Adoption Crossroads
PO Box 9025
Schenectady, NY 12309
(518) 377-5936

Adoption Identity Movement of Grand Rapids (AIM)
(Kentwood Recreation Center, 355 48th Street, S.E.—location)
PO Box 9783 (mailing address)
Grand Rapids, MI 49509
(616) 531-1380 (24-hour answering service)
Peg Richer, Director
(serves western Michigan; adoption searches and support)
one-time $30.00 donation for membership

Adoption Information and Direction, Inc. (AID)
PO Box 174
Coon Valley, WI 54623
(608) 452-3146 (8:00 A.M.–10:00 P.M., will return calls collect)
Pat Helgerson, Director, LaCrosse Area
(serves Wisconsin, Iowa and Minnesota; adoption search and support for adoptee, birthparent, adoptive parent, concerned others)
$20.00 per year membership; search fees: depending on services rendered

Adoption Information and Direction, Inc. (AID)
PO Box 2043
Oshkosh, WI 54903
(920) 233-6487 (Carroll); (920) 233-2608 (Carol)
meetings last Thur 7:00 at Presbyterian Church, 110 Church Avenue

(serves Oshkosh, Wisconsin; search and support)

Adoption Information and Direction, Inc. (AID)
4308 Heffron Street
Stevens Point, WI 54481-5538
(715) 345-1290 (President)
Fireworks@charter.net
Doug Henderson, Group Leader
meetings at Frame Presbyterian Church, Main and Church Streets: first Mon 7:00
(serves central Wisconsin; adoption search for all sides of triad served)

Adoption Information Exchange
PO Box 1917
Matthews, NC 28106-1917
(704) 537-5919; (704) 846-5123
mzchrislee@aol.com
http://kinsolving.com
Chris Lee
9:00–5:00
(serves North Carolina, Tennessee and Virginia; free North Carolina reunion registry)
search fee varies, "no find, no fee"

Adoption Insight
PO Box 171
Portage, MI 49081
(616) 324-9987
Carol Gray; Elaine Meints
evenings
("Adoption search aid")
donation

Adoption Network Cleveland
291 East 222
Cleveland, OH 44123-1751
(216) 261-1551 (24-hour voice mail); (216) 261-1164 FAX
http://pages.prodigy.com/adoptreform/anc.com
Betsie Norris, Executive Director
Mon–Fri 9:00–5:00, Sat 10:00–2:00
Pub. *Adoption Network News*, bimonthly
("Specializing in Cleveland area searches (adoption); services include support, education and advocacy.")
$30.00 per year membership; search fee: $25.00

Adoption Option
PO Box 429327
Cincinnati, OH 45242
(513) 244-7072; (513) 793-7268
Carole Adlard
(serves southwest Ohio)

Adoption Reality/Adoption Research Services
2180 Clover Street
Simi Valley, CA 93065
(805) 526-2289; (526) 2920 FAX
beckars 2000@yahoo.com
Gayle L. Beckstead, ISC
("California only")
search fee

Adoption Records Search Program
Department of Health and Family Services
(1 West Wilson Street, Room 465—location)
Box 8916 (mailing address)
Madison, WI 53708-8916
(608) 266-7163; (608) 264-9852
http://www.dhfs.state.wi.us
Theodora A. Christensen, MSSW, Adoption Search Specialist, Bureau of Programs and Policies, Division of Children and Family Services
8:00–4:30

(prepares closed adoption record in nonidentifying fashion, searches for birth parents and updated medical/genetic information, and maintains files for birth parents who are willing to disclose their identities should the adopted person request a search)

Adoption Reform Movement of Michigan
95 North Whitesbridge Road
Belding, MI 48809
(616) 897-5342
Bob Schafer, Co-Director
24 hours
Pub. *Newsletter*, irregularly
(adoption reform activist organization, legislative reform, support group referral)

Adoption Resource Center of Children's Home Society of Washington
(3300 N.E. 65th Street—location)
PO Box 15190 (mailing address)
Seattle, WA 98133
(206) 524-6020
Mon–Fri 8:30–5:30
("Provide search services for those adopted through CHSW, or for those who relinquished their children through CHSW; provide information and referral for others")
call for information on search fees

Adoption Resource Service, Inc.
1904 North Avenue
Burlington, VT 05401

Adoption Reunion Connection
263 Lemonade Road
Pacolet, SC 29372
(864) 474-3479
Pollie Robinson, Search Consultant and Co-Director
(serves South Carolina, offers adoption search help)
$35.00 per year membership

Adoption Search and Reconciliation
14320 S.E. 170th Street
Renton, WA 98058
(425) 228-6179

Adoption Search Consultants
8539 Monroe Road, Suite 25
Charlotte, NC 28212-7150
(704) 537-5919

Adoption Search for Life
PO Box 66
Anderson, SC 29622
(864) 224-8020
cpwalters@aol.com
Cynthia P. Walters, Coordinator
meetings at AnMed Resource Center, Anderson Mall, Anderson
("Adoption search/support group. Volunteer organization. No paid staff.")
donation only

Adoption Search/Support Network
Rural Route 1, Box 83
East Calais, VT 05650
(802) 456-8850
beleaf4u@aol.com
Marge Garfield, Director
Mon–Fri 9:00–5:00

Adoption Support Group
PO Box 2316
Ketchum, ID 83340
(208) 726-8543

Adoption Triad Midwest

PO Box 37273
Omaha, NE 68137
(402) 895-3706 (6:00 P.M.–8:00 P.M., long distance calls will be returned collect)
Nancy Sullivan
(adoption search support)
$25.00 per year membership

Adoption Triangle
PO Box 384
Park Forest, IL 60466
(708) 365-0574
Beth Duensing, Independant Search Consultant
Mon–Fri noon–5:00
(search and support group for adoptees, birth parents and adoptive parents)
send LSASE for information

Adoption with Truth
66-C Panoramic Way
Berkeley, CA 94704
Sara Vick

The Adoptive Experience
2690 Meadow Street
Osceola, IA 50213
(641) 342-4803
Marianne Lippold
(serves Iowa)

Adoptive Parents for Open Records
PO Box 193
Long Valley, NJ 07853
(908) 850-1706

Advocating Legislation for Adoptive Reform Movement (ALARM) Network
9203 S.W. Cree Circle
Tualatin, OR 97062
(503) 692-5794

American Adoption Congress
PO Box 42730
Washington, DC 20015
(202) 483-3399; (636) 225-8998 (Membership)
wmintert@aol.com
http://www.americanadoptioncongress.org
Whitney Mintert, Membership
24 hours
Pub. *The Decree*, quarterly
$50.00 per year membership

Americans for Open Records (AmFOR)
PO Box 401
Palm Desert, CA 92261
(900) LOCATOR, ext. 11 ($2.50 per minute, must be 18 years of age or older and have a touchtone phone)
http://www.genealogymall.com
Lori Carangelo, President
Pub. *The Open Record*, irregularly, depending on available funds
(a nonprofit, international, voluntary civil liberties network, established to promote the inherent right of Americans to information about themselves without court or agency intervention; no fee for search help—10,000 families reunited since 1989; pro se legal help, referrals and other information; civil liberties legal advocacy; publishes client case histories with permission; publishes *The Ultimate Search Book: From the Files of Americans For Open Records (AmFOR) (how to find anyone, with or without a name, in 50 states and 200 countries,* $69.95)
$5.00 total fee covers Registry, computer-matching, materials, postage

Arkansas Adoption Triad
5900 Scenic Drive
Little Rock, AR 72202

B.K.I.D.S.
PO Box 43
Erin, NY 14838
(607) 739-2957

Baccus Genealogical Research
5817 144 Street East
Puyallup, WA 98373-5221
(253) 537-8288
janetgb@worldnet.att.net
Janet G. Baccus, Owner
(adoptions, Pierce County, and Washington state research)

Birthparents Adoptees Adoptive Parents United in Support (B.U.S.)
PO Box 299
Victor, NY 14564-0299
(716) 924-0410
Marcia Brady-Cohen, Founder and Director
9:00 A.M.–10:00 P.M.
Pub. *B.U.S. Bulletin*, quarterly
(serves eastern, central, and upstate New York; adoption, twelve-step self-help group)
$20.00 per year membership

Birthright of Greater Kansas City
6309 Walnut
Kansas City, MO 64113
(816) 444-7090; (800) 550-4900
Glenda Merten, Director
Mon–Tue & Thur–Fri 10:00–2:00, Tue 6:00–8:00, Wed 2:00–8:00
Pub. *Heartbeat*, quarterly
(emotional support and practical assistance to pregnant women; international organizaiton based in Toronto, Ontario)

Bonding by Blood, Unlimited
Foess Family Farm
5845 Waterman Road
Vassar, MI 48768-9790
(989) 823-8248
kharput1913@hotmail.com
Mary Louise Foess, Founder and President
weekdays 9:00–8:00
("I will help anyone any way I can, just as others once helped me. My reward is your loving reunion with your lost loved ones!")
SASE for mail replies; $5.00 for initial 1995 Confidential Intermediary Open Records Law and other search tips packet

Catholic Social Service
2546 20th Street
Great Bend, KS 67530
(620) 792-1393; (620) 792-1399 FAX
slytle@cpcis.net
Shirley Lyte, Post Adoption/Search Coordinator
Mon–Fri 9:00–5:00
(adoption, search and reunion; serves southwest Kansas)
$120.00 (includes one active hour of searching), $40.00 per hour thereafter

Center for Family Connections
350 Cambridge Street
Cambridge, MA 02141
(617) 547-0909; (800) KINNECT; (617) 497-5952 FAX
http://www.kinnect.org
Dr. Joyce Maguire Pavao; Assistant
Mon–Thur 9:00–7:00, Fri 9:00–5:00, Sat 9:00–2:00
(serves U.S.; specializing in adoption, foster

care, kinship, families by alternative reproductive technologies, and other blended and complex families)
$50.00 per year membership

Central Coast Adoption Support Group
94 Manchester Place
Goleta, CA 93117
(805) 968-4351
Susan Bott
(serves Southern California)

Children and Families First
2005 Baynard Boulevard
Wilmington, DE 19802
(302) 658-5177; (302) 658-5170 FAX
Sally Decker, Search Coordinator
Mon–Fri 9:00–5:00
(search only for adoptees and birth parents who used agency adoption services)
sliding-scale fees

Chosen Children
31 Springbrook Boulevard
Dayton, OH 45405
(937) 274-8017
Joanne Gall, Director
10:00–6:00

Circle of Hope
PO Box 127
Somersworth, NH 03878
(603) 692-5917
Karen Amos
9:00–5:00
(adoption search and support group, some missing relatives (i.e. aunt, father, daughter, etc.); serves New Hampshire and New England)
$30.00 per year membership; search fees vary

Colorado Confidential Intermediary Service
PO Box 260460
Lakewood, CO 80226
(303) 237-6919

Colorado Department of Public Health and Environment
4300 Cherry Creek Drive, South
Denver, CO 80222-1530
(303) 692-2188
theresa.salazar@state.co.us
Theresa Salazar, Adoption Registry Coordinator
Mon–Fri 8:30–4:30, except holidays
$15.00 registration fee

Concerned United Birthparents (CUB)
National Headquarters
2000 Walker Street
Des Moines, IA 50317
(800) 822-2777 (24-hours); (515) 263-9541 FAX
http://www.webnations.com/cub
Bonnie Bis, President
Pub. *CUB Communicator*, monthly
$50.00 initial year's membership in support group, $35.00 per year renewal

Concerned United Birthparents (CUB)
7105 Shoresin Circle
Anchorage, AK 99504
(907) 333-2272

Concerned United Birthparents (CUB)
10801 San Paco Circle
Fountain Valley, CA 92708
(714) 962-8866

Concerned United Birthparents (CUB)

1008 West Kensington Road
Los Angeles, CA 90026
Patti Prickett

Concerned United Birthparents (CUB)
10511 104th Avenue
Broomfield, CO 80021
(303) 466-8554
Vickie Ransier

Concerned United Birthparents (CUB)
130 33rd Avenue, S.W.
Cedar Rapids, IA 52404
(319) 363-6929
Judy Wilkins

Concerned United Birthparents (CUB)
500 Kimberly Lane
Des Moines, IA 50317
(515) 262-2334

Concerned United Birthparents (CUB)
14914 Nighthawk Lane
Bowie, MD 20716
(301) 249-8135

Concerned United Birthparents (CUB)
PO Box 380-396, Harvard Square
Cambridge, MA 02238
(617) 328-3005 (anytime)
Libbi Campbell, Coordinator
meetings at Plymouth Congregational Church, Edgell Road, Framingham Center; hotline anytime
Pub. *CUB Communicator*, monthly
(support for birthparents and other adoption-affected people; search referrals, advocacy and education)
$50.00 initial year's membership, $35.00 per year membership thereafter

Concerned United Birthparents (CUB)
Twin City Metro-Area Branch
6429 Mendelssohn Lane
Edina, MN 55343-8424
(952) 930-9058
Sandra L. Sperrazza, Branch Coordinator
Mon–Fri 9:00–5:00
Pub. *Cub Communicator* (out of CUB headquarters), monthly
(searcher for those separated by adoption as well as for those looking for heirs to finalize estates)
$50.00 for first-year membership, $35.00 per year membership renewal

Concerned United Birthparents (CUB)
7000 Jackson
Kansas City, MO 64132

Concerned United Birthparents (CUB)
4589 Hopewell Road
Wentzville, MO 63385
(636) 828-5726

Concerned United Birthparents (CUB)
25371 Perkins Road
Veneta, OR 97487-9783
Janet Appleford

Cooperative Adoption Consulting
54 Wellington Avenue
San Anselmo, CA 94960
(415) 453-0902 voice & FAX
Ellen Roseman, Director
Mon–Fri 9:00–5:00
(Serves Japan, Europe and the U.S.; helps with searching; special focus on bonding/attachment issues; service is international, serving both couples and singles across the United States and abroad—mainly U.S. military families in

foreign locations; infant open adoption placement)

Coping with Adoption
61 County Farm Road
Peru, IN 46970
(765) 472-7425

Department of Children and Family Services
Director's Office, Closed Records
406 East Monroe
Springfield, IL 62701-1498
(217) 785-2509

Department of Children's Services
Post Adoption Services
436 Sixth Avenue
North Nashville, TN 37243-1290
(615) 532-5637
8:00–4:30
fee for services

Division of Child and Family Services—Nevada Adoption Registry
711 East Fifth Street
Carson City, NV 89710-5092
(775) 684-4415
Deborah Gottschalk, Administrative Assistant II
8:00–5:00
("The Nevada Adoption Registry registers all adoptees and birth parents and relatives. If an applicant moves and does not notify us of their new address, we do not search for them.")

Division of Youth and Family Services, Adoption Unit
Adoption Registry
(50 East State Street—location)
PO Box 717 (mailing address)
Trenton, NJ 08625-0717
(609) 292-8816
Gerald R. Gioglio, Adoption Registry Coordinator
9:00–4:00
(post adoption services, registry for DYFS clients—adoptees, birth family members, and adoptive parents—only)
no charge

Donor's Offspring
PO Box 37
Sarcoxie, MO 64862
(417) 548-3679
Candace Turner
(serves the U.S. and the world for DI/Adoptees, the southwest and Missouri)

Families First
1105 West Peachtree Street, N.E.
Atlanta, GA 30305
(404) 853-2800

Family Court, First Circuit
Adoption Records Clerk
(777 Punchbowl Street, Second Floor/First Circuit Court—location)
PO Box 3498 (mailing address)
Honolulu, HI 96811-3498
(808) 539-4424 (calls returned collect)
Mon–Fri 7:45–4:30

Family Ties
4537 Souza Street
Eugene, OR 97402-6122
(541) 461-0752
Helen Gallagher, Independent Search Consultant
9:00 A.M.–9:00 P.M.
(adoption support group, also helps children

of divorce, separated families, etc.;
includes information regarding Orphan
Train riders)
search fees negotiable, depending upon
services

Finders Keepers
PO Box 748
Bear, DE 19701-0748
(302) 834-8888
Ginger Farrow
(serves Delaware, Maryland, New Jersey and
Pennsylvania)

Group for Openness in Adoption
518 General George Patton Road
Nashville, TN 37221-2449
(615) 646-8116
Sandra
(support group for adoptee and birthparents
in search, primarily addressing feelings
involved when searching)

Heritage Searching
4308 San Mateo Street
North Las Vegas, NV 89030-2822
Mary Buckley
("adoption researcher and support to people
in search")

Independent Search Consultant (ISC)
20111 Riverside Drive
Santa Ana, CA 92707
(714) 669-8100

Independent Search Consultant (ISC)
1602 Cole Street
Birmingham, MI 48009
Mrs. Chris Spurr, ISC
(serves Michigan)

Independent Search Consultant (ISC)
512 Wayside
Albert Lea, MN 56007
(507) 377-0517

**Independent Search Consultants (ISC),
Inc.**
PO Box 10192
Costa Mesa, CA 92627
(949) 225-9245
http://www.rmci.net/isc
Pat Sanders, Executive Director
Pub. *The ISC Searchbook*, annually, $10.00
per issue
(referrals to adoption search consultants,
U.S., Canada and Germany; certification
of consultants)

Indiana Adoption Coalition
PO Box 76
Oakford, IN 46965
(765) 453-4427; (765) 453-7418 FAX
Candy Jones, Co-director
("Post adoption in Indiana")

**International Soundex Reunion Registry
(I.S.R.R.)**
PO Box 2312
Carson City, NV 89702-2312
(702) 882-7755
Marri Rillera, Registrar
Mon–Fri 9:00–4:00
("to serve and promote, through the Reunion
Registry, the interests of any adult persons
desiring and seeking a reunion with next-
of-kin by birth; adoption, divorce,
foster—any cause of separation")
free, but donation accepted

Iowa Reunion Registry
PO Box 8

Blairsburg, IA 50034-0008
Doris Smith
(serves Iowa and surrounding states)
free, donation accepted, LSASE requested

Jewish Family Services
Birth Parent Support Group
229 Waterman Street
Providence, RI 02906
(401) 331-1244
8:30–4:30

Kansas City Adult Adoptees Organization
(Kansas City Public Library, 311 East 12th
Street, Kansas City, MO 64106—location)
PO Box 11576 (mailing address)
Kansas City, MO 64138-9998
(816) 229-4075
Sandy Hassler, President
$35.00 one-time fee

**Kentucky Department for Social
Services—Adult Adoptees**
275 East Main Street
Frankfort, KY 40621
(502) 564-2147
http://members.tripod.com/ABORN.
Webring/State/NotAnswered/Kentucky.
html
Virginia Nester, Program Specialist
Mon–Fri 8:00–4:30

**Kinsolving Investigations/Adoption
Information Exchange**
PO Box 1917
Matthews, NC 28106-1917
(704) 537-5919; (704) 846-5123 FAX
mzchrislee@aol.com
http://kinsolving.com
Chris Lee
10:00–4:00
Pub. *The Vanguard*, quarterly (online)
(adoption searches for the U.S. and Canada,
"reunification of adoptees, birthparents,
and all adoptive triad members")
search fees based on case

**L.A.S.S.O. (Lafayette Adoption
Search/Support Organization)**
5936 Lookout Drive
West Lafayette, IN 47906
(765) 567-4139
Sue Madden, Convener
Bethany Presbyterian Church, 3305 Longlois
Drive, Lafayette, IN 47905: second &
fourth Thur (except Thanksgiving or
Maundy Thursday) 7:30–9:30
(adoptive search and support)
free-will donation

Life Adoption Ministry
1350 Placer Street
Redding, CA 96001-1013
(800) 57 ADOPT
Donna Lessard Pratt
Mon–Fri 8:30–5:30
Pub. *Prose & Coos Adoption News*,
bimonthly

Lifeline International
702 Brandywine Boulevard
Wilmington, DE 19809

**Lincoln County Department of Social
Services**
PO Box 130
Lincolnton, NC 28093-0130
(704) 732-0738
Pat Hovis
(serves Lincoln County)

Locators Unlimited

PO Box 1218
Nicholasville, KY 40340
(859) 885-6634

**Los Angeles County Adoption Search
Association**
PO Box 1461
Roseville, CA 95678
(916) 784-2711
Vikki Schummer
Tue–Fri 10:00–4:30
(specializing in California searches)
search fees dependent on service needed

Lutheran Social Services of North Dakota
Post Adoption Coordinator
(1325 South 11th Street—location)
PO Box 389 (mailing address)
Fargo, ND 58107-0389
(701) 235-7341
8:00–5:00
(nonidentifying information or identifying
search)
research: $75.00 for nonidentifying
information, $300.00 for identifying
search (including nonidentifying
information)

**Maryland Mutual Consent Voluntary
Adoption Registry**
Social Services Administration
311 West Saratoga Street
Baltimore, MD 21201
(410) 767-7663; (410) 333-0922 FAX
msmith11@dhr.state.md.us
7:30–4:00
$25.00 registration

Mendo Lake Adoption Triad
620 Walnut Avenue
Ukiah, CA 95482
(707) 468-0648

Minnesota Department of Human Services
Adoption/Guardianship Section
444 Lafayette Road
Saint Paul, MN 55155-3831
(612) 297-1949
8:00–4:30

**Minnesota Reunion Registry/Liberal
Education for Adoptive Families**
23247 Lofton Court North
Scandia, MN 55073-9752
(651) 636-7031; (651) 433-5211

New York Foundling Hospital
Record Information Office
590 Avenue of the Americas
New York, NY 10011
Gloria Rella, Director, Public Relations
(Orphan Trains in the late 1800s)

**Oasis, Inc. (Organized Adoption Search
Information Services, Inc.)**
PO Box 53-0761
Miami Shores, FL 33153
(305) 758-5196
Rachel S. Rivers, Director
Mon–Fri 9:00–6:00
(specializes in research and reunification,
serves the U.S. and abroad; maintains
match-up system by date and place of
birth: OASIS Birth Registry)
$70.00 per year membership; search help in
adoption to adults

Operation Identity
1818 Somervell, N.E.
Albuquerque, NM 87112-2836
(505) 275-9952
Barbara Free, Newsletter Editor

Pub. *Operation Identity Newsletter*, quarterly ("adoption triad support group open to all with adoption connections") $20.00 per year membership

Oregon Adoptive Rights Association (OARA)
PO Box 882
Portland, OR 97207
(503) 235-3669
Delores Teller, President
Pub. *OARA Newsletter*, quarterly
(adoption and reunion registry; search and support)
$40.00 for first year's membership, $25.00 per year membership renewal

Orphan Train Heritage Society of America, Inc. (OTHSA)
614 East Emma Avenue, Suite 115
Springdale, AR 72764-4634
(501) 756-2780; (501) 756-0769 FAX
Mary Ellen Johnson, Editor
Mon–Fri 8:00–1:00, and by appointment
Pub. *Crossroads*, quarterly
(orphan train riders, 1854–1929)
$25.00 per year membership

Orphan Trains of Kansas
http://kuhttp.cc.ukans.edu/carrie/kancoll/
    articles/orphans/index.html
Connie DiPasquale

Orphan Voyage
1305 Augustine Court
College Station, TX 77840
(979) 764-7157
Linda Crenwelge, U.S. Search Assistant
after 6:00 and on weekends
(serves the U.S., adoption searchers, free assistance/referrals for all states)

Orphan Voyage of Houston
5811 Southminster
Houston, TX 77035
(713) 723-1762

Overseas Brats
PO Box 47112
Wichita, KS 67201-7112

Parents and Adoptees Liberty Movement
861 Mitchell's Lane
Middletown, RI 02840
(401) 437-1811

Pittsburgh Adoption Lifeline
Altoona Chapter
414 28th Avenue
Altoona, PA 16601

Pittsburgh Adoption Lifeline
PO Box 52
Gibsonia, PA 15044
(724) 443-3370 (anytime)
Jean Vincent, Coordinator
Pub. *Lifeline*, three or four times per year
(adoption search and emotional support)
$15.00 per year membership

Post Adoption Center for Education and Research (P.A.C.E.R.)
PO Box 309
Orinda, CA 94563-0309
Virginia Keeler Wolf

Post Adoption Center Support Group
8600 Wurzbach Road, Suite 1110
San Antonio, TX 78240-4334
(serves San Antonio and surrounding area)

Pure, Inc.

PO Box 638
Westminster, CA 92684
(The Surname/Birthdate Index—over 100,000 listings of birth dates, birthplaces, surnames, given names, and the originating source of the data, listed in Triadoption Services computerized Database; collection of newsletters; etc.)

Rainbow Families, Inc.
734 Pahumele Place
Kailua, HI 96734

Reunion
PO Box 112
Salinda, CO 81201

Reunions, Ltd.
2611 East 25th Street
Topeka, KS 66605-3237
(785) 267-0827
Bonnie Warren, Founder
(search and support for adoptees and birthparents)

ROOTS
7110 Westway Circle
Knoxville, TN 37919
(865) 691-7412
Susie Thompson
(serves Eastern Tennessee)

Search Consultant
6475-B East Pacific Coast Highway
Long Beach, CA 90803
(562) 427-0463; (562) 596-2466 FAX
Mary Ann Dunkinson
(serves California)

Search-Finders of California
PO Box 24595
San Jose, CA 95154-4595
(408) 356-6711 (24-hour answering machine and FAX)
searchfinders@earthlink.net
http://www.searchfinders.org
Dorothy Yturriaga, Director
Pub. *Lost & Found*, quarterly
(serves Northern California)
$50.00 per year membership

Search-Finders of Idaho
PO Box 7941
Boise, ID 83707
(208) 375-9803
Lois Wight, Chairman
(nonprofit organizaiton; search and support group)
$35.00 per year

Search for Tomorrow
PO Box 441
New Haven, IN 46774-0441
(219) 749-4392
NY4211NY@aol.com
Martha Barrow, Executive Director
Mon, Wed & Fri 5:00–9:00, Thur 4:30–9:00
(maintains a registry of over 4,000 adoptees, birthmothers, adopted parents and separated siblings)
$35.00 application fee; negotiable fee for search

Search Line of Texas, Inc.
1516 Old Orchard
Irving, TX 75061
(972) 445-7005
Pat Palmer
daily 9:00 A.M.–10:00 P.M.
(serves Texas)
$200.00 for adoptees, $350.00 for birthparents

Search Triad, Inc.
PO Box 1432
Litchfield Park, AZ 85340
(623) 834-7417 (24-hour message machine)
searchtriad@att.net
http://searchtriad.org
Karen Tinkham, Search Assistant Coordinator
(participates in the free International Soundex Reunion Registry)
$75.00 membership the first year, $35.00 renewal, free reunion registry

Seek
2410 Manhattan Street
Michigan City, IN 46360-6050
Faith

South Coast Adoption Research and Support
PO Box 039
Harbor City, CA 90710
(310) 833-5822
Marilyn Miller, ISC
8:00 A.M.–8:00 P.M.
$35.00 per year membership

Sunshine Reunions
1175 Virginia Avenue
Akron, OH 44306-3545
(330) 773-4691
Jean Batis, Founder
Tue–Sat 10:00–7:00
("Reuniting families separated by adoption, since 1977; individual counseling, search assistance, referrals, resources, speakers, legislation (open records and open adoption advocates), totally confidential, serves all adoption triad members")
$25.00 life membership; research: fees by individual case ("For a birth family member to search, amount seldom exceeds $75.00, but for an adopted person to search, fee may be higher.")

Support for Birthparents
35 Demorest Road
Columbus, OH 43204
(614) 274-4492

T.R.I.A.D.
7155 East Freestone Drive
Tucson, AZ 85730
(520) 790-6320

Ties That Bind
PO Box 3119
Milford, CT 06460
(203) 874-2023

Tracers Company of America, Inc.
183 Waverly Avenue
Medford, NY 11763
(631) 654-0091; (212) 558-6550
Robert Eisenberg, President
10:00–4:00
(specialty: adoption reunion registry and missing persons)
adoption reunion registry one-time fee $50.00

Tracers, Ltd.
(9141 East 38th Street, Tucson, AZ 85731-1851—location)
PO Box 18511 (mailing address)
Tucson, AZ 85731-8511
(520) 885-5958
Gari-Sue Greene, Owner
9:00–5:00

Tri-County Genealogical Society
(21715 Brittany, Eastpointe, MI 48021-

2503—location)
15492 MacArthur (mailing address)
Redford Township, MI 48239
(313) 255-7319
Karen Mehlberg
(adoption search)

Triad Research
300 Golden West
Shafter, CA 93263

Truth Seekers in Adoption
PO Box 366
Prospect Heights, IL 60070-0366
(847) 342-8742 (24-hour answering
    machine)
http://www.truthseekers/adoption
Barbara Gonyo, Reunion Consultant
meetings at Lutheran General Hospital, 1775
    Dempster Street, Park Ridge, Illinois: last
    Mon 7:00–10:00
(experienced intermediaries; a support group
    for adoption triad members, search
    referrals worldwide)
meeting fee: $10.00

**TRY Resource/Referral Center and
Library for Adoption Issues**
Today Reunites Yesterday
(116 Pleasant Street, Easthampton, MA
01027—location)
PO Box 989 (mailing address)
Northampton, MA 01061-0989
(413) 527-1388; (413) 527-1387
try@try.org
http://www.try.org
Ann Henry, LSW Program Director
9:00–5:00
Pub. *Adoption Newsletter*, quarterly, $15.00
    per year subscription
(nationwide, adoption issues for TRIAD
    members; largest adoption library in
    Massachusetts)
$30.00 per year membership; library loans to
    nonmembers; $3.00; photocopies: 5¢ each

University of Southern Maine
Project Director, Human Services
Development Institute
Law Building 516
96 Falmouth Street
Portland, ME 04103
(207) 780-4403

Utah Department of Health
Bureau of Vital Records and Health Statistics
(288 North 1460 West, Salt Lake
City—location)
PO Box 142855 (mailing address)
Salt Lake City, UT 84114-2855
(801) 538-6363 (Adoption Clerk)
Barry E. Nangle, Bureau Director
Mon–Fri 8:00–5:00
(Utah Voluntary Mutual Consent Adoption
    Registry)
$25.00 registration fee; preparation of new
    birth certificate after adoption: $40.00

**Washington Adoption Reunion Movement
(WARM)**
5950 Sixth Avenue, South, Suite 107
Seattle, WA 98108-3317
(206) 767-9510 (to reach a "real person" and
    24-hour voice mail system); (206) 763-
    4803 FAX
warm@wolfenet.com
http://www.warmsearch.org
Margaret LeClair
Office: by appointment, call for scheduling
Pub. *WARM Journeys*
("WARM is a nonprofit organization
    dedicated since 1976 to serving the needs

of adult adoptees and their families.
Services for Washington births or
adoptions are: a Free Birth Registry, court
and noncourt searches, support groups
and educational materials.")

Wichita Adult Adoptees
4551 South Osage
Wichita, KS 67217
(316) 522-8772 (Director, 11:00 A.M.–9:00
    P.M.); (316) 729-7474 (Assistant Director,
    11:00 A.M.–9:00 P.M.)
http://www2.southwind.net/~1peters/
    waaindex.html
Rochelle Harris, Director; Tanya Sultz,
    Assistant Director
Pub. *News 'n' Views*, bimonthly
(serves Kansas; postadoption search)
$25.00 per year membership; search fees:
    expenses

Yesterday's Children
77 Homer Street
Providence, RI 02903

Immigration Research Centers

The first Act, in 1790, made naturalization
possible for any free, white adult with four
years of U.S. residency. From then, until
1906, any federal, state or local Court of
Record could confer citizenship. At that
time, the Immigration and Naturalization
Service, established to bring order to the
process, began reporting its findings to the
judge of the relevant court, who then signed
the Order. Naturalization of women and
children differed in that, before 1952,
children under 21 years of age received
derivative citizenship and have no separate
file. Women, on the other hand, received
automatic citizenship by marriage, after one
year of residency, and needed no Declaration
of Intent.

Many persons were granted citizenship
outside the normal process. Blacks became
citizens by constitutional amendment in
1868. Indians, who were wards of the state
until 1924, became citizens by an Act of
Congress. Citizens who were living in
territories which were brought into the U.S.
as a block, by treaty, were often awarded
citizenship *en masse*. The incorporation of
Texas in 1845 is a case in point.

The forms used for Naturalization
documents have also varied. Before 1906,
each court had its own form, usually one
which required only the foreswearing of
allegiance to the Head of the State from
which the applicant came, and the signature
of two witnesses. The Immigration and
Naturalization Service required forms to
include name, age, date and place of birth,
occupation, physical description, current and
former residences, Ports of Debarkation and
Arrival, name of the ship, date of arrival in
the U.S. In 1912, names and birth dates of
spouses and children were added. Beginning
in 1930, photographs were often included.

The normal process has required two
classes of documents. The Declaration of
Intent was often filed upon arrival in order to
begin establishment of residency without
delay. With a copy of this filing in hand,
final papers could be obtained from any court
after residency requirements had been met. A
two-to-seven-year lapse between the
Declaration and final papers is common. The
final paper has four parts: Petition, which
carries the most information; Affidavits of
witnesses and petitioner; Oath of Allegiance;
and Court Orders of admitting, denial, or
continuance. Name changes often occurred at
this time.

**Balch Institute for Ethnic Studies of The
Historical Society of Pennsylvania**
Center for Immigration Research
(see Ethnic Archives, Libraries, and
Societies—General, Part 3)

**Center for Migration Studies of New
York, Inc.**
209 Flagg Place
Staten Island, NY 10304
(718) 351-8800; (718) 667-4598 FAX
http://www.cmsny.org
Olha della Cava, Ph.D., Archivist
Pub. *International Migration Review*,
    quarterly

Genealogical Institute
(see Independent Publications, Part 1)

Great Migration Study Project

The New England Historic Genealogical Society (NEHGS)
PO Box 5089
Framingham, MA 01701
(888) 296-3447; (508) 788-9500 FAX
greatmigration@nehgs.org
http://www.NewEnglandAncestors.org
9:00–5:00
Pub. *Great Migration Newsletter*, quarterly,
$10.00 per year online subscription for
NEHGS members
(immigration to New England, 1620-1643)

Immigrant Genealogical Society
Immigrant Library
(1310-B West Magnolia
Boulevard—location)
PO Box 7369 (mailing address)
Burbank, CA 91510-7369
(818) 848-3122; (818) 716-6300 FAX; (818)
991-9475 (Editor's home)
lural@juno.com
http://feefhs.org/igs/frq-igs.html
Lura Perkins, Corresponding Secretary; Jean
Nepsund, Editor
Wed & Sun noon–5:00, Sat 10:00–5:00;
meetings: second Sun 2:00
Pub. *German American Genealogy*,
semiannually; *Immigrant Genealogical
Society Newsletter*, monthly
(especially German and Swiss)
$20.00 per year membership; library
admission: $2.00 for nonmembers

Immigration History Research Center
University of Minnesota
311 Andersen Library
222 21st Avenue South
Minneapolis, MN 55455-0439
(612) 625-4800; (612) 626-0018 FAX
ihrc@umn.edu
http://www.umn.edu/ihrc
Judith Rosenblatt, Public Relations
Mon–Fri 8:30–4:30
Pub. *Spectrum*, irregularly, $8.50 per issue;
IHRC News, two times per year, free upon
request; *Headline News*, posted monthly
at mid-month on the web site
(Resources focus on immigration from and
ethnic groups originating in eastern,
central, and southern Europe; fraternal
society, immigrant/refugee services
agency, and church records, newspapers
and serials, but no ship manifests or
naturalization records, concentration on
second wave [turn of the century]
immigrants, including from the Near East)
$15.00 per year membership in Friends of
the IHRC; research: responses to inquiries
available (see web site for details)

Immigration History Society
University of Cincinnati
3410 Bishop Street
Cincinnati, OH 45220
(513) 861-7462; (513) 556-7901 FAX
Pub. *The Immigration History Newsletter*,
semiannually (M. Mark Stolarik, Editor,
The Balch Institute for Ethnic Studies,
Immigration History Research Center, 18
South Seventh Street, Philadelphia, PA
19106); *Journal of American Ethnic
History*, semiannually (Ronald H. Bayor,
Editor)
$17.00 per year membership (includes both
publications)

KinShips
(see Miscellaneous—Products and Services,
Part 4)

The Historical Society of Lawrence and Its

People
Immigrant City Archives
(see Massachusetts, Part 2)

**Institute for Migration and Ancestral
Research**
mecklenburg@imar-mv.com
http://www.imar-mv.com

**The Statue of Liberty-Ellis Island
Foundation, Inc.**
American Family Immigration History
Center
292 Madison Avenue
New York, NY 10017
(212) 363-5804 (Museum); (212) 363-6307
(Library); (212) 363-3200 (History
Center); (212) 363-8347 FAX (Museum);
(212) 363-6302 FAX (Library)
historycenter@ellisisland.org
http://www.ellisisland.org;
http://ellisislandrecords.org
Jeffrey Dosik and Barry Moreno, Librarians
Mon–Fri 9:00–5:00
Pub. *Ellis Island and Statue of Liberty
Magazine*, annually, free
(history of Ellis Island, Castle Garden,
immigration and Statue of Liberty;
holdings include books, manuscripts,
photographs, clippings; currently no
genealogical or immigration records on
site)

**Swenson Swedish Immigration Research
Center**
(see Ethnic Archives, Libraries and
Societies—Swedish, Part 3)

Texas Seaport Museum
(see Texas, Part 2)

Computer Interest

America on Line
http://www.aol.com/webchannels/
families/html
(genealogical resources to subscribers only)

The American Local History Network
(ALHN)
webmaster@alhn.org
http://www.alhn.org/index.htm
(nationwide links to resources)

Ancestral File™ Operations
Family History Library
35 North West Temple
Salt Lake City, UT 84150
(801) 240-2585; (801) 240-2466; (801) 240-
2584 (for general FamilySearch®
questions)
Jayare Roberts, Specialist, Ancestral File™
Expansion
Mon 7:30 A.M.–6:00 P.M., Tue–Sat 7:30
A.M.–10:00 P.M.
(database not online)

Ancestry, Inc.
Genealogical Computing
(see Publishers, Part 4)

**Arizona Genealogy Computer Interest
Group (AGCIG)**
(see Arizona, Part 2)

Colorado Genealogical Society
Computer Interest Group
6437 Arbor Drive
Littleton, CO 80123-3827

Comgenes
(209 North Bayard Street—location)
PO Box 1581 (mailing address)
Silver City, NM 88062
Barbara Holley Rock, Genealogy Manager
Pub. *Grassroots Catalog*, semiannually (Jan,
July)
$20.00 per year membership

Commonwealth Network
http://www.gentree.com;
http://www.gentree.com/gentree.html
(Online Genealogical Database Index)
Tim Doyle
(links to all known searchable genealogical
databases on the Web)

The Genealogy Forum on CompuServe
(5000 Arlington Centre Boulevard,
Columbus, OH 43220—corporate
headquarters location)
PO Box 5273 (mailing address)
Billerica, MA 01822-5273
(978) 663-6510 (Forum Manager); (800)
848-8199 (Customer Service)
roots@compuserve.com
http://www.rootscomputing.com
Richard W. Eastman, Forum Manager;
Martha Reamy, Book Review Editor
Mon–Sun 24 hours
(worldwide online genealogy club, online
database of queries, message capabilities
accessed through local access numbers
which connect into the network)
$9.95 per month

Compute-A-Tree
2238 Cimmaron Pass Road
Fort Wayne, IN 46815
Karen Cavanaugh, Editor
Pub. *Compute-A-Tree*

Computer Genealogy Society of Long

Island
10 Beal Court
Huntington, NY 11743
(631) 549-3731
jbrower@optonline.net
http://freepages.genealogy.rootsweb.com/
~gfli/computer.html
James Brower, President
$15.00 per year membership

**Computer Genealogy Society of San Diego
(CGSSI)**
PO Box 370357
San Diego, CA 92137-0357
(619) 670-0960; (619) 670-0960 (Hotline)
cgssd-board@ucsd.edu; ctatina1@san.rr.com
http://www.cgssd.org
Carl Tatina, President
meetings at the Tierrasanta Christian Church,
11445 Tierrasanta Boulevard, San Diego:
third Sat (except Dec) 9:00–noon
(FTM, Legacy, PAF, TMG, Mac)
$20.00 per year membership

Computer Interest Group
Minnesota Genealogical Society
5768 Olson Memorial Highway
Golden Valley, MN 55422
(763) 595-9347 (Library)
mgsray@mtn.org
http://mtn.org/mgs/computer
Ray Kleinow
third Tue (except Dec) 7:00–9:00
$7.50 per year membership

Computer Rooters
PO Box 161693
Sacramento, CA 95816
(916) 363-8403; (916) 988-1125 (Mr.
Sissell)
Joy Huskey; Alton Sissell
meetings fourth Wed (odd-numbered
months) 7:30 at SMUD Auditorium, 6201
S Street, Sacramento; PAF® Users Group
(even-numbered months; Roots II™ SIG
first Wed
Pub. *Computer Rooters*, quarterly

**Cyndi's List of Genealogy Sites on the
Internet**
cyndihow@oz.net
http://www.CyndisList.com
Cyndi Howells

Datatrace Systems
(see Miscellaneous, Part 4)

**Digital Librarian: A Librarian's Choice of
the Best of the Web (Genealogy)**
mvail@digital-librarian.com
http://www.digital-
librarian.com/genealogy.html
Margaret Vail Anderson

**DistantCounsin.com: Uniting Cousins
Worldwide**
taxpod@yahoo.com
http://www.distantcousin.com
David Podmajersky, Webmaster
("I am not a professional genealogist nor one
who holds himself out to perform
genealogical research.")

**Firstmom's Genealogy Resources and
Records**
AnoleLady@aol.com
http://members.tripod.com/~KHuish
Kathy Huish
("huge site with many categorized pages
such as U.S., AL, IN, ME, NY, PA, SC,
WV, Non-USA, Ireland, Germany,
military resources for genealogists,

freebies for genealogists [links to free
forms, letters, software, etc.], ship
passenger lists," etc.)
free

GENDEX
14 Landing Lane
Port Jefferson, NY 11777
support@gendex.com
http://www.gendex.com
Eugene W. Stark
24/7 ("There are no services provided in
'realtime' by a human being.")
("The services currently provided are: (1)
GENDEX WWW genealogical index: an
index consisting of links to data pages for
over 40 million names. The data pages are
located on the contributors' sites. Basic
access is free of charge. Some enhanced
search features are available for a small
fee. See the site pages for more details. (2)
GED2HTML GEDCOM to HTML
conversion program. Windows and Unix-
compatible software for generating HTML
from standard GEDCOM files.
Shareware: registration fee $20.00. (3)
Web site service. Customers can rent the
services of the GENDEX web server to
publish their genealogy-related Web site.
Rate based on disk storage consumed
[currently $2.00/MB/year for the first
25MB and $1.25/MB/year for the amount
in excess of 25MB]. Customers choose
the content of their own pages—no
advertising is inserted.")

The Gene Pool
PO Box 41552
Eugene, OR 97404-0369
genepool@attbi.com
http://www.rootsweb.com/~genepool
Joanne Todd Rabun
(an eclectic collection of links and resources,
including "Quaker Corner," "Oregon
Genealogy" [no longer being updated],
"NJ Founders," Surnames," "Research
Aids," "Favorite Websites," etc.)

Genealogical Computer Society of Georgia
Western Maryland Center
1500 Pennsylvania Avenue
Hagerstown, MD 21742
(301) 766-9155; (301) 791-4435 FAX
noahsark@mindspring.com
http://www.mindspring.com/~noahsark/
gcsga.html
Noah Linn Hendershot

**Genealogical Computer Society of Western
Maryland**
genealogy@wc-link.org
http://www.mindspring.com/~noahsark/
guest-md.html

**Genealogical Computing Association of
Pennsylvania (GENCAP)**
51 Hillcrest Road
Barto, PA 19504
(610) 438-2858 BBS
gencap@libertynet.org
http://libertynet.org/~gencap
M. A. Miller, Treasurer

The Genealogy Home Page
http://www.genhomepage.com
Stephen A. Wood

Genealogy Special Interest Group
(Rescue Squad Building, Bartle Avenue,
Scotch Plains, NJ—location)
PO Box 773 (mailing address)
New Providence, NJ 07974

(908) 665-0481
Helen Wolf
fourth Thur (Sept–June) 7:30
Pub. *Amateur Computer Group of N.J. News*
(includes "Genealogy Helpline" column),
ten times per year (monthly, Sept–June)
$20.00 per year membership in the Amateur
Computer Group, includes all special
interest groups

Genealogy Today
74 Forest Road
New Providence, NJ 07974
(908) 963-1277
editor@genealogytoday.com
http://genealogytoday.com
Illya D'Addezio
Mon–Fri 10:00–6:00
("Extensive article library. Free research
tools via signup called Team Roots. Meta-
Search Engine.")

Genealogy Toolbox
(217) 352-1309
info@FamilyToolbox.net
http://genealogytoolbox.com
Matthew L. Helm
(publishes representations of original records
on CD-ROM and will soon be introducing
a new line of books)

H-Net
Humanities and Social Sciences Online
310 Auditorium Building
Michigan State University
East Lansing, MI 48824
(517) 355-9300; (517) 355-8363 FAX
http://www2.h-net.msu.edu
(includes history; discussion networks for
California, Indiana, Ohio, Michigan,
Texas, and local history issues)

**Milwaukee PAF® Users Group
(MPAFUG)**
PO Box 268
Muskego, WI 53150
http://www.execpc.com/~bheck/mpafug.
html

Mission Oaks Genealogy Club
PAF® User's Group
(see California, Part 2)

National Genealogical Society (NGS)
NGS/CIG Digest
(see Virginia, Part 2)

NGS-GENTECH
(A Division of the National Genealogical
Society)
4527 17th Street, North
Arlington, VA 22207-2399
(703) 525-0050; (800) 473-0060; (703) 525-
0052 FAX
http://www.gentech.org
Wendy Herr
("NGS-GENTECH facilitates
communication among persons interested
in genealogy and technology. Through
presenting national conferences,
sponsoring programs with other societies,
and publishing white papers based on
analyses of problems of common interest
to genealogists and technologists, we seek
to maximize the movement of knowledge
among the members of our
constituencies.")

**New York Genealogical and Biographical
Society Library**
(see New York, Part 2)

PAF® Users Unlimited
2463 Ledgewood Drive
West Jordan, UT 84084-5738
(801) 967-8400; (801) 963-4604 FAX
Vance C. Parker, Editor
Pub. *PAF® Users Unlimited Quarterly*
(Personal Ancestral File computer
software), $15.00 per year subscription

Personal Computer Club of Charlotte
Genealogy Special Interest Group
PO Box 114
Paw Creek, NC 28130-0114
http://www.chem.uncc.edu/pccc/gensig

Rand Genealogy Club
http://www.rand.org

Roots Users Group of Portland, Oregon
28750 S.E. Haley Road
Boring, OR 97009-9440
(503) 663-6387
Ruth Mickelson, President
meetings at U.S. Bank, 15900 S.W. 116th
Avenue, King City, OR: third Sat (except
July & Dec) 9:00–noon
Pub. *Root Users Group of Portland, Oregon,
Newsletter*, ten times per year (monthly,
except Dec & July)
(for users of COMMSOFT's ROOTS III™,
ROOTS IV™, ROOTS V™, Family
Gathering, genealogical software
programs)
$15.00 per year membership

RootsWeb
http://www.rootsweb.com
(cooperative database, nationwide links to
resources)

RUNGS
2193 Wisconsin
Eugene, OR 97402
Juanite Beagley, Treasurer
Pub. *The Ladder*, quarterly, $12.00 per year
(prorated) subscription

Toolbox Internet Marketing Services, Inc.
editor@onlinegenealogy.com
http://www.onlinegenealogy.com
Pub. *Journal of Online Genealogy*
(a free e-zine which focuses on the use of
online resources and techniques in
genealogy and family history)

University of Idaho
University Library
Special Collections
(see Idaho, Part 2)

The USGenWeb Project
IsaiahHarrison@cs.com;
admin@usgenweb.com
http://www.usgenweb.org
National Coordinator
(links to individual states in the U.S.)

Utah Blue Chips
PO Box 510811
Salt Lake City, UT 84151
(801) 281-8339; (801) 281-8770 BBS
sysop@ucs.org
http://www.ucs.org

Utah Genealogical Association
Computer Chapter
(see Utah, Part 2)

Utah Valley PAF® Users Group
490 East 600 South
Orem, UT 84058
(801) 224-1167

http://www.genealogy.org/~ovpafug
Jay P. Markham, President

Utah Valley PC Users Group
PO Box 1834
Provo, UT 84603
http://www.xmission.com/~uvpcug
**Utah Valley Regional Family History
Center**
Brigham Young University
4386 Harold B. Lee Library
Provo, UT 84603
(801) 378-6200
Diane R. Parkinson, Director
Mon–Sat 8:00 A.M.–10:00 P.M., second &
fourth Sun 9:00–7:00.
Pub. *Newsletter*, bimonthly
BYLINE (database not online, accessed
through Library Gateway)
(no research by correspondence, assistance
for patrons on site only; depository
library, photo archives, special collections
pertaining to U.S. western history)

**Western Pennsylvania Genealogical
Society**
(see Pennsylvania, Part 2)

Genealogical Computer Software

Adventures in Ancestry, Inc.
10714 Hepburn Circle
Culver City, CA 90232-3717
(800) 237-5333; (310) 842-7443 FAX
http://www.aia-and.com
Ancestors and Descendants

Ancestral File™ Operations
Family History Library
35 North West Temple
Salt Lake City, UT 84150
(801) 240-2585; (801) 240-2466; (801) 240-
2584 (for general FamilySearch®
questions)
Jayare Roberts, Specialist, Ancestral File™
Expansion
Mon 7:30 A.M.–6:00 P.M., Tue–Sat 7:30
A.M.–10:00 P.M.
Personal Ancestral File™ (PAF, version 5.0)

B. K. Times
501 East 63rd North, #12 Sioux
Wichita, KS 67219-1213
Pub. *B. K. Times*
(a newsletter for Brother's Keeper™ software
users)

Birthwrite
birthwrite@rogers.com (usally responds
within 48 hours)
http://www.birthwrite.com
Richard McDonald
Birthwrite (Version 2.6 for Windows®)

Black´Fire Technology
info@blackfire.com.au
http://www.blackfire.com.au
Peter Kortge
Mon–Fri 9:00–5:00 AEST
My Family History (Version 1.02 for
Windows®)

Brøderbund Software, Inc.
Banner Blue Division
39500 Stevenson Place, Suite 204
Fremont, CA 94539-3103
(510) 794-6850; (800) 315-0672; (510) 795-
4488 FAX
http://www.familytreemaker.com
Family Tree Maker™ (10.0 for Windows®);

Biography Maker™ (for DOS);
Generations Family Tree Plus

Brother's Keeper
6907 Childsdale Avenue
Rockford, MI 49341
(616) 364-5503; (616) 866-3345 FAX
75745.1371@compuserve.com
http://www.bkwin.com
John Steed
Brother's Keeper® (Version 5.2 for
Windows®)

Citius Software
CitiusNet, Inc.
genus.helpdesk@citius.net
http://www.citiussoftward.com
GENUS Senior (Version 2.21 for
Windows®)

Common Sense Software
2068 Trailwood Drive
Cincinnati, OH 45230
(513) 841-7099
Family Tree Print Utility™

Cumberland Family Software
385 Idaho Springs Road
Clarksville, TN 37043
(931) 647-4012 (6:00–8:00 P.M.)
ira.lund@cf-software.com
http://www.cf-software.com
Ira J. Lund
Cumberland Family Tree for Windows®
(Version 3.11)

Data Base Systems (DBS)
(295 Mohawk Road, Brownsboro,
AL—location)
PO Box 7263 (mailing address)
Huntsville, AL 35807
(256) 518-9957
Paul I. Gulick, Owner
Mon–Fri 9:00–5:00
The Genealogical Data Base System™
(GDBS™, software to develop, maintain
and store genealogy)

**Family History Network (formerly
Everton Publishers)**
PO Box 368
Logan, UT 84323-0368
(800) 443-6325, (435) 752-7979 FAX
http://www.familyhistorynetwork.net
Mon–Fri 8:00–5:00
GENContacts

Family Tree
6180 Via Real, S-25
Carpinteria, CA 93013-2863
(805) 684-3366
Robert M. Merrill, Owner
Mon–Sat 9:00–1:00
Family Tree, a Genealogists Program™
(Apple IIe enhanced or better, text-based
database with GEDCOM™ support)

Flying Pigs Software
PO Box 688
Saint George, UT 84771
(435) 628-5713
Generation Gap™

**Genie Speak-Genealogy Workshop and
Family Research Resources**
PO Box 475
Slippery Rock, PA 16057
(724) 794-4627
http://www.geniespeak.com
Helen Staiger
("Website listing upcoming genealogy
events, speakers bureau, researchers

bureau, vendors bureau, society listings, family page links, webrings, helpful hints, and more.")

Genius Family Tree
http://www.gensol.com.au/genius.htm
Peter Resch
Genius Family Tree (Version 1.5 for Windows®)

The Harbinger Group
6253 BenMore Drive
Fridley, MN 55432
Hyper-Genealogy™

IMSI
1895 Francisco Boulevard East
San Rafael, CA 94901-5506
(415) 257-3000; (415) 257-3565 FAX
http://www.imsisoft.com/familyheritage
Family Heritage Deluxe (Version 2.0 for Windows®)

Incline Software
PO Box 17788
Salt Lake City, UT 84117-0788
(801) 278-5886; (800) 825-8864; (801) 273-1535 FAX
ancquest@ancquest.com
http://www.ancquest.com
Ancestral Quest (Version 3.0); Family Trees Quick & Easy (Version 5.0)

Kindred Konnections, Inc.
MyTrees.com
PO Box 1882
Orem, UT 84059
(801) 229-7967
feedback@mytrees.com
http://www.kindredkonnections.com
Ron Bremer, President
(seminars, lectures, workshops, databases, Internet genealogical research services through parent company, Kindred Konnections)
$5.00 for ten days, $15.00 per month, $100.00 per year, with a one-time free month when you submit a GEDCOM of your family history with at least fifteen families and sixty individuals

MatterWare
3522 Sandy Ridge Trail
DeLand, FL 32724
(386) 736-8030
Ray@matterware.com
http://www.matterware.com
Ray Nicklas
Mon–Fri 7:00 P.M.–10:00 P.M., Sat–Sun all day
Family Matters® 97 (for Windows®)

MicroFox Company
PO Box 447
Richfield, OH 44286-0447
(330) 659-9489; (330) 659-9489 FAX
http://ourworld.compuserve.com/
homepages/microfox
EZ-Tree (Version 2.3 for DOS)

Millennia Corporation
PO Box 1800
Duvall, WA 98019
(800) 753-3453; (425) 940-1610 FAX
Info@MillenniaCorp.Com
http://www.legacyfamilytree.com
9:00–5:00
Legacy (Version 4.0 for Windows®)

Millisecond Publishing Company, Inc.
Family Forest Department
PO Box 6168

Kamuela, HI 96743
(888) 4-R-FORESTS; (808) 885-7171 voice & FAX
forest@aloha.net
http://www.familyforest.com
(Family Forest Odyssey Edition)

NickleWare
PO Box 393
Orem, UT 84059
nickleware@cs.Com
http://www.nickleware.com
Bradley Nicholes
Parents (Version 5 for Windows®)

Palladium Interactive
900 Larkspur Landing Circle, Suite 295
Larkspur, CA 94939
(415) 464-5500; (415) 464-5530
Ultimate Family Tree (for Windows 95®)

PRO-GEN
http://www.pi.net/~progen/home.html
PRO-GEN (Version 2.3C for DOS)

Quinsept, Inc.
1080 North Holliston Avenue
Pasadena, CA 91104-3014
(626) 794-7973
kathryn@bassett.net
http://freepages.misc.rootsweb.com/
~kathryn/famroots/familyroots.htm
Kathryn Rhinehart Bassett
("Family Roots™ is no longer sold. With the blessing of Steve Vorenberg [the program developer], Kathryn provides all available support and has tips on her website on how to salvage your data for use in other programs.")

RF Corporation
308 Devon Lane
West Chester, PA 19380
Genealogical Application for dBASE III +©

RootsMagic, Inc.
PO Box 495
Springville, UT 84663
(877) 766-8762
webmaster@rootsmagic.com
http://www.rootsmagic.com
Bruce Buzbee
RootsMagic genealogy software

SKY Software
4675 York Road #1
Manchester, MD 21102
(800) 776-0137; (410) 374-3484 FAX
http://www.sky-software.com/about.htm
Kamm or Bette Schreiner, Co-owners
10:00–6:00
SKY Index™ version 3.1 (for back-of-book indexing, for Windows®); SKY Catalog™ version 1.1 (for cataloging home libraries); SKY Filer™ version 1.0 (for keeping track of data collected, for Windows®); SKY Address™ (for maintaining correspondent's list)

SpanSoft
SpanSoft@compuserve.com
http://ourworld.compuserve.com/
homepages/SpanSoft
Kith and Kin (Version 3.11 for Windows®)

Wholly Genes Software
5144 Flowertuft Court
Columbia, MD 21044
(877) TMG-FAMILY (toll free)
support@whollygenes.com
http://www.whollygenes.com
Tim Shaw

Mon–Fri 9:00–5:00
Pub. *Wholly Genes Newsletter*, free
The Master Genealogist (TMG), Family Tree SuperTools (FTST) ("Power tools for the family historian"); Chartform Delivery ("Wall chart printing service")

Win-Family
support@winfamily.com
Win-Family (Version 5.01 for Windows®)

Professional Bodies

American Historical Association
400 A Street, S.E.
Washington, DC 20003-3889
(202) 544-2422; (202) 544-8307 FAX
http://chnm.gmu.edu/chnm/aha
Gretchen Miller, Executive Office
Pub. *American Historical Review*;
    Perspectives
(A membership organization for historians)

American Society of Genealogists
PO Box 1515
Derry, NH 03038-1515
Cameron Allen, F.A.S.G., President; Roger
    D. Joslyn, C.G., F.A.S.G., Secretary; Col.
    Charles M. Hansen, U.S.A. (ret.),
    F.A.S.G., Editor, Gale Ion Harris, Ph.D.,
    F.A.S.G., Editor
Pub. *The Genealogist*, semiannually, $25.00
    per year subscription, $45.00 for two-year
    subscription, $65.00 for three-year
    subscription to libraries and institutions
(honorary organization; membership by
    election only; to advance genealogical
    research standards and to encourage
    publication of scholarly studies, to secure
    recognition of genealogy as a serious
    subject of research in historical and social
    fields of learning)

**Association for the Promotion of
Scholarship in Genealogy, Ltd.**
255 North Second West
Salt Lake City, UT 84103-4545
(801) 521-4732
Neil D. Thompson, Ph.D., F.A.S.G.,
    Executive Director

Association of Professional Genealogists
PO Box 40393
Denver, CO 80204-0393
(504) 766-3018 (Executive Secretary)
apg-editor@apgen.org
http://www.apgen.org/~apg
Sharon DeBarotollo, C.G.R.S., Editor; James
    L. Hansen, President; Barbara C.
    Strickland, Executive Secretary
Pub. *Association of Professional
    Genealogists Quarterly* (*APG Quarterly*)
    (Mar, June, Sept, Dec)
$35.00 per year membership

Association of Professional Genealogists
Northern California Chapter
PO Box 4153
Mountain View, CA 94040-4153
(650) 967-2017
sjshafer@compuserve.com
http://www.apgen.org/localchapters/
    northerncalifornia/index.html
Sandra Shafer

Association of Professional Genealogists
San Jacinto Chapter
(currently inactive)
http://www.apgen.org/localchapters/
    sanjacinto/index.html

Association of Professional Genealogists
Southern California Chapter (SCC-APG)
PO Box 9486
Brea, CA 92822-9486
barbzr@msn.com
http://www.compuology.com/sccapg
Barbara Renick

**Colorado Chapter Association of
Professional Genealogists**
PO Box 740637
Arvada, CO 80006-0637

nratay@ng-tek.com
http://www.rootsweb.com/~coapg
Nancy Ratay, Secretary

Association of Professional Genealogists
Florida Chapter
4825 North Galloway Road
Lakeland, FL 33810-6722
(863) 858-6745
floridasearch@tampabay.rr.com
http://www.apgen.org/localchapters/
    florida/index.html
Alvie L. Davidson

Association of Professional Genealogists
Idaho Chapter
11668 West Huckleberry Drive
Nampa, ID 83651
(208) 461-8866
juvanne@earthlink.net;
    vhix@snackteam.com
http://www.rootsweb.com/~idapg
Juvanne Clezie Martin, Southwest Idaho
    Coordinator; Veldon Hix, Ph.D.,
    Southeast Idaho Coordinator

Association of Professional Genealogists
Chicago Area Chapter
4166 Arthur avenue
Brookfield, IL 60513
(708) 485-3970
purplonyon@aol.com
http://www.apgen.org/localchapters/
    chicago/index.html
Holly K. Meany

Association of Professional Genealogists
Louisiana Chapter
PO Box 1320
Winnfield, LA 71483-1320
(318) 628-6768; (318) 628-6673 FAX
annettewomack@aol.com
http://homepages.rootsweb.com/
    ~acwomack/apg2.htm
Annette Carpenter Womack

Association of Professional Genealogists
Greater Boston Chapter
PO Box 550115
Waltham, MA 02455-0115
(781) 424-1467
bmathews@gis.net
http://www.apgen.org/localchapters/
    boston/index.html
Barbara J. Mathews

Association of Professional Genealogists
Heartland Chapter
307 West 109 Street
Kansas City, MO 64114-4907
(816) 941-7545
eviebresette@everestkc.net
http://www.rootsweb.com/~mohcapg/
    index.htm
Evie Bresette

Association of Professional Genealogists
New York Metro Chapter
240 West End Avenue #15A
New York, NY 10023-3613
(212) 787-4371; (201) 387-2855 FAX
eileenpolakoff@avotaynu.com
http://www.apgen.org/localchapters/
    newyork/index.html

Association of Professional Genealogists
North Carolina Chapter
Professional Genealogists' Network (PGN)
4013 Spruce Road
Raleigh, NC 27612
(919) 783-5322
jhilke@mindspring.com

http://www.ncprogen.org
Ann C. Hilke

Association of Professional Genealogists
Great Lakes Chapter
PO Box 38314
Olmsted Falls, OH 44138-0314
GenealogyTalk@aol.com
http://members.cox.net/talkgenealogy
Gary M. Smith, Secretary/Treasurer

Association of Professional Genealogists
Oregon Chapter
10411 S.W. 41st Street
Portland, OR 97219-6984
(503) 244-4357; (503) 245-4723 FAX
clenzen@dialoregon.net
http://www.apgen.org/localchapters/
    oregon/index.html
Connie Lenzen, President

Association of Professional Genealogists
Philadelphia Area Chapter
407 North Fifth Avenue
Royersford, PA 19468
(610) 948-2161
LindaCourt@aol.com
http://www.apgen.org/localchapters/
    philadelphia/index.html
Linda Craig Courtemanche

Association of Professional Genealogists
Salt Lake Chapter
972 South Saratoga Drive
Saratoga Sprngs, UT 84043
(801) 766-8106
jwhsearch@aol.com
http://www.slcapg.com
Judith Hansen

Association of Professional Genealogists
Hampton Roads Chapter
1721 Indian River Road
Virginia Beach, VA 23456-3816
(757) 426-9045
donald.moore@cox.net
http://www.apgen.org/localchapters/
    hampton/index.html
Donald W. Moore

Association of Professional Genealogists
National Capital Area Chapter
2853 Rosemary Lane
Falls Church, VA 22042
(703) 536-4820
molye@erols.com
http://www.apgen.org/localchapters/
    nationalcapital/index.html
Susan Nusbaum Molyé

Association of Professional Genealogists
Puget Sound Chapter
18309 155th Place S.E.
Renton, WA 98058
(206) 280-1010
lauren@family-branches.com
http://www.apgen.org/localchapters/
    pugetsound/index.html
Luaren H. Richardson

Board for Certification of Genealogists
PO Box 14291
Washington, DC 20044
office@bcgcertification.org
http://www.bcgcertification.org
Lynn C. McMillion, CLS℠, Executive
    Director
Pub. *OnBoard*, three times per year; *The
    BCG Genealogical Standards Manual*;
    The BCG Application Guide (last revised
    in 2001); *The BCG Certification Roster*
    (published every two years, updated in

interim by inserts to *OnBoard* newsletter)

Connecticut Professional Genealogists Council
PO Box 4273
Hartford, CT 06147-4273
cpgc@aol.com; tvhowsearch@snet.net
http://www.rootsweb.com/~ctpgc
Robert Rafford, President; Thomas Howard,
    Corresponding Secretary
Pub. *CPGC Newsletter*, monthly
("Connecticut research, southern New
    England")
$15.00 per year; research: fees vary with
    each professional genealogist

Council of Genealogy Columnists
(see Newspaper Columns, Part 4)

Family History Library of The Church of Jesus Christ of Latter-day Saints
(see Utah, Part 2)

Federation of Genealogical Societies
(see Genealogical Societies [National
Focus], Part 1)

Genealogical Research Associates
203 Locust Street, S.W.
Vienna, VA 22183
(703) 938-0974
Robert E. Thompson, A.G., Owner
hours: various
(offers advanced research courses and mini-
    seminars)
hourly or daily fees for research, plus
    expenses: National Archives, Library of
    Congress, DAR Library, and Virginia
    courthouses and archives, etc.

Houston Area Professional Genealogists
1001 West Loop, North, #144
Houston, TX 77055-7215
(713) 684-4633
Mic Barnette, President

The International Genealogy Consumer Organization
4329 South Stafford Way
West Valley City, UT 84119
R. Clayton Brough, President
Pub. *International Genealogy Consumer
    Report*, semiannually (Jan–June,
    July–Dec), $8.00 for four-issue
    subscription (two years)

National Institute on Genealogical Research (NIGR)
PO Box 14274
Washington, DC 20044-4274
NatGenInst@aol.com
http://NatGenInst.genealogy.org
Claire Mire Bettag, CGRS℠, CGL℠,
    Director
(Educational institute which holds a week-
    long seminar, second week of July at the
    National Archives, enrollment limited to
    44)

New England Historical Research Associates
225 South Road
Fremont, NH 03044
(603) 895-4032
Matthew E. Thomas, President
Mon–Fri 9:00–5:00
(lecturers and researchers of New England
    city/town history and genealogy)

The Ohio Academy of History
1465 Mount Vernon Avenue
Marion, OH 43302-5695

(740) 389-2361
Vladimir Steffel, Ph.D., Secretary-Treasurer
10:00–3:00
Pub. *OAH Newsletter*, three times per year
$10.00 per year membership

The Organization of American Historians (OAH)
112 North Bryan Street
Bloomington, IN 47408-4199
(812) 855-7311
Arrita A. Jones, Executive Director
8:00–5:00
Pub. *Journal of American History*, quarterly;
    OAH Newsletter (not genealogical),
    quarterly; *Magazine of History*, quarterly,
    $25.00 per year subscription
from $30.00–$90.00 per year membership

Professional Business Services
450 Potter Street
Wauseon, OH 43567
(419) 335-6485
Howard V. Fausey, Owner
8:00–5:00
Pub. *The Family Tree*, twelve times per year,
    $12.00 per year subscription
limited search

Professional Genealogists of California
5048 J Parkway
Sacramento, CA 95823

The Society of American Archivists
600 South Federal, Suite 504
Chicago, IL 60605
(312) 922-0140; (312) 347-1452 FAX
info@archivists.org
http://www.archivists.org
Susan E. Fox, Executive Director
Mon–Fri 8:00–5:00
Pub. *The American Archivist*, two times per
    year, $85.00 per year subscription in the
    U.S., $100.00 per year subscription
    elsewhere
(professional organization)

The Society of American Historians, Inc.
Columbia University
610 Fayerweather
New York, NY 10027
(212) 854-2555
Kenneth T. Jackson, Ph.D., Executive
    Secretary

Society of Georgia Archivists
(address withheld upon request)
Pub. *Provenance*, semiannually; *SGA
    Newsletter*, quarterly
(scholarly articles of archival issues, news of
    educational opportunities, meetings. "The
    Society's mission is to serve archivists'
    educational and professional needs, and is
    not set up for referral to researchers.")
$15.00 per year membership

Society of Ohio Archivists
(address withheld upon request)
Pub. *Society of Ohio Archivists Newsletter*,
    semiannually

Wallace State Community College Library
(see Alabama, Part 2)

Newspaper Columns

Hundreds of additional columns in
newspapers and magazines may be found in
Anita Cheek Milner's book, *Newspaper
Genealogical Column Directory*.

Council of Genealogy Columnists
158 Lafayette Circle
Ocean Springs, MS 39564
(228) 875-4920
Regina Hines Ellison, C.G.R.S
("The organization is a professional group
    for journal and newspaper columnists.")
Pub. *The Columns*, quarterly
$15.00 per year membership

AntiqueWeek
"Genealogy Sources" and "Genealogy
Week"
Eastern Edition
(27 North Jefferson Street—location)
PO Box 90 (mailing address)
Knightstown, IN 46148-9900
(800) 876-5133
Shirley Richardson, Genealogy Editor
8:00–4:30
weekly

***Centreville Press and Marion Times
Standard***
22 First Street North
Centreville, AL 35042-2749
Elia Daws

Cherokee County Herald
"Tracing Southern Families"
Route 5, Box 109
Piedmont, AL 36272-8709
KYencer@CherokeeHerald.com
Mrs. Frank Ross Stewart, Sr.

Arkansas Democrat Gazette
PO Box 303
Conway, AR 72033
(501) 470-1120 voice & FAX
desmond@intellinet.com
http://biz.ipa.net/arkresearch
Desmond Walls Allen, Editor
(queries related to southern Kansas, northeast
    Oklahoma, and Arkansas)
weekly (Sunday)

The Record
"Ancestor Ambling"
145 West 200 North, Apartment 5
Salt Lake City, UT 84103-4522
Ann McDanell
(Delano, California)

Los Angeles Times Syndicate
"Shaking Your Family Tree"
Times-Mirror Square
Los Angeles, CA 90053
Myra Vanderpool Gormley

Florida Times Union
"Out on a Limb"
1 Riverside Avenue
Jacksonville, FL 32207
LaViece Smallwood

Pensacola News Journal
"It's All Relative"
PO Box 12710
Pensacola, FL 32574
(850) 435-8538 (*PNJ*)
relativenews@aol.com
Linda Reinauer, Freelance Writer and
    Columnist
weekly (Sunday, Life Section); queries
    accepted, announcements of family

reunions, topics of interest to genealogists everywhere with special emphasis on genealogy in Florida and other southern states"

"Searching Yesteryear"
Genealogy and Local History Department
201 South Coffee Avenue
Douglas, GA 31533
(912) 384-1033 (home)
Winifred Merier Gourley
weekly

The Albany Herald
"Ancestors"
1006 Sixth Avenue
Albany, GA 31701
(229) 435-4032
mdelamar362@juno.com
Marie DeLamar
monthly (third Sunday); queries accepted, books reviewed

Atlanta Journal-Constitution
"Genealogy"
(PO Box 4689, Atlanta, GA 30302—newspaper's address)
PO Box 901 (mailing address)
Decatur, GA 30031
Kenneth H. Thomas, Jr.
weekly (Sunday), $2.00 per issue (column is not in mailed editions), no queries accepted

The La Grange Daily News
"History and Your Family"
PO Box 2291
La Grange, GA 30241
Shirley W. Bowen

The Newnan Times Herald
"Norma's Coweta Chatter"
8031 Highway 54, Route 1
Sharpsburg, GA 30277
Norma Gunby

The Thomasville Times-Enterprise
"Genealogy Today"
401 Tuxedo Drive
Thomasville, GA 31792
Annette J. Stewart

The Valdosta Daily Times
"About Genealogy"
201 North Troup Street
Valdosta, GA 31601
(229) 244-0464
Lillian Newham McRee, Columnist
weekly

Idaho Post Register
"Out on a Limb"
(333 Northgate Mile—location)
PO Box 1800 (mailing address)
Idaho Falls, ID 83403
LaViece Smallwood

The News Gazette
"Illinois Ancestors"
(PO Box 677, Champaign, IL 61824-0677—location)
105 Poland Road (mailing address)
Danville, IL 61834-7462
(217) 446-6339
Joan A. Griffis
weekly, Saturday; free queries

Commercial-News
"Illiana Ancestors"
105 Poland Road
Danville, IL 61834-7462
(217) 446-6339

Joan A. Griffis
weekly, Sunday; free queries

Antique and Collectible News
"Ancestoritis"
705 Cathy Lane
Mount Prospect, IL 60056
(847) 398-1884
Carol Sims Rademacher
10:00–4:00
monthly

The Petersburg Observer
"Genealogical Corner"
Weaver Genealogical Publications
27 Timber Valley
Petersburg, IL 62675
(217) 632-3543
Jeanne Crain Weaver, Publisher-Researcher
Office: 8:00–7:00
(specializing in Menard County, Illinois, names)
bimonthly (also printed in *The Menard County Review*); free queries

STAR Newspapers
"It's All Relative"
6901 West 159 Street
Tinley Park, IL 60477
Linda Swisher
free queries pertaining to south Cook County or north Will County, Illinois

Hoosier Times
"Family Tree Leaves"
1717 East Hunter Avenue
Bloomington, IN 47401-5232
jcrobins@indiana.edu
Mona Robinson, Columnist
(southwestern Indiana counties)
weekly; free queries up to 35 words plus name and address

Montgomery County Magazine
"Family Roots"
(*The Crawfordsville Journal-Review*, 119 North Green Street, Crawfordsville, IN 47933—publisher's location)
PO Box 235 (mailing address)
Waveland, IN 47989
Karen Zach
(Montgomery and surrounding counties)
queries free

The Indianapolis Star
"Indiana Ancestors"
PO Box 145
Indianapolis, IN 46206-0145
(317) 444-6160
indianaancestors@aol.com
Vicktoria Hizer, Columnist
weekly (Sunday), $4.00 per issue

The National Jewish Post and Opinion
"Your Name"
238 South Meridian Street, Room 502
Indianapolis, IN 46225-1024
Jpost@jewishpostopinion.com
http://www.jewishpostopinion.com
David L. Gold
(mail inquiries only, no telephone or personal inquiries)
weekly

Kokomo Tribune
7 Green Hills Court
Greentown, IN 46936
Judy Lausch

The Dearborn County Register and Alsino Sun Recorder
PO Box 328

Lawrenceburg, IN 47025
Chris McHenry

The Loogootee Tribune
1230 Rowin Road
Indianapolis, IN 46220
Robert Conalty-Webber

The Madison Courier
"Family Trees, Twigs, Chips"
2729 Arbor Avenue
Cincinnati, OH 45209-2206
(513) 351-8639
http://www.seidata.com/~bhoggatt/ruth/ ingenweb/spiry.html (column archives)
Al and Margaret Spiry, Genelogists and Columnists
weekly, Tuesdays in *The Madison Courier* and Fridays in *The Weekly Herald*, both published at 310 Courier Square, Madison, IN 47250, no charge for genealogical queries

Milford Mail-Journal
"Relatively Speaking"
PO Box 214
Warsaw, IN 46581-0214
(219) 267-4271
Doris McManis Camden
(also printed in *The Paper*)
twice per month

The North Vernon Plain Dealer
(528 East O&M Avenue, PO Box 410, North Vernon, IN 47265—location)
3345 South County Road 800 East (mailing address)
Dupont, IN 47231
(812) 346-3973 (Office); (812) 873-6494 (Home, Mon–Fri after 6:00 and all day weekends); (812) 346-8368
lcarmer@seidata.com
Lilian Hall Carmer
Office: 8:00–4:00
Pub. *The North Vernon Plain Dealer*, weekly, $32.00 per year subscription locally
queries accepted free for Jennings and surrounding counties

The Scott County Journal and Chronicle
5764 South State Road 203
Lexington, IN 47138-8365
(812) 889-2044 voice & FAX
Jeannie Noe Carlisle, Editor
(published in Scottsburg)
every four to eight weeks; free queries related to Scott, Washington, Jefferson, Clark, Jennings and Jackson counties; search fee: $10.00 per hour plus expenses

The South Bend (Ind) Tribune
"Michiana Roots"
PO Box 634
Granger, IN 46530
(616) 641-7985 (Michigan)
BHarman6@aol.com
Barbara S. Harman
(specializing in Michigan-Indiana genealogical-historical research and photography)
weekly on Sun; subscription $5.00 per month; free queries

Sunday Gazette
"Dear Genie"
PO Box 175
Cedar Rapids, IA 52406

Cotton and Quail Antique Trail
"About Genealogy"
PO Box 1050

Dubuque, IA 52004-1050
Lillian Newham McRee, Columnist
monthly

Appalachian News-Express
"Genealogy Notes"
(563 Lower Pompey Road, Shelbiana, KY
41562—columnist's location)
PO Box 802 (newspaper mailing address)
Pikeville, KY 41501
(606) 432-4904 (Home)
Sharon D. Warrix
weekly (Fridays), $39.00 per year
subscription in Pike County, $49.00 per
year subscription in Floyd and Letcher
counties, $65.00 per year elsewhere; free
queries, also photos (include SASE for
return)

Sunday Advocate Magazine
"Louisiana Ancestors"
PO Box 588
Baton Rouge, LA 70821
(225) 383-1111
ancestorslaveach@yahoo.com;
bookman@intersurf.com
http://www.theadvocate.com (click on
Entertainment, then Louisiana Ancestors)
Damon Veach
Mon–Sat 1:00–6:00
("Queries should have a Louisiana
connection but note that Louisiana at one
time covered a large area of the
Mississippi Valley, and also at one time
covered much of the South, when it was
known as Spanish West Florida and
included southern Mississippi, Alabama,
and the Florida panhandle; books and
magazines reviewed if sample copies are
submitted with each request; notices of
genealogical meetings, seminars and other
activities are included; also appears in *The
Times-Picayune*, New Orleans.")
weekly (Sunday Living section)

Shreveport Journal
"Ancestor Hunting"
PO Box 303
Conway, AR 72033
(501) 470-1120 voice & FAX
desmond@intellinet.com
http://biz.ipa.net/arkresearch
Desmond Walls Allen, Editor
(queries related to northern Louisiana,
eastern Texas and southern Arkansas)
weekly (Monday)

"Old Pike Travelers"
PO Box 3103
LaVale, MD 21504

Tri-City Record
"Family Heirlooms"
(PO Box 7—newspaper mailing
address/location)
PO Box 81 (columnist's mailing address)
Watervliet, MI 49098
Carole Kiernan
(no geographical limitations, free queries)

The Times
"Roots and Branches"
(4 Willow Point—location)
PO Box 15
Hattiesburg, MS 39402
rootsandbranches39074@yahoo.com
http://www.thetimeswire.com

The Sun Herald
"Genealogy"
PO Box 4567
Biloxi, MS 39532

(228) 875-8144 (Office); (228) 875-4920
(Home, after 5:00)
Regina Hines, C.G.R.S.
Office: 7:00–3:00

Advertiser News
"Meet Your Ancestors"
806 South 17th Avenue
Hattiesburg, MS 39401-7587
(601) 583-0336
Dr. Betty Drake
weekly, free newspaper, no charge for
genealogical/historical queries on south
Mississippi families, no searches done for
the public

The Mississippi Press
"Branches and Twigs"
1222 Highway 90 East
Ocean Springs, MS 39564
(228) 875-8144 (Office); (228) 875-4920
(Home, after 5:00)
Regina Hines, C.G.R.S.
Office: 7:00–3:00
(Also appears in the *Sun Herald*, Biloxi-
Gulfport)
weekly

"Family Roots"
5560 Gibson Road
Vicksburg, MS 39180
Lamar Roberts
(appears in six newspapers)

Reynolds County Courier
"Kinfolks Search"
c/o Reynolds County Genealogy and
Historical Society, Inc.
PO Box 281
Ellington, MO 63638
Lee Sylcox, Treasurer

The Kansas City Times
"Shaking Your Family Tree"
PO Box 64316
Tacoma, WA 98464
Myra Vanderpool Gormley
weekly (Saturday)

Rolla Daily News
"Ancestors Column"
c/o Phelps County Genealogical Society
PO Box 571
Rolla, MO 65402-0571
(573) 265-7401
Mona Hale, Secretary
weekly (Sunday)

West Plains
"Family Tree"
939 Nichols Drive
West Plains, MO 65775
Irene Kimberlin

Pilot Tribune
"Digging for Roots"
2145 Wright Street
Blair, NE 68008
Diane Stier
irregularly; also published in the Blair
Enterprise

Cortland Standard
"Times Past"
Courthouse Building
46 Greenbush Street, Suite 1001
Cortland, NY 13045-3702
(607) 753-5360; (607) 758-5500 FAX
cbarber@cortland-co.org
http://www.cortlandny.com/community/
history/historians
Cathy A. Barber, Cortland County Historian

Tri-Town News
(Sidney, NY—location)
335 State Highway 41 (mailing address)
Afton, NY 13730
(607) 639-2720
Charles J. Decker, Afton Town and Village
Historian
by appointment
weekly

Herald-American
"Genealogy"
PO Box 4915
Syracuse, NY 13221-4915
Sheila M. Byrnes
(central and upper New York State)
free, biweekly in Sunday newspaper

The Lawton Constitution
"Tree Tracers"
3607 Arlington
Lawton, OK 73505-6138
(580) 355-7432; (580) 355-7053 FAX
http://www.lawton-constitution.com
Aulena Scearce Gibson, Columnist
(queries relating to southwest Oklahoma
published free; in cooperation with the
Southwest Oklahoma Genealogical
Society, which has volunteers who assist
out-of-town researchers)
weekly column in daily newspaper

Pond Creek Herald
"Bits and Pieces of Grant County History"
PO Box 31
Medford, OK 73759-0031
(580) 395-2888
Nina L. Pond

The Oklahoman
"We The People" and "In Search of Family"
PO Box 25125
Oklahoma City, OK 73125-5125
http://www.oklahoman.net/connections/
familysearch/home.htm
Sharon King Burns
weekly, Saturday; no charge for queries with
Oklahoma connections

The Poteau News and Spiro Graphic
"Family Finder"
c/o Poteau Valley Genealogical Society
(Buckley Public Library, 408
Dewey—research library location)
PO Box 1031 (mailing address)
Poteau, OK 74953
Arlene LeMaster, President
weekly; free queries

The Spiro Graphic
"Know Your Kin"
Spiro, OK 74959

Old Huntsville Magazine
716 East Clinton Avenue
Huntsville, AL 35801
(256) 534-0502
oldhuntsville@knology.net
http://oldhuntsville.com
Cathey or Tom Carney
8:00–5:00
Pub. *Old Huntsville Magazine*, monthly,
$15.00 per year subscription
(has a genealogy section)

The Daily News
"Our Keystone Families"
PO Box 43
Rehrersburg, PA 19550
(717) 933-4630
Schuyler C. Brossman
(published in Lebanon, Pennsylvania, now in

The Genealogist's Address Book

its thirty-first year)
weekly, $22.00 in Pennsylvania, $34.00 out
of state

Press and Journal
"Our Keystone Families"
PO Box 43
Rehrersburg, PA 19550
(717) 933-4630
Schuyler C. Brossman
(published in Middletown, PA)
weekly

Sullivan County News
"Steps to the Past—A Guide to Genealogy"
c/o Sullivan County Library
PO Box 510
Blountville, TN 37617

Amarillo (TX) News-Globe
"Kinsearching"
PO Box 6825
Lubbock, TX 79493-6825
kinsearch@door.net
Marleta Childs
(column is national in scope; circulation
includes twenty-eight Texas counties,
western Oklahoma, northeastern New
Mexico, and southwestern Kansas)
weekly; free queries and announcements of
reunions and conferences

Northeast Texas Chronicle
"Genealogy Corner"
1559 Florence Court
Manteca, CA 95336
Jewel Dixon Johnston
(published in Daingerfield, TX)

The Dallas Morning News
"Family Tree"
PO Box 655237
Dallas, TX 75265
(214) 670-1406
Lloyd DeWitt Bockstruck
weekly (Saturday) (also *Index to 1987
Family Tree Columns from the Dallas
Morning News*)

The El Paso Times
"All in Your Family"
PO Box 20
El Paso, TX 79999
(915) 546-6397; (800) 351-6007, ext. 6397
Mary Margaret Davis, Community News
Editor
monthly (first Sun), free queries

Galveston Daily News
Texas City Ancestry Searchers
(Moore Memorial Library, 1701 Ninth
Avenue, North, Texas City, TX
77590—location)
PO Box 3301 (mailing address)
Texas City, TX 77592-3301
(409) 935-5343
Zora A. Evans, Editor and Newspaper
Column Chairman
8:00–4:00 or evenings

The Henderson Daily News
"Footprints"
Rusk County Genealogical Society
PO Box 1314
Henderson, TX 75653-1314
Len Rives

The Houston Chronicle
"Your Family Tree"
6323 Crakston Street
Houston, TX 77084
(281) 550-7935

mic@barnettesbooks.com
http://www.chron.com/deaths (current
column, see link on Deaths web page);
http://www.geocities.com/barnette_geo
(online version)
Mic Barnette
Mon–Sat 10:00–6:00
(worldwide in scope, no queries accepted)
weekly (Saturday)

The Texas Spur
"Family Corner"
PO Box 344
Jayton, TX 79528

The Longview Morning Journal
"East Texas Heritage"
PO Box 1792
Longview, TX 75601
Nancy Ruff

Nacogdoches Daily Sentinel
"Kissin Kuzzins"
1614 Redbud Street
Nacogdoches, TX 75961-2936
(936) 564-3625; (936) 552-8999 FAX
Carolyn Ericson, Editor
weekly, free Texas queries

Newton County News
"Historical Newsletter"
PO Box 1383
Newton, TX 75966
(409) 379-2109
Pauline Hines
weekly

The Pampa News
"Gena on Genealogy"
PO Drawer 2198
Pampa, TX 79066-2198

The Panola Post and Panola Watchman
"Know Your Heritage"
Rural Route 2, Box 138AA
Carthage, TX 75633-9624
Leila B. LaGrone

The Lamar County Echo
"The Family Tree"
PO Box 1078
Paris, TX 75460

"Window on San Marcos"
c/o The Heritage Association of San Marcos,
Inc.
(308 East Hopkins Street—location)
20 Timbercrest Street (mailing address)
San Marcos, TX 78666-3018
(512) 392-9997; (512) 393-3735 FAX
http://www.centuryinter.net/smheritage
Frances E. Stovall, Coordinator Heritage
Tourism

The Seguin Gazette Enterprise
"Family Tree"
208 North Roosevelt Avenue
Nixon, TX 78140-2717
(830) 582-2876
Mary C. Bond
weekly (Wednesday); free queries;
newspaper subscription from PO Box
1200, Seguin, TX 78155

The Liberty Gazette
"Tracing Roots"
PO Box 16
Wallisville, TX 77597-0016
(409) 389-2252
Kevin R. Ladd
weekly (Wednesday); queries on Liberty or
Chambers counties or southeast Texas

The Weatherford Democrat
"Kissin' Kin"
512 Palo Pinto Street
Weatherford, TX 76086
Evlyn Broumley
free queries, reviews upon receipt of book or
material

The Kenbridge-Victoria Dispatch
4037 Tanglewood Trail
Chesapeake, VA 23325
Mildred W. Steltzner

Times-Mirror
"Loudoun's Legacy"
Loudoun County Genealogy Club
PO Box 254
Leesburg, VA 22075
Mary Fishback, President
biweekly

Spokesman Review
"Heritage Hunting"
West 999 Riverside
Spokane, WA 99210
mitzi@arias.net
Donna Potter Phillips
"Pastfinding" column also appears in *Tri-
City Herald*, Kennewick, and "Family
History" in *The Columbian*

The Washington News Tribune
"Shaking Your Family Tree"
PO Box 64316
Tacoma, WA 98464
Myra Vanderpool Gormley

Nisqually Valley News
"Routes to Roots"
PO Box 597
Yelm, WA 98597
Janet Nixon Baccus, Genealogist

Morgan Messenger
"Warm Spring Echoes"
6 Rockwell Center
Berkeley Springs, WV 25411
Frederick T. Newbrough

**The West Virginia Advocate, Cacapon
Bridge**
"Genealogical Queries"
4715 North 38th Place
Arlington, VA 22207
Wilmer Kerns, Ph.D.

Publishers

Many historical and genealogical societies, as well as publishers of independent periodicals, produce original books and reprints. For an exhaustive list of genealogical books and their publishers see the current edition of *Genealogical & Local History Books in Print* (*GBIP*), edited by Marian R. Hoffman, published by Genealogical Publishing Company. Many publishers operate outlet stores for their own books and also stock titles by other publishers.

Acadian House Publishing
(see Louisiana, Part 2)

American Heritage Publishing
1500 North Kansas Avenue
Marceline, MO 64658
(660) 376-2301

Ancestry
MyFamily.com, Inc.
PO Box 476
Salt Lake City, UT 84110-0476
(800) ANCESTRY (262-3787); (800) 531-1790 (*Genealogical Computing*); (801) 531-1798 FAX
http://www.ancestry.com
Dean R. Zimmerman, Director of Marketing and Sales; Dennis Sampson, Editor, *Genealogical Computing*
8:00–5:00
Pub. *Ancestry* (instructional, international genealogy, how-to articles, regular columns), bimonthly, $4.95 per issue for nonmembers, $21.00 per year subscription for nonmembers, $38.00 two-year subscription for nonmembers, $54.00 three-year subscription for nonmembers; *Genealogical Computing*, quarterly, $25.00 per year subscription; over fifty books, Family Tree software; CD-ROMs
$24.95 membership in Ancestry Research Club (includes subscription)

Boyd Publishing Company
(see Booksellers, Part 4)

Clearfield Company
200 East Eager Street
Baltimore, MD 21202
(410) 625-9004; (800) 296-6687; (410) 752-8492 FAX; (800) 599-9561 FAX
http://www.ClearfieldCompany.com
Roger J. Sherr, President

Closson Press
1935 Sampson Drive
Apollo, PA 15613-9209
(724) 337-4482; (724) 337-9484 FAX
rclosson@nb.net
http://www.clossonpress.com
Mary Closson, Correspondent
8:00–noon & 1:15–4:00
Pub. *Catalog*, annually, $1.00 per issue or free with book order
(Genealogical and historical specialty books and records: Pennsylvania, Ohio, Virginia, West Virginia and European emigration. "We specialize in printing family histories and offer free advertising on our web site and in one annual catalog.")

Deseret Book Company
PO Box 30178
Salt Lake City, UT 84130-0178
(801) 534-1515; (800) 453-3876; (800) 453-4532 (Deseret Book Direct, Orders);
(801) 578-3392 FAX (Deseret Book Direct, Orders)
http://www.deseretbook.com

Dome Shadow Press
51905 Courtland East
South Bend, IN 46637
(574) 273-0232 voice & FAX
francoeur@domeshadowpress.com
http://www.domeshadowpress.com
Joan Francoeur, Publicity Manager
("We are tapping into a new area of Irish genealogy: pre-Famine sources that can be used as census substitutes for the destroyed censuses of Ireland.")

Betterway Books
F&W Publications, Inc.
4700 East Galbraith Road
Cincinnati, OH 45236
(513) 531-2690; (800) 289-0963; (513) 531-4082 FAX
http://www.fwpublications.com/genealogy.asp
Sharon DeBartolo Carmack
Pub. *Family Tree Magazine*, bimonthly, $19.96 per year subscription

Family Historian Books
404 Tule Lake Road South
Tacoma, WA 98444-1952
(253) 535-0108; (800) 535-0118; (253) 537-8998 FAX
http://www.familyhistorianbooks.com
Jeff and Kerstin Horning, Owners
Mon–Fri 8:00–5:00
(includes Missouri, Cherokee and adoption titles)

Family History Educators
PO Box 510606
Salt Lake City, UT 84151-0606
(801) 359-7391
Elizabeth L. Nichols
(instruction in genealogy how-to; genealogy and computers; wholesale and retail mail order)

Family History Network (formerly Everton Publishers)
PO Box 368
Logan, UT 84323-0368
(800) 443-6325; (435) 752-7979 FAX
customer_service@familyhistorynetwork.net
http://www.familyhistorynetwork.net
Bob Arbon, Manager
Mon–Fri 8:00–5:00
Pub. *Everton's Family History Magazine*, bimonthly, $28.95 per year subscription
(queries, classified advertisements; directories of genealogical researchers, periodical publications, etc.; computerized database of ancestor data: Computerized "Roots Cellar"; computerized Family File; computerized Pedigree Library)
Roots Cellar registration: $5.00 for one name, $1.00 for each additional name

Family Times Publishing
PO Box 901653
Kansas City, MO 64190-1653
familynewsletters4u@yahoo.com

Family Tree Press
5700 Oaktree Lane North
Plymouth
Minneapolis, MN 55442-1534
(612) 557-7138
http://feefhs.org/pub/frg-ftp.html
Fay Dearden, President

Frontier Press
(see Booksellers, Part 4)

Genealogical Institute
(see Independent Publications, Part 1)

Genealogical Publishing Company, Inc.
1001 North Calvert Street
Baltimore, MD 21202-3897
(410) 837-8271; (800) 296-6687; (410) 752-8492 FAX; (800) 599-9561 FAX
http://www.genealogical.com
Michael Tepper, Editor-in-Chief
Mon–Fri 8:30–4:30

Genealogy Publishing Service
573 Beasley Mine Road
Franklin, NC 28734-4144
(828) 524-7063
http://www.gpsbooks.com
Jane S. Moyer, Co-owner
9:00–6:00

Hearthside Press
PO Box 4029
Alexandria, VA 22303-0029
(703) 960-0086; (703) 960-0087 FAX
Stuart and Tammy Nixon, Owners
Mon–Sat 10:00–5:00, Thur 5:00–8:00

Heritage Books, Inc.
1540 Pointer Ridge Place #E
Bowie, MD 20716
(800) 398-7709; (800) 276-1760 FAX
info@heritagebooks.com
http://www.heritagebooks.com
Darren, Customer Service
Mon 9:00–4:00
Pub. *Heritage Book News*, monthly, free; *Heritage News*, two times per month, free (e-zine)
(online library, books, CD-ROMs)

Higginson Book Company
(148 Washington Street—location)
PO Box 778 (mailing address)
Salem, MA 01970
(978) 745-7170; (978) 745-8025 FAX
acquisitions@higginsonbooks.com
http://www.higginsonbooks.com
Laura Bjorklund, Acquisitions Director
Mon–Fri 10:00–7:00, Sat by appointment
Pub. *Family History Catalog*, annually (genealogy); *Source Catalog*, annually (local history); *Historic Map Catalog* (map reprints), $4.00 for the set
(reprints and sells over 12,000 family and local histories; reprints current, out-of-print books under its "Royalty Program"; publishes new books under its "New Book Publishing Program" [not a vanity press]; does customer reprinting for local historical and family socieites who do not wish to sell their books privately, with no minimum; does preservation reprinting for libraries and other collections whose valuable work is disintegrating)

Historical Research Associates
PO Box 242
Marshfield Hills, MA 02051
(781) 834-7329
Cynthia Hagar Krusell, Proprietor
(Mayflower lineages—Plymouth, Bristol and Barnstable counties)
research: $20.00 per hour

Hope Farm Press and Bookshop
252 Main Street
Saugerties, NY 12477
(845) 246-3522; (800) 883-5778
hopefarm@hopefarm.com
http://www.hopefarm.com/geneatop.htm

Mon–Sat 10:00–6:00
("Specializing in New York Books since
1959. Over 2,600 titles.")

Hunterdon House
38 Swan Street
Lambertville, NJ 08530
(609) 397-2523
tombwilson@aol.com
Thomas B. Wilson, General Manager

Iberian Publishing Company
1071 Elder Heights Drive
Bishop, GA 30621-1233
(706) 310-1393 (Customer service, Mon–Fri
1:00–6:00); (877) 569-9742 (Orders
only); (706) 310-0959 FAX
books@iberian.com
http://www.iberian.com
Chris Alexander, CEO
Mon–Fri 9:00–9:00, Sat noon–6:00
(over 500 titles, specializing in Virginia,
West Virginia, the Carolinas, Georgia and
other states, as well as general reference
and military records; publication services
with press runs from 25-2,500 copies)

Hank Jones Publishing Company
PO Box 261388
San Diego, CA 92196-1388
Henry Z Jones, Jr., Fellow, American Society
of Genealogists

Kinship—Sources for Kith and Kin
60 Cedar Heights Road
Rhinebeck, NY 12572
(845) 876-4592; (845) 518-9955
Louise Gay Rogers Till, Editor
Mon–Sun 9:00–9:00
(publishes New York source records;
Palatine transcripts)

The Linden Tree
1204 West Prospect Street
Cloquet, MN 55720-1332
(218) 879-5727
http://feefhs.org/pub/frg-lt.html
Marilyn Lind, Owner
(free catalog on request, mostly German and
how-to titles)

Marietta Publishing Company
2115 North Denair Avenue
Turlock, CA 95382
(209) 634-9473
Janet G. Parker, Publisher; J. Carlyle Parker,
Editor
Mon–Sat 8:00 A.M.–9:00 P.M.
(seven titles in print)

Mary and John Clearing House
5602 305th Street, Suite AB
Toledo, OH 43611
(419) 726-4192
Burton W. Spear, President
9:00–3:00
(publishes volumes on the English families
who came to New England by 1643 from
the west country of England, counties of
Somerset, Dorset, Devon and Cornwall,
approximately annually, fourteen in print)
$1.00 for publication list

Mountain Press
(4503 Anderson Pike—location)
PO Box 400 (mailing address)
Signal Mountain, TN 37377-0400
(423) 886-6369 (Office); (423) 886-5312
FAX
James L. Douthat, Owner
daily 9:00–5:00

**Native American Genealogical Research
and Publishing Company with Oklahoma
Yesterday Publications**
PO Box 908
Hixson, TN 37343
(423) 870-5960; (423) 870-1796 FAX
http://www.nagrpubco.net
Jeff Bowen, Owner and Publisher; Dorothy
T. Mauldin, Owner and Publisher
Mon–Fri 9:00–6:00 (Eastern time)
(Native American and Civil War; catalog
available upon request)

**The New England Historic Genealogical
Society (NEHGS)**
PO Box 5089
Framingham, MA 01701
(888) 296-3447; (508) 788-9500 FAX
sales@nehgs.org
http://www.NewEnglandAncestors.org
Erin Nikitchyuk, Director of Sales
Mon–Fri 9:00–5:00
Pub. *Catalog*, three to four times per year
(genealogies, histories, reference works, vital
records, software, and CD-ROMs)

New England History Press
9 Lakeview Drive
Somersworth, NH 03878-2003

Picton Press
(120 Union Street—location)
PO Box 250 (mailing address)
Rockport, ME 04856-0250
(207) 236-6565
sales@pictonpress.com
http://www.pictonpress.com
Stephanie McMahan, Mail Clerk
Mon–Fri 8:30–5:00
Pub. *Genealogical and Historical Catalog*
("We are publishers of many genealogical
and historical books.")

ProQuest
(see Antiquarian Book Dealers—Copy
Services, Part 4)

The Reprint Company, Publishers
(611 Perrin Drive, Spartanburg, SC
29307—location)
PO Box 5401 (mailing address)
Spartanburg, SC 29304
(864) 579-4433; (864) 579-4969 FAX
tom_rep@bellsouth.net
Thomas E. Smith, Owner and Publisher
Mon–Fri 9:00–5:00
(reprint editions of local history and
genealogy of the southeast; offers self-
publishing services to authors and
organizations)

Scholarly Resources, Inc.
(see Miscellaneous—Products and Services,
Part 4)

Jonathan Sheppard Books
PO Box 2020, Empire State Plaza Station
Albany, NY 12220
http://www.jonathansheppardbook.com
Meldon J. Wolfgang, Owner
(European and North American map reprints;
out-of-print local histories and
genealogies)

Simmons Historical Publications
(see Tennessee, Part 2)

Southern Historical Press, Inc.
(375 West Broad Street, Greenville, SC
29601—location)
PO Box 1267 (mailing address)
Greenville, SC 29602-1267

(864) 233-2346; (800) 233-0152; (864) 233-
2349 FAX
LaBruce M. S. Lucas
Mon–Fri 9:00–5:00
Pub. *The Georgia Genealogical Magazine*,
quarterly, $35.00 per year subscription
("Alabama, Arkansas, Georgia, Kentucky,
Louisiana, Mississippi, Missouri, North
Carolina, South Carolina, Tennessee,
Texas, and Virginia")

**Southwest Pennsylvania Genealogical
Services**
PO Box 253
Laughlintown, PA 15655
(724) 238-3176
William L. Iscrupe, Editor/Publisher

Summit Publications
Ye Olde Genealogie Shoppe
(see Booksellers, Part 4)

TLC Genealogy
PO Box 403369
Miami Beach, FL 33140-1369
(800) 858-8558; (305) 531-1158 FAX
http://tlcgenealogy.com
Nancy Bradley
24/7
(primary record abstracts from Kentucky,
Maryland, Mississippi, Missouri, New
Jersey, North Carolina, Ohio,
Pennsylvania, Virginia, West Virginia and
Wisconsin; original books, not reprints,
mostly covering the 1700s)

Virginia Book Company
(216 South Buckmarsh Street—location)
PO Box 431 (mailing address)
Berryville, VA 22611
(540) 955-1428; (540) 955-1162 FAX
Mrs. L. F. Myers
by appointment
(Virginiana, Clarke County, Virginia,
Pocahontas and Patsy Cline)

Willow Bend Books
(see Booksellers, Part 4)

Microform Publishers

InfoTech Publications
(see Missouri, Part 2)

Library Microfilms
Division of Bay Microfilm, Inc.
1115 East Arques Avenue
Sunnyvale, CA 94086
(408) 736-7444; (800) 359-FILM
Jan Hawley, Director
8:00–5:00
Pub. *Catalog*

Micro Specialties
19925 Stevens Creek Boulevard
Cupertino, CA 95014
(408) 973-7872
Dennis Lewandowski

Microform Books
(see Massachusetts, Part 2)

ProQuest
(see Antiquarian Book Dealers—Copy
Services, Part 4)

Electronic Publishers

Accessible Archives, Inc.
697 Sugartown Road
Malvern, PA 19355

(610) 296-7441; (610) 725-1745 FAX
jnagy@accessible.com
http://www.accessible.com
John C. Nagy
(publishes items of genealogical importance
from major 19th-century newspapers from
southeastern Pennsylvania, Delaware,
northern Maryland, and southern New
Jersey on CD-ROM)

ProQuest
(see Antiquarian Book Dealers—Copy
Services, Part 4)

Self-Publishing

Following is a list of publishers and
printers who are experienced in producing
family histories and genealogical reference
books. These firms can help an author design
an attractive book and may also offer him
some limited editorial advice. They print and
bind books (or produce microform copies)
for an agreed fee. Distribution and publicity
are usually a self-publisher's own
responsibility, unless stated otherwise in the
publishing contract.

Ancestor Research and Analysis
13727 North Amiss Road
Baton Rouge, LA 70810-5042
(225) 766-0140; (225) 766-3018
Danell Spillman and Barbara Comeaux
Strickland, Owners
Mon–Sat 8:00–5:00
(provides all aspects of genealogical services:
research, consultation, publishing, mailing
services, word processing for manuscripts,
indexing, lecturers, seminar coordinator)

The Anundsen Publishing Company
(108 Washington Street—location)
PO Box 230 (mailing address)
Decorah, IA 52101
(563) 382-4295
John K. Anundsen, President

The Bookmark
(see Booksellers, Part 4)

Closson Press
(see Publishers, Part 4)

Curtis Media Corporation
530 Bedford Road, Suite 112
Bedford, TX 76022-6554

Dogwood Printing
(Campbell City Shopping Center, Highway
65 and CC—location)
PO Box 716 (mailing address)
Ozark, MO 65721-0716
(417) 581-8585; (800) 862-8382; (417) 581-
5858 FAX
Betty R. Braden and Peggy L. Taylor,
Owners
Mon–Fri 8:30–5:00
(specializes in family histories, records,
newsletters, quarterlies)

F & M Enterprises
(see Mississippi, Part 2)

Family History Network
(see Publishers, Part 4)

Family History Publishers
845 South Main Street
Bountiful, UT 84010
(801) 295-7490
Jay L. Long, Editor-Publisher

Gateway Press, Inc.
1001 North Calvert Street
Baltimore, MD 21202-3897
(410) 837-8271; (800) 296-6687
Ann Hughes, Publishing Director

Genealogy Publishing Service
(see Publishers, Part 4)

The Gregath Publishing Company
PO Box 505
Wyandotte, OK 74370
(918) 542-4148; (800) 955-5232
http://www.gregathcompany.com

Fredrea Gregath Cook, President; Carrie
Cook, Vice President/Webmaster
Mon–Fri 9:00–noon & 1:00–4:00
(specializes in genealogy, folklore, family
history, local history, military history;
prints on demand, produces E-books and
web sites)

Heart of the Lakes Publishing
(2989 State Route 96A—location)
PO Box 299 (mailing address)
Interlaken, NY 14847-0299
(607) 532-4204; (607) 532-4684 FAX
hlpbooks@aol.com
http://www.hlpbooks.com
Walt Steesy
by appointment
(production services with emphasis on family
history and local studies)

Heirloom Publishing Services
PO Box 3011
Lake Placid, FL 33852

Higginson Book Company
(see Publishers, Part 4)

Iberian Publishing Company
(see Publishers, Part 4)

Lightning Source
1246 Heil Quaker Boulevard
La Vergne, TN 37086
(615) 213-5815; (615) 213-4426 FAX
Newaccounts@lightningsource.com
http://www.lightningsource.com
Mon–Fri 8:00–5:00
(print-on-demand and e-book services, no
editorial assistance)

Newbury Street Press
101 Newbury Street
Boston, MA 02116-3007
(617) 536-5740; (617) 536-7307 FAX
nsp@nehgs.org
http://www.NewEnglandAncestors.org
Christopher Hartman, Editorial Director
Mon–Fri 9:00–5:00
("publishers of compiled genealogies and
family narratives)

Picton Press
(see Publishers, Part 4)

Publishers Press, Inc.
1900 West 2300 South
Salt Lake City, UT 84119
(801) 972-6600; (800) 456-6600

The Reprint Company, Publishers
(see Publishers, Part 4)

Timbercreek, Ltd.
Route 1, Box 242
Miami, OK 74354
(918) 542-4148; (800) 955-5232
Fredrea Gregath Cook, President

Walking the Line Publications
sales@walkingthelinebooks.com
http://www.walkingthelinebooks.com
(Self-publishing services)

Wolfe Publishing
PO Box 8036
Fernandina Beach, FL 32035-8036
(904) 277-0555
Betty Wolfe, Owner

Booksellers

Appleton's Books and Genealogy
8700 Pineville-Matthews Road, Suite 590-151
Charlotte, NC 28226-4715
shopping@appletons.com
http://www.appletons.com
Jennifer Schmidt
("Appleton's features a wide variety of genealogy books, CDs, software, and supplies.")

Barnette's Family Tree Book Company
PO Box 2360
McKinney, TX 75070
(281) 550-7935
mic@barnettesbooks.com
http://barnettesbooks.com (online bookstore)
Mic Barnette, Proprietor
Mon–Sun 10:00–6:00
("We purchase from over 150 different publishers and authors. We sell how-to reference guides, plus books about all states east of the Mississippi River, Texas, Oklahoma, Arkansas, Louisiana, Native Americans, African Americans.")

The Bookmark
(36 Public Square—location)
PO Box 90 (mailing address)
Knightstown, IN 46148-9900
(765) 345-5133; (800) 876-5133, ext. 170; (800) 695-8153 FAX
Bookmark.Mayhill@Spitfire.net
http://www.the-bookmark.com
Bonnie Manche, Secretary/Clerk
Mon–Fri 8:00–noon & 12:30–4:30
(publishes atlases and county histories)

Boyd Publishing Company
PO Box 367
Milledgeville, GA 31061
(478) 452-4020; (800) 452-4035 (Orders only); (478) 452-6380 FAX
tignall@accucomm.net
http://www.boydpublishing.com
Brenda D. Phillips
("Annual catalog of over 3,000 genealogical source materials for all states: books, CDs, pamphlets. Listings from over 200 vendors. Largest mail order genealogical book supplier. Also genealogical publishers.")

Deseret Book Company
(see Publishers, Part 4)

The Family Tree Bookshop
406 Parker Road
Salisbury, MD 21804-9012
(410) 749-8835; (888) 525-3966; (410) 749-4419 FAX
neilkeddie@beast.toad.net
http://www.familytreebookshop.com
Leslie & Neil Keddie

Family Tree Genealogy Book Store
books@genealogy.theshoppe.com
http://genealogy.theshoppe.com/index.htm

Family Tree House
(in the Antique Trove, 232 Vernon Street, Roseville, CA 95678—location)
PO Box 2262 (mailing address)
Granite Bay, CA 95746
(916) 791-2050; (916) 791-8920 FAX
gregory.bragg@gbbragg.com
http://www.abebooks.com/home/FTHBOOKS
Gregory B. Bragg, Owner
Mon–Sun 10:00–6:00

(genealogy and family history how-to books, computer software, CD-ROMs, and supplies)
$20.00 per year membership in discount club (20%)

Fort Laramie Historical Association
(Western books, see Wyoming, Part 2)

Frontier Press
PO Box 126
Cooperstown, NY 13326
(607) 547-1970; (800) 772-7559 (order line); (607) 547-9415 FAX
kgfrontier@aol.com;
    karen@frontierpress.com
http://www.frontierpress.com
Karen Mauer Green, Owner
(largest genealogical bookstore on the Internet)

Genealogy House
10950 Spoon Ridge
Minneapolis, MN 55347
(952) 920-6990; (800) 920-6992
jhaase@genealogyhouse.com
http://www.genealogyhouse.com/index.html
Jan Haase, President
by appointment

Genealogy Publishing Service
(see Publishers, Part 4)

Genealogy Unlimited, Inc.
Interlink Bookshop and Genealogical Services
(1060 South 500 East, American Fork, UT 84003-9723—location)
PO Box 537 (mailing address)
Orem, UT 84059-0537
(801) 763-7132; (800) 666-4363; (801) 763-7185 FAX
info1@genealogyunlimited.com
http://www.genealogyunlimited.com
Carol Mehr Schiffman, President
Mon–Fri 10:00–4:00
("Genealogical and archival supplies; importer of European maps and atlases, free catalog available")
free semiannual mail-order catalog

The Gregath Publishing Company
(see Self-Publishing, Part 4)

Heritage Quest, from ProQuest Company
PO Box 540670
North Salt Lake, UT 84054
(801) 298-5358; (800) 760-2455 (Orders); (801) 299-0082 FAX
sales@heritagequest.com
http://www.heritagequest.com
Jerry Millar, Sales Manager
8:00–5:00
(over 250,000 titles—books, CD-ROMs, microfilm, and microfiche—for sale; heritagequestonline.com available through libraries only)

Heritage Quest Research Library and Bookstore
(see Washington, Part 2)

Higginson Book Company
(see Publishers, Part 4)

History House
PO Box 30093
Raleigh, NC 27622
(919) 755-3952; (919) 781-7240
Mrs. H. A. Smith, Editor
Mon–Fri 10:00–5:00

Hope Farm Press and Bookshop
(see Publishers, Part 4)

The Memorabilia Corner
1312 McKinley Avenue
Norman, OK 73072
(405) 321-8366; (405) 321-3444 FAX
TMCorner@aol.com
http://members.aol.com/TMCorner
Henry C. Hensel, Proprietor

The New England Historic Genealogical Society (NEHGS)
(see Publishers, Part 4)

New York Genealogical and Biographical Society Library
(see New York, Part 2)

Origins
4327 Milton Avenue
Janesville, WI 53546-9322
(608) 757-2777
Origins@OriginsBooks.com
http://www.angelfire.com/biz/origins1
Wendy Uncapher, Owner; Linda Herrick, Owner
Mon–Fri 9:00–5:00, Sat 11:00–3:00
(genealogy supplies, maps, acid-free preservation products)
free catalog upon request

Stagecoach Library for Genealogical Research
1840 South Wolcott Court
Denver, CO 80219
(303) 922-8856
Donna J. Porter, Owner
Pub. *Catalog* (mail order rental/sale), $10.00 per issue

Stevenson's Genealogy Center
230 West 1230 North
Provo, UT 84604
(801) 374-9600; (801) 374-9622 FAX
cs@sgenealogy.com
http://www.sgenealogy.com
Mon–Sat 8:00–8:00

Thomsen's Genealogical Center
PO Box 588
Bountiful, UT 84011
(801) 294-5105; (801) 292-7952 (Barbara)
Barbara Ann Orris, Manager
(genealogical supplies, maps and atlases; Scandinavian)

Virginia Book Company
(see Publishers, Part 4)

Willow Bend Books, A Division of Heritage Books, Inc.
65 East Main Street
Westminster, MD 21157-5026
(800) 876-6103
bookorder@WillowBendBooks.com
http://www.WillowBendBooks.com
Craig Roberts Scott, C.G.R.S., Proprietor
Mon–Fri 9:00–5:00
Pub. *Catalog*, quarterly; *Heritage News* (free); *Living History News* (free); *The Town Crier* (free)
("Bookstore specializing in currently in-print genealogy books; publishes over 200 titles per year.")

Ye Olde Genealogie Shoppe
(9605 Vandergriff Road—location)
PO Box 39128 (mailing address)
Indianapolis, IN 46239-0128
(317) 862-3330; (800) 419-0200; (317) 862-2599 FAX

yogs@iquest.net
http://www.yogs.com
Ray Gooldy and Pat Gooldy, Co-owners
Mon–Sat 9:00–3:30
(Genealogy forms, supplies, resources, CDs,
    charts, Genealogist Mini Binder. "We are
    the home of books by Jana Broglin, Fran
    Carter-Walker, Colleen Alice Ridlen,
    Charles Franklin, and, of course, Ray &
    Pat Gooldy.")

Antiquarian Book Dealers

Abebooks, Inc.
PMB 185
1574 Gulf Road
Port Roberts, WA 98281-9007
http://www.abebooks.com
("The world's largest online marketplace for
    books")

Aceto Bookmen
(see Independent Publications, Part 1)

Americana Books
723 Fifth Avenue, South
Saint Cloud, MN 56301
(American history)

Andover Books
41 Chandler Circle
Andover, MA 01810
(local history)

Bibliofind
http://www.amazon.com/exec/obidos/
    subst/books/misc/bibliofind.html/103-
    7935271-8400608

Book Hawk
236 West East Avenue
Chico, CA 95926
(530) 343-4183

Osee H. Brady, Books
12 Elm Street
Assonet, MA 02702
(508) 644-5073
Althea H. Brady, Owner
10:00–5:00 by appointment
(a general stock out-of-print/antiquarian
    shop, with a good selection of New
    England material and limited genealogical
    material)

Vernon and Zona Braun Booksellers
9004 Rosewood Drive
Sacramento, CA 95826
(local history)

Cabin in the Pines Bookshop
Route 5, Box 409
Potsdam, NY 13676
(Saint Lawrence and Franklin counties
    history)

A. Eileen Smith Cunningham
(1208 South Fifth Street, also Route
267—location)
Route 2, Box 10 (mailing address)
Carrollton, IL 62016
(217) 942-3868
(genealogy, local history of central-western
    Illinois and the Illinois River Valley)

Q. M. Dabney & Co.
PO Box 849
Princeton Junction, NJ 08550-0849
Michael E. Schnitter, General Manager
Mon–Fri 9:00–5:30, Sat by appointment
Pub. *Catalog*, two or three times per year,
    $3.00 per issue
(old books on American history, including
    some genealogy)

Thomas S. DeLong
RDG Box 336
Sinking Spring, PA 19608
(PA local history)

Fine Books Division
1550 West Mockingbird
Dallas, TX 75235

Pub. *The Americana Catalog*, annually, free

Lawrence Golder Rare Books, ABAA
PO Box 144
Collinsville, CT 06022
(860) 693-8631; (860) 693-8110 FAX
Lawrence Golder
by appointment only
Pub. *Catalog*, annually
(rare general Americana, West, Colonial,
    South, Indians, Canadiana, Arctic, world
    voyages and travels)

Great Bridge Books, Inc.
301 Woodberry Drive
Chesapeake, VA 23322-5739
(VA & NC local history)

Klaus Gruneweld Bookdealer
807 West 87 Terrace
Kansas City, MO 64114
(816) 333-7799
by appointment
(Kansas, Missouri, and Kansas City local
    history)

Haunted Bookshop
(73 Lincoln Street—location)
PO Box 34 (mailing address)
Paris, ME 04271
(207) 743-6216
Wini Mott, Owner
(Maine town histories and a few books on
    genealogy)

Paul Henderson Books
466 Penacook Road
Hopkinton, NH 03229
(603) 746-3396
Joanna Henderson, Owner
by appointment
(local history and family genealogies)

Peter Hennessey Bookseller
PO Box 393
Peconic, NY 11958
(631) 734-5650; (631) 298-1790 FAX
hennesseybkslr@aol.com
http://www.NorthFork.Net/com/Hennessey
Peter Hennessey
(free out-of-print book search service)

Higginson Book Company
(see Publishers, Part 4)

Hoenstine Rental Library
(see Lending Libraries, Part 4)

Dan Jones Research
PO Box 177
Department GA
Salt Lake City, UT 84110-0177
Dan Jones
$5.00 plus LSASE for price list of out-of-
    print and hard-to-find family and local
    histories, fee refunded as $10.00 on first
    order); genealogical research services
    offered

Light of Parnell Bookshop
3362 Mercersburg Road
Mercersburg, PA 17236-9609
(717) 328-3478
Nathan O. Heckman
by appointment
(Franklin County local history)

Lindsay's Books, Inc.
(106 East Meeting Street—location)
PO Box 1075 (mailing address)
Lancaster, SC 29721
(803) 285-9455 (Office); (803) 547-5383

(Home)
D. Lindsay Pettus, Owner
(historical books, manuscripts, old postcards
of Lancaster County, South Carolina)

MacDonalds Military Memorabilia and Maine Mementoes
PO Box 65
Eustis, ME 04936-0065
(207) 246-5999
Tommac@somtel.com
Thomas L. MacDonald, Owner
by appointment only
(books, local history, military, Maine)

Madigan's Books
(16707 E CR 1600 N—location)
PO Box 62 (mailing address)
Charleston, IL 61920-9339
(217) 345-3657
mmadigan@advant.com
http://www.madigansbooks.com
Matt Madigan
by appointment
Pub. *Catalog*, three to five times per year,
free
(county, town, family histories, plat books,
vital records; maintains a book-wanted
file)

Robert Murphy Bookseller
3113 Bunker Hill Road
Marietta, GA 30062
(county local history)

New Englandiana
(121 Ben Mont Avenue—location)
PO Box 589 (mailing address)
Bennington, VT 05201
(802) 447-1695
Roger D. Harris, Owner
Mon 8:00–4:30, Tue–Fri by chance
(bimonthly used book list, includes
genealogy)
six issues for $2.00

Nu-tique Shop
Main Street
Newfane, VT 05345
(genealogy and local history)

Otzinachson Bookshop
Kelly Court Apartments #B8
Lewisburg, PA 17837
Duane Edward Steininger
(PA)

Dick Perier—Books
PO Box 1
Vancouver, WA 98666
(360) 676-2033 (mail order only)
Dick Perier
9:00 A.M.–10:00 P.M.
(Washington, Oregon, Idaho and Montana
state, county and local history)

Seven Oak Press
405 South Seventh Street
Saint Charles, IL 60174
(American history)

Tan Bark Books
120 Reist Street
Buffalo, NY 14221-5322
(county and town history)

Tuttle Antiquarian Books, Inc.
28 South Main Street
Rutland, VT 05701
(802) 773-8229; (802) 773-1493 FAX
tuttbook@sover.net
http://tuttlebooks.com

Apr–Dec: Mon–Fri 9:00–5:00, Sat
9:00–4:00; Jan–Mar: by appointment
Pub. *Catalog of Genealogy; Catalog of
Regional Americana*, every 1-2 years,
$7.50 per issue

Unicorn Limited, Inc.
PO Box 397
Bruceton Mills, WV 26525
(304) 379-8803; (304) 379-8923 FAX
Dr. W. R. McLeod, President
Pub. *Catalog*, bimonthly, $12.50 per year
subscription (genealogy catalog issued
every Jan–Mar period)
(history, folklore, children's language,
bagpipe music, genealogy, and related
areas of Scottish, Celtic and Norse
peoples)

Wootens Old and Rare Books
G 3311
Cheyenne Burton, MI 48529
(American history)

The Yankee Book and Art Gallery
10 North Street
Plymouth, MA 02360
(508) 747-2691
Charles F. Purro, Owner
Mon–Sat 11:00–5:00; Sun noon–4:00
(Pilgrims and Plymouth history, *The
Mayflower*)

**George A. Young—Books of Colonial
America**
3611 Janet Road
Wheaton, MD 20906
(301) 946-6490
George A. Young, Owner
(genealogy, history, local history, church
history)
free search by mail or phone only

Search Service

Booksearch, Inc.
(612) 292-1842; (612) 292-1742 FAX
booksearch@booksearch.com
http://www.booksearch.com
(search form available online)

Copy Services

**Photoduplication Service, Library of
Congress**
Washington, DC 20540-4570
(202) 707-5640
photoduplication@loc.gov
http://www.loc.gov/preserv/pds
Sandra Lawson, Acting Head, Public
Services Section
Mon–Fri 9:00–4:45
("The Photoduplication Service provides
access to one of the largest collections of
genealogical materials, including over
40,000 genealogical charts, tables, and
family trees, and the nation's most
extensive holdings of local and state
histories.")

ProQuest
UMI/Books on Demand
300 North Zeeb Road
Ann Arbor, MI 48106-1346
(800) 521-0600
http://www.umi.com
Karen Kaltz, Product Manager
8:00–5:00
Pub. *Books on Demand*
(specializes in out-of-print books, genealogy;
microfilming of books, documents,
newspapers; microfilm and microfiche

duplication in both silver and diazo;
publisher of original records, indexes, and
other materials in Internet, CD-ROM,
book, and microform formats)

Periodicals

AntiqueWeek
(27 North Jefferson Street—location)
PO Box 90 (mailing address)
Knightstown, IN 46148-9900
(765) 345-5133; (800) 876-5133
connie@antiqueweek.com (Eastern Edition);
thoepf@antiqueweek.com (Central
Edition)
http://www.antiqueweek.com (AntiqueWeek
Online)
Pub. *AntiqueWeek*, weekly, Eastern Edition
$3.70 for eight-week subscription, $12.20
for thirty-week subscription, $22.70 for
sixty-week subscription

Lending Libraries

Many of the libraries and societies listed elsewhere participate in the Interlibrary Loan program on a selective basis, depending on the condition of the books requested. Many more allow only their members to borrow books by mail.

American Family Records Association (AFRA)
Alexander Mitchell Public Library
Genealogy Circulation Collection
519 South Kline Street
Aberdeen, SD 57401-2596
(605) 626-7097 (Library)
Shirley Arment, Reference and Genealogy Librarian
Library: Mon–Thur 9:00–9:00, Fri 9:00–6:00, Sat 1:00–5:00, Sun (Sept–June) 1:00–5:00

Becker's Bookshelf
1314 Prospect Avenue
Norfolk, NE 68701
Charlene K. Becker, Owner
(sends "new on shelf" lists 3-4 times per year)
20% of the value of the book, plus postage (special 4th class rate)

The Connecticut Historical Society (CHS)
(see Connecticut, Part 2)

Sherry Foresman Library
2787 335th Street
Menlo, IA 50164
(641) 524-5110
Sherry Foresman
(30-day book rentals and publications for sale, $.75 for catalog)

Genealogical Center Library
(see Georgia, Part 2)

Hoenstine Rental Library
10 Harbor Court
Groton, CT 06340-5618
http://ourworld.compuserve.com/homepages/LLewis/hoenstin.htm
Barbara Ann Hoenstine
Mon–Fri 9:00–noon & 1:00–4:00
(sales of new and used books on Pennsylvania history and genealogy; collection of over 4,000 books for rent)

Micro Quix
5615 176th S.W.
Lynwood, WA 98037-2816
free one-year membership

Mid-Continent Public Library
(see Missouri, Part 2)

National Archives Microfilm Rental Program
PO Box 30
Annapolis Junction, MD 20701-0030
(federal population census schedules 1790–1920, American Revolutionary War service records and pension and bounty-land warrant application files)

National Genealogical Society (NGS)
(see Virginia, Part 2)

The New England Historic Genealogical Society (NEHGS)
PO Box 5089
Framingham, MA 01701
(888) 296-3447; (508) 788-9500 FAX
bookloan@nehgs.org
http://www.NewEnglandAncestors.org
Alex Woodle, Circulating Library Director
Mon–Fri 9:00–5:00
Circulating Library Catalogs (Vol. I: Genealogies, Vol. II: Histories and Research Aids), $10.00 each or $15.00 for the set (allows NEHGS members to borrow family genealogies, local histories, abstracted records and reference works from a 30,000 volume circulating collection, $15.00 for three books for two-week loan, including shipping and handling, catalog and order forms also on web site)
$50.00 per year membership

Stagecoach Library for Genealogical Research
(see Booksellers, Part 4)

University of California—Los Angeles
University Research Library
(see California, Part 2)

Miscellaneous

General

American Association for State and Local History
530 Church Street, #600
Nashville, TN 37219-2325
(615) 255-2971; (615) 255-2979 FAX
http://www.nashville.net/~aaslh
John-Paul Richiuso, Director of Publications and Archives
9:00–5:00
Pub. *History News*, bimonthly; *History News Dispatch*, monthly, $55.00 per year subscription (includes both *History News* and *History News Dispatch*); *Directory of Historical Organizations in the United States and Canada*, about every four years
("AASLH is a nonprofit, membership organization providing educational assistance to professionals and amateurs doing local and state history.")
$30.00 per year membership (does not include *Directory*)

American Association of University Women
Genealogy Division
6564 DeMuth Circle
Sacramento, CA 95842-2413
(916) 332-9419
Carrol L. Camomile, Chairman Genealogy Division

The American College of Heraldry
PO Box 710
Cottondale, AL 35453
davidwu10@sbcglobal.net
http://www.americancollegeofheraldry.org/acheraldry.html
David Robert Wooten
hours: various
Pub. *The Armiger's News*, quarterly; *The Heraldic Register of America*, occasionally, $7.00 per issue postpaid, special rates for libraries
(coats of arms rightfully borne in America, biographical listings of armigers)
$25.00 per year membership (includes only *The Armiger's News*)

American Independence Museum
1 Governors Lane
Exeter, NH 03833-2420
(603) 772-2622; (603) 772-0861 FAX
aim@nh.ultranet.com
http://www.nh.ultranet.com/~aim

American Medical Association
Executive Vice President
515 North State Street
Chicago, IL 60610
(312) 464-5000
http://www.social.com/health/nhic/data/hr1800/hr1817.html
(database on 350,000 deceased U.S. physicians, 1878–1969)

American Name Society
Modern Languages
Baruch College
Modern Languages Box G-1224
New York, NY 10010
(212) 387-1570; (212) 387-1591 FAX
Wayne H. Finke, Executive Secretary/Treasurer
9:00–5:00
Pub. *Names*, quarterly
$35.00 per year membership

American Police Center and Museum
1717 South State Street
Chicago, IL 60616-1215
(312) 431-0005

American Society/French Legion of Honor
22 East 60th Street
New York, NY 10022-1077
Pub. *Laurels*, three times per year
$10.00 per year membership

American Studies Association
1120 19th Street, N.W., Suite #301
Washington, DC 20036
(202) 467-4783; (202) 467-4786 FAX; (800)
548-1784 (The Johns Hopkins University
Press)
http://www.georgetown.edu/crossroads
John F. Stephens, Executive Director
9:00–5:00
Pub. *American Quarterly* (Mar, June, Sept,
Dec), $69.00 per year subscription for
institutions, $18.00 per issue (from The
Johns Hopkins University Press, Journals
Publishing Division, 2715 North Charles
Street, Baltimore, MD 21218-4319)
$15.00 per year membership

The American Victorian Museum
(325 Spring Street—location)
PO Box 328 (mailing address)
Nevada City, CA 95959
(530) 265-5804
David S. Osborn, President
(primarily historical, not genealogical)

**American West Research Center and
Historical Society, Inc.**
(see Ohio, Part 2)

TheAmericanWest.com
12691 Apple Valley Road
Apple Valley, CA 92308
(760) 240-2401
webmaster@americanwest.com
http://www.americanwest.com

Anglo-American Genealogical Society
2686 Claybourne Road
Shaker Heights, OH 44122
Mrs. John Schaltinger

Association for Gravestone Studies
278 Main Street, Suite 207
Greenfield, MA 01301-3230
(413) 772-0836
info@gravestonestudies.org
http://www.gravestonestudies.org
Pub. *Association for Gravestone Studies
Newsletter*, quarterly; *Markers—Journal
of the Association for Gravestone Studies*,
annually, $20.00 per issue to members,
$25.00 per issue to nonmembers
$20.00 per year membership

**Broad Top Area Coal Miners Historical
Society, Inc.**
Reality Theatre
Main Street
Robertsdale, PA 16674
(814) 635-3807 voice & FAX
ebtminer@nb.net
Ronald Morgan, President, Board of
Directors; Margaret Duvall, Office
Manager
Fri–Sat 10:00–5:00, Sun 1:00–5:00
Pub. *Coal Miners Journal*, quarterly
("The Broad Top Area Coal Miners
Historical Society, Inc. is a nonprofit
historical and educational organization.
Museum and Entertainment Center.")
$15.00 per year membership; admission:

$3.00 for adults

Carter-Coile Country Doctors Museum
(111 Marigold Lane—location)
PO Box 306 (mailing address)
Winterville, GA 30683
(706) 742-8600; (706) 742-5476 FAX

Center for Historical Population Studies
211 Carlson Hall
Salt Lake City, UT 84112
Pub. *Center for Historical Population
Studies Newsletter*, annually

Center for Human Genetics
Umbilical Line Project
Municipal Building
PO Box 770
Bar Harbor, ME 04609-0770
(207) 288-3371
thr@jax.org
http://feefhs.org/misc/frg-chg.html
Thomas H. Roderick, Ph.D., Project Director

**The Center for Thanatology Research and
Education, Inc.**
391 Atlantic Avenue
Brooklyn, NY 11217-1701
(718) 858-3026; (718) 852-1846
rhalporn@pipeline.com
Roberta Halporn, Director
noon–5:00
(Gravestone studies of interest to historians,
genealogists and those devoted to
American folk art. Also rubbing
materials.)
$30.00 per year membership (members
receive 10% discount on purchases, plus
tax deduction)

Communal Studies Association
PO Box 122
Amana, IA 52203
(319) 622-6446 voice & FAX
csa@netins.net
http://www.ic.org/csa
Susan Shoup, Office Manager
Pub. *Communal Societies*, annually, $15.00
per year subscription
$25.00 per year membership

Datatrace Systems
PO Box 1587
Stephenville, TX 76401
(254) 965-6979
James Pylant, Editor
Mon–Fri 9:00–5:00
Pub. *American Genealogy Magazine*,
quarterly (Mar, June, Sept, Dec), $22.50
per year subscription, $43.00 for two-year
subscription, $3.75 sample issue (Texas
residents add 8.25% sales tax)
(Indian records, pension files, Black Dutch
ancestry; also transmitted electronically
on nationwide satellite)

Public Library of Des Moines
(National Bar Association Archives, see
Iowa)

Direct Line Software
Land Record Reference
71 Neshobe Road
Newton, MA 02468
(617) 527-9566
deeds@rcn.com
http://users.rcn.com/deeds/landref.htm
(Land history for Indiana, Ohio,
Pennsylvania, Tennessee and Virginia,
plus informative land-related articles.)

Freedom of Information Center

127 Neff Annex
University of Missouri-Columbia
Columbia, MO 65211
(573) 882-4856; (573) 882-9002 FAX
M. Kathleen Edwards, Manager
Mon–Fri 8:00–5:00
(collects materials on the freedom,
documents controls)

**Friends of the Middle Border Museum of
American Indian and Pioneer Life**
(see Ethnic Archives, Libraries and
Societies—Native American, Part 3)

Gangster Chronicles
13509 Pendleton Street
Oxon Hill, MD 20022
Shannon Bridget Murphy
Pub. *Gangster Chronicles*, quarterly, $14.00
per year subscription

**Genealogical and Heraldic Institute of
America**
American Italian Congress
(see Ethnic Archives, Libraries and
Societies—Italian, Part 3)

The Guild of One Name Studies
2204 West Houston
Spokane, WA 99208-4440
Donna Potter Phillips

Heraldica
velde@heraldica.org
http://www.heraldica.org
François R. Velde
(information and links)

Holocaust Library and Research Center
557 Bedford Avenue
Brooklyn, NY 11211
(718) 599-5833

**Holocaust Memorial and Resource Center
of Central Florida**
851 North Maitland Avenue
Maitland, FL 32751
(407) 628-0555; (407) 628-1079 FAX
http://www.holocaustedu.org
Mon–Thur 9:00–4:00, Fri 9:00–1:00

**The Holocaust Center of United Jewish
Federation, Pittsburgh**
5738 Darlington Road
Pittsburgh, PA 15217
(412) 421-1500; (412) 422-1996 FAX
lhurwitz@ujf.net
http://www.ujfhc.net
Linda F. Hurwitz, Director
Mon–Fri 9:00–5:00, and by appointment

Hudson's Bay Company Archives
(204) 945-4949; (204) 948-3236 FAX
hbca@gov.mb.ca
http://www.gov.mb.ca/chc/archives/hbca/
index.html

Isle a la Cache Museum
(501 East Romeo Road, Romeoville, IL
60441—location)
Will County Forest Preserve, PO Box 1069
(mailing address)
Joliet, IL 60434-1069
(815) 886-1467
Jack MacRae, Museum Coordinator
(French and Indian Fur Trade, 17th and 18th
century)

Kendall Whaling Museum
27 Everett Street
Sharon, MA 02067
(781) 784-5642

http://www.boston.com/arts/museums/
muskwm.htm

Klondike Gold Rush National Historical Park—Seattle Unit
(see Washington, Part 2)

Lincoln Group of Boston
27 Forest Trail
East Bridgewater, MA 02333
(508) 697-1387
Professor Thomas R. Turner, President
$20.00 per year membership

Mount Diablo Surveyors Historical Society (MDSHS)
5042 Amethyst Drive
San Jose, CA 95136-2601
http://www.mdshs.org/first.html
("The Mount Diablo Surveyors Historical Society was created to enrich the general public by collecting, preserving and displaying the knowledge, technology and artifacts of the land surveying profession.")
$25.00 per year membership

Museum Association of the American Frontier
(3½ miles east of Chadron, on U.S. 20—location)
HC 74, Box 18 (mailing address)
Chadron, NE 69337
(308) 432-3843
Charles E. Hanson, Jr., Director
Pub. *Museum of the Fur Trade Quarterly*
("North American fur trade 1500–1900; emphasis is on objects as well as people.")
$6.00 per year membership; research: $10.00 per hour

Museum of Jewish Heritage—A Living Memorial to the Holocaust
18 First Place
Battery Park City
New York, NY 10004
(212) 968-1800
communications@mjhnyc.org
http://jewishheritage.citysearch.com
Esther Brumberg, Research Coordinator
Mon–Wed & Sun 9:00–5:00, Thur 9:00–8:00, Fri and eve of Jewish Holidays 9:00–5:00
Pub. *Newsletter*, quarterly
(not genealogical)

National Trust for Historic Preservation Library Collection
Hornbake Library
University of Maryland
College Park, MD 20742
(301) 405-6320; (301) 314-2709 FAX
NT_Library@umail.umd.edu
http://www.lib.umd.edu/UMCP/NTL/ntl.html
Sally Sims Stokes, Curator
Mon–Fri 10:00–5:00 (appointment suggested)
(materials on certain historic landmarks)

Southwest Field Office-National Trust for Historic Preservation
500 Main Street, Suite 1036
Fort Worth, TX 76102
(817) 332-4398; (817) 332-4512 FAX
Mon–Fri 9:00–5:00
Pub. *Preservation Magazine*, bimonthly
(New Mexico, Texas, Oklahoma)

National United States Marshals Museum
Wyoming Territorial Park
975 Snowy Range Road

Laramie, WY 82070
(307) 745-6161; (800) 845-2287; (307) 745-8620 FAX
questions@wyoprisonpark.org
http://www.wyoprisonpark.org/marshals.shtml
Annette Amerman, Office Manager and Curator
May–Oct: 9:00–6:00

The Old Time Historical Association
(9161 N.C. Highway 22—location)
PO Box 220 (mailing address)
Climax, NC 27233
(336) 685-4253
James S. Ferree, Jr., President
by appointment
Pub. *Bulletin Board*, quarterly
(specializes in Frick Steam Engines and old machinery, worldwide)
$10.00 per year membership

Oral History Association
1093 Braxton Avenue
Los Angeles, CA 90024
Pub. *Oral History Association Annual Report and Membership Directory*, annually

Oral History Association
Old Capitol Annex
Frankfort, KY 40601
(502) 564-3016
Kim Lady Smith, Manager
8:00–4:30
Pub. *Oral History Review*, semiannually, $20.00 per year subscription

Pioneer America Society
Southeast Missouri State University
Department of Earth Science
Cape Girardeau, MO 63701
(573) 651-2354
Michael Roark, Ph.D., Executive Director
Pub. *Material Culture*

Pioneer Genealogy Society
PO Box 11488
Salt Lake City, UT 84147
Michel L. Call, President
(specializes in royal ancestry, Mayflower, New England colonial and pre-colonial, Mormon pioneer ancestry)
$2.00 plus SASE for list of colonists with royal descent and price list for indexes and other services

Plantation Society in the Americas
University of New Orleans/University of South Florida
Department of History
University of New Orleans
New Orleans, LA 70148-2550
(504) 280-6886; (504) 286-5505 FAX
Professor Edward Lazzerini
daily
Pub. *Plantation Society in the Americas*, two or three times per year, three issues per volume
(West Indies, plantations, families, Creole studies, Southern U.S., Caribbean, Mississippi Valley, Afro-American)
$25.00 per year membership

Presidential Libraries and Historic Homes
The Hermitage, Home of President Andrew Jackson (see Tennessee, Part 2)
Fillmore House (see New York, Part 2)
The Pierce Brigade and Hillsborough Historical Society, Inc. (see New Hampshire, Part 2)
Abraham Lincoln Library and Museum (see

Ohio, Part 2)
Abraham Lincoln Presidential Library (see Illinois, Part 2)
President Andrew Johnson Museum and Library (see Tennessee, Part 2)
Ulysses Simpson Grant Birthplace (see Ohio, Part 2)
Rutherford B. Hayes Presidential Center Library (see Ohio, Part 2)
Garfield Farm Museum (see Illinois, Part 2)
President Benjamin Harrison Home (see Indiana, Part 2)
McKinley Memorial Library and Museum (see Ohio, Part 2)
Theodore Roosevelt Association (see New York, Part 2)
The Herbert Hoover Presidential Library and Museum (see Iowa, Part 2)
Franklin D. Roosevelt Library and Digital Archives (see New York, Part 2)
Harry S Truman Library and Harry S. Truman National Historic Site (see Missouri, Part 2)
Dwight D. Eisenhower Library and Museum (see Kansas, Part 2)
John Fitzgerald Kennedy Library and Museum (see Massachusetts, Part 2)
Lyndon B. Johnson Library (see Texas, Part 2)
Nixon Presidential Materials (see Maryland, Part 2)
Gerald R. Ford Library (see Michigan, Part 2)
Jimmy Carter Library (see Georgia, Part 2)
The Ronald Reagan Presidential Library and Museum (see California, Part 2)
The George Bush Presidential Library and Museum (see Texas, Part 2)
William J. Clinton Presidential Materials Project (see Arkansas, Part 2)
(primarily historical, not genealogical)

Radcliffe College
Arthur and Elizabeth Schlesinger Library on the History of Women in America
3 James Street
Cambridge, MA 02138
(617) 495-8647; (617) 496-8340
slref@radcliffe.edu
http://www.radcliffe.edu/schles
Wendy Thomas, Public Service Librarian
Mon–Fri 9:00–5:00
Pub. *Schlesinger Library Newsletter*, two times per year
$25.00 per year Active Friend membership

ROOTS Dictionary of Genealogy and Archaic Terms
randyj2222@yahoo.com
http://freepages.genealogy.rootsweb.com/~randyj2222/gendict.html
Randy Jones

Sag Harbor Whaling and Historical Museum
Main and Garden Streets
Sag Harbor, NY 11963
(631) 725-0770
George A. Finckenor, Sr., Curator/Secretary/Treasurer
(primarily historical, not genealogical)

Salem Witch Museum
19½ Washington Square, North
Salem, MA 01970
(978) 744-1692
facts@salemwitchmuseum.com
http://www.salemwitchmuseum.com

San Francisco State University
Labor Archives and Research Center
(see California, Part 2)

Underground Railroad Operators Directory
http://www.ugrr.org//names/map-in.htm (Indiana); http://www.ugrr.org//names/map-ia.htm (Iowa); http://www.ugrr.org//names/map-ks.htm (Kansas)

United States Board on Geographic Names
Domestic Geographic Names
United States Department of the Interior
U.S. Geological Survey
523 National Center
Reston, VA 22092
(703) 648-4544
http://www~nmd.usgs.gov/www/gnis
Roger L. Payne, Executive Secretary, U.S. Board on Geographic Names
8:00–5:00
(free research inquiries)

United States Holocaust Memorial Museum
100 Raoul Wallenberg Place, S.W.
Washington, DC 20024-2150
(202) 488-0400; (202) 488-2690 FAX; (202) 828-9583 (Registry)
research@ushmm.org; archives@ushmm.org
http://www.ushmm.org
Radu Ioanid, Ben and Vladka Meed National Registry of Jewish Holocaust Survivors

The Victorian Society in America
219 South Sixth Street
Philadelphia, PA 19106
(215) 627-4252
Judith Snyder, Executive Director
Pub. *The Victorian: Newsletter of the Victorian Society in America*, quarterly; *Classic America*
(primarily historical, not genealogical)

Victorian Society in America, Iowa Chapter
2940 Cottage Grove
Des Moines, IA 50311
(515) 274-4996 (evenings and weekends)
Patrice Beam, Executive Director
Pub. *Hope & Glory*, annually; *Newsletter*, quarterly

Victorian Society in America, New England Chapter
137 Beacon Street
Boston, MA 02116
(617) 267-6338
Peter Ambler, President

Victorian Society of America, Savannah Chapter
10 West Jones Street
Savannah, GA 31401
Dean Owens

Victorian Society of America
Northern New Jersey Chapter
PO Box 717
Montclair, NJ 07042
(973) 744-8267

Western Museum of Mining and Industry
1025 North Grate Road
Colorado Springs, CO 80921
(719) 598-8850
Linda Lemieux, Director
Pub. *WMMI Newsletter*
(primarily historical, not genealogical)

Women and Leadership Archives
Gannon Center for Women and Leadership
Loyola University Chicago
Sullivan Center/Science Library, Room 200
6525 North Sheridan Road
Chicago, IL 60626
(773) 508-8837; (773) 508-8492 FAX
gannonarchives@luc.edu
http://www.luc.edu/orgs/gannon/archives
Valerie Gerrard Brown, Director/Archivist
Mon–Fri 8:30–5:00 (call ahead to assure staff availability)
Pub. *Linkage*, semiannually (Gannon Center newsletter), free
("Archives with local, state, and national holdings relating to women, with special emphasis on women as leaders. Mundelein College affiliated with Loyola University Chicago in 1991. The Archives of Mundelein College are now part of the Women and Leadership Archives of the Gannon Center for Women and Leadership of Loyola University Chicago.")

Fraternal Organizations

The Ancient Free and Accepted Masons (Freemasons)
The Philalethes Society
nking@freemasonry.org (E-M@ason)
http://www.freemasonry.org
Nelson King, FPS, Editor
("Each Grand Lodge keeps its own records; we do not have access to those records")

Iowa Masonic Library
The Grand Lodge of Iowa, A.F. & A.M.
813 First Avenue, S.E.
Cedar Rapids, IA 52401-5001
(319) 365-1438
http://freemasonry.org/gl-ia/index.html

Hays Masonic Bodies (A.F. & A.M.)
107 West 11th
Hays, KS 67601
(785) 625-3127
http://spidome.net/~masons/index.html

Masonic Historical Society and Museum, Minnesota
200 East Plato Boulevard
Saint Paul, MN 55107
(612) 222-6051; (612) 222-6144 FAX

Ancient Free and Accepted Masons
Grand Lodge of New Mexico
Po Box 25004
Albuquerque, NM 87125-0004
http://204.134.124.1/leon/gmm.htm

Allen E. Roberts Masonic Library and Museum
4115 Nine Mile Road
Richmond, VA 23223-4926
(804) 222-3110; (804) 222-4253 FAX
grandlodge@rcn.com
http://leo.vsla.edu/reposit/sites/aerml.html
Marie M. Barnett
Mon, Wed & Fri 9:00–4:00
Pub. *The Virginia Masonic Herald*, quarterly
("Masonic history of Virginia and Virginia Masons. Records before 1940 contain mainly Masonic history of member, very little biographical information [death date].")

Benevolent and Protective Order of Elks of the USA (B.P.O.E.)
2750 North Lakeview Avenue
Chicago, IL 60614-1889
(773) 755-4708; (773) 755-4790 FAX
grandlodge@elks.org
http://www.elks.org
Jack Jensen, Grand Secretary
(a fraternal organization, formed in 1868 in New York City)

Order of De Molay
DeMolay International Service and Leadership Center
10200 N.W. Ambassador Drive
Kansas City, MO 64153
(800) DEMOLAY, (816) 891-9062 FAX
demolay@demolay.org
http://www.demolay.org/home/index.shtml
Bengamin W. Johnson, II, Executive Director
(a fraternal organization for young men, founded in 1919)

Order of the Eastern Star
easternstar@erols.com
http://www.easternstar.org
(a fraternal organization, originally the women's auxiliary to Freemasonry)

Fraternal Order of Eagles
Grand Aerie, F.O.E.
PO Box 250972
Milwaukee, WI 53225-0972
(414) 781-7585; (414) 781-5046 FAX
assistance@foe.com
http://foe.com
Bill Loffer, Membership Director
(a fraternal organization, founded in 1898)

Improved Benevolent and Protective Order of Elks
postmaster@ibpoe.com
http://www.ibpoe.com
(a charitable fraternal organization)

International Genealogy and Heraldry Fellowship of Rotarians
I.F.R. Genealogy
PO Box 62
Cooperstown, NY 13326-0062
James R. High
Pub. *Roto-Gene*, quarterly, $15.00 per year subscription

International Order of Odd Fellows (IOOF)
SGL/IARA Headquarters
422 North Trade Street
Winston-Salem, NC 27101
(336) 725-5955, (800) 235-8358, (336) 722-7317 FAX (Sovereign Grand Lodge); (336) 725-6037, (800) 766-1838, (336) 773-1066 FAX (International Association of Rebekah Assemblies)
IOOFSGL@aol.com
http://www.ioof.org
(a fraternal organization established in America in 1819, separated from its English parent organization in 1843, established the Rebekah Lodges for women in 1851)

International Order of Job's Daughters
233 West Sixth Street
Papillion, NE 68046-2210
(402) 592-7987; (402) 592-2177 FAX
sgc@iojd.org
http://www.iojd.org
Susan M. Goolsby, Executive Manager
(a fraternal organization for young women, founded in 1920)

Kiwanis International
3636 Woodview Trace
Indianapolis, IN 46268-3196
(317) 875-8755, ext. 325; (317) 879-0204 FAX
http://www.kiwanis.org
Karen Yakovac, Public Relations Manager
(a fraternal service organization founded in 1915)

Knights of Columbus Museum
1 State Street
New Haven, CT 06511-6702
(203) 865-0400, ext. 224
http://www.kofc.org
Susan Brosnan, Archivist
generally Mon–Sun 10:00–5:00; Archivst:
Mon–Fri by appointment
Pub. *Columbia*
(Roman Catholic fraternal organization)

The Order of Knights of Pythias
Supreme Lodge Knights of Pythias
59 Coddington Street, Suite 202
Quincy, MA 02169-4150
(617) 472-8800
pythianwebsite@yahoo.com
http://www.pythias.org
(a fraternal organization, founded in 1864;
auxiliaries: the Pythian Sisters, the
Dramatic Order Knights of Khorassan,
and the Junior Order Princes of Syracuse)

Lions Clubs International Headquarters
300 West 22nd Street
Oak Brook, IL 60523-8842
(630) 571-5466
IT@LIONSCLUBS.org
http://www.lionsclubs.org
(a fraternal organization, founded in 1917)

Loyal Order of Moose
Moose International, Inc.
(address withheld upon request)
(a fraternal organization, founded in 1888)

Masonic Museum
curator@phoenixmasonry.org
http://www.phoenixmasonry.org/
masonicmuseum
(an online museum including information on
many fraternal organizations)

Modern Woodmen of America
(1701 First Avenue—location)
PO Box 2005 (mailing address)
Rock Island, IL 61204-2005
(309) 786-6481; (800) 447-9811
glevis@modern-woodmen.org
http://www.modern-woodmen.org
Gail Ann Hodges Levis, Historian
Mon–Fri 8:00–4:30
Pub. *The Modern Woodmen* (official
publication for members)
(a fraternal life insurance society founded by
Joseph Cullen Roon in 1883 in Lyons,
Iowa; maintains its own archives which
includes historical documents,
photographs and films, and memorabilia
from 1883 to the present day; records are
used to assist historians, genealogists and
librarians in documenting family and
community histories)
no cost for research services

P.E.O. Executive Office
3700 Grand Avenue
Des Moines, IA 50312
(515) 255-3153; (515) 255-3820 FAX
http://www.peointernational.org
(a fraternal organization, originally founded
in 1869 as a sorority at Iowa Wesleyan
College)

Rosicrucian Order
Ancient Mystic Order Rosae Crucis
(AMORC)
North American-English Grand Lodge
1342 Naglee Avenue
San Jose, CA 95191
(408) 947-3600; (408) 947-3677
http://www.rosicrucian.org

(founded in the U.S. in 1693)

Rotary International
1 Rotary Center
1560 Sherman Avenue
Evanston, IL 60201
(847) 866-3000; (847) 866-3193 (Rotary
Archives); (847) 328-8554 FAX; (847)
328-8281 FAX
http://www.rotary.org
Cyndi Beck
8:30–5:00
(a fraternal organization, founded in 1905)

**Scottish Rite Masonic Library and
Museum**
Van Gorden-Williams Library
National Heritage Museum
33 Marrett Road
Lexington, MA 02421
(781) 861-6559; (781) 861-9846 FAX
library@monh.org
http://www.vgw.library.net
Nancy Wilson, Head Librarian
Library Reading Room: Mon–Sat
10:00–5:00; Museum: Mon–Sat
10:00–5:00 & Sun noon–5:00
("Our collections focus on Freemasonry and
other fraternal orders, American history,
and Americana.")

The Shrine of North America
International Shrine Headquaraters
2900 Rocky Point Drive
Tampa, FL 33607-1460
(813) 281-0300
http://www.shrinershq.org;
http://www.quetzalcoatl.org (Order of
Quetzalcoatl);
http://www.daughtersofthenile.com/index.
html (Daughters of the Nile)
(a fraternal organization, founded in 1872,
supported by the Daughters of the Nile,
founded in 1913, and by the Order of
Quetzalcoatl, founded in 1945)

Woodmen of the World
(address withheld upon request)
(fraternal organization; because of privacy
laws, no longer provides genealogical
information)

Transportation (Maritime, Canal, Steamship, Railroad, Bridges, Trails)

Bellefonte Historical Railroad Society
Train Station
Bellefonte, PA 16823
(814) 355-0311

Bridge Line Historical Society
Historical Society for the Delaware &
Hudson Railroad
PO Box 7242, Capitol Station
Albany, NY 12224
http://www.fileshop.com/personal/
jashaw/rhs/blhs.html

**California State Railroad Museum
Library**
111 I Street
Sacramento, CA 95814-2265
(916) 323-8073; (916) 327-5655 FAX
library@californiastaterailroadmuseum.org
http://californiastaterailroadmuseum.org
Tue–Sat 1:00–5:00
("The California State Railroad Museum
Library has several archival collections
which contain employee information.
These documents cover specific railroads,

for specific occupations, during specific
periods. The Library does not have
complete employee records for any
railroad. Some materials are stored off-
site. Please call in advance for an
appointment to search manuscript
sources.")

Canal Society of New York State
7308 Jamesville Road
Manlius, NY 13104
(315) 682-8378 (Home); (315) 478-6551
(Work); (315) 682-8124 FAX
acottr9528@aol.com
http://www.canalsnys.org
Anita Cottrell, Secretary-Treasurer
$25.00 per year membership

**Charlotte-Genesee Lighthouse Historical
Society**
70 Lighthouse Street
Rochester, NY 14612
(716) 621-6179

Chesapeake Bay Maritime Museum
(Mill Street—location)
PO Box 636 (mailing address)
Saint Michaels, MD 21663
(410) 745-2916
http://www.cbmm.org

**Chicago and East Illinois Railroad
Historical Society**
PO Box 606
Crestwood, IL 60445-0606
(708) 385-8182
http://www.justnet.com/cei/index.html

**Chicago and Northwestern Railroad
Historical Soc**
(1812 Hood Avenue, Chicago, IL
60660—Archives location)
8703 North Olcott Avenue (mailing address)
Niles, IL 60648-2023
(773) 794-5633 (Society); (773) 743-1159
(Archives)

Chisholm Trail Historical Museum
(Highways 70 and 81, just east of 81 on
70—location)
Box 262
Waurika, OK 73573
(580) 228-2166; (580) 228-3290 FAX
Gin Dodson, Director
Sat 10:00–4:00, Sun (except first Sun)
1:00–4:00

**Clark County Historical Society and
Howard Steamboat Museum, Inc.**
(see Indiana, Part 2)

**Columbia River Maritime Museum
Library**
1792 Marine Drive
Astoria, OR 97103-3525
(503) 325-2323

Conneaut Historical Railroad Society
363 Depot Street
Conneaut, OH 44030-2468
(440) 599-7878

**Delaware & Hudson Canal Historical
Society**
(Mohonk Road—location)
PO Box 23 (mailing address)
High Falls, NY 12440
(845) 687-9066
Susan Ingalls Lewis, Director
Pub. *D&H Canal Society Newsletter*
(primarily historical, not genealogical)

East Ely Railroad Depot Museum
1100 Avenue
Ely, NV 89301
(775) 289-1663; (775) 289-1664 FAX
http://www.clan.lib.nv.us/docs/
MUSEUM/ELY/mus-ely.htm

Fennimore Railroad Historical Society/Museum
610 Lincoln Avenue
Fennimore, WI 53809
(608) 822-6144

Fort Wayne Railroad Historical Society, Inc.
PO Box 11017
Fort Wayne, IN 46855
(219) 493-0765

The Great Lakes Historical Society
(480 Main Street—location)
PO Box 435 (mailing address)
Vermilion, OH 44089-0435
(440) 967-3467; (440) 967-1519
http://www.inlandseas.org
William A. O'Brien, Executive Director
10:00–5:00
Pub. *Inland Seas* (Great Lakes history), quarterly
$44.00 per year membership

Association for Great Lakes Maritime History
PO Box 25
Lakeside, OH 43440
D. Glick
(primarily historical, not genealogical)

Hawaii Maritime Center Library and Photo Archives
Pier 7
Honolulu, HI 96813
(808) 523-6151; (808) 536-6373; (808) 536-1519 FAX

Hinton Railroad Museum
217 Seventh Avenue
Hinton, WV 25951
(304) 466-1433

Historic Pullman Foundation
Pullman Historic District
614 East 113th Street
Chicago, IL 60628
(773) 785-3828; (773) 785-8901 (Tours); (773) 785-8181 (Business Office); (773) 785-8182 FAX
foundation@pullmanil.org; tours@ pullmanil.org; publicity@pullmanil.org
http://pullmanil.org
Cynthia McMahon, President
Mon–Fri noon–2:00, Sat 11:00–2:00, Sun noon–3:00
Pub. *Update*, quarterly
(historic preservation, tours, architecture)
$20.00 per year membership

Hudson Valley Railroad Society
(Hyde Park Railroad Station, River Road—location)
PO Box 135 (mailing address)
Hyde Park, NY 12538
(845) 331-9233

Collis P. Huntington Railroad Historical Society, Inc.
(At end of 14th Street West, Huntington, WV—museum location)
PO Box 451 (mailing address)
Kenova, WV 25530
(304) 453-1641
railtwo@aol.com

http://www.newrivertrain.com
Don Maxwell, Vice President and Trip Director
Museum: Sat–Sun, and by appointment; Excursions in Oct
Pub. *Gondola Gazette*, monthly
$12.00 per year membership

Huron Valley Railroad Historical Society
3487 Broad Street
Dexter, MI 48130
(734) 426-5100

Iron Horse Historical Society
PO Box 8
Parsons, KS 67357
(620) 421-1959

Lawrence County Railroad Historical Society
1420 I Street
Bedford, IN 47421

Marine Historical Society of Detroit
Department W
606 Laurel Avenue
Port Clinton, OH 43452
http://www.oakland.edu/~ncschult/mhsd

Maybrook Railroad Historical Society
Route 208E
Maybrook, NY 12543
(845) 427-2845

Missouri Pacific Historical Society
Museum of Transportation
3015 Barrett Station
Saint Louis, MO 63122
(314) 937-7941; (314) 234-8622
http://library.wustl.edu/~spec/archives/
aslaa/mopac-historical.html

Mountain State Railroad and Logging Historical Association
PO Box 89
Cass, WV 24927

National Frontier Trails Center Archives and Library
318 West Pacific Street
Independence, MO 64050
(816) 325-7577; (816) 836-7101 FAX
http://www.frontiertrailscenter.com
John Mark Lambertson, Director
Mon–Sat 9:00–4:30, Sun 12:30–4:30
Pub. *The Trail Scout*, six times per year, $10.00 per year
("Research library pertaining to the Oregon, California and Santa Fe Trails. Library available to researchers, but we are unable to conduct research for patrons.")

National Historic Trails Interpretive Center
500 North Center Street
Casper, WY 82601
(307) 265-8030
http://w3.trib.com/~rlund/NHTIC.html

National Maritime Historical Society
5 John Walsh Boulevard
Peekskill, NY 10566
(914) 737-7878
http://www.seahistory.org
Pub. *Sea History*
$35.00 per year membership

National Maritime Museum and Library
Fort Mason Center, Building E
860 Beach Street
San Francisco, CA 94123
(415) 556-3002; (415) 556-9870 (Library;

(415) 556-8177 (Museum)
http://www.apl.com/nmma/safrpg.html

National Railway Historical Society
100 North 17th Street
Philadelphia, PA 19102
(215) 557-6606

National Railway Historical Society
Chicago Chapter
PO Box 53
Oak Park, IL 60303-0053
(708) 386-2809

National Railway Historical Society
Mohawk/Hudson Chapter
74 Brookline Avenue
Albany, NY 12203
(518) 489-2829

Ontario & Western Railway Historical Society, Inc.
PO Box 713
Middletown, NY 10940

Oregon-California Trails Association (OCTA)
(524 South Osage Street, Independence, MO 64050—location)
PO Box 1019 (mailing address)
Independence, MO 64051-0519
(816) 252-2276; (816) 836-0989 FAX
lethene@theofficenet.com
http://OCTA-trails.org
Jeanne Miller, Executive Director; Lethene Parks, Secretary
Mon–Fri 9:00–3:00
Pub. *Overland Journal*, quarterly
(The Oregon Trail extended from the vicinity of Independence, Missouri, to Fort Vancouver, Washington; the California Trail branched off the Oregon Trail, toward Sacramento. OCTA web site includes links to its eleven chapters.)
$35.00 per year membership

Oregon Electric Railway Historical Society
PO Box 702
Forest Grove, OR 97116
reyn@reed.edu
http://www.reed.edu/~reyn/oerhs.html

Oregon Trail
http://www.isu.edu/~trinmich/
Oregontrail.html

Overland Trail Museum (Logan County Historical Society, Inc.)
(see Colorado, Part 2)

Philadelphia Maritime Museum
321 Chestnut Street
Philadelphia, PA 19106
(215) 925-5439

Phillips Library
American Neptune
(see Massachusetts, Part 2)

National Pony Express Association (NPEA)
xptom@xphomestation.com
http://www.xphomestation.com (Pony Express Home Station)
Tom Crews
Pub. *News From the Trail*
("The National Pony Express Association is an all-volunteer, nonprofit historical organization for the purpose of identifying, reestablishing and marking the original Pony Express trail through the

eight states it served: California, Nevada, Utah, Wyoming, Colorado, Nebraska, Kansas, and Missouri. The Pony Express Home Station is a compilation of information [fact, fiction and lore] of the Pony Express. Of particular interest to genealogists would be the list of Pony Express Riders.")

Puget Sound Maritime Historical Society
Museum of History and Industry
2700 24th Avenue, East
Seattle, WA 98112
(206) 524-5013; (206) 938-2397; (206) 324-1126 (Museum); (206) 324-1346 FAX (Museum)
http://www.psmaritime.org (Kitsap County); http://www.historymuse-nw.org (Museum)
Robert McNeil, President

Puget Sound Railway Historical Association
PO Box 459
Snoqualmie, WA 98065-0459
(425) 888-0373

Rails and Trails Museum
914 Washington Street
Montpelier, ID 83254

Reading Company Technical and Historical Society
PO Box 15143
Reading, PA 19612
(610) 372-5513
http://www.vicon.net/~reading

Saginaw River Marine Historical Society
PO Box 2051
Bay City, MI 48707
http://www.concentric.net/~Djmaus/srmhs.htm
Pub. *MODOC Whistle*, quarterly
$10.00 per year membership

Salem Maritime National Historic Site
174 Derby Street
Salem, MA 01970
(978) 744-4323

San Diego Maritime Museum
1492 North Harbor Drive
San Diego, CA 92101
(619) 234-9153
Peter S. Branson, Executive Director
(primarily historical, not genealogical)

San Francisco Maritime National Historical Park
J. Porter Shaw Library
Building E, Fort Mason Center
San Francisco, CA 94123
(415) 556-0793; (415) 556-1659; (415) 556-1624 FAX; (415) 556-9870 (Library)
Lynn Cullivan, Publications
Park: Mon–Sat 8:00–5:00; Library: Tue 5:00–8:00, Wed–Fri 1:00–5:00, Sat 10:00–5:00 by appointment
Pub. *Sea Letter*, semiannually
(major research library: 22,000 volumes, including backruns of 500 periodicals (including *Lloyds*, *Record of American and Foreign Shipping* and *Merchant Vessels of the United States* from 1764 into the 1980s), and over 100 bibliographies, 400 oral history interviews, and ephemeral collection of 50,000 items, also West Coast commercial maritime history)
free admission to library

Santa Fe Trail Association
Santa Fe Trail Center
Rural Route 3
Larned, KS 67550
(316) 285-2054; (316) 285-7491 FAX
trailassn@larned.net
http://www.santafetrail.org
Linda Revello, Office Manager
daily 9:00–5:00
Pub. *Wagon Tracks*
membership fees for joining the association

Santa Fe Train Museum of Gray County
Main Street
Ingalls, KS 67853
(620) 335-5220
Hester Kendall, President
(primarily historical, not genealogical)

Society for Preservation of Covered Bridges
1611 Sandcastle Road
Sanibel, FL 33957
David A. Topham, Treasurer
Pub. *Covered Bridge Topics*, quarterly
$15.00 per year membership

Sons and Daughters of Pioneer Rivermen
126 Seneca Drive
Marietta, OH 45750
http://s-and-d.hspsi.org
Mrs. J. W. Rutter, Secretary
Pub. *S & D Reflector*, quarterly
("S&D is an organization of like-minded people with a common interest in boats of the past and the people who operated them, with a special emphasis toward paddlewheel and steam-powered vessels of America's inland rivers. While S&D is not specifically a genealogy-based organization, it does pay homage to those rivermen and women who pioneered the inland rivers.")
$15.00 per year membership

Southwest Railroad Historical Society
Age of Steam Railroad Museum
(Fair Park—location)
PO Box 153259 (mailing address)
Dallas, TX 75315
(214) 428-0101
http://www.startest.net/homes/railroad

Steamboat Masters and Associates, Inc.
(2316 Northwestern Parkway, Louisville, KY 40212-1024—location)
PO Box 3046 (mailing address)
Louisville, KY 40201-3046
(502) 778-6784; (502) 776-9006 FAX
Sandra Miller Custer, President
Mon–Fri 9:00–5:00 by appointment only
Pub. *The Egregious Steamboat Journal*, bimonthly, $5.00 per issue, $20.00 per year U.S. subscription, $24.00 per year Canadian subscription, $40.00 per year foreign subscription
(extensive library and archives of books, indices, model plans, and videos pertaining to steamboating, history of steamboats and the people who worked and traveled on them, on the inland rivers of America)
will quote price for finding information; catalogue of resources: $4.00

Steamship Historical Society of America, Inc.
SSHSA Collection
University of Baltimore
Langsdale Library
1420 Maryland Avenue
Baltimore, MD 21201

(410) 625-3134
ahouse@UBmail.UBalt.edu
http://www.ubalt.edu/www//anglib/index.html
Henry T. Bishop; Ann House, Librarian
by appointment only
Pub. *Steamboat Bill*, quarterly
(200,000 photos and 5,000 maritime titles; does not have passenger lists)
$25.00 per year membership

Steamship Historical Society of America
Hudson Valley Chapter
55 Indian Ledge Road
Voorheesville, NY 12186
(518) 765-4446

Sunbelt Railroad Historical Society
110 West A Street
Jenks, OK 74037
(918) 298-7246

Ulster and Delaware Railroad Historical Society, Inc.
Po Box 404
Margaretville, NY 12455-0404

Union Pacific Historical Society
PO Box 4006
Cheyenne, WY 82003
http://www.uphs.org/uphs.html

United Association of Railroad Veterans
187 Illinois Street
Paterson, NJ 07503

United Railroad Historical Society
W-11 Avon Drive
East Windsor, NJ 08520-5647

Washington State Railroads Historical Society
PO Box 552
Pasco, WA 99301
http://home1.gte.net/jimbowe/WSRHS1.htm

Waterways Journal
650 Security Building
319 North Fourth Street
Saint Louis, MO 63102
(314) 241-7354
info@waterwaysjournal.net
http://www.waterwaysjournal.net
H. Nelson Spencer, III, Publisher
8:00–4:30
Pub. *Waterways Journal*, weekly, $32.00 per year subscription
(emphasis on inland waterways)

Wisconsin Marine Historical Society
814 West Wisconsin Avenue
Milwaukee, WI 53233-2385
(414) 286-3074
wmhs@execpc.com
http://www.execpc.com/~wmhs
Suzette Lopez
Tue (volunteer's day)
Pub. *Soundings*

Military

Air Force Historical Research Agency
HQ AFHRA/RSA
600 Chennault Circle
Maxwell AFB, AL 36112-6424
http://www.au.af.mil/au/afhra

Americal Division Veterans Association
Army Awards
gnoller@aol.com
http://www.americal.org/awards
Gary Noller, ADVA Past National

Commander
(Information on awards with lists of
recipients for Americal Division, plus
links to sources for other recipients.)

**The American Battle Monuments
Commission**
Courthouse Plaza II, Suite 500
2300 Clarenden Boulevard
Arlington, VA 22201
http://www.abmc.gov
(information about American cemeteries and
memorials located in foreign countries;
can provide specific information/photos
of gravesites and inscriptions on
memorials

The American Civil War Home Page
hoemann@utk.edu
http://sunsite.utk.edu/civil-war
Dr. George H. Hoemann

The American Civil War
An Indexed Guide to Resources on the Net
Dakota State University
(605) 256-5848
jim.janke@dsu.edu
http://homepages.dsu.edu/jankej/civilwar/
civilwar.htm
Jim Janke

The American Legion Library
(700 North Pennsylvania, Indianapolis, IN
46204—location)
PO Box 1055 (mailing address)
Indianapolis, IN 46206
(317) 630-1367
tal@legion.org
http://www.legion.org
Joseph J. Hovish, Librarian and Curator
8:00–4:00
("Almost no information for the
genealogist.")

American Merchant Marine Museum
U.S.M.M.A.
Kings Point, NY 11024
(516) 773-5515

American Society of Military History
1816 South Figueroa Street, Suite 200
Los Angeles, CA 90015
(213) 746-1776

American Veterans Historical Museum
PO Box 115
Pleasantville, NY 10570
(914) 769-5297

Andersonville Guild
(114 Church Street—location)
PO Box 6 (mailing address)
Andersonville, GA 31711
(229) 924-2558
Peggy Sheppard, President
9:00–5:00; festivals: Memorial Day weekend
& first full weekend of Oct
$10.00 per year membership

Andersonville National Historic Site
Route 1, Box 800
Andersonville, GA 31711
(229) 924-0343; (229) 928-9640 FAX
http://www.nps.gov/ande

National Society of Andersonville
PO Box 48
Andersonville, GA 31711
(229) 924-2558 voice & FAX
Peggy Sheppard, President
daily 9:00–5:00
(published *Atwater Report—List of Dead at*

Andersonville Confederate Prison,
$12.00)
$15.00 per year membership

Arizona Military Museum
(52nd Street and McDowell Road—entrance
location)
5636 East McDowell Road (mailing address)
Phoenix, AZ 85008-3495
(602) 267-2676
Col. (Ret.) John L. Johnson, Director
Tue & Thur 9:00–2:00, Sat–Sun 1:00–4:00
Pub. *The Courier*, quarterly
("Wartime casualty data, Arizona only)
$15.00 per year membership

Army Knowledge Network Directorate
Rodler Morris
10 Meade Avenue
Fort Leavenworth, KS 66027-1350
(913) 684-2919; (913) 684-4387 FAX
George Gernert, Director
daily
(military command documents and images)

Arnold Expedition Historical Society
(Arnold Road, Pittston—location)
Rural Route 4, Box 6895 (mailing address)
Gardiner, ME 04345-9112
(207) 582-7080
http://www.rootsweb.com/~aehs/aehs.htm
Daniel H. Warren, Jr., President
July–Aug: weekends 10:00–5:00 (subject to
change), and by appointment
Pub. *Newsletter*, three to four times per year
(to promote and advance research,
preservation and publication projects
related to the Arnold Expedition to
Quebec in 1775, including biographical
and historical records pertaining to the
participants)
$10.00 per year membership

**Association for Preservation of Civil War
Sites**
11 Public Square, Suite 200
Hagerstown, MD 21740-5510
(301) 665-1400; (301) 665-1416 FAX
Tamela Baker, Editor
Pub. *Hallowed Ground*, quarterly
$35.00 per year membership

Atlanta History Center
Civil War Manuscript Collections
(see Georgia, Part 2)

Battle of Lexington State Historic Site
(see Missouri, Part 2)

**Bentonville Battlefield Historical
Association**
(5466 Harper House Road, Four Oaks, NC
27524—location
PO Box 432 (mailing address)
Newton Grove, NC 28366
(910) 594-0789

http://www.ah.dcr.state.nc.us/sections/hs/
bentonvi/bentonvi.htm
$20.00 per year membership

Blue & Gray Enterprises
PO Box 28685
Columbus, OH 43228
Pub. *Blue & Gray Magazine*, bimonthly,
$19.00 per year subscription
(specializes in Civil War military)

Blue and Gray Memorial Association
(see Georgia, Part 2)

Eleanor S. Brockenbrough Library

The Museum of the Confederacy
1201 East Clay Street
Richmond, VA 23219-1615
(804) 649-1861, ext. 27/28; (804) 644-7150
FAX (Museum)
library@moc.org
http://www.moc.org/moc-lib.htm
Dr. John M. Coski, Historian
Mon–Fri 10:00–4:45 by appointment only
Pub. *The Museum of the Confederacy
Journal*, annually
(library has no genealogy collection, per se,
but has documents of some soldiers,
officers, and commands that may be
helpful in genealogical research, but does
not have Confederate military
service/pension records; has Jefferson
Davis Collection, Southern Women's
History Collection, Confederate Memorial
period collections, papers of Confederate
units and commands, wartime objects and
manuscripts)
$35.00 per year resident membership
(residents of Richmond, Petersburg and
the counties of Henrico, Chesterfield,
Hanover, Goochland, Charles City, Prince
George, New Kent, King William, and
Dinwiddie), otherwise $20.00 per year
membership; admission: $4.00 for
nonmembers; photocopies: 25¢ each

California Veterans Museum
PO Box 1200
Yountville, CA 94599-1297
(707) 944-4918 (Workshop); (707) 944-4919
(Museum)
Suzel Ho, Assistant Curator
Fri–Sun noon–2:00
research: $15.00 suggested donation;
museum admission by donation

Camp Dennison Civil War Museum
SR 126
Camp Dennison, OH 45111
http://intcom.net/~tomt/dennison/
dennison.html

Campbellsville University
American Civil War Institute
1 University Drive
Campbellsville, KY 42718

Cantigny First Division Foundation
The First Division Museum
1 South 151 Winfield Road
Wheaton, IL 60187
(630) 668-5185
John F. Votaw, Director

Center for the Study of the Korean War
(1401 West Truman Road—location)
PO Box 456 (mailing address)
Independence, MO 64050
(816) 832-0524 (4303)
PEDWARDS@GRACELAND.edu
Paul M. Edwards, Executive Director
by appointment
Pub. *The Proceedings*
(materials on the Korean War, 1950–1953,
and the armistice period)

Champlin Fighter Museum
4636 Fighter Aces Drive
Mesa, AZ 85205
(480) 830-4540
Doug Champlin, President
(WW I through Vietnam)

The Citadel
Daniel Library
171 Moultrie Street
Charleston, SC 29409

(803) 953-2569 (Reference); (803) 953-5190 FAX
http://www.citadel.edu/citadel/otherserv/library/index.htm
(military history)

Civil Engineer Corps—Seabee Museum
Code 22M NCBC
Port Hueneme, CA 93043
(805) 982-5163
Y. H. Ketels, Director

Civil War at Charleston
10 Resolute Lane, Suite 202-E
Mount Pleasant, SC 29464-2672
(843) 216-2646 (Work); (843) 849-8481 (Home); (843) 870-5299 (Cell); (843) 216-2644 FAX
http://www.awod.com/hamilton
William J. Hamilton, III, Author and Web Editor

Civil War Museum of Jackson County, Missouri
Lone Jack, MO 64070
(816) 881-4431
Sally Schweick, Site Administrator

Civil War Round Table of Arkansas
PO Box 7281
Little Rock, AR 72217
(501) 225-3996
L. A. Russell, Treasurer
Pub. *CWRTA Newsletter*
(no genealogical information)

The Civil War Round Table of Kansas City
1130 Westport Road
Kansas City, MO 64111
(816) 931-6620
Milton F. Perry, President
Pub. *Border Bugle*

Civil War Sons
Sons of Sherman's March to the Sea
2193 East Arrowhead Lane
Cottonwood, AZ 86316-5022
Stan Schirmacher, National Director
Pub. *The National Hobby News*, "Potpourri Page," quarterly, $4.00 per year subscription, c/o PO Box 612, New Philadelphia, OH 44663
(membership in Sons of Sherman's March to the Sea open to all "buffs," not limited to direct descendants)
$3.00 lifetime membership; ancestors' war veterans records information: $1.00

Coast Guard Museum/Northwest
1519 Alaskan Way, South
Seattle, WA 98134
(206) 442-5019

Combined Arms Research Library-Archives
Commandant
ATTN: ATZL-SWS-L (Archives)
Fort Leavenworth, KS 66027-6900
(913) 768-3139
http://www-cgsc.army.mil/cgsc/CARL/archive.htm
Martha Davis, Director; Ed Burgess, Archives Manager
Mon–Fri 7:00–5:00
(Fort Leavenworth institutional archives; rare books, special collections)

The Commonwealth of Massachusetts
Military Division History Research and Museum
Massachusetts National Guard Supply

Depot, Building 2
143 Speen Street
Natick, MA 01760-2599
(508) 651-5700
James Fahey, Archivist
Mon–Fri 9:00–4:00

Company of Military Historians
North Main Street
Westbrook, CT 06498
(860) 399-9460

Confederate Corner
ConfederateH@aol.com
http://www.mindspring.com/~graysky1/page4.html
Shelby B. Pittman, Webmaster
(Kershaw and Lancaster counties, South Carolina)

Confederate Historical Institute
PO Box 7388
Little Rock, AR 72217
(501) 225-3996
Jenny Russell, Chairman
Pub. *Confederate Historical Institute Dispatch*, bimonthly
(Confederate history and battlefield preservation; no genealogical information)
$20.00 per year membership

Confederate Memorial Association, Inc.
The Confederate Embassy
Confederate Memorial Hall
1322 Vermont Avenue, N.W.
Washington, DC 20005
(202) 483-5700
John Edward Hurley, President
Mon–Fri 10:00–4:00, and by appointment
Pub. *Confederate Embassy News*, quarterly
(museum and library)
$25.00 per year membership

Confederate Memorial Hall
929 Camp Street
New Orleans, LA 70130
(504) 523-4522; (504) 523-4595 FAX
Patricia Ricci, Curator

Confederate Memorial Hall (Bleak House)
3148 Kingston Pike, S.W.
Knoxville, TN 37919
(865) 522-2371
Marjorie R. Yeomans, Librarian
Tue–Fri 1:00–4:00
(Southern Americana and Confederate period)

The Confederate Museum-Museum of Southern History
2740 Farm Road, #359
Richmond, TX 77406
(281) 342-8787 FAX
Jim Pearson, Director; Joella Morris, President Emeritus
Tue–Thur 10:00–2:00, Sat–Sun 1:00–4:00
Pub. *Newsletter*, two or three times per year
$35.00 per year membership

Confederate Veteran
8506 Braesdale
Houston, TX 77071
(713) 850-5031
James N. Vogler, Jr., Editor-in-Chief
Mon–Fri 8:00–5:00
Pub. *Confederate Veteran*, bimonthly, $13.00 per year subscription in the U.S., $16.00 per year subscription in Canada, $25.00 per year foreign subscription

Confederated Memorial State Historic Site

211 West First
Higginsville, MO 64037
(660) 584-2853
Kurt Senn, Site Administrator
Mon–Sat 10:00–4:00, Sun noon–5:00
(genealogical services, emphasis on Civil War; "Missouri Confederate pensions and confederate home applications on microfilm.")
copies: 10¢ per page

Cowles Magazines
6405 Flank Drive
Harrisburg, PA 17105
(717) 657-9555
Ed Holm, Editor
Pub. *Civil War Times Illustrated*, bimonthly, $20.00 per year subscription

Custer Battlefield Historical Association
PO Box 902
Hardin, MT 59034
(406) 665-2060
by appointment
Pub. *The Dispatch*, quarterly
$7.50 per year membership

David Library of the American Revolution
(1201 River Road—location)
PO Box 748 (mailing address)
Washington Crossing, PA 18977
(215) 493-6776; (215) 493-9276 FAX
http://www.libertynet.org/~dlar/dlar.html

De Anza Trek Lancer Society
20739 Sunrise Drive
Cupertino, CA 95014
(408) 252-6065
Joseph Adamo, Commander
(emphasis on early California Spanish Cavalry)

18th Century Society
Route 1, Box 264
New Alexandria, PA 15670
Pub. *F & I War Magazine*, quarterly, $10.00 per year

Electric Cemetery Home Page
800 Buckhill Drive
McKinney, TX 75070-5373
deone@pearcy.com
http://www.electriccemetery.com
Deone Pearcy
(Civil War union soldiers and sailors buried in Oklahoma, the 8th Iowa Cavalry, the sinking of the steamship *Sultana*, Cahaba federal prison, the 19th Kansas Cavalry, etc.)

Factor's Walk Historical Commission, Inc.
Factor's Walk Military Museum
PO Box 10041
Savannah, GA 31412
(912) 232-8003; (912) 232-5457

Family Publications
5628 60th Drive, N.E.
Marysville, WA 98270-9509
Rose Caudle Terry, Publisher
Pub. *Military Sources, Queries & Reviews*, two to four times per year, $8.95 per volume subscription, plus $1.50 postage per order
(information on military records, all wars)

1st Cavalry Division Museum
Building 2218, Headquarters Avenue
Fort Hood, TX 76545-5101
(254) 287-3626
Michael P. Bellafaire, Director

Fort Douglas Military Museum
32 Potter Street
Fort Douglas, UT 84110
(801) 588-5188 voice & FAX
Jess McCall, Curator
Tue–Sat 10:00–noon & 1:00–4:00
Pub. *Fort Douglas Vedette and the Museum Association Bulletin*, quarterly, free while supply lasts
(history of the founding of Fort Douglas, of the military in Utah, of the military exploration of the Utah Territory, and of the early Mormon military organizations)

Fort Frederica National Monument
Route 9, Box 286-C
Saint Simons Island, GA 31522-9710
(912) 638-3639 voice & FAX
fofr_superintendent@nps.gov
http://www.nps.gov/fofr

Fort Gibson Military Park
(110 East Ash Avenue—location)
PO Box 457 (mailing address)
Fort Gibson, OK 74434
(918) 478-2669

Fort Larned Historical Society, Inc.
Santa Fe Trail Center
(see Kansas, Part 2)

Fort Leavenworth Historical Society
Frontier Army Museum
20 Reynolds Avenue
Fort Leavenworth, KS 66027-5072
(913) 684-3191; (913) 684-3767; (913) 684-3624 FAX
http://leav-www.army.mil/museum
Stephen J. Allie, Director
Mon–Fri 9:00–4:00, Sat 10:00–4:00, Sun & holidays (except New Year's Day, Easter, Thanksgiving, Christmas) noon–4:00
(1,500 volumes on the history of Fort Leavenworth and the military aspect of the western frontier from 1827)

Fort McAllister Historic Park
3894 Fort McAllister Road
Richmond Hill, GA 31324
(912) 727-2339
http://fortmcallister.org

Fort McKavett State Historic Site
PO Box 867
Fort McKavett, TX 76841
(915) 396-2358
David Bischofhausen, Park Superintendent

Fort Point and Army Museum Association
Fort Point National Historic Site
(Funsten Avenue and Lincoln Boulevard—location)
PO Box 29163 (mailing address)
Presidio of San Francisco, CA 94129
(415) 921-8193
Milton B. Halsey, Jr., Executive Director
Pub. *Fort Point SALVO* (1776 to the present, but primarily Civil War-era)

Fort Polk Military Museum
South Carolina Avenue, Building 917
PO Box 3916
Fort Polk, LA 71459-0916
(337) 531-7905
David S. Bingham, Historian/Curator
Wed–Fri 10:00–2:00; Sat–Sun 9:00–4:00

Fort Ticonderoga
Thompson-Pell Research Center
(Fort Road—location)
PO Box 390 (mailing address)
Ticonderoga, NY 12883

(518) 585-2821; (518) 585-2210 FAX
http://www.fort-ticonderoga.org
Christopher D. Fox, Director/Curator
weekdays by appointment only
Pub. *Bulletin of the Fort Ticonderoga Museum*, annually, $10.00 per issue
(Colonial history, military and Native American; topical finding aids to the collection are available)
from $20.00 per year membership in Friends organization

45th Infantry Division Museum
2145 N.E. 36th Street
Oklahoma City, OK 73111
(405) 424-5313
Tue–Fri 9:00–5:00, Sat 10:00–5:00, Sun 1:00–5:00

Fraser's 78th Highland Regiment
PO Box 214
Topsfield, MA 01983
Walter H. McIntosh
(information regarding Fraser's 78th Highland Regiment who fought the French at Louisbourg and Quebec in 1758 and 1760)

Grand Army of the Republic
(see Lineage, Hereditary and Patriotic Societies—Civil War, Part 4)

Historical Museum at Fort Missoula
Building 322, Fort Missoula
Missoula, MT 59804
(406) 728-3476; (406) 728-5063 FAX
ftmslamuseum@marsweb.com
Dr. Robert M. Brown, Director
Tue–Sun noon–5:00; Memorial Day–Labor Day: Mon–Sat 10:00–5:00, Sun noon–5:00

Confederate Research Center
The Harold B. Simpson Hill College History Complex
Hood's Texas Brigade Association
(112 Lamar Drive—location)
PO Box 619 (mailing address)
Hillsboro, TX 76645-0619
(254) 582-2555
http://hill-college.cc.tx.us/crc/Complex/complex.html
Peggy Fox, Director
Mon–Fri 9:00–3:00
("Time period: War Between the States 1861–1865. We have a beautiful research center/library and have been here for over 35 years.")
research: $15.00 per person (to be billed)

Illinois Association for the Preservation of Historic Arms and Armamemts, Inc.
1800 Western Avenue
Flossmoor, IL 60422-0339
(708) 798-1109

Illinois in the Civil War
ilcivilwar@outfitters.com
http://www.illinoiscivilwar.org
(Brief instruction and links to other sites.)
research: will try to facilitate research but not do research for correspondents

Indiana in the Civil War
kris@IndianaintheCivilWar.com;
larry@IndianaintheCivilWar.com
http://www.indianainthecivilwar.com
Kristopher & Larry Ligget

Jackson Barracks Military Library
Office of the Adjutant General
Building 53, Jackson Barracks

New Orleans, LA 70146-0330
(504) 278-8241; (504) 278-6554 FAX

Journals Division
University of North Texas Press
PO Box 13856
Denton, TX 76203
(940) 565-2124
Jane Tanner, Director Journals
Mon–Fri
Pub. *Military History of the West* (Military history west of the Mississippi), semiannually
$12.00 per year membership

Jerome B. Kelley Memorial Museum
501 Willow Avenue
Ithaca, NY 14850
(607) 272-7314
Danny L. Wheeler, Past Commander in Chief, Sons of Union Veterans of the Civil War
by appointment
("Private Museum. Not for profit. Dedicated to the Grand Army of the Republic, 1861–1865. Headquarters for Sydney Camp #41 Sons of Union Veterans.")

Kennesaw Civil War Museum
2829 Cherokee Street
Kennesaw, GA 30144
(770) 427-2117; (770) 429-4559 FAX
http://www.ngeorgia.com/history/kewm.html

Kennesaw Mountain Historical Association
Kennesaw Mountain National Battlefield Park
(see Georgia, Part 2)

The Kent State University Press
Journals Department
(307 Lowry Hall, Terrace Drive—location)
PO Box 5190 (mailing address)
Kent, OH 44242-0001
(330) 672-7913; (330) 672-3104 FAX
Sandy Clark, Journals Manager
7:30–5:00
Pub. *Civil War History* (includes slavery, abolition, antebellum and reconstruction politics, diplomacy, social and cultural developments in mid-19th-century America, and military history), quarterly (Mar, June, Sept, Dec), $6.00 per issue or $21.00 per year subscription

Kentucky Civil War, Confederate States of America, Orphan Brigade
http://bl-12.rootsweb.com/~orphanhm
(First Kentucky Brigade, CS, "The Orphan Brigade")

Kentucky in the Civil War
http://www.dsenter.com/~trice/ky/civilwar.html

Kentucky Military History Museum
(Capitol Avenue and Main Street—location)
PO Box 1792 (mailing address)
Frankfort, KY 40602-1792
(502) 564-1792, ext. 4498
http://www.kyhistory.org/index.htm
Bill Bright, Curator
Mon–Sat 9:00–4:00, Sun noon–4:00, by appointment (at least 24 hours ahead)

Knoxville Civil War Roundtable
PO Box 313
Knoxville, TN 37901

Liberty Memorial Museum of World War I

100 West 26th Street
Kansas City, MO 64108
(816) 221-1918
Lynn M. Ward
Museum: Wed–Sun 9:30–4:30, please call
for museum/off-site exhibit hours;
Archives: by appointment
(archives includes unit rosters of individual
war participants; if researcher knows unit
of individual being studied, archives can
identify the battle activities of the unit and
possibly find the name of the individual in
a roster; archives has no information
regarding WW II)
copies: 10¢ per page; photograph
reproduction charges

Lincoln Memorial Shrine
125 West Vine Street
Redlands, CA 92373
(909) 798-7632; (909) 798-7636; (909) 798-
7566 FAX
http://www.akspl.org
Donald McCue, Curator
Tue–Sun 1:00–5:00, closed holidays except
12 Feb; Heritage Room: 9:00–noon &
1:00–5:00
Pub. *LMA Newsletter*, quarterly
(not primarily genealogical, but has books,
manuscripts, photographs, etc., on
Lincoln and the Civil War; research Civil
War relatives)
$15.00, $25.00, $35.00 per year membership

**Louisiana Historical Association
Confederate Museum**
929 Camp Street
New Orleans, LA 70130
(504) 523-4522

Maine Military Historical Society/Museum
Camp Keyes
Upper Winthrop Street
Augusta, ME 04330
(207) 626-4338

Manassas Museum
(9101 Prince William Street—location)
PO Box 560 (mailing address)
Manassas, VA 22110
(703) 368-1873; (703) 257-8406 FAX
http://leo.vsla.edu/reposit/sites/mm.html

March Field Museum
(16222 I-215, March Air Force Base,
Intersection of I-215 and Van Buren
Boulevard—location)
PO Box 6463 (mailing address)
March AFB, CA 92518
(909) 697-6600
Steven P. Clark, Director
Mon–Sun 10:00–4:00
Pub. *Newsletter*, quarterly
(not genealogical, except concerning people
associated with the base or units stationed
there; "military aviation history and
memorabilia")
$25.00 per year membership; admission:
$3.00 for adults

Marine Corps Historical Center
Washington Navy Yard
1254 Charles Morris Street S.E.
Washington, DC 20374-5040
(202) 433-3483
http://www.history.usmc.mil
MS. Evie Englander, Head Librarian
Mon–Fri 10:00–4:00
Pub. *Fortitudine*, quarterly, minimal cost
("Military History, Service Museum.")

Maryland Loyalists and the American

Revolution
http://www.erols.com/candidus/index.htm

Master Index of Army Records
http://www.army.mil/cmh-pg/records.html

General D. L. McBridge Museum
New Mexico Military Institute
(101 West College Boulevard—location)
PO Box J (mailing address)
Roswell, NM 88201
(505) 622-3155; (505) 624-8220; (505) 624-
8222; (505) 624-8107 FAX
http://www.nmmi.cc.nm.us/home/
campustour.html

Medals of Honor Index
http://www.army.mil/cmh-pg/moh1.htm
(information about each honoree)

**Members of Quantrill's Guerillas in the
Civil War**
(see The Genealogy Home Page, Computer
Interest, Part 4)

Michigan in the Civil War
http://users.aol.com/dlharvey/cwmireg.htm

Military Historical Society of Australia
astaunto@pcug.org.au
http://www.pcug.org.au/~astaunto/mhsa.htm
Federal Secretary
Pub. *Sabretache*, quarterly, $40.00 per year
subscription
(military history with Australian emphasis)

Military Information Enterprises, Inc.
MIE Publishing
PO Box 17118
Spartanburg, SC 29301-0101
Debra A. Knox, Vice President
Mon–Fri 8:00–5:00
Pub. *How to Locate Anyone Who Is or Has
Been in the Military, Armed Forces
Locator Directory*, annually, $19.95 per
issue
(all military bases in the U.S. and every
conceivable place to obtain military
records or information)

**Military Order of the Loyal Legion of the
United States**
Civil War Library and Museum
(see Lineage, Hereditary and Patriotic
Societies, Part 4)

**Military Order of the Purple Heart of the
U.S.A., Inc.**
5413-B Backlick Road
Springfield, VA 22151
(703) 642-5360
Jay Phillips, Adjutant General
8:00–5:00
Pub. *Purple Heart Magazine*, bimonthly
("veterans organization for combat
wounded")
$12.00 per year membership

**Military Order of the Purple Heart of the
U.S.A., Inc.**
Ladies Auxiliary
419 Franklin Street
Reading, MA 01867
(781) 944-1844
Nancy C. Klare, National Secretary
9:00–6:00
Pub. *Purple Heart Magazine*, bimonthly

Military Records and Research Branch
Kentucky Department of Military Affairs
Division of Veterans Affairs
1121 Louisville Road

Frankfort, KY 40601-6169
(502) 564-4883; (502) 564-4437 FAX
http://www.state.ky.us/agencies/military/
mrrb.htm
C. L. McDaniels, Manager
8:30–4:30
no charge

Mississippi Civil War History Sources
http://home.teclink.net/~moorerga/cw/list-
hx.html

**National Guard Association of the United
States Library**
1 Massachusetts Avenue, N.W.
Washington, DC 20001
(202) 789-0031

National Temple Hill Association, Inc.
(Revolutionary War, see New York)

Naval Historical Center
Washington Navy Yard
805 Kidder Breese, S.E.
Washington, DC 20374-5060
(202) 433-4132 (Library); (202) 433-4882
(Museum); (202) 433-3643 (Ships History
Branch); (202) 433-9553 FAX (Library);
(202) 433-8200 FAX (Museum); (202)
433-6677 FAX (Ships History Branch);
(202) 433-2833 FAX (Operational
Archives)
http://www.history.navy.mil

New England Civil War Museum
Vernon Town Hall, Second Floor
14 Park Place
Vernon, CT
ne.civilwar.mus@snet.net
http://pages.cthome.net/ne.civilwar.mus
(New England Civil War Museum)
Ross S. Dent, Executive Director
Thur 1:00–3:00, second Sun noon–3:00, and
by appointment
admission: donation

**New York Division of Military and Naval
Affairs**
330 Old Niskayuna Road
Latham, NY 12110
(518) 436-0218

The New York Public Library
Military History Collection
(see New York, Part 2)

19th Louisiana Volunteer Infantry
2519 June Street
Baton Rouge, LA 70808
(225) 387-4296

Ohio in the Civil War
http://infinet.com/~lstevens/a/civil.html

Ohio Society of Military History Museum
316 Lincoln Way, East
Massillon, OH 44646
(330) 832-5553

141st Military History Detachment
Washington Army National Guard State
Historical Society
Camp Murray
Tacoma, WA 98430
(253) 581-8498
William Woodward, Ph.D., Historian

Order of Confederate Rose
West Virginia Chapter
Rural Route 9, Box 67
Princeton, WV 24740
(304) 487-0829

Anna B. Belcher, President
Pub. *Parshandatha Papers*, monthly
(for women loving Southern culture and
history)
$7.00 per year membership; research: $10.00

Order of the Indian Wars
PO Box 7401
Little Rock, AR 72217
(501) 225-3996
http://lbha.org/oiw.html
Jerry L. Russell, National Chairman
Pub. *OIW Communique*
(primarily historical, no specifically
genealogical information)
$20.00 per year membership

Oregon Military Museum
Camp Withycombe
Clackamas, OR 97015-9150
(503) 557-5359; (503) 557-6713 FAX
Maj. (Ret) Stephen C. McGeorge, Director
Fri–Sat 9:00–5:00, and by appointment

Pearl Harbor Casualty List
ftp://ftp.rootsweb.com/pub/usgenweb/
hi/military/pearl.txt

John Pelham Historical Association
7 Carmel Terrace
Hampton, VA 23666
Peggy Vogtsberger
Pub. *Cannoneer*, bimonthly
(emphasis on the War Between the States;
Lt.-Col. John Pelham)

Pennsylvania Military Museum
28th Division Shrine
(Business Route 322 and Route
45—location)
PO Box 160A (mailing address)
Boalsburg, PA 16827
(814) 466-6263; (814) 466-6618
wleech@state.pa.us
William J. Leech, Administrator
Tue–Sat 9:00–5:00, Sun noon–5:00

Presidio Army Museum
Building 2, Presidio of San Francisco
San Francisco, CA 94129
(415) 561-4115; (415) 561-3319
Elizabeth A. Poulliot, Director

Presidio Lancers
715 Morningside, N.E.
Albuquerque, NM 87110
(505) 268-2896

Pricketts Fort Memorial Foundation
Pricketts Fort State Park
Route 3
Fairmont, WV 26554
(304) 363-3030

Rosehill Cemetery Civil War Museum
5800 North Ravenswood Avenue
Chicago, IL 60660
(773) 561-5940
David Wendell
Mon–Fri 9:00–5:00, Sat–Sun 9:00–4:00
(Chicago's Civil War history)

San Diego Military Heritage Society
PO Box 33672
San Diego, CA 92163

2nd Armored Division Museum
(418 Battalion Avenue—location)
PO Box 5009 (mailing address)
Fort Hood, TX 76546
(254) 287-8812

Signal Archives
Command Historian
U.S. Army Signal Center and Fort Gordon
ATZH-MH, Fort Gordon
Fort Gordon, GA 30905
(706) 791-5212; (706) 791-5777 FAX

Sixth Cavalry Museum
2 Barnhardt Circle
Fort Oglethorpe, GA 30742
(706) 861-2860

Society of Civil War Historians
PO Box 7401
Little Rock, AR 72217
(501) 225-3996
Jerry L. Russell, Executive Secretary
Pub. *CWH Newsletter*
(no genealogical information)

Society of the Cincinnati Library
(see Lineage, Hereditary and Patriotic
Societies—Revolutionary War, Part 4)

Society of World War I Aero Historians
10443 South Memphis Avenue
Whittier, CA 90604

Soldiers' Memorial Military Museum
1315 Chestnut Street
Saint Louis, MO 63103
(314) 622-4550

Stones River National Battlefield
3501 Old Nashville Highway
Murfreesboro, TN 37129
(615) 893-9501; (615) 893-9508 FAX
STRI_Information@nps.gov
http://www.nps.gov/stri
James B. Lewis, Park Ranger
by appointment
(Civil War)

Tennessee and the Civil War
civilwar@tngenweb.org
http://www.tngennet.org/civilwar/index.html
Mitzi Freeman, TNGenWeb Civil War Host
(online databases, research tools, and links)

**Texas State Library and Archives
Commission**
Confederate Pensions Index
Texas Adjutant General Service Records
(see Texas, Part 2)

3rd Cavalry Museum
PO Box 12721
Colorado Springs, CO 80913
Paul D. Martin

U.S. Air Force in Utah Historical Society
Directorate of Material Management
Hill Air Force Base
Ogden, UT 84056
(801) 777-5076

United States Army Institute of Heraldry
9235 Gunston Road, Room S-112
Fort Belvoir, VA 22060-5579
(703) 806-4968; (703) 806-4969

**United States Army Military History
Institute**
22 Ashburn Drive
Carlisle, PA 17013-5008
(717) 245-3611; (717) 245-3205 (Online
Resources); (717) 245-4370 FAX (Online
Resources)
http://carlisle-www.army.mil/usamhi
John Slonaker, Chief, Reference Branch
Mon–Fri 8:00–4:30 (except federal holidays)
(electronic database containing 3,000

bibliographic references to MHI holdings
pertaining to specialized aspects of
military history; army unit histories; is
compiling a photographic collection of
those who fought in the Civil War)

United States Cavalry Association
(Building 247—location)
PO Box 2325 (mailing address)
Fort Riley, KS 66442
(785) 784-5797 voice & FAX
cavalry@flinthills.com
http://www.uscavalry.org
Patricia Spurrier Bright, Executive Director
Mon–Fri 8:00–4:00 and by appointment
Pub. *The Cavalry Journal*, quarterly; *The
Crossed Sabers*, quarterly
$30.00 per year membership

U.S. Cavalry Museum
(Building 205—location)
PO Box 2160 (mailing address)
Fort Riley, KS 66442
(785) 239-2737
Terry Van Meter, Museum Director
(specializes in First Infantry Division,
Cavalry)

United States Civil War Center
Louisiana State University
Raphael Semmes Drive
Baton Rouge, LA 70803
(225) 578-3151; (225) 578-4876 FA
http://www.cwc.lsu.edu
Mon–Fri 8:00–4:30
Newsletter, quarterly
("interdisciplinary study of Civil War")
Pub. $25.00+ per year membership

United States Coast Guard Academy
15 Mohegan Avenue
New London, CT 06320-4195
(860) 444-8501

**United States Coast Guard Historian's
Office (G-IPA-4)**
2100 Second Street, S.W.
Washington, DC 20593
(202) 267-2596; (202) 267-4309 FAX
sprice@comdt.uscg.mil
http://www.uscg.mil/hq/g-
cp/history/collect.html
Scott Price

United States Military Academy
Museum and Archives
Building 2107
Pershing Center
West Point, NY 10996-2099
(845) 938-7052
http://www.usma.edu/Museum

United States Mormon Battalion, Inc.
Californian Southern Division
6477 Elmhurst Drive
San Diego, CA 92120
(619) 582-7243

United States Naval Academy
Nimitz Library
589 McNair Road
Annapolis, MD 21402-5029
(410) 293-2220 (Special Collections); (410)
293-2178 (Archives)
cummings@nadn.navy.mil
http://www.nadn.navy.mil/Library

United States Naval Institute
United States Naval Academy Campus
118 Maryland Avenue
Annapolis, MD 21402-5035
(410) 268-6110

Part 4. Miscellaneous—Products and Services

http://www.usni.org

United States Naval War College
Library
Code 1E3
686 Cushing Road
Newport, RI 02841-1207
(401) 841-1435; (401) 841-3397; (401) 841-
4345 (Government Documents)
libref@usnwc.edu
http://users.ids.net/~nwcird

U.S. Navy Supply Corps Museum
U.S. Navy Supply Corps School
1425 Prince Avenue
Athens, GA 30606-2205
(706) 354-7349; (706) 354-7239 FAX
dan.roth@cnet.navy.mil
http://www.nscs.com
Dan Roth, Curator/Director
Mon–Fri 9:15–5:15
("Navy and Supply Corps directories, helpful
in tracing service records.")

Vallejo Naval and Historical Museum
734 Marin Street
Vallejo, CA 94590
(707) 643-0077; (707) 643-2443 FAX
valmuse@pacbell.net
http://www.vallejomuseum.org
James Kern, Executive Director
Pub. *VNHM Newsletter*, bi-monthly
(historical, not genealogical)
$25.00 per year membership

Department of Veterans Affairs
National Cemetery Administration (402B)
810 Vermont Avenue, N.W.
Washington, DC 20420
public.inquiry@mail.va.gov
http://www.cem.va.gov
Peggy McGee(402B)
7:00–4:30
(For national cemetery burial records during
and after the Civil War, supply full name,
dates and places of birth and death, state
from which entered military service, rank
and military unit in which served on
active duty.)
no charge

**Virginia Polytechnic Institute and State
University**
(see Virginia, Part 2)

Products and Services

All Topo Maps
iGage Mapping Corporation
(801) 412-0011; (888) 450-4922; (801) 412-
0022 FAX; (888) 450-4983 FAX
info7@igage.com
http://www.igage.com/whereto.htm
(includes list of topographical map dealers,
nationwide)

American Research
PO Box 4043
Salt Lake City, UT 84110-4043
(800) 488-6929
http://www.american-research.com
Rod Stucker, Accredited Genealogist

The Brinkley Press
7345 47th, N.E.
Seattle, WA 98115
(206) 524-1910
Allen Norris, President
9:00–5:30

Discount Equipment Sales
PO Box 222

Linn, TX 78563
(956) 383-8669
(microfiche readers)

Duplitech
(1560 Fir Street, South—location)
PO Box 4154 (mailing address)
Salem, OR 97302
(503) 378-0751
Jeff Murray, Owner
(photo restoration; photographic copy
service)

European Focus
508 Pineapple Avenue
Sarasota, FL 34236
(941) 330-0877; (800) 401-7802; (941) 330-
0878 FAX
EuroFocus@aol.com
http://www.eurofocus.com
James Derheim, Owner
(photos of ancestral towns and private
genealogical research tours)

Family History Company
PO Box 15905
Fort Wayne, IN 46885-5905
FamHistCo@aol.com
("Master genealogical forms set which can
be photocopies.")

Family Tree DNA
Genealogy by Genetics, Ltd.
1919 North Loop West, Suite 110
Houston, TX 77008
(713) 828-4200; (713) 868-4584 FAX
info@FamilyTreeDNA.com
http://www.familytreedna.com
Bennett Greenspan

Genealogy Unlimited, Inc.
(see Booksellers, Part 4)

The Gold Bug
PO Box 588
Alamo, CA 94507
(925) 838-MAPS
Art Lassagne
(old map reproductions)

The Heritage Project
PO Box 600
Franconia, NH 03580
(603) 823-5848
http://www.heritageproject.com
Sybil C. Carey
(publishes *The Heritage Project*, a complete
do-it-yourself oral-history package,
containing a booklet and two self-guiding
cassettes with tips on collecting oral
history, including sample interview
questions and pages to record
information)
$39.00 per unit plus $5.00 shipping and
handling in the U.S.

Just Black & White
(54 York Street—location)
PO Box 4628 (mailing address)
Portland, ME 04112
(207) 761-5861 (in Maine); (800) 827-5881
http://www.maine.com/photos
Tracey Mousseau
Mon–Fri 8:00–5:00
(copies, restoration and enhancements of old
photos, salt and albumen prints, tintypes,
daguerreotypes, ambrotypes)

KinShips
455 Morris, S.E.
Grand Rapids, MI 49503
ships@KinShipsPrints.com

http://kinshipsprints.com

MAPS
PO Box 119
Washington Court House, OH 43160-0119
(740) 335-0266; (740) 333-3530 FAX
Ms. Sandy Fackler, Owner
(specializes in maps)
price list for two first-class stamps and SAE

Old Photo Copying
3860 Weston Place
Long Beach, CA 90807-3317
(562) 427-8165
knatz@bcf.usc.edu
http://feefhs.org/photo/opc/frg-opc.html
John Mulvey
(reproduction, restoration and enlargements)

S & N Genealogy Supplies
100064.737@compuserve.com
http://www.genealogy.demon.co.uk
Nigel Bayley
24 hour information and ordering
(the leading genealogy supplier and
publisher for UK data and programs; free
catalog)

Sampubco
http://www.wasatch.com/~dsam/sampubco
W. David Samuelsen
(supplies photocopies of will record
including any attached proceedings, not a
mere transcription, from selected counties
in Alabama, Idaho, Iowa, Kansas, New
York, Ohio, Oregon, Pennsylvania, and
Texas)

Scholarly Resources, Inc.
104 Greenhill Avenue
Wilmington, DE 19805-1897
(302) 654-7713; (800) 772-8937; (302) 654-
3871 FAX
sales@scholarly.com
Roger Strong, Sales Manager
9:00–5:00
(authorized distributor for the National
Archives and Records Administration
[NARA], also publishes books)

Travel Genie Maps
3815 Calhoun Avenue
Ames, IA 50010-4106
(515) 232-1070
travgenie@aol.com
http://showcase.netins.net/web/travelgenie
Elaine Larson
primarily mail-order and online
(map grid brochures available online or by
mail: detailed sectional maps for Britain,
Denmark, Germany, Ireland, Norway,
Poland and Sweden)

Radio Programs

DearMYRTLE's Family History Hour
Internet Radio
(877) 638-7234
DearMYRTLE@aol.com
http://www.DearMYRTLE.com
broadcasts Tue–Thur 9:00–10:00 P.M.
   (Eastern Time)
("Live call-in talk radio show.")

Eagles Byte Historical Research
(see New York, Part 2)

Family History Show
PO Box 116605
Carrollton, TX 75011-6605
(972) 306-8000; (800) 765-1080
http://familyhistory.flash.net
Michael Matthews
broadcast live on KRLD 1080 AM: Sun
   10:00–midnight

Index

The Genealogist's Address Book

Dale E. Berger 470
Dalesburg-Hub City Historical Society 482
Dalesburg Scandinavian Association 616
Dallam-Hartley Counties Historical
  Association, Inc. 508
Dallas County East Genealogical Society
  514
Dallas County Genealogical Society 162
Dallas County Heritage Society, Inc. 508
Dallas County Historical Commission 508
Dallas County Historical Society 274
Dallas County Library 269
Dallas Genealogical Society 514
Dallas Historical Society 508
Dallas Jewish Historical Society 597
Dallas Morning News 688
Dallas Public Library 448
Dallas Public Library, Genealogy Section
  500
Dallas Public Library, Texas-Dallas History
  and Archives Division 500
Dalles-Wasco County Public Library 448
Dalton Community Historical Society 423
Dalton Historical Commission 217
Dalton Historical Society 300
Dalton Public Library 287
Dan Jones Research 693
Danbury Public Library 63
Danbury Scott-Fanton Museum and
  Historical Society, Inc. 67
Dancing Rabbit Genealogical Society 266
Dandridge Memorial Library 486
Dane County Genealogical Society 567
Dane County Historical Society 560
Daniels County Museum and Pioneer Town
  285
Danish American Fellowship 583
Danish-American Genealogical Group 583
Danish American Heritage Society 583
Danish Emigration Archives 583
Danish Immigrant Museum 583
Dansville Area Historical Society 349
Dansville Public Library 328
Danvers Historical Commission 217
Danvers Historical Society 112, 225
Danville-Boyle County Historical Society
  185
Danville Historical Archives 525
Danville Public Library 105, 131, 530
Darby Free Library 456
Darien Historical Society 67, 112
Darien Library 63
Darke County Genealogical Society 432
Darke County Historical Society, Inc. 423
Darke County Ohio Genealogical
  Researchers 437
Darlington County Historical Commission
  476
Darlington County Library 475
Darlington Public Library 131
Darnestown Historical Society 211
Dartford Historical Society 560
Dartmouth College 297
Data Base Systems (DBS) 682
Datatrace Systems 696
Daughters of American Pioneers 672
Daughters of Charity Archives—Albany 648
Daughters of Hawaii 670
Daughters of Old Westport 671
Daughters of the American Revolution 663
Daughters of the American Revolution,
  Francis Vigo Chapter DAR Genealogical
  Library 662
Daughters of the American Revolution, Ohio
  663
Daughters of the Cincinnati 663
Daughters of the Republic of Texas 671
Daughters of the Republic of Texas Library
  500
Daughters of the Union, 1861–1865 666
Daughters of Union Veterans of the Civil
  War, 1861–1865 666, 667

Daughters of Utah Pioneers Relic Hall 671
Davenport Historical Society 349
Davenport Public Library 153
David A. Howe Public Library 330
David Library of the American Revolution
  703
David Lipscomb University 627
David M. Roth Center for Connecticut
  Studies 63
Davidson County Historian 491
Davidson County Historical Association 403
Davidson County Historical Museum 399
Davidson County Public Library 399
Davidson University 399
Davie County Historical and Genealogical
  Society 403
Daviess County Historian 141
Daviess County Historical Society 141, 274
Davis and Elkins College 550
Davis County Genealogical Society 162
Davis County Historical Society 158
Davis Genealogy Club and Library 49
Dawes County Historical Society Museum
  290
Dawson County Historical and Genealogical
  Society 90
Dawson County Historical Society 290
Dawson County Library—Chestatee
  Regional Library 85
Dayton and Montgomery County Public
  Library 415
DCGenWeb 74
De Anza Trek Lancer Society 703
De Kalb County Historian 141
De Kalb County Historical Society 141
De Kalb County Indiana Genealogy Society
  149
De Pere Historical Society 561
De Soto Historical and Genealogical Society
  195
Dead River Area Historical Society 201
Deadwood Public Library 481
Deaf Smith County Genealogical Society
  514
Deaf Smith County Museum 500
Dearborn County Historian 141
Dearborn County Historical Society 141
*Dearborn County Register and Alsino Sun
  Recorder* 686
Dearborn Genealogical Society 246
Dearborn Historical Commission 241
DearMYRTLE's Family History Hour
  Internet Radio 708
Decatur County Chapter (IGS) 162
Decatur County Genealogical Society 94
Decatur County Genealogy Society 177
Decatur County Historian 141, 491
Decatur County Historical Society 90, 158
Decatur Genealogical Society 124
Decatur Public Library 105, 131
Decatur Township Historical Society 141
Decorah Genealogy Association 162
Decorah Public Library 153
Dedham Historical Society 225
Deer Isle-Stonington Historical Society 201
Deer Lodge Historical Society 491
Deer Park Independent School District
  Historical Museum 500
Deer Park Public Library 500
Deer Trail Pioneer Historical Society 59
Deerfield Area Historical Society 112
Deerfield Heritage Commission 300
Deerfield Historical Society 300
Defense Language Institute Historical
  Holding (Museum) 32
Defiance County County, Ohio Genealogical
  Society 432
Defiance County Historical Society-Au
  Glaize Village 423
Defiance Public Library 415
DeForest Area Historical Society 560
DeGenWeb 73

Dekalb County Historian 491
DeKalb County Historical-Genealogical
  Society 112
DeKalb County Historical Society 274
DeKalb County Public Library 85
DeKalb Historical Society, Inc. 90
DeKalb Public Library 105, 263
Del Mar Historical Society 41
Del Norte County Historical Society 41
DeLand Area Public Library 75
Delano Historical Society and Heritage Park
  41
Delaware & Hudson Canal Historical Society
  699
Delaware County Chapter (IGS) 162
Delaware County Genealogical Society 162,
  432, 445
Delaware County Historian 141, 350
Delaware County Historical Association 350
Delaware County Historical Society 141,
  158, 423, 461
Delaware County (Oklahoma) Historical
  Society 442
Delaware Genealogical Society 73
Delaware Geographic Names Committee 73
Delaware Public Archives 72
Delaware Society Daughters of the American
  Revolution 662
Delaware Society for the Preservation of
  Antiquities 73
Delaware Society, Sons of the American
  Revolution 664
Delaware State Library 72
Delaware State University 72
Delaware Swedish Colonial Society 615
Delhi Township Historical Society 423
Dells County Historical Society 561
Delphi Falls 370
Delphi Public Library 132
Delphos Historical Association 423
Delray Beach Historical Society 79
Delta County Genealogical Society 246
Delta County Historical Society 59
Delta Cultural Center 24
Delta Genealogical Interest Group 49
Delta Genealogical Society 94
DeMotte Public Library 132
Denison Historical Society 508
Denison Library Historical and Genealogical
  Society 508
Denison Public Library 508
Denison Society, Inc. 67
Denmark SIG 597
Dennis Historical Society 225
Dennis Memorial Library 306
Dennis Memorial Library Association 217
Dent County Historical Society 274
Denton County Genealogical Society 514
Denton County Historical Commission 508
Denton Public Library System-Emily Fowler
  Central Library 500
Denver City Museum 519
Denver Public Library 57
Denville Historical Society 310
Department of Children and Family Services
  676
Department of Children's Services 676
Department of Defense 3
Department of Homeland Security 3
Department of State 3
Department of Transportation and
  Development 197
Department of Veterans Affairs 707
DePaul University Archives 105
Depauville Library 350
DePauw University 132
Depreciation Lands Association 462
Derby Historical Society 67, 525
Derring Historical Society 300
Derry Area Historical Society 462
Derry Historical Society and Museum 300
Derry Township Historical Society 462

Double Check Research 673
Dougherty County Public Library 85
Douglas County Genealogical Society 124, 260
Douglas County Historical and Genealogical Society, Inc. 274
Douglas County Historical Society 59, 90, 172, 254, 482, 561
Douglas County, Kansas, Genealogical Society 177
Douglas County Library 295
Douglas County Library System 448
Douglas Historical Society, Inc. 226
Douglas Public Library District 57
Douglass Historical Museum 167
Douglaston and Little Neck Historical Society 350
Dover Area Historical Society 310
Dover-Foxcroft Historical Society 202
Dover Historical Society 158, 226, 423
Dover Public Library 72, 297
Downers Grove Park District Museum 105
Downey City Library 32
Downey Historical Society/Downey History Center 41
Downington Historical Commission 462
Downingtown Historical Society 462
Downriver Genealogical Society 246
Downs Carnegie Library 167
Downs Park Historical Society 211
Downstate Delaware Genealogical Society 73
Dr. Andrew T. Udvardy Reference Library 594
Dr. Asa Fitch Historical Society 354
Dr. Edwards Memorial Church 617
Dracut Historical Society, Inc. 226
Drake University 153
Draper Historical Society 522
Dresden Historical Society 202
Drew County Historical Society 26
Drummond Historical Society 442, 561
Drummond Island Historical Society 241
Drumright Historical Society, Inc. 442
Dryden Town Historical Society 350
Du Pont Historical Museum 541
Duarte Historical Society, Museum, and Friends of the Duarte Library 41
Dublin Historical Society 300, 423
Dublin Public Library 132
DuBois Area Historical Society 462
DuBois County Genealogical Society 149
DuBois County Historian 141
DuBois County Historical Society, Inc. 141
Dubuque County-Key City Genealogical Society 162
Duck Creek Historical Society 73
Duck's Old Time Journal 496
Duke University 399
Duke University Press 613
Dulany Memorial Library 269
Dull Knife Community College 285
Duluth Public Library 250
Dumas Genealogical and Historical Society 514
Dummer Historical Society 300
Dunbarton Historical Society 300
Duncan Cottage Museum 19
Duncan Lamont Clinch Historical Society 79
Duncanville Historical Commission 508
Duncanville Public Library 500
Dundalk-Patapsco Neck Historical Society 211
Dundee Area Historical Society 350
Dundee Township Historical Society 113
Dundee Township Library 105
Dundee Woman's Study Club and Library 328
Dunedin Historical Society/Museum 79
Dunellen Historical Society 310
Dunham Historical Society 482

Dunkirk Historical Museum 328
Dunklin County Genealogical Society 279
Dunklin County Library 269
Dunn County Genealogical Society 567
Dunn County Historical Society 411, 561
DuPage County Genealogical Society 124
DuPage County Historical Society 113
Duplin County Historical Society 403
Duplitech 707
DuQuoin Public Library 105
Durham Center Museum 328, 351
Durham County Library 399
Durham Historic Association, Inc. 300
Durham Historical Society 67, 202
Durham-Orange Genealogical Society 406
DuSable Museum of African American History, Inc. 578
Dutch Family Heritage Society 583
Dutch Fork Chapter (SCGS) 478
Dutch Settlers Society of Albany 393, 584
Dutchess County Genealogical Society 393
Dutchess County Historian 351
Dutchess County Historical Society 351
Duvall Historical Society 544
Duxbury Historical Commission 217
Duxbury Rural and Historical Society 226
Dwight D. Eisenhower Library and Museum 179
Dwight Historical Society 113
Dyer County Historian 491
Dyer Historical Society 141
Dyer Library Association 199
Dyer Memorial Library 217
Dyersville Historical Society 158

— E —

E. C. Scranton Memorial Library 65
E. G. Fisher Public Library 486
Eagle Historical Society 18
Eagle Public Library 99
Eagle River Historical Society 561
Eagle Rock Valley Historical Society 41
Eagle Valley Historical Society 59
Eagles Byte Historical Research 395
Eagleswood Historical Society 310
Earl Park Public Library 132
Earlham College 640
Earlville Community Historical Society 113
Early American Museum 105
Early American SIG 597
Early County Historical Society, Inc. 90
Early Mormon Research Institute 626
East Arkansas Community College 24
East Ascension Genealogical and Historical Society 196
East Baton Rouge Parish Library 191
East Baton Rouge Park and Recreation Commission 197
East Bay Genealogical Society 49
East Bell County Genealogical Society 514
East Benton County Historical Society 544
East Bridgewater Historical Commission 217
East Bridgewater Public Library 217
East Brunswick Historical Society 310
East Brunswick Museum Corporation 306
East Carroll Parish Library 191
East Chicago Historical Society 141
East Chicago Public Library 132
East Cuyahoga Chapter OGS 432
East Ely Railroad Depot Museum 700
East End Historical Association (Galveston County) 508
East Europe Connection 612
East Fork Valley Consortium 437
East Georgia Genealogical Society 94
East Granby Public Library 63
East Greenwich Free Library 472
East Haddam Historical Society 67
East Hampton Historical Society 351
East Hampton Library 328

East Hanover Historical Society 311
East Hartford Public Library System 63
East Haven Historical Society 67
East Hillsborough Historical Society 79
East Hounsfield Free Library 328
East Islip Historical Society 352
East Kentuckian 190
East Kern Genealogical Society 49
East LA/Orange County Region 48
East Liverpool Historical Society 423
East Longmeadow Historical Commission 217
East Machias Historical Society 202
East Orange Public Library 306
East Palestine Historical Society 423
East Point Historical Society, Inc. 90
East Quogue Historical Group 352
East Side Historical Society 113
East Springwater Historical Society 352
East Tennessee Heritage Foundation 496
East Tennessee Historical Society 491
East Tennessee Society for the Preservation of Friends (Quaker) History 640
East Texas Genealogical Society 514
East Texas Historical Association 508
East Troy Area Historical Society 561
East Windsor Historical Society, Inc. 67
East Yuma County Historical Society 59
Eastchester Historical Society 352
Eastern Arizona Museum and Historical Society 21
Eastern Band of Cherokee Office Headquarters 604
Eastern Baptist Theological Seminary 622
Eastern Cabarrus Historical Society and Museum 403
Eastern California Museum 32
Eastern Colorado Historical Society (Cheyenne County) 59
Eastern Illinois University 102
Eastern Kentucky Genealogical Society 188
Eastern Kentucky University 181
Eastern Lewis County Historical Society 544
Eastern Nebraska Genealogical Society 292
Eastern New Mexico University (ENMU) 321
Eastern Oklahoma Historical Society and Carl Albert State College 442
Eastern Oregon Museum 454
Eastern Oregon State College 448
Eastern Shawnee Tribe of Oklahoma 604
Eastern Shore of Virginia Historical Society 534
Eastern Shore of Virginia Public Library 530
Eastern Slovakia, Slovak and Carpatho-Rusyn Genealogical Research Page 612
Eastern Washington Genealogical Society 547
Eastern Washington Genealogical Society, Metis Genealogical Society Chapter 547
Eastford Historical Society 67
Eastham Historical Society, Inc. 226
Eastham Public Library 217
Easthampton Historical Commission 217
Easton Area Public Library 456
Easton Historical Commission 217
Easton Historical Society 202, 226
Eastside Genealogical Society 547
Eastville Community Historical Society 352
Eaton County Genealogical Society 246
Eaton Florida History Room 75
Eatonton-Putnam County Historical Society, Inc. 90
Eatontown Historical Committee 311
Eatonville Historical Society 544
Eckhart Public Library 132
Eckles Memorial Library 153
Ecorse Public Library 236
Ector County Library 500
Ed Nugent's Family Tree 673

American Indian and Pioneer Life 604
Friends of the Mitchell Public Library
Research Committee 246
Friends of the North Country, Inc. 329
Friends of the Nyacks, Inc. 355
Friends United Meeting 641
Friends University 167, 641
Friendship Free Library 329
Friendship Hill Association 462
Friendship Museum, Inc. 207
Frisco Historical Society 59
Frisian Roundtable 584
Frontenac Historical Society 355
Frontier County Genealogical Society 293
Frontier Heritage Library 154
Frontier Historical Society (Garfield County)
59
Frontier Museum 413
Frontier Press 692
Frontier Researchers Genealogical Society
29
Frontier Times Museum 519
Fruitlands Museums, Inc. 234
Fryeburg Historical Society/Museum 202
Fryer Memorial Museum 329
Fulda Heritage Society 254
Full Gospel Assemblies International 633
Full Gospel Fellowship of Churches and
Ministers International 633
Fulton County/Atlanta-Fulton Public Library
85
Fulton County Chapter OGS 432
Fulton County Genealogical Society 188
Fulton County Historian 355
Fulton County Historical and Genealogical
Society 114
Fulton County Historical Society 142, 424,
463
Fulton County-Johnson Township Public
Library 132
Fulton County Public Library 181
Fulton Public Library 329
Furnas County Genealogical Society 293
Furnas County Historical Society 290

— G —

G.A.R. Memorial and Veterans' Military
Museum 667
G-Tree 673
Gadsden-Etowah County Public Library 11
Gage County Historical Society 290
GaGenWeb 95
Gahanna Historical Society 424
Gail Borden Public Library District 103
Gainesville Heritage Group 90
Galax-Carroll Regional Library 531
Gale Free Library 218
Galen Historical Society 355
Galena/Jo Daviess County Historical Society
and Museum 114
Galena Mining and Historical Museum
Association, Inc. 167
Galena Public Library 106, 167
Galesburg Memorial Library 236
Galesburg Public Library 106
Galewood-Mont Clare Historical Society
114
Galion Historical Society, Inc. 424
Galizien German Descendants (GGD) 588
Gallacia Historical Society 114
Gallatin County Historical Society 114, 185
Gallatin County Historical Society and
Pioneer Museum 283
Gallatin County Public Library 181
Gallatin Genealogy Society 285
Gallia County Historical/Genealogical
Society 424
Gallier House Museum 192
Galloway Township Historical Society 311
Galt Historical Society 41
Galva Historical Society/Wiley House

Museum 114
Galveston County Genealogical Society 514
Galveston County Historical Museum 501
Galveston Daily News 688
Galveston Historical Foundation 508
Gangster Chronicles 696
Gann Museum of Saline County 24
Garden City Historical Commission 242
Garden City Public Library 99, 329
Garden Prairie Genealogical and Historical
Society 125
Garden Valley Library 99
Gardena Library 580
Gardiner Public Library 199
Garfield County Genealogical Society 445
Garfield County Historical Society 290, 442
Garfield County Museum 285
Garfield Farm Museum 128
Garfield Heritage Society 114
Garland County Historical Society 27
Garland County Library 24
Garland Genealogical Society 515
Garnavillo Historical Society 158
Garner Public Library 154
Garrard County Historical Society 185
Garrard County Public Library 181
Garretson Area Historical Society 482
Garrett County Historical Society, Inc. 211
Garrett Historical Society 142
Garrett Public Library 132
Gary Historical and Cultural Society 142
Gary Historical Association 482
Gary Public Library 133
Gas City Historical Society 142
Gas City-Mill Township Public Library 133
Gasconade County Historical Society 275
Gassaway Public Library 550
Gastineau Channel Historical Society 18
Gastineau Genealogical Society 19
Gaston County Historical Society, Inc. 403
Gaston-Lincoln Genealogical Society 406
Gaston-Lincoln Regional Library 399
Gates County Historical Society 403
Gates Mills Historical Society 424
Gates Public Library 329
Gatesville Public Library 501
Gateway Press, Inc. 691
Gateway to the Panhandle 439
Gay-Kimball Public Library 297
Gaylord Fact-Finders Genealogical Society
246
Gaylordsville Historical Society 67
Geary County Historical Society (Museum)
172
Geauga County Chapter OGS 432
Geauga County Historical Society 424
Gem County Historical Society 100
Gem Village Museum 57
GENCOM PC User Group of Shreveport
198
GENDEX 681
Gene Pool 681
Genealogical Advisor 62
Genealogical and Heraldic Institute of
America 595
Genealogical and Historical Council of
Sacramento Valley 51
Genealogical and Historical Society of
Caldwell County 513
Genealogical Association of English
Speaking Researchers in Europe 9, 585
Genealogical Association of Sacramento 51
Genealogical Center Library 85
Genealogical Computer Society of Georgia
681
Genealogical Computer Society of Western
Maryland 681
Genealogical Computing Association of
Pennsylvania (GENCAP) 681
Genealogical Council of Oregon 452
Genealogical Forum of Elmhurst, Illinois
124

Genealogical Forum of Oregon, Inc. 452
Genealogical Friends of the Pasadena Public
Library 51
Genealogical Institute, Inc. 10
Genealogical Institute of Oklahoma 444
Genealogical Publishing Company, Inc. 689
Genealogical Queries Magazine 10
Genealogical Questers 125
Genealogical Research and Consultation
437
Genealogical Research Associates 685
Genealogical Research Center and Library of
Southeast Texas 504
Genealogical Research Directory 10
Genealogical Research in Caldwell County,
N.C. 408
Genealogical Research Institute of Virginia
"GRIVA" 537
Genealogical Research Society of Durango
61
Genealogical Research Society of Eau Claire
567
Genealogical Research Society of New
Orleans 197
Genealogical Research Society of
Northeastern Pennsylvania (GRSNP) 470
Genealogical Roundtable 233
Genealogical Roundtable of Monroe County
394
Genealogical Society: Fayette and Raleigh
Counties, Inc. 554
Genealogical Society of Adams County 266
Genealogical Society of Bergen County, N.J.
318
Genealogical Society of Broward County 81
Genealogical Society of Butler County,
Missouri, Inc. 278
Genealogical Society of Carlton County 260
Genealogical Society of Carter County 278
Genealogical Society of Cecil County 213
Genealogical Society of Central Missouri
278
Genealogical Society of Coachella Valley 48
Genealogical Society of Collier County 81
Genealogical Society of Cumberland and
Coles County 124
Genealogical Society of Davidson County
406
Genealogical Society of DeSoto County,
Mississippi 266
Genealogical Society of Douglas County
453
Genealogical Society of East Alabama 15
Genealogical Society of Finland 585
Genealogical Society of Flemish-Americans
581
Genealogical Society of Greater Miami 81
Genealogical Society of Hancock County,
Kentucky 188
Genealogical Society of Henry and Clayton
Counties, Inc. 94
Genealogical Society of Henry County
Indiana 149
Genealogical Society of Hispanic America
614
Genealogical Society of Iredell County 406
Genealogical Society of Kendall County 516
Genealogical Society of Linn County, Iowa
163
Genealogical Society of Madera County 50
Genealogical Society of Marion County 149
Genealogical Society of Minnesota 260
Genealogical Society of Monroe County, MI
247
Genealogical Society of Morongo Basin 50
Genealogical Society of New Jersey 318
Genealogical Society of North Brevard
(GSNB) 82
Genealogical Society of North Orange
County California (GSNOCC) 49
Genealogical Society of Okaloosa County
82

Indian and Colonial Research Center 604
Indian City U.S.A., Inc. 604
Indian Grinding Rock State Historic Park 54
Indian Heritage Museum 604
Indian Hill Historical Society 425
Indian Lake Museum 396
Indian Museum of the Carolinas, Inc. 605
Indian Pueblo Cultural Center, Inc. 605
Indian River County Historical Society 79
Indian River County Main Library 76
Indian River Genealogical Society 81
Indian Temple Mound Museum 605
Indian Territory Genealogical Society 605
Indian Territory Society—Military Order of the Stars and Bars 668
Indian Village Association 605
Indian Wells Valley Genealogical Society 49
Indiana Adoption Coalition 677
Indiana Department of Transportation 152
Indiana Genealogical Society, Inc. 148
Indiana German Heritage Society, Inc. 591
Indiana Historical Bureau 129
Indiana Historical Society 129, 578
Indiana in the Civil War 704
Indiana Junior Historical Society 143
Indiana Province Archives Center 649
Indiana Religious History Association 620
Indiana Society, Sons of the American Revolution 664
Indiana State Archives 129
Indiana State Department of Health 5
Indiana State Library 129
Indiana State University 133
Indiana University 641
Indiana University—Bloomington 133
Indiana University Folklore Institute 152
Indiana University Northwest 143
Indiana University of Pennsylvania 463
Indiana University-Purdue University at Fort Wayne 133
Indianapolis-Marion County Public Library 133
Indianapolis Star 686
Indianola Public Library 154
Information Center (Petersburg, Virginia) 531
InfoTech Publications 281
InGenWeb 152
Ingham County Commission on History 249
Ingleside-On-The-Bay Historical Society/Museum 509
Inman Heritage Association 173
Institute for American Indian Studies 605
Institute for Boston Studies 234
Institute for Massachusetts Studies 234
Institute for Migration and Ancestral Research 680
Institute of Family History and Genealogy 233
Institute of Scottish Studies 611
Institutions Lily Dale 345
Interlaken Historical Society 359
International Association of Jewish Genealogical Societies (IAJGS) 598
International Church of the Foursquare Gospel 634
International Communion of the Charismatic Episcopal Church 632
International Council of Community Churches 620
International District, Sons of the American Revolution 664
International Genealogical Directory 673
International Genealogy and Heraldry Fellowship of Rotarians 698
International Genealogy Consumer Organization 685
International Museum of Cultures 575
International Order of Job's Daughters 698
International Order of Odd Fellows (IOOF) 698

International Pentecostal Church of Christ 634
International Pentecostal Holiness Church 634
International Society, Daughters of Utah Pioneers 671
International Society for British Genealogy and Family History 585
International Society of the Descendants of Charlemagne 672
International Soundex Reunion Registry (I.S.R.R.) 677
Interstate Library Contract 12
Iola Historical Society 562
Iola Public Library 168
Ionia County Genealogical Society 247
Ionia County Historical Society 242
Iosco-Arenac District Library 237
Iosco County Historical Society and Museum 242
Iowa City Genealogical Society 163
Iowa City Public Library 154
Iowa County Genealogical Society 568
Iowa County Genealogy Society 163
Iowa County Historical Society 158, 562
Iowa Department of Public Health 5
Iowa Department of Transportation 165
Iowa Genealogical Society (IGS) 160
Iowa Historical Information 165
Iowa Lakes Genealogical Society 163
Iowa Masonic Library 698
Iowa Reunion Registry 677
Iowa Society Daughters of the American Revolution 662
Iowa Society of Mayflower Descendants 660
Iowa Society, Sons of the American Revolution 664
Iowa State University 154
Iowa Welsh Society-Cymdeithas Gymreig Iowa 618
Ipswich Historical Society 227
Iredell County Public Library 400
Irish America Magazine/Irish Voice Newspaper 594
Irish American Cultural Institute (IACI) 594
Irish American Heritage Center 594
Irish Cultural Center Library 595
Irish Family Group Sheet Exchange (IFGSX) 673
Irish Family History Forum, Inc. 595
Irish Family History Foundation 595
Irish Genealogical Foundation 595
Irish Genealogical Society, International (IGSI) 595
Irish Genealogical Society of Wisconsin 595
Irish Interest Group of Portland 595
Iron County Historical and Museum Society 242
Iron County Historical Society 275, 522, 562
Iron Horse Historical Society 700
Iron Range Historical Society 255
Iron Range Research Center Library and Archives 251
Irondequoit Historical Office and Museum 359
Irondequoit Public Library 330
Ironwood Historical Society 242
Iroquois County Genealogical Society 125
Iroquois County Historical Society 115
Iroquois Indian Museum 605
Irvine Historical Society and Museum 42
Irving Genealogical Society 516
Irving Park Historical Society 115
Irving Public Library 502
Irvington Historical Society 143, 312, 359
Irvington Public Library 306
Isaac Franck Jewish Public Library 597
Isabella Community Council 255
Isanti County Historical Society 255
Ischua Valley Historical Society 359

Islamic Center of New York 634
Islamic Center of North America 634
Islamic Center of Washington 634
Island County Historical Society 545
Island Falls Historical Society 202
Island Heights Cultural and Heritage Association 319
Island Pond Historical Society, Inc. 526
Isle a la Cache Museum 696
Isle La Motte Historical Society 526
Islesboro Historical Society 202
Islesford Historical Society 203
Islip Hamlet Historical Society 359
Issaquah Historical Society 545
Italian American Cultural Society 595
Italian Cultural Center 595
Italian Cultural Society 595
Italian Genealogical Group 595
Italian Genealogy Homepage 595
Italian Genealogy Interest Group 595
Italian Genealogy Society of America 596
Italo-Albanian Home Page 596
Itasca County Genealogical Club 260
Itasca County Historical Society 255
Itasca Historical Society 115
Itawamba County Historical Society 265
Iuka Public Library 263
IUPUI 133
Izard County Historical and Genealogical Society 27

— J —

J & W Publications 198
J. B. Cain Archives of Mississippi Methodism 652
J. C. Holliday Memorial Library 400
J. Robert Jamerson Memorial Library 531
J. T. & E. J. Crumbaugh Memorial Public Library 104
J. V. Fletcher Library 218
Jackman-Moose River Historical Society 203
Jackson Assembly, Inc. 195
Jackson Barracks Military Library 704
Jackson Center Historical Society 425
Jackson City Library 416
Jackson County Chapter OGS 433
Jackson County Genealogical Chapter (IGS) 163
Jackson County Genealogical Society 15, 150, 247, 266, 279, 407
Jackson County Historian 143, 492
Jackson County Historical Association 14, 403
Jackson County Historical Society 27, 91, 115, 143, 158, 173, 265, 275, 552, 562
Jackson County Historical Society and Museum 255
Jackson County Public Library 76, 133, 182, 550
Jackson County Public Library/Main Branch 448
Jackson County, WI, Genealogy 569
Jackson District Library 237
Jackson-George Regional Library System 263
Jackson Heritage Museum and Fine Arts Association 192
Jackson Historical Society 301, 562
Jackson Homestead 219
Jackson/Madison County Library 486
Jackson Township Historical Society 425
Jacksonville Area Genealogical and Historical Society 125
Jacksonville Genealogical Society, Inc. 81
Jacksonville Public Libraries 76
Jacksonville Public Library 502
Jacob and Bernard Hostert Log Cabins 128
Jacob S. Mauney Memorial Library 400
Jacobsburg Historical Society 463
Jacques Timothé Boucher de Montbrun

Liberal Memorial Library 169
Liberty County Historical Commission 509
Liberty County Historical Society 91
Liberty County Museum 285
Liberty Gazette 688
Liberty Hall Historic Center 165
Liberty Historical Society 203
Liberty Memorial Museum of World War I 704
Libertyville-Mundelein Historical Society, Inc. 117
Library and Historical Museum (Shaw Island) 543
Library and Museum of Slovak Language, History, Literature, and Culture 612
Library Company of Philadelphia 458
Library District #1, Doniphan County 167
Library Microfilms 690
Library of Congress 74
Library of Hattiesburg, Petal and Forrest County 263
Library of Michigan 235
Library of the Boston Athenaeum 216
Library of the Chathams 306
Library of Virginia 529
Licking County Genealogical Society 433
Licking County Historical Society 426
Lietuvos Bajoru Karaliskoji Sajunga (LBKS) 602
Life Adoption Ministry 677
Lifeline International 677
Light of Parnell Bookshop 693
Lightning Source, Inc. 691
Ligonier Public Library 134
Ligonier Valley Historical Society 464
Liles Memorial Library 12
Lima Historical Society 362
Lima Public Library 417
Limaville Historical Society, Inc. 426
Lime Creek/Winnebago County Genealogical Society 163
Limerick Historical Society 203
Limerick Township Historical Society 464
Limestone County Archives 12
Limestone County Historical Society 14
Limington Historical Society 203
Lincoln City Libraries 288
Lincoln County Archives 487
Lincoln County Cultural and Historical Association 203
Lincoln County Department of Social Services 677
Lincoln County Genealogical Society 279, 495, 554
Lincoln County Historical Association 403
Lincoln County Historical Museum and Society 291
Lincoln County Historical Society 60, 91, 173, 186, 256, 442, 451, 493, 545, 571
Lincoln County Library 282
Lincoln County Montana Genealogical Society 285
Lincoln County Museum 296
Lincoln County Public Library 263, 400
Lincoln County Tennessee Pioneers 497
Lincoln Courtroom and Museum 107
Lincoln Group of Boston 697
Lincoln Historical Commission 219
Lincoln Historical Society 227, 526
Lincoln-Lancaster County Genealogical Society 293
Lincoln/Lancaster Historical Society 291
Lincoln Library 107
Lincoln Memorial Shrine 705
Lincoln Parish Library 192
Lincoln Park Historical Museum and Society 243
Lincoln Park Historical Society 212
Lincoln Public Library 472
Lincoln University 578
Lincolnville Historical Society and School House Museum 203

Lincolnwood Public Library District 107
Linden Carnegie Public Library 135
Linden Historical Society 562
Linden-Madison Township Historical Society 144
Linden Tree 690
Lindenhurst Historical Society 362
Lindsay's Books, Inc. 693
Lindsborg Community Library 169
Lindstrom Historical Society 256
Lineage Search Associates 539
Lineages, Inc. 539
Linebaugh Public Library 487
Linesville Historical Society 464
Linfield College Library 622
Link O Mania Scotland on the Web 611
Links Genealogy Publications 592
Linn County Historical and Genealogical Society 173
Linn County Historical Museum and Moyer House 449
Linn County Historical Society 159, 451
Linn County, Missouri Genealogy Researchers 279
Linn Genealogical Society 453
Linn Library 270
Linwood Historical Society 313
Lions Clubs International Headquarters 699
Lipscomb County Historical Commission 509
Lisbon Historical Society 203, 426
Lisle Heritage Society 117
Litchfield Carnegie Public Library 107
Litchfield Historical Society 68
Lithuanian Research List 602
Lithuanian Special Interest Group, Inc. (LitvakSIG) 600
Lititz Historical Foundation, Inc. 464
Little Beaver Historical Society, Inc. 464
Little Canada Historical Society 256
Little Compton Historical Society 473
Little Dixie Regional Libraries 270
Little Falls Historical Society 313
Little Falls Historical Society Museum 362
Little Falls Public Library 307, 331
Little Falls Township Historical Society 313
Little Landers Historical Society 43
Little Nine Partners 362
Little Norway, Inc. 608
Little Red Schoolhouse 331
Little Red Schoolhouse Association 234
Little Red Schoolhouse Historical Society 362
Little Silver Historical Society 313
Little Thompson Valley Pioneer Museum 60
Little Traverse Regional Historical Society 243
Littleton Area Historical Society 302
Littleton/Edwin A. Bemis Public Library 56
Littleton Historical Museum 57
Littleton Historical Society 227
Live Oak Public Libraries 86
Livermore-Amador Genealogical Society (LAGS) 49
Livermore Heritage Guild 43
Livermore Public Library 155
Liverpool Township Historical Society 426
Living History Farms 165
Living Museum of Avon 64
Livingston County Genealogical Society 247, 279, 394
Livingston County Historian 362
Livingston County Historical Society 117, 362
Livingston County Library 270
Livingston Historical Society 313
Livingston Parish Library 192
Livingston-Park County Public Library 282
Livonia Area Preservation and Historical Society 362
Livonia Historical Society 243
Lloyd Harbor Historical Society 363

Lloyd Historical Society 363
Locators Unlimited 677
Locke History Explorers 363
Lockport Public Library 331
Locust Valley Historical Society 363
Locust Valley Library 331
Lodi Historical Society 363
Logan County District Library 417
Logan County Genealogical Society 61, 186, 433, 445, 554
Logan County Historical Society 27, 291, 411, 442
Logan County Historical Society and Museum 426
Logan County Public Library 182
Logan Library 521
Logansport-Cass County Public Library 135
Lohefener House Museum and Gifts 270
Lombard Historical Society 117
Lomita Historical Society 43
Lompoc Public Library 34
Lompoc Valley Genealogical Society (formerly Vandenberg Genealogical Society) 49
Lompoc Valley Historical Society, Inc. 43
Londonderry Historical Society 302, 526
Lone Star Junction 519
Long Beach Historical Society 363
Long Beach Island Historical Association 313
Long Beach Public Library 34
Long Branch Free Public Library 307
Long Branch Historical Museum 307
Long Grove Historical Society 117
Long Hill Township Historical Society 313
Long Island University 331
Longmeadow Historical Society 227
Longmire Museum 549
Longmont Genealogical Society 61
Longmont Public Library 57
Longport Historical Society 313
Longview Morning Journal 688
Longview Public Library 502, 542
Longwood Public Library 331
Longyear Museum 624
Lonoke County Historical Society 27
Loogootee Public Library 135
Loogootee Tribune 686
Looking Glass 30
Lopez Island Historical Society and Museum 545
Lorain County Chapter OGS 433
Lorain County Historical Society 426
Lorain Public Library 417
Lorenzo State Historic Site 331
Los Alamos County Historical Society 322
Los Alamos Genealogical Association 323
Los Altos Hills Historical Society 43
Los Altos Historical Commission 43
Los Angeles City Historical Society 43
Los Angeles Corral of Westerners 55
Los Angeles County Adoption Search Association 677
Los Angeles Public Library 34
Los Angeles Times Syndicate 685
Los Angeles Westside Genealogical Society 50
Los Banos Genealogical Society, Inc. 50
Los Bexareños Genealogical Society 516
Los Californianos, Hispanic Ancestors of Alta California 614
Los Descendientes del Presidio de Tucson 614
Los Fundadores, The Founders and Friends of Santa Clara County 54
Los Pobladores 200 54
Lost and Found National Genealogical Query Newsletter 10
Lost City Museum 296
Lost Creek Lineage Company 152
Lost Nation Public Library 155
Loudon County Heritage Association 493

Phillipsburg City Library 169
Phillipsburg Free Public Library 308
Philomathean Free Library 334
Phippsburg Historical Society, Inc. 204
Phoenix Genealogical Society 23
Phoenix Museum of History 20
Phoenix Public Library 21
Photoduplication Service, Library of
    Congress 694
Piatt County Historical and Genealogical
    Society 119
Piatt County Museum 108
Pickaway County Historical Society Chapter
    OGS 428
Pickens County Cooperative Library 12
Pickens County Historical Society 477
Pickens County Library 476
Pickering-Beach Historical Museum 334
Pickett County Historian 493
Picton Press 690
Piedmont Historical and Genealogical
    Society 14
Piedmont Historical Society 477
Piedmont Regional Genealogy Society 95
Piedmont Regional Library 87
Pierce Brigade 305
Pierce County Historical Association 564
Pierceton and Washington Township Public
    Library 137
Piermont Historical Society 303
Piermont Public Library 334
Pierre-Fort Pierre Genealogical Society
    (SDGS) 483
Pierrepont Museum 397
Pieter Claesen Wyckoff House Museum 337
Pig's Eye's Notepad—Historical
    Encyclopedia of Saint Paul 1830–1850
    262
Piggott Public Library 25
Pike-Amite-Walthall Library System 264
Pike and Calhoun Counties Genealogical
    Society 127
Pike County Archives 30
Pike County Genealogical Society 280, 434
Pike County Historian 146
Pike County Historical and Genealogical
    Society 14
Pike County Historical Society 466
Pike County Historical Society and Museum
    119, 146
Pike County Public Library 137
Pike County Society for Historical and
    Genealogical Research 187
Pike Heritage Foundation 418
Pikes Peak Genealogical Society 61
Pikes Peak Library District 58
Pikeville Public Library 183
Pilesgrove-Woodstown Historical Society
    315
Pilgrim Society 221
Pilgrims of the United States 662
Pillar of Fire 638
Pillsbury Free Library 298
Pilot Point Community Library 503
Pilot Tribune 687
Pimeria Alta Historical Society 22
Pinal County Historical Society, Inc. 22
Pinckney Area Historical Society 244
Pinckney District Chapter (SCGS) 479
Pine Bluff/Jefferson County Public Library
    25
Pine County Historical Society 257
Pine Grove Historical Society 466
Pine Mountain Regional Library 87
Pinellas County Historical Society 80
Pinellas Genealogy Society, Inc. 82
Piney Woods Pioneer Genealogical Society
    517
Pioneer America Society 697
Pioneer and Historical Society of
    Muskingum County 436
Pioneer Association/Pioneer Women 670

Pioneer City/County Museum 503
Pioneer Club of Western South Dakota 484
Pioneer Daughters 671
Pioneer Genealogical Society 446
Pioneer Genealogy Society 697
Pioneer Heritage Public Library 156
Pioneer Historic Society 92
Pioneer Historical Society 60, 160, 412, 443
Pioneer Historical Society for Sheridan
    County 412
Pioneer Historical Society of Bedford
    County 460
Pioneer Historical Society of Riverside 44
Pioneer Memorial Museum 286
Pioneer Museum and Art Center 440
Pioneer Publications 71, 73, 152, 166, 409,
    437, 595
Pioneer Sons and Daughters Chapter (IGS)
    164
Pioneer Town 520
Pioneer, Trail Driver and Former Texas
    Rangers Association, Inc. 503
Pioneer Trails Historical Society 412
Pioneer Utah's Online Electronic Library
    671
Pioneer Village Commission 166
Piper City Community Historical Society
    119
Pipestone County Genealogical Society 261
Pipestone County Historical Society and
    Museum 257
Piscataqua Pioneers 304, 670
Piscataway Historical and Heritage Society
    315
Piseco Lake Historical Society 375
Pitt County Family Researchers 407
Pitt County Historical Society 404
Pittsburg County Genealogical and Historical
    Society 446
Pittsburg Historical Society 303
Pittsburg Public Library 169
Pittsburgh Adoption Lifeline 678
Pittsburgh History and Landmarks
    Foundation 458
Pittsfield Historical Society 204, 303, 527
Pittsford Historical Society 527
Pittstown Historical Society 375
Pittsylvania Historical Society 536
Placer County Archives and Research Center
    (Department of Museums) 36
Placer County Genealogical Society 51
Plainfield-Guilford Township Public Library
    137
Plainfield Historical Society 230, 303
Plainfield Historical Society Museum 119
Plainfield Public Library 108
Plains and Emigrant Tribes of Kansas 606
Plains Genealogical Society 293
Plains Historic Preservation Trust, Inc. 96
Plains Historical Society 291
Plains Indians and Pioneers Historical
    Foundation 443
Plainsboro Historical Society, Inc. 315
Plainview-Old Bethpage Public Library 334
Plainville Historical Society, Inc. 69
Plaistow Historical Society 303
Plano Community Library District 108
Plano Public Library System 503
Plantagenet Society 672
Plantation Society in the Americas 697
Plaquemines Deep Delta Genealogical
    Society 197
Plaquemines Parish Library 193
Platte County Genealogical Society 280
Platte County Historical Society 291
Platte County Historical Society and
    Museum 277
Platte County Public Library 570
Platte Valley Kin Seekers 293
Plattsburgh Public Library 334
Plattsburgh State University of New York
    336

Pleasant Grove Historical Commission 14
Pleasant Hill Historical Society, Inc. 277
Pleasant Hill Historical Society of the
    Cumberlands, Inc. 493
Pleasanton Library 36
Pleasants County Historical Society 553
Pleasants County Public Library 551
Plumas County Historical Society 44
Plumas County Museum Association 36
Plymouth Area Historical Society 428
Plymouth Cambrian Society 616
Plymouth County Genealogists, Inc. 233
Plymouth County Historical Museum 166
Plymouth Hereditary Society 670
Plymouth Historical Museum 238, 305
Plymouth Historical Society 69, 257, 303,
    466
Plymouth Meeting Historical Society 466
Plymouth Public Library 137, 221, 559
Pocahontas County Historical Society 160,
    553
Pocahontas Public Library 156
Pocahontas Trails Genealogical Society 51,
    453
Pocatello Branch Genealogical Society 101
Poestenkill Historical Society 375
Poinsett County Historical Society 27
Point Coupee Parish Library 193
Point Pleasant Historical Society 315
POINT/POINTers (Pursuing Our Italian
    Names Together) 596
Pointe de l'Eglise: Acadia Genealogical and
    Historical Society, Inc. 197
Pokrajinski Arhiv Maribor 612
Polish American Cultural Center 609
Polish American Cultural Institute of
    Minnesota 609
Polish American Historical Association 609
Polish American Museum 609
Polish Genealogical Society of America 609
Polish Genealogical Society of California
    609
Polish Genealogical Society of Greater
    Cleveland 609
Polish Genealogical Society of
    Massachusetts 609
Polish Genealogical Society of Michigan
    609
Polish Genealogical Society of Minnesota
    609
Polish Genealogical Society of New York
    State (PGSNYS) 609
Polish Genealogical Society of the Northeast
    609
Polish Genealogical Society of Wisconsin
    609
Polish Historical Commission 610
Polish Museum of America Library 610
Polish National Alliance 610
Polish National Catholic Church
    Commission on History and Archives
    637
Polish National Catholic Church of America
    637
Polish Nobility Association Foundation 610
Polishville Cemetery and Grotto Association
    and Esther Johanna Peck Museum 610
Polk County Genealogical Society 453
Polk County Genealogical Society (PCGS)
    29
Polk County Heritage Society 510
Polk County Historian 493
Polk County Historical and Genealogical
    Library 77
Polk County Historical and Genealogical
    Society 493
Polk County Historical Association 80
Polk County Historical Society 92, 160,
    257, 451, 564
Polk County Library 25
Polk County Museum Historical Society 291
Polk County North Carolina Genealogical

Putnam County Historical Society 120, 146, 429
Putnam County Historical Society and Foundry School Museum 376
Putnam County Library 271, 488, 551
Putnam County Library System 77
Putnam County Public Library 137
Putnam Museum Library 156
Putnam Valley Historical Society 376
Putney Historical Society 527

— Q —

Q. M. Dabney & Co. 693
Quaker Corner 641
Quaker Queries 641
Quaker Yeomen 641
Quakertown Historical Society, Inc. 466
Quapaw Tribal Business Committee 607
Quechan Indian Museum 607
Queen Anne's County Free Library 209
Queen Anne's County Historical Society 212
Queens Borough Public Library 334
Queens County Historian 376
Queens Historical Society (QHS) 376
Questing Heirs Genealogical Society 51
Quincy Historic Commission 221
Quincy Historical Society 230
Quincy Museum 108
Quincy Public Library 108
Quinsept, Inc. 683
Quitman-Brooks County Genealogical Society 95
Quitman Public Library 504
Quogue Historical Society 376

— R —

R. C. Baker Memorial Museum, Inc. 31
R. T. Elethorp Historical Society 352
Rabbinic Genealogy Special Interest Group (Rav-SIG) 601
Rabun County Historical Society 92
Racine County Historical Society and Museum, Inc. 565
Racine Heritage Museum 559
Racine Public Library 559
Radford Public Library 532
Radio Prague History Online 583
Radnor Heritage Society 617
Radnor Historical Society 466
Ragersville Historical Society, Inc. 429
Rahway Historical Society, Inc. 316
Rails and Trails Museum 701
Rainbow Families, Inc. 678
Rainy River Valley Genealogical Society 261
Raleigh County Historical Society 553
Ralls County Historical Society 277
Ralls Historical Museum 504
Ralph L. Milliken Museum 34
Ramapogue Historical Society 230
Ramona Museum of California History 36
Ramona Pioneer Historical Society and Guy B. Woodward Museum 45
Ramsey County Historical Society 257
Ramsey County Library 251
Ramsey Free Public Library 308
Ramsey Historical Association 316
Rancho Bernardo Genealogy Group 51
Rancho Cordova Community Library 36
Rancho Los Cerritos Historic Site 55
Rancho Santa Fe Historical Society 45
Rand Genealogy Club 682
Randall Library 221
Randolph Area Genealogical Society 517
Randolph County Archives and Museum 108
Randolph County Genealogical Society 127
Randolph County Genealogical Society 407
Randolph County Historian 146

Randolph County Historical/Genealogical Society 146
Randolph County Historical Society 120, 277, 404, 553
Randolph County Library 25
Randolph Historical Commission 221
Randolph Historical Society, Inc. 92, 527
Randolph Southern Historical Society 146
Range Genealogical Society 261
Rangeley Lakes Region Historical Society 204
Rankin County Historical Society, Inc. 265
Rankin Museum 504
Ransom County Historical Society 412
Rapid City Public Library 481
Rapid City Society for Genealogical Research, Inc. (SDGS) 483
Rapides Parish Library 193
Rappahannock Historical Society/Library 536
Rathbun Free Memorial Library 65
Raton Museum 321
Raupp Memorial Museum 108
Ravenna Genealogical and Historical Society 294
Ravenswood-Lake View Historical Association 120
Rawlins County Genealogical Society 179
Rawlins County Historical Society 175
Rawlins Municipal Library 481
Ray County Genealogical Association 280
Ray County Historical Society and Museum, Inc. 277
Ray County Library 271
Raymond-Casco Historical Society 205
Raymond E. Baldwin Museum of Connecticut History 63
Raymond Historical Society, Inc. 303
Readfield Historical Society 205
Reading Antiquarian Society 230
Reading Company Technical and Historical Society 701
Reading Historical Commission 221
Reading Historical Society Museum 527
Reading Public Library 221, 458
Reading Public Museum and Art Gallery 471
Readsboro Historical Society 527
Reagan County Historical Association 510
Rebecca Winters Genealogical Society 294
Record 685
Records Management Bureau 282
Records Management Division 214, 262
Rector Public Library 25
Red Bank Public Library 308
Red Bird Missionary Conference Archives 654
Red Clay State Historic Park 607
Red Dragon Welsh Society of Greater Hazelton 619
Red Lake County Historical Society 258
Red Lion Area Historical Society 466
Red Mill Museum Village 308
Red Oak Public Library 156
Red River County Texas Genealogical Society 517
Red River Crossroads Historical and Cultural Association, Inc. 195
Red River Historical Museum of Sherman 504
Red River Historical Society 187
Red River Meeting House and Cemetery Association 190
Red River Parish Library 193
Red River Valley Genealogical Society Library 413
Red River Valley Heritage Society 258
Red River Valley Historical Association 443
Red River Valley Museum 520
Reddick Library 108
Redding Historical Society, Inc. 69
Redding Museum and Art Center 36

Redlands Area Historical Society, Inc. 45
Redondo Beach Historical Society 45
Redwood City Public Library 36
Redwood County Historical Society 258
Redwood Genealogical Society, Inc. 51
Reed City Area Genealogical Society 248
Reed City Area Public Library 238
Reed Gold Mine Library 401
Reed Memorial Library 419
Reedley Historical Society 45
Reedsburg Area Historical Society, Inc. 565
Reese Resource Center 624
Reform Public Library 12
Reformed Church in America 640
Reformed Church in the United States 640
Reformed Episcopal Church 632
Reformed Methodist Union Episcopal Church 627
Reformed Presbyterian Church of North America 639
Refugio County Historical Society 510
Regional Council of Historical Agencies 325
Registry Division (Massachusetts, City of Boston) 5
Registry of Vital Records (Massachusetts) 5
Rehoboth Antiquarian Society 230
Rehoboth Beach Historical Society, Inc. 73
Rehoboth Capel Cymraeg, Delta, Pa. 617
Reidsville Library 401
Religious Society of Friends 641
Remick Country Doctor Museum and Farm 305
Remington-Carpenter Township Public Library 137
Remsen-Steuben Historical Society 376
Rend Lake College 109
Renegade Root Diggers 51
Reno County Genealogical Society 179
Reno County Historical Society 175
Rensselaer County Historian 376
Rensselaer County Historical Society 377
Rensselaer Falls Historical Association 377
Rensselaer Falls Library 334
Rensselaer Public Library 334
Rensselaerville Historical Society 377
Renton Historical Society and Museum 546
Renville County Genealogical Society 261
Renville County Historical Society 258, 412
Reppert Publications 129
Reprint Company, Publishers 690
Republic County Historical Society 175
Researchers 190
Researchers Surname Index 673
Restore Our County, Inc. 497
Resurrection Bay Historical Society Museum 18
Reunion 678
Reunions, Ltd. 678
Reunions Magazine 10
Revere Historical Commission 221
Reynolds Center 288
Reynolds Community Museum 413
Reynolds County Courier 687
Reynolds County Historical Society 277
Reynolds Historical Society 412
Reynoldsburg Truro Historical Society 429
RF Corporation 683
Rhea County Historian 494
Rhea County Historical Society 494
Rhinebeck Historical Society 377
Rhinelander District Library 559
Rhinelander Historical Society/Museum 568
Rhoades Valley Camp, Daughters of Utah Pioneers 671
Rhode Island Black Heritage Society 579
Rhode Island Cemeteries Database 474
Rhode Island Department of Library Services 472
Rhode Island Department of Transportation 474
Rhode Island Families Association 474

Rose City Area Historical Society, Inc. 244
Roseau County Historical Museum and Interpretive Center 251
Rosebud County Historical Society 284
Rosehill Cemetery Civil War Museum 706
Roseland Historical Society 316
Roselle Historical Foundation 120
Roselle Historical Society, Inc. 316
Roselle Park Historical Society 316
Rosemead Library 36
Rosemount Area Historical Society 258
Rosenbach Museum and Library 471
Rosenberg Library 504
Roseville Genealogical Society 51
Roseville Historical and Genealogical Society 244
Roseville Historical Society 45, 258
Roseville Public Library 36, 238
Rosicrucian Order 699
Roslindale Historical Society 230
Roslyn Historical Museum Society 546
Ross County Chapter OGS 435
Ross County Historical Society 429
Ross Township Historical Society 466
Rossville Historical Society 120
Rossville Public Library 87
Roswell Genealogical Society 323
Roswell Historic Preservation Commission 96
Roswell Historical Society 93
Roswell New Mexico Genealogical Group 323
Roswell P. Flower Memorial Library 329
Roswell Public Library 321
Rotary International 699
Rough and Tumble Engineers Historical Association, Inc. 471
Round Rock Public Library System 504
Routes to Roots 601
Rowan County Historical Society 187
Rowan County Public Library 183
Rowan County Register 409
Rowan Public Library 401
Rowan University Library 308
Rowayton Historical Society 69
Rowe Historical Society, Inc. 230
Rowley Historical Society 230
Roxborough-Manayunk-Wissahickon Historical Society 466
Roxbury Burrough's Club 378
Roxbury Historical Society 69, 230
Roxbury Library Association 335
Roxbury Public Library 308
Roxbury Township Historical Society 316
Royal Center-Boone Township Public Library 137
Royal Oak Public Library 238
Royalston Historical Society 230
Royalton Historical Society 258, 527
Ruby M. Sisson Memorial Library 58
Rufus M. Reed Public Library 183
Ruggles House Society 207
Rumford Historical Association 230
Rumford Historical Society 205
Rumson Historical Society 316
RUNGS 682
Rush County Historian 146
Rush County Historical Society 146, 175
Rushford Area Historical Organization 258
Rushford Museum 397
Rushville Public Library 137, 288
Rusin Association of Minnesota 582
Rusk County Genealogical Society 517
Rusk County Historical Foundation 511
Rusk County Historical Society 565
Russell Collection of Vermontiana 524
Russell County Historical Commission 14
Russell County Historical Society 175, 187
Russell Library 65
Russell Public Library 335
Russian-American Genealogical Archival Source (RAGAS) 611

Russian Heraldry 611
Russian Heritage Society 611
Russian Nobility Association 611
Russian Orthodox Church Outside of Russia 638
Rutgers University 308
Ruth Enlow Library of Garrett County 209
Ruth L. Rockwood Memorial Library 308
Rutherford B. Hayes Presidential Center Library 416
Rutherford County Archives 489
Rutherford County Historian 494
Rutherford County Historical Society 404, 494
Rutland Free Library 524
Rutland Historical Society 527
Ryder Historical Society 412
Rye Historical Society 303, 378

— S —

S & N Genealogy Supplies 707
S.S. Lipscomb Arkansas History and Genealogy Room 25
SAAAB Wing, Costa Mesa Historical Society 45
Sabbathday Lake Shaker Library 650
Sabine Parish Library 193
Sac County Genealogical Society 164
Sackets Harbor Historical Society 378
Sacramento Archives and Museum Collection Center 36
Sacramento Branch Genealogical Library 37
Sacramento City Cemetery Archives 37
Sacramento County Historical Society 45
Sacramento Cylch Cymraeg 617
Sacramento Genealogical Society—Root Cellar 51
Sacramento German Genealogy Society 593
Sacramento Historical Museum 37
Sacramento Mountains Historical Society, Inc. 322
Sacramento Public Library 37
Sacramento Trust for Historic Preservation 55
Sacramento Valley Museum 37
Sacramento Valley Region 48
Sacred Heart Area Historical Society 258
Saddleback Area Historical Society 45
Safety Harbor Museum of History and Fine Arts 77
Safety Harbor Public Library 77
Sag Harbor Historical Society 378
Sag Harbor Whaling and Historical Museum 697
Sagadahoc Preservation, Inc. 205
Saginaw County Historical Society 244
Saginaw Genealogical Society, Inc. 248
Saginaw River Marine Historical Society 701
Sagtikos Manor Historical Society 397
Saint Albans Free Library 524
Saint Albans Historical Society 527, 553
Saint Andrew's Society of Philadelphia 611
Saint Anne's Episcopal Church Historical Commission 632
Saint Augustine Genealogical Society 82
Saint Augustine Historical Society 80, 195
Saint Basil's College 616
Saint Bernard Parish Genealogical Society, Inc. 197
Saint Charles Avenue Association 195
Saint Charles City-County Library District 271
Saint Charles County Genealogical Society 280
Saint Charles County Historical Society 277
Saint Charles Heritage Center 120
Saint Charles Parish Library 193
Saint Charles Public Library District 109
Saint Clair County Genealogical Society 127

Saint Clair County Historical Society 120, 277
Saint Clair County Library 239, 271
Saint Clair Family History Group Inc. 248
St. Clair Historical Society 14
Saint Clair Shores Historical Commission 244
Saint Clair Shores Public Library 239
Saint Clairsville Public Library 419
Saint Cloud Area Genealogists, Inc. 261
Saint Croix County Historical Society 565
Saint Croix Landmarks Society 573
Saint Croix Valley Genealogical Society 568
Saint David's Society 617
Saint David's Society of Connecticut 617
Saint David's Society of Emporia 617
Saint David's Society of Georgia 617
Saint David's Society of Greater Buffalo, N.Y. 617
Saint David's Society of Greater Saint Louis 617
Saint David's Society of Lackawanna County 618
Saint David's Society of Lyon County 617
Saint David's Society of Minnesota 617
Saint David's Society of Nebraska 617
Saint David's Society of New York 617
Saint David's Society of Oshkosh, Wisconsin and Winnebago County, Welsh Settlement 618
Saint David's Society of Pittsburgh 618
Saint David's Society of Poultney 618
Saint David's Society of Racine 618
Saint David's Society of Rochester and Genesee Region 618
Saint David's Society of Schuylkill and Carbon Counties 618
Saint David's Society of South Carolina 618
Saint David's Society of Texas 618
Saint David's Society of the Capital District 617
Saint David's Society of the Inland Empire 618
Saint David's Society of the State of Kansas 617
Saint David's Society of Utica, Inc. 618
Saint David's Society of Waukesha County 618
Saint David's Society of Wyoming Valley 618
Saint David's Society of Youngstown 618
Saint David's Welsh-American Society of Washington, DC 618
Saint David's Welsh Society of Greater Kansas City 617
Saint David's Welsh Society of Nebraska 617
Saint David's Welsh Society of Saint Petersburg and the Suncoast 617
Saint David's Welsh Society of the Slate Belt, Bangor, Pennsylvania 618
Saint Ephrem Educational Center 638
Saint Francis Historical Society 565
Saint Francois County Historical Society 277
Saint George's Society of New York 585
Saint Helena Historical Association 195
Saint James Historical Society 196
Saint James Parish Library 193
Saint John Historical Society 146
Saint John the Baptist Parish Library 194
Saint John's University 251
Saint Johns County Public Library 77
Saint Johnsbury Athenaeum 524
Saint Josaphat's Ukrainian Catholic Seminary 638
Saint Joseph County Historian 146
Saint Joseph County Public Library 137
Saint Joseph Museum 271
Saint Joseph Public Library 239
Saint Joseph's Historic Foundation, Inc. 579
Saint Lawrence County Historian 378

Washington News Tribune 688
Washington Parish Library System 194
Washington Public Library 156, 272
Washington Society, Sons of the American Revolution 666
Washington State Archives 541
Washington State Archives, Central Regional Branch 541
Washington State Archives, Eastern Regional Branch 541
Washington State Archives, Northwest Region 541
Washington State Archives, Southwest Regional Branch 541
Washington State Department of Transportation 549
Washington State Genealogical Society 547
Washington State Historical Society 541
Washington State Library 541
Washington State Railroads Historical Society 701
Washington State Society Daughters of the American Revolution 663
Washington State University 543
Washington Township Historical Society 47, 317, 430
Washington-Wilkes Historical Foundation, Inc. 93
Washita County Historical Society 444
Washoe Archive and Cultural Resource Center 295
Washoe County Historical Society 296
Washoe County Library System 295
Washtenaw County Historical Society 245
Washtenaw County History District Commission 245
Wasilla-Knik-Willow Creek Historical Society 18
Watauga Association of Genealogists—Upper East Tennessee 496
Watauga County Historical Society 405
Watchung Hills Historical Society 317
Watchung Historical Society 317
Waterborough Historical Society 206
Waterbury Historical Society Museum 528
Waterford Foundation, Inc. 537
Waterford Historical Museum and Cultural Center 337
Waterford Historical Society 70, 206
Waterloo Area Historical Society 245, 566
Waterloo Library and Historical Society 389
Waterloo Public Library 156
Watertown Free Public Library 222
Watertown Historical Society 70, 566
Watertown Regional Genealogical Society (SDGS) 484
Waterville Historical Society 206, 430
Waterville Public Library 200
Watervliet Historical Society 389
Waterways Journal 701
Watkins Mill Association 278
Watkinson Library 585
Watonga Public Library 441
Watonwan County Historical Society 259
Wattsburg Area Historical Society 468
Wauconda Township Historical Society 122
Waukegan Historical Society 122
Waukesha County Genealogical Society 569
Waukesha County Historical Society 566
Waukesha County Museum 559
Waukesha Public Library 559
Waupaca Area Genealogical Society 569
Waupaca County Historical Society 566
Waupaca Historical Society 566
Waupun Historical Society 566
Waushara County Historical Society 566
Wauwatosa Historical Society 566
Wauwatosa Public Library 559
Waveland Brown Township Public Library 139
Waverly Genealogical and Historical Society 128

Wawina Area Historical Society 259
Way Public Library 420
Wayland Baptist University 506
Wayland Free Public Library 222
Wayland Historical Commission 222
Wayland Historical Society 231
Wayland Tree Tracers Genealogy Society 249
Wayne County Genealogical Organization 267
Wayne County Genealogical Society 165, 294, 435
Wayne County Historian 148, 495
Wayne County Historian's Office 389
Wayne County Historical and Genealogical Society 187
Wayne County Historical Association 405
Wayne County Historical Museum 139
Wayne County Historical Society 93, 122, 292, 390, 468, 495
Wayne County (IN) Genealogical Society 149
Wayne County Public Library 184, 401, 420, 490
Wayne Historical Society 206, 245
Wayne Public Library 289, 308, 420
Wayne State University 239
Wayne Township Historical Commission 317
Wayne Township Historical Society 148
Waynesboro Historical Society 468
Waynesboro Memorial Library 264
Waynesboro Public Library 534
Waynesville-Kinderhook Library 272
Waynoka Historical Society 444
Waynoka Public Library 441
Wayzata Historical Society 259
Wead Library 337
Weakley County Genealogical Society 496
Weakley County Historian 495
Weare Historical Society 304
Weatherford Democrat 688
Weatherford Public Library 441, 506
Weathersfield Historical Society 528
Weaver Genealogical Publications 129
Weaverville Joss House State Historic Park 55
Webb City Area Genealogy Society 280
Webb County Heritage Foundation 512
Webb Shadle Memorial Library 156
Weber County Library 522
WebLUIS! 74
Webster County Genealogical Society 165
Webster County Historical and Genealogical Society 187
Webster County Historical Museum 292
Webster County Historical Society 266, 278, 553
Webster County Library 272
Webster Dudley Historical Society 231
Webster Groves Historical Society 278
Webster Museum and Historical Society 390
Webster Parish Library 194
Webster University 272
Weeping Water Valley Historical Society 292
Weimar Heritage Society/Museum 512
Weirton Historical Landmarks Commission 555
Welcome Historical Society 259
Welcome Society of Pennsylvania 662
Weld County Genealogical Society 62
Weld Historical Society, Inc. 206
Weld Library District 58
Welles-Turner Memorial Library 66
Wellesley Historical Society 231
Wellfleet Historical Society Museum 232
Wellington Genealogy Group 436
Wellington Public Library 58
Wells County Historian 148
Wells County Historical Society 148, 412
Wells County Public Library 139

Wells Fargo Bank History Department 55
Wells Historical Society 528
Wells Memorial Library 337
Wellsville Historical Society 430
Welsh-American Family History Association (W.A.F.H.A.) 618
Welsh-American Genealogical Society (WAGS) 618
Welsh American Heritage Museum 618
Welsh-American Heritage Museum 618
Welsh American Society of Dallas 618
Welsh American Society of Northern California 618
Welsh American Society of Southern California 618
Welsh Harp Society of Kansas City 618
Welsh National Gymanfa Ganu Association, Inc. 618
Welsh Saint David's Society of Spokane 618
Welsh Society 619
Welsh Society of Berks County 619
Welsh Society of Central New Jersey 619
Welsh Society of Central Ohio 619
Welsh Society of Cincinnati 619
Welsh Society of Columbus 619
Welsh Society of Delaware 618
Welsh Society of Detroit 619
Welsh Society of Fredericksburg, VA 619
Welsh Society of Grand Rapids 619
Welsh Society of Greater Boston 619
Welsh Society of Greater Cincinnati 619
Welsh Society of Greater Harrisburg, Pa. 619
Welsh Society of Madison 619
Welsh Society of New Mexico 619
Welsh Society of Philadelphia 619
Welsh Society of Richville 619
Welsh Society of the Carolinas 619
Welsh Society of the Monterey Peninsula 618
Welsh Society of the Southern Tier 619
Welsh Society of West Virginia 619
Wenatchee Area Genealogical Society 548
Wendell Historic Commission 222
Wenham Historic District Commission 234
Wenham Historical Association and Museum, Inc. 232
Wenonah Historical Society 317
Wentzville Community Historical Society/Archives 278
Weslaco Public Library 506
Wesley College 72
Wesleyan Church Archives and Local History Library 657
Wesleyan College 88
Wesleyan University 66
West Allis Historical Society 566
West Augusta Historical and Genealogical Society 553
West Baden Historical Society 148
West Bank Genealogy Society 197
West Baton Rouge Genealogical Society 197
West Baton Rouge Historical Association 196
West Baton Rouge Parish Library 194
West Bell Genealogical Society 519
West Bend Community Memorial Library 559
West Bend Historical Society 160
West Boylston Historical Society, Inc. 232
West Branch Public Library 239
West Brookfield Historical Commission 232
West Carrollton Historical Society 430
West Central Georgia Genealogical Society, Inc. 95
West-Central Kentucky Family Research Association 189
West Central Minnesota Historical Center 250
West Central Missouri Genealogical Society

Printed in the United States
42493LVS00001B/39-104